# COMBAT FLEETS OF THE WORLD 1988/89

## Their Ships, Aircraft, and Armament

Edited by
JEAN LABAYLE COUHAT
and
BERNARD PRÉZELIN

English language version prepared by
A. D. BAKER III

NAVAL INSTITUTE PRESS
Annapolis, Maryland

WORKS BY JEAN LABAYLE COUHAT

- *French Warships of World War I* } Published by Ian Allan, London. Sold in France by Éditions
- *French Warships of World War II* } Maritimes et d'Outre-Mer
- Articles for *"La Revue Maritime," "Marine," "Revue de Défense Nationale,"* and *"Armées d'aujourdhui"*
- Monographs on the French, American, British, and Soviet navies, published by Éditions Ozanne.
- *Flottes de Combat 1974* in collaboration with H. Le Masson
- *Flottes de Combat 1976*
- *Flottes de Combat 1978*
- *Flottes de Combat 1980*
- *Flottes de Combat 1982*
- *Flottes de Combat 1984*
- *Flottes de Combat 1986*
- *Flottes de Combat 1988* in collaboration with B. Prézelin



This seventh English-language edition is published by arrangement with Éditions Maritime et d'Outre-Mer.



Library of Congress Catalog Card Number: 78-50192

ISBN: 0-87021-194-3

Printed in the United States of America.

Published in the U.S.A. by
Naval Institute Press,
United States Naval Institute
Annapolis, Maryland 21402.

# CONTENTS

# TERMS AND ABBREVIATIONS

Most ships' characteristics are given in the following sample:

| | Bldr | Laid down | L | In serv. |
|---|---|---|---|---|
| D 602 SUFFREN | Lorient | 12-62 | 15-5-65 | 1967 |

**D:** 5,090 tons (6,090 fl) **S:** 34 kts
**Dim:** 157.6 (148.0 pp) 15.54 × 7.25 (max.)
**A:** 1/Masurca system (II × 1)—4/MM 38 Exocet—2/100-mm, Model 1953 (I × 2)—4/20-mm AA (I × 4)—1/Malafon system (13 missiles)—2/catapults for L-5 torpedoes (10 torpedoes)
**Electron Equipt:** Radar: 1/DRBI-23, 1/DRBV-50, 2/DRBR-51, 1/DRBC-32A, 1/DRBN-32
Sonar: 1/DUBV-23, 1/DUBV-43—SENIT-1,2 Syllex systems
**M:** 2 Rateau double-reduction GT; 2 props; 72,500 hp
**Boilers:** 4 multitube, automatic-control; 45 kg/cm$^2$, 450°C
**Electric:** 3,440 kw (2 × 1,000-kw turbogenerators, 3 × 480-kw diesel alternators)
**Range:** 2,000/30; 2,400/29; 5,100/18
**Man:** 23 officers, 164 petty officers, 168 men

Ships' hull numbers and names are in capitals and small capitals. Hull dimensions are in meters, calibers in millimeters, speeds in knots, ranges in nautical miles; speeds and ranges of aircraft are in kilometers/hour and kilometers, unless otherwise indicated.

**D:** Displacment. In most cases, standard displacement, as defined by the Treaty of Washington (1922), is given. Where possible, full load (fl) is given; otherwise, normal (avg) displacement or trial displacement is given. In the case of most submarines, two displacements are given: the first figure is surfaced displacement; the second is submerged displacement. When available, the figure for standard displacement precedes the surfaced and submerged figures.

**S:** Speed. This is given in knots and generally refers to maximum speed; in some cases trial speed is given. For submarines, surfaced speed is given first and is followed by submerged speed.

**Dim:** Hull dimensions are given as follows: length overall × beam × draft (full load, unless otherwise stated). Length between perpendiculars is given as "pp"; length at the waterline as "wl." In cases where two figures are given for one of the dimensions, e.g., the beam of the flight deck and of the hull of an aircraft carrier, the hull measurement is given as "hull."

**A:** Armament. Number of guns/bore diameter; or number of torpedo tubes or launchers with diameter. Figures in parentheses show the number of mounts and whether they are single, double, triple, etc.; e.g., (III × 2) indicates two triple mounts.

**M:** Machinery. Geared turbine is shown as GT; in some cases, the type or manufacturer of turbine is given, e.g., Parsons, etc. COSAG, CODAG/CODOG, COGAG/COGOG are used when such combinations of machinery have to be shown. "Props" indicates propellers. "CP" indicates controllable-pitch.

**Boilers:** In most cases, number and type are shown. Steam pressure is expressed in kilograms/square centimeter and steam superheat in degrees centigrade.

**Electric:** Electric generating power, in kilowatts (kw) or kilovolt-amperes (kVA).

**Armor:** Armor protection, thickness given in millimeters.

**Range:** Cited in nautical miles at a given speed.

**Man:** Ship's company. Where not broken down into "officers" and "men" (i.e., noncommissioned personnel), a total complement figure is given as "tot."

**Dates:** Dates are given in the following sequence: day-month-year.

| | |
|---|---|
| A | Armament |
| AA | Antiaircraft |
| A & C, AT & Ch | Shipbuilding yard *(Atelier & Chantiers)* |
| AAW | Anti-air warfare |
| ADAWS | Action Data Automation Weapon System |
| AEW | Airborne early warning |
| ARM | Anti-radiation missile |
| ASM | Anti-ship missile |
| Ast Nav | Shipyard *(Astilleros Navales)* |
| ASW | Antisubmarine warfare |
| Author. | Authorized |
| avg | Average, normal |
| BB | Boatbuilding |
| Bldr | Builder |
| BPDMS | Basic Point Defense Missile System |
| BW | Boat Works |
| BY | Boat Yard |
| CAAIS | Computer-Assisted Action Information System |
| CH, Ch. Nav. | Builder, shipyard *(Chantier, Chantier Navals)* |
| CIWS | Close-In Weapon System (U.S.) |
| CN, Cant. Nav. | Naval shipyard *(Cantière Navale)* |
| COD | Carrier Onboard Delivery |
| COGAG/CODAG/COSAG/COGOG/CODOG | Combined propulsive machinery systems, gas turbine, diesel, steam. *CO* means *combined, A* means *and, O* means *or.* For example, CODOG means *combined diesel or gas turbine* |
| CP | Controllable-pitch |
| D | Displacement |
| d.c. | Depth charge |
| d.c.t. | Depth-charge thrower |
| DD, DDM | Dry dock, dry dock company (Dutch) |
| DECM | Deceptive Electronic Countermeasures |
| Dim | Dimensions |
| DP | Dual-purpose |
| DSRV | Deep Submergence Rescue Vessel |
| dwt | Deadweight tonnage |
| ECM | Electronic countermeasures |
| ECCM | Electronic counter-countermeasures |
| Electron Equipt | Electronic equipment |
| ELINT | Electronic intelligence |
| Eng. | Engineering |
| E/O | Electro-Optical |
| ESM | Electronic support measures (i.e., passive EW) |
| EW | Electronic Warfare |
| FF, FFG | Frigate, guided-missile frigate |
| f.c.s. | Fire-control system |
| fl | Full load |
| freq. | Frequency |
| FRAM | Fleet Rehabilitation and Modernization (U.S.) |
| fwd | Forward |
| G.E. | General Electric Company |
| GFCS | Gunfire-control system |
| G.M. | General Motors Corp. |
| grt | Gross registered tons |
| GT | Geared turbine |
| GWS | Guided Weapon System (U.K.) |
| HF | High frequency |
| HMDY | Her Majesty's Dockyard |
| H.S.A. | Hollandse Signaal Apparaaten |
| hp | Horsepower |
| IFF | Identification Friend or Foe |
| kg | Kilogram |
| Kon. Mij. | Royal Company (Dutch) |
| KT | Kiloton |
| kts | Knots |
| kVA | Kilovolt-ampere |
| kw | Kilowatt |
| L | Launched |
| LAMPS | Light Airborne Multi-Purpose System (U.S.N. helicopter) |
| LF | Low frequency |
| loa | Length overall |
| LRMP | Long-Range Maritime Patrol (U.S.) |
| M | Machinery |
| MAD | Magnetic Anomaly Detection |
| Man | Manpower on board ship, crew, ship's company |
| MAP | Military Assistance Program (U.S. and allies) |
| MCM | Mine Countermeasures |
| MF | Medium frequency |
| mg | Machine gun |
| mm | Millimeters |
| MSC | Military Sealift Command |
| MTU | Motoren and Turbinen Union |
| N.B. | New Brunswick |
| NBC | Nuclear, biological, and chemical |
| NDY | Naval dockyard |
| n.m. | Nautical miles |
| nrt | Net registered tons |
| N.S. | Nova Scotia |
| NTDS | Naval Tactical Data System |
| NY | Navy Yard |
| o.a. | Overall |
| PADLOC | Passive/Active Detection and Location |
| PDMS | Point-Defense Missile System |
| pp | Between perpendiculars |
| PUFFS | Passive Underwater Fire-Control System |
| RAS | Replenishment-At-Sea |
| RDY | Royal dockyard |
| RL | Rocket launcher |
| rpm | Revolutions per minute or rounds per minute |
| S | Speed |

| | |
|---|---|
| SAM | Surface-to-air missile |
| SAR | Search and rescue |
| SB | Shipbuilding |
| S.F.C.N. | Société Française de Construction Navale |
| SINS | Ships' Inertial Navigation System |
| SLBM | Submarine-Launched Ballistic Missile |
| SLEP | Service Life Extension Program |
| SSBN | Nuclear-powered fleet ballistic-missile submarine |
| SSM | Surface-to-surface missile |
| STIR | Separate Track and Illumination Radar |
| SURTASS | Surface Towed Array Surveillance System |
| SY | Shipyard |
| syst | System |
| TACAN | Tactical Air Navigation beacon |
| TACTASS | Tactical Towed Acoustic Sensor System |
| TASS | Towed-Array Surveillance System |
| TT | Torpedo tubes/launchers |
| tot. | Total |
| VDS | Variable-depth sonar |
| VLS | Vertical-Launch System |
| Wks. | Works |
| wl | Waterline |

# CONVERSION TABLES

## ◆ METERS (m.) to FEET (ft.)
**based on 1 inch = 25.4 millimeters**

| m | 0 | 1 | 2 | 3 | 4 | 5 | 6 | 7 | 8 | 9 |
|---|---|---|---|---|---|---|---|---|---|---|
| | ft. | ft. | ft. | ft. | ft. | ft. | ft. | ft. | ft. | ft. |
| — | — | 3.28084 | 6.5617 | 9.8425 | 13.1234 | 16.4042 | 19.6850 | 22.9659 | 26.2467 | 29.5276 |
| **10** | 32.8084 | 36.0892 | 39.3701 | 42.6509 | 45.9317 | 49.2126 | 52.493 | 55.774 | 59.005 | 62.336 |
| **20** | 65.617 | 68.898 | 72.178 | 75.459 | 78.740 | 82.021 | 85.302 | 88.583 | 91.863 | 95.144 |
| **30** | 98.425 | 101.706 | 104.987 | 108.268 | 111.549 | 114.829 | 118.110 | 121.391 | 124.672 | 127.953 |
| **40** | 131.234 | 134.514 | 137.795 | 141.076 | 144.357 | 147.638 | 150.919 | 154.199 | 157.480 | 160.761 |
| **50** | 164.042 | 167.323 | 170.604 | 173.884 | 177.165 | 180.446 | 183.727 | 187.008 | 190.289 | 193.570 |
| **60** | 196.850 | 200.131 | 203.412 | 206.693 | 209.974 | 213.255 | 216.535 | 219.816 | 223.097 | 226.378 |
| **70** | 229.659 | 232.940 | 236.220 | 239.501 | 242.782 | 246.063 | 249.344 | 252.625 | 255.905 | 259.186 |
| **80** | 262.467 | 265.748 | 269.029 | 272.310 | 275.590 | 278.871 | 282.152 | 285.433 | 288.714 | 291.995 |
| **90** | 295.276 | 298.556 | 301.837 | 305.118 | 308.399 | 311.680 | 314.961 | 318.241 | 321.522 | 324.803 |
| **100** | 328.084 | 331.365 | 334.646 | 337.926 | 341.207 | 344.488 | 347.769 | 351.050 | 354.331 | 357.611 |
| **10** | 360.892 | 364.173 | 367.454 | 370.735 | 374.016 | 377.296 | 380.577 | 383.858 | 387.139 | 390.420 |
| **20** | 393.701 | 396.982 | 400.262 | 403.543 | 406.824 | 410.105 | 413.386 | 416.667 | 419.947 | 423.228 |
| **30** | 426.509 | 429.790 | 433.071 | 436.352 | 439.632 | 442.913 | 446.194 | 449.475 | 452.756 | 456.037 |
| **40** | 459.317 | 462.598 | 465.879 | 469.160 | 472.441 | 475.722 | 479.002 | 482.283 | 485.564 | 488.845 |
| **50** | 492.126 | 495.407 | 498.688 | 501.97 | 505.25 | 508.53 | 511.81 | 515.09 | 518.37 | 521.65 |
| **60** | 524.93 | 528.22 | 531.50 | 534.78 | 538.06 | 541.34 | 544.62 | 547.90 | 551.18 | 554.46 |
| **70** | 557.74 | 561.02 | 564.30 | 567.59 | 570.87 | 574.15 | 577.43 | 580.71 | 583.99 | 587.27 |
| **80** | 590.55 | 593.83 | 597.11 | 600.39 | 603.67 | 606.96 | 610.24 | 613.52 | 616.80 | 620.08 |
| **90** | 623.36 | 626.64 | 629.92 | 633.20 | 636.48 | 639.76 | 643.04 | 646.33 | 649.61 | 652.89 |
| **200** | 656.17 | 659.45 | 662.73 | 666.01 | 669.29 | 672.57 | 675.85 | 679.13 | 682.41 | 685.70 |
| **10** | 688.98 | 692.26 | 695.54 | 698.82 | 702.10 | 705.38 | 708.66 | 711.94 | 715.22 | 718.50 |
| **20** | 721.78 | 725.07 | 728.35 | 731.63 | 734.91 | 738.19 | 741.47 | 744.75 | 748.03 | 751.31 |
| **30** | 754.59 | 757.87 | 761.15 | 764.44 | 767.72 | 771.00 | 774.28 | 777.56 | 780.84 | 784.12 |
| **40** | 747.40 | 790.68 | 793.96 | 797.24 | 800.52 | 803.81 | 807.09 | 810.37 | 813.65 | 816.93 |
| **50** | 820.21 | 823.49 | 826.77 | 830.05 | 833.33 | 836.61 | 839.89 | 843.18 | 846.46 | 849.74 |
| **60** | 853.02 | 856.30 | 859.58 | 862.86 | 866.14 | 869.42 | 872.70 | 875.98 | 879.26 | 882.55 |
| **70** | 885.83 | 889.11 | 892.39 | 895.67 | 898.95 | 902.23 | 905.51 | 908.79 | 912.07 | 915.35 |
| **80** | 918.63 | 921.92 | 925.20 | 928.48 | 931.76 | 935.04 | 938.32 | 941.60 | 944.88 | 948.16 |
| **90** | 951.44 | 954.72 | 958.00 | 961.29 | 964.57 | 967.85 | 971.13 | 974.41 | 977.69 | 980.97 |
| **300** | 984.25 | 987.53 | 990.81 | 994.09 | 997.38 | 1000.66 | 1003.94 | 1007.22 | 1010.50 | 1013.78 |
| **10** | 1017.06 | 1020.34 | 1023.62 | 1026.90 | 1030.18 | 1033.46 | 1036.75 | 1040.03 | 1043.31 | 1046.59 |
| **20** | 1049.87 | 1053.15 | 1056.43 | 1059.71 | 1062.99 | 1066.27 | 1069.55 | 1072.83 | 1076.12 | 1079.40 |
| **30** | 1082.68 | 1085.96 | 1089.24 | 1092.52 | 1095.80 | 1099.08 | 1102.36 | 1105.64 | 1108.92 | 1112.20 |
| **40** | 1115.49 | 1118.77 | 1122.05 | 1125.33 | 1128.61 | 1131.89 | 1135.17 | 1138.45 | 1141.73 | 1145.01 |
| **50** | 1118.29 | 1151.57 | 1154.86 | 1158.14 | 1161.42 | 1164.70 | 1167.98 | 1171.26 | 1174.54 | 1177.82 |

## ◆ MILLIMETERS (mm.) to INCHES (in.)
**based on 1 inch = 25.4 millimeters**

| mm | 0 | 1 | 2 | 3 | 4 | 5 | 6 | 7 | 8 | 9 |
|---|---|---|---|---|---|---|---|---|---|---|
| | in. | in. | in. | in. | in. | in. | in. | in. | in. | in. |
| — | — | 0.03937 | 0.07874 | 0.11811 | 0.15748 | 0.19685 | 0.23622 | 0.27559 | 0.31496 | 0.35433 |
| **10** | 0.39370 | 0.43307 | 0.47244 | 0.51181 | 0.55118 | 0.59055 | 0.62992 | 0.66929 | 0.70866 | 0.74803 |
| **20** | 0.78740 | 0.82677 | 0.86614 | 0.90551 | 0.94488 | 0.98425 | 1.02362 | 1.06299 | 1.10236 | 1.14173 |
| **30** | 1.18110 | 1.22047 | 1.25984 | 1.29921 | 1.33858 | 1.37795 | 1.41732 | 1.45669 | 1.49606 | 1.53543 |
| **40** | 1.57480 | 1.61417 | 1.65354 | 1.69291 | 1.73228 | 1.77165 | 1.81102 | 1.85039 | 1.88976 | 1.92913 |
| **50** | 1.96850 | 2.00787 | 2.04724 | 2.08661 | 2.12598 | 2.16535 | 2.20472 | 2.24409 | 2.28346 | 2.32283 |
| **60** | 2.36220 | 2.40157 | 2.44094 | 2.48031 | 2.51969 | 2.55906 | 2.59843 | 2.63780 | 2.67717 | 2.71654 |
| **70** | 2.75591 | 2.79528 | 2.83465 | 2.87402 | 2.91339 | 2.95276 | 2.99213 | 3.03150 | 3.07087 | 3.11024 |
| **80** | 3.14961 | 3.18898 | 3.22835 | 3.26772 | 3.30709 | 3.34646 | 3.38583 | 3.42520 | 3.46457 | 3.50394 |
| **90** | 3.54331 | 3.58268 | 3.62205 | 3.66142 | 3.70079 | 3.74016 | 3.77953 | 3.81890 | 3.85827 | 3.89764 |
| **100** | 3.93701 | | | | | | | | | |

### CONVERSION FACTORS

| Meter | Yard | Foot | Inch | Centimeter | Millimeter |
|---|---|---|---|---|---|
| 1 | 1.093 61 | 3.280 84 | 39.370 1 | 100 | 1 000 |
| 0.914 4 | 1 | 3 | 36 | 91.44 | 914.4 |
| 0.304 8 | 0.333 333 | 1 | 12 | 30.48 | 304.8 |
| 0.254 | 0.027 777 8 | 0.083 333 | 1 | 2.54 | 25.4 j |
| 0.01 | 0.010 936 1 | 0.032 808 4 | 0.393 701 | 1 | 10 |
| 0.001 | 0.001 093 61 | 0.003 280 84 | 0.039 370 4 | 0.1 | 1 |

| Nautical mile | | Statute mile | | Meters |
|---|---|---|---|---|
| 1 | = | 1.151 52 | = | 1 853.18 |

◆ Boiler working pressure

| *Kilogram per square centimeter (atmosphere)* | | *Pounds per square inch* |
|---|---|---|
| 1 | equivalent → | 14.223 3 |
| 0.070 307 | ← equivalent | 1 |

◆ Conversion for Fahrenheit and centigrade scales

1 degree centigrade = 1.8 degrees Fahrenheit
1 degree Fahrenheit = 5/9 degree centigrade
$t$ °F = 5/9($t$ − 32)°C.
$t$ °C = (1.8 $t$ + 32)°F.

◆ Weights

1 kilogram = 2.204 62 *pounds* (av)
1 *pound* = 0.453 592
1 ton (metric) = 0.984 21 *ton*
1 *ton* = 1.016 05 *metric ton*

◆ Power

1 CV = 0.986 32 *horsepower* (HP) 0.735 88 kilowatt (Greenwich) (75 kgm s)
1 *horsepower* (HP) = 1.013 87 (CV) 0.746 08 kilowatt (Greenwich)

# PREFACE TO THE ENGLISH-LANGUAGE EDITION

The 1988–89 *Combat Fleets* is one hundred twenty-five pages longer than the previous edition, primarily because of increased coverage of existing fleets, but also because of new naval and coast guard services that have come into being. Thus, welcomed to these pages are the naval and paramilitary ships of Anguilla, the Central African Republic, the Cook Islands, Dubai, the Faeroe Islands, the Falkland Islands, Laos, Mali, the Marshall Islands, the Turks and Caicos Islands, Tuvalu, and Zimbabwe. We have also added greatly to the coverage of the various Italian marine security forces, the U.S. Army's Transportation Corps, and the ever-growing U.S. Ready Reserve Force. And, of course, photographic coverage of the ships and aircraft of the fleets of the world has continued to expand.

*Combat Fleets* itself is now "only" in its seventh edition, but our parent publication in France, *Flottes de Combat,* first appeared in 1897. Although the shape and size of the book have altered over the years, there has been a general adherence to a format that permits the maximum concentration of information within a given space. The 1974 edition of *Flottes de Combat* marked a transition of great importance in the history of that venerable publication, for the by-line of its editor since 1943, Henri Le Masson, was for the first time shared. The time has now come for the editorship of "*Flottes*" to change again, and once again there is a transitional sharing of the editorial duties. Jean Labayle Couhat, who had compiled eleven editions during a period of vast technological and geopolitical change, shares the editorial duties for this edition with Bernard Prézelin, who has for some time performed the duties of proofreader, as well as contributing his own excellent photography to the work. M. Labayle Couhat has wrought a revolution in the detailing and chronicling of the combat fleets of the world, as well as enthusiastically embracing the concept of sharing the French edition with a worldwide, English-language audience. M. Labayle Couhat's valedictory introductory essay in this edition is of special significance, as he judges the changes that have evolved in the major navies during his tenure. His careful work, thoughtful introductory essays, and helpful guidance with the English edition have been greatly appreciated and will be sorely missed. At the same time, M. Prézelin, who will have sole proprietorship of the next edition, is enthusiastically welcomed as he settles in to his difficult task.

Users are directed to the Terms and Abbreviations sections on the preceding pages; a short study will assist in understanding the condensed data format used in the book. Conversion tables between the English measurements system and the metric system employed here are also given. One deviation has been made from the metric system, however. Because so many of the users are U.S. citizens, *displacements for U.S. Navy ships have been retained in long tons of 2,240 lbs.* For those seeking to make "exact" comparisons between U.S. Navy ships and a similar foreign vessel, it will be necessary to convert the U.S. displacement to metric by multiplying by 1.01605 or by converting the metric displacement to English long tons by multiplying by 0.98421. Major naval weapons systems, sensors, and naval aircraft are described at the beginning of each country-of-origin entry. The volume concludes with an index to all ships names (and also class codenames for the navies of the People's Republic of China, U.S.S.R., and other Warsaw Pact fleets) used in the book. There is also an addenda, to which the user's attention is drawn for late-arriving information received through February 1988.

A word on the sources of information used in the preparation of this book: all information has been derived from unclassified, open publications and correspondence received from around the world. The official publications of many navies have been consulted, especially the material released by the Western nations on the fleet of the Soviet Union. Nonetheless, some data, particularly that on the submarines and major surface combatants of the U.S.S.R. is estimative in nature, based on measurement of dimensions, the study of photography, and reasonable engineering and naval architectural estimates. Fortunately for the editors, there is a vast body of authentic data on warships constantly appearing in professional publications, and even the more secretive navies have been increasingly generous with data as they have come to realize that a threat unknown is a threat that may be discounted.

Particularly valuable as sources for and checks on information have been the following periodicals: *Air International, Alle Hens, Aviation Week, Flight, International Defense Review, Jane's Defence Weekly, Marine Rundschau, Maritime Defence, The Navy, Navy International, Pacific Defense Reporter, Ships of the World, Soldat und Technik, Surface Warfare, Warship International,* and *Warship World.* Our sister references, *Almanacco Navale, Jane's Fighting Ships,* and *Weyers Flottentaschenbuch,* edited by Giorgio Giorgerini, John E. Moore, and Gerhard Albrecht, respectively, also were frequently consulted. To John Moore, who joins M. Lebayle Couhat in retirement this year, go the very best of wishes and admiration for a job supremely well done; to his successor, Richard Sharpe, a hearty "Welcome Aboard!"

The majority of the new photographs in *Combat Fleets* continue to come from the diverse and comprehensive collection of Leo and Linda Van Ginderen; without their almost weekly packages of photography of ships from around the world, production of this book would be almost impossible.

Many others, however, have also assisted with this edition, some with only a single photograph or item of information and others with a constant stream of invaluable information or new photography. Some of these more than helpful individuals have been professionals in the offices of shipbuilders or various government agencies, while the majority have been "amateurs" in name only but in reality individuals with an intense interest in the navies of the world and, thank goodness, the knack of taking ship photography from just the right angle to catch the details so necessary for illustration and to allow the editors to extract data on minute changes in equipment. *All* information and photography sent to *Combat Fleets* is carefully studied and employed in the preparation of the final manuscript.

Those who have helped with this edition include: CAPT Kendall Allen, USNR; Dr. Yves J. Alloucherie; Dr. Giorgio Arra, one of the world's leading ship portrait photographers; Victor M. Baca, for many excellent photos from the U.S. West Coast; George I. Baldwin, Director, Communications Services, Bath Iron Works; Bob Bennett, of NAVSEA; Eric Berryman, of CHINFO; Jay Berry for data on USN yardcraft; J.H. Bih, editor, *Defense Technology,* for sharing photos and information; John Bouvia, for photos of ships and craft in the Persian Gulf area; Mary Breig, editor of the Canadian Coast Guard's excellent quarterly, *Fleet News;* M. Brescia; the late CDR Joseph Z. Brown, USN, commanding officer, USS *Constitution;* Bob Bryan, of the Maritime Administration, for data on the ships of the Ready Reserve Force; LT Kippy Burns, USN, of CHINFO; Charles Cart, of NAVSEA; Fred Cassaday, of NAVSEA; Clarke E. Castle, for photos; CDR Richard Y.K. Chen, ROCN, for excellent photos of the ships of the ROC fleet; Raymond Cheung, London correspondent for *Defence Technology,* for invaluable information and photography on the PRCN and the ROCN; Ashley M. Clarke, of Swiftships, Inc., for photos and data cheerfully provided; Walter Cloots, submarine enthusiast; Bill Cooper, Pacer Systems, Inc., who kept me straight on the AVT 16; Robert Cressman, the U.S. Navy's "Namer of Ships" at the Naval Historical Center; Göran Damstrom, of Wärtsilä, Helsinki Shipyard; Gary Davies, of Maritime Photographic, whose camera has now joined the RN to see the world; Fred Dittmer, for data on former merchant ships; Wilhelm Donko, correspondent, intrepid photographer of the U.S. Navy, and now author of excellent books on the U.S. fleet; Leslie M. Dury, faithful correspondent on Royal Navy and European developments; Russell D. Egnor and Pat Toombs of the Still Photos Branch, CHINFO, for unfailing assistance; Dipl.-Ing. Hartmut Ehlers, prolific photographer and correspondent on the Turkish Navy and the navies of Africa and elsewhere; Ron Elias, of Ingalls Shipbuilding, whose color photographs dramatize his company's ships so well; William M. Ellsworth, vice president, E & SA, Inc., for data on *High Point;* John R. Forster, of Lantana Boatyard, Inc.; Dr. Norman Friedman, consummate expert on all things naval and many things not, and a friend when one is needed; Roger J.L. Fry, who provided great assistance in understanding RN countermeasures systems and a good deal of other useful data; Andy Ferguson, of NAVSEA; Ross Gillett, editor of the Australian Navy League's *The Navy,* author of authoritative works on the R.A.N., and provider of much useful photography; T.K. Glenn, recently retired from R.C.A. Government and Commercial Systems; Luciano Grazioli, for sending not only his own excellent photos, but also those of his colleagues; CDR Alvin H. Grobmeier, USN (Ret.), who provided much assistance on the U.S. Navy's small craft and the ships and craft of the U.S. Army, as well as asking the right questions of the editors; Gilbert Gyssels, for box after box of superb ship photography; William E. Haggett, chairman of the board, Bath Iron Works; RADM Francisco Herrera Balduz, Venezuelan Navy, naval attaché, Washington; Ken Hum, of NAVSEA; CDR Edward Hunter, USN; Kohji Ishiwata, editor of the world's leading magazine on contemporary warships, *Ships of the World;* John Jedrlinic, for advice on merchant ships; Vic Jeffery, Command Public Relations Officer, R.A.N., Rockingham, for supplying the superb photography taken by the R.A.N.'s staff photographers in Western Australia; Florian Jentsch, for many unusual and well-documented ship photos and for authoritative data on the conversion of the *Mudyug;* Tony Kendrick, of the Military Sealift Command's public affairs office; Pete Kilroy, of NAVSEA; Teddy Kilbourne, of Ingalls Shipbuilding; Luana R. King, of of Marinette Marine; Dane Konop, public affairs officer for the National Oceanic and Atmospheric Administration (NOAA), who quickly supplied all new photos of NOAA's fleet; Gerhard Koop, principal and frequent correspondent on the *Bundesmarine* and its many developments; Jürg Kürsener, for U.S. Navy photos; Michel Louagie, whose camera knows no peer; Bill Malacrida, of Swiftships, Inc., who supplied much of interest on small combatant developments; Michael Mally; Charles W. Mann, MonArk Boat Co.; Paul J. Martineau, of Ingalls Shipbuilding, who quickly obtained much useful photography; Roy T. McMillan, Todd Shipyards Corp.; Jim Meason, for help on Africa; Edward A. Michalski, director, Audiovisual Div., DDI, Office of the Assistant Secretary of Defense (Public Affairs); Michael A. Milam, of Tampa Shipyards, Inc.; ENS Peter W. Miller, USN, for data on Fiji; Ted Minter, faithful correspondent on the U.S. Navy; Dennis P. Moore, for useful photography from the Vancouver area; Jurrien S. Noot; Michael W. Oehler, Master, M/V *Falcon Leader;* Gunnar Olsen, for photos of ships of the Danish Navy and other Baltic fleets; Ronald E. Parkinson, for photography of USN ships; Norman Polmar, editor of *Ships and Aircraft of the U.S. Fleet* and *Guide to the Soviet Navy,* and director of the U.S. Naval Institute's Military Database, who supplied many photos and much useful guidance; John C. Reilly, head, Ship's Histories Branch, Naval Historical Center; Bram Risseeuw, correspondent on the Netherlands and South American navies, without whose constant help this book would have been considerably less comprehensive and accurate; A.J. Rizzo, of Anderson and Rizzo; Robert Rowe, for photos and data; F. Sadek, for many unusual photos from unusual places; Ray Saenz, Defense Systems Division, General Electric Co.; Tom Saponas, of Hewlitt-Packard; Walter Sartori; Dr. Robert L. Scheina, official historian, U.S. Coast Guard, for obtaining most of the new information in the U.S. Coast Guard section, as well as providing advice and guidance on South American navies; Antonio Scrimali; Adam Śmigielski; Steve Snowden, of Moss Point Marine,

Inc.; Ben Sullivan, recently retired Royal Marine, for very useful photos and information; Arne Ingar Tandberg, for data on ships built in Norway; Rev. Albert T. Tappman; Clive and Sue Taylor, portrait photographers of ships; Dipl.-Ing. Stefan Terzibaschitsch, West Germany's leading expert on the U.S. Navy, prolific photographer, and correspondent on baroque music; Linda Turgeon, of NAVSEA; Giuseppe Valentini; LT L.R. Tye, RNZN, Public Relations Officer, Royal New Zealand Navy; Christophe Van Oyen; Dr. Milan Vego, for help on the Serbo-Croatian language and the Yugoslav Navy; Dr. Michael Vlahos, for much useful data on the Indian Navy and developments in the Middle East; LT Thomas D. Walczyk, USN; LCDR William A. Weronko, USN; Mark Willis, of Maritime Photographic; CAPT Linton Wells, USN, for translations from the Japanese; CAPT Hugh D. Wisely, USN; Lillian Wong, of Singapore Shipbuilding and Engineering; Christopher C. Wright, editor *Warship International* and compiler of the authoritative annual chronicle of the U.S. Navy in the Naval Institute's *Naval Review;* Thomas-Durell Young, for information on the Royal New Zealand Navy; Jürgen Zeitelhofer, for many useful photos; and Andrej Zioko, for several very unusual photos. To all those others who helped as well, my deepest thanks—and apologies to any who may have been overlooked.

Others who have made significant contributions to the production of this edition include meticulous proofreader Joanna Taylor, Professor Kendall Lappin, retired professor of the U.S. Naval Academy, who expertly and gracefully translated M. Labayle Couhat's introductory essay, and the staff in Pennsylvania and Singapore of Syntax, Inc., who swiftly and accurately set the type and laid out the pages.

My gratitude to the senior manuscript editor at the Naval Institute Press, Carol Swartz, cannot possibly be expressed fully enough; Carol has cheerfully endured endless phone calls, hand-scrawled notes, reams of paper, piles of photography, and frantic requests for assistance, while at the same time expertly presiding over the assembly of this extremely complex publication. Her editing has been impeccable, her questions diplomatic, and her productivity truly amazing.

Many of my other colleagues at the U.S. Naval Institute deserve grateful mention for their assistance and encouragement in the preparation of this edition: Jim Barber, the Executive Director of the Naval Institute, and Tom Epley, the Director of the Naval Institute Press, urged me onward when it looked as though this project might not be able to be completed. Fred Rainbow, editor of the *Proceedings,* was generous with advice, photos, and information. Mark Gatlin, assistant editor of the *Proceedings,* not only provided an expert clipping service but also acted as proofreader and "sanity checker" for the entire text, a truly thankless task. Photo librarian Patty Maddocks and her associate Linda Cullen were ever generous with their time and energy in tracking down obscure illustration sources. Debbie Reid worked with Carol Swartz in the difficult task of compiling the thousands of entries in the index, while Moira M. Megargee kept track of the enormous production problems inherent in dealing with far over a thousand manuscript pages and well over 3,600 illustrations. I thank them all.

I would also like to express my appreciation to a number of naval professionals for urging me to continue this project when others were seeking its demise. These true gentlemen include RADM Bill Studeman, Rich Haver, CAPT Bill Cracknell, Dr. Bruce Watson, and CAPT Peter Swartz, among others best nameless. Appreciation is also due to my former employer, John Lehman, without whose incredible efforts there would have been no "600-ship Navy" to describe in these pages.

Finally, I must again express my heartfelt gratitude to my wife, Anne-marie, and my daughter, Alexandra, for their assistance, patience, and moral support through the ten months of evening and weekend labor that resulted in transposing *Flottes de Combat* into *Combat Fleets.*

*Combat Fleets* appears on a two-year cycle, but the work of the editors of the French and English versions is never-ending. Any user who has information to update or correct the information herein or photographs which could be used to illustrate the next edition is urged to contact the editors via the Naval Institute Press, Annapolis, Md. 21402. Dates and locations for all photographs are highly desirable, and all illustrations used will be credited to the contributors. *Your* assistance in making *Combat Fleets* and *Flottes de Combat* as accurate, thorough, and timely as possible is once again urgently solicited.

A.D. Baker III
1-1-88

# PREFACE TO THE FRENCH EDITION

As I announced in the preface to the 1986 edition of "Flottes de Combat," the present edition is appearing under the name of my successor, M. Bernard Prézelin, and for the last time, under my own. Obviously it is not without some regret that I sever my ties with a publication to which I have devoted myself so wholeheartedly since 1974; but I do so without bitterness, for one must know how to stop when the time comes and pass the torch to a younger person, one who I am certain will do his utmost to raise this publication to an ever-higher level of international renown; so I wish him "fair wind and a following sea."

In the course of my work on the seven editions for which I alone have been entirely responsible, I have had nothing but the best from all those who have assisted me to execute this difficult assignment:

- the officers of the Etat-Major de la Marine in Paris, in whose presence I have always encountered cordiality, good counsel and assistance;
- the officers of the French Navy's Press Information Service;
- the Defense Attachés and Naval Attachés accredited to Paris;
- the various foreign Admiralties who have always responded so amiably to my requests;
- Capitaine de Corvette L. Gassier and M. Robert Dumas, the creators of the marvelous sketches that are a specialty of *Flottes de Combat* appreciated by everyone.

I wish to thank also all the persons who across the years have sent me documents in abundance so very faithfully, and in particular Messrs. Aldo Fraccaroli, Armin Wetterhahn, Carlo Martinelli, Giorgio Arra, Gerhard Koop, Hannsjörg Kowark, Jean-Claude Bellonne, Louis Van Cant, Norman Polmar, Martin Prevel, W.J. Goss, Maurice Voss, Peter Voss, Pradignac et Léo, Siegfried Breyer, Stefan Terzibaschitsch, and Wilhelm Donko, for their friendly collaboration, without which *Flottes de Combat* would not have become what it is today, a valuable work of reference.

Of course I must mention also the authors of analogous works published abroad: Captain John Moore of *Jane's Fighting Ships* (who, like me, is retiring), Gerhard Albrecht of *Weyers Flotten Taschenbuch,* Giorgio Giorgerini of the Italian *Almanacco Navale,* and the editor of the famous journal *Ships of the World,* Koji Ishiwata, to whom I have always been indebted for the photographic illustrations used in chapters devoted to the Japanese Navy.

I must also mention here my high regard for Mr. A.D. Baker III, who bears the heavy responsibility, under the auspices of the U.S. Naval Institute in Annapolis, of preparing the American edition of *Flottes de Combat*—translating it, supplementing it when necessary, and adapting it to the needs of the American public and the U.S. Navy.

Finally I wish to thank my editor, Mme. Nicole Lattès, as charming as she is authoritative; first M. Courtin, then M. Piassale; and especially Mme. Renelle Setton, all of whom have helped me constantly, with the utmost amiability and efficiency, to solve the multifarious problems posed by the production of a work of this magnitude.

J.L.C.

# PANORAMA OF THE GREAT NAVIES AND OTHERS: THEIR SITUATION AND DEVELOPMENT

At the moment of passing the torch to my successor, I have deemed it useful to present in this preface a synthesis on the world's great navies. The text which follows is a résumé of the formal and informal lectures I have had occasion to deliver to naval and military audiences and in various military schools during my career. I want to stress the fact that the judgments expressed here and there are strictly my personal opinions.

## THE UNITED STATES NAVY

In the United States, the Navy is the key element in military policy, and therefore in the American government's foreign policy. The foundations of this policy are a strategic deterrent force consisting today of 36 strategic submarines (SSBN); an all-purpose force of 390 combat, amphibious, auxiliary, and logistic ships centered around 15 large aircraft carriers, of which 5 are nuclear-powered; and a force of 94 nuclear-powered attack submarines. The total displacement represented by these ships is about 4,200,000 Washington tons. This enormous fleet is manned by nearly 590,000 officers, petty officers, quartermasters, and enlisted men, not counting a Marine Corps contingent of a little under 200,000 men.

Since 1970, the budget of the Navy, including that of the Marine Corps, has been the largest of the three armed services. The operating budget for 1988 represents 33.6 percent of total military expenditures.

Reorganized after the defeat of Japan to facilitate the projection of American airborne troops onto the Eurasian continent, American naval policy had been modified under President Carter, who, believing there would be no major conflict anywhere but in Europe, had accepted a decline in naval operational capabilities. For President Reagan and his administration, the United States must be ready to participate not only in a conflict limited to Europe, but also in a major war anywhere in the world. Such enlargement of the areas of possible conflict considerably increases the responsibilities of the Navy. This is why a plan was set up to equip the Navy, between now and the year 2000, with a fleet of 600 ships of all types. This fleet would then comprise, in operational configuration, an adequate number of strategic submarines (SSBN); 15 carrier groups (CVBG), each consisting of one carrier supported by two large missile cruisers; four surface-ship groups (BBSAG), each centered on a battleship; an amphibious force capable of transporting the assault echelons of one and a half "Marine Expeditionary Forces"; seven escort groups for military convoys; the ten escort groups for provisioning at sea.

By the end of the century, this plan calls for a combat fleet strength of 100 nuclear-powered attack submarines (SSN), 15 large nuclear-powered or conventional aircraft carriers, four modernized battleships, 137 cruisers and destroyers, and 101 frigates. Since 1981, five-year naval plans have been worked out on the basis of these numbers, with provision for revision each year.

A word about the organization of Defense and of the Navy.

What strikes the interested observer is the amount of overlap existing between the political power and the military command, in decision making as well as in the sharing of intelligence information.

Equally striking is an extremely stripped-down chain of command, leaving the decision makers with reduced staffs and supplied with synthesized intelligence reports by groups outside the hierarchy and totally isolated from problems of management and administration.

At the top, the President of the United States, the head of the executive branch of the government, is also commander-in-chief of the armed forces in time of peace as well as in time of war. He does not delegate to anyone the powers and responsibilities he holds. The decisions he makes regarding the employment of forces and weapons are not subject to appeal.

The prerogatives of Congress are no less broad. It alone has the power to declare war and to provide for the common defense. It levies and supports troops and authorizes expenditures. If emergencies arise, they do not preclude consultation. For instance, a 1973 law obliges the President to report to the Congress within 48 hours any military action involving American armed forces, to indicate the reasons therefor and the duration thereof. Barring a direct attack on the United States, the armed forces are to be withdrawn from the conflict within 60 days if Congress has not declared war.

In order to determine what his military policy will be, the President consults the National Security Council. The latter is composed of four members: the President, the Vice President, the Secretary of State (Minister of Foreign Affairs), and the Secretary of Defense; this body, before any decision is made, has working documents prepared by ad hoc working groups.

The Joint Chiefs of Staff (JCS), which comprises the chiefs of staff of the Navy, the Army, the Air Force, and the Marine Corps under the chairmanship of the Chairman of the Joint Chiefs, has a dual function: an advisory role and the planning of operations. It advises the President, the Secretary of Defense, and the National Security Council. As a general staff, it is an intermediate echelon between the Secretary of Defense on the one hand and the major operational commands on the other. The Secretary of Defense exercises his authority over the armed forces via two entirely distinct chains of command: an operational chain of command and an organic, administrative chain of command. The former, the only one that concerns us here, functions through the JCS; seven major interservice commands (Unified Commands): the Atlantic Command (LANTCOM), the Pacific Command (PACCOM), the Southern Command (SOUTHCOM), the European Command (EUCOM), the Central Command (CENTCOM), the U.S. Space Command (SPACECOM), and the Transport Command (TRANSCOM); one specialized command, that is, specific to a single service, the Strategic Air Command (SAC); and finally, one command charged with supplying reinforcements to the five interservice commands, the Readiness Command (READCOM). The fleets, reduced to four after World War II, are divided between the Pacific and Atlantic Commands.

The U.S. Navy includes an oceanic strategic force, which is a part of the American "deterrent," and general-purpose forces. The oceanic strategic component consists of 36 SSBNs: 16 *Lafayette* class each carrying 16 Poseidon missiles, 12 *Lafayette* class carrying 16 Trident-1 C4 missiles, and 8 *Ohio* class carrying 24 Trident-1 C4. The Poseidon is a two-stage, solid-propellant ballistic missile that can deliver at a range of 2,500 nautical miles (4,625 km) a military payload of fourteen 50-kiloton nuclear warheads with independent trajectories (MIRV), or at a range of 3,900 nautical miles (6,475 km), ten nose-cones of this type. As for the Trident-I C4, it is a three-stage solid-propellant missile whose range is 4,350 nautical miles (8,050 km). Its payload consists of eight 100-kiloton warheads. This SSBN force represents a theoretical strike capacity of 640 submarine-launched ballistic missiles, all armed with multiple warheads with independent trajectories. Since our last edition, two *Ohio*-class boats, *Alaska* and *Nevada,* have been commissioned; but in order to remain within the limits set by Soviet-American agreements on strategic arms limitation, three SSBNs armed with Poseidon have been disarmed. *Nevada* is the last *Ohio*-class boat to carry the Trident-1 C4; *Tennessee,* which will join the fleet in 1989, will be the first to be armed with the Trident-II D5, capable of reaching targets 11,000 kilometers away within a circle of probable error 120 meters in diameter! Five Trident-II SSBNs are in the yard, ordered or budgeted for, and five others are programmed for 1988–1992; it appears that this program will be continued on beyond the 20 units originally projected; furthermore, the first eight SSBNs of this class will be rearmed with Trident-II early in the 1990s. The *Ohio* class, which displaces 18,750 tons submerged, is considered a complete success, the results obtained having often surpassed predictions and specifications.

The big aircraft carrier remains and will remain for a long time the keystone of the American fleet and the symbol of its capacity to project its power more than 500 km inland from the ocean, anywhere in the world; for it is a well-known fact that most of the cities and industries on our planet are located within a coastal strip 500 kilometers in width. There are at present 15 aircraft carriers in commission, of which 5 are nuclear-powered; 2 others, also nuclear, are under construction, to be commissioned in late 1989 and late 1991, and budgeting approved for 1988–1992 envisions the ordering of the sixth and seventh vessels of this type. It is noteworthy that *Midway,* the oldest aircraft carrier in the U.S. Navy, has undergone a remodeling that will ostensibly enable her to last until the end of the century, when she will be more than 50 years old. One of the 15 aircraft carriers in commission is not operational, for it is undergoing extensive remodeling under SLEP (Service Life Extension Program), which will prolong its life by 15 to 20 years. The total number of aircraft embarked on all these ships is more than a thousand.

The U.S. Navy possesses 94 nuclear-powered attack submarines (SSN), 37 of the *Los Angeles* class, 37 of the *Sturgeon* class, and 20 older or experimental; 29 more *Los Angeles* class are in the yard, ordered, budgeted, or programmed. These boats, which displace 6,000 tons submerged and have a speed of over 30 knots, are probably the best nuclear attack submarines in the world. True, they are not as fast as the Soviet Alfa class and cannot go as deep, but they are quieter, and their underwater detection gear certainly performs more efficiently. In addition to torpedoes, which are getting better and better, the *Los Angeles* class are beginning to employ the Tomahawk missile in its two versions, anti-land-target and antiship. On older submarines, it is fired from the torpedo tubes. Those now being commissioned are fitted with vertical launching tubes installed in their forward framing, outside the pressure hull, between the latter and the sonar sphere. *Sturgeon*-class SSNs are also armed with the Tomahawk.

With the antiship version of this missile, American SSNs have acquired the capability of firing from beyond the range of Soviet surface ships' ASW weapons. To replace Subroc, which is beginning to age and may be losing its reliability, the U.S. Navy is developing a new weapon, the ASW SOW (Antisubmarine Warfare Stand Off Weapon), which it plans to install on a new class of SSN whose prototype will bear the name *Seawolf.* This will be a very large submarine (9,150 tons submerged), very deep, very fast, and very quiet, that will be able to carry up to 40 weapons (torpedoes, Tomahawk, Sub Harpoon, SOW, etc.); it will be equipped with an integrated combat system and with detection gear considerably improved over that of *Los Angeles.* Five SSNs of this class, including the prototype, are programmed for 1988–1992.

*Wisconsin,* the fourth and last battleship of the *Iowa* class to be reactivated, will join the fleet late in 1988; these very heavily armored old ships, thanks to the

Tomahawk cruise missiles they carry, are capable of bringing nuclear fire to bear on a potential enemy's heartland or sinking his ships.

The U.S. Navy has 9 nuclear and 27 conventional cruisers, 9 of which are of the recent *Ticonderoga* class of 9,500 tons. Eighteen more cruisers of this class are in the yard, ordered, or budgeted. These ships, equipped with the AEGIS system, the SM-2 MR surface-to-air missile, and Harpoon (and from CG 52 onward, with Tomahawk) have no equivalent anywhere in the world; they are zonal air-defense ships whose principal mission is the protection of aircraft carriers against aerial attack, antiship missiles, and submarines.

The U.S. Navy has available 69 destroyers, of which 37 are area defense surface-to-air missile-firing. To replace the oldest of these ships, construction of 29 units of the 8,500-ton *Arleigh Burke* class is envisioned, and 3 have already been ordered; they will have AEGIS, the SM-2 MR, Tomahawk, and the new vertically launched version of the ASROC ASW missile. This destroyer class is being rather severely criticized, notably in Congress; it is charged with being expensive and too much like the *Ticonderoga* class with respect to weapons and equipment; so it is possible that the full program may not come to fruition. In the category of large destroyers designed primarily for ASW, the 31 recent *Spruance* class are already being modernized with Tomahawk, the very-low-frequency passive towed array sonar SQR-19, etc. This will pose no problem, since there is plenty of room aboard these ships, the engineers and command personnel having had the foresight, when the project was being delineated, to anticipate their remodeling in mid-life. It is noteworthy that these splendid destroyers are the immediate ancestors of the *Ticonderoga*-class cruisers: same hull, same propulsion equipment, but different armament.

There are at present 115 frigates in service. The most numerous and most recent series is the FFG 7 class, of which there are 50. This is the largest series of frigates built since the Second World War. It is an excellent escort ship—sturdy, fast, and well-armed. In the rather near future, some thought will have to be given to replacing the oldest frigates of the *McCloy, Garcia,* and *Brooke* classes, already more than 20 years old. The author of these lines—who may be mistaken—thinks the Americans are eventually going to have to adopt for these ships of the future the MEKO concept originated by the German firm of Blohm + Voss. This concept offers the possibility, starting from a standard hull and a standard power train, of numerous combinations of weapons and systems, thanks to interchangeable modules of normalized and standardized dimensions and articulations. This would make it possible to produce, from the same design of 4,000 to 5,000 tons, two ships with different missions, one for ASW and the other for antiaircraft duty; this would resolve the problem posed by the excessive cost of the *Arleigh Burke.*

After years of neglect, the U.S. Navy is again taking an interest in ships designed specifically for mine warfare. The mooring of mines in the Persian Gulf and the necessity of calling on foreigners to get rid of them was enough to bring the Navy face to face with reality in this regard. Until that time, anti-mine warfare had been of little concern to the naval command, which had counted on using RH-53D Sea Stallion and MH-53E Sea Dragon helicopters for minesweeping.

In its effort to remedy its backwardness in this field, the Navy has been wise enough to adopt some well-tested materiel. For instance, the American firm Raytheon has associated itself with the French company Thomson/CSF in producing a towed mine-hunting sonar christened AMSS (Advanced Minehunting Sonar System) and designated AN/SQQ-32. This system will be used by two types of anti-mine ships now being built: an oceangoing sweeper-hunter of American design and a minehunter derived from the Italian *Lerici,* the plans for an air-cushion minehunter having been abandoned.

The American amphibious fleet includes a large number of ships: LHA helicopter attack carriers, LPH helicopter carriers, LSD landing craft transports, LPD landing craft and personnel transports, LST and assorted vehicles, all of which enable the Navy to conduct, with the Marine Corps, intervention operations over long distances—several thousand kilometers—operations that may be of tremendous scope and may involve thousands of men. This is one of the great, original innovations of the U.S. Navy. To replace the oldest of its ships, it has set up a vast program, notably envisaging the construction of at least ten *Wasp*-class large helicopter assault ships and 12 more *Whidbey Island*- and LSD 49-class LSDs. The *Wasp* is a cross between the LHA and the LPD; displacing, like the former, more than 40,000 tons and having a speed of 24 knots, it is fitted with a *wet well,* a flight deck, and a starboard island, and it can also carry an increased number of Marines; its hospital facilities are considerable; its hangar deck can accommodate up to 42 helicopters, but its air group can also consist of the AV-8B Harrier attack plane, which the Marine Corps has adopted. To replace most of its LCU landing barges, the Navy plans to build 90 LCAC surface-effect amphibious vehicles; thanks to its speed of 54 knots versus the 10 knots of the present LCU, the LCAC is capable of achieving surprise in an intervention operation by considerably reducing transit time between the mother ship and the landing beaches.

All these amphibious ships are designed to transport and then put ashore soldiers of the Marine Corps, often called the fourth armed force of the United States. Its manpower potential amounts to nearly 200,000 men, and it has at its disposal over 1,100 aircraft; Marine Corps combat aircraft are capable of operating from aircraft carriers.

The U.S. Navy still possesses throughout the world a number of main bases, operating bases, and other facilities that, even without counting those of its allies, provide it with very effective assistance in fleet deployments overseas. It also has a number of logistic and auxiliary ships that give it a strategic mobility of tremendous importance. Some of these ships belong directly to the Navy, others to the Military Sealift Command, a body that belongs to the Navy but is distinct from it. MSC administers some 100 ships of all categories, which are manned by civilian personnel.

A number of these ships, whether they belong to the Navy or to the MSC, are of late World War II vintage and urgently need to be replaced. To this end, a program calling for the construction of 4 *Supply*-class large oiler-storeships for the Navy and 18 *Kaiser*-class large oilers for the MSC has been set up, to be completed in the next decade.

Forming a part of the naval logistic support fleet are the ships placed at the disposal of the "Afloat Prepositioning Force," which the U.S.A. has set up to enable its forces to intervene quickly wherever such intervention might prove to be necessary. In order to reduce delays, the material, spare parts, and munitions that such a force might require are permanently embarked aboard ships belonging to or chartered by the Navy or MSC. Several ships of this "Afloat Prepositioning Force" are deployed overseas in the vicinity of sensitive areas, notably at Diego Garcia atoll in the Indian Ocean, where the Americans have built a large operating base.

Naval aviation comprises some 5,000 aircraft on line and in reserve. The planes and helicopters of the Marine Corps are included in this total. Shipborne aviation, as reported above in discussing aircraft carriers, is well over 1,000 aircraft strong, including helicopters. The material employed is in all respects remarkable and among the finest in performance: F-14 Tomcat all-weather interceptors, F/A-18 Hornet and A-6E Intruder attack planes, EA-6B Prowler offensive and E-2C Hawkeye defensive electronic-warfare planes, and S-3A Viking ASW planes, for example. Several hundred Tomcats and Hornets are in service, under construction, and on order, while construction of Prowlers and Hawkeyes is proceeding at a steady pace, and their performance parameters are being steadily improved. It is obvious that these programs have been assigned a very high priority. The helicopter plays a considerable role in the U.S. Navy. It is utilized in ASW, minesweeping, transport, liaison, search and rescue, ground attack, etc. The most recent all-purpose helicopter is the Seahawk SH-60B, embarkable on cruisers, destroyers, and frigates; more than 200 are planned. As for maritime patrol aviation, the total is about 400 P-3Bs and P-3C Orions, the latter considered one of the best patrol planes in the world.

In the field of weapons and equipment, the Navy's effort is being brought to bear essentially on four great programs: the cruise missile Tomahawk, air defense at sea with the AEGIS system, VLF underwater detection, and space and communications. The Tomahawk system is now operational aboard several types of ships: battleships, cruisers, destroyers, and submarines; and by 1995 the U.S. Navy will have available 190 launching platforms armed with this missile, 106 of them on nuclear attack submarines and 84 on surface units. Fired massively in successive or simultaneous salvos, the Tomahawk, combined with other means, is an extremely formidable weapon because it can complicate, even saturate, the opposing defense. It is all the more dangerous because one cannot be sure whether it is being fired from a submarine or a surface ship, and because the targets selected in the course of a single operation may include land targets as well as ships. This is no doubt what the Americans have attempted to achieve by assigning high priority to the Tomahawk program, for they think it will take the Soviets a long time to come up with an effective response to this multiform, imprecise threat.

Faced with the threat of Soviet Backfire and other Blackjack bombers, the Navy has developed and continues to perfect the AEGIS air-defense system. Designed to be installed aboard the 27 *Ticonderoga*-class cruisers and 29 *Burke*-class destroyers, this system is linked with the latest version of the Standard surface-to-air missile, the SM-2 MR, which can hit an aircraft 120 kilometers away. AEGIS is in essence an integrated system of zonal air defense, to which has been added fire control and controlled response to other threats, surface and submarine. It ensures automatic detection, tracking, firing decision, and weapon operation. The main element of the system is a radar consisting of four hexagonal antennas that cover the entire horizon. This radar can identify 256 targets and can track 18 at a time. The installation aboard the *Ticonderoga* class, from CG 52 on, of 122 vertical launching cells for SM-2 MR, Tomahawk, and ASROC considerably strengthens the effectiveness of AEGIS in all aspects of combat, for it makes it possible to engage several highly varied targets at a time in rapid sequence.

The U.S. Navy's third major program in the field of equipment has to do with underwater detection at very low acoustic frequencies. In this field it has taken and still maintains a tremendous lead over other navies, although the latter are trying hard to catch up. A large number of surface units are now equipped with SQR-18-series sonar: this consists of a towed antenna called TASS, which carries hydrophones guarding the VLF range; signals received are analyzed and matched with information already gathered on the sound signatures of foreign ships, such intelligence being systematically researched. Over the next few years the SQR-18 is to be gradually replaced by the more elaborate SQR-19; this will equip 150 ships. There exists also a version of TASS designed for SSBNs and SSNs; it is integrated with the multipurpose sonar of these submarines. In order to exploit TASS to the full and to prevent the collection of information on its own noises, the carrier of this system must itself be as quiet as possible. The U.S. Navy has seized the initiative in this field by applying itself systematically to the reduction of noise from all sources aboard its surface ships and submarines (soundproofing the suspension of main and auxiliary engines, blowing air along the hull and into the propellers, large propeller blades turning slowly, the latter to be replaced on the most recent submarines by pump-propellers ["pump jet"] to reduce cavitation sounds, etc.).

Another version of this type of underwater detection, designed for surveillance of large zones in oceanic areas, is now operational. Called SURTASS, it complements the SOSUS fixed listening system, whose performance parameters are also being improved. SOSUS consists of hydrophones suspended under water or anchored on the bottom and connected by cable to stations ashore, which process and exploit the signals received. As for SURTASS, it is deployed from vessels called T-AGOS, which tow slowly astern a long antenna crammed with hydrophones; the data collected is transmitted immediately via satellite to a processing center ashore. Ten T-AGOS are in service, of a total 19 on order; they are attached to the Military Sealift Command and are manned by civilian personnel.

The U.S. Navy's fourth major program involves space and communications. It utilizes surveillance, navigational-aid and telecommunications satellites, which are probably administered by the U.S. Space Command, one of the major interservice commands reporting to the Secretary of Defense. For surveillance of the oceans, it employs EORSAT satellites capable of locating a ship by its electromagnetic emissions and RORSATs, which make it possible to locate targets by radar and to identify them by the signature of their emissions as collected by the EORSAT. For navigational aid, since 1974 it has been using the TRANSIT system, which is to be replaced by NAVSTAR. This system with its worldwide coverage will consist of 18 satellites in circular, 12-hour orbits; its accuracy will be on the order of 15 meters.

In order to increase the capacity of its $C^3$ strategic system (command, control, communications) to survive a massive, unexpected nuclear strike, as well as all attempts to strike obliquely at the U.S. via other forms of aggression (neutralization by electromagnetic impulse of an exoatmospheric nuclear explosion [IEM], terrorism, action by Spetznaz-type commandos, etc. . . .), the Reagan administration has been pursuing a vast program of modernization and hardening ever since it took office. This program, which directly concerns the Navy and its SSBNs, includes notably improved protection of the command centers of the NCA (National Command Authority) against nuclear attack. This is why the strategic telegraphic network SACDIN, linking NCA to different forces and communications stations, is in the process of being reinforced by GWEN (Ground Wave Emergency Network); this will ultimately include some 300 LF stations hardened against IEM, and a portion of it will evidently provide communication with submerged SSBNs within radar range. In addition to these national means, the Navy has available, for communication with its SSBNs, eight fixed VLF stations and (since 1974) 18 EC-130Q TACAMO airplanes. Upon receiving messages on LF, HF, UHF, and VLF from shore stations or from satellites, these aircraft retransmit them on VLF to SSBNs on patrol. Their mission is strictly limited to retransmitting engagement orders to these submarines and is in no case to replace normal means of communication when the submarines are neutralized, since the invulnerability of aircraft in flight is dependent on their radio discretion. The present fleet of TACAMO planes makes it possible to keep two planes constantly in the air and two others on the runway ready to take off. Thanks to these two planes' being kept constantly in the air, the TACAMO system is considered the U.S. Navy's means of communication having the greatest chance of survival in the event of a surprise nuclear attack. It is therefore to be modernized in the near future by replacement of the EC-130Q with another aircraft, the E-6A Hermes, of which some fifteen will probably be ordered. This plane will have new equipment hardened against IEM and protected against jamming; it will be capable of receiving messages originating from DSCS III and from the MILSTAR system.

In addition to the modernized TACAMO system, the U.S. Navy envisages utilizing other forms of aeromobile transmission, such as a VLF/LF antenna deployed by aerostat, while studies are in progress to develop a satellite carrying a blue-green laser, making it possible to communicate with submerged submarines; this is the SLC project (Submarine Laser Communication). It seems, however, that this system is limited by meteorological conditions, by its inability to penetrate sea water beyond a hundred meters or so in depth, and by the necessity of knowing a submarine's approximate orientation with respect to the direction of the laser beam.

The TACAMO system is complemented by an ELF transmission network from two stations, one at Clam Lake, Wisconsin, the other at K.I. Sawyer AFB in Michigan; the former covers the Atlantic, the latter the Pacific. These stations are not protected, but they might, in the long run, become a part of an ELF network with stations buried far underground, and therefore quasi-invulnerable. This configuration, originally conceived as the *Sanguine* project, was abandoned by the Carter administration.

Two systems of telecommunication via satellite are used by the Navy: FLEETSATCOM and DSCS II (Defense Satellite Communications System). The former, which functions on UHF and utilizes four geostationary satellites, covers only a part of the globe; it is used for communication with surface ships and submarines, but it is not secure nor well protected against jamming. The DSCS system, on the other hand, is well protected; it operates in the SHF range.

DSCS II is to be replaced progressively by DSCS III 6, consisting of geostationary satellites, four activated and two in reserve. Fourteen satellites have been ordered; their service life is to be seven years, and they are to be shielded strongly against jamming and the effects of nuclear weapons. The FLEETSATCOM system is to be replaced, starting in 1990, by the interservice system MILSTAR (Military Strategic Tactical Relay); operating in the EHF range and very well shielded against IEM, it will complement DSCS III for a time and will finally replace it, when DSCS III reaches the end of its service life. Consisting of five geostationary satellites, three of them activated, and of three satellites in polar orbit, MILSTAR will cover the planet almost completely.

Roughly speaking, the American fleet is distributed half in the Pacific theater and half in the Atlantic. At the operational level, the Pacific fleet is under CINCPACFLEET, who has his headquarters at Pearl Harbor and who is himself subordinate to the Pacific Command, the largest of the American interservice commands, since it extends over the whole Pacific, the Bering Sea, and the Indian Ocean (excepting the Red Sea and the Persian Gulf, which are under CENTCOM). The Pacific fleet is subdivided in two large groupings:

### The 7th Fleet

Its normal theater of operations is the Western Pacific, but it also carries out deployments in the Indian Ocean; even in peacetime, with its 50 ships including 2 aircraft carriers, it is the most powerful continuously operational fleet in the world.

### The 3rd Fleet

Stationed on the West Coast of the United States and in the Hawaiian Islands, it plays the role of a reserve for the 7th Fleet, and is charged with operational instruction of units. It includes five aircraft carriers and two battleships, with their support.

The Atlantic theater is likewise under an admiral who wears two hats, that of area commander (CINCLANT) and that of commander of allied naval forces (SACLANT) within NATO.

In the Atlantic theater the fleet is likewise roughly divided between two big commands:

### The 6th Fleet

Its normal theater of operations is the Mediterranean. It is under the European Command via the admiral commanding American naval forces in Europe (CINCUSNAVEUR), who is at the same time, within the NATO organization, Supreme Allied Commander Europe (SACEUR).

This 6th Fleet consists in normal times of some 20 combat ships, including one or two aircraft carriers, five SSNs, and a dozen amphibious ships with a "Marine Expeditionary Unit" aboard, some 3,000 men. All are supported logistically by about ten large supply ships, which are totally integrated into the fleet. Like the 7th Fleet, the 6th Fleet is completely operational at all times.

### The 2nd Fleet

It is based on the East Coast and serves as a reserve for the 6th Fleet. This 2nd Fleet also constitutes the naval striking force of the interservice Atlantic Command (LANTCOM).

The most remarkable thing about the personnel of the U.S. Navy is that, while they are basically volunteers insofar as enlisted men and petty officers are concerned, 50 percent of the officer corps are reservists, serving in the Navy for periods of varying duration. Another noteworthy peculiarity is that more than 70 percent of the officers, whatever their origin, leave the Navy after ten years of service, so that the Navy loses more than 13 percent of its officers every year. This virtual exodus to civilian life is a particularly sore point when it comes to naval aviators and officers with nuclear qualification.

Officers are classified into four groups: one group destined for command, *Unrestricted Line;* a group of specialized officers, *Restricted Line,* which includes intelligence officers, code and cipher specialists, naval architects, aviation engineers, etc.; a category of noncombatant officers, the *Staff Corps* (supply officers, doctors, dentists, pharmacists, judges, etc.); and a group of technicians, *Warrant Officers,* corresponding to the technical officers, specialized officers, and crew officers of the French Navy.

The two traits most characteristic of American officers are youth and a lack of specialization. A 7,000-ton cruiser may be commanded by a captain in his mid-40s, and an ensign aboard such a ship may go from the billet of ASW officer to that of chief propulsion engineer or detection officer by the time he is made a lieutenant. Such a system is nevertheless efficient, thanks to constant training and to a different concept of the role of the commanding officer. The American concept is that of a rigorous vertical hierarchy that excludes any advisory function on the part of officers; so it suffices that they do a good job of carrying out orders. On the other hand, the commanding officer must have a thorough knowledge of his ship and must know how to handle her in combat.

The recruitment of personnel, easy during hard times, is susceptible of being slowed down by economic recovery. In order to cope with this, therefore, the Navy has worked out a whole series of incentives, notably in the area of pay and benefits.

In general, U.S. Navy personnel display deep patriotic feelings and a highly developed professionalism, based on their understanding and willing acceptance of necessary discipline. Officers of high rank are characterized by a broad competence in all fields, a competence acquired by frequent training periods in schools and even university, and by extensive experience in command at sea.

Like all navies, the U.S. Navy has its strengths, but it also has some weaknesses. Among the former must be cited: *Ohio*-class SSBNs and *Los Angeles*-class SSNs; 15 big aircraft carriers, 5 of them nuclear, symbolic of the projection of American armed forces' power from the sea; 230 other surface warships, displacing 2,000 tons or more; the amphibious fleet; the logistic and auxiliary fleet, which gives the fighting forces an unequaled strategic flexibility; the over 400 naval long-range patrol planes; a technical and technological advantage in almost every field: Tomahawk cruise missiles, VLF underwater detection, space communications, etc.; highly qualified career personnel among petty officers and crew, and "super-competent" cadres.

As for weaknesses—and of course everything is relative in this area—one must mention: a divided fleet, half in the Atlantic and half in the Pacific; an officer corps more than 50 percent reservists on active duty, plus the fact that after ten years of service, 70 percent of officers leave the Navy; the lack of a real anti-mine force, for some time to come; and a kind of superiority complex at the top of the hierarchy that could be the cause of some surprises in case of conflict, as it was for the British versus the Argentines in the Falkland Islands affair.

## THE SOVIET NAVY

The continental land-mass occupied by the U.S.S.R. borders on two oceans, the Arctic and the Pacific, with very harsh climatic conditions, and on two almost landlocked seas, the Baltic and the Black Sea, which are linked with the open sea only by restricted passages, the Belts and the Turkish straits, controlled by foreign powers. Despite this very unfavorable geostrategic situation, there has always been a Russian Navy since the time of Peter the Great—a Soviet Navy since the 1917 revolution.

With its tonnage of over 3,500,000 tons and its 1,700-plus combat vessels, of which over 350 are submarines, the Soviet Navy constitutes a formidable force close on the heels of the U.S. Navy; but within the armed forces of the U.S.S.R. it ranks only fifth in importance, after the land army, the strategic missile forces, the territorial defense forces, and the air forces. The fact is that the concept of "naval strategy," in the broad sense given to that expression in the West, does not exist in U.S.S.R. military doctrine. In this doctrine, which is considered to be integral, a particularized strategy for each armed force is out of place, and the Navy is looked upon as just one means among others contributing to the U.S.S.R.'s global strategy, whose ultimate goal still remains the triumph of communist ideology.

Like every important institution in the U.S.S.R., the Navy has at its head a collective directorate, and its commander-in-chief must have all his decisions approved by the Military Defense Council under the Minister of Defense.

The Military Council of the Navy includes, under the chairmanship of the commander-in-chief, the latter's deputy, the highest-ranking staff officer, and finally the individuals responsible for the various directorates charged with new construction, logistics, naval aviation, personnel, and schools, etc. Alongside the Navy's commander-in-chief, but not subject to the latter's authority, is the chief of the Navy's political directorate, who exerts his influence within the staffs, ships, and units of the Navy via the intermediation of political officers, who are present everywhere, even aboard the smallest vessels.

The Soviet Navy is articulated into four fleets, one attached to each of its maritime theaters: Arctic, Baltic, Black Sea, and Pacific fleets. Each fleet includes naval forces and naval air forces, as well as the shore installations located within its zone of operations; so a fleet constitutes at the same time an operational command and a territorial command. As in the uppermost echelons of Defense, each fleet commander is assisted by a military council, a general staff, and of course by a high-ranking political officer who receives his directives from the chief of the political directorate of Defense via that of the Navy. Each fleet commander has four or five high-ranking subordinates in charge of submarines, surface forces, naval aviation, logistics, and coastal defense.

Soviet doctrine in command matters is, therefore, to maintain a highly centralized organization. Very specific directives are given to each subordinate echelon, and it appears that not very much is left to subordinates' initiative.

The submarine force is enormous and constitutes more than half the tonnage of the fleet; but impressive as it may appear, its size should be somewhat discounted because it includes a large number of old conventional submarines of classes now totally out of date, which would be easy prey for modern ASW equipment and weapons. Even among its nuclear submarines, the November, Echo, and Echo II classes, as well as the Yankee-class strategic missile-launchers, cannot be considered front-line combat vessels. Most of these are gradually being withdrawn from service, assigned to training, or, as in the case of the Yankee, progressively deactivated as new SSBNs are commissioned, in order to comply with the 1972 Soviet-American agreements on the limitation of strategic arms.

Since our 1986 edition, three Delta IV-class SSBNs have joined the fleet, while two others are under construction to go into service about 1990; a fifth gigantic Typhoon (25,000 tons submerged) is in the process of completion. In order to comply with the 1972 agreements, the Soviets have had to disarm 5 Yankees, and another was lost in the Atlantic. Taking into account these additions and withdrawals, the number of SSBNs in service, 60, and the number of missiles embarked on them, 900, are within the limits agreed upon; on the other hand, the number of SLBM with "MIRVed" warheads has gone from 304 to 352, resulting in a marked increase in the capabilities of the naval component of the Soviet strategic deterrence forces.

Of these various missiles, only the SS-N-17 (experimental) and the SS-N-20 are solid-fueled, but it is said that a new solid-propellant missile is in the experimental stage. All other SLBMs, including the very recent SS-N-23, are propelled by liquid fuel, which, as the accident aboard one Yankee has demonstrated, may be a source of vulnerability for the carrying submarine. In order to provide shelter for their Typhoon and Delta submarines, the Soviets are fitting out some shelter-pens dug out of solid rock on the Kola Peninsula. It has been determined that Soviet SSBN ratio of time at sea vs. time at base is far inferior to that of their Western counterparts. Various explanations for this have been given: unreliability of materiel, maintenance problems, and lack of qualified personnel. The decision to construct shielded, hardened submarine bases, dug out of solid rock on the Kola Peninsula, will enable the U.S.S.R. to preserve the overall invulnerability of its strategic submarine force by putting it out of reach of a nuclear or sub-nuclear strike, whether its SSBNs are at sea or at base, leaving them available at any moment for massive deployment, even though at reduced strength and for a limited time, within their coastal firing zone, since the great range of their new missiles no longer obliges them to approach enemy coasts in order to fire. Soviet engineers are constantly refining the accuracy of these ballistic missiles, from model to model. This is why the SS-N-20, they say, is probably capable of dropping from a range of 8,300 km into a circle less than 600 meters in diameter; and the new solid-propellant missile being tested would be even more accurate (a 150-meter circle).

The nuclear attack submarine force totals nearly 130 units, but as noted above, the November, Echo, and Echo II classes, 41 units, cannot be considered first-line submarines. Soviet SSNs, although they are all currently equipped to fire aerodynamic missiles, have for the sake of convenience been classified by NATO into two distinct groups: those equipped with missiles fired from tubes outside the pressure hull (SSGN) and those that launch from their torpedo tubes (SSN).

Since our last edition, two Oscar-class SSGNs have been added to the two that were in service in 1986, and several more are under construction; these submarines, displacing 11,500 tons surfaced, carry 24 aerodynamic SS-N-19 missiles capable of hitting a surface target more than 500 kilometers away by utilizing a relay (aircraft or satellite) to verify the target's location. The most recent serially built SSNs are of the Victor III class. These are very sturdy boats comparable to the first generation of American nuclear attack submarines and therefore relatively noisy; but on the big Akula- and Sierra-class SSNs that are now beginning to join the fleet, Soviet engineers have made a great effort to make them as quiet as possible vis-à-vis passive sonar; their construction program could therefore turn out to be more time consuming and less productive in numbers than that of the Victor III, perhaps explaining why construction of the Victor III-class submarines has been resumed (it was believed to have been discontinued after the 20th unit went into active service). Two Akula and two Sierra are now in service, and several more are to be built, it is believed, to replace the oldest SSNs of the Victor I, Victor II, and November classes. Like the Victor III, these new submarines are armed with the recent SS-N-21 missile, which resembles the U.S. Navy's Tomahawk but could be used only against land targets; it would not be surprising, however, if it gives rise sooner or later to an anti-ship missile similar to the TASM-C version of Tomahawk.

To conclude this all-too-rapid survey of the Soviet submarine force, let us note that although the U.S. Navy has definitively renounced conventional submarines, its rival continues to show an interest in them. The Kilo class, with diesel-electric drive, now coming into service at a steady pace, concedes nothing to the best of Western models. Fourteen are already in service in the Soviet fleet; others, in an export version, have been acquired or ordered by India (5 units), Poland (4), Romania (1 or 2), and Algeria (2); other countries also are interested in this type of submarine. It is noteworthy that the Soviets also seem to be interested in submarines of 2,000 to 3,000 tons (the Uniform and Beluga projects), realizing that by the end of the century, ASW will have to resort to active detection against ever-quieter submarines, and that from that time on, a weak silhouette will again become an important trump card for future submarines.

In the field of surface ships, the highest of priorities is being given to construction, at the Nikolayev shipyards on the Black Sea, of the nuclear aircraft carrier *Leonid Brezhnev* and the second ship of this class, which was laid down in the same yard immediately after the former was launched. From what one can find out today about these ships' future characteristics, it appears that the primary mission of these 60,000- to 65,000-ton ships will be air defense of forces at sea, but that a certain capability of power-projection will not be excluded. It seems *Leonid Brezhnev* will have no catapults but will, like the British *Invincible* class, be equipped at the forward end of its axial runway with a ski jump to facilitate the takeoff of light planes. *Brezhnev*'s sister ship may, on the contrary, be equipped with catapults and arresting gear, the Soviets having had the time, between now and the first ship's commissioning, to master this technique and to build some true carrier aircraft. However this may be, with these two aircraft carriers and the support of four *Kirov*-class missile cruisers, the Soviet Navy will be able to deploy to sensitive zones nuclear "task groups" capable of remaining in place for many weeks, as the Americans did a few years ago in the Arabian Sea when the Iranians took their people hostage.

As a result of the priority given to constructing these two aircraft carriers, and also because of the complexity of new surface ships, there has been evident for some time a perceptible slowing down in the rate of new commissionings. During the past two years, only one large surface ship, the missile cruiser *Marshal Ustinov,* the second unit of the *Slava* class, has joined the fleet. Two *Sovremennyy*-class destroyers and three others of the *Udaloy* class have also been commissioned; others are under construction. In the Baltic, construction in Leningrad's Baltiyskiy shipyard of the third nuclear cruiser of the *Kirov* class is proceeding afloat, and a fourth is being assembled. In the Black Sea, the third and presumed last cruiser of the *Slava* class was to have begun its trials, as was the aircraft carrier *Baku,* which everyone had for a long time been expecting to see join the fleet; but it is true that this ship is quite different from its "sister ships" *Kiev, Minsk,* and *Novorossiysk* in weaponry and equipment, which may account for the stretching out of its construction time.

In the category of amphibious and auxiliary ships, there is not much that is new. One LSD derived from the *Ivan Rogov* class is reported to be under construction, but work on the Ropucha-class LSTs in Poland has been stopped after the commissioning of the 20th unit. On the other hand, the Navy continues to take a great interest in air-cushioned amphibious vehicles, and in the two Pomornik ACVs put into service in 1986–87 it possesses the largest and heaviest vehicles of this type; others are in the yard or planned. One may therefore suppose that the Soviets, finding them satisfactory for whatever type of amphibious operations they envisage in Europe, are content just to modernize the means they now have at their disposal.

As for anti-mine vessels, it is noteworthy that a new class christened Pelikan is under construction in the Baltic, for coastal minesweeping. This is, moreover, the only really new anti-mine vessel that has appeared in the Soviet Navy in a long time; but the Soviets are continuing to construct Natya-class minesweepers and Yevgenya-class minehunters for export. A new type of oceanic minesweeper, however, is expected to appear soon, to relieve the Natya class.

To assist friendly countries in difficulty or to support movements favorable to its interests, the U.S.S.R. can count on its merchant fleet of container ships and cargo carriers, which it continues to reinforce; it does not hesitate to use them for transporting materials and equipment discreetly to countries whose régimes or political activity it supports. This is no doubt one reason why modernization of its operational-support forces is proceeding at a slackened pace. A second large multipurpose supply ship of the *Berezina* class is in the yard, and the fleet has been augmented by a new transport for ballistic missiles, the *Aleksandr Brykin.*

About 1,500 aircraft strong, the vast majority of them based ashore, Soviet naval aviation continues to be modernized. The very formidable Backfire long-range bomber is replacing the aging Badger; it is believed that at least 120 are now in service. The new Helix all-weather helicopter is also coming on line. Some new long-range air-to-surface missiles, such as the AS-15, are being added to the assortment of nuclear-warhead missiles long in service, the Kipper and Kitchen. The AS-15 is a "cruise missile" resembling the American Tomahawk; subsonic, it flies at low altitude and can reach a target 3,000 kilometers away; it is currently deployed aboard the Bear H, a four-turboprop-engined plane that is getting old but possesses a considerable autonomy and radius of action.

No ASW patrol plane such as the American Orion or the French Navy's Atlantique has as yet made an appearance in naval aviation to replace the May and the seaplane Mail, but the Bear has in some instances been modified for this role.

The Forger, whose performance parameters are rather modest compared to those of the British Sea Harrier, has not yet been replaced by a more modern plane on *Kiev*-class aircraft carriers; but it is possible that *Leonid Brezhnev,* thanks to its ski-jump ramp, may be using a derivative of this aircraft with superior characteristics.

In technique and technology, the Soviet Navy continues to make great progress, and, as even the Americans say, it may have developed some materials, equipment, and weapons systems that did not previously exist or that have been more or less disregarded by Western navies. For example, its modern antisubmarine and antiship torpedoes are armed with nuclear warheads; Soviet engineers may have succeeded in perfecting a wake-detecting torpedo, very dangerous to surface ships.

In the field of long-range (greater than 500 km) aerodynamic missiles, the Soviet Navy continues to show an interest in those with a sea-high-low flight trajectory; in fact, a new anti-land-target missile, the SSN-X-24, is in the experimental stage. Aware that its antiship missiles (SS-N-12 and SS-N-19) of this type are vulnerable while flying at altitude, the Soviet Navy is now turning to "cruise missiles," which fly only a few meters above the ground or sea throughout all stages of their flight trajectory. On the other hand, they do not yet seem to be interested in surface-skimming missiles like the Exocet, but they are concerned about them, and their most recent surface ships are armed with anti-missile weapons systems and countermeasures equipment to defend themselves against them.

Modern pulse-compression and phased-array radars are beginning to appear on new ships, but since these ships lack the necessary high-powered computers, it seems unlikely that they have data-processing systems as sophisticated as those in use in the West, and certainly there are no systems analogous to the AEGIS found on the most recent American cruisers. The Soviet Navy is beginning to remedy its acknowledged shortcomings in underwater detection; it has developed some up-to-date medium- and low-frequency sonars, and towed VLF sonars may now be making their appearance on submarines, but not as yet on surface ships. There is general agreement, however, that the Soviets still have room for improvement in the fields of acoustic discretion and the collection and analysis of sounds to exploit fully all the capabilities of passive detection.

Finally, the Soviet Navy is far ahead of the Western nations in the field of air-cushion vehicles.

In order to ensure still further its effective control of subordinate echelons, the Soviet Navy has developed to a considerable degree a reliable, secure communications system, which it is constantly improving. Whether tactical or strategic, its transmissions rely on a network of stations scattered all over the territory of the Union but also established in countries friendly to or allied with the U.S.S.R. For instance, there are important radio centers at Lourdes, near Havana, at Aden, and at Cam Ranh Bay. Shielded, hardened, and redundant, these stations, fixed or mobile, utilize very diversified procedures, from the simple (HF) to the most complex (VLF, ELF, satellites). As a complement to these means, the Navy has quite recently converted some Bear airplanes into airborne VLF relay stations whose role is comparable to that of the U.S. Navy's TACAMO.

It is developing also a vast ocean-surveillance system to collect operational data in peacetime and thereby to facilitate the conduct of operations in case of crisis or war. Contributing to this vast network are optical and radar satellites whose performance is constantly being improved, long-range aircraft, warships, information-gathering ships, and of course merchant ships and fishing vessels. The data collected by these multifarious means are transmitted to and analyzed by special centers in the U.S.S.R.

At 18 percent, the Soviet Navy's proportion of officers to total manpower is the highest of all the great navies. This is due to the nature of the fleet's enlisted crews. The latter are composed almost entirely of recruits called up for service, who serve for three years instead of the 24 months served in the other Soviet armed forces. The technical and educational level of these conscripts being on the whole rather low, they receive only operator training, and very rare are those who stay in the Navy upon completion of their obligatory service. The result is that the number of career petty officers is extremely low, about 8 percent, whereas it is around 30 percent in most of the great Western navies. This is a serious handicap that is not taken sufficiently into account in analyzing the strengths and weaknesses of the Soviet fleet, for it cannot be other than detrimental to that fleet's true effectiveness. This situation makes it implicit that within individual ships and units, tasks normally entrusted to petty officers in other navies are being performed by officers in the Soviet Navy. Such activities as the handling, maintenance, and upkeep of materiel can only divert them from their principal role of conducting operations.

Life aboard Soviet ships is more austere than aboard Western ships; discipline is more rigorous, and living conditions in general are not as good.

Although few enlisted men reenlist, the recruitment of officers poses no problem whatever, since their social position in their country is quite prestigious. A young man with a diploma roughly comparable to the French *baccalauréat* can, after surviving difficult competition, enter one of the five naval schools in the U.S.S.R.: Frunze in Leningrad, Kaliningrad, Nakhimov in Sevastopol, Makarov in Vladivostok, and Kirov in Baku; the first-named is considered the most prestigious. The course lasts five years; political instruction figures prominently in it, and being a faithful, highly regarded Party member can favorably influence an officer's career. The education afforded is comparable in quality to that offered by naval schools abroad. Upon graduation from these schools, young officers go to their assigned billets. These first assignments are generally of extremely long duration, sometimes as long as ten years or more; so an effort is made, not to train their minds by giving them frequent changes of duty, nor to prepare them for dealing with a great variety of problems, but rather to exploit thoroughly each officer's training by restricting that training to a single type of assignment: submarine, cruiser, destroyer, naval aviation, etc. Advancement is selective, and the selection upon which it is based takes place for the most part at the ship or unit level. Thus, an officer's entire career may be spent in the same fleet, or even aboard the same ship. This is not the kind of system calculated to develop initiative in officers, but they do come to know very well the strong and weak points of their materiel. Certain officers, however, whose intellectual, scientific, or technical capacity surpasses that of their comrades—if they are also convinced communists—may be authorized to pursue a broader, more thorough education in staff schools and may aspire thereafter to high-level command; but most of the rest remain narrowly specialized to the end of their careers. Advancement is rapid, and it is possible to be promoted captain at 42; but after that, one either stagnates in that rank until retirement, or moves up into the corps of general officers, where it seems the tendency is not to manifest too much independence—whether this be due to a desire to take maximum advantage of the tremendous benefits such rank procures, or to escape excessive responsibility and possible harassment that might disrupt one's personal tranquility; the collective nature of high-level command, control, and direction can only encourage this tendency toward ultra-conservatism. General officers occupying the most important posts are often older than in other navies, and although Fleet Admiral Chernavin, who replaced the famous Admiral Gorshkov as head of the Navy, is only 59, several of his subordinates are well into their sixties. Will Mr. Gorbachev succeed in imposing a rejuvenation of the Navy's upper ranks? Admiral Chernavin's retirement at the age limit for his rank, and his replacement by an officer as young as or younger than Chernavin was two years ago when he became head of the Navy, might constitute a test in this regard.

The Soviet Navy's activity during the two years that have elapsed since our 1986 edition has conformed to its usual pattern. Their deployments in the Mediterranean and the Indian Ocean have not at any time taken on any exceptional character, and though there were the usual large-scale exercises in the North Atlantic and the Pacific, it must be noted that the Navy has abstained since 1975 from organizing large-scale maneuvers of the "Okean" variety, wherein it put into action simultaneously the four fleets and all elements then deployed in the Indian Ocean and the Mediterranean. It is not impossible, however, political contingencies permitting, that we may see another manifestation of similar scope, if only to test the new communications and ocean-surveillance systems already alluded to. The Soviet Navy is greatly handicapped in overseas deployment by a scarcity of bases it can really rely on; but the U.S.S.R. has succeeded in obtaining by agreement the use of some facilities here and there, and at Camranh it has at its disposal an advanced operating base, well organized and well positioned to support an intervention in the Indian Ocean or the Pacific.

The Soviet Navy has some strengths but also some undeniable weaknesses. Its strong points are: the size of its submarine fleet, notably the nuclear, which is improving in quality from year to year; the long-distance striking power of its naval aviation; the truly formidable armament of its large surface ships; and an advantage in certain technical fields such as wake-detecting torpedoes and the use of satellites to designate targets for ships armed with long-range aerodynamic missiles. Its weaknesses are: heavy geographical constraints from which it cannot escape; a really crucial shortage of career petty officers, which can only be prejudicial to its efficiency; lack of initiative in junior, senior, and general officers; a temporary lack of true aircraft carriers; lack of maritime patrol planes and of ASW aircraft worthy of the name; some backwardness in the fields of underwater detection and ships' acoustic signature reduction, and also in the field of high-powered computers, which compromises the utilization of the modern sound sensors now coming into service; the relative insufficiency of its logistic and operational support fleet, which as of today is in danger of restricting the freedom of action of its surface forces in case of crisis and, *a fortiori,* of war. Once the "aircraft carrier" program has been realized, perhaps the Navy will be directing its greatest efforts toward improvement in the latter field.

The concept of a sudden, all-out nuclear attack on Western naval forces, that "one shock strategy" that certain observers attributed to the Soviet Navy when the theories of Marshal Sokolovskiy were dictating military doctrine in the U.S.S.R., is today no longer believed in by most specialists; but that concept cannot be dismissed *a priori,* any more than can participation by the Soviet Navy in an all-out conflict in Europe without the use of nuclear weapons. There has been a lot of heated argument—and it still goes on—about the essential nature of the Soviet Navy. Is it defensive or is it offensive? Its composition does not provide a definitive solution to this dilemma. The author of these lines, basing his judgment on its peacetime activities, exercises, external deployments, etc., thinks—but he may be mistaken—that it has two essential missions in Soviet military doctrine: a totally defensive mission, and a mission of external action—that is, a political mission. The first of these, in addition to participating with its SSBNs in the Union's nuclear umbrella, consists of protecting the northern and southern flanks of the "West" theater of operations, and, in the Pacific, the eastern provinces of the Soviet Union, against Western naval air attack. Note that the Pacific Fleet could be used offensively against China. In Europe, this defensive mission could be preceded by initial offensive actions to assist in the conquest of Norway, the Belts, the Turkish Straits, etc., to facilitate subsequent defense. The latter would employ, in the form of defensive barriers echeloned in depth, the Navy's SSNs, large surface ships, bomber squadrons in successive waves, and, as a last resort, coastal defense. This hypothesis envisages the use of nuclear weapons as possible, with a strong effort being made to limit their use at sea. Strikes against Western sea communications are merely subsidiary to this defensive mission.

The second mission of this Navy is to support countries linked with the U.S.S.R. by friendship or mutual interest, to show the flag in the world's trouble spots in support of U.S.S.R. policy—in short, to implement the strategy of external action and crisis control that supports its interests, economic as well as political. Large surface ships, soon to be joined by nuclear aircraft carriers with the direct support of SSNs, are the forces assigned to this mission, which is perhaps, in view of the nuclear stalemate in Europe, the Navy's principal mission as a part of the U.S.S.R's global strategy.

## THE ROYAL NAVY

The security of Great Britain depends essentially on its membership in NATO. It devotes most of its forces and some 98 percent of its defense budget to the Alliance. It is the only European nation to contribute to all three of the pillars on which NATO rests: strategic nuclear power, tactical nuclear power, and what is improperly termed "conventional" power.

In an effort to profit from the lessons learned in the Falklands, the U.K.'s defense organization has been progressively modified in the direction of still more thorough integration of the three services, at the highest level. The result, as of today, is a rather complex military-civilian organization in which, on the military side, the Chief of Defence Staff (CDS) plays a preponderant role, at the expense of the chiefs of the Navy, Army, and Air Force. He is the government's principal advisor in defense matters (policy, major orientations, employment of forces). Charged with the planning, organization, and conduct of military operations, he has an integrated staff, the "Defence Staff," which has arrogated to itself many of the prerogatives and responsibilities that formerly devolved upon the commanders-in-chief of the various services; the latter have in fact lost all authority in matters of military planning and programming. The CDS chairs the committee of chiefs of staff and receives their opinions and advice.

The organization of the Royal Navy rests on the following principles: peacetime organization is valid for times of crisis or war, with no *a priori* changes in personnel or structuring; as a matter of fact, this organization is specifically designed to deal with a continuing, unresolved crisis. There is total separation between command of forces and command of the "Naval Establishment" ashore; ashore, there is no dichotomy between staffs and services—hence unity of command.

At the central echelon, administration of the Navy is handled by the Navy Department, itself subordinate to the integrated echelon administering the three armed forces within the Ministry of Defence (M.O.D.). The Navy Department, which continues to be called the Admiralty, includes: a general staff in the true sense, directed by the Chief of Naval Staff and First Sea Lord, assisted by the Vice Chief of Naval Staff and by the Commandant General Royal Marines; three big directorates, one responsible for the management, schooling, and training of military personnel (except naval aviation personnel), another for the administration of naval dockyards, upkeep of the fleet, and provisioning and logistic support at sea, and a third for new construction and aeronautical materiel in close liaison with M.O.D.'s Chief of Defence Procurement, who is responsible for the British armament industry.

Operations are determined in accordance with the directives of the Committee of Chiefs of Staff, of which the top naval authority, the Chief of Naval Staff and First Sea Lord, is a member. Subject to the authority of the First Sea Lord, command of Royal Navy forces and means is exercised by two admirals, commanders-in-chief: the Commander-in-Chief Naval Home (CINCNAVHOME) based at Portsmouth and commanding the Naval Establishment ashore, and the Commander-in-Chief Fleet (CINCFLEET), based at a shielded command post at Northwood on the western outskirts of London and commanding naval forces afloat. The first-named is principally responsible for the functioning of the Navy's establishments ashore (including dockyards), for the on-shore training of active-duty personnel, for the training of reserves ashore, and also afloat, through delegation by CINCFLEET, and for public-relations activities; he exercises command through the intermediation of three subordinates with geographical jurisdiction: Flag Officer Plymouth, Flag Officer Portsmouth, and Flag Officer Scotland and Northern Ireland (FOSNI, at Rosyth). CINCNAVHOME is therefore a kind of maritime super-prefect whose jurisdiction embraces all the British Isles. The second (CINCFLEET) is: theater commander, with responsibility for the Royal Navy's areas of operation in the aggregate—that is, for the entire world; and commander of all forces at sea, including strategic nuclear submarines. In his role as theater commander, his principal subordinates or area commanders are Flag Officer Plymouth for the Central Atlantic, the English Channel, and the southern North Sea, FO Portsmouth for the immediate approaches to that great port, and FOSNI; to these three subordinates, who for the "maritime prefect" aspect of their job also serve under CINCNAVHOME, must be added Flag Officer Gibraltar for the western Mediterranean. In his role as commander of forces, CINCFLEET has six major subordinates at his disposal "at sea": Flag Officer First Flotilla (FOF 1, CP afloat or at Devonport); Flag Officer Second Flotilla (FOF 2, CP afloat or at Portsmouth); Flag Officer Third Flotilla (FOF 3, CP afloat or at Fort Southwick); Flag Officer Submarines (FOSM, CP at Northwood); Captain Mine Countermeasures (CMCM); Captain Fishery Protection (CFP); and finally Flag Officer Sea Training or FOST (training admiral), based at Portland on the south coast; the latter's mission is to put ships into operational condition before they first enter active service or are returned to it, and specialty instruction and training at sea. CINCFLEET bears some important responsibilities within NATO. As CINCCHAN he is responsible for the Channel area; as CINCEASTLANT he is a major subordinate of SACLANT. Finally, he is charged with integrating British strategic submarines into the NATO organism. Thus the national and NATO responsibilities of CINCFLEET are closely intermeshed. The NATO command posts (CINCCHAN, CINCEASTLANT) and the national (CINCFLEET) are both located at Northwood.

The potential of the Royal Navy amounts to 153 combat ships, to which must be added 10 amphibious ships and 20 large auxiliary and operational-support vessels. This represents a total of something over 588,000 standard displacement tons. The fighting fleet is composed essentially of 4 SSBNs of the *Resolution* class, 3 small *Invincible*-class aircraft carriers, 15 nuclear attack submarines, 11 conventional submarines, 13 destroyers, 37 frigates, and 45 mine-countermeasures vessels.

The *Resolution*-class SSBNs constitute the U.K.'s only deterrent force; they are at the disposal of NATO, which determines their targets, but the British government may (under the Nassau accords of 1962) withdraw them if doing so is deemed necessary in the nation's best interest. These submarines were thoroughly remodeled between 1982 and 1986; the 16 Polaris missiles each carries were "remotorized" and their initial payload of three 200-kiloton warheads replaced by a new one consisting of six 40-kiloton re-entry vehicles with a greatly enhanced power of penetration; like those they replaced, these warheads are of British design and manufacture. The reactor, the navigation system, and the equipment of these submarines have been improved, as have their acoustic signature characteristics. Thanks to this remodeling, it will be possible to keep these SSBNs in active service until late in the 1990s, when they will have been replaced by four boats of a new generation. The first of these, *Vanguard,* was laid down 3 September 1986; it will join the fleet in 1994, and the program is in principle to be completed in 1997. Adopted in 1980 by the Conservatives, it has since been bitterly contested by the Labourites, who have consistently sworn that they would abandon it if they were returned to power, despite the considerable sums already expended toward its realization. The Conservatives having won the recent elections, the program will henceforth be following its planned course. The *Vanguard* class will be submarines of 14,900 tons carrying 16 American Trident-IIC missiles, but the latter's nose cones will also contain eight warheads of British design and manufacture. The agreement concerning acquisition of the Trident-IIC, effectively identical to the Nassau agreement, was signed 15 July 1980.

Vertical takeoff and landing aircraft carriers are ships having a continuous flight deck, but no catapults or arresting gear. They can handle helicopters as well as airplanes, but the latter can be only of the short-takeoff-and-landing variety. To facilitate takeoff for such aircraft, the British came up with the idea of equipping these ships with a springboard ("ski jump") at the forward end of the flight deck; this is inclined at an angle of 7° on *Invincible* and *Illustrious* and at 12° on *Ark Royal.* Architecturally, these ships of roughly 20,000 tons displacement and 28-knot speed are less than a complete success, notably because of the poor placement of their elevators, an oblique runway that is almost nonexistent, and a poorly conceived hangar deck that limits the total number of aircraft each of the first two ships can embark to five *Sea Harrier* and nine helicopters; the more recent *Ark Royal* (9 planes and 12 helicopters) is a little better in this respect. *Invincible* is currently undergoing major remodeling to bring her up to the level of *Ark Royal;* then it will be *Illustrious*'s turn, and in principle, two of the three ships will be kept operational.

The Royal Navy has the largest fleet of nuclear attack submarines in Western Europe. These SSNs, which it calls "fleet submarines," as opposed to diesel-propelled "patrol submarines," are divided into three classes:

- 5 *Valiant* class, commissioned from 1966 to 1981,
- 6 *Swiftsure* class, dating from 1973–1981,
- 4 *Trafalgar* class, plus 3 more in the yard or on order.

All these SSNs, whatever their class, are characterized by the care taken to make them more quiet from one series to the next, quietness being the essential quality in view of the passive sonars the Soviets are developing. The *Trafalgar* class, notably, have an anechoic coating on their hulls and are equipped with a "pump-jet" (pump-propeller) system that resolves the phenomena of cavitation. The armament of these various SSNs comprises 5 to 6 torpedo tubes, with a total of 20 to 26 antisubmarine and antiship torpedoes or a mix of the latter and American Sub Harpoon antiship missiles. All of them have, or will be getting, a towed VLF passive linear array sonar, which improves their antisubmarine detection capability. In addition to these SSNs, the Royal Navy has 11 conventional attack submarines of the *Oberon* class, completed between 1962 and 1967; the most recent of these are in the process of modernization, including installation of a towed passive hydrophone array and the capability of carrying a few American Sub Harpoon missiles.

The Royal Navy, unlike the U.S. Navy, believes that conventional but high-performance submarines can still prove very useful; for example, to conduct surveillance of obligatory passages or to perform certain missions that do not require using nuclear attack submarines, thereby freeing the latter for high-priority missions such as hunting down enemy SSBNs and SSNs and scouting operational surface groups. It has therefore decided to replace its *Oberons* by beginning construction of eight high-performance submarines, whose prototype, *Upholder*, is being fitted out; three others are on order, to be commissioned between now and 1993. It is noteworthy that these 2,400-ton boats will be equipped with a partially French sonar (the *Argonaute* sonar, derived from Thomson/CSF's *Eledone*).

The guided-missile destroyer *Bristol*, which had been scheduled for a long time to be scrapped, is going to be kept in service after all, to be used as a school ship. The 12 *Sheffield*-class destroyers are good antiaircraft ships, but they cannot be considered usable for zonal air defense because of their small size and insufficient equipment for detecting and countering the threat of submarines; the oldest are to be modernized to raise them to the level of the most recent with a new air-search radar, new sonar, and a more sophisticated data-processing system.

Sixteen of the 37 frigates in service are already 20 years old, and several of them are to be disarmed in the near future. The most recent frigates, those of the Type 22 class, of which several are still under construction, are characterized by a high displacement (more than 4,500 tons) and a relatively light armament for that tonnage, which gives a visitor aboard them the impression that they are rather empty; but all that room will be eventually filled by the new weapon systems and equipment expected to appear at mid-life. To replace the aging *Leander* class, the Royal Navy has conceived in the Type 23 class a new kind of frigate, with a new kind of propulsion system very different from that used habitually heretofore; this system, called CODLAG (for Combined Diesel Electric and Gas Turbine) consists of four diesel-electric units feeding two electric motors for silent running during operations, complemented by two gas turbines to attain great speed; another peculiarity of the Type 23 class is that it will be the first in the Royal Navy to be equipped with a vertical-launching self-defense antiaircraft weapon system; as on the Type 22 class, ASW detection will be ensured by a combination of low-frequency sonars and towed passive linear hydrophone arrays. The Royal Navy has announced that it would like to build 20 ships of this class, but the cost of the *Vanguard* program will probably oblige it to scale down its requests; be that as it may, four frigates of the Type 23 class have been ordered, and the first, *Norfolk,* was launched last July 10.

Conscious of the increasingly serious threat of mines against the great European ports and its own harbor approaches, the Royal Navy has begun a great effort to revive and renew its mine-warfare forces. To modernize in this area, three types of ships have been conceived:

- a minehunter-sweeper of 625 standard tons, relatively expensive, the "Hunt" class,
- a smaller, more economical minehunter, the SRMH ("Single Role Mine Hunter"), the "Racecourse" class,
- a ship of 770 tons, specially equipped for sweeping mines moored at great depths—the "River"-class ships of the EDATS program ("Extra Deep Team Sweepers").

It is noteworthy that, with respect to minesweepers, the Royal Navy has declined to subscribe to the Tripartite minesweeper program conceived in common by France, Belgium, and the Netherlands, but has determined to go it alone and develop its own ideas in the field of mine warfare. Eleven of the 13 projected "Hunt" class are now in service, as are 12 of the 16 planned EDATS; on the other hand, only the prototype of the SRMH has been laid down, though 20 are programmed.

As far as interservice combined operations are concerned, the British had envisaged, before the Falklands affair, only a token participation in operations on the northern flank of NATO; so their two landing-craft transports *Fearless* and *Intrepid* were definitely to be decommissioned. Today these two ships still figure in the Royal Navy's order-of-battle, and there are even plans to modernize them. To replace the *Sir Galahad* sunk in the Falklands, a new type of LST by the same name has been delivered, while the badly damaged *Sir Tristram* has been returned to service after a long period under repairs.

As for troops truly specially trained for amphibious operations, there are only the four "commandos" of Royal Marines, professional soldiers whose formidable efficiency the Argentines learned about to their cost in the Falklands.

The operational-transport and logistic-support fleet constitutes what is called the Royal Fleet Auxiliary (RFA). Until 1985, ships of the RFA were subject to the regulations of the Shipping Naval Acts of 1911 and to Lloyd's standards of construction; they were then considered merchant ships and required no authorization to enter a foreign port. The Navy having decided to equip them with some light armament to counter any acts of terrorism, the ships of this auxiliary fleet have now become government ships and are therefore subject to diplomatic accord whenever they put in at a foreign port. All are manned by civilian personnel, about 3,600 men in all. This force now includes nine oiler-storeships, four large all-purpose provisioning ships, four chartered oilers, one auxiliary helicopter carrier, and one repair ship. Construction of 6 to 12 *Fort Victoria*-class large squadron storeships is projected, and the first of these ships has been ordered; they will replace the oldest oiler-storeships and the chartered oilers.

Shipborne aviation, or the Fleet Air Arm, is the only aviation properly belonging to the Royal Navy; ASW on the high seas and maritime patrolling are the province of the Royal Air Force, which has a specialized unit for this purpose called the Maritime Command, employing about thirty Nimrods. The Fleet Air Arm includes, counting those under construction, about 50 Sea Harriers; this VTOL/VSTOL-type plane proved itself in the Falklands, but from the standpoint of performance, carrying capacity, and autonomy, it cannot compare with present-day carrier-borne fighters and assault planes. The bulk of the Fleet Air Arm still consists of helicopters, about 150 on line and 100 or so in second-line service. These include Sea Kings for ASW and transport, Lynx for ASW and surface-ship attack, and still a few old Wessex transport helicopters. In addition, eight Sea Kings have been converted to early-warning aircraft (AEW). To replace Sea King in the 1990s, the Royal Navy has chosen the EH.101 helicopter, designed jointly by the Italian firm Agusta and the English firm Westland.

In the field of weapons and equipment, the Royal Navy does not hesitate to call on items of foreign materiel when they are high-performance and look interesting from the standpoint of cost-efficiency. For instance, it has adopted the French Exocet, the American Harpoon, the Italian 76 OTO-Melara Compact, and many other items of materiel. This policy enables it to avoid bottlenecks and concentrate its efforts on the projects it considers most important: nuclear power, of course, with the *Vanguard* program; passive listening devices, heavy submarine torpedoes, electronic warfare, data processing, etc.

In the field of communications, the Royal Navy has for several years been exploiting the Scot communications system via Skynet satellite, for its surface ships as well as its submarines. For communication with its SSBNs and SSNs, it utilizes, in support of its own VLF stations, a number of civilian stations that can be plugged into its network at any time. In addition, Great Britain will also be developing an ELF communications system in Scotland.

The personnel of the Royal Navy consist entirely of volunteers. There are no problems in this respect, but there is some concern that too many sailors may leave the service prematurely after acquiring skills and knowledge that qualify them for attractive careers in civilian life.

Officer personnel represents about 14 percent of total strength, so the Royal Navy is particularly well staffed; this partially explains its universally recognized high quality. More than 35 percent of all effectives serve aboard ship, and about 7,600 serve in naval aviation. The officers fall into three different categories: the General List, the Supplementary List, and the Special Duties List. Those in the first category pass through the mould of the Britannia Royal Naval College at Dartmouth, for which one must be at least 17 years of age to enter; the education imparted there is a judicious blend of naval tradition and the most modern educational methods.

Those on the Supplementary List sign a contract with the Navy for a limited period: five to ten years. In principle, they can rise no higher than the rank of lieutenant commander; but the most brilliant among them may, if they so desire, transfer to the General List.

Special Duties officers, whose career is of normal duration, come from the enlisted ranks and may attain the rank of commander, or under certain conditions may transfer to the General List.

Officers up to and including the rank of lieutenant commander constitute the following fractions of the officer corps: General List, 4/10; Supplementary List, 3/10; Special Duties, 3/10.

Three parallel careers are offered to officers: deck (X); machinery (Engineer), weapons & equipment (Weapons Engineer); commissary (Supply).

The Royal Navy considers that the first two of these careers call for further specialization. It is noteworthy that the Engineer's career covers a wide range of technical fields: machinery, electricity, electronics, weapons. Officers with this specialty may aspire to accede to posts of great responsibility.

When they reach the rank of commander, officers of the General List are classified into two categories (although this distinction has disappeared from the directory, leading one to think it has perhaps been abolished): the Wets, who will have access to command at sea, and the Drys, whose future assignments will be to shore billets, assuring them greater geographic stability.

In principle, the prospects for advancement of these two lists are the same, and this proves true in practice, up to and including the rank of captain. But it becomes less true with respect to promotions to the rank of general officer. The average ages of promotion to commander and above are as follows: commander 36 years, captain 42 years, flag officer 51 years.

The duration of assignments to command at sea is never less than 18 months, and it must be noted that an inexorable rule prevents "digging in." After nine years in grade, whatever his age, a captain who is not promoted leaves the Navy. The First Sea Lord himself must retire four years after being promoted to that position.

In summary, one may say that everything is organized in such a way that the highest ranks, and then the posts of highest responsibility, are accessible only to officers who have distinguished themselves during their careers, not only by their technical competence and seamanship but perhaps still more by their character and their dynamism. Everything is done with one end in view: efficiency.

Third largest but far behind the Soviet Navy in size, the Royal Navy nevertheless remains a very great navy, not only because of the forces it can deploy, but also and especially because of the skill and valor of its personnel. The Falklands crisis enabled them once again to demonstrate their remarkable aptitude and their no less amazing versatility and resilience by bringing to a victorious conclusion, thousands of miles from the homeland, an affair whose outcome was by no means a foregone conclusion.

The Royal Navy has its strengths but also its weaknesses. Among the former must be cited:

- its organization, which enables it to pass quickly from peacetime to a time of crisis or war without making any structural change;
- its career personnel, one of the best-officered in existence;
- its training, very thorough and as realistic as possible (more than 35 percent at sea);
- its glorious past and the prestige deriving therefrom;
- its magnificent fleet of nuclear attack submarines; designed for attacking enemy submarines, their anti-surface-ship capability has been considerably enhanced by adoption of Sub Harpoon and some sophisticated new torpedoes;
- its well-balanced logistic fleet.

Among the negative factors must be noted:

- a stretching out of new construction time, due of course to financing problems but also very often to social problems, resulting in numerous strikes in naval and private shipyards;
- the lack of true aircraft carriers, the *Invincible* class being able to operate only in areas where threat from the air is minimal, or under the protection of large American aircraft carriers; their attack capability is also very limited.

## THE FRENCH NAVY

The reader might very well think I would hesitate to pass judgment on the French Navy, to which I have belonged in a civilian capacity for more than 30 years, and which I have served and still love passionately. Nevertheless, I shall take the risk and shall begin, perhaps surprisingly, by saying that for the first time since the time of Louis XVI, the French Navy is in the process of acquiring, with its nuclear-powered ballistic-missile submarines lurking in the ocean depths, its nuclear-powered attack submarines, which can go thousands of miles without surfacing, and its aircraft carriers such as *Clémenceau* (currently deployed in the Indian Ocean), a truly oceanic dimension. That will be still more true with the advent of *Charles de Gaulle* and subsequently the second ship of that class, which we hope will appear in the next enabling legislation and will be named *Richelieu*, for the founder of our Navy and one of our greatest statesmen.

The defense of France rests essentially on two strategies: a strategy of deterrence and a strategy of action. The first is aimed at preventing any aggression in Europe, be it nuclear or conventional, via the threat of nuclear retaliation. This policy is endorsed today by the majority of Frenchmen. The strategy of action is a logical concomitant of deterrence. It is the symbol of a nation that has chosen to control its own destiny by means of deterrence. It contributes to the stature of the French nation by enabling her to become a world nuclear power with a presence in the Pacific, a space power with a presence in the Atlantic, and an indispensable partner in dialogue between North and South, notably in Africa, the Mediterranean, and the Indian Ocean. The Navy plays a privileged role in all this, with its "presence" capabilities being emphasized by occasional deployments of shipborne aviation and nuclear attack submarines.

*Le Tonnant,* first of the four *Le Redoutable*-class SSBNs to be remodeled to carry M4 missiles, joined the Oceanic Strategic Force (FOST) this year, and the last of the four will be returned to service in 1993. Counting those embarked on *L'Inflexible,* the French Navy will then possess 80 M4 missiles, with a total of 480 individualized warheads, and its strategic retaliation capacity from the sea will be three times greater than it was two years ago. Programming for 1987–91 projects the construction of two *Le Triomphant*-class SSBNs, bigger, deeper, and quieter. The first of these new strategic submarines will join FOST in 1994, and the second will be ordered in 1989. These two submarines will be carrying a new version of M4 that will make it possible to reach still more distant targets, and consequently to expand their areas of patrol and launch. Subsequently, these submarines will receive the M5 missile, for which they will be prepared in advance. The M5 missile will be armed with a large number of so-called "stealthy" warheads. Thanks to this planning, the strategy of deterrence will therefore retain its credibility throughout the next decade and the one after that. In this field, then, the French Navy's situation can be deemed entirely satisfactory. The same is true of *Rubis*-class nuclear attack submarines: three are in service, a fourth, *Emeraude*, in process of completion, and the eighth and last of the series provided for in the 1987–91 programming. Starting with *Améthyste* (No. 5), these SSNs will feature some important improvements in the fields of acoustic signature, underwater detection, weapons control, and communications (the Syracuse II satellite communications system)—improvements that will subsequently be extended to their four predecessors. As for SSN No. 8, it should be joining the fleet in 1997. The *Rubis* class will thus acquire an ASW mission, which they did not have originally. Furthermore, their relatively small size, far from being a defect, will very probably prove to be—come the year 2000 when a return to active detection will have become necessary in ASW—an extra trump card, for which a number of their peers will envy them.

The mission of *Rubis* is more modest than that of the American or Soviet SSNs: protection of French SSBNs on France's sea approaches, attack on surface forces, and information-gathering or action in localized conflict—a role analogous to that of the British *Conqueror* during the Falklands crisis. Studies are to be made, however, of a new class of SSN, which will probably be larger, to replace the diesel submarines still in service; two of these might be ordered when the time is right.

Insofar as the small number of surface ships is concerned, the situation, while not alarming, is nonetheless a cause for concern, since the number of new ships under construction or programmed is not great enough to replace all the ships that must soon be struck off the list because of their age; but every effort will be made, by modernizing existing units, to maintain somehow or other the fleet's operational capability. Because of the unavailability of the antiaircraft weapons system desired, construction of corvettes Nos. 3 and 4 of the *Cassard* class has had to be abandoned. So by the end of the 1987–91 program, the French Navy will have only five antiaircraft "corvettes": two new *Cassard* class, two modernized *Suffren* class, and the cruiser *Colbert*, also modernized but more than 33 years old by that time.

The situation is a little better for ASW corvettes: five are in service, one ready for commissioning, and a seventh, *Latouche-Treville,* is in the yard. In addition, the three *Tourville* class are to be modernized with new radar and countermeasures systems, Crotale EDIR SAM system, TASS, and new ASW weapons.

Charged with participation in emergency crisis control, France's eight aviso-escorts are beginning to age and are in urgent need of replacement. As a half-hearted effort in this direction, three light frigates are projected in the 1987–91 programming, but this is not enough.

The Tripartite minehunter program is under way, but the program has been cut back from 15 units to 10; 7 are in service and 3 in various stages of completion; the 5 *Circé* class are to be modernized, but several of the older minesweepers are to be decommissioned. In order to cope with the new deep-water moored mines, the programming calls for the building of six oceanic minesweepers of about 950 tons, of fiberglass construction and with a catamaran hull. This is a bold innovation, since the largest ships of this type, the Australian *Rushcutter* class, scarcely exceed 150 tons. These BAMO [*bâtiments anti-mines océaniques*] are primarily designed to ensure the safety of French SSBNs during their transit of the continental shelf.

The logistic-transport and operational-support fleet, often neglected when the Navy was seeing little action anywhere outside the Mediterranean, has in recent years been the focus of a great effort, which is now bearing fruit. All new, it is well adapted to its requirements, notably for deployment overseas. But because other programs, such as that of the BAMO, have proved more urgent, construction of *Foudre*-class LSDs Nos. 2 and 3 has been provisionally abandoned.

In order to take account of the diminution of the French surface fleet, which may become serious enough by 1992 to compromise seriously the second aspect of the strategy on which the nation's defense policy is based, the forthcoming bill of programming for 1992–96, insofar as the Navy (outside of FOST) is concerned, should provide for a second nuclear aircraft carrier to replace *Foch,* which will reach the age limit in the year 2000, and should give top priority to the replacement of antiaircraft support ships; *Colbert* will effectively disappear early in the 1990s; the last *Tartar* SAM T47 will have been decommissioned, likewise the two *Suffren* class, by the turn of the century. Successors to these could be a 6,000-ton ship with diesel-engine propulsion, the Navy having acquired great expertise and some technical advantage over other nations in this method of propulsion, thanks to the French low-compression diesel concept. As an antiaircraft weapon the new ship could have, in place of the SM-1 MR that will have had to be abandoned, a medium-range weapons system that could be derived from the very promising SAAM anti-missile system developed for self-defense of large ships, beginning with *Charles de Gaulle*. For very short range self-defense, the Navy has developed the Mistral missile, which can be employed either in a centralized mode aboard large ships or autonomously from simpler mounts aboard small units. The armament of these future ships could be supplemented by the antiship weapon that is to succeed Exocet, a helicopter or two, the weapon that is to replace Malafon, the towed linear hydrophone array, etc. In the field of ship signature reduction, the Navy has made great progress: the most recent *Georges Leygues*-class corvettes, for example, are as good in this respect as the very best to be found abroad. On French ships of the future the Navy must not scrimp on tonnage, as has so often been done in the past: an extra 200 or 300 tons increases the cost of a ship only slightly, but it may facilitate the ship's subsequent modernization, especially if the deck space and volume needed for it have been envisaged in advance, as, for example, the British have done on their Type 22-class frigates and the Americans on their *Spruance* class. The added initial expense would be more than compensated for by the lower costs of repair and modernization made possible by this policy.

Facing up to the new threats, notably chemical, which are appearing in the developing countries, recent French ships are certainly among the best-conceived with respect to protection against NBC warfare.

The effort to arm ships with light weapons with which to counter unsophisticated naval threats should be pursued.

Nothing need be said about Exocet; it proved itself in the Falklands and continues to do so in the Persian Gulf. Its successor is the Franco-German ANS, whose first trials have been very promising.

In the field of very-low-frequency underwater detection, the Frency Navy has caught up with the U.S. Navy and the Royal Navy in materiel, but it still needs to improve its employment procedures. The ASW capability of present-day ships will be improved with the advent of the Murène torpedo and the weapon to be associated with it to replace Malafon.

The adaptation of Super-Étendard to ASW and patrol will strengthen considerably the nuclear operational capabilities of shipborne aviation by giving it the range it formerly lacked. Replacement of the Crusader interceptor and the Étendard IVP reconnaissance plane remains to be accomplished. Both will have to be withdrawn from service in 1993. Their replacement should be the navalized version of the fighter plane derived from Rafale; but this aircraft will not be available until 1996 at the earliest. French aircraft carriers are therefore in danger of being short of interceptors and reconnaissance planes for a period of three to four years under the best of circumstances. Several solutions for this are said to be under study.

As far as maritime patrol planes (PATMAR) are concerned, a difficult situation will arise in 1991–92. By then the Atlantic will have to be withdrawn from service more rapidly than the more elaborate Atlantique destined to replace it will be delivered. The programming for 1987–91 nevertheless envisages a considerable effort on behalf of PATMAR, for the latter contributes to the security of SSBNs, and ensures long-distance air coverage of sea approaches to France as well as of her overseas departments and territories. The Atlantic, moreover, during operation "Epervier," demonstrated that it was indispensable to the air forces deployed to Chad by providing them with operational guidance and security.

A total of 42 Atlantiques are projected, 27 of them in the 1987–1991 plan plus 5 whose fabrication was begun under the preceding program. The PATMAR situation will therefore improve in operational capability with the delivery in 1989 of the first Atlantique in the series and the formation in 1990 of the first flotilla using that aircraft.

Like the other nuclear powers, France has undertaken to modernize its system of command and communications for putting into action its strategic and pre-strategic forces: SSBNs and aircraft carriers armed with nuclear weapons. Only the first of these forces to be deployed at sea will have a good chance of being able to retaliate after an unexpected nuclear strike, and its second-strike capacity depends on the survival of the communications system to give the order to engage after that attack. This communications survival, which is vital for the nation, is achieved or will be improved by a judicious combination of interservice means with strictly naval means. This system has at its disposal, to ensure command liaison between metropolitan France and her strategic and conventional forces, means of communication that rely on the twin concepts of interlocking networks and mobility of stations (i.e., the Astarte aircraft). In addition, vital operational communications centers are hardened against IEM effects, but also against a broad spectrum of nuclear, biological, chemical, and conventional attack and against the new threats posed by terrorism or the action of specially trained military commandos—threats that must henceforth be taken into account.

Among the means utilized by the Navy to communicate with its forces at sea, the Syracuse I interservice satellite telecommunications system is now operational and is rendering invaluable service, but it does not make possible communication with submarines. It consists of a number of fixed or mobile shore stations and of others embarked on surface ships, including replenishment vessels. The Syracuse II system, designed to succeed it, will cover the same area (from the Caribbean to Pakistan), but will provide increased communications capacity, notably by increasing the number of stations and adding new types of ships. The Navy will have stations installed aboard *Le Triomphant*-class SSBNs, SSNs, light frigates, and if feasible, A69-class avisos. As for observation satellites, the Helios program is supposed in principle to be operational by 1993; it will provide images even more precise than those of the civilian satellite Spot, itself already far advanced in comparison with other civilian satellites; the press has shown some extraordinary shots of the secret Soviet SSBN bases along the Kola Peninsula.

As I have done for the preceding navies, I must also say a word about the personnel of the French Navy. In this area, the French Navy is much less well off for officer personnel than are the other great Western navies; officers represent only 6.8 percent of its military personnel, as compared with more than 12 percent in the other navies. Thanks to its petty officer corps, probably superior to those abroad, this handicap has been manageable thus far; but the unacceptability of this situation must be recognized, for it obliges officers of shore-based staffs to perform several kinds of duties simultaneously, which is not a good thing. The solution, if there is one, would perhaps be to increase the budgetary allotment for personnel, in order to retain a greater number of officers on active duty, or to do as the Americans and the British do, and call upon civilian employees.

## OTHER NAVIES

For lack of space, I find it difficult to say as much here about other navies as I would have liked. So in the lines that follow I shall content myself with mentioning briefly only those whose development over the past two years has seemed to me the most significant.

The Japanese Maritime Self-Defense Force occupies fifth place in the hierarchy of great navies. The number of its units remains approximately the same, since ships newly constructed are merely replacing others that are being struck off the list or reduced to auxiliary functions; but the new ships are nevertheless more powerful and better equipped, with the result that the Navy's operational capabilities are being constantly improved. It possesses as many conventional submarines as the French Navy, but these are larger and on the whole more recent. Japan's surface fleet in the categories of missile destroyers, destroyers, frigates, and other escort ships is also more numerous, and especially more recent, than France's. Worthy of note is the forthcoming construction of four destroyers equipped with the AEGIS system and with the American SM-2 MR vertical-launching system; the first of these may be ordered in the 1988–89 budget. Deployed in the Sea of Japan, these ships would be a part of the nation's advance air-defense system.

Naval aviation, an integral part of the Navy, consists only of helicopters and maritime-patrol planes, the latter being both land-based and seaplanes. The helicopters, about 90 in number, are either shipborne or shore-based; most of them are assigned to ASW duty. Japanese maritime-patrol aircraft, the most numerous and best-equipped after the U.S. Navy's force, total 225 fixed-wing planes, of which 69 or more are of the American P-3C Orion type. Ten planes of this designation figure in the 1986–87 budget, one of which is an electronic-warfare plane.

The equipment with which Japanese ships and aircraft are provided is for the most part of American design, manufactured under permit; but some items of Japanese design, notably in electronics, are making their appearance. The Navy's personnel, exclusively career in nature, include 20 percent officers and 50 percent petty officers; everyone agrees that it is very responsible and competent.

The increase in power of the Indian Navy in recent years has been spectacular, and it now occupies seventh place in the hierarchy of great navies. Since our 1986 edition, it has been enriched by the ex-British aircraft *Hermes,* a fourth Kashin-class DDG, two submarines of the Soviet Kilo class, and two Type 1500-class submarines ordered in West Germany. A fifth Kashin and three or four more Kilo are expected. A series of three large *Godavari*-class frigates is on the verge of completion; and more Type 1500-class submarines, as well as four *Khukri*-class light frigates, are in the yard at Bombay.

Naval aviation is on the rise. Already boasting 8 Sea Harriers, 10 Alizés for ASW security, and some 40 helicopters, it has 11 Sea Harrier and 20 Sea King helicopters on order. There are plans also for developing maritime patrol aviation by acquiring aircraft from abroad.

Officer personnel, trained in the British fashion, are responsible and competent; but the number of petty officers is notoriously insufficient because of the nation's rather low educational level; a great effort is being made, however, to remedy this situation as quickly as possible.

The Indian Navy is already the most powerful among the states bordering on the Indian Ocean, and it apparently intends to remain so, since it plans to build in the years to come, in its own shipyards, a 25,000- to 30,000-ton aircraft carrier to replace *Vikrant* (dating from 1961) and several 5,000- to 6,000-ton destroyers for antiaircraft and anti-surface-ship duties.

The Royal Saudi Navy is at the stage where it must thoroughly familiarize itself with the superb materiel with which it is now equipped. So far as the future is concerned, it is still trying to decide whether it will acquire a submarine force or whether it will develop its surface fleet, notably by adding antiaircraft ships.

The Federal German Navy or *Bundesmarine,* remarkably well organized, commanded, and trained, is well adapted to the missions assigned to it by NATO in the Baltic and on the North Sea approaches. Its fleet, relatively recently built, possesses various types of forces in a good balance; its equipment, whether of German or foreign origin, is excellent. Naval aviation, with its modern Tornado fighter-bombers and its maritime patrol aviation consisting of 19 Atlantics, looks very good but will soon reach the point where the latter aircraft will have to be replaced; the *Bundesmarine* will probably make its choice in this regard next year. For the future, it envisages building eight large frigates to replace the *Lütjens*- and *Hamburg*-class destroyers now in service, and modernizing its submarine force.

One of the essential characteristics of the Italian Navy is its strong integration into NATO. Within this framework, it is charged with the protection of Italian and allied maritime shipping in the Mediterranean, surveillance of the Adriatic, and defense of the peninsula's coasts and ports. It can also provide effective support for the U.S. Sixth Fleet with its missile-firing ships.

The increased importance of the Italian Navy in this context has been underscored by the assignment of Italian admirals to posts of high responsibility within NATO: that of naval command in the Mediterranean (COMNAVSOUTH), and that of naval commander in the central Mediterranean (COMEDCENT).

The fleet is on the whole modern and well adapted to its normal theater of operations. Now that the helicopter carrier *Giuseppe Garibaldi* and eight large *Maestrale*-class frigates have been completed, the fleet's renovation program will concentrate on the two missile destroyers *Animoso* and *Ardimentono* of 4,800 tons, which will replace *Impavido* and *Intrepido,* which are more than 20 years old. Construction of a new class of light frigates is also well along, as are two large amphibious ships; the latter will soon be joining the fleet. The *Lerici*-class minehunter program, which had been interrupted for the sake of orders from foreign navies, is to be resumed. The last two of six 1,450-ton *Sauro*-series submarines will join the fleet next year. In the long-term, the Italian Navy envisages building four additional, somewhat larger submarines.

Italian law long forbade the Navy to possess fixed-wing aircraft weighing more than 1,500 kg, and the Navy has only helicopters, some 90 of them. In order to remedy this situation, which dates from long before World War II and which has proved such a handicap to its operations, the Navy has done its utmost to get this law modified, encountering resistance from the Air Force. Nonetheless, it has prevailed and will now acquire a small number of Sea Harrier or AV-8B Harrier V/STOL fighter-bombers, embarkable with no problems aboard the helicopter carrier *Garibaldi,* since that ship was designed with this eventuality in mind. Speaking of helicopters, it must be remembered that the Italian and British aeronautical industries are working jointly on production of a helicopter, the EH.101, meant to replace the Sea Kings now in service.

The Italian Air Force's Atlantic planes are being modernized by modification of their weapon systems and installation of some new equipment.

The Royal Spanish Navy has entered a renovation phase with a relatively extensive program of new construction. Its centerpiece is the aircraft carrier *Principe de Asturias.* Derived from a project dear to the heart of Admiral Zumwalt, CNO of the U.S. Navy a few years ago, her commissioning, which has been delayed several years, is being awaited with a great deal of interest. In addition to this ship, the naval program includes construction of *Santa Maria*-class frigates, a Spanish copy of the American FFG 7. Along with these sizeable projects, the Spanish Navy has begun modernization of its recent *Baleares*- and *Descubierta*-class units, equipping them with the Meroka close-in defense gun system and with the Tritan combat data control system, both of Spanish design.

The Air Arm of the Navy, consisting of Matador (the Spanish name for the McDonnell Douglas AV-8A Harrier) and some 50 helicopters, is being modernized by the acquisition of 12 additional V/STOL AV-8B Harriers for *Principe de Asturias* and the conversion of four Sea King helicopters into early-warning aircraft (AEW), following the installation of British Searchwater radar.

The Brazilian Navy, with its total standard displacement of some 76,000 tons, is the foremost in South America. It may become the sixth in the world to have nuclear-powered ships. The government in Brasilia has in fact decided to entrust to the Navy the task of building a nuclear-powered attack submarine of about 2,700 tons submerged. It believes that Brazilian engineers and the naval industry are entirely capable of carrying through to completion a project of this magnitude.

In this connection it should be noted that the Canadian Navy desires to have some 8–12 nuclear attack submarines, the design for which it plans to acquire from abroad.

J. Labayle-Couhat
Académie de la Marine
October 1987

(Translated by Kendall Lappin)

# ALBANIA

## People's Socialist Republic of Albania

PERSONNEL (1986): 1,500 men, with about 300 Coast Guard troops

MERCHANT MARINE (1986): 20 ships—56,138 grt

Neither the U.S.S.R. nor China is now supporting Albania, and the material condition of the ships listed below must be suffering. All former Soviet equipment was transferred prior to 1961.

◆ **3 Soviet Whiskey-class submarines**

**D:** 1,050/1,350 tons **S:** 17/13.5 kts **Dim:** 76.0 × 6.3 × 4.8
**A:** 6/533-mm TT (4 fwd, 2 aft)—12 torpedoes or 24 mines
**Electron Equipt:** Radar: 1/Snoop Plate—Sonar: Tamir-5 MF active
**M:** 2 Type 37-D, 2,000-hp diesels, electric motors; 2 props; 2,500 hp (sub.)
**Range:** 6,000/5 (snorkel) **Endurance:** 40–45 days **Man:** 50 tot.

REMARKS: All reported out of service in 1980, but two have reportedly been made operational. A fourth is a mere hulk.

◆ **2 Soviet Kronshtadt-class patrol boats**

**D:** 300 tons (330 fl) **S:** 18 kts **Dim:** 52.1 × 6.5 × 2.2
**A:** 1/85-mm DP—2/37-mm AA (I × 2)—6/12.7-mm mg (II × 3)—2/d.c.t.—2/d.c. rack—2/RBU-900 ASW RL—mines
**M:** 3 Type 9-D diesels; 3 props; 3,300 hp **Range:** 3,500/14 **Fuel:** 20 tons
**Man:** 40 tot.

REMARKS: Two others have been discarded.

◆ **6 Chinese Shanghai-II-class patrol boats**

**D:** 122.5 tons (135 fl) **S:** 28 kts **Dim:** 38.78 × 5.41 × 1.55 (props)
**A:** 4/37-mm AA (II × 2)—4/25-mm AA (II × 2)
**Electron Equipt:** Radar: 1/Pot Head
**M:** 2/1,200-hp diesels, 2/910-hp diesels; 4 props; 4,220 hp **Man:** 36 tot.
**Electric:** 39 kw **Endurance:** 7 days **Range:** 750/16.5

REMARKS: Transferred 1974–75; probably operational.

◆ **30 Chinese Huchuan-class hydrofoil torpedo boats**

**Huchuan-class hydrofoil torpedo boat in Albanian service** 1976

**D:** 39 tons (45.8 fl) **S:** 50 kts **Dim:** 22.30 × 3.80 (6.26 over fenders) × 1.15
**A:** 2/533-mm TT—4/14.5-mm mg (II × 2)
**Electron Equipt:** Radar: 1/Skin Head
**M:** 3 M50F-4 diesels; 3 props; 3,600 hp
**Electric:** 5.6 kw **Range:** 500/30 **Man:** 11 tot.

REMARKS: Bow foils only; stern planes on surface. Transferred 1974–75.

◆ **1 Soviet T-43-class ocean minesweeper**

**D:** 500 tons (570 fl) **S:** 14 kts **Dim:** 58.0 × 8.6 × 2.3 (3.5 sonar)
**A:** 4/37-mm AA (II × 2)—8/12.7-mm mg (II × 4)—2/d.c.t.—mines
**Electron Equipt:** Radar: 1/Ball End—Sonar: Tamir-11
**M:** 2 Type 9-D diesels; 2 props; 2,200 hp **Range:** 3,200/10

REMARKS: A sister has been stricken.

◆ **4 Soviet T-301-class coastal minesweepers**

**D:** 145.8 tons (160 fl) **S:** 12.5 kts **Dim:** 38.0 × 5.1 × 1.6
**A:** 1/45-mm AA—4/12.7-mm mg (II × 2)—mines
**M:** 36-cyl. diesels; 3 props; 1,440 hp **Range:** 2,500/8 **Man:** 32 tot.

REMARKS: Two others have been discarded.

◆ **1 Soviet Khobi-class small oiler**

PATOS (ex-Sov. *Linda*)

**D:** 1,525 tons (fl) **S:** 12 kts **Dim:** 62.0 × 10.0 × 4.4
**M:** 2 diesels; 2 props; 1,600 hp

REMARKS: Transferred 2-59. 795 grt. Sister *Semani* is civil.

◆ **1 Soviet Toplivo-I-class fuel lighter**—450 tons (fl)

◆ **1 Soviet Sekstan-class degaussing tender**

**D:** 280 tons (345 fl) **S:** 10 kts **Dim:** 40.8 × 9.3 × 4.2
**M:** 1 diesel; 1 prop; 400 hp **Range:** 1,200/10.5 **Man:** 24 tot.

◆ **2 Soviet Tuger-class coastal tugs**

MUJOULQINAKU N . . .

**D:** 300 tons (fl) **S:** 12 kts **Dim:** 30.7 × 7.7 × 2.3
**M:** 1 set reciprocating steam; 1 prop; 500 hp
**Boilers:** 2

◆ **1 Soviet Nyryat-1-class diving tender**

**D:** 120 tons (fl) **S:** 12 kts **Dim:** 29.0 × 5.0 × 1.7
**M:** 1 diesel; 1 prop; 450 hp **Range:** 1,600/10 **Man:** 15 tot.

◆ **4 Soviet Poluchat-I-class torpedo retrievers**

SKENDERBEU + 3 others

**D:** 90 tons (fl) **S:** 18 kts **Dim:** 29.6 × 5.8 × 1.5
**A:** 2/14.5-mm mg (II × 1) **M:** 2 M50 diesels; 2 props; 2,400 hp
**Range:** 450/17; 900/10 **Man:** 20 tot.

◆ **2 Soviet Shalanda-class cargo lighters**

◆ **1 Soviet Duna-class power barge**

# ALGERIA

## Democratic and Popular Republic of Algeria

PERSONNEL (1984): 3,800 men with about 300 to 350 officers, not necessarily on full-time active duty with the navy.

MERCHANT MARINE (1986): 145 ships—881,670 grt
(tankers: 17—119,079 grt)

NAVAL AVIATION: The Algerian Air Force uses 3 Fokker F-27 (Maritime) Mk 400 and 2 Beech Super King Air 200 patrol aircraft for maritime surveillance.

### SUBMARINES

◆ **2 Soviet Romeo class** Bldr: Baltic SY, Leningrad (In serv. 1957–60)

**One of two Algerian Romeos** U.S. Navy, 1986

**D:** 1,330/1,700 tons **S:** 15.5/13 kts **Dim:** 77.0 × 6.7 × 4.9
**A:** 8/533-mm TT (6 fwd, 2 aft)—14 torpedoes or 28 mines
**Electron Equipt:** Radar: 1/Snoop Plate—EW: 1/Stop Light
Sonar: 1/med. freq.; passive array
**M:** 2 Type 37-D diesels; electric motors; 2 props; 3,000 hp (sub.)
**Endurance:** 45 days **Range:** 7,000/5 **Man:** 56 tot.

REMARKS: On 5-year loan; 1 transferred 1-82, second in 2-83. Diving depth, 270–300 meters. One has lower portion of forward edge of sail projecting forward.

### FRIGATES

◆ **3 Soviet Koni class** Bldr: Zelenodolsk SY

901 MOURAD RAÏS (In serv. 20-12-80) 902 RAÏS KELLIK (In serv. 24-3-82)
903 RAÏS KORFO (In serv. 10-84)

**Raïs Kellik (902)** French Navy, 9-80

**D:** 1,440 tons (1,600 fl) **S:** 30 kts **Dim:** 96.40 × 12.55 × 3.48 (hull)
**A:** 1/SAN-4 SAM syst. (II × 1; 20 missiles)—4/76.2-mm DP (II × 2)—4/30-mm AA (II × 2)—2/RBU-6000—2/d.c. racks—mines

FRIGATES *(continued)*

**Electron Equipt:** Radar: 1/Strut Curve, 1/Don-2, 1/Pop Group, 1/Hawk Screech, 1/Drum Tilt
IFF: 2/Square Head, 1/High Pole B (Salt Pot C on 902)
EW: 2/Watch Dog passive—1/Cross Loop A (D/F), 2/chaff RL(XVI × 2)
**M:** CODAG: 1/19,000-hp gas turbine, 2 Type 68-B, 9,000-hp diesels, 3 props; 35,000 hp
**Range:** 1,800/14 **Man:** 130 tot.

REMARKS: In service dates reflect delivery dates. Have two chaff launchers, deckhouse abaft stack, unlike earlier examples. D.C. racks bolt to mine rails. Believed to be the 5th, 7th, and 10th units of the class.

## GUIDED-MISSILE CORVETTES

◆ **3 (+1) Soviet Nanuchka-II class** Bldr: Petrovskiy SY, Leningrad

801 RAÏS HAMIDOU 802 SALAH RAÏS 803 RAÏS ALI

**Raïs Ali (803)** VP-23, U.S. Navy, 5-82

**Raïs Hamidou (801)** French Navy, 1980

**D:** 675 tons (fl) **S:** 30 kts **Dim:** 59.3 × 12.6 × 2.4
**A:** 4/SS-N-2C (II × 2)—1/SA-N-4 SAM syst. (II × 1; 20 missiles)—2/57-mm DP (II × 1)
**Electron Equipt:** Radar: 1/Mius, 1/Square Tie, 1/Pop Group, 1/Muff Cob
EW: 1/Bell Tap, 1/Cross Loop (D/F), 2/chaff RL (XVI × 2)
IFF: 2/Square Head, 1/Salt Pot B
**M:** 3 M517 diesels; 3 props; 30,000 hp **Range:** 900/30; 2,500/12 **Man:** 60 tot.

REMARKS: 801 arrived in Algeria 4-7-80, 802 in 2-81, 803 in 5-82. The Square Tie radar antenna is mounted within the Band Stand radome atop the bridge. Contract to reengine with MTU diesels signed 5-83, but not known if accomplished.

## GUIDED-MISSILE PATROL BOATS

◆ **9 Soviet Osa-II class**

644 645 646 647 648 649 650 651 974

**D:** 215 tons (240 fl) **S:** 36 kts **Dim:** 38.6 × 7.6 × 1.9
**A:** 4/SS-N-2B Styx SSM (I × 4)—4/30-mm AA (II × 2)
**Electron Equipt:** Radar: 1/Square Tie, 1/Drum Tilt
IFF: 2/Square Head, 1/High Pole B
**M:** 3 M504 diesels; 3 props; 15,000 hp **Range:** 430/34; 790/20 **Man:** 30 tot.

REMARKS: Transferred 1976–78, except 974: 12-80. Contract for replacement of engines by MTU diesels discussed 1983.

◆ **2 Soviet Osa-I class**

641 642

**D:** 185 tons (209 fl) **S:** 36 kts **Dim:** 38.6 × 7.6 × 1.8
**A:** 4/SS-N-2A Styx SSM (I × 4)—4/30-mm AA (II × 2)
**Electron Equipt:** Radar: 1/Square Tie, 1/Drum Tilt
IFF: 2/Square Head, 1/High Pole B
**M:** 3 M503A diesels; 3 props; 12,000 hp **Man:** 30 tot.

REMARKS: Transferred 1967. No. 643 lost in explosion 1981.

## PATROL BOATS

◆ **0 (+1 + 2) Bulgarian C-58 design** Bldr: ONCN/CNE, Mers el-Kébir

N . . . (L: 3-2-85) N . . . (L: . . .) N . . . (L: . . .)

**D:** 500 tons (fl) **S:** 35 kts **Dim:** 58.00 × 8.4 × . . .
**A:** 1/76-mm Oto Melara DP—2/40-mm Breda AA (II × 1)
**Electron Equipt:** Radar: . . .
**M:** 3 MTU 20V538 series diesels; 3 props; 12–15,000 hp
**Range:** . . ./. . . **Man:** . . .

REMARKS: Ordered 7-83; difficulties in fitting out the prototype forced suspension of work on the other pair prior to launch. Were to have optronic director for the 76-mm gun, optical director for the twin 40-mm. Trials for first, mid-1987.

NOTE: Two T-43-class ocean minesweepers have been discarded; their eventual replacement by European-built ships is planned.

## AMPHIBIOUS WARFARE SHIPS

◆ **2 British Brooke Marine-design landing ships**

| | Bldr | Laid down | L | In serv. |
|---|---|---|---|---|
| 472 KALAAT BENI HAMMED | Brooke Marine, Lowestoft | . . . | 18-4-84 | 4-84 |
| 473 KALAAT BENI RACHED | Vosper-Thornycroft, Woolston | 20-12-82 | 15-5-84 | 10-84 |

**Kalaat Beni Rached (473)** Walles Foto, 9-84

**Kalaat Beni Hammed (472)** L. & L. Van Ginderen, 1984

**D:** 2,130 tons (fl) **S:** 16 kts **Dim:** 93.0 (80.00 pp) × 15.0 × 2.5
**A:** 2/40-mm Breda AA (II × 1)—2/20-mm AA (I × 2)
**Electron Equipt:** Radar: 1/Decca TM 1229, 1/Marconi S800
**M:** 2 MTU 12V7763 TB92 diesels; 2 props; 6,000 hp
**Range:** 3,000/12 **Endurance:** 28 days (10 with troops)
**Man:** 81 tot. + 240 troops

REMARKS: 472 ordered 10-81; 473 sub-contracted to Vosper-Thornycroft 18-10-82. Naja optronic gun director. Helicopter deck aft. Pontoon sections stowed on deck forward. The vehicle deck is 75 m long by 7.4 m wide and is served by a 30-m by 7-m hatch. The bow ramp extends to 18 m and is 4–5 m wide, while the stern

**AMPHIBIOUS WARFARE SHIPS** *(continued)*

ramp measures 5 m by 4 m. The traveling crane has a 16-ton capacity. Minimum beaching gradient is 1:40. Can carry 650 tons of cargo, but beaching limit is 450.

◆ **1 Soviet Polnocny-A-class medium landing ship** (transferred 9-76)

471 N . . .

**471** 1982

**D:** 770 tons (fl) **S:** 18 kts **Dim:** 73.0 × 8.6 × 2.0
**A:** 2/30-mm AA (II × 1)—2/140-mm barrage RL (XVIII × 2)
**Electron Equipt:** Radar: 1/Don-2, 1/Drum Tilt
IFF: 1/Square Head, 1/High Pole A
**M:** 2 diesels; 2 props; 5,000 hp **Range:** 1,500/14 **Man:** 40 tot.

**MISCELLANEOUS**

◆ **1 Soviet Poluchat-1-class torpedo retriever**

A 641

**D:** 90 tons (fl) **S:** 18 kts **Dim:** 29.6 × 5.8 × 1.5
**M:** 2 M50 diesels; 2 props; 2,400 hp **Man:** 20 tot.

◆ **1 Soviet Nyryat-1-class diving tender** (transferred 1965)

VP 650 Yavdezan

**D:** 120 tons (fl) **S:** 12 kts **Dim:** 29.0 × 5.0 × 1.7
**M:** 1 diesel; 1 prop; 450 hp **Range:** 1,600/10

◆ **1 survey craft** Bldr: Matsukara, Hirao, Japan

A 673 El Idrissi (L: 17-4-80) **D:** 250 grt

COAST GUARD

◆ **6(+ 6) British Brooke Marine 37.5-meter-design patrol boats**

Bldr. 341, 342: Brooke Marine, Lowestoft; others: ONCN/CNE, Mers el-Kébir

| | In serv. | | In serv. |
|---|---|---|---|
| 341 El Yadekh | 12-82 | 347 N . . . | . . . |
| 342 El Morakeb | 4-83 | 348 N . . . | . . . |
| 343 N . . . | 5-84 | 349 N . . . | . . . |
| 344 N . . . | 1985 | 350 N . . . | . . . |
| 345 N . . . | 10-11-85 | 351 N . . . | . . . |
| 346 N . . . | 1986 | 352 N . . . | . . . |

**D:** 166 tons (250 fl) **S:** 27 kts **Dim:** 37.50 (34.74 pp) × 6.86 × 1.78
**A:** 2/25-mm Soviet AA (II × 1) (341, 342: 1/76-mm OTO Melara DP)—2/14.5-mm Soviet mg (I × 2)
**Electron Equipt:** Radar: 1/Decca 1226
**M:** 2 MTU 12V538 TB92 diesels; 2 props; 6,000 hp
**Range:** 2,500/15 **Man:** 3 officers, 24 men

**El Yadekh (341)** French Navy, 9-84

**El Morakeb (342)** Skyfotos, 1983

Remarks: Also known as "Kebir" class. Program replaced indigenous missile boat program in 1981. Laurence Scott optronic GFCS. Nos. 347–349 ordered 1984, three more in 1986.

◆ **6 Mangusta-class patrol boats** Bldr: Baglietto, Italy (In serv. 1977–78)

| | | |
|---|---|---|
| 323 Ombrine | 324 Dorade | 331 Requin |
| 332 Espadon | 333 Marsouin | 334 Murene |

**D:** 91 tons (fl) **S:** 32 kts **Dim:** 30.0 × 5.84 × 2.1
**A:** 2/25-mm AA (II × 2)—2/23-mm AA (II × 1)
**Electron Equipt:** Radar: 1/3RM 20 SMA
**M:** 3 diesels; 3 props; 4,050 hp **Range:** 800/24; 1,400/12.5
**Man:** 3 officers, 11 men

**Requin** (now renumbered and armed) C. Martinelli, 1977

◆ **10 Type 20-GC-class patrol craft** Bldr: Baglietto, Italy (In serv. 8-76 to 12-76)

100 112 113 114 221 222 235 236 237 325

**Baglietto**—20-GC class C. Martinelli, 1977

**D:** 44 tons (fl) **S:** 36 kts **Dim:** 20.4 × 5.2 × 1.7 **A:** 1/20-mm AA
**M:** 2 CRM 18DS diesels; 2 props; 2,700 hp **Range:** 445/20 **Man:** 11 tot.

◆ **12 18-ton patrol craft** Bldr: ONCN/CNE, Mers el-Kébir (In serv. 1982–83)

Djebel Antar Djebel Handa 10 others

**ALGERIA** *(continued)*

CUSTOMS SERVICE

◆ **3 P 1200 Mk II class patrol craft** Bldr: Watercraft, Shoreham, U.K. (In serv. 21-11-85)

Bouzagza Djurdjura Hodna

**D:** 38.5 tons (fl) **S:** 35 kts **Dim:** 20.80 (18.00 wl) × 5.59 × 1.52
**A:** 2/7.62-mm mg (1 × 2) **Electron Equipt:** Radar: 1/Decca 170
**M:** 2 M.A.N. V10 D2450 MLE diesels; 2 props; 1,300 hp
**Range:** 300/21 **Man:** 4 tot.

Remarks: Glass-reinforced plastic construction.

◆ **2 P 802-class patrol craft** Bldr: Watercraft, Shoreham, U.K. (In serv. 21-11-85)

Aures Hoggar

Remarks: 8.00 m overall, powered by two Volvo AQAD 40 inboard/outboard diesels for 30+ kts. GRP construction.

# ANGOLA

## People's Republic of Angola

Personnel (1986): about 1,500 total

Merchant Marine (1986): 100 ships—92,285 grt (tankers: 3—2,052 grt)

Naval Aviation: One Fokker F-27 Maritime and two EMB 111 patrol aircraft

Note: The ex-Portuguese craft were located in Angola in 1975 and were transferred on independence.

### GUIDED-MISSILE PATROL BOATS

◆ **6 Soviet Osa-II class**

**D:** 215 tons (245 fl) **S:** 36 kts **Dim:** 39.0 × 7.7 × 1.8
**A:** 4/SS-N-2 Styx (I × 4)—4/30-mm (II × 2) **Man:** 30 tot.
**Electron Equipt:** Radar: 1/Square Tie, 1/Drum Tilt
IFF: 2/Square Head, 1/High Pole B
**M:** 3 Type M504 diesels; 3 props; 15,000 hp **Range:** 430/34; 790/20

Remarks: Delivered in pairs, 10-82, 12-82, and 11-83 by RO/FLO cargo ship *Stakhanovets Petrash.*

### TORPEDO BOATS

◆ **4 Soviet Shershen class**

**D:** 145 tons (170 fl) **S:** 45 kts **Dim:** 34.0 × 6.8 × 1.5
**A:** 4/30-mm AA (II × 2)—4/533-mm TT
**Electron Equipt:** Radar: 1/Pot Drum, 1/Drum Tilt
IFF: 1/Square Head, 1/High Pole A
**M:** 3 M503A diesels; 3 props; 12,000 hp **Range:** 450/34; 700/20

Remarks: Delivered 12-77 to 11-79. Unlike many recent transfers to this class, all retained torpedo tubes.

### PATROL BOATS

◆ **2 Soviet Zhuk class** (transferred 23-1-77)

**D:** 50 tons (60 fl) **S:** 34 kts **Dim:** 26.0 × 4.9 × 1.5
**A:** 4/14.5-mm mg (II × 2) **M:** 2 M50 diesels; 2 props; 2,400 hp

◆ **2 Soviet Poluchat-I class** (transferred 12-79)

**D:** 90 tons (fl) **S:** 18 kts **Dim:** 29.6 × 5.8 × 1.5 **Range:** 450/17; 900/10
**A:** 2/14.5-mm mg (II × 1) **M:** 2 M50 diesels; 2 props; 2,400 hp **Man:** 20 tot.

◆ **5 Portuguese Argos class** Bldr: Castelo SY (P 375, P 1130: Alfeite Navy Yd, Lisbon) In serv. 1963–65

P 361 (ex-*Lira*) P 375 (ex-*Escorpido*) P 1130 (ex-*Centauro*)
P 362 (ex-*Orion*) P 379 (ex-*Pegaso*)

**D:** 180 tons (210 fl) **S:** 18 kts **Dim:** 41.6 × 6.2 × 2.2 **Fuel:** 16 tons
**A:** 2/40-mm AA (I × 2) **M:** 2 Maybach diesels; 2 props; 2,000 hp **Man:** 24 tot.

Remarks: Two others, *Argos* and *Dragao,* transferred for cannibalization. Several of the above may now be out of service.

◆ **1 Portuguese Jupiter class** Bldr: Mondego SY (In serv. 1965)

P 1133 (ex-*Venus*)

**D:** 32 tons (43.5 fl) **S:** 20 kts **Dim:** 20.7 × 5.0 × 1.3 **A:** 1/20-mm AA
**M:** 2 Cummins diesels; 2 props; 1,270 hp

◆ **5 Portuguese Bellatrix class** Bldr: Bayerische Schiffsbaugesellschaft, West Germany (In serv. 1961–62)

P 366 (ex-*Espiga*) P 368 (ex-*Pollux*) P 378 (ex-*Rigel*)
P 367 (ex-*Fomelhaut*) P 377 (ex-*Altair*)

**D:** 23 tons (27.6 fl) **S:** 15 kts **Dim:** 20.5 × 4.6 × 1.2
**A:** 1/20-mm AA—1/37-mm RL (atop 20-mm AA)
**M:** 2 Cummins diesels; 2 props; 470 hp **Man:** 7 tot.

### AMPHIBIOUS WARFARE SHIPS

◆ **2 commercial-design vehicle landing craft** Bldr: Scheepswerf Ton Bodewes, Franeker, Neth. (In serv. 1979)

47 10 Diciembre 48 11 Noviembre

**D:** 850 (fl) **S:** 10 kts **Dim:** 53.0 (pp) × 11.5 × 2.2
**M:** 2 Caterpillar diesels; 2 props; . . . hp

Remarks: 446 grt/575 dwt. May be engaged in civil cargo-carrying tasks.

◆ **3 Soviet Polnocny-B-class medium landing ships** Bldr: Polnocny SY, Gdansk, Poland

**D:** 800 tons (fl) **S:** 19 kts **Dim:** 74.0 × 8.6 × 2.0
**A:** 2/30-mm AA (II × 1)—2/140-mm barrage RL (XVIII × 2)
**Electron Equipt:** Radar: 1/Don 2, 1/Drum Tilt
IFF: 1/Square Head
**M:** 2 diesels; 2 props; 5,000 hp **Range:** 1,500/14 **Man:** 40 tot.

Remarks: First transferred 16-12-77, second 16-12-78, third 1-12-79.

◆ **1 Portuguese Alfange-class medium landing ship** Bldr: Mondego SY (In serv. 1965)

N . . . . . . . (ex-*Alfange*)

**D:** 500 tons (fl) **S:** 11 kts **Dim:** 57.0 × 11.8 × 1.9 **A:** 2/20-mm AA
**M:** 2 diesels; 2 props; 1,000 hp **Range:** 1,500/9 **Man:** 14 tot. + 35 troops

Remarks: A second unit was not placed in service. Design based on British LCT (4) class of World War II.

◆ **5 Soviet T-4-class landing craft** (Transferred 1976)

**D:** 70 tons (fl) **S:** 10 kts **Dim:** 19.0 × 4.3 × 1.0
**M:** 2 diesels; 2 props, 600 hp **Man:** 5 tot.

◆ **Up to 9 Portuguese LDM-400-class landing craft**

**D:** 56 tons (fl) **S:** 9 kts **Dim:** 17.0 × 5.0 × 1.2 **A:** 1/20-mm AA
**M:** 2 Cummins diesels; 2 props; 450 hp

# ANGUILLA

Merchant Marine (1986): 14 ships—3,966 grt

MARINE POLICE

◆ **1 Huntsman-class patrol craft** Bldr: Fairey Marine, U.K.

Lapwing (In Serv. 1984)

Remarks: GRP construction. Also in use is a Fairey Intercepter craft for search and rescue; powered by two 280-hp outboard engines for 30+ kts, the craft carries eight 25-person liferafts.

# ANTIGUA-BARBUDA

Merchant Marine (1986): 5 ships—1,048 grt

COAST GUARD

◆ **1 U.S. 65-ft Commercial Cruiser-class patrol craft** Bldr: Swiftships, Inc., Morgan City, Louisiana

P-01 Liberta (In serv. 30-4-84)

**D:** 36 tons (fl) **S:** 23 kts **Dim:** 19.96 × 5.59 × 1.52
**A:** 1/12.7-mm mg **Electron Equipt:** Radar: 1/Raytheon 1210

**ANTIGUA-BARBUDA** *(continued)*
**COAST GUARD** *(continued)*

**M:** 2 G.M. 12V71 TI diesels; 2 props; 1,350 hp
**Electric:** 20 kw **Range:** 500/18 **Man:** 6 tot.

REMARKS: Aluminum construction. U.S. Grant-Aid.

**Liberta (P-01)** Swiftships, 1984

# ARGENTINA

## Argentine Republic

PERSONNEL (1985): 23,400 men, including 2,300 officers and 3,000 Marines

MERCHANT MARINE (1986): 454 ships—2,117,917 grt (tankers: 60—653,964 grt)

NOTE: Fiscal constraints have forced cutting new programs, the disposal of older ships, the reduction of manpower by 7,500 (including 500 officers and 3,000 Marines), and a severe restriction in annual steaming days.

NAVAL AVIATION: In 1987, the aircraft for shipboard service included: 14 Super Étendard (4 in storage, remainder now flown from land), 4 A-4Q Skyhawk fighter-bombers, and 7 S-2E ASW aircraft. Helicopters: 5 SH-3D, 2 SH-3H, 2 WG-13 Mk 23 Lynx, 6 Hughes 500M Cayuse, 2 Sikorsky S-61NR, and 8 Alouette-III. Three S-2A Trackers perform COD duties.

For land-based duties: 3 Aeromacchi MB-339AA and 8 MB-326GB attack/trainers; 3 Fokker F-28-3000, 1 BAe 125 Series 400A, 12 Lockheed L-188 Electra transports (2 with Exocet capability, 2 with maritime search radars and EW gear), 12 EMB-326GB Xavante, and 2 Short Skyvan transports; 8 Beech Super King Air 200, 5 Beech B80 Queen Air, and 3 Fairchild Porter light transports; 11 Beech T-34 C-1 trainers; 2 AS332 Super Puma, and 2 Puma helicopters.

Because it has proven difficult to operate the Super Étendard on the small, slow *Veinticinco de Mayo,* 12 ex-Israeli A-4E Skyhawks were ordered in 12-84, but were still not delivered as of 5-87. One Boeing 707 transport for EW duties was ordered from Israel, 1986. The new IA-63 Pampa fighter trainer may be ordered in a navalized version to replace the MB-339AA and MB-326GB aircraft. Four Agusta A-109 helicopters were ordered 1-87 for service on the MEKO 360 class in lieu of non-delivered Lynxes, and four SH-3H ASW helicopters were also ordered from Agusta. Twelve Kaman SH-2F Sea Sprite ASW helicopters may be ordered for shipboard service.

**Super Étendard 3-A-204,** one of two aircraft in the attack on HMS *Sheffield*
R. Scheina, 1982

### AIRCRAFT CARRIER

NOTE: A 30,000-ton replacement for *Veinticinco de Mayo* is planned, finances permitting.

◆ **1 British Colossus-class**

| | Bldr | Laid down | L | In serv. |
|---|---|---|---|---|
| VEINTICINCO DE MAYO (ex-*Karel Dorman,* ex-*Venerable*) | Cammell Laird | 3-12-42 | 30-12-43 | 17-1-45 |

**Veinticinco De Mayo** R. Scheina, 1982

**D:** 15,892 tons (19,896 fl) **S:** 24.5 kts (limited to 18.0)
**Dim:** 212.67 (192.04 pp) × 24.49 (40.66 flight deck) × 7.5
**A:** 9/40-mm AA (I × 10)—4 A-4E Skyhawk, 5 S-2E Tracker, 3–4 SH-3D or H helo
**Electron Equipt:** Radar: 2/LW-02, 1/SGR-109 (height-finding), 1/SGR-105 (DA-05), 1/SGR-103 (ZW-01), 1/SMA MM/SPN-720 air control—TACAN: URN-20

**M:** 2 sets Parsons GT; 2 props; 40,000 hp **Electric:** 2,500 kw
**Boilers:** 4 Admiralty 3-drum type; 30.23 kg/cm² (since refit), 371°C
**Fuel:** 3,200 tons **Range:** 6.200/23; 12,000/14
**Man:** 1,509 tot.

REMARKS: Purchased by the Netherlands from the British Navy in 1948. Rebuilt from 1955 to 1958 by Wilton-Fijenoord; 165.80-meter angled flight deck, steam catapult, mirror optical landing equipment, new antiaircraft guns, and new radar equipment of Dutch conception and construction. Modified for service in the tropics. Partially air-conditioned. In 1967 new boilers were installed from the British aircraft carrier *Leviathan,* which was never completed. Purchased in 1968 by Argentina and again refitted, recommissioning 22-8-69. She is equipped with the British C.A.A.I.S. data display system, compatible with the ADAWS-4 data system on the *Sheffield*-class destroyers. 1980 refit enlarged flight deck to permit deck-parking three additional aircraft. Altered 1982–83 to permit operating Super Étendard fighter/bombers; 1/40-mm AA removed. Super Étendards replaced by Skyhawks, 1985. Persistent engineering problems have left her inactive since 6-86.

### SUBMARINES

◆ **2 (+3) TR-1700-class diesel-electric attack submarines**

| | Bldr | Laid down | L | In serv. |
|---|---|---|---|---|
| S 41 SANTA CRUZ | Thyssen Noordseewerke, Emden | 6-12-80 | 28-9-82 | 14-12-84 |
| S 42 SAN JUAN | Thyssen Noordseewerke, Emden | 18-3-82 | 20-6-83 | 18-11-85 |
| S 43 SANTA FE | Manuel Domecq Garcia, Buenos Aires | 14-10-83 | . . . | 1991 |
| S 44 SANTAGO DEL ESTERO | Manuel Domecq Garcia, Buenos Aires | . . . | . . . | . . . |
| S 45 N . . . . . . . . | Manuel Domecq Garcia, Buenos Aires | | | |

**Santa Cruz (S 41)**—on trials Thyssen, 1984

**D:** 1,770 tons (2,150 surf./2,364 sub. fl)
**S:** 25 kts (sub)—13 snorkel, 15 kts (surf) **Dim:** 66.00 × 7.30 × 6.50
**A:** 6/533-mm TT, 22 SST-4 wire-guided torpedoes
**Electron Equipt:** Radar: 1/MM/BPS-704
Sonar: Krupp Atlas . . .
**M:** diesel-electric: 4/MTU 16V652 MB80 1,100-kw generator sets; 1 6,600-kw motor; 1 prop, 8,970 hp (8,000 sust.)
**Fuel:** 314 tons **Endurance:** 30 days **Man:** 30 tot.
**Range:** 20/25, 50/20, 110/15, 460/6 sub.—12,000/8 surf.

## SUBMARINES *(continued)*

**TR-1700 class** L. & L. Van Ginderen, 5-87

REMARKS: Ordered 30-11-77. Originally only the first to be built in Germany. Two smaller Type TR-1400 replaced by 2 TR-1700 in the 2-82 change to order. 300-m depth. Battery has eight groups of 120 cells, 5,858-amp/10-hr. H.S.A. SINBADS weapons control system, SAGEM plotting table. Pressure hull 48.0 m long. Torpedoes auto-reload in 50 seconds.

Permission to sell *all* of these submarines to a third country was given in 6-86 by West Germany; the Argentine-built ships have been for sale since 1984. No work seems to have been done on the planned 6th unit, and progress is slow on the others.

◆ **German Type 209-class diesel-electric coastal submarines**

| | Bldr | Laid down | L | In serv. |
|---|---|---|---|---|
| S 31 SALTA | Howaldtswerke, Kiel | 3-4-70 | 9-11-72 | 7-3-74 |
| S 32 SAN LUIS | Howaldtswerke, Kiel | 1-10-70 | 3-4-73 | 24-5-74 |

**Salta (S 31)** Argentine Navy, 1982

**D:** 980 tons standard, 1,105 surfaced, 1,230 submerged
**Dim:** 55.9 × 6.20 × 5.50 **S:** 23 max. submerged, 12 snorkel, 11 surf.
**A:** 8/533-mm TT (14 German SST-4 and U.S. Mk 37 torpedoes)
**M:** 4 MTU 12V493 TY60, 600-hp diesels, 4/405-kw generators, Siemens electric motor; 1 prop; 5,000 hp
**Endurance:** 40 days **Fuel:** 63 tons **Man:** 5 officers, 26 men
**Range:** 230/8; 400/4 submerged; 6,000/8 snorkel

REMARKS: Built in four sections at Kiel and assembled at the Navy Yard in Rio Santiago. *San Luis* fired 6 torpedoes, without success, in the Falklands War; *Salta* did not take part. H.S.A. M8 fire-control system. *Salta* reported for sale, 1986.

## DESTROYERS

◆ **2 British Sheffield-class guided-missile destroyers**

| | Bldr | Laid down | L | In serv. |
|---|---|---|---|---|
| D 1 HERCULES | Vickers, Barrow | 1971 | 24-10-72 | 10-5-76 |
| D 2 SANTISIMA TRINIDAD | Ast. Nav., Rio Santiago | 2-72 | 9-11-74 | -81 |

**Hercules (D 1)**—note Exocets abreast stack Argentine Navy, 1984

**D:** 3,150 tons (4,100 fl) **S:** 28 kts **Dim:** 125.0 (119.5 pp) × 14.34 × 4.2 (hull)
**A:** 4/Exocet MM 38 SSM (I × 4)—1/Sea Dart Mk 30 Mod. 2 SAM syst. (II × 1, 20 missiles)—1/114-mm DP Mk 8—2/20-mm AA—1/helicopter—6/324-mm ASW TT (III × 2, A224S torpedoes)
**Electron Equipt:** Radar: 1/965M, 1/992Q, 2/909, 1/1006
Sonar: 1/184M, 1/162M—EW: intercept array
**M:** COGOG 2 Olympus TM 3B gas turbines, 27,200 hp each for boost; 2 Tyne RM 1A gas turbines, 4,100 hp each for cruising; 2 CP, 5-bladed props
**Electric:** 4,000 kw **Range:** 4,000/18 **Man:** 270 tot.

REMARKS: Ordered 18-5-70. D 2 was sabotaged on 22-8-75 and was delayed, running initial trials on 7-3-80. D 1, refitted 1980, had MM 38 Exocet missiles added atop the hangar; these were relocated in place of the boats abreast the stack in both, early 1982, when EW gear was also fitted. Have ADAWS-4 data system and NATO Link 10 data link. Both reported to be for sale in 9-84, due to inability to obtain spares from Britain; offered to Turkey, mid-1986.

## FRIGATES

◆ **4 MEKO 360 H2 Class** Bldr: Blohm + Voss, Hamburg

| | Laid down | L | In serv. |
|---|---|---|---|
| D 10 ALMIRANTE BROWN | 8-9-80 | 28-3-81 | 2-2-83 |
| D 11 LA ARGENTINA | 31-3-81 | 25-9-81 | 19-7-83 |
| D 12 HEROINA | 24-8-81 | 17-2-82 | 7-11-83 |
| D 13 SARANDI | 9-3-82 | 31-8-82 | 27-4-84 |

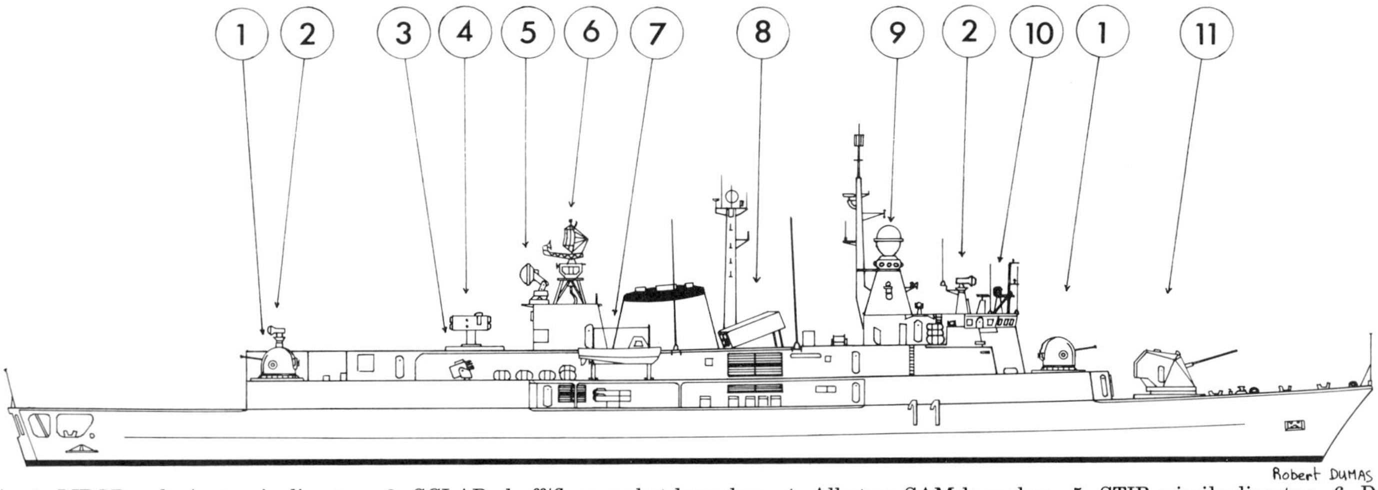


1. Twin 40-mm AA 2. LIROD radar/optronic director 3. SCLAR chaff/flare rocket launcher 4. Albatros SAM launcher 5. STIR missile director 6. DA-08 long-range radar antenna 7. triple ASW torpedo tubes 8. quadruple MM 40 Exocet ramps (under shield) 9. WM-25 track-while-scan radar 10. ZW-06 navigational radar 11. 127-mm dual-purpose gun mount

**FRIGATES** *(continued)*

**Sarandi (D 13)** P. Voss, 5-84

**Heroina (D 12) and sister** L. & L. Van Ginderen, 10-85

**D:** 2,900 tons (3,360 fl) **S:** 30.5 kts
**Dim:** 125.9 (119.0 pp) × 15.0 × 4.32 (5.80 sonar)
**A:** 8/MM 40 Exocet SSM (IV × 2)—1 Albatros SAM syst. (VIII × 1; 24 Aspide missiles)—1/27-mm OTO Melara DP—8/40-mm Breda AA (II × 4)—6/324-mm ILAS-3 ASW TT (III × 2; 18 torp.)—2/helicopters (10 ASW torp.)
**Electron Equipt:** Radar: 1/H.S.A. ZW-06, 1/H.S.A. DA-08A, 1/H.S.A. WM-25, 1/STIR, 2/H.S.A. LIROD
Sonar: Krupp Atlas KAE 80, hull-mounted
EW: AEG-Telefunken syst., 2/SCLAR chaff (XX × 2)
**M:** COGOG: 2 Olympus TM 3B gas turbines, 25,800 hp each; 2 Tyne RM 1C, 5,100 hp each for cruise; 2 Escher-Wyss CP props; 51,600 hp max.
**Electric:** 2,600 kw (2/940-kw sets, 2/360-kw) **Range:** 4,500/18
**Man:** 26 officers, 84 petty officers, 90 men

**Almirante Brown and La Argentina on trials** Schulz-Alex/Blohm + Voss, 1983

REMARKS: Considered to be destroyers by Argentine Navy. Ordered 11-12-78 as a class of *six,* four of which were to be built in Argentina, but altered to four when MEKO 140-series frigate program was introduced. Albatros system has a 16-missile Aspide SAM rapid-reload magazine nearby. SEWACO weapons data/control system. The two H.S.A. LIROD radar/optronic GFCS each control two twin 40-mm AA, for which 10,752 rounds can be carried. Graseby G1738 towed torpedo decoy system. Four Lynx helicopters for these ships canceled by U.K., 1982, and one Alouette-III is normally carried. The MEKO concept calls for modularized weapons and electronics systems, to permit rapid modernization and repair. Nigeria's *Aradu* is very similar.

◆ **1 (+5) MEKO 140 A16 class** Bldr: AFNE, Rio Santiago, Ensenada

| | Laid down | L | In serv. |
|---|---|---|---|
| F 10 Espora | 10-3-80 | 23-1-82 | 5-7-85 |
| F 11 Rosales | 7-1-81 | 4-3-83 | 14-11-86 |
| F 12 Spiro | 1-4-82 | 24-6-83 | 24-11-87 |
| F 13 Parker | 9-2-82 | 31-3-84 | . . . |
| F 14 Robinson | 6-6-83 | 2-85 | . . . |
| F 15 Gomez Roca (ex-*Seaver*) | 1-12-83 | 14-11-86 | . . . |

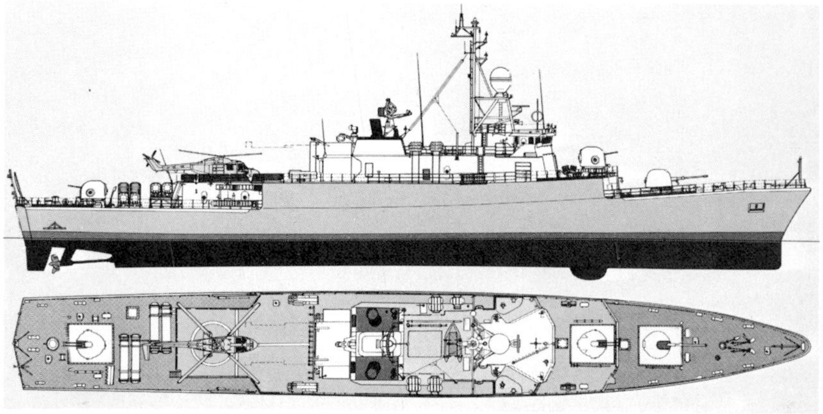

**MEKO 140 A 16 class with hangar** Blohm + Voss

**Espora (F 10) on trials** Blohm + Voss, 1984

**D:** 1,560 tons (1,790 fl) **S:** 27 kts **Dim:** 91.2 (86.4 pp) × 11.0 × 3.33 (hull)
**A:** 4/MM 40 Exocet SSM (II × 2)—1/76-mm DP OTO Melara—4/40-mm AA Breda (II × 2), 2/12.7-mm mg (I × 2)—6/324-mm ASW TT (III × 2)—1/helo
**Electron Equipt:** Radar: 1/Decca TM 1226, 1/H.S.A. DA-05/2, 1/H.S.A. WM-28, 2/H.S.A. LIROD
Sonar: 1/ASO-4
EW: RDC-2ABC and RCM-2 systems, 2/Dagaie chaff RL
**M:** 2 SEMT-Pielstick 16 PC2-5V400 diesels; 2/5-bladed props; 22,600 hp
**Electric:** 1,410 kVA (3 × 470 kVA diesel sets) **Range:** 4,000/18
**Fuel:** 230 tons **Man:** 11 officers, 46 petty officers, 36 men

REMARKS: All reported to be available for sale, late 1984. Ordered 8-79. Blohm + Voss design, based on Portuguese *João Coutinho* class. Have fin stabilizers. LIROD radar/electro-optical system controls 40-mm AA. Carry Whitehead A244S ASW torpedoes. To carry 5 tons aviation fuel, 70 tons fresh water. H.S.A. DAISY data system. Telescoping helo hangar on F 13–F 15 only. F 13 flooded out 2-10-86, delaying completion.

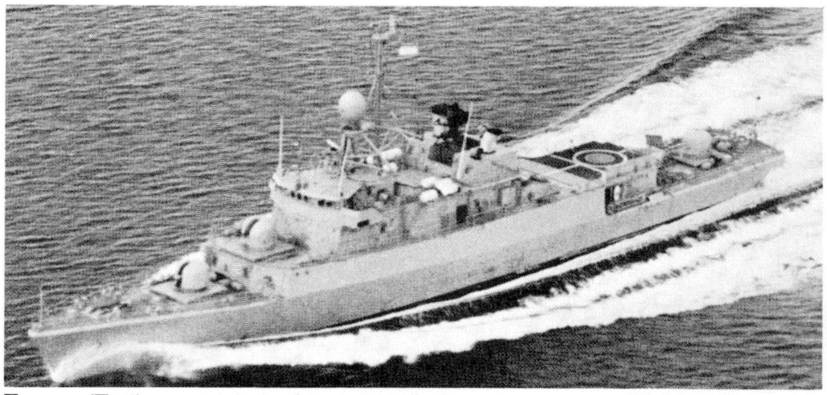

**Espora (F 10)**—on trials (no-hangar version) Blohm + Voss, 1984

◆ **3 French Type A-69 class** Bldr: Lorient DY

| | Laid down | L | In serv. |
|---|---|---|---|
| P 1 Drummond (ex-*Good Hope,* F 432, ex-*Lieutenant de Vaisseau le Henaff,* F 784) | 12-3-76 | 5-3-77 | 10-78 |
| P 2 Guerrico (ex-*Transvaal,* F 102, ex-*Commandant l'Herminier,* F 791) | 1-10-76 | 9-77 | 10-78 |
| P 3 Granville | end-78 | 28-6-80 | 22-6-81 |

**D:** 1,100 tons (1,250 fl) **S:** 23.3 kts
**Dim:** 80.5 (76.0 pp) × 10.3 × 3.0 (5.2 sonar)
**A:** 4/MM 38 Exocet (II × 2)—1/100-mm DP Mod. 1968—2/40-mm AA (II × 1)—2/20-mm AA (I × 2)—6/324-mm ASW TT (III × 2)
**Electron Equipt:** Radar: 1/Decca RM 1226, 1/DRBV-51A, 1/DRBC-32E
Sonar: Diodon
**EW:** DR 2000 S3 intercept, Alligator 51 jammer, 2 chaff RL
**M:** 2 SEMT-Pielstick 12 PC 2 V400 diesels; 2 CP props; 12,000 hp

**FRIGATES** *(continued)*

**Granville (P 3)** Argentine Navy, 1984

**Electric:** 840 kw **Range:** 3,000/18; 4,500/15 **Endurance:** 15 days
**Man:** 5 officers, 79 men

Remarks: The first two were originally ordered by South Africa, but delivery was embargoed. Purchased by Argentina, 25-9-78, to augment fleet in case of war with Chile. Armament and some electronic gear differ from French Navy version. P 3 has Breda twin 40-mm AA controlled by a CSEE Naja optronic GFCS; the others have older Bofors L60 mountings. Have fin stabilizers. P 3 has Dagaie chaff system. P 2 damaged on 7-4-82 during the invasion of South Georgia; repaired.

## CORVETTES

◆ **2 U.S. Achomawi class** Bldr: Charleston SB & DD Co.

| | Laid down | L | In serv. |
|---|---|---|---|
| A 1 Comandante General Irigoyen (ex-*Cahuilla*, ATF 152) | 16-6-44 | 2-11-44 | 10-3-45 |
| A 3 Francisco De Churruca (ex-*Luiseno*, ATF 156) | 7-11-44 | 17-3-45 | 16-6-45 |

**Comandante General Irigoyen (A 1)** R. Scheina, 1980

**D:** 1,235 tons (1,675 fl) **S:** 16.5 kts **Dim:** 62.48 (59.44 wl) × 11.73 × 4.67
**A:** 4/40-mm AA (II × 2, I × 2)—2/20-mm AA (I × 2)
**M:** 4 G.M. 12-278A diesels, electric drive; 1 prop; 3,000 hp
**Fuel:** 363 tons **Electric:** 400 kw **Range:** 7,000/15; 15,000/8 **Man:** 85 tot.

Remarks: A 1 transferred 1961 as an ocean tug; rerated a patrol ship in 1966. A 3 purchased 1-7-75. Retain tug and salvage facilities. A 3: 2/40-mm AA (II × 1) only. Were to be discarded on completion of MEKO 140 class.

◆ **Murature Class** Bldr: Rio Santiago Nav. Base

| | Laid down | L | In serv. |
|---|---|---|---|
| P 20 Murature | 3-40 | 7-43 | 4-45 |
| P 21 King | 6-38 | 11-43 | 11-46 |

**D:** 913 tons (1,032 fl) **S:** 18 kts **Dim:** 77.0 × 8.8 × 2.3
**A:** 3/105-mm DP (I × 3)—4/40-mm AA (II × 1, I × 2)—5/12.7-mm mg (I × 5)
**Electron Equipt:** Radar: 1/. . . navigational
**M:** 2 Werkspoor 4-cycle diesels; 2 props; 2,500 hp
**Range:** 6,000/12 **Fuel:** 90 tons **Man:** 100 tot.

Remarks: Riveted construction patrol gunboats now limited to sheltered waters and used primarily as cadet training ships. Scheduled to be replaced by MEKO 140-class frigates. Guns are obsolete German weapons.

## PATROL BOATS

◆ **2 Intrepida class** (Lürssen TNC 45 design)

| | Bldr | L | In serv. |
|---|---|---|---|
| P 85 Intrepida | Lürssen, Bremen-Vegesack | 2-12-73 | 20-7-74 |
| P 86 Indomita | Lürssen, Bremen-Vegesack | 8-4-74 | 12-74 |

**Indomita (P 86)** L. & L. Van Ginderen, 1986

**D:** 240 tons (265 fl) **S:** 37.8 kts **Dim:** 44.9 (42.3 pp) × 7.4 × 2.28 (prop.)
**A:** 1/76-mm DP OTO Melara—2/40-mm AA (I × 2)—2/533-mm wire-guided TT (German SST-4 torp.)
**Electron Equipt:** Radar: 1/Decca 101, 1/H.S.A. WM-22—EW: Decca Cutlass
**M:** 4 MTU MD872 diesels; 4 props; 14,400 hp **Electric:** 330 kw
**Range:** 640/36; 1,700/16 **Man:** 5 officers, 37 men

Remarks: Anti-rolling stabilizers. Plans to acquire two more canceled.

◆ **4 Israeli Dabur class** Bldr: Israeli Aircraft Industries, Israel (In serv. 1978)

P 61 Baradero P 62 Barranqueras P 63 Clorinda
P 64 Concepcion Del Uruguay

**D:** 26.8 tons (34.2 fl) **S:** 22 kts **Dim:** 19.8 × 5.4 × 1.75
**A:** 2/20-mm AA (I × 2)—4/12.7-mm mg (II × 2)
**Electron Equipt:** Radar: Decca 101
**M:** 2 G.M. 12V71 T diesels; 2 props; 1,200 hp **Range:** 700/16 **Man:** 8 tot.

## MINE WARFARE SHIPS

◆ **6 British "Ton"-class minesweepers/minehunters**

| | L | | L |
|---|---|---|---|
| M 1 Neuquen (ex-*Hickleton*) | 26-1-55 | M 4 Tierra del Fuego (ex-*Bevington*) | 17-3-53 |
| M 2 Rio Negro (ex-*Tarlton*) | 10-11-54 | M 5 Chaco (ex-*Rennington*) | 27-11-58 |
| M 3 Chubut (ex-*Santon*) | 18-8-55 | M 6 Formosa (ex-*Ilmington*) | 8-3-54 |

**Three Argentine "Tons";** minehunter at left L. & L. Van Ginderen, 4-84

**D:** 370 tons (425 fl) **S:** 15 kts **Dim:** 46.33 (42.68 pp) × 8.76 × 2.50
**A:** 1/40-mm AA **Electron Equipt:** Radar: Type 978
**M:** 2 Paxman Deltic 18A-7A diesels; 2 props; 3,000 hp **Fuel:** 45 tons
**Range:** 2,300/13; 3,000/8 **Man:** 27 tot. (M 5, M 6: 36 tot.)

Remarks: M 5 and M 6 refitted as minehunters in 1968, with Plessey Type 193M sonar. The others may retain Mirrlees JVSS-12 diesels, totaling 2,500 hp. In poor condition, may soon be stricken.

## AMPHIBIOUS WARFARE SHIPS

NOTE: Construction of a 3,770-ton landing ship reported ordered in 1982 from South Korea does not appear to have taken place, although one source records that *two* were ordered, the first being laid down in 1984.

**◆ 1 Modified U.S. DeSoto County-class tank landing ship**

| | Bldr | L | In serv. |
|---|---|---|---|
| Q 42 CABO SAN ANTONIO | AFNE, Rio Santiago | 1968 | 2-11-78 |

**Cabo San Antonio (Q 42)** Argentine Navy, 1983

**D:** 4,300 tons (8,000 fl) **S:** 16 kts **Dim:** 134.72 (129.8 wl) × 18.9 × 5.5
**A:** 12/40-mm AA (IV × 3)—2/20-mm AA (I × 2)
**Electron Equipt:** Radar: 1 navigational, 1/Plessey AWS-1 air search
**M:** 6 diesels; 2 CP props; 13,700 hp **Electric:** 900 kw **Man:** 124 tot.

REMARKS: Differs from U.S. Navy version primarily in armament and in having a 60-ton Stülcken heavy-lift kingpost set amidships. Carries 4 LCVP. Tank deck 88-m long can stow 23 medium tanks. 700 troops can be carried. Three U.S. Mk 51 Mod. 2 optical GFCS.

**◆ 4 U.S. LCM(6)-class landing craft** (In serv. 6-71)

EDM 1 EDM 2 EDM 3 EDM 4

**D:** 24 tons (56 fl) **S:** 10 kts **Dim:** 17.07 × 4.37 × 1.17 (aft)
**A:** 2/12.7-mm mg **M:** 2 Gray Marine 64 HN9 diesels; 2 props; 330–450 hp
**Range:** 130/10 **Cargo:** 30 tons

**◆ 8 U.S. LCVP-class landing craft**

EDVP 30–37

**D:** 13 tons (fl) **S:** 9 kts **Dim:** 10.90 × 3.21 × 1.04 (aft)
**M:** 1 Gray Marine 64 HN9 diesel; 225 hp **Range:** 110/9

REMARKS: It is not known whether the above list includes the four LCVP carried by *Cabo San Antonio.* Cargo: 36 troops or 3.5 tons. Five others discarded post-1982.

## HYDROGRAPHIC SHIPS

**◆ 1 Puerto Deseado class**

| | Bldr | Laid down | L | In serv. |
|---|---|---|---|---|
| Q 20 PUERTO DESEADO | Astarsa, San Fernando | 17-3-76 | 4-12-77 | 26-2-79 (trials) |

**D:** 2,133 tons **S:** 15 kts **Dim:** 70.81 (67.0 pp) × 13.2 × 4.5
**M:** 2 Fiat-GMT diesels; 2 props; 2,700 hp **Electric:** 1,280 kVA
**Range:** 12,000/12 **Man:** 12 officers, 53 men, 9 scientists, 10 technicians

**Puerto Deseado (Q 20) nested with Comodoro Rivadavia (Q 11), Cormoran (Q 15), and Petrel (Q 16)** R. Scheina, 1982

REMARKS: Used for hydrometeorological reporting. Four Hewlett-Packard 2108-A computers for data analysis/storage. Has seismic, gravimetric, and magnetometer equipment. Omega- and NAVSAT-equipped. Has geology laboratory. Ice-reinforced. The previously listed *Alvaro Alberto,* completed 1983, is subordinate to the Ministry of Marine, as is the *Capitan Oca Balda* (598 dwt), completed 1983.

**◆ 1 Comodoro Rivadavia class**
Bldr: Mestrina, el Tigre (L: 29-11-73, in serv. 6-12-76)

Q 11 COMODORO RIVADAVIA

**D:** 655 tons (830 fl) **S:** 12 kts **Dim:** 52.2 × 8.8 × 2.6 **Man:** 27 tot.
**M:** 2 Werkspoor Stork RHO-218K diesels; 1,160 hp **Range:** 6,000/12

**◆ 2 inshore survey craft** Bldr: Cadenazzi, el Tigre (In serv. 1965)

Q 16 PETREL

**Petrel** L. & L. Van Ginderen, 1986

**D:** 52 tons (fl) **S:** 9 kts **Dim:** 19.7 × 4.5 × 1.7
**M:** 2 diesels; . . . props; 340 hp **Man:** 9 tot.

Q 15 CORMORAN Bldr: AFNE, Rio Santiago (In serv. 20-2-64)

**D:** 82 tons (102 fl) **S:** 11 kts **Dim:** 25.3 × 5.0 × 1.8
**M:** 2 diesels; 2 props; 440 hp **Man:** 19 tot.

## ICEBREAKER

**◆ 1 antarctic support ship** Bldr: Wärtsilä, Helsinki, Finland

| | Laid down | L | In serv. |
|---|---|---|---|
| Q 5 ALMIRANTE IRIZAR | 4-7-77 | 3-2-78 | 15-12-78 |

**Almirante Irizar (Q 5)**—red hull and stack, white superstructure Wärtsilä, 1978

**D:** 11,811 (14,900 fl) **S:** 16.5 kts **Dim:** 119.3 × 25.0 × 9.5
**A:** 2/40-mm AA (I × 2)—2/Agusta A-109 helicopters
**Electron Equipt:** Radar: 1 Plessey AWS-2, 2/navigational
**M:** diesel-electric; 4 SEMT-Pielstick 8 PC 2.5 L/400 diesels; 2 Stromberg motors; 2 props; 16,200 hp
**Electric:** 2,640 kw **Man:** 123 crew plus 100 scientists

REMARKS: Ordered 17-12-75. Canadian RAST helicopter downhaul winch system, 2 helicopters. Wärtsilä bubbler system to keep ice from hull bottom. Sixty-ton towing winch. Two 16-ton cranes. Used as a hospital ship during Falklands War.

## AUXILIARY SHIPS

◆ **1 antarctic supply ship** Bldr: Principe & Menghe SY, Maciel Isl.

| | Laid down | L | In serv. |
|---|---|---|---|
| Q 6 Bahia Paraiso | 27-2-79 | 3-7-80 | 11-12-81 |

**Bahia Paraiso**—as a hospital ship during Falklands War Argentine Navy, 1982

**D:** 9,200 tons (fl) **S:** 18 kts **Dim:** 130.7 (120.0 pp) × 19.5 × 7.0 **A:** none
**M:** 2 diesels; 2 CP props; 15,000 hp **Fuel:** 300 tons **Man:** 180 tot.

Remarks: To carry up to 82 passengers or 252 troops, 3,500 $m^3$ dry and 250 $m^3$ refrigerated stores, plus 1,200 tons cargo fuel. Two helicopters plus hangar. Icebreaking hull form. Used as hospital ship during Falklands War.

◆ **3 "Costa Sur"-class transports** Bldr: Principe & Menghe SY, Maciel Isl.

| | Laid down | L | In serv. |
|---|---|---|---|
| B 3 Canal Beagle | 10-1-77 | 14-10-77 | 28-4-78 |
| B 4 Bahia San Blas | 11-4-77 | 29-4-78 | 27-11-78 |
| B 5 Cabo De Hornos (ex-*Bahia Camarones*) | 29-4-78 | 4-11-78 | 18-7-79 |

**Cabo de Hornos (B 5)** L. & L. Van Ginderen, 11-82

**D:** 7,640 tons (fl) **S:** 15 kts **Dim:** 119.9 × 17.5 × 6.4 **A:** none
**M:** 2 AFNE-Sulzer diesels; 2 props; 6,400 hp

Remarks: To supply remote stations. 4,600 grt/5,800 dwt. 9,700 cubic meters cargo. Also carry passengers and cargo in commercial service.

Note: The Argentine Navy no longer has any underway replenishment oilers of its own, but, as was done during the Falklands War, it has access to two state-owned merchant tankers that have been equipped with an alongside refueling capability.

◆ **2 merchant tankers** Bldr: Italcantiere, Castellamare

Puerto Rosales Campo Duran

**D:** approx. 37,000 tons (fl) **S:** 16.5 kts **Dim:** 170.2 (161.53 pp) × 25.94 × 11.02
**M:** 2 GMT diesels; 1 CP prop; 14,400 hp **Electric:** 7,000 kw

Remarks: 18,012 grt/30,884 dwt.

◆ **1 coastal tanker** Bldr: Puerto Belgrano SY

B 12 Punta Alta (In serv. 1938)

**D:** 1,900 tons (fl) **S:** 8 kts **Dim:** 64.0 × 10.3 × 3.8
**M:** 1 set reciprocating steam; 1,850 hp **Fuel:** 146 tons
**Man:** 40 tot.

Remarks: 800 dwt. Used primarily for harbor storage service at Puerto Belgrano.

◆ **1 lighthouse supply ship** Bldr: Wheeler SB Co., Freeport, N.Y.

B 7 San Julian (ex-U.S. Army FS 281, L: 1-45)

**San Julian (B 7)** L. & L. Van Ginderen, 8-84

**D:** 900 tons (fl) **S:** 12 kts **Dim:** 53.49 (49.99 pp) × 9.75 × 3.05
**M:** 2 G.M. 6-278A diesels; 2 props; 1,000 hp **Fuel:** 57 tons
**Range:** 4,300/9.5 **Man:** 30 tot.

Remarks: Purchased after WW II. Reported stricken early 1980s, but retained for lighthouse and navigational aid/buoy-tending services. Cargo: 595 $m^3$.

◆ **2 auxiliary ocean tugs** Bldr: Ast. Vicente Forte, Buenos Aires

R 2 Querandi (In serv: 22-8-78) R 3 Tehuelche (In serv: 2-11-78)

**Querandi (R 2)** R. Scheina, 1980

**D:** 370 tons (fl) **S:** 12 kts **Dim:** 33.6 × 8.4 × 3.0
**M:** 2 M.A.N. 6V 23.5/33 diesels; 1,200 hp
**Range:** 1,200/12 **Man:** 30 tot.

◆ **1 training ship** Bldr: Union Naval de la Levante, Valencia, Spain

Q 31 Piloto Alsina (ex-*Ciudad de Formosa*) (In serv. 1963)

**D:** 2,800 tons (fl) **S:** 14 kts **Dim:** 105.60 (99.98 pp) × 17.89 × 2.52
**M:** 3 Maquinista-Burmeister & Wain 8-cyl. diesels: 1 prop; 4,800 hp
**Electric:** 480 kw **Fuel:** 224 tons

Remarks: Former passenger/cargo ferry purchased and commissioned 17-3-81 for training duties. 3,986 grt/720 dwt. See photo in addenda.

◆ **1 sail-training vessel**

| | Bld | L | In serv. |
|---|---|---|---|
| Q 2 Libertad | AFNE, Rio Santiago | 30-5-56 | 1962 |

**D:** 3,025 tons (3,625 fl) **S:** 12 kts **Dim:** 94.25 (79.9 pp) × 13.75 × 6.75
**M:** diesels; 2 props; 2,400 hp **Range:** 12,000
**Man:** 222 men and 140 cadets.

Note: The former sail-training ship *Presidente Sarmiento* (1898) and the sail corvette *Uruguay* (1874) are maintained by the Navy as museums at Buenos Aires.

## AUXILIARY SHIPS *(continued)*

**Libertad (Q 2)** L. & L. Van Ginderen, 9-87

◆ **5 small sail-training yachts**

Q 73 Itati II Bldr: Cadenazzi SY, 1979 **D:** 80 tons (fl) **S:** 15 kts
Q 25 Fortuna I Bldr: Tandanor, Buenos Aires **D:** 17 tons
Q 26 Fortuna II Bldr: Tandanor, Buenos Aires **D:** 31.5 tons
Q 72 Tequara
Q . . . Adhara

## YARD AND SERVICE CRAFT

◆ **6 U.S. YTL-422-class small harbor tugs** (In serv. 1944–45)

Bldrs: R 5, 16, 18: Robt. Jacobs, City Isl., NY; R 6, 19: H.C. Grebe Co; R 10: Everett Pacific BY, Everett, Wash.

R 5 Mocovi (ex-YTL 441)
R 6 Calchaqui (ex-YTL 445)
R 10 Chulupi (ex-YTL 426)
R 16 Capayan (ex-YTL 443)
R 18 Chiquillan (ex-YTL 444)
R 19 Morcoyan (ex-YTL 448)

**Mocovi (R 5)** L. & L. Van Ginderen, 4-81

**D:** 70 tons (80 fl) **S:** 10 kts **Dim:** 20.16 × 5.18 × 2.44
**M:** 1 Hoover-Owens-Rentschler diesel; 300 hp **Electric:** 40 kw
**Fuel:** 7 tons **Man:** 5 tot.

Remarks: R 16, 18, 19 leased 3-65, others 3-69; purchased outright 16-6-77.

◆ **4 floating dry docks**

Y 1 (ex-U.S. ARD 23): 3,500-ton capacity; 14.9 × 24.7 × 1.73 (light) (In serv. 1944)
Y 2: 1,500-ton capacity; 91.5 × 18.3 (In serv. 1913)
Y 3, Y 4: 750-ton capacity; 65.8 × 14
A: 12,000-ton capacity; 172.5 × 26 (In serv. 1958)
B: 2,800-ton capacity; 110.0 × 18.0 (In serv. 1956)
C: 1,000-ton capacity; 75.0 × 15.7

◆ **4 floating cranes**

PREFECTURA NAVAL ARGENTINA
(COAST GUARD)

Note: Ships and craft painted white. Attached aircraft include 2 Puma helicopters and several Short Skyvan transports. The *Prefectura Naval* was transferred from naval control to the Ministry of Defense in 10-84.

## PATROL SHIPS AND BOATS

◆ **5 "Halcon"-class ocean patrol ships** Bldr: Bazán, El Ferrol, Spain

| | Laid down | L | In serv. |
|---|---|---|---|
| GC 24 Doctor Manuel Mantilla | 16-2-81 | 29-6-81 | 15-5-82 |
| GC 25 Azopardo | 1-4-81 | 14-10-81 | 1-83 |
| GC 26 Thompson | 6-81 | 7-12-81 | 20-6-83 |
| GC 27 Prefecto Fique | 9-81 | 24-2-82 | 29-7-83 |
| GC 28 Prefecto Derbes | 11-81 | 16-6-82 | 16-11-83 |

**Doctor Manuel Mantilla (GC 24)** Bazán, 1982

**D:** 767 tons normal (900 fl) **S:** 21.5 kts **Dim:** 67.0 (63.0 pp) × 10.0 × 3.06
**A:** 1/40-mm AA Breda-Bofors—1 Alouette-III helo
**Electron Equipt:** Radar: 1 Decca AC 1226 **Electric:** 710 kw
**M:** 2 Bazán-MTU 16V956 TB91 diesels; 2 props; 9,000 hp (7,500 sust.)
**Range:** 5,000/18 **Man:** 9 officers/24 men/4 cadets

Remarks: Ordered 3-79 to patrol 200-nautical-mile economic zone. Endurance 20 days. Carry 144 rounds 40-mm. Same class built for Mexico. Helicopters, when aboard, would be on loan from Navy.

◆ **1 former whaler, used for ocean patrol** (In serv. 1958; purchased 1975)

GC 13 Delfin

**Delfin (GC 13)** L. & L. Van Ginderen, 1986

**D:** 1,000 tons **S:** 15 kts **Dim:** 60.0 × 9.0 × 4.7 **A:** 1/20-mm AA
**M:** diesel; 2,300 hp **Man:** 32 tot.

◆ **1 Dorado class** Bldr: Rio Santiago Navy Base

GC 43 Mandubi (In serv. 1940)

**D:** 208 tons (fl) **S:** 11 kts **Dim:** 33.2 × 4.0 × 1.9
**M:** 2 G.M. diesels; 2 props; 880 hp **Man:** 10

Remarks: Sister *Dorado* (GC 34) and the similar *Robalo* (GC 45) stricken 1985-86.

**ARGENTINA** *(continued)*

**PATROL CRAFT**

◆ **18 Z-28 class** Bldr: Blohm + Voss, Hamburg (All in serv. 9-79/1-80)

GC 64 Mar Del Plata
GC 65 Martin Garcia
GC 66 Rio Lujan
GC 67 Rio Uruguay
GC 68 Rio Paraguay
GC 69 Rio Parana
GC 70 Rio Plata
GC 71 La Plata
GC 72 Buenos Aires
GC 73 Cabo Corrientes
GC 74 Quequen
GC 75 Bahia Blanca
GC 76 Ingeniero White
GC 77 Golfo San Matias
GC 78 Madryn
GC 79 Rio Deseado
GC 80 Ushuaia
GC 81 Canal De Beagle

**Buenos Aires (GC 72)** L. & L. Van Ginderen, 1984

**D:** 81 tons (fl) **S:** 22 kts **Dim:** 27.65 (26.0) × 5.30 × 1.65
**A:** 1/20-mm AA—2/7.62-mm mg (I × 2)
**M:** 2 MTU 8V331 TC92 diesels; 2 props; 2,100 hp (1,770 sust.)
**Electric:** 90 kVA **Range:** 780/18; 1,200/12 **Man:** 15–23 tot.

Remarks: Ordered 24-11-78. Fin stabilizers fitted. During the Falklands War, *Rio Iguaza* (GC 83) was lost, and *Islas Malvinas* (GC 82) was captured and renamed *Tiger Bay* by British forces. Not all units have the 20-mm gun.

◆ **3 Lynch-class** Bldr: AFNE, Rio Santiago (In serv. 1964–67)

GC 21 Lynch GC 22 Toll GC 23 Erezcano

**D:** 100 tons (117 fl) **S:** 22 kts **Dim:** 27.44 × 5.80 × 1.85
**A:** 1/20-mm AA **M:** 2 Maybach diesels; 2 props; 2,700 hp **Man:** 16 tot.

◆ **14 patrol craft** Bldr: Cadenazzi SY, Tigre, 1978–79

GC 48 through GC 61

**D:** 13 tons **S:** 25 kts **Dim:** 12.54 × 3.57 × 1.1 **A:** 1 mg
**M:** 2 G.M. diesels; 2 props; 560 hp

◆ **1 tug** Bldr: Sanym SA, San Fernando (In serv. 21-10-77)

GC 47 Tonina

**D:** 200 tons (fl) **S:** 11 kts **Dim:** 25.5 × 3.3 × 2.1 **A:** 1/20-mm AA
**M:** 1 diesel; 500 hp **Range:** 3,400/10 **Man:** 11 tot.

◆ **Approx. 28** smaller patrol craft for harbor duty: GC 88–94, GC 102, 103, 105–108, GC 110–114; ST 4; SB 2, 3; SI 2.

◆ **17 pilot boats**—no data available

SP 14 Lago Alumine
SP 15 Lago Traful
SP 16 Lago Colhue
SP 17 Lago Mascardi
SP 18 Lago Argentino
SP 19 Lago Nahuel Huapi
SP 20 Lago Viedma
SP 21 Lago San Martin
SP 22 Lago Buenos Aires
SP 23 Lago Faviano
SP 24 Lago Lacar
SP 25 Lago Cardiel
SP 26 Lago Musters
SP 27 Lago Quillen
SP 28 Lago Roca
SP 29 Lago Puelo
SP 30 Lago Futalaufquen

Remarks: Some (SP 19–21, 30) are of Dutch construction. Displacements run 20–30 tons (fl).

**Lago Buenos Aires (SP 22)** L. & L. Van Ginderen, 1986

◆ **1 pilot station ship** Bldr: Bartram & Sons, Sunderland

Recalada (ex-*Recalada Light,* ex-*Juanita Halkias,* ex-*Ioannis,* ex-*Prodomis*) (In serv. 1969)

**Recalada**—under conversion L. & L. Van Ginderen, 1986

**D:** . . . . tons (fl) **S:** 14 kts **Dim:** 141.05 (134.17 pp) × 20.48 × 8.86
**M:** 2 single-acting, 5-cyl. Clark-Sulzer diesels; 1 prop; 5,500 hp
**Electric:** 654 kw **Fuel:** 984 tons heavy oil/122 tons diesel

Remarks: Former five-hold cargo vessel of 8,946 grt/15,266 dwt acquired for conversion and use as a pilot station vessel. Helicopter flight deck added aft. Retains eight 10-ton and two 5-ton cargo booms.

◆ **1 sail-training craft**

Esperanza (L: 12-68) D: 32 tons

# AUSTRALIA

**Commonwealth of Australia**

Personnel (1986): 15,536 total including about 1,000 women. Civilians operate many service craft.

Merchant Marine (1986): 673 ships—2,368,462 grt (tankers: 20—622,352 grt)

Naval Aviation: After announcing the cancellation of plans to acquire a new carrier and striking the old *Melbourne* on 14-3-83, the new government announced the transfer of all naval fixed-wing aircraft assets to the R.A.A.F. by 30-6-84. Two HS-748 transports have been retained for EW training.

Helicopters in service include: 2 Mk 50A Sea King helicopters delivered in 1983, 5 Sea King Mk 50, 14 Wessex 31B helicopters, and 6 AS-350B Écureuil light helicopters. Three additional Wessex 31B helicopters are in storage.

The Sikorsky S-70B2 (U.S. Navy SH-60B LAMPS III-equivalent) was selected 10-84 for use on the FFG 7-class frigates; eight were ordered for delivery late 1987, late 1988, with M.E.L. "Super Searcher" radar in place of the U.S. LN-66; eight more to be ordered later. No. 816 Squadron was reestablished 1984 to operate the 14 Wessex helicopters retrieved from storage. The Écureuils are for interim use on the FFG 7s.

**NAVAL AVIATION** *(continued)*

**Sea King Mk 50 helicopter**—decorated for 75th anniversary of the R.A.N.
R.A.N., 10-86

The R.A.A.F. operates 20 P-3C Orion with AQS-901 receiver/processors for the Australian-developed "Barra" sonobuoy.

Weapons and Systems: The Australian Navy uses U.S. equipment and systems on its U.S.-built warships and British weapons and systems on its other ships, but some of its air-search and fire-control radars have been purchased in the Netherlands (LW-02, M-20, etc.). Some 71 U.S. Mk 48 torpedoes have been purchased for use by submarines, with an additional batch ordered in 1980. U.S. Harpoon antiship missiles are to be carried by the submarines, FFG 7-class frigates, and R.A.A.F. P-3C, F-18, and F-111 aircraft.

Except for the U.S.-built ships, the sonars are of British or Australian (Mulloka) origin. Mulloka is a high-frequency set tailored to Australian coastal water-sound propagation conditions. The "Karrawarra" towed passive sonar array entered service in 1985. The "Winnin" countermeasures system with "Hoveroc" chaff/IR decoy rockets began trials in 1985; it will use the same Mk 137 6-tubed launcher as the U.S. Mk 36 SRBOC system, with the Winnin tubes added. The Australian Ikara is a Mk 46 torpedo coupled with a guided missile and guidance equipment and has a maximum range of about 20,000 yards.

## SUBMARINES

◆ **0 (+6 + 2) Kockums Type 471, new construction** Bldr: Australian Submarine Corporation, Port Adelaide

| | Laid down | L | In serv. |
|---|---|---|---|
| . . . N . . . | | | 1994 |
| . . . N . . . | | | |
| . . . N . . . | | | |
| . . . N . . . | | | |
| . . . N . . . | | | |
| . . . N . . . | | | 2000 |

**Kockums Type 471 model** Kockums, 1987

**D:** 2,500 tons (sob.) **S:** 21 kts (sub.) **Dim:** 70 × 7.0 × . . .
**A:** 6/533-mm TT fwd. (23 Harpoon SSM and Mk 48 torpedoes)
**Electron Equipt:** Radar: . . .—EW: . . .
Sonar: Thomson-Sintra Eledone-derivative
**M:** diesel-electric: 4 SEMT-PIELSTICK diesels, Jeumont-Schneider motors; 1 prop; 5,000 hp
**Range:** 11,500/. . . (see remarks); 32.6/21 (sub.); 480/4 (sub.)
**Endurance:** 75 days **Man:** 46 tot.

Remarks: Contract announced 18-5-87 for six, with option for two more. Kockums, Sweden, design. Australian Submarine Corp. is a consortium of Kockums, U.S. CBI Industries, and Australian firms. Electronics/weapons control is to be by a consortium of Rockwell International, Singer Librascope, Computer Science (Aust.), and Thompson-CSF. They will have the Singer Librascope SCCS Mk 2 f.c.s.

To be the quietest, most shock-resistant diesel-electric submarines in the world. Modular construction. Intended to meet a mission requirement of 3,500 n.m. radius at 10 kts submerged, plus 47 days on station at 4 kts. Battery capacity gives 120 hours at 4 kts.

◆ **6 British Oberon-class** Bldr: Scotts' SB & Eng., Greenock

| | Laid down | L | In serv. |
|---|---|---|---|
| S 57 Oxley | 2-7-64 | 24-9-65 | 27-3-67 |
| S 59 Otway | 29-6-65 | 29-11-66 | 22-4-68 |
| S 60 Onslow | 26-5-67 | 29-8-68 | 22-12-69 |
| S 61 Orion | 6-10-72 | 16-9-74 | 15-6-77 |
| S 62 Otama | 28-5-73 | 3-12-75 | 27-4-78 |
| S 70 Ovens | 17-6-66 | 5-12-67 | 18-4-69 |

**Orion (S 61)** ABPH P. Kalajzich, R.A.N., 7-87

**Ovens (S 70)** POPH E. Pitman, R.A.N., 3-87

**D:** 1,610/2,196/2,417 tons **S:** 17.5/15 kts
**Dim:** 89.92(87.45 pp) × 8.07 × 5.48 **Man:** 6 officers, 57 men
**A:** 6/533-mm TT for Sub-Harpoon and U.S. Mk 48 Mod. 3 torpedoes (fwd)—12 reloads
**Electron Equipt:** Radar: 1/1006—Sonar: 1/187 C, 1/197, 1/2007, "Micro-Puffs"
**M:** two 1,840-hp Admiralty Standard Range 16 VVS-ASR1 diesel engines; diesel-electric propulsion; 2 props; 6,000 hp
**Endurance:** 56 days **Fuel:** 298 m$^3$ (446 emergency)

Remarks: *Oxley* recommissioned 22-2-80 with U.S. Singer/Librascope SFCS Mk 1 digital computer fire-control system with a UYK-20 computer, and a new sonar suit incorporating a Krupp/Atlas CSU-3-41 active/passive system (active transducer in sail, passive array in enlarged dome on bow), U.K. Type 2007 LF passive array, and Type 2004 sound velocity meter. The two short 533-mm torpedo tubes aft are no longer used. All are to receive Sub-Harpoon antiship missiles under the 1985–89 Defense Program, and U.S. Mk 48 Mod. 3 torpedoes have replaced all the Mk 37 type formerly carried. S 62 began trials with the "Karrawarra" towed linear passive hydrophone array in 1984, and S 59 received the first definitive version of this "clip-on" array in 4-85. S 70 first R.A.N. sub to launch Harpoon, 12-85.

All six R.A.N. *Oberons* received the *Oxley* mid-life modernization: S 59 in 1-79 to 1981, S 70 from 3-80 to mid-1983, S 60 from 8-82 to 12-84, S 61 from 11-81 to 8-83, and S 62 from 1984 to 11-85. S 57 completed long refit 8-5-87 to bring her up to the definitive standard. 448 battery cells deliver 5,000 amp/hr. at 1-hr. rate, 7,420 amp/hr. at 5-hr. rate. Maximum operating depth: 200 m.

## DESTROYERS

◆ **3 U.S. Charles F. Adams-class guided-missile destroyers** Bldr: Defoe SB, Bay City, Michigan

| | Laid down | L | In serv. |
|---|---|---|---|
| D 38 Perth (ex-U.S. DDG 25) | 21-9-62 | 26-9-63 | 17-7-65 |
| D 39 Hobart (ex-U.S. DDG 26) | 26-10-62 | 9-1-64 | 18-12-65 |
| D 41 Brisbane (ex-U.S. DDG 27) | 15-2-65 | 5-5-66 | 16-12-67 |

**Perth (D 38)**—*Canberra* (F 02) and *Parramatta* beyond R.A.N., 10-86

**Hobart (D 39)** U.S. Navy, 7-86

**D:** 3,370 tons (4,618 fl) **S:** 35 kts **Dim:** 134.18 (128.0 pp) × 14.32 × 6.0
**A:** 1/Mk 13 system for Harpoon SSM and Standard SM-1A SAM (40 missiles)—2/127-mm DP Mk 42 (I × 2)—2/Ikara ASW missile systems (. . . missiles)—6/324-mm ASW TT Mk 32 (III × 2)
**Electron Equipt:** Radar: 1/978, 1/SPS-40C, 1/SPS-10F, 1/SPS-52B, 2/SPG-51C, 1/SPG-53A, 1/Ikara control
Sonar: 1/SQS-23F—TACAN: 1/URN-20
EW: WLR-1F, WLR-6, URD-4 (UHFD/F)
**M:** 2 sets GT; 2 props; 70,000 hp **Fuel:** 900 tons
**Boilers:** 4 Babcock & Wilcox, 84 kg/cm$^2$—superheat 520°C
**Electric:** 2,200 kw **Range:** 1.600/30; 6,000/14 **Man:** 21 officers, 312 men

Remarks: D 38 modernized in the U.S. 3-9-74 to 2-1-75 with SM-1A Standard missiles, NTDS, and Mk 42 Mod. 10 guns. The other two were refitted to the same standard in Australia. Missile fire control is Mk 74 Mod. 8 with two radar directors; guns are controlled by one Mk 68 radar director (optical range-finder removed). Further modernization began mid-1985, with D 41, to include substituting U.S. SLQ-32(V)2 EW gear and Mk 36 SRBOC decoy launchers; the gunfire control system was replaced by the U.S. Mk 86, and the Mk 13 missile system was updated to handle Harpoon missiles. D 41 completed modernization late 1987.

## FRIGATES

◆ **0 (+6 to 12) new-construction frigates** Bldr: . . .

**D:** . . . **S:** . . . **Dim:** . . . × . . . × . . .
**A:** provision for SSM—1/75-mm or larger DP gun—CIWS—provision for ASW TT—1 or 2 Sea Hawk helos (with ASM)
**Electron Equipt:** Radar: 1/. . . nav., 1/. . . 3-D air search, 2/fire control
Sonar: Mulloka hull-mounted, . . . towed array
EW: . . .
**M:** . . . **Range:** 6,000/18 **Man:** . . .

Remarks: Request for proposals issued 1-87. Replaces earlier proposal to build four additional *Oliver Hazard Perry*-class frigates and a new class of destroyers. Intended to replace the "River"-class frigates. To minimize costs, much combat equipment is specified only as "weight and space for." To be built entirely in Australia. To be built in cooperation with New Zealand, which plans to acquire four. Short list of competitors announced 9-87: Blohm + Voss MEKO 200, Dutch *Karel Doorman*, and Yarrow light patrol frigate.

◆ **4 (+2) U.S. Oliver Hazard Perry-class guided-missile frigates**

| | Bldr | Laid down | L | In serv. |
|---|---|---|---|---|
| F 01 Adelaide (ex-FFG 17) | Todd, Seattle | 29-7-77 | 21-6-78 | 6-11-80 |
| **F 02 Canberra (ex-FFG 18)** | Todd, Seattle | 1-3-78 | 1-12-78 | 21-3-81 |
| F 03 Sydney (ex-FFG 35) | Todd, Seattle | 16-1-80 | 26-9-80 | 29-1-83 |
| F 04 Darwin (ex-FFG 44) | Todd, Seattle | 2-7-81 | 26-3-82 | 21-7-84 |
| F 05 Melbourne | Williamstown DY, Melbourne | 12-7-85 | . . . | 1991 |
| F 06 N . . . . . . . | Williamstown DY, Melbourne | . . . | . . . | 1993 |

**Adelaide (F 01)** POPH E. Pitman, R.A.N., 7-85

**Darwin (F 04)**—note lengthened stern, Écureuil helo R.A.N., 1986

**Canberra (F 02)** R.A.N., 1986

**D:** 2,769 tons light (3,678 fl)—F 04: 2,851 tons (3,740 fl) **S:** 29 kts
**Dim:** 135.64 (125.9 wl) × 13.72 × 4.52 (7.47 max.) (F 04 and later: 138.80 o.a.)
**A:** 1/Mk 13 Mod. 4 launcher for Standard SM-1A SAM and Harpoon (40 missiles)—1/76-mm DP OTO Melara Compact (U.S. Mk 75)—1/20-mm Mk 15 CIWS—6/324-mm ASW TT Mk 32 for Mk 46 torpedoes (III × 2)—2 helicopters (see remarks)
**Electron Equipt:** Radar: 1/SPS-55, 1/SPS-49(V)2, 1/Mk 92, 1/SPG-60 STIR
Sonar: 1/SQS-56—EW: SLQ-32(V)2, Mk 36 SRBOC (VI × 2)
TACAN: URN-25
**M:** 2 G.E. LM-2500 gas turbines; 1 CP prop; 41,000 hp; 2/350-hp aux. propulsors
**Electric:** 3,000 kw **Fuel:** 587 tons (plus 64 tons helo fuel)
**Range:** 4,200/20; 5,000/18 **Man:** 226 tot.

**FRIGATES** *(continued)*

Remarks: First two ordered 27-2-76 in lieu of Australian DDL design. The third was ordered 23-1-79 and the fourth on 28-4-80. In 1980 two more were authorized for construction in Australia, and four more were to be ordered later (now cancelled). The first two Australian-built ships were ordered 12-10-83. Two drop-down, diesel-electric-driven propellers are located forward beneath the hull for emergency propulsion and maneuvering. Crew larger than in U.S. sisters. (F 04 arrived Australia 25-10-85.

The selection of the Sikorsky S-70B2 helicopter for these ships will require that the first three be lengthened and have fin stabilization systems added at Garden Island Dockyard; F 01–F 04 will all require the RAST helicopter downhaul and traversing system to be added. During 1984-88 an Écureuil light liaison helicopter is being carried. The S-70B2 will be able to carry two antiship missiles (Penguin Mk 2 Mod. 7 or Sea Skua).

The Australian-built units will have Mulloka sonars in place of SQS-56, an Australian-developed towed-array sonar, the Winnin countermeasures system, with Hoveroc decoys, and, possibly, box-launcher-mounted Ikara ASW missiles. F 01 and 02 had their two Mk 24 target designators atop the pilothouse and EW systems added after delivery; their Mk 15 Vulcan-Phalanx Close-in Weapon Systems were ordered during 1984. All carry the SLQ-25 towed torpedo decoy and WSC-3 SATCOMM.

◆ **5 "River"-class frigates**

| | Bldr | Laid down | L | In serv. |
|---|---|---|---|---|
| DE 46 Parramatta | Cockatoo D. & Eng. Co. | 3-1-57 | 31-1-59 | 4-7-61 |
| DE 48 Stuart | Cockatoo D. & Eng. Co. | 20-3-59 | 8-4-61 | 28-6-63 |
| DE 49 Derwent | Williamstown Nav. DY | 18-8-65 | 16-12-67 | 20-1-70 |
| DE 50 Swan | Williamstown Nav. DY | 18-8-65 | 16-12-67 | 20-1-70 |
| DE 53 Torrens | Cockatoo D. & Eng. Co. | 18-8-65 | 28-9-68 | 19-1-71 |

**D:** 2,100 tons (2,750 fl) **S:** 30 kts **Dim:** 112.75 (109.75 pp) × 12.5 × 3.9
**A:** 2/114-mm DP Mk 6 (II × 1)—1/Sea Cat/SAM syst. (IV × 1, 24 missiles)—1/Ikara ASW missile launcher—6/324-mm Mk 32 ASW TT (III × 2)
**Electron Equipt:** Radar: 1/978, 1/LW-02, 1/WM-22, 1/Ikara control, DE 50, 53: 1/M 45 also
Sonar: 1/Mulloka—EW: intercept arrays
**M:** 2 sets GT; 2 props; 34,000 hp **Fuel:** 400 tons
**Electric:** 1,140 kw (DE 46: 1,500 kw) **Man:** 13 officers, 238 men
**Boilers:** 2 Babcock & Wilcox, 38.7 kg/cm$^2$, 450°C **Range:** 4,500/12

Remarks: Sister *Yarra* (DE 45) was stricken 22-11-85 and hulked as a spares source. Improved versions of the British *Rothesay* class. Profiles of the DE 50 and DE 53 differ from those of other three, resembling more the British *Leander* class. DE 46, DE 48, and DE 49 given an extensive mid-life overhaul, receiving two triple Mk 32 ASW torpedo tubes in place of the Limbo mortar, Mulloka sonar in place of part of their original suits, H.S.A. M 22 gunfire-control systems with LIROD optronic backup director, having their boilers converted to use diesel fuel, and having their accommodations improved; DE 46 completed 8-81, DE 48 on 29-7-83, and DE 49 began work in 7-81, with completion 3-86. DE 50 and DE 51 are now to receive only normal refits and will not be modernized; DE 50 is to become training ship in 1990. The Ikara missile carries a U.S. Mk 46 ASW torpedo as its payload. Variable-depth sonars have been removed, where fitted. Sea Cat has optical GWS 20 system in early units, H.S.A. M4 radar director (M 45 radar) in DE 50, 53.

**Parramatta (DE 46)** R. Gillett, 1986

**Derwent (DE 49)**—post-modernization, with new stack, LW-02 radar antenna lowered, triple ASW TT, etc. R.A.N., 3-86

**Torrens (DE 53)** R.A.N., 9-86

**Swan (DE 50)** LSPH E. Pitman, R.A.N., 1-87

**PATROL BOATS**

◆ **15 Fremantle class** Bldr: North Queensland Eng. and Agents, Cairns (P 203: Brooke Marine, Lowestoft)

| | L | In serv. | | L. | In serv. |
|---|---|---|---|---|---|
| P 203 Fremantle | 15-2-79 | 8-10-79 | P 211 Bendigo | 9-4-83 | 28-5-83 |
| P 204 Warrnambool | 25-10-80 | 14-3-81 | P 212 Gawler | 9-7-83 | 30-8-83 |
| P 205 Townsville | 16-5-81 | 18-7-81 | P 213 Geraldton | 22-10-83 | 10-12-83 |
| P 206 Wollongong | 17-10-81 | 28-11-81 | P 214 Dubbo | 21-1-84 | 10-3-84 |
| P 207 Launceton | 23-1-82 | 1-3-82 | P 215 Geelong | 14-4-84 | 2-6-84 |
| P 208 Whyalla | 22-5-82 | 3-7-82 | P 216 Gladstone | 28-7-84 | 8-9-84 |
| P 209 Ipswich | 25-9-82 | 13-11-82 | P 217 Bunbury | 3-11-84 | 15-12-84 |
| P 210 Cessnock | 15-1-83 | 5-3-83 | | | |

**Gawler (P 212)** L. & L. Van Ginderen, 5-86

**Townsville (P 205)** R.A.N., 9-86

**PATROL BOATS** *(continued)*

**D:** 200 tons (230 fl) **S:** 30 kts **Dim:** 42.0 × 7.15 × 1.8
**A:** 1/40-mm AA—1/81-mm mortar—212.7-mm mg (II × 2)
**Electron Equipt:** Radar: 1/Kelvin-Hughes 1006
**M:** 2 MTU MD 16V538 TB91 diesels; 2 CP props; 7,200 hp—1 Dorman 12JTM diesel; 1 prop; . . . hp for cruising (removed from P 206)
**Range:** 1,450/28; 4,800/8 **Man:** 3 officers/19 men

REMARKS: Brooke Marine PCF-420 design. Ordered 9-77. Five more (*Ballarat, Mildura, Armidale, Bundaberg, Pirie*) authorized 1980, but canceled 1982. P 203 was built as pattern craft. The 40-mm AA was to be replaced with newer weapons, but will now be retained for reasons of economy; all 40-mm guns are being modernized by the Government Ordnance Factory to improve firing rate and elevation and train speeds. P 203: 26 tons overweight (246 fl), later reduced to 20 tons; all later units 10 tons over original 220-tons design fl. P 206 aground 31-5-85, later salved; cruise engine removed during repairs.

◆ **5 Attack-class coastal-patrol boats**

| | Bldr | Laid down | L | In serv. |
|---|---|---|---|---|
| P 82 ADROIT | Evans Deakin | 8-67 | 3-2-68 | 17-8-68 |
| P 83 ADVANCE | Walkers, Ltd. | 3-67 | 16-8-67 | 24-1-68 |
| P 87 ARDENT | Evans Deakin | 10-67 | 27-4-68 | 26-10-68 |
| P 91 AWARE | Walkers, Ltd. | 7-67 | 7-10-67 | 21-6-68 |
| P 101 BAYONET | Walkers, Ltd. | 10-68 | 6-11-68 | 22-2-69 |

**Advance (P 83)** R. Gillett, 11-84

**D:** 146 tons (fl) **S:** 24 kts **Dim:** 32.76 (30.48 pp) × 6.2 × 1.9
**A:** 1/40-mm Mk 7 AA—2/7.62-mm machine guns **Radar:** 1/Decca RM 916
**M:** 2 Davey-Paxman Ventura 16 YJCM diesels; 2 props; 3,500 hp (2,460 sust.)
**Range:** 1,220/13 **Man:** 3 officers, 19 men

REMARKS: Steel hull; light-alloy superstructure; air-conditioned. All assigned to R.A.N. Reserve training. Sisters P 84 *Aitape*, P 92 *Ladava*, P 93 *Lae*, P 94 *Madang*, P 85 *Samarai* transferred to Papua New Guinea in 1974. P 86 *Archer* and P 95 *Bandolier* sold in 1973 to Indonesia and transferred in 1973 and 1974, respectively. P 88 *Arrow* sank 25-12-74 in Cyclone Tracey. Transferred to Indonesia were *Barricade* (P 98) on 22-4-82, *Bombard* (P 99) in 11-83, and *Acute* (P 81) on 6-5-83. *Barbette* (P 97) stricken 15-6-84, *Buccaneer* (P 100) decommissioned to material reserve 27-7-84, *Attack* (P 90) stricken 21-2-85, for transfer to Indonesia 24-5-85; P 97 transferred to Indonesia 22-2-85, P 100 in 5-85, and P 90 in 1-86. *Assail* (P 89) stricken 18-10-85 and transferred to Indonesia 30-1-86.

**MINE WARFARE SHIPS**

◆ **2 (+1 + 3) "Bay"-class catamaran minehunters** Bldr: Carrington Slipway, Tomago

| | Laid down | L | In serv. |
|---|---|---|---|
| M 80 RUSHCUTTER | 31-5-84 | 8-5-86 | 1-11-86 |
| M 81 SHOALWATER | 17-9-85 | 20-6-87 | -87 |
| M 82 N . . . | 1987 | . . . | . . . |

**D:** 100 tons (170 fl) **S:** 10 kts **Dim:** 31.0 (28.0 wl) × 9.0 × 1.8
**A:** 2/12.7-mm mg (I × 2)—2/PAP-104 disposal vehicles
**Electron Equipt:** Radar: 1/Kelvin-Hughes Type 1006(4)
Sonar: Krupp Atlas DSQS-11H
**M:** 2 SACM-Poyaud 325-hp diesels, electric drive; 2 Schottel props; 180 hp
**Range:** 1,200/10 **Man:** 2 officers, 11 men

REMARKS: Ordered late 1981. Glass-reinforced plastic construction. If first pair successful, had planned construction of four (originally to have been six) more, beginning in mid-1988, for delivery by mid-91, but funds for yard to begin third made available 2-87, prior to official order. Sonar transducer beneath port hull. Sonar/mine-countermeasures control room in dismountable deckhouse. Main engines drive propulsion generators *and* ships service generators. Carry two PAP-104 remote-controlled, tethered minehunting submersibles.

**Rushcutter (M 80)** L. & L. Van Ginderen, 1-87

**Rushcutter (M 80)** L. & L. Van Ginderen, 1-87

◆ **1 British "Ton"-class coastal minehunter**

| | Bldr | Laid down | L | In serv. |
|---|---|---|---|---|
| M 1121 CURLEW (ex-*Chediston*) | Montrose SY | 30-4-53 | 6-10-53 | 28-9-54 |

**D:** 375 tons (445 fl) **S:** 15 kts **Dim:** 46.33 (42.68 pp) × 8.76 × 2.50
**A:** removed
**Electron Equipt:** Radar: 1/978—Sonar: Type 193
**M:** Napier Deltic 18A-7A diesels; 2 props; 3,000 hp **Fuel:** 45 tons
**Range:** 2,300/13; 3,500/8 **Man:** 3 officers, 35 men

REMARKS: Bought in 1962. Converted to minehunter during refit. Air-conditioned and stabilized. M 1121 equipped as minehunter, with Type 193 sonar and four divers, only 1/40-mm AA. Proposal to replace these two survivors of a group of six ex-RN minesweepers with a new class of two oceangoing minehunters in the mid-1980s deferred for lack of funds. Sisters *Snipe* (M 1102) stricken 3-6-83, *Ibis* (M 1183) stricken 4-5-84. *Curlew* disposal extended to 1989 to permit use during *Rushcutter*'s trials, and plans for acquiring further seagoing minehunters have been shelved.

**Curlew (M 1121)**—gun removed 1985 R. Gillett, 11-84

## AMPHIBIOUS WARFARE SHIPS

◆ **1 modified British Sir Bedivere class**

| | Bldr | Laid down | L | In serv. |
|---|---|---|---|---|
| L 50 Tobruk | Carrington Skipways, Tomago | 7-2-79 | 1-3-80 | 23-4-81 |

**Tobruk (L 50)** ABPH P. Kalajzich, R.A.N., 8-87

**D:** 3,400 tons (6,000 fl) **S:** 17 kts **Dim:** 129.5 × 19.6 × 4.3
**A:** 2/40-mm AA (I × 2)
**Electron Equipt:** Radar: 1/Decca RM 916, 1/Decca 1226
**M:** 2 Mirrlees-Blackstone KDM8 diesels; 2 props; 9,600 hp
**Electric:** 1,990 kw **Man:** approx. 18 officers, 50 men

Remarks: Announced 8-76 as a replacement for the *Sydney*. Can carry Wessex Mk 31B troop helicopters operating from platform amidships and aft, and can carry 300–500 troops, Leopard tanks, and other military vehicles. Bow and stern ramps fitted. Two LCVP carried. Can carry two LCM 8 on deck. Two 4.5-ton cranes fwd.; 60-ton heavy lift boom before bridge. Home-ported at Sydney, 1986.

◆ **6 Balikpapan-class utility landing craft** Bldr: Walkers Ltd., Maryborough

| | Laid down | L | In serv. |
|---|---|---|---|
| L 126 Balikpapan | 5-71 | 15-8-71 | 27-9-74 |
| L 127 Brunei | 7-71 | 15-10-71 | 5-1-73 |
| L 128 Labuan | 10-71 | 29-12-71 | 9-3-73 |
| L 129 Tarakan | 12-71 | 16-3-71 | 15-6-73 |
| L 130 Wewak | 3-72 | 18-5-72 | 10-8-74 |
| L 133 Betano | 9-72 | 5-12-72 | 8-2-74 |

**D:** 316 tons (503 fl) **S:** 10 kts **Dim:** 44.5 × 10.1 × 1.9
**A:** 2/7.62-mm mg (I × 2) **M:** 2 G.M. 6-71 diesels; 2 props; 675 hp
**Electron Equipt:** Radar: 1/Decca RM 916
**Range:** 3,000/10 **Man:** 2 officers, 11 men

Remarks: In service 1971–74. *Salamaua* (L 131) and *Buna* (L 132) were transferred to Papua New Guinea in 1974. Can carry three Leopard tanks. Originally Army-subordinated. L 127 and L 133 used in inshore survey work. L 128 is used for Reserve training. L 126, L 129, L 130 placed in storage ashore at Cairns after decommissioning 1985.

**Betano (L 133)** L. & L. Van Ginderen, 9-84

## HYDROGRAPHIC SHIPS

◆ **1 Cook class**

| | Bldr | Laid down | L | In serv. |
|---|---|---|---|---|
| A 291 Cook | Williamstown Nav. DY | 30-9-74 | 27-8-77 | 28-10-80 |

**Cook (A 291)**—as reviewing ship for R.A.N. 75th anniversary review, HMNZS *Canterbury* beyond R.A.N., 10-86

**D:** 1,910 tons (2,550 fl) **S:** 17 kts **Dim:** 96.6 (91.2 pp) × 13.41 × 4.6
**Electron Equipt:** Radar: 1/Decca TM 829c—Sonar: 1/Simrad SU-2
**M:** 4 Caterpillar D398TA diesels; 2 props; 3,400 hp **Fuel:** 640 tons
**Range:** 11,000/14 **Man:** 137 crew, 13 scientists

Remarks: Intended for oceanographic research and hydrographic survey. Carries one inshore survey launch. Survey equipment includes Decca Hi-Fix 6, Mini-Ranger MRS3, Atlas DESC-10 echo-sounder, and Harris narrow-beam echo-sounders. Unsatisfactory design, not fully operational until mid-82.

◆ **1 Moresby class**

| | Bldr | Laid down | L | In serv. |
|---|---|---|---|---|
| A 573 Moresby | State DY, Newcastle, NSW | 1-7-62 | 7-9-63 | 6-3-64 |

**D:** 1,714 tons (2,340 fl) **S:** 19 kts **Dim:** 95.7 (86.7 pp) × 12.8 × 4.6
**Electron Equipt:** Radar: 1/Decca TM 829C—Sonar: 1/Simrad SU-2
**M:** diesel-electric propulsion: 3/1,330-hp diesels; 3 CSVM generator sets, each 1,330 kw/800 rpm; 2 electric motors, 2 props; 5,000 hp
**Man:** 13 officers, 133 men

Remarks: A small helicopter can be carried. Ship is air-conditioned. 2/40-mm AA removed, exhaust pipe added on foredeck, stack heightened 1973-74. Three inshore survey launches carried.

**Moresby (A 573)** POPH E. Pitman, R.A.N., 1982

◆ **1 Flinders class**

| | Bldr | Laid down | L | In serv. |
|---|---|---|---|---|
| A 312 Flinders | Williamstown Nav. DY | 11-6-71 | 29-7-72 | 27-4-73 |

**D:** 765 tons (fl) **S:** 13.5 kts **Dim:** 49.1 × 10.05 × 3.7
**Electron Equipt:** Radar: Decca TM 829C—Sonar: Simrad SU-2
**M:** 2 Paxman Ventura diesels; 2 props; 1,680 hp **Range:** 5,000/9
**Man:** 4 officers, 34 men

Remarks: Similar to the Philippine ship *Atyimba*. Replaced the *Paluma*, stricken in 1974. Operates along Barrier Reef. Received new survey launch named *Bramble* in 1982. To strike 1993.

◆ **0 (+4) inshore survey boats** (In serv. 1988–89)

A . . . N . . . A . . . N . . . A . . . N . . . A . . . N . . .

**D:** 120 tons (fl) **S:** . . . **Dim:** 33.0 × . . . × . . .
**M:** diesels; 2 props; . . . hp **Range:** 1,800/. . .
**Man:** 1 officer, 9 men

Remarks: Programmed construction, bids out 6-86. Planned as catamarans, to work with *Flinders* in North Queensland area. Still not ordered, mid-1987.

HYDROGRAPHIC SHIPS *(continued)*

**Flinders (A 312)** R.A.N., 1980

## AUXILIARIES

◆ **1 modified French Durance-class replenishment oiler**

| | | Bldr | Laid down | L | In serv. |
|---|---|---|---|---|---|
| AOR 304 | Success | Vickers, Cockatoo DY | 9-8-80 | 3-3-84 | 23-4-86 |

**Success (AOR 304)** L. & L. Van Ginderen, 12-85

**Success (AOR 304)** R.A.N., 12-85

**D:** 17,993 tons (fl) **S:** 18 kts **Dim:** 157.3 (149.0 pp) × 21.2 × 10.8
**A:** 3/40-mm AA (I × 3)—4/12.7-mm mg (I × 4)
**Electronic Equipt:** Radar: 3 navigational sets
**M:** 2 SEMT-Pielstick 16 PC 2.5 diesels; 1 CP prop; 20,000 hp **Electric:** 5,440 kw
**Range:** 9,000/15 **Man:** 16 officers, 12 CPO, 22 PO, 127 men **Fuel:** 750 tons

Remarks: Ordered 9-79 from design prepared by DTCN, France. Second proposed 1980, but will not be built. To carry 8,220 tons distillate fuel, 1,131 tons aviation fuel, 170 tons munitions, 183 tons provisions, 259 tons water, and 45 tons of spare parts. Will carry 2 stores-handling land craft in davits and will be able to refuel three ships simultaneously. Helicopter platform. Construction progress slow and costs tripled. In mid-1987 the R.A.N. began looking for an existing 6,000 to 9,000 dwt tanker to convert for underway replenishment purposes.

◆ **1 destroyer tender** Bldr: Cockatoo D & E, Sydney

| | Laid down | L | In serv. |
|---|---|---|---|
| AD 215 Stalwart | 6-64 | 7-10-66 | 4-2-68 |

**Stalwart (AD 215)** R.A.N., 1986

**D:** 10,000 tons (15,500 fl) **S:** 20 kts **Dim:** 157.12 (143.25 pp) × 20.57 × 9.0
**A:** 4/40-mm AA (II × 2) **Electric:** 3,200 kw
**Electron Equipt:** Radar: 1/978, 1/293Q
**M:** 2 Scott-Sulzer 6 cyl. Mk RD 68 diesels; 2 props, 14,400 hp
**Range:** 12,000/12 **Man:** 396 tot.

Remarks: Helicopter platform and hangar for two Wessex or one Sea King. Workshops and foundry (400 m$^2$); boiler shop (100 m$^2$); electric shop; electronic shop (300 m$^2$); mechanical workshop (500 m$^2$); and shops for precision equipment and plastic-boat repairs. Four 3-ton and two 6-ton cranes. Carries spare missiles for destroyers and frigates. Acts as R.A.N. Fleet Flagship.

◆ **1 training ship**

| | Bldr | Laid down | L | In serv. |
|---|---|---|---|---|
| AGT 203 Jervis Bay (ex-*Australian Trader*) | State DY, Newcastle | 18-8-67 | 17-2-69 | 17-6-69 |

**D:** 8,915 tons (fl) **S:** 17 kts **Dim:** 135.7 (123.5 pp) × 21.5 × 6.1
**A:** none **Electron Equipt:** Radar: 1/Decca RM 916, 1/Kelvin-Hughes 1006
**M:** 2 Crossley-Pielstick 16 PC 2V400 diesels; 2 props; 13,000 hp
**Fuel:** 820 tons **Electric:** 2,000 kw
**Man:** 111 crew plus 40 trainees

Remarks: A former roll-on/roll-off cargo ferry converted to a training ship to replace the destroyer *Duchess*. Commissioned 25-8-77. Name commemorates a Royal Navy armed merchant cruiser of World War II. Can also serve as a transport and

**Jervis Bay (AGT 203)** L. & L. Van Ginderen, 10-84

**AUXILIARIES** *(continued)*

vehicle cargo ship. U.S. WSC-3 SATCOMM gear added 1984. Helicopter deck added 6-87.

Note: Modified *Daring*-class destroyer *Vampire* (D 11), used as a training ship since 1981, was stricken 13-8-86, may become a museum ship. Hulk of sister *Vendetta* sold for scrap, 12-86, along with oiler *Supply* (AOR 195) and research ship *Kimbla* (AGOR 314).

◆ **2 general-purpose tenders** Bldr: Walkers, Ltd, Maryborough

| | Laid down | L | In serv. |
|---|---|---|---|
| AG 244 Banks | 11-58 | 15-12-59 | 16-2-60 |
| AG 247 Bass | 11-58 | 26-3-60 | 15-11-60 |

**Bass (AG 247)** R. Gillett, 1985

**D:** 207 tons (255 fl) **S:** 10 kts **Dim:** 30.8 (27.5 pp) × 6.7 × 2.5
**M:** diesels; 2 props; . . . hp **Man:** 2 officers, 12 men

Remarks: AG 247 was originally equipped as a hydrographic ship and AG 244 for fisheries protection, but both were used primarily for reserve training until 1983. AG 247: 260 tons fl. AG 247 to Darwin 18-10-85 for reserve training.

◆ **1 sail-training brigantine** Bldr: . . . , U.K. (In serv. 6-87) N . . .

**D:** 200 tons (fl) **S:** 14 kts (sail)/10 kts (diesel)
**Dim:** 43.0 × . . . × . . . **M:** 2 diesels; 1 prop; . . . hp
**Man:** 8 naval crew plus 24 youth trainees

Remarks: Gift of the U.K. for Australia's Bicentennial.

◆ **5 small training yachts** Bldr: Swarbrick Bros., Osbourne Park, West Australia (In serv. 1984)

3807 Alexander of Cresswell
3808 Friendship of Leeuwin
3809 Lady Peryhyn of Nirimba
3810 Charlotte of Cerberus
3811 Scarborough of Cerberus

**D:** 4.35 tons (fl) **S:** . . . **Dim:** 11.10 × 3.20 × 1.95
**M:** 1 Yanmar diesel; 22 hp **Man:** 8 to 10

Remarks: Many other small sailboats are also used for training.

**YARD AND SERVICE CRAFT**

Note: Letters in the pendant numbers ceased to be painted on hulls in 1984–85 as these units were named.

◆ **2 British "Ham"-class diving tenders, former inshore minesweepers** Bldr: J. Samuel White, Cowes

DTV 1001 Seal (ex-*Wintringham*) (L: 24-5-55)
DTV 1002 Porpoise (ex-*Neasham*) (L: 14-3-55)

**Seal (DTV 1001)** L. & L. Van Ginderen, 3-84

**D:** 120 tons (159 fl) **S:** 14 kts **Dim:** 32.43 (30.48 pp) × 6.45 × 1.75
**M:** 2 Paxman YHAXM diesels; 2 props; 1,100 hp **Fuel:** 15 tons
**Range:** 2,000/9 **Man:** 7 crew + 14 divers

Remarks: Transferred in 1966, but not converted until 12-68 (*Seal*) and 1973. Assigned to the school of diving and underwater demolition in Sydney. Can support fourteen divers. Sister *Popham* (Y 299) sold 1974. Large deckhouse replaced sweep winch and cable reel.

◆ **1 coastal tug** Bldr: Australian SB Industries, South Coogee, West Australia

| | Laid down | L | In serv. |
|---|---|---|---|
| OT 2601 Tammar | 20-4-83 | 10-3-84 | 15-3-84 |

**Tammar (OT 2601)** LSPH S. Given, R.A.N., 3-84

**D:** 265 tons (300 fl) **S:** 11.5 kts **Dim:** 25.68 (23.63 pp) × 8.42 × 2.00
**Electron Equipt:** Radar: 1/Furuno navigational
**M:** 2 G.M. 16V149 TI diesels; . . . props; 2,560 hp
**Range:** 1400/10 **Man:** 6 tot.

Remarks: Ordered 30-3-83 for use at HMAS *Sterling,* Cockburn Sound. 160 grt. Bollard pull 40 tons.

◆ **1 medium harbor tug** Bldr: Shoreline Eng., Portland, Victoria

OT 1801 Quokka (L: 10-83)

**Quokka (OT 1801)** LSPH S. Given, R.A.N., 3-84

**D:** 110 tons (fl) **S:** 9 kts **Dim:** 18.17 (16.84 pp) × 5.91 × 2.55
**Electron Equipt:** Radar: 1/Furuno navigational
**M:** 2 G.M. 8V53 diesels; 633 hp

Remarks: Used at Cockburn Sound, West Australia. Bollard pull 8.5 tons

◆ **3 501-class harbor tugs** Bldr: Stannard Bros., Sydney (504: Perrin Eng., Brisbane)

HTS 501 Bronzewing (In serv. 12-68)
HTS 502 Currawong (In serv. 1969)
HTS 504 Mollymawk (In serv. 1972)

**D:** 34 tons (47.5 fl) **S:** 9 kts **Dim:** 19.4 × 4.6 × . . .
**M:** 2 G.M. diesels; 2 props; 340 hp **Range:** 710/9.5 **Man:** 3 tot.

Remarks: Sister 503 to Papua New Guinea 1974. Civilian-manned. Named 1983.

YARD AND SERVICE CRAFT *(continued)*

**Mollymawk (HTS 504)** L. & L. Van Ginderen, 2-86

◆ **2 wooden-hulled harbor tugs** (In serv. 1946)

TB 9 SARDIUS TB 1536 CERBERUS V

**Sardius (TB 9)** L. & L. Van Ginderen, 8-83

**D:** 60 tons (fl) **S:** 8 kts **Dim:** 13.7 × 4.6 × 2.0
**M:** 1 Hercules diesel; 240 hp **Range:** 500/8 **Man:** 4 tot.

REMARKS: TB 9 to be retained into 1990s; TB 1536 laid up 1983, rehabilitated by Port of Melbourne Authority, 1987; engineroom automated.

◆ **3 torpedo-recovery craft** Bldr: Williamstown DY (In serv. 1970–71)

TRV 801 TAILOR TRV 802 TREVALLY TRV 803 TUNA

**Tuna (TRV 803)** G. Gyssels, 11-82

**D:** 91.6 tons **S:** 13 kts **Dim:** 27.0 × 6.4 × 1.4
**M:** 3 G.M. 6-71 diesels; 3 props; 684 hp **Range:** 500/8 **Man:** 1 officer, 8 men

REMARKS: TRV 802 previously used as a diving tender. All named 1982.

NOTE: The torpedo recovery launch *Bincleaves* (TRB 586) was stricken in 1985.

◆ **1 Seaward Defense Boat general-purpose tender**

| | Bldr | In serv. |
|---|---|---|
| SDB 1325 | E. Jack, Launceton, Tasmania | 4-11-43 |

**SDB 1325** LSPH S. Given, R.A.N., 2-83

**D:** 47 tons (58 fl) **S:** 12 kts **Dim:** 24.4 × 4.9 × 1.3
**M:** 2 Buda diesels; 2 props; 390 hp **Range:** 2,000/10 **Man:** 2 officers, 10 men

REMARKS: Last of 28 lengthened versions of the British "72-ft. HDML." Wooden hull.

NOTE: Water tender/cargo lighter/training ships *Gayundah* (MRL 253), MWL 254, and MWL 257 were stricken late in 1982, along with the General-Purpose Vessel GPV 958 and the tank-cleaning vessel TCV *Colac.*

◆ **4 liquid-cargo lighters** Bldr: Williamston DY

WFL 8001 WARRIGAL (In serv. 10-84) WFL 8003 WOMBAT (In serv. 10-2-83)
WFL 8002 WALLABY (In serv. 3-2-83) WFL 8004 WYULDA (In serv. 10-84)

**Wallaby (WFL 8002)** L. & L. Van Ginderen, 5-85

**D:** 265 tons light (1,206 fl) **S:** 9 kts **Dim:** 38.0 × 10.2 × 3.98
**M:** 2 G.E.C. diesels; 1 Harbourmaster outdrive prop fwd., 1 aft; 564 hp
**Range:** 100/9 **Man:** 5 tot.

REMARKS: Cargo: 564 tons diesel fuel, 107 tons feedwater, 104 tons distilled water, 93 tons waste, and 73 tons ballast. Civilian manned. Replaced fuel oil barges OFL 1201–1204, 1207, 1208 in 1984. Known as WFL, Water Fuel Lighters.

◆ **3 stores lighters** Bldr: Cockatoo DY, Sydney

CSL 01 WATTLE (In serv. 15-8-72) CSL 02 BORONIA (In serv. 25-9-72)
CSL 03 TELOPEA (In serv. 31-10-72)

**Wattle (CSL 01)** L. & L. Van Ginderen, 1-86

YARD AND SERVICE CRAFT *(continued)*

**D:** 145.1 tons (fl) **S:** 8 kts **Dim:** 23.7 × 9.75 × 2.0
**M:** 2 G.M. 6-71 diesels; 2 props; 600 hp **Range:** 320/8 **Man:** 4 (civil.)

REMARKS: Catamarans. One 3-ton electric crane. Based on AWL 304 design, but with pilothouse aft.

◆ **1 aircraft lighter** Bldr: Cockatoo DY, Sydney

AWL 304 (In serv. 16-1-67)

**AWL 304** R. Gillett, 1985

**D:** 175 tons (fl) **S:** 8.8 kts **Dim:** 23.7 × 9.75 × 2.0
**M:** 2 G.M. 6-71 diesels; 2 props; 600 hp **Range:** 320/8 **Man:** 3 (civil.)

REMARKS: Built 1967 to carry 2 Skyhawk or 1 Tracker to service the *Melbourne*. Similar to CSL 01 class, but with A-frame aft and low pilothouse forward, to port. Now used as a general stores lighter and cable layer.

◆ **2 Harbor Personnel Launches** Bldr: Bertram, U.S.A. (In serv. 1966)

38101 38102

**D:** 12 tons (fl) **S:** 22 kts **Dim:** 11.5 × 3.9 × . . .
**M:** 2 G.M. 8V53M diesels; 2 props; 500 hp **Range:** 200/22 **Man:** 2 tot.

REMARKS: Originally purchased as air-sea rescue boats.

◆ **15 Navy Work Boats** Bldr: North Queensland Engineers, Cairns

NWB 1280–1294 (In serv. 1980–81)

Known names: NWB 1281, *Otter*; NWB 1282, *Walrus*; NWB 1283, *Beaver*; NWB 1285, *Grampus*; NWB 1286, *Dolphin*; NWB 1287, *Dugong*; NWB 1292, *Turtle*

**Walrus (NWB 1282)** L. & L. Van Ginderen, 2-82

**D:** 12.5 tons **S:** 12 kts **Dim:** 12.0 × . . . × . . . **M:** 2 diesels; 2 props; . . . hp

REMARKS: Army operates 7 additional. Some (including NWB 1288) are configured as diving tenders. Aluminum construction.

◆ **32 wooden-hulled work boats** (In serv. 1944–46)

AWB 404, 411, 413, 416–424, 426, 428, 430, 433–436, 440–442, 444, 445, 1658, 4001–4003, 4006, 4007, 4010, 4011

**AWB 4003** R. Gillett, 1985

**D:** 10 tons light (22 fl) **S:** 8 kts **Dim:** 12.2 × 3.81 × 1.37
**M:** 1 Gray Marine 64 HN 9 diesel; 175 hp **Range:** 600/8

REMARKS: Superstructures vary. Some have names (AWB 420, *Amethyst*).

Other self-propelled service craft include:
1 7-m Range Clearance Boat: RCV 0701
1 8-m "Shark Cat" for Naval Police: DV 0801
1 10.6-m Fast Motor Boat: FMB 3501
10 10.0-m Fast Utility Boats: FUB 3310–3319
1 7.9-m Fast Utility Boat: FUB 2603
7 10.0-m Harbor Personnel Boats: HPB 3350–3356
1 9.1-m Harbor Personnel Boat: HPB 30102
7 7.9-m Harbor Personnel Boat: HPB 2620–2626
1 7.6-m Harbor Personnel Boat: HPB 25101
20 Light Utility Boats in 3 types: LUB 20 . . . series
4 Firefish Radio-Controlled Surface Targets: RCST 02–05
10 10.0-m Sea Boats: SB 3330–3339
3 Survey Motor Boats: SMB 3401 (*Fantome*), 3405, 3411
1 training yacht: *Franklin*
1 7.9-m workboat: WB 2601
Other non-self-propelled service craft include:
8 300-ton Concrete Ammunition Lighters: CAL 201–206, 208, 209
8 100-ton Concrete Ammunition Lighters: CAL 101, 102, 10010–10015
8 50-ton Concrete Ammunition Lighters: CAL 501–504, 508, 5010–5012
4 Container Pontoons: 1–4
1 Deperming Lighter: DGL 1
3 Dry Dock Caissons: DCI 1, 2; DC 219
21 60-ton Flat-Top Lighters: FTL 60101–60121
1 Flat-Top Lighter: FTL 764
1 1,000-ton-capacity Floating Dock: FD 1002

**Survey Motor Boat SMB 3405** R. Gillett, 1984

**Survey Motor Boat SMB 3411** L. & L. Van Ginderen, 5-85

**YARD AND SERVICE CRAFT** *(continued)*

**100-ton Concrete Ammunition Lighter CAL 10012**
L. & L. Van Ginderen, 11-81

**Fast Utility Boat Platypus (FUB 3311)** L. & L. Van Ginderen, 8-83

**Harbour Personnel Boat HPB 3352** L. & L. Van Ginderen, 7-85

ROYAL AUSTRALIAN ARMY CORPS OF ENGINEERS

Personnel: Approx. 300

◆ **16 U.S. LCM (8)-class landing craft** Bldrs: AB 1050–1061: North Queensland Engineers, Cairns; others: Dillingham SY, Fremantle (In serv. 1967)

AB 1050–1053, 1055, 1056, 1058–1067

**AB 1051**—green-painted L. & L. Van Ginderen, 9-84

**D:** 34 tons light (116 fl) **S:** 12 kts (9 loaded) **Dim:** 22.70 × 6.41 × 1.37
**M:** 2 G.M. 12V71 diesels; 2 props; 600 hp **Range:** 200/9
**Man:** 5 tot.

Remarks: Cargo: 55 tons. Some kept in land storage. Sister AB 1057 transferred to Tonga in 1982; AB 1054 stricken 1984. LCVPs 752, 755–757: stricken 1984. The Army plans to replace the LCMs with a larger type of utility landing craft.

◆ **2 harbor tugs** (In serv. 1963)

AT 2700 Joe Mann AT 2701 The Luke

**Joe Mann (AT 2700)**—with NLE (Naval Lighterage Equipment) pontoon *Castor*
R. Gillett, 8-82

**D:** 54.5 tons (60 fl) **S:** 10 kts **Dim:** 17.06 × 5.20 × 1.60
**M:** 2 G.M. 6-71 diesels; 1 prop; 333 hp **Man:** 3 tot.
**Range:** 5,700/8

Remarks: AT 2700 based at Sydney, AT 2701 at Brisbane. AT 2701 has smaller pilothouse. Both fitted for firefighting.

◆ **2 NLE (Naval Lighterage Equipment) self-propelled pontoons**

201 Castor 202 Pollux

**D:** 32.6 tons **S:** 4 kts **Dim:** 25.5 × 6.4 × . . .
**M:** 2 portable diesel outdrives

◆ **7 Navy work boats** Bldr: North Queensland Engineers, Cairns (In serv. 1979–80)

AM 417 Oolah
AM 418 Kewal
AM 419 Sea Horse One
AM 420 Boongaree
AM 421 Mena II
AM 422 Akuna
AM 423 Gabinga

**Oolah (AM 417)**—with portable cover over passenger deck R. Gillett, 1984

Remarks: Data as for naval version. Crew: 2.

◆ **2 Shark Cat launches** Bldr: Shark Cat, Queensland (In serv. 1980)

AM 215 AM 216

**AUSTRALIA** *(continued)*
**ROYAL AUSTRALIAN ARMY CORPS OF ENGINEERS** *(continued)*

**"Shark Cat" AM 215**—sisters are operated by the R.A.N. and R.A.A.F.
L. & L. Van Ginderen, 11-83

REMARKS: Glass-reinforced plastic, 60-knot, radar-equipped catamarans, for landing craft command and control. **D:** About 4 tons. Several sisters are operated by the R.A.A.F. Marine Section.

◆ **2 diving tender/survey craft** (In serv. 1979)

AB 251 AFRICAN QUEEN    AB 252

NOTE: Also in service are over 70 U.S. Army-design LARC 5, 5-ton amphibious lighters and a variety of river-crossing craft and small assault boats.

ROYAL AUSTRALIAN AIR FORCE

**WORK BOATS**

REMARKS: The following craft are in service for search-and-rescue duties:

016–100 WARANA—49 tons, 23 m, range 400/18
. . . MAX EISE II—14.7 m, 18.4 kt, waterjet-propelled
Four Shark Cat catamarans:
07-001—7.0 m, 2 × 175-hp outboards, 35 kts
08-001, 08-002, 08-003—8.3 m, 2 × 135-hp outboards, 35 kts

CUSTOMS SERVICE

**PATROL CRAFT**

◆ **3 (+ . . .) Jabiru class** (In serv. 1985)

JABIRU    JACANA    JERBOA

**D:** 17 tons (fl) **S:** 23 kts **Dim:** 14.0 × . . . × . . .
**M:** 2 Cummins diesels; 2 props; 740 hp

◆ **3 glass-reinforced plastic craft** (In serv. 1981–82)

PERCY WHITTEN    EDWIN ABBOT    E.T. HALL

REMARKS: 12.8 m o.a., 540 n.m. at 17 kts. Also in use are six 7.0-m. trailer-transportable boats delivered 1981–82.

◆ **1 Cocos Islands patrol craft**

SIR ZELMAN COWAN

**D:** . . . **S:** 20 kts **Dim:** 14.6 × 3.0 × . . . **Man:** 7 off., 10 men
**M:** 2 Cummins diesels; 2 props; . . . hp **Range:** 400/17

REMARKS: Subordinated to the Western Australia Department of Harbours and Lights.

# AUSTRIA

**Republic of Austria**

AUSTRIAN ARMY DANUBE FLOTILLA

PERSONNEL (1986): 1 officer, 26 men

MERCHANT MARINE (1986): 26 ships—124,794 grt

◆ **2 patrol craft for the Danube**    Bldr: Korneuberg Werft AG

| | Laid down | L | In serv. |
|---|---|---|---|
| A 604 NIEDERÖSTERREICH | 31-3-69 | 26-7-69 | 16-4-70 |

**D:** 73 tons (fl) **S:** 22 kts **Dim:** 29.67 × 5.41 × 1.1
**A:** 1/20-mm AA—2/12.7-mm mg—2/7.62-mm mg—1/84-mm mortar

**Niederösterreich (A 604)**

**M:** 2 MWM V-16 diesels; 1,620 hp **Fuel:** 9.3 tons
**Range:** 900/. . . **Man:** 1 officer, 11 men

A 601 OBERST BRECHT    Bldr: Korneuberg Werft AG (In serv. 14-1-58)

**D:** 10 tons **S:** 14 kts **Dim:** 12.30 × 2.51 × 0.75
**A:** 1/12.7-mm mg—1/84-mm mortar
**M:** 2 Graf & Stift 6-cyl. diesels; 290 hp
**Range:** 160/10 **Man:** 5 tot.

◆ **10 M-boot 80 class launches**    Bldr: Schottel Werft, Spay, West Germany (In serv. 1984)

**D:** 4.7 tons (fl) **S:** 14 kts **Dim:** 7.5 × 2.5 × 0.6
**M:** 1 Klöckner-Humboldt-Deutz V-12 diesel; . . . hp

REMARKS: Push-boat/personnel launches. Replaced 10 U.S. Army M-3 Series launches discarded 1984.

◆ **several motorized pontoons**

**D:** 8.5 to 40 tons (fl) **Dim:** 19.0 × 17.0 (some 30.0) × 0.7

# THE BAHAMAS

**Commonwealth of the Bahamas**

MERCHANT MARINE (1986): 302 ships—5,985,011 grt (tankers: 71—4,111,082 grt)

POLICE MARINE DIVISION

◆ **3 "Protector" class**    Bldr: Fairey Marine, Cowes, U.K.

P 03 YELLOW ELDER (In serv. 14-7-86)    P 05 SAMANA (In serv. 9-86)
P 04 PORT NELSON (In serv. . . . -86)

**Yellow Elder (P 03)**    M. Louagie, 8-86

**Port Nelson (P 04)**    L. & L. Van Ginderen, 8-86

**THE BAHAMAS** *(continued)*
**POLICE MARINE DIVISION** *(continued)*

**D:** 100 tons (fl) **S:** 30 kts (26 sust.)
**Dim:** 33.00 (28.96 wl) × 6.73 × 1.95 (props)
**A:** 1/20-mm Oerlikon Mk 7A AA—2/7.62-mm mg (I × II)
**Electron Equipt:** Radar: 1/Furuno FR-701
**M:** 3 G.M. Detroit Diesel 16V149 TIB diesels; 3 props; 5,400 hp
**Fuel:** 16 tons **Range:** 300/24; 1,400/14 **Man:** 2 officers, 18 men

REMARKS: Ordered 1985. Steel construction. All delivered by ship 6-10-86. Racal MNS 2000 navigation system.

◆ **1 103-foot patrol boat** Bldr: Vosper Thornycroft

| | Laid down | L | In serv. |
|---|---|---|---|
| P 01 MARLIN | 22-11-76 | 20-6-77 | 23-5-78 |

**Marlin (P 01)** Vosper, 1978

**D:** 100 tons (125 fl) **S:** 24 kts **Dim:** 31.5 × 5.9 × 1.6
**A:** 1/20-mm AA **M:** 2 Paxman Ventura diesels; 2 props; 2,900 hp
**Range:** 2,000/13 **Man:** 3 officers, 16 men

REMARKS: Fin stabilizers, steel hulls. Two 50-mm flare launchers. Sister *Flamingo* sunk 11-5-80 by Cuban MiG-21 aircraft.

◆ **5 Keith Nelson patrol craft** Bldr: Vosper Thornycroft. First four in serv. 5-3-71, last three 10-12-77

P 22 ANDROS P 25 EXUMA P 27 INAGUA
P 23 ELEUTHERA P 26 ABACO

**D:** 30 tons (37 fl) **S:** 19.5 kts **Dim:** 18.29 (17.07 pp) × 5.03 × 1.53
**A:** 2/7.62-mm mg (I × 2) **Electron Equipt:** Radar: 1/Decca 110
**M:** 2 Caterpillar 3408 TA diesels; 2 props; 950 hp
**Fuel:** 4 tons **Electric:** 29 kVA **Range:** 650/16 **Man:** 11 tot.

REMARKS: Fiberglass construction, air-conditioned. First unit, *Acklins* (P 21), destroyed by fire, 1980. *San Salvador* (P 24) stricken 1982.

◆ **1 Standard Arctic-24-class rigid inflatable rescue craft** Bldr: Osbourne, Littlehampton (In serv: 10-86)

REMARKS: 7-m o.a., two Yamaha ABTL outboards, 180 hp, 3-man crew; has self-righting buoyancy bag.

◆ **1 Spear-class patrol craft** Bldr: Fairey, Cowes, U.K. . . . (In serv. 1985)

**D:** 4.8 tons (fl) **S:** 30 kts **Dim:** 9.10 × 2.75 × 0.84
**A:** small arms **Electron Equipt:** Radar: 1/Decca . . .
**M:** 2 diesels; 2 props; 360 hp **Range:** 200/26

REMARKS: GRP construction. Delivery uncertain.

◆ **4 small patrol craft** Bldr: Phoenix Marine, Florida, U.S.A.

P 30, P 31 (In serv. 6-81) P 32, P 33 (In serv. 12-81)

**D:** 8 tons (fl) **S:** 24 kts **Dim:** 8.8 × 3.0 × 0.7
**A:** 2/7.62-mm mg (I × 2) **Range:** 350/21
**M:** 2 Volvo TAMD 40 diesel outdrives; . . . hp **Man:** 4 tot.

REMARKS: Glass-reinforced plastic construction.

◆ **1 support craft, former fishing boat** (Purchased 21-10-81)

AO 2 FORT CHARLOTTE (ex-. . .)

**D:** 150 tons (fl) **S:** 12 kts **Dim:** 45.1 × 6.1 × 2.1
**A:** 2/7.62-mm mg (I × 2) **Range:** 3,500/12
**M:** 1 G.M. Detroit Diesel 16-71 diesel; 1 prop; 800 hp **Man:** 16 tot.

REMARKS: Used for constabulary transport and supply.

◆ **1 support craft, former fishing boat** (Purchased 6-8-80)

AO 1 FORT MONTAGUE (ex-. . .)

**D:** 90 tons (fl) **S:** 10 kts **Dim:** 28.6 × 7.0 × 1.8
**A:** 2/7.62-mm mg (I × 2) **Range:** 3,000/10
**M:** 1 G.M. 12-71 diesel; 1 prop; . . . hp **Man:** 16 tot.

◆ **4 miscellaneous launches**

P 101—8.53 m o.a., 2/235-hp Johnson outboards
P 102—8.64 m o.a., 2/235-hp Mercury outboards
P 103—9.14 m o.a., 2/350-hp Mercury outboards
P 104—11.68 m o.a., 2/235-hp Mercury outboards

◆ **3 former fishing boats about 15 m o.a.**

P 34 (ex-*Carmen Rosa*) P 35 (ex-*Carey*)
P 36 (ex-*Maria Mercedes*)

# BAHRAIN

**State of Bahrain**

MERCHANT MARINE (1986): 98 ships—51,713 grt (tankers: 5—3,308 grt)

DEFENSE FORCES

PERSONNEL (1986): About 350 Navy; 250 Coast Guard

## CORVETTES

◆ **1 (+1) Type FPB 62-001** Bldr: Lürssen, Vegesack, West Germany

| | Laid down | L | In serv. |
|---|---|---|---|
| . . . N . . . | . . . | -86 | 12-87 |
| . . . N . . . | . . . | . . . | 1988 |

**Type 62-001 Number One**—on trials P. Voss, 12-86

**D:** 632 tons (fl) **S:** 34.7 kts (32.25 sust.)
**Dim:** 62.95 (59.90 pp) × 9.30 × 2.6
**A:** 4/Harpoon SSM (II × 2)—1/76-mm OTO Melara Compact DP—2/40-mm Breda AA (II × 1)—2/20-mm AA (I × 2)—1/Dauphin helicopter (AST-15 missiles)
**Electron Equipt:** Radar: 1/Decca 1226, 1/Philips 9LV200, 1/Philips . . .
EW: Cygnus jammer, Cutlass intercept, Dagaie RL
**M:** 4 MTU . . . diesels; 4 props; 19,600 hp **Fuel:** 120 tons
**Range:** 4,000/16 **Electric:** 408 kw (3 × 136 kw)
**Man:** 43 tot.

REMARKS: Contract announced 5-85. The raised helicopter platform incorporates an elevator to lower the helicopter to the hangar below. Eight AST-15 antiship missiles are carried for the helicopter. Philips 9LV-331 weapons-control system with one I/J-band air/surface-search radar, one J-band tracking radar (with t.v./laser/infrared backup), one helicopter control and navigational radar and two Panda Mk 2 optronic directors.

## PATROL BOATS

◆ **4 TNC 45-class guided-missile boats** Bldr: Lürssen, Vegesack, West Germany

20 AHMED AL FATEH (In serv. 5-2-84) 21 AL JABERI (In serv. 5-84)

22 ABDUL RAHMAN AL-FADEL (In serv. 9-86) 23 N . . . (In serv. . . .-87)

**D:** 203 tons light (259 fl) **S:** 40.5 kts
**Dim:** 44.9 (42.3 fl) × 7.3 × 2.05 (2.31 props)
**A:** 4/MM 40 Exocet SSM (II × 2)—1/76-mm OTO Melara DP—2/40-mm Breda AA (II × 1)—2/12.7-mm M3 mg (I × 2)
**Electron Equipt:** Radar: 1/Decca . . . nav.; 1/. . . search radar; 1/PEAB 9 LV223 f.c.s.
EW: Decca RDL-2 ABC passive warning, 1/Dagaie chaff RL (X × 1)
**M:** 4 MTU 16V538 TB92 diesels; 4 props; 15,600 hp (13,460 sust.) **Fuel:** 45 tons
**Electric:** 405 kVA **Range:** 500/38.5; 1,500/16 **Man:** 6 officers, 30 men

**PATROL BOATS** *(continued)*

**Abdul Rahman Al-Fadel** (22)—note added radar aft P. Voss, 1-86

Remarks: First pair ordered 1979, second pair in 5-85; no third pair yet on order. Very similar to TNC 45 class for the United Arab Emirates. Panda backup director for 40-mm guns. Carry 250 rds 76-mm, 1,800 rds. 40-mm, 6,000 rds. 12.7-mm ammunition.

◆ **2 FPB 38-class patrol boats** Bldr: Lürssen, Vegesack, West Germany

| | L | In serv. | | L | In serv. |
|---|---|---|---|---|---|
| 10 Al Riffa | 4-81 | 3-3-82 | 11 Hawar | ... | 3-3-82 |

**Al Riffa (10)** J. Bouvia, 1987

**D:** 188 tons normal (205 fl) **S:** 34 kts **Dim:** 38.5 (36.0 pp) × 7.0 × 2.2 (props)
**A:** 2/40-mm AA Breda AA (II × 1)—2/mine rails
**Electron Equipt:** Radar: 1/Decca . . . nav.; 1/9GR 600 **Electric:** 130 kVA
**M:** 2 MTU diesels; 2 props; 9,000 hp
**Range:** 550/31.5; 1,100/16 **Man:** 3 officers, 24 men

Remarks: Ordered 1979. 2/3-pdr. saluting cannon. CSEE Lynx optical GFCS. 57-mm flare rocket/chaff launcher abaft mast.

◆ **2 65-ft Commercial Cruiser class** Bldr: Swiftships, Morgan City, La., U.S.A.

30 Al Jarim (In serv. 9-2-82) 31 Al Jasrah (In serv. 26-2-82)

**Al Jarim (30)** J. Bouvia, 1987

**D:** 33 tons (fl) **S:** 30 kts **Dim:** 19.17 × 5.56 × 1.98
**A:** 1/20-mm AA **Electron Equipt:** Radar: 1/Decca 110
**M:** 2 G.M. 12V71 TI diesels; 2 props; 1,200 hp **Range:** 1,200/18

Remarks: Aluminum construction.

MINISTRY OF THE INTERIOR
COAST GUARD

**PATROL BOATS AND CRAFT**

◆ **1 30-meter Wasp class** Bldr: Souter, Cowes, U.K.

Al Yusrah (Laid down: 15-11-84—In serv. 12-8-85)

**Al Yusrah** J. Bouvia, 1987

**D:** 10.5 tons (fl) **S:** 23.6 kts **Dim:** 30.0 (26.75 wl) × 6.40 × 1.60
**A:** 1/20-mm AA, 1/7.62-mm mg
**M:** 2 G.M. 16V149 TI diesels; 2 props; 3,100 hp **Fuel:** 17 tons
**Electric:** 47 kVA **Range:** 500/22; 1,000/12 **Man:** 16 tot.

Remarks: Enlarged version of standard 20-m Wasp, ordered 3-8-84. Glass-reinforced plastic construction. A VIP lounge is built over the stern. Outfitted as a yacht.

◆ **2 20-meter Wasp class fiberglass-hulled** Bldr: Souter, Cowes, U.K. (Ord. 1-83; in serv. 1983)

Dera'a 4 Dera'a 5

**Dera'a 4** J. Bouvia, 1987

**D:** 34 tons (fl) **S:** 21 kts **Dim:** 20.0 (16.0 wl) × 5.0 × 1.5
**A:** 2/7.62-mm mg (I × 2)
**M:** 2 G.M. 12V71 TI diesels; 2 props; 1,200 hp **Man:** 8 tot.

◆ **3 11-meter Wasp class fiberglass-hulled** Bldr: Souter, Cowes, U.K. (Ord. 20-8-82; in serv. 1983)

Sahem 1 Sahem 2 Sahem 3

**D:** 7.25 tons (fl) **S:** 24 kts **Dim:** 11.0 × 3.2 × 0.56
**A:** 1/7.62-mm mg **M:** 2 Perkins TV8.450 diesels; 2 waterjets; 612 hp

◆ **4 Sword class fiberglass-hulled** Bldr: Fairey Marine, Cowes, U.K.

Saif 1 Saif 2 Saif 3 Saif 4 (In serv. 1980)

**D:** 15.2 tons **S:** 28 kts **Dim:** 13.7 × 4.1 × 1.32
**M:** 2 G.M. 8V71 TI diesels; 2 props; 850 hp **Range:** 500/. . . **Man:** 6 tot.

◆ **3 patrol craft** Bldr: Vosper, Singapore (In serv. 1977)

Al Bayneh Junnan Quaimas

**D:** 6.3 tons (fl) **S:** 27 kts **Dim:** 11.1 × 3.3 × 0.9
**M:** 1 Sabre diesel; 210 hp

◆ **3 Tracker class** Bldr: Fairey Marine, U.K.

Dera'a 1 (In serv. 1975) Dera'a 2 (In serv. 1980) Dera'a 3 (In serv. 1980)

**D:** 26 tons (fl) **S:** 28 kts **Dim:** 19.6 × 4.9 × 1.5 **A:** 1/20-mm AA
**M:** 2 G.M. diesels; 2 props; 1,120 hp **Range:** 500

◆ **2 Spear class fiberglass-hulled** Bldr: Fairey Marine, U.K. (In serv. 1975)

Sahem 4 5 Khataf

**D:** 4.5 tons (10 fl) **S:** 26 kts **Dim:** 9.1 × 2.75 × 0.84
**A:** 2/7.62-mm mg **M:** 2 Perkins diesels; 2 props; 290 hp
**Range:** 220/26 **Man:** 3 tot.

◆ **3 27-foot** Bldr: Cheverton, Cowes, U.K. (In serv. 1977)

15 Noon 16 Askar 17 Suwad

**D:** 8.3 tons **S:** 15 kts **Dim:** 8.23 × 2.44 × 0.81
**M:** 2 diesels; 1 prop; 150 hp

◆ **1 50-foot** Bldr: Cheverton, Cowes, U.K. (In serv. 1976)

6 Mashtan

**D:** 9 tons **S:** 22 kts **Dim:** 15.2 × 4.3 × 1.4
**M:** 2 G.M. 8V TI diesels; 2 props; 900 hp **Range:** 660/12

◆ **1 utility landing craft** Bldr: Swiftships, Inc., Morgan City, La.

41 Ajirah (In serv. 21-10-82)

**BAHRAIN** *(continued)*
**PATROL BOATS AND CRAFT** *(continued)*

**Ajirah (41)** Swiftships, Inc., 11-82

**D:** 428 tons (fl) **S:** 12 kts **Dim:** 39.62 × 10.97 × 1.30
**A:** none **Electron Equipt:** Radar: 1/Decca . . . nav.
**M:** 2 G.M. Detroit Diesel 16V71N diesels; 2 props; . . . hp
**Fuel:** 20 tons **Range:** 1,500/10 **Man:** 2 officers, 6 men

Remarks: Aluminum construction. Cargo: vehicles, supplies, up to 100 tons cargo fuel and 88 tons water. Bow ramp. 15-ton crane. Turning radius: 77 m. Two sisters in Venezuelan Navy.

### MISCELLANEOUS

◆ **1 Loadmaster II-class landing craft** Bldr: Fairey Marine, Cowes, U.K. (In serv. 1981)

40 Safra II

**D:** 150 tons (fl) **S:** 8 kts **Dim:** 22.5 × 7.5 × 1.2
**M:** 2 G.M. 8V92N diesels; 2 props; 776 hp **Range:** 500/. . . **Man:** 6 tot.

◆ **1 Loadmaster-class landing craft** Bldr: Cheverton, Cowes, U.K. (In serv. 1976)

7 Safra I

**D:** 90 tons (fl) **S:** 10 kts **Dim:** 18.23 × 6.1 × 1.0
**M:** 2 diesels; 2 props; 240 hp **Range:** 600/9 **Man:** 13 tot.

Remarks: Can carry 40 tons of vehicles or dry cargo, or 60 tons of liquid cargo.

◆ **10 wooden motor dhows for logistics and patrol duties**

◆ **1 utility hovercraft** Bldr: Tropimere, U.K. (In serv. 1977)

**D:** 4.23 tons (fl) **S:** 45 kts **Dim:** 8.9 × 4.5 × 3.6 high

◆ **1 tug** (In serv. 1981)

N . . . . . . .

**D:** 12 tons (fl) **S:** . . . kts **Dim:** 11.0 × . . . × . . .
**M:** 1 G.M. 6V71 diesel; 300 hp

# BANGLADESH

**People's Republic of Bangladesh**

Personnel (1986): About 7,500 men (600 officers)

Merchant Marine (1986): 274 ships—378,563 grt (tankers: 44—39,640 grt)

### FRIGATES

◆ **2 British Leopard-class (Type 41) frigates**

| | Bldr | Laid down | L | In serv. |
|---|---|---|---|---|
| F 15 Abu Bakr (ex-*Lynx,* F 27) | John Brown, Clydebank | 13-8-53 | 12-1-55 | 14-3-57 |
| F 17 Ali Haider (ex-*Jaguar,* F 37) | Wm. Denny, Dumbarton | 2-11-53 | 30-7-57 | 12-12-59 |

**D:** 2,300 tons (2,520 fl) **S:** 23 kts **Dim:** 103.63 (100.58 pp) × 12.19 × 4.8 (fl)
**A:** 4/114-mm Mk 6 DP (II × 2)—1/40-mm Mk 9 AA
**Electron Equipt:** Radar: 1/965, 1/978, 1/993, 1/275 fire-control
**M:** 8 Admiralty 16 VVS ASR 1 diesels; 2 CP props; 12,400 hp
**Electric:** 1,500 kw **Fuel:** 230 tons
**Range:** 2,300/23; 7,500/16 **Man:** 10 officers, 200 men

**Abu Bakr (F 15)** 1982

Remarks: F 17 purchased 6-7-78; arrived Bangladesh 11-78 after overhaul. F 15 purchased 12-3-82, commissioned 19-3-82. Squid ASW mortar and sonars removed while in Royal Navy. Fin stabilizers. 1/Mk 6 GFCS with Type 275 radar for 114-mm guns; 40-mm, local control only.

◆ **1 ex-British Salisbury-class (Type 61) aircraft direction frigate**

| | Bldr | Laid down | L | In serv. |
|---|---|---|---|---|
| F 16 Umar Farooq (ex-*Llandaff,* F 61) | Hawthorn Leslie | 27-8-53 | 30-11-55 | 11-4-58 |

**Umar Farooq (F 16)** 1979

**D:** 2,170 tons (2,408 fl) **S:** 24 kts **Dim:** 103.6 (100.58 pp) × 12.19 × 4.8
**A:** 2/114-mm Mk 6 Dp (II × 1)—2/40-mm Mk 5AA (II × 1)—1/Mk 4 Squid ASW mortar (III × 1)
**Electron Equipt:** Radar: 1/985, 1/993, 1/277Q, 1/982, 1/975, 1/275
Sonar: 1/174, 1/170B
**M:** 8 Admiralty 16 VVS ASR 1 diesels; 2 props; 12,400 hp
**Range:** 2,300/24; 7,500/16 **Man:** 14 officers, 223 men

Remarks: Transferred 10-12-76. Mk 6 GFCS for 114-mm mount. Major machinery casualty during 1985; may be non-operational.

### PATROL BOATS AND CRAFT

◆ **4 Chinese Hoku-class guided-missile patrol boats**

P 8111 Duranta P 8112 Durbar P 8113 Duruedya P 8114 Durdam

**D:** 68 tons (79 fl) **S:** 37 kts **Dim:** 27.00 × 6.50 × 1.80 (1.3 hull)
**A:** 2/CSS-N-1 SSM (I × 2)—2/25-mm AA (II × 1)
**Electron Equipt:** Radar: 1/Square Tie **Electric:** 65 kw
**M:** 4 M50 F-4 diesels; 4 props; 4,800 hp **Range:** 500/24 **Man:** 16 tot.

Remarks: First two delivered 6-4-83; others in 10-83. Steel construction. Have 5-day endurance.

◆ **2 fisheries protection patrol boats** Bldr: Vosper Pty, Tanjong Rhu, Singapore

P 316 Megna (L: 19-1-84) P 317 Jamuna (L: 19-3-84)

**D:** 410 (fl) **S:** 20 kts **Dim:** 46.5 × 7.5 × 2.0 (hull)
**A:** 2/40-mm AA (I × 2)—2/7.62-mm mg (I × 2)
**Electron Equipt:** Radar: 1/Decca 1229 **Range:** 2,000/16
**M:** 2 Paxman Valenta 12 CM diesels; 2 props; 6,000 hp **Man:** 44

**Megna (P 316)**—fitting out 1984

## PATROL BOATS AND CRAFT *(continued)*

REMARKS: Operated for the Ministry of Agriculture by the Navy for 200-nautical-mile economic zone patrol.

◆ **6 Chinese Hainan-class submarine chasers**

P 811 DURJOY (In serv. 10-9-82) P 814 N . . . (In serv. 8-84)
P 812 N . . . (In serv. 8-84) P 815 N . . . (In serv. 1985)
P 813 N . . . (In serv. 8-84) P 816 NIRBHOY (In serv. 1-12-85)

**D:** 375 tons normal (400 fl) **S:** 30.5 kts **Dim:** 58.77 × 7.20 × 2.20 (hull)
**A:** 4/57-mm AA (II × 2)—4/25-mm AA (II × 2)—4/RBU-1200 ASW RL (V × 4)—2/BMB-2 d.c. mortars—2/d.c. racks—mines
**Electron Equipt:** Radar: 1/Pot Head—Sonar: 1/Tamir-11 HF
**M:** 4 diesels; 4 props; 8,800 hp **Range:** 2,000/14 **Man:** 70 tot.

◆ **4 Soviet P-4-class torpedo boats** (In serv. mid-1950s)

T 8221 T 8222 T 8223 T 8224

**D:** 19.3 tons (22.4 fl) **S:** 55 kts **Dim:** 19.3 × 3.7 × 1.0
**A:** 2/14.5-mm mg (II × 1)—2/450-mm TT **Man:** 12 tot.
**Electron Equipt:** Radar: 1/Skin Head **M:** 2 M50 diesels; 2 props; 2,400 hp

REMARKS: Delivered from China 6-4-83 along with the two Hoku-class missile boats. Aluminum construction. Thoroughly obsolescent.

◆ **1 Japanese-built patrol boat**

| | Bldr | L | In serv. |
|---|---|---|---|
| SHAMJALA | Sumidagawa, Tokyo | 2-7-81 | 1982 |

**D:** 160 tons (fl) **S:** 26.5 kts **Dim:** 30.0 × . . . × . . . **A:** . . .
**M:** 2 diesels; 2 props; . . . hp

REMARKS: Apparently a variant of the Japanese Maritime Safety Agency's *Akagi* (130-ton) class. Six patrol boats of this size were planned, but further orders did not materialize. *Shamjala* may have been stricken during 1986.

◆ **2 ex-Yugoslav Kraljevica-class patrol boats** (In serv. 1956)

P 314 KARNAPHULI (ex-Yugoslav PBR 502) P 315 TISTNA (ex-Yugoslav PBR 505)

**Tistna (P 315)** 1976

**D:** 190 tons (202 fl) **S:** 18 kts **Dim:** 41.0 × 6.3 × 2.2
**A:** 2/40-mm AA (I × 2)—4/20-mm AA (I × 4)—2/Mk 6 d.c. throwers—2/d.c. racks—2/128-mm RL (V × 2)
**Electron Equipt:** Radar: 1/Decca 1229—Sonar: QCU-2 **Range:** 1,000/12
**M:** 2 M.A.N. W8V 30/38 diesels; 2 props; 3,300 hp
**Man:** 4 officers, 40 men

REMARKS: Transferred 6-6-75. New navigational radar.

◆ **8 Chinese Shanghai-II-class patrol boats**

P 411 SHAHEED DAULAT P 415 TOWHEED
P 412 SHAHEED FARID P 416 TOWFIQ
P 413 SHAHEED MOHIBULLAH P 417 TAMJEED
P 414 SHAHEED AKHTARUDDIN P 418 TANVEER

**Shaheed Farid (old number) and sister** 1980

**D:** 122 tons (135 fl) **S:** 28.5 kts **Dim:** 38.78 × 5.41 × 1.55 (max.)
**A:** 4/37-mm AA (II × 2)—4/25-mm AA (II × 2) **Man:** 36 tot.
**Electron Equipt:** Radar: 1/Pot Head **Electric:** 39 kw
**M:** 2 M50F-4/1,200-hp and 2/910-hp diesels; 4 props; 4,220 hp **Range:** 750/16.5

REMARKS: 101–104 delivered 6-7-80. 105–108 delivered 5-82. Two earlier units, delivered 1974, now stricken.

◆ **1 salvaged Pakistani patrol boat** Bldr: Brooke Marine, Lowestoft, U.K.

P 311 BISHKALI (ex-*Jessore*)—In serv. 20-5-65

**D:** 115 tons (143 fl) **S:** 24 kts **Dim:** 32.62 (30.48 pp) × 6.10 × 1.55 **Man:** 30
**A:** 2/40-mm AA (I × 2) **M:** 2 MTU 12V538 diesels; 2 props; 3,400 hp

REMARKS: Sunk in 1971 War of Independence; salvaged and repaired, Khulna SY; recommissioned 23-11-78.

◆ **2 Ajay-class patrol boats** Bldr: Hooghly D & E, Calcutta (In serv. 1-62)

P 312 PADMA (ex-*Akshay,* P 3136) P 313 SURMA (ex-*Ajay,* P 3135)

**D:** 120 tons (151 fl) **S:** 18 kts **Dim:** 35.75 (33.52 pp) × 6.1 × 1.9
**A:** 8/20-mm AA (IV × 2)
**M:** 2 Paxman YHAXM diesels; 2 props; 1,000 hp—1 Foden FD-6 cruise diesel; 100 hp
**Range:** 500/12; 1,000/8 **Man:** 3 officers, 32 men

REMARKS: Indian version of British "Ford" class, donated and commissioned 12-4-73 and 26-7-74, respectively. Recently rearmed with Yugoslav weapons.

◆ **5 river patrol boats** Bldr: DEW Narayengonj, Dacca

P 111 PABNA (6-72) P 113 PATUAKHALI (11-74) P 115 RANGAMATI (6-77)
P 112 NOAKHALI (7-72) P 114 BOGRA (6-77)

**D:** 69.5 tons (fl) **S:** 10 kts **Dim:** 22.9 × 6.1 × 1.9 **A:** 1/40-mm AA
**M:** 2 Cummins diesels; 2 props **Range:** 700/8 **Man:** 3 officers, 30 men

REMARKS: Last two differ in configuration, gun forward.

◆ **1 small patrol craft, former Thai fishing boat**

P . . . SHAH JALAL (ex-*Gold 4*)

## AUXILIARIES

◆ **2 Chinese Yuchin (Type 069)-class landing craft employed as inshore survey craft** (In serv. 1984)

A 581 DARSHAK A 582 TALLESHI

**D:** 83 tons (fl) **S:** 11.5 kts **Dim:** 24.1 × 5.2 × 1.1
**M:** 2 Type 12V150 diesels; 2 props; 600 hp

◆ **1 small underway-replenishment ship** Bldr: . . . SY, Japan

A 515 KHANJAHAN ALI

**D:** 2,900 tons (fl) **S:** 12 kts **Dim:** 76.1 × 11.4 × 5.3
**M:** 1 6-cyl. diesel; 1 prop; 1,350 hp **Man:** 3 officers, 23 men

REMARKS: Transferred 1983 from state-owned shipping line and equipped for underway refueling. 1,342 grt. Cargo: 1,500 tons.

◆ **1 transport, former passenger/cargo ship** Bldr: Ch. & At. de St. Nazaire (Penhöet), France (In serv. 1953)

A 514 SHAHEED SALAHUDDIN (ex-*Hizbal Bahr,* ex-*Eastern Queen,* ex-*General Mangan*)

**D:** 8,800 light (14,800 fl) **S:** 16 kts **Dim:** 162.01 × 19.72 × 6.94
**M:** 2 Penhöet/Burmeister & Wain 9-62 BTF-115 diesels; 2 props; 9,600 hp
**Electric:** 1,500 kw **Fuel:** 1,045 tons **Range:** 9,750/13
**Man:** 25 officers, 125 men

REMARKS: 11,684 grt/6,383 nrt/5,882 dwt. Purchased 18-2-81 from Bangladesh Shipping Corp. and commissioned 10-4-81. Used as a stationary barracks.

◆ **1 small repair ship**

A 512 SHAHAYAK

REMARKS: Former riverine passenger ship, 55 m. overall. Purchased, re-engined, and commissioned as a tender in 1978.

◆ **1 training ship** Bldr: Atlantic SB, Montreal, Canada (1957)

A 511 SHAHEED RUHUL AMIN (ex-*Anticosti,* Canadian merchant)

**D:** 710 tons (fl) **S:** 11.5 kts **Dim:** 47.5 × 11.1 × 3.1 **A:** 1/40-mm AA
**M:** 1 Caterpillar diesel **Range:** 4,000/10 **Man:** 8 officers, 72 men

REMARKS: Transferred 1972 from relief agency; recommissioned after conversion, 10-12-74.

◆ **1 floating drydock** Bldr: Tito SY, Trogir, Yugoslavia

A 701 SUNDARBAN (In serv. 15-8-80)

**Lift capacity:** 3,500 tons **Dim:** 117.0 × 27.6 × 0.3 loaded.

REMARKS: Self-docking type with 7 sectional pontoons. 17.6 m between dock walls, which are 101.4 m long. A second dry dock, 16,500 tons capacity, 182.9 m o.a., delivered 1981, is available.

**BANGLADESH** *(continued)*
**AUXILIARIES** *(continued)*

◆ **1 Chinese Dinghai-class seagoing tug** Bldr: Wuhu SY

A 721 KHADEM (In serv. 1984)

**Khadem (A 721)** 1984

**D:** 1,472 tons (fl) **S:** . . . **Dim:** 60.22 × 11.60 × 4.44
**A:** 4/14.5-mm mg (II × 2) **Electron Equipt:** Radar: 2/. . . nav.
**M:** 2 diesels; 2 props; 2,640 hp **Man:** 4 officers, 28 men
**Range:** 7,200/. . .

REMARKS: 980.28 grt.

◆ **3 small Chinese-built landing craft, used as tenders**

LCVP 011 LCVP 012 LCVP 013

◆ **1 ex-Thai fishing boat**

MFDV 55 MFV 66

REMARKS: Confiscated fishing poacher, used as harbor tender; steel hull.

# BARBADOS

COAST GUARD

PERSONNEL (1986): 92 (11 officers, 81 men); to increase to 120

MERCHANT MARINE (1986): 34 ships—7,572 grt

◆ **1 patrol boat** Bldr: Brooke Marine, Lowestoft, U.K.

| | L | In serv. |
|---|---|---|
| P 01 TRIDENT | 14-4-81 | 11-81 |

**Trident (P 01)** Brooke Marine, 1981

**D:** 165 tons (200 fl) **S:** 25 kts **Dim:** 37.50 × 6.86 × 1.78
**A:** 1/40-mm AA—1/20-mm AA **Man:** 25 tot.
**Electron Equipt:** Radar: 1/Decca TM 1226C
**M:** 2 Paxman Valenta 12 RP 200 diesels; 2 props; 4,000 hp **Range:** 3,000/12

◆ **2 converted shrimp boats** Bldr: Desco Marine

P 02 ENTERPRISE (In serv. 8-81) P 03 EXCELLENCE (In serv. 7-1-82)

**D:** 130 tons (fl) **S:** 12 kts **Dim:** 22.8 × 6.2 × 1.8
**A:** 1/20-mm AA **M:** 1 Caterpillar diesel; . . . hp **Man:** 2 officers, 8 men

REMARKS: Wooden-hulled craft, converted for use as seagoing patrol boats by Swan Hunter, Trinidad.

◆ **1 Halmatic 20-meter Guardian-class police patrol craft** Bldr: Aquarius Boat, U.K.

P 04 GEORGE FERGUSON (In serv. 12-74)

**D:** 30 tons (fl) **S:** 24 kts **Dim:** 20.0 × 5.25 × 1.5
**M:** 2 G.M. 12V71 TI diesels; 2 props; 1,300 hp **Range:** 650/12 **Man:** 11 tot.

REMARKS: Fiberglass hull. Can carry 2/7.62-mm mg.

◆ **2 Halmatic 12-meter Guardian-class police patrol craft** Bldr: Aquarius Boat, U.K. (In serv. 12-73 to 2-74)

P 05 COMMANDER MARSHALL P 06 J.T.C. Ramsay

**D:** 11.5 tons **S:** 21 kts **Dim:** 12.0 × 3.7 × 1.0
**M:** 2 Caterpillar Mk 334 TA diesels; 2 props; 580 hp **Man:** 4 tot.

REMARKS: Like P 04, used for search and rescue. Can carry 1/7.62-mm mg. Glass-reinforced plastic hull from Halmatic.

# BELGIUM

**Kingdom of Belgium**

PERSONNEL (1985): 300 officers, 4,191 men (including 1,116 draftees)

MERCHANT MARINE (1986): 355 ships—2,419,661 grt (tankers: 11—115,417 grt)

NAVAL AVIATION: Three Alouette-IIIB helicopters.

**FRIGATES**

◆ **4 Wielingen class, Type E 71**

| | Bldr | Laid down | L | In serv. |
|---|---|---|---|---|
| F 910 WIELINGEN | Boëlwerf, Temse | 5-3-74 | 30-3-76 | 20-1-78 |
| F 911 WESTDIEP | Cockerill, Hoboken | 2-9-74 | 8-12-75 | 20-1-78 |
| F 912 WANDELAAR | Boëlwerf, Temse | 5-3-75 | 21-6-77 | 27-10-78 |
| F 913 WESTHINDER | Cockerill, Hoboken | 8-12-75 | 31-1-77 | 27-10-78 |

**D:** 1,880 tons (2,283 fl) **S:** 25 kts on gas turbine
**Dim:** 106.38 (103 pp) × 12.3 × 5.3 (over sonar)
**A:** 4 MM 38 (II × 2) Exocet—1/100-mm Model 1968 DP—1/NATO Sea Sparrow SAM syst. (8 AIM-7M missiles)—1/375-mm Bofors ASW RL (II × 1)—2 launching racks for L-5 ASW torpedoes

**Wandelaar (F 912)** L. & L. Van Ginderen, 8-86

**Westdiep (F 911)** G. Gyssels, 9-86

**FRIGATES** *(continued)*

**Westdiep (F 911)** G. Gyssels, 10-86

**Electron Equipt:** Radar: 1/Raytheon TM 1645/9X, 1/DA-05, 1/H.S.A. WM-25
Sonar: 1/SQS-505A
EW: Elcos-1 intercept—2/Mk 36 SRBOC chaff (VI × 2)
**M:** CODOG: 2 Cockerill CO-240V-12 diesels, each 3,000 hp; 1 Rolls-Royce Olympus TM 3B gas turbine, 28,000 hp; 2 CP props
**Fuel:** 250 tons diesel **Electric:** 2,000 kw (4 × 500 kw diesel sets)
**Range:** 4,500/18; 6,000/16 **Man:** 15 officers, 145 men

REMARKS: Vosper fin stabilizers. 15 knots max. on one diesel, 20 knots on two. Belgian-Dutch automatic surface- and air-search radar system, including fire control and SEWACO-IV automatic tactical data system. Two Panda optical gun directors. The ASW rocket launcher carries six 103-mm rocket flare rails. U.S. SLQ-25 NIXIE ASW decoys. Plan to add 30-mm Goalkeeper AA system, probably in place of other armament, in abeyance, due to shortage of funds. F 913 in refit, 1986. Have lost 3 kts below original 28-kt trial speeds after modifications.

**PATROL CRAFT**

◆ **2 Leie-class river gunboats** Bldr: Hitzler, Regensburg

P 902 LIBERATION (In serv. 4-8-54) P 903 MEUSE (In serv. 20-8-53)

**Liberation (P 902)** L. & L. Van Ginderen, 9-86

**D:** 25 tons (27.5 fl) **S:** 19 kts **Dim:** 23.25 × 3.8 × 0.9
**A:** 2/12.7-mm mg (I × 2) **M:** 2 MWM diesels; 2 props; 440 hp
**Man:** 1 officer, 6 men

REMARKS: P 902 is 26 meters in length, 4 meters in beam, 30 tons (fl). Sisters *Rupel* (P 907, ex-*Tresignies*) and *Ourthe* (P 908) were sold 8-9-83; *Leie* (P 901) and *Semois* (P 906) were sold 21-2-85; *Sambre* (P 904) was donated to the Sea Scouts, and *Schelde* (P 905) given to a museum in 1984. P 902 used for public relations and recruiting, P 903 is guard ship at Antwerp.

**MINE WARFARE SHIPS**

Although a consortium of Boelwerf, Beliard Mercantile, and ACEC had been formed to study a minehunter design to follow the "Tripartite" program, this was superseded in a 12-9-86 announcement that Belgium would join the Netherlands and Norway in a study of a plan to produce a joint minehunter program for 17 total ships for the three countries. The first is somewhat optimistically intended to be delivered in 1992.

◆ **5 (+5) Tripartite-class minehunters** Bldr: Béliard, Ostend and Antwerp

| | Laid down | L | In serv. |
|---|---|---|---|
| M 915 ASTER | 24-2-83 | 26-6-84 | 18-12-85 |
| M 916 BELLIS | 15-2-83 | 21-2-85 | 18-9-86 |
| M 917 CROCUS | 4-10-84 | 3-10-85 | 18-9-86 |
| M 918 DIANTHUS | 1-4-85 | 16-4-86 | 15-6-87 |
| M 919 FUCHSIA | 28-10-85 | 20-5-86 | -87 |
| M 920 IRIS | 1-12-86 | ... | ... |
| M 921 LOBELIA | ... | ... | ... |
| M 922 MYOSOTIS | ... | ... | ... |
| M 923 NARCIS | ... | ... | ... |
| M 924 PRIMULA | ... | ... | ... |

**Aster (M 915)** M. Louagie, 3-87

**Bellis (M 916)**—divers' decompression van aboard L. &. L. Van Ginderen, 8-86

**Dianthus (M 918)**—without van M. Louagie, 6-87

**D:** 511 tons (595 fl) **S:** 15 kts **Dim:** 51.6 (47.1 pp) × 8.96 × 2.49 (hull)
**A:** 1/20-mm AA **Electron Equipt:** Radar: Decca 1229—Sonar: DUBM-21B
**M:** 1 Brons/Werkspoor A-RUB 215X 12 diesel; 1 CP prop; 1,900 hp (1,200 rpm); 2 120-hp maneuvering props (active rudder); bow-thruster
**Electric:** 880 kw **Range:** 3,000/12 **Man:** 34 tot. (49 accommodations)

REMARKS: Same as French *Eridan* and Dutch *Alkmaar* classes. Original construction consortium, Polyship, dissolved. Ships reordered 12-2-81 from Béliard; hulls launched at Ostend and fitted out by Béliard Mercantile at Rupelmonde, Antwerp. Three Astazou-IV, 320-kw gas-turbine generators; 1 140-kw diesel set. Two PAP-104 remote-controlled mine locators; automatic pilot; automatic track-plotter; TORAN and Sydelis navigation systems; conventional wire sweep also. Glass-reinforced-plastic construction. Carry portable divers' decompression van aft on 01 deck just above forecastle break.

◆ **6 U.S. Dash-class oceangoing minesweeper/minehunters**

| | L | In serv. |
|---|---|---|
| M 902 VAN HAVERBEKE (ex-MSO 522) | 29-10-59 | 7-11-60 |
| M 903 A. F. DUFOUR (ex-*Lagen*, ex-MSO 498) | 13-8-54 | 27-9-55 |
| M 904 DE BROUWER (ex-*Nansen*, ex-MSO 499) | 15-10-54 | 1-11-55 |
| M 906 BREYDEL (ex-AM 504) | 25-3-55 | 24-1-56 |
| M 908 GEORGES TRUFFAUT (ex-AM 515) | 1-11-55 | 21-9-56 |
| M 909 FRANÇOIS BOVESSE (ex-AM 516) | 28-2-56 | 21-12-56 |

Bldrs: M 902: Peterson Bldrs, Sturgeon Bay, Wisc.; M 903, 904: Bellingham BY, Bellingham, Wash.; M 906: Tacoma BY, Tacoma, Wash.; M 908, 909: Tampa SB, Tampa, Fla.

## MINE WARFARE SHIPS *(continued)*

**De Brouwer (M 904)** L. & L. Van Ginderen, 10-86

**François Bovesse (M 909)** M. Louagie, 3-87

**D:** 720 tons (780 fl) **S:** 14 kts
**Dim:** 52.42 (50.3 pp) × 10.97 × 4.20 **A:** 2/12.7-mm mg (II × 1, not in M 906)
**Electron Equipt:** Radar: 1/Decca 1229—Sonar: SQQ-14
**M:** 4 G.M. 8-268A diesels; 2 CP props; 1,520 hp **Fuel:** 53 tons diesel
**Range:** 3,000/10; 2,400/12 **Man:** 5 officers, 67 men

Remarks: Transferred 1955-60, except M 903 and M 904 transferred from Norway in 1966. Equipped as minehunters, with PAP-104 remote-control minehunting submersibles. Wooden hulls. *Artevelde* (M 907) stricken 1-2-85. M 909 used as schoolship for mine warfare reservists.

◆ **5 U.S. Adjutant-class coastal minesweepers** Bldr: Béliard, Ostend (M 928: Boëlwerf, Temse)

| | L | In serv. | | L | In serv. |
|---|---|---|---|---|---|
| M 928 Stavelot | 26-3-55 | 1-7-55 | M 932 Nieuwpoort | 12-3-55 | 9-1-56 |
| M 929 Heist | . . . | 4-4-56 | M 933 Koksijde | 4-6-55 | 29-11-55 |
| M 930 Rochefort | 5-6-54 | 28-11-55 | | | |

**Rochefort (M 930)** M. Louagie, 2-85

**D:** 330 tons (390 fl) **S:** 13.5/12 kts **Dim:** 44.0 (42.1 pp) × 8.3 × 2.6
**A:** 1/40-mm AA
**Electron Equipt:** Radar: 1/Decca 1229—Sonar: AN/UQS-1
**M:** 2 G.M. 8-268A diesels; 2 props; 880 hp **Fuel:** 40 tons
**Range:** 2,700/10.5 **Man:** 4 officers, 17 petty officers, 19 men

Remarks: M 928, stricken 1979, restored to service 1982–83. M 929, converted to degaussing tender (A 964) in 1978, restored as a minesweeper 6-85. Two minehunter conversions, *Verviers* (M 934, ex-U.S. AMS 259) and *Veurne* (M 935, ex-U.S. AMS 260) stricken 6-85. M 932 has a lengthened forward deckhouse.

◆ **11 Herstal-class inshore minesweepers** Bldr: Mercantile Marine Yd., Kruibeke

| | L | In serv. | | L | In serv. |
|---|---|---|---|---|---|
| M 474 Turnhout | 7-9-57 | 29-9-58 | M 480 Seraing | 16-3-57 | 24-3-58 |
| M 475 Tongeren | 16-11-57 | 9-12-58 | M 482 Vise | 7-9-57 | 11-9-58 |
| M 476 Merksem | 5-4-58 | 6-2-59 | M 483 Ougrée | 16-11-57 | 10-11-58 |
| M 477 Oudenaerde | 3-5-58 | 25-4-59 | M 484 Dinant | 5-4-58 | 14-1-59 |
| M 478 Herstal | 6-8-56 | 14-10-57 | M 485 Andenne | 3-5-58 | 20-4-59 |
| M 479 Huy | 17-11-56 | 14-10-57 | | | |

**Ougrée (M 483)**—aground near Antwerp L. & L. Van Ginderen, 1-87

**D:** 160 tons (190 fl) **S:** 15 kts **Dim:** 34.5 (32.5 pp) × 6.7 × 2.1
**A:** 2/12.7-mm mg (II × 1) **Electron Equipt:** Radar: 1/Decca 1229
**M:** 2 Fiat-Mercedes Benz MB 820 diesels; 2 props; 1,260 hp
**Fuel:** 24 tons **Range:** 2,300/10 **Man:** 1 officer, 7 petty officers, 9 men

Remarks: Wooden hulls. Intended to sweep the Schelde River. Fitted for magnetic, acoustic, and mechanical sweeping to a depth of 4.50 to 10 m. M 471, 472, 478 were designated RDS-Ready Duty Ship, sweep gear removed, deckhouse in place of cable reel, and pollution cleanup gear and special cranes added aft; M 471, 478 restored as minesweepers, 1983, but without large cable drum. Modified version of British "Ham" class. M 478 to M 485, built with U.S. funds, are ex-U.S. MSI 90–97. Sister *Hasselt* (M 471) towed away for scrap, 11-9-86; *Lokeren* (M 473) stricken 1987, as was *Kortijk* (M 472), which had served as a research ship.

## AUXILIARIES

◆ **2 "command and logistics support ships" for mine countermeasures**

| | Bldr | Laid down | L | In serv. |
|---|---|---|---|---|
| A 961 Zinnia | Cockerill (Hoboken) | 8-11-66 | 6-5-67 | 5-9-67 |

**Zinnia (A 961)** L. & L. Van Ginderen, 12-86

**D:** 1,705 tons (2,685 fl) **S:** 18 kts (20 on trials)
**Dim:** 99.5 (94.2 wl) × 14.0 × 3.6 **Range:** 14,000/12.5

**AUXILIARIES** *(continued)*

**A:** 3/40-mm (I × 3)—1/Alouette-IIIB helicopter
**Electron Equipt:** Radar: 2/Decca navigational
**M:** 2 Cockerill-Ougrée V 12 TR 240 CO diesels; 1 CP prop; 5,000 hp
**Fuel:** 150 $m^3$ diesel; 300 $m^3$ for supply to minesweepers—500 tons total
**Man:** 13 officers, 46 petty officers, 64 men

REMARKS: Fin stabilizers, telescoping helicopter hangar.

| | Bldr | Laid down | L | In serv. |
|---|---|---|---|---|
| A 960 GODETIA | Boelwerf, Temse | 15-2-65 | 7-12-65 | 23-5-66 |

**Godetia (A 960)** M. Louagie, 6-87

**D:** 1,700 tons (2,500 fl) **S:** 18 kts **Dim:** 91.83 (87.85 pp) × 14.0 × 3.5
**A:** 1/40-mm AA **Electron Equipt:** Radar: 2/nav.
**M:** 4 ACEC-M.A.N. diesels; 2 CP props; 5,400 hp
**Fuel:** 294 tons **Range:** 2,250/15; 8,700/12
**Man:** 10 officers, 37 petty officers, 48 men

REMARKS: 15 knots on one diesel. Passive tank stabilization. Protected closed-circuit ventilation. Can accommodate oceanographic research personnel and has space for laboratory. Minesweeping cables are stowed on reels on the helicopter deck, which has been extended aft to continue to permit one Alouette-III to land. 8/12.7-mm mg (II × 4) removed 1983; quickly remountable.

◆ **1 new-construction oceanographic research ship**

| | Bldr | Laid down | L | In serv. |
|---|---|---|---|---|
| A. 962 BELGICA | Boelwerf, Temse | 17-10-83 | 6-1-84 | 5-7-84 |

**Belgica (A 962)** L. & L. Van Ginderen, 5-86

**D:** 835 tons (fl) **S:** 12 kts **Dim:** 50.90 (44.95 pp) × 10.00 × 4.40
**M:** 1 ABC 6M DZC-1000-150 diesel; 1 Kort-nozzle prop; 1,570 hp **Fuel:** 158 tons
**Electron Equipt:** Radar: 1/Decca . . . nav.
**Electric:** 640 kw **Range:** 20,000/12 **Man:** 15 crew + 11 scientists

REMARKS: For use in North and Irish Seas or for fisheries or hydrographic research. Can carry two laboratory containers on deck. 150-hp thrusters fore and aft. Very bluff hull lines, bulbous bow.

NOTE: Former "Ham"-class inshore minesweeper *Kortrijk* (M 472), used for research, stricken 1987. The 80-grt research ship *Ter Streep,* launched 28-6-85 by Langerbragge, Ghent, is not naval.

◆ **1 U.S. Adjutant-class former minesweeper** Bldr: Boëlwerf, Temse

| | In serv. |
|---|---|
| A 963 SPA (ex-M 927)—Missile/munitions transport for frigates | 1-1-56 |

REMARKS: Data as for minesweeper sisters. Retains 1/40-mm AA.

**Spa (A 963)** L. & L. Van Ginderen, 6-86

◆ **1 oceanographic research and sail-training craft**

| | Bldr | Laid down | L | In serv. |
|---|---|---|---|---|
| A 958 ZENOBE GRAMME | Boëlwerf, Temse | 7-10-60 | 23-10-61 | 1962 |

**Zenobe Gramme (A 958)**—now carries hull number L. & L. Van Ginderen, 3-84

**D:** 149 tons **S:** 10 kts **Dim:** 28.15 (23.10 wl) × 6.85 × 2.64
**M:** 1 MWM 518A diesel; 232 hp **Man:** 14 tot.

REMARKS: Fitted out as Bermudian ketch (240 $m^3$ sail area). Visited U.S.A., 7-86.

◆ **1 seagoing tug** Bldr: Ch. Navals & Atelier Const. de Hemixem

A 954 ZEEMEEUW (In serv. 1971)

**D:** 400 tons (fl) **S:** 10 kts **Dim:** 27.94 (26.60 pp) × 7.29 × 3.37
**M:** 2 ABC 6-cyl. diesels; 2 props; . . . hp **Electric:** 96 kw **Man:** . . .

**Zeemeeuw (A 954)** L. & L. Van Ginderen, 2-83

**BELGIUM** *(continued)*
**AUXILIARIES** *(continued)*

REMARKS: 146 grt/24 nrt. Acquired from another Belgian government agency, 1982. Based at Zeebrugge and used on pollution control duties.

◆ **2 seagoing tugs** Bldr: H. Bodewes, Millengen a/d Ryn (In serv. 1960)

A 950 VALCKE (ex-*Astronoom*, ex-*Schouwenbank*)
A 998 EKSTER (ex-*Astrodom*, ex-*Steenbank*)

**Ekster (A 998)** G. Davies, 3-87

**D:** 420 tons (fl) **S:** 13 kts **Dim:** 30.08 × 7.55 × 2.99
**Electron Equipt:** Radar: 1/Decca 1229
**M:** 24-cycle, single-acting 8-cyl. diesels, electric drive; 1 prop; 1,250 hp

REMARKS: 183 grt. Purchased 1980 from A. Smit. Based at Zeebrugge on pollution-control duties. A 950 in collision 1985, out of service for many months.

**YARD AND SERVICE CRAFT**

◆ **2 Bij-class small harbor tugs**

| | Bldr | In serv. |
|---|---|---|
| A 953 BIJ | Akerboom, Lisse | 1959 |
| A 956 KREKEL | Rupelmonde SY | 1961 |

**Bij (A 953)** M. Louagie, 3-87

**D:** 60 tons (71 fl) **S:** 10 kts **Dim:** 17.65 (16.0) × 5.2 × 2.0
**M:** 2 MWM RHS 518A diesels; 2 Voith-Schneider vertical cycloidal props; 300 hp

◆ **1 small fireboat tug** A 959 MIER Bldr: Liège SY (1962): 12.5 m o.a., 17.5 tons, 90 hp

◆ **1 personnel launch** SPIN (1958)—32 tons, 14.6 m., 1 diesel; Voith-Schneider prop; 250 hp; 8 kts—can also be used as a tug.

NOTE: Small tug *Mier* (A 959) sold 12-4-86 to German firm.

**Spin** L. & L. Van Ginderen, 8-85

◆ **2 small Royal yachts**

A 981 AVILA (In serv. 1963) A 982 TREFOGLIU (In serv. . . .)

REMARKS: A 981, a small cabin cruiser, is kept at Motril, Spain.

# BELIZE

PERSONNEL (1985): 33 total

MERCHANT MARINE (1986): 3 ships—620 grt

AVIATION: 2 Pilatus-Britten-Norman BN 2B Defender.

◆ **2 20-meter Wasp-class patrol craft** Bldr: Souter, Cowes, U.K. (In serv. 19-9-84)

PB 01 DANGRIGA PB 02 TOLEDO

**Dangriga (PB 01)** L. Dury, 8-83

**D:** 36.25 tons (fl) **S:** 23 kts **Dim:** 20.00 (16.00 pp) × 5.00 × 1.50
**A:** 1/12.7-mm mg—4/7.62-mm mg (I × 4)
**Electron Equipt:** Radar: 1/Decca 150
**M:** 2 G.M. 16V71 TI diesels; 2 props; 2,400 hp **Man:** 2 officers, 6 men
**Range:** 430/18 **Electric:** 37 kw (2 × 18.5 kw) **Fuel:** 5 tons

REMARKS: Glass-reinforced plastic construction. Completed 8-84, not commissioned in-country until 19-9-84.

NOTE: 15-ton patrol craft *Belmopan* (PBM 02) stricken 1985 after only 3 years' service.

# BENIN

**People's Republic of Benin**

PERSONNEL: About 100

MERCHANT MARINE (1986): 15 ships—4,887 grt

BENIN *(continued)*

**Four Zhuks in the port of Cotonou, with "P 4" moored ahead** 1-84

◆ **1 38-m, GRP patrol boat** Bldr: SBCN, France

**D:** . . . **S:** 36 kts **Dim:** 38.0 × . . . × 0.85 **A:** . . .
**M:** 3 Baudouin 12 P 15-25R-3 diesels; waterjets; . . . hp

REMARKS: Reported building 1986 for delivery 1987; no other information available.

◆ **2 ex-North Korean, Soviet P 4-class torpedo boats** (transferred 1979)

**D:** 19.3 tons (22.4 fl) **S:** 54 kts **Dim:** 19.3 × 3.7 × 1.0
**A:** 2/14.5-mm mg (II × 1)
**Electron Equipt:** Radar: 1/. . . nav. **M:** 2 M50 diesels; 2 props; 2,400 hp

REMARKS: Aluminum-construction hydroplanes. May in fact be newer craft of similar design to P 4 from North Korea. Torpedo tubes removed. In poor condition.

◆ **4 Soviet Zhuk-class patrol craft**

**D:** 60 tons (fl) **S:** 34 kts **Dim:** 24.0 × 5.0 × 1.5 (props)
**A:** 4/14.5-mm mg (II × 2) **M:** 2 M50 diesels; 2 props; 2,400 hp
**Electron Equipt:** Radar: 1/Spin Trough

REMARKS: Transferred: 2 in 1979, 1 in 5-80, 1 in 9-80. Have twin mg in side-by-side, enclosed mountings.

# BERMUDA

**The Crown Colony of Bermuda**

MERCHANT MARINE (1986): 97 ships—1,208,276 grt (17 tankers—301,229 grt)

BERMUDIAN POLICE

◆ **1 sport cruiser** Bldr: Harris Boat, Newburyport, Mass., U.S.A.

BLUE HERON (In serv. 22-5-78)

**D:** 7 tons **S:** . . . **Dim:** 10.9 × . . . × . . .
**M:** 2 G.M. diesels; 2 props; 260 hp **Man:** 3

◆ **2 small craft** Bldr: Mako Marine, Florida, U.S.A.

HERON II (In serv. 7-81) HERON III (In serv. 4-78)

REMARKS: 7.1 and 6.7 m overall, about 1 ton, powered by one 235-hp Evinrude outboard each.

# BOLIVIA

**Republic of Bolivia**

PERSONNEL (1986): 4,000 including 600 Almirante Grau Battalion marines

MERCHANT MARINE (1986): 2 ships—14,913 grt

NAVAL AVIATION: 1 Cessna U206 and 3 Cessna 402C light transports.

◆ **1 aluminum-hulled patrol boat** Bldr: Hope/Progressive Shipbuilders, Houma, Louisiana, U.S.A. (In serv. 1985)

PR 51 SANTA CRUZ DE LA SIERRA

**Santa Cruz de la Sierra (PR 51)** Hope, 1985

**D:** . . . **S:** . . . **Dim:** 20.4 × . . . × . . .
**A:** 1/20-mm AA **Electron Equipt:** Radar: 1/Furuno . . .
**M:** 2 G.M. diesels; 2 props; . . . hp

REMARKS: Journeyed to South America under own power.

◆ **1 seagoing cargo ship** Bldr: Fairfield, U.K., 1951

TM-01 LIBERTADOR BOLÍVAR (ex-*Simon Bolívar*, ex-*Ciudad de Barquisimeto*)

**D:** 9,000 tons **S:** 14.5 kts **Dim:** 128.3 (120.4 pp) × 16.76 × 6.7
**M:** 1 Doxford diesel; 4,350 hp **Range:** 7,000/14

REMARKS: Donated by Venezuela, 1977. Home-ported in Argentina. Used to generate revenue and for training in preparation for possible ceding to Bolivia of a "corridor to the sea" between Peru and Chile. 4,214 grt/6,390 dwt/2,352 nrt.

◆ **8 river patrol craft/transports**

| | |
|---|---|
| MO 1 ALMIRANTE GRAU, 52 tons | MO 5 COMANDANTE ARANDIA, 82 tons |
| MO 2 NICOLAS SUAREZ, 26 tons | MO 6 TOPATER |
| MO 3 MARISCAL SANTA CRUZ, 52 tons | MO 7 BRUNO RACUA |
| MO 4 PRESIDENTE BUSCH, 52 tons | MO 8 CORONEL EDUARDO AVAROA, 82 tons |

REMARKS: Iron- or wooden-hulled, raftlike craft with high superstructures and speeds of 8–10 knots.

◆ **1 or more Brown-class patrol launches** (In serv. 1978- . . .)

ALMIRANTE GUILLERMO BROWN

**D:** 4 tons **S:** 12 kts **Dim:** 7.0 × 2.3 × 1.0
**M:** 1 Ford Penta diesel; 116 hp **Man:** 12 tot.

◆ **2 ex-U.S. PBR Mk-II patrol boats** (Transferred 4-74)

**D:** 8.9 tons **S:** 24 kts **Dim:** 9.73 × 3.53 × 0.81
**A:** 3/12.7-mm mg (II × 1, I × 1)—1/60-mm mortar
**Electron Equipt:** Radar: 1/Raytheon 1900
**M:** 2 G.M. 6V53N diesels; 2 water jets; 430 hp **Range:** 150/23 **Man:** 4 tot.

REMARKS: On Lake Titicaca. GRP construction.

◆ **24 miscellaneous Lake Titicaca and river service launches** (several oar-propelled)

◆ **2 hospital launches**

AH-1 JULIAN APAZA AH-02 RIO MAMORE

REMARKS: Launched 1977–78; 17 tons. *Apaza* a gift of the U.S.A.

# BRAZIL

**Federative Republic of Brazil**

PERSONNEL (1987): 4,100 officers, 41,900 men (plus 650 officers, 10,850 marines in the Fuzileiros Navais, and reservists).

MERCHANT MARINE (1986): 697 ships—6,212,287 grt (tankers: 63–1,877,026 grt)

NAVAL AVIATION: Uses 4 SH-3D and 4 SH-3H (with 4 more ordered in 1984) Sea King, 9 Westland Wasp HAS.1 (UH-2), 17 Bell 206B JetRanger II (SAH-11) helicopters, 9 Westland Mk 21 Lynx (equipped with Sea Skua missiles), 11 AS.350 Esquilo (UH-12), and 3 AS.330 Super Puma (with 3 more on order). In 3-85, 16 used Bell 206Bs were ordered in the U.S. in lieu of purchasing a planned 15 AS.332F Super Puma with AM-39 missiles. Planned purchases include 15 more Super Puma, 11 AS.350 Esquilo, 4 Sea King, and additional Lynx.

The Air Force makes available to the Navy: 3 RC-130E Hercules, and 20 EMB 111 (P-95) Bandeirante in a sea-surveillance version. Eight Grumman S-2E Tracker aircraft are available for use on *Minas Gerais*, and 5 S-2A are used for training and transport. To support the Navy, the Air Force also operates 2 Piper/Embraer Seneca II and 15 Neiva T-25 Universal aircraft. The Air Force Coastal Command also has 6 Puma helicopters for search-and-rescue purposes.

WEAPONS AND SENSORS: Avibrás Indústria Aerospacial is developing the Barracuda antiship missile. The SM-70 version will be quadruple-mounted on trucks for coastal defense, and the MM-70 is for shipboard use. Range: 70 km. Length: 5 m; dia.: 30 cm. Also referred to as the "Astros II/Ms."

WARSHIPS IN SERVICE OR UNDER CONSTRUCTION AS OF 1 JANUARY 1988

| | L | Tons | Main armament |
|---|---|---|---|
| ◆ **1 light aircraft carrier (A SW)** | | | |
| MINAS GERAIS | 1944 | 15,890 | 10/40-mm AA, 18–22 aircraft |
| ◆ **7 (+4) submarines** | | | |
| 0 (+4) Type 1400 | 1987 | 1,400 | 8/533-mm TT |
| 3 OBERON | 1971–75 | 1,610 | 8/533-mm TT |
| 2 Guppy III | 1945 | 1,650 | 10/533-mm TT |
| 2 Guppy II | 1944–45 | 1,517 | 10/533-mm TT |
| ◆ **7 destroyers** | | | |
| 2 GEARING, FRAM I | 1944–45 | 2,425 | 2/127-mm DP, 6 ASW TT ASROC |
| 4 ALLEN M. SUMNER, FRAM II | 1944 | 2,200 | 6/127-mm DP, 6 ASW TT |
| 1 ALLEN M. SUMNER | 1944 | 2,200 | 6/127-mm DP, 1 Sea Cat SAM, 6 ASW TT |
| ◆ **6 (+4) frigates** | | | |
| 0 (+4) new construction | 1986– | 1,600 | 4 Exocet, 1/114-mm DP, 6 ASW TT, 1 helicopter |
| 4 NITEROI | 1974–75 | 3,200 | 1/114-mm DP, 2/40-mm AA, 1 Branik system, 2 Sea Cat systems, 1 Bofors ASW RL, 6 ASW TT, 1 helicopter |
| 2 CONSTITUCÃO | 1976–77 | 3,200 | 2/114-mm DP, 2/40-mm AA, 4 Exocet, 2 Sea Cat systems, 1 Bofors ASW RL, 6 ASW TT, 1 helicopter |
| ◆ **9 corvettes** | | | |
| 9 IMPERIAL MARINHEIRO | 1954–55 | 911 | 1/76.2-mm DP |

## LIGHT AIRCRAFT CARRIER (ASW)

NOTE: Long-range plans for replacing *Minas Gerais* with one or two small carriers have been canceled.

◆ **1 British Colossus class**

| | Bldr | Laid down | L | In serv. |
|---|---|---|---|---|
| A 11 MINAS GERAIS (ex-*Venegeance*) | Swan Hunter, Wallsend-on-Tyne | 16-11-42 | 23-3-44 | 15-1-45 |

**D:** 15,890 tons (19,890 fl) **S:** 24 kts
**Dim:** 211.25 × 36.44 (24.50 hull) × 7.15
**A:** 10/40-mm AA (IV × 2, II × 1)—6–8/S-2E aircraft—4–6/SH-3, 2/SAH-11, 3/UH-12 helicopters
**Electron Equipt:** Radar: 1/SPS-40B, 1/SPS-4, 1/Raytheon 1402, 2/SPG-34 fire control—EW: SLR-2
**M:** Parsons GT; 2 props; 42,000 hp

**Minas Gerais (A 11)** U.S. Navy, 1985

**Minas Gerais (A 11)** U.S. Navy, 1985

**Minas Gerais (A 11)** 1985

**Boilers:** 4 Admiralty 3-drum; 28 kg/cm$^2$, 371° C **Fuel:** 3,200 tons
**Electric:** 2,500 kw **Range:** 12,000/14; 6,200/23
**Man:** 1,000 ship's company plus 300 aviation personnel

REMARKS: Purchased from Great Britain in 12-56; refitted in Rotterdam, completing in 1960 with new weapons, steam catapult, angled flight deck (8.5°), mirror optical landing equipment, new radars, and 2 new elevators. GFCS for the 40-mm AA include 2 Mk 63 (with SPG-34 radar on the quadruple mounts) and 1 Mk 51 Mod. 2. Hangar 135.6 × 15.8 × 5.3 high; 2 elevators 13.7 × 10.4. Catapult can launch 15-ton aircraft. A data link system for cooperation with the *Niteroi* class has been installed, and U.S. SPS-40B radar has replaced SPS-12. Plans to purchase 12 A-4 Skyhawk fighter-bombers for use from this ship were announced in 1984 and canceled early in 1985. The SPS-8B height-finding radar was removed during 1984. Now planned for retention in service until 2000. Laid up in 1987 with catapult problems.

## SUBMARINES

NOTE: On 29-11-84 the Navy announced plans to build a 2,200-ton "NAC-1"- class submarine of Brazilian design following the construction of the two IKL Type 1400 submarines in Brazil. Long-range plans also call for construction of nuclear-powered submarines, but in 4-87, it was stated that such ships are many years off.

◆ **0 (+4) West German Type 1400 class**

| | Bldr | Laid down | L | In serv. |
|---|---|---|---|---|
| S . . . TUPI | Howaldtswerke, Kiel | 8-3-85 | 28-4-87 | 7-88 |
| S . . . TAMOIO | Ast. Ilha das Cobras, Rio | 15-7-86 | . . . | . . . |
| S . . . TIMBIRA | Ast. Ilha das Cobras, Rio | 1988 | . . . | . . . |
| S . . . TABAJOS | Ast. Ilha das Cobras, Rio | . . . | . . . | . . . |

**D:** 1,400 tons surf., 1,900 sub. **S:** 21.5 sub. **Dim:** 61.0 × 6.2 × 5.5
**A:** 8/533-mm TT fwd.—16 Mk 24 Mod. 1 Tigerfish torpedoes
**Electron Equipt:** Radar: . . .
Sonar: Krupp-Atlas CSU-83/1
EW: Thomson-CSF DR-4000
**M:** 4 MTU 12V493 TY60, 600 bhp diesels, 4 AEG 420-kw generators, electric drive; 1 prop; 5,000 hp
**Range:** 8,200/8 snorkel; 50/16; 400/4 submerged **Fuel:** 118 tons **Man:** 30 tot.

REMARKS: The largest version of the Type 209 yet ordered; order placed 8-82. Will have Ferranti KAFS A10 action data system, 2 Kollmorgen periscopes, Sperry MK 29 Mod. 2 Ships Inertial Navigation System (SINS). Can make 25 knots for brief period. Diving depth: 250 m. Endurance: 50 days. 480-cell battery.

◆ **3 British Oberon class**

| | Bldr | Laid down | L | In serv. |
|---|---|---|---|---|
| S 20 HUMAITA | Vickers-Barrow | 3-11-70 | 5-10-71 | 18-6-73 |
| S 21 TONELERO | Vickers-Barrow | 18-21-70 | 22-11-72 | 8-9-78 |
| S 22 RIACHUELO | Vickers-Barrow | 26-5-73 | 6-9-75 | 12-3-77 |

**Riachuelo (S 22)** L. & L. Van Ginderen, 7-77

**SUBMARINES** *(continued)*

**D:** 1,610 tons standard, 2,030 surf., 2,400 sub.
**S:** 17.5/15 kts **Dim:** 89.9 × 8.07 × 5.48
**A:** 6/533-mm TT forward (18 U.K. Mk 24 and U.S. Mk 37 torpedoes)
**Electron Equipt:** Sonar: 1/187, 1/2007, DUUG-1, AUUD-1
**M:** 2 Admiralty Standard Range 16 VVS-ASR1 diesels; 2 electric generators, each 1,280 kw; 2 electric motors; 2 props; 6,000 hp
**Range:** 11,000/11 snorkel **Endurance:** 56 days **Man:** 5 officers, 57 men

Remarks: S 21 several years late entering active service due to a fire on board during construction. Batteries made up of 224 elements in two sections, with a 7,240-ampere capacity for five hours. "One-man control" system for immersion and diving. Satellite navigation receiver installed. Two short torpedo tubes aft are no longer used. Receiving U.K. DCH torpedo f.c.s.

◆ **2 ex-U.S. Guppy III class**

| | Bldr | Laid down | L | In serv. |
|---|---|---|---|---|
| S 15 Goiás (ex-*Trumpetfish,* SS 425) | Cramp S.B. | 23-8-43 | 13-5-45 | 29-1-46 |
| S 16 Amazonas (ex-*Greenfish,* SS 351) | Electric Boat Co. | 29-1-44 | 21-12-45 | 7-6-46 |

**Goiás (S 15)** 1975

**D:** 1,650 tons standard, 1,975 surf., 2,450 sub. **S:** 17.2/14.5 kts (9.4 snorkel)
**Dim:** 99.52 × 8.23 × 5.18 **A:** 10/533-mm TTs, 6 fwd, 4 aft (24 torpedoes)
**Electron Equipt:** Radar: 1/SS-2A—Sonar: BQG-4 PUFFS, BQR-2B
**M:** diesel-electric propulsion; 4 diesel generator sets (6,400 hp); 2 electric motors (5,400 hp)
**Range:** 12,000/10 surf., 95/5 sub. **Man:** 86 tot.

Remarks: S 15 purchased 17-10-73, S 16 on 19-12-73. S 15 converted to Guppy-II in 1948, lengthened to Guppy III in 1962; S 16 to Guppy II 1948, Guppy III in 1961. S 15 has Fairbanks-Morse 38D 8⅛-10 diesels, S 16 has G.M. 16-278A. Two 126-cell batteries.

◆ **2 ex-U.S. Guppy II class**

| | Bldr | Laid down | L | In serv. |
|---|---|---|---|---|
| S 12 Bahia (ex-*Sea Leopard,* SS 483) | Portsmouth NSY | 7-11-44 | 2-3-45 | 11-6-45 |
| S 14 Ceara (ex-*Amberjack,* SS 522) | Boston NSY | 8-2-44 | 15-12-44 | 4-3-46 |

**D:** 1,525 tons standard, 1,848 surf., 2,440 sub. **S:** 17.4/14 kts (9.4 snorkel)
**Dim:** 93.36 × 8.18 × 5.04 **A:** 10/533-mm TT, 6 fwd, 4 aft (24 torpedoes)
**Electron Equipt:** Radar: 1/SS-2A—Sonar: BQR:2B, BQS-4
**M:** diesel-electric propulsion; 3 Fairbanks-Morse 38D 8⅛-10 generator groups; 2 electric motors; 2 props; 4,800/5,400 hp
**Fuel:** 330 tons diesel **Range:** 10,000/10 surf., 95/5 sub. **Man:** 86 tot.

Remarks: Purchased 27-3-73 and 17-10-73. One generator set removed on conversion. Two 126-cell batteries. Converted from fleet submarines 1947-49. S 14 has auxiliary rudder atop hull. Sisters *Rio Grande do Sul* (S 11, ex-*Grampus,* SS 523) and *Rio de Janeiro* (S 13, ex-*Odax,* SS 484) stricken 1978: *Guanabara* (S 10, ex-*Dogfish,* SS 350) stricken late 1983.

**DESTROYERS**

◆ **2 ex-U.S. Gearing class, FRAM I**

| | Bldr | Laid down | L | In serv. |
|---|---|---|---|---|
| D 25 Marcilio Diaz (ex-*Henry W. Tucker,* DD 875) | Consolidated Steel Corp | 29-5-44 | 8-11-44 | 10-3-45 |
| D 26 Mariz E. Barros (ex-*Brinkley Bass,* DD 887) | Consolidated Steel Corp | 20-6-44 | 26-5-45 | 1-10-45 |

**D:** 2,425 tons (3,600 fl) **S:** 30 kts
**Dim:** 119.17 × 12.52 × 4.61 (6.4 over sonar)
**A:** 4/127-mm (II × 2)—1/ASROC ASW syst. (VIII × 1; 12 total missiles)—6/324-mm Mk 32 ASW TT (III × 2)—1/Wasp helicopter
**Electron Equipt:** Radar: 1/SPS-10, 1/SPS-40, 1/Mk 25 fire control
Sonar: 1/SQS-23—EW: WLR-1, ULQ-6
**M:** 2 sets GT; 2 props, 60,000 hp
**Boilers:** 4 Babcock & Wilcox, 43.3 kg, 454°C **Electric:** 1,200 kw
**Fuel:** 750 tons **Range:** 2,400/25; 4,800/15 **Man:** 14 officers, 260 men

Remarks: Purchased 3-12-73 and reached Brazil in 6-74. Mk 37 GFCS. Former DASH drone ASW helicopter hangar used for Westland Wasp.

**Marcilio Diaz (D 25)** G. Gyssels, 1981

◆ **5 ex-U.S. Allen M. Sumner class**

| | Bldr | Laid down | L | In serv. |
|---|---|---|---|---|
| D 34 Mato Grosso (ex-*Compton,* DD 705) | Federal SB, Kearny | 28-3-44 | 17-9-44 | 4-11-44 |
| D 35 Sergipe (ex-*James C. Owens,* DD 776) | Bethlehem, San Pedro | 9-4-44 | 1-10-44 | 17-2-45 |
| D 36 Alagaos (ex-*Buck,* DD 761) | Bethlehem, San Fran. | 1-2-44 | 11-3-44 | 28-6-46 |
| D 37 Rio Grande do Norte (ex-*Strong,* DD 758) | Bethlehem, San Fran. | 25-7-43 | 23-4-44 | 8-3-45 |
| D 38 Espirito Santo (ex-*Lowry,* DD 770) | Bethlehem, San Pedro | 1-8-43 | 6-2-44 | 28-7-44 |

**Rio Grande do Norte (D 37)** U.S. Navy, 1985

**Espirito Santo (D 38) and a sister** L. & L. Van Ginderen, 10-85

**D:** 2,200 tons (3,320 fl) **S:** 30 kts **Dim:** 114.75 × 12.45 × 5.8
**A:** 6/127-mm (II × 3)—(D 34 only: 1/quadruple Sea Cat SAM)—2/Hedgehog ASW RL (XXIV × 2)—6/324-mm Mk 32 ASW TT (III × 2)—1/Wasp helicopter (not on D 34)
**Electron Equipt:** Radar: 1/SPS-10, 1/SPS-40 (D 34: 1/SPS-6, D 38: 1/SPS-29), 1 Mk 25 fire-control—
EW: WRL-1 or 3 intercept
Sonar: 1/SQS-44 (D 34: SQS-31); D 35 also: SQA-10 VDS
**M:** 2 sets GT; 2 props; 60,000 hp
**Boilers:** 4 Babcock & Wilcox, 43.3 kg/cm², 454°C **Fuel:** 460 tons
**Electric:** 1,200 kw **Range:** 1,260/30; 4,600/15 **Man:** 15 officers, 260 men

Remarks: All except D 34 had FRAM II modernization. D 34 transferred 27-9-72, the others in 1973. Mk 37 GFCS. Sea Cat system added in D 34 uses M 20 optical director. D 38 has ULQ-6 jamming gear. D 35 collided with a merchant ship 11-84, out of service for 8 months or more.

◆ **3 ex-U.S. Fletcher class** (In reserve)

| | Bldr | Laid down | L | In serv. |
|---|---|---|---|---|
| D 31 Piaui (ex-*Lewis Hancock,* DD 675) | Federal SB & DD | 31-3-43 | 1-8-43 | 29-9-43 |
| D 32 Santa Catarina (ex-*Irwin,* DD 794) | Bethlehem, San Pedro | 2-5-43 | 31-10-43 | 14-2-44 |
| D 33 Maranhão (ex-*Shields,* DD 596) | Puget Sound B & DD | 10-8-44 | 29-4-44 | 8-2-45 |

DESTROYERS *(continued)*

**Piaui (D 31)** L. & L. Van Ginderen, 5-83

**D:** 2,050 tons (2,850 fl) **S:** 33 kts **Dim:** 114.85 × 12.03 × 5.5
**A:** 5/127-mm DP (I × 5)—10/40-mm AA (IV × 2, II × 2—D 33: none)
**Electron Equipt:** Radar: 1/SPS-10, 1/SPS-66, 1/Mk 25 fire-control
**M:** 2 sets GT; 2 props; 60,000 hp **Electric:** 880 kw
**Boilers:** 4 Babcock & Wilcox, 43.3 kg/cm², 454°C **Fuel:** 450 tons
**Range:** 1,260/30; 3,600/14 **Man:** 15 officers, 247 men

REMARKS: D 31 transferred on loan under Mutual Aid Agreement on 2-8-67, D 32 on 10-5-68. D 33 purchased 1-7-72; the other two were bought outright on 11-4-73. ASW armament and sonar were to have been deleted and the ships used for 200-n.m. economic zone patrol, but were placed in Special Reserve in 1983 with quintuple 533-mm TT mount, 2 Hedgehog ASW spigot mortars and a d.c. rack still aboard. Unlikely now to see further service. Mk 37 GFCS for 127-mm, 3 Mk 5/Mod. 1 GFCS for 40-mm.

## FRIGATES

◆ **0 (+4 + 12) new-construction ocean patrol frigates** Bldr: First two: Ast. Ilha das Cobras, Rio; others: Verolme do Brasil, Puerto Alegre

| | Laid down | L | In serv. |
|---|---|---|---|
| V30 INHAUMA | 23-9-83 | 3-12-86 | 1989 |
| V31 JACEGUARI | 15-10-84 | 8-6-87 | 1990 |
| V32 JULIO DE NORONHA | 1-87 | . . . | . . . |
| V33 FRONTIN | 2-87 | . . . | . . . |

**Inhauma (V 30)**—artist's impression, old hull number 1985

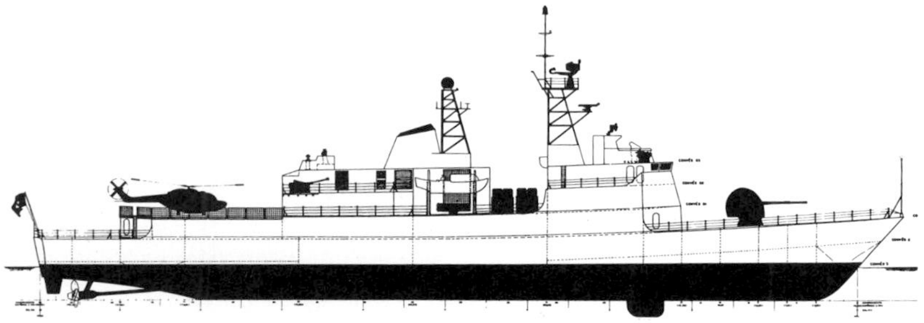

**New ocean patrol frigate**

**D:** 1,670 tons (1,970 fl) **S:** 26 kts **Dim:** 95.77 (90.00 pp) × 11.40 × 3.64
**A:** 4/MM 40 Exocet SSM—1/114-mm Vickers Mk 8 DP—2/40-mm Bofors L 70 AA (I × 2)—6/324-mm ASW TT for Mk 46 torpedoes (III × 2)—1/Lynx helicopter
**Electron Equipt:** Radar: 1/navigational, 1/Plessey AWS-4, 1/Orion RTN-10X
Sonar: Krupp-Atlas ASO-4-2
EW: . . . passive, 2/Plessey Shield chaff RL (VI × 2)
**M:** CODOG: 1 G.E. LM 2500 gas turbine, 27,000 hp; 2 MTU 16V956 TB91 diesels, 7,880 hp; 2 CP props
**Electric:** 2,000 kw (4 Siemens 500-kw alternators)
**Range:** 4,000/15. **Man:** 14 officers, 33 petty officers, 79 men

REMARKS: Originally to have been a program of 12 smaller "corvettes," intended for Coast Guard service. Four were authorized 11-81, with the possibility of more later, and the first two were ordered 15-2-82; second pair ordered 9-6-86 for delivery 1989. Will have Ferranti CAAIS 2-50 (Computer-Assisted Information System). The projected 7th through 16th ships are to carry the Brazilian-designed Barracuda SSM in place of Exocet and will also have eight Avibras SSA-N-1 SAMs.

◆ **6 British Vosper Thornycroft Mk 10 class**

| ASW: | Bldr | Laid down | L | In serv. |
|---|---|---|---|---|
| F 40 NITEROI | Thornycroft, Woolston | 8-6-72 | 8-2-74 | 20-11-76 |
| F 41 DEFENSORA | Thornycroft, Woolston | 14-12-72 | 27-3-75 | 5-3-77 |
| F 44 INDEPENDENCIA | Ast. Ilha das Cobras, Rio | 11-6-72 | 2-9-74 | 3-9-79 |
| F 45 UNIÃO | Ast. Ilha das Cobras, Rio | 11-6-72 | 14-3-75 | 12-9-80 |
| General-purpose: | | | | |
| F 42 CONSTITUCÃO | Thornycroft, Woolston | 13-3-74 | 15-4-76 | 31-3-78 |
| F 43 LIBERAL | Thornycroft, Woolston | 2-5-75 | 7-2-77 | 18-11-78 |

**Constitucão (F 42)**—general-purpose version L. & L. Van Ginderen, 7-86

**Liberal (F 43)**—general-purpose version L. & L. Van Ginderen, 7-85

**Defensora (F 41)**—ASW version L. & L. Van Ginderen, 10-85

**D:** 3,200 tons (3,800 fl)
**S:** 30.5 kts (28 cruising on gas turbines, 22 on diesels)
**Dim:** 129.24 (121.92 pp) × 13.52 × 4.20 (5.94 sonar)
**A:** ASW type: 4/MM 40 Exocet SSM (II × 2)—1/114-mm Mk 8 Vickers automatic DP—2/40-mm Bofors AA (I × 2)—2/Sea Cat SAM systems (III × 2)—Branik ASW system—1/375-mm, Bofors ASW RL (II × 1)—6/324-mm ASW TT (III × 2)—1/Lynx helicopter—1/d.c. rack (5 charges)
General-purpose type: similar but without the Branik system and with a second 114-mm Mk 8 aft and 4 launchers (II × 2) for the MM 38 Exocet SSM system
**Electron Equipt:** Radar: 1/Plessey AWS-2 air search, 1/H.S.A. ZW-06, 2/Orion RTN-10 X f.c.—1/Ikara tracker (not in F 42, 43)
Sonar: 1/EDO 610 E; ASW ships also have 1/EDO 700 E VDS
EW: Decca RDL-2/3 intercept—2/Plessey Shield RL (VI × 2)

**FRIGATES** *(continued)*

**M:** CODOG: 2 Rolls-Royce Olympus TM3B gas turbines, 28,000 hp each; 4 MTU 16V956 TB91 diesels, 3,940 hp each; 2 Escher-Wyss CP props; 56,000 hp max.
**Endurance:** 45 days **Electric:** 4,500 kw **Fuel:** 480 tons
**Range:** 1,300/29; 5,300/17 **Man:** 21 officers, 180 men

REMARKS: Ordered 20-9-70. Fitted with retractable fin stabilizers. Branik is the name of the system devised for handling the Australian Ikara ASW missile in these ships. All have CAAIS action data system (Ferranti 1600B computers) and are equipped with Decca EW gear. The Brazilian-built units experienced considerable delays in fitting out. F40–45 to receive 4 MM 40 Exocet SSM ordered 1986.

## CORVETTES

◆ **0 (+16) patrol corvettes**—programmed

**D:** 400–500 tons (fl) **S:** . . . **Dim:** . . . × . . . × . . .
**A:** . . .
**Electron Equipt:** . . .
**M:** . . .

REMARKS: Program announced 2-86 but later reported as 8 of 450 tons and 4 of 1,000. To be built in Brazil for 200-n.m. economic zone patrol and SAR duties. May delay for financial reasons.

◆ **9 Imperial Marinheiro class** Bldr: L. Smit, Kinderdijk, Netherlands

| | L | In serv. |
|---|---|---|
| V 15 IMPERIAL MARINHEIRO | 24-11-54 | 8-6-55 |
| V 16 IGUATEMI | 1954 | 17-9-55 |
| V 18 FORTE DE COIMBRA | 11-6-54 | 26-7-55 |
| V 19 CABOCLO | 28-8-54 | 4-55 |
| V 20 ANGOSTURA | 1955 | 1955 |
| V 21 BAHIANA | 11-54 | 26-6-55 |
| V 22 MEARIM | 8-54 | 3-8-55 |
| V 23 PURUS | 6-11-54 | 4-55 |
| V 24 SOLIMÕES | 24-11-54 | 1955 |

**Imperial Marinheiro (V 15)** 1971

**D:** 911 tons (960 fl) **S:** 15 kts **Dim:** 55.72 × 9.55 × 3.6
**A:** 1/76.2-mm DP—4/20-mm AA (I × 4)
**M:** 2 Sulzer diesels; 2 props; 2,160 hp **Fuel:** 135 tons diesel **Man:** 60 tot.

REMARKS: Oceangoing tug design. Were intended to be convertible for minesweeping or minelaying. V 15 is used as a submarine tender. Officially designated "vedettes" and used in district patrols and in support of the 200-mile economic zone. Sister *Iparanga* (V 17) stricken 1983.

NOTE: The three former U.S. Navy patrol tugs *Tritão* (R 21), *Tridente* (R 22), and *Triunfo* (R 23) have been replaced by new tugs with the same names and numbers; see later page.

## PATROL BOATS AND CRAFT

◆ **6 Piratini-class patrol boats** Bldr: Ast. Ilha das Cobras, Rio

| | In serv. | | In serv. |
|---|---|---|---|
| P 10 PIRATINI (ex-PGM 109) | 30-11-70 | P 13 Parati (ex-PGM 119) | 7-71 |
| P 11 PIRAJÁ (ex-PGM 110) | 3-71 | P 14 PENEDO (ex-PGM 120) | 9-71 |
| P 12 PAMPEIRO (ex-PGM 118) | 6-71 | P 15 POTI (ex-PGM 121) | 10-71 |

**Penedo (P 14)** 1985

**D:** 105 tons (fl) **S:** 18.0 kts (15.5 sust.) **Dim:** 28.95 × 6.1 × 1.55
**A:** 1/81-mm mortar with 12.7-mm mg atop—2/12.7-mm mg (I × 2)
**M:** 4 Cummins VT-12M diesels; 2 props; 1,100 hp
**Electric:** 40 kw **Range:** 1,000/15; 1,700/12 **Man:** 2 officers, 14 men

REMARKS: These patrol craft are based on the 95-foot WPBs of the U.S. Coast Guard and were funded by the U.S.

◆ **0 (+16) Tracker-20-class patrol craft** Bldr: Asteleiros du Sud, Porto Alegre

**D:** 31 tons (34.5 fl) **S:** 27 kts **Dim:** 20.0 (19.3 pp) × 5.18 × 1.45
**A:** 1/30-mm AA **Electron equipt:** Radar: 1/. . . navigational
**M:** 2 G.M. 12V71 TI diesels; 2 props; 1,300 hp **Range:** 650/20
**Electric:** 30 kw **Man:** 11 tot.

REMARKS: Licensed construction GRP craft designed by Fairey Marinteknik, Cowes, U.K. License agreed 4-87. Engines may differ from Royal Navy version described above.

◆ **10 U.S. Swift Mk II patrol craft** Bldr: R 61–64: Swiftships, Morgan City, La.; others: DM-Commercio, Importacão & Maintencão de Producto Nauticas

R 61 through R 76

**D:** 22.5 tons (fl) **S:** 22 kts **Dim:** 15.66 × 4.55 × 1.1 **A:** 1/12.7-mm mg
**M:** 2 G.M. 12V71 TI diesels; 2 props; 850 hp
**Range:** 400/22 **Man:** 6 tot **Electric:** 6 kw

REMARKS: Employed by naval police and port captains. Six ordered 16-1-81 in Brazil. Four earlier units built in U.S., transferred under AID program in 1972–73.

## RIVER PATROL SHIPS

◆ **0 (+3) new-construction river patrol ships**

| | Bldr | Laid down | L | In serv. |
|---|---|---|---|---|
| P . . . PORTO ESPERANÇA | Ars. de Marinha, Rio | 14-1-85 | . . . | . . . |
| P . . . N . . . | . . . | . . . | . . . | . . . |
| P . . . N . . . | . . . | . . . | . . . | . . . |

**D:** 270 tons (380 fl) **S:** 12 kts **Dim:** 49.33 (45.57 pp) × 8.45 × 1.40
**A:** 2/40-mm AA (I × 2)—6/12.7-mm mg (I × 6)—2/81-mm mortars (I × 2)
**M:** 2 diesels; 2 props; . . . hp **Man:** 8 officers, 54 men

REMARKS: Replaces program for ships named *Cascaval* and *Jararaca,* announced 1981. All for use on Paraguay River; second two to build at private yards. Will have a helo deck and can carry 2 LCVP. Program delayed by financial problems.

◆ **3 Roraima class** Bldr: MacLaren, Niteroi

| | L | In serv. | | L | In serv. |
|---|---|---|---|---|---|
| P 30 RORAIMA | 9-11-72 | 21-2-75 | P 32 AMAPA | 9-3-73 | 1-76 |
| P 31 RONDÔNIA | 10-1-73 | 3-12-75 | | | |

**D:** 340 tons (365 fl) **S:** 14.5 kts **Dim:** 46.3 × 8.45 × 1.37
**A:** 1/40-mm AA—6/12.7-mm mg (I × 6)—2/81-mm mortars (I × 2)
**Electron Equipt:** 3/navigational radars

**Rondônia (P 31)** Brazilian Navy, 1983

**Amapa (P 32)** 1985

**RIVER PATROL SHIPS** *(continued)*

**M:** 2 M.A.N. V6V16/18 TL diesels; 2 props; 1,824 hp
**Range:** 6,000/11
**Man:** 9 officers, 54 men

Remarks: In Amazon Flotilla. Carry one LCVP.

◆ **2 Pedro Teixeira class**

| | Bldr | L | In serv. |
|---|---|---|---|
| P 20 Pedro Teixeira | Ilha das Cobras, Rio | 11-6-72 | 17-12-73 |
| P 21 Raposo Tavares | Ilha das Cobras, Rio | 11-6-72 | 17-12-73 |

**Pedro Teixeira (P 20)**—note hangar offset to starboard 1985

**D:** 690 tons (fl) **S:** 16 kts **Dim:** 63.55 × 9.71 × 1.70
**A:** 1/40-mm AA—6/12.7-mm mg (I × 6)—2/81-mm mortars (I × 2)—1/SAH-11 helicopter
**Electron Equipt:** Radar: 2/navigational
**M:** 2 MEP-M.A.N. V6V16/18 TLS diesels; 2 props; 3,840 hp
**Range:** 6,800/10
**Man:** 6 officers, 72 men

Remarks: In Amazon Flotilla. Carry two LCVP.

◆ **1 old river monitor**

| | Bldr | Laid down | L | In serv. |
|---|---|---|---|---|
| U 17 Parnaiba | Arsenal de Marinha, Rio | 11-6-36 | 2-9-37 | 11-37 |

**Parnaiba (U 17)** 1976

**D:** 620 tons (720 fl) **S:** 12 kts **Dim:** 55.0 × 10.1 × 1.6
**A:** 1/76.2-mm DP—2/47-mm—2/40-mm AA (I × 2)—6/20-mm AA (I × 6)
**M:** 2 sets triple-expansion reciprocating steam; 2 props; 1,300 hp
**Boilers:** 2/3-drum **Fuel:** 90 tons
**Range:** 1,350/10 **Man:** 90 tot.

Remarks: In Mato Grosso Flotilla. To be replaced by *Porto Esperança*.

## MINE WARFARE SHIPS

◆ **6 German Schütze-class (Type 340a) patrol minesweepers** Bldr: Abeking and Rasmussen, Lemwerde, West Germany

| | L | In serv. | | L | In serv. |
|---|---|---|---|---|---|
| M 15 Aratu | 27-5-70 | 5-5-71 | M 18 Aracatuba | 1971 | 13-12-72 |
| M 16 Anhatomirim | 4-11-70 | 30-11-71 | M 19 Abrolhos | 7-5-74 | 16-4-75 |
| M 17 Atalaia | 14-4-71 | 13-12-72 | M 20 Albardão | 9-74 | 21-7-75 |

**D:** 241 tons (280 fl) **S:** 24 kts **Dim:** 47.44 × 7.16 × 2.4 **A:** 1/40-mm AA
**M:** 4 Maybach diesels; 2 Escher-Wyss vertical cycloidal props; 4,500 hp
**Electric:** 120 kw plus 340-kw sweep generator **Fuel:** 22 tons
**Range:** 710/20 **Man:** 39 tot.

**Anhatomirim** 1972

Remarks: Four ordered 4-69, two 11-73. Fitted for magnetic, mechanical, and acoustic minesweeping. Wooden hulls. A new series of minesweepers is planned.

## AMPHIBIOUS WARFARE SHIPS

Note: Long-range plans call for acquisition of two new landing ships to replace those listed.

◆ **1 U.S. De Soto County-class tank landing ship** Bldr: Avondale, New Orleans

| | L | In serv. |
|---|---|---|
| G 26 Duque de Caxias (ex-*Grant County,* LST 1174) | 12-10-56 | 8-11-57 |

**D:** 4,164 tons (7,800 fl) **S:** 16 kts **Dim:** 135.7 (129.8 wl) × 18.9 × 5.3
**A:** 2/76.2-mm DP (II × 1) **Electron Equipt:** Radar: 1/SPS-21
**M:** 4 Fairbanks-Morse 38D $8\frac{1}{8}$ × 12 diesels; 2 CP props; 13,900 hp
**Electric:** 900 kw **Range:** 13,000/10
**Man:** 11 officers, 164 men

Remarks: Transferred 15-1-73; purchased 12-17-78. Can carry 700 men. Air-conditioned. Tank deck 88 m long. Four LCVP in davits; can carry four causeways (pontoon sections). Platform for helicopter. Stülcken 60-ton lift gear reported added forward in place of 4/76.2-mm. Mk 51 Mod. 2 GFCS for guns.

◆ **1 U.S. LST 542-class tank landing ship** Bldr: Bethlehem, Hingham, Mass.

| | Laid down | L | In serv. |
|---|---|---|---|
| G 28 Garcia D'Avila (ex-*Outagamie County,* LST 1073) | 20-2-45 | 22-3-45 | 17-4-45 |

**D:** 1,490 tons light (4,100 fl) **S:** 11.6 kts **Dim:** 100.0 × 15.25 × 4.29
**A:** 8/40-mm AA (II × 2, I × 4)
**M:** 2 G.M. 2-278A diesels; 2 props; 1,700 hp **Electric:** 300 kw

Remarks: Loaned 25-5-71; purchased 1-12-73. Beaching displacement: 2,336 tons. Carries 2 LCVP.

◆ **3 U.S. LCU 1610-type landing craft** Bldr: Navy Yard, Rio, 1974–78

L 10 Guarapari L 11 Timbau L 12 Camboriu

**Guarapari (L 10)** 1978

**D:** 200 tons (396 fl) **S:** 11 kts **Dim:** 41.0 × 8.42 × 2.0
**A:** 3/12.7-mm mg. (I × 3) **Electron Equipt:** Radar: 1/. . . nav.
**M:** 2 G.M. 12V71 diesels; 2 props; 1,000 hp
**Range:** 1,200/8

Remarks: Typed EDCG—"Embarcaçao de Desembarque de Carga Generales." Can carry 172 tons cargo. The uncompleted *Tramandai* (L 13) was scrapped in 1983.

◆ **21 LCVP** built in Japan, 1959–60
501–521

◆ **15 EDVP** built in Brazil, 1971

**Dim:** 11.0 × 3.2 × 0.6 (fwd), 1.0 (aft)
**M:** Brazilian Scania diesel

Remarks: Glass-reinforced plastic construction. Can carry 36 men with full pack or one jeep with trailer and 17 men or 1/105-mm howitzer or an anti-tank gun and 18 men. Japanese-built craft similar, but are wooden. At least one U.S. LCM (6) design landing craft is also in service.

## HYDROGRAPHIC AND OCEANOGRAPHIC SHIPS

◆ **1 U.S. Robert D. Conrad-class oceanographic ship** Bldr: Marietta Co., Pt. Pleasant, West Virginia (In serv. 8-2-65)

H 41 Almirante Camara (ex-*Sands,* T-AGOR 6)

**D:** 1,020 tons (1,370 fl) **S:** 13.5 kts **Dim:** 63.7 (59.7 pp) × 12.2 × 4.9 mean
**Electron Equipt:** Radar: 1/RCA CRM-N1A-75
**M:** 2 Caterpillar D-378 diesels, electric drive; 1 prop; 1,000 hp
**Electric:** 850 kw (plus 620 kw)
**Fuel:** 211 tons **Range:** 10,000/12
**Man:** 8 officers, 18 men, 15 oceanographers

Remarks: Loaned 1-7-74. An auxiliary 620-hp gas turbine powers a small electric maneuvering propeller for stationkeeping purposes at extremely low rpm; also has bow-thruster. Has echo-sounders capable of measuring 11,000-meter depths.

## HYDROGRAPHIC AND OCEANOGRAPHIC SHIPS *(continued)*

**Almirante Camara (H 41)** 1974

◆ **1 Antarctic exploration support ship** Bldr: Aalborg Vaerft, Denmark (In serv. 10-57)

H 42 Barão de Teffé (ex-*Thala Dan*)

**D:** approx. 5,500 tons (fl) **S:** 12 kts **Dim:** 75.14 (65.54 pp) × 13.77 × 6.30
**M:** 1 Burmeister & Wain 7-cyl. diesel; 1 CP prop; 1,970 hp
**Electric:** 680 kw **Fuel:** 457 tons **Man:** 50 tot.

Remarks: 2,183 grt/2,164 dwt. Purchased 5-82 from J. Lauritzen in lieu of the Royal Navy ice patrol ship, *Endurance.* Conversion completed 28-9-82 as Antarctic support ship, including helicopter deck over stern (added overall length not included above). Ice-reinforced-hulled former cargo ship. To be replaced by a Brazilian-built polar icebreaker.

◆ **2 Sirius class**

| | Bldr | Laid down | L | In serv. |
|---|---|---|---|---|
| H 21 Sirius | Ishikawajima, Tokyo | 12-56 | 30-7-57 | 1-1-58 |
| H 22 Canopus | Ishikawajima, Tokyo | 12-56 | 20-11-57 | 15-3-58 |

**Canopus (H 22)**

**D:** 1,463 tons (1,900 fl) **S:** 15 kts **Dim:** 77.9 × 12.03 × 3.7
**M:** 2 Sulzer 7T6-36 diesels; 2 CP props; 2,700 hp **Range:** 12,000/11
**Fuel:** 343 tons **Man:** 102 tot.

Remarks: 1 SAH-11 helicopter, 1 LCVP, 3 small survey craft. Fully equipped. Armament removed.

◆ **6 wooden-hulled hydrographic boats** Bldr: Bormann, Rio de Janeiro

| | In serv. | | In serv. |
|---|---|---|---|
| H 11 Paraibano | 10-68 | H 15 Itacurussá | 3-71 |
| H 12 Rio Branco | 10-68 | H 16 Camocim | 1971 |
| H 14 Nogueira da Gama (ex-*Jaceguai*) | 3-71 | H 17 Caravelas | 1971 |

**Nogueira da Gama (H 14)** 1971

**D:** 32 tons (50 fl) **S:** 11 kts **Dim:** 16.0 × 4.6 × 1.3 **Range:** 600/11
**M:** 2 G.M. 6-71 diesels; 2 props; 330 hp **Man:** 2 officers, 9 men

Remarks: In Amazon Flotilla.

◆ **1 former sail-training ship**

| | Bldr | L | In serv. |
|---|---|---|---|
| H 10 Almirante Saldanha | Vickers, Barrow | 19-12-33 | 6-34 |

**Almirante Saldanha (H 10)** 1975

**D:** 3,325 tons (3,825 fl) **S:** 11 kts **Dim:** 93.6 × 15.8 × 5.5
**M:** 1 Sulzer diesel; 1 CP prop; 1,400 hp **Range:** 12,000/10
**Fuel:** 390 tons **Electric:** 550 kw **Man:** 210 tot.

Remarks: Former 4-masted schooner, refit completed in 7-61 as an oceanographic research ship and for training. Refitted again for zooplankton research, completed 6-80; received NAVSAT and Omega navigation systems, new current and salinity meter systems.

◆ **3 Argus-class coastal survey ships**

| | Bldr | L | In serv. |
|---|---|---|---|
| H 31 Argus | Ars. de Marinha, Rio | 6-12-57 | 29-1-59 |
| H 32 Orion | Ars. de Marinha, Rio | 5-2-58 | 11-6-59 |
| H 33 Taurus | Ars. de Marinha, Rio | 7-1-58 | 23-4-59 |

**Taurus (H 33)** 1985

**D:** 250 tons (350 fl) **S:** 15 kts **Dim:** 44.67 (41.14 pp) × 6.50 × 2.80
**M:** 2 Caterpillar DT 379 diesels; 2 props; 1,200 hp **Fuel:** 35 tons
**Range:** 3,000/. . . **Endurance:** 20 days **Man:** 34 tot.

Remarks: Based on the Portuguese *Azevia*-class gunboat. H 32 modernized in 1973/74, with new propulsion machinery, auxiliaries, and electronic equipment.

◆ **1 fisheries research oceanographic ship** Bldr: INACE, Fortaleza

U 15 Suboficial Oliveira (In serv. 22-5-81)

**D:** 108 tons (120 fl) **S:** 10 kts **Dim:** 35.5 × 6.7 × . . .
**M:** 2 diesels; . . . props; 740 hp **Range:** 1400/8 **Man:** 10 tot.

Remarks: For use by the Naval Research Institute in "Capo Frio Project" for shrimp cultivation.

## AUXILIARY SHIPS

◆ **1 cadet training ship, modified Mk 10 frigate**

| | Bldr | Laid down | L | In serv. |
|---|---|---|---|---|
| U 27 Brasil | Ast. Ilha das Cobras, Rio | 18-9-81 | 23-9-83 | 21-8-86 |

**Brasil (U 27)** L. & L. Van Ginderen, 9-87

**AUXILIARY SHIPS** *(continued)*

**D:** 2,380 tons (3,400 fl) **S:** 18 kts **Dim:** 131.25 × 13.52 × 4.21 mean (fl)
**A:** 2/40-mm Bofors L70 AA (I × 2)
**Electron Equipt:** Radar: 2/navigational
**M:** 2 Ishikawajima Brazil-Pielstick 6 PC. 2 L400 diesels; 2 props; 7,800 hp
**Range:** 7,000/15 **Man:** 26 officers, 69 petty officers, 120 men, 200 cadets

Remarks: Uses hull of the Mk 10 frigate design, but has less powerful plant and simpler weapons and electronics. Electro-optical GFCS only. Fin stabilizers. Replaces *Custódio de Mello* (U 26) for training cadets from Naval and Merchant Marine Academies. Master CIC with 3 satellite training CICs, navigational training compartment for 40 trainees, 2 other classrooms. A planned 76-mm OTO Melara Compact mount forward has not been installed, nor was planned hangar.

◆ **4 Custódio de Mello-class transports**

| | Bldr | Laid down | L | In serv. |
|---|---|---|---|---|
| G 26 Custódio de Mello | Ishikawajima, Tokyo | 12-53 | 10-6-54 | 1-12-54 |
| G 16 Barroso Pereira | Ishikawajima, Tokyo | 12-53 | 7-8-54 | 1-12-54 |
| G 21 Ary Parreiras | Ishikawajima, Tokyo | 12-55 | 24-8-56 | 29-12-56 |
| G 22 Soares Dutra | Ishikawajima, Tokyo | 12-55 | 13-12-56 | 23-3-57 |

**Custódio de Mello (as U 26)** G. Gyssels, 9-86

**D:** 4,800 tons (8,600 fl) **S:** 16 kts **Dim:** 119.2 (110.4 pp) × 16.0 × 6.1
**A:** 2/76.2-mm DP (I × 2)—2/20-mm AA (I × 2)—U 26: 4/76.2-mm DP (I × 4)
**Electron Equipt:** Radar: U 26: 1/navigational, 1/SPS-4—others: 2/navigational
**M:** GT; 2 props; 4,800 hp **Boilers:** 2 Foster-Wheeler; 350°C **Fuel:** 880 tons
**Man:** 118 tot. Can carry 1,972 troops (497 normal)

Remarks: 4,200 dwt/4,879 grt. Living spaces mechanically ventilated and partially air-conditioned. *Custódio de Mello,* used as training ship, replaced in that role by *Brasil* (U 30). Others have a helicopter platform aft, can carry 497 troops, and are occasionally used in commercial service; all have 425 $m^3$ refrigerated cargo space.

◆ **1 U.S. Aristaeus-class small repair ship** Bldr: Maryland DD, Baltimore

| | Laid down | L | In serv. |
|---|---|---|---|
| G 24 Belmonte (ex-*Helios,* ARB 12, ex-LST 1127) | 23-11-44 | 14-2-45 | 26-2-45 |

**Belmonte (G 24)**

**D:** 2,030 tons (4,100 fl) **S:** 9 kts **Dim:** 100.0 (96.3 wl) × 15.25 × 3.36
**A:** 8/40-mm AA (IV × 2) **M:** 2 G.M. 12-567A diesels; 2 props; 1,800 hp
**Electric:** 600 kw **Fuel:** 584 tons **Range:** 6,000/9

Remarks: 1-62; purchased 28-12-67. 1/60-ton winch crane, 2/10-ton booms. Used mainly as a transport.

◆ **0 (+1) fleet supply ship** Bldr: Lenin SY, Gdansk, Poland (In serv. 1971)

G 29 Almirante Gastão Motta (ex-*Itatinga*)

**D:** approx. 12,000 tons (fl) **S:** 20.5 kts **Dim:** 161.02 (150.02 pp) × 22.99 × 9.72
**A:** . . . **Electron Equipt:** Radar: . . .
**M:** 1 Sulzer diesel; 1 prop; 18,400 hp **Electric:** 1,200 kw
**Man:** 25 officers, 36 petty officers, 153 men **Fuel:** 1,727 tons

Remarks: Cargo vessel purchased 1984 from Lloydd Brasileiro Steamship Co. Under conversion 1985–. . . at Rio de Janeiro Naval Arsenal to act as fleet supply ship to replace *Marajo* (G 27). Will carry cargo fuel and water, as well as ammunition for underway transfer. Helicopter deck and facilities for two Sea King. Extensive medical and dental facilities. Total accommodations: 214. Sister *Itacpuca* acquired 5-85, but conversion is not to be carried out.

◆ **1 fleet replenishment oiler** Bldr: Ishikawajima do Brasil, Rio

| | Laid down | L | In serv. |
|---|---|---|---|
| G 27 Marajo | 13-12-66 | 31-1-68 | 22-10-68 |

**Marajo (G 27)** U.S. Navy, 1985

**D:** 16,000 tons (fl) **S:** 13.6 kts **Dim:** 137.1 (127.69 pp) × 19.22 × 7.35
**M:** 1 Sulzer GRD 68 diesel; 8,000 hp **Cargo capacity:** 7,200 tons
**Fuel:** 700 tons **Electric:** 1,200 kw **Range:** 9,200/14.5 **Man:** 80 tot.

Remarks: 6,600 grt/11,119 dwt. Two liquid replenishment stations per side. Has always had engineering problems.

◆ **1 river oiler**

G 17 Potengi Bldr: Papendrecht, Holland (L: 16-3-38)

**D:** 600 tons **S:** 10 kts **Dim:** 54.5 × 7.5 × 1.8
**M:** 2 diesels; 2 props; 550 hp **Range:** 600/8 **Man:** 20 tot.

Remarks: In Mato Grosso Flotilla. Cargo capacity: 450 tons

◆ **1 U.S. Penguin-class submarine rescue ship**

| | Bldr | Laid down | L | In serv. |
|---|---|---|---|---|
| K 10 Gastão Moutinho (ex-*Skylark,* ASR 20; ex-*Yustaga,* ATF 165) | Charleston SB & DD | 23-7-45 | 19-3-46 | 19-7-46 |

**Gastão Moutinho (K 10)**

**D:** 1,780 tons (2,140 fl) **S:** 14.5 kts
**Dim:** 62.48 (59.44 wl) × 11.96 × 4.72 **A:** 2/20-mm AA (I × 2)
**Radar:** 1/SPS-5 **M:** 4 G.M. 12-278A diesels; electric drive; 1 prop; 3,000 hp
**Electric:** 400 kw **Fuel:** 301 tons **Range:** 15,000/8

Remarks: Begun as an *Achomawi*-class fleet tug. Purchased 30-6-73. Has rescue bell, salvage equipment, pumps, 4 pontoons, etc. Often employed as a hydrographic survey ship and as a diving tender.

◆ **3 ocean patrol tugs, former oilfield supply tugs** Bldr: ESTENAVE, Manaus (In serv. 1987–. . .)

R 21 Tritão (ex-*Sarandi*)
R 22 Tridente (ex-*Sambaiba*)
R 23 Triunfo (ex-*Sorocaba*)

**D:** 950 tons (fl) **S:** . . . **Dim:** 53.52 (50.02 pp) × 11.61 × 3.35
**A:** 2/12.7-mm mg (I × 2) **Electron Equipt:** Radar: . . .
**M:** diesels; . . . props; . . . hp **Man:** 16 tot.

Remarks: Begun as oilfield supply tugs for PETROBRAZ but purchased 5-86 while still under construction as replacements for the three former U.S. Navy *Sotoyomo*-class ocean tugs. Will have a helicopter flight deck. Intended for 200-n.m. economic zone patrol and SAR duties.

◆ **2 oceangoing tugs** Bldr: Sumitomo Heavy Industries, Japan (Both L: 1976)

R 24 Almirante Guilhem (ex-. . .)
R 25 Almirante Guillobel (ex-. . .)

**D:** 2,400 tons (fl) **S:** 14 kts **Dims:** 63.15 × 13.40 × 4.50 **A:** . . .
**M:** 2 G.M. 20-645 ET diesels; 2 CP props; 7,200 hp **Electric:** 550 kw
**Fuel:** 670 tons **Man:** 40 tot.

Remarks: Purchased 1980 from Superpesa Maritime Transport, Ltd., and commissioned 22-1-81. Former oilfield supply tugs. 84-ton bollard pull. 525-hp bow-thruster.

**AUXILIARY SHIPS** *(continued)*

◆ **1 lighthouse and buoy tender**

| | Bldr | Laid down | L | In serv. |
|---|---|---|---|---|
| H 34 Graça Aranha | Elbin, Niteroi | end 1970 | 23-6-74 | 9-9-76 |

**Graça Aranha (H 34)** 1976

**D:** 1,253 tons (2,300 fl) **S:** 13 kts **Dim:** 75.57 × 13.0 × 3.71
**M:** diesel; 1 CP prop; 2,000 hp; 1 bow-thruster **Man:** 101 tot.

Remarks: Telescoping helicopter hangar for one SAH-11. Two LCVP carried as supply lighters.

**YARD AND SERVICE CRAFT**

◆ **1 large yard tug**

R 14 Laurindo Pitta Bldr: Vickers (In serv. 1910, rebuilt 1969)

**D:** 514 tons **S:** 11 kts **Dim:** 39.04 × 7.77 × 4.6
**M:** 2 sets reciprocating steam; 2 props; . . . hp **Man:** 33 tot.

◆ **4 Comandante Marriog-class yard tugs** Bldr: Turn-Ship Ltd., U.S.A. (In serv. 1981)

R 14 Comandante Didier R 17 Tenente Magalhaes
R 15 Comandante Marriog R 18 Cabo Schram

**D:** 115 tons (fl) **S:** 10 kts **Dim:** 19.8 × 7.0 × 2.0
**M:** 2 G.M. diesels; . . . props; 900 hp **Man:** 6 tot.

◆ **4 yard tugs** Bldr: Holland Nautic Yard, Haarlem (In serv. 1953)

R 32 Centauro R 34 Lamego R 35 Passo De Patria R 36 Voluntario

**D:** 220 tons (fl) **S:** 11 kts **Dim:** 27.6 × 7.2 × 3.1
**M:** 1 Krupp Womag diesel; 765 hp **Man:** 12 tot.

Remarks: Sisters *Audaz* (R 31) and *Guarani* (R 33) stricken 1986.

◆ **3 Isaias de Noronha-class tugs** (1972–74)

R . . . Isaias De Noronha R . . . D.N.O.G.
R . . . Teniente Lahmeyer

**D:** 200 tons (fl) **Dim:** 47.0 × . . . × . . .

Remarks: Latter pair reported as only 100 tons, 32.0 m o.a.

◆ **1 personnel and stores transport** Bldr: Embrasa, Itajai, Santa Catarina (L: 29-8-74)

R 47 Sargento Borges

**D:** 108.5 tons **S:** 10 kts **Dim:** 28.0 × 6.5 × 1.5
**M:** 2 diesels; 2 props; 480 hp **Cargo:** 106 passengers **Range:** 400/10

◆ **4 Rio Pardo-class harbor passenger ferries** Bldr: Inconav Niteroi Shipbuilders (In serv. 1975–76)

U 40 Rio Pardo U 42 Rio Chui
U 41 Rio Negro U 43 Rio Oiapoque

**D:** 150 tons **S:** 14 kts **Dim:** 35.38 × 6.5 × 1.9
**M:** 2 diesels; 2 props; 1,096 hp **Cargo:** 400 passengers

◆ **6 Rio Doce-class river transports** Bldr: G. deVries Leutsch, Amsterdam (In serv. 1956)

U 20 Rio Doce U 22 Rio Formoso U 24 Rio Turvo
U 21 Rio Das Contas U 23 Rio Real U 25 Rio Verde

**D:** 150 tons (200 fl) **S:** 14 kts **Dim:** 36.6 × 6.5 × 2.1
**M:** 2 Sulzer diesels; 2 props; 450 hp **Cargo:** 600 passengers
**Range:** 700/14 **Man:** 10 tot.

◆ **7 Anchova-class personnel launches** Bldr: Brazil (1965–67)

R 54 Anchova R 55 Arenque R 56 Atum R 57 Acará
R 58 Agulha R 59 Aruana R 60 Argentina

**D:** 11 tons (13 fl) **S:** 25 kts **Dim:** 13.0 × 3.8 × 1.2
**M:** 2 diesels; 280 hp **Cargo:** 12 passengers **Range:** 400/20 **Man:** 3 tot.

◆ **1 command ship**

G 15 Paraguassu (ex-*Guarapuava*)

**D:** 285 tons **S:** 12 kts **Dim:** 40.0 × 7.0 × 1.2
**M:** diesel; 1 prop **Range:** 2,500/10

Remarks: Former river transport ship, bought in 1971, refitted for the Mato Grosso Flotilla, and used as a river buoy tender and flagship.

◆ **1 river transport/despatch boat for the Mato Grosso Flotilla** Bldr: Estaliero SNBP, Mato Grosso

U 29 Piraim (In serv. 1982)

**D:** 73.3 tons (91.5 fl) **S:** 7 kts **Dim:** 25.0 × 5.5 × 0.97
**M:** 2 MWM diesels; 2 props; 400 hp **Range:** 700/7
**Electric:** 60 kVA **Man:** 2 officers, 13 men, 2 civil pilots

◆ **2 small service transports**

Tenente Fabio Tenente Raul

**D:** 55 tons **S:** 10 kts **Dim:** 20.28 × 5.1 × 1.2 **M:** diesel; 135 hp
**Cargo capacity:** 22 tons **Range:** 350

◆ **6 munitions lighters**

São Francisco Dos Santos (1964), Ubirajara Dos Santos (1968), Operatīo Luis Leal (1968), Miguel Dos Santos (1968), Aprendiz Lédio Conceição (1968), U 30 Almirante Hess (In serv. 27-10-83)

**D:** 88.2 tons (fl) **S:** 13.5 kts **Dim:** . . . × . . . × . . .

Remarks: Last three for torpedoes.

◆ **1 yard oiler** (purchased 1973)

R 11 Martins De Oliviera (ex-*Gastão Moutinho*)

**D:** 588 tons **S:** 10.3 kts **Dim:** 49.4 × 7.0 × 2.4

◆ **1 yard oiler:** Anita Garibaldi—no data

◆ **2 water tankers** (L: 1957)

R 43 Paulo Afonso R 42 Itapura

**D:** 485.3 tons **Dim:** 42.8 × 7.0 × 2.5 **M:** 1 diesel **Cargo:** 389 tons

◆ **3 miscellaneous small water tankers**

R 38 Doctor Gondim R 40 Guairia R 41 Iguaçu

**Iguaçu (R 41)** G. Gyssels, 1981

Remarks: R 38 is 485 tons (fl), 42.8 × 7.0 × 2.5, capacity: 380 tons.

◆ **5 Comandante Varella-class navigational aid tenders**

| | Bldr | Laid down | L | In serv. |
|---|---|---|---|---|
| H 18 Comandante Varella | Ast. Ilha das Cobras, Rio | 1-8-78 | 18-9-81 | 30-9-82 |
| H 19 Comandante Menhaes | Sao João de Nilo SY | . . . | . . . | . . . |
| H 20 Tenente Castelho | Sao João de Nilo SY | . . . | . . . | . . . |
| H . . . Tenente Boanerges | Sao João de Nilo SY | . . . | . . . | 1985 |
| H 26 Faroleiro Mario Seixax | . . . | . . . | . . . | . . . |

**Comandante Varella (H 18)** 1985

**BRAZIL** *(continued)*
**YARD AND SERVICE CRAFT** *(continued)*

**D:** 300 tons light (440 fl) **S:** 12 kts **Dim:** 37.51 (34.5 pp) × 8.60 × 2.56
**M:** 2 8-cyl. diesels; 2 props; 1,300 hp **Range:** 2,880/12 **Man:** 22 tot.

◆ **8 130-ton navigational aid tenders**

| | |
|---|---|
| H 13 Mestro João Dos Santos | H 30 Faroleiro Nascimento |
| H 24 Castelhanos | H . . . Cabo Branco |
| H 27 Faroleiro Areas | H . . . Cabo Callanhar |
| H 28 Faroleiro Santana | H . . . Cabo Frio |

Remarks: No data available. Also in use are H 21 *Sirius* and captured U.S. fishing poachers *Sea Horse* and *Condor*.

◆ **2 river hospital shops** Bldr: Naval Arsenal, Rio de Janeiro

| | Laid down | L | In serv. |
|---|---|---|---|
| U 18 Oswaldo Cruz | 1981 | 11-7-83 | 31-5-84 |
| U 19 Carlos Chagas | 1982 | 16-4-84 | 12-84 |

**D:** 500 tons (fl) **S:** 9 kts **Dim:** 47.18 (45.0 pp) × 8.45 × 1.75
**M:** 2 diesels; 2 props; 714 hp **Range:** 4,000/9 **Electric:** 420 kVA
**Man:** 4 officers, 21 men, 6 doctor/dentists, 15 health personnel

Remarks: Intended to serve in Amazon Flotilla with the similar *Roraima*-class gunboats. Helo deck for one AS 350. Two sick bays (6 total beds), operating theater, two clinics, dental laboratory, x-ray facilities.

◆ **3 Voga Picada-class training craft** Bldr: CARBRASMAR, Rio de Janeiro (All in serv. 17-1-84)

U 31 Voga Picada U 32 Rosca Fina U 33 Leva Ariba

**Rosca Fina (U 32)** 1985

**D:** 50 tons (fl) **S:** 11 kts **Dim:** 18.60 × 4.70 × 1.20
**M:** 1 MWM diesel; 1 prop; 650 hp **Range:** 200/11
**Man:** 5 crew + 11 trainees

◆ **3 Aspirante Nascimento-class training craft** Bldr: Embrassa Itajai, Santa Catarina (In serv. 1980–81)

U 10 Aspirante Nascimento U 11 Guardia Marinha Jansen
U 12 Guardia Marinha Brito

**Aspirante Nascimento (U 10)** 1985

**D:** 130 tons (fl) **S:** 10 kts **Dim:** 28.0 (25.0 pp) × 6.50 × 1.80
**A:** 1/12.7-mm mg **M:** 2 MWM D232V12 diesels; 2 props; 650 hp
**Range:** 700/10 **Man:** 2 officers, 10 men, 24 midshipmen

Remarks: Used for navigation and seamanship training at the Naval Academy. Also used for training are sail yacht *Cisne Branco* and ex-U.S. fishing boat *Night Hawk*.

**FLOATING DRY DOCKS**

◆ **1 U.S. AFDL 34 class** Bldr: V.P. Loftis (In serv. 10-44)

G 27 Cidade De Natal (ex-U.S. AFDL 39, ex-ARDC 6)

**Lift capacity:** 2,800 tons **Dim:** 118.6 × 25.6 × 2.84 (light)

Remarks: Loaned 10-11-66; purchased 28-12-77. Concrete construction. 17.7-m clear width inside, 105.2-m length on blocks.

◆ **1 U.S. AFDL 1 class** Bldr: Chicago Bridge & Iron (In serv. 12-43)

G 26 Almirante Jeronimo Goncalves (ex-*Goiaz,* ex-AFDL 4, ex-AFD 4)

**Lift capacity:** 1,000 tons **Dim:** 60.96 × 19.51 × 1.04 (light)

Remarks: Loaned 10-11-66; purchased 28-7-77. Steel construction. 13.7-m clear width inside, 56.4-m length on blocks.

◆ **1 U.S. ARD 12 class** Bldr: Pacific Bridge, Alameda, Cal. (In serv. 11-43)

G 25 Afonso Pena (ex-*Ceara,* ex-ARD 14)

**Lift capacity:** 3,500 tons **Dim:** 149.86 × 24.69 × 1.73 (light)

Remarks: Loaned 1963; purchased 28-12-77. Steel construction, pointed ship-type bow. 18.0-m clear with inside, 118.6-m length on blocks.

◆ **1 U.S. dry dock companion craft** Bldr: Bushell Lyons Ironwks, Tampa, Fla. (In serv. 22-3-45)

. . . (ex-YFN 903)

**D:** 170 tons (590 fl) **Dim:** 33.53 × 10.36 × 2.74

Remarks: Converted non-self-propelled cargo barge. Loaned 1963; purchased 28-12-77.

# BRUNEI DARUSSALEM

Personnel (1987): 388 (including 38 officers and "Special Combat Squadron" of 6 officers and 114 men for river duties)

Merchant Marine (1986): 5 ships—1,973 grt (1 tanker—382 grt)

FLOTILLA OF THE ROYAL BRUNEI ARMED FORCES

Note: Brunei plans to purchase three 75-m o.a. patrol boats and will also acquire eight 8-m craft for the Special Combat Squadron. Three 35-ton patrol boats listed in the previous edition do not appear to have ever been acquired.

◆ **3 guided-missile patrol boats** Bldr: Vosper Thornycroft, Singapore

| | L | In serv. |
|---|---|---|
| P 02 Waspada | 3-8-77 | 7-78 |
| P 03 Pejuang | 3-78 | 1979 |
| P 04 Seteria | 22-6-78 | 1979 |

**Waspada (P 02)** G. Arra, 1984

**Seteria (P 04)**—note open bridge G. Arra, 1984

**BRUNEI DARUSSALEM** *(continued)*
**FLOTILLA OF THE ROYAL BRUNEI ARMED FORCES** *(continued)*

**D:** 150 tons (fl) **S:** 32 kts **Dim:** 36.88 (33.53 pp) × 7.16 × 1.8
**A:** 2/MM 38 Exocet SSM—2/30-mm AA (II × 1)—4/7.62-mm mg (II × 2)
**Electron Equipt:** Radar: 1/Decca AC 1229—EW: Decca RDL intercept
**M:** 2 MTU 20V538 TB91 diesels; 2 props; 9,000 hp (7,500 sust.)
**Fuel:** 16 tons **Range:** 1,200/14 **Man:** 4 officers, 20 men

REMARKS: P 02 has enclosed upper bridge (open on other two) and facilities for training. All have Sperry Sea Archer fire-control system and two 50-mm rocket-flare launchers. The 30-mm mount is BMARC/Oerlikon GCM-BO1. Modernizing with new EW suite, twin mg; planned 2-m stretch canceled.

◆ **3 Periwa-class patrol craft**

| | Bldr | L | In serv. |
|---|---|---|---|
| P 14 PERIWA | Vosper, Singapore | 5-74 | 9-9-74 |
| P 15 PEMBURU | Vosper, Singapore | 30-1-75 | 17-6-75 |
| P 16 PENYARANG | Vosper, Singapore | 20-3-75 | 24-6-75 |

**Periwa (P 14)** 1974

**D:** 30 tons (38.5 fl) **S:** 32 kts **Dim:** 21.7 × 6.1 × 1.2
**A:** 2/20-mm AA (I × 2)—2/7.62-mm mg
**Electron Equipt:** Radar: Decca RM 916 (P 14, 15: Decca 1216A)
**M:** 2 MTU 12V331 TC81 diesels; 2,700 hp **Range:** 600/20; 1,000/16

◆ **3 Bendahara-class river patrol craft**

P 21 BENDAHARA P 23 KEMAINDERA P 22 MAHARAJALELA

**D:** 10 tons (fl) **S:** 20 kts **Dim:** 14.1 × 3.6 × 0.9
**A:** 2/7.62-mm mg **Electron Equipt:** Radar: Decca RM 616
**M:** 2 6-71 G.M. diesels; 334 hp **Range:** 200/18 **Man:** 6 tot.

◆ **2 Loadmaster-class landing craft** Bldr: Cheverton, Cowes, U.K.

L 31 DAMUAN (5-76) L 32 PUNI (2-77)

**D:** 64.3 tons (light) **S:** 8.5 kts **Dim:** 22.86 × 6.1 × 1.07
**Electron Equipt:** Radar: Decca RM 1216
**M:** 2 G.M. 6-71 diesels; 2 props; 348 hp **Cargo:** 30 tons
**Range:** 300/8.5; 1,000/6 **Man:** 8 tot.

REMARKS: L 31: 19.8 m overall, 60 tons light.

◆ **3 FPB 512-class landing craft** Bldr: Rotork, U.K.

S 24 (In serv. 11-80) S 25 (In serv. 5-81) S 26 (In serv. 5-81)

**D:** 8.8 tons (fl) **S:** 27 kts **Dim:** 12.7 × 3.2 × . . . **A:** 3/7.62-mm mg (I × 3)
**Electron Equipt:** Radar: 1/Decca 060 **Range:** 100/12
**M:** 2 Ford Mermaid diesels; 2 Castoldi waterjets; 430 hp **Man:** 3 tot.

REMARKS: Glass-reinforced plastic hulls, bow ramps. For patrol and transport duties.

◆ **25 small armed river craft for the Special Combat Squadron**

**A:** 1/7.62-mm mg **M:** 100 hp

◆ **3 support tenders** Bldr: Cheverton, Cowes, U.K. (In serv. 1982)

BURONG NURI N . . .

**D:** 23 tons (fl) **S:** 12 kts **Dim:** 17.0 × 4.3 × . . .
**M:** 2 G.M. diesels, 2 props; 400 hp

REMARKS: Used as tugs, target tugs, diving tenders, or for anti-pollution duties. Glass-reinforced plastic construction.

MARINE POLICE

◆ **7 14.5-m patrol craft** Bldr: Singapore SB & Eng. (In serv. 6-87 to 12-87)

**D:** 20 tons (fl) **S:** 30 kts **Dim:** 14.54 × 4.23 × 1.20 (props)
**A:** 1/7.62-mm mg **Electron equipt:** Radar: 1/. . . nav.
**M:** 2 M.A.N. D 2840 diesels; 2 props; 1,270 hp
**Range:** 310/22 **Fuel:** 1,800 litres **Man:** 7 tot.

REMARKS: Aluminum construction craft similar to Singapore Marine Police Force's PT 1 class. Ordered 28-10-86 for delivery at one-month intervals from 6-87.

◆ **4 patrol craft** Bldr: Vosper Thornycroft, Singapore, 1978–80

TENANG ABADI N . . . . . . . N . . . . . . .

**D:** 14 tons (fl) **S:** 28 kts **Dim:** 18.0 × 4.88 × 0.79
**A:** machine guns **M:** 2 MTU diesels; 2 water jets

REMARKS: Glass-reinforced plastic hulls. The second pair was ordered early in 1979.

# BULGARIA

**People's Republic of Bulgaria**

PERSONNEL (1987): approx. 8,500 men, including 2,200 coast defense troops

MERCHANT MARINE (1986): 197 ships—1,282,962 grt (tankers: 18—311,735 grt)

NAVAL AVIATION: Up to six Mi-14 Haze A, land-based ASW helicopters may be in service.

## SUBMARINES

◆ **4 Soviet Romeo class**

13 SLAVA 14 POBIEDA . . . N . . . . . . N . . .

**D:** 1,330/1,700 tons **S:** 15.5/13 kts **Dim:** 77.0 × 6.7 × 4.9
**A:** 8/533-mm TT (6 fwd, 2 aft)—14 torpedoes or 24 mines
**Electron Equipt:** Radar: 1/Snoop Plate—Sonar: MF active; passive array
**M:** 2/2,000-hp diesels; electric drive; 3,000 hp
**Range:** 7,000/5 (snorkel)
**Endurance:** 45 days
**Man:** 60 tot.

REMARKS: First pair, transferred 1971-72, replaced two Whiskey class with same names. Third unit transferred 1985, fourth in 1986. Can dive to 300 meters.

## FRIGATES

◆ **3 Soviet Riga class**—Transferred 1957, 1958, and 11-85

12 SMELY 13 BODRY 16 DRUZKI (ex-*Kobchik*)

**D:** 1,260 tons (1,480 fl) **S:** 30 kts **Dim:** 91.0 × 10.2 × 3.2 (4.4 sonar)
**A:** 3/100-mm DP—3/533-mm TT (III × 1)—2/RBU-1200 ASW RL (V × 2)—1/MBU-600 Hedgehog
**Electron Equipt:** Radar: 1/Slim Net, 1/Neptune, 1/Sun Visor—IFF: 2/Square Head, 1/High Pole
Sonar: 1/MF hull-mounted—EW: 2/Watch Dog intercept
**M:** 2 sets GT; 2 props; 20,000 hp
**Boilers:** 2; 27 kg/cm², 360°C
**Range:** 550/28; 2,000/13 **Electric:** 450 kw
**Fuel:** 230 tons **Man:** 180 tot.

REMARKS: Third ship transferred 1986; was at Varna 8-86, probably has more modern equipment, including 4/25-mm AA (II × 2).

## CORVETTES

◆ **3 Soviet Poti class**—Transferred 12-75 (In serv. 1961–68)

41 N . . . 42 N . . . 43 N . . .

**D:** 400 tons (fl) **S:** 38 kts **Dim:** 59.4 × 7.9 × 2.0 (mean hull)
**A:** 2/57-mm AA (II × 1)—2/RBU-6000 rocket launchers—4/400-mm ASW TT
**Electron Equipt:** Radar: 1/Spin Trough, 1/Strut Curve, 1/Muff Cob
IFF: 2/Square Head, 1/High Pole B
Sonar: 1 high frequency—EW: 2 Watch Dog
**M:** CODAG: 2 M503A diesels of 4,000 hp each plus 2 gas turbines of 20,000 hp each; 2 props plus waterjet thrust
**Range:** 520/37; 4,500/10
**Man:** 50 tot.

REMARKS: One is named *Khabri.*

## GUIDED-MISSILE, PATROL, AND TORPEDO BOATS

◆ **6 Soviet Osa-II-class guided-missile patrol boats**—Transferred 1978, 1982, . . .

**D:** 190 tons (240 fl) **S:** 35 kts **Dim:** 38.6 × 7.6 × 2.0 mean
**A:** 4/SS-N-2B Styx—4/30-mm AA (II × 2)
**Man:** 30 tot.

BULGARIA *(continued)*
GUIDED-MISSILE, PATROL, AND TORPEDO BOATS *(continued)*

**Electron Equipt:** Radar: 1/Square Tie, 1/Drum Tilt—IFF: 2/Square Head, 1/High Pole B
**M:** 3 Type M504 diesels; 3 props; 15,000 hp **Range:** 500/34; 750/25

◆ **4 Soviet Osa-I-class guided-missile patrol boats**—Transferred 1970–71.

**D:** 175 tons (215 fl) **S:** 36 kts **Dim:** 38.6 × 7.6 × 1.8
**A:** 4/SS-N-2A Styx—4/30-mm (II × 2) **Man:** 30 tot.
**Electron Equipt:** Radar: 1/Square Tie, 1/Drum Tilt—IFF: 2/Square Head, 1/High Pole B
**M:** 3 Type M503A diesels; 3 props; 12,000 hp **Range:** 500/34; 750/25

◆ **6 Soviet Shershen-class torpedo boats**—Transferred 1970

**D:** 150 tons (170 fl) **S:** 45 kts **Dim:** 34.7 × 6.7 × 1.5
**A:** 4/533-mm TT—4/30-mm AA (II × 2) **Man:** 20 tot.
**Electron Equipt:** Radar: 1/Drum, 1/Drum Tilt
**M:** 3 Type M503A diesels; 3 props; 12,000 hp **Range:** 460/42; 850/30

NOTE: Six SO-1-class subchasers, transferred 1963, are no longer in service.

◆ **6 Soviet Zhuk-class patrol boats**—Transferred 1980–81

511–516

**D:** 60 tons (fl) **S:** 34 kts **Dim:** 24.0 × 5.0 × 1.8 (props)
**A:** 4/14.5-mm mg (II × 2) **Man:** 12 tot.
**M:** 2 Type M50F diesels; 2 props; 2,400 hp **Range:** 700/30; 1,100/15

### MINE WARFARE SHIPS

◆ **4 Soviet Sonya-class coastal minesweepers** Bldr: Petrozavodsk SY

**D:** 380 tons (450 fl) **S:** 15 kts **Dim:** 48.8 × 8.8 × 2.1
**A:** 2/30-mm AA (II × 1)—2/25-mm AA (II × 1)
**Electron Equipt:** Radar: 1/Spin Trough nav.
IFF: 1/High Pole, 2/Square Head
**M:** 2 diesels; 2 props; 2,400 hp **Range:** 1,600/14; 3,000/10
**Man:** 40 tot.

REMARKS: Wooden hull with plastic sheathing. Date of transfer uncertain, but were in service by 1986.

◆ **7 Soviet Vanya-class minesweepers**—Two transferred 1971–72, others recently

**D:** 220 tons (245 fl) **S:** 16 kts **Dim:** 40.2 × 7.9 × 1.7
**A:** 2/30-mm AA (II × 1)
**Electron Equipt:** Radar: 1/Don-2—IFF; 1/Square Head, 1/High Pole B
**M:** 2 diesels; 2 props; 2,200 hp **Range:** 10/2,400 **Man:** 30 tot.

◆ **4 Soviet Yevgenya-class inshore minesweepers**—Transferred 1977–. . .

**D:** 80 tons (90 fl) **S:** 11 kts **Dim:** 26.2 × 6.1 × 1.5 **A:** 2/14.5-mm AA (II × 1)
**Electron Equipt:** Radar: 1/Spin Trough—IFF: 1/High Pole B
**M:** 2 diesels; 2 props; 600 hp **Range:** 300/10 **Man:** 12 tot.

REMARKS: Plastic hull. Equipped with towed television minehunting and marking system effective to 30-meter depths. Probably replaced PO 2 class. Pendant numbers sighted include 51 and 52.

NOTE: Two T-43-class minesweepers, transferred 1953, have been stricken.

### AMPHIBIOUS WARFARE SHIPS

◆ **23 Soviet Vydra-class landing craft**—Transferred 1970–79

**D:** 600 fl **S:** 11 kts **Dim:** 54.9 × 7.6 × 2.0
**Electron Equipt:** Radar: 1/Spin Trough **M:** 2 diesels; 2 props; 1,040 hp
**Range:** 2,700/10 **Cargo:** 220 tons

### AUXILIARIES AND SERVICE CRAFT

◆ **1 Mesar-class replenishment oiler** Bldr: Bulgaria (In serv. 1980)

11 DIMITRI A. DIMITROV

**Dimitri A. Dimitrov** 6-80

**D:** 3,500 (fl) **S:** 20 kts **Dim:** 97.5 × 13.2 × 5.0
**A:** 4/30-mm AA (II × 2) **M:** 2 diesels; 2 props; 12,000 hp

REMARKS: Deployed to Mediterranean 1980 with the two Rigas. Over-the-stern underway refueling; also has dry stores cargo. Unusually fine hull lines for an oiler.

◆ **1 Soviet Moma-class survey ship/buoy tender** Bldr: Poland (1977)

401 ADMIRAL BRANIMIR ORMANOV

**D:** 1,260 tons (1,540 fl) **S:** 17 kts **Dim:** 73.3 × 10.8 × 3.8
**Electron Equipt:** Radar: 2/Don-2—IFF: 1/High Pole A
**M:** 2 Sgoda-Sulzer 6 TD 48 diesels; 2 CP props; 3,600 hp
**Endurance:** 35 days **Range:** 8,700/11 **Man:** 56 tot.

◆ **1 East German Type-700 salvage tug**—(In serv. 4-64)

JUPITER

**D:** 700 tons (792 fl) **S:** 13 kts **Dim:** 44.7 × 10.7 × 3.9
**M:** 2 Type 12 KVD 21 diesels, electric drive; 2 props; 1,680 hp
**Range:** 4,000/12 **Man:** 39 tot.

◆ **1 inshore survey craft** (In serv. 1973)

GENERAL VLADIMIR ZAIMOV—**D:** 600 tons (fl), 48.0 m o.a., 12 kts.

REMARKS: A craft named *Kiril Khalachev* is also in use.

◆ **1 small degaussing tender**—No. 317

◆ **4 Type 024 yard oilers** (In serv. 1956)

**D:** 450 tons (fl) **S:** 9 kts **Dim:** 46.0 × 6.1 × 2.5

◆ **2 small tugs**

◆ **2 diving tenders**

◆ **6 torpedo retrievers**

◆ **6 barracks barges**

FRONTIER POLICE

The Bulgarian Frontier Police operate 12 ex-naval PO 2-class launches and two 25-knot patrol craft with a range of 350 n.m.

# BURMA

**The Socialist Republic of the Union of Burma**

PERSONNEL: approx. 7,000, including reserves and 800 naval infantry

MERCHANT MARINE (1986): 106 ships—125,524 grt (tankers: 5—2,935 grt)

### CORVETTES

◆ **1 U.S. PCER 848 class** Bldr: Willamette Iron & Steel, Portland, Ore.

| | Laid down | L | In serv. |
|---|---|---|---|
| 41 YAN TAING AUNG (ex-*Farmington,* PCER 894) | 7-12-42 | 15-5-43 | 10-8-44 |

**D:** 640 tons (903 fl) **S:** 15 kts **Dim:** 56.24 (54.86 wl) × 10.08 × 2.87 (hull)
**A:** 1/76.2-mm DP Mk 26—6.40-mm AA (II × 3)—8/20-mm AA (II × 4)—1/Mk 10 Hedgehog—2/Mk 6 d.c. launcher—2/d.c. rack
**Electron Equipt:** Radar: 1/SPS-5
Sonar: 1/QCU-2
**M:** 2 G.M. 12-567A diesels; 2 props; 1,800 hp **Electric:** 240 kw
**Fuel:** 125 tons **Range:** 9,000/10 **Man:** 100 tot.

REMARKS: Transferred 18-6-55.

◆ **1 U.S. Admirable-class former fleet minesweeper** Bldr: Willamette Iron & Steel, Portland, Ore.

| | Laid down | L | In serv. |
|---|---|---|---|
| 42 YAN GYI AUNG (ex-*Creddock,* MSF 356) | 10-11-43 | 22-7-44 | 18-12-45 |

**D:** 650 tons (905 fl) **S:** 14 kts **Dim:** 56.24 (54.86) × 10.08 × 2.87 (hull)
**A:** 1/76.2-mm DP Mk 26—2/40-mm AA (II × 1)—4/20-mm AA (II × 2)—1/Mk 10 Hedgehog—2/Mk 6 d.c. launcher—2/d.c. rack
**Electron Equipt:** Radar: 1/SPS-5
Sonar: QCU-2
**M:** 2 Busch-Sulzer Type 539 diesels; 2 props; 1,710 hp
**Electric:** 280 kw **Fuel:** 140 tons **Range:** 9,300/10 **Man:** 100 tot.

REMARKS: Minesweeping gear removed prior to transfer 21-3-67.

### PATROL BOATS

◆ **2 (+2) PGM 412 class** Bldr: Burma Naval Dockyard, Rangoon

PGM 412 (In serv. 1983) PGM . . . (In serv. 1984) PGM . . . PGM . . .

**PATROL BOATS** *(continued)*

**D:** 128 tons (fl) **S:** 16 kts **Dim:** 33.5 × 6.7 × 2.0
**A:** 2/40-mm AA (I × 2) **Range:** 1,400/14 **Man:** 17 tot.
**M:** 2 Deutz SBA 16MB216 LLKR diesels; 2 props; 2,720 hp

◆ **6 U.S. PGM 43 class** Bldrs: 401–404: Marinette Marine, Marinette, Wisc.; 405, 406: Peterson Bldrs, Sturgeon Bay, Wisc.

| | In serv. | | In serv. |
|---|---|---|---|
| 401 (ex-PGM 43) | 8-59 | 404 (ex-PGM 46) | 9-59 |
| 402 (ex-PGM 44) | 8-59 | 405 (ex-PGM 51) | 6-61 |
| 403 (ex-PGM 45) | 9-59 | 406 (ex-PGM 52) | 6-61 |

**D:** 100 tons (141 fl) **S:** 17 kts **Dim:** 30.81 × 6.45 × 2.30
**A:** 1/40-mm AA—4/20-mm AA (II × 2)—2 mg (I × 2)
**Electron Equipt:** Radar: EDO 320 (405, 406: Raytheon 1500)
**M:** 8 G.M. 6-71 diesels; 2 props; 2,040 hp **Fuel:** 16 tons
**Range:** 1,000/16 **Man:** 17 tot.

**RIVERINE PATROL VESSELS**

◆ **2 improved 301 class** Bldr: Similak, Burma (In serv. 1967)

Y 311 Y 312

**D:** 250 tons **S:** 14 kts **Dim:** 37.0 × 7.3 × 1.1
**A:** 2/40-mm AA (I × 2)—2/20-mm AA (I × 2)
**M:** 2 Mercedes-Benz diesels; 2 props; 1,000 hp

◆ **2 Nawarat class** Bldr: Dawbon DY, Rangoon (In serv. 1961)

Nawarat Nagakyay

**Nawarat**

**D:** 400 tons (450 fl) **S:** 12 kts **Dim:** 49.7 × 8.23 × . . .
**A:** 2/25-pounder guns (Army ordinance)—2/40-mm AA
**M:** 2 Paxman-Ricardo diesels; 2 props; 1,160 hp **Man:** 43 tot.

◆ **10 Y 301 class** Bldr: Uljanik, Pula, Yugoslavia (In serv. 1957–60)

Y 301–Y 310

**Y 301 class**

**D:** 120 tons **S:** 13 kts **Dim:** 32.0 × 7.25 × 0.8
**A:** 2/40-mm AA (I × 2)—2/20-mm AA (I × 2)
**M:** 2 Mercedes-Benz diesels; 2 props; 1,100 hp **Man:** 29 tot.

◆ **6 U.S. PBR Mk II-class patrol craft** Bldr: Uniflite, Bellingham, Washington (In serv. 1978)

PBR 211–216

**D:** 8.9 tons (fl) **S:** 24 kts **Dim:** 9.73 × 3.53 × 0.81
**A:** 3/12.7-mm mg (II × 1, I × 1)—1/60-mm mortar
**Electron Equipt:** Radar: 1/Raytheon 1900
**M:** 2 G.M. GV53N diesels; 2 water jets; 430 hp
**Range:** 150/23 **Man:** 4–5 tot.

**AUXILIARIES**

◆ **10 30- to 40-ton river boats** Bldr: Burma (In serv. 1951–52)

◆ **25 30- to 40-ton river boats** Bldr: Yugoslavia (In serv. 1965)

◆ **1 hydrographic survey ship** Bldr: Tito SY, Belgrade, Yugoslavia

Thu Tay Thi (In serv. 1965)

**D:** 1,100 tons (1,271 fl) **S:** 15 kts **Dim:** 62.21 (56.80 pp) × 11.00 × 3.60
**M:** 2 MB820 Db diesels; 2 props; 1,710 hp **Man:** 99 tot.

**Thu Tay Thi**

Remarks: Helicopter platform. Carries 2 inshore survey craft. Can be armed with 1/40-mm AA, 2/20-mm AA (I × 2).

◆ **1 inshore survey boat** Bldr: Netherlands (In serv. 1957)

Yay Bo **D:** 108 tons **Man:** 25 tot.

◆ **4 landing craft** Bldr: Yokohama Yacht, Japan (L: 3-69)

Aiyar Maung Aiyar Mai
Aiyar Min Thar Aiyar Min Tha Mee

**Aiyar Maung** Yokohama Yacht, 1969

**D:** 250 tons (fl) **S:** 10 kts **Dim:** 38.25 × 9.14 × 1.4
**M:** 2 Kubota diesels; 2 props; 560 hp **Cargo:** 100 tons **Man:** 10 tot.

◆ **2 landing craft** Bldr: Yokohama Yacht, Japan (In serv. 1978)

Sinde Htonbo

**D:** 220 tons (fl) **S:** 10 kts **Dim:** 29.5 × 6.72 × 1.4
**M:** 2 Kubota diesels; 2 props; 300 hp **Cargo:** 50 tons, 30 passengers

◆ **1 U.S. LCU 1610-class utility landing craft** Bldr: Southern SB, U.S.

Aiyar Lulin (ex-U.S. LCU 1626)

**D:** 190 tons (390 fl) **S:** 11 kts **Dim:** 41.0 × 9.0 × 2.0
**A:** 2/20-mm AA (I × 2) **M:** 4 G.M. 6-71 diesels; 2 props; 1,200 hp

Remarks: Used as a transport. Transferred on completion, 10-67.

◆ **1 diving and repair tender** Bldr: Japan (In serv. 1967)

Yan Long Aung **D:** 520 tons

Remarks: Formerly a torpedo retriever and torpedo boat tender.

PEOPLE'S PEARL AND FISHERIES MINISTRY

◆ **3 Danish "Osprey"-class fisheries protection ships**

| | Bldr | In serv. |
|---|---|---|
| In Daw | Frederikshavn SY | 5-80 |
| In Ma | Frederikshavn SY | 25-3-82 |
| In Ya | Frederikshavn SY | 25-3-82 |

**D:** 385 tons (505 fl) **S:** 20 kts
**Dim:** 49.95 (45.80 pp) × 10.5 (8.8 wl) × 2.75
**A:** 2/40-mm AA (II × 1)—1/20-mm AA **Electric:** 359 kVA
**M:** 2 Burmeister & Wain "Alpha" 16V23L-VO diesels; 2 CP props; 4,640 hp
**Range:** 4,500/16 **Man:** 15 or more tot.

Remarks: Sister to Danish *Havornen,* armed in Burma. Helicopter hangar and flight deck aft. Rescue launch recessed into inclined ramp at stern. Second pair arrived in Burma 24-5-82.

◆ **6 "Carpentaria"-class fisheries patrol boats** Bldr: deHavilland, Australia (1979–80)

**D:** 27 tons (fl) **S:** 27 kts **Dim:** 16.0 × 5.0 × 1.2
**A:** 2/7.62-mm mg (I × 2) **Electron Equipt:** Radar: 1/Decca 110
**M:** 2 G.M. 12V71 TI diesels; 2 props; 1,120 hp **Range:** 700/22
**Man:** 8 tot.

**BURMA** *(continued)*
**AUXILIARIES** *(continued)*

**Burmese "Carpentaria"-class patrol boat on trials** G. Gyssels, 1980

REMARKS: Ordered 12-78. Sisters in Indonesian and Solomon Islands forces. Aluminum construction.

◆ **3 105-ft. Commercial Cruiser-type patrol craft** Bldr: Swiftships, Morgan City, La.

421 (In serv. 31-3-79) 422 (In serv. 31-3-79)
423 (In serv. 28-9-79)

**D:** 103 tons (111 fl) **S:** 24 kts **Dim:** 31.5 × 7.2 × 2.1
**A:** . . . **Electron Equipt:** Radar: 1/. . . navigational
**M:** 2 diesels; 2 props; . . . hp **Range:** 1,200/18 **Man:** 16 tot.
**Fuel:** 21.6 tons

REMARKS: Aluminum construction. These are the craft incorrectly described in earlier editions as being of Vosper, Singapore construction, 32.3 m o.a.

# CAMEROON

## United Republic of Cameroon

PERSONNEL (1986): 667 total (38 officers, 214 petty officers, 415 enlistees), plus one company paracommandos.

MERCHANT MARINE (1986): 49 ships—76,650 grt

NAVAL AVIATION: Three Dornier 128-6 Maritime Patrol aircraft with MEL Marec radar.

### GUIDED-MISSILE PATROL BOATS

◆ **1 French P 48S class** Bldr: Soc. Française Constructions Navales (SFCN), Villeneuve-la-Garenne

| | Laid down | L | In serv. |
|---|---|---|---|
| BAKASSI | 12-81 | 22-10-82 | 8-10-83 |

**D:** 270 tons (308 fl) **S:** 26 kts **Dim:** 50.0 (47.0 pp) × 7.45 × 2.35
**A:** 8/MM 40 Exocet (IV × 2)—2/40-mm AA (I × 2)
**Electron Equipt:** Radar: 1/Decca TM1229C, 1/Decca RM1230

**Bakassi** SFCN, 1983

**M:** 2 SACM 195V16 CZSHR diesels; 2 props; 6,400 hp **Electric:** 280 kw
**Range:** 2,000/16 **Man:** 6 officers, 21 petty officers, 12 men

REMARKS: Ordered 14-12-80; enlarged version of P 48 class. Two CSEE Naja optronic sights for 40-mm AA, with RADOP ranging system using the navigation radars. Racal CANE 100 (Command and Navigation Equipment) fitted. To receive new radars.

### PATROL BOATS

◆ **0 (+3) 55-m patrol boats**—planned

REMARKS: Construction of three 55-meter patrol boats is planned, with Swiftships, Morgan City, Louisiana, U.S.A. apparently offering the best arrangement. Contracts were being finalized during 1987. They are expected to displace 400–500 tons full load and should be delivered in 1990.

◆ **1 French P 48 class** Bldr: SFCN, Villeneuve-la-Garenne

| | Laid down | L | In serv. |
|---|---|---|---|
| L'AUDACIEUX | 10-2-75 | 31-10-75 | 11-5-76 |

**L'Audacieux**

**D:** 250 tons (fl) **S:** 18.5 kts **Dim:** 47.5 (45.5 pp) × 7.1 × 2.5
**A:** 2/40-mm AA (I × 2) **M:** 2 MGO AGO V12 CZSHR diesels; 2 props; 4,200 hp
**Electric:** 100 kw **Range:** 2,000/15 **Man:** 4 officers, 30 men

◆ **2 Chinese Shanghai-II class**—Transferred 16-10-76

101 CAP CAMEROON 102 MAN O'WAR BAY

**D:** 122 tons (135 fl) **S:** 28.5 kts **Dim:** 38.78 × 5.41 × 1.55
**A:** 4/37-mm AA (II × 2)—4/25-mm AA (II × 2)
**Electron Equipt:** Radar: 1/Pot Head **Endurance:** 7 days
**M:** 2 M50F diesels of 1,200 hp, 2 12D6 diesels of 910 hp; 4 props; 4,220 hp
**Range:** 750/165 **Electric:** 39 kw **Man:** 25 tot.

REMARKS: Re-engining planned.

### PATROL CRAFT

◆ **20 38-ft. patrol boats** Bldr: Swiftships, Morgan City, La.

**D:** 11.7 tons (fl) **S:** 33 kts **Dim:** 11.58 × 3.81 × . . .
**A:** 2/12.7-mm mg (I × 2)—2/7.62-mm mg (I × 2)
**Electron Equipt:** Radar: 1/. . . navigational
**M:** 2 Stewart & Stevenson-G.M. 6V 92 MTA diesels; 2 props; 1,100 hp
**Range:** 216/20 **Man:** 4 tot.

REMARKS: A contract for thirty of these craft (10 for the Gendarmerie) was signed 29-8-86, with all deliveries to be made by end 1987. For use on the Chad River, based at Doula. Aluminum construction. Hull of 1.90-m moulded depth. The first 10 arrived in Cameroon 3-87, the second 10 in 9-87.

**38-foot patrol craft on trials** Swiftships, 9-86

**CAMEROON** *(continued)*
**PATROL CRAFT** *(continued)*

◆ **2 small coastal surveillance craft**

Le Valeureux Bldr: Chantiers Navals de l'Estérel, Nice (In serv. 19-11-70)

**D:** 45 tons **S:** 25 kts **Dim:** 26.8 × 4.97 × 1.55 **A:** 2/20-mm AA
**M:** 2 G.M. 12V71 diesels; 2 props; 960 hp **Man:** 1 officer, 8 men

Quartier Maître Alfred Motto Bldr: A.C.R.E., Libreville, Gabon (In serv. 12-11-73)

**Quartier Maître Alfred Motto** L. & L. Van Ginderen, 1986

**D:** 96 tons (fl) **S:** 15.5 kts **Dim:** 29.1 × 6.2 × 1.85 (aft)
**A:** removed **M:** 2 Baudouin diesels; 2 props; 1,290 hp
**Man:** 2 officers, 15 men

## AMPHIBIOUS WARFARE CRAFT

◆ **1 LCM** Bldr: Carena, Abidjan, Ivory Coast (In serv. 1973)

**D:** 57 tons (fl) **S:** 9 kts **Dim:** 17.5 × 4.28 × 1.3
**M:** 2 Baudouin diesels; 490 hp

◆ **5 LCVP-type landing craft** Bldr: A.C.R.E., Libreville, Gabon

Souellaba Indépendance Réunification Manoka Machtigal

**D:** 11 tons **S:** 10 kts

## SERVICE CRAFT

◆ **2 10-ton harbor launches**

Sanaga Bimbia

◆ **6 FAC 408-class Seatrucks** Bldr: Rotork Marine, Poole, U.K. (In serv. 1978)

**D:** 2 tons **S:** 10 to 35 kts **Dim:** 7.37 × 2.74 × . . .
**M:** 1 or 2 inboard/outboard motors

Remarks: For patrolling rivers and lagoons. Two similar 12-m craft were delivered 1-82 by Tanguy Marine, France, along with two 17-m "Seatrucks."

◆ **3 Raider-class landing craft** Bldr: NAPCO Intl., U.S.A. (In serv. 1987)

**D:** . . . **S:** 40 kts **Dim:** 7.0 × . . . × . . .
**A:** 2/12.7-mm mg (I × 2) **Range:** 200/. . .
**M:** 2 outboard engines; 2 props; 280 hp **Man:** 3

Remarks: Ordered 2-87. Use well-known "Boston Whaler" GRP hull. Thirty more are planned.

GENDARMERIE

◆ **10 38-ft. patrol boats** Bldr: Swiftships, Morgan City, La.

Remarks: For characteristics, see above under naval entry.

Note: Police forces also operate 12 Type 650 and 800 launches of 3.5 tons delivered 1977–1982 by Chantiers Plascoa, Cannes. Dim: 8.50 × 3.00 × 0.72.

**Plascoa launch Sanaga (PN 2)** L. & L. Van Ginderen, 1986

# CANADA

The Canadian Armed Forces are completely unified. There are six operational commands: Mobile Command, Maritime Command, Air Transport Command, Air Defense Command, Training Command, and Material Command. The Maritime Command is in charge of the naval ships, the ship-based aircraft, and all of the units of the former Maritime Air Command (RCAF). Its principal role is ASW, but it can also be called upon to transport men and equipment for the Mobile Command.

Personnel (1987): about 10,000 total active, plus 2,900 in the Naval Reserve, and 7,400 civil employees.

Merchant Marine (1986): 1,248 ships—3,160,043 grt (tankers: 48—260,192 grt)

Naval Aviation: Made up of ship-based ASW helicopters, maritime patrol aircraft, and ASW aircraft, formerly carrier-based but now maintained at land bases.

Primary strength as follows:

—31 ASW CH-124A Sea King helicopters (see U.S.A. section), armed with Mk 44 or Mk 46 torpedoes and AQS-13 sonar. Several are used in logistics service aboard the replenishment oilers. All based on the East Coast, at Shearwater, Nova Scotia, until 7-87, when 4 transferred to West Coast. Being fitted with Emerson *Calypso* acoustic processors. To be replaced by 28 to 51 new EH.101 helicopters in 1990s.

—18 CP-140 Aurora maritime patrol aircraft, based on the U.S. Navy's P-3 Orion. The first plane was delivered 28-5-80, with the remaining arriving by 3-81. The Canadian version of the plane is fitted not only for reconnaissance, ASW, and electronic warfare, but also for detecting atmospheric and maritime pollution and for analyzing oil spills at sea. It has a crew of twelve. The Aurora has the Orion's A-NEW system, based on the miniaturized Univac ASQ-114 computer, which can store 65,000 words of 30 bits and has a retrieval time of 4 microseconds. There are 36 launching chutes for dropping active and passive sonobuoys and racks for 120 reserve sonobuoys. Other principal systems are: 2ASN-84 inertial navigation computers; Doppler radar; tactical recorder flight-control director; tactical data link system: FLIR (Forward-Looking Infrared); SLAR (Side-Looking Airborne Radar) antennas; detectors for lasers; a low-light television pod. Six more may be acquired.

**CP-140 Aurora, low-visibility gray paint scheme** C.A.F., 1986

—15 CP-121 (CS-2F) Tracker former carrier-based ASW aircraft, now used as land-based maritime surveillance aircraft, with additional fuel in the former weapons bay. Omega navigation systems were added during 1979–80, and a wing-mounted camera pod is installed. Planned to modernize as "Turbo Trackers" with 2 Pratt Whitney PT6A-67R engines, new radar, MAD, IR sensors; prototype delivered 8-87. Twelve are based at Shearwater, Nova Scotia, while the 3 Pacific Coast units also perform ship target service duties, along with several CT-33A Silver Star jet trainers. Eight Canadian Challenger 600/601 corporate jets were ordered 1985 to supply naval and land forces with EW training. Three CH-113A Labrador helicopters (rehabilitated CH-76) entered service 1986 for SAR duties.

WEAPONS AND SYSTEMS

## A. MISSILES

◆ **Surface-to-air missiles.** The Canadian Navy has adopted the short-range surface-to-air NATO Sea Sparrow for its four *Iroquois*-class destroyers. The missile is designed to attack aircraft or missiles flying at a low altitude or at a transonic speed. Its characteristics are:

**Length:** 3.660 m **Diameter:** 0.200 m
**Wingspan:** .020 m **Weight:** 204 kg
**Speed:** Mach 3.5 **Practical antiaircraft range:** 8,000 to 10,000 m

The launching system on the *Iroquois* class, designed by Raytheon Canada, is made up of two loaders and two launchers. The launchers are fixed one to port and one to starboard, perpendicular to the axis of the ship. They are retractable, can be trained and elevated, and are housed in the structure forward of the bridge. Each launcher has four missiles ready to be fired. A new Raytheon vertical-launch system for Sea Sparrow underwent trials aboard *Huron* in 2-81 at Roosevelt Roads, Puerto

**WEAPONS AND SYSTEMS** *(continued)*

Rico, and will be used on the *Halifax* class. Vertically launched Standard SM-2MR will replace Sea Sparrow in the *Iroquois* class.

Canada is purchasing the U.S. Harpoon missile for use by CP-140 Aurora aircraft, submarines, and surface ships. In 1984, 34 RGM-84D shipboard versions were ordered.

## B. GUNS

The following guns are currently in use:

**57-mm Bofors SAK Mk 2.** Single mount, to be used on the *Halifax* class. See Swedish section for data.

**76.2-mm Mk 22.** Twin DP (U.S. Mk 34 mount) mounted behind a GRP spray shield.
**Length:** 50 calibers **Muzzle velocity:** 822 m/s
**Maximum firing rate:** 50 rounds per minute per barrel
**Arc of elevation:** 115° to +85°
**Maximum effective antiaircraft range:** 4,000 to 5,000 m
Fitted on the *St. Laurent, Restigouche, Mackenzie,* and *Annapolis* class of frigates.

**76.2-mm Mk 6.** Twin barrel, automatic (British model).
**Length:** 70 calibers. **Muzzle velocity:** . . . m/s. **Maximum firing rate:** 60 rounds per minute per barrel.
**Maximum effective antiaircraft range:** 5,000 m.
Installed forward on the *Restigouche* and *Mackenzie* classes of frigates.

**127-mm OTO-Melara** (*see* Italy section)
Installed on the *Iroquois*-class destroyers, to be replaced by the OTO Melara 76-mm DP gun.

## C. ASW WEAPONS

### ◆ Depth-charge and torpedo launchers

—British Mk 10 Limbo triple-barreled mortar on frigates.
—U.S. ASROC on 4 *Restigouche*-class frigates.
—U.S. Mk 32 ASW triple torpedo tubes on all destroyers and frigates.

### ◆ Torpedoes

—U.S. Mk 44 and 46 ASW torpedoes aboard ships, and on Sea King helicopters and maritime patrol aircraft.
—U.S. Mk 37 aboard submarines, in Northrop NT37C improved version.
—U.S. Mk 48 Mod. 4 on submarines; 48 ordered 1985

## D. ELECTRONICS

### ◆ Radars:

—SPS-12 long-range air search.
—SPS-49(v), U.S. (Raytheon) 2-D air-search radar on *Halifax* class.
—SPS-501 long-range air search (version of Dutch LWO-3) installed in *Iroquois*-class destroyers. Uses LWO-3 antenna, SPS-12 transmitter.
—SPS-503, Canadian-made radar using the Plessey AWS-4's antenna, for 8 modernized frigates.
—SPS-10 and Sperry Mk 2 navigation/surface search.
—SPQ-2D combination search (Italian radar) installed in the *Iroquois* class.
—Sea Giraffe HC 150, Ericsson surface search on the *Halifax* class.

### ◆ Sonars:

—SQS-501 for detection of submarines lying on the sea bottom.
—SQS-503 hull-mounted MF.
—SQS-504 towed MF, Type 503 transducer.
—SQS-505 hull-mounted LF installed in the *Iroquois* and *Halifax* classes.
—SQS-505 towed LF installed in the *Iroquois* class (SQA-502 hoist). SQS-505 TASP with digital acoustic processing and SHINPADS display tested in an *Iroquois*-class ship in 1984.
—SQR-501 CANTASS towed passive linear hydrophone array for the *Halifax* class; uses "wet end" of U.S. AN/SQR-18A system with Canadian receiver/processor.

## SUBMARINES

Note: What had originally been planned as a program for four diesel-electric submarines to replace the present *Oberon*-class in the mid-1990s, possibly employing some form of closed-cycle auxiliary propulsion, has now been vastly expanded into a program to construct from eight to twelve *nuclear*-powered submarines, to cost some $400–500 million (Can.) each. These ships would be intended to defend Canada's Arctic sovereignty. A firm decision will apparently not be made until 1990, which means that the present trio of diesel submarines will probably have to be operated into the next century.

### ◆ 3 British Oberon class

| | Bldr | Laid down | L | In serv. |
|---|---|---|---|---|
| SS 72 Ojibwa (ex-*Onyx*) | H.M. DY, Chatham | 27-9-62 | 29-2-64 | 23-9-65 |
| SS 73 Onandaga | H.M. DY, Chatham | 18-6-64 | 25-9-65 | 22-6-67 |
| SS 74 Okanagan | H.M. DY, Chatham | 25-3-65 | 17-9-66 | 22-6-68 |

**D:** 1,610/2,070/2,410 tons **Dim:** 17.5/15 kts
**Dim:** 89.92(87.45 pp) × 8.07 × 5.48
**A:** 8/533-mm TT (6 fwd, 2 aft)—22 NT37C torpedoes—see Remarks

**Okanagan (SS 74)** L. & L. Van Ginderen, 10-86

**Electron Equipt:** Radar: 1/1006
Sonar: British 2007, Krupp-Atlas CSU3-41, BGQ-501 Micropuffs
**M:** 2 Admiralty Standard Range 16VVS-AS21 diesels, diesel-electric drive; 2 props; 6,000 hp

Remarks: The *Ojibwa* was begun under the name of *Onyx* for the Royal Navy and transferred while still under construction. The living spaces have been modified for Canadian weather conditions. Modernized under "SOUP" (Submarine Operational Update Program), beginning in 1980 with SS 72, getting Singer-Librascope Mk 1 Mod. 0 fire-control system using Sperry UYK-20 computer and new sonar suit with the Krupp-Atlas CSU3-41 active-passive system for the passive array, and an active transducer in the sail replacing the original Type 187, 197, and 719 sets. The Type 2007 long-range passive search array was retained. Able to employ U.S. Mk 48 torpedoes and Sub-Harpoon missiles. SS 72 completed 6-82, SS 73 in 4-84, and SS 74 in 5-86. Two Thorn-EMI Pertel low light-level t.v. periscopes in each. The aft tubes can only be employed for NT37C torpedoes. To be replaced 1995–99.

## DESTROYERS

### ◆ 4 Iroquois DDH 280 class

| | Bldr | Laid down | L | In serv. |
|---|---|---|---|---|
| DDH 280 Iroquois | Marine Industries, Sorel | 15-1-69 | 28-11-70 | 29-7-72 |
| DDH 281 Huron | Marine Industries, Sorel | 15-1-69 | 3-4-71 | 16-12-72 |
| DDH 282 Athabascan | Davie S.B., Lauzon | 1-6-69 | 27-11-70 | 30-11-72 |
| DDH 283 Algonquin | Davie S.B., Lauzon | 1-9-69 | 23-4-71 | 30-9-73 |

**D:** 3,551 tons (4,200 fl) **S:** 30/29 kts
**Dim:** 128.92 (121.31 pp) × 15.24 × 4.42
**A:** 2/Canadian Sea Sparrow SAM syst. (IV × 2; 32 AIM-7E missiles)—1/127-mm OTO Melara DP—1/Mk 10 Limbo ASW mortar (III × 1)—6/324-mm Mk 32 TT (III × 2)—2/Sea King ASW helicopters.

**Algonquin (DDH 283)**—prior to modernization M. Louagie, 6-87

**Iroquois (DDH 280)**—with new URN-25 TACAN G. Gyssels, 3-85

**DESTROYERS** *(continued)*

**Huron (DDH 281)**—with CANEWS EW array L. & L. Van Ginderen, 9-86

**Electron Equipt:** Radar: 1/navigational, 1/SP-501, 1/SPQ-2D; 2/WM-22 dir.
Sonar: 1/SQS-505, 1/SQS-505(VDS), 1/SQS-501
EW: WLR-1, ULQ-6 jammer—1/6-rail flare and chaff RL—2/Knebworth/Corvus chaff RL (VIII × 2)—TACAN: URN-25

**M:** COGOG: 2 FT 4A2 Pratt & Whitney gas turbines, 25,000 hp each, 2 Solar Mk FT 12H gas turbines, 3,700 hp each; 2 five-bladed CP props; 50,000 hp

**Electric:** 2,750 kw **Range:** 4,500/20 **Man:** 27 officers, 258 men

Remarks: Two paired stacks, angled to avoid corrosion of the antennas by stack gases. Bear Trap positive-control helicopter landing system. Passive-tank anti-rolling system fitted to improve stability at low speeds. *Huron* tested the Raytheon vertical-launch Sea Sparrow SAM system in 2-81. U.S. WSC-3 SATCOMM capability added 1982; 2 OE-82 antennas. Have H.S.A. ASWDS computerized data display system. DDH 283 tested the AN/SAR-8 IRSTD (Infrared Search and Target Designation) system atop her pilothouse in 1984. *Huron* to West Coast 7-87.

Modernization Notes: These ships are being updated under the TRUMP (Tribal Update and Modernization Program) under a design prepared by Litton Systems Canada. DDH 283 began reconstruction 11-87, to complete 5-89; to follow with DDH 280, 282, 281, completing 1993 at Versatile Davie SB, Lauzon, Que. ASW systems are to be basically unchanged, except for removal of the Limbo mortar. The U.S. Mk 41 VLS (Vertical Launch System) for 32 Standard SM 2 Block II SAMs will replace the 127-mm forward, while an OTO Melara 76-mm DP gun will be installed in the former Sea Sparrow magazine area. A Mk 15 CIWS (Vulcan-Phalanx) will be placed atop the hangar, and ASW torpedo stowage and handling will be improved. The 76-mm gun and Standard missiles will be controlled by two H.S.A. STIR 1.8 fire-control illuminator/trackers. The LW-08 long-range air-search radar will be retained, supplemented by a DA-06 medium-range radar atop the mast. Harpoon anti-ship missiles are no longer planned to be carried. Plessey's Shield decoy RL (VI × 2) will replace Knebworth/Corvus, and the CANEWS EW system (with Ramses jammer) will replace WLR-1 (already done in DDH 281). The SHINPADS command and control system will be added, as will the U.S. SLQ-25 Nixie torpedo decoy.

The cruise turbines will be replaced by two G.M. Allison 570KF gas turbines, each generating 6,394 shp, and the twin stacks will be integrated into a single, larger structure; yet to be decided is whether the boost engines will be replaced with G.E. LM-2500 gas turbines. A new G.M. 1,000-kw diesel generator will be fitted. An inertial navigation system is planned. Ships to remain active to post-2004.

**Iroquois (DDH 280) after modernization** Litton Canada, 1985

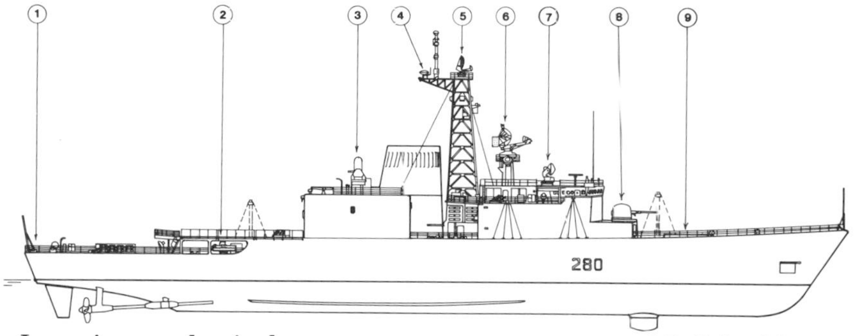


**Iroquois as modernized:** A.D. Baker III, 6-85
1. VDS housing 2. Triple Mk 32 ASW TT 3. Mk 15 CIWS 20-mm gatling AA
4. URN-25 TACAN 5. DA-08 radar 6. LW-08 long-range search radar
7. 2 STIR 1.8 fire-control tracker/illuminator radars
8. 76-mm OTO Melara Compact DP 9. Standard SM-2 VLS launcher Ex-41

**FRIGATES**

◆ **0 (+6 + 6) Halifax, or "City" class**

| | Bldrs | Laid down | L | In serv. |
|---|---|---|---|---|
| FFH 330 Halifax | St. Johns SB, New Brunswick | 8-85 | ... | 11-89 |
| FFH 331 Vancouver | Marine Ind., Sorel, Que. | ... | ... | 9-90 |
| FFH 332 Ville de Quebec | St. Johns SB, New Brunswick | 4-87 | ... | 9-90 |
| FFH 333 Toronto | Marine Ind., Sorel, Que.* | ... | ... | 3-91 |
| FFH 334 Regina | St. Johns SB, New Brunswick, Que. | ... | ... | 3-91 |
| FFH 335 Calgary | Marine Ind., Sorel, Que.* | ... | ... | 3-92 |

* To fit out at Versatile Vickers, Montreal

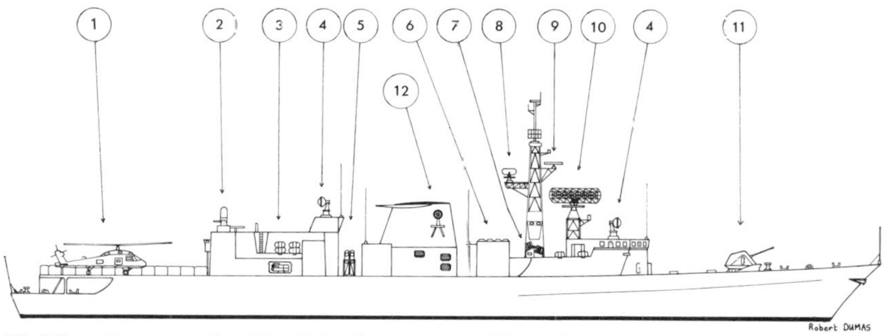


**Halifax class** 1. Sea Hawk helicopter 2. Mk 15 CIWS 3. helicopter hangar
4. STIR weapon-control radars 5. Harpoon antiship missiles (IV × 2)
6. Sea Sparrow vertical launchers 7. Shield decoy RL 8. Sea Giraffe radar
9. 1629C navigational radar 10. SPS-49 long-range air-search radar
11. 57-mm SAK Mk 2 DP mount 12. OE-82 SATCOMM antennas

**D:** 3,866 tons (4,254 fl) **S:** 29.2 kts (27 sust.)

**Dim:** 135.5(124.50 pp) × 16.40(14.80 wl) × 4.64(5.85 max.)

**A:** 8/Harpoon SSM (IV × 2)—Sea Sparrow VLS syst. (16 ready, plus 12 reload)—1/57-mm Bofors SAK Mk 2 DP—1/20-mm Mk 15 CIWS—6/324-mm Mk 32 ASW TT(III × 2)—1/CH-124A helicopter

**Electron Equipt:** Radar: 1/Raytheon 1629C nav., 1/Ericsson Sea Giraffe 150HC search, 1/SPS-49 (V) long-range air search, 2 H.S.A. STIR 1.8 f.c.
Sonar: SQS-510 hull-mounted, SQR-501 CANTASS towed array
EW: Ramses jammer, M.E.L. CANEWS intercept, 4/Shield RL (VI × 4)—TACAN: URN-25

**M:** CODOG: 2 G.E. LM-2500 gas turbines/1 S.E.M.T.-Pielstick 20PA6-V280-BTC diesel (11,780 hp); 2 CP props; 50,000 hp

**Electric:** 4,880 kVA (4 MWM TBO-602 V-16K diesel generator sets)

**Fuel:** 479 tons **Range:** 4,500/20; 5,700/15

**Man:** 180 tot. (225 accommodations)

Remarks: First six ordered 29-7-83 from consortium of St. Johns Shipbuilding and Dry Dock, Paramax Electronics, and Sperry. Announced 19-11-84 that a second group of six are to be built. FFH 330 was to have been laid down 12-84, but program (first announced 22-12-77!) continues to experience delays. Work suspended 3-86 to 5-86 when inferior steels discovered. Six more (first to be named *Montreal*) authorized 1986, with contract to be let late 1987.

Will have Bear Trap helicopter recovery system. Fin stabilizers. The U.S./Canadian AN/SAR-8 IRSTD (Infrared Search and Target Designation) system is to be carried. SQR-501 CANTASS towed tactical passive hydrophone system uses the "wet end" of the U.S. SQR-18A TACTASS. Will have AN/SLQ-25 Nixie towed torpedo decoys and a bubbler noise-reduction system. The Signaal SHINPADS (Shipboard Integrated Processing And Display System) data system will be fitted, as will the UYS-503 sonobuoy processor.

**FRIGATES** *(continued)*

**Halifax (FFH 330)**—official model C.A.F., 1984

**Halifax (FFH 330)**—artist's rendering 1986

NOTE: A "Destroyer Life Extension Program" (DELEX) was approved 7-8-80. All 16 older frigates are receiving: ADLIPS (Automated Data Link Processing System), hull and machinery overhaul and repair, new underwater telephones, the Mk 12 IFF system, secure UHF communications, and a new navigational radar. Additional features are being added to the various ships in proportion to their future value, with $22 million per ship being spent on the 1964-vintage *Annapolis* class, down to only $5 million for the *St. Laurent*-class ships, which, as the oldest, are the first to be worked on. Individual class DELEX features are listed in the Remarks sections.

◆ **2 Annapolis class**

| | Bldr | Laid down | L | In serv. |
|---|---|---|---|---|
| DDE 265 ANNAPOLIS | Halifax Shipyards Ltd | 7-60 | 27-4-63 | 19-12-64 |
| DDE 266 NIPIGON | Marine Industries, Sorel | 4-60 | 10-12-61 | 30-5-64 |

**Annapolis (DDE 265)**—note new stern shape L. & L. Van Ginderen, 9-87

**D:** 2,463 tons (3,063 fl) **S:** 28 kts **Dim:** 113.1 × 12.8 × 4.4
**A:** 2/76.2-mm DP Mk 33 (II × 1)—6/324-mm ASW TT (III × 2) Mk 32—1/CH-124A Sea King helicopter
**Electron Equipt:** Radar: 1/nav., 1/SPS-503, 1/SPS-10D, 1/Mk 60 fire control
Sonar: SQS-505(V), DDE 265 also: SQR-501 CANTASS
EW: CANEWS intercept, 4/Mk 36 SRBOC RL(VI × 4)—TACAN: URN-25
**M:** 2 sets English-Electric GT; 2 props; 30,000 hp
**Boilers:** 2 Babcock & Wilcox; 43.3 kg/cm², 454°C **Electric:** 1,400 kw
**Range:** 4,750/14 **Man:** 18 officers, 210 men

REMARKS: Have Litton CCS-280 data system. Under DELEX received SPS-503 (CMR-1820) air-search radar with Plessey AWS-4 antenna, new EW system, fire-control syst., and navigational radar; SQS-503 sonar replaced by SQS-505. SLQ-25 Nixie torpedo decoys added. DDE 266, refitted 27-6-83 to 22-8-85, will get SQR-50 CANTASS in 1988 in place of SQS-504 VDS and SQS-510 in lieu of SQS-505. SPS-503's antenna not a success, will be replaced. DDE 265 DELEX refit 8-85 to 8-86, received CANEWS, lengthened stern for SQR-501. Mk 60 f.c. radar is a digital version of the U.S. GFCS Mk 69. Both have two Litton ADLIPS data displays. New masts in both. Both on East Coast. To remain in service until 1994–96.

◆ **4 Mackenzie-class frigates**

| | Bldr | Laid down | L | In serv. |
|---|---|---|---|---|
| DDE 261 MACKENZIE | Canadian-Vickers | 15-12-58 | 25-5-61 | 6-10-62 |
| DDE 262 SASKATCHEWAN | Victoria Machinery | 16-7-59 | 1-2-61 | 16-2-63 |
| DDE 263 YUKON | Burrard, Vancouver | 25-10-59 | 27-7-61 | 25-5-63 |
| DDE 264 QU'APPELLE | Davie S.B., Lauzon | 14-1-60 | 2-5-62 | 14-19-63 |

**Saskatchewan (DDE 262)** L. & L. Van Ginderen, 10-86

**Yukon (DDE 263)** R.A.N., 9-86

**D:** 2,380 tons (2,890 fl) **S:** 28 kts **Dim:** 111.5 × 12.8 × 4.1
**A:** 4/76.2-mm DP (II × 2—see remarks)—2/Mk 10 Limbo mortars (III × 2)—6/324-mm ASW TT Mk 32 (III × 2)
**Electron Equipt:** Radar: 1/SPS-12, 1/SPS-10, 1/Sperry Mk 2, 1/SPG-48, 1/SPG-34
Sonar: 1/SQS-505—EW: WLR-1
**M:** 2 sets English-Electric GT; 2 props; 30,000 hp
**Boilers:** 2 Babcock & Wilcox; 43 kg/cm², 454°C **Range:** 4,750/14
**Man:** 11 officers, 199 men

REMARKS: All employed in the Pacific. U.S. Mk 69 gunfire control forward, Mk 63 aft. DDE 264 has had British Mk 6, 76.2-mm/70-cal. gun mount forward replaced by U.S. Mk 34, 76.2-mm/50-cal. mount, which is mounted aft on all. Under DELEX received SQS-505 in place of SQS-503, a new navigational radar in place of Mk 2, 2 ADLIPS displays, LINK 11, and the SLQ-25 Nixie torpedo decoy. Will remain in service until 1990-93. Refit of DDE 264 completed 1-84; DDE 263 completed 1-85, DDE 262 in 2-86 and DDE 261 in 1987, all by Burrard Yarrows, Victoria.

◆ **4 (+3 reserve) modified Restigouche-class ASW frigates**

4 active:

| | Bldr | Laid down | L | In serv. |
|---|---|---|---|---|
| DDE 236 GATINEAU | Davie SB, Lauzon | 30-4-53 | 3-6-57 | 17-2-59 |
| DDE 257 RESTIGOUCHE | Canadian-Vickers | 15-7-53 | 22-11-54 | 7-6-58 |
| DDE 258 KOOTENAY | Burrard, Vancouver | 21-8-52 | 15-6-54 | 7-3-59 |
| DDE 259 TERRA NOVA | Victoria Machinery | 14-11-52 | 21-6-55 | 6-6-59 |

3 reserve, unmodified:

| | Bldr | Laid down | L | In serv. |
|---|---|---|---|---|
| DDE 235 CHAUDIÈRE | Halifax SY | 30-7-53 | 13-11-57 | 14-1-59 |
| DDE 256 ST. CROIX | Marine Ind., Sorel | 15-10-54 | 17-11-57 | 4-10-58 |
| DDE 260 COLUMBIA | Burrard, Vancouver | 11-6-53 | 1-11-56 | 7-11-59 |

**FRIGATES** *(continued)*

**St. Croix (DDE 256)**—in reserve as engineering training hulk. A: 4/76.2-mm DP (II × 2), 2 LIMBO L. & L. Van Ginderen, 11-86

**Kootenay (DDE 258)**—post-DELEX modernization G. Arra, 1983

**D:** 2,390 tons (2,900 fl) **S:** 28 kts **Dim:** 113.1 × 12.8 × 4.3
**A:** 2/76.2-mm DP Mk 6 (II × 1) fwd—1/ASROC syst. (VIII × 1, 8 reloads)—1/Mk 10 Limbo mortar (III × 1)—6/324-mm ASW TT (III × 2)
**Electron Equipt:** Radar: 1/nav., 1/SPS-503, 1/SPS-10D, 1/Mk 60 f.c.
Sonar: 1/SQS-501, 1/SQS-503, 1/SQS-505 (VDS)
EW: CANEWS passive, ULQ-6 jammer, 4 Mk 36 SRBOC RL (VI × 4)
**M:** 2 sets English-Electric GT; 2 props; 30,000 hp
**Boilers:** 2 Babcock & Wilcox, 43.3 kg/cm², 454°C **Electric:** 1,800 kw
**Range:** 4,750/14 **Man:** 13 officers, 201 men

REMARKS: All on Pacific Coast except DDE 236, transferred east 7-87. Reconstruction with lengthened hull for VDS and ASROC in place of aft 76.2-mm mount and one Limbo completed 1968–73. Unmodified sisters *Chaudière, Columbia,* and *St. Croix* were reduced to disposal reserve in 1974; *Columbia* remains in use as a stationary training ship at Esquimault, and *St. Croix* refitted 1986 as engineering training ship at Halifax. DDE 258 completed DELEX modernization 11-83, DDE 259 in 1984. SPS-503 radar replaced SPS-12, a new navigational radar was added, U.S. WSC-3 SATCOMM gear (two OE-82 antennas) was added, Mk 32 ASW TT replaced the Knebworth/Corvus chaff RL on the upper deck aft, and four Mk 137 launchers for the U.S. Mk 36 SRBOC chaff system replaced the flare rocket launcher atop the ASROC reload magazine. The GFCS was updated to GFCS Mk 60, data link capability improved, SLQ-25 Nixie torpedo decoys added, and a 400-kw generator was added. Data in listing are for ships post-DELEX; to be retained to 1994–96.

◆ **6 St. Laurent-class helicopter frigates** (3 in reserve 1987*)

| | Bldr | Laid down | L | In serv. |
|---|---|---|---|---|
| DDE 206 SAGUENAY* | Halifax Shipyards | 4-4-51 | 30-7-53 | 15-12-56 |
| DDE 207 SKEENA | Burrard, Vancouver | 1-6-51 | 19-8-52 | 30-3-57 |
| DDE 229 OTTAWA | Canadian-Vickers | 8-6-51 | 29-4-53 | 10-11-56 |
| DDE 230 MARGAREE* | Halifax Shipyards | 12-9-51 | 29-3-56 | 5-10-57 |
| DDE 233 FRASER | Burrard, Vancouver | 11-12-51 | 19-2-53 | 28-6-57 |
| DDE 234 ASSINIBOINE* | Marine Industries, Sorel | 19-5-52 | 12-2-54 | 16-8-56 |

**D:** 2,260 tons (2,630 fl) **S:** 28 kts **Dim:** 111.5 × 12.8 × 4.2
**A:** 2/76.2-mm DP Mk 33—1/Mk 10 Limbo mortar (III × 1)—6/324-mm Mk 32 ASW TT (III × 2)—1/Sea King helicopter
**Electron Equipt:** Radar: 1/SPS-12, 1/SPS-10, 1 navigational, 1/SPG-48 f.c.
Sonar: 1/SQS-503, 1/SQS-501, 1/SQS-504 VDS
EW: WLR-1—TACAN: URN-20
**M:** 2 sets English-Electric GT; 2 props; 30,000 hp

**Fraser (DDE 233)**—post-DELEX—TACAN on lattice L. & L. Van Ginderen, 10-85

**Assiniboine (DDE 234)** C.A.F., 1986

**Boilers:** 2 Babcock & Wilcox; 43.3 kg/cm², 454°C
**Electric:** 1,400 kw **Range:** 4,750/14 **Man:** 18 officers, 210 men

REMARKS: *St. Laurent* (DDE 205) stricken in 1974. *Fraser,* which was completed by Yarrow, Ltd., has a lattice mast between her funnels to support the TACAN dome; the others carry their TACAN atop a pole mast. Nos. 207, 229, and 233 given major overhauls 1977–78. DELEX overhaul begun 1980 on 207, 229, 230, and 233; DDE 206, 230, 234 refitted 9-7-84 to 8-85: no major updates. DDE 207, 229, 233 were to refit again 1986–87, losing Limbo and VDS to a towed array sonar system; the others were to decommission to reserve during 1987.

## OCEANOGRAPHIC AND HYDROGRAPHIC SHIPS

◆ **2 oceanographic research ships**

| | Bldr | Laid down | L | In serv. |
|---|---|---|---|---|
| AGOR 172 QUEST | Burrard DD, Vancouver | 1967 | 9-7-68 | 21-8-69 |

**Quest (AGOR 172)** L. & L. Van Ginderen, 7-81

**D:** 2,130 tons (fl) **S:** 15 kts **Dim:** 77.2 (71.62 pp) × 12.8 × 4.6
**Electron Equipt:** Radar: 1/Decca 838, 1/Decca 929 **Fuel:** 256 tons
**Range:** 10,000/12 **Man:** 37 tot.

REMARKS: A modification of the *Endeavour* (AGOR 171) with the same machinery. Can land a small helicopter. See remarks on the *Endeavour.*

| | Bldr | L | In serv. |
|---|---|---|---|
| AGOR 171 ENDEAVOUR | Yarrow, Ltd., Victoria | 17-8-61 | 9-3-65 |

**D:** 1,560 tons (fl) **S:** 16 kts **Dim:** 71.85 (65.53 wl) × 11.73 × 4.0
**M:** 2 Fairbanks-Morse 38D8⅛, 9-cylinder diesels, G.E. electric drive; 2 props; 2,960 hp
**Electron Equipt:** Radar: 1/Decca 838, 1/Decca 929 **Fuel:** 256 tons
**Range:** 10,000/12 **Man:** 37 crew plus 14 scientists

## OCEANOGRAPHIC AND HYDROGRAPHIC SHIPS *(continued)*

**Endeavour (AGOR 171)** 1985

Remarks: (for both ships): Reinforced hulls for navigation in icefields. Two electro-hydraulic 5- and 9-ton cranes. Bulbous bows. Anti-rolling and anti-pitching devices. Civilian crews.

◆ **1 former minelayer**

| | Bldr | Laid down | L | In serv. |
|---|---|---|---|---|
| AGOR 114 Bluethroat | Geo. T. Davie, Lauzon | 31-10-52 | 15-9-55 | 28-11-55 |

**Bluethroat (AGOR 114)** L. & L. Van Ginderen, 1985

**D:** 785 tons (870 fl) **S:** 13 kts **Dim:** 47.0 × 9.9 × 3.0
**M:** 2 diesels; 2 props; 1,200 hp **Man:** 27 tot.

Remarks: Completed as a mine and magnetic loop layer; redesignated a cable layer in 1959 and as a research ship in 1964.

## DEEP SUBMERGENCE EXPERIMENTAL SHIP

◆ **1 former Italian stern-haul trawler** Bldr: Marelli, Italy (L: . . .)

ASXL 20 Cormorant (ex-*Aspa Quarto*) (In serv. 10-11-78)

**Cormorant (ASXL 20)** C.A.F., 1978

**D:** 2,350 tons (fl) **S:** 15 kts **Dim:** 74.6 (72.0 pp) × 11.9 × 5.3
**Electron Equipt:** Radar: 1/Decca TM 1229, 1/RM 1229
**M:** 3 Marelli-Deutz ACR 12456 CV, 950-hp diesels, electric drive; 1 CP prop; 2,100 hp
**Electric:** 730 kVA + 250 kw **Range:** 11,800/15; 13,000/12

Remarks: Ex-Italian stern-haul trawler bought in 1975 and adapted to handle and service the SDL-1 submersible, which can dive to 600 m. A large hangar for submersibles and a gallows crane have been built on the stern. The ship can also support conventional and saturation divers and has extensive compressor facilities, decompression chambers, etc. Numerous specialized echo-sounders fitted.

## REPLENISHMENT OILERS

◆ **2 Protecteur-class multi-purpose underway replenishment ships**

| | Bldr | Laid down | L | In serv. |
|---|---|---|---|---|
| AOR 509 Protecteur | St. John SB & DD (NB) | 17-10-67 | 18-7-68 | 30-8-69 |
| AOR 510 Preserver | St. John SB & DD (NB) | 17-10-67 | 29-5-69 | 30-7-70 |

**Protecteur (AOR 509)** L. & L. Van Ginderen, 6-87

**D:** 8,380 tons light (24,700 fl) **S:** 21 kts
**Dim:** 172.0 (166.42 pp) × 23.16 × 9.15
**A:** guns: see remarks—3/CH-124A Sea King helicopters
**Electron Equipt:** Radar: 1/Decca . . . , 1/Decca TM 969—TACAN: URN-20
Sonar: 1/SQS-505
**M:** 1 set Canadian G.E. GT; 1 prop; 21,000 hp **Boilers:** 2 **Electric:** 3,500 kw
**Cargo capacity:** 13,250 tons, with 12,000 tons of distillate fuel, 600 tons of diesel oil, 400 tons of jet fuel, frozen and dry foods, spare parts, munitions, etc.
**Range:** 4,100/20; 7,500/11.5 **Man:** 15 officers, 212 men, 57 passengers

Remarks: Four replenishment-at-sea stations, one elevator abaft the navigation bridge, two 15-ton cranes on the afterdeck. One bow-thruster. Daily fresh-water distillation capacity is 80 tons. Twin 76.2-mm gun mount, formerly carried at the extreme bow, was removed in both in 1983; locally controlled, it was of little use and had several times been washed overboard. Can be used to carry military vehicles and troops for commando purposes. Carry four LCVPs. Both operate in the Atlantic.

◆ **1 Provider-class multi-purpose underway replenishment ship**

| | Bldr | Laid down | L | In serv. |
|---|---|---|---|---|
| AOR 508 Provider | Davie SB, Lauzon | 1-5-61 | 5-7-62 | 28-9-63 |

**Provider (AOR 508)**—servicing USS *Berkeley* (DDG 15) and HMAS *Darwin* (FFG 04) PH2 P. Thompson, USN, 5-86

**D:** 7,300 tons (22,000 fl) **S:** 20 kts
**Dim:** 168.0 (159.4 pp) × 23.17 × 9.15 **M:** GT; 1 prop; 21,000 hp
**Boilers:** 2 **Fuel:** 1,200 tons **Range:** 5,000/20
**Electric:** 2,140 kw **Man:** 15 officers, 151 men

Remarks: 14,054 grt. Platform and hangar for two Sea King helicopters. Can carry 12,000 tons of distillate fuel, 1,200 tons of diesel, 1,000 tons of aviation gas, 250 tons of provisions, munitions, and various spare parts. Operates in the Pacific. Refitted 1982.

## SMALL OILERS

◆ **1 "Dun" class** Bldr: Canadian Bridge Co., Walkerville, Ont.

| | Laid down | L | In serv. |
|---|---|---|---|
| AOTL 502 Dundurn | 27-1-43 | 18-9-43 | 25-11-43 |

**D:** 950 tons (1,500 fl) **S:** 10 kts **Dim:** 54.5 × 9.8 × 3.9
**M:** 1 Fairbanks-Morse diesel; 1 prop; 700 hp **Man:** 24 tot.

Remarks: Sister *Dundalk* (AOTL 501) stricken 17-2-82. Cargo: 792 tons liquid, 25 tons dry.

## REPAIR SHIP

◆ **1 "Park"-class dépôt repair ship** Bldr: Burrard DD, Vancouver

| | Laid down | L | In serv. |
|---|---|---|---|
| ARE 100 Cape Breton (ex-*Flamborough Head*) | 5-7-44 | 7-10-44 | 25-4-45 |

**D:** 8,450 tons (11,270 fl) **S:** 11 kts **Dim:** 134.6 (129.4) × 17.4 × 6.96
**M:** 1 set triple-expansion, reciprocating; 2,500 hp
**Boilers:** 2 Foster-Wheeler 17.6 kg/cm², 316°C **Fuel:** 709 tons
**Range:** 5,000/9

Remarks: Purchased from the Royal Navy in 1951. Used as training ship 1953–58. Refitted 1958–59. Equipped for pierside service at Esquimault and not expected ever to steam again. Sister *Cape Scott* (ARE 101) discarded in 1977.

## RESERVE TRAINING SHIPS AND CRAFT

Note: In addition to the ships and craft listed below, the four *Mackenzie*-class frigates are used primarily for training, and the research ship *Fort Steele* is used to train Reserves. The units below retain hull numbers associated with their former functions.

The *Bay* and *Porte* classes are planned to be replaced by a new class of 46-m, 484-ton "coastal class" units that can be converted to mine countermeasures vessels through the addition of portable modules. The smaller training craft are to be replaced by 30-m, 244-ton "harbor-class" craft with a diving tender capability. The first 10 of these ships were to be requested in 1985–86, but the program was delayed for lack of funds.

◆ **1 ex-Royal Canadian Mounted Police patrol boat** Bldr: Canadian SB & Eng. Co.

FS 140 Fort Steele (L: 18-7-59, in serv. 11-59)

**Fort Steele (PB 140)** L. & L. Van Ginderen, 10-82

**D:** 85 tons (110 fl) **S:** 18 kts **Dim:** 35.97 × 6.4 × 2.1
**M:** Paxman Ventura 12 YJCM diesels; 2 CP props; 2,800 hp
**Range:** 1,200/16 **Man:** 16 tot.

Remarks: Taken over 1973. Although designated a research ship, primarily acts as training ship for Reserves at Halifax. Originally had Napier Deltic diesels. Refitted 1986.

◆ **6 Bay-class former minesweepers**

| | Bldr | Laid down | L | In serv. |
|---|---|---|---|---|
| PB 159 Fundy | Davie S.B., Lauzon | 3-55 | 14-6-56 | 27-11-56 |
| PB 160 Chignecto | Davie S.B., Lauzon | 10-55 | 26-2-57 | 1-8-57 |
| PB 161 Thunder | Port Arthur S.B., Ont. | 9-55 | 27-10-56 | 3-10-57 |
| PB 162 Cowichan | Yarrows Ltd., Victoria | 7-56 | 26-2-57 | 19-12-57 |
| PB 163 Miramichi | Victoria Machinery | 2-56 | 22-2-57 | 28-10-57 |
| PB 164 Chaleur | Marine Industries, Sorel | 2-56 | 17-11-56 | 12-9-57 |

**Chaleur (PB 164)**—note deckhouse aft now in all L. Akin, 6-84

**D:** 370 tons (415 fl) **S:** 15 kts **Dim:** 50.0 (46.05 pp) × 9.21 × 2.8
**Electron Equipt:** Radar: 1/Sperry Mk 2 **Electric:** 690 kw
**M:** 2 12-278A G.M. diesels; 2 props; 2,500 hp
**Fuel:** 53 tons **Range:** 4,500/11 **Man:** 3 officers, 35 men

Remarks: Reclassified as patrol escorts in 1972 and used for training reserve personnel. They took the names of minesweepers transferred to France in 1954. The *Gaspé* (143), *Comox* (146), *Ungava* (148), and *Trinity* (157) were transferred to Turkey in 1958. Hull of composite construction. One 40-mm AA removed, deckhouse added in place of former sweep winch.

◆ **5 Porte class** Bldrs: 180, 183: Davie, Lauzon; 184: Victoria Mach. & DD; 185: Burrard DD; 186: Pictou Foundry

| | In serv. | | In serv. |
|---|---|---|---|
| YMG 180 Porte St. Jean | 4-6-52 | YMG 185 Porte Quebec | 28-8-52 |
| YMG 183 Porte St. Louis | 28-8-52 | YMG 186 Porte Dauphine | 10-12-52 |
| YMG 184 Porte De La Reine | 19-9-52 | | |

**Porte St. Louis (YMG 183)** L. & L. Van Ginderen, 10-84

**D:** 300 tons (429 fl) **S:** 12 kts **Dim:** 38.0 × 8.5 × 3.9
**M:** 1 Fairbanks-Morse 6-cyl. diesel, electric drive; 1 prop; 600 hp
**Fuel:** 47 tons **Range:** 4,100/10 **Man:** 38 tot.

Remarks: Launched 1950–52. Built as auxiliary minesweepers and net tenders.

◆ **2 ex-Canadian Coast Guard R-Class patrol craft**

PB 141 Rally (In serv. 1963) PB 142 Rapid (In serv. 1963)

**Rally (PB 141)**—with *Rapid* (PB 142) beyond G. Gyssels, 10-85

**D:** 105 tons (fl) **S:** 13.5 kts **Dim:** 29.03(27.34 pp) × 6.10 × 1.96
**M:** 4 Cummins VT-12-M-700 diesels; 2 props; 2,400 hp
**Electric:** 76 kw **Fuel:** 12 tons **Range:** 1,050/16; 1,500/12.5 **Man:** 12 tot.

Remarks: Transferred 1983 from Coast Guard for $1 each. Sisters in Coast Guard.

◆ **5 former Mounted Police patrol craft** Bldr: Smith & Rhulorel, Lunenburg, N.S. (In serv. 1957–59)

PB 191 Adversus PB 193 Captor PB 195 Sidney
PB 192 Detector PB 194 Acadian

**Captor (PB 193)** L. & L. Van Ginderen, 9-81

### RESERVE TRAINING SHIPS AND CRAFT *(continued)*

**D:** 48 tons **S:** 12 kts **Dim:** 19.8 × 4.6 × 1.2
**M:** 1 Cummins diesel; 410 hp **Range:** 1,000/10.5

◆ **1 former Mounted Police patrol craft** Bldr: Smith & Rhulorel, Lunenburg, N.S.

PB 196 Nicholson (In serv. 1968, transferred from Coast Guard, 1976)

**D:** 85 tons (fl) **S:** 16 kts **Dim:** 36.0 × 6.4 × 2.1 **Man:** 18 tot.
**M:** 2 Paxman YJCM diesels; 2 CP props; 2,800 hp **Range:** 900/13

◆ **6 Ville-class former tugs** Bldr: Russell Bros. (In serv. 1944)

YTL 578 Cavalier (ex-*Listerville*)

YTL 582 Burrard (ex-*Lawrenceville*) YTL 586 Queensville YTL 587 Plainsville YTL 588 Youville YTL 589 Loganville

**D:** 25 tons **S:** . . . **Dim:** 12.2 × 3.2 × 1.5 **M:** 1 diesel; 150 hp

Remarks: Sister *Beamsville* (YTL 583) remains in use as a tug.

◆ **3 miscellaneous reserve training craft**

YAG 116 (18 tons) YFL 104 (102 tons) YDT 2 (70 tons)

◆ **1 sailing ketch for cadet training**

YAC 3 Oriole (In serv. 1920)

**D:** 78.2 tons **S:** 8 kts (power) **Dim:** 31.1 × 5.8 × 2.7
**M:** 1 Cummins diesel; 1 prop; 165 hp **Man:** 24 tot.

Remarks: Based at Esquimault. Also in use is the 11.0-m GRP sloop *Tuna,* at the Fleet Training School, Halifax.

### SEAGOING TUGS

◆ **2 Saint-class oceangoing tugs** Bldr: St. John DD

ATA 531 Saint Anthony (In serv. 22-2-57) ATA 532 Saint Charles (In serv. 7-6-57)

**Saint Charles (ATA 532)** L. & L. Van Ginderen, 11-86

**D:** 840 tons (1,017 fl) **S:** 14 kts **Dim:** 46.2 (40.7 pp) × 10.0 × 5.2
**M:** 1 Fairbanks-Morse diesel; 1 prop; 1,920 hp **Man:** 21 tot.

### YARD AND SERVICE CRAFT

◆ **5 Glen-class harbor tugs** (In serv. 1975–77)

Bldrs: 640, 641: Yarrow, Esquimault; others: Georgetown SY, Prince Edward Isl.

YTB 640 Glendyne YTB 641 Glendale YTB 642 Glenevis YTB 643 Glenbrook YTB 644 Glenside

**Glenbrook (YTB 643)** L. & L. Van Ginderen, 5-82

**D:** 255 tons (400 fl) **S:** 11.5 kts **Dim:** 28.2 × 8.5 × 3.8
**M:** 2 Ruston AP-3 diesels; 2 vertical cycloidal props; 1,750 hp **Man:** 6 tot.

◆ **5 new Ville-class harbor tugs** Bldr: YTL 590, 591: Vito Steel & Barge Co.; others: Georgetown SY, Prince Edward Isl. (In serv. 1974)

YTL 590 Lawrenceville YTL 591 Parksville YTL 592 Listerville YTL 593 Merrickville YTL 594 Marysville

**Listerville (YTL 592)** L. & L. Van Ginderen, 1983

**D:** 70 tons (fl) **S:** 9.8 kts **Dim:** 13.6 × 4.5 × 2.4
**M:** 1 diesel; 370 hp **Man:** 3 tot.

◆ **1 Wood-class harbor tug** Bldr: Falconer Marine (In serv. 1944)

YTL 553 Wildwood

**D:** 65 tons (fl) **S:** 10 kts **Dim:** 18.3 × 4.9 × 1.5
**M:** 1 diesel; 250 hp **Man:** 3 tot.

◆ **1 old Ville-class tug** Bldr: Russell Bros. (In serv. 1944)

YTL 583 Beamsville

Remarks: Rest of class used for reserve training; see earlier entry for data.

### DIVING TENDERS

◆ **2 steel-hulled** Bldr: Ferguson, Pictou, N.S. (In serv. 1962–63)

YDT 11 (In serv. 1-62) YDT 12 (In serv. 7-8-63)

**YDT 12** 1980

**D:** 70 tons (132 fl) **S:** 11 kts **Dim:** 38.3 × 8.0 × . . .
**M:** 1 G.M. 6-71 diesel; 228 hp **Man:** 3 officers, 20 men

◆ **4 wooden-hulled**

YDT 6 YDT 8 YDT 9 YDT 10

**YDT 8 at Halifax** G. Gyssels, 1984

**DIVING TENDERS** *(continued)*

**D:** 70 tons (fl) **Dim:** 22.9 × 5.6 × . . . **M:** 2 G.M. diesels; 2 props; 330 hp

REMARKS: YDT 6 has a larger after deckhouse. Also in use is the small *Caribou* (YDT 2).

**FIREBOATS**

◆ **2 130-ton**

YFB 561 FIREBIRD YFB 562 FIREBRAND

**Firebird (YFB 561)** L. & L. Van Ginderen, 8-79

◆ **2 48-ton**

YFB 556 FIRE TUG 1 YFB 557 FIRE TUG 2

**TORPEDO RETRIEVERS**

NOTE: The first of a new class of 30-m, 215-ton torpedo-retriever "range vessels" was to be requested in 1985–86 to replace the craft below; order delayed by lack of funds.

◆ **2 Songhee class** Bldr: Falconer Marine (In serv. 1944)

YPT 1 SONGHEE YPT 120 NIMPKISH

**D:** 162 tons (fl) **Dim:** 22.8 × . . . × . . . **M:** 2 diesels; 2 props; 400 hp

**MISCELLANEOUS SERVICE CRAFT**

◆ Approximately 12 self-propelled units in the categories of fuel-oil lighter, water tanker, degaussing tender, water tender, floating crane, etc., plus a number of non-self-propelled cargo and fuel barges, power barges, sludge-removal craft, etc. Known names/numbers: *Tayut* (YAG 1), *Guillemot* (YAG 2), *Egret* (YAG 3), . . . (YAG 4), *Admiral's Lady* (YFL 100), . . . (YFL 101), *Pogo* (YFL 104), *Flamingo* (YFL 847), *Black Duck* (YFL 872), and *Gannet* (YFL 873).

**Self-propelled ammunition lighter YE 218** (sister is YFNL 220)
L. & L. Van Ginderen, 7-86

**Support barge YRC 62** L. & L. Van Ginderen, 5-82

COAST GUARD

Created in 1972 from a number of government agencies, the Canadian Coast Guard is a civilian organization in the Federal Transportation Ministry. It mans some 150 ships, 20 icebreakers, and 37 helicopters.

Canadian icebreakers and major service ships are broken down into the following categories:

| Type | Designation | Ice-thickness | No. in service |
|---|---|---|---|
| 1500 | Polar Icebreaker | 3-m | 0 |
| 1400 | Sub-Polar Icebreaker | 1.6-m | 0 |
| 1300 | Heavy Gulf Icebreaker | 1.2-m | 1 |
| 1200 | River Icebreaker | 0.7-m | 8 |
| 1100 | Light Icebreaker/Navaids Tender | 20–40-ton* | 11 |
| 1050 | Navaids Tender | 15-ton* | 2 |
| 1000 | Ice-Strengthened Navaids Tender | 10–20-ton* | 12 |
| 900 | Small Ice-Strengthened Navaids Tender | 5–10-ton* | 3 |
| 800 | Small Navaids Tender | 2–5-ton* | 9 |
| 700 | Special River Navaids Tender | 5–10-ton* | 5 |
| 600 | Large Search & Rescue Cutter | — | 5 |
| 500 | Intermediate Search & Rescue Cutter | — | 0 |
| 400 | Small Search & Rescue Cutter | — | 9 |
| 300 | Search & Rescue Lifeboat | — | 18 |
| 200 | Small Search & Rescue Cutter | — | 2 |
| 100 | Small Search & Rescue Craft | — | 8 |

* Buoy derrick capacity

AVIATION: The Canadian Coast Guard operates one Douglas DC-3 transport and 37 helicopters: 1 Sikorsky S-61N, 2 Alouette-III, 5 Bell 212, 6 Bell 206B, 7 Bell 206L, and 16 MBB BO-105CBS; 12 of the latter delivered 1986–87. Helicopters are painted red, with a white stripe.

**POLAR ICEBREAKERS (Type 1500)**

◆ **0 (+1) Polar 8 Project** Bldr: Versatile Pacific SY, North Vancouver

N . . . (In serv. 1992)

**Polar 8**—artist's impression Official, 1984

**D:** 35,000 tons (fl) **S:** 15 kts **Dim:** 194.0 × 32.3 × 11.9
**M:** CODAGE: 2 gas turbines, 4 diesel generator sets; 2 props; 88,000 hp
**Range:** 30,000/. . . **Man:** 175 tot.

REMARKS: Construction contract offered 3-87. For use in asserting Canadian Arctic sovereignty. To cost $320M (Can.). Originally to have had 100,000 hp; still will be world's most powerful icebreaker. Intended to break 2.45-m ice in continuous steaming or up to 2.0-m ice by ramming. Combined diesel and gas turbine electric (CODAGE) propulsion. Ordered 12-8-87, with work to start 1-89.

**HEAVY GULF ICEBREAKERS (Type 1300)**

◆ **1 turbo-electric drive**

| | Bldr | L | In serv. |
|---|---|---|---|
| LOUIS S. ST. LAURENT | Canadian Vickers, Montreal | 3-6-66 | 8-69 |

**Louis S. St. Laurent** L. & L. Van Ginderen, 3-82

**HEAVY GULF ICEBREAKERS** *(continued)*

**D:** 14,509 tons (fl) **S:** 17.7 kts **Dim:** 111.70 (101.80 pp) × 24.38 × 9.45
**Electron Equipt:** Radar: 2/Kelvin-Hughes 14-12, 1/Kelvin-Hughes 14-9
**M:** 3 sets GT, electric drive; 3 props; 24,000 hp
**Electric:** 4,300 kw **Boilers:** 4 Babcock & Wilcox; 42.2 $kg/cm^2$, 449°C
**Fuel:** 3,632 tons **Range:** 16,000/13 **Man:** 81 tot.

REMARKS: 10,907 grt. Accommodations for 216 total. Two helicopters with hangar below flight deck served by an elevator. Flume passive stabilization tanks. Carries two 15.2-m stores landing craft. Operates off Maritime Provinces. Serious fire 3-82 and again 30-12-85. To receive new bow during modernization 1987–89.

**RIVER ICEBREAKERS (Type 1200)**

◆ **1 new construction** Bldr: Versatile Pacific, North Vancouver

| | Region | Laid down | L | In serv. |
|---|---|---|---|---|
| HENRY LARSEN | Maritimes | 15-8-85 | 3-1-87 | 7-87 |

**Henry Larsen**—fitting out G. Gyssels, 1-87

**D:** 8,290 tons (fl) **S:** 16.5 **Dim:** 99.80 (93.00 pp) × 19.70 × 7.24
**Electron Equipt:** Radar: 2/nav.
**M:** diesel-electric, 3 Wärtsilä Vasa V32, 8,160-hp diesels; 2 props; 16,300 hp
**Electric:** 840-kw aux. **Fuel:** . . .
**Range:** 15,000/13.5 **Man:** 72 tot. accommodations

REMARKS: Ordered 25-5-84. Design based on *Pierre Radisson* class. 5,910 grt, 2,490 dwt. Has Wärtsilä bubbler system, with two associated 600-kw generators.

◆ **3 Pierre Radisson river icebreakers**

| | Bldr | Region | L | In serv. |
|---|---|---|---|---|
| PIERRE RADISSON | Burrard DD, Vancouver | Laurentian | 3-6-77 | 6-78 |
| SIR JOHN FRANKLIN | Burrard DD, Vancouver | Newfoundland | 10-3-78 | 3-79 |
| DES GROSEILLIERS | Port Weller DD, Ont. | Laurentian | 20-2-82 | 7-8-82 |

**D:** 6,400 tons (7,721 fl) **S:** 16.2 kts **Dim:** 98.15 (87.90 pp) × 19.50 × 7.16
**Electron Equipt:** Radar: 1/TR-611-1, 1/TR-311-S1 **Electric:** 2,250 kw
**M:** diesel-electric: 6 Montreal Loco MLW 251V-16F diesels (17,580 hp total); 6 G.E.C. alternators (11,100 kw); 2 G.E.C. motors; 2 props; 13,600 hp
**Fuel:** 2,215 tons **Range:** 15,000/13.5 **Man:** 55 tot. (76 accom.)

REMARKS: 5,910 grt/2,820 dwt; 440 $m^3$ cargo capacity. *Franklin:* 6,100 grt, range: 16,500/135. Bow-thruster-equipped. Telescopic hangar and flight deck for one Bell-212 helicopter. Passive-tank stabilization. Used on St. Lawrence River and Great Lakes in winter, in Arctic in summer. Third unit ordered 1981.

**Pierre Radisson** L. & L. Van Ginderen, 6-86

◆ **1 river icebreaker**

NORMAN MCLEOD ROGERS Bldr: Vickers, Montreal (In serv. 6-69)

**Norman McLeod Rogers** L. & L. Van Ginderen, 4-82

**D:** 6,506 tons (fl) **S:** 15.0 kts **Dim:** 89.92 (81.10 pp) × 19.05 × 6.10
**Electron Equipt:** Radar: 2/Kelvin-Hughes 14/12
**M:** 2 Ruston-Paxman HP 16 RKC diesels, electric drive; 2 props; 8,000 hp
**Electric:** 1,615 kw **Fuel:** 1,095 tons **Range:** 12,000/12
**Cargo:** 900 tons **Man:** 78 tot.

REMARKS: 4,179 grt/2,320 dwt. Also navigation tender. One helicopter, telescoping hangar. Operates in Laurentian Region. Re-engined during refit 7-11-83 to 14-9-84.

◆ **1 cable-laying river icebreaker** Bldr: Vickers, Montreal

JOHN CABOT (In serv. 31-5-65)

**John Cabot** L. & L. Van Ginderen, 6-86

**D:** 4,180 tons light (6,502 fl) **S:** 15 kts **Dim:** 95.50 (84.13 pp) × 18.29 × 6.73
**Electron Equipt:** Radar: 1/Decca 969, 1/Decca 2400
**M:** 4 Fairbanks-Morse 38D8-12 diesels, electric drive; 2 props; 9,000 hp
**Electric:** 1,060 kw **Fuel:** 719 tons
**Range:** 10,000/12 **Man:** 76 tot.

REMARKS: 5,097 grt/2,220 dwt. Carries 400 miles of cable in 3 tanks. Flume passive stabilization and heeling tanks, telescoping helo hangar, 1,000-hp bow-thruster, 70-ton towing winch (50-ton bollard pull). Operates in Newfoundland Region. Received new bow sheaves in refit ending mid-1987, to handle transatlantic fiber-optic cable.

◆ **1 river icebreaker** Bldr: Davie SB, Lauzon, Que.

**John A. MacDonald** L. & L. Van Ginderen, 10-82

JOHN A. MACDONALD (In serv. 9-60)

**D:** 9,307 tons (fl) **S:** 15.5 kts **Dim:** 96.01 (88.40 pp) × 21.30 × 8.58
**M:** 9 Fairbanks-Morse $38D8\frac{1}{8}$ diesels, electric drive; 3 props; 15,000 hp
**Fuel:** 2,245 tons **Range:** 20,000/10 **Man:** 80 tot.

REMARKS: 6,186 grt/3,380 dwt. Three helicopters, fixed hangar. 221-$m^3$ cargo space. Four stores landing craft. Operates in Maritime Provinces Region. Modernization commenced 9-87.

NOTE: *Labrador* stricken 5-87.

## LIGHT ICEBREAKER/NAVIGATIONAL AIDS TENDERS (Type 1100)

◆ **6 new construction**

| | Bldr | Laid down | L | In serv. |
|---|---|---|---|---|
| Martha L. Black | Burrard Yarrows, Vancouver, B.C. | 3-84 | 6-9-85 | 3-4-86 |
| George R. Pearkes | Burrard Yarrows, Victoria, B.C. | 3-84 | 30-11-85 | 17-4-86 |
| Ann Harvey | Halifax SY | 1984 | 12-12-85 | 2-87 |
| Sir William Alexander | Marine Industries, Sorel, Que. | 24-2-86 | 23-10-86 | 13-2-87 |
| Edward Cornwallis | Marine Industries, Sorel, Que. | 5-7-84 | 22-2-86 | 14-8-86 |
| Sir Wilfrid Laurier | Collingwood SY | 14-5-85 | 6-12-85 | 15-11-86 |

**George R. Pearkes**—derrick stepped at bridge face, telescoping hangar extended
L. & L. Van Ginderen, 7-86

**Sir William Alexander**—kingposts forward L. & L. Van Ginderen, 2-87

**D:** 3,140 tons light (4,662 fl) **S:** 15.3 kts **Dim:** 83.00 (75.00 pp) × 16.20 × 5.75
**Electron Equipt:** Radars: 2/nav.
**M:** diesel-electric: 3 Bombardier/Alco 12V-251 diesels (2,950-hp each) 3 Can. G.E. generators, 2,000 kw each, 2 Can. G.E. motors; 2 props; 8,000 hp—bow-thruster
**Fuel:** 693 tons **Range:** 6,500+/15 **Man:** 44 (+6 spare accom.)

Remarks: 1,950 grt/1,522 dwt. Will carry one Bell 212 helicopter. Cargo capacity is 400 tons in forward hold, 50 tons aft. Carry 670 tons water ballast. Construction of pair assigned to Marine Industries delayed by strike; both have derricks on king posts, while on the others the derricks are stepped on the bridge face. To operate from Prince Rupert, Victoria, St. Johns, Dartmouth, and Quebec City, respectively.

◆ Griffon Bldr: Davie 5B, Lauzon, Que. (In serv. 12-70)

**D:** 2,959 tons (fl) **S:** 14.0 kts **Dim:** 71.32 × 14.94 × 4.73
**Electron Equipt:** Radar: 2/Kelvin-Hughes 14-12 **Electric:** 422 kw
**M:** 4 Fairbanks-Morse 38D8⅛-8 diesels, electric drive; 2 props; 4,000 hp
**Fuel:** 345 tons **Range:** 5,500/11 **Man:** 38 tot.

Remarks: 160-ton cargo capacity. Flume passive tank stabilization. Helicopter landing platform, no hangar; 10- and 20-ton buoy derricks. Plans were announced during 1982 to order two similar ships. Operates in Central Region (Great Lakes).

**Griffon** L. & L. Van Ginderen, 8-78

◆ J.E. Bernier Bldr: Davie SB, Lauzon, Que. (In serv. 8-67)

**J.E. Bernier**—with hangar extended L. & L. Van Ginderen, 12-85

**D:** 3,150 tons (fl) **S:** 13.5 kts **Dim:** 70.48 (64.62 pp) × 14.94 × 4.91
**Electron Equipt:** Radar: Kelvin-Hughes; 1/14-12, 1/14-9
**M:** 2 diesels, electric drive; 2 props; 4,250 hp **Fuel:** 450 tons
**Range:** 8,000/11 **Man:** 37 tot.

Remarks: Similar to *Griffon* and *Montcalm* classes, but thinner plating. Has telescoping helo hangar. Flume passive stabilization tanks. Operates in Laurentian Region.

◆ Narwhal Bldr: Canadian Vickers, Montreal (In serv. 7-63)

**Narwhal**—as reconstructed F. Jentsch, 7-86

**D:** 2,222 tons (fl) **S:** 12 kts **Dim:** 76.66 (69.80 pp) × 12.80 × 3.75
**M:** 2 Cooper-Bessemer direct-drive diesels, fluid couplings; 2 props; 2,000 hp
**Electric:** 796 kw **Fuel:** 399 tons
**Range:** 9,200/11 **Man:** 35 tot.

Remarks. 2,064 grt/697 dwt. Originally typed "Depot Ship/Lighthouse and Buoy Tender"; and intended for summer use as an Arctic supply ship carrying 60 stevedores, 20 stores landing craft crew, and 20 administrators. During rest of year, based at Dartmouth, N.S. Has 40-ton buoy derrick. Mid-life refit at Halifax Shipyard, 1984 to 8-86: helicopter deck and telescoping hangar added, new engines.

## LIGHT ICEBREAKERS/NAVIGATIONAL AIDS TENDERS *(continued)*

◆ Sir Humphrey Gilbert  Bldr: Davie SB, Lauzon, Que. (In serv. 6-59)

**D:** 3,053 tons (fl) **S:** 13 kts **Dim:** 67.06 (61.53 pp) × 14.63 × 4.98
**M:** 2 2,400 hp diesels, electric drive; 4,250 hp **Fuel:** 552 tons
**Range:** 10,000/11 **Man:** 40 tot.

Remarks: 1,931 grt. Home-ported at Quebec City. Telescoping helicopter hangar. No landing craft. Refitted 1983 to 1-86 at Halifax SY, with new bow, Wärtsilä bubbler system, new 20-ton crane.

Note: Of the Type 1100 light icebreakers listed in the previous edition, *Wolfe* was stricken 22-11-85, *Camsell* placed in reserve 7-86 and stricken 7-87, *Alexander Henry* stricken 9-85, *Montcalm* in 1987, *Walter E. Foster* in 12-85, and *Edward Cornwallis* in 9-86. *Sir William Alexander* was to have been stricken 5-87, but was temporarily retained, renamed *William.*

## NAVIGATIONAL AIDS TENDERS (Type 1050)

◆ **2 Samuel Risley class**

| | Bldr | L | In serv. | Based |
|---|---|---|---|---|
| Samuel Risley | VITO Corp., Vancouver | . . . | 6-85 | Thunder Bay |
| Earl Grey | Ferguson Ind., Pictou, N.S. | 21-10-85 | 30-5-86 | Charlottetown |

**Earl Grey** C.C.G., 1986

**D:** 2,935 tons (fl) **S:** 12 kts **Dim:** 69.73 × 13.70 × 5.20
**Electron Equipt:** Radar
**M:** 4 Bombardier/Wärtsilä diesels; 2 Kort-nozzle CP props; 8,800 hp—750-hp bow-thruster—400-hp stern-thruster
**Fuel:** . . . tons **Range:** . . . **Man:** 31

Remarks: Design based on offshore supply vessel technology. Able to break 0.6-m ice. Computerized directional control. Buoy crane capacity 15 ton at 8.0-m radius/8.5 tons at 20 m. Two fire monitors produce 600 $m^3$/hr to 75-m range

## ICE-STRENGTHENED NAVIGATIONAL AIDS TENDERS (Type 1000)

◆ **0 (+2) programmed new construction**

Remarks: To order 1987–88, to break ice to 3 m. Crew 25. To handle 5.4-ton buoys.

◆ **2 Provo Wallis class**  Bldr: Marine Industries, Sorel, Que.

Provo Wallis (In serv. 10-69)  Bartlett (In serv. 12-69)

**Provo Wallis** L. & L. Van Ginderen, 10-85

**D:** 1,722 tons (fl) **S:** 12.5 kts **Dim:** 57.68 × 12.95 × 3.66
**Electron Equipt:** Radar: 2/Kelvin-Hughes 14-12
**M:** 2 direct-drive diesels; 2 CP props; 1,760 hp **Fuel:** 102 tons
**Range:** 3,300/11 **Man:** 29 tot.

Remarks: 1,313 grt. Carry one 9.1-m landing craft. Have 15-ton derrick. *P. Wallis* based at St. John's, *Bartlett* at Central District (1987). *P. Wallis* crew: 30 tot.

◆ Tracy  Bldr: Port Weller DD, Ltd. (In serv. 17-4-68)

**Tracy** L. & L. Van Ginderen, 1-84

**D:** 1,320 tons (fl) **S:** 13 kts **Dim:** 55.17 (50.29 pp) × 11.58 × 3.66
**Electron Equipt:** Radar: 1/Kelvin-Hughes 14-12 **Electric:** 402 kw
**M:** 2 Fairbanks-Morse $38D8\frac{1}{8}$-8 diesels, electric drive; 2 props; 2,000 hp
**Fuel:** 131 tons **Range:** 5,000/11.5 **Man:** 30 tot.

Remarks: 960 grt. Based at Sorel, Quebec.

◆ Montmagny  Bldr: Russell Bros., Owen Sound, Ont. (In serv. 5-63)

**Montmagny** L. & L. Van Ginderen, 6-86

**D:** 625 tons (fl) **S:** 12 kts **Dim:** 45.11 × 8.84 × 2.59
**M:** 2 Werkspoor diesels; 2 props; 1,048 hp **Fuel:** 48 tons
**Range:** 4,000/10 **Man:** 22 tot.

Remarks: 497 grt. Based at Sorel, Quebec. One 7-ton derrick.

◆ Nicolet  Bldr: Collingwood SY, Collingwood, Ont. (In serv. 12-66)

**Nicolet** L. & L. Van Ginderen, 6-84

**D:** 901 tons (fl) **S:** 13 kts **Dim:** 51.74 × 11.10 × 3.05
**Electron Equipt:** Radar: 1/Kelvin-Hughes 14-9
**M:** 2 diesels; 2 props; 1,350 hp **Fuel:** 76 tons
**Range:** 3,000/10 **Man:** 26 tot.

Remarks: 887 grt. Based at Sorel, Que., for use as a hydraulic survey and soundings ship on the St. Lawrence Ship Channel. An updated *Beauport.*

## ICE-STRENGTHENED NAVIGATIONAL AIDS TENDERS *(continued)*

◆ SIMCOE Bldr: Canadian Vickers, Montreal (In serv. 1962)

**Simcoe** F. Jentsch, 7-86

**D:** 1,392 tons (fl) **S:** 13 kts **Dim:** 54.62 × 11.58 × 3.83
**M:** 2 diesels, electric drive; 2 props; 2,000 hp **Fuel:** 156 tons
**Range:** 5,000/10 **Man:** 34 tot.

REMARKS: 961 grt. Based on Lake Ontario at Prescott.

◆ THOMAS CARLETON Bldr: St. John's DD (In serv. 1960)

**Thomas Carleton** C.C.G., 1986

**D:** 1,636 tons (fl) **S:** 12 kts **Dim:** 50.84 × 12.83 × 4.15
**M:** 2 diesels, electric drive; 2 props; 2,900 hp **Fuel:** 178 tons
**Range:** 2,200/11 **Man:** 38 tot.

REMARKS: 1,217 grt. Home-ported at St. John, New Brunswick. Helicopter platform, no hangar; has 20-ton buoy derrick.

◆ BEAUPORT Bldr: Davie SB, Lauzon, Que. (In serv. 1960)

**D:** 789 tons (fl) **S:** 13 kts **Dim:** 51.05 × 10.36 × 2.74
**Electron Equipt:** Radar: 1/LN-47 **M:** 2 diesels; 2 props; 1,280 hp
**Fuel:** 63 tons **Range:** 3,000/10 **Man:** 26 tot.

**Beauport**—broad bow, like *Nicolet* L. & L. Van Ginderen, 5-85

REMARKS: 813 grt. Based at Sorel, Que., as a hydraulic survey and soundings ship on the St. Lawrence Ship Channel. 8-ton electric buoy crane.

◆ TUPPER Bldr: Marine Ind., Sorel, Que. (In serv. 12-59)

**D:** 1,380 tons (fl) **S:** 13.5 kts **Dim:** 62.36 × 12.80 × 4.23
**M:** 2 diesels, electric drive; 2 props; 2,900 hp **Fuel:** 206 tons
**Range:** 5,000/11 **Man:** 37 tot.

REMARKS: 1,358 grt. Based at Charlottetown, Prince Edward Isl. Helicopter deck, no hangar. 15-ton buoy derrick.

◆ MONTMORENCY Bldr: Davie SB, Lauzon, Que. (In serv. 8-57)

**D:** 980 tons (fl) **S:** 12 kts **Dim:** 50.14 × 9.75 × 3.35
**M:** 2 diesels; 2 props; 1,200 hp **Fuel:** 142 tons
**Range:** 3,500/11 **Man:** 30 tot.

REMARKS: 751 grt. Operates in Maritimes District. 12-ton buoy derrick.

◆ **1 Alexander McKenzie class** Bldr: Burrard DD, Vancouver, B.C.

SIR JAMES DOUGLAS (In serv. 11-56)

**D:** 768 tons (fl) **S:** 11.5 kts **Dim:** 46.00 × 9.22 × 3.17
**M:** 2 diesels; 2 props; 1,000 hp **Fuel:** 86 tons
**Range:** 6,000/10.5 **Man:** 29 tot.

REMARKS: *McKenzie:* 560 grt; based at Dartmouth, N.S., since 1982. *Douglas:* 564 grt; based at Prince Rupert, British Columbia. 10-ton buoy boom. *Douglas* is 45.87 o.a. by 9.45 beam; range: 5,500/10.5 on 89 tons fuel. Sister *Alexander McKenzie* stricken 1987, *Douglas* soon to follow.

## SMALL ICE-STRENGTHENED NAVIGATIONAL AIDS TENDERS (Type 900)

NOTE: One new Type 900 tender is to be ordered during 1988 for delivery in 1990. Will carry up to 4,428-kg buoys and have a crew of 12 to 15.

◆ NAMAO Bldr: Riverton Boatwks, Manitoba (In serv. 1975)

**D:** 386 tons (fl) **S:** 12 kts **Dim:** 33.53 × 8.53 × 2.13
**M:** 2 diesels; 2 props; 1,350 hp **Fuel:** 34.5 tons **Range:** 2,000/11
**Man:** 10 tot.

REMARKS: Employed as buoy tender on Lake Winnipeg.

◆ ROBERT FOULIS Bldr: St. John DD, N.B. (In serv. 24-11-69)

**D:** 332 tons (fl) **S:** 11 kts **Dim:** 31.70 × 7.62 × 2.44
**M:** 2 diesels; 2 props; 960 hp **Fuel:** 21 tons **Range:** 1,500/10
**Man:** 12 tot.

REMARKS: 258 grt. Employed on St. John River, New Brunswick.

◆ KENOKI Bldr: Erieu Dry Dock, Frien, Ont. (In serv. 5-64)

**D:** 274 tons (438 fl) **S:** 10.5 kts **Dim:** 33.22 × 9.75 × 1.85
**Electron Equipt:** Radar: 1/Kelvin-Hughes 14-9 **M:** 2 diesels; 2 props; 800 hp
**Fuel:** 40 tons **Range:** 1,000/10 **Man:** 12 tot.

REMARKS: 310 grt. Barge-like hull with four hydraulic pilings for precise positioning while working as a shallow-water buoy tender. Two 5-ton cranes. Based at Prescott, Ont.

## SMALL ICE-STRENGTHENED NAVIGATIONAL AIDS TENDERS
*(continued)*

**Kenoki**—with pilings retracted 1969

NOTE: Type 900 Small Navigational Aids Tenders *Skidegate* and *Verendrye* were stricken 6-87 and 12-85, respectively.

## SMALL NAVIGATIONAL AIDS TENDERS (Type 800)

◆ **4 Partridge Island class** Bldr: Breton Industrial & Marine, Hawkesbury, N.S.

| | Laid down | L | In serv. |
|---|---|---|---|
| PARTRIDGE ISLAND | 1-11-84 | 2-7-85 | 31-10-85 |
| ÎLE DES BARQUES | 1-11-84 | 3-7-85 | 26-11-85 |
| ÎLE SAINT OURS | 7-5-85 | 25-4-86 | 15-5-86 |
| CARIBOU ISLE | 7-5-85 | 7-5-86 | 16-6-86 |

**Caribou Isle** L. & L. Van Ginderen, 6-86

**D:** 133 tons (fl) **S:** 10 kts **Dim:** 23.00 (22.50 wl) × 6.00 × 1.35
**Electron Equip:** Radar: 1/Sperry Mk. 1270 navigational
**M:** 2 G.M. 8V92 diesels; 2 props; 640 hp **Electric:** 70 kw (2 gen.)
**Range:** 1,800/8 **Fuel:** 26,000 l **Man:** 5 tot.

REMARKS: The first pair, ordered 23-7-84, are considered to be Type 800 tenders and operate at St. John, New Brunswick, and the Laurentian Region, respectively. The other pair, ordered 23-11-84, are considered to be "day boats." Cargo capacity is 20 tons. Have a fire monitor with 2,500-l/min. capacity to 60-m range.

◆ **2 Cove Isle class** Bldr: Canadian Dredge & Dock, Kingston, Ont.

COVE ISLE (In serv. 1980) GULL ISLE (In serv. 1980)

**D:** 116 tons (fl) **S:** 10 kts **Dim:** 20.00 × 6.00 × 1.35
**M:** 2 diesels; 2 props; 470 hp **Range:** 2,500/8 **Man:** 5 tot.
**Fuel:** 20.5 tons

REMARKS: Both operate on Great Lakes, in Central Region.

◆ F. G. OSBOURNE (In serv. 1974)—workboat

**D:** . . . tons **S:** 8 kts **Dim:** 15.85 × 5.18 × 1.22
**M:** diesels; . . . hp **Man:** 4 tot.

NOTE: Type 800 navigational aids tenders *Nokomis* and *Barge 501* stricken 12-85 and 11-85, respectively.

## SPECIAL RIVER NAVIGATIONAL AIDS TENDERS (Type 700)

NOTE: All below serve in the Western Region, mostly on the Mackenzie River, Northwest Territories.

◆ DUMIT Bldr: Allied SB, Vancouver, B.C. (In serv. 7-79)

**Dumit** C.C.G., 1985

**D:** 628 tons (fl) **S:** 12 kts **Dim:** 48.80 × 12.20 × 1.64
**M:** diesel-electric; . . . props; 1,140 hp
**Fuel:** 175 tons **Range:** 9,000/10 **Man:** 10 tot.

◆ NAHIDIK Bldr: Allied SB, Vancouver, B.C. (In serv. 1974)

**D:** 1,122 tons (fl) **S:** 14 kts **Dim:** 53.35 × 15.24 × 1.98
**M:** diesel-electric: 2 diesels; 2 props; 4,360 hp
**Fuel:** 331 tons **Range:** 1,000/11 **Man:** 15 tot.

◆ TEMBAH Bldr: Allied SB, Vancouver, B.C. (In serv. 9-63)

**D:** 181 tons (fl) **S:** 13 kts **Dim:** 37.51 × 7.92 × 0.91
**M:** 2 diesels; 2 props; 680 hp **Fuel:** 21 tons **Range:** 1,000/11 **Man:** 9 tot.

◆ ECKALOO Bldr: Allied SB, Vancouver, B.C. (In serv. 1961)

**Eckaloo** C.C.G., 1986

**D:** 135 tons (fl) **S:** 10 kts **Dim:** 25.26 × 6.71 × 1.22
**M:** 2 diesels; 2 props; 600 hp **Fuel:** 17.3 tons **Range:** 600/9.5 **Man:** 9 tot.

◆ **1 Dumit class** Bldr: Allied SB, Vancouver, B.C. (In serv. 1958)

MISKANAW (operates on the Hay River)

**D:** 99.6 tons (fl) **S:** 10 kts **Dim:** 19.51 × 5.97 × 1.22
**M:** 2 diesels; 2 props; 300 hp **Fuel:** 9.9 tons **Range:** 300/9.5 **Man:** 9 tot.

## LARGE SEARCH-AND-RESCUE CUTTERS (Type 600)

NOTE: Two new Type 600 to be ordered, one in 1988, one 15 months later.

◆ **1 modified offshore anchor-handling vessel** Bldr: Marystown SY, Marystown, Newfoundland

| | Laid down | L | In serv. |
|---|---|---|---|
| MARY HICHENS (ex-*Beau Bois*) | 23-5-83 | 5-11-83 | 19-4-85 |

## LARGE SEARCH-AND-RESCUE CUTTERS *(continued)*

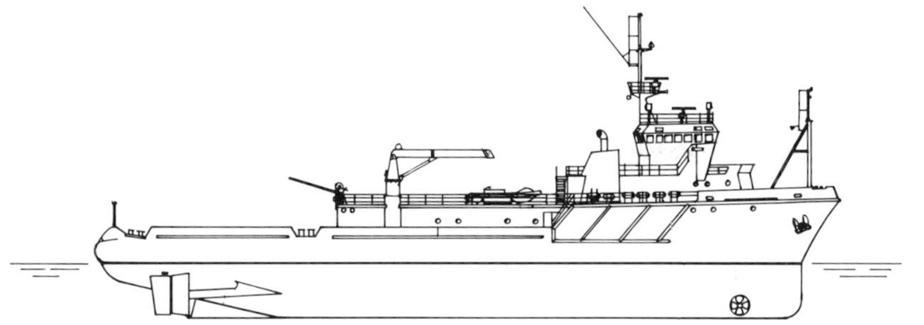

**Mary Hitchens**

**D:** 3,262 tons (fl) **S:** 15 kts **Dim:** 64.40 (56.40 pp) × 13.80 × 5.91
**M:** 2 B & W Alpha 14-U28L-VO diesels; 2 Kort-nozzle CP props; 7,420 hp—2 bow-thrusters; 1,000 hp
**Fuel:** . . . tons **Range:** 8,000/15
**Man:** 7 officers, 2 cadets, 11 men, and up to 85 survivors

REMARKS: Ulstein Type 704 oilfield supply-tug design purchased on completion, 31-3-84. Based at Dartmouth, N.S. Carries 8,000 liters foam concentrate and fire monitors. Can pump 5,000 lit./min. Two 6.7-m rigid inflatable rescue boats. Tank stabilization. A 4,150-ton near-sister from the same builder was being studied for possible purchase during 1986.

◆ **1 former oilfield supply tug** Bldr: Bel-Aire SY, North Vancouver, B.C. (In serv. 1972)

GEORGES A. DARBY (ex-. . .)

**D:** 2,204 tons (fl) **Dim:** 56.08 × 13.72 × 4.72
**M:** 2 Ruston diesels; 2 props; 4,380 hp **Range:** 6,500/11.5 **Man:** 16 tot.

REMARKS: Purchased 1-82 and refitted for Coast Guard at Vancouver for Pacific service. 885 grt. Similar to *Grenfell.*

◆ **2 former oilfield supply ships** Bldr: Bel-Aire SY, North Vancouver, B.C.

JACKMAN (ex-M/V *Hudson Service,* ex-*Nordic IV*) (In serv. 8-73)

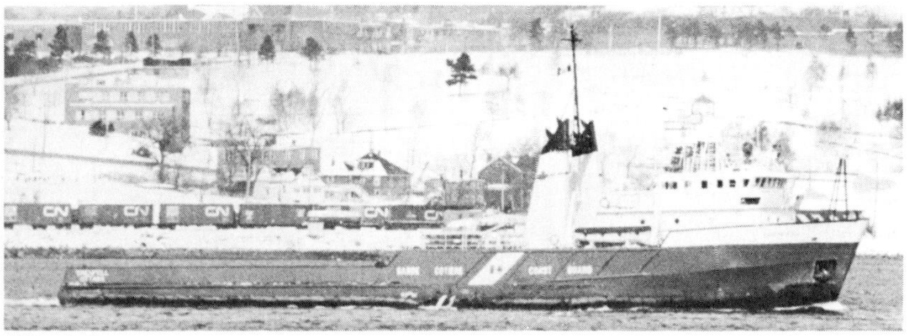

**Grenfell** L. & L. Van Ginderen, 1981

**D:** 2,106 tons (fl) **S:** 13 kts **Dim:** 56.10 (51.94 pp) × 13.70 × 4.42
**M:** 4 G.M. 16-565C diesels; 2 props; 6,400 hp **Electric:** 360 kw
**Fuel:** 587 tons **Range:** 6,500/12 **Man:** 16 tot.

REMARKS: 877 grt/452 dwt. Acquired from Nordic Offshore Services in 1979 and based at St. Johns, Newfoundland. Typical oilfield supply tugs with long, low, open cleared fantail. Main engines built 1950, rebuilt in 1972 for shipboard use. Ice-strengthened hulls. *Grenfell:* 2,113 tons, 457 tons fuel. *Grenfell* unsatisfactory, to be replaced by uncompleted oilfield boat "Hull 37" bought 1987; to be named *Sir William Grenfell.*

◆ ALERT Bldr: Davie SB, Lauzon, Que. (In serv. 20-11-69)

**Alert** L. & L. Van Ginderen, 12-82

**D:** 2,164 tons (fl) **S:** 18.7 kts **Dim:** 71.40 × 12.12 × 4.94 **Fuel:** 275 tons
**M:** 2 diesels; electric drive; 2 props; 9,716 hp **Range:** 6,000/14.5 **Man:** 38 tot.

REMARKS: 1,752 grt. Was to have been a class of six. Telescoping hangar for helicopter. Operates in Atlantic. To be given life-extension modernization.

◆ SIMON FRASER Bldr: Burrard DD, Vancouver (In serv. 2-60)

**D:** 1,375 tons (fl) **S:** 13.5 kts **Dim:** 62.26 × 12.80 × 4.27 **Range:** 5,000/10
**M:** 2 diesels, electric drive; 2 props; 2,900 hp **Fuel:** 178 tons **Man:** 38 tot.

REMARKS: 1,352 grt. Based at Quebec City. Helicopter deck and telescoping hangar. Very similar to *Tupper.* Refitted at Versatile Vickers SY, Montreal, 1985 to 4-86; hangar removed, extra lifeboats added for search-and-rescue duties; retyped from Type 1000 navigational aids tender.

Note: The only Intermediate Search-and-Rescue Cutter (Type 500), *Ville Marie,* was stricken 11-85.

NOTE: Two Type 500 rescue cutters are to order 1988 for delivery 1990.

## SMALL SEARCH-AND-RESCUE CUTTERS (Type 400)

N . . . (In serv. 6-87)

**D:** . . . **S:** . . . **Dim:** 22-74 (19.00 wl) × 6.12 × 1.50 **M:** . . .

REMARKS: To replace *Spume,* operating from Medford, Central Region (Great Lakes). Kevlar hull.

◆ **4 Point Henry class** Bldr: Breton Industry & Machinery, Point Hawkesbury, N.S.

CG 123 POINT HENRY CG 125 POINT RACE
CG 124 ÎLE ROUGE CG 126 CAPE HURD

**D:** 77 tons (97 fl) **S:** 24 kts **Dim:** 21.30 × 5.50 × 1.70
**M:** 2 MTU 8V396 TC2 diesels; 2 props; 1,300 hp
**Fuel:** 7 tons **Range:** 1,000/12 **Man:** 5 tot.

REMARKS: CG 123, 125 proceeded from Nova Scotia to the Pacific Coast under own power. CG 126 based in Central Region, CG 124 in Laurentian Region. First two completed 1980, other pair 4-82.

◆ **2 R class, based on U.S. Coast Guard 95-ft. design**

| | Bldr | In serv. |
|---|---|---|
| CG 140 RACER | Yarrow, Esquimault, B.C. | 1963 |
| CG 143 READY (ex-*Hunter Point*) | Burrard DD, Vancouver, B.C. | 1963 |

**D:** 105 tons (fl) **S:** 16 kts **Dim:** 29.03 (27.34 pp) × 6.10 × 1.96
**M:** CG 140, 143: 2 KHD Deutz SBA 8M8-16CR diesels; 2 props; 1,480 hp; CG 145: 4 Cummins VT-12-M-700 diesels; 2 props; 1,820 hp
**Electric:** 76 kw **Fuel:** 12 tons **Range:** 1,050/16; 1,500/12.5 **Man:** 12 tot.

REMARKS: Sisters *Rally* (CG 141), *Rapid* (CG 142), and *Relay* (CG 144) to Navy, 1983. CG 140, 143 re-engined in refits 9-84 to 12-2-85 and 11-84 to 29-3-85. See photo of *Rally* in Navy section. Sister *Rider,* unmodified and in reserve, deleted 1986.

◆ **2 S class—for Great Lakes service**

| | Bldr | In serv. |
|---|---|---|
| SPRAY | J.J. Taylor & Son, Toronto, Ont. | 1964 |
| SPINDRIFT | Cliff Richardson BY, Medford, Ont. | 1964 |

**Spindrift** 1969

**D:** 57 tons (fl) **S:** 14 kts **Dim:** 21.88 × 5.11 × 1.40
**M:** 2 diesels; 2 props; 1,050 hp
**Fuel:** 5.3 tons **Range:** 500/13.5 **Man:** 4 tot.

REMARKS: Sister *Spume* stricken 7-87; others to go soon.

## SEARCH-AND-RESCUE LIFEBOATS (Type 300)

◆ **2 self-righting motor lifeboats** Bldr: Hike Metal, Wheatly, Ont. (In serv. 1985)

CAP GOELANDS SOURIS

REMARKS: No data available.

## SEARCH-AND-RESCUE LIFEBOATS *(continued)*

◆ **15 U.S. Coast Guard 44-ft. motor lifeboat class**

| | In serv | Region | | In serv. | Region |
|---|---|---|---|---|---|
| CG 102 Westport | 1969 | Mar. | CG 114 Burgeo | 1973 | Newf. |
| CG 103 Bickerton | 1969 | West. | CG 115 Shippegan | 1975 | Mar. |
| CG 104 Bamfield | 1970 | West. | CG 116 Clark's Harbour | 1975 | Mar. |
| CG 105 Tofino | 1970 | West. | CG 117 Sambro | 1975 | Mar. |
| CG 106 Bull Harbour | 1970 | West. | CG 118 Louisburg | 1975 | Mar. |
| CG 107 Burin | 1974 | Newf. | CG 140 Port Mouton | 1982 | Mar. |
| CG 108 Tobermory | 1974 | Central | CG 141 Cap Aux Meules | 1982 | Mar. |
| CG 109 Thunder Bay | 1974 | Cent. | | | |

**D:** 17.9 tons (fl) **S:** 14 kts **Dim:** 13.45 × 3.86 × 1.01
**Electron Equipt:** Radar: 1/Raytheon 1900
**M:** 2 G.M. 6-71 diesels; 2 props; 360 hp (294 hp sust.) **Range:** 150/10.5
**Fuel:** 1.2 tons **Man:** 3 tot.

Remarks: First unit built U.S.C.G. Yard, Curtis Bay, Md., in 1967; remainder built in Canada, CG 140 and 141 by Georgetown SY, Prince Edward Isl. CG 107 and later are 485 hp. Sister *Souris* (CG 101) renamed *Westmount* and used for training at Coast Guard College.

◆ **2 Type 200 ice-strengthened rescue craft** Bldr: Georgetown SY

| | Laid down | L | In serv. |
|---|---|---|---|
| Harp | 15-12-85 | 20-9-86 | 12-12-86 |
| Hood | 15-12-86 | 5-11-86 | 12-12-86 |

**D:** 225 tons (fl) **S:** 11 kts **Dim:** 24.5 (21.50 pp) × 7.50 × 2.40
**Electron Equipt:** Radar: 1/Sperry Mk. 1270E nav.
EW: Taiyo MF/DF, Raytheon VHF/DF
**M:** 2 Caterpillar 3408-BDITA diesels; 2 CP, Kort-nozzle props; 850 hp
**Range:** 500/10 **Fuel:** 50,000-1 **Man:** 7 (10 spare accom.)
**Electric:** 80 kw (2/40 kw sets, Perkins 635A diesels)

Remarks: Ordered 26-4-85. Steel rescue ships to operate up to 100 n.m. from land. Have towing, firefighting, and medical evacuation capability. Red hull, yellow superstructure.

## SMALL RESCUE CRAFT (Type 100)

◆ **4 U.S. Coast Guard 41-ft. Utility Boat Class** Bldr: Matsumoto, Vancouver

CG 156 Osprey (In serv. 3-5-86) CG 157 Bittern (In serv. 1982)
CG . . . Mallard (In serv. 28-2-86) CG . . . Skua (In serv. 14-3-86)

**Skua** L. & L. Van Ginderen, 7-86

**D:** 12.8 tons (fl) **S:** 26 kts **Dim:** 12.40 × 4.11 × 1.24 **Range:** 300/26
**M:** 2 Mitsubishi S6B diesels: 2 props; 640 hp **Man:** 3 tot.

Remarks: 207 built for U.S. Coast Guard 1973 – 82. Canadian units all on West Coast.

◆ **4 miscellaneous**

| | In serv. | Region |
|---|---|---|
| CG 120 Teal | 1967 | West |
| CG . . . Swift | 1981 | West |
| CG 119 Grebe | 1973 | Cent. |
| CG 121 Sora | 1982 | Cent. |

◆ **1 rigid inflatable rescue boat** Bldr: Hurricane Rescue Craft, Vancouver

CGR-100 (In serv. 1986)

**D:** 10.5 tons (fl) **S:** 30 kts **Dim:** 12.40 × . . . × . . .
**M:** 2 Caterpillar 3208 diesels; 2 P.P. 140 waterjets; . . . hp

Remarks: World's largest rigid-hull inflatable craft when delivered, has deep-vee hull.

## AIR CUSHION VEHICLES

◆ **1 AP-1-88-class rigid sidewall air-cushion vehicle** Bldr: BHC, Cowes, **U.K. (In serv. 1987)**

**D:** . . . **S:** 40 kts **Dim:** 24.4 × 11.0 × . . .
**M:** 4 Deutz diesels; 2 props; . . . hp **Man:** 12

Remarks: Ordered 2-86, for use as a tender. Replaces Bell-built *Voyageur* at Montreal. Hull by Aluminium SB, Cowes.

◆ **3 British Hovercraft SRN-6 class**

CG 045 CG 039 CG 086—based on West Coast

Note: The following small craft were also in use in 1987: 19 Type Al work-boat/lifeboats (8–9 m o.a.), 2 Type A2 workboats (8–9 m), 3 Type B workboats (10–14 m), 2 Type C Self-Propelled Barges (7–8 m), 23 Type D Self-Propelled Barges (9–12 m), 3 Type E Landing Craft (15–17 m), and 2 Type F Utility Craft.
For training at the Coast Guard College, the following are used: *Mikula* (the former lightship *Lurcher*), *Westmount* (ex-*Souris,* U.S. Coast Guard lifeboat type), a lifeboat, a Zodiac boat, the launch *Mink*, 3 8.2-m workboats, 3 Boston Whalers, a self-propelled barge, and a small launch.

DEPARTMENT OF FISHERIES AND OCEANS

## FISHERIES PATROL SHIPS

◆ **1 seagoing patrol ship** Bldr: West Coast Manly SY, Vancouver, B.L.

| | Laid down | L | In serv. |
|---|---|---|---|
| Leonard J. Cowley | 15-1-84 | 24-10-84 | 4-85 |

**Leonard J. Cowley** West Coast Manly, 1985

**D:** 1,470 tons light (2,080 fl) **S:** 12.25 kts
**Dim:** 72.00 (67.60 pp) × 14.00 × 4.50 (4.90 max.)
**M:** 2 Nohab Polar F312A diesels; 1 Kort-nozzle CP prop; 3,140 hp
**Fuel:** 400 tons **Range:** 12,000/12 **Man:** 30 crew + 10 spare

Remarks: 1,730 grt. Helo deck. Bow-thruster. For Pacific Region. Ordered 8-11-83.

◆ **1 research vessel** Bldr: Bel-Aire SY, Vancouver

| | Laid down | L | In serv. |
|---|---|---|---|
| John P. Tully | 30-1-84 | 27-10-84 | 5-85 |

**D:** 2,200 tons (fl) **S:** 14 kts **Dim:** 68.90 (60.00 pp) × 14.00 × 4.50
**M:** 2 Deutz SBV-628 diesels; 1 CP prop; 3,120 hp
**Fuel:** 400 tons **Range:** 12,000/12 **Man:** 25 crew + 15 scientists

Remarks: 1,750 grt. For oceanographic/fisheries research and hydrographic survey.

◆ **1 aluminum construction** Bldr: John Manly SY, Vancouver

James Sinclair (In serv. 4-81)—Pacific Region

**D:** . . . **S:** 16.5 kts **Dim:** 37.8 × 8.4 × . . .
**M:** 2 MTU 12V538 TB91 diesels; 2 props; 4,600 hp
**Electron Equipt:** Radar: 2/Sperry navigational

FISHERIES PATROL SHIPS *(continued)*

**James Sinclair** Manly SY, 1981

◆ **1 seagoing patrol ship** Bldr: Marystown SY, Newfoundland

CYGNUS (In serv. 1981)—Newfoundland Region

**Cygnus** 1981

**D:** 1,461 tons (fl) **S:** 16 kts **Dim:** 62.5 × 12.2 × . . .
**M:** 2 Nohab diesels; 1 prop; . . . hp

◆ **1 seagoing patrol ship** Bldr: Ferguson, Pictou, N.S.

CAPE ROGER (In serv. 1977)—Maritime Region

**Cape Roger**—note telescoping helo hangar Pictou SB, 1979

**D:** approx. 1,500 tons **S:** 15 kts **Dim:** 62.49 (57.31 pp) × 12.22 × 4.13
**M:** 2 Bofors Nohab diesels; 2 CP props; 4,410 hp—bow-thrusters
**Electric:** 575 kw (1 × 250 kw, 1 × 75 kw) **Man:** 42 tot.

REMARKS: 1,255 grt.

◆ **2 fisheries research boats** Bldr: Ferguson, Pictou (In serv. 1981)

ALFRED NEEDLER WILFRED TEMPLEMAN

REMARKS: 50 m. o.a.; no other data available. One based at Halifax, the other at St. Johns, Newfoundland.

◆ **2 Louisbourg-class patrol/survey ships** Bldr: . . . (In serv. 1977)

LOUISBOURG LOUIS M. LAURIER (ex-*Cape Harrison*)

**Louisbourg** L. & L. Van Ginderen, 10-82

**D:** 450 tons (fl) **S:** 20 kts **Dim:** 38.1 (36.6 pp) × 8.2 × 2.5
**M:** 2 MTU 12V538 TB91 diesels; 2 props; 4,500 hp

REMARKS: *Louisbourg* patrols the Maritime Provinces Region, *Laurier* was renamed 1984 after conversion as a survey boat by Breton Industrial & Marine, Port Hawkesbury, N.S.

◆ **1 seagoing patrol ship** Bldr: Yarrow, Esquimault

TANU (In serv. 7-9-68)—Pacific Region

**D:** 880 tons (925 fl) **S:** 15 kts **Dim:** 54.69 (50.06 pp) × 32.00 × 3.35 mean
**M:** 2 Fairbanks-Morse $38D8\frac{1}{8}$-8 diesels; 1 CP prop; 2,400 hp
**Range:** 5,000/12 **Electric:** 500 kw **Man:** 34 tot.

REMARKS: Has 125-hp Pleuger active rudder. Aluminum superstructure. Similar to *Chebucto*.

◆ **1 seagoing patrol ship** Bldr: Ferguson, Pictou, N.S.

CHEBUCTO (In serv. 1966)—Maritime Region

**Chebucto**—gun no longer carried L. & L. Van Ginderen, 11-71

**D:** 865 tons normal **S:** 15 kts **Dim:** 54.6 × 9.45 × . . .
**M:** 2 Fairbanks-Morse $38D8\frac{1}{8}$-8 diesels; 1 CP prop; 2,560 hp
**Range:** 6,000/12 **Electric:** 300 kw **Man:** 35 tot.

## PATROL BOATS

◆ **1 catamaran** Bldr: Georgetown SY

F. C. G. Smith (L: 14-11-85; In serv. 17-1-86)

**D:** 326 tons **S:** 11 kts **Dim:** 34.80 (32.80 pp) × 14.0 × 1.90
**M:** 2 diesels; 2 props; 800 hp **Electric:** 270 kw
**Range:** 1,500/11 **Fuel:** 24 tons **Man:** 10 tot.

The units below run from 40 ft. (12.2 m) to 116 ft. (35.5 m) in length and are listed in descending length. Several of the older units may have been stricken.

| | Displacement | Length | | Beam | Year | Region |
|---|---|---|---|---|---|---|
| GOLDEN BAY | 136 grt | 30.5 | × | 5.4 | 1975 | Que. |
| . . . | 148 grt | 25 | × | . . . | 1984 | . . . |
| CUMELLA | 80 | 23.17 | × | 5.1 | 1983 | . . . |
| GROSWATER BAY | 80 | 23.17 | × | 5.1 | 1984 | . . . |
| CRATENA | 94 | 20.9 | × | 4.8 | 1953 | Mar. |
| SOOKE POST | 59 grt | 20.7 | × | 5.2 | 1973 | Pac. |
| GOOSE BAY | 44 | 20.1 | × | 4.8 | 1968 | Newfdl. |
| HAWKE BAY | 44 | 20.1 | × | 4.8 | 1965 | Newfdl. |
| PISTOLET BAY | 44 | 20.1 | × | 4.8 | 1966 | Newfdl. |

CANADA *(continued)*
PATROL BOATS *(continued)*

| | | | | |
|---|---|---|---|---|
| Burin Bay | 44 | 20.1 × 4.8 | 1967 | Newfdl. |
| Atlin Post | 57 grt | 19.8 × 5.2 | 1975 | Pac. |
| Kitimat II | 57 grt | 19.8 × 5.2 | 1974 | Pac. |
| Comox Post | 57 grt | 19.8 × 5.2 | 1975 | Pac. |
| Chilco Post | 57 grt | 19.2 × 5.2 | 1975 | Pac. |
| Gander Bay | 44 | 18.6 × 4.9 | 1969 | Newfdl. |
| Garia Bay | 49 | 18.6 × 5.8 | 1961 | Newfdl. |
| Badger Bay | 42 | 17.4 × 4.7 | 1954 | Newfdl. |
| Baso Reef | 48 grt | 17.1 × 5.1 | 1984 | Pac. |
| Cutter Rock | 36 grt | 16.1 × 4.3 | 1967 | Pac. |
| Christie Bay I | 35 | 15.8 × . . . | 1972 | West. |
| Stuart Post | 37 grt | 15.8 × 4.6 | 1973 | Pac. |
| Babine Post | 37 grt | 15.8 × 4.6 | 1972 | Pac. |
| North Rock | 31 grt | 15.2 × 4.6 | 1975 | Pac |
| Surge Rock | 33 grt | 14.6 × 4.3 | 1964 | Pac. |
| Boltenia | 29 grt | 14.6 × 3.7 | 1951 | Newfdl. |
| Bonilla Rock | 41 grt | 14.6 × 4.6 | 1971 | Pac. |
| Lomond | 24 grt | 14.3 × 4.3 | 1959 | Newfdl. |
| Beaver Rock | 31 grt | 14.3 × 4.3 | 1961 | Pac. |
| Pillar Rock | 31 grt | 14.3 × 4.3 | 1961 | Pac. |
| Falcon Rock | 28 grt | 14.3 × 5.8 | 1960 | Pac. |
| Buctouche Light | 20 grt | 14.0 × 4.0 | 1963 | Mar. |
| Kla-Wichen | . . . | 13.8 × . . . | 1986 | Pac. |
| Temple Rock | 23 grt | 13.4 × 3.6 | 1960 | Pac. |
| 11A-6538 | 36 | 13.1 × 4.0 | 1969 | Mar. |
| 11A-6539 | 36 | 13.1 × 4.0 | 1969 | Mar. |
| Seal Rock | 24 grt | 13.1 × 3.6 | 1959 | Pac. |
| . . . | 9.25 grt | 12.8 × 3.9 | 1984 | Mar. |
| Rustico Light | 17 grt | 12.8 × 4.0 | 1965 | Mar. |
| 11A-6204 | 45 | 12.8 × 4.0 | 1969 | Mar. |
| 11A-6206 | 45 | 12.8 × 4.0 | 1969 | Mar. |
| 11A-5831 | 46 | 12.8 × 4.0 | 1968 | Mar. |
| 11A-5832 | 46 | 12.8 × 4.0 | 1968 | Mar. |
| Marilla | 10 grt | 12.8 × . . . | 1955 | West. |
| 1B-1284 | . . . | 12.8 × 4.6 | 1975 | Mar. |
| 1B-1452 | 45 | 12.8 × 4.0 | 1979 | Mar. |
| Brama | 20 grt | 12.5 × 3.7 | 1955 | Pac. |
| Gavia | 17 grt | 12.5 × 3.4 | 1955 | Pac. |
| Walker Rock | 15 grt | 12.2 × 4.0 | 1976 | Pac. |
| Star Rock | 18 grt | 12.2 × 3.4 | 1957 | Pac. |
| 7C-109 | 30 | 12.2 × 3.4 | 1966 | Mar. |
| 17A-601 | 23 | 12.5 × 4.0 | 1976 | Mar. |

Regions: Pac.—Pacific; Que.—Quebec; Mar.—Maritimes; Newfdl.—Newfoundland; West.—Western

PATROL CRAFT

The craft listed below by region are all less than 40 ft (12.2 m) in length. There are, in addition, some 500 craft of 20 ft (6.1 m) or less in service. Maritimes: *Stikine, La Bradelle, Johnny Hoe,* 11A-5743, 11A-5830, 20A-1138, 20A-1139, 20A-1141, 20A-1142, 20A-1152, 20A-1153—Western Region: *Sangstercraft*—Pacific: *FD202, Petrel Rock, Anchor Rock, Babine River, Canoe Rock, Crescent Rock, Gale Rock, Bertram, Beluga, Gull Rock, Heron Rock, Legace Bay, Little Atlin, Little Brama, Little Crescent, Little Falcon, Little Nahmint, Little Pillar, Little River, Little Rock, Mission Jet, Nimpkish, RD 105, Roanna, Tatchie River, Vancouver Sport Fishing, Vedder Rock, Warrior Rock, 13K49012, 13K56195, 13K76101, 13K76026, 13K76149.*

Note: The Canadian Department of Energy, Mines and Resources operates a number of oceangoing survey and oceanographic research ships, which, for reasons of space, cannot be listed here.

# CAPE VERDE ISLANDS

**Republic of Cape Verde**

Personnel: approx. 100 total

Merchant Marine (1984): 24 ships—13,690 grt

PATROL BOATS

◆ **2 Soviet Shershen-class former torpedo boats**

451 452

**D:** 180 tons (fl) **S:** 45 kts **Dim:** 34.0 × 7.2 × 1.5
**A:** 4/30-mm AA (II × 2) **Electron Equipt:** Radar: 1/Pot Head, 1/Drum Tilt
**M:** 3 M503A diesels; 3 props; 12,000 hp **Range:** 450/34, 700/20

Remarks: Transferred 3-, and 7-79. Torpedo tubes removed prior to transfer.

◆ **3 Soviet Zhuk class**—transferred 1980

**D:** 60 tons (fl) **S:** 34 kts **Dim:** 24.0 × 5.0 × 1.8 **A:** 4/14.5-mm mg (II × 2)
**Electron Equipt:** Radar: 1/Spin Trough **M:** 2 M50 diesels; 2 props; 2,400 hp

◆ **1 Soviet Biya class survey ship** Bldr: Gdansk SY, Poland

**5th July (A 450)**—with two Shershens astern 1982

A 450 5th July (In serv. 1968–72)

**D:** 750 tons (fl) **S:** 13 kts **Dim:** 55.0 × 9.2 × 2.6
**Electron Equipt:** Radar: 1/Don-2 **Range:** 4,700/11
**M:** 2 diesels; 2 CP props; 1,200 hp **Man:** 25 tot. **Endurance:** 15 days

Remarks: Transferred 1980 for use as a training ship. Also capable of acting as a navigational buoy tender. One 5-ton crane. Misidentified as a Kamenka in previous edition.

◆ **1 oceanographic and fisheries research ship**

N . . . (ex-*Fengur*)

**D:** . . . **S:** . . . **Dim:** 27.3 × 7.4 × . . .
**M:** diesels; . . . hp

Remarks: Transferred 6-5-84 by Icelandic Government. 140 grt/60 dwt.

# CENTRAL AFRICAN REPUBLIC

ARMY

Remarks: Delivered from Tanguy Marine, Le Havre, France, in 5-86 were a 12-m, GRP landing craft and two 5.45-m raiding craft. No further details available.

# CHILE

**Republic of Chile**

Personnel (1986): 28,610 total (1,995 officers; 23,935 men; 2,680 naval infantry). Civil Service personnel number about 6,600.

Merchant Marine (1986): 255 ships—566,881 grt (tankers: 2—582 grt)

Naval Aviation: The naval air arm has 24 aircraft (6 Embraer EMB 111 Bandeirante and 3 Embraer 110 Bandeirante maritime surveillance aircraft, 10 Pilatus PC-7 trainers, and 5 Casa 212 Aviocar) and 19 helicopters (10 Alouette-III, 6 Bell 206A JetRanger, and 3 AS.332 Super Puma). The principal air base is at El Belloto, near Valparaiso. Several MBB Bo-105 helicopters are to be acquired. Chilean Air Force Halcón A-36 jet trainers may be equipped with Sea Eagle missiles for maritime strike duties.

SUBMARINES

◆ **2 IKL Type 1300** Bldr: Howaldtswerke, Kiel, West Germany

| | Laid down | L | In serv. |
|---|---|---|---|
| S 20 Thomson | 1-11-80 | 28-2-82 | 31-8-84 |
| S 21 Simpson | 15-2-81 | 29-7-83 | 18-9-84 |

SUBMARINES *(continued)*

**Simpson (S 21)** P. Voss, 7-84

**Thomson (S 20)** HDW, 1984

**D:** 1,285 tons surf./1,390 submerged. **S:** 10/22 kts
**Dim:** 61.00 × 6.20 × 5.50 (surf.)
**A:** 8/533-mm TT fwd. (16 SST-4 and A-184 torpedoes)
**Electron Equipt:** Radar: 1/Calypso II
Sonar: Krupp-Atlas CSU-3 system
**M:** 4 MTU 12V-493 AZ-80 diesels; 4/450-kw AEG generators; 1 Siemens electric motor; 5,000 hp
**Fuel:** 110 tons **Range:** 400/4; 16/21.5 sub.; 8,200/8 snorkel
**Endurance:** 50 days **Man:** 5 officers, 26 men

Remarks: Ordered 12-80; construction encountered political opposition in West Germany. Utilized components from canceled Iranian order. Maximum snorkel speed is 12 kts. S 21, damaged in collision 29-3-84 on trials, was completed 18-9-84. S 20 was completed 7-5-84. Have larger casing than earlier IKL-designed submarines. Sail and masting .5 m higher than on other ships of this class, to cope with heavy seas in Chilean operating areas.

◆ **2 British Oberon class**

| | Bldr | Laid down | L | In serv. |
|---|---|---|---|---|
| S 22 O'Brien | Scott Lithgow | 17-1-71 | 21-12-72 | 4-76 |
| S 23 Hyatt | Scott Lithgow | 16-1-72 | 26-9-73 | 27-9-76 |

**O'Brien (S 22)** G. Arra, 1977

**D:** 1,650/2,070/2,450 tons **S:** 15/17.5 kts **Dim:** 89.92 (87.45 pp) × 8.07 × 5.48
**A:** 8/533-mm TT (6 fwd, 2 aft)—22 A-184 and . . . torpedoes
**Electron Equipt:** Radar: 1/1006—Sonar: 1/2007, 1/187, 1/197, 1/719
**M:** 2 1,840-hp Admiralty Standard Range 16 VVS-AS21 diesels, diesel-electric drive; 2 props; 6,000 hp
**Man:** 65 tot.

Remarks: Delivery of these submarines was a year late because of a number of malfunctions in the electrical equipment. The after two "short" torpedo tubes were for countermeasures weapons and may no longer be in use. Collided with each other on surface, 4-87, repaired.

Note: U.S. *Brooklyn*-class cruiser *Chacabuco* (03, ex-*Prat*, ex-*Nashville*, CL 43) were stricken in 1984. Ex-Swedish cruiser *Almirante Latorre* (ex-*Göta Lejon*) decommissioned 9-84 and sold for scrap 1986. *O' Higgins* (02, ex-*Brooklyn*, CL40), inactivated 1986, is being retained for possible conversion to a helicopter carrier.

DESTROYERS

◆ **4 British "County"-class guided-missile destroyers**

| | Bldr | Laid down | L | In serv. |
|---|---|---|---|---|
| 11 Capitan Prat (ex-*Norfolk*) | Swan Hunter, Wallsend-on-Tyne | 15-3-66 | 16-11-67 | 7-3-70 |
| 12 Almirante Cochrane (ex-*Antrim*) | Fairfield SB & Eng., Govan | 20-1-66 | 19-10-67 | 14-7-70 |
| 13 Almirante Latorre (ex-*Glamorgan*) | Fairfield SB & Eng., Govan | 13-9-62 | 9-7-64 | 11-10-66 |
| 14 Blanco Encalada (ex-*Fife*) | Vickers-Armstrong | 1-6-62 | 9-7-64 | 21-6-66 |

**Almirante Cochrane (12)** L. & L. Van Ginderen, 8-84

**Blanco Encalada (14)**—no Sea Slug system L. & L. Van Ginderen, 8-87

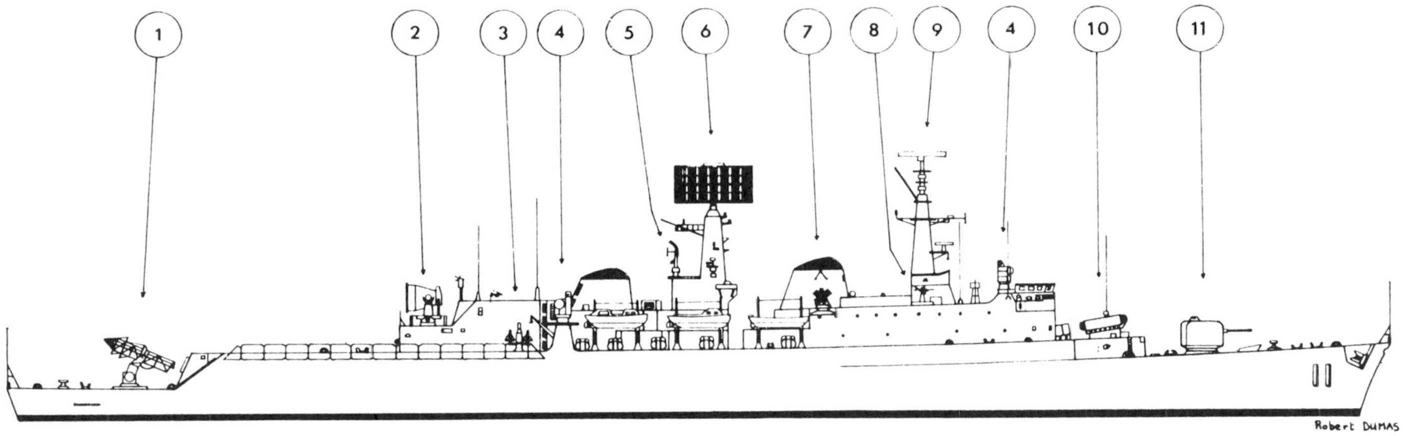


**Capitan Prat (11):** 1. Sea Slug launcher 2. Type 901 radar director 3. Sea Cat launcher 4. MRS. 3 radar director for Sea Cat 5. Type 278 height-finding radar 6. Type 965M air early-warning radar 7. Knebworth/Corvus chaff RL 8. 20-mm AA 9. Type 9920 search radar 10. Exocet launchers 11. 114-mm Mk 6 gun mounts

DESTROYERS *(continued)*

**Almirante Latorre (13)**—note no Sea Cat system G. Gyssels, 11-86

**D:** 5,440 tons (6,200 fl) **S:** 32.5 kts (30 sust.)
**Dim:** 158.55 (153.9 pp) × 16.46 × 6.3 (max.)
**A:** 4/MM 38 Exocet—1/Sea Slug Mk 2 syst. (II × 1, 30 missiles)—2/Sea Cat GWS 22 Syst. (IV × 2, . . . missiles)—2/114-mm Mk 6 DP (II × 1)—2/20-mm AA (I × 2)—1/helicopter [13: No Sea Cat—2/40-mm AA (I × 2)—6/20-mm AA (II × 2, I × 2); no Sea Slug system]
**Electron Equipt:** Radar: 1/978, 1/965M, 1/992Q, 1/277, 1/901 (not in 14), 1/903, 2/904 (not in 13)
Sonar: 1/184, 1/162
EW: UA-8/9 passive, jammers, 2 Knebworth/Corvus chaff RL (VIII × 2)
**M:** COSAG: 2 sets A.E.I. GT (15,000 hp each) and 4 English Electric G6 gas turbines (7,500 hp each); 2 props; 60,000 hp
**Boilers:** 2 Babcock & Wilcox; 49.2 kg/cm$^2$, 510°C **Fuel:** 600 tons
**Electric:** 4,750 kw **Range:** 3,500/28 **Man:** 33 officers, 438 men

REMARKS: *Prat* purchased by Chile, left U.K. 17-2-82, transferred 6-4-82 in Chile; *Cochrane* purchased 22-6-84, commissioned 25-6-84. *Latorre* transferred by sale 3-10-86, arriving 12-86. *Blanco Encalada* purchased and transferred 12-8-87, possibly as a replacement for *Prat*, reportedly damaged by fire early 1986. Four pair fin stabilizers. Twin rudders. Sea Slug magazine runs 80-m long through ship, with two parallel rows of 15 missiles. SCOT SATCOMM equipment deleted. Have ADAWS-1 data system.

In this class, each propeller is driven by one steam turbine for cruise, adding one or two gas turbines for boost. There are 3 steam turbo alternators and 3 gas-turbine generators. *Latorre*, damaged in Falklands War, has 2/40-mm AA in place of the Type 904 Sea Cat missile directors, has no Sea Cat launchers, and has two twin 20-mm AA mounts added on platforms on the deckhouse sides, forward. One boiler was non-functional at time of transfer.

The Sea Slug Mk 2 short-range SAM system is now used only by Chile, which bought all remaining missiles during 1986.

Length: 5.94 m — Speed: Mach 1.8
Diameter: 0.41 m — Range: 15 n.m.
Wingspan: 1.42 m — Altitude: 500 to 50,000 ft.
Weight: 900 kg (2,000 kg with boosters)
Propulsion: Solid fuel, with four solid-fuel boosters
Guidance: Beam-rider, using the one Type 901 radar.

NOTE: Sea Slug can also be used against surface targets.

◆ **2 Almirante Williams class**

| | Bldr | Laid down | L | In serv. |
|---|---|---|---|---|
| D 18 ALMIRANTE RIVEROS | Vickers-Armstrong | 12-4-57 | 12-12-58 | 31-12-60 |
| D 19 ALMIRANTE WILLIAMS | Vickers-Armstrong | 20-6-56 | 5-5-58 | 26-3-60 |

**Almirante Riveros (D 18)** Chilean Navy, 11-83

**D:** 2,730 tons (3,300 fl) **S:** 34.5 kts **Dim:** 122.5 (113.99 pp) × 13.1 × 3.9
**A:** 4/MM 38 Exocet—2/Sea Cat SAM systems (IV × 2)—4/102-mm DP (I × 4)—4/40-mm AA (I × 4)—6/324-mm Mk 32 ASW TT (III × 2)—2/Squid ASW mortars (III × 2)
**Electron Equipt:** Radar: 1/Decca 629, 1 Plessey AWS-1, 1 Marconi SNW-10, 1/SWW-20, 2/SGR-102, 2/SNG-20
Sonar: 1/164B—EW: WLR-1 intercept
**M:** 2 sets Parsons-Pamatreda GT; 2 props; 50,000 hp
**Boilers:** 4 Babcock & Wilcox; 43.3 kg/cm$^2$, 454°C **Range:** 7,800
**Man:** 17 officers, 249 men

REMARKS: Refitted in Great Britain, D 18 in 1973–75 and D 19 in 1971–74. Dutch M-4 radar directors for Sea Cat. Exocet replaced four 533-mm TT (IV × 1); 2 Exocet removed from each and placed on *Allen M. Sumner* class, 1980. The 114-mm guns are unique to this class; gunhouse weight is 26 tons, muzzle velocity is 900 m/sec., firing rate is 46 rpm, range is 18,500 m, and maximum altitude is 12,000 m.

◆ **2 U.S. Allen M. Sumner FRAM II class**

| | Bldr | Laid down | L | In serv. |
|---|---|---|---|---|
| D 16 MINISTRO ZENTENO (ex-*Charles S. Sperry,* DD 697) | Federal SB & DD, Kearny, N.J. | 19-10-43 | 30-9-44 | 26-12-44 |
| D 17 MINISTRO PORTALES (ex-*Douglas H. Fox,* DD 779) | Todd Pacific SY, Tacoma, Wash. | 31-1-44 | 13-3-44 | 17-5-44 |

**Ministro Zenteno (D 16)**—with added AA guns U.S. Navy, 1982

**D:** 2,200 tons (3,300 fl) **S:** 30 kts **Dim:** 114.75 × 12.45 × 5.8 (sonar)
**A:** 2/MM 38 Exocet—6/127-mm DP 38-cal. (II × 3)—2/40-mm AA (I × 2)—2/20-mm AA (I × 2)—6/324-mm Mk 32 ASW TT (III × 2)—2/Hedgehogs—1 SH-57A helicopter
**Electron Equipt:** Radar: 1/SPS-40 (D 17) or SPS-29 (D 16), 1/SPS-10, 1/Mk 25
Sonar: 1/SQS-40—EW: WLR-1
**M:** 2 sets GT; 2 props; 60,000 hp
**Boilers:** 4 Foster-Wheeler and Babcock & Wilcox; 43.3 kg/cm$^2$, 454°C
**Fuel:** 650 tons **Range:** 1,260/30; 4,600/15 **Man:** 14 officers, 260 men

REMARKS: Purchased 8-1-74. VDS removed 1980; 2 Exocet SSM from *Williams* class mounted on 01 deck between stacks. By 1982, the Exocet missiles appear to have been removed, and 40-mm AA guns have been added at the forward corners of the helicopter platform. Mk 37 GFCS.

FRIGATES

◆ **2 British Leander class**

| | Bldr | Laid down | L | In serv. |
|---|---|---|---|---|
| PF 06 CONDELL | Yarrow & Co | 5-6-71 | 12-6-72 | 21-12-73 |
| PF 07 LYNCH | Yarrow & Co | 6-12-72 | 6-12-73 | 25-5-74 |

**Condell (PF 06)**—in camouflage paint Chilean Navy, 1983

**Lynch (PF 07)** U.S. Navy, 1985

**FRIGATES** *(continued)*

**D:** 2,500 tons (2,962 fl) **S:** 27 kts **Dim:** 113.38 (109.73 pp) × 13.12 × 5.49 (fl)
**A:** 4/MM 38 Exocet—2/114-mm Mk VI DP (II × 1)—1/Sea Cat SAM system (IV × 1; 16 missiles)—2/20-mm AA (I × 2)—6/324-mm ASW TT (III × 2)—1 helicopter
**Electron Equipt:** Radar: 1/978, 1/965, 1/992 Q, 1/903, 1/904
Sonar: 1/177, 1/170B, 1/162—EW: UA-8/9 intercept, 2/Knebworth/Corvus chaff RL (VIII × 2)
**M:** 2 sets GT; 2 props; 30,000 hp
**Boilers:** 2 Babcock & Wilcox; 38.7 kg/cm², 450°C **Electric:** 2,500 kw
**Fuel:** 500 tons **Range:** 4,500/12 **Man:** 263 tot.

Remarks: Ordered 14-1-70. GWS 22 FCS for Sea Cat, MRS 3 GFCS for 114-mm. Exocet missiles at stern in lieu of Limbo ASW mortar. The Chilean Navy has expressed a desire to purchase two ex-RN units of this class, when available.

## CORVETTES

◆ **1 U.S. Abnaki-class former fleet tug** Bldr: Charleston SB & DD Co., S.C.

| | Laid down | L | In serv. |
|---|---|---|---|
| 63 Sergente Aldea (ex-*Arikara,* ATF 98) | 28-11-42 | 22-4-43 | 15-11-43 |

**Sergente Aldea (63)** Chilean Navy

**D:** 1,235 tons (1,675 fl) **S:** 15 kts **Dim:** 62.48 (59.44 wl) × 11.73 × 4.67
**A:** 1/76.2-mm DP Mk 26—2/20-mm AA (I × 2)
**Electron Equipt:** Radar: 1/SPS-5
**M:** diesel-electric: 4 Busch-Sulzer BS539 diesels; 1 prop; 3,000 hp
**Electric:** 400 kw **Fuel:** 363 tons **Range:** 7,000/15; 15,000/8 **Man:** 85 tot.

Remarks: Transferred 1-7-71 on lease.

◆ **1 U.S. Sotoyomo-class former auxiliary ocean tug** Bldr: Levingston, SB, Orange, Texas

| | Laid down | L | In serv. |
|---|---|---|---|
| 62 Lautaro (ex-ATA 122) | 19-10-42 | 27-11-42 | 10-6-43 |

**D:** 534 tons (835 fl) **S:** 13 kts **Dim:** 43.59 (41.00 pp) × 10.31 × 4.01
**A:** 1/76.2-mm DP Mk 26—4/20-mm AA (II × 2)
**Electron Equipt:** Radar: 1/Decca 505
**M:** 2 G.M. 12-278A diesels, electric drive; 2 props; 1,500 hp
**Electric:** 90–120 kw **Fuel:** 171 tons **Range:** 16,500/18 **Man:** 46 tot.

Remarks: Purchased 9-47. Sister *Lientur* (60, ex-ATA 177) sold 1986 for scrap.

## GUIDED-MISSILE BOATS

◆ **2 (+2 to 4) Israeli Reshev (Sa'ar IV) class** Bldr: Israeli SY, Haifa

| | L | In serv. | Transferred |
|---|---|---|---|
| ... Casma (ex-*Romach*) | 1-74 | 3-74 | 12-79 |
| ... Chipana (ex-*Keshet*) | 23-8-73 | 10-73 | 1-81 |

**D:** 415 tons (450 fl) **S:** 32 kts **Dim:** 58.10 × 7.60 × 2.40
**A:** 6/Gabriel SSM (I × 6)—2/76-mm DP OTO Melara (I × 2)—2/20-mm AA (I × 2)—2/12.7-mm mg (I × 2)
**Electron Equipt:** Radar: 1/Neptune, 1/EL/M-2221 f.c. (Orion)
EW: passive syst.—4 large/72 small chaff RL
**M:** 4 MTU MD 871 diesels; 4 props; 14,000 hp **Range:** 1,500/30; 4,000/17
**Man:** 45 tot.

Remarks: Harpoon SSM removed prior to transfer. Transfer of three additional units canceled, but in 6-86 it was announced that 2 to 4 may be built under license at ASMAR, Talcahuano, beginning in 1987.

## TORPEDO BOATS

◆ **4 Guacolda (Lürssen 36-m design) class** Bldr: Bazán, Cadiz, Spain (In serv. 1965–66)

81 Fresia 82 Guacolda 83 Quidora 84 Tehualda

**Guacolda class** Chilean Navy, 1985

**D:** 134 tons (fl) **S:** 30 kts **Dim:** 36.2 (34.0 wl) × 5.6 × 1.68
**A:** 2/40-mm AA—4/533-mm TT (British Mk IV)
**Electron Equipt:** Radar: 1/Decca 505
**M:** 2 Mercedes-Benz MB839Bb diesels; 2 props; 4,800 hp
**Electric:** 90 kVA **Range:** 1,500/15 **Man:** 20 tot.

## PATROL BOATS

◆ **1 U.S. PC 1638-class submarine chaser** Bldr: ASMAR, Talcahuano

| | In serv. |
|---|---|
| P 37 Papudo (ex-U.S. PC 1646) | 27-11-71 |

**Papudo (P 37)** 1977

**D:** 313 tons (417 fl) **S:** 20 kts **Dim:** 52.9 × 7.0 × 3.1
**A:** 1/40-mm AA—4/20-mm AA (II × 2)—1/trainable Mk 15 Hedgehog—4/Mk 6 d.c. throwers—1 d.c. rack
**M:** 2 G.M. 16-567 diesels; 2 props; 2,800 hp **Fuel:** 60 tons **Range:** 5,000/10
**Man:** 69 tot.

Remarks: The construction of two additional units of this class, to be named *Abtao* (P 36) and *Pisaqua* (P 38), was canceled.

## HYDROGRAPHIC SURVEY AND RESEARCH SHIPS

◆ **1 U.S. Cherokee-class former fleet tug** Bldr: Commercial Iron Wks, Portland, Ore.

| | Laid down | L | In serv. |
|---|---|---|---|
| AGS 64 Yelcho (ex-USS *Tekesta,* ATF 93) | 7-9-42 | 20-3-43 | 16-8-43 |

**Yelcho (AGS 64)** 1970

**D:** 1,235 tons (1,675 fl) **S:** 15 kts **Dim:** 62.48 (59.44 wl) × 11.73 × 4.67
**A:** 1/76.2-mm Mk 26 DP—2/20-mm AA **Electric:** 260 kw
**M:** 4 G.M. 12-278 diesels, electric drive; 1 prop; 3,000 hp
**Fuel:** 363 tons **Range:** 7,000/15; 15,000/8 **Man:** 5 officers, 59 men

Remarks: Used for oceanographic research. Loaned 15-5-60. Carries survey launch on fantail.

## HYDROGRAPHIC SURVEY AND RESEARCH SHIPS *(continued)*

◆ **1 Antarctic patrol, transport, and research ship**

| | Bldr | Laid down | L | In serv. |
|---|---|---|---|---|
| AP 45 Piloto Pardo | Haarlemsche Scheepsbouw | 1957 | 1958 | 8-58 |

**Piloto Pardo (AP 45)** 1977

**D:** 1,250 tons (2,545 fl) **S:** 14 kts **Dim:** 83.0 × 11.9 × 7.4 (fl)
**M:** diesel-electric propulsion; 1 prop; 2,000 hp **Range:** 6,000/10
**Man:** 44 crew, 24 passengers

Remarks: Armament removed; can carry 2 Bell 47-G helicopters.

## AUXILIARY SHIPS AND SERVICE CRAFT

◆ **1 U.K. "Later Tide"-class replenishment oiler** Bldr: Hawthorn Leslie, Hebburn-on-Tyne

| | Laid down | L | In serv. |
|---|---|---|---|
| AO 52 Almirante Montt (ex-*Tidepool*) | 4-12-61 | 11-12-62 | 28-6-63 |

**Almirante Montt (AO 52) as Tidepool** L. & L. Van Ginderen, 7-81

**D:** 8,531 tons light (27,400 fl) **S:** 18.3 kts
**Dim:** 177.60 (167.65 pp) × 21.64 × 9.75
**Electron Equipt:** Radar: 1/Kelvin-Hughes 14/12, 1 Kelvin-Hughes 14/16
**M:** 1 set Pametrada GT; 1 prop; 15,000 hp
**Boilers:** 2 Babcock & Wilcox, 60 kg/cm$^2$, 510°C **Man:** 110 tot.

Remarks: Sold to Chile and was to have been transferred 2-4-82 at Valparaiso; repossessed because of Argentine invasion of Falklands, returned and commissioned in Chilean Navy 8-82. 14,130 grt/18,900 dwt. Cargo: approx. 18,000 tons liquid. Hangar and flight deck for one large helicopter.

◆ **1 replenishment oiler** Bldr: Burmeister & Wain, Copenhagen

| | L | In serv. |
|---|---|---|
| AO 53 Araucano | 21-6-66 | 10-1-67 |

**Araucano (AO 53)** 1977

**D:** 23,000 tons (fl) **S:** 17 kts **Dim:** 160.93 × 21.95 × 8.8 **A:** removed
**M:** Burmeister & Wain diesel, type 62 VT 2 BF 140, 9-cyl.; 1 prop; 10,800 hp
**Range:** 12,000/14.5

Remarks: Can replenish two ships at sea simultaneously. Carries 21,126 cu. meters liquid and 1,444 cu. meters dry cargo. Can carry 8/40-mm AA (II × 4).

◆ **1 small tanker** Bldr: Marco SY, Iquique (In serv. 1966)

AO 55 Guardian Brito (ex-*Silvia*)

**D:** 482 tons (fl) **S:** 10 kts **Dim:** 39.60 × 7.44 × 3.30 (max.)
**M:** MWM diesel; . . . hp **Range:** 3,000/8 **Man:** 1 officer, 7 men

Remarks: Acquired 13-1-83 from the Ultramar Co. Based at Punta Arena.

◆ **3 French BATRAL-class landing ship/transports** Bldr: ASMAR, Talcahuano

| | L | In serv. | | L | In serv. |
|---|---|---|---|---|---|
| R 91 Maipo | 26-9-81 | 12-82 | R 93 Chacabuco | 16-7-85 | 4-86 |
| R 92 Rancagua | 26-3-82 | 1-7-83 | | | |

**Maipo (R 91)** Chilean Navy, 12-82

**D:** 770 tons (1,330 fl) **S:** 16 kts (13 sustained)
**Dim:** 80.0 (68.0 pp) × 13.0 × 3.0 (max.) **A:** 2/20-mm AA (I × 2)
**M:** 2 SACM V-12 diesels; 2 props; 3,600 hp **Range:** 4,500/13 **Man:** 40 tot.

Remarks: Constructed with French technical assistance. Cargo: 350 tons. Bow ramp, helicopter platform. Can carry 138 troops.

◆ **1 transport and disaster relief ship**

| | Bldr | Laid down | L | In serv. |
|---|---|---|---|---|
| AP . . . Aquiles | ASMAR, Talcahuano | 27-5-86 | . . . | 12-87 |

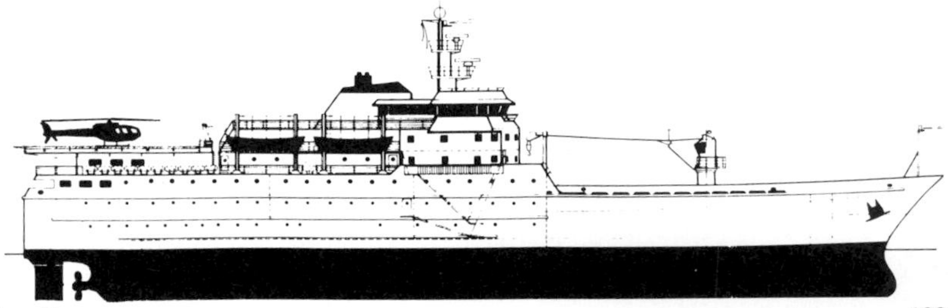

**Aquiles** 1986

**D:** 2,767 tons light (4,550 fl) **S:** 18 kts
**Dim:** 103.0 (97.0 pp) × 17.0 × 5.50 **A:** . . .
**Electron Equipt:** Radar: . . . **Man:** 80 crew + 200 troops
**M:** 2 MaK 8M453B diesels; 2 CP props; 7,200 hp—bow-thruster
**Electric:** 1,375 kw (1 × 500 kw, 2 × 400 kw, 1 × 75 kw)

Remarks: 1,550 dwt. Intended as replacement for *Aquiles* (AP 47), completed 1953 and purchased 1967. Has two cargo holds, one electric crane. Helicopter deck.

◆ **2 Orompello-class landing ships**

AP 94 Orompello Bldr: Dade DD Co., Miami, Fla. (In serv. 15-9-64)
AP 95 Elicura Bldr: ASMAR, Talcahuano (In serv. 10-12-63)

**D:** 290 tons (750 fl) **S:** 12 kts **Dim:** 43.9 (42.05 pp) × 10.3 × 6.9
**A:** 3/20-mm AA **Electron Equipt:** Radar: 1 Raytheon 1500B
**Electric:** 120 kw **M:** 2 Cummins VT-17-700M diesels; 2 props; 900 hp
**Fuel:** 71 tons **Range:** 2,900/10.5 **Cargo:** 350 tons **Man:** 20 tot.

◆ **1 Meteoro-class coastal ferry** Bldr: ASMAR, Talcahuano

AP 110 Meteoro (In serv. 1967)

**D:** 205 tons (fl) **S:** 8 kts **Dim:** 24.4 × 6.7 × . . . **M:** diesel
**Man:** 220 passengers

Remarks: Sister *Grumete Perez Huemel* (AF 112) has been stricken.

◆ **1 submarine tender** Bldr: Orenst & Koppel, Germany (In serv. 1966)

70 Angamos (ex-*Puerto Montt,* ex-*Pres. Aguirre,* ex-*Cerda,* ex-*Kobenhavn,* ex-*Paquet Ferry*)

**D:** 3,560 tons **S:** 16 kts **Dim:** 93.92 × 16.2 × 4.5
**M:** 2 Lind-Pielstick V-8 diesels; 2 props; 6,500 hp

Remarks: Former car and passenger ferry, purchased from Empresa Maritime del Estado 4-77 and in service in 1979. Now fitted with workshops, spare parts stores, ammunition and torpedo magazines. 4,616 grt. Also used as a transport.

**CHILE** *(continued)*
**AUXILIARY SHIPS AND SERVICE CRAFT** *(continued)*

**Esmeralda (BE 43)** Chilean navy

◆ **1 sail-training ship**

| | Bldr | L | In serv. |
|---|---|---|---|
| BE 43 ESMERALDA (ex-*Don Juan de Austria*) | Bazán, Cadiz | 12-5-53 | 9-54 |

**D:** 3,673 tons **S:** 11 kts **Dim:** 94.1 × 13.1 × 8.7
**A:** 4/47-mm saluting **M:** Fiat diesel; 1,400 hp **Range:** 8,000/8
**Man:** 271 crew, 80 midshipmen

REMARKS: Four-masted schooner, ordered by Spain, sold to Chile in 1953. Similar to the Spanish *Juan Sebastian de Elcano*. Refitted in South Africa, 1977. The small yacht *Blanco Estella* (14 crew) is also used for training.

◆ **1 buoy tender and lighthouse-servicing ship**

ATA 73 COLO COLO Bldr: Bow, McLachlan, Paisley, U.K. (In serv. 1929)

**D:** 790 tons **S:** 11 kts **Dim:** 41.38 × 8.72 × 4.07
**M:** 1 set triple-expansion, reciprocating; 1 prop; 1,050 hp **Boilers:** 2
**Fuel:** 155 tons

◆ **1 tug**

YT 115 GALVEZ Bldr: Southern Shipbuilders, U.K. (In serv. 1975)

**D:** 112 grt **S:** . . . **Dim:** 25.5 × 7.3 × 2.8

REMARKS: Subordinated to ASMAR, Talcahuano, which also has two small tugs of 200 hp and 500 hp.

◆ **1 harbor fuel lighter** Bldr: Svendborg, Denmark (In serv. . . .)

AP 48 AGUILA (ex-*Australgas)*

**D:** . . . tons **S:** 10 kts **Dim:** 51.3 × 8.7 × 4.2 **Range:** 6,000/10

REMARKS: 397 dwt. Origins uncertain.

◆ **1 10,000-ton-capacity floating dry dock** Bldr: ASMAR, Talcahuano

VALPARAISO III (L: 8-10-83)

**D:** 4,150 tons (light)
**Dim:** 167.0 (151.2 on blocks) × 32.1 (26.1 interior width) × 3.95

REMARKS: Built for shipyard, rather than naval service, but available to the Navy.

◆ **2 U.S. ARD 24-class floating dry docks** (In serv. 1944)

131 INGENIERO MERY (ex-ARD 25) 132 MUTILLA (ex-ARD 32)

**Capacity:** 3,500 tons **Dim:** 149.86 × 24.69 × 1.73 (light)

REMARKS: 131 leased 15-12-60; 132 transferred 20-8-73. Both at Talcahuano. Dock inside dimensions: 118.6 m on blocks, 18.0-m clear width, 6.3-m draft over blocks. Bow end pointed.

◆ **1 small floating dry dock** (In serv. 1908)

MANTEROLA

**Capacity:** 1,000 tons **Dim:** 66.0 × 12.8 × . . .

## CHILEAN COAST GUARD

### GENERAL DIRECTORATE OF THE MARITIME TERRITORY

Founded 1848 and now responsible for regulating the Chilean merchant marine, water sport, coastal and port patrol, and for navigational aid maintenance. Also intended to organize the merchant marine as a potential naval reserve. In addition to the units listed below, there are also a large number of very small launches, rigid inflatable boats, etc.

**PATROL CRAFT**

◆ **10 "Anchova"-class patrol craft** Bldr: MacLaren, Niteroi, Brazil (In serv. 1980–82)

| | | |
|---|---|---|
| GC 1801 PILLAN | GC 1805 CORCOVADO | GC 1808 OSORNO |
| GC 1802 TRONCADOR | GC 1806 LLAINA | GC 1809 CHOSHUENCO |
| GC 1803 RANO-KAU | GC 1807 ANTUCO | GC 1810 COPAHUE |
| GC 1804 VILLARRICA | | |

**D:** 31 tons (43 fl) **S:** 25 kts **Dim:** 18.60 × 5.25 × 1.62
**A:** 2/20-mm AA (I × 2)—2/d.c. racks **Electron Equipt:** Radar: 1/Decca 110
**M:** 2 MTU 8V331 TC 81 diesels; 2 props; 1,800 hp
**Range:** 700/15 **Electric:** 10 kw

REMARKS: Ordered 1977. Wooden construction. Named for volcanoes. ("Anchova" is the builder's class name. Last pair delivered 16-11-82.)

◆ **2 small trawler-type patrol boats** Bldr: ASMAR, Talcahuano (In serv. 1966–67)

PC 75 MARINHEIRO FUENTALBAS PC 76 CABO ODGER

**D:** 215 tons **S:** 9 kts **Dim:** 24.4 × 6.4 × 2.75
**A:** 1/20-mm AA **M:** 1 Cummins diesel; 340 hp **Range:** 2,600/9

REMARKS: Purchased 1966, used primarily as buoy tenders. Also in use is the 9-kt, 80-ton *Castor,* built 1964.

◆ **2 patrol launches** Bldr: MacLaren, Niteroi, Brazil (In serv. 11-82)

ONA YAGAN

**D:** 14 tons (fl) **S:** 19 kts **Dim:** 13.2 × 3.6 × 1.1
**A:** . . . **M:** 2 MTU 6V 331 TC82 diesels; 2 props; 1,320 hp

REMARKS: Built as compensation for the late delivery of the "Anchova"-class patrol boats. One based at Puerto Montt, the other at Chiloe.

◆ **1 hospital craft** Bldr: ASMAR, Talcahuano (In serv. 1964)

CG 111 CIRUJANO VIDELA
**D:** 140 tons (fl) **S:** 14 kts **Dim:** 31.0 × 6.5 × 2.0
**M:** 2 Cummins VT-12-700M diesels; 2 props; 1,400 hp **Electric:** 60 kw

REMARKS: Modified U.S. PGM 59 gunboat design, with enlarged superstructure. Originally used by Navy for civil assistance programs but later transferred to Coast Guard for same function.

◆ **13 search-and-rescue craft** Bldr: ASENAV, Valdivia (In serv. 1981–84)

LPM 1901–1913

**D:** 14 tons (fl) **S:** 18 kts **Dim:** 13.3 × 3.5 × 1.0
**M:** 2 MTU 6V331 TC92 diesels; 2 props; 1,320 hp

REMARKS: Names include: *Aquila, Arica, Calle-Calle, Corrae, Punta Gruesa.* Also in use is the 20-ton LPM 1914, built 1953.

◆ **1 service launch for search and rescue at Easter Island**

KIMITAHI (In serv. 1981)—**D:** 14 tons **S:** 20 kts. **Dim:** 19.5 × . . . × . . .
**Man:** 1 officer, 6 men, 50 passengers

# CHINA

## People's Republic of China

PERSONNEL: 176,000 men in the following categories:
Regular naval: 24,000 afloat/80,000 ashore
Naval air arm: 40,000, Marine Corps: 42,500. There are also about 1,000,000 paramilitary personnel in the Naval Militia.

MERCHANT MARINE (1986): 1,562 ships—11,131,129 grt (tankers: 161 ships—1,634,692 grt)

NOTE: This does not include the large number of merchant ships involved only in domestic coastal trade.

NAVAL AVIATION: Under the operational control of the Navy, the Naval Air Arm consists of a force of some 700–750 aircraft, including:
—500 interceptors of types Jian 5 (MiG 17), Jian 6 (MiG 19), and Jian 7 (MiG 21)
—about 20 Jian 8 interceptors (a modified version of the MiG 21F)
—about 100 H 5 bombers (copy of the Soviet Il 28)
—about 50 H 6 bombers (copy of the Tu 16 Badger), many equipped to carry two HY 4 antiship missiles (version B 6D)
—about 12 Soviet Be 6 Madge amphibians
—7 or more Harbin SH 5 amphibians, powered by four 3,150-hp turboprops for a cruising speed of 300 kts and a 2,850-n.m. range (1,200-n.m. patrol radius at 45 tonnes max. takeoff weight); 10-tonne payload (including 6 tonnes depth bombs). Equipped with MAD boom, guns, and radar. First flight 3-4-76. Can operate 12 hours on 4 engines or 15 on 2 at 6,000-ft altitude.

**NAVAL AVIATION** *(continued)*

**Shui Hong 5 ASW amphibian** China Features, 1986

—13 French-supplied Super Frélon heavy helicopters (2 or 3 equipped with Thomson-Sintra HS 3125 dipping sonars), with additional Zhi 8 copies being built since 1985
—26 or more Zhi 9 (copy of SA 375 Dauphin) light helicopters out of 50 licensed for production

China continues to study acquisition of improved ASW helicopters for shipboard use, including the Sikorsky S 76, Kaman SH-2F LAMPS I, Dauphin variants, and the Super Puma.

WARSHIPS IN SERVICE OR UNDER CONSTRUCTION AS OF 1 JANUARY 1988

| | L | Tons (Surfaced) | Main armament |
|---|---|---|---|
| ◆ **116 (+ . . .) submarines** | | | |
| 2 (+2) Xia | 1981– | . . . | 12 CSS-NX-3, TT |
| 3–4 (+1) HAN | 1971–83 | . . . | TT |
| 1 GOLF | 1964 | 2,300 | 3 ballistic missiles, 10/533-mm TT |
| 3 MING | 1975–82 | 1,500 | 8/533-mm TT |
| 91 ROMEO | 1964 on | 1,330 | 8/533-mm TT |
| 15 WHISKEY | 1960–64 | 1,050 | 6/533-mm TT |
| ◆ **19 destroyers** | | Tons | |
| 15 LUDA | 1970–83 | 3,960 | 4/130-mm, 6 Styx |
| 4 GORDYY | 1938–40 | 1,660 | 4/130-mm, 4 Styx |
| ◆ **48 frigates** | | | |
| 1 (+ . . .) JIANGHU IV | 1986– | 1,600 | 1/100-mm, 2 HY-2 SSM, helo |
| 2 JIANGHU III | 1986–87 | 2,100 | 1/100-mm, 4 SSM |
| 21 (+ . . .) JIANGHU I, II | 1974–84 | 1,600 | 2 or 4/100-mm, 4 Styx |
| 2 JIANGDONG | 1972–75 | 1,586 | 4/100-mm, 2 SAM |
| 5 JIANGNAN | 1966–68 | 1,400 | 3/100-mm |
| 4 RIGA | 1953–56 | 1,186 | 3/100-mm, 2 Styx |

◆ **190-195 guided-missile patrol boats**

◆ **220 torpedo boats**

◆ **500+ patrol boats and craft**

◆ **115-120 minesweepers**

◆ **500+ amphibious ships and craft**

WEAPONS AND SENSORS

The ballistic missiles on the Xia-class SSBNs and the majority of the other weapons on Chinese ships are of Chinese manufacture, with many being copies of or derivations of Soviet systems.

ANTISHIP CRUISE MISSILES:

—Hai Ying-1 ("Sea Eagle-1")—a direct copy of the Soviet SS-N-2a Styx (P-15)
—Hai Ying-2 (CSS-N-2)—improved Styx

**Length:** 6.25 m **Weight:** 2,998 kg **Range:** 90 km
**Wingspan:** 2.75 m **Speed:** Mach 0.9 **Altitude:** 90–100 m

Hai Ying-2 (HY-2) is used aboard Luda destroyers and Jianghu-class frigates and uses a jettisonable solid rocket booster. Guidance is by gyro autopilot, with radar terminal homing. A land-launched version (Western "Silk Worm") is also available. All have a 500-kg warhead. Other versions include:

◆ Hai Ying-2A—infrared, vice radar, terminal homing

◆ Hai Ying-2G—radar altimeter-equipped, with 20-m cruise altitude, descending to 8 m during radar terminal homing

◆ Hai Ying-4—air-launched version, carried two per H-6 (Badger) bomber. Turbojet engine 7.36 m long, 0.76 m diameter

—C 801 Yinji ("Hawk Attack")—wholly Chinese weapon, using a box launcher similar to that of Exocet MM 38

Propelled by solid rocket, with two solid boosters.

**Length:** 5.2 m **Range:** 75 km
**Wingspan:** 1.0 m **Weight:** approx. 1,000 kg

Land- and air-launched (C 601) versions are in development.

—C 101—Program announced 1985. Propelled by two solid rockets for a range of 120 km (64.8 n.m.). C 101A is a proposed air-launched version.

SURFACE-TO-AIR MISSILES:

—HQ-61 (CSA-N-1)—Naval version of land-based SAM in development since 1960s and used only aboard the two Jiangdong frigates.

**Length:** 3.99 m **Range:** 10 km max./3 km min.
**Diameter:** 0.286 m **Altitude:** 8 km **Wingspan:** 1.66 m
**Guidance:** command, using radar tracker/illuminator, semi-active homing
**Speed:** Mach 3.0 **Propulsion:** single-stage, solid-fuel rocket

Guns are all versions of Soviet equipment of 130-mm, 100-mm, 57-mm, 37-mm, and 25-mm caliber, except for two French Creusot-Loire 100-mm mounts, one of which is on the Jianghu-III frigate 544. Torpedoes and mines are of Soviet or local design, with negotiations ongoing to manufacture the U.S. Mk-46 lightweight ASW torpedo. China may also acquire the U.S. Mk-15 20-mm CIWS for air defense.

Radars are, with a few exceptions, known by their Western nicknames:

| Name | Origin | Band | Function |
|---|---|---|---|
| Ball End | U.S.S.R. | E/F | Surface search |
| Bean Sticks | China | S | Early warning |
| Eye Shield | China | E/F | Surface search (Chinese name: MX-902) |
| Fin Curve | U.K. | I | Nav. (Decca 707 copy) |
| Fog Lamp | China | H/I | SAM f.c. |
| Neptun | U.S.S.R. | I | Nav. |
| Pot Head | U.S.S.R. | I | Nav./surface search |
| Rice Lamp | China | I | Gun control |
| Rice Screen | China | G | 3-D phased-array air search (Chinese "Sea Eagle")—in two versions |
| Skin Head | U.S.S.R. | I | Surface search |
| Slim Net | U.S.S.R. | E/F | Air/surface search |
| Square Tie | U.S.S.R. | . . . | Surface search (Chinese name: Type 331) |
| Sun Visor | U.S.S.R. | I | Gun f.c. |
| Type 756 | China | S | Nav. |
| Type 354 | China | C | low-altitude air search |

IFF systems have only come into general use since the early 1980s and are still not universally fitted. The equipment includes the Soviet Square Head interrogation antenna and the High Pole A transponder. Sonars are of Soviet design, with an active program under way to acquire modern Western systems.

CLASS NAMES AND PENDANTS

The class names used below are generally those assigned by Western intelligence services; the Chinese Navy uses a numbered system, for which few of the designations are known.

For combatants, three-digit hull numbers are assigned. Small combatants have a four-digit pendant, the first number of which signifies area subordination. Auxiliaries have three-digit numbers preceded by a letter signifying function:

| | |
|---|---|
| B—Cable layer | Q—Crane |
| C—Icebreaker | S—Research ship |
| E—Diving tender | T—Tug (all types) |
| H—Buoy tender | U—Repair |
| J—Salvage and rescue (submarine-associated) | W—Dredge |
| K—Hydrographic survey | X—Liquid cargo |
| L—Dry cargo/stores | Y—Dry cargo/transport |

In addition, the numerous ships subordinated to the various districts of the Maritime Border Defense Force have four-digit pendants preceded by a letter signifying the district; known prefixes include "S" for Shenyang, "N" for Nanjing (commonly seen in the Shanghai area), and "G" for Guangzhou.

**BALLISTIC MISSILE SUBMARINES**

◆ **2 (+2) Xia class** Bldr: Huludao SY (In serv. 1986–87- . . .)

**BALLISTIC MISSILE SUBMARINES** *(continued)*

406 (L: 4-81) . . . (L: 1982)

**D:** 7,000 tons submerged **S:** 20 kts sub. **Dim:** 120.0 × 10.0 × . . .
**A:** 12 CSS-NX-3 strategic missiles—. . ./TT
**M:** 1 pressurized-water nuclear reactor, turbo-electric drive; 1 prop; . . . hp

Remarks: The first "Xia" (Western nickname)-class submarine was launched in 4-81 from the same facility that builds the Han-class nuclear-powered attack submarine—Huludao shipyard, 200 km northeast of Peking in Liao Ning province. At least two additional units are expected. The first CSS-NX-3 submerged launch took place on 12-10-82 to a range of 1,600 km from the Golf-class trials submarine. The missile is believed to have 2 solid-propulsion stages and to have a range of 1,500 n.m. (2,795 km).

◆ **1 Soviet Golf Class**

**D:** 2,300/2,700 tons **S:** 12 kts submerged **Dim:** 100.0 × 8.5 × 6.6
**A:** 3 ballistic missiles—10/533-mm TT (6 fwd, 4 aft)
**M:** 3 diesels, electric drive; 3 props; 6,000 hp **Range:** 9,000/5

Remarks: Plans furnished by the Soviet Union at a time when relations between the two countries were good. Launched first Chinese SLBM on 12-10-82.

**NUCLEAR-POWERED ATTACK SUBMARINES**

◆ **3 (+1) Han class, nuclear**

| | Bldr | Laid down | L | In serv. |
|---|---|---|---|---|
| 401 | Huludao SY | 1965–68 | 1972 | 1974 |
| 402 | Huludao SY | . . . | 1977 | 1980 |
| 403 | Huludao SY | . . . | 1983 | 21-9-84 |
| 404 | Huludao SY | . . . | . . . | . . . |

**Han 402, the second unit** China Features

**D:** 4,500 tons submerged **S:** 25 kts surf./30 kts sub. **Dim:** 90.0 × 8.0 × . . .
**A:** . . ./TT
**M:** 1 pressurized-water nuclear reactor, turbo-electric drive; 1 prop (?); . . . hp

Remarks: The trials series for the first unit was very protracted. Considering that the first Xia SSBN is numbered 406, there may be intended to be five Hans built.

**CRUISE MISSILE SUBMARINES**

◆ **1 (+ . . .) E5SG class** Bldr: . . . (In serv. 1986–. . .)

**Project E5SG submarine launching C 801 missile** CPMIEC, 1987

**D:** 1,650 tons surf./2,100 sub. **S:** 15/17 kts **Dim:** 74.0 × 7.6 × 5.3
**A:** 6 C 801 SSM (I × 6)—8/533-mm TT (6 fwd, 2 aft; 18 torpedoes or 28 mines)
**Electron Equipt:** Radar: Snoop Plate
Sonar: Herkules active/passive, Feniks passive
**M:** diesel-electric, 2 diesels; 2 props; 2,500 hp
**Range:** 8,000/8 (snorkel); 330/4 (sub.) **Endurance:** 60 days
**Man:** 10 officers, 48 men

Remarks: A *surface*-launched cruise-missile-carrying version of the Ming (Project E5SE) attack submarine. Each of the six tubes elevates separately to fire one C 801 Yinji Missile. Diving depth: 300 m. Offered for foreign sale.

**ATTACK SUBMARINES**

◆ **3 Ming (Project E5SE) class** Bldr: . . .

**D:** 1,584 tons surf./2,113 tons sub. **S:** 15 surf./10 snorkel/18 sub.
**Dim:** 76.0 × 7.6 × 5.10
**A:** 8/533-mm TT (6 fwd, 2 aft; 16 torpedoes or 32 mines)
**Electron Equipt:** Radar: 1/Snoop Plate
Sonar: Herkules active/passive, Feniks passive
**M:** diesel-electric, 2 diesels; 2 props; 2,500 hp
**Range:** 8,000 (8 snorkel; 330/4 sub.) **Endurance:** 60 days
**Man:** 8 officers, 48 men

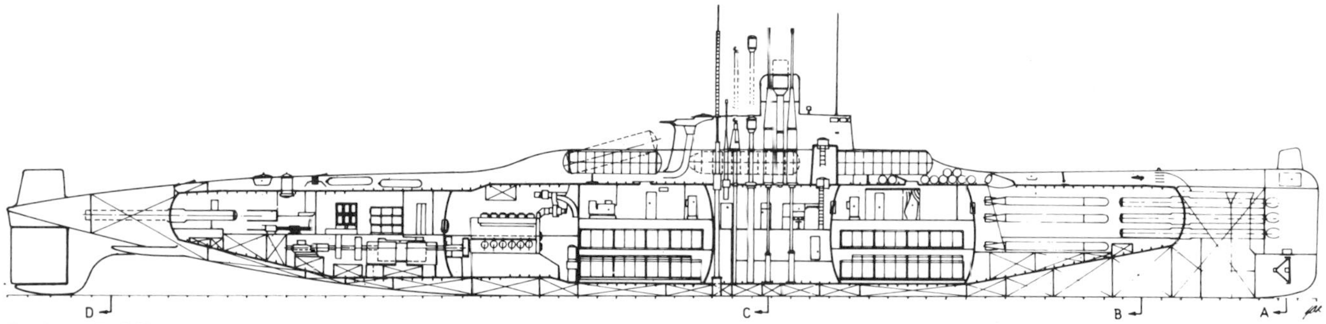

**Project E5SG**

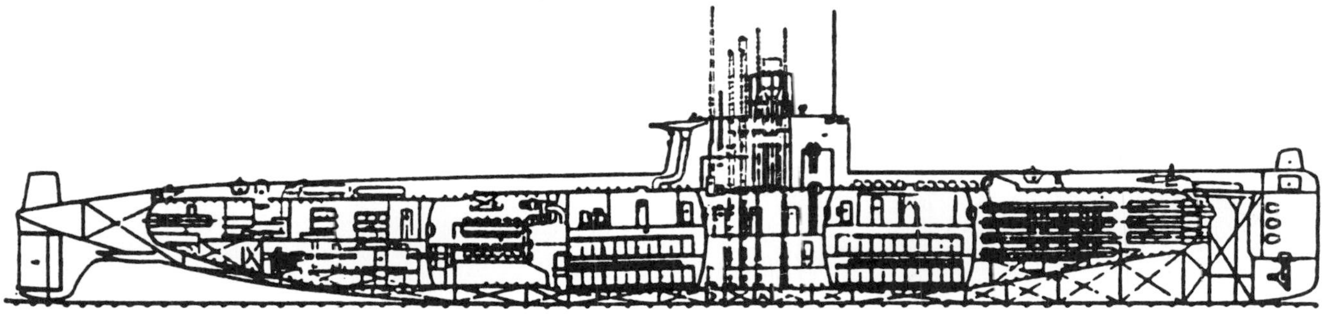
**Ming class**

**ATTACK SUBMARINES** *(continued)*

Remarks: First two launched 1975, third in 1982. Based on Romeo design, but with different propulsion plant (possibly of foreign origin) and fuller hull form. Design offered for export. Diving depth: 300 m.

◆ **91 Soviet Romeo (Chinese ES3B) class** Bldr: Wuzhang SY, Guangzhou SY, Jiangnan SY, Huludao SY (In serv. 1960–82)

**Romeo 267** R. Gillett, 9-84

**Romeo 260** 5-84

**D:** 1,319/1,712 tons **S:** 15.2/13 kts **Dim:** 76.60 × 6.70 × 4.95
**A:** 8/533-mm TT (6 fwd/2 aft)—14 torpedoes or 28 mines
**Electron Equipt:** Radar: 1/Snoop Plate—Sonar: Tamir-5L active, Feniks passive (two units: DUUX-5)
**M:** diesel-electric: 2 Type 1Z38 diesels, 2,400 hp each; 2 props; 2,700 hp—2 electric creep motors: 100 hp
**Endurance:** 60 days
**Range:** 14,000/9 surf.; 350/9 sub. **Man:** 8 officers, 43 men

Remarks: Diving depth: 300 meters. Foreign transfers include 7 to North Korea between 1973 and 1975, 4 to Egypt in 1982–83. 224-cell battery: 6,600 amp hr. Chinese project E3SB, also called T-33 class. One unit has one of two Thomson-Sintra DUUX-5 passive sonar suites delivered in 1983, and export version is offered with that gear plus an enlarged chin sonar dome.

◆ **15 Soviet Whiskey class** Bldr: 15 at Jiangnan SY, 6 at Wuzhang, SY

**D:** 1,050/1,350 tons **S:** 17/13.5 **Dim:** 76.0 × 6.3 × 4.8
**A:** 6/533-mm TT (4 fwd, 2 aft)—12 torpedoes or 24 mines
**Electron Equipt:** Radar: 1/Snoop Plate—Sonar: Tamir-5L active; . . . passive
**M:** diesel-electric: 2 Type 37D diesels; 2,000 hp each; 2,500 hp
**Range:** 8,300/8 snorkel

Remarks: A few were delivered by the U.S.S.R., the others were built in China (1960–64), probably at the Jiangnan Shipyard near Shanghai. Several retain a twin 25-mm AA in a semi-enclosed mount at the base of the forward end of the sail. About 6 are believed to have been stricken.

**DESTROYERS**

Note: An export version of the Luda, powered by a CODOG plant including two U.S. LM-2500 gas turbines, has been offered. Shown armed with 8 SSM (U.S. Harpoon or Chinese C 801), a box-type SAM launcher, a U.S. 127-mm Mk 45 DP gun, a Mk 15 20-mm CIWS, 2 sets triple ASW TT, and having a helicopter hangar, the Project EF5 can be taken as the next step in Chinese surface combatant development. Range is given as 5,000/16, and the crew as only 220. The first of these 4,200-ton (fl) ships is to be delivered in 1990 by Jiangnan SY, Shanghai.

◆ **15 Luda (Project EF4) class** Bldr: Hongqi SY, Luda SY, Donglang SY, Guangzhou and Zhonghua SY, Shanghai (In serv., 1972–1987)

105, 106, 107, 108, 109, 110, 111, 112, 131, 132, 133, 161, 163, 164, 165

**Luda 132**—with 8/57-mm AA, two f.c. radars R.N.Z.N., 1980

**Luda 110**—with 8/37-mm AA R. Gillett, 9-84

**Luda 105** *Ships of the World,* 1984

**D:** 3,250 tons (3,960 fl) **S:** 32 kts
**Dim:** 132.0 (127.5 pp) × 12.8 × 4.0 (5.2 sonar)
**A:** 6/HY-2 SSM (III × 2)—4/130-mm DP (II × 2)—8/57-mm (on 105, 108, 132) or 37-mm AA (II × 4)—4/25-mm AA (II × 2)—2 12-tubed ASW RL—4/BMB-2 d.c. mortars—2/d.c. racks—mines
**Electron Equipt:** Radar: 1/Fin Curve or Type 756 navigational, 1/Eye Shield (MX-902) short-range air-search, 1 Bean Sticks or Pea Sticks (antenna variant) long-range air-search, 1/Square Tie, 1/Sun Visor (not on all) 2/Rice Lamp for 57-mm f.c. (not on all); 132: Rice Screen also
Sonar: . . . EW: 2/Jug Pair
IFF: 3/Square Head interrogators, 1/High Pole A transponder
**M:** 2 sets GT; 2 props; 60,000 hp **Boilers:** 4 **Range:** 3,475/18 **Man:** 300 tot.

Remarks: Superficially resembles Soviet Kotlin, but is larger and has a flat transom stern, larger superstructure, etc. Ships in 100 series built at Luda, 110 series at Shanghai, 160 series at Guangzhou. Some systems of Soviet design; the ASW rocket launchers are derived from the Soviet RBU-1200 design, but have more tubes. Equipment varies greatly from ship to ship, with only a small number having fire-control radar systems, even on the Soviet Wasp Head 130-mm GFCS. The SSM used is derived from the Soviet SS-N-2 Styx, but is longer. One ship of this class (probably 162) lost 8-78 near Zanjiang through explosion. All equipped for underway fueling.

Ludas 105, 108, and 132 are the only units confirmed to mount twin 57-mm vice 37-mm AA; they also carry the Rice Lamp AA fire-control radars not mounted on the others. Pea Sticks long-range air search is carried by 107, 131, 132, and 162; the remainder have Bean Sticks. 132 has a larger variant of the Rice Screen (Sea Eagle) 3-D phased-array air-search radar atop the after mast and may receive

**DESTROYERS** *(continued)*

a new SAM system for evaluation. Sun Visor fire-control radars are mounted on the Wasp Head directors for the 130-mm DP guns only on 105, 108, 131, 161, and 162. Plans to modernize these basically excellent platforms with British equipment fell through in 1983. In 1985 it was announced that U.S. Mk 15 CIWS (Vulcan/Phalanx) would be added, along with U.S. Mk 46 ASW torpedoes and, possibly, ASW helicopters (Kaman SH-2F Lamps I) in a few.

◆ **4 Soviet Gordyy-class**

| | Bldr | L | In serv. |
|---|---|---|---|
| 101 Anshan (ex-*Razyaschiy*) | Dalzavod SY, Vladivostok | 1938 | 1940 |
| 102 Zhangzhun (ex-*Reshitel'nyy*, ex-*Pritkiy*) | Dalzavod SY, Vladivostok | 1939 | 1941 |
| 103 Ji Lin (ex-*Retivyy*) | Komsomolsk SY | 1940 | 1941 |
| 104 Fu Zhun (ex-*Rezkiy*, ex-*Pospenshnyy*) | Komsomolsk SY | 1939 | 1942 |

**D:** 1,657 tons (2,039 fl) **S:** 38 kts when built, certainly much less today
**Dim:** 112.86 × 10.20 × 3.8 **Range:** 800/38; 2,600/20 **Man:** 197 tot.
**A:** 4/HY-2 SSM (II × 2)—4/130-mm (I × 4)—8/37-mm AA (II × 4)—mines
**Electron Equipt:** Radar: 1/Fin Curve, 1/Square Tie—Sonar: none
**M:** 2 sets GT; 2 props; 48,000 hp **Boilers:** 3 **Fuel:** 500 tons

Remarks: All assembled in Far East from prefabrications by 61 Kommuna SY, Nikolayev. Transferred by the U.S.S.R., two in 12-54, the others in 7-55. The SSM, derived from the Soviet SS-N-2 Styx, replaced 6/533-mm TT (III × 2) between 1972 and 1974. No ASW armament.

**FRIGATES**

Note: An export frigate design, the Type EF3C, has been offered and may indicate the intended follow-on design to the Jianghu series:

**D:** 1,700 tons **S:** 28 kts **Dim:** 110.0 × 11.5 × . . . (8.0 moulded depth)
**A:** 4/C 801 SSM (II × 2)—2/100-mm DP (II × 1)—8/30-mm (II × 2)—2/RBU-1200 ASW RL (V × 2)—6/324-mm ASW TT (III × 2)—1/Zhi-9 (SA-365N Dauphin) helicopter
**Electron Equipt:** Radar: 1/Type 956 nav., 1/Eye Shield air search, 1/Square Tie f.c., 1/Rice Lamp f.c., 1/ Sun Visor f.c.
Sonar: 1/MF bow-mounted (Raytheon 1160 series)
EW: . . . intercept, 2 chaff RL
**M:** 2 diesels; 2 props; 24,000 hp **Man:** approx. 180 tot.
**Range:** 2,500/18 **Electric:** 1,720 kw (4 × 400 kw, 1 × 120 kw)

Remarks: Would have China's first computerized weapons data and control system.

◆ **1 (+?) Jianghu IV class** Bldr: Hudong SY, Shanghai

544 (In serv. 11-86)

**544 as completed** *Ships of the World,* 11-86

**544 fitting out** K. Ikeda, *Ships of the World,* 6-86

**D:** 1,600 tons (2,000 fl) **S:** 25.5 kts **Dim:** 103.2 × 10.2 × 3.05 (hull)
**A:** 2/HY-2 SSM (II × 1)—1/100-mm Creusot-Loire Compact DP—8/37-mm AA (II × 4)—2/RBU-1200 ASW RL (V × 2)—1/Zhi-9 (SA-365N Dauphin) helicopter
**Electron Equipt:** Radar: 1/Type 956 nav., 1/Eye Shield air search, 1/Square Tie missile f.c.
Sonar: 1/MF hull-mounted—EW: . . .
IFF: 2/Square Head interrogators, 1/High Pole A transponder
**M:** 2 SEMT-Pielstick 12 PA6 diesels; 2 props; 16,000 hp
**Range:** 4,000/15; 1,750/25 **Electric:** 1,320 kw (3 × 400 kw, 1 × 120 kw)
**Endurance:** 15 days **Man:** approx. 200 tot.

Remarks: Pendant 544, launched 9-85, was the first Chinese combatant to incorporate a helicopter. A second is probably under construction to utilize the other one of two French 90 round/min. 100-mm automatic guns purchased. Adding the helicopter facility to the Jianghu design cost the after 100-mm gun and twin SSM positions. The 100-mm gun is controlled by a CSEE Naja laser-electro-optical director.

◆ **2 (+ . . .) Jianghu III class** Bldr: Hudong SY, Shanghai

535 (In serv. 1986) 536 (In serv. 1987)

**536 fitting out** *Ships of the World,* 11-86

**535** China Features, 1986

**D:** approx. 2,100 tons (fl) **S:** 25.5 kts **Dim:** 103.2 × 10.2 × 3.05 (hull)
**A:** 8/C 801 SSM (II × 4)—4/100-mm DP (II × 2)—8/37-mm AA (II × 4)—2/RBU-1200 ASW RL (V × 2)—2/BMB-2 d.c. mortars
**Electron Equipt:** Radar: 1/Type 756 nav., 1/Eye Shield (MX-902) air search, 1/Rice Lamp f.c. (aft), 1/Square Tie, 1/Sun Visor
Sonar: bow-mounted MF
EW: 4 spherical radomes
IFF: 2/Square Head interrogators, 1/High Pole transponder
**M:** 2 SEMT-Pielstick 12 PA6 diesels; 2 props; 16,000 hp
**Electric:** 1,720 kw (4 × 400 kw, 1 × 120 kw) **Endurance:** 15 days
**Range:** 4,000/15; 1,750/25 **Man:** approx. 200 tot.

Remarks: An improved version of the Jianghu I/II series, apparently on the same hull and propulsion plant, but with a full shelter deck amidships supporting four pairs of SSM launchers. Wasp Head optical GFCS forward (with Sun Visor radar) for surface gunfire, and Rice Lamp radar director aft for AA.

◆ **23 (+ . . .) Jianghu I and II class, guided-missile** Bldr: Hudong SY and Jiangnan SY, Shanghai (1975– . . .) 509–516, 518, 521, 524–527, 533, 534, 535, 543, 545, 551, 553–555

**FRIGATES** *(continued)*

**Dandong (543) Jianghu II**—with twin 100-mm, round stack *Ships of the World,* 1985

**Jianghu II 533**—with twin 100-mm mounts, Eye Shield radar, and rounded stack Chinese Navy, 1983

**Jianghu II 553** L. & L. Van Ginderen, 1-87

**D:** 1,586 tons (1,900 fl) **S:** 25.5 kts **Dim:** 103.2 × 10.2 × 3.05 (hull)
**A:** 4/HY-2 SSM (II × 2)—2 or 4/100-mm DP (I or II × 2)—8 or 12/37-mm AA (II × 4 or 6)—2 or 4/RBU 1200 (V × 2 or 4)—4/BMB-2 d.c. mortars—2/d.c. racks—mines (533, 534 have 2 twin 100, only 4 twin 37-mm)
**Electron Equipt:** Radar: 1/Eye Shield (MX-902) air search, 1/Square Tie f.c., 1/Type 756 navigational
Sonar: 1/medium-freq.—EW: none or 2 Jug Pair
IFF: 2/Square Head, 1/High Pole A
**M:** 2/SEMT-Pielstick 12 PA6 diesels; 2 props; 16,000 hp
**Range:** 4,000/15; 1,750/25 **Endurance:** 15 days
**Man:** 195 tot. **Electric:** 1,320 kw (3 × 400 kw, 1 × 120 kw)

REMARKS: First launched 1975. Chinese Project EF3H, or Changsha class. Units with square stacks (510–514, 518, 526, 551) built by Jiangnan SY; the others have rounded stacks. Ships with twin 100-mm mounts (531, 533, 534, 543, 553) are referred to as Jianghu II; they omitted two twin 37-mm AA as partial weight compensation. Most have only two RBU-1200, while 515, 516, and 5 ships in the 521 series have four. 100-mm fire control is by a simple stereoscopic rangefinder. Two sisters with twin 57-mm guns vice 100-mm were delivered to Egypt in 1984–85. 543 is named *Dandong;* 511 is named *Kaifeng.*

◆ **2 Jiangdong-class, guided missile** Bldr: Hudong SY, Shanghai

531 ZHONGDONG (In serv. 1972) 535 N . . . (In serv. 1975)

**D:** 1,568 tons (1,900 fl) **S:** 25.5 kts **Dim:** 103.2 × 10.2 × 3.05 (hull)
**A:** 2/HQ-61 SAM systems—4/100-mm DP (II × 2)—8/37-mm AA (II × 4)—2/RBU-1200 (V × 2)—2/BMB-2 d.c. mortars—2/d.c. racks
**Electron Equipt:** Radar: 1/Type 756 nav., 1/Rice Screen, 2/Fog Lamp, 1/Rice Lamp, 1/Sun Visor
Sonar: 1/MF hull-mounted—EW: 2 Jug Pair intercept
IFF: 1/High Pole A transponder
**M:** 2 SEMT-Pielstick 12 PA6 diesels; 2 props; 16,000 hp
**Range:** 4,000/15; 1,750/25 **Endurance:** 15 days
**Man:** 195 tot. **Electric:** 1,720 kw (4 × 400 kw, 1 × 120 kw)

**Zhongdong (531)** *Ships of the World,* 1983

**Jianghu I 514**—square stack, bow bulwarks, single 100-mm DP mounts R. Gillett, 9-84

FRIGATES *(continued)*

**Zhongdong (531)** *Ships of the World,* 1983

REMARKS: SAM system, of Chinese design, only achieved operational status in the mid-1980s. A Fog Lamp missile f.c. radar is mounted on the foremast, with a second aft. A Rice Screen ("Sea Eagle") phased-array 3-D air-search radar antenna surmounts the foremast, and a Rice Lamp gun f.c. radar is atop the aftermast.

◆ **5 Jiangnan class** Bldr: Shantou SY and Jiangnan SY, Shanghai (In serv. 1964–68)

501 502 503 504 508

**Jiangnan-class frigate 504** U.S. Navy, 1983

**D:** 1,400 tons (fl) **S:** 28 kts **Dim:** 92.0 × 10.2 × 3.15 (hull)
**A:** 3/100-mm (I × 3, 1 fwd, 2 aft)—8/37-mm AA (II × 4)—4/14.5-mm mg (II × 2)—2/RBU-1200 (V × 2)—4/BMB-2 d.c. mortars—2/d.c. racks—mines
**Electron Equipt:** Radar: 1/Fin Curve nav.—Sonar: MF hull-mounted
**M:** 2 diesels; 2 props; 16,000 hp

REMARKS: Chinese version of the Soviet Riga class, with diesel propulsion. One built at Shanghai 1968, the others at Shantou. Lack sensors and radar f.c., but do have optical director for 100-mm guns.

◆ **4 Soviet Riga class**

| | Bldr | L | In serv. |
|---|---|---|---|
| 505 GUIYANG | Hudong SY, Shanghai | 26-9-56 | 1958 |
| 506 KUNMING | Guangzhou SY | 1957 | 1959 |
| 507 CHENGDU | Hudong SY, Shanghai | 28-4-56 | 1958 |
| 509 GUILIN | Guangzhou SY | 1957 | 1959 |

**D:** 1,186 tons (1,415 fl) **S:** 28 kts
**Dim:** 91.58 (88.00 wl) × 10.20 × 3.15 (4.40 sonar)
**A:** 2/SSM (II × 1)—3/100-mm DP (I × 3)—4/37-mm AA (II × 2)—4/14.5-mm mg (II × 2)—4/BMB-2 d.c. mortars—2/d.c. racks—mines

**Kunming (506)** 1980

**Chengdu (507)** 1982

**Electron Equipt:** Radar: 1/Type 756 nav., 1/Slim Net, 1/Square Tie, 1/Sun Visor
Sonar: Pegas-2M MF hull-mounted—EW: none
IFF: 2/Square Head, 1/High Pole A
**M:** 2 sets GT; 2 props; 20,000 hp **Boilers:** 2: 27 kg/cm$^2$, 360°C **Fuel:** 230 tons
**Electric:** 450 kw **Range:** 550/28; 2,000/13 **Man:** 175 tot.

REMARKS: Twin, trainable CSS-N-1 Styx launcher replaced torpedo tube mount during early 1970s. Very limited endurance.

NOTE: The remaining World War II former Japanese and British corvettes were stricken in 1986.

GUIDED-MISSILE PATROL BOATS

◆ **1 Hola class** (In serv. 1970)

**D:** 300 tons **S:** . . . kts **Dim:** 43.0 × . . . × . . .
**A:** 2/HY-2 SSM (I × 2)—2/37-mm AA (II × 2)

REMARKS: An enlarged version of Osa-I, and at one time equipped with a large radome. Apparently unsuccessful. Two additional SSM also removed by 1980s.

◆ **120 Huangfeng (Soviet Osa-I) class** Bldr: Jiangnan SY, Shanghai, 1960–. . .

**No. 7130, with radome**—note differences in detail from 3115 below: porthole pattern, missile tube supports L. & L. Van Ginderen, 1-87

**No. 3115, with radome aft and 30-mm AA**

**D:** 175 tons, 186.5 normal (205 fl) **S:** 35 kts **Dim:** 38.75 × 7.60 × 1.7 (mean)
**A:** 4/HY-1 or 2 SSM—4/25-mm or 30-mm AA (II × 2)
**Electron Equipt:** Radar: 1/Square Tie—IFF: 2/Square Head, 1/High Pole A
**M:** 3 M503A diesels; 3 props; 12,000 hp
**Electric:** 65 kw **Range:** 800/30 **Man:** 28 tot.

REMARKS: At least four were transferred by the U.S.S.R. circa 1960 and have 4/30-mm AA (II × 2) but no Drum Tilt gun fire-control radar. Most Chinese-built units had two twin 25-mm AA until early 1980s, when increasing numbers with a Chinese-built version of the Soviet AK-230, 30-mm AA began to appear; more recently, several have had a radome installed aft for a probable f.c. radar for the 30-mm AA. The 1980s have also seen the introduction of IFF equipment. Considerable numbers of the craft have been seen in an incomplete state in the Shanghai area in recent years, and not all of the listed total are operational.

## GUIDED-MISSILE PATROL BOATS *(continued)*

**No. 3113, with 25-mm AA, no IFF or gun f.c. radar** Chinese Navy, 1979

**No. 5102, with 30-mm AA, but no radome aft** R. Gillett, 9-84

◆ **1 Homa (Project EM1B) class** (In serv. circa 1970)

**D:** 85 tons (fl) **S:** 38 kts **Dim:** 28.00 × 6.60 × . . . (3.10 moulded depth)
**A:** 2/HY-1 SSM (I × 2)—4/25-mm AA (II × 2)
**Electron Equipt:** Radar: 1/Square Tie
**M:** 4 M50 series diesels; 4 props; 5,600 hp
**Range:** 500/25 **Man:** 20 tot.

Remarks: A single, apparently unsuccessful prototype with lengthened hull over the Hoku design, an extra twin 25-mm AA mount aft, and uprated engines. Design offered for foreign sale 1986.

◆ **70–75 Hoku (Project EM1A) class** (In serv. circa 1968–74)

**Hoku-class guided-missile patrol boats** Poly Technologies, 1986

**D:** 68 tons (74 normal/79.19 fl) **S:** 37 kts
**Dim:** 27.0 × 6.50 (6.30 wl) × 1.8 (1.295 mean hull)
**A:** 2/HY-1 SSM—2/25-mm AA (II × 1)
**Electron Equipt:** Radar: 1/Square Tie **M:** 4 M50 diesels; 4 props; 4,800 hp
**Electric:** 65 kw **Endurance:** 5 days **Range:** 500/24 **Man:** 16 tot.

Remarks: Steel-hulled improvement on Komar. Also referred to as "Hegu" class. Offered for export with 4 C-801 missiles.

Note: The H-3 missile boat project described in the previous edition has not progressed.

## TORPEDO BOATS

◆ **120 Huchuan-class hydrofoils** Bldr: Hudong SY, Shanghai (In serv. 1966–1980)

**D:** 39 tons (45.8 fl) **S:** 50 kts **Dim:** 22.50 × 3.80 (6.26 over foils) × 1.146
**A:** 2/533-mm TT—4/14.5-mm mg (II × 2)
**Electron Equipt:** Radar: 1/Type 756
**M:** 3 M50 diesels; 3 props; 3,600 hp **Electric:** 5.6 kw
**Range:** 500/30 **Man:** 11 tot.

Remarks: Identical to the hydrofoils delivered to Albania, Pakistan, and Tanzania. Also built in Romania. Not all units have the foils fitted; no foils aft, as stern planes on surface. In most, both gun mounts are aft, but in a few, one mount is forward. Some have Skin Head radar, while later ships have a Type 756 slotted-waveguide radar antenna.

**Chinese Huchuan class**—unit in foreground (3214) has no hydrofoils; craft in background to left does

◆ **40–50 Soviet P 6-class wooden-hulled** Bldr: China, 1960s

**D:** 56 tons (66.5 fl) **S:** 43 kts **Dim:** 25.3 × 6.1 × 1.7
**A:** 2/533-mm TT—4/25-mm AA (II × 2)
**Electron Equipt:** Radar: 1/Skin Head
**M:** 4 M50 diesels; 4 props; 4,800 hp **Man:** 20 tot.

Remarks: Beginning to be retired.

◆ **30–40 Soviet P 4-class aluminum-hulled hydroplanes (1950s)**

**D:** 19.3 tons (22.4 fl) **S:** 55 kts **Dim:** 19.3 × 3.7 × 1.0
**A:** 2/14.5-mm mg (II × 1)—2/450-mm TT **Man:** 12 tot.
**Electron Equipt:** Radar: 1/Skin Head **M:** 2 M50 diesels; 2 props; 2,400 hp

Remarks: Majority believed to be in reserve. Four transferred to Bangladesh, 1983.

## PATROL BOATS

◆ **44 Hainan class** (In serv. 1964– . . .)

**Hainan-class patrol boat 642** R. Gillett, 9-84

## PATROL BOATS *(continued)*

**D:** 375 tons (400 fl) **S:** 30.5 kts **Dim:** 58.77 × 7.20 × 2.20 (hull)
**A:** 4/57-mm AA (II × 2)—4/25-mm AA (II × 2)—4/RBU-1200 (V × 4)—2/BMB-2 d.c. mortars—2/d.c. racks—mines
**Electron Equipt:** Radar: 1/Pot Head—IFF; 1/High Pole A transponder
Sonar: Tamir-11 HF
**M:** 4 diesels; 4 props; 8,800 hp **Range:** 2,000/14 **Man:** 70 tot.

REMARKS: Hull numbers in 600s and 800s. Early units had 2/76.2-mm DP U.S. Mk 26 vice 4/57-mm AA and Skin Head radars. Two sets of Thomson-Sintra SS12 VDS lightweight variable depth sonars for this class were delivered 1986; more may be acquired after trials 1986–87. Two were transferred to Pakistan, 1976, and two more in 1980; eight delivered to Egypt 1983–85; eight to Bangladesh 1982–85.

NOTE: An enlarged version of Hainan, nicknamed the Haiju class, has been reported. On an overall length of 64 m, the armament is 4/57-mm AA (II × 2), 4/30-mm AA (II × 2), 4/RBU-1200 ASW RL (V × 4). No confirmation available.

**Hainan-class patrol boat 729** L. & L. Van Ginderen, 1-87

◆ **20 Soviet Kronshtadt class** (In serv. 1956–57)

**Chinese Kronshtadt** 1970

**D:** 300 tons (330 fl) **S:** 18 kts **Dim:** 52.1 × 6.5 × 2.2
**A:** 1/85-mm DP—2/37-mm AA—6/14.5-mm mg (II × 3)—2/BMB-1 d.c. projectors—2/d.c. racks. Some: 2/RBU-1200 ASW RL (V × 2)
**Electron Equipt:** Radar: 1/Ball End **M:** 3 diesels; 3 props; 3,300 hp
**Fuel:** 20 tons **Range:** 3,500/14 **Man:** 50 tot.

REMARKS: Six could have been delivered by the U.S.S.R., the others built in Shanghai and Canton. Other information indicates that only two were built in China, the balance in the Soviet Union. Hull numbers in 600s. Probably soon to strike.

◆ **325–330 Shanghai-II class** (In serv. 1962–. . .)

**Shanghai-II**—late version *Ships of the World,* 1986

**D:** 122.5 tons (134.8 fl) **S:** 28.5 kts **Dim:** 38.78 × 5.41 × 1.49 (hull; 1.554 full load)

**Shanghai-II class**—early version with squared-off bridge 1976

**A:** 4/37-mm AA (II × 2)—4/25-mm AA (II × 2)—depth charges—mines. Some: 2 RBU-1200 ASW RL (V × 2)
**Electron Equipt:** Radar: Pot Head or Skin Head—Sonar: HF on some
**M:** 2 M50F-4, 1,200-hp, and 2/12D6, 910-hp diesels; 4 props; 4,220 hp
**Endurance:** 7 days **Electric:** 39 kw **Range:** 750/16.5 **Man:** 36 tot.

REMARKS: Still being constructed. A large number have been transferred to foreign navies. Very unsophisticated and sparsely equipped. Shanghai-I class was smaller and had 2/57-mm (II × 1) forward; a few of the 12 built 1959–60 may remain in service: 125 tons (fl); 36.0 × 5.5 × 1.4; propulsion as for Shanghai-II.

NOTE: All Shantou (formerly Swatow)-class gunboats have been deleted from this edition, due to age and lack of sightings.

## PATROL CRAFT

◆ **1 (+ . . .) Cougar catamarans** Bldr: . . .

**D:** 5 tons **S:** 35 kts **Dim:** 14.0 (13.50 wl) × 5.15 × 1.30 **A:** . . .
**M:** 2 MWM diesels; 2 props; 1,230 hp **Range:** 500/35

REMARKS: Prototype and moulds for this GRP design delivered 2-87 by Cougar Marine, Hamble, U.K. for license production in China.

◆ **. . . 25-meter class** Bldr: . . . (In serv. 1980s)

**D:** 53.5 tons normal (55.77 fl) **S:** 38 kts **Dim:** 25.0 × 5.0 × . . .
**A:** 4/25-mm AA (II × 2) **Electron Equipt:** Radar: 1/Pot Head
**M:** 3 M50-series diesels; 3 props; 3,600 hp **Electric:** 12 kw
**Endurance:** 5–7 days **Range:** 300/27; 490/. . . **Man:** 20 tot.

REMARKS: Official data for a class of patrol craft that has yet to receive a Western nickname. Apparently a production successor to the Beihai class.

◆ **30 Beihai-class patrol craft** Bldr: . . . (1960s)

**Beihai class** 1966

**D:** 80 tons (fl) **S:** 18 kts **Dim:** 27.5 × 5.5 × 1.6
**A:** 4/25-mm AA (II × 2) **M:** 3 diesels; 3 props; 900 hp

REMARKS: Majority subordinated to Naval Militia of the various "Military Maritime Districts."

◆ **15 Huangpu-class patrol craft** Bldr: . . . (In serv. 1970s)

REMARKS: Data as for Beihai class, except A: 4/14.5-mm mg (II × 2). Have low superstructure fore and aft, providing additional accommodations for police or troops.

◆ **40 Yulin-class patrol craft** Bldr: . . . (In serv. 1964–68)

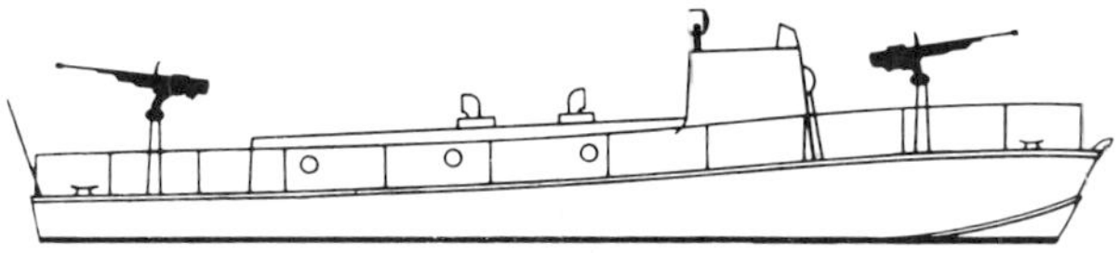
**Yulin class**

**D:** 9.8 tons (fl) **S:** 20 kts **Dim:** 13.0 × 2.9 × 1.1
**A:** 2/12.7-mm mg (I × 2) **M:** 1 diesel; 1 prop; 300 hp

REMARKS: Craft of this class also transferred to Kampuchea, Congo, and Tanzania.

◆ **1 or more Yingkou-class patrol craft** Bldr: . . . (In serv. 1960–65)

**D:** 40 tons (fl) **S:** 18 kts **Dim:** 20.0 × . . . × . . . **A:** 2/12.7-mm mg
**M:** 2 diesels; 2 props; 600 hp

REMARKS: Subordinated to "Military Maritime District" in South China militia.

**PATROL CRAFT** *(continued)*

◆ **several hundred armed fishing trawlers**

REMARKS: Many Chinese fishing trawlers are armed with 1 or 2/12.7-mm mg and perform dual service as fisheries patrol craft and fishing trawlers. There are several classes of these Militia-subordinated, steel-hulled, single-screwed craft displacing 200–450 tons (fl).

**Yingkou class** 1967

**Chinese armed fishing trawler T 710** 1973

**Customs Patrol 301 at Shanghai** R. Gillete, 9-84

The above craft, armed with 4/14.5-mm mg (II × 2), is one of a number operated by customs and piloting agencies. This particular unit displaces 245 tons (fl), has a max. speed of 28 knots (27 continuous), an endurance of 2,000 n.m. at 16 kts, and has dimensions of 44.50 × 7.00 × 1.85.

## MINE WARFARE SHIPS

◆ **23 Soviet T-43-class fleet minesweepers** Bldrs: Wuzhang SY, Guangzhou SY (In serv. 1956–1970s)

**D:** 500 tons (590 fl) **S:** 14 kts **Dim:** 60.0 × 8.6 × 2.16
**A:** 4/37-mm AA (II × 2)—4/25-mm AA (II × 2)—4/12.7-mm mg (II × 2)—2/d.c. projectors—mines
**Electron Equipt:** Radar: 1/Ball End—IFF: 1/Square Head, 1/High Pole A
**M:** 2/Type 9D diesels; 2 props; 2,200 hp
**Fuel:** 70 tons **Electric:** 550 kw **Range:** 3,200/10 **Man:** 65–80 tot.

**Chinese T-43-class minesweeper** R. Gillett, 9-84

**T-43-class 830** L. & L. Van Ginderen, 1-87

REMARKS: A few shorter-hulled, 58-meter, 570-ton units were transferred from the U.S.S.R.; the majority are long-hulled ships and were built in China. Several were built or converted as surveying ships, civilian research ships, and submarine rescue ships (J 124). At least one minesweeper has an 85-mm DP gun forward. Current hull numbers in the 800s.

◆ **up to 80 auxiliary Lienyun-class minesweepers converted from fishing boats**

**Auxiliary minesweepers**—subordinated to the Shanghai area Military Maritime District. Sometimes referred to as the Lien Yun class, these ships displace about 400 tons, are armed with 12.7-mm machine guns, and are based on a steel-hulled trawler design 1970

◆ **20 Fushun-class coastal minesweepers** (In serv. 1976–. . .)

**D:** 275 tons **S:** . . . **Dim:** 40.0 × 5.5 × . . .
**A:** 2/37-mm AA (II × 1)
**M:** 2 M50F-4 diesels, 2 12D6 diesels; 4 props; 4,220 hp

◆ **. . . Yenkuan and Wochang classes**

REMARKS: Shanghai II-class patrol boats adopted as minesweepers. Class differentiation not available.

◆ **60 Type 312 drone minesweepers** (In serv. late 1960s–. . .)

**Type 312 drone minesweeper** Chinese Navy, 1984

**D:** 46.95 tons (fl) **S:** 2 kts **Dim:** 20.94 × 4.20 × 1.30
**M:** 1 Type 3D12 diesel; 1 CP prop; 300 hp

REMARKS: Normally operated by radio control to a range of 3 n.m., but can be manned. Electric propulsion for sweeping at 1 to 5 kts. Diesel generator amidships powers integral electromagnet for magnetic sweeping and a noisemaker for actuating acoustic mines. All equipment shock-mounted. Laser precision navigation system. Officially stated not to be good sea boats; large numbers have been built, however.

## AMPHIBIOUS WARFARE SHIPS

◆ **4 Yukan-class landing ships** Bldr: Zhonghua SY, Shanghai (In serv. 1978–80)

927 928 928 934

**Yukan No. 927**—and a sister R. Gillett, 9-84

**Yukan No. 927 and sister**—note lowered stern ramp R. Gillett, 9-84

**D:** 3,110 tons (fl) **S:** 17 kts **Dim:** 119.5 × 15.6 × 2.9
**A:** 8/57-mm AA (II × 4)—8/25-mm AA (II × 4)
**Electron Equipt:** Radar: 2/nav.—IFF: 1/High Pole A
**M:** 2 SEMT-Pielstick 12 PA6 diesels; 2 props; 16,000 hp

REMARKS: Evidently built to replace aging World War II-built U.S. LSTs, these ships are larger and considerably faster than their predecessors. Carry two U.S.-design LCVPs. Bow and stern ramps.

◆ **15 ex-U.S. LST 1- and LST 542-class tank landing ships** (In serv. 1943–45)

355, 361, 901, 902, 903, 906, 907, 921, 922, 923, 924, 925, 926, 927, 928

**LST 1-class 903**—76.2-mm guns fore and aft, one radar *Ships of the World,* 1986

**LST 1-class 901**—2 twin 37-mm on bow, two radars *Ships of the World,* 1986

**D:** 1,625 tons (4,080 fl) **S:** 11 kts **Dim:** 99.98 × 15.24 × 4.36
**A:** 2-3/76.2-mm DP (I)—6-12–8/37-mm AA (II)
**M:** 2 G.M. 12-278A or 12-567A diesels; 2 props; 1,800 hp

REMARKS: Cargo capacity: 2,100 tons. Some are immobile as accommodations ships or tenders for submarines. Most rearmed during late 1950s with U.S. 76.2-mm guns and Soviet twin 37-mm AA. Hull numbers in 900s.

◆ **4 Yudao-class medium landing ships** (In serv. 1980–. . .)

**D:** 1,000 tons (fl) **S:** . . . **Dim:** 65.0 × . . . × . . .
**A:** 8/25-mm AA (II × 4) **M:** diesels

REMARKS: Smaller, but apparently faster than the Yu Ling class. Probably intended as replacements for World War II-era U.S. LSM 1 class. Resemble a smaller version of the LST 1 design.

◆ **14 ex-U.S. LSM 1-class medium landing ships** (In serv. 1944–45)

352, 353, 354, 393, 511, 809, 810, 811, 931, 932, 933, 934, 935, 936

**LSM 1-class 936**, showing mine port aft R. Gillett, 9-84

**D:** 743 tons (1,095 fl) **S:** 12.5 kts **Dim:** 62.03 × 10.52 × 2.54
**A:** 6/37-mm AA (II × 3)—4/25-mm AA (II × 2)—mines
**Electron Equipt:** Radar: 1/Fin Curve
**M:** 2 Fairbanks-Morse 38D8$\frac{1}{8}$-10 or G.M. 16-278A diesels; 2 props; 2,800 hp
**Range:** 2,500/12

REMARKS: Rearmed with Soviet weapons late 1950s. Most have two mine-laying ports in the stern. Several have superstructure built over the open tank deck.

◆ **23 Yuling-class utility landing craft** (In serv. 1971–75)

**D:** 600 tons (fl) **S:** 12 kts **Dim:** 50.0 × 7.0 × 2.0
**A:** 8/14.5-mm mg (II × 4) **Electron Equipt:** Radar: 1/Type 756 nav.
**M:** 2 diesels; 2 props; . . . hp

**Yuling-class N 1122 of the Nanjing Maritime Border Defense Force** 1983

◆ **6–8 U.S. LCT (6)-class utility landing craft** (In serv. 1943–45)

**U.S. LCT (6)-class landing craft Y 698** R. Gillett, 9-84

**D:** 143 tons (309 fl) **S:** 10 kts **Dim:** 36.3 × 9.6 × 1.2
**A:** 4/145-mm mg (I × 4)
**M:** 3 G.M. 6-71 diesels; 3 props; 675 hp **Range:** 1,200/7

AMPHIBIOUS WARFARE SHIPS *(continued)*

Remarks: Acquired 1949. Cargo: 150 tons. Sterns since enclosed and pilothouses greatly enlarged. Several LCT (5) of similar design may also survive. Now considered to be "transports" and have "Y"-series pendants.

◆ **300 Yunnan-class landing craft** Bldr: Huangzhou SY (In serv. 1968–72)

**Yunnan-class No. 5561** R. Gillett, 9-84

**D:** 133.2 tons (fl) **S:** 10.5 kts **Dim:** 27.50 (24.07 pp) × 5.40 × 1.40
**A:** 2–4/14.5-mm mg (I or II × 2) **M:** 2 diesels; 2 props; 600 hp
**Range:** 500/10 **Man:** 6 tot.

Remarks: Cargo: 46 tons (1 tank). Cargo deck 15.0 × 4.0 m

◆ **40–50 Yuchin-class landing craft** (In serv. 1962–72)

**Yuchin-class No. N 3015 of the Nanjing Maritime Border Defense Force** R. Gillett, 9-84

**D:** 60 tons light (110 fl) **S:** 11.5 (9 loaded) kts **Dim:** 24.1 × 5.2 × 1.1
**A:** 2/14.5-mm mg (I × 2) **M:** 2 diesels; 2 Type 12V50 props; 600 hp

Remarks: Two transferred to Bangladesh in 1984 as survey craft.

◆ **20–30 Yuchai-class landing craft** (In serv. 1960s)

**Yuchai class Y 761** R. Gillett, 9-84

**D:** 70 tons (fl) **S:** 10 kts **Dim:** 20.0 × 4.3 × 1.0
**A:** 4/14.5-mm mg (II × 2) **M:** 2 diesels; 2 props; 600 hp

Remarks: Some, including unit shown above, have "Y"-pendants, indicating service as "transports" rather than as landing craft *per se.*

◆ **approx. 50 copies U.S. LCM(6)-class landing craft** (In serv. 1950s–1960s)

**D:** 24 tons (56 fl) **S:** 9 kts **Dim:** 17.0 × 4.4 × 1.2
**A:** 2/12.7-mm mg (I × 2) **M:** 2 diesels; 2 props; 300 hp

◆ **1 Dagu-A-class air-cushion landing craft prototype**

**D:** 61 tons (fl) **S:** 55 kts **Dim:** 27.2 × 13.8 × 9.6 (high)
**M:** 2 turboprop propulsion engines; 1 gas-turbine lift engine, geared also to 2 auxiliary propellers

**Dagu-A air-cushion vehicle**—note bow door 1981

Remarks: Cargo: 16.8 tons. Designed by Shanghai SB Research and Development Institute. The function of the small airscrews amidships is uncertain; they may aid in maneuvering. There are six centrifugal lift-fans. Appears to be an engineering prototype rather than an operational combatant. Other hovercraft designs reported include the 15-meter Payi and 70-ton Jingoah designs.

## AUXILIARY SHIPS

There is no comprehensive information on the Chinese fleet's logistic support, but China has designated and built large numbers of auxiliary vessels, running the spectrum of logistics support, repair, hydrographic survey, and research types, including a great many tugs and small oilers.

### ICEBREAKERS

◆ **2 Haiping class** Bldr: Jiu Shin SY, Shanghai

C 721 Haiping 101 (L: 26-12-69) C 723 Haiping 102 (L: 1972)

**Haiping 102 (C 723)** 3-85

**D:** 3,200 tons **S:** 16 kts **Dim:** 84.0 × 15.0 × 5.0
**A:** 8/37-mm AA (II × 4)—8/25-mm AA (II × 4)
**M:** 2 diesels; 2 props; 5,200 hp

Remarks: Differ in details of superstructure. Can also be used as ocean tugs.

### HYDROGRAPHIC SURVEY SHIPS

◆ **1 Kanzhu class** (In serv. 1973)

K 420

**Kanzhu-class No. K 420** 1975

**HYDROGRAPHIC SURVEY SHIPS** *(continued)*

**D:** 1,000 tons (fl) **S:** 20 kts **Dim:** 65.0 × 9.0 × 3.0
**A:** 4/37-mm AA (II × 2)—4/25-mm AA (II × 2)—4/14.5-mm mg (II × 2)
**M:** 4 diesels; 2 props; 4,400 hp **Man:** 120 tot.

REMARKS: Operates in South China waters.

◆ **3 Yanlai class** (In serv. early 1970s)

K 629 K 512 K . . .

**D:** 1,100 tons (fl) **S:** 16 kts **Dim:** 72.0 × 9.8 × 3.0
**A:** 4/37-mm AA (II × 2)—4/25-mm AA (II × 2)
**M:** 2 diesels; 2 props; 2,200 hp

REMARKS: Funnel amidships; large crane aft.

◆ **2 Modified T-43-class minesweepers** (In serv. late 1960s)

**T-43-class research ship S 994** R. Gillett, 9-84

**D:** 500 tons (590 fl) **S:** 14 kts **Dim:** 60.0 × 8.6 × 2.16
**A:** 2/37-mm AA (II × 1)—4/14.5-mm AA (II × 2)
**Electron Equipt:** Radar: 1/Fin Curve **Range:** 3,200/10
**M:** 2 Type 9D diesels; 2 props; 2,200 hp **Fuel:** 70 tons

REMARKS: "S" pendant indicates research role, rather than hydrographic survey. Extended after deckhouse, no minesweeping equipment. Four-point mooring capability.

◆ **2 Hace-class coastal survey ships** (In serv. 1960s)

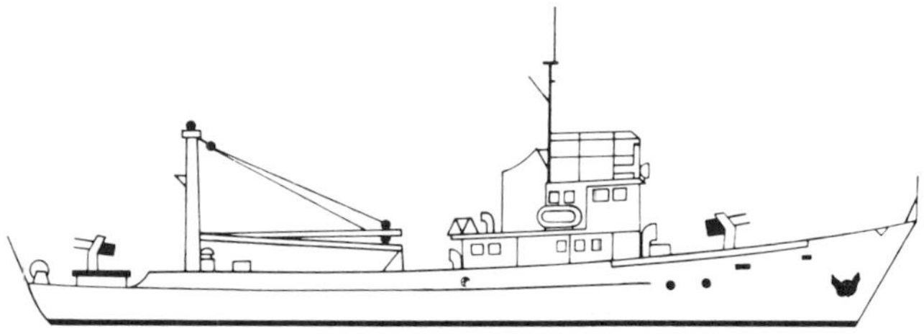

**Hace class**

**D:** 400 tons **S:** 12 kts **Dim:** 38.0 × 7.6 × 3.4 **A:** 4/14.5-mm mg (II × 2)
**M:** 1 diesel; 1 prop; 400 hp

REMARKS: Design derived from that of a coastal cargo ship.

◆ **1 Yanlun class** (In serv. 1965)—no data available

◆ **up to 10 additional naval survey ships**

**OCEANOGRAPHIC RESEARCH SHIPS**

◆ **2 Haiyang class** (In serv. 1972–73)

HAIYANG 01 HAIYANG 02

**D:** 3,295 tons **S:** 20 kts **Dim:** 104.0 × 13.8 × 5.0
**A:** 6/37-mm AA (II × 3) **M:** 2 diesels; 2 props; 9,000 hp

REMARKS: Resemble passenger liners; white-painted.

◆ **3 Shukuang class** (In serv. late 1960s)

SHUKUANG 01 SHUKUANG 02 SHUKUANG 03

**D:** 500 tons (590 fl) **S:** 14 kts **Dim:** 60.0 × 8.4 × 2.15
**A:** 1/37-mm AA **M:** 2 diesels; 2 props; 2,200 hp
**Range:** 3,200/10

REMARKS: Design closely derived from T-43-class minesweeper. White-painted. There is also *Shukuang* 04, a more modern-appearing ship about the same size.

◆ **2 Shihjian class** Bldr: Hutung SY, Shanghai (In serv. 1968–69)

SHIHJIAN N . . . . . . .

**D:** 2,955 tons **S:** 16.2 kts **Dim:** 94.73 (87.00 pp) × 14.04 × 4.75
**A:** 8/14.5-mm mg (II × 4) **Electric:** 1,065 kw
**M:** 2 Type 6 ESD(2) 48/82 diesels; 2 props; 4,000 hp **Range:** 7,500/14.5

REMARKS: 2,500 grt/1,000 dwt. Enlarged version of *Dong Fang Hong* class.

◆ **2 Dong Fang Hong class** Bldr: Hutung SY, Shanghai (In serv. 1964–66)

N . . . . . . . DONG FANG HONG

**Dong Fang Hong** 1978

**D:** 2,900 tons **S:** 14 kts **Dim:** 86.00 × 11.50 × 4.75 **A:** none
**M:** 2 diesels; 2 props; 4,000 hp

NOTE: Subordinated to the Shandong Oceanographic College. There are also large numbers of civilian-agency-subordinated research vessels for oil exploration, fisheries research, etc.

**EXPERIMENTAL SHIPS**

◆ **2 Yuanwang-class satellite and missile-tracking ships** Bldr: Hutung SY, Shanghai (In serv. 1980)

YUANWANG 1 YUANWANG 2

**Yuanwang 2** R.N.Z.N., 1980

**D:** 17,100 tons (21,000 fl) **S:** 20 kts **Dim:** 190.0 × 22.6 × 7.5
**M:** 1 diesel; 1 prop; . . . hp

REMARKS: First observed during the 5-80 Chinese ICBM tests in the Central Pacific. Have one large parabolic tracking antenna, two log-periodic HF ("fish-spine") antennas, several precision theodolite optical tracking stations, and two smaller missile-tracking radars, as well as positions for later installation of equipment. Large helicopter deck, but no hangar. Have a bow-thruster and retractable fin stabilizers.

NOTE: The Xiang Yang Hong ("East is Red"—the title of the Chinese national anthem)—series ships are mainly disparate in size and characteristics; all are capable of a variety of experimental duties (including general oceanography), particularly in support of missile and satellite research and hydrometeorology. All are under the general subordination of the Academy of Sciences.

◆ **1 Antarctic research and support ship** Bldr: . . . , Finland

XIANG YANG HONG . . . (ex-*Ji Di*, ex-*Rhea*) (In serv. 1971)

**D:** 15,000 tons (fl) **S:** . . . **Dim:** . . . × . . . × . . .
**M:** . . .

REMARKS: 7,890 grt/10,000 dwt. Acquired 10-85. Has helicopter deck and hangar. Carried 126 scientists to Antarctica 12-86, traveling 26,700 n.m. on a 200-day journey.

## EXPERIMENTAL SHIPS *(continued)*

◆ **1 weather reporting ship**

Xiang Yang Hong 14

Remarks: No data available; participated in joint U.S.–Chinese Western Pacific research cruise 12-85 to 2-86.

◆ **1 general oceanographic research ship** (In serv. 1982)

Xiang Yang Hong 16

**D:** 4,000 tons (fl) **S:** . . . **Dim:** . . . × . . . × . . .

Remarks: Operated for the East China Branch of the National Bureau of Oceanography, for biological and mineral bottom sampling. Possibly a sister to *Xiang Yang Hong 9.*

◆ **1 Xiang Yang Hong 10 class** Bldr: Hutung SY, Shanghai (In serv. 1980)

Xiang Yang Hong 10

**Xiang Yang Hong 10**—Super Frélon helicopter on deck aft; a weather-balloon tracking radar has since been added atop the bridge. R.N.Z.N., 1980

**D:** 10,975 tons **S:** 20 kts **Dim:** 156.2 × 20.6 × 6.8
**M:** 2 Xin Zhong-M.A.N. K9Z60/105E diesels; 2 props; . . . hp

Remarks: Operated by the East China Sea Branch, State Oceanographic Bureau. Uses same hull and propulsion as the Dajiang-class submarine tenders, but has twin, side-by-side funnels and hangar space for only one French Super Frélon helicopter; the crane forward is smaller, and the kingposts abaft the stacks and the heavy foremast support large log-periodic HF antennas. Has retractable fin stabilizers. Departed for 150-day Antarctic expedition 20-11-84 to 10-4-85 with submarine tender J 121 and a landing ship named *Great Wall 2.*

◆ **1 Xiang Yang Hong 9 class** Bldr: Hutung SY, Shanghai (In serv. 1979)

Xiang Yang Hong 9

**Xiang Yang Hong 9** U.S. Navy, 1982

**D:** 4,400 tons **S:** . . . kts **Dim:** 110.0 × . . . × . . . **M:** diesels; 4,000 hp
**Range:** 11,000/. . . **Man:** 145 tot.

◆ **1 Polish Francesco Nullo-class (Type B-41)**—former cargo ship
Bldr: Paris Commune SY, Gdynia, Poland (In serv. 1967)

Xiang Yang Hong 5 (ex-*Chang Niy*)

**Xiang Yang Hong 5** R.N.Z.N., 1980

**D:** 14,500 tons (fl) **S:** 16 kts **Dim:** 152.6 (141.6 pp) × 19.5 × 8.75
**M:** 1 Ciegielski-Sulzer 6RD68 diesel; 1 prop; 7,200 hp **Range:** 15,000/16

Remarks: Extensively rebuilt as a hydrometeorological-research and radiosonde-balloon tracking ship at Canton in 1970–72, and altered again after 1976, with a two-level superstructure replacing the after two hatches. Has one large log-periodic HF antenna forward. One of her four Chinese-operated merchant sisters briefly served as an unaltered support ship as *Xiang Yang Hong 10* in the late 1970s (not the same ship as the new unit above).

◆ **1 Xiang Yang Hong 2 class** (In serv. 1971)

Xiang Yang Hong 2

**D:** 1,000 tons (fl) **S:** . . . kts **Dim:** 72.5 × 8.7 × . . .
**M:** 2 diesels; 2 props; . . . hp

◆ **3 Xiang Yang Hong 1 class** (In serv. 1972–74)

Xiang Yang Hong 1 Xiang Yang Hong 4 Xiang Yang Hong 6

**Xiang Yang Hong 6** U.S. Navy, 1979

**D:** approx. 1,000 tons (fl) **S:** . . . kts **Dim:** 67.0 × 10.0 × . . .
**M:** 2 diesels; 2 props; . . . hp

Remarks: Carried 2/37-mm AA (II × 1), 8/14.5-mm mg (II × 4) as completed.

## SUBMARINE SUPPORT SHIPS

Note: A new submarine tender was officially reported completed 1985; no data available.

◆ **3 Dajiang class** Bldr: Hudong SY, Shanghai (In serv. 1978–80)

J 302 R 327 (ex-J 506) J 121

**J 302**—note rescue submersible on deck beside crane R. Gillett, 9-84

**R 327**—note 2 Super Frélon helicopters (old number) R.N.Z.N., 1980

## SUBMARINE SUPPORT SHIPS *(continued)*

**D:** 10,087 tons (fl) **S:** 20 kts **Dim:** 156.2 × 20.6 × 6.8 **A:** none
**A:** none **Electron Equipt:** Radar: 2/Fin Curve, 1/Eye Shield (MX-902)
**M:** 2 Xin Zhong-M.A.N. K9Z60/105E diesels; 2 props; . . . hp

REMARKS: Carry two French Super Frélon heavy helicopters in a double hangar. J 301 differs in not having the deep recesses at the stern (evidently intended to permit a 4-point moor). The huge crane forward tends two trainable cradles just forward of the bridge; the cradles are semicircular in section and support salvage-and-rescue submersibles. The ships share the hull and propulsion of the research ship *Xiang Yang Hong 10* and probably also have fin stabilizers. Former J 506 transferred to Academy of Sciences, 1983, and renumbered R 327; large log-periodic antenna added.

◆ **1 Dalang class** Bldr: Guangzhou SY (In serv. 1975)

J 503

**No. J 503**—Dalang class 1980

**D:** 4,000 tons (fl) **S:** 16 kts **Dim:** 130.0 × 14.0 × 4.0
**A:** 8/37-mm AA (II × 4)—4/14.5-mm mg (II × 2)
**M:** 2 diesels; 2 props; 4,000 hp

REMARKS: Primarily intended for general salvage and towing duties in support of submarines.

◆ **1 Dazhi class** Bldr: Hudong SY, Shanghai (In serv. mid-1960s)

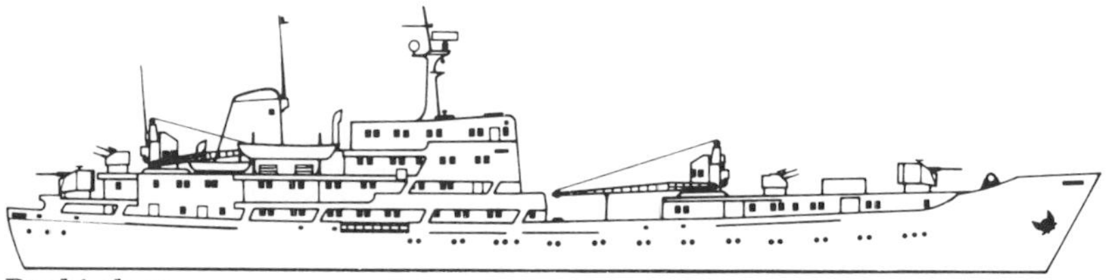

**Dazhi class**

**D:** 5,800 tons (fl) **S:** 14 kts **Dim:** 106.7 × 15.3 × 6.1
**A:** 4/37-mm AA (II × 2)—8/25-mm AA (II × 4)
**M:** 1 diesel; 1 prop; . . . hp

◆ **1 Hudong class** Bldr: Hudong SY, Shanghai (In serv. 1969)

J 301

**Hudong-class submarine tender J 301** R. Gillett, 9-84

**D:** 5,000 tons (fl) **S:** . . . kts **Dim:** 95.0 × 17.0 × 4.5
**A:** 4/37-mm AA (II × 2)—4/14.5-mm mg (II × 2) **M:** 1 diesel; 1 prop; . . . hp
**Electron Equipt:** Radar: 1/Fin Curve

REMARKS: Has large gantry over stern for lowering a submarine rescue chamber.

NOTE: There are several other small submarine support classes, including the 1,100-ton Dazhou class (J 502, J 504) and the 2,800-ton, 82-meter Dadong class (J 304, . . .). At least one T-43 minesweeper (J 124) is used in a submarine support role.

## REPAIR SHIPS

◆ **1 Romanian Galati class** Bldr: Galati SY (In serv. early 1970s)

**D:** 5,200 tons (fl) **S:** 12.5 kts **Dim:** 100.60 (93.70 pp) × 13.92 × 6.60 **A:** . . .
**M:** 1 Sulzer 5TAD56 diesel; 1 prop; . . . hp **Electric:** 345 kw
**Fuel:** 250 tons **Range:** 5,000/12.5

REMARKS: Converted from a cargo ship, with minimal external alterations. Of nine sisters purchased by China, two others serve the navy as cargo ships.

◆ **1 U.S. Achelous class** Bldr: Kaiser Co., Vancouver, Wash.

| | Laid down | L | In serv. |
|---|---|---|---|
| TAKUSHAN (ex-*Hsing An*, ex-*Achilles*, ARL 41, ex-LST 455) | 3-8-42 | 17-10-42 | 30-1-43 |

**Takushan (U 891)** R. Gillett, 9-84

**D:** 4,100 tons (fl) **S:** 11 kts **Dim:** 99.98 × 15.24 × 3.40
**A:** 12/37-mm AA (II × 6) **M:** 2 G.M. 12-567A diesels; 2 props; 1,800 hp
**Electric:** 350 kw **Range:** 9,000/9 **Man:** 290 tot.

REMARKS: Acquired 1949. Has 60-ton A-frame gantry, plus several cranes. Generally immobile at Shanghai. Bow doors still functional.

## CABLE SHIPS/BUOY TENDERS

◆ **3 or more Youzhong class** Bldr: Zhonghua SY, Shanghai (In serv. (1982– . . .)

G 2693 N 2304 N 2404

**Cable layer N 2304**—note quadrantial gantry aft R. Gillett, 9-84

**D:** 750 tons (fl) **S:** 14.5 kts **Dim:** 59.0 × 10.50 × 2.8
**A:** 4/14.5-mm mg (II × 2) **Electron Equipt:** Radar: 1/Fin Curve
**M:** 2 Type 8300Z diesels; 2 props; 2,200 hp

REMARKS: Smaller version of Youdien class, shallower draft, with only 50 $m^3$ of cable stowage.

◆ **4 or more Youdian class** Bldr: Zhonghua SY, Shanghai (In serv. late 1970s)

B 765 B 873 H 263 N . . .

**Cable layer B 873 with Yuchai LCM alongside**—note fixed gantry aft
R. Gillett, 9-84

## CABLE SHIPS/BUOY TENDERS *(continued)*

**Buoy tender H 263**—note lack of bow sheaves, buoy crane, and handling deck, with reinforced hull sides R. Gillett, 9-84

**D:** 1,550 tons (fl) **S:** 14 kts (sust.)
**Dim:** 71.40 (63.00 pp) × 10.50 × 3.60
**A:** 4/37-mm AA (II × 2)—4/14.5-mm mg *or* 8/14.5-mm mg (II × 2) *or* none
**M:** 2 Type 8300Z diesels; 2 props; 2,200 hp
**Electron Equipt:** Radar: 1/Fin Curve

REMARKS: Design built for both military and civil use. Cable tank has 187-$m^3$ capacity; ship can lay cable up to 100 mm thick. Those with "B" pendants serve as cable layers; those with "H" pendants are used as mooring buoy tenders. Several ("N" pendants) also serve the Nanjing Maritime Border Defense Force.

## REPLENISHMENT OILERS

◆ **3 Fuqing class** Bldr: Dalien SY (In serv. 1980–82)

X 575 X 615 X950

**X 615**—streamlined stack L. & L. Van Ginderen, 1-87

**X 950**—rectangular stack, no armament positions L. & L. Van Ginderen, 1-87

**D:** 14,600 tons (21,740 fl) **S:** 18.6 kts **Dim:** 160.82 × 21.80 × 9.40 **A:** none
**Electron Equipt:** Radar: 2/Fin Curve—IFF: 1/High Pole A
**Electric:** 2,480 kw **M:** 1/Dalian-Sulzer 8RLB 66 diesel; 1 prop; 17,400 hp
**Range:** 18,000/14.6 **Man:** 26 officers, 120 men

REMARKS: Equipment similar to U.S. Navy transfer systems. Two liquid replenishment stations per side, with constant-tension solid transfer stations each side just forward of the stack. Helo deck, but no hangar. Provision for four twin 37-mm AA gun mounts. X 615 has a rounded stack and a higher aft superstructure than X 950. Both have 4 small electric cranes for stores handling. Carry 11,000 tons fuel oil, 1,000 tons diesel fuel, 200 tons feedwater, 200 tons potable water, and 50 tons lube oil.

## TRANSPORT OILERS

◆ **2 or more new construction** (In serv. 1981–. . .)

X 620 X 621

**D:** 4,940 tons (fl) **S:** 14 kts **Dim:** 101.0 (92.0 pp) × 13.8 × 5.5
**M:** 1 diesel; 1 prop; 2,600 hp **Range:** 2,400/14

REMARKS: 3,318.5 dwt. Cargo: 3,002 tons fuel oil (4,240 $m^3$). Most are for commercial service, but two also employed by the navy.

◆ **6 or more Fulin class** Bldr: Hudong SY, Shanghai (In serv. 1972)

**D:** 2,200 tons (fl) **S:** 10 kts **Dim:** 66.0 × 10.0 × 4.0
**A:** 4/25-mm AA (II × 2) **Electron Equipt:** Radar: 1/Fin Curve
**M:** 1 diesel; 1 prop; 600 hp **Range:** 1,500/8 **Man:** 30 tot.

REMARKS: Part of a series of 20, most of which went into merchant service. Several reported to have a single underway replenishment rig. At least one (N 1104) is subordinated to the Nanjing Maritime Border Defense Force. Resemble an enlarged Fuzhou.

◆ **14 or more Fuzhou class** Bldr: Hudong SY, Shanghai (In serv. 1964–70)

**Fuzhou-class N 1101 of the Nanjing Maritime Border Defense Force** R. Gillett, 9-84

**D:** 1,200 tons (fl) **S:** 10–12 kts **Dim:** 60.0 (55.0 pp) × 9.0 × 3.5
**A:** 4.25-mm AA (II × 2)—4/14.5-mm mg (II × 2)
**Electron Equipt:** Radar: 1/Fin Curve or Type 756
**M:** 1 diesel; 1 prop; 600 hp **Man:** 30 tot.

REMARKS: Cargo: 600 tons. Five also built in a water-tanker version. Many of the oilers are subordinated to Maritime Border Defense Force. Some are not armed.

◆ **5 Leizhou class** (In serv. early 1960s)

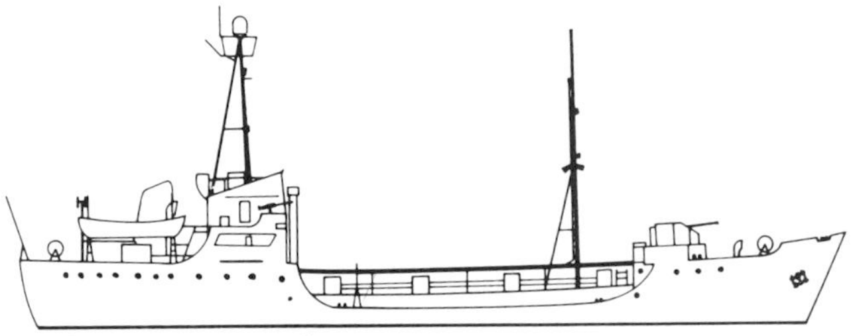

**Leizhou transport oiler**

**D:** 900 tons **S:** 10–12 kts **Dim:** 53.0 (48.0 pp) × 9.8 × 3.0
**A:** 4/37-mm AA (II × 2)—2/12.7-mm mg (I × 2) **M:** 1 diesel; 1 prop; 600 hp
**Man:** 30 tot.

REMARKS: Four also built in a water-tanker version, and another was built as a cargo ship (Y 737) with a single kingpost and two cargo holds amidships.

## WATER TANKERS

◆ **5 Fuzhou class** Bldr: Hudong SY, Shanghai (In serv. 1964–70)

**Fuzhou-class water or gasoline tanker X 629**—no armament R. Gillett, 9-84

## WATER TANKERS *(continued)*

Remarks: Data generally as for transport oiler version. Armament distributed differently and lack raised cargo expansion tank top amidships. Formerly armed with 4/25-mm AA (II × 2)—4/14.5-mm mg (II × 2).

◆ **4 Leizhou class** (In serv. early 1960s)

Remarks: Appearance similar to transport oiler version, but lack raised tank top in well-deck area.

◆ **. . . harbor oilers** (In serv. . . .)

N 1143 N 11 . . .

**Harbor tanker N 1143 and a sister** R. Gillett, 9-84

Two small liquid cargo transports subordinated to the Nanjing District of the Maritime Border Defense Force. Capacity is about 50–70 tons. The total number of craft of this design and the Western nickname are unavailable.

## TRANSPORTS

◆ **4 Qiongsha Class** Bldr: Guangzhou SY (In serv. 1980– . . .)

Y 832 Y . . . Y . . . Y . . .

**Qiongsha-class transport Y 832** U.S. Navy, 5-83

**D:** 2,150 tons (fl) **S:** 16.2 kts **Dim:** 86.0 (76.0 pp) × 13.4 × 3.9
**A:** 8/14.5-mm mg (II × 4) **Electron Equipt:** Radar: 2/Fin Curve
**M:** 3 8NVD48A-2U diesels; 3 props; 3,960 hp
**Fuel:** 195 tons **Electric:** 575 kw **Man:** 59 tot.

Remarks: Built for South Seas Fleet service. Carry about 400 troops. Cargo holds fore and aft, each tended by two 1-ton derricks, can hold 350 tons.

## CARGO SHIPS

◆ **1 or more . . . class** (In serv. 1980)

**Cargo ship L 201** 1980

Remarks: A cargo ship of about 1,000 dwt, armed with 2/37-mm AA (II × 1) and 4/14.5-mm mg (II × 2) and equipped with a Fin Curve navigational radar. Three holds, served by two electrohydraulic cranes. Class name not available.

◆ **3 or more Hongoi 081 class** Bldr: . . . (In serv. 1970s)

Y 443 Y 755 Y 756

**D:** 1,950 tons (fl) **S:** 10–12 kts **Dim:** 62.0 (58.0 wl) × 12.0 × 4.5
**A:** 4/25-mm AA **M:** 1 diesel; . . . hp

Remarks: 875 grt/1,100 dwt. Sisters in commercial service.

◆ **2 Romanian Galati class** (In serv. early 1970s)

Remarks: Characteristics as for the repair-ship version described earlier.

◆ **1 Zhandou 59 class** (In serv. 1959–65)

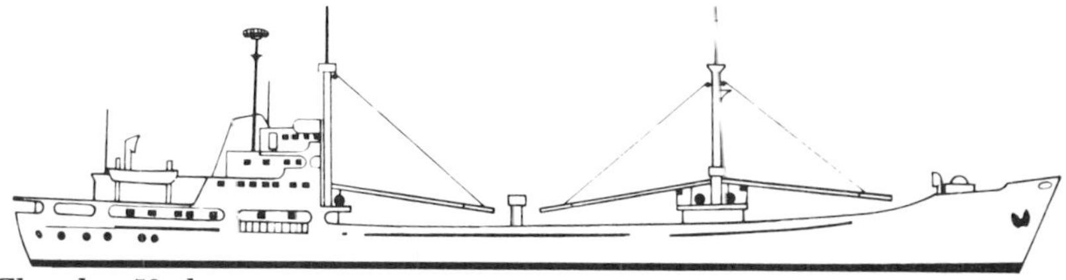

**Zhandou 59 class**

**D:** 4,735 tons (fl) **S:** 12.5 kts **Dim:** 99.4 × 13.0 × 5.5 **A:** none
**M:** 1 diesel; 1 prop; . . . hp **Man:** 50 tot.

Remarks: 2,798 grt/3,200 dwt. One of a class of 20 built for merchant marine service; two were combined to produce an oil-drilling platform in the mid-1970s.

◆ **3 Danlin class** (In serv. mid-1960s)

L 202 L 591 L 790

**Danlin-class L 202** R. Gillett, 9-84

**D:** 1,150 tons (fl) **S:** 10–12 kts **Dim:** 60.0 × 9.1 × 3.5
**A:** 2/37-mm AA (I × 2)
**M:** 1 diesel; 1 prop; 600 hp **Cargo:** About 600 tons

**Small cargo transport N 1127** R. Gillett, 9-84

Remarks: One of a number of units of this design (including N 1121 and N 3215), most of which seem to be subordinated to the Maritime Border Defense Force districts of about 450 tons (fl) displacement, they have a single cargo hold amidships, are equipped with a Type 756 navigational radar, and are armed with two twin side-by-side 14.5-mm mg mounts. Maximum speed is about 9 kts on a single 300-hp diesel.

## TRAINING SHIP

◆ **1 naval cadet training ship** Bldr: Qiuxin SY, Shanghai

V 856 (L: 12-7-86)

**D:** 5,500 tons (fl) **S:** . . . **Dim:** 142.0 (132.0 × 16.0 × . . . pp)
**A:** 4/57-mm AA (II × 2)—4/30-mm AA (II × 2)
**Electron Equipt:** Radar: . . .
**M:** diesels **Man:** 170 crew, 30 instructors, 200 cadets

Remarks: Resembles a coastal passenger ship. Helicopter deck aft. Officially stated to employ British navigation and radar systems.

CHINA *(continued)*

### SEAGOING TUGS

◆ **3 or more Hujia-class seagoing** Bldr: . . . (In serv. 1980s)

T 155 T 867 T . . .

**Hujia-class tug T 867** R. Gillett, 9-84

**D:** 750 tons (fl) **S:** 13.5 kts **Dim:** 49.0 (44.5 pp) × 9.5 × 3.7 **A:** . . .
**M:** 2 LVP 24 diesels; 2 CP props; 1,800 hp **Fuel:** 135 tons
**Electric:** 336 kVA **Range:** 2,200/13.5; 1,100/9 (towing)

◆ **2 Tuzhong-class salvage tugs** Bldr: Zhonghua SY, Shanghai (In serv. late 1970s)

T 164 T 710

**Tuzhong-class salvage tug T 710** 1980

**D:** 3,600 tons (fl) **S:** 18.5 kts **Dim:** 84.90 (77.00 pp) × 14.00 × 5.50
**A:** none **M:** 2/9 ESDZ 43/82B diesels; 2 CP props; 9,000 hp
**Range:** 18,000/. . . **Electron Equipt:** Radar: 1/Fin Curve, 1/Square Tie

Remarks: Powerful salvage tug equipped for firefighting, emergency repairs, and with high-capacity pumps. Has 35-ton-capacity towing winch. T 710 has Square Tie missile fire-control radar on foremast, possibly for weapons trials purposes. There is provision for mounting at least two twin 37-mm AA.

◆ **2 Dinghai class** Bldr: Wuhu SY (In serv. late 1970s)

T 837 T 717

**Dinghai-class tug T 717** L. & L. Van Ginderen, 1-87

**D:** 1,472 tons (fl) **S:** . . . kts **Dim:** 60.22 × 11.60 × 4.44 **A:** . . .
**M:** 2 diesels; 2 props; 2,460 hp **Range:** 7,200/. . .

Remarks: Also built for civil use. 980.28 grt. 25-ton-capacity towing winch. Equipped for firefighting. One transferred to Bangladesh Navy, 1984.

◆ **3 Yanting class—D:** 450 tons—trawler-type hull

◆ **3 FT 14-class converted trawlers—D:** 400 tons (fl)

◆ **16 Soviet Gromovoy class** Bldr: China (early 1960s)

**Gromovoy-class tug T 802**—outboard two T-43-class minesweepers
R. Gillett, 9-84

**D:** 900 tons (fl) **S:** 11 kts **Dim:** 45.7 (41.5 pp) × 9.45 × 4.6
**A:** 2/12.7-mm mg (I × 2) **M:** 2 diesels; 2 props; 1,200 hp

Remarks: Soviet commercial tug design, built under license.

◆ **4 Soviet Roslavl class** Bldr: See remarks (In serv. 1958–64)

**D:** 750 tons (fl) **S:** 11 kts **Dim:** 44.5 × 9.5 × 3.5
**M:** 2 diesels, electric drive; 2 props; 1,200 hp

Remarks: One transferred from the U.S.S.R.; the other built circa 1964–65 in China.

### YARD AND SERVICE CRAFT

There are a reported 380 units in this category, but the true total number is probably far larger and would include yard oilers, tugs, barges, floating dry docks, dredges, and the like. No details are available.

**Two Chinese Navy harbor tugs** R. Gillett, 9-84

# COLOMBIA

**Republic of Colombia**

Personnel (1986): 700 officers, 6,500 enlisted, 2,500 marines

Merchant Marine (1986): 90 ships—380,074 grt (tankers: 8 ships—31,954 grt)

### SUBMARINES

◆ **2 German Type 209 Mod. 1 class**

| | Bldr | L | In serv. |
|---|---|---|---|
| SS 28 Pijao | Howaldtswerke, Kiel | 10-4-74 | 17-4-75 |
| SS 29 Tayrona | Howaldtswerke, Kiel | 16-7-74 | 18-7-75 |

**D:** 990 tons std./1,180 surf./1,290 sub. **S:** 11/22 kts (1 hr.)
**Dim:** 56.10 × 6.20 × 5.50 (surf.)
**A:** 8/533-mm TT fwd (6 reloads, SUT SST-4 torpedoes)
**Electron Equipt:** Radar: 1/Calypso II
Sonar: Krupp-Atlas CSU 3-2 active/PRS 3-4 passive
**M:** 4 MTU 12V493 TY60 diesels, 600 hp each; 4 A.E.G. 405-kw generators; 1 Siemens motor, 5,000 hp
**Fuel:** 100 tons **Endurance:** 30 days **Range:** 8,000/8 (snorkel), 400/4 (sub.)
**Man:** 5 officers, 26 men

SUBMARINES *(continued)*

**Tayrona (S 29)** G. Gyssels, 10-81

REMARKS: Have H.S.A. Mk 8 Mod. 24 torpedo f.c.s. Diving depth: 250 m.

◆ **2 Italian S.X. 506 midgets** Bldr: Cosmos, Livorno, Italy (1972–74)

SS 20 Intrepido SS 21 Indomable

**D:** 58/70 tons **S:** 8.5 kts **Dim:** 23.0 × 2.0 × 4.0
**Cargo capacity:** 2,050 kg of explosives; 8 frogmen fully equipped; 2 submarine vehicles (for the frogmen) supported by a fixed system on lower part of the hull, one on each side.
**Range:** 1,200/7 **Man:** 5 tot.

REMARKS: Similar submarines have been bought by the Pakistani and Taiwanese navies. Sisters *Roncador* (SS 23) and *Quita Sueno* (SS 24) are no longer in service.

## FRIGATES

◆ **4 FS 1500 class** Bldr: Howaldtswerke, Kiel, W. Germany

| | Laid down | L | In serv. |
|---|---|---|---|
| 51 Almirante Padilla | 3-81 | 8-1-82 | 31-10-83 |
| 52 Caldas | 1981 | 14-6-82 | 14-2-84 |
| 53 Antioquia | 22-6-81 | 28-8-82 | 30-4-84 |
| 54 Independiente | 22-6-81 | 21-1-83 | 27-7-84 |

**D:** 1,600 tons (1,850 fl) **S:** 27 kts **Dim:** 95.3 (90.0 pp) × 11.3 × 3.5 (hull)
**A:** 8/MM-40 Exocet SSM—1/76-mm OTO Melara DP—2/40-mm Breda AA (II × 1)—6/324-mm Mk 32 ASW TT (III × 2)—1/BO-105 helicopter
**Electron Equipt:** Radar: 1/navigational, 1/Sea Tiger air search, 1/Castor IIB f.c.
Sonar: Krupp Atlas ASO4-2—EW: Scimitar jammer; Phoenix-II, SUSIE passive; 2/Dagaie chaff RL
**M:** 4 MTU 20V1163 TB82 diesels; 2 CP props; 23,000 hp (21,000 sust.)
**Fuel:** 200 tons **Range:** 5,000/14 **Electric:** 2,120 kw **Man:** 92 tot.

**Independiente (54)** HDW, 1984

**Almirante Padilla (51)**—with 8 MM 40 Exocet added R. Scheina, 7-84

REMARKS: Ordered 1980, with the first originally scheduled for delivery 20-7-82. Fin stabilizers, helicopter hangar. Engines are a new model not previously installed in a ship. Thomson-CSF Vega II f.c.s. for the 76-mm gun, 2 Canopus optronic directors. Torpedo tubes, Exocet, 30-mm AA, and Dagaie chaff not yet mounted at time of commissioning. Either the Israeli Barak or French 4-cell Crotale SAM system is planned for later installation forward of the bridge.

## CORVETTES

◆ **4 U.S. Cherokee- and Abnaki-class* former fleet tugs** Bldr: Charleston SB & DD Co.

| | Laid down | L | In serv. |
|---|---|---|---|
| RM 72 Pedro De Heredia (ex-*Choctaw,* ATF 70) | 4-4-42 | 18-10-42 | 21-4-43 |
| RM 73 Sebastian De Belalcazar (ex-*Carib,* ATF 82) | 7-9-42 | 7-2-43 | 24-7-43 |
| RM 74 Rodrigo De Bastedas (ex-*Hidatsa,* ATF 102)* | 8-8-43 | 29-12-43 | 25-4-44 |
| RM 76 Bahia Solano (ex-*Jacarilla,* ATF 104)* | 25-8-43 | 25-2-44 | 26-6-44 |

**Pedro de Heredia (RM 72)** R. Neth. N., 1983

**D:** 1,235 tons (1,675 fl) **S:** 16.5 kts **Dim:** 62.48 × 11.73 × 4.67
**A:** 1/76.2-mm DP
**M:** 4 G.M. 12-278 diesels (ex-ATF 102, ex-ATF 104: 4 Busch-Sulzer B5-539 diesels, electric drive); 1 prop; 3,000 hp
**Electric:** 300 kw **Range:** 15,000/8 **Man:** 75 tot.

REMARKS: RM 76, 73, 74 reactivated from U.S. Maritime Commission reserve fleet and transferred 15-3-79 for use as patrol and rescue ships. RM 72 transferred 1961; purchased 31-3-78.

## PATROL BOATS

◆ **2 U.S. Asheville class**

| | Bldr | Laid down | L | In serv. |
|---|---|---|---|---|
| P 111 Quito Sueño (ex-*Tacoma,* PG 92) | Tacoma Boat, Tacoma, Wash. | 24-7-67 | 13-4-68 | 14-7-69 |
| P 112 Albuquerque (ex-*Welch,* PG 93) | Peterson, Sturgeon Bay, Wisc. | 8-8-67 | 25-7-68 | 8-9-69 |

**D:** 225 tons (245 fl) **S:** 40 kts (16 cruising)
**Dim:** 50.14 (46.94 wl) × 7.28 × 2.9
**A:** 1/76.2-mm 50 DP Mk 34—4/12.7-mm mg (II × 2)
**Electron Equipt:** Radar: 1/LN-66, 1/SPG-50 **Electric:** 100 kw
**M:** CODOG: 1 G.E. 7LM-1500-PE 102 gas turbine; 13,300 hp (12,500 sust.) 2 Cummins VT 12-875M diesels, 1,650 hp (1,450 sust.); 2 CP props

### PATROL BOATS *(continued)*

**Albuquerque (P 112)** W. Donko, 7-83

REMARKS: Leased 16-5-83, towed to Jonathan Corp., Norfolk, Va., for reactivation. Used on anti-drug patrol. Mk 63 GFCS for 76.2-mm gun. Offer of two more not taken up due to difficulty of maintaining engineering plant.

◆ **7 miscellaneous captured drug runners**

. . . TURBU, . . . TOLU, . . . SERRANILLA (ex-*Tropic Ace*), . . . TENIENTE DE NAVIO JOSE MARIA PALAS, . . . TENIENTE DE NAVIO ALEJANDRO BAL DOMERO SALGADO, . . . TENIENTE PRIMO ALCALA, TENIENTE LUIS GUILLERMO ALCALA (ex-*Joanna*)

REMARKS: Characteristics unknown; placed in service 1981 to help combat drug traffic in the Caribbean. Most are ex-drug runners. *Rigel,* a former trawler used in this service, was lost 15-8-82.

### RIVER PATROL BOATS AND CRAFT

◆ **2 Rio Hacha class** Bldr: Unial Barranquilla (In serv. 1955)

CF 35 RIO HACHA CF 37 ARAUCA

**Arauca (CF 37)**

**D:** 170 tons (184 fl) **S:** 13 kts **Dim:** 47.25 × 8.23 × 1.0
**A:** 2/76.2-mm DP (I × 2)—4/20-mm AA (I × 4)
**M:** 2 Caterpillar diesels; 2 props; 800 hp **Range:** 1,000/12 **Man:** 27–43 tot.

REMARKS: Sister *Leticia* disarmed and equipped as a hospital boat.

◆ **CF 33 Cartagena** Bldr: Yarrow, Glasgow (In serv. 1930)

**Cartagena (CF 33)**

**D:** 142 tons **S:** 15.5 kts **Dim:** 41.9 × 7.16 × 0.8
**A:** 2/76.2-mm—1/20-mm AA—4/7.7-mm mg **Range:** 2,100/15 **Man:** 39 tot.
**M:** 2 Gardner diesels; 2 props (in tunnels); 600 hp **Fuel:** 24 tons

REMARKS: Principal parts of the ship protected against small arms.

### OCEANOGRAPHIC RESEARCH SHIPS

◆ **2 Malpelo class** Bldr: Martin Jansen, Leer, W. Germany

BO 155 PROVIDENCIA (In serv. 5-81) BO 156 MALPELO (In serv. 4-81)

**Malpelo (BO 156)** 1983

**D:** 1,090 tons (fl) **S:** 13 kts **Dim:** 50.3 (44.0 pp) × 10.0 × 4.0
**M:** 2 M.A.N. 6-cyl. diesels; 1 Kort-nozzle prop; 1,570 hp
**Range:** 16,000/11.5 **Man:** 9 officers, 18 men, 6 scientists

REMARKS: Delivered 1981 for DIMAR (Dirección General Maritima Portuario), one for geophysical research, one for fisheries. White-painted. Naval manned. Bow-thruster, flapped Becker rudder. Prime contractor: Ferrostaal, Kiel. Both commissioned 24-7-81.

NOTE: Oceanographic ship *San Andres* (BO 151, ex-US. *Rockville,* PCER 851) stricken by 1986.

◆ **1 U.S. former refrigerated stores lighter** Bldr: Niagara SB, Buffalo, N.Y.

BO 153 QUINDIO (ex-U.S. YFR 433) (In serv. 11-11-43)

**D:** 380 tons (600 fl) **Dim:** 40.4 × 9.10 × 2.5 **M:** 1 Union diesel; 600 hp
**Man:** 17 tot.

REMARKS: Leased 7-64; purchased 31-3-78. Used on coastal survey duties.

### AUXILIARY SHIPS

◆ **1 U.S. Patapsco-class tanker, former gasoline tanker**

| | Bldr | Laid down | L | In serv. |
|---|---|---|---|---|
| BT 67 TUMACO (ex-U.S. *Chewaucan,* AOG 50) | Cargill, Inc., Savage, Minn. | 23-12-43 | 22-7-44 | 19-2-45 |

**Tumaco (BT 67)** 1976

**D:** 4,570 tons (fl) **S:** 14 kts **Dim:** 94.7 (89.0 pp) × 14.78 × 4.9
**A:** 2/76.2-mm DP (I × 2) **M:** 2 G.M. 16-278A diesels; 2 props; 3,300 hp
**Range:** 8,350/11.5 **Man:** 45 tot.

REMARKS: Purchased 1-7-75. Foremast deleted, small lattice mast stepped for navigational radar. Cargo: 2,575 tons. Retains one Mk 52 radar GFCS (with Mk 26 radar) and one Mk 51 GFCS.

◆ **1 seagoing cargo ship** Bldr: At. Ch. dela Rochelle-Pallice (In serv. 1979)

TM . . . JURADO (ex-Chilean *Tocopila)*

**D:** . . . **S:** 12 kts **Dim:** 90.12 (80.29 pp) × . . . × 6.00
**M:** 2 M.A.N. diesels; 1 prop; 2,130 hp

REMARKS: 1,979 grt/3,249 dwt. Acquired 1985.

◆ **1 coastal cargo ship** Bldr: Schiffswerft H. Rancke, Hamburg (In serv. 1956)

TM . . . SAN ANDRES (ex-*Philip P.*, ex-*Marga B.*, ex-*Margaret Oltmann*, ex-*Ruth*, ex-*Nadir*, ex-*Elbstrom*)

**D:** . . . **S:** 9 kts **Dim:** 51.85 (46.18 pp) × 8.41 × 3.46
**M:** 1 diesel; 1 prop; 300 hp

COLOMBIA *(continued)*
AUXILIARY SHIPS *(continued)*

REMARKS: 432 grt/680 dwt. Former Honduran coaster detained for smuggling and taken over for Navy 1986.

◆ **1 small transport/cargo ship** Bldr: Sander, Delfzijl, Netherlands (In serv. 1953)

TM 43 CIUDAD DE QUIBDO (ex-M/V *Shamrock*)

**D:** 633 tons **S:** 11 kts **Dim:** 50.3 × 7.2 × 2.8
**M:** 1 M.A.N. diesel; 1 prop; 390 hp **Fuel:** 32 tons
**Man:** 11 tot.

REMARKS: Purchased 1953.

◆ **2 hospital boats**

BD 36 LETICIA Former river patrol boat, see under *Rio Hacha* class. Has 6 beds, surgery facilities, etc.

BD 33 SOCORRO Bldr: Cartagena Naval DY, 1956

**D:** 70 tons **S:** 9 kts **Dim:** 25.0 × 5.5 × 0.75 **M:** 2 G.M. diesels; 270 hp
**Man:** 10 tot.

REMARKS: Originally fitted to carry 56 troops on the rivers, now used for surgery.

### TUGS

◆ **1 U.S. Sotoyomo-class auxiliary ocean tug** Bldr: Levingston SY, Orange, Texas

| | Laid down | L | In serv. |
|---|---|---|---|
| RM 75 BAHIA UTRIA (ex-*Kalmia*, ATA 184) | 27-7-44 | 29-8-44 | 26-10-44 |

**D:** 534 tons (835 fl) **S:** 13 kts **Dim:** 43.6 × 10.3 × 4.0
**A:** 1/76.2-mm DP Mk 26 **Electric:** 120 kw
**M:** 2 G.M. 12-278A diesels, electric drive; 1 prop; 1,500 hp **Range:** 8,000/8

REMARKS: Transferred 1-7-71. Sister *Bahia Honda* lost 2-75.

◆ **1 ex-U.S. small harbor tug** Bldr: Henry C. Grebe (In serv. 2-9-43)

RM 73 TENIENTE RICARDO SORZANO (ex-YTL 231)

**D:** 70 tons (80 fl) **S:** 9 kts **Dim:** 20.2 × 5.2 × 1.5 **Electric:** 15 kw
**M:** 1 Cooper-Bessemer diesel; 240 hp **Fuel:** 7 tons

REMARKS: Loaned 1963; purchased 31-3-78.

◆ **6 Capitan Castro class**—for river use

| | |
|---|---|
| RR 81 CAPITAN CASTRO | RR 86 CAPITAN RIGOBERTO GIRALDO |
| RR 82 CANDIDO LEGUIZAMO | RR 87 CAPITAN VLADIMIR VALEK |
| RR 84 CAPITAN ALVARO RUIS | RR 88 TENIENTE LUIS BERNAL |

**D:** 50 tons **S:** 10 kts **Dim:** 20.0 × 4.25 × 0.75 **M:** 2 G.M. diesels; 260 hp

◆ **1 floating dry dock for river force use**

JAIME ARIAS—D: 700 tons (fl) Capacity: 165 tons

◆ **1 school sailing ship** Bldr: Celaya, Bilbao, Spain (In serv. 7-9-68)

GLORIA

**Gloria** G. Gyssels, 7-85

**D:** 1,300 tons (fl) **S:** 10.5 kts (on diesel) **Dim:** 64.7 × 10.6 × 6.6
**M:** 1 diesel; 500 hp **Sail areas:** 1,400 m² (bark-rigged)

COAST GUARD
(Cuerpo del Guardacosta)

Established 1981. The surviving craft of the former Customs Service fleet have been refitted and incorporated. A major function is anti-drug patrol.

### PATROL BOATS

◆ **2 U.S. 105-ft. Commercial Cruiser class** Bldr: Swiftships Inc., Berwick, La.

AN 101 OLAYA HERRERA (In serv. 16-10-81)
AN 102 RAFAEL DEL CASTILLO Y RADA (In serv. 2-83)

**Rafael del Castillo y Rada (102)** 1983

**D:** 103 tons (fl) **S:** 25 kts **Dim:** 31.5 × 6.6 × 2.1
**A:** 1/40-mm AA—2/12.7-mm mg
**M:** 2 MTU 12V331 TC92 diesels; 2 props; 7,000 hp **Range:** 1,600/25; 2,400/15
**Electric:** 113 kw **Man:** 3 officers, 16 men

◆ **2 Jorge Soto del Corval class** Bldr: Rauma Repola SY, Rauma, Finland (In serv. 1971)

A 208 CARLOS ALBAN A 209 NITO RESTREPO

**D:** 100 tons (130 fl) **S:** 18 kts **Dim:** 34.0 × 6.0 × 1.9 **A:** 1/20-mm AA
**M:** 2 MTU diesels; 2 CP props; 2,500 hp

REMARKS: A 208 recommissioned 1980, A 209 in 1981. Sister *J.S. del Corval* hulked.

◆ **1 Pedro Gaul class** Bldr: F. Schürenstedt, Bardenfleth, W. Germany

A 206 CARLOS E. RESTREPO (In serv. 1964)

**D:** 85 tons (fl) **S:** 26 kts **Dim:** 34.7 × 5.5 × 1.8 **A:** 1/20-mm AA
**M:** 2 Maybach 12-cyl. diesels; 2 props; 2,500 hp

REMARKS: Sisters *Pedro Gaul* (AN 204) and *Estaban Jaramillo* (A 205) hulked. A 206 recommissioned 1981.

# COMOROS

## Republic of the Comoros

MERCHANT MARINE (1986): 3 ships—1,261 grt

### PATROL CRAFT

◆ **2 Japanese Yamayuri class** Bldr: Ishihara, Takasago (In serv. 10-81)

KASTHALA NTRINGHUI

**D:** 27 tons (40.3 fl) **S:** 20.7 kts **Dim:** 18.0 × 4.3 × 0.82 (1.1 prop) **A:** . . .
**M:** 2 Type RD 10T diesels; 2 props; 900 hp **Man:** 6 tot.

REMARKS: Identical to craft in the Japanese Maritime Safety Agency.

### AUXILIARIES

◆ **1 former French transport** Bldr: Toulon DY (In serv. 1957)

VILLE DE NIMACHOVA (ex-*Issole*)

**D:** 600 tons (fl) **S:** 12 kts **Dim:** 49.0 × 7.0 × 2.2
**M:** 2 diesels; 2 props; 1,000 hp **Fuel:** 36 tons **Range:** 2,600/10.8

REMARKS: Stricken from French Navy and acquired by Comoros in 1981. Former "regional transport" with bow doors and beaching ramp for vehicle cargo. Cargo: 240 tons plus 60 tons on deck.

**COMOROS** *(continued)*
**AUXILIARIES** *(continued)*

◆ **1 British LCT(8)-class tank-landing ship** (In serv. 1945)

N . . . . . . . (ex-Fr. LCT 9061, ex-Br. *Buttress,* LCT(8) 4099)

**L 9061** C. Limonier, 1975

**D:** 657 tons (1,000 fl) **S:** 12 kts **Dim:** 70.48 × 11.9 × 1.8
**A:** 2/20-mm AA (I × 2)—1/120-mm mortar, Army model
**M:** 4 Paxman diesels; 2 props; 1,840 hp **Man:** 29 tot.

Remarks: Bought 7-65 by France, transferred by France, 1976. Present serviceability doubtful.

# CONGO
## People's Republic of the Congo

Personnel (1986): 250 total

Merchant Marine (1986): 21 ships—8,548 grt

COASTAL NAVY

The naval forces are divided into coastal navy and the river navy. Plans to acquire three additional seagoing patrol boats began during 1985; under consideration are three 357-ton Spanish "Cormoran"-class gunboats.

◆ **3 Spanish "Piraña"-class patrol boats** Bldr: Bazán, Cadiz—ordered 1980

| | In serv. |
|---|---|
| P 601 Marien Ngouabi (ex-*L'Intrépide*) | 10-11-82 |
| P 602 Les Trois Glorieuses (ex-*Le Vaillant*) | 1-83 |
| P 603 Les Maloango (ex-*Le Terrible*) | 3-83 |

**Marien Ngouabi (P 601)** Bazán, 1983

**D:** 125 tons (138 fl) **S:** 34 (29 sust.) **Dim:** 32.70 (30.60 pp) × 6.15 × 1.55
**A:** 1/40-mm—1/20-mm AA—2/12.7-mm mg (I × 2)
**Electron Equipt:** Radar: 1/Raytheon RM 1220/6 × 8
**M:** 2 MTU 12V538 TB92 diesels; 2 props; 6,120 hp (5,110 sust.)
**Electric:** 210 kw **Range:** 1,000/17 **Man:** 3 officers, 16 men

Remarks: CSEE Panda optronic GFCS. Renamed on delivery; arrived in Congo 1-6-83; by 8-84 badly needed overhaul, which began at builders in 1985.

◆ **6 Soviet Zhuk-class patrol boats** (3 transferred 1982, 3 in 2-84)

V 301 V 302 V 303 V 304 V 305 V 306

**D:** 48 tons (60 fl) **S:** 34 kts **Dim:** 24.0 × 5.0 × 1.2 (1.8 props)
**A:** 4/14.5-mm mg (II × 2) **Fuel:** 10 tons **Man:** 12 tot.
**M:** 2 M50F-4 diesels; 2 props; 2,400 hp **Range:** 700/28; 1,100/15

◆ **1 Soviet Shershen-class former torpedo boat**

**D:** 145 tons (165 fl) **S:** 45 kts **Dim:** 34.0 × 6.8 × 1.5
**A:** 4/30-mm AA (II × 2) **Electron Equipt:** Radar: 1/Pot Drum, 1/Drum Tilt
**M:** 3 M503A diesels; 3 props; 12,000 hp **Range:** 460/42; 850/30

Remarks: Transferred 1979; torpedo tubes removed prior to delivery.

◆ **3 ex-Chinese Shanghai-II-class patrol boats** (Transferred 3-75)

P 401 P 402 P 403

**D:** 122.5 tons (135 fl) **S:** 28.5 kts **Dim:** 38.78 × 5.41 × 1.55
**A:** 4/37-mm AA (II × 2)—4/25-mm AA (II × 2)
**Electron Equipt:** Radar: 1/Pot Head
**M:** 2 M50F-4, 1,200 hp and 2/12D6 diesels; 4 props; 4,220 hp **Man:** 36 tot.
**Endurance:** 7 days **Electric:** 39 kw **Range:** 750/16.5

RIVER NAVY

◆ **2 13-m and 2 11.4-m Arcor (France)-built patrol craft** (In serv. 1982)

◆ **4 ex-Chinese Yu Lin-class patrol craft** (Transferred 1966)

**D:** 9.8 tons (fl) **S:** 25 kts **Dim:** 13.0 × 2.9 × 1.1 **A:** 1/12.7-mm mg
**M:** 1 diesel; 1 prop; 300 hp

◆ **2 locally built small craft**

◆ **10 outboard-powered small craft**

# COOK ISLANDS

Merchant Marine (1986): . . . ships—. . . grt

**PATROL BOAT**

◆ **0 (+1) Australian ASI 315 class** Bldr: Australian SB Ind. (WA), South Coogie, W. Australia

N . . . (In serv. 10-89)

**D:** 165 tons (fl) **S:** 20 kt (sust.) **Dim:** 31.50 (28.60 wl) × 8.10 × 2.12
**A:** small arms
**Electron Equipt:** Radar: 1/Furuno 1011
EW: 1 Furuno 120 MF-HFD/F, 1 Furuno 525 VHFD/F
**M:** 2 Caterpillar 3516 diesels; 2 props; 2,820 hp (2,400 sust.)
**Range:** 2,500/12 **Fuel:** 27.9 tons **Endurance:** 8–10 days
**Electric:** 116 kw (2 × 50 kw, 1 × 16 kw) **Man:** 3 officers, 14 men

Remarks: A unit of the Australian "Pacific Patrol Boat" foreign aid program. Extremely well equipped with navaids: SATNAV receiver, doppler log, etc. Will carry a 5-m Stressl aluminum boarding boat with a 40-hp outboard.

# COSTA RICA
## Republic of Costa Rica

Personnel: 100 men

Merchant Marine (1986): 29 ships—13,329 grt

CIVIL GUARD

**PATROL BOATS AND CRAFT**

◆ **1 105-foot Commercial Cruiser class** Bldr: Swiftships, Morgan City, Louisiana

SP 1055 Isla del Coco (In serv. 2-78)

COSTA RICA *(continued)*
PATROL BOATS AND CRAFT *(continued)*

**D:** 118 tons (fl) **S:** 36 kts **Dim:** 31.73 × 7.1 × 2.16
**A:** 2/12.7-mm mg (I × 2) **Electron Equipt:** Radar: 1/Decca RM 916
**M:** 3 MTU 12V331 TC92 diesels; 3 props; 10,500 hp **Range:** 1,200/18
**Fuel:** 21 tons **Electric:** 80 kw (2 × 40 kw) **Man:** 21 tot.

REMARKS: Refitted 1984 to 3-85 by builders. Aluminum construction.

**Isla del Coco (SP 1055)** Swiftships, 4-85

◆ **4 65-foot Commercial Cruiser class** Bldr: Swiftships, Morgan City, Louisiana (In serv. 1978)

SP 656 SP 657 SP 658 SP 659

**65-ft. patrol boat SP 657** Swiftships, 4-85

**D:** 24.9 tons (33 fl) **S:** 24 kts **Dim:** 19.77 (17.90 wl) × 5.56 × 1.98
**A:** 2/12.7-mm mg **Electron Equipt:** Radar: 1/Decca RM 916
**M:** 2 MTU 8V331 diesels; 2 props; 1,400 hp **Fuel:** 4.8 tons
**Range:** 1,200/18 **Electric:** 20 kw **Man:** 7 tot.

REMARKS: Aluminum construction. Refitted by builder, 1985.

◆ **1 42-ft. aluminum patrol craft** Bldr: Swiftships, Morgan City, La.

SP 421 PUNTARENA (In serv. 9-86)

**D:** 16.2 tons (fl) **S:** 34 kts **Dim:** 12.80 × 4.26 × . . .
**A:** 2/12.7-mm mg (I × 2)—2/7.62-mm mg (I × 2)
**M:** 2 G.M. 8V92 TI diesels; 2 props; . . . hp **Range:** 300/30

◆ **2 36-ft. aluminum patrol craft** Bldr: Swiftships, Morgan City, La.

SP 361 SP 362 (Both in serv. 3-86)

**D:** 10.7 tons (fl) **S:** 24 kts **Dim:** 10.97 × 3.05 × . . .
**A:** 2/12.7-mm mg (I × 2)—2/7.62-mm mg (I × 2)—1/60-mm mortar
**M:** 2 G.M. DD8240 MT diesels; 2 props; . . . hp **Range:** 300/20

# CUBA

## Republic of Cuba

PERSONNEL: Approx. 9,000 men, including 1,000 naval infantry

MERCHANT MARINE (1986): 422 ships—958,663 grt (tankers: 16—68,184 grt)

### SUBMARINES

◆ **3 Soviet Foxtrot class**

**D:** 1,900/2,400 tons **S:** 16/15.5 kts **Dim:** 91.5 × 7.5 × 6.0
**A:** 10/533-mm TT (6 fwd, 4 aft)—22 torpedoes or 44 mines
**Electron Equipt:** Radar: 1/Snoop Tray
Sonar: 1/MF active, passive
**M:** 3/2,000-hp diesels, 3 electric motors; 3 props; 5,300 hp **Endurance:** 70 days
**Range:** 11,000/8 (snorkel); 350/2 (sub.) **Man:** 78 tot.

REMARKS: Transferred 1-79, 1-80, and 2-84. A non-operational Whiskey-class submarine was transferred 4-79 for use as a battery-charging barge.

### FRIGATES

◆ **2 Soviet Koni class** Bldr: Zelenodolsk SY

350 MARIEL 356 N . . .

**Cuba's second Koni (356)** U.S. Navy, 2-84

**D:** 1,440 tons (1,600 fl) **S:** 30 kts **Dim:** 96.40 × 12.55 × 3.48 (hull)
**A:** 1/SAN-4 SAM syst. (II × 1; 20 missiles)—4/76.2-mm DP (II × 2)—4/30-mm AA (II × 2)—2/RBU-6000—mines
**Electron Equipt:** Radar: 1/Strut Curve, 1/Don-2, 1/Pop Group, 1/Hawk Screech, 1/Drum Tilt—IFF: 2/Square Head, 1/High Pole A
Sonar: 1/MF, hull-mounted
EW: 2 Watch Dog, 2/chaff RL (XVI × 2)
**M:** CODAG: 1 19,000-hp gas turbine, 2 Type 68D, 8,000-hp diesels; 3 props; 35,000 hp
**Range:** 1,800/14 **Man:** 120 tot.

REMARKS: *Mariel* delivered 23-9-81; second unit arrived 2-84. Like the Algerian units, have a continuous deckhouse amidships.

### GUIDED-MISSILE PATROL BOATS

◆ **13 Soviet Osa-II class**

**Cuban Osa-II**—note man with SA-7 Grail missile amidships U.S. Navy, 7-84

**D:** 190 tons (240 fl) **S:** 35 kts **Dim:** 38.6 × 7.6 × 2.0
**A:** 4/SS-N-2 Styx (I × 4)—4/30-mm AA (II × 2)
**Electron Equipt:** Radar: 1/Square Tie, 1/Drum Tilt
IFF: 2/Square Head, 1/High Pole A
**M:** 3 M504 diesels; 3 props; 15,000 hp **Range:** 500/34; 750/25 **Man:** 30 tot.

REMARKS: Transferred: 2 in 1977, 3 in 1978, 2 in 1979, 2 in 11-81, 2 in 1-82, 2 in 2-82. Carry SA-7 Grail (Strela) surface-to-air missiles in hand-held launchers.

GUIDED-MISSILE PATROL BOATS *(continued)*

◆ **5 Soviet Osa-I class**

**D:** 175 tons (210 fl) **S:** 36 kts **Dim:** 38.6 × 7.6 × 1.8
**A:** 4/SS-N-2 Styx (I × 4)—4/30-mm AA (II × 2)
**Electron Equipt:** Radar: 1/Square Tie, 1/Drum Tilt
IFF: 2/Square Head, 1/High Pole A
**M:** 3 M503A diesels; 3 props; 12,000 hp **Range:** 500/34; 750/25 **Man:** 30 tot.

REMARKS: Two were delivered in 1972, two in 1973, and two in 1974; one deleted in 1981.

PATROL BOATS AND CRAFT

◆ **4 Soviet Stenka class**

**D:** 170 tons (210 fl) **S:** 36 kts **Dim:** 39.5 × 7.6 × 1.8
**A:** 4/30-mm AA (II × 2)
**Electron Equipt:** Radar: 1/Pot Drum, 1/Drum Tilt
EW: 2/chaff RL (XVI × 2)
IFF: 1/Square Head, 1/High Pole B
**M:** 3 M503A diesels; 3 props; 12,000 hp
**Range:** 550/34; 750/25 **Man:** 20 tot.

REMARKS: Transferred two in 2-85, two in 9-85. Do not have the 4/400-mm ASW TT and stern-mounted dipping sonar found on standard Soviet Navy version.

◆ **4 Soviet S.O.-1 class**

**Cuban S.O.-1** U.S. Navy, 1972

**D:** 190 tons (215 fl) **S:** 28 kts **Dim:** 42.0 × 6.1 × 1.9
**A:** 4/25-mm AA (II × 2)—4/RBU-1200 ASW RL—2/d.c. racks (24 d.c.)
**Electron Equipt:** Radar: 1/Pot Head **M:** 3 Type 40D diesels; 3 props; 7,500 hp
**Range:** 340/28; 1,900/7 **Man:** 30 tot.

REMARKS: Six were transferred in 1964 and six in 1967. Three additional believed discarded by 1983 and an additional 5 by 1985.

◆ **20 Soviet Zhuk class**

**Cuban Navy Zhuk patrol boat** U.S. Navy, 7-84

**D:** 48 tons (60 fl) **S:** 34 kts **Dim:** 24.0 × 5.0 × 1.2 (1.8 props)
**A:** 4/14.5-mm mg (II × 2) **Fuel:** 10 tons **Man:** 12 tot.
**M:** 2 M50 F-4 diesels; 2 props; 2,400 hp **Range:** 700/28; 1,100/15

REMARKS: Transferred 1 in 12-71, 1 in 7-74, 4 in 10-75, 2 in 12-76, 4 in 1977-79, 6 in 1980 (including 3 in 12-80), 3 in 1984, and four in 9-85; at least 5 have been passed on to Nicaragua, however.

TORPEDO BOATS

◆ **9 Soviet Turya-class semi-hydrofoils**

**Cuban Navy Turya 193** U.S. Navy, 7-84

**D:** 215 tons (250 fl) **S:** 40 kts
**Dim:** 39.0 × 7.6 (12.5 over foils) × 2.0 (4.0 over foils)
**A:** 2/57-mm AA aft (II × 1)—2/25-mm AA (II × 1)—4/533-mm TT (I × 4)
**Electron Equipt:** Radar: 1/Pot Drum, 1/Muff Cob
IFF: 1/Square Head, 1/High Pole B
**M:** 3 M504 diesels; 3 props; 15,000 hp **Range:** 400/38; 650/25 **Man:** 24 tot.

REMARKS: First two delivered 2-79, the first foreign transfer of this class; 2 in 2-80, 2 in 1-81, 2 in 1-83, and 1 in 11-83. ASW capability omitted. Semi-retractable forward hydrofoils; stern planes on surface. Uses Osa-II hull and propulsion. Hand-held SA-7 Grail ("Sa-N-5") surface-to-air missiles were carried by mid-1984.

NOTE: The six remaining P-6- and six P-4-class torpedo boats have been deleted due to age and hard usage.

MINE WARFARE SHIPS

◆ **4 Soviet Sonya-class coastal minesweepers**

**Cuban Sonya on delivery voyage** U.S. Navy, 1-85

**D:** 380 tons (450 fl) **S:** 14 kts **Dim:** 48.8 × 8.8 × 2.1
**A:** 2/30-mm AA (II × 1)—2/25-mm AA (II × 1)
**Electron Equipt:** Radar: 1/Spin Trough
IFF: 1/High Pole B, 1/Square Head
**M:** 2 diesels; 2 props; 2,400 hp **Range:** 1,600/14; 3,000/10 **Man:** 40 tot.

REMARKS: Delivered 8-80, 10-80, 1-85, and 12-85—all by tow. Wooden hulls, sheathed in glass-reinforced plastic.

MINE WARFARE SHIPS *(continued)*

◆ **9 Soviet Yevgenya-class inshore minesweepers** Bldr: Srednyy Neva SY, Kolpino

**D:** 80 tons (90 fl) **S:** 11 kts **Dim:** 26.2 × 6.1 × 1.5 **A:** 2/25-mm AA (II × 1)
**Electron Equipt:** Radar: 1/Spin Trough—IFF; 1/High Pole B
**M:** 2 diesels; 600 hp **Range:** 300/10 **Man:** 12 tot.

REMARKS: Two transferred 1978, two in 1979, two in 12-80, 1 in 11-82, and 2 in 11-84; two others, delivered 9-84, were transferred to Nicaragua. Equipped to search for mines in depths of up to 30 m using towed television, marker buoys, and standard wire cable gear. Glass-reinforced plastic construction.

AMPHIBIOUS WARFARE SHIPS AND CRAFT

◆ **2 Soviet Polnocny B class** Bldr: Polnocny SY, Gdansk (In serv. circa 1968)

**Polnocny B under tow to Cuba** Skyfotos, 10-82

**D:** 800 tons (fl) **S:** 19 kts **Dim:** 74.0 × 8.6 × 2.0 (aft)
**A:** 4/30-mm AA (II × 2)—2/140-mm artillery RL (XVIII × 2)
**Electron Equipt:** Radar: 1/Spin Trough, 1/Drum Tilt
IFF: 1/Square Head, 1/High Pole B
**M:** 2 diesels; 2 props; 5,000 hp **Range:** 900/18; 1,500/14
**Man:** 30 tot. plus 200 troops

REMARKS: The first, wearing transfer pendant, arrived in 9-82; the second, number 442, arrived 4-12-82. These particular units are configured for troop carrying, as evidenced by the large number (23) of 10-man life rafts carried. Cargo: 180 tons (5 tanks).

◆ **7 Soviet T-4-class landing craft** (In serv. 1950s–1970s)

**D:** 70 tons (fl) **S:** 10 kts **Dim:** 19.0 × 4.3 × 1.0
**M:** 2 diesels; 2 props; 600 hp **Man:** 5 tot.

REMARKS: Transferred 1967–74. Used as utility lighters.

HYDROGRAPHIC SURVEY SHIPS

◆ **1 Soviet Biya class** Bldr: Gdansk, Poland (1972–76)

H 103 GUAMA (ex-GS 186)

**D:** 750 tons (fl) **S:** 13 kts **Dim:** 55.0 × 9.2 × 2.6
**Electron Equipt:** Radar: 1/Don-2 **M:** 2 diesels; 2 CP props; 1,200 hp
**Range:** 4,700/11 **Fuel:** 90 tons **Man:** 25 tot.

REMARKS: Transferred 11-80. Carries one survey launch. Also useful as a buoy tender; one 5-ton crane.

◆ **1 Spanish-built** Bldr: Maritime del Musel, Gijon

H 102 TAINO (In serv. 1979)

**D:** 1,100 tons **S:** 12 kts **Dim:** 53.0 (42.0 pp) × 10.4 × 3.5
**M:** 2 diesels; 2 props; 1,550 hp **Electric:** 360 kw

REMARKS: Primarily a buoy tender. 669 grt/572 dwt.

◆ **1 converted trawler** Bldr: Ast. Talleres de Celaya, Bilbao, Spain

H 101 SIBONEY (In serv. 1968)

**D:** 600 tons (fl) **S:** 11.4 kts **Dim:** 40.2 × 8.3 × 2.6
**M:** 2 Stork-Werkspoor RHD-216K diesels; 1 prop; 910 hp
**Electric:** 160 kw **Man:** . . .

◆ **3 Lamda-class converted wooden fishing boats** (In serv. 1960s)

H 76 H 77 H 78

**D:** 150 tons (fl) **S:** 10 kts **Dim:** 29.0 × 6.0 × 2.1
**M:** 1 diesel; 1 prop; 250 hp

◆ **6 Soviet Nyryat-1 class.** (In serv. 1962-69)

H 91 H 92 H 93 H 94 H 95 H 96

**D:** 120 tons (fl) **S:** 12 kts **Dim:** 29.0 × 5.0 × 1.7
**M:** 1 diesel; 2 props; 450 hp **Radar:** 1/Spin Trough **Range:** 1,600/10
**Man:** 15 tot.

REMARKS: Date of transfer not known. Known in U.S.S.R. as GPB 480 class. Some, with different equipment, also used as diving tenders.

AUXILIARIES

◆ **1 replenishment oiler** Bldr: Niigata Iron Wks., Japan

LAS GUASIMAS (In serv. 1978)

**D:** 8,300 tons (fl) **S:** 12.75 kts **Dim:** 106.99 (100.01 pp) × 14.34 × 6.99
**M:** 1 diesel; 1 CP prop; 4,000 hp **Fuel:** 862 tons **Electric:** 900 kw

REMARKS: Ostensibly for the fishing fleet, but can refuel under way alongside or astern.

◆ **1 cargo ship:** ARENAL (1965) 763 grt. Acquired 12-82. No other data available.

◆ **1 Soviet Pelym-class degaussing tender**

**Pelym-class degaussing tender en route Cuba** 2-82

**D:** 1,300 tons (fl) **S:** 16 kts **Dim:** 65.5 × 11.6 × 3.4
**A:** none **Electron Equipt:** Radar: 1/Don-2
**M:** 2 diesels; 2 props; . . . hp **Range:** 4,500/12 **Man:** 70 tot.

REMARKS: Arrived in Cuba 2-82 under tow. Probably intended to support the Foxtrot-class submarines.

◆ **1 intelligence collector, former fishing boat** Bldr: Sociedad Española de Construcción Naval, Bilbao (In serv. 1967)

ISLA DE LA JUVENTUD (ex-*Arminza*)

**Isla de la Juventud** U.S. Navy, 7-84

**D:** 1,556 grt **S:** 13 kts **Dim:** 70.0 × 12.6 × 5.4
**M:** 1 MWM diesel; 1 prop; 2,200 hp

REMARKS: Equipped with a variety of electronic collection antennas. Converted around 1980.

**CUBA** *(continued)*
**AUXILIARIES** *(continued)*

◆ **1 yacht**

A 11 GRANMA

REMARKS: Small cabin cruiser in which Fidel Castro returned to Cuba in 1956. Maintained by the navy as a museum.

◆ **1 Soviet Okhtenskiy-class seagoing tug** (In serv. 1960s)

CARIBE

**D:** 663 tons (926 fl) **S:** 13.3 kts **Dim:** 47.3 (43.0 pp) × 10.3 × 5.5 (4.1 mean)
**M:** electric drive: 2 Type 5D50 diesels; 1 prop; 1,500 hp **Range:** 7,800/7
**Man:** 40 tot. **Fuel:** 197 tons **Electric:** 340 kw

REMARKS: Transferred 1976.

◆ **3 Soviet Prometey-class large harbor tugs**

**D:** 319 tons (fl) **S:** 12 kts **Dim:** 29.8 (28.2 pp) × 8.30 × 3.20
**A:** 3/12.7-mm mg (I × 3) **Electron Equipt:** Radar: 1/Spin Trough
**M:** 2 Type 6D30/50.4 diesels; 2 CP props; 1,200 hp
**Electric:** 50 kw (2 × 25 kw) **Man:** 8 tot.

REMARKS: Two transferred 1967, one in 1972. Bollard pull: 14 tons

◆ **2 Soviet Yelva-class diving tenders**

**D:** 295 tons (fl) **S:** 12.4 kts **Dim:** 40.9 (37.0 pp) × 8.0 × 2.1
**Electric:** 200 kw **M:** 2 3D12A diesels; 2 props; 600 hp
**Radar:** 1/Spin Trough **Man:** 20 tot.

REMARKS: Transferred 1978. Can support 7 divers to 60-m depths.

◆ **1 or more Soviet Poluchat-I-class torpedo retrievers**

**Cuban Navy Poluchat-I** 1983

**D:** 90 tons (fl) **S:** 18 kts **Dim:** 29.6 × 6.1 × 1.9
**A:** 4/14.5-mm mg (II × 2)
**Electron Equipt:** Radar: 1/Spin Trough—IFF: 1/High Pole A
**M:** 2 M50-F1 diesels; 2 props; 1,800 hp
**Range:** 450/17; 900/10 **Electric:** 14 kw **Man:** 20 tot.

REMARKS: Transfer data uncertain. Equipped for patrol boat duties as well as for retrieving torpedoes via a stern ramp.

◆ **1 Soviet Whiskey-class battery-charging barge**

**D:** 1,050 tons **Dim:** 75.0 × 6.3 × 4.8 **Electric:** 3,000 kw

REMARKS: Former submarine, transferred under tow 4-79 with propellers removed, torpedo tubes sealed, and periscopes removed, for use as a charging station for the Foxtrot-class submarines.

COAST GUARD

◆ **7 craft**

GF 528 GF 725 GF 825 GF 720 Similar to 40-foot U.S. Coast Guard small craft

GF 101 GF 102 GF 701 Similar to U.S. Coast Guard small craft

REMARKS: Assigned to the Department of the Interior. Hull numbers painted in red to distinguish these boats from naval ships.

◆ **1 patrol craft**

GUANABACOA Bldr: Cadiz, Spain (L: . . .)

**S:** 22 kts

◆ **6 fast launches** Bldr: Spain, 1971–72

CAMILO CIENFUEGOS MACEO MARTI
ESCAMBRAY CUARTEL MONCADA FINLAY

REMARKS: No other information available.

# CYPRUS

**Republic of Cyprus**

MERCHANT MARINE (1986): 940 ships—10,616,809 grt (tankers: 164—4,397,519 grt)

Two Agusta-Bell 47G helicopters are assigned coastal patrol duties.

◆ **2 Type 32L patrol boats** Bldr: Ch. Navals de l'Estérel, Cannes

APHRODITE (In serv. 12-82) SALAMIS (In serv. 24-5-83)

**D:** 96 tons (fl) **S:** 32 kts **Dim:** 32.1 × 6.45 × 1.9
**A:** 1/40-mm AA—1/20-mm AA
**M:** 2 MTU diesels; 2 props; 4,000 hp **Range:** 1,500/15

REMARKS: Wooden construction. First unit ordered 9-81. *Salamis* powered by SACM diesels producing 4,640 hp.

# DENMARK

**Kingdom of Denmark**

PERSONNEL (1986): 6,200 (1,700 officers, 3,300 enlisted, 1,200 conscripts), plus 2,600 civilians. There are 10,000 Naval Reservists and 5,200 members of the Home Guard.

MERCHANT MARINE (1986): 1,063 ships—4,651,224 grt
(tankers: 37 ships—1,830,270 grt)

NAVAL AVIATION: Eight Mk 80 Lynx helicopters, the first of which was delivered 15-5-80; these are to be updated with the Racal RAMS 4000 data system. The air force took delivery of three U.S. Gulfstream G III Maritime Patrol Aircraft during 1981–82.

**Danish Westland Mk 80 Lynx** Danish Navy

## SUBMARINES

◆ **0 (+3) ex-Norwegian Kobben class** Bldr: Rheinstahl Nordseewerke, Emden, West Germany

| | | | L | In serv. | Conv. |
|---|---|---|---|---|---|
| S . . . | N . . . | (ex-*Utvaer,* S 303) | 30-6-65 | 1-12-65 | -88 |
| S . . . | N . . . | (ex-*Uthaug,* S 304) | 8-10-65 | 16-2-66 | -88 |
| S . . . | N . . . | (ex-. . .) | . . . | . . . | -89 |

**D:** 370/482 tons **S:** 13.5/17 kts **Dim:** 45.11 × 4.60 × 3.80
**A:** 8/533-mm TT, fwd (8 Swedish TP 613 torpedoes)
**Electron Equipt:** Radar: Thomson-CSF Calypso
Sonar: . . .
EW: . . .
**M:** 2 MTU MB820 Db, 600-hp diesels, 2/405-kw generators, 1/1,100-kw motor; 1 prop (2.3 m dia.); 1,700 hp max. **Man:** 17 tot.

REMARKS: West German IKL Type 207 design, based on Type 205 but deeper diving: 190 m max. Purchased by Denmark 1986. Refitting at Mjellum & Karlsen, Bergen, 1987–89 with new Thorn-EMI D3 fire-control system, sonar, and a propulsion overhaul. Danish Navy desires to acquire two more, but funding is lacking. The three Danish boats are the second, fourth, and sixth to be modernized in the series. Norway's *Stadt* (S 307) was to have been the third boat transferred but was damaged beyond economic repair in the spring of 1987.

◆ **2 German Type 205**

| | Bldr | Laid down | L | In serv. |
|---|---|---|---|---|
| S 320 NARHVALEN | RDY Copenhagen | 16-2-65 | 10-9-68 | 27-2-70 |
| S 321 NORDKAPEREN | RDY Copenhagen | 20-1-66 | 18-12-69 | 22-12-70 |

**SUBMARINES** *(continued)*

**Narhvalen (S 320)** L. & L. Van Ginderen, 5-87

**D:** 370 light/430 surf./480 tons **S:** 10/17 kts **Dim:** 45.41 × 4.60 × 3.80 (surf.)
**A:** 8/533-mm TT fwd (. . . Swedish TP 61 torpedoes) **Man:** 22 tot.
**Electron Equipt:** Radar: 1/Thomson-CSF Calypso
Sonar: 1/SRS-M1H, 1/GHG AN5039A1
**M:** 2 MTU 820 Db, 600-hp diesels; 2/405-kw generators, 1/2,300-hp motor

Remarks: Modeled on the German Type 205 and Norwegian Type 207 (*Kobben* class).

◆ **1 Delfinen class**

| | Bldr | Laid down | L | In serv. |
|---|---|---|---|---|
| S 329 Springeren | RDY Copenhagen | 3-1-61 | 26-4-63 | 22-10-64 |

**Springeren (S 329)** H. Ehlers, 5-87

**D:** 595/643 tons **S:** 13/12 kts **Dim:** 54.0 × 4.7 × 3.8
**A:** 4/533-mm TT fwd
**M:** Burmeister & Wain 12-cyl. diesels, 2 motors; 2 props; 1,200 hp
**Range:** 4,000/8.5 **Man:** 33 tot.

Remarks: S 329 built with U.S. "Offshore" funds, as U.S. SS 554. Diving depth: 100 m. Sister *Tumleren* (S 328) stricken 8-81, and *Delfinen* (S 326) was decommissioned 1983 and stricken 11-9-84. *Spaekhuggeren* (S 327), badly damaged in dry dock 21-9-79 and repaired, was to be discarded during 1987; S 329 to discard 1988.

## FRIGATES

◆ **2 Peder Skram class**

| | Bldr | Laid down | L | In serv. |
|---|---|---|---|---|
| F 352 Peder Skram | Helsingør Vaerft | 25-9-64 | 20-5-65 | 30-6-66 |
| F 353 Herluf Trolle | Helsingør Vaerft | 18-12-64 | 8-9-65 | 16-4-67 |

**Peder Skram (F 352)** L. & L. Van Ginderen, 5-86

**Herluf Trolle (F 353)** P. Voss, 10-85

**D:** 2,030 tons (2,720 fl) **S:** 28 kts (16.5 diesel)
**Dim:** 112.5 (108.0 pp) × 12.0 × 3.6
**A:** 8/Harpoon SSM (IV × 2)—1 NATO Sea Sparrow SAM system (VIII × 1)—2/127-mm 38-cal. DP, U.S. Mk 30 (II × 1)—4/40-mm AA (I × 4)—4/20-mm AA (I × 4)—4/533-mm TT (I × 4)—1 d.c. rack
**Electron Equipt:** Radar: 1 Skanter 009, 1/CWS-2, 1/CWS-3, 3 M 46 fire-control, 1/Mk 91 Mod. 1 fire-control (2 radar directors)
Sonar: 1 Plessey PMS 26—EW: Decca Racal Cutlass intercept
**M:** CODOG propulsion: 2 G.M. 16-567D diesels (4,800 hp); 2 Pratt & Whitney PWA GG 4A-3 gas turbines (44,000 hp); 2 CP props
**Man:** 200 tot.

Remarks: Danish design, built with U.S. "Offshore" funds. Speed with diesels: 16 knots. There are two radar directors for the Mk 91 Mod. 1 Sea Sparrow system, which, along with Harpoon, was added 1977-79, as was the CEPLO computerized tactical data system. The torpedo tubes fire Swedish Type 61 wire-guided torpedoes. F 353 had a serious engine-room fire, 15-7-82, recommissioning after repairs in 10-83. Both to reserve, early 1987.

Note: Plans call for replacing these ships in the 1990s with two "Standard-flex 2,000" frigates, but funding is not likely to be provided.

◆ **3 Nils Juel (Type KV 72) class** Bldr: Aalborg Vaerft

| | Laid down | L | In serv. |
|---|---|---|---|
| F 354 Nils Juel | 20-10-76 | 27-9-78 | 22-8-80 |
| F 355 Olfert Fischer | 6-12-78 | 15-1-80 | 16-10-81 |
| F 356 Peter Tordenskjold | 3-12-79 | 2-81 | 2-4-82 |

**Peter Tordenskjold (F 356)**—with 8 Harpoon aboard H. Ehlers, 5-87

**Olfert Fischer (F 355)**—note d.c. door through stern L. & L. Van Ginderen, 5-87

**FRIGATES** *(continued)*

**D:** 1,100 tons (1,320 fl) **S:** 30 kts (20 on diesel)
**Dim:** 84.0 (80.0 pp) × 10.3 × 3.1
**A:** 8/Harpoon SSM (IV × 2)—1 NATO Sea Sparrow SAM (VIII × 1)—1/76-mm OTO Melara Compact DP—1 d.c. rack
**Electron Equipt:** Radar: 1/Plessey AWS-5, 2/Skanter 009, 1/Phillips 3-cm, 1 Phillips 9 LV 200 GFCS (with Type 771 low-light t.v. tracker), 1/Mk 91 Mod. 1 MFCS (2 dir.)
Sonar: Plessey PMS-26
EW: Decca-Racal Cutlass passive
**M:** CODOG: 1 G.E. LM-2500 gas turbine (26,600 hp), 1 MTU 20V956 TB82 diesel (4,800 hp); 2 CP props
**Range:** 800/28; 2,500/18 **Electric:** 1,500 kw (3,500-kw diesel sets)
**Fuel:** 130 tons **Man:** 18 officers, 9 CPOs, 63 men

REMARKS: Ordered 5-12-75. Planned ASW torpedo system not installed. Two Breda SCLAR chaff/flare RL not yet added. NATO Sea Sparrow system, with no reloads, has two radar directors. DataSAAB CEPLO data system. F 355 commissioning delayed by fire 5-81. Planned to receive U.S. RAM (Rolling Airframe Missile) SAM system, using two lightweight, 8–10 missile launchers per ship.

## FISHERIES PROTECTION FRIGATES

◆ **0 (+1 + 3) projected** Bldr: . . .

| | | Laid down | L | In serv. |
|---|---|---|---|---|
| F 357 | N . . . | . . . | . . . | 1989 |

**F 357 concept**—artist's rendering Y-ARD, 1986

**D:** 2,400 tons (3,500 fl) **S:** 22 kts **Dim:** 100.0 × 14.0 × . . .
**A:** 1/76-mm OTO Melara DP—1/Lynx helicopter
**Electron Equipt:** Radar: 1/Plessey AWS-6, 1/. . . nav.
**M:** 4 diesels; 2 CP props; 12,000 hp
**Endurance:** 21+ days **Man:** 60–65 tot.

REMARKS: Designed with Y-ARD assistance. Tenders to construct the first of a planned four out 6-86; no award as of 6-87. Class will replace the *Hvidbjørnen* class.

◆ **1 modified Hvidbjørnen class** Bldr: Aalborg Vaerft

| | Laid down | L | In serv. |
|---|---|---|---|
| F 340 BESKYTERREN | 15-12-74 | 27-5-75 | 27-2-76 |

**Beskyterren (F 340)**—with radome atop crow's nest P. Voss, 9-86

**D:** 1,970 tons (fl) **S:** 18 kts **Dim:** 74.4 × 11.8 × 4.5
**A:** 1/76.2-mm DP—1/Lynx helicopter **Man:** 60 tot.
**Electron Equipt:** Radar: 1/Skanter 009, 1/Plessey AWS-6
Sonar: 1/Plessey PMS-26
**M:** 4 Burmeister & Wain Alpha diesels; 1 CP prop; 7,440 hp **Range:** 6,000/13 (one engine)

REMARKS: Serves as a fisheries-protection ship. An OTO Melara Compact 76-mm gun was to have been fitted.

◆ **4 Hvidbjørnen class**

| | Bldr | Laid down | L | In serv. |
|---|---|---|---|---|
| F 348 HVIDBJØRNEN | Aarhus Flydedok | 6-61 | 23-11-61 | 12-62 |
| F 349 VAEDDEREN | Aalborg SY | 10-61 | 6-4-62 | 3-63 |
| F 350 INGOLF | Svendborg Skibsvaerft | 12-61 | 27-7-62 | 6-63 |
| F 351 FYLLA | Aalborg SY | 6-62 | 18-12-62 | 7-63 |

**Fylla (F 351)** L. & L. Van Ginderen, 11-85

**Vaedderen (F 349)**—with new radome L. & L. Van Ginderen, 6-86

**D:** 1,345 tons (1,650 fl) **S:** 18 kts **Dim:** 72.6 × 11.6 × 4.9
**A:** 1/76.2-mm DP—1/Lynx helicopter **Man:** 10 officers, 60 men
**Electron Equipt:** Radar: 1/Skanter 009, 1/CWS-1 (F 349: Plessey AWS-6)
Sonar: 1 Plessey PMS-46
**M:** 4 G.M. 16-567C diesels; 1 CP prop; 6,400 hp **Range:** 6,000/13

REMARKS: Reinforced bow. Plessey AWS-6 to replace CWS-1 radar (already in F 349, 1985).

## GUIDED-MISSILE BOATS

◆ **10 Willemoes class** Bldr: Frederikshavn SY

| | In serv. | | In serv. |
|---|---|---|---|
| P 540 BILLE | 10-76 | P 545 NORBY | 22-11-77 |
| P 541 BREDAL | 21-1-77 | P 546 RODSTEEN | 16-2-78 |
| P 542 HAMMER | 1-4-77 | P 547 SEHESTED | 19-5-78 |
| P 543 HUITFELDT | 15-6-77 | P 548 SUENSON | 10-8-78 |
| P 544 KRIEGER | 22-9-77 | P 549 WILLEMOES | 7-10-76 |

**Bille (P 540)**—with 8 Harpoon SSM L. & L. Van Ginderen, 5-87

## GUIDED-MISSILE BOATS *(continued)*

**Sehested (P 547)**—only 2 Harpoon aboard H. Ehlers, 5-87

**D:** 232 tons (265 fl) **S:** 40 kts (36 normal)—diesels: 12 kts
**Dim:** 46.1 (42.4 pp) × 7.4 × 2.1 (2.7 over props)
**A:** 4/Harpoon SSM—1/76-mm OTO Melara Compact—2/533-mm TT
**Electron Equipt:** Radar: 1/9GA-208, 1/NWS-3, 1/9LV 200 fire-control
**M:** CODOG: 3 Rolls-Royce Proteus 52M/544 gas turbines; 2 G.M. 8V-71 diesels; 3 Liaan CP props; 12,750/800 hp
**Electric:** 420 kw **Range:** 400/36 **Man:** 5 officers, 21 men

Remarks: Based on the Swedish Lürssen-designed Spica class and ordered in 1972. The torpedoes are Swedish Type 61, wire-guided, with a range of 20,000 meters. Endurance is normally 36 hours. Two triple 103-mm flare rocket rails on pilothouse sides. Decca-Racal Cutlass intercept system ordered 1980 for all. Have TORCI torpedo f.c.s. and CEPLO tactical data system. Normally operate with only two Harpoon aboard. Can carry 20 mines in lieu of SSM and torpedoes or 6 torpedo tubes and no SSM. Five are to receive a new Terma tactical data system.

## TORPEDO BOATS

◆ **6 Søløven class**

| | Bldr | Laid down | L | In serv. |
|---|---|---|---|---|
| P 510 Søløven | Vosper, Portsmouth | 8-62 | 19-4-63 | 12-2-65 |
| P 511 Søridderen | Vosper, Portsmouth | 10-62 | 22-8-63 | 10-2-65 |
| P 512 Søbjornen | RDY Copenhagen | 7-63 | 19-8-64 | 9-65 |
| P 513 Søhesten | RDY Copenhagen | 8-63 | 31-3-65 | 6-66 |
| P 514 Søhunden | RDY Copenhagen | 2-64 | 12-1-66 | 1-67 |
| P 515 Søulven | RDY Copenhagen | 6-64 | 27-4-66 | 3-67 |

**Søløven (P 510)**—with 1/40-mm, 4/TT, 1/20-mm L. & L. Van Ginderen, 6-85

**D:** 95 tons (114 fl) **S:** 50 kts (10 on diesel)
**Dim:** 30.26 (27.44 pp) × 7.3 × 2.15
**A:** 1 or 2/40-mm AA (I × 2)—2 or 4/533-mm TT
**Electron Equipt:** Radar: 1/NWS-1
**M:** 3 Rolls-Royce Marine Proteus gas turbines; 3 props; 10,500 hp (12,750 max.); 2 G.M. 6V-71 diesels, 530 hp, for cruising
**Man:** 4 officers, 22 men

Remarks: A modification of the British Brave class. All normally in reserve. Four 50-mm flare RL on fwd 40-mm shield. P 510 was built as PT 821 with U.S. funds. Four of these craft were to be refitted, the other two discarded, in 1984–85; they will receive RADAMEC Type 409 optronic gun directors. Can be configured with 2/40-mm and 2 TT or 1/40-mm and 4 TT. A 20-mm AA can be carried aft. To discard on completion of the Stanflex 300 class.

## PATROL BOATS

◆ **0 (+7 + 9) "Stanflex 300"-class multifunction** (first unit: hull by Karlskrona) Bldr: Aalborg Vaerft

| | Laid down | L | In serv. |
|---|---|---|---|
| P . . . Flyve Fisken | 15-8-85 | 26-4-86 | 10-87 |
| P . . . Hajen | . . . | . . . | . . . |
| P . . . Havkatten | . . . | . . . | . . . |
| P . . . Laxen | . . . | . . . | . . . |
| P . . . Makrelen | . . . | . . . | . . . |
| P . . . Stoeren | . . . | . . . | . . . |
| P . . . Swaerdfisken | . . . | . . . | . . . |

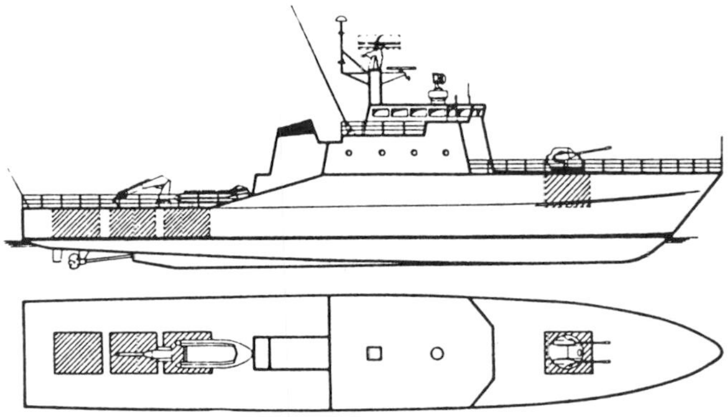

**Standard-flex 300 in patrol-boat configuration** (Shaded areas show interchangeable mission module locations)

**Artist's rendering of Stanflex 300 in missile-boat configuration** Aalborg Vaerft, 1986

**D:** 320 tons **S:** 35 kts gas turbine/19 diesel/6 electric
**Dim:** 54.0 (50.0 pp) × 9.0 × 3.0
**A:** Patrol boat: 2/30-mm AA
Torpedo boat: 1/76-mm OTO Melara Super Rapid DP, 4/Harpoon SSM (II × 2), 2/533-mm TT, SAM syst.
Minelayer: 1/20-mm AA, SAM syst.
Minesweeper: 2/30-mm AA
**Electron Equipt:** Radar: 1/nav., 1/9GA-208, 1/9LV-200
Sonar: . . . EW: . . .
**M:** CODAG: 1 G.E.-Fiat LM-2500 gas turbine, 2 MTU 16V396 TB94, 3,480-hp diesels; 3 props; 31,960 hp—hydraulic drive for minesweeping/laying—bow-thruster
**Man:** 15–17 tot. (28 accom.) **Range:** . . .

Remarks: Glass-reinforced plastic construction concept intended to replace *Daphne*-class patrol boats, existing minesweepers, and the *Søløven*-class torpedo boats. As patrol boats (the initial configuration) will carry a twin AA mount forward and a rigid inflatable inspection boat aft; as torpedo boats will carry a 76-mm gun forward with missiles and torpedo tubes aft; as a minelayer will carry an undetermined SAM system forward, a light AA aft, mine rails, and a crane; in mine countermeasures configuration, will have a twin AA forward, sweep gear aft, and a SAM system. All configurations are intended to be interchangeable, using modular, plug-in equipment. First seven units ordered 27-7-85 to a Karlskronavarvet design. Diesel propellers are controllable-pitch. Three rudders, with the outboard pair acting as stabilizers. Passive tank stabilization at low speeds.

◆ **3 Agdlek class for fisheries protection** Bldr: Svendborg Vaerft

| | In serv. |
|---|---|
| Y 386 Agdlek | 12-3-74 |
| Y 387 Agpa | 14-5-74 |
| Y 388 Tulugaq | 26-6-79 |

**PATROL BOATS** *(continued)*

**Agpa (Y 387)** H. Ehlers, 4-86

**D:** 330 tons (fl) **S:** 12 kts **Dim:** 31.4 × 7.7 × 3.3 **A:** 2/20-mm AA (I × 2)
**Electron Equipt:** Radar: 1/Terma 20T48 (NWS-3), 1/Skanter 009 nav.
**M:** 1 Burmeister & Wain Alpha diesel; 800 hp **Man:** 15 tot.

REMARKS: For fisheries patrol service in Greenland waters. Can carry two survey launches. Y 388 has only the small navigational radar, is .3-m longer, and can make 14 kts.

◆ **9 Barsø class** Bldr: Svendborg Vaerft

Y 300 BARSØ, Y 301 DREJØ, Y 302 ROMSØ, Y 303 SAMSØ, Y 304 THURØ, Y 305 VEJRØ, Y 306 FARØ, Y 307 LAESØ, Y 308 ROMØ

**Laesø (Y 307)**—with decompression chamber H. Ehlers, 7-86

**D:** 155 tons (fl) **S:** 11 kts **Dim:** 25.5 × 6.0 × 2.8 **A:** 2/20-mm AA (I × 2)
**Electron Equipt:** Radar: 1/Skanter 009 **M:** 1 diesel; 1 prop; 385 hp

REMARKS: The first six were completed in 1969 and the last three 1972–73. For fisheries-protection duties. Y 307, with decompression chamber forward, is used as a diving tender. Y 306–308 have broader pilothouses.

◆ **2 Maagen-class fisheries patrol boats** Bldr: Helsingør (In serv. 5-60)

Y 384 MAAGEN Y 385 MALLEMUKKEN

**D:** 175 tons (190 fl) **S:** 10 kts **Dim:** 27.0 × 7.2 × 2.75
**A:** 2/20-mm AA (I × 2)
**Electron Equipt:** Radar: 1/Terma 20T48 (NWS-3), 1/Skanter 009
**M:** diesel; 1 prop; 350 hp

REMARKS: Based in Greenland.

**Maagen (Y 384)** S. Terzibaschitsch, 6-85

◆ **8 Daphne-class antisubmarine patrol boats** Bldr: RDY, Copenhagen

| | Laid down | L | In serv. |
|---|---|---|---|
| P 530 DAPHNE | 4-60 | 10-11-60 | 19-12-61 |
| P 531 DRYADEN | 7-60 | 1-3-61 | 4-4-62 |
| P 533 HAVFRUEN | 3-61 | 4-10-61 | 20-12-62 |
| P 534 NAJADEN | 9-61 | 20-6-62 | 26-4-63 |
| P 535 NYMFEN | 4-62 | 1-11-62 | 4-10-63 |
| P 536 NEPTUN | 9-62 | 29-5-63 | 18-12-63 |
| P 537 RAN | 12-62 | 10-7-63 | 15-5-64 |
| P 538 ROTA | 6-63 | 26-11-63 | 20-1-65 |

**Dryaden (P 531)** Danish Navy, 1983

**D:** 150 tons (170 fl) **S:** 20 kts **Dim:** 38.0 × 6.75 × 2.0
**A:** 1/40-mm AA—2 d.c. projectors—2 d.c. racks **Man:** 23 tot.
**Electron Equipt:** Radar: 1/NWS-3—Sonar: Plessey PMS 26
**M:** 2 Maybach diesels, 1,300 hp, and 1 Foden cruise FD-6 diesel, 100 hp; 3 props

REMARKS: P 530, P 534, and P 536, which were paid for with U.S. "Offshore" funds as PGM 47, PGM 49, and PGM 50, are now completely disarmed. *Havmanden* (P 532) was struck in 1978; others to follow on completion of Stanflex 300 units.

## PATROL CRAFT

◆ **3 Y 377 class** Bldr: Botved (In serv. 1975)

Y 377 Y 378 Y 379

**D:** 9 tons (fl) **S:** 27 kts **Dim:** 9.8 × 3.3 × 0.9
**Electron Equipt:** Radar: 1/NWS-3
**M:** 2 Volvo Penta inboard/outboard diesels; 2 props; 600 hp

◆ **2 Y 375 class** Bldr: Botved (In serv. 1974)

Y 375 Y 376

**PATROL CRAFT** *(continued)*

**Y 376** 1978

**D:** 12 tons (fl) **S:** 26 kts **Dim:** 13.3 × 4.5 × 1.1
**Electron Equipt:** Radar: 1/NWS-3 **M:** 2 diesels; 2 props; 680 hp

PATROL CRAFT MANNED BY
THE HOME GUARD

Note: Funding for 25 new patrol craft for the Home Guard was requested 1987.

◆ **6 MHV 20 class** Bldr: Ejvinds, Plastikbodevaerft Svendborg (In serv. 1974–81)

MHV 20 MHV 21 MHV 22 MHV 23 MHV 24 MHV 25

**MHV 25** H. Ehlers, 4-85

**D:** 60 tons (fl) **S:** 15 kts **Dim:** 16.5 × 4.2 × 2.0 **A:** 1/12.7-mm mg
**M:** 2 MTU diesels; 2 props; 500 hp **Radar:** 1/NWS-3

Remarks: Additional units of these craft were intended to replace the older MHV units, but no further units were authorized. Glass-reinforced plastic hulls.

◆ **7 MHV-90 class** (In serv. 1974–75)

MHV 90 MHV 91 MHV 92 MHV 93 MHV 94 MHV 95 MHV 96

**MHV 95** H. Ehlers, 4-85

**D:** 85 tons (130 fl) **S:** 10.7 kts **Dim:** 19.8 × 5.7 × 1.6 **A:** 1/20-mm AA
**M:** 1 Burmeister & Wain diesel; 400 hp **Radar:** 1/NWS-3

◆ **3 MHV 70 class** Bldr: Navy Yard, Copenhagen (In serv. 1958)

MHV 70 MHV 71 MHV 72

**MHV 71**—with new, enlarged pilothouse Danish Navy, 1983

**D:** 78 tons (130 fl) **S:** 10 kts **Dim:** 20.1 × 5.1 × 2.5 **A:** 1/20-mm AA aft
**Electron Equipt:** Radar: 1/NWS-3 **M:** 1 diesel; 200 hp

◆ **6 MHV 80 class** (In serv. 1941)

MHV 81 (ex-Askø) MHV 83 (ex-Manø) MHV 85 (ex-Hjortø)
MHV 82 (ex-Enø) MHV 84 (ex-Baagø) MHV 86 (ex-Lyø)

**MHV 84** H. Ehlers, 4-85

**D:** 74 tons **S:** 11 kts **Dim:** 24.4 × 4.9 × 1.6 **A:** 1/20-mm AA
**Electron Equipt:** Radar: 1/NWS-3 **M:** 1 diesel; 350 hp

Remarks: In Home Guard service 1958. Former inshore minesweepers. Wooden hulls. The gun mount is not normally aboard.

◆ **32 smaller craft, including:**

MHV 51, MHV 52, MHV 54, HMV 56 through 64, MHV 65 through 68, MHV 73, 74, 75, 76, 80. Small, wooden-hulled fishing boat designs. Most have a Skanter 009 radar. No fixed armament.

**MHV 62** L. & L. Van Ginderen, 11-86

**PATROL CRAFT** *(continued)*

**MHV 75** H. Ehlers, 7-86

**MHV 73** H. Ehlers, 7-86

## MINE WARFARE SHIPS

◆ **4 Falster-class minelayers**

| | Bldr | Laid down | L | In serv. |
|---|---|---|---|---|
| N 80 Falster | Nakskov Skibsvaerft | 4-62 | 19-9-62 | 7-11-63 |
| N 81 Fyen | Frederikshavn Vaerft | 4-62 | 3-10-62 | 18-9-63 |
| N 82 Møen | Frederikshavn Vaerft | 10-62 | 6-6-63 | 20-4-64 |
| N 83 Sjaelland | Nakskov Skibsvaerft | 1-63 | 14-6-63 | 7-7-64 |

**D:** 1,880 tons (fl) **S:** 16.5 kts **Dim:** 77.0 (72.5 pp) × 12.8 × 3.4
**A:** 4/76.2-mm DP U.S. Mk 33 (II × 2)—400 mines (4 minelaying tracks)
**Electron Equipt:** Radar: 1/CWS-2, 1/NWS-2, 1/NWS-3, 1/M-46
EW: . . .
**M:** 2 G.M. 16-567D3 diesels; 2 CP props; 4,800 hp **Fuel:** 130 tons
**Man:** 10 officers, 108 men

Remarks: NATO design. The Turkish ship *Nusret* is identical. N 82 is training ship for naval cadets. N 83 converted to submarine tender in 1976, to replace *Henrik Gerner* (can still lay mines). N 80 and N 82 built with U.S. "Offshore" funds as MMC 14 and MMC 15. Have 2/57-mm multiple chaff launchers. All to be refitted for service through 2000.

**Fyen (N 81)** L. & L. Van Ginderen, 10-86

**Møen (N 82)**—with EW van aft L. & L. Van Ginderen, 5-87

◆ **2 Lindormen-class coastal minelayers** Bldr: Svendborg

| | Laid down | L | In serv. |
|---|---|---|---|
| N 43 Lindormen | 20-1-77 | 7-6-77 | 26-10-77 |
| N 44 Loussen | 2-77 | 9-9-77 | 30-1-78 |

**Loussen (N 44)** H. Ehlers, 5-87

**D:** 575 tons (fl) **S:** 14 kts **Dim:** 43.3 (40.0 pp) × 9.0 × 2.65
**A:** 2/20-mm AA (I × 2)—50 to 60 mines **Electron Equipt:** Radar: 1/NWS-3
**M:** 2 Wichmann 7AX diesels; 2 props; 4,200 hp **Electric:** 192 kw
**Man:** 27 tot.

Remarks: Built to replace the *Lougen* class. 20-mm AA not always mounted. Controlled minefield planters.

◆ **6 ex-U.S. Adjutant- and Redwing*-class coastal minesweepers**

| | Bldr | In serv. |
|---|---|---|
| M 572 Alssund (ex-MSC 128)* | Hiltebrand DD, Kingston, NY | 5-4-55 |
| M 573 Egernsund (ex-MSC 129)* | Hiltebrand DD, Kingston, NY | 3-8-55 |
| M 574 Grønsund (ex-MSC 256) | Stephen Bros. SY | 21-9-56 |
| M 575 Guldborgsund (ex-MSC 257) | Stephen Bros. SY | 11-11-56 |
| M 577 Ulvsund (ex-MSC 263) | Harbor BY, Terminal Isl., Cal. | 20-9-56 |
| M 578 Vilsund (ex-MSC 264) | Harbor BY, Terminal Isl., Cal. | 15-11-56 |

**D:** 350 tons (376 fl) **S:** 13 kts (8 sweeping)
**Dim:** 43.89 (41.50 pp) × 7.95 × 2.55 **A:** 1/40-mm AA
**Electron Equipt:** Radar: 1/NWS-3—Sonar: 1/UQS-1 **Man:** 38 tot.
**M:** 2 G.M. 8-268A diesels; 2 props; 1,000 hp **Fuel:** 40 tons **Range:** 2,500/10

**MINE WARFARE SHIPS** *(continued)*

**Grønsund (M 574)**—standard configuration H. Ehlers, 11-86

**Vilsund (M 578)**—enlarged superstructure H. Ehlers, 11-86

**Guldborgsund (M 575)**—survey ship M. Willis, 5-85

Remarks: Hull entirely of wood. The first two are 405 tons (fl); they have davits abreast the stack to handle noisemakers. M 575 has a charthouse between the stack and bridge so that she can act as a survey ship; she still has minesweeping equipment. M 578 also has an enlarged superstructure, after modernization at Svendborg, 1985. *Aarøsund* (M 571) stricken 1981, and *Omøsund* (M 576) placed in reserve for use as cannibalization spares. In 3-83 it was announced that three of these ships will be modernized.

## AUXILIARY SHIPS

◆ **4 SKA 11-class inshore survey launches** (In serv. 1981–82)

SKA 11 SKA 12 SKA 13 SKA 14

**D:** 52 tons (fl) **S:** 12 kts **Dim:** 20.0 × 5.2 × 2.1
**M:** 1 G.M. diesel; 540 hp **Man:** 6 tot.

Remarks: Stationed in Greenland. GRP construction.

◆ **4 inshore survey launches** (In serv. 1958–68)

SKA 5 SKA 6 SKA 7 SKA 8

**SKA 7** S. Terzibaschitsch, 6-84

**D:** 27 tons **S:** 9 kts **Dim:** 13.0 × . . . × . . . **Man:** 6 tot.
**M:** 1 diesel; . . . hp **Electron Equipt:** Radar: 1/Skanter 009

Remarks: Minesweeper *Guldborgsund* and frigate *Ingolf* also used in survey work, the latter being able to transport four of this class.

◆ **2 U.S. YO 65-class coastal oilers** Bldr: Jeffersonville Boat & Machine, Indiana

| | Laid down | L | In serv. |
|---|---|---|---|
| A 568 Rimfaxe (ex-YO 226) | 21-4-45 | 20-7-45 | 22-10-45 |
| A 569 Skinfaxe (ex-YO 229) | 25-5-45 | 28-8-45 | 7-12-45 |

**Skinfaxe (A 569)** D. Koop, 5-84

**D:** 440 tons (1,390 fl) **S:** 10 kts **Dim:** 53.0 × 9.75 × 4.0 **A:** 1/20-mm AA
**Electron Equipt:** Radar: 1/NWS-3 **Electric:** 40 kw **Man:** 23 tot.
**M:** 1 G.M. 8-278A diesel; 1 prop; 640 hp **Fuel:** 25 tons **Range:** 2,000/8

Remarks: Transferred 2-8-62. Cargo: 900 tons.

◆ **1 torpedo transport/retriever**

A 558 Sleipner

**Sleipner (A 558)** 1980

**AUXILIARY SHIPS** *(continued)*

**D:** 150 tons (200 fl) **S:** 9 kts **Dim:** 30.0 (26.0 pp) × 6.5 × 2.0 **Man:** 7 tot.
**Electron Equipt:** Radar: 1/Skanter 009 **M:** 1 Callesen diesel; . . . hp

Remarks: Former coastal cargo ship. Refitted and re-engined 1986.

◆ **1 small torpedo retriever**

TO 9 Munin—no data available

◆ **1 royal yacht** Bldr: Royal DY, Copenhagen

| | L | In serv. |
|---|---|---|
| A 540 Dannebrog | 10-10-31 | 1932 |

**Dannebrog (A 540)** 1980

**D:** 1,130 tons **S:** 14 kts **Dim:** 74.9 × 10.4 × 3.7
**Electron Equipt:** Radar: 1/Skanter 009 **Electric:** 507 kVA
**M:** 2 Burmeister & Wain Alpha 6 T23L-KVO diesels; 2 CP props; 1,600 hp

Remarks: Re-engined, new electrical generating plant winter 1980–81. Does not wear pendant number assigned.

◆ **2 small sail-training yawls**

Y 101 Svanen Y 102 Thyra

MINISTRY OF FISHERIES

◆ **1 "Osprey" FV 710-class fisheries patrol ship** Bldr: Frederikshavn SY (In serv. 7-79)

Havørnen

**Havørnen** L. & L. Van Ginderen, 6-86

**D:** 320 tons (506 fl) **S:** 18 kts **Dim:** 49.98 (45.8 pp) × 10.50 × 2.75
**Electron Equipt:** Radar: 1/Skanter 009, 1/NWS-3
**M:** 2 Burmeister & Wain Alpha 16V23L-VO diesels; 2 CP props; 4,640 hp
**Range:** 4,500/16 **Man:** 15 tot. (accommodations for 35)

Remarks: Has small stern ramp for a 6.5-m rubber inspection dinghy. Built to mercantile specifications, a modified British "Osprey" design. Helicopter deck and hangar facilities not used.

◆ **1 fisheries research ship** Bldr: Dannebrog, Aarhus

Dana (In serv. 1982)

**D:** 2,483 grt **S:** 15.5 kts **Dim:** 78.43 × 14.7 × . . .
**M:** 2 diesels; 1 CP prop; 4,600 hp **Man:** 27 crew, plus 12 scientists

◆ **1 fisheries oceanographic ship** (In serv. 1960)

Jens Vaever

**D:** 280 tons (fl) **S:** 11.5 kts **Dim:** 30.53 × 6.35 × 3.15
**M:** 1 Burmeister & Wain 406 VD diesel; 1 prop; 420 hp **Fuel:** 20 tons
**Range:** 2,600/9 **Man:** 10 tot.

◆ **2 Nordsøen-class salvage & rescue tugs** Bldr: Frederikshavn DY (In serv. 1968)

Nordylland Nordsøen

**D:** 900 tons (fl) **S:** 14.5 kts **Dim:** 52.35 (45.75 pp) × 10.00 × 3.35
**M:** 2 Burmeister & Wain 8-23MTBF-308G diesels; 1 CP prop; 1,960 hp
**Electric:** 472 kw **Man:** 12 tot.

MINISTRY OF TRADE AND SHIPPING

**ICEBREAKERS**

Note: Danish icebreakers all civilian-manned and are subordinate to the Ministry of Trade and Shipping. During summer months they are maintained by the Danish Navy at Frederikshavn.

◆ **1 new construction** Bldr: Svendborg (L: 6-80)

Thorbjørn

**Thorbjørn** H. Ehlers, 4-85

**D:** 2,250 tons (fl) **S:** 16.5 kts **Dim:** 67.5 × 15.3 × 4.70
**M:** 4 Burmeister & Wain Alpha diesels, electric drive; 2 props; 6,800 hp

Remarks: Can be used for hydrographic surveys by the navy when not needed for icebreaking, and can also act as a tug.

◆ **2 Danbjørn class** Bldr: Lindø Vaerft, Odense

Danbjørn (In serv. 1965) Isbjørn (In serv. 1966)

**Isbjørn** L. & L. Van Ginderen, 6-86

**D:** 3,685 tons (fl) **S:** 14 kts **Dim:** 76.8 × 16.8 × 6.0
**M:** diesel-electric; 2 props; 11,880 hp **Man:** 34 tot.

◆ **1 Elbjørn class** Bldr: Frederikshavn Vaerft (In serv. 1953)

Elbjørn

**D:** 898 tons (1,400 fl) **S:** 12 kts **Dim:** 47.0 × 12.1 × 4.35
**M:** diesel-electric; 2 props; 3,600 hp

Remarks: Used by Danish Navy for survey work in the summer.

**DENMARK** *(continued)*
**ICEBREAKERS** *(continued)*

**Elbjørn** Danish Navy

MINISTRY OF THE ENVIRONMENT
(These units are manned by naval and civil personnel)

**POLLUTION-CONTROL SHIPS AND CRAFT**

◆ **2 Gunnar Thorson class** Bldr: Ørnskov SY, Frederikshavn

Gunnar Thorson (In serv. 8-5-81) Gunnar Seidenfaden (In serv. 2-7-81)

**Gunnar Thorson** Danish Navy, 1981

**D:** 672 tons (750 fl) **S:** 14.5 kts **Dim:** 55.6 (47.9 pp) × 12.3 × 3.9
**M:** 2 Burmeister & Wain Alpha 8V-23L-VO diesels; 2 CP props; 2,320 hp

◆ **2 "Sea Truck" design**

| | Bldr | In serv. |
|---|---|---|
| Mette Miljo | Carl B. Hoffman SY, Esbjerg | 22-2-80 |
| Marie Miljo | Søren Larsen SY, Nykøbing Mors | 22-2-80 |

**Mette Miljo** H. Ehlers, 4-85

**D:** 157 tons **S:** 10 kts **Dim:** 29.8 × 8.0 × 1.6
**M:** 2 Grenaa diesels; 2 props; . . . hp **Man:** 8 tot.

◆ **2 Miljo 101 class** Bldr: Eljvinds, Svendborg

Miljo 101 (In serv. 1-11-77) Miljo 102 (In serv. 1-12-77)

**Miljo 101** Danish Navy, 1982

**D:** 16 tons **S:** 15 kts **Dim:** 16.2 × 4.2 × 2.2
**M:** 1 MWM TBD232 V12 diesel; 1 prop; 454 hp
**Range:** 350/8 **Man:** 3 tot. (naval crew)

Remarks: Glass-reinforced plastic construction. Carry spill containment gear.

# DJIBOUTI

**Republic of Djibouti**

Merchant Marine (1986): 7 ships—3,051 grt

◆ **2 patrol craft** Bldr: Plascoa, France

P 10 Moussa Ali (In serv. 8-6-85) P 11 Mont Arreh (In serv. 16-2-86)

**Moussa Ali (P 10)** Plascoa, 6-85

**D:** 30 tons (35 fl) **S:** 24.5 kts **Dim:** 23.30 × 5.50 × 1.50
**A:** 1/20-mm GIAT AA—1/12.7-mm mg
**Electron Equipt:** Radar: 1/Decca 36 MN
**M:** 2 UNI Diesel V12-520 M25 diesels; 2 props; 1,700 hp
**Range:** 750/12; 460/15 **Man:** 15 tot.

Remarks: GRP construction. Ordered 10-84. Used for coastal surveillance.

◆ **1 ex-French patrol craft** Bldr: Tecimar (In serv. 1974)

Zena

**D:** 30 tons (fl) **S:** 25 kts **Dim:** 13.3 × 4.1 × 1.1
**A:** 1/12.7-mm and 1/7.5-mm mg **M:** 2 G.M. 6V71 diesels; 2 props; 240 hp

Remarks: Transferred 1977 from the French colonial police at Djibouti. Glass-reinforced plastic construction.

Note: Three small personnel launches, ex-French, are also in use.

# DOMINICA

MERCHANT MARINE (1986): 7 ships—2,013 grt

COAST GUARD

◆ **1 U.S. 65-ft Commercial Cruiser-class patrol boat** Bldr: Swiftships, Inc., Morgan City, Louisiana, U.S.A.

P-04 MELVILLE (In serv. 2-5-84)

**D:** 34 tons (fl) **S:** 23 kts **Dim:** 19.96 × 5.58 × 1.52
**A:** small arms **Electron Equipt:** Radar: 1/Raytheon 1210
**M:** 2 G.M. 12V71 TI diesels; 2 props; 1,350 hp
**Range:** 500/18 **Electric:** 20 kw **Man:** 6 tot.

REMARKS: One of three sisters presented to Caribbean Island republics by the U.S. government, the others going to Antigua-Barbuda (see photo) and St. Lucia. Aluminum construction. Blue hull, white upperworks.

# DOMINICAN REPUBLIC

PERSONNEL (1986): 4,050 officers and men

MERCHANT MARINE (1986): 35 ships—42,241 grt (tanker: 1 ship—674 grt)

## FRIGATE

◆ **1 Canadian "River" class**

| | Bldr | L | In serv. |
|---|---|---|---|
| 451 MELLA (ex-*Presidente Trujillo,* ex-*Carlplace*) | Davie, S.B., Lauzon, Quebec | 6-7-44 | 13-12-44 |

**Mella (F 451)** 1981

**D:** 1,445 tons (2,300 fl) **S:** 19 kts **Dim:** 92.35 × 11.45 × 4.3
**A:** 1/76.2-mm DP—2/40-mm AA (II × 1)—4/20-mm AA—2/47-mm saluting guns
**Electron Equipt:** Radar: 1/SPS-64
**M:** 2 sets triple-expansion; 2 props; 5,500 hp **Boilers:** 2 (3-drum)
**Fuel:** 645 tons **Range:** 7,700/12 **Man:** 15 officers, 135 men

REMARKS: Bought in 1947. Serves as fleet flagship and as a training ship; can carry 50 cadets.

## CORVETTES

◆ **3 ex-U.S. Cohoes-class former net tenders**

| | Bldr | L | In serv. |
|---|---|---|---|
| P 207 CAMBIASO (ex-*Etlah,* AN 79) | Marietta Mfg., W. Va. | 16-12-44 | 16-4-45 |
| P 208 SEPARACIÓN (ex-*Passaconaway,* AN 86) | Marine Iron & Ry, Duluth | 30-6-44 | 27-4-45 |
| P 209 CALDERAS (ex-*Passaic,* AN 87) | Leatham B. Smith, Wisc. | 29-6-44 | 6-3-45 |

**D:** 650 tons (785 fl) **S:** 12.3 kts **Dim:** 51.36 (44.5 pp) × 10.31 × 3.3
**A:** 2/76.2-mm DP (I × 2)—3/20-mm AA (I × 3)
**Electron Equipt:** Radar: 1/SPS-64 **Fuel:** 88 tons **Man:** 48 tot.
**M:** diesel-electric: 2 Busch-Sulzer B5-539 diesels, 1 motor; 1 prop; 1,200 hp
**Electric:** 120 kw

REMARKS: Recommissioned from the U.S. Maritime Commission's reserve fleet, where they had been laid up since 1963, and transferred 9-76. Despite low speed and general unsuitability, they are employed as patrol ships and tugs. Also used in general support, navigational tender, and hydrographic survey duties. P 207 and P 208 have had the net tender "horns" at the bow removed and a new, curved stem added; they also received a second 76.2-mm gun on the forecastle.

◆ **2 ex-U.S. Admirable-class former minesweepers** Bldr: Associated SB, Seattle, Wash.

| | Laid down | L | In serv. |
|---|---|---|---|
| BM 454 PRESTOL BOTELLO (ex-*Separación,* ex-*Skirmish,* MSF 303) | 8-4-43 | 16-8-43 | 30-6-44 |
| BM 455 TORTUGERO (ex-*Signet,* MSF 302) | 8-4-43 | 16-8-43 | 20-8-44 |

**D:** 600 tons (903 fl) **S:** 15 kts **Dim:** 54.24 × 10.06 × 4.4
**A:** 1/76.2-mm DP—2/40-mm AA (I × 2)—6/20-mm AA (I × 6)
**Electron Equipt:** Radar: 1/SPS-69
**M:** 2 Cooper-Bessemer GSB-8 diesels; 2 props; 1,710 hp **Electric:** 240 kw
**Fuel:** 260 tons **Range:** 5,600/9 **Man:** 100 tot.

REMARKS: Transferred in 1-65. BM 454 renamed 1976. All minesweeping equipment and ASW armament removed from both.

## PATROL BOATS AND CRAFT

◆ **2 110-ft Commercial Cruiser class** Bldr: Swiftships, Inc., Morgan City, Louisiana

GC 108 CANOPUS (In serv. 6-84) GC 109 ORION (In serv. 8-84)

**Orion (GC 109)** Swiftships, 8-84

**D:** 93.5 tons (fl) **S:** 23 kts (20 sust.) **Dim:** 33.53 × 7.32 × 1.83
**A:** . . . **Electron Equipt:** Radar: . . .
**M:** 3 G.M. 12V92 TI diesels; 3 props; 2,700 hp
**Electric:** . . . **Range:** 1,500/12 **Man:** . . .

REMARKS: Aluminum construction. Acquisition of a third has been proposed.

NOTE: The three early-1930s-vintage former U.S. Coast Guard *Argo*-class patrol boats have been placed "in reserve" and are unlikely to see further service: *Independencia* (P 204, ex-*Icarus*), *Libertad* (P 205, ex-*Rafael Atoa,* ex-*Thetis*), and *Restauración* (P 206, ex-*Galatea*).

◆ **1 ex-U.S. PGM 71 class** Bldr: Peterson SB, Sturgeon Bay, Wisc.

GC 102 BETELGEUSE (ex-PGM 77)

**D:** 130 tons (145.5 fl) **S:** 16 kts **Dim:** 30.8 (30.2 pp) × 6.4 × 1.85
**A:** 1/20-mm AA—2/12.7-mm mg (I × 2)
**M:** 2 Caterpillar D-348TA diesels; 2 props; 1,450 hp **Range:** 1,000/12
**Man:** 20 tot.

REMARKS: Transferred 14-1-66. One of many gunboats of this class transferred to smaller navies by the United States. Re-engined and armament reduced, 1980.

◆ **1 former U.S. Army aircraft-rescue launch**

GC 105 CAPITÁN ALSINA (L: 1944)

**D:** 100 tons (fl) **S:** 17 kts **Dim:** 31.5 × 5.8 × 1.75 **A:** 2/20-mm AA (I × 2)
**M:** 2 G.M. diesels; 2 props; 1,000 hp **Man:** 20 tot.

REMARKS: Wooden hull. Used as Naval Academy training craft, refitted 1977.

◆ **4 U.S. 85-ft Commercial Cruiser-class patrol craft** Bldr: Sewart Seacraft, Berwick, La.

| | In serv. | | In serv. |
|---|---|---|---|
| GC 103 PROCION | 1972 | GC 106 BELLATRIX | 1967 |
| GC 104 ALDEBARÁN | 1967 | GC 108 CAPELLA | 1968 |

**D:** 60 tons (fl) **S:** 21.7 kts **Dim:** 25.9 × 5.7 × 2.1 **A:** 3/12.7-mm mg (I × 3)
**M:** 2 G.M. 16V71N diesels; 2 props; 1,400 hp **Range:** 800/20 **Man:** 9 tot.

◆ **1 former U.S. 63-ft aircraft-rescue launch** (In serv. 1953)

GC 101 RIGEL

**D:** 27 tons (fl) **S:** 18.5 kts **Dim:** 19.3 × 4.7 × 1.2 **A:** 2/12.7-mm mg
**M:** 2 G.M. 6V71 diesels; 2 props; 800 hp **Range:** 450/15 **Man:** 9 tot.

**PATROL BOATS AND CRAFT** *(continued)*

**Capella (GC 108)** L. & L. Van Ginderen, 3-84

◆ **4 small patrol craft** Bldr: Dominican NY (In serv. 1975)

BA 3 Carite BA 6 Atón BA 9 Picúa BA 15 Jurel

**D:** 30 tons (fl) **S:** 12 kts **Dim:** 12.7 × 4.0 × 1.8 **A:** 1/76.2-mm mg
**M:** 2 G.M. diesels; 200 hp

Remarks: Have auxiliary sail power. Sisters *Albacora* and *Bonito* discarded.

## AUXILIARY SHIPS

◆ **1 converted U.S. LSM 1-class cargo carrier** Bldr: Brown Bros., Houston, Tex.

| | Laid down | L | In serv. |
|---|---|---|---|
| BDM 301 Sirio (ex-LSM 483) | 17-2-45 | 10-3-45 | 13-4-45 |

**D:** 734 tons (1,100 fl) **S:** 12 kts **Dim:** 62.8 × 10.4 × 2.1 **Man:** 30 tot.
**M:** 2 G.M. 16-278A diesels; 2,800 hp **Electric:** 240 kw **Fuel:** 164 tons

Remarks: Transferred 3-58. Decked over, bow doors plated up, bridge re-sited on centerline, 1970.

◆ **1 utility landing craft** Bldr: Dominican NY (In serv. 1958)

LDM 302 Samana

**D:** 128 tons (310 fl) **S:** 8/7 kts **Dim:** 36.4 × 11.0 × 1.15 **A:** 1/12.7-mm mg
**M:** 3 G.M. 64HN9 diesels; 3 props; 450 hp **Fuel:** 80 tons **Man:** 17 tot.

Remarks: U.S. LCT(5) design, used for logistics duties. Sister *Enriquillo* discarded 1979.

◆ **1 small buoy tender**

BA 10 Neptuno (ex-*Toro*) Bldr: J.H. Mathis, U.S.A., 1954

**D:** 72.2 tons (fl) **S:** 10 kts **Dim:** 19.5 × 5.7 × 2.4
**M:** 1 G.M. diesel; 225 hp **Man:** 7 tot.

◆ **1 survey ship, former 110-ft U.S. Coast Guard buoy tender**

| | Bldr | Laid down | In serv. |
|---|---|---|---|
| FB 1 Capotillo (ex-*Camelia,* WAGL 206) | Racine Boat Co., Muskegon, Mich. | 18-10-09 | 13-7-11 |

**D:** 327 tons (377 fl) **S:** 10 kts **Dim:** 33.53 × 7.32 × 2.44
**M:** 2 diesels; 2 props; 220 hp **Range:** 1,700/9; 2,100/7 **Man:** 23 tot.

Remarks: Stricken from U.S. Coast Guard 18-8-47 and purchased 29-12-47 by the Dominican Republic. Re-engined and rehabilitated early 1970s for use as a hydrographic survey ship.

◆ **2 U.S. YO 153-class small oilers** Bldr: Ira S. Bushey, Brooklyn, N.Y.

| | Laid down | L | In serv. |
|---|---|---|---|
| BT 4 Capitan W. Arvelo (ex-U.S. YO 213) | 3-2-45 | 21-6-45 | 8-11-45 |
| BT 5 Capitan Beotegui (ex-U.S. YO 215) | 23-4-45 | 30-8-45 | 17-12-45 |

**D:** 370 tons (1,076 fl) **S:** 8 kts **Dim:** 47.63 × 9.32 × 3.66
**A:** 2/20-mm AA (I × 2)
**M:** 1 Union diesel; 1 prop; 525 hp **Cargo:** 6,071 barrels fuel (660 tons)
**Electric:** 39 kw **Man:** 25 tot.

Remarks: Both were loaned 4-64; lease extended 31-12-80.

◆ **1 small survey ship, converted sport-fishing boat**

BA 8 Atlantida

**D:** . . . **S:** . . . **Dim:** 12.1 × 3.6 × 1.8
**M:** 2 G.M. 4-71 diesels; 2 props; 300 hp

◆ **1 U.S. Cherokee-class fleet tug** Bldr: Charleston SB & DD, S. Carolina

| | Laid down | L | In serv. |
|---|---|---|---|
| RM 21 Macorix (ex-*Kiowa,* ATF 72) | 22-6-42 | 5-11-42 | 7-6-43 |

**D:** 1,235 tons (1,675 fl) **S:** 15 kts **Dim:** 62.48 (59.44 wl) × 11.73 × 4.67
**A:** 1/76.2-mm DP—2/20-mm AA (I × 2) **Electron Equipt:** Radar: 1/SPS-5D
**M:** 4 G.M. 12-278 diesels, electric drive; 1 prop; 3,000 hp
**Electric:** 260 kw **Fuel:** 295 tons **Man:** 85 tot.

Remarks: Transferred 16-10-72; lease extended 31-12-80. Has what appear to be multiple mg mounts abreast after tripod mast.

◆ **2 U.S. Sotoyomo-class auxiliary ocean tugs**

| | Bldr | Laid down | L | In serv. |
|---|---|---|---|---|
| RM 18 Caonabo (ex-*Sagamore,* ATA 208) | Gulfport Boiler, Port Arthur, Tex. | 27-11-44 | 19-1-45 | 19-3-45 |
| RM 22 Enriquillo (ex-*Stallion,* ATA 193) | Levingston SB, Orange, Tex. | 26-10-44 | 24-11-44 | 1-2-45 |

**Caonabo (RM 18)** 1981

**D:** 534 tons (860 fl) **S:** 13 kts **Dim:** 43.59 × 10.31 × 3.96
**A:** 1/76.2-mm DP—2/20-mm AA (I × 2)
**Electron Equipt:** Radar: 1/Raytheon 1500B
**M:** 2 G.M. 12-278A diesels, electric drive; 1 prop; 1,500 hp
**Electric:** 120 kw **Fuel:** 160 tons **Range:** 8,000/8 **Man:** 45 tot.

Remarks: RM 18 leased 1-2-72, extended 31-12-80. RM 22 purchased 30-10-80.

◆ **2 Hercules-class harbor tugs** Bldr: Dominican NY (In serv. 1960)

RP 12 Hercules RP 13 Guacanagarix

**D:** 200 tons (fl) **S:** . . . kts **Dim:** 21.4 × 4.8 × 2.7
**M:** 1 Caterpillar diesel; 1 prop; 500 hp **Man:** 8 tot.

◆ **1 former landing craft**

RDM 303 Ocoa Bldr: U.S.A.

**D:** 50 tons (fl) **S:** 9 kts **Dim:** 17.1 × 4.3 × 1.2
**M:** 2 G.M. 6-71 diesels; 2 props; 450 hp **Range:** 130/9

Remarks: Modified as a tug about 1976. Retains bow ramp.

◆ **3 small harbor tugs**

RP 20 Isabela RP 19 Calderas RP 22 Puerto Hermoso—no data

◆ **1 U.S. YTL 422-class small tug** Bldr: Robt. Jacob, City Isl., NY

RP 16 Bohechio (ex-*Mercedes,* ex-YTL 600) (In serv. 25-7-45)

**D:** 70 tons (80 fl) **S:** 10 kts **Dim:** 20.1 × 5.5 × 2.4
**M:** 1 Hoover-Owens-Rentschler diesel; 1 prop; 375 hp **Fuel:** 7 tons

Remarks: Transferred 1-71.

## TRAINING CRAFT

◆ **1 sail-training ship for Naval Academy** (In serv. 1979)

BA 7 Nube Del Mar (ex-*Catuan*)

**D:** 40 tons (fl) **S:** 12 kts **Dim:** 12.8 × 3.6 × . . .
**M:** 1 Volvo Penta 21A diesel; 1 prop; 75 hp

◆ **1 training launch** (In serv. . . .)

BA . . . Duarte

**D:** 60 tons (fl) **S:** . . . kts **Dim:** 22.9 × 5.7 × 2.1
**M:** 1 G.M. 6-71 diesel; 1 prop; 325 hp **Man:** 30 tot.

◆ **2 small fishing boats** (In serv. 1979)

BA 11 Alto Velo BA 12 Saona

Remarks: BA 11 is a two-masted sailing craft.

◆ **floating dry dock** Bldr: Chicago Bridge & Iron

N . . . (ex-*Endeavor,* AFDL 1) (In serv. 1943)

**Lift Capacity:** 1,000 tons **Dim:** 60.96 × 19.51 × 1.07 (light)

Remarks: Leased from U.S. 8-3-86. Length on blocks: 56.39 m; clear width: 13.72 m; draft over blocks: 4.42 m; max-draft: 8.23 m.

# DUBAI

NOTE: In addition to Dubai's participation in the federated naval force of the United Arab Emirates (U.A.E.), Dubai also operates two patrol boats for customs purposes.

◆ **2 U.S. 65-ft Commercial Cruisers** Bldr: Swiftships, Morgan City, Louisiana (In serv. 12-12-77)

**D:** 24.9 tons (36.3 fl) **S:** 24 kts **Dim:** 19.77 (17.9 wl) × 5.56 × 1.98
**M:** 2 MTU 8V331 diesels; 2 props; 1,400 hp
**Range:** 1,200/18 **Fuel:** 4.8 tons **Electric:** 20 kw **Man:** 7 tot.

# ECUADOR

**Republic of Ecuador**

PERSONNEL (1984): 3,800 total (300 officers, 3,500 men), plus 1,500 naval infantry

MERCHANT MARINE (1986): 155 ships—436,743 grt (tankers: 22 ships—154,725)

NAVAL AVIATION: A small detachment with 2 French Alouette-III helicopters, 3 Israeli Arava light transports, 4 Cessna T-37, 2 T-41D, 1 Cessna 320E, one Cessna 177, 3 Beech T-34C-1 trainers, and one Beech Super King Air light transport.

## SUBMARINES

◆ **2 German Type 209** Bldr: Howaldtswerke, Kiel

| | Laid down | L | In serv. |
|---|---|---|---|
| S 11 SHYRI | 5-8-74 | 6-10-76 | 6-11-77 |
| S 12 HUANCAVILCA | 20-1-75 | 15-3-77 | 16-3-78 |

**Huancavilca (S 12)** P. Voss, 4-84

**D:** 1,285 tons surf./1,390 sub. **S:** 21.4 kts (1 hr.) **Dim:** 59.50 × 6.20 × 5.50
**A:** 8/533-mm TT (fwd.)—14 torpedoes **Fuel:** 110 tons
**Electron Equipt:** Radar: 1 Thomson-CSF Calypso
Sonar: 1/Atlas A526 passive, 1/CSUAN 407 A9 active, 1/DUUX-2
**M:** 4 MTU 12V493 TY60 diesels, 4 Siemens 405-kw generators, electric drive: 1 Siemens motor; 1 prop; 5,000 hp
**Endurance:** 45 days **Range:** 400/4 sub.; 8,400/8 snorkel
**Man:** 5 officers, 26 men

REMARKS: Ordered 1974. Hollandse Signaal M8 Mod. 24 torpedo f.c.s. S 11 refitted at her builders, 1983, S 12 in 1984.

## DESTROYER

◆ **1 U.S. Gearing FRAM-I class**

| | Bldr | Laid down | L | In serv. |
|---|---|---|---|---|
| DD 01 PRESIDENTE ELOY ALFARO (ex-*Holder,* DD 819) | Consolidated Steel, Orange, Tex. | 23-4-45 | 25-8-45 | 18-5-46 |

**D:** 2,425 tons (3,500 fl) **S:** 30 kts **Dim:** 119.1 × 12.4 × 5.8
**A:** 4/127-mm DP (II × 2)—6/324-mm Mk 32 ASW TT (III × 2)—1/helicopter
**Electron Equipt:** Radar: 1/LN-66, 1/SPS-10, 1/SPS-40, 1/Mk 25 fire-control
Sonar: SQS-23—EW: WLR-1
**M:** 2 sets GT; 2 props; 60,000 hp
**Boilers:** 4 Babcock & Wilcox; 43.3 kg/cm², 454°C **Electric:** 1,200 kw
**Fuel:** 650 tons **Range:** 2,400/25; 4,800/15 **Man:** 270 tot.

**Presidente Eloy Alfaro (DD 01)** J. Jedrlinic, 1980

REMARKS: Transferred by sale on 1-9-78, the *Alfaro* began overhaul in the U.S. 8-78; recommissioning 27-6-80. ASROC deleted. Has Mk 37 GFCS.

## FRIGATE

◆ **1 U.S. Charles Lawrence-class fast transport**

| | Bldr | Laid down | L | In serv. |
|---|---|---|---|---|
| DD 03 MORAN VALVERDE (ex-*26 de Julio,* ex-*Enright,* APD 66) | Phila. Navy Yd | 22-2-43 | 29-5-43 | 21-9-43 |

**Moran Valverde (DD 03)** U.S. Navy, 1974

**D:** 1,400 tons (2,130 fl) **S:** 23 kts **Dim:** 93.27 × 11.27 × 4.7
**A:** 1/127-mm DP—6/40-mm AA (II × 3)—2 d.c. racks
**Electron Equipt:** Radar: 1/SPS-6, 1/navigational
**M:** G.E. turbo-electric drive; 2 props; 12,000 hp **Electric:** 680 kw
**Boilers:** 2 Foster-Wheeler "D" Express; 30.6 kg/cm², 399°C **Fuel:** 350 tons
**Range:** 2,000/23; 5,000/15 **Man:** 212 tot.

REMARKS: Transferred 7-67. Could carry 162 troops when in U.S. Navy. Davits can handle four LCPR/LCVP, but ship carries only two to reduce top weight. Has a raised helicopter deck over the stern area.

## CORVETTES

◆ **6 Italian modified Wadi M'ragh class**

| | Bldr | Laid down | L | In serv. |
|---|---|---|---|---|
| CM 11 Esmeraldas | CNR, Muggiano | 27-9-79 | 5-10-80 | 7-8-82 |
| CM 12 Manabi | CNR, Ancona | 1-2-80 | 5-2-81 | 21-6-83 |
| CM 13 Los Rios | CNR, Muggiano | 1-9-79 | 28-2-81 | 1-10-83 |
| CM 14 El Oro | CNR, Ancona | 1-3-80 | 5-2-81 | 10-12-83 |
| CM 15 Galapagos | CNR, Muggiano | 20-10-80 | 5-7-81 | 26-5-84 |
| CM 16 Loja | CNR, Ancona | 6-2-81 | 27-2-82 | 26-5-84 |

**Esmeraldas (CM 11)** CNR, 1982

**El Oro (CM 14)** U.S. Navy, 1985

**D:** 620 tons (700 fl) **S:** 37 kts **Dim:** 62.3 (57.8 pp) × 9.3 × 2.8
**A:** 6/MM 40 Exocet SSM (III × 2)—1 Albatros SAM system (IV × 1; Aspide missiles)—1/76-mm OTO Melara DP—2/40-mm Breda AA (II × 1)—6/324-mm ILAS-3 ASW TT (III × 2)
**Electron Equipt:** Radar: 1/Decca TM1226, 1/RAN-10S, 1/Orion 10X, 1/Orion 20X
Sonar: Diodon—EW: Gamma syst., 1/SCLAR chaff RL
**M:** 4 MTU 20V956 TB92 diesels; 4 props; 24,400 hp (20,400 sust.)
**Electric:** 750 kw **Fuel:** 126 tons
**Range:** 1,200/31; 4,000/18 **Man:** 51 tot.

Remarks: Ordered 1978 from CNR del Tirreno. More powerful engines than earlier Libyan units of class, helicopter platform added. Selenia IPN-10 data system, with NA 21 Mod. 0 radar f.c.s. and two CO3 directors for guns and SAM system. Have a helicopter platform, but no aircraft have been acquired, and there is no hangar. CM 14 badly damaged by fire, 18-4-85.

## GUIDED-MISSILE PATROL BOATS

◆ **3 Quito class** Bldr: Lürssen, Vegesack, West Germany

| | L | In serv. |
|---|---|---|
| LM 21 Quito | 20-11-75 | 13-7-76 |
| LM 22 Guayaquil | 5-4-76 | 22-12-77 |
| LM 24 Cuenca | 12-76 | 17-7-77 |

**Quito (LM 21)** G. Koop, 1976

**D:** 250 tons (265 fl) **S:** 35 kts **Dim:** 47.0 × 7.0 × 2.4
**A:** 4/MM 38 Exocet SSM (II × 2)—1/76-mm OTO Melara—2/35-mm AA (II × 1)
**Electron Equipt:** Radar: 1/Decca TM 1226, 1/Thomson-CSF Triton, 1/Thomson-CFS Pollux f.c.
**M:** 4 MTU 16V538 diesels; 4 props; 14,000 hp **Electric:** 330 kw
**Fuel:** 39 tons **Range:** 600/30 **Man:** 34 tot.

Remarks: Carry 250 rounds of 76-mm and 1,100 rounds of 35-mm ammunition. Thomson-CSF Vega fire-control system.

◆ **3 Manta class** Bldr: Lürssen, Vegesack, W. Germany

LM 25 Manta (In serv. 11-6-71) LM 26 Tulcan (In serv. 2-4-71) LM 27 Nueva Rocafuerte (ex-*Tena*) (In serv. 23-6-71)

**Manta (LM 25)** U.S. Navy, 1981

**D:** 119 tons (134 fl) **S:** 35 kts **Dim:** 36.2 × 5.8 × 1.7
**A:** 4/Gabriel II SSM (I × 4)—2/30-mm AA Emerlec (II × 1)
**Electron Equipt:** Radar: 1/navigational, 1/Thomson-CSF Pollux
**M:** 3 Mercedes-Benz diesels; 3 props; 9,000 hp **Fuel:** 21 tons
**Range:** 700/30; 1,500/15 **Man:** 19 tot.

Remarks: Similar to Chilean *Guacolda* class, but faster. New guns added 1979; Gabriel missiles and Thomson-CSF Vega fire-control system (without Triton search radar) replaced 2/533-mm TT 1980-81. Replacements for these three units being sought in 1987 with the Spanish Piraña class under consideration.

## PATROL CRAFT

◆ **3 Port Director class** Bldr: Halter, New Orleans, 1975

Comandancia De Balao Comandancia De Salinas
Comandancia De Guayaquil

**D:** 34 tons (fl) **S:** 25 kts **Dim:** 19.66 × 5.18 × 1.24 **A:** . . .
**M:** 2 G.M. 12V71 TI diesels; 2 props; 960 hp

◆ **3 LPI class** Bldr: F. Schürenstedt, Bardenfleth, W. Germany (In serv. 1954–55)

LC 81 Baba Hoyo (ex-*10 de Agosto*) LC 83 Portoviejo (ex-*3 de Noviembre*)
LC 82 Pichincha (ex-*9 de Octubre*)

**D:** 45 tons (64 fl) **S:** 20 kts **Dim:** 23.4 × 4.6 × 1.8 **A:** 1 or 2 mg
**M:** 2 Böhn & Kahler diesels; 2 props; 1,200 hp **Range:** 556/16 **Man:** 9 tot.

◆ **2 ex-U.S. Coast Guard utility boats**—transferred 1971

UT 111 Rio Napo UT 112 Isla Puna

**D:** 10.6 tons **S:** 19 kts **Dim:** 12.27 × 3.45 × 1.0 **A:** . . .
**M:** 2 G.M. diesels; 2 props; 380 hp **Range:** 280/18 **Man:** 4–5 tot.

## AMPHIBIOUS WARFARE SHIPS

◆ **1 ex-U.S. LST 542-class tank landing ship** Bldr: Chicago Bridge & Iron

| | Laid down | L | In serv. |
|---|---|---|---|
| T 55 Hualcopo (ex-*Summit County,* LST 1146) | 15-2-45 | 23-5-45 | 1-6-45 |

**D:** 1,650 tons (4,080 fl) **S:** 11.6 kts **Dim:** 100.04 × 15.24 × 4.3
**A:** 8/40-mm (II × 2, I × 4) **M:** 2 G.M. 12-567A diesels; 2 props; 1,700 hp
**Electric:** 300 kw **Range:** 7,200/10 **Man:** 119 tot.

Remarks: Bought 2-77. Used as transport; has ice-reinforced waterline. To be replaced by a new transport to be built by ASTINAVE.

◆ **1 ex-U.S. LSM 1-class medium landing ship** Bldr: Charleston NY, S.C.

| | Laid down | L | In serv. |
|---|---|---|---|
| T 52 Tarqui (ex-LSM 555) | 3-3-45 | 22-3-45 | 24-9-45 |

**AMPHIBIOUS WARFARE SHIPS** *(continued)*

**D:** 513 tons (1,095 fl) **S:** 12.5 kts **Dim:** 62.0 × 10.5 × 2.2
**A:** 2/40-mm AA (II × 1) **M:** 2 G.M. 16-278A diesels; 2 props; 2,800 hp
**Range:** 2,500/12 **Man:** 60 tot.

Remarks: Built 1945, transferred 11-58. Used as transports. Sister *Jambeli* (T 51, ex-LSM 539) stricken 1983.

◆ **6 "Sea Trucks"** Bldr: Rotork, U.K. (In serv. 1979)

LF 91 LF 92 LF 93 LF 94 LF 95 LF 96

**D:** 5 tons (9 fl) **S:** 26 kts (light) **Dim:** 12.65 × 3.20 × . . .
**M:** 2 Volvo AQD 40A diesels; 2 outdrive props; 240 hp **Cargo:** 4 tons

**AUXILIARY SHIPS**

◆ **1 oceanographic research ship** Bldr: Ishikawajima Harima, Tokyo (In serv. 21-10-81)

HI 92 Orion (ex-*Dometer*)

**Orion (HI 92)** Ishikawajima Harima, 1981

**D:** 1,105 grt **S:** 12.6 kts **Dim:** 70.17 (64.20 pp) × 10.70 × 3.6 (5.40 max.)
**Electron Equipt:** Radar: 2/Decca 1226 **Electric:** 700 kw
**M:** 3 G.M. 16V92 TI diesels, electric drive (2 motors); 1 prop; 950 hp
**Range:** 6,000/12 **Man:** 6 officers, 25 men, 19 scientists

Remarks: *Dometer* was delivery name, changed to *Orion* on arrival for commissioning. Equipped to conduct physical and biological oceanography, geophysical research, and hydrographic surveys.

◆ **1 inshore oceanographic research craft**

O 112 Rigel Bldr: Halter Marine, New Orleans (In serv. 1975)

**D:** 50 tons **Man:** 10 tot.

◆ **1 ex-U.S. Army FS 381-class small cargo ship** Bldr: Higgins, New Orleans (In serv. 1944)

T 12 Calicuchima (ex-FS 525)

**D:** 650 tons (930 fl) **S:** 11.5 kts **Dim:** 54.86 (52.37 pp) × 9.75 × 3.05
**M:** 2 G.M. 6-278A diesels; 2 props; 1,000 hp **Fuel:** 100 tons
**Range:** 4,000/11 **Man:** 30 tot.

Remarks: Used to supply the Galápagos Islands. Leased 8-4-63; purchased 30-8-78.

◆ **1 ex-U.S. small water tanker**

T 41 Atahualpa (ex-YW 131) Bldr: Leatham D. Smith, Wisc. (In serv. 17-9-45)

**D:** 440 tons (1,390 fl) **S:** 7 kts **Dim:** 53.1 × 9.8 × 4.6
**M:** 1 G.M. diesel; 1 prop; 640 hp **Fuel:** 25 tons **Man:** 20 tot.

Remarks: Transferred 2-5-63; purchased 1-12-77. Cargo: 930 tons water.

◆ **2 U.S. Abnaki- and Achomawi-class fleet tugs** Bldr: Charleston SB & DD, Charleston, S.C.

| | Laid down | L | In serv. |
|---|---|---|---|
| R 101 Cayambe (ex-*Los Rios*, ex-*Cusabo*, ex-ATF 155) | 18-9-44 | 26-2-45 | 19-5-45 |
| R 71 Chimborazo (ex-R 105, ex-*Chowanoc*, ATF 100) | 24-4-43 | 20-8-43 | 21-2-44 |

**D:** 1,235 tons (1,675 fl) **S:** 16.5 kts **Dim:** 62.48 (59.44 wl) × 11.73 × 4.67
**A:** 1/76.2-mm DP—2/40-mm AA (I × 2)—2/20-mm AA (I × 2)
**Electron Equipt:** Radar: 1/Decca 916
**M:** 4 G.M. 12-278A diesels, electric drive; 1 prop; 3,000 hp **Electric:** 400 kw
**Fuel:** 376 tons **Range:** 16,000/8; 7,000/15 **Man:** 85 tot.

**Cayambe**—now new number 1966

Remarks: R 71: **A:** 2/12.7-mm mg; **M:** 4 Busch-Sulzer B5-539 diesels; pipe *vice* stack. *Cayambe* leased 2-11-60, purchased 30-8-78. *Chimborazo* purchased 1-10-77.

◆ **1 medium harbor tug** (In serv. 1952)

R 102 Sangay (ex-*Losa*)

**D:** 295 tons (390 fl) **S:** 12 kts **Dim:** 32.6 × 7.9 × 4.25
**M:** 1 Fairbanks-Morse diesel; 1 prop; . . . hp

Remarks: Bought 1964.

◆ **1 former U.S. Army tug** Bldr: Equitable Bldg. (In serv. 1945)

R 103 Cotopaxi (ex-*R. T. Ellis*)

**D:** 150 tons **S:** 9 kts **Dim:** 25.0 × 6.62 × 2.9 **M:** diesel; 1 prop; 650 hp

Remarks: Bought 1947.

◆ **2 small tugs**

R . . . Tungurahua R 104 Antizana—no data

◆ **1 sail-training bark** Bldr: Ast. Celaya SY, Bilbao, Spain

| | L | In serv. |
|---|---|---|
| BE 01 Guayas | 23-9-76 | 23-7-77 |

**Guayas (BE 01)** Ecuadoran Navy, 11-83

**D:** 934 grt **S:** 10.5 kts **Dim:** 76.2 × 10.6 × 4.2
**M:** 1 G.M. 12V-149 diesel; 1 prop; 700 hp

◆ **1 repair barge**

BT 62 Putamayo (ex-YR 340) Bldr: New York Navy Yard, 1944

**D:** 520 tons (770 fl) **Dim:** 45.7 × 10.4 × 1.8 **Electric:** 330 kw

Remarks: Transferred 7-62; purchased 1-12-77.

◆ **1 ex-U.S. auxiliary repair dock** (In serv. 1944)

DF 121 Amazonas (ex-ARD 17)

**Capacity:** 3,500 tons **Dim:** 149.9 × 24.7 × 1.7 (light)

Remarks: Transferred 7-1-61. Pointed bow. Length over blocks: 118.6 m; 18.0-m clear width. Dry dock companion craft YFND 20 leased 2-11-61 to support.

## COAST GUARD
Established 1980

Personnel (1982): 13 officers, 257 enlisted men

**ECUADOR** *(continued)*
**COAST GUIDE** *(continued)*

◆ **2 (+6) 13-m class** Bldr: (first four) Halter Marine, New Orleans; remainder: . . . , Ecuador

**D:** . . . **S:** . . . **Dim:** 13.0 × . . . × . . .
**A:** 3/12.7-mm mg (I × 3) **M:** 2 G.M. diesels; 2 props; 690 hp

Remarks: Two in service in Galápagos by 1986; new order for six announced 2-87, with four to be assembled in Ecuador from kits. Aluminum construction. Replaced a contract with Neville Boatyard, Louisiana, for six 15-m boats.

◆ **14 U.S. Baycraft 40-ft. patrol craft** (In serv. 1979–80)

Remarks: Fiberglass hulls; modified sport-fishing boat design. No other data available.

# EGYPT

## Arab Republic of Egypt

Personnel (1985): Approx. 30,000 total

Merchant Marine (1986): 422 ships—1,063,020 grt
(tankers: 46 ships—98,141 grt)

Naval Aviation: The Navy operates 18 Westland Sea King Mk 47 helicopters and 12 Aerospatiale SA 342 L Gazelle helicopters; another 12 Gazelles are on order. The Sea Kings are to be fitted to guide Otomat anti-ship missiles, and the Gazelles can carry AS.12 wire-guided missiles. The Air Force ordered two Beech 1900C light coastal surveillance aircraft with Litton radar, 1987.

Coast Defenses: The Navy is responsible for coastal defenses. Fifty Coast Defense, truck-mounted versions of the Otomat missile were purchased 1983. Targeting performed by land-based Sea King helicopters. Some Soviet Samlet coast-defense missiles remain in service also.

### SUBMARINES

◆ **8 Soviet and Chinese Romeo class**

4 Soviet-built: 834, 837, 840, 843
4 Chinese-built: 831, 842, 852, . . .

**Chinese-built Romeo** (old number) L. & L. Van Ginderen, 2-83

**D:** 1,320/1,712 tons **S:** 15.2/13 kts **Dim:** 77.60 × 6.70 × 4.95
**A:** 8/533-mm TT (6 fwd, 2 aft)—14 torpedoes or 28 mines
**Electron Equipt:** Radar: 1/Snoop Plate—Sonar: Hercules (Chinese units: Tamir-5L active, Feniks)
**M:** diesel-electric, 2 Type 37D diesels, 2,000 hp each; 2 props; 2,700 hp—2/50-hp creep motors **Range:** 350/4 sub.; 14,000/9 surf.; 7,000/5 (snorkel)
**Endurance:** 60 days **Man:** 56 tot.

Remarks: The Soviet-built units were transferred—5 in 1966, 1 in 1969, and began refitting with European equipment in 1981. They had been constructed between 1957 and 1960 at Baltic Shipyard, Leningrad; two Soviet-built units have been discarded. Two units, launched in 1980, were delivered from China on 28-3-83; the second Chinese pair were delivered 3-1-84 and commissioned 21-5-84. The Chinese-built units have sonar domes atop their bows. All have 224 battery cells, producing 6,000 amp/hr. Operating depth is 270 m (300 max.). The Soviet-built units are to be updated by Thyssen Nordseewerke, under a contract signed 1984, and the Chinese units are to receive U.S. Singer Librascope f.c.s.

◆ **3 Soviet Whiskey class**

810 816 819

**D:** 1,050/1,350 tons **S:** 17/16 kts **Dim:** 75.0 × 6.3 × 4.8
**A:** 6/533-mm TT (4 fwd, 2 aft)—12 torpedoes or 28 mines
**Electron Equipt:** Radar: 1/Snoop Plate
Sonar: Hercules, passive array
**M:** 2 Type 37D diesels; 2,000 hp each; 2 electric motors; 2 props; 2,500 hp
**Endurance:** 40–45 days **Range:** 6,000/5 (snorkel) **Man:** 50 tot.

**Egyptian Whiskey** (old number) L. & L. Van Ginderen, 1980

Remarks: Survivors of six transferred from 6-57 to 8-62. Reported in poor condition. Refitted 1978–79; were to get British electronic intercept equipment. Two others survive as hulks.

### FRIGATES

◆ **2 Chinese Jianghu class** Bldr: Jiangnan SY, Shanghai

951 Najim Al Zafir (In serv. 27-10-84) 956 El Nasser (In serv. 16-4-85)

**Najim al Zafir (951)** H. Ehlers, 5-86

**El Nasser (956)** L. & L. Van Ginderen, 4-86

**D:** 1,586 tons (1,900 fl) **S:** 25.5 kts **Dim:** 103.20 × 10.20 × 3.05 (hull)
**A:** 4/HY-2 SSM (II × 2)—4/57-mm AA (II × 2)—12/37-mm AA (II × 6)—4/RBU-1200 ASW RL (V × 4)—4/BMB-2 d.c. mortars—2/d.c. racks—mines
**Electron Equipt:** Radar: 1/Decca . . . , 1/Type 756, 1/Eye Shield, 1/Square Tie
Sonar: MF, hull-mounted
EW: Elettronica . . .—IFF: 2/Square Head, 1/High Pole A
**M:** 2 SEMT-Pielstick 12 PA 6 diesels; 2 props; 16,000 hp **Electric:** 1,320 kw
**Range:** 1,750/25; 4,000/15 **Endurance:** 15 days **Man:** 195 tot.

Remarks: Ordered 1982. 951 completed 7-84, arriving in Egypt in 10-84. 952 completed 12-84, arriving in Egypt 3-85. There are plans to update the armament suits and sensors. Differ from Chinese Navy units in having twin 57-mm guns vice single or twin 100-mm mounts fore and aft, and in having an enclosed housing for the optical rangefinder atop the bridge. There is no radar fire-control equipment for the eight gun mounts, all of which are locally controlled via on-mount sights. Elettronica EW equipment added after delivery, also a second navigational radar.

◆ **2 Spanish Descubierta class** Bldr: Bazán, Cartagena

| | Laid down | L | In serv. |
|---|---|---|---|
| 936 El Suez (ex-*Centinela*) | 31-10-78 | 6-10-79 | 21-5-84 |
| 941 El Aboukir (ex-*Serviola*) | 28-2-79 | 20-12-79 | 27-10-84 |

**D:** 1,363 tons (1,575 fl) **S:** 26 kts **Dim:** 88.88 (85.80 pp) × 10.40 × 3.70
**A:** 8/Harpoon SSM (IV × 2)—1/Mk 29 SAM launcher (VIII; 24 NATO Sea Sparrow missiles)—1/76-mm OTO Melara Compact—2/40-mm AA (I × 2)—1/375-mm Bofors ASW RL (II × 1)—6/324-mm Mk 32 ASW TT (III × 2, Stingray torpedoes)

**FRIGATES** *(continued)*

**El Aboukir (941)**—fitting out; note VDS position aft L. & L. Van Ginderen, 10-84

**El Aboukir (941)**—fitting out L. & L. Van Ginderen, 10-84

**Electron Equipt:** Radar: 1/H.S.A. ZW-06/Z, 1/H.S.A. DA-05/2, 1/H.S.A. WM-25 f.c.
Sonar: Raytheon 1160B hull-mounted, Raytheon 1167 VDS
EW: Elettronica Beta intercept
**M:** 4 MTU-Bazán 16 MA656 TB91 diesels; 2 CP props; 18,000 hp
**Electric:** 1,810 kw **Fuel:** 250 tons **Range:** 6,000/18
**Man:** 10 officers, 106 men (146 accom.)

REMARKS: Originally ordered 25-5-76 for the Spanish Navy, but sold 1982. 936 completed 28-2-84 and 941 on 6-9-84. Have fin stabilizers, plus U.S. "Prairie/Masker" bubble system to reduce sound radiation below the waterline. Carry 600 rds. 76-mm ammunition. H.S.A. SEWACO weapons-control system. The U.S. supplied the Harpoon missiles in 1984.

◆ **1 British Black Swan Class** Bldr: Yarrow, Glasgow

| | Laid down | L | In serv. |
|---|---|---|---|
| 931 TARIQ (ex-*Malek Farouk,* ex-*Whimbrel*) | 31-10-41 | 25-8-42 | 13-1-43 |

**Tariq (931)** L. & L. Van Ginderen, 2-87

**D:** 1,471 tons (1,925 fl) **S:** 19 kts **Dim:** 91.29 × 11.73 × 3.45
**A:** 6/102-mm Mk 19-DP (II × 3)—4/40-mm AA (II × 2)—4/d.c. projectors—2/d.c. racks
**Electron Equipt:** Radar: 2/. . . nav., 1/285 f.c.—Sonar: . . .
**M:** 2 sets Parsons GT; 2 props; 4,300 hp **Fuel:** 390 tons
**Boilers:** 2 Admiralty 3-drum **Range:** 5,700/15; 9,200/10 **Man:** 180 tot.

REMARKS: Bought 12-49. Thought to be non-operational but was in good steaming condition early 1987. Used for training and of little combat value. Last of the British "sloop" type to survive in near-original appearance.

NOTE: British Hunt I-class frigate *Port Said* (ex-*Mohammed Ali el Kebit,* ex-*Cottesmore*) is an inoperable hulk used for accommodations at pierside. British "Z"-class destroyer *El Fateh* (ex-*Zenith,* ex-*Wessex*), last used as cadet training ship in 1985, has ceased operating.

## GUIDED-MISSILE PATROL BOATS

NOTE: Still planned is the acquisition of a further six Western-designed guided-missile patrol boats. A repeat of the *Ramadan* class, Spain's Bazán "Cormoran" design, and a 61-m, 465-ton, 38-kt. PSSM-200 design from Tacoma Boatyard, Tacoma, Washington are leading contenders; the latter would have 8/Harpoon, a 76-mm OTO Melara compact, and a 30-mm gatling gun. Funds to order these ships are expected to become available in 1988.

◆ **6 Chinese Hoku class** Bldr: . . . (In serv. 27-10-84)

401 402 403 404 405 406

**D:** 68 tons, 73.88 normal (79.19 fl) **S:** 37 kts
**Dim:** 27.0 × 6.50 × 1.80 (1.295 hull)
**A:** 2/HY-2 SSM (I × 2)—2/25-mm AA (II × 1)
**Electron Equipt:** Radar: 1/Square Tie
**M:** 4 M50F-4 diesels; 4 props; 4,800 hp **Electric:** 65 kw
**Endurance:** 5 days **Range:** 500/24 **Man:** 16 tot.

REMARKS: Delivered 9-84 and commissioned together the following month; did not have missiles aboard during public display. Steel construction.

◆ **6 Ramadan class** Bldr: Vosper Thornycroft, Portchester, U.K.

| | Laid down | L | In serv. |
|---|---|---|---|
| 670 RAMADAN | 22-9-78 | 6-9-79 | 20-7-81 |
| 672 KHYBER | 23-2-79 | 31-1-80 | 15-9-81 |
| 674 EL KADESSEYA | 23-4-79 | 19-2-80 | 6-4-82 |
| 676 EL YARMOUK | 15-5-79 | 12-6-80 | 18-5-82 |
| 678 BADR | 29-9-79 | 17-6-81 | 17-6-82 |
| 680 HETTEIN | 29-2-80 | 25-11-80 | 28-10-82 |

**El Kadesseya (674)** L. & L. Van Ginderen, 6-87

**El Yarmouk (676)** L. & L. Van Ginderen, 6-82

## GUIDED-MISSILE PATROL BOATS *(continued)*

**D:** 262 tons (312 fl) **S:** 35 kts **Dim:** 52.0 (48.0 pp) × 7.6 × 2.0 (hull)
**A:** 4/Otomat SSM (II × 2)—1/76-mm OTO Melara Compact DP—2/40-mm Breda AA (II × 1)
**Electron Equipt:** Radar: Marconi: 1/S820, 1/S810, 2/ST802
EW: Decca-Racal Cutlass and MEL Matilda passive, Decca-Racal Cygnus jammer, Mel Protean chaff RL (VI × 2)
**M:** 4 MTU 20V538 TB91 diesels; 4 props; 16,000 hp **Fuel:** 43 tons
**Electric:** 420 kw **Range:** 2,000/15 **Man:** 31 tot.

Remarks: Ordered 4-9-77. Have Marconi Sapphire fire-control system with two ST 802 radar/t.v. directors, two Lawrence Scott optical directors. Ferranti CAAIS automated data system. First pair arrived Egypt 13-11-81, second 23-7-82, third in 12-82.

◆ **6 6 October class** Bldr: Egypt/Vosper Thornycroft (In serv. 1980–81)

783 785 787 789 790 791

**6 October class (791)**—Otomat racks empty L. & L. Van Ginderen, 7-82

**D:** 71 tons (82 fl) **S:** 40 kts **Dim:** 25.3 × 6.0 × 1.8
**A:** 2/Otomat SSM—4/30-mm AA Type A32 (II × 2)
**Electron Equipt:** Radar: Marconi: 1/S810, 1/ST802
EW: MEL Matilda passive, MEL Protean chaff RL (VI × 2)
**M:** 4 CRM 18V-12D/55 YE diesels; 4 props; 5,400 hp **Range:** 400/30
**Man:** 20 tot.

Remarks: Wooden hulls, built at Alexandria DY, Egypt, 1969–75. Completed by Vosper Thornycroft at Portchester, Portsmouth, 1979–81, with Italian-French missiles and British guns; diesels are Italian. Basic design is that of the Soviet Komar class. Use Marconi Sapphire radar/t.v. fire-control system. 791 was lost overboard during delivery 16-12-80, salvaged, returned to U.K. 30-6-81, and completed repairs 13-8-82.

◆ **7 ex-Soviet Osa-I class**

631 633 635 637 639 641 643

**Egyptian Osa-I** 1975

**D:** 175 tons (209 fl) **S:** 35 kts **Dim:** 38.6 × 7.6 × 1.8
**A:** 4/SS-N-2A Styx SSM (I × 4)—1/SA-7 Grail position—4/30-mm AA (II × 2)
**Electron Equipt:** Radar: 1/Square Tie, 1/Drum Tilt, 1/Decca 916
IFF: 2/Square Head, 1/High Pole A
**M:** 3 M503A diesels; 3 props; 12,000 hp **Range:** 500/34; 750/25

Remarks: Transferred 1966. Reported being refitted with 3 MTU diesels. All carry shoulder-launched SA-7 Grail (SA-N-5) SAMs, launched from a tub amidships. Passive warning equipment now fitted.

## PATROL BOATS

◆ **8 Chinese Hainan class**

| | In serv. | | In serv. |
|---|---|---|---|
| 430 Al Nour | 23-10-83 | 442 Al Salam | 21-5-84 |
| 433 Al Hadi | 23-10-83 | 445 N . . . | 6-84 |
| 436 Al Hakim | 21-5-84 | 448 N . . . | 6-84 |
| 439 Al Wakil | 21-5-84 | 451 N . . . | 6-84 |

**D:** 375 tons normal (400 fl) **S:** 30.5 kts **Dim:** 58.77 × 7.20 × 2.20 (hull)
**A:** 4/57-mm AA (II × 2)—4/25-mm AA (II × 2)—4/RBU-1200 ASW RL (V × 4)—2/BMB-2 d.c. mortars—2/d.c. racks—mines
**Electron Equipt:** Radar: 1/Pot Head
Sonar: Tamir-11
**M:** 4 diesels; 4 props; 8,800 hp **Man:** 70 tot. **Range:** 2,000/14

Remarks: First pair arrived 10-83, next three in 2-84, and final trio in 6-84. All were delivered aboard the Chinese float-on cargo ship *Shamekou*. Four are to receive 6 324-mm ASW TT (III × 2) and Stingray torpedoes.

◆ **4 Chinese Shanghai-II class**

**Egyptian Navy Shanghai-II** 1984

**D:** 122.5 tons normal (134.8 fl) **S:** 28.5 kts **Dim:** 38.78 × 5.41 × 1.55
**A:** 4/37-mm AA (II × 2)—4/25-mm AA (II × 2)
**Electron Equipt:** Radar: 1/Pot Head
**M:** 2 M50F-4, 1,200-hp diesels; 2/12D6, 910-hp diesels; 4 props; 4,220 hp
**Electric:** 39 kw **Range:** 750/16.5 **Man:** 36 tot. **Endurance:** 7 days

Remarks: Transferred 1984 with transfer numbers E 601–604. Do not have depth charges, as on Chinese Navy examples.

## TORPEDO BOATS

◆ **6 Soviet Shershen class**

310 321 332 343 354 365

**Shershen 343**—with 122-mm rocket launchers, Grail tub abaft Drum Tilt

**D:** 150 tons (180 fl) **S:** 45 kts **Dim:** 34.0 × 6.8 × 1.5
**A:** 4/30-mm AA (II × 2)—4/533-mm TT (I × 4) or 2/122-mm RL (XX × 2)
**Electron Equipt:** 1/Square Tie, 1/Drum Tilt
**M:** 3 M503A diesels; 3 props; 12,000 hp

Remarks: Transferred 1967–68. Three are armed with two 20-tubed 122-mm artillery rocket launchers instead of torpedoes. Most carry shoulder-launched SA-7 Grail (SA-N-5) missiles as well.

## MINE WARFARE SHIPS

Note: The acquisition of two Dutch-built "Tripartite" minehunters as *Mecca* (ex-*Middleberg*) and *Medina* (ex-*Hellevoetsluis*) was canceled 1986 for lack of funds.

◆ **4 ex-Soviet Yurka-class minesweepers**

530 Assuan 533 Guizan 536 Qena 539 Suhag

**D:** 400 tons (460 fl) **S:** 16 kts **Dim:** 52.0 × 9.3 × 2.0
**A:** 4/30-mm AA (II × 2)—10 mines **Electron Equipt:** Radar: 1/Don-2
**M:** 2 diesels; 2 props; 4,000 hp **Range:** 2,000/14; 3,200/10

**MINE WARFARE SHIPS** *(continued)*

REMARKS: Delivered new 1969. Do not have Drum Tilt radar fire-control system. Low-magnetic alloy steel construction.

◆ **2 Soviet T-301-class minesweepers** (In serv. circa 1950)

EL FAYOUD EL MANUFIEH

**D:** 145.8 tons (160 fl) **S:** 12.5 kts **Dim:** 38.0 × 5.1 × 1.6
**A:** 2/45-mm—2/12.7-mm mg **M:** 3 6-cyl. diesels; 3 props; 1,440 hp
**Fuel:** 20 tons **Range:** 2,500/8

REMARKS: Transferred 1962–63. No radars. Used in harbor service only.

## AMPHIBIOUS WARFARE SHIPS

◆ **3 Soviet Polnocny A-class LSM** Bldr: Polnocny SY, Gdansk, Poland

301 303 305

**D:** 770 tons (fl) **S:** 19 kts **Dim:** 73.0 × 8.6 × 2.0
**A:** 2/30-mm AA (II × 1)—2/140-mm artillery RL (XVIII × 2)
**Electron Equipt:** Radar: 1/Don-2, 1/Drum Tilt
**M:** 2 Type 40D diesels; 2 props; 4,000 hp
**Range:** 900/18; 1,500/14 **Man:** 40 tot.

REMARKS: Transferred 1974. Cargo: 3 tanks or 180 tons.

◆ **9 ex-Soviet Vydra-class LCUs**

330 332 334, etc.

**Egyptian Vydra with rocket launchers** (old number) 1976

**D:** 425 tons (600 fl) **S:** 11 kts **Dim:** 54.9 × 7.6 × 2.0
**A:** 4/40-mm AA (II × 2)—8/15-tubed artillery RL—see remarks
**Electron Equipt:** Radar: 1/Spin Trough removed
**M:** 2 diesels; 2 props; 800 hp
**Range:** 2,700/10 **Man:** 20, plus 200 troops

REMARKS: Transferred 1967–69. Armament now removed. Some had 37-mm AA vice 40-mm. Cargo: 200 tons.

◆ **4 ex-Soviet SMB-I-class LCUs**

660 664 666 679

**D:** 180 tons (335 fl) **S:** 10 kts **Dim:** 48.2 × 6.5 × 2.0
**Electron Equipt:** Radar: none **M:** 2 diesels; 2 props; 600 hp
**Range:** 400/8 **Man:** 16 tot.

REMARKS: Transferred 1965. Cargo: 180 tons.

◆ **8 U.S. "Seafox"-class swimmer delivery craft** Bldr: Uniflite, Bellingham, Wash.

**D:** 11.3 tons (fl) **S:** 30+kts **Dim:** 11.0 × 3.0 × 0.84
**A:** small arms **Electron Equipt:** Radar: 1/LN-66
**M:** 2 G.M. 6V92 TA diesels; 2 props; 900 hp **Man:** 3 tot.

REMARKS: Ordered 1982. Glass-reinforced plastic construction.

◆ **10 to 12 small landing craft of various origins**

## AUXILIARY SHIPS

◆ **8 Soviet Toplivo-2-class coastal tankers** Bldr: Alexandria SY, Egypt

**D:** 466 tons (1,180 fl) **S:** 10 kts
**Dim:** 54.26 (49.40 pp) × 9.40 × 3.10 (3.40 max.)
**Electron Equipt:** Radar: 1/Spin Trough
**M:** 1 Russkiy Dizel 6 DR 30/50-5-2 diesel; 1 prop; 600 hp **Electric:** 250 kw
**Fuel:** 19 tons **Range:** 1,500/10 **Man:** . . . tot.

REMARKS: 308 grt/508 dwt. Part of a series of 26 ordered in Egypt for the U.S.S.R. prior to that country's expulsion. Cargo: 606 m$^3$ (500 tons diesel oil).

◆ **4 Soviet Okhtenskiy-class tugs**

AL ISKANDARANI EL MAKS
EL AGAMI EL DIKHILA

**D:** 700 tons (950 fl) **S:** 13.3 kts **Dim:** 47.3 × 10.3 × 5.5
**Electron Equipt:** Radar: 1/Don-2 or Spin Trough
**M:** 2 diesels, electric drive; 1 prop; 1,500 hp **Range:** 7,800/7 **Man:** 40 tot.

REMARKS: Two transferred 1966; two assembled in Egypt.

◆ **1 British "River"-class former frigate**

| | Bldr | Laid down | L | In serv. |
|---|---|---|---|---|
| 511 RACHID (ex-*Spey*) | Smith's Dock Co., Ltd. | 7-41 | 18-12-41 | 19-5-42 |

**Rachid (511)** 1978

**D:** 1,460 tons (2,175 fl) **S:** 19 kts **Dim:** 91.90 (86.26 pp) × 11.13 × 4.37
**A:** 1/102-mm—4/40-mm AA (II × 2)—1/SA-N-5 Grail SAM system
**M:** triple-expansion; 2 props; 5,500 hp **Boilers:** 2 Admiralty watertube
**Fuel:** 640 tons **Range:** 7,700/12; 5,000/16 **Man:** 110 tot.

REMARKS: Bought in 12-49. Used as a submarine tender.

◆ **2 Soviet Nyryat-I-class diving tenders**

**D:** 120 tons (fl) **S:** 12 kts **Dim:** 29.0 × 5.0 × 1.7
**Electron Equipt:** Radar: 1/Spin Trough **M:** 1 diesel; 1 prop; 450 hp
**Range:** 1,600/10 **Man:** 15 tot.

REMARKS: Transferred 1964.

◆ **2 Soviet Poluchat-I-class torpedo retrievers**

**D:** 80 tons (90 fl) **S:** 18 kts **Dim:** 29.6 × 5.8 × 1.5
**Electron Equipt:** Radar: 1/Spin Trough
**M:** 2 M50 diesels; 2 props; 2,400 hp **Range:** 450/17; 900/10 **Man:** 20 tot.

◆ **2 Soviet PO-2-class general-purpose launches**

**D:** 50 tons (fl) **S:** 9 kts **Dim:** 21.0 × . . . × . . .
**M:** 1 diesel; 1 prop; 150 hp

◆ **1 Soviet Sekstan-class degaussing tender**

**D:** 408 tons (fl) **S:** 10.5 kts **Dim:** 41.0 × 9.3 × 4.2
**M:** 1 diesel; 1 prop; 400 hp **Range:** 1,200/10

REMARKS: Wooden construction.

## TRAINING SHIPS

◆ **1 former yacht** Bldr: Samuda, Scotland (In serv. 1865)

EL HORRIA (ex-*Mahroussa*)

**El Horria** G. Garier, 1976

**D:** 4,561 tons (fl) **S:** 16 kts **Dim:** 145.6 (121.9 pp) × 13.0 × 5.3
**A:** Several mg **M:** 3 sets GT; 3 props; 5,500 hp

REMARKS: World's oldest active naval ship; carried President Sadat in naval review, 12-80. Used as a training ship.

◆ **1 navigational training ship for the Naval Academy**

EL KOUSSER **D:** 1,000 tons

**EGYPT** *(continued)*
**TRAINING SHIPS** *(continued)*

◆ **1 former yacht, attached to the Naval Academy**

INTISAR **D:** 500 tons

COAST GUARD
The Coast Guard is a branch of the naval service in Egypt

### PATROL BOATS

◆ **9 U.S. Commercial Cruiser design** Bldr: (1st 3) Swiftships, Inc., Morgan City, La.; others: . . . SY, Egypt.

335–343 (In serv.: first 3: 15-1-85; 338: 9-9-85; 339: 24-10-85; 340: 24-11-85; others: 1986)

**Egyptian Coast Guard patrol boats** Swiftships, 1985

**D:** 102 tons (fl) **S:** 27 kts **Dim:** 28.30 × 5.66 × 1.60
**A:** 1/20-mm AA (aft)—1/12.7-mm mg (fwd) **Electron Equipt:** Radar: . . .
**M:** 2 MTU 12V331 TC92 diesels; 2 props; 2,660 hp
**Range:** 1,000/12 **Fuel:** 11.7 tons **Man:** 2 officers, 12 men

REMARKS: Ordered 11-83. First 3 built in U.S., remainder assembled in Egypt from U.S.-supplied components. Steel construction.

◆ **0 (+6) Timsah-II class** Bldr: Timsah SY, Ismailia (In serv. . . .)

**D:** 99 tons **S:** 24 kts **Dim:** 29.0 × 5.2 × 1.48
**A:** 2/20-mm Oerlikon GAM-B01 AA (I × 2)
**Electron Equipt:** Radar: . . .
**M:** 2 MTU 12V331 TC92 diesels; 2 props; 2,660 hp
**Range:** 600/. . . **Fuel:** 10 tons **Man:** 13 tot.

REMARKS: Revised version of Timsah class, with different engines, waterline exhausts vice stack. Ordered 1-85.

◆ **6 Timsah class** Bldr: Timsah SY, Alexandria (In serv. 1981–84)

**Timsah-class unit at launch** 1983

**D:** 100 tons (fl) **S:** 25 kts **Dim:** 29.0 × 5.2 × 1.48
**A:** 2/30-mm Oerlikon A32 AA (II × 1)—1/20-mm AA
**M:** 2 MTU 8V331 diesels; 2 props; 2,960 hp
**Fuel:** 10 tons **Range:** 600/. . . **Man:** 13 tot.

REMARKS: Based on *Nisr*-class design. First unit laid down 1-1-80, launched 11-81, delivered 12-81.

◆ **3 Nisr class** Bldr: de Castro BY, Port Said (In serv. 1963)

NIMR NISR THAR

**D:** 110 tons (fl) **S:** . . . **Dim:** 31.0 × 5.2 × 1.5 **A:** 1/20-mm AA
**M:** 2 Maybach diesels; 2 props; . . . hp

**Nisr class** F. Sadek, 1-86

### PATROL CRAFT

◆ **4 small patrol craft** Bldr: Canal Naval Const., Port Fuad, Egypt

**D:** 10 tons **S:** . . . **Dim:** 10.49 × . . . × . . . **M:** 1 Thornycroft diesel

REMARKS: Ordered 12-12-83. No further data available. Last two delivered 1986.

◆ **6 MV70 class** Bldr: Crestitalia, Ameglia (La Spezia), Italy

**D:** 33 tons (41.5 fl) **S:** 34 kts **Dim:** 21.0 × 5.2 × 0.9
**A:** 2/30-mm Oerlikon A32 (II × 1)—1/20-mm AA—2/12.7-mm mg
**M:** 2 MTU 12V331 TC92 diesels; 2 props; 2,800 hp **Range:** 500/3

REMARKS: Fiberglass hulls.

◆ **30 DC-35 class** Bldr: Dawncraft, Wroxham, U.K. (In serv. 1977)

**D:** 4 tons (fl) **S:** 25 kts **Dim:** 10.7 × 3.5 × 0.8
**M:** 2 Perkins T6-354 diesels; 2 props; 390 hp **Man:** 4 tot.

REMARKS: Fiberglass hulled. For harbor police duties.

◆ **20 28-ft. "Enforcer" class** Bldr: Bertram Yacht, Miami, Fla. (In serv. 1973)

**D:** 8 tons (fl) **S:** 24 kts **Dim:** 8.5 × . . . × . . .
**A:** 2/12.7-mm mg (I × 2) **M:** 2 diesels; 2 props; 300 hp

REMARKS: Formerly naval, had 4/122-mm RL on sides of hull. Fiberglass construction.

NOTE: The Customs Service received twelve 19.8-m Sea Spectre-class patrol craft in 1980–81.

# EL SALVADOR

**Republic of El Salvador**

PERSONNEL (1986): 350 officers and men plus 500-man Marine battalion

MERCHANT MARINE (1986): 14 ships—3,819 grt

### PATROL CRAFT

◆ **1 U.S. 77-ft Commercial Cruiser** Bldr: Swiftships, Inc., Morgan City, La.

GC 11 (In serv. 6-5-85)

**GC 11** Swiftships, 6-85

**EL SALVADOR** *(continued)*
**PATROL CRAFT** *(continued)*

**D:** 48 tons (fl) **S:** 26 kts **Dim:** 23.47 × 6.10 × 1.52
**A:** 2/12.7-mm mg (I × 2) **Electron Equipt:** Radar: . . .
**Range:** . . . **M:** 3 G.M. 12V71 TI diesels; 3 props; 1,200 hp

REMARKS: Aluminum construction.

◆ **1 U.S. 65-ft Commercial Cruiser class** Bldr: Swiftships Inc., Morgan City, La.

GC 10 (In serv. 14-6-84)

**D:** 36 tons (fl) **S:** 23 kts **Dim:** 19.96 × 5.59 × 1.52
**A:** 2/12.7-mm mg (I × 2) **Electron Equipt:** Radar: 1/. . . nav.
**M:** 2 G.M. 12V71 TI diesels; 2 props; 1,350 hp
**Electric:** 20 kw **Range:** 500/18 **Man:** 6 tot.

REMARKS: Aluminum construction.

◆ **3 aluminum-hulled** Bldr: Camcraft, Crown Pt., Louisiana

GC 6 (In serv. 24-10-75) GC 7 (In serv. 3-12-75) GC 8 (In serv. 11-75)

**D:** 100 tons (fl) **S:** 25 kts **Dim:** 30.5 × 6.4 × 1.5 **A:** 3/12.7-mm mg (I × 3)
**M:** 3 G.M. 12V71 TI diesels; 3 props; 1,200 hp **Range:** 780/24 **Man:** 10 tot.

REMARKS: See addenda for photo.

◆ **1 U.S. 65-ft Commercial Cruiser class** Bldr: Sewart Seacraft, Berwick, La.

GC 5 (In serv. 9-67)

**D:** 33 tons (36 fl) **S:** 25 kts **Dim:** 19.8 × 5.5 × 1.3 **A:** 3/12.7-mm mg (I × 3)
**M:** 2 G.M. 12V71 diesels; 2 props; 1,860 hp **Range:** 1,360/17

REMARKS: Overhauled, redelivered 1-2-85 by Swiftships, Inc.

◆ **6 40-ft river patrol craft** Bldr: Lantana Boatyard, Lantana, Fla. (In serv. 2-87)

**40-ft patrol craft** Lantana, 1987

**D:** 9 tons (fl) **S:** 26 kts (22 sust.) **Dim:** 12.19 × 3.05 × 0.53
**A:** 2/12.7-mm mg (I × 2)—2/7.62-mm mg (I × 2)
**Electron Equipt:** Radar: 1/Furuno 3600 nav.
**M:** 2 Caterpillar 3208 TA diesels; 2 props; 630 hp
**Endurance:** 5 days **Man:** 5 tot.

REMARKS: Aluminum construction with Kevlar plastic armor. Lengthened version of 8-unit class built for Honduras, 1986.

◆ **6 Outrage-class patrol craft** Bldr: Boston Whaler, U.S.A.

**D:** 2.2 tons (fl) **S:** 35 kts **Dim:** 7.62 × 2.40 × 0.40
**A:** 1/12.7-mm mg—1/7.62-mm mg **M:** 2 outboard motors; 2 props; 300 hp
**Range:** 200/35 **Man:** 4 tot.

REMARKS: GRP foam sandwich construction.

◆ **25 small launches with outboard motors**

NOTE: Ten patrol craft were ordered mid-1987 from Mercougar, North Miami, Florida; see addenda for details.

# EQUATORIAL GUINEA

**Republic of Equatorial Guinea**

PERSONNEL (1986): Approx. 60 tot.

MERCHANT MARINE (1986): 2 ships—6,412 grt

◆ **1 68-ft patrol boat** Bldr: Lantana Boatyard, Lantana, Fla.

N . . . (In serv. 11-87)

**D:** . . . **S:** 24 kts **Dim:** 20.73 × . . . × . . .
**A:** 2/12.7-mm mg (I × 2)—2/7.62-mm mg (I × 2)
**Electron Equipt:** Radar: 1/Furuno 3600 nav.
**M:** 2 diesels; 2 props; . . . hp **Range:** 800/15

REMARKS: Aluminum construction. U.S. Grant Aid.

◆ **1 ex-Nigerian P/20-class patrol craft** Bldr: Van Mill Marine Service, Hardinxveld-Giessendam, the Netherlands

RIOWELE (ex-P 220) (In serv. 17-1-86)

**D:** 45 tons (fl) **S:** 32.5 kts **Dim:** 20.26 (18.00 wl) × 5.30 × 1.75
**A:** 1/20-mm Rheinmetall AA—2/7.62-mm mg (I × 2)
**Electron Equipt:** Radar: 1/Decca . . .
**M:** 3 G.M. 12V71 TI diesels; 3 props; 2,100 hp
**Range:** 950/25; 1,200/11 **Man:** 12 tot.

REMARKS: Transferred as a gift 27-6-86. GRP construction.

NOTE: All earlier craft discarded by 1986.

# ETHIOPIA

PERSONNEL: 1,500 men including 250 officers

MERCHANT MARINE (1986): 23 ships—66,926 grt (tankers: 1 ship—1,317 grt)

NAVAL AVIATION: Still in service may be 4 DHC Otter and 3 DHC Twin Otter light transports, and 6 UH-1 Huey helicopters. Several Soviet Mi-14 Haze A ASW helicopters reported in service, 1987.

## FRIGATES

◆ **2 Soviet Petya-II class**

F 1616 (In serv. 20-7-83) F 1617 (In serv. 20-3-84)

**D:** 950 tons light, 1,020 tons std (1,160 fl) **S:** 29 kts (16 on diesel)
**Dim:** 81.8 (78.00 pp) × 9.20 × 2.97
**A:** 4/76.2-mm DP (II × 2)—2/RBU-6000 ASW RL (XII × 2)—10/400-mm ASW TT (V × 2)—2/d.c. racks—mines
**Electron Equipt:** Radar: 1/Don-2, 1/Strut Curve, 1/Hawk Screech
Sonar: 1/HF hull-mounted
EW: 2/Watch Dog intercept—IFF: High Pole B
**M:** CODAG: 2/15,000-hp gas turbines, 1 Type 61-D3, 6,000-hp diesel; 3 props (CP on centerline); 36,000 hp—2 active rudders; 100 hp
**Range:** 450/29; 1,800/16 (diesel); 4,800/10 **Man:** 8 off., 84 crew

REMARKS: In service dates above are those of arrival at Massawa. Believed to be standard Petya-IIs, i.e., not "export model" with 3/533-mm TT and 4/RBU-2500. Hawk Screech gunfire control radar has two associated target designators on the open bridge.

## GUIDED-MISSILE PATROL BOATS

◆ **4 Soviet Osa-II class**

FMB 160 FMB 161 FMB 162 FMB 163

**D:** 210 tons (240 fl) **S:** 35 kts **Dim:** 38.6 × 7.6 × 2.0
**A:** 4/SS-N-2B Styx SSM—4/30-mm AA (II × 2)
**Electron Equipt:** Radar: 1/Square Tie, 1/Drum Tilt
IFF: 2/Square Head, 1/High Pole B
**M:** 3 M504 diesels; 3 props; 15,000 hp **Range:** 500/34; 750/25 **Man:** 30 tot.

REMARKS: First unit transferred 1978, second 10-80, third 13-1-81, the fourth in 1982.

## TORPEDO BOATS

◆ **1 Soviet Turya-class semi-hydrofoil** Bldr: . . .

**D:** 215 tons (250 fl) **S:** 40 kts
**Dim:** 39.0 × 7.6 (12.5 over foils) × 2.0 (4.0 over foils)

**ETHIOPIA** *(continued)*
**TORPEDO BOATS** *(continued)*

**A:** 2/57-mm DP aft (II × 1)—2/25-mm AA (II × 1)—4/533-mm TT (I × 4)
**Electron Equipt:** Radar: 1/Pot Drum, 1/Muff Cob
IFF: 1/Square Head, 1/High Pole B
**M:** 3 M504 diesels; 3 props; 15,000 hp
**Range:** 400/38; 650/25 **Man:** 24 tot.

Remarks: Transferred 2-85. Probably does not have the normal helicopter-type dipping sonar and may not have the torpedo tubes.

◆ **2 Soviet Mol class**

FTB 110 FTB 111

**D:** 175 tons (220 fl) **S:** 36 kts **Dim:** 38.6 × 7.6 × 1.9
**A:** 4/533-mm TT (I × 4)—4/30-mm AA (II × 2)
**Electron Equipt:** Radar: 1/Pot Head, 1/Drum Tilt
IFF: 1/Square Head, 1/High Pole B
**M:** 3 M503A diesels; 3 props; 12,000 hp **Man:** 30 tot.

Remarks: Transferred 1978.

### PATROL BOATS

◆ **2 Soviet Zhuk class** (In serv. 18-10-82)

PC 16 PC 17

**D:** 48 tons (60 fl) **S:** 34 kts **Dim:** 24.0 × 5.0 × 1.8 (props)
**A:** 4/14.5-mm (II × 2) **Electron Equipt:** Radar: 1/Spin Trough
**M:** 2 M50F-4 diesels; 2 props; 2,400 hp

◆ **3 aluminum-hulled boats** Bldr: Swiftships, Morgan City, La.

P 201 P 203 P 204

**P 203**—with 23-mm AA 1978

**D:** 118 tons (fl) **S:** 32 kts **Dim:** 31.73 × 7.1 × 2.16
**A:** 4/30-mm Emerlec AA (II × 2) **Electron Equipt:** Radar: Decca RM 916
**M:** 2 MTU MB 16V538 TB90 diesels; 2 props; 7,000 hp
**Range:** 1,200/18 **Man:** 21 tot.

Remarks: Ordered 1976, delivered 4-77; two additional units were canceled by the U.S. arms embargo. P 203 and P 204 have four 23-mm AA (II × 2) and two 12.7-mm machine guns (II × 1). P 202 defected to Somalia, 1984.

◆ **1 ex-U.S. Coast Guard Cape design** Bldr: Peterson Bldrs, Sturgeon Bay, Wisc. (In serv. 5-62)

PC 15 (ex-U.S. PGM 58)

**PC 14** (since discarded)

**D:** 80 tons (105 fl) **S:** 18 kts **Dim:** 28.95 × 6.1 × 1.55
**A:** 1/40-mm AA—1/20-mm AA
**M:** 4 Cummins VT-12M700 diesels; 2 props; 2,200 hp **Electric:** 40 kw
**Fuel:** 12 tons **Range:** 460/20; 1,500/10 **Man:** 15 tot.

Remarks: PC 11 lost in action, 4-77. PC 12–14 discarded 1984.

◆ **1 ex-Dutch Wildervank-class former minesweeper**

| | Bldr | Laid down | L | In serv. |
|---|---|---|---|---|
| MS 41 (ex-M 829 *Elst*) | Pot Bros., Bolnes | 10-5-55 | 21-3-56 | 6-12-56 |

**D:** 373 tons (417 fl) **S:** 14 kts **Dim:** 46.62 × 8.75 × 2.28
**A:** 2/40-mm AA (I × 2) **Electron Equipt:** Radar: 1/ZW-04
**M:** 2 Werkspoor diesels; 2 props; 2,500 hp **Range:** 2,500/10 **Man:** 40 tot.

Remarks: Bought in 1970. All minesweeping gear removed. Wooden construction. Present utility doubtful.

### PATROL CRAFT

◆ **4 aluminum-hulled craft** Bldr: Sewart Seacraft, Berwick, La. (In serv. 1965–67)

GB 21 GB 22 GB 23 GB 24 (ex-*John, Caroline, Patrick, Jacqueline*)

**D:** 15 tons (fl) **S:** 20 kts **Dim:** 13.1 × 3.9 × 0.9 **A:** 2/12.7-mm mg
**M:** 2 G.M. 6-71 diesels; 2 props; 500 hp **Man:** 7 tot.

### AMPHIBIOUS SHIPS

◆ **2 Soviet Polnocny-B class** Bldr: Polnocny SY, Gdansk, Poland

LTC 1037 LTC 1038

**D:** 800 tons (fl) **S:** 19 kts **Dim:** 74.0 × 8.6 × 2.0
**A:** 4.30-mm AA—2/140-mm RL (XVIII × 2)
**Electron Equipt:** Radar: 1/Spin Trough, 1/Drum Tilt
IFF: 1/Square Head, 1/High Pole
**M:** 2 diesels; 2 props; 4,000 hp **Range:** 900/18; 1,500/14 **Man:** 40 tot.

Remarks: Transferred 11-81 and 1-83. Cargo: 180 tons.

◆ **2 French EDIC-class LCU** Bldr: SFCN, Villeneuve la Garonne (L: 5-77)

LTC 1035 LTC 1036

**D:** 250 tons (670 fl) **S:** 8 kts **Dim:** 59.0 × 11.95 × 1.3
**A:** 2/20-mm AA (I × 2) **M:** 2 MGO diesels; 2 props; 1,000 hp
**Range:** 1,800/8 **Man:** 1 officer, 15 men

Remarks: Cargo: 11 trucks or 5 light armored vehicles.

◆ **6 Soviet T-4-class landing craft**

**D:** 70 tons (fl) **S:** 10 kts **Dim:** 19.0 × 4.3 × 1.0
**M:** 2 diesels; 2 props; 600 hp **Man:** 5 tot.

Remarks: Four transferred 1977–78, two in 1984.

### AUXILIARIES

◆ **1 cargo ship** (In serv. 1961)

A . . . Ras Dedgen (ex-. . .)

Remarks: Former merchant ship acquired 1985. No data available except 6,615 grt. May also serve as training ship.

Note: Also in service are a tug, AO 2, transferred from the U.S.S.R., 1979, and a small service launch, TR 74. Training ship *Ethiopia* (A 01, ex-U.S. *Orca*, AVP 49) has been deleted from this edition due to age and lack of spares support.

# FAERO ISLANDS

**(Semi-Autonomous Danish Dependency)**

Merchant Marine (1986): 195 ships—115,394 grt (tankers: 1 ship—499 grt)

COAST GUARD AND FISHERY PROTECTION SERVICE

◆ **1 fisheries protection ship and rescue tug** Bldr: Svolvaer, Norway

N . . . (In serv. 1976)

**D:** . . . **S:** 14.5 kts **Dim:** 44.50 × 10.10 × 4.02
**A:** 1/57-mm single-fire **Electron Equipt:** Radar: . . .
**M:** 2 MWM 6-cyl. diesels; 1 prop; 2,400 hp

Remarks: Acquired 1987. 437 grt. Gun manufactured 1896 at Royal Dockyard, Copenhagen.

# FALKLAND ISLANDS

**(British Colony)**

Merchant Marine (1986): 55 ships—6,307 grt

Aviation: In addition to R.A.F. assets stationed in the Falklands, the local government has acquired a Dornier Do. 228–200 maritime surveillance aircraft with Sperry Primus radar.

## FALKLAND ISLANDS *(continued)*

### FISHERIES PATROL SHIPS

◆ **1 former seismic survey vessel** Bldr: Hall, Russell, Aberdeen

FALKLANDS DESIRE (ex-*Seisella,* ex-*Southella*) (In serv. 2-69)

**D:** . . . **S:** 15 kts **Dim:** 74.50 (64.32 pp) × 12.68 × 4.57
**A:** . . . **Electron Equipt:** Radar: . . .
**M:** 1 Mirrlees National diesel; 1 prop; 2,880 hp **Fuel:** 400 tons
**Range:** 15,000/15 **Electric:** 750 kw (3 × 250 kw) **Man:** 32 tot.

REMARKS: 1,496 grt. Chartered from J. Marr 1-2-87 for fisheries patrol. Former stern-haul trawler, converted 1986 as a seismic survey and oilfield standby safety vessel. Has helicopter deck and accommodations for 15 spare personnel.

◆ **1 former stern-haul trawler** Bldr: Stocznia Gdynia, Poland

FALKLANDS RIGHT (ex-*G.A. Reay,* ex-*Arctic Privateer*) (In serv. . . .)

**D:** . . . **S:** 14.5 kts **Dim:** 69.15 (60.30 pp) × 11.99 × 4.99
**A:** . . . **Electron Equipt:** Radar: . . .
**M:** 1 diesel; 1 prop; 2,500 hp **Electric:** 750 kw (1 × 400 kw, 1 × 350 kw)
**Range:** . . . **Fuel:** 329 tons **Man:** 23 tot. (+6 spare)

REMARKS: 1,878 grt. Chartered 1-2-87; had been on charter since 26-9-84 for South Atlantic service.

◆ **1 former Argentine oilfield-supply tug** Bldr: Hitzler SY, Lauenburg

FALKLAND SOUND (ex-*Yehuin,* ex-*Millerntor*) (In serv. . . .)

**D:** 1,200 tons (fl) **S:** 12.5 kts **Dim:** 53.52 (49.20 pp) × 11.26 × 3.35
**A:** . . . **Electron Equipt:** Radar: . . . **Electric:** 336 kw
**M:** 2 MWM diesels; 2 CP props; 1,900 hp **Fuel:** 254 tons

REMARKS: Captured 6-82; transferred to Falklands Government 12-86. 495 grt/756 dwt.

# FIJI

**Dominion of Fiji**

PERSONNEL (1986): 168 men total (26 officers)

MERCHANT MARINE (1986): 57 ships—29,954 grt (6 tankers—4,933 grt)

### PATROL BOATS

◆ **0 (+4) ASI-315 class** Bldr: Australian SB Industries (WA), South Coogie, W. Australia

| | | | |
|---|---|---|---|
| . . . N . . . | (In serv. 2-89) | . . . N . . . | (In serv. 6-90) |
| . . . N . . . | (In serv. 2-90) | . . . N . . . | (In serv. 10-90) |

**D:** 165 tons (fl) **S:** 21 kts **Dim:** 31.50 (28.60 wl) × 8.10 × 2.12 (1.80 hull)
**A:** 1/20-mm AA—2/12.7-mm mg (I × 2)
**Electron Equipt:** Radar: 1/Furuno 1011 (I/J-band)
EW: Furuno 120 MF-HF/DF, Furuno 525 VHF/DF
**M:** 2 Caterpillar 3516 diesels; 2 props; 2,820 hp (2,400 sust.)
**Range:** 2,500/12 **Fuel:** 27.9 tons **Electric:** 116 kw (2 × 50 kw, 1 × 16 kw)
**Endurance:** 8–10 days **Man:** 3 officers, 14 men

REMARKS: Ordered 3-10-85 for delivery as above as replacements for remaining *Redwing*-class units. Will be 7th and 10th–12th units of this "Pacific Patrol Boat" class designed for Australian foreign aid program. See photo in Papua New Guinea section. Will carry extensive navigational equipment (SATNAV, omega, doppler log, etc.) and a 5-m Stressl aluminum boarding boat with 40-hp outboard. Aluminum construction. Carry 21 days' dry stores and spares, 6,500 liters water. 20 kt sustained speed, 7-kt minimum.

◆ **2 ex-U.S. Redwing-class minesweepers** Bldr: Bellingham SY, Washington

**Kula (205)**—with Bell 222 helicopter 9-84

| | In serv. |
|---|---|
| 204 KIKAU (ex-*Woodpecker,* MSC 209) | 3-2-56 |
| 205 KULA (ex-*Vireo,* MSC 205) | 7-6-55 |

**D:** 370 tons (fl) **S:** 13 kts **Dim:** 43.9 × 8.5 × 2.6
**A:** 1/20-mm AA—2/12.7-mm mg
**M:** 2 G.M. 8-268A diesels; 2 props; 880 hp **Range:** 2,500/10 **Man:** 39 tot.

REMARKS: Both transferred 10-75. All minesweeping gear removed. *Kula* has a small flight deck built over the fantail for one Bell 222 helicopter. Sister *Kiro* (206, ex-*Warbler,* MSC 206) stricken late 1985.

### SCIENTIFIC SHIPS

◆ **1 hydrographic survey ship** Bldr: Gov't Yard, Suva

RUVE (ex-*Vuniwai*) (In serv. 1970)

**D:** 150 tons (fl) **S:** 10 kts **Dim:** 28.0 × 6.7 × 2.0
**Electron Equipt:** Radar: 1/. . . nav.
**M:** 2 Rolls-Royce diesels; 2 props; . . . hp **Range:** 1,900/10 **Man:** 17 tot.

REMARKS: 303 grt. Former fishing boat acquired for conversion and recommissioned 12-9-79.

◆ **1 hydrographic survey launch**

BELO

REMARKS: No date available, except: 8 tons (fl).

◆ **1 oceanographic research craft** Bldr: Gov't Yard, Suva

LATUI (ex-*Bulikula*) (In serv. 1978)

**D:** . . . **S:** 9 kts **Dim:** 20.4 × 5.2 × 2.1
**Electron Equipt:** Radar: 1/. . . nav.
**M:** 1 G.M. 8V71 diesel; 1 prop; 325 hp **Man:** 10 tot.

REMARKS: 85 grt. Built for Mineral Resources Dept. and transferred to Navy 1-82.

# FINLAND

**Republic of Finland**

The naval force, limited by the Treaty of Paris to 10,000 tons and 4,500 men, is a separate establishment under the orders of the chief of the armed forces. Submarines and torpedo boats are excluded from the fleet, and there is no naval aviation. A Fokker F-27 MK 400M Maritime Patrol aircraft was delivered to the Air Force 31-1-84.

PERSONNEL (1986): about 2,500, including 200 officers and 600 Frontier Guards

MERCHANT MARINE (1986): 276 ships—1,461,927 grt (tankers: 23 ships—557,640 grt)

### WEAPONS

The *Turunmaa*-class corvettes and the minelayer *Pohjanmaa* have a single-barrel automatic Bofors 120-mm gun with the following characteristics:

| | |
|---|---|
| weight without munitions: 28.5 tons | arc of elevation: −10° to +80° |
| length: 46 calibers | maximum rate of fire: 80 rounds/min |
| muzzle velocity: 800 m/sec | projectile weight: 35 kg |
| training speed: 40°/sec | maximum effective range, surface fire: 12,000 m |
| elevation speed: 30°/sec | |

The other major weapons employed are Soviet SS-N-2 Styx missiles, Bofors 40-mm L70 AA guns, Soviet twin 30-mm AA guns, and 23-mm AA in twin mountings. Swedish RBS-15 antiship missiles were ordered in 1983 to equip the *Helsinki* class and also for shore-based defense, using trucks.

### CORVETTES

◆ **2 Turunmaa class**

| | Bldr | Laid down | L | In serv. |
|---|---|---|---|---|
| 03 TURUNMAA | Wärtsilä, Helsinki | 3-67 | 11-7-67 | 29-8-68 |
| 04 KARJALA | Wärtsilä, Helsinki | 3-67 | 16-8-67 | 21-10-68 |

**Turunmaa (03)**—with new mast, RBU-1200 launcher deployed H. Ehlers, 6-86

**CORVETTES** *(continued)*

**Turunmaa (03) from astern**—note gas-turbine exhaust trunks flanking 40-mm AA, d.c. rack port through stern S. Terzibaschitsch, 6-86

**D:** 605 tons (770 fl) **S:** 35 kts **Dim:** 74.1 × 7.8 × 2.83
**A:** 1/120-mm Bofors DP—2/40-mm AA (I × 2)—4/23-mm AA (II × 2)—2/RBU-1200 ASW RL (V × 2)—2/d.c. racks
**Electron Equipt:** Radar: 1/H.S.A. M22, 1/navigational, 1/. . . surface search
Sonar: . . .
EW: . . .
**M:** CODOG propulsion: 1 Bristol-Siddeley Olympus TM3B, 22,000-hp gas turbine; 3 Mercedes-Benz 1,100-hp diesels; 3 CP props
**Electric:** 880 kVA **Fuel:** 120 tons **Range:** 2,500/14 **Man:** 70 tot.

REMARKS: Cruise on the diesels at 17 knots. Have Vosper fin stabilizers. Soviet ASW rocket launchers are behind doors in main-deck superstructure, abreast the mast; the d.c. racks are internal, at the stern. Six 103-mm flare RL rails on 120-mm mount. Both refitted 1984–86 by Wärtsilä, Turku; received Data Saab EOS-400 optronic f.c.s, new radars, EW gear and sonar.

## GUIDED-MISSILE PATROL BOATS

◆ **0 (+4) Helsinki-II class** Bldr: Hollming, Rauma

| | In serv. | | In serv. |
|---|---|---|---|
| . . . N . . . | 1990 | . . . N . . . | . . . |
| . . . N . . . | . . . | . . . N . . . | 1992 |

**D:** 200 tons (fl) **S:** 30 kts **Dim:** 40.0 × 7.0 × . . .
**A:** 4 RBS-15 FN SSM (II × 2)—1/57-mm Bofors DP—. . .
**Electron Equipt:** Radar: 1/nav.; 1/9GA208; 1/9L V225
EW: MEL Matilda passive, 2/decoy RL (XXXII × 2)
**M:** 2 MTU 16V538 TB92 diesels; 2 props; 8,000 hp

REMARKS: Construction approved 2-87, with the first to be laid down fall 1987. To be shorter and shallower in draft than *Helsinki* class and will normally carry only two missiles. A second group of four is planned. PEAB 96V200 Mk 3 f.c.s. with 9EW300 EW system. See drawing in addenda.

◆ **4 Helsinki (PB 80) class** Bldr: Wärtsilä, Helsinki

| | Laid down | L | In serv. (scheduled) |
|---|---|---|---|
| 60 HELSINKI | 3-9-80 | 5-11-80 | 1-9-81 |
| 61 TURKU | 1-84 | 1985 | 1-6-85 |
| 62 OULU | . . . | . . . | 1-10-85 |
| 63 KOTKA | . . . | . . . | 16-6-86 |

**Helsinki (60)**—on trials Finnish Navy, 1981

**Kotka (63)**—with four RBS-15FN missiles Wärtsilä, 6-86

**D:** 250 tons (280 fl) **S:** 30 kts **Dim:** 45.0 × 8.9 × 3.0 (props)
**A:** 4/RBS-15FN SSM (II × 2)—1/57-mm Bofors Mk 1 DP—4/23-mm AA (II × 2)
**Electron Equipt:** Radar: 1/navigational, 1/9GA208, 1/9L V225 f.c.
Sonar: Simrad SS 304
**M:** 3 MTU 16V538 TB92 diesels; 3 props; 12,000 hp
**Range:** . . . **Man:** 30 tot.

REMARKS: Prototype ordered 5-10-78. Three additional ordered 13-1-83. Aluminum hull. ata Saab EOS-400 optronic f.c.s. on 61–63, which have a revised pilothouse shape. Can carry up to 8 RBS-15FN missiles. Further construction deferred to new "Helsinki-II" class above.

◆ **4 Soviet Osa-II class**

11 TUIMA 12 TUISKU 14 TUULI 15 TYRSKY

**Tyrsky (15)** Finnish Navy, 1984

**D:** 210 tons (240 fl) **S:** 35 kts **Dim:** 38.6 × 7.6 × 2.0
**A:** 4/SS-N-2B Styx—4/30-mm AA (II × 2)
**Electron Equipt:** Radar: 1/Square Tie, 1/Drum Tilt, 1/navigational
**M:** 3 M504 diesels; 3 props; 15,000 hp **Range:** 500/34; 750/25
**Man:** 30 tot.

REMARKS: Transferred in 1975. Some Western electronic equipment has been added, including a navigational radar. Engines reported to be unreliable.

◆ **Sea-sled hull type** Bldr: Reposaaren Konepaja, Pori

| | Laid down | L | In serv. |
|---|---|---|---|
| 16 ISKU | 11-68 | 4-12-69 | 1970 |

**Isku (16)** 1979

**D:** 115 tons (140 fl) **S:** 15 kts **Dim:** 26.35 × 8.70 × 2.00
**A:** 4/SS-N-2A Styx (I × 4)—2/30-mm AA (II × 1)
**Electron Equipt:** Radar: 1/navigational, 1/Square Tie
**M:** 4 Soviet M50-series diesels; 4 props; 4,800 hp **Man:** 25 tot.

### GUIDED-MISSILE PATROL BOATS *(continued)*

REMARKS: Barge-like hull, designed for more powerful propulsion plant. Used primarily for training.

### PATROL BOATS

◆ **1 prototype** Bldr: Fiskar's Turan, Veneveistamo SY/Laivateollisuus

33 HURJA

**D:** 54 tons (60 fl) **S:** 42 kts **Dim:** 21.7 × 5.0 × . . . **A:** . . .
**M:** diesels; waterjets; . . . hp

REMARKS: Glass-reinforced plastic prototype hull delivered 1-7-80 to Laivateollisuus for fitting out. This class was intended to replace at least seven of the Nuoli class during the 1980s, but no further orders have materialized. A "Nuoli 90" class is still in the planning stages.

◆ **6 Nuoli class** Bldr: Laivateollisuus, Turku (In serv. 1961–66)

| | In serv. | | In serv. |
|---|---|---|---|
| 35 NUOLI 5 | 6-7-62 | 41 NUOLI 11 | 5-5-64 |
| 38 NUOLI 8 | 10-10-62 | 42 NUOLI 12 | 30-11-64 |
| 40 NUOLI 10 | 5-5-64 | 43 NUOLI 13 | 12-10-66 |

**Nuoli 5 (35)** Finnish Navy, 1983

**D:** 40 tons (64 fl) **S:** 40 kts **Dim:** 22.0 × 6.65 × 1.5
**A:** 1/40-mm AA—1/20-mm AA **Electron Equipt:** Radar: Decca 707
**M:** 3 Soviet M50 diesels; 3,600 hp **Man:** 15 tot.

REMARKS: Nuoli 10–13 have a lower superstructure. Sisters *Nuoli-1–3, 6,* and *9* discarded by 1984; survivors being modernized.

◆ **3 Ruissalo class** Bldr: Laivateollisuus, Turku

| | L | In serv. |
|---|---|---|
| 53 RUISSALO | 16-6-59 | 11-8-59 |
| 54 RAISIO | 2-7-59 | 12-9-59 |
| 55 RÖYTTA | 2-6-59 | 14-10-59 |

**Ruissalo (53)**—bow gun mount now twin 23-mm Finnish Navy, 1979

◆ **2 Rihtniemi class** Bldr: Rauma-Repola, Rauma

| | | |
|---|---|---|
| 51 RIHTNIEMI | 1956 | 21-2-57 |
| 52 RYMATTLYA | 1956 | 20-5-57 |

**D:** 115 tons (135 fl) **S:** 18 kts **Dim:** 34.0 × 6.0 × 1.8
**A:** 4/23-mm AA (II × 2)—2/RBU-1200 ASW RL (V × 2)—mines
**M:** 2 Mercedes-Benz diesels; 2 CP props; 2,500 hp **Man:** 20 tot.

REMARKS: *Ruissalo* and *Rihtniemi* classes are former convertible minesweeper/gunboats, modernized 1977–80. 51 and 52 originally only 31 meters overall and are 5.7 meters in beam. All five now have bow bulwarks.

### MINE WARFARE SHIPS

◆ **1 minelayer/training ship** Bldr: Wärtsilä, Helsinki

| | Laid down | L | In serv. |
|---|---|---|---|
| 01 POHJANMAA | 5-78 | 28-8-78 | 8-6-79 |

**Pohjanmaa (01)** L. & L. Van Ginderen, 6-87

**D:** 1,100 tons (fl) **S:** 20 kts **Dim:** 78.3 × 11.6 × 3.0
**A:** 1/120-mm Bofors DP—2/40-mm AA (I × 2)—8/23-mm AA (II × 4)—2/RBU-1200 ASW RL (II × 2)—mines
**Electron Equipt:** Radar: 1/navigational, 1/H.S.A. DA 05 air search, 1/9GA 208, 1/9LV100
Sonar: 2 sets
**M:** 2 Wärtsilä-Vasa 16V22 diesels; 2 CP props; 5,800 hp
**Electric:** 1,040 kVA **Range:** 3,500/17 **Man:** 80 crew plus 70 cadets

REMARKS: Training facilities fitted in portable containers mounted on the two internal mine rails, easily removable if the ship is required for combat. Bow-thruster. Six 102-mm flare RL rails mounted on 120-mm mount.

◆ **1 coastal minelayer** Bldr: Valmet Oy, Helsinki (L: 16-3-57)

05 KEIHASSALMI

**Keihassalmi (05)** L. & L. Van Ginderen, 1982

**D:** 290 tons (360 fl) **S:** 15 kts **Dim:** 56.0 × 7.7 × 2.0
**A:** 4/30-mm AA (II × 2)—2/20-mm AA (I × 2)—100 mines
**Electron Equipt:** Radar: 1/navigational, 1/Drum Tilt
**M:** 2 Wärtsilä diesels; 2 props; 2,000 hp **Man:** 60 tot.

REMARKS: Given Soviet guns 1972, Drum Tilt f.c. radar 1976. A replacement is projected under the 1986–91 program.

NOTE: Soviet Riga-class minelayer (former frigate) *Hameenmaa* stricken at end 1985.

◆ **6 Kuha-class inshore minesweepers** Bldr: Laivateollisuus, Turku

| | In serv. | | In serv. | | In serv. |
|---|---|---|---|---|---|
| KUHA 21 | 28-6-74 | KUHA 23 | -75 | KUHA 25 | 17-6-75 |
| KUHA 22 | -74 | KUHA 24 | 7-3-75 | KUHA 26 | 13-11-75 |

**D:** 90 tons (fl) **S:** 12 kts **Dim:** 26.6 × 6.9 × 2.0
**A:** 2/23-mm AA (II × 1)—1/12.7-mm mg **Man:** 2 officers, 12 men
**M:** 2 Cummins NT-380M diesels; 2 outboard-drive props; 600 hp

REMARKS: Glass-reinforced plastic hulls. Plans for eight additional canceled. Engines, flexibly mounted, drive rudder/propellers through hydrostatic transmissions. Can tow Type F-82 electrode sweep while also controlling a *Kiskii* drone with a similar sweep deployed. A follow-on mine countermeasures craft class is planned under the 1986–91 program.

## MINE WARFARE SHIPS *(continued)*

**Kuha 22** Finnish Navy, 1984

◆ **7 Kiskii-class drone minesweepers** Bldr: Fiskars Turun, Turku

| | Laid down | L | In serv. |
|---|---|---|---|
| 521 Kiskii 1 | ... | ... | 1983 |
| 522 Kiskii 2 | 20-1-83 | 21-10-83 | 4-11-83 |
| 523 Kiskii 3 | 14-2-83 | 10-11-83 | 28-11-83 |
| 524 Kiskii 4 | 5-4-83 | 28-11-83 | 12-12-83 |
| 525 Kiskii 5 | 16-5-83 | 2-5-84 | 24-5-83 |
| 526 Kiskii 6 | 29-8-83 | 9-5-84 | 24-5-83 |
| 527 Kiskii 7 | 12-9-83 | 10-5-84 | 24-5-83 |

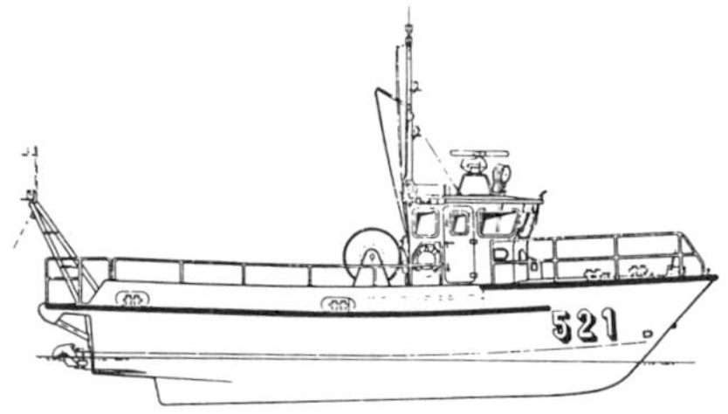


**Kiskii class** Finnish Navy, 1983

**D:** 17.7 tons (20 fl) **S:** 10.7 kts **Dim:** 15.18 (13.00 pp) × 4.10 × 1.20
**A:** 1/20-mm AA **Range:** 250/10 **Man:** 4 tot.
**M:** 2 Valmet 611 CSMP diesels; 2 Hamilton Model 1341 waterjets; 340 hp

Remarks: Can be operated by crews or under remote control by *Kuha*-class inshore minesweepers. Glass-reinforced plastic construction. Tow a Type F-82 electrode sweep to counter magnetic mines and can also counter acoustic mines. *Kiskii 1* was a trials prototype.

Note: Two small non-self-propelled minelaying barges were ordered from Lehtinen SY, Rauma, in 12-84.

## AMPHIBIOUS WARFARE SHIPS

◆ **4 landing craft/patrol boats** Bldr: 2 by Hollming, 2 by Rauma-Repola, Rauma

**D:** 28 tons (38 fl) **S:** 24 kts **Dim:** 20.50 × 5.90 × 1.00
**A:** 1/20-mm AA—mines **Range:** 240/24 **Man:** 4 tot.
**M:** 2 Wizeman-MTU diesels; 2 KaMeWa waterjets; 1,100 hp

Remarks: Ordered 17-1-83; laid down 8-9-83.

◆ **3 Kampela-class utility landing craft** Bldr: Enso-Gutzeit, Savonlinna

Kampela 1 (In serv. 29-7-76) Kampela 2 (In serv. 21-10-76)
Kampela 3 (In serv. 23-10-79)

**Kampela class** Finnish Navy, 1984

**D:** 90 tons (260 fl) **S:** 9 kts **Dim:** 32.5 × 8.0 × 1.5 **Man:** 10 tot.
**A:** 4/23-mm AA (II × 2)—mines **M:** 2 Scania diesels; 2 props; 460 hp

Remarks: *Kampela 3* built by Finnmekano, Teija.

◆ **6 Kala-class utility landing craft** Bldr: Rauma-Repola, Rauma (In serv. 1956–59)

Kala 1–Kala 6

**D:** 60 tons (200 fl) **S:** 9 kts **Dim:** 27.0 × 8.0 × 1.8 **Man:** 10 tot.
**A:** 1/20-mm AA—34 mines **M:** 2 Valmet diesels; 2 props; 360 hp

◆ **5 Kave-class landing craft** Bldr: Hollming, Rauma (In serv. 1956–60)

Kave 1 Kave 2 Kave 3 Kave 4 Kave 6

**D:** 27 tons (60 fl) **S:** 9 kts **Dim:** 18.0 × 5.0 × 1.3 **A:** 1/20-mm AA
**M:** 2 Valmet diesels; 2 props; 360 hp **Man:** 3 tot.

Remarks: *Kave 1* built by Haminen Konepaja Oy.

◆ **9 Meriusko-class assault boats** Bldr: Alumina Varvet, Kokkola (In serv. 1986)

**D:** 8.5 tons (10.2 fl) **S:** 36 kts (30 loaded)
**Dim:** 11.3 × 3.5 × . . . **Man:** 48 troops
**M:** 2 Volvo TAMD70E diesels; 2 Hamilton 291 waterjets; 600 hp

Remarks: An earlier series, built in 1983, carries 24 troops at 25 kts, 10.72 tons full load; number built not available; known as the Vietivisko class, they have the same propulsion plant as the Meriusko class.

## AUXILIARY SHIPS

Note: A new naval tug was ordered 12-84 from Lehtinen SY, Rauma; no data available.

◆ **1 pollution cleanup ship**

| | Bldr | Laid down | L | In serv. |
|---|---|---|---|---|
| Halli | Hollming, Rauma | 18-3-86 | 25-6-86 | -86 |

**D:** . . . **S:** . . . **Dim:** . . . × . . . × . . . **M:** . . .

Remarks: 1,400 grt, probably similar to *Hylse*. Built for the Ministry of Ecology.

◆ **2 buoy-tender/pollution control ships** Bldr: Rauma-Repola (Both in serv. 31-5-85)

Kummeli Sektori

**D:** . . . **S:** 10 kts **Dim:** 28.2 × 7.9 × 2.5
**M:** 2 diesels; 1 prop; 700 hp

◆ **1 pollution cleanup ship** Bldr: Laivateollisuus, Turku

99 Hylse (In serv. 3-6-81)

**D:** 1,500 (fl) **S:** 7 kts **Dim:** 49.9 × 12.5 × 3.0
**M:** 2 Saab-Scania DSI-14 diesels; 2 retractable, steerable props; 680 hp

Remarks: Owned by Board of Navigation, operated by Navy, with civilian crew. Has bow ramp on rectangular hull and can be used to transport 100 tons of deck cargo. Storage tanks can hold 550 $m^3$ of recovered seawater/oil slurry and 850 $m^3$ recovered oil. One 10-m and one 13-m oil-skimming boats carried.

◆ **1 cable ship** Bldr: Rauma-Repola (L: 15-12-65)

Putsaari

**D:** 430 tons (fl) **S:** 10 kts **Dim:** 45.5 × 8.9 × 2.3
**M:** 1 Wärtsilä diesel; 1 prop; 450 hp **Man:** 20 tot.

◆ **1 salvage tender**

220 Parainen (ex-*Pellinki*, ex-*Meteor*)

**D:** 700 tons **S:** 12 kts **Dim:** . . . × . . . × . . . **M:** diesels

**Parainen (220)** 1978

AUXILIARY SHIPS *(continued)*

Remarks: 352 grt. Purchased 1978. Former rescue tug, has diving and fire-fighting facilities.

Note: The patrol-boat tender *Louhi* (ex-*Sisa*) was stricken at the end of 1985.

## SERVICE CRAFT

◆ **1 modified Valas-class diving tender** Bldr: Hollming SY, Rauma

. . . Mersu (In serv. 10-80)

**D:** 300 tons (fl) **S:** 12 kts **Dim:** 30.65 × 8.1 × 3.4
**A:** 2/23-mm AA (II × 1)—1/12.7-mm mg
**M:** 1 Wärtsilä Vasa 22 diesel; 1 prop; 1,450 hp **Man:** 1 officer, 6 crew; 20 divers

Remarks: Can also be used to transport 300 personnel. Appearance generally as the *Valas* class.

◆ **4 Valas-class general-service tenders** Bldr: Hollming Oy, Rauma (In serv. 1979–81)

220 Valas 221 Vahakari 222 Vaarlehti 223 Vänö

**Vahakari (221)** 1980

**D:** 100 tons (275 fl) **S:** 12 kts **Dim:** 30.65 × 7.85 × 3.40
**A:** 2/23-mm AA (II × 1)—1/12.7-mm mg—20 mines
**M:** 1 Wärsilä Vasa 22 diesel; 1 prop; 1,300 hp **Man:** 11 tot.

Remarks: Ordered 1978. Can break .4-meter ice. Carry 30 tons of cargo or 150 passengers. Stern ramp for vehicle-loading or minelaying.

◆ **3 Pukkio-class general-service tenders** Bldr: Valmet, Turku (In serv. 1947–48)

420 Pansio 421 Porkkala 422 Pyharänta

**Pyharänta (422)** L. & L. Van Ginderen, 3-86

**D:** 162 tons **S:** 10 kts **Dim:** 28.5 × 6.0 × 2.7
**M:** 1 Wärtsilä diesel; 1 prop; 300 hp **Man:** 10 tot.

Remarks: Used as tugs, transports, minelayers, and patrol boats, with armament of 1/40-mm AA, 1/20-mm AA, and up to 20 mines.

◆ **6 Hauki-class personnel transports** Bldr: 1–3: Linnan Telakka, Turku; 4–6: Valmet, Kolka (In serv. 1978–80)

133 Havouri 232 Hauki 235 Hirsala
334 Hankoniemi 431 Hakuni 436 Houtskär

**Hankoniemi (334)** 1980

**D:** 46 tons (fl) **S:** 10 kts **Dim:** 14.4 × 4.6 × 2.2
**M:** 2 Valmet 611 CSM diesels; 1 prop; 280 hp **Man:** 2 tot.

Remarks: Cargo: 45 personnel or 6 tons supplies. Can break .2-meter ice. Operated for the Coast Artillery.

◆ **2 Lohi-class personnel transports** Bldr: Savonlinna SY (In serv. 7-9-84)

Lohi Lohm

**D:** 28 tons (38 fl) **S:** 24 kts **Dim:** 20.50 × 5.90 × 1.00
**A:** 1/20-mm AA—mines
**M:** 2 Wizeman-Mercedes Benz diesels; 2 KaMeWa waterjets; 1,000 hp
**Range:** 240/24 **Man:** . . .

Remarks: Have a near-vertical bow door and ramp for landing personnel embarked. Ordered 17-1-83 and laid down 8-83 and 9-83. Aluminum construction. Used as VIP transports, patrol hospital launches, etc.

◆ **1 presidential yacht** Bldr: Uusikaupanki SY (In serv. 5-84)

Kultaranta VII

**D:** 15 tons (fl) **S:** 25 kts **Dim:** 12.5 × 4.0 × 1.4 **M:** 2 diesels; 2 props; 700 hp

Remarks: Described as a "communications ship" and used as a presidential yacht in summer and for search and rescue and medical transport in winter.

◆ **6 Ahven-class training tenders** Bldr: Valmet, Kotka

A1 Ahven A2 N . . . . . . . A3 N . . . . . . . A4 N . . . . . . . A5 N . . . . . . .
A6 N . . . . . . .

**D:** . . . **S:** . . . **Dim:** 10.3 × 3.2 × . . .
**M:** 1 Valmet 611 diesel; . . . hp

Remarks: Glass-reinforced plastic construction. First unit delivered 1980. Intended as tugs, buoy tenders, and navigational training craft.

◆ **57 (+12) service launches, K, Y, L, YM, and H and new construction**

**D:** 2 to 34 tons **S:** 7 to 10 kts

**Coast Artillery service launch** 1982

**SERVICE CRAFT** *(continued)*

Remarks: For local transport, primarily in support of Coast Artillery. Four 9-ton launches were ordered 12-84 from Unden Kaupungin SY, Uusikaupunki, and 8- to 10-ton launches were ordered from Valkoisen SY, Paimio.

Note: A 115-ton tender named *Harun* was delivered 14-5-86 by Rauma-Repola, Savonlinna; no further data available.

## COAST GUARD

Operated by the Ministry of the Interior. All ships now have black hull with a red-white-red diagonal stripe, as on U.S. Coast Guard ships. Upperworks are white.

Aviation: Three Soviet Mi-8 helicopters were purchased 12-80 for search-and-rescue duties, and three Agusta Bell AB 212 helicopters were acquired in 1985. Two Super Puma helicopters with Thomson-Sintra HS12 sonar are being acquired.

**PATROL BOATS** ("Outer Sea Patrol Ships")

◆ **2 improved Turva class**

| | Bldr | Laid down | L | In serv. |
|---|---|---|---|---|
| Tursas | Rauma-Repola, Uusikaupunki | 4-9-85 | 31-1-86 | 6-6-86 |
| N . . . | Rauma-Repola, Uusikaupunki | 4-4-86 | 19-6-86 | 2-87 |

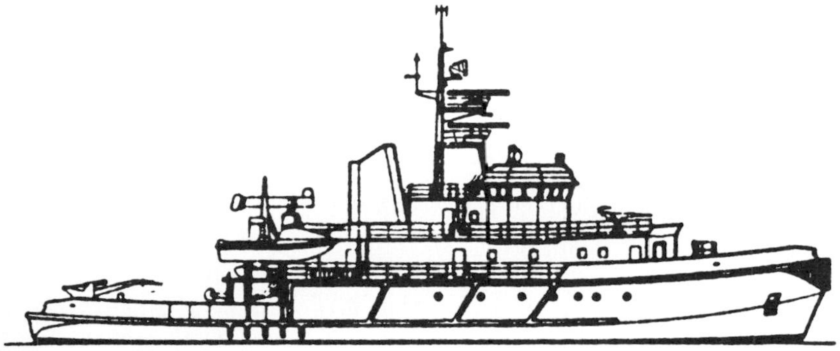

**Tursas**—builder's drawing Rauma-Repola, 1986

**D:** 750 tons (fl) **S:** 15.5 kts **Dim:** 49.00 (43.80 pp) × 10.40 × 4.00
**A:** 1/20-mm AA **Electron Equipt:** Radar: . . .
**M:** 2 Wärtsilä Vasa 8-R22 diesels; 2 props; 3,200 hp
**Electric:** 1,070 kw (1 × 750 kw, 2 × 160 kw) **Fuel:** 73 tons **Man:** 32 tot.

Remarks: First unit ordered 12-12-84, second on 20-3-86. Ice-strengthened hulls. Have hull-mounted sonars.

◆ **1 (+4) new construction**

| | Bldr | Laid down | L | In serv. |
|---|---|---|---|---|
| Kiisla | Hollming, Rauma | 12-2-86 | 18-9-86 | 25-5-87 |

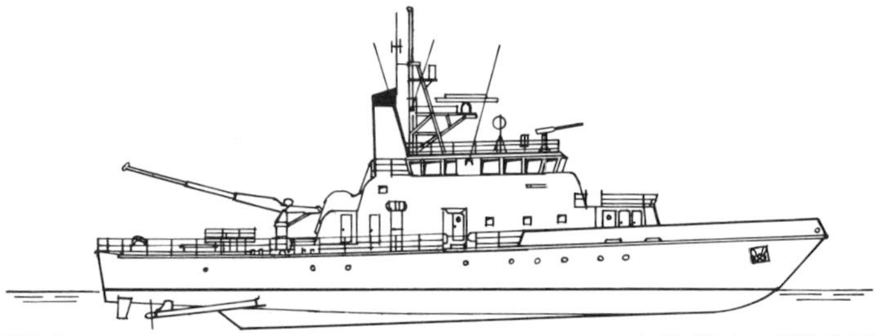

**Kiisla** A.D. Baker III, 5-85

**D:** 250 tons (270 fl) **S:** 25 kts **Dim:** 43.80 (38.50 pp) × 8.80 × 2.20
**A:** 1/20-mm AA **Fuel:** 53 tons **Electric:** 264 kw **Man:** 22 tot.
**M:** 2 MTU 16V538 TB93 diesels; 2 KaMeWa waterjets; 7,500 hp

Remarks: Ordered 21-11-84. Aluminum construction. Four more planned. Has a variable-depth sonar. Can also act as a minesweeper, minelayer, or ASW escort.

◆ **1 improved Valpas class** Bldr: Laivateollisuus, Turku

Turva (In serv. 15-12-77)

**D:** 550 tons **S:** 16 kts **Dim:** 48.5 × 8.6 × 3.9 **A:** 1/20-mm AA
**M:** 2 Wärtsilä diesels; 1 prop; 2,000 hp

Remarks: Ordered 24-6-75. An improved *Valpas,* similar in appearance.

◆ **1 Valpas class** Bldr: Laivateollisuus, Turku

| | Laid down | L | In serv. |
|---|---|---|---|
| Valpas | 20-5-70 | 22-12-70 | 21-7-71 |

**D:** 545 tons **S:** 15 kts **Dim:** 48.3 × 8.7 × 4.0 **A:** 1/20-mm AA
**M:** 1 Werkspoor TMABS-398 diesel; 1 CP prop; 2,000 hp **Man:** 22 tot.

Remarks: Ice-strengthened, equipped with Simrad Subsea sonar.

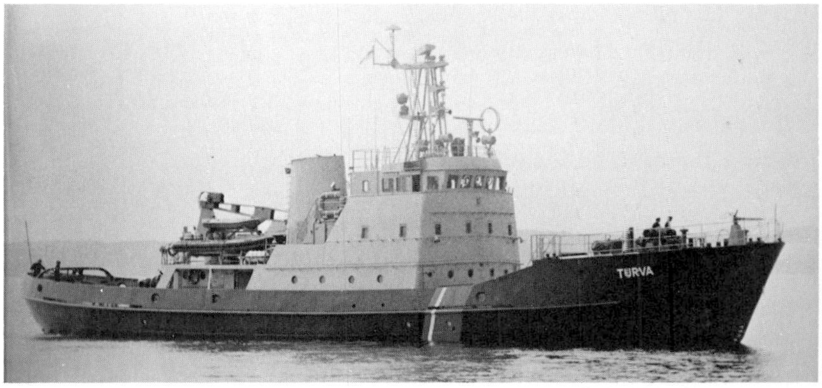



**Turva** L. & L. Van Ginderen, 1984

**Valpas** 1974

◆ **1 Viima class** Bldr: Laivateollisuus, Turku

| | L | In serv. |
|---|---|---|
| Viima | 20-7-64 | 12-10-64 |

**D:** 135 tons **S:** 23 kts **Dim:** 35.7 × 6.6 × 2.0 **A:** 1/20-mm AA
**M:** 3 Maybach diesels; 3 CP props; 4,050 hp **Man:** 12 tot.

Remarks: A variant of the Finnish Navy *Ruissalo* class.

◆ **1 Silma class** Bldr: Laivateollisuus, Turku

| | Laid down | L | In serv. |
|---|---|---|---|
| Silma | 30-8-62 | 23-3-63 | 19-8-63 |

**D:** 530 tons **S:** 15 kts **Dim:** 48.3 × 8.3 × 4.3 **A:** 1/20-mm AA
**M:** 1 Werkspoor diesel; 1 prop; 1,800 hp **Man:** 22 tot.

◆ **1 Uisko class** Bldr: Valmet, Helsinki (In serv. 1959)

Uisko

**D:** 370 tons **S:** 15 kts **Dim:** 43.4 × 7.3 × 3.83 **A:** 1/20-mm AA
**M:** 1 Werkspoor diesel; 1 prop; 1,800 hp **Man:** 20 tot.

◆ **3 (+3) Türa class** Bldr: Valmet-Laivateollisuus, Turku

| | Laid down | L | In serv. |
|---|---|---|---|
| Türa | 11-3-85 | 5-9-85 | 1-11-85 |
| Kajava | 25-11-85 | 25-3-86 | 28-8-86 |
| Kihu | 7-4-86 | 7-86 | 17-12-86 |
| N . . . | . . . | . . . | . . . |
| N . . . | . . . | . . . | . . . |
| N . . . | . . . | . . . | . . . |

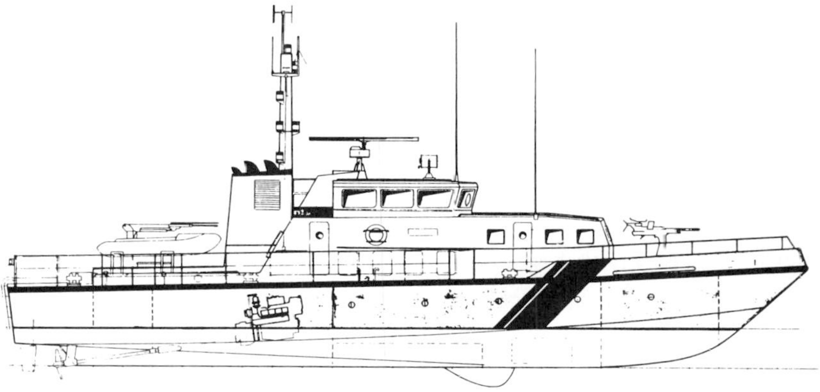

**Türa class** Valmet, 1986

## PATROL BOATS *(continued)*

**D:** 65 tons (fl) **S:** 24 kts **Dim:** 26.80 (24.20 pp) × 5.50 × 1.40 (1.85 props)
**A:** 1/20-mm AA **Electron Equipt:** Radar: 1/. . . nav.—Sonar: Simrad SS-242
**M:** 2 MTU 8V396 TB83 diesels; 2 props; 2,040 hp **Electric:** 62 kVA
**Fuel:** 8 tons **Man:** 2 officers, 6 men

REMARKS: Development of *Lokki* design, with hard-chine vice round-bilged hull form. Aluminum construction. Can be fitted with a second 20-mm AA.

◆ **1 Lokki class** Bldr: Valmet-Laivateollisuus, Turku

LOKKI (In serv. 27-11-81)

**Lokki** Laivateollisuus, 1981

**D:** 53 tons (60 fl) **S:** 25 kts **Dim:** 26.80 × 5.20 × 1.40 (1.85 props)
**A:** 1/20-mm AA **M:** MTU 8V396 TB83 diesels; 2 props; 2,040 hp
**Electric:** 62 kVA **Man:** 8 tot.

REMARKS: Aluminum construction. Prototype ordered 17-5-80. To replace *Koskelo* class.

◆ **1 Koskelo class** Bldr: Valmet, Helsinki (In serv. 1960)

TELKKÄ

**D:** 75 tons (97 fl) **S:** 23 kts **Dim:** 29.42 × 5.02 × 1.5 **A:** 1/20-mm AA
**M:** Mercedes-Benz diesels; 2 props; 2,700 hp **Man:** 11 tot.

REMARKS: Used as training ship. Modernized and re-engined 1970–74 by Laivateollisuus, Turku. Sisters *Kaakkuri, Koskelo, Kuovi, Kiisla, Kuikka, Kurki,* and *Tavi* stricken 1986–87.

## SERVICE CRAFT

◆ **98 small craft, Series RV, NV, and PV**

**D:** 1.1 to 20 tons **S:** most, 9 to 13 kts **Dim:** 8 to 14 overall

REMARKS: The newest are RV 37 to RV 39, delivered 1978 by Hollming.

**D:** 20 tons **S:** 12 kts **Dim:** 14.3 × 3.5 × . . . **M:** 1 MTU diesel; 300 hp

## ICEBREAKERS (Under Board of Navigation)

◆ **2 new construction** Bldr: Wärtsilä, Helsinki

| | L | In serv. |
|---|---|---|
| OTSO | 12-7-85 | 30-1-86 |
| KONTIO | 30-7-86 | 29-1-87 |

**Otso** Wärtsilä, 1986

**D:** 8,500 tons (fl) **S:** 17 kts **Dim:** 99.0 (90.0 pp) × 24.20 (23.50 wl) × 7.30
**M:** 4 Wärtsilä Vasa 16V32 diesels (7,425 hp each); Kymi-Stromberg a.c. cyclo-converters, 2 props; 17,700 hp.
**Man:** 28 tot.

REMARKS: Ordered 29-3-84. Have 2 transverse thrusters, bow propeller, Wärtsilä "bubbler" system. Replaced the three *Karhu*-class icebreakers, *Karhu, Murtjala* and *Sampo.*

◆ **2 Urho class** Bldr: Wärtsilä, Helsinki

URHO (In serv. 5-3-75) SISU (In serv. 28-1-76)

**Urho** Wärtsilä, 1975

**D:** 7,960 tons (9,500 fl) **S:** 18 kts **Dim:** 104.6 × 23.8 × 8.3 **Man:** 45 tot.
**M:** 5 SEMT-Pielstick 5,000-hp diesels, electric drive; 4 props; 22,000 hp

REMARKS: Sisters to Swedish *Atle* class. One helicopter. Two props forward, two aft.

◆ **3 Tarmo class** Bldr: Wärtsilä, Helsinki

TARMO VARMA APU

**Varma** Wärtsilä

**Voima** 1979

**FINLAND** *(continued)*
**ICEBREAKERS** *(continued)*

**D:** 4,890 tons **S:** 17 kts **Dim:** 85.7 × 21.7 × 6.8
**M:** 4 Sulzer diesels, electric drive; 4 props; 10,000 hp **Man:** 45–55 tot.

REMARKS: In service 1963, 1968, and 1970, respectively. Two props forward, two aft.

◆ **1 Voima class** Bldr: Wärtsilä, Helsinki (In serv. 1954)

VOIMA

**D:** 4,415 tons **S:** 16.5 kts **Dim:** 83.6 × 19.4 × 6.8
**M:** 6 Wärtsilä Vasa 16V22 diesels (17,460 hp), electric drive; 4 props; 14,000 hp

REMARKS: Reconstructed and re-engined 1978–79 by Wärtsilä; expected to serve until 1994.

NOTE: The Board of Navigation also owns the pollution-control ship *Hylse* (99), operated by the Navy; see entry on Navy pages.

# FRANCE

## French Republic

PERSONNEL (1987): 66,160 men and women on active duty, including 4,518 officers, 29,711 chief petty officers and petty officers, and 31,931 other enlisted personnel.

NAVAL AVIATION: Principal aircraft in service (numbers in parentheses indicate first-line units) include: 27 (12) F-8E Crusader interceptors, 63 (38) Super-Étendard fighter-bombers, 12 (8) Étendard IVP photo-reconnaissance aircraft, 22 (16) modernized Alizé shipboard ASW aircraft, 31 (28) Atlantic Mk 1, and 5(5) Gardian surveillance aircraft, 17 (13) Super-Frélon heavy helicopters, and 38 (28) WG-13 Lynx light ASW helicopters. Also in naval service are 147 other support and training aircraft and helicopters.

MERCHANT MARINE (1987): 984 ships—5,936,268 grt (tankers: 54 ships—2,588,580 grt)

WARSHIPS IN SERVICE OR UNDER CONSTRUCTION AS OF 1 JANUARY 1988

| | L | Tons | Main armament |
|---|---|---|---|
| ◆ **3 (+1) aircraft carriers** | | | |
| CHARLES DE GAULLE | 1992 | 34,600 | SAAM, Sadral, 35–40 aircraft |
| 2 CLEMENCEAU (fixed-wing) | 1957–60 | 22,000 | 8/100-mm DP, 40 aircraft |
| 1 JEANNE D'ARC (helicopter) | 1961 | 10,000 | 4/100-mm DP, 6/MM 38 Exocet, 8 heavy helicopters |
| ◆ **22 (+5) submarines** | | | |
| 1 L'INFLEXIBLE (nuclear) | 1982 | 8,000 | 16 missiles, 4 TT |
| 5 LE REDOUTABLE (nuclear) | 1967–77 | 8,000 | 16 missiles, 4 TT |
| 0 (+4) "AMÉTHYSTE" | 1988–94 | 2,400 | 4 TT |
| 3 (+1) RUBIS (nuclear) | 1979–87 | 2,265 | 4 TT |
| 4 AGOSTA | 1974–76 | 1,200 | 4 TT |
| 9 DAPHNÉ | 1959–67 | 700 | 12 TT |
| 1 NARVAL | 1954–58 | 1,320 | 6 TT |
| ◆ **1 guided-missile cruiser** | | | |
| 1 COLBERT | 1956 | 8,500 | 1 Masurca, 4/MM 38, 2/100-mm DP, 12/57-mm AA |
| ◆ **15 (+4) destroyers** | | | |
| 0 (+2) CASSARD | 1985–87 | 4,000 | Mk 13 launcher, 8/MM 40, 2/100-mm DP, 2 TT |
| 5 (+2) GEORGES LEYGUES | 1975–87 | 3,800 | 1/100-mm DP, 4/MM 38, 2 TT 2 WG 13 Lynx helicopters |
| 3 TOURVILLE | 1972–74 | 4,800 | 1 Malafon, 6/MM 38, 1 Crotale, 2/100-mm DP, 2 TT, 2 WG 13 Lynx helicopters |
| 2 SUFFREN | 1965–66 | 5,090 | 1 Masurca, 2/100-mm DP, 1 Malafon, 4/MM 38 |
| 1 ACONIT | 1970 | 3,500 | 8/MM 40, 2/100-mm DP, 1 Malafon, ASW mortar, 2 TT |
| 1 LA GALISSONNIÈRE | 1960 | 2,750 | 2/100-mm DP, 1 Malafon, 1 helicopter |
| 1 DUPERRÉ | 1956 | 2,750 | 1/100-mm DP, 4/MM 38 |
| 1 D'ESTRÉES | 1954 | 2,750 | 2/100-mm DP, 1 Malafon, ASW weapons |
| 1 KERSAINT | 1954 | 2,750 | 1 SM-1 MR, 6/57-mm AA, 1 ASW RL, 6 TT |
| ◆ **25 frigates** | | | |
| 0 (+3) FL 25 | | | |
| 17 D'ESTIENNE D'ORVES | 1973–80 | 1,100 | 1/100-mm DP, 2/MM 38, 1 ASW rocket launcher, 4 TT |
| 1 BALNY | 1962 | 1,750 | 2/100-mm DP, 1 ASW mortar, 6 TT |
| 7 COMMANDANT RIVIÈRE | 1958–63 | 1,750 | 4/MM 38, 2/100-mm DP, 1 ASW mortar, 6 TT |
| ◆ **20 patrol boats and craft** | | | |
| 10 P 400 | 1984– | 320 | 1/40-mm AA |
| 4 TRIDENT | 1976 | 115 | 1/40-mm 6/SS 12 SSM |
| 1 STERNE | 1979 | 270 | 2 mg |
| 1 LA COMBATTANTE | 1963 | 180 | 2/40-mm AA, 4/SS 12 SSM |
| 1 MERCURE | 1957 | 365 | 2/200-mm AA |
| 2 "Ham" | 1954–55 | 140 | 1/20-mm AA |
| 1 trawler type | 1965 | 1,800 | 1/40-mm AA |
| ◆ **24 (+2) minehunters and minesweepers** | | | |
| 8 (+2) TRIPARTITE (minehunters | 1979–88 | 500 | 1/20-mm AA |
| 5 CIRCÉ (minehunters) | 1970–72 | 460 | 1/20-mm AA |
| 7 U.S. MSO (3 minehunters) | 1953–56 | 700 | 1/40-mm AA |
| 4 SIRIUS | 1955–56 | 400 | 1 or 2/20-mm AA |
| ◆ **18 (+1) amphibious warfare ships** | | | |
| 0 (+1) TCD 90 | 1968 | 9,300 | 2 Sadral, 1/40-mm AA |
| 2 OURAGAN | 1963–67 | 5,800 | 4/40-mm AA |
| 1 ARGENS | 1958 | 1,750 | 3/40-mm AA |
| 5 CHAMPLAIN (Batral) | 1973–85 | 750 | 2/40-mm AA |
| 5 CDIC | 1987 | ... | ... |
| 4 EDIC | 1958–68 | 250 | 2/20-mm AA |

WEAPONS AND SYSTEMS

### A. MISSILES

◆ **strategic ballistic**

**M 20**

This missile, which has replaced the M 2, has two stages, is aerodynamically unstable, and has the following characteristics:

| | | | |
|---|---|---|---|
| Total height | 10.40 m | Launch | compressed air |
| Height 1st stage | 5.20 m | Launch weight | 20 tons |
| Height 2nd stage | 2.60 m | Max. range | 3,000 km |
| Diameter | 1.50 m | | |

The thermonuclear warhead is in the megaton range and has been especially "hardened" to facilitate penetration and to counter nuclear anti-missile defenses.

**M 4, Improved M 4 (M 45)**

This missile entered service in 1985 aboard *L'Inflexible* and has three stages. Characteristics include:

| | | | |
|---|---|---|---|
| Total height | 11.05 m | Launch | powder charge |
| Diameter | 1.93 m | Launch weight | around 36 tons |
| | | Max. range | 4,000 km (M 4B: 5,000) |

The payload is 6 warheads of around 150 kt, of great precision and with improved penetration over the already excellent M 20. The launch interval is shorter between missiles than with the M 20 and is capable of being carried out at greater depths. The first at-sea firings took place in early 3-82. M 4 will be backfitted into all earlier submarines except *Le Redoutable*. To effect installation, it is necessary to replace the existing missile tubes. The M 4 has 6 TN-70 warheads, which spread over a 150- × 350-km area at a range of 4,000 km; The Improved M 4 uses the TN-71 reentry vehicle to a range of 5,000 km, although one was officially reported to have traveled 6,000 km on 4-3-86.

**M 5**

A new weapon being developed for the "second generation" ballistic-missile submarines. To have a range of 6,000 km (3,240 n.m.), with 8–12 TN-75 independently targeted warheads (MIRV). The first to carry it will be the third ship of the class.

◆ **surface-to-air**

**SAAM (Système Surface Anti-Air Missiles)** Manufacturer: Aerospatiale

Intended to become operational in 1995 aboard the carrier CHARLES DE GAULLE. To have a 15-km range, it will be vertically launched from 8-missile modular cell groups. Aerospatiale is developing the "Aster 15" missile, which will be highly maneuverable. Guidance will be supported by the Thomson-CSF I/J-band missile detection radar.

**Masurca**

A medium-range missile (30 nautical-mile range, intercept between 100 ft and 75,000 ft) launched by a solid-propellant booster, which in a few seconds brings it

**MISSILES** *(continued)*

to a speed close to Mach 3; a slower-burning solid propellant maintains this speed throughout the flight. The missile and booster together are 8.6 m long and weigh 2,098 kg. Other characteristics are:

| | Missile | Booster |
|---|---|---|
| Length | 5.38 m | 3.32 m |
| Diameter | 0.406 m | 0.57 m |
| Span of fins | — | 1.5 m |
| Weight | 950.0 kg | 1,148.0 kg |
| Warhead | 100.0 kg | — |

Mod. 3, a semiactive homing missile, is the only one now in service. It follows a trajectory determined by proportional navigation, keeping its antenna pointed at the target, which is illuminated by the launching ship's radar transmitter.

Masurca, which is installed in the *Suffren*-class guided-missile destroyers and in the guided-missile cruiser *Colbert,* consists of (1) a target-designator and weapon-assignment console, including a computer, which uses the shipboard search radar and the Senit automatic tactical data system, and (2) two guidance systems, each with: DRBC 51 tracking radar, a director carrying the rear-reference beam and illumination beam for the control system, an illumination beam, a twin launcher, storage and maintenance facilities, including two horizontal ready-service drums containing 18 missiles in addition to reserve missiles in the magazines, and IFF and control equipment.

The Masurca systems aboard *Colbert* and the *Suffren* class were modernized 1983–85 to keep the system up-to-date to the end of its expected service life (1998–2000).

**Standard SM-1 MR**

A one-stage U.S.-designed-and-manufactured missile with solid fuel. Characteristics:

Length: 4.60 m — Guidance: semiactive homing, proximity fuze
Diameter: .41 m — Range: 50,000 m, max.
Weight: 590 kg — Interception altitude: 60 ft to 80,000 ft

The complete system consists of, in addition to the missile:

1 single Mk 13 launcher, 1 vertical stowage-loader containing 40 missiles, various computers, SPS 39B height-finding radar, and 2 SPG 51C tracking radars.

SM-1 MR is mounted on T-47-type destroyers modified for Tartar and the C-70 AAW-type destroyers, which have the DRBJ 11B height-finding radar. It has replaced the earlier Tartar ITR and SM-1A in French naval service.

**Crotale**

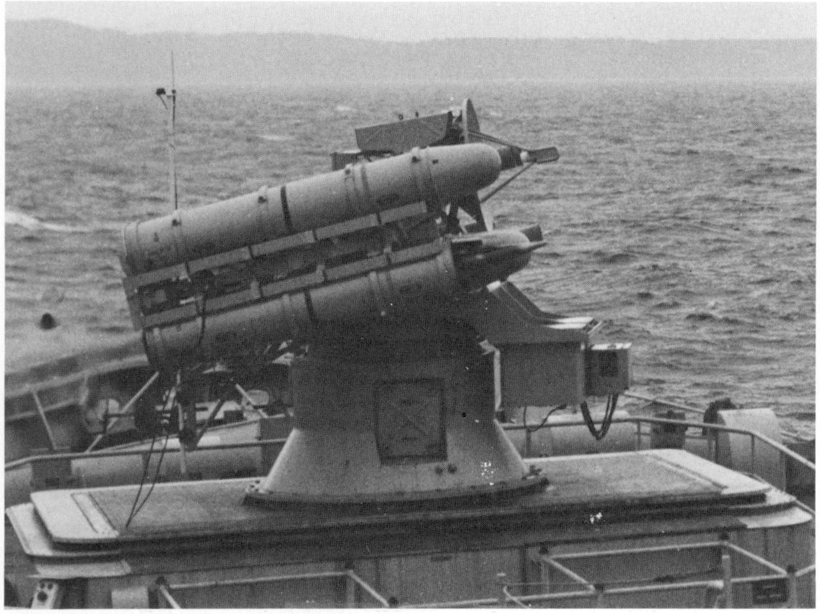
**Crotale system at moment of launch** French Navy

A French Air Force missile adapted for naval use. Electronics are by Thomson-CSF and the missile by Matra. Characteristics for the R440N missile are:

Length: 2.930 m
Diameter: 0.156 m
Span: cruciform (0.54 m with fins extended), antipitching canards forward
Weight: 85.1 kg
Range: 8,000 m
Interception altitudes: 150 ft to 12,000 ft
Warhead: 14 kg
Guidance: beam-riding, then detonation by infrared fuze incorporated in the missile
Launcher: octuple

Crotale is installed on the F 67 and C 70 destroyer classes. It is used with DRBV 51C radar and has a Thomson tracking radar in the KU band. Eighteen reload missiles are carried in the magazine. The prototype was installed in the test ship *Île d'Oléron* in May 1977, while the first operational installation was aboard *Georges Leygues* in 1978.

Crotale is being updated to enable it to handle Mach 2.0 targets at altitudes down to 4 m. The missiles, named Crotale EDIR *(Écartometrie Différentielle Infra Rouge),* are being equipped with a new proximity fuze, and an infrared tracker is being added to the launcher/director; range is increased to 13,000 m. Will be carried by *Clemenceau* and *Foch* and by the 7th C 70-class ASW destroyer and will be backfitted in earlier Crotale ships by 1990.

**SADRAL** (System d'Auto Défense Rapprochée Anti-aérienne Leger)—Manufacturer: Matra

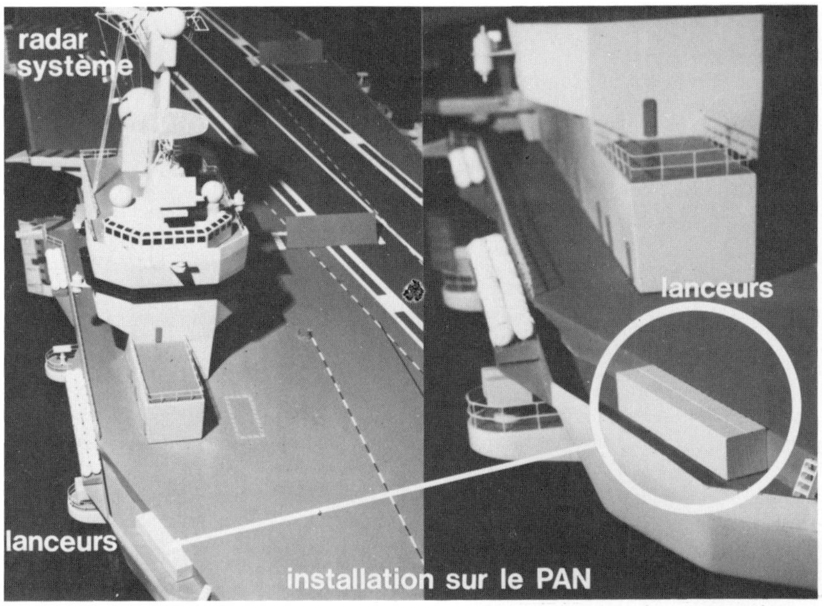

**Installation of vertical launchers for the SADRAL system aboard Richelieu** DCN, 1987

SATCP *(Surface-Air, á Très Courte Portie).* The system has a C.S.E.E. automatic director and IR homing, with laser-backup proximity and impact fuzing. The missile itself, called "Mistral," has:

Length: 1.80 m — Warhead: 3 kg, 1,500 tungsten balls
Diameter: 0.90 m — Range: under 500 to around 6,000 m, at altitudes down to 3 m.
Weight: 18 kg
Speed: Mach 2.7

The missiles are installed in a 6-missile, rapid-reload, lightweight launcher. The system should be operational about 1988 in the antiaircraft destroyers of the C 70 AAW type. First "operational" firing 23-10-86 from *Île d'Oléron.*

### ◆ Surface-to-surface

**MM 38 Exocet** Manufacturer: Aerospatiale

A homing missile with solid-fuel propulsion. Characteristics:

Weight: 700 kg, approx. (explosive charge: more than 150 kg)
Speed: Mach 1 — Diameter: 0.35 m
Range: 37 km, min — Wingspan: 1.00 m
Length: 5.20 m — Cylindrical body with a pointed nose, cruciform wings with arrow shape.

The fire-control solution requires a fix on the target provided by the surface radar of the firing ship and uses the necessary equipment for launching the missile and determining the correct range and height bearing of the target.

The missile is launched at a slight elevation (about 15°). After the boost phase, it reaches its flight altitude and is stabilized at between 3 and 15 meters. Altitude is maintained by a radar altimeter.

During the first part of the flight, the missile is automatically guided by an inertial system that has received the azimuth of the target. When within a certain distance from the target, an automatic homing radar begins to seek the target, picks it up, and directs the missile. Great effort has been made to protect the missile from countermeasures during this phase. A new "Super ADAC" seeker, with improved anti-jamming features, is offered for backfit to earlier missiles.

Detonation takes place upon impact or by pseudo-proximity fuze, according to interception conditions, size of the target ship, and the condition of the sea.

**SM 39 Exocet** Manufacturer: Aerospatiale

A submarine torpedo-tube-launched version of the Exocet concept, SM 39 began in 1981 aboard the *Narval*-class submarine *Requin.* It has a range of 50 km. The missile is 4.7 m long by 350 mm in diameter and weighs 650 kg. With its solid-fueled

**MISSILES** *(continued)*

launch/ejection capsule, the missile is 5.8 m long, weighs 1,350 kg, and fits within a 533-mm torpedo tube. The system became operational 1985 on *Saphir*. Thirty-six ordered 1986.

**MM 40 Exocet** Manufacturer: Aerospatiale

An improved version of the MM 38 and the AM 39, the MM 40 is an over-the-horizon missile whose range is adapted to radar performance and is able to use fire-control data relayed by an outside source. Instead of the usual metal launcher, it has a fiberglass, cylindrical one, which, because it is lighter and has less fittings, increases firepower by allowing more missiles to be carried.

Length: 5.80 m — Weight: 850 kg
Diameter: 0.35 m — Speed: Mach .95
Wingspan: 1.135 m — Range: 65 km

**SS 12 M** Manufacturer: Aerospatiale

Wire-guided, solid-fueled missile. Characteristics:

Length: 1.870 m — Weight: 75 kg (upon firing)
Diameter: 0.210 m — Warhead: 30 kg (about)
Wingspan: 0.650 — Range: 5,500 m

No longer used on French Navy ships but is used by foreign fleets.

## B. AVIATION MISSILES

### ◆ Air-to-ground

**ANL (Anti-Navire Léger)** Manufacturer: Aerospatiale and MBB of West Germany

Will be launchable from helicopters and aircraft.

Weight: 200 kg — Warhead: 50 kg
Length: . . . — Range: 180 km
Guidance: inertial, with radar terminal homing. Ram jet propulsion.

**STAR (Supersonique Tactique Anti-Radiation)** Manufacturer: Matra and ONERA

Intended as a Martel replacement, this project envisions 4 missiles per Super Étendard. With a range of 150 km, it is to weigh about 220 kg.

**ASMP (Air-Surface à Moyenne Porte)** Manufacturer: Aerospatiale

To enter service in 1990–91 on the Super Étendard, the ASMP has a 300-kt nuclear warhead. It uses inertial guidance, has a radar altimeter, and is very resistant to countermeasures. Operational 1-5-86 on the land-based Mirage IV.

Length: 8.3 m — Weight: 840 kg
Diameter: 0.35 m — Range: 100–350 km
Wingspan: 0.956 m — Speed: Mach 2.4

**AM 39** Manufacturer: Aerospatiale

This is the air-to-sea version of the MM 38. After being launched, it has the same flight characteristics as the MM 38.

Length: 4.633 m
Diameter: 0.348 m
Wingspan: 1.004 m
Weight: 650 kg (before launching)
Range: 50–70 km, according to altitude and speed at launch
Radar: active home-seeking head (EMD)

Operational since 1978, AM 39 is a "fire and forget" missile that permits an aircraft that has fired to renew its attack or to seek a new target. It is used with the Atlantique Mk 2 patrol aircraft, the Super Étendard aircraft, and the Super Frélon helicopter.

**AS 11** Manufacturer: Aerospatiale

A wire-guided system with optical alignment on the target. Used for training by CM 175 aircraft.

Length: 1.210 m — Wingspan: 0.50 m
Diameter: 0.164 m — Weight: 29.900 kg

**AS 12** Manufacturer: Aerospatiale

A wire-guided system with optical alignment on the target. Used by WG-13 Lynx helicopter.

Length: 1.870 m — Wingspan: 0.650 m
Diameter: 0.210 m — Weight: 75 kg
Range: maximum 7,500 to 8,000 m; minimum 1,500 m

**AS 15 TT** Manufacturer: Aerospatiale

Length: 2.16 m — Range: 15 km
Weight: 96 kg

For use by light helicopters (Dauphin, Lynx); developed under the Saudi Arabian "Sawari" program. First production deliveries 3-85.

**AS 20** Manufacturer: Aerospatiale

Length: 2.60 m — Weight: 140 kg
Diameter: 0.25 m — Guidance: radio command
Wingspan: 0.80 m — Range: 4,000 m to 8,000 m

Used in firing training for the AS 30.

**AS 30** Manufacturer: Aerospatiale

System developed for firing from a maneuvering aircraft at middle, low, or very low altitude. Used by the Super Étendard.

Length: 3.785 m — Wingspan: 1.000 m
Diameter: 0.342 m — Total weight: 528 kg
Range: maximum 9 to 12,000 m; minimum 1,500 m
Guidance: radio command or laser designation (AS 30L)

**AS 37 Martel** Manufacturers: Matra and British Aerospace

Two types, television and anti-radar. Only the latter is used in the French Navy.

Length: 4.122 m — Total weight: 531 m
Diameter: 0.40 m — Range: over 20,000 m
Wingspan: 1.192 m

Passive homing head (EMD); the missile homes on the radar emissions of the enemy vessel. Immediately after being fired, the missile is on its own, permitting the aircraft to depart or evade. Used with Atlantic Mk 1 aircraft.

### ◆ Air-to-air

**R 530** Manufacturer: Matra

There are two versions of this missile: infrared (IR) and radar-homing (EMD).

Length: IR type: 3.198 m; EMD type: 3.284 m
Diameter: 0.263 m
Wingspan: 1.103 m
Weight: IR type: 193.5 kg, EMD type: 192 kg
Range: maximum 10,000 m: minimum 5,000 m
Guidance: Semi-passive-homing (MD) or infrared-homing

**Sidewinder**

The French Navy uses this air-to-air American missile (*see* U.S.A. section).

**R 550 Magic** Manufacturer: Matra

Length: 2.900 m — Weight: 89 kg
Diameter: 0.157 m — Range: 300/8,000 m
Wingspan: 0.660 m — Guidance: infrared-homing

## C. GUNS

**100-mm Compact (USINOR/Creusot-Loire)**

Single-barrel automatic, for export only.

Weight of mount: 17.3 tons
Length of barrel: 55 calibers
Range: 17,200 m
Muzzle-velocity: 870 m/sec.
Max. effective range for surface fire: 12,000 m
Max. effective range for antiaircraft fire: 6,000 m
Max. rate of fire: 20, 45, or 90 rpm, or single file
Arc of elevation: $-15°$ to $+80°$
Max. speed: training 50°/sec, elevation, 33°/sec

Most installations have a 42-round magazine, while those for Malaysia had 90-round magazines. Used by Saudi Arabian frigates; two sold to China.

**100-mm, Models 1953 and 1968**

**100-mm Model 1968 DP gun** — M. Louagie, 7-85

**GUNS** *(continued)*

Single-barrel automatic, for use against aircraft, surface vessels, or land targets. Model 1968 is a lighter version of Model 1953. The ammunition is the same. Characteristics of Model 1968:

Weight of mount: 22 tons
Length of barrel: 55 calibers
Range at 40° elevation: 17,000 m
Maximum effective range for surface fire: 15,000 m
Maximum effective range for antiaircraft fire: 8,000 m
Maximum rate of fire: 60 rounds/minute (78 rds/min in recent models)
Arc of elevation: −15° to +80°
Maximum speed: training, 40°/sec, elevation, 25°/sec

Model 1953 uses an analog fire-control system with electro-mechanical and electronic equipment for the fire-control solution. The director can be operated in optical and radar modes. Used in *Jeanne d'Arc,* the *Suffren* class, *La Galissonnière, Surcouf* T-47 ASW destroyers, and the *Cdt. Rivière* class.

Model 1968 used a digital fire-control system, with central units, and memory disks or magnetic tape for data storage. Light radar gun director. Optical direction equipment can be added. Used in the *Colbert, Tourville* class, *Georges Leygues* class, *Aconit, Duperré,* and A-69 class.

**57-mm Model 1951**

Twin-barrel automatic:

Length of barrel: 60 calibers
Muzzle velocity: 865 m/sec
Maximum range: 13,000 m
Effective antiaircraft range: 5,000 m
Maximum rate of fire: 60 rounds/min per barrel
Arc of elevation: −8° to 90°

**30-mm**

Single-barrel automatic:

| | |
|---|---|
| Length: 2.440 m | Maximum effective range: 2,800 m |
| Weight: 4 tons | Maximum rate of fire: 650 rounds/minute |
| Muzzle velocity: 1,000 m/sec | |

Used only on the frigates *Balny, Enseigne de Vaisseau Henry, Protet,* and *Victor Schoelcher.*

Also in service are typical 40-mm guns based on Bofors designs and 20-mm guns of Oerlikon design.

A new 20-mm mounting has been designed by DCAN for the GIAT CN-MIT-20F2 gun, which has a 650–720 rd/min firing rate. Two 150-round magazines are carried on the mount. Weight: 322 kg empty. Length: 2.6 m.

## D. ANTISUBMARINE WEAPONS

**Malafon**

A glider that carries L-4 torpedoes and is launched with the assistance of a double booster. It is stabilized by automatic pilot and guided by radio command.

Glider: speed, 230 m/sec; range, 12,000 m
Missile: length, 6.15 m; diameter, 0.65 m; span, 3.30 m; weight, including torpedo, 1,500 kg

The Malafon, initially built by Latécoère in partnership with St. Trôpez, is installed in the two *Suffren*-class destroyers, *La Galissonnière,* the Type T-47 ASW conversions, the *Aconit,* and the *Tourville*-class destroyers.

A successor to Malafon is planned, using the Murène homing torpedo as a payload.

**Malafon on launcher** M. Louagie, 6-84

**375-mm Rocket Launchers, Models 1964 or 1972**

Sextuple mount. Automatic loading in vertical position. Firing rate, 1 rocket/second. Range: 1,600 m. Time or proximity fuze. Based on Bofors quadruple mounting. Normally has six illumination-flare rocket rails mounted also.

**375-mm sextuple ASW rocket launcher**—with flare rails M. Louagie, 7-85

**305-mm Mortar**

Quadruple mount; automatic loading. ASW projectile weight: 230 kg; range: 400 to 3,000 m. Can also fire a 100-kg projectile against land targets; range: 6,000 m. Normally has four illumination-flare rocket rails mounted on the face of the rotating housing. Used only on the *Commandant Rivière* class (removed from *Aconit*).

## E. TORPEDOES

◆ **For surface ships**

| | Weight in kg | Diameter in mm | Speed in kts |
|---|---|---|---|
| L 3 | 900 | 550 | 25 |
| L 5, Mod. 1 and Mod. 4 | 1,000 | 533 | 35 |

◆ **For submarines**

| | Weight in kg | Diameter in mm | Speed in kts |
|---|---|---|---|
| L 5, Mod. 1 | 1,000 | 533 | 35 |
| L 5, Mod. 3 | 1,300 | 533 | 35 |
| F 17, Mod. 1 | 1,300 | 533 | 35 |
| F 17, Mod. 2 | 1,300 | 533 | 40 |

◆ **For aircraft**

**Murène**

A new multipurpose ASW torpedo to enter service about 1990 as a replacement for the U.S. Mk 46.

| | |
|---|---|
| Length: 3.00 m | Speed: 50 kts (38 kt. cruise) |
| Diameter: 0.324 m | Depth: over 1,000 m max. |
| Weight: 285 kg | |

In addition to the U.S. Mk 46 torpedo, French naval aircraft use the L 4 torpedo.

## F. SONARS

◆ **For surface ships**

| | Type | Frequency | Average range |
|---|---|---|---|
| DUBA 3 | Hull | HF | 3,000 m |
| DUBV 24 | Hull | LF | 6,000 m |
| DUBV 23 | Bow | LF | *see* Remarks |
| DUBV 24C | Hull | LF (5 kHz) | *see* Remarks |
| DUBV 43C | Towed | LF (5 kHz) | *see* Remarks |
| DUBA 25 | Hull | MF (9 kHz) | *see* Remarks |
| DUBA 26 | Hull | MF | *see* Remarks |
| DUBM 20 | Hull—on *Circé*-class minehunters | | |
| DUBM 21 | Hull—on new Tripartite and modernized MSO minehunters | | |
| DUBM 41 | Towed—on modernized MSO; sidescan minehunting | | |
| DSBV 61 | A towed passive linear array system, VLF | | |
| DSBV 62 | Towed linear array, in development | | |
| Diodon | A 12 kHz hull-mounted sonar developed for export. Is also available in 11 and 13 kHz models. | | |
| SQS-505 | Hull—Canadian set on aircraft carriers | | |
| SQS-17 | U.S. mid-frequency set on *Cdt. Rivière* class | | |

**SONARS** *(continued)*

**DUBV 43 VDS fish and hoist gear on Dupleix (D 641)** L. Grazioli, 3-87

REMARKS: DUBV 23 and DUBV 43 are used simultaneously and, under normal sound-propagation conditions, achieve ranges of 8,000 and 10,000 meters; the DUBV 43C operates at depths of up to 700 m; when used with DUBV 43C, hull-mounted sonar becomes DUBV 24. In certain bathymetric conditions, the range is 20,000 meters. DUBA 25 is a new sonar designed for the A-69 class and the C 70 AA destroyers. The DUBM 41B can be towed at 10 kts and covers a 400-m swath, compared to the 4-kt/50-m capability of the DUBM 41.

◆ **For submarines**

Listening devices, active-passive sonars, and underwater telephone equipment, including:

| | |
|---|---|
| DUUA 1 | On the *Daphné* and *Agosta* classes: active |
| DUUA 2 | On modernized *Daphné, Agosta,* and *Rubis* classes (DUUA 2B in latter): active |
| DSUV 2 | Hydrophone array on *Narval* and *Daphné* classes |
| DSUV 22 | Hydrophone array on the *Rubis* and *Agosta* classes |
| DUUV 23 | Panoramic passive array on the ballistic-missile submarines |
| DSUX 21 | Multifunction system for *L'Inflexible* and earlier missile submarines |
| DSUV 61 | Towed passive array for the ballistic-missile submarines |
| DSUV 62 | Towed passive array for the *Agosta* and *Rubis* classes |
| DUUX 2 | Passive hull array |
| DUUX 5 | Passive hull array |

◆ **For helicopters**

| | Frequency | Remark |
|---|---|---|
| AQS-13 | HF | U.S. sonar |
| DUAV 4 | HF | In the WG-13 Lynx |

## G. SENIT COMBAT INFORMATION SYSTEMS

This system serves four principal purposes:

It establishes the combat situation from the manual collection of information derived from detection equipment on board and from the automatic or manual collection of information from external sources.

It disseminates the above data to the ship and to other vessels by automatic means (Links 11 and 14).

It assists in decision making and transmits to the target-designation console all the information it requires.

The several versions of the SENIT are similar in general concept but differ in construction and programming in order to ensure fulfillment of the various missions assigned to each type of ship.

SENIT 1: A system with one or two computers. Installed in the *Suffren,* the *Duquesne,* and the *Colbert.*

SENIT 2: A single-computer system. Installed in the T-47 type *Kersaint*-class destroyers, as well as in the *Duperré,* which uses a version with two computers.

SENIT 3: A central system consisting of two computers and two memory banks, the entire group designed for the control of various weapons (guns, Malafon ASW system, torpedoes). Installed in the *Aconit,* and the three *Tourville*-class ships.

The above three systems are based on equipment of U.S. origin, some built in France under license.

SENIT 4: A system conceived by the French Navy's programming center and designed around the French Iris N 55 computer. Fitted in the *Georges Leygues* class.

SENIT 5: Also designed by the French Navy's programming center, this system will be fitted on small ships. It uses the French M 15 minicomputer.

SENIT 6: Another system designed by the French Navy's programming center. It will equip the future C-70 AAW version of the *Georges Leygues* class. It combines a number of M 15 computers and a new generation of display devices particularly adapted for command purposes.

SISC (Système d'Intégration du Système de Combat)
New data system being developed for the carrier *Charles de Gaulle.*

### DLT D3

All submarines use the Direction de Lancement Torpilles DLT D3. There are three identical data displays for current and historical target data, and the system can be used to launch torpedoes and missiles.

## H. RADARS

◆ **Air search**

| | |
|---|---|
| DRBV 20C: | Metric, long-range. Mounted on aircraft carriers and *Colbert.* |
| DRBV 22A: | Mounted in T-47 ASW version destroyers, frigates, *Duperré, Aconit,* and *La Galissonnière.* L-band (23 cm). |
| DRBV 22C: | *Île d'Oléron.* |
| DRBV 22D: | *Jeanne d'Arc, Henri Poincaré.* |
| DRBV 22E: | *Rance.* |
| DRBV 23B: | On aircraft carriers. |
| DRBV 23C: | Mounted in *Colbert.* |
| DRBV 26: | Mounted in the *Tourville* and first 4 *Georges Leygues* class and aboard AA destroyers. 150-n.m. range. Commercial name: Jupiter. |
| DRBV 27: | New radar in development for the new carrier. |

◆ **Height-finding/three-dimensional**

| | |
|---|---|
| DRBI 10: | Mounted in aircraft carriers, *Colbert, Île d'Oléron.* "Nodding"-type antenna with "Robinson" feed. |
| DRBI 23: | Mounted in the *Duquesne* and *Suffren;* monopulse. |
| SPS-39B: | American radar. Mounted on Standard-equipped T-47-class destroyer. |
| DRBJ 11B: | Pulse-coded radar for the C-70 AAW-class guided-missile destroyers and the new nuclear-powered carrier. |

◆ **Surface and low-altitude air search**

| | |
|---|---|
| DRBV 15: | Pulse-doppler design, with pulse-compression and frequency agility, intended to replace the DRBV 51. Commercial name: Sea Tiger. Replaced DRBV 13 in *Aconit* and will replace DRBV 50 in the *Suffren* class, in the *Jeanne d'Arc,* and in the final three C 70 ASW destroyers. |
| DRBV 31: | Mounted on the Standard-equipped T-47-class destroyer. |
| DRBV 50: | Mounted on aircraft carriers, *Jeanne d'Arc,* T-47 ASW destroyer, the *Rhin, Île d'Oléron, Colbert,* and *La Galissonnière.* |
| DRBV 51A: | Mounted on A-69 class and the *Duperré.* |
| DRBV 51B: | Mounted on the *Georges Leygues* class. |
| DRBV 51C: | Mounted on the *Tourville* class. |

◆ **Navigational**

Decca RM 416, 1229, etc.: Commercial radars used on smaller units.
DRBN 32: French Navy designator for Decca 1226 navigational radar.

◆ **Fire-control**

| | |
|---|---|
| DRBC 31: | For the 57-mm guns of the *Colbert* and T-47 Tartar destroyer. |
| DRBC 32A: | For the 100-mm guns on ASW-modified T-47-class destroyer, some frigates, the *Jeanne d'Arc, Clemenceau,* and *La Galissonnière.* |
| DRBC 32B: | For 100-mm guns on the *Aconit.* |
| DRBC 32C: | Mounted on the *Colbert,* carriers, and the A-69 class. |
| DRBC 32D: | Mounted on the *Tourville* class. |
| DRBC 32E: | Mounted on the A-69-class frigates. X-band. |
| DRBC 33: | A monopulse, frequency-agile system in development for the C 70 AA class and for backfit on the *Suffren* class. |
| SPG-51C: | U.S. tracking radar used with the Standard system on the T-47-type AAW destroyer. |
| DRBC 51: | Tracking radar for the Masurca on the *Colbert, Suffren,* and *Duquesne.* C-band (5-cm) tracker, 7-cm command signal. |

Also in use is the DIBV 1A Vampir, an infrared detection and fire-control system built by Thomson-CSF.

## I. COUNTERMEASURES

—The French Navy uses the eight-barreled Syllex chaff launcher (a version of the British Knebworth/Corvus), which is being replaced by the Sagaie, a long-range system. Smaller ships will receive the Dagaie system, and some major classes will get both. Both Sagaie and Dagaie are fired automatically by the electronic intercept system. Sagaie has a range of 8 km for chaff or 3 km for chaff/IR deception rounds.

—Electronics intercept systems in use include:

ARBR/ARBA 10C/D, ARBR 16, and ARBR 17 for surface ships; ARUR 10B/C, ARUR 11, ARUR 12, and ARUX 1 for submarines; and ARAR 10B, ALR-8, ARAR 12, and ARAR 13 for aircraft.

—Jammers: ARBB 32, ARBB 33

### J. COMMUNICATIONS

Recent construction or recently modified major ships are receiving radome-mounted antennas for the Syracuse satellite communications transmission system. The system became fully operational in 1987. Syracuse operates at 7–8 gHz and transmission rate is 2400-bit voice/75-baud telemetry per sec. Syracuse II in development.

To ensure communications with submerged ballistic-missile submarines, the ELF Astarte system is being developed, with a transmitter at Rosnay. Also being developed is an airborne system using U.S. VLF equipment mounted in four Transall aircraft. Astarte will enter service 1988–89.

### NUCLEAR-POWERED AIRCRAFT CARRIER

◆ **0 (+1) Charles de Gaulle class** Bldr: Brest Naval Arsenal

| | Laid down | L | In serv. |
|---|---|---|---|
| R 91 Charles de Gaulle | 1989 | 1992 | 1996 |

**Charles De Gaulle**—artist's view, showing revised bridge, mast, and SAAM installation DCN, 1987

**D:** 34,000 tons (36,000 fl) **S:** 27 kts
**Dim:** 261.50 (238.00 wl) × 64.36 (31.50 wl) × 8.45
**A:** 35 to 40 aircraft (including fixed-wing fighters and helicopters)—56 SAAM vertical-launch SAM (VIII × 7)—3/Sadral point-defense SAM (VI × 3)—possible 4/20-mm AA (I × 4)
**Electron Equipt:** Radar: 2/Decca nav., 1/DRBJ 11B, 1/DRBV 15, 1/DRBV 27, 1/Arabel
EW: 1/ARBR 17, 2/ARBB 33 jammers, 4/Sagaie RL
IR: DIBV 10 Vampir
**M:** 2 150-megawatt, type K15 pressurized-water reactor plants; double-reduction geared steam turbines; 2 5-bladed props; 83,000 hp
**Electric:** 13,100 kw (4/2,000-kw and 6/850-kw turbo alternators)
**Man:** 1,150 total ship's crew, plus 550 air group personnel (1,850 total accom.)

Remarks: General: Ordered 4-2-86. This ship represents an expansion on the abortive PH 74/PH 75 nuclear carrier program of the 1970s and is intended as replacement for *Clemenceau,* which will be 35 years old when the "PAN" (Porte-Avions Nuclear) enters service. A second unit to replace *Foch* falls outside the current 1984–88 planning program and would complete around 2001.

Hull: Design based on *Clemenceau,* but with more robust construction and protection systems. Four fin stabilizers and an air filtration system will be installed.

Aviation installations: The flight deck will be 261.5 m long, with a 195-m, 8.3-degree angled-deck portion. Maximum flight deck width is 64.36 m for an area of 12,300 $m^2$. There will be two 75-m U.S. Type C13 F steam catapults, one on the angled deck and the other on the port side of the bow, an arrangement that emphasizes parking arrangements over an ability to launch and land simultaneously. There will be two 35-ton deck-edge elevators, both to starboard amidships. The nuclear propulsion arrangement allows the island to be mounted much farther forward than is standard practice, ahead of both elevators, and permits more efficient deck utilization. The 138-m-long by 29-m-broad by 6.1-m-high (4,600 $m^2$) hangar will be lower than on the *Clemenceau* class, but considerably larger in area and better protected. The initial combat aircraft will be the Super-Étendard, but a new fighter bomber, the ACM *(Avion de Combat Maritime)* may be developed to replace the Super-Étendard by 1999. The U.S. F-18 Hornet may be purchased as an interim replacement for the F-8E and Étendard IVP. Aviation fuel capacity: 3,000 $m^3$; munitions magazines: 4,900 $m^3$.

Propulsion: The plant will be located in five compartments.

Electronics: Will have the SISC data system. There will be a rocket-launched torpedo decoy system. Arabel is the missile detection radar for the SAAM missiles.

Note: As part of the development of this complex ship, a 20-ton, 19.83-m model of *Charles de Gaulle* was built by Le Perrière, Lorient. Ordered 22-4-86, it was laid down 3-8-86, launched 30-1-87 and delivered 2-87. Powered by two 50-kw electric motors, it has a crew of three.

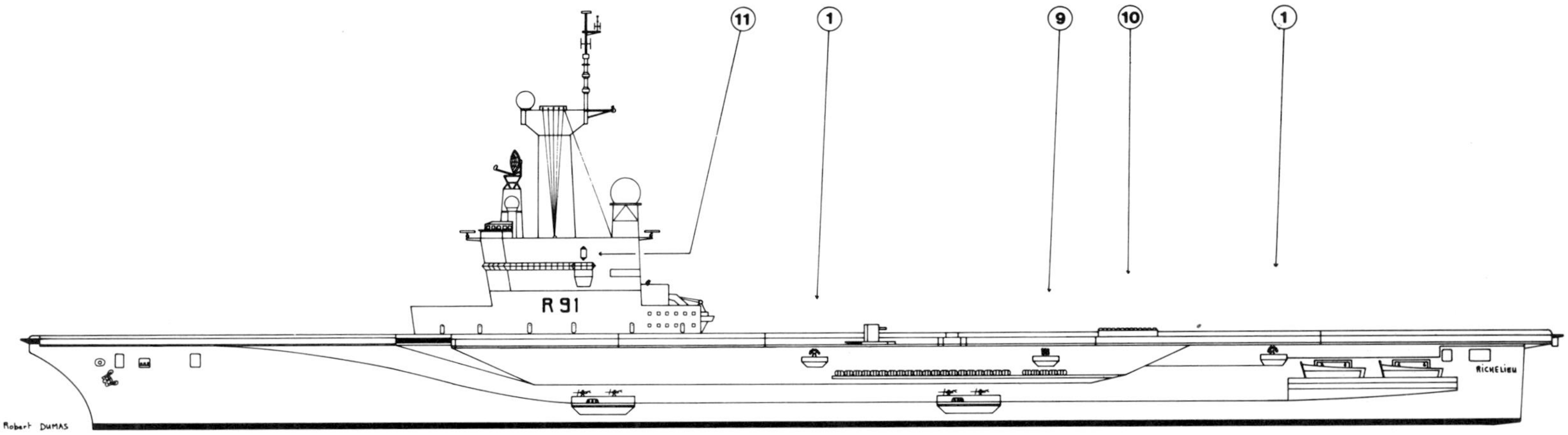


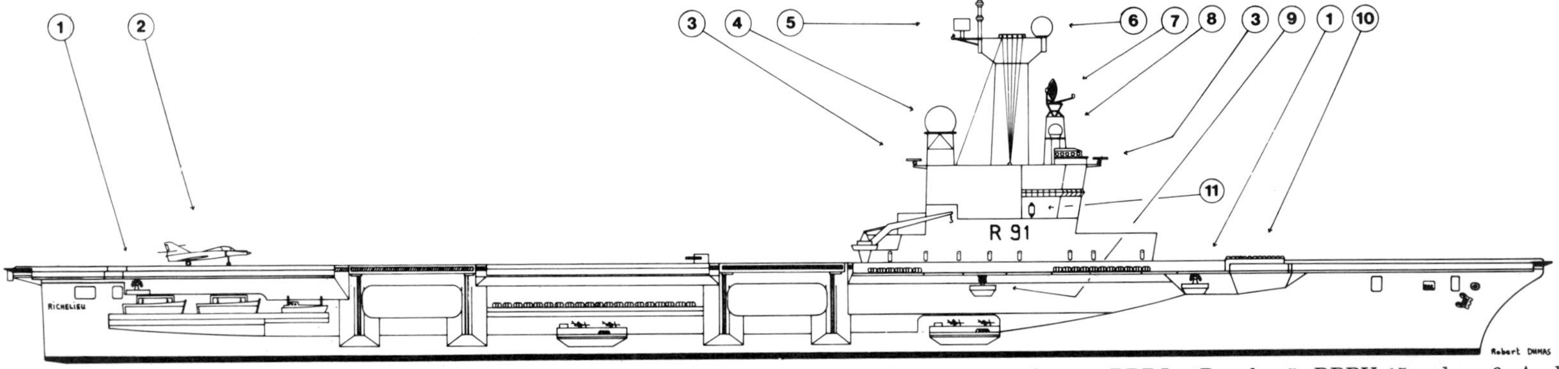


**Charles De Gaulle (R 91)** 1. Sagaie decoy launchers 2. Super-Etendard fighter-bomber 3. Decca nav. radar 4. DRBJ 11B radar 5. DRBV 15 radar 6. Arabel radar 7. DRBV 27 early-warning radar 8. Syracuse SATCOMM antenna 9. SADRAL point-defense SAM 10. SAAM vertical launchers 11. ARBB 33 jammers

## AIRCRAFT CARRIERS

### ◆ 2 Clemenceau class

| | Budget | Bldr | Laid down | L | In serv. |
|---|---|---|---|---|---|
| R 98 CLEMENCEAU | 1953 | Brest Arsenal | 11-55 | 21-12-57 | 22-11-61 |
| R 99 FOCH | 1955 | Ch. Atlantique | 2-57 | 28-7-60 | 15-7-63 |

**D:** 22,000 tons (27,307 mean, 32,700 fl) **S:** 32 kts
**Dim:** 265.0 (238.0 pp) × 31.72 beam × 51.2 flight deck × 7.8 light draft × 8.6 fl
**A:** R 98: 2/Crotale EDIR SAM syst. (VIII × 2; 36 missiles)—4/100-mm Model 1953 DP—16/Super-Étendard, 10/F-8E Crusader, 3/Étendard IVP, 7/Alizé, 2 or more/helicopters
**Electron Equipt:** Radar: 1/Decca 1226, 1/DRBV 23B, 1/DRBV 15, 2/DRBI 10, 2/DRBC 32C, 1/NRBA 51
Sonar: SQS-503—TACAN: SRN-6
EW: ARBR 16, ARBR 17, ARBX 10, 2 Dagaie RL, 2 Sagaie RL
**M:** 2 sets Parsons GT; 2 props; 126,000 hp **Electric:** 14,000 kw
**Boilers:** 6; 45 kg/cm$^2$, 450°C **Fuel:** 3,720 tons **Endurance:** 60 days
**Armor:** Reinforced flight deck, armored bulkheads in engine room and magazines, reinforced-steel bridge superstructure
**Range:** 4,800/23; 7,500/18

Clemenceau (R 98) — L. & L. Van Ginderen, 6-87

**Foch (R 99)**—prior to modifications — M. Bar, 9-86

**Clemenceau (R 98)**—with Crotale SAM system — J.-C. Bellonne, 1987

**Man:** Peacetime: as aircraft carriers: 64 officers, 476 petty officers, 798 other enlisted. Total: 1,338 men
As helicopter carriers: 45 officers, 392 petty officers, 547 other enlisted. Total: 984

REMARKS: Flight deck 257 m in length; deck angled at 8°, 165.5 × 29.5; deck forward of the angled deck: 93 × 28; width of the deck abreast the island: 35. Hangar dimensions, 180 × 22 to 24 × 7 (height). Two elevators 16 m long, 11 m in width, one forward on the main flight deck, one slightly abaft the island, able to raise a 15-ton aircraft 8.50 m in 9 seconds. Two 50-meter Mitchell-Brown type BS5 steam catapults, able to launch 15/20-ton aircraft at 110 knots, one forward, another on the angled deck. New catapult mechanisms installed in the mid-1980s. Optical-mirror landing equipment of French manufacture.

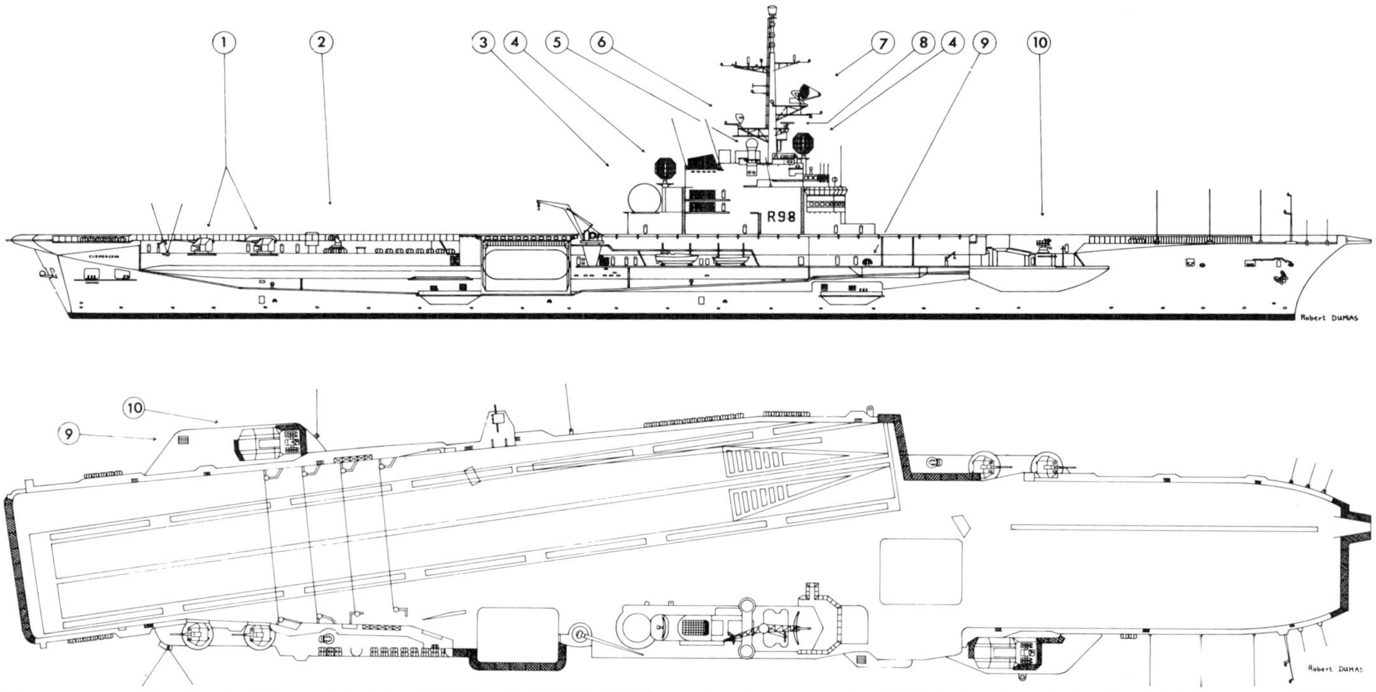


**Clemenceau (R 98)** 1. 100-mm Model 1953 DP 2. DRBC 32C f.c. radar directors 3. NRBA 51 aircraft landing-aid radar 4. DRBI 10 height-finding radar 5. Syracuse SATCOMM antenna radomes 6. DRBV 15 search radar 7. DRBV 23B early-warning radar 8. Decca 1226 nav. radar 9. Sagaie decoy RL 10. Crotale EDIR SAM launchers

**AIRCRAFT CARRIERS** *(continued)*

The propulsion machinery was built by the Chantiers de l'Atlantique. Living spaces are air-conditioned. Medium-sized island with three bridges: flag, navigation, aviation. Communication systems, especially with fighter aircraft, are a significant aspect of the ships' capabilities.

The *Foch,* built in a special dry dock at St. Nazaire, was towed to Brest for the installation of her armament.

*Aviation fuel:* 1,800 $m^3$ of jet fuel and 109 $m^3$ of aviation gasoline carried by the *Foch;* 1,200 $m^3$ of jet fuel and 400 $m^3$ of aviation gasoline by the *Clemenceau.*

Between September 1977 and November 1978, *Clemenceau* underwent a significant refit in the Toulon dockyard. The work consisted of a general overhaul of her installations and living spaces, modernization of the flight deck, reinforcement of the arresting gear, strengthening of the catapults, machinery overhaul, and the addition of two auxiliary boilers. Her electronic systems were modernized, and she was given the SENIT 2 combat data system removed from the inactivated destroyer *Jaurreguibery.* On the *Clemenceau,* this system has three main functions: establishment of a situation based on information from external sources (land-based radars, aircraft, ships); dissemination of those data to the ship and to other ships; and assistance in decision making. The ship was equipped with a closed-circuit television system that displays needed information in interested parts of the ship: flight-deck control, the combat operations center, the ready rooms, the air operations office. To operate the Super-Étendard, the *Clemenceau* has been fitted with a central inertial guidance system that transfers information to the inertial guidance system in each plane. Her magazines have been modified to carry AN-52 tactical nuclear weapons. The *Foch* underwent a similar overhaul 15-7-80 to 4-12-81, receiving SENIT 2 from the inactivated destroyer *Tartu. Clemenceau* received the DALLAS laser landing aid early in 1988 as a prototype for *Charles De Gaulle.*

*Clemenceau* refitted 1-9-85 to 31-8-86 to improve sensor and defensive systems, including the substitution of two Crotale EDIR systems for four of the 100-mm guns and catapult overhaul. *Foch* began modernization to a similar standard in 2-87. Both received Syracuse SATCOMM systems during refits ending in 1984. *Clemenceau* to strike 1996, *Foch* in 2001.

◆ **1 helicopter-carrier and cadet training ship**

| | Budget | Bldr | Laid down | L | In serv. |
|---|---|---|---|---|---|
| R 97 Jeanne d'Arc (ex-*La Résolue*) | 1957 | Brest Ars. | 7-7-60 | 30-9-61 | 30-6-64 |

**D:** 10,000 tons (12,365 fl) **S:** 26.5 kts (cruising)
**Dim:** 182.0 (172.0 wl) × 24.0 × 22.0 (wl) × 6.6 (7.3 aft)
**A:** 6/MM 38 Exocet—4/100-mm DP Model 1953 (I × 4)—3/WG-13 Lynx helicopters—3/Alouette-III helicopters
**Electron Equipt:** Radar: 1/DRBV 22D, 1/DRBV 50, 1/DRBN 32, 3/DRBC 32A
Sonar: DUBV 24—TACAN: SRN-6
EW: ARBR 16, 2 Syllex RL (VIII × 2)
**M:** 2 sets Rateau-Bretagne GT; 2 props; 40,000 hp **Electric:** 4,400 kw
**Boilers:** 4 asymmetric, multitube, 45 kg/$cm^2$—superheat 450°C
**Fuel:** 1,360 tons **Range:** 3,000/26.5; 3,750/25; 5,500/20; 6,800/16
**Man:** Ships company: 31 officers, 182 petty officers, 414 other enlisted

Remarks: Replaced the former cruiser *Jeanne d'Arc* as a training ship for officer cadets; when on this mission, she carries only the aircraft listed above. In wartime, she would be used for ASW missions, amphibious assault, or as a troop transport. The number of Super-Frélon heavy helicopters can be quickly augmented by simple structural changes.

**Jeanne d'Arc (R 97)**—at end of refit LSPH E. Pitman, R.A.N., 2-86

**Jeanne d'Arc (R 97)** L. & L. Van Ginderen, 7-86

Aviation facilities include: a 62 × 21-m flight deck aft of the island structure, which permits the simultaneous takeoff of two helicopters, while two machines can be stationed forward of the takeoff area and two others astern, one on each side of the elevator. An elevator (12-ton capacity) is located at the after end of the flight deck.

The hangar deck can, if some of the living quarters used by midshipmen are removed, accommodate eight helicopters. At the after end of the hangar deck there are machine shops for maintenance and repair, including helicopter electronic equipment and an area for inspection. The compartments for handling weapons and ammunition (torpedoes, missiles, etc.) are there also.

In addition to the navigation bridge, the superstructure contains a helicopter-control bridge, a modular-type information-and-operations center, and a combined control center for amphibious operations. Two LCVP landing craft are carried.

The engineering spaces are divided into two compartments, each with two boilers and a turbine, separated by a bulkhead.

The *Jeanne d'Arc* was in refit during 1983–84; the DRBI 10 height-finding radar was removed. DRBV 51 f.c. radar is to replace DRBV 50. Installation of SENIT-2 data system no longer planned.

## NAVAL AVIATION

The Naval Air establishment is made up of combatant flotillas, maintenance squadrons or sections, bases, schools, and the special services necessary to ensure the efficient operation of the flight components. First aircraft received 26 December 1910.

Administration is handled by the Aeronautical Division of the Naval General Staff and the Central Service Branch of Naval Air, both headed by flag officers. Operational and training matters are directed by the Navy Staff, whose various bureaus include aviation officers.

Primary training in fixed-wing planes is provided by the Air Force; helicopter pilots are given initial training by the Army as well as the Air Force. Specialization of pilots in multi-engine aircraft or in carrier-based fixed-wing and rotary aircraft is provided by Naval Air. The latter also trains navigators and maintenance crews at the Naval Air School, Rochefort.

The combat flotillas are:

(a) those embarked, which, flying from aircraft carriers or helicopter carriers, carry out intercept, attack, reconnaissance, or CAP missions and engage in antisubmarine warfare;

(b) maritime patrol flotillas and antisubmarine warfare flotillas that are land-based.

The service support squadrons and sections have various missions: schools, training exercises, transportation, logistical support for seagoing forces, experimental and salvage operations.

Authority over embarked flotillas and squadrons is assigned to a rear admiral, commander, aircraft carriers and seagoing aviation (ALPA).

Maritime patrol squadrons are commanded by a rear admiral (ALPATMAR).

Shore-based flotillas, squadrons, and sections are commanded by the Préfets Maritimes (Naval District Commandants) through the regional aviation commanders.

Bases: Nîmes-Garon, Saint-Mandrier (helicopters), Saint-Raphaël (experimental station), Hyères, Cuers (maintenance), Ajaccio-Aspretto (training), Lorient-Lann Bihoué, Lanvéoc-Poulmic (helicopters), Landivisiau.

Fixed-wing combat aircraft in service at end 1986 were: 27 F-8E Crusader interceptors, 64 Super-Étendard fighter-bombers, 13 Étendard IVP reconnaissance fighters, 22 Alizé ASW aircraft, 31 Atlantic Mk 1 land-based ASW aircraft, and 5 Gardian patrol aircraft. Combat helicopters included 16 Super-Frélon heavy helicopters, 38 WG-13 Lynx ASW helicopters, and 13 Alouette-III. Support aircraft included 19 Étendard IVM fighter trainers, 12 CM-175 Zephyr jet trainers, 9 MS-760 Paris trainers, 6 Falcon 10 MER communications jets, 23 Nord 23 trainer/transports, 17 EMB 121 Xingu light transports, 12 Piper Navajo light transports, 11 Socata 100 and 10 Robin HR 100 light communications, 6 CAP 10B air experience aircraft, and 7 Alouette-II helicopters.

NAVAL AVIATION *(continued)*

**Super-Étendard** J.M. Guhl, 1984

**Super-Étendard**—in new camouflage paint scheme B. Prézelin, 1987

FIRST-LINE OPERATIONAL COMBAT ORGANIZATIONS

| Flotilla | Subordination | Bases | Equipment | Missions |
|---|---|---|---|---|
| **4 F** | ALPA | Lann-Bihoué | **8 Alizé** | ASW |
| **6 F** | ALPA | Nîmes-Garons | **8 Alizé** | ASW |
| **11 F** | ALPA | Landivisiau | **12 Super-Étendard** | Attack |
| **12 F** | ALPA | Landivisiau | **12 Crusader (F-8E)** | Interception |
| **14 F** | ALPA | Landivisiau | **14 Super-Étendard** | Attack |
| **16 F** | ALPA | Landivisiau | **8 Étendard IV P** | Reconnaissance |
| **17 F** | ALPA | Hyères | **12 Super-Étendard** | Attack |
| **21 F** | ALPATMAR | Nîmes-Garons | **7 Atlantic Mk 1** | Maritime patrol |
| **22 F** | ALPATMAR | Nîmes-Garons | **7 Atlantic Mk 1** | Maritime patrol |
| **23 F** | ALPATMAR | Lann-Bihoué | **7 Atlantic Mk 1** | Maritime patrol |
| **24 F** | ALPATMAR | Lann-Bihoué | **7 Atlantic Mk 1** | Maritime patrol |
| **31 F** | ALPA | St. Mandrier | **14 WG-13 Lynx** | ASW |
| **32 F** | ALPA | Lanvéoc-Poulmic | **6 Super-Frélon** | ASW & troop transport |
| **33 F** | ALPA | St. Mandrier | **7 Super-Frélon** | Troop transport |
| **34 F** | ALPA | Lanvéoc-Poulmic | **11 WG-13 Lynx** | ASW |
| **35 F** | ALPA | *Jeanne d'Arc* or Lanvéoc-Poulmic | **3 WG-13 Lynx**<br>**3 Alouette-III** | |
| **12 S** | ALPATMAR | Faaa, Tahiti | **3 Gardian** | Maritime patrol |
| **4 S** | ALPATMAR | Tontouta, New Caledonia | **2 Gardian** | Maritime patrol |

**Étendard IVP**—in new camouflage B. Prézelin, 5-86

A new ACM *(Avion de Combat Marine)* fighter-bomber to replace the Super-Étendard in the late 1990s is in the planning stages. A flight-demonstrator prototype, the Rafale (ACX) flew in 1986, powered by two G.E. F404 engines; the production aircraft would be powered by two SNECMA M88 engines of 7,500-lb thrust each.

A total of 42 Atlantique Mk 2 patrol aircraft are planned, 16 in the 1984–88 Plan. The prototype was completed in mid-1981, but the first production aircraft is to be delivered in 1989.

**F-8E Crusader** 1987

**Alizé**—with radome extended 1987

**Gardian (Falcon 20)** French Navy, 1984

**Super-Frélon** B. Prézelin, 5-86

## NAVAL AVIATION *(continued)*

**Alouette-III** B. Prézelin, 5-86

**Atlantique Mk 2 prototype**

**WG-13 Lynx** B. Prézelin, 5-86

**Atlantic Mk I**

| Type | Mission | Wingspan | Length | Height | Weight (max.) kilos | Engine | Max. speed in Mach or in knots | Maximum ceiling | Range | Weapons | Remarks |
|---|---|---|---|---|---|---|---|---|---|---|---|
| ◆ **SHIP-BASED PLANES** | | | | | | | | | | | |
| **CRUSADER F8-E (FN)** (Ling-Temco-Vought) | All-weather interceptor | 10.72 | 16.61 | 4.80 | 13,000 | 1 J57 P20 *A* Pratt & Whitney turbojet with after-burner | Mach 1.8 | 50,000 ft | 1,500 miles 2 hr 30 min | 4/20-mm guns, M 530 air-to-air missiles | (1) 2 Flotilles are modified to carry the ANT 52 nuclear bomb. Fifty to carry ASMP.<br>(2) Modernized 1980–84 with Iguane radar, Omega radio-navigation equipment, and ARAR 12-A intercept gear.<br>(3) Can be outfitted with a small photo pod for reconnaissance missions.<br>The Atlantique Mk 2, which will enter service in 1989, will have the same airframe, engines, and characteristics as the Mk I but its weapon system will be entirely new, built around a Type 15 M digital tactical computer. It will be able to transport 3 tons of weapons, e.g., 4 Martel under the wings or 2 AM 39 inboard.<br>(4) Localization, classification, and attack of contacts picked up by an antisubmarine ship. Carries DUAV-4 dipping sonar.<br>(5) Detection, identification, and neutralization of small surface vessels with weak antiaircraft defense. 4 equipped with MAD for ASW. |
| **SUPER-ÉTENDARD** (Dassault) (1) | Fleet air defense, attack | 9.60 | 14.35 | 3.85 | 11,900 | 1 8 K 50 SNECMA turbojet developing 5 tons of thrust | Mach 1 at 11,000 m; Mach 0.97 at low altitude | | | 2/30-mm guns, bombs, rockets, or one AM 39 | |
| **Étendard IVP** (Dassault) | Photo-reconnaissance | 9.60 | 14.50 | 3.85 | 10,200 | 1 SNECMA Atar 8 turbojet | Mach 1.3 | 35,000 ft | 750 miles 1 hr 45 or 2 hr 15 with supplemental reserve tank | 100-mm rockets, 68-mm rockets, photo-flash bombs flash bombs | |
| **Alizé** (BR 1050) (Bréguet) (2) | AEW, ASW | 15.60 | 13.66 | 5 | 8,200 | 1 Rolls-Royce Dart 21 turboprop (1,925 hp + 230 kts of thrust) | 240 kts | 11,000 ft | 685 miles 3 hr 45 | Air-to-surface missiles, Mk 46 torpedoes, 100-mm rockets, ASW depth charges 50- to 250-kg bombs, acoustic buoys, mortar-type projectiles | |
| ◆ **LAND-BASED PLANES** | | | | | | | | | | | |
| Gardian (Bréguet) | Maritime surveillance, search & rescue | 16.3 | 17.15 | 5.32 | 15,200 | 2 Garrett ATF3 turbojets | Mach 0.86 | 42,000 ft | 2,200 n. miles 5 hr 30 min | Varan radar, ventral chute to launch rescue gear | |
| **Atlantic Mk 1** (Br 1150) (Bréguet) (3) | Patrol, ASW (2) | 36.30 | 31.75 | 11.33 | 43,500 | 2 Rolls-Royce Tyne 20 turboprops, 6,000 hp each | 300 kts | 30,000 ft | 4,300 miles 17 hr | Air-to-surface missiles, L 4 or Mk 46 torpedoes, ASW depth charges, sonobuoys, mortar-type projectiles (ASW), photo-flash bombs | |
| ◆ **HELICOPTERS** | | | | | | | | | | | |
| **Super-Frélon** (S.N.I.A.S.) | ASW (2 used as transports) | 18.90 (rotor diameter) | 23 | 6.35 | 13,000 | 3 C3 Turboméca III turboshafts, each with 1,500 hp | 145 kts | 10,000 ft | 420 miles 3 hr 30 min | Mk 46 ASW torpedoes | |
| **Lynx (WG-13)** (Westland S.N.I.A.S.) (4) | ASW (3) and surface attack aircraft (4) | 12.80 (rotor diameter) | 15.2 | 3.20 | 4,150 | 2 BS 360 Rolls-Royce Gem turboshafts, of 900 or 750 hp each | 150 kts | 12,000 ft | 1 hr 30, half hovering, half in flight 2 hr 30 min with 3 men and 4 missiles | Mk 46 torpedoes, air-to-surface missiles | |
| **Alouette-III** (S.N.I.A.S.) (5) | ASW (6) | 11.02 (rotor diameter) | 12.8 | 3.0 | 2,200 | 1 Turbomeca Astazou turboshaft, 870 hp | 110 kts | 10,000 ft | 325 miles 2 hr 30 min | Mk 46 torpedoes | |

NAVAL AVIATION *(continued)*

**Xingu multi-engine trainer** French Navy, 1983

## BALLISTIC-MISSILE SUBMARINES

General Note for Submarines: Names and pendant numbers ceased to be displayed on 1-1-83, to augment security.

◆ **0 (+1 + 2) SNLE-NG new design** Bldr: DCAN, Cherbourg

| | Laid down | L | In serv. |
|---|---|---|---|
| S . . . Le Triomphant | 1988 | . . . | 1994 |

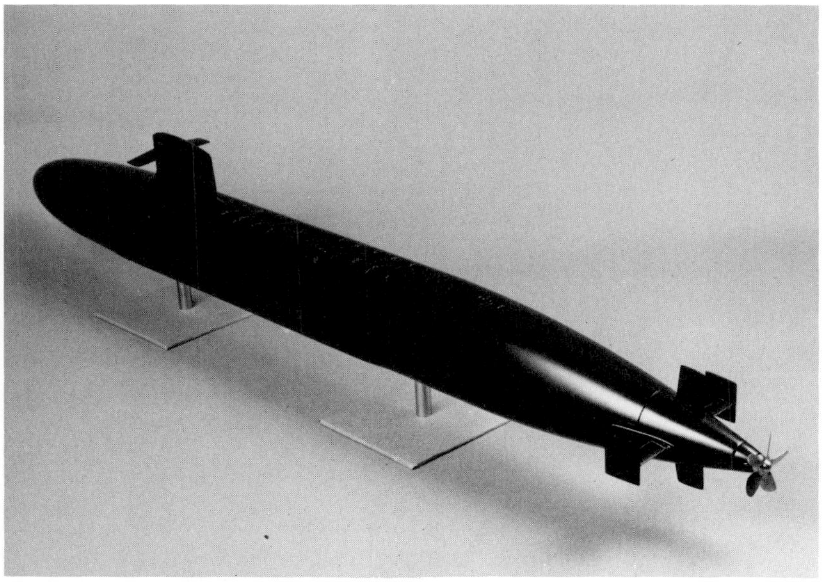

**Model of the "SNLE-NG"** STCAN, 1987

**D:** 12,700 tons/14,200 submerged **S:** over 25 kts (sub.)
**Dim:** 138.00 × 12.50 × . . .
**A:** 16/M 4S ballistic missiles—. . ./533-mm TT (SM 39 missiles, torpedoes)
**Electron Equipt:** Radar: . . .—EW: . . .
Sonar: . . .
**M:** 1 Type K15, 150-megawatt pressurized-water reactor; 1 large-diameter prop; 41,500 hp
**Man:** 2 crews, 100–110 total each

Remarks: First of a "new generation," first announced 1981. Will use new NLES 100, high-elasticity steel for pressure hull and a potential 500-m diving depth. Careful attention to radiated noise reduction, including "rafted" (isolated) propulsion plant and large-diameter, low rpm propeller. Sail-mounted bow planes and vertical surfaces at ends of stern planes.

The initial ship will have the M 45 missile, with TN-71 warheads. The third ship will have the M 5 missile with TN-75 warheads, to be backfitted into the first two.

◆ **1 L'Inflexible class**

| | Bldr | Laid down | L | In serv. |
|---|---|---|---|---|
| S 615 L'Inflexible | DCAN, Cherbourg | 27-3-80 | 23-6-82 | 1-4-85 |

**D:** 8,080/8,920 tons **S:** over 20 kts (sub.) **Dim:** 128.70 × 10.60 × 10.00
**A:** 16/M 4 ballistic missiles—4/533-mm TT fwd (12 torpedoes or SM 39 missiles)
**Electron Equipt:** Radar: DRUA 33—EW: radar detector
Sonar: DSUX 21 multifunction, DUUX 5, DSUV 61 towed array
**M:** 1 pressurized-water reactor, 2 steam turbines; turbo-reduction drive; 1 prop; 16,000 hp—electric emergency propulsion with 5,000-n.m. range
**Man:** 2 crews in rotation, each of 15 officers, 120 men

Remarks: Ordered 9-78, *L'Inflexible* has most characteristics in common with the five preceding SSBNs of *Le Redoutable* class, but takes advantage of many technological advances in propulsion, sonar systems, navigation systems, etc., and is able to dive 100 m deeper. The ship was equipped from the outset with the M 4 missile, which has six TN-70 150-kt Multiple Independent Re-entry Vehicle (MIRV) warheads. Sail planes higher on more streamlined sail than in *Le Redoutable* class. First patrol began 25-5-85.

◆ **5 nuclear-powered Le Redoutable class** Bldr: DCAN, Cherbourg

| | Laid down | L | Trials | In serv. |
|---|---|---|---|---|
| S 611 Le Redoutable | 11-64 | 29-3-67 | 7-69 | 1-12-71 |
| S 612 Le Terrible | 22-6-67 | 12-12-69 | 1971 | 1-1-73 |
| S 610 Le Foudroyant | 12-12-69 | 4-12-71 | 5-73 | 6-6-74 |
| S 613 L'Indomptable | 4-12-71 | 17-9-74 | 12-75 | 23-12-76 |
| S 614 Le Tonnant | 10-74 | 17-9-77 | 4-79 | 3-4-80 |

**Le Terrible (S 612)** E.C.P.A., 1978

**Le Foudroyant (S 610)** L. & L. Van Ginderen, 2-83

**D:** 8,000/9,000 tons **S:** 20 kts max. **Dim:** 128.0 × 10.6 × 10.0
**A:** 16 M 20 or M 4 ballistic missiles—4/550-mm TT fwd (18 L 5 and F 17 torpedoes)
**Electron Equipt:** Radar: 1/DRUA 33—EW: radar detector
Sonar: 1/DUUV 23, 1/DUUX 2

**Le Triomphant (S 615)** J. Biaugeaud, 1985

**BALLISTIC-MISSILE SUBMARINES** *(continued)*

**M:** Principal: 1 pressurized-water reactor, 2 steam turbines with 1 set turboreduction gears; 1 prop; 16,000 hp
Secondary: 1 electric motor driven by batteries powered by 1 SEMT-Pielstick 16 PA4, 850-kw diesel generator set (sufficient fuel for 5,000 n.m.)
**Man:** Twin crews of 15 officers and 120 men for each ship, manning in rotation

REMARKS: *Le Redoutable* (authorized in March 1963) and other submarines of this class are the principal elements of the French naval deterrent. They can dive more than 200 meters. All, with the exception of *Le Redoutable,* are being backfitted to carry the M 4 missile. The substitution will not require replacing the existing missile tubes. The sonar suit will be upgraded by the installation of DSUX 21, and other equipment will be modernized. S 614 began modernization 1-2-85 at Cherbourg, completing 17-6-86. S 613 followed, with S 612 and then S 610 last to complete in late 1987.

NOTE: Trials ballistic-missile submarine *Gymnote* (S 655) stricken 17-7-86.

**NUCLEAR-POWERED ATTACK SUBMARINES**

◆ **0 (+4) "Améthyste" class** Bldr: DCAN, Cherbourg

| | | Laid down | L | Trials | In serv. |
|---|---|---|---|---|---|
| S 605 | AMÉTHYSTE | 31-10-83 | 1988 | ... | 3rd quarter '91 |
| S 606 | N... | 27-3-87 | 1990 | ... | 4th quarter '92 |
| S... | N... | ... | 1993 | ... | 3rd quarter '95 |
| S... | N... | ... | ... | ... | ... |

**D:** 2,400/2,660 tons **S:** 25 kts (sub.) **Dim:** 73.6 × 7.60 × 6.40
**A:** 4/533-mm TT, rapid-loading (14 weapons: F 17 Mod. 2 and L 5 Mod. 3 torpedoes, SM 39 Exocet, FG 29 mines)
**Electron Equipt:** Radar: . . .—EW: ARUR, ARUD
Sonar: DSUV 62 towed array; multifunction hull array
**M:** 1 48-megawatt natural circulation, pressurized-water reactor turboelectric drive; 2 turboalternator sets; 1 electric motor; 1 prop; 9,500 hp—emergency backup system: 200 kw
**Endurance:** 90 days **Man:** 8 officers, 58 men

REMARKS: S 605 and 606 ordered 17-10-84. Will employ all improved, body-of-revolution hull form of HLES 80 steel, with lengthened bow. Will have two crews, improved combat data, sensor, and communications systems. Syracuse II SATCOMM capability. "Améthyste" is an acronym for "Amélioration Tactique Transmission Écoute," i.e. reduced radiated noise transmission.

◆ **3 (+1) Rubis class, Type SNA 72** Bldr: DCAN, Cherbourg

| | Laid down | L | Trials | In serv. |
|---|---|---|---|---|
| S 601 RUBIS (ex-*Provence*) | 11-12-76 | 7-7-79 | 1-4-81 | 23-2-83 |
| S 602 SAPHIR (ex-*Bretagne*) | 1-9-79 | 1-9-81 | 1-7-83 | 6-7-84 |
| S 603 CASABIANCA (ex-*Bourgogne*) | 9-81 | 22-12-84 | 4-86 | 21-4-87 |
| S 604 ÉMERAUDE | 10-82 | 12-4-86 | 10-87 | 11-88 |

**D:** 2,265 std./2,385 surf./2,670 tons sub. **S:** 25 kts **Dim:** 72.10 × 7.60 × 6.40
**A:** 4/533-mm TT fwd (14 torpedoes, SM 39 missiles, or mines)
**Electron Equipt:** Radar: 1/DRUA 33—EW: ARUR, ARUD
Sonar: 1/DSUV 22, 1/DUUA 2B, 1/DUUX 5, TUUM, DSUV 62
**M:** Principal: 1 48-megawatt pressurized-water reactor; two turboalternator sets; 1 electric motor; 1 prop; 9,500 hp

**Casabianca (S 603)** 1987

**Saphir (S 602)** J. Pradignac, 5-85

Secondary: 1 electric motor driven by batteries powered by 1 SEMT-Pielstick 16PA4, 85-kw diesel generator set
**Endurance:** 45 days **Man:** 8 officers, 35 chief petty officers, 22 other enlisted

REMARKS: Names for the first two changed 11-80. Fire-control, torpedo-launching, and submarine-detection systems are the same as for the *Agosta* class. *Rubis* was financed under the Third Military Equipment Plan. The second through the fourth came under the Fourth Plan (1977–82). *Rubis's* reactor became operational early 2-81, and trials started 6-81. S 602 the first to carry the SM 39 Exocet missile. All have the Pivair optronic periscope and employ the SADE automated combat data system. Diving depth: 300 m. Hull of HLES 80 steel. Two crews per submarine.

**ATTACK SUBMARINES**

◆ **4 Agosta class** Bldr: DCAN, Cherbourg

| | Laid down | L | In serv. |
|---|---|---|---|
| S 620 AGOSTA | 10-11-72 | 19-10-74 | 28-7-77 |
| S 621 BÉVÉZIERS | 17-5-73 | 14-6-75 | 27-9-77 |
| S 622 LA PRAYA | 1974 | 15-5-76 | 9-3-78 |
| S 623 OUESSANT | 1974 | 23-10-76 | 27-7-78 |

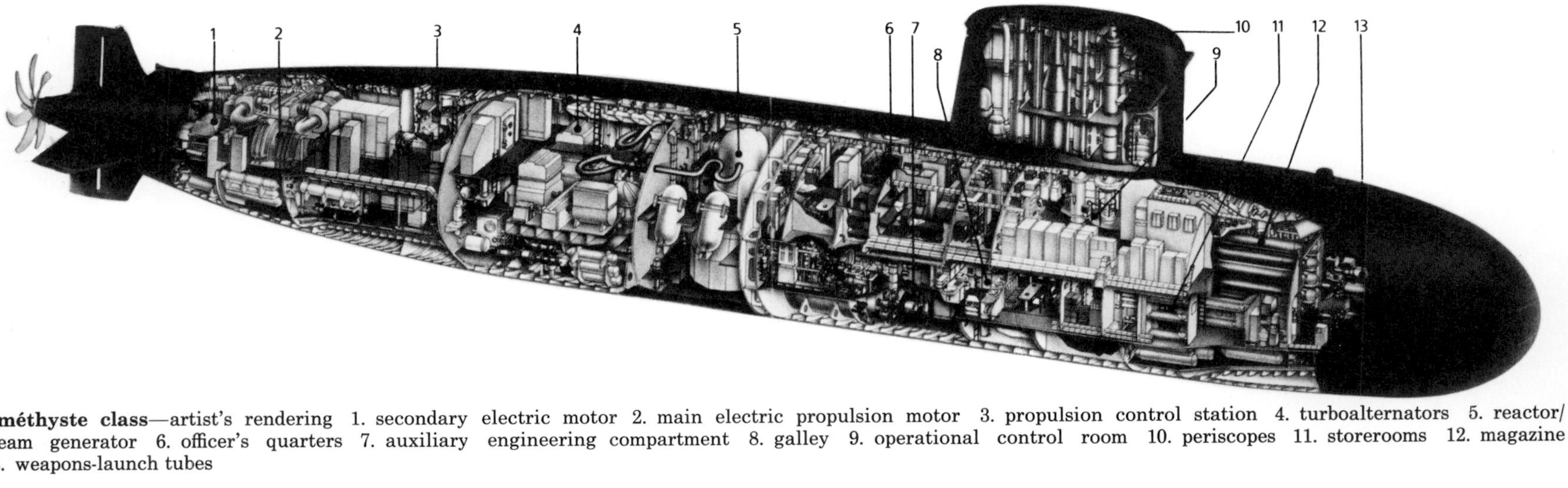


**Améthyste class**—artist's rendering 1. secondary electric motor 2. main electric propulsion motor 3. propulsion control station 4. turboalternators 5. reactor/steam generator 6. officer's quarters 7. auxiliary engineering compartment 8. galley 9. operational control room 10. periscopes 11. storerooms 12. magazine 13. weapons-launch tubes

ATTACK SUBMARINES *(continued)*

**Agosta (S 620)** L. & L. Van Ginderen, 3-87

**Ouessant (S 623)** Pradignac & Leo, 6-86

**D:** 1,230/1,490/1,740 tons (fl) **S:** 12.5 kts/20.5 kts for 5 min., 17.5 kts for 1 hr.
**Dim:** 67.57 × 6.8 × 5.4
**A:** 4/550-mm TT fwd (20 L 5 Mod. 3 and F 17 torpedoes, SM 39 Exocet)
**Electron Equipt:** Radar: 1/DRUA 33—EW: ARUR, ARUD
Sonar: 1/DUUA 1D, 1/DUUA 2A, 1/DUUA 2D, 1/DSUV 22, 1/DUUX 2A, DSUV 62
**M:** 2 SEMT-Pielstick 320-16 PA 4 185 diesel generator sets (850 kw each); 1 × 3,500-kw propulsion motor; 1 prop; 4,600 hp (1 × 23-hp creep motor)
**Fuel:** 185 tons **Endurance:** 45 days **Man:** 7 officers, 47 men
**Range:** 8,500/9 (snorkel); 178/3.5 (creep motor), 7,900/. . . surf. (1 engine)

REMARKS: Oceangoing submarines, authorized in the 1970–75 program. Weapons and equipment similar to the refitted *Daphné* class. DLA D3 fire control centralized in one computer bank. Air-conditioned. Retractable deck fittings on hull exterior. Advanced techniques for quiet operations both inboard and outboard. The torpedo tubes accept torpedoes of either 550-mm or 533-mm diameter. S 621 used in SM 39 Exocet trials. 320-cell battery with twice the capacity of the *Daphné* class. Diving depth 300 m. Spain built four of this class of submarine, and Pakistan has two—from an embargoed South African order.

◆ **9 Daphné class**

| | Budget | Bldr | Laid down | L | In serv. |
|---|---|---|---|---|---|
| S 641 DAPHNÉ | 1955 | Dubigeon, Nantes | 3-58 | 20-6-59 | 1-6-64 |
| S 642 DIANE | 1955 | Dubigeon, Nantes | 7-58 | 4-10-60 | 20-6-64 |
| S 643 DORIS | 1955 | Cherbourg Ars. | 1-9-58 | 14-5-60 | 26-8-64 |
| S 645 FLORE | 1956 | Cherbourg Ars. | 1-9-58 | 21-12-60 | 21-5-64 |
| S 646 GALATÉE | 1956 | Cherbourg Ars. | 1-9-58 | 22-9-61 | 25-7-64 |
| S 648 JUNON | 1960 | Cherbourg Ars. | 7-61 | 11-5-64 | 25-2-66 |
| S 649 VÉNUS | 1960 | Cherbourg Ars. | 8-61 | 24-9-64 | 1-1-66 |
| S 650 PSYCHÉ | 1964 | Brest Arsenal | 5-65 | 28-6-67 | 1-7-69 |
| S 651 SIRÈNE | 1964 | Brest Arsenal | 5-65 | 28-6-67 | 1-3-70 |

**D:** 700 std./869 surf./1,043 tons sub. **S:** 13.5/16 kts
**Dim:** 57.75 × 6.76 × 5.25 (max.)
**A:** 12/550-mm TT, 8 fwd, 4 aft (no reloads)
**Electron Equipt:** Radar: 1/DRUA 33
Sonar: 1/DUUA 2B, 1/DSUV 2, 1/DUUX 2
**M:** 2 SEMT-Pielstick/Jeumont-Schneider 450-kw diesel generator sets; 2 × 1,000-hp (1,300 for a brief period) electric motors; 2 props—*see* Remarks
**Range:** 4,300/7.5 (snorkel) **Man:** 6 officers, 39 men

REMARKS: Development of the *Aréthuse* class. Very quiet when submerged. Modernized, beginning in 1971, with special attention given to detection equipment and weapons. S 650 and S 651 were the last modernized, in 1981. S 641, not fully modernized, does not have the large bow sonar dome. Can submerge to 300 meters. Have DLT D3 torpedo fire-control system. The first seven have Type 12 PA1 diesels, while S 650 and S 651 use Type 12 PA4-135. This class of submarine has been purchased by the following countries: Portugal, four in 1964; Pakistan, four in 1966, South Africa, three in 1967. Spain built four with French technical assistance. One Portuguese unit was sold to Pakistan in 1976. S 651 flooded and sank 11-10-72 but was salvaged; sisters *Minerve* (S 647) and *Eurydice* (S 644) lost 27-1-68 and 4-3-70.

**Galatée (S 646)** H. Ehlers, 2-87

**Vénus (S 649)** L. & L. Van Ginderen, 3-87

◆ **1 Narval-class trials submarine**

| | Bldr | Laid down | L | In serv. |
|---|---|---|---|---|
| S 633 DAUPHIN | Cherbourg Ars. | 5-52 | 17-9-55 | 1-8-58 |

**Dauphin (S 633)**—with experimental bow M. Bar, 9-86

**D:** 1,320 std./1,635 surf./1,910 tons sub. **S:** 15/18 kts
**Dim:** 80.50 × 7.82 × 5.40 **A:** . . .
**Electron Equipt:** Radar: DRUA 33
Sonar: . . .
**M:** 3 SEMT-Pielstick 12 PA4 motor generator sets; 2 electric motors; 2 props; 3,000 hp (2 × 40-hp creep motors)
**Endurance:** 45 days **Range:** 15,000/8 (snorkel) **Man:** 7 officers, 57 men

REMARKS: Rebuilt from 1966 to 1970; re-engined, with complete modernization of detection devices and weapons. Of sisters, *Requin,* modified 1980 for trials with the SM 39 submerged-launch missile, discarded 11-85; *Marsouin* (S 632) decommissioned 8-11-82 for cannibalization; *Narval* (S 631), which had a special swimmer-delivery vehicle housing on deck aft, stricken spring 1983; *Espadon* (S 637)

## ATTACK SUBMARINES *(continued)*

stricken 1985 as a museum exhibit; and *Morse* (S 638) was discarded 9-86. S 633 is used in trials of materials and equipment for future submarines, having had the bow for the new "Améthyste" series SSNs grafted on in 1986, extending her length 2.97 m.

## GUIDED-MISSILE CRUISER

| | Budget | Bldr | Laid down | L | In serv. |
|---|---|---|---|---|---|
| C 611 Colbert | 1953 | Brest | 12-53 | 24-3-56 | 5-5-59 |

**D:** 8,500 tons (11,300 fl) **S:** 31.5 kts
**Dim:** 180.80 (175.00 pp) × 20.20 (19.70 wl) × 7.90 (max.)
**A:** 4/MM 38 Exocet—1/Masurca SAM syst. (II × 1, 48 missiles)—2/100-mm DP, Model 1968 (I × 2)—12/57-mm AA (II × 6)
**Electron Equipt:** Radar: 1/DRBN 32, 1/DRBV 50, 1/DRBV 23C, 1/DRBV 20C, 2/DRBR 51, 1/DRBR 32C, 2/DRBC 31, 1/DRBI 10D
EW: ARBB 31, ARBB 32, ARBR 10F, 2/Syllex countermeasures RL—TACAN: SRN-6
**M:** 2 sets C.E.M. Parsons GT; 2 props; 86,000 hp **Electric:** 4,920 kw
**Boilers:** 4 asymmetric, multitube; 45 kg/cm$^2$, 450°C **Range:** 4,000/25
**Man:** 25 officers, 208 petty officers, 329 men
**Armor:** Deck: 50 mm, Belt: 50 to 80 mm

Remarks: Converted into a surface-to-air guided-missile cruiser between 4-70 and 10-72. The SENIT 1 tactical data system enables real-time control of the surface and air situation at the center of a widely dispersed formation, making this an excellent command ship, able also to coordinate the air defense of the formation. The ship can be used as a command post for an interservice operation overseas. During the 1970–72 refit the bridge superstructure was rebuilt, the electronic equipment for command and control was modernized, the electric power increased, and living spaces were improved, including air-conditioning. Four MM 38 Exocet antiship missiles were installed in 1980. In addition to the two DRBR 31 radar directors for the 57-mm AA guns, there are also four lead-computing visual directors. Machinery and boilers are installed in two separate compartments, each with two boilers and a turbine, separated by an 18-meter-long watertight compartment. Refitted 9-81 to 11-82, during which the Syracuse satellite communications system was fitted and the Masurca system updated. Flagship, Mediterranean Squadron. Scheduled for disposal in 1997.

## GUIDED-MISSILE DESTROYERS

### ◆ 0 (+2) Cassard (C 70 AA) class

| | Bldr | Laid down | L | In serv. |
|---|---|---|---|---|
| D 614 Cassard | DCAN, Lorient | 3-9-82 | 6-2-85 | 3-88 |
| D 615 Jean Bart | DCAN, Lorient | 5-84 | 1986 | 3-90 |

**Colbert (C 611)** Pradignac & Leo, 6-86

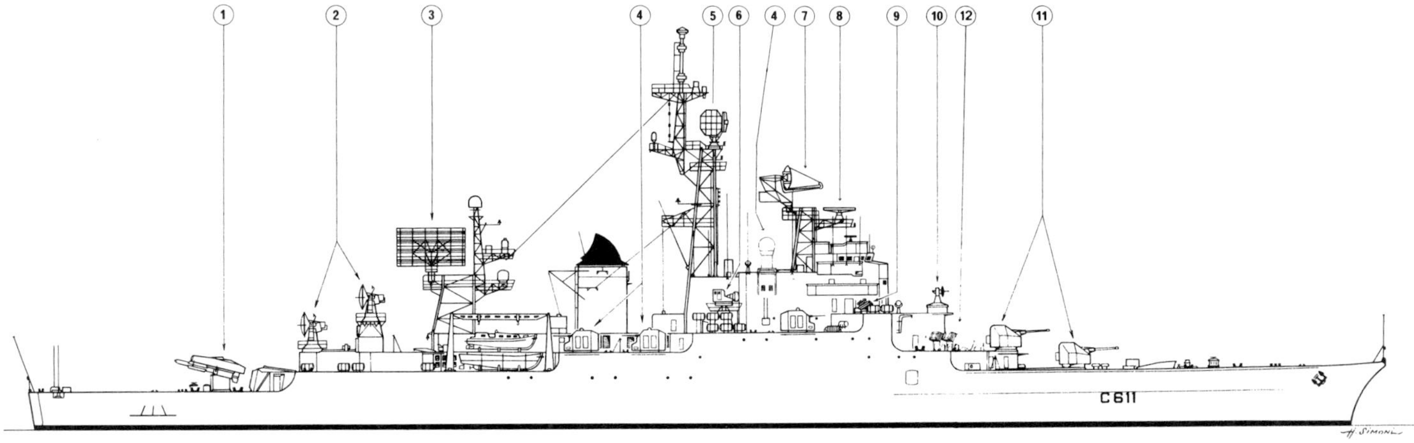


**Colbert** 1. Masurca twin launcher 2. DRBR 51 Masurca tracker/illuminator radars 3. DRBV 20C early-warning radar 4. Twin 57-mm AA mounts 5. DRBI 10D height-finding radar 6. DRBC 31 radar director for 57-mm AA 7. DRBV 23C stabilized air-search radar 8. DRBV 50 surface/air-search radar 9. Syllex chaff RL (VIII × 2) 10. DRBC 32C radar director for 100-mm guns 11. 10-mm Model 1968 dual-purpose guns 12. MM 38 Exocet launch cells (Note that the forward arrow marked "4" points to the Syracuse SATCOMM antenna radome rather then the forwardmost 57-mm AA mount.)

**GUIDED-MISSILE DESTROYERS** *(continued)*

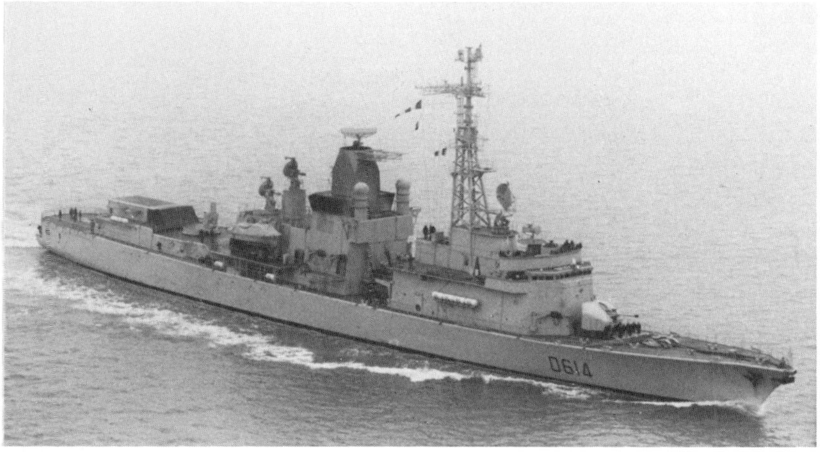

**Cassard (D 614)**—on trials B. Prézelin, 1-87

**D:** 3,820 tons (4,340 fl) **S:** 29.6 kts **Dim:** 139.00 (129.00 pp) × 14.00 × 5.50
**A:** 8/MM 40 SSM—1/Mk 13 launcher (40 Standard SM-1 MR missiles)—2/SADRAL systems (VI × 2)—1/100-mm Model 1968 DP—2/20-mm AA (I × 2)—2 fixed catapults for Type L-5 ASW torpedoes (10 torpedoes)—1/light helicopter
**Electron Equipt:** Radar: 2/Decca 1229, 1/DRBJ 11B, 1/DRBV 26, 2 SPG-51C, 1/DRBC 33
Sonar: 1/DUBA 25A—IR: DIBV 10 Vampir
EW: ARBB 33, ARBR 17, 2 Dagaie and 2 Sagaie countermeasures RL
**M:** 4 SEMT-Pielstick 18 PA 6 BTC diesels; 2 props; 42,300 hp
**Electric:** 3,400 kw **Fuel:** 600 tons **Range:** 4,800/24; 8,000/17
**Man:** 12 officers, 124 petty officers, 105 men (251 accom.)

Remarks: 1977–82 program; the first was authorized under the 1978 budget, the second under the 1979 budget. A third and fourth were authorized in 1983 but have since been canceled.

The Mk 13 launchers and missile fire-control systems are being taken from the *Kersaint* (converted T-47)-class destroyers. The design has been recast, with a second 100-mm mount aft being replaced by a helicopter shelter for a small, AS.15 missile-equipped helicopter, flanked on either side by launchers for SADRAL system short-range point-defense missiles. The space beneath the helicopter deck may eventually accommodate the DSBV 61 towed linear passive hydrophone array. The ships have the SENIT 6 digital data system, and the new DRBC 33 radar fire-control director is aided by a Piranha III t.v./laser attachment. Also installed are 2 CSEE Lynx and 2 Naja optronic directors. A SAMAHE deck traversing system will be fitted for the helicopter. The Model 1968 gun has a 78 rd/min firing capability.

**Cassard (D 614)** DCAN, 7-87

**Cassard (D 614)** H. Ehlers, 6-87

◆ **5 (+2) Georges Leygues (C 70 ASW) class** Bldr: Brest Arsenal

| | Laid down | L | In serv. |
|---|---|---|---|
| D 640 Georges Leygues | 16-9-74 | 17-12-76 | 10-12-79 |
| D 641 Dupleix | 17-10-75 | 2-12-78 | 16-6-81 |
| D 642 Montcalm | 5-12-75 | 31-5-80 | 28-5-82 |
| D 643 Jean de Vienne | 26-10-79 | 17-11-81 | 25-5-84 |
| D 644 Primauguet | 19-11-81 | 17-3-84 | 5-11-86 |
| D 645 La Motte-Picquet | 9-2-82 | 6-2-85 | 1988 |
| D 646 Latouche-Treville | 31-5-85 | ... | 1990 |

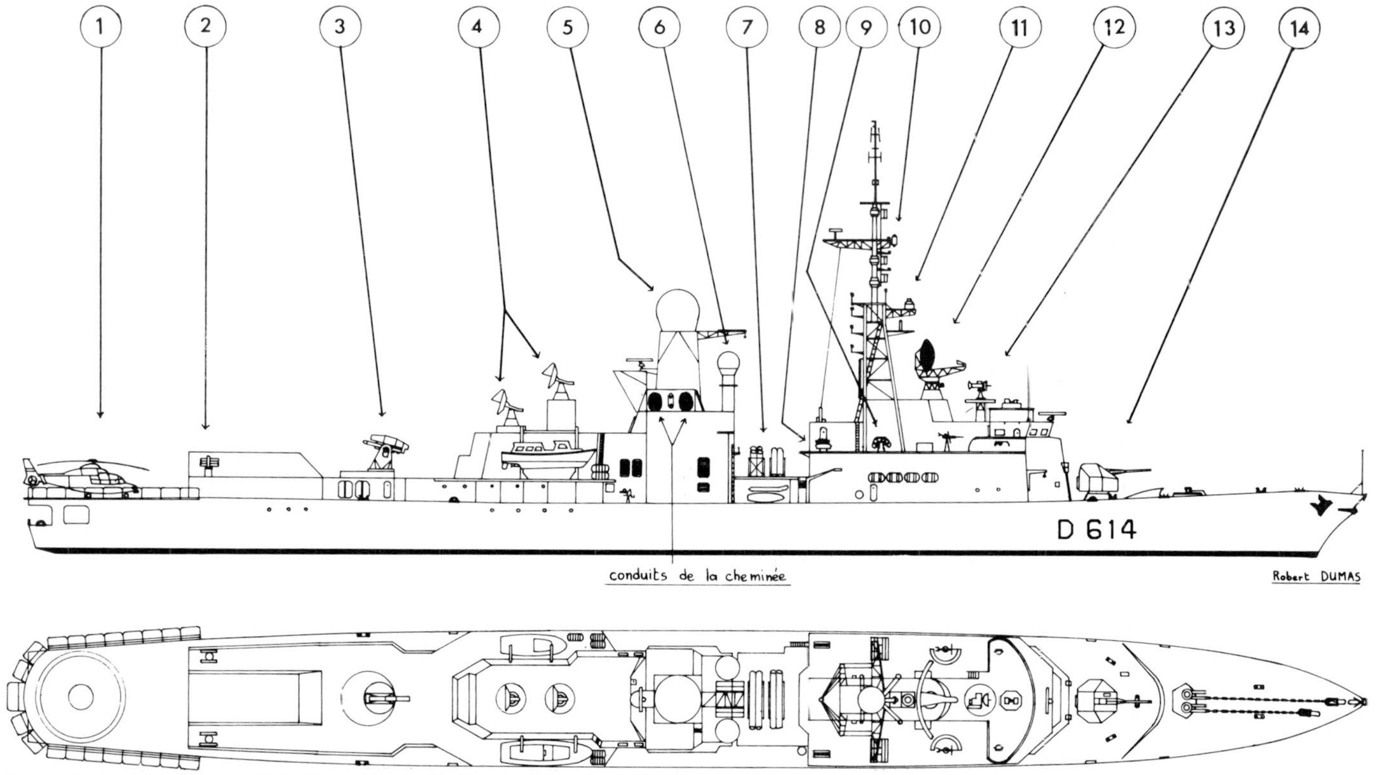


**Cassard (D 614)** 1. small helicopter 2. SADRAL launcher (VI × 2) 3. Mk 13 missile launcher for Standard SM-1 MR 4. SPG-51C tracker/illuminator radars 5. DRBJ 11B 3-D radar (DRBV 15 provisionally, as completed) 6. Syracuse SATCOMM antennas 7. MM 40 Exocet launch cells 8. Dagaie countermeasures launcher 9. Sagaie countermeasures launcher 10. DIBV 10 Vampir IR system 11. ARBR 17 EW antenna 12. DRBV 26 radar 13. DRBC 33 f.c. radar director 14. 100-mm DP

**GUIDED-MISSILE DESTROYERS** *(continued)*

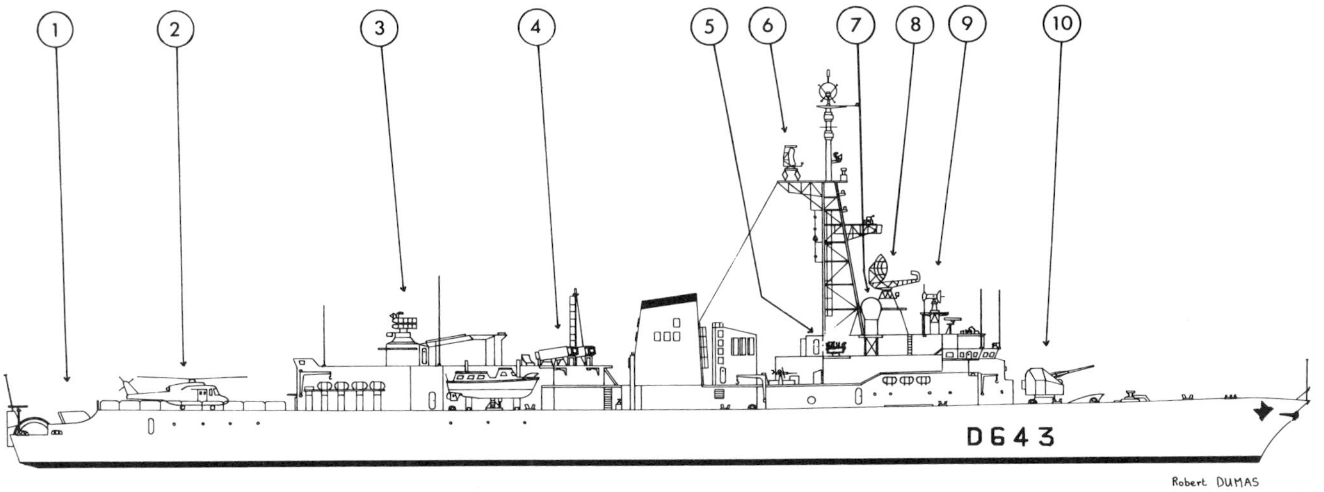


**Jean de Vienne (D 643)** 1. DUBV 43 towed sonar 2. Lynx helicopter 3. Crotale SAM system 4. MM 40 Exocet 5. Dagaie decoy launcher 6. DRBV 51C radar 7. Syracuse SATCOMM radome 8. DRBC 33 f.c. radar 9. 100-mm Model 1968 DP

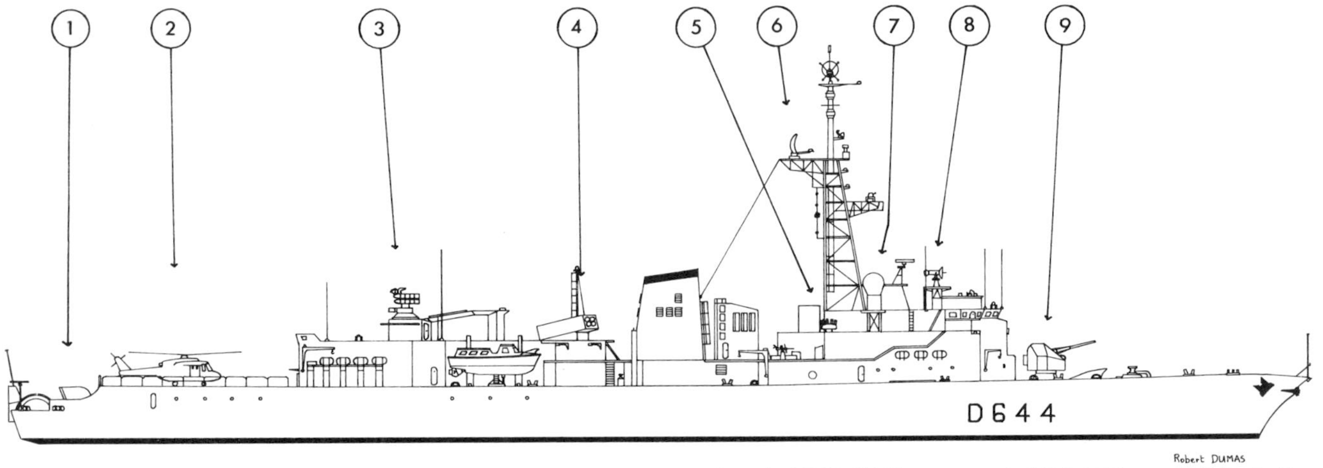


**Primauguet (D 644)** 1. DUBV 43 towed sonar 2. Lynx helicopter 3. Crotale EDIR SAM system 4. MM 40 Exocet SSM 5. Dagaie decoy launcher 6. DRBV 15 surveillance radar 7. Syracuse SATCOMM radome 8. DRBC 33 f.c. radar 9. 100-mm Model 1968 DP

**Primauguet (D 644)** Skyfotos, 10-86

**Dupleix (D 641)**—with MM 38 missiles L. & L. Van Ginderen, 6-87

**D:** 3,830 tons (4,170 fl) **S:** 30 kts (GT), 21 kts (diesels)
**Dim:** 139.00 (129.00 pp) × 14.00 × 4.10 (hull); 5.73 (props); 5.50 (sonar)
**A:** 4/MM 38 Exocet (D 642 and later: 8 MM 40)—1/Crotale system (VIII × 1; 26 missiles)—1/100-mm DP, Model 1968—2/20-mm AA (I × 2)—2 catapults for L-5 ASW torpedoes (10 torpedoes)—2/WG-13 Lynx helicopters
**Electron Equipt:** D 640–643: Radar: 2/DRBN 32 (Decca 1226), DRBV 26, DRBV 516C, 1/DRBC 32D
Sonar: DUBV 23 hull-mounted; DUBV 43B VDS
EW: ARBR 16, ARBR 11B (D/F), ARBB 32, 2/Syllex (D 643: Dagaie) countermeasures RL
D 644–646: Radar: 2/DRBN 32 (Decca RM 1226), DRBV 15A, 1/DRBC 33 with optronics
Sonar: DUBV 24C hull-mounted, DUBV 43B VDS, DSBV 61 towed array
EW: ARBR 17, HF monitoring syst, 2/Dagaie RL
**M:** CODOG: 2 Rolls-Royce Olympus TM3B gas turbines; 2 SEMT-Pielstick 16 PA 6 CV 280 diesels; 2 CP props; 52,000 hp (gas turbine), 10,400 hp (diesel)
**Electric:** 3,400 kw (4 × 850-kw alternator sets) **Fuel:** 600 tons distillate
**Range:** 1,000/30; 9,500/17 diesels
**Man:** Peacetime: 18 officers, 127 petty officers, 83 men (accommodations for 250 total)

**GUIDED-MISSILE DESTROYERS** *(continued)*

**Montcalm (D 642)**—with MM 40 missiles L. & L. Van Ginderen, 6-87

Remarks: Units 6 and 7 built at Brest and fitted out at Lorient Dockyard. Main propulsion and auxiliary equipment is divided among four compartments from forward to aft: forward auxiliary room, turbine room, diesel room with the reduction gears, and after auxiliary room. On diesel power and with the DUBV 43 sonar in the water, maximum speed is 19 knots. Centralized control of the propulsion machinery from the bridge greatly reduces the engineering staff required (3 officers, 23 petty officers, 24 men).

As in the *De Grasse,* much attention has been given to habitability, which caused the addition of 5 meters of length and 150 tons to the original plans. Denny Brown automatic stabilizers fitted. Have SENIT 4 data system. Dagaie rocket launchers replace Sagaie in D 643 and later ships. Have 1 CSEE Panda optronic backup director for the 100-mm gun. The helicopters can be used for ASW with Mk 46 torpedoes or Mk 54 depth bombs or for antiship duties with AS-12 missiles.

The final three have a modified sensor suit and the pilothouse placed one deck higher. D 640–643 will eventually have their sonar suits updated to match the others, but will retain the original radars. Beginning with D 644, the Crotale EDIR SAM system is installed. All have the SENIT 4 combat data system and Syracuse SATCOMM equipment. The DIBV 10 Vampir IR system is to be added.

◆ **3 Tourville class, Type F 67, ex-C 67A** Bldr: Lorient Arsenal

| | Budget | Laid down | L | In serv. |
|---|---|---|---|---|
| D 610 Tourville | 1967 | 3-70 | 13-5-72 | 21-6-74 |
| D 611 Duguay-Trouin | 1967 | 1-71 | 1-6-73 | 17-9-75 |
| D 612 De Grasse | 1970 | 1972 | 30-11-74 | 1-10-77 |

**D:** 4,800 tons (5,800 fl) **S:** 32 kts
**Dim:** 152.75 (142.0 pp) × 15.3 × 5.70 (hull) (6.48 props)
**A:** 6/MM 38 Exocet—1/Crotale syst. (VIII × 1, 24 missiles)—2/100-mm DP, Model 1968 (I × 2)—2/20-mm AA (I × 2)—1/Malafon ASW syst. (13 missiles)—2/catapults for L-5 antisubmarine torpedoes (10 torpedoes)—2/WG-13 Lynx helicopters
**Electron Equipt:** Radar: 2 DRBN 32 (Decca 1226), 1/DRBV 26, 1/DRBV 51B, 1/DRBC 32D
Sonar: 1/DUBV 23, 1/DUBV 43—E/O: DIBV 1A
EW: ARBB 32, ARBR 16, 2/Syllex countermeasures RL
**M:** 2 sets Rateau double-reduction GT; 2 props; 54,400 hp
**Electric:** 4,440 kw (2 × 1,500-kw turbogenerators, 3 × 480-kw diesel alternators)
**Boilers:** 4 asymmetric, multitube, automatic-control; 45 kg/cm$^2$, 450°C
**Range:** 1,900/30; 4,500/18 **Man:** 17 officers, 122 petty officers, 143 men

**Duguay-Trouin (D 611)** H. Ehlers, 12-86

**Tourville (D 610)** DCAN, Brest, 4-87

**De Grasse (D 612)** L. & L. Van Ginderen, 1-87

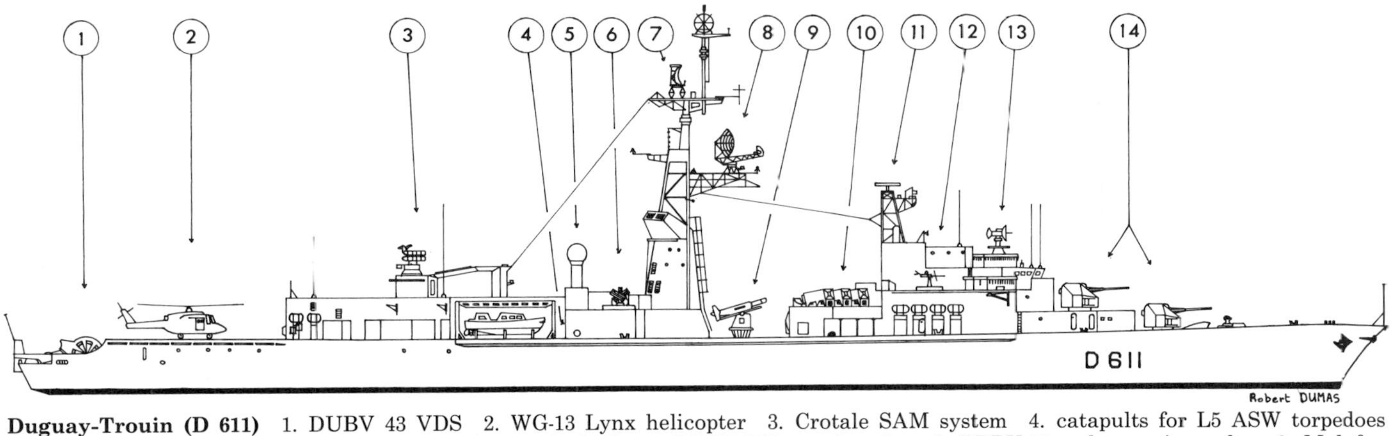


**Duguay-Trouin (D 611)** 1. DUBV 43 VDS 2. WG-13 Lynx helicopter 3. Crotale SAM system 4. catapults for L5 ASW torpedoes 5. Syracuse SATCOMM antenna radomes 6. Syllex chaff RL 7. DRBV 51B search radar 8. DRBV 26 early-warning radar 9. Malafon ASW system 10. MM 38 Exocet launchers 11. Decca 1226 nav. radar 12. 20-mm AA 13. DRBC 32D f.c. radar director 14. 100-mm Model 1968 DP

## GUIDED-MISSILE DESTROYERS *(continued)*

REMARKS: SENIT 3 data system fitted. *Duguay-Trouin* was equipped with the Crotale antiaircraft missile system during 1979, *Tourville* in 1980, and *De Grasse* in 1981. In preparation for Crotale, the third 100-mm gun mount atop the helicopter hangar on *Tourville* and *Duguay-Trouin* was removed; it was never carried by *De Grasse*. During her Crotale installation refit, the *Tourville* had her boilers converted to burn distillate fuel, which has been burned by *De Grasse* from the outset. Fin stabilizers are fitted. These ships, particularly *De Grasse,* have a very high standard of habitability and seakeeping qualities on a par with those of the *Suffren* class. The Syllex countermeasures launchers are to be replaced by 2 Dagaie systems, the Crotale EDIR missile substituted about 1990, and a major modernization may commence by 1992. D 610 will receive a very low frequency (VLF) towed sonar to operate at 600-m depths; it will have both MF and VLF transducers and a towed linear VLF array.

### ◆ 2 Suffren class

| | Bldr | Budget | Laid down | L | In serv. |
|---|---|---|---|---|---|
| D 602 SUFFREN | Lorient Ars. | 1960 | 12-62 | 15-5-65 | 20-7-67 |
| D 603 DUQUESNE | Brest Ars. | 1960 | 11-64 | 11-2-66 | 1-4-70 |

**Suffren (D 602)** L. & L. Van Ginderen, 6-87

**Duquesne (D 603)** Pradignac & Leo, 2-87

**D:** 5,090 tons (6,090 fl) **S:** 34 kts
**Dim:** 157.60 (148.00 pp) × 15.54 × 7.25 (max.)
**A:** 1/Masurca SAM syst. (II × 1; 48 missiles)—4/MM 38 Exocet SSM—2/100-mm, Model 1953 (I × 2)—4/20-mm AA (I × 4)—1/Malafon ASW syst. (13 missiles)—2/catapults for L-5 torpedoes (10 torpedoes)
**Electron Equipt:** Radar: 1/DRBN 32, 1/DRBI 23, 1/DRBV 50 (D 603: DRBV 15) 2/DRBR 51, 1/DRBC 32A
Sonar: 1/DUBV 23, 1/DUBV 43—TACAN: . . .
EW: ARBB 31, ARBB 32, 2 Syllex countermeasures RL
**M:** 2 sets Rateau double-reduction GT; 2 props; 72,500 hp
**Electric:** 3,440 kw (2 × 1,000-kw turbogenerators, 3 × 480-kw diesel alternators)
**Boilers:** 4 multitube, automatic-control; 45 kg/cm$^2$, 450°C
**Range:** 2,000/30; 2,400/29; 5,100/18
**Man:** 23 officers, 164 petty officers, 168 men

REMARKS: Built under the 1960–65 plan, these ships are extremely seaworthy; they roll and pitch only slightly and vibrate very little. Three pairs of nonretractable, anti-rolling stabilizers. Living and operating spaces are air-conditioned. SENIT 1 data system fitted. The DRBC 33 gunfire-control radar with Piranha III optronic attachment is to be installed in place of DRBC 32A in 1987. Two Dagaie and two Sagaie countermeasures launchers will replace Syllex. DRBV 15 surveillance radar replaced DRBV 50 in D 603 in 1985.

### ◆ 1 C 65 class

| | Bldr | Laid down | L | In serv. |
|---|---|---|---|---|
| D 609 ACONIT | Lorient Ars. | 1967 | 7-3-70 | 30-3-73 |

**D:** 3,500 tons (3,840 fl) **S:** 27 kts **Dim:** 127.00 × 13.40 × 4.05 (5.80 props)
**A:** 8/MM 40 Exocet SSM (IV × 2)—2/100-mm DP, Model 1968 (I × 2)—1/Malafon ASW system (13 missiles)—2/catapults for L-5 ASW torpedoes (10 torpedoes)
**Electron Equipt:** Radar: 1/DRBN 32, 1/DRBV 15, 1/DRBV 22A, 1/DRBC 32B
Sonar: 1/DUBV 23, 1/DUBV 43 VDS
EW: ARBB 32, ARBR 16, 2/Syllex countermeasures RL
**M:** 1 set Rateau double-reduction GT; 1 prop; 28,650 hp (31,500 hp for short periods)
**Boilers:** 2 asymmetric, multitube, automatic-control; 45 kg/cm$^2$, 450°C
**Electric:** 2,960 kw **Range:** 1,600/27; 5,000/18
**Man:** 15 officers, 103 petty officers, 114 men

REMARKS: One computer controls the SENIT 3 data system functions and the weapons. Propulsion machinery is very compact and produced 31,500 hp on trials. Equipped with fin stabilizers. During a major refit in 1984–85 she received 8/MM 40 Exocet positions in place of the 305-mm mortar and DRBV 15 in place of DRBV 13. DSBV 61 or DSBV 62 towed linear hydrophone array may be fitted.

**Aconit (D 609)** B. Prézelin, 6-86

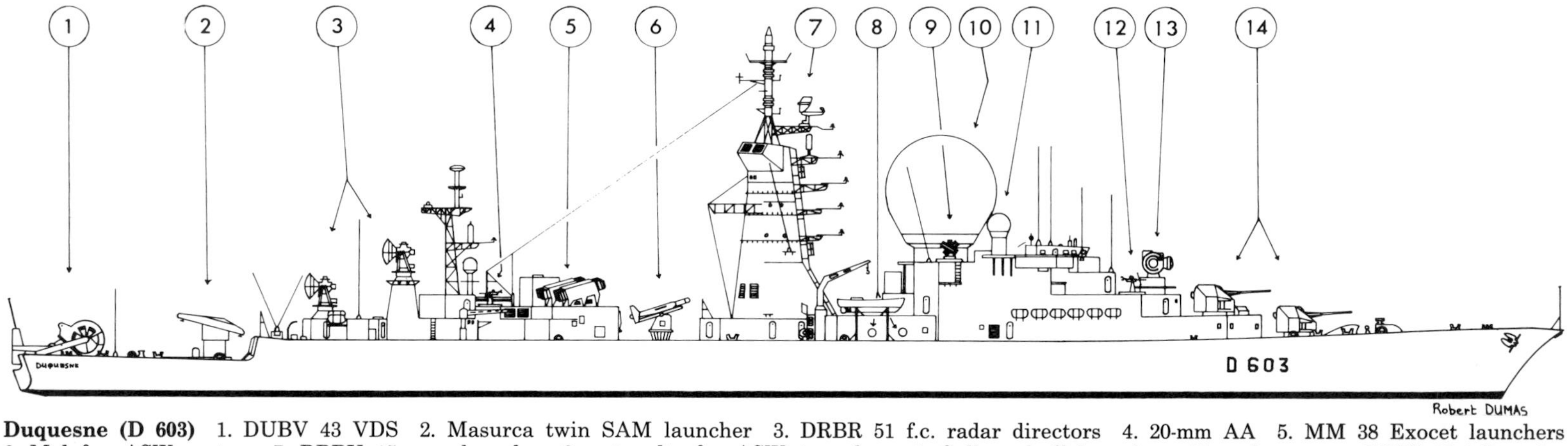


**Duquesne (D 603)** 1. DUBV 43 VDS 2. Masurca twin SAM launcher 3. DRBR 51 f.c. radar directors 4. 20-mm AA 5. MM 38 Exocet launchers 6. Malafon ASW system 7. DRBV 15 search radar 8. catapults for ASW torpedoes 9. Syllex chaff launcher 10. radome over DRBI 23 3-D radar 11. Syracuse SATCOMM antenna radomes 12. 20-mm AA 13. DRBC 32A f.c. radar director 14. 100-mm Model 1953 DP

## GUIDED-MISSILE DESTROYERS *(continued)*

**Aconit (D 609)** B. Prézelin, 6-86

### ◆ 1 T-56 class, ASW

| | Bldr | Laid down | L | In serv. |
|---|---|---|---|---|
| D 638 La Galissonnière | Lorient Ars. | 11-58 | 12-3-60 | 9-7-62 |

**D:** 2,750 tons (3,740 fl) **S:** 34 kts (32 fl)
**Dim:** 132.80 × 12.70 × 5.40 (fwd) 5.90 (props)
**A:** 2/100-mm DP, Model 1953 (I × 2)—1/Malafon ASW syst. (13 missiles)—6/550-mm TT (III × 2) for L-3 torpedoes—1/Alouette-III ASW helicopter
**Electron Equipt:** Radar: 1/DRBN 32, 1/DRBV 22A, 1/DRBV 50, 1/DRBC 32A
Sonar: 1/DUBV 23, 1/DUBV 43 VDS—TACAN: SRN-6
EW: ARBR/ARBA 10C
**M:** 2 sets Rateau GT; 2 props; 63,000 hp
**Boilers:** 4 ACB-Indret; 35 kg/cm², 385°C **Fuel:** 800 tons
**Range:** 1,500/30; 5,000/18
**Man:** Peacetime: 15 officers, 92 petty officers, 165 men

Remarks: Formerly an experimental vessel for ASW sonar, with two bow-mounted sonars. A quadruple 305-mm ASW mortar and six torpedo tubes (III × 2) have been removed. The hangar unfolds to become the helicopter flight deck. Due for disposal in 1990.

**La Galissonnière (D 638)**—with hangar opened to create a flight deck
L. & L. Van Ginderen, 6-84

**La Galissonnière (D 638)**—with hanger open and Alouette-III on deck
L. & L. Van Ginderen, 6-87

### ◆ 1 modified T-53 class, ASW

| | Bldr | Laid down | L | In serv. |
|---|---|---|---|---|
| D 633 Duperré | Lorient Ars. | 11-54 | 23-6-56 | 8-10-57 |

**D:** 2,750 tons (3,740 fl) **S:** 34 kts (32 fl) **Dim:** 132.8 × 12.7 × 5.9 (props)
**A:** 4/MM 38 Exocet—1/100-mm DP, Model 1968—2/20-mm AA (I × 2)—2/catapults for L-5 torpedoes (8 torpedoes)—1/WG-13 Lynx helicopter
**Electron Equipt:** Radar: 2/DRBN 32, 1/DRBV 22A, 1/DRBV 51, 1/DRBC 32C,
Sonar: 1/DUBV 23, 1/DUBV 43 VDS
EW: ARBR 16, 2/Syllex countermeasures RL
**M:** 2 sets Rateau GT; 2 props; 64,000 hp **Electric:** 1,640 kw
**Boilers:** 4/ACB-Indret; 35 kg/cm², 385°C **Fuel:** 800 tons
**Range:** 1,500/30; 5,000/18
**Man:** Peacetime: 15 officers, 102 petty officers, 142 men

Remarks: From 1967 to 1971, the *Duperré* was unarmed and was used for towed-sonar research, using the huge array later mounted in the auxiliary *Aunis*. Reconverted at Brest from 1972 to 21-5-74, as the final step in the long evolution of the T-47, *Surcouf*-class destroyer design. The hangar is fixed and has maintenance facilities, and the flight deck has a harpoon helicopter-recovery system similar to that on the *Tourville* and *Georges Leygues* classes. SENIT 2 data system fitted. The ship ran aground 13-4-78 and was badly damaged, but was repaired using

**Duperré (D 633)** J.-C. Bellonne, 1986

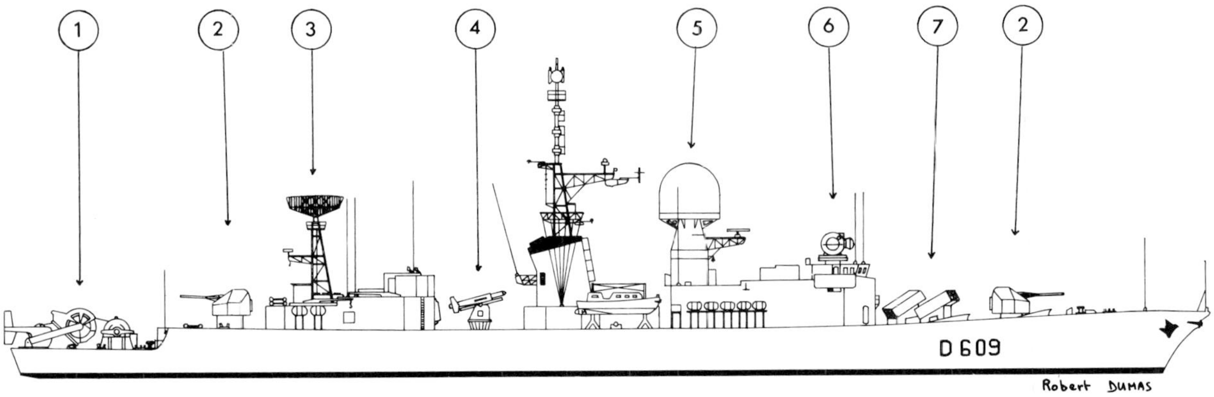


**Aconit** 1. DUBV 43 sonar 2. 100-mm DP mounts 3. DRBV 22A radar 4. Malafon launcher 5. DRBV 15 radar 6. 100-mm gun director with DRBC 32B radar 7. MM 40 Exocet launch cells

GUIDED-MISSILE DESTROYERS *(continued)*

**Duperré (D 633)** L. Grazioli, 3-87

components cannibalized from the inactivated *La Bourdonnais,* recommissioning 2-80. Flagship for destroyer squadron in the Atlantic; now due for disposal 1990.

◆ **1 D'Estrées class, converted Type T-47, ASW**

| | Bldr | Laid down | L | In serv. |
|---|---|---|---|---|
| D 627 Maille Brézé | Lorient Ars. | 10-53 | 26-9-54 | 4-5-57 |

**Maille Brézé (D 627)** L. & L. Van Ginderen, 11-84

**Maille Brézé (D 627)** L. & L. Van Ginderen, 11-84

**D:** 2,750 tons (3,740 fl) **S:** 32 kts **Dim:** 132.5 × 12.72 × 5.9 (props)
**A:** 2/100-mm DP, Model 1953 (I × 2)—2/20-mm AA (I × 2)—1/Malafon ASW syst. (13 missiles)—1/375-mm Bofors ASW RL (VI × 1)—6 TT (III × 2) for L-3 ASW torpedoes
**Electron Equipt:** Radar: 1/DRBN 32, 1/DRBV 22A, 1/DRBV 50, 2/DRBC 32A
Sonar: 1/DUBV 23, 1/DUBV 43 VDS
TACAN: URN 20 or . . .—EW: ARBR/ARBA 10C
**M:** 2 sets Rateau GT; 2 props; 63,000 hp **Electric:** 1,440 kw
**Boilers:** 4/ACB-Indret; 35 kg/cm$^2$, 385°C **Fuel:** 800 tons
**Range:** 1,500/30; 5,000/18
**Man:** Peacetime: 15 officers, 103 petty officers, 151 men

REMARKS: ASW conversions completed between 1-68 and 1-71: weapon system renewed, living spaces air-conditioned, electrical system and safety installations completely redesigned. These ships do not have the SENIT system. The *D'Estrées* has carried the British SCOT satellite-communications system as an experiment. Sisters *Casabianca* (D 631) stricken 1984, *D'Estrées* (D 629) in 8-85, and *Guépratte* (D 632) on 5-7-85; *Vauquelin* (D 628) on 6-11-86. D 627 to strike during 1988.

◆ **1 Kersaint class, converted Type T-47**

| | Bldr | Laid down | L | In serv. |
|---|---|---|---|---|
| D 630 Du Chayla | Brest Ars. | 7-53 | 27-11-54 | 4-6-57 |

**Du Chayla (D 630)** B. Prézelin, 6-87

**D:** 2,750 tons (3,850 fl) **S:** 32 kts **Dim:** 128.50 × 12.96 × 5.00 (6.30 sonar)
**A:** 1/Mk 13 launcher (40 Standard SM-1 MR missiles)—6/57-mm AA (II × 3)—1/375-mm ASW RL (VI × 1) Model 1954—6/550-mm TT (III × 2) for L-3 ASW torpedoes
**Electron Equipt:** Radar: 1/DRBV 22A, 1/SPS-39 B, 1/DRBV 31, 2/SPG-51B, 1/DRBC 31
Sonar: 1/DUBA 1, 1/DUBV 24
EW: ARBR/ARBA 10C—TACAN: SRN-6
**M:** 2 sets Rateau GT; 2 props; 63,000 hp **Electric:** 1,600 kw
**Boilers:** 4 ACB-Indret; 35 kg/cm$^2$, 385°C
**Range:** 1,200/32; 3,500/20; 4,100/14
**Man:** Peacetime: 15 officers, 87 petty officers, 173 men

REMARKS: Converted to carry U.S. Tartar missile system, 1961–65. DRBV 20 air-search radar replaced by later DRBV 22A. Sisters *Bouvet* (D 624) and *Kersaint* (D 622) stricken 1-1-82 and 1-12-83, respectively, to provide missile systems for the 1st and 2nd C-70AA-class destroyers under construction. Sister *Dupetit Thouars* (D 625) stricken 1987, and D 625 is to strike 1988. Has SENIT 2 data system.

## FRIGATES

◆ **0 (+3) FL 25 class** Bldr: . . .

| | Laid down | L | In serv. |
|---|---|---|---|
| F . . . N . . . | . . . | . . . | . . . |
| F . . . N . . . | . . . | . . . | . . . |
| F . . . N . . . | . . . | . . . | . . . |

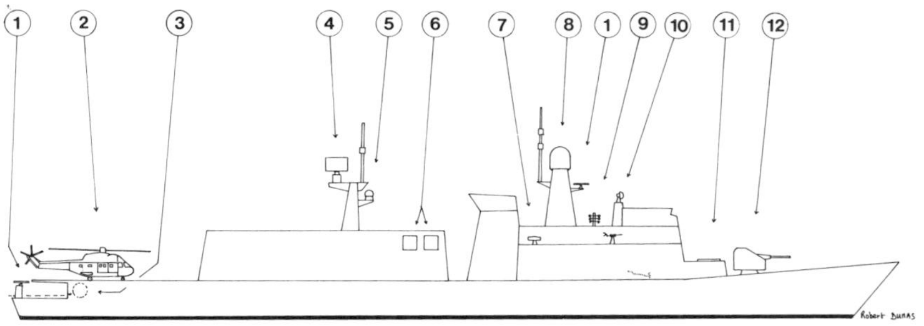


1. Decca radars 2. helicopter (with AM 39 SSM or Murène ASW torpedoes) 3. towed passive sonar array 4. DRBV 15 radar 5. Syracuse SATCOMM radome 6. MM 40 launchers 7. Dagaie decoy RL 8. Arabel radar 9. Mistral SAM launcher 10. fire-control director 11. SAAM vertical-launch SAM installation 12. 100-mm DP gun

**D:** 3,200 tons (trials) **S:** 27 kts **Dim:** 123.0 (115.0 pp) × 13.8 × 4.0 (hull)
**A:** to include: 8/MM 40 Exocet (IV × 2)—1/100-mm DP—1/helicopter with AM 39 Exocet (see Remarks)
**Electron Equipt:** Radar: 2/Decca . . . nav., 1/Arabel, 1/DRBV 15

**FRIGATES** *(continued)*

**M:** CODEOD (diesel-electric or diesel): 2 SEMT-Pielstick 18 PA 6 BTC diesels, 2 1MW electric motors; 2 fixed-pitch props; . . . hp
**Range:** 9,000/. . . **Man:** 175 crew + 24 commandoes

REMARKS: Under consideration during the 1987–91 program. Will have the Syracuse SATCOMM system. Superstructure surfaces will be sloped about 10 degrees to reduce radar cross section. The weapons suite will probably include SAAM vertical-launch and Mistral close-range missiles. Decision to build may await French decision of the NATO NFR-90 program in 10-87; France did not join.

◆ **17 D'Estienne d'Orves class, Type A-69** Bldr: Lorient Arsenal

| | Laid down | L | In serv. |
|---|---|---|---|
| F 781 D'ESTIENNE D'ORVES | 1-9-72 | 1-6-73 | 10-9-76 |
| F 782 AMYOT D'INVILLE | 9-73 | 30-11-74 | 13-10-76 |
| F 783 DROGOU | 10-73 | 30-11-74 | 30-9-76 |
| F 784 DÉTROYAT | 12-74 | 31-1-76 | 4-5-77 |
| F 785 JEAN MOULIN | 15-1-75 | 31-1-76 | 11-5-77 |
| F 786 QUARTIER-MAÎTRE ANQUETIL | 1-8-75 | 7-8-76 | 4-2-78 |
| F 787 COMMANDANT DE PIMODAN | 1-9-75 | 7-8-76 | 20-5-78 |
| F 788 SECOND MAÎTRE LE BIHAN | 1-11-76 | 13-8-77 | 7-7-79 |
| F 789 LIEUTENANT DE VAISSEAU LE HENAFF | 3-77 | 16-9-78 | 13-2-80 |
| F 790 LIEUTENANT DE VAISSEAU LAVALLÉE | 11-11-77 | 29-5-79 | 16-8-80 |
| F 791 COMMANDANT L'HERMINIER | 7-5-79 | 7-3-81 | 1985 |
| F 792 PREMIER MAÎTRE L'HER | 15-12-78 | 28-6-80 | 15-12-81 |
| F 793 COMMANDANT BLAISON | 15-11-79 | 7-3-81 | 28-4-82 |
| F 794 ENSEIGNE DE VAISSEAU JACOUBET | 4-79 | 26-9-81 | 23-10-82 |
| F 795 COMMANDANT DUCUING | 1-10-80 | 26-9-81 | 17-3-83 |
| F 796 COMMANDANT BIROT | 23-3-81 | 22-5-82 | 14-3-84 |
| F 797 COMMANDANT BOUAN (ex-*Commandant Levasseur*) | 12-10-81 | 23-4-83 | 11-5-84 |

**Commandant de Pimodan (F 787)**—with MM 38 Exocet, but still lacking Dagaie launchers J. Jedrlinic, 12-86

**D:** 1,100 tons (1,250 fl) **S:** 23.3 kts
**Dim:** 80.0 (76.0 pp) × 10.3 × 3.0 (5.3 sonar)
**A:** F 781, 783, 785, 786, 787: 2/MM 38 Exocet (I × 2); F 792—797: 4/MM 40 Exocet (II × 2)—1/100-mm DP, Model 1968—2/20-mm AA (I × 2)—1/375-mm ASW rocket launcher (VI × 1)—4/TT for L-3, (F 782: L-5) ASW torpedoes (no reloads)

**Détroyat (F 784)**—with two MM 38 and Dagaie launchers H. Ehlers, 7-87

**Commandant Ducuing (F 795)**—with four MM 40 missiles and Dagaie launchers Pradignac & Leo, 1985

**Electron Equipt:** Radar: 1/DRBN 32, 1/DRBV 51A, 1/DRBC 32E
Sonar: 1/DUBA 25
EW: ARBR 16, 2/Dagaie RL (in final 7 ships, plus refitted ships)
**M:** 2 SEMT-Pielstick 12 PC 2 V400 diesels; 2 CP props; 11,000 hp
**Electric:** 840 kw **Endurance:** 15 days **Range:** 4,500/15
**Man:** 7 officers, 42 petty officers, 56 men

REMARKS: Very economical and seaworthy ships designed for coastal antisubmarine warfare, but available for scouting missions, instruction, and showing the flag. Can carry a troop detachment of one officer and seventeen men. The control system for the 100-mm gun consists of a DRBC 32E monopulse, X-band radar, and a semi-analog, semi-digital computer; it also has an optical sight. F 781, F 783, F 786, and F 787 of the Mediterranean Squadron have 2 MM 38 Exocet. All have fin stabilizers except F 795 and F 797, which have a "dynamic" stabilization system. Stacks and masts were modified from the *Jean Moulin* (F 785) onward; the heightened stack was backfitted in earlier units. Plans to add a helicopter facility to F 793 and F 794 were abandoned. F 791 has 2 SEMT-Pielstick 12 PA 6 BTC diesels totaling 14,400 hp, with infrared signature suppression features; protracted trials delayed commissioning. The original *Lieutenant de Vaisseau Le Henaff* and *Commandant L'Herminier* were completed to a slightly modified design for South Africa and then sold to Argentina, which also ordered an additional unit. F 782 completed refit 11-86 with new 100-mm gun, U.S. SLQ-25 Nixie torpedo decoy, upgraded sonar, Dagaie launchers, L-5 ASW torpedo capability (first in class), and waste processing system. One unit had lightweight Crotale launcher in place of the 100-mm gun, for trials, 1986.

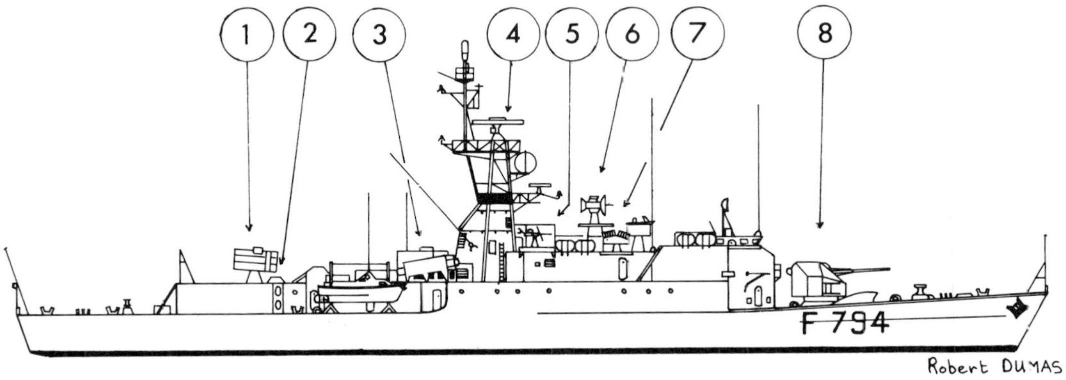


**Enseigne de Vaisseau Jacoubet** 1. Sextuple Bofors ASW RL, Model 1954 2. ASW torpedo tubes 3. Exocet launchers 4. 20-mm AA gun mounts 5. DRBC 32E f.c. radar 6. 100-mm DP gun mount, Model 1968 7. DRBV 51A search radar

**FRIGATES** *(continued)*

**Commandant Birot (F 796)**—with MM 38 Exocet, Dagaie (Note widened superstructure forward) L. & L. Van Ginderen, 3-87

◆ **1 Modified Commandant Rivière class**

| | Bldr | Laid down | L | In serv. |
|---|---|---|---|---|
| F 729 Balny | Lorient Ars. | 3-60 | 17-3-62 | 1-2-70 |

**Balny (F 729)** E.C.P.A., 1985

**D:** 1,750 tons (2,230 fl) **S:** 26 kts **Dim:** 102.7 (98.0 pp) × 11.8 × 5.0 (prop)
**A:** 2/100-mm DP, Model 1953 (I × 2)—2/30-mm AA (I × 2)—1/305-mm ASW mortar (IV × 1)—6/TT for L-3 ASW torpedoes (III × 2)
**Electron Equipt:** Radar: DRBN 32, 1/DRBV 22A, 1/DRBC 32C
Sonar: 1/DUBA 3, 1/SQS 17—EW: ARBR 16
**M:** CODAG: 1 Turbomeca M 38 gas turbine (11,500 hp), 2 AGO V-16 diesels (3,600 hp each); 1 CP prop; 18,700 hp
**Electric:** 1,280 kw **Range:** 13,000/10
**Man:** 9 officers, 67 petty officers, 93 men

Remarks: Allocated for trials in 1964 with the French Navy's first combined gas-turbine *and* diesel plant (CODAG). The gas turbine is a version of the Atar-8 turbojet used in the Étendard fighter, reduced in rating from 15,000 shp to 11,500 hp. Both diesels and the gas turbine can be clutched together to drive the single propeller, which is 3.6 meters in diameter and extends 1 meter beneath the keel. The compactness of the *Balny's* propulsion plant, compared with that of the all-diesel plants in her half-sisters of the *Commandant Rivière* class, permits her to carry approximately 100 more tons of fuel, which accounts for her great endurance on diesels alone. Because one of her 100-mm guns is mounted atop the lengthened after superstructure, it has not been possible to install Exocet antiship missiles.

◆ **7 Commandant Rivière class** Bldr: Lorient Arsenal

| | Laid down | L | In serv. |
|---|---|---|---|
| F 725 Victor Schoelcher | 10-57 | 11-10-58 | 15-10-62 |
| F 726 Commandant Bory | 3-58 | 11-10-58 | 5-3-64 |
| F 727 Amiral Charner | 11-58 | 12-3-60 | 14-12-62 |
| F 728 Doudart de Lagrée | 3-60 | 15-4-61 | 1-5-63 |
| F 740 Commandant Bourdais | 4-59 | 15-4-61 | 10-3-63 |
| F 748 Protet | 9-61 | 7-12-62 | 1-5-64 |
| F 749 Enseigne de Vaisseau Henry | 9-62 | 14-12-63 | 1-1-65 |

**Commandant Bourdais (F 740)** LSPH E. Pitman, R.A.N., 2-86

**Commandant Bory (F 726)** M. Bar, 6-86

**D:** 1,750 tons (2,070 normal, 2,230 fl) **S:** 26 kts (26.6 on trials)
**Dim:** 102.7 (98.0 pp) × 11.8 × 4.35 (max.)
**A:** 4/MM 38 Exocet—2/100-mm DP, Model 1963 (I × 2)—2/30- or 40-mm AA—1/305-mm ASW mortar (IV × 1)—6/TT L-3 ASW torpedoes (III × 2)
**Electron Equipt:** Radar: 1/DRBN 32, 1/DRBV 22A, 1/DRBC 32C
Sonar: 1/DUBA 3, 1/SQS-17
EW: ARBR 16, 2/Dagaie countermeasures RL
**M:** 4 SEMT-Pielstick 12 PC-series diesels; 2 props; 16,000 hp
**Electric:** 1,280 kw **Fuel:** 210 tons **Range:** 2,300/26; 7,500/16.5
**Endurance:** 45 days **Man:** 9 officers, 66 petty officers, 91 men

Remarks: Designed for escort duty in various climates; air-conditioned. Can embark a flag officer and staff or an 80-man commando unit. F 726 originally had free-piston generators driving turbines, but these were replaced with a standard diesel plant in 1974–75. Beginning in the mid-1970s, four Exocet missiles replaced a 100-mm gun atop the after superstructure. F 728 replaced *Forbin* as cadet training ship in 1981. F 726 was the first ship to carry the Dagaie countermeasures rocket-launching system. F 725, F 748, and F 749 have 30-mm AA, the others have 40-mm AA. Sister *Commandant Rivière* (F 733) rerated as an auxiliary and converted

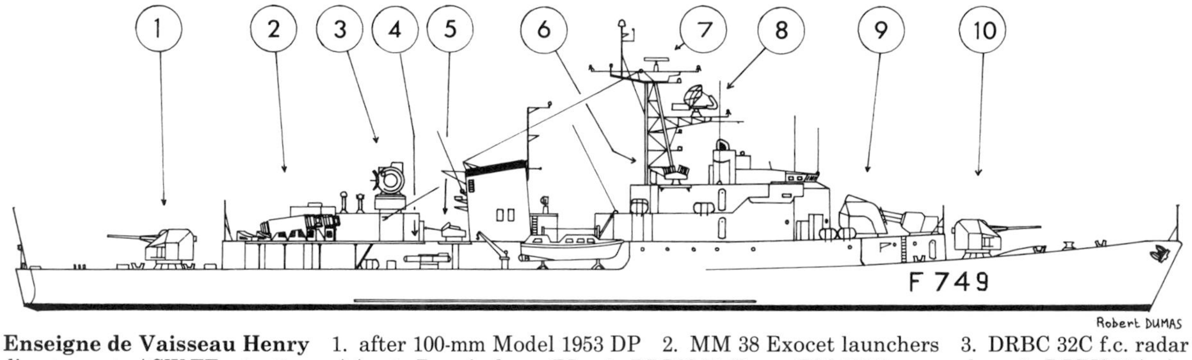


**Enseigne de Vaisseau Henry** 1. after 100-mm Model 1953 DP 2. MM 38 Exocet launchers 3. DRBC 32C f.c. radar director. 4. ASW TT 5. 40-mm AA 6. Dagaie decoy RL 7. DRBN 32 (Decca RM 1226) nav. radar 8. DRBV 22A air-search radar 9. 305-mm quadruple mortar 10. forward 100-mm DP

**FRIGATES** *(continued)*

1985 as sonar trials ship. F 725 to be stricken 1988, F 740 in 1990, the others in 1990–92.

**PATROL BOATS**

◆ **10 P 400 (Super PATRA) class** Bldr: CMN, Cherbourg

| | Laid down | L | In serv. | Op. Area |
|---|---|---|---|---|
| P 682 L'Audacieuse | 11-4-83 | 21-3-84 | 21-3-85 | Indian Ocean |
| P 683 La Boudeuse | 15-6-83 | 21-5-84 | 25-7-86 | Nouméa |
| P 684 La Capricieuse | 12-4-83 | 31-10-84 | 26-9-86 | Papeete |
| P 685 La Fougeuse | 25-11-83 | 17-12-84 | 19-2-87 | Indian Ocean |
| P 686 La Glorieuse | 21-2-84 | 25-1-85 | 25-3-87 | Papeete |
| P 687 La Gracieuse | 26-4-84 | 26-3-85 | 1987 | Papeete |
| P 688 La Moqueuse | 4-10-84 | 8-4-86 | 25-3-87 | Fr. Guyana |
| P 689 La Railleuse | 27-12-84 | 2-9-86 | 24-4-87 | Fr. Guyana |
| P 690 La Rieuse | 14-3-85 | 17-10-86 | 15-5-87 | Cherbourg |
| P 691 La Tapageuse | 13-8-85 | . . . | -87 | Cherbourg |

**L'Audacieuse (P 682)** L. & L. Van Ginderen, 7-87

**L'Audacieuse (P 682)** M. Bar, 9-85

**D:** 337.5 tons light (422.5 fl) **S:** 24.5 kts
**Dim:** 54.50 (50.0) × 8.0 (7.7 wl) × 2.54
**A:** 1/40-mm AA—1/20-mm AA—1/7.62-mm mg
**Electron Equipt:** Radar: 1/DRBN 32 (Decca 1226)
**M:** 2 Alsthom/SEMT-Pielstick 16 PA 4V200 VGDS diesels; 2 props; 8,000 hp
**Electric:** 360 kw **Range:** 4,200/15 **Endurance:** 15 days
**Man:** 3 officers, 21 men + 20 passengers **Fuel:** 73 tons

Remarks: First six ordered 5-82, remainder on 6-3-84. Four were originally to have been part of the *Force de Service Public* (Public Service Force) under the designation SP 400 class; they were to have had firefighting, search-and-rescue, and antipollution equipment. All will now be identical. Last two to relieve *Glaive* (P 671) and *Pertuisane* (P 673) on Atlantic Coast. Carry 840 rds. 40-mm and 2,100 rds. 20-mm ammunition; equipped for later addition of two Exocet missiles and a fire-control radar. Maximum permissible displacement is 446 tons. P 686 carried Thomson-CSF VDS-12 small variable-depth sonar for trials in 1985. Propulsion problems with P 682 greatly delayed entire program.

◆ **4 Trident ("PATRA") class**

| | Bldr | L | In serv. |
|---|---|---|---|
| P 670 Trident | Auroux, Arcachon | 31-5-76 | 17-12-76 |
| P 671 Glaive | Auroux, Arcachon | 25-8-76 | 3-77 |
| P 672 Épée | C.N.M. Cherbourg | 31-3-76 | 9-10-76 |
| P 673 Pertuisane | C.N.M. Cherbourg | 2-6-76 | 20-1-77 |

**Épée (P 672)** B. Prézelin, 4-87

**Pertuisane (P 673)** L. & L. Van Ginderen, 5-85

**D:** 115 tons (148 fl) **S:** 28 kts **Dim:** 40.70 (38.5 wl) × 5.90 × 1.55
**A:** 1/40-mm AA—2/12.7-mm mg (I × 2)
**Electron Equipt:** Radar: 1/DRBN 32 (Decca 1226)
**M:** 2 AGO 195 V 12 CZSHR diesels; 2 CP props; 5,000 hp (4,400 sust.)
**Electric:** 120 kw **Range:** 750/20; 1,500/15; 1,750/10
**Man:** 2 officers, 5 petty officers, 12 men

Remarks: Thirty were planned, then fourteen, but only four were finally built. Two sisters have been built for the Ivory Coast, and another, initially commissioned as *Rapière* (P 674) in the French Navy, was sold to Mauritania in 1982. P 670 and P 672 serve the Gendarmerie Maritime. Carry 500 rounds of 40-mm, 2,000 rounds 12.7-mm ammunition. Six SS-12 wire-guided missile launchers atop the superstructure have been replaced by a single 12.7-mm mg.

◆ **1(+1) Sterne class** Bldr: A & C. de la Perrière, Lorient

| | Laid down | L | In serv. |
|---|---|---|---|
| P 680 Sterne (ex-PM 41) | 18-5-79 | 31-10-79 | 18-7-80 |
| P . . . N . . . | 1988 | . . . | . . . |

**Sterne (P 680)** M. Louagie, 9-85

**D:** 270 tons (380 fl) **S:** 20 kts **Dim:** 49.00 (43.60 pp) × 7.50 × 2.80
**A:** 2/12.7-mm mg (I × 2) **Electron Equipt:** Radar: 1/DRBN-32, 1/Decca. . . .
**M:** 2 SACM V12 CZSHR diesels; 2 props; 4,200 hp **Electric:** 160 kw
**Endurance:** 15 days **Range:** 1,500/19; 4,900/12 **Man:** 16 tot.

Remarks: Constructed to merchant marine specifications for fisheries patrol duties within the 200-nautical-mile economic zone, including rescue services. Equipped with a large infirmary. Passive tank stabilization system. Can patrol at speeds up to 6.5 knots on an electrohydraulic drive system connected to the starboard propeller. Two rubber inspection dinghies are carried. Accommodations for 23 persons. The second unit was to be ordered late 1987.

## PATROL BOATS *(continued)*

◆ **1 former stern-haul trawler** Bldr: Le Trait (1965–67)

P 681 Albatros (ex-*Nevé*) (In serv. 23-3-84)

**Albatros (P 681)** J.-C. Bellonne, 1-84

**D:** 1,800 tons (2,800 fl) **S:** 15 kts **Dim:** 85.0 (75.0 pp) × 13.5 × 6.0
**A:** 1/40-mm AA—2/12.7-mm mg (I × 2)
**Electron Equipt:** Radar: 2/navigational
**M:** diesel-electric drive; 1 prop, 2,200 hp
**Range:** 12,000/15 **Man:** 6 officers, 20 petty officers, 16 men + 15 passengers

Remarks: Purchased 1982 from Société Naval Caenaise for use in Antarctic area fisheries-patrol duties, off Kerguelen, Crozet, St. Paul, and Amsterdam islands. Based at La Réunion.

◆ **1 Combattante-I class**

| | Bldr | Laid down | L | In serv. |
|---|---|---|---|---|
| P 730 La Combattante | CMN, Cherbourg | 4-62 | 20-6-63 | 1-3-64 |

**La Combattante (P 730)** 1987

**D:** 180 tons (202 fl) **S:** 23 kts **Dim:** 45.0 × 7.35 × 2.45 (fl)
**A:** 1/40-mm AA—2/12.7-mm mg (I × 2)
**M:** 2 SEMT-Pielstick 8 PA4 200 VGDS diesels; 2 CP props; 3,600 hp
**Electric:** 120 kw **Range:** 2,000/12
**Man:** 3 officers, 22 men

Remarks: Anti-magnetic, laminated wood and plastic hull. Re-engined 1978. Launcher for 4 SS-12 wire-guided missiles removed. Formerly based at Tahiti; now operates in Mediterranean for the Gendarmerie Maritime.

◆ **1 Type DB-1 former minesweeper** Bldr: Const. Méc. de Normandie, Cherbourg

| | Laid down | L | In serv. |
|---|---|---|---|
| P 765 Mercure | 1-55 | 21-2-57 | 20-12-58 |

**D:** 365 tons (400 fl) **S:** 15 kts **Dim:** 44.35 (42.0 pp) × 8.27 × 4.04
**A:** 2/20-mm AA (II × 1) **Electron Equipt:** Radar: 1/DRBN 32
**M:** 2 MGO diesels; 2 KaMeWa CP props; 5,000 hp **Range:** 6,200/10
**Man:** 5 officers, 14 petty officers, 18 men

Remarks: The *Mercure* was converted to a fisheries-protection ship, re-entering service 22-12-80. Minesweeping equipment removed. Insulated against cold climate. Habitability modernized. Carries two 6-man rubber inspection boats with 20-hp motors. Physician and dentist carried; accommodations for 44 personnel. Former pendant number M 765. Construction financed by U.S. as MSC 254. Six sisters built for West Germany have since been transferred to Turkey.

**Mercure (P 765)** LV (R) B. Prézelin, French Navy, 11-84

◆ **2 British "Ham"-class ex-minesweepers**

| | Bldr | In serv. |
|---|---|---|
| P 742 Paquerette (ex-*Kingham*) | J.S. White | 14-8-54 |
| P 784 Géranium (ex-*Tibenham*) | McGruer | 23-7-55 |

**Géranium (P 784)** L. & L. Van Ginderen, 5-86

**D:** 140 tons (170 fl) **S:** 14 kts **Dim:** 33.43 × 6.45 × 1.7 **A:** 1/20-mm AA
**M:** 2 Paxman YHAXM diesels; 2 props; 550 hp **Fuel:** 15 tons
**Endurance:** 4 days **Man:** 1 officer, 10 petty officers, 2 men

Remarks: Manned by the Gendarmerie. Built with U.S. Offshore Procurement funds as USN MSI 82 and MSI 84. Sisters *Jonquille* (P 787) stricken 1984, *Violette* (P 788) in 1985; *Jasmin* (P 661) and *Petunia* (P 662) in 1986.

## PATROL CRAFT

◆ **3 P 778 class** Bldr: CMN, Cherbourg (In serv. 1974)

P 779 P 780 *(Karukera)* P 781 *(Gugane)*

**D:** 20 tons (30 fl) **S:** 25 kts **Dim:** 24.9 × 5.3 × . . . **A:** 1/12.7-mm mg
**M:** 2 diesels; 2 props; . . . hp

Remarks: *P 779* at La Réunion, *P 780* at Cayenne, *P 781* at Pointe à Pitre. Manned by Gendarmerie Marine. Names in parentheses are unofficial. Sister P 778 stricken 1986.

◆ **2 Volte 43 class** Bldr: Tecimar (In serv. 1975)

P 772 P 774

**P 772** Tecimar, 1974

PATROL CRAFT *(continued)*

**D:** 14 tons **S:** 21 kts **Dim:** 13.30 × 3.90 × 1.10
**A:** 1/12.7-mm mg—1/7.62-mm mg **M:** 2 G.M. 8V71 diesels; 2 props; 670 hp
**Electron Equipt:** Radar: 1/Decca 1229 **Range:** 400/20 **Man:** 4 tot.

Remarks: Hull molded of glass-reinforced plastic. Manned by the Gendarmerie, P 772 and 774 at Brest. P 771 transferred to Djibouti, P 770 stricken.

## MINE WARFARE SHIPS

Note: The tender *Loire* (A 615) is, in effect, a mine countermeasures support ship. However, because she has an auxiliary "A" pendant, and for convenience, she is listed with her *Rhin*-class sisters under Support Tenders.

◆ **0 (+1 + 9) oceangoing mine countermeasures ship** Bldr: Arsenal de Lorient

| | Laid down | L | In serv. |
|---|---|---|---|
| M . . . N . . . | . . . | . . . | 1992 |

**D:** 830 tons (trials) **S:** 15 kts **Dim:** 46.60 (pp) × 14.80 × . . .
**A:** 1/20-mm AA—1/12.7-mm mg
**Electron Equipt:** Radar: 1/. . . nav.—Sonar: DUBM 42
**M:** 2 . . . diesels; 2 CP props; 2,720 hp—2 electric auxiliary motors—bow- and stern-thrusters
**Range:** 5,000/10 **Man:** 46 tot.

Remarks: Prototype for a new class of up to 10 ocean mine countermeasures units, with six to be ordered under the 1987–92 program. Catamaran hull of GRP construction. Will carry remote-controlled mine localization vehicles.

◆ **8 (+2) Tripartite-class minehunters** Bldr: Lorient Arsenal

| | Laid down | L | In serv. |
|---|---|---|---|
| M 641 Eridan | 20-12-77 | 2-2-79 | 16-4-84 |
| M 642 Cassiopée | 26-3-79 | 28-9-81 | 5-5-84 |
| M 643 Andromède | 6-3-80 | 22-5-82 | 19-10-84 |
| M 644 Pégase | 22-10-80 | 23-4-83 | 30-5-85 |
| M 645 Orion | 17-8-81 | 6-2-85 | 14-1-86 |
| M 646 Croix du Sud | 22-4-82 | 6-2-85 | 14-11-86 |
| M 647 Aigle | 2-12-82 | 8-3-86 | -87 |
| M 648 Lyre | 14-10-83 | 15-11-86 | -87 |
| M 649 Persée | 30-10-84 | -87 | 1988 |
| M 650 Sagittaire | 13-11-85 | -88 | 1989 |

**Croix du Sud (M 646)** M. Louagie, 3-87

**Orion (M 645)** B. Prézelin, 12-86

**Eridan (M 641)**—with portable decompression chamber aboard, abaft stack G. Gyssels, 3-87

**D:** 500 tons (562 fl) **S:** 15 kts on main engine, 7 kts while hunting
**Dim:** 51.6 (47.1 pp) × 8.96 × 2.49 (hull) 2.64 (max.)
**A:** 1/20-mm AA—2/12.7-mm mg (I × 2)—2/PAP-104 remote-control mine-locators
**Electron Equipt:** Radar: 1/Decca 1229, 1/automatic track-plotter with numerical calculator, automatic pilot, Toran and Syledis radio navigation systems, Decca HiFix
Sonar: DUBM 21B
**M:** 1 Brons-Werkspoor A-RUB 215 × 12 diesel; 1 CP prop, 1,900 hp; 2 electric maneuvering props, 120 hp each; bow-thruster
**Electric:** 750 kw **Range:** 3,000/12 **Man:** 5 officers, 29 petty officers, 21 men

Remarks: Hull built of glass-reinforced polyester plastic. Program well behind schedule; last five canceled in favor of a larger design. Will have one mechanical drag sweep. France, Belgium, and the Netherlands are cooperating in building these ships for the requirements of the three countries. French examples are rated at a heavier displacement (562 fl vice 544), with 595 tons given as limiting displacement. Have the EVEC 20 automatic plotting table and other precision navigation equipment. In 1985 began to receive the AP-4 acoustic sweep.

◆ **5 Circé-class minehunters** Bldr: Const. Méc. de Normandie, Cherbourg

| | Laid down | L | In serv. |
|---|---|---|---|
| M 712 Cybèle | 15-9-70 | 2-3-72 | 28-9-72 |
| M 713 Calliope | 4-4-70 | 20-10-71 | 28-9-72 |
| M 714 Clio | 4-9-69 | 10-6-71 | 18-5-72 |
| M 715 Circé | 30-1-69 | 15-12-70 | 18-5-72 |
| M 716 Cérès | 2-2-71 | 10-8-72 | 8-3-73 |

**Circé (M 715)** G. Davies, Maritime Photographic, 4-87

**Cérès (M 716)** L. & L. Van Ginderen, 2-87

## MINE WARFARE SHIPS *(continued)*

**D:** 460 tons (495 fl) **S:** 15 kts **Dim:** 50.9 (46.5 pp) × 8.9 × 3.6 (max.)
**A:** 1/20-mm AA—2 PAP-104 remote-control mine-locators
**Electron Equipt:** Radar: Decca 1229—Sonar: DUBM 20 (minehunting)
**M:** 1 MTU diesel; 1 prop; 1,800 hp
**Range:** 3,000/12 **Man:** Peacetime: 4 officers, 19 petty officers, 24 men

REMARKS: Designed for the detection and destruction of mines laid as deep as 60 meters. Hull made of laminated wood. Stress is on anti-magnetism and silence. Two independent propulsion systems, one for navigation, the other for minesweeping, both with remote control. Special rudders with small propellers mounted at the base of the rudder's after end and powered by a 260-hp electric motor, giving a speed of 7 knots and permitting exceptional maneuverability. Mines are destroyed either by divers (six in each crew) or by the PAP-104 *(poisson auto-propulsé)* wire-guided sled device, which is 2.7 meters long, 1.1 meters in diameter, weighs 700 kg, is moved by two electric motors that drive it at 6 knots for a distance of up to 500 meters, and has a television camera that displays an image of the mine. It can deposit its explosive charge of 100 kg near the mine. When the sled has been recovered, the charge is detonated by ultrasonic waves. These ships do not have minesweeping gear. *Cérès* carried the prototype EVEC automatic plotting table, now aboard all. All received updated DUBM 20A sonar with coherent processing feature during mid-1980s refits.

◆ **3 ex-U.S. Agile class, converted to minehunters** Bldr: Bellingham Shipyard, Bellingham, Washington

| | In serv. | Converted |
|---|---|---|
| M 615 CANTHO (ex-MSO 476) | 14-10-55 | 1-9-78 |
| M 617 GARIGLIANO (ex-MSO 452) | 30-10-54 | 18-9-79 |
| M 619 VINH-LONG (ex-MSO 477) | 14-10-55 | 10-4-78 |

**Dompaire (M 616)**—now stricken G. Gyssels, 2-85

**D:** 700 tons (780 fl) **S:** 13.5 kts (14 kts on trials) **Dim:** 50.29 × 10.67 × 3.15
**A:** 1/40-mm AA—2/PAP-104 remote-control mine-locators
**Electron Equipt:** Radar: 1/Decca 1229
Sonar: DUBM 21
**M:** 2 G.M. 8-278A diesels; 2 CP props; 1,600 hp; bow-thruster
**Range:** 3,000/10
**Man:** Peacetime: 4 officers, 22 petty officers, 28 men

REMARKS: Modified as minehunters, completing 1-9-78, 18-9-79, and 10-4-78, respectively. Mechanical minesweeping capability retained. All have new bridge superstructure. Have EVEC 11 automatic plotting tables. Sisters *Dompaire* (M 616, ex-MSO 454) and *Mytho* (M 618, ex-MSO 475) stricken 1987. M 619 to strike 1988.

◆ **4 ex-U.S. Agile-class ocean minesweepers**

| | Bldr | In serv. |
|---|---|---|
| M 610 OUISTREHAM (ex-MSO 513) | Peterson Bldrs., Sturgeon Bay, Wisc. | 8-56 |
| M 612 ALENÇON (ex-MSO 453) | Bellingham SY, Wash. | 6-54 |
| M 613 BERNEVAL (ex-MSO 450) | Bellingham SY, Wash. | 12-53 |
| M 623 BACCARAT (ex-MSO 505) | Tacoma Boat, Wash. | 3-56 |

**D:** 700 tons (780 fl) **S:** 13.5 kts (14 kts on trials) **Dim:** 50.29 × 10.67 × 3.15
**A:** 1/40-mm AA **Electron Equipt:** Radar: Decca 1229—Sonar: DUBM 41B
**M:** 2 G.M. 8-268A diesels; 2 CP props; 1,600 hp **Fuel:** 47 tons
**Range:** 3,000/10
**Man:** 5 officers, 53 men

REMARKS: Conversion of these ships to minehunters was canceled. However, they began receiving the new DUBM 41B sonar in 1978. M 620 recommissioned 3-80, M 613 in 7-80, M 612 in 1-81, and M 610 on 1-7-81. M 612 and M 613 have short stacks. Sister *Narvik* (M 609) was reclassified A 769 1-1-76 as a trials ship for the AP-4 acoustic sweep and the DUBM 21 sonar—*see* Experimental Ships. Sister *Berlaimont* (M 620, ex-MSO 500) stricken 1987; M 613 to strike 1988.

**Alençon (M 612)**—short stack L. & L. Van Ginderen, 9-87

**Baccarat (M 623)**—tall stack version L. & L. Van Ginderen, 2-87

◆ **4 Sirius-class coastal minesweepers** Bldr: CMN, Cherbourg

| | L | In serv. |
|---|---|---|
| M 737 CAPRICORNE | 8-8-56 | 11-7-58 |
| M 749 PHÉNIX | 23-5-55 | 21-12-56 |
| M 756 CÉPHÉE | 3-1-56 | 11-6-56 |
| M 757 VERSEAU | 26-4-56 | 10-9-56 |

**Verseau (M 757)** G. Gyssels, 2-87

**D:** 400 tons (440 fl) **S:** 15 kts (11.5 kts when sweeping)
**Dim:** 46.4 (42.7 pp) × 8.55 × 2.5 **A:** 1/20-mm AA
**Electron Equipt:** Radar: 1/DRBN 31
**M:** 2 SEMT-Pielstick 16 PA1-175 diesels; 2 props; 1,600 hp **Fuel:** 48 tons
**Range:** 3,000/10 **Man:** 3 officers, 35 men

REMARKS: French-built versions of the British "Ton" class. Engines built by S.G.C.M. Hull laminated wood and light aluminum alloy. Keel and stem in heavy wood. Have gear for sweeping mechanical, magnetic, and acoustic mines. The

## MINE WARFARE SHIPS *(continued)*

*Capricorne* (M 737) has greater degaussing capability than the others. All have one diesel sweep-generator (500 hp). *Aries* (M 758) was loaned to Morocco in 1975. *Bételgeuse* (A 747) was reclassified 1-5-77 as an experimental ship and used for trials with the DUBM 41 sonar and its computer; stricken 1987. M 749 through M 757 were financed under the U.S. Offshore Procurement program as MSC 232 to MSC 235. Sister *Capella* (M 755) badly damaged in collision 4-87 and stricken; the remainder to strike 1988, except M 749 in 1989.

### ◆ 4 mine countermeasures divers' tenders

| | Bldr: | Laid down | L | In serv. |
|---|---|---|---|---|
| M 611 VULCAIN | La Perrière, Lorient | 15-5-85 | 17-1-86 | 1-10-86 |
| M 612 PLUTON | La Perrière, Lorient | 11-10-85 | 13-5-86 | 12-12-86 |
| M 613 ACHÉRON | CMN, Cherbourg | 5-2-86 | 19-11-86 | 21-4-87 |
| M 614 STYX | CMN, Cherbourg | 20-5-86 | 3-3-87 | 6-87 |

**Pluton (M 612)** J.-C. Bellonne, 1987

**Vulcain (M 611)** L. & L. Van Ginderen, 2-87

**D:** 375 tons light (500 fl) **S:** 13.7 kts **Dim:** 41.60 (36.96 pp) × 7.50 × 3.20
**A:** 1/12.7-mm mg **Electron Equipt:** Radar: 1/Decca 1226
**M:** 2 S.A.C.M. MGO V16 AFHR diesels, 2 Kort-nozzle CP props; 2,200 hp—750-hp bow-thruster
**Range:** 2,850/13.5; 7,400/9 **Electric:** 176 kw
**Fuel:** 92 m³ **Man:** 10 officers, 8 petty officers, 6 men

REMARKS: Derived from the *Chamois*-class local support tender design as replacements for the U.S. *Adjutant*-class former minesweepers used as mine-clearance diver support tenders. First two ordered 11-10-84, other pair 7-85 on subcontract. Can support up to 15 divers. Hydraulic crane on fantail can lift 5 tons at 6-m radius, 3.5 tons at 10 m.

## AMPHIBIOUS WARFARE SHIPS

### ◆ 0 (+1) TCD 90 dock landing ship

| | Bldr | Laid down | L | In serv. |
|---|---|---|---|---|
| L 9011 FOUDRE | Brest Ars. | 26-3-86 | late 1987 | 1990 |

**Foudre (L 9011)**—official model DCN, 1987

**D:** 9,300 tons (11,880 fl) **S:** 21 kts
**Dim:** 168.00 (160.00 pp) × 23.50 (22.00 wl) × 5.2 (9.10 flooded)
**A:** 2/SADRAL SAM syst (VI × 2, . . . Mistral missiles)—1/40-mm AA—2/20-mm AA (I × 2)—4/Super Puma helicopters
**Electron Equipt:** Radar: 2/Decca . . . 1/*Rodeo* (French Army radar)
EW: . . . intercept;
**M:** 2 SEMT-Pielstick 16 PC 2.5-V400 diesels; 2 CP props; 21,600 hp—700-hp bow-thruster
**Electric:** 4,250 kw **Range:** 11,000/15 **Fuel:** . . .
**Man:** 210 crew + 350 passengers or 1,200 troops (470 extra emergency)

REMARKS: TCD = *Transport de Chalands de Débarquement* intended to carry one mechanized, 350-man regiment plus 1,080 tons combat vehicles and cargo for the Rapid Action Force; will also be able to act as logistics support ship. Docking well 122.0 × 13.50 × 7.70 high for 2 CDIC (EDIC replacement) or 10 CTM landing craft or one P 400 patrol boat: 1,740 m². Helo platform 1,080 m² with two spots, plus third spot on rolling dock-well cover; hangar for 4 helicopters. Vehicle cargo area of 1,360 m² can be extended by using dock floor; 60-ton elevator connects dock floor and cargo decks. Side loading doors. Will have Syracuse SATCOMM system. Propulsion plant same as in *Meuse*-class replenishment ships.

First ordered 5-11-84; two others were to order 1986 and 1988 but have been deferred; the second was to have been built at NORMED, La Seyne. See drawing on next page.

NOTE: The smaller dock landing ship, *Bougainville,* ordered 12-83 to support the Pacific nuclear-weapons testing facility, is described in the auxiliary pages with other ships subordinated to the same agency.

### ◆ 2 Ouragan-class dock landing ships

| | Budget | Bldr | Laid down | L | In serv. |
|---|---|---|---|---|---|
| L 9021 OURAGAN | 1960 | Brest Ars. | 6-62 | 9-11-63 | 1-6-65 |
| L 9022 ORAGE | (22-7-65) | Brest Ars. | 6-66 | 22-4-67 | 1-3-68 |

**Orage (L 9022)** Pradignac & Leo, 6-85

AMPHIBIOUS WARFARE SHIPS *(continued)*

**Orage (L 9022)** H. Ehlers, 6-87

**D:** 5,800 tons (8,500 fl) **S:** 17.3 kts
**Dim:** 149.0 (144.5 pp) × 21.5 × 5.4 (8.7 max.)
**A:** 4/40-mm AA (I × 4)—2/120-mm mortars (on L 9021 only)
**Electron Equipt:** Radar: 1/DRBN 32—Sonar: 1/SQS-17 on L 9021
**M:** 2 SEMT-Pielstick diesels; 2 CP props; 8,640 hp **Electric:** 2,650 kw
**Range:** 4,000/15 **Man:** 10 officers, 66 petty officers, 135 men

REMARKS: Bridge to starboard of permanent helicopter deck. L 9022 is assigned to the Pacific Test Center and acts as transport to and from France, as well as floating headquarters, employing a modular structure within the well deck. Both have repair facilities. Can carry 349 troops, including 14 officers, or 470 troops for a short distance. A 120-meter-long well with a 14-by-5.5-meter stern gate can be submerged by 3 meters. When ships are ballasted down, displacement reaches 14,400 tons. Movement of the sluices and valves is automatic, using pumps (3,000 $m^3/h$) controlled from a central position. A removable deck in six sections covers 36 meters of the after part of the well and allows the landing and takeoff of heavy helicopters. A 90-meter-long temporary deck in 15 sections can be used to stow cargo or vehicles, but its use reduces the number of landing craft that can be carried, because the well is then diminished by half.

If used as transports, they can embark either two EDIC landing craft for infantry and tanks, carrying 11 light tanks or trucks, or 18 LCM Mk 6 with tanks or vehicles and, in addition, heavy helicopters on a landing platform. If used as cargo-carriers, they can embark 1,500 tons of material. Lifting equipment includes two 35-ton cranes. A combined command center permits the simultaneous direction of helicopter and amphibious operations. To be discarded in 1990 and 1993, respectively.

◆ **1 Argens-class tank landing ship**

| | Bldr | Laid down | L | In serv. |
|---|---|---|---|---|
| L 9007 TRIEUX (BDC-1) | A.C. de Bretagne | 12-57 | 6-12-58 | 18-3-60 |

**D:** 1,750 tons light (4,225 fl) **S:** 11 kts **Dim:** 102.12 (96.6 pp) × 15.54 × 3.2
**A:** 3/40-mm AA (I × 3)—1/120-mm mortar
**Man:** 5 officers, 24 petty officers, 45 men
**Electron Equipt:** Radar: DRBN 32
**M:** 2 SEMT-Pielstick 16 PA1 diesels; 2 props; 2,000 hp **Range:** 18,500/10

REMARKS: Design derived from U.S. LST 1 class. Can carry 1,800 tons of cargo, 4 LCVP landing craft, and a maximum of 807 passengers (normally 170 troops). MacGregor-type loading hatches. *Trieux* modified with a hangar for two Alouette-III helicopters. The mortar is mounted at the bow. Sisters *Blavet* (L 9009) and *Argens* (L 9003) stricken 1985; *Bidassoa* (L 9004) and *Dives* (L 9008) stricken 1986. L 9007 to strike 1988.

◆ **5 Champlain-class medium landing ships** Bldrs: L 9030, 9031: Brest Arsenal; others: At. Francais de L'Ouest, Grand-Querilly

| | Laid down | L | In serv. |
|---|---|---|---|
| L 9030 CHAMPLAIN | 1973 | 17-11-73 | 5-10-74 |
| L 9031 FRANCIS GARNIER | 1973 | 17-11-73 | 21-6-74 |
| L 9032 DUMONT D'URVILLE | 4-81 | 27-11-81 | 5-2-83 |
| L 9033 JACQUES CARTIER | 10-81 | 28-4-82 | 23-9-83 |
| L 9034 LA GRANDIÈRE | 27-8-84 | 11-12-85 | 20-1-87 |

**La Grandière (L 9034)**—high superstructure, longer helo deck J.-C. Bellonne, 12-86

**Jacques Cartier (L 9033)** 16 Flot., French Navy, 1984

**D:** 750 tons (1,330 fl; L 9032–9034: 1,386 fl) **S:** 16 kts (13 cruising)
**Dim:** 80.0 (68.0 pp) × 13.0 × 3.0 (2.50 hull) **Electric:** 360 kw
**A:** L 9030, 9031: 2/40-mm AA (I × 2)—2/81-mm mortars (I × 2)—2/12.7-mm mg—others: 2/20-mm AA (I × 2)—2/81-mm mortars (I × 2)—2/12.7-mm mg
**Electron Equipt:** Radar: 1/DRBN 32
**M:** 2 SACM V-12 diesels; 2 CP props; 3,600 hp **Range:** 3,500/13
**Man:** 3 officers, 15 petty officers, 26 enlisted

REMARKS: Bow-door design, embarkation ramp and helicopter platform aft. Cargo: 350 tons. Living quarters for a landing team (5 officers, 15 noncommissioned officers, 118 men) and its 12 vehicles, including Leopard armored personnel carriers. L 9032 through L 9034 are able to transport 180 men; they have a 40-ton capacity bow ramp, improved accommodations, and carry 1 LCVP and 1 LCP landing craft. Their superstructure is one deck higher, and they can carry a 330-ton vehicle cargo for beaching and 208 tons of potable water. All have a helicopter deck for one Alouette-III. A sister ship has been built for Gabon. L 9034, built on speculation, then acquired for French Navy; has a longer helicopter deck.

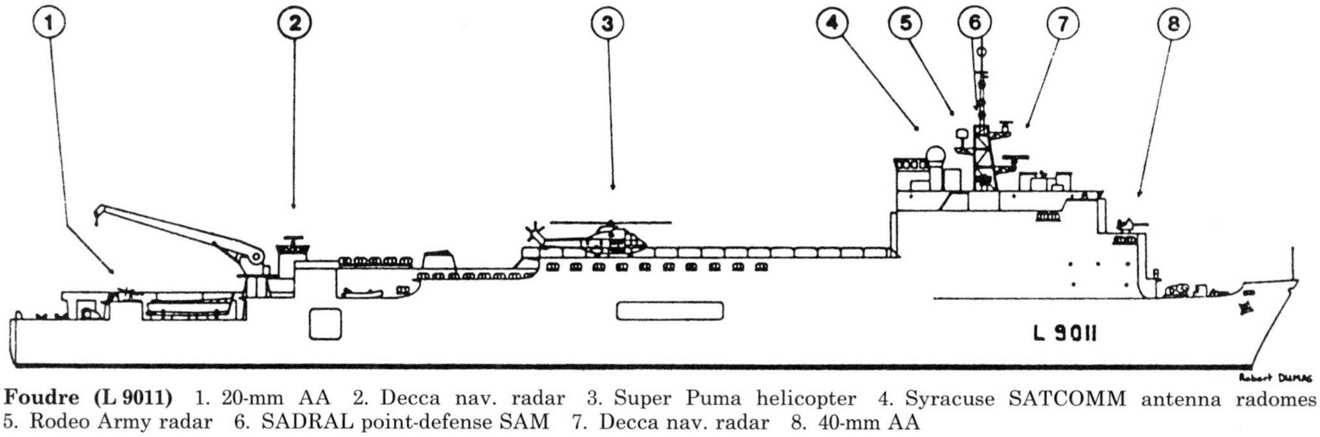


**Foudre (L 9011)** 1. 20-mm AA 2. Decca nav. radar 3. Super Puma helicopter 4. Syracuse SATCOMM antenna radomes 5. Rodeo Army radar 6. SADRAL point-defense SAM 7. Decca nav. radar 8. 40-mm AA

**AMPHIBIOUS WARFARE SHIPS** *(continued)*

**Francis Garnier (L 9031)**—low superstructure L. & L. Van Ginderen, 3-84

◆ **0 (+5) CDIC tank and infantry landing craft**
Bldr: SFCN, Villeneuve-la-Garenne

L . . . N . . . L . . . N . . . L . . . N . . . L . . . N . . . L . . . N . . .

**D:** 326 tons light (710 fl) **S:** 10 kts
**Dim:** 59.40 (55.45 pp) × 11.90 × 1.10 (1.76 max.)
**A:** 2/20-mm F2 AA (I × 2)—2/12.7-mm mg
**M:** 2 diesels; 2 props; 1,080 hp **Range:** 1,000/10 **Man:** 18 tot.

Remarks: CDIC = *Chalands de Débarquement d'Infantrie et de Chars.* In 1987–92 program. Cargo: 336 tons. Will replace surviving EDIC-I class. First unit ordered 18-3-87.

◆ **5 EDIC-class tank landing craft**

| | L | | L | | L |
|---|---|---|---|---|---|
| L 9091 | 7-1-58 | L 9096 | 11-10-58 | L 9072 | 1968 |
| L 9093 | 17-4-58 | L 9070 | 30-3-67 | | |

**L 9096**—broken deck line H. Ehlers, 6-87

**L 9070**—note flush deck H. Ehlers, 6-87

**D:** 250 tons (670 fl) **S:** 8 kts **Dim:** 59.0 × 11.95 × 1.3 (1.62 fl)
**A:** 2/20-mm AA (I × 2) **M:** 2 MGO diesels; 2 props; 1,000 hp
**Range:** 1,800/8 **Man:** 5 petty officers, 12 men

Remarks: EDIC = *Engins de débarquement pour infanterie et chars.* Can carry 11 trucks or 5 LVTs. Two each can be carried aboard the *Ouragan* and the *Orage.* L 9095 transferred to Senegal, 1-7-74. L 9071 stricken 19-4-77, L 9092 and L 9082 stricken 1981. L 9084 reclassified BAME (repair barge). L 9096 was loaned to Lebanon 7-11-83 and returned in 1-85: L 9073, L 9074, L 9083 stricken 1986; L 9094 stricken 1987; L 9091, L 9093, L 9096 to strike 1988, L 9072 in 1989. The similar "EDIC III," L 9051, was launched 10-3-87 for DIRCEN; see auxiliary pages.

◆ **21 repeat U.S. LCM (8)-class landing craft** Bldr: CMN, Cherbourg (CTM 4, 5, 11: C.N. Auroux, Arcachon)

| | In serv. | | In serv. | | In serv. | | In serv. |
|---|---|---|---|---|---|---|---|
| CTM 1 | 19-10-82 | CTM 5 | 21-12-82 | CTM 9 | 25-5-83 | CTM 13 | 11-4-84 |
| CTM 2 | 27-10-82 | CTM 6 | 16-2-83 | CTM 10 | 22-6-83 | CTM 14 | 8-8-84 |
| CTM 3 | 12-82 | CTM 7 | 3-83 | CTM 11 | 20-7-83 | CTM 15 | 25-10-84 |
| CTM 4 | 2-12-82 | CTM 8 | 1983 | CTM 12 | 11-8-83 | CTM 16 | 1985–86 |
| | | | | | | CTM 17 | 13-8-86 |
| | | | | | | CTM 18-21 | . . . |

**CTM 17** H. Ehlers, 6-87

**D:** 56 tons light (150 fl) **S:** 9.5 kts **Dim:** 23.80 × 6.35 × 1.25
**M:** 2 Poyaud 520 V8 diesels; 2 props; 480 hp
**Range:** 380/8.0 **Fuel:** 3.4 tons **Man:** 6 tot.

Remarks: Repeat version of earlier CTM 1–16. Cargo capacity: 90 tons. A small navigational radar is fitted. Endurance: 48 hours at half power.

◆ **6 U.S. LCM (3) class**

LCM 1035, 1036, 1055–1058

**L 1055** G. Gyssels, 6-82

**D:** 26 tons (52 fl) **S:** 8 kts **Dim:** 15.25 × 4.3 × 1.2
**M:** 2 Gray Marine 64 HN9 diesels; 2 props; 450 hp **Cargo:** 30 tons

Remarks: Transferred 6-58, except for LCM 1057 and 1058, built at La Réunion and delivered 3-83 for local service at Mayotte Naval Base. LCM 1031, 1045, 1052, 1074, and 1076 stricken 1984–85.

## EXPERIMENTAL SHIPS

Note: For smaller experimental trials tenders with Y-series pendants, see Miscellaneous Service Craft entry at end of France section.

◆ **0 (+1) Mine countermeasure experimental ship**

| | Bldr | Laid down | L | In serv. |
|---|---|---|---|---|
| A 785 Thetis (ex-*Néreide*) | Lorient Ars. | 3-86 | 15-11-86 | 1988 |

**D:** 720 tons (970 fl) **S:** 15 kts **Dim:** 59.00 (53.00 pp) × 10.90 × 3.55
**A:** . . . **Electric:** 750 kw (3 × 250 kw)
**Electron Equipt:** Radar: . . .—Sonar: DUBM 42
**M:** 2 SACM MGO 175-V12-RVR diesels; 2 CP props; 2,860 hp—2/122 electric motors

Remarks: Typed BEGM—*Bâtiment d'Expérimentation de la Guerre des Mines.* Ordered 11-10-84. Use same hull and machinery as the new hydrographic survey ships. A second unit was in the 1984-88 Plan; canceled. Will do trials with DUBM 42, new remotely operated mine-disposal vehicle, and AD-4 acoustic sweep. To replace *Narvik.*

◆ **1 missile-range tracking ship** Bldr: Cantieri Riuniti de Adriatico, Monfalcone, Italy

| | L | In serv. |
|---|---|---|
| A 603 Henri Poincaré (ex-*Maina Morasso*) | 10-60 | 1-3-68 |

**D:** 22,640 tons (23,430 fl) **S:** 15 kts **Dim:** 180.00 (160.00 pp) × 22.20 × 9.40
**A:** 2/20-mm AA **Electron Equipt:** Radar: 1/DRBV 22D, 2/Gascogne, 1/Savoie
**M:** 1 set Parsons GT; 1 prop; 10,000 hp; bow-thruster **Electric:** 7,355 kw
**Boilers:** 2 Foster-Wheeler; 48 kg/cm², 445°C **Range:** 11,800/13.5
**Man:** 22 officers, 144 petty officers, 159 men, and several civilian technicians

Remarks: Flagship of Group M (the Naval Test and Measurement Group), which makes at-sea tests, takes measurements, and conducts experiments, as requested

## EXPERIMENTAL SHIPS *(continued)*

**Henri Poincaré (A 603)** — 16 F., French Navy, 1983

by the Navy or any other organization, civilian or military. The chief mission of the *Henri Poincaré* is to measure the trajectory of ballistic missiles (MSBS and SSBS) fired from the experimental station at Landes or from missile-carrying nuclear submarines and to compute their flight characteristics, especially from re-entry to impact. Her secondary mission is to assist the flag officer in controlling the naval and air elements in the test area, particularly recovery and security.

A former Italian tanker, the ship was entirely rebuilt by DCAN at Brest between 1964 and 1967, during which time she was given three radars for tracking and trajectory-measuring in ballistic tests and a sonar dome. She also has: an automatic tracking station; celestial position-fixing equipment; a camera-equipped theodolite; infrared equipment; a Transit navigational system; aerological, meteorological, and oceanographic equipment; excellent communications equipment; a programming and transcribing center for all experiments and installations; and a platform and hangar for two heavy or five light helicopters. Refitted 1-8-79 to 1-6-80, with 2 Gascogne tracking radars in place of original 2 Bearn, as well as other alterations. Received Syracuse SATCOMM system in 1983.

◆ **1 Commandante Rivière-class sonar trials ship, former frigate**

| | Laid down | L | In serv. |
|---|---|---|---|
| A 733 Commandant Rivière (ex-F 733) | 4-57 | 11-10-58 | 4-12-62 |

**Commandant Rivière (A 733)** — DCAN Lorient, 12-85

**Commandant Rivière (A 733)** — M. Bar, 5-86

**D:** 2,100 tons (fl) **S:** 16 kts **Dim:** 103.00 × 12.52 (11.8 wl) × . . .
**A:** 1/40-mm AA—2/12.7-mm mg (I × 2)
**Electron Equipt:** Radar: 1/Decca 1226, 1/DRBV 22A
Sonar: DSBV 61 towed passive array; DUBV 43B VDS
**M:** 4 SEMT-Pielstick 12 PC-series diesels; 2 props; 16,000 hp
**Man:** 9 officers, 14 chief petty officers, 34 petty officers, 58 men + 37 technicians
**Electric:** 1,280 kw **Fuel:** . . . **Range:** . . .

Remarks: Converted during 1985 as replacement for the former frigate *L'Agenais* (A 784) in towed sonar array trials. The 100-mm guns and MM 38 Exocet missiles were removed, and a 40-mm AA replaced the 305-mm ASW mortar. A new, broader stern of about 20-m length replaced the original and supports the DUBV 43 variable-depth sonar hoist equipment removed from the stricken destroyer *Casabianca* (D 631). The original hull-mounted SQS-17 sonar has been replaced possibly by DUBV 24. Original 26-kt speed either reduced or restricted. Intended to test interface between hull-mounted VDS and passive linear towed hydrophone array sonars. To recommission 1-86.

◆ **1 guided-missile trials ship** Bldr: A. G. Weser, Bremen

| | L | In serv. |
|---|---|---|
| A 610 Île d'Oléron (ex-*Lazarettschiff München,* ex-*Sperrbrecher 32,* ex-*Mur*) | 1939 | 29-8-45 |

**Île d'Oléron** — Pradignac & Leo, 11-86

**D:** 5,500 tons (6,500 fl) **S:** 14.5 kts **Dim:** 115.05 (107.00 pp) × 15.24 × 6.50
**A:** 1/SADRAL SAM system (V × 1)—1/100-mm DP Model 1968 (78 rds/min.)
**Electron Equipt:** Radar: 1/DRBN 32, 1/DRBV 22C, 1/DRBV 50, 1/DRBI 10
**M:** 2 M.A.N. 6-cyl. diesels; 1 prop; 3,500 hp **Electric:** 1,240 kw
**Fuel:** 340 tons **Range:** 5,900/14; 7,200/19
**Man:** 9 officers, 46 petty officers, 113 men

Remarks: Taken from the Germans as a prize of war and used as a transport until converted, 1957-58, to an experimental ship for missiles. Besides the radars listed, she carries guidance radars for the systems under test. Used for MM 38 Exocet trials and, since 1977, for Crotale. Trials with Mistral SAM began 5-86. Helicopter deck aft.

◆ **1 electronics experimental ship**

| | Bldr | L | In serv. |
|---|---|---|---|
| A 644 Berry (ex-*Medoc*) | Roland Werft, Bremen | 10-9-58 | 26-11-64 |

**Berry (A 644)** — M. Bar, 4-85

**D:** 1,150 tons (2,700 fl) **S:** 15 kts **Dim:** 86.7 (78.5 pp) × 11.6 × 4.6
**A:** 2/20-mm AA (I × 2) **M:** 2 MWM diesels; 1 prop; 2,400 hp
**Range:** 7,000/15

Remarks: An ex-stores ship, converted 1976-77 at Toulon and recommissioned 2-77. Used for trials with electronic-warfare equipment. Painted white. Former sister *Aunis,* a sonar-trials ship, was stricken 1-7-81 and sunk as an AS-30 target, 4-87.

**EXPERIMENTAL SHIPS** *(continued)*

◆ **1 ex-U.S. Agile-class ocean minesweeper** Bldr: Peterson Builders, Sturgeon Bay, Wisc. In serv. 3-2-57

A 769 Narvik (ex-M 609, ex-MSO 512)

**Narvik (A 769)** LV (R) B. Prézelin, French Navy, 6-85

Remarks: Since recommissioning 1-1-76, conducts experiments with the AP-4 acoustic sweep and the DUBM 21 series. For data, see ex-U.S. *Agile* class under Mine Warfare Ships. Retains 1/40-mm AA.

Note: The *Sirius* class mine countermeasures trials ship *Bételgeuse* (A 747) was still in service in 1987; see photo in addenda.

◆ **1 underwater-research ship**

| | Budget | Bldr | Laid down | L | In serv. |
|---|---|---|---|---|---|
| A 646 Triton | 1967 | Lorient Ars. | 1967 | 7-3-70 | 20-1-72 |

**Triton (A 646)** Pradignac & Leo, 11-86

**D:** 1,410 tons (1,510 fl) **S:** 13 kts **Dim:** 74.00 (68.00 pp) × 11.85 × 3.65
**M:** 2 MGO V-12 ASHR diesels, electric drive; aft: 1/Voith-Schneider 30 G cycloidal propeller; 880 hp; forward: 2 electric motors, 1/Voith-Schneider 26 G cycloidal propeller; 530 hp
**Electric:** 640 kw **Range:** 4,000/13
**Man:** Ship's company: 4 officers, 44 men; divers: 5 officers, 12 men

Remarks: Assigned to GISMER (*Groupe d'Intervention sous la Mer*) for deep-sea diving and observation. Has a decompression chamber, laboratories, television, navigational radar, sonar for deep-water area search, etc. Helicopter platform. Good maneuverability at very slow speeds; capable of remaining positioned above a point 300 meters deep. Can be used in submarine-rescue operations. Her 15-ton crane can lower and raise: (a) a 13.5-ton tethered bell that can be sunk to 250 meters and can carry two four-man diving teams; (b) the two-man submarine *Griffon,* which is capable of diving to 600 meters for underwater exploration; (c) diving devices, sleds (troika, automatically guided). The *Griffon* has a manipulator arm, and other characteristics are:

**D:** 14.2 to 16.7 tons **Dim:** 7.8 × 2.3 × 3.1 (height) **M:** 1 electric motor
**Range:** 24 hours/4 kts

Note: The *Chamois*-class local support tender *Isard* is also subordinated to GISMER and supports the ERIC *(Engin de Recherche et d'Intervention par Cable)* wire-guided submersible. For data, see the *Chamois* class under Miscellaneous Auxiliary Ships.

◆ **1 ASW weapons-trials support tender**

| | Bldr | L | In serv. |
|---|---|---|---|
| A 743 Denti | DCAN, Toulon | 7-10-75 | 15-7-76 |

**Denti (A 743)** G. Gyssels, 6-85

**D:** 170 tons (fl) **S:** 12 kts **Dim:** 34.70 (30.00 pp) × 6.60 × 2.27
**Electron Equipt:** Radar: 1/Decca . . .
**M:** 2 Baudouin DP 8 diesels; 2 props; 960 hp
**Range:** 800/12 **Man:** . . .

Remarks: Employed by DCAN Toulon in support of weapons trials. Essentially a recovery craft, with an overhead rail gantry aft. Carries divers also.

**OCEANOGRAPHIC RESEARCH SHIPS**

◆ **1 expeditionary ship**

| | Bldr | Laid down | L | In serv. |
|---|---|---|---|---|
| A 757 D'Entrecasteaux | Brest | 7-69 | 30-5-70 | 10-10-70 |

**D'Entrecasteaux (A 757)** Skyfotos, 3-82

**D'Entrecasteaux (A 757)** L. & L. Van Ginderen, 5-82

**D:** 2,058 tons (2,440 fl) **S:** 15 kts
**Dim:** 95.65 (89.00 pp) × 13.00 × 4.20 (5.50 props)
**Electron Equipt:** Radar: 2/Decca 1226
**M:** 2 diesel engines, electric drive; 2 CP props; 2,720 hp; for extremely slow maneuvering: 2 retractable Schöttel propellers, 1 fwd, 1 aft

### OCEANOGRAPHIC RESEARCH SHIPS *(continued)*

**Range:** 12,000/12
**Man:** 6 officers, 31 petty officers, 41 men, up to 38 Hydrographic Service scientists and technicians

REMARKS: For oceanographic research and hydrographic duties. Has a dynamic mooring/maneuvering system permitting station-keeping in 5,000-m depths. Can take soundings and surveys to a depth of 5,000 meters. Helicopter platform and hangar (Alouette-III helicopter). Electrohydraulic oceanographic equipment cranes, one landing craft, three hydrographic launches, hull-mounted scanning sonar. Painted white. Three echo-sounders (one stabilized). Has Trident, Syledis, Toran, Transit, Omega, and Global Positioning System navigation equipment, plus Hydrac and Hydrai automatic data systems.

◆ **1 underwater archeological research ship**

| | Bldr | L |
|---|---|---|
| A 789 ARCHÉONAUTE | Auroux, Arcachon | 25-8-67 |

**Archéonaute (A 789)** J.-C. Bellonne, 1972

**D:** 100 tons (120 fl) **S:** 12 kts **Dim:** 29.3 × 6.0 × 1.7
**M:** 2 Baudouin diesels; 2 CP props; 600 hp
**Man:** 2 officers, 4 men, 3 scientific research personnel, 6 divers

REMARKS: Ordered by the Office of Cultural Affairs, manned by Navy personnel. Laboratory and workshops, decompression chamber, underwater television.

### HYDROGRAPHIC SURVEY SHIPS

◆ **0 (+4) new construction**

| | Bldr | Laid down | L | In serv. |
|---|---|---|---|---|
| A 791 LA PÉROUSE | Lorient Arsenal | 11-6-85 | 15-11-86 | . . . |
| A 792 BORDA | Lorient Arsenal | 2-9-85 | 15-11-86 | . . . |
| A 793 LA PLACE | Normandie, Gran Querilly | 22-1-86 | . . . | . . . |
| A 794 ARAGO | . . . | . . . | . . . | . . . |

**Borda (L 792)**—with *La Pérouse* beyond, fitting out B. Prézelin, 4-87

**D:** 720 tons light (970 fl) **S:** 15 kts **Dim:** 59.00 (53.00 pp) × 10.90 × 3.63 (max.)
**M:** 2 S.A.C.M. MGO Type 175 V 16SHR diesels; 1 CP prop; 2,200 hp—plus a 200-hp swivelling propulsor
**Range:** 6,000/12 **Man:** 27 crew + 11 hydrographic survey party
**Electric:** 620 kw

REMARKS: First two ordered 24-7-84. This program replaces the one 2,000-ton Type BH1 and two 800-ton Type BH2 described in the previous edition. The ships will carry the Thomson-CSF TSM 5425 wreck-identification sonar. They will replace four older coastal survey ships. Two 9-m hydrographic survey launches are carried. A near-sister will serve as a mine-warfare trials ship. A 791 alone has a sidescan sonar for wreck location.

◆ **2 converted ex-trawlers** Bldr: Gdynia, Poland

| | L | In serv. with French Navy |
|---|---|---|
| A 756 L'ESPÉRANCE (ex-*Jacques Coeur*) | 1962 | 12-7-69 |
| A 766 L'ESTAFETTE (ex-*Jacques Cartier*) | 1962 | 16-11-72 |

**L'Espérance (A 756)** Skyfotos, 4-86

**D:** 900 tons (1,300 fl) **S:** 13.5 kts **Dim:** 63.45 (59.75 pp) × 9.82 × 5.85 (fl)
**M:** 2 M.A.N. diesels; 1 prop; 1,870 hp **Range:** 7,500/13
**Man:** 3 officers, 11 petty officers, 29 enlisted

REMARKS: Former oceangoing fishing trawlers, purchased 1968–69. Carry one survey launch. Large oceanographic winch on stern, articulated crane amidships. Painted white.

| | Bldr | L | In serv. |
|---|---|---|---|
| A 758 LA RECHERCHE (ex-*Guyane*) | Ziegler, Dunkerque | 4-51 | 19-3-62 (in French Navy) |

**La Recherche (A 758)** G. Valentini, 6-86

**D:** 810 tons (910 fl) **S:** 13.5 kts **Dim:** 67.5 (62 pp) × 10.4 × 4.5
**M:** 1 Werkspoor MABS 398 diesels; 1 prop; 1,535 hp
**Range:** 3,100/10 **Man:** 2 officers, 10 petty officers, 26 men

REMARKS: Operated for the French Overseas Ministry. Bought in 1960. Hull bulged for improved stability. Carries two inshore survey launches. Painted white.

◆ **2 Astrolabe-class survey ships**

| | Bldr | Laid down | L | In serv. |
|---|---|---|---|---|
| A 780 ASTROLABE | Seine Maritime | 1962 | 27-5-63 | 7-64 |
| A 781 BOUSSOLE | Seine Maritime | 6-62 | 11-4-63 | 7-64 |

**D:** 330 tons (440 fl) **S:** 12.5 kts **Dim:** 42.7 (36.65 pp) × 8.45 × 2.9
**M:** 2 Baudouin DV 8 diesels; 1 CP prop; 800 hp
**Range:** 4,000/12 **Man:** 1 officer, 32 men

REMARKS: Air-conditioned. Carry two 8.8-m Type VH8 survey launches equipped with the Trident radiolocation system; they are later to be fitted with Toran. Painted white. Formerly had "P"-series pendants, and A 780 at one time carried 1/40-mm AA, 2/12.7-mm mg. See photo next page.

◆ **1 inshore survey ship**

| | Bldr | L | In serv. |
|---|---|---|---|
| A 794 CORAIL (ex-*Marc Joly*) | Thuin, Belgium | 1967 | 11-4-75 (French Navy) |

**HYDROGRAPHIC SURVEY SHIPS** *(continued)*

**D:** 54.78 tons (light) **S:** 10.3 kts **Dim:** 17.8 × 4.92 × 1.83
**M:** 1 Caterpillar diesel; 1 prop; 250 hp **Man:** 7 tot.

REMARKS: Ex-fishing boat, operates in the Pacific. Painted white.

**Astrolabe (A 780)** M. Louagie, 3-87

## SUPPORT TENDERS

◆ **1 multipurpose repair ship**

| | Budget | Bldr | Laid down | L | In serv. |
|---|---|---|---|---|---|
| A 620 JULES VERNE (ex-*Achéron*) | 1961 | Brest Ars. | 1969 | 30-5-70 | 1-6-76 |

**Jules Verne (A 620)** J.-C. Bellonne, 1982

**D:** 6,485 tons (10,250 fl) **S:** 18 kts **Dim:** 147.0 × 21.56 × 6.5
**A:** 2/40-mm AA (I × 2)
**M:** 2 SEMT-Pielstick T2 PC diesels; 1 prop; 11,200 hp
**Electric:** 3,800 kw **Range:** 9,500/18
**Man:** 16 officers, 150 petty officers, 116 men

REMARKS: Six years after being launched as an ammunition ship, the uncompleted *Jules Verne* was converted to a floating workshop to provide support to a force of from three to six surface warships. Has significant capabilities for both regular maintenance and battle-damage repair: mechanical, engine, electrical, sheet-metal, electronic workshops, etc. She carries a stock of torpedoes and other munitions. Has a platform and hangar for two Alouette-III helicopters. Operates in support of the Indian Ocean Flotilla.

◆ **5 Rhin class** Bldr: Lorient Arsenal (differences as noted)

| | Budget | Purpose | Laid down | L | In serv. |
|---|---|---|---|---|---|
| A 615 LOIRE | 1962 | Minesweepers | 9-7-65 | 1-10-66 | 10-10-67 |
| A 621 RHIN | 1959 | Electronics | 24-4-61 | 17-3-62 | 1-3-64 |
| A 622 RHÔNE | 1960 | Submarines | 23-2-62 | 8-12-62 | 1-12-64 |

**Loire (A 615)**—helicopter hangar, 3 radars, IFF interrogator
L. & L. Van Ginderen, 9-85

**Rhône (A 622)**—helo deck, no hangar (A 615 similar)
L. & L. Van Ginderen. 1-85

**D:** 2,075 tons (2,445 fl) **S:** 16.5 kts **Dim:** 101.05 (92.05 pp) × 13.1 × 3.65
**A:** 3/40-mm AA (I × 3) **Electron Equipt:** Radar: 2/DRBN 32
**M:** 2 SEMT-Pielstick 16 PA 2V diesels; 1 prop; 3,200 hp
**Electric:** 920 kw **Range:** 13,000/13
**Man:** A 621, 622: 6 officers, 42 petty officers, 76 men (A 615: 9 officers, 131 men)

| | Budget | Purpose | Laid down | L | In serv. |
|---|---|---|---|---|---|
| A 618 RANCE | 1964 | Experimental | 8-64 | 5-5-65 | 5-2-66 |

**Rance (A 618)** G. Gyssels, 6-82

**A:** none **Electron Equipt:** Radar: 1/DRBN 32, 1/DRBV 22E
EW: ARBR/ARBA 10
**M:** SEMT-Pielstick 12 PA 4 diesels; 3,600 hp
**Man:** 10 officers, 39 petty officers, 69 men

| | Budget | Purpose | Bldr | Laid down | L | In serv. |
|---|---|---|---|---|---|---|
| A 617 GARONNE | 1964 | Repair | Lorient | 11-63 | 8-8-64 | 9-65 |

**Garonne (A 617)** J.-C. Bellonne, 1977

**D:** 2,320 tons **S:** 15 kts **Dim:** 101.5 (92.05 pp) × 13.8 × 3.7
**A:** 1/40-mm AA—2/20-mm AA **Electron Equipt:** Radar: 1/DRBN 32
**M:** 2 SEMT-Pielstick 12 PA 4 diesels; 1 prop; 3,600 hp **Range:** 13,000/13
**Man:** 6 officers, 39 petty officers, 69 men

REMARKS: *Rhin* has 1,700 $m^3$ of store rooms and 700 $m^3$ of workshops, many air-conditioned. She has a hangar and flight deck for one helicopter, which is equipped to serve minesweepers with spare sweep gear, cable, and repairs. *Rhône* is fitted to service submarines; helicopter deck but no hangar. *Loire* has a helicopter deck and hangar. All have one 5-ton crane with a 12-meter reach. The profile of the *Rance* is different from that of the other ships of this group; an additional deck has been fitted between her navigating bridge and her stack. She has a laboratory, radioactive decontamination stations, and carries up to three Alouette helicopters, using both the stern and her hangar roof as landing platforms. *Garonne* was designed for overseas service. She has metalworking and carpentry shops, an extra deck with lower overhead, and a 30-ton crane mounted in the center of her fantail; no helicopter facilities.

## FLEET REPLENISHMENT SHIPS

◆ **4(+1) Durance-class fleet oilers** Bldr: Brest Arsenal

| | Laid down | L | In serv. |
|---|---|---|---|
| A 629 Durance | 10-12-73 | 6-9-75 | 1-12-76 |
| A 607 Meuse | 2-6-77 | 2-12-78 | 2-8-80 |
| A 608 Var | 12-78 | 9-5-81 | 29-1-83 |
| A 630 Marne | 4-8-82 | 6-2-85 | 16-1-87 |
| A . . . N . . . | 3-5-85 | 3-10-87 | 1-89 |

**Var (A 608)**—Syracuse SATCOMM antennas atop bridge superstructure J.-C. Bellonne, 1987

**Meuse (A 607)** L. Grazioli, 1-87

**Marne (A 630)** J.-C. Bellonne, 1987

**D:** 7,600 tons (17,800 fl) **S:** 19 kts
**Dim:** 157.3 (149.0 pp) × 21.2 × 8.65 (10.8 fl)
**A:** 1/40-mm AA—2/20-mm AA (I × 2)—A 629: 2/40-mm AA (I × 2)—no 20-mm
**M:** 2 SEMT-Pielstick 16 PC 2.5 V400 diesels; 2 CP props; 20,000 hp
**Electric:** 5,400 kw **Fuel:** 750 tons **Range:** 9,000/15
**Man:** 8 officers, 62 petty officers, 89 men (*Var:* 10 officers, 62 p.o., 90 men)

Remarks: Two dual solids/liquids underway-replenishment stations per side. Can supply two ships alongside and one astern. *Durance:* 7,500 tons fuel oil, 1,500 tons diesel fuel, 500 tons JP-5, 130 tons distilled water, 170 tons fresh provisions, 150 tons munitions, 50 tons spare parts; *Meuse:* 5,090 tons fuel oil, 4,014 tons diesel, 1,140 tons JP-5, 250 tons distilled water, 180 tons provisions, 122 tons munitions, and 45 tons spare parts. *Var* and *Marne:* 5,090 tons fuel oil, 3,310 tons diesel, 1,090 tons JP-5, 260 tons distilled water, 170 tons ammunition, 180 tons provisions, 15 tons spares. Hangar for one Alouette-III (*Var:* Lynx) and flight deck for larger helicopters. Superstructure before the bridge one deck higher in *Meuse*. In *Meuse* the 40-mm AA is aft; in *Var* it is forward. *Var* and *Marne* are equipped as flagships for a major area commander and can accommodate 257 persons. The forward superstructure block is extended aft by 8 meters to provide increased staff accommodations, and the two beam-mounted stores cranes immediately abaft the bridge are replaced by a single, centerline crane; the Syracuse SATCOMM system is fitted. A fifth ship, which will resemble A 608 and A 630, was ordered 3-84 from CNM, La Seyne, on speculation and purchased 10-87 for the French Navy; the ship is identical to A 608 and A 630. A fifth for the French Navy was to have been ordered in 1986 under the 1984-88 Plan. A near sister was built in Australia for the R.A.N.

## TRANSPORT OILERS

◆ **2 chartered freighting tankers** Bldr: Ch. de l'Atlantique, St. Nazaire

| | Laid down | L | In serv. |
|---|---|---|---|
| Mascarin | 10-9-85 | 20-3-86 | 11-7-86 |
| Penhors | 2-86 | 9-9-86 | 23-11-86 |

**D:** approx 42,000 tons (fl) **S:** 14.25 kts
**Dim:** 178.17 (165.02 pp) × 27.50 × 11.38
**A:** none **Electron Equipt:** Radar: . . .
**M:** 1 SOCATRA-B & W 6L-67 GBE diesel; 1 CP prop; 11,110 hp (7,440 sust.)—1,210-hp bow-thruster
**Range:** 21,000/14
**Electric:** 4,000 kw (3 × 1000-kw diesel; 1 × 1,000-kw shaft-driven)
**Man:** 18 tot. (civil)

Remarks: 18,900 grt/32,000 dwt. First unit ordered 20-3-85 for charter to French Navy for use between Persian Gulf and La Réunion in support of Indian Ocean activities. Twelve centerline cargo tanks, flanked by wing ballast tanks. Can carry up to four different types of liquid cargo: 35,160 $m^3$. Ballast: 9,160 $m^3$. Four 800 $m^3$/hr. cargo pumps; two 250 $m^3$/hr. ballast pumps; two 150 $m^3$/hr. stripping pumps. Tanks have heating coils. One underway-replenishment station per side. These are *not* officially considered to be French Navy ships.

◆ **1 chartered tanker** Bldr: Brodogradititse, Uljanik, Yugoslavia

Port Vendres (ex-*Mont-Agel, ex-Wiiri*) (L: 17-2-73; in serv. 3-73)

**Port Vendres** G. Gyssels, 7-87

**D:** approx. 31,000 tons (fl) **S:** 15.5 kts
**Dim:** 175.10 (163.20 pp) × 25.05 × 9.68
**M:** 1 Burmeister & Wain 6K74EF diesel; 1 prop; 10,600 hp
**Electric:** 1,544 kw **Man:** 27 tot.

Remarks: 15,285 grt/25,253 dwt. Chartered 4-8-82 and to be returned to owners, SOFLUMAR (Societé d'Armament Fluvial et Maritime), by 1988. Cargo capacity 32,088 $m^3$ liquid. Has a 1,200-hp KaMeWa tunnel bow-thruster. Can refuel over the stern.

◆ **2 Punaruu class** Bldr: Trosvik Verkstad, Brevek, Norway

| | In serv. (French Navy) |
|---|---|
| A 625 Papenoo (ex-*Bow Queen*) | 9-11-71 |
| A 632 Punaruu (ex-*Bow Cecil*) | 16-11-71 |

**Papenoo (A 625)** French Navy, 1983

**D:** 1,195 tons light (4,050 fl) **S:** 13 kts **Dim:** 83.00 (70.70 pp) × 13.85 × 5.50
**Electron Equipt:** Radar: 1/Decca RM 316
**M:** 2 Normo LSMC-8 diesels; 1 CP prop; 2,050 hp **Electric:** 290 kw
**Fuel:** 174 tons **Range:** 8,000/11.5 **Man:** 2 officers, 20 men

**TRANSPORT OILERS** *(continued)*

Remarks: 1,119 grt, 2,889 dwt. Former Norwegian solvent tankers purchased at the end of 1969. Highly automated ships. Capacity: 2,554 m$^3$. Ten washable "inox" cargo tanks that can accept any liquid. Astern fueling capability. Bow-thruster equipped (530 kw). Operate primarily in the Pacific.

**LIGHT-FUELS TANKER**

| | Bldr | Laid down | L | In serv. |
|---|---|---|---|---|
| A 619 Aber Wrach | CNM, Cherbourg | 11-62 | 11-63 | 27-3-66 |

**Aber Wrach (A 619)** L. & L. Van Ginderen, 1984

**D:** 1,220 tons (3,500 fl) **S:** 12 kts **Dim:** 86.55 (80.0 pp) × 12.2 × 4.8
**A:** 1/40-mm AA **M:** 1 SEMT-Pielstick 6 PL diesel; 1 CP prop; 2,000 hp
**Electron Equipt:** Radar: 1/DRBN 32—EW: ARBR/ARBA 10
**Range:** 5,000/12 **Man:** 3 officers, 45 men

Remarks: Cargo capacity: 2,200 tons. Carries diesel oil, jet fuel, and gasoline in point-to-point service. Capable of astern underway fueling, or anchored alongside.

**SUPPORT SHIPS FOR NUCLEAR WEAPONS TESTING**

Note: The seven ships described below were financed by and are operated for DIRCEN—*Direction des Centres d'Expérimentation Nuclear*—the French nuclear-weapon testing agency, in support of activities at Muraroa in the South Pacific. They are manned by the French Navy.

◆ **1 BTMS small dock landing ship**

| | Bldr | Laid down | L | In serv. |
|---|---|---|---|---|
| L 9077 Bougainville | Dubigeon, Nantes | 28-1-86 | 3-10-86 | 12-87 |

**Bougainville (L 9077)** L. & L. Van Ginderen, 11-87

**D:** 4,200 tons (4,870 fl) **S:** 14.6 kts
**Dim:** 113.50 (105.00 pp) × 17.00 × 4.24
**A:** no weapons—2/Super Puma helicopters
**Electron Equipt:** Radar: 1/navigational
**M:** 2 SACM MGO 195 V12 RVR diesels; 2 CP props; 4,800 hp—side-thruster
**Electric:** 1,600 kw **Range:** 6,000/12
**Fuel:** . . . **Endurance:** 30 days
**Man:** 6 officers, 17 petty officers, 29 enlisted + 50 passengers or 500 troops

Remarks: BTMS—*Bâtiment de Transport Moyen et de Soutien;* intended for Directorate of Nuclear Experimentation for use between Papeete and the Muraroa Test Center. Ordered 12-83; completed after launch by Ch. de l'Atlantique, St. Nazaire when building yard closed. Miniature LSD design with 78.0 × 11.8 (10.2 clear)-m docking well for landing craft or 40 20-ft containers. Draft aft 9.20 when flooded, providing 3.15 m clear over deck. 37-ton crane aft to starboard. Six-meter ramp to starboard can accommodate 53 tons. Has 70 m$^3$ helicopter fuel. Can also act as a repair and stores ship.

◆ **1 EDIC type 700 landing craft**

| | Bldr | L | In serv. |
|---|---|---|---|
| L 9051 | SFCN, Villeneuve la Garenne | 10-3-87 | 6-87 |

**L 9051** H. Ehlers, 6-87

**D:** 315 tons light (726 fl) **S:** 12 kts **Dim:** 59.00 (52.90 pp) × 11.90 × 1.69 (max)
**A:** 2/20-mm AA (I × 2)—2/12.7-mm mg (I × 2)
**Electron Equipt:** Radar: 1/. . . nav.
**M:** 2 UNI UD.30 V12 diesels; 2 props; 1,400 hp
**Range:** 1,800/8 **Man:** 7 petty officers, 9 men

Remarks: 320 grt. Ordered 9-86 as standard version of current EDIC design ("EDIC-III") to serve the French nuclear test site. Cargo: 340 tons. Can carry 11 trucks. Previous designation for main engines: S.A.C.M. MGO 175-V12.

Note: The following six ships were originally ordered to support *Force de Surface à Missions Civiles* (Civil Missions Surface Force) duties on the Atlantic coast of France.

◆ **2 Type RR 4000 class tug/supply vessels** Bldr: Breheret, Coneron, Nantes

| | L | In serv. | | L | In serv. |
|---|---|---|---|---|---|
| A 634 Rari | 16-4-84 | 5-2-85 | A 635 Revi | 15-5-84 | 6-2-85 |

**Rari (A 634)** B. Prézelin, 7-84

**D:** 1,057 tons light (1,557 fl) **S:** 14.5 kts **Dim:** 51.00 (49.50 wl) × 12.60 × 4.10
**Electron Equipt:** Radar: 1/Decca 1226 nav. **Range:** 6,000/12
**M:** 2 SACM Type 195 V12 RVR; 2 CP props; 4,000 hp
**Man:** 2 officers, 16 men **Fuel:** 300 tons **Electric:** 600 kw (2 × 300 kw)

Remarks: Can carry 18 passengers. Bollard pull: 47 tons. Two 2.5-ton thrust side-thrusters. Have a 14-ton crane aft, plus a quadrantial gantry at the extreme stern. Two water cannons for firefighting. Can carry fuel cargo.

◆ **1 Type RR 2000 (Modified Chamois) class tug/supply vessel**

| | Bldr | Laid down | L | In serv. |
|---|---|---|---|---|
| A 633 Taape | de la Perrière, Lorient | 22-10-82 | 14-4-83 | 30-6-83 |

**Taape (A 633)** BAN Lanveoc-Poulmic, French Navy, 1984

**D:** 383 tons (505 fl) **S:** 14.2 kts **Dim:** 41.02 (38.50 pp) × 7.5 × 3.18
**M:** 2 SACM M60 V16 ASHR diesels; 2 CP Kort-nozzle props; 2,200 hp
**Range:** 7,200/12 **Man:** 2 officers, 18 men

Remarks: A variation of the FISH-class design also used in the *Chamois*-class tenders. 24.8 bollard pull. Can carry 100 tons of cargo on the long, open afterdeck. Transported to Muraroa in the landing ship *Orage* in 4-84.

SUPPORT SHIPS FOR NUCLEAR WEAPONS TESTING *(continued)*

◆ **3 seagoing tugs** Bldr: SFCN, Villeneuve-la-Garenne

| | Laid down | L | In serv. |
|---|---|---|---|
| A 636 Maito | 24-6-83 | 6-1-84 | 27-2-84 |
| A 637 Maroa | 30-8-83 | 20-1-84 | 30-3-84 |
| A 638 Manini | 15-11-84 | 19-4-85 | 12-9-85 |

**Maroa (A 637)** 1984

**D:** 245 tons (278 fl) **S:** 11 kts **Dim:** 27.60 (24.50 wl) × 8.90 × 3.50
**M:** 2 SACM Type 175 6L RVR diesels; 2 Voith-Schneider vertical cycloidal props; 1,280 hp
**Range:** 1,200/10 **Man:** 6 tot. + 4 passengers.

Remarks: For service at Muraroa. Bollard pull: 12 tons. Have a firefighting water cannon.

MISCELLANEOUS AUXILIARY SHIPS

◆ **6 Chamois-class local support or diving tenders** Bldr: Ch. de la Perrière, Lorient

| | Laid down | L | In serv. |
|---|---|---|---|
| A 767 Chamois | . . . | 30-4-76 | 24-9-76 |
| A 768 Elan | 16-3-77 | 28-7-77 | 7-4-78 |
| A 774 Chevreuil | 15-9-76 | 8-5-77 | 7-10-77 |
| A 775 Gazelle | 30-12-76 | 7-6-77 | 13-1-78 |
| A 776 Isard | 2-11-77 | 2-5-78 | 15-12-78 |
| A 779 Tapatai (ex-*Silver Fish*) | . . . | 1971 | 27-3-81 |

**D:** 305 tons light (505 fl) **S:** 14.5 kts **Dim:** 41.60 (36.96 pp) × 7.5 × 3.20
**M:** 2 SACM MGO V16 AFHR diesels; 2 CP Kort-nozzle props; 2,200 hp
**Fuel:** 92 m$^3$ **Range:** 7,200/12 **Man:** 2 officers, 16 petty officers, 2 men

Remarks: Except for a 5.6-ton crane, the first four are identical to the 14 merchant FISH class designed for the supply of petroleum platforms. Hydraulic 50-ton stern crane mounted on A 767, A 774. All but A 776 can carry 100 tons dry cargo on deck or 125 tons fuel and 40 tons water (or 65 tons fuel/125 tons water). A 768 and A 775 primarily used as water tankers. Can be used for coastal towing and cleaning up oil spills. Two rudders and an 80-hp bow-thruster. After winch with 28-ton bollard pull. Can be used as transports for 28 passengers, as minelayers, or as torpedo retrievers. *Isard* is equipped as a divers' support ship and tender for the ERIC wire-guided submersible (2 tons, 4 m overall, 600-m diving depth). She has a ULISM decompression chamber capable of simulating pressures to a water depth of 150 m. She also has a longer aft structure, supporting divers' rubber dinghys and a small helicopter deck; the ship is subordinated to GISMER. A 779, a former merchant unit of this class, was purchased at Noumea in 1979 and commissioned for service in support of the Pacific Test Center.

Four additional modified units, intended to replace the U.S. MSC-class mine-clearance, diver-support ships, were ordered 11-10-84. They are listed with the mine warfare ships.

**Chevreuil (A 774)** L. & L. Van Ginderen, 4-86

**Isard (A 776)**—white-painted divers' support ship M. Louagie, 8-86

NET TENDERS

◆ **1 seagoing net tender**

| | Bldr | Laid down | L | In serv. |
|---|---|---|---|---|
| A 731 Tianée | Brest Ars. | 1-4-73 | 1-11-73 | 8-7-75 |

**Tianée (A 731)** 1974

**D:** 842 tons (905 fl) **S:** 12 kts **Dim:** 54.3 × 10.6 × . . .
**M:** 2/480-kw diesel generator sets, 1/880-kw electric motor; 1 prop; 1,200 hp
**Range:** 5,200/12 **Man:** 1 officer, 12 petty officers, 24 men

Remarks: Living quarters air-conditioned, transverse bow-thruster. Used primarily as a mooring-buoy tender. Stationed at Papeete.

◆ **5 U.S. AN 93 class**

| | Bldr | L | In serv. |
|---|---|---|---|
| A 760 Cigale (ex-AN 98) | A.C. de la Rochelle-Pallice | 23-9-54 | 24-6-55 |
| A 761 Criquet (ex-AN 96) | A.C. Seine Maritime | 3-6-54 | 25-3-55 |
| A 762 Fourmi (ex-AN 97) | A.C. Seine Maritime | 6-7-54 | 24-6-55 |
| A 763 Grillon (ex-AN 95) | Penhoët | 18-2-54 | 25-3-55 |
| A 764 Scarabée (ex-AN 94) | Penhoët | 21-11-53 | 15-2-55 |

**Grillon (A 763)** B. Prézelin, 4-87

**NET TENDERS** *(continued)*

**D:** 770 tons (850 fl) **Dim:** 46.28 (44.5 pp) × 10.2 × 3.2
**Electron Equipt:** Radar: 1/Decca . . . nav.
**M:** 2 SEMT-Pielstick PA-1 diesels, electric drive; 1 prop; 1,600 hp
**Fuel:** 125 m³ diesel oil **Range:** 5,200/12
**Man:** 1 officer, 36 men

Remarks: U.S. "Offshore" mutual assistance. One sister built for Spain, two others built in Italy. Used as mooring-buoy and salvage tenders, except A 760, used as a torpedo retriever. Formerly carried 1/40-mm AA, 4/20-mm AA (I × 4).

◆ **3 La Prudente-class port netlayers**

| | Bldr | L | In serv. |
|---|---|---|---|
| Y 749 La Prudente | A.C. de la Manche | 13-5-68 | 27-7-69 |
| Y 750 La Persévérante | A.D. de la Rochelle-Pallice | 14-5-68 | 3-3-69 |
| Y 751 La Fidèle | A.C. de la Manche | 26-8-68 | 10-6-69 |

**Persévérante (Y 750)** G. Gyssels, 7-82

**D:** 446 tons (626 fl) **S:** 10 kts **Dim:** 43.5 (42.0 pp) × 10.0 × 2.8
**M:** 2 Baudouin diesels, electric drive; 1 prop; 620 hp **Electric:** 440 kw
**Range:** 4,000/10 **Man:** 1 officer, 8 petty officers, 21 men

Remarks: Used as mooring-buoy tenders. Lifting power via pivoting gantry forward: 25 tons.

◆ **1 small mooring-buoy tender** Bldr: IMC, Rochefort sur Mer

Y 692 Telenn Môr (L: 4-4-85; in serv. 16-1-86)

**Telenn Môr (Y 692)** L. & L. Van Ginderen, 9-86

**D:** 518 tons (fl) **S:** 8 kts **Dim:** 41.40 (37.00 pp) × 9.10 × 1.88
**M:** 2 diesels; 2 props; 900 hp **Electric:** 350 kw **Man:** 10 tot.

◆ **1 Tupa-class mooring-buoy tender** (In serv. 16-3-74)

Y 667 Tupa

**D:** 292 tons light **S:** 6 kts **Dim:** 28.5 × 8.3 × 0.85
**M:** 1 diesel; 1 prop; 210 hp

Remarks: Based at Muraroa.

◆ **1 Calmar-class small mooring-buoy tender** (In serv. 12-8-70)

Y 698 Calmar

**D:** 270 tons light **S:** 9.5 kts **Dim:** . . . × . . . × . . .
**M:** 1 Baudouin diesel; 1 prop; . . . hp

Remarks: Based at Lorient. Former tug.

**Tupa (Y 667)** French Navy, 1983

**DIVING TENDERS**

◆ **1 base tender**

| | Bldr | L | In serv. |
|---|---|---|---|
| A 722 Poseidon | SIGNAV, St.-Malo | 5-12-74 | 14-1-77 |

**Poseidon (A 722)** J.-C. Bellonne, 1977

**D:** 200 tons (220 fl) **S:** 13 kts **Dim:** 40.5 (38.5 pp) × 7.2 × 2.2
**M:** 1 diesel; 600 hp **Endurance:** 8 days **Man:** 42 tot.

Remarks: Used for training combat frogmen. Based at Toulon.

Note: The four remaining U.S. *Adjutant*-class former minesweepers used as diving tenders in support of mine-clearance divers and for training, were to have been stricken by end 1987: *Ajonc* (A 701, ex-M 667, ex-MSC 71), *Gardenia* (M 711, ex-A 711, ex-M 676, ex-MSC 114), *Liseron* (A 723, ex-M 683, ex-MSC 98), and *Magnolia* (M 770, ex-A 770, ex-M 685, ex-MSC 87). They were replaced by new units of the *Vulcain* class.

**TORPEDO RECOVERY SHIPS**

Note: The net tender *Cigale* (A 760) is also used as a torpedo retriever, and some of the tenders of the *Chamois* class can be employed as such.

◆ **1 former tuna-fishing boat**

A 699 Pélican (ex-*Kerfany*) Bldr: Avondale, U.S.A., 1951

**Pélican (A 699)** Pradignac & Leo, 9-86

**D:** 362 tons (425 fl) **S:** 11 kts **Dim:** 37.0 × 8.55 × 4.0
**M:** 1 Burmeister & Wain diesel; 1 prop; 650 hp **Man:** 5 petty officers, 14 men

Remarks: Purchased 1965. 550-mm torpedo tube at stern.

## TORPEDO RECOVERY SHIPS *(continued)*

◆ **2 small torpedo retrievers for use at the St. Tropez trials center**

PÉGASE Bldr: SFCN (In serv. 1975)—880-hp catamaran with one 550-mm torpedo tube aft

SAMBRACITE (In serv. 1974)

## COASTAL TRANSPORTS

◆ **1 transport/miscellaneous service craft** Bldr: . . .

Y . . . GAPEAU (In serv. . . .-86)

**D:** 509 tons light (1,058 fl) **S:** 10 kts **Dim:** 64.00 × 12.20 × 3.30
**M:** . . .
**Man:** 6 crew + 30 passengers

REMARKS: Replaced EDIC L 9092 and L 9093 as tender to the *Centre d'Essais de la Marine*. Cargo: 460 tons.

◆ **9 Ariel class** Bldr: A: SFCN, Franco-Belges; B: DCAN, Brest

| | Bldr | L | | Bldr | L |
|---|---|---|---|---|---|
| Y 604 ARIEL | A | 27-4-63 | Y 700 NÉRÉIDE | B | 17-2-77 |
| Y 613 FAUNE | A | 8-9-71 | Y 701 ONDINE | B | 4-10-79 |
| Y 622 DRYADE | A | 1973 | Y 702 NAIADE | B | 4-10-79 |
| Y 661 KORRIGAN | A | 6-3-64 | Y 741 ELFE | A | 14-4-70 |
| Y 696 ALPHÉE | A | 10-6-69 | | | |

**Naiade (Y 702)** G. Gyssels, 6-85

**D:** 195 tons (225 fl) **S:** 15 kts **Dim:** 40.5 × 7.45 × 3.3
**M:** 2 MGO (1,640 hp) or Poyaud (1,730 hp) diesels; 2 props
**Man:** 9 tot.

REMARKS: Can carry 400 passengers (250 seated). All based at Brest, except *Ariel* and *Naiade* at Toulon.

◆ **1 small personnel transport:** TREBERON (In serv. 26-11-79)—at Brest

◆ **3 Merlin class**

Bldrs: Y 735 and Y 736: C.N. Franco-Belges; Y 671: A du Mourillon

Y 735 MERLIN (L: 8-11-67) Y 736 MÉLUSINE (L: 23-12-63) Y 671 MORGANE (L: 14-6-73)

**Mélusine (Y 736)** L. & L. Van Ginderen, 8-84

**D:** 170 tons **S:** 11 kts **Dim:** 31.5 × 7.06 × 2.4
**M:** MGO diesels; 2 props; 960 hp **Man:** 400 passengers

REMARKS: All based at Toulon.

◆ **1 Sylphe class** Bldr: C.N. Franco-Belges (In serv. 1960)

Y 710 SYLPHE

**Sylphe (Y 710)** 1976

**D:** 142 tons (189 fl) **S:** 12 kts **Dim:** 38.5 (36.75 pp) × 6.9 × 2.5
**M:** 1 MGO diesel; 1 prop; 425 hp **Man:** 9 tot.

REMARKS: Has operated from Brest since 1981.

## SALVAGE AND RESCUE TUGS

NOTE: The French government leased four powerful salvage tugs as a result of the *Amoco Cadiz* disaster; *Abeille Normandie* and *Abeille Provence* were returned to the owners in 1986 and replaced by *Mérou* and *Girelle* in 1987.

◆ **1 Mérou class** Bldr: B.V. Scheepswerf Waterhuizen J. Pattje, Groningen (In serv. 1982)

MÉROU (ex-*King Fish*)

**D:** . . . **S:** 14.2 kts **Dim:** 59.35 × 15.00 × 5.32 **Electron Equipt:** Radar: . . .
**M:** 4 Wichmann diesels; 2 CP props. 8,000 hp—500-hp thruster
**Endurance:** 50 days **Range:** 13,000/14.2
**Man:** 8 officers, 18 men, 12 passengers

REMARKS: 1,471 grt. Leased from Fish International. Based at Toulon. Two water cannon, 1/1,200-$m^3$/hr. pump. See photo in addenda.

◆ **1 Girelle class** Bldr: B.V. Scheepswerf Waterhuizen J. Pattje, Groningen (In serv. 1981)

GIRELLE (ex-*Moon Fish*)

**D:** . . . **S:** 13 kts **Dim:** 53.55 × 11.54 × 4.56
**Electron Equipt:** Radar: . . .
**M:** 2 Wichmann diesels; 2 CP props; 4,000 hp—400-hp thruster
**Range:** 13,248/13 **Man:** 5 officers, 14 men, 12 passengers

REMARKS: 851 grt. Leased from Fish International. Bollard pull: 50 tons. See photo in addenda.

◆ **2 Abeille Flandre class** Bldr: Ulstein Hatlo A/S, Ulsteinvik, Norway

ABEILLE FLANDRE (In serv. 1978) (ex-*Neptun Suecia*) ABEILLE LANGUEDOC (In serv. 1978) (ex-*Neptun Gothia*)

**Abeille Languedoc** M. Louagie, 3-87

**D:** . . . **S:** 17 kts **Dim:** 63.40 (58.60 pp) × 14.74 × 6.90 **Fuel:** 1,450 tons
**M:** 4/8-cyl. Atlas diesels; 2 CP props; 23,000 hp **Electric:** 1,280 kw

REMARKS: 1,577 grt. *A. Flandre* at Brest, *A. Languedoc* at Cherbourg. Ice-strengthened; have bow-thrusters.

## SEAGOING TUGS

◆ **3 Tenace class**

| | Bldr | L | In serv. |
|---|---|---|---|
| A 664 MALABAR | Oelkers, Hamburg | 16-4-75 | 3-2-76 |
| A 669 TENACE | Oelkers, Hamburg | 12-71 | 15-11-73 |
| A 674 CENTAURE | de la Rochelle-Pallice | 8-1-74 | 15-11-74 |

**D:** 970 tons (1,440 fl) **S:** 13.5 kts **Dim:** 51.0 × 11.5 × 5.7
**M:** 2 diesels; 1 Kort-nozzle CP prop; 4,600 hp—see Remarks **Fuel:** 500 tons
**Range:** 9,500/13 **Man:** 2 officers, 30 petty officers, 24 men
**Electric:** 502 kw (A 674: 766 kw)

SEAGOING TUGS *(continued)*

**Tenace (A 669)** L. & L. Van Ginderen, 6-86

REMARKS: Bollard-pull capacity: 60 tons. Living quarters air-conditioned. All based at Brest. A 644 and A 669 are powered by two MaK 9-cylinder diesels, while A674 is powered by two S.A.C.M. AGO 240 V12 diesels. A 674 has 3 × 227-kw and 1 × 85-kw generators; the others have 2 × 227-kw and 1 × 48-kw sets. Pumps include onee of 350 $m^3$/hr (serving two fire monitors with a range of 60 m) and one of 120 $m^3$/hr, plus numerous smaller salvage and firefighting pumps. Carry two semi-rigid boats.

### COASTAL TUGS

NOTE: A program is under way to replace the older existing coastal tugs. The initial units were ordered in 3-85 in two series:

◆ **1 (+ . . .) 358-ton** Bldr: IMC, Rochefort

| | Laid down | L | In serv. |
|---|---|---|---|
| A . . . N . . . | 6-85 | 2-86 | 1986 |

**D:** 358 tons **S:** 14 kts **Dim:** 33.30 (30.20 pp) × 8.60 × 3.40
**M:** 2 diesels; 1 prop; 3,420 hp **Electric:** 180 kw (2 × 90 kw)
**Man:** 8 tot.

◆ **2 (+ . . .) 248 ton** Bldr: IMC, Rochefort

| | Laid down | L | In serv. |
|---|---|---|---|
| A . . . N . . . | 3-85 | 8-85 | 12-85 |
| A . . . N . . . | 4-85 | 9-85 | 2-86 |

**D:** 248 tons (285 fl) **S:** 12.75 kts **Dim:** 30.20 (28.30 pp) × 8.40 × 3.20
**M:** 2 S.A.C.M. AGO 195 V12 RVR diesels; 1 prop; 2,236 hp
**Electric:** 160 kw (2 × 80 kw) **Man:** 7 tot.

◆ **3 Belier class** Bldr: Cherbourg Arsenal

| | L | In serv. |
|---|---|---|
| A 695 BELIER | 4-12-79 | 25-7-80 |
| A 696 BUFFLE | 18-1-80 | 19-7-80 |
| A 697 BISON | 20-11-80 | 16-4-81 |

**Buffle (A 696)** G. Gyssels, 6-85

**D:** 500 tons (800 fl) **S:** 11 kts **Dim:** 32.0 × 8.8 × . . .
**M:** 2 SACM AGO 195 V8 CSHR diesels, electric drive; 2 Voith-Schneider vertical cycloidal props; 2,600 hp
**Man:** 1 officer, 7 petty officers, 4 men

REMARKS: Based at Toulon. Bollard pull: 25 tons. Have two firefighting monitors atop bridge.

◆ **11 Actif group**

| | Bldr | D: light/fl | In serv. |
|---|---|---|---|
| A 667 HERCULE | Franco-Belges | 194/240 | 21-3-60 |
| A 671 LE FORT | FCG, Bordeaux | 248/311 | 12-7-71 |
| A 672 UTILE | FCG, Bordeaux | 226/288 | 8-4-71 |
| A 673 LUTTEUR | . . . | 226/288 | 19-7-63 |
| A 685 ROBUSTE | Franco-Belges | 194/239 | 4-4-60 |
| A 686 ACTIF | FCM, Le Havre | 226/288 | 11-7-63 |
| A 687 LABORIEUX | FCM, Le Havre | 226/287 | 14-3-63 |
| A 688 VALEUREUX | Franco-Belges | 196/247 | 17-10-60 |
| A 692 TRAVAILLEUR | FCM, Le Havre | 226/288 | 11-7-63 |
| A 693 ACHARNÉ | La Perrière, Lorient | 218/293 | 5-7-74 |
| A 694 EFFICACE | La Perrière, Lorient | 230/. . . | 17-10-74 |

**Lutteur (A 673)** L. & L. Van Ginderen, 6-86

**D:** see name list **S:** 11.8 kts **Dim:** 28.3 (25.3 pp) × 7.9 × 4.3
**M:** 1 MGO ASHR diesel; 1,100 to 1,450 hp **Range:** 2,400/1

REMARKS: Bollard pull: 17 tons. Similar, but not identical, ships. *Courageux* (A 706) stricken 1980.

### HARBOR TUGS

◆ **20 pusher tugs** Bldr: La Perrière, Lorient (In serv. 1976–1983)

P. 1–P. 20

**P. 7**—24-ton pusher tug G. Gyssels, 6-83

**D:** 24 tons (fl) **S:** 9.2 kts **Dim:** 11.50 (11.25 wl) × 4.30 × 1.45
**M:** 2 Poyaud 520 V8M diesels; 2 props; 440 hp **Fuel:** 1.7 tons
**Range:** 191/9.1, 560/8 **Man:** 2 tot.

REMARKS: For dockyard use. Primarily for pushing, but have 4.1-ton bollard pull. No names or NATO pendant numbers assigned.

NOTE: The tugs listed below have two-letter contractions of names on bows instead of official pendant numbers.

◆ **2 Bonite class** Bldr: SFCN, Châlon-sur-Seine

Y 634 ROUGET (In serv. 1974) Y 630 BONITE (In serv. 1975)

**D:** 93 tons (fl) **S:** 11 kts **M:** 380 hp

REMARKS: Bollard-pull capacity: 7 tons.

HARBOR TUGS *(continued)*

**Bonite (Y 630)** J.-C. Bellonne, 1975

◆ **28 Acajou class** (alphabetical listing; pendant numbers not borne)

| | | | |
|---|---|---|---|
| Y 601 Acajou | Y 618 Érable | Y 638 Marronier | Y 740 Papayer |
| Y 607 Balsa | Y 635 Equeurdreville | Y 668 Mélèze | Y 688 Peuplier |
| Y 623 Charme | Y 644 Frêne | Y 669 Merisier | Y 689 Pin |
| Y 620 Chataigner | Y 654 Hêtre | Y 739 Noyer | Y 695 Platane |
| Y 624 Chêne | Y 655 Hevea | Y 682 Okoumé | Y 720 Santal |
| Y 629 Cormier | Y 663 Latanier | Y 719 Olivier | Y 708 Saule |
| Y 717 Ébène | Y 666 Manguier | Y 686 Palétuvier | Y 704 Sycomore |

**Noyer (Y 739)** H. Ehlers, 6-87

**D:** 105 tons **S:** 11 kts **Dim:** 21.0 × 6.9 × 3.2 **M:** 1 diesel; 700 hp

Remarks: Bollard-pull capacity: 10 tons. *Bouleau* (Y 612) stricken 1980.

◆ **29 Oiseau class** (alphabetical listing, pendant numbers not borne)

| | | | |
|---|---|---|---|
| Y 602 Aigrette | Y 723 Engoulevent | Y 725 Marabout | Y 691 Pinson |
| Y 720 Alouette | Y 687 Fauvette | Y 675 Martin Pêcheur | Y 694 Pivert |
| Y 730 Ara | Y 748 Gelinotte | Y 636 Martinet | Y 724 Sarcelle |
| Y 611 Bengali | Y 648 Goeland | Y 670 Merle | Y 726 Toucan |
| Y 625 Cigogne | Y 728 Grand Duc | Y 621 Mésange | Y 722 Vanneau |
| Y 628 Colibri | Y 653 Héron | Y 673 Moineau | |
| Y 632 Cygne | Y 747 Loriot | Y 617 Mouette | |
| Y 729 Eider | Y 727 Macreuse | Y 687 Passereau | |

**Toucan (Y 726)** G. Gyssels, 6-85

**D:** 65 tons **S:** 9 kts **Dim:** 18.4 × 5.7 × 2.5
**M:** 1 Poyaud diesel; 250 hp **Range:** 1,700/9

Remarks: Bollard-pull capacity: 3.5 tons. *Ibis* (Y 658) on loan to Senegal.

## TRAINING SHIPS AND CRAFT

Note: In addition to the designated ships and craft below, the French Navy operates a number of other units primarily in training roles. These include the helicopter carrier *Jeanne d'Arc* (R 97), frigate *Doudart de Lagrée* (F 728), and the diving tender *Poseidon* (A 722).

◆ **8 Léopard class**

| | Bldr | Laid down | L | In serv. |
|---|---|---|---|---|
| A 748 Léopard | de la Manche, St.-Malo | 6-4-81 | 4-6-81 | 4-12-82 |
| A 749 Panthère | de la Manche, St.-Malo | 9-6-81 | 3-9-81 | 4-12-82 |
| A 750 Jaguar | de la Manche, St.-Malo | 27-9-81 | 29-10-81 | 18-12-82 |
| A 751 Lynx | La Perrière, Lorient | 23-7-81 | 27-2-82 | 18-12-82 |
| A 752 Guépard | de la Manche, St.-Malo | 11-10-82 | 1-12-82 | 1-7-83 |
| A 753 Chacal | de la Manche, St.-Malo | 11-10-82 | 11-2-83 | 10-9-83 |
| A 754 Tigre | La Perrière, Lorient | 16-4-82 | 8-10-82 | 1-7-83 |
| A 755 Lion | La Perrière, Lorient | 21-2-82 | 13-12-82 | 10-9-83 |

**Tigre (A 754)** L. & L. Van Ginderen, 6-87

**Panthère (A 749)** L. & L. Van Ginderen, 3-87

**D:** 463 tons (fl) **S:** 15 kts **Dim:** 43.00 (40.15 pp) × 8.30 × 3.21
**A:** 2/20-mm AA (I × 2) **Electron Equipt:** Radar: 1/Decca . . .
**M:** 2 SACM 75 V16 ASHR diesels; 2 props; 2,200 hp **Range:** 4,100/12
**Man:** 1 officer, 13 men, plus 17 trainees and 4 instructors

Remarks: First four authorized 1980, second group 1981. Replaced the minesweepers of the U.S. *Adjutant* class in training duties. Also for patrol use if required.

◆ **2 ex-trawlers**

A 772 Engageante (ex-*Cayolle*) A 773 Vigilante (ex-*Iseran*)

**D:** 286 tons fl (156 grt) **S:** 11 kts **Dim:** 30.0 (25.0 pp) × 6.7 × 3.8 (aft)
**Electron Equipt:** Radar: 1/Decca . . . **M:** 1 Deutz diesel; 1 prop; 560 hp

Remarks: Built 1964; purchased 1975. Used by petty officers' navigation school.

◆ **2 tenders** Bldr: Bayonne (In serv. 1971)

Y 706 Chimère Y 711 Farfadet

**D:** 100 tons **S:** 11 kts **M:** 1 diesel; 200 hp

Remarks: Used by the Naval Academy for training in maneuvering.

Note: The two "Ham"-class former inshore minesweepers used as training craft at Cherbourg have been stricken 1986–87: *Hibiscus* (A 735, ex-*Sparham,* ex-MSI-85) and *Dahlia* (A 736, ex-*Whippinham,* ex-MSI-88).

**TRAINING SHIPS AND CRAFT** *(continued)*

**Vigilante (A 773)** L. & L. Van Ginderen, 11-82

**Farfadet (Y 711)** Pradignac & Leo, 1983

◆ **2 auxiliary barkentines** Bldr: Chantiers de Normandie, Fécamp (In serv. 1932)

A 649 L'Étoile A 650 La Belle Poule

**D:** 225 tons (275 fl) **S:** 6 kts **Dim:** 32.25 × 7.0 × 3.2
**M:** Sulzer diesel; 125 hp

Remarks: Assigned to the Naval Academy.

**La Belle Poule (A 650)** L. & L. Van Ginderen, 7-85

◆ **1 sail-training yawl** (L: 1932)

A 653 La Grande Hermine (ex-*La Route Est Belle,* ex-*Menestrel*)

Remarks: Fourteen-meter yawl purchased in 1964 for the reserve officers' school. D: 7 tons (13 fl).

◆ **1 sail-training craft** Bldr: C.N. de Vendée (l: 1927)

A 652 Mutin

**D:** 40 tons (55 fl) **S:** . . . **Dim:** 33.0 (22.0 hull) × 6.5 × 3.2 (1.5 fwd)
**M:** 1 Baudouin 6-cyl. diesel; 1 prop; 112 hp

Remarks: Assigned to the annex of the Seamanship School. 240 $m^3$ sail area.

**MISCELLANEOUS SERVICE CRAFT**

◆ **1 ASW trials tender** Bldr: . . .

L'Aventurière II (In serv. 1985)

**D:** . . . **S:** . . . **Dim:** 24.5 × 7.9 × 3.1
**M:** 1 Poyaud diesel; 1 prop; 650 hp

Remarks: No hull number. Used by GESMA *(Group d'Etudes Sous Marines de l'Atlantique)* at Brest.

◆ **2 weapons range-safety patrol boats** Bldrs: C.N. de L'Estérel

| | L | In serv. |
|---|---|---|
| A 712 Athos | 20-11-79 | 22-11-79 |
| A 713 Aramis | 9-9-80 | 22-9-80 |

**Athos (A 712)** L. & L. Van Ginderen, 9-83

**D:** 80 tons (99.5 fl) **S:** 28 kts **Dim:** 32.1 × 6.5 × 1.9
**A:** 1/20-mm AA **Electron Equipt:** Radar: 1/Decca . . .
**M:** 2 SACM Type 195 V12 diesels; 2 props; 4,640 hp **Range:** 1,500/15
**Man:** 1 officer, 6 petty officers, 10–11 men (including 6 divers)

Remarks: Operate at the Landes Test Center, both as range-safety craft and for weapons-recovery duties. Wooden hulls.

◆ **1 trials support tender**

DCAN 164 Mérou

**Mérou (DCAN 164)** G. Gyssels, 6-85

Remarks: A diving tender with bow-door arrangement for lowering test equipment. Based at Toulon and civilian-operated.

◆ **1 range-safety patrol craft**

A 702 Girelle

**D:** 42 tons (45 fl) **S:** . . . **M:** . . .

Remarks: Wooden construction. Operates from St. Raphaël.

MISCELLANEOUS SERVICE CRAFT *(continued)*

**Girelle (A 702)** H. Ehlers, 5-86

◆ **1 range-safety patrol boat** Bldr: C.N. de L'Estérel (In serv. 14-2-74)

A 714 Tourmaline

**Tourmaline (A 714)** 1974

**D:** 37 tons (45 fl) **S:** 15 kts **Dim:** 26.8 × 4.97 × 1.53
**M:** 2 diesels; 2 props; 480 hp

Remarks: Wooden construction. Can carry 1/20-mm AA.

◆ **6 fireboats**

| | | |
|---|---|---|
| Y 745 Aiguière | Y 618 Cascade | Y 746 Embrun |
| Y 645 Gave | Y 646 Geyser | Y 684 Oued |

**Aiguière (A 745)**—red-painted, no pendant number G. Gyssels, 7-85

**D:** 70 tons (85 fl) **S:** 11.3 kts **Dim:** 23.8 × 5.3 × 1.7
**M:** 2 Poyaud 6 PZM diesels; 2 props; 405 hp

◆ **1 degaussing (deperming) tender**

Y 732

**Y 732** DCAN, 1970

**D:** 260 tons **S:** 10 kts **Dim:** 38.2 × 4.3 × 2.4
**M:** 1 diesel; 1 prop; 375 hp **Man:** 5 tot.

◆ **1 radiological monitoring ship** (In serv. 1969)

Y 743 Palangrin

**D:** 44 tons **S:** 9 kts **M:** 1/220-hp diesel

**Palangrin (Y 743)** Pradignac & Leo, 1984

◆ **18 motor lighters, converted from LCM (3)-class landing craft**

CHA 1, 2, 6, 7, 8, 9, 13, 14, 15, 16, 17, 18, 19, 22, 23, 24, 25, 26

**D:** 20 tons (50 fl) **S:** 7 kts **Dim:** 15.2 × 4.4 × 1.6
**M:** 1 diesel; 100 hp (CHA 1, CHA 6: 115 hp)

◆ **18 water lighters**

1 to 18

◆ **5 self-propelled floating cranes** Bldr: . . .

GFA 1–5 (In serv. . . .)

**GFA 3** G. Gyssels, 6-83

Remarks: Lift capacity: 15 tons maximum. GFA—*Grue Flottante Automotrice.* Two each at Brest and Toulon, one at Cherbourg.

◆ **1 floating dry dock** (In serv. 1975)

Remarks: Capacity: 3,500 tons. Based at Papeete.

**D:** . . . **S:** 9 kts **Dim:** . . . × . . . × . . . **M:** 1 diesel; 430 hp

Remarks: Nos. 5 and 6 in Tahiti, No. 2 at Brest, Nos. 1 and 11 at Toulon, No. 12 at Lorient, others at the CEP (*Centre d'Expérimentation Pacifique*).

◆ **4 water lighters for SSBNs**

1 2 3 4

**D:** 44 tons light **S:** 6 kts **Dim:** . . . × . . . × . . . **M:** 1 diesel; 496 hp

Remarks: Two at Brest, two at Cherbourg. Also remaining in service is the pre–World War II water tender *Ondée* (Y 683).

**FRANCE** *(continued)*
**MISCELLANEOUS SERVICE CRAFT** *(continued)*

**CHA 13** L. & L. Van Ginderen, 8-84

# GABON
## Gabonese Republic

PERSONNEL (1986): approx. 350

MERCHANT MARINE (1982): 23 ships—97,967 grt (tankers: 2 ships—74,471 grt)

NAVAL AVIATION: One Embraer EMB 111 Bandeirante maritime patrol aircraft is operated by the Air Force.

### PATROL BOATS AND CRAFT

◆ **0 (+2) French "Super PATRA" class** Bldr: CMN, Cherbourg

N . . . N . . .

**D:** 371.5 tons light (422.5 fl) **S:** 24 kts
**Dim:** 54.50 (50.0 pp) × 8.0 (7.7 wl) × 2.54 (2.08 hull)
**A:** one unit: 1/57-mm Bofors SAK 57 Mk 2—1/20-mm Oerlikon AA; other: 2/20-mm Oerlikon AA (I × 2)
**Electron Equipt:** 1/Decca-Racal 1226
**M:** 2 SEMT-Pielstick 16PA4V200 VGDS diesels; 2 CP props; 8,000 hp
**Electric:** 360 kw **Fuel:** 73 tons **Range:** 4,000/15
**Endurance:** 15 days **Man:** 3 officers, 22 men + 23 passengers

REMARKS: Ordered 11-84. Limiting displacement 446 tons. Carries 840 rds 40-mm, 2,100 rds 20-mm ammunition. Can carry two MM 40 Exocet SSM. For search-and-rescue use, carries inflatable launch and can accommodate 23 rescued personnel. Have two contraband storerooms. Engines to be built by Uni-Diesel. First unit laid down 2-7-86.

◆ **1 wooden-hulled** Bldr: de l'Estérel, Cannes (In serv. 12-1-78)

GC 05 GENERAL NAZAIRE BOULINGUI KOUNBA (ex-*President el Haj Omar Bongo*)

**General Nazaire Boulingui Kounba** de l'Estérel, 1977

**D:** 100 tons (fl) **S:** 32 kts **Dim:** 42.0 × 7.8 × 1.9
**A:** 4/SS-12M SSM (II × 2)—1/40-mm Bofors AA—1/20-mm AA
**Electron Equipt:** Radar: Decca RM 1226
**M:** 3 SACM AGO 195 12CSNR diesels; 3 props; 5,400 hp
**Fuel:** 28.4 tons **Range:** 1,000/18 **Man:** 3 officers, 20 men

REMARKS: Wire-guided, optically aimed antiship missiles. Reported re-engined at Port-Gentil, completing early 1985; the original 3 MTU 16V538 TB91 diesels produced 40 kts on 10,500 hp.

◆ **1 N'Golo class** Bldr: Intermarine, Sarzana, Italy

GC 04 N'GOLO (In serv. 1981)

**N'Golo (GC 04)**—the first; the second is identical Intermarine, 1978

**D:** 65 tons (88 fl) **S:** 43 kts **Dim:** 27.3 × 6.8 × 2.1
**A:** 1/40-mm AA—2/20-mm AA **Electron Equipt:** Radar: 1/Decca RM 916
**M:** 2 MTU diesels; 2 props; 7,000 hp **Man:** 13 tot.

REMARKS: Replaces the original *N'Golo,* which was destroyed by fire 13-3-80. This design uses the largest glass-reinforced plastic hull of any high-speed craft in the world.

◆ **1 U.S. aluminum-hulled design** Bldr: Swiftships, Morgan City, La. (In serv. 2-76)

GC 03 N'GUENE

**D:** 118 tons (fl) **S:** 27 kts **Dim:** 32.17 (29.18 pp) × 2.3 (props)
**A:** 2/40-mm AA (I × 2)—2/20-mm AA (I × 2)—2/12.7-mm mg (I × 2)
**Electron Equipt:** Radar: Decca RM 916 **Range:** 825/25 **Man:** 21 tot.
**M:** 3 G.M. 16V149 TE diesels; 3 props; 4,800 hp **Electric:** 80 kw

◆ **1 32-m wooden-hulled** Bldr: de l'Estérel, Cannes (In serv. 3-72)

GC 02 COLONEL DJOUÉ DABANY (ex-*Président Albert Bernard Bongo*)

**Colonel Djoué Dabany (GC 02)** de l'Estérel, 1972

**D:** 80 tons **S:** 30 kts **Dim:** 32.0 × 5.8 × 1.5 **A:** 2/20-mm AA (I × 2)
**M:** 2 MTU diesels; 2,700 hp **Man:** 17 tot.

◆ **1 Gabonese design** Bldr: Libreville DY, Gabon (In serv. 16-1-68)

GC 01 PRÉSIDENT LÉON M'BA

**D:** 85 tons **S:** 12.5 kts **Dim:** 28.0 × 6.2 × 1.54
**A:** 1/75-mm recoilless rifle—1/12.7-mm mg **Man:** 1 officer, 15 men
**M:** 2 Baudouin diesels; 2 props; 540 hp **Range:** 1,000/12

### AMPHIBIOUS WARFARE SHIPS AND CRAFT

◆ **1 French Champlain-class landing ship** Bldr: Atelier Français de l'Ouest, Grand Quevilly, Rouen, France

| | Laid down | L | In serv. |
|---|---|---|---|
| LO 5 PRÉSIDENT EL HADJ OMAR BONGO | 7-3-83 | 16-4-84 | 24-10-84 |

**Président El Hadj Omar Bongo (L 05)** 6-85

**D:** 770 tons (1,336 fl) **S:** 16 kts **Dim:** 80.0 × 13.0 × 2.40
**A:** 2/40-mm AA (I × 2)—1/81-mm mortar—2/12.7-mm mg (I × 2)
**Electron Equipt:** Radar: 1/DRBN-32 (Decca 1226)
**M:** 2 SACM 195V12 diesels; 2 CP props; 3,600 hp
**Range:** 4,500/13 **Man:** 47

**GABON** *(continued)*
**AMPHIBIOUS WARFARE SHIPS AND CRAFT** *(continued)*

Remarks: Purchase announced 28-2-84. Capacity: 340 tons stores, plus 138 troops and 7 combat vehicles. Helicopter platform aft. Carries one LCVP and one personnel landing craft

◆ **1 transport** Bldr: DCAN, Dakar (In serv. 11-5-76)

GC . . . Manga

**D:** 152 tons **S:** 9 kts **Dim:** 24.0 × 6.4 × 1.3 **A:** 2/12.7-mm mg
**Electron Equipt:** Radar: Decca 101
**M:** 2 Poyaud V8-520 diesels; 2 props; 480 hp **Man:** 10 tot.

Remarks: Landing craft design, equipped with bow ramp.

◆ **2 harbor launches** Bldr: Tanguy Marine, Le Havre (In serv. 1985)

**D:** 2.5 tons (7.5 fl) **S:** . . . **Dim:** 12.00 × 2.95 × 0.30
**M:** 2 Volvo Penta AQAD-40B diesel outdrives; 165 hp

Remarks: One unit is only 10.00 m o.a., 2.25 tons (6.25 fl). Ordered 10-84.

Note: In 6-85, ten small GRP craft were ordered from Simonneau, Foutenay, France. These included one 11.8-m and two 8.10-m patrol craft, each powered by a Volvo Penta TAMD-608 inboard/outboard diesel of 235 hp, and seven 6.8-m personnel landing craft powered by a 110-hp Volvo Penta AQAD-30/DP diesel.

COAST GUARD

◆ **2 harbor patrol craft** Bldr: La Manche, Dieppe (In serv. 24-11-77)

Omboué Ndjole

**D:** 18 tons (fl) **S:** 10 kts **Dim:** 12.4 × 3.7 × 0.9 **M:** 1 diesel; 1 prop; 170 hp

◆ **1 Arcoa 960 launch**—**S:** 25 kts

◆ **6 Arcoa launches**—**S:** 15 kts

◆ **1 buoy tender** Bldr: La Manche, Dieppe (In serv. 24-11-77)

N'Gombe

**D:** 60 tons (fl) **S:** 10 kts **Dim:** 17.0 × 4.5 × 1.3
**M:** 1 Baudouin DNP-6-diesel; 1 prop; 215 hp

# THE GAMBIA

**Republic of the Gambia**

Note: The "unification" of the Gambia with Senegal on 1-2-82 was supposed to have unified the armed forces of both countries, but this has not yet occurred to any appreciable extent.

Merchant Marine (1986): 6 ships—2,588 grt

HARBOR POLICE—BANJUL

**PATROL CRAFT**

◆ **3 Tracker Mk-2 class** Bldr: Fairey Marine, U.K. (In serv. 1977–78)

P 2 Jato P 3 Challenge P 4 Champion

**D:** 31.5 tons (fl) **S:** 29 kts **Dim:** 19.25 × 4.98 × 1.45
**A:** 1/20-mm AA—2/7.62-mm mg
**M:** 2 G.M. 12V-71 TI diesels; 2 props; 1,290 hp
**Range:** 650/20 **Man:** 11 tot.

◆ **1 Lance class** Bldr: Fairey Marine, U.K. (In serv. 28-10-76)

P 1 Sea Dog

**D:** 17 tons (fl) **S:** 24 kts **Dim:** 14.81 × 4.76 × 1.3
**A:** 1/20-mm AA—3/7.62-mm mg (I × 3)
**M:** 2 G.M. 8V-71 TI diesels; 2 props; 850 hp **Range:** 500/15
**Man:** 6 crew plus 10-man boarding party

◆ **1 Keith Nelson 75-foot class** Bldr: Camper & Nicholson, U.K. (In serv. 1974)

Mansa Kila IV

**D:** 70 tons (fl) **S:** 24.5 kts **Dim:** 22.9 × 6.0 × 1.6 **A:** 2/20-mm AA (I × 2)
**M:** 2 diesels; 2 props; 1,840 hp **Range:** 800/20 **Man:** 11 men

# GERMANY (EAST)

**German Democratic Republic**

Personnel: 17,000 total, including approx. 1,800 officers and 3,000 Frontier Guards personnel. A 1,250-man Naval Infantry was formed in 1987 at Rügen.

Merchant Marine (1986): 403 ships—1,518,944 grt (tankers: 8 ships—35,860 grt)

Naval Aviation: Helicopters in naval service include 8 Mi-14 Haze-A for land-based ASW, and 13 Mi-8 Hip-F and 7 Mi-8 Hip-C transport helicopters. A naval squadron of Su-22 Fitter-N bombers was formed at Laage in 1986.

Weapons and Systems: Nearly all of Soviet design. *See* U.S.S.R. section for details.

Warships In Service Or Under Construction As Of 1 January 1988

| | L | Std. Tons | Main armament |
|---|---|---|---|
| ◆ **3 frigates** | | | |
| 3 Koni | 1977–85 | 1,440 | 1/SA-N-4, 4/76.2-mm, 4/30-mm, 2 ASW RL |
| ◆ **16 corvettes** | | | |
| 16 Parchim | 1980–84 | 800 | 2/57-mm AA, 4 ASW TT, 2 ASW RL |
| ◆ **49 missile and torpedo boats** | | | |
| 5(+. . .) Tarantul I | 1984 | 480 | 4 Styx, 1/76-mm AA |
| 13 Osa-I | 1964– | 175 | 4 Styx, 4/30-mm AA |
| 11 Shershen | 1966– | 150 | 4/30-mm AA, 4/533-mm TT |
| 20 Libelle | 1975–79 | 20 | 2/533-mm TT |
| ◆ **45 minesweepers** | | | |
| 45 Kondor I, II | 1968–79 | 22/310 | 2 or 6/25-mm AA |
| ◆ **12 landing ships** | | | |

Note: Ships and craft in auxiliary status have pendant numbers beginning with a letter denoting the general function:

A: Salvage ships and tugs
B: Torpedo retrievers
C: Liquid cargo carriers
D: Ships and craft of the SHD
E: Dry-cargo carriers
F: Fireboats (*Feuerlöschboot*)
G: Coastal Border Brigade (GBK—*Grenzbrigade Küste*) units
H: Barracks ships
S: Training units (*Schulschiff*)
V: Experimental units (*Versuch*)

Navigational service and hydrographic survey units are operated by the civilian-manned Naval Hydrographic Service (SHD-*Seehydrographischer Dienst*): The ships wear "SHD" on a band on their stacks and do not carry pendant numbers; they do display their names.

**FRIGATES**

◆ **3 Soviet Koni class** Bldr: Zelenodolsk SY

141 Rostock (In serv. 25-7-78) 142 Berlin (In serv. 10-5-79)
143 Halle (In serv. 28-1-86)

**Rostock (141)** M.O.D., Bonn, 5-83

**Halle (143)** M.O.D., Bonn, 4-86

**FRIGATES** *(continued)*

**D:** 1,440 tons (1,900 fl) **S:** 30 kts **Dim:** 96.40 × 12.55 × 3.48 (hull)
**A:** 1/SA-N-4 SAM system (II × 1, 20 missiles)—4/76.2-mm DP (II × 2)—4/30-mm AA (II × 2)—2/RBU-6000 ASW RL (XII × 2)—2/d.c. racks (24 d.c.)—20 mines
**Electron Equipt:** Radar: 1/TSR-333, 1/Strut Curve, 1/Pop Group, 1/Hawk Screech, 1/Drum Tilt
Sonar: med.-freq., hull-mounted
IFF: 2/Square Head, 1/High Pole-A
EW: 2/Watch Dog, 2 decoy RL (XVI × 2)
**M:** CODAG: 1 19,000 hp gas turbine; 2 Type 68B, 8,000-hp diesels; 3 props; 35,000 hp
**Range:** 1,800/14 **Man:** 130 tot.

REMARKS: TSR-333 substituted for Don-2. Depth-charge racks bolt to mine rails. Chaff/decoy RL added to first pair in 1986.

**CORVETTES**

◆ **16 Parchim class** Bldr: Peenewerft, Wolgast (In serv. 1981–85)

| | In serv. | | In serv. |
|---|---|---|---|
| 241 BÜTZOW | 9-4-81* | 231 LUDWIGSLUST | 1982* |
| 242 PARCHIM | 3-9-81 | 232 RIBNITZ-DAMGARTEN | 1982* |
| 243 PERLEBERG | 1981* | 233 TETEROW | 1984* |
| 244 BAD DOBERAN | 1981 | 234 DIRNA | 1984 |
| 221 LÜBZ | 1981* | 211 GÄDEBUSCH | 6-85 |
| 222 WISMAR | 1982 | 212 ANGERMÜNDE | 1985 |
| 223 GÜSTROW | 1982* | 213 BERGEN | 6-85 |
| 224 WAREN | 1982* | 214 N . . . | 7-85* |

* Name/number correlation tentative

**D:** 800 tons (950 fl) **S:** 28 kts **Dim:** 72.5 × 9.4 × 3.0 (hull)
**A:** 2/57-mm AA (II × 1)—2/30-mm AA (II × 1)—2/SA-N-5 SAM systems (IV × 2)—4/400-mm ASW TT (I × 4)—2/RBU-6000 ASW RL (XII × 2)—2/d.c. racks—mines
**Electron Equipt:** Radar: 1/TSR-333, 1/Strut Curve, 1/Muff Cob
Sonar: MF hull-mounted; high-freq. dipping sonar
IFF: 1/High Pole-B
EW: 2/Watch Dog, 2/chaff RL (XVI × 2)
**M:** 2 Type M504 diesels; 2 props; 14,250 hp **Man:** 60 tot.

**Güstrow (223)** G. Koop, 1986

**Ribnitz-Damgarten (232)** M.O.D., Bonn, 7-84

**Teterow (233)** M.O.D., Bonn, 3-84

REMARKS: Two began trials 1980, 4 in 1981, 2 in 1982, 4 in 1983. Intended to replace the Hai-III class. Previously referred to by NATO as the "Bal-Com-4" and by the press as the "Koralle" class. Helicopter dipping sonar deploys through door on starboard side of main deck superstructure. D.C. racks exit through doors in stern.

NOTE: An improved version of the *Parchim* class, NATO "Parchim II," is being built for the U.S.S.R.; see that chapter.

**GUIDED-MISSILE CORVETTES**

◆ **5 (+ . . .) Soviet Tarantul-I class** Bldr: Petrovskiy SY, Leningrad

771 ALBIN KÖBIS (In serv. 24-9-84)
772 RUDOLF EGELHOFER (In serv. 2-4-85)
773 N . . . (In serv. 6-7-85)
774 N . . . (In serv. 1-86)
775 N . . . (In serv. 10-86)

**Rudolf Egelhofer (772)** M.O.D., Bonn, 11-86

**Rudolf Egelhofer (772)** M.O.D., Bonn, 11-86

**GUIDED-MISSILE CORVETTES** *(continued)*

**D:** 480 tons (540 fl) **S:** 35 kts
**Dim:** 56.60 (52.50 pp) × 10.50 max. (9.4 wl) × 2.50
**A:** 4/SS-N-2C Styx SSM (II × 2)—1/76.2-mm DP—1/SA-N-5 SAM syst. (IV × 1; . . . SA-7 Grail missiles)—2/30-mm, 6-barreled gatling AA (I × 2)
**Electron Equipt:** Radar: 1/Krivach (or TSR-333) nav., 1/Plank Shave missile targeting, 1/Bass Tilt gun f.c.
EW: 4/intercept antenna, 2 decoy RL (XVI × 2)
IFF: 1/Square Head, 1/High Pole-B
**M:** COGOG: 2 probable NK-12MV gas turbines (12,000 hp each), 2 diesel or gas-turbine cruise engines (approx. 2–3,000 hp each); probable 2 props
**Range:** . . . **Man:** 50 tot.

REMARKS: Export version of Tarantul design, with simplified electronics. May be intended to replace the aged Osa-Is. The main propulsion gas turbines exhaust through the transom stern, adding their residual thrust to the power. The cruise engines exhaust through a small stack. The SA-N-5 launcher is on the stern, flanked by the two decoy rocket launchers.

### GUIDED-MISSILE PATROL BOATS

◆ **13 or fewer Soviet Osa-I-class missile boats** Bldr: U.S.S.R

711 ALBERT GAST
712 HEINRICH DORRENBACH
714 JOSEPH SCHARES
715 PAUL EISENSCHNEIDE
731 OTTO TOST
732 KARL MESEBERG
733 AUGUST LÜTGENS
734 ANTON SÄFKOW
735 FRITZ BEHN
751 PAUL WIEKZOREK
753 RICHARD SORGE
754 FRITZ GAST
755 MAX REICHPIETSCH

**Richard Sorge (753)** M.O.D., Bonn, 11-86

**D:** 185 tons (215 fl) **S:** 35 kts **Dim:** 38.6 × 7.6 × 1.8
**A:** 4/Styx (SS-N-2)—4/30-mm AA (II × 2)
**Electron Equipt:** Radar: 1/Square Tie, 1/Drum Tilt
IFF: 2/Square Head, 1/High Pole-A
**M:** 3 M503A diesels; 3 props; 12,000 hp **Range:** 500/34; 750/25 **Man:** 30 tot.

REMARKS: Transferred 1966. Until 1981–82, boats 711–714 bore "S"-series training squadron pendants. Nearing end of useful lives. Three or more stricken by 1987, including *Albin Köbis* (. . .) and *Rudolf Egelhofer* (752); one source indicated that only 11 remained.

### TORPEDO BOATS

◆ **11 or fewer Soviet Shershen-class torpedo boats** Bldr: U.S.S.R.

Hull numbers in 800s—see Remarks

**Heinz Biemler (853)** M.O.D., Bonn, 11-86

**D:** 145 tons (170 fl) **S:** 45 kts **Dim:** 34.0 × 6.8 × 1.5
**A:** 4/Styx (SS-N-2)—4/30-mm AA (II × 2)
**Electron Equipt:** Radar: 1/Pot Drum, 1/Drum Tilt
IFF: 1/Square Head, 1/High Pole-A
**M:** 3 M503A diesels; 3 props; 12,000 hp **Range:** 460/42; 850/30

REMARKS: Transferred 1968–76. No d.c. racks, unlike Soviet Navy units. Nearing end of useful lives; seven stricken by 1987.

◆ **20 or fewer Libelle-class light torpedo boats** Bldr: East Germany (In serv. 1975–78)

911–915, 921–925, 931–935, 941–945, 951–955, 991–995

**Libelle class No. 993** M.O.D., Bonn, 1976

**D:** 28 tons (fl) **S:** 50 kts **Dim:** 18.96 × 4.50 × 2.00
**A:** 2/533-mm TT—2/23-mm ZSU-23/2 AA (II × 1)—2 mine launchers
**Electron Equipt:** Radar: 1/TSR-333
**M:** 3 M50F-3 to 7 diesels; 3 props; 3,600 hp **Man:** 10 tot.

REMARKS: Can quickly convert to commando/frogman carriers. Torpedoes discharged over stern; short tubes on deck eject mines. At least ten stricken by end-1986. Two enginerooms, one forward, one aft.

### PATROL CRAFT

◆ **15 Bremse (GB 23) class** Bldr: VEB Yachtswerft, Berlin (In serv. 1971– . . .)

G 30 to G 39, G 71 to G 75

**Bremse class No. G 39.** 1978

**D:** 25 tons **S:** 14 kts **Dim:** 23.13 (20.97 pp) × 4.58 × 1.50 (max.)
**A:** Small arms **M:** 1 Type 6VD 18/15 diesel; 1 prop; 496 hp
**Electron Equipt:** Radar: 1/TSR-333

REMARKS: Operated by the Border Guard on rivers and inland waterways. Some exported.

◆ **6 SAS-class fishing cutter-type** (In serv. 1965–67)

G 60 to G 65

**D:** 90 tons (fl) **S:** 11 kts **Dim:** 21.0 × 5.5 × . . .
**A:** small arms **Electron Equipt:** Radar: 1/. . . nav.
**M:** 1 Type 4NVD 36 diesel; 1 prop; 150 hp

REMARKS: Typical Baltic steel-hulled fishing cutters built 1965 and converted 1967 for Border Guard use.

### MINE WARFARE SHIPS

◆ **27 Kondor-II-class patrol minesweepers** Bldr: Peenewerft, Wolgast (In serv. 1970–78)

311 URANIENBURG
312 GENTHIN
313 ZERBST
314 BITTERFELD
315 ROSSLAU
316 DESSAU
321 KYRITZ
322 RIESA
323 TIMMENDORF
324 RÖBEL
325 GUBEN
326 RATHENOW
331 KLÜTZ
332 TORGAU
333 TANGERHÜTTE

**MINE WARFARE SHIPS** *(continued)*

| | | |
|---|---|---|
| 334 Pössnick | 342 Boltenhagen | 346 Strasburg |
| 335 Altenburg | 343 Bernau | 351 Stralsund |
| 336 Freiberg | 344 Meiningen | 352 Kamenz |
| 341 Eilensburg | 345 Neuruppin | 353 Pritzwalk |

**Guben (325)** L. & L. Van Ginderen, 1984

**Zerbst (313)** M.O.D., Bonn, 6-84

**D:** 260 tons light (414 fl) **S:** 19 kts **Dim:** 56.73 × 7.50 × 2.35
**A:** 6/25-mm AA (II × 3)—mines **Electron Equipt:** Radar: 1/TSR-333
**M:** 2 Type 40DM diesels; 2 CP Kort-nozzle props; 4,000 hp (sust.)
**Man:** 40 tot.

Remarks: Typed "High Seas Minesweepers-Long" by the East German Navy. Those units with a deckhouse aft (including 313–315, 321, 325, and 332) carry within them the cable reel/winch for the Type 1-Ss/e "Fernräumgerät" (a magnetic minesweeping array) added since 1982. All may carry a small sonar. Three, with "S" pendants, served as training ships. Three additional units are trials craft.

◆ **18 Kondor-I-class inshore minesweepers, used as patrol boats**
Bldr: Peenewerft, Wolgast (In serv. 1968–70)

| | | |
|---|---|---|
| G 411 Stendal | G 421 Ahrenskoop | G 441 Malchin |
| G 412 Bergen | G 422 Demmin | G 442 Ückermünde |
| G 413 Greifswald | G 423 Prerow | G 443 Templin |
| G 414 Pasewalk | G 424 Graal-Müritz | G 444 Weisswasser |
| G 415 Meissen | G 425 Zingst | G 445 Neustrelitz |
| G 416 Prenzlau | G 426 Witte | G 446 Bansiln |

**Bansiln (G 446)** M.O.D., Bonn, 11-86

**D:** 225 tons light (327 fl) **S:** 19 kts **Dim:** 52.00 × 6.70 × 2.40
**A:** 2/25-mm AA (II × 1)—mines **Electron Equipt:** Radar: 1/TSR-333
**M:** 2 Type 40DM diesels; 2 Kort-nozzle CP props; 4,000 hp (sust.) **Man:** 30 tot.

Remarks: Originally typed "MSR-*Kurz*" (Minensuch-und-räumschiffe) but reclassified "Küstenminenabwehrschiffe" in 1985. Attached to Border Guard as patrol boats, but retain minesweeping gear. Three served as training units, with "S" numbers until early 1980s: 814–816. Two have been converted as torpedo- recovery craft; two others, *Komet* and *Meteor,* altered as intelligence collectors; another is the state yacht *Ostseeland; Ernst Thaelmann* was converted to a youth-training ship in 1977. The now-stricken prototype Kondor I (V 85) was launched 6-6-68 and completed 30-12-68; of 283 tons (fl), she was 47.25 × 6.60 × 1.91 and was powered by two Type 12 KVD 20/21 diesels (1,350 hp each).

**AMPHIBIOUS SHIPS AND CRAFT**

◆ **12 Frosch-class landing ships** Bldr: Peenewerft, Wolgast (In serv. 1976–79)

| | | |
|---|---|---|
| 611 Hoyerswerda | 615 Eisenhüttenstadt | 633 Hettstadt |
| 612 Eberswalde-Finow | 616 Neubrandenburg | 634 Grimmen |
| 613 Lübben | 631 Cottbus | 635 Schwerin |
| 614 Anklam | 632 Frankfurt/Oder | 636 Schwedt |

**Schwerin (635)**—with two 40-tubed, 122-mm artillery RL U.S. Navy, 1986

**Eberswalde-Finow (612)**—note mine rails aft L. & L. Van Ginderen, 10-83

**D:** 1,744 tons normal (1,900 fl) **S:** 19 kts **Dim:** 98.0 (90.7 pp) × 11.2 × 2.8
**A:** 4/57-mm AA (II × 2)—4/30-mm (II × 2)—2/122-mm artillery RL (XL × 2)—mines
**Electron Equipt:** Radar: 1/Strut Curve, 1/Muff Cob, 1/TSR-333—IFF: 1/High Pole-B
**M:** 2 Type 61B diesels; 2 CP props; 12,000 hp

Remarks: Cargo capacity 400 to 600 tons or 11 tanks and a company of troops. Similar in general form to Soviet Ropucha class, but smaller and with a blunter bow, heavier armament, etc. Two 40-tubed rocket launchers of the type carried by the Soviet ship *Ivan Rogov* are mounted forward of the bridge. Two additional units have been completed as Frosch-II-class supply ships—see under Auxiliaries.

**INTELLIGENCE COLLECTION SHIPS**

◆ **1 Darss class** Bldr: VEB Schiffswerft Neptun, Rostock

D 41 Jasmund (In serv. 6-85)

**D:** 2,200 tons (fl) **S:** 12 kts **Dim:** 76.29 × 12.09 × 4.15
**A:** provision for 2/25-mm Type 2-M-3 (II × 1)
**Electron Equipt:** Radar: 1/TSR-33
EW: . . .
**M:** 1 Type 40DM diesel; 1 CP Kort-nozzle prop; 2,000 hp
**Electric:** 520 kw (4 × 130 kw) **Man:** approx. 140 tot.

Remarks: Sister to cargo-ship class, with radome aft and deckhouse over second hold. Replaced *Hydrograph* (Okean trawler class), stricken 1985.

## INTELLIGENCE COLLECTION SHIPS *(continued)*

**Jasmund (D 41)** M.O.D., Bonn, 11-86

◆ **2 modified Kondor-I class** Bldr: Peenewerft, Wolgast (In serv. 1968–70)

D 42 Komet (ex-. . .)
D 43 Meteor (ex-. . .)

**Komet (D 42)** M.O.D., Bonn, 1984

Remarks: No armament. Collection antennas added; data otherwise as for Kondor-I-class minesweepers.

## HYDROGRAPHIC SURVEY SHIPS

Note: All survey ships and buoy tenders are operated under SHD, the Naval Hydrographic Service, and are civilian-manned. The ships display their names and do not carry pendant numbers.

◆ **1 Soviet Finik (Projekt 872) class** Bldr: Polnocny SY, Gdansk, Poland (In serv. 12-80)

Dornbusch

**D:** 1,200 tons (fl) **S:** 13 kts **Dim:** 61.30 × 11.80 (10.80 wl) × 3.27
**Electron Equipt:** Radar: 2/Don-2—IFF: 1/High Pole-B
**M:** 2 Cegielski-Sulzer diesels; 2 CP props; 1,920 hp (plus two 75-kw electric motors for quiet, 6-kt operations)
**Electric:** 675 kVA **Endurance:** 15 days **Range:** 3,000/13
**Man:** 5 officers, 23 men

Remarks: Replaced a navigational buoy tender/light cable layer of the same name. Intended for navigational buoy tending and hydrographic survey, for which 4 echo-sounders are fitted. Bow-thruster of 176 hp.

◆ **1 modified Kondor-II class** Bldr: Peenewerft, Wolgast

C.F. Gauss (In serv. 1976)

Remarks: No armament; white-painted. Data as for Kondor-II-class minesweepers. Has more extensive superstructure, twin kingposts aft for handling boats, buoys, etc. D: 490 tons (fl), 19 kts.

◆ **1 Soviet Kamenka class** Bldr: Stocznia Pólnocna, Gdansk

Buk II (In serv. 1969)

**Buk II** 1983

**D:** 703 tons (fl) **S:** 12 kts **Dim:** 53.5 × 9.1 × 2.6
**M:** 2 Zgoda-Sulzer 6 NVD 48 A2U diesels; 2 CP props; 1,765 hp
**Range:** 4,000/10

Remarks: 480-grt buoy tender and survey ship; one 5-ton crane.

◆ **3 Arkona class** (Projekt 601) (In serv. 1977)

Arkona Darsser Ort Gellen

**D:** 155 tons **S:** 10 kts **M:** diesel

Remarks: Also act as navigational buoy tenders. Improved *Breitling* design.

◆ **10 Breitling (SK 64)-class buoy tenders** Bldr: Peenewerft, Wolgast

Breitling, Esper Ort, Golwitz, Grass Ort, Landtieff, Palmer Ort, Ramzow, Rosen Ort, Kollicker Ort, Stubbenkammer (In serv. 12-67 to 12-68)

**Breitling**—note "SHD" logo on kingpost-stack 1983

**D:** 151.8 tons **S:** 11.0 kts **Dim:** 29.5 × 6.2 × 1.86
**M:** 1 diesel; 1 prop; 580 hp

## EXPERIMENTAL SHIPS V = *Versuch* (Research)

Note: Two *Darss*-class cargo ships have V-pendants—see opposite.

◆ **1 ex-civilian research ship** Bldr: Volkswerft, Stralsund

V 84 Rügen (ex-V 71, ex-*Meteor*) (acquired 1974)

**Rügen (V 84)**—with old number 1976

**D:** 470 tons **S:** 10 kts **Dim:** 39.15 × 7.30 × 2.70 **Range:** 5,000/9
**Man:** 30 tot. **Electron Equipt:** Radar: 1/TSR-333
**M:** 1 Type R6DV 148 diesel; 1 prop; 400 hp

Remarks: Built as a fisheries research lugger, late 1950s.

◆ **3 Kondor-II-class minesweepers** (In serv. 1971–78)

V 381 Jüterbog V 382 Wittstock V 383 Schönebeck

**Schönebeck (V 383)**—note deckhouse aft 1978

**EXPERIMENTAL SHIPS** *(continued)*

REMARKS: Involved in trials of new mine-countermeasures equipment, including the 1-Ss/e array for the Kondor-II class. Data otherwise as for minesweeper-designated sisters.

NOTE: Of other trials craft, Libelle-class torpedoboat V 87 was stricken in 1983, and Kondor-I prototype V 87 (ex-V 85) was deleted 1984.

## AMPHIBIOUS WARFARE SUPPORT SHIPS

◆ **2 Frosch-II class** Bldr: Peenewerft, Wolgast

E 35 NORDPERD (In serv. 3-10-79) E 36 SÜDPERD (In serv. 26-2-80)

**Nordperd (E 35)**—note 2 twin 25-mm AA at bow PH1 (SW) J. Hilton, USN, 9-86

**D:** 2,000 tons (fl) **S:** 16 kts **Dim:** 98.0 (90.7 pp) × 11.12 × 2.80
**A:** 4/57-mm AA (II × 2)—4/25-mm AA (II × 2)—mines
**Electron Equipt:** Radar: 1/TSR-333, 1/Strut Curve, 1/Muff Cob
IFF: 1/Square Head, 1/High Pole-A
**M:** 2 Type 61D diesels; 2 CP props; 12,000 hp **Man:** 120 tot.

REMARKS: Differ from Frosch-I in having an 8-ton Type 2Hy SWK8 crane amidships and two cargo hatches, and in having 25-mm (mounted right forward to cover the beach) in place of 30-mm AA. Although they have an auxiliary-series pendant number, the bow ramp is retained to permit a beaching capability, and they presumably can be used as assault landing ships if needed. Believed to carry munitions, at least in peacetime. Chaff rocket launchers (XVI × 2) added 1986, just forward of bridge.

## STORES SHIPS

◆ **6 Darss class** Bldr: Neptunwerft, Rostock (In serv. 1982–84)

| | In serv. | | In serv. |
|---|---|---|---|
| E 41 DARSS | 1982 | P 41 KÜHLUNG | 1984 |
| E 11 MÖNCHGUT | 1983 | V 85 GRANITZ | 1984 |
| E 61 WITTOW | 1983 | V 86 WERDAU | 1984 |

**Darss (E 41)** M.O.D., Bonn, 8-83

**Wittow (E 61)** M.O.D., Bonn, 1984

**D:** 2,292 tons (fl) **S:** 12 kts **Dim:** 76.29 × 12.09 × 4.15
**A:** provision for 6/25-mm AA (II × 3)
**Electron Equipt:** Radar: 1/TSR-333—IFF: 1/High Pole-B
**M:** 1 Type 40 DM diesel; 1 CP Kort-nozzle prop; 2,000 hp **Man:** 60 tot.
**Electric:** 520 kw (4 × 130 kw)

REMARKS: E 41 laid down 14-12-81, launched 27-7-82. Cargo: Approx. 800 tons missiles, ammunition, dry stores, etc., plus about 200 tons cargo fuel. Intended for dead-in-the-water replenishment at sea, as indicated by the heavy rubbing strakes on the hull sides and the 12 rubber fenders carried. Can refuel two ships simultaneously over stern. Crane between the two holds is the same 8-ton model used on the Frosch-II class. "V" pendant for *Werdau* and *Granitz* indicates trials employment. Sister *Jasmund* (D 41) is equipped as an intelligence collector, no crane, 5-m radome abaft stack.

## OILERS

◆ **1 Soviet Baskunchak class** Bldr: Kamysh Burun SY, Kerch' (In serv. 1964–68)

C 42 USEDOM (ex-C27)

**Usedom (C 42)** 1982

**D:** 2,940 tons **S:** 13.2 kts **Dim:** 83.6 (74.0 pp) × 12.0 × 4.6
**Electron Equipt:** Radar: 1/TSR-333
**M:** 1 Zgoda-Sulzer 8DR43/61 W diesel; 1 prop; 2,220 hp **Electric:** 325 kw
**Range:** 5,000/12.6 **Man:** 30 tot. **Fuel:** 124 tons

REMARKS: 1,770 grt/1,660 dwt. Cargo: 1,490 tons (9,993 barrels fuel oil). Has provision for mounting 4/25-mm AA (II × 2), one mount forward, one aft.

◆ **3 Riems (Klasse 600) class** Bldr: Peenewerft, Wolgast (In serv. 1960–61)

C 11 HIDDENSEE C 43 POEL C 61 RIEMS (L: 24-6-59)

**Poel (C 43)** L. & L. Van Ginderen, 9-83

**D:** 1,206 tons (fl) **S:** 17 kts **Dim:** 59.6 (53.7 pp) × 9.0 × 3.9
**Electron Equipt:** Radar: 1/TSR-333 **M:** 2 8NVD 26/20 AU diesels; 1,400 hp
**Man:** 26 tot.

REMARKS: Cargo: 650 tons. Provision for 4/25-mm AA (II × 2), one mount forward, one aft. C 11 re-engined and partially automated in 1984, reducing crew to 12 total.

## TRAINING SHIPS S = *Schulschiff* (Schoolship)

◆ **1 Polish Wodnik class** Bldr: Gdansk SY (In serv. 6-7-76)

S 61 WILHELM PIECK

**D:** 1,800 tons (fl) **S:** 17 kts **Dim:** 73.0 × 12.0 × 4.0
**A:** 4/30-mm AA (II × 2)—4/25-mm AA (II × 2)
**Electron Equipt:** Radar: 2/TSR-333, 1/Drum Tilt **Man:** 80 tot.
**M:** 2 Cegielski-Sulzer 6 TD48 diesels; 2 props; 3,600 hp **Electric:** 530 kw

### TRAINING SHIPS *(continued)*

**Wilhelm Pieck (S 61)**—at Piraeus, Greece L. & L. Van Ginderen, 1984

REMARKS: In service 6-7-76. Sister to *Wodnik* and *Gryf* in Polish Navy and *Oka* and *Luga* in Soviet Navy. Design developed from that of the Soviet Moma-class surveying ships.

### SALVAGE SHIP

◆ **1 Polish Piast class** Bldr: Gdansk SY, 1977

A 46 OTTO VON GÜRICKE

**Otto Von Güricke (A 46)** M.O.D., Bonn, 1983

**D:** 1,560 tons (1,732 fl) **S:** 16.5 kts **Dim:** 73.2 × 10.0 × 4.0
**M:** 2 Cegielski-Sulzer 6DT48 diesels; 2 props; 3,600 hp **Range:** 3,000/12
**Electron Equipt:** Radar: 1/TSR-333 **A:** 8/25-mm AA (II × 4)

REMARKS: Sister to Polish *Piast* and *Lech*. Armed 1983. Has diving bell. Built on Soviet Moma-class survey-ship hull and propulsion plant.

### AIR/SEA RESCUE SHIP

◆ **1 converted Havana-class fishing trawler** Bldr: Rosslauer Schiffswerft

A 15 HUGO ECKENER (In serv. 1970, rebuilt 1971)

**Hugo Eckener (A 15)**—old number 1977

**D:** 384 tons (488 fl) **S:** 10.6 kts **Dim:** 37.66 (32.95 pp) × 8.20 × 3.63 max.
**M:** 1 type 8 NVD36A1 diesel; 578 hp **Electric:** 280 kw **Man:** 20 tot.
**Range:** 6,500/10 **Electron Equipt:** Radar: 1/TSR-333

REMARKS: Rebuilt from stern-haul trawler by Peenewerft, Wolgast.

### MISCELLANEOUS SHIPS

◆ **6 Ohre-class self-propelled barracks ships** Bldr: Peenewerft, Wolgast

| | In serv. | | In serv. |
|---|---|---|---|
| H 11 N . . . | 1985 | H72 ALTMARK | 1984 |
| H31 HARZ | 1983 | H91 N . . . | 1985 |
| H51 N . . . | 1986 | | |
| H71 VOGTLAND | 5-9-84 | | |

**Vogtland (H 71)** EGN, 1985

**D:** 2,400 tons (fl) **S:** . . . **Dim:** 89.41 × 13.22 × 2.36
**A:** 4/25-mm AA (II × 1) **Electron Equipt:** Radar: 1/TSR-333
**M:** 2 Type 6VD 18/51 Al-1 diesels; 2 CP props; . . . hp
**Man:** . . .

REMARKS: Built to replace the non-self-propelled Jugend-class barracks/base ships and officially described as "Wohn-und-Kampfschiff." Equipped with bow-thruster, one electrohydraulic crane.

◆ **2 Kondor-I-class torpedo retriever/target ships**

B 82 LIBBEN (ex-B 74, ex-B 62) B 81 N . . . (ex-B 73)

**Libben (B 82)**—old number 1980

REMARKS: Converted Kondor-I-class minesweepers, which they basically resemble. No armament. Ramp at stern for torpedo recovery. Radar reflector array on mast, below TSR-333 radar. See data under minesweepers.

◆ **1 state yacht** Bldr: Peenewerft, Wolgast

OSTSEELAND (In serv. 1971)

**D:** 623 tons (fl) **S:** 16 kts **Dim:** 60.90 × 7.77 × 3.36
**M:** 2 Type 40 DM diesels; 2 CP props; 4,000 hp
**Electric:** 300 kw (5 × 60 kw) **Man:** . . .

REMARKS: Lengthened Kondor-II minesweeper hull, rakish superstructure. Used by head of state. Unlike half-sisters, does not have Kort-nozzle props.

◆ **1 state yacht** Bldr: Warnow Werft, Warnemünde

OSTSEELAND II (L: 28-6-61)

**MISCELLANEOUS SHIPS** *(continued)*

**Ostseeland II** L. & L. Van Ginderen, 9-81

**D:** 342 tons (fl) **S:** 13 kts **Dim:** 40.56 × 7.95 × 2.51
**M:** 1 Type 8NVD 48 A-20 diesel; 1 prop; 1,320 hp
**Electric:** 180 kw (2 × 90 kw) **Man:** . . .

REMARKS: Renamed from *Ostseeland* in 4-71. Re-engined 1981.

◆ **1 small cable tender**

FREESENDORF Built 1962—No data available

◆ **1 Soviet Prometey class** (Type KM U1) **tug** Bldr: Gorokhovets SY, Leningrad

A 16 (In serv. 1983)

**D:** 319 tons (fl) **S:** 12 kts **Dim:** 29.8 (28.2 pp) × 8.3 × 3.2
**M:** 2 Type 6D30/50-4 diesels; 2 Kort-nozzle CP props; 1,200 hp
**Range:** 1,800/12 **Electric:** 50 kw **Man:** 3–5 tot.

REMARKS: Has ice-strengthened hull, 14-ton bollard pull. Over 100 sisters built in U.S.S.R. since 1971.

◆ **1 Type 700 seagoing tug (also salvage tug)** Bldr: Peenewerft, Wolgast (In serv. 1963)

A 14 THALE

**Thale (A 14)** 1978

**D:** 700 tons (792 fl) **S:** 12.8 kts **Dim:** 44.7 × 10.7 × 3.9
**Electron Equipt:** Radar: 1/TSR-333 **Range:** 4,000/12
**M:** 2 12KVD 21 diesels, electric drive; 2 props; 1,760 hp
**Man:** 6 officers, 33 men

REMARKS: 505 grt. Sister to Bulgarian *Jupiter*. Bollard pull: 16 tons. Provision made for 2/25-mm AA (II × 1).

◆ **6 Type 270 harbor tugs** Bldr: Peenewerft, Wolgast (In serv. 1959–60)

| | | |
|---|---|---|
| A 11 PEENE | A 13 BELT | A 71 ODER |
| A 12 SPEE | A 22 HAVEL | A 72 ERICH KRENKEL |

**D:** 270 tons **S:** 12 kts **Dim:** 30.0 × 5.5 × 2.5
**M:** 1 Buckau-Wolf LR6DV 148 diesel; 1 prop; 550 hp **Man:** 12 tot.

REMARKS: Provision for 2/25-mm AA (II × 1). Refitted 1983, new auxiliary machinery.

◆ **1 or more Warnow-class small tugs** Bldr: Yachtswerft, Berlin (In serv. 1973–. . .)

**D:** 25.5 tons (fl) **S:** . . . kts **Dim:** 15.25 × 3.97 × 0.92
**M:** 1 Type 6VD 14.5/12-1 diesel; 1 prop; 140 hp

◆ **1 small harbor tug** Bldr: Yachtswerft, Berlin

A23 ELBE (In serv. 1964)

**Elbe (A 23)** 1980

**D:** 18 tons **S:** . . . **Dim:** 14.20 × 3.25 × 0.99
**M:** 1 Type 4 NVD 21/2 diesel; 1 prop; 90 hp

◆ **6 FLB-class fireboats** Bldr: Schiffswerft, Berlin (In serv. 1959–60)

F 31 F 32 F 45 F 46 F 82 F 83

**FLB class F 46** L. & L. Van Ginderen, 1980

**D:** 124 tons **S:** 12 kts **Dim:** 32.3 (29.3 pp) × 5.9 × 1.6
**M:** 2 Buckau-Wolf 6NVD26A diesels; 1 prop; 540 hp
**Man:** 3 officers, 10 men

REMARKS: Three fire monitors. Can also act as tugs. Three sisters built for Egypt, 1961. FLB—Feuerlöschboot.

◆ **5 Gustav Koenigs-class river fuel lighters** Bldr: VEB Rosslau/Elbe

C 16 C 17 C 25 C 76 C 77 (all in serv. 1960)

**D:** 1,010 tons (fl) **S:** 8 kts **Dim:** 67.00 × 8.16 × 2.18
**M:** 1 Type R8DV 148 diesel; 1 prop; 420 hp

REMARKS: Typed "Binnentanker." Low freeboard, with folding masts to pass beneath bridges.

◆ **2 or more self-propelled cranes**

M 11 M 34

REMARKS: Built late 1970s to lift Libelle-class torpedoboats for servicing. Capacity: approx. 30 tons.

**GERMANY-GERMAN DEMOCRATIC REPUBLIC** *(continued)*
**MISCELLANEOUS SHIPS** *(continued)*

SOCIETY FOR SPORTS AND MECHANICS

The Naval College of this paramilitary youth organization maintains a number of craft for training, the largest of which is the *Ernst Thaelmann.*

◆ **1 converted Kondor-I-class minesweeper**

Ernst Thaelmann

Remarks: Conversion completed 19-8-77. Superstructure enlarged; carries 10 crew and 28 trainees.

◆ **1 sail-training ship** Bldr: Warnow Werft, Warnow (In serv. L: 2-8-51)

Wilhelm Pieck

**Wilhelm Pieck** 1978

**D:** 290 tons (fl) **S:** 12 kts (5 on diesel) **Dim:** 41.0 (29.5 pp) × 7.6 × 3.60
**M:** 1 diesel; 100 hp **Fuel:** 16 tons
**Man:** 13 crew plus 32 trainees

Remarks: 178 grt/29 nrt. Sail area: 580 m$^2$.

◆ **There are also a number of small craft used for youth training, including:**
**. . . MAB-14 (Type 407) class** Bldr: Yachtswerft, Berlin (In serv. 1976–79)

**D:** 18–24 tons (fl) **S:** . . . **Dim:** 14.55 (13.13 wl) × 3.97 × 1.05
**M:** 1 Type 6VD15.4/12-1 diesel; 1 prop; 140 hp

# GERMANY (WEST)
## Federal Republic of Germany

Personnel (1987): 37,540 men (including 5,640 officers, 15,300 noncommissioned officers and 16,600 non-rated personnel)

Merchant Marine (1986): 1,752 ships—5,565,214 grt
(tankers: 59 ships—593,213 grt)

Ships In Service, Under Construction, Or Ordered
As Of 1 January 1988

| | L | Tons | Main armament |
|---|---|---|---|
| ◆ **24 submarines** | | | |
| 18 Type 206 | 1972–74 | 450 | 8/533-mm TT |
| 6 Type 205 | 1961–68 | 370 | 8/533-mm TT |
| ◆ **7 destroyers** | | | |
| 3 Charles F. Adams | 1967–69 | 3,370 | 1/Tartar, 2/127-mm DP, 1/ASROC |
| 4 Hamburg | 1960–63 | 3,400 | 4/MM 38, 3/100-mm, 8/40-mm AA, 4/ASW TT |
| ◆ **9 frigates** | | | |
| 6 Type 122 | 1979–82 | 2,900 | 8/Harpoon, 1/Sea Sparrow, 1/76-mm, 4/ASW TT, 2/helicopters |
| 3 Köln | 1958–62 | 1,750 | 2/100-mm DP, 6/40-mm AA, 2/ASW RL, 4/ASW TT |
| ◆ **5 corvettes** | | | |
| 5 Thetis | 1960–62 | 604 | 2/40-mm AA, 1/ASW RL, 4/ASW TT |
| ◆ **40 guided-missile boats** | | | |
| 10 Type 143A | 1981–83 | 300 | 4/MM 38, 1/76-mm DP, 1/RAM system, mines |
| 10 Type 143 | 1973–76 | 295 | 4/MM 38, 2/76-mm DP, 2/533-mm TT |
| 20 Type 148 | 1972–75 | 234 | 4/MM 38, 1/76-mm DP, 1/40-mm AA |

◆ **64 (+10 + 20) minesweepers/minehunters**

Naval Aviation:

1 squadron of 19 Bréguet Atlantic-1150 aircraft, of which 5 have been modified for electronic warfare. The ASW aircraft underwent modernization in 1981–83.

1 squadron of 22 Mk 43 Sea King helicopters for search-and-rescue operations. Twenty Sea Kings are being upgraded to permit carrying 4 Sea Skua antiship missiles, a Sea Spray Mk 3 search radar, electronic intercept gear, chaff, and LINK 11 computer data system. The first two were to have completed by 1984 and all by 1988, but delays moved initial redeliveries to 1987, with the last to deliver during 1989. Procurement of up to 80 NH-90 helicopters to replace the SH-3D is anticipated for the 1990s.

On 7-4-76 the German government decided to begin construction of 112 MRCA Tornado variable-geometry fighter-bombers for the Navy. The first four entered service in 7-82 and 47 were operational by 7-84. Characteristics are:

Length: 17.2 meters
Wingspan: 13.90 meters max./8.40 meters min.
Maximum takeoff weight: 26,000 kg
Maximum speed: Mach 2.2
Ceiling: 15,200 m
Weapons: 4 Kormoran ASM or 10 Mk 83 or Mk 82 bombs or 8 BL 755 cluster bombs—plus 2 AIM 9 Sidewinder and a 23-mm gun

Deliveries were scheduled for: 1 in 1981, 26 in 1982, 22 in 1983, 32 in 1986, 16 in 1987, and 15 in 1988, but total production may cease at 95. U.S. HARM missiles were ordered 1986 to replace the Kormorans.

**Tornado** 1982

Fourteen Westland/Bréguet WG-13 Lynx Mk 88 ASW helicopters were bought for the new Type 122 frigates. The Bendix DAQS-18 dipping sonar is employed. First 4 delivered 1981, 8 in 1982, 4 in 1983, and 2 in 1986. Five Mk 88 Lynx ordered 1986 for delivery beginning in 7-88.

There are also 20 Dornier DO-28D-2 liaison aircraft, an HFB 32 EW aircraft, a small number of Piaggio P 149D basic trainers, and 4 IAI Westwind target tugs.

Two more Dornier DO-28D2 delivered 15-1-86 for oil-pollution spotting, and a DO-228-201 was acquired 10-1-86 for a 6-month trial.

**Lynx Mk 88 of the West German Navy** P. Voss, 8-84

WEAPONS AND SYSTEMS

With a few exceptions, such as torpedoes, West German ships have weapons and systems of foreign origin.

### (A) MISSILES

◆ **Surface-to-air**

Standard Tartar SM-1 MR on board the 3 *Charles F. Adams*-class destroyers

In conjunction with the U.S.A., the General Dynamics RIM-116A RAM (Rolling Air-frame Missile) is being developed as a close-in defense weapon. The system will carry 21 missiles per EX-31 launcher. A total of 63 launchers are programmed for purchase.

◆ **Surface-to-surface**

MM 38 Exocet on board *Hamburg*-class destroyers and Types 143A, 143, and 148 guided-missile patrol boats. The U.S. Harpoon (RGM-84A) is carried by the Type 122 frigates and by refitted units of the *Charles F. Adams*-class destroyers. The Anglo-French ANS missile will replace both MM 38 Exocet and the Kormoran air-launched SSM from the mid-1990s.

◆ **Air-to-surface**

Kormoran missiles, carried by Tornado aircraft. To be replaced by U.S. HARM missiles delivered 1987–89. Kormoran II, with a new digital seeker, is in development.

### (B) GUNS

Automatic 127-mm U.S. Mk 42 Mod. 10 on *Adams*-class destroyers
French Model 1953 100-mm dual-purpose on *Hamburg*-class destroyers, *Köln*-class frigates, *Rhein*-class tenders, and the training ship *Deutschland*
OTO Melara Compact 76-mm guns on board Types 143, 143A, and 148 guided-missile patrol boats
40-mm (70-caliber) Bofors, in single or twin mounts on many types of ships. Replaced by open Breda mountings in combatants. Bofors "Trinity" elevating masses and 100-round ready-service magazines ordered 1986 to update existing 40-mm mounts.
20-mm Oerlikon and Rheinmetall

### (C) ANTISUBMARINE WARFARE

◆ **Rocket launchers**

Quadruple 375-mm Bofors, automatically loaded in a vertical position
The U.S. ASROC system, with a Mk 112 octuple launcher for missiles having a Mk 46 ASW torpedo payload

◆ **Torpedoes**

U.S. Mk 37 Mod. 0 on submarines (possibly no longer in use)
U.S. Mk 44 and Mk 46 on *Charles F. Adams*-class destroyers, Type 122 frigates, and Bréguet Atlantic-1150 ASW patrol aircraft

Wire-guided "Seeal (SST-4)" type (20,000-m range) on Type 143 missile boats, and submarines (DM-1)
Wire-guided "Seeschlange" type on Type 206 submarines; range; 10,000 m (DM 2A1)
Wire-guided "Seehecht" (DM 2A3) in development. DM 2A4 version will be deeper diving.

### (D) ELECTRONICS

In addition to the U.S. radars mounted in the *Charles F. Adams*-class destroyers, the West German Navy uses the following Dutch radars (Hollandse Signaal-Apparaaten):

LW-02-long-range-air search (Band D)
SGR-105 multi-purpose search (Band E-F)
SGR-103 surface search (Band I)
Band X for 100-mm and 40-mm fire control

Type 148 missile patrol boats have a Thomson-CSF Triton target-designation radar and Vega fire-control system with Pollux radar.

Type 143 missile patrol boats carry the AGIS fire-control system combined with Dutch H.S.A. WM 27 M radar. AGIS has two UNIVAC computers, one for fire control and the other for real-time threat-processing. WM 27 has two antennas within its dome, one for search and one for tracking. An automatic data link permits AGIS to relay information with other units of the Type 143, *Charles F. Adams*-class, and with future combatants destined for service with the fleet operating from Glücksberg-Meierwik. The *Adams*-class destroyers have received the Lockheed-built Mk 86 gunfire-control system, with SPQ-9 and SPG-60 radar.

Aside from the SQS-23 on the *Adams* class, sonars are of West German origin.

## SUBMARINES

◆ **0 (+6) Type 212**

REMARKS: Project to develop a smaller submarine to replace the six Type 205 in the late 1990s. To be 800 tons (surfaced).

◆ **0 (+12 + 6) Type 211** Bldr: . . .

**D:** 1,040 tons surf./1,300 sub. **S:** 11/23 kts
**Dim:** 59.00 × 5.40 × 4.50 (surf.)
**A:** 8/533-mm TT—(14 Seeal-3 ASW and DM 2A3 torpedoes)
**Electron Equipt:** Radar: . . .—Sonar: Krupp-Atlas DBSQS-21
**M:** 2 MTU 16V396 SB83, 1,260-bhp diesels; 2/870-kw generators; electric drive; 1 prop; 6,000 hp
**Fuel:** 100 tons **Range:** 5,000/8 snorkel
**Endurance:** 40 days **Man:** 20 tot.

REMARKS: Six of this general type ordered from Thyssen Nordseewerke for Norway as the "Type 210," for delivery beginning 1989. Diving depth 250 m. In German Navy will replace Type 205 and some Type 206, with first delivering 1995. To use a Norwegian-developed, Kongsberg MSI-90U fire-control system. Program remained in concept planning through 1987 and may be canceled due to funding constraints. May receive a surface-to-air missile system.

◆ **18 Type 206** Bldrs: (A)—Howaldtswerke-Deutsche Werft, Kiel; (B)—Rheinstahl Nordseewerke, Emden

| | Bldr | Laid down | L | In serv. |
|---|---|---|---|---|
| S 192 U 13 | A | 24-11-69 | 28-9-71 | 19-4-73 |
| S 193 U 14 | B | 10-9-70 | 1-2-72 | 19-4-73 |
| S 194 U 15 | A | 29-5-70 | 15-6-72 | 17-4-74 |
| S 195 U 16 | B | 22-4-71 | 29-8-72 | 9-11-73 |
| S 196 U 17 | A | 19-10-70 | 10-10-72 | 28-11-73 |
| S 197 U 18 | B | 28-7-71 | 31-10-72 | 19-12-73 |
| S 198 U 19 | A | 14-1-71 | 15-12-72 | 9-11-73 |
| S 199 U 20 | B | 15-2-72 | 16-1-73 | 24-5-74 |
| S 170 U 21 | A | 14-4-71 | 9-3-73 | 16-8-74 |
| S 171 U 22 | B | 3-5-72 | 27-3-73 | 26-7-74 |
| S 172 U 23 | B | 21-8-72 | 22-5-73 | 2-5-75 |
| S 173 U 24 | B | 10-7-72 | 26-6-73 | 16-10-74 |
| S 174 U 25 | A | 6-10-71 | 23-5-73 | 14-6-74 |
| S 175 U 26 | B | 17-11-72 | 20-11-73 | 13-3-75 |
| S 176 U 27 | A | 11-1-72 | 21-8-73 | 16-10-74 |
| S 177 U 28 | B | 26-1-72 | 22-1-74 | 18-12-74 |
| S 178 U 29 | A | 29-2-72 | 5-11-73 | 27-11-74 |
| S 179 U 30 | B | 27-4-73 | 26-3-74 | 13-3-75 |

**U 13 (S 192)** P. Voss, 5-86

**U 23 (S 172)** L. & L. Van Ginderen, 6-87

**U 25 (S 174)** L. & L. Van Ginderen, 1-87

**SUBMARINES** *(continued)*

**D:** 450 tons surf./500 tons sub. **S:** 10 surf./17 kts sub. (5 snorkel)
**Dim:** 48.6 × 4.6 × 4.3
**A:** 8/533-mm TT—(16 DM-1 and DM-2A1 torpedoes)—24 mines in external container
**Electron Equipt:** Radar: 1/Thomson-CSF Calypso
Sonar: 1/WSU AN 410A4, 1/GHG AN 5039A1, 1/DBQS-21D, 1/DUUX-2
**M:** 2 MTU 12V493AZ diesels; 600 hp each, 2/405-kw generators; 1/2,300-hp electric motor
**Range:** 4,500/5 (snorkel); 200/5 submerged **Man:** 4 officers, 18 men

REMARKS: *U 13* to *U 24* authorized in 1969, *U 25* to *U 30* in 2-70. An external "mine-belt" container has been developed for these submarines to permit them to carry a full complement of torpedoes plus 24 mines. Three batteries, 92 cells each. Now have H.S.A. Mk 8; new Krupp-Atlas sonars and CSU 83 fire-control systems and DM 2A3 torpedoes are to be installed in 12 of the 18 by HDW and Thyssen. Modernized units to be typed 206A and will be distinguished by a new sail shape. *U 29* began modernization at HDW 9-6-87 for completion 12-87; *U 23* first at Thyssen 18-7-87, to complete 7-88. Last to complete 2-92.

◆ **6 Type 205** Bldr: Howaldtswerke, Kiel

| | Laid down | L | In serv. |
|---|---|---|---|
| S 180 U 1 | 1-2-65 | 17-2-67 | 6-6-67 |
| S 181 U 2 | 1-19-64 | 15-7-66 | 11-10-66 |
| S 188 U 9 | 10-12-64 | 20-10-66 | 11-4-67 |
| S 189 U 10 | 15-7-65 | 5-6-67 | 28-11-67 |
| S 190 U 11 | 1-4-66 | 9-2-68 | 21-6-68 |
| S 191 U 12 | 1-9-66 | 10-9-68 | 14-1-69 |

**U 2 (S 181)**—in refit F. Jentsch, 6-86

**U 10 (S 189)** Marineamt, 1981

**D:** 419 tons surf./450 sub. **S:** 10 surf./17 kts sub. **Dim:** 43.5 × 4.6 × 3.8
**A:** 8/533-mm TT
**Electron Equipt:** Radar: 1/Thomson-CSF Calypso
Sonar: 1/SRS-M1H, 1/GHG AN5039A1
**M:** 2 MTU 12V493AZ, 600-hp diesels, 2/405-kw generators, 1/2,300-hp electric motor **Man:** 4 officers, 17 men

REMARKS: *U 10* is 43.8 m overall; *U 11, 12:* 45.8 m overall. Diving depth: 150 m. The poor quality of the antimagnetic steel used in the first six of this class caused serious pitting, which made it necessary to rebuild the *U 1* and *U 2* (originally launched 21-10-61 and 25-1-62) with regular steel. Beginning with the *U 9,* laid down in 1964, these submarines were built with a new antimagnetic steel. Have H.S.A. Mk 8 torpedo f.c.s. The *U 3* was stricken in 1968, the *U 4* and *U 8* in 1974, the *U 5* in 1975, and the *U 6* and *U 7* in 1974. *U 1* refitted at HDW, Kiel, 19-3-87 to 11-87 for trials with oxygen/hydrogen fuel-cell closed-cycle propulsion system.

**GUIDED-MISSILE DESTROYERS**

◆ **3 U.S. Charles F. Adams (Type 103B) class** Bldr: Bath Iron Works, Bath, Maine

| | Laid down | L | In serv. |
|---|---|---|---|
| D 185 LÜTJENS (ex-DDG 28) | 1-3-66 | 11-8-67 | 22-3-69 |
| D 186 MÖLDERS (ex-DDG 29) | 12-4-66 | 13-4-68 | 20-9-69 |
| D 187 ROMMEL (ex-DDG 30) | 22-8-67 | 1-2-69 | 2-5-70 |

**Mölders (D 186)**—as modernized L. & L. Van Ginderen, 9-85

**Mölders (D 186)**—as modernized L. & L. Van Ginderen, 4-87

**D:** 3,550 tons (4,720 fl) **S:** 35 kts **Dim:** 134.4 (128.1 pp) × 14.38 × 6.4 (max)
**A:** 1/Tartar Mk 13 missile launcher (40 Harpoon and Standard SM-1 MR missiles)—2/127-mm Mk 42 DP (I × 2)—6/324-mm Mk 32 ASW TT (III × 2, Mk 46 torpedoes)—1 Mk 112 ASROC ASW RL (VIII × 1)
**Electron Equipt:** Radar: 1/SPS-40, 1/SPS-10, 1/SPS-52, 1/Kelvin-Hughes 14/9, 2/SPG-51C, SPQ-9, 1/SPG-60
Sonar: 1/SQS-23—EW: FL-1800S, 2/Mk 36 RBOC chaff—TACAN: URN-20
**M:** GT; 2 props; 70,000 hp **Electric:** 3,000 kw
**Boilers:** 4 Combustion Engineering, 84 kg/cm² pressure, superheat 500°C
**Fuel:** 950 tons **Range:** 1,600/30; 4,030/18 **Man:** 21 officers, 319 men

REMARKS: Authorized 1964. They differ in several ways, especially in profile, from the *Charles F. Adams* design, on which they are based. Installation of the SM-1 MR system and digitalization of some computer equipment was completed 1981–82. All three were further modernized, with most of the improvements originally planned for the U.S. Navy units of the class: the Mk 13 missile system was revised to permit carrying Harpoon antiship missiles, the Mk 68 gunfire-control system was replaced by the Mk 86 GFCS with SPQ-9 and SPG-60 radars (the latter permitting a third SAM fire-control channel as well), the U.S. SYS-1 computerized data systems, the Mk 36 Super RBOC chaff system, and the substitution of the German FL-1800S EW system for WLR-6. D 185 began modernization 5-85, completing 16-12-86. D 186 refitted 12-83 to 29-3-84, and D 187 12-83 to 26-7-85. Have Satir-1 NTDS data link. Will later receive two RAM launchers (XXI × 2) and DSQS-21B (2) sonar in place of SQS-23. To strike: one in 2002, two in 2003.

◆ **4 Hamburg class (Type 101B)** Bldr: H. C. Stülcken, Hamburg

| | Laid down | L | In serv. |
|---|---|---|---|
| D 181 HAMBURG | 29-1-59 | 26-3-60 | 23-3-64 |
| D 182 SCHLESWIG-HOLSTEIN | 20-8-59 | 20-8-60 | 12-10-64 |
| D 183 BAYERN | 14-9-60 | 14-8-62 | 6-7-65 |
| D 184 HESSEN | 15-2-61 | 4-5-63 | 8-10-68 |

## GUIDED-MISSILE DESTROYERS *(continued)*

**Hamburg (D 181)** L. & L. Van Ginderen, 8-86

**Hessen (D 184)** L. & L. Van Ginderen, 9-86

**D:** 3,500 tons (4,700 fl) **S:** 35 kts **Dim:** 133.7 (128.0 pp) × 13.4 × 5.2 (max.)
**A:** 4/MM 38 Exocet SSM—3/100-mm Mod. 1953 DP (I × 3)—8/40-mm Breda AA (II × 4)—4/533-mm ASW TT—2/375-mm Bofors ASW RL (IV × 2)—2/d.c. racks (12 d.c.)—60–80 mines
**Electron Equipt:** Radar: 1/Kelvin-Hughes 14/9, 1/DA-08, 1/LW-04, 1/SGR-103, 3/M 45
Sonar: 1/Atlas ELAC 1BV med. freq.
EW: WLR-6, 2/SCLAR chaff RL
**M:** 2 sets GT; 2 props; 68,000 hp **Boilers:** 4/59 kg/cm$^2$, 465°C
**Fuel:** 810 tons **Electric:** 5,400 kw **Range:** 920/34; 3,400/18
**Man:** 270 tot.

REMARKS: Between the beginning of 1975 and the end of 1977, refitted with 4/MM 38 to replace mount C, in the following order: D 184, D 181, D 182, and D 183. Five fixed antiship torpedo tubes (3 in bows, 2 aft) removed, 40-mm replaced by later model, new air-search radar. There are three H.S.A. M4 radar directors for the 100-mm guns. The d.c. racks are bolted to the mine rails. Further modernization, beginning with D 184, is planned, including the installation of 2/21-missile EX-31 launchers for the RAM SAM system, and a new computer data system. Planned for disposal: two in 1997, two in 1998.

## GUIDED-MISSILE FRIGATES

### ◆ 0 (+6) Type 124 class

REMARKS: In project definition through the end of 1987 was a program for six new guided-missile frigates, to be based in part on the successful Type 122 design. A delay may permit adopting the NFR 90 "NATO Frigate." The ships will rationally replace the four *Hamburg*-class destroyers and the three remaining *Köln*-class frigates in the 1990s. May also be canceled altogether in favor of additional Type 122 construction.

### ◆ 6 (+2) Bremen (Type 122) class

| | Bldr | Laid down | L | In serv. |
|---|---|---|---|---|
| F 207 Bremen | Bremer-Vulkan | 9-7-79 | 27-9-79 | 7-5-82 |
| F 208 Niedersachsen | AG Weser, Bremen | 9-11-79 | 9-6-80 | 15-10-82 |
| F 209 Rheinland-Pfalz | Blohm + Voss, Hamburg | 25-9-79 | 3-9-80 | 9-5-83 |
| F 210 Emden | Nordseewerke, Emden | 23-6-80 | 17-12-80 | 9-10-83 |
| F 211 Köln | Blohm + Voss, Hamburg | 16-6-80 | 29-5-81 | 19-10-84 |
| F 212 Karlsruhe | Howaldtswerke, Kiel | 10-3-81 | 8-1-82 | 19-4-84 |
| F 213 Augsburg | Bremer Vulkan | 4-4-87 | 17-9-87 | 9-89 |
| F 214 Lübeck | Thyssen, Emden | 1-6-87 | 15-10-87 | 3-90 |

**Karlsruhe (F 212)**—with Lynx on deck L. & L. Van Ginderen, 5-86

**Rheinland-Pfalz (F 209)** M.O.D., Bonn, 1986

**GUIDED-MISSILE FRIGATES** *(continued)*

**Emden (F 210)** L. & L. Van Ginderen, 6-87

**D:** 2,950 tons (3,800 fl) **S:** 30 kts
**Dim:** 130.0 (121.8 wl) × 14.4 × 4.26 (6.0 sonar)
**A:** 8/Harpoon SSM (IV × 2)—1/NATO Sea Sparrow SAM system (VIII × 1, Mk 29 launcher, 24 RIM-7M missiles)—1/76-mm OTO Melara DP—4/324-mm Mk 32 ASW TT (I × 4)—2/Lynx Mk 88 ASW helicopters
**Electron Equipt:** Radar: 1/3RM 20, 1/DA-08, 1/WM-25, 1/STIR
Sonar: 1/DSQS-21B(Z) (bow-mounted)
EW: FL 1800S intercept array (7.5-17 GHz), Mk 36 Super RBOC chaff RL (VI × 4)
**M:** CODOG: 2 G.E.-Fiat LM 2500 GT (50,000 hp); 2 MTU 20V956 TB92 diesels (10,400 hp); 2/5-bladed Escher-Wyss CP props
**Electric:** 3,000 kw (4/750-kw diesel sets) **Range:** 5,700/17 **Fuel:** 610 tons
**Man:** 21 officers, 160 men (plus 6-officer/12-man air complement)

REMARKS: Germanized version of Dutch *Kortenaer* class. Ordered 7-77; two additional canceled. The helicopters will be equipped with DAQS-13D dipping sonar. Two RAM point-defense SAM launchers are to be added atop the hangar. Fin stabilizers fitted. Have SATIR tactical data system, and H.S.A. Vesta helicopter transponder. Fitted with U.S. Prairie/Masker bubbler system to reduce radiated noise, fin stabilizers, a citadel nuclear-biological-gas protection system, and the U.S. SLQ-25 Nixie towed torpedo decoy. F 212 has a revised engine air intake system. Carry 16 torpedoes for helos, 8 for tubes. Construction of two additional units was approved by the government 12-6-85; F 214 to be last ship built by Bremer Vulkan. F 14 fitted out by Bremer-Vulkan. Both will get W.K. SCOT SATCOMM gear. Four more may build in lieu of NFR 90 program.

## FRIGATES

◆ **3 Köln class (Type 120)** Bldr: H.C. Stülcken, Hamburg

| | Laid down | L | In serv. |
|---|---|---|---|
| F 222 AUGSBURG | 29-10-58 | 15-8-59 | 7-4-62 |
| F 224 LÜBECK | 28-10-59 | 23-7-60 | 6-7-63 |
| F 225 BRAUNSCHWEIG | 28-7-60 | 3-2-62 | 16-6-64 |

**D:** 2,425 tons (2,970 fl) **S:** 30 kts (20 on diesels)
**Dim:** 109.83 (105.0 pp) × 10.5 × 4.61 (fl)
**A:** 2/100-mm Mod. 1953 DP (I × 2)—6/40-mm AA (II × 2, I × 2)—2/375-mm Bofors ASW RL (IV × 2; 70 rockets)—4/533-mm ASW TT (I × 4)—2/d.c. racks (12 d.c.)—82 mines
**Electron Equipt:** Radar: 1/DA-02, 1/SGR-103, 1/Kelvin-Hughes 14/9, 2/M 44 fire-control, 1/M 45 fire-control
Sonar: 1/PAE/CWE MF hull-mounted—EW: . . . intercept
**M:** CODAG: 4 M.A.N. V-16-cylinder diesels (each 3,000 hp); 2 Brown-Boveri gas turbines (each 13,000 hp); 2 CP props; 36,000 hp
**Man:** 17 officers, 193 men

REMARKS: The rocket-launcher magazines carry 72 projectiles. Two diesels and one gas turbine on each of the two shafts. Made 33 knots on trials. Three sisters disposed of: *Köln* (F 220) on 17-12-82 for damage-control static training at the Naval Technical School until 1988–89; *Karlsruhe* (F 223) on 27-12-82, to Turkey 28-3-83; and *Emden* (F 221) on 23-9-83 for transfer to Turkey late 1983. F 225 heavily damaged in collision with HMS *Plymouth,* 11-4-84. F 222 and F 224 to be renamed if retained past completion of new Type 122 frigates with same names; currently planned disposal is 1990, with F 225 to discard in 1996.

**Augsburg (F 222)** L. & L. Van Ginderen, 3-87

**Lübeck (F 224)** M. Louagie, 3-87

## CORVETTES

◆ **0 (+3) Type 423**

REMARKS: Programmed class for delivery 1990–93 to replace the *Thetis* (Type 420) class. No data available; program probably canceled or deferred.

◆ **5 Thetis class (Type 420)** Bldr: Roland Werft, Bremen-Hemelingen

| | Laid down | L | In serv. |
|---|---|---|---|
| P 6052 THETIS | 19-6-59 | 22-3-60 | 1-7-61 |
| P 6053 HERMES | 8-10-59 | 9-8-60 | 16-12-61 |
| P 6054 NAJADE | 22-3-60 | 6-12-60 | 12-5-62 |
| P 6055 TRITON | 15-8-60 | 5-8-61 | 10-11-62 |
| P 6056 THESEUS | 1-7-61 | 20-3-62 | 15-8-63 |

**D:** 575 tons (658 fl) **S:** 23.5 kts **Dim:** 69.78 (65.5 pp) × 8.2 × 2.65
**A:** 2/40-mm AA (II × 1)—1/Bofors 375-mm ASW RL (IV × 1)—4/533-mm ASW TT (I × 4)—2/d.c. racks (12/d.c.)—mines
**Electron Equipt:** Radar: 1/Kelvin-Hughes 14/9, 1/TRS-N
Sonar: ELAC 1BV—EW: . . . intercept
**M:** 2 M.A.N. V84V diesels; 2 props; 6,800 hp **Electric:** 540 kw
**Range:** 2,760/15 **Man:** 5 officers, 43 men **Fuel:** 78 tons

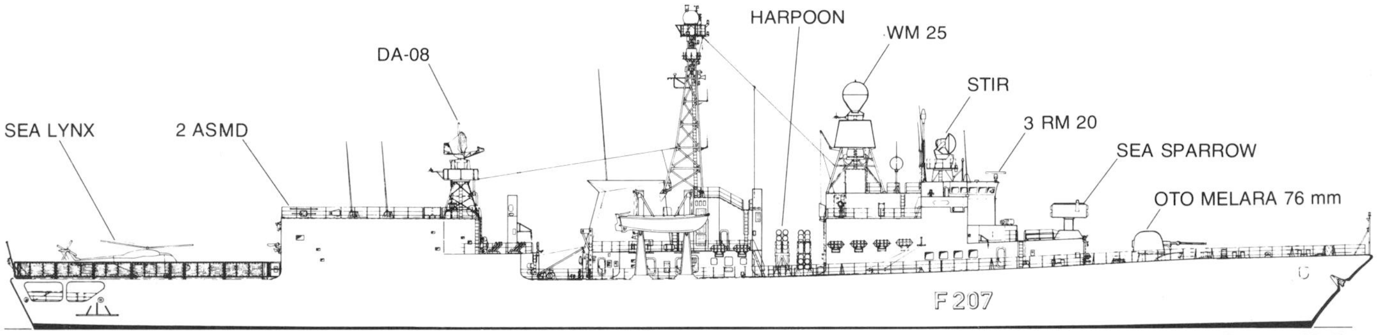


**Bremen** Bremer-Vulkan

**CORVETTES** *(continued)*

**Triton (P 6055)** L. & L. Van Ginderen, 5-87

**Theseus (P 6056)** Marineamt, 5-84

Remarks: Former torpedo-recovery boats, well designed for operations in the Belts and the Baltic. Have H.S.A. Mk 9 torpedo f.c.s. and an optical lead-computing gun f.c.s. P 6054 has forward superstructure extended toward bow to accommodate a medical facility. Carry 20 ASW RL projectiles.

**GUIDED-MISSILE PATROL BOATS**

◆ **10 Type 143A** Bldrs: A: Lürssen, Vegesack; B: Kröger, Rendsburg

| | | Laid down | L | In serv. |
|---|---|---|---|---|
| P 6121 S71 Gepard | A | 11-7-79 | 25-9-81 | 7-12-82 |
| P 6122 S72 Puma | A | 17-12-79 | 8-2-82 | 24-2-83 |
| P 6123 S73 Hermelin | B | 1-2-80 | 8-12-81 | 28-4-83 |
| P 6124 S74 Nerz | A | 24-7-80 | 18-8-82 | 14-7-83 |
| P 6125 S75 Zobel | B | 3-7-80 | 30-6-82 | 29-9-83 |
| P 6126 S76 Frettchen | A | 22-12-80 | 26-1-83 | 15-12-83 |
| P 6127 S77 Dachs | B | 9-3-80 | 14-12-82 | 1-3-84 |
| P 6128 S78 Ozelot | A | 25-6-81 | 7-6-83 | 3-5-84 |
| P 6129 S79 Wiesel | A | 5-10-80 | 8-8-83 | 12-7-84 |
| P 6130 S80 Hyäne | A | 7-12-81 | 5-10-83 | 13-11-84 |

**D:** 300 tons (390.6 fl) **S:** 36 kts (32 fl)
**Dim:** 57.6 (54.4 pp) × 7.76 × 2.99 (2.56 hull)
**A:** 4/MM 38 Exocet—provision for 1/RAM ASMD (XXI × 1, RIM-116A missiles)—1/76-mm OTO Melara DP—mines
**Electron Equipt:** Radar: 1/3RM 20, 1/H.S.A. WM-27—EW: FL 1800 intercept, chaff
**M:** 4 MTU 16V956 SB80 diesels; 4 props; 16,000 hp **Electric:** 540 kw
**Fuel:** 116 tons **Range:** 600/30; 2,600/16 **Man:** 4 officers, 18 p.o., 12 men

Remarks: Ordered 1978. A repeat Type 143 with the much-delayed RAM point-defense SAM system intended to replace the after 76-mm gun, and mine rails in place of the wire-guided torpedoes. Wood-planked hull on steel frame. Have AGIS integrated data system. Lack after optical GFCS found on Type 143/143B. Constitute the 7th Fast Patrol Boat Squadron. RAM to become operational circa 1989 after many delays.

**Zobel (P 6125)** L. & L. Van Ginderen, 4-85

**Frettchen (P 6126)** L. & L. Van Ginderen, 4-85

◆ **10 Type 143/143B** Bldrs: A: Lürssen, Vegesack; B: Kröger, Rendsburg

| | Bldr | Laid down | L | In serv. |
|---|---|---|---|---|
| P 6111 S61 Albatros | A | 4-5-72 | 22-10-73 | 1-11-76 |
| P 6112 S62 Falke | A | 25-10-72 | 21-3-74 | 13-4-76 |
| P 6113 S63 Geier | A | 14-2-73 | 18-9-74 | 2-6-76 |
| P 6114 S64 Bussard | A | 4-7-73 | 14-4-75 | 14-8-76 |
| P 6115 S65 Sperber | B | 18-1-73 | 15-1-74 | 27-9-76 |
| P 6116 S66 Greif | A | 12-12-73 | 4-9-75 | 25-11-76 |
| P 6117 S67 Kondor | B | 19-6-73 | 6-3-75 | 17-12-76 |
| P 6118 S68 Seeadler | A | 12-6-74 | 17-11-75 | 28-3-77 |
| P 6119 S69 Habicht | B | 25-1-74 | 5-6-75 | 23-12-77 |
| P 6120 S70 Kormoran | A | 26-11-74 | 14-4-76 | 29-7-77 |

**Albatros (P 6111)** L. & L. Van Ginderen, 5-86

**Greif (P 6116)** L. & L. Van Ginderen, 5-85

**GUIDED-MISSILE PATROL BOATS** ***(continued)***

**D:** 300 tons (393 fl) **S:** 36 kts (32 fl)
**Dim:** 57.6 (54.4 pp) × 7.76 × 2.82 (2.56 hull)
**A:** 4/MM 38 Exocet—2/76-mm OTO Melara AA (I × 2)—2/533-mm TT (aft-launching, for Seeal wire-guided torpedoes)
**Electron Equipt:** Radar: 1/3RM 20, 1/H.S.A. WM-27—EW: . . . intercept, chaff
**M:** 4 MTU 16V956 TB91 diesels; 4 props; 16,000 hp **Electric:** 540 kw
**Fuel:** 116 tons **Range:** 600/30; 2,600/16 **Man:** 4 officers, 18 p.o., 12 men

REMARKS: Wood-planked hull on steel frame. To be refitted to Type 143A standard, becoming Type 143B. There is a secondary OGR-7/3 optical f.c.s. for the aft 76-mm gun. PG 119 carried a *mockup* RAM launcher aft during 1983. EW equipment is less elaborate than on the Type 143A; both classes have a chaff-dispensing mast abaft the mainmast central leg. To receive FL 1800 EW system, delete torpedo tubes, add the RAM SAM system, and receive mine rails by 1990–92.

◆ **20 Type 148, steel-hulled** Bldrs: A: Constructions Mécaniques de Normandie, Cherbourg; B: Lürssen, Vegesack

| | Bldr | Laid down | L | In serv. |
|---|---|---|---|---|
| P 6141 S41 TIGER | A | 11-10-71 | 27-9-72 | 30-10-72 |
| P 6142 S42 ILTIS | A | 2-2-72 | 12-12-72 | 8-1-73 |
| P 6143 S43 LUCHS | A | 23-3-72 | 7-3-73 | 9-4-73 |
| P 6144 S44 MARDER | A | 15-4-72 | 5-5-73 | 14-7-73 |
| P 6145 S45 LEOPARD | A | 13-9-72 | 3-7-73 | 21-8-73 |
| P 6146 S46 FUCHS | B | 10-3-72 | 21-5-73 | 17-10-73 |
| P 6147 S47 JAGUAR | A | 29-11-72 | 20-9-73 | 13-11-73 |
| P 6148 S48 LÖWE | B | 10-7-72 | 10-9-73 | 9-1-74 |
| P 6149 S49 WOLF | A | 23-1-73 | 11-1-74 | 26-2-74 |
| P 6150 S50 PANTHER | B | 30-9-72 | 10-12-73 | 27-3-74 |
| P 6151 S51 HÄHER | A | 5-4-73 | 26-4-74 | 12-6-74 |
| P 6152 S52 STORCH | B | 12-3-73 | 25-3-74 | 17-7-74 |
| P 6153 S53 PELIKAN | A | 11-9-73 | 4-7-74 | 24-9-74 |
| P 6154 S54 ELSTER | B | 29-6-73 | 8-7-74 | 14-11-74 |
| P 6155 S55 ALK | A | 9-4-74 | 15-11-74 | 7-1-75 |
| P 6156 S56 DOMMEL | B | 13-12-73 | 30-10-74 | 12-2-75 |
| P 6157 S57 WEIHE | A | 2-7-74 | 13-2-75 | 3-4-75 |
| P 6158 S58 PINGUIN | B | 11-3-74 | 26-2-75 | 22-5-75 |
| P 6159 S59 REIHER | A | 8-11-74 | 15-5-75 | 24-6-75 |
| P 6160 S60 KRANICH | B | 9-5-74 | 26-5-75 | 6-8-75 |

**Alk (P 6155)**—new 40-mm mount aft L. & L. Van Ginderen, 10-86

**Weihe (P 6157)** H. Ehlers, 5-86

**D:** 234 tons (264 fl) **S:** 35.8 kts **Dim:** 47.0 (45.9 pp) × 7.1 × 2.66 (fl)
**A:** 4/MM 38 Exocet—1/76-mm DP OTO Melara (fwd)—1/40-mm Bofors AA (aft)—8 mines in place of the 40-mm AA
**Electron Equipt:** Radar: 1/3RM 20 navigation, 1/Triton, 1/Pollux
**M:** 4 MTU MD 872 16-cyl. diesels; 4 props; 14,400 hp (12,000 sust.)
**Electric:** 270 kw **Range:** 570/30; 1,600/15 **Fuel:** 39 tons
**Man:** 4 officers, 15 p.o., 18 men

REMARKS: All hulls fitted out at Cherbourg. Ordered 18-12-70, as CMN's type *Combattante II* A4L. Steel construction. Thomson-CSF Vega fire-control system with Pollux radar; Triton is used for target designation. P 6152 received Triton II search radar and Castor II fire-control radar, the latter with a Piranha optronic attachment in 1980. Another ship conducted trials with the CSEE Naja optronic and CSEE Panda optical directors during 1982–83. Castor-II ordered for rest of class in 1986, for installation in all by 1990, along with EW equipment. All have the PALIS (Passive-Active-Link) system for data sharing and can use NATO LINK 11. An enclosed Mauser 40-mm gun mounting is replacing the open mount aft.

## MINE WARFARE SHIPS

◆ **0 (+12) Type 355 pressure-mine sweepers**

REMARKS: Remains a project to design a ship capable of detecting and disposing of the "unsweepable" pressure mine. If successful, may be built during 1990s.

◆ **0 (+10 + 10) Type 332 coastal minehunters** Bldr: . . .

**Type 332 minehunter**—artist's impression 1986

**D:** 635 tons (fl) **S:** 24.5 kts **Dim:** 54.4 (51.0 pp) × 9.2 × 2.6 (3.3 props)
**A:** 1/40-mm AA—possible 1/RAM launcher aft (XXI × 1)
**Electron Equipt:** Radar: 1/ . . . nav.
Sonar: . . .
**M:** 2 MTU 16V396 TB84 diesels; 2 CP props; 6,140 hp—low-speed drive
**Range:** . . . **Electric:** . . . **Man:** 48 tot.

REMARKS: Minehunter version of Type 343 with slightly different hull form, minehunting sonar and low-speed drive. Intended to carry the Pinguin B3 remote-controlled mine location/destruction submersible and mine-clearance divers. First increment of 10 planned for delivery 1992; second group, 1996–99, may have "Troika" control systems.

◆ **0 (+10) Type 343 minesweepers** Bldr: 4 by Lürssen, Vegesack; 3 by Abeking & Rasmussen, Lemwerde; 3 by Krögerwerft, Rendsburg (In serv. 1988–90)

| | Bldr | Laid down | L | In serv. |
|---|---|---|---|---|
| M 1092 N . . . | Lürssen | 18-6-86 | 9-87 | 12-88 |
| M 1093 N . . . | Lürssen | . . . | . . . | . . . |
| M 1094 N . . . | . . . | . . . | . . . | . . . |
| M 1095 N . . . | Abeking & Rasmussen | 15-12-86 | . . . | . . . |
| M . . . N . . . | . . . | . . . | . . . | . . . |
| M . . . N . . . | . . . | . . . | . . . | . . . |
| M . . . N . . . | . . . | . . . | . . . | . . . |
| M . . . N . . . | . . . | . . . | . . . | . . . |
| M . . . N . . . | . . . | . . . | . . . | . . . |
| M . . . N . . . | . . . | . . . | . . . | 4-91 |

**Type 343 minesweeper**—artist's impression 1984

**MINE WARFARE SHIPS** *(continued)*

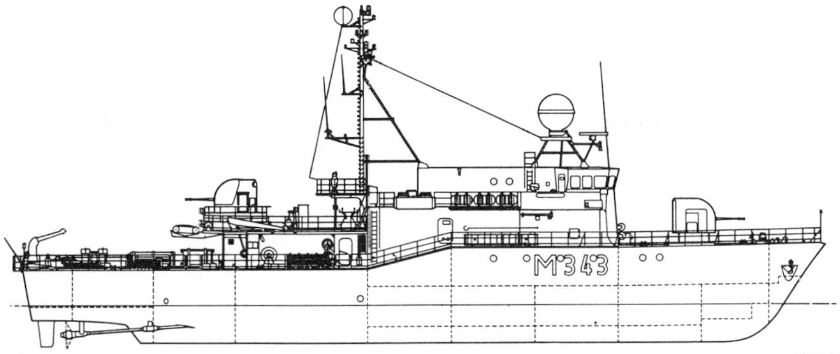


**Type 343 class** 1986

**D:** 600 tons (fl) **S:** 24.5 kts **Dim:** 54.4 (51.0 pp) × 9.2 × 2.5 (3.2 props)
**A:** 2/40-mm Bofors AA (I × 2)—2/Stinger point-defense SAM positions—up to 60 mines
**Electron Equipt:** Radar: 1/Raytheon SPS-64, 1/H.S.A. WM-20/1
Sonar: DSQS-11
EW: DR 2000 intercept, 2/Silver Dog decoy RL
**M:** 2 MTU 16V396 TB84-DB51L diesels; 2 Escher-Wyss CP props; 6,080 hp
**Range:** . . ./. . . **Electric:** 3 gens., . . . kw **Man:** 38 tot.

Remarks: Messerschmidt-Bölkow-Blohm (MBB) was selected as prime contractor 10-1-85. The Type 343s will be configured for mechanical, acoustic, and magnetic minesweeping to replace Type 340/341 (Schütze)-class patrol minesweepers. The later two series of Type 332-class minehunters will be very similar, except for carrying remote-controlled minehunting submersibles. Have PALIS data link. All-steel construction of low-magnetic alloy. The M 20 radar systems come from stricken *Zobel*-class torpedoboats.

◆ **6 Type 351 drone minesweeper-control ships** Bldr: Burmester, Bremen

| | L | In serv. | Conversion completed |
|---|---|---|---|
| M 1073 Schleswig | 2-10-57 | 30-10-58 | 19-3-81 |
| M 1076 Paderborn | 5-12-57 | 16-12-58 | 17-9-81 |
| M 1079 Düren | 12-6-58 | 22-4-59 | 7-11-83 |
| M 1081 Konstanz | 30-9-58 | 23-7-59 | 24-5-82 |
| M 1082 Wolfsburg | 10-12-58 | 8-10-59 | 4-3-82 |
| M 1083 Ulm | 10-2-59 | 7-11-59 | 11-11-81 |

**Schleswig (M 1073)** G. Davies/Maritime Photographic, 6-87

**Düren (M 1079)**—with brood, Seehunds 13–15 L. & L. Van Ginderen, 8-86

**D:** 488 tons (fl) **S:** 16.5 kts **Dim:** 47.5 × 8.5 × 2.75 **A:** 1/40-mm AA
**Electron Equipt:** Radar: 1/TRS-N—Sonar: DSQS-11A
**M:** 2 MD 871 UM/1D diesels; 2 CP props; 3,300 hp **Range:** 2,200/16
**Electric:** . . . **Man:** 44 tot.

Remarks: Type 320 minesweepers, each converted to control three F-1 "Troika" drone magnetic/acoustic/mechanical minesweepers. Also carry and tow an Oropesa sweep rig and stow numerous channel-marking ("dan") buoys.

◆ **18 Type HL 351 "Troika" drones** Bldr: MAK, Kiel

| | In serv. | | In serv. | | In serv. |
|---|---|---|---|---|---|
| Seehund 1 | 1-8-80 | Seehund 7 | 17-9-81 | Seehund 13 | 1-9-82 |
| Seehund 2 | 1-8-80 | Seehund 8 | 17-9-81 | Seehund 14 | 1-9-82 |
| Seehund 3 | 1-8-80 | Seehund 9 | 17-9-81 | Seehund 15 | 1-9-82 |
| Seehund 4 | 17-7-81 | Seehund 10 | 11-11-81 | Seehund 16 | 13-5-82 |
| Seehund 5 | 17-7-81 | Seehund 11 | 11-11-81 | Seehund 17 | 13-5-82 |
| Seehund 6 | 17-7-81 | Seehund 12 | 11-11-81 | Seehund 18 | 13-5-82 |

**Seehund 7** M. Louagie, 3-87

**D:** 91 tons (96.5 fl) **S:** 9.4 kts **Dim:** 24.92 × 4.46 × 1.8 **A:** none
**M:** 1 MWM TRHS 518A diesel; Schöttel prop; 445 hp **Electric:** 208 kw
**Range:** 520/8.8 **Man:** 3 tot.

Remarks: Ordered 1977, to operate three-apiece with the Type 351 control ships. Essentially remote-controlled, self-propelled magnetic minesweeping solenoids with all machinery highly shock-protected. Also able to carry two Type SDG-21 Oropesa mechanical minesweeping gear. Dates given are completions; were originally commissioned in groups of three on same date as Type 351 control ships were recommissioned (see above). Three earlier trials craft in this series, *Seekuh 1–3,* are no longer in service.

◆ **12 Type 331 A* and 331 B minehunters** Bldr: Burmester, Bremen

| | L | In serv. | | L | In serv. |
|---|---|---|---|---|---|
| M 1070 Göttingen | 1-4-57 | 31-5-58 | M 1078 Cuxhaven | 11-3-58 | 11-3-59 |
| M 1071 Koblenz | 6-5-57 | 8-7-58 | M 1080 Marburg | 4-8-58 | 11-6-59 |
| M 1072 Lindau | 16-2-57 | 24-4-58 | M 1084 Flensburg* | 7-4-59 | 3-12-59 |
| M 1074 Tübingen | 12-8-57 | 25-9-58 | M 1085 Minden | 9-6-59 | 22-1-60 |
| M 1075 Wetzlar | 24-6-57 | 20-8-58 | M 1086 Fulda* | 19-8-59 | 5-3-60 |
| M 1077 Weilheim | 4-2-59 | 28-1-59 | M 1087 Völklingen | 20-10-59 | 21-5-60 |

**D:** 388 tons (402 fl) **S:** 17 kts **Dim:** 47.45 × 8.5 × 3.68 (sonar down)
**A:** 1/40-mm AA
**Electron Equipt:** Radar: 1/TRS-N or Kelvin-Hughes 14/9
Sonar: DSQS-11 (Type 331A: Plessey 193M Mk 20G)
**M:** 2 Maybach diesels; 2 CP props; 3,340 hp **Electric:** 220 kw
**Range:** 1,400/16; 3,950/9 **Man:** 46 tot.

Remarks: All are conversions from the Type 320, *Lindau*-class, wooden-hulled minesweepers. The Type 331As were converted 1968–72, the Type 331Bs in 1975–79. None have mechanical sweep gear. Minehunting speed is 6 kts, on two 50-kw electric motors. Six divers and 2 French PAP-104 remote-controlled minehunting devices are carried.

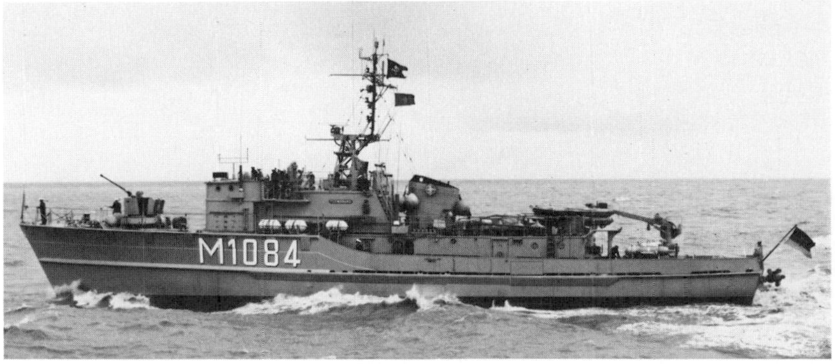


**Flensburg (M 1084)**—Type 331A, with Kelvin-Hughes radar—note auxiliary propulsors raised at stern M. Louagie, 3-87

**MINE WARFARE SHIPS** *(continued)*

**Göttingen (M 1070)**—Type 331B, with TRS-N radar L. & L. Van Ginderen, 10-86

◆ **19 Type 340 and Type 341 patrol minesweepers** Bldr: Abeking & Rasmussen, Lemwerde (except: Schürenstedt, Bardenfleth: M 1064, 1065, 1092, 1094; Schlichting, Travemünde: M 1067, 1090, 1095)

| Type 340 | L | In serv. | | L | In serv. |
|---|---|---|---|---|---|
| M 1051 Castor | 12-7-62 | 11-12-62 | M 1064 Deneb | 11-9-61 | 7-12-61 |
| M 1054 Pollux | 15-9-60 | 28-4-61 | M 1065 Jupiter | 15-2-61 | 30-5-61 |
| M 1055 Sirius | 15-3-61 | 5-10-61 | M 1067 Atair | 20-4-61 | 27-9-61 |
| M 1056 Rigel | 2-4-62 | 19-9-62 | M 1069 Wega | 10-10-62 | 8-4-63 |
| M 1057 Regulus | 18-12-61 | 20-6-62 | M 1090 Perseus | 22-9-60 | 16-3-61 |
| M 1058 Mars | 1-12-60 | 18-7-61 | | | |
| M 1059 Spica | 25-5-60 | 10-5-61 | M 1093 Neptun | 9-6-60 | 29-9-60 |
| M 1060 Skorpion | 21-5-63 | 9-10-63 | M 1094 Widder | 12-3-59 | 26-9-60 |
| Type 341 | | | | | |
| M 1062 Schütze | 20-5-58 | 14-4-59 | M 1096 Fische | 14-7-59 | 12-1-60 |
| M 1063 Waage | 9-4-59 | 19-3-62 | M 1097 Gemma | 6-10-59 | 5-7-60 |

**Fische (M 1096)**—Type 341 M. Louagie, 10-86

**Schütze (M 1062)** H. Ehlers, 7-87

**Rigel (M 1056)** H. Ehlers, 7-87

**D:** 241 tons (280 fl) **S:** 24.6 kts **Dim:** 47.44 × 7.2 (6.96 wl) × 2.4
**A:** 1/40-mm AA (*see* Remarks) **Electron Equipt:** Radar: 1/TRS-N
**M:** Maybach or Mercedes-Benz diesels; 2 Escher-Wyss cycloidal props; 4,000/4,200 hp
**Electric:** 120 kw plus 340-kw sweep generator **Fuel:** 22 tons
**Range:** 640/22; 1,000/18 **Man:** 39 tot.

Remarks: Multipurpose ships that can be employed as minesweepers, coastal patrol craft (2/40-mm AA), and minelayers (2 mine rails), the minesweeping gear to be removed in the latter two instances. Have appeared only in the minesweeper configuration for many years. *Stier* (former M 1061), used as a submarine-rescue ship, has been given a new hull number and disarmed; decompression chamber in new stern deckhouse. Eight with Mercedes-Benz diesels are Type 340; the remainder, with Maybach diesels, are Type 341. Sisters *Capella* (ex-M 1098), *Krebs* (ex-M 1052), *Orion* (ex-M 1053), *Steinbock* (ex-M 1091), and *Uranus* (ex-M 1099) have been operated by the *Deutscher Marinebund* youth organization since the mid-1970s; *Algol* (ex-M 1068) is used by the naval damage-control school, and *Mira* (ex-M 1050), formerly used by the Naval Technical School, was sold for scrap in 1984. *Pluto* (M 1092) stricken 1-7-87, *Herkules* (M 1095) on 25-8-87. Planned for disposal: 4, including M 1069, in 1988, 4 in 1989, 6 in 1990, 5 in 1991.

◆ **10 Type 394 inshore minesweepers** Bldr: Krögerwerft, Rendsburg

| | L | In serv. | | L | In serv. |
|---|---|---|---|---|---|
| M 2658 Frauenlob | 26-2-65 | 27-9-66 | M 2663 Minerva | 25-8-66 | 16-6-67 |
| M 2659 Nautilus | 19-5-65 | 26-10-66 | M 2664 Diana | 13-12-66 | 21-9-67 |
| M 2660 Gerion | 19-6-65 | 17-2-67 | M 2665 Loreley | 14-3-67 | 29-3-68 |
| M 2661 Medusa | 25-1-66 | 17-2-67 | M 2666 Atlantis | 20-6-67 | 29-3-68 |
| M 2662 Undine | 16-5-66 | 20-3-67 | M 2667 Acheron | 11-10-67 | 10-2-68 |

**Atlantis (M 2666)** H. Ehlers, 4-86

**D:** 238 tons (246 fl) **S:** 14.3 kts **Dim:** 38.01 × 8.03 × 2.1
**A:** 1/40-mm AA **Electron Equipt:** Radar: 1/TRS-N
**M:** 2 Mercedes-Benz MB 820 Db diesels; 2 props; 2,000 hp
**Electric:** 554 kw **Fuel:** 30 tons **Range:** 648/14; 1,770/7
**Man:** 4 officers, 20 men

Remarks: Wooden construction. Differ from Type 393 in having a 260-kw diesel sweep-current generator. Formerly had "Y,"- and earlier "W,"-series pendants.

◆ **8 Type 393 inshore minesweepers** Bldr: Krögerwerft, Rendsburg

| | L | In serv. | | L | In serv. |
|---|---|---|---|---|---|
| M 2650 Ariadne | 23-4-60 | 23-10-61 | M 2654 Nymphe | 20-9-62 | 8-5-63 |
| M 2651 Freya | 25-6-60 | 6-1-62 | M 2655 Nixe | 3-12-62 | 20-6-63 |
| M 2652 Vineta | 17-9-60 | 9-4-62 | M 2656 Amazone | 27-2-63 | 4-9-63 |
| M 2653 Herta | 18-2-61 | 7-6-62 | M 2657 Gazelle | 14-8-63 | 9-12-63 |

**Herta (M 2653)** L. & L. Van Ginderen, 6-86

## MINE WARFARE SHIPS *(continued)*

**D:** 199–205 tons light (252 fl) **S:** 14.3 kts **Dim:** 38.01 × 8.03 × 1.99
**A:** 1/40-mm AA **Electron Equipt:** Radar: 1/TRS-N
**M:** 2 Mercedes-Benz MB 820 Db diesels; 2 props; 2,000 hp **Electric:** 554 kw
**Fuel:** 30 tons **Range:** 830/12 **Man:** 4 officers, 20 men

REMARKS: Similar to Type 394, but have a 260-kw gas-turbine sweep-current generator.

## AMPHIBIOUS WARFARE CRAFT

◆ **22 Type 520 utility landing craft** Bldr: Howaldtswerke, Hamburg, 1965–66 (launch dates in parentheses)

| | | |
|---|---|---|
| L 760 FLUNDER (6-1-66) | L 767 TÜMMLER (14-6-66) | L 792 DORSCH (17-3-66) |
| L 761 KARPFEN (5-1-66) | L 768 WELS (15-6-66) | L 793 FELCHEN (19-4-66) |
| L 762 LACHS (17-2-66) | L 769 ZANDER (13-7-66) | L 794 FORELLE (20-4-66) |
| L 763 PLÖTZE (16-2-66) | L 788 BUTT (28-3-65) | L 795 INGER (14-7-66) |
| L 764 ROCHEN (18-3-66) | L 789 BRASSE (28-3-65) | L 796 MAKRELE (22-8-66) |
| L 765 SCHLEI (17-5-66) | L 790 BARBE (26-11-65) | L 797 MURÄNE (23-8-66) |
| L 766 STÖR (18-5-66) | L 791 DELPHIN (25-11-65) | L 798 RENKE (22-9-66) |
| | | L 799 SALM (23-9-66) |

**Wels (L 768)** H. Ehlers, 5-86

**D:** 166 tons (403 fl) **S:** 11 kts **Dim:** 40.04 (36.7 pp) × 8.8 × 1.6 (2.1 max.)
**A:** 2/20-mm Rheinmetall Rh 202 AA (II × 1) **Range:** 1,200/11
**Electron Equipt:** Radar: 1/Kelvin-Hughes 14/9
**M:** 2 MWM 12-cyl. diesels; 2 props; 1,200 hp **Electric:** 130 kVA
**Man:** 17 tot.

REMARKS: Design based on the American LCU 1646 class. *Renke* (L 798) and *Salm* (L 799) in reserve; *Inger* (L 795) used for reserve training. Cargo: 237 tons max.; 141.6 normal.

◆ **24 Type 521 landing craft** Bldr: Rheinwerft, Walsum (LCM 1, 2: Blohm + Voss, Hamburg) (In serv. 1964–67)

| | |
|---|---|
| LCM 1 through LCM 11 | L 780 LCM 21 HUMMER |
| L . . . LCM 12 SPROTTE | L 781 LCM 22 KRILLE |
| L . . . LCM 13 SARDINE | L 782 LCM 23 KRABBE |
| L . . . LCM 14 SARDELLE | L 783 LCM 24 AUSTER |
| L . . . LCM 16 ORFE | L 784 LCM 25 MUSCHEL |
| L . . . LCM 18 SAITLING | L 785 LCM 26 KORALLE |
| L . . . LCM 19 STINT | |
| L . . . LCM 20 ÄSCHE | |

**Saitling (LCM 18)**—with tripod mast L. & L. Van Ginderen, 10-85

**D:** 116 tons (168 fl) **S:** 10.6 kts **Dim:** 23.56 × 6.40 × 1.46
**M:** 2 MWM 8-cyl. diesels; 2 props; 684 hp **Range:** 690/10; 1,430/7 **Man:** 7 tot.

REMARKS: Design based on U.S. LCM (8). LCM 1 to LCM 11 are in reserve. LCM 11–20 have a 20-kw diesel generator and a 2-ton cargo boom; they can be used to carry up to 18 torpedoes. Cargo: 60 tons or 50 troops. During 1981, six were reclassified as auxiliaries: LCM 21 as A 1423, and LCM 22–26 as A 1430–A 1434; LCM 15 reclassified A 1408 in 1985. LCM pendants belong to base commands; A pendants belong to schools. In 1987 LCM 21–26 were reclassified as landing craft and given L-pendants; they are used by the Beachmaster Company at Eckenförde for training.

## AUXILIARY SHIPS

## HYDROGRAPHIC SURVEY SHIP

◆ **1 Type 750** Bldr: J.R. Köser Norderwerft, Hamburg

| | Laid down | L | In serv. |
|---|---|---|---|
| A 1452 PLANET (ex-Y 843) | 30-4-64 | 23-9-65 | 15-4-67 |

**Planet**—pendant A 1452 not painted on P. Voss, 6-85

**D:** 1,513 tons (1,917 fl) **S:** 13.9 kts **Dim:** 80.43 (74.0 pp) × 12.60 × 3.97
**M:** 4 MWM 12-cyl., 850-hp diesels, electric drive; 1 prop; 1,390 hp
**Electric:** 650 kw **Range:** 9,300/13.4 **Man:** 39 crew plus 13 scientists

REMARKS: Operated for the Ministry of Communications by a civilian crew. Hangar for one helicopter. Capable of conducting geophysical, meteorological, biological, chemistry, and hydrographic research. Denny-Brown stabilizers, 125-hp Pleuger active rudder and bow-thruster fitted. Main engines provide 560 kw of the electrical power. Painted white, with buff stack and mast.

## SUPPORT TENDERS

◆ **10 Rhein-class Types 401, 402, and 403**

(*a*) Type 401, for missile boats

| | Bldr | L | In serv. |
|---|---|---|---|
| A 58 RHEIN | Schlieker, Hamburg | 10-12-59 | 6-11-61 |
| A 61 ELBE | Schlieker, Hamburg | 5-5-60 | 17-4-62 |
| A 63 MAIN | Lindenauwerft, Kiel | 23-7-60 | 29-6-63 |
| A 66 NECKAR | Lürssen, Vegesack | 26-6-61 | 7-12-63 |
| A 68 WERRA | Lindenauwerft, Kiel | 26-3-63 | 2-9-64 |
| A 69 DONAU | Schlichting, Travemünde | 26-11-60 | 23-5-64 |
| (*b*) Type 402, for mine-countermeasures ships | | | |
| A 65 SAAR | Norderwerft, Hamburg | 11-3-61 | 11-5-63 |
| A 67 MOSEL | Schlieker, Hamburg | 15-12-60 | 8-6-63 |
| (*c*) Type 403, for submarines | | | |
| A 55 LAHN | Flenderwerke, Lübeck | 21-11-61 | 24-3-64 |
| A 56 LECH | Flenderwerke, Lübeck | 4-5-62 | 8-12-64 |

**Werra (A 68)**—Type 401 small combatant tender P. Voss, 9-86

**SUPPORT TENDERS** *(continued)*

**Lahn (A 55)**—Type 403 submarine tender L. & L. Van Ginderen, 2-87

**Saar (A 65)**—Type 402 minecraft tender L. & L. Van Ginderen, 10-86

**D:** (a): 2,370 tons (3,000 fl); (b): 2,330 tons (3,000 fl); (c) 2,400 tons (2,956 fl)
**S:** 20 kts (trials, 22) **Dim:** 98.2 × 11.83 × 5.20
**A:** 2/100-mm AA (I × 2) (not in A 55, A 56)—4/40-mm AA (I × 4, except II × 2 in A 55 and A 56)—mines
**Electron Equipt:** Radar: 1/Kelvin-Hughes 14/9, 1/SGR-105, 1/SGR-103, 2/Mk 45 fire control; A 55 and A 56: 14/9 and SGR-103 only
**M:** 6 Maybach diesels (Mercedes-Benz 839Db in A 54–56, 65, 67); 2 props; 11,400 hp
**Electric:** 2,250 kw **Fuel:** 334 tons **Range:** 2,500/16
**Man:** 98 tot. (space for 40 officers, 40 petty officers, 130 nonrated men)

REMARKS: Slight variations in length: Type 402 are 98.5 m o.a., Type 403 are 98.6 m o.a. Type 401 have one crane to port, Type 402 have two side by side farther aft. A 54, A 55, A 56, A 65, A 67 have electric drive; the others have diesel-reduction drive, CP props. Tenders carry 200 tons of fuel oil, 40 reserve torpedoes; A 55, A 56, and A 58 have an additional 200 tons of stores; A 66, A 68, and A 69 can be used as training ships. *Weser* (A 62) and *Ruhr* (A 64) transferred to the Greek and Turkish navies in 1975 and 1976, respectively. *Isar* (A 54), long in reserve, was transferred to Turkey 30-9-82 and delivered under tow. Two of the combatant-tender version are to be re-equipped to support the new Type-143A missile boats as Type-401D tenders. Type 401 and 402 have two M4 radar GFCS. The Type 401 and 402 units are scheduled to receive the RAM point-defense missile system. A 66 hit by Polish Navy 30-mm shells during exercise, 15-6-87.

## UNDERWAY REPLENISHMENT SHIPS

◆ **0 (+5) KSV 90 combat support ships**

**D:** 12–14,000 tons (fl) **S:** . . . **Dim:** . . . × . . . × . . .
**A:** . . . **M:** . . .

REMARKS: Planned as multipurpose ships to carry fuel, munitions, supplies and to provide helicopter support. Will replace the various Type 701-series ships in the mid-to-late 1990s.

NOTE: The following classes (Type 701, Type 760, Type 762) are grouped together here because, despite their dissimilar functions, they are variations on the same basic design.

◆ **8 Type 701A, Type 701C, and 701E supply ships**

| | Bldr | Laid down | L | In serv. |
|---|---|---|---|---|
| *(a)* Type 701A | | | | |
| A 1411 LÜNEBURG | Flensburger SY | 8-7-64 | 3-5-65 | 31-1-66 |
| A 1416 NIENBURG | Flensburger SY | 16-11-65 | 28-7-66 | 1-8-68 |
| A 1417 OFFENBURG | Blohm + Voss, Hamburg | 1966 | 10-9-66 | 27-5-68 |
| *(b)* Type 701C | | | | |
| A 1412 COBURG | Flensburger SY | 9-4-65 | 15-12-65 | 9-7-68 |
| A 1414 GLÜCKSBURG | Flensburger SY | 18-8-65 | 3-5-66 | 9-7-68 |
| A 1415 SAARBURG | Blohm + Voss, Hamburg | 1-3-66 | 15-7-66 | 30-7-68 |
| A 1418 MEERSBURG | Flensburger SY | 5-8-65 | 22-3-66 | 25-6-68 |
| *(c)* Type 701E | | | | |
| A 1413 FREIBURG | Blohm + Voss, Hamburg | 1965 | 15-4-66 | 27-5-68 |

**Nienburg (A 1416)**—Type 701A L. & L. Van Ginderen, 10-86

**Meersburg (A 1418)**—Type 701C L. & L. Van Ginderen, 6-83

**Freiburg (A 1413)**—Type 701E—note helo deck, new crane to port
L. & L. Van Ginderen, 10-86

**D:** Type 701A: 1,896 tons light (3,483 fl); Type 701C: 3,709 tons (fl); Type 701E: 3,900 tons (fl)
**S:** 17 kts
**Dim:** 104.15 (98.00 pp) × 13.2 × 4.2 (Type 701C: 114.9 overall; Type 701E: 118.3 overall)
**A:** 4/40-mm AA (II × 2) in preservation (fwd. mount active in A 1415, A 1413)
**M:** 2 Maybach MD 872 diesels; 2 CP props; 5,600 hp **Electric:** 1,935 kw
**Range:** 3,000/17; 3,200/14 **Man:** 82 tot.

REMARKS: Originally configured to carry more than 1,100 tons of cargo, including 640 tons fuel, 205 tons ammunition, 100 tons spare parts (10,000 separate items), and 131 tons fresh water, plus 267 $m^3$ refrigerated stores. A 1415 lengthened 11.5 meters in 1974–75 to carry spare Exocet missiles and other supplies for the new Type 143 and Type 148 classes; stowage for spare parts increased to 30,000 items, with inventory management by the Nixdorf computer system. A 1412, A 1414, A 1418 also converted to Type 702C standard, 1975–77. A 1413, converted 1981–84 to support Type 122 frigates, is equipped with helicopter facilities to permit vertical replenishment, 9 spare Harpoon missiles, repair facilities for Mk 88 Lynx helicopters and a new articulated crane, to port. A 1412 has a bow-thruster. All are equipped with fin stabilizers, one 3-ton and two 2-ton cranes.

◆ **2 Type 760 ammunition ships** Bldr: Orenstein & Koppel, Lübeck

| | Laid down | L | In serv. |
|---|---|---|---|
| A 1435 WESTERWALD | 3-11-65 | 25-2-66 | 11-2-67 |
| A 1436 ODENWALD | 3-11-65 | 5-5-66 | 23-3-67 |

**D:** 3,460 tons (4,014 fl) **S:** 17 kts **Dim:** 105.3 × 14.0 × 4.6
**A:** 4/40-mm AA (II × 2) in preservation
**M:** 2 Maybach MD 872 diesels; 2 CP props; 5,600 hp **Electric:** 1,285 kw
**Range:** 3,500/17 **Man:** 60 tot. (A 1436: 45 tot.)

REMARKS: Similar to Type 701, but carry only ammunition. A 1436 had the forward 40-mm AA mount removed 1981. Cargo: 1,080 tons.

### UNDERWAY REPLENISHMENT SHIPS *(continued)*

**Odenwald (A 1436)** F. Jentsch, 6-86

◆ **2 Type 762 mine-supply ships** Bldr: Blohm + Voss, Hamburg

| | Laid down | L | In serv. |
|---|---|---|---|
| A 1437 SACHSENWALD | 1-8-66 | 10-12-66 | 20-8-69 |
| A 1438 STEIGERWALD | 9-5-66 | 10-3-67 | 20-8-69 |

**Steigerwald (A 1438)** L. & L. Van Ginderen, 6-86

**D:** 2,962 tons (3,380 fl) **S:** 17 kts **Dim:** 110.7 × 13.9 × 3.79
**A:** 4/40-mm AA (II × 2)—mines
**M:** 2 Maybach MD 872 diesels; 2 CP props; 5,600 hp **Electric:** 1,300 kw
**Range:** 3,500/17 **Man:** 65 tot.

REMARKS: The designation "supply ships" is something of a euphemism, since these ships have four mine ports at the stern and are actually minelayers, capable of carrying 668 to 1,048 mines, depending on type. Construction of a torpedo-transport version was canceled.

### REPAIR SHIPS

◆ **2 Type 726, former U.S. Aristaeus class**

| | Bldr | L | In serv. |
|---|---|---|---|
| Y 847 ODIN (ex-*Ulysses,* ARB 9) | Bethlehem, Hingham | 2-12-44 | 27-12-44 |
| Y 848 WOTAN (ex-*Diomedes,* ARB 11) | Chicago Bridge & Iron | 11-11-44 | 23-1-45 |

**Wotan (Y848)**—with old number L. & L. Van Ginderen, 4-87

**D:** 3,435 tons (3,455 fl) **S:** 11 kts **Dim:** 101.0 × 15.28 × 2.80
**M:** 2 G.M. 12-278A (A 513: 12-567A) diesels; 2 props; 1,800 hp
**Fuel:** 438 tons **Range:** 13,200/11 **Man:** 143 tot. (civilian personnel)

REMARKS: Modified former LST 967 and LST 1119, respectively, transferred in 6-61. A 10-ton traveling crane moves on rails between the bridge and the forward sheer. Have accommodations for 187. Renumbered from A 512, A 513 in 1987.

### REPLENISHMENT OILERS

◆ **2 Type 704 former merchant tankers**

| | Bldr | L | In serv. |
|---|---|---|---|
| A 1443 RHÖN (ex-*Okene*) | Kröger, Rendsburg | 23-8-74 | 5-9-77 |
| A 1442 SPESSART (ex-*Okapi*) | Kröger, Rendsburg | 13-2-75 | 23-9-77 |

**Spessart (A 1442)** L. & L. Van Ginderen, 3-85

**D:** 14,260 tons (fl); 6,209 grt/10,950 dwt **S:** 16 kts **Dim:** 130.2 × 19.3 × 8.20
**M:** 1 MAK 12-cyl. diesel; CP prop; 8,000 hp **Electric:** 2,000 kw **Man:** 42 tot.

REMARKS: 6,200 grt. Converted while building. Purchased from Bulk Acid Carriers, Monrovia, in 1976. Fitted with one underway-replenishment station per side. Cargo: 9,500 $m^3$ distillate fuel, 1,650 $m^3$ fuel oil, 400 $m^3$ water. Pronounced bulbous bow. Replenishment facilities are to be upgraded.

◆ **4 Type 703** Bldr: Lindenauwerft, Kiel

| | Laid down | L | In serv. |
|---|---|---|---|
| A 1424 WALCHENSEE | 12-10-64 | 10-7-65 | 29-6-66 |
| A 1425 AMMERSEE | 28-3-66 | 9-7-66 | 2-3-67 |
| A 1426 TEGERNSEE | 21-4-66 | 22-10-66 | 23-3-67 |
| A 1427 WESTENSEE | 28-10-66 | 8-4-67 | 6-10-67 |

**Westensee (A 1427)** L. & L. Van Ginderen, 5-87

**D:** 2,174 tons (fl) **S:** 12.5 kts **Dim:** 71.9 × 11.2 × 4.28
**M:** 2 MWM 12-cyl. diesels; 1 CP prop; 1,200 hp **Electric:** 635 kw
**Cargo capacity:** 1,130 $m^3$ **Range:** 3,250/12 **Man:** 21 tot.

◆ **1 Type 763 former merchant tanker** Bldr: Lindenauwerft, Kiel

| | Laid down | L | In serv. |
|---|---|---|---|
| A 1407 WITTENSEE (ex-*Sioux*) | 15-2-58 | 23-9-58 | 5-12-58 |

**Wittensee (A 1407)** L. & L. Van Ginderen, 6-86

**D:** 1,237 tons (1,854 fl) **S:** 12 kts **Dim:** 67.45 × 9.84 × 4.25
**M:** 1 MAK 6-cyl. diesel; 1,250 hp **Electric:** 216 kw **Cargo:** 1,238 tons
**Range:** 6,240/12 **Man:** 21 tot. (civilian crew) **Cargo capacity:** 1,250 $m^3$

REMARKS: Purchased 26-3-59. Sister *Bodensee* transferred to Turkey 8-77. 998 grt.

◆ **1 Type 766 former merchant tanker** Bldr: Norderwerft, Hamburg

| | Laid down | L | In serv. |
|---|---|---|---|
| A 1429 EIFEL (ex-*Friedrich Jung*) | 5-11-57 | 2-4-58 | 26-7-58 |

**REPLENISHMENT OILERS** *(continued)*

**Eifel (A 1429)** L. & L. Van Ginderen, 10-86

**D:** 6,720 tons (fl) **S:** 13 kts **Dim:** 101.76 × 14.43 × 7.1
**M:** 2 M.A.N. 8-cyl. diesels; 1 prop; 3,360 hp **Electric:** 760 kVA
**Cargo:** 6,500 $m^3$ **Range:** 7,300/12 **Man:** 40 tot.

REMARKS: 3,444 grt. Purchased and commissioned 27-5-63. Equipped for underway replenishment. One fueling station per side, plus over-the-stern capability.

◆ **1 Type 766 former merchant tanker** Bldr: Norderwerft, Hamburg

| | Laid down | L | In serv. |
|---|---|---|---|
| A 1428 HARZ (ex-*Claere Jung*) | 31-3-53 | 2-9-53 | 26-11-53 |

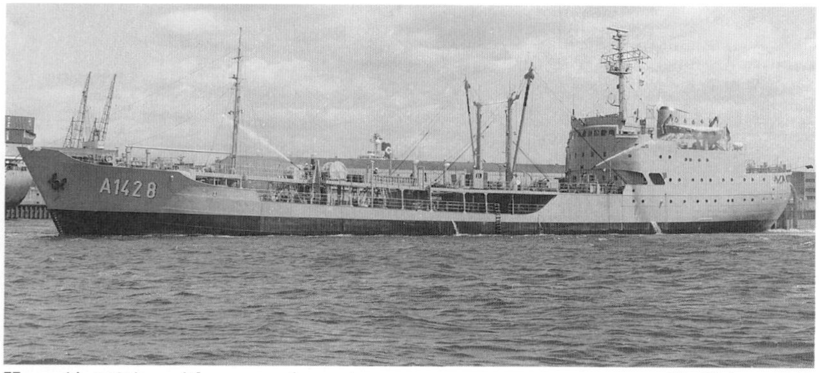

**Harz (A 1428)**—with new mainmast H. Ehlers, 7-87

**D:** 5,380 tons (fl) **S:** 12 kts **Dim:** 92.40 × 13.60 × 6.70
**M:** 2 OEW 8-cyl. diesels; 1 prop; 2,520 hp **Electric:** 380 kVA
**Cargo:** 5,000 $m^3$ **Range:** 7,200/11 **Man:** 28 tot.

REMARKS: 2,800 grt. Purchased and commissioned 27-5-63. Equipped for underway replenishment, one station per side.

**INTELLIGENCE COLLECTORS**

◆ **1 (+2) Type 143 new construction** Bldr: Flensburger Schiffsbau, Flensburg

| | Laid down | L | In serv. |
|---|---|---|---|
| A 52 OSTE | 16-12-86 | 15-5-87 | 9-87 |
| A 53 OKER | 16-12-86 | 24-9-87 | 2-88 |
| A 51 ALSTER | . . . | . . . | . . . |

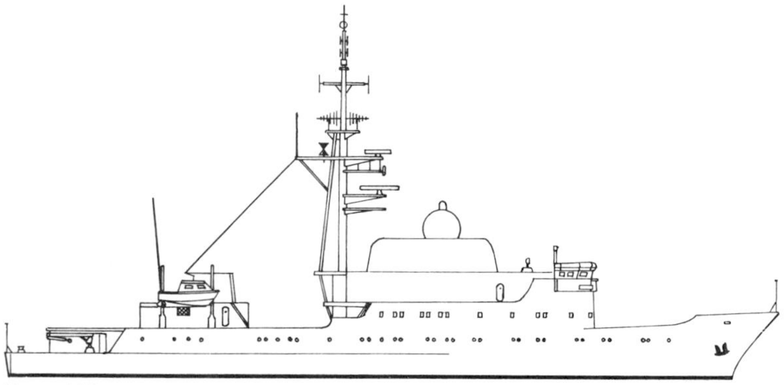

**Type 143** Robert Dumas

**D:** 2,375 tons (fl) **S:** 18 kts **Dim:** 83.50 (75.70 pp) × 14.60 × 4.18
**A:** none **Electron Equipt:** . . .
**M:** 2 Deutz diesels; 2 props; 6,500 hp **Man:** 40

REMARKS: First two ordered 3-7-85 as replacements for the Type 442B converted trawlers with the same names (A 50, A 53). Planned construction of a third was announced 10-86, as a replacement for the original *Oste* (A 52). Built to commercial (Germanischer Lloyd) standards. Third unit ordered 15-12-86.

◆ **2 Type 442B converted trawlers** Bldr: Unterweser, Bremerhaven

| | L | In serv. | Conv. |
|---|---|---|---|
| A 50 ALSTER (ex-*Mellum*) | 21-11-60 | 21-3-61 | 19-10-71 |
| A 53 OKER (ex-*Hoheweg*) | 29-8-60 | 19-10-60 | 11-2-72 |

**Oker (A 53)** B. Prézelin, 5-86

**D:** 1,187 tons (1,497 fl) **S:** 15 kts **Dim:** 72.83 (68.35 pp) × 10.50 × 5.60
**M:** 1 Klöckner-Humboldt-Deutz 8-cyl., 1,800-hp diesel, electric drive; 1 KHD 8-cyl. auxiliary propulsion diesel, 400-hp electric drive; 1 prop

REMARKS: For disposal 1988.

◆ **1 Type-740 converted inshore minesweeper** Bldr: Abeking & Rasmussen, Lemwerde

| | Laid down | L | In serv. |
|---|---|---|---|
| A 836 HOLNIS | 15-8-64 | 20-5-65 | 31-3-66 |

**Holnis (A 1400)** H. Ehlers, 6-87

**D:** 150 tons (180 fl) **S:** 16.5 kts **Dim:** 36.87 × 7.40 × 1.80
**M:** 2 Mercedes-Benz MB 820Db diesels; 2 props; 2,000 hp
**Electric:** 380 kw **Fuel:** 13 tons **Man:** 27 tot.

REMARKS: Wooden construction, prototype of a class of 20 Type 390 inshore minesweepers, the other 19 of which were canceled. Altered circa 1968 as an intelligence collector. Renumbered from Y 836 to A 836 in 1985, and to A 1400 in 1987.

NOTE: Type 422A intelligence collector *Oste* (A 52, ex. *Puddefjord*) stricken 12-6-87.

**SEAGOING TUGS**

◆ **3 Baltrum (Type 722) class** Bldr: Schichau, Bremerhaven

| | Laid down | L | In serv. |
|---|---|---|---|
| A 1451 WANGEROOGE | 1-10-65 | 4-7-66 | 9-4-68 |
| A 1452 SPIEKEROOG | 20-11-65 | 26-9-66 | 14-8-68 |
| A 1455 NORDERNEY | 29-5-67 | 28-2-68 | 15-10-70 |

SEAGOING TUGS *(continued)*

**Wangerooge (A 1451)** P. Voss, 9-86

**D:** 854 tons (1,039 fl) **S:** 13.6 kts **Dim:** 51.78 × 12.11 × 4.2
**A:** 1/40-mm AA (preserved)
**M:** 4 MWM 16-cyl. diesels, electric drive; 2 props; 2,400 hp
**Electric:** 540 kw **Range:** 5,000/10 **Man:** 31 tot.

REMARKS: A 1451 is used at Cuxhaven in survival training for aircrew. Also employed as salvage tugs and port icebreakers. Sister *Baltrum* has been used as a diving-training tender since 1974; *Juist* and *Langeoog* were reconfigured for training duties during 1977–78; see page 192.

◆ **2 Helgoland (Type 720)-class salvage tugs** Bldr: Schichau, Bremerhaven

| | Laid down | L | In serv. |
|---|---|---|---|
| A 1457 HELGOLAND | 24-7-64 | 9-4-65 | 8-3-66 |
| A 1458 FEHMARN | 23-4-65 | 25-11-65 | 1-2-67 |

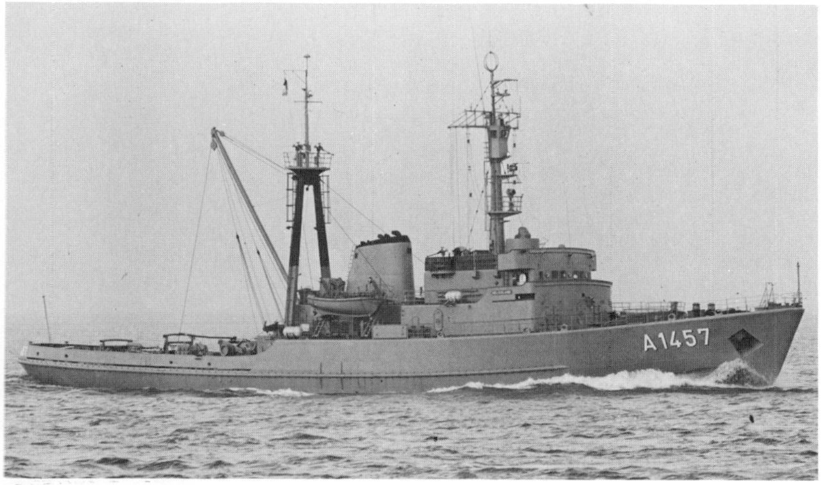

**Helgoland (A 1457)** P. Voss, 11-86

**D:** 1,304 tons (1,558 fl) **S:** 16.6 kts **Dim:** 67.9 × 12.74 × 4.20
**A:** 2/40-mm AA (II × 1)—in preservation
**M:** 4 MWM 12-cyl. diesels, electric drive; 2 props; 3,300 hp
**Electric:** 1,065 kw **Range:** 6,400/16 **Man:** 34 tot.

REMARKS: *Fehmarn* serves as a tender to the submarine training establishment. Equipped to serve as mine planters, if required.

◆ **2 Eisvogel (Type 721)-class icebreaking tugs** Bldr: Hitzler, Lauenburg

| | Laid down | L | In serv. |
|---|---|---|---|
| A 1401 EISVOGEL | 10-3-59 | 28-4-60 | 11-3-61 |
| A 1402 EISBÄR | 12-5-59 | 9-6-60 | 1-11-61 |

**D:** 496 tons (641 fl) **S:** 13 kts **Dim:** 37.8 × 9.7 × 4.2
**Electron Equipt:** Radar: 1/Kelvin-Hughes 14/9
**M:** 2 Maybach 12-cyl. diesels; 2 CP props; 2,400 hp **Electric:** 180 kw
**Range:** 2,000/12 **Man:** 16 tot.

REMARKS: Provision for 1/40-mm AA aft.

**Eisvogel (A 1401)** L. & L. Van Ginderen, 4-87

EXPERIMENTAL SHIPS

◆ **0 (+2) Type 749 trials ships** Bldr: . . .

| | | Laid down | L | In serv. |
|---|---|---|---|---|
| A . . . | N . . . | . . . | . . . | . . . |
| A . . . | N . . . | . . . | . . . | . . . |

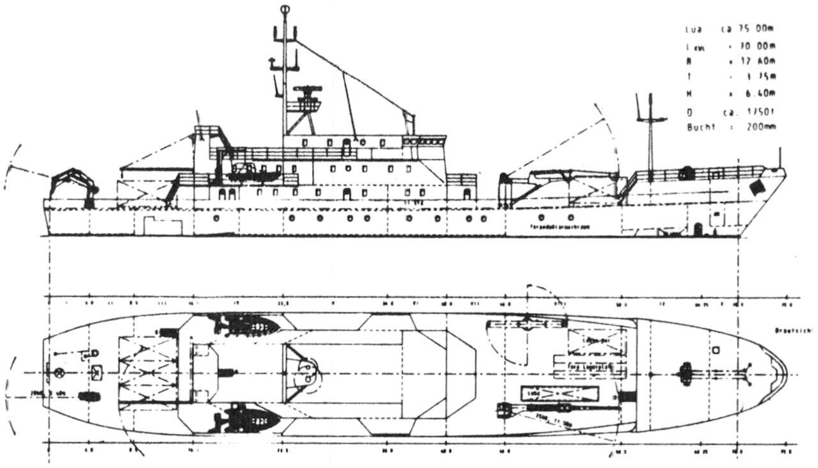

**Type 749** 1987

**D:** approx. 1,750 tons (fl) **S:** . . . **Dim:** 75.00 (70.00 pp) × 12.60 × 3.75
**A:** 2/533-mm TT (1 trainable, above water, to port: 1 fixed, submerged)
**Electron Equipt:** Radar: 2/. . . nav.—Sonar: . . .
**M:** 2 . . . diesels; . . . props; . . . hp
**Range:** . . . **Man:**

REMARKS: Torpedo and other weapons and sensors trials ships programmed to replace *Hans Bürkner* (A 1449) and *Heinz Roggenkamp* (Y 871) after 1990. Hydraulic cranes on stern and to starboard, forward, for weapons retrieval. Three portable van positions aft.

◆ **1 Type 421 former corvette** Bldr: Atlaswerke, Bremen

| | Laid down | L | In serv. |
|---|---|---|---|
| A 1449 HANS BÜRKNER | 12-10-60 | 6-6-61 | 18-5-63 |

**Hans Bürkner (A 1449)** H. Ehlers, 8-87

## EXPERIMENTAL SHIPS *(continued)*

**D:** 983 tons (1,348 fl) **S:** 24 kts **Dim:** 80.6 × 9.42 × 3.50
**A:** 1/375-mm Bofors 4-barreled ASW RL (*see* Remarks)
**M:** 4 M.A.N. 16-cyl. diesels; 2 CP props; 13,600 hp **Electric:** 520 kVA
**Range:** 2,180/15 **Man:** 50 tot.

Remarks: Employed as an ASW trials ship. Has recently carried a small variable-depth sonar. Position for two 40-mm AA (II × 1) retained, and has previously carried two 533-mm ASW torpedo tubes. Fitted with mine rails. Conducted trials with Raytheon MBAR Beam Acquisition Radar, 1985–86.

## TRAINING SHIPS

◆ **1 Type 440 cruiser type**

| | Bldr | Laid down | L | In serv. |
|---|---|---|---|---|
| A 59 Deutschland | Nobiskrug, Rendsburg | 17-9-59 | 5-11-60 | 25-5-63 |

**Deutschland (A 59)** L. Grazioli, 4-87

**D:** 4,880 tons (5,684 fl) **S:** 22 kts (18 cruising) **Range:** 6,000/17
**Dim:** 138.2 (130.0 pp) × 16.0 × 5.0 **Man:** 33 officers, 521 men (250 cadets)
**A:** 4/100-mm AA (I × 4)—8/40-mm AA (II × 2, 1 × 4)—4/533-mm ASW TT—2/375-mm Bofors ASW RL (IV × 2)
**Electron Equipt:** Radar: 1/LW-08, 1/SGR-114, 1/SGR-105, 1/SGR-103, 4/M 45 f.c.—Sonar: 1/ELAC 1BV (med. freq.)
**M:** 4/2,000-hp Maybach diesels; 1 set Wahodag 8,000-hp GT; 3 props (2 CP); 16,000 hp
**Boilers:** 2 Wahodag, 450°C **Electric:** 1,500 kw **Fuel:** 640 tons

Remarks: Quarters for 7 instructors and 250 cadets. Can be used as a minelayer. Two Mercedes-Benz diesels replaced by Maybach engines in 1979.

◆ **1 Type 441 sail-training ship** Bldr: Blohm + Voss, Hamburg

| | Laid down | L | In serv. |
|---|---|---|---|
| A 60 Gorch Fock | 24-2-58 | 23-8-58 | 17-12-58 |

**Gorch Fock**—pendant number, A 60, not painted on P. Voss, 7-86

**D:** 1,819 tons (2,005 fl) **S:** 10 kts (15 kts under sail)
**Dim:** 89.32 (81.44 hull, 70.20 pp) × 12.02 × 5.25
**M:** 1 M.A.N. 6-cyl. diesel; 1 prop; 890 hp **Electric:** 266 kw
**Range:** 1,100/10 **Man:** 74 tot. plus 200 cadets

Remarks: 1,904 $m^2$ sail area. Carries 350 tons permanent ballast. Has made 296 nautical miles progress in one day.

## YARD AND SERVICE CRAFT
### HARBOR TUGS

◆ **3 (+ . . .) Type 725 large harbor tugs** Bldr: Orenstein & Koppel, Lübeck

| | L | In serv. |
|---|---|---|
| Y 816 Vogelsand | 30-1-87 | 14-4-87 |
| Y 817 Nordstrand | 24-10-86 | 20-1-87 |
| Y 819 Langeness | 28-11-86 | 15-5-87 |

**Vogelsand (Y 816)** H. Ehlers, 7-87

**D:** 445 tons (fl) **S:** 12 kts **Dim:** 30.25 (28.00 pp) × 9.10 × 2.55
**Electron Equipt:** Radar: 1/. . . nav.
**M:** 2 Deutz SBV6M628 diesels; 2 Voith-Schneider Model 24 G-11/165 vertical cycloidal props; 2,230 hp
**Range:** . . . **Man:** . . .

Remarks: 212 grt. Bollard pull: 25 tons. Class intended to replace *all* present harbor tugs, with eventual total of 15 planned. Launched via crane. All laid down 1-4-86.

◆ **3 Heppens (Type 724)-class tugs** Bldr: Schichau, Bremerhaven

| | Laid down | L | In serv. |
|---|---|---|---|
| Y 1680 Neuende | 29-12-70 | 2-6-71 | 27-10-71 |
| Y 1681 Heppens | 19-3-71 | 15-9-71 | 17-12-71 |
| Y 1682 Ellerbek | 29-12-70 | 2-6-71 | 26-11-71 |

**Heppens (Y 1681)** L. & L. Van Ginderen, 9-86

**D:** 232 tons (319 fl) **S:** 12 kts **Dim:** 26.6 × 7.4 × 2.6
**M:** 1 MWM 8-cyl. diesel; 800 hp **Electric:** 120 kw **Man:** 6 tot.

◆ **4 Sylt (Type 724)-class tugs** Bldr: Schichau, Bremerhaven

| | L | In serv. | | L | In serv. |
|---|---|---|---|---|---|
| Y 820 Sylt | 29-4-61 | 5-7-62 | Y 822 Amrum | 6-10-61 | 25-1-63 |
| Y 821 Föhr | 13-5-61 | 11-10-62 | Y 823 Neuwerk | 12-10-61 | 5-4-63 |

## YARD AND SERVICE CRAFT HARBOR TUGS *(continued)*

**Sylt (Y 820)** H. Ehlers, 7-87

**D:** 266 tons (282 fl) **S:** 12 kts **Dim:** 30.2 × 7.9 × 4.0
**M:** 1 MAK 8-cyl. diesel; 1,000 hp **Range:** 1,775/12 **Man:** 10 tot.

REMARKS: All four to be discarded shortly.

◆ **5 Lütje Hörn (Type 723) class**

| | L | | L |
|---|---|---|---|
| Y 812 LÜTJE HÖRN | 9-5-58 | Y 815 SCHÄRNHORN | 9-5-58 |
| Y 813 MELLUM | 23-10-58 | Y 818 TRISCHEN | 27-2-59 |
| Y 814 KNECHTSAND | 3-12-58 | | |

**Schärnhorn (Y 815)**—Lütje Hörn class P. Voss, 9-86

**D:** 52.2 tons (57.5 fl) **S:** 10 kts **Dim:** 15.2 × 5.06 × 2.2
**M:** 2 Deutz 8-cyl. diesels; 2 Voith-Schneider cycloidal props; 340 hp
**Range:** 550/9 **Man:** 4 tot.

REMARKS: *Vogelsand* (Y 816) stricken 16-2-87; *Nordstrand* (Y 817) stricken 1-11-86; *Langeness* (Y 819) 15-1-87.

## HARBOR OILER

◆ **1 Class 763 harbor oiler** Bldr: Flenderwerke, Lübeck

| | L | In serv. |
|---|---|---|
| Y 824 BORKUM (ex-A 54, ex-U.S.N. 105, ex-*Borkum*) | 25-3-36 | 19-5-36 |

**D:** 268 tons (light) **S:** 8 kts **Dim:** 37.52 (34.50 pp) × 7.60 × 3.60 (max.)
**Electron Equipt:** Radar: 1/. . . nav. **Electric:** 24 kw
**M:** 1 8-cyl. MWM diesel; 1 prop; 150 hp **Man:** 6 tot.

**Borkum (Y 824)** H. Ehlers, 9-85

REMARKS: Served U.S. Navy 1954 until recommissioned in Bundesmarine 1-11-56. Stationed at Wilhelmshaven. Cargo: 286 tons.

## WATER TANKERS

◆ **4 FW 1 (Type 705) class**

| | Bldr | Laid down | L | In serv. |
|---|---|---|---|---|
| A . . . FW 1 | Schichau, Bremerhaven | 5-4-63 | 22-7-63 | 30-11-63 |
| A . . . FW 4 | Jadewerft, Wilhemshaven | 14-6-63 | 14-3-64 | 28-7-64 |
| A 1405 FW 5 | Ranke, Hamburg | 26-7-63 | 26-11-63 | 21-2-64 |
| Y 869 FW 6 | Ranke, Hamburg | 4-11-63 | 25-2-64 | 19-6-64 |

**FW 1**—with old number L. & L. Van Ginderen, 8-86

**D:** 598 tons (647 fl) **S:** 9.5 kts **Dim:** 44.03 (41.1 pp) × 7.80 × 2.63
**M:** 1 MWM 12-cyl. diesel; 230 hp **Electric:** 130 kVA **Fuel:** 15 tons
**Range:** 2,150/9 **Man:** 12 tot.

REMARKS: Cargo: 343 tons. Sister FW 2 to Turkey in 1975, FW 3 to Greece in 1976. FW 6 is in reserve. Active units given A pendants 1987; formerly Y 864, 867, 868.

## TORPEDO-RECOVERY BOATS

NOTE: Some of the ten surviving torpedo retrievers, including TF 104 (Y 886) are to be replaced by the new Type 745 trials tenders. Small retrievers Y 883 and Y 884 stricken 1985–86.

◆ **9 TF 1 (Type 430) class** Bldr: Burmester, Bremen and Schweers, Bardenfleth

| | L | | L | | L |
|---|---|---|---|---|---|
| Y 851 TF 1 | 13-10-65 | Y 854 TF 4 | 21-10-65 | Y 872 TF 106 | 10-6-66 |
| Y 852 TF 2 | 22-9-65 | Y 855 TF 5 | 28-2-66 | Y 873 TF 107 | 13-9-65 |
| Y 853 TF 3 | 13-10-65 | **Y 856 TF 6** | 4-5-66 | Y 874 TF 108 | 22-9-65 |

**TF 5 (Y 855)** P. Voss, 6-85

**D:** 56 tons (63.5 fl) **S:** 17 kts **Dim:** 25.22 × 5.40 × 1.60
**M:** 1 MWM 12-cyl. diesel; 1 prop; 1,000 hp **Man:** 6 tot.

◆ **1 TF 104 (Type 438) class** Bldr: Kröger, Warnemünde

Y 886 TF 104 (ex-*Süderoog*) (In serv. 1-10-59)

**D:** 41 tons **S:** . . . kts **Dim:** 24.05 × 4.60 × 1.50
**M:** 1 MWM 8-cyl. diesel; 320 hp

## AIR-SEA RESCUE CRAFT

◆ **7 KW 15 (Type 369) class**

| | Bldr | L |
|---|---|---|
| Y 827 KW 15 (ex-BG 1, ex-KW 15, ex-H 15, ex-U.S.N. 57) | Schweers, Bardenfleth | 6-10-52 |
| Y 830 KW 16 (ex-BG 2, ex-KW 16, ex-H 16, ex-U.S.N. 54) | Lürssen, Vegesack | 1952 |
| Y 832 KW 18 (ex-H 18, ex-U.S.N. 55) | Abeking & Rasmussen | 17-11-51 |
| Y 845 KW 17 (ex-BG 3, ex-KW 17, ex-H 17, ex-U.S.N. 58) | Schürenstedt | 27-3-53 |
| Y 846 KW 20 (ex-BG 4, ex-KW 20, ex-H 20, ex-U.S.N. 56) | Lürssen, Vegesack | 1953 |
| Y 857 H 11 (ex-FL 5, ex-KW 11, ex-H 11, ex-P 1) | . . . | 1952 |
| Y 859 H 13 (ex-FL 7, ex-KW 13, ex-H 13, ex-P 3) | . . . | 1952 |

### AIR-SEA RESCUE CRAFT *(continued)*

**H 11 (Y 857) and H 13 (Y 859)** H. Ehlers, 7-86

**D:** 59.5 tons (69.6 fl) **S:** 25.0
**Dim:** 28.90 × 4.70 × 1.42
**Electron Equipt:** Radar: 1/Kelvin-Hughes 14/9
**M:** 2 MTU 12-cyl. diesels; 2 props; 2,000 hp
**Electric:** 10 kw **Man:** 17 tot.

REMARKS: Built as patrol boats for U.S. Navy, taken over 30-11-56. Served in Border Guard 1963–1969/70. Y 857 and Y 859, stricken 17-10-75, re-acquired 8-12-85 for use as safety boats at Todendorf Firing Range.

### SUBMARINE RESCUE CRAFT

◆ **1 converted *Schütze*-class former patrol minesweeper**

| | Bldr | L | In serv. |
|---|---|---|---|
| M 1092 STIER (ex-Y 849) | Abeking & Rasmussen | 30-10-58 | 28-6-61 |

**Stier (M 1092)** H. Ehlers, 8-87

REMARKS: Data as for Type 341 class. Retains 40-mm AA. Converted 1969. Deckhouse with decompression chamber added on fantail; also carries two rubber Gemini dinghies. Renumbered to original M 1092 from Y 849 in 1987.

### EXPERIMENTAL AND TRIALS CRAFT

◆ **2 (+1 + 1) Type 748 multipurpose trials craft**

| | Bldr | Laid down | L | In serv. |
|---|---|---|---|---|
| Y 860 SCHWEDENECK | Nobiskrug, Rendsburg | 11-86 | 19-2-87 | 8-87 |
| Y . . . KRONSORT | Krögerwerft, Rendsburg | 6-10-86 | 9-5-87 | 6-87 |
| Y . . . HELMSAND | Elsflether Werft, Elsfleth | -86 | . . . | 7-87 |

**D:** 999 tons (fl) **S:** 12.6 kts
**Dim:** 56.50 × 10.80 × 3.65
**Electron Equipt:** Radar: 2/. . . nav.
**M:** 2 diesels, electric drive; 1 prop; 1,490 hp
**Range:** 2,400/12 **Man:** 13 crew + 10 technicians

REMARKS: Ordered 14-12-85 with Lürssen as prime contractor, subcontracted to yards above, as replacements for *Adolf Bestelmeyer* (Y 881), *Rudolf Diesel* (Y 889), *Hans Christian Oersted* (Y 877), and *Friedrich Voge* (Y 888). Will have side-thrusters fore and aft. Space for four modular trials equipment containers, two on fantail, two amidships. Quadrantial scientific equipment gallows crane at stern. A fourth is planned to replace *Walther von Ledebur* (Y 841).

**Schwedenech (Y 860)** H. Ehlers, 8-87

◆ **0 (+5 + 2) Type 745 small multipurpose trials tenders**

| | | Bldr | Laid down | L | In serv. |
|---|---|---|---|---|---|
| Y . . . | N . . . | . . . | . . . | . . . | 1989 |
| Y . . . | N . . . | . . . | . . . | . . . | . . . |
| Y . . . | N . . . | . . . | . . . | . . . | . . . |
| Y . . . | N . . . | . . . | . . . | . . . | . . . |
| Y . . . | N . . . | . . . | . . . | . . . | . . . |

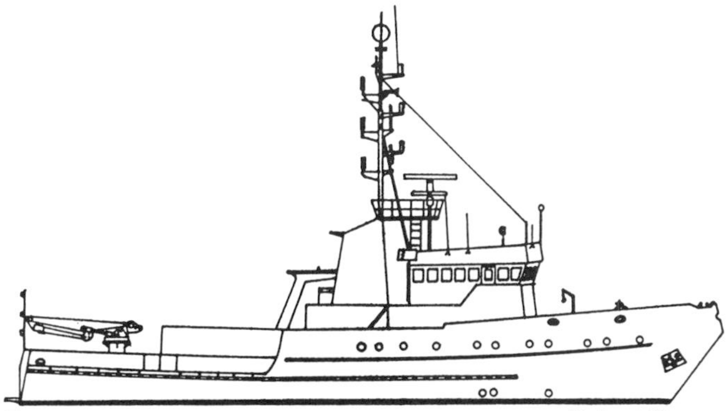

**Type 745** Robert Dumas

**D:** 450 tons (fl) **S:** 12 kts **Dim:** 38.00 × 9.20 × 3.50
**Electron Equipt:** Radar: 1/. . . nav.—Sonar: . . .
**M:** 1 diesel; 1 prop; 1,080 hp—also 2 omnidirectional thrusters
**Man:** 6 crew + 6 technicians

REMARKS: First five intended to replace diving tender TB 1 (Y 1678), radio trials craft KW 3 (Y 829), and five of the Type 430 torpedo retrievers. Two more planned for delivery post-1995 to replace *Wilhelm Pullwer* (Y 838) and two more torpedo retrievers. Nine were originally programmed. Torpedo recovery ramp to starboard through transom stern, divers' stage to port. Space for two trials equipment vans on stern. Ducted rudder.

NOTE: An air-cushion vehicle trials craft is planned for delivery after 1990. No details available.

◆ **1 Type 742 magnetic research ship**

| | Bldr | L | In serv. |
|---|---|---|---|
| A 1410 WALTHER VON LEDEBUR | Burmester, Bremen | 30-6-66 | 21-12-67 |

**Walther Von Ledebur (A 1410)**—old number P. Voss, 6-87

**EXPERIMENTAL AND TRIALS CRAFT** *(continued)*

**D:** 775 tons (825 fl) **S:** 19 kts **Dim:** 63.2 × 10.6 × 3.0
**M:** 2 Maybach 16-cyl. diesels; 2 props; 5,200 hp **Electric:** 1,620 kw
**Man:** 19 crew plus technicians

REMARKS: One of the largest wooden ships built in modern times. Used in mine-warfare research and can be employed as a minesweeper. Two 600-kw sweep current generators. Renumbered from Y 841 in 1987.

◆ **2 Type 741 net tenders** Bldr: Schürenstedt K.G., Bardenfleth

| | Laid down | L | In serv. |
|---|---|---|---|
| A 1408 SP 1 | 7-9-65 | 21-6-66 | 29-6-67 |
| A 1409 WILHELM PULLWER (ex-SP 2) | 4-10-65 | 16-8-66 | 22-12-67 |

**Wilhelm Pullwer (A 1409)** H. Ehlers, 9-87

**D:** 132 tons (160 fl) **S:** 12.5 kts **Dim:** 31.54 × 7.5 × 2.2
**M:** 2 Mercedes-Benz 8-cyl. diesels; 2 Voith-Schneider cycloidal props; 792 hp
**Electric:** 120 kw **Man:** 17 crew plus trials personnel

REMARKS: Used in experimental trials. Wooden hulls. SP 1 pendant changed 1985 from Y 837 to Y 838, renumbered again 1987, as was A 1409 (from Y 838).

◆ **1 Type 740 torpedo-trials ship** Bldr: AG Weser, Bremerhaven

| | Laid down | L | In serv. |
|---|---|---|---|
| Y 871 HEINZ ROGGENKAMP (ex-*Greif*) | 23-8-52 | 8-11-52 | 30-12-52 |

**Heinz Roggenkamp (Y 871)** L. & L. Van Ginderen, 2-75

**D:** 935 tons (996 fl) **S:** 12 kts **Dim:** 57.19 (51.5 pp) × 9.04 × 3.10
**A:** 2/533-mm torpedo tubes (1 ASW, on deck; 1 underwater)—3/324-mm Mk 32 ASW TT (III × 1)
**Electric:** 192 kw **Man:** 19 crew plus trials personnel
**M:** 1 Klöckner-Humboldt-Deutz 8-cyl. diesel; 1 prop; 1,145 hp (800 sust.)

REMARKS: Former trawler purchased 1963; commissioned after reconstruction 25-9-64. Civilian crew. To be replaced by a Type 749 trials ship post-1990.

◆ **1 weapons-trials barge** Bldr: Howaldtswerke, Kiel (In serv. 26-6-64)

Y 844 BARBARA

**Barbara (Y 844)**—with legs retracted H. Ehlers, 8-87

**D:** 3,500 tons (fl) **Dim:** 62.1 × 24.2 × 3.0 **Electric:** 1,650 kVA

REMARKS: Non-self-propelled. Eight extending legs to anchor ship to bottom. Used to test guns. Civilian crew. Helicopter deck, 12-ton crane. Named for the patron saint of artillerists.

◆ **1 former fishing cutter** Bldr: Lürssen, Vegesack (L: 6-47)

Y 882 OTTO MEYCKE (ex-*Meteor II*)

**D:** 50 tons **S:** 9 kts **Dim:** 17.45 (14.95 pp) × 5.0 × 1.9
**M:** 1 Modag SRB55 diesel; 1 prop; 150 hp **Man:** 6 tot.

REMARKS: Wooden craft, purchased 1960; commissioned 5-8-60. Primarily a diving tender. Civilian crew. Pendant number not painted on. To be replaced shortly.

◆ **1 former Swedish submarine** Bldr: Karlskrona

| | Laid down | L | In serv. |
|---|---|---|---|
| Y . . . JONAS (ex-*Valen*) | | 24-4-55 | 4-3-57 |

**Jonas (Y . . .)** H. Ehlers, 8-87

**D:** 785 tons surf. (1,000 sub.) **S:** . . . **Dim:** 66.0 × 5.1 × 5.5
**A:** 4/533-mm TT fwd—deactivated **Electron Equipt:** Radar: . . .—Sonar: . . .
**M:** 2 Hedemora-Pielstick 16V-12PA diesels, 830 hp each; 2 electric motors; 1 prop; 1,500 hp—inoperable
**Man:** . . .

REMARKS: Former Swedish Navy *Hajen*-class submarine stricken 1978. Hulk purchased 1984 and towed to Kiel for conversion to tethered target and underwater trials platform for Trials Station 71 at Eckenförde to replace *Wilhelm Bauer*.

◆ **1 ex-U.S. YMS-class minesweeper** Bldr: Weaver Bros., Orange, Texas

| | Laid down | L | In serv. |
|---|---|---|---|
| Y 877 HANS CHRISTIAN OERSTED (ex-*Vinstra*, ex-NYMS 247, ex-YMS 247) | 27-5-42 | 14-10-42 | 13-5-43 |

**D:** 260 tons (302 fl) **S:** 16 kts **Dim:** 41.53 (39.62 pp) × 7.52 × 2.40
**M:** 2 Maybach diesels, electric drive; 2 props; 1,800 hp
**Electric:** 120 kw (plus 680 kw from main engines)
**Man:** 16 crew plus trial personnel

REMARKS: Operated in Norwegian Navy from completion to 1959; acquired 1960 and reconstructed and re-engined, recommissioning 12-7-62. Initially used as a degaussing tender, but since 1974 used in research. To be replaced by a Type 748 trials tender, 1988. The similar *Adolf Bestelmeyer* (Y 881, ex-BYMS 2213, ex-YMS 213) stricken 26-6-87, and *Rudolf Diesel* (Y 889, ex-BYMS 2279, ex-YMS 279) stricken 28-11-86.

## EXPERIMENTAL AND TRIALS CRAFT *(continued)*

**H.C. Oersted (Y 877)** L. & L. Van Ginderen, 10-87

◆ **5 Type 740 trials craft** Bldr: . . . (In serv. . . .)

Y 1673 AK 5 (ex-AM 4)
Y 1674 AM 6 — Y 1683 AK 6
Y 1675 AM 8 — Y 1684 Peter Bachmann

**Workboat AK 5** S. Terzibaschitsch, 6-87

**D:** 18.5 tons (fl) **S:** 18.5 kts **Dim:** 15.50 (14.40 wl) × 3.14 × 1.37
**Electron Equipt:** Radar: 1/. . .
**M:** 2 Klöckner-Humboldt-Deutz 6-cyl diesels;
2 Schottel vertical cycloidal props; 500 hp.

Remarks: Sisters ST 1, ST 2, and AM 1 served as navigational training craft until sold 1978–81. Y 1673 is used in radar trials, the others as general-purpose launches. Another MT-BOOT has no pendant number.

◆ **1 Type 740 trials craft, former motor torpedo boat** Bldr: Schlichting-werft, Travemünde (L: 21-10-43)

Y 840 EF 3 (ex-UW-10, ex-Brit. FPB 5030, ex-Ger. S 130)

**D:** 92 tons (112 fl) **S:** . . . **Dim:** 34.94 × 5.28 × . . .
**M:** 3 diesels; 3 props; 3,300 hp **Man:** . . .

**EF 3 (Y 840)** H. Ehlers, 10-86

Remarks: Re-acquired from Great Britain and commissioned 7-3-57; stricken as a warship 15-8-63 but retained for trials duties. Originally powered by 3 Daimler-Benz 12-cylinder diesels. A classic "S-boot."

Note: Radio calibration craft KW 3 (Y 829) of the WWII KFK class was scheduled for disposal 1987–88 and is to be replaced by a Type 745 trials craft. Trials tender *Friedrich Voge* (Y 888) was stricken 8-5-87.

## DIVING TENDERS

◆ **3 Baltrum (Type 754)-class converted seagoing tugs** Bldr: Schichau, Bremerhaven

| | Laid down | L | In serv. |
|---|---|---|---|
| A . . . Baltrum (ex-Y 1661, ex-A 1454) | 29-6-66 | 2-6-67 | 8-10-68 |
| A . . . Juist (ex-A 1456) | 23-9-67 | 15-8-68 | 1-10-71 |
| A 1441 Langeoog (ex-Y 1665, ex-A 1453) | 12-7-66 | 2-5-67 | 14-8-68 |

**Baltrum (A 1661)** P. Voss, 6-86

Remarks: Data as for seagoing tug sisters; can be armed with 1/40-mm AA. Y 1661 converted 1974, others in 1978. Used to train mine-clearance divers.

◆ **1 Type-732 small diving tender** Bldr: Burmester, Bremen

M 1050 TB 1 (ex-Y 1678) (In serv. 21-6-72)

**D:** 70 tons **S:** 14 kts **Dim:** 27.75 × 5.77 × 1.90
**M:** 1 MWM 12-cyl. diesel; 950 hp **Electric:** 36 kw

Remarks: Also used for research. To be replaced by a Type 745 trials tender. Diving boat MB 8 at Wihelmshaven is the ex-AM 3 (Y 1685). AM 11 and AM 12 are diving floats. M 1050 renumbered 1987.

◆ **1 Type 392 former inshore minesweeper** Bldr: Kröger, Rendsburg

| | Laid down | L | In serv. |
|---|---|---|---|
| M 1052 Hansa (ex-Y 806, ex-W 22, ex-M 2662) | 7-8-57 | 18-11-57 | 23-7-58 |

**Hansa (M 1052)** H. Ehlers, 8-87

**D:** 155 tons (175 fl) **S:** 14 kts **Dim:** 35.18 × 6.84 × 1.95 **A:** 1/40-mm AA
**M:** 1 Mercedes-Benz MB 820Db diesel; 1 prop; 1,000 hp **Electric:** 180 kw
**Range:** 1,500/12 **Man:** 20 tot.

### DIVING TENDERS *(continued)*

Remarks: Wooden hull. Converted 1968–69 as a training tender for mine-clearance divers. 40-mm AA forward removed by 1986, restored 1987 when ship was renumbered M 1052.

### MISCELLANEOUS SERVICE CRAFT

◆ **1 Type 743 support tender** Bldr: Fritz Staack, Lübeck (In serv. 1980)

Y 1679 AM 7

**AM 7 (Y 1679)** P. Voss, 10-84

**D:** . . . **S:** . . . **Dim:** 16.3 × 4.1 × . . .
**M:** 1 MWM diesel; 1 prop; 180 hp

Remarks: Glass-reinforced plastic construction.

◆ **1 pollution-control ship** Bldr: C. Lühring, Brake

| | Laid down | L | In serv. | To Navy |
|---|---|---|---|---|
| Y 1643 Bottsand | 14-11-83 | 22-9-84 | 26-10-84 | 24-1-85 |

**Bottsand (Y 1643)** H. Ehlers, 8-87

**D:** approx. 1,100 tons (fl) **S:** 10 kts **Dim:** 46.30 × 12.00 × 3.10
**A:** none **Electron Equipt:** Radar: 1 navigational
**M:** 2 diesels, 2 rudder-props, 1,600 hp—2 omnidirectional bow-thrusters; 400 hp
**Man:** 3 officers, 3 men

Remarks: 500 grt/650 dwt. Twin hulls, hinged near the stern to open scissors-fashion to 65-deg., leaving a 42-m wide Vee opening to collect oil spills at the rate of approx. 140 $m^3$/hr, at a speed of 1 knot. When folded can also be used as a coastal tanker and bunkerage craft. Concept known as THOR (Twin Hull Oil Recovery), which is also the name of a smaller civil-operated prototype completed in 1983. Built for the Niedersachsen Ministry for the Environment, but turned over to the Bundesmarine on loan, 24-1-85. Six cargo/spill tanks totalling 790 $m^3$.

◆ **2 Type 710 tank-cleaning craft** Bldr: Deutsche Werft, Hamburg

| | Laid down | L | In serv. |
|---|---|---|---|
| Y 1641 Förde | 12-1-67 | 10-3-67 | 14-12-67 |
| Y 1642 Jade | 18-5-67 | 19-7-67 | 6-11-67 |

**D:** 1,830 tons (fl) **S:** 8 kts **Dim:** 58.46 × 10.40 × 4.1 (light)
**M:** 1 MWM 16-cyl. diesel; 1 prop; 390 hp **Range:** 750/8 **Man:** 16 tot.

Remarks: For steam-cleaning fuel tanks and for sludge removal. Civilian crews.

**Jade (Y 1642)** H. Ehlers, 9-85

◆ **2 Type 711 self-propelled floating cranes** Bldr: Rheinwerft, Walsum

Y 875 Hiev (In serv. 2-10-62) Y 876 Griep (In serv. 15-5-63)

**Hiev (Y 875)** L. & L. Van Ginderen, 1981

**D:** 1,830 tons (1,875 fl) **S:** 6 kts **Dim:** 52.9 × 22.0 × 2.1
**M:** 3 MWM 600-hp diesels, electric drive; 3 vertical cycloidal props; 1,425 hp
**Electric:** 358 kVA **Man:** 12 tot.

Remarks: Electric-crane capacity: 100 tons. Civilian crews.

◆ **3 Type 718 battery-charging craft** Bldrs: Jadewerft, Wihelmshaven (LP 2: Oelkers, Hamburg)

LP 1 (In serv. 18-2-64) LP 2 (In serv. 17-4-64) LP 3 (In serv. 16-9-74)

**LP 3** L. & L. Van Ginderen, 8-85

### MISCELLANEOUS SERVICE CRAFT *(continued)*

**D:** 192 tons (234 fl) **S:** 8 kts **Dim:** 27.6 × 7.0 × 1.6
**M:** 1 MTU diesel; 250 hp **Electric:** 960 kw (LP 3: 1,110 kw) **Man:** 6 tot.

REMARKS: Each has two 405-kw generators and one (LP 3: two) 150-kw generator for charging submarine batteries. LP 3 is 7.5 m in beam, 1.8 m draft, 267 tons (fl).

### TRAINING CRAFT

NOTE: Also included in this category are the three *Baltrum*-class former seagoing tugs and the diving tender *Hansa* listed under diving tenders. The three Type 945/740 training cutters in the previous edition, ST 1 (Y 1669), ST 2 (Y 1670), and AM 1 (Y 1671) were in fact discarded by 1981.

◆ **4 Type 521 landing craft** Bldr: Rheinwerft, Wolsam (In serv. 1966–67)

A 1406 GARNELE (ex-LCM 27)
A 1408 HERING (ex-LCM 15)
A 1409 MAREENE (ex-LCM 17)
A 1410 LANGUSTE (ex-LCM 28)

**Languste (A 1410)** H. Ehlers, 7-87

REMARKS: Characteristics the same as the 18 sisters listed as landing craft on page 183. A 1408 and A 1409 have tripod masts, a 2-ton cargo boom, and a separate 20-kw diesel generator; they are attached to the Seamanship School, Borkum. A 1406 and A 1410 are attached to the Coastal Services School, Grossenbrode.

◆ **1 Type 368 ketch, former patrol fishing cutter** (In serv. 1942–44?)

Y 834 NORDWIND (ex-W 43)

**Nordwind (Y 834)** H. Ehlers, 6-86

**D:** 100 tons (110 fl) **S:** 11 kts
**Dim:** 27.00 (24.00 hull, 21.48 pp) × 6.39 × 2.94
**Electron Equipt:** Radar: 1/Kelvin-Hughes 14/9
**M:** 1 Demag 5-cyl. diesel; 1 prop; 137 hp **Range:** 1,200/7 **Man:** 10 tot.

REMARKS: Taken over by U.S. Navy 1945; acquired 1-7-56 by German Navy. Wooden hull; 195 $m^2$ sail area. Operated for the Mürwik Naval School.

NOTE: There are also 70 smaller sail-training craft, all bearing names. Included are 26 Type 914 class, 5 m long, 10 Type 913 class, 7.64 m long, 25 Type 910 (most 10.46 m o.a.), 6 Type 911, and 1 Type 912.

### ACCOMMODATIONS BARGE (Type 130)

NOTE: New accommodation barges are planned. *Knurrhahn* (Y 811) was sold in the Netherlands in 1986.

### FLOATING DRY DOCKS

◆ **2 Type 712** Bldr: Krupp, Rheinhausen

HEBEWERK 2 (In serv. 15-3-61) HEBEWERK A (In serv. 13-1-61)

**D:** 1,000 tons **Dim:** 66.01 × 21.10 × . . .

REMARKS: Serviced by 4 Type-713 "Hebeponton": 500 tons, 56 m by 14.8 m.

◆ **1 Type 714 self-propelled** Bldr: Flenderwerft, Lübeck (In serv. circa 1945)

Y 879 SCHWIMMDOCK B

**D:** 4,500 tons **S:** . . . **Dim:** 156.00 × 25.00 × 3.50
**M:** 4 MWM 16-cyl. diesels, electric drive; 2 Schöttel props; 500 hp

REMARKS: In German naval service 26-10-63 at Kiel. The propellers are at the starboard forward and port aft corners.

◆ **1 Type 715** Bldr: Howaldtswerke, Hamburg (In serv. 1961)

Y 842 SCHWIMMDOCK 3

**D:** 8,000 tons **Dim:** 164.0 × 30.0 × 3.5

REMARKS: Seven pontoon sections.

◆ **1 Type 715** Bldr: Flenderwerke, Lübeck (In serv. 8-9-67)

DRUCKDOCK *("Dock C")*

**D:** . . . tons **Dim:** 93.0 × 26.5 × 3.6

The compression floating dry dock used at Kiel for testing submarine pressure-hull integrity. An entire Type 205 or 206 submarine can fit inside.
L. & L. Van Ginderen, 5-84

## SEA BORDER PATROL
*(Bundesgrenzschutz-See)*

NOTE: A separate paramilitary force of 1,000 men.

### PATROL BOATS

◆ **8 Neustadt class** Bldrs: Lürssen, Vegesack, except BG 13: Schlichting, Travemünde

| | Laid down | L | In serv. |
|---|---|---|---|
| BG 11 NEUSTADT | 25-11-68 | 27-2-69 | 25-11-69 |
| BG 12 BAD BRAMSTEDT | 10-1-69 | 2-4-69 | 1969 |
| BG 13 UELZEN | 17-5-69 | 25-7-69 | 24-2-70 |
| BG 14 DUDERSTADT | 21-2-69 | 3-6-69 | 1970 |
| BG 15 ESCHWEGE | 27-3-69 | 16-9-69 | 19-3-70 |
| BG 16 ALSFELD | 31-5-69 | 11-11-69 | 1970 |
| BG 17 BAYREUTH | 15-9-69 | 9-1-70 | 1970 |
| BG 18 ROSENHEIM | 8-11-69 | 12-3-70 | 11-70 |

**D:** 191 tons (218 fl) **S:** 30 kts **Dim:** 38.50 (36.00 pp) × 7.00 × 2.15
**A:** 2/40-mm AA (I × 2) **Electron Equipt:** Radar: 1/Kelvin-Hughes 14/9
**M:** 2 Maybach 16-cyl. diesels; 2 props; 7,200 hp **Fuel:** 15 tons
**Electric:** 195 kVA **Range:** 450/27 **Man:** 23 tot.

**PATROL BOATS** *(continued)*

**Rosenheim (BG 18)** H. Ehlers, 7-86

REMARKS: Have an additional centerline propeller for cruising, powered by a 685-hp MWM diesel. Two additional units canceled. Hulls painted blue, superstructure white. A new "North Sea Patrol Boat" is to be ordered in 1988.

◆ **1 tug** Bldr: Mützelbeldt-Werft, Cuxhaven (L: 29-1-76)

BG 5 RETTIN

**Rettin (BG 5)** L. & L. Van Ginderen, 4-87

**D:** 99.9 grt **S:** 9 kts **Dim:** 22.5 (20.0 pp) × 6.6 × 2.9
**M:** 2 MWM diesels; 1 prop; 590 hp

FISHERIES PROTECTION SHIPS

NOTE: Operated by the Ministry of Agriculture and Fisheries. Have black hulls with "Fischereischutz" (Fisheries Protection) on sides of most, grey superstructures, buff-colored masts, and orange boats.

◆ **7 patrol ships**

SEEFALKE Bldr: Orenstein & Koppel (In serv. 4-8-81)

**Seefalke**—note folding edge to helo deck P. Voss, 24-8-82

**D:** 2,386 tons (fl) **S:** 20 kts **Dim:** 83.10 (76.20 pp) × 12.80 × 4.70
**M:** 2 MWM TBD 510 L8 diesels; 2 CP props; 8,000 hp **Man:** 29 tot.

REMARKS: 1,980 grt. Equipped to operate in East Greenland Sea; fin stabilizers, elaborate navigation equipment, helicopter platform, bow-thruster.

MEERKATZE Bldr: Lürssen, Vegesack (In serv. 1976)

**Meerkatze** P. Voss, 3-84

**D:** 2,386 tons **S:** 15 kts **Dim:** 76.5 × 11.8 × 5.5
**M:** 3 MWM diesels, electric drive; 2 props; 2,300 hp **Man:** 30 tot.

SOLEA Bldr: Sieghold, Bremerhaven (In serv. 1974)

**Solea** L. & L. Van Ginderen, 10-75

**D:** 337 grt **S:** 12 kts **Dim:** 33.5 × 9.0 × 3.6 **M:** 1 Deutz diesel; 640 hp
**Man:** 11 tot.

WALTHER HERWIG Bldr: Schlichting, Travemünde (In serv. 1972)

**Walther Herwig** P. Voss, 9-83

**D:** 2,500 tons **S:** 15.5 kts **Dim:** 77.0 × 14.9 × 5.2
**M:** 2 M.A.N. diesels; 2 props; 3,380 hp **Man:** 35 tot.

**FISHERIES PROTECTION SHIPS** *(continued)*

FRITHJOF Bldr: Schlichting, Travemünde (In serv. 1967)

**Frithjof** P. Voss, 1-85

**D:** 2,140 tons **S:** 15 kts **Dim:** 76.0 × 11.8 × 5.2
**M:** 3 Maybach diesels, electric drive; 2 props; 2,650 hp **Man:** 35 tot.

ANTON DOHRN (ex-*Walther Herwig*) Bldr: Seebeck, Bremerhaven (In serv. 1963)

**Anton Dohrn** P. Voss, 12-82

**D:** 1,986 grt **S:** 15 kts **Dim:** 83.0 × 12.5 × 5.2
**M:** Maybach diesels; 2,210 hp **Man:** 38 tot.

REMARKS: Late note: stricken 2-87.

POSEIDON Bldr: Mützelfeldt, Cuxhaven (In serv. 1957)

**Poseidon** L. & L. Van Ginderen, 5-81

**D:** 934 grt **S:** 12 kts **Dim:** 58.8 × 10.2 × . . .
**M:** 1 Verschure diesel; 800 hp **Man:** 20 tot.

GOVERNMENT CIVIL RESEARCH SHIPS

NOTE: Operated by the German Hydrographic Institute, which is subordinate to the Ministry of Transport.

◆ **1 polar research ship and transport**

| | Bldr | Laid down | L | In serv. |
|---|---|---|---|---|
| POLARSTERN | Howaldtswerke, Kiel | 22-9-81 | 8-1-82 | 8-12-82 |

**Polarstern** L. & L. Van Ginderen, 12-86

**D:** 15,000 tons (fl) **S:** 15.5 kts **Dim:** 117.55 (102.20 pp) × 25.00 × 10.50
**M:** 4 Deutz diesels, electric drive; 2 Kort-nozzle CP props; 21,120 hp
**Electric:** 5,400 kVA × 2,580 kw
**Man:** 36 crew, 40 scientists, 30 relief staff

REMARKS: 3,900 dwt. Built for the Alfred Wegener Institute for Polar Research, Bremerhaven. Capable of carrying 1,500 tons of liquid cargo, plus stores to support Germany's Antarctic research station; 100 tons of provisions are carried in refrigerated vans on the forecastle. Helicopter deck and hangar. Can break 2-m ice; shell plating 43.5-mm at waterline. Has bow and stern side-thrusters. INDAS V system ("Integrated Navigation system with Data Acquisition and automatic ship's Steering").

◆ **9 oceanographic and hydrographic survey ships**

ATAIR Bldr: Krögerwerft, Rendsburg (In serv. 7-87)

**Atair** P. Voss, 2-8-83

**D:** . . . **S:** 11.6 kts **Dim:** 49.8 × . . . × . . .
**M:** diesel-electric: 2 463-kw generator sets; 1 Kort-nozzle CP prop; 800 hp
**Range:** . . ./. . . **Man:** 16 crew + 7 scientists

REMARKS: Intended as a coastal survey and shipwreck search ship. Keel laid 4-87. Replaces earlier ship of the same name. 999 grt.

PROFESSOR MINTHROP (ex-*Bremen*) (In serv. 15-4-86)

**D:** . . . **S:** . . . **Dim:** . . . × . . . × . . . **M:** diesel-electric

REMARKS: Stern trawler acquired 28-11-85 and converted by Lindenau, Kiel.

METEOR Bldr: Schlichting Werft, Travemünde (In serv. 15-3-86)

**Meteor** P. Voss, 7-86

## GOVERNMENT CIVIL RESEARCH SHIPS *(continued)*

**D:** 3,128 tons (fl) **S:** 14 kts **Dim:** 98.0 × 17.0 × 4.8
**M:** diesel-electric; 1 prop, 4,760 hp **Range:** 10,000/14
**Man:** 38 crew, 29 scientific party

REMARKS: Intended to replace *Meteor*. Has asymetrical stern form and "Grim Wheel," free-wheeling prop abaft regular propeller to improve performance by roughly 10 percent. Launched 3-9-85. Previous *Meteor* sold 12-85 to New Zealand.

GAUSS Bldr: Schlichtingwerft, Travemünde (In serv. 1980)

**Gauss** P. Voss, 7-84

**D:** 1,372 tons (1,813 fl) **S:** 13.5 kts **Dim:** 68.7 (61.0 pp) × 13.0 × 4.25
**Electron Equipt:** Radar: 1 Raytheon 1660/12SR, 1 Raytheon RM1650/9 × R
**M:** 3 MAK 331 AK 800-hp diesels, electric drive; 1 prop; 1,647 hp
**Electric:** 220 kVA **Range:** 4,000/13.5 **Man:** 19 crew plus 12 scientists

REMARKS: Has special free-wheeling prop aft of propulsion propeller. Equipped with Becker flap-rudder, Denny-Brown fin stabilizers, and a 725-hp drop-down bow-thruster. Ship's service power from main engine generators. Grim Wheel propeller substituted, added 9 percent to fuel efficiency.

POSEIDON Bldr: Schichau, Unterweser (In serv. 1976)

**D:** 1,050 grt **S:** 15 kts **Dim:** 58.0 × 11.4 × . . . **M:** MWM diesels; 1,800 hp

VICTOR HENSEN Bldr: Schichau, Bremerhaven (L: 1975)

**Victor Hensen** L. & L. Van Ginderen, 8-75

**D:** 423 grt **S:** 12 kts **Dim:** 37.04 (33.99 pp) × 9.50 × 3.07
**M:** 2 MTU 6-cyl. diesels; 1 prop; . . . hp **Man:** 28 tot.

SENCKENBERG Bldr: . . . (In serv. 1976)

REMARKS: 165 grt. No other data available.

KOMET Bldr: Jadewerft, Wilhelmshaven (In serv. 1969)

**D:** 1,253 grt **S:** 15 kts **Dim:** 68.0 × 11.5 × 4.0
**M:** 2 Maybach diesels; 1 prop; 2,650 hp **Man:** 42 tot.

WEGA Bldr: Schlichting, Travemünde (In serv. 1962)

**D:** 157 grt **S:** 10.5 kts **Dim:** 31.7 × 6.5 × 2.3 **M:** 1 Deutz diesel: 205 hp
**Man:** 13 tot.

REMARKS: Sister *Atair* stricken 1987.

**Komet**—note six survey launches P. Voss, 11-83

VALDIVIA (ex-*Viking Bank*) Bldr: A.G. Weser, Bremerhaven (In serv. 1961)

**D:** 1,317 grt **S:** 13 kts **Dim:** 73.46 (63.99 pp) × 11.03 × 5.23
**M:** 1 M.A.N. 6L 52/74 diesel; 1 prop; 2,160 hp
**Man:** 24 crew plus 16 scientists

REMARKS: Purchased 1981 and converted at A.G. Weser, completing 5-82 as a submersible tender. Former stern-haul trawler. Also in government service are the research ships *Uthorn* (200 tons, 12 kts, in serv. 8-9-82) and *Bulse* (1982).

### WATER AND NAVIGATION BOARD
*(Schiffartpolizei)*

## POLLUTION-CONTROL SHIPS

◆ **1 seagoing** Bldr: Elsflether Werft

MELLUM (In serv. 4-7-84)

**Mellum** P. Voss, 5-86

**D:** approx. 3,600 tons (fl) **S:** 16 kts **Dim:** 71.5 × 15.0 × 5.8
**M:** 4 Mak diesels; 2 CP props; 9,000 hp

REMARKS: 2,157 grt.

◆ **1 converted offshore supply vessel** Bldr: Rheinwerft, Walsum

SCHARNHÖRN (ex-*Ostertor*)

**D:** approx. 2,100 tons (fl) **S:** 14 kts **Dim:** 56.1 × 14.3 × 4.6
**M:** 2 Deutz diesels; 2 props; 3,500 hp

REMARKS: 933 grt. Converted by Elsflether Werft, 1981–82. Large crane aft.

◆ **1 modified dredge** Bldr: Orenstein & Koppel, Lübeck

NORDSEE (In serv. 25-5-78)

**D:** approx. 12,500 tons (fl) **S:** 11 kts **Dim:** 131.8 × 23.0 × 6.7
**M:** 1 Mak diesel; 1 prop; 14,506 hp

REMARKS: 8,785 grt. Converted 1983 for pollution clearance.

◆ **1 small suction dredge** Bldr: Husumer Werft

OLAND (In serv. 1985)

**D:** . . . **S:** 10 kts **Dim:** 26.0 × 7.2 × 1.5
**M:** 2 Deutz diesels; 1 prop; 850 hp

REMARKS: 134 grt.

**GERMANY—FEDERAL REPUBLIC** *(continued)*
**POLLUTION-CONTROL SHIPS** *(continued)*

**Oland** L. & L. Van Ginderen, 8-86

GERMAN SOCIETY FOR THE RESCUE OF THE SHIPWRECKED
SEARCH AND RESCUE SERVICE

**Rescue Cutters**

NOTE: Two 27.5-meter rescue cutters ordered 1987 from Lürssen, Vegesack, for delivery spring 1988.

◆ **3 44.2-meter class** Bldr: . . . (In serv. . . .)

JOHN T. ESSBERGER HERMANN RITTER WILHELM KAISEN

**John T. Essberger** MTU

**D:** 170 tons (fl) **S:** 26 kts **Dim:** 44.20 × 8.05 × 2.75
**M:** 1 4,500-hp diesel centerline, 2 1,350-hp diesels; 3 props; 7,200 hp

REMARKS: Equipped with helicopter deck, extensive navigational aids, firefighting gear. Carry "daughter boat" rescue craft: 8.8 × 2.5 × 0.9 m; 150-hp diesel = 9 kts.

◆ **2 27.5-meter class** Bldr: . . .

BERLIN (In serv. 29-5-85) HERMANN HELMS (In serv. . . .)

**D:** 100 tons (fl) **S:** 24 kts **Dim:** 27.5 × 6.53 × 1.65
**M:** 1 1,632-hp diesel centerline, 2 781-hp diesels; 3 props; 3,194 hp

REMARKS: "Daughter-boat" rescue craft: 7.5 × 2.5 × 0.75 m; 165-hp diesel = 17 kts. Extensive rescue and navigational equipment, 2,200 ton/hr firefighting pump system.

◆ **3 26.6-meter class** Bldr: . . . (In serv. . . .)

GEORG BREUSING ADOLPH BERMPOHL ARWED EMMINGHAUS

**D:** 85 tons **S:** 19 kts **Dim:** 26.60 × 5.60 × 1.80
**M:** 1 1,350-hp diesel centerline, 2 525-hp diesels; 3 props; 2,400 hp

REMARKS: Carry "daughter-boat" rescue craft recessed into stern ramp: 8.5 × . . . × 0.75-m; 100 hp = 10 kts. Have medical, firefighting, and salvage pump facilities, extensive navigational equipment.

◆ **4 23.3-meter class** Bldr: . . . (In serv. . . .)

EISWETTE FRITZ BEHRENS MINDEN VORMANN LEISS

**D:** 60 or 66 tons (fl) **S:** 20 kts **Dim:** 23.3 × 5.64 (or 5.50) × 1.70
**M:** 2 1,038- or 972-hp diesels; 2 props; 2,076 or 1,944 hp

REMARKS: Two slightly different designs. Carry "daughter-boat" rescue craft at stern: 7.0 × . . . 0.6-m (or 6.9 × . . . 0.67 m) with 68-hp or 165-hp diesels for 10 or 17 kts. Have 380-ton/hr firefighting pump capacity, medical, rescue, salvage, and extensive navigational equipment.

◆ **4 18.9-meter class** Bldr: . . . (In serv. . . .)

OTTO SCHÜLKE HANS LÜKEN H.J. KRATSCHKE GÜNTER KUCHENBECKER

**D:** 30 tons **S:** 16 kts **Dim:** 18.90 × 4.30 × 1.40
**M:** 1 diesel; 1 prop; 830 hp

REMARKS: Carry a 5.5-m, 54-hp, 8-kt rescue craft. Equipped for firefighting, salvage; have extensive navigational equipment.

◆ **1 16.8-meter class** Bldr: . . . (In serv. . . .)

PAUL DENKER

**D:** 25 tons (fl) **S:** 15 kts **Dim:** 16.80 × 3.80 × 1.35
**M:** 1 diesel; 1 prop; 665 hp

REMARKS: Carries an 18-kt, semi-rigid inflatable rescue boat; has salvage and fire-fighting capability.

◆ **2 12.2-meter class** Bldr: . . . (In serv. . . .)

SIEGFRIED BOYSEN EDUARD NEBELTHAU

**D:** 10 tons **S:** 15 kts **Dim:** 12.20 × 3.00 × 1.00
**M:** 1 diesel; 1 prop; 240 hp

◆ **5 9.0-meter class** Bldr: . . . (In serv. . . .)

WILHELM HÜBOTTER CARL A. WUPPESAHL WALTHER MÜLLER
HERNUM ARTHUR MENGE

**D:** 5 tons **S:** 13 kts **Dim:** 9.00 × 2.70 × 0.90
**M:** 1 diesel; 1 prop; 150 hp

◆ **13 7.0-meter class** Bldr: . . . (In serv. . . .)

TAMINA MARTJE GESINA SWANTJE UMMA DORTJE ILKA
ELTJE KAATJE BRUNTJE TRIENTJE GRIETJE MAX CARSTENSEN

**D:** 2 tons **S:** 10 kts **Dim:** 7.00 × 2.34 × 0.60 **M:** 1 diesel; 45 hp

# GHANA

**Republic of Ghana**

PERSONNEL (1984): 750 total

MERCHANT MARINE (1986): 137 ships—165,644 grt (tankers: 1 ship—965 dwt)

## CORVETTES

◆ **2 Vosper Mk 1 class**

| | Bldr | L | In serv. |
|---|---|---|---|
| F 17 KROMANTSE | Vosper Ltd, Portsmouth, U.K. | 5-9-63 | 9-64 |
| F 18 KETA | Vickers Ltd, Newcastle, U.K. | 18-1-65 | 8-65 |

**D:** 435 tons (500 fl) **S:** 18 kts **Dim:** 53.95 (49.38 pp) × 8.7 × 3.05
**A:** 1/102-mm—1/40-mm AA—1/Squid ASW mortar (III × 1)
**Electron Equipt:** Radar: 1/Type 978 nav., 1/Plessey AWS-1
Sonar: 1/Type 164 (med. freq.)

**Keta (F 18)** G. Arra, 1975

**GHANA** *(continued)*
**CORVETTES** *(continued)*

**M:** 2 Bristol Siddeley-Maybach 16-cyl. diesels; 2 props; 5,720 hp
**Electric:** 360 kw **Fuel:** 60 tons **Range:** 1,100/18; 2,900/14
**Man:** 5 officers, 49 men

REMARKS: Fin stabilizers fitted. Quarters are air-conditioned. Both refitted 1974–75 and again in 1983–84.

### PATROL BOATS

◆ **2 FBP 57 class** Bldr: Lürssen, Vegesack

| | Laid down | L | In serv. |
|---|---|---|---|
| P 28 ACHIMOTA | 1978 | 14-3-79 | 27-3-81 |
| P 29 YOGAGA | 1978 | 14-3-79 | 27-3-81 |

**Yogaga (P 29)** L. & L. Van Ginderen, 7-86

**D:** 380 tons (410 fl) **S:** 30 kts **Dim:** 58.10 × 7.62 × 2.83
**A:** 1/76-mm OTO Melara DP—1/40-mm Bofors AA
**Electron Equipt:** Radar: 1/Decca 1226, 1/Thomson-CSF Canopus-A
**M:** 3 MTU 16V538 TB91 diesels; 3 props; 10,800 hp **Man:** 40 tot.

REMARKS: Have LIOD optronic gun director atop pilothouse. Carry 250 rounds 76-mm, 750 rounds 40-mm. Carry rubber dinghy for air/sea rescue and inspection purposes.

◆ **2 FPB 45 class** Bldr: Lürssen, Vegesack

| | Laid down | L | In serv. |
|---|---|---|---|
| P 26 DZATA | 16-1-78 | 19-9-79 | 4-12-79 |
| P 27 SEBO | 1-78 | 19-9-79 | 2-5-80 |

**Sebo (P 27) and Dzata (P 26)**—prior to arming G. Gyssels, 1979

**D:** 212 tons (252 fl) **S:** 30 kts **Dim:** 44.90 (42.25 wl) × 7.00 × 2.50 (props)
**A:** 2/40-mm Bofors AA (I × 20)
**Electron Equipt:** Radar: 1/nav.
**M:** 2 MTU 16V538 TB91 diesels; 2 props; 7,200 hp (6,000 sust.)
**Electric:** 408 kVA **Range:** 1,100/25; 2,000/15
**Man:** 5 officers, 30 men

REMARKS: Flare RL on sides of both 40-mm mounts. Planned Thomson-CSF Canopus-A radar not mounted.

◆ **2 Sahene class** Bldr: Ruthoff, Mainz, Germany (In serv. 1976)

P 24 SAHENE P 25 DELA

**Dela (P 25)** 1976

**D:** 160 tons (fl) **S:** 30 kts **Dim:** 35.2 × 6.5 × 1.8
**A:** 1/40-mm AA (with flare launchers attached)
**M:** 2 MTU 16V538 TB90 diesels; 2 props; 3,000 hp
**Range:** 1,000/30 **Man:** 32 tot.

REMARKS: Ordered 1973; builder went bankrupt, and four others were not delivered. Designed for rescue and fisheries protection. Rescue equipment aft. Refitted 1981 by Lürssen.

◆ **2 British Spear-class patrol craft** Bldr: Fairey Marine, Hamble (In serv. 1978)

**D:** 4.5 tons (fl) **S:** 29 kts **Dim:** 9.1 × 2.9 × 0.8
**M:** 2 diesels; 2 props; 360 hp **Range:** 250/26 **Man:** 3 tot.

REMARKS: GRP construction.

### MISCELLANEOUS

◆ **2 Sea Truck service craft** Bldr: Rotork, U.K. (In serv. 1981)

**D:** 5 tons **S:** 25 kts **Dim:** 12.65 × 3.20 × . . .
**M:** 2 Volvo AQD YOA diesels, 2 props; 240 hp

REMARKS: GRP construction, with bow door. One is builder's model FPB 512 for patrol duties; the other is a Model STW 408.

NOTE: The two British "Ford"-Class patrol boats, *Elmina* (P 13) and *Komenda* (P 14) are no longer in service.

# GREAT BRITAIN

**United Kingdom of Great Britain and Northern Ireland**

PERSONNEL (4-87):

| | Officers | Non-officers | Total |
|---|---|---|---|
| Royal Navy | | | |
| Men | 8,900 | 47,000 | 55,900 |
| Women | 400 | 2,900 | 3,300 |
| Royal Marines | | | |
| Men | 700 | 7,100 | 7,800 |
| Total | 10,000 | 57,000 | 67,000 |

In addition, there were about 22,900 (300 women) Regular Reservists and 5,300 (1,200 women) Royal Naval Volunteer Reserves and 3,300 Royal Marine Reservists (of whom 1,050 are in the Volunteer & Auxiliary). There were also 2,680 members of the Royal Naval Auxiliary Service (RNAS). About 75,000 civilians are employed, including those who man the ships and craft of the Royal Fleet Auxiliary Service (1,000 officers, 100 cadets, 1,150 ratings, 260 Hong Kong Chinese) and the Royal Maritime Auxiliary Service. During 1985–86, Royal Naval Volunteer Reservists rose to 7,800 total, Royal Marine Volunteer Reservists to 1,580, and the Royal Naval Auxiliary Service to 3,242 men and women.

MERCHANT MARINE (1986): 2,256 ships—11,567,117 grt (tankers: 261—4,302,604 grt)

WARSHIPS IN SERVICE, UNDER CONSTRUCTION, OR ON ORDER AS OF 1 JANUARY 1988

| ◆ **3 aircraft carriers** | L | Tons | Main armament |
|---|---|---|---|
| 3 INVINCIBLE | 1977–81 | 16,000 | 1/Sea Dart, 5/Sea Harrier, 9/Sea King |

| ◆ **31 (+9) submarines** | | Tons (surfaced) | |
|---|---|---|---|
| 0 (+4) VANGUARD (nuclear ballistic missile) | 1992– | . . . | 16/Trident D5, 4/533-mm TT |
| 4 RESOLUTION (nuclear ballistic missile) | 1966–68 | 7,500 | 16/Polaris A3, 6/533-mm TT |
| 4 (+3) TRAFALGAR (nuclear attack) | 1981– | 4,200 | 5/533-mm TT |

**WARSHIPS IN SERVICE** *(continued)*

| | | | |
|---|---|---|---|
| 6 SWIFTSURE (nuclear attack) | 1971–79 | 4,200 | 5/533-mm TT |
| 5 VALIANT (nuclear attack) | 1963–70 | 4,000 | 6/533-mm TT |
| 0 (+4 . . .) UPHOLDER | 1986– | 2,160 | 6/533-mm TT |
| 11 OBERON | 1959–66 | 2,030 | 8/533-mm TT |
| ◆ **13 guided-missile destroyers** | | | |
| 4 MANCHESTER | 1980–83 | 3,450 | 1/Sea Dart, 1/114-mm DP, 1/Lynx |
| 8 SHEFFIELD | 1971–80 | 3,150 | 1/Sea Dart, 1/114-mm DP, 1/Lynx |
| 1 BRISTOL | 1969 | 6,100 | 1/Sea Dart, 1/Limbo, 1/Ikara, 1/114-mm DP |
| ◆ **38 (+9 + . . .) frigates** | | | |
| 0 (+4 + . . .) "Duke" | 1987– | 3,000 | Sea Wolf, 1/114-mm AA, 8 Harpoon, 1 helo |
| 1 (+3) CORNWALL | 1984– | 4,200 | 8 Harpoon, Sea Wolf, 1/114-mm AA, 2/Lynx |
| 4 (+2) BOXER | 1981–85 | 4,100 | 4/Exocet, 2/Sea Wolf, 2/40-mm AA, 1/Lynx |
| 4 BROADSWORD | 1976–80 | 3,500 | 4/Exocet, 2/Sea Wolf, 2/40-mm AA, 1/Lynx |
| 6 AMAZON | 1971–75 | 2,750 | 4/MM 38 Exocet, 1/Sea Cat, 1/114-mm DP, 1/Lynx or Wasp |
| 19 LEANDER | 1961–71 | 2,450–650 | 1, 2, or 3/Sea Cat, or 1/Sea Wolf, 2/114-mm and/or 40-mm, 1/Wasp, 4/MM 38 Exocet or Ikara in 15, ASW weapons |
| 2 ROTHESAY | 1957–60 | 2,380 | 2/114-mm DP, 1/Sea Cat, 1/Wasp, 1/Limbo |

◆ **30 (+8) patrol ships, boats, and craft**

◆ **41 (+3) mine warfare ships**

◆ **9 amphibious warfare ships**

## WEAPONS AND SYSTEMS

### A. MISSILES AND BOMBS

◆ **strategic ballistic missiles**

**Trident 2D-5** Bldr: Lockheed

U.S. missile with a delivery vehicle and payload of British design and manufacture, with an independent trajectory capability (MIRV). The agreement for the acquisition of Trident was signed 14–15 July 1980. The submarines to carry Trident will not be ready until the mid-1990s; 80 Trident missiles are to be acquired.

**Polaris A-3TK**

The nuclear-powered ballistic-missile submarines of the *Resolution* class employ Polaris A-3 missiles with a payload package of entry vehicles of British design and manufacture. The payload is designated Chevaline and is composed of six 150-kT warheads with greatly improved penetration aids. Chevaline employs post-boost guidance to improve accuracy and entered service late in 1982, the missile thus being typed Polaris A-3TK.

◆ **surface-to-air missiles**

**Sea Dart (GWS.30)** Bldr: British Aerospace Dynamics Group

Medium-range system (35 miles, interception altitudes from 100 to 60,000 ft)

Length: 4.40 m Diameter: 0.42 m Wingspan: 0.91 m Weight: 550 kg
Propulsion: solid-propellant booster, ramjet sustainer
Guidance: semi-active homing Fire control: Type 909 radar

Fitted on the *Bristol, Sheffield, Manchester,* and *Invincible* classes.
Mk 30 Mod. 0 launcher on the *Bristol;* the lighter Mk 30 Mod. 2 on the *Sheffield* and *Invincible* classes. Improvements in low-altitude capability and response time are being made. 1,000 delivered by 1985. 100 with G.Mk. 39 A1 fragmentation warheads ordered 3-86. 500 had been fired by late 1986. The Type 909 fire-control radars to be updated under 5-87 contract with Marconi.

**Sea Darts and launcher on Liverpool (D 92)** L. & L. Van Ginderen, 11-83

**Sea Wolf (GWS.25)** Bldr: British Aerospace Dynamics Group

Short-range missile system (5,000 m)

Length: 1.9 m Wingspan: 0.56 m Warhead: 13.4 kg
Diameter: 0.3 m Weight: 82 kg
Guidance: radar Speed: Mach 2.5
Fire control: Marconi Type 910 pulse-doppler radar, which permits control of 2-missile salvos, or by electro-optical tracker

Fitted on *Broadsword*-class frigates; being installed on some *Leander* class. Launcher contains six missiles (total weight with missiles: 3,500 kg). Target designation is via the combined Type 967-968 radar. A vertical-launch version (GWS.26) is in development, and a new GWS.25 Mod. 3 fire-control system employing the Marconi Type 911 (ex-805SW) search-and-track radar, with DN 181 Blindfire guidance, and upgraded features to the Type 967-968 radar is now being delivered. A simplified 4-missile adaptation, using the Sea Cat quadruple launcher was being developed with government assistance in 1985.

**Sextuple Sea Wolf launcher** G. Davies, Maritime Photographic, 8-86

**Sea Cat (GWS.20, 22, and 24)** Bldr: Short Bros. and Harland

Length: 1.47 m Wingspan: 0.65 m Range: 5,300 m (max.)
Diameter: 0.2 m Weight: 68 kg
Propulsion: 2-stage solid propellant
Guidance: GWS.22 or GWS.24 radar, or GWS.20 optical system

Launcher normally carries 4 missiles, although a 3-missile, lightweight launcher has been exported.

## MISSILES AND BOMBS *(continued)*

**Quadruple Sea Cat launcher**—with two drill missiles
G. Davies, Maritime Photographic, 8-86

**Javelin (GWS. . . .)** Bldr: Short Bros. and Harland

The Royal Navy began purchase of the hand-held Javelin (successor to Blowpipe) in 6-84 and conducted initial at-sea firings shortly thereafter in HMS *Phoebe*. Guidance is semi-autonomous, line-of-sight. The weapon will be issued to deployed units of all types for terminal defense. The Javelin missile is 1.4 m long, has a range of 4,000 m, and employs a 2-stage rocket motor. A 5-round mount is being developed.

NOTE: The Royal Marines employ mobile Rapier area-defense SAMs.

### ◆ surface-to-surface missiles

The Royal Navy has purchased the MM 38 Exocet GWS.50 (see section on France). It is employed on the *Amazon, Broadsword,* and some units of the *Leander* class.

Two twin trailer-mounted MM 38 Exocet launchers built by Vosper Thornycroft are maintained at Gibraltar by Royal Navy personnel.

In August 1977, it was announced that the U.S. Sub-Harpoon system would be bought for use from all nuclear attack submarines. 300 have been purchased. Additional Harpoons have been procured for use on RAF Nimrod aircraft. Harpoon 1C, for surface launching, is being purchased for "Duke"- and *Cornwall*-class frigates.

### ◆ air-to-surface missiles

AS 12 (see section on France) wire-guided is used from Wasp helicopters on frigates.

**Sea Skua (CL 834)** Bldr: British Aerospace Dynamics Group

Solid propellant

Length: 2.50 m Wingspan: 0.72 m
Diameter: 0.25 m Weight: 145 kg
Speed: Mach 0.8 Range: 15,000 m
Guidance: semi-active Warhead: 20 kg high explosive

Developed for use by Lynx helicopters, which can carry 2 or 4. An export surface ship version is being developed for small combatant use.

**Sea Eagle (P3T)** Bldr: British Aerospace Dynamics Group

Developed from the Anglo-French, television-guided Martel. Sea Eagle is intended for use as an antiship weapon by carrier-based Sea Harrier V/STOL aircraft as well as by land-based Tornado GR-1 and Buccaneer attack aircraft. Using active radar guidance, it employs the French Microturbo/Toulouse TRI-60 engine for propulsion. First aerial launchings took place in the spring of 1981. A Mk 2 version is not to be proceeded with. First launching of a shipboard version 3-87, using solid boosters developed for Indian Sea King helicopter version.

Length: 4.0 m Weight: 600 kg
Diameter: 0.4 m Range: 36+ km
Wingspan: 1.2 m

### ◆ bombs

500- and 1,000-lb conventional bombs are carried on *Invincible*-class carriers for use by Sea Harrier fighter-bombers; nuclear bombs for these aircraft are also available, it was officially stated in 1985.

### ◆ air-to-air missiles

**Sidewinder-1B (AIM-9L)** Bldr: Philco-Ford

Infrared-homing, solid-fueled, Mach 2.5 lightweight weapon employed with Sea Harrier V/STOL aircraft aboard *Invincible*-class carriers and *Hermes*.

Range: 12 nautical miles Weight: 84.4 kg Diameter: 0.127 m
Wingspan: 0.61 m Length: 2.90 m Speed: Mach 2.5

The American AMRAAM (AIM-120A) missile is to be carried by the Sea Harrier FRS.2.

## B. GUNS

**114-mm Mk 6**

Double-barreled, semi-automatic, dual-purpose.

Muzzle velocity: 850 m/sec
Maximum effective range in surface fire: 17,000 m
Maximum effective range in antiaircraft fire: 6,000 m
Rate of fire: 10–12 rounds/min/barrel

Installed on some *Leander*- and all *Rothesay*-class frigates. Uses variable-fuzed shells with proximity and point-detonating fuzes of variable sensitivity.

**114-mm Mk 8**

**Vickers, 114-mm Mk 8 gun and Exocet launchers aboard Alacrity (F 174)**
G. Arra, 1980

Single-barreled, automatic, dual-purpose; has a muzzle brake

Length of barrel: 55 calibers
Maximum effective range in surface fire: 23,000 m
Maximum effective range in antiaircraft fire: 6,000 m
Rate of fire: 25 rounds/min
Arc of elevation: $-10° + 53°$ Shell weight: 21.0 kg

Light gun mount with glass-reinforced plastic housing. Installed on the *Bristol, Sheffield*-class destroyers, and *Amazon*- and *Cornwall*-class frigates.

**Oto Melara 76-mm Compact**

This lightweight weapon is installed in the *Peacock*-class Hong Kong patrol corvettes. See Italian section for characteristics. 80-rpm version in use.

**Bofors 40-mm**

60-caliber guns are used on single Mk 7 and Mk 9 powered mounts; rate of fire on these obsolete weapons is only about 120 rpm.

**Oerlikon 30-mm**

Twin GCM-A02 mounts. Eight procured 1982 from BMARC as emergency close-defense weapons for *Sheffield*-class destroyers. Shared among class, used on units deployed to South Atlantic. Optical lead-computing sights.

**Oerlikon GCM-A02 30-mm gun mount** J. Goss, NavPic

**GUNS** *(continued)*

**Rarden 30-mm LS-30B**

A stabilized Lawrence-Scott single mounting for the BMARC/Oerlikon KCD-30, 30-mm gun. Twenty-five were ordered 9-84 for the "Duke"-class frigates and to begin replacement of old 40-mm mounts. Rate of fire: 650 rpm.

**Goalkeeper 30-mm SGE-30**

General Electric GAU-8A, 30-mm gatling gun in EX-30 mounting co-mounted with H.S.A. radar detect-and-track fire-control system. Six mounts ordered 1984 for close-defense in the *Cornwall*-class frigates; nine more ordered 2-86 for the *Invincible* class. See additional details in Netherlands section.

**Oerlikon 20-mm**

Large numbers of single-barrel GAM-B01 mountings procured 1982–83 to augment close defense on a variety of classes. An 85-caliber weapon with 1,000-rpm firing rate and optical, lead-computing sight on mount.

**General Dynamics Vulcan/Phalanx 20-mm**

Six U.S. Mk 15 Mod. 0 CIWS (Close-In Weapon System) mounts purchased 5-82 for use on the *Invincible*-class carriers. Additional mountings have since been ordered for the *Invincible* class. Uses 6-barreled G.E. Vulcan gatling gun.

**20-mm**

Standard Mk 4 Oerlikon single mounts and a few twin mounts, all of World War II origin, remain in many classes.

**7.62-mm machine guns**

Standard NATO 7.62-mm light machine guns, having been found very useful in the Falklands War for disrupting low-level air attack, have been added in considerable numbers to frigates and destroyers, using simple pintle mountings.

## C. ANTISUBMARINE WEAPONS

**Mk 10 Mortar (Limbo)**

Triple-barreled mortar based on the Squid of World War II. Range: 700 to 1,000 m. Fitted on four *Leander* and both *Rothesay*-class frigates.

**Ikara GWS. 41**

U.S. Mk 46 torpedo below an Australian-designed guided missile launched by a solid-fuel rocket motor. A "super Ikara," with 90-km range, is under development by British Aerospace to meet a Royal Navy requirement for a long-range weapon. No funds were authorized for this program for 1987–88, however.

Maximum range: 18,000 m. See Australia section for further details.

Fitted only on two *Leander*-class frigates.

**Mk 11 depth charge**

Dropped from helicopters against shallow targets. Officially reported that there are also nuclear depth bombs for ASW.

## D. TORPEDOES AND MINES

Triple STWS.1 ASW torpedo tubes on Type 42 destroyer accommodate U.S. Mk 44 and Mk 46 or U.K.-built Stingray torpedoes. Note the swinging bulletproof plate outboard the warhead end of the tubes—another Falklands War lesson learned
L. & L. Van Ginderen, 1984

U.S. Mk 44 and Mk 46 Mod. ASW torpedoes on surface ships and helicopters

The principal torpedoes of British origin are:

- the 50-year-old, straight-running Mk 8 for submarines; replaced by Sub-Harpoon in most nuclear attack submarines
- the wire-guided, submarine-launched Mk 23 for ASW, being phased out
- the wire-guided Mk 24 Tigerfish (ex-Ongar) for submarines; entered service 1980, with 2,000 on order by 1986. To improve reliability, the 600 Mod. 1 in service are to update by mid-1988. Mod. 0 Is ASW only, Mod. 1 is dual-purpose; Mod. 2 entered service 1986 with 134-kg warhead.

  Length: 6.47 m  Speed: 26 kts
  Diameter: .533 m  Range: 16,000 m
  Weight: 1,600 kg

- the NST 75 11, Stingray, lightweight torpedo, which entered service in 1983, for launch by helicopters and by RAF Nimrod ASW aircraft and for surface ships.

  Length: 2.597 m  Speed: 45 kts
  Diameter: 324 mm  Range: 7,000 m
  Weight: 266 kg  Depth: 800 m

  Stingray uses seawater-activated batteries powering an electrically driven pump-jet propulsor and employs active/passive acoustic homing. 2,500 ordered 1-86.
- the heavyweight Spearfish, in development since 1981 to replace the Mk 24 Tigerfish. It has achieved over 70 kts in trials. Weighing some 2,000 kg, it is 8.5 m long and uses a Sundstrand turbine engine; range: about 65 km. To enter service in the late 1980s.
- the air-, ship-, and submarine-launchable Stonefish medium-depth, modular mine and the Dragonfish shallow-water, anti-invasion mine with an 85-kg charge are being procured to replace earlier mines.

  Length: 2.4 m (1.9 exercise)  Warhead: 600 kg
  Diameter: .53 m  Life: 90 days
  Weight: 990 kg (440 kg exercise)  Shelf life: 20 years

- the Hammerhead Advanced Sea Mine is being jointly developed by Marconi and Goodyear (U.S.) for ASW and antiship use for production by mid-1990s. It will have a .53-m diameter.

## E. SONARS

**Type 2031(1) towed passive hydrophone array winch and reel aboard Sirius (F 40)**
L. & L. Van Ginderen, 3-84

◆ **On surface ships**

| No. | Type | Frequency band | Average range (above layer) |
|---|---|---|---|
| **162, 162M** | Sidelooking classification | High | . . . |
| **170B** | Hull, searchlight | High | 2,500 m |
| **174** | Hull, searchlight | High | 2,500 m |
| **177** | Hull, 360° scan | Medium | 6,000 m |
| **184** | Hull, 360° scan | Medium | 7,000 m |
| **185** | Underwater telephone | High | . . . |
| **193, 193M** | Minehunting | High | . . . |
| **199*** | Towed VDS | Medium | 7,000 m |
| **2008** | Underwater telephone | High | . . . |
| **2016** | Hull, 360° scan | Multiple (5.5–6.5–7.5 kHz) | . . . |
| **2031*** | Towed passive array | . . . | . . . |
| **2050** | Hull, 360° scan | 5.5–7.5 kHz | . . . |
| **2059** | PAP-104 tracker | High | . . . |

* 199 is the British version of the Canadian SQS-504. Two versions of the Type 2031 towed passive linear array have been developed: Type 2031(1) for use on four "Exocet *Leander*" frigates, and Type 2031(2) on the "Duke," *Boxer,* and *Cornwall* classes.

Trials with Ferranti's Type 2050 began 1986 on *Jupiter*. Type 2059 is used by minehunters, as an adjunct to Type 193M.

◆ **On submarines**

| | | | |
|---|---|---|---|
| **186** | Passive ("Knout") | Medium | . . . |
| **187** | Active-Passive mine-detection | Low-Medium | . . . |
| **197** | Passive direction-finding | Medium-High | . . . |
| **2001** | Active-Passive | Low | . . . |
| **2007** | Passive | Medium-H/F | . . . |

**SONARS** *(continued)*

**2019**—Active/Passive/Intercept, "PARIS" (Passive/Active Range and Intercept Sonar) in SSNs, SSBNs, *Upholder* class.
**2020**—a 360-degree coverage, low-frequency passive system for *Trafalger*-class nuclear-powered submarines; to be refitted to older classes. Sub version of 2016.
**2023**—a towed linear passive array, based on the U.S. BQR-15, for SSBNs.
**2024**—a towed, linear passive array for use on nuclear-powered attack submarines.
**2040**—under development for the *Upholder*-class diesel-electric submarine; based on the Thomson-CSF "Argonaute" passive system.
**2051**—"Triton"—new Plessey suite on *Oberon*-class diesel submarines; incorporates a "clip-on" towed array and a new, streamlined bowdome.
**2052**—Interim, "clip-on" towed array for SSNs.
**2054**—Plessey-built suite (active/passive/towed passive) for Trident ballistic-missile submarines.

Note: British Aerospace commenced trials 1987 with the ATAS towed linear active/passive array, with a 900-m transmitter section and a 300-mm section for receiving. If adopted, it would succeed the Type 2031 system.

### ◆ On helicopters

| | | | |
|---|---|---|---|
| **195, 195 M** | Dipping | Medium | 3,000 m |

### ◆ Sonobuoys

In use are the Australian SSQ-981 "Barra" (7,000 ordered 1986), the SSQ-904 "Jezebel," and SSQ-954 Miniature DIFAR.

## F. DATA SYSTEMS

**ADA (Action Data Automation):**
**ADAWS 1** Aerial defense system. Fitted on "County"-class destroyers.
**ADAWS 2** Integrated AAW and ASW defense system. Fitted on the *Bristol*.
**ADAWS 4** Integrated AAW and ASW defense system. Fitted on the *Sheffield*- and *Manchester*-class destroyers.
**ADAWS 5** Aerial and ASW defense. Fitted on the *Invincible*-class aircraft carriers.
**CAAIS (Computer-Assisted Action Information System)**
In *Amazon*- and *Broadsword*-class frigates for tactical data-handling; linked to WSA 4 fire-control system.
**CACS 1 (Computer-Assisted Command System)**
To be employed in the *Cornwall*-class frigates. Two Ferranti FM 1600E computers, 12 Argus M700 miniprocessors.

Note: Only the *Invincible*-class carriers and the destroyer *Bristol* have equipment compatible with the LINK 11/NTDS system of the U.S. Navy or the French Navy's SENIT system and other analogous NATO systems.

## G. RADARS

### ◆ Navigation

**978**—(3 cm, I-band), obsolescent, being replaced.
**1002**—(9,650 MHz) for *Porpoise*-class submarines.
**1003**—(. . .) in *Resolution*-, *Swiftsure*-, and *Valiant*-class submarines.
**1006**—(9,445 MHz) in newest surface ships and submarines; navalized Kelvin-Hughes 19/9A.
**1007**—Kelvin-Hughes Series 1600 + Red Pac, I-band (3-cm) nav. radar with manual plot, to replace Type 1006.

Note: Auxiliaries use a number of different commercial navigational radars, primarily the Decca-Racal 1226 and 1229 models.

### ◆ Combined air and surface search

**967/968**—pulse-doppler, paired back-to-back antennas; 967 in D-band (1–2 GHz); 968 in E-band (2–3 GHz). Employed with GWS.25 Sea Wolf system in the *Broadsword* class. Type 967M in development, 1984. Rotates at 30 rpm.
**992Q** (E–F band)—stabilized medium range for low-altitude air-search, surface-search, and target designation. To be replaced by 996/2.
**993** (S-band)—short-range air-search/surface-search and target-detection radar in *Leander*- and *Rothesay*-class frigates; uses wedge-shaped "cheese" antenna.
**994**—Plessey AWS-4; uses 993's antenna. Replacing Type 993.
**996**—Replacement for 992Q in older ships (996/2) and 996/1 version for Type 23 class frigates. Replaces Type 1030 STIR program. Also for target designation. Plessey to manufacture, chosen 9-83; variant of Plessey AWS-9.

### ◆ Air search, early warning

**965**—Metric radar, long-range early warning. On some *Leander*-class frigates.
**965M**—Employs two stacked antennas from the Type 965, with an integral Mk 10 SIF IFF interrogator.
**1022**—Dutch H.S.A. LW-08 radar with a Marconi antenna, on *Invincible*-class, and *Manchester*- and *Sheffield*-class destroyers. Incorporates Cossor 850 IFF interrogator.

Note: Marconi and Thomson-CSF/Selenia are jointly developing a multi-function phased-array radar for the NATO NFR-90 frigate program.

### ◆ Height-finding

**277** (E-band)—controlled by ADAWS 1 computer for fire control of Sea Slug system in the "County" class.

### ◆ Gun-direction

**903** (I-band)—is used in all Mk 6 and Mk 5, 114-mm gun directors (MRS 3).

### ◆ Missile-guidance

**904**—MRS 3 and GWS.22 fire control for the Sea Cat.
**909**—Sea Dart system (also 114-mm Mk 8 gun in the *Sheffield*-class destroyers)
**910**—Tracking radar used with the Sea Wolf (GWS.25) system; also does vertical search in I-/J-band (8–15 GHz)
**911**—Marconi ST805 SW for Sea Wolf GWS.25 Mod. 3 system in *Cornwall* class; uses part of antenna array for the land-based "Blindfire" radar. Also used with GWS.26 (I/K-band). 911(2) version for vertical-launch Sea Wolf.
**912**—Used for Sea Cat (GWS.24) and 114-mm gun control in *Amazon*-class frigates. British designation for Selenia RTN-10X system.

### ◆ For aircraft

**Sea Spray**—For Lynx helicopters—surface-search and target designation
**Blue Fox**—For Sea Harrier—a development of Sea Spray. To be replaced by Blue Vixen.
**Sea Searcher**—For Sea King Mk 5 ASW helicopters, for use in interrogating the LAPADS sonobuoy system.
**Searchwater**—For surface search in Nimrod patrol aircraft and air- and surface-search in Sea King Mk 2 AEW helicopters. Frequency-agile.

## H. COUNTERMEASURES

### ◆ Active Countermeasures

The various active countermeasures systems are described as "outfits":

DLA—6-tubed Sea Gnat multipurpose decoy rocket launcher.
DLB—Plessey Shield 6-tubed launcher, equipped to fire Corvus chaff or infrared decoy rockets.
DLC—Knebworth/Corvus 8-tubed launcher, often with 50-mm flare launcher atop.
DLD—U.S. Hycor Mk 137, 6-tubed launcher for U.S. Mk 36 SRBOC system; several different configurations.
DLE—Plessey Shield launcher for R.F.A. auxiliaries.
DLF—Irvin "Rubber Duck" floating corner reflectors.

**DLC**—Knebworth/Corvus launcher at left and two DLD; Mk 137 launchers at right on *Bristol* (D 23) (1986)

### ◆ Electronic warfare systems

UAA-1—"Abbeyhill," covers 1–18 GHz. Used on most modern destroyer and frigate classes. Passive intercept.
UA-8/9—older passive intercept system. 1–10 GHz
UA-13—passive array covering 12–18 GHz
RCM-3—gate-stealing jammer by Decca—being added to large surface combatants.
670—jammer
675—Thorn EMI Guardian low-cost intercept system under evaluation 1985–87 to replace 670.
Matilda—Microwave Analysis Threat Indication and Launch Direction Apparatus; lightweight, low-cost intercept system by MEL

## I. COMMUNICATIONS

The Royal Navy employs the Skynet Super-High-Frequency (SHF) satellite communications system in carriers, destroyers, and frigates, although since there are not sufficient sets, only units deploying or fully operational carry the twin SCOT (Satellite Communications Terminal) radomes, which are 1–2 m in diameter and operate in the 500-MHz band. Royal Fleet auxiliaries, hydrographic ships, and corvettes of the "Castle" class carry the commercial MARISAT SATCOMM system. Shipboard LF/MF/HF/VHF systems are increasingly integrated and are among the best in the world; single-sideband is extensively employed.

## AIRCRAFT CARRIERS

### ◆ 3 Invincible class

| | Bldr | Laid down | L | In serv. |
|---|---|---|---|---|
| R 05 Invincible | Vickers, Barrow | 20-7-73 | 3-5-77 | 11-7-80 |
| R 06 Illustrious | Swan Hunter, Wallsend | 7-10-76 | 14-12-78 | 20-6-82 |
| R 07 Ark Royal | Swan Hunter, Wallsend | 14-12-78 | 4-6-81 | 1-11-85 |

**D:** R 05: 16,256 tons (19,960 fl); others: 16,860 tons (20,600 fl) **S:** 28 kts
**Dim:** 206.6 (192.87 wl) × 31.89 (27.5 wl) × 6.4 (mean; 8.8 over sonar dome)
**A:** 1/Sea Dart GWS.30 Mod.2 system (II × 1; 22 missiles)—2 or 3/20-mm Mk 15 CIWS (I × 2; R 07: 3)—2/20-mm AA (I × 2)—Aircraft: 5/Sea Harrier—9/Sea King Mk 2/5 (R 05: 8/Sea Harrier—12/Sea King)—see remarks
**Electron Equipt:** Radar: 2/1006, 1/992R, 1/1022, 2/909
Sonar: 1/2016 (R 06: 184), 1/762 echo-sounder, 1/185 telephone
EW: UAA-1 Abbeyhill, 4 DLA RL (VI × 4)
R 06: 2 DLC RL (VIII × 2), 4 DLD (VI × 4)
**M:** 4 Rolls-Royce Olympus TM3B gas turbines; 2 props; 112,000 hp (94,000 sust.)
**Electric:** 14,000 kw **Range:** 7,000/18
**Man:** 131 officers, 869 men (plus 318 aircrew)

Remarks: Redesignated "ASW aircraft carriers" in 1980, previously having been, for political reasons, considered to be a type of cruiser. Only two will be operational at any one time. *Invincible,* ordered 17-4-73 and *Illustrious* had a 7-degree "ski jump" to assist Sea Harrier aircraft in making rolling takeoffs at full combat load. The ramp on *Ark Royal* is 12 degrees and is 12 meters longer. The 183-meter-long by 13.5-m-wide flight deck is slightly angled to port to clear the Sea Dart launcher, which is awkwardly located on the ship's centerline and has been given an elaborate blast shield to protect the aircraft aboard. The single-level hangar has three separate bays, with the amidships bay narrower to permit passage of the gas-turbine exhausts. There are two 9.7 by 16.7-m elevators. The Type 1022 long-range air-search radar uses a Marconi antenna, but has the same electronics as the H.S.A. LW-08. Four MM 38 Exocet launchers were deleted from the design. The electrical generating plant consists of 8 General Electric 1,750-kw alternators driven by Paxman Valenta 16-RPM 200A diesels of 2,700 hp each. *Invincible* deployed with 10 Sea Harrier and 11 Sea King to the Falklands in 4-82, and the ships can accommodate up to 22 Sea King-sized helicopters (with no Sea Harriers) if required, 16 of them in the hangar. Can embark 960 Marines for short periods. *Ark Royal* was completed with 3 Mk 15 CIWS (Vulcan/Phalanx). *Ark Royal* ran first sea trials on 22-10-84; she has the CACS data system; the others had ADAWS-5 as completed.

*Invincible* entered refit at Portsmouth 17-3-86 for modernization. Received hangar modifications to permit stowing 8 Sea Harrier and 12 Sea King, magazine spaces enlarged by 50%, Type 2016 sonar in place of Type 184, Type 996 radar in place of 992R, the CACS data system, the flight deck reconfigured to *Ark Royal*-type 12-degree ramp configuration, and three 30-mm Goalkeeper CIWS in place of the Mk 15 Phalanx—adding 600 tons to her displacement. To complete 1-7-88. *Illustrious* will be similarly updated, followed by *Ark Royal.* All receiving NATO LINK 11.

**Illustrious (R 06)** L. & L. Van Ginderen, 6-87

**Illustrious (R 06)**—shorter ski-jump, Mk 15 CIWS on flight deck aft
G. Davies, Maritime Photographic, 6-87

**Ark Royal (R 07)**—longer ramp, Mk 15 CIWS at extreme bow
G. Davies, Maritime Photographic, 6-87

**Ark Royal (R 07)**—showing port quarter Mk 15 CIWS installation
P. Voss, 11-86

Note: The Improved *Centaur*-class V/STOL carrier *Hermes,* stricken 1-7-85, was transferred to India 14-11-86 and commissioned 12-5-87 as *Viraat.*

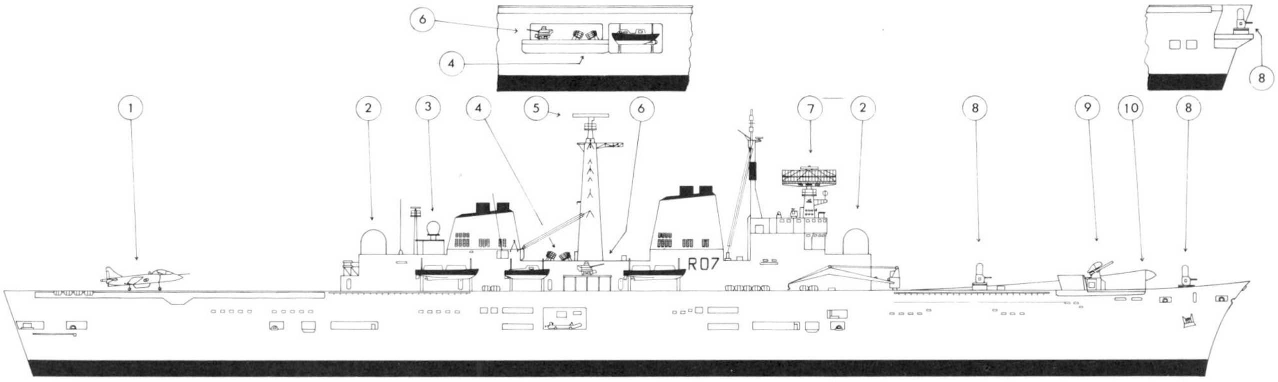


**Ark Royal (R 07)** 1. Sea Harrier FRS.1 2. Type 909 missile-control radar 3. SCOT SHF SATCOMM antenna 4. Shield decoy RL 5. Type 992R radar 6. starboard Mk 15 CIWS location (single 20-mm shown is actually on platform farther forward; "6" in port scrap view is a single 20-mm GAM-B01) 7. Type 1022 early-warning radar 8. Mk 15 CIWS, 20-mm Vulcan/Phalanx AA gun 9. Sea Dart launcher 10. 12-degree "ski-jump" takeoff ramp

AIRCRAFT CARRIERS *(continued)*

**Illustrious (R 06)**—with 5 Sea King, 1 Sea Harrier on deck R.A.N., 9-86

**Ark Royal (R 07)**—showing Mk 15 CIWS mounted right forward
L. &. L. Van Ginderen, 7-87

NAVAL AVIATION

The Flag Officer Naval Air Command (F.O.N.A.C.) is located at the principal naval air facility, Yeovilton, and is chiefly responsible for training and maintenance. Land-based ASW aircraft belong to the RAF and, since the reorganization of the latter, have constituted the Eighteenth, or Maritime, Group of Strike Command. While the group is part of the RAF as regards personnel and equipment, its employment is determined by the Royal Navy's commander in chief.

The Fleet Air Arm consists of:

- First-line squadrons (designation characterized by a group of three figures beginning with an 8) whose missions are: attack, ASW, and helicopter assault.
- Second-line squadrons (designation characterized by a group of three figures beginning with a 7) that are used in schools, tests, and maintenance.

Aircraft of the Royal Navy include (as of 7-87):

| | | Function | Squadron Assignment |
|---|---|---|---|
| 35 (+9) | Sea Harrier FRS.1/2 | attack/interceptor | 800, 801, 899 |
| 2 (+3) | Sea Harrier T.4(N)/T.4 | training | 899 |
| 1 (+1) | Harrier T.4A | training | 899 |
| 77 (+7) | Sea King 2A/5 | ASW, logistics | 706, 810, 814, 819, 820 |
| 33 | Sea King HC.4 | troop-carrying | 707, 846 |
| 10 | Sea King HAS.2A (AEW) | early warning | 849 |
| 28 | Lynx HAS.2 | ASW, attack, training | 702, 815 |
| 50 (+1) | Lynx HAS.3 | ASW, attack | 702, 815 |
| 10 | Wasp HAS.1 | ASW, liaison | 829 |
| 31 | Gazelle Mk 2 | liaison, training | 705 |
| 15 | Wessex HU.5 | training, SAR, troop-carrying | 707, 845, 771 |
| 20 | Jetstream T.2, T.3 | training | 750 |
| 4 | Canberra T.22, T.4 | radar training | Airwork Ltd. (contractor) |
| 24 | Hunter T.8M | training | Airwork, Ltd. |
| 10 (+6) | Falcon 20 | training, transport | FR Aviation, Ltd. |
| 13 | Chipmunk T.10 | training | Flying Grading Unit, Roborough |
| 2 | HS.125 | VIP transport | RAF detachment |
| 3 | Sea Devon | liaison | . . . |
| 1 | Turbine Defender | ASW research | Dir. General Underwater weapons |

**NAVAL AVIATION** *(continued)*

NOTE: All Wessex HU.5 were to strike by 1-4-88, and all Wasp helicopters were to be discarded by 1-1-88. Remaining Sea King HAS.2/2A are converting to HAS.5. All Lynx to update to Lynx Mk 8 from 1989, with 360-degree radar, ASQ-504(V) MAD gear, and Sea Owl EW, but funds may be lacking. ASW-504 and new EW gear will go on Sea King HAS.6 conversions 1989-on. In 1987, 3 Sea King HC.4 and HAS.6 were ordered for delivery 1989 on. The Royal Marines operate 12 Gazelle AH.1 and 4 Lynx AH.2 helicopters. Royal Air Force Maritime Patrol Aircraft of No. 18 (Maritime) Group (as of 1987):

| | Function | Squadron Assignment |
|---|---|---|
| 34 Nimrod MR.2 | Maritime patrol | 42, 120, 201, 206, 236(OCU) |
| 65 Buccaneer S.2 | Maritime strike | 12, 208, 237(OCU) |

**Lynx HAS.3**—with Mk 46 practice torpedo Marconi, 1986

**Sea Harrier FRS.1** L. & L. Van Ginderen, 7-84

**Sea King HAS.5** Westland, 1980

**EH.101**—model Westland, 1986

**Gazelle, of the Royal Marines** M.O.D., 1982

**Sea King HAS. Mk 2** R.N., 12-84

**Nimrod MR.2** 1981

## COMBAT AIRCRAFT

| Type and builder | Mission | Wingspan | Length | Height | Weight | Engine | Max. speed in Mach or in knots | Practical maximum ceiling in feet | Range | Weapons | Remarks |
|---|---|---|---|---|---|---|---|---|---|---|---|
| ◆ **FIXED-WING** | | | | | | | | | | | |
| **Sea Harrier FRS.1** (British Aerospace) | Attack fighter/ interceptor | 7.6 | 14.5 | 3.71 | 10,500 | 1 Rolls-Royce Pegasus 104 vectored-thrust turbojet with 9,750 kg thrust | Mach 0.96; Mach 1.2 (diving) | 50,000+ | VTOL: 50 n.m. STOL: 250 n.m. | 2,270 kg, max total: 4/AIM-9L Sidewinder, 2/30-mm Aden guns, 454-kg bombs (normal load), nuclear weapons | For the *Invincible* class. FRS.2 version (delayed) to receive Blue Vixen radar, AMRAAM air-to-air missiles, and the Pegasus 105 engine. FRS.1 has Blue Fox navigation/ attack radar. |
| **Nimrod MR.2** (British Aerospace) (RAF-operated) | ASW detection and engagement | 35.30 | 38.63 | 9.08 | 80,510 to 87,090 | 4 Rolls-Royce Spey (RB 168-20) Mk 250 jet engines, 5,200-hp thrust each | 450 kts | 42,000 | 12 hrs | Bomb bay for 15-m weapons (6 torpedoes + 10 buoys) 2/Harpoon, 4 Sidewinder | Can carry nuclear depth charges. Last of 34 delivered 1985. |
| ◆ **HELICOPTERS** | | | | | | | | | | | |
| **Wasp HAS.1** (Westland) | ASW, antisurface | Rotor diam. 9.82 | 12.29 | 3.56 | 2,495 | 1 Rolls-Royce Nimbus 503 turboshaft, 710 hp | 104 kts 96 kts (cruising) | 12,000 | 234 n.m. | 1–2/Mk 44 torpedo or 2/AS 12 ASM | On *Amazon*, *Rothesay*, and *Leander* frigates, and survey ships. To discard 1988. |
| **Lynx HAS.2, 3** (Westland) | ASW, antisurface | 12.80 | 15.16 | 3.60 | 4,763 | 2 Rolls-Royce Gem Z turboshafts, 750 hp each (HAS.3: Gem 4; 1,120 hp each) | 145 kts | 12,000 | 1 hr 30 min. (half hovering, half cruising) (approx. 340 n.m.) | 2/Mk 44 or Mk 46 torpedoes 2–4 Sea Skua air-surface missiles | On *Sheffield*, *Amazon*, and *Broadsword* classes. |
| **Wessex HU-5** (Westland) | transport assault, SAR | 17.06 | 20.03 | 4.93 | 5,800 (6,120 max.) | 2 linked Bristol-Siddeley Gnome H 1400 turboshafts with 1,400 hp each | 130 kts | 6,000 hovering 14,000 cruising | 3 hrs (664 n.m. normal) | 14 troops, 2/AS 11 or 12 missiles or 2/50-mm rocket pods | Most have MIR.2 "orange-crop" ESM system. |
| **Sea King** (Westland) **HAS.2, 2A** **HC.4** **HAS.5/6** **HAS.2 (AEW)** | ASW, cargo troop-carrying ASW AEW | 18.9 | 22.15 | | 9,525 | 2 Rolls-Royce Gnome H 1400-1 turboshafts, 1,660 hp each driving a 5-bladed rotor and a tail rotor | 122 kts | 10,000 | 3 hr 15 min | 4/Mk 44, 46 or Stingray torpedoes or 4/Mk 11 depth charges or nuclear depth charges; (HC.4: 2,727 kg stores or 22 troops) | Sea King HAS.2 and 2A have Type 195 sonar, AW 392 radar, and Marconi-Elliot AD580 doppler navigation systems. HAS.5 has Sea Searcher radar (initially: ARI 5955), LAPADS sonobuoy system. HAS.2A has Searchwater air/ surface-search radar. Many now have MIR-2 "Orangecrop" EW system. HAS.6 updates HAS.5 and is to get Canadian ASQ-504(V) MAD gear 1989–91. |
| **Gazelle Mk 2** (Westland/SNIAS) | reconnaissance, liaison | 10.5 | 11.97 | 3.18 | 917/975 | 1 Turbomeca Astazou, turboshaft, 850 hp | 167 kts (140 kts cruise) | . . . | 190 n.m. | rockets | Used by Royal Marines in attack/reconn. duties and by R.N. for training. |
| **EH.101** (Agusta-Westland) | ASW | 18.59 | 22.85 (15.85 folded) | 6.5 | 13,000 (6,917 empty) | 2 General Electric T 700/CT-0 turboshafts, 1,723 hp each | 160 kts | . . . | 4.5 hr on station 100 n.m. operational radius | 4 Stingray torpedoes (2.5 hr at 100 n.m. radius); or 24 troops over 200 n.m. radius; a 4,500 kg underslung | May use Rolls-Royce/Turbomeca RTMK-322 engines. To enter service 1992-on; to acquire 50. |

## BALLISTIC-MISSILE SUBMARINES

NOTE: Royal Navy submarines no longer wear hull numbers. The assigned numbers are included here for reference only.

◆ **0 (+4) Trident D5-carrying** Bldr: Vickers Shipbldg. & Eng., Ltd. (VSEL), Barrow-in-Furness

| | Ordered | Laid down | L | In serv. |
|---|---|---|---|---|
| S . . . VANGUARD | 30-4-86 | 3-9-86 | . . . | 1994 |
| S . . . VICTORIOUS | 10-87 | . . . | . . . | 1995 |
| S . . . N . . . | . . . | . . . | . . . | 1996 |
| S . . . N . . . | . . . | . . . | . . . | 1997 |

**Vanguard**—artist's rendering M.O.D., 1986

**BALLISTIC-MISSILE SUBMARINES** *(continued)*

**D:** 15,850 tons (submerged) **S:** . . . kts **Dim:** 149.30 × 12.80 × 10.10
**A:** 16/Trident D5 ballistic missiles—4/553/mm TT (Sub-Harpoon and torpedoes)
**Electron Equipt:** Radar: 1/1007
Sonar: Type 2054 suite: active, passive, intercept; 2046 towed array; 2019
**M:** 1 Vickers/Rolls-Royce PWR 2 pressurized-water reactor, GEC steam turbines; 1 pump-jet prop; 22,500 hp
**Man:** 130 tot.

Remarks: Use of the Trident D5 missile with 8 multiple, independent re-entry vehicle (MIRV) warheads decided 3-82, necessitating use of U.S. *Ohio*-class midsection (although it will be shorter, as eight fewer missiles will be carried). Will replace *Resolution* class and require refit only every 8–9 years. To have anechoic hull coating. U.S. Rockwell SINS Mk 2 inertial navigation system, TDHSI (Tactical Data Handling System, Improved). Program experiencing delays and cost-overruns.

◆ **4 Resolution class**

| | Bldr | Laid down | L | In serv. |
|---|---|---|---|---|
| S 22 Resolution | Vickers-Armstrong, Barrow | 26-2-64 | 15-9-66 | 2-10-67 |
| S 23 Repulse | Vickers-Armstrong, Barrow | 12-3-65 | 4-11-67 | 28-9-68 |
| S 26 Renown | Cammell Laird, Birkenhead | 25-6-64 | 25-2-67 | 15-11-68 |
| S 27 Revenge | Cammell Laird, Birkenhead | 19-5-65 | 15-3-68 | 4-12-69 |

**Repulse (S 23)** L. & L. Van Ginderen, 10-76

**Renown (S 26)** M.O.D., 1986

**D:** 7,600/8,500 tons **S:** 20/25+ kts **Dim:** 129.54 × 10.06 × 9.15
**A:** 16/Polaris A3TK—6/533-mm TT (bow) **Man:** 156 tot.
**Electron Equipt:** Radar: 1/1003
Sonar: 1/2001, 1/2007, 2023 or 2024 towed passive array, 2019 intercept
**M:** 1 Rolls-Royce PWR 1 pressurized-water reactor; 1 English-Electric turbine; 1 prop; 15,000 hp

Remarks: Characteristics are very similar to those of the U.S. *Lafayette* class, including the propulsion machinery, the launching and guidance systems, and the inertial navigation system. The original A3TK missiles were furnished by the U.S., but the 6 Cheveline MRV warheads of 150 kilotons each re-entry vehicles are of British conception and construction; introduced 1982 on S 26; S 22 (in refit 8-82 to 10-84) in 1984, and S 23 (refit 10-84 to 4-87) in 1986. Each ship has two crews, as in U.S. Navy SSBNs. Main ship's service turboalternator produces 1,700 kw. Have diesel generator-driven electric emergency drive.

**NUCLEAR-PROPELLED ATTACK SUBMARINES**

◆ **0 (+1 + . . .) SSN 20 class** Bldr: Vickers (VSEL), Barrow-in-Furness

Remarks: Design study contract 1-87 to Rolls-Royce for PWR 2 reactor derivative to power the first of a new class of SSNs to be ordered in 1990.

◆ **4 (+3) Trafalgar class** Bldr: Vickers, Barrow-in-Furness

| | Ordered | Laid down | L | In serv. |
|---|---|---|---|---|
| S 107 Trafalgar | 7-4-77 | 25-4-79 | 1-7-81 | 27-5-83 |
| S 110 Turbulent | 28-7-78 | 8-5-80 | 1-12-82 | 28-4-84 |
| S 117 Tireless | 5-7-79 | 1981 | 13-7-84 | 5-10-85 |
| S 118 Torbay | 26-6-81 | 12-82 | 8-3-85 | 7-2-87 |
| S 91 Trenchant | 22-3-83 | 28-10-85 | 4-11-86 | 1989 |
| S 92 Talent | 10-9-84 | . . . | 1989 | 1990 |
| S 93 Triumph | 3-1-86 | . . . | . . . | 1991 |

**Turbulent (S 110)** L. & L. Van Ginderen, 8-86

**Tireless (S 117)** L. & L. Van Ginderen, 9-86

**Trafalgar (S 107)**—in dry dock, showing submerged bow planes, bow form, and sonar window L. & L. Van Ginderen, 8-84

**D:** 4,700 tons surf. (5,208 sub.) **S:** 30 submerged **Dim:** 85.38 × 9.83 × 8.25
**A:** 5/533-mm TT fwd (20 Mk 24 torpedoes/UGM-84B2 Sub-Harpoon)
**Electron Equipt:** Radar: 1/1006—Sonar: 2001, 2020, 2026 towed array, 197, 183
**M:** 1 reactor, 2 English Electric turbines; 1 shrouded pump-jet prop; 15,000 hp (1 Paxman 400-hp auxiliary propulsion diesel, electric drive)
**Man:** 14 officers, 116 men **Endurance:** 85 days

Remarks: An improved version of the *Swiftsure* class. Coated with rubber compound anechoic tiles to reduce radiated and reflected noise. S 107 has a standard, 7-bladed propeller. Diving depth: 300 m operating/590 m max.

◆ **6 Swiftsure class** Bldr: Vickers, Barrow-in-Furness

| | Ordered | Laid down | L | In serv. |
|---|---|---|---|---|
| S 104 Sceptre | 1-11-71 | 25-10-73 | 20-11-76 | 14-2-78 |
| S 108 Sovereign | 16-5-69 | 18-9-70 | 22-2-73 | 22-7-74 |
| S 109 Superb | 20-5-70 | 16-3-72 | 30-11-74 | 13-11-76 |
| S 111 Spartan | 7-2-73 | 26-3-76 | 7-4-78 | 22-9-79 |
| S 112 Splendid (ex-*Severn*) | 26-5-76 | 23-11-77 | 5-10-79 | 21-3-81 |
| S 126 Swiftsure | 3-11-67 | 6-6-69 | 7-9-71 | 17-4-73 |

**D:** 4,000 light/4,200/4,500 tons **S:** 20/28 kts **Dim:** 82.90 × 9.83 × 8.25
**A:** 5/533-mm bow TT (20 Mk 8 and Mk 24 torpedoes/UGM-84B2 Sub-Harpoon)
**Electron Equipt:** Radar: 1/1003
Sonar: 2001 or 2020 active/passive, 2007 active/passive, 2019 intercept, 2024 towed passive array, 197, 183
**M:** 1 reactor; 2 English Electric turbines; 1 prop or pump-jet; 15,000 hp (1 Paxman 400-hp auxiliary propulsion diesel, electric drive)
**Man:** 12 officers, 85 men (berthing)—but 120 normally aboard

## NUCLEAR-PROPELLED ATTACK SUBMARINES *(continued)*

**Spartan (S 111)** S. Terzibaschitsch, 6-86

**Sovereign (S 108)** P. Voss, 7-86

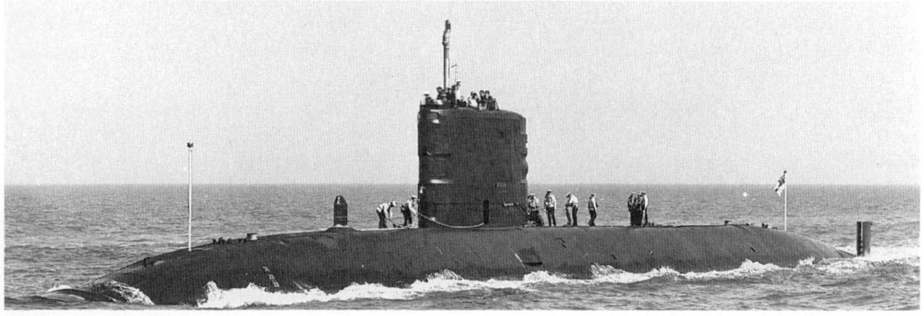

**Superb (S 109)**—with anechoic coating L. & L. Van Ginderen, 8-87

REMARKS: High-performance, very quiet submarines with excellent passive sonars. Have 112-cell battery. The forward diving planes are below the surfaced waterline and retract within the outer hull. DCB weapons-control system, with two Ferranti 1600B computers. To receive Type 2020 sonar in place of 2007, beginning with S 109 in refit ending 28-9-85. S 108 refitted 1983 to 24-11-84. S 104 refit 1986–87, S 111 13-10-86 to 7-87, both with 2020, new 12-year reactor cores, 2024 towed array, new decoy system.

### ◆ 5 Valiant class

| | Bldr | Laid down | L | In serv. |
|---|---|---|---|---|
| S 46 CHURCHILL | Vickers, Barrow | 30-6-67 | 20-12-68 | 15-7-70 |
| S 48 CONQUEROR | Cammell Laird | 5-12-67 | 29-8-69 | 9-11-71 |
| S 50 COURAGEOUS | Vickers, Barrow | 15-5-68 | 7-3-70 | 16-10-71 |
| S 102 VALIANT | Vickers, Barrow | 22-1-62 | 3-12-63 | 18-7-66 |
| S 103 WARSPITE | Vickers, Barrow | 10-12-63 | 25-9-65 | 18-4-67 |

**Conqueror (S 48)** L. & L. Van Ginderen, 3-87

**Conqueror (S 48)** L. & L. Van Ginderen, 10-86

**D:** 3,500/4,200/4,900 tons **S:** 20/28 kts **Dim:** 86.87 × 9.83 × 8.25
**A:** 6/533-mm TT fwd (26 Mk 8 and Mk 24 torpedoes/UGM-84B2 Sub-Harpoon)
**Electron Equipt:** Radar: 1/1003
Sonar: 2001, 2007, 197, 183, 2052 towed array, 2019 intercept
**M:** 1 pressurized-water reactor; 2 English-Electric GT; 1 prop; 15,000 hp
**Man:** 13 officers, 90 men

REMARKS: The propulsion plant is of entirely British design and construction. Diving depth: 300 m. Have a 112-cell emergency battery. The hull form of this class is a development of the *Dreadnought.* In 1967 the *Valiant* made a nonstop, submerged cruise from Singapore to Great Britain in 28 days (12,000 miles). S 46 completed trials with Sub-Harpoon missiles in 2-80 and was in "Long Refit" until 7-5-83. All but S 103 eventually to get Type 2020 sonar in place of 2001. S 46 has anechoic rubber coating on sail and hullsides. S 50, used for Spearfish torpedo trials, completed second major refit 26-9-86. S 102 in refit 1986–87. S 103 began refit 12-87. S 48 completed short refit 10-87 with new prototype sonars, displays, and computers for 2-year trial period.

## TORPEDO ATTACK SUBMARINES

### ◆ 0 (+4 + . . .) Upholder class (Type 2400)

| | Bldr | Laid down | L | In serv. |
|---|---|---|---|---|
| S 40 UPHOLDER | VSEL, Barrow-in-Furness | 2-86 | 2-12-86 | 3-88 |
| S . . . UNSEEN | Cammell-Laird, Birkenhead | 12-8-87 | 1988 | 1991 |
| S . . . URSULA | Cammell-Laird, Birkenhead | . . . | . . . | 1992 |
| S . . . UNICORN | Cammell-Laird, Birkenhead | . . . | . . . | 1993 |

**D:** 1,870 standard/2,185 surfaced/2,400 submerged tons **S:** 12/20 kts
**Dim:** 70.26 (47.5 pressure hull) × 7.60 × 5.50
**A:** 6/533-mm TT fwd (18 tot. Mk 24 and/or Spearfish torpedoes, UGM-84B2 Sub-Harpoon)

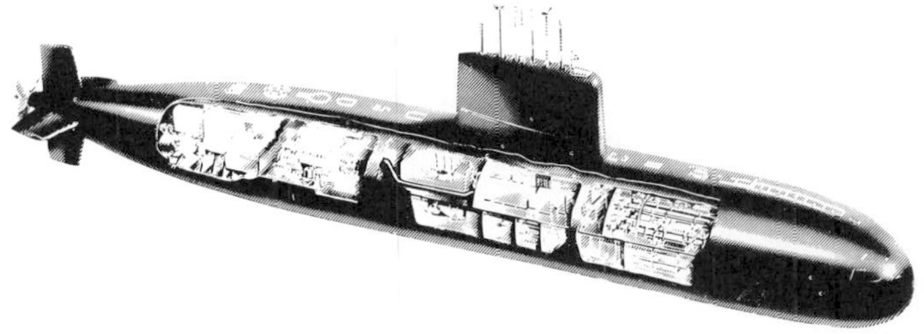

**Upholder (Type 2400)** Vickers, 1981

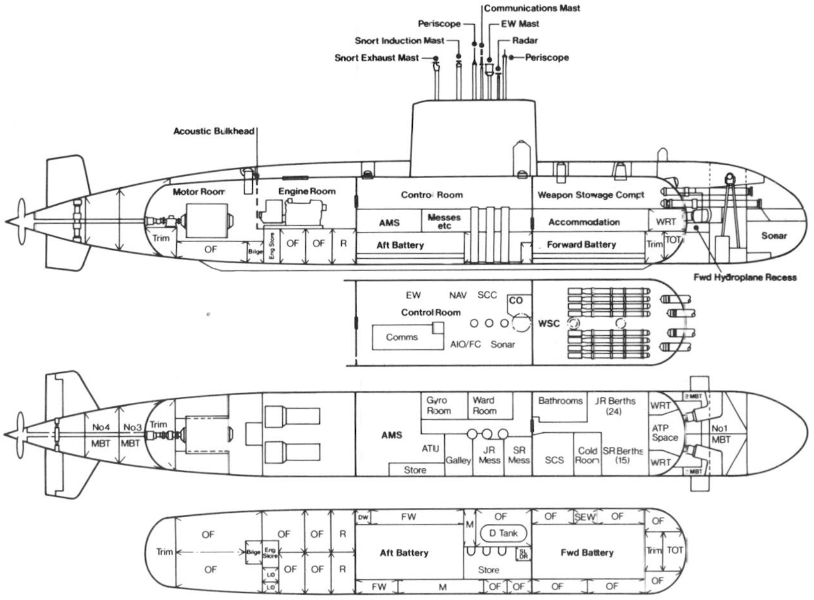


**Layout of Upholder** Royal Institute of Naval Architects

**TORPEDO ATTACK SUBMARINES** *(continued)*

**Electron Equipt:** Radar: 1/1007—EW: Decca Porpoise
Sonar: Type 2040 active/passive, Micropuffs passive, 2046 towed array, 2019 (PARIS) intercept
**M:** 2 Paxman Valenta 16 RPA 200SZ 16-cyl. diesel generators, 2,035 hp each, 2 G.E.C. 2,500-kw alternators; 1/7-bladed prop; 5,400 hp
**Endurance:** 49 days **Fuel:** 200 tons **Range:** 10,000+/. . . (snorkel)
**Man:** 7 officers, 37 men

Remarks: All to have names beginning with "U." Based on the Vickers commercial Type 2400 design and are intended to provide successors to the *Oberon* class. The first unit was ordered late 1983, the next three on 3-1-86. No more to be ordered until 1989; was to be a class of 12. Have rubber anechoic hull coating. Class intended to operate 15,000 hrs (7 years) between overhauls. Have 11 percent reserve buoyancy when surfaced. Two 240-cell lead-acid batteries, 6,080 amp/hr at one-hour rate, 8,800 amp/hr. at five-hour rate. Barr & Stroud CK 35 search periscope with Decca EW array; CH 85 attack scope with infrared capability. Will be able to snorkel at 19 kts 250+ m diving depth. DCC weapons control, with two Ferranti FM 1600E computers, Thorn E.M.T. 1553B data system. Inertial navigation system. Type 2040 sonar is a version of the Thomson-CSF Argonaute system. The 2040's cylindrical array is at the bow, with intercept hydrophones arranged along the sides. The sail has a glass-reinforced plastic skin. The fifth and later units may be of a stretched 3,000-ton surfaced displacement version to obtain longer endurance; will also have a more powerful propulsion plant.

◆ **11 Oberon class**

| | Bldr | Laid down | L | In serv. |
|---|---|---|---|---|
| S 10 Odin | Cammell Laird | 27-4-59 | 4-11-60 | 3-5-62 |
| S 12 Olympus | Vickers-Armstrong | 4-3-60 | 14-6-61 | 7-7-62 |
| S 13 Osiris* | Vickers-Armstrong | 26-1-62 | 29-11-62 | 11-1-64 |
| S 14 Onslaught | HM Dockyard, Chatham | 8-4-59 | 24-9-60 | 14-8-62 |
| S 15 Otter* | Scotts SB, Greenock | 14-1-60 | 15-5-61 | 20-8-62 |
| S 16 Oracle* | Cammell Laird | 26-4-60 | 26-9-61 | 14-2-63 |
| S 17 Ocelot | HM Dockyard, Chatham | 17-11-60 | 5-5-62 | 31-1-64 |
| S 18 Otus | Scotts, SB, Greenock | 31-5-61 | 17-10-62 | 5-10-63 |
| S 19 Opossum* | Cammell Laird | 21-12-61 | 23-5-63 | 5-6-64 |
| S 20 Opportune | Scotts SB, Greenock | 26-10-62 | 14-2-64 | 29-12-64 |
| S 21 Onyx | Cammell Laird | 16-11-64 | 18-8-66 | 20-11-67 |

* modernized units

**Onslaught (S 14)**—standard bow dome L. & L. Van Ginderen, 11-86

**Opossum (S 19)**—with new bow dome L. & L. Van Ginderen, 9-86

**Osiris (S 13)**—after modernization B. Sullivan, 5-87

**D:** 1,650/2,080/2,450 tons **S:** 17.5 kts **Dim:** 89.92 (87.45 pp) × 8.07 × 5.48
**A:** 8/533-mm TT (6 fwd, 2 short aft; 18 Mk 8 and Mk 24 torpedoes)
**Electron Equipt:** Radar: 1/1006 (S 07, 08: 1/1002)
Sonar: 2007, 186, 187 (S 15, S 19, S 21: 2051 in place of 2007)
**M:** 2/1,840-hp Admiralty Standard Range 16VVS-AS21, 1,740-hp diesels, electric drive; 2 props; 6,000 hp
**Endurance:** 56 days **Fuel:** 298 m³ (446 m³ emergency)
**Man:** 6 officers, 62 men (S 08: 65 tot., S 07: 71 tot.)

Remarks: Conventional propulsion and hull form. Streamlined sail. Maximum depth: 200 meters. Snorkel. Air-conditioned. Excellent living spaces. Batteries with 448 total cells provide 5,300 amp/hr at 1-hr rate; 7,420 amp/hr at 5-hr rate. *Olympus* completed a 2-year refit 7-84 with a new aluminum alloy sail and a 5-man exit chamber for Special Boat Service swimmers. The two after torpedo tubes, for Mk 23 short ASW torpedoes, are no longer used. The first *Onyx* transferred to Canada (1-64) and renamed the *Ojibwa;* another *Onyx* was built. Canada ordered three ships of this class, Australia six, Chile two, and Brazil three. The *Grampus* (S 04) of the *Porpoise* class was stricken in 1976, *Rorqual* (S 02) in 1976, *Narwhal* (S 03), *Cachelot* (S 06) in 1977, *Finwhale* (S 05) in 1978, and *Porpoise* (S 01) in 8-82, sunk 10-85 as Stingray target. Sale of the *Cachelot* to Egypt was canceled.

All but S 12 and S 20 are being modernized with the Type 2051 sonar forward and Type 2046 "clip-on" passive towed array, Ferranti-Gresham Lion Oberon Dual Guidance System (to permit firing 2 Mk 24 torpedoes at once), and MEL Manta EW intercept gear. *Oberon* (S 09) stricken 10-12-86 and sold 2-87 to Seaforth Group for foreign sale. *Orpheus* (S 11) stricken 6-87. *Sealion* (S 07) stricken 12-87; *Walrus* (S 08) stricken 10-12-86 and sold to Seaforth Group 2-87 for refurbishment for foreign sale.

## GUIDED-MISSILE DESTROYERS

◆ **4 Manchester class (Type 42C)**

| | Bldr | Laid down | L | In serv. |
|---|---|---|---|---|
| D 95 Manchester | Vickers, Barrow | 19-5-79 | 24-11-80 | 16-12-82 |
| D 96 Gloucester | Vosper Thornycroft | 26-10-79 | 2-11-82 | 9-85 |
| D 97 Edinburgh | Cammell Laird | 8-9-80 | 14-4-83 | 18-12-85 |
| D 98 York | Swan Hunter | 18-1-80 | 21-6-82 | 9-8-85 |

**York (D 98)** G. Arra, 1986

**Manchester (D 95)**—still with old decoy launchers; note square stern, compared to earlier Type 42B group L. & L. Van Ginderen, 6-87

**Edinburgh (D 97)** L. & L. Van Ginderen, 7-86

**GUIDED-MISSILE DESTROYERS** *(continued)*

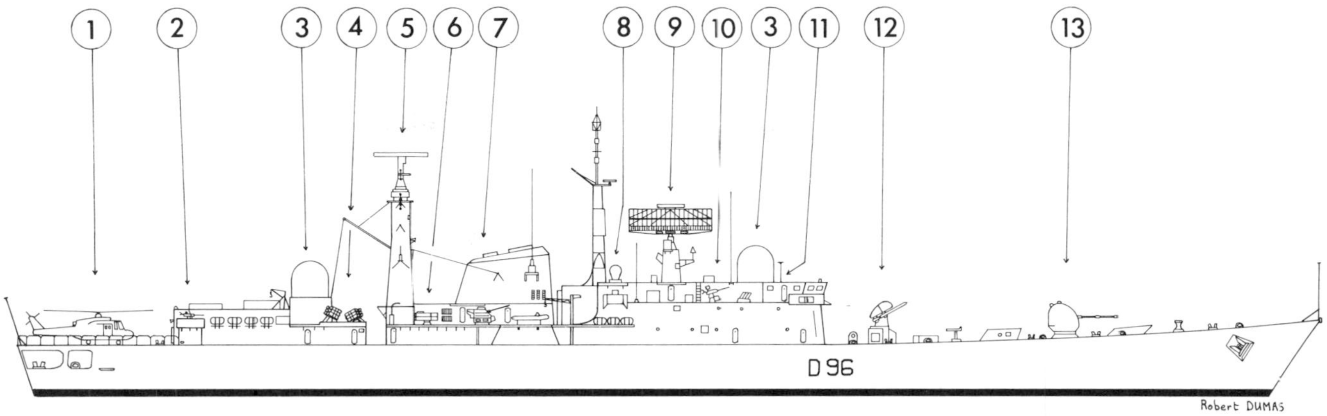


**Gloucester (D 96)** 1. Lynx helicopter 2. 20-mm Mk 4 AA 3. Type 909 f.c. radar 4. DLA decoy RL 5. 992Q radar 6. STWS.1 ASW TT 7. twin 30-mm Oerlikon GCM-A02 AA 8. SCOT SATCOMM antenna for Skynet 9. Type 1022 search radar 10. 20-mm GAM-B01 AA 11. Mk 137 decoy RL for Mk 36 SRBOC system (only on D 95) 12. Sea Dart launcher 13. 114-mm Mk 8 DP gun

**D:** 4,100 tons (4,775 fl) **S:** 29.5 kts (18 cruising)
**Dim:** 141.12 (132.3 wl) × 14.90 × 5.80 (4.20 hull)
**A:** 1/Sea Dart GWS.30 syst. (II × 1, 40 missiles)—1/114-mm Mk 8 DP—4/30-mm Oerlikon AA (II × 2)—4/20-mm AA (I × 4)—6/324-mm STWS.1 ASW TT (III × 2)—1/Lynx helicopter
**Electron Equipt:** Radar: 1/1006, 1/992Q, 1/1022, 2/909
Sonar: 1/2016 (D 95: 1/184M, 1/162M)
EW: UAA-1 passive, 2/Type 670 active, 4/DLA chaff RL (VI × 4)—D 35: 2/DLC Knebworth/Corvus, (VIII × 2), 2/DLD Mk 36 SRBOC (VI × 2)
**M:** COGOG: 2 Rolls-Royce Olympus TM3B gas turbines of 27,200 hp each for boost, 2 Rolls-Royce Tyne RM1C of 5,340 hp each for cruise; 2/5-bladed CP props; 54,400/10,680 hp
**Electron Equipt:** 4,000 kw (4/1,000-kw diesel sets) **Range:** 4,750/18
**Fuel:** 610 tons **Man:** 26 officers, 81 senior petty officers, 194 men

Remarks: A lengthened version of the *Sheffield* class intended to provide better seaworthiness, endurance, and habitability, but having no change in armament despite the additional 16-m overall length. Have larger Sea Dart magazine. The ADAWS 7 combat data system is carried. Have LINK 11 data link system. D 95 ordered 10-11-78, D 96 on 27-3-79, and D 97 and D 104 on 25-4-79. No additional ships of this class are planned. Completion of D 97 delayed by strike at yard. D 96 delivered 16-5-85.

All are to have Type 992Q radar replaced by Type 996. The close-in AA suite is temporary, consisting of 4/20-mm AA (two each Mk 4 aft and Oerlikon GAM-B01 abreast bridge) and two twin 30-mm amidships; this *may* be replaced with Sea Wolf and/or a modern close-defense gun. D 95 has older sonar suite and earlier decoy rocket launchers. Several 7.62-mm mg are carried, including one on each bridge wing. Active EW jammers flank the Type 1022 radar's pylon. All will receive three refits during planned 22-year service and will get Type 2050 sonar in place of their present hull-mounted sets.

◆ **8 Sheffield class (Type 42)**

| | Bldr | Laid down | L | In serv. |
|---|---|---|---|---|
| D 86 Birmingham | Cammell Laird | 28-3-72 | 30-7-73 | 3-12-76 |
| D 87 Newcastle | Swan Hunter | 21-2-73 | 24-4-75 | 23-3-78 |
| D 88 Glasgow | Swan Hunter | 7-3-74 | 14-4-76 | 24-5-79 |
| D 89 Exeter | Swan Hunter | 22-7-76 | 25-4-78 | 19-9-80 |
| D 90 Southampton | Vosper Thornycroft | 21-10-76 | 29-1-79 | 23-7-81 |
| D 91 Nottingham | Vosper Thornycroft | 6-2-78 | 12-2-80 | 8-4-83 |
| D 92 Liverpool | Cammell Laird | 5-7-78 | 25-9-80 | 9-7-82 |
| D 108 Cardiff | Vickers, Barrow | 3-11-72 | 22-2-74 | 19-10-79 |

**D:** 3,150 tons (4,100 fl) **S:** 28 kts (18 cruising)
**Dim:** 125.0 (119.5 pp) × 14.34 × 5.8 (4.2 hull)
**A:** 1/Sea Dart GWS.30 Mod. 2(II × 1, 20 missiles)—1/114-mm Mk 8 DP—4/30-mm Oerlikon AA (II × 2) (D 86, D 87, D 89: 2/20-mm Mk 15 CIWS)—4/20-mm AA (I × 4)—6/324-mm STWS.1 ASW TT (III × 2)—1/Lynx helicopter—see Remarks
**Electron Equipt:** Radar: 1/1006, 1/1022, 1/992Q, 2/909
Sonar: 1/184M (D 88: 2016), 1/162M
EW: UAA-1 passive, 2/Type 670 active (some), 2/DLC Knebworth/Corvus chaff RL (VIII × 2), 2/DLD Mk 36 SRBOC (VI × 2)
**M:** COGOG; 2 Rolls-Royce Olympus TM3B gas turbines, 27,200 hp each for high speed; 2 Rolls-Royce Tyne RM1A gas turbines, 4,100 hp each for cruising; 2/5-bladed CP props (D 89 and later Tyne RM1C, 5,340 hp each)
**Electric:** 4,000 kw (4/1,000-kw diesel sets) **Range:** 650/30; 4,500/18
**Man:** 26 officers, 273 men maximum (normal 250–280 tot.)

Remarks: Have ADAWS 4 tactical data system. *Cardiff,* delayed by labor problems, was completed by Swan Hunter. Completion of *Glasgow* delayed by fire 9-76. All

**Glasgow (D 88)** Pradignac & Leo, 10-86

**Southampton (D 90)** G. Davies, Maritime Photographic, 6-87

**Exeter (D 89)**—U.S. Mk 15 Phalanx CIWS abreast stack, radomes temporarily off Type 909 f.c. radars L. & L. Van Ginderen, 3-87

**Nottingham (D 91)** L. & L. Van Ginderen, 2-87

**GUIDED-MISSILE DESTROYERS** *(continued)*

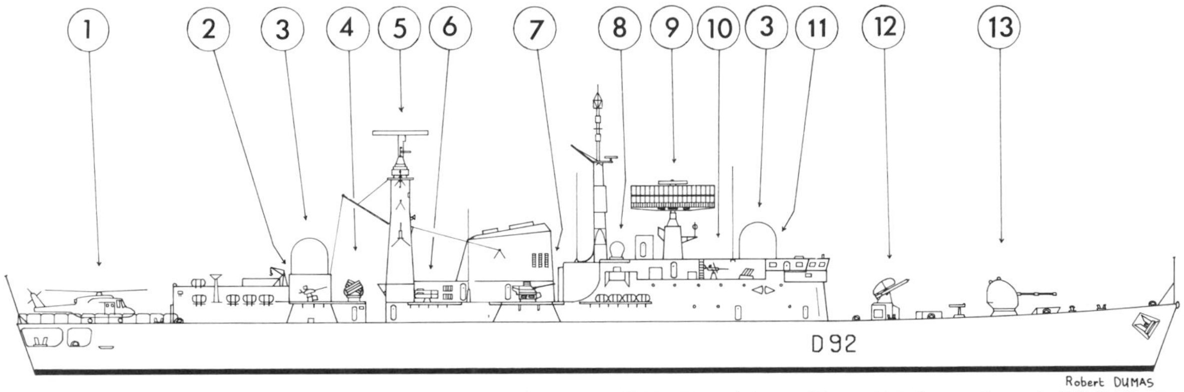


**Liverpool (D 92)** 1. Lynx helicopter 2. 20-mm Oerlikon GAM-B01 AA 3. Type 909 f.c. radar 4. DLC Knebworth/Corvus chaff RL 5. Type 992Q surface/air-search radar 6. triple STWS.1 ASW TT 7. twin 30-mm Oerlikon GCM-A02 AA 8. SCOT SATCOMM antenna for Skynet 9. Type 1022 air-search radar 10. 20-mm Mk 4 AA 11. DLD Mk 137 decoy launcher for Mk 36 SRBOC system 12. Sea Dart launcher 13. 114-mm Mk 8 DP gun

can carry SCOT radomes for Skynet SHF satellite communications system. Very cramped ships. Helicopter used for surveillance and attack (Sea Skua missiles) as well as ASW. Have "Agouti" bubble ejector system for propellers (which rotate inwardly) to reduce cavitation noise. Two pair fin stabilizers fitted. D 89 and later had a taller mainmast and Type 1022 radar forward vice Type 965M; Type 965M was replaced in 4 early ships, beginning with D 108 and D 87 in 1984. Those same ships are updated with the ADAWS 7 data system and stack water spray equipment to reduce IR signature. In 1987 it was announced that this class would be given three lifetime refits, guaranteeing 22-year retention; the Sea Dart system is to be improved.

Class prototype, *Sheffield* (D 80), foundered 10-5-82, having been hit by an Argentine AM 39 Exocet missile on 4-5-82. *Coventry* (D 118) was lost to bombs on 25-5-82. This class was found to be deficient in damage-control during the Falklands War and also to be limited in sensor capability and self-defense, although the Sea Dart system functioned effectively.

As an interim measure, all ships have had 2/20-mm Oerlikon GAM-B01 AA mounts added on platforms abreast the after Type 909 radome, while deploying ships mount twin Oerlikon GCM-A02 30-mm mounts (on-mount sights only) on platforms that replaced the boats, abreast the stack. U.S.-supplied Mk 137 chaff rocket launchers (DLD) are now mounted just abaft the pilothouse, and some ships are receiving enhanced electronic warfare suites. The Type 992Q radar is to be replaced by the new Type 996, and Type 2016 sonar is to replace the Type 184M. All received 2/7.62-mm mg on the bridge wings. U.S. Mk 15 Vulcan/Phalanx CIWS replaced 30-mm AA in D 86, D 89 in 1987; will be added to others as well.

◆ **1 Bristol (Type 82) class (Cadet Training Ship)**

| | Bldr | Laid down | L | In serv. |
|---|---|---|---|---|
| D 23 Bristol | Swan Hunter | 15-11-67 | 30-6-69 | 31-3-73 |

**D:** 6,100 tons (7,100 fl) **S:** 28 kts
**Dim:** 154.60 (149.90 wl) × 16.77 × 5.20 (6.85 over sonar)
**A:** 1/Sea Dart GWS.30 (II × 1, 40 missiles)—1/114-mm Mk 8 DP—4/30-mm AA (II × 2)—4/20-mm AA (I × 4)—2 Mk 7, 2 GAM-B01
**Electron Equipt:** Radar: 1/1006, 1/1022, 1/992Q, 2/909
Sonar: 1/184M, 1/162M
EW: UAA-1 intercept, 970 jammers, 4/DLD Mk 36 SRBOC RL (VI × 4), 2/DLC Knebworth/Corvus RL (VIII × 2)
**M:** COSAG; 2 A.E.I. GT (15,000 hp each) and 2 Rolls-Royce Olympus TM1A gas turbines (22,300 hp each); 2 props; 74,600 hp
**Boilers:** 2 Babcock & Wilcox, 49.2 kg/cm² pressure, 510°C superheat
**Electric:** 7,000 kw **Range:** 5,000/18 **Man:** 29 officers, 378 men, 100 cadets

Remarks: Designed as an escort for the 50,000-ton aircraft carrier *Furious* when construction of the latter was being considered. There were to be eight in the class, but this ship, ordered in 10-66, was the only one built. Four pair fin stabilizers. Although nominally commissioned in 1973, she had not been accepted for active service by the time of her first refit in 1976–78. Equipped with the LINK 11 automated action data communications system, for the U.S. NTDS or French SENIT systems, the British LINK 10 and LINK 14. Equipped with the ADAWS 2 data system. Designated flagship of the Third Flotilla in 1980 and given U.S. WSC-3 satellite communications equipment. Can land a helicopter, but has no hangar. Limbo triple ASW mortar removed 1978. Generally considered an expensive failure, but is now Britain's largest non-carrier surface combatant. Was to have been stricken in 1985, but will now be retained and equipped with a new point-defense gun system. U.S. Mk 36 Super RBOC chaff, two twin Oerlikon GCM-A02, 30-mm AA, and two Oerlikon GAM-B01, 20-mm AA added 1983. Boats removed. Had boiler explosion 17-7-84, just prior to entering refit, 984 to 2-86,

**Bristol (D 23)** C. & S. Taylor, 6-86

**GUIDED-MISSILE DESTROYERS** *(continued)*

**Bristol (D 23)** C. & S. Taylor, 6-86

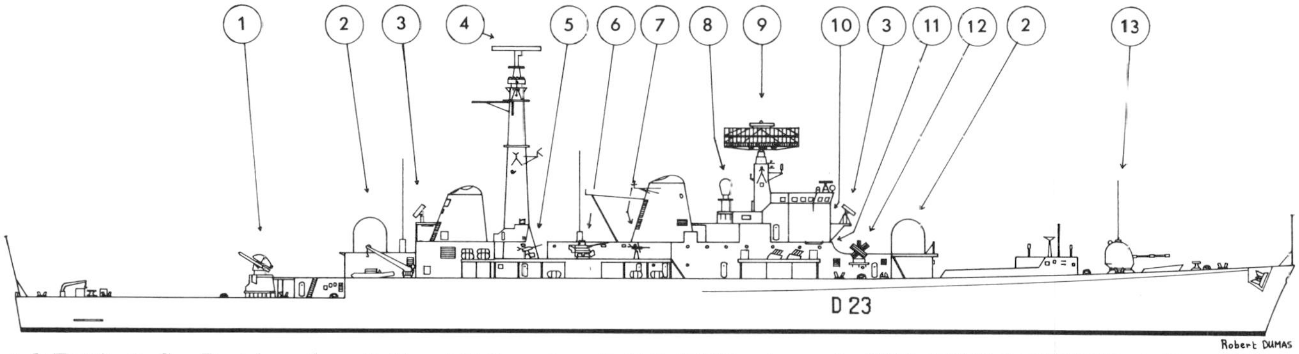


**Bristol (D 23)** 1. Sea Dart launcher 2. Type 909 f.c. radar 3. U.S. OE-82 antenna for WSC-3 UHF SATCOMM 4. Type 992Q radar 5. 20-mm Oerlikon GAM-B01 AA 6. twin 30-mm Oerlikon GCM-A02 AA 7. 20-mm Mk 4 AA 8. SCOT antenna for Skynet SHF SATCOMM 9. Type 1022 radar 10. bridge area 11. DLD Mk 137 chaff RL for Mk 36 SRBOC system 12. DLC Knebworth/Corvus chaff RL 13. 114-mm Mk 8 DP gun

when Ikara ASW missile system was removed (leaving ship with no ASW weapons!) and Type 1022 early-warning radar in place of 965M. Was to get 2 U.S. Mk 15 Vulcan/Phalanx CIWS in place of 30-mm AA and Type 2050 in place of 184M, but due to reassignment 9-87 as Dartmouth Training Ship, this may not be done. Additional accommodations added 1987 for 100 cadets.

Note: Of the two surviving active "County"-class units, *Glamorgan* (D 19), was stricken 7-9-86 for sale to Chile, and *Fife* (D 20) transferred to Chile 12-8-87 as *Blanco Encalada*. Sister *Kent* (D 12) is an accommodations hulk at Portsmouth.

### FRIGATES

**◆ 0 (+4 + 4) "Duke" (Type 23) general-purpose class**

| | Bldr | Laid down | L | In serv. |
|---|---|---|---|---|
| F 230 Norfolk | Yarrow, Scotstoun | 19-12-85 | 10-7-87 | 1989 |
| F 231 Marlborough | Swan Hunter | 11-87 | . . . | . . . |
| F 232 Argyll | Yarrow, Scotstoun | 1-87 | . . . | . . . |
| F 233 Lancaster | Yarrow, Scotstoun | 10-87 | . . . | . . . |

**D:** 3,000 tons (3,700 fl) **S:** 28 kts (17 kts electric drive)
**Dim:** 133.0 (123.0 pp) × 16.1(15.0 wl) × 4.3 (hull)
**A:** 8/Harpoon SSM (IV × 2)—1/Sea Wolf GWS.26 vertical-launch group (32 missiles)—1/114-mm Mk 8 DP—1/30-mm Goalkeeper gatling AA—2/30-mm Rarden AA (I × 2)—4/324-mm TT (II × 2, fixed)—1/EH.101 ASW helicopter
**Electron Equipt:** Radar: 1/1007, 1/996 Mod. 1, 2/911 Sea Wolf control
Sonar: 1/2050, 1/2031(2) towed linear passive array
EW: UAF-1 (Decca Cutlass) passive, 675 jammer, 4/DLB chaff RL (VI × 4)
**M:** CODLAG (Combined Diesel-Electric and Gas turbine): 2 Rolls-Royce SM1A Spey gas turbines (37,540 hp); 4 Paxman Valenta 12 RPA 200CZ diesel generator sets (5,200 kw total)—2/2,000-hp electric motors; 2 props; 41,540 hp

**Norfolk (F 230)**—artist's rendering M.O.D.

**Range:** 8,000/15 **Fuel:** 800 tons **Electric:** —see Remarks
**Man:** 12 officers, 41 petty officers, 90 men

Remarks: First unit ordered 29-10-84; letter-of-intent for second signed 28-1-85, but second through fourth ordered 15-7-86. F 232 has been offered to Pakistan, with two sisters to build at Karachi. *Norfolk* was originally to have been named *Daring*. Intended as lineal replacements for the remaining *Leander*-class frigates. Prototype design assigned to Yarrow. Flush-decked hull, with large helicopter hangar, helo in-haul system, fin stabilizers. Design grew considerably as a result of Falklands "Lessons-Learned." Will have first bow-mounted sonars in the Royal Navy. Have Marconi ICS3 integrated communications system. Planned third group (units 12–20) may be 7 m longer.

The propulsion system permits running the shaft-concentric electric propulsion motors with the power from any combination of the four 1,300-kw ship's service

**FRIGATES** *(continued)*

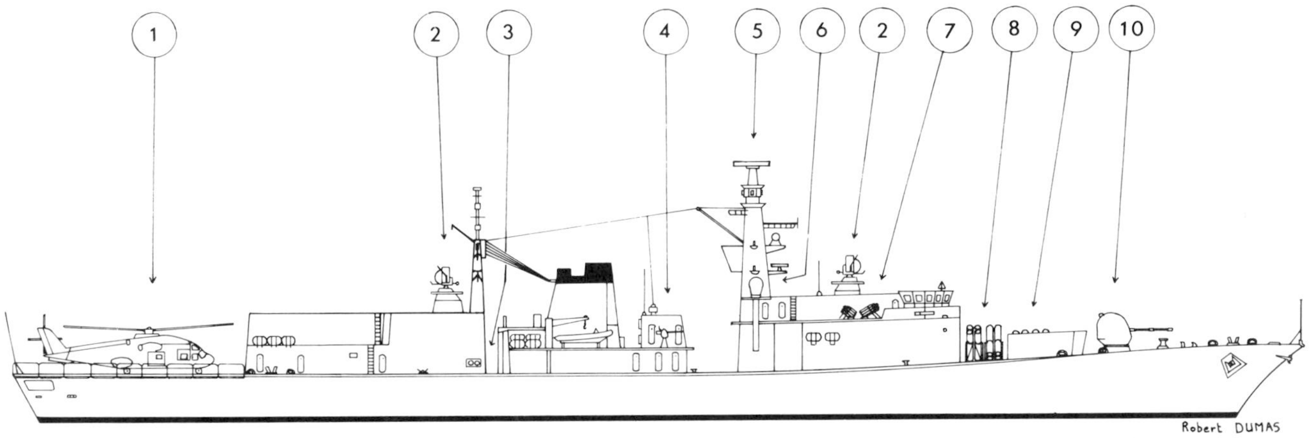


**"Duke" class** 1. EH.101 helicopter 2. Type 911 radar director 3. ASW TT 4. 30-mm Rarden gun 5. Type 996 radar 6. SCOT SHF SATCOMM antenna 7. DCA decoy RL 8. Harpoon SSM (IV × 2) 9. 32 vertical-launch Sea Wolf missiles 10. 114-mm Vickers Mk 8 DP gun

generators; power from both the gas turbines and the electric motors can be obtained. There is also a 250-kw diesel emergency generator. Fixed-pitch props, with astern power available only by electric drive. Numerous improvements in damage control, as a result of Falklands War lessons. There will be accommodations for 15 officers, 57 petty officers, and 105 junior ratings, but crew size may grow. May carry 2 U.S. Mk 15 CIWS AA vice Goalkeeper. The Ferranti CACS 4 weapons-control system for these ships was canceled 7-87; it will be replaced either by the Ferranti-Logica CS500 or a Plessey-Software Science system, which will not be available until 1990-91. The first two ships will thus commission without an integrated weapons-control system. Long-lead equipment for units 5 through 8 in this class was ordered during 1987. There is a GSA-8/GPEOD Sea Archer optronic/infrared director for the 114-mm gun.

**Norfolk (F 230)**—artist's rendering 1985

◆ **1 (+3) Cornwall (Type 22 Batch 3) general-purpose class**

| | Bldr | Laid down | L | In serv. |
|---|---|---|---|---|
| F 99 Cornwall | Yarrow, Scotstoun | 12-9-83 | 14-10-85 | 12-87 |
| F 85 Cumberland | Yarrow, Scotstoun | 12-10-84 | 21-6-86 | 1988 |
| F 86 Campbeltown | Cammell Laird | 4-12-85 | 10-87 | 6-89 |
| F 87 Chatham | Swan Hunter, Neptune | 12-5-86 | -88 | 1990 |

**D:** 4,380 tons (5,250 fl) **S:** 30 kts
**Dim:** 148.10(135.65 pp) × 14.75 × 5.35 hull (6.00 max.)
**A:** 2/Sea Wolf GWS.25 Mod. 3 systems (VI × 2)—8/Harpoon. SSM (IV × 2)—1/114-mm Vickers Mk 8 DP—1/30-mm Goalkeeper AA gun syst.—2/30-mm LS-30B AA (I × 2)—6/324-mm STWS.2 ASW TT (III × 2)—2/Lynx (Sea Skua ASM, Stingray ASW torpedoes) or 1/EH.101 or Sea King helicopters
**Electron Equipt:** Radar: 1/1006, 1/967M-968, 2/911 f.c., 2/Goalkeeper f.c.
Sonar: Type 2050 hull-mounted, Type 2031(2) towed linear passive array
EW: UAA-1 passive, 2/675 jammer, 4/DLB chaff RL (VI × 4)
**M:** COGAG: 2 Rolls-Royce Spey SM.1A DR gas turbines (18,770 hp each) *and* 2 Rolls-Royce Tyne RM.1C gas turbines (5,340 hp each); 2 Stone Manganese CP props; 48,220 hp
**Electric:** 4,000 kw (4/Paxman Valenta 12PA 200CZ diesel sets)
**Man:** 286 tot. (accommodations for 320)
**Range:** 7,000/18 (on Tyne gas turbines); 12,000/14 (one shaft)
**Fuel:** 700 tons, plus 80 tons aviation fuel

Remarks: Third series in the Type 22/*Broadsword*-class design, with same basic hull as Batch 2/*Boxer* class, but with a 114-mm gun on the forecastle, the antiship missile launchers moved to abaft the pilothouse and oriented athwartships. Will have EASAMS' Sea Archer GSA-8/GPEOD (Gun System Automation 8/General-Purpose Electro-Optical Director)T.V./IR/laser back-up directors for the 114-mm gun. The Goalkeeper gatling AA gun mount has its own integral I-band search/tracker and I/K-band tracking radars. Maximum generator output is 5,200 kw. All will have the CACS-1 Computer-Assisted Command System.

The first pair were ordered 14-12-82 and the third and fourth on 28-1-85. Launch of F 99 delayed from 3-6-85 by strikes. There are to be no additional units of what is the world's largest "frigate" design.

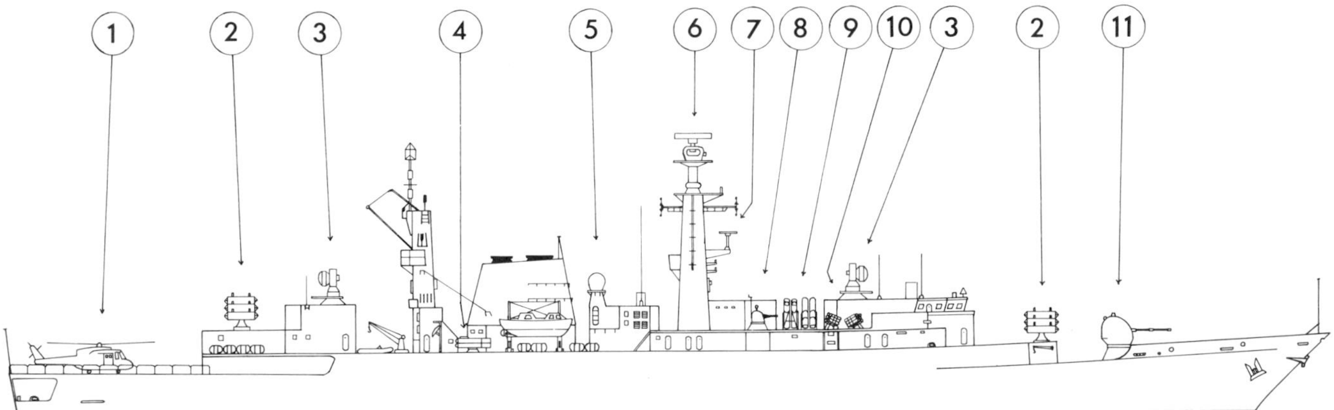


**Cornwall (F 99) Type 22 Batch 3** 1. Lynx helicopter 2. Sea Wolf launchers 3. Type 911 missile f.c. radars 4. triple STWS.1 ASW TT 5. SCOT SHF SATCOMM radomes 6. Type 967/968 radar antenna 7. Type 1006 nav. radar 8. a single Goalkeeper 30-mm AA should be shown atop deckhouse 9. Harpoon SSM 10. Shield decoy RL 11. 114-mm Vickers Mk 8 DP gun

FRIGATES *(continued)*

◆ **4 (+2) Boxer (Type 22 Batch 2)-class ASW frigates**

| | Bldr: | Laid down | L | In serv. |
|---|---|---|---|---|
| F 92 Boxer | Yarrow, Scotstoun | 5-11-79 | 17-6-81 | 14-1-84 |
| F 93 Beaver | Yarrow, Scotstoun | 20-6-80 | 8-5-82 | 13-12-84 |
| F 94 Brave | Yarrow, Scotstoun | 24-5-82 | 19-11-83 | 4-7-86 |
| F 95 London | Yarrow, Scotstoun | 7-2-83 | 27-10-84 | 5-6-87 |
| F 96 Sheffield | Swan Hunter, Wallsend | 29-3-84 | 26-3-86 | -88 |
| F 97 Coventry | Swan Hunter, Wallsend | 29-3-84 | 8-4-86 | -88 |

**London (F 95)**—on trials M. Adams, Maritime Photographic, 2-87

**Beaver (F 93)** L. & L. Van Ginderen, 6-87

**Beaver (F 93)**—note bullnose for Type 2031(2) towed array to port on fantail R.A.N., 9-86

**D:** 4,250 tons (4,850 fl) **S:** 30 kts (F 94: 28 kts)—18 kts on cruise engines
**Dim:** 145.00; F 94–97: 148.10 (140.0 pp) × 14.75 × 4.3 hull (6.0 max.)
**A:** 4/MM 38 Exocet (I × 4)—2/Sea Wolf GWS.25 Mod. 0 (F 94–97: Mod. 3) syst. (VI × 2)—2/40-mm Mk 7 AA (I × 2)—6/324-mm STWS.1 ASW TT (III × 2)—2/Lynx helicopters (Sea Skua ASM, Stingray torpedoes)
**Electron Equipt:** Radar: 1/1006, 1/967M–968, 2/910 (F 94–97: 2/911)
Sonar: Type 2016 hull-mounted, Type 2008, 1/Type 2031(2) towed linear passive array
EW: UAA-1 passive, 2/670 active, 4/DLD decoy RL (VI × 4) chaff RL (F 92, 93: 670 4/DLB), DLF (VIII × 2)

**Brave (F 94)**—the unique COGOG-powered ship in the diverse Type 22 Batch 2 series; the ship also has 4 U.S. Mk 137 chaff launchers (outfit DLD), vice the four Plessey Shield launchers on F 92, 93. Note higher hangar, larger flight deck than F 92, 93, later missile radar directors C. & S. Taylor, 6-86

**Boxer (F 92)**—low hangar G. Davies, Maritime Photographic, 5-87

**Brave (F 94)**—note taller hangar, overhanging flight deck L. & L. Van Ginderen, 6-86

**FRIGATES** *(continued)*

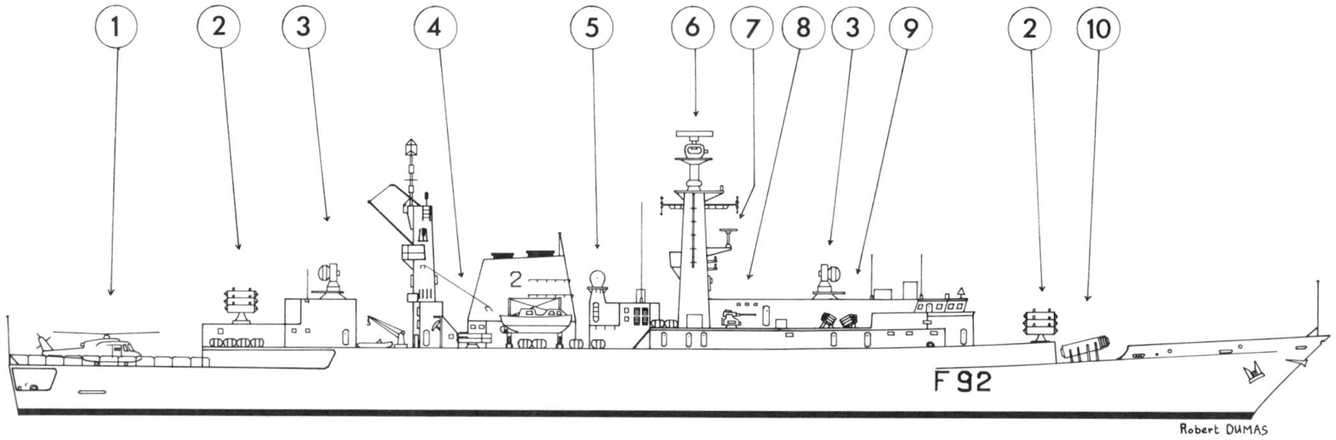


**Boxer (F 92)**—Batch 2 Type 22 class 1. Lynx helicopter 2. Sea Wolf launchers 3. Type 911 radar directors 4. triple STWS.1 ASW TT 5. SCOT SHF SATCOMM radome 6. Type 967/968 radar 7. Type 1006 nav. radar 8. 40-mm AA 9. DLB decoy/chaff RL 10. MM 38 Exocet SSM

**M:** F 92, F 93: COGOG: 2 Rolls-Royce Olympus TM.3B gas turbines (27,300 hp each), *or* 2 Rolls-Royce Tyne RM.1C gas turbines (5,340 hp each); 2 Stone Manganese CP props; 54,600 hp max.
F 95–F 97: COGAG: 2 Rolls-Royce Spey SM.1A gas turbines (18,770 hp each), or 2 Rolls-Royce Tyne RM.1C max. gas turbines (5,340 hp each); 2 CP props; 48,220 hp max. (F 94 same plant, but COGOG: 37,540 hp max.)
**Range:** 7,000/18 12,000/14 (one shaft) **Electric:** 4,000 kw
**Fuel:** 700 tons, +80 tons aviation fuel
**Man:** 19 officers, 246 men (berths for 320)

REMARKS: "Batch 2" employs a lengthened hull over the *Broadsword* class to improve seaworthiness, endurance, and habitability and to provide space for handling the Type 2031 towed linear passive hydrophone array (not yet aboard F 92). F 92 and F 93 ordered 25-4-79, F 94 (with Spey gas turbines substituted for the less-economical Olympus) ordered 27-8-81, F 95 on 23-2-82, and the other two (as Falklands war-loss replacements) on 14-12-82. To have Type 2016 hull-mounted sonar replaced by Type 2050 during first major refits. Names *Bloodhound, Boadicea,* and *Bruiser* originally selected for final three. Two 30-mm Rarden AA will replace the 40-mm AA.

Have CACS 1 data system, with 26 operators and 16 displays. F 94 is first with lightweight Marconi 805-SW (Type 911) missile directors, but the CACS 1 action data system, which has been plagued with developmental delays, was not installed at time of commissioning. Her hull has greater flare at the stern to permit a larger helicopter deck for the EH.101 helo, producing an overall length of 146.5 m; the hangar is also higher. F 92 commissioned in 1984 for 3-year trials with the CACS 1 data system. Water-displacement fuel tanks are used, and the ships are said to have twice the range of the "Batch 1" *Broadsword* class.

There are four 1,000-kw diesel generator sets. Two auxiliary boilers and two 50-ton/day flash evaporators are installed. F 94 is to receive improved Spey SM1C engines during a 1989 refit, increasing available power, but will remain unique in not being able to gear all four main engines to the shafts. All planned to receive three major refits during 22-year lifetimes.

◆ **4 Broadsword (Type 22)-class ASW frigates** Bldr: Yarrow, Scotstoun

| | Ordered | Laid down | L | In serv. |
|---|---|---|---|---|
| F 88 BROADSWORD | 8-2-74 | 7-2-75 | 12-5-76 | 3-5-79 |
| F 89 BATTLEAXE | 4-9-75 | 4-2-76 | 18-5-77 | 28-3-80 |
| F 90 BRILLIANT | 7-9-76 | 24-3-77 | 15-12-78 | 10-4-81 |
| F 91 BRAZEN (ex-*Boxer*) | 21-10-77 | 19-8-78 | 4-3-80 | 2-7-82 |

**Brazen (F 91)**—with 20-mm AA and Mk 36 SRBOC amidships
L. & L. Van Ginderen, 8-86

**Brilliant (F 90)**—low stack G. Davies, Maritime Photographic, 5-87

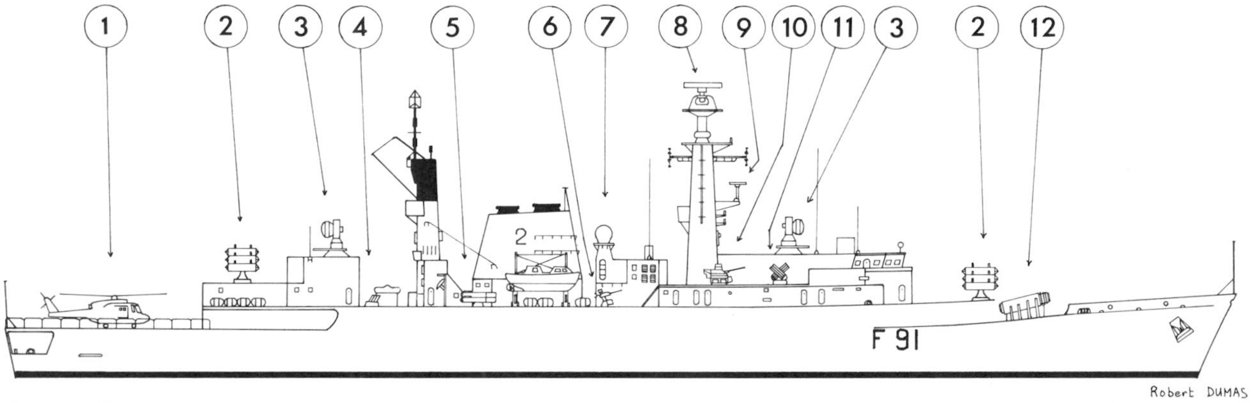


**Brazen (F 91)**—Type 22 Batch 1 1. Lynx helicopter 2. Sea Wolf launchers 3. Type 910 radar/electro-optical directors 4. Mk 137 launchers for Mk 36 SRBOC system 5 triple STWS.1 ASW TT 6. 20-mm GAM-B01 AA 7. SCOT SHF SATCOMM radome 8. Type 967/968 radar 9. Type 1006 nav. radar 10. 40-mm AA 11. chaff RL 12. MM 38 Exocet launchers

**FRIGATES** *(continued)*

**Battleaxe (F 89)**—high stack G. Davies, Maritime Photographic, 5-87

**Broadsword (F 88)** L. & L. Van Ginderen, 4-87

**D:** 3,500 tons (4,400 fl) **S:** 29 kts (18 cruise)
**Dim:** 131.2 (125.0 wl) × 14.8 × 4.3 (6.0 sonar)
**A:** 4/MM 38 Exocet—2/Sea Wolf GWS.25 syst. (VI × 2)—2/40-mm Mk 9 AA (I × 2)—2/20-mm Oerlikon GAM-B01 AA (I × 2; not always aboard)—6/324-mm STWS.1 ASW TT (III × 2)—1 or 2 Lynx helicopters
**Electron Equipt:** Radar: 1/1006, 1/967-968, 2/910 (GWS.25)
Sonar: 1/2008, 1/2016
EW: UAA-1, passive, 2/Type 670 active, 2 DLC chaff RL (VIII × 2)—see Remarks
**M:** COGOG; 2 Olympus TM3B gas turbines, 27,300 hp each for high speed; 2 Tyne RM1A, 4,100 hp each for cruising; 2 CP props; 54,600 hp max.
**Electric:** 4,000 kw (4 Paxman Ventura diesel sets; 450 v., 3 ph., 60 Hz)
**Range:** 4,500/18 (on Tyne); 1,200/29 (on Olympus) **Man:** 18 officers, 205 men

REMARKS: Originally to have been a class of 26. Type 2016 is a multiple-frequency sonar. The Lynx can carry both ASW and antiship weapons; two were to have been carried, but only one is normally aboard. CAAIS combat data system. The 967–968 radar is a back-to-back array with track-while-scan features. To be backfitted with Sea Wolf GWS.25 Mod. 3 system (Type 911 trackers) beginning in 1988 with F 88, which will also get Type 2050 sonar in place of 2016. First two have higher, more elaborate stacks. Two 20-mm AA added 1982–83; locations vary. F 89 has 4/Mk 137 chaff RL (Outfit DLD) in addition to standard Outfit DLC.

◆ **6 Amazon (Type 21) class**

| | Bldr | Laid down | L | In serv. |
|---|---|---|---|---|
| F 169 AMAZON | Vosper Thornycroft | 6-11-69 | 26-4-71 | 11-5-74 |
| F 171 ACTIVE | Vosper Thornycroft | 23-7-71 | 23-11-72 | 17-6-77 |
| F 172 AMBUSCADE | Yarrow, Scotstoun | 1-9-71 | 18-1-73 | 5-9-75 |
| F 173 ARROW | Yarrow, Scotstoun | 28-9-72 | 5-2-74 | 29-7-76 |
| F 174 ALACRITY | Yarrow, Scotstoun | 5-3-73 | 18-9-74 | 2-4-77 |
| F 185 AVENGER | Yarrow, Scotstoun | 30-10-74 | 20-11-75 | 15-4-78 |

**D:** 2,850 tons (3,350 fl) **S:** 32 kts
**Dim:** 117.04 (109.70 pp) × 12.7 × 4.6 (6.2 over sonar)
**A:** 4/MM 38 Exocet—1/Sea Cat GWS.24 system (IV × 1)—1/114-mm Mk 8 DP—4/20-mm Mk 4 AA (I × 4)—1/Lynx helicopter—F 172, 184, 185 only: 6/324-mm STWS.1 ASW TT (III × 2)
**Electron Equipt:** Radar: 1/1006, 1/992Q, 2/912 (RTN-10X Orion)
Sonar: 1/184M, 1/162M
EW: UAA-1 passive or none, 2/DLC chaff RL (VIII × 2), FH-12 HF/DF
**M:** COGOG; 2 Olympus TM.3B gas turbines, 25,000 hp each; 2 Tyne RM.1A gas turbines, 4,250 hp each; 2 CP props; 50,000 hp max.
**Electric:** 3,000 kw **Range:** 4,500/18; 1,200/30
**Endurance:** 60 days
**Man:** 13 officers, 164 men

**Amazon (F 169)**—Lynx helo D. Moore, 5-86

**Arrow (F 173)**—Lynx on deck G. Gyssels, 1986

**Amazon (F 169)** L. & L. Van Ginderen, 7-87

**Alacrity (F 174)**—with Exocet, 4/20-mm AA, no ASW TT, SCOT, or UAA-1—note hull reinforcement amidships G. Davies, Maritime Photographic, 2-86

**FRIGATES** *(continued)*

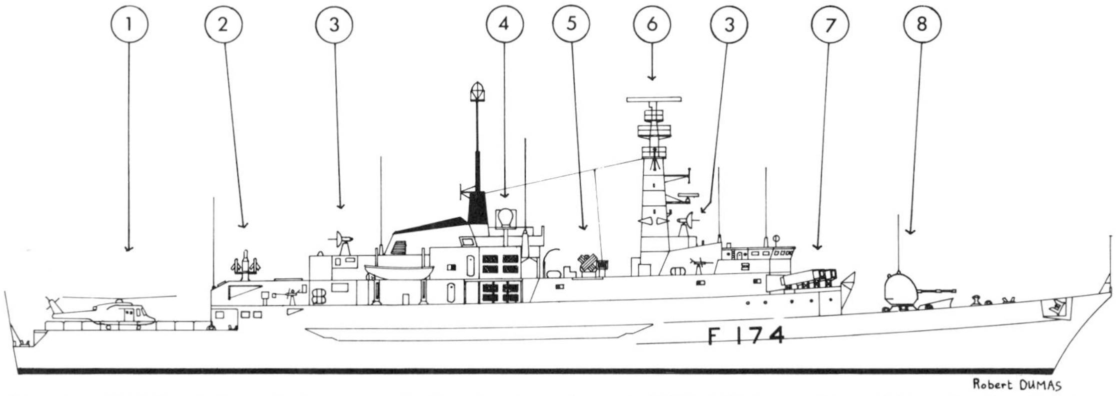


**Alacrity (F 174)** 1. Lynx helicopter 2. Sea Cat launcher 3. RTN-10X Orion (Type 912) radar f.c. directors 4. SCOT SHF SATCOMM radomes 5. Knebworth/Corvus chaff RL 6. Type 992Q radar 7. MM 38 Exocet launchers 8. 114-mm Vickers Mk 8 DP gun

**Avenger (F 185)**—with ASW TT, 20-mm aft at forward end of helo deck
L. & L. Van Ginderen, 7-85

Remarks: Designed jointly by Vosper Thornycroft and Yarrow. The ships have been criticized for fragility, vulnerability, and for being overloaded and top-heavy; permanent ballast had to be added, but none can carry the full originally intended weapon and sensor suite. Hulls strengthened, due to cracking during the Falklands War; doubler plates added amidships, beginning with F 173, completed 6-83; modifications added 100+ tons to displacement. All are based at Devonport, with F 185 as flagship. F 169, 172 did not receive Exocet until 1984–85.

Remote control of engine room from the bridge. Ferranti WSA 4 digital system used in fire control, employing two Selenia RTN-10X radar directors (Type 912) for both Sea Cat and the 114-mm gun; there is also a backup optical director for each. The CAAIS combat data system is a separate entity, whose data are automatically transmitted to WSA 4; both use a single FM-1600B computer. The Exocet launchers are paired, toed-in, and forward of the bridge. All can carry two SCOT radomes for the Skynet SHF communications satellite system. Four 750-kw diesel generator sets supply the 450-volt, 3-phase, 60-Hz electrical current. Type 992Q radar to be replaced by Type 996. A separate Cossor Type 1010 IFF interrogator is mounted below the Type 992Q. Several still lack UAA-1 Abbey Hill intercept arrays.

*Ardent* (F 184) of this class was lost to multiple bomb and rocket hits 21-5-82, and *Antelope* (F 170) sank 24-5-82 after an unexploded bomb detonated, causing uncontrolled fires and eventual magazine explosions.

◆ **19 Leander class**

Note: For convenience in describing the numerous appearances and functional variations in this class, they have been divided into six separate listings, in general order of construction and conversion.

◆ **(a) 5 Sea Wolf antiaircraft missile conversions**

| | Bldr | Laid down | L | In serv. | Conv. |
|---|---|---|---|---|---|
| F 57 Andromeda | HMDY/Portsmouth | 25-5-66 | 24-5-67 | 2-12-68 | 4-81 |
| F 58 Hermione | Stephen/Yarrow | 6-12-65 | 26-4-67 | 11-7-69 | 21-6-83 |
| F 60 Jupiter | Yarrow, Scotstoun | 3-10-66 | 4-9-67 | 9-8-69 | 21-10-83 |
| F 71 Scylla | HMDY, Devonport | 17-5-67 | 8-8-68 | 12-2-70 | 7-12-84 |
| F 75 Charybdis | Harland & Wolff | 27-1-67 | 28-2-68 | 2-6-69 | 6-8-82 |

**D:** 2,640 tons (3,100 fl) **S:** 27 kts
**Dim:** 113.38 (109.73) × 13.12 × 4.60 (5.60 props)
**A:** 4/MM 38 Exocet SSM (I × 4)—1/Sea Wolf GWS.25 syst. (VI × 1)—4/20-mm AA (I × 4)—6/324-mm STWS.1 ASW TT (III × 2)—1/Lynx helicopter (Sea Skua ASM, Stingray torpedoes)
**Electron Equipt:** Radar: 1/1006, 1/967–968, 1/910
Sonar: Type 2016 (F 60: 2050), Type 2008, Type 162M
EW: UAA-1 passive, 2/Type 670 jammer, 2/DLC chaff RL (VIII × 2), 2/DLF (VIII × 2)

**Charybdis (F 75)** L. & L. Van Ginderen, 3-86

**Hermione (F 58)** G. Davies, Maritime Photographic, 6-87

**Scylla (F 71)** L. & L. Van Ginderen, 3-87

**Jupiter (F 60)** G. Davies, Maritime Photographic, 4-86

**FRIGATES** *(continued)*

**M:** 2 sets White-English Electric GT, 2/5-bladed props; 30,000 hp
**Boilers:** 2 Babcock & Wilcox 3-drum; 38.7 kg/cm$^2$, 450°C
**Fuel:** 500 tons **Electric:** 2,500 kw **Range:** approx. 4,500/12
**Man:** 19 officers, 241 men

Remarks: F 58 launched by Alex Stephens, completed by Yarrow. Conversions from "Broad-beam Leanders" to improve warfare capabilities in all areas. Five sisters *not* converted, for economy reasons (see below). Sea Wolf, manually loaded launcher and 4 Exocet and twin 114-mm gun mount, hangar enlarged to take Lynx, sonar replaced. Limbo mortar and Type 965 radar deleted, Type 967–968 radar stepped atop new foremast, and Type 910 Sea Wolf director placed atop bridge. All now have 2 Mk 4 20-mm and 2 20-mm GAM-B01 AA. F 58 tested Thorn-EMI Guardian (Type 675) jammer in 1985. F 60 began trials with Type 2050 hull-mounted sonar in 10-86.

◆ **(b) 4 unmodified "Broad-beamed Leander" general-purpose**

| | Bldr | Laid down | L | In serv. |
|---|---|---|---|---|
| F 12 Achilles | Yarrow, Scotstoun | 1-12-67 | 21-11-68 | 9-7-70 |
| F 16 Diomede | Yarrow, Scotstoun | 30-1-68 | 15-4-69 | 2-4-71 |
| F 70 Apollo | Yarrow, Scotstoun | 1-5-69 | 15-10-70 | 28-5-72 |
| F 72 Ariadne | Yarrow, Scotstoun | 1-11-69 | 10-9-71 | 10-2-73 |

**Apollo (F 70)** L. & L. Van Ginderen, 10-85

**Ariadne (F 72)**—with UA-13 array at masthead, single 20-mm aft
L. & L. Van Ginderen, 10-87

**Achilles (F 12)**—FH-12 at masthead, 20-mm aft
G. Davies, Maritime Photographic, 5-87

**D:** 2,660 tons (3,120 fl) **S:** 27 kts
**Dim:** 113.38 (109.73 pp) × 13.12 × 4.50 (5.49 props)
**A:** 2/114-mm Mk 6 DP (II × 1)—1/Sea Cat GWS.22 syst. (IV × 1)—3 or 4/20-mm AA (I × 3; F 16, 70: II × 1, I × 2)—1/Limbo Mk 10 ASW mortar (III × 1)—1/Wasp helicopter (AS.12 ASM, Mk 44/46 torpedoes)—see Remarks

**Electron Equipt:** Radar: 1/978 or 1006, 1/994, 1/965, 1/903, 1/904
Sonar: Type 184, Type 170B, Type 162
EW: UA-8/9 passive, Type 668 or 669 active, 2/DLC chaff RL (VIII × 2)—F 70, 72 also: UA-13 passive, others: FH-12 HFD/F
**M:** 2 sets White-English Electric GT; 2/5-bladed props; 30,000 hp
**Boilers:** 2 Babcock & Wilcox 3-drum; 38.7 kg/cm$^2$, 450°C
**Electric:** 2,500 kw **Fuel:** 500 tons **Range:** approx. 4,500/12
**Man:** 19 officers, 241 men

Remarks: The newest of the Royal Navy's Leanders, conversion of these ships to "Sea Wolf Leander" configuration was canceled for reasons of economy. A fifth unmodified "Broad-beam Leander," *Bacchante* (F 69), was sold to New Zealand 4-10-82. A single Oerlikon GAM-B01 20-mm AA gun was mounted on the starboard side of the stern in 1982–83 in F 12 and F 72; F 16 and F 70 received a twin 20-mm mount. F 12 entered major refit 4-6-84, F 70 on 30-7-84, and F 72 refitted 1-85 to 11-85. All are now to be retained to at least 1989. These are the last RN ships with the twin 114-mm Mk 6 gun mount. Wasp helicopter to delete by 4-88. All but F 70 to strike by 31-3-89; F 12 and F 72 for foreign sale.

◆ **(c) 4 "Exocet Leander" Batch 2TA conversions with towed arrays**

| | Bldr | Laid down | L | In serv. | Conv. |
|---|---|---|---|---|---|
| F 28 Cleopatra | HMDY, Devonport | 19-6-63 | 25-3-64 | 4-1-66 | 11-75 |
| F 40 Sirius | HMDY, Portsmouth | 9-8-63 | 22-9-64 | 15-6-66 | 10-77 |
| F 42 Phoebe | Alex Stephens & Sons | 3-6-63 | 8-7-64 | 15-4-66 | 4-77 |
| F 56 Argonaut | Hawthorne Leslie | 27-11-64 | 8-2-66 | 17-8-67 | 10-78 |

**Cleopatra (F 28)**—towed array without sponson, UA-13 at masthead, SCOT radomes aboard
French Navy, 7-86

**Sirius (F 40)**—towed array sponson G. Gyssels, 6-87

**Sirius (F 40)**—FH-12 at masthead, Lynx on deck L. & L. Van Ginderen, 6-87

**FRIGATES** *(continued)*

**D:** 2,750 tons (3,300 fl) **S:** 28 kts
**Dim:** 113.38 (109.73 pp) × 12.50 × 5.00 (6.40 props)—see Remarks
**A:** 4/MM 38 Exocet (I × 4)—2 Sea Cat GSW.22 syst. (IV × 2—only one director)—2/20-mm Mk 4 AA (I × 2)—6/324-mm STWS.1 ASW TT (III × 2)—1/Lynx helicopter (Sea Skua ASM, Stingray torpedoes)
**Electron Equipt:** Radar: 1/1006, 1/994, 1/904
Sonar: Type 184M, Type 162M, Type 2031 (1) towed passive linear array
EW: UA-8/9 passive, Type 668 or 669 active, 2/DLC chaff RL (VIII × 2), also: F 28, 42: UA-13; F 40, 56: FH-12 HFD/F
**M:** 2 sets White-English Electric GT; 2/5-bladed props; 30,000 hp
**Boilers:** 2 Babcock & Wilcox 3-drum; 38.7 kg/cm², 450°C
**Electric:** 1,900 kw **Fuel:** 460 tons **Range:** approx. 4,000/12
**Man:** 20 officers, 203 men

Remarks: Original conversion completion dates in table. These four ships are typed "Exocet Leander Group 2A" and have been further modified from "Exocet Leander" configuration by the deletion of the forward Sea Cat launcher and director, the lowering of the Exocet installation to the main-deck level, the substitution of 20-mm Mk 4 AA for the 40-mm AA, the removal of the Type 965 early-warning radar (replaced by a Cossor Type 1010 IFF interrogator), and the addition of the Type 2031 (1) towed passive linear hydrophone array on the starboard quarter. F 42, completing first in 7-82, mounted 4/20-mm AA while awaiting the Type 2031 equipment; one AA gun was placed atop the former forward director platform and the other on the starboard quarter. F 28, completing reconversion in 1983, had the Type 2031, SCOT SHF SATCOMM antennas, and only 2/20-mm AA, F 56, damaged in the Falklands War, replaced *Minerva* (F 45) in the towed array conversion program, recommissioning 1984. On all but F 28, the Type 2031 (1) reel/winch is on a sponson projecting to starboard and astern, adding about 1 meter to the overall length.

◆ **(d) 3 "Exocet Leander" Batch 2B conversions**

| | Bldr | Laid down | L | In serv. | Conv. |
|---|---|---|---|---|---|
| F 45 Minerva | Vickers, Armstrong | 25-7-63 | 19-12-64 | 14-5-66 | 9-79 |
| F 47 Danae | HMDY, Devonport | 16-12-64 | 31-10-65 | 7-9-67 | 9-80 |
| F 127 Penelope (ex-*Coventry*) | Vickers-Armstrong | 14-3-61 | 17-8-62 | 31-10-63 | 1-82 |

**Danae (F 47)** L. & L. Van Ginderen, 6-87

**Danae (F 47)** Royal Navy, 1987

**D:** 2,650 tons (3,200 fl) **S:** 28 kts
**Dim:** 113.38 (109.73 pp) × 12.50 × 4.80 (6.20 props)
**A:** 4/MM 38 Exocet SSM (I × 4)—3/Sea Cat GWS.22B syst. (IV × 3—2 directors)—2/40-mm AA (I × 2)—3/20-mm GAM-B01 AA—6/324-mm STWS.1 ASW TT (III × 2)—1/Lynx helicopter (Sea Skua ASM, Stingray torpedoes)
**Electron Equipt:** Radar: 1/1006, 1/994, 1/965, 2/904
Sonar: Type 184M, Type 162M
EW: UA-8/9 passive, Type 668 or 669 jammer, 2/DLC chaff RL (VIII × 2), 2 DLD (VI × 2), FH-12 HFD/F
**M: and Boilers:** as in "Exocet Leander" Batch 2A
**Electric:** 1,900 kw **Fuel:** 460 tons **Range:** approx. 4,000/12
**Man:** 20 officers, 203 men

Remarks: Converted from standard "Leander" configuration, except for F 127, which reconverted from Sea Wolf trials ship, recommissioning 22-1-82. Sea Cat launcher and 4 Exocet replaced twin 114-mm gun forward, single Sea Cat launcher augmented by a second launcher atop enlarged hangar, Limbo ASW mortar replaced by 2 sets ASW TT. Will not be further altered, as in Batch 2A above. Have CAAIS combat data system. F 45 is, technically speaking, a "Batch 2A" conversion unit.

◆ **(e) 2 "Ikara Leander" conversions**

| | Bldr | Laid down | L | In serv. | Conv. |
|---|---|---|---|---|---|
| F 15 Euryalus | Scotts SB&E | 2-11-61 | 6-6-63 | 16-9-64 | 3-76 |
| F 38 Arethusa | J. Samuel White | 7-9-62 | 5-11-63 | 24-11-65 | 4-77 |

**Arethusa (F 38)**—with Type 2031 towed array Pradignac & Leo, 12-86

**Euryalus (F 15)**—Ikara on launcher Royal Navy, 1982

**D:** 2,610 tons (3,020 fl) **S:** 27 kts
**Dim:** 113.38(109.73 pp) × 12.50 × 4.60 (5.70 props)
**A:** 2/Sea Cat GWS.22B syst. (IV × 2, 1 director)—2/40-mm AA (I × 2)—1/Ikara GWS.40 syst. (I × 1)—1/Limbo Mk 10 ASW mortar (III × 1, not in F 38)—1/Wasp helicopter (AS.12 ASM, Mk 44/46 torpedoes)
**Electron Equipt:** Radar: 1/1006, 1/994, 1/904, 1/Ikara tracker
Sonar: Type 170B, Type 184M, Type 162M
EW: UA-8/9 passive, Type 668/669 jammers, 2/DLC chaff RL (VIII × 2)
**M:** 2 sets White-English Electric GT; 2/5-bladed props; 30,000 hp
**Boilers:** 2 Babcock & Wilcox 3-drum, 38.7 kg/cm², 450°C
**Electric:** 2,000 kw **Fuel:** 460 tons **Range:** approx. 4,500/12
**Man:** 19 officers, 238 men

Remarks: Conversions from standard "Leanders," with the Australian ASW torpedo-carrying Ikara antisubmarine cruise-missile system replacing the twin 114-mm gun mount, the number of Sea Cat launchers doubled, and the Type 965 radar removed (necessitating the installation of a Type 1010 IFF interrogation

**FRIGATES** *(continued)*

antenna atop the after pylon mast). Fitted for 2 SCOT antennas for the Skynet SHF SATCOMM system on platforms on the foremast. Retention of Limbo limits flight deck to Wasp helicopter. Have ADAWS 5 data system and LINK 10 data link. Type 994 radar (Plessey AWS.4 with Type 993's antenna retained) has replaced Type 993 in the survivors, and Type 199 VDS has been removed.

Sister *Dido* (F 104) sold to New Zealand, transferred 18-7-83. *Ajax* (F 114), stricken 31-5-85, was scrapped 1986. *Galatea* (F 18) to reserve 30-7-86 and stricken 3-87, along with *Leander* (F 109, ex-*Weymouth*), which had decommissioned 1-8-86. *Aurora* (F 10) struck 30-4-87 and *Naiad* on 29-4-87. The surviving pair (despite F 15 having undergone a 49-week refit in 1984–85) are to be paid off 1988. F 38 carries the prototype Type 2031 towed linear passive hydrophone array, removed from the *Rothesay*-class frigate *Lowestoft* (F 103) in 1985 and necessitating removal of the Limbo ASW mortar.

◆ **(f) 1 unmodified "Leander"**

| | Bldr | Laid down | L | In serv. |
|---|---|---|---|---|
| F 52 Juno | Thornycroft, Woolston | 16-7-74 | 24-11-65 | 18-7-67 |

**Juno (F 52)** L. & L. Van Ginderen, 5-87

**D:** 2,400 tons (2,800 fl) **S:** 28 kts
**Dim:** 113.38 (109.73 pp) × 12.50 × 4.40 (5.4 props)
**A:** 2/20-mm Mk 4 AA (I × 2)—6/324-mm STWS.1 ASW TT (III × 2)
**Electron Equipt:** Radar: 1/1006, 1/994
Sonar: Type 184M, Type 162
EW: . . . passive, 2/DLC chaff RL (VIII × 2)
**M: and Boilers:** as for "Ikara Leander" class
**Electric:** 1,600 kw **Fuel:** 460 tons **Range:** approx. 4,500/12
**Man:** 17 officers, 245 men

Remarks: *Juno* was the last unmodified early "Leander." She entered refit 9-81 at Rosyth for conversion as a navigational training ship to replace *Torquay* in 3-84. Economics forced delay of the plan, and the ship was given a regular overhaul ending in 10-82 and placed in ready reserve. In 1984–85 the work was completed: the 114-mm mount, Limbo mortar, and Sea Cat systems removed, Type 965 radar and most EW equipment deleted; ASW TT, new navigational gear, and Type 1010 IFF interrogation added. Primarily a training ship, with little combat value. Fin stabilizers removed 1986. The helicopter hangar is used as a workshop.

General Remarks: ("Leander" class): The design is an improvement on the *Rothesay* class, of which *Dido* (F 104), F 109, F 114, and F 127 were originally to have been members. Have twin rudders and one pair of fin stabilizers, set well aft of amidships. The "Broad-beamed Leanders" incorporated engineering plant improvements and were the first to be fitted with Sea Cat missiles on completion, earlier ships having had 2/40-mm AA (I × 2). All were intended to carry Type 199 variable-depth sonars, but these were installed in only a few of the class.

◆ **2 Rothesay class (Type 12)**

| | Bldr | Laid down | L | In serv. |
|---|---|---|---|---|
| F 107 Rothesay | Yarrow, Scotstoun | 6-11-56 | 9-12-57 | 23-4-60 |
| F 126 Plymouth | HMDY, Devonport | 1-7-58 | 20-7-59 | 11-5-61 |

**Plymouth (F 126)** L. & L. Van Ginderen, 11-86

**D:** 2,380 tons (2,800 fl) **S:** 26 kts
**Dim:** 112.78 (109.73 pp) × 12.5 × 4.50 (5.30 sonar)
**A:** 2/114-mm Mk 6 DP (II × 1)—4/20-mm AA (I × 4)—1/Sea Cat GWS.20 system (IV × 1)—1/Mk 10 Limbo ASW mortar (III × 1)—1/Wasp helicopter (AS.12 ASM, Mk 44/46 torpedoes)
**Electron Equipt:** Radar: 1/1006, 1/993, 1/903
Sonar: 1/174, 1/170B, 1/162M
EW: FH-5 HFD/F, 2/DLC chaff RL (VIII × 2)
**M:** 2 sets English Electric GT; 2 props; 30,000 hp
**Electric:** 1,460 kw **Boilers:** 2 Babcock & Wilcox, 38.7 kg/cm$^2$, 450°C
**Fuel:** 400 tons **Range:** 4,500/12 **Man:** 155 officers, 220 men

Remarks: Improved version of the *Whitby* class. Original nine ships all modernized 1966–72 with Sea Cat GWS.20 system (no radar) and helicopter facility in place of one Limbo ASW mortar. MRS.3 fire-control system replaced the original Mk 6 director, and new electronics and air-conditioning were installed. Two/20-mm Mk 4 in bridge area; 2/20-mm GAM-B01, one on quarterdeck to starboard, one amidships to port on F 126.

F 107 completed refit 11-84 to extend service to 1988. F 126 completed 26-week refit 18-4-86, had boiler explosion 7-86, in repair to 11-86. Of seven sisters, *Brighton* (F 106) was stricken 1-81. *Falmouth* (F 113), in reserve 7-80 and stricken 12-81, was recommissioned 23-4-82 for Falklands service and was decommissioned 27-11-84 for harbor training service, stricken 1987. *Rhyl* (F 129), on Sales List since 2-82, recommissioned 18-6-82 and was stricken 2-85 and sunk as a target 8-85. *Lowestoft* (F 103), used for trials with towed passive linear hydrophone arrays since 1978, first with DA-5 and later with Type 2031, paid off for disposal 29-3-85 and sunk as a target 8-6-86. *Londonderry* (F 108), a disarmed electronics trials ship since recommissioning from conversion 11-10-79, was paid off 29-3-84 for use by HMS *Sultan* as a training hulk, stricken due to funding cuts. *Berwick* (F 115), placed in reserve 1-81, stricken 12-81, recommissioned 5-8-82, was stricken 17-10-85 and sunk as a target 3-10-86. *Yarmouth* (F 101) was stricken 30-4-86 and sunk as target 6-87. The survivors are to be paid off in 1988.

**CORVETTES**

Note: Plans to acquire an OPV 3 (Offshore Patrol Vessel, Mk 3) design were placed in abeyance 6-85, although design work will continue. The Royal Navy may instead lease a vessel (or airship) to perform this function.

◆ **5 Peacock class** Bldr: Hall Russell, Aberdeen

| | Laid down | L | In serv. |
|---|---|---|---|
| P 239 Peacock | 29-1-82 | 1-12-82 | 12-10-83 |
| P 240 Plover | 13-5-82 | 12-4-83 | 20-7-84 |
| P 241 Starling | 9-9-82 | 7-9-83 | 10-8-84 |
| P 242 Swallow | 24-4-83 | 30-3-84 | 16-11-84 |
| P 243 Swift | 23-9-83 | 11-9-84 | 3-5-85 |

**D:** 662 tons (710 fl) **S:** over 28 kts (trials)
**Dim:** 62.60 (60.00 pp) × 10.00 × 2.72
**A:** 1/76-mm OTO Melara Compact DP—4/7.62-mm mg (I × 4)
**Electron Equipt:** Radar: 1/1006
**M:** 2 APE-Crossley SEMT-Pielstick 18PA6V280 diesels; 2/3-bladed props; 14,188 hp—1/Schottel S103 LSVEST drop-down, shrouded loiter prop; 181 hp
**Range:** 2,500/. . . **Fuel:** 44 tons **Electric:** 755 kw
**Man:** 7 officers, 36 men

Remarks: Replaced the five "Ton"-class former minesweepers used for patrol duties at Hong Kong, whose government has paid 75 percent of the construction costs. Carry two Avon Sea Raider 5.4-m, 30-kt, 10-man semi-rigid rubber inspection dinghies. Some 450 rds 76-mm ammunition can be carried, with the gun controlled by a GSA7 Sea Archer Mk 1 electro-optical director, to which a G.E.C. V3800 thermal imager was added in 1987. The auxiliary drive employs a Schöttel retractable, steerable shrouded thruster. Accommodations for 44 total. Have 2/50-mm rocket flare projectors. Maximum sustained speed: 25 kts. Two rudders. Reported to be bad rollers, with deeper bilge keels having had to be fitted. Propulsion problems occurred with P 239. Two were to be leased to Brunei in 1987, but all will remain at Hong Kong at China's request.

**Peacock (P 239)** LSPH E. Pitman, R.A.N., 2-87

**CORVETTES** *(continued)*

**Swallow (P 242)**—with *Peacock* (P 239) beyond G. Arra, 7-85

◆ **2 "Castle"-class offshore patrol vessels** Bldr: Hall Russell, Aberdeen

| | Laid down | L | In serv. |
|---|---|---|---|
| P 258 Leeds Castle | 18-10-79 | 22-10-80 | 12-81 |
| P 265 Dumbarton Castle | 25-6-80 | 3-6-81 | 12-3-82 |

**Leeds Castle (P 258)**—MARISAT SATCOMM antenna fitted L. & L. Van Ginderen, 3-86

**Dumbarton Castle (P 265)** L. & L. Van Ginderen, 3-84

**D:** 1,250 tons (1,450 fl) **S:** 20 kts **Dim:** 81.0 (75.0 pp) × 11.5 × 3.42
**A:** 1/40-mm AA—2/7.62-mm mg (I × 2)—mines—helicopter platform
**Electron Equipt:** Radar: 1/1006
**M:** 2 Ruston 12 RK 320DM diesels; 2 CP props; 5,640 hp (4,380 sust.)
**Electric:** 890 kw **Fuel:** 380 tons **Range:** 10,000/12
**Man:** 7 officers, 43 men (plus 25 Marine detachment as required)

Remarks: Ordered 8-8-80, *after* both had been laid down. P 265 operated at over 2,000 tons displacement during the Falklands War. Can carry acoustic and mechanical mine-sweeping gear as well as being able to lay mines. The helicopter deck is large enough to accommodate either Lynx or Sea King helicopter. Carry two 50-mm rocket flare launchers. Can carry 19.5 tons helicopter fuel and 30 tons of oil-spill dispersant detergent. Have Decca CANE-2 (Computer-Assisted Navigation Equipt.) NAVSAT, and Omega systems. Two Avon "Sea Raider" rubber rescue/inspection dinghies carried. Have one fire monitor and two oil-dispersing spray booms. Intended for 21-day patrols. P 258, equipped with MARISAT, conducted minelaying trials in mid-1983. P 265 given new surveillance radar above bridge prior to S. Atlantic patrol, 1986.

◆ **7 "Isles"-class offshore patrol vessels** Bldr: Hall Russell, Aberdeen

| | L | In serv. |
|---|---|---|
| P 277 Anglesey | 18-10-78 | 1-6-79 |
| P 278 Alderney | 27-2-79 | 6-10-79 |
| P 295 Jersey | 18-3-76 | 15-10-76 |
| P 297 Guernsey | 17-2-77 | 28-10-77 |
| P 298 Shetland | 22-11-76 | 14-7-77 |
| P 299 Orkney | 29-6-76 | 25-2-77 |
| P 300 Lindisfarne | 1-6-77 | 26-1-78 |

**Shetland (P 298)** G. Gyssels, 9-86

**Anglesey (P 277)** G. Davies, Maritime Photographic, 2-86

**D:** 1,000 tons (1,280 fl) **S:** 16.5 kts **Dim:** 61.10 (51.97 pp) × 11.00 × 4.27
**A:** 1/40-mm AA Mk 3—2/7.62-mm mg (I × 2)
**Electron Equipt:** Radar: 1/1006—Sonar: 1/Simrad SU "Sidescan"
EW: MR-2 Orange Crop intercept
**M:** 2 Ruston 12 RK 3 CM diesels (750 rpm); 1/CP prop; 4,380 hp
**Electric:** 536 kw **Fuel:** 310 tons **Range:** 11,000/12
**Man:** 5 officers, 29 men (plus Marine detachment)

Remarks: Near duplicates of the Scottish Department of Fisheries ships *Jura* and *Westra*. *Jura* (as P 296) was loaned to the Royal Navy from 1975 to 1-77 for use in patrolling offshore oil rigs and the 200-nautical-mile economic zone, the purpose for which the "Isles" class were built. First five ordered 11-2-75, other pair 21-10-77. P 277 and P 278 had fin stabilizers on completion, back-fitted in the others. Can maintain 12–15 kts in a Force 8 gale. Have Decca CANES-2 Navaid. Avon Sea Raider semi-rigid dinghies are replacing the original Geminis for inspection purposes. Carry 28.6 tons detergent (a 6-hr supply) for oil-spill cleanup.

◆ **1 submarine escort ship, former oilfield supply tug**

| | Bldr | L | In serv. |
|---|---|---|---|
| P 246 Sentinel (ex-*Seaforth Warrior*, ex-*Edda Sun*) | Husumer SY, Husumer, W. Germany | 1975 | 27-6-75 (14-1-84 RN) |

**CORVETTES** *(continued)*

**Sentinel (P 246)** L. & L. Van Ginderen, 8-86

**D:** 1,100 tons (fl) **S:** 14 kts **Dim:** 60.50 (52.80 pp) × 13.00 × 4.50
**A:** 2/40-mm Mk 9 AA (I × 2)—3/7.62-mm mg (I × 3)
**Electron Equipt:** Radar: 2/Krupp-Atlas nav.
**M:** 2 MaK 12M453 A4 diesels; 2 Kort-nozzle CP props; 7,760 hp
**Electric:** 692 kVA **Man:** 26 tot.

Remarks: 934 grt/733 dwt tug purchased 3-83 for service as patrol ship, supply ship, and moorings tender for duty in the Falkland Islands. Two Becker flapped rudders, 500-hp bow-thruster, 150-ton towing winch, 87-ton bollard pull. Two 50-mm rocket flare projectors, enhanced communications suite, and two SeaRaider semi-rigid boats with electrohydraulic derrick added. Refitted 1986–87 as replacement for *Wakeful* (A 236) as submarine security vessel at Faslane.

Note: Two oilfield supply tugs purchased 3-83 for conversion as Falkland Islands patrol vessels, were sold commercial mid-1987: sisters *Protector* (P 244, ex-*Seaforth Saga*) and *Guardian* (P 245, ex-*Seaforth Champion*). They have been replaced by two Falkland Islands Government-chartered trawlers (see Falkland Islands entry).

## PATROL BOATS

◆ **5 Kingfisher class** Bldr: Richard Dunston, Hessle (P 259: Fairmile Const., Berwick-on-Tweed)

| | Laid down | L | In serv. |
|---|---|---|---|
| P 259 Redpoll (ex-RAF *Sea Otter*) | ... | ... | 1970 |
| P 260 Kingfisher | 7-73 | 20-9-74 | 8-10-75 |
| P 261 Cygnet | 10-73 | 26-10-75 | 8-7-76 |
| P 262 Peterel | 11-73 | 14-5-76 | 7-7-77 |
| P 263 Sandpiper | 12-73 | 20-1-77 | 16-9-77 |

**Cygnet (P261)**—40-mm AA replaced by boat L. & L. Van Ginderen, 9-87

**D:** 187 tons **S:** 25 kts **Dim:** 36.6 (33.8 pp) × 7.0 × 2.0
**A:** 1/40-mm AA—2/7.62-mm mg (I × 2)—see Remarks
**M:** 2 Paxman 16 YCJM diesels (1,500 rpm); 2 props; 4,000 hp
**Range:** 2,000/14 **Man:** 4 officers, 10 men

Remarks: Unsuccessful design based on RAF *Seal*-class air-sea-rescue craft. P 259 was transferred to the RN 30-10-84 and towed to Brooke Marine, Lowestoft, 2-2-85 for refit, arming, and conversion to naval standard. A large number of additional sisters were canceled. P 262 and P 263 are used for naval officer training at Dartmouth; P 260 and P 261 were employed in patrol work in the North Sea, but P 261 is now assigned as tender to the mine countermeasures squadron at Rosyth. Have fin stabilizers, but evidently still have stability problems. Only P 260 has hull portholes; P 262 and P 263 have enclosed pilothouses. 40-mm gun replaced by Zodiac boat and crane, exhaust stacks raised in 1985 refit to P 260, which, with P 259, operates in North Irish waters. 40-mm gun removed from all by mid-1987.

◆ **2 Spitfire class, ex-R.A.F.** Bldr: James & Stone, Brightlingsea

| | In serv. |
|---|---|
| P 256 Cormorant (ex-*Sunderland,* 4000) | 1976 |
| P 257 Hart (ex-*Stirling,* 4001) | 1976 |

**D:** 48 tons (60 fl) **S:** 22 kts **Dim:** 23.70 (22.15 wl) × 5.50 × 1.50
**A:** small arms **Electron Equipt:** Radar: 1/Decca AC1226
**M:** 2 Paxman 8YJCM4 diesels; 2 props; 2,000 hp
**Range:** 500/21; 1,000/15 **Fuel:** 10 tons
**Electric:** 30 kVA **Man:** 1 officer, 8 men

Remarks: Transferred 28-8-85 and stationed at Gibraltar. Six sisters remain in air/sea rescue service for the R.A.F.

Note: The P.2000-class and Tracker-class "patrol craft" formerly listed here are now found on the training craft pages, as that is their principal function. The two "Loyal"-class tenders formerly used as patrol craft in Northern Ireland were returned to the Royal Maritime Auxiliary Service in 1986 for use as tenders: *Alert* (P 252, ex-*Loyal Governor,* A 510) and *Vigilant* (P 254, ex-*Loyal Factor,* A 382) as *Lydford* (A 251, rededicated 16-9-86) and *Meary* (A 254, rededicated 25-10-86), respectively.

◆ **0 (+5 + 7) "Single-Role Minehunter" (SRMH) design** Bldr: Vosper Thornycroft, Portchester

| | Laid down | L | In serv. |
|---|---|---|---|
| M 132 Sandown | 2-87 | ... | 3-89 |
| M ... Inverness | ... | ... | ... |
| M ... Cromer | ... | ... | ... |
| M ... Walney | ... | ... | ... |
| M ... Bridport | ... | ... | ... |

**Single-Role Minehunter—artist's impression** Vosper Thornycroft, 1984

**D:** 450 tons (fl) **S:** 13 kts
**Dim:** 52.50 (50.00 pp) × 10.50 (9.00 waterline) × 2.10
**A:** 1/30-mm Rarden LS-30B AA
**Electron Equipt:** Radar: 1/Decca TM 1229—Sonar: 1/2093
**M:** 2 Paxman Valenta 6RP 200E 1500 diesels; 2 Voith-Schneider vertical cycloidal props; 3,000 hp—2/200-hp electric motors (6.5 kts)—2 bow-thrusters
**Electric:** 750 kw (3 diesel sets) **Man:** 7 officers, 26 men
**Range:** 3,500/12.

Remarks: First unit ordered 28-8-85 for a design contracted to Vosper in 1983. Class to be named for race courses. Glass-reinforced plastic construction. Will use electric drive for low-speed, quiet operation. Plessey's Type 2093 sonar uses a variable-depth vertical lozenge-shaped towed body lowered beneath the hull; it has search, depth-finder, classification, and route survey modes. The ships will carry two Remote-Controlled Mine Disposal System Mk 2 (improved PAP 104 Mk 5) submersibles for identification and disposal and will carry a mine-clearance diver team NAUTIS-M navigational $C^3$ system. Capable of dealing with mines to 200-m depths. Will replace "Ton"-class minehunters. Four ordered 23-7-87, but not funded until 1988–89. A total of twelve to be built, announced 1987.

**PATROL BOATS** *(continued)*

◆ **12 (+0 + 4) "River"-class "Extra Deep Armed Team Sweeps" (MSM/EDATS)** Bldr: Richards (Shipbuilders) Ltd.; Lowestoft (L) or Great Yarmouth (G)

| | Bldr | Laid down | L | In serv. | Station |
|---|---|---|---|---|---|
| M 2003 Waveney (ex-*Amethyst*) | L | 21-2-83 | 8-9-83 | 29-9-84 | S. Wales |
| M 2004 Carron | G | 21-2-83 | 23-9-83 | 29-9-84 | Severn |
| M 2005 Dovey | G | 3-3-83 | 1-12-83 | 30-3-85 | Clyde |
| M 2006 Helford | G | 12-10-83 | 16-5-84 | . . .-5-85 | Ulster |
| M 2007 Humber | G | 21-10-83 | 17-5-84 | 7-6-85 | London |
| M 2008 Blackwater | G | 16-1-84 | 29-8-84 | 20-6-85 | RN |
| M 2009 Itchen | L | 26-3-84 | 16-11-84 | 12-10-85 | Solent |
| M 2010 Helmsdale | L | 21-5-84 | 11-1-85 | 1-3-86 | Tay |
| M 2011 Orwell | G | 4-6-84 | 7-2-85 | . . .-86 | Tyne |
| M 2012 Ribble | G | 17-9-84 | 7-5-85 | 28-6-86 | Mersey |
| M 2013 Spey | L | 12-11-84 | 22-5-85 | 19-7-86 | Forth |
| M 2014 Arun | L | 4-2-85 | 20-8-85 | 29-8-86 | Sussex |

**Blackwater (M 2008)**—Fisheries Protection L. & L. Van Ginderen, 1-87

**Arun (M 2014)** L. & L. Van Ginderen, 10-86

**Spey (M 2013)** L. & L. Van Ginderen, 9-86

**D:** 770 tons (fl) **S:** 14 kts (15 on trials; 12 sustained)
**Dim:** 47.60 (42.00 pp) × 10.50 × 3.10 (3.75 max.)
**A:** 1/40-mm Mk 3 AA—2/7.62-mm mg (I × 2)
**Electron Equipt:** Radar: 2/Decca TM 1226—Sonar: none
**M:** 2 Ruston 6 RKCM diesels; 2 4-bladed CP props; 3,040 hp
**Range:** 4,500/10 **Fuel:** 88 tons **Electric:** 460 kw
**Man:** 7 officers, 7 petty officers, 16 men

Remarks: 638 grt. First four ordered 27-9-82, next six in 5-83, and last two on 25-2-84, to form the 10 Mine Countermeasures Squadron. Built to commercial standards, following the design of a North Sea oilfield supply vessel. Single-compartment damage standard. Intended to work in pairs, operating the BAJ-Vickers Wire Sweep Mk 9 Team Sweep System, essentially a wire catenary stretched between the ships. Navigation gear includes 2 Kelvin-Hughes MS 48 echo-sounders. Decca QM 14 (1), Decca Hifix Mk 6, and a satellite navigation receiver. All manned by Royal Naval Reserve personnel, except M 2007, used by RN for Fisheries Protection Squadron. Announced 1985 that 12 more may be built; later reduced to four, but still not ordered as of 11-87.

◆ **11 (+2) "Hunt"-class minehunters**

| | Bldr | Laid down | L | In serv. |
|---|---|---|---|---|
| M 29 Brecon | Vosper Thornycroft | 15-9-75 | 21-6-78 | 21-3-80 |
| M 30 Ledbury | Vosper Thornycroft | 5-10-77 | 5-12-79 | 11-6-81 |
| M 31 Cattistock | Vosper Thornycroft | 20-6-79 | 22-1-81 | 16-6-82 |
| M 32 Cottesmore | Yarrow, Scotstoun | 27-9-79 | 9-2-82 | 24-6-83 |
| M 33 Brocklesby | Vosper Thornycroft | 8-5-80 | 12-1-82 | 3-2-83 |
| M 34 Middleton | Yarrow, Scotstoun | 1-7-80 | 27-4-83 | 15-8-84 |
| M 35 Dulverton | Vosper Thornycroft | 1-6-81 | 3-11-82 | 4-11-83 |
| M 36 Bicester | Vosper Thornycroft | 2-1-85 | 4-6-85 | 14-2-86 |
| M 37 Chiddingfold | Vosper Thornycroft | . . . | 6-10-83 | 26-10-84 |
| M 38 Atherstone | Vosper Thornycroft | 9-1-84 | 1-3-86 | 20-1-87 |
| M 39 Hurworth | Vosper Thornycroft | 1-83 | 25-9-84 | 19-7-85 |
| M 40 Berkeley | Vosper Thornycroft | 9-9-85 | 3-12-86 | 1988 |
| M 41 Quorn | Vosper Thornycroft | 2-6-86 | -87 | 1988 |

**Atherstone (M 38)** M. Louagie, 2-87

**Dulverton (M 35)** L. & L. Van Ginderen, 7-87

**Bicester (M 36)** G. Davies, Maritime Photographic, 3-87

**PATROL BOATS** *(continued)*

**D:** 625 tons (725 fl) **S:** 17 kts **Dim:** 60.0 (56.6 pp) × 9.85 × 2.2
**A:** 1/40-mm Mk 9 AA (M 32: 1/30-mm LS-30B AA)—see Remarks
**Electron Equipt:** Radar: 1/1006—Sonar: 1/193M Mod. 1, 1/2059
**M:** 2 Ruston-Paxman Deltic 9-59K diesels (1,600 rpm); 2 props; 1,900 hp (1,770 sust.); slow-speed hydraulic drive for hunting (8 kts)—bow-thruster
**Electric:** 1,140 kw (3 Foden FD 12 Mk 7 diesel alternators of 200 kw each for ship's service plus one 480-kw Deltic 9-55B diesel alternator for magnetic minesweeping and one 60-kw emergency set)
**Man:** 6 officers, 39 men

Remarks: Equipped for both hunting and sweeping mines. Hull constructed of glass-reinforced plastic. Carry 6 or 7 divers and 2 French PAP 104 wire-guided, remote-controlled mine locators. Have Sperry "Osborn" TA 6 acoustic, M.M. Mk 11 magnetic loop and M. Mk 3 Mod. 2 Orepesa wire sweeping gear as well. Equipped with CAAIS data system and Decca Mk 21 "Hi-Fix" navigation system. M 33 laid down *prior* to ordering on 19-6-80. Twelfth and thirteenth ordered 4-6-85. M 29–M 35 are 1st Mine Countermeasures Squadron (M 29 leader); rest in 3rd MCM Sq. M 29, 33, 36, 39 to Persian Gulf 1987 with 2/20-mm BMARC AA, 2/7.62-mm mg, Matilda intercept, 2/DLF-2 (VIII × 2), 2/Barricade chaff RL added.

◆ **1 prototype glass-reinforced plastic minehunter** Bldr: Vosper Thornycroft

| | Ordered | L | In serv. |
|---|---|---|---|
| M 1116 Wilton | 11-2-70 | 18-2-72 | 25-4-73 |

**Wilton (M 1116)** L. & L. Van Ginderen, 9-86

**D:** 450 tons (fl) **S:** 15 kts **Dim:** 46.33 × 8.76 × 2.6
**A:** 1/40-mm AA Mk 7 **M:** as for "Ton" class
**Electric:** 240 kw (4/60-kw sets) **Man:** 5 officers, 32 men

Remarks: First large warship with an all-glass-reinforced plastic hull. Machinery and fittings are from *Derriton,* scrapped in 1970. Two 6-tubed chaff launchers added 1984. Acts as leader of 2nd Mine Countermeasures Squadron.

◆ **9 "Ton"-class minehunters** (3 in reserve)

| | Bldr | Laid down | L | In serv. |
|---|---|---|---|---|
| M 1113 Brereton* | Richard Ironworks | 25-9-51 | 14-5-53 | 9-7-54 |
| M 1114 Brinton | Cook, Welton & Gemmell | 30-5-51 | 8-8-52 | 4-3-54 |
| M 1115 Bronington | Cook, Welton & Gemmell | 30-5-51 | 19-3-53 | 4-6-54 |
| M 1147 Hubberston | Fleetlands SY, London | 29-1-53 | 14-9-54 | 14-10-55 |
| M 1151 Iveston | Philip & Son, Dartmouth | 22-10-52 | 1-6-54 | 20-6-55 |
| M 1153 Kedleston* | Wm. Pickersgill & Son | 26-11-52 | 21-12-53 | 2-7-55 |
| M 1154 Kellington* | Wm. Pickersgill & Son | 5-1-54 | 12-10-54 | 4-11-55 |
| M 1166 Nurton | Harland & Wolff, Belfast | 31-8-55 | 22-10-56 | 21-8-57 |
| M 1181 Sheraton | White's SY, Southhampton | 23-2-54 | 20-7-55 | 24-8-56 |

*Reserve Training

**Sheraton (M 1181)**—divers' semi-rigid boats to starboard of stack, larger pilothouse as leader, 3rd MCM Sq. L. & L. Van Ginderen, 2-87

**Bronington (M 1115)** M. Louagie, 3-87

**Hubberston (M 1147)**—minehunter, without divers' boats
G. Davies, Maritime Photographic, 4-87

◆ **4 "Ton"-class minesweepers**

| | Bldr | Laid down | L | In serv. |
|---|---|---|---|---|
| M 1124 Crichton* | J.S. Doig, Grimsby | 21-4-52 | 17-3-53 | 23-4-54 |
| M 1125 Cuxton | Camper & Nicholson's | 23-7-52 | 4-11-53 | 13-10-54 |
| M 1187 Upton | J.I. Thornycroft | 14-2-55 | 15-3-56 | 24-7-56 |
| M 1200 Soberton* | Fleetlands SY, Gosport | 11-3-55 | 20-11-56 | 17-9-57 |

* Coastal Division, Fisheries Protection Squadron

**Soberton (M 1200)**—Fisheries Protection Sq. B. Prézelin, 6-87

**D:** 370 tons (425 fl) **S:** 15 kts (cruising) **Dim:** 46.33 (42.68 pp) × 8.76 × 2.50
**A:** 1/40-mm Mk 7 AA
**Electron Equipt:** Radar: 1/978—Sonar: 1/193 (hunters only)
**M:** 2 Paxman Deltic 18A-7A diesels; 2 props; 3,000 hp
**Fuel:** 43 tons (minehunters: 36 tons) **Range:** 3,000/8; 2,300/13
**Electric:** minehunters: 240 kw **Man:** 5 officers, 33 men (sweepers: 24 men)

Remarks: Survivors of a class of 118 completed 1952–58. All minehunters are equipped with active rudders for low-speed operations, have a Type 193 sonar, and carry mine-clearance divers. The minehunter conversions were completed 1964–69.

All have wooden hulls, sheathed with nylon below the waterline. Fin stabilizers are fitted. M 1125 was first commissioned 10-75, having gone into reserve on completion in 1953. Some (but not all) fisheries protection units have a searchlight aft.

The minehunters are being refitted for retention until the new "Single-Role Mine-hunters" are ready; 6-tubed shield chaff rocket launchers were fitted on the forecastle, just forward of the break in 1984–85, but were removed in 1986.

**PATROL BOATS** *(continued)*

Disposals since last edition: Minesweepers: *Alfriston* (M 1103) paid off 11-7-86; *Bickington* (M 1109) on 31-7-86; *Walkerton* (M 1188) on 20-6-86; *Stubbington* (M 1204) on 30-7-86, and *Hodgeston* (M 1146) on . . . 86, all ostensibly for the "Standby Squadron" but in fact for scrapping. Minehunters: Paid off for scrapping were *Gavinton* (M 1140) on 4-12-86 and *Bossington* (M 1133) on 2-3-87. For retention in the "Standby Squadron," *Kirkliston* (M 1157) and *Maxton* (M 1165) were paid off in 7-86, and *Bildeston* (M 1110) paid off 30-11-86 for scrapping; the reserve units are unlikely to see further service.

## MINE COUNTERMEASURES SUPPORT SHIP

◆ **1 exercise minelayer and tender**

| | Bldr | Laid down | L | In serv. |
|---|---|---|---|---|
| N 21 Abdiel | Thornycroft, Woolston | 23-5-66 | 22-1-67 | 17-10-67 |

**Abdiel (N 21)**—note two mineports — L. & L. Van Ginderen, 6-84

**D:** 1,375 tons (1,460 fl) **S:** 16 kts **Dim:** 80.42 (74.67 pp) × 11.74 × 2.85
**A:** 2/20-mm AA—44 mines **Electron Equipt:** Radar: 1/1006
**M:** 2 Paxman Ventura 16-YSCM diesels; 2 props; 2,690 hp
**Electric:** 1,225 kw **Man:** 8 officers, 90 men

Remarks: Carries and repairs spare sweeping equipment and cable. Used primarily as an exercise minelayer, using two mine ports at the stern. Gun added 1984. To be discarded 31-3-88 without replacement, after Mideast service with Matilda intercept gear, Barricade chaff RL.

## AMPHIBIOUS WARFARE SHIPS

### ASSAULT SHIPS

Note: Landing ships and craft subordinated to the Royal Corps of Transport are covered in the Royal Army entry at the conclusion of the Great Britain section, on page 244. *Invincible*-class carriers can also carry troops.

Four new amphibious warfare ships are to be built in the 1990s to replace existing units, according to a 5-86 announcement. Two LPD type will replace *Fearless* and *Intrepid,* and two assault helicopter carriers are to follow. Swan Hunter has proposed a 175.0 × 24.0 × 19.0-m (moulded depth) LPD that would carry two air-cushion landing craft in its docking well and would be powered by four 5,400-hp diesels driving 2 CP propellers. Conversions have also been considered, including the commercial vehicle cargo ships *Contender Argent* and *Seaspeed America.*

◆ **2 Fearless class** (1 in reserve)

| | Bldr | Laid down | L | In serv. |
|---|---|---|---|---|
| L 10 Fearless* | Harland & Wolff | 25-7-62 | 19-12-63 | 25-11-65 |
| L 11 Intrepid | J. Brown (Clyde) | 11-12-62 | 5-6-64 | 11-3-67 |

* In reserve

**Intrepid (L 11)** — L. & L. Van Ginderen, 4-87

**Intrepid (L 11)** — G. Davies, Maritime Photographic, 6-87

**D:** 11,060 tons (12,120 fl) (16,950 tons, draft 9.15, with well deck flooded)
**S:** 21 kts **Dim:** 158.5 (152.4 pp) × 24.38 × 6.2
**A:** 4/Sea Cat GWS.20 systems (IV × 4) (L 11: IV × 2)—2/40-mm AA (I × 2)—L 11: 4/30-mm Oerlikon GCM-A02 AA (II × 2), 2/20-mm GAM-B01 AA (I × 2)
**Electron Equipt:** Radar: 1/978, 1/994—IFF: 1/1010 interrogator
EW: passive system, 2 DLC chaff RL (VIII × 2)
**M:** English-Electric GT; 2 props; 22,000 hp **Electric:** 4,000 kw
**Boilers:** 2 Babcock & Wilcox, 38.66 $kg/cm^2$, 454°C superheat
**Range:** 5,000/20 **Man:** 36 officers, 520 men, 380-700 troops

Remarks: Equivalent to U.S. LPD type, and have excellent command and communication facilities for amphibious operations. CAAIS combat data system fitted. They can launch four to six assault helicopters (landing platform but no hangar). On board are four LCVP Mk 2 landing craft, which can transport 35 men or a half-ton vehicle, and four LCM (9) landing craft carrying two Chieftain tanks or four vehicles or 100 tons of supplies; four additional tanks can be carried on the tank deck. The vehicles are divided between the tank deck, a lower deck, and a half-deck reserved for jeeps. The active unit has normally been assigned as officer cadet training ship at the Royal Naval College, Dartmouth, but has been immediately available for amphibious operations as required. Two twin 30-mm AA replaced the after two Sea Cat launchers in L 11 1985, and two 20-mm AA were added forward. *Fearless,* in reserve at Portsmouth 1985, will reactivate with 2/20-mm Mk 15 Phalanx CIWS in place of the after Sea Cat launchers and is to receive the Plessey NAUTIS-L navigation/action data system, with seven display consoles. May be refitted to last past mid-1990s vice building new ships, announced 5-87.

## TANK LANDING SHIPS

| | Bldr | Laid down | L | In serv. |
|---|---|---|---|---|
| L 3066 Sir Galahad | Swan Hunter, Wallsend | 12-7-85 | 13-12-86 | 7-12-87 |

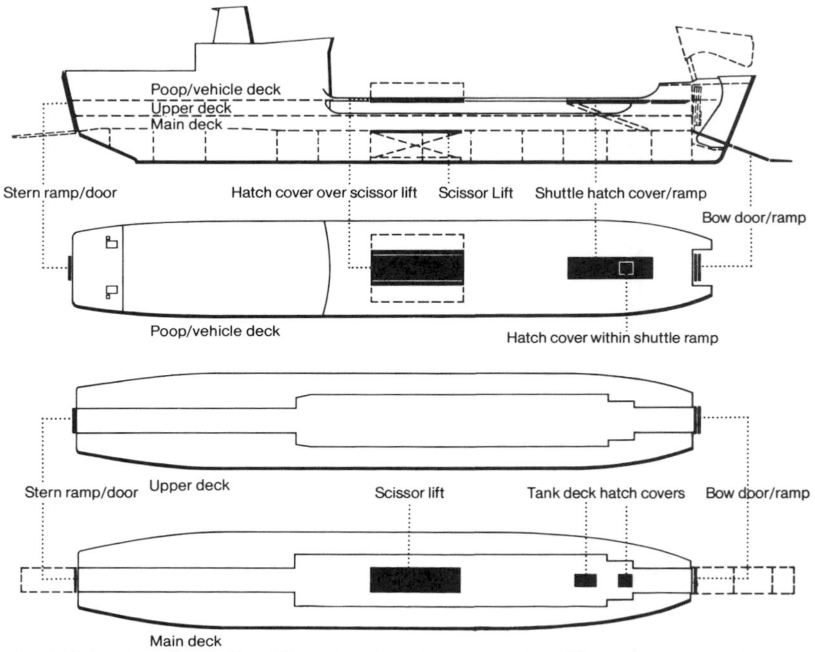


**Sir Galahad**—schematic of interior, showing cargo-handling arrangement
MacGregor-Navire, 1985

**D:** 7,400 tons light (8,585 fl) **S:** 18 kts
**Dim:** 140.46 (126.00 pp) × 19.50 × 4.50 (3.97 light)
**A:** 2/40-mm AA (I × 2)—2/20-mm GAM-B01 AA (I × 2)
**Electron Equipt:** Radar: 1/1007, 1/. . . X-band nav.,
1/. . . S-band nav.
EW: . . . intercept, 4 DLB RL (VI × 4)

## TANK LANDING SHIPS *(continued)*

**M:** 2 Mirrlees-Blackstone K9 Major diesels; 2 CP props; 13,320 hp
**Range:** 13,000/15 **Fuel:** 1,260 tons
**Electric:** 2,460 kw (4 × 540 kw, 1 × 300 kw sets)
**Man:** 52 crew, plus 340 troops—see Remarks.

REMARKS: 3,055 dwt. Ordered 6-9-84 as replacement for ship of the same name lost in the Falklands War. Has Decca-Racal CANE navigational system. Type 182 torpedo decoy installed. One 25-ton crane forward of the bridge, two 8.5-ton cranes forward. Bow and stern ramps, visor-type bow door 20-ton scissor lift amidships to forward vehicle/helicopter deck; 20-ton traveling crane on upper of two vehicle decks within 8.57-m moulded-depth hull. Can accommodate an additional 133 troops in public spaces, plus another 64 without berths, for a maximum of 537. Completed trials 10-7-87.

◆ **1 chartered merchant ship** Bldr: Trosvik Verksted, Brevik, Norway

| | L | In serv. |
|---|---|---|
| L 3522 SIR CARADOC (ex-*Gray Master*) | 8-11-72 | 1-73 |

**Sir Caradoc (L 3522)** G. Gyssels, 3-87

**D:** 5,980 tons (fl) **S:** 17.5 kts **Dim:** 124.20 (114.33) × 16.03 × 4.85
**A:** removed **Electron Equipt:** Radar: 2/navigational
**M:** 4 Bergens-Normo LSM-9 diesels; 2 CP props; 5,040 hp
**Range:** 10,600/16 **Fuel:** 500 tons
**Electric:** 625 kw **Man:** 33 crew + 24 RFA personnel

REMARKS: 1,899 grt/3,480 dwt. Chartered 14-1-83 from Norwegian Nitre Shipping Co. and put in service 26-3-83 as replacement (with *Sir Lamorak*) for the sunken *Sir Galahad* and the damaged *Sir Tristram*. Crew augmented, armament added, and MARISAT system installed. Two 350-hp side-thrusters, bow and stern vehicle cargo ramps fitted. **A:** 2/20-mm AA removed 1984. Refitted 1987, apparently for further RFA service, although was due for return to owners.

NOTE: The similar chartered vehicle cargo ship *Sir Lamorak* (L 3532) was returned to owners in 11-85 and now operates commercially as *Merchant Trader*.

◆ **5 Sir Bedivere class** (logistic lift ships in peacetime)

| | Bldr | Laid down | L | In serv. |
|---|---|---|---|---|
| L 3004 SIR BEDIVERE | Hawthorn Leslie | 10-65 | 20-7-66 | 18-5-67 |
| L 3027 SIR GERAINT | Alexander Stephen | 6-65 | 26-1-67 | 12-7-67 |
| L 3029 SIR LANCELOT | Fairfield | 3-62 | 25-6-63 | 16-1-64 |
| L 3036 SIR PERCIVALE | Hawthorn Leslie | 4-66 | 4-10-67 | 23-3-68 |
| L 3505 SIR TRISTRAM | Hawthorn Leslie | 2-66 | 12-12-66 | 14-9-67 |

**Sir Geraint (L 3027)** G. Davies, Maritime Photographic, 6-87

**Sir Lancelot (L 3029)**—class prototype, with four cranes and raised gun platforms
G. Gyssels, 7-86

**Sir Tristram (L 3505)**—lengthened, kingposts supporting electronics arrays
L. & L. Van Ginderen, 5-86

**D:** 3,270 tons (5,674 fl) (L 3505: 5,800 fl) **S:** 17 kts
**Dim:** 126.45 (L 3505: 134.84) × 17.7 × 3.8 **A:** removed
**Electron Equipt:** Radar: 2 or 3/navigational
EW: 2/DLC chaff RL (VIII × 2)
**M:** 2 Mirrlees 10-ALSSDM 10-cyl. diesels; 2 props; 9,400 hp (L 3029: 2 Denny-Sulzer diesels; 9,520 hp)
**Fuel:** 811 tons **Range:** 8,000/15 **Man:** 18 officers, 51 men

REMARKS: 2,443 dwt. In 1963 the Ministry of Transportation ordered the first of six specially designed LST-type ships for the Army, chartered in peacetime to various private maritime firms. In 1970 these ships came under the control of the Royal Fleet Auxiliary Service. Beaching cargo capacity is 340 tons. Bow and stern ramps for vehicles, interior ramps connect the two decks. Quarters for 402 men. Helicopter platform and three cranes (two 4.5, one 8.5 tons). All have MARISAT gear. L 3029 has four cranes, and is 5,550 tons full load. L 3505 badly damaged 8-6-83, but was carried home in 6-83 and repaired by Tyne Shiprepair, South Shields, 7-84 to 7-85; a new 120-ton, 8.915-m midsection being added, along with rehabilitated accommodations and larger helicopter deck. The rebuilding was not entirely successful, as the ship trims down by the stern and can no longer load tanks on the after trunk space. L 3505 carried 2/20-mm AA and was equipped with 4 DLB (shield) decoy RL; in refit again 1986–87. L 3036 in major refit 1986–87. Falklands War armament of 2/40-mm Mk 3 AA (I × 2) removed 1984. *Sir Galahad* (L 3005) was fatally damaged on 8-6-82 and was scuttled 24-6-82. L 3029 may strike 1988.

## LANDING CRAFT

◆ **15 LCM (9) class** (In serv. 1963–66; L 713–715: 1986)

L 700–L 702 (Bldr: Brooke Marine, Lowestoft) L 710, L 711 (Bldr: J. Bolson, Poole)
L 704–L 709 (Bldr: Richard Dunston, Thorne) L 3508 (Bldr: Vosper)
L 713–715 (Bldr: McTay Marine, Liverpool)

**L 709**—attached to *Intrepid* L. & L. Van Ginderen, 5-85

**L 704**—hull built up amidships and inflatable personnel shelter on tank deck
L. & L. Van Ginderen, 2-87

**D:** 75 tons (176 fl) **S:** 9 kts **Dim:** 25.7 × 6.5 × 1.7
**Electron Equipt:** Radar: 1/Decca 101
**M:** 2 Paxman YHXAM diesels; Kort-nozzle props; 624 hp **Man:** 6 tot.

REMARKS: Can carry two Centurion tanks or 70 tons of cargo. All naval-manned. *Fearless* (L 10) and *Intrepid* (L 11) can each carry four of this class. L 703 (F4-*Fearless* No. 4) lost to bomb 8-6-82. L 713–L 715 have Dorman 8 JTM diesels; 540 hp.

LANDING CRAFT *(continued)*

◆ **17 LCVP Mk 4 Class** Bldrs: 8301 by Fairey Allday Marine, Hamble; 8401–8418 by W.A. Souter, Cowes

| | In serv. | | In serv. |
|---|---|---|---|
| 8301 | 1982 | 8411 | 3-12-85 |
| 8401 | 5-3-85 | 8412 | 15-1-86 |
| 8403 | 29-3-85 | 8413 | 1986 |
| 8404 | 1-5-85 | 8414 | 1986 |
| 8405 | 30-5-85 | 8415 | 1986 |
| 8406 | 10-7-85 | 8416 | 1986 |
| 8407 | 18-7-85 | 8417 | 1986 |
| 8408 | 12-8-85 | 8418 | 1987 |
| 8410 | 11-10-85 | | |

**LCVP Mk 4 8404** L. & L. Van Ginderen, 7-85

**D:** 10 tons (fl) **S:** 20 kts (16 loaded) **Dim:** 13.00 (11.90 pp) × 3.20 × 0.80
**A:** 2/7.62-mm mg (I × 2)
**M:** 2 Perkins 76-3544 diesels; 2 props; 440 hp (8416–18: 2 Dorman diesels; 2 CP props; . . . hp)
**Range:** 200/12 (8416–18: 300/12) **Man:** 3 crew + 35 troops

Remarks: Prototype, ordered 6-2-80, is 13.50 long by 3.50 beam. Series units ordered 21-8-84. Have cargo well 8.80 × 2.13 and a cargo capacity of 5.5 tons. Aluminum construction. Replacing LCVP (1) through LCVP (3). 8416–8418 can reach 22 kts. Four others serve the Army's Royal Corps of Transport.

◆ **3 Ferryman 18 class** Bldr: Freezer Aluminum Boats, Hayling Island (In serv. 1 on 13-8-84, 2 on 16-8-84)

LCR 5506–5508

**D:** 2.5 tons **S:** 20 kts **Dim:** 5.48 × 2.21 × 0.40
**M:** 1 OMC gasoline outboard; 140 hp **Cargo:** 10 troops

Remarks: New series of raider boats for Royal Marines, ordered 16-5-84. Additional aluminum and rigid inflatable raider boats of this size are also available.

◆ **8 LCVP (2)**

LCVP (2): 142–149

**LCVP (2)** L. & L. Van Ginderen, 7-85

**D:** 8.5 tons (13.5 fl) **S:** 8–10 kts **Dim:** 12.7 or 13.1 × 3.1 × 0.8
**M:** 2 Foden diesels; 2 props; 130 or 200 hp

Remarks: The eight LCVP (2) were carried in *Fearless* and *Intrepid.* Four fitted for mine countermeasures in the Falklands War, 5-82. 16 earlier LCVP (1) and LCVP (3) discarded 1986–87. Late note: all discarded 1987.

◆ **35 or more "Mexiflote" self-propelled pontoons**

A "Mexiflote" self-propelled pontoon in use during the recovery of the Falkland Islands, 6-82. Each *Sir Bedivere*-class LST can carry two of these low-freeboard craft mounted vertically on the hull sides. Powered by 2 Sykes Marine Harbormaster F 725 units: 150 hp. Sixty-seven more propulsion units ordered 1985, using Ford 2725 diesels.

### AUXILIARY SHIPS

Most auxiliary and supply vessels are responsible to the Royal Fleet Auxiliary (RFA), an organization peculiar to the Royal Navy. Built to the specifications of Lloyds of London (compartmentation, security, habitability), they also meet the standards of the Shipping Naval Acts of 1911 and of the Ministry of Transportation. In 1985, it was decided to reclassify all RFA ships as "Government-Owned Vessels." Manned by the Civil Service, they fly the blue ensign of the reserve, rather than the white ensign. In addition, about 40 tugs, salvage vessels, cable layers, research vessels, etc., are assigned to the Royal Maritime Auxiliary Service (RMAS), whose personnel are also civil servants. The former Port Auxiliary Service (PAS) was absorbed by the RMAS on 1-10-76. An additional group of service craft are operated by the Royal Naval Auxiliary Service (RNXS). Ships not listed below as either RFA, RNXS, or RMAS are manned by the Royal Navy. RMAS ships have black hulls and buff upperworks, while RNXS units have black hulls and gray upperworks. They often do not display hull numbers; pendant numbers are listed hereafter in parentheses for reference only.

### HYDROGRAPHIC SHIPS

Note: All Royal Navy survey ships are painted white, with buff-colored stacks and masts.

◆ **1 improved Hecla class**

| | Bldr | Laid down | L | In serv. |
|---|---|---|---|---|
| (A 138) Herald | Robb Caledon | 9-11-72 | 4-10-73 | 31-10-74 |

**Herald (A 138)** B. Sullivan, 10-87

**D:** 2,125 tons (2,945 fl) **S:** 14 kts **Dim:** 79.3 × 14.9 × 4.7
**Electron Equipt:** Radar: 1/1006, 1/. . . nav. **Man:** 128 tot.
**M:** diesel-electric propulsion (identical to the *Hecla* class); 1 prop

Remarks: Improved version of the *Hecla* class. Carries one Wasp helicopter. Has Type 2034 Sidescan charting sonar. On ice-patrol duties, 6-83 to 2-84, gray-painted and with 2/20-mm AA. Has MARISAT. Has Type 2034 mapping sonar.

◆ **2 Hecla class**

| | Bldr | Laid down | L | In serv. |
|---|---|---|---|---|
| (A 133) Hecla | Yarrow, Blythswood | 6-5-64 | 21-12-64 | 9-9-65 |
| (A 137) Hecate | Yarrow, Scotstoun | 26-10-64 | 31-3-65 | 20-12-65 |

**D:** 1,915 tons (2,733 fl) **S:** 14 kts **Dim:** 79.25 (71.63 pp) × 14.94 × 4.0
**M:** diesel-electric propulsion: 3 Paxman Ventura diesels (12 cyl.), each 1,280 hp; 2 electric motors; 1 prop; 2,000 hp
**Fuel:** 450 tons **Range:** 20,000/9; 12,000/11 **Man:** 14 officers, 104 men

Remarks: Based on the oceanographic research vessel *Discovery.* Air-conditioned hull, reinforced against ice; bow-thruster for navigation in narrow waters. Hangar and platform for one Wasp helicopter. Excellent scientific laboratories; usually carry seven civilian scientists in addition to crew. Two survey launches. Have

## HYDROGRAPHIC SHIPS *(continued)*

Type 2034 Sidescan charting sonar. Have Type 2034 mapping sonars. Sister *Hydra* (A 144) stricken 18-4-86 and sold to Indonesia. The surviving two were to be paid off in late 1987 (*Hecla*) and early 1988 (*Hecate*) but striking delayed during search for a commercial charter successor.

**Hecla**—in survey colors L. & L. Van Ginderen, 9-86

◆ **1 Roebuck-class coastal survey ship** Bldr: Brooke Marine, Lowestoft

| | Laid down | L | In serv. |
|---|---|---|---|
| (A 130) Roebuck | . . . | 14-11-85 | 30-10-86 |

**Roebuck** M.O.D., 5-87

**Roebuck** L. & L. Van Ginderen, 5-87

**D:** 1,521 tons (fl) **S:** 15 kts **Dim:** 63.89 (57.60 pp) × 13.00 × 3.82
**Electron Equipt:** Radar: 2/nav.
Sonar: Marconi Hydrosearch, Waverley Sidescan
**M:** 4 Mirrlees ES-8 Mk 1 diesels; 2 CP props; 3,040 hp
**Range:** 4,000/10 **Man:** 6 officers, 10 senior P.O., 31 ratings

Remarks: Ordered 21-5-84 as first of a planned quartet; other three no longer in program. Has replaced *Hydra.* Has Qubit SIPS (Survey Information Processing System). Hydrosearch sonar provides high-definition imaging to 600-m depths. Has A-frame at stern to tow magnetometer and Waverley Sidescan sonar. Carries two survey launches, *Batchellor Delight* and *Jolly Prize,* described next page.

◆ **4 Bulldog-class coastal survey ships** Bldr: Brooke Marine, Lowestoft

| | L | In serv. |
|---|---|---|
| (A 317) Bulldog | 12-7-67 | 21-3-68 |
| (A 319) Beagle (ex-*Barracuda*) | 7-9-67 | 9-5-68 |
| (A 320) Fox | 6-11-67 | 11-7-68 |
| (A 335) Fawn | 29-2-68 | 10-9-68 |

**Bulldog** L. & L. Van Ginderen, 11-85

**D:** 800 tons (1,088 fl) **S:** 15 kts **Dim:** 60.95 × 11.43 × 3.6
**M:** 4 Lister-Blackstone ERS-8-M diesels; 2 KaMeWa CP props; 2,640 hp
**Electric:** 720 kw **Range:** 4,600/12 **Man:** 5 officers, 34 men

Remarks: Hulls built to commercial specifications and reinforced against ice damage. Carry one 8.7-meter survey launch. Passive tank stabilization. Decca "Hi-Fix" precision plot. Can be equipped with 2/20-mm AA on bridge wings (I × 2). Carry one 8.7-m survey boat. Have Type 2034 mapping sonars, except *Bulldog,* refitted 1985 with prototype Marconi Hydrosearch and a new radar.

◆ **1 chartered trawler** Bldr: Mathias Thesen Werft, Wismar, East Germany
Bon Esprit (ex-*Ernst Haeckel*) (In serv. 1963)

**D:** 1453 grt **S:** 12 kts **Dim:** 67.70 (60.00 pp) × 11.82 × 4.90
**Electron Equipt:** . . .
**M:** 2 Görlitz diesels: 1/8-cyl.; 1/6-cyl.; 1 CP prop; 1,420 hp
**Electric:** 372 kw (1/160 kw, 1/132 kw, 1/80 kw)
**Range:** . . . **Fuel:** 289.5 tons **Man:** . . .

Remarks: Ice-strengthened, stern-haul trawler chartered 5-86 for three years from J. McKee and Partners for coastal surveys in British waters. Propulsion plant employs "mother/daughter" concept with 6-cyl. cruise diesel. In 1985 the Royal Navy chartered M/V *Proud Seahorse* and M/V *Bon Esprit* for coastal survey work, using owner's crews plus Hydrographic Service survey parties.

◆ **1 inshore survey craft** Bldr: Emsworth SY, Emsworth

| | L | In serv. |
|---|---|---|
| (A 86) Gleaner | 18-10-83 | 5-12-84 |

**Gleaner** Maritime Photographic, 2-85

**D:** 22 tons (fl) **S:** 14 kts **Dim:** 14.81 × 4.55 × 1.30
**Electron Equipt:** Radar: 1/Decca 110
**M:** 2 Rolls-Royce CG M-310 diesels; 2 props; 524 hp; 1 Perkins 4.236 M cruise diesel; 1 prop; 72 hp
**Range:** 450/10 **Man:** 1 officer, 4 men

### HYDROGRAPHIC SHIPS *(continued)*

REMARKS: Smallest commissioned "ship" in the RN, intended for survey work in the Solent-Portsmouth area and in the Channel Islands. Glass-reinforced plastic hull by Halmatic. Speed on cruise engine: 3 to 7 kts.

◆ **3 survey boats** Bldr: Halmatic, Havant (In serv. 1986)
BATCHELLOR DELIGHT JOLLY PRIZE N . . .

**D:** 8.75 tons (fl) **S:** 13 kts **Dim:** 8.94 (8.10 wl) × 3.60 × 0.99
**M:** 2 Perkins 6.3544 diesels; 2 props; 230 hp
**Range:** 200/13 **Man:** 4 tot.

REMARKS: GRP construction; builder's "Serviceman" class ordered 12-84. First two carried by *Roebuck*, third (with wood-sheathed hull for ice protection) carried by *Endurance.*

NOTE: The *Echo*-class inshore survey boats *Echo* (A 70), *Enterprise* (A 71), and *Egeria* (A 72) were paid off 12-84 but retained. *Egeria* was loaned to the Maritime Society as *Jonas Hanway* in 1986 and borrowed back 1987 as a training craft for the RNXS; the other two are retained for spares.

### EXPERIMENTAL SHIPS

◆ **0 (+1) chartered sonar trials ship** Bldr: . . .

**N:** . . .
**D:** . . . **S:** . . . **Dim:** . . . × . . . × . . .
**Electron Equipt:** Radar: . . . —Sonar: 2093
**M:** . . .

REMARKS: Ship sought for charter for delivery 1-1-88 for trials with Type 2093 minehunting sonar. To have centerline "moonpool" for 2,900-kg "fish," plus side lift for 1,200-kg PAP-104 Mk 5 minehunting submersible.

◆ **1 sonar-trials ship**

| | Bldr | Laid down | L | In serv. |
|---|---|---|---|---|
| A 285 AURICULA | Ferguson Bros. | 16-2-79 | 22-11-79 | 6-11-80 |

**Auricula (A 285)** L. & L. Van Ginderen, 1985

**D:** 1,200 tons (fl) **S:** 12 kts **Dim:** 60.0 (52.0 pp) × 11.0 × 3.6
**M:** 2 Mirrlees-Blackstone ESL-6-MGR diesels; 2 props; 1,300 hp
**Man:** 7 officers, 15 men, 10 technicians

REMARKS: Ship operated by RMAS. Ordered 5-1-78. "Trials and Experimental Tender" to Admiralty Underwater Weapons Establishment, Portland; replaced *Steady*. Has a bow-thruster.

◆ **1 sonar-research ship**

| | Bldr | Laid down | L | In serv. |
|---|---|---|---|---|
| A 367 NEWTON | Scott-Lithgow, Greenock | 19-12-73 | 26-6-75 | 17-6-76 |

**Newton (A 367)** L. & L. Van Ginderen, 8-84

**D:** 3,940 tons (fl) **S:** 14 kts **Dim:** 98.6 (88.7 pp) × 16.15 × 4.7
**Electron Equipt:** Radar: 1/1006—Sonar: 1/182, 1/185, 1/2010, 1/2013
**M:** 3 Mirrlees-Blackstone EWSL-12 MA 1,450-hp diesels, electric drive; 1 Kort-nozzle prop; 2,680 hp
**Electric:** 2,150 kw **Fuel:** 244 tons **Range:** 5,000/9
**Man:** 61 men (including 12 technicians)

REMARKS: Intended for sonar-propagation trials and also fitted to lay cable over the bows. Equipped with 350-hp retractable bow-thruster and passive tank stabilization system. Propulsion plant extremely quiet, with a 300-hp electric motor for low speeds. Has four laboratories and seven special winches. Can carry and lay 400 tons of undersea cable and 361 tons cable repeaters. Navigation equipment includes SINS, satellite receivers, two optical range-finders, Decca Mk 21, and considerable other equipment. RMAS-operated. Optical rangefinder atop pilothouse. Refitted 1986 to 3-87 to test new equipment.

◆ **1 torpedo-research vessel**

A 364 WHITEHEAD Bldr: Scotts SB, Greenock (L: 5-5-70)

**Whitehead (A 364)** 1971

**D:** 3,040 tons (fl) **S:** 15.5 kts **Dim:** 97.23 (88.7 pp) × 14.63 × 5.2
**A:** 1/533-mm TT (bow, submerged)—3/324-mm S.T.W.S.1 ASW TT (III × 1)
**M:** 2 Paxman 12 YLCM diesels; 1 prop; 3,400 hp
**Range:** 4,000/12 **Man:** 10 officers, 47 men and scientists

REMARKS: Designed not only to launch and recover exercise torpedoes but also to perform precision tracking in three dimensions, using passive hydrophone arrays, and post-firing checkout and maintenance on torpedoes. RMAS-operated. May replace *Abdiel* (N 21) as exercise minelayer.

◆ **1 sonar-research barge**

| | Bldr | L | In serv. |
|---|---|---|---|
| (RDV 01) CRYSTAL | HMDY, Devonport | 22-3-71 | 30-11-71 |

**Crystal** L. & L. Van Ginderen, 7-85

**D:** 3,040 tons (fl) **Dim:** 126.0 × 17.0 × 1.7 **Man:** 60 tot.

REMARKS: No propulsion plant. Assigned to test new sonars at Admiralty Underwater Weapons Establishment, Portland. RMAS-operated.

◆ **1 vertical-launch missile trials barge**

LONGBOW (ex-*Dynamic Servant*, ex-*Ocean Servant* 2) (In serv. 1976)

**Longbow**—with tender *Grasmere* (A 402) L. & L. Van Ginderen, 7-85

## EXPERIMENTAL SHIPS *(continued)*

**D:** 12,600 tons (fl) **S:** . . . **Dim:** 109.0 (108.0 pp) × 30.0 × . . .
**A:** 6/Sea Wolf VLS launchers **Electron Equipt:** Radar: 2/. . . nav., 1/911 f.c.
**M:** 2 Bolnes diesels; 2 Schottel props; 1,200 hp **Man:** 10 tot. (contractor)

REMARKS: Delivered post-conversion 23-7-85. Originally chartered by British Aerospace late 1984; converted from float-on/float-off cargo barge at Govan. Crew are British Aerospace personnel. Bo-105 helicopter used for support.

## REPAIR SHIP

◆ **1 former oilfield support tender** Bldr: Øresundvarvet, Landskrona, Sweden

| | L | In serv. (RN) |
|---|---|---|
| A 132 DILIGENCE (ex-*Stena Inspector*) | 1981 | 12-3-84 |

**Diligence (A 132)** W. Sartori, 7-87

**Diligence (A 132)** B. Sullivan, 6-87

**D:** approx. 10,900 tons (fl) **S:** 16 kts **Dim:** 111.47 (101.30 pp) × 20.97 × 8.30
**A:** 4/20-mm Oerlikon GAM-B01 AA (I × 4)
**Electron Equipt:** Radar: 3/. . . nav.—EW: 4 DLB RL (VI × 4)
**M:** 5 Nohab 16-cyl. diesels, electric drive (4 motors); CP prop; 1,800 hp—2 side-thrusters forward, 2 rotatable thrusters aft
**Man:** RFA: 15 officers, 24 men + 155-man naval repair party **Fuel:** 3,150 tons

REMARKS: 6,060-grt former North Sea oilfield support ship chartered during Falklands War for emergency, war-zone repairs. Purchased outright 31-10-83 and commissioned 12-3-84. Has MARISAT SATCOMM terminal, large helicopter deck (no hangar) atop massive superstructure, moon-pool for divers. Ice-strengthened hull. Cranes include four 20- to 40-ton, one 20-ton, one 15-ton and one 5-ton. Capable of firefighting, towing, and salvage. Very maneuverable; can make 6 kts sideways. Had long refit 9-83 to 6-84. Near-sister *Stena Seaspread* chartered early 1987 during 2-month refit in U.K..

## ACCOMMODATIONS SHIPS

◆ **1 "County"-class former guided-missile destroyer**

| | Bldr | Laid down | L | In serv. |
|---|---|---|---|---|
| D 12 KENT | Harland & Wolff, Belfast | 1-3-60 | 27-9-61 | 15-8-63 |

**Kent (D 12)** W. Donko, 8-85

**D:** approx. 5,400 tons **S:** . . . **Dim:** 158.55 (153.90 pp) × 16.46 × . . .
**A:** 4/114-mm DP Mk 6 (II × 2; inactivated)
**Electron Equipt:** Radar: 1/978, 1/965, 1/992Q, 1/277, 1/901, 1/903—inactivated
Sonar: 184M, 162M—inactivated
**M:** COSAG: 2 sets A.E.I. GT (15,000 hp each), 4 G6 gas turbines (7,500 hp each); 2 props; 60,000 hp—inactivated
**Electric:** 4,750 kw **Fuel:** 600 tons **Range:** 3,500/28
**Boilers:** 2 Babcock & Wilcox; 49.21 kg/cm$^2$, 510°, 510°C superheat

REMARKS: Decommissioned, relegated to harbor training, again decommissioned 16-5-83. Converted 30-10-84 to 6-8-85 to act as accommodations hulk for cadets.

NOTE: The Head-class former repair ship *Rame Head* was discarded 13-3-87; her sister *Berry Head*, formerly used as floating office space at Devonport, was scrapped *in situ* during 1986-87.

## FLEET-REPLENISHMENT SHIPS

◆ **2 Fort-class ammunition, explosives, food, and stores ships** Bldr: Scott-Lithgow, Greenock

| | Laid down | L | In serv. |
|---|---|---|---|
| A 385 FORT GRANGE | 9-11-73 | 9-12-76 | 6-4-78 |
| A 386 FORT AUSTIN | 9-12-75 | 9-3-78 | 11-5-79 |

**Fort Grange (A 385)** L. & L. Van Ginderen, 10-86

**Fort Austin (A 386)** Skyfotos, 9-85

**D:** 22,749 tons (fl) **S:** 20 kts **Dim:** 183.8 (170.0 pp) × 24.1 × 8.6
**A:** 2/20-mm AA (I × 2)—1 or 2/Sea King helicopters
**Electron Equipt:** Radar: 1/Kelvin-Hughes 21/16 P, 1/Kelvin-Hughes 14/12
EW: 2/DLC RL (VIII × 2)
**M:** 1 Sulzer 8 RND 90 diesel; 1 prop; 23,200 hp **Electric:** 4,120 kw
**Range:** 10,000/20 **Man:** 140 Royal Fleet Auxiliary personnel, plus 45 naval.

REMARKS: Ordered 11-71 and 4-72; 16,009 grt/8,300 dwt/6,729 nrt. In addition to the flight deck on the stern, the roof of the hangar can land helicopters. One Sea King is normally carried (although four can be accommodated), and the ships have ASW torpedoes and other ASW stores for use if needed. Carry 3,500 tons of ammunition, food, and spares. Bow-thruster. Three sliding-stay, constant-tension, alongside-replenishment stations on each beam. Have 2/10-ton and 4/5-ton electric stores cranes. Platforms for two SCOT satellite communications radomes atop superstructure, but received MARISAT commercial system instead, and 20-mm AA were mounted on the SCOT platforms in 1982. Have Type 182 towed torpedo decoys. RFA-operated.

**FLEET-REPLENISHMENT SHIPS** *(continued)*

◆ **2 Resource-class ammunition, explosives, food, and stores ships**

| | Bldr | Laid down | L | In serv. |
|---|---|---|---|---|
| A 480 Resource | Scotts SB, Greenock | 6-64 | 11-2-66 | 18-5-67 |
| A 486 Regent | Harland & Wolff, Belfast | 9-64 | 9-3-66 | 6-6-67 |

**Regent (A 486)** H. Ehlers, 11-86

**Regent (A 486)** L. & L. Van Ginderen, 4-84

**D:** 22,890 tons (fl) (18,029 grt) **S:** 17 kts
**Dim:** 195.07 (182.88 pp) × 23.47 × 7.95
**Electron Equipt:** Radar: 1/Kelvin-Hughes 21/16P, 1/Kelvin-Hughes 14/12
EW: 2/DLC chaff RL (VIII × 2)
**M:** 1 set A.E.I. GT; 1 prop; 20,000 hp **Boilers:** 2 Foster-Wheeler
**Man:** 119 Royal Fleet Auxiliary, 52 civilian, plus airgroup

Remarks: RFA-operated. Three sliding-stay, constant-tension, alongside-replenishment stations per side. Carry one Sea King helicopter.

**FLEET OILERS**

◆ **0 (+2 + 4 + 6) Fort Victoria-class replenishment ships**

| | Bldr | Laid down | L | In serv. |
|---|---|---|---|---|
| A . . . Fort Victoria | Harland & Wolff, Belfast | . . . | . . . | 1990 |
| A . . . N . . . | . . . | . . . | . . . | . . . |

**Fort Victoria**—artist's rendering Y-ARD, 1986

**D:** 31,565 (fl) **S:** 20 kts **Dim:** 203.50 (195.00 wl) × 28.50 × . . .
**A:** 32 Sea Wolf GWS.26 vertical-launch SAM—4/30-mm LS-30B AA (I × 4)—3/EH.101 or Sea King helicopters
**Electron Equipt:** Radar: 1/1007, 1/. . . nav, 1/996, 2/911
EW: intercept array; 4/DLB RL (VI × 4)
**M:** 2 Crossley-Pielstick medium-speed diesels; 2 props; 25,000 hp
**Electric:** 9,600 kw (6 × 1,600-kw diesel sets) **Range:** . . .
**Man:** 120 RFA, 100 naval, 30 spare accom.

Remarks: Intended to carry about 70,000 barrels (12,000 m$^3$) liquid cargo and 6,000 m$^3$ of munitions, dry stores, and refrigerated cargo. Will replace present generation of replenishment ships. The first was ordered 8-5-86; the second was to be ordered from Swan Hunter in 1987. There will be two fueling stations per side, plus an astern refueling capability. Two dual-purpose liquid/solid replenishment stations per side, plus vertical replenishment. The ships will carry ASW ordnance for their three helicopters. Will have SCOT antennas for the SHF SATCOMM Skynet IV system. To have Type 182 towed torpedo decoys. One 25-ton, two 10-ton, and two 5-ton electric cranes will be fitted, with one 10-ton crane capable of supporting an additional underway-refueling rig.

The second series of six will be of a simplified version, primarily intended for point-to-point service as replacements for the "Leaf" series.

◆ **3 Olwen class**

| | Bldr | L | In serv. |
|---|---|---|---|
| A 122 Olwen (ex-*Olynthus*) | Hawthorn Leslie | 10-7-64 | 21-6-65 |
| A 123 Olna | Hawthorn Leslie | 28-7-65 | 1-4-66 |
| A 124 Olmeda (ex-*Oleander*) | Swan Hunter | 19-11-64 | 18-10-65 |

**Olmeda (A 124)**—showing hangar to port L. & L. Van Ginderen, 7-87

**Olna (A 123)** L. & L. Van Ginderen, 9-86

**D:** 10,890 tons light (36,000 fl) **S:** 20 kts
**Dim:** 197.51 (185.92 pp) × 25.6 × 10.5 **A:** 2/20-mm AA (I × 2)—see Remarks
**Electron Equipt:** Radar: 1 Kelvin-Hughes 14/12, 1 Kelvin-Hughes 14/16, 1/1006
EW: 2/DLC chaff RL (VIII × 2)
**M:** 1 set Pamatreda GT; 1 prop; 26,500 hp
**Boilers:** 2 Babcock & Wilcox, 60 kg/cm$^2$, 510°C
**Man:** 25 officers, 62 men, plus naval air group

Remarks: Hull reinforced against ice, living space air-conditioned, advanced automation, excellent facilities for replenishment at sea; 25,000 dwt, 18,600 grt. Helicopter platform; hangar to port recently enlarged to hold two Sea King helicopters, but normally only one is carried. Can carry 18,400 tons fuel oil, 1,720 tons diesel, 3,730 tons aircraft fuel, and 130 tons lube oil. RFA-operated. Now have MARISAT commercial communications satellite system. Chaff RL and guns added 1982; latter now not normally carried (were atop hangar).

◆ **1 later Tide class** Bldr: Hawthorn Leslie, Hebburn-on-Tyne

| | Laid down | L | In serv. |
|---|---|---|---|
| A 75 Tidespring | 24-7-61 | 3-5-62 | 18-1-63 |

**Tidespring (A 75)** G. Davies, Maritime Photographic, 6-87

**FLEET OILERS** *(continued)*

**D:** 8,531 tons light (27,400 fl) **S:** 18.3 kts
**Dim:** 177.6 (167.65 pp) × 21.64 × 9.75 **A:** removed
**Electron Equipt:** Radar: 1 Kelvin-Hughes 14/12, 1 Kelvin-Hughes 14/16
EW: 2/DLC Chaff RL (VIII × 2)
**M:** 1 set Pamatreda GT; 1 prop; 15,000 hp **Boilers:** 2
**Man:** 30 officers, 80 men, plus air group

Remarks: RFA-operated; 18,900 dwt, 14,130 grt. As built, carried 17,400 tons fuel oil and 700 tons diesel, but with RN dependence on gas-turbine propulsion, proportions may have changed. Hangar and flight deck for 1 large helicopter. Sister *Tidepool* (A 76) sold to Chile, transferred 4-82 to Chile, repossessed for Falklands War, turned over permanently 8-82. MARISAT SATCOMM, armament, and chaff RL added 1982; 2/20-mm Mk 4 AA subsequently removed again. Was scheduled for disposal 1984, but is being retained, completing a refit 22-12-84; pilothouse rebuilt like *Olwen* class.

**SMALL FLEET OILERS**

◆ **5 Rover class** Bldr: Swan Hunter, Hebburn-on-Tyne

| | L | In serv. |
|---|---|---|
| A 268 Green Rover | 19-12-68 | 15-8-69 |
| A 269 Grey Rover | 17-4-69 | 10-4-70 |
| A 270 Blue Rover | 11-11-69 | 15-7-70 |
| A 271 Gold Rover | 7-3-73 | 22-3-74 |
| A 273 Black Rover | 30-10-73 | 23-8-74 |

**Gold Rover (A 271)**—MARISAT aft L. & L. Van Ginderen, 5-86

**Black Rover (A 273)** L. & L. Van Ginderen, 10-86

**D:** 4,700 tons light (11,522 fl) **S:** 19.25 kts **Dim:** 140.5 × 19.2 × 7.3
**Electron Equipt:** Radar: 3/navigational—EW: 2/DLC RL (VIII × 2)
**M:** 2 SEMT-Pielstick 16PA 4 diesels; 1 CP prop; 15,300 hp **Electric:** 2,720 kw
**Fuel:** 965 tons **Range:** 15,000/15 **Man:** 16 officers, 31 men

Remarks: RFA-operated; 6,822 dwt (A 271, A 273: 6,692 dwt), 7,510 grt. Carry 6,600 tons of fuel plus water, dry stores, and provisions. Helicopter deck but no hangar. A 271 is used in supporting the training squadron at Portland. First three re-engined 1973–74. Not all carry chaff RL. Stern shapes vary, early units having two stern anchors and later units one.

**SUPPORT OILERS**

◆ **4 Appleleaf class** Bldr: Cammell Laird, Birkenhead

| | L | In serv. |
|---|---|---|
| A 79 Appleleaf (ex-*Hudson Cavalier*) | 24-7-75 | 11-79 |
| A 81 Brambleleaf (ex-*Hudson Deep*) | 22-1-76 | 3-80 |
| A 109 Bayleaf (ex-*Hudson Progress*) | 27-10-81 | 26-3-82 |
| A 110 Orangeleaf (ex-*Balder London*) | . . . | 2-5-84 (RN) |

**D:** 40,200 tons (fl) **S:** 16.4 kts **Dim:** 170.69 (163.51 pp) × 25.94 × 11.56
**A:** 2/20-mm AA (I × 2) **Electron Equipt:** Radar: 2/. . . nav.
**M:** 2 Crossley-Pielstick 14PC2V-400 diesels; 1 CP prop; 14,000 hp
**Fuel:** 2,498 tons **Man:** 65 tot.

**Bayleaf (A 109)** LSPH E. Pitman, R.A.N., 10-86

Remarks: RFA-operated. A 79 chartered 1978 and refitted 12-78 to 11-79 at Wallsend Dry Docks; stack raised 3.5 m, dry cargo hold added forward, replenishment-at-sea working deck added amidships, and superstructure enlarged aft. A 81 given similar refit by Cammell Laird after charter in 1979, completing 1980. A 109, on which work had been suspended while still on the ways, was chartered 3-4-81 and similarly altered. A 110, on charter since 4-82, was purchased 26-3-84 and initially operated without replenishment equipment, receiving a similar conversion to that of her sisters in 1985 to 2-5-86. Average 20,440 grt, 33,750 dwt. All now have one refueling station per side, over-the-stern fueling, and MARISAT.

◆ **1 ex-Norwegian tanker** Bldr: Uddevallavarvet, Uddevalla, Sweden

| | L | In serv. |
|---|---|---|
| A 111 Oakleaf (ex-*Oktania*) | 1981 | 14-8-86 (in RFA) |

**Oakleaf (A 111)** L. & L. Van Ginderen, 9-87

**D:** 49,310 tons (fl) **S:** 15.75 kts (14.5 sust.)
**Dim:** 173.69 (168.00 wl) × 32.26 × 10.22
**A:** . . . **Electron Equipt:** Radar: 2/. . . nav.
**M:** 1 Uddevalla-Burmeister & Wain 4-cyl., 2-stroke diesel; 1 CP prop; 12,250 hp
**Electric:** 2,472 kw. **Man:** 36 tot.

Remarks: 21,999 grt/34,800 dwt. Leased 7-85 to replace *Plumleaf* (A 78). Ice-strengthened hull, with tunnel side-thrusters fore and aft. Cargo: 43,020 m$^3$. Converted for naval support service by Falmouth Ship Repairers, 17-2-86 to 14-8-86. Received two alongside fueling stations (one per side) with raised working deck, astern refueling capability; two additional generator sets, additional communications, NAVSAT equipment and MARISAT SATCOMM. Retained sauna. Non-manned engine spaces when under way. Hull reinforced for ice navigation.

**MISCELLANEOUS AUXILIARY SHIPS**

◆ **1 aviation support ship** Bldr: Breda SY, Venice

| | L | In serv. |
|---|---|---|
| A 135 Argus (ex-*Contender Bezant*) | 1981 | 28-10-87 (RN) (accepted) |

**D:** 22,256 tons light (28,163 fl) **S:** 22 max. (19.25 sust.)
**Dim:** 175.12 (163.60 wl, 160.00 pp) × 30.40 × 8.20
**A:** 6/Sea King helicopters—12 Sea Harrier V/STOL (8 operational)—4/30-mm A-32 AA (II × 2)—2/20-mm GAM-B01 AA (I × 2)
**Electron Equipt:** Radar: 1/1007, 1/1006, 1/. . . air search
Sonar: 1/2068
EW: . . . intercept, . . . jammer, 4/DLB RL (VI × 4)
**M:** 2 Lindholmen-Pielstick 18PC2.5 V400 diesels; 2 props; 23,400 hp
**Range:** 20,000/19 **Fuel:** 4,515 tons heavy oil/1,565 tons diesel
**Electric:** 4,800 kw (4 GMT BL230-8V diesels)
**Man:** 23 officers, 56 men RFA; 3 officers, 25 men RN; 42 officers, 95 men in training detachment (up to 750 troops in emergency)

Remarks: Purchased 2-3-84, having been on charter since 5-82, when she was used as an aircraft transport to the Falklands. Conversion at Harland and Wolff,

**MISCELLANEOUS AUXILIARY SHIPS** *(continued)*

Belfast was to complete 1986, with vehicle cargo decks converted to a hangar and elevators added. Intended to replace *Engadine* (K 08) as helicopter training ship or to act as a transport for Harrier/Sea Harrier aircraft. Plans to purchase sister *Contender Argent* dropped late 1984. Originally a combined container/vehicle cargo ship, with vehicle ramps to starboard at bow and stern. Has space for 8 Sea Harriers and 3 helicopters on the hangar deck and 3 helicopters on deck, aft. There are two aircraft elevators. Hangar segregates into four sections. The flight deck, some 1.9 m *thick* for ballast and stability purposes, measures 113.52 × 28 but is encumbered by stack and superstructure to starboard. Carries 1,000 tons aviation fuel, plus 3,500 tons fuel for transfer to other ships. Racal supplied the sensors, data system, communications, and weapons control package, which includes the CANE action data system. Passive tank stabilization added, watertight compartmentation improved. Despite "auxiliary" status, can obviously be employed in a combat role—although lack of ski jump inhibits V/STOL operations.

**Argus (A 135)**—artist's rendering — P. Hogan/Harland & Wolff, 6-86

Note: The helicopter support ship *Reliant* (A 131, ex-*Astronomer*) was paid off 25-5-86; the ARAPAHO aviation support system was removed, and the ship was sold commercial (as *Admiralty Island*) in 7-86.

◆ **1 helicopter training ship**

| | Bldr | Laid down | L | In serv. |
|---|---|---|---|---|
| K 08 Engadine | Henry Robb Ltd. | 9-8-65 | 16-9-66 | 15-12-67 |

**Engadine (K 08)**—with lengthened flight deck, MARISAT, chaff launchers — L. & L. Van Ginderen, 11-86

**D:** 3,875 tons light (9,105 fl) **S:** 16 kts **Dim:** 141.20 × 17.86 × 6.73
**Electron Equipt:** Radar: 3/nav.—EW: 2/DLC chaff RL(VIII × 2)
**M:** 1 Sulzer 5RD68, 5-cyl. diesel; 1 prop; 5,500 hp **Electric:** 1,200 kw
**Fuel:** 450 tons **Man:** 61 RFA plus 14 RN (and air group: 29 officers, 84 men)

Remarks: Intended to train flight crews in ASW helicopter procedures at sea. The hangar can hold either four Wessex or two Sea King and two Wasp. A smaller hangar atop the superstructure serves a target-drone launch facility. Equipped with Denny-Brown fin stabilizers and has remote bridge control for all engineering plants. Many internal compartments are voids. RFA-operated. 6,384 grt, 4,520 dwt. Flight deck extended aft 11.9 m at Gibraltar, early 1984, to permit two Sea King on deck at once; original length 129.31 m. Was to be replaced by the much-delayed *Argus* in 1986; now to be relieved spring 1988. Officially on Sales List 1987, but still in use.

◆ **1 antarctic patrol ship**

| | Bldr | L | In serv. |
|---|---|---|---|
| A 171 Endurance (ex-*Anita Dan*) | Krögerwerft, Rendsburg | 25-5-56 | 12-56 |

**Endurance (A 171)** — B. Sullivan, 10-87

**D:** 3,600 tons (fl) **S:** 14.5 kts **Dim:** 93.58 (82.9 pp) × 14.03 × 5.03
**A:** 2/20-mm Mk 4 AA (I × 2)—1/Lynx helicopter
**Electron Equipt:** Radar: 2/Decca TM 829
**M:** 1 Burmeister & Wain 550VTBF, 5-cyl. diesel; 1 prop; 3,220 hp (plus a bow-thruster)
**Range:** 12,000/14 **Man:** 13 officers, 106 men, up to 12 scientists

Remarks: Purchased 20-2-67. Hull painted red, superstructure white. Carried two Wasp helicopters and two survey launches. Converted 1967–68 by Harland & Wolff, Belfast, to support the British Antarctic Survey and act as guard ship in the Falkland Islands; 2,641 grt. MARISAT added 1978. Was to have been discarded 1982, but performed with distinction in Falklands War and will be retained. Refitted 9-6-86 to 6-87; new hangar for Lynx helicopter, enlarged superstructure, converted to a.c. power, new Halmatic 8.94-m survey launch (see earlier entry for data). Expected to operate to 1995.

◆ **1 royal yacht**

| | Bldr | Laid down | L | In serv. |
|---|---|---|---|---|
| (A 00) Britannia | J. Brown (Clydebank) | 7-52 | 16-4-53 | 14-1-54 |

**Britannia** — G. Gyssels, 5-85

**D:** 3,990 tons (4,961 fl) **S:** 21 kts **Dim:** 125.9 (115.82 pp) × 16.76 × 4.86
**Electron Equipt:** Radar: 2/1006 **M:** 2 sets GT; 2 props; 12,000 hp
**Boilers:** 2 **Fuel:** 510 tons **Range:** 3,100/20 **Man:** 21 officers, 256 men

Remarks: 5,769 grt. Naval-manned. In wartime, would become a hospital ship (200 beds and 60 medical personnel) and have a helicopter platform. Gyrofin stabilizers. Reboilered during 1980 refit; equipped to burn distillate fuel 1984. Equipped with MARISAT 1982. Refitted 1986–87, wooden decking deleted. To last 10-15 more years.

◆ **1 submarine-support ship**

Note: *Wakeful* (A 236), a former tug used as submarine security and target vessel at Faslane, was replaced by *Sentinel* (P 246) in 1987 and paid off 15-10-87.

◆ **1 seabed operations tender**

| | Bldr | Laid down | L | In serv. |
|---|---|---|---|---|
| K 07 Challenger | Scotts SB, Govan | 25-1-80 | 19-5-81 | 3-8-84 |

**D:** 6,500 tons (7,185 fl) **S:** 15 kts **Dim:** 134.0 (130.5 pp) × 18.0 × 5.4
**Electron Equipt:** Radar: 1/1006, 1/Decca . . .—Sonar: 1/2008, 1/2013, 1/193M
**M:** 5 Ruston 16 RK3CZ diesels (3,430 hp each), electric drive; 2 Voith-Schneider vertical cycloidal props aft; 10,200 hp (three bow-thrusters)
**Electric:** 1,500-kw harbor service **Range:** 8,000/. . . **Man:** 186 tot.

Remarks: Ordered 28-9-79. Royal Navy manned. Dynamic positioning system capable of maintaining a constant location in 50- to 60-kt winds, in a sea state of 5. Carries a submersible decompression chamber for 12 divers and is equipped for saturation diving. Twelve divers and their equipment are handled through a "moon-pool" amidships by a 25-ton crane, while a gallows crane on the stern will handle Towed Unmanned Submersibles (TUMS). Passive tank stabilization

**MISCELLANEOUS AUXILIARY SHIPS** *(continued)*

system. The integrated navigational system, with a GEC 4070 computer, incorporates Decca "Hi-Fix," Omega, navigational satellite reception, and a Decca radio navaid receiver. The helo platform will accept a Sea King. Completion delayed by faulty wiring. Can move at 3.5 kts sideways and can lift 25-ton objects from the bottom.

Modified 4-86 to 12-86 to correct problems with diving system. Phoenix hyperbaric lifeboat added; has decompression chamber to sustain 12 men for 5 days. Diving bell and divers' gas systems also rehabilitated.

**Challenger (K 07)**—new lifeboat to starboard — L. & L. Van Ginderen, 5-87

**Challenger (K 07)**—note stern gallows crane, helicopter deck abaft paired stacks — M.O.D., 6-85

NOTE: Offshore support and salvage ship *Seaforth Clansman,* on charter since 1978, was returned to owners 17-6-87.

## MOORING, SALVAGE, AND NET TENDERS

◆ **3 "Sal" class** Bldr: Hall Russell, Ltd., Aberdeen

| | Laid down | L | In serv. |
|---|---|---|---|
| A 185 SALMOOR | 19-4-84 | 8-5-85 | 12-11-85 |
| A 186 SALMASTER | 17-9-84 | 12-11-85 | 12-5-86 |
| A 187 SALMAID | 29-6-84 | 22-5-86 | 28-10-86 |

**Salmoor (A 185)** — L. & L. Van Ginderen, 8-87

**D:** 1,700 tons (fl) **S:** 15 kts **Dim:** 77.10 (65.80 pp) × 14.80 × 3.80
**Electron Equipt:** Radar: . . . nav.
**M:** 2 Ruston-Paxman 8RKCM diesels; 1 CP prop; 4,000 hp
**Man:** 4 officers, 17 men, 27 spare **Range:** . . .

REMARKS: 1,967 grt. Ordered 29-1-84 as replacements for "Kin" class. R.M.A.S.-manned. Capable of mooring, buoy tending, salvage, diving support, and firefighting. Have 400-ton tidal lift/200-ton deadlift capacity. Can carry 14-man salvage party. Based in the Clyde, at Rosyth, and at Portsmouth, respectively. A 187 conducted trials 1987 with 20-ton submersible LR 5.

◆ **2 Pochard class**

| | Bldr | L | In serv. |
|---|---|---|---|
| A 164 GOOSANDER (ex-P 196) | Robb Caledon Ltd. | 12-4-73 | 10-9-73 |
| A 165 POCHARD (ex-P 197) | Robb Caledon Ltd. | 21-6-73 | 11-12-73 |

**Pochard (A 165)** — L. & L. Van Ginderen, 1-86

**D:** 750 tons (1,200 fl) **S:** 10 kts **Dim:** 55.4 (48.8 pp) × 12.2 × 5.5
**M:** 2 Paxman RPHXM 16-cyl. diesels; 550 hp **Range:** 3,250/9.5 **Man:** 26 tot.

REMARKS: RMAS-operated. All moorings, salvage, and boom vessels are multipurpose and are capable of transporting and servicing moorings, performing salvage duties, and, in wartime, handling harbor-defense nets. Can dead-lift 200 tons over bow horns.

◆ **4 Wild Duck class**

| | Bldr | L | In serv. |
|---|---|---|---|
| P 192 MANDARIN | | | |
| P 193 PINTAIL | Cammell Laird | 17-9-63 | 5-3-64 |
| P 194 GARGANEY | Cammell Laird | 3-12-63 | 3-64 |
| P 195 GOLDENEYE | Brooke Marine Ltd. | 13-12-65 | 20-9-66 |
| | Brooke Marine Ltd. | 31-3-66 | 21-12-66 |

**Goldeneye (P 195)** — G. Gyssels, 6-85

**D:** 850 tons (1,300 fl) (P 192, P 193: 941/1,622 tons) **S:** 10.8 kts
**Dim:** 57.86 (47.24 pp) × 13.0 × 3.2 (P 192, P 193: 60.23 × 12.22 × 4.21)
**M:** Davey-Paxman 16-cyl. diesels; 1 CP prop; 50 hp (P 192, P 193: 750 hp)
**Electric:** P 194, P 195: 640 kw; P 921, P 193: 405 kw **Range:** 3,000/10
**Man:** 7 officers, 18 men

REMARKS: RMAS-operated. *Pintail* has extra accommodations for divers in 2-level deckhouse abaft stack. 200-ton deadlift capacity over bow. Retain "P" (Patrol-series) pendant numbers.

◆ **1 "Kin" class** (in reserve)

| | Bldr | Laid down | L | In serv. |
|---|---|---|---|---|
| A 281 KINBRACE | Alex. Hall, Aberdeen | 20-4-44 | 17-1-45 | 30-4-45 |

**D:** 950 tons (1,050 fl) **S:** 9 kts **Dim:** 54.0 × 10.6 × 3.6
**M:** 1 Atlas Polar M44M diesel; 630 hp **Man:** 34 tot.

REMARKS: RMAS-operated; 200-ton lift. Originally had reciprocating steam engines; diesels fitted 1964–67. 775 grt, 262 dwt. Sisters *Uplifter* (A 507) stricken 10-85, *Kingarth* (A 232) in 4-86, *Kinloss* (A 482) in 1986—the first two for scrap, the latter to become a shock test barge at Rosyth. A 281 to reserve 5-87.

NOTE: The "Insect" class fleet tender *Scarab* is also equipped as a moorings tender (10-ton lift).

## MOORING, SALVAGE, AND NET TENDERS *(continued)*

**Kinbrace (A 281)** L. & L. Van Ginderen, 5-87

## SEAGOING TUGS

◆ **3 Roysterer class** Bldr: C.D. Holmes, Beverley, Humberside

| | L | In serv. |
|---|---|---|
| A 361 Roysterer | 20-5-70 | 25-4-72 |
| A 502 Rollicker | 29-1-71 | 2-73 |
| A 366 Robust | 7-10-71 | 6-4-74 |

**Robust (A 366)** L. & L. Van Ginderen, 1-87

**D:** 1,630 tons (fl) **S:** 15 kts **Dim:** 54.8 (49.4 pp) × 11.6 × 5.5
**M:** 2 Mirrlees KMR6 diesels; 2 CP props; 4,500 hp
**Electron Equipt:** Radar: 2/Decca nav. **Range:** 13,000/12
**Man:** 10 officers, 21 men (plus 10-man RN salvage party if needed)

Remarks: RMAS-operated; 50-ton bollard pull. Although designed for long-distance towing, have been used primarily in port service, A 361 at Greenock, A 502 at Portland, A 366 at Devonport. Have heavy tripod mast, with after legs containing engine exhausts.

◆ **1 Typhoon class** (in reserve) Bldr: H. Robb, Leith

| | L | In serv. |
|---|---|---|
| A 95 Typhoon | 14-10-58 | 1960 |

**D:** 800 tons (1,380 fl) **S:** 17 kts **Dim:** 60.5 × 12.3 × 4.0
**Electron Equipt:** Radar: 1/978 **Range:** 15,000/16
**M:** 2 12-cyl. Vickers-Armstrong diesels; 1 CP prop; 2,750 hp **Man:** 27 tot.

**Typhoon (A 95)** L. & L. Van Ginderen, 10-82

Remarks: 32-ton bollard pull. Refitted spring 1986 and placed in reserve; was RMAS-operated.

Note: The last *Confiance*-class seagoing tug, *Confident* (A 290), was stricken late 1985 and scrapped beginning 11-8-86.

## SERVICE CRAFT

Note: Most service craft are operated by the Royal Maritime Auxiliary Service (RMAS), a civilian organization, with some operated by the reservists of the Royal Naval Auxiliary Service (RNXS). Increasingly, pendant numbers are being displayed; in the listings below, where the numbers are not borne, they are given in parentheses.

## AMMUNITION TRANSPORTS

◆ **2 Throsk class** (1 in reserve)

| | Bldr | Laid down | L | In serv. |
|---|---|---|---|---|
| A 378 Kinterbury | Cleland SB, Wallsend | 1980 | 8-11-80 | 20-1-81 |
| A 379 Throsk | Cleland SB, Wallsend | 25-8-76 | 31-3-77 | 20-9-77 |

**Throsk (A 379)** L. & L. Van Ginderen, 5-85

**D:** 2,193 tons (fl) **S:** 14 kts **Dim:** 70.57 (64.31 pp) × 11.9 × 4.57
**M:** 2 Mirrlees-Blackstone diesels; 1 prop; 3,000 hp **Range:** 1,500/14; 5,000/10
**Electron Equipt:** Radar: 1/Decca . . . **Man:** 10 officers, 22 men

Remarks: RMAS-operated. Two holds, two 5-ton cranes; 1,150 dwt. Two cargo holds: 750 $m^3$ total. Can transport 760 tons in holds plus 25 tons of cargo on deck. A 378 has improved accommodations and two electric cranes; A 379 has two cargo boom cranes. Sister *St. George* (in serv. 4-81) operated by Army's Royal Corps of Transport. A 379 is normally kept in reserve at Portsmouth.

## DEGAUSSING TENDERS

◆ **2 Magnet class** (1 in reserve) Bldr: Cleland, Wallsend

| | Laid down | L | In serv. |
|---|---|---|---|
| A 114 Magnet | 3-11-78 | 12-7-79 | 15-11-79 |
| A 115 Lodestone | 22-12-78 | 15-11-79 | 4-80 |

**Magnet (A 114)** L. & L. Van Ginderen, 2-87

**D:** 950 grt **S:** 12 kts **Dim:** 54.8 (50.0 pp) × 11.4 × 3.0
**Electron Equipt:** Radar: 1/978
**M:** 2 Mirrlees-Blackstone ESL-6-MGR diesels, electric drive; 2 props; 1,650 hp
**Electric:** 245 kw **Fuel:** 40 tons **Range:** 1,750/12 **Man:** 15 tot.

Remarks: Built to commercial standards. RMAS-operated. Use two 800-cell, 400-V battery banks and two variable-resistance capacitors to provide 4,000 amps d.c.

### DEGAUSSING TENDERS *(continued)*

for 40 seconds. Can deperm a 60,000-ton ship. A 115 completed a refit 21-12-84; normally in reserve, she was activated 6-86 to 12-2-87, when another refit began. A 114 refitted 1985, received new crane aft.

### TORPEDO RETRIEVERS

◆ **4 Tornado class** Bldr: Hall Russell, Aberdeen

| | Laid down | L | In serv. | Based |
|---|---|---|---|---|
| A 140 Tornado | 2-11-78 | 24-5-79 | 15-11-79 | Clyde |
| A 141 Torch | 5-12-78 | 7-8-79 | 12-2-80 | Portland |
| A 142 Tormentor | 19-3-79 | 6-11-79 | 29-4-80 | Plymouth |
| A 143 Toreador | 14-6-79 | 14-2-80 | 1-7-80 | Clyde |

**Tormentor (A 142)** L. & L. Van Ginderen, 7-87

**D:** 660 tons (698 fl) **S:** 14 kts **Dim:** 47.47 (40.0 pp) × 8.53 × 3.0
**Electron Equipt:** Radar: 1/978
**M:** 2 Lister-Blackstone ESL-8-MGR diesels; 2 props; 2,200 hp
**Fuel:** 110 tons **Range:** 3,000/. . . **Man:** 14 tot.

Remarks: RMAS-operated. Stern ramp for weapon recovery. A 140 used in trials 1987 with Qubit TRAC IV B track recording system and Bathymetrics Bathyscan 300 precision side-looking sonar/echo sounder.

◆ **2 Torrent class**

| | Bldr | L | In serv. |
|---|---|---|---|
| A 127 Torrent | Cleland SB, Wallsend | 29-3-71 | 10-9-71 |
| A 128 Torrid | Cleland SB, Wallsend | 7-9-71 | 1-72 |

**Torrid (A 128)** L. & L. Van Ginderen, 7-81

**D:** 468 tons (685 fl) **S:** 11.5 kts **Dim:** 49.55 (44.2 pp) × 9.72 × 3.05
**Electron Equipt:** Radar: 1/978
**M:** Paxman 16 RPHM diesel; 1 prop; 700 hp **Electric:** 300 kw **Fuel:** 49 tons
**Range:** 1,500/11 **Man:** 19 tot.

Remarks: Can stow 32 torpedoes in hold and 10 on deck and perform post-firing maintenance. Stern ramp for recovery. RMAS-operated; both based on the Clyde.

◆ **1 converted customs craft**

Endeavor Bldr: R. Dunston, Thorne (In serv. 1966)

**D:** 88 tons (fl) **S:** 10.5 kts **Dim:** 23.2 × 4.4 × 2.0
**M:** 1 Lister-Blackstone diesel; 337 hp

Remarks: RMAS-operated. Resembles a small tug; cannot bring recovered torpedoes aboard. Also used as range safety craft at Portland.

◆ **3 torpedo recovery launches** Bldr: R. Dunston, Thorne (In serv. 1979)

**D:** 15 tons **S:** 9 kts **Dim:** 13.8 × 2.98 × 0.76
**M:** 1 Perkins 6-354 diesel; 1 prop; 104 hp **Man:** 4 tot.

◆ **1 ex-RAF RTTL Mk 2-class former target-tow launch**

Osprey (ex-RAF 2770) (In serv. 1940s)

**Osprey** L. & L. Van Ginderen, 10-82

**D:** 34.6 tons (fl) **S:** 30 kts **Dim:** 20.7 × 5.8 × 1.8
**M:** 2 Rolls-Royce Sea Griffon gasoline engines; 2 props; 2,200 hp **Man:** 9 tot.

◆ **1 ex-RAF 1300 series former air/sea rescue launch**

L 72 (ex-RAF . . .) (In serv. 1955–56)

**D:** 28.3 tons (fl) **S:** 13 kts **Dim:** 19.2 × 4.7 × 1.5
**M:** 2 Rolls-Royce C8 diesels; 2 props; 190 hp

### DIVING TENDERS

◆ **5 modified Cartmel class** Bldr: Gregson, Blyth

A 308 Ilchester
A 309 Instow
A 310 Invergordon
A 311 Ironbridge (ex-*Invergordon*)
A 318 Ixworth

**Instow (A 309)** L. & L. Van Ginderen, 7-84

**Datchet (A 357)**—see next page L. & L. Van Ginderen, 8-85

Remarks: RMAS-operated, except A 308 and A 309, by Navy. All in service 1974, except A 310, ordered 7-80. Details and appearance as for *Cartmel*-class tenders, except for a decompression chamber on deck forward, beneath a stowage platform for a Gemini dinghy. Can be used for harbor mine clearance. Displacement is 150 tons (fl).

**DIVING TENDERS** *(continued)*

◆ **1 Datchet class** Bldr: Vosper, Singapore (In serv. 1968)

A 357 Datchet

**D:** 70 tons (fl) **S:** 12 kts **Dim:** 22.86 × 5.79 × 1.22
**Electron Equipt:** Radar: 1/978
**M:** 2 Gray Marine diesels; 2 props; 500 hp **Range:** 500/12

Remarks: Was RMAS, but now RN-manned; based at Plymouth. To be replaced.

◆ **4 diver support craft** Bldr: Tough, Teddington (In serv. 1981–82)

**D:** 10 tons (fl) **S:** 8.5 kts **Dim:** 11.7 × 4.3 × 1.4
**M:** 1 Perkins 6-354.4 diesel; 120 hp **Man:** 2 crew, 12 divers

Remarks: Glass-reinforced plastic construction. One unit, unofficially named *Reclaim,* is attached to HMS *Vernon.*

**LOCAL TRAINING SHIPS AND CRAFT**

Note: In addition to the units listed below, the following ships are used for training: *Bristol* (D 23), *Juno* (F 52), 11 of the "River"-class minesweepers, "Ton"-class minehunters *Kedleston* (M 1153) and *Kellington* (M 1154), "Ton"-class minesweepers *Cuxton* (M 1125) and *Upton* (M 1187), patrol boats *Peterel* (P 262) and *Sandpiper* (P 263), and tenders *Clovelly* (A 389), *Cromarty* (A 488), *Froxfield* (A 354), *Hever* (A 1767), *Headcorn* (A 1776), *Aberdovey* (Y 10), *Alnmouth* (Y 13), and *Sultan Venturer* (A 103). Harbor training ships (former frigates) *Falmouth* (F 113), *Ashanti* (F 117), *Londonderry* (F 108), and *Ajax* (F 114) were stricken 1986–87. *Cartmel* (A 350) and *Glencoe* (A 392) were transferred to the RNXS 1987.

◆ **1 chartered trawler** Bldr: Clelands, Wallsend
Northella (In serv. 7-73)

**Northella**—orange hull, white superstructure H. Ehlers, 6-87

**D:** . . . **S:** 16.5 kts **Dim:** 70.20 (65.20 pp) × 12.60 × 4.90
**Electron Equipt:** Radar: 2/. . . nav.
**M:** 1 Mirrlees-Blackstone KMR-7 diesel; 1 CP prop; 3,246 hp

Remarks: 1,238 grt. Chartered 10-83 for navigational training and submarine target and security duties at Faslane. Transferred to Devonport for navigational training 1985. Stern-haul trawler, originally acquired 4-82 for use as a minesweeper in the Falklands.

◆ **1 chartered trawler** Bldr: Goole SB & Repair, Goole
Arctic Freebooter (In serv. 2-66)

**D:** . . . **S:** . . . **Dim:** 67.79 (64.62 wl) × 12.63 × . . .
**Electron Equipt:** Radar: . . .
**M:** 1 6-cyl., 4-stroke Mirrlees National diesel; 1 CP prop; 2,380 hp **Man:** . . .

Remarks: Chartered fall 1985 to relieve *Northella* at Faslane. Employed in navigational training and submarine target and security duties.

◆ **5 (+5) P.2000 class** Bldr: Watercraft, Shoreham-by-Sea/Fairey Marinteknik, Cowes

| | In serv. | | In serv. |
|---|---|---|---|
| A 153 Example | 18-10-85 | P 272 Smiter | 7-2-86 |
| A 154 Explorer | 16-1-86 | P 273 Pursuer | . . . |
| A 163 Express | . . . | P 279 Blazer | . . . |
| P 264 Archer | 1-3-86 | P 280 Dasher | . . . |
| P 270 Biter | 5-11-85 | P 291 Puncher | . . . |

**D:** 38 tons (43 fl) **S:** 22.5 kts **Dim:** 20.80 (18.00 pp) × 5.80 × 1.50
**A:** 1/20-mm AA (fitted for) **Electron Equipt:** Radar: 1/Decca AC121C
**M:** Perkins CV M800T diesels; 2 props; 1,590 hp (1,380 sust.)
**Electric:** 62 kVA **Range:** 330/20; 500/15 **Man:** 11 tot.

Remarks: Glass-reinforced plastic craft ordered 7-84, primarily for peacetime training: 6 for Royal Navy Reserve training, 4 for the Universities of Glasgow, Liverpool, Southampton, and Aberdeen, and 4 with "A" pendants for the Royal Naval Auxiliary Service. Nine incomplete (P 273 ready for trials) when Water-

**Biter (P 270)**—RNR unit L. & L. Van Ginderen, 8-86

**Explorer (A 154)**—RNXS unit M. Louagie, 8-86

craft closed. Fourteen were ordered, but only the five nearest completion were to be finished under an 8-87 contract; *Exploit* (A 167), *Charger* (P 292), *Ranger* (P 293), and *Trumpeter* (P 294) have been canceled.

◆ **5 Tracker Mk I and II class** Bldr: Fairey Allday Marine, Cowes and Hamble

| | In serv. | | In serv. |
|---|---|---|---|
| P 281 Attacker | 11-3-83 | P 284 Hunter | 21-3-83 |
| P 282 Chaser | 11-3-83 | P 285 Striker | 7-83 |
| P 283 Fencer | 21-3-83 | | |

**Striker (P 285)** M. Louagie, 7-85

**D:** 31 tons (34.5 fl) **S:** 21 kts **Dim:** 20.0 (19.3 pp) × 5.18 × 1.45
**A:** 1/20-mm AA (fitted for) **Electron Equipt:** Radar: 1/Decca 150
**M:** 2/G.M. 12V71 TI diesels; 2 props; 1,300 hp **Range:** 650/20
**Man:** 3 officers, 2 petty officers, 6 men **Electric:** 30 kw

Remarks: Glass-reinforced plastic craft procured primarily for reserve training duties, with a wartime local patrol function. P 281 operates from HMS *Graham* for the Clyde Division, RNR; P 282 operates for the Tay Div., RNR; P 283 operates from HMS *President* for the London Div., RNR; and P 284 operates from HMS

## LOCAL TRAINING SHIPS AND CRAFT *(continued)*

*Solent* for the London Div., RNR. P 281, built at Cowes, is a Tracker Mk I with an open lattice mast; the others, built at Hamble, have "solid" masts. Speed with engine governors lifted: 24 kts.

◆ **4 modified "Loyal" class** Bldr: R. Dunston, Thorne

| | Laid down | L | In serv. |
|---|---|---|---|
| A 92 Manly | 18-9-80 | 23-7-81 | 2-3-82 |
| A 94 Mentor | 20-10-80 | 7-10-81 | 6-4-82 |
| A 97 Milbrook | 30-1-81 | 16-12-81 | 24-6-82 |
| A 107 Messina | 7-4-81 | 5-3-82 | 1-9-82 |

**Messina (A 107)** L. & L. Van Ginderen, 6-86

**D:** 128 tons (150 fl) **S:** 11.5 kts **Dim:** 24.00 × 6.40 × 2.33
**Electron Equipt:** Radar: 1/978 **Fuel:** 4.5 tons
**M:** 1 Lister-Blackstone ES4MGR diesel; 1 cycloidal prop; 330 hp
**Range:** 700/10 **Man:** 6 tot. (plus trainees)

Remarks: First three serve HMS *Raleigh* training facility; last for Royal Marine training.

◆ **1 Echo-class former survey ship** Bldr: W. Weatherhead, Cockenzie

| | Laid down | L | In serv. |
|---|---|---|---|
| Jonas Hanway (ex-*Egeria*, A 72) | 17-5-57 | 13-9-58 | 18-6-59 |

**D:** 120 tons (160 fl) **S:** 12 kts **Dim:** 32.55 × 6.98 × 2.10
**Electron Equipt:** Radar: 1/Decca TM 629
**M:** 2 Paxman diesels; 2 CP props; 700 hp **Fuel:** 15 tons
**Range:** 1,600/10 **Man:** 18 tot. (22 accom.)

Remarks: Wooden-hull design, based on "Ham"-class inshore minesweeper. On loan from the Marine Society in 1987 as RNXS training craft, having been stricken 12-84 from the RN. Flies Blue Ensign and is based at Gravesend. Sister *Echo* (A 70) renamed *Earl of Romney* by Marine Society in 1987, and *Enterprise* (A 71) is retained as a spare-parts source.

◆ **3 target craft, ex-side-haul trawlers** Bldr: Goole SB & Repair, Goole. (In serv. 1961)

Bullseye (ex-*Tokio*) Magpie (ex-*Honda*) Targe (ex-*Erimo*)

**Magpie**—controller unit R.J.L. Fry, 7-85

**D:** 600 tons (fl) **S:** 12 kts **Dim:** 35.85 × 7.73 × 3.70
**M:** 1 Mirrlees 6-cyl. diesel; 1 prop; 700 hp **Fuel:** 57 tons
**Man:** 1 officer, 12 men

Remarks: 273 grt/91 nrt. First two acquired 6-82 and third in 6-84 for use as radio-controlled targets at Portland. Royal Navy-manned. "T.V." on hull before name means "Target Vessel." Radar corner reflectors mounted forward, and television camera placed on stub mast forward of stack. *Magpie* is the controller unit and has a large radome atop the pilothouse.

Note: Two new target craft were ordered 8-86 from Souter, Cowes. To be of GRP construction, with 12-80 "trihedral" hulls.

◆ **3 training tenders** (In serv. 1944–46) (1 in reserve).

Oliver Twist Smike Uriah Heep

**Uriah Heep** L. & L. Van Ginderen, 8-83

**D:** . . . **S:** 8 kts **Dim:** 15.2 × . . . × . . . **M:** 1 diesel; . . . hp

Remarks: 20 grt. Wooden-hulled fishing-boat-type craft transferred from the Royal Corps of Transport in 1974–81 for use as Royal Naval Reserve training tenders. Sisters *Martin* and *Raddle* used in civil youth programs. *Oliver Twist* is based at London, *Uriah Heep* at Southampton; *Smike* is in reserve.

## SALVAGE CRAFT

◆ **2 self-propelled lifting lighters** Bldr: . . .

| | Laid down | L | In serv. |
|---|---|---|---|
| A . . . Moorhen | . . . | . . . | . . . |
| A . . . Moorfowl | . . . | . . . | . . . |

**D:** . . . **S:** . . . **Dim:** . . . × . . . × . . .
**M:** . . .

Remarks: Were to have been ordered 1987 from Scott-Lithgow, but contract was delayed.

## FUEL LIGHTERS

◆ **6 Oil class** (1 in reserve) Bldr: Appledore SB (All in serv. 1979)

| | L | | L |
|---|---|---|---|
| (Y 21) Oilpress | 10-6-68 | (Y 24) Oilfield | 5-9-68 |
| (Y 22) Oilstone | 11-7-68 | (Y 25) Oilbird | 21-11-68 |
| (Y 23) Oilwell | 20-1-69 | (Y 26) Oilman | 18-2-69 |

**Oilwell** G. Davies, Maritime Photographic, 5-87

**D:** 250 tons (535 fl) **S:** 10 kts **Dim:** 42.26 (39.62 pp) × 7.47 × 2.51
**Electron Equipt:** Radar: 1/978
**M:** 1 Lister-Blackstone ES-6-MGR diesel; 405 hp **Electric:** 225 kw
**Fuel:** 15 tons **Range:** 1,500/10 **Man:** 4 officers, 7 men

Remarks: First three carry diesel fuel and are 247 tons (527 fl); other three carry fuel oil. RMAS-operated. Y 24 to reserve, 9-5-87.

## WATER LIGHTERS

◆ **7 Water class** Bldr: Drypool, Hull, except A 146: R. Dunston, Hessle

| | In serv. | | In serv. |
|---|---|---|---|
| Y 17 Waterfall | 1967 | Y 30 Watercourse | 1974 |
| Y 18 Watershed | 1967 | Y 31 Waterfowl | 25-5-74 |
| Y 19 Waterspout | 1967 | A 146 Waterman | 6-78 |
| Y 20 Waterslide | 1968 | | |

**Waterfall (Y 17)** L. & L. Van Ginderen, 7-85

**D:** 344 tons (fl) **S:** 11 kts **Dim:** 40.02 (37.5 pp) × 7.5 × 2.44
**Electron Equipt:** Radar: 1/978
**M:** 1 Lister-Blackstone ERS-8-MGR diesel; 600 hp **Electric:** 155 kw
**Range:** 1,500/11 **Man:** 11 tot.

Remarks: RMAS-operated. Built 1966–73. Carry 150 tons water cargo. Resemble Oil class. Y 30, Y 31, and A 146 have deckhouse over after cargo tanks, others do not.

## GENERAL-PURPOSE TENDERS

◆ **7 100-foot "Insect" class** Bldr: C.D. Holmes, Beverley (In serv. 1970–73)

| | | | |
|---|---|---|---|
| A 216 Bee | A 230 Cockchafer | A 253 Ladybird | A 272 Scarab |
| A 229 Cricket | A 239 Gnat | A 263 Cicada | |

**Bee (A 216)** G. Davies, Maritime Photographic, 6-87

**D:** 213 tons (450 fl) **S:** 10.5 kts **Dim:** 34.06 (30.48 pp) × 8.53 × 3.2
**Electron Equipt:** Radar: 1/978
**M:** 1 Lister-Blackstone ERS-8-HGR diesel; 660 hp **Man:** 10 tot.

Remarks: RMAS-operated; 200 tons cargo, one 3-ton crane. *Scarab,* with 5-ton winch and bow horn, is used as a moorings tender, *Bee, Gnat,* and *Ladybird* transport ammunition.

◆ **10 "Loyal" class** Bldr: R. Dunston, Thorne

| | In serv. | | In serv. |
|---|---|---|---|
| A 157 Loyal Helper | 1978 | A 251 Lydford (ex-*Alert,* P 252; ex-*Loyal Governor,* A510) | 1975 |
| A 158 Supporter (ex-*Loyal Supporter)* | 1977 | A 254 Meavy (ex-*Vigilant,* P 254; ex-*Loyal Factor,* A 382) | 1974 |
| A 159 Loyal Watcher | 1977 | A 1770 Loyal Chancellor | 1972 |
| A 160 Loyal Volunteer | 1977 | A 1771 Loyal Proctor | 1973 |
| A 161 Loyal Mediator | 1978 | | |
| A 220 Loyal Moderator | 1973 | | |

Remarks: RNXS-operated except A 251, A 254: RMAS; these were recommissioned and renamed 16-9-86 and 25-10-86, respectively, after service as Royal Navy patrol boats off Ulster. Details as for *Cartmel* class, but equipped to carry up to 200 personnel in cargo hold for short distances (except *Loyal Moderator,* training craft, 12 extra berths instead). A 158 operates as a stores carrier from Belfast. Four very similar craft built as training tenders; see above.

**Loyal Volunteer (A 160)** L. & L. Van Ginderen, 9-86

◆ **32 Cartmel class** Bldr: (A): Isaac Pimblott & Sons, Northwich; (B): C.D. Holmes, Beverley; (C): John Lewis, Aberdeen; (D): R. Dunston, Thorne; (E): J. Cook, Wivenhoe

| | Bldr | In serv. | | Bldr | In serv. |
|---|---|---|---|---|---|
| A 350 Cartmel | A | 1968 | A 381 Cricklade | B | 1970 |
| A 389 Clovelly | A | 1971 | A 488 Cromarty | C | 1970 |
| A 391 Criccieth | A | 1971 | A 363 Denmead | B | 1970 |
| A 490 Dornoch | C | 1970 | A 1769 Hambledon | D | 1972 |
| A 393 Dunster | D | 1970 | A 1768 Harlech | D | 1972 |
| A 353 Elkstone | E | 1969 | A 1776 Headcorn | D | 1972 |
| A 277 Elsing | E | 1970 | A 1767 Hever | D | 1972 |
| A 355 Epworth | E | 1970 | A 1772 Holmwood | D | 1973 |
| A 274 Ettrick | E | 1970 | A 1773 Horning | D | 1973 |
| A 348 Felsted | D | 1970 | A 208 Lamlash | D | 1973 |
| A 394 Fintry | C | 1970 | A 211 Lechlade | D | 1973 |
| A 341 Fotherby | D | 1970 | A 207 Landovery | D | 1973 |
| A 354 Froxfield | D | 1970 | A 83 Melton | D | 21-8-81 |
| A 365 Fulbeck | B | 1969 | A 84 Menai | D | 4-11-81 |
| A 392 Glencoe | A | 1971 | A 87 Meon | D | 9-11-82 |
| A 402 Grasmere | C | 1970 | A 91 Milford | D | 11-1-83 |

**Froxfield (A 354)** G. Davies, Maritime Photographic, 3-86

**D:** 143 tons (fl) **S:** 10.5 kts **Dims:** 24.38 (22.86 pp) × 6.40 × 1.98
**Electron Equipt:** Radar: 1/978 (not on all)
**M:** 1 Lister-Blackstone ERS-4-MGR diesel; 330 hp **Electric:** 106 kw
**Range:** 700/10 **Man:** 6 tot.

Remarks: RMAS-operated, except *Ettrick* and *Elsing,* which are RN-manned and used for patrol at Gibraltar. Improved version of *Aberdovey* class; 25 tons cargo. First two, 5.49-meter beam. Carry stores, personnel, food. Can tow. *Clovelly, Cromarty, Froxfield, Hever,* and *Headcorn* are also used for training, and *Dornoch* and *Fotherby* have been used as diving tenders. The last four were ordered 25-2-80.

## GENERAL-PURPOSE TENDERS *(continued)*

Sister *Cawsand* (A 351) for sale 10-85. A 350 and A 392 transferred to RNXS as training craft 1987.

◆ **6 Aberdovey class** Bldr: (A): Isaac Pimblott & Sons, Northwich; (B): J.S. Doig, Grimsby

| | Bldr | In serv. | | Bldr | In serv. |
|---|---|---|---|---|---|
| Y 10 Aberdovey | A | 1963 | A 101 Bembridge | B | 1968 |
| Y 13 Alnmouth | A | 1966 | A 103 Sultan Venturer (ex-*Bibury*) | B | 1969 |
| A 99 Beaulieu | B | 1966 | A 104 Blakeney | B | 1970 |

**Sultan Venturer (A 103)** L. & L. Van Ginderen, 6-87

**D:** 117.5 tons (fl) **S:** 10.5 kts **Dim:** 24.16 (22.86 pp) × 5.79 × 1.68
**Electron Equipt:** Radar: 1/978 or Decca 150
**M:** 1 Lister-Blackstone ER-4-MGR diesel; 225 hp **Range:** 700/10 **Man:** 6 tot.

Remarks: RMAS-operated, except for Y 10, RNXS. Carry 25 tons cargo. *Aberdovey* used for training Royal Marines; *Abinger* (Y 11) attached to Aberdeen University for officer candidate training, was paid off in 1985. Sisters *Alness* (Y 12), *Ashcott* (Y 16), and *Brodick* (A 105) for sale 10-85. *Appleby* (Y 14) and *Beddgelert* (A 100) stricken 1986 and transferred to Sea Cadets, the former with a deckhouse added amidships. A 103 renamed 1986 as tender to HMS *Sultan,* Portsmouth.

◆ **1 new construction range mooring tender**

| | Bldr: | L | In serv. |
|---|---|---|---|
| A . . . Warden | . . . | . . . | . . . |

**D:** . . . **S:** . . . **Dim:** . . . × . . . × . . .
**M:** . . .

Remarks: Was to have been ordered 1987 from Scott-Lithgow to replace *Dolwen* (A 362), but contract delayed.

◆ **1 range mooring tender** Bldr: P.K. Harris, Appledore (In serv. 1962)

A 362 Dolwen (ex-*Hector Gull*)

**Dolwen (A 362)** L. & L. Van Ginderen, 1980

**D:** 602 tons (fl) **S:** . . . kts **Dim:** 39.65 (36.73 pp) × 9.12 × 4.40
**Electron Equipt:** Radar: 1/1006
**M:** 1 National FSSM-6 diesel; 1 CP prop; 1,160 hp

Remarks: Converted stern trawler. Gallows at stern for laying buoys; used as air bombardment safety range craft for the Royal Aircraft Establishment, Aberforth. Operated by a private contractor.

◆ **1 "Ham"-class former inshore minesweeper**

M 2781 Portisham

**Portisham (M 2781)** L. & L. Van Ginderen, 8-85

**D:** 115–120 tons (150–160 fl) **S:** 14 kts **Dim:** 32.47 × 6.10 × 1.75
**Electron Equipt:** Radar: 1/978 **Range:** 2,350/9
**M:** 2 Paxman YHAXM 12-cyl. diesels; 2 props; 1,100 hp
**Electric:** 108 kw **Fuel:** 15 tons **Man:** . . .

Remarks: *Portisham,* RNXS-operated, was to be replaced in 1986 by P.2000-class training patrol boat. Built 1953–57. Carries passengers and stores. Last of once-numerous class in British service.

◆ **2 trials craft, former harbor tugs**

(A 126) Cairn (A 328) Collie

Remarks: Converted 1987 to serve as trials tenders at Kyle of Lochalsh. Towing gear removed. Completed between 1962 and 1972 as units of the "Dog" class, which see for data.

◆ **15 motor fishing vessel tenders**

6 store carriers: MFV.7 (1943), MFV.15 (1942), MFV.96 (1944), MFV.256 (1944), MFV.740 (1945), MFV.911 (1945)
5 general-purpose: MFV.140 (1946), MFV.175 (1945), MFV.609 Apollo, MFV.622 Gambia, MFV.816 (1945)
4 diving tenders: MFV.119 (1944), MFV.642 Hannibal (1945), MFV.775 Merchant Venturer (1945), MFV.1077 (1944)

**MFV.15**—stores carrier L. & L. Van Ginderen, 10-81

**Hannibal, MFV.642**—diving tender L. & L. Van Ginderen, 7-85

**GENERAL-PURPOSE TENDERS** *(continued)*

**MFV.119**—diving tender G. Gyssels, 4-83

Remarks: Wooden-hulled fishing boats of varying characteristics. Most have "double-ended" hulls, engines and pilothouse aft.

### LARGE HARBOR TUGS

◆ **9 Adept-class "Twin-Unit Tractors"** Bldr: R. Dunston, Hessle

| | Laid down | L | In serv. | Based |
|---|---|---|---|---|
| A 221 Forceful | 30-3-84 | . . . | 29-3-85 | Devonport |
| A 222 Nimble | 27-4-84 | 21-3-85 | 25-6-85 | Rosyth |
| A 223 Powerful | 21-6-84 | 3-6-85 | 3-10-85 | Portsmouth |
| A 224 Adept | 22-7-79 | 27-8-80 | 28-10-80 | Portsmouth |
| A 225 Bustler | 28-11-79 | 20-2-80 | 15-4-81 | Portsmouth |
| A 226 Capable | 5-9-80 | 2-7-81 | 11-9-81 | Gibraltar |
| A 227 Careful | 15-1-81 | 12-1-82 | 12-3-82 | Plymouth |
| A 228 Faithful | 30-11-84 | . . . | 13-12-85 | Plymouth |
| A 231 Dexterous | 18-4-85 | 25-2-86 | 24-4-86 | Rosyth |

**Powerful (A 223)** G. Davies, Maritime Photographic, 6-87

**D:** 450 tons **S:** 12.5 kts **Dim:** 38.82 (37.00 pp) × 9.10 × 4.20 (3.40 mean)
**Electron Equipt:** Radar: 1/Decca . . .
**M:** 2 Ruston 6 RKCM diesels; 2 Voith-Schneider vertical-cycloidal props; 2,640 hp
**Electric:** 294 kw **Fuel:** 49 tons **Man:** 11 tot.

Remarks: RMAS-operated. Ordered 22-2-79. 28-ton bollard pull. Also used for coastal towing. The five later units were ordered 8-2-84 to replace the *Confiance*-class seagoing tugs.

◆ **16 "Dog" class** Bldrs: Various (In serv. 1962–72)

| | | |
|---|---|---|
| (A 106) Alsatian | (A 162) Elkhound | (A 188) Pointer |
| (A 327) Basset (ex-*Beagle*) | (A 326) Foxhound (ex-*Boxer*) | (A 182) Saluki |
| | | (A 187) Sealyham |
| (A 330) Corgi | (A 169) Husky | (A 189) Setter |
| (A 129) Dalmatian | (A 168) Labrador | (A 250) Sheepdog |
| (A 155) Deerhound | (A 180) Mastiff | (A 201) Spaniel |

**D:** 206 tons (248 fl) **S:** 12 kts **Dim:** 28.65 (25.91 pp) × 7.72 × 3.51
**Electron Equipt:** Radar: 1/978
**M:** 2 Lister-Blackstone ERS-86-MGR diesels; 1 prop; 1,320 hp
**Electric:** 80 kw **Man:** 8 tot.

Remarks: RMAS-operated. 18.7-ton bollard pull. *Foxhound* renamed 22-10-77. Appearances vary, some having streamlined upper pilothouse structures, others higher pilothouses. Sister *Airedale* (A 102) sold commercially at Gibraltar, 12-84. *Cairn* (A 126) and *Collie* (A 328) converted 1987 as trials craft for use at Kyle of Lochalsh; towing gear deleted. *Basset* and *Dalmatian* in reserve.

**Dalmatian (A 129)**—no radar, low pilothouse L. & L. Van Ginderen, 7-83

**Setter (A 189)**—high pilothouse with windows, Decca radar
G. Davies, Maritime Photographic, 4-86

### MEDIUM HARBOR TUGS

◆ **8 Felicity-class water tractors** Bldrs: R. Dunston, Thorne (A 148, A 152, A 196, A 198: Hancock, Pembroke)

| | In serv. | | In serv. |
|---|---|---|---|
| (A 112) Felicity | 1969 | (A 150) Genevieve | 29-10-80 |
| (A 147) Frances | 5-80 | (A 152) Georgina | 1973 |
| (A 148) Fiona | 1973 | (A 196) Gwendoline | 1974 |
| (A 149) Florence | 8-8-80 | (A 198) Helen | 1974 |

**Fiona (A 148)** L. & L. Van Ginderen, 7-85

**D:** 220 tons (fl) **S:** 10.2 kts **Dim:** 22.25 (20.73 pp) × 6.40 × 2.97 (2.10 hull)
**M:** 1 Lister-Blackstone ERS-8-MGR diesel; cycloidal prop; 615 hp
**Fuel:** 12 tons **Range:** 1,800/8 **Man:** 6 tot.

Remarks: RMAS-operated, 138 grt. 5.9 to 6.1-ton bollard pull. Final three ordered 13-12-78.

◆ **7 modified "Girl" class** Bldrs: (A): Isaac Pimblott & Sons, Northwich; (B): R. Dunston, Thorne

| | Bldr | In serv. | | Bldr | In serv. |
|---|---|---|---|---|---|
| (A 210) Charlotte | A | 1966 | (A 252) Doris | B | 1969 |
| (A 217) Christine | A | 1966 | (A 173) Dorothy | B | 1969 |
| (A 145) Daisy | B | 1968 | (A 178) Edith | B | 1969 |
| (A 156) Daphne | B | 1969 | | | |

**MEDIUM HARBOR TUGS** *(continued)*

**Dorothy (A 173)** G. Davies, Maritime Photographic, 5-87

**D:** 100 tons (fl) **S:** 10.5 kts **Dim:** 20.57 × 6.25 × 2.9
**Electron Equipt:** Radar: 1/978 or none
**M:** 1 Lister-Blackstone ERS-8-MGR diesel; 495 hp
**Range:** 900/10 **Man:** 4 tot.

REMARKS: RMAS-operated. *Celia* (A 206) sold commercially, 1971, *Clare* (A 218) in 12-85. 50 grt; 6.5-ton bollard pull.

◆ **1 "Girl" class** Bldr: P.K. Harris, Appledore

(A 121) AGNES (In serv. 1961)

**D:** 66.5 tons (81 fl) **S:** 10 kts **Dim:** 18.75 (17.3 pp) × 5.11 × 2.36
**M:** 1 Lister-Blackstone ERS-6-MGR diesel; 495 hp
**Range:** 980/9.8 **Man:** 4 tot.

REMARKS: RMAS-operated. 40 grt; 6.5-tons bollard pull. Sisters *Agatha* (A 116), *Alice* (A 113), *Audrey* (A 117), and *Barbara* (A 324) stricken 1982. *Betty* (A 232) was stricken 1983. *Brenda* (A 335) and *Bridget* (A 322) transferred to the Royal Corps of Transport, 19-8-83.

## SMALL HARBOR TUGS

◆ **12 Triton-class water tractors** Bldr: R. Dunston, Thorne (In serv. 1972–73)

| | | |
|---|---|---|
| (A 181) IRENE | (A 166) KATHLEEN | (A 175) MARY |
| (A 183) ISABEL | (A 170) KITTY | (A 199) MYRTLE |
| (A 190) JOAN | (A 172) LESLEY | (A 202) NANCY |
| (A 193) JOYCE | (A 174) LILAH | (A 205) NORAH |

**Irene** G. Davies, Maritime Photographic, 4-87

**D:** 107.5 tons (fl) **S:** 7.75 kts **Dim:** 17.65 (16.76 pp) × 5.26 × 2.8
**M:** 1 Lister-Blackstone ERS-4-M diesel; cycloidal prop; 330 hp
**Man:** 4 tot.

REMARKS: RMAS-operated; 50 grt; 3-ton bollard pull. Voith vertical cycloidal prop to provide instant mobility and full power in any direction.

## FLOATING DRYDOCKS

NOTE: "AFD" indicates Admiralty Floating Dock

AFD 60 Bldr: Portsmouth Dockyard (In serv. 1966)
Capacity: 13,500 tons Dim: 149.7 × 28 (17.7 wide × 10.7 depth interior)

AFD 59 Bldr: Portsmouth Dockyard (In serv. 1960)
Capacity: 12,000 tons Dim: 148.4 × 23.5 (15.5 wide × 10.4 depth interior)

AFD 58 Bldr: Furness Shipbldg, Teeside (In serv. 1957)
Capacity: 8,000 tons Dim: 137.2 × 28.0 (18.9 wide × 6.4 depth interior)

AFD 26 Bldr: Bombay Dockyard (In serv. 1944)
Capacity: 7,750 tons Dim: 115.8 × 28.0 (15.2 wide by 5.6 depth interior)

**AFD 26**—with tug *Foxhound* L. & L. Van Ginderen, 9-84

NOTE: AFD 26 is at Rosyth, AFD 58 at Devonport, AFD 59 at Barrow-in-Furness, and AFD 60 at the Gareloch. Most Royal Navy dockings are performed at permanent, fixed dry docks at Royal Dockyards and, recently, at private repair facilities.

## HARBOR SERVICE CRAFT

NOTE: Little information is available on the hundreds of smaller self-propelled service craft or on non-self-propelled units such as cargo, fuel, and water barges in service with the Royal Navy, Royal Dockyards, or the Royal Maritime Auxiliary Service. Some typical examples and recent classes are shown below.

◆ **3 hydrophone array tenders** Bldr: McTay Marine, Bromsborough (In serv. 1986) TRV 8611 (In serv. 3-86) TRV 8612 (In serv. 1986) TRV 8613 (In serv. . . .)

**TRV 1** J. Goss, NavPic, 1986

**D:** . . . **S:** 12.5 kts **Dim:** 20.10 (19.88 wl) × 6.00 × . . .
**Electron Equipt:** Radar: 1/Decca . . . **Man:** 8 tot.
**M:** 2 Perkins 6/3544 diesels; 2 Kort-nozzle props; 400 hp

REMARKS: Aluminum hulls built by Hall's Aluminium Shipbuilders, Portchester. Intended to service "clip-on" linear hydrophone arrays for submarines. Not initially accepted; could not make design speed. Basic design under evaluation 1986 for use as personnel launches.

◆ **7 harbor launches** Bldr: R. Dunston, Hessle (In serv. 1981)

**D:** 40 tons (fl) **S:** 9.9 kts **Dim:** 13.90 × 4.50 × 1.21
**M:** 1 Dorman 8 JTM diesel; 1 prop; 270 hp **Man:** 3 tot.

REMARKS: Can carry 40 passengers or act as tug; 2-ton bollard pull.

◆ **2 (+2) 260-ton dumb barges** Bldr: Dunston, Hessle

REMARKS: First two ordered 19-12-85; two more planned.

◆ **2 (+2) generator test barges** Bldr: R. Dunston, Hessle

| | Laid down | L | In serv. |
|---|---|---|---|
| MAC. 1020 | 24-4-86 | 22-7-86 | 5-2-87 |
| MAC. 1021 | 2-5-86 | 17-11-86 | -87 |

**HARBOR SERVICE CRAFT** *(continued)*

REMARKS: Ordered 19-12-85; two more planned. 260 tons (fl).

NOTE: Of the units listed under the Ministry of Defence heading in the previous edition, transport *Keren* was placed up for sale 18-11-85, accommodations barge *Pursuivant* was put up for sale in 6-87, and the larger *Safe Dominia* and *Safe Esperia* were placed out of service in 1987.

**Harbor Service Launch Sparrow** B. Sullivan, 7-87

**R.N.A.L. 54 aircraft transport barge**—with tugs *Irene* and *Foxhound* L. & L. Van Ginderen, 11-86

**Portsmouth Dockyard service launch D 57** L. & L. Van Ginderen, 7-84

**Portland-area service launch Penguin** L. & L. Van Ginderen, 7-84

**Power Barge M.A.C. 1002 at Portsmouth** L. & L. Van Ginderen, 7-81

**Harbor Launch RMAS 6807** G. Davies, Maritime Photographic, 5-87

**Sludge treatment barge 1901** L. & L. Van Ginderen, 10-86

ROYAL ARMY
ROYAL CORPS OF TRANSPORT

### MEDIUM LANDING SHIPS

◆ **2 Ardennes-class logistic landing craft** Bldr: Brooke Marine, Lowestoft

| | Laid down | L | In serv. |
|---|---|---|---|
| L 4001 ARDENNES | 27-8-75 | 29-7-76 | 1977 |
| L 4003 ARAKAN | 16-2-76 | 23-5-77 | 9-6-78 |

**Ardennes (L 4001)**—with deck load of containers L. & L. Van Ginderen, 1-87

**D:** 870 tons (1,663 fl) **S:** 10.0 kts **Dim:** 72.16 (69.95 pp) × 15.03 × 2.01
**M:** 2 Mirrlees-Blackstone GWSL 8-MGR 2 diesels; 2 props; 2,000 hp
**Fuel:** 150 tons **Range:** 2,500/10 **Man:** 4 officers, 31 men

REMARKS: Replacements for the LCT(8) class, operated by the Royal Corps of Transport. Can carry 5 70-ton tanks or 24 standard 20-foot containers (254 tons) as well as 6 officers and 28 troops. No armament.

### LANDING CRAFT

◆ **9 Arromanches class**

| | Bldr: | L | In serv. |
|---|---|---|---|
| L 105 ARROMANCHES | Brooke Marine, Lowestoft | 6-1-81 | 31-7-81 |
| L 106 ANTWERP | Brooke Marine, Lowestoft | 9-3-81 | 14-8-81 |
| L 107 ANDALSNES | James & Stone, Brightlingsea | 16-3-84 | 22-5-84 |

**LANDING CRAFT** *(continued)*

| | | | |
|---|---|---|---|
| L 108 Abbeville | James & Stone, Brightlingsea | 28-8-84 | 9-11-84 |
| L 109 Akyab | James & Stone, Brightlingsea | 20-11-84 | 21-12-84 |
| L 110 Aachen | James & Stone, Brightlingsea | 25-6-86 | 26-1-87 |
| L 111 Arezzo | James & Stone, Brightlingsea | 18-11-86 | 2-3-87 |
| L 112 Agheila | James & Stone, Brightlingsea | 27-4-87 | 12-6-87 |
| L 113 Audemer | James & Stone, Brightlingsea | 24-6-87 | 8-87 |

**Aachen (L 110)** L. & L. Van Ginderen, 2-87

**Andalsnes (L 107)** G. Arra, 1-87

**D:** 290 tons (fl) **S:** 9.25 kts **Dim:** 33.26 (30.00 pp) × 8.30 × 1.45 loaded
**Electron Equipt:** Radar: 1/Decca 110
**M:** 2 Doorman 8 JTCWM diesels; 2 props; 660 hp
**Range:** 900/9 **Fuel:** 17 tons **Man:** 6 tot.

Remarks: First two ordered 18-3-80 to begin replacement of *Avon* class. Next three ordered 31-3-83, and four more in 3-85. L 105 and L 106 displace 282 tons (fl) and can make 10 kts at light load; they operated in the Falklands 1982–83 and are now based at Cyprus.

◆ **3 Avon class** Bldr: Saunders-Roe, Isle of Wight (In serv. 1961–67)

RPL 05 Eden RPL 06 Forth RPL 12 Medway

**Eden (RPL 05)** L. & L. Van Ginderen, 3-87

**D:** 61 tons (100 fl) **S:** 8 kts **Dim:** 22.0 × 6.1 × 1.7
**M:** 2 diesels; 2 props; 870 hp **Man:** 6 tot.

Remarks: RPL—Ramped Powered Lighter: Rotate on duty at Belize. Sisters *Clyde* (RPL 03), *Dart* (RPL 04), *Itchen* (RPL 09), *Kennet* (RPL 10), and *Lodden* (RPL 11) stricken 1987.

◆ **4 LCVP 4-class landing craft** Bldr: W.A. Souters & Sons, Cowes

LCVP 8402 (In serv. 15-3-85) LCVP 8619 (In serv. 1987)
LCVP 8409 (In serv. 18-9-85) LCVP 8620 (In serv. 1987)

**D:** 10 tons (fl) **S:** 20 kts (16 loaded) **Dim:** 13.00 (11.90 pp) × 3.20 × 0.80
**A:** 2/7.62-mm mg (I × 2; provision for)
**M:** 2 Perkins 76-3544 diesels; 2 props; 440 hp
**Range:** 200/12 **Man:** 3 crew + 35 troops

Remarks: Cargo well 8.80 × 2.13, with 5.5-ton capacity. Aluminum construction. Seventeen in RN service. Two serve in Falklands, one in Belize, one in U.K..

## CARGO SHIP

◆ **1 Throsk class** Bldr: Appledore SB

| | Laid down | L | In serv. |
|---|---|---|---|
| A 382 St. George | 9-11-80 | 3-81 | 7-81 |

**St. George (A 382)** L. & L. Van Ginderen, 2-87

**D:** 2,193 tons (fl) **S:** 14 kts **Dim:** 70.57 (64.31 pp) × 11.90 × 4.57
**M:** 2 Mirrlees-Blackstone diesels; 1 prop; 3,000 hp **Range:** 1,500/14; 5,000/10
**Electron Equipt:** 1/1006 **Man:** 10 officers, 22 men

Remarks: Sister to RMAS-operated munitions carriers *Kinterbury* and *Throsk*, with improved accommodations. Two holds, two 5-ton cranes; 1,150 dwt. Ordered 2-10-79.

## SERVICE CRAFT

◆ **2 Spitfire-class range safety boats** Bldr: James & Stone, Brightlingsea

Alfred Herring, V.C. (In serv. 1978) Michael Murphy, V.C. (In serv. 10-3-83)

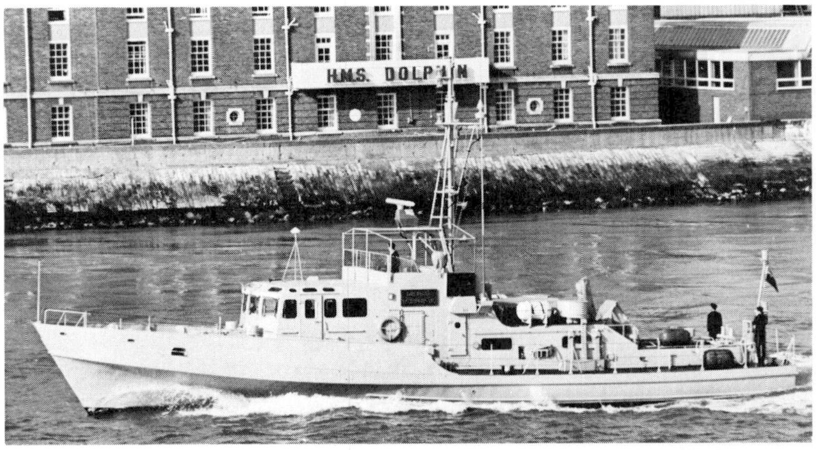

**Michael Murphy, V.C.** L. & L. Van Ginderen, 3-83

**D:** 48 tons (60 fl) **S:** 22 kts **Dim:** 23.70 × 5.50 × 1.50
**M:** 2 Paxman 8YJCM4 diesels; 2 props; 2,100 hp **Man:** 9 tot.

Remarks: Sisters to RAF target tow launches. *Herring* operates in Outer Hebrides at Royal Artillery Range, *Murphy* at Cyprus.

**SERVICE CRAFT** *(continued)*

◆ **13 Samuel Morley, V.C.-class range safety craft** Bldrs: *Morley:* Fairey Marine, Hamble (except *Dalton, Masters, Hughes:* A.R.P. Whitstable); others: Halmatic, Havant.

| | In serv. | | In serv. |
|---|---|---|---|
| Samuel Morley, V.C. | 1980 | Sir William Roe | 1983 |
| James Dalton, V.C. | 1981 | Sir Reginald Kerr | 17-3-83 |
| Richard Masters, V.C. | 1981 | Sir Humphrey Gale | 8-4-83 |
| Joseph Hughes, G.C. | 1981 | Geoffrey Rackham, G.C. | 19-12-85 |
| Sir Paul Travers | 20-10-82 | Walter Cleal, G.C. | 1986 |
| Sir Cecil Smith | 6-7-82 | Sir Evan Gibb | 8-86 |
| Sir John Potter | 24-8-82 | | |

**Geoffrey Rackham, G.C.** L. & L. Van Ginderen, 8-86

**D:** 20.6 tons (23.6 fl) **S:** 20-22 kts **Dim:** 14.94 × 4.65 × 1.30
**M:** First four and last three: 2 Rolls-Royce C8M410 diesels; 2 props; 820 hp. Remainder: 2 Fiat 828SM diesels; 2 props; 880 hp
**Range:** 320/17 (300/18, last three)
**Electron Equipt:** Radar: 1/Decca . . . **Man:** 3 tot.

Remarks: Glass-reinforced plastic hulls by Halmatic, Havant. *Hughes* and *Potter* based at Hong Kong. Design based on "Talisman 49" hull. Last three ordered 11-4-85.

◆ **8 workboats** Bldr: Anderson, Rigden & Perkins, Whitstable

HL 1 through HL 7 (In serv. 2-3-81) HL 8 (In serv. 2-6-81)

**D:** 8 tons (fl) **S:** 11 kts **Dim:** 11.2 × 3.5 × . . .
**M:** 1 Perkins T6-354 M diesel; 129 hp **Man:** 2 tot.

Remarks: Glass-reinforced plastic construction. Five also built for RN.

◆ **1 (+1) general-purpose workboat** Bldr: James & Stone, Brightlingsea

| | Laid down | L | In serv. |
|---|---|---|---|
| WB 08 Mill Reef | 17-3-86 | 17-11-86 | 16-2-87 |

**D:** 25 tons (fl) **S:** . . . **Dim:** 14.75 × . . . × . . .
**M:** 2 diesels; 2 props; . . . hp **Electron Equipt:** Radar: 1/Decca . . .

Remarks: Prototype of design to replace class below. Ordered 6-12-85. Four more planned.

◆ **4 general-purpose workboats** (In serv. 1966–71)

WB 03 Bream WB 05 Roach WB 06 Perch WB 07 Pike

**D:** 19 tons (fl) **S:** 8 kts **Dim:** 14.3 × . . . × . . .

Remarks: Sister *Barbel* (WB 04) stricken 1987.

◆ **1 command and control craft** Bldr: Nelson, Cowes (In serv. 1971)

L 02 Tern

**D:** 12 tons (fl) **S:** 15 kts **Dim:** 12.5 × . . . × . . .

Remarks: Sisters *Petrel* (L 01) stricken 1985, *Fulmar* (L 03), *Skua* (L 04), and *Shearwater* (L 05) in 1986-87.

◆ **2 air-cushion vehicles** Bldr: Air Vehicles, Cowes

SH 01 (In serv. 11-5-82) SH 02 (In serv. 15-7-82)

**D:** 1 ton (fl) **S:** 34 kts **Dim:** 8.45 × 4.57 × 2.18 (high)
**M:** 1 diesel; 1 air screw; 1 lift fan; 200 hp
**Crew:** 1, plus 11 passengers

Note: Training ship *Yarmouth Navigator* stricken 1987. Tugs *Bridget* and *Brenda* transferred from R.M.A.S. on 19-8-83, sold commercial in 1987.

**Mill Reef (WB 08)** L. & L. Van Ginderen, 6-87

**Perch (WB 06)** L. & L. Van Ginderen, 3-87

**Shearwater**—now stricken L. & L. Van Ginderen, 7-83

**Brenda (A 325)**—now sold L. & L. Van Ginderen, 6-86

**SERVICE CRAFT** *(continued)*

ROYAL AIR FORCE MARINE BRANCH

Personnel (1984): 430 RAF, 80 civilian

### LONG-RANGE RECOVERY AND SUPPORT CRAFT (LRRSC)

Note: Craft have black hulls, gray upperworks, RAF roundel on hull sides and top of pilothouse. The Royal Air Force Marine Branch, established 1-4-1918, was disbanded 31-3-86, with afloat assets now operated for the RAF by James Fisher, Ltd., with civil crews. Based at Plymouth, Invergordon, Holyhead, and Great Yarmouth. Fly Blue Ensign with gold eagle holding anchor.

◆ **2 Seal class**

| | Bldr | In serv. |
|---|---|---|
| 5000 Seal | Brooke Marine, Lowestoft | 8-67 |
| 5001 Seagull | Fairmile Const., Berwich-on-Tweed | 1970 |

**Seal (5000)** L. & L. Van Ginderen, 6-83

**D:** 159 tons (fl) **S:** 21 kts **Dim:** 36.6 (33.8 pp) × 7.0 × 2.0
**Electron Equipt:** Radar: 1/978
**M:** 2 Paxman 16 YJCM diesels; 2 props; 4,000 hp
**Electric:** 110 kw
**Fuel:** 31 tons **Range:** 2,200/12
**Man:** 2 officers, 15 men

Remarks: Design similar to Royal Navy's *Kingfisher*-class patrol boats. Used for search and rescue, target towing, and recovering guided missiles and other air-dropped ordnance. Sister *Sea Otter* (5002) transferred to Royal Navy 30-10-84 and renamed *Redpole*. Both based at Invergordon.

### RESCUE AND TARGET-TOWING LAUNCHES (RTTL)

◆ **6 Spitfire (RTTL Mk 3) class** Bldr: James & Stone, Brightlingsea

| | In serv. | | In serv. |
|---|---|---|---|
| 4000 Spitfire | 1972 | 4005 Hurricane | 1980 |
| 4003 Halifax | 1977 | 4006 Lancaster | 1981 |
| 4004 Hampden | 1980 | 4007 Wellington | 25-5-81 |

**Halifax (4003)** B. Sullivan, 5-87

**Spitfire (4000)** G. Gyssels, 9-85

**D:** 48 tons (60 fl) **S:** 22 kts **Dim:** 23.70 (22.15 wl) × 5.50 × 1.50
**Electron Equipt:** Radar: 1/Decca . . .
**M:** 2 Paxman 8YJCM4 diesels; 2 props; 2,000 hp **Electric:** 30 kVA
**Fuel:** 10 tons **Range:** 500/21; 1,000/15 **Man:** 1 officer, 8 men

Remarks: *Spitfire* is 20.6 m overall and has two side-by-side stacks; the series-construction units discharge exhaust through ports in the stern. Sisters *Sunderland* (4001) and *Stirling* (4002) to Royal Navy 8-85 as *Hart* (P 257) and *Cormorant* (P 256).

◆ **1 aviation trials support ship** Bldr: Hall Russell, Aberdeen (In serv. 1966)

Colonel Templar (ex-*Criscilla*)

**Colonel Templar** L. & L. Van Ginderen, 11-82

**D:** . . . **S:** . . . **Dim:** 56.6 × 11.0 × 4.1
**M:** 2 diesels; 1 prop; . . . hp

Remarks: 952 grt/411 nrt. Former stern-haul trawler purchased 1980 to support the Royal Aircraft Establishment, Farnborough.

◆ **5 1300-series rescue pinnaces** Bldrs: Groves & Gutteridge, Robertsons, Poole, and Dorset Yacht Co., Poole (In serv. 1955–65)

1374 1387 1389 1390 1392

**Rescue Pinnace 1389** B. Sullivan, 5-87

**RESCUE AND TARGET-TOWING LAUNCHES (RTTL)** *(continued)*

**D:** 28.3 tons (fl) **S:** 13 kts **Dim:** 19.2 × 4.7 × 1.5
**M:** 2 Rolls-Royce C6 diesels; 2 props; 190 hp **Man:** 5 tot.

REMARKS: Wooden construction. 1387 and 1390 in storage.

## DEPARTMENT OF AGRICULTURE AND FISHERIES FOR SCOTLAND

AVIATION: In late 1984, a Cessna Titan with Racal ASR 360 radar and aerial cameras was purchased for surveillance, to replace a Turbine Islander chartered in 1982. Three Dornier 228–200, one with Bendix RDR 1500 color radar, were acquired 1986.

### FISHERIES PROTECTION SHIPS

◆ **2 (+1) Sulisker class**

| | Bldr | Laid down | L | In serv. |
|---|---|---|---|---|
| SULISKER | Ferguson Brothers, Port Glasgow | . . . | 8-80 | 1980 |
| VIGILANT | Ferguson Ailsa, Port Glasgow | . . . | 26-3-82 | 9-82 |
| NORNA | Richards, Lowestoft | 5-1-87 | 11-9-87 | 7-88 |

**Sulisker** L. & L. Van Ginderen, 2-81

**D:** 1,580 tons (fl) **S:** 18 kts **Dim:** 71.33 (64.00 pp) × 11.60 × 4.66
**Electron Equipt:** Radar: 1/Sperry Mk 3012X-59, 1/Sperry Mk 3012S-312
**M:** 2 Ruston 12RKCM diesels; 2 CP props; 5,640 hp **Electric:** 638 kw
**Fuel:** 198 tons **Range:** 7,000/14 **Man:** 8 officers, 17 men

REMARKS: 1,250 grt. Equipped with 450-hp bow-thruster, Denny-Brown fin stabilizers. 1,177 grt/337 dwt. Equipped for rescue, firefighting, and oil-spill cleanup. Elaborate navigational equipment, particularly in *Vigilant.* Third unit ordered 11-6-86.

◆ **2 Jura class** Bldr: Hall Russell & Co., Aberdeen

JURA (In serv. 1973) WESTRA (In serv. 1975)

**Jura** L. & L. Van Ginderen, 10-81

**D:** 778 tons (1,285 fl) **S:** 17 kts **Dim:** 59.6 × 10.7 × 4.4
**M:** 2 British Polar SP112VS-F diesels; 1 prop; 4,200 hp **Man:** 28 tot.

REMARKS: Design (with different engines) employed for Royal Navy's "Isles"-class offshore patrol vessels. *Jura,* chartered by Royal Navy 1973–77, had 1/40-mm AA.

◆ **2 fisheries patrol boats** Bldr: Cheverton, Cowes (In serv. 31-1-83)

MORVEN MOIDART

**D:** 37 tons (44 fl) **S:** 24 kts **Dim:** 19.8 (17.9 pp) × 5.77 × 1.63
**M:** 3 G.M. 8V92 TI diesels; 3 props; 1,530 bhp **Electric:** 75 kw
**Endurance:** 7 days **Man:** 2 officers, 3 men

REMARKS: Glass-reinforced plastic construction. Use Murray, Cormack "North Cape 65" hulls, built at Cheverton, Newport, and fitted out at Cowes. Carry Avon Sea-Raider semi-rigid inflatable inspection dinghy.

**Moidart, home-ported at Leith** L. & L. Van Ginderen, 1-84

◆ **1 fisheries patrol boat** Bldr: Osbourne, Littlehampton (In serv. 4-84)

OSPREY

**D:** 6.25 tons **S:** 28 kts **Dim:** 10.06 × 3.05 × 1.12
**M:** 2 Rolls-Royce Sabre 212 diesels; 2 props; 424 hp
**Range:** 200/. . . **Man:** 3 tot.

REMARKS: Combines rigid hull with inflatable flotation/fender collar, which increases dimensions to 11.20 × 3.73 when inflated.

◆ **2 13-m patrol craft** Bldr: Cheverton, Cowes (In serv. 1981)

N. . . . . . . N. . . . . .

◆ **1 7.9-m patrol craft** Bldr: Horne Bros. (In serv. 1981)

SKUA

NOTE: The Scottish Department of Agriculture and Fisheries also operates the research trawlers *Brenda* (460 grt, 1951) and *Scotia.*

**Scotia** L. & L. Van Ginderen, 5-82

## H.M. CUSTOMS AND EXCISE MARINE DIVISION
Headquartered at HMS *Vernon,* Portsmouth

### PATROL BOATS AND CRAFT

◆ **0 (+3) Protector-class patrol boats** Bldr: Fairey Marintechnik, Cowes

| | Laid down | L | In serv. |
|---|---|---|---|
| N . . . | 7-87 | . . . | 1988 |
| N . . . | . . . | . . . | 1988 |
| N . . . | . . . | . . . | 1988 |

**D:** 100 tons (fl) **S:** 25 kts **Dim:** 25.7 × 6.2 × 1.7
**Electron Equipt:** Radar: 2/Decca . . . nav.
**M:** 2 Paxman SET-CW diesels; 2 props; 2,880 hp—1 Perkins T6. 3544 diesel-driven Hamilton waterjet; 200 hp (for speeds to 8 kts)
**Range:** . . . **Fuel:** 16 tons **Man:** . . .

REMARKS: Ordered 23-4-87, to begin replacement of Tracker-series. Smaller than Bahamian units of class, and with different propulsion plant; waterjet adds 1 kt to maximum speed.

◆ **2 33-m-class patrol boats** Bldr: Brooke Marine, Lowestoft (In serv. 1979)

SEARCHER SEEKER

**D:** 140 tons (160 fl) **S:** 21 kts **Dim:** 36.6 (33.8 pp) × 7.0 × 2.0
**Electron Equipt:** Radar: 1/978
**M:** 2 Paxman 16YJCM diesels; 2 props; 4,000 hp **Electric:** 110 kw
**Fuel:** 31 tons **Range:** 2,600/12 **Man:** 10 tot.

**GREAT BRITAIN** *(continued)*
**PATROL BOATS AND CRAFT** *(continued)*

**Searcher** L. & L. Van Ginderen, 1-86

REMARKS: Generally similar to RAF's *Seal* class and Royal Navy's *Kingfisher* class, but have more extensive superstructures. Fin stabilizers. Used in Scottish waters.

◆ **6 Tracker Mk II patrol craft** Bldr: Fairey Marine, Hamble (In serv. 1978–. . .)

ACTIVE ALERT CHALLENGE CHAMPION SAFEGUARD SWIFT

**Safeguard** L. & L. Van Ginderen, 2-87

REMARKS: Data as for units of this class in the Royal Navy (*Attacker* class). *Alert* is a Tracker Mk I with pilothouse farther forward.

◆ **5 service launches** Bldr: Fairey Cheverton, Cowes (In serv. 8-84 to 1986)

ANTELOPE AVOCET BITTERN N . . . N . . .

**D:** 3.75 tons (fl) **S:** 15 kts **Dim:** 8.23 × 2.74 × 0.81
**M:** 2 Perkins 4.236 diesels; 2 props; 140 hp **Range:** 100/13 **Man:** 2 tot.

◆ **40 smaller craft, including Avon Surfrider semi-rigid inflatables**

Four 5.5-m and one 6.5-m TF 550-series craft were delivered 1985–86 by Task Force Boats; capable of 25 kts on their 110-hp Turbo Merlin diesel-powered P 90 waterjets.

# GREECE

## Hellenic Republic

PERSONNEL (1984): 19,500 men, including 2,500 officers

MERCHANT MARINE (1986): 2,255 ships—28,390,800 grt (tankers: 391 ships —10,234,774 grt

NAVAL AVIATION: Greek naval aviation began in April 1975, when four Alouette-III ASW helicopters fitted with AS-12 antiship, wire-guided missiles went into service. Subsequently, 16 Agusta-Bell AB-212 helicopters were ordered from Italy in 1977; these are based at Eleusis, with the first two having been delivered 19-7-79. The Air Force has 14 HU-16B Grumman Albatross amphibian planes remaining for maritime reconnaissance; these carry mixed Navy/Air Force crews and have been modernized by Grumman with MEC Super Searcher radars, IFF gear, Marconi LAPADS sonobuoy signal processors, and new radars. Three ex-Dutch Breguet Atlantic 1 patrol aircraft may be purchased from France to replace some HU-16B Albatross.

**Greek Navy AB-212 helicopter** Official

SUBMARINES

◆ **8 German Type 209** Bldr: Howaldtswerke, Kiel

| | Laid down | L | In serv. |
|---|---|---|---|
| S 110 GLAVKOS | 1-9-68 | 15-9-70 | 5-11-71 |
| S 111 NEREUS | 15-1-69 | 7-6-71 | 10-2-72 |
| S 112 TRITON | 1-6-69 | 19-10-71 | 23-11-72 |
| S 113 PROTEUS | 1-10-69 | 1-2-72 | 23-11-72 |
| S 116 POSEIDON | 15-4-76 | 21-3-78 | 22-3-79 |
| S 117 AMFRITITI | 16-9-76 | 14-6-78 | 14-8-79 |
| S 118 OKEANOS | 1-10-76 | 16-11-78 | 15-11-79 |
| S 119 PONTOS | 15-1-77 | 22-3-79 | 29-4-80 |

**Glavkos (S 110)**—original version 1977

**Amfrititi (S 117)**—second group, with higher bow L. & L. Van Ginderen, 1987

**D:** 980/1,105/1,230 **S:** 22 kts (max. sub. for 15 min.), 12 kts, snorkel
**Dim:** 55.0 (116–118: 56.1) × 6.6 × 5.9
**A:** 8/533-mm TT fwd (+6 reserve torpedoes)
**Electron Equipt:** Radar: Thomson-CSF Calypso
Sonar: Atlas AN 526 passive, CSU AN 406 A9 active, DUUX-2
**M:** diesel-electric propulsion; 4 MTU 12V493 TY60 diesels, each linked to an AEG generator of 420 kw; 1 Siemens motor; 1 prop; 5,000 hp
**Range:** 25/30; 230/8; 400/4 submerged **Man:** 5 officers, 26 men

REMARKS: Diving depth 250 m. The second group of four are 56.1 m overall, 1,185 tons surfaced/1,285 tons submerged, have a higher bow, and H.S.A. SINBADS weapons control with Mk 8 torpedo f.c.s. The first four had a CSU3-2 and PRS-3-4 sonar suite; they are being modernized with a KANARIS tactical data system employing 2 Sperry displays and a UYK-44 computer.

## SUBMARINES *(continued)*

◆ **1 ex-U.S. Guppy III class** Bldr: Portsmouth Naval SY, New Hampshire

| | Laid down | L | In serv. |
|---|---|---|---|
| S 115 Katsonis (ex-*Remora,* SS 487) | 5-3-45 | 12-7-45 | 3-1-46 |

**Katsonis (S 115)** D. Dervissis, 9-79

**D:** 1,660/1,975/2,540 tons **S:** 17.2/14.5 kts **Dim:** 99.52 × 8.23 × 5.18
**A:** 10/533-mm TT (6 fwd, 4 aft; 24 torpedoes)
**Electron Equipt:** Radar: 1/SS-2A—EW: WLR-1
Sonar: BQG-4 (PUFFS), BQR-2B
**M:** 4 Fairbanks-Morse $38D8\frac{1}{8}$ 10-cyl. diesels (1,600 hp each), electric drive; 2 props; 6,400/5,480 hp
**Range:** 10,000–12,000/10; 95/5 submerged **Man:** 85 tot.

Remarks: Purchased 29-10-73. Guppy III conversion completed 1962 at Pearl Harbor SY.

◆ **1 ex-U.S. Guppy IIA class** Bldr: Manitowoc SB, Wisconsin

| | Laid down | L | In serv. |
|---|---|---|---|
| S 114 Papanikolis (ex-*Hardhead,* SS 365) | 7-7-43 | 12-12-43 | 18-4-44 |

**Papanikolis (S 114)** D. Dervissis, 9-79

**D:** 1,517/1,870/2,440 tons **S:** 18/13.5 kts **Dim:** 93.6 × 8.2 × 5.2
**A:** 10/533-mm TT (6 fwd, 4 aft, 24 torpedoes)
**Electron Equipt:** Radar: 1/SS-2A—Sonar: BQR-2R—EW: WLR-1
**M:** 3 G.M. 16-278A diesels (1,600 hp each), 2 electric motors; 2 props; 3,430/5,480 hp

Remarks: Purchased 26-7-72. The fourth diesel generator was removed to permit enlargement of the sonar compartment during Guppy II conversion completed 1953. Two 126-cell batteries. *Triana* (S 86), ex-*Scabbardfish* (SS 397), is now used for pierside training.

## DESTROYERS

◆ **6 ex-U.S. Gearing FRAM I class**

| | Bldr | Laid down | L | In serv. |
|---|---|---|---|---|
| D 212 Kanaris (ex-*Stickell,* DD 888) | Consolidated Steel | 5-1-45 | 16-6-45 | 26-9-45 |
| D 213 Kontouriotis (ex-*Rupertus,* DD 851) | Bethlehem, Quincy | 2-5-45 | 21-9-45 | 8-3-46 |
| D 214 Sachtouris (ex-*Arnold J. Isbell,* DD 869) | Bethlehem, Quincy | 14-3-45 | 6-8-45 | 5-1-46 |
| D 215 Toumbazis (ex-*Gurke,* DD 783) | Todd SY, Seattle | 1-7-44 | 15-4-45 | 5-12-45 |
| D 216 Apostolis (ex-*Charles P. Cecil,* DD 835) | Bath Iron Wks. | 2-12-44 | 22-2-45 | 29-6-45 |
| D 217 Kriezis (ex-*Myles C. Fox,* DD 829) | Bath Iron Wks. | 14-8-44 | 13-1-45 | 20-3-45 |

**Toumbazis (D 215)** Pradignac & Leo, 10-84

**Sachtouris (D 214)** G. Gyssels, 1985

**Sachtouris (D 214)** L. Grazioli, 10-84

**D:** 2,425 tons (3,500 fl) **S:** 30 kts
**Dim:** 119.03 × 12.52 × 4.45 (6.40 over sonar)
**A:** 4/127-mm, 38-cal. (II × 2)—1/76-mm OTO Melara DP—1/40-mm AA—2/12.7-mm mg—1/ASROC system (VIII × 1, 14 missiles)—6/324-mm Mk 32 ASW TT (III × 2)—1/d.c. rack
**Electron Equipt:** Radar: 1/navigational, 1/SPS-10, 1/SPS-40 (SPS-29 on 212, 215, 216), 1/Mk 25, 1/Orion RTN-20X
Sonar: SQS-23D—EW: WLR-1 intercept, ULQ-6 active
**M:** GT; 2 props; 60,000 hp **Electric:** 1,200 kw
**Boilers:** 4 Babcock & Wilcox; 43.3 kg/cm$^2$, 454°C superheat **Fuel:** 650 tons
**Range:** 2,400/25; 4,800/15 **Man:** 14 officers, 260 men

Remarks: D 212 transferred 1-7-72; D 213 on 10-7-73 (purchased 11-7-78); D 214 on 4-12-73 (purchased 11-7-78); D 215 purchased 17-3-77; D 216 purchased 2-8-80 originally for cannibalization; and D 217 purchased 8-7-81. All have been given an Elsag NA-21 fire-control system aft, 1/76-mm OTO Melara Compact on the helicopter deck, and a 40-mm AA before the bridge; equipment for D 216 and D 217 ordered 4-85 and completed 12-86 and -87, respectively. In D 215, which was equipped as Fleet Flagship 1980–81, two of the boilers are Foster-Wheeler. The 1980–81 purchase ships had LN-66 navigational radars. Also purchased were *Corry* (DD 817) and *Dyess* (DD 880), on 8-7-81; they are being cannibalized for spares.

◆ **1 ex-U.S. Gearing DDR FRAM II class**

| | Bldr | Laid down | L | In serv. |
|---|---|---|---|---|
| D 210 Themistocles (ex-*Frank Knox,* DD 742) | Bath Iron Wks. | 8-5-44 | 17-9-44 | 11-12-44 |

**D:** 2,425 tons (3,500 fl) **S:** 30 kts
**Dim:** 119.03 × 12.52 × 4.45 (6.40 over sonar)
**A:** 6/127-mm DP (II × 3)—4/30-mm AA Emerlec (II × 2)—6/324-mm Mk 32 ASW TT (III × 2)—2 Hedgehog—1/AB 212 ASW helicopter
**Electron Equipt:** Radar: 1/navigational, 1/SPS-10, 1/SPS-29, 1/Mk 25
Sonar: SQS-23, SQA-10 VDS—EW: WLR-1

**DESTROYERS** *(continued)*

**Themistocles (D 210)** L. & L. Van Ginderen, 1980

**M:** 2 sets GT; 2 props; 60,000 hp **Electric:** 1,200 kw
**Boilers:** 2 Babcock & Wilcox; 43.3 kg/cm², 454°C superheat
**Fuel:** 650 tons **Range:** 2,400/25; 4,800/15 **Man:** 16 officers, 253 men

REMARKS: Purchased 30-1-71, having been extensively rebuilt after a grounding in 1966. Radar picket features deleted and helicopter hangar added in Greece by 1978 in place of the after 01 level deckhouse. 30-mm AA substituted for 20-mm single mounts in 1980. Receiving 3-section 19.17-m long telescoping hangar and enlarged flight deck for AB 212 helicopter during 1987.

◆ **1 ex-U.S. Allen M. Sumner class** Bldr: Federal SB & DD, Kearny, New Jersey

| | Laid down | L | In serv. |
|---|---|---|---|
| D 211 MIAOULIS (ex-*Ingraham,* DD 694) | 4-4-43 | 16-1-44 | 10-3-44 |

**Miaoulis (D 211)** Official

**D:** 2,200 tons (3,320 fl) **S:** 30 kts
**Dim:** 114.76 × 12.49 × 4.39 (5.79 over sonar)
**A:** 6/127-mm, 38-cal. DP (II × 3)—2/40-mm AA (I × 2)—6/20-mm AA (I × 6)—2 Hedgehogs—6/324-mm Mk 32 ASW TT (III × 2)—1/AB-212 ASW helicopter
**Electron Equipt:** Radar: 1/navigational, 1/SPS-10, 1/SPS-40, 1/Mk 25
Sonar: SQS-29, SQA-10 VDS—EW: WLR-1
**M:** 2 sets GT; 2 props; 60,000 hp **Electric:** 1,200 kw
**Boilers:** 4 Babcock & Wilcox; 43.3 kg/cm², 454°C **Fuel:** 495 tons
**Range:** 2,400/25; 4,800/15 **Man:** 14 officers, 260 men

REMARKS: Transferred 16-7-71. Mk 37 gunfire-control system for 127-mm mounts. Modernization commenced 11-86 at Eleusis SY; receiving helicopter facilities as on *Themistocles* (D 210)

◆ **6 ex-U.S. and West German Fletcher class**—all in reserve

| | Bldr | Laid down | L | In serv. |
|---|---|---|---|---|
| D 06 ASPIS (ex-*Conner,* DD 582) | Boston NSY | 16-4-42 | 18-9-42 | 8-6-43 |
| D 16 VELOS (ex-*Charette,* DD 581) | Boston NSY | 20-2-42 | 3-6-42 | 18-5-43 |
| D 42 KIMON (ex-German Z-2, ex-*Ringgold,* DD 500) | Federal SB & DD | 25-6-42 | 11-11-42 | 24-12-42 |
| D 58 LONCHI (ex-*Hall,* DD 583) | Boston NSY | 16-4-42 | 18-7-42 | 6-7-43 |
| D 65 NEARCHOS (ex-German Z 3, ex-*Wadsworth,* DD 516) | Bath Iron Wks. | 18-8-42 | 10-1-43 | 16-3-43 |
| D 85 SPHENDONI (ex-*Aulick,* DD 569) | Consolidated SB | 14-5-41 | 2-3-42 | 27-10-42 |

**D:** 2,050 tons (2,850 fl) **S:** 32/30 kts **Dim:** 114.85 × 12.03 × 5.5
**A:** 4/127-mm, 38 cal. (I × 4)—6/76.2-mm DP, 50-cal. (II × 3)—5/533-mm TT (V × 1, see Remarks)—6/324-mm Mk 32 ASW TT (II × 2)—2 Hedgehogs—1/d.c. rack (not in D 42, D 65)—D 42, D 65: mine rails

**Velos (D 16)** G. Arra

**Kimon (D 42)**—en route Greece as Z 2 (D 171) Skyfotos, 8-81

**Electron Equipt:** Radar: 1/navigational, 1/SPS-10, 1/SPS-6, 1/Mk 25, 2/Mk 34, 1/Mk 35
Sonar: SQS-4 or 29 series—EW: SLR-1 or WLR-1
**M:** 2 sets GT; 2 props; 60,000 hp **Electric:** 580 kw
**Boilers:** 4 Babcock & Wilcox; 43.3 kg/cm², 454° **Fuel:** 650 tons
**Range:** 1,260/30; 4,400/15 **Man:** 350 tot.

REMARKS: D 06 loaned 15-9-59, D 16 on 15-6-69, D 58 on 9-2-60, and D 85 on 21-8-59; all purchased 25-4-77, along with *Thyella* (D 28, ex-*Bradford,* DD 545), stricken 2-81, and *Navarinon* (D 63, ex-*Brown,* DD 546) stricken 1981. D 65 purchased and transferred from West Germany on 30-10-80, and D 42 was purchased 9-81, originally for cannibalization. Have Mk 37 GFCS for 127-mm, Mk 56 GFCS for aft 76.2-mm, and 2 Mk 63 GFCS for amidships 76.2-mm guns. The ex-German ships had 2/533-mm ASW TT vice Mk 32 ASW TT and were equipped with mine rails; they had Kelvin-Hughes 14/9 navigational radars. Acquired for cannibalization and scrapping were ex-German Z 1 (ex-*Anthony,* DD 515) in 1979, Z 4 (ex-*Claxton,* DD 571) on 26-2-80, and Z 5 (ex-*Dyson,* DD 572) in 9-81. All in reserve by 1987. D 42, D 65, and one other were to be modernized, it was announced in 5-85.

## FRIGATES

NOTE: Plans to construct four new frigates in Greece have been under discussion since 1985. Under consideration are the Blohm + Voss MEKO 200, Italian *Lupo,* British modernized Leander, and U.S. Todd "Superior" designs. The latter has the following characteristics:

**D:** 1,874 tons **S:** 30 kts (18 on diesel)
**Dim:** 105.6 (100.00 pp) × 12.15 × 3.33 (hull)
**A:** 8/Harpoon SSM (IV × 2)—16/vertical-launch sea sparrow SAM—1/76-mm OTO Melara Compact DP—4/40-mm Breda AA (II × 2)—1/20-mm Mk 15 CIWS gatling—6/324-mm ASW TT (III × 2)—1/AB-212 ASW helo
**Electron Equipt:** Radar: 1/. . . nav., 1/. . . air-search, 1/H.S.A. WM-25, 1/STIR
Sonar: . . .
EW: . . . intercept, 4/Mk 36 SRBOC (VI × 4)
**M:** CODAG: 1 LM-2500 gas turbine (28,000 hp), 2/2,000-hp diesels; 2 CP props; 32,000 hp
**Range:** 4,500/15 **Electric:** 2,250 kw (3 × 750 kw) **Man:** 120 tot.

REMARKS: Will be built by Hellenic SY, Skaramanga, if project progresses.

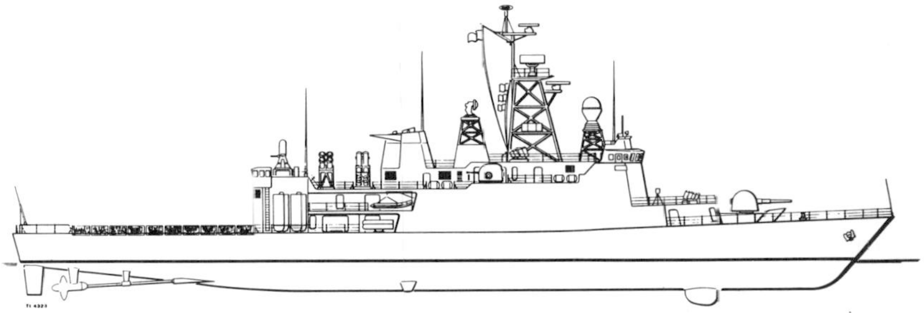

**Todd "Superior" frigate** Todd SY, 1986

**FRIGATES** *(continued)*

◆ **2 Dutch Kortenaer class** Bldr: de Schelde, Vlissingen

| | Laid down | L | In serv. |
|---|---|---|---|
| F 450 Elli (ex-*Pieter Floresz*) | 2-7-77 | 15-12-79 | 10-10-81 |
| F 451 Limnos (ex-*Witte de With*) | 13-6-78 | 27-10-79 | 18-9-82 |

**Elli (F 450)** L. & L. Van Ginderen, 10-81

**Limnos (F 451)** L. & L. Van Ginderen, 9-82

**D:** 3,000 tons (3,786 fl) **S:** 30 kts
**Dim:** 130.2 (121.8 pp) × 14.4 × 4.4 (6.0 props)
**A:** 8/Harpoon SSM (IV × 2)—1 Mk 29 SAM syst. (VIII × 1; 24 Aspide missiles)—2/76-mm OTO Melara DP—4/324-mm Mk 32 ASW TT (II × 2)—1/AB-212 ASW helicopter
**Electron Equipt:** Radar: 1/ZW-06, 1/LW-08, 1/WM-25, 1/STIR
Sonar: SQS-505
EW: Elektronica Sphinx intercept syst., 2 Knebworth/Corvus chaff RL (VIII × 2)
**M:** COGOG: 2 Rolls-Royce Tyne RM-1C cruise gas turbines, 4,900 hp each, 2 Rolls-Royce Olympus TM-3B gas turbines, 25,800 hp each; 2 LIPS CP props; 51,600 hp max.
**Electric:** 3,000 kw (4 SEMT-Pielstick PA4 diesel generator sets)
**Range:** 4,700/16 (on one Tyne turbine) **Man:** 17 officers, 182 men

Remarks: *Elli* was officially turned over to Greece on 26-6-81 at the commencement of sea trials, having been ordered 7-81, along with the second unit. Both were taken from production for the Dutch Navy, in order to speed delivery. Plans to build a third ship in Greece were canceled. Have Denny-Brown fin stabilizers. *Elli* had been equipped with racks to hold 8 Harpoon SSM containers (IV × 2), but these were removed prior to transfer in 1983; 32 Harpoon were ordered from the U.S. for these ships and others. One U.S. Mk 15 CIWS 20-mm gatling AA is being added for close-in defense. Hangar lengthened 2.2 m to accept Italian-built helicopter vice Lynx used by Dutch Navy. Have SEWACO II combat data system. See also class notes in Netherlands section.

◆ **1 German Rhein-class former tender** Bldr: Elsflether Werft, West Germany

| | Laid down | L | In serv. |
|---|---|---|---|
| D 03 Aegeon (ex-*Weser,* A 62) | 1-8-59 | 11-6-60 | 14-7-62 |

**D:** 2,370 tons (2,740 fl) **S:** 20.5 kts **Dim:** 98.18 (92.8 pp) × 11.8 × 3.9
**A:** 2/76-mm OTO Melara Compact DP (I × 2)—4/40-mm AA (I × 4)—70 mines
**Electron Equipt:** Radar: 1/nav.—see Remarks
**M:** 6 Maybach 16-cyl. diesels; 2 CP props; 12,600 hp **Electric:** 2,250 kVA
**Range:** 2,500/16 **Man:** 110 tot.

Remarks: Transferred 6-7-76. A small combatant tender used by Greece as a frigate. Still can act as a tender. Contracted late 1986 with Hellenic SY to modernize armament (replacing 2/100-mm DP), add new air- and surface-search radars and fire-control system.

◆ **4 ex-U.S. Cannon class**

| | Bldr | Laid down | L | In serv. |
|---|---|---|---|---|
| D 01 Aetos (ex-*Ebert,* DE 768) | Tampa Shipbldg, Tampa, Florida | 1-4-43 | 11-5-44 | 12-7-44 |
| D 31 Hierax (ex-*Slater,* DE 766) | Tampa Shipbldg, Tampa, Florida | 9-3-43 | 13-2-44 | 1-5-44 |
| D 54 Leon (ex-*Garfield Thomas,* DE 193) | Federal, Port Newark, New Jersey | 23-9-43 | 12-12-43 | 24-1-44 |
| D 67 Panthir (ex-*Eldridge,* DE 173) | Federal, Port Newark, New Jersey | 22-2-43 | 25-6-43 | 27-8-43 |

**Hierax (D 31)** L. & L. Van Ginderen, 7-80

**D:** 1,300 tons (1,750 fl) **S:** 19 kts **Dim:** 93.0 (91.5 pp) × 11.17 × 3.25
**A:** 3/76.2-mm DP—6/40-mm AA (II × 3)—14/20-mm AA (II × 7)—6/324-mm Mk 32 ASW TT (III × 2)—1 Hedgehog—8/d.c. projectors—2/d.c. racks
**Electron Equipt:** Radar: 1/navigational, 1/Mk 26 f.c.
Sonar: QCU-2
**M:** 4 G.M. 16-278A diesels, electric drive; 2 props; 6,000 hp
**Electric:** 680 kw **Fuel:** 300 tons **Range:** 5,500/19; 11,500/11
**Man:** Peacetime: 150 men; wartime: 185 men

Remarks: Transferred in 1951. Have Mk 52 GFCS for 76.2-mm guns (plus separate rangefinder), 3 Mk 51 Mod. 2 GFCS for 40-mm AA. Obsolete SA radar removed by 1980. Thoroughly obsolete; to be replaced by new construction.

**GUIDED-MISSILE PATROL BOATS**

Note: Three (with nine more planned) 45-m patrol boats were reportedly ordered 1984 from Olympic Marine, Lavrio. Apparently supersede the planned order for additional units of the Combattante III N class. No progress or data reported by 7-87. This program, in turn, may have been superseded by the following: Plans and support services for the construction of two 55-meter "patrol boats" in Greece were ordered from Danyard, Denmark, in 8-87, similar to unit built for Senegal.

◆ **10 Combattante III N class** Bldr: (A) Hellenic SY, Skaramanga; (B) Constr. Méc. de Normandie, Cherbourg

| | Bldr | L | In serv. |
|---|---|---|---|
| P 20 Antipliarchos Lascos | B | 6-7-76 | 2-4-77 |
| P 21 Antipliarchos Blessas | B | 10-11-76 | 19-7-77 |
| P 22 Antipliarchos Troupakis | B | 6-1-77 | 8-11-77 |
| P 23 Antipliarchos Mykonios | B | 5-5-77 | 10-2-78 |
| P 24 Simaiforos Kavalouthis | A | 10-11-79 | 14-7-80 |
| P 25 Antipliarchos Kostakos | A | 1-3-80 | 9-9-80 |
| P 26 Ipopliarchos Deyiannis | A | 14-7-80 | 12-80 |
| P 27 Simaiforos Xenos | A | 8-9-80 | 31-3-81 |
| P 28 Simaiforos Simitzopoulos | A | 12-10-80 | 6-82 |
| P 29 Simaiforos Starakis | A | 1981 | 12-10-81 |

**D:** 385 tons (447 fl) **S:** 36.5 kts (2nd group: 32.6)
**Dim:** 56.65 (53.00 pp) × 8.00 × 2.70 (props)
**A:** First four: 4/MM 38 Exocet SSM (II × 2)—2/76-mm OTO Melara DP (I × 2)—4/30-mm Emerlec AA (II × 2)—2/533-mm TT (2 SST-4 wire-guided torpedoes)
Later six: 6 Penguin SSM (I × 6)—2/76-mm OTO Melara Compact DP (I × 2)—4/30-mm Emerlec AA (II × 2)—2/533-mm TT (2 SST-4 torpedoes)
**Electron Equipt:** Radar: 1/Decca 1226, 1/Thomson-CSF Triton, 1/Thomson-CSF Castor
**M:** First four: 4 MTU 20V538 TB92 diesels; 4 props; 20,800 hp (18,000 sust.)
Later six: 4 MTU 20V538 TB91 diesels; 4 props; 15,000 hp (13,400 sust.)
**Electric:** 450 kw **Range:** 800/32.5; 2,000/15 **Man:** 7 officers, 36 men

Remarks: First four ordered 22-5-75. Second group, built in Greece, and with less expensive weapon, sensor, and propulsion systems, ordered 22-12-76. Each 76-mm gun has 350 rounds, with 80 in ready service. The Emerlec 30-mm mounts are furnished with 3,200 rounds and fire at 700 rounds/barrel/minute. Ships have excellent habitability; accommodations and operations spaces are air-conditioned.

**Simaiforos Kavalouthis (P 24)**—second group Hellenic SY, 1981

## GUIDED-MISSILE PATROL BOATS *(continued)*

**Antipliarchos Lascos (P 20)**—first group CMN, 1976

There are 3 Jeumont-Schneider 150-kw generator sets (440v., 3-ph., 60-Hz.). First group has Thomson-CSF Vega weapon-control system, later ships Vega II. All have 2 CSEE Panda directors for the 30-mm AA.

◆ **4 Combattante II class** Bldr: Constr. Méc. de Normandie (CMN), Cherbourg

| | L | In serv. |
|---|---|---|
| P 14 Ipopliarchos Arliotis (ex-*Evniki*) | 26-4-71 | 4-72 |
| P 15 Ipopliarchos Anninos (ex-*Navsithoi*) | 8-9-71 | 6-72 |
| P 16 Ipopliarchos Konidis (ex-*Kimothoi*) | 20-12-71 | 7-72 |
| P 17 Ipopliarchos Batsis (ex-*Kalypso*) | 26-1-71 | 12-71 |

**Ipopliarchos Arliotis (P 14)** P. Voss, 10-86

**D:** 234 tons (255 fl) **S:** 36.5 kts **Dim:** 47.0 (44.0 pp) × 7.1 × 2.5 (fl)
**A:** 4/MM 38 Exocet SSM (II × 2)—4/35-mm Oerlikon AA (II × 2)—2/533-mm wire-guided TT aft
**Electron Equipt:** Radar: 1/Decca 1226, 1/Thomson-CSF Triton, 1/Thomson-CSF Castor
**M:** 4 MTU MD 872 diesels; 4 props; 12,000 hp **Fuel:** 39 tons
**Range:** 850/25; 2,000/15 **Man:** 4 officers, 36 men

Remarks: Steel hull, light steel alloy superstructure. Ordered 1969. Thomson-CSF Vega weapon-control system.

◆ **2 Kelefstis Stamou class** Bldr: Chantiers Navales de l'Estérel, Cannes

P 286 Kelefstis Stamou (In serv. 28-7-75)
P 287 Diopos Antoniou (In serv. 4-12-75)

**D:** 80 tons (115 fl) **S:** 30 kts **Dim:** 32.0 × 5.8 × 1.5
**A:** 4/SS-12 wire-guided SSM—1/20-mm AA—2/12.7-mm mg (I × 2)
**M:** 2 MTU 12V331 TC81 diesels; 2 props; 2,700 hp **Range:** 1,500/15
**Electron Equipt:** Radar: 1/Decca . . . nav. **Man:** 17 tot.

Remarks: These wooden-hulled ships were ordered by Cyprus, but acquired by Greece. Pendant numbers were P 28 and P 29 until 1980.

**Kelefstis Stamou (P 286)** L. & L. Van Ginderen, 8-84

## TORPEDO BOATS

◆ **5 ex-German Type 141 class** Bldrs: (A) Lürssen, Vegesack; (B) Krögerwerft, Rendsburg

| | Bldr | Laid down | L | In serv. |
|---|---|---|---|---|
| P 50 Esperos (ex-*Seeadler*) | A | 23-9-57 | 1-2-58 | 29-8-58 |
| P 53 Kyklon (ex-*Grief*) | A | 5-2-58 | 28-6-58 | 3-3-59 |
| P 54 Laiaps (ex-*Kondor*) | A | 2-1-58 | 17-5-58 | 24-2-59 |
| P 55 Scorpios (ex-*Kormoran*) | B | 2-2-59 | 16-7-59 | 9-11-59 |
| P 56 Tyfon (ex-*Geier*) | A | 27-5-58 | 1-10-58 | 3-6-59 |

**Kentauros (P 52)**—now stricken D. Dervissis, 9-80

**D:** 195 tons (221 fl) **S:** 42.5 kts **Dim:** 42.62 × 7.10 × 2.39
**A:** 2/40-mm AA (I × 2)—4/533-mm TT (I × 4)
**M:** 4 Maybach 16-cyl. diesels; 4 props; 14,400 hp **Electric:** 192 kw
**Range:** 500/39; 1,000/32

Remarks: Transferred 1976–77. Three others, ex-*Albatros*, ex-*Bussard*, and ex-*Sperber*, were transferred to be cannibalized for spares. Wooden-planked hull skin on metal frame. ***Kataigis*** **(P 51, ex-P 197, ex-*Falke*) stricken late 1981. *Kentauros* (P 52, ex-*Habicht*) stricken 1985, for cannibalization.**

## PATROL CRAFT

◆ **3 (+2) Dilos class** Bldr: Hellenic SY, Skaramanga (In serv. 1977–79; 1987–88)

P 267 Dilos P 268 Lindos P 269 Knossos P . . . N . . . P . . . N . . .

**Knossos (P 269)** L. & L. Van Ginderen, 7-79

**PATROL CRAFT** *(continued)*

**D:** 75 tons (86 fl) **S:** 27 kts **Dim:** 29.0 (27.0 wl) × 5.0 × 1.62
**A:** 2/20-mm AA (I × 2)
**M:** 2 MTU 12V331 TC81 diesels; 2 props; 2,720 hp **Range:** 1,600/25
**Man:** 15 tot.

REMARKS: Designed by Abeking & Rasmussen, West Germany. Used for air/sea rescue. Three each also built for Customs Service and Coast Guard. Two more ordered 12-86 from same builder.

◆ **3 Panagopoulos I class** Bldr: Hellenic SY, Skaramanga

P 61 E. PANAGOPOULOS I (In serv. 23-6-76)
P 62 E. PANAGOPOULOS II (In serv. 1980)
P 63 E. PANAGOPOULOS III (In serv. 1981)

**E. Panagopoulos I (P 61)** Hellenic SY

**D:** 35 tons (fl) **S:** 38 kts **Dim:** 23.0 (21.00 wl) × 5.0 × 0.97
**A:** 1/20-mm AA **Electron Equipt:** Radar: 1/Decca . . .
**M:** 2 MTU 12V331 TC92 diesels; 2 props; 3,060 hp **Man:** 6 tot.

◆ **1 Goulandris I class** Bldr: Neozioh SY, Syros

| | In serv. |
|---|---|
| P 290 N.I. GOULANDRIS II | 6-6-77 |

**N.I. Goulandris II (P 290)** 1981

**D:** 38.5 tons **S:** 30 kts **Dim:** 24.0 × 6.2 × 1.1 **A:** 2/20-mm AA (I × 2)
**M:** 2 diesels; 2 props; 2,700 hp **Range:** 1,600/. . . **Man:** 10 tot.

REMARKS: *N.I. Goulandris I* (P 289) blew up and sank 24-6-83.

NOTE: Two former British *Scimitar*-class fast target craft, sold to Greek interests in 1985–86, were for private use as yachts.

## MINE WARFARE SHIPS

◆ **9 U.S. Falcon (MSC 294)-class coastal minesweepers** Bldr: Peterson Bldrs, Sturgeon Bay, Wisconsin (except M 246: Tacoma Boatbldg, Tacoma, Washington)

| | In serv. | | In serv. |
|---|---|---|---|
| M 211 ALKYON (ex-MSC 314) | 3-12-68 | M 242 KISSA (ex-MSC 309) | 1-9-64 |
| M 213 KLIO (ex-*Argo*, ex-MSC 317) | 7-8-68 | M 246 AIGLI (ex-MSC 299) | 4-1-65 |
| M 214 AVRA (ex-MSC 318) | 3-10-68 | M 247 DAFNI (ex-MSC 307) | 23-9-64 |
| M 240 PLEIAS (ex-MSC 319) | 22-6-67 | M 248 AEDON (ex-MSC 310) | 13-10-64 |
| M 241 KICHLI (ex-MSC 308) | 14-7-64 | | |

**D:** 300 tons (394 fl) **S:** 13 kts **Dim:** 44.32 × 8.29 × 2.55
**A:** 2/20-mm AA (II × 1) **M:** 2 Waukesha L-1616 diesels; 2 props; 1,200 hp
**Electron Equipt:** Radar: 1/. . . nav.—Sonar: UQS-1D
**Fuel:** 40 tons **Range:** 2,500/10 **Man:** 4 officers, 27 men

REMARKS: Built for Greece under the Military Aid Program; transferred on completion. Sister *Doris* (A 475, ex-M 245, ex-MSC 298) is employed as a hydrographic survey ship. Original Decca 707 radar replaced by 1984.

**Alkyon (M 211)**—painted olive green G. Gyssels, 6-86

◆ **5 ex-Belgian U.S. Adjutant-class coastal minesweepers**
Bldrs: Consolidated SB, Morris Heights, N.Y. (M 205, M 206: Hodgdon Bros., East Boothbay, Maine)

| | In serv. |
|---|---|
| M 202 ATALANTI (ex-*St. Truiden,* ex-MSC 169) | 2-54 |
| M 205 ANTIOPI (ex-*Herve,* ex-MSC 153) | 3-54 |
| M 206 PHEDRA (ex-*Malmedy,* ex-MSC 154) | 5-54 |
| M 210 THALIA (ex-*Blankenberge,* ex-MSC 170) | 5-54 |
| M 254 NIOVI (ex-*Laroche,* ex-MSC 171) | 8-54 |

**Antiopi (M 205)** G. Arra, 1973

**D:** 330 tons (402 fl) **S:** 13 kts (8 sweeping)
**Dim:** 43.0 (41.50 pp) × 7.95 × 2.55 **A:** 2/20-mm AA (II × 1)
**M:** 2 G.M. 8-268A diesels; 2 props; 880/1,000 hp **Fuel:** 40 tons
**Range:** 2,500/10 **Man:** 4 officers, 27 men

REMARKS: Transferred to Belgium on completion; re-transferred to Greece 7-9-69. M 202 was configured as a hydrographic survey ship from the late 1970s to 1982.

◆ **4 ex-U.S. 50-ft-class minesweeping launches**

**D:** 21 tons (fl) **S:** 8 kts **Dim:** 15.20 × 4.01 × 1.31
**M:** 1 Navy DB diesel; 60 hp **Range:** 150/8 **Man:** 6 tot.

REMARKS: Wooden-hulled former personnel launches loaned in 1972 and purchased during 1981.

◆ **2 minelayers, former U.S. LSM 1-class landing ships** Bldr: Charleston Naval SY

| | Laid down | L | In serv. |
|---|---|---|---|
| N 04 AKTION (ex-LSM 301) | 18-10-44 | 19-11-44 | 1-1-45 |
| N 05 AMVRAKIA (ex-LSM 303) | 8-10-44 | 14-11-44 | 6-1-45 |

**Amvrakia (N 05)**

**D:** 720 tons (1,100 fl) **S:** 13 kts **Dim:** 62.0 × 10.5 × 2.4
**A:** 8/40-mm AA (II × 4)—6/20-mm AA (I × 6)—100 to 300 mines, depending upon type
**M:** 2 G.M. 16-278A diesels; 2 props; 2,800 hp **Range:** 3,500/12 **Man:** 65 tot.

## MINE WARFARE SHIPS *(continued)*

REMARKS: Transferred in 1953. Four derricks, two forward and two aft, for handling mines. Two minelaying rails. Four 30-cm searchlights, 1 of 60 cm. Four Mk 51 Mod. 2 optical GFCS for the 40-mm AA. Twin rudders. Three of the same class ships were transferred to Turkey and two to Norway, who passed them on to Turkey in 1961.

## AMPHIBIOUS WARFARE SHIPS

### ◆ 1 ex-U.S. Cabildo-class dock landing ship Bldr: Boston Naval SY

| | Laid down | L | In serv. |
|---|---|---|---|
| L 153 NAFKRATOUSSA (ex-*Fort Mandan*, LSD 21) | 16-12-44 | 6-4-45 | 31-10-45 |

**D:** 4,790 tons (9,375 fl) **S:** 15 kts **Dim:** 139.5 × 21.9 × 5.49
**A:** 8/40-mm AA (IV × 2) **Electron Equipt:** Radar: 1/SPS-5, 1/SPS-6
**M:** 2 sets GT; 2 props; 7,000 hp **Electric:** 600 kw
**Boilers:** 62/30.6 kg/cm², 393°C **Fuel:** 1,758 tons **Range:** 8,000/15
**Man:** 254 tot.

REMARKS: Modernized under the FRAM program and transferred 1-71. Flagship of the amphibious forces. Helicopter deck. Well deck: 103.0 × 13.3. Two 35-ton cranes. Can carry 18 LCMs, each with an LCVP nested in it. SPS-6 air-search radar recently added.

### ◆ 0 (+5) new construction tank landing ships Bldr: Eleusis SY

| | Laid down | L | In serv. |
|---|---|---|---|
| L . . . N . . . | 4-87 | . . . | . . . |
| L . . . N . . . | . . . | . . . | . . . |
| L . . . N . . . | . . . | . . . | . . . |
| L . . . N . . . | . . . | . . . | . . . |
| L . . . N . . . | . . . | . . . | 6-90 |

**D:** 4,400 tons (fl) **S:** 17 kts **Dim:** 114.00 (106.00 pp) × 15.30 × 3.34 (mean)
**A:** 8/40-mm AA (II × 2) **Electron Equipt:** Radar: . . .
**M:** 2 diesels; 2 props; 10,600 hp **Man:** . . .

REMARKS: Ordered 12-86 as replacements for U.S. LST 1/LST 511 class. Similar arrangement, with raised helicopter deck aft, racked bow, ramp from upper deck to bow ramp.

### ◆ 2 ex-U.S. Terrebonne Parish-class LSTs

| | Bldr | Laid down | L | In serv. |
|---|---|---|---|---|
| L 104 OINOUSSAI (ex-*Terrell County*, LST 1157) | Bath Iron Wks. | 3-3-52 | 6-12-52 | 19-3-53 |
| L 116 KOS (ex-*Whitfield County*, LST 1169) | Christy Corp. | . . . | 22-8-53 | 14-9-54 |

**Kos (L 116)** L. & L. Van Ginderen, 1982

**D:** 2,590 tons (6,225 fl) **S:** 12 kts **Dim:** 112.35 × 16.7 × 3.7
**A:** 6/76.2-mm AA (II × 3)—4/20-mm AA (I × 4)
**Electron Equipt:** Radar: 1/. . . nav., 1/SPS-10, 2/Mk 34
**M:** 4 G.M. diesels; 2 CP props; 6,000 hp **Man:** 115 crew, 395 troops

REMARKS: Purchased 17-3-77. Two Mk 63 GFCS.

### ◆ 5 ex-U.S. LST 1 and LST 511-class tank landing ships

| | Bldr | Laid down | L | In serv. |
|---|---|---|---|---|
| L 144 SYROS (ex-LST 325) | Philadelphia NY | 10-8-42 | 27-10-42 | 1-2-43 |
| L 154 IKARIA (ex-*Potter County*, LST 1086) | American Bridge, Ambridge, Pa. | 5-12-44 | 28-1-45 | 24-2-45 |
| L 157 RODOS (ex-*Bowman County*, LST 391) | Newport News SB & DD | 14-7-42 | 28-10-42 | 3-12-42 |
| L 171 KRITI (ex-*Page County*, LST 1076) | Bethlehem Steel, Hingham, Mass. | 16-3-45 | 14-4-45 | 1-5-45 |
| L 172 LESBOS (ex-*Boone County*, LST 389) | Newport News SB & DD | 20-6-42 | 15-10-42 | 24-11-42 |

**Ikaria (L 154)** L. & L. Van Ginderen, 1982

**D:** 1,653 tons (4,080 fl) **S:** 11.6 kts **Dim:** 99.98 × 15.24 × 3.4
**A:** 8/40-mm AA (II × 2, I × 4)—4/20-mm AA (II × 2)
**Electron Equipt:** Radar: 1/. . . nav.
**M:** 2 G.M. 12-567A (L 171: 16-278A) diesels; 1,700 hp
**Electric:** 300 kw **Fuel:** 569 tons **Range:** 15,000/9 **Man:** 125 tot.

REMARKS: L 144 (with reinforced waterline belt for ice operations!) was transferred 29-5-64 after a complete refit and modernization; L 154, L 157, and L 172 transferred 9-8-60; L 171 transferred 3-71 (purchased 11-7-78). All have tripod masts and carry 4 LCVP in Welin davits. Cargo: 2,100 tons. To discard by 1990–91.

### ◆ 5 ex-U.S. LSM 1-class medium landing ships

Bldrs: L 161, 162, 165: Brown Bros. SB, Houston; L 163: Dravo Corp, Wilmington, Del.; L 164: Charleston NSY

| | Laid down | L | In serv. |
|---|---|---|---|
| L 161 IPOPLIARCHOS GRIGOROPOULOS (ex-LSM 45) | 6-6-44 | 30-6-44 | 31-7-44 |
| L 162 IPOPLIARCHOS TOURNAS (ex-LSM 102) | 23-9-44 | 14-10-44 | 9-11-44 |
| L 163 IPOPLIARCHOS DANIOLOS (ex-LSM 227) | 17-7-44 | 9-9-44 | 5-10-44 |
| L 164 IPOPLIARCHOS ROUSEN (ex-LSM 399) | 29-12-44 | 18-1-45 | 13-8-45 |
| L 165 IPOPLIARCHOS KRYSTALLIDIS (ex-LSM 541) | 7-7-45 | 18-8-45 | 7-12-45 |

**D:** 1,095 tons (fl) **S:** 12.5 kts **Dim:** 62.03 × 10.52 × 2.54
**A:** 2/40-mm AA (II × 1)—4/20-mm AA (I × 4)
**Electron Equipt:** Radar: 1/Decca . . . nav.
**M:** 2 Fairbanks-Morse 38D1/8-10 (L 164: G.M. 16-278A) diesels; 2 props; 2,800 hp
**Electric:** 240 kw **Fuel:** 161 tons **Range:** 4,900/12 **Man:** 60 tot.

REMARKS: Transferred 3-11-58 (L 165: 30-10-58).

### ◆ 6 ex-U.S. LCU 501-class utility landing craft

Bldrs: L 145, 146, 147: Mare Island NSY, Cal.; L 149; Missouri Valley Bridge & Iron, Leavenworth, Kan.; L 150: Pidgeon-Thomas Iron, Memphis, Tenn.; L 152: Kansas City Steel, Kansas City, Missouri

| | In serv. | | In serv. |
|---|---|---|---|
| L 145 KASSOS (ex-LCU 1382) | 30-11-44 | L 149 KYTHNOS (ex-LCU 763) | 24-12-43 |
| L 146 KARPATHOS (ex-LCU 1379) | 17-11-44 | L 150 SIFNOS (ex-LCU 677) | 11-3-44 |
| L 147 KIMONOS (ex-LCU 971) | 1-2-44 | L 152 SKYATOS (ex-LCU 827) | 10-4-44 |

**D:** 143 tons (309 fl) **S:** 8 kts **Dim:** 36.3 × 9.96 × 1.14
**A:** 2/20-mm AA (I × 2) **M:** 3 G.M. 6-71 diesels; 675 hp **Man:** 13 tot.

REMARKS: Transferred 1959–62.

### ◆ 2 ex-British LCT(4)-class utility landing craft Bldrs: . . . , U.K. (In serv. 1944–45)

L 185 KYTHERA (ex-LCT 1198) L 189 MILOS (ex-LCT 1300)

**D:** 280 tons light (640 fl) **S:** 9.5 kts **Dim:** 57.07 × 11.79 × 1.30 (aft)
**A:** 2/20-mm AA **M:** 2 Paxman diesels; 2 props; 1,000 hp
**Range:** 500/9.5; 3,100/7 **Man:** 12 tot.

REMARKS: Transferred 1946; survivors of a group of 12. Cargo: 350 tons.

### ◆ 11 ex-U.S. LCM(6)-class landing craft

**D:** 24 tons light (56 fl) **S:** 10 kts **Dim:** 17.07 × 4.37 × 1.17 (aft)
**M:** 2 Gray Marine 64HN9 diesels; 2 props; 330 hp **Range:** 130/10

REMARKS: Cargo: 30 tons. Transferred: 5 in 3-56, remainder in 3-58.

### ◆ 7 LCVP-type landing craft Bldr: Viking Marine, Hellas, Piraeus (In serv. 1-80)

**D:** 13 tons (fl) **S:** 8 kts **Dim:** 10.90 × 3.21 × 1.04 (aft)
**M:** 1 G.M. 6-71 diesel; 200 hp

### ◆ 34 ex-U.S. LCVP-type landing craft

**D:** 13 tons (fl) **S:** 9 kts **Dim:** 10.90 × 3.21 × 1.04 (aft)
**M:** 1 Gray Marine 64HN9 diesel; 225 hp **Range:** 110/9

REMARKS: Carried by LSTs and the LSD. Cargo 36 troops or 3.5 tons cargo. Transferred: 10 in 11-56, 4 in 7-58, 10 in 1-62, 4 in 6-64, 3 in 10-69, and remainder in 3-71.

## HYDROGRAPHIC SHIPS

◆ **1 oceanographic survey ship** Bldr: Anastassiadis Tsortanidis, Perama

| | L | In serv. |
|---|---|---|
| A 474 Pytheas | 19-9-83 | 12-83 |

**D:** 670 tons (840 fl) **S:** 15 kts **Dim:** 50.00 (44.91 pp) × 9.60 × 4.22
**M:** 2 G.M. diesels; 2 props; 1,800 hp **Man:** 40 tot.

Remarks: Programmed 1979, ordered 5-82.

◆ **1 Naftilos-class hydrographic survey ship**

| | Bldr | L | In serv. |
|---|---|---|---|
| A 478 Naftilos | Anastassiadis Tsortanidis, Perama | 19-11-75 | 3-4-76 |

**Naftilos (A 478)** Greek Navy

**D:** 1,380 tons (1,480 fl) **S:** 15 kts **Dim:** 63.1 (56.5 pp) × 11.6 × 4.0
**M:** 2 Burmeister & Wain SS28LH diesels; 2 props; 2,640 hp **Man:** 57 tot.

Remarks: In service 3-4-76. Sisters *St. Lykoudis* (A 481) and *I. Theophilopoulos Karavoyiannos* (A 485) are lighthouse tenders. Helicopter landing platform.

◆ **1 coastal survey ship** Bldr: Khalkis SY

| | Laid down | L | In serv. |
|---|---|---|---|
| A . . . Aigeo | 30-9-84 | 15-3-85 | 9-12-85 |

**D:** 650 tons **S:** . . . **Dim:** . . . × . . . × . . .
**M:** . . .

◆ **1 modified U.S. Falcon-class coastal minesweeper**

| | Bldr | In serv. |
|---|---|---|
| A 475 Doris (ex-M 245, ex-MSC 298) | Tacoma Boatbldg. | 9-11-64 |

Remarks: Transferred on completion; converted late 1970s. Man: 3 officers, 32 men; other details as for minesweeper version.

◆ **2 ex-German KW1-class coastal survey ships**

A 476 Archikelefstis Maliopoulos (ex-Ger. KW 8, ex-H 8, ex-W 17)
A 477 Archikelefstis Stasis (ex-Ger. KW 2, ex-H 2, ex-W 2, ex-*Inger*, ex-*Concordia*, ex-K 613, ex-M 3253)

**D:** 112 tons (fl) **S:** 9 kts **Dim:** 22.30 (20.57 pp) × 6.40 × 2.75
**M:** 1 Demag 5-cyl. diesel; 150 hp **Electric:** 10 kVA
**Range:** 1,200/7 **Man:** 16 tot.

Remarks: Wooden construction, fishing-cutter hulls. Construction yard unknown; entered West German service 10-4-52. Transferred 30-8-75 as patrol boats. A 476 converted to replace sister *Anemos* (A 469), stricken 1977, while A 477 was converted in 1981 to replace the minesweeper *Atalanti* (M 202), returned to mine countermeasures duties.

## AUXILIARY SHIPS

◆ **1 training ship** Bldr: Anastassiadis Tsortanidis, Perama

| | Laid down | L | In serv. |
|---|---|---|---|
| A 74 Aris | 10-76 | 4-10-78 | 1-81 |

**Aris (A 74)** L. & L. Van Ginderen, 7-87

**Aris (A 74)** L. & L. Van Ginderen, 7-87

**D:** 3,100 tons (4,500 fl) **S:** 17.8 kts **Dim:** 100.0 (95.0 pp) × 11.0 × 4.5
**A:** 2/76.2-mm U.S. Mk 26 DP (I × 2)—2/40-mm AA (I × 2)—4/20-mm AA (I × 4)—1 Alouette-III or AB-212 helicopter
**M:** 2 MAK diesels; 2 props; 10,000 hp **Man:** 21 officers, 94 men, 359 cadets

Remarks: Largest naval ship built in Greece. Resembles a small passenger ship and can serve as a hospital ship or transport in wartime. Completion delayed by payment dispute. Two lead-computing GFCS for the 40-mm AA. During 1986 refit received new command center, and helicopter facility was reactivated.

◆ **2 personnel ferries** Bldr: Anastassiadis Tsortanidis, Perama

A 419 Pandora (In serv. 26-10-73) A 420 Pandrosos (In serv. 1-12-73)

**Pandrosos (A 420)** L. & L. Van Ginderen, 9-86

**D:** 350 tons (390 fl) **S:** 11 kts **Dim:** 46.8 × 8.3 × 1.9
**M:** 2 diesels; 2 props; . . . hp

Remarks: Can carry up to 500 personnel.

◆ **1 netlayer and mooring buoy tender** Bldr: Krögerwerft, Rendsburg

A 307 Thetis (ex-U.S. AN 103) (In serv. 4-60)

**Thetis (A 307)** D. Dervissis, 7-79

**D:** 560 tons (975 fl) **S:** 12.8 kts **Dim:** 48.5 (51.7 over horns) × 10.6 × 3.7
**A:** 1/40-mm AA—3/20-mm AA (I × 3) **Electron Equipt:** Radar: 1/Decca 707
**M:** 1 M.A.N. G7V 40/60 diesel; 1 prop; 1,470 hp **Fuel:** 134 tons
**Range:** 6,500/10.2 **Man:** 5 officers, 45 men

## AUXILIARY SHIPS *(continued)*

REMARKS: Launched 1959. Transferred 4-60. Has 152 tons water ballast. The 40-mm AA is normally not aboard; can carry 1,600 rds 40-mm, 25,200 rds 20-mm ammunition.

### ◆ 2 ex-U.S. Patapsco-class oilers     Bldr: Cargill SY, Savage, Minn.

| | Laid down | L | In serv. |
|---|---|---|---|
| A 377 ARETHOUSA (ex-*Natchaug,* AOG 54) | 15-8-44 | 6-12-44 | 11-6-45 |
| A 414 ARIADNI (ex-*Tombigbee,* AOG 11) | 23-10-42 | 18-11-43 | 13-7-44 |

**Arethousa (A 377)**—note 76.2-mm gun off centerline to stbd. Official

**D:** 1,850 tons (4,335 fl) **S:** 13 kts **Dim:** 94.72 (89.0 pp) × 14.78 × 4.78
**A:** A 377: 4/76.2-mm AA (I × 4)—A 414: 2/76.2-mm AA (I × 2)
**Electron Equipt:** Radar: 1/navigational, 1/SPS-5, 1/Mk 26
**M:** 2 G.M. 16-278A diesels; 2 props; 3,300 hp **Electric:** 460 kw
**Fuel:** 295 tons **Man:** 46 tot.

REMARKS: Former gasoline tankers. Cargo: 2,040 tons. One Mk 52 radar GFCS and one Mk 51 GFCS.

### ◆ 0 (+3) coastal tankers     Bldr: Hellenic SY, Skaramanga

A 374 N . . . (In serv. . . .) A . . . N . . . (In serv. . . .)
A . . . N . . . (In serv. . . .)

**D:** . . . **S:** . . . **Dim:** . . . × . . . × . . .
**M:** . . .

REMARKS: 2,100 dwt. Ordered: one in 1-86, two in 9-86.

NOTE: Five oil barges were "projected" for construction by Eleusis SY, 1-87. No details available.

### ◆ 2 coastal tankers     Bldr: Kynossoura SY, Piraeus

A 416 OURANOS (In serv. 29-1-77) A 417 HYPERION (In serv. 27-2-77)

**D:** 1,200 tons (fl) **S:** 13 kts **Dim:** 67.7 × 10.0 × 4.7
**M:** 1 MWM TPD-484BU diesel; 1,750 hp

### ◆ 1 small harbor oiler

A 471 VIVIES

REMARKS: Cargo: 187 tons; S: 11 kts.

NOTE: *Kronos* (A 373), built in 1943, still exists as a fuel lighter, unpowered; cargo: 110 tons.

### ◆ 1 ammunition ship     Bldr: Dubigeon, Nantes

| | Laid down | L | In serv. |
|---|---|---|---|
| A 415 EVROS (ex-German *Schwarzwald,* ex-French *Amalthée*) | 30-6-55 | 31-1-56 | 7-6-56 |

**D:** 2,395 tons **S:** 15 kts **Dim:** 80.18 × 11.99 × 4.65
**A:** 4/40-mm AA (II × 2)
**M:** 1 Sulzer 6-SD-60 diesel; 3,000 hp **Electric:** 500 kw **Range:** 4,500/15
**Man:** 32 tot.

REMARKS: Purchased 2-60 by the German Navy and converted for naval use, commissioning 11-10-61; transferred to Greece 2-6-76. 1,667 grt.

### ◆ 0 (+1) new-construction water tanker     Bldr: Khalkis SY

| | Laid down | L | In serv. |
|---|---|---|---|
| A . . . N . . . | 15-4-85 | 20-8-85 | . . . |

**D:** . . . **S:** . . . **Dim:** 67.0 × . . . × . . .
**M:** . . .

REMARKS: 2,100 dwt. Ordered 30-12-85. Suspended when builder closed. Completion contracted to Hellenic SY, Skaramanga, late 1986.

### ◆ 3 Doirani-class water lighters

A 434 PRESPA (ex-*Doirani*) (In serv. 10-10-72) A 467 DOIRANI (In serv. 1972)
A 468 KALIROI (In serv. 26-10-72)

**Prespa (A 434)** P. Voss, 10-86

**D:** 850 tons (fl) **S:** 13 kts **Dim:** 54.77 × 7.95 × 3.87
**M:** 1 MWM 6-cyl. diesel; 1,300 hp

REMARKS: A 467 is 58.88 m overall, 4.02 m draft; 765 dwt. A 434 is 600 dwt, A 468 is 671 dwt and has a 1,005-hp MWM diesel. A 434 taken over from another government agency 1979. Very low freeboard.

### ◆ 1 ex-German FW 1-class water lighter

| | Bldr | Laid down | L | In serv. |
|---|---|---|---|---|
| A 433 KERKINI (ex-FW 3) | Jadewerft, Wilhelmshaven | 14-6-63 | 15-10-63 | 11-5-64 |

**Kerkini (A 433)** L. & L. Van Ginderen, 12-84

**D:** 598 tons (624 fl) **S:** 9.5 kts **Dim:** 44.03 (41.10 pp) × 7.80 × 2.63
**M:** 1 MWM 12-cyl. diesel; 1 prop; 230 hp **Electric:** 83 kw
**Range:** 2,150/9 **Man:** 12 tot.

REMARKS: Transferred 22-4-76. Cargo: 350 $m^3$.

### ◆ 2 miscellaneous small water lighters

A 470 KASTORIA (In serv. . . .)—Cargo: 520 tons
A 473 TRICHONIS (In serv. 1980)—Cargo: 650 tons

### ◆ 1 British Bustler-class salvage tug     Bldr: Henry Robb, Leith

| | Laid down | L | In serv. |
|---|---|---|---|
| A 428 ATLAS (ex-*Nisos Zakynthos,* ex-HMS *Mediator*) | 18-10-43 | 21-6-44 | 8-11-44 |

**D:** 1,118 tons (1,630 fl) **S:** 16 kts **Dim:** 62.48 (59.4 pp) × 12.32 × 5.18
**A:** . . . **M:** 2 Atlas diesels; 2 props; 3,200 hp **Fuel:** 340 tons
**Range:** 3,400/11 **Man:** 42 tot.

REMARKS: Purchased from Royal Navy 1965 by private owner. Acquired 1-8-79 by Greek Navy and commissioned 12-79.

### ◆ 2 new-construction coastal tugs

Bldr: Hellenic SY, Skaramanga

**D:** . . . **S:** . . . **Dim:** . . . × . . . × . . .
**M:** . . .

REMARKS: Ordered 1-86. No data available.

### ◆ 3 Heraklis-class coastal tugs     Bldr: Anastassiadis Tsortanidis, Perama

A 423 HERAKLIS (In serv. 6-4-78) A 425 ODISSEUS (In serv. 28-6-78)
A 424 JASON (In serv. 6-3-78)

**D:** 345 tons **S:** 12 kts **Dim:** 30.0 × 7.9 × 3.4
**M:** 1 MWM diesel; 1,200 hp

**AUXILIARY SHIPS** *(continued)*

◆ **6 harbor tugs**

A 410 Atromitos } (In serv. 20-6-68)—1,260 hp, D: 310 tons
A 411 Adamastos } Dim: 30.0 × 7.9 × 3.0
A 412 Aias (ex-U.S. *Ankachak,* YTM 767) (Transferred 1972)—650 hp
A 421 Minotauros (ex-U.S. Army ST 539) (Transferred 1962)—650 hp
A 431 Titan (In serv. 1962)—240 hp
A 432 Gigas (In serv. 26-11-61)—1,200 hp

◆ **2 lighthouse tenders** Bldr: Anastassiadis Tsortanidis, Perama

A 479 I. Theophilopoulos Karavoyiannos (In serv. 2-1-76)
A 481 St. Lykoudis (In serv. 17-3-76)

**I. Theophilopoulos Karavoyiannos (A 479)** L. & L. Van Ginderen, 12-84

**D:** 1,350 tons (1,450 fl) **S:** 15 kts **Dim:** 63.24 (56.50 pp) × 11.6 × 4.0
**M:** 1 MWM TBD-500-8UD diesel; 2,400 hp **Man:** 40 tot.

Remarks: Near sisters to hydrographic survey ship *Naftilos.* Have a helicopter deck.

◆ **5 miscellaneous floating cranes**

◆ **0 (+1) planned 6,000-ton-capacity floating dry dock**

Remarks: Programmed for construction by Eleusis SY, to deliver 1991.

◆ **1 relic, former armored cruiser**

| | Bldr | L | In serv. |
|---|---|---|---|
| Averoff | Orlando, Livorno | 12-3-10 | 5-11 |

**Averoff** L. & L. Van Ginderen, 10-86

**D:** 9,960 tons **S:** . . . **Dim:** 140.8 × 21.0 × 7.6
**A:** 4/234-mm 50-cal. (II × 2)—8/190-mm 45-cal. (II × 4)
**M:** 2 sets 4-cyl. triple expansion steam; 2 props; 19,000 hp
**Boilers:** 22 Belleville type **Fuel:** 1,500 tons coal

Remarks: Survivor of World War II. Maintained at Paleon Farilon. Could make 14 kts when last operational in 1941 (22.5 on trials, 1911). Had crew of 620. Originally also mounted 16/76-mm and 4/47-mm guns.

## COAST GUARD
## HARBOR CORPS

The Greek Coast Guard has some 4,000 personnel, most of whom are shore-based. There are some 80 small craft, the largest and newest of which are three units of the *Dilos*-class patrol boats, as described above. Five Cessna light aircraft are used for coastal patrol. The Greek Customs Service also operates about 20 boats in its Anti-Smuggling Flotilla. "LS" stands for "patrol boat."

**LS 81**—*Dilos*-class patrol boat H. Ehlers, 4-84

**Patrol Boat LS 52**—LS 51–55 are of the same class H. Ehlers, 5-84

**13.50-m patrol craft LS 88 of the OL 44 class** H. Ehlers, 6-86

**GREECE** *(continued)*
**AUXILIARY SHIPS** *(continued)*

**8.23-m patrol craft LS 72** H. Ehlers, 5-84

**Pollution-collection boat LS 24** H. Ehlers, 5-84

**High-speed landing craft LS 69** H. Ehlers, 5-86

CUSTOMS SERVICE

◆ **3 Dilos-class patrol craft** Bldr: Hellenic SY, Skaramanga (In serv. 1977–79)

**A/L 18** L. & L. Van Ginderen, 6-86

Remarks: Data as for sisters in naval service.

◆ **10 0L 76 class** Bldr: Olympic Marine S.A., Lavrio (In serv. 1986–87)

**Small patrol craft A/L 04** H. Ehlers, 6-86

**D:** 50 tons (fl) **S:** 28 kts **Dim:** 23.16 (19.50 pp) × 5.03 × 1.00
**A:** 2/20-mm AA (I × 2)—2/127-mm mg (I × 2)
**M:** 2 MTU diesels; 2 props; 2,600 hp **Man:** 11 tot.

# GRENADA

Merchant Marine (1984): 3 ships—425 grt

◆ **1 U.S. 106-ft patrol boat** Bldr: Lantana Boatyard, Florida

PB 01 Tyrrel Bay (In serv. 21-11-84)

**Tyrrel Bay (PB 01)** Lantana, 11-84

**D:** 94 tons (fl) **S:** 24 kts **Dim:** 32.31 × 6.25 × 2.13 (props)
**A:** 2/12.7-mm mg (I × 2)—2/7.62-mm mg (I × 2)
**Electron Equipt:** Radar: 1/Furuno . . . nav.
**M:** 3 G.M. Detroit Diesel 12V71 TI diesels; 3 props; 2,250 hp
**Electric:** 100 kw **Fuel:** 21 tons **Man:** 4 officers, 12 men

Remarks: Laid down 1-84 to U.S. Gov't order. Aluminum construction. Has a Magnavox MX4102 NAVSAT receiver.

GRENADA *(continued)*

◆ **1 patrol craft** Bldr: Brooke Marine, Lowestoft (In serv. 1972)

PB 2

**D:** 15 tons (fl) **S:** 22 kts **Dim:** 12.2 × 3.7 × 0.6 **A:** 3/7.62-mm mg (I × 3)
**M:** 2 Caterpillar diesels; 2 props; 740 hp

◆ **3 Spear-class patrol craft** Bldr: Fairey Marine, Hamble, U.K. (In serv. 1978)

**D:** 10 tons (fl) **S:** 26 kts **Dim:** 9.10 × 2.75 × 0.84
**A:** 2/7.62-mm mg (I × 2) **M:** 2 diesels; 2 props; 580 hp **Man:** 3 tot.

Note: PB 1 and the three Spear-class patrol craft were derelict at the time of the U.S. "invasion" in 1983; they have since been rehabilitated and put back in service.

# GUATEMALA

**Republic of Guatemala**

Personnel (1987): 1,000 total: 125 officers, 875 enlisted, including 700 Marines

Merchant Marine (1986): 8 ships—9,432 grt

### PATROL BOATS AND CRAFT

◆ **1 U.S. Broadsword class** Bldr: Halter Marine, Chalmette, La.

P-1051 Kukulkan (In serv. 4-8-76)

**Kukulkan**—on trials with the *Bitol* (P-655), *Picuda* (P-361), and *Barracuda* (P-362) Halter, 1976

**D:** 90.5 tons light (110 fl) **S:** 32 kts **Dim:** 32.0 (29.4 wl) × 6.3 × 1.9 (props)
**A:** 2/75-mm recoilless rifles—4/12.7-mm mg (I × 4)—2/12.7-mm mg (I × 2)
**M:** 2 G.M. 16V149 TI diesels; 3,200 hp **Electric:** 60 kw **Range:** 1,150/20
**Fuel:** 16 tons **Man:** 5 officers, 15 men

◆ **2 U.S. 85-foot Commercial Cruiser class** Bldr: Sewart Seacraft, Berwick, La.

P 851 Utatlan (In serv. 5-67) P 852 Subteniente Osorio Saravia (In serv. 11-72)

**D:** 43.5 tons (54 fl) **S:** 23 kts **Dim:** 25.9 × 5.8 × 2.2 (props)
**A:** 3/12.7-mm mg (I × 3)—1/75-mm recoilless rifle
**M:** 2 G.M. 16 V71 TI diesels; 2 props; 2,200 hp **Range:** 780/15 **Fuel:** 8 tons
**Man:** 7 officers, 10 men **Electric:** 40 kw

Remarks: Aluminum construction. Photo in addenda.

◆ **6 U.S. Cutlass class** Bldr: Halter Marine, New Orleans, La.

| | In serv. | | In serv. |
|---|---|---|---|
| P 651 Tecunuman | 26-11-71 | P 654 Tzacol | 8-76 |
| P 652 Kaibilbalan | 8-2-72 | P 655 Bitol | 8-76 |
| P 653 Azumanche | 8-2-72 | P 656 Gukamatz | -81 |

**D:** 34 tons (45 fl) **S:** 25 kts **Dim:** 19.7 × 5.2 × 0.9
**A:** 1/12.7-mm mg—3/7.62-mm mg (I × 3) **Man:** 6 tot.
**M:** 2 G.M. 12V71 diesels; 2 props; 1,020 hp **Electric:** 20 kw **Range:** 400/15

◆ **30 river patrol craft** Bldr: Trabejos Baros SY, Guatemala (In serv. 1979)

**D:** . . . tons **S:** 19 or 28 kts **Dim:** 9.14 × 3.66 × 0.61
**A:** 2/7.62-mm mg (I × 2)
**M:** 1 diesel; 1 prop; 150 or 300 hp **Range:** 400–500 n.m.

Remarks: Wooden construction—in two series, with different engines.

### AMPHIBIOUS WARFARE CRAFT

◆ **2 U.S. Machete class** Bldr: Halter Marine, New Orleans, La. (In serv. 4-8-76)

P 361 Picuda P 362 Barracuda

**D:** 6 tons **S:** 36 kts **Dim:** 11.0 × 4.0 × 0.76
**M:** 2 G.M. 6V53 PI diesels; 2 water jets; 540 hp

Remarks: Troop carriers. Square bows, aluminum construction.

◆ **1 ex-U.S. LCM (6) class**

561 Chinaltenango

**D:** 24 tons (56 fl) **S:** 10 kts **Dim:** 17.07 × 4.37 × 1.17 (aft)
**A:** 2/12.7-mm mg (I × 2)
**M:** 2 Gray Marine 64HN9 diesels; 2 props; 450 hp **Range:** 130/10

Remarks: Transferred in 12-65. Cargo: 30 tons.

# GUINEA

**Republic of Guinea**

Personnel (1984): 600 total

Merchant Marine (1986): 19 ships—7,179 grt

### PATROL BOATS AND CRAFT

◆ **1 U.S. 77-ft class** Bldr: Swiftships, Morgan City, La. (In serv. 18-12-86)

P-328 Intrepide

**Intrepide (P-328)** L. Turgeon, 12-86

**D:** 39.8 tons (47.6 fl) **S:** 24 kts **Dim:** 23.47 × 6.10 × 1.52
**A:** 2/12.7-mm mg (I × 2)—2/7.62-mm mg (I × 2)
**Electron Equipt:** Radar:1/. . . nav.
**M:** 3 G.M. 12V71 T1 diesels; 3 props; 2,385 hp
**Range:** 1,800/15 **Man:** 10 tot.

Remarks: Ordered 7-85. Aluminum construction.

◆ **1 U.S. 65-ft class** Bldr: Swiftships, Inc., Morgan City, La. (In serv. 6-85)

P-300 Vigilante

**Vigilante (P-300)** Swiftships, 6-85

GUINEA *(continued)*
**PATROL BOATS AND CRAFT** *(continued)*

**D:** 31.7 tons (36.3 fl) **S:** 24 kts **Dim:** 19.96 × 5.61 × 1.52
**A:** 2/12.7-mm mg (I × 2)—2/7.62-mm mg (I × 2)
**Electron Equipt:** Radar: 1/. . . nav.
**M:** 2 G.M. 12V71 TI diesels; 2 props; 1,590 hp
**Range:** 500/18 **Man:** 10 tot.

REMARKS: Aluminum construction. Resembles El Salvador's GC-11.

◆ **2 U.S. Stinger class** Bldr: MonArk, Monticello, Arkansas (In serv. 3-6-85)

P-30 P-35

**Guinea's two Stinger-class patrol craft** MonArk, 1985

**D:** 2.7 tons (fl) **S:** 35 kts **Dim:** 7.92 × 3.25 × 0.91
**A:** 2/12.7-mm (I × 2) **Electron Equipt:** Radar: 1/Raytheon 1200 nav.
**M:** 2 OMC 55 XL "Commercial" outboard motors; 310 hp **Man:** 4 tot.

REMARKS: Ordered 10-84. Camouflaged in three shades of green.

◆ **1 French 28-m class** Bldr: Chantiers Navals de l'Estérel, Cannes

P-400 ALMARIY BOCAR BIRO BARRY (In serv. 8-79)

**Almariy Bocar Biro Barry (P-400)** French Navy, 1984

**D:** 56 tons (fl) **S:** 35 kts **Dim:** 28.0 × 5.2 × 1.6 **A:** 1/7.62-mm mg
**M:** 2 MTU 12V331 TC82 diesels; 2 props; 2,600 hp **Range:** 750/15
**Man:** 12 tot.

◆ **2 ex-Soviet Poluchat-I class**

**D:** 70 tons (90 fl) **S:** 18 kts **Dim:** 29.6 × 5.8 × 1.5
**A:** 2/14.5-mm mg (II × 1) **Man:** 20 tot.
**Electron Equipt:** Radar: 1/Spin Trough
IFF: 1/High Pole A
**M:** 2 M50-series diesels; 2 props; 2,400 hp **Range:** 450/17; 900/10

◆ **1 1,500-ton-capacity floating dry dock**

NOTE: The former Soviet 7-58-class corvette, ex-minesweeper *Lamine Sadji Kaba* (F-79), six Chinese Shanghai-class patrol boats (P-733 to P-778) and 3 ex-Soviet Shershen-class patrol boats (ex-torpedo boats) were all out of service by early 1987 and unlikely to be restored.

# GUINEA-BISSAU

**Republic of Guinea-Bissau**

PERSONNEL (1986): approx. 250 total

MERCHANT MARINE (1986): 17 ships—4,070 grt

NAVAL AVIATION: One Cessna 337 for coastal surveillance.

## PATROL BOATS AND CRAFT

◆ **1 Dutch PT 1903 Mk III class** Bldr: Le Comte, Vianen, The Netherlands

NAGA (In serv. 5-81)

**D:** 30 tons (33 fl) **S:** 30 kts **Dim:** 19.27 × 4.95 × 1.25
**A:** 2/12.7-mm mg (I × 2) **Range:** 1,650/17; 2,300/12 **Man:** 10 tot.
**M:** 2 MTU 8V331 TC92 diesels; 2 props; 1,770 hp

◆ **1 ex-Soviet Shershen-class former torpedo boat**

**D:** 150 tons (170 fl) **S:** 45 kts **Dim:** 34.7 × 6.7 × 1.5
**A:** 4/30-mm AA (II × 2) **Man:** 24 tot.
**Electron Equipt:** Radar: 1/Pot Drum, 1 Drum Tilt
IFF: 1/Square Head, 1/High Pole A
**M:** 3 M503A diesels; 3 props; 12,000 hp **Range:** 460/42; 850/30

REMARKS: Transferred 12-78. Torpedo tubes removed prior to transfer.

◆ **2 French Plascoa-1900 class** (In serv. 8-78)

CABO ROXO ILHA DE POILÃO

**D:** 30 tons (fl) **S:** 25 kts **Dim:** 19.0 × 5.35 × 1.2
**A:** 2/12.7-mm mg (I × 2) **M:** 2 G.M. diesels; 2 props; 1,050 hp
**Range:** 650/25; 1,500/9

◆ **2 ex-Soviet Poluchat-I class**

**D:** 70 tons (90 fl) **S:** 18 kts **Dim:** 29.6 × 5.8 × 1.5
**A:** 2/14.5-mm mg (II × 1) **Electron Equipt:** Radar: 1/Spin Trough
**M:** 2 M50-series diesels; 2 props; 2,400 hp **Range:** 450/17; 900/10
**Man:** 20 tot.

REMARKS: Transferred 1977.

◆ **2 Chinese Shantou class** (In serv. 1955–60)

**D:** 80 tons (fl) **S:** 28 kts **Dim:** 25.1 × 6.0 × 1.8
**A:** 4/37-mm AA (II × 2)—2/14.5-mm mg (I × 2)
**Electron Equipt:** Radar: 1/Skin Head
**M:** 2 M50 series, 1,200-hp and 2 Type 3D12, 300-hp diesels; 4 props; 3,000 hp

REMARKS: Transferred late 1983; previously thought to have been units of the Shanghai-class. Steel construction. Of little value, due to age.

◆ **3 Spanish LVC-1 class** Bldr: Aresa, Barcelona (In serv. 1979)

**D:** 20.8 tons (fl) **S:** 23.3 kts **Dim:** 16.00 × 4.36 × 1.30
**A:** 1/12.7-mm mg **M:** 2 Baudouin DNP-8 M1R diesels; 2 props; 700 hp
**Range:** 400/18 **Man:** 6 tot.

## AUXILIARIES AND SERVICE CRAFT

◆ **1 ex-Soviet Biya-class survey ship and buoy tender** Bldr: Gdansk, Poland

**D:** 750 tons (fl) **S:** 13 kts **Dim:** 55.0 × 9.2 × 2.6
**Electron Equipt:** Radar: 1/Don-2 **M:** 2 diesels; 2 CP props; 1,200 hp
**Range:** 4,700/11 **Man:** 25 tot.

REMARKS: Transferred 6-78. One 5-ton buoy crane; one inshore survey launch; one 15-$m^2$ oceanographic laboratory.

◆ **4 ex-Soviet T-4-class landing craft**

**D:** 70 tons (fl) **S:** 10 kts **Dim:** 19.0 × 4.3 × 1.0
**M:** 2 diesels; 2 props; 600 hp **Man:** 5 tot.

REMARKS: Employed in logistics support duties. Delivered 2 in 1975, 2 in 1978.

# GUYANA

**Cooperative Republic of Guyana**

PERSONNEL (1986): 150 total

MERCHANT MARINE (1986): 103 ships—22,731 grt (tankers: 1 ship—125 grt)

## PATROL BOATS

NAVAL AVIATION: 1 Embraer EMB111 Bandeirante for coastal surveillance

◆ **2 ex-North Korean patrol boats**

**D:** 35 tons (fl) **S:** 40 kts **Dim:** 18.3 × 3.4 × 1.7 **A:** 2/14.5-mm mg (I × 2)
**M:** 2 gasoline engines; 2 props; . . . hp **Man:** 9 tot.

REMARKS: Transferred 1980.

◆ **1 103-foot British patrol boat**

| | Bldr | L | In serv. |
|---|---|---|---|
| DF 1010 PECCARI | Vosper Thornycroft, Portsmouth, U.K. | 26-3-76 | 26-1-77 |

**GUYANA** *(continued)*
**PATROL BOATS** *(continued)*

**D:** 96 tons (109 fl) **S:** 27 kts **Dim:** 31.4 × 6.0 × 1.6
**A:** 2/20-mm AA (I × 2)
**M:** 2 Paxman Ventura 12-cyl. diesels; 2 props; 3,500 hp
**Range:** 1,400/14 **Man:** 22 tot.

Remarks: A second unit was ordered in 1977, but was canceled because of lack of funds.

◆ **3 patrol boats** Bldr: Vosper Thornycroft, U.K.

Jaguar (In serv. 28-4-71) Margay (In serv. 21-5-71) Ocelot (In serv. 22-6-71)

**D:** 10 tons **S:** 20 kts **Dim:** 14.0 × 3.4 × 2.0 **A:** 1/7.62-mm mg
**M:** 2 Cummins D366A diesels; 2 props; 270 hp **Range:** 150/12 **Man:** 6 tot.

Remarks: Fiberglass hull; light-alloy superstructure.

◆ **3 45-foot boats, supplied by the U.S.**

Camoudie Labana Rattler

◆ **2 ex-fishing boats**

Ekereku Number 2

Note: Guyana also received the ex-U.S. Navy tug YTM 190 and the covered barge YFN 960, both operated by the Guyana Harbor Board. The 600-grt ramped cargo ship *Kimbla,* delivered to the Guyana government by Damen, the Netherlands, in 1981, is also non-naval.

# HAITI

**Republic of Haiti**

Personnel (1984): 40 officers, 260 men

Merchant Marine (1986): 8 ships—2,688 grt

## PATROL BOATS AND CRAFT

◆ **1 U.S. Sotoyomo-class former auxiliary ocean tug**

| | Bldr | Laid down | L | In serv. |
|---|---|---|---|---|
| MH 20 Henri Christophe (ex-*Samoset,* ATA 180) | Levingston SB, Orange, Tx. | 5-6-44 | 14-7-44 | 27-9-44 |

**D:** 689 tons (835 fl) **S:** 13 kts **Dim:** 43.6 (40.75 pp) × 10.37 × 3.65
**A:** 2/40-mm AA (I × 2)—2/12.7-mm mg (I × 2)
**M:** 2 G.M. 12-278A diesels, electric drive; 1 prop; 1,500 hp
**Electric:** 120 kw **Fuel:** 154 tons **Range:** 16,500/9 **Man:** 40 tot.

Remarks: MH 20 transferred 18-9-78. One 40-mm on fantail, one forward.

◆ **3 U.S. 65-foot Commercial Cruiser class** Bldr: Sewart, Louisiana (In serv. 1976)

MH 21 (In serv. 22-6-72) MH 22 (In serv. 14-9-72) MH 23 (In serv. 20-3-73)

**D:** 33 tons (fl) **S:** 25 kts **Dim:** 21.3 × 5.2 × 1.0
**A:** 1/20-mm AA—2/12.7-mm mg (I × 2)
**M:** 2 G.M. 12V-71 diesels; 2 props; 1,300 hp

Remarks: MH 21, cannibalized 1982 for parts, refitted for service 11-84.

◆ **9 U.S. 3812-VCF class** Bldr: MonArk, Monticello, Arkansas (In serv. 1980–81)

MH 11 Le Maroon
MH 12 Oge
MH 13 Chavannes
MH 14 Capois La Mort
MH 15 Bauckman
MH 16 Makandal
MH 17 Charlemagne Perrault
MH 18 Sonthonax
MH 24 Boisrond Tonneree

**Oge (MH 12)** MonArk Boat Co., 1980

**D:** 8.5 tons (9.0 fl) **S:** 25 kts **Dim:** 12.34 × 4.11 × . . .
**A:** 1/12.7-mm mg—2/7.62-mm mg (I × 2)
**M:** 2 G.M. 6V-71N diesels; 2 props; 480 hp **Man:** 4 tot.

◆ **1 U.S. Enforcer class** Bldr: Bertram, Miami

MH 6

**Dim:** 9.5 × . . . × . . . **M:** 2 Caterpillar 3160 diesels; 2 props; 420 hp

# HONDURAS

**Republic of Honduras**

Personnel: approx. 250 total

Merchant Marine (1986): 424 ships—555,202 grt (tankers: 42 ships—67,255 grt)

Naval Aviation: Four Embraer EMB111 Bandeirante delivered 1983 for coastal surveillance; flown by naval crews. Two Lake Seawolf amphibians delivered 1987.

## PATROL BOATS AND CRAFT

◆ **2 U.S. 106-foot class** Bldr: Lantana Boatyard, Lantana, Florida

FNH 106 Copan (In serv. 6-86)
FNH 107 Tegucigalpa (ex-FNH 105) (In serv. 1983)

**Copan (FNH 106)** G. Arra, 7-86

**D:** 94 tons (fl) **S:** 35 kts **Dim:** 32.31 × 6.25 × 2.13 (props)
**A:** 1/20-mm Sea Vulcan 20 gatling gun—2/12.7-mm mg (I × 2)
**Electron Equipt:** Radar: 1/Furuno . . . nav.
**M:** 3 G.M. Detroit Diesel 16V92 TI diesels; 3 props; 3,900 hp
**Electric:** 100 kw **Fuel:** 21 tons **Man:** 4 officers, 12 men

Remarks: Aluminum construction. Have Magnavox MX 4102 NAVSAT receiver and two echo-sounders. HSV-20NCS optronic control system for 20-mm gun. A third unit, to have been named *Comayguela,* was canceled and became Jamaica's *Paul Bogle.*

◆ **3 U.S. 105-foot class** Bldr: Swiftships, Morgan City, Louisiana

FNH 101 Guaymuras (In serv. 4-77)
FNH 102 Honduras (In serv. 3-80)
FNH 103 Hibures (In serv. 3-80)

**Honduras (FNH 102)**—old number Swiftships, Inc., 3-80

**HONDURAS** *(continued)*
**PATROL BOATS AND CRAFT** *(continued)*

**D:** 103 tons (111 fl) **S:** 24 kts **Dim:** 32.00 × 7.20 × 3.1 (props)
**A:** 1/20-mm Sea Vulcan 20 gatling gun—2/12.7-mm mg (I × 2)
**Electron Equipt:** Radar: 1/. . . nav.
**M:** 2 MTU diesels; 2 props; 7,000 hp **Electric:** 80 kw
**Range:** 1,200/18 **Fuel:** 21 tons **Man:** 16 tot.

Remarks: Aluminum construction. Gatling gun and HSV-20NCS f.c.s. added 1987.

◆ **1 U.S. 85-foot Commercial Cruiser class** Bldr: Swiftships, Morgan City, Louisiana

FNH 851 Chamelecon (ex-*Rio Kuringwas*) (In serv. 1967)

**D:** 50 tons (54 fl) **S:** 23 kts **Dim:** 25.9 (23.1 wl) × 5.8 × 1.0 (hull)
**A:** 1/20-mm Sea Vulcan 20 gatling—2/12.7-mm mg (I × 2)
**Electron Equipt:** Radar: 1/. . . nav.
**M:** 2 G.M. 12V71 TI diesels; 2 props; 1,400 hp **Electric:** 40 kw
**Range:** 780/15 **Man:** 12 tot.

Remarks: Craft defected from Nicaragua in 1979. Aluminum construction. Received gatling gun and HSV-20NCS f.c.s. in 1987.

◆ **5 U.S. 65-foot Commercial Cruiser class** Bldr: Swiftships, Morgan City, Louisiana

| | In serv. | | In serv. |
|---|---|---|---|
| FNH 651 Nacaome (ex-*Aguan*, ex-*Gral*) | 12-73 | FNH 654 Ulua | 1980 |
| FNH 652 Goascoran (ex-*J.T. Cabanas*) | 1-74 | FNH 655 Chuluteca | 1980 |
| FNH 653 PETULA 1980 | | | |

**D:** 33 tons (36 fl) **S:** 24 or 36 kts **Dim:** 19.9 (17.4 wl) × 5.6 × 1.6 (props)
**A:** 2/12.7-mm mg (I × 2) **Electron Equipt:** Radar: 1/Decca . . .
**M:** 2 G.M. 12V71 TI or MTU diesels; 2 props; 1,300 or 1,590 hp
**Range:** 2,000/22 **Fuel:** 5 tons **Man:** 7 tot.

Remarks: First pair were originally ordered for Haiti and were delivered to Honduras in 1977. The others, ordered 1979, have more powerful diesels. Aluminum construction.

◆ **8 river patrol craft** Bldr: Lantana Boatyard, Lantana, Florida (In serv. 3-2-86)

**Lantana 11-m patrol craft** Lantana, 1-86

**D:** 8.16 tons (fl) **S:** 26 kts (22 sust.) **Dim:** 11.00 (10.06 wl) × 3.05 × 0.53
**A:** 2/12.7-mm mg (I × 2)—2/7.62-mm mg (I × 2)
**Electron Equipt:** Radar: 1/Furuno . . .—EW: VHF D/F
**M:** 2 Caterpillar 3208 TA diesels; 2 props; 630 hp
**Endurance:** 5 days **Man:** 5 tot.

Remarks: Aluminum construction, with Kevlar armor.

◆ **6 Outrage-class inshore patrol craft** Bldr: Boston Whaler (In serv. 1982)

**D:** 2.2 tons **S:** 35 kts **Dim:** 7.62 × 2.40 × 0.40
**A:** 1/12.7-mm mg—1/7.62-mm mg
**Electron Equipt:** Radar: 1/Furuno 3600
**M:** 2 outboard gasoline engines; 2 props; 300 hp
**Range:** 200/35 **Man:** 4 tot.

◆ **1 inshore patrol craft** Bldr: Ampela Marine, Honduras (In serv. 1981)

FNH 251 N . . . . . . .

**D:** 3 tons (fl) **S:** 24 kts **Dim:** 7.62 × 2.74 × 0.38
**A:** 1/12.7-mm mg—1/7.62-mm mg
**M:** 1 Chrysler 6M655 TI diesel, waterjet drive; . . . hp
**Range:** 250/18 **Man:** 4 tot.

Remarks: Built of wood and glass-reinforced plastic.

**AUXILIARY AND SERVICE CRAFT**

◆ **1 utility landing craft** Bldr: Lantana Boatyard, Fla.

| | Laid down | L | In serv. |
|---|---|---|---|
| FNH . . . N . . . | 11-86 | . . . | 12-1-88 |

**D:** . . . **S:** . . . **Dim:** 45.42 × . . . × . . .
**A:** . . . **M:** . . .

◆ **1 ex-U.S. Coast Guard Hollyhock-class buoy tender**

| | Bldr | In serv. |
|---|---|---|
| FNH . . . Yogoa (ex-*Walnut*) | Moore Drydock Co., Oakland, Cal. | 27-6-39 |

**D:** 825 tons (986 fl) **S:** 12 kts **Dim:** 53.4 × 10.4 × 3.7
**M:** 2 diesels; 2 props; 1,350 hp **Range:** 6,500/12; 10,000/7.5
**Man:** 40 tot.

Remarks: Transferred 1-7-82 for navigational support duties. One 20-ton buoy crane.

◆ **6 miscellaneous ex-fishing boats for logistics support**

| | | |
|---|---|---|
| FN 7501 Juliana | FN 7503 Carmen | FN 7505 Yosuro |
| FN 7502 San Rafael | FN 7504 Mairy | FN 7506 Jose Gregori |

# HONG KONG

**British Crown Colony of Hong Kong**

Merchant Marine (1986): 416 ships—8,179,670 grt (tankers: 31 ships—846,155 grt)

Note: In addition to the craft listed below, the Royal Navy maintains five *Peacock*-class corvettes at Hong Kong. The Royal Hong Kong Auxiliary Air Force operates one BN-42B/T Maritime Defender and 2 SA Bulldog 128 aircraft for coastal patrol, and 3 SA.365C Dauphin helicopters for rescue work.

ROYAL HONG KONG POLICE FORCE
MARINE DISTRICT

Personnel (1984): 160 officers, 3,105 men

**PATROL BOATS**

◆ **15 King Lai class** Bldr: Chung Wah SB & Eng, Kowloon

| | Laid down | L | In serv. |
|---|---|---|---|
| PL 70 King Lai | 28-2-84 | 14-7-84 | 29-10-84 |
| PL 71 King Yee | 28-2-84 | 17-7-84 | 29-11-84 |
| PL 72 King Lim | 28-2-84 | 29-7-84 | 17-12-84 |
| PL 73 King Hau | 15-3-84 | 2-11-84 | 31-1-85 |
| PL 74 King Dai | 15-3-84 | 8-11-84 | 28-2-85 |
| PL 75 King Chung | 15-3-84 | 12-11-84 | 1-4-85 |
| PL 76 King Shun | 17-8-84 | 26-1-85 | 17-5-85 |
| PL 77 King Tak | 25-8-84 | 4-2-85 | 10-6-85 |
| PL 78 King Chi | 17-8-84 | 1-2-85 | 2-7-85 |
| PL 79 King Tai | 1-12-84 | 29-4-85 | 19-8-85 |
| PL 80 King Kwan | 1-12-84 | 4-5-85 | 18-9-85 |
| PL 81 King Mei | 1-12-84 | 8-5-85 | 7-10-85 |
| PL 82 King Yan | 8-3-85 | 19-8-85 | 4-11-85 |
| PL 83 King Yung | 8-3-85 | 30-8-85 | 25-11-85 |
| PL 84 King Kan | 8-3-85 | 2-9-85 | 18-12-85 |

**D:** 85 tons (97 fl) **S:** 25 kts **Dim:** 26.50 (24.27 pp) × 5.80 × 1.80
**A:** 1/7.62-mm mg **Electron Equipt:** Radar: 1/. . . nav.
**M:** 2 MTU 12V396 TC83 diesels (1,483 hp each); 1/M.A.N. MB OM-424A V-12 cruise diesel (465 hp); 2 props, 1 waterjet
**Range:** 600/14; 1,400/8 **Man:** 17 tot.

Remarks: PL 70–78 ordered 10-83; PL 79–81 ordered 1/12/84. Modified version of the PL 60 class; Damen Stan Patrol 2600/Chung Wah Mk 3 design. Can make up to 7 kts on the centerline waterjet. Carry an Avon SeaRaider semi-rigid inspection boat. Three near sisters built for Hong Kong Customs.

**PATROL BOATS** *(continued)*

**King Chung (Police 75)** G. Arra, 7-86

◆ **2 command boats** Bldr: Hong Kong United DY (In serv. 1965)

PL 1 Sea Lion PL 2 Sea Tiger

**Sea Lion (Police Launch 1)** G. Arra, 11-86

**D:** 222 tons (fl) **S:** 11.8 kts **Dim:** 33.9 × 7.3 × 3.2
**A:** 1/12.7-mm mg **M:** 2 Cummins diesels; 2 props; 674 hp **Range:** 5,200/11.8
**Man:** 29 tot.

◆ **10 Damen-design** Bldr: Chung Wah SB & Eng, Kowloon

| | In serv. | | In serv. |
|---|---|---|---|
| PL 60 N . . . . . . . | 2-80 | PL 65 Cetus | 2-9-80 |
| PL 61 Pisces | 2-80 | PL 66 Dorado | 8-9-80 |
| PL 62 N . . . . . . . | 2-80 | PL 57 Mercury | 26-1-82 |
| PL 63 N . . . . . . . | 1980 | PL 58 Vulcan | 22-3-82 |
| PL 64 N . . . . . . . | 1980 | PL 59 Ceres | 29-3-82 |

**Cetus (Police 65)** G. Arra, 11-86

**Mercury (Police 57)**—cargo version G. Arra, 1984

**D:** 86 tons (normal) **S:** 23 kts **Dim:** 26.2 × 5.9 × 1.80
**A:** 1/12.7-mm mg **Electron Equipt:** Radar: 1 Decca 150
**M:** 2 MTU 12V396 TC82 diesels (1,300 hp each), 1 M.A.N. D2566 cruise diesel (195 hp); 3 props (Schottel on centerline); 2,600 hp
**Range:** 1,400/8 **Man:** 1 officer, 13 men

Remarks: First unit laid down 9-79 to a Dutch design. Cruise engine provides 7–8-kt max. speeds. PL 57–59 ordered 3-81 for logistics support duties, with same engines, but waterjet vice Schottel propeller for cruise (2 to 7 kts): have restricted patrol range, but have a cargo hold; also differ in lacking bow bulwarks and in having smaller pilothouse.

◆ **7 78-foot craft** Bldr: Vosper Thornycroft, Singapore (In serv. 5-72 to 5-73)

PL 50 Sea Cat PL 53 Sea Eagle PL 55 Sea Lynx
PL 51 Sea Puma PL 54 Sea Hawk PL 56 Sea Falcon
PL 52 Sea Leopard

**Sea Eagle (PL 53)** G. Arra, 1980

**D:** 82 tons (fl) **S:** 20.7 kts **Dim:** 23.7 × 5.2 × 1.7 **A:** 1/12.7-mm mg
**M:** 2 Cummins diesels; 2 props; 1,500 hp **Range:** 4,000/20 **Man:** 16 tot.

◆ **7 45-foot converted wooden tugs** Bldr: Australia (In serv. 1944–45)

PL 9 Snipe PL 11 Wren PL 14 Tern PL 16 Kestrel
PL 10 Puffin PL 13 Gull PL 15 Cormorant

**D:** 27.7 tons **S:** 9 kts **Dim:** 13.7 × 4.6 × 2.1
**A:** small arms **M:** 1 Gardner diesel **Range:** 1,700/8 **Man:** 5 tot.

**Kestrel (PL 16)** G. Arra

HONG KONG *(continued)*
PATROL BOATS *(continued)*

◆ **3 40-foot patrol launches** Bldr: Cheoy Lee SY (In serv. 1971)

PL 6 JETSTREAM (In serv. 17-4-86) PL 8 TIDESTREAM (In serv. 12-6-86)
PL 7 SWIFTSTREAM (In serv. 25-5-86)

**D:** 24 tons (fl) **S:** 18 kts **Dim:** 16.4 × 4.5 × 0.85
**M:** 2 MTU diesels; 2 Hamilton 421 waterjets; 455 hp
**Range:** 300/15 **Man:** 8 tot.

REMARKS: GRP construction. Replace trio by same builder with same names.

◆ **9 30-foot Spear class** Bldr: Fairey Allday Marine, Hamble (In serv. 1981)

PL 37 to PL 45

**D:** 4.5 tons (fl) **S:** 28 kts **Dim:** 9.10 × 2.89 × 0.84
**A:** 1/7.62-mm mg **M:** 2 Perkins T6.3544 diesels; 2 props; 370 hp
**Range:** 250/25 **Man:** 4 tot.

REMARKS: Glass-reinforced plastic construction.

### MISCELLANEOUS CRAFT

◆ **1 support launch** Bldr: Reliance Marine, Salisbury, U.K.

PL . . . N . . . . . . . (In serv. 5-82)

**D:** 3 tons (fl) **S:** 25 kts **Dim:** 8.8 × 2.9 × 0.76
**M:** 1 Volvo Penta AQAD-40/280 diesel; 155 hp **Man:** 4 tot.

◆ **1 personnel launch** Bldr: Hip Hing Cheung SY (In serv. 1975)

PL 7 DRAGON

**D:** 18.5 tons **S:** 23.5 kts **Dim:** 16.0 × . . . × . . .
**A:** small arms **M:** 2 diesels; 2 props; 700 hp **Range:** 300/20 **Man:** 6 tot.

◆ . . . **7-meter Typhoon rigid inflatable craft** Bldr: Task Force Boats, U.K.

REMARKS: Ordered 1987. Powered by two outboard motors for 35 kts.

CUSTOMS SERVICE

### PATROL BOATS

◆ **3 Damen 26-meter class** Bldr: Chung Wah SB & Eng., Hong Kong

6 SEA GLORY (In serv. 28-7-86) 8 SEA LEADER (In serv. 3-11-86)
7 SEA GUARDIAN (In serv. 28-8-86)

**D:** 96 tons (fl) **S:** 24 kts **Dim:** 26.50 (24.79 pp) × 5.80 × 1.80
**A:** . . . **Electron Equipt:** Radar: 1/Decca RM 1290
**M:** 2 MTU 12V396 TB93 diesels; 2 props; 3,000 hp
**Range:** . . . **Electric:** 120 kVA **Man:** . . .

REMARKS: Similar to Police *King Lai* class, but lack waterjet cruise system and have a higher pilothouse with open bridge atop it.

# HUNGARY
**Hungarian People's Republic**

PERSONNEL: Approx. 500 total

MERCHANT MARINE (1986): 22 ships—86,395 grt

HUNGARIAN ARMY MARITIME FORCE

◆ **1 Yugoslav Nestin-class minesweeper/patrol boat** Bldr: Brodotehnika, Belgrade

**D:** 66 tons (78 fl) **S:** 15 kts **Dim:** 27.00 × 6.50 × 1.15 max.
**A:** 5/20-mm AA (III × 1, I × 2)—24 small mines
**Electron Equipt:** Radar: 1/Decca 101 **Man:** 17 tot.
**M:** 2 diesels; 2 props; 520 hp **Range:** 860/11

REMARKS: Has 2 flare/chaff RL. Sweep gear includes PEAM magnetic/acoustic sweep, AEL-1 explosive sweep, and MDL-1 and -2 mechanical wire sweeps. Sisters in Yugoslav and Iraqi navies. Transferred circa 1982–83. There are also several other small river minesweepers.

◆ **1 river patrol boat** Bldr: Hamilton Marine, New Zealand

RENDORSEG (In serv. 1986)

**D:** . . . **S:** . . . **Dim:** 8.7 × 2.9 × . . .
**M:** 1 Caterpillar 3208 TA diesel; 1 Hamilton waterjet; 350 hp

◆ **10 river patrol craft** (In serv. early 1960s)

**D:** 10 tons **S:** . . . **Dim:** . . . × . . . × . . . **A:** 1/14.5-mm mg **M:** 2 diesels

◆ **5 landing craft**

◆ **several small tugs**

◆ **several river transports—of up to 1,000 tons**

# ICELAND
**Republic of Iceland**

PERSONNEL: 160 men

MERCHANT MARINE (1986): 389 ships—176,409 grt (tankers: 3 ships—1,539 grt)

AVIATION: One Fokker F-27 Mk 200 Friendship patrol aircraft, 1 Hughes 500D helicopter, and 1 SA-365N Dauphin II helicopter.

COAST GUARD

### FISHERIES-PROTECTION SHIPS

◆ **2 Aegir class**

| | Bldr | L | In serv. |
|---|---|---|---|
| AEGIR | Aalborg SY, Denmark | 1967 | 1968 |
| TYR | Dannebrog Vaerft, Aarhus, Denmark | 10-10-74 | 15-3-78 |

Aegir — B. Olafsson, 3-87

Tyr — B. Olafsson, 3-87

**D:** 1,150 tons (1,500 fl) **S:** 20 kts **Dim:** 69.84 (62.18 pp) × 10.02 × 5.02
**A:** 1/57-mm (6-pdr.) low-angle, single-fire
**M:** 2 M.A.N. R8V 40/54 diesels; 2 KaMeWa CP props; 8,600 hp
**Electric:** 630 kVA **Range:** 10,000/19 **Man:** 22 tot.

REMARKS: Although built ten years apart, these two ships are nearly identical. Helicopter hangar between twin stacks. Three radar sets, fish-finding sonar. 20-ton bollard-pull towing winch, passive rolling tanks. *Tyr* is 70.90 m o. a.

◆ **1 Odinn class**

| | Bldr. | Laid down | L | In serv. |
|---|---|---|---|---|
| ODINN | Aalborg SY, Denmark | 1-59 | 9-59 | 1-60 |

**D:** 1,000 tons (fl) **S:** 18 kts **Dim:** 63.63 (56.61 pp) × 10.0 × 4.8
**A:** 1/57-mm (6-pdr.) low-angle **Range:** 10,000/18
**M:** 2 Burmeister & Wain diesels; 2 props; 5,050 hp **Man:** 22 tot.

REMARKS: Rebuilt in 1975 with hangar, helicopter deck, and passive antirolling tanks.

**ICELAND** *(continued)*
**FISHERIES-PROTECTION SHIPS** *(continued)*

◆ **1 former lighthouse tender** Bldr: Bodewes, Netherlands (In serv. 1962)

ARVAKUR

**D:** 716 tons (fl) **S:** 12 kts **Dim:** 32.3 × 10.0 × 4.0
**A:** 1/12.7-mm mg **M:** 1 Deutz diesel; 1,000 hp **Man:** 12 tot.

REMARKS: Transferred to the Coast Guard in 1969.

◆ **1 Nelson 45-foot customs launch** Bldr: W. S. Souter, Cowes, U.K. (In serv. 1978)

**S:** 17 kts **M:** 2 Cummins V555M diesels

◆ **. . . 21-SS Smuggler-class patrol launches** Bldr: Norway, 1975

**S:** 36 kts **M:** Castoldi water jets

# INDIA

## Republic of India

PERSONNEL (1986): Approx. 46,000 total

MERCHANT MARINE (1986): 736 ships—6,540,121 grt
(tankers: 65 ships—1,241,904 grt)

NAVAL AVIATION: Shipboard aircraft include 14 Magic air-to-air missile-equipped Sea Harrier FRS.Mk 51 V/STOL fighters (with 10 more ordered 25-11-85 and a further 8 to 10 more planned); 11 Bréguet Alizé ASW aircraft, 19 Sea King helicopters (3 Mk 42A delivered 8-80, 10 Mk 42, 6 Mk 42C transports delivered from 5-2-87); on order for delivery 1987–88 were an additional 20 Mk 42B, equipped with Sea Eagle antiship missiles and Sintra-Alcatel MS-12 dipping sonars, at least 1 Ka 27 Helix-A ASW helicopter (with 8 more ordered during 1986), 5 Ka 25 Hormone-A ASW helicopters, and 19 Chetak (Alouette-III) light ASW/liaison helicopters. For land-based maritime surveillance 3 Soviet Il-38 May and 5 Lockheed Constellations are in use, with delivery of two Soviet Tu-142M Bear-F scheduled for 1988. Five of a planned total of 26 Dornier 228 coastal surveillance aircraft were to be in service by end-1987; the first three were built in West Germany, the rest by HAL, and some of the 26 will enter Coast Guard service. Twelve BN-42B/T Maritime Defender coastal patrol aircraft are also in use. Training and logistics support aircraft include 3 Mk 60 Harrier V/STOL trainers, 2 Devon transports, 4 Hughes 300 helicopters, 4 Vampire T55 jet trainers, and 7 HAL Kiran trainers. The Indian Navy may order the Mk 42D air early-warning version of the Sea King helicopter. The Alizé aircraft "came ashore" in 10-87 and are to be discarded during 1989.

**Indian Navy Sea Harrier FRS.51** British Aerospace

**Indian Navy Il-38 May ASW aircraft** U.S. Navy, 1981

WEAPONS AND SENSORS: A mixture of Western (primarily British and Dutch) and Soviet weapons and sensors, with Western designs built in India under license. Hindustan Aeronautics Ltd. is developing an air-to-ground missile for Air Force and Navy use; it will have a range of 100 km at Mach 4 to Mach .85 at 30,000-foot altitude and will have a 35-kg payload.

WARSHIPS IN SERVICE, UNDER CONSTRUCTION, OR PROJECTED AS OF 1 JANUARY 1988

◆ **2 aircraft carriers**

| | L | Tons, std. | Main Armament |
|---|---|---|---|
| 1 HERMES | 1953 | 23,900 | 15 aircraft |
| 1 GLORY | 1945 | 15,700 | 15 aircraft |

◆ **0 (+3?) cruisers**

| | | | |
|---|---|---|---|
| 0 (+3?) KRESTA-II | . . . | 6,000 | . . . |

◆ **12 (+7) submarines**

| | | Tons (submerged) | |
|---|---|---|---|
| 2 (+4) TYPE 1500 | 1985– | 3,200 | 6/533-mm TT |
| 2 (+3) KILO | 1984– | 1,860 | 8/533-mm TT |
| 8 FOXTROT | 1965–72 | 2,400 | 10/533-mm TT |

◆ **4 (+6) destroyers**

| | | Tons, std. | |
|---|---|---|---|
| 4 (+6) KASHIN | 1979–. . . | 3,950 | 2/Goa SAM, 4/SSN-2C, 2/76-mm, ASW Weapons, 1/helicopter |

◆ **13 (+6) frigates**

| | | | |
|---|---|---|---|
| 0 (+6) Project 15 | . . . | 4,000 | . . . |
| 3 GODAVARI | 1980–84 | 3,500 | 4/SS-N-2C, 1/SA-N-4, 2/57-mm, 1-2 helicopters |
| 6 LEANDER | 1968–77 | 2,250 | 2/114-mm, 1 or 2/Sea Cat, 1 helicopter |
| 2 LEOPARD | 1958–59 | 2,250 | 2/114-mm DP, 1/Squid |
| 2 WHITBY | 1958 | 2,144 | 3/SS-N-2, 2/Limbo |

◆ **13 (+35) corvettes**

| | | | |
|---|---|---|---|
| 1 (+23) TARANTUL | 1986– | 480 | 4/SS-N-2C, 1/76-mm |
| 0 (+112) KHUKRI | 1986– | 900 | 4/SS-N-2C, 1/76-mm |
| 3 NANUCHKA | 1977–78 | 600 | 4/SS-N-2C, 1/SA-N-4, 2/57-mm |
| 9 PETYA-II | 1968–74 | 950 | 4/76.2-mm DP, 3/533-mm TT |

◆ **13 guided-missile patrol boats**

◆ **18 (+4) minesweepers**

◆ **11 (+7) amphibious ships**

### AIRCRAFT CARRIERS

◆ **1 Hermes class** Bldr: Vickers-Armstrong, Barrow-in-Furness

| | Laid down | L | In serv. |
|---|---|---|---|
| R 22 VIRAAT (ex-*Hermes*) | 21-6-44 | 16-2-53 | 18-11-59 |

**D:** 23,900 tons (28,706 fl) **S:** 28 kts
**Dim:** 226.85 (198.12 pp) × 48.78 (27.43 wl) × 8.80
**A:** 2/Sea Cat GWS. 22 SAM systems (IV × 2), 6/Sea Harrier FRS.Mk 51, 3/Sea King Mk 426, 6/Sea King Mk 42B—see Remarks
**Electron Equipt:** Radar: 2/1006, 1/965, 1/993
TACAN: FT13-S/M
EW: . . . intercept; 2 Corvus RL (VIII × 2)
**M:** 2 sets Parsons GT; 2 props; 76,000 hp **Electric:** 9,000 kw
**Boilers:** 4 Admiralty 3-drum **Range:** 6,500/14
**Fuel:** 4,200 tons, plus 320 tons aviation fuel
**Man:** approx. 140 officers, 1,030 men

REMARKS: Purchased 19-4-86, having been paid off 12-4-84 from the Royal Navy and stricken 1-7-85. Turned over to Indian control 14-11-86 during reactivation and minor modernization overhaul and commissioned 12-5-87 at Devonport. The name means "Mighty." Had been converted from a standard carrier to a helicopter commando carrier 1971–73 and converted again 1976–77 as an ASW helicopter carrier; again modified 5-80 to 9-5-81 to operate Sea Harrier V/STOL attack fighters, receiving a 230-ton, 45.7-m-long by 13.7-m-wide by 4.9-m-high 12-degree "ski-jump" takeoff ramp. Retained commando transport capability for 750 troops and continues to carry four LCVP landing craft aft. Has two elevators.

During the Falkland War (when she was the last RN warship still using black oil fuel), the ship operated as many as 12 Harriers and a large number of helicopters. The air group in the Indian Navy includes at least one 6-aircraft Sea Harrier squadron, plus 3 Sea King Mk 42C logistics helicopters and probably 6 Sea King Mk 42B ASW helicopters, which are also equipped to launch Sea Eagle antiship missiles. During reactivation new Type 1006 navigational radars were

**AIRCRAFT CARRIERS** *(continued)*

**Viraat (R 22)** W. Sartori, 7-87

**Viraat (R 22)** B. Sullivan, 6-87

added, and an Italian TACAN system (replacing the U.K. system removed in 4-82) was added. EW equipment will be added in India. Has limited steaming endurance.

◆ **1 Glory class** Bldr: Vickers-Armstrong, Barrow-in-Furness

| | Laid down | L | In serv. |
|---|---|---|---|
| R 11 VIKRANT (ex-*Hercules*) | 14-10-43 | 22-9-45 | 4-3-61 |

**Vikrant (R 11)**—prior to addition of ski jump Indian Navy, 1986

**D:** 15,700 tons (19,500 fl) **S:** 24 kts (max.), 17 kts cruising
**Dim:** 211.25 (198.0 wl) × 24.29 × 7.15
**A:** 8/40-mm (I × 8)—6/Sea Harrier, 3/Sea King Mk 42C, 6/Sea King Mk 42B
**Electron Equipt:** Radar: 1/ZW-06, 1/DA-05, 1/LW-08
**M:** 2 sets Parsons GT; 2 props; 40,000 hp
**Boilers:** 4 Admiralty; 28 kg/cm² **Fuel:** 3,200 tons
**Range:** 6,200/23; 12,000/14 **Man:** Peacetime: 1,075 tot.; wartime: 1,340 tot.

REMARKS: Bought in Great Britain in 1-57 while still incomplete. Air-conditioned. One hangar, two elevators, angled flight deck, steam catapult. Flight deck: 210 × 34. Modernized 1979 to 3-1-82 with new boilers, engines, new CIC, and new Dutch-design radars. Bofors L 70 single 40-mm AA in place of original British Mk 5 twin and Mk 9 single mountings. A further refit from 12-82 to 2-83 made the ship ready for its Sea Harrier complement, but did not include a planned ski-jump ramp. Catapult and arrester gear were retained to permit continued use of Alizé ASW aircraft. With the delivery of additional Sea Harriers in 1984 and later, the Alizés are moving ashore. The ship also carries Chetak (Alouette-III) helicopters equipped for ASW and *may* carry Sea Kings, although the latter cannot be accommodated in the hangar. The ship received the IPN-10 combat data system in 1985, and four lightweight directors were added for the 40-mm AA.

NOTE: A 30,000–40,000-ton replacement for *Vikrant,* to be built in India, is under design, but would not be available until the late 1990s. *Vikrant* is to be used as an attack carrier, with an all-Sea Harrier complement. *Vikrant* will have a commando function.

**SUBMARINES**

◆ **2 (+2 + 2) West German Type SSK-1500**

| | Bldr | Laid down | L | In serv. |
|---|---|---|---|---|
| S 44 SHISHUMAR | Howaldtswerke, Kiel | 1-5-82 | 13-12-84 | 28-9-86 |
| S 45 SHANKUSH | Howaldtswerke, Kiel | 1-9-82 | 11-5-84 | 20-11-86 |
| S 45 N . . . | Mazagon DY, Bombay | 5-6-84 | . . . | 1990 |
| S 47 N . . . | Mazagon DY, Bombay | . . . | . . . | 1991 |

**Shankush (S 45)** HDW, 1986

**Shishumar (S 44)**—note rescue sphere housing in deck before sail P. Voss, 7-85

**D:** 1,450 tons std.; 1,660 tons surf./1,860 sub. **S:** 11/22.5 kts
**Dim:** 64.40 × 6.50 × 6.20
**A:** 8/533-mm (fwd—14 torpedoes)—mines (see Remarks)
**Electron Equipt:** Radar: Kelvin-Hughes . . .
Sonar: Krupp Atlas search and attack, Alcatel DUUX-5
**M:** 4 MTU 12V493 TY60 (AZ 80) diesels (600 hp each), 4/430 kw generators, 2 Siemens motors; 1 prop; 5,000 hp
**Fuel:** 146 tons **Range:** 13,000/10 (surf.); 8,200/8 (snorkel), 524/4 (sub.)
**Endurance:** 50 days **Man:** 8 officers, 28 men

**SUBMARINES** *(continued)*

Remarks: Final order, signed 11-12-81, includes an option to build 2 additional units in India. A variant of the Type 209 design. Have Singer-Librascope SFCS Mk 1 weapons control system and the Gäbler spherical escape chamber. Varta batteries, two Kollmorgen periscopes. Strap-on minelaying pods were purchased for these ships. Indian-built units reported far behind schedule, with little accomplished; trials for first now scheduled for 9-90.

◆ **2 (+3) Soviet Kilo class** Bldr: Sudomelch SY, Leningrad

| | In serv. | | In serv. |
|---|---|---|---|
| S 55 Sindhugosh | 6-86 | S 58 N . . . | . . . |
| S 56 Sindhudhvaj | 7-87 | S 59 N . . . | . . . |
| S 57 N . . . | . . . | S 60 N . . . | . . . |

**Sindhugosh (S 55)** French Navy, 7-86

**Sindhugosh (S 55)** L. Grazioli, 7-86

**D:** 2,300 tons (surf.)/2,900 tons (sub.) **S:** 16/20 kts
**Dim:** 73.0 × 9.9 × 6.5
**A:** 6/533-mm TT fwd (12 torpedoes)
**Electron Equipt:** Radar: 1/Snoop Tray
Sonar: passive array; low-freq. active
**M:** . . . diesels, electric drive; 1/6-bladed prop; . . . hp
**Range:** . . . **Man:** 60 tot.

Remarks: S 55 arrived in India 17-9-86. These ships may be intended to replace, rather than augment, the Foxtrot class. Apparent delivery rate is one per year. A nuclear-powered submarine was delivered from the U.S.S.R. in 1988.

◆ **8 Soviet Foxtrot class**

| | In serv. | | In serv. |
|---|---|---|---|
| S 20 Kursura | 12-70 | S 40 Vela | 31-8-73 |
| S 21 Karanj | 10-70 | S 41 Vagir | 3-11-73 |
| S 22 Kandheri | 1-69 | S 42 Vagli | 10-8-74 |
| S 23 Kalvari | 16-7-68 | S 43 Vagsheer | 26-12-74 |

**Vagli (S 42)** G. Arra, 1982

**D:** 1,950/2,400 tons **S:** 16/15.5 kts **Dim:** 91.5 × 7.5 × 6.0
**A:** 10/533-mm TT (6 fwd, 4 aft)—22 torpedoes or 44 mines
**Electron Equipt:** Radar: 1/Snoop Tray
Sonar: 1/MF active, passive array
**M:** 3 diesel generator sets (2,000 hp each), 3 motors; 3 props; 5,300 hp
**Range:** 11,000/8 (snorkel) **Endurance:** 70 days **Man:** 8 officers, 70 men

**CRUISERS**

◆ **0 (+3) Soviet Kresta-II/Sovremennyg class (?)**

Remarks: Reportedly ordered 20-12-82. If new construction (rather than transfers from Soviet Navy inventory), will probably differ considerably from Soviet Navy units, due to the age of the Kresta-II design (early 1960s). Because of the uncertainties surrounding the program, no characteristics data are given here; see U.S.S.R. section for Kresta-II. Also reported, up to five *Sovremennyy*-class destroyers may be ordered, vice Kresta-II.

**GUIDED-MISSILE DESTROYERS**

◆ **4 (+2) Soviet Kashin class** Bldr: 61 Kommuna SY, Nikolayev

| | In serv. | | In serv. | | In serv. |
|---|---|---|---|---|---|
| D 51 Rajput | 10-80 | D 52 Rana | 28-6-82 | D 53 Ranjit | 21-11-83 |
| D 54 Ranvir | 6-86 | D . . . N . . . | . . . | D . . . N . . . | . . . |

**Rajput (D 51)** U.S. Navy, 3-87

**Rana (D 52)** French Navy, 1986

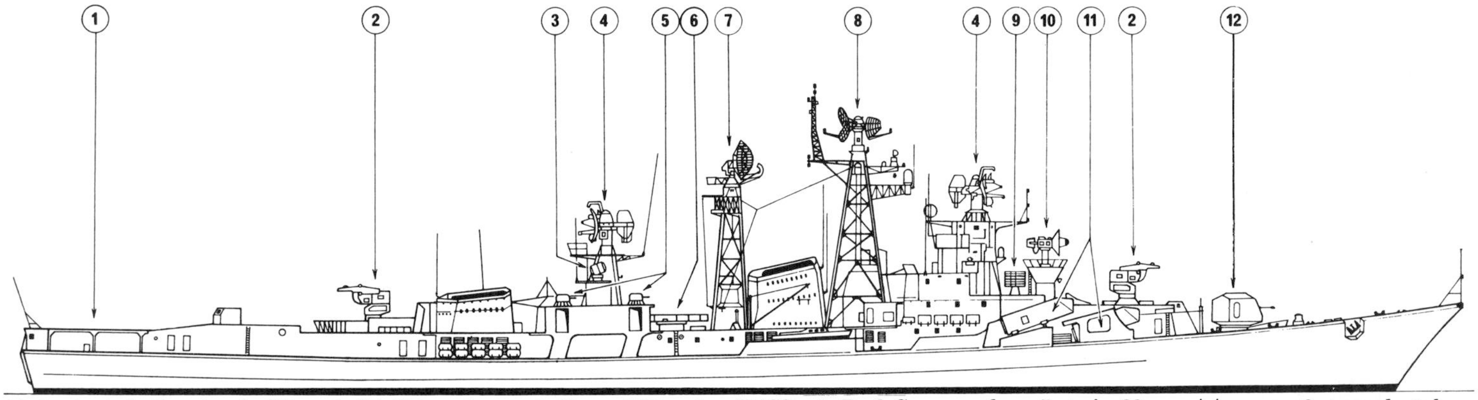


**Rajput** 1. helicopter facility 2. SA-N-1 systems 3. Drum Tilt radar GFCS 4. Peel Group radar 5. twin 30-mm AA guns 6. torpedo tubes (V × 1) 7. Big Net radar 8. Head Net-C radar 9. RBU-6000 ASW RL 10. Owl Screech radar GFCS 11. SS-N-2C SSM 12. 76.2-mm DP (II × 1)

## GUIDED-MISSILE DESTROYERS *(continued)*

**Ranvir (D 54)**—with Helix helo on deck and hangar open 8-86

**D:** 3,950 tons (4,950 fl) **S:** 36–39 kts **Dim:** 147.0 × 15.8 × 5.0 (hull)
**A:** 4/SS-N-2C SSM (I × 4)—2/SA-N-1 SAM syst. (II × 2; 44 Goa missiles)—2/76.2-mm DP (II × 1)—8/30-mm AA (II × 4) (D 54: 4/30-mm gatling AA)—5/533-mm TT (V × 1)—2/RBU-6000 ASW RL (XII × 2)—1/Ka-25 Hormone-A ASW helicopter (D 54: Ka-27 Helix-A)
**Electron Equipt:** Radar: 2/Don Kay, 1/Big Net, 1/Head Net C, 2/Peel Group, 1/Owl Screech, 2/Drum Tilt (D 54: Bass Tilt)
IFF: 2/High Pole B transponders
Sonar: 1/hull-mounted med. freq., 1/med.-freq. VDS
EW: 2/Watch Dog, 2 Top Hat A, 2 Top Hat B, 4/chaff RL (XVI × 4)
**M:** 4 gas turbines; 2 props; 94,000 hp **Range:** 900/35; 5,000/18
**Man:** 35 officers, 330 men

Remarks: New construction units, not conversions from former Soviet Navy units. In contrast to Soviet Navy "Modified Kashins," the SS-N-2C missiles are mounted forward and fire forward, while the after twin 76.2-mm gun mount has been omitted in favor of a hangar for the helicopter. Program for first three was far behind delivery schedule; 3 more ordered 20-12-82. D 54 carries the latter 6-barrelled 30-mm gatling AA weapon with Bass Tilt radar directors in place of the twin 30-mm/Drum Tilt of the initial trio and was delivered with a Helix helicopter aboard; the hangar, below the main deck level in the location occupied by an aft 76-mm magazine in Soviet units, is accessed by an elevator.

## FRIGATES

◆ **0 (46) Project 15 class** Bldr: Mazagon DY, Bombay

| | Laid down | L | In serv. |
|---|---|---|---|
| F . . . N . . . | 3-87 | . . . | 1991-92 |
| F . . . N . . . | . . . | . . . | . . . |
| F . . . N . . . | . . . | . . . | . . . |
| F . . . N . . . | . . . | . . . | . . . |
| F . . . N . . . | . . . | . . . | . . . |
| F . . . N . . . | . . . | . . . | . . . |

**Godavari (F 20)**—see entry next page L. & L. Van Ginderen, 7-86

**Godavari (F 20)** U.S. Navy, 7-86

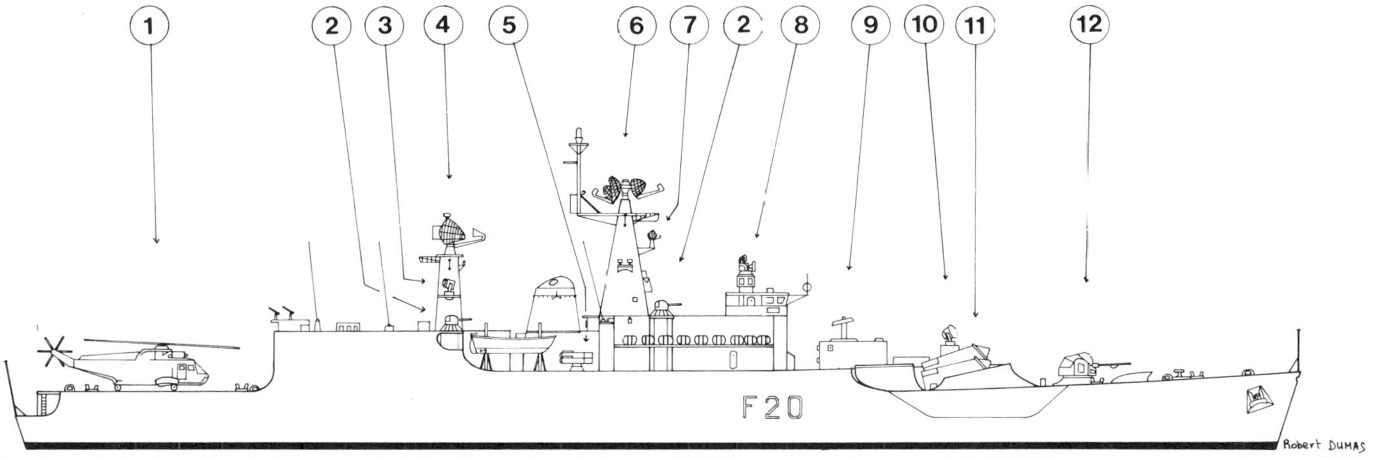


**Godavari** 1. Sea King helicopter 2. twin 30-mm AA 3. Drum Tilt 30-mm control radar 4. RALW-02 early-warning radar 5. ASW TT (III × 2) 6. Head Net-C (MR.310) air/surface-search radar 7. ZW-06A navigational/surface-search radar 8. Pop Group missile-control radar director 9. SA-N-4 (ZIF-122) launch group 10. Muff Cob 57-mm gun-control radar 11. SS-N-2C (P. 21) SSM launch tubes 12. twin 57-mm automatic DP

**FRIGATES** *(continued)*

**D:** 5,000 tons (fl) **S:** . . . **Dim:** . . . × . . . × . . . **Range:** . . . **Man:** . . .
**A:** . . . SSM—. . . SAM
**Electron Equipt:** Radar: . . .
Sonar: APSOH (active/passive)
EW: . . .
**M:** CODOG: 2 MTU . . . diesels, 2 HAL-G.E. LM-2500 gas turbines; 2 CP props; 54,000 hp

REMARKS: First unit ordered 3-86 as a follow-on to the *Godavari* class. Will have fin stabilizers. License to build U.S. gas turbines granted 1986. Will have Soviet weapons and European-designed/Indian-improved-and-manufactured electronics, including Bharat Electronics APSOH (Advanced Panoramic Sonar).

◆ **3 Godavari class** Bldr: Mazagon Docks, Bombay

| | Laid down | L | In serv. |
|---|---|---|---|
| F 20 GODAVARI | 2-6-78 | 15-5-80 | 10-12-83 |
| F 21 GANGA | 1980 | 15-11-81 | 1-1-86 |
| F 22 GOMATI | 1981 | 20-3-84 | . . .-87 |

**Ganga (F 21)**—on trials Indian Navy, 1986

**D:** 3,500 tons (4,100 fl) **S:** 27 kts **Dim:** 126.4 (123.6 pp) × 14.5 × 4.5 (hull)
**A:** 4/SS-N-2C SSM (I × 4)—1/SA-N-4 SAM syst. (II × 1; 20 Gecko missiles)—2/57-mm DP (II × 1)—8/30-mm AA (II × 4)—6/324-mm ASW TT (III × 2; NST-58 torpedoes)—1/Sea King ASW helicopter—1/Chetak helicopter
**Electron Equipt:** Radar: 1/ZW-06, 1/Head Net C (MR.310), 1/RALW-02, 1/Pop Group, 2/Drum Tilt, 1/Muff Cob
Sonar: 1 U.K. Type 184 (D 21, 22: APSOH)
EW: . . .—TACAN: FT13-S/M
**M:** 2 sets GT; 2 five-bladed props; 30,000 hp **Range:** 4,500/12
**Boilers:** 2 Babcock & Wilcox, 3-drum; 38.7 kg/cm$^2$, 450°C
**Man:** 51 officers, 262 men (362 accommodations)
**Electric:** 2/750-kw turbogenerators, 3/. . . kw diesel sets

REMARKS: Design derived from the *Leander* class, with the same propulsion plant but larger hull. Electronics and weapons systems a very diverse selection of Western European-designed/Indian-built and Soviet systems. The hull is an enlarged and improved version of the *Leander* form. Steel superstructure. Two pairs Vosper fin stabilizers. Bharat's RALW-02 radar uses the same antenna as the H.S.A. DA-08. There are two backup manual directors for the twin AK-230 30-mm AA guns and two for the AK-57 57-mm mount. The hangar is sized for two Sea King, but only one (often with a Chetak light helo aboard also) is normally carried for stability reasons. The Bear Trap helicopter landing and traversing system is fitted to F 22 and will be backfitted to F 21. The Selenia IPN-10 combat data system is fitted, as is a comprehensive EW sensor suite—but no decoy launchers. These ships are a remarkable technical achievement.

◆ **6 British Leander class** Bldr: Mazagon Docks, Bombay

| | Laid down | L | In serv. |
|---|---|---|---|
| F 33 NILGIRI | 10-66 | 23-10-68 | 3-6-72 |
| F 34 HIMGIRI | 1967 | 6-5-70 | 23-11-74 |
| F 35 UDAYGIRI | 14-9-70 | 24-10-72 | 18-2-76 |
| F 36 DUNAGIRI | 1-73 | 9-3-74 | 5-5-77 |
| F 41 TARAGIRI | 1974 | 25-10-76 | 16-5-80 |
| F 42 VINDHYAGIRI | 1976 | 12-11-77 | 8-7-81 |

**Udaygiri (F 35)** G. Gyssels, 1977

**Vindhyagiri (F 42)** 1984

**D:** 2,250 tons (2,800 fl); later units: 3,250 tons (fl) **S:** 30 kts
**Dim:** 113.38 × 13.1 × 4.27 (avg.)
**A:** 2/114-mm DP (II × 1)—F 33: 1/Sea Cat GWS 22; others; 2/Sea Cat with M-4 directors—1/Limbo Mk 10 ASW mortar (not on F 41 and F 42, which have 1/375-mm Bofors ASW RL (II × 1))—2/20-mm AA (I × 2)—1/Chetak ASW helicopter (Sea King on F 41 and F 42)—F 41, 42: 6/324-mm ILAS-3 ASW TT (III × 2; A 184 torpedoes)
**Electron Equipt:** Radar: F 33: 1/965, 1/993, 1/978, 2/903
F 34 on: 1/Decca navigational, 1/ZW-06, 1/LW-08, 1/M 44, 2/M 45
Sonar: 1/184 plus 1/199 VDS on F 33; F 41, 42: Thomson-CSF hull-mounted
**M:** 2 sets GT; 2 five-bladed props; 30,000 hp **Electric:** 2,500 kw
**Boilers:** 2 Babcock & Wilcox, 3-drum; 38.7 kg/cm$^2$, 450°C **Fuel:** 500 tons
**Range:** approx. 4,500/12

REMARKS: The first two are very similar to British versions of the *Leander* class, but later units have been progressively improved, using H.S.A. radars and an ever-greater proportion of Indian-built components. F 41 and F 42 have very large telescoping hangars situated much nearer the stern and requiring removal of the three-barreled Limbo ASW mortar (replaced by a twin Bofors ASW RL on the forecastle); the new hangar holds a Westland Sea King ASW helicopter, and the flight deck incorporates Canadian Bear Trap haul-down gear. F 41 and F 42 also have openings in the hull sides beneath the helicopter deck at the stern. F 33 and F 34 received Type 199 variable-depth sonar; later units did not. The single Sea Cat quadruple SAM launcher in the F 33 has one MRS-3 director; later ships have two Dutch M-4 directors (with M-45 radar). F 41 and F 42 may receive SS-N-2 missiles, but are already overloaded. Later units have Decca-Racal Cutlass EW gear. All have Graseby G1738 towed torpedo decoys. F 33–36 are receiving U.S. Westinghouse sonar equipment (including VDS) in place of their original British equipment. F 41 and F 42 have the FT13-S/M TACAN system. F 34 has the prototype APSOH (Advanced Panoramic Sonar) active/passive system vice Type 184 hull-mounted.

◆ **2 British Leopard (Type 41) class**

| | Bldr | Laid down | L | In serv. |
|---|---|---|---|---|
| F 37 BEAS | Vickers-Armstrong | 1957 | 9-10-58 | 24-5-60 |
| F 38 BETWA | Vickers-Armstrong | 1957 | 15-9-59 | 8-12-60 |

**D:** 2,250 tons (2,515 fl) **S:** 25 kts
**Dim:** 103.63 (100.58 pp) × 12.19 × 4.80 (hull)
**A:** 2/114-mm DP Mk 6 (II × 1)—2/40-mm AA Mk 5 (II × 1)—1/Squid ASW mortar (III × 1)
**Electron Equipt:** Radar: 1/293, 1/978, 1/275
Sonar: 1/177, 1/162, 1/174B
**M:** 8 Admiralty 16 VVS ASR1 diesels; 2 props; 12,380 hp
**Electric:** 1,200 kw **Range:** 7,500/15 **Man:** 240 tot.

**FRIGATES** *(continued)*

**Brahmaputra (F 31)**—now stricken, others similar French Navy, 4-85

REMARKS: Beginning in 1978 with *Brahmaputra* (F 31, stricken 30-6-86), all had their after 114-mm twin gun mounts replaced by an accommodations deckhouse to act as cadet training ships. F 37 was modernized during 1980, F 38 in 1981. The 40-mm radar GFCS was removed.

◆ **2 British Whitby class**

| | Bldr | Laid down | L | In serv. |
|---|---|---|---|---|
| F 40 TALWAR | Cammell Laird | 1957 | 18-7-58 | 4-60 |
| F 43 TRISHUL | Harland & Wolff | 1957 | 18-6-58 | 1-60 |

**Trishul (F 43)** U.S. Navy, 3-87

**D:** 2,144 tons (2,560 fl) **S:** 30 kts **Dim:** 112.7 × 12.5 × 5.4 (over sonar)
**A:** 3/SS-N-2 Styx SSM (I × 3)—8/30-mm AA (II × 2)—6/324-mm ASW TT (III × 2)—1/Limbo triple ASW mortar—1/Chetak light ASW helicopter
**Electron Equipt:** Radar: 1/ZW-06A, 1/RALW-04, 1/Square Tie, 2/Drum Tilt
Sonar: 1/177, 1/174B, 1/162 (possibly updated)
EW: . . . intercept
**M:** 2 sets GT; 2 props; 30,000 hp **Electric:** 1,140 kw
**Boilers:** 2 Babcock & Wilcox; 38.7 kg/cm², 450°C
**Fuel:** 370 tons
**Range:** 4,500/12
**Man:** 11 officers, 220 men

REMARKS: Three SS-N-2 Styx launchers—removed from Osa-I-class, guided-missile patrol boats—replaced the twin 114-mm Mk 6 gun mount in these two ships. Soviet Square Tie radar associated with Styx replaced the gun director, atop the pilothouse. Further refitted 1982–83 at Mazagon Dockyard, Bombay, with larger hangar and haul-down system at the expense of the one Limbo ASW mortar; new radars, and Soviet AA guns. Modernization of F 43 reported delayed by yard problems, 7-85, but completed by early 1987.

**CORVETTES**

◆ **0 (+4 + 8) Khukri class**

| | Bldr | Laid down | L | In serv. |
|---|---|---|---|---|
| P . . . KHUKRI | Mazagon DY, Bombay | 27-9-85 | 3-12-86 | . . . |
| P . . . N . . . | Mazagon DY, Bombay | 9-86 | . . . | . . . |
| P . . . N . . . | Mazagon DY, Bombay | . . . | . . . | . . . |
| P . . . N . . . | Mazagon DY, Bombay | . . . | . . . | . . . |
| P . . . N . . . | Garden Reach DY, Calcutta | . . . | . . . | . . . |
| P . . . N . . . | Garden Reach DY, Calcutta | . . . | . . . | . . . |

**D:** 1,200 tons (fl) **S:** 27 kts **Dim:** 90.0 × . . . × . . .
**A:** 4/SS-N-2C SSM (II × 2)—1/76-mm DP—4/30-mm AA (II × 2) or 2/30-mm gatling AA (I × 2)—6/324-mm ASW TT (III × 2)—1/light helicopter (deck only)
**Electron Equipt:** Radar: 1/Square Tie, 1/ZW-06A(?), 1/Bass Tilt
Sonar: . . .—EW: . . .
**M:** 2 SEMT-Pielstick 18 PA6 BTC diesels; 2/306 rpm CP props; 16,920 hp (12,800 sust.)
**Range:** . . . **Man:** . . .

REMARKS: Known also as DP 25 class. First four are to be of an ASW-capable version, the next four (plus four more projected) to be of general-purpose configuration. Intended to replace the Petya class. Later units may incorporate gas turbines in the propulsion system and may have a Soviet-supplied SA-N-4 SAM system.

◆ **1 (+5 + 18) Soviet Tarantul-I class** Bldr: K 40–45: . . . SY, U.S.S.R.; others. Mazagon DY, Bombay

| | In serv. | | In serv. |
|---|---|---|---|
| K 40 VEER | 5-87 | K 43 N . . . | . . . |
| K 41 N . . . | . . . | K 44 N . . . | . . . |
| K 42 N . . . | . . . | K 45 N . . . | . . . |

**D:** 480 tons (580 fl) **S:** 36 kts **Dim:** 56.5 × 10.5 × 2.5
**A:** 4/SS-N-2C SSM (II × 2)—1/76.2-mm DP—1/SA-N-5 SAM syst. (IV × 1; . . . Grail missiles)—2/30-mm gatling AA (I × 2)
**Electron Equipt:** Radar: 1/Krivach nav., 1/Bass Tilt, 1/Plank Shave
EW: . . .—IFF: 1/High Pole, 1/Square Head
**M:** CODOG or COGOG: 2 NK-12MV gas turbines (12,000 hp each) two cruise gas turbines or diesels (3–4,000 hp each); 2 props
**Range:** . . . **Man:** . . .

REMARKS: First five (or six?) ordered 1984 for delivery 1986–89 from the U.S.S.R. Six to be built by Mazagon Dockyard ordered 1-87. To replace Osa-I and Osa-II missile boats, taking their names.

◆ **3 Soviet Nanuchka-II class** Bldr: Petrovskiy SY, Leningrad

K 71 VIJAYDURG (In serv. 12-76)
K 72 SINDHURDURG (In serv. 5-77)
K 73 HOSDURG (In serv. 1-78)

**D:** 675 tons (fl) **S:** 32 kts **Dim:** 59.3 × 12.6 × 2.4
**A:** 4/SS-N-2C (II × 2)—1/SA-N-4 SAM system (II × 1, 2 Gecko missiles)—2/57-mm AA (II × 1)
**Electron Equipt:** Radar: 1/Square Tie, 1/Pop Group, 1/Muff Cob, 1/Don-2
IFF: 2/Square Head, 1/High Pole (probably replaced)
EW: passive syst., 2 chaff RL (XVI × 2)
**M:** 3 Type M521-TM5 diesels; 3 props; 25,996 hp
**Range:** 900/30; 2,500/12 **Man:** 60 tot.

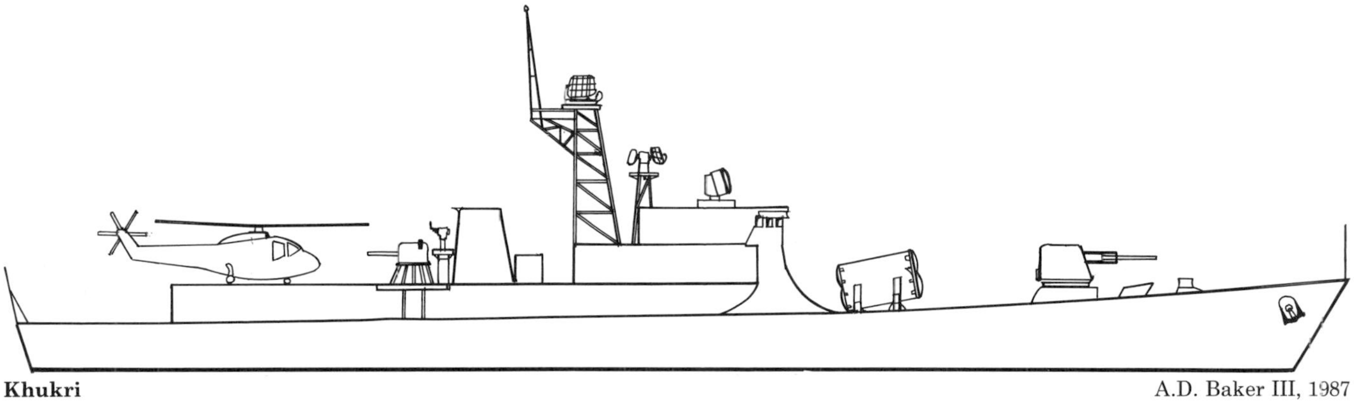

**Khukri** A.D. Baker III, 1987

**CORVETTES** *(continued)*

**Sindhurdurg (K 72)** 4-79

REMARKS: Arrived in India 3-77, 8-77, and 3-78. Three or more additional units were reportedly ordered 20-12-82, but no deliveries have taken place. Poor sea boats. The "Band Stand" radome covers a Square Tie antenna in these export units. The diesels each are composed of two coupled M504 diesel engines.

◆ **9 Soviet Petya-II class** Bldr: U.S.S.R.

| | | |
|---|---|---|
| P 68 ARNALA | P 74 ANDAMAN | P 78 KADMATH |
| P 69 ANDROTH | P 75 AMINI | P 79 KILTAN |
| P 73 ANJADIP | P 77 KAMORTA | P 81 KATCHAL |

**Andaman (P 74)** G. Arra, 1982

**D:** 950 tons (1,150 fl) **S:** 29 kts **Dim:** 81.8 (78.0 pp) × 9.2 × 2.9 (hull)
**A:** 4/76.2-mm DP (II × 2)—4/RBU-2500 ASW RL (XVI × 4)—3/533-mm TT (III × 1)—2/d.c. racks—2/mine rails
**Electron Equipt:** Radar: 1/Don-2, 1/Slim Net, 1/Hawk Screech
Sonar: 1 Hercules med.-freq.
**M:** CODOG: 1 Type 61-D3 diesel (6,000 hp), 2 gas turbines (15,000 hp each); 3 props; 36,000 hp
**Range:** 450/29; 4,800/10 **Man:** 98 tot.

REMARKS: Transferred in 1969, 1972, and 1975. Were new-construction, export-version ships. Sister *Kavaratti* (P 80) stricken 8-86. To be replaced by *Khukri* class.

**GUIDED-MISSILE PATROL BOATS**

◆ **8 Soviet Osa-II class**

| | | | |
|---|---|---|---|
| K 90 PRACHAND | K 92 PRABAL | K 94 CHAMAK | K 96 CHAPAK |
| K 91 PRALAYA | K 93 PRATAP | K 95 CHAPAL | K 97 CHARAG |

**Prabal (K 92)**—note EW antenna atop mast, Soviet IFF gear deleted
French Navy, 1986

**D:** 215 tons (240 fl) **S:** 35 kts **Dim:** 38.6 × 7.6 × 2.0
**A:** 4/SS-N-2B Styx (I × 4)—4/30-mm AA (II × 2)
**Electron Equipt:** Radar: 1/Square Tie, 1/Drum Tilt—EW: . . .
**M:** 3 M504 diesels; 3 props; 15,000 hp **Range:** 500/34; 750/25 **Man:** 30 tot.

REMARKS: To be equipped with modern EW system. First four in service 17-2-76, second four on 5-11-76.

◆ **5 Soviet Osa-I class** (In serv. 1971)

| | | |
|---|---|---|
| K 83 VIDYUT | K 86 NIPAT | K 89 NIRGHAT |
| K 85 VINASH | K 88 NIRBHIK | |

**D:** 175 tons (209 fl) **S:** 36 kts **Dim:** 38.6 × 7.6 × 1.8
**A:** 4/SS-N-2A Styx (I × 4)—4/30-mm AA (II × 2)
**Electron Equipt:** Radar: 1/Square Tie, 1/Drum Tilt—EW: . . .
**M:** 3 M503A diesels; 3 props; 12,000 hp **Range:** 500/34; 750/25 **Man:** 30 tot.

REMARKS: Transferred 1971. *Vijeta* (K 84) and *Nashat* (K 87) had their missile tubes removed and three from each placed on the frigates *Talwar* (F 40) and *Trishul* (F 43). Both, however, remained in service as patrol boats. Sister *Veer* (K 82) apparently stricken 1987, as name is now borne by a Tarantul.

**PATROL BOATS**

◆ **7 SDB Mk 3 class**

| | Bldr | Laid down | L | In serv. |
|---|---|---|---|---|
| T 58 N . . . | Garden Reach, Calcutta | 17-2-83 | 20-12-83 | 26-3-85 |
| T 59 N . . . | Goa SY | 24-3-83 | 17-1-84 | 13-7-85 |
| T 60 N . . . | Garden Reach, Calcutta | . . . | 20-3-84 | 24-8-85 |
| T 61 N . . . | Goa SY | . . . | 17-1-86 | 1985 |
| T 62 N . . . | Garden Reach, Calcutta | . . . | . . . | 1986 |
| T 63 RAJKAMAL | Goa SY | . . . | . . . | 10-86 |
| T 64 N . . . | Garden Reach, Calcutta | . . . | . . . | 1986 |

**D:** 210 tons (fl) **S:** 34 kts **Dim:** 37.80 × . . . × 1.30 (hull)
**A:** 1/40-mm AA—. . .
**Electron Equipt:** Radar: 1/. . . nav.—Sonar: . . .
**M:** 2 MTU diesels; 2 props; 9,200 hp **Man:** 34 tot.

REMARKS: Intended as an improved version of the SDB Mk 2 with better hull form, less rake to propeller shafts. Probably also have a centerline cruise engine. Speed also reported as 28 kts for Goa-built units.

◆ **5 SDB Mk 2 class** Bldr: Garden Reach SB & Eng., Calcutta

| | L | In serv. | | L | In serv. |
|---|---|---|---|---|---|
| T 51 N . . . . . . . | 31-12-75 | 17-11-78 | T 56 RAJTARANG | 2-81 | 1984 |
| T 52 N . . . . . . . | 16-7-76 | 3-9-77 | T 57 RAJSHREE | 27-5-83 | 1984 |
| T 53 N . . . . . . . | 12-4-78 | 17-11-78 | | | |

**D:** 160 tons (203 fl) **S:** 29 kts **Dim:** 37.50 × 7.50 × 1.75
**A:** 1/40-mm CT AA—2/d.c. racks (18 Mk 7 d.c.)
**M:** 2 Deltic 18-42K diesels; 2 props; 6,240 hp; 1 Kirloskar Cummins NH-220 cruise diesel, 165 hp (for 6-kt cruising)
**Electric:** 220 kVA **Range:** 1,400/14 **Man:** 4 officers, 26 men

◆ **2 Soviet Osa-I class** (In serv. 1971)

. . . VIJETA (ex-K 84) . . . NASHAT (ex-K 87)

REMARKS: Missile tubes removed, as noted above. *Nashat* was converted to carry frogmen in 1980.

**MINE WARFARE SHIPS**

◆ **0 (+10) new-construction minehunters** Bldr: Goa SY and . . .

REMARKS: Construction of a license-built version of a standard modern Western European minehunter is contemplated. To be built of GRP and twin-screwed, the first two would be built in Europe. The Tripartite, Karlskrona *Landsort,* Vosper *Sandown,* and Intermarine *Lerici* are in competition.

◆ **8 (+4) Soviet Natya class** Bldr: Ust Izhora SY, Kolpino

| | | | |
|---|---|---|---|
| M 61 PONDICHERY | M 63 BEDI | M 65 ALLEPPY | M 67 KAMAR |
| M 62 PORBANDAR | M 64 BHAVNAGAR | M 66 RATNAGIRI | M 70 KAKINADA |

**Kakinada (M 70)** L. & L. Van Ginderen, 5-87

**MINE WARFARE SHIPS** *(continued)*

**Alleppy (M 65)** French Navy, 7-80

**D:** 650 tons (750 fl) **S:** 20 kts **Dim:** 61.0 × 9.8 × 3.0
**A:** 4/30-mm AA (II × 2)—4/25-mm AA (II × 2)—2/RBU-1200 ASW RL (V × 2)—mines
**Electron Equipt:** Radar: 1/Don-2, 1/Drum Tilt—Sonar: 1/HF hull-mounted
IFF: 2/Square Head, 1/High Pole B
**M:** 2 diesels; 2 props; 8,000 hp **Range:** 1,800/16; 5,200/10 **Man:** 80 tot.

REMARKS: Of first batch, two transferred in 1978, two in 1979, and two in 1980. Differ from the units in the Soviet Navy in that they do not have a ramp at the stern. Can be used as ASW escorts. Six additional units ordered 20-17-82. Aluminum/steel alloy construction. M 67 delivered 10-86; M 70, in 5-87, appears to mount Soviet SA-N-5 SAM systems abreast mast.

◆ **6 Soviet Yevgenya-class inshore minesweepers** (First 3 in serv. 15-5-83, others: 2-84)

| | | |
|---|---|---|
| M 83 MAHE | M 85 MANGALORE | M 87 MULKI |
| M 84 MALWAN | M 86 MALPE | M 88 MAGDALA |

**D:** 80 tons (90 fl) **S:** 11 kts **Dim:** 26.2 × 6.1 × 1.5
**A:** 2/14.5-mm mg (II × 1) **Electron Equipt:** Radar: 1/Spin Trough
**M:** 2 diesels; 2 props; 600 hp **Range:** 300/10 **Man:** 10 tot.

REMARKS: Glass-reinforced plastic construction. Equipped for shallow-water mine-hunting with a towed television and marker-buoy dispenser.

◆ **4 British "Ham"-class inshore minesweepers**

| | Bldr | L |
|---|---|---|
| M 79 BIMLIPATHAM (ex-*Hildersham*) | Vosper, Portsmouth | 5-2-54 |
| M 80 BASSEIN (ex-*Littleham*) | Brooke Marine, Lowestoft | 4-5-54 |
| M 81 BHATKAL | Mazagon DY, Bombay | 5-67 |
| M 82 BULSAR | Mazagon DY, Bombay | 17-5-69 |

**Bhatkal (M 81)**—old pendant number 1968

**D:** 120 tons (159 fl) **S:** 14 kts (9, sweeping)
**Dim:** 32.43 (30.48 pp) × 6.45 × 1.7 **A:** 1/20-mm AA
**Electron Equipt:** Radar: 1/978 **Man:** 2 officers, 13 men
**M:** 2 Paxman YHAXM diesels; 2 props; 1,000 hp **Fuel:** 25 tons

REMARKS: M 79 and M 80 were transferred in 1955. The Indian-built units have teakwood hulls but are otherwise almost identical.

**AMPHIBIOUS WARFARE SHIPS**

◆ **1 (+7) Magar-class tank landing ships** Bldr: Garden Reach Dockyard, Calcutta

| | Laid down | L | In serv. |
|---|---|---|---|
| L.11 MAGAR | . . . | 7-11-84 | 10-87 |

**D:** 3,200 tons (fl) **S:** 17 kts **Dim:** 126.4 × 17.7 × 3.8
**A:** . . . **Electron Equipt:** Radar: . . .
**M:** 2 SEMT-Pielstick diesels; 2 props; 8,560 hp
**Range:** . . . **Man:** . . .

REMARKS: Design based on British *Sir Bedivere* class. Seven more planned. Has bow doors and helicopter deck aft. Second unit ordered 1985.

◆ **8 Soviet Polnocny-C class** Bldr: Polnocny SY, Gdansk, Poland

| | | | |
|---|---|---|---|
| L 14 GHORPAD | L 15 KESARI | L 16 SHARDUL | L 17 SHARABH |
| L 18 CHEETAH | L 19 MAHISH | L 20 GULDAR | L 21 KUMBHIR |

**Kumbhir (L 21)** French Navy, 2-86

**Mahish (L 19)** L. Grazioli, 7-85

**D:** 1,150 (fl) **S:** 18 kts **Dim:** 81.3 × 10.1 × 2.1
**A:** 4/30-mm AA (II × 2)—2/140-mm rocket launchers (VIII × 2)
**Electron Equipt:** Radar: 1/Don-2 (Krivach in L 18—L 21)
**M:** 2 diesels; 2 props; 5,000 hp
**Range:** 900/17; 1,500/14 **Man:** 60 tot.

REMARKS: L 14 transferred in 1975, L 17 in 1976, L 18 in 12-84, L 19 in 7-85, rest by end 1986. First four do not have a helicopter platform as on other export Polnocny-Cs. Cargo: 350 tons and up to 140 troops. L 19 delivered 7-85, L 20 in 11-86, and L 21 in 2-86.

◆ **1 Soviet Polnocny-A class** Bldr: Polnocny SY, Gdansk, Poland

L 12 GHARIAL

**D:** 770 tons (fl) **S:** 19 kts **Dim:** 73.0 × 8.6 × 2.0
**A:** 2/25-mm AA (II × 1)—2/140-mm rocket-launchers (XVIII × 2)
**Electron Equipt:** Radar: 1/Don-2 **M:** 2 diesels; 2 props; 5,000 hp
**Range:** 900/18; 1,500/14 **Man:** 40 tot.

REMARKS: Transferred 1966. Cargo: 180 tons. Sister *Guldar* (L 13) stricken 1984.

◆ **6 (+1) Vasco da Gama-class utility landing craft**

| | Bldr | L | In serv. |
|---|---|---|---|
| L 34 VASCO DA GAMA | Goa SY, Goa | 29-11-78 | 28-1-80 |
| L 35 N . . . . . . . | Hooghly DY, Calcutta | 16-3-80 | 17-12-83 |
| L 36 N . . . . . . . | Goa SY, Goa | 13-1-79 | 1-12-80 |
| L 37 N . . . . . . . | Goa SY, Goa | 22-7-85 | 1986 |
| L 38 MIDHUR | Goa SY, Goa | 2-86 | 1987 |
| L 39 MANGALA | Goa SY, Goa | 2-86 | 25-5-87 |
| L 40 N . . . . . . . | Goa SY, Goa | . . . | . . . |

**D:** 500 tons (fl) **S:** 9 kts **Dim:** 55.96 × 7.94 × 1.71 (aft)
**A:** 2/40-mm AA (I × 2)—mines
**M:** 3 Kirloskar-M.A.N. W8V 17.5/22 AMAL diesels; 3 Kort-nozzle props; 1,245 hp
**Range:** 1,000/8

REMARKS: Cargo: 250 tons or 150 men.

### HYDROGRAPHIC SURVEY SHIPS

◆ **3 (+2) Sandhayak class** Bldr: Garden Reach SB & Engineers, Calcutta

| | | L | In serv. | | L | In serv. |
|---|---|---|---|---|---|---|
| J . . . | SANDHAYAK | 6-4-77 | 26-2-81 | J . . . N . . . | . . . | . . . |
| J . . . | NIRDESHAK | 16-11-78 | 4-10-83 | J . . . N . . . | . . . | . . . |
| J . . . | NIPURAK | 10-7-81 | 14-8-85 | | | |

**D:** 1,200 tons (1,820 fl) **S:** 16.75 kts **Dim:** 85.77 (78.80 pp) × 12.30 × 3.34
**A:** 2/40-mm AA (I × 2)—1/Chetak helicopter
**Electron Equipt:** Radar: 1/Decca TM-series navigational
**M:** 1 GRSE-M.A.N. G8V 30/45 ATL diesel; 1 prop; 3,920 hp (plus 1 Pleuger 200-hp active rudder; 5 kts)
**Fuel:** 264 tons **Range:** 6,000/14 **Man:** 12 officers, 134 men

REMARKS: 2,050 grt. Telescoping hangar. Four inshore survey launches with "Hydrodist" fixing system. Have 3 precision depth-finders, Decca "Navigator," Decca "Hi-Fix," taut-wire measuring gear, and a gravimeter. Carry 169 tons water and 5 tons aviation fuel. Construction of 4th unit approved under 1985 Budget, and a fifth is planned. Fourth laid down 1987.

◆ **1 hydrographic survey ship**

| | Bldr | L | In serv. |
|---|---|---|---|
| J 14 DARSHAK | Hindustan SY, India | 2-11-59 | 28-12-61 |

**Darshak (J 14)** 1974

**D:** 2,790 tons **S:** 16 kts **Dim:** 97.3 × 14.94 × 5.8
**A:** 1/40-mm AA—1/Chetak helicopter
**M:** 2 diesels, electric drive; 2 props; 3,000 hp **Man:** 150 tot.

◆ **4 inshore survey ships** Bldr: Goa SY, Vasco da Gama (In serv. 1984–85)

J 33 N . . . . . . . J 34 N . . . . . . . J 35 N . . . . . . . J 36 N . . . . . . .

**D:** 185 **S:** 12.5 kts **Dim:** 37.5 × 7.5 × 1.75
**M:** diesels **Range:** 1,500/12.5

REMARKS: J 34 launched 28-5-83 and J 35 on 10-8-83. Steel-hulled. Same hulls as SDB Mk 2 patrol-boat class.

◆ **2 Gaveshani-class small inshore survey craft**

J . . . GAVESHANI J . . . N . . . . . . .

REMARKS: Launched 2-76.

NOTE: The modern and elaborately equipped research ships operated by the National Oceanographic Institute are non-naval. They include: *Sagar Kanya, Sagar Sampada, Samudra Manthan, Samudra Sarveshak, Samudra Nidhi,* and *Samudra Sandhari.*

### AUXILIARY SHIPS

◆ **1 Soviet Ugra-class submarine tender** Bldr: U.S.S.R. (In serv. 28-12-68)

A 54 AMBA

**Amba (A 54)** 1968

**D:** 6,750 tons (9,600 fl) **S:** 20 kts **Dim:** 145.0 × 17.7 × 6.4
**A:** 4/76.2-mm DP (II × 2)
**Electron Equipt:** Radar: 1/Don-2, 1/Slim Net, 2/Hawk Screech
**M:** 4 diesels; 2 props; 8,000 hp **Range:** 21,000/10

REMARKS: Helicopter platform. Quarters for 750 men. Two 6-ton cranes, one 10-ton crane.

◆ **1 Soviet T 58-class submarine-rescue ship**

A 55 NISTAR

**D:** 930 tons (fl) **S:** 17 kts **Dim:** 71.7 × 9.1 × 2.7
**Electron Equipt:** Radar: 1/Don-2 **M:** 2 diesels; 2 props; 4,000 hp
**Range:** 2,500/12 **Man:** 60 tot.

REMARKS: Built during late 1950s, transferred 1971. Two rescue chambers, port and starboard sides of the stern. Decompression chamber, diving bells.

NOTE: Two new submarine rescue ships are programmed to be built in India.

◆ **1 repair ship** Bldr: Foundation Maritime, Canada (L: 25-7-44)

A 52 DHARINI (ex-*La Petite Hermine,* ex-*Ketowna Park*)

**D:** 6,000 tons (fl) **S:** 9 kts **Dim:** 99.0 × 13.9 × 4.0
**M:** triple-expansion reciprocating steam; 1 prop; 800 hp **Fuel:** 620 tons

REMARKS: Sold to India for cargo use, 1953; in service in Indian Navy 5-60.

◆ **1 transport** Bldr: Mazagon DY, Bombay

. . . N . . . . . . .

**D:** 1,800 grt **S:** 20 kts **Dim:** 74.0 (pp) × 14.4 × . . .
**M:** 2 diesels; 2 props; 8,000 hp

REMARKS: Ordered 3-81. No other details available.

◆ **1 hospital ship** Bldr: Hindustan SY, Calcutta

LAKSHADWEEP (L: 28-8-81)

**D:** . . . **S:** 12 kts **Dim:** 52.0 (46.8 pp) × 9.5 × 3.0
**M:** 2 diesels; 2 props; 900 hp
**Man:** 19 crew, plus 15 medical staff (90 hospital berths)

REMARKS: Laid down 2-81.

◆ **1 (+1) training ships** Bldr: Mazagon DY, Bombay

| | Laid down | L | In serv. |
|---|---|---|---|
| TIR | . . . | 15-4-83 | 21-2-86 |
| N . . . | . . . | . . . | . . . |

**D:** . . . **S:** . . . **Dim:** 107.0 × . . . × . . . **A:** 4/. . . **M:** diesels

REMARKS: *Tir* ordered 1981, was intended to supplement the *Leopard* class and carries approximately 120 cadets. Was to have completed 3-84, delayed by yard problems. Second ship ordered 5-86 from same builder. Helicopter facilities.

### OILERS

◆ **2 (+2) Deepak class** Bldr: Bremer Vulkan Schiffbau, Bremen-Vegesack, West Germany (Third ship: Garden Reach SB & Eng., Calcutta)

A 50 DEEPAK (In serv. 20-11-72) A 57 SHAKTI (In serv. 21-2-76)

**Shakti (A 57)** French Navy, 1986

**D:** 6,785 tons (22,000 fl) **S:** 20 kts **Dim:** 168.43 (157.50 pp) × 23.0 × 9.14
**A:** 3/40-mm AA (I × 3)—2/20-mm AA (I × 2) **M:** 1 set GT; 1 prop; 16,500 hp
**Boilers:** 2 Babcock & Wilcox **Range:** 5,500/18.5 **Man:** 169 tot.

REMARKS: 12,690 grt/15,800 dwt. Two liquid-replenishment stations per side, with British-style rigs. Telescoping hangar and flight deck for one helicopter. Carry 12,624 tons fuel oil, 1,280 tons diesel fuel, 1,495 tons aviation fuel, 812 tons fresh water, and some dry cargo. Third unit, ordered 1987, may differ. Fourth planned.

◆ **1 former merchant tanker** Bldr: Japan (In serv. 1959)

DESH DEEP

**D:** 16,400 tons (fl) **S:** 13 kts **Dim:** 145.0 (135.0 pp) × 19.5 × 7.8
**M:** 2 Sulzer 6-cyl. diesels; 2 props; 8,200 hp **Electric:** 320 kw
**Fuel:** 1,056 tons **Range:** 23,000/13 **Man:** . . . tot.

REMARKS: 8,324 grt, 12,177 dwt. Taken over 1972 and operated as a freighting tanker. Cargo: 11,800 tons (100,048 $m^3$).

### TUGS

◆ **2 Gaj-class oceangoing tugs** Bldr: Garden Reach SB & Eng., Calcutta

A 51 GAJ (In serv. 20-9-73) A. . . MATANGA (L: 29-10-77; in serv. 1983)

**D:** 1,465 tons (1,600 fl) **S:** 15 kts **Dim:** 66.0 (60.0 pp) × 11.6 × 4.0
**A:** none **M:** 2 GRSE-M.A.N. G7V diesels; 2 CP props; 3,292 hp
**Range:** 8,000/12

**TUGS** *(continued)*

**Gaj (A 51)** 1977

Remarks: Fitted for salvage work. 40-ton bollard pull. *Matanga* reported as 62.0 m overall by 12.3 beam, 3,920 hp.

### YARD AND SERVICE CRAFT

◆ **1 coastal tanker** Bldr: Central Inland Water Transport Corp., Rajabagan SY, Calcutta

Palan (In serv 5-86)

**D:** approx. 1,200 tons (fl) **S:** . . . **Dim:** 57.94 (54.39 pp) × 9.10 × 3.10
**M:** 2 M.A.N. diesels; 1 prop; 1,440 hp

Remarks: 624 grt/715 dwt.

◆ **1 fuel lighter** Bldr: Rajabagan SY, Bombay

Poshak (In serv. 4-82)

**D:** 600 tons **S:** 8 kts **Dim:** 36.3 × 7.6 × 2.4
**M:** 1 M.A.N. diesel; 255 hp **Cargo:** 200 tons dwt.

◆ **2 fuel lighters** Bldr: Rajabagan SY, Bombay

Purak (In serv. 3-6-77) Pradhayak (In serv. 2-78)

**D:** 960 tons (fl) **S:** 9 kts **Dim:** 49.7 × 8.1 × 3.0
**M:** 1 diesel; 1 prop; 560 hp **Cargo:** 376 tons dwt.

◆ **3 water lighters** Bldr: 1 by Rajabagan SY, Bombay; others: Mazagon DY, Bombay

**D:** 200 tons **S:** 9 kts **Dim:** 32.0 × . . . × 2.4
**M:** 1 diesel; 1 prop; . . . hp

◆ **1 torpedo trials and retrieval craft** Bldr: P.S. & Co., Bombay

A 71 Astravahini (In serv. 8-9-83)

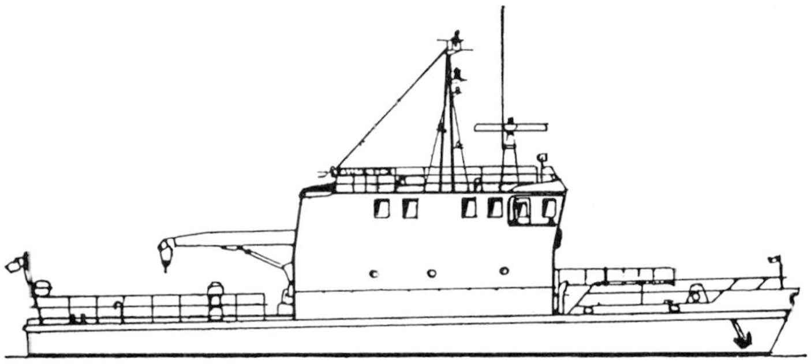

**Astravahini (A 71)** P.S. & Co., 1983

Remarks: No details available.

◆ **2 torpedo retrievers** Bldr: Goa SY, Vasco da Gama

A 71 N . . . . . . . (In serv. 16-9-82) A 72 N . . . . . . . (L: 5-11-80)

**D:** 110 tons (fl) **S:** 11 kts **Dim:** 28.5 × 6.1 × 1.4
**M:** 1 Kirlasker-M.A.N. 12-cyl. diesel; 1 prop; 300 hp

◆ **3 diving tenders** Bldr: Cleback SY (In serv. 1979, 2-84, 8-84)

**D:** 36 tons (fl) **S:** 12 kts **Dim:** 14.89 (13.37 pp) × 4.40 × 1.21
**M:** 2 Premier Auto-Meadows diesels; 2 props; 130 hp **Fuel:** 2 tons

◆ **1 coastal tug** Bldr: Garden Reach S.B. & Eng., Calcutta

Rajaji (In serv. 7-82)

**D:** 428 tons **S:** 12.5 kts **Dim:** 30.5 × 9.5 × 3.8
**M:** 2 Garden Reach-M.A.N. diesels; 2 Kort-nozzle props; 2,120 hp

Note: Construction of four new tugs was authorized under the 1985 Budget.

◆ **3 large harbor tugs** Bldr: Mazagon Dock, Bombay (In serv. 1973–74)

Ajaral Arjun Balshil

◆ **1 sail-training craft** Bldr: Alcock Ashdown, Bhavnagar

Varuna (In serv. 20-4-81) **D:** 130 tons (fl) **Dim:** 30.5 × . . . × . . .

Remarks: Two-masted brig for training Sea Cadets. Construction of a second sail-training ship has been proposed; to carry 90 cadets.

Note: There are undoubtedly a large number of other yard and service craft, for which no names or data are available. A new floating dry dock for Ft. Blair in the Andaman Islands was announced 1986.

## COAST GUARD

Personnel (1986): 80 officers, 400 men

The Coast Guard was established 1-2-77 to ensure surveillance of India's 200-nautical-mile economic zone. Commanded by an admiral, it consisted initially of ships and craft transferred from the Indian Navy. The Indian Customs Service was merged with the Coast Guard in April 1982. The name "Coast Guard" is written in large black letters on the sides of ship hulls, which are painted white.

Coast Guard Aviation: In service are 2 Fokker F-27 Friendship transports, 3 or more Dornier Do-228 for surveillance, and six Chetak (Alouette-III) helicopters. Thirty-six Do-228 and 34 helicopters are expected to be in service by 2000.

### PATROL SHIPS

◆ **0 (+7) new construction** Bldr: Korea Tacoma SY, Masan, South Korea, and . . .

| | Laid down | L | In serv. |
|---|---|---|---|
| 39 N . . . | . . . | . . . | . . . |
| 40 N . . . | . . . | . . . | . . . |
| 41 N . . . | . . . | . . . | . . . |

**D:** approx. 1,600 fl **S:** . . . **Dim:** 85.0 × . . . × . . . **A:** . . . **M:** . . .

Remarks: Ordered 27-3-87. Four sisters to be built under license in India in lieu of the expanded versions of the unsatisfactory *Vikram* class that were to have been ordered in 1986.

◆ **3 (+3) Vikram class** Bldr: Mazagon DY, Bombay

| | Laid down | L | In serv. |
|---|---|---|---|
| 33 Vikram | 3-81 | 26-9-81 | 20-12-83 |
| 34 Visaya | . . . | . . . | 13-4-84 |
| 35 Veera | . . . | 30-6-84 | 3-5-86 |
| 36 Varuna | . . . | 1-2-86 | 3-88 |
| 37 Vajira | . . . | 31-1-87 | . . . |
| 38 N . . . | . . . | . . . | . . . |

**Visaya (34)** Mazagon DY, 1984

**D:** 940 tons (1,100 fl) **S:** 22 kts **Dim:** 74.10 × 11.40 × 3.00 (3.48 props)
**A:** 1/40-mm AA—1/Chetak (Alouette-III) helicopter
**Electron Equipt:** Radar: 1/Decca 1230, 1/Decca . . .
**M:** 2 SEMT-Pielstick 16 PA6 V80 diesels; 2 CP props; 12,800 hp
**Electric:** 880 kw **Fuel:** 108 tons **Range:** 3,500/14
**Man:** 10 officers, 12 chief petty officers, 52 men

Remarks: First 3 ordered 1979; second three ordered 1983. Have fin stabilizers, hangar for Chetak (license-built Alouette-III) helicopter. Have pollution-control equipment, diving gear, and firefighting monitors. *Varuna* has training facilities on the fantail in lieu of the anti-pollution equipment.

◆ **2 British Blackwood-class former ASW frigates**

| | Bldr | Laid down | L | In serv. |
|---|---|---|---|---|
| 31 Kirpan | Alex. Stephen, Glasgow | 1957 | 9-8-58 | 7-59 |
| 32 Kuthar | Samuel White, Cowes | 1957 | 14-10-58 | 1960 |

**D:** 1,180 tons (1,456 fl) **S:** 23 kts **Dim:** 94.5 (91.44 pp) × 10.05 × 4.7
**A:** 3/40-mm AA (I × 3)—
**Electron Equipt:** Radar: 2/navigational—EW: Decca-Racal Cutlass intercept
**M:** 1 set GT; 1 prop; 15,000 hp **Electric:** 1,108 kw
**Boilers:** 2 Babcock & Wilcox; 38.7 kg/cm$^2$; 450°C **Range:** 4,500/12

**INDIA** *(continued)*
**PATROL SHIPS** *(continued)*

**Kirpan (31)**—in naval service 1969

Remarks: Transferred to the Coast Guard 1-7-77. Sister *Khukri* sunk 9-12-71 by a Pakistani submarine. Sonars and two Mk 10 Limbo triple ASW mortars removed by 1983.

### PATROL BOATS

◆ **2 (+4) Tara Bai class** Bldr: 71,72: Singapore SB & Eng., Ltd; others: Garden Reach SB & Eng., Ltd., Calcutta

| | L | In serv. | | L | In serv. |
|---|---|---|---|---|---|
| 71 Tara Bai | 4-87 | 20-5-87 | 74 N . . . | . . . | . . . |
| 72 Ahalya Bai | 5-87 | 7-87 | 75 N . . . | . . . | . . . |
| 73 N . . . | . . . | . . . | 76 N . . . | . . . | . . . |

**Tara Bai (71)**—on trials Singapore SB & Eng., 5-87

**D:** 173 tons normal (195 fl) **S:** 26 kts **Dim:** 44.90 (42.30 wl) × 7.00 × 1.89 (2.59 props)
**A:** 1/40-mm AA—2/7.62-mm mg (I × 2) **Electron Equipt:** Radar: 1/. . . nav.
**M:** 2 MTU 12V 538 TB82 diesels; 2 props; 4,400 hp (4,000 sust.)
**Range:** 2,400/14 **Fuel:** 30 tons **Endurance:** 7 days
**Man:** 5 officers, 27 men, 2 passengers
**Electric:** 260 kw (2 × 100 kw; 1 × 60 kw)

Remarks: Ordered 6-86, with license for the four to build in India. Air-conditioned. Five-ton towing hook. Rigid inflatable boat. Ten tons fresh water, with 3 ton/day distiller. HF/DF, echo-sounder, autopilot. Intended for SAR, fisheries patrol, sovereignty patrol, etc. Hull design based on standard Lürssen 45-m hull; steel construction.

◆ **7 (+8) Japanese design** Bldr: T 64: Sumidagawa SY, Tokyo; others: Garden Reach SB & Eng., Calcutta

| | In serv. | | In serv. |
|---|---|---|---|
| T 64 Jija Bai | 20-6-83 | T 72 N . . . | . . . |
| T 65 Rani Jindan | 1985 | T 73 N . . . | . . . |
| T 66 Kittur Chinnama | 1985 | T 74 N . . . | . . . |
| T 67 Ramadevi | 1985 | T 75 N . . . | . . . |
| T 68 Habbah Khatun | 1985 | T 76 N . . . | . . . |
| T 69 Avvaiyar | 19-10-85 | T 77 N . . . | . . . |
| T 70 N . . . | 1986 | T 79 N . . . | . . . |
| T 71 N . . . | . . . | | |

**D:** 273 tons (fl) **S:** 25 kts (sust.) **Dim:** 44.02 (41.10 pp) × 7.40 × 1.50 (hull)
**A:** 1/40-mm AA **Electron Equipt:** Radar: 1/nav. **Man:** 34
**M:** 2 MTU 12V538 TB82 diesels; 2 props; 4,030 hp **Range:** 2,375/14

**Jija Bai (T 64)** Sumidigawa, 1983

Remarks: Same basic design as Philippine Coast Guard's *Bessang Pass* class. Two additional units authorized in 1985 Budget.

◆ **6 SDB MK 2 class** Bldr: Garden Reach SB & Eng., Calcutta (T58, 59: Goa SY)

| | In serv. | | In serv. |
|---|---|---|---|
| T 54 Rajhans | 23-12-80 | T 57 Rajkamal | 10-86 |
| T 55 Rajtarang | 26-11-81 | T 58 N . . . | . . . |
| T 56 N . . . | 1985 | T 59 Rajshri | . . . |

**D:** 160 tons (203 fl) **S:** 29 kts **Dim:** 37.50 × 7.50 × 1.75
**A:** 1/20-mm AA **Electron Equipt:** Radar: . . .
**M:** 2 Deltic 18-42K diesels; 2 props; 6,240 hp; 1 Kirlaskar-Cummins NH-220 cruise diesel; 165 hp (6 kts)
**Range:** 1,400/14 **Man:** 4 officers, 26 men **Electric:** 220 kVA

Remarks: There is considerable confusion as to which boats of this class are assigned to the Coast Guard and which (if any) of these and the improved SDB Mk 3 design may belong to the Navy, due to overlapping of hull numbers and names.

Note: The five Soviet Poluchat-class patrol boats have been stricken—*Ponaji* (51) and *Panvel* (52) in 1985, and *Pamban* (53), *Puli* (54), and *Pulicat* (55) in 1986. Also discarded has been the SDB 1-class patrol boat *Abhay* (. . .).

### PATROL CRAFT

◆ **8 South Korean patrol craft** Bldr: Swallow Craft, Pusan (In serv. 1980–82)

C01–C08

**D:** 32 tons (35 fl) **S:** 26 kts **Dim:** 20.0 × 4.8 × 1.3
**A:** 1/7.62-mm mg **Electron Equipt:** Radar: 1/nav.
**M:** 2 MTU diesels; 2 props; 1,350 hp
**Range:** 600/20 **Man:** 12 tot.

Remarks: First six in service 24-7-80; last two taken over from India Oil Corp. 22-5-82.

◆ **5 12.5-meter class** Bldr: Mandovani Marine, . . . (In serv. 198. . .)

**D:** 10 tons (fl) **S:** 18 kts **Dim:** 12.5 × . . . × . . .
**M:** 2 Cummins diesels; 2 Hamilton waterjets; 550 hp

Remarks: GRP construction, deep-vee hull form.

◆ **. . . Norwegian SM-43 Smuggler-class launches** Bldr: GRW, India

**D:** . . . **S:** 36 kts **Dim:** 13.4 × . . . × . . .
**M:** 2 Castoldi waterjets; . . . hp **Man:** 4 tot.

Remarks: Acquired when the Coast Guard merged with the Customs Service in 4-82. Glass-reinforced plastic construction. Original design by Båtservice, Mandal, Norway.

# INDONESIA

Personnel (1986): 35,800, including 5,000 Marines and 1,000 Naval Aviation

Merchant Marine (1986): 1,707 ships—2,085,635 grt (tankers: 193 ships—603,394 grt)

Naval Aviation: The Indonesian Navy has a coastal-surveillance and logistic-support force consisting of 12 Australian N22B and 6 N22SL Searchmaster maritime surveillance aircraft, 6 C-47 Dakota transports, 3 Aero Commander light transports, and 4 CASA-212 light transports, plus 5 BO-105, 1 Alouette-III, and 14 Wasp helicopters. The first of 26 Nuritanio-built AS-332 Puma (NAS 132) helicopters was delivered 29-12-84, with all to deliver by end 1986, all to be fitted with AS.39 Exocet antiship missiles, Omega ORB-22 radar, Thomson-Sintra HS-12 dipping sonar and ASW torpedoes; unfortunately, only two had been delivered by 1-87. Four older Bell Model 476 helicopters were re-engined with

**NAVAL AVIATION** *(continued)*

turbines in 1984–85. The Air Force has 2 Boeing 737 Surveiller long-range maritime patrol aircraft (first delivered 6-83) with "Slammer" side-looking radar; a third was to convert by 1987. Also used are 3 C-130H-MP in a surveillance role. Six ITPN-Casa CN-235 light maritime surveillance aircraft were ordered 30-6-86.

WARSHIPS IN SERVICE OR UNDER CONSTRUCTION AS OF 1 JANUARY 1988

| | L | Tons (Surfaced) | Main armament |
|---|---|---|---|
| ◆ **2 submarines** | | | |
| 2 TYPE 209 | 1980 | 980 | 8/533-mm TT |
| ◆ **14 (+1) frigates** | | | |
| 1 TRAINING FRIGATE | 1980 | 1,850 | 4/Exocet, 1/57-mm DP |
| 3 FATAHILAH | 1977–79 | 1,160 | 4/Exocet, 1/120-mm DP, 1/40-mm |
| 3 (+1) VAN SPEIJK | 1965–66 | 2,200 | 8/Harpoon, 2/Sea Cat, 1/76-mm DP, ASW weapons, helicopter |
| 3 TRIBAL | 1960–62 | 2,300 | 2/114 mm DP, 2/Sea Cat, ASW weapons |
| 4 CLAUD JONES | 1958–59 | 1,450 | 1 or 2/76-mm, 6/Mk 32 TT |
| ◆ **4 guided-missile patrol boats** | | | |
| ◆ **22 (+ . . .) patrol boats** | | | |
| ◆ **2 (+2) minesweepers** | | | |
| ◆ **11 amphibious-warfare ships** | | | |

NOTE: The names of Indonesian ships are preceded by the designation KRI (*Kapalperang Republik Indonesia,* or Warship of the Republic of Indonesia).

## SUBMARINES

◆ **2 West German Type 209** Bldr: Howaldtswerke, Kiel

| | Laid down | L | In serv. |
|---|---|---|---|
| 401 CAKRA | 25-11-77 | 10-9-80 | 18-3-81 |
| 402 NANGGALA (ex-*Candrasa*) | 14-3-78 | 10-9-80 | 6-7-81 |

**Cakra (401)**—at builders for overhaul G. Gyssels, 6-86

**D:** 980/1,150/1,440 tons **S:** 11 (snorkel)/21.5 kts
**Dim:** 61.00 × 6.20 × 5.50 **A:** 8/533-mm TT (fwd)—14 total torpedoes
**Electron Equipt:** Radar: 1/Thompson-CSF Calypso
Sonar: 1/Atlas AN 526 passive, 1/CSU AN 407 A9 passive, DUUX-2
**M:** 4 MTU 12V493AZ diesels (600 hp each), 2 electric motors; 1 prop; 5,000 hp
**Range:** 16/21.5; 25/20; 230/8; 400/4—8,200/11 (snorkel)
**Man:** 6 officers, 28 men

REMARKS: Ordered 2-4-77. Can dive to 250 m. H.S.A. Sinbads weapons control. Ordering of a third has been postponed.

NOTE: Whiskey-class submarine *Pasopati* (410) listed in previous edition, was reportedly stricken during 1983.

## FRIGATES

◆ **1 training frigate** Bldr: Uljanic SY, Yugoslavia

| | Laid down | L | In serv. |
|---|---|---|---|
| HAJAR DEWANTARA | 11-5-79 | 11-10-80 | 20-8-81 |

**Hajar Dewantara (364)** 10-81

**D:** 1,850 tons (fl) **S:** 27 kts **Dim:** 96.70 (92.00 wl) × 11.20 × 3.55
**A:** 4/MM 38 Exocet SSM (II × 2)—1/57-mm Bofors—2.20-mm AA (I × 2)—2/ASW TT (2/SUT wire-guided torpedoes)—mines—1 BO-105 helicopter
**Electron Equipt:** Radar: 1/Decca 1229, 1/H.S.A. WM-28
Sonar: PHS-32
EW: SUSIE-I system—2/128-mm flare RL (II × 2)
**M:** CODOG: 1 Rolls-Royce Olympus TM-3B gas turbine, 27,250 hp; 2 MTU 16V956 TP91 diesels, 7,000 hp; 2 CP props
**Fuel:** 338 tons **Range:** 1,150/27 (gas turbine); 4,000/20 (diesels)
**Man:** 92 crew + 100 students

REMARKS: Same basic design as ship laid down in 1977 for Iraq. Ordered 14-3-78. SEWACO GM 101-41 computerized data system. Fin stabilizers, 114 tons water ballast, 50 tons potable water, 7 tons helo fuel. Carries two LCVP-type landing craft. 1,000 rounds 57-mm, 3,120 rounds 20-mm ammunition. Gas turbine rated at 22,300 hp in tropics. WM-28 track-while-scan fire-control radar not fitted at time of delivery. Second unit, reported ordered 7-83, has apparently *not* materialized.

◆ **3 Fatahilah class** Bldr: Wilton-Fijenoord, Schiedam, the Netherlands

| | Laid down | L | In serv. |
|---|---|---|---|
| 361 FATAHILAH | 31-1-77 | 22-12-77 | 16-7-79 |
| 362 MALAHAYATI | 28-7-77 | 19-6-78 | 21-3-80 |
| 363 NALA | 27-1-78 | 11-1-79 | 8-80 |

**Malahayati (362)** R. Gillett, 11-84

**Nala (363)**—with hangar in folded state 1980

**D:** 1,160 tons (1,450 fl) **S:** 30 kts (21 diesel) **Dim:** 83.85 × 11.10 × 3.30
**A:** 361,362: 4/MM 38 Exocet SSM (II × 2)—1/120-mm Bofors L-46 DP—1/40-mm Bofors L-70—2/20-mm AA (I × 2)—2/375-mm Bofors SR-375A ASW RL (II × 1)—6/324-mm Mk 32 ASW TT (III × 2); 363: 4/MM 38 Exocet (II × 2)—1/120-mm Bofors L-46 DP—2/40-mm AA (I × 2)—2/20-mm AA (I × 2)—1/BO-105 helicopter
**Electron Equipt:** Radar: 1/Decca AC 1229, 1/DA-05/2, 1/WM-28
Sonar: PHS-32
EW: SUSIE-I syst.—2/Knebworth/Corvus chaff RL
**M:** CODOG: 1 Rolls-Royce Olympus TM-3B gas turbine, 22,360 hp (tropical); 2 MTU 16V956 TB81 diesels; 800 hp; 2 CP props
**Electric:** 1,350 kw **Range:** 4,250/16 (diesels)
**Man:** 11 officers, 71 men

REMARKS: Ordered 8-75. *Nala* has a new type of helicopter deck that folds around the helicopter to form a hangar, two single 40-mm AA instead of one, and ASW torpedo tubes. DAISY computerized data system. Have an NBC warfare citadel.

**FRIGATES** *(continued)*

**Malahayati (362)** R. Gillett, 11-84

Living spaces air-conditioned. Fin stabilizers. Ammunition supply: 400 rounds 120-mm, 3,000 rounds 40-mm, 12 ASW torpedoes, 54 Nelli and Erica ASW rockets, 50 rounds chaff. The GFCS has a LIROD t.v./laser/infrared backup director.

◆ **3 (+1) Dutch Van Speijk class**

| | Bldr | Laid down | L | In serv. |
|---|---|---|---|---|
| 351 Ahmad Yani (ex-*Tjerk Hiddes,* F 804) | Nederlandsche DSM | 1-6-64 | 17-12-65 | 16-8-67 |
| 352 Slamet Riyadi (ex-*Van Speijk,* F 802) | Nederlandsche DSM | 1-10-63 | 5-3-65 | 14-2-67 |
| 353 Yos Sudarso (ex-*Van Galen,* F 803) | Kon. Mih. de Schelde | 25-7-63 | 19-6-65 | 1-3-67 |
| 354 N . . . . (ex-*Van Nes,* F 805) | Kon. Mih. de Schelde | 25-7-63 | 23-6-66 | 9-8-67 |

**D:** 2,200 tons (2,835 fl) **S:** 28.5 kts **Dim:** 113.42 (109.75 pp) × 12.48 × 4.57
**A:** 8/Harpoon SSM (IV × 2—see Remarks)—2/Sea (at SAM systems (IV × 2)—1/76-mm OTO Melara DP—6/324-mm ASW TT (III × 2)—1/light helicopter

**Ahmad Yani (351)** L. & L. Van Ginderen, 11-86

**Slamet Riyadi (352)** L. & L. Van Ginderen, 11-86

**Electron Equipt:** Radar: 1/Decca TM 1229C, 1/DA-05/2, 1/LW-03 2/M-44 (for Sea Cat), 1/M-45 (for 76-mm)
Sonar: 1/CWE-610, 1/PDE-700
EW: passive intercept, FH-12 HFD/F, 2/Knebworth/ Corvus decoy RL (VIII × 2)
**M:** 2 sets Werkspoor-English Electric double-reduction GT; 2 props; 30,000 hp
**Boilers:** 2/Babcock & Wilcox; 38.7 kg/cm$^2$, 450°C
**Range:** 4,500/12 **Electric:** 1,900 kw **Man:** 180–200 tot.

Remarks: 351 decommissioned 6-1-86 from Dutch Navy, 352 on 13-9-86; both transferred to Indonesia 13-10-86 and 1-11-86, respectively. 353 decommissioned 2-87 for transfer 2-11-87, and 354 decommissioned 2-87 for transfer 2-88.

Design based on British *Leander* class, but with broader enclosed bridge and *two* Sea Cat SAM systems, each with a director. Major modifications begun 1977, during which the twin, Mk 6, 114-mm DP gun mount was replaced by the OTO Melara Compact 76-mm weapon, the Limbo ASW mortar was deleted and two triple ASW TT were added, the hangar was enlarged, new sonars, radars, and the SEWALD-II data system was added; provision was made for carrying up to 8 Harpoon, but only two were normally aboard (these were probably removed prior to transfer), and the crew complement was reduced from 247 to 180. Conversions took place: 351: 15-12-78 to 1-6-81; 352: 24-12-76 to 3-1-78; 353: 15-7-77 to 30-11-79; and 354: 31-3-78 to 1-8-80. New infrared suppression stack caps added early 1980s.

**FRIGATES** *(continued)*

◆ **3 ex-U.K. "Tribal" class**

| | Bldr | Laid down | L | In serv. |
|---|---|---|---|---|
| 331 Martha Khristina Tiyahahu (ex-*Zulu,* F 124) | Alex. Stephens & Sons | 13-12-60 | 3-7-62 | 17-4-64 |
| 332 Wilhelmus Zakarias Yohannes (ex-*Gurkha,* F 122) | Thornycroft, Woolston | 3-11-58 | 11-7-60 | 13-2-63 |
| 333 Hasanuddin (ex-*Tartar,* F 133) | HMDY, Devonport | 22-10-59 | 19-9-60 | 26-2-62 |

**Martha Khristina Tiyahahu (331)** L. & L. Van Ginderen, 4-85

**Wilhelmus Zakarias Yohannes (332)** L. & L. Van Ginderen, 1-86

**Hassanuddin (333)** Maritime Photographic, 5-86

**D:** 2,300 tons (2,700 fl) **S:** 24 kts **Dim:** 109.73 (106.68 pp) × 12.95 × 3.80 (5.30 props)
**A:** 2/114-mm Mk 5 DP (I × 2)—2/Sea Cat GWS.21 syst. (IV × 2, 2 directors)—2/20-mm AA (I × 2)—1/Limbo Mk 10 ASW mortar (III × 2)—1/Wasp helicopter (AS.12 ASM, Mk 44/46 torpedoes)
**Electron Equipt:** Radar: 1/978, 1/993, 1/965, 1/903, 2/262
Sonar: Type 170B, Type 177, Type 162
EW: intercept equipt., 2/Knebworth/Corvus chaff RL (VIII × 2)
**M:** COSAG: 1 set Metrovik GT (15,000 hp) and 1 A.E.I. gas turbine (7,500 hp); 1/5-bladed prop; 22,500 hp
**Boilers:** 1 Babcock & Wilcox 3-drum; 38.7 kg/cm$^2$, 450°C
**Man:** 13 officers, 240 men (in R.N. service)

Remarks: Survivors of a class of seven Royal Navy "General-Purpose" frigates, stricken 3-84 after having been recommissioned because of the Falklands War. Purchased by Indonesia 16-4-84 and towed to Vosper Thornycroft, Woolston, for overhaul/modernization during April-June 1984. 331 began post-refit trials 22-3-85 and recommissioned 2-5-85; 332 recommissioned 21-10-85. 333 redelivered 22-1-86 and commissioned 3-4-86.

Twin rudders, one pair fin stabilizers. The helicopter fight deck has a small hangar beneath, into which the aircraft is lowered by elevator; the resultant hole is covered with segmented panels normally stowed beside the Limbo mortar position. MRS.3 director with Type 903 radar for the 114-mm guns, two modified MRS.8 directors with Type 262 radars for the Sea Cat systems. 332 had Type 199 variable-depth sonar removed prior to transfer.

◆ **4 ex-U.S. Claud Jones class** Bldrs: 341, 343: Avondale Marine, Westwego, La.; 342, 344: American SB, Toledo, Ohio

| | | In serv. |
|---|---|---|
| 341 Samadikun (ex-*John R. Perry,* DE 1034) | 29-7-58 | 5-5-59 |
| 342 Martadinata (ex-*Charles Berry,* DE 1035) | 17-3-59 | 25-11-60 |
| 343 Monginsidi (ex-*Claud Jones,* DE 1033) | 27-5-58 | 10-2-59 |
| 344 Ngurah Rai (ex-*McMorris,* DE 1036) | 26-5-59 | 4-3-60 |

**Ngurah Rai (344)** R. Gillett, 11-84

**D:** 1,720 tons (1,970 fl) **S:** 22 kts
**Dim:** 95.10 (91.75 wl) × 11.84 × 3.70 (hull)/5.54 (sonar)
**A:** 1 or 2/76.2-mm DP (I × 1 or 2)—0 or 2/37-mm AA (II × 1)—0 or 2/25-mm AA (II × 1)—6/324-mm ASW Mk 32 TT (III × 2)
**Electron Equipt:** Radar: 1/Decca 1226, 1/SPS-10 1/SPS-6, 1/SPG-52
Sonar: SQS-42 series—EW: WLR-1 (not in 341)
**M:** 4 Fairbanks-Morse 38ND8$\frac{1}{8}$ diesels; 1 prop; 9,240 hp **Electric:** 600 kw
**Fuel:** 296 tons **Range:** 3,590/22; 10,300/9 **Man:** 15 officers, 160 men

Remarks: No. 341 was transferred on 20-2-73, No. 342 on 31-1-74, Nos. 343 and 344 on 16-12-74. Nos. 341 and 342 have a twin Soviet 37-mm AA in place of one 76.2-mm on fantail and a twin 25-mm at the forecastle break. Navigational radar added 1980–81. Have Mk 70 Mod. 2 GFCS, Mk 105 ASW FCS.

**GUIDED-MISSILE PATROL BOATS**

◆ **4 PSK Mk 5 class** Bldr: Korea-Tacoma SY

| | In serv. | | In serv. |
|---|---|---|---|
| 621 Mandau | 7-79 | 623 Badek | 2-80 |
| 622 Rencong | 7-79 | 624 Keris | 2-80 |

**Rencong (622)** R. Gillett, 11-84

**D:** 250 tons (290 fl) **S:** 41 kts **Dim:** 53.58 × 8.00 × 1.63 (hull)
**A:** 4/MM 38 Exocet (II × 2)—1/57-mm Bofors DP—1/40-mm Bofors AA—2/20-mm AA (I × 2)
**Electron Equipt:** Radar: 1/Decca AC 1229, 1/H.S.A. WM-28
**M:** CODOG: 1 G.E.-Fiat LM-2500 gas turbine, 25,000 hp; 2 MTU 12V331 TC81 diesels, 1,120 hp each; 2 CP props
**Fuel:** 65 tons **Range:** 2,500/17 **Electric:** 400 kw **Man:** 5 officers, 34 men

Remarks: First unit laid down 5-77. Modification of U.S. *Asheville*-class design. A second group of four were not ordered as planned.

## PATROL BOATS AND CRAFT

◆ **2 (+6) Lürssen PB 57 design** Bldr: Lürssen, Vegesack, and P.T. PAL SY, Surabaja

| | In serv. | | In serv. |
|---|---|---|---|
| ... ANDAU | 15-4-86 | ... N ... | ... |
| ... N ... | 1-10-86 | ... N ... | ... |
| ... N ... | ... | ... N ... | ... |
| ... N ... | ... | ... N ... | ... |

**D:** 423 tons (fl) **S:** 27.25 kts **Dim:** 58.10 (54.40 wl) × 7.62 × 2.78
**A:** 1/57-mm Bofors DP—1/40-mm Bofors AA—2/20-mm AA (I × 2)—2/324-mm ASW TT (fixed at stern; 2 reloads)
**Electron Equipt:** Radar: 1/. . . nav., 1/H.S.A. WM-25
Sonar: . . .—EW: . . .
**M:** 2 MTU 16V956 TB92 diesels; 2 props; 8,260 hp
**Range:** 2,200/27; 4,200/17 **Fuel:** 110 tons
**Electric:** 324 kw (3 × 108 kw) **Man:** 42 tot.

REMARKS: Midbody for *Andau* shipped from West Germany 1984 for completion in Indonesia. Small helicopter platform aft. Armament for a total of six more was ordered 19-5-84 for delivery 1986–88. Lighter-armed version also building for the Indonesian Customs Service.

◆ **5 Jetfoil Model 929 hydrofoils**

| | Bldr | L | In serv. |
|---|---|---|---|
| ... BIMA SAMUDERA I | Boeing, Seattle | 22-10-81 | 14-12-81 |
| ... N ... | Boeing/P.T. PAL | 1984 | 1986 |
| ... N ... | Boeing/P.T. PAL | 6-1-84 | 1986 |
| ... N ... | Boeing/P.T. PAL | 6-3-86 | 1-10-86 |
| ... N ... | Boeing/P.T. PAL | 23-7-86 | 1-10-86 |

**Bima Samudera I** Boeing Marine Systems, 1981

**D:** 115 tons (fl) **S:** 46 kts
**Dim:** 27.4 (foils down) × 9.1 × 1.9 (5.2 foils down, 2.0 max. foiling)
**A:** 1/40-mm AA—1/20-mm AA (none on *Bima Samudera I*)
**Electron Equipt:** Radar: 1/Decca . . .
**M:** 2 Allison 501-K20A gas turbines; 2 Rocketdyne R-20 waterjet pumps; 7,560 hp—2 G.M. 8V92 TI diesels; 2 props; 900 hp for hull-borne cruise
**Range:** 900/40; 1,500/15 **Fuel:** 33.4 tons
**Man:** 6 tot. plus 260 passengers

REMARKS: *Bima Samudera I* was purchased by the Indonesian Agency for the Development and Application of Technology for evaluating such a craft in naval patrol, logistics support, and civil roles. Naval-manned. Delivered in-country 2-82. Has enhanced fuel tankage over standard commercial model. Aluminum construction.

The hydrofoil contract with Boeing Marine Services called for two each of two versions of the basic Jetfoil design, with completion taking place at P.T. Pabrik

**Troop-carrying hydrofoil on trials** Boeing, 1-85

Kapal (P.T. PAL), Indonesia. Another six craft were on option, and a total of 47 was once foreseen. The first four series craft were built by Boeing, Seattle, and delivered to Indonesia for fitting out. The two troop transport versions (the first two series units) carry up to 100 troops and are armed with a 20-mm AA and 2/12.7-mm mg (I × 2). The first production boat was laid down 10-12-83. The first two were delivered 1-85 to P.T. PAL for outfitting and completion by 1986. Numbers 3 and 4, intended as gunboats, were completed by Boeing 6-3-86 and 23-7-86. Further craft of this type are no longer programmed.

◆ **4 Carpentaria class** Bldr: De Havilland Marine, Australia

| | In serv. | | In serv. |
|---|---|---|---|
| 851 SAMADAR | 8-76 | 855 SADARIN | 12-76 |
| 854 SAWANGI | 11-76 | 856 SALMANETI | 7-77 |

**Samadar (851)** 1981

**D:** 27 tons (fl) **S:** 25 kts **Dim:** 15.7 × 5.0 × 1.3
**A:** 2/12.7-mm mg (I × 2) **Electron Equipt:** Radar: 1/Decca 110
**D:** 2 MTU 8V331 diesels; 2 props; 1,400 hp **Range:** 950/18 **Man:** 10 tot.

REMARKS: Grant-aid from Australia. Aluminum construction. Sisters *Sasila* (852) and *Sabola* (853) transferred to Sea Police 1981.

◆ **8 Australian Attack class**

| | Bldr | Laid down | L | In serv. |
|---|---|---|---|---|
| 847 SIBARU (ex-*Bandolier*) | Walkers, Ltd. | 7-68 | 2-10-68 | 14-12-68 |
| 848 SULIMAN (ex-*Archer*) | Walkers, Ltd. | 7-67 | 2-12-67 | 15-5-68 |
| 857 SIGALU (ex-*Barricade*) | Evans Deakin | 12-67 | 29-6-68 | 26-10-68 |
| 858 SILEA (ex-*Acute*) | Evans Deakin | 4-67 | 29-8-67 | 26-4-68 |
| 8 . . . SIRIBUA (ex-*Bombard*) | Walkers, Ltd. | 4-68 | 6-7-68 | 5-11-68 |
| 8 . . . SIADA (ex-*Barbette*) | Walkers, Ltd. | 11-67 | 10-4-68 | 16-8-68 |
| 8 . . . SIKUDA (ex-*Attack*) | Evans Deakin | 9-66 | 8-4-67 | 17-11-67 |
| 8 . . . SIGUROT (ex-*Assail*) | Evans Deakin | . . . | 18-11-67 | 12-7-68 |

**Suliman (848)** 10-81

**D:** 146 tons (fl) **S:** 21 kts **Dim:** 32.76 (30.48 pp) × 6.2 × 1.9
**A:** 1/40-mm AA—2/7.65-mm mg (I × 2)
**Electron Equipt:** Radar: 1/Decca RM 916
**M:** 2 Davey-Paxman Ventura 16 YJCM diesels; 3,460 hp **Fuel:** 20 tons
**Range:** 1,220/13 **Man:** 3 officers, 19 men

REMARKS: Light-alloys superstructure. Air-conditioned. 847 transferred 16-11-73, 848 in 1974, 857 on 22-4-82, 858 on 6-5-83, and ex-*Bombard* later in 1983. Ex-*Barbette* transferred 22-85, ex-*Attack* on 24-5-85, and ex-*Assail* on 30-1-86.

◆ **3 ex-Yugoslav PBR-500 class**

819 KAYANG 822 DORANG 823 TODAK

**D:** 190 tons (202 fl) **S:** 18 kts **Dim:** 41.0 × 6.3 × 2.2
**A:** 1/76.2-mm—1/40-mm AA—6/20-mm AA (II × 3)—2/Mousetrap Mk 22 ASW RL—2/d.c. projectors—2/d.c. racks
**Electron Equipt:** Radar: 1/Decca 45—Sonar: U.S. QCU-2
**M:** 2 M.A.N. W8V 30/38 diesels; 2 props; 3,300 hp **Fuel:** 15 tons
**Range:** 1,000/12 **Man:** 54 tot.

## PATROL BOATS AND CRAFT *(continued)*

**Kayang (819)** 10-81

Remarks: Transferred in 1959. *Krapu* (821) and *Dorang* (822) stricken 1980 and *Lemadang* in 1984. Rest to strike shortly.

◆ **2 Soviet Kronshtadt class** Bldr: U.S.S.R., 1951–52

814 Pandrong 815 Sura

**Sura (815)** 1978

**D:** 300 tons (330 fl) **S:** 18 kts **Dim:** 52.1 × 6.5 × 2.2
**A:** 1/85-mm—2/37-mm AA (I × 2)—6/14.5-mm—2/MBU 1200 ASW RL (V × 2)—2/d.c. projectors—2/d.c. racks—mines
**M:** 3 9D diesels; 3 props; 3,300 hp **Fuel:** 20 tons **Range:** 3,500/14
**Man:** 50 tot.

Remarks: Transferred 1958–59. A number of others have been stricken, including *Kakap* (816) in 1981 and *Barakuda* (817) in 1985. Late note: Both reported stricken 1986.

## MINE COUNTERMEASURES SHIPS

◆ **1 (+1 + 4) Alkmaar ("Tripartite")-class minehunters** Bldr: Van der Giessen de Noord, Alblasserdam, the Netherlands

| | Laid down | L | In serv. |
|---|---|---|---|
| 7 . . . Pulau Rengat (ex-*Willemstad*) | 13-12-85 | . . . | 8-87 |
| 7 . . . Pulau Rupat (ex-*Vlardingen*) | . . . | . . . | . . . |

**D:** 510 tons (568 fl) **S:** 15.5 kts
**Dim:** 51.50 (47.10 pp) × 8.90 × 2.47 (2.62 max.) **A:** 2/20-mm AA (I × 2)
**Electron Equipt:** Radar: 1/Decca AC 1229
Sonar: Thomson Sintra TSM 2022
**M:** 2 MTU 12V396 TCDb51 diesels; 2 props; 1,900 hp—2/75-hp bow-thrusters; 2/120-hp Schottel active rudders (7 kts)
**Electric:** 910 kw (3 × 250 kw, 1 × 160 kw) **Range:** 3,500/10; 3,000/12
**Man:** 45 tot.

Remarks: Ordered 29-3-85 and 30-8-85; taken from Royal Netherlands Navy production. Glass-reinforced plastic construction. Carry two PAP-104 MK5 remote-controlled minehunting/destruction submersibles. Have TSM 2060 plot, TMV628 Trident III radio location system. Sweep equipment includes Fiskars F-82 magnetic sweep tail, SA Marine AS203 acoustic gear, and OD-3 mechanical sweep; there are two sweep gear cranes. The minehunting system is the Thomson-CSF IBIS V. Plan construction of up to ten more in Indonesia, plus possible two more in the Netherlands.

◆ **2 ex-Soviet T-43-class minesweepers**

701 Pulau Rani 702 Pulau Ratewo

**D:** 500 tons (570 fl) **S:** 14 kts **Dim:** 58.0 × 8.6 × 2.3
**A:** 4/37-mm AA (II × 2)—8/12.7-mm mg (II × 4)—2/d.c. projectors—2/mine rails
**M:** 2 Type 9D diesels; 2 props; 2,200 hp **Fuel:** 70 tons **Range:** 3,200/10

Remarks: Transferred 1962–64. Used on patrol duties. Three others lost or stricken 1980–81. To be replaced by the *Alkmaar*-class units.

## AMPHIBIOUS WARFARE SHIPS

◆ **6 Teluk Semangka-class landing ships** Bldr: Hyundai SY, South Korea

| | In serv. | | In serv. |
|---|---|---|---|
| 512 Teluk Semangka | 20-1-81 | 515 Teluk Sampit | 1981 |
| 513 Teluk Penyu | 20-1-81 | 516 Teluk Banten | 5-82 |
| 514 Teluk Mandar | 7-81 | 517 Teluk Ende | 2-9-82 |

**Teluk Ende (517)**—with helicopter hangar, enlarged superstructure
R.A.N., 1982

**Teluk Penyu (513)** R.A.N., 1985

**D:** 1,800 tons (3,770 fl) **S:** 15 kts **Dim:** 100.0 × 15.4 × 4.2 (3.0 mean)
**A:** 2/40-mm AA (I × 2)—2/20-mm AA (I × 2)
**M:** 2 diesels; 2 props; 6,860 hp (5,600 sust.) **Electric:** 750 kw
**Range:** 7,500/13 **Man:** 13 officers, 104 men, plus 202 troops

Remarks: First four ordered 6-79, two more in 6-81. Near duplicates of U.S. LST 542-class design. Beaching load: 690 tons (17 main battle tanks), or up to 1,800 tons max. Helicopter decks amidships and aft. Carry 2 LCVP landing craft. There is a 50-ton-capacity turntable in the tank deck and an elevator to the upper deck. 516 and 517 have a large hangar incorporated in the superstructure, the helicopter deck raised one level, the forward helicopter positions deleted, the landing craft davits moved forward of the superstructure, and increased command facilities to act as flagships; they can carry three AS.332 Super Puma helicopters.

◆ **5 ex-U.S. LST 542-class tank landing ships** Bldr: Chicago Bridge & Iron Wks., Seneca, Ill. (except 509 and 511: American Bridge, Ambridge, Pa.)

| | Laid down | L | In serv. |
|---|---|---|---|
| 501 Teluk Langsa (ex-LST 1128) | 23-11-44 | 19-2-45 | 9-3-45 |
| 504 Teluk Kau (ex-LST 652) | 24-7-44 | 19-10-44 | 1-1-45 |
| 509 Teluk Sindoro (ex-M/V *Inagua Shipper*, ex-*Presqul Isle*, APB 44, ex-LST 678) | 29-4-44 | 16-6-44 | 30-6-44 |
| 510 Teluk Saleh (ex-*Clarke County*, LST 601) | 21-10-43 | 4-3-44 | 25-3-44 |
| 511 Teluk Bone (ex-*Iredell County*, LST 839) | 25-9-44 | 12-11-44 | 6-12-44 |

**D:** 1,650 tons light (4,080 fl) **S:** 11.6 kts **Dim:** 99.98 × 15.24 × 4.29
**A:** 6 or 7/40-mm or 37-mm AA
**M:** 2 G.M. 12-567A diesels; 2 props; 1,800 hp **Electric:** 300 kw
**Fuel:** 590 tons **Range:** 6,000/9 (loaded)
**Man:** 119 crew + 264 passengers

Remarks: Transferred in 3-60, 1961, and Nos. 510 and 511 in 7-70 under the Military Assistance Program. Can carry 2,100 tons of cargo. Sisters *Teluk Bayer* and *Teluk*

### AMPHIBIOUS WARFARE SHIPS *(continued)*

*Tomani* are in the Military Sealift Command, as is the Japanese-built near-sister *Teluk Amboina.*

### HYDROGRAPHIC SHIPS

◆ **1 Burudjulasad class** Bldr: Schlichtingwerft, Travemünde (L: 8-65; In serv. 1967)

931 Burudjulasad

**Burudjulasad (931)** 1981

**D:** 1,800 tons (2,150 fl) **S:** 19 kts **Dim:** 82.0 (78.0 pp) × 11.4 × 3.5
**M:** 4 M.A.N. V6V 22/30 diesels; 2 CP props; 6,400 hp **Electric:** 1,008 kw
**Fuel:** 600 tons **Range:** 14,500/15.7
**Man:** 13 officers, 88 men, 28 technicians

Remarks: Launched in 8-65. Can accommodate 28 scientists and can carry one helicopter.

◆ **1 U.K. Hecla class** Bldr: Yarrow, Blythswood

| | Laid down | L | In serv. |
|---|---|---|---|
| 932 Dewa Kembar (ex-*Hydra,* A144) | 14-5-64 | 14-7-65 | 5-5-66 |

**Dewa Kembar (932)** L. & L. Van Ginderen, 9-86

**D:** 1,915 tons (2,733 fl) **S:** 14 kts **Dim:** 79.25 (71.63 pp) × 14.94 × 4.00
**Electron Equipt:** Radar: 1/. . .
Sonar: Type 2034 sidescan
**M:** diesel-electric: 3 Paxman Ventura diesels (12 cyl.) 1,280 hp each; 2 electric motors; 1 prop; 2,000 hp
**Range**: 12,000/11; 20,000/9 **Fuel**: 450 tons **Man**: 118 tot.

Remarks: Purchased 18-4-86, refitted by Vosper Thornycroft, Southampton, 24-4-86 to 16-7-86. Recommissioned 10-9-86 and left for Indonesia 1-10-86. Bow-thruster, hangar, and platform for light helicopter. Retains MARISAT SATCOMM gear. Carries two survey launches.

◆ **1 hydrometeorological and oceanographic research ship** Bldr: Sasebo Heavy Industries, Japan (In serv. 12-1-63)

1005 Jalanidhi

**Jalanidhi (1005)** 1972

**D:** 740 tons (985 fl) **S:** 12.7 kts **Dim:** 53.9 (48.5 pp) × 9.5 × 4.3
**M:** 1 M.A.N. G6V 30/42 diesel; 1,000 hp **Electric:** 261 kw
**Fuel:** 165 tons **Range:** 7,200/10.5

Remarks: Weather-balloon facility aft.

◆ **1 ex-Soviet PO-2-class inshore survey craft**

1008 Aries

**D:** 56 tons (fl) **S:** 12 kts **Dim:** 21.3 × 3.8 × 2.0
**M:** 1 3D12 diesel; 300 hp **Man:** 13 tot.

Remarks: Transferred in 1964.

◆ **1 hydrographic survey ship** Bldr: De Waal Scheepswerf, Nijmegen (L: 6-9-52; In serv. 7-53)

1002 Burdjamhal

**D:** 1,200 tons (1,500 fl) **S:** 13 kts **Dim:** 64.5 (58.5 pp) × 10.1 × 3.3
**M:** 2 Werkspoor TMAB-278 diesels; 2 props; 1,160 hp
**Fuel:** 150 tons **Man:** 90 tot.

### AUXILIARY SHIPS

◆ **1 ex-Soviet Don-class submarine tender** Bldr: U.S.S.R., 1960

301 Ratulangi (ex-Sov. 441)

**Ratulangi (301, ex-441)** 1979

**D:** 6,700 tons (fl) **S:** 21 kts **Dim:** 139.9 × 17.6 × 5.4
**A:** 4/100-mm DP(I × 4)—8/57-mm AA (II × 4)—8/25-mm AA (II × 4)
**Electron Equipt:** Radar: 1/navigational, 1/Slim Net, 1/Sun Visor A
**M:** 4 diesels; 2 props; 8,000 hp **Range:** 21,000/10 **Man:** 300 tot.

Remarks: Transferred in 1962. Because of heavy armament and extensive sensors, is used for patrol duties.

◆ **1 command ship** Bldr: Ishikawajima, Japan (L: 13-6-61)

561 Multatuli

**Multatuli (561)** J. Jedrlinic, 1982

**D:** 4,500 tons (fl) **S:** 18.5 kts **Dim:** 111.35 (103.0 pp) × 16.0 × 6.98
**A:** 8/37-mm AA (II × 2, I × 4)—4/14.5-mm AA (II × 2)
**M:** 1 Burmeister & Wain diesel; 5,500 hp **Fuel:** 1,400 tons **Range:** 6,000/16
**Man:** 134 tot.

Remarks: Built as a submarine-support ship, converted as a fleet command ship in the late 1960s. Has a helicopter platform aft. Construction of two similar ships of about 10,000 tons, to carry fuel, troops, and hospital facilities, is planned.

◆ **1 ex-U.S. Achelous-class repair ship** Bldr: Chicago Bridge & Iron, Seneca, Illinois

| | Laid down | L | In serv. |
|---|---|---|---|
| 921 Jaja Widjaja (ex-*Askari,* ARL 30, ex-LST 1131) | 8-12-44 | 2-3-45 | 15-3-45 |

**D:** 2,130 (3,640 fl) **S:** 11 kts **Dim:** 99.98 × 15.24 × 4.25
**A:** 8/40-mm AA (IV × 2) **M:** 2 G.M. 12-267A diesels; 2 props; 1,800 hp
**Electric:** 520 kw **Fuel:** 590 tons **Man:** 280 tot.

Remarks: Leased 31-8-71; purchased 22-2-79. Cargo capacity: 300 tons. 60-ton lift rig.

◆ **1 replenishment oiler** Bldr: Yugoslavia, 1965

911 Sorong

**D:** 5,100 (dwt) **S:** 15 kts **Dim:** 112.17 × 15.4 × 6.6
**A:** 8/12.7-mm mg (II × 4) **M:** 1 diesel; 1 prop; . . . hp

## AUXILIARY SHIPS *(continued)*

**Jaja Widjaja (921)** 1981

**Sorong (911)** 1979

Remarks: Cargo: 3,000 tons fuel/300 tons water. Can conduct underway replenishments.

◆ **1 ex-Soviet Khobi-class oiler**

909 Pakan Baru

**D:** 1,525 tons (fl) **S:** 12.7 kts **Dim:** 67.4 (63.7 pp) × 10.0 × 4.4
**M:** 2 diesels; 2 props; 1,600 hp **Range:** 2,500/12.5

Remarks: Cargo: 700 tons fuel oil.

◆ **1 sail-training ship** Bldr: Stülcken, Hamburg (L: 21-1-52)

Dewarutji

**Dewarutji** W. Donko, 7-86

**D:** 810 tons (1,500 fl) **S:** 9 kts **Dim:** 58.3 (41.5 pp) × 9.5 × 4.23
**M:** 1 M.A.N. diesel; 575 hp **Man:** 110 men, 78 cadets

Remarks: Sail area: 1,091 m$^2$.

◆ **1 ex-U.S. Cherokee-class fleet tug** Bldr: United Eng., Alameda, California

| | Laid down | L | In serv. |
|---|---|---|---|
| 922 Rakata (ex-U.S. *Menominee*, ATF 73) | 27-9-41 | 14-2-42 | 25-9-42 |

**D:** 1,640 tons (fl) **S:** 15 kts **Dim:** 62.5 × 11.7 × 4.7
**A:** 1/76.2-mm DP—2/40-mm AA (I × 2)—4/25-mm AA (II × 2)
**M:** 4 G.M. 12-278A diesels, electric drive; 1 prop; 3,000 hp

Remarks: Transferred 3-61.

◆ **1 coastal tug** Bldr: P.T. PAL SY, Surabaja (L: 6-6-79)

**D:** . . . **S:** 10 kts **Dim:** 24.25 × 6.5 × . . .
**M:** diesel; 1 prop; . . . hp **Man:** 10 tot.

◆ **1 coastal tug** Bldr: Ishikawajima Harima, Tokyo (L: 4-61)

934 Lampo Batang

**D:** 250 tons **S:** 11 kts **Dim:** 28.1 × 7.6 × 2.6
**M:** 2 M.A.N. diesels; 2 props; 600 hp **Fuel:** 18 tons
**Range:** 1,000/11 **Man:** 13 tot.

◆ **2 Tambora-class coastal tugs** Bldr: Ishikawajima Harima, Tokyo

935 Tambora 936 Bromo (both L: 6-61)

**D:** 250 tons (fl) **S:** 10.5 kts **Dim:** 24.1 × 6.6 × 3.0
**M:** 2 M.A.N. diesels; 2 props; 600 hp **Fuel:** 9 tons
**Range:** 690/10.5 **Man:** 15 tot.

### MILITARY SEALIFT COMMAND (KOLINLAMIL)

Formed in 1978 to coordinate the Indonesian Navy's logistic support for its far-flung bases and outposts in the Indonesian archipelago. Some of the units have been taken over from the Indonesian Army and others from the Navy.

◆ **1 tank landing ship** Bldr: Sasebo Heavy Industries (L: 17-3-61)

9 . . . Teluk Amboina

**D:** 4,145 tons (fl) **S:** 13 kts **Dim:** 99.9 × 15.2 × 4.6
**A:** 4/40-mm AA—1/37-mm AA
**M:** 2 M.A.N. V6V 22.30 diesels; 2 props; 3,200 hp (2,850 sust.)
**Electric:** 135 kw **Fuel:** 1,200 tons **Range:** 4,000/13
**Man:** 88 men + 212 passengers

Remarks: Built as reparations. Near duplicate of U.S. LST 542 design. Guns may have been removed. Can carry 654 tons water. Has a 30-ton crane.

◆ **2 ex-U.S. LST 542-class tank landing ships**

| | Bldr | Laid down | L | In serv. |
|---|---|---|---|---|
| 9 . . . Teluk Bayer (ex-LST 616) | Chicago Bridge & Iron, Seneca, Ill. | 12-2-44 | 12-5-44 | 29-5-44 |
| 9 . . . Teluk Ratai (ex-*Teluk Tomani,* ex-*Inagua Crest,* ex-*Brunei,* ex-*Bledsoe County,* LST 356) | Charleston Naval Shipyard | 7-9-42 | 16-11-42 | 22-12-42 |

**D:** 1,650 tons (4,080 fl) **S:** 11 kts **Dim:** 99.98 × 15.24 × 4.29
**A:** none **M:** 2 G.M. 12-567A diesels; 2 props; 1,800 hp
**Fuel:** 590 tons **Range:** 6,000/9 (loaded) **Man:** 119 men + 264 passengers

Remarks: *Teluk Ratai* is used as a cattle-carrier and does not carry passengers (by mutual agreement?). Both acquired around 1961.

◆ **3 Krupang-class utility landing craft** Bldr: Surabaja DY

9 . . . Krupang (In serv. 3-11-78) 9 . . . Dili (In serv. 27-2-79) 9 . . . Nusantara (In serv. 1980)

**D:** 400 tons (fl) **S:** 11 kts **Dim:** 42.9 (36.27 pp) × 9.14 × . . .
**M:** 2 diesels; 2 props; . . . hp **Range:** 700/11 **Man:** 17 tot.

Remarks: Based on U.S. LCU 1610 class. Cargo: 200 tons.

◆ **2 Amurang-class landing craft** Bldr: Korneuberg SY, Austria (In serv. 1968)

9 . . . Amurang 9 . . . Dore

**D:** 182 tons (275 fl) **S:** 8 kts **Dim:** 38.3 × 10.0 × 1.8
**M:** 2 diesels; 2 props; 420 hp **Man:** 17 tot.

Remarks: Sister *Banten* and one other in merchant service. 200 grt.

Note: Small oiler *Balikpapan* (901) stricken 1984.

◆ **1 small oiler** Bldr: . . . . , Indonesia (In serv. 1979)

902 Sambu

**D:** . . . **S:** . . . **Dim:** approx. × 70.0 × 10.0 × 4.6 m
**A:** 4/14.5-mm mg (II × 2) **Electron Equipt:** Radar: 1/ . . . nav.
**M:** 1 diesel; 1 prop; . . . hp

Remarks: No further data available.

**MILITARY SEALIFT COMMAND (KOLINLAMIL)** *(continued)*

**Sambu (902)**—with missile boats *Keris* (624) and *Rencong* (622) alongside
R. Gillett, 11-84

◆ **6 Hungarian Tisza-class cargo ships** Bldr: Angyalfold SY, Budapest

| | | |
|---|---|---|
| 951 Telaud | 953 Natuna | 957 Karimundsa |
| 952 Nusatelu | 956 Teluk Menitawi | 960 Karamaja |

**D:** 2,000 tons (fl) **S:** 12 kts **Dim:** 74.5 (67.4 pp) × 11.3 × 4.6
**A:** some ships: 4/14.5-mm mg (II × 2) **M:** 1 Lang 8-cyl. diesel; 1,000 hp
**Electric:** 746 kw **Fuel:** 98 tons **Range:** 4,200/10.7 **Man:** 26 tot.

Remarks: Transferred 1963–64. Taken over from the Army in 1978. Had originally been naval. 1,296 grt/1,280 dwt. Cargo: 1,100 tons.

◆ **1 former pilgrim transport** Bldr: Blohm + Voss, Hamburg (In serv. 1936)

971 Tanjung Pandan (ex-*Genung Djati,* ex-*Empire Orwell,* ex-*Empire Doon,* ex-*Pretoria*)

**D:** . . . **S:** . . . **Dim:** 167.6 × 22.0 × . . .
**M:** 8 sets GT; 4 props; . . . hp

Remarks: 17,362 grt. German liner, used as a barracks during W.W. II, to U.K. in 1945, used as a troopship, then transport for religious pilgrims. Sold to Indonesia 1962. Acquired 1981 for Kolinlamil, but has remained immobile at Tanjung Priok.

◆ **1 former passenger-cargo ship** Bldr: N.V. Scheepswerfen Machinefabrick de Merwede, Hardinxveld, the Netherlands

931 Tansung Pandan (ex-*Tjut Njak Dhien,* ex-*Prinses Irene*) (In serv. 1965)

**D:** . . . **S:** 16.5 kts **Dim:** 139.92 × 18.67 × 8.61
**M:** diesels; 1 prop; 8,600 hp

Remarks: 8,456 grt/8,618 dwt. Purchased 1978 for use as a transport.

◆ **1 former passenger-cargo ship** Bldr: . . .

932 Tansung Oisina (ex-*Gunungjati*) (In serv. . . .)

Remarks: Approx. 6,000–8,000 grt. Purchased 1978 for use as a transport. No further data available.

◆ **. . . coastal cargo lighters** Bldr: Fasharkan DY, Manokwari, Irian

**D:** . . . **S:** 8 kts **Dim:** 31.1 × 6.26 × 1.80
**M:** diesels

Remarks: 200 dwt. First unit delivered 7-3-82. Others may be built.

SEA COMMUNICATIONS AGENCY

Established in 1978 to patrol Indonesia's 200-nautical-mile economic zone and to maintain navigational aids. Full name: Indonesian Directorate General of Sea Communication/Department of Transport, Communications and Tourism.

## PATROL BOATS

◆ **4 Golok class** Bldr: Schlichtingwerft, Harmsdorf, W. Germany

| | In serv. | | In serv. |
|---|---|---|---|
| PAT 206 Golok | 12-3-82 | PAT 208 Pedang | 12-5-82 |
| PAT 207 Panah | 12-3-82 | PAT 209 Kapak | 12-5-81 |

**D:** 200 tons (fl) **S:** 28 kts **Dim:** 37.50 × 7.00 × 2.00
**A:** 1/20-mm AA **Range:** 1,500/18 **Man:** 18 tot.
**M:** 2 MTU 16V652 TB61 diesels; 2 props; 4,200 hp

Remarks: Intended for search-and-rescue duties. 120³/hr. fire pump and water monitor, rescue launch, 8-man sick bay. Hulls built by Deutsche Industrie Werke, Berlin.

◆ **5 Kujang class** Bldr: SFCN, Villeneuve-la-Garenne, France

| | Laid down | L | In serv. |
|---|---|---|---|
| PAT 201 Kujang | 5-80 | 17-10-80 | 19-8-81 |
| PAT 202 Parang | 7-80 | 18-11-80 | 19-8-81 |
| PAT 203 Celurit | 9-80 | 20-3-81 | 1981 |
| PAT 204 Cundrik | 7-9-80 | 10-11-80 | 1981 |
| PAT 205 Belati | 2-81 | 21-5-81 | 10-81 |

**Kujang (PAT 201)** SFCN, 1981

**D:** 126 tons (162 fl) **S:** 28 kts
**Dim:** 38.32 (35.46 pp) × 6.00 × 1.78 (2.60 props) **A:** 1/20-mm AA
**M:** 2 S.A.C.M. AGO V12 195 CZ SHR T5; 2 props; 4,400 hp
**Range:** 1,500/18 **Man:** 18 tot.

Remarks: Intended for search-and-rescue duties.

◆ **6 PAT-01-class patrol craft** Bldr: Tanjung Priok SY, 1978–79

PAT 01 to PAT 06

**D:** 12 tons (fl) **S:** 14 kts **Dim:** 12.15 × 4.25 × 1.0
**A:** mg **M:** 1 Renault diesel; 260 hp

## TRANSPORTS

◆ **2 Lawit class** Bldr: Meyerwerft, Papenburg, West Germany

Lawit (In serv. 7-86) Kelimutu (In serv. 7-86)

**Kelimutu** Meyerwerft, 7-86

**D:** . . . **S:** 14 kts (sust.) **Dim:** 99.80 × 18.00 × 4.20
**Electron Equipt:** Radar: 2/. . . nav. (1 X-band, 1 S-band)
**M:** 2 Mak 6 MU453 diesels; 2 props; 4,352 hp—653-hp CP bow-thruster
**Range:** 4,000/14 **Electric:** 2,310 kVA (4 × 525 kVA, 1 × 210 kVA)
**Man:** 84 crew, 920 passengers

Remarks: 5,700 grt. Eleven watertight compartments, 8 motor lifeboats, 20 rafts. *Lawit* named for mountain on Borneo, *Kelimutu* a mountain on Flores. Intended as inter-island passenger ships in peacetime and as military transports in time of war.

◆ **Kerinci class** Bldr: Meyerwerft, Papenburg, West Germany

| | |
|---|---|
| Kerinci (In serv. 6.83) | Rinjani (In serv. 10-84) |
| Kambuna (In serv. 8-83) | Umsini (In serv. 1985) |

**D:** . . . **S:** 20 kts **Dim:** 144.0 (130.0 pp) × 23.4 × 5.9
**M:** 2 Mak 6MU601 diesels; 2 props; 17,000 hp **Electric:** 3,520 kw
**Range:** 5,500/20 **Man:** 119 crew + 1,596 to 1,737 passengers

Remarks: 13,861 + 13,954 grt/3,400 dwt. Intended for inter-island revenue passenger-carrying in peacetime and as military transports in time of war. Accommodations

TRANSPORTS *(continued)*

**Rinjani** Meyerwerft, 1984

for approximately 100 first-class, 200 second, 300 third, 496 fourth-class, and 500-plus economy passengers. Bow-thruster.

## NAVIGATIONAL AID TENDERS

◆ **0 (+11) lighthouse and buoy tenders** Bldr: Carrington Slipway, Tomago, Australia

REMARKS: Ordered 12-84. To fit out in Indonesia. No data available.

◆ **2 coastal service** Bldr: . . . , Japan (In serv. 1976)

KARAKATA KUMBA

**D:** 569 grt/552 dwt **S:** 13 kts **Dim:** 50.50 (47.43 pp) × 10.00 × 3.71
**M:** 2 Niigata diesels; 1 prop; 850 hp

◆ **2 seagoing buoy tender/cargo ships** Bldr: . . . (In serv. 1963)

MAJANG MIZAN

**D:** 2,150 tons (fl) **S:** 14 kts **Dim:** 78.0 (71.0 pp) × 13.7 × 4.0
**M:** 1 set 4-cyl. compound reciprocating steam; 1 prop; 1,800 hp
**Boilers:** Two 16 kg/cm$^2$ **Fuel:** 376 tons **Man:** 70 tot.

REMARKS: 1,705 grt/1,170 dwt. Resemble small cargo ships, with bridge forward, engine aft, and holds amidships

◆ **1 seagoing buoy tender and cable layer** Bldr: . . . . , the Netherlands

BIDUK (L: 30-10-51; In serv. 7-52)

**D:** 1,250 dwt **S:** 12 kts **Dim:** 65.0 × 12.0 × 4.5 **Boilers:** two 16-kg/cm$^2$
**M:** 1 set triple-expansion reciprocating steam; 1 prop; 1,600 hp **Man:** 66 tot.

REMARKS: Cable sheaves over bow. Transferred from Navy, 1978 (ex-pendant 1003).

◆ **2 split-hopper dredges** Bldr: Tanjung Priok SY, Jakarta

N . . . . . . . (In serv. 1983) N . . . . . . . (In serv. 1983)

**D:** 1,600 tons (fl) **S:** 10.7 kts **Dim:** . . . × . . . × 4.05 m
**M:** 2 Bolnes 6DNL 150 diesels; 2 CP props; 1,692 hp
**Electric:** 1,280 kwt **Man:** 25 tot.

REMARKS: 1,000 m$^3$ capacity, able to dredge to 14 m. 272-hp bow-thruster. Built with assistance from IHC Holland. Ordered 1981, laid down 1982.

◆ **1 suction hopper dredge** Bldr: Orenstein & Koppel, Lübeck, West Germany

IRIAN (L: 26-6-81)

**D:** 9,500 tons (fl) **S:** 12 kts **Dim:** 110.0 × 18.0 × 7.1
**M:** 2 MWM diesels; 2 props; 7,700 hp

# CUSTOMS SERVICE

Note: The Indonesian Customs Service is currently undergoing an ambitious expansion, with patrol boats and craft constructed in Western Europe and at home.

## PATROL BOATS

◆ **2 (+1 + . . .) Lürssen PB 57 design** Bldr: Lürssen, Vegesack, and P.T. PAL SY, Surabaja

. . . N . . . (In serv. 1986) . . . N . . . (In serv. 1-10-86)

**D:** 342 tons (416 fl) **S:** 28.0 kts **Dim:** 58.10 (54.40 pp) × 7.62 × 2.73
**A:** 1/40-mm Bofors AA—1/20-mm Rheinmetall AA
**Electron Equipt:** Radar: . . .
**M:** 2 MTU 16V956 TB92 diesels; 2 props; 8,260 hp
**Range:** 2,200/28; 4,200/17 **Electric:** 324 kw (3 × 108 kw)
**Fuel:** 110 tons **Man:** 41 crew, plus 5 spare

REMARKS: Naval-manned for the Customs Service; more heavily armed versions serve in Navy. Mid-body for first unit shipped to Indonesia for completion during 1984. May have small helicopter platform aft.

◆ **30 (+5) Lürssen FPB 28 class**

| | | |
|---|---|---|
| BC 4001 through BC 4006 | Lürssen, Vegesack | 4-81 to . . .-81 |
| BC 5001 through BC 5006 | Lürssen, Vegesack | . . . to . . . |
| BC 6001 through BC 6005 | BSC, Belgium | 11-81 to 8-82 |
| BC 7001 through BC 7006 | BSC, Belgium | 8-2-82 to 8-82 |
| BC 8001 through BC 8006 | P.T. PAL SY, Surabaja | 1-85 to -86 |
| BC 9001 through BC 9006 | P.T. PAL SY, Surabaja | . . . |

**BC 7002** B. Risseeuw, 10-86

**D:** 61 tons (68.5 fl) **S:** 30 kts **Dim:** 28.0 (26.0 wl) × 5.4 × 1.6
**A:** 1/12.7-mm mg
**M:** BC 4001–4003 and BC 6001–6005: 2 Deutz SBA 16M 816LCK-R diesels; 2 props; 2,720 hp—others: 2MTU diesels; 2 props; 2,620 hp
**Electric:** 36 kVA
**Fuel:** 10 tons
**Range:** 700/27.5; 1,050/17
**Man:** 6 officers, 13 men

REMARKS: Building to replace a series of very similar craft built by Lürssen in 1962–63. A collaborative effort by Lürssen, Abeking and Rasmussen of West Germany, and BSC—Belgium Shipbuilding Corp., a consortium of Fulton Marine, Ruisbrock, and Scheepswerven Van Langebrugge—delivering prefabricated sections to PAL shipyard, Surabaja, in addition to building complete boats. BC 5001–5003 rated at 30.6 kts. BC 6001 and 7001 series ordered 1980; BC 8001 and 9001 series ordered 1-81; program well behind schedule, with only two launched by 12-84.

◆ **7 BC 2001 class** Bldr: CMN, Cherbourg

| | L | In serv. | | L | In serv. |
|---|---|---|---|---|---|
| BC 2001 | 27-9-79 | 8-2-80 | BC 2005 | 19-8-80 | 5-9-80 |
| BC 2002 | 20-12-79 | 8-2-80 | BC 2006 | 14-10-80 | 7-11-80 |
| BC 2003 | 4-3-80 | 3-4-80 | BC 2007 | 9-12-80 | 10-2-81 |
| BC 2004 | 14-5-80 | 9-6-80 | | | |

**BC 2001** J. Jedrlinic, 2-84

**D:** 58.5 tons (70.3 fl) **S:** 29.7 kts (at 64.4 tons)
**Dim:** 28.5 (26.5 wl) × 5.4 × 1.3 (1.65 props)
**A:** 1/12.7-mm mg
**M:** 2 MTU 12V331 TC92 diesels; 2 props; 2,440 hp
**Man:** . . . tot.

◆ **7 BC 3001 class** Bldr: Chantiers Navals de l'Estérel, Cannes

| | In serv. | | In serv. |
|---|---|---|---|
| BC 3001 | 9-7-79 | BC 3005 | 22-10-80 |
| BC 3002 | 24-1-80 | BC 3006 | 22-1-81 |
| BC 3003 | 24-4-80 | BC 3007 | 3-4-81 |
| BC 3004 | 12-6-80 | | |

**INDONESIA** *(continued)*
**PATROL BOATS** *(continued)*

**BC 3006** L. & L. Van Ginderen, 10-86

**D:** 57 tons (71 fl) **S:** 34 kts **Dim:** 28.2 × 5.2 × 1.6
**A:** 1/12.7-mm mg **M:** 2 MTU 12V331 TC81 diesels; 2 props; 2,700 hp
**Range:** 800/15 **Man:** 2 officers, 16 men

Remarks: Similar design to BC 1001 class; also built of wood.

◆ **3 BC 1001 class** Bldr: Chantiers Navals de l'Estérel, Cannes

BC 1001 (In serv. 4-75) BC 1002 (In serv. 6-75) BC 1003 (In serv. 11-75)

**BC 1002** J. Jedrlinic, 5-84

**D:** 56 tons (fl) **S:** 34 kts **Dim:** 28.0 (26.6 wl) × 5.3 × 1.6
**A:** 1/12.7-mm mg **M:** 2 MTU 12V331 TC81 diesels; 2 props; 2,700 hp
**Fuel:** 10 tons **Range:** 750/15 **Man:** 15 tot.

◆ **up to 24 BC 401 series** Bldr: Lürssen, Vegesack (In serv. 1960–62)

Remarks: Data as for BC 4001 series, with Deutz engines. BC 401, BC 502, BC 703, and others remain in service pending completion of duplicate replacements.

MARITIME POLICE

**PATROL BOATS**

◆ **9 DKN 908 class** Bldr: Baglietto, Italy; Riva Trigoso, Italy (In serv. 1961–64)

DKN 908 DKN 911 DKN 914
DKN 909 DKN 912 DKN 915
DKN 910 DKN 913 DKN 916

**D:** 139 tons (159 fl) **S:** 21 kts **Dim:** 42.0 × 6.5 × 1.8
**A:** 3/20-mm AA (I × 3) **M:** 2 Maybach MD655 diesels; 2 props; . . . hp
**Range:** 1,500/17 **Man:** 22 tot.

◆ **10 DKN 504 class** Bldrs: DKN 504–508: Ishikawajima Harima, Tokyo; others: Uraga Dockyard, Yokosuka (In serv. 1963–64)

DKN 504 DKN 507 DKN 510 DKN 513
DKN 505 DKN 508 DKN 511
DKN 506 DKN 509 DKN 512

**D:** 314 tons light (390 std., 444 fl) **S:** 15.3 kts
**Dim:** 48.1 (44.0 pp) × 7.5 × 2.9 **A:** 1/20-mm AA, 2/12.7-mm mg (I × 2)
**M:** 2 M.A.N. W8V 22/30 ALU diesels; 2 props; 1,400 hp **Electric:** 126 kw
**Fuel:** 41 tons **Range:** 2,700/14 **Man:** 35 tot.

Remarks: Cargo hold with 75 tons capacity.

◆ **2 Carpentaria class** Bldr: De Havilland Marine, Australia

DKN . . . (ex-*Sasila*) DKN . . . (ex-*Sabola*)

Remarks: Transferred from Indonesian Navy 1981, under which see for data.

**DKN 507** 1981

**PATROL CRAFT**

◆ **32 chase boats** Bldr: P.T. Kodjo, Jakarta (In serv. 1982–86)

**D:** 3.7 tons (fl) **S:** 28.3 kts **Dim:** 7.6 × 2.7 × · · ·
**A:** small arms **Man:** 3 tot. **Fuel:** 150 lit.
**M:** 1 Caterpillar 3208T diesel; 1 Hamilton 1031 waterjet; 260 hp

Remarks: Trihedral form, GRP hull. Converted from original propeller drive.

INDONESIAN ARMY (ADRI)

At one time the Indonesian Army operated a great variety of ships, including up to 29 units in the ADRI-I series, most of which were old passenger-cargo ships acquired for use as troop transports. Most of its serviceable ships were turned over to the new Military Sealift Command in 1977 and 1978, but a new series of logistics landing craft is under construction.

◆ **28 utility landing craft** Bldr: Koja SY, Tanjung Priok (In serv. 1978–1982)

Adri XXXI to Adri LVIII

**D:** 580 tons (fl) **S:** 10 kts **Dim:** 42.0 (38.0 wl) × 10.7 × 1.8
**M:** 2 G.M. 6-71 diesels; 2 props; 680 hp **Electric:** 100 kw
**Fuel:** 40 tons **Range:** 1,500/10 **Man:** 15 tot.

Remarks: 300 dwt. Construction continues. Cargo: 122 tons vehicles/stores; 120 tons water. Two 150-dwt landing craft were also completed during 1980, while in 1982 the first of several 30-dwt landing craft and 180-dwt cargo lighters were acquired.

INDONESIAN AIR FORCE (AURI)

The Indonesian Air Force operates six passenger-cargo logistics ships that were completed in the mid-1960s. Of about 600 dwt, they are intended to beach and are equipped with bow doors.

# IRAN

## Islamic Republic of Iran

Personnel (1987): Approx 1,100 officers, 11,400 men, plus Revolutionary Guards

Merchant Marine (1986): 359 ships—2,911,359 grt (tankers: 33 ships—1,241,904 grt)

Maritime Aviation: On hand before the revolution and war with Iraq were: 7 SH-3D Sea King, 7 AB-212, 5 AB-205A, 14 AB-206A, and 2 Sikorsky RH-53D helicopters. Fixed-wing assets remaining include 2 P-3F Orion long-range patrol aircraft; 4 Fokker F-27 Mk 400M Friendship transports; 4 Falcon 20 and 4 Aero Commander utility transports.

Weapons: Three Iranian destroyers use General Dynamics-developed fixed-train, elevatable box-launchers to fire U.S.-supplied Standard SM-1 MR surface-to-*air* missiles; these have a secondary antiship capability. Target tracking and illumination is supplied by shipboard gunnery radars. Four Vosper Mk 5 frigates carry a quintuple-position, trainable launcher for Italian Sea Killer Mk 2 antiship missiles:

| | |
|---|---|
| Length: 4.70 m | Range: 25 km |
| Diameter: 20.6 cm | Speed: 300 m/sec. |
| Span: 99.9 cm (cruciform) | Guidance: beam-rider/command with optical backup |
| Weight: . . . | Engine: 100-kg-thrust solid-fuel with 4,400-kg-thrust solid booster |

Also used are Short Bros. & Harland Sea Cat short-range SAMs. Guns and torpedoes are of U.S., Italian, Swedish, and British origin. Only a dozen of U.S. Harpoon missiles were supplied, and all are believed to have been expended or are unserviceable.

**WEAPONS** *(continued)*

Note: Pendant numbers are no longer displayed. Although reporting on the current conflict between Iran and Iraq seems anything but accurate, the following ships appear to have been lost:

- 2 U.S. PF 103-class frigates, with another possibly lost in 1983
- 2 Combattante-II-class guided-missile patrol boats (including *Peykan*)
- 5 patrol boats
- 4 mine countermeasures ships

The two Combattante-II class and one of the PF 103 class were sunk by AM 39 Exocet missiles launched from Super Frélon helicopters.

## SUBMARINES

Note: The U.S. *Tang*-class submarine *Kusseh* (ex-*Trout*, SS 566) was abandoned at Groton, Connecticut, in 5-79. In 11-82 the Ayatollah Khomeini announced that he wished to renew the canceled 1978 contract for 6 West German Type 209 submarines; the West German government was still deciding its position as of 8-87. A claim by Iran to have launched its own submarine during 1987 was apparently a reference to a type of swimmer transport.

## GUIDED-MISSILE DESTROYERS

◆ **1 ex-British Battle class** Bldr: Cammell Laird, Birkenhead

| | Laid down | L | In serv. |
|---|---|---|---|
| Damavand (ex-*Artemiz*, ex-*Sluys*, D 60) | 24-11-43 | 28-2-45 | 30-9-46 |

**Damavand**—wearing old number Thornycroft, 1969

**D:** 2,325 tons (3,360 fl) **S:** 31 kts **Dim:** 115.32 (108.2 pp) × 12.95 × 5.2 (fl)
**A:** 4/Standard SM-1 MR SAM box launchers (8 missiles)—4/114-mm DP (II × 2, fwd)—4/40-mm AA (I × 4)—1/Sea Cat SAM (IV × 1)—1/Squid ASW mortar (III × 1)
**Electron Equipt:** Radar: 1/Decca . . . nav., 1/Plessey AWS-1 air-search, 1/Contraves Sea Hunter RTN-10X fire-control
Sonar: Plessey MS-26—EW: 1 Decca RDL-1
**M:** 2 sets Parsons GT; 2 props; 50,000 hp **Boilers:** 2 Admiralty 3-drum
**Fuel:** 680 tons **Range:** 3,200/20 **Man:** 260 tot.

Remarks: Modernized before transfer on 20-1-67. Antiship missiles added after refit in South Africa, 1975–76. Sea Cat system NSCS optical director only. Standard missiles are SAM version, vice SSM, using Sea Hunter for fire control. Renamed 1985.

◆ **2 ex-U.S. Allen M. Sumner, FRAM II, class**

| | Bldr | Laid down | L | In serv. |
|---|---|---|---|---|
| Babr (ex-*Zellars*, DD 777) | Todd, Pacific | 24-12-43 | 19-7-44 | 25-10-44 |
| Palang (ex-*Stormes*, DD 780) | Federal SB, Kearny | 25-2-44 | 4-11-44 | 27-1-45 |

**Palang**—old number—forward box-launcher raised 1975

**D:** 2,200 tons (3,320 fl) **S:** 30 kts **Dim:** 114.75 × 12.45 × 5.6
**A:** 4/Standard SM-1 MR SAM box-launchers (8 missiles)—4/127-mm DP (II × 2)—6/324-mm Mk 32 ASW TT (III × 2)—2/Hedgehogs—1/AB-204 helicopter
**Electron Equipt:** Radar: 1/SPS-10, 1/SPS-29, 1/Mk 25
Sonar: 1/SQS-29—EW: WLR-1, ULQ-6
**M:** 2 sets GT; 2 props; 60,000 hp
**Boilers:** 4 Babcock & Wilcox; 43.3 kg/cm$^2$, 454°C **Fuel:** 650 tons
**Range:** 1,260/30; 4,600/14 **Man:** 14 officers, 260 men

Remarks: Purchased in 3-71 and delivered in 10-73 and 1974. The *Bordelon* (DD 881) and the *Kenneth D. Bailey* (DD 713) were transferred for cannibalization. The Standard missile launchers are on a platform between the stacks and also on the 01 level forward of the bridge. Mk 37 fire control for the 127-mm guns. VDS now removed from the *Babr*. Both believed to be inoperable.

## FRIGATES

◆ **4 Saam (Vosper Mk 5) class**

| | Bldr | Laid down | L | In serv. |
|---|---|---|---|---|
| Alvand (ex-*Saam*) | Vosper Thornycroft | 22-5-67 | 25-7-68 | 20-5-71 |
| Alborz (ex-*Zaal*) | Vickers, Newcastle | 3-3-68 | 25-7-68 | 1-3-71 |
| Sabalan (ex-*Rastam*) | Vickers, Barrow | 10-12-67 | 4-3-69 | 28-2-72 |
| Sahand (ex-*Faramarz*) | Vosper Thornycroft | 25-7-68 | 30-7-69 | 28-2-72 |

**Sahand** G. Davies, Maritime Photographic, 9-87

**D:** 1,250 tons (1,540 fl) **S:** 40/30 kts (17.5 with diesel)
**Dim:** 94.5 (88.4 pp) × 11.07 × 3.25
**A:** 1/Sea Killer SSM system (V × 1)—1/Sea Cat SAM system (III × 1) 1/114-mm DP Mk 8—2/35-mm AA (II × 1)—1/Limbo Mk 10 ASW mortar (III × 1)—2/23-mm AA (II × 1)—2/12.7-mm mg (I × 2)
**Electron Equipt:** Radar: 1/Plessey AWS-1 air-search, 2/Contraves Sea Hunter RTN-10X fire control
EW: Decca RDL-1 intercept
**M:** CODOG: 2 Rolls-Royce Olympus TM3A gas turbines; 2 Paxman 16-cyl. Ventura diesels for cruising; 2 CP props; 46,000 hp (turbines), 3,800 hp (diesels)
**Fuel:** 150 tons (250 with overload) **Range:** 5,000/15 **Man:** 135 tot.

Remarks: Air-conditioned. Retractable fin stabilizers. All now carry Mk 8 guns in place of original Mk 6. One or two believed to be operable, but status of combat systems uncertain; were used in attacks on merchant ships, 1987. All renamed 1985.

◆ **1 or 2 U.S. PF 103 class** (see Remarks) Bldr: Levingston SB, Orange, Texas

| | Laid down | L | In serv. |
|---|---|---|---|
| Bayandor (ex-PF 103) | 20-8-62 | 7-7-63 | 18-5-64 |
| Naghdi (ex-PF 104) | 12-9-62 | 10-10-63 | 22-7-64 |

**D:** 900 tons (1,135 fl) **S:** 20 kts **Dim:** 83.82 × 10.06 × 3.05 (4.27 sonar)
**A:** 2/76.2-mm DP (I × 2)—2/40-mm AA (II × 1)—2/23-mm AA (II × 1)—4/d.c. projectors—2/d.c. racks
**Electron Equipt:** Radar: 1/SPS-6, 1/Raytheon navigational, 1/Mk 34
Sonar: SQS-17A
**M:** 4 Fairbanks-Morse 38D8$\frac{1}{8}$-10 diesels; 2 props; 5,300 hp
**Electric:** 750 kw **Fuel:** 110 tons **Range:** 2,400/18; 3,000/15 **Man:** 133 tot.

Remarks: Transferred under the Military Aid Program. Twin Soviet 23-mm AA have been added forward of the bridge in place of the single Hedgehog ASW mortar. Mk 63 GFCS for 76.2-mm guns (radar on fwd gun mount); Mk 51 Mod. 2 GFCS for 40-mm mount. Sisters *Milanian* (83, ex-PF 105) and *Kahnamuie* (84, ex-PF 106) reported lost to Iraqi forces by 1982, with a third reported lost in 1983.

## PATROL BOATS

◆ **11 Combattante-II class** Bldr: Constr. Méc. de Normandie, Cherbourg

| | L | In serv. | | L | In serv. |
|---|---|---|---|---|---|
| Kaman | 8-1-76 | 6-77 | Gorz | 28-12-77 | 15-9-78 |
| Zoubin | 14-4-76 | 6-77 | Gardouneh | 23-2-78 | 23-10-78 |
| Khadang | 15-7-76 | 15-3-78 | Khanjar | 27-4-78 | 1-8-81 |
| Joshan | 21-2-77 | 31-3-78 | Neyzeh | 5-7-78 | 1-8-81 |
| Falakhon | 2-6-77 | 31-3-78 | Tabarzin | 15-9-78 | 1-8-81 |
| Shamshir | 12-9-77 | 31-3-78 | | | |

**D:** 249 tons (275 fl) **S:** 36 kts **Dim:** 47.0 × 7.1 × 1.9
**A:** 1/76-mm OTO Melara DP—1/40-mm AA
**Electron Equipt:** Radar: 1/Decca 1226, 1/H.S.A. WM-28
EW: TSF TMV-433 suite: DR-2000 receiver, DALIA analyzer, Alligator 5-A jammer
**M:** 4 MTU 16V538 TB91 diesels; 4 props; 14,400 hp **Electric:** 350 kw
**Fuel:** 41 ton **Range:** 700/33.7s **Man:** 31 tot.

PATROL BOATS *(continued)*

**Zoubin** CMN, 1977

**Khadang**—with 4 Harpoon launchers 1978

Remarks: Contracted 19-2-74 and 14-10-74. The last three were embargoed at Cherbourg 4-79 and released 22-6-81. P 232 captured off Spain 13-8-80 by anti-Khomeini forces but abandoned later at Toulon. P 231 and 232 had no Harpoon tubes on delivery, and all missiles delivered by the U.S. are believed to have been expended. Two, including *Peykan* (P 224), reported lost to Iraqi forces 11-80.

◆ **1 U.S. Coast Guard Cape class** Bldr: U.S. Coast Guard, Curtis Bay, Md. (In serv. 1956–59)

Keyvan

**D:** 85 tons (107 fl) **S:** 20 kts **Dim:** 29.0 × 6.2 × 2.0
**A:** 1/40-mm AA—2/Mk 22 Mousetrap ASW RL—2/d.c. racks
**M:** 4 Cummins VT-12-M700 diesels; 2,200 hp **Electric:** 40 kw
**Range:** 1,500/15 **Man:** 15 tot.

Remarks: Sisters *Mehran* (P 203), *Mahvan* (P 204), and *Tiran* (P 202) lost 1980–83, as were the three U.S. PGM 71-class patrol boats *Parvin* (P 211), *Bahram* (P 212), and *Nahid* (P 213).

## SPECIAL FORCES CRAFT

◆ **29 (+11) special forces craft** Bldr: Boghammar Marin, Stockholm, Sweden (In serv. 1986–. . .)

**D:** 5.5 tons **S:** 45 kts **Dim:** 12.80 × 2.66 × 0.90
**A:** 1/106-mm recoilless rifle and/or RPG-7 anti-tank rocket launchers—machine guns
**Electron Equipt:** Radar: none
**M:** 2 Volvo Penta TAMD-OE diesels; 2 props; 610 hp
**Range:** 500/38 **Man:** 5–6 tot.

Remarks: Ordered 1984; 29 delivered by 7-87 for use by Revolutionary Guards in attacks on undefended merchant ships. Aluminum construction. Resemble small patrol craft, not pleasure boats. Reported based at al-Farisiyah Island, Sirri Island, Abu Musa Island, Larak Island, and from a disused oil-drilling platform.

Note: The Revolutionary Guards also employ a number of rigid inflatable craft for raiding parties in shallow water areas.

## MINE WARFARE SHIPS

◆ **1 ex-U.S. Falcon-class minesweeper** Bldr: Peterson (L: 1958)

Shahrokh (ex-MSC 276)

**D:** 320 tons (378 fl) **S:** 12.5 kts (8, sweeping)
**Dim:** 43.0 (41.5 pp) × 7.95 × 2.55
**A:** 2/20-mm AA (II × 1) **Range:** 2,500/10 **Man:** 3 officers, 35 men
**Electron Equipt:** Radar: 1/Decca 707 Sonar: UQS-1 **Fuel:** 27 tons
**M:** 2 G.M. 8-268A diesels; 2 props; 890 hp

Remarks: Sisters *Shabaz* lost through fire in 1975, *Simorgh* (302) and *Karkas* (303) to Iraqi forces 1980–81.

## AMPHIBIOUS WARFARE SHIPS

◆ **4 Hengam-class LSTs** Bldr: Yarrow & Co., Scotstoun

| | L | In serv. | | L | In serv. |
|---|---|---|---|---|---|
| Hengam | 27-9-73 | 12-8-74 | Lavan | 12-6-78 | 16-1-85 |
| Larak | 7-5-74 | 12-11-74 | Tonb | 6-12-79 | 7-85 |

**Larak**—wearing old number 1976

**Tonb**—laid up at builders L. & L. Van Ginderen, 8-82

**D:** 2,940 tons (fl) **S:** 14.5 kts **Dim:** 92.96 (86.87 wl) × 14.94 × 3.00 max.
**A:** 4/40-mm Bofors AA (I × 4)—8/23-mm AA (II × 4)
**Electron Equipt:** Radar: 1/Decca TM 1229
**M:** 511, 512: 4 Paxman Ventura 12 YJCM diesels; 2 CP props; 5,600 hp
513, 514: 4 MTU 12V562 TB61 diesels; 2 CP props; 5,800 hp
**Range:** 3,500/12 **Fuel:** 295 tons **Electric:** 1,280 kw
**Man:** 75 crew + 168 troops

Remarks: 513, 514, laid up since completion, were released by the British Government 5-10-84 on the excuse that they would be used in the unlikely role of hospital ships; delivered without armament. Negotiations continued into 1985 for the construction of two more, originally ordered 7-77, for which considerable material had been accumulated.

Flight deck for one Sea-King-sized helicopter aft. Cargo capacity of 600 tons on 39.6 × 8.8 × 4.5m (high) vehicle deck, with 15-m-long bow ramp. Can also carry up to 300 tons liquid cargo in lieu of some vehicle stowage. Can stow 12 Soviet T-55 or 6 British Chieftain battle tanks. Upper deck forward has a 10-ton crane to handle two Uniflote cargo lighters (LCVP) and twelve Z-boat rubber personnel landing craft. Intended for logistics support (when ten 20-ton or thirty 10-ton containers would be carried) or for amphibious assault. Magazines hold 8,000 rounds 40-mm; guns are locally controlled. 513 has an additional Decca 1216 nav. radar. 513 and 514 have a U.S. URN 25 TACAN system. 23 mm AA added circa 1986.

◆ **3 Iran Hormuz 24-class landing ships** Bldr: Inchon SB & Eng., Inchon, South Korea (all L: 20-12-85, In serv. 2-86)

Iran Hormuz 24 Iran Hormuz 25 Iran Hormuz 26

**D:** 2,014 tons (fl) **S:** 12 kts **Dim:** 73.06 (68.00 pp) × 14.23 × 2.50
**A:** . . . **Electron Equipt:** Radar: . . .
**M:** 2 Daihatsu diesels; 2 props; 2,530 hp **Electric:** 450 kw

Remarks: 1,010 grt/750 dwt. Nominally under the control of the Iranian Merchant Marine Ministry. Have bow doors, large amidships superstructures. Allegedly intended for coastal transportation. Berths for 146, plus 150 on deck. *Iran Hormuz 23* is a small oilfield exploration ship, unrelated in design.

◆ **2 medium landing ships** Bldr: Ravenstein SY, Deest, Netherlands (In serv. 1-85)

Iran Hormuz 21 Iran Hormuz 22

**D:** 1,400 tons (fl) **S:** 9 kts **Dim:** 65.03 (58.43 pp) × 12.01 × 2.60
**A:** . . . **Electron Equipt:** Radar: 1/. . . nav.
**M:** 2 M.A.N. V12V-12.5/14 diesels; 2 props; 730 hp
**Man:** . . .

Remarks: 906 grt/750 dwt. Delivered via U.K. as merchant ships, but bore naval pendants. Cargo capacity about 600 tons. Freight-barge design, with bow ramps.

◆ **2 tank landing ships** Bldr: Teraoka SY, Japan (In serv. 1978)

Iran Asr (ex-*Arya Akian*) Iran Ghadr (ex-*Arya Dokht*)

**D:** 614 tons light (2,274 fl) **S:** 11 kts
**Dim:** 53.65 (48.01 pp) × 10.81 × 5.70 (moulded depth)
**A:** 2/12.7-mm mg (I × 2)—mines, small arms **Electron Equipt:** Radar: 1/. . .
**M:** 2 diesels; 2 props; 2,200 hp **Man:** 30 tot.

Remarks: 984 grt/1,660 dwt. Blunt-bowed, commercial landing craft with bow ramp; single-hulled with sliding hatch cover. One 10-ton cargo boom. Mines are deck-

**AMPHIBIOUS WARFARE SHIPS** *(continued)*

stowed atop the hatch cover and launched over the side. Sister *Iran Ajr* (ex-*Arya Rakhsh*) captured 21-9-87 by U.S. forces while laying mines in international waters and scuttled 26-9-87. Sisters *Iran Bahr* (ex-*Arya Sahand*) and *Iran Badr* (ex-*Arya Boum*) lost 1980. See addenda for photo.

## HOVERCRAFT

◆ **4 BH.7 Wellington class** Bldr: British Hovercraft, Cowes, U.K. (In serv. 1970–75)

**D:** 50 to 55 tons (fl) **S:** 65 kts **Dim:** 23.9 × 13.8 × 10.36 (high)
**A:** several mg **Electron Equipt:** Radar: 1/Decca 914
**M:** 1 Rolls-Royce Proteus 15M549 gas turbine; 1 6.4-m-diameter prop; 4,250 hp
**Electric:** 110 kVA **Fuel:** 9 tons **Range:** 400/56

REMARKS: Four were of the logistics-support version, with a 14-ton payload. Two were of the Mk 4 version with recess for two SSM, which were not mounted. The Mk 4 uses the Gnome 15M541 engine of 4,750 hp and can carry 60 troops in side compartments as well as assault vehicles on its 56-m$^2$ cargo deck. Speed in both versions is reduced to 35 kts in a 1.4-meter sea. Overhauled at builders beginning with two in 2-84 and two more in 1985; new engines, skirts, etc. Two others, plus 8 SR-N6 Winchester-class hovercraft are inoperable.

## AUXILIARY SHIPS

◆ **1 large replenishment oiler**

| | Bldr | Laid-down | L | In serv. |
|---|---|---|---|---|
| KHARG | Swan Hunter, Wallsend | 1-76 | 3-2-77 | 25-4-80 |

**Kharg**—prior to rearming French Navy, 1985

**D:** 33,014 tons (fl) **S:** 21.5 kts **Dim:** 207.15 (195.00 pp) × 25.50 × 9.14
**A:** 1/76-mm OTO Melara compact DP—8/23-mm AA (II × 4)—3 helicopters
**M:** 1 set Westinghouse GT; 1 prop; 26,870 hp **Electric:** 7,000 kw
**Boilers:** 2 Babcock & Wilcox 2-drum **Man:** 248 tot.

REMARKS: Ordered 10-74. 21,100 grt/20,000 dwt. Carries fuel and ammunition. Design is greatly modified version of the Royal Navy's *Olwen* class. Ran initial trials 11-78, but delays in fitting out made delivery before the revolution impossible; remained at builders until released 5-10-84; ran trials again 4-9-84. Has U.S. URN-20 TACAN equipment. Delivered without armament; originally had an OTO Melara 76-mm Compact forward. One 40-mm AA was installed on the former 76-mm pedestal, the other on the helo deck during 1985, replaced by present armament 1986.

◆ **2 Bandar Abbas-class small replenishment oilers** Bldr: C. Lühring, Brake, West Germany

BANDAR ABBAS (L: 14-8-73) BOOSHEHR (L: 22-3-74)

**Booshehr**—composite photo G. Koop, 1974

**D:** 5,000 tons (fl) **S:** 15 kts **Dim:** 108.0 × 16.6 × 4.5
**A:** 2/40-mm AA (I × 2)—1/helicopter
**M:** 2 M.A.N. diesels; 2 props; 6,000 hp **Man:** 60 tot.

REMARKS: 3,250 dwt. Telescoping hangar. Carry fuel, food, ammunition, and spare parts. Armed after delivery. Used for patrol duties 1984-on, due to lack of operable combatants.

◆ **2 water tankers** Bldr: Mazagon Dock, Bombay, India

KANGAN (L: 4-78) TAHERI (L: 17-9-78)

**Kangan** 1979

**D:** 12,000 tons (fl) **S:** 12 kts **Dim:** 147.95 (140.0 pp) × 21.5 × 5.0
**M:** 1 M.A.N. 7L52/55A diesel; 7,385 hp

REMARKS: 9,430 dwt. Intended to supply Arabian Gulf islands. Liquid cargo: 9,000 m$^3$. Used in patrol duties 1984–on.

◆ **1 U.S. 174-foot-class water tanker** Bldr: Zenith Dredge, Duluth, Minn.

| | Laid down | L | In serv. |
|---|---|---|---|
| LENGEH (ex-U.S. *YW 88*) | 18-3-43 | 18-5-43 | 17-10-43 |

**D:** 440 tons light (1,390 fl) **S:** 10 kts **Dim:** 53.04 × 10.01 × 4.27
**M:** 2 Union diesels; 2 props; 580 hp **Electric:** 80 kw
**Fuel:** 25 tons **Man:** 22 tot.

REMARKS: Purchased in 1964. Cargo: 930 tons.

◆ **1 ex-U.S. Amphion-class repair ship** Bldr: Tampa SB, Florida

| | Laid down | L | In serv. |
|---|---|---|---|
| CHAH BAHAR (ex-*Amphion*, AR 13) | 20-9-44 | 15-5-45 | 30-1-46 |

**D:** 8,670 tons light (14,450 fl) **S:** 16 kts **Dim:** 150.0 × 21.4 × 8.4
**A:** 2/76.2-mm DP (I × 2) **M:** 1 set GT; 1 prop; 8,500 hp **Electric:** 3,600 kw
**Boilers:** 2 Foster-Wheeler "D"; 30.6 kg/cm$^2$, 382°C **Fuel:** 1,850 tons
**Man:** Quarters for 921 men

REMARKS: Transferred in 10-71. Primarily stationary, but can steam.

◆ **1 former imperial yacht for Caspian Sea** Bldr: Boele's SW, Bolnes, the Netherlands

CHAH SEVAR

**D:** 530 tons **S:** 15 kts **Dim:** 53.0 × 7.65 × 3.2
**M:** 2 Stork diesels; 2 props; 1,300 hp

◆ **1 former imperial yacht for Arabian Gulf** Bldr: Burmester, W. Germany (In serv. 1970)

KISH

**D:** 175 tons **Dim:** 37.0 × 7.6 × 2.2 **M:** 2 MTU diesels; 2 props; 2,920 hp

## YARD AND SERVICE CRAFT

◆ **1 barracks ship**

| | Bldr | L | In serv. |
|---|---|---|---|
| RAFFAELLO | CRDA, Monfalcone | . . . | 7-7-65 |

**D:** 42,000 tons (fl) **S:** 29 kts **Dim:** 275.8 (244.0 pp) × 31.0 × 9.3
**M:** 4 sets GT; 4 props; 65,000 hp **Boilers:** 4 Foster-Wheeler

REMARKS: Former cruise liner, purchased 12-12-76. Arrived July/August 1977 at Bandar Abbas for use as floating barracks for Iranian naval personnel and their families. *Raffaello* seriously damaged by Iraqi missile, 20 or 21-11-82. Sister *Michelangelo* for sale 1986.

◆ **2 harbor tugs** Bldr: B.V. Scheepswerf K. Damen, Hardinxveld-Giessendam, Netherlands (In serv. 1985)

ARAS ATRAK

**D:** 91 grt **S:** . . . **Dim:** 22.00 × 7.12 × 2.65
**M:** 2 MTU diesels; . . . hp

◆ **2 harbor tugs**

| | Bldr | L | In serv. |
|---|---|---|---|
| HAMOON | Deltawerf, Sliedrecht, Neth. | . . . | 4-84 |
| HIRMAND | Damen, Hardinxveld, Neth. | 1-8-84 | . . . |

**D:** 300 tons (fl) **S:** 12 kts **Dim:** 25.63 (23.53 pp) × 6.81 × 3.19
**M:** 2 MTU GV396 TC62 diesels; 2 props; 1,200 hp

REMARKS: 122 grt. There may be three other craft in this group.

◆ **1 ex-U.S. Army tug** (transferred 2-62)

45 BAHMAN SHIR (ex-ST 2001)

**D:** 150 tons

IRAN *(continued)*
YARD AND SERVICE CRAFT *(continued)*

◆ **2 ex-German tugs**

1 (ex-*Karl*) 2 (ex-*Ise*)

**D:** 134 tons

REMARKS: Built in 1962-63, and transferred 17-6-74.

◆ **2 ammunition lighters** Bldr: Karachi SY & Eng. Wks. (In serv. 1978)

N . . . . . . . CHIROO

**D:** 840 grt **S:** 11 kts **Dim:** 64.0 × 10.5 × 3.2
**M:** 2 M.A.N. G6V-23.5/33ATL diesels; 2 props; 1,560 hp

◆ **2 water barges** Bldr: Karachi SY & Eng. Wks (In serv. 1977–78)

1701 1702

**D:** 1,410 grt **Dim:** 65.0 × 13.0 × 2.6

◆ **2 large fuel lighters** Bldr: Karachi SY & Eng. Wks (In serv. 1981)

1718 DAYERE N . . . DAYLAM

**D:** 1,300 tons (fl) **S:** 9 kts **Dim:** 63.45 (58.48 pp) × 11.00 × 3.03
**M:** 2 M.A.N. diesels; 2 props; 1,560 hp

REMARKS: 933 grt/850 dwt

◆ **2 small fuel lighters** Bldr: Karachi SY & Eng. Wks. (In serv. 1981)

1703 N . . . . . . . 1704 N. . . . . . .

**D:** . . . **S:** . . . **Dim:** 30.51 × 9.30 × 1.83
**M:** 2 M.A.N. diesels; 2 props; 326 hp

REMARKS: 195 grt/200 dwt.

NOTE: In addition to the eight units immediately above, Karachi Shipyard and Engineering Works delivered 10 other yard and service craft between 1977 and 7-81. All were designed in Great Britain. A variety of craft were built, all initially numbered 1701 through 1718. Types included a self-propelled dredge, (1711), a pontoon barge (1710), a diving tender (1705), and garbage lighter (120 $m^3$ hopper with compacter). Two cargo lighters were reportedly similar to the ammunition lighters described above.

◆ **3 coastal tankers** Bldr: Scheepswerf Ravestein, Deest, the Netherlands (In serv. 1983)

IRAN PARAK IRAN SHALAK IRAN YOUSHAT

**D:** approx. 800 fl **S:** 6 kts **Dim:** 40.01 (38.82 pp) × 10.01 × 2.6
**M:** 2 G.M. 6-71 diesels; 2 props; 730 hp
**Fuel:** 5 tons **Electric:** 12 kw

REMARKS: 400 grt/540 dwt. Originally purchased for commercial purposes.

◆ **1 modified U.S. 174-foot-class yard oiler** Bldr: Nav. Mec. Castellammare (In serv. 2-56)

HORMUZ (ex-U.S. *YO 247*)

**Hormuz** 1974

**D:** 1,400 tons (fl) **S:** 9 kts **Dim:** 54.4 × 9.8 × 4.3
**A:** 2/20-mm AA (I × 2) **Electron Equipt:** Radar: 1/Decca 707
**M:** 1 Ansaldo Q370 diesel; 600 hp **Fuel:** 25 tons

REMARKS: Built under U.S. Military Aid Program. Cargo: 900 tons

◆ **1 large floating dry dock** Bldr: M.A.N.-G.H.H., Nordenham/Blexen, West Germany

DOLPHIN (L: 22-11-85)

**D:** 28,000 tons lift **Dim:** 240.00 × 52.50 × . . .

REMARKS: Docking well 230.00 m over keel blocks, 41.00 m free width, 8.50 m flood-able overblocks.

◆ **1 floating dry dock** Bldr: Pacific Bridge, Alameda, Cal. (In serv. 7-44)

400 (ex-ARD 28)

**D:** 3,500 tons lift **Dim:** 149.8 × 25.6 × 1.7 (light)

REMARKS: Transferred 1-3-77.

PATROL CRAFT

◆ **up to 81 U.S. 50-ft. class** Bldr: Peterson Bldrs., Sturgeon Bay, Wisc. (In serv. 1975–78)

**D:** 22 tons (fl) **S:** 28 kts **Dim:** 15.24 × 4.80 × 1.9
**A:** 1/12.7-mm mg **Range:** 500/30
**M:** 2 G.M. 8V71 TI diesels; 3 props; 850 hp **Man:** 6 tot.

REMARKS: Twenty were ordered in 1973 and 61 more in 1976. Shipped as kits for assembly in Iran, at Boghammar, where they were still being assembled into the 1980s. Some have probably been lost, and some may be under Revolutionary Guards' control.

◆ **20 U.S. Swift Mk II class** Bldr: Peterson Bldrs., Sturgeon Bay, Wisc. (In serv. 1976–77)

1201 to 1220

**D:** 22 tons (fl) **S:** 26 kts **Dim:** 15.3 × 4.8 × 1.9
**A:** none **M:** 2 G.M. 12V71 diesels; 2 props; 900 hp **Man:** 6 tot.

REMARKS: Equipped to carry extra personnel and have no fixed armament.

◆ **6 U.S. 40-ft. class** Bldr: Sewart Seacraft, Louisiana (In serv. 1963)

MAHMAVI-HAMARAZ MAHMAVI-VANEDI MORDARID
MAHMAVI-TAHERI MARDJAN SADAF

**D:** 10 tons **S:** 30 kts **Dim:** 12.2 × 3.4 × 1.1
**A:** 2/7.62-mm mg **M:** 2 G.M. diesels; 2 props; 600 hp

REMARKS: Four given to Sudan in 1978, two stricken.

◆ **40 + U.S. Bertram Enforcer harbor patrol craft** **Dim:** 9.5 and 6.1 o.a.

◆ **10 Medina-class motor lifeboats** Bldr: Fairey Marine, Hamble (In serv. 1978)

1601 to 1610

**D:** 15.5 tons (fl) **S:** 16 kts **Dim:** 14.0 × 3.7 × 1.1
**M:** 2 Ford Sabre Turbo-Plus diesels; 2 props; 500 hp **Range:** 150/12
**Man:** 4 tot. (plus 12 passengers)

# IRAQ

## Republic of Iraq

PERSONNEL (1987): about 3,000 men, including 400 officers

MERCHANT MARINE (1986): 149 ships—1,016,343 grt (tankers: 27 ships—775,280 grt)

NAVAL AVIATION: The Air Force operates eight French-supplied Super Frélon helicopters, armed with AM 39 Exocet antiship missiles, and in 10-83 France loaned 5 Super Étendard fighter-bombers with AM 39 missiles; returned 10-85. Some of the newly delivered 83 Mirage F.1EQ fighter-bombers also carry one or two AM 39. Five Agusta AB 212 and 10 A 103A helicopters were ordered 1984.

NOTE: Losses to date during the war with Iran reportedly include:

- 4 Osa-II-class guided-missile patrol boats (two to Iranian naval ships and two to aircraft)
- 6 P 6-class torpedo boats
- 1 Polnocny-C-class landing ship

FRIGATES

◆ **4 Italian Lupo class** Bldr: Fincantieri, Ancona (A) and Riva Trigoso (B)

| | Yard | Laid down | L | In serv. |
|---|---|---|---|---|
| F 14 HITTIN | A | 31-3-82 | 27-7-83 | 3-85 |
| F 15 TMI QAR | A | 9-82 | 19-12-84 | -85 |
| F 16 AL QADISSIYA | A | 15-4-83 | 31-3-84 | -85 |
| F 17 AL YARMOOK | B | 12-3-84 | 20-6-85 | -86 |

**Hittin (F 14)** A. Fraccaroli, 10-86

**FRIGATES** *(continued)*

**Tmi Qar (F 15)**—laid up at builders A. Scrimali, 4-87

**D:** 2,213 tons (2,525 fl) **S:** 35 kts (20.5 diesel)
**Dim:** 112.8 (106.0 pp) × 11.98 × 3.84
**A:** 8/Otomat Mk II SSM (I × 8)—1/Albatros SAM syst. (VIII × 1; no reloads)—1/127-mm DP OTO Melara—4/40-mm AA Breda Dardo (II × 2)—6/324-mm ASW TT (III × 2)—2/AB 212 ASW helicopters
**Electron Equipt:** Radar: 1/3RM20 navigational, 1/RAN-11X surf./air search, 1/RAN-10S air search, 2/Orion RTN-10XRCT f.c., 2/Orion RTN-20X f.c.
Sonar: Edo 610E or Raytheon 1160B
EW: Lambda F passive syst.—2/SCLAR chaff RL
**M:** CODOG: 2 Fiat/G.E. LM-2500 gas turbines (25,000 hp each); 2 GMT A230-20M diesels (3,900 hp each); 2 CP props
**Electric:** 4,000 kVA **Range:** 900/35; 3,450/20.5 **Man:** 185 tot.

Remarks: Ordered 2-81. 127-mm gun and SAM fire control by two Elsag Mk 10 Mod. 0 systems with NA-10 radar directors; 40-mm f.c. by two Dardo systems. Selenia IPN-10 combat data system. SAM system will use Aspide missiles rather than NATO Sea Sparrow. Fin stabilizers fitted. Fixed hangar, as on Venezuelan and Peruvian units of the class, to which this version will in other ways be similar. U.S. objection to the sale of major components of the LM-2500 gas turbines was overcome. *Hittin* delivered 11-84, commissioned 3-85, but had not sailed for Iraq by 8-87, nor had any of the others.

◆ **1 training frigate** Bldr: Uljanic SY, Yugoslavia

| | Laid down | L | In serv. |
|---|---|---|---|
| 507 Ibn Khaldum | 1977 | 1978 | 21-3-80 |

**Ibn Khaldum (507)** 1980

**D:** 1,850 tons (fl) **S:** 26 kts **Dim:** 96.7 × 11.2 × 3.55
**A:** 1/57-mm Bofors SAK 57 AA—1/40-mm AA—8/20-mm AA (II × 4)—1/d.c. rack
**Electron Equipt:** Radar: 2/navigational, 1/surface search, 1/Philips 9LV200 Mk II f.c.
Sonar: . . .
**M:** CODOG: 1 Rolls-Royce Olympus TM-3B gas turbine, 22,360 hp; 2 MTU 16V956 TB61 diesels, 7,500 hp; 2 CP props
**Range:** 4,000/20 (diesels) **Man:** 93 men + 100 students

Remarks: Same basic design as the ship laid down in 1979 for Indonesia. To provide experience in operating larger ships for future expansion of the Iraqi fleet and has served as a transport during the Iranian war. No helicopter facilities.

**GUIDED-MISSILE CORVETTES**

◆ **4 modified Wadi M'ragh class** Bldr: Fincantieri, Marghera

| | Laid down | L | In serv. |
|---|---|---|---|
| F 214 Abdullah ibn ari Serh | 22-3-82 | 5-7-83 | 1987 |
| F 216 Kalid ibn al Walid | 3-6-82 | 5-7-83 | 1987 |
| F 218 Saad ibn ali Wakkad | 17-8-82 | 30-12-83 | 1987 |
| F 220 Sala al din Ayubi | 17-9-82 | 30-3-84 | 1987 |

**Abdullah ibn ari Serh (F 214)** C. Martinelli, 12-86

**Kalid ibn al Walid (F 216)** L. Grazioli, 1-87

**D:** 600 tons (675 fl) **S:** 37.5 kts **Dim:** 62.3 (57.8 pp) × 9.3 × 2.8 (hull)
**A:** 6/Otomat Mk II SSM (III × 2)—1/Albatros SAM system (IV × 1, plus 8 reload Aspide missiles)—1/76-mm OTO Melara DP—2/40-mm Breda Dardo AA (II × 1)—6/324-mm ILAS-3 ASW TT (III × 2)
**Electron Equipt:** Radar: 1/3RM 20, 1/RAN-12 L/X, 1/Orion RTN-10X
Sonar: Diodon
EW: Electronica Gamma syst., 2/SCLAR chaff RL (XX × 2)
**M:** 4 MTU 20V956 TB92 diesels; 4 props; 24,400 hp (20,400 sust.)
**Electric:** 650 kw **Fuel:** 126 tons **Range:** 1,200/31; 4,000/18 **Man:** 51 tot.

Remarks: Ordered 2-81. Attack variant of leader version listed below. Aspide reload via manual crane. Selenia IPN-10 data system with 2 radar directors and 2 CO3 optical directors for guns. Probably exceed 700 tons displacement on completion. Trials began 4-84 with first ship, but none delivered in Iraq as of 8-87.

◆ **2 helicopter-equipped** Bldr: Fincantieri, Muggiano

| | Laid down | L | In serv. |
|---|---|---|---|
| F 210 Mussa Ben Nussair | 15-1-82 | 16-12-82 | 17-9-86 |
| F 212 Tariq Ibn Ziad | 20-5-82 | 8-7-83 | 29-10-86 |

**D:** 610 tons (685 fl) **S:** 37.5 kts **Dim:** 62.3 (57.8 pp) × 9.3 × 2.9 (hull)
**A:** 2/Otomat Mk II SSM (I × 2)—1/Albatros SAM syst. (IV × 1, plus 4 reload Aspide missiles)—1/76-mm OTO Melara DP—6/324-mm ILAS-3 ASW TT (III × 2)—1/A 109A helicopter
**Electron Equipt:** Radar: 1/3RM 20, 1/RAN-12L/X, 2/Orion RTN-10X
Sonar: Diodon
EW: Electronica Gamma syst., 1/SCLAR chaff RL (XX × 1)

Remarks: Remaining data as per attack version above. Telescopic hangar for the helicopter. Remained in Italian waters through 8-87. ASW TT may not be mounted.

## GUIDED-MISSILE CORVETTES *(continued)*

**Tariq Ibn Ziad (F 212)** M. Louagie, 7-87

## GUIDED-MISSILE PATROL BOATS

◆ **6 Soviet Osa-II class**

**D:** 210 tons (240 fl) **S:** 36 kts **Dim:** 38.6 × 7.6 × 2.0
**A:** 4/SS-N-2B Styx (I × 4)—4/30-mm AA (II × 2)
**Electron Equipt:** Radar: 1/Square Tie, 1/Drum Tilt
IFF: 2/Square Head, 1/High Pole A
**M:** 3 M504 diesels; 3 props; 15,000 hp **Range:** 500/34; 750/25 **Man:** 30 tot.

REMARKS: Two transferred in 1974 and two in each year through 1977. Four reported lost 1980-81. Two replacements delivered 11-84.

◆ **4 Soviet Osa-I class**

**D:** 180 tons (215 fl) **S:** 36 kts **Dim:** 38.6 × 7.6 × 1.8
**A:** 4/SS-N-2 Styx—4/30-mm AA (II × 2)
**Electron Equipt:** Radar: 1/Square Tie, 1/Drum Tilt
IFF: 2/Square Head, 1/High Pole A
**M:** 3 M503A diesels; 3 props; 12,000 hp
**Range:** 500/34; 750/25 **Man:** 30 tot.

REMARKS: Two transferred 1971–72, two in 1973, and two in 1974. Of these, two have been "retired from service."

NOTE: Names reported for both Osa-I and Osa-II craft include: *Al Walid, Hazirani, Kanun Ath-Tani, Khalid Ibn, Nisan, Sa'd,* and *Tamuz.*

NOTE: The last four Soviet P 6-class torpedo boats are believed to have been stricken.

## PATROL BOATS AND CRAFT

◆ **3 ex-Soviet S.O.-1 class**

210 211 212

**D:** 190 tons (215 fl) **S:** 28 kts **Dim:** 42.0 × 6.1 × 1.9
**A:** 4/25-mm AA (II × 2—4/RBU-1200 ASW RL (V × 4)—2/d.c. racks—mines
**Electron Equipt:** Radar: 1/Pot Head
Sonar: high-frequency
**M:** 3 Type 40D diesels; 3 props; 7,500 hp **Range:** 340/28; 1,920/7
**Man:** 3 officers, 27 men

REMARKS: Delivered in 1962. Probably in only marginal operating condition.

◆ **5 Soviet Zhuk class**

**D:** 50 tons (60 fl) **S:** 34 kts **Dim:** 24.0 × 5.0 × 1.8 (props)
**A:** 4/14-mm AA (II × 2) **Electron Equipt:** Radar: 1/Spin Trough
**M:** 2 M50 diesels; 2 props; 2,400 hp

REMARKS: Transferred in 1975.

◆ **2 Soviet Poluchat-I class**

**D:** 80 tons (90 fl) **S:** 18 kts **Dim:** 29.6 × 6.1 × 1.9 (props)
**A:** 2/14.5-mm AA **Electron Equipt:** Radar: 1/Spin Trough
**M:** 2 M50 diesels; 2 props; 2,400 hp **Range:** 450/17; 900/10 **Man:** 20 tot.

REMARKS: Transferred in 1966. May in fact be torpedo-recovery versions of the Poluchat class.

## MINE WARFARE SHIPS

◆ **1 Soviet T-43-class fleet minesweeper**

467 AL KADISIA

**D:** 500 tons (570 fl) **S:** 14 kts **Dim:** 58.0 × 8.6 × 2.3
**A:** 4/37-mm AA (II × 2)—8/12.7-mm mg (II × 4)—2/d.c. projectors—mines
**Electron Equipt:** Radar: 1/Ball End—IFF: 1/Square Head, 1/High Pole A
**M:** 2 Type 9D diesels; 2 props; 2,200 hp **Range:** 3,200/10

REMARKS: Transferred in 1969. Sister *Al Yarmouk* stricken 1984.

◆ **3 Yevgenya-class inshore minesweepers**

**D:** 80 tons (90 fl) **S:** 11 kts **Dim:** 26.2 × 6.1 × 1.5 **A:** 2/25-mm AA (II × 2)
**Electron Equipt:** Radar: 1/Spin Trough
**M:** 2 diesels; 2 props; 600 hp **Range:** 300/10

REMARKS: Transferred in 1975 as "oceanographic research craft." Have heavier guns than their Soviet Navy sisters.

◆ **4 Yugoslav Nestin-class river minesweepers** Bldr: Brodotehnika, Belgrade

**D:** 66 tons (78 fl) **S:** 15 kts **Dim:** 27.0 × 6.5 × 1.15
**A:** 5/20-mm AA (III × 1, I × 2)—24 mines
**M:** 2 diesels; 2 props; 520 hp **Range:** 860/11 **Man:** 17 tot.

REMARKS: Transferred 1978–79. Have acoustic, magnetic, and mechanical sweep gear.

## AMPHIBIOUS WARFARE SHIPS

◆ **3 modified roll-on/roll-off cargo ships** Bldr: Helsingor Vaerft, Denmark

| | Laid down | L | In serv. |
|---|---|---|---|
| 426 AL ZAHRAA | 7-7-81 | 19-3-82 | 18-3-83 |
| 428 KHAWLA | 19-11-81 | 8-82 | 7-83 |
| 429 BALQUSES | 21-4-82 | 11-82 | 10-83 |

**Al Zahraa (426)** MacGregor-Navire, 1983

**D:** 5,800 tons (fl) **S:** 15.5 kts **Dim:** 106.0 (96.1 pp) × 18.8 × 5.25
**A:** . . . **M:** 2 MTU 12V1163 TB62 diesels; 2 CP props; 6,000 hp
**Electric:** 1,280 kw **Man:** 35 crew plus 250 troops

REMARKS: 3,681 grt/3,500 dwt. Modified vehicle cargo ship design with military features. 880 $m^2$ vehicle cargo space. Slewing ramp aft can handle 55-ton tanks or place tanks up to 41 tons in water. Side ramps with 50-ton capacity. Helicopter deck, 55-ton elevator to upper deck. 1,200-ton automated water ballast system.

◆ **3 Soviet Polnocny-C class** Bldr: Polnocny SY, Gdansk, Poland

**D:** 1,150 tons (fl) **S:** 18 kts **Dim:** 81.3 × 10.1 × 2.1
**A:** 4/30-mm AA (II × 2)—2/122-mm rocket launchers (XL × 2)
**Electron Equipt:** Radar: 1/Don-2, 1/Drum Tilt
**M:** 2 Type 40D diesels; 2 props; 5,000 hp **Range:** 900/17; 1,500/14

REMARKS: Have a helicopter platform forward of the superstructure. Barrage rocket launchers differ from others of this class, which use 140-mm rockets. Two transferred in 1977, one in 1978, and one in 9-79. Names of first three: *Atika, Ganda,* and *Nouh.* One lost to Iranian Harpoon missiles, 11-80.

## AUXILIARY SHIPS AND CRAFT

◆ **1 Italian Stromboli-class replenishment oiler**

| | Bldr | Laid down | L | In serv. |
|---|---|---|---|---|
| A 102 AGNADEEN | Castellamare di Stabia, Naples | 29-1-82 | 22-10-82 | 29-10-84 |

**IRAQ** *(continued)*
**AUXILIARY SHIPS AND CRAFT** *(continued)*

**Agnadeen (A 102)** C. Martinelli, 12-83

**D:** 8,706 tons (fl) **S:** 19.5 kts (18 sust.)
**Dim:** 129.0 (118.5 pp) × 18.0 × 6.5 **A:** 1/76-mm OTO Melara DP
**Electron Equipt:** Radar: 1/3RM7-250, 1/Orion RTN-10X
**M:** 2 GMT A428SS diesels; 1 CP prop; 11,200 hp (9,600 sust.)
**Electric:** 4,200 kw **Range:** 10,000/16 **Man:** 124 tot.

Remarks: Ordered 2-81. Will probably be modified from the Italian Navy version as to cargo and equipment. Capable of serving two ships alongside while underway. Delivered 20-12-83 after fitting out at Muggiano, La Spezia. Moored at Alexandria, Egypt, 1986.

◆ **1 Yugoslav Spasilac-class salvage ship** Bldr: Tito SY, Belgrade

A 51 Aka (In serv. 1978)

**D:** 1,590 tons (fl) **S:** 13.4 kts **Dim:** 55.50 × 12.00 × 4.34
**A:** 4/14.5-mm mg (II × 2) **M:** 2 diesels; 2 Kort-nozzle props; 4,340 hp
**Man:** 53 tot.

Remarks: Can carry up to 250 tons deck cargo, 490 tons cargo fuel, 48 tons cargo water. Can support divers to 300 m. Can lay a 4-point moor. Sisters in Yugoslav and Libyan navies.

◆ **1 transport** Bldr: Wärtsilä, Turku, Finland (In serv. 3-83)

Al Mansur

**D:** . . . **S:** . . . **Dim:** 121.01 (96.50 pp) × 17.53 × 5.51
**A:** . . . **M:** 2 Wärtsilä diesels; 2 CP props; 11,994 hp
**Fuel:** 693 tons

Remarks: 7,359-grt/3,795-dwt troop transport with helicopter deck, hangar. Light armor on hull sides, bulletproof portholes. Has bow-thruster.

◆ **1 presidential yacht** Bldr: Elsinore SB & Eng., Denmark

Qadissayat Saddam (L: 10-80; In serv. 1981)

**Qadissayat Saddam**—artist's rendering Elsinore SY, 1980

**D:** 1,660 tons (fl) **S:** 19.3 kts **Dim:** 82.00 × 13.00 × 3.30
**M:** 2 MTU 12V1163 TB82 diesels; 2 CP props; 6,000 hp
**Electric:** 1,095 kVA

Remarks: 2,282 grt. Can carry 56 passengers (74 additional on short cruises). Sperry retractable fin stabilizers. 300-hp bow-thruster. Helicopter deck aft above swimming pool.

◆ **1 presidential barge** Bldr: Elsinore SB & Eng., Denmark

Al Qadissiya

**D:** . . . **S:** . . . **Dim:** 67.0 × . . . × 1.2 **M:** . . .

Remarks: Ordered 1981. Luxurious barge-type yacht for use on the Tigris.

◆ **1 diving tender** Bldr: Gorter, the Netherlands (In serv. 10-80)

N . . . . . . .

**D:** 200 tons (fl) **S:** 15 kts **Dim:** 28.5 (27.8 pp) × 6.4 × 1.8
**M:** 1 MTU 8V396 TC82 diesel; 1 prop; 870 hp

◆ **4 Soviet Nyryat-2-class diving tenders**

**D:** 56 tons (fl) **S:** 12 kts **Dim:** 21.3 × 3.8 × 2.0 **M:** 1 3D12 diesel; 300 hp

Remarks: May also be used as tugs.

◆ **1 Soviet Pozharney-I-class fireboat**

**D:** 180 tons (fl) **S:** 17 kts **Dim:** 35.0 × 6.2 × 2.0
**M:** 2 diesels; 2 props; 1,800 hp

◆ **1 Soviet Prometey-class tug** Bldr: Okhtenskiy SY, Leningrad

**D:** 319 tons (fl) **S:** 12 kts **Dim:** 29.8 (28.2 pp) × 8.3 × 3.2
**M:** 2 6D30/50-4 diesels; 2 Kort-nozzle props; 1,200 hp **Electric:** 50 kw
**Range:** 1,800/12 **Man:** 3 tot.

Remarks: Delivered mid-1970s. Has firefighting monitor.

◆ **1 new-construction floating dry dock** Bldr: Italcantiere, Trieste (In serv. 7-84)

Remarks: Ordered 2-81. 6,000-ton capacity. Moored at Alexandria, Egypt.

CUSTOMS SERVICE

◆ **1 yacht used as a pilot station** (In serv. 1929)

Al Thawra (ex-*Malike Aliyah*)

**D:** 746 tons **S:** 14 kts **M:** diesels; 2 props; 1,800 hp

◆ **9 Tana-class pilot launches** Bldr: Kone-Jyraa Oy, Jyvasky, Finland (In serv. 1980–81)

**D:** . . . **S:** 33 kts **Dim:** 9.45 × 2.44 × . . .
**M:** 2 MTU diesels; 2 props; . . . hp

Remarks: Delivery delayed by war.

◆ **8 pilot launches** Bldr: Thornycroft, 1961–62

**D:** 10 tons **S:** . . . **Dim:** 11.0 × . . . × . . . **M:** 1 diesel; 125 hp

◆ **4 pilot launches** Bldr: Thornycroft

**Dim:** 6.4 × . . . × . . . **M:** 40 hp

◆ **6 SRN. Mk 6C-class hovercraft** Bldr: British Hovercraft, Cowes

**D:** 17 tons **S:** 50 to 55 kts **Dim:** 18.3 × 8.5 × . . .
**A:** 2/20-mm GAM-BO1 AA—1/7.62-mm mg
**M:** 1 Rolls-Royce Gnome gas turbine; 2 CP airscrews; 1,285 hp

Remarks: Ordered 1981. Six-ton payload; 6- to 11-hour endurance.

# IRELAND

**Eire**

Personnel (31-7-87): 874 active, plus 300 reserves

Merchant Marine (1986): 154 ships—149,308 grt (3 tankers—8,754 grt)

Naval Aviation: The Irish Air Force operates 3 Beech A200 Maritime Patrol Aircraft. Two longer-range maritime patrol aircraft are planned. Two Air Force-manned SA-365 Dauphin II helicopters were delivered in 1985.

## FISHERIES-PROTECTION SHIPS

◆ **1 P 31 class** Bldr: Verolme DY, Cork

| | Laid down | L | In serv. |
|---|---|---|---|
| P 31 Eithne | 15-12-82 | 19-12-83 | 7-12-84 |

**Eithne (P 31)** L. & L. Van Ginderen, 7-86

**IRELAND** *(continued)*
**FISHERIES-PROTECTION SHIPS** *(continued)*

**D:** 1,760 tons (1,915 fl) **S:** 19 kts **Dim:** 81.0 × 12.0 × 4.30
**A:** 1/57-mm Bofors SAK 57/70 Mk 1 DP—2/20-mm Rheinmetall AA—1/SA-365 Dauphin II helicopter
**Electron Equipt:** Radar: 1/Decca TM 1229C, 1/Decca AC 1629C, 1/H.S.A. DA-05/4
Sonar: Plessey PMS 26L
**M:** 2 Ruston Paxman 12RKCM diesels; 2 CP props; 7,200 hp (6,640 sust.)
**Electric:** 1,625 kVA (3 × 400 kw, 1 × 100 kw)
**Range:** 7,000/15 **Man:** 13 officers, 69 men, plus 4 cadets

Remarks: P 31 ordered 23-4-82. Construction of a second unit deferred, in part because yard closed in 1983 for financial reasons. Has H.S.A. LIOD t.v./laser/IR fire-control system and 2 H.S.A. t.v./optical target designators for the 57-mm gun. Denny-Brown fin stabilizers. Considerable firefighting capability and can be replenished underway at sea. Boats include a 7.3-m crew boat, 5.5-m inspection boat, and 2 Avon Searaider semi-rigid inflatable boats with 90-hp outboard motors. Harpoon landing system for the helicopter. MEL RRB helo transponder. Carries 2 Wallop 57-mm flare RL. Has three firefighting water monitors.

◆ **3 Emer class** Bldr: Verolme, Cork

| | L | In serv. |
|---|---|---|
| P 21 Emer | 1977 | 18-1-78 |
| P 22 Aoife | 12-4-79 | 21-11-79 |
| P 23 Aisling | 3-10-79 | 21-5-80 |

**Aoife (P 22)** Irish Navy, 1986

**D:** 1,003 tons (fl) **S:** 18.5 kts **Dim:** 65.20 (58.50 pp) × 10.40 × 4.36
**A:** 1/40-mm AA—2/20-mm AA (I × 2)
**Electron Equipt:** Radar: 2/Decca . . .
Sonar: Simrad SU side-scan
**M:** 2 SEMT-Pielstick 6 PA6L-280 diesels; 1 CP prop; 4,800 hp **Fuel:** 170 tons
**Range:** 4,500/18; 6,750/12 **Man:** 5 officers, 41 men

Remarks: Developed version of the *Deirdre* with raised forecastle instead of bow bulwarks, to improve sea-keeping. Have advanced navigational aids, fin stabilizers. P 22 and P 23 have satellite navigation receivers, a 225-kw bow-thruster, a computerized plotting table, and a new-pattern KaMeWa propeller. Only P 23 has evaporators. All have three Pamou-Markon alternators.

◆ **1 Deirdre class** Bldr: Verolme, Cork

| | L | In serv. |
|---|---|---|
| P 20 Deirdre | 29-12-71 | 19-6-72 |

**Deirdre (P 20)** M. Louagie, 7-87

**D:** 966 tons (fl) **S:** 17.5 kts (15.5 cruising)
**Dim:** 62.61 (56.20 pp) × 10.40 × 4.35
**A:** 1/40-mm AA—2/52-mm flare launchers
**M:** 2 British Polar SF 112 VS-F diesels; 1 CP prop; 4,200 hp
**Fuel:** 150 tons **Range:** 3,000/15.5; 5,000/12 **Man:** 5 officers, 41 men

Remarks: Vosper fin stabilizers. New KaMeWa CP propeller fitted 1980.

Note: The former Royal Navy "Ton"-class minesweepers *Grainne* (CM 10) and *Fola* (CM 12) have been laid up, unmaintained since 1985–86. Plans to replace them with four French P.400-class patrol boats were announced 8-86 but have been deferred for lack of funds. Similar plans to acquire two Dutch *Alkmaar* ("Tripartite") minehunters have also been found to be unattainable.

### AUXILIARIES AND SERVICE CRAFT

◆ **1 stores tender** Bldr: R. Dunston, U.K. 1934

John Adams

**D:** 94 grt **S:** 10 kts **Dim:** 25.9 × 5.6 × 2.1 **M:** 1 diesel; 216 hp

◆ **1 inshore survey launch** Bldr: Fairey Marine, Hamble (In serv. 11-78)

Hydrafix

Remarks: No data available.

◆ **1 sail-training craft** Bldr: J. Tyrell, Arklow (In serv. 7-3-81)

Asgard II

**D:** 120 tons (fl) **S:** . . . **Dim:** 25.6 (21.3 wl) × 6.4 × 2.9
**M:** 1 Kelvin 6-cyl. diesel; 1 prop; 150 hp/418.2 $m^2$ sail area
**Man:** 4 crew plus 20 cadets

Remarks: Operates for both the Navy and Merchant Marine. *Tatlye,* a French-built Dufour 10.7-m sailboat, is also in service.

◆ **4 passenger and service launches**

Colleen II (In serv. 1972) Raven II (In serv. 1938)
Sir Cecil Romer (In serv. 1938) Jackdaw (In serv. 1938)

◆ **1 fuel barge**

Chowl—**D:** 100 tons **M:** 1 diesel; 50 hp

Note: In 1985, the Irish Naval Reserve (*An Slua Muiri*) operated the 13.7-m motorboat *Kathleen Roma,* bermuda ketches *Creidne* (15.8 m) and *Nancy Bet* (14.6 m), and five 5.5-m sail/oar boats.

# ISRAEL

**State of Israel**

Personnel (1986): Active: 3,500, of whom 250 officers and 500 men are especially trained as commandos and frogmen. Reserves: 500 total.

Merchant Marine (1986): 64 ships—556,628 grt (tankers: 4 ships—991 grt)

Naval Aviation: During 1978 the Israeli Navy put into service three IAI Westwind 1124 Sea Scan maritime-reconnaissance aircraft, whose mission is to cooperate with surface forces. Range: 1,350 n.m. at 270 kts. Carry sonobuoys. Two SA 365 G (ex-U.S. Coast Guard HH-65A Dolphin prototypes) were delivered 7-85; 12 to 20 more ordered from France, 5-87.

### WEAPONS AND SYSTEMS

The Israeli Navy uses foreign equipment, such as 76-mm OTO Melara Compact, Breda 40-mm, and Oerlikon guns, and it has perfected the Gabriel antiship missile systems.

Gabriel is a 560-kg, solid-propellant, surface-to-surface missile. After being fired, it climbs about 100 meters, then, at 7,500 meters from the launcher, descends slowly to an altitude of 20 meters. Optical or radar guidance is provided in azimuth, and a radio altimeter determines altitude. At a distance of 1,200 meters from the target, the missile descends to 3 meters, under either radio command or semiactive homing. The explosive charge is a 75-kg conventional warhead.

The Gabriel II carries a television camera and a transceiver for azimuth and altitude commands. The television is energized when the missile has attained a certain height and sends to the firing ship a picture of the areas that cannot be picked up by shipboard radar. The operator then can send any necessary corrections during the middle and final phases of the missile's flight, and thus find a target that cannot be seen either by the naked eye or on radar. The range of the Gabriel II is about 40,000 meters.

The Gabriel III system now entering service employs a frequency-agile, home-on-jam active radar seeker. An air-launched "Mk 3A/S" version is in development for launch from F-4, Mirage, Kfir, and A-4 Skyhawk aircraft. The sea-launched version has a range of 36,000 m at Mach .73, weighs 560 kg, and is 3.8 m long. Mk 3A/S weighs 600 kg, and has a range of 60,000 m, being launchable at 300 to 30,000-foot altitudes.

The Barak surface-to-air point-defense system, originally developed for use with an elevatable/trainable 8-cell box-launcher, will now use a 32-cell vertical launch group:

| | |
|---|---|
| Weight: 86 kg | Speed: Mach 1.6 |
| Length: 2.175 m | Guidance: Semiactive homing |
| Warhead: 22 kg | Range: 10 km |

## WEAPONS AND SYSTEMS *(continued)*

Barak's system weight with 32 rounds requires 1.3 $m^2$ deck space plus 2 $m^3$ below-decks volume. The intended fire-control system employs the AMDR (Advanced Missile Detection Radar), an S-band, pulse-doppler set capable of tracking 250 Mach 0.3 to 3.0 targets. To become operational 1990.

Also in use are U.S.-supplied Redeye hand-held, IR-homing missiles.

The U.S. Harpoon was acquired beginning in 1978 and is used on guided-missile patrol boats in a mix with Gabriel, in both block 1B and 1C versions.

Israeli Aircraft Industries and Oerlikon were cooperating in the development of a 30-mm antiaircraft gun mounting, the PCM-30. The system would replace 40-mm AA guns in earlier Israeli missile combatants, but it may have been canceled. Fourteen U.S. Vulcan/Phalanx 20-mm close-in weapon systems were delivered for use in various units of the Sa'ar classes.

**A Barak SAM being fired from an early octuple launcher on a Reshev-class unit** I.A.I., 1982

## SUBMARINES

◆ **0 (+3) new construction**

| | Bldr | Laid down | L | In serv. |
|---|---|---|---|---|
| N . . . | . . . | . . . | . . . | 1992 |
| N . . . | . . . | . . . | . . . | 1993 |
| N . . . | . . . | . . . | . . . | 1994 |

**D:** . . . **S:** . . . **Dim:** . . . × . . . × . . .
**A:** . . ./533-mm torpedo tubes (NT-37 torpedoes & Sub-Harpoon missiles)
**Electron Equipt:** Radar: . . .—Sonar: EDO passive flank array
**M:** diesel-electric: . . .
**Range:** . . .

REMARKS: Construction contingent upon cancellation of the Lavi fighter aircraft, which occurred 30-8-87. Funded by U.S., first submarine would be built in West Germany, the other two at Haifa. Ostensibly to replace the relatively recent Type 206 submarines to track 16 targets simultaneously.

◆ **3 German Type 206** Bldr: Vickers, Barrow, U.K.

| | Laid down | L | In serv. |
|---|---|---|---|
| GAL | 1973 | 2-12-75 | 12-76 |
| TANIN | 1974 | 25-10-76 | 6-77 |
| RAHAV | 1975 | 1977 | 12-77 |

**Gal** 1982

**D:** 420/600 tons **Dim:** 17/11 kts **S:** 45.0 × 4.7 × 3.8
**A:** 8/533-mm TT, fwd (10 U.S. NT-37E torpedoes, Sub-Harpoon missiles)
**M:** 2 MTU 12V493 TY60 diesels (600 hp each); AEG generators; 1 prop; 1,800 hp
**Man:** 22 tot.

REMARKS: Ordered in 4-72. Vickers Type 500. Carry two spare torpedoes. These submarines do *not* carry the Vickers SLAM submarine-launched antiaircraft missile systems, although provision was made for its installation. U.S. Sub-Harpoon missiles provided and fire-control systems altered, 1983. NT-37E torpedoes ordered 1986.

## GUIDED-MISSILE CORVETTES

◆ **0 (+4) Sa'ar V class** Bldr: . . .

**Sa'ar V**—artist's concept B. Bichler/I.A.I., 1986

**D:** 1,150 tons (fl) **S:** 35 kts **Dim:** 76.2 × . . . × . . .
**A:** Harpoon and Gabriel III/IV missiles—Barak SAM system (32 vertical-launch missiles)—guns—ASW torpedoes—1/SA-365G helicopter
**Electron Equipt:** Radar: . . .
Sonar: . . .—EW: . . .
**M:** CODOG: 1 LM-2500 gas turbine, 2 . . . diesels; 30,000 hp
**Range:** . . . **Man:** . . .

REMARKS: Construction contingent on cancellation of Lavi fighter program in 8-87. U.S. Ingalls Shipbuilding and Todd Shipyards (the latter in bankruptcy 8-87) competing as project managers. Up to *eight* ships actually programmed. Design to emphasize radar, infrared and noise signature reduction, high sea-state operations, and resistance to nuclear or chemical attack. If built, first unit would probably be constructed in the U.S., with keel-laying during 1990, completion circa 1992.

## GUIDED-MISSILE PATROL BOATS

◆ **2 (+1) Romat class** Bldr: Israeli SY, Haifa

| | L | In serv. |
|---|---|---|
| ROMAT | 1981 | 10-81 |
| KESHET | 10-82 | 1982 |
| N . . . . . . . | . . . | . . . |

**Keshet** 1984

**D:** 500 tons (fl) **S:** 31 kts **Dim:** 61.7 × 7.6 × 2.4
**A:** 8/Harpoon SSM (IV × 2)—6/Gabriel III (I × 6)—1/76-mm OTO Melara DP—1/20-mm Mk 15 CIWS (Vulcan-Phalanx gatling AA)—2/20-mm AA (I × 2)—2/12.7-mm mg (I × 2)
**Electron Equipt:** Radar: 1/TH-D 1040 Neptune, 1/Orion RTN-10X
EW: MN-53 intercept system—1/45-tube chaff RL, 4/24-tube chaff RL, 4/single chaff RL
**M:** 4 MTU 16V956 TB91 diesels; 4 props; 14,000 hp
**Range:** 1,500/30; 4,000/17 **Man:** 45 tot.

REMARKS: Employ the lengthened *Aliyah*-class hull, substituting additional armament for the helicopter facility. Apparently only three are to be built; fate of third unit, under construction during 1984, uncertain.

GUIDED-MISSILE PATROL BOATS *(continued)*

◆ **2 Aliyah (Sa'ar 4.5) class** Bldr: Israeli SY, Haifa

| | L | In serv. |
|---|---|---|
| ALIYAH | 10-7-80 | 8-80 |
| GEOULA | 10-80 | 31-12-80 |

**Aliyah**—with Mk 15 CIWS forward, 8 SSM 11-84

**D:** 500 tons (fl) **S:** 31 kts **Dim:** 61.7 × 7.6 × 2.4
**A:** 4/Harpoon SSM (II × 2)—4/Gabriel SSM (I × 4)—1/20-mm Mk 15 CIWS—2/20-mm AA (I × 2)—4/12.7-mm mg (I × 4)—1/helicopter
**Electron Equipt:** Radar: 1/TH-D 1040 Neptune, 1/Orion RTN-10X
EW: MN-53 intercept system—1/45-tube chaff RL, 4/24-tube chaff RL, 4/single chaff RL
**M:** 4/MTU 16V956 TB91 diesels; 4 props; 14,000 hp
**Range:** 1,500/30; 4,000/17 **Man:** 53 tot.

REMARKS: The helicopters were intended to provide an over-the-horizon targeting capability to utilize fully the range capabilities of the Harpoon missiles, which are mounted athwartships in the gap between the fixed hangar and the bridge superstructure. Each *Aliyah* was to lead a group of missile boats. U.S. Mk 15 CIWS replaced original 40-mm mount forward.

◆ **8 Reshev (Sa'ar IV) class** Bldr: Israeli SY, Haifa

| | L | In serv. | | L | In serv. |
|---|---|---|---|---|---|
| RESHEV | 19-2-73 | 4-73 | NITZAHON | 10-7-78 | 9-78 |
| KIDON | 7-74 | 9-74 | HATZMAAT | 3-12-78 | 2-79 |
| TARSHISH | 1-75 | 3-75 | MOLEDET | 22-3-79 | 5-79 |
| YAFO | 2-75 | 4-75 | KOMEMIYUT | 19-7-79 | 8-80 |

**A Reshev**—with 4 Harpoon, 6 Gabriel, and Mk 15 CIWS forward 11-83

**A Reshev**—with 2 Harpoon, 6 Gabriel, two speedboats on davits, and Mk 15 CIWS 1983

**D:** 415 tons (450 fl) **S:** 32 kts **Dim:** 58.1 × 7.6 × 2.4
**A:** 2/Harpoon SSM (I or II × 2 or IV × 1)—4–6 Gabriel SSM (I)—1/76-mm OTO Melara Compact—1/20-mm Mk 15 CIWS gatling AA—2/20-mm AA (I × 2)—2/12.7-mm mg (I × 2)
**Electron Equipt:** Radar: 1/Thomson-CSF Neptune TH-D 1040, 1 Selenia Orion RTN-10X
EW: Elta MN-53 intercept—0 or 1/45-tube chaff RL, 4 or 6/24-tube chaff RL, 4/single chaff RL
**M:** 4 MTU 16V956 TB91 diesels; 4 props; 14,000 hp (10,680 sust.)
**Range:** 1,650/30; 4,000/17.5 **Man:** 45 tot.

REMARKS: Quarters are air-conditioned. The *Tarshish* had a temporary helicopter deck in place of the after 76-mm gun for experiment with over-the-horizon targeting for Harpoon in 1979. Original missile armament was seven Gabriel. The Gabriel launchers are fixed. The 76-mm guns have been specially adapted for shore bombardment. The forward 76-mm mount was replaced by a 40-mm AA in *Nitzahon* and *Komemiyut,* pending availability of the U.S. Vulcan/Phalanx CIWS, the first of which was fitted to a *Reshev* in 2-83; all had it by 1985. Sisters *Keshet* and *Romach* were transferred to Chile 1979–80; with planned transfer of *Reshev* and one other in 1984 canceled. Three were built in Israel for South Africa, with others built under license at Durban. The elaborate ECM/ESM system was designed by the Italian firm Eletronica and manufactured by Israel's Elta.

◆ **6 Sa'ar III class** Bldr: Constr. Méc. de Normandie, Cherbourg

| | L | | L |
|---|---|---|---|
| SA'AR | 25-11-69 | HEREV | 20-6-69 |
| SOUFA | 4-2-69 | HANIT | 1969 |
| GAASCH | 24-6-69 | HETZ | 14-12-69 |

**A Sa'ar III**—with 2 Harpoon, 3 Gabriel, 1/76-mm gun French Navy, 1983

◆ **6 Sa'ar II class** Bldr: Constr. Méc. de Normandie, Cherbourg

| | L | | L |
|---|---|---|---|
| MIVTACH | 11-4-67 | EILATH | 14-6-68 |
| MIZNAG | 1967 | HAIFA | 14-6-68 |
| MISGAV | 1967 | AKKO | 1968 |

**EDO 780 variable-depth sonar on a Sa'ar II** French Navy, 1982

**Miznag**—Sa'ar II with 5 Gabriel, 1/40-mm AA 1978

## GUIDED-MISSILE PATROL BOATS *(continued)*

**D:** 220 tons (250 fl) **S:** 40 kts **Dim:** 45.0 × 7.0 × 1.8 (2.5 fl)
**A:** *Sa'ar II:* 5/Gabriel SSM (III × 1, I × 2)—2/40-mm AA Breda (I × 2)—2/12.7-mm mg—see Remarks
*Sa'ar III:* 2/Harpoon SSM (I × 2)—3/Gabriel SSM (III × 1)—1/76-mm DP OTO Melara—4/12.7-mm mg (I × 4)
**Electron Equipt:** Radar: 1/Thomson-CSF Neptune TH-D 1040, 1/Selenia Orion RTN-10X
EW: VHFD/F and Elta MN-53 or NS 9000 intercept gear—6/24-tube chaff RL, 4/1-tube chaff RL
**M:** 4 MTU MD871 diesels; 4 props; 14,000 hp **Fuel:** 30 tons
**Range:** 1,000/30; 1,600/20; 2,500/15 **Man:** 5 officers, 30-35 men

Remarks: Excellent sea qualities and endurance. *Sa'ar I* is the name that was used for these ships in an all-gun configuration. Four units of the *Sa'ar II* variant now carry an EDO 780 variable-depth sonar and 2/324-mm Mk 32 single ASW TT (Mk 46 torpedoes) aft and have no after gun mount. *Sa'ar III* has no ASW capability. Armaments now fairly standardized, but triple Gabriel launchers can be interchanged with the after 40-mm mountings.

## GUIDED-MISSILE HYDROFOILS

◆ **3 Grumman Mk II/M 161 class**

| | Bldr | L | In serv. |
|---|---|---|---|
| Shimrit | Lantana BY, Lantana, Fla. | 26-5-81 | 7-82 |
| Livnit | Israeli SY, Haifa | 1983 | 1983 |
| Snapirit | Israel, SY, Haifa | . . . | 6-85 |

**Shimrit**—on trials Grumman, 1981

**Livnit, at rest, foils down, no Gabriel aboard** French Navy, 11-83

**D:** 71 tons light (103.5 fl) **S:** 45 kts (47 trials)
**Dim:** 31.79 foils retracted (25.62 hull; 23.40 wl) × 12.95 (7.32 hull) × 4.75 at rest (1.93 foiling; 1.52 foils retracted)
**A:** 4/Harpoon SSM (II × 2)—2/Gabriel SSM (I × 2)—2/30-mm BMARC AA (II × 1)—2/12.7-mm mg (I × 2)
**M:** 1 Allison 501-KF gas turbine; 1 CP, 4-bladed prop; 5,400 hp—2 G.M. 6V53 diesels driving retractable 80-hp hydraulic motors for hull-borne maneuvering
**Electric:** 400 kw (2 Pratt & Whitney ST-6 gas turbines)
**Fuel:** 21 tons **Endurance:** 3 to 5 days **Range:** 750/42 foiling
**Man:** 15 tot.

Remarks: Ordered 1978 from Grumman, with prototype construction subcontracted to Lantana. Numerous delays in program. *Livnit* built simultaneously at Haifa. Aluminum construction. Pineapple-shaped radome conceals intercept array. Maximum speed on auxiliary system: 10 kts. Turning radius at 45 kts: 200 m. Design based on U.S. Navy's *Flagstaff* (PGH 2). *Livnit* has navigational radar atop radome, different engine air intakes. Original plans for 15 cut to 3 in 1982; did not make 52-kt. designed speed.

## PATROL CRAFT

◆ **1 (+5) Super Dvora class** Bldr: RAMTA-Israeli Aircraft Industries, Be'er Sheva (In serv. 8-87)

**Super Dvora prototype** I.A.I., 8-87

**D:** 46 to 54 tons (fl) **S:** 40 kts **Dim:** 21.64 × 5.49 × 1.00
**A:** 2/20-mm AA (I × 2)—2/12.7-mm mg (I × 2)—provision for SSM
**Electron Equipt:** Radar: 1/. . .
**M:** 2 diesels; 2 props; . . . hp **Electric:** 30 kw
**Range:** 500/. . . **Man:** 8–10 tot.

Remarks: Improved version of basic Dvora design. Ordered by Israeli Navy and Sri Lanka during 1987. Depending on engine selected, can make 25 to 40 kts maximum speed. Maximum displacement would be as a missile boat. Aluminum construction.

◆ **1 Dvora class** Bldr: Israeli Aircraft Industries, 1978

**D:** 47 tons (fl) **S:** 36 kts **Dim:** 21.62 × 5.49 × 0.94 (1.82 props)
**A:** 2/20-mm AA (I × 2)—2/12.7-mm mg **Electron Equipt:** Radar: 1/Decca 926
**M:** 2 MTU 12V331 TC81 diesels; 2 props; 2,720 hp
**Electric:** 30 kw **Range:** 700/32 **Man:** 8-10 tot.

Remarks: Privately funded prototype, acquired in 1979. The design has been offered with two Gabriel SSM and has been exported to Nicaragua, Argentina, and Chile without missiles.

◆ **37 Dabur class** Bldrs: 12 by Sewart Seacraft, U.S.A.; others by Israeli Aircraft Industries, Be'er Sheva (In serv. 1973–77)

**Dabur class** U.S. Navy, 3-82

**D:** 25 tons (35 fl) **S:** 25 kts **Dim:** 19.8 × 5.8 × 0.8
**A:** 2/20-mm (I × 2)—2/12.7-mm mg (I × 2)
**Electron Equipt:** Radar: 1/Decca 101 or 926
**M:** 2 G.M. 12V71 TI diesels; 2 props; 960 hp
**Electric:** 20 kw **Range:** 1,200/17 **Man:** 1 officer, 5 men

Remarks: Quarters air-conditioned and spacious. Five given to Christian forces in Lebanon in 1976.

◆ **up to 28 Yatush class (U.S. PBR type)**

**D:** 6.5 tons (8.9 fl) **S:** 25 kts **Dim:** 9.73 × 3.53 × 0.81
**A:** 2/7.62-mm mg **M:** 2 G.M. 6V53N diesels; Jacuzzi water jets; 430 hp
**Range:** 150/23 **Man:** 5 tot.

Remarks: Early units built by Uniflite, Bellingham, Washington, bought in the United States in 1968, later ones built in Israel. Several may be stationed in the Red Sea. Two given to Lebanese Christians, 1975–76.

ISRAEL *(continued)*

## AMPHIBIOUS WARFARE SHIPS

◆ **1 former commercial landing craft** Bldr: . . . , West Germany

Bat Sheva (In serv. 1967)

**Bat Sheva** 1969

**D:** 900 tons (1,150 fl) **S:** 10 kts **Dim:** 95.1 × 11.2 × . . .
**A:** 4/20-mm—4/12.7-mm mg **M:** diesels; 2 props **Man:** 26 tot.

Remarks: Bought in South Africa in 1968. Construction of two new landing ships is planned: approx. 117.0 × 17.0 × 2.2, helicopter platform, facilities for several hundred troops.

◆ **3 LCT type** Bldr: Israeli SY, Haifa (In serv. 1966–67)

Ashdod Ashkelon Ahziv

**Ashdod** 1971

**D:** 400 tons (730 fl) **S:** 10.5 kts **Dim:** 62.7 × 10.0 × 1.8
**A:** 2/20-mm AA (I × 2) **M:** 3 MWM diesels; 3 props; 1,900 hp
**Fuel:** 37 tons **Man:** 20 tot.

◆ **3 Etziongueber class** Bldr: Israeli SY, Haifa (In serv. 1965)

Etziongueber Shikmona Kessaraya

**Etziongueber**

**D:** 182 tons (230 fl) **S:** 10 kts **Dim:** 30.5 × 5.9 × 1.3
**A:** 2/20-mm AA (I × 2) **M:** diesels; 2 props; 1,280 hp **Man:** 10 tot.

◆ **4 U.S. LCSR swimmer-delivery boats** (In serv. 1964)

**D:** 16.5 tons (24.3 fl) **S:** 35 kts **Dim:** 16.00 × 4.35 × 1.68 (loaded)
**A:** 2/12.7-mm mg (I × 2)
**M:** 2 Saturn T-1000 gas turbines; 2 props; 2,000 hp
**Range:** 200/35 **Man:** 8 crew, 22 troops

Remarks: Transferred from U.S. Navy late 1960s. Can also transport about 1 ton of supplies.

Note: The Israeli Army also employs several 54-ton (light) river-crossing craft capable of transporting 130-ton loads.

## VARIOUS SHIPS

◆ **1 training ship**

Nogah

Remarks: Former small cargo vessel equipped as a training ship for the merchant marine.

◆ **1 small missile-boat tender**

Naharya

Remarks: Base craft for the missile craft stationed at Eilath.

◆ **1 missile-boat tender** Bldr: Todd SY, Seattle (In serv. 1976)

Ma'oz

Remarks: 4,000-ton oilfield-supply type used as a missile-boat tender in the Mediterranean.

# ITALY

**Italian Republic**

Personnel (1987): 44,500, including 5,200 officers and the San Marco (Marine) battalion

Merchant Marine (1986): 1,569 ships—7,896,569 grt
(tankers: 187 ships: 2,513,197 grt)

Naval Aviation: The Marinavia operates only helicopters, of which some 64 are in service: 25 SH-3D Sea King heavy ASW (shore-based and aboard *Giuseppe Garibaldi*), 27 AB-212 light ASW helicopters for service aboard frigates and destroyers, and 12 AB-204B light ASW helicopters for training. Plans call for an eventual total of 48 AB-212 and 36 SH-3D. In 12-84, the Navy requested authorization for 22 Sea Harrier V/STOL fighter-bombers, receiving Ministry of Defense approval for 12 to 18 late in 1986.

The Air Force conducts fixed-wing maritime ASW patrol, using 18 Bréguet Atlantics ordered in 1968 and delivered by 1973, and 8 Grumman S-2F Tracker medium-range aircraft. The Atlantics are based at Catania (No. 86 Squadron) and Cagliari/Elmas (No. 88 Squadron), and No. 87 Tracker Squadron is based at Catania. The Atlantics are being modernized to Atlantique Mk 2 standard; 17 are to be equipped with Iguane radar, Litton inertial navigation systems, a new acoustic processor, and sonobuoy dispensers. The first aircraft was scheduled to redeliver 15-2-88, the last in 1990. Fifteen Agusta-built variants of the U.S. Coast Guard Sikorsky HH-3F Pelican helicopter were ordered 1987 for the *Protezione Civile* for search-and-rescue service.

The Bell AB-204B and AB-212 are built under license from Bell Helicopter by Agusta in Italy. Principal characteristics are:

AB-204B

| | |
|---|---|
| Ceiling: 10,800 ft | Length: 17.4 m |
| Range: 2 hr 5 min without torpedoes<br>1 hr 15 min with torpedoes | Rotor: 14.6 m |
| Armament: 2 Mk 46 or A-244 torpedoes or<br>4 AS-12 missiles | Max. weight: 4,310 kg |
| Electronics: ASQ-13 sonar | Motor: 1 turboshaft, 1,200 hp |
| Crew: 3 | Max. speed: 104 kts |
| | Cruising speed: 90 kts |

AB-212

| | |
|---|---|
| Ceiling: 5,000 ft | Length: 17.4 m |
| Range: 4 hr 15 min (360 n.m. at 100 kts) | Rotor: 14.6 |
| Armament: 2 Mk 46 or A-244 torpedoes, depth<br>charges, or 2 AS-12 ASM missiles | Max. weight: 5,086 kg;<br>3,240 light |
| Electronics: ASQ-13B sonar | Motor: 1 turboshaft, 1,290 hp |
| Crew: 3 | Max. speed: 130 kts |
| | Cruising speed: 100 kts |

Note: A new ASW helicopter, the EH-101, is being jointly developed by Agusta and Westland in Great Britain to succeed the SH-3D in the late 1980s; see page 207 for data. The Italian Navy plans to acquire 39, powered by General Electric CT7-6A, a variant of T-700-CT7 turboshaft engines.

**Italian Navy AB-212** Italian Navy, 1986

NAVAL AVIATION *(continued)*

**Italian Air Force Atlantic Mk 1** U.S. Navy, 1981

WARSHIPS IN SERVICE, UNDER CONSTRUCTION, OR AUTHORIZED AS OF 1 JANUARY 1988

| | L | TONS | MAIN ARMAMENT |
|---|---|---|---|
| ◆ **1 helicopter carrier** | | | |
| GIUSEPPE GARIBALDI | 1983 | 10,000 | 4/Otomat, 2/Albatros, 16/helicopters |
| ◆ **10 (+1) submarines** | | | |
| | | Tons (surfaced) | |
| 1 (+1) SALVATORE PELOSI | 1986–87 | 1,476 | 6/533-mm TT |
| 4 NAZARIO SAURO | 1976–80 | 1,456 | 6/533-mm TT |
| 4 ENRICO TOTI | 1967–68 | 535 | 4/533-mm TT |
| 1 TANG | 1951 | 2,100 | 8/533-mm TT |
| ◆ **3 cruisers** | | | |
| | | Tons | |
| 1 VITTORIO VENETO | 1967 | 7,500 | 1/missile launcher, 8/76.2-mm, 9/helicopters |
| 2 ANDREA DORIA | 1962–63 | 6,500 | 1/missile launcher, 8/76.2-mm, 4/helicopters |
| ◆ **4 (+2) destroyers** | | | |
| 0 (+2) ANIMOSO | 1989–90 | 4,400 | 1/missile launcher, 2/127-mm, ASW weapons |
| 2 AUDACE | 1971 | 3,950 | 1/missile launcher, 2/127-mm, ASW weapons |
| 2 IMPAVIDO | 1962 | 3,201 | 1/missile launcher, 2/127-mm, ASW weapons |
| ◆ **14 frigates** | | | |
| 8 MAESTRALE | 1981– | 3,040 | 4/Otomat, 1/Sea Sparrow, 1/127-mm, ASW weapons |
| 4 LUPO | 1976–79 | 2,208 | 8/Otomat, 1/Sea Sparrow, 1/127-mm, ASW weapons |
| 2 ALPINO | 1967 | 2,000 | 6/76-mm, ASW weapons |
| ◆ **8 (+6) Corvettes** | | | |
| 2 (+6) MINERVA | 1986– | 1,029 | 4/Otomat, 1/Albatros, 1/76-mm, ASW weapons |
| 4 PIETRO DE CRISTOFARO | 1964–65 | 850 | 2/76-mm, ASW weapons |
| 2 ALBATROS | 1954 | 800 | 2/40-mm, ASW weapons |
| ◆ **7 missile hydrofoils** | | | |
| ◆ **27 (+6) mine countermeasures ships** | | | |
| ◆ **2 (+2) amphibious ships** | | | |

WEAPONS AND SYSTEMS

## A. MISSILES

### ◆ Surface-to-air

**Idra** Bldr: Selenia

A planned vertical-launch replacement for Aspide to enter service 1993–94. First flight of this private-venture design planned for 1988. Guidance will use an active pulse-doppler radar with J-band terminal homer:

Weight: . . .
Length: 3.65 m
Span: 0.644 m
Diameter: 0.212 m
Propulsion: 2-step booster/sustainer
Range: . . .
Warhead: . . .
Guidance: active-homing

Standard SM-1 ER and SM-1 MR (see under U.S.A.)

**Aspide** (Italian version of the Sea Sparrow) Bldr: Selenia

Ceiling: 15 m (min); 5,000 m (max.)
Length: 3.65 m
Wingspan: 0.644 m
Range: 10,000 m
Diameter: 0.212 m
Weight: 204 kg
Guidance: semiactive homing

This equipment employs an octuple Albatros launcher built by OTO Melara and weighing 7 tons; elevation: 5 to +65 degrees. Controlled by NA-30 system. A quadruple launcher has been produced for use on export corvettes.

### ◆ Surface-to-surface

**Otomat Mk 1** Bldr: OTO Melara/Matra

Length: 4,820 m
Wingspan: 1.19 m
Range: 60–80 km
Diameter: 1,060 m (with boosters); 460 m (without boosters)
Weight: 750 kg
Guidance: Thomson-CSF active homing, 3-axis

This missile flies almost at sea level after firing, climbs at a steep angle to a predetermined height, and strikes its target during descent.

**Otomat Mk 2** (also known as "Teseo")

This model differs from the Mk 1 in having an Italian (SMA) active radar homing head, instead of a French one. It is also a "sea-skimmer"; that is, it flies close to the water after firing. Its explosive charge is about 200 kg and its ramjet propulsion system allows it to be used at ranges limited only by its guidance system and its target designation. Range: 150 km; speed: 300 m/sec.

Two additional projects are in development: "Briaero," a Mach 1.0 weapon with a 200–400-km range, and "Otomach," a Mach 2, turbojet-powered weapon being developed by OTO Melara and Alfa-Romeo.

### ◆ Air-to-surface

The French S.N.I.A.S. AS-12 wire-guided antishipping missile has been adopted for use by helicopters, and the Marte Mk 2 is in production for use by Sea King helicopters:

Length: 4.84 m (with 1.09-m booster)
Diameter: 31.6 cm
Span: 98.7 cm (cruciform)
Weight: 340 kg
Speed: Mach 0.8
Range: over 20 km
Warhead: 70 kg

Guidance is by gyro autopilot and radar altimeter over mid-course, with active pseudo-monopulse radar homing, using the Otomat's seeker. Fuzing is influence and impact. The airframe is that of the Sistel Sea Killer surface-launched antiship missile.

## B. GUNS

**40-mm Breda/Bofors Compact twin**

Length: 70 calibers
Muzzle velocity: 1,000 m/sec
Max. effective range, antiaircraft fire: 3,500–4,000 m
Rate of fire: 300 rounds/min/barrel
Projectile weight: 0.96 kg
Number of ready-service rounds: 444 or 736 (depending on installation)
Fire control: Dardo system (Selenia RTN-20X radar)
Impact or proximity fusing

**76-mm OTO Melara**

Single- or twin-barreled, automatic, for air, surface, and land targets

Length: 62 calibers
Muzzle velocity: 850 m/sec
Max. effective range, surface fire: 8,000 m
Max. effective range, antiaircraft fire: 4,000–5,000 m
Rate of fire: 60 rounds/min/barrel

**76-mm OTO Melara Compact**

Single-barreled light antiaircraft automatic fire; entirely remote control with muzzle brake and cooling system. Research is continuing on a course-corrected shell for this weapon, using a shipboard data link to the projectile.

Length: 62 calibers
Muzzle velocity: 925 m/sec
Max. effective range, surface fire: 8,000 m
Max. effective range, antiaircraft fire: 4,000–5,000 m
Rate of fire: 85 rounds/min
Weight of mount: 7.35 tons, because of the use of light alloys and fiberglass; 80 ready-service rounds in the drum.

The current "Super Rapid" version of the weapon weighs 7.5 tons and fires at 1, 10, or 120 rds/min, with 85 rds on mount.

**127-mm OTO Melara Compact**

Single-barreled automatic, remote control

Length: 54 calibers
Muzzle velocity: 807 m/sec
Max. effective range, surface fire: 15,000 m
Max. effective range, antiaircraft fire: 7,000 m
Rate of fire: 45 rounds/min, automatic setting

**GUNS** *(continued)*

Weight of the mount: 32 tons because of the use of light alloys and a fiberglass shield. The gun has a muzzle brake; it can automatically fire 66 rounds, thanks to 3 loading drums, each with 22 rounds. Two hoists serve two loading trays with rounds coming from the magazine, and a drum may be loaded even while the gun is firing. An automatic selection system allows a choice of ammunition (antiaircraft, surface target, pyrotechnics, chaff for cluttering radar).

This equipment has also been purchased by the Canadian Navy for its *Iroquois*-class destroyers.

## C. ANTISUBMARINE WEAPONS

OTO Melara and France's Engins Matra are developing a vertical-launch ASW weapon for the NATO NFR-90 frigate program, using the Otomat propulsion section and carrying a homing torpedo payload; range: 20–30 km.

### K113 Menon mortar

The system has a single 305-mm barrel some 4.6 m long, with automatic loading. Fire control is usually directed in the underwater battery plot. The mortar is fired at a 45-degree angle, with the range fixed by a system similar to that of the no-longer-used triple-barreled Menon; firing 160-kg depth charges round by round; gas relief valves from three powder chambers have adjustable vents; range varies from 400 to 900 m. The weapon is automatically reloaded from the magazine by hoist and a loading drum.

### Torpedoes

American Mk 46 and Italian Whitehead Motofides A-244 small ASW torpedoes are used on ships (using the triple ILAS-3 tube mount, a version of the U.S. Mk 32 ASW torpedo tube set) and helicopters.

The Whitehead Motofides A-184 (6.0 m long; 1,245 kg) wire-guided torpedo is a 533-mm weapon with a range of over 15,000 m. A-290, a 50-knot weapon using the A-244's seeker has been in development since 1981 and was to begin trials in 1984; it will use a lithium battery.

## D. RADARS

The Italian Navy has used a number of American radars (SPS-6, SPS-12, SPS-52, etc.) but now primarily uses a number of systems developed in Italy, including:

| Type | Band | Remarks |
|---|---|---|
| RTN-10X Orion | I/J(X) | Gun and missile fire control (Argo system) |
| RTN-20X Orion | I/J(X) | With Dardo system (40-mm gun) |
| SPQ-2D | I/J(X) | Combined surveillance |
| RAN-3L | D(S) | Air search, 3-dimensional |
| RAN-10S | E/J (S/X) | Combined surveillance |
| RAN-11X | 1/J(X) | Combined air/surface search |
| RAN-12X | I/J(X) | Combined air/surface search (in development) |
| RAN-20S | E/F(S) | Air search |
| RTN-30X | I/J(X) | Target acquisition (Albatros system) |
| 3 RM series | I/J(X) | Navigation and surface search |
| MM/SPN-749(V) | I(X) | Navigation set on *Garibaldi;* 2 antennas |
| MM/SPN-728 | . . . | Unstabilized surface search |
| MM/SPS-702 | X | Frequency-agile, sea-skimmer detector |
| MM/SPS-703 | X | Navigational radar |
| MM/SPN-704 | X | Version of SPN-703 for submarines |
| MM/SPN-720 | . . . | Landing-aid radar |
| MM/SPN-749 | X | Navigational |

## E. SONARS

Most of the newest equipment is American or Dutch.

| | Type | Frequency | | Type | Frequency |
|---|---|---|---|---|---|
| CWE 610 | Hull | LF (Dutch) | SQS-10 | Hull (U.S.) | MF |
| DE 1160B | Hull | MF (U.S.) | SQA-10 | VDS (U.S.) | MF |
| DE 1164 | Hull or VDS | MF (U.S.) | SQS-36 | VDS (U.S.) | HF |
| SQS-23 | Hull | MF (U.S.) | SQQ-14 | Minehunting (U.S.) | HF |
| SQS-29 | Hull | MF (U.S.) | P2072 | Minehunting | HF |
| SQS-11A | Hull | MF (U.S.) | | | |
| SQS-39 | Hull | MF (U.S.) | | | |

## F. TACTICAL INFORMATION SYSTEM

The Italian Navy has developed the SADOC system, which is compatible with the American NTDS and the French SENIT.

## G. COUNTERMEASURES

A wide variety of intercept arrays, many with stabilized cylindrical radome antennas, are in use. The Breda SCLAR chaff rocket-launching system is used on frigates and larger ships; it has 20 tubes for 105-mm rockets in a trainable, elevatable launcher. A number of Wallops Barricade chaff rocket launchers were ordered 1984, and the French Sagaie is being used on the new *Animoso*-class guided-missile destroyers.

## HELICOPTER CARRIER

### ◆ 1 Garibaldi class

| | Bldr | Laid down | L | In serv. |
|---|---|---|---|---|
| C 551 Giuseppe Garibaldi | Italcantieri, Monfalcone | 26-3-81 | 7-6-83 | 30-9-85 |

**D:** 9,360 tons (13,240 fl) **S:** 29.5 kts
**Dim:** 180.2 (162.8 pp) × 30.4 (23.8 wl) × 6.7
**A:** 4/Otomat-Teseo Mk 2 SSM (I × 4)—2/Albatros SAM (VIII × 2; 46 Aspide missiles)—6/40-mm AA Breda Dardo (II × 3)—6/324-mm ILAS-3 ASW TT (III × 2)—16/SH-3D Sea King helicopters (see Remarks)
**Electron Equipt:** Radar: 1/MM/SPN-749(V) nav. (2 antennas), 1/SPS-702 surf.-search, 1/RAN-3L (SPS-768) air early warning, 1/RAN-10S (SPS-774) air search, 1/SPS-52C 3-D air search, 3/RTN-20X f.c., 2/RTN-30X f.c.
Sonar: Raytheon DE 1164
EW: 4 Elettronica D/F-intercept arrays, receiver/jammer system, 2/SCLAR decoy RL (XX × 2)
TACAN: . . .

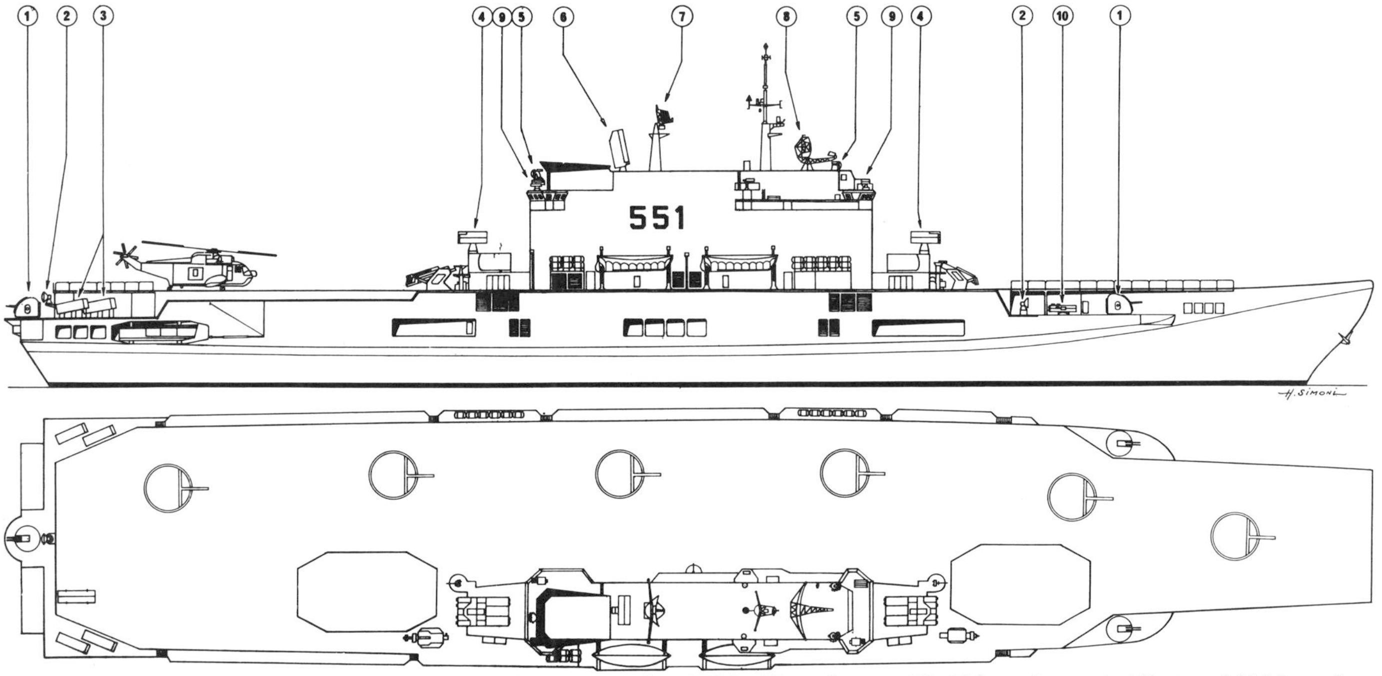


**Giuseppe Garibaldi** 1. Twin 40-mm AA 2. Dardo system radar (RTN-20X) 3. Otomat Mk II launchers 4. Albatros SAM launchers 5. RTN-30X radar for Albatros/Aspide 6. RAN-3L (SPS-768) 3-D air-search radar 7. RAN-10S (SPS-774) surface/air-search radar 8. SPS-52C 3-D air-search radar 9. SCLAR chaff launcher 10. triple ILAS-3 ASW TT

**HELICOPTER CARRIER** *(continued)*

**Giuseppe Garibaldi (C 551)** M. Louagie, 7-87

**Giuseppe Garibaldi (C 551)** Italian Navy, 1986

**M:** 4 G.E./Fiat LM 2500 gas turbines; 2 CP props; 80,000 hp
**Electric:** 9,360 kw (6 GMT B230-12M diesel alternator sets)
**Range:** 7,000/20 **Man:** 560 tot. (accommodations for 825)

REMARKS: Began sea trials 1-85; delivered 31-7-85. Ship type: *Incrociatore Porto-Aeromobili.* The *Garibaldi* is essentially an ASW ship for helicopters, although the design permits the handling of V/STOL aircraft as well. The flight deck is 173.8 meters long. There are two elevators, one forward of and one

**Giuseppe Garibaldi (C 551)** Italian Navy, 1986

HELICOPTER CARRIER *(continued)*

**Giuseppe Garibaldi (C 551)** Italian Navy, 1986

abaft the island. There are six flight-deck spaces for flight operations. The hangar (110 × 15 × 6 meters) can accommodate 12 Sea King, or 10 Sea Harrier and 1 Sea King. Permission to begin acquisition of Sea Harrier/Harrier aircraft given 1987. Steel superstructure and hull. To permit helicopter operations in heavy weather, much attention was given to stability, and the ship has two pairs of fin stabilizers; the bow has a small "ski-jump" sheer, officially to improve deck dryness. There are five decks; the flight deck; the hangar deck, which is also the main deck; and two decks and a platform deck below the hangar deck. Thirteen watertight bulkheads divide the ship into 14 sections. Has IPN-20 computerized data system, capable of handling 200 threat tracks simultaneously.

Carries two GRP personnel transports, MEN 215 and MEN 216, each capable of carrying up to 250 persons in SAR, commando, disaster relief duties; see full description of these craft on later page.

## SUBMARINES

NOTE: Planned are 4 to 6 S-90-class submarines to replace the *Toti* and *Tang* classes. Of some 1,500–2,000 tons submerged displacement, the first is planned to be delivered in 1993–94. Will have 22-kt submerged speed and carry 12 torpedoes (6 tubes).

◆ **2 Salvatore Pelosi class** Bldr: Fincantiere, Monfalcone

| | Laid down | L | In serv. |
|---|---|---|---|
| S 522 SALVATORE PELOSI | 3-83 | 29-11-86 | 10-87 |
| S 523 GIULIANO PRINI | 24-7-86 | 12-12-87 | 5-88 |

**Salvatore Pelosi (S 522)** Fincantiere, 11-86

**D:** 1,476 tons surf./1,680 sub. **S:** 11 kts surf./12 kts snorkel/19 sub.
**Dim:** 64.35 × 6.83 × 6.00
**A:** 6/533-mm TT fwd (12 Type A-184 torpedoes)
**Electron Equipt:** Radar: 1/3RM-20
Sonar: USEA/Selenia IPD-70/3, Velox M5
EW: Elettronica MM/BLD-727
**M:** 3 GMT A210 16NM, 895-kw diesel generator sets, 1 twin 3,140-kw motor (2,400-kw sust.); 1/7-bladed prop; 4,270 hp max.
**Range:** 3,000/11 surf.; 2,500/12 snorkel; 250/4 sub.
**Fuel:** 144 tons **Endurance:** 45 days **Man:** 6 officers, 43 men

REMARKS: Improved version of *Sauro* class, with .5 m added amidships, one watertight bulkhead. Have capability to launch U.S. Sub-Harpoon SSM. Two Kollmorgen S76 models 322 and 323 periscopes (one with laser range finder), Litton PZ-41 inertial navigation system, improved combat data-weapons control system. Do not have "crash-dive" ballast tank as in *Sauro* class. Pressure hull of U.S. HY-80 steel.

◆ **4 Nazario Sauro class** Bldr: C.R.D.A., Monfalcone (last two: Italcantiere, Monfalcone)

| | Laid down | L | In serv. |
|---|---|---|---|
| S 518 NAZARIO SAURO | 26-6-74 | 9-10-76 | 1-3-80 |
| S 519 CARLO FECIA DI COSSATO | 15-7-76 | 16-11-77 | 1-3-80 |
| S 520 LEONARDO DA VINCI | 1-7-76 | 20-10-79 | 6-11-82 |
| S 521 GUGLIERMO MARCONI | 23-10-79 | 20-9-80 | 16-10-82 |

**Gugliermo Marconi (S 521)** G. Gyssels, 11-85

**Carlo Fecia di Cossato (S 519)** C. Martinelli, 3-83

**D:** 1,450 surf./1,637 tons sub. **S:** 11 kts surf./12 kts snorkel/19 kts sub.
**Dim:** 63.85 × 6.83 × 5.70 (12.38 keel to top of sail)
**A:** 6/533-mm B.512 TT fwd (12 Type A-184 torpedoes)
**Electron Equipt:** Radar: 1/3 RM-20
Sonar: USEA/Selenia IPD-70/S system, Velox M5
EW: MM/BLD-727
**M:** 3 GMT A210 16NM, 895-kw diesel generators, 1 twin, 3,140-kw (2,400 kw cont.) motor; 1 prop; 4,270 hp
**Fuel:** 144 tons **Endurance:** 45 days
**Range:** 6,150/11 surf.; 2,500/12 snorkel, 250/4 sub.
**Man:** 6 officers, 43 men

REMARKS: First two authorized 1972; second pair ordered 12-2-76. Third pair (to have longer tubes to accommodate U.S. Harpoon missiles) ordered 7-3-83. Can travel 20 knots submerged for 1 hour, or 100 hours at 4 knots. Maximum diving depth is 300 meters. Seven-bladed propeller. Completion of first pair delayed by need to replace original batteries. Batteries: 2 148-cell, 6,000 amp/hr, one hour rate. Can maintain 19.3 kts for one hour submerged. Have SISU-1 fire-control system, which can track 4 targets simultaneously. Sonar system operates 200 Hz—7 kHz passive, 8–15 kHz active, and has active, passive, passive-ranging, and surveillance modes. S 521 has a smaller "crash-dive" ballast tank than the others

◆ **4 Enrico Toti class** Bldr: C.R.D.A., Monfalcone

| | Laid down | L | In serv. |
|---|---|---|---|
| S 505 ATTILIO BAGNOLINI | 15-4-65 | 28-8-67 | 22-6-68 |
| S 506 ENRICO TOTI | 15-4-65 | 12-3-67 | 22-1-68 |
| S 513 ENRICO DANDOLO | 10-3-67 | 16-12-67 | 29-9-68 |
| S 514 LAZZARO MOCENIGO | 12-6-67 | 20-4-68 | 11-1-69 |

**Lazzaro Mocenigo (S 514)** C. Martinelli, 1985

**SUBMARINES** *(continued)*

**Enrico Dandolo (S 513)** G. Gyssels, 3-83

**D:** 536 tons surf./593 sub. **S:** 9.7 kts surf./14 sub.
**Dim:** 46.20 × 4.75 × 3.99 **A:** 4/533-mm TT (6 A-184 torpedoes)
**Electron Equipt:** Radar: 1/3 RM-20/SMG
Sonar: JP-64 active, Velox passive
**M:** diesel-electric propulsion: 2 Fiat/MB 820 diesels; 1 electric motor; 1 prop; 2,200 hp
**Range:** 7,500/4.5 **Man:** 4 officers, 22 men

REMARKS: Can make 15 kts for one hour submerged. Diving depth: 180 m. Have IPD-60/64 combat data/fire-control system.

◆ **1 U.S. Tang class** Bldr: Electric Boat, Groton, Connecticut

| | Laid down | L | In serv. |
|---|---|---|---|
| S 516 ROMEO ROMEI (ex-*Harder,* SS 568) | 30-6-50 | 3-12-51 | 19-8-52 |

**Romeo Romei (S 516)** G. Valentini, 5-86

**D:** 2,055 surf./2,585 sub. tons **S:** 14 surf./14 kts sub.
**Dim:** 87.5 × 8.3 × 6.2 **A:** 8/533-mm TT (6 long fwd, 2 short aft)
**Electron Equipt:** Radar: 1/BPS-12—Sonar: BQR-3, BQS-4, BQG-4
**M:** diesel-electric propulsion: 3 Fairbanks-Morse 38ND8$\frac{1}{8}$ × 10, 1,500-hp diesels; 2 Westinghouse motors; 2 props; 5,600 hp
**Range:** 7,600/15; 14,000/9 snorkels; 17/9 (sub.)
**Man:** 7 officers, 71 men

REMARKS: Transferred on 20-2-74. Has BQG-4 "PUFFS" passive ranging sonar, U.S. Mk 106 Mod. 14 fire-control system. Aft tubes no longer used. Addition stabilizing fins added aft, angled upward at 45 deg. Sister *Livio Piomarta* (S 515, ex-*Trigger,* SS 564) stricken 28-2-86; S 516 will strike on completion of *Giuliano Prini* (S 523).

## CRUISERS

◆ **1 Vittorio Veneto class**

| | Bldr | Laid down | L | In serv. |
|---|---|---|---|---|
| C 550 VITTORIO VENETO | Cant. Riuniti Castellammare | 10-6-65 | 5-2-67 | 12-7-69 |

**D:** 8,130 tons (9,500 fl) **S:** 30.5 kts
**Dim:** 179.60 (170.61 pp) × 19.42 (hull) × 5.50 (7.9 max.)
**A:** 1/Mk 20 Mod. 7 Aster launch system (20 ASROC and 40 Standard SM-1 ER)—4/Otomat-Tesio Mk II SSM (I × 4)—8/76-mm OTO Melara DP (I × 8)—6/40-mm Breda Dardo AA (II × 3)—6/324-mm ILAS-3 ASW TT (III × 2)—6/AB-212 ASW helicopters
**Electron Equipt:** Radar: 1/RAN-20X, 1/SPS-52C, 1/MM/SMA-702, 1/3RM-7, 2/SPG-55C, 4/RTN-10X, 2/RTN-20X
Sonar: SQS-23
EW: . . . —TACAN: SRN-15A

**Vittorio Veneto (C 550)** L. Grazioli, 11-86

**Vittorio Veneto (C 550)** Italian Navy, 1986

**M:** 2 sets Tosi GT; 2 props; 73,000 hp **Electric:** 6,800 kw tot.
**Boilers:** 4 Foster-Wheeler; 43 kg/cm$^2$, 450°C **Fuel:** 1,200 tons
**Range:** 3,000/28; 6,000/20 **Man:** 53 officers, 504 men

**CRUISERS** *(continued)*

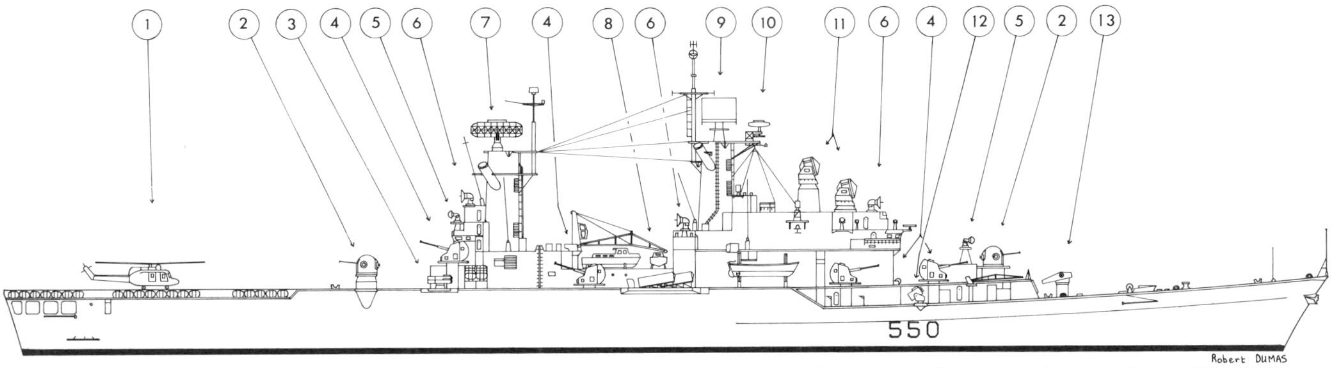


**Vittorio Veneto** 1. AB-212 helicopter 2. 40-mm Breda Dardo twin AA 3. ILAS-3 triple ASW TT 4. 76-mm DP 5. RTN-20X f.c. radar (for 40-mm AA) 6. RTN-20X f.c. radar (for 76-mm DP) 7. RAN-20X early-warning radar 8. Tesio/Otomat Mk 2 SSM 9. SPS-52C 3-D radar 10. MM/SM-702 surface-search radar 11. SPG-55B f.c. radar tracker illuminators (for Standard) 12. SCLAR RL 13. Mk 20 Aster launcher.

Remarks: Underwent modernization 1981–83 with 4 Otomat Mk 2 (Teseo) missiles and 3 Dardo 40-mm AA gun systems added. The radar suite was updated, the SPS-40 being replaced by the Italian RAN-20X. The flight deck (40 × 18.5) is served from a hangar immediately below by two elevators (18 × 5.3). The hangar (27.5 × 15.3) is two decks in depth. Very extensive, stabilized electronic intercept arrays. Two sets anti-rolling fin stabilizers. The Aster system can launch either ASROC ASW or Standard SM-1 ER SAM and has a total capacity of 60 missiles on three magazine drums. Beam listed does not include projections around SCLAR launchers fwd or flight deck aft.

### ◆ 2 Andrea Doria class

| | Bldr | Laid down | L | In serv. |
|---|---|---|---|---|
| C 553 Andrea Doria | C. Nav. Tirreno, Riva Trigoso | 11-5-58 | 27-2-63 | 23-2-64 |
| C 554 Caio Duilio | Navalmeccanica Castellammare | 16-5-58 | 22-12-62 | 30-11-64 |

**Andrea Doria (C 553)** G. Arra, 8-84

**Andrea Doria (C 553)** C. Martinelli, 7-85

**Caio Duilio (C 554)**—training cruiser P. Voss, 7-83

**Caio Duilio (C 554)** G. Gyssels, 8-86

**D:** 6,500 tons (7,300 fl) **S:** 30 kts **Dim:** 149.3 (144.0 pp) × 17.25 × 4.96 (7.5 fl)
**A:** 1/Mk 10 launcher (40 Standard SM-1 ER—6 or 8/76-mm AA (I × 6 or 8)—6/324-mm ASW TT (III × 2)—3/AB-212 helicopters (C 554:2)
**Electron Equipt:** Radar: 1/RAN-20S (SPS-768), 1/SPQ-2D, 1/SPS-39, 2/SPG-55C, 3 or 4/RTN-10X (Argo system)
TACAN: SRN-15—Sonar: SQS-23 (C 554:SQS-39)
EW: passive arrays, 2/SCLAR chaff launchers (XX × 2)
**M:** 2 sets GT; 2 props; 60,000 hp **Electric:** 4,700 kw
**Boilers:** 4 Foster-Wheeler; 43 kg/cm², 450°C **Fuel:** 1,100 tons
**Range:** 6,000/15 **Man:** 47 officers, 437 men (C 554:418 men)

Remarks: The flight deck is 30 × 16 meters on C 553. Hangar on main deck. Fin anti-rolling stabilizers fitted. The engineering spaces are divided into two groups, forward and aft: each has a boiler room with two boilers and a turbine compartment separated by living spaces. In each turbine space are two 1,000-kw turbo-alternators; there are also two 350-kw emergency diesel alternators. The engineering groups are automatic and remote-controlled. Listed beam does not include platforms extending from sides aft. C 554 refitted 1979–80 as training cruiser to replace *San Giorgio* (D 562). The after two 76-mm guns and the aft NA-9 gunfire-control system were removed, and the hangar was converted to accommodations and classrooms; a new, lower hangar was built on abaft the old one, reducing the flight-deck length and limiting the ship to two helicopters. A small navigational radar was added atop the hangar for helicopter control.

Both received Standard SM-1 ER missiles and associated electronics during refits in the latter 1970s. Have four (C 554:3) Argo NA-9 GFCS.

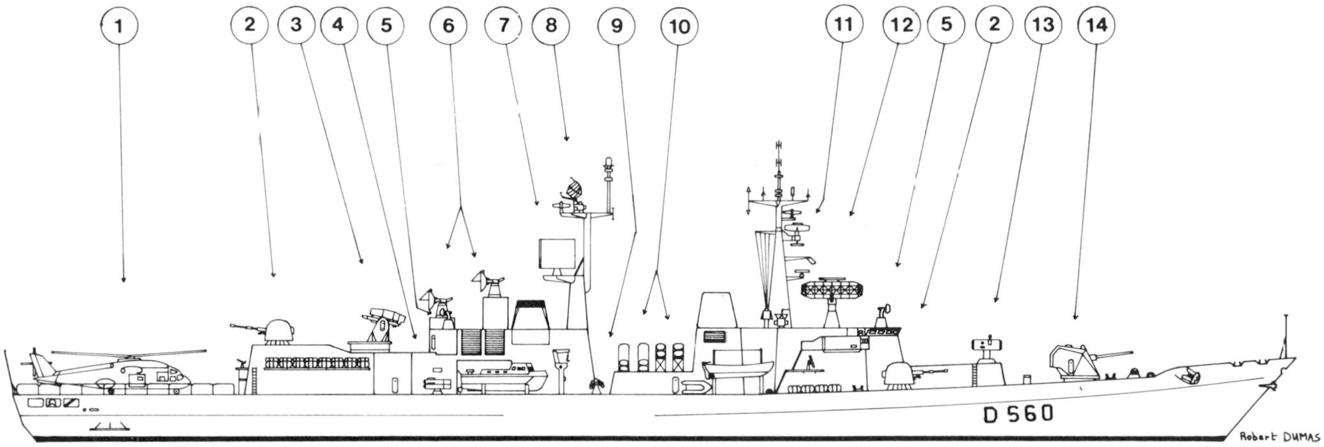


**Animoso** 1. EH-101 helicopter 2. 76-mm OTO Melara Super Rapid DP 3. Mk 13 launcher for Standard SAM 4. triple ILAS-3 ASW TT 5. RTN-20X f.c. directors (port and starboard) 6. SPG-51D radar SAM directors 7. SPS-52C 3-D radar 8. RAN-10S air-search radar 9. Sagaie decoy RL 10. Otomat/Teseo SSM launchers 11. RAN-11L/X radar 12. SPS-768 (RAN-3L) air-search radar 13. Albatros SAM system launcher 14. 127-mm OTO Melara DP

## GUIDED-MISSILE DESTROYERS

◆ **0 (+2) Animoso class** Bldr: Fincantieri, Riva Trigoso (to fit-out at Muggiano)

| | Laid down | L | In serv. |
|---|---|---|---|
| D 560 ANIMOSO | ... | ... | 1992 |
| D 561 ARDIMENTOSO | ... | ... | 1992 |

**D:** 4,500 tons (5,250 fl) **S:** 31.5 kts **Dim:** 135.60 × 16.10 (15.00 wl) × . . .
**A:** 8/Otomat-Teseo SSM (II × 4)—1/U.S. SM-1 MR Standard system, Mk 13 launcher (40 missiles)—1/Albatros point-defense SAM (VIII × 1; . . . Aspide missiles)—1/127-mm OTO Melara DP—3/76-mm OTO Melara Super Rapid DP (I × 3)—6/324-mm ASW TT (III × 2, ILAS-3)—2/EH-101 helicopters (with Marte Mk 2 SSM)
**Electron Equipt:** Radar: 1/SPN-702, 1/SPN-703, 1/SPS-768 (RAN-3L), 1/RAN-11L/X, 1/SPS-774 (RAN-103), 1/SPS-52C, 2/SPG-51D (for SAM), 4/RTN-30X (NA-30E GFCS)
Sonar: Raytheon DE 1164—TACAN: . . .
EW: . . . intercept, 2 Sagaie decoy RL
**M:** CODOG: 2 Fiat/G.E. LM-2500 gas turbines, 2 GMT BL230-20DVM diesels; 2 CP props; 55,000/12,600 hp
**Range:** 7,000/18 (diesel) **Electric:** . . . **Fuel:** . . . **Man:** 400 tot.

REMARKS: Ordered 9-3-86 as replacements for *Impavido* class. Steel superstructure, with Kevlar armor. Two pair fin stabilizers. Twin helicopter hangar, 18.5 m long; flight deck 24.0 × 13.0, with Italian Navy's first haul-down system. SADOC combat data/weapons control system. Four NA-30 weapons control systems handle the Albatros SAM and the four guns. U.S. Prairie noise-masking system to be installed.

◆ **2 Audace class**

| | Bldr | Laid down | L | In serv. |
|---|---|---|---|---|
| D 550 ARDITO | Nav. Mec. Castellammare | 19-7-68 | 27-11-71 | 5-12-73 |
| D 551 AUDACE | C. Nav. del Tirreno | 27-4-68 | 2-10-71 | 16-11-72 |

**D:** 3,600 light/3,950 tons (4,554 fl) **S:** 33 kts **Dim:** 140.7 × 14.65 × 4.60 (hull)
**A:** 1/Mk 13 missile launcher (40 Standard SM-1 MR)—2/127-mm OTO Melara Compact DP (I × 2)—4/76-mm AA OTO Melara Compact DP (I × 4)—6/324-mm ASW TT (II × 2)—4/533-mm TT (I × 4, AS-184 wire-guided torpedoes)—2/AB-212 or 1/SH-3D Sea King ASW helicopter
**Electron Equipt:** Radar: 1/3 RM-20, 1/RAN-20S (SPS-768), 1/SPQ-2, 1/SPS-52, 2/SPG-51C, 3/RTN-10X (Argo systems)
Sonar: CWE 610A
EW: passive arrays, 1/SCLAR chaff RL (XX × 2)

**Audace (D 551)** G. Arra, 1984

**Ardito (D 550)** G. Arra, 1984

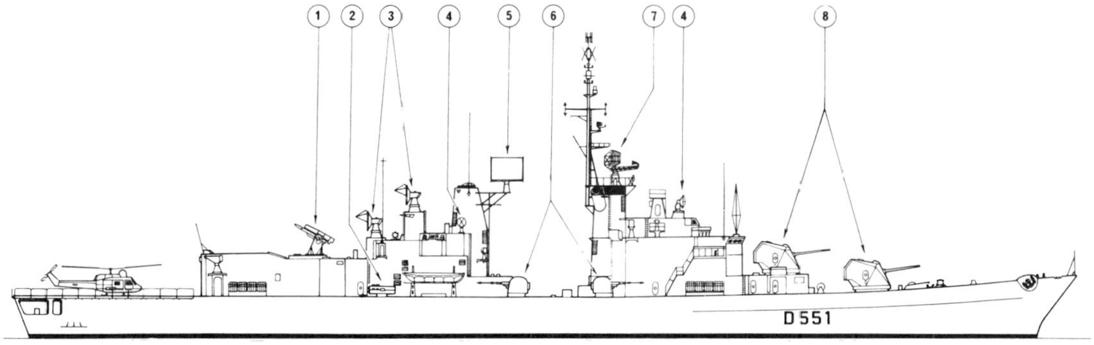


**Audace (D 551)** 1. Mk 13 launcher 2. triple ASW TT 3. SPG-51B radars 4. RTN-10X f.c. radars 5. SPS-52C radar 6. 76-mm DP 7. RAN-20S radar 8. 127-mm DP H. Simoni

**GUIDED-MISSILE DESTROYERS** *(continued)*

**Ardito (D 550)**—note torpedo-tube recesses at stern L. & L. Van Ginderen, 5-84

**M:** 2 sets GT; 2 props; 73,000 hp
**Boilers:** 4 Foster-Wheeler; 43 kg/cm², 450°C **Electric:** 5,200 kw
**Range:** 4,000/25 **Man:** 30 officers, 350 men

REMARKS: Habitability has been given much attention in the design of these very fine ships. The four single 533-mm torpedo tubes are mounted at the extreme stern, below the fantail, and launch A-184 wire-guided torpedoes aftward. Both now have RAN-20S air-search radar, replacing SPS-12 (D 550) or RAN-3 (D 551). The missile system is to be modernized; the upper 127-mm gun is to be replaced by an Albatros SAM system. Have fin stabilizers.

◆ **2 Impavido class**

| | Bldr | Laid down | L | In serv. |
|---|---|---|---|---|
| D 570 IMPAVIDO | C.N. del Tirreno, Riva Trigoso | 10-6-57 | 25-5-62 | 16-11-63 |
| D 571 INTREPIDO | Ansaldo, Livorno | 16-5-59 | 21-10-62 | 18-7-64 |

**Impavido (D 570)** L. & L. Van Ginderen, 2-86

**Impavido (D 570)** Pradignac & Leo, 1986

**D:** 3,201 tons (3,851 fl) **S:** 33.5 kts **Dim:** 131.3 × 13.65 × 4.43
**A:** 1/Mk 13 launcher aft (40 Standard SM-1 MR missiles)—2/127-mm 38-cal. DP (II × 1) fwd—4/76-mm DP (I × 4)—6/324-mm ASW TT (III × 2)
**Electron Equipt:** Radar: 1/SPS-12, /SPQ-2, 1/SPS-39, 2/SPG-51C, 3/RTN-10X (Argo systems)
Sonar: 1/SQS-39
EW: passive arrays, 2/SCLAR chaff RL (XX × 2)
**M:** 2 sets Tosi GT; 2 props; 70,000 hp
**Boilers:** 4 Foster-Wheeler; 43 kg/cm², 450°C **Fuel:** 650 tons
**Range:** 3,300/20; 2,900/25; 1,500/30 **Man:** 22 officers, 313 men

REMARKS: Refitted (D 571 in 1974–75, D 570 in 1976–77) with new fire control for guns and new missiles. Have fin stabilizers. To be replaced by the *Animoso* class.

**GUIDED-MISSILE FRIGATES**

◆ **8 Maestrale class** Bldr: CNR, Riva Trigoso (F 571: CNR, Muggiano)

| | Laid down | L | In serv. |
|---|---|---|---|
| F 570 MAESTRALE | 8-3-78 | 2-2-81 | 7-3-82 |
| F 571 GRECALE | 21-3-79 | 12-9-81 | 5-2-83 |
| F 572 LIBECCIO | 1-8-79 | 7-9-81 | 5-2-83 |
| F 573 SCIROCCO | 26-2-80 | 17-4-82 | 20-9-83 |
| F 574 ALISEO | 26-2-80 | 29-10-82 | 20-9-83 |
| F 575 EURO | 15-4-81 | 25-3-83 | 7-4-84 |
| F 576 ESPERO | 1-8-82 | 19-11-83 | 4-5-85 |
| F 577 ZEFFIRO | 15-3-83 | 19-5-84 | 4-5-85 |

**D:** 2,700 tons light (3,040 normal) **S:** 33 kts (21 max. diesel/3,200 fl)
**Dim:** 122.73 (116.4 pp) × 12.88 × 4.10 (hull: 5.95 max.)
**A:** 4/Teseo Otomat Mk 2 SSM (I × 4)—1/Albatros SAM system (VIII × 1, 24 Aspide missiles)—1/127-mm DP OTO Melara—4/40-mm Breda Dardo AA (II × 2)—2/533-mm TT (A-184 torpedoes)—6/324-mm ILAS-3 ASW TT (III × 2)—2/AB-212 helicopters
**Electron Equipt:** Radar: 1/MM/SPS-702, 1/RAN-10S (SPS-774), 1/RAN-11L/X, 1/RTN-30X (NA-30A system), 2/RTN-20X (Dardo system)
Sonar: 1/Raytheon DE 1160B, 1/Raytheon DE 1164 VDS
EW: Elettronica Newton active/passive suite, 2/SCLAR chaff launchers (XX × 2)
**M:** CODOG: 2 G.E./Fiat LM-2500 gas turbines, 50,000 hp; 2 GMT B 230-20 DV diesels, 10,146 hp; 2 CP props
**Electric:** 3,120 kw **Endurance:** 90 days
**Range:** 1,500/30; 3,800/22; 6,000/15 **Man:** 24 officers, 201 men

**Zeffiro (F 577)** L. & L. Van Ginderen, 2-87

**Grecale (F 571)**—showing VDS well at stern L. Grazioli, 3-87

**GUIDED-MISSILE FRIGATES** *(continued)*

**Maestrale (F 570)** Italian Navy, 1986

**Aliseo (F 574)** G. Arra, 7-85

REMARKS: An enlarged version of *Lupo* with better seaworthiness and two helicopters at the expense of four antiship missiles and about 2.5 knots maximum speed. Have SADOC-2 (IPN-20) computerized data system. There is a Galileo OG-30 optronic backup director to the NA-30A GFCS system and two MM 59 optical backup directors for the 40-mm guns. Helo deck is 12 × 27 m. D 1164 is a VDS version of DE 1160 and operates on the same frequencies. The hull sonar is a commercial version of the U.S. Navy SQS-56 as used in the *Oliver Hazard Perry* (FFG 7) class. FF 576 and FF 577 ordered 10-80, 572–575 in 12-76, 576 and 577 in 10-80. Have U.S. Prairie/Masker bubbler noise-suppression system and SLQ-25 Nixie towed torpedo decoys. There are plans to lengthen the VDS tow cable from 600 m to 900 m and to attach a towed passive linear hydrophone array to the VDS fish; trials to take place with F 570. F 571 and F 573 got 2/20-mm AA in 9-87 for Persian Gulf duty.

◆ **4 Lupo class** Bldr: C.N. Riuniti, Riva Trigoso (F 567; CNR Muggiano)

| | Laid down | L | In serv. |
|---|---|---|---|
| F 564 LUPO | 8-10-74 | 29-7-76 | 20-9-77 |
| F 565 SAGITTARIO | 4-2-76 | 22-6-77 | 18-11-78 |
| F 566 PERSEO | 28-2-77 | 8-7-78 | 1-3-80 |
| F 567 ORSA | 1-8-77 | 1-3-79 | 1-3-80 |

**Lupo (F 564)** L. Grazioli, 2-86

**Orsa (F 567)**—hangar extended P. Voss, 6-85

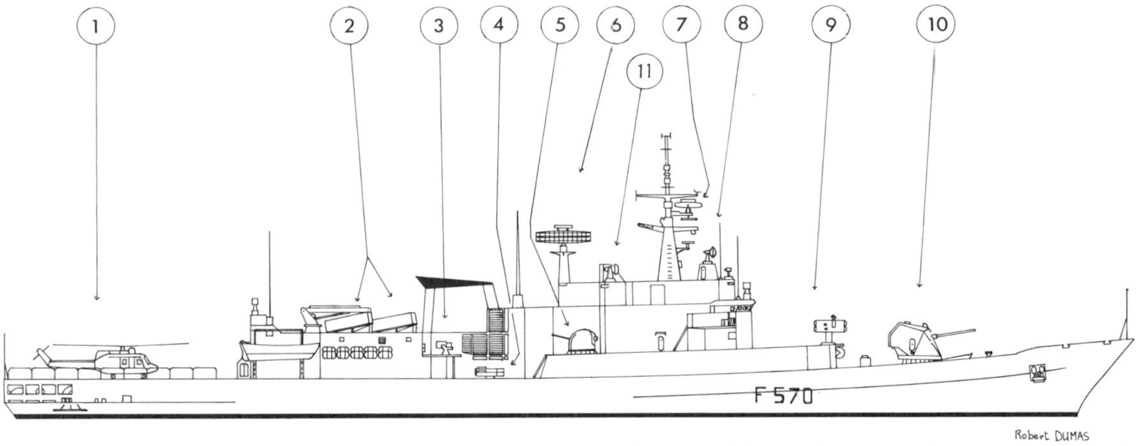


**Maestrale class** 1. AB-212 helicopter 2. Otomat SSM launchers 3. SCLAR chaff rocket launchers 4. ILAS-3 triple ASW TT 5. Breda Dardo twin 40-mm AA 6. RAN-10S radar antenna 7. RAN-11L/X surface-search radar antenna 8. RTN-30X gun/missile-control radar 9. Albatros launcher (VIII × 1) 10. 127-mm dual-purpose gun 11. RTN-20X radar directors

## GUIDED-MISSILE FRIGATES *(continued)*

**D:** 2,208 tons (2,340 trials; 2,525 fl)
**S:** 35.23 kts (trials, *Lupo*); 32 kts at 80% power; 20.3 kts on 2 diesels
**Dim:** 113.55 (106.00 pp) × 12.00 × 3.54 (hull)
**A:** 8/Otomat Mk 2 SSM (I × 8)—1/Nato Sea Sparrow system (VIII × 1)—1/127-mm OTO Melara DP—4/40-mm Breda AA (II × 2)—6/324-mm Mk 32 ASW TT (III × 2)—1/AB-212 helicopter
**Electron Equipt:** Radar: 1/SMA-703, 1/RAN-10S (SPS-774) combined search, 1/SPQ-2F, 1/RAN-11/LX combined search, 1/Orion RTN-10X (NA-10 mod. 2 Argo f.c. system), 1/Mk 91 Mod. 1, 2/Orion RTN-20X (Dardo system)
Sonar: Raytheon 1160B
EW: active and passive systems, 2/SCLAR chaff RL (XX × 2)
**M:** CODOG: 2 G.E./Fiat LM-2500 gas turbines, 50,000 hp; 2 GMT A 230-20M diesels, 7,900 hp; 2 CP props
**Electric:** 3,120 kw (4 Fiat 236 SS diesel alternator sets)
**Range:** 900/35; 3,450/20; 4,350/16 (diesels) **Man:** 17 officers, 177 men

Remarks: Fin stabilizers. Telescopic hangar. The Otomat Mk-II (Teseo) launchers are mounted two per side abreast the hangar and two per side on the forward superstructure. The *Lupo* had her radar antennae redistributed 1978–79 and a new mast added at the after end of the stack. The SAM system uses the U.S. Mk 29 launcher and a U.S. director, rather than the later Albatros system with the similar Aspide missiles of the *Maestrale* class. The highly automated machinery plant is mounted in four compartments: auxiliaries, gas turbines, reduction gearing, and diesel alternator sets. Six ships of the same class were ordered for Venezuela, four for Peru, and four for Iraq.

## FRIGATES

◆ **2 Alpino class** Bldr: C.N. del Tirreno, Riva Trigoso

| | Laid down | L | In serv. |
|---|---|---|---|
| F 580 Alpino (ex-*Circe*) | 27-2-63 | 10-6-67 | 14-1-68 |
| F 581 Carabiniere (ex-*Climene*) | 9-1-65 | 30-9-67 | 28-4-68 |

**Carabiniere (F 581)**—showing VDS installation G. Arra, 1982

**Alpino (F 580)** A. Fraccaroli, 9-84

**D:** 2,000 tons (2,689 fl) **S:** 28 kts **Dim:** 113.3 (106.4 pp) × 13.3 × 3.80 (hull)
**A:** 6/76-mm 62-cal. DP (I × 6)—1/305-mm Menon K113 ASW mortar (I × 1)—6/324-mm ASW TT (III × 2)—1/AB-212 helicopter
**Electron Equipt:** Radar: MM/SPN-728(V)2 nav., 1/SPS-12, 1/SPQ-2, 1/RTN-30X (NA-30 system), 3/RTN-10X (Argo systems), F 580 also: 1/MAD
Sonar: 1/SQS-43 (F 581: DE 1164), 1/SQA-10 VDS
EW: MM/SPR-A intercept, 2/SCLAR chaff RL (XX × 2)
**M:** CODAG: 4 Tosi OTV-320 diesels, 4,200 hp each; 2 Tosi-Metrovik G6 gas turbines, 7,700 hp each; 2 props; 31,800 hp
**Electric:** 2,400 kw **Fuel:** 275 tons **Range:** 4,200/17
**Man:** 19 officers, 228 men

Remarks: Fin stabilizers. Cruising, 22 knots on diesels. F 580 fitted with experimental MAD gunfire-control radar 1975. F 581 received bow-mounted sonar, improved combat data system and EW equipment during refit ended 7-85.

◆ **2 Carlo Bergamini class** Bldr: Castellammare, Stabia

| | Laid down | L | In serv. |
|---|---|---|---|
| F 594 Virgilio Fasan | 6-3-60 | 9-10-60 | 10-10-62 |
| F 595 Carlo Margottini | 25-5-57 | 12-6-60 | 5-5-62 |

**Carlo Margottini (F 595)** L. & L. Van Ginderen, 4-85

**Virgilio Fasan (F 584)** L. & L. Van Ginderen, 6-86

**D:** 1,140 tons (1,650 fl) **S:** 25 kts **Dim:** 93.95 (86.51) × 11.35 × 3.20 (hull)
**A:** 2/76-mm 62-cal. DP (1 × 2)—1/single-barreled Menon K113 ASW mortar—6/324-mm ILAS—3/ASW TT (III × 2)—1/AB-212 helicopter
**Electron Equipt:** Radar: 1/nav., 1/SPQ-2, 1/SPS-12, 1/RTN-10X
Sonar: SQS-40
EW: MM/SPR-A intercept
**M:** 4 high-speed Fiat 3012 diesels; 2 props; 16,000 hp
**Range:** 3,600/18; 4,500/16 **Electric:** 204 kw
**Man:** 12 officers, 163 men

Remarks: Were to have been stricken 1982–83. Sisters *Luigi Rizzo* (F 593) and *Carlo Bergamini* (F 593) stricken 30-11-80 and 11-81, respectively. Have Denny-Brown fin stabilizers, telescoping hangar; flight deck enlarged 1968–71, requiring removal of a third 76-mm gun. OGS.3 GFCS.

## CORVETTES

Note: The new corvettes of the "Constellazione" *Cassiopea* class are being built for the Ministry of the Merchant Marine, apparently for the Port Captains Corps. See later page for details. They will be Navy-manned.

◆ **3 (+5) Minerva class** Bldr: Fincantieri, Muggiano and Riva Trigoso, Laspezia

| | Yard | Laid down | L | In serv. |
|---|---|---|---|---|
| F 551 Minerva | Riva Trigoso | 20-2-84 | 25-3-86 | 28-2-87 |
| F 552 Urania | Riva Trigoso | 20-2-84 | 21-6-86 | 10-10-87 |
| F 553 Daniade | Muggiano | 20-8-84 | 18-10-86 | 10-87 |
| F 554 Sfinge | Muggiano | 20-8-84 | 13-5-87 | 1988 |
| F 555 Driade | ... | ... | ... | ... |
| F 556 Chimera | ... | ... | ... | ... |
| F 557 Fenice | ... | ... | ... | ... |
| F 558 Sibilla | ... | ... | ... | ... |

**Minerva (F 551)** A. Fraccaroli, 5-87

CORVETTES *(continued)*

**Minerva (F 551)** G. Valentini, 5-87

**Urania (F 552)**—at launch, 21-6-86 C. Martineli, 6-86

**D:** 1,029 tons (1,285 fl) **S:** 24 kts **Dim:** 86.60 (80.00 pp) × 10.50 × 3.16 (hull)
**A:** 1/Albatros SAM system (VIII × 1, 8 Aspide missiles)—1/76-mm OTO Melara Super Rapid DP—6/324-mm ILAS-3 ASW TT (III × 2)
**Electron Equipt:** Radar: 1/MM/SPN-703 nav., 1/MM/SPS-774 combined air/surface search, 1/RTN-20X f.c. (Dardo E f.c.s.)
Sonar: 1/Raytheon DE 1167 (MF, hull-mounted)
EW: Elettronica Newton INS-3 active/passive suite, 2 Type 207/E chaff RL
**M:** 2 GMT BM 230.20 DVM diesels; 2 CP props; 11,000 hp
**Electric:** 2,080 kw (4 Isotta Fraschini ID36 S12V diesel sets)
**Range:** 3,500/18 **Man:** 9 officers, 112 men

Remarks: First four authorized 1983 to begin replacement of earlier corvettes; names for second planned group released 1985; ships ordered 1-87. Intended for surveillance, coastal escort, fisheries protection, training, and search-and-rescue duties. Weight and space reserved for addition of Aspide reload facility, four Teseo-Otomat Mk 2 SSM, variable-depth sonar. Will have Selenia SADOC-2 combat data system, with two computers and three displays. Elsag NA-16 optronic GFCS for the 76-mm gun, with the Dardo E radar f.c.s. controlling the SAM system or the gun. Sonars will be the first to be built (though under license) in Italy. Fin stabilizers, satellite navigation systems fitted.

◆ **4 Pietro de Cristofaro class**

| | Bldr | Laid down | L | In serv. |
|---|---|---|---|---|
| F 540 Pietro de Cristofaro | C.N. del Tirreno | 20-4-63 | 29-5-65 | 19-12-65 |
| F 541 Umberto Grosso | Ansaldo, Livorno | 21-10-62 | 12-12-64 | 25-4-66 |
| F 546 Licio Visintini | C.R.D.A., Monfalcone | 30-9-63 | 30-5-65 | 10-8-66 |
| F 550 Salvatore Todaro | Ansaldo, Livorno | 21-10-62 | 24-10-64 | 25-4-66 |

**D:** 850 tons (1,020 fl) **S:** 22 kts **Dim:** 80.37 (75.0 pp) × 10.28 × 2.80 (hull)
**A:** 2/76-mm DP (I × 2)—1/305-mm K113 Menon ASW mortar (I × 1)—6/324-mm ASW TT (III × 2)
**Electron Equipt:** Radar: 1/SPQ-2B, 1/Orion RTN-7A (OG-3 system), 1/BX-732 nav.
Sonar: 2/SQS-36 (1 hull, 1 in SQA-13 VDS hoist)
EW: MM/SPR-A intercept
**M:** 2 diesels (see Remarks); 2 props; 8,400 hp **Fuel:** 100 tons
**Electric:** 600 kw **Range:** 4,600/18 **Man:** 7 officers, 122 men

**Licio Visintini (F 546)** L. & L. Van Ginderen, 2-86

**Pietro de Cristofaro (F 540)** L. Grazioli, 11-85

Remarks: High-speed diesels; Fiat 3012 RSS on F 540, F 541, and F 550; Tosi on F 546, with reduction gears and Tosi-Vulcan hydraulic linkage. OG-3 gun director forward, U.S. Mk 51 director aft. The VDS uses an SQA-13 hoist. No VDS on F 540; no ASW TT on F 541.

◆ **3 Albatros class** Bldr: Nav. Mec. Castellammare di Stabia (except F 542: Breda, Marghera-Mestre, Venice)

| | Laid down | L | In serv. |
|---|---|---|---|
| F 542 Aquila (ex-Dutch *Lynx*) | 25-7-53 | 31-7-54 | 2-10-56 |
| F 544 Alcione | 1953 | 19-9-54 | 23-10-55 |
| F 545 Airone | 1953 | 21-11-54 | 29-12-55 |

**Airone (P 545)** L. Grazioli, 5-87

**D:** 800 tons (950 fl) **S:** 19 kts **Dim:** 76.3 (69.49 pp) × 9.65 × 2.72 (hull)
**A:** 3/40-mm AA (II × 1, I × 1)—2/Mk 11 Hedgehog (XXIV × 2)—F 542, F 545: 6/324-mm ILAS ASW TT (III × 2)—F 542, F 545: 1/d.c. rack
**Electron Equipt:** Radar: 1/BX-732 nav., 1/SPQ-2—Sonar: QCU-2
**M:** 2 Fiat M 409 diesels; 2 props; 5,200 hp (3,500 sust.) **Fuel:** 100 tons
**Electric:** 1,200 kw **Range:** 2,988/18 **Man:** 6 officers, 96 men

**CORVETTES** *(continued)*

Remarks: Ships built with U.S. "Offshore" funds (ex-U.S. PC 1626, PC 1620, and PC 1921). One similar ship was delivered to the Netherlands (F 542, returned to Italy in 10-61 and commissioned 9-11-61) and four to Denmark. Originally had two 76-mm DP, two 40-mm AA (II × 1); rearmed 1963. F 544 is equipped for minesweeping, having rubber dinghies, 2 paravanes, and equipment davits on the stern. All were to be decommissioned 1982–83, but were retained until the *Minerva* class entered service. *Albatros* (F 543) decommissioned 30-4-86.

**GUIDED-MISSILE PATROL BOATS**

◆ **1 private-venture DA-360T design** Bldr: Fincantieri, Muggiano

| | Laid down | L | In serv. |
|---|---|---|---|
| "920" Saettia | 6-84 | 12-84 | 12-85 |

**Saettia (920)** C. Martinelli, 6-86

**D:** 330 tons (370 normal, 400 fl) **S:** 40 kts (37.5 sust.)
**Dim:** 51.70 (47.20 pp) × 8.10 × . . . (5.40 moulded depth)
**A:** 4/Otomat Mk 2 SSM—1/76-mm OTO Melara Compact DP—2/40-mm Breda Dardo AA (II × 1)
**Electron Equipt:** Radar: 1/. . . nav., 1/RAN-11 L/X, 1/Orion RTN-10X f.c.
EW: Elettronica Farad A1 intercept; 2 Breda 6105, 105-mm chaff RL
**M:** 4 MTU 16V538 TB93 diesels; 4 props; 17,600 hp (16,560 hp sust.)
**Range:** 2,200/16 **Endurance:** 12 days **Man:** 4 officers, 29 men
**Electric:** 450 kw (3 × 150 kw; 3 Isotta Fraschini ID38 SS6V diesels)

Remarks: *Not* a unit of the Italian Navy. Built in hopes of sales and to test concept. Has fin stabilizers. Elsag NA 21 weapons control system with RTN-10X radar has NA 12 optronic backup director. Selenia's IPN-10 combat data system. EW system includes ELT/521 jammer, ELT/261 signal analyzer. Hull number is unofficial.

◆ **7 Sparviero-class hydrofoils** Bldr: CNR, Muggiano (P 420: Alinavi, La Spezia)

| | Laid down | L | Delivered | In serv. |
|---|---|---|---|---|
| P 420 Sparviero | 4-71 | 9-5-73 | . . . | 15-7-74 |
| P 421 Nibbio | 1-8-77 | 29-2-80 | 10-11-80 | 7-3-82 |
| P 422 Falcone | 1-10-77 | 27-10-80 | 1-3-82 | 7-3-82 |
| P 423 Astore | 1-7-78 | 20-7-81 | 6-8-82 | 5-2-83 |
| P 424 Griffone | 15-11-78 | 1-12-81 | 16-9-82 | 5-2-83 |
| P 425 Gheppio | 16-5-79 | 24-6-82 | 11-5-83 | 20-9-83 |
| P 426 Condore | 21-3-80 | 25-1-83 | 19-1-84 | 7-4-84 |

**Griffone (P 424)** C. Martinelli, 5-84

**Sparviero (P 420)** L. Grazioli, 3-86

**D:** 63.0 tons (fl) **S:** 43 kts (heavy sea), 50 kts (calm sea)
**Dim:** 22.95 (24.56, foils retracted) × 7.01 (12.06 max. over foils) × 1.87 (1.45 over foils at speed, 4.37 over foils at rest)
**A:** 2 Otomat Mk II SSM (I × 2)—1/76-mm OTO Melara Compact
**Electron Equipt:** Radar: 1/SPN-701 (P 420: 3RM7-250), 1/RTN-10X (NA-10 Mod. 3 system)
**M:** CODOG: 1 Rolls-Royce Proteus 15 M560 gas turbine; 1 waterjet; 5,044 hp (P 420: 4,500); 1 G.M. 6V-53N diesel; 1 prop; 180 hp
**Fuel:** 11 tons **Range:** 1,050/8 (diesels); 400/45
**Man:** 2 officers, 8 men

Remarks: Prototype studied by the Alinavi Society, which was formed in 1964 by Boeing, U.S.A., the Italian government's I.R.I., and Carlo Rodriguez of Messina, builder of commercial hydrofoils. Six more (of eight planned) were ordered 1977. The three hydrofoils are raised when cruising, and the diesel engine is engaged. All-aluminum construction. Used for short-duration operations, have no berths. Design based on U.S. *Tucumcari*. F 421 onward have a later navigational/surface-search radar, incorporating an IFF interrogator. All except P 420 have water injection to increase gas-turbine power output, but they are basically underpowered. There are plans to replace the Proteus with a G.M. Allison 570 KF turbine producing 6,394 hp.

Note: The two *Freccia*-class convertible torpedo-gunboats have been stricken: *Freccia* (P 493) on 15-9-84 and *Saetta* (P 494) on 9-10-86. Former motor torpedo boats MS 441 and MS 443 were stricken 31-10-85.

**MINE WARFARE SHIPS**

◆ **0 (+6) Lerici-II class** Bldr: Intermarine, Sarzana

| | L | In serv. | | L | In serv. |
|---|---|---|---|---|---|
| M 5554 Gaeta | . . . | 1989 | M 5557 Numano | . . . | . . . |
| M 5555 Termoli | . . . | . . . | M 5558 Crotone | . . . | . . . |
| M 5556 Alghero | . . . | . . . | M 5559 Viareggio | . . . | 1991 |

**D:** 510 tons (542 fl) **S:** 15 kts **Dim:** 51.00 (46.50 pp) × 9.56 × 2.75
**A:** 1/20-mm AA
**Electron Equipt:** Radar: 1/MM/SPN-703
Sonar: FIAR P2072
**M:** 1 GMT B230-8M diesel; 1 prop; 1,840 hp (3 retractable 120-hp Riva Calzoni thrusters, 360 hp, for 7-kt hunting speed
**Electric:** 900 kw (3/250-kw sets, ID 36SS diesels; 1/150-kw set, ID 36N diesel)
**Range:** 2,500/12 **Fuel:** 49 tons **Man:** 40 tot.

Remarks: Names announced 1980, but ships not ordered until 3-87. Lengthened version of *Lerici* design, with new minehunting auxiliary thruster system and new sonar (an Italian-built version of the SQQ-14 with digital processor) a Plessey Speedscan, sidescan route-mapping sonar, and an additional generator set. Carry one MIN-77 and one Gaymarine Pluto remote-controlled mine disposal submersibles and Oropesa MKA mechanical sweep gear. Have the MM/SSN-714 command and control system. Carry 2-man decompression chamber and are fitted with passive tank stabilization (using tanks for fuel, range can be extended by 1,500 mm at 12 kts). Two more are planned.

◆ **4 Lerici-class minehunter/minesweepers** Bldr: Intermarine, Sarzana

| | L | In serv. | | L | In serv. |
|---|---|---|---|---|---|
| M 5550 Lerici | 3-9-82 | 4-5-85 | M 5552 Milazzo | . . . | 14-12-85 |
| M 5551 Sapri | . . . | 14-12-85 | M 5553 Vieste | . . . | 14-12-85 |

**D:** 488 tons (520 fl) **S:** 15 kts **Dim:** 49.98 (45.50 pp) × 9.56 × 2.70
**A:** 1/20-mm AA
**Electron Equipt:** Radar: MM/SPN-703—Sonar: SQQ-14
**M:** 1 GMT B230-8M diesel; 1 prop; 1,840 hp (2 retractable auxiliary thrusters; 470 hp for 7 kts)
**Electric:** 650 kw (2/250-kw sets, ID 36SS diesels; 1/150-kw set)
**Range:** 1,500/14; 2,500/12 **Fuel:** 49 tons **Man:** 40 tot.

**MINE WARFARE SHIPS** *(continued)*

**Lerici (M 5550)** M. Louagie/Plokker, 6-87

**Vieste (M 5553)** L. & L. Van Ginderen, 6-87

REMARKS: Ordered 4-78. Sisters built for Nigeria and Malaysia, and the U.S. Navy MHC 51 class is based on this design. Glass-reinforced, shock-resistant plastic construction throughout. Hull material 140-mm thick. SQQ-14 is a high-frequency minehunting sonar with a retractable transducer. While minehunting, speed is 7 knots, using the two drop-down, shrouded thrusters. Carry 6–7 divers, who use CAM mine destructor charges. One Pluto remote-controlled submersible disposal and one MIN-77 locating submersible carried by each ship, along with Oropesa Mk 4 mechanical sweep gear. Have Motorola MHS-1A navigation system and MM/SSN-714 command and control system. Range at 12 knots can be extended to 4,000 nautical miles by using the passive roll stabilization tanks to carry fuel. Delivery of these ships delayed by the presence of a bridge blocking the seaward exit from the yard.

◆ **4 ex-U.S. Agile-class fleet minesweepers**

| | Bldr | L | In serv. |
|---|---|---|---|
| M 5430 SALMONE (ex-MSO 507) | Martinolich, San Diego | 19-2-55 | 15-5-56 |
| M 5431 STORIONE (ex-MSO 506) | Martinolich, San Diego | 13-11-54 | 23-2-56 |
| M 5432 SGOMBRO (ex-MSO 517) | Tampa Marine | 1954 | 12-5-57 |
| M 5433 SQUALO (ex-MSO 518) | Tampa Marine | 1955 | 20-6-57 |

**Squalo (M 5433)** C. Martinelli, 9-86

**D:** 665 tons (750 fl) **S:** 14 kts **Dim:** 52.27 × 10.71 × 4.0 (fl)
**A:** 1/40-mm AA
**Electron Equipt:** Radar: 1/MM/SPN-703, 1/BX-732—Sonar: UQS-1
**M:** 2 G.M. 8-278ANW diesels; 2 CP props; 1,600 hp **Fuel:** 46 tons
**Range:** 3,000/10 **Man:** 4 officers, 58 men

REMARKS: Had been scheduled for disposal 1982–83. Wooden construction.

◆ **19 U.S. Adjutant-class minesweepers** (9 converted as minehunters*)

| | Bldr | In serv. |
|---|---|---|
| M 5504 CASTAGNO (ex-MSC 74)* | H. Grebe, New York | 7-8-55 |
| M 5505 CEDRO (ex-MSC 88)* | Berg SY, Wash. | 9-11-53 |
| M 5508 FRASSINO (ex-MSC 89)* | Berg SY, Wash. | 15-2-54 |
| M 5509 GELSO (ex-MSC 75)* | H. Grebe, New York | 8-3-54 |
| M 5516 PLATANO (ex-MSC 136)* | Bellingham BY, Wash. | 16-10-54 |
| M 5519 MANDORLO (ex-MSC 280)* | Tacoma BY, Wash. | 16-12-60 |
| M 5521 BAMBU (ex-MSC 214) | CRDA, Monfalcone | 8-9-56 |
| M 5522 EBANO (ex-MSC 215) | CRDA, Monfalcone | 8-11-56 |
| M 5523 MANGO (ex-MSC 216)* | CRDA, Monfalcone | 5-12-56 |
| M 5524 MOGANO (ex-MSC 217) | CRDA, Monfalcone | 9-1-57 |
| M 5525 PALMA (ex-MSC 238)* | CRDA, Monfalcone | 28-2-57 |
| M 5527 SANDALO (ex-MSC 240) | CRDA, Monfalcone | 17-4-57 |
| M 5531 AGAVE | CRDA, Monfalcone | 1-2-56 |
| M 5533 EDERA | CRDA, Monfalcone | 7-56 |
| M 5535 GELSOMINO | Baglietto, Varezze | 5-56 |
| M 5536 GIAGGIOLO | Picchiotti, Viareggio | 6-56 |
| M 5538 LOTO* | Celli, Venice | 21-1-56 |
| M 5540 TIMO | Costaguta, Voltri | 8-56 |
| M 5542 VISCHIO | C. Mediterraneo, Piera | 8-56 |

**Cedro (M 5505)**—minehunter with pole mast C. Martinelli, 11-86

**Gelsomino (M 5535)**—minesweeper L. Grazioli, 4-87

**Mandorlo (M 5519)**—minehunter with unique bridge, tall stack
C. Martinelli, 3-86

**MINE WARFARE SHIPS** *(continued)*

**Loto (M 5538)**—prototype minehunter conversion, with short forecastle, lattice mast — Pradignac & Leo, 6-87

**D:** 375 tons (405 fl) **S:** 12 kts **Dim:** 43.92 (42.1 pp) × 8.23 × 2.68
**A:** 2/20-mm AA (II × 1)
**Electron Equipt:** Radar: 1/BX-732—(minehunters: 1/MM/SPN-703)
Sonar: UQS-1 (minehunters: SQQ-14)
**M:** 2 G.M. 8-268A diesels; 2 props; 1,200 hp (see Remarks) **Fuel:** 40 tons
**Range:** 2,500/10 **Man:** 2 officers, 29 men (minehunters: 3 officers, 38 men)

REMARKS: M 5531 to M 5542 were built with "Offshore" procurement funds and did not receive MSC-series hull numbers; the others were built under the U.S. Military Aid Program. M 5519 is of a later design than the others, with a lower bridge and larger stack; she was converted as a minehunter in 1975 and displaces 370 tons; her dimensions are 44.12 × 8.50 × 2.30, and her two 900-hp diesels provide a 12-kt max. speed. Eight others have since been similarly altered, with the forecastle being lengthened; they have a standard displacement of 354.5 tons and have a single 310-hp Voith-Schneider vertical cycloidal prop for minehunting. The minehunters' main engines produce 810 hp total, for 11.4 kts. The minehunters employ the Pluto remote-controlled submersible, capable of 4.5-kt speeds; the divers aboard use CAM-T destruction charges. All have wooden hulls and nonmagnetic fittings. M 5521 to M 5527 have Fiat diesels. *Mirto* (ex-M 5539) and *Pioppo* (ex-M 5515) have been converted to survey ships, and *Alloro* (M 5532) became an auxiliary during 1986. *Noce* (M 5511) and *Larice* (M 5510) stricken 30-9-83. Twelve others were discarded 1974 to 1980.

NOTE: The five British-design *Aragosta*-class inshore minesweepers were reclassified as administrative tenders and navigational training craft during 1984–85.

## AMPHIBIOUS WARFARE SHIPS

◆ **1 (+1) San Giorgio-class amphibious warfare ships** Bldr: Fincantieri, Riva Trigoso

| | Laid down | L | In serv. |
|---|---|---|---|
| L 9892 SAN GIORGIO | 26-6-85 | 25-2-87 | 9-10-87 |
| L 9893 SAN MARCO | 28-6-86 | 10-10-87 | . . . |

**San Giorgio (L 9892)**—at launch, 25-2-87 — C, Martinelli

**D:** 5,000 tons (7,665 fl) **S:** 21 kts (sust.)
**Dim:** 133.30 (118.00 pp) × 20.50 × 5.25
**A:** 1/76-mm OTO Melara DP—2/20-mm AA (I × 2)—2/12.7-mm mg (I × 2)—5/CH-47 or SH-3D helicopters
**Electron Equipt:** Radar: 1/. . . nav., 1/SPS-774 (RAN-10S), 1/RTN-30X (NA 21 GFCS)
EW: . . . intercept, . . . chaff RL
TACAN: . . .
**M:** 2 GMT A420.12, 12-cyl., 4-stroke diesels; 2 CP props; 16,800 hp—1,000-hp bow-thruster
**Range:** 4,500/20; 7,500/16
**Electric:** 3,330 kw (4 × 770 kw, 1 × 250 kw)
**Man:** 160 crew, plus 400 troops

**San Giorgio (L 9892)**—left, and *San Marco* (L 9893) on the ways — Italian Navy

REMARKS: L 9892, initially requested in 1980, was approved in 1983 and ordered 5-3-84. L 9893, ordered 26-3-85 with funds from the Ministry of Civil Protection, is intended for disaster-relief service and has more extensive medical facilities than her sister. Both were to fit out at Muggiano.
Both carry three 18.5-m LCM (see below), launched via a 20.5 × 7.0 m docking well aft, plus three 13.0 m LCVP on deck. The helicopters are stowed on deck, not in the 100 × 20.5-m vehicle hangar below, which can hold up to 30 or more personnel carriers; the ships can beach and offload vehicles via a bow ramp. The flight deck is served by a 13.5 × 3.5-m, 30-ton elevator and a 16-ton crane. There is stowage for 99 m³ of refrigerated and 300 m³ dry stores and 60 tons aviation fuel. Evaporators producing 90 tons water per day are fitted. Have passive tank stabilization. The old-model 76-mm gun is served by an NA-21 f.c.s.

◆ **2 ex-U.S. De Soto County-class LST**

| | Bldr | L |
|---|---|---|
| L 9890 GRADO (ex-*De Soto County,* LST 1171) | Avondale SY, New Orleans, La. | 28-2-57 |
| L 9891 CAORLE (ex-*York County,* LST 1175) | Newport News SB & DD | 5-9-57 |

**Grado (L 9890)** — H. Ehlers, 5-86

**D:** 4,164 tons (7,804 fl) **S:** 16 kts **Dim:** 134.7 × 18.9 × 5.5 max.
**A:** 6/76.2-mm 50-cal. DP (II × 3) **Electron Equipt:** Radar: 1/3 RM-7, 1/BX-732
**M:** 6 Fairbanks-Morse 38C8⅛ diesels; 2 CP props; 14,400 hp
**Man:** 13 (L 9891: 11) officers, 147 men + 700 troops

REMARKS: Three Mk 51 gunfire-control systems, two forward, one aft. Carry four LCVPs each. Leased 15-7-72, purchased outright 1981. Planned for disposal on completion of *San Giorgio* and *San Marco.*

◆ **8 new-construction LCM** Bldr: Fincantieri, Muggiano
MTM . . . to . . . (In serv. 1987–88)

**D:** 62 tons (fl) **S:** 9 kts **Dim:** 18.5 × . . . × . . . **M:** . . .

REMARKS: For service three each in *San Giorgio* and *San Marco,* plus two spare. MTM = *Mototrasporti Medi.* Cargo: 30 tons.

◆ **13 U.S. LCM(6)-class LCM**

**D:** 24 tons (56 fl) **S:** 10 kts **Dim:** 17.07 × 4.37 × 1.17 (aft)
**M:** 2 diesels; 2 props; 330 hp **Range:** 130/10

## AMPHIBIOUS WARFARE SHIPS *(continued)*

REMARKS: Transferred 1953. Cargo: 30 tons. Until 1986 were numbered as MTM 9908, 9921, 9922 etc; now numbered MTM 542, 554 etc.

◆ **. . . new-construction LCVP** Bldr: Cantiere Tecnomatic, Ancona (In serv. 1987–88)

MTP . . . to . . .

**D:** 14 tons (fl) **S:** 15 kts **Dim:** 13.5 × . . . × . . . **M:** . . .

REMARKS: For use on *San Giorgio.* To carry 45 troops. MTP = *Mototrasporti Personale.*

◆ **6 U.S. LCVP class**

**D:** 7 tons (11 fl) **S:** 9 kts **Dim:** 10.9 × 3.2 × 1.03
**M:** 1 Gray Marine 64 HN9 diesel; 165 hp **Range:** 110/9

REMARKS: Transferred 1953. Two stricken 1979, three in 1980, and 28 others in 1982. Were numbered MTP 9726, 9731, 9748–9751 until 1986 when renumbered in MTP 523–539 series.

## HYDROGRAPHIC SHIPS

◆ **1 Ammiraglio Magnaghi class** Bldr: C. N. del Tirreno, Riva Trigoso

| | Laid down | L | In serv. |
|---|---|---|---|
| A 5303 AMMIRAGLIO MAGNAGHI | 13-6-73 | 11-9-74 | 2-5-75 |

**Ammiraglio Magnaghi (A 5303)** L. & L. Van Ginderen, 10-84

**D:** 1,550 tons (1,700 fl) **S:** 17 kts **Dim:** 82.70 (76.80 pp) × 13.70 × 3.60
**A:** 1/40-mm—1/AB-212 helicopter **Electron Equipt:** Radar: 1/2RM-20
**M:** 2 GMT B306 SS diesels; 1 CP prop; 3,000 hp; 1 electric auxiliary engine; 240 hp (4 kts)
**Range:** 5,500/12; 4,200/16 **Man:** 15 officers, 120 men, 15 scientists.

REMARKS: Equipped for survey and oceanographic studies and for search-and-rescue duties. Passive tank stabilization. Bow-thruster. Part of 1972 program. Has chemistry, physical, oceanography, photo, and hydrology labs, computerized data loggers, underwater TV. To receive Qubit TRAC 100/CHART 100 integrated hydrographic data acquisition system in 1988.

◆ **2 ex-U.S. Adjutant-class minesweepers**

| | Bldr | In serv. |
|---|---|---|
| A 5306 MIRTO (ex-M 5539) | Breda, Marghera | 4-8-56 |
| A 5307 PIOPPO (ex-M 5515, ex-MSC 135) | Bellingham SY, Washington | 30-7-54 |

**Pioppo (A 5307)** C. Martinelli. 4-85

REMARKS: Characteristics generally as for minesweeper version; displacement: 322 tons std. Superstructure enlarged, stack raised. Both can carry two 20-mm AA (II × 1). Man: 3 officers, 31–35 men. Special survey equipment includes Elac Deneb Special scanning sonar, Atlas scanning sonar, TORAN F, Raydist, Mini Ranger III, and LORAN-C. To be replaced by two new 1,000-ton ships.

## REPLENISHMENT OILERS

◆ **2 Stromboli-class oilers** Bldr: C.N. del Tirreno, Riva Trigoso

| | Laid down | L | In serv. |
|---|---|---|---|
| A 5327 STROMBOLI | 1-10-73 | 20-2-75 | 31-10-75 |
| A 5329 VESUVIO | 1-7-74 | 4-6-77 | 18-11-78 |

**Stromboli (A 5327)**—with ELINT hut on helo deck Pradignac & Leo, 1985

**Vesuvio (A 5329)** C. Martinelli, 10-85

**D:** 4,200 tons (8,706 fl) **S:** 19.5 kts
**Dim:** 129.0 (118.5 pp) × 18.0 × 6.5 (3.17 light) **A:** 1/76-mm DP
**Electron Equipt:** Radar: 1/3RM7-250, 1/Orion RTN-10X
**M:** 2 GMT C428 SS diesels: 1 LIPS 4-bladed CP prop; 11,200 hp (9,600 sust.)
**Electric:** 2,350 kw **Range:** 10,000/16 **Man:** 10 officers, 114 men

REMARKS: Cargo: 1,370 tons fuel oil, 2,830 tons diesel, 480 tons aviation fuel, and 200 tons miscellaneous (torpedoes, missiles, projectiles, spare parts). Capable of serving two units simultaneously alongside while under way with constant-tension fueling rigs, each capable of pumping 650 $m^3$/hr of fuel oil and 480 $m^3$/hr of diesel fuel or aviation fuel. Can also refuel over the stern at the rate of 430 $m^3$/hr. There are also constant-tension cargo transfer rigs on either side, each capable of transferring 1.8-ton loads, as well as two stations for lighter loads. The ships can also replenish via helicopters, although they do not have hangars. Two single 40-mm AA can be added abreast the stack. Twenty repair-party personnel can also be accommodated, and the ships can carry up to 250 passengers. NA-10 Argo GFCS. Sister built for Iraq.

## EXPERIMENTAL SHIPS

◆ **1 weapons systems trials craft** Bldr: Picchiotti, Viareggio

| | L | In serv. |
|---|---|---|
| A 5315 RAFFAELE ROSSETTI | 21-7-86 | 20-12-86 |

**Raffaele Rossetti (A 5315)** C. Martinelli, 4-87

**D:** 282 tons (320 fl) **S:** 14.5 kts **Dim:** 44.60 (40.00 pp) × 7.90 × 2.10
**A:** 2/533-mm TT (1 submerged, *Sauro*-type; 1 surface, *Maestrale*-type, for A 184-series wire-guided torpedoes)—3/324-mm ILAS-3 ASW TT (III × 1)
**Electron Equipt:** Radar: 1/. . . nav.—Sonar: . . .
**M:** 2 Isotta Fraschini ID 36 N 12V diesels; 2 CP props; . . . hp
**Electric:** . . . kw (2 gen.) **Range:** 12,000/12
**Man:** 1 officer, 8 men, 8 technicians

**EXPERIMENTAL SHIPS** *(continued)*

REMARKS: Ordered 3-84. For torpedo, sonar, and electronic warfare equipment trials.

◆ **1 ex-landing ship** Bldr: Taranto Naval Base

| | Laid down | L | In serv. |
|---|---|---|---|
| A 5314 QUARTO | 19-3-66 | 18-3-67 | 18-3-68 |

**Quarto (A 5314)**—note blunt bow G. Arra, 7-85

**D:** 764 tons (820 fl) **S:** 13 kts **Dim:** 66.6 × 9.55 × 1.95
**A:** 2/Otomat Mk 2 SSM (I × 2)—2/40-mm AA (II × 1)
**Electron Equipt:** Radar: 1/3ST-7, 1/SQS-20, 1/RAN-111/X, 1/RTN-10X
**M:** 3 diesels; 3 props; 2,280 hp **Range:** 1,300/13 **Man:** 4 officers, 38 men

REMARKS: Unsuccessful landing ship used as a trials ship since early 1970s. Blunt bow restricts speed and seaworthiness. Sisters *Marsala* (hull used as a pontoon) and *Caprara* canceled. Retains visor-type bow door.

◆ **1 converted fishing boat** Bldr: C.N. Castracani, Ancona

A 3315 BARBARA

**D:** 185 tons (195 fl) **S:** 12 kts **Dim:** 30.50 × 6.30 × 1.50
**M:** 2 diesels; 2 props; 600 hp **Man:** 7 tot.

REMARKS: Purchased 1975. Used for oceanographic research. Has 7.5-ton crane.

◆ **1 Aragosta-class former inshore minesweeper**

A 5305 MURENA (ex- . . .)

REMARKS: Characteristics generally as for minesweeper version. New superstructure, with enclosed bridge. Stern area bare.

◆ **2 former minelayers** (In serv. circa 1939–41)

GIS 59 GIS 61

**GIS 61** C. Martinelli, 1983

**D:** 230 tons **S:** 7 kts **Dim:** . . . × . . . × . . .
**A:** 1/533-mm TT

REMARKS: Used for torpedo firing trials.

**SUPPORT TENDERS**

◆ **1 supply ship** Bldr: Lake Washington SY, Houghton, Washington

| | Laid down | L | In serv. |
|---|---|---|---|
| A 5301 PIETRO CAVEZZALE (ex-*Oyster Bay*, AGP 6, ex-AVP 28) | 17-4-42 | 23-5-43 | 17-11-43 |

**Pietro Cavezzale (A 5301)** G. Arra, 7-85

**D:** 1,766 tons (2,800 fl) **S:** 16 kts **Dim:** 94.6 × 12.58 × 3.7
**A:** 1/76.2-mm 50-cal. DP—2/40-mm AA (II × 1)
**Electron Equipt:** Radar: 1/3RM7-250, 1/SPS-6C
**M:** 2 Fairbanks-Morse $38D8\frac{1}{8}$ × 10 diesels; 2 props; 6,000 hp
**Electric:** 600 kw **Fuel:** 400 tons **Range:** 10,000/11
**Man:** 7 officers, 105 men

REMARKS: Transferred 23-10-57. Serves as tender to assault swimmers and amphibious support craft.

**SALVAGE SHIPS**

◆ **1 salvage ship**

| | Bldr | Laid down | L | In serv. |
|---|---|---|---|---|
| A 5309 ANTEO | C.N. Breda, Mestre | 1977 | 11-11-78 | 31-7-80 |

**Anteo (A 5309)**—hangar extended C. Martinelli, 7-86

**Salvage submersible Usel on Anteo (A 5309)** A. Fraccaroli, 2-81

**D:** 2,178 tons (3,070 fl) **S:** 18.3 kts **Dim:** 98.4 (93.0 pp) × 15.8 × 5.18
**A:** 2/20-mm AA (II × 1)—1/AB-212 helicopter
**Electron Equipt:** Radar: 1/3RM-7-250, 1/MM/SPN-748
**M:** 3 GMT A-230-12V diesels (4,050 hp each), electric drive (2 motors); 1 prop; 6,000 hp (5,360 sust.)
**Fuel:** 270 tons **Range:** 4,000/14 **Man:** 9 officers, 104 men

REMARKS: Ordered 1977. Carries U.S. Navy-style submarine rescue equipment, including a McCann rescue bell capable to 150 meters, and two decompression chambers. A Type MSM-1/S, 22-ton salvage submersible named *Usel* is also carried; 9.0 × 2.5 × 2.7 meters, it can submerge to 600 meters and has a 120-hour autonomous endurance with a 4-kt max. speed. The ship supports saturation

**SALVAGE SHIPS** *(continued)*

diving to 350 meters and has a 27-ton bollard pull at 10 kts. A bow-thruster is fitted.

◆ **1 U.S. AN 93-class former netlayer**

| | Bldr | Laid down | L | In serv. |
|---|---|---|---|---|
| A 5304 Alicudi (ex-AN 99) | Ansaldo, Livorno | 4-54 | 11-7-54 | 1955 |

**Alicudi (A 5304)**—with experimental radar in place of 1/20-mm AA G. Gyssels, 1985

**D:** 680 tons (832 fl) **S:** 13 kts **Dim:** 46.28 × 10.26 × 3.2
**A:** 1/40-mm AA—4/20-mm AA (I × 4) **Electron Equipt:** Radar: 1/BX-732
**M:** 2 Maybach MBA 6H/D650/655 diesels, electric drive; 1 prop; 1,700 hp
**Fuel:** 105 tons **Range:** 8,300/12 **Man:** 3 officers, 41 men

Remarks: Sister *Filicudi* (A 5305) stricken 1979. Used for salvage work and mooring-buoy laying.

◆ **1 former submarine rescue ship** Bldr: CNR, Ancona

| | Laid down | L | In serv. |
|---|---|---|---|
| A 5310 Proteo (ex-*Perseo*) | 1943 | 1944 | 24-8-51 |

**Proteo (A 5310)** C. Martinelli, 1981

**D:** 1,865 tons (2,147 fl) **S:** 16 kts **Dim:** 75.70 × 11.70 × 6.10
**A:** 2/20-mm AA (I × 2) **Electron Equipt:** Radar: 1/MM/SPN-748
**M:** 2 Fiat diesels; 1 prop; 4,800 hp
**Range:** 7,500/13 **Man:** 8 officers, 106 men

Remarks: Seized by German forces after launch, towed to Trieste; returned to Ancona, and fitting out resumed 1949. Relieved by *Anteo* (A 5309) as submarine rescue ship, but is retained as an ocean tug and salvage ship. Has submersible decompression chamber, extensive divers' support equipment, and 4-point mooring capability. Refitted 1984–85 with new stack and an electrohydraulic crane.

## WATER TANKERS

◆ **1 water tanker** Bldr: CINET, Molfetta

A . . . Simeto (In serv. . . .)

**D:** 1,858 tons (fl) **S:** 13 kts **Dim:** 68.35 × 10.06 × 3.90
**A:** . . . **Electron Equipt:** Radar: 1/. . .
**M:** 2 GMT B 230.6 diesels; 1 prop; 2,400 hp
**Electric:** 420 kw (3 × 140 kw) **Man:** 2 officers, 25 men

Remarks: Cargo: 1,200 tons. Replaces the canceled *Tevere* (A 5355), which was scrapped incomplete in 1985 when her builder, Ferbex, went bankrupt. *Simeto* design based on *Basento* class. A second new water tanker was authorized in 1982, but has yet to be ordered.

◆ **1 Piave class**

| | Bldr | L | In serv. |
|---|---|---|---|
| A 5354 Piave | Orlando, Livorno | 18-12-71 | 23-5-73 |

**Piave (A 5354)** L. & L. Van Ginderen, 8-86

**D:** 5,003 tons (fl) **S:** 13.6 kts **Dim:** 97.8 (86.7 pp) × 13.4 × 5.9 **A:** removed
**Electron Equipt:** Radar: 1/3RM-7 **M:** 2 diesels; 2,560 hp
**Cargo capacity:** 3,500 tons **Range:** 1,500/12 **Man:** 5 officers, 42 men

Remarks: Sister *Tevere* (A 5355) sold commercially, 1976. Formerly carried 4/40-mm AA (II × 2).

◆ **3 Basento class** Bldr: Inma, La Spezia

A 5356 Basento (In serv. 19-7-71)
A 5357 Bradano (In serv. 29-12-71)
A 5358 Brenta (In serv. 18-4-72)

**Bradano (A 5357)** M. Louagie, 7-87

**D:** 1,930 tons (fl) **S:** 12.5 kts **Dim:** 68.65 × 10.07 × 3.90
**A:** removed **Electron Equipt:** Radar: 1/3RM-7
**M:** 2 Fiat LA-230 diesels; 1,730 hp **Cargo Capacity:** 1,200 tons
**Range:** 1,650/12.5 **Man:** 2 officers, 25 men

Remarks: Can carry 2/20-mm AA (I × 2). Can make 13.1 kts in light condition.

◆ **1 small water tanker** Bldr.: La Spezia Naval Dockyard

A 5359 Bormida (In serv. 1975)

**Bormida (A 5359)** C. Martinelli

**WATER TANKERS** *(continued)*

**D:** 736 tons (fl) **S:** . . . **Dim:** 40.2 × 7.2 × 3.2
**M:** 2 diesels; 130 hp **Cargo:** 260 tons **Man:** 6 tot.

◆ **1 U.S. Army 327E class** Bldr: Zenith Dredge, Duluth, Minn.

| | Laid down | L | In serv. |
|---|---|---|---|
| A 5369 ADIGE (ex-YW 92) | 19-5-43 | 31-7-43 | 21-11-43 |

**D:** 476 tons (1,517 fl) **S:** 8 kts **Dim:** 55.63 × 9.14 × 4.29
**A:** 3/20-mm AA (I × 3) **Electron Equipt:** Radar: 1/3RM7
**M:** 2 diesels; 2 props; 315 hp
**Range:** 2,560/7 **Fuel:** 32 tons **Man:** 2 officers, 24 men

REMARKS: Transferred 1948 to Italy. Transferred from U.S. Army to Navy while building. Sister *Ticeno* (A 5377) stricken 30-6-85 and *Tanaro* (A 5376) stricken 1985 also.

◆ **1 small water tanker** Bldr: C. N. di Venezia

A 5374 MINCIO (In serv. 1930)

**D:** 645 tons **S:** 6 kts **Dim:** 43.1 × 8.00 × 3.00
**M:** 1 diesel; 350 hp **Man:** 23 tot.

**TRAINING SHIPS**

NOTE: The cruiser *Ciao Duilio* (C 554) serves as a training ship also.

◆ **5 Aragosta-class former inshore minesweepers**

| | Bldr | L | In serv. |
|---|---|---|---|
| A 5378 ARAGOSTA (ex-M 5450) | CRDA, Monfalcone | 8-56 | 19-7-57 |
| A 5379 ASTICE (ex-M 5452) | CRDA, Monfalcone | 16-1-57 | 19-7-57 |
| A 5380 MITILO (ex-M 5459) | Picchiotti, Viareggio | 1-6-57 | 11-7-57 |
| A 5381 POLIPO (ex-M 5463) | Costaguta, Voltri | 15-6-57 | 10-7-57 |
| A 5382 PORPORA (ex-M 5464) | Costaguta, Voltri | 1-6-57 | 10-7-57 |

**Porpora (A 5382)** C. Martinelli, 10-85

**D:** 120 tons (178 fl) **S:** 13.5 kts **Dim:** 32.35 × 6.47 × 2.14 **A:** none
**Electron Equipt:** Radar: 1/MLN-1A
**M:** 2 Fiat/MTU MB 820D diesels; 2 props; 1,000 hp **Electric:** 340 kw
**Fuel:** 15 tons **Range:** 2,000/9 **Man:** 2 officers, 13 men

REMARKS: Based on British "Ham"-class design. Originally 20 in class. Built with U.S. Military Assistance Program funds. Wooden construction. Single 20-mm AA fwd removed. Reclassified 1984–85 for use as administrative tenders and navigational training craft. Two sisters serve as ferries (GLS 501, GLS 502) and one as a weapons trials craft, *Murena* (A 5305)

◆ **1 sail-training ship** Bldr: Nav. Mec. Castellammare

| | Laid down | L | In serv. |
|---|---|---|---|
| A 5312 AMERIGO VESPUCCI | 12-5-30 | 22-2-31 | 15-5-31 |

**D:** 3,545 tons (4,146 fl) **S:** 10 kts (under power)
**Dim:** 101.00 over bow sprit/82.38 (70.72 pp) × 15.56 × 6.7
**A:** 4/40-mm AA (I × 4)—1/20-mm AA
**Electron Equipt:** Radar: 2/MM/SPN-748
**M:** 2 Tosi E6 diesels, electric drive; 1 prop; 1,900 hp
**Range:** 5,450/6.5 **Man:** 13 officers, 228 men, 150 cadets

REMARKS: Sail area: 2,100 m$^2$. Steel construction, including masts. Refitted 1984.

◆ **1 sail-training barkentine** Bldr: Dubigeon, France (In serv. 1920)

A 5311 PALINURO (ex-*Cdt Louis Richard*)

**D:** 1,042 tons (1,341 fl) **S:** 10 kts **Dim:** 68.9 (59.0 pp) × 10.1 × 4.8
**A:** 2/76-mm (saluting battery) **M:** 1 M.A.N. G8V23.5/33 diesel; 450 hp
**Range:** 5,385/7.5 **Man:** 4 officers, 44 men

REMARKS: Former French cod-fishing craft bought in 1951, refitted and recommissioned 16-7-55. Steel hull.

**Amerigo Vespucci (A 5312)** L. & L. Van Ginderen, 7-87

**Palinuro (A 5311)** Italian Navy, 1986

◆ **1 sail-training yawl** Bldr: Costaguta, Genoa (In serv. 5-1-61)

A 5316 CORSARO II

**D:** 41 tons **Dim:** 20.9 × 4.7 **M:** 1 auxiliary engine; 96 hp
**Electron Equipt:** Radar: 1/Decca 060 **Man:** 2 officers, 14 men

REMARKS: Based at Naval Academy, Livorno. Very similar to *Stella Polare* (A 5313). Sail area: 205 m$^2$.

◆ **1 RORC-class cruising yacht** Bldr: Sangermani, Chiavari (In serv. 7-10-65)

A 5313 STELLA POLARE

**D:** 41 tons (47 fl) **S:** . . . **Dim:** 20.9 × 4.7 × 2.9
**M:** 1 Mercedes-Benz diesel; 1 prop; 96 hp **Man:** 2 officers, 4 men

REMARKS: Sail area: 197 m$^2$. Based at Naval Academy, Livorno.

◆ **1 sail-training yawl** Bldr: Baglietto Varazze (In serv. 1948)

A 5302 CAROLY

**D:** 60 tons (fl) **S:** 9 kts (6.5 power) **Dim:** 26.60 (23.75 pp) × 4.80 × 3.10
**M:** 1 G.M. diesel; 100 hp **Man:** 13 officers, 3 men

REMARKS: Donated to Navy 25-4-83. There are also a number of smaller sail-training craft in use.

**SERVICE CRAFT**

◆ **2 personnel transports** Bldr: Crestitalia, Ameglia, La Spezia (In serv. 1986)

MEN 215 MEN 216

SERVICE CRAFT *(continued)*

**MEN 216** C. Martinelli, 6-86

**D:** 82 tons (fl) **S:** 28 kts (23 sust.) **Dim:** 27.28 × 6.98 × 1.10
**Electron Equipt:** Radar: 1/. . . nav.
**M:** 2 Isotta Fraschini diesels; 2 props; 3,200 hp
**Range:** 250/14 **Electric:** 50 kVA (2 × 25 kVA gen.)
**Man:** 4 crew, plus 250 passengers

REMARKS: Built to be carried by the carrier *Giuseppe Garibaldi* as commando transports, for search-and-rescue, disaster relief, and other transport duties. GRP construction.

◆ **1 U.S. Adjutant-class former minesweeper**

| | Bldr | In serv. |
|---|---|---|
| . . . ALLORO (ex-M5532) | CRDA, Monfalcone | 1-2-56 |

REMARKS: Reclassified as a personnel ferry/transport in 1985–86. Characteristics under minesweeper/hunter version.

◆ **2 Aragosta-class former inshore minesweepers**

GLS 501 (ex- . . .) GLS 502 (ex-*Riccio,* M 5465)

REMARKS: Retyped as personnel transports 1979-80. Characteristics under administrative tender/navigational training craft sisters.

◆ **2 swimmer support craft** Bldr: Crestialia, Ameglia, La Spezia

| | Laid down | L | In serv. |
|---|---|---|---|
| MEN 213 MARIO MARINO | 8-9-83 | . . . | 23-10-84 |
| MEN 214 ALCIDE PEDRETTI | 8-9-83 | . . . | 21-12-84 |

**Alcide Pedretti (MEN 214)** C. Martinelli, 10-85

**D:** 69.5 tons light (96.6 fl) **S:** 28 kts **Dim:** 25.85 × 6.90 × 1.06 (1.50 max.)
**Electron Equipt:** Radar: 2/. . . nav.
**M:** 2 Isotta Fraschini ID 36 SS 12V diesels; 2 props; 3,040 hp
**Range:** MEN 213: 236/28; 264/23—MEN 214: 450/23.5
**Man:** 1 officer, 7 men

REMARKS: Built for San Marco Battalion assault swimmers (COMSUBIN), based at La Spezia. GRP construction. Recessed stern for diver recovery, divers' stage, decompression chamber fitted. Two near-sisters built for U.A.E.

◆ **1 yacht/ambulance craft** Bldr: Picchiotti, Viareggio

R. PAOLUCCI (In serv. 12-9-70)

**D:** 70 tons (fl) **S:** 21.3 kts **Dim:** 27.72 × 7.40 × . . .
**M:** 2 diesels; 2 props; . . . hp **Man:** 1 officer, 7 men

REMARKS: White-painted, streamlined yacht, with red crosses painted on sides.

◆ **4 torpedo-recovery craft** Bldr: Crestitalia, Ameglia, La Spezia (In serv. 1984)

MEN 212 MEN . . . MEN . . . MEN . . .

**MEN 212 and smaller MCN 1595** H. Ehlers, 5-86

**D:** . . . **S:** 23 kts **Dim:** 11.65 × 3.9 × . . .
**M:** 2 diesels; 2 props; 470 hp **Range:** 250/20 **Man:** . . .

REMARKS: Can stow 3 torpedoes. Glass-reinforced plastic construction.

◆ **0 (+4) MTF-class coastal transports** Bldr: C.N Mario Morini, Ancona

| | In serv. | | In serv. |
|---|---|---|---|
| MTF . . . | . . . | MTF . . . | . . . |
| MTF . . . | . . . | MTF . . . | . . . |

**D:** 608 tons (fl) **S:** 14+kts **Dim:** 56.72 × 10.00 × 2.50
**A:** provision for 2/7.62-mm mg (I × 2)
**Electron Equipt:** Radar: 1/. . . nav.
**M:** 2 Isotta Fraschini ID 36 SS 8V diesels; 2 props; 1,760 hp
**Range:** 1,500/14 **Electric:** 464 kw (2 × 232 kw)
**Man:** 2 officers, 32 men

REMARKS: MTF-*Mototrasporti Fari,* i.e. ferry. Very similar to MTC 1011 design; to replace MTF 1301–1303. One 15-ton hydraulic crane aft for mooring buoy handling; one 1.5-ton crane forward.

◆ **6 MTC 1011-class coastal transports** Bldr: C.N Mario Morini, Ancona

| | L | In serv. | | L | In serv. |
|---|---|---|---|---|---|
| MTC 1011 | 12-7-86 | 23-12-86 | MTC 1014 | 31-1-87 | . . . |
| MTC 1012 | 9-86 | 2-3-87 | MTC 1015 | . . . | . . . |
| MTC 1013 | 11-86 | 10-4-87 | MTC 1016 | . . . | . . . |

**D:** 631 (fl) **S:** 14+kts **Dim:** 56.72 × 10.00 × 2.50
**A:** provision for 1/20-mm AA—2/7.62-mm mg (I × 2)—mine rails
**Electron Equipt:** Radar: 1/. . . nav.
**M:** 2 CRM 12D/SS diesels; 2 props; 1,520 hp
**Range:** 1,500/14 **Electric:** 484 kw (2 × 192 kw, 1 × 100 kw)
**Man:** 4 officers, 28 men

REMARKS: MTC 1011 laid down 12-7-86, MTC 1014 on 31-1-87. MTC = *Mototrasporti Costieri.* Two electrohydraulic cranes. Intended to carry palletized cargo on their open decks. Replacing World War II-era MTC of the MZ class.

◆ **6 ex-British LCT(3)-class coastal transports** (In serv. 1943–44)

A 5331 MOC 1201 A 5334 MOC 1204
A 5332 MOC 1202 A 5335 MOC 1205
A 5333 MOC 1203 A 5337 MOC 1207

**MOC 1201 (A 5331)**—torpedo retriever/workshop G. Arra, 1981

## SERVICE CRAFT *(continued)*

**D:** 711–752 tons (fl) **Dim:** 58.25 × 9.22 × 2.0–2.2
**A:** 2/20-mm AA (I × 2; not in all) **Electron Equipt:** Radar: 1/BX-732
**M:** 2 diesels; 2 props; 1,000 hp **Man:** 1–2 officers, 20–26 men

Remarks: MOC 1201 is used for torpedo recovery; MOC 1207 is an ammunition transport; the remainder serve as repair craft for minesweepers and small combatants. The bow door/ramp has been welded closed. Similar MTF 1301 (A 5301), MTF 1302 (A 5362), and MTF 1303 (A 5363) stricken 1986–87.

◆ **1 ex-German MFP-D cargo lighter, former landing craft** (In serv. 1942)

A 5341 MTC 1101

**D:** 218 tons (fl) **S:** 10 kts **Dim:** 49.8 × 6.6 × 1.12
**A:** 2/20-mm AA **M:** 3 Deutz diesels; 3 props; 450 hp **Range:** 540/9

Remarks: Built 1942. Can carry 150 tons cargo; beaching capability retained. Can lay mines. To be stricken soon.

◆ **3 MZ-class cargo lighters** (In serv. 1942)

A 5344 MTC 1004    A 5346 MTC 1006
A 5350 MTC 1010

**MTC 1006 (A 5346)** G. Arra, 1982

**D:** 218 tons (240 fl) **S:** 10.5 kts **Dim:** 47.0 × 6.55 × 1.13
**A:** 2 or 3/20-mm AA (I × 2 or 3) **Electron Equipt:** Radar: 1/BX-732
**M:** 3 diesels; 3 props; 450 hp **Man:** 15–16 tot.

Remarks: Former Italian-built landing craft. Similar to MFP-D class, but hull has sheer fore and aft. Can carry 150 tons cargo. Sisters MTC 1007–1009 (A 5347–5350) stricken 1983; MTC 1005 stricken 30-4-87; these craft, plus MTC 1101, will soon follow.

◆ **4 fuel lighters** Bldr: Cantieri Ferrari, La Spezia

| | In serv. | | In serv. |
|---|---|---|---|
| A 5370 MCC 1101 | -86 | A 5372 MCC 1103 | . . . |
| A 5371 MCC 1102 | 6-12-86 | A 5373 MCC 1104 | . . . |

**D:** 863 tons (fl) **S:** 13 kts **Dim:** 47.30 × 10.00 × 3.30
**M:** 2 Isotta Fraschini ID 36 SSV6 diesels; 2 props; 1,320 hp

Remarks: Cargo: 550 tons. MMC = *Motocisterne Combustibili* (fuel lighter). MCC 1102 in service 6-12-86.

◆ **5 harbor fuel lighters**

GRS 172    GRS 173    GRS 175    GRS 178    XI

Remarks: All of about 500 tons capacity.

Note: There are a large number of harbor service craft, launches, etc., with hull numbers in the GAS, GAA, GTM, GGS, MDN, VS, GT, MCC and MCM series.

## SEAGOING TUGS

◆ **4 (+2) Ciclope Class seagoing tugs** Bldr: Ferrari, La Spezia

| | L | In serv. | | L | In serv. |
|---|---|---|---|---|---|
| A 5319 Ciclope | 20-2-85 | 9-85 | A 5328 Gigante | . . . | 18-7-86 |
| A 5324 Titano | 2-3-85 | 7-12-85 | A . . . Saturno | . . . | -88 |
| A 5325 Polifemo | 15-6-85 | 21-4-86 | A . . . Tenace | . . . | -88 |

**Ciclope (A 5319)** H. Ehlers, 5-86

**D:** 600 tons (658 fl) **S:** 14.5 kts **Dim:** 38.95 (32.30 pp) × 9.85 × 3.32
**Electron Equipt:** Radar: 1/. . . nav.
**M:** 2 GMT BL 230 diesels; 1 CP prop; 3,300 hp **Range:** 3,000/14.5
**Electric:** 500 kw (2 × 200 kw, 1 × 100 kw) **Man:** . . .

Remarks: Bollard pull: 45 tons (36 tons sustained at 8.3 kts). Two 130-m/hr. water cannon, 23-ton-capacity foam tank. Enlarged and improved version of *Atlante* class.

◆ **2 Atlante class** Bldr: Visitini, Donada (Both in serv. 14-8-75)

A 5317 Atlante    A 5318 Prometeo

**Atlante (A 5317)** L. & L. Van Ginderen, 9-83

**D:** 478 tons light (750 fl) **S:** 13.5 kts **Dim:** 38.9 × 9.6 × 3.70
**M:** 1 Tosi QT 320/8SS diesel; 1 CP prop; 2,670 hp (3,000 max.)
**Man:** 25 tot. **Range:** 4,000/12

◆ **1 U.S. Army 293-design class**

A 5321 Forte (ex-LT 159)

**Forte (A 5321)** L. & L. Van Ginderen, 9-83

**D:** 525 tons (835 fl) **S:** 11 kts **Dim:** 38.6 × 8.53 × 3.89
**M:** 2 Fairbanks-Morse 38D8$\frac{1}{8}$ diesels, electric drive; 2 props; 1,690 hp
**Fuel:** 112 tons **Range:** 3,800/8

Remarks: Built during World War II; transferred 1948. Sister *Colosso* (A 5320) stricken 31-7-86.

◆ **1 San Giusto class** Bldr: CNR, Palermo (In serv. 1941)

A 5326 San Giusto

**D:** 370 tons (486 fl) **S:** 12 kts **Dim:** 38.7 × 7.1 × 3.8
**M:** triple-expansion reciprocating steam; 900 hp **Range:** 2,460/9

◆ **1 Gagliardo class**

| | L |
|---|---|
| A 5322 Gagliardo | 1938 |

**D:** 389 tons (506 fl) **S:** 8 kts **Dim:** 33.2 × 7.1 × 3.6
**M:** triple-expansion reciprocating steam; 1,000 hp

Remarks: Sister *Robusto* (A 5323) stricken 31-3-87.

## SEAGOING TUGS *(continued)*

**San Giusto (A 5326)** L. & L. Van Ginderen, 11-82

◆ **6 (+3) Porto class** Bldr: first six: De Poli, Pellestrina; others: Ferbex, Naples

| | L | In serv. |
|---|---|---|
| Y 421 PORTO EMPEDOCLE | 4-12-85 | 19-3-86 |
| Y 422 PORTO PISANO | 22-10-85 | 20-8-85 |
| Y 423 PORTO CONTE | 21-11-85 | 28-9-85 |
| Y 425 PORTO FERRAIO | 21-7-85 | 3-4-85 |
| Y 426 PORTO VENERE | 13-5-85 | 12-2-85 |
| Y 428 PORTO SALVO | 13-9-85 | 4-7-85 |
| Y . . . PORTO FOSSONE | . . . | . . . |
| Y . . . PORTO TORRES | . . . | . . . |
| Y . . . PORTO CORSINI | . . . | . . . |

**Porto Conte (Y 423)** C. Martinelli, 10-86

**D:** 412 tons (fl) **S:** 11.5 kts **Dim:** 32.36 (28.00 pp) × 8.50 × 3.32
**Electron Equipt:** Radar: 1/. . . nav.
**M:** 1 GMT B230-8M diesel; 1 CP prop; 1,600 hp
**Range:** 1,800/11.5 **Fuel:** 46 tons
**Electric:** 200 kw (2 × 100 kw) **Man:** 12 tot.

REMARKS: Bollard pull: 25 tons (15 tons at 5 kts). Two water cannons, two 130-m/hr pumps. First six ordered 2-6-83; other three in 1986.

◆ **2 Ercole class** (In serv. 1971)

A 5388 ERCOLE Y 451 VIGOROSO (ex-A 5394)

**D:** 506 tons (fl) **S:** 8 kts **Dim:** 33.2 × 7.1 × 3.6
**M:** diesels; 850 hp

REMARKS: Flushed-deck diesel version of *Gagliardo* class.

◆ **2 Porto d'Ischia class** Bldr: CNR, Riva Trigoso (In serv. 1969–70)

Y 436 PORTO D'ISCHIA Y 443 RIVA TRIGOSO

**D:** 250 tons (296 fl) **S:** 12 kts **Dim:** 25.5 × 7.1 × 3.3
**M:** 1 diesel; 1 CP prop; 850 hp

**Porto d'Ischia (Y 436)** G. Arra, 1982

◆ **3 miscellaneous coastal tugs**

Y 431 PANARIA (In serv. 1945): 240 tons, 8 kts
Y 429 MONTECRISTO (ex-U.S. . . .) (In serv. 1946): 285 tons
Y 448 USTICA (In serv. 1973)

**D:** 270 tons **S:** 13 kts **Dim:** 35.0 × 9.0 × 4.0
**M:** diesel; 1 prop; 1,200 hp

REMARKS: *Favignana* (Y 424) stricken 31-1-86.

## SMALL HARBOR TUGS

◆ **10 RP 125 class** Bldr: (A) C.N. Vittoria, Adria; (B) C.N. Ferrari, La Spezia; (C) CINET, Molfetta

| | Bldr | In serv. | | Bldr | In serv. |
|---|---|---|---|---|---|
| Y 478 RP 125 | A | 1983 | Y . . . RP 130 | B | 10-8-84 |
| Y 479 RP 126 | A | 24-9-83 | Y . . . RP 131 | B | 28-8-84 |
| Y 480 RP 127 | B | 29-3-84 | Y . . . RP 132 | C | 7-7-84 |
| Y . . . RP 128 | B | 4-84 | Y . . . RP 133 | C | 3-11-84 |
| Y . . . RP 129 | B | 5-6-84 | Y . . . RP 134 | B | -85 |

**RP 134** C. Martinelli, 10-86

**D:** 78 tons (120 fl) **S:** 9.5 kts **Dim:** 19.85 (17.00) × 5.20 × 2.10
**M:** 1 Fiat AIFO 828-SM diesel; 1 prop; 368 hp **Man:** 3 tot.
**Range:** 400/9.5 **Electric:** 28 kw

REMARKS: First six ordered 18-8-83. 76 grt. One 120-$m^3$/hr. water cannon.

◆ **10 RP 113 class** Bldr: Visitini, Donada (In serv. 1978–1981)

| | In serv. | | In serv. |
|---|---|---|---|
| Y 463 RP 113 | 1978 | Y 471 RP 120 | 1980 |
| Y 464 RP 114 | 1980 | Y 472 RP 121 | 1980 |
| Y 465 RP 115 | 1980 | Y 473 RP 122 | 1980 |
| Y 466 RP 116 | 1980 | Y 474 RP 123 | 1980 |
| Y 470 RP 119 | 1980 | Y 475 RP 124 | 1981 |

REMARKS: Characteristics similar to RP 101 class below, but have a larger superstructure. Details differ. RP 117 (Y 467) and RP 118 (Y 468) deleted, date not available.

## SMALL HARBOR TUGS *(continued)*

**RP 121** G. Valentini, 5-86

◆ **12 RP-101 class** Bldr: CN Visitini-Loreo, Donado (In serv. 1972–75)

| | | |
|---|---|---|
| Y 403 RP 101 | Y 408 RP 105 | Y 456 RP 109 |
| Y 404 RP 102 | Y 410 RP 106 | Y 458 RP 110 |
| Y 406 RP 103 | Y 413 RP 107 | Y 460 RP 111 |
| Y 407 RP 104 | Y 452 RP 108 | Y 462 RP 112 |

**RP 110 (Y 458)** C. Martinelli, 1980

**D:** 36 tons (75 fl) **S:** 12 kts **Dim:** 18.8 × 4.5 × 1.9
**M:** 1 diesel; 500 hp

◆ **5 miscellaneous harbor tugs**

Y 412 Albenga Y 430 Linaro Y 435 Mesco
Y 446 San Benedeto Y . . . Tarantola

Remarks: *Arzachena* (Y 414) stricken 31-1-87; *Boeo* (Y 417) stricken 30-4-86. Y 446 is a coal-burner.

## FLOATING DRY DOCKS

◆ **13 miscellaneous**

| | In serv. | Capacity (tons) | | In serv. | Capacity (tons) |
|---|---|---|---|---|---|
| GO 52 | 1979 | 6,000 | GO 17 | 1917 | 500 |
| GO 51 | 1971 | 2,000 | GO 11 | 1911 | 2,700 |
| GO 23 | 1935 | 1,000 | GO 10 | 1900 | 2,000 |
| GO 22 | 1935 | 1,000 | GO 8 | 1904 | 3,800 |
| GO 20 | 1935 | 1,600 | GO 5 | 1893 | 100 |
| GO 18B | 1920 | 600 | GO 1 | 1942 | 1,000 |
| GO 18A | 1920 | 800 | | | |

Remarks: GO 52 is 150.5 m long by 29.6 m (21.6-m internal width).

## PORT CAPTAIN CORPS
*(Corpo delle Capitanerie di Porto)*

The Port Captain Corps comes under the control of the Ministry of the Merchant Marine in peacetime and has police, fisheries protection, oil spill recovery, and SAR duties. There are 80 Detachments at various Italian ports, operating some 140 large and 60 smaller patrol craft. The Corps is to acquire a number of Piaggio P166 DL3/SEM aircraft for surveillance duties.

## CORVETTES

◆ **0 (+5) "Constellazione"/Cassiopea class** Bldr: Fincantieri, Muggiano

| | Laid down | L | In serv. |
|---|---|---|---|
| F . . . Cassiopea | . . . | . . . | . . . |
| F . . . Libra | . . . | . . . | . . . |
| F . . . Orione | . . . | . . . | . . . |
| F . . . Spiga | . . . | . . . | . . . |
| F . . . Vega | . . . | . . . | . . . |

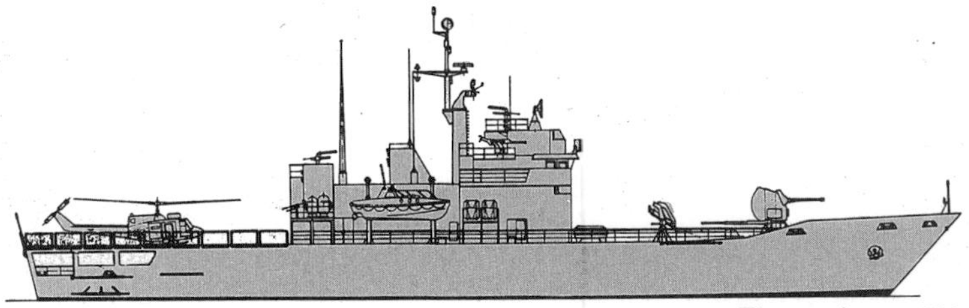

**Cassiopea** Fincantiere, 1986

**D:** 1,002 tons (1,450 fl) **S:** 19.5 kts (15 kts cruise)
**Dim:** 79.80 × 11.80 (11.40 wl) × 3.50
**A:** 1/76-mm DP—2/20-mm AA (I × 2)—1/AB-212 helicopter
**Electron Equipt:** Radar: 1/I-band, 1/S-band, 1/RTN-20X
EW: Intercept gear
**M:** 2 GMT BL 230.16 diesels; 2 CP props; 7,490 hp (6,745 sust.)
**Range:** 3,300/17 **Fuel:** 165 tons **Man:** 8 officers, 70 men
**Electric:** 1,500 kVA (3/ID6 SSV6 gen. sets)

Remarks: Construction authorized 31-12-82; first three ordered 12-86. The 76-mm will be older-model weapons removed from scrapped naval ships. Designed to merchant ship standards. Telescopic hangar and 22.0 × 8.0-m helicopter deck. Will be manned by Italian Navy personnel.

## SEAGOING PATROL AND RESCUE BOATS

◆ **0 (+8) CP 400 class** Bldr: Baglietto, Varazze

**D:** 100 tons (fl) **S:** 22 kts **Dim:** 28.3 × . . . × . . .
**A:** none **Man:** . . . **M:** 2 CRM 12D/S diesels; 1 prop; 750 hp

Remarks: Unsinkable lifeboat-type. Up to 18 more are planned. First unit out-of-mould 2-87. Carry 20 rescued persons; have 4-berth sick-bay.

◆ **1 Vosper-Thornycroft design** Bldr: Nelson, Viareggio

CP 313 Dante Novarro (In serv. 1977)

**Dante Novarro (CP 313)** 1977

**D:** 57 tons (fl) **S:** 24.5 kts **Dim:** 22.8 × 6.1 × 1.7
**A:** small arms **Electron equipt:** Radar: 1/. . . nav.
**M:** 2 diesels; 2 props; 2,760 hp **Range:** 1,000/. . .

◆ **1 seagoing rescue lifeboat** Bldr: Scheerswerft, W. Germany

CP 312 Bruno Gregoretti (In serv. 1972)

**D:** 65 tons (fl) **S:** 19 kts **Dim:** 22.5 × 5.3 × 1.4
**Electron Equipt:** Radar: 1/. . . nav.
**M:** 3 diesels; 3 props; 1,750 hp **Range:** 1,000/19

Remarks: Typical West German lifeboat design with Maierform hull and stern ramp for 6.5-m rescue boat CVP 312/5.

◆ **1 seagoing rescue lifeboat** Bldr: Pellegrino, Naples

CP 307 Michelle Fiorillo (In serv. 1968)

**D:** 84 tons (fl) **S:** 17 kts **Dim:** 26.6 × 5.6 × 1.6
**A:** 2/12.7-mm mg (I × 2) **Electron Equipt:** Radar: 1/. . . nav.
**M:** 3 diesels; 3 props; 2,350 hp **Range:** 1,000/17

## SEAGOING PATROL AND RESCUE BOATS *(continued)*

**Michelle Fiorillo**—Maierform German-built lifeboat

REMARKS: Another German-style rescue boat with Maierform hull and stern ramp for 8.5-m rescue boat CP 307/5.

◆ **7 CP 301 class** Bldr: Groves, Cowes, U.K.

CP 301, CP 305–306, CP 308–311 (In serv. 1962–70)

**D:** 29 tons (fl) **S:** 8.5 kts **Dim:** 15.8 × 4.3 × 1.6
**M:** 2 diesels; 2 props; 144 hp **Range:** 600/8

REMARKS: Barnett design "unsinkable," self-righting lifeboats.

◆ **2 U.S. Coast Guard 44-ft class lifeboats** Bldr: U.S. Coast Guard Yard, Curtis Bay, Md.

CP 303, CP 304 (In serv. 1965)

**CP 303**—U.S. Coast Guard lifeboat L. & L. Van Ginderen, 1982

**D:** 16 tons (fl) **S:** 13 kts **Dim:** 13.06 × 3.86 × 0.93
**M:** 2 Cummins diesels, 1 prop; 370 hp **Range:** 350/13
**Fuel:** 1.2 tons **Man:** 3 tot.

## FAST PATROL BOATS

◆ **1 CP 256 class** Bldr: Italcraft, Gaeta

CP 256 (In serv. 9-7-85)

**D:** 20.75 tons (fl) **S:** 30 kts **Dim:** 16.00 × 5.25
**A:** . . . **Electron Equipt:** Radar: 1/. . . nav.
**M:** 2 Isotta Fraschini ID 36-55-6V diesels; 2 Riva-Calzoni waterjets; 750 hp
**Range:** 350/24 **Fuel:** 3,500 l. **Man:** . . .

◆ **2 CP 254 class** Bldr: Picchiotti, Viareggio

CP 254 CP 255 (In serv. 1984–85)

**CP 254** L. Grazioli, 3-85

**D:** 22.5 tons (fl) **S:** 31 kts **Dim:** 15.10 × 5.25 × 0.98
**A:** 2/12.7-mm mg (I × 2) **Electron Equipt:** Radar: 1/. . . nav.
**M:** 2 Isotta-Fraschini ID 36-55-6V diesels; 2 Riva-Calzoni IRC-43-DL waterjets; 1,520 hp
**Range:** 350/24 **Man:** 7 tot.

◆ **8 CP 246 class** Bldr: CP 246: Navaltechnica, Anzio; others: Coop. Navale, Ostia

CP 246 (In serv. 1977) CP 247–253 (In serv. 1980–81)

**CP 246** G. Valentini, 4-87

**D:** 21.5 tons (fl) **S:** 29.5 kts **Dim:** 15.0 × 4.8 × 1.6 **A:** 1/20-mm AA
**Electron Equipt:** Radar: 1/. . . nav. **M:** 2 diesels; 2 props; 1,380 hp
**Range:** 325/. . . **Man:** 7 tot.

◆ **7 CP 239 class** Bldr: Rodriguez, Messina

CP 239–245 (In serv. 1971)

**D:** 25 tons (fl) **S:** 30 kts **Dim:** 16.8 × 5.0 × 1.7 **A:** 1/12.7-mm mg
**Electron Equipt:** Radar: 1/. . . nav. **M:** 2 diesels; 2 props; 1,380 hp
**Range:** 450/. . . **Man:** 9 tot.

◆ **8 CP 231 (Super Speranza) class** Bldr: Rodriguez, Messina

CP 231–238 (In serv. 1966–69)

**D:** 14 tons (fl) **S:** 26 kts **Dim:** 13.4 × 4.8 × 1.3 **A:** 2/12.7-mm mg
**Electron Equipt:** Radar: 1/. . . nav. **M:** 2 diesels; 2 props; 850 hp
**Range:** 400/. . . **Man:** 7 tot.

◆ **5 CP 226 class** Bldr: Navaltechnica, Anzio

CP 226–230 (In serv. 1966)

**D:** 18–20 tons (fl) **S:** 24 kts **Dim:** 13.1 × 4.7 × 1.2
**A:** 2/12.7-mm mg (I × 2) **Electron Equipt:** Radar: 1/. . . nav.
**M:** 2 diesels; 2 props; 600 hp **Range:** 400/. . . **Man:** 7 tot.

FAST PATROL BOATS *(continued)*

**CP 244** C. Martinelli, 10-82

**CP 237** L. Grazioli, 1986

**COASTAL PATROL CRAFT**

◆ **12 CP 6001 class** Bldr: Crestitalia, Ameglia

CP 6001 to 6010 (In serv. 25-3-86)
CP 6011, CP 6012 (In serv. 21-11-86)

**CP 6005** L. Grazioli, 3-87

**D:** . . . **S:** . . . **Dim:** 9.0 × . . . × . . . **M:** . . .

REMARKS: GRP construction.

◆ **13 Keith Nelson GRP design** Bldr: Balsamo, Brindisi

CP 2069–2081 (In serv. 1980–85)

**CP 2073** M. Brescia, 5-86

**D:** 13 tons (fl) **S:** 23 kts **Dim:** 12.5 × 3.5 × 1.0
**A:** 1/12.7-mm mg **Electron Equipt:** Radar: 1/. . . nav.
**M:** 2 diesels; 2 props; 600 hp **Range:** 400/. . .

REMARKS: CP 2078 and 2079 (delivered 26-4-85) and CP 2080 and 2081 (delivered 11-6-85) built by Mericraft. Some 70 units (see below for others still in service) of this British hull design craft have been built for the *Capitanerie di Porto.*

◆ **4 waterjet-propelled GRP** Bldr: Crestitalia, Ameglia, La Spezia

CP 502–505 (In serv. 1981)

**D:** 6.6 tons **S:** 30 kts **Dim:** 8.9 × 2.8 × 0.8 **A:** small arms
**M:** 2 diesels; 2 waterjets; 270 hp **Range:** 245/. . .

◆ **5 CP 601 series** Bldrs: Crestitalia, Ameglia and Italcraft, Gaeta

CP 601–605 (In serv. 1978–85)

**D:** 3 tons (fl) **S:** 12 kts **Dim:** 3.7 × 2.6 × 0.7 **A:** small arms.
**M:** 1 diesel; 110 hp **Range:** 250/12

REMARKS: Minor differences in characteristics.

◆ **1 CP 501 class** Bldr: Crestitalia, Ameglia, La Spezia

CP 501 (In serv. 1978)

**D:** 3 tons (fl) **S:** 31 kts **Dim:** 8.3 × 2.8 × 0.4 **A:** small arms
**M:** 2 diesels; 2 Castoldi waterjets; 130 hp **Range:** 186/. . .

◆ **18 CP 2049-class Nelson GRP launches** Bldrs: CP 2049–2051, 2060–2065: Balsamo, Brindisi; CP 2053–2058: Nelson, Viareggio; CP 2066–2068; Bianchi & Cecchi, Cogoleto

CP 2049–51, 2053–2058, 2060–2068 (In serv. 1977–80)

**CP 2067** L. & L. Van Ginderen, 2-81

**D:** 12.5 tons (fl) **S:** 23 kts **Dim:** 12.5 × 3.6 × 1.1
**A:** 1/7.62-mm mg **Electron Equipt:** Radar: 1/. . . nav.
**M:** 2 diesels; 2 props; 600 hp **Range:** 400/. . .

◆ **5 CP 2043-class GRP Nelson launches** Bldrs: Nelson, Viareggio, and Motomar, Palermo

CP 2043–2047 (In serv. 1977–78)

COASTAL PATROL CRAFT *(continued)*

**D:** 12.4 tons (fl) **S:** 21 kts **Dim:** 12.5 × 3.6 × 1.2
**A:** 1/7.62-mm mg **Electron Equipt:** Radar: 1/. . .
**M:** 2 diesels; 2 props; 600 hp **Range:** 400/. . .

◆ **6 CP 1001 class** Bldr: Crestitalia, Ameglia, La Spezia

CP 1001–1006 (In serv. 1974–76)

**CP 1004** C. Martinelli, 7-84

**D:** 5.2 tons (fl) **S:** 24 kts **Dim:** 9.0 × 2.6 × 0.5
**M:** 2 diesels; 2 props; 320 hp **Range:** 240/. . .

Remarks: Builder's Azteca design; GRP monohedron hull.

◆ **3 CP 2033-class GRP Nelson launches** Bldr: Motomar, Lavagna

CP 2033–2035 (In serv. 1975–76)

**D:** 12 tons (fl) **S:** 21.5 kts **Dim:** 12.5 × 3.6 × 1.1
**A:** 1/7.62-mm mg **Electron Equipt:** Radar: 1/. . . nav.
**M:** 2 diesels; 2 props; 600 hp **Range:** 414/. . .

◆ **8 CP 2010-class GRP Nelson launches** Bldr: Balsamo, Brindisi

CP 2010–2017 (In serv. 1973–75)

**CP 2011** C. Martinelli, 1982

**D:** 10 tons (fl) **S:** 22 kts **Dim:** 12.3 × 3.6 × 1.0
**M:** 2 diesels; 2 props; 420 hp **Range:** 400/. . .

◆ **1 GRP Nelson launch** Bldr: Navaltechnica, Messina

CP 2024 (In serv. 1975)

**D:** 15 tons (fl) **S:** 24 kts **Dim:** 13.7 × 3.8 × 1.3
**M:** 2 diesels; 2 props; 700 hp **Range:** 400/. . .

Remarks: Has two radio direction finders.

◆ **32 CP 2006-series GRP Nelson launches** Bldrs: CP 2006–2009, 2018–2023: Bianchi & Cecchi, Cogoleto; CP 2025–2031, 2036–2048: Nelson, Viareggio; CP 2032: Motomar, Lavagna

CP 2006–2009, 2018–2023, 2025–2032, 2036–2048 (In serv. 1973–79)

**D:** 10–11 tons (fl) **S:** 21–23 kts **Dim:** 12.5 × 3.6 × 1.0
**M:** 2 diesels; 2 props; 570–600 hp **Range:** 320–414/. . .

**CP 2021** L. & L. Van Ginderen, 8-84

Remarks: Characteristics vary by builder. CP 2032 is 12 tons (fl). All have a radio direction finder, as well as radar.

MISCELLANEOUS

◆ **1 salvage tug** Bldr: Felszegia, Muggia

CP 305 Audax (In serv. . .)

**Audax (CP 305)** A. Scrimali, 4-87

**D:** 78 tons (fl) **S:** 9.5 kts **Dim:** 19.9 × 4.5 × 2.6
**M:** 1 diesel; 1 prop; 500 hp **Range:** 740/9.5

Note: Also in service are 5 CP 100-series launches, 50 CP 5000-series outboard motor boats (25–30 kts), 10 CP 6000-series small motor boats, and 6 semi-rigid inflatable boats.

CUSTOM SERVICE
*(Guardia di Finanza)*

The Ministry of Finance is organized into 15 administrative areas and 48 squadrons. Most of the large units have 7.62- or 12.7-mm AA armament. The *Guardia di Finanza* also operates 3 Agusta A 109 and several Breda Nardi NH 500 helicopters.

◆ **2 (+4) CNL 39 class** Bldr: CN Liguri, Riva Trigoso

G. . . . . . . .
G. . . . . . . .

**D:** 210 tons (fl) **S:** 28 kts (26 sust)
**Dim:** 40.40 (36.20 pp) × 7.60 × 2.46 (1.88 hull)
**A:** 2/30-mm Breda AA (II × 1)—2/7.62-mm mg (I × 2)
**Electron Equipt:** Radar: 1/. . .
**M:** 2 CRM 18D-55-1500 diesels; 2 props; 6,000 hp **Fuel:** 54 tons
**Range:** 1300/20; 23,000/15 **Electric:** 380 kw **Man:** 1 officer, 20 men

Remarks: First two ordered 1-84; four more planned.

◆ **1 U.S. 105-ft Commercial-Cruiser class** Bldr: Swiftships, Morgan City, Louisiana

G.96 Genna (In serv. 1980)

**CUSTOM SERVICE** *(continued)*

**Genna (G. 96)** H. Ehlers, 5-86

**D:** 120 tons (fl) **S:** 35 kts **Dim:** 32.2 × 7.2 × 3.1 (moulded depth)
**A:** 1/20-mm AA—2/7.62-mm mg
**Electron Equipt:** Radar: 2/Furuno FR-711
**M:** 3 MTU 12V331 TC92 diesels; 3 props; 2,940 hp
**Range:** 1,380/30 **Fuel:** 24.4 tons **Man:** 11 tot.
**Electric:** 80 kw (2 × 40 kw)

Remarks: Acquired 1984. Aluminum construction. Has SATNAV and LORAN-C, Raytheon F720-D echo sounder.

◆ **1 . . . class** Bldr: Italcraft, Gaeta

G . . . N . . . (In serv. 1985)

**D:** 39 tons (43.5 fl) **S:** 46 kts **Dim:** 22.15 × 5.25 × 1.36
**A:** 1/30-mm AA **Electron Equipt:** Radar: 1/. . . nav.
**M:** 2 MTU diesels; 2 surface-piercing props; 2,800 hp
**Range:** 300/28 **Fuel:** . . . tons **Man:** 10 tot. **Electric:** 20 kw

Remarks: GRP construction. Made 52 kts on trials.

◆ **2 (+10) Bigliani class** Bldr: Crestitalia, La Spezia

G.35 Bigliani (In serv. . . . . . .) G.374 Cavaglia (In serv. . . .)

**D:** . . . **S:** 45 kts **Dim:** 26.40 × . . . . . × . . . . .
**A:** 1/30-mm Breda AA—2/12.7-mm mg
**Electron Equipt:** Radar: 1/Gem nav.
**M:** 2 MTU 16V369 TB84 diesels; 2 props; 7,000 hp

Remarks: Trials for first pair 2-87. Ten more were to order 6-87. Planned to replace the *Meattini* class.

◆ **58 Meattini class** Bldr: Baglietto, Varazze; Picchiotti; Viareggio; Italcraft, Gaeta; Navaltechnica, Messina; Cantiere di Pisa; Cantiere di Lavagna; Cantiere di Chiavari (In serv. 1970–85)

| | | |
|---|---|---|
| G. 10 Meattini | G. 11 Amici | G. 12 Di Bartolo |
| G. 13 R.D.36 | G. 14 Gori | G. 15 Ramaci |
| G. 16 Denaro | G. 17 Bambaci | G. 18 Arcioni |
| G. 19 Steri | G. 20 Cotugno | G. 21 Manoni |
| G. 22 Giannotti | G. 23 Carrubba | G. 24 Guglielmi |
| G. 25 Salone | G. 26 Esposito | G. 27 Russo |
| G. 28 Zara | G. 29 Rando | G. 30 Cicalese |
| G. 31 Di Sessa | G. 32 Coppola | G. 33 Rizzi |
| G. 34 D'Aleo | G. 35 Baccile | G. 36 Cavatorto |
| G. 37 Fusco | G. 38 De Turris | G. 39 Chiaramida |
| G. 40 Cav. D'Oro | G. 41 Bianca | G. 42 Nuvoletta |
| G. 43 Preite | G. 44 Mazzeo | G. 46 Silanos |
| G. 47 Ignesti | G. 48 Barreca | G. 49 Ciraulo |
| G. 50 D'Agostino | G. 51 Fiore | G. 52 Nuziale |
| G. 53 Tavano | G. 54 De Alexandris | G. 55 Stefannini |
| G. 56 Tridenti | G. 57 Fazio | G. 58 Atzei |
| G. 59 Cicale | G. 60 Fidone | G. 61 Sguazzin |
| G. 62 Tavormina | G. 63 Colombina | G. 64 Darida |
| G. 65 Pizzighella | G. 66 Sciuto | G. 67 N . . . |
| G. 68 N . . . | | |

**D:** 40 tons (fl) **S:** 34 kts **Dim:** 20.1 × 5.2 × 0.9 (hull)
**A:** 1/20-mm AA—2/7.62-mm mg (I × 2)
**Electron Equipt:** Radar: 1/3RM 20
**M:** 2 CRM 18D-S2 DS-2 diesels; 2 props; 2,500 hp
**Range:** 560/21 **Fuel:** 5.8 tons **Man:** 11 tot.
**Electric:** 48 kw (2 × 24 kw)

Remarks: GRP construction. Constructed as a continuing series.

◆ **2 Gabrielle class** Bldr: Picchiotti, Viareggio

G. 70 Gabrielle (In serv. 1966) G. 71 Grasso (In serv. 1967)

**D:** 54 tons (fl) **S:** 34 kts **Dim:** 23.2 × 6.6 × 2.0
**A:** 1/20-mm AA **Electron Equipt:** Radar: 1/3RM 20
**M:** 3 CRM 18D-S2 DS2 diesels; 3 props; 2,100 hp **Fuel:** 9 tons
**Range:** 730/20 **Man:** 12 tot.

**Darida (G. 64)** M. Louagie, 7-87

◆ **6 British Dark-class former torpedoboats** Bldr: Saunders-Roe, Beaumaris, Wales (In serv. 1955–59)

| | |
|---|---|
| G. 72 Calabrese (ex-*Dark* . . .) | G. 76 Urso (ex-*Dark* . . .) |
| G. 73 Inzucchi (ex-*Dark* . . .) | G. 77 Vitali (ex-*Dark* . . .) |
| G. 75 Sanna (ex-*Dark* . . .) | G. 79 Lagana (ex-*Dark* . . .) |

**D:** 57 tons (fl) **S:** 28 kts **Dim:** 21.8 × 5.8 × 1.1
**A:** 1/20-mm AA **Electron Equipt:** Radar: 1/3RM 20
**M:** 2 CRM 18-DS diesels; 2 props; 2,500 hp
**Range:** 493/19 **Man:** 11 tot. **Fuel:** 6.7 tons

Remarks: Purchased 1969; converted for coastal patrol service, completed 1970. Original Napier Deltic diesels replaced. Composite hull construction, with wooden skinning.

**PATROL CRAFT**

◆ **2 GL. 432 class** Bldr: Picchiotti, Viareggio (In serv. 1968)

GL. 432 GL. 434

**D:** 13.3 tons (fl) **S:** 33 kts **Dim:** 16.5 × 5.1 × 0.9
**A:** 1/7.62-mm mg **Electron Equipt:** Radar: 1/. . . nav.
**M:** 2 CRM 12-D52 diesels; 2 props; 1,800 hp
**Range:** 390/25 **Fuel:** 3.4 tons **Man:** 7 tot.

◆ **4 GL. 103 class** Bldr: Navaltechnica, Anzio

GL. 103–106 (In serv. 1964)

**D:** 7.1 tons (fl) **S:** 34 kts **Dim:** 10.9 × 3.8 × 1.1
**A:** 1/7.62-mm mg **Electron Equipt:** Radar: 1/Sperry Mk 7 AL
**M:** 2 diesels; 2 props; 872 hp **Range:** 380/18
**Man:** 7 tot. **Fuel:** 1.2 tons

Remarks: Wooden construction.

◆ **11 GL. 313 class** Bldr: Baglietto, Varazze; Picchiotti, Viareggio; Fincantieri, Monfalcone

GL. 313–321, GL. 324–326 (In serv. 1957–59)

**D:** 16.4 tons (fl) **S:** 31 kts **Dim:** 15.5 × 4.9 × 1.1
**A:** 1/7.62-mm mg **Electron Equipt:** Radar: 1/Raytheon 2502
**M:** 2 AIFO SRM-828 diesels; 2 props; 880 hp
**Range:** 485/20 **Fuel:** 2 tons **Electric:** 2.5 kw **Man:** 7 tot.

**INSHORE PATROL CRAFT**

◆ **44 . . . class** Bldr: Baia SY, Naples

V . . .

**D:** 4 tons (fl) **S:** 35 kts **Dim:** 8.10 (6.58 pp) × 2.48 × 0.65
**M:** 2 G.M.692HT-9 diesels; 2 waterjets; 296 hp
**Range:** . . ./. . . **Man:** 3 tot.

Remarks: GRP construction. For harbor, river, and lake service.

◆ **82 V. 5500 class** Bldr: Crestitalia, Ameglia, La Spezia

V. 5500–5581 (In serv. 1979–81)

**D:** 7.8 tons (fl) **S:** 32 kts **Dim:** 12.0 × 3.8 × 0.5
**A:** small arms **Electron Equipt:** Radar: 1/BX-732
**M:** 2 AIFO 8361 SM diesels; 2 Castoldi 06 waterjets; 640 hp
**Range:** 224/28 **Fuel:** 0.6 tons **Man:** 5 tot.

Remarks: GRP construction. One lost.

## INSHORE PATROL CRAFT *(continued)*

**V. 5504** L. & L. Van Ginderen, 5-86

◆ **15 V. 4000 class** Bldr: Lucchese, Venice

V. 4000–4014 (In serv. 1980–83)

**D:** 6.9 tons (fl) **S:** 47.7 kts **Dim:** 13.1 × 3.0 × 0.7
**A:** small arms **Electron Equipt:** Radar: 1/BX-732
**M:** 2 Isotta-Fraschini ID 32-55-61 diesels; 2 props; 700 hp
**Range:** 290/37 **Fuel:** 0.7 ton **Man:** 4 tot.

REMARKS: Wooden construction.

◆ **34 V. 5800 class** Bldr: Motomar, Lavagna

V. 5800–5833 (In serv. 1979–82)

**D:** 15 tons (fl) **S:** 26 kts **Dim:** 12.6 × 3.6 × 1.2
**A:** 1/7.62-mm mg **Electron Equipt:** Radar: 1/BX-732
**M:** 2 Fiat AIFO 828-SM diesels; 2 props; 1,000 hp
**Range:** 537/25 **Fuel:** 0.4 ton **Man:** 5 tot.

REMARKS: GRP construction.

◆ **3 V. 5300 class** Bldr: Motomar, Lavagna

V. 5300–5302 (In serv. 1979–82)

**D:** 5.1 tons (fl) **S:** 36 kts **Dim:** 8.3 × 2.8 × 0.5
**M:** 1 AIFO 8361-SM diesels; 1 prop; 480 hp
**Range:** 154/36 **Fuel:** 0.5 ton **Man:** 3 tot.

◆ **1 V. 3000 class** Bldr: SAL Ambrosini, Oristano

V. 3000 (In serv. 1978)

**D:** 2.9 tons (fl) **S:** 40 kts **Dim:** 7.5 × 2.5 × 0.6
**M:** 1 BPM-Vulcano gasoline engine; Castoldi 06 waterjet; 450 hp
**Range:** 330/22 **Fuel:** 0.6 ton **Man:** 3 tot.

◆ **1 V. 1640 class** Bldr: Abbate, Como

V. 1640 (In serv. 1979)

**D:** 6.5 tons (fl) **S:** 42 kts **Dim:** 9.5 × 3.1 × 0.5
**M:** 1 BPM-Vulcano gasoline engine; 760 hp
**Range:** 189/40 **Fuel:** 0.8 ton **Man:** 3 tot.

REMARKS: For Lake Como service.

◆ **1 V. 1630 class** Bldr: Italcraft, Gaeta

V. 1630 (In serv. 1974)

**D:** 6.8 tons (fl) **S:** 50 kts **Dim:** 13.0 × 2.6 × 0.9
**M:** 1 Cummins VT-8 gasoline engine; 740 hp
**Range:** 360/40 **Fuel:** 0.6 ton **Man:** 3 tot.

◆ **2 V. 5901 class** Bldr: Motomar, Lavagna

V. 5901–5902 (In serv. 1977)

**D:** 10.5 tons (fl) **S:** 23 kts **Dim:** 12.3 × 3.3 × 1.0
**M:** 1 Fiat-AIFO CP3-SM diesel; 380 hp
**Range:** 630/20 **Fuel:** 1.6 tons **Man:** 3 tot.

◆ **3 V. 2911 class** Bldr: Fiart, Naples

V. 2911–2913 (In serv. 1973–74)

**D:** 4.9 tons (fl) **S:** 26 kts **Dim:** 9.5 × 3.3 × 1.6
**M:** 1 OM-CP3-SM gasoline engine; 380 hp
**Range:** 200/24 **Fuel:** 0.6 ton **Man:** 3 tot.

◆ **4 V. 2901 class** Bldr: Chris-Craft, Fiumicino

V. 2901–2904 (In serv. 1969)

**D:** 1.8 tons (fl) **S:** 28 kts **Dim:** 7.9 × 2.8 × 0.6
**M:** 1 BPM-Oceanic 235C gasoline engine; 370 hp
**Range:** 149/23 **Fuel:** 0.1 ton **Man:** 4 tot.

REMARKS: Builder's Cavilier Futura model; wooden construction.

NOTE: Also in service are around 210 smaller craft for port, river, and lake service.

## TRAINING SHIPS

◆ **1 former yacht** Bldr: Lucchese, Venice

GIORGIO CINI (In serv. 1971)

**Giorgio Cini** H. Ehlers, 5-86

**D:** 800 tons (fl) **S:** 14 kts **Dim:** 54.0 × 10.0 × 2.9
**Electron Equipt:** Radar: . . .
**M:** 1 Fiat B306-SS diesel; 1 prop; 1,500 hp **Fuel:** 65 tons
**Range:** 800/14 **Man:** . . .

REMARKS: Acquired 1981 and refitted for training; operational 1982.

◆ **1 former fishing boat** Bldr: Benetti, Viareggio

G. 95 PAOLINI (In serv. 1967)

**D:** 348 tons **S:** 11 kts **Dim:** 36.8 × 7.7 × 2.3
**A:** 1/20-mm AA **M:** 1 Ansaldo 326-R diesel; 1 prop; 530 hp
**Fuel:** 33 tons **Range:** 350/10 **Man:** . . .

REMARKS: Acquired 1977 for student training.

MARINE POLICE
*(Comando Generale dell'Arma dei Caribinieri Servizio Navale)*

Established 1969 for patrol out to the 3-nautical-mile limit, search-and-rescue, research and police duties.

## PATROL CRAFT

◆ **6 700 class** Bldr: . . .

**D:** 22 tons (fl) **S:** 21 kts **Dim:** 15.07 × 4.91 × . . .
**A:** 1/7.62-mm mg **Electron Equipt:** Radar: 1/. . . nav.
**M:** 2 AIFO 8280 diesels; 2 props; 808 hp **Man:** 5 tot.

◆ **21 600-series** Bldrs: Posillipo, Sabandia (In serv. 1984–85)

**CC. 612** L. Grazioli, 8-86

**D:** 11–12 tons (fl) **S:** 20–21 kts **Dim:** 12.54 × 3.61 × . . .
**A:** small arms **Electron Equipt:** radar: 1/. . . . . nav.
**M:** 2 AIFO CP3-SRM or 8361-SRM diesels; 2 props; 380 or 480 hp
**Range:** 350/18 **Man:** 5 tot.

ITALY *(continued)*
PATROL CRAFT *(continued)*

*** 30 N500 class** Bldr: Italcraft, Gaeta (In serv. 23-5-85 to 20-9-85)

**N 525** L. & L. Van Ginderen, 5-86

**D:** 5.8 tons (fl) **S:** 22 kts **Dim:** 9.10 × 2.95 × . . .
**A:** small arms **Electron Equipt:** Radar: 1/. . . nav.
**M:** 2 AIFO 8061-SM diesels; 2 props; 280 hp
**Range:** 200/18 **Man:** 3 tot.

◆ **3 S500 class** Bldr: . . .

**D:** 7 tons (fl) **S:** 22 kts **Dim:** 10.00 × 3.40 × . . .
**A:** small arms **Electron Equipt:** Radar: 1/. . . nav.
**M:** 2 AIFO 8361-SRM diesels; 2 props; 430 hp
**Range:** 200/18 **Man:** 3 tot.

Remarks: Equipped to support frogmen.

◆ **23 500 class** Bldr: . . .

**D:** 2.6 tons (fl) **S:** 20 kts **Dim:** 6.46 × 2.37 ×
**M:** 1 AIFO 806-M diesel; . . . hp **Range:** 100/20 **Man:** 2 tot.

◆ **54 400 class** Bldr: . . .

**D:** 1.4 tons (fl) **S:** 25 kts **Dim:** 5.50 × 2.10 × . . .
**M:** 1 AIFO 804-M diesel; . . . hp **Man:** 2 tot.

# IVORY COAST

## Republic of the Ivory Coast

Personnel (1986): 545 total (45 officers, 500 enlisted)

Merchant Marine (1986): 58 ships—120,679 grt (2 tankers—789 grt)

### PATROL BOATS

◆ **2 French Patra class** Bldr: Auroux, Arcachon

| | Laid down | L | In serv. |
|---|---|---|---|
| L'Ardent | 15-4-77 | 21-7-78 | 6-10-78 |
| L'Intrepide | 7-7-77 | 21-7-78 | 6-10-78 |

**L'Ardent** Auroux, 1978

**D:** 125 tons (148 fl) **S:** 26.3 kts **Dim:** 40.70 (38.50 pp) × 5.90 × 1.55
**A:** 1/40-mm AA—1/20-mm AA—2/7.62-mm mg
**Electron Equipt:** Radar: 1/Decca 1226
**M:** 2 AGO 195 V12CZ SHR diesels; 2 CP props; 5,000 hp (4,400 sust.)
**Electric:** 120 kw

Remarks: Ordered 1-77 and 4-77, respectively. Planned addition of Exocet missiles did not occur.

◆ **2 PR-48 class** Bldr: SFCN, Villeneuve-la-Garenne

| | Laid down | L | In serv. |
|---|---|---|---|
| Vigilant | 2-67 | 23-5-67 | 1968 |
| Le Valeureux | 28-10-75 | 8-3-76 | 25-9-76 |

**D:** 250 tons (fl) **S:** 23 kts **Dim:** 47.5 (45.5 pp) × 7.0 × 2.25
**A:** 2/40-mm AA (I × 2)
**M:** 2 MGO diesels with Masson reduction gear; 2 props; 4,200 hp
**Range:** 2,000/16 **Man:** 4 officers, 30 men

Remarks: *Vigilant* refitted at Brest, France, 1981. *Le Valeureux* requires new engines and was out of service in 1987.

### AMPHIBIOUS WARFARE SHIPS

◆ **1 French BATRAL-E-class medium landing ship** Bldr: Dubigeon, Normandy

Éléphant (In serv. 2-2-77)

**D:** 750 tons (1,330 fl) **S:** 16 kts **Dim:** 80.0 (68.0 pp) × 13.0 × 3.0 (max.)
**A:** 2/40-mm AA (I × 2) **M:** 2 SACM diesels; 2 CP props; 1,800 hp
**Range:** 4,500/13 **Man:** 4 officers, 35 men

Remarks: Ordered 2-8-74. Similar to the French Navy's *Champlain.* Helicopter platform aft. Refitted at Brest, 1981.

◆ **10 Type 412 fast assault boats** Bldr: Rotork, U.K. (In serv. 1979–80)

**D:** 5.2 tons (8.9 fl) **S:** 21 kts **Dim:** 12.65 × 3.20 × . . .
**M:** 2 Volvo AQD 40A outdrive diesels; 2 props; 240 hp

◆ **1 Barracuda-class launch** Bldr: Halter, New Orleans, U.S.A. (In serv. 1976)

**D:** 6 tons (8.35 fl) **S:** 36 kts **Dim:** 11.0 × 3.8 × 0.6
**M:** 2 G.M. 6V-53PI diesels; 2 water jets; 540 hp **Capacity:** 20 men

◆ **2 LCVP** Bldr: Abidjan, 1970

**D:** 7 tons (9 fl) **S:** 9 kts **Dim:** 10.9 × 3.2 × 1.0
**M:** 1 Mercedes-Benz diesel

◆ **7 Arcor 24 launches** Bldr: Arcor, La Teste (In serv. 1982)

**D:** 2 tons (fl) **Dim:** 7.92 × 3.04 × 0.80 **M:** 2 Renault diesels; 2 props; 320 hp

GENDARMERIE

◆ **1 small patrol craft** Bldr: DCAN Cherbourg

Le Barracuda (In serv. 1974)

**D:** 15 tons **S:** 18 kts **Dim:** 9.0 × 3.0 × . . . **A:** 1/12.7 mm mg
**Man:** 2 crew, 18 troops **M:** diesels; . . . hp

◆ **1 Arcor-30 launch** Bldr: Arcor, La Teste, France (In serv. 1985)

**D:** 5 tons **S:** 20 kts **Dim:** 9.25 (8.30 pp) × 3.50 × 0.82
**M:** 2 Renault RC-160-D3 diesels; 2 props; 320 hp **Man:** 2 tot.

◆ **4 Arcor-31 launches** Bldr: Arcor, La Teste, France (In serv. 1982)

**Dim:** 9.45 × 3.50 × 0.82 **M:** 2 Renault diesels; 2 props; 240 hp

# JAMAICA

DEFENCE FORCE COAST GUARD

Personnel (1984): 18 officers, 150 men (plus reserves: 16 officers, 30 men)

Merchant Marine (1986): 13 ships—9,419 grt

### PATROL BOATS

◆ **1 Guardian class** Bldr: Lantana Boatyard, Lantana, Fla.

P 8 Paul Bogle (ex-*Comayguela*) (In serv. 26-9-85)

**Paul Bogle (P 8)**—20-mm AA added later J. Forster, 1986

**JAMAICA** *(continued)*
**PATROL BOATS** *(continued)*

**D:** 93 tons (fl) **S:** 33 kts **Dim:** 32.31 × 6.25 × 1.24 (2.13 props)
**A:** 1/20-mm AA—2/12.7-mm mg (I × 2)
**Electron Equipt:** Radar: 2/Furuno . . .
**M:** 3 MTU 8V 396 TB 92 diesels; 3 props; 3,600 hp
**Endurance:** 7 days **Electric:** 100 kw (2 G.M. 4-71 diesels)
**Man:** 4 officers, 16 men

Remarks: Begun and launched for Honduras, then purchased by Jamaica. Was originally to have been renamed *Cape George*. Aluminum construction. Sisters in Grenadian and Honduran service. The 20-mm AA was added by 7-86.

◆ **1 Fort Charles class** Bldr: Teledyne Sewart, Berwick, La. (In serv. 1974)

P 7 Fort Charles

**Fort Charles (P 7)** J. Forster, 1986

**D:** 103 tons (fl) **S:** 32 kts **Dim:** 31.5 × 5.7 × 2.1
**A:** 1/20-mm AA—2/12.7 mm mg (I × 2)
**Electron Equipt:** Radar: 1/Sperry 4016
**M:** 2 MTU MB 16V538 TB90 diesels; 2 props; 6,000 hp
**Range:** 1,200/18
**Man:** 3 officers, 14 men

Remarks: Can carry 24 soldiers and serve as an 18-bed floating dispensary. Refitted 1979–81 at Jacksonville, Florida, and again 1985–86 at Atlantic Marine, Florida.

◆ **3 85-foot Commercial Cruiser design** Bldr: Sewart Seacraft, Berwick, La., U.S.A., 1966–67

P 4 Discovery Bay P 5 Holland Bay P 6 Manatee Bay

**Discovery Bay (P 4)** J. Forster, 1986

**D:** 60 tons **S:** 30 kts **Dim:** 25.9 × 5.68 × 1.83
**A:** 3/12.7-mm mg(I × 3) **Electron Equipt:** Radar: 1/Sperry 3012
**M:** 3 MTU 8V331 TC81 diesels; 3 props; 3,000 hp
**Fuel:** 13 tons
**Range:** 800/20 **Man:** 3 officers, 10 men

Remarks: Re-engined three times, most recently from 1981 to 1983, by Swiftships, Inc., more than quadrupling the original horsepower. P 4 has MTU 8V396-series engines for 2,700 hp max.

Note: Also used by the Coast Guard is a 12-meter sail-training craft. The Kingston Constabulary operates CG-121, a 12-meter Bertram patrol craft acquired in 1984, and a 19.8-m search-and-rescue boat was to be purchased from Swiftships, U.S.A., in 1986.

# JAPAN

Personnel (1987): 10,225 officers, 33,360 enlisted, plus 300 reservists and approx. 4,300 civilian employees

Merchant Marine (1986): 10,011 ships—38,487,773 grt
(tankers: 1,220 ships—12,116,867 grt)

The Maritime Self-Defense Force (MSDF), or Kaiso Jeitai, was created in 1954. In Article 9 of its constitution, Japan waived the right of belligerence and declared peaceful intentions. Consequently, the armed forces are designed to carry out purely defensive tasks.

In addition to the MSDF, Japan has a large and recently modernized Maritime Safety Agency (Kaijo Hoancho), which, in function, is roughly comparable to the U.S. Coast Guard and which, in time of war, would come under the control of the Navy. Its ships are listed at the end of this section.

Construction Programs:
1984 Budget:
3 3,400-ton DDG (152 . . . , 153 . . . , 154 . . .), 1 SS (581, *Yukishio*), 2 MHC (664, 665), 1 8,300-ton AOE (423, *Towada*)
1985 Budget:
3 3,400-ton DDG 155 . . . , 156 . . . , 157 . . .), 1 SS (582 . . .), 2 MHC (666 . . . , 667 . . .), and 1 service craft
1986 Budget
1 3,400-ton DDG (158 . . .), 2 1,900-ton FF (229, 230), 1 SS (583 . . .), 2 MHC (668 . . . , 669 . . .), 1 2,200-ton training ship, 1 420-ton LCU, 3 service craft
1987 Budget:
2 1,900-ton FF (231, 232), 1 2,400-ton SS (584), 2 490-ton MHC (668, 669), 2 8,300-ton AOE (423, 424), 7 service craft
1988 Budget (Request):
1 6,500-ton DDG (. . .), 1 2,400-ton SS (585), 2 490-ton MHC, . . .

Naval Aviation: Naval air is an integral part of the Navy and has about 8,000 men assigned. Its headquarters are in Atsugi, and it has twelve bases along the coasts of Japan. The Air Training Command has several centers at Shimofusa. Some 20 helicopters serve on board the destroyers and frigates. As of mid-1987, the naval air arm consisted of 212 aircraft including:
78 P-2J patrol planes
75 HSS-2 Sea King ASW helicopters
69 P-3C patrol planes
7 KV-107-II minesweeping helicopters
6 PS-1 ASW seaplanes
81 miscellaneous aircraft, including 62 KM-2 trainers and 10 US-1 SAR amphibians

Originally set at 45, the force-level goal for P-3C long-range patrol aircraft was announced in 5-85 as 103, as the P-2J is slowly phased out; all will be able to launch

**P-3C Orion** JMSDF, 1986

**PS-1 of the Iwakuni-based Fleet Air Wing** JMSDF, 1986

**NAVAL AVIATION** *(continued)*

**EP-2J Neptune** JMSDF, 1986

**SH-60J prototype** JMSDF, 1986

**HSS-2B Sea King** JMSDF, 1986

U.S. Harpoon missiles and those acquired from FY 88 on will be of the Update III version. Three P-2Js have been converted to EP-2J ELINT collectors and 4 to UP-2J trainers; three Learjet U-36A aircraft have replaced the UP-2Js as radar and sonobuoy trainers between 10-85 and 3-87. The Shin-Meiwa PS-1 ASW seaplanes are being modernized with Litton APS-504 radars, cargo doors, cameras, and drop ports. A plan to acquire U.S. MH-53E imnesweeping helicopters to replace the dwindling numbers of KV-107-IIs has been deferred for several years, but in 5-85 it was announced that a new goal of 12 had been set, and the first 4 were ordered during FY 86. The SH-60B (S-70B) helicopter will replace the HSS-2 Sea Kings beginning 1991; the first fully equipped prototype flew 9-87.

Planned for acquisition FY 86 through FY 90 were 50 P-3C, 36 SH-60J, 30 HSS-2B, 12 MH-53E, 3 US-1 amphibians. and 3 Learjet U-36A. The FY 85 Budget included finding for 7 P-3C, 1 US-1A, 7 HSS-2B, 1 U-36A, 1 S-61A SAR helicopter, and 1 SH-60B. The FY 86 Budget funded 10 P-3C, 1 US-1A, 1 KM-2 trainer, 1 TC-90 trainer, 13 HSS-2B, and 4 MH-53E. The FY 87 Budget provided 9 P-3C; 1 EP-3C, 1 U-36A, 1 TC-90, 2 KM-2D, 2 MH-53E, 17 HSS-2B, and 2 OH-6D helicopter trainers.

### Warships In Service Or Under Construction As Of 1 January 1988

| | L | Tons (Surfaced) | Main armament |
|---|---|---|---|
| **◆ 14 (+3) submarines** | | | |
| 8 (+3) Yushio | 1979–89 | 2,200 | 6/533-mm TT |
| 6 Uzushio | 1970–75 | 1,850 | 6/533-mm TT |
| **◆ 34 (+9) destroyers** | | (Std.) | |
| 0 (+8) Asagiri DDG | 1986–89 | 3,400 | Harpoon, Sea Sparrow, ASROC, 1/76-mm DP, ASW TT, 1 helo |
| 1 (+1) Hatakaze | 1984–87 | 4,500 | Harpoon, 1/Standard launcher, 1/127-mm, ASROC, ASW TT |
| 12 Hatsuyuki | 1980– | 2,900 | Harpoon missiles, Sea Sparrow, ASROC, 1/76-mm DP, ASW TT, 1/helo |
| 2 Shirane | 1978–79 | 5,200 | 2/127-mm DP, 3 helicopters |
| 3 Tachikaze | 1974–81 | 3,850 | 1/Standard launcher, 2/127-mm, ASROC, 6 TT |
| 2 Haruna | 1971–73 | 4,700 | 2/127-mm DP, 6/324-mm TT, ASROC, 3 helicopters |
| 6 Yamagumo | 1965–77 | 2,100 | 4/76-mm DP, 4/375-mm TT |
| 3 Minegumo | 1967–69 | 2,066 | 4/76-mm DP, 1 rocket launcher, 6/324-mm TT |
| 4 Takatsuki | 1966–69 | 3,200 | 2/127-mm DP, ASROC |
| 1 Amatsukaze | 1963 | 3,050 | 1/Standard launcher, 4/76-mm DP, ASROC |
| **◆ 17 (+4) frigates** | | | |
| 0 (+4) 1,900-ton | 1988– | 1,900 | Harpoon missiles, 1/76-mm DP |
| 2 Yubari | 1982 | 1,400 | Harpoon missiles, 1/76-mm DP |
| 1 Ishikari | 1980– | 1,200 | Harpoon missiles, 1/76-mm DP |
| 11 Chikugo | 1970–76 | 1,470 | 2/76-mm DP, 2/40-mm AA, ASROC |
| 3 Isuzu | 1961–63 | 1,490 | 4/76-mm DP, ASW weapons |
| **◆ 5 torpedo boats** | | | |
| **◆ 37 (+4) mine warfare ships and craft** | | | |
| **◆ 8 amphibious warfare ships** | | | |

### WEAPONS AND SYSTEMS

Until the 1970s, most weapons and detection gear were of American design, built under license in Japan. Subsequently, ships have been equipped with Japanese-designed, long-range, pulse-compression air-search radars and with the 76-mm OTO Melara gun. The latter is built under license. U.S. Vulcan/Phalanx 20-mm CIWS (Close-In Weapon System) and Harpoon antiship missiles are being procured in quantity.

In Japan, the U.S. SPS-10 radar is referred to as OPS-1, SPS-6 as OPS-15, and SPS-12 as OPS-16. Similarly, the U.S. SQS-23 sonar, when built in Japan, is referred to as the OQS-3, while the OQS-1 and -2 were license-built SQS-4/29-series equipments. The OQS-4 is an indigenous, low-frequency design, as is OQS-101.

Weapons are also produced in Japan. Mitsubishi has a license to build the U.S. Mk 46 Mod. 5 "Neartips" ASW torpedo, while the indigenously designed GRX-2 high-speed homing torpedo for submarine service and the GRX-3 short-range ASW torpedo for aircraft are in development. The U.S. Standard SM-1 MR and AIM-7E surface-to-air missiles are in use, while submarines, surface ships, and aircraft are being equipped with the U.S. Harpoon antiship missile.

For shore defense, 56 6-tubed trucks are to be delivered beginning in 1989 to launch the Mitsubishi SSM-1 missile, powered by a TSM-2 turbojet. ASM-2 will be the air-launched variant. Details for SSM-1:

| | |
|---|---|
| Length: 5.0 m | Weight: 660 kg |
| Diameter: 35 cm | Warhead: 224 kg |
| Span: 1.2 m | Range: 150 km |

A new antiship missile, SSM-B, is to replace the Harpoon, with first trials in 1988.

### SUBMARINES (SS)

**◆ 0 (+2 + . . .) 2,400-ton class**

| | Bldr | Laid down | L | In serv. |
|---|---|---|---|---|
| 584 N . . . | Kawasaki, Kobe | -88 | -90 | 1991 |
| 585 N . . . | Mitsubishi, Kobe | -89 | -91 | 1992 |

**D:** 2,400 tons (surf.) **S:** 12/20 kts **Dim:** 77.0 × 10.0 × . . .
**A:** 6/533-mm TT (. . . torpedoes and Harpoon missiles)
**Electron Equipt:** Radar: . . . —Sonar: . . .
**M:** diesel-electric; 1 prop; 7,200 hp
**Man:** . . .

Remarks: First unit authorized 30-12-86; second requested under FY 88 Budget. Improved version of *Yushio* class.

SUBMARINES (SS) *(continued)*

◆ 8 (+3) Yushio class

| | Bldr | Laid down | L | In serv. |
|---|---|---|---|---|
| 573 Yushio | Mitsubishi, Kobe | 3-12-76 | 29-3-79 | 26-2-80 |
| 574 Mochishio | Kawasaki, Kobe | 28-4-78 | 12-3-80 | 5-3-81 |
| 575 Setoshio | Kawasaki, Kobe | 28-4-79 | 12-2-81 | 17-3-82 |
| 576 Okishio | Kawasaki, Kobe | 17-4-80 | 5-3-82 | 1-3-83 |
| 577 Nadashio | Mitsubishi, Kobe | 16-4-81 | 27-1-83 | 6-3-84 |
| 578 Hamashio | Kawasaki, Kobe | 8-4-82 | 1-2-84 | 5-3-85 |
| 579 Akishio | Mitsubishi, Kobe | 15-4-83 | 21-1-85 | 5-3-86 |
| 580 Takeshio | Kawasaki, Kobe | 3-4-84 | 19-2-86 | 3-3-87 |
| 581 Yukishio | Mitsubishi, Kobe | 11-4-85 | 23-1-87 | 31-3-88 |
| 582 N. . . . . . . | Kawasaki, Kobe | 11-4-86 | 2-88 | 30-3-89 |
| 583 N. . . . . . . | Mitsubishi, Kobe | 21-4-87 | 7-89 | 12-90 |

**Akishio (SS 579)** JMSDF, 1986

**Hamashio (SS 578)** L. & L. Van Ginderen, 1986

**Nadashio (SS 577)** L. & L. Van Ginderen, 7-85

**D:** 2,200–2,250 tons (surf.) **S:** 12/20 kts
**Dim:** 76.20 × 9.9 × 7.5 **A:** 6/533-mm TT
**Electron Equipt:** Radar: ZPS-6—Sonar: SQS-36J active, ZQQ-4 passive suite
**M:** 2 Mitsubishi/M.A.N. V8/V24-30 AMTL, 1,700-hp Kawasaki diesel generator sets (2,840 kw tot.), 1 Fuji electric motor; 1 prop; 7,220 hp
**Man:** 10 officers, 70 men

Remarks: Deeper-diving than the *Uzushio* class and have more modern electronic equipment. 577 and later are equipped with U.S. Sub-Harpoon missiles. Double-hull design. 579–583 displace 2,250 tons surfaced. Use Nihon-Denchi batteries.

◆ 6 Uzushio class

| | Bldr | Laid down | L | In serv. |
|---|---|---|---|---|
| 567 Makishio | Mitsubishi, Kobe | 21-6-69 | 27-2-71 | 2-2-72 |
| 568 Isoshio | Kawasaki, Kobe | 9-7-70 | 18-3-72 | 25-11-72 |
| 569 Narushio | Mitsubishi, Kobe | 8-5-71 | 22-11-72 | 28-9-73 |
| 570 Kuroshio | Kawasaki, Kobe | 5-7-72 | 22-2-74 | 27-11-74 |
| 571 Takashio | Kawasaki, Kobe | 6-7-73 | 30-6-75 | 30-1-76 |
| 572 Yaeshio | Kawasaki, Kobe | 14-4-75 | 19-5-77 | 7-3-78 |

**Kuroshio (SS 570)** L. & L. Van Ginderen, 1-87

**D:** 1,850/3,600 tons **S:** 12/20 kts **Dim:** 72.0 × 9.9 × 7.5 **A:** 6/533-mm TT
**Electron Equipt:** Radar: 1/ZPS-4—Sonar: ZQQ-4 passive suite, SQS-36J active
**M:** diesel-electric propulsion; 2 Kawasaki-M.A.N. V8/V24-30 AMTL, 1,700-hp diesels; 1 prop; 7,200 hp
**Man:** 10 officers, 70 men

Remarks: Tear-drop hull. Double-hull construction, bow sonar array, torpedo tubes amidships, as in modern U.S. Navy submarines. Maximum depth: 200 m. Sister *Uzushio* (566) stricken 24-3-87 after only 16 years service; 567 to strike 1988.

Note: The last *Asashio*-class submarine, *Arashio* (565), was stricken 27-3-86.

HELICOPTER-CARRYING DESTROYERS (DDH)

◆ 2 Shirane class

| | Bldr | Laid down | L | In serv. |
|---|---|---|---|---|
| 143 Shirane | Ishikawajima, Tokyo | 25-2-77 | 18-9-78 | 17-3-80 |
| 144 Kurama | Ishikawajima, Tokyo | 17-2-78 | 20-9-79 | 27-3-81 |

**D:** 5,200 tons (6,800 fl) **S:** 32 kts **Dim:** 158.8 × 17.5 × 5.3 (hull)
**A:** 2/127-mm Mk 42 DP (I × 2)—1/Mk 29 launcher (VIII × 24 Sea Sparrow)—144 only; 2/20-mm Mk 15 CIWS AA (I × 2)—1/ASROC ASW RL (VIII × 1, 16 missiles)—6/324-mm Type 68 ASW TT (III × 2)—3/HSS-2B ASW helicopters
**Electron Equipt:** Radar: OPS-22 nav., 1/OPS-12, 1/OPS-28, 1/WM-25 (H.S.A.), 2/GFCS-1A, 1/CCA (helo control)
TACAN: URN-25
EW: NOLQ-1 passive/active, OLR-9B passive
Sonar: OQS-101 (hull), SQS-35 VDS, SQR-18A towed array
**M:** 2 sets GT; 2 props; 70,000 hp **Boilers:** 2; 60 kg/cm², 480°C **Man:** 370 tot.

Remarks: Modified *Haruna* class. Both received U.S. SQR-18A TACTASS passive towed hydrophone arrays during 1981. Have "Masker" bubble-generating system to reduce radiated noise. WM-25 controls the Sparrow missiles. Will eventually receive Harpoon missiles. Have *two* stacks, slightly staggered, compared to one on the *Haruna* class. DDH 143 still lacked Vulcan/Phalanx in late 1986. Both have TDPS-Target Data Processing System, with a U.S. UYK-20 computer and OYQ-5 display. Have LINK 11 and LINK 14 data transmission systems. A landing control radar is mounted to port of the after stack. Two pair fin stabilizers fitted.

**Shirane (DDH 143)**—with 2 SATCOMM radomes, no CIWS
*Ships of the World,* 11-84

HELICOPTER-CARRYING DESTROYERS (DDH) *(continued)*

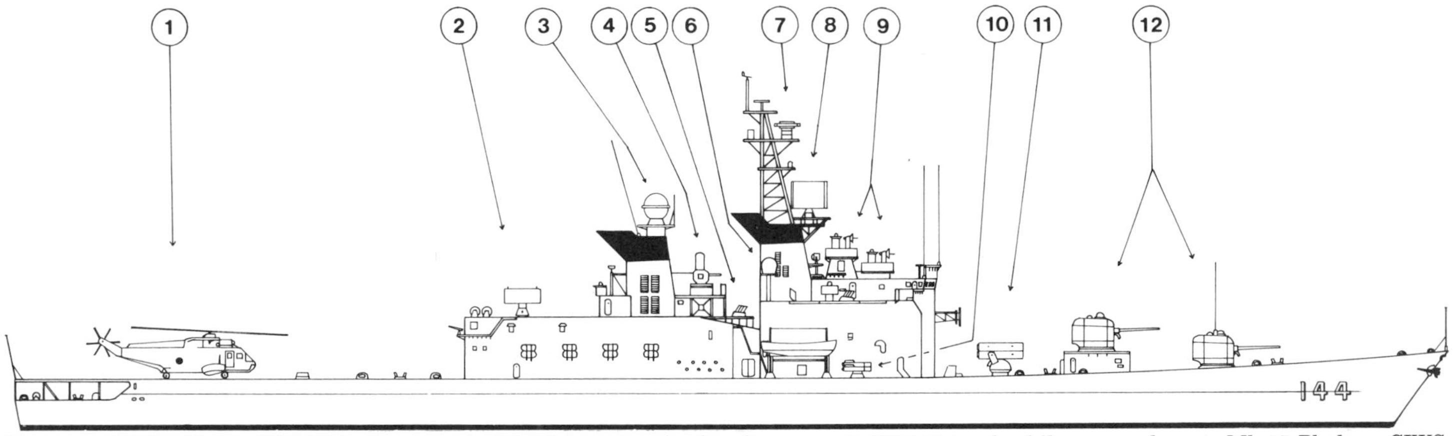


**Kurama (DDH 144)** 1. HSS-2B helicopter 2. Mk 29 launcher for Sea Sparrow 3. WM-25 track-while-scan radar 4. Mk 15 Phalanx CIWS 5. Mk 36 SRBOC decoy launchers 6. SATCOMM antennas 7. OPS-28 surface-search radar 8. OPS-12 3-D radar 9. GFCS-1A radar directors 10. Mk 68 triple ASW TT 11. Mk 112 ASROC ASW RL (XIII × 1) 12. 127-mm Mk 42 DP guns

**Kurama (DDH 144)** *Ships of the World,* 1984

**Kurama (DDH 144)**—with 2 Mk 15 CIWS (Vulcan/Phalanx) JMSDF, 1986

◆ **2 Haruna class**

| | Bldr | Laid down | L | In serv. |
|---|---|---|---|---|
| 141 Haruna | Mitsubishi, Nagasaki | 19-3-70 | 1-2-72 | 22-3-73 |
| 142 Hiei | Ishikawajima-Harima | 8-3-72 | 13-8-73 | 27-12-74 |

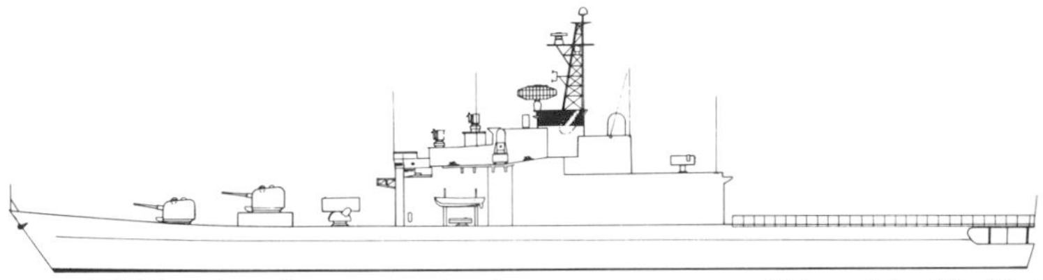

**Haruna (DDH 141)**—after modernization *Ships of the World,* 1987

**Hiei (DDH 142)**—with 2 SATCOMM antennas L. & L. Van Ginderen, 7-85

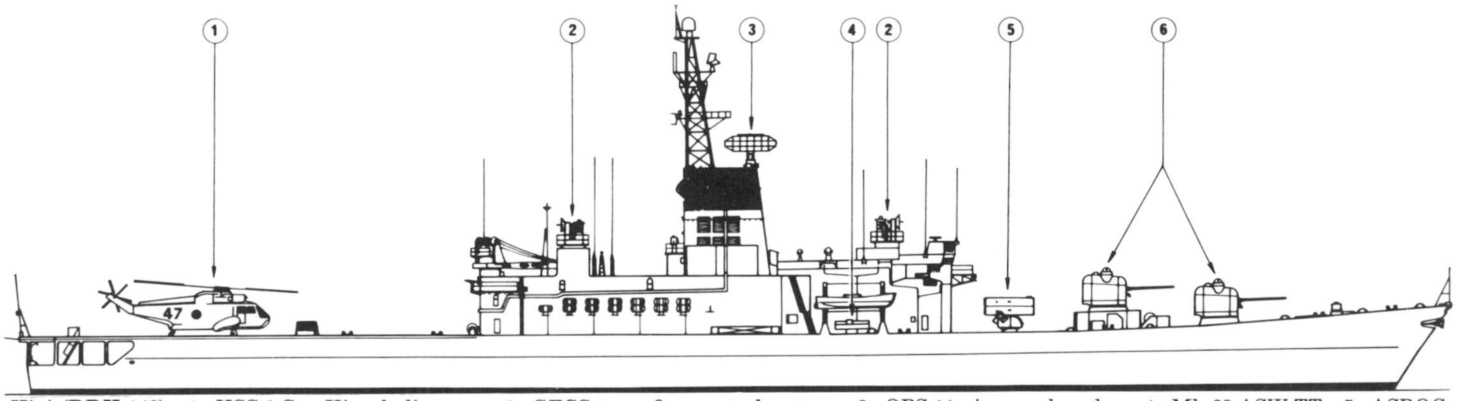


**Hiei (DDH 142)** 1. HSS-2 Sea King helicopter 2. GFCS-1 gunfire-control system 3. OPS-11 air-search radar 4. Mk 68 ASW TT 5. ASROC ASW rocket launcher 6. 127-mm 54-caliber, dual-purpose guns, Mk 42 Mod. 10

**HELICOPTER-CARRYING DESTROYERS (DDH)** *(continued)*

**D:** 4,700 tons (6,300 fl) **S:** 32 kts **Dim:** 153.0 × 17.5 × 5.1
**A:** 141: 2/127-mm Mk 42 DP (I × 2)—1/Mk 29 launcher for Sea Sparrow (VIII × 1; . . . reloads)—2/20-mm Mk 15 CIWS (I × 2)—6/324-mm Mk 68 ASW TT (III × 2)—1/Mk 112 ASROC launcher (VIII × 1; . . . reloads)—3/HSS-2B ASW helicopters
142: 2/127-mm Mk 42 DP (I × 2)—1/Mk 112 ASROC launcher (VIII × 1; . . . reloads)—6/324-mm Mk 68 ASW TT (III × 2)—3/HSS-2B ASW helicopters
**Electron Equipt:** 141: Radar: 1/OPS-28, 1/OPS-11C, 1/FCS-2-12, 2/FCS-1A
Sonar: OQS-3—TACAN: ORN-6
EW: NOLQ-1-3, OPN-7B, OPN-11B, 4/Mk 36 SRBOC decoy RL (V1 × 4)
142: Radar: 1/OPS-17, 1/OPS-11, 2/FCS-1A
Sonar: OQS-3—TACAN: ORN-6
EW: NOLR-6, OLR-9
**M:** 2 sets GT; 2 props; 70,000 hp **Boilers:** 2; 60 kg/cm², 480°C
**Man:** 36 officers, 304 men

Remarks: Modernization of DDH 141, provided in FY 83 Budget, began 1986 for completion by early 1988. Modernization of DDH 42 funded FY 84. Superstructure enlarged to accommodate additional electronics, Sea Sparrow launcher added atop hangar, with FCS-2-12 director abaft "mack," 2 Mk 15 Phalanx CIWS flank superstructure, aft GFCS-1A moved to atop bridge, new EW gear added (including Mk 36 decoy RL). The OYQ-6 Combat Direction System (using the U.S. UYK-20A computer) was installed, replacing the OYQ-3. Planned addition of VDS does not seem to have been accomplished, and Harpoon missile launchers were not added. The single combined mast/stack is off centerline, to port. Have two pair fin stabilizers. A helicopter haul-down system is installed in the flight deck.

**GUIDED-MISSILE DESTROYERS**

◆ **0 (+1 + 3) Aegis destroyers**

| | Bldr | Laid down | L | In serv. |
|---|---|---|---|---|
| . . . N . . . | . . . | . . . | . . . | 1993 |

**D:** 6,500 tons (approx. 8,500 fl) **S:** . . . **Dim:** . . . × . . . × . . .
**A:** 8/Harpoon SSM (IV × 2)—1/Mk 41 VLS (90 Standard SM-2 MR block 2 missiles)—1/127-mm OTO Melara DP—2/20-mm Mk 15 CIWS (I × 2)—6/324-mm ASW TT Mk 68 (III × 2)—platform for 1/HSS-2B or SH-60J ASW helicopter
**Electron Equipt:** Radar: 1/OPS-28D, 1/SPY-1D Aegis, 4/Mk 99 illuminator
Sonar: OQS-101C, SQR-19 TASS
EW: NOLQ-1, NOLQ-2, 4/Mk 36 SRBOC decoy RL (VI × 4)
**M:** 4 gas turbines; 2 CP props; approx. 80,000 hp
**Range:** . . . **Man:** . . . **Electric:** . . .

Remarks: First ship of four requested under FY 88 Budget, with three more to follow at 2-year intervals. Great expense has caused considerable resistance to program, delaying start by two years. Either U.S. General Electric LM-2500 or British Rolls-Royce Spey SM-1C engines will be used. The ships are intended to assist in the aerial defense of Japan, vice acting as AAW escorts for task forces.

◆ **0 (+8) Asagiri class (DDK)**

| | Bldr | Laid down | L | In serv. |
|---|---|---|---|---|
| 151 Asagiri | Ishikawajima-Harima, Tokyo | 13-2-85 | 19-9-86 | 31-3-88 |
| 152 N . . . | Sumitomo, Uraga | 5-2-86 | -10-87 | 1-89 |
| 153 N . . . | Mitsui, Tamano | 25-2-86 | -9-87 | 2-89 |
| 154 N . . . | Ishikawajima-Harima | 3-3-86 | -8-87 | 3-89 |
| 155 N . . . | Hitachi, Maizuru | 20-1-87 | 6-88 | 30-1-90 |
| 156 N . . . | Sumitomo, Uraga | 9-3-87 | 9-88 | 28-2-90 |
| 157 N . . . | Mitsubishi, Nagasaki | 14-1-87 | 8-88 | 30-3-90 |
| 158 N . . . | Ishikawajima-Harima, Tokyo | 8-88 | 9-89 | 3-91 |

**D:** 3,400 tons (4,200 fl) **S:** 30 kts **Dim:** 136.5 × 14.6 × 4.45 (mean)
**A:** 8/Harpoon SSM (IV × 2)—1/Mk 29 missile launcher (VIII × 1; 18 Sea Sparrow missiles)—1/76-mm OTO Melara Compact—2/20-mm Mk 15 CIWS AA (I × 2)—1/Mk 112 ASROC ASW RL (VIII × 1; . . . rockets)—6/324-mm Type 68 ASW TT (III × 2 H.O.S. 301 for Mk 46 Mod 5 torpedoes)—1/HSS-2B helicopter
**Electron Equipt:** Radar: 1/OPS-28C, 1/OPS-14C, 1/FCS-2-21A, 1/FCS-2-12E
Sonar: OQS-4A, SQR-18B TASS—TACAN: URN-25
EW: OLR-9C passive, OLR-6C active/passive, OLT-3 D/F, 2 Mk 36 SRBOC chaff RL (VI × 2)
**M:** COGAG: 4 Kawasaki-Rolls-Royce Spey SM-1A gas turbines; 2 CP props; 59,000 hp (68,400 max.)
**Range:** . . . **Electric:** . . . **Fuel:** . . . **Man:** 230 tot.

Remarks: Authorized: 1 in FY 83, 3 in FY 84, 3 in FY 85, 1 in FY 86. An improved *Hatsuyuki*. DDK 151 ordered 29-3-84; 152–154 ordered 23-3-85, DDK 155–157 ordered 3-86. DDK 158, ordered 3-87, was the only ship authorized of two requested under FY 86. Will have the OYQ-6 Combat Direction System, employing the U.S.-built UYK-20A computer and the Japanese OJ-194B Digital Display Indicator.

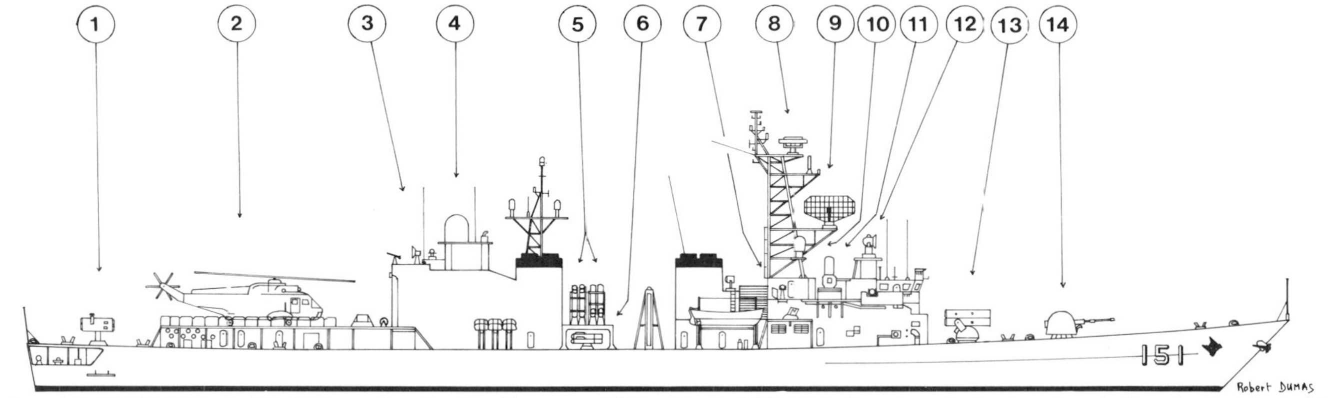

**Asagiri (DDK 151)** 1. Mk 29 launcher for Sea Sparrow (VIII × 1) 2. HSS-2B helicopter 3. horizon bar helicopter landing aid 4. FCS-2-12E missile-control radar 5. Harpoon SSM (IV × 2) 6. triple Mk 68 ASW TT 7. Mk 36 SRBOC decoy launchers 8. OPS-28C surface/air search radar 9. OPS-14C air-search radar 10. EW antenna radomes 11. Mk 15 Phalanx CIWS 12. FCS-2-21A gun director 13. Mk 112 ASROC launcher 14. 76-mm OTO Melara Compact DP gun (*Note*: Aft stack configuration changed.)

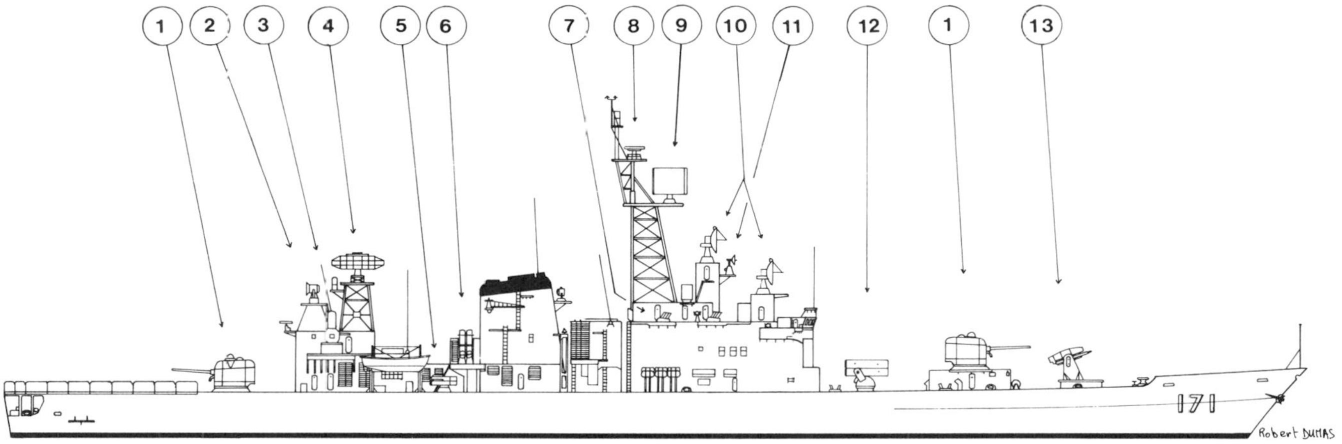

**Hatakaze (DDG 171)** 1. helicopter platform 2. 127-mm Mk 42 DP guns 3. FCS-2-21C for 127-mm guns 4. Mk 15 Phalanx CIWS 5. OPS-11C air-search radar 6. Harpoon SSM (IV × 2) 7. OPS-28B surface/air search radar 8. U.S. SPS-52C 3-D radar 9. SPG-51C missile directors 10. Mk 112 ASROC launcher (VIII × 1) 11. Mk 13 Mod. 4 launcher for Standard SM-1 MR SAMs

## GUIDED-MISSILE DESTROYERS *(continued)*

The combat system is designated OYQ-5. U.S.-built SLQ-25 Nixie torpedo decoys and the Prairie/Masker bubble countermeasures system are fitted. Will have fin stabilizers, and a Beartrap/RAST-type helicopter landing and deck-handling system.

### ◆ 1 (+1) Hatakaze class (DDG)

| | Bldr | Laid down | L | In serv. |
|---|---|---|---|---|
| 171 Hatakaze | Mitsubishi, Nagasaki | 20-5-83 | 9-11-84 | 27-3-86 |
| 172 Shimakaze | Mitsubishi, Nagasaki | 30-1-85 | 30-1-87 | 31-3-88 |

**Hatakaze (DDG 171)** JMSDF, 1986

**Hatakaze (DDG 171)** *Ships of the World,* 1986

**Hatakaze (DDG 171)** JMSDF, 1986

**D:** 4,650 tons (5,600 fl) **S:** 32 kts (30 sust.) **Dim:** 150.0 × 16.4 × 4.80 (hull)
**A:** 1/Mk 13 Mod. 4 missile launcher (I × 1, 40 Standard SM-1 MR missiles)—8/Harpoon SSM (IV × 2)—2/127-mm Mk 42 DP (I × 2)—2/20-mm Vulcan/Phalanx Mk 15 Mod. 2 AA (I × 2)—1/ASROC Mk 116 ASW RL (VIII × 1)—6/324-mm Type 68 ASW TT (III × 2)—1/HSS-2B helicopter (no hangar)
**Electron Equipt:** Radar: 1/OPS-28B, 1/OPS-11C, 1/SPS-52C, 2/SPG-51C, 2/FCS-2-21C
Sonar: OQS-4 Mod. 1—TACAN: URN-25
EW: NOLQ-1-3 active/passive, OLR-9B passive, Mk 36 SRBOC chaff RL (VI × 4)
**M:** COGAG: 2 Rolls-Royce Spey SM-1A and 2 Olympus TM-3D gas turbines; 2 CP props; 72,000 hp
**Range:** . . . **Man:** 260 tot.

Remarks: No hangar for helicopter. U.S. Mk 74 Mod. 13 missile fire-control system (2/SPG-51C radar directors) for the Standard missile system. DDG 171 in 1981 Budget, 172 in 1983; 173 requested 1985 but denied. DDG 172 ordered 29-3-84. Have LINK 11 and LINK 14 data links, OYQ-4 Mod. 1 combat data system, NYPX-2 IFF system.

### ◆ 12 Hatsuyuki class (DDK)

| | Bldr | Laid down | L | In serv. |
|---|---|---|---|---|
| 122 Hatsuyuki | Sumitomo, Uraga | 14-3-79 | 7-11-80 | 23-3-82 |
| 123 Shirayuki | Hitachi, Maizuru | 3-12-79 | 4-8-81 | 8-2-83 |
| 124 Mineyuki | Mitsubishi, Nagasaki | 7-5-81 | 17-10-82 | 26-1-84 |
| 125 Sawayuki | Ishikawajima-Harima, Tokyo | 22-4-81 | 21-6-82 | 15-2-84 |
| 126 Hamayuki | Mitsui, Tamano | 4-2-81 | 27-5-82 | 18-11-83 |
| 127 Isoyuki | Ishikawajima-Harima, Tokyo | 20-4-82 | 19-9-83 | 23-1-85 |
| 128 Haruyuki | Sumitomo, Uraga | 11-3-82 | 6-9-83 | 14-3-85 |
| 129 Yamayuki | Hitachi, Maizura | 25-2-83 | 10-7-84 | 3-12-85 |
| 130 Matsuyuki | Ishikawajima-Harima, Tokyo | 7-4-83 | 25-10-84 | 19-3-86 |
| 131 Setoyuki | Mitsui, Tamano | 26-1-84 | 3-7-85 | 31-1-87 |
| 132 Asayuki | Sumitomo, Uraga | 22-12-83 | 16-10-85 | 20-2-87 |
| 133 Shimayuki | Mitsubishi, Nagasaki | 8-5-84 | 29-1-86 | 31-3-87 |

**Asayuki (DDK 132)** JMSDF, 1987

**Isoyuki (DDK 127)** JMSDF, 1986

**Yamayuki (DDK 129)** L. & L. Van Ginderen, 8-87

**GUIDED-MISSILE DESTROYERS** *(continued)*

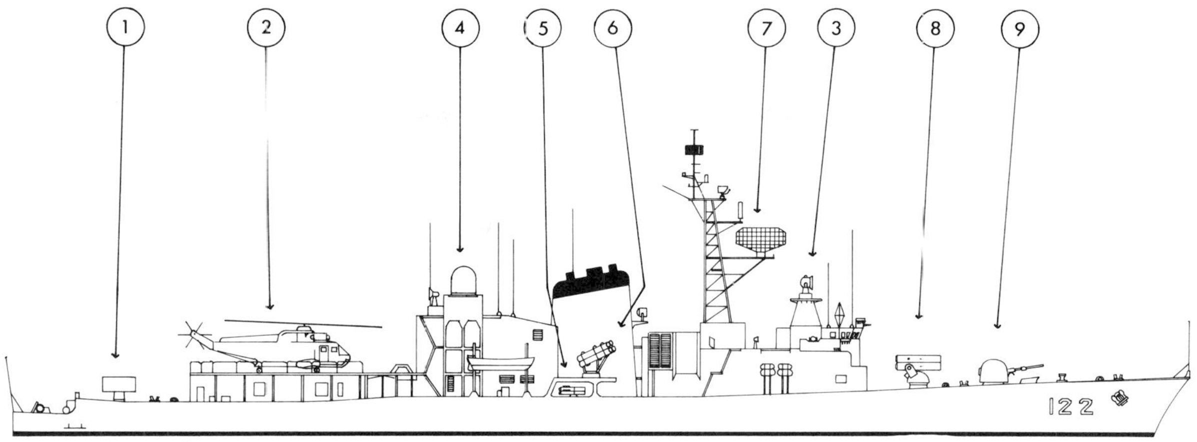


**Hatsuyuki (DDG 122)** 1. Mk 29 launcher for Sea Sparrow 2. HSS-2B helicopter 3. GFCS-2-21 fire-control radar 4. GFCS-2-12 radome 5. Mk 68 ASW TT (III × 2) 6. Harpoon SSM (IV × 2) 7. OPS-14B radar antenna 8. ASROC ASW RL (VIII × 1) 9. 76-mm OTO Melara Compact dual-purpose gun

**Hatsuyuki (DDK 122)**—neither Mk 15 CIWS nor Mk 36 SRBOC
L. & L. Van Ginderen, 7-85

**D:** DDK 122–128: 2,950 tons (3,700 fl) DDK 129–133: 3,050 tons (3,800 fl)
**S:** 30 kts **Dim:** 131.7 (126.0 wl) × 13.7 × 4.1 (129 and later: 4.3)(hull)
**A:** 8/Harpoon SSM (IV × 2)—1/Mk 29 missile launcher (VIII × 1, 18 Sea Sparrow missiles)—1/76-mm OTO Melara Compact DP—2/20-mm Mk 15 CIWS AA (I × 2)—1/ASROC ASW RL (VIII × 1, 16 missiles)—6/324-mm Type 68 ASW TT (III × 2)—1/HSS-2B ASW helicopter
**Electron Equipt:** Radar: 1/OPS-18-1, 1/OPS-14B, 1/GFCS-2-21 (76-mm), 1/GFCS-2-12 (Sea Sparrow)
Sonar: OQS-4—TACAN: URN-25
EW: NOLR-6C passive, (OLR-9B also in DDK 131–133) OLT-3 D/F, 2 Mk 36 SRBOC chaff RL (VI × 2)

**Shirayuki (DDK 123)**—no Mk 15 CIWS JMSDF, 1984

**M:** COGOG: 2 Kawasaki-Rolls-Royce Olympus TM-3B gas turbines, 28,390 hp each; 2 Tyne RM-1C gas turbines, 5,340 hp each; 2 CP props; 45,000 hp (50,000 max.)
**Man:** 190–195 tot.

Remarks: Have fin stabilizers, DDK 122 in 1977 budget, 123 in 1978, 124–126 in 1979, 129 and 130 in 1981, and 131–133 in 1982. The Olympus engines are rated at 22,500 hp for cruise, 25,000-hp limit, while the Tyne cruise engines are rated at 4,620-hp cruise/5,000-hp max. and provide speeds up to 19.5 kts. Helicopter deck

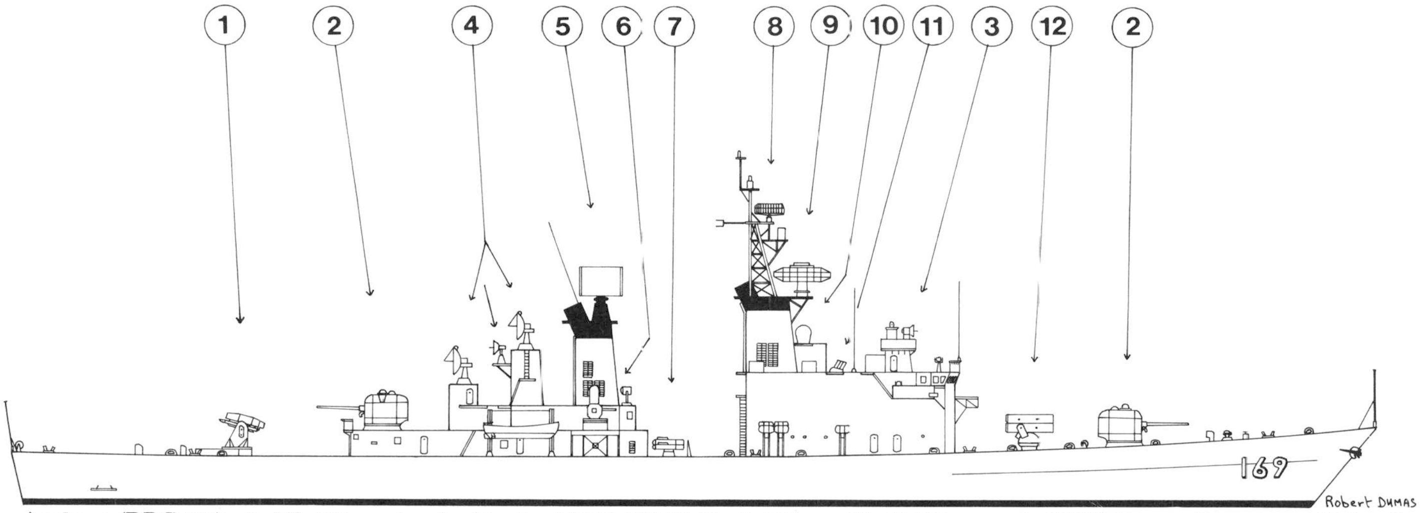


**Asakaze (DDG 169)** 1. Mk 13 launcher for Standard SM-1 MR SAM 2. 127-mm Mk 42 DP guns 3. GFCS-1A gun director 4. SPG-51C missile directors 5. SPS-52B 3-D radar 6. Mk 15 Phalanx 20-mm CIWS 7. triple Mk 68 ASW TT 8. OPS-17 surface-search radar 9. OPS-11B air-search radar 10. OLT-3 EW radomes 11. Mk 36 SRBOC decoy RL 12. Mk 112 ASROC launcher

**GUIDED-MISSILE DESTROYERS** *(continued)*

has the Canadian Beartrap traversing/landing system. All are programmed to receive U.S. SQR-18 or 19 TACTASS towed passive linear arrays. Have OYQ-5 TDPS—Tactical Data Processing System—with a U.S. UYK-20 computer. Have LINK 14 data relay receiver only. Stack incorporates passive infrared cooling features and a water-spray system. DDK 129 and later have steel vice aluminum superstructures. DDK 122 lacks Mk 15 CIWS and Mk 36 SRBOC chaff RL; DDK 123 lacks CIWS. DDK 131–133 have later EW equipment. All have NYPX-2 IFF systems.

◆ **3 Tachikaze class (DDG)**

| | Bldr | Laid down | L | In serv. |
|---|---|---|---|---|
| 168 Tachikaze | Mitsubishi, Nagasaki | 19-6-73 | 12-12-74 | 26-3-76 |
| 169 Asakaze | Mitsubishi, Nagasaki | 27-5-76 | 15-10-77 | 27-3-79 |
| 170 Sawakaze | Mitsubishi, Nagasaki | 14-9-79 | 4-6-81 | 30-3-83 |

**Asakaze (DDG 169)**—with two Mk 15 CIWS, new EW *Ships of the World,* 4-85

**Sawakaze (DDG 170)** *Ships of the World,* 1984

**D:** 3,850 tons (4,800 fl) **S:** 32 kts **Dim:** 143.0 × 14.3 × 4.6
**A:** 1/Mk 13 Mod. 4 missile launcher (40 Standard SM-1 MR SAM/Harpoon SSM)—2/127-mm Mk 42 DP (I × 2)—2/20-mm Mk 15 CIWS gatling AA (I × 2)—1 Mk 112 ASROC ASW RL (VIII × 1)—6/324-mm Type 68 ASW TT (III × 2)
**Electron Equipt:** Radar: OPS-17 (170: OPS-28), 1/OPS-11B, 1/SPS-52B, 2/SPG-51C, 1/GFCS-1A
Sonar: OQS-3 (170: OQS-4)
EW: OLT-3 system, 4/Mk 36 Mod. 2 Super RBOC chaff RL
**M:** 2 sets GT; 2 props; 70,000 hp **Boilers:** 2; 60 kg/cm², 480°C
**Man:** 277 tot.

Remarks: U.S. Vulcan/Phalanx gatling guns and Harpoon were added to 168 under 1981 Budget, as well as improvements to SAM system. Same improvement made to DDG 169 in 1984–85 and to DDG 170 under 1985 Budget. The missile-control system is Mk 74 Mod. 13 and uses the two SPG-51C radars. The propulsion plant is identical to that of the *Haruna* class. Have a LINK 14 data transmission system. The ASROC launcher has a reload magazine below the bridge.

◆ **1 Amatsukaze class (DDG)**

| | Bldr | Laid down | L | In serv. |
|---|---|---|---|---|
| 163 Amatsukaze | Mitsubishi, Nagasaki | 29-11-62 | 5-10-63 | 15-2-65 |

**D:** 3,050 tons (4,000 fl) **S:** 33 kts **Dim:** 131.0 × 13.4 × 4.2 (mean)
**A:** 1/Mk 13 launcher (40 Standard SM-1 MR SAM)—4/76.2-mm 50-cal. Mk 33 DP (II × 2)—1 Mk 112 ASROC ASW RL (VIII × 1)—6/324-mm Type 68 ASW TT (III × 2)—2/Mk 15 trainable Hedgehog
**Electron Equipt:** Radar: 1/OPS-17, 1/SPS-29, 1/SPS-52C, 2/SPG-51B, 1/GFCS-2-21
Sonar: SQS-23—EW: OLT-1
**M:** 2 sets Ishikawajima-G.E. GT; 2 props; 60,000 hp **Fuel:** 900 tons
**Boilers:** 2 Ishikawajima-Foster-Wheeler; 38 kg/cm², 438°C
**Electric:** 2,700 kw **Range:** 7,000/18 **Man:** 290 tot.

**Amatsukaze (DDG 163)** L. & L. Van Ginderen, 7-85

Remarks: Refitted in 1967 with ASW TT and SPS-52C radar. Crane at stern handles boats stowed in a below-decks hangar. One GFCS-2-21 radar director replaced the original two U.S. Mk 63 GFCS in 1982–83, but planned replacement of the guns by two 76-mm OTO Melara mounts and EW updates were not carried out. There are no reloads for the ASROC.

◆ **4 Takatsuki class (DD)**

| | Bldr | Laid down | L | In serv. |
|---|---|---|---|---|
| 164 Takatsuki | Ishikawajima, Tokyo | 8-10-65 | 7-1-66 | 15-3-67 |
| 165 Kikizuki | Mitsubishi, Nagasaki | 15-3-66 | 25-3-67 | 27-3-68 |
| 166 Mochizuki | Ishikawajima, Tokyo | 25-11-66 | 15-3-69 | 25-3-69 |
| 167 Nagatsuki | Ishikawajima, Tokyo | 2-3-68 | 19-3-69 | 12-2-70 |

**Takatsuki (DD 164)**—as modernized *Ships of the World,* 11-85

**Kikizuki (DD 165)**—as modernized, smooth hull sides
*Ships of the World,* 12-86

**Nagatsuki (DD 167)**—hull knuckle, TACAN, no VDS *Ships of the World,* 1986

**GUIDED-MISSILE DESTROYERS** *(continued)*

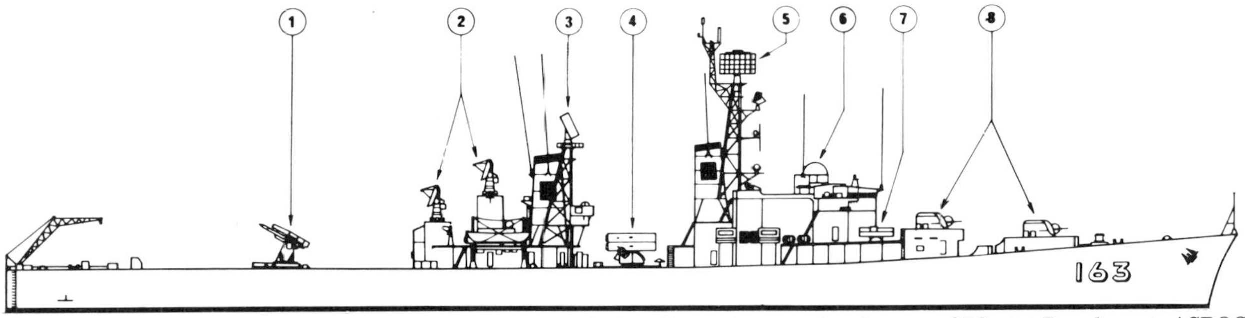


**Amatsukaze (DDG 163)** 1. Mk 13 missile launcher 2. SPG-51C missile-control radars 3. SPS-52 3-D radar 4. ASROC ASW rocket launcher 5. SPS-29 air-search radar 6. GFCS-2-21 gunfire-control director 7. Mk 68 ASW TT 8. 76.2-mm, 50-caliber, U.S. Mk 33, dual-purpose gun mounts

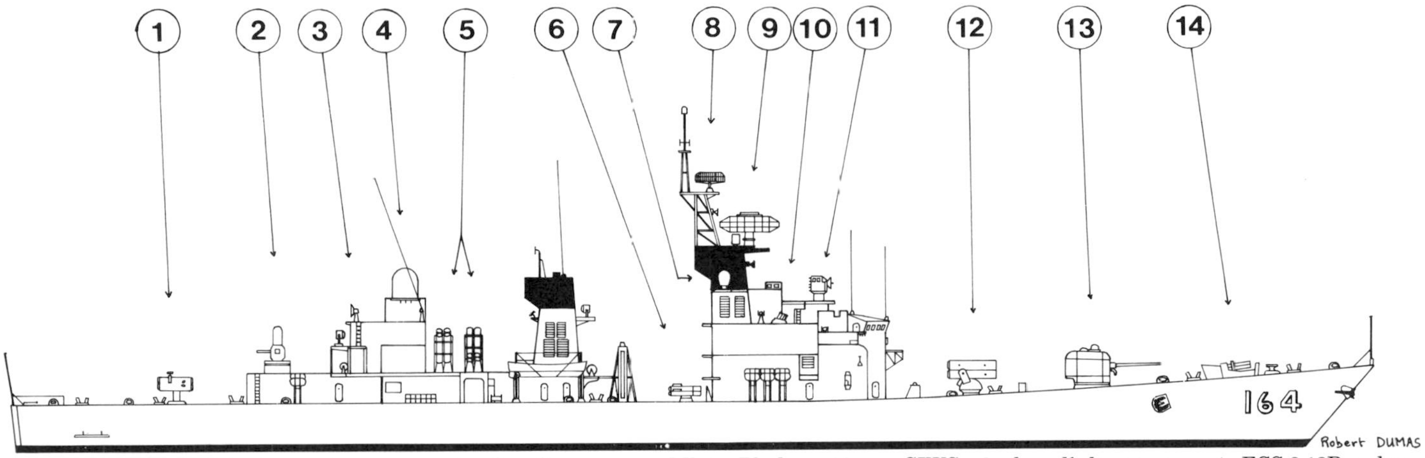


**Takatsuki (DD 164)** 1. Mk 29 launcher for Sea Sparrow 2. Mk 15 Phalanx 20-mm CIWS 3. data link antenna 4. FCS-2-12B radar director for Sea Sparrow 5. Harpoon SSM (IV × 2) 6. triple Mk 68 ASW TT 7. OLT-3 EW radomes 8. OPS-17 surface-search radar 9. OPS-11B-Y air-search radar 10. Mk 36 SRBOC chaff RL 11. Mk 56 GFCS 12. Mk 112 ASROC ASW rocket launcher (VIII × 1) 13. 127-mm Mk 42 DP gun 14. 375-mm ASW RL (IV × 1)

**D:** 3,200 tons (4,500 fl) **S:** 32 kts **Dim:** 136.0 (131.0 pp) × 13.4 × 4.4 (mean)
**A:** 164, 165: 8/Harpoon SSM (IV × 2)—1/Mk 29 SAM launcher (VIII × 1, 16 Sea Sparrow missiles)—1/127-mm Mk 42 DP—1/20-mm Mk 15 CIWS—1/Mk 112 ASROC ASW RL (VIII × 1, no reloads)—1/375-mm Bofors ASW RL (IV × 1)—6/324-mm Mk 32 ASW TT (IV × 2); 166, 167: 2/127-mm Mk 42 DP (I × 2)—1/Mk 112 ASROC ASW RL (VIII × 1)—1/375-mm Bofors ASW RL (IV × 1)—6/324-mm ASW TT (III × 2)
**Electron Equipt:** Radar: 1/OPS-11B-Y, 1/OPS-17, 1/GFCS-2-12B, 1/Mk 35 (167: 2/GFCS-1)
Sonar: SQS-23 (166, 167: OQS-3), 164, 165: SQS-35 (J) VDS
EW: OLT-3, NOLR-6C (167: NOLR-9C), Mk 36 SRBOC (VI × 2, not in 167)
TACAN: 167 only: ORN-6
**M:** 2 sets Mitsubishi GT; 2 props; 60,000 hp
**Boilers:** 2 Mitsubishi-Combustion Eng.; 43 kg/cm$^2$, 454°C
**Fuel:** 900 tons **Range:** 7,000/20 **Man:** 270 tot.

REMARKS: Originally carried three U.S. DASH drone ASW helicopters, removed in 1977 and hangar not used. DD 166 and 167 have a knuckle in the hull sides forward; the earlier two do not. DD 165 has fin stabilizers. DD 164 authorized under 1981–82 Budget to receive extensive modernization, completing in 10-85, DD 165 refitted under 1983–84 Budget, completing 10-86. The other two are no longer planned to be modernized. DD 167 acts as naval cadet training ship with *Katori* (TV 3501). On DD 164 and 165 the DASH hangar and after 127-mm gun were removed. Gained was a Mk 29 launcher aft for Sea Sparrow, 8 Harpoon missiles (IV × 2), 1/Mk 15 CIWS (Vulcan/Phalanx) gatling AA gun, upgrading of the OQS-3 sonar, provision for U.S. SQR-18A TACTASS towed passive hydrophone array, replacement of the after Mk 56 GFCS with GFCS-2-12, substitution of the NOLR-6C EW system, addition of LINK 14 digital data link equipment, installation of the U.S. Mk 36 Super RBOC chaff launching system. DD 166 and DD 167 do not have VDS.

◆ **6 Yamagumo class (DDK)**

| | Bldr | Laid down | L | In serv. |
|---|---|---|---|---|
| 113 YAMAGUMO | Mitsui, Tamano | 23-3-64 | 27-2-65 | 29-1-66 |
| 114 MAKIGUMO | Uraga, Yokosuka | 10-6-64 | 26-7-65 | 19-3-66 |
| 115 ASAGUMO | Maizuru, Heavy Ind. | 24-6-65 | 25-11-66 | 29-8-67 |
| 119 AOKUMO | Sumitomo, Uraga | 2-10-70 | 30-3-72 | 25-11-72 |
| 120 AKIGUMO | Sumitomo, Uraga | 7-7-72 | 23-10-73 | 24-7-74 |
| 121 YUGUMO | Sumitomo, Uraga | 4-2-76 | 31-5-77 | 24-3-78 |

**Makigumo (DDK 114)**—raised fantail for VDS, tripod mainmast
L. & L. Van Ginderen, 7-84

**Yugumo (DDK 121)**—lattice mainmast L. & L. Van Ginderen, 1986

**D:** 2,100 tons (2,700 fl) **S:** 27 kts **Dim:** 114.9 × 11.8 × 4.0 (hull)
**A:** 4/76.2-mm 50-cal. Mk 33 DP (II × 2)—1/ASROC ASW RL (VIII × 1)—1/375-mm Bofors ASW RL (IV × 1)—6/324-mm Mk 116 ASW TT (III × 2)
**Electron Equipt:** Radar: 1/OPS-11, 1/OPS-17, 2/GFCS 1 (*see* Remarks)
Sonar: DDK 113–115: SQS-23; later: OQS-3; also SQS-35(J) VDS (not in DDK 115)
EW: NORL-1B (119–121: NOLR-5)
**M:** 6 Mitsubishi 12UEV 30/40N diesels; 2 props; 26,500 hp
**Range:** 7,000/20 **Man:** 210–220 tot.

## GUIDED-MISSILE DESTROYERS *(continued)*

Remarks: Version of the *Minegumo* class completed with ASROC instead of DASH. DK 113–115 and 119 were given U.S. Mk 56 gun director forward (Mk 35 radar) and Mk 63 GFCS aft (Mk 34 radar on after gun mount); DDK 120 and 121 got two Japanese GFCS-1 systems instead. DDK 113 has Mitsui diesels. DDK 113 and 114 have raised sterns to house VDS; on DDK 119–121 the VDS was installed during construction, and, therefore, the stern was not raised. Final three have lattice mainmasts and a bulwark above the pilothouse.

◆ **3 Minegumo class (DDK)**

| | Bldr | Laid down | L | In serv. |
|---|---|---|---|---|
| 116 Minegumo | Mitsui, Tamano | 14-3-67 | 16-12-67 | 21-8-68 |
| 117 Natsugumo | Uraga, Yokosuka | 26-6-67 | 25-7-68 | 25-4-69 |
| 118 Murakumo | Maizuru, Heavy Ind. | 19-10-68 | 15-11-69 | 21-8-70 |

**Natsugumo (DDK 117)**—ASROC aft *Ships of the World,* 1984

**Murakumo (DDK 118)**—with OTO Melara gun and ASROC aft JMSDF, 1984

**D:** 2,100 tons (2,750 fl) **S:** 27 kts **Dim:** 114.9 × 11.8 × 4.0 (hull)
**A:** DDK 116, 117: 4/76.2-mm 50-cal. Mk 33 DP (II × 2); DDK 118: 1/76-mm OTO Melara Compact, 2/76.2-mm Mk 33 DP (II × 1)—1/Mk 116 ASROC ASW RL (VIII × 1, with reloads)—1/375-mm Bofors ASW RL (IV × 1)—6/324-mm Type 68 ASW TT (III × 2)
**Electron Equipt:** Radar: 1/OPS-11, 1/OPS-17; DDK 116: 1/Mk 35, 1/SPG-34; DDK 118: 1/GFCS-2-12, 1/GFCS-1; DDK 117: 1/GFCS-1, 1/SPG-34
Sonar: OQS-3—DDK 118: SQS-35(J) VDS also
EW: NOLR-5
**M:** 6 Mitsubishi 12UEV 30/40 diesels; 2 props; 26,500 hp
**Range:** 7,000/20 **Man:** 19 officers, 196 men

Remarks: Originally differed from the *Yamagumo* class in having a DASH drone-helicopter facility instead of ASROC, but DASH is no longer carried. In 1976, DDK 118 had an OTO Melara 76-mm gun and the prototype GFCS-2-12 radar director substituted for her after 76.2-mm twin mount and U.S. Mk 63 control system; in 1979, she received an ASROC launcher on what had been her DASH flight deck. DDK 116 and 117 received ASROC in 1982–83. DDK 116 has a U.S. Mk 56 GFCS (with Mk 35 radar) forward; the other two have a Japanese GFCS-1, and DDK 116 and 117 have a Mk 63 GFCS aft. DDK 118, with VDS, is 1.0 m longer and displaces 50 tons more.

Note: *Akizuki*-class destroyer *Teruzuki* (DD 162) was reclassified as auxiliary ASU 7012 on 27-3-86. The *Ayanami*-class destroyers *Onami* (DD 111) and *Makinami* (DD 112) were reclassified as ASU 7013 and ASU 7014 on 20-2-87.

## FRIGATES (DE)

◆ **0 (+4 + 2) 1,900-ton class**

| | Bldr | Laid down | L | In serv. |
|---|---|---|---|---|
| 229 N . . . | Mitsui, Tamano | 3-88 | 12-88 | 12-89 |
| 230 N . . . | Hitachi, Kanegawa | 4-88 | 1-89 | 3-90 |
| 231 N . . . | . . . | . . . | . . . | . . . |
| 232 N . . . | . . . | . . . | . . . | . . . |

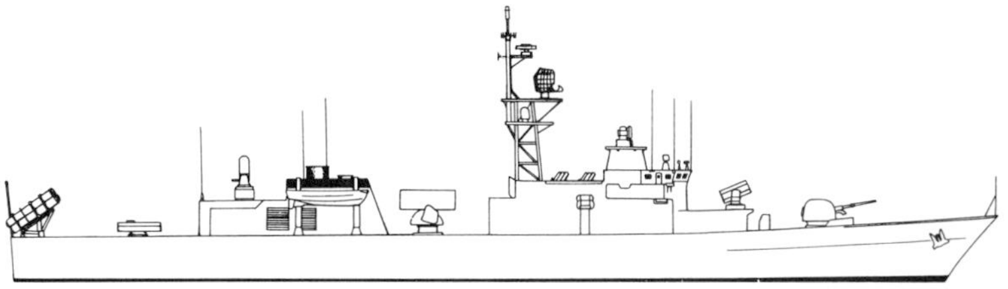

**DE 229** *Ships of the World,* 1987

**D:** 1,900 tons (approx. 2,300 fl) **S:** 27 kts **Dim:** 104.0 × 12.5 × 3.8 (hull)
**A:** 8/Harpoon SSM (IV × 2)—1/76-mm OTO Melara Compact DP—1/Mk 31 launcher for RAM (XXI × 1)—1/20-mm Mk 15 Phalanx CIWS—1/Mk 112 ASROC ASW RL (VIII × 1)—6/324-mm Mk 68 ASW TT
**Electron Equipt:** Radar: 1/OPS-28, 1/OPS-14C, 1/FCS-2-21A
Sonar: OQS-4A, possible SQR-19A TASS
EW: NOLQ-6C intercept, OLT-3 jammer, 4/Mk 36 SRBOC (VI × 4)
**M:** CODOG: 1 Kawasaki-Rolls-Royce Spey SM-1C gas turbine, 2 Mitsubishi 6DRV-35/44 diesels; 2 CP props; 24,000/10,000 hp
**Range:** . . . **Man:** 132 tot.

Remarks: First pair authorized under FY 86 Budget; second pair under FY 87. Two more to be requested by FY 90. The RAM (RIM-116A) point-defense SAM is planned, although Japan has yet to order the system from the U.S. or West Germany. The design has considerable improvements in sensors and firepower over the austere *Yubari* and *Ishikari* designs. First two ordered 26-3-87.

◆ **2 Yubari class**

| | Bldr | Laid down | L | In serv. |
|---|---|---|---|---|
| 227 Yubari | Sumitomo, Uraga | 9-2-81 | 22-2-82 | 18-3-83 |
| 228 Yubetsu | Hitachi, Maizuru | 14-1-82 | 25-1-83 | 14-2-84 |

**Yubari (DE 227)** JMSDF, 1984

**Yubetsu (DE 228)** *Ships of the World,* 1987

**D:** 1,470 tons (1,760 fl) **S:** 25 kts **Dim:** 91.0 × 10.8 × 3.6 (hull)
**A:** 8/Harpoon SSM (IV × 2)—1/76-mm OTO Melara DP—1/375-mm Bofors ASW RL (IV × 1)—6/324-mm Type 68 ASW TT (III × 2)
**Electron Equipt:** Radar: 1/OPS-19 nav., 1/OPS-28, 1/GFCS-2-21
Sonar: OQS-4—EW: NOLQ-6C passive, OLT-3 jammer, 2/Mk 36 SRBOC chaff RL (VI × 2)
**M:** CODOG: 1 Kawasaki-Rolls-Royce Olympus TM-3B gas turbine, 28,390 hp; 1 Mitsubishi 6DRV 35/44 diesel, 5,000 hp; 2 CP props
**Range:** . . . **Man:** 98 tot.

Remarks: An enlarged version of the *Ishikari* class, presumably as the earlier ship is too cramped for the mission requirements. Greater length permits later addition of a Vulcan/Phalanx gatling AA gun aft. DE 227 ordered under 1979 Budget, DE 228 under the 1980 Budget. A third was requested for the 1982 Budget, but was not authorized. Planned installation of a U.S. Mk 15 CIWS (Vulcan/Phalanx) aft has not occurred.

◆ **1 Ishikari class**

| | Bldr | Laid down | L | In serv. |
|---|---|---|---|---|
| 226 Ishikari | Mitsui, Tamano | 17-5-79 | 18-3-80 | 30-3-81 |

**FRIGATES (DE)** *(continued)*

**Ishikari (DE 226)**—Harpoon missiles aft *Ships of the World,* 1987

**D:** 1,200 tons (1,450 fl) **S:** 25 kts **Dim:** 84.5 × 10.0 × 3.5 (mean hull)
**A:** 8/Harpoon SSM (IV × 2)—1/76-mm DP OTO Melara—1/375-mm Bofors ASW RL (IV × 1)—6/324-mm Type 68 ASW TT
**Electron Equipt:** Radar: 1/OPS-19 nav., 1/OPS-28, 1/GFCS-2-21
Sonar: OQS-4
EW: NOLQ-6C passive, OLT-3 jammer, 2/Mk 36 SRBOC chaff RL (VI × 2)
**M:** CODOG: 1 Kawasaki-Rolls-Royce Olympus TM-3B gas turbine, 28,390 hp; 1 Mitsubishi 6DRV 35/44 diesel, 5,000 hp; 2 CP props
**Man:** 90 tot.

Remarks: Smaller, more lightly armed, faster, and with fewer sensors than the preceding *Chikugo* class. Aluminum superstructure. Either the gas turbine *or* the single diesel will drive both propellers. Ordered under 1977 program. 19 kts max. on diesel. The Combat Information Center (CIC) is below the waterline. Highly automated ship with very small crew.

◆ **11 Chikugo class**

| | Bldr | Laid down | L | In serv. |
|---|---|---|---|---|
| 215 Chikugo | Mitsui, Tamano | 9-12-68 | 13-1-70 | 31-7-70 |
| 216 Ayase | Ishikawajima, Tokyo | 5-12-69 | 16-9-70 | 20-7-71 |
| 217 Mikumo | Mitsui, Tamano | 17-3-70 | 16-2-71 | 26-8-71 |
| 218 Tokachi | Mitsui, Tamano | 11-12-70 | 25-11-71 | 17-5-72 |
| 219 Iwase | Mitsui, Tamano | 6-8-71 | 29-6-72 | 12-12-72 |
| 220 Chitose | Hitachi, Maizuru | 7-10-71 | 25-1-73 | 21-8-73 |
| 221 Niyodo | Mitsui, Tamano | 20-9-72 | 28-8-73 | 8-2-74 |
| 222 Teshio | Hitachi, Maizuru | 11-7-73 | 29-5-74 | 10-1-75 |
| 223 Yoshino | Mitsui, Tamano | 28-9-73 | 22-8-74 | 6-2-75 |
| 224 Kumano | Hitachi, Maizuru | 29-5-74 | 24-2-75 | 19-11-75 |
| 225 Noshiro | Mitsui, Tamano | 27-1-76 | 23-12-76 | 31-8-77 |

**D:** 1,470–1,530 tons (1,700–1,800 fl) **S:** 25 kts **Dim:** 93.0 × 10.8 × 3.5 (hull)
**A:** 2/76.2-mm 50-cal. Mk 33 DP (II × 1)—2/40-mm AA (II × 1)—1/Mk 116 ASROC ASW RL (VIII × 1)—6/324-mm Type 68 ASW TT (III × 2)

**Teshio (DE 222)** L. & L. Van Ginderen, 1983

**Tokachi (DE 218)** *Ships of the World,* 1986

**Kumano (DE 224)**—with VDS *Ships of the World,* 1986

**Electron Equipt:** Radar: 1/OPS-16, 1/OPS-14, 1/GFCS-1B—EW: NOLR-5
Sonar: OQS-3, SQS-35(J) (*see* Remarks)
**M:** 4 Mitsubishi-Burmeister & Wain UEV 30/40 or Mitsui 28VBC-38 diesels; 2 props; 16,000 hp
**Range:** 10,700/12; 12,000/9 **Man:** 13 officers, 152 men

Remarks: To date, SQS-35(J) towed, variable-depth sonar has been mounted in only five units; it is stowed in an open well at the stern, offset to starboard. These are the smallest ships in any navy to carry ASROC. A Mk 51 director (no radar) controls the twin 40-mm mount. DE 215 and 220 are 1,480 tons std., DE 216–219 and 221 are 1,470 tons std.; later units 1,500 tons std. DE 215, 217–219, 221, 223, 225 have the Mitsubishi diesels.

◆ **4 Isuzu class (DE and TV)**

| | Bldr | Laid down | L | In serv. |
|---|---|---|---|---|
| 211 Isuzu | Mitsui, Tamano | 16-4-60 | 17-1-61 | 29-7-61 |
| Mogami TV 3505 (ex-DE 212) | Mitsubishi, Nagasaki | 4-8-60 | 13-3-61 | 28-10-61 |
| 213 Kitakami | Ishikawajima, Tokyo | 7-6-62 | 21-6-63 | 27-2-64 |
| 214 Ohi | Maizuru, Heavy Ind. | 10-6-62 | 15-6-63 | 22-1-64 |

**D:** 1,490 tons (1,790 fl) **S:** 25 kts **Dim:** 94.0 × 10.4 × 3.5 (hull)
**A:** 4/76.2-mm 50-cal. Mk 33 DP (II × 2)—1/375-mm Bofors ASW RL (IV × 1)—6/324-mm Type 68 ASW TT (III × 2)—1/d.c. rack (not on DE 212 and 213)
**Electron Equipt:** Radar: 1/OPS-1, 1/OPS-16, 2/Mk 34—EW: NOLR-1
Sonar: OQS-12 or -14; DE 213: OQA-1 VDS also
**M:** diesels; 2 props; 16,000 hp (*see* Remarks) **Man:** 180 tot.

**Mogami (TV 3505)**—with VDS now removed *Ships of the World,* 1987

**Isuzu (DE 211)** *Ships of the World,* 1986

### FRIGATES (DE) *(continued)*

Remarks: Each has a different diesel propulsion plant: DE 211: 4 Mitsui 35 VBU 45V; DE 212: 2 Mitsubishi UET 52/65; DE 213: 4 Mitsubishi UEV 30/40; and DE 214: 4 Mitsui 28 VBU 38. Have two U.S. Mk 63 GFCS (Mk 34 radar on gun mounts) for the guns. All now have ASW torpedo tubes. *Mogami* redesignated a training ship 1987 and should be listed with the auxiliaries; VDS removed.

Note: The last *Mizutori*-class submarine chaser, *Hiyodori* (PC 320), was rebuilt as a yacht and redesignated ASY 92 on 27-4-87.

### GUIDED-MISSILE PATROL BOATS

◆ **0 (+3 + 15) new construction**

| | Bldr | Laid down | L | In serv. |
|---|---|---|---|---|
| . . . N . . . . . . . | . . . | . . . | . . . | 1989 |

**D:** 250 tons (. . . fl) **S:** 40 kts **Dim:** . . . × . . . × . . .
**A:** 4/SSM (II × 2)—. . . **Electron Equipt:** Radar: . . .
**M:** . . . **Man:** 20 tot.

Remarks: First unit of a 250-ton planing hull design was to have been in 1983 Budget, but has been continually postponed to permit further design definition. Class of six planned to replace the PT 11 class. In 10-86 there were reports that the Italian *Sparveiro* 65-ton hydrofoil design had been selected and that up to 18 would be acquired, equipped to launch the SSM-B antiship missile. The first three would be delivered by 1990.

### TORPEDO BOATS (PT)

◆ **5 PT 11 class** Bldr: Mitsubishi, Shimonoseki

| | Laid down | L | In serv. | | Laid down | L | In serv. |
|---|---|---|---|---|---|---|---|
| 811 PT 11 | 17-3-70 | 10-70 | 23-3-71 | 814 PT 14 | 23-3-72 | . . . | 10-7-73 |
| 812 PT 12 | 22-4-71 | 7-72 | 8-72 | 815 PT 15 | 23-4-74 | . . . | 8-1-75 |
| 813 PT 13 | 28-3-72 | 7-72 | 12-72 | | | | |

**PT 12 (PT 812)** *Ships of the World,* 1987

**D:** 100 tons (125 fl) **S:** 40 kts **Dim:** 35.0 × 9.2 × 1.2
**A:** 2/40-mm AA (I × 2)—4/533-mm TT (I × 4)
**Electron Equipt:** Radar: 1/OPS-13 **Man:** 26 tot.
**M:** CODAG: 2 Ishikawajima IM-300 gas turbines, 2 Mitsubishi 24 WZ-31MC diesels; 3 props; 11,000 hp
**Range:** 300/40; 1,000/18

Remarks: Class planned for disposal commencing 3-89.

### PATROL CRAFT (PB)

◆ **9 PB type** Bldr: Ishikawajima, Yokohama

PB 19 to PB 27 (PB 19–24 in serv. 31-3-72; others, 29-3-73)

**PB 22 (PB 922)** *Ships of the World,* 1986

**D:** 18 tons **S:** 20 kts **Dim:** 17.0 × 4.3 × 0.8 **A:** 1/20-mm AA (aft)
**Electron Equipt:** Radar: 1/OPS-29 nav. **Range:** 400/20 **Man:** 5 tot.
**M:** 2 Isuzu 17T-MF RCOR diesels; 2 props; 760 hp

Remarks: Fiberglass hulls. Hull numbers run 919 through 927. Two additional units delivered 3-79 and 28-3-80 for use as radio-controlled surface gunnery target-towing craft; 850 hp, 25 kts.

### MINE WARFARE SHIPS

◆ **1 minelayer (MMC)** Bldr: Hitachi, Maizuru

| | Laid down | L | In serv. |
|---|---|---|---|
| 951 Souya | 9-7-70 | 31-3-71 | 30-9-71 |

**Souya (MMC 951)** *Ships of the World,* 1987

**D:** 2,150 tons (3,250 fl) **S:** 18 kts **Dim:** 99.0 × 15.0 × 4.2 (hull)
**A:** 2/76.2-mm Mk 33 DP (II × 1)—2/20-mm AA (I × 2)—6/324-mm Type 68 ASW TT (III × 2)—200 mines
**Electron Equipt:** Radar: 1/OPS-14, 1/OPS-16C, 1/GFCS-1
Sonar: SQS-11A, 1/ZQS-1B
**M:** 4 Kawasaki-M.A.N. V6V 22/30 ATL diesels; 2 props; 6,400 hp
**Range:** 7,500/14 **Man:** 185 tot.

Remarks: Platform for KV-107-II mine-countermeasures helicopter, six mine rails, two external, four through the transom stern. Can also act as an ASW escort. Often acts as flagship for mine countermeasures forces. Two hull-mounted sonar domes, with that for the ZQS-1B forward.

◆ **1 mine-countermeasures support ship/minelayer (MST)**

| | Bldr | Laid down | L | In serv. |
|---|---|---|---|---|
| 462 Hayase | Ishikawajima, Haruna | 16-9-70 | 21-6-71 | 6-11-71 |

**Hayase (MST 462)** *Ships of the World,* 1987

**D:** 2,000 tons (3,050 fl) **S:** 18 kts **Dim:** 99.0 × 13.0 × 3.8
**A:** 2/76.2-mm 50-cal. DP (II × 1)—2/20-mm AA (I × 2)—6/324-mm Type 68 ASW TT (III × 2)—200 mines
**Electron Equipt:** Radar: 1/OPS-16C, 1/OPS-14, 1/Mk 34
Sonar: SQS-11A, 1/ZQS-1B
**M:** 4 Kawasaki-M.A.N. V6V 22/30 ATL diesels; 2 props; 6,400 hp

Remarks: The *Hayase* is similar to the *Souya* but has no forecastle, and has five mine rails exiting through the transom stern. She has a U.S. Mk 63 gun-control system. Fantail cleared as a platform for KV-107-II mine-countermeasures helicopters.

◆ **1 Takami-class mine countermeasures support ship (MST)**

| | Bldr | L | In serv. |
|---|---|---|---|
| 475 Utone | Hitachi, Kanagawa | 6-4-70 | 3-9-70 |

**D:** 380 tons (approx. 530 fl) **S:** 14 kts **Dim:** 52.0 × 8.8 × 2.4
**A:** 1/20-mm AA **Electron Equipt:** Radar: OPS-9—Sonar: ZQS-2
**M:** 2 Mitsubishi YV12ZC-15/20 diesels; 2 CP props; 1,440 hp **Man:** . . .

Remarks: Reclassified as tender to MSB 707-class inshore minesweepers on 16-12-86, replacing *Kasado*-class unit *Otsu* (MST 474, ex-MSC 621), stricken the same date. Other than removal of most portable sweep gear, retains MSC appearance.

MINE WARFARE SHIPS *(continued)*

Utone (MST 475) *Ships of the World,* 1987

◆ **0 (+1 + 5) new-construction deep-sea minesweepers**

| | Bldr | Laid down | L | In serv. |
|---|---|---|---|---|
| . . . N . . . | . . . | . . . | . . . | . . . |

**D:** 1,000 tons **S:** 18 kts **Dim:** . . . × . . . × . . . **A:** . . .
**Electron Equipt:** . . . **M:** diesels; . . . hp **Man:** 70 tot.

REMARKS: First unit now programmed for FY 89 Budget, with one per year thereafter to a total of six. Intended to deploy Type S-7 deep-sea minehunting system and Type S-8 deep-sea moored minesweeping system. Also planned are eight 600-ton minehunters, to be ordered two per year from FY 90.

◆ **0 (+2 + . . .) glass-reinforced plastic minehunters**

| | Bldr | Laid down | L | In serv. |
|---|---|---|---|---|
| 668 N . . . | Nippon Kokan, Tsurumi | 5-87 | 6-88 | 12-88 |
| 669 N . . . | Hitachi, Kanagawa | 5-87 | 5-88 | 12-88 |

**D:** 490 tons **S:** 14 kts **Dim:** . . . × . . . × . . .
**A:** 1/20-mm JM-61-MB gatling AA
**Electron Equipt:** Radar: 1/. . .—Sonar: . . .
**M:** 2 diesels; 2 CP props; 1,440 hp **Man:** . . .

REMARKS: Essentially a GRP-hulled version of the *Hatsushima* class. First two in 1987 Budget.

◆ **19 Hatsushima-class minehunter/minesweepers (MSC)**

| | Bldr | Laid down | L | In serv. |
|---|---|---|---|---|
| 649 HATSUSHIMA | Nippon Kokan, Tsurumi | 6-12-77 | 30-10-78 | 30-3-79 |
| 650 NINOSHIMA | Hitachi, Kanagawa | 8-5-78 | 9-8-79 | 19-12-79 |
| 651 MIYAJIMA | Nippon Kokan, Tsurumi | 8-11-78 | 18-9-79 | 29-1-80 |
| 652 NENOSHIMA | Nippon Kokan, Tsurumi | 4-10-79 | 25-7-80 | 25-12-80 |
| 653 UKISHIMA | Hitachi, Kanagawa | 15-5-79 | 11-7-80 | 27-11-80 |
| 654 OSHIMA | Hitachi, Kanagawa | 2-6-80 | 17-6-81 | 26-11-81 |
| 655 MIIJIMA | Nippon Kokan, Tsurumi | 4-8-80 | 2-6-81 | 26-11-81 |
| 656 YAKUSHIMA | Nippon Kokan, Tsurumi | 15-6-81 | 22-6-82 | 17-12-82 |
| 657 NARUSHIMA | Hitachi, Kanagawa | 29-5-81 | 7-6-82 | 17-12-82 |
| 658 CHICHIJIMA | Hitachi, Kanagawa | 2-6-82 | 13-7-83 | 16-12-83 |
| 659 TOROSHIMA | Nippon Kokan, Tsurumi | 30-6-82 | 23-6-83 | 16-12-83 |
| 660 HAHAJIMA | Nippon Kokan, Tsurumi | 20-5-83 | 27-6-84 | 18-12-84 |
| 661 TAKASHIMA | Hitachi, Kanagawa | 7-6-83 | 18-6-84 | 18-12-84 |
| 662 NEWAJIMA | Hitachi, Kanagawa | 21-5-84 | 5-6-85 | 12-12-85 |
| 663 ETAJIMA | Nippon Kokan, Tsurumi | 22-5-84 | 17-6-85 | 12-12-85 |
| 664 KAMISHIMA | Nippon Kokan, Tsurumi | 10-5-85 | 20-6-86 | 16-12-86 |
| 665 HIMESHIMA | Hitachi, Kanagawa | 16-5-85 | 10-6-86 | 16-12-86 |
| 666 OGOSHIMA | Hitachi, Kanagawa | 16-5-86 | -6-87 | 19-12-87 |
| 667 MOROSHIMA | Nippon Kokan, Tsurumi | 22-5-86 | -6-87 | 19-12-87 |

**D:** 440 tons (approx. 620 fl) **S:** 14 kts **Dim:** 55.0 × 9.4 × 2.4
**A:** 1/20-mm AA (*see* Remarks)
**Electron Equipt:** Radar: OPS-9—Sonar: ZQS-2B
**M:** 2 Mitsubishi YV12ZC-15/20 diesels; 2 CP props; 1,440 hp **Man:** 45 tot.

Himeshima (MSC 665) *Ships of the World,* 1986

Miyajima (MSC 651) L. & L. Van Ginderen, 11-84

REMARKS: Expansion of the *Takami* design. Being equipped with Type-54 mobile minehunting devices, which carry and lay their own disposal charges. MSC 653 and later have a 20-mm Type JM-61-MB gatling gun AA. Wooden construction. MSC 666 and 667 have Mitsubishi 6NMU-TAI diesels. MSC 664 and 665 have Mitsubishi 122C-15/22 diesels.

◆ **12 Takami-class minehunter/minesweepers**

| | Bldr | L | In serv. |
|---|---|---|---|
| 636 TEURI | Nippon Kokan, Tsurumi | 10-71 | 10-3-72 |
| 637 MUROTSU | Hitachi, Kanagawa | 10-71 | 3-3-72 |
| 638 TASHIRO | Nippon Kokan, Tsurumi | 2-4-73 | 30-7-73 |
| 640 TAKANE | Nippon Kokan, Tsurumi | 8-3-74 | 28-8-74 |
| 641 MUZUKI | Hitachi, Kanagawa | 5-4-74 | 28-8-74 |
| 642 YOKOSE | Nippon Kokan, Tsurumi | 21-7-75 | 15-12-75 |
| 643 SAKATE | Hitachi, Kanagawa | 5-8-75 | 17-12-75 |
| 644 OUMI | Nippon Kokan, Tsurumi | 28-5-76 | 18-11-76 |
| 645 FUKUE | Hitachi, Kanagawa | 12-7-76 | 18-11-76 |
| 646 OKITSU | Nippon Kokan, Tsurumi | 4-3-77 | 20-9-77 |
| 647 HASHIRA | Hitachi, Kanagawa | 8-11-77 | 28-3-78 |
| 648 IWAI | Nippon Kokan, Tsurumi | 8-11-77 | 28-3-78 |

Tashiro (MSC 638) JMSDF, 1987

Iwai (MSC 648) *Ships of the World,* 1987

**D:** 380 tons (approx. 530 fl) **S:** 14 kts **Dim:** 52.0 × 8.8 × 2.4
**A:** 1/20-mm AA **Electron Equipt:** Radar: OPS-9—Sonar: ZQS-2
**M:** 2 Mitsubishi YV12ZC-15/20 diesels; 2 CP props; 1,440 hp **Man:** 45–47 tot.

REMARKS: ZQS-2 sonar is a license-built version of the British Type 193-M minehunting sonar. OPS-9 radar, used in conjunction with a Mk 20 plotter, is a Japanese version of the British Type 978. These ships are of wooden construction, and they carry four divers for mine clearance. Sister *Miyato* (MSC 639) stricken 31-3-82. Carry U.S. Mk 4 acoustic noisemaker gear and S2 wire sweep. Six sisters

## MINE WARFARE SHIPS *(continued)*

have been reclassified to other functions: *Takami* (MSC 630) and *Iou* (MSC 631) to YAS 82 and YAS 83 on 27-3-86; *Miyake* (MSC 632) to YAS 84 on 16-12-86; *Utone* (MSC 633) to MST 475 on 16-12-86; and *Awaji* (MSC 634) and *Toushi* (MSC 635) to YAS 85 and YAS 86 on 24-3-87. MSC 637 and MSC 638 will likely reclassify as YAS on the commissioning of MSC 666 and 667.

◆ **6 inshore minesweepers (MSB)** Bldrs: Odd-numbered craft: Hitachi, Kanagawa; even-numbered craft: Nippon Kokan, Tsurumi

| | In serv. | | In serv. | | In serv. |
|---|---|---|---|---|---|
| MSB 707 | 30-3-73 | MSB 709 | 28-3-74 | MSB 711 | 10-5-75 |
| MSB 708 | 27-3-73 | MSB 710 | 29-3-74 | MSB 712 | 24-4-75 |

**MSB 709** *Ships of the World*

**D:** 58 tons (fl) **S:** 10 kts **Dim:** 22.5 × 5.4 × 1.1 **A:** none
**M:** 2 Mitsubishi 4ZV20 diesels; 2 props; 480 hp **Man:** 10 tot.

REMARKS: Wooden construction. Supported by *Utone* (MST 475). No radar.

NOTE: Eight former minesweepers (three *Kasado* class and five *Takami* class) serve as mine-disposal divers' tenders and are designated as yardcraft (YAS-Special Service Craft); see service craft section.

## AMPHIBIOUS WARFARE SHIPS

NOTE: Construction of a 3,500-ton standard displacement LST was projected in the FY 86–90 acquisition plan. Funds had not been requested through FY 87. Originally, *two* of these ships had been sought.

◆ **3 Miura-class landing ships (LST)** Bldr: Ishikawajima Harima, Tokyo

| | Laid down | L | In serv. |
|---|---|---|---|
| 4151 MIURA | 26-11-73 | 13-8-74 | 29-1-75 |
| 4152 OJIKA | 10-6-74 | 2-9-75 | 27-3-76 |
| 4153 SATSUMA | 26-5-75 | 12-5-76 | 17-2-77 |

**Satsuma (LST 4153)**—beached L. & L. Van Ginderen, 2-86

**Satsuma (LST 4153)**—note 2 LCM and launching gantry *Ships of the World,* 1987

**D:** 2,000 tons (3,200 fl) **S:** 14 kts **Dim:** 98.0 (94.0 pp) × 14.0 × 3.0
**A:** 2/76.2-mm 50-cal. Mk 33 DP (II × 1)—2/40-mm AA (II × 1)
**Electron Equipt:** Radars: 1/OPS-14, 1/OPS-16, 1/GFCS-1 **Man:** 118 tot.
**M:** 2 Kawasaki-M.A.N. V8V 22/30 AMTL diesels; 2 props; 4,400 hp

REMARKS: Carry 180 troops, 1,800 tons cargo, LST 4153 has carried prototype OTO Melara Compact gun at bow. All have two LCVP in davits and two LCM(6) on deck, the latter served by a traveling gantry with folding rails that can be extended over the sides. GFCS-1 fwd controls 76.2-mm guns; U.S. Mk 51 Mod. 2 GFCS aft controls 40-mm mount. Tank deck can hold 10 Type 74 battle tanks.

◆ **3 Atsumi class (LSTs)** Bldr: Sasebo Heavy Industries

| | Laid down | L | In serv. |
|---|---|---|---|
| 4101 ATSUMI | 7-12-71 | 13-6-72 | 27-11-72 |
| 4102 MOTOBU | 23-4-73 | 3-8-73 | 21-12-73 |
| 4103 NEMURO | 18-11-76 | 16-6-77 | 27-10-77 |

**Atsumi (LST 4101)** JMSDF, 1986

**D:** 1,480 tons (2,400 fl) **S:** 14 kts **Dim:** 89.0 × 13.0 × 2.7
**A:** 4/40-mm AA (II × 2) **Electron Equipt:** Radar: 1/OPS-9
**M:** 2 Kawasaki-M.A.N. V8V 22/30 AMTL diesels; 2 props; 4,400 hp
**Range:** 4,300/12 **Man:** 100 tot.

REMARKS: Can carry 120 men and 20 vehicles or 400 tons cargo. LST 4102 and 4103 are 1,550 tons standard and have a max. speed of 13 kts. Have 2 U.S. Mk 51 Mod. 2 GFCS, two LCVP in davits, and can carry one LCVP on deck, amidships. 4103 has an electric crane forward of the bridge; the other two have a simple king post and boom.

◆ **2 Yura-class utility landing ships (LSU)** Bldr: Sasebo Heavy Industries

| | Laid down | L | In serv. |
|---|---|---|---|
| 4171 YURA | 23-4-80 | 10-8-80 | 27-3-81 |
| 4172 NOTO | 23-4-80 | 1-11-80 | 27-3-81 |

**Yura (LSU 4171)**—gatling AA gun atop pilothouse L. & L. Van Ginderen, 8-84

**D:** 500 tons (590 fl) **S:** 12 kts **Dim:** 58.0 × 9.5 × 1.7 (aft)
**A:** 1/20-mm JM 61-MB gatling AA
**M:** 2 Fuji 6L 27.5X diesels; 2 CP props; 3,000 hp **Man:** 32 tot.

REMARKS: Both in 1979–80 Budget; request for a third in 1981 Budget denied. Bow doors and ramp.

◆ **0 (+1 + 2) 420-ton utility landing craft (LCU)**

| | Bldr | Laid down | L | In serv. |
|---|---|---|---|---|
| . . . N . . . | Sasebo DY | 5-87 | 10-87 | 3-88 |

**D:** 420 tons **S:** 12 kts **Dim:** 50.2 × 9.0 × . . . (3.9 moulded depth)
**A:** 1/20-mm JM-61-MB gatling gun **Electron Equipt:** Radar: 1/. . .
**M:** 2 diesels; 2 props; 3,000 hp **Man:** 32 tot.

REMARKS: First unit approved under FY 86 Budget. Two more projected under FY 86–90 Budgets. First unit ordered 24-3-87.

AMPHIBIOUS WARFARE SHIPS *(continued)*

◆ **15 U.S. LCM(6)-class landing craft**

**D:** 24 tons (56 fl) **S:** 10 kts **Dim:** 17.07 × 4.37 × 1.17 (aft)
**M:** 2 Yanmar diesels; 2 props; 450 hp

REMARKS: Total includes 6 units carried aboard the *Miura*-class LSTs. Built in Japan.

◆ **22 U.S. LCVP-class landing craft**

**D:** 13 tons (fl) **S:** 8 kts **Dim:** 10.90 × 3.21 × 1.04 (aft)
**M:** 1 Yanmar diesel; 1 prop; 180 hp

REMARKS: Japanese-built, most with GRP hulls. Total includes the 12-15 carried by the 6 LSTs.

### HYDROGRAPHIC SHIPS

◆ **2 Futami class (AGS)**

| | Bldr | Laid down | L | In serv. |
|---|---|---|---|---|
| 5102 FUTAMI | Mitsubishi, Shimonoseki | 20-1-78 | 9-8-78 | 27-2-79 |
| 5104 WAKASA | Hitachi, Maizuru | 21-8-84 | 25-5-85 | 25-2-86 |

**Futami (AGS 5102)**—low stack L. & L. Van Ginderen, 6-84

**Wakasa (AGS 5104)**—tall stack *Ships of the World,* 1986

**D:** 2,050 tons (3,175 fl) **S:** 16 kts **Dim:** 96.80 (90.00 pp) × 15.00 × 4.50
**A:** none **Electron Equipt:** Radar: 1/OPS-18
**M:** 5102: 2 Kawasaki-M.A.N. V8V 22/30 ATL diesels; 2 CP props; 4,400 hp
5104: 2 Fuji 6LS 27-5XF diesels; 2 CP props; 4,580 hp
**Fuel:** 556 tons **Electric:** 1,800 kw **Man:** 105 tot.

REMARKS: Configured for both hydrographic surveying and cable-laying. Bow-thruster. Have three diesel and one gas-turbine generator sets. Carry one RCV-225 remote-controlled unmanned submersible. AGS 5104, ordered 29-3-84 under FY 83 Budget, has a taller stack and differs somewhat in equipage.

◆ **1 Suma class (AGS)** Bldr: Hitachi Heavy Ind., Maizuru

| | Laid down | L | In serv. |
|---|---|---|---|
| 5103 SUMA | 24-9-80 | 1-9-81 | 30-3-82 |

**Suma (AGS 5103)** L. & L. Van Ginderen, 1986

**D:** 1,180 tons **S:** 15 kts **Dim:** 72.0 × 12.8 × 3.4
**A:** none **M:** 2 Fuji 6 LS 27.5X diesels; 2 CP props; 3,000 hp **Man:** 65

REMARKS: Built under 1979–80 Budget to begin replacement of the *Kusado*-class former minesweepers used as coastal survey ships. Carries one 7.9-m boat and one 11-m inshore survey launch. Passive tank stabilization, bow-thruster fitted. Operated by the "Ocean Management Group."

◆ **1 Akashi class (AGS)**

| | Bldr | Laid down | L | In serv. |
|---|---|---|---|---|
| 5101 AKASHI | Nippon Kokan, Tsurumi | 21-9-68 | 30-5-69 | 25-10-69 |

**Akashi (AGS 5101)** *Ships of the World,* 1984

**D:** 1,420 tons **S:** 16 kts **Dim:** 74.0 × 12.9 × 4.3
**A:** none **Electron Equipt:** Radar: OPS-9—EW: NOLR-5
**M:** 2 Kawasaki-M.A.N. V8V 22/30 ATL diesels; 2 CP props; 3,800 hp
**Range:** 16,500/14 **Man:** 70 crew, 10 scientists

REMARKS: Bow-thruster. Two cranes; one 5-ton and one 1-ton. Has extensive electronics intercept arrays, new radar.

NOTE: The last *Kasado*-class survey ship, ex-minesweeper AGS 5 (5115, ex-*Hario,* MSC 618) was stricken 27-3-86.

### EXPERIMENTAL SHIP

◆ **1 Kurihama class (AGE)**

| | Bldr | Laid down | L | In serv. |
|---|---|---|---|---|
| 6101 KURIHAMA | Sasebo Heavy Industries | 23-3-79 | 20-9-79 | 8-4-80 |

**Kurihama (AGE 6101)** *Ships of the World*

**D:** 959 tons **S:** 15 kts **Dim:** 68.0 × 11.6 × 3.3
**A:** various **Electron Equipt:** Radar: 1/OPS-9B
**M:** 2 Fuji 6S 30B diesels; 2 CP props; 2,600 hp (plus 2 electric auxiliary propulsors; 400 hp)
**Man:** 42 crew + 13 technicians

REMARKS: For testing mines, torpedoes, and sonars. In 1979 Budget. Has Flume-type passive stabilization tanks and gas-turbine generators in superstructure. Retractable bow-thruster. Can be rigged for silent operation. Has extra accommodations for trials personnel.

### CABLE-LAYER

◆ **1 Muroto class (ARC)**

| | Bldr | Laid down | L | In serv. |
|---|---|---|---|---|
| 482 MUROTO | Mitsubishi, Shimonoseki | 28-11-78 | 25-7-79 | 27-3-80 |

**CABLE-LAYER** *(continued)*

**Muroto (AGS 482)** JMSDF, 1980

**D:** 4,544 tons **S:** 17 kts **Dim:** 131.0 × 17.4 × 5.7
**A:** none **Electron Equipt:** Radar: 1/OPS-9
**M:** 2 Mitsubishi MTU V8V 22/30 diesels; 2 CP props; 4,400 hp **Man:** 122 tot.

Remarks: Intended to replace *Tsugaru* as naval cable layer. Able to lay cable over bow or stern at 2–6 knots. Bow-thruster. Similar to commercial *Kuroshio Maru.* Has extensive facilities for oceanographic research.

Note: The former cable-layer *Tsugaru* (ARC 481) was redesignated ASU 7001 in 1979 and is listed with the special use auxiliaries.

**SUBMARINE RESCUE SHIPS**

◆ **1 Chiyoda class (ASR)**

| | Bldr | Laid down | L | In serv. |
|---|---|---|---|---|
| 405 Chiyoda | Mitsui, Tamano | 19-1-83 | 7-12-83 | 27-3-85 |

**Chiyoda (ASR 405)** *Ships of the World,* 1985

**D:** 3,690 tons (4,450 fl) **S:** 17 kts (16 sust.)
**Dim:** 112.5 (106.0 pp) × 17.6 (18.0 max.) × 4.8
**A:** none **Electron Equipt:** Radar: 1/OPS-16
**M:** 2 Mitsui 8LV42M diesels; 2 CP props; 11,500 hp **Man:** 120 tot.

Remarks: In 1981 Budget as a replacement for *Chihaya.* Carries a deep-submergence rescue vehicle (DSRV) launched 15-10-84 by Kawasaki, Kobe:

**D:** 40 tons **S:** 4 kts **Dim:** 12.4 × 3.2 × 4.3 (high)
**M:** electric motors; 40 hp **Man:** 12 passengers

The DSRV is deployed over the sides, using hoist equipment similar to that of the U.S. Navy's *Pigeon* (ASR 21) class. There is also a deep-diving rescue bell. The helicopter platform can accommodate an HSS-2 Sea King. Has bow and stern thrusters.

◆ **1 Fushimi class (ASR)**

| | Bldr | Laid down | L | In serv. |
|---|---|---|---|---|
| 402 Fushimi | Sumitomo, Uraga | 5-11-68 | 10-9-69 | 10-2-70 |

**Fushimi (ASR 402)** *Ships of the World,* 1984

**D:** 1,430 tons **S:** 16 kts **Dim:** 76.0 × 12.5 × 3.8
**Electron Equipt:** Radar: OPS-9—Sonar: SQS-11A
**M:** 1 Kawasaki-M.A.N. V6V 22/30 ATL diesel; 1 prop; 3,000 hp **Man:** 102 tot.

Remarks: Has one rescue bell, two decompression chambers; one 12-ton crane. Employed as support ship for the First Submarine Flotilla.

Note: Submarine rescue ship *Chihaya* (ASR 401) was redesignated ASU 7011 on 27-3-85 on completion of *Chiyoda* (ASR 405).

**REPLENISHMENT OILERS (AOE/AO)**

◆ **1 (+2) new construction**

| | Bldr | Laid down | L | In serv. |
|---|---|---|---|---|
| 422 Towada | Hitachi, Maizuru | 17-4-85 | 25-3-86 | 24-3-87 |
| 423 N . . . . . . . | . . . | | | |

**Towada (AOE 422)** *Ships of the World,* 3-87

**Towada (AOE 422)** *Ships of the World,* 3-87

**D:** 8,300 tons (15,850 fl) **S:** 22 kts
**Dim:** 167.00 (160.00 pp) × 22.0 × 8.40 (15.90 moulded depth)
**A:** none **Electron Equipt:** Radar: 1/OPS-18-1
**M:** 2 Mitsui 16V42M-A diesels; 2 props; 26,400 hp
**Range:** 10,500/20 **Fuel:** 1,659 tons
**Electric:** 3,200 kw (4 × 800 kw diesel sets) **Man:** 140 tot.

Remarks: AOE 422 authorized under FY 84 Budget, to replace *Hamana* (AO 411). AOE 423 and 424 authorized under FY 87. Are all-purpose liquid, solid stores, and ammunition ships, with two liquid and one solid transfer stations per side. Helicopter deck aft for vertical replenishment. No provision for armament.

◆ **1 Sagami class (AOE)**

| | Bldr | Laid down | L | In serv. |
|---|---|---|---|---|
| 421 Sagami | Hitachi, Maizuru | 28-9-77 | 4-9-78 | 30-3-79 |

**D:** 5,000 tons (11,600 fl) **S:** 22 kts **Dim:** 146.0 (140.0 pp) × 19.0 × 7.3
**A:** none **Electron Equipt:** Radar: 1/OPS-16
**M:** 2 Type 12 DRV diesels; 2 props; 18,600 hp **Range:** 9,500/20
**Man:** 130 tot.

Remarks: Has three stations per side, two for liquid transfers, one for solid. Large helicopter deck but no hangar. In addition to fuel oil, diesel fuel, and JP-5 aviation fuel, carries food and ammunition. 1975 Budget.

Note: The oiler *Hamana* (AO 411) was stricken 24-3-87.

**REPLENISHMENT OILERS (AOE/AO)** *(continued)*

**Sagami (AOE 421)** JMSDF, 1984

### TRAINING SHIPS (TV)

Late Note: Former destroyer *Teruzuki* (ASU 7012) and frigate *Mogami* (DE 212) redesignated TV 3504 and TV 3505 in 1987. See pages 337 and 344 for descriptions.

◆ **1 Katori-class cadet-training ship (TV)**

| | Bldr | Laid down | L | In serv. |
|---|---|---|---|---|
| 3501 Katori | Ishikawajima Harima, Tokyo | 8-12-67 | 19-11-68 | 10-9-69 |

**Katori (TV 3501)** L. & L. Van Ginderen, 8-87

**D:** 3,372 tons (4,100 fl) **S:** 25 kts **Dim:** 127.5 (122.0 pp) × 15.0 × 4.35
**A:** 4/76.2-mm DP Mk 23 (II × 2)—1/375-mm Bofors ASW RL (IV × 1)—6/324-mm Mk 32 ASW TT (III × 2)
**Electron Equipt:** Radar: 1/OPS-2, 1/OPS-15, 1/Mk 34
Sonar: OQS-3—EW: NOLR-1B
**M:** 2 sets Ishikawajima GT; 2 props; 20,000 hp **Boilers:** 2
**Range:** 7,000/18 **Man:** 295 crew + 165 cadets

Remarks: U.S. Mk 63 GFCS system for 76.2-mm guns. After superstructure contains an auditorium. Helicopter deck is also used for ceremonial functions and calisthenics. An Intelset satellite communication system was added in mid-1979.

◆ **2 Ayanami-class former destroyers (TV)**

| | Bldr | Laid down | L | In serv. |
|---|---|---|---|---|
| 3502 Isonami (ex-DD 104) | Mitsubishi, Kobe | 14-12-56 | 30-9-57 | 14-3-58 |
| 3503 Shikinami (ex-DD 106) | Mitsui, Tamano | 24-12-56 | 25-9-57 | 15-3-58 |

**Shikinami (TV 3503)** *Ships of the World*, 3-86

**D:** 1,700 tons (2,400 fl) **S:** 32 kts **Dim:** 109.0 × 10.7 × 3.7 (mean)
**A:** 6/76.2-mm 50-cal. U.S. Mk 33 DP (II × 3)—2/Mk 15 trainable Hedgehog ASW mortar—6/324-mm Type 68 ASW TT (III × 2)—3503 only: 2/depth-charge racks
**Electron Equipt:** Radar: 1/OPS-15, 1/OPS-2, 2/Mk 34
Sonar: OQS-12 or 14—EW: BLR-1
**M:** 2 sets Mitsubishi-Escher-Wyss GT; 2 props; 3,500 hp
**Boilers:** 2 Mitsubishi (TV 3503: Hitachi-Babcock & Wilcox); 43 kg/cm$^2$, 454°C
**Range:** 6,000/18 **Man:** 175 crew + 50 cadets

Remarks: Reclassified as training ships on 30-3-83, a duty they had performed as destroyers since 13-6-75, when their quadruple 533-mm antiship torpedo-tube mount was replaced by a classroom deckhouse and they were designated the First Training Unit. Variable-depth sonar removed from TV 3502 in 1983. There are two U.S. Mk 63 GFCS for the three gun mounts, the Mk 34 radars being mounted on two of the gun mounts. OPS-2 is the Japanese designation for the U.S. SPS-6 air-search radar. *Late note:* Stricken 1987, replaced by *Teruzuki* (TV 3504) and *Mogami* (TV 3505).

◆ **1 new-construction target service ship**

| | Bldr: | Laid down | L | In serv. |
|---|---|---|---|---|
| 4202 N . . . | Nippon Kokan, Tsurumi | 31-7-87 | 5-88 | 30-3-89 |

**D:** 2,200 tons (approx. 3,200 fl) **S:** 20 kts **Dim:** 100.0 × 16.5 × 3.5
**A:** 1/76-mm OTO Melara Compact DP—. . .
**Electron Equipt:** Radar: . . .
Sonar: . . .
**M:** 4 . . . diesels; 2 props, 9,200 hp
**Range:** . . . **Man:** 147 tot.

Remarks: Approved under FY 1986 Budget as a replacement for *Azuma* (ATS 4201).

◆ **1 Azuma-class target service ship (ATS)**

| | Bldr | Laid down | L | In serv. |
|---|---|---|---|---|
| 4201 Azuma | Hitachi, Maizuru | 15-7-68 | 14-4-69 | 26-11-69 |

**Azuma (ATS 4201)** *Ships of the World*, 1983

**D:** 1,950 tons (2,400 fl) **S:** 18 kts **Dim:** 98.0 (94.0 pp) × 13.0 × 3.8
**A:** 1/76.2-mm Mk 34 DP—2/Mk 4 torpedo launchers (U.S. Mk 32 torpedoes)
**Electron Equipt:** Radar: 1/OPS-15, 1/SPS-40, 1/TCATS
Sonar: SQS-11A
**M:** 2 Kawasaki-M.A.N. V8V 23/30 ATL diesels; 2 props; 4,000 hp
**Electric:** 700 kw
**Man:** 185 tot.

Remarks: Has ten KD2R-5 and four BQM-34-AJ drones. Portable catapult on helicopter deck for launching. Hangar is used for drone check-out and storage. Has the only SPS-40 radar in Japanese service. TCATS (Target Control and Tracking System) radar in large radome atop bridge replaced earlier radar, 1983. Mk 51 Mod. 2 director for gun (no radar).

### SPECIAL USE AUXILIARIES (ASU)

◆ **5 target-support craft (ASU)** Bldr: ASU 81–83: Sasebo Heavy Industries; Others: . . .

| | Laid down | L | In serv. |
|---|---|---|---|
| ASU 81 (ex-YAS 101) | 10-10-67 | 18-1-68 | 30-3-68 |
| ASU 82 (ex-YAS 102) | 25-9-68 | 20-12-68 | 31-3-69 |
| ASU 83 (ex-YAS 103) | 2-4-71 | 24-5-71 | 30-9-71 |
| ASU 84 (ex-YAS 104) | 4-2-72 | 15-6-73 | 19-9-73 |
| ASU 85 (ex-YAS 105) | 20-2-73 | 16-7-73 | 19-9-73 |

**ASU 83** *Ships of the World*, 1984

**SPECIAL USE AUXILIARIES (ASU)** *(continued)*

**D:** 490 tons (543 fl) **S:** 14.5 kts **Dim:** 51.5 × 10.0 × 2.6
**Electron Equipt:** Radar: OPS-10 (ASU 84: OPS-29; ASU 85: OPS-19)
**M:** 2 Akasaka UH-527-42 diesels; 2 props; 1,600 hp
**Range:** 2,500/12 **Man:** 26 men + 14 passengers

REMARKS: ASU 82 is configured as a rescue ship. The others are intended to carry, control, recover, and service up to six KD2R-5 drone target aircraft. ASU 81: 480 tons std.; ASU 85: 500 tons std. Crane and mast configurations aft differ; early units have pole and derrick, later ones have a crane, with a tripod mast stepped on the stack.

◆ **1 former submarine rescue ship (ASU)**

| | Bldr | Laid down | L | In serv. |
|---|---|---|---|---|
| 7011 CHIHAYA (ex-ASR 401) | Mitsubishi, Yokohama | 15-3-60 | 4-10-60 | 15-3-61 |

**Chihaya (ASU 7011)** *Ships of the World,* 1986

**D:** 1,340 tons (1,800 fl) **S:** 15 kts **Dim:** 73.0 × 12.0 × 3.9
**Electron Equipt:** Radar: OPS-4—Sonar: SQS-11A
**M:** 1 Yokohama-M.A.N. G6Z S170 diesel; 1 prop; 2,700 hp
**Range:** 5,000/12 **Man:** 90 tot.

REMARKS: Reclassified as a utility service ship on 27-3-85 after being replaced on submarine rescue duties by the new *Chiyoda* (ASR 405). Has a McCann rescue bell for six persons, 12-ton crane, four flotation pontoons, and a 4-point mooring system.

◆ **2 Akizuku-class former destroyers (ASU and TV)**

| | Bldr | Laid down | L | In serv. |
|---|---|---|---|---|
| ASU 7010 AKIZUKI (ex-DD 161) | Mitsubishi, Nagasaki | 31-7-58 | 26-6-59 | 13-2-60 |
| TV 3504 TERUZUKI (ex-ASU 7010, ex-DD 162) | Shin-Mitsubishi, Kobe | 15-8-58 | 24-6-59 | 29-2-60 |

**Akizuki (ASU 7010)** *Ships of the World,* 1986

**Teruzuki (ASU 7012)—now TV 3504** *Ships of the World,* 1986

**D:** 2,300 tons (3,100 fl) **S:** 32 kts **Dim:** 118.0 (115.0 pp) × 12.0 × 4.02
**A:** 3/127-mm 54-cal. DP Mk 39 (I × 3)—4/76.2-mm 50-cal. DP Mk 33 (II × 2)—1/375-mm Bofors ASW RL (IV × 1)—2/Mk 15 trainable Hedgehog ASW RL—6/324-mm Type 68 ASW TT (III × 2)
**Electron Equipt:** Radar: 1/OPS-1, 1/OPS-15, 3/Mk 34
Sonar: SQS-23—EW: NOLR-1
**M:** DD 161: 2 sets Mitsubishi-Escher-Wyss GT; DD 162: 2 sets Westinghouse GT; 2 props; 45,000 hp
**Boilers:** 4; 43 kg/cm$^2$, 454°C **Man:** 170 tot.

REMARKS: Weapons and ASW sensors modernized in 1976–77, the Bofors ASW RL replacing a U.S. Mk 108 "Weapon Alfa," VDS being added, and SQS-23 replacing SQS-29. The 127-mm guns were removed from U.S. *Midway*-class carriers. Two U.S. Mk 57 and one Mk 63 gunfire-control systems are carried. *Akizuki* (DD 161) served as Fleet Flagship until 27-3-85 when reclassified as an auxiliary (ASU). *Teruzuki* reclassified as ASU on 27-3-86. Variable-depth sonar and 4/533-mm TT (IV × 1) removed from both on reclassification. *Teruzuki* again reclassified, as a training ship, in 1987.

◆ **2 Murasame-class former destroyers (ASU)**

| | Bldr | Laid down | L | In serv. |
|---|---|---|---|---|
| 7006 MURASAME (ex-DD 107) | Mitsubishi, Nagasaki | 17-12-57 | 31-7-58 | 28-2-59 |
| 7008 HARUSAME (ex-DD 109) | Uraga DY,Yokosuka | 17-6-58 | 18-6-59 | 15-12-59 |

**Harusame (ASU 7008)** L. & L. Van Ginderen, 1986

**D:** 1,800 tons (2,400 fl) **S:** 30 kts **Dim:** 109.73 × 10.97 × 3.7 (mean)
**A:** 3/127-mm 54-cal. U.S. Mk 39 DP (II × 3)—4/76.2-mm 50-cal. U.S. Mk 33 DP (II × 2)—1/Mk 15 trainable Hedgehog ASW mortar (XXXIV × 1)—ASU 7008 only: 6/324-mm Type 68 ASW TT (III × 2)—ASU 7006: 1/Y-gun d.c. mortar (II × 1)—1/d.c. rack
**Electron Equipt:** Radar: 1/OPS-15, 1/OPS-1, 1/Mk 34, 2/Mk 35
Sonar: SQS-29—EW: NORL-1B
**M:** 2 sets Kampon (ASU 7008: Mitsubishi-Escher-Wyss) GT; 2 props; 35,000 hp
**Boilers:** 2 Foster-Wheeler-D (ASU 7008: Mitsubishi); 43 kg/cm$^2$, 454°C
**Range:** 6,000/18 **Man:** 170 tot.

REMARKS: ASU 7006 reclassified 30-3-84 from destroyer, ASU 7008 on 5-3-85. ASU 7008 serves as support ship for the First Submarine Flotilla. Hull and machinery spaces similar to those of the *Ayanami* class. Have two U.S. Mk 57 and one U.S. Mk 63 GFCS to control the five gun mounts, U.S. Mk 105 underwater battery fire-control system. OPS-1 is a Japanese equivalent to one variant of the U.S. SPS-6 air-search radar. Sister *Yudachi* (ASU 7007, ex-DD 108), reclassified ASU on 30-3-84 and stricken 24-3-87.

◆ **3 Ayanami-class former destroyers (ASU)**

| | Bldr | Laid down | L | In serv. |
|---|---|---|---|---|
| 7009 TAKANAMI (ex-DD 110) | Mitsui, Maizuru | 8-11-58 | 8-8-59 | 30-1-60 |
| 7013 ONAMI (ex-DD 111) | Ishikawajima, Tokyo | 20-3-59 | 13-2-60 | 29-8-60 |
| 7014 MAKINAMI (ex-DD 112) | Iino, Maizuru | 20-3-59 | 25-4-60 | 30-10-60 |

**Takanami (ASU 7009)** *Ships of the World,* 1985

## SPECIAL USE AUXILIARIES (ASU) *(continued)*

**D:** 1,700 tons (2,400 fl) **S:** 32 kts **Dim:** 109.0 × 10.7 × 3.7 (mean)
**A:** 6/76.2-mm Mk 33 DP (II × 3)—2/Mk 15 trainable Hedgehog—6/324-mm Type 68 ASW TT (III × 2)—ASU 7013, 7014: 2/d.c. racks
**Electron Equipt:** Radar: 1/OPS-15, 1/OPS-2, 2/Mk 34
Sonar: OQS-12 or 14—EW: NORL-1B
**M:** 2 sets Mitsubishi-Escher-Wyss GT; 2 props; 35,000 hp
**Boilers:** 2 Mitsubishi (ASU 7009: Hitachi-Babcock & Wilcox); 43 kg/cm$^2$, 454°C
**Range:** 6,000/18 **Man:** 170 tot.

REMARKS: ASU 7009, reclassified as utility service ship on 27-3-85, when the quadruple 533-mm TT were removed. ASU 7013 and 7014 reclassified from DD on 20-2-87 and similarly modified. There are two U.S. Mk 63 GFCS for the three gun mounts. OPS-2 is the Japanese designation for the U.S. SPS-6 radar. Sisters *Ayanami* (ASU 7004, ex-DD 103) and *Uranami* (ASU 7005, ex-DD 105) reclassified as auxiliaries on 30-3-83 and were stricken 25-12-86.

**◆ 1 Tsugaru class (ASU, ex-ARC)**

| | Bldr | Laid down | L | In serv. |
|---|---|---|---|---|
| 7001 TSUGARU (ex-ARC 481) | Yokohama SY | 18-12-54 | 19-7-55 | 15-12-55 |

**Tsugaru (ASU 7001)** L. & L. Van Ginderen, 8-85

**D:** 2,150 tons **S:** 13 kts **Dim:** 103.0 × 14.6 × 4.9
**A:** 2/20-mm AA (I × 2) **Electron Equipt:** Radar: 1/OPS-16
**M:** 2 Sulzer diesels; 2 props; 3,200 hp **Man:** 103 tot.

REMARKS: Originally completed as a minelayer/cable-layer; between 10-7-69 and 30-4-70 she was lengthened and the amidships part of her hull widened by 2.2 meters at Nippon Kokan, Tsurumi. Also, her cable facilities were greatly enlarged. Redesignated ASU (Auxiliary, Special Use) in 1979.

**◆ 2 Mizutori-class former patrol boat (ASU and ASY)**

| | Bldr | Laid down | L | In serv. |
|---|---|---|---|---|
| ASU 66 SHIRATORI (ex-PC 319) | Sasebo DY | 29-2-64 | 8-10-64 | 26-2-65 |
| ASY 92 HIYODORI (ex-PC 320) | Sasebo DY | 26-2-65 | 26-9-65 | 28-2-66 |

**Shiratori (ASU 66)** *Ships of the World,* 3-86

**D:** 420 tons (450 fl) **S:** 20 kts **Dim:** 60.00 × 7.10 × 2.35
**A:** 2/40-mm AA (II × 1)—1/Mk 10 Hedgehog ASW mortar (XXIV × 1)—6/324-mm ASW TT (III × 2)—1/d.c. rack (ASY 92: none)
**Electron Equipt:** Radar: 1/OPS-36, 1/Mk 34
Sonar: SQS-11A—EW: BLR-1
**M:** 2 Kawasaki-M.A.N. V8V diesels; 2 props; 3,800 hp **Fuel:** 24 tons
**Range:** 3,000/12 **Man:** 80 tot.

REMARKS: ASY 92 reclassified for training duties 19-3-86; redesignated 27-4-87 after conversion as yacht, now resembling the stricken *Hayabusa* (ASY 91). The unit of the class remaining designated PC may be retyped later as well. Mk 63 GFCS for 40-mm AA. Sisters *Kasasagi* (ASU 87, ex-PC 314), *Mizutori* (ASU 88, ex-PC 311), and *Yamadori* (ASU 90, ex-PC 312) stricken 3-85; *Otori* (ASU 61, ex-PC 313) and *Hatsukari* (ASU 62, ex-PC 315) stricken 31-10-86; and *Umidori* (ASU 63, ex-PC 316) stricken 24-3-87.

**◆ 2 Umitaka-class former patrol boats (ASU)**

| | Bldr | Laid down | L | In serv. |
|---|---|---|---|---|
| ASU 64 WAKATAKA (ex-PC 317) | Kure SY | 5-3-62 | 13-11-62 | 30-3-63 |
| ASU 65 KUMATAKA (ex-PC 318) | Fujinagata, Osaka | 20-3-63 | 21-10-63 | 25-3-64 |

**Wakataka (ASU 64)** *Ships of the World,* 3-86

**D:** 490 tons (530 fl) **S:** 20 kts **Dim:** 60.0 × 7.1 × 2.4 (hull)
**A:** 2/40-mm AA (II × 1)—6/324-mm Type 68 ASW TT (III × 2)—1/Mk 10 Hedgehog—1/d.c. rack
**Electron Equipt:** Radar: ASU 64: 1/OPS-36; ASU 65: 1/OPS-16; both: 1/Mk 34
EW: BLR-1
Sonar: SQS-11A
**M:** 2 Mitsui-Burmeister & Wain V8V diesels; 2 props; 4,000 hp
**Fuel:** 24 tons **Range:** 3,000/12 **Man:** 80 tot.

REMARKS: Reclassified 27-3-85. Mk 63 GFCS for 40-mm AA. Sister *Umitaka* (ASU 86, ex-PC 309) was stricken 20-2-85 and sister *Ootaka* (ASU 88, ex-PC 310) on 3-85.

## ICEBREAKER (AGB)

**◆ 1 Shirase class (AGB)**

| | Bldr | Laid down | L | In serv. |
|---|---|---|---|---|
| 5002 SHIRASE | Nippon Kokan, Tsurumi | 5-3-81 | 11-12-81 | 12-12-83 |

**Shirase (AGB 5002)** L. & L. Van Ginderen, 4-85

**D:** 11,660 tons (18,900 fl) **S:** 19 kts **Dim:** 134.0 × 28.0 × 9.2
**M:** 6 M.A.N.-Mitsui 12V42M diesels, electric drive; 3 props; 30,000 hp
**Electron Equipt:** Radar: OPS-18, OPS-22—TACAN: URN-25
**Range:** 25,000/15 **Man:** 37 officers, 137 men, plus 60 passengers

REMARKS: Built under 1979–80 budget to replace *Fuji* (AGB 5001). Cargo capacity: 1,000 tons. Hangar and flight deck for 2 S-61A and 1 OH-6 helicopters.
The icebreaker *Fuji* (AGB 5001), inactive since her final deployment in 1982–83, was stricken 11-4-84.

NOTE: The yacht *Hayabusa* (ASY 91, ex-PC 308) was stricken 28-2-87.

## SERVICE SHIPS AND CRAFT

NOTE: All Japanese Navy service ships and craft are listed below in the alphabetical order of the two- or three-letter designator system employed to define their functions. Self-propelled units have 2-digit hull numbers following the letter designator (as in "YO 01"). Non-self-propelled craft with the same functions have 3-digit numbers starting with "1" (as in "YO 102"). Self-propelled units that have returned to an original type designation *after* an initial type change receive 3-digit numbers beginning with "2" (as in "YG 202," ex-YO 20, ex-YG 08).

## MINE TRIALS AND SERVICE CRAFT (YAL)

**◆ 1 YAL 01 class**

YAL 01 (In serv. 22-3-76)

**D:** 240 tons (265 fl) **S:** 12 kts **Dim:** 37.00 × 8.00 × 1.90
**A:** mine rails **M:** 2 Type 64 H 19-E-4A diesels; 2 props; 800 hp **Man:** 16 tot.

**◆ 3 former U.S. LCU 1466-class landing craft**

YAL 02 (L: 23-1-55) YAL 03 (L: 5-1-55) YAL 04 (L: 13-12-54)

**D:** 180 tons (347 fl) **S:** 9 kts **Dim:** 35.08 × 10.36 × 1.60 (aft)
**A:** 2/20-mm AA (I × 2)—mines
**M:** 3 Gray Marine 64YTL diesels; 3 props; 675 hp
**Fuel:** 11 tons **Range:** 1,200/6 **Man:** . . .

## MINE TRIALS AND SERVICE CRAFT (YAL) *(continued)*

**YAL 03** *Ships of the World,* 1984

REMARKS: Three of the six-unit LCU 2001 class (ex-U.S. LCU 1602–1607), built in Japan under the Offshore Procurement Program, reconfigured to serve as exercise mine planters.

## SPECIAL SERVICE CRAFT (YAS)

◆ **5 Takami-class former minesweeper/minehunters**

| | Bldr | L | In serv. |
|---|---|---|---|
| YAS 82 Takami (ex-MSC 630) | Nippon Kokan, Tsurumi | 15-7-69 | 15-12-69 |
| YAS 83 Iou (ex-MSC 631) | Hitachi, Kanagawa | 12-8-69 | 22-1-70 |
| YAS 84 Miyake (ex-MSC 632) | Nippon Kokan, Tsurumi | 3-6-70 | 19-11-70 |
| YAS 85 Awaji (ex-MSC 634) | Nippon Kokan, Tsurumi | 11-12-70 | 29-3-71 |
| YAS 86 Toushi (ex-MSC 635) | Hitachi, Kanagawa | 13-12-70 | 18-3-71 |

**Miyake (YAS 84)**—prior to reclassification L. & L. Van Ginderen, 1985

**D:** 380 tons (510 fl) **S:** 14 kts **Dim:** 52.0 × 8.8 × 2.4 (mean)
**A:** 1/20-mm AA **Electron Equipt:** Radar: OPS-9—Sonar: ZQS-2
**M:** 2 Mitsubishi: YV122C-15/20 diesels; 2 CP props; 1,440 hp
**Range:** . . . **Man:** . . .

REMARKS: Reclassified and now used as mine-disposal divers' tenders. Wooden construction. Reclassified YAS 82 and YAS 83 on 27-3-86, YAS 84 on 16-12-86, and YAS 85 and YAS 86 on 24-3-87. Twelve sisters remain as minesweeper/hunters, and one, *Utone* (MST 475, ex-MSC 633) acts as inshore minesweeper tender.

◆ **5 Kasado-class former coastal minesweepers**

| | Bldr | L | In serv. |
|---|---|---|---|
| YAS 77 Amami (ex-MSC 625) | Nippon Kokan, Tsurumi | 13-10-66 | 6-3-67 |
| YAS 78 Urume (ex-MSC 626) | Hitachi, Kanagawa | 12-11-66 | 30-1-67 |
| YAS 79 Minase (ex-MSC 627) | Nippon Kokan, Tsurumi | 10-1-67 | 25-3-67 |
| YAS 80 Ibuki (ex-MSC 628) | Hitachi, Kanagawa | 2-12-67 | 27-2-68 |
| YAS 81 Katsura (ex-MSC 629) | Nippon Kokan, Tsurumi | 18-9-67 | 15-2-68 |

**Amami (YAS 77)** *Ships of the World,* 1984

**D:** 330–340 tons (350–360 fl) **S:** 14 kts **Dim:** 45.7 × 8.38 × 2.30
**A:** 1/20-mm AA **Electron Equipt:** Radar: 1/OPS-9 **Range:** 2,000/10
**M:** 2 Mitsubishi YV102-DE diesels; 2 props; 1,200 hp **Man:** 40 tot.

REMARKS: YAS 77, 78, and 80 serve as mine-disposal divers' support ships. Wooden construction. Sister *Koshiki* (YAS 63, ex-MSC 615) stricken 1981; YAS 62 *Shisaka* and YAS 64 *Sakito* were stricken during 1982; YAS 66 *Tsukumi* and YAS 70 *Hotaka* in 3-83, YAS 65 *Kanawa* on 10-2-84, and YAS 68 *Shikine* on 30-3-84. YAS 79–81 redesignated from MSC on 21-6-84. Not all are armed. Sisters *Mikura* (YAS 67, ex-MSC 612), *Karato* (YAS 71, ex-MSC 67), and *Reshiri* (YAS 75, ex-MSC 623) stricken 1985; *Mutusure* (YAS 72, ex-MSC 619) stricken 4-6-86; *Chiburi* (YAS 73, ex-MSC 620) stricken 24-5-86; and *Kudako* (YAS 74, ex-MSC 622) and *Rebun* (YAS 76, ex-MSC 624) stricken 24-3-87.

## OIL SLUDGE REMOVAL CRAFT (YB)

◆ **1 YB 01-class lighter (L: 31-3-75)**

YB 01

**YB 01** *Ships of the World*

**D:** 177 tons **S:** 9 kts **Dim:** 27.5 × 5.2 × 1.9
**M:** 1 diesel; 230 hp **Cargo:** 100 dwt

◆ **4 YB 101-class barges** (In serv. 1975–76)

YB 101–104

**D:** 100 dwt **Dim:** 17.0 × 5.2 × 2.0 **M:** non-self-propelled

## SELF-PROPELLED FLOATING CRANES (YC)

◆ **1 YC 09 class**

YC 09 (In serv. 25-2-74)

**YC 09** L. & L. Van Ginderen, 4-85

**D:** 260 tons **S:** 6 kts **Dim:** 26.0 × 14.0 × 0.9 **M:** 2 diesels; 2 props; 280 hp

◆ **3 YC 06 class**

YC 06 (In serv. 31-3-69) YC 07 (In serv. 28-2-70) YC 08 (In serv. 29-3-72)

**D:** 150 tons **S:** 5 kts **Dim:** 24.0 × 10.0 × 0.8 **M:** 2 diesels; 2 props; 240 hp

REMARKS: In service 1969–72.

◆ **1 YC 05 class**

YC 05 (In serv. 27-3-67)

**D:** 110 tons **S:** 5 kts **Dim:** 22.0 × 10.0 × 0.9 **M:** 2 diesels; 180 hp

## SELF-PROPELLED FLOATING CRANES (YC) *(continued)*

**YC 05**—pontoon hull, crawler crane *Ships of the World*

## DOCKYARD SERVICE CRAFT (YD)

YD 01, 02: 0.8 tons, 7.60 × 1.90, rowboats in serv. 25-3-75; YD 03: 1.7 tons, same dimensions, in service 1978; YD 04: 0.5 tons, in serv. 25-12-79.

## FIREBOAT (YE)

◆ **1 Shobo class** Bldr: Azumo, Yokosuka (In serv. 28-2-64)

YE 41 SHOBO 1 (ex-*Kosuko* 6)

**D:** 45 tons **S:** 19 kts **Dim:** 22.9 × 5.5 × 1.0 **M:** 3 diesels; 3 props; 1,300 hp

REMARKS: Employed as air/sea rescue boat and fireboat at Iwakuni Air Station for seaplanes. Three firefighting monitors. Re-engined 1977; originally made 30 kts on 2,800 hp.

## COMMUNICATIONS BOATS (YF)

◆ **66 miscellaneous service boats**

YF 1029 YF 1030 (Both in serv. 1982)

**D:** 11 tons **S:** 18 kts **Dim:** 13.5 (12.3 pp) × 3.8 × 0.7
**M:** 2 Type 6BDITC-MRD diesels; 2 props; 360 hp

YF 1022 through YF 1028 (In serv. 1980)

**D:** 9 tons (11 fl) **S:** 14 kts **Dim:** 13.00 × 3.80 × 0.60
**M:** 2 Type E 120 T-MF6RE diesels; 2 props; 280 hp **Cargo:** 73 passengers

Others in service are:

| | Tons | Dim: | S (kts): | Hp. |
|---|---|---|---|---|
| YF 1021 | 11 | 13.0 × 3.6 × 0.6 | 14 | 350 |
| YF 2097, 2098, 2100 2103–2105, 2108, 2109 | 11 | 17.0 × 4.2 × 0.8 | 10 | 450 |
| YF 2060, 2062 | 11 | 15.0 × 3.6 × 0.6 | 10 | 160 |
| YF 2066–2074, 2078–2081, 2083–2087, 2091, 2096, 2110, 2116 | 8 | 10.5 × 3.2 × 0.6 | 9 | 180 |
| YF 2075 | 22 | 17.0 × 3.7 × 0.7 | 10 | 400 |
| YF 2076, 2077 | 0.8 | 7.0 × 2.2 × 0.3 | 8 | 22 |
| YF 2082 | 5 | 11.0 × 3.2 × 0.6 | 9 | 90 |
| YF 2088–2090, 2092, 2095, 2111–2115, 2117–2119, 2122 | 5.9 | 11.0 × 3.2 × 0.6 | 10 | 135 |
| YF 2120 | 12.6 | 15.0 × 3.6 × 0.7 | 10 | 230 |
| YF 2121 | 33 | 17.0 × 4.3 × 0.7 | 10 | 480 |
| YF 2123 | 14.3 | 15.0 × 4.2 × 1.6 | 10 | 460 |
| YF 2124 | 11 | . . . | . . . | . . . |

REMARKS: YF 2097 series and YF 2075 designs are essentially U.S. LCM(6) landing craft adapted as utility craft. YF 2066 series are of the U.S. LCVP design. Smaller units are of wooden or glass-reinforced plastic construction. YF 2123, built of GRP, in service 30-1-87, has two UM 6-BDI diesels. YF 2124 authorized under FY 87.

**YF 2108**—U.S. LCM(6) type *Ships of the World*

## JET ENGINE FUEL CRAFT (YG)

◆ **2 (+1) YG 07-class lighters**

YG 201 (ex-YG 07; in serv. 30-3-73) YG 202 (ex-YO 20, ex-YG 08; in serv. 29-3-77) YG 09 (In serv. . . .)

**YG 202 (as YG 08)** 1977

**D:** 270 dwt **S:** 10 kts **Dim:** 36.7 × 6.8 × 2.6
**M:** 1 diesel; 1 prop; 350 hp

REMARKS: YG 08 reclassified YO 20 in 1979, then again reclassified YG 202 in 1981. YG 09 authorized under FY 87.

## CARGO CRAFT (YL)

◆ **1 new construction** Bldr: . . .

YL 11 (In serv. . . .)

**D:** 50 dwt **S:** . . . **Dim:** . . . × . . . × . . . **M:** . . .

REMARKS: Authorized under FY 87.

◆ **2 YL 09-class lighters**

| | Laid down | L | In serv. |
|---|---|---|---|
| YL 09 | 24-11-79 | 3-3-80 | 28-3-80 |
| YL 10 | . . . | 17-12-82 | 28-2-83 |

**YL 09** *Ships of the World*, 1980

**D:** 126 tons (fl) **S:** 9–10 kts **Dim:** 27.00 × 7.00 × 1.04
**M:** 2 Type E 120 T-MF6 RE diesels; 2 props; 560 hp **Man:** 5 tot.

REMARKS: 50 dwt. Resemble a U.S. LCM(8) and have a bow ramp, two 2-ton stores cranes.

◆ **1 YL 08-class lighter**

YL 08 (In serv. 10-3-67)

**D:** 50 dwt **S:** 8 kts **Dim:** 22.40 × 5.10 × 1.20 **M:** 1 diesel; 1 prop; 180 hp

◆ **4 YL 02-class lighters**

YL 03 (In serv. 31-5-54) YL 06 (In serv. 30-11-54)
YL 04 (In serv. 31-5-54) YL 07 (In serv. 30-11-54)

**CARGO CRAFT (YL)** *(continued)*

**D:** 50 dwt **S:** 8 kts **Dim:** 20.00 × 5.10 × 1.20
**M:** 1 diesel; 1 prop; 100 hp

◆ **1 YL 01-class lighter**

YL 01 (In serv. 30-5-53)

**D:** 50 dwt **S:** 7 kts **Dim:** 20.00 × 5.50 × 1.20
**M:** 1 diesel; 1 prop; 90 hp

◆ **1 YL 119-class barge**

YL 119 (In serv. 20-3-71)

**D:** 200 dwt **Dim:** 34.00 × 13.00 × 1.00

◆ **3 YL 116-class barges**

YL 116 (In serv. 21-12-63) YL 117 (In serv. 25-2-64) YL 118 (In serv. 31-3-66)

**D:** 100 dwt **Dim:** 21.50 × 8.40 × 1.00

◆ **2 YL 114-class barges**

YL 114 (In serv. 20-2-63) YL 115 (In serv. 12-3-63)

**D:** 80 dwt **Dim:** 18.40 × 7.40 × 0.90

**FUEL LIGHTERS (YO)**

Note: YO is now applied to all fuel carriers except jet fuel carriers, which are typed YG.

◆ **4 (+2) YO 21 class** Bldr: Yoshiura Shipbuilding

| | Laid down | L | In serv. |
|---|---|---|---|
| YO 21 | . . . | 15-3-80 | 31-3-80 |
| YO 22 | 11-11-80 | 26-2-81 | 28-2-81 |
| YO 23 | 26-11-82 | 12-3-83 | 31-3-83 |
| YO 24 | 4-11-83 | 20-1-84 | 29-2-84 |
| YO 25 | . . . | . . . | . . . |
| YO 26 | . . . | . . . | . . . |

**YO 24** *Ships of the World,* 2-84

**D:** 490 tons (694 fl) **S:** 10 kts **Dim:** 45.5 × 7.8 × 2.9
**M:** 2 Yanmar 6 MA diesels; 2 props; 460 hp **Cargo:** 520 m³

Remarks: YO 25 and 26 authorized under FY 87.

◆ **1 YO 19-class former diesel fuel lighter**

YO 19 (ex-YG 06; in serv. 20-6-63)

**D:** 270 dwt **S:** 9 kts **Dim:** 34.4 × 6.8 × 2.8 **M:** 2 diesels; 2 props; 330 hp

Remarks: Reclassified under FY 1979–80. YO 290 (ex-YG 08) reclassified YG 202 in 1981.

◆ **3 YO 15-class former diesel fuel lighters**

| | In serv. |
|---|---|
| YO 15 (ex-YG 01) | 20-5-53 |
| YO 16 (ex-YG 02) | 15-10-53 |
| YO 18 (ex YG 04) | 10-1-55 |

**D:** 100 dwt **S:** 8 kts **Dim:** 23.0 × 5.0 × 2.0 **M:** 1 diesel; 1 prop; 90 hp

Remarks: Reclassified 1979–80. Sister YO 17 (ex-YG 03) stricken 30-3-84.

◆ **1 YO 14-class lighter**

YO 14 (In serv. 31-3-76)

**D:** 490 dwt **S:** 9 kts **Dim:** 45.0 × 7.8 × 2.9 **M:** 2 diesels; 2 props; 460 hp

Remarks: Very similar to YO 21; officially considered same class.

◆ **4 YO 10-class lighters**

YO 10 (In serv. 31-3-65) YO 12 (In serv. 21-3-67)
YO 11 (In serv. 14-3-66) YO 13 (In serv. 31-3-67)

**D:** 290 dwt **S:** 9 kts **Dim:** 36.5 × 6.8 × 2.6 **M:** 2 diesels; 2 props; 360 hp

**YO 14** L. & L. Van Ginderen, 9-86

◆ **3 YO 07-class lighters**

YO 07 (In serv. 28-2-63) YO 08 (In serv. 29-2-64) YO 09 (In serv. 15-3-65)

**D:** 490 dwt **S:** 9 kts **Dim:** 43.9 × 7.8 × 3.1 **M:** 2 diesels; 400 hp

◆ **4 YO 03-class lighters**

YO 03 (In serv. 15-4-55) YO 05 (In serv. 15-3-56)
YO 04 (In serv. 15-4-55) YO 06 (In serv. 15-3-56)

**D:** 300 dwt **S:** 7 kts **Dim:** 33.0 × 7.0 × 2.6
**M:** 2 diesels; 150 hp

◆ **1 YO 107-class barge** (non-self-propelled)

YO 108 (In serv. 15-3-54)

**D:** 100 dwt **Dim:** 17.00 × 5.20 × 2.20

◆ **1 YO 106-class barge** (non-self-propelled)

YO 106 (In serv. 20-5-53)

**D:** 250 dwt **Dim:** 23.00 × 7.00 × 2.50

**DEBRIS CLEARANCE CRAFT (YS)**

◆ **1 catamaran "sweeper boat"**

YS 01 (In serv. 30-3-79)

**YS 01** *Ships of the World*

**D:** 80 tons **S:** 9 kts **Dim:** 22.0 × 7.80 × 1.40
**M:** 2 diesels; 2 props; 460 hp **Man:** 6 tot.

Remarks: Stationed at Iwakuni Air Station seaplane base; used to clear floating debris in seaplane landing lanes and as a marker-buoy tender.

**TUGS (YT)**

◆ **9 (+1) YT 58-class large harbor tugs** Bldr: Yokohama Yacht

YT 58 (In serv. 31-10-78) YT 65 (In serv. 20-9-84) YT 68 (In serv. 9-9-87)
YT 63 (In serv. 27-9-82) YT 66 (In serv. 20-9-85) YT 69 (In serv. 16-9-87)
YT 64 (In serv. 30-9-83) YT 67 (In serv. 4-9-86) YT 70 (In serv. . . .)

**D:** 262 tons **S:** 11 kts **Dim:** 28.40 × 8.60 × 2.50
**M:** 2 Niigata 6L25B diesels; 2 pivoting Kort-nozzle props; 1,800 hp

Remarks: YT 66, in 1984 Budget, ordered 17-12-84. YT 67 in 1985 Budget; YT 68 and 69 in FY 86; YT 70 in FY 87 Budget. Have two water cannon for firefighting. YT 67 laid down 3-3-86, launched 7-6-86; YT 68 laid down 3-3-87, launched 7-6-87; YT 69 laid down 3-3-87, launched 15-6-87.

**TUGS (YT)** *(continued)*

**YT 64** *Ships of the World,* 9-83

◆ **4 YT 53-class large harbor tugs**

YT 53 (In serv. 1974) YT 56 (In serv. 13-7-76)
YT 55 (In serv. 22-8-75) YT 57 (In serv. 22-8-77)

**YT 55** L. & L. Van Ginderen, 1986

**D:** 195 tons (200 fl) **S:** 11 kts **Dim:** 25.70 × 7.00 × 2.30
**M:** 2 Kubota M6D20BUCS diesels; 1 prop; 1,500 hp **Man:** 10 tot.

◆ **8 YT 35-class harbor tugs**

YT 35 (In serv. 28-2-63) YT 41 (In serv. 31-3-66) YT 46 (In serv. 29-3-67)
YT 37 (In serv. 31-3-65) YT 44 (In serv. 29-3-67) YT 48 (In serv. 31-3-68)
YT 40 (In serv. 31-3-66) YT 45 (In serv. 30-3-67)

**YT 40** L. & L. Van Ginderen, 1-86

**D:** 100 tons **S:** 10 kts **Dim:** 23.80 × 5.40 × 1.80
**M:** 2 diesels; 2 props; 400 hp

◆ **3 YT 60-class harbor pusher tugs** Bldr: Yokohama Yacht

YT 60 (In serv. 31-3-80) YT 62 (In serv. 16-3-81)
YT 61 (In serv. 26-3-80)

**YT 61** *Ships of the World,* 1980

**D:** 30 tons (37 fl) **S:** 8.6 kts **Dim:** 15.50 × 4.20 × 1.50 (0.97 hull)
**M:** 2 Isuzu E 120-MF64A diesels; 2 cycloidal props; 380 hp

◆ **11 YT 34-class harbor pusher tugs**

YT 34 (In serv. 20-3-63) YT 42 (In serv. 31-3-65) YT 51 (In serv. 28-2-72)
YT 36 (In serv. 14-3-64) YT 43 (In serv. 29-3-66) YT 54 (In serv. 24-3-75)
YT 38 (In serv. 31-3-65) YT 47 (In serv. 20-1-67) YT 59 (In serv. 16-1-79)
YT 39 (In serv. 31-3-65) YT 49 (In serv. 5-3-68)

**YT 34** L. & L. Van Ginderen, 10-86

**D:** 28 tons (30 fl) **S:** 9 kts **Dim:** 14.50 × 4.00 × 1.00
**M:** 2 diesels; 2 props; 320 hp **Man:** 3 tot.

Remarks: Conventional tugs. Sisters YT 27 and 33 stricken 1979, and YT 32 during 1981. YT 59 displaces 30 tons std.

◆ **2 YT 25-class pusher tugs** (In serv. . . .)

YT 25 YT 29

**D:** 26 tons **S:** 11 kts **Dim:** 14.0 × 4.0 × 1.0
**M:** 2 diesels; 2 props; 320 hp **Man:** 3 tot.

Remarks: Sister YT 30 discarded 30-6-84; YT 28 on 15-5-85; YT 31 on 14-1-87.

**TRAINING TENDERS (YTE)**

◆ **1 minesweeper construction experimental craft** Bldr: Hitachi, Kanegawa

| | Laid down | L | In serv. |
|---|---|---|---|
| YTE 12 Tokiwa | 1980 | 12-1-82 | 12-1-83 |

**D:** 110 tons light, 142 std. (180 fl) **S:** 14 kts **Dim:** 35.0 × 7.5 × 1.5
**M:** 2 diesels; 2 props; 1,100 hp **Man:** 18 tot.

Remarks: Built to test glass-reinforced plastic construction techniques for building future mine countermeasures ships and for testing shock resistance and sound transmission properties. Lines based on former inshore minesweeper *Atada;* flush deck, no minesweeping gear as completed.

◆ **1 navigational training tender** Bldr: Ando Iron Works

YTE 11 (In serv. 31-3-73)

TRAINING TENDERS (YTE) *(continued)*

YTE 11 *Ships of the World,* 1979

**D:** 120 tons (170 fl) **S:** 13 kts **Dim:** 33.0 × 7.0 × 1.5
**M:** 2 Shinko-Zoki SG175/CM diesels; 2 props; 1,400 hp

REMARKS: Based at Etajima Naval Academy to teach officer cadets ship handling and navigation. Can carry 25 cadets.

**SEAPLANE BUOY TENDERS (YV)**

◆ **3 YV 01 class**

YV 01 (In serv. 30-3-68) YV 02 (In serv. 28-3-69) YV 03 (In serv. 20-3-70)

YV 02—with *Asagumo* (DDK 115) in background *Ships of the World,* 1986

**D:** 45 tons **S:** 10 kts **Dim:** 20.0 × 4.40 × 1.00 **M:** 2 diesels; 2 props; 240 hp

REMARKS: Maintain seaplane fairway marker buoys. YV 02 and YV 03 have a single hydraulic crane; YV 01 has two smaller davits.

**WATER LIGHTERS (YW)**

◆ **5 YW 12 class**

YW 12 (In serv. 14-3-64) YW 15 (In serv. 20-3-67)
YW 13 (In serv. 28-3-66) YW 16 (In serv. 20-3-67)
YW 14 (In serv. 30-3-66)

YW 12 *Ships of the World,* 1979

**D:** 160 dwt **S:** 8 kts **Dim:** 30.5 × 5.7 × 2.2 **M:** 1 diesel; 180 hp

◆ **1 (+1) YW 11 class**

YW 11 (In serv. 25-3-64) YW 17 (In serv. . . .)

**D:** 310 dwt **S:** 10 kts **Dim:** 36.7 × 6.8 × 2.8 **M:** 2 diesels; 2 props; 360 hp

REMARKS: YW 17 authorized under FY 87 as replacement for YW 02.

◆ **1 YW 10 class**

YW 10 (In serv. 20-3-63)

**D:** 100 dwt **S:** 8 kts **Dim:** 23.5 × 5.1 × 1.0 **M:** 1 diesel; 160 hp

◆ **7 YW 03 class**

YW 03 (In serv. 22-3-54) YW 06 (In serv. 20-12-54) YW 09 (In serv. 20-12-54)
YW 04 (In serv. 31-3-54) YW 07 (In serv. 11-12-54)
YW 05 (In serv. 20-12-54) YW 08 (In serv. 20-12-54)

**D:** 150 dwt **S:** 8 kts **Dim:** 27.0 × 5.5 × 2.1 **M:** 1 diesel; 75 hp

◆ **1 YW 02 class**

YW 02 (In serv. 20-5-53)

**D:** 150 dwt **S:** 9 kts **Dim:** 27.0 × 5.5 × 2.1 **M:** 1 diesel; 90 hp

**MOTOR BOATS (B)**

◆ **12 miscellaneous**

B 4006: 8 tons—13.00 × 3.20 × 0.50—14 kts (In serv. 16-3-76)
B 4007–4013: 1 ton—5.00 × 2.10 × 0.40—22 kts (All in serv. 26-1-76)
B 4014–4016: 8 tons—13.00 × 3.20 × 0.50—14 kts (In serv. 1978–80)
B 4017: 16 tons—17.4 × 3.9 × 1.5—10 kts (In serv. 28-3-85)

REMARKS: Fiberglass-hulled. B 4016 capable of 18 kts. B 4006 basically the same as B 4014–4016. B 4017 replaced the wooden-hulled B 4005 (stricken 30-3-85) and has a glass-reinforced plastic hull with pilothouse offset to port; 180 hp.

**ROWING CRAFT AND SAILBOATS**

**64 "C" group rowing boats:** C 5094–5157

**D:** 1.5 tons **Dim:** 9.0 × 2.5 × . . .

**39 "T" group rowing punts:** T 6063–6102 (T 6058–6062 stricken '85, but T 6098–6102 added 26-2-85)

**D:** .5 tons **Dim:** 6.0 × 1.6 × . . .

**13 "Y" group sailboats:** Y 7010–7022 (Y 7021, 22 added 26-2-85)

MARITIME SAFETY AGENCY
*(Kaijo Hoancho)*

PERSONNEL (1984): 11,944 men (approx. 2,500 officers)

The Maritime Safety Agency, which was organized in 1948, underwent a massive expansion in the 1970s, which by 1982 made it the world's largest and best-equipped coast guard. In peacetime, it is directed by the Department of Transportation. Although most of its ships are armed, they are not considered part of the Navy; they fly only the national colors (a red disk on a white background), not the flag flown by naval ships. A stylized blue stripe has recently been added to the hull sides of larger units. In wartime, the ships would be under naval control. Under the FY 87 Budget authorized on 30-12-86, the MSA was to build one 1,000-ton large patrol ship, one 500-ton medium patrol ship, one 180-ton patrol boat, one 17-m buoy boat, two 12-m buoy boats, and two 10-m buoy boats.

AVIATION: In 1987, the MSA operated 21 fixed-wing aircraft (5 YS-11A transports, 2 SC-7 Skyvan, and 14 Beech 200T light transports) and 38 helicopters (31 Kawasaki-Bell 212, 1 Bell 206G, 4 Bell 206B, and 2 Hughes 369-HS).
Under FY 87, two French Falcon 90 transports, equipped as long-range maritime patrol aircraft (ordered 8-87), and one Bell 212 helicopter were authorized.

**HIGH-ENDURANCE HELICOPTER-CARRYING CUTTERS (PLH)**

◆ **1 Mizuho class**

| | Bldr | Laid down | L | In serv. |
|---|---|---|---|---|
| PLH 21 MIZUHO | Mitsubishi, Shimonoseki | 27-8-84 | 5-6-85 | 19-3-86 |

**D:** 4,960 tons (5,300 fl) **S:** 23.3 kts **Dim:** 130.00 (123.00 wl) × 15.50 × 5.25
**A:** 1/35-mm Oerlikon AA—1/20-mm JM-61-MB gatling AA—2/Kawasaki-Bell 212 helicopters
**Electron Equipt:** Radar: 3 navigational sets
**M:** 2 SEMT-Pielstick 14 PC 2.5V diesels; 2 CP props; 18,200 hp
**Range:** . . ./. . . **Electric:** 1,875 kVA **Man:** 130 tot.

REMARKS: Ordered under the 1984 program. Design is a reduced version of a 5,900-std.-ton patrol and rescue ship intended for Indian Ocean service: is the first MSA unit to carry two helicopters. Has a flight deck traversing system, a bow-thruster, and two pairs of fin stabilizers. Based at Yokohama. Second unit requested FY 86, but denied.

## HIGH-ENDURANCE HELICOPTER-CARRYING CUTTERS (PLH) *(continued)*

**Mizuho (PLH 21)** MSA, 1986

**Mizuho (PLH 21)** L. & L. Van Ginderen, 5-86

◆ **6 Tsugaru class**

| | Bldr | Laid down | L | In serv. |
|---|---|---|---|---|
| PLH 02 Tsugaru | Ishikawa-Harima, Tokyo | 18-4-78 | 6-12-78 | 17-4-79 |
| PLH 03 Oosumi | Mitsui, Tamano | 1-9-78 | 1-6-79 | 18-10-79 |
| PLH 04 Uraga | Hitachi, Maizuru | 14-3-79 | 12-10-79 | 5-3-80 |
| PLH 05 Zaō | Mitsubishi, Nagasaki | 23-10-80 | 29-10-81 | 19-3-82 |
| PLH 06 Chikuzen | Kawasaki, Kobe | 20-4-82 | 18-3-83 | 28-9-83 |
| PLH 07 Settsu | Sumitomo, Uraga | 5-4-83 | 21-4-84 | 27-9-84 |

**Tsugaru (PLH 02)** L. & L. Van Ginderen, 5-86

**Zaō (PLH 05)** L. & L. Van Ginderen, 5-86

**D:** 3,730 tons (4,037 fl) **S:** 22 kts **Dim:** 105.4 (100.0 wl) × 14.6 × 4.8
**A:** 1/40-mm AA—1/20-mm AA (not in PL 03, 04)—PL 04, 05, 06: 1/35-mm AA—all: 1/Bell 212 helicopter
**M:** 2 Pielstick 12PC2-5V400 diesels; 2 CP props; 15,600 hp (13,260 hp sust.)
**Electric:** 1,450 kVA **Fuel:** 650 tons **Range:** 5,700/18
**Man:** 21 officers, 7 warrant officers, 28 men, 15 spare

Remarks: Have bow-thruster, 2 pair fin stabilizers, normal ship bow for operations in ice-free waters. Also have: flume-type passive stabilization tanks in superstructure. Have 3 radars. Engines manufactured by different builders. PLH 03, 04 built under 1978 program, PLH 05 under 1979 program, PLH 06 under 1981 program, and PLH 07 under the 1983 program. Redesignated from PL on 12-2-86, 4-9-85, 22-11-85, 8-3-86, 17-7-85, and 18-10-85, respectively. PLH 02 has a MARISAT SATCOMM installation.

◆ **1 Soya class**

| | Bldr | Laid down | L | In serv. |
|---|---|---|---|---|
| PLH 01 Soya | Nippon Kokan, Tsurumi | 12-9-77 | 3-7-78 | 22-11-78 |

**Soya (PLH 01)** L. & L. Van Ginderen, 1986

**D:** 3,562 tons (4,089 fl) **S:** 21 kts **Dim:** 98.6 × 15.6 × 5.2
**A:** 1/40-mm AA—1/20-mm AA—1/Bell 212 helicopter
**M:** 2 Nippon Kokan-Pielstick 12PC2-5V400 diesels; 2 CP props; 16,000 hp (13,260 hp sust.)
**Electric:** 1,450 kVA **Fuel:** 650 tons
**Range:** 5,700/18 **Man:** 71 tot.

Remarks: The *Soya* was built under the 1977 program. The *Soya* has an icebreaking bow and operates in the north. Passive tank stabilization only, no bow-thruster. Rounded stern, vice squared on *Tsugaru* class. Four radars (one aft for helo control). Redesignated PLH from PL on 13-12-85.

## HIGH ENDURANCE CUTTERS (PL)

◆ **28 (+1 + . . .) Shiretoko class**

| | Bldr | L | In serv. |
|---|---|---|---|
| PL 101 Shiretoko* | Mitsui, Tamano | 13-7-78 | 8-11-78 |
| PL 102 Esan | Sumitomo, Oshima | 8-78 | 16-11-78 |
| PL 103 Wakasa* | Kawasaki, Kobe | 8-78 | 29-11-78 |
| PL 104 Yahiko | Mitsubishi, Shimonoseki | 8-78 | 16-11-78 |
| PL 105 Motobu | Sasebo Dockyard | 8-78 | 29-11-78 |
| PL 106 Rishiri | Shikoku DY | 27-3-79 | 12-9-79 |
| PL 107 Matsushima* | Tohoku DY | 11-4-79 | 14-9-79 |
| PL 108 Iwaki* | Naikai, Innoshima | 28-3-79 | 10-8-79 |
| PL 109 Shikine | Usuki SY, Usuki | 27-4-79 | 20-9-79 |
| PL 110 Suruga* | Kurushima DY, Onishi | 20-4-79 | 28-9-79 |
| PL 111 Rebun* | Narasaki SY, Muroran | 6-79 | 21-11-79 |
| PL 112 Chokai* | Nipponkai Heavy Ind., Toyama | 6-79 | 30-11-79 |
| PL 113 Ashizuri* | Sanoyasu DY, Oshima | 6-79 | 31-10-79 |
| PL 114 Oki | Tsuneishi SY, Numakuma | 6-79 | 16-11-79 |
| PL 115 Noto | Miho SY, Shimuzu | 7-79 | 30-11-79 |
| PL 116 Yonakuni | Hiyashigane SY, Nagasaki | 6-79 | 31-10-79 |
| PL 117 Daisetsu* | Hakodate DY | 22-8-79 | 31-1-80 |
| PL 118 Shimokita | Ishikawajima, Tokyo | 9-79 | 12-3-80 |
| PL 119 Suzuka | Kanasashi SY, Toyohashi | 4-10-79 | 7-3-80 |
| PL 120 Kunasaki | Koyo DY, Mihara | 8-10-79 | 29-2-80 |
| PL 121 Genkai* | Oshima SY, Oshima | 9-79 | 31-1-80 |
| PL 122 Goto* | Onomichi SY, Onomishi | 10-79 | 29-2-80 |
| PL 123 Koshiki | Kasado DY, Kasado | 9-79 | 25-1-80 |
| PL 124 Hateruma* | Osaka DY | 11-79 | 12-3-80 |
| PL 125 Katori | Tohoku DY, Shiogama | 5-80 | 17-10-80 |
| PL 126 Kunigami | Kanda SY, Kawashiri | 28-3-80 | 21-10-80 |
| PL 127 Etomo* | Naikai, Innoshima | 30-9-81 | 17-3-82 |
| PL 128 Mashiyu | Shikoku DY, Kochi, Takamatsu | 14-10-81 | 12-3-82 |
| PL 129 Mikura | . . . | . . . | . . . |

## HIGH ENDURANCE CUTTERS (PL) *(continued)*

**D:** 974 tons (1,350–1,360 fl) **S:** 20 kts **Dim:** 77.8 (73.6 pp) × 9.6 × 3.42
**A:** 1/40-mm AA—1/20-mm AA—*see* Remarks
**M:** 2 Niigata 8MA 40 or Fuji 8 S40B diesels; 2 CP props; 7,000 hp
**Electric:** 625 kVA **Fuel:** 191 tons **Range:** 4,406/17 **Man:** 41 tot.

REMARKS: Program helped small shipyards to stay in business. Intended to patrol the 200-nautical-mile economic zone. Starred units have Fuji 8 S40B diesels. PL 106 and later have no 20-mm AA, while PL 118, 122, 124–128 have an Oerlikon 35-mm in place of the 40-mm AA. Carry 153 tons water. Fuel capacities and endurances vary. Use passive tank stabilization, with tanks in superstructure. Range greater for some: PL 127: 5,200/17. PL 120 had a serious fire 15-2-82. PL 129, authorized under FY 87, may be of a different design. PL 130, if authorized, is to be named *Shikoku*.

Noto (PL 115) L. & L. Van Ginderen, 5-86

Yahiko (PL 104) MSA, 1986

◆ **2 Izu class**

| | Bldr | L | In serv. |
|---|---|---|---|
| PL 31 IZU | Hitachi, Mukaishima | 1-67 | 31-7-67 |
| PL 32 MIURA | Maizuru DY | 11-68 | 15-3-69 |

Izu (PL 31) L. & L. Van Ginderen, 5-86

**D:** 2,081 tons (2,200 fl) **S:** 24.6 kts **Dim:** 95.5 (86.45 pp) × 11.6 × 3.8
**A:** 1/76.2-mm DP **M:** 2 SEMT-Pielstick 12PC2V diesels; 2 CP props; 10,400 hp
**Electric:** 800 kVA **Range:** 5,000/20.5; 14,500/12.7 **Man:** 72 tot.

REMARKS: Large weather radar in dome aft removed in 1978 and gun added forward. Passive stabilization, with Flume-type tanks in superstructure.

◆ **4 Erimo class**

| | Bldr | L | In serv. |
|---|---|---|---|
| PL 13 ERIMO | Hitachi, Mukaishima | 14-8-65 | 30-11-65 |
| PL 14 SATSUMA | Hitachi, Mukaishima | 4-66 | 30-7-66 |
| PL 15 DAIO | Hitachi, Maizuru | 19-6-73 | 28-9-73 |
| PL 16 MUROTO | Naikai, Taguma | 5-8-74 | 30-11-74 |

**D:** 980 tons (1,009 fl) **S:** 19.5 kts **Dim:** 76.6 (73.0 pp) × 9.2 × 3.0
**A:** 1/76.2-mm Mk 26 DP—1/20-mm AA
**M:** 2 Burmeister & Wain 635V 2 BU 45 diesels; 2 props; 4,800 hp
**Electric:** 320 kVA **Range:** 5,000/18 **Man:** 72 tot.

REMARKS: The hull of PL 13 is reinforced against ice. PL 15 and PL 16:

**D:** 1,206 tons **Dim:** beam 9.6, draft, 3.18
**A:** 1/40-mm AA—1/20-mm AA **M:** 7,000 hp for 20.4 kts
**Electric:** 500 kVA **Range:** 6,600/18 **Man:** 50 tot.

Erimo (PL 13) MSA, 1986

◆ **2 Nojima class** Bldr: Uraga Dock Co., Ltd.

| | L | In serv. |
|---|---|---|
| PL 11 NOJIMA | 12-2-62 | 30-4-62 |
| PL 12 OJIKA | . . . | 10-6-63 |

Nojima (PL 11) MSA, 1986

**D:** 980 tons (1,009 fl) **S:** 18.1 kts **Dim:** 69.0 × 9.18 × 3.2
**M:** 2 Uraga-Sulzer 6 MD 42 diesels; 2 props; 3,000 hp
**Electric:** 310 kVA **Range:** 6,000/16.5 **Man:** 73 tot.

REMARKS: Used for meteorological reporting. Passive tank stabilization.

◆ **1 Kojima-class training cutter**

| | Bldr | In serv. |
|---|---|---|
| PL 21 KOJIMA | Kure DY | 21-5-64 |

Kojima (PL 21) L. & L. Van Ginderen, 5-85

**D:** 1,066 tons (1,206 fl) **S:** 17.3 kts **Dim:** 69.6 × 10.3 × 3.53
**A:** 1/40-mm AA—2/20-mm AA (I × 2)
**M:** 1 Uraga-Sulzer 7 MD 51 diesel; 1 prop; 2,600 hp
**Electric:** 550 kVA **Range:** 6,120/13 **Man:** 17 officers, 42 crew, 47 cadets

REMARKS: Used as a training ship at Kure Academy. 76.2-mm DP replaced by relocated 40-mm AA, and second 20-mm AA added between 1982 and 1985.

## MEDIUM-ENDURANCE CUTTERS (PM)

◆ **13 (+1) Teshio (500-ton) class**

| | Bldr | L | In serv. |
|---|---|---|---|
| PM 01 TESHIO | Shikoku DY, Kochi | 30-5-80 | 30-9-80 |
| PM 02 OIRASE | Naikai, Taguma, Innoshima | 15-5-80 | 29-8-80 |
| PM 03 ECHIZEN | Usuki Iron Wks., Usuki | 2-6-80 | 30-9-80 |
| PM 04 TOKACHI | Narazaki, Muroran | 21-11-80 | 24-3-81 |
| PM 05 HITACHI | Tohoku SY, Shiogoma | 15-11-80 | 19-3-81 |
| PM 06 OKITSU | Usuki Iron Wks. | 5-12-80 | 17-3-81 |
| PM 07 ISAZU | Naikai, Taguma, Innoshima | 29-10-81 | 18-2-82 |

## MEDIUM-ENDURANCE CUTTERS (PM) *(continued)*

| | | | |
|---|---|---|---|
| PM 08 Chitose | Shikoku DY, Kochi | 7-7-81 | 17-11-82 |
| PM 09 Kumano | Naikai, Taguma, Innoshima | 8-81 | 10-3-83 |
| PM 10 Sorachi | Tohoku SY, Shiogama | 27-4-84 | 27-9-84 |
| PM 11 Yubari | . . . | 20-8-85 | 28-11-85 |
| PM 12 Motoura | Shikoku DY, Takamatsu | 7-8-86 | 21-11-86 |
| PM 13 Kano | Naikai, Taguma, Innoshima | 7-8-86 | 13-11-86 |
| PM 14 N . . . | . . . | . . . | . . . |

**Hitachi (PM 05)** L. & L. Van Ginderen, 5-86

**Yubari (PM 11)** MSA, 11-85

**D:** 630 tons (670–692 fl) **S:** 18 to 18.6 kts **Dim:** 67.80 (63.00 pp) × 7.90 × 2.65
**A:** 1/20-mm JN-61B gatling AA **Electron Equipt:** Radar: 2/JMA-159B
**M:** 2 Fuji 6S 32F diesels; 2 props; 3,000 hp **Electric:** 240 kVA
**Endurance:** 15 days **Range:** 3,200/16 **Man:** 33 tot.

Remarks: 540 grt. Three built under 1979–80 program, three under 1980–81 program, one under 1981, 1983, and 1984 programs. Some have Arakata 6 M31 EX diesels. PM 07 also used for training and has a lengthened after deckhouse. PM 12 and 13 approved in 1985 Budget. PM 12 has Niigata 6-M31 diesels, a range of 3,900 n.m. at 16 kts, and a full load displacement of 692 tons. PM 14 authorized under FY 87 Budget.

### ◆ 2 Takatori (350-ton) class

| | Bldr | L | In serv. |
|---|---|---|---|
| PM 89 Takatori | Naikai, Taguma, Innoshima | 8-12-77 | 24-3-78 |
| PM 94 Kumano | Naikai, Taguma, Innoshima | 2-11-78 | 23-2-79 |

**Kumano (PM 94)** L. & L. Van Ginderen, 5-84

**D:** 634 tons normal **S:** 15.7 kts **Dim:** 45.70 (44.25 pp) × 9.20 × 3.88
**A:** none **M:** 2 Niigata 6M31EX diesels; 1 CP prop; 3,000 hp
**Electric:** 200 kVA **Range:** 750/15 **Man:** 34 tot.

Remarks: 469 grt. Rescue-tug types. Equipped for fire-fighting and salvage duties. Two water cannon (3,000 lit./min. each). Carry an 8-m rescue boat and a 4.6-m speedboat.

### ◆ 20 Bihoro (350-ton) class

| | Bldr | In serv. |
|---|---|---|
| PM 73 Bihoro | Tohoku SY, Shiogama | 28-2-74 |
| PM 74 Kuma | Usuki Iron Wks., Usuki | 28-2-74 |
| PM 75 Fuji | Usuki Iron Wks., Usuki | 7-2-75 |
| PM 76 Kabashima | Usuki Iron Wks., Usuki | 25-3-75 |
| PM 77 Sado | Tohoku SY, Shiogama | 1-2-75 |
| PM 78 Ishikari | Tohoku SY, Shiogama | 13-3-76 |
| PM 79 Abakuma | Tohoku SY, Shiogama | 30-1-76 |
| PM 80 Isuzu | Nakai, Taguma | 10-3-76 |
| PM 81 Kikuchi | Usuki Iron Wks., Usuki | 6-2-76 |
| PM 82 Kuzuryu | Usuki Iron Wks., Usuki | 18-3-76 |
| PM 83 Horobetsu | Tohoku SY, Shiogama | 21-1-77 |
| PM 84 Shirakami | Tohoku SY, Shiogama | 3-3-77 |
| PM 85 Sagami | Naikai SY, Taguma | 30-11-76 |
| PM 86 Tone | Usuki Iron Wks., Usuki | 30-11-76 |
| PM 87 Yoshino | Usuki Iron Wks., Usuki | 28-1-77 |
| PM 88 Kurobe | Shikoku DY, Kochi | 15-2-77 |
| PM 90 Chikugo | Naikai, Taguma | 27-1-78 |
| PM 91 Yamakuni | Usuki Iron Wks., Usuki | 26-1-78 |
| PM 92 Katsura | Shikoku DY, Kochi | 15-2-77 |
| PM 93 Shinano | Tohoku SY, Shiogama | 23-2-78 |

**Isuzu (PM 80)** L. & L. Van Ginderen, 5-85

**Abakuma (PM 79)** L. & L. Van Ginderen, 5-85

**D:** 636 tons (657 fl) **S:** 18 kts **Dim:** 63.35 × 7.80 × 2.53 **A:** 1/20-mm AA
**Electron Equipt:** Radar: 2/JMA-159B or 1/JMA 1576, 1/JMA 1596
**M:** 2 Niigata 6M31EX diesels; 2 CP props; 3,000 hp **Electric:** 200 kVA
**Range:** 3,260/16 **Man:** 34 tot.

### ◆ 7 Kunashiri (350-ton) class

| | Bldr | In serv. |
|---|---|---|
| PM 65 Kunashiri | Maizuru DY | 28-3-69 |
| PM 66 Minabe | Maizuru DY | 28-3-70 |
| PM 67 Sarobetsu | Maizuru DY | 30-3-71 |
| PM 68 Kamishima | Usuki Iron Wks., Usuki | 31-1-72 |
| PM 70 Miyake | Tohoku SY, Shiogama | 25-1-73 |
| PM 71 Awaji | Usuki Iron Wks., Usuki | 25-1-73 |
| PM 72 Yaeyama | Usuki Iron Wks., Usuki | 20-12-72 |

## MEDIUM-ENDURANCE CUTTERS (PM) *(continued)*

**Miyake (PM 70)** *Ships of the World,* 1986

**D:** 498 tons (574 fl) **S:** 17.5 kts **Dim:** 58.04 × 7.38 × 2.40
**Electron Equipt:** Radar: 2/JMA 1576 or 1596
**A:** 1/20-mm AA **M:** 2 Niigata 6MF32H diesels; 2 props; 2,600 hp
**Electric:** 120 kVA **Range:** 3,040/16 **Man:** 40 tot.

Remarks: PM 70 to PM 72 have 6M31EX diesels, 3,000 hp. PM 72 has controllable-pitch propellers. PM 70–72 have JMA 1596 radars.

◆ **3 Matsuura (350-ton) class** Bldrs: PM 60, PM 61: Osaka SB; Others: Hitachi SY, Mukaishima

| | In serv. |
|---|---|
| PM 62 Amami | 29-3-65 |
| PM 63 Natori | 20-1-66 |
| PM 64 Karatsu | 29-3-67 |

**Karatsu (PM 64)** *Ships of the World,* 1986

**D:** 425 tons **S:** 16.5 kts (PM 64: 18 kts; PM 63: 16.8 kts)
**Dim:** 55.33 × 7.00 × 2.30 **A:** 1/20-mm AA
**M:** 2 Ikegai 6MSB31S diesels; 2 props; 1,400 hp (PM 63: 2 Type 6MSB31HS diesels; 1,800 hp—PM 64: 2 Type 6MA31X diesels; 2,600 hp)
**Electric:** 140 kVA **Range:** 3,500/12–13 **Man:** 37–40 tot.

Remarks: Sisters *Matsuura* (PM 60) stricken 1986, *Sendai* (PM 61) stricken 1987.

Note: The last two *Yahagi*-class (350-ton) patrol boats were stricken on 5-3-87: *Horonai* (PM 59) and *Okinawa* (PM 69).

## PATROL BOATS (PS)

◆ **1 new-construction (180-ton) class**

| | Bldr | Laid down | L | In serv. |
|---|---|---|---|---|
| PS 104 N . . . | . . . | . . . | . . . | . . . |

**D:** 180 tons (normal) **S:** . . . **Dim:** . . . × . . . × . . . **A:** . . .
**Electron Equipt:** Radar: . . . **M:** . . . **Range:** . . . **Man:** . . .

Remarks: Authorized under FY 87 Budget.

◆ **3 Akagi (130-ton) class**

| | Bldr | Laid down | L | In serv. |
|---|---|---|---|---|
| PS 101 Akagi | Sumidigawa, Tokyo | 31-7-79 | 5-12-79 | 26-3-80 |
| PS 102 Tsukuba | Sumidigawa, Tokyo | 7-7-81 | 29-10-81 | 24-2-82 |
| PS 103 Kongo | Ishikawa DY, Takasago | 1-8-86 | 17-12-86 | 16-3-87 |

**D:** 127.7 tons normal (134 fl) **S:** 26.5 kts **Dim:** 35.0 (33.0 wl) × 6.3 × 1.3
**A:** 1/12.7-mm mg **M:** 2 Pielstick 16PA 4V-185 VG diesels; 2 props; 4,400 hp
**Electric:** 40 kVA **Range:** 570/20 **Man:** 12 tot.

Remarks: PS 101 in 1979 Budget, PS 102 in 1981. Glass-reinforced plastic hull; 4-day endurance. Carry a 25-man rubber rescue dinghy. PS 103 authorized under FY 86 Budget and made 28 kts on trials.

**Kongo (PS 103)** *Ships of the World,* 1987

◆ **2 Bizan (130-ton) class**

| | Bldr | In serv. |
|---|---|---|
| PS 47 Asama | Mitsubishi, Shimonoseki | 31-1-69 |
| PS 48 Shiramine | Mitsubishi, Shimonoseki | 15-12-69 |

**Shiramine (PS 48)** *Ships of the World,* 1984

**D:** 42–48 tons (83–85 fl) **S:** 21.6 kts (PS 48: 25 kts) **Dim:** 26.0 × 5.6 × 1.0
**A:** 1/12.7-mm mg **Electron Equipt:** Radar: 1/MD 808
**M:** 2 Mitsubishi 12 HD 2 OMTK diesels; 2 props; 1,140 hp (PS 48: 2 MTU diesels; 2,200 hp)
**Electric:** 2 kw **Range:** 400/18; PS 48: 250/25 **Man:** 14 tot.

Remarks: Sister *Bizan* (PS 42) stricken 26-2-87.

◆ **14 Hidaka (130-ton) class**

| | Bldr | In serv. |
|---|---|---|
| PS 32 Hidaka | Azuma SY, Yokosuka | 23-4-62 |
| PS 33 Hiyama | Hitachi SY, Mukaishima | 13-3-63 |
| PS 34 Tsurugi | Hitachi SY, Mukaishima | 13-3-63 |
| PS 35 Rokko | Shikoku DY, Shimonoseki | 31-1-64 |
| PS 36 Takanawa | Hayashigane SY, Shimonoseki | 27-1-64 |
| PS 37 Akiyoshi | Hashihama SY, Imabaki | 29-2-64 |
| PS 38 Kunimi | Hayashigane SY, Shimonoseki | 15-2-65 |
| PS 39 Takatsuki | Kurashima DY, Onishi | 30-3-65 |
| PS 41 Kamui | Hayashigame SY, Shimonoseki | 15-2-66 |
| PS 43 Ashitaka | Usuki Iron Wks., Usuki | 10-2-67 |
| PS 44 Kurama | Usuki Iron Wks., Usuki | 28-2-67 |
| PS 45 Ibuki | Usuki Iron Wks., Usuki | 5-3-68 |
| PS 46 Toumi | Usuki Iron Wks., Usuki | 20-2-68 |
| PS 49 Nobaru | Hitachi SY, Mukaishima | 10-12-68 |

**Kurama (PS 44)** *Ships of the World,* 1984

**PATROL BOATS (PS)** *(continued)*

**D:** 169 tons normal **S:** 13.7 kts **Dim:** 31.72 (30.5 wl) × 6.29 × 1.80
**A:** 1/12.7-mm mg (usually not mounted)
**M:** 1 6MSB 31S diesel; 1 prop; 700 hp **Electric:** 60 kVA
**Range:** 1,100/12 **Man:** 17 tot.

Remarks: PS 44 replaced in training role by *Isazu* (PM 07) on 20-4-82.

**COASTAL PATROL BOATS (PC)**

◆ **23 Murakomo (30-meter) class**

| | Bldr | In serv. |
|---|---|---|
| PC 201 Murakomo | Mitsubishi, Shimonoseki | 24-3-78 |
| PC 202 Kitagumo | Hitachi, Kanagawa | 17-3-78 |
| PC 203 Yukigumo | Hitachi, Kanagawa | 27-9-78 |
| PC 204 Asagumo | Mitsubishi, Shimonoseki | 21-9-78 |
| PC 205 Hayagumo | Mitsubishi, Shimonoseki | 30-1-79 |
| PC 206 Akigumo | Hitachi, Kanagawa | 28-2-79 |
| PC 207 Yaegumo | Mitsubishi, Shimonoseki | 16-3-79 |
| PC 208 Natsugumo | Hitachi, Kanagawa | 22-3-79 |
| PC 209 Yamagiri | Hitachi, Kanagawa | 29-6-79 |
| PC 210 Kawagiri | Hitachi, Kanagawa | 27-7-79 |
| PC 211 Teruzuki | Maizuru Heavy Ind. | 26-6-79 |
| PC 212 Natsuzuki | Maizuru Heavy Ind. | 26-7-79 |
| PC 213 Miyazuki | Hitachi, Kanagawa | 13-3-80 |
| PC 214 Nijigumo | Mitsubishi, Shimonoseki | 29-1-81 |
| PC 215 Tatsugumo | Mitsubishi, Shimonoseki | 19-3-81 |
| PC 216 Hamayuki | Hitachi, Kanagawa | 27-2-81 |
| PC 217 Isonami | Mitsubishi, Shimonoseki | 19-3-81 |
| PC 218 Nagozuki | Hitachi, Kanagawa | 29-1-81 |
| PC 219 Yaezuki | Hitachi, Kanagawa | 19-3-81 |
| PC 220 Yamayuki | Hitachi, Kanagawa | 16-2-82 |
| PC 221 Komayuki | Mitsubishi, Shimonoseki | 10-2-82 |
| PC 222 Asagiri | Mitsubishi, Shimonoseki | 17-2-82 |
| PC 223 Umigiri | Hitachi, Kanagawa | 23-2-83 |

**Asagumo (PC 204)** L. & L. Van Ginderen, 5-86

**D:** 88 tons (125 fl) **S:** 31 kts **Dim:** 31.0 (28.5 pp) × 6.3 × 1.17
**A:** 1/12.7-mm mg **M:** 2 Ikegai MTU 16V652 TB81 diesels; 2 props; 4,800 hp
**Electric:** 40 kVA **Range:** 350/28
**Man:** 11 tot.

Remarks: PC 201 to PC 204 built under 1977–78 program. PC 205–208 under 1978–79, PC 209–212 under 1978–79 supplementary program, PC 213 under 1979–80 program, PC 214–219 under 1980–81 program, PC 220–221 under 1981–82.

◆ **15 Akizuki (23-meter) class** Bldr: Mitsubishi, Shimonoseki (except PC 83–85: Hitachi, Kanagawa)

| | In serv. | | In serv. |
|---|---|---|---|
| PC 64 Akizuki | 28-2-74 | PC 79 Shimanami | 23-12-77 |
| PC 65 Shinonome | 25-2-74 | PC 80 Yuzuki | 22-3-79 |
| PC 72 Urayuki | 31-5-75 | PC 81 Hanayuki | 27-3-81 |
| PC 73 Iseyuki | 31-7-75 | PC 82 Awagiri | 27-12-82 |
| PC 75 Hatayuki | 19-3-75 | PC 83 Shimagiri | 7-2-84 |
| PC 76 Hatagumo | 21-2-76 | PC 84 Setogiri | 22-3-85 |
| PC 77 Hamazuki | 29-11-76 | PC 85 Hayagiri | 22-2-85 |
| PC 78 Isozuki | 18-3-77 | | |

**D:** 77 tons normal **S:** 22.1 kts **Dim:** 26.00 (23.00 pp) × 6.30 × 1.12
**A:** PC 85 only: 1/20-mm AA **Electron Equipt:** Radar: 1/FRA 10 Mk 2
**M:** 3 Mitsubishi 12 DM 20 MTK diesels; 3 props; 3,000 hp
**Electric:** 40 kVA **Range:** 290/21.5 **Man:** 10 tot.

Remarks: Superstructure on PC 83 and later differs (see photos); they also use the Mitsubishi 12V175RTC diesel of 1,000 hp.

**Shimagiri (PC 83)**—low bridge *Ships of the World,* 1986

**Urayuki (PC 72)**—high bridge L. & L. Van Ginderen, 6-84

**Matsunami (PC 53)** *Ships of the World,* 1984

◆ **1 Matsunami (23-meter) class** Bldr: Hitachi, Kanagawa

PC 53 Matsunami (In serv. 30-3-71)

**D:** 59 tons normal **S:** 20.7 kts **Dim:** 24.96 × 6.0 × 1.33
**M:** 2 Mercedes-Benz MB820Db diesels; 2 props; 2,200 hp; 2 DA640 cruise diesels: 180 hp
**Electric:** 3 kw **Range:** 270/18 **Man:** 30 tot.

Remarks: Especially configured for Emperor Hirohito for oceanographic research. Two cruise diesels can be geared to the props.

◆ **17 Shikinami (23-meter) class**

| | Bldr | In serv. |
|---|---|---|
| PC 54 Shikinami | Mitsubishi, Shimonoseki | 24-2-71 |
| PC 55 Tomonami | Mitsubishi, Shimonoseki | 20-3-71 |
| PC 56 Wakanami | Mitsubishi, Shimonoseki | 30-10-71 |
| PC 57 Isenami | Hitachi, Kanagawa | 29-2-72 |
| PC 58 Takanami | Mitsubishi, Shimonoseki | 30-11-71 |
| PC 59 Mutsuki | Hitachi, Kanagawa | 18-12-72 |
| PC 60 Mochizuki | Hitachi, Kanagawa | 18-12-72 |
| PC 61 Haruzuki | Mitsubishi, Shimonoseki | 30-11-72 |

## COASTAL PATROL BOATS (PC) *(continued)*

| | | |
|---|---|---|
| PC 62 Kiyozuki | Mitsubishi, Shimonoseki | 18-12-72 |
| PC 63 Urazuki | Mitsubishi, Shimonoseki | 30-1-73 |
| PC 66 Uranami | Hitachi, Kanagawa | 22-12-73 |
| PC 67 Tamanami | Mitsubishi, Shimonoseki | 25-12-73 |
| PC 68 Minegumo | Mitsubishi, Shimonoseki | 30-11-73 |
| PC 69 Kiyonami | Mitsubishi, Shimonoseki | 30-10-73 |
| PC 70 Okinami | Hitachi, Kanagawa | 8-2-74 |
| PC 71 Wakagumo | Hitachi, Kanagawa | 25-3-74 |
| PC 74 Asoyuki | Hitachi, Kanagawa | 16-6-75 |

**Haruzuki (PC 61)** *Ships of the World,* 1984

**D:** 46 tons normal **S:** 25.8 kts **Dim:** 21.0 × 5.3 × 1.22
**A:** 1/12.7-mm mg (usually not mounted) **Electron Equipt:** Radar: 1/MD 806
**M:** 12 Mercedes-Benz MB820Db diesels; 2 props; 2,200 hp **Electric:** 2 kw
**Range:** 240/23.8 **Man:** 10 tot.

◆ **1 Hamanami (23-meter) class** Bldr: Sumidagawa, Tokyo

PC 52 Hamanami (In serv. 22-3-71)

**Hamanami (PC 52)** *Ships of the World,* 1987

**D:** 60 tons (fl) **S:** 20.9 kts **Dim:** 21.0 × 5.1 × 1.22
**Electron Equipt:** Radar: 1/MD 808
**M:** 2 Mercedes-Benz MB820Db diesels; 2 props; 2,200 hp
**Electric:** 2 kw **Range:** 290/20.9 **Man:** 10 tot.

◆ **1 Hamagiri (23-meter) class** Bldr: Sumidagawa, Tokyo

PC 48 Hamagiri (In serv. 19-3-70)

**D:** 51 tons (fl) **S:** 14.6 kts **Dim:** 21.0 × 5.1 × 1.11
**Electron Equipt:** Radar: 1/MD 808
**M:** 2 Mitsubishi 12DH 20TK diesels; 2 props; 1,140 hp
**Electric:** 2 kw **Range:** 270/12.9 **Man:** 10 tot.

Note: The 5 *Umigiri*-class patrol boats, *Umigiri* (PC 46), *Asagiri* (PC 47), *Sagiri* (PC 49), *Setogiri* (PC 50), and *Hayagiri* (PC 51) were stricken 1982–85.

## PATROL CRAFT (CL)

◆ **63 Yamayuri (15-meter) class**

| | Bldr | In serv. |
|---|---|---|
| CL 201 Yamayuri | Ishihara, Takasago | 27-1-78 |
| CL 202 Tachibana | Ishihara, Takasago | 24-2-78 |
| CL 203 Komakusa | Ishihara, Takasago | 30-1-79 |
| CL 204 Shiragiku | Ishihara, Takasago | 22-2-79 |
| CL 205 Yaguruma | Sumidagawa, Tokyo | 31-7-79 |
| CL 206 Hamanasu | Sumidagawa, Tokyo | 29-9-79 |
| CL 207 Suzuran | Sumidagawa, Tokyo | 31-7-79 |
| CL 208 Isogiku | Sumidagawa, Tokyo | 12-9-79 |
| CL 209 Isegiko | Sumidagawa, Tokyo | 31-8-79 |
| CL 210 Ayame | Yokohama Yacht | 29-10-79 |
| CL 211 Ajisai | Yokohama Yacht | 26-9-79 |
| CL 212 Himawari | Yokohama Yacht | 29-10-79 |
| CL 213 Hazakura | Yokohama Yacht | 29-8-79 |
| CL 214 Hinagiku | Ishihara, Takasago | 9-7-79 |
| CL 215 Hamagiku | Yokohama Yacht | 19-9-79 |
| CL 216 Fuyume | Ishihara, Takasago | 30-7-79 |
| CL 217 Tsubaki | Ishihara, Takasago | 10-8-79 |
| CL 218 Sazanka | Ishihara, Takasago | 30-8-79 |
| CL 219 Aoi | Sumidagawa, Tokyo | 31-10-79 |
| CL 220 Suisen | Yokohama Yacht | 29-10-79 |
| CL 221 Yaezakura | Ishihara, Takasago | 25-9-79 |
| CL 222 Akebi | Ishihara, Takasago | 29-10-79 |
| CL 223 Shirahagi | Sumidagawa, Tokyo | 25-1-80 |
| CL 224 Benibana | Sumidagawa, Tokyo | 25-1-80 |
| CL 225 Muratsubaki | Ishihara, Takasago | 20-12-79 |
| CL 226 Tsutsuji | Sumidagawa, Tokyo | 22-2-80 |
| CL 227 Ashibi | Ishihara, Takasago | 20-12-79 |
| CL 228 Satozakura | Ishihara, Takasago | 26-2-80 |
| CL 229 Yukitsubaki | Ishihara, Takasago | 28-2-80 |
| CL 230 Satsuki | Shinki SY, Osaka | 22-2-80 |
| CL 231 Ezogiku | Yokohama Yacht | 18-11-80 |
| CL 232 Akashio | Sumidagawa, Tokyo | 18-11-80 |
| CL 233 Kozakura | Yokohama Yacht | 18-11-80 |
| CL 234 Shirame | Ishihara, Takasago | 28-11-80 |
| CL 235 Sarubia | Ishihara, Takasago | 28-11-80 |
| CL 236 Suiren | Shinki SY, Osaka | 19-12-80 |
| CL 237 Hatsugiku | Ishihara, Takasago | 29-1-81 |
| CL 238 Hamayura | Ishihara, Takasago | 29-1-80 |
| CL 239 Airisu | Yokohama Yacht | 18-2-82 |
| CL 240 Yamabuki | Sumidagawa, Tokyo | 17-12-81 |
| CL 241 Shirayuri | Nobutaka | 1-2-82 |
| CL 242 Karatachi | Ishihara, Takasago | 17-12-81 |
| CL 243 Kobai | Ishihara, Takasago | 18-2-82 |
| CL 244 Hamayūū | Ishihara, Takasago | 29-1-82 |
| CL 245 Sasayuri | Sumidagawa, Tokyo | 25-1-83 |
| CL 246 Kosumosu | Ishihara, Takasago | 17-2-83 |
| CL 247 Shiogiku | Sumidagawa, Tokyo | 29-11-82 |
| CL 248 Yamahagi | Yokohama Yacht | 29-11-82 |
| CL 249 Mokuren | Shinki SY, Osaka | 25-1-83 |
| CL 250 Isobuji | Ishihara, Takasago | 7-3-83 |
| CL 251 Tamatsubaki | Sumidagawa, Tokyo | 26-1-84 |
| CL 252 Yodoki | Shinki SY, Osaka | 22-11-83 |
| CL 253 Iozakura | Ishihara, Takasago | 25-11-83 |
| CL 254 Himetsubaki | Ishihara, Takasago | 18-1-84 |
| CL 255 Tokikusa | Sumidagawa, Tokyo | 24-2-84 |
| CL 256 Mutsugiku | Sumidagawa, Tokyo | 15-11-84 |
| CL 257 Terugiko | Shiga, Sagai | 19-12-84 |
| CL 258 Mayazakura | Ishihara, Takasago | 20-12-84 |
| CL 259 Yamagiko | Yokohama Yacht | 22-1-85 |
| CL 260 Tobiume | Ishihara, Takasago | 24-1-85 |
| CL 261 Kotozakura | Sumidagawa, Tokyo | 28-2-85 |
| CL 262 Minogiku | Ishihara, Takasago | 14-2-85 |
| CL 263 Kuroyuri | Yokohama Yacht | 15-11-84 |

**Isobuji (CL 250)** *Ships of the World,* 1987

**PATROL CRAFT (CL)** *(continued)*

**D:** 27 tons normal (35.7 fl) **S:** 20.7 kts
**Dim:** 18.00 (16.60 wl) × 4.30 × 0.82 (1.10 props)
**M:** 2 RD10T AO6 diesels; 2 props; 900 hp
**Range:** 180/19 **Man:** 6 tot.

Remarks: Three water cannon for fire-fighting. CL 251–263 have waterjets, vice propellers, and can make 21.9 kts; their engines are type S6A-MTK (450 hp each).

◆ **4 Nogekaze class** Bldr: Sumidagawa, Tokyo

| | In serv. | | In serv. |
|---|---|---|---|
| CL 99 Nogekaze | 10-72 | CL 107 Itokaze | 11-72 |
| CL 105 Kusukaze | 10-72 | CL 128 Kawakaze | 10-73 |

**Itokaze (CL 107)** *Ships of the World,* 1984

**D:** 22.5 tons normal **S:** 16.6 kts **Dim:** 16.00 × 4.10 × 0.80 (hull)
**M:** 2 Type UDV816 diesels; 2 props; 500 hp **Electric:** 5 kVA
**Range:** 160/14.7 **Man:** 6 tot.

◆ **95 Chiyokaze class**

Bldrs: Ishihara, Nobotuka, Yokohama Yacht, Sumidagawa, 1968–76

| | | |
|---|---|---|
| CL 44 Chiyokaze | CL 89 Kishikaze | CL 125 Tonekaze |
| CL 50 Suzukaze | CL 90 Mayakaze | CL 126 Shizukaze |
| CL 51 Urakaze | CL 91 Kikukaze | CL 127 Murokaze |
| CL 53 Sugikaze | CL 92 Hirokaze | CL 129 Yamakaze |
| CL 54 Fujikaze | CL 93 Kibikaze | CL 130 Hikokaze |
| CL 55 Miyakaze | CL 94 Ashikaze | CL 131 Takakaze |
| CL 57 Chinukaze | CL 95 Otokaze | CL 132 Murakaze |
| CL 59 Nachikaze | CL 96 Kurikaze | CL 133 Nomokaze |
| CL 65 Tomakaze | CL 97 Imakaze | CL 134 Kumokaze |
| CL 66 Hibakaze | CL 98 Terukaze | CL 135 Yanakaze |
| CL 67 Yurikaze | CL 100 Tokitsukaze | CL 136 Yurakaze |
| CL 68 Sumikaze | CL 101 Tsukikaze | CL 137 Washikaze |
| CL 69 Kashima | CL 102 Awakaze | CL 138 Kushikaze |
| CL 70 Takekaze | CL 104 Miokaze | CL 139 Hoshikaze |
| CL 71 Kinukaze | CL 106 Kilkaze | CL 140 Gettō |
| CL 72 Shigikaze | CL 108 Tamatsukaze | CL 141 Iwakaze |
| CL 73 Uzukaze | CL 109 Miyokaze | CL 142 Matsukaze |
| CL 74 Akikaze | CL 110 Ayakaze | CL 143 Oitsukaze |
| CL 75 Setokaze | CL 111 Mitsukaze | CL 144 Arakaze |
| CL 76 Kurekaze | CL 112 Hatakaze | CL 145 Tanikaze |
| CL 77 Mojikaze | CL 113 Numakaze | CL 146 Kochikaze |
| CL 78 Satakaze | CL 114 Soyokaze | CL 147 Okikaze |
| CL 79 Kirikaze | CL 115 Minekaze | CL 148 Suwakaze |
| CL 80 Kamikaze | CL 116 Okitsukaze | CL 149 Sachikaze |
| CL 81 Umikaze | CL 117 Deigo | CL 150 Natsukaze |
| CL 82 Yumekaze | CL 118 Yuuna | CL 151 Harukaze |
| CL 83 Makikaze | CL 119 Adan | CL 152 Rindō |
| CL 84 Hakaze | CL 120 Horokaze | CL 153 Sawakaze |
| CL 85 Shachikaze | CL 121 Somakaze | CL 154 Kaidō |
| CL 86 Himekaze | CL 122 Hatsukaze | CL 155 Nadeshiko |
| CL 87 Isekaze | CL 123 Sasakaze | CL 156 Yamazakura |
| CL 88 Komakaze | CL 124 Hagikaze | |

**D:** 19.5 tons normal **S:** 18.4 kts **Dim:** 15.00 × 4.10 × 0.76 (hull)
**M:** 2 Mitsubishi DH24MK diesels; 2 props; 500 hp **Range:** 180/16.1
**Man:** 6 tot.

Remarks: *Nomakaze* (CL 103) was lost in 1978. CL 69 is named for her home port; CL 117 to CL 119 are home-ported in Okinawa.

**Kirikaze (CL 79)** L. & L. Van Ginderen, 5-85

**HYDROGRAPHIC SHIPS**

◆ **1 Tenyo class**

| | Bldr | Laid down | L | In serv. |
|---|---|---|---|---|
| HL 04 Tenyo | Sumitomo, Uraga | 11-4-86 | 5-8-86 | 27-11-86 |

**Tenyo (HL 04)** MSA, 11-86

**D:** 770 tons (. . . fl) **S:** 13.5 kts **Dim:** 56.0 × 9.8 × 2.9
**Electron Equipt:** Radar: 2/SMA 1596
**M:** 2 Asakasa MH23 diesels; 2 CP props; 1,300 hp **Range:** 5,400/13
**Electric:** 320 kVA (2 × 160 kVA diesel sets) **Man:** . . .

Remarks: 430 grt. Carries one 10-m survey boat.

◆ **1 Takuyo (2,600-ton) class** Bldr: Nippon Kokan, Tsurumi

| | Laid down | L | In serv. |
|---|---|---|---|
| HL 02 Takuyo | 14-4-82 | 24-3-83 | 31-8-83 |

**Takuyo (HL 02)** L. & L. Van Ginderen, 5-85

**D:** 2,979 tons (3,370 fl) **S:** 18.2 kts
**Dim:** 96.00 (90.00 wl) × 14.20 × 4.51 mean (4.91 max. over sonar)
**M:** 2 Fuji 6S40B diesels; 2 CP props; 5,200 hp **Electric:** 965 kVA
**Range:** 12,800/16.9 **Endurance:** 50 days
**Man:** 39 crew + 22 survey party

Remarks: 2,481 grt. In 1981 program to replace earlier unit with same name. Has bow-thruster, side-looking, contour-mapping sonars, precision echo-sounders, etc. Carries two survey launches.

## HYDROGRAPHIC SHIPS *(continued)*

◆ **1 Shoyo (1,900-ton) class** Bldr: Hitachi, Maizuru

HL 01 Shoyo (In serv. 26-2-72)

**Shoyo (HL 01)** *Ships of the World,* 1987

**D:** 2,200 tons normal **S:** 17.4 kts **Dim:** 81.70 (78.60 wl) × 12.60 × 4.20
**M:** 2 Fuji 12VM 32 H2F diesels; 1 prop; 4,800 hp **Electric:** 1,250 kVA
**Range:** 12,000/14 **Man:** 73 tot.

Remarks: 1,900 grt. Has bow-thruster.

◆ **1 Meiyo class** Bldr: Nagoya SY

HL 03 Meiyo (In serv. 15-3-63)

**Meiyo (HL 03)** 1975

**D:** 486 tons normal **S:** 12 kts **Dim:** 44.80 (40.50 pp) × 8.05 × 2.88
**M:** 1 Asakasa TR 655 diesel; 1 prop; 700 hp **Electric:** 140 kVA
**Range:** 5,280/11 **Man:** 40 tot.

## COASTAL HYDROGRAPHIC SHIP

◆ **1 Kaiyo class** Bldr: Ishikawajima Harima, Nagoya

HM 06 Kaiyo (In serv. 14-5-64)

**Kaiyo (HM 06)** *Ships of the World,* 1984

**D:** 380 tons normal **S:** 12 kts **Dim:** 44.53 × 8.05 × 2.39
**M:** 1 Sumiyoshi Tekko S 6 NBS diesel; 1 prop; 450 hp
**Electric:** 90 kVA **Range:** 3,160/10 **Man:** 31 tot.

Note: Two smaller coastal survey ships were stricken 30-6-86: *Tenyo* (HM 05) and *Heiyo* (HM 04).

## INSHORE HYDROGRAPHIC CRAFT

◆ **1 Kerama (15-meter) class** Bldr: Ito Tekko SY, Sasebo

HS 32 Kerama (In serv. 28-11-73)

**D:** 23.2 tons normal **S:** 11 kts **Dim:** 15.0 × 4.0 × 0.86
**M:** 1 UDV 816 diesel; 250 hp **Range:** 450/10 **Man:** 7 tot.

Remarks: Glass-reinforced plastic construction.

◆ **4 Akashi (15-meter) class** Bldrs: Various (In serv. 1973–77)

HS 31 Akashi HS 33 Hayatomo HS 34 Kurihama HS 35 Kurushima

**D:** 21 tons normal **S:** 10.2 kts **Dim:** 15.0 × 4.0 × 0.84
**M:** 1 Nissan-MTU UD626 diesel; 180 hp **Range:** 630/9.7 **Man:** 7 tot.

Remarks: Glass-reinforced plastic hull. Resemble CL 44-class patrol craft, but have bulwarks surrounding upper deck of the hull.

◆ **11 Hamashio class** Bldr: Nippon Hikaki, Yokosuka (In serv. 1969–72)

| | | | |
|---|---|---|---|
| HS 01 Hamashio | HS 04 Uzushio | HS 07 Takashio | HS 10 Oyashio |
| HS 02 Iseshio | HS 05 Hayashio | HS 08 Wakashio | HS 11 Kuroshio |
| HS 03 Setoshio | HS 06 Isoshio | HS 09 Yukishio | |

**Hamashio (HS 01)** L. & L. Van Ginderen, 5-83

**D:** 6 tons normal **S:** 8.9–9.3 kts **Dim:** 10.15 × 2.65 × 0.81
**M:** 1 Nissan-MTU UD326 diesel; 90 hp **Range:** 343/8.5 **Man:** 7 tot.

Remarks: Glass-reinforced plastic construction.

## NAVIGATIONAL AID TENDERS

◆ **1 Tsushima class** Bldr: Mitsui, Tamano

| | Laid down | L | In serv. |
|---|---|---|---|
| LL 01 Tsushima | 10-6-76 | 7-4-77 | 9-9-77 |

**Tsushima (LL 01)** *Ships of the World,* 1987

**D:** 1,865 tons normal **S:** 16 kts (17.6 trials)
**Dim:** 75.00 (70.00 wl) × 12.50 × 4.15
**M:** 1 Fuji-Sulzer 8S 40C diesel; 1 CP prop; 4,200 hp **Electric:** 900 kVA
**Fuel:** 477 tons **Range:** 10,000/15 **Man:** 54 tot.

Remarks: Intended for use as a lighthouse supply ship. Has Flume-type passive stabilization tanks, bow-thruster.

◆ **3 Hokuto-class buoy tenders**

| | Bldr | Laid down | L | In serv. |
|---|---|---|---|---|
| LL 11 Hokuto | Sasebo DY | 19-10-78 | 20-3-79 | 29-6-79 |
| LL 12 Kaio | Sasebo DY | 17-7-79 | 20-10-79 | 11-3-80 |
| LL 13 Ginga | Kawasaki, Kobe | 13-6-79 | 16-11-79 | 18-3-80 |

**D:** 620 tons light (839 fl) **S:** 13.8 kts **Dim:** 55.00 (51.00 wl) × 10.60 × 2.65
**M:** 2 Asakasa MH23 (LL 11: Hanshin 6L 24SH) diesels; 2 props; 1,400 hp
**Electric:** 300 kVA **Fuel:** 62 tons **Range:** 3,460/13
**Man:** 9 officers, 20 men, 2 technicians

## NAVIGATIONAL AID TENDERS *(continued)*

**Hokuto (LL 11)** L. & L. Van Ginderen, 5-84

◆ **1 Zuiun (270-ton) class**

| | Bldr | Laid down | L | In serv. |
|---|---|---|---|---|
| LM 101 Zuiun | Usuki Iron Wks., Usuki | 19-1-83 | 27-4-83 | 27-7-83 |

**Zuiun (LM 101)** *Ships of the World,* 1987

**D:** 370 tons normal (398 fl) **S:** 15.1 kts **Dim:** 46.00 (41.40 pp) × 7.50 × 2.23
**M:** 2 Mitsubishi-Akasaka MH 23-series diesels; 2 CP props; 1,300 hp
**Range:** 1,440/14.5 **Electric:** 120 kw **Fuel:** 34 $m^3$ **Man:** 20 tot.

Remarks: Lighthouse service vessels. Cargo: 85 tons. One diesel is model MH23F, other is MH23. Second unit requested under FY 85 Budget but not approved.

◆ **1 Miyojo-class buoy tender** Bldr: Ishikawajima, Tokyo

LM 11 Miyojo (In serv. 25-3-74)

**Miyojo (LM 11)** F. Lauga, 1976

**D:** 248 tons (303 normal) **S:** 11 kts **Dim:** 27.0 × 12.0 × 2.58
**M:** 2 Niigata 6MG 16HS diesels; 2 CP props; 600 hp **Electric:** 135 kVA
**Fuel:** 15 tons **Range:** 1,360/10 **Man:** 18 tot.

Remarks: Has catamaran hull. Replaced a very similar ship with same name and number, which was lost in 4-72.

◆ **4 Hakuun class** Bldr: Sumidagawa, Tokyo (LM 107, 114; Yokohama Yacht)

| | |
|---|---|
| LM 106 Hakuun (In serv. 28-2-78) | LM 107 Toun (In serv. 3-79) |
| LM 114 Tokuun (In serv. 23-3-82) | LM 201 Shoun (In serv. 26-3-86) |

**Hakuun (LM 106)** *Ships of the World,* 1984

**D:** 57.6 tons (92.7 fl) **S:** 15 kts **Dim:** 24.00 (23.00 pp) × 6.00 × 1.00
**Electron Equipt:** Radar: 1/FRA-10 Mk III
**M:** 2 G.M. 12V71 TI diesels; 2 props; 1,080 hp **Electric:** 30 kVA
**Range:** 420/13 **Man:** 10 tot.

◆ **1 Ayabane class** Bldr: Shimoda DY, Shimoda

LM 112 Ayabane (In serv. 25-12-72)

**Ayabane (LM 112)** *Ships of the World,* 1987

**D:** 187 tons normal **S:** 12.3 kts **Dim:** 32.70 × 6.5 × 1.8
**M:** 1 Hanshin 6 L24SH diesel; 1 prop; 500 hp **Electric:** 70 kVA
**Range:** 2,330/11.9 **Man:** 18 tot.

◆ **5 23-meter group** Bldrs: Various

| | In serv. | | In serv. |
|---|---|---|---|
| LM 102 Reiun | 11-71 | LM 111 Houn | 3-70 |
| LM 105 Sekiun | 3-70 | LM 113 Genun | 3-73 |
| LM 110 Seiun | 3-68 | | |

**Genun (LM 113)** *Ships of the World,* 1987

**D:** 67–74 tons (normal) **S:** 9.7–10.5 kts **Dim:** 22.1 × 4.65 × 1.4
**M:** 1 Yanman or G.M. diesel; 120–200 hp **Range:** 760–1,060/9.5
**Man:** 11–12 tot.

Remarks: Minor variations but all similar. The original LM 108, *Reimei,* completed in 1962, was replaced in 1982. *Shoun* (LM 109) stricken 10-3-86.

## NAVIGATIONAL AID TENDERS *(continued)*

◆ **12 (+1) 17-meter class** Bldr: Yokohama Yacht

| | In serv. | | In serv. |
|---|---|---|---|
| LS 204 Hatsuhikari | 3-79 | LS 210 Shimahikari | 17-12-79 |
| LS 205 Nahahikari | 2-79 | LS 211 Akihikari | 27-2-81 |
| LS 206 Matsuhikari | 3-79 | LS 212 Wakahikari | 5-3-82 |
| LS 207 Michihikari | 14-7-79 | LS 213 Miohikari | 18-3-83 |
| LS 208 Nishihikari | 14-7-79 | LS 214 Urahikari | 27-1-84 |
| LS 209 Kamihikari | 17-12-79 | LS 215 Tamahikari | 24-2-84 |
| | | LS . . . N . . . | . . . |

**Kamihikari (LS 209)** *Ships of the World,* 1980

**D:** 25 tons normal **S:** 16.3 kts **Dim:** 17.50 × 4.30 × 0.80
**M:** 2 E12OT-MF6R diesels; 2 props; 560 hp **Endurance:** 2 days
**Range:** 230/14.5 **Man:** 8 tot.

Remarks: One unit approved under FY 87 Budget.

◆ **6 Urahikari (17-meter) class** Bldrs: Various (In serv. 1972–75)

| | | |
|---|---|---|
| LS 115 Fusahikari | LS 184 Tomohikari | LS 202 Takahikari |
| LS 156 Sekihikari | LS 201 Haruhikari | LS 203 Setohikari |

**Takahikari (LS 202)** *Ships of the World,* 1984

**D:** 16 tons (20 fl) **S:** 17.2 kts **Dim:** 17.00 × 3.50 × . . .
**M:** 1 MTU UD 626 diesel; 180 hp **Range:** 320/5 **Man:** 10 tot.

◆ **10 (+2) 12-meter class** Bldr: Nippon Hikoki, Yokosuka (LS 186–193: Ishikawajima, Tokyo)

| | In serv. | | In serv. | | In serv. |
|---|---|---|---|---|---|
| LS 181 Keiko | 29-6-79 | LS 188 Taiko | 24-1-85 | LS 192 Suiko | 30-1-87 |
| LS 185 Shoko | 26-2-79 | LS 189 Choko | 20-12-85 | LS 193 Saiko | 2-2-87 |
| LS 186 Toko | 30-6-79 | LS 190 Miyoko | 24-12-85 | LS 194 N . . . | . . . |
| LS 187 Getsuko | 30-6-79 | LS 191 Kyoko | 21-1-86 | LS 195 N . . . | . . . |

**D:** 9.4 tons (10 fl) **S:** 15 kts **Dim:** 12.00 × 3.20 × 0.60
**M:** 1 diesel; 1 prop; 210 hp **Range:** 120/13.5 **Man:** 6 tot.

Remarks: Two more approved in FY 87 Budget.

◆ **1 Taiko (12-meter) class** Bldr: Tsubo Yacht, Nagoya

LS 183 Haruko (In serv. 10-3-73)

**D:** 8 tons (12 fl) **S:** 14.8 kts **Dim:** 12.0 × 3.2 × 1.6
**M:** 1 MTU UD 626 diesel; 180 hp **Range:** 130/12.5 **Man:** 6 tot.

Remarks: Sister *Taiko* (LS 152) stricken 1-10-84; *Kyoko* (LS 151) on 8-1-86, *Myoko* (LS 171) on 9-12-85, and *Choko* (LS 218) on 4-12-85; *Meiko* (LS 122) on 1-2-87, and *Suiko* (LS 153) and *Saiko* (LS 219) on 14-1-87.

**Choko (LS 189)** *Ships of the World,* 1986

◆ **1 (+2) No. 1 Reiko (10-meter) class** Bldr: . . .

LS 168 No. 1 Reiko (In serv. 2-12-86)
LS 169 No. 2 Reiko (In serv. . . .)
LS 170 No. 3 Reiko (In serv. . . .)

**No. 1 Reiko (LS 168)** *Ships of the World,* 1987

**D:** 4.9 tons **S:** 15 kts **Dim:** 9.9 × 2.5 × 1.1
**M:** 1 diesel; 1 prop; 115 hp **Range:** 140/13

Remarks: GRP construction. Two more authorized under FY 87. LS 168 laid down 1-10-86, launched 21-11-86.

◆ **5 No. 1 Zuiko (10-meter) class** Bldr: . . .

| | Laid down | L | In serv. |
|---|---|---|---|
| LS 161 No. 1 Zuiko | 20-9-85 | 20-11-85 | 5-12-85 |
| LS 164 No. 2 Zuiko | 29-9-85 | 26-11-85 | 12-12-85 |
| LS 165 No. 3 Zuiko | 8-10-85 | 2-12-85 | 18-12-85 |
| LS 166 No. 4 Zuiko | 16-10-85 | 19-12-85 | 17-1-86 |
| LS 167 No. 5 Zuiko | 24-10-85 | 9-1-86 | 24-1-86 |

**No. 2 Zuiko (LS 164)** *Ships of the World,* 1986

## NAVIGATIONAL AID TENDERS *(continued)*

**D:** 4–5 tons **S:** 14 kts **Dim:** 9.9 × 2.8 × 1.6
**M:** 1 diesel; 1 prop; 115 hp **Range:** 130/13 **Man:** 8 tot.

REMARKS: GRP construction.

◆ **10 No. 1 Kaiko (10-meter) class** Bldr: Nippon Hikoki, Yokosuka

LS 144 No. 1 KAIKO (In serv. 5-3-81)
LS 145 No. 2 KAIKO (In serv. 12-3-81)
LS 146 No. 3 KAIKO (In serv. 19-3-81)
LS 148 No. 4 KAIKO (In serv. 10-12-81)
LS 149 No. 5 KAIKO (In serv. 1982)
LS 154 No. 6 KAIKO (In serv. 1982)
LS 155 No. 7 KAIKO (In serv. 12-1-84)
LS 157 No. 8 KAIKO (In serv. 17-1-84)
LS 158 No. 9 KAIKO (In serv. 13-2-84)
LS 160 No. 10 KAIKO (In serv. 21-2-84)

**No. 3 Kaiko (LS 146)** *Ships of the World,* 1984

**D:** 5.2 tons **S:** 13 kts **Dim:** 9.00 × 2.25 × . . .
**M:** 2 Nissan FD606 diesels; 1 prop; 230 hp **Range:** 130/12.5 **Man:** 6 tot.

REMARKS: Glass-reinforced plastic construction.

◆ **6 No. 1 Yoko (10-meter) class** Bldr: IHI Craft, Yokohama (In serv. 1975–79)

LS 114 No. 3 YOKO
LS 180 No. 1 YOKO
LS 182 No. 2 YOKO
LS 141 No. 4 YOKO
LS 142 No. 5 YOKO
LS 143 No. 6 YOKO

**D:** 3 tons (5 fl) **S:** 16.2 kts **Dim:** 7.3 × 2.45 × 0.5
**M:** 1 G.M. 3-53N diesel; 112 hp **Range:** 100/12 **Man:** 8 tot.

◆ **2 No. 1 Shinko (10-meter) class** Bldr: . . .

LS 147 No. 1 SHINKO (In serv. 20-10-72)
LS 132 No. 2 SHINKO (In serv. 10-12-72)

**D:** 10 tons **S:** 8.7 kts **Dim:** 9.5 × 2.6 × 1.1
**M:** 1 diesel; 1 prop; 90 hp **Range:** 100/8.7

REMARKS: Wooden construction. To be replaced by the two FY 87 10-meter boats.

◆ **4 Wako No. 4 class** Bldr: Yanmar Diesel, Arai

LS 123 WAKO No. 4 (In serv. 31-1-74)
LS 116 WAKO No. 1 (In serv. 11-10-78)
LS 117 WAKO No. 2 (In serv. 11-10-78)
LS 118 WAKO No. 3 (In serv. 24-3-79)

**D:** 2 tons **S:** 17 kts **Dim:** 5.99 × 2.41 × . . .
**M:** 1 Yanmar diesel; 115 hp **Range:** 70/17

REMARKS: Same design as the *Orion*-class oil-spill surveillance craft.

◆ **5 Tenko No. 1 class** Bldr: Yanmar Diesel, Arai

LS 125 TENKO No. 1 (In serv. 28-7-70)
LS 102 TENKO No. 2 (In serv. 30-9-71)
LS 103 TENKO No. 3 (In serv. 30-9-71)
LS 137 TENKO No. 4 (In serv. 30-9-72)
LS 105 TENKO No. 5 (In serv. 4-12-73)

**D:** 0.6 tons **S:** 9 kts **Dim:** 5.6 × 1.6 × . . .
**M:** 1 Yanmar outboard; 12 hp **Range:** 20/9

REMARKS: Wooden outboard motor boats.

NOTE: All units of the *Eko No. 1* class have been stricken: *Eko No. 1* (LS 106) on 5-12-85; *Eko No. 2* (LS 113) on 12-12-85; *Eko No. 3* (LS 163) on 31-3-86; *Eko No. 4* (LS 174) on 18-12-85; and *Eko No. 5* (LS 112) in 1985–86.

## FIREBOATS

NOTE: Most patrol ships, boats, and craft are fitted for fire-fighting.

◆ **5 Hiryu class** Bldr: Nippon Kokan, Yokohama (FL 05: Yokohama Yacht)

| | In serv. | | In serv. |
|---|---|---|---|
| FL 01 HIRYU | 4-3-69 | FL 04 KAIRYU | 18-3-77 |
| FL 02 SHORYU | 4-3-70 | FL 05 SUIRYU | 24-3-78 |
| FL 03 NANRYU | 4-3-71 | | |

**D:** 199 tons (251 normal) **S:** 13.7 kts **Dim:** 27.5 × 10.4 × 2.1
**M:** 2 Ikegai-MTU MB820Db diesels; 2 props; 2,200 hp **Electric:** 70 kVA
**Range:** 400/13 **Man:** 14 tot.

**Hiryu (FL 01)** L. & L. Van Ginderen, 1985

REMARKS: Catamaran hulls. For fighting fires on board supertankers. 14.5 $m^3$ tank for fire-fighting chemicals. One 45-meter-range chemical sprayer; seven 60-meter-range water cannon.

◆ **10 Ninobiki class**

Bldrs: FM 02, FM 06, FM 08, FM 10: Sumidagawa, Tokyo; Others: Yokohama Yacht

| | In serv. | | In serv. |
|---|---|---|---|
| FM 01 NINOBIKI | 25-2-74 | FM 06 NACHI | 14-2-76 |
| FM 02 YODO | 30-3-75 | FM 07 KEGON | 29-1-77 |
| FM 03 OTOWA | 25-12-74 | FM 08 MINOO | 27-1-78 |
| FM 04 SHIRAITO | 25-2-75 | FM 09 RYUSEI | 24-3-80 |
| FM 05 KOTOBIKI | 31-1-76 | FM 10 KYOTAKI | 25-3-81 |

**Kegon (FM 07)** *Ships of the World,* 1987

**D:** 89 tons (99 normal) **S:** 13.4 kts **Dim:** 23.00 × 6.00 × 1.55
**M:** 1 Ikegai MTU MB820Db and 2 Nissan UDV 816 diesels; 3 props; 1,600 hp
**Electric:** 40 kVA **Range:** 234/13.4
**Man:** 12 tot.

REMARKS: Four fire pumps: one of 6,000 lit./min., two of 3,000 lit./min., and one of 2,000 lit./min. Have two 750-liter and one 5,000-liter foam tanks.

## ENVIRONMENTAL-PROTECTION CRAFT

◆ **1 Katsuren-class radiation monitoring craft** Bldr: Ishihara, Takasago

MS 03 KATSUREN (In serv. 13-12-75)

**D:** 30 tons (46 fl) **S:** 12.3 kts **Dim:** 16.50 × 5.50 × 1.10
**M:** 2 UDV 816 diesels; 2 props; 500 hp **Range:** 190/10.8 **Man:** 9 tot.

◆ **2 Kinagusa-class radiation monitoring craft** Bldr: Sumidagawa, Tokyo

MS 01 KINAGUSA (In serv. 25-9-70)
MS 02 SAIKAI (In serv. 1-10-70)

**D:** 16 tons (23 fl) **S:** 8.1 kts **Dim:** 10.50 × 5.00 × 0.63
**M:** 2 UD 326 diesels; 2 props; 180 hp **Range:** 170/7.6
**Man:** 8 tot.

ENVIRONMENTAL-PROTECTION CRAFT *(continued)*

**Katsuren (MS 03)** *Ships of the World,* 1987

**Kinagusa (MS 01)** *Ships of the World,* 1987

◆ **1 Sazankurosu-class oil-spill surveillance craft**

SS 35 Sazankurosu (In serv. 20-9-84)

**D:** 4.7 tons **S:** 25 kts **Dim:** 7.0 × 2.3 × . . .
**M:** 1 AQ 260A inboard/outboard motor; 130 hp
**Range:** 70/25 **Man:** . . . tot.

Remarks: GRP unsinkable lifeboat design.

◆ **32 Orion-class oil-spill surveillance craft** Bldr: Yokohama Yacht and Yanmar Diesel, Arai (In serv. 1972–1979)

| | | | |
|---|---|---|---|
| SS 01 Orion | SS 10 Carina | SS 19 Rigel | SS 27 Hercules |
| SS 02 Pegasus | SS 11 Capella | SS 20 Cygnus | SS 28 Gemini |
| SS 04 Neptune | SS 12 Spica | SS 21 Deneb | SS 29 Aries |
| SS 05 Jupiter | SS 13 Sirius | SS 22 Mercury | SS 30 Comet |
| SS 06 Venus | SS 14 Vega | SS 23 Perseus | SS 31 Regulus |
| SS 07 Cassiopeia | SS 16 Procyon | SS 24 Centaurus | SS 32 Betelgeuse |
| SS 08 Phoenix | SS 17 Leo | SS 25 Andromeda | SS 33 Aldebaran |
| SS 09 Serpens | SS 18 Polaris | SS 26 Altair | SS 34 Pleiades |

**D:** 2.1 tons (5 fl) **S:** 28.0 kts **Dim:** 5.99 × 2.44 × . . .
**M:** 1 AQ 200 inboard/outboard motor; 130 hp **Range:** 85/25 **Man:** 6 tot.

**Polaris (SS 18)** *Ships of the World,* 1984

Remarks: Propulsion and speeds vary: 16–28 kts from 130–210 hp. Four sisters serve as navigational aid tenders (LS 116–118, 123).

◆ **1 Antares-class oil-spill surveillance craft** Bldr: Sajima Marina, Aburappo

SS 15 Antares (In serv. 1-7-75)

**D:** 1.6 tons **S:** 25 kts **Dim:** 5.49 × 2.41 × . . .
**M:** 1 Yanmar YA-19J2 diesel; waterjet; 220 hp **Range:** 170/24 **Man:** 6 tot.

◆ **5 Shirasagi-class oil-spill clearance boats** Bldr: Various (In serv. 1977–79)

| | | |
|---|---|---|
| OR 01 Shirasagi | OR 03 Mizunagi | OR 05 Isoshigi |
| OR 02 Shiratori | OR 04 Chidori | |

**Shiratori (OR 02)** *Ships of the World,* 1984

**D:** 78.5 tons (153 fl) **S:** 6.8 kts **Dim:** 22.0 × 6.4 × 0.9
**M:** 2 UD 626 diesels; water-jet drive; 390 hp **Range:** 160/6 **Man:** 7 tot.

◆ **3 Uraga-class oil-skimmer boats** Bldr: Lockheed, U.S.A. (In serv. 1975–76)

OS 01 Tsurumi (ex-*Uraga*) OS 02 Bisan OS 03 Naruto

**Bisan (OS 02)** *Ships of the World,* 1987

**D:** 11 tons (fl) **S:** 6 kts **Dim:** 8.26 × 5.00 × 0.70
**M:** 1 HR-6 diesel; 2 props; 90 hp **Range:** 90/4.5 **Man:** 4 tot.

◆ **18 M-101-class oil-boom-extender barges** Bldrs: Various (In serv. 1974–76)

OX 01 to OX 06, OX 08 to OX 19 (M 101 to M 119)

**D:** 48 tons **Dim:** 22.00 × 7.20 × 0.45

**M 101 (OX 01)** 1975

**JAPAN** *(continued)*
**ENVIRONMENTAL-PROTECTION CRAFT** *(continued)*

◆ **2 miscellaneous wooden oil-spill craft** Bldr: Eidai Sangyo (In serv. 1967)

M 603 No. 02 M 804 No. 34

**D:** 1.1 tons **S:** 23.4 kts **Dim:** 6.0 × 2.1 × . . .
**M:** 1 outboard motor; 80 hp **Range:** 80/23

**TRAINING CRAFT**

◆ **1 A-class** (In serv. 12-75)

Aoba

**Aoba** *Ships of the World,* 1987

**D:** 15 tons **S:** 15.5 kts **Dim:** 14.0 × 3.6 × . . .
**M:** 1 diesel; 325 hp **Range:** 243/15.5

◆ **2 C-I class** Bldr: Yanmar Diesel, Arai (In serv. 9-75)

C-I C-II

**D:** 1 ton **S:** 28 kts **Dim:** 4.9 × 2.1 × . . .
**M:** 1 gasoline engine; 380 hp **Range:** 80/28

Remarks: Small GRP open, runabout launches of commercial design.

# JORDAN

**Hashemite Kingdom of Jordan**

COASTAL GUARD

Personnel: 300 men, including those at the base at Aqaba and frogmen

Merchant Marine (1986): 5 ships—42,365 grt

Note: Plans to acquire larger patrol craft from Greece or Great Britain have not reached fruition.

◆ **4 U.S.-supplied GRP smallcraft** Bldr: Bertram, Miami

Faysal Han Hasayu Muhammed

**D:** 8 tons **S:** 25 kts **Dim:** 11.6 × 4.0 × 0.5 **Man:** 8 tot.
**A:** 1/12.7-mm mg—2/7.62-mm mg **M:** 2 diesels; 2 props; 600 hp

◆ **2 U.S.-supplied GRP smallcraft** Bldr: Bertram, Miami

Abdullah Al Hussein

**D:** 6.5 tons **S:** 25 kts **Dim:** 9.26 × 3.26 × 0.46
**A:** 1/12.7-mm mg—1/7.62-mm mg **Man:** 8 tot.
**M:** 2 diesels; 2 props; 430 hp

# KAMPUCHEA

**Democratic Kampuchea**

Merchant Marine (1980): 3 ships—3,558 grt (No recent data available)

Note: The units listed below have been delivered to forces subservient to the Vietnamese government. A few craft left behind in 1975 by fleeing forces may still exist, but no reliable details are available.

**PATROL BOATS**

◆ **3 Soviet Turya-class hydrofoils**

**D:** 215 tons (250 fl) **S:** 40 kts
**Dim:** 39.0 × 7.6 (12.5 over foils) × 2.0 (4.0 over foils)
**A:** 2/57-mm AA aft (II × 1)—2/25-mm AA fwd (II × 1)
**Electron Equipt:** Radar: 1/Pot Drum, 1/Muff Cob
IFF: 1/High Pole B, 1/Square Head interrogator
**M:** 3 M504 diesels; 3 props; 15,000 hp
**Range:** 400/38; 650/25 **Man:** 24 tot.

Remarks: One unit delivered 3-84, two on 23-2-85 to Kampong Song. Torpedo tubes and helicopter-type dipping sonar deleted. Fixed hydrofoils forward, with stern planning on surface. Use Osa-II hull and propulsion.

**RIVER PATROL BOATS**

◆ **4 Soviet Shmel class**

**D:** 60 tons (fl) **S:** 22 kts **Dim:** 28.3 × 4.6 × 0.9
**A:** 1/76.2-mm, 48-cal. gun fwd. in tank turret (with one coaxial 7.62-mm mg)—2/25-mm AA aft (II × 1)—5/76.2-mm mg (I × 5)—1/122-mm RL (XVIII × 1)—mines
**M:** 2 M50-F4 diesels; 2 props; 2,400 hp **Range:** 240/20; 600/10
**Man:** 15–20 tot.

Remarks: Delivered 1984–85.

**AMPHIBIOUS CRAFT**

◆ **2 Soviet landing craft**

**D:** 70 tons (fl) **S:** 10 kts **Dim:** 19.0 × 4.3 × 1.0
**M:** 2 diesels; 2 props; 600 hp **Man:** 5 tot.

Remarks: Probable T4 class, delivered 1984–85.

# KENYA

**Republic of Kenya**

Personnel: (1986) approx. 650 total

Merchant Marine (1986): 29 ships—9,040 grt

**GUIDED-MISSILE PATROL BOATS**

◆ **2 "Province" class** Bldr: Vosper-Thornycroft, Portchester, U.K.

| | Laid down | L | In serv. |
|---|---|---|---|
| P 3126 Nyayo | 11-84 | 20-8-86 | 23-7-87 |
| P 3127 Umoja | 11-84 | 5-3-87 | 7-9-87 |

**D:** 311 tons light (363 fl) **S:** 40 kts **Dim:** 56.7 (52.0 pp) × 8.2 × 2.1
**A:** 4/Otomat Mk II SM (II × 2)—1/76-mm OTO Melara Compact DP—2/30-mm BMARC/Oerlikon GCM A02 AA (II × 1)—2/20-mm GAM-B01 AA (I × 2)
**Electron Equipt:** Radar: 1/Decca AC 1226, 1/Plessey AWS-4, 1/Marconi ST-802 f.c.
EW: MEL Matilda intercept, 2/Barricade RL (IX × 2)
**M:** 4 Paxman Valenta 18 RP 200 CM diesels; 4 props; 17,900 hp (15,000 sust.)—2 electric outdrives; 160 hp
**Electric:** 420 kw **Fuel:** 45.5 tons **Range:** 2,000/15 **Man:** 40 tot.

Remarks: Ordered 9-84. Generally similar to craft built for Oman and Egypt. Use Ferranti WSA.423 combat data/fire-control system. Carry a semi-rigid inspection boat on the stern. To replace the Vosper 31-m patrol boats in 1988 when fully operational.

**Nyayo (P 3126)**—on trials L. & L. Van Ginderen, 9-87

**KENYA** *(continued)*
**GUIDED-MISSILE PATROL BOATS** *(continued)*

**Umoja (P 3127)**—on trials G. Davies, Maritime Photographic, 12-87

◆ **3 32-meter class** Bldr: Brooke Marine, Lowestoft, U.K.

| | L | In serv. |
|---|---|---|
| P 3121 Madaraka | 28-1-75 | 16-6-75 |
| P 3122 Jamhuri | 14-3-75 | 16-6-75 |
| P 3123 Harambee | 2-5-75 | 28-8-75 |

**Jamhuri (P 3122)**—with Gabriel missiles
G. Davies, Maritime Photographic, 2-11-87

**D:** 120 tons (145 fl) **S:** 25.5 kts **Dim:** 32.6 × 6.1 × 1.7
**A:** 4/Gabriel SSM (I × 4)—2/30-mm AA BMARC GCM-AO AA (II × 1)
**M:** 2 Paxman Valenta 16-cyl. diesels; 2 props; 5,400 hp
**Electron Equipt:** Radar: 1/Decca 1226, 1/Orion RTN-10X
**Range:** 2,300/12 **Man:** 3 officers, 18 men

Remarks: Ordered 10-5-73. P 3121 and 3123 received Gabriel missiles during 1982; P 3122 in 1983, with 2/40-mm AA removed. Have radar/optronic director.

◆ **1 37.5-meter class** Bldr: Brooke Marine, Lowestoft, U.K.

| | Laid down | L | In serv. |
|---|---|---|---|
| P 3100 Mamba | 17-2-72 | 6-11-73 | 7-2-74 |

**Mamba (P 3100)**—prior to modernization 1975

**D:** 130 tons (160 fl) **S:** 25 kts **Dim:** 37.5 × 6.86 × 1.78
**A:** 4/Gabriel SSM (I × 4)—2/30-mm BMARC GCM-AO AA (II × 1)
**Electron Equipt:** Radar: 1/Decca 1226, 1/Orion RTN-10X
**M:** 2 Paxman Valenta 16-cyl. diesels; 2 props; 4,000 hp
**Range:** 3,500/13 **Man:** 3 officers, 22 men

Remarks: Rearmed 1982, with 2/40-mm AA removed. Have radar/optronic director.

**PATROL BOATS**

◆ **1 Vosper 31-meter class** Bldr: Vosper Portsmouth, U.K.

| | L | In serv. |
|---|---|---|
| P 3110 Simba | 9-9-65 | 23-5-66 |

**D:** 96 tons (109 fl) **S:** 24/23 kts **Dim:** 31.25 (28.95 pp) × 5.95 × 1.65
**A:** 2/40-mm AA Mk 7 (I × 2) **Electron Equipt:** Radar: 1/Decca 914
**M:** 2 Paxman Ventura 12-cyl. diesels; 2 props; 2,900 hp **Fuel:** 14 tons
**Range:** 1,500/16 **Man:** 3 officers, 20 men

Remarks: Sisters *Chui* (P 3112) and *Ndovu* (P 3117) laid up inoperable by 1986; *Simba* to be stricken 1988 on arrival of new missile boats.

**AUXILIARIES**

◆ **1 large harbor tug** Bldr: James Lamont, Port Glasgow, U.K.

Ngamia (In serv. 1969)

**D:** . . . **S:** 14 kts **Dim:** 35.3 × 9.3 × 3.9 **M:** diesels; 1 prop; 1,200 hp

Remarks: 298 grt. Transferred to Navy from Mombasa Port Authority, 1-83.

CUSTOMS SERVICE

**PATROL CRAFT**

◆ **2 Dutch-built** Bldr: Akerboom, Leyden (In serv. 1983)

Kiongozi

**D:** 55 tons (fl) **S:** 12 kts **Dim:** 22.5 × 5.3 × 1.8
**M:** 2 Kelvin TAS-6 diesels; 2 props; 560 hp **Man:** 8 tot.

Remarks: Used primarily as pilot boats, carrying four pilots.

◆ **2 17-meter workboats** Bldr: Cheverton, Cowes, U.K. (In serv. 10-82)

M'chunguzi M'linzi

**D:** 25 tons (fl) **S:** 24 kts **Dim:** 17.0 × 4.4 × 1.5
**M:** 2 diesels; 2 props; 688 hp **Man:** 8 tot

◆ **1 14-m launch** Bldr: Tremlett Powerboats, Topsham, U.K. (In serv. 1986)

**D:** . . . **S:** 20 kts **Dim:** 14.0 × . . . × . . . **M:** 2 Perkins diesels; 2 props; . . . hp

Remarks: Ordered 20-6-86, for use at Mombasa.

◆ **2 12-m launches** Bldr: Tremlett Powerboats, Topsham, U.K. (In serv. 1986)

**D:** . . . **S:** 20 kts **Dim:** 12.0 × . . . × . . .
**M:** 2 Perkins diesels; 2 props; . . . hp

Remarks: Ordered 20-6-86 for use on Lake Victoria.

# KIRIBATI

**(formerly Gilbert Islands)**

Merchant Marine (1986): 6 ships—3,197 grt

**PATROL CRAFT**

◆ **1 17-meter glass-reinforced plastic patrol craft** Bldr: Cheverton, Cowes (In serv. 1980)

**D:** 22 tons (fl) **S:** 23.6 kts **Dim:** 17.0 × 4.5 × 1.2
**A:** 1/7.62-mm mg **M:** 2 G.M. 8V-71 TI diesels; 2 props; 800 hp
**Range:** 790/18; 1,000/12 **Man:** 7 tot.

# KOREA, NORTH

**Democratic People's Republic of Korea**

Personnel: Approximately 9,000 men, plus reserves (*Note:* Other sources give as many as 30,000 active)

Merchant Marine (1986): 71 ships—407,253 grt (tankers: 3 ships—58,781 grt) (*Note:* This represents only ships engaged in international trade.)

**SUBMARINES**

◆ **16 Soviet Romeo class** (In serv. 1973–. . .)

**D:** 1,320/1,712 tons **S:** 15.2/13 kts **Dim:** 76.60 × 6.70 × 4.95
**A:** 8/533-mm TT (6 fwd, 2 aft)—14 torpedoes or 28 mines
**Electron Equipt:** Radar: 1/Snoop Plate
Sonar: Tamir-5L active, Feniks passive array
**M:** 2 Type 37D diesels of 2,000 hp, electric drive; 2 props; 2,700 hp—2 electric creep motors; 100 hp
**Endurance:** 60 days **Range:** 14,000/9 surf.; 7,500/5 snorkel; 350/sub.
**Man:** 8 officers; 43 men

SUBMARINES *(continued)*

Remarks: Seven are of Chinese construction, transferred in 1973 (two), 1974 (two), and 1975 (three). The others have been built at Mayang Do in North Korea. One lost off each coast 20-2-85. Max. diving depth: 300 m (270 normal). Batteries have 224 cells, are rated at 6,000-amp/hr.

◆ **4 Soviet Whiskey class**

**D:** 1,050/1,350 tons **S:** 16/17 kts **Dim:** 76.0 × 6.3 × 4.8
**A:** 6/533-mm TT (4 fwd, 2 aft)—12 torpedoes or 24 mines
**Electron Equipt:** Radar: 1/Snoop Plate
Sonar: Herkules, passive array
**M:** 2 Type 37D diesels of 2,000 hp, diesel-electric drive; 2 props; 2,500 hp
**Endurance:** 60 days **Range:** 4,000/5 (snorkel) **Man:** 50 tot.

Remarks: Transferred from the U.S.S.R. during 1960s.

Note: Also in use are as many as 19 locally built midget submarines, intended primarily for the transport of commandos. One is reported to be 41 m overall, but the others are probably much smaller. In addition, some eight "semi-submersibles" built at Wonsan since 1985 are in use:

**D:** 5 tons **S:** 50 kts (surf.) **Dim:** 8.60 × 2.50 × . . .
**M:** . . . **Man:** 6 tot.

Remarks: Intended for saboteur delivery to South Korea, traveling surfaced until near insertion point and then ballasting down to run in awash. Sighted at Pusan 20-10-85.

FRIGATES

◆ **2 Najin class** Bldr: North Korea

3025 (In serv. 1973) 3026 (In serv. 1975)

**D:** 1,200 tons (1,500 fl) **S:** 25 kts **Dim:** 100.0 × 10.0 × 2.7
**A:** 2/SS-N-2 Styx SSM (II × 1)—2/100-mm DP (I × 2)—4/57-mm AA (II × 2)—4/25-mm AA (II × 2)—8/14.5-mm mg (II × 4)—4/d.c. projectors—30 mines
**Electron Equipt:** Radar: 1/Skin Head, 1/Pot Head, 1/Slim Net
Sonar: . . .
**M:** 2 diesels; 2 props; 15,000 hp **Range:** 4,000/14 **Man:** 155 tot.

Remarks: Very primitive design, crude in finish and appearance. Trainable missile launcher mount (Chinese?) replaced 3/533-mm TT (III × 1) in early 1980s. Reports of two others apparently incorrect. There is also reported another frigate class nicknamed "Soho," but this may be an alternate name for the Najin class.

CORVETTES

◆ **3 Sariwan class** Bldr: North Korea, 1965

**D:** 475 tons (600 fl) **S:** 21 kts **Dim:** 62.1 × 7.3 × 2.4
**A:** 1/76-mm DP—2/57-mm AA (II × 2)—4/25-mm AA (II × 2)—4/d.c. projectors
**M:** 2 diesels; 2 props; 3,000 hp

Remarks: Data dubious. Design based on Soviet Tral-class minesweeper. Possible pendant numbers: 725, 726, 727, 728.

Note: There is a new corvette design nicknamed the "Mayang" class; no data available.

GUIDED-MISSILE PATROL BOATS

◆ **8 (+ . . .) Soju class** Bldr: North Korea

**D:** approx. 220 tons (fl) **S:** 34 kts **Dim:** 43.0 × . . . × . . .
**A:** 4/SS-N-2 Styx SSM . . .
**M:** 3 Type M503A diesels; 3 props; 12,000 hp
**Range:** . . . **Man:** . . .

Remarks: North Korean version of Osa-I. Some reports indicate only four in service.

◆ **4 (+ . . .) So Hung class** Bldr: North Korea

**D:** 80 tons (fl) **S:** 40 kts **Dim:** 26.8 × 6.2 × 1.5
**A:** 2/SS-N-2 Styx SSM—2/25-mm AA (II × 1)
**Electron Equipt:** Radar: probably 1/Square Tie
**M:** 4 M50-F4 diesels; 4 props; 4,800 hp **Man:** 19 tot.

Remarks: Steel-hulled version of Soviet Komar class. With only four built, may not have been successful. May use the Chaho-class patrol boat hull.

◆ **8 Soviet Osa-I class**

**D:** 170 tons (209 fl) **S:** 35 kts **Dim:** 38.6 × 7.6 × 1.8
**A:** 4/SS-N-2A Styx SSM (I × 4)—4/30-mm AA (II × 2)
**Electron Equipt:** Radar: 1/Square Tie, 1/Drum Tilt
IFF: 2/Square Head, 1/High Pole
**M:** 3 M503A diesels; 3 props; 12,000 hp **Range:** 500/34; 750/25 **Man:** 30 tot.

◆ **8 Soviet Komar class**

**D:** 71 tons (82 fl) **S:** 40 kts **Dim:** 25.3 × 7.0 × 1.9
**A:** 2/SS-N-2A Styx SSM (I × 2)—2/25-mm AA (II × 1)
**Electron Equipt:** Radar: 1/Square Tie
**M:** 4 M50-F4 diesels; 4 props; 4,800 hp **Range:** 400/30 **Man:** 18 tot.

Remarks: Wooden construction; hull same as P 6 torpedo boat.

PATROL BOATS

◆ **7 (+ . . .) Taechong class** Bldr: North Korea (In serv. 1975– . . .)

**D:** 140 tons (165 fl) **S:** . . . **Dim:** 44.2 × 5.5 × 2.4 (props)
**A:** 2/57-mm AA (II × 1)—1/37-mm AA—2/25-mm AA (II × 1)—4/14.5-mm mg (II × 2)—2/RBU-1200 ASW RL—2/d.c. racks
**Electron Equipt:** Radar: 1/Pot Head—Sonar: Tamir-11 (HF)
**M:** Diesels; . . . props; . . . hp **Range:** . . . **Man:** . . .

◆ **6 Chinese Hainan class**

**D:** 375 tons (400 fl) **S:** 30.5 kts **Dim:** 58.77 × 7.20 × 2.20 (hull)
**A:** 4/57-mm AA (II × 2)—4/25-mm AA (II × 2)—4/RBU-1200 ASW RL (V × 4)—2/d.c. projectors—2/d.c. racks—mines
**Electron Equipt:** Radar: 1/Pot Head—Sonar: Tamir 11 **M:** 4 Type 9D diesels; 4 props; 8,800 hp
**Man:** 70 tot. **Range:** 2,000/14

Remarks: Two transferred in 1975; two in 1976; and two in 1978.

◆ **66 Chaho class** Bldr: North Korea

**D:** 80 tons (fl) **S:** 40 kts **Dim:** 27.7 × 6.1 × 1.8
**A:** 4/14.5-mm AA (II × 2)—1/200-mm artillery RL (40 tubes)
**M:** 4 M50 diesels; 4 props; 4,800 hp

Remarks: Based on P 6 design, but have steel hull.

◆ **45 Chong Jin and Chong Ju classes** Bldr: North Korea

Remarks: Data as for Chaho class, except armaments include: one 85-mm tank gun and four 14.5-mm antiaircraft guns (II × 2). Chong Ju variant substitutes a multiple 122-mm rocket launcher (XI × 1) for the tank turret.

◆ **15 Chinese Shanghai II class**

**D:** 122.5 tons (134.8 fl) **S:** 28.5 kts **Dim:** 38.78 × 5.41 × 1.49 (hull)
**A:** 4/37-mm AA (II × 2)—4/25-mm AA (II × 2)—d.c.—mines
**Electron Equipt:** Radar: 1/Pot Head
**M:** 2 M50F-4, 1,200-hp and 2/12D6, 910-hp diesels; 4 props; 4,220 hp
**Range:** 750/16.5 **Electric:** 39 kw **Endurance:** 7 days **Man:** 36 tot.

Remarks: Transferred circa 1967–69.

◆ **18 Soviet S.O. 1 class**

**D:** 190 tons (215 fl) **S:** 28 kts **Dim:** 42.0 × 6.1 × 1.9
**A:** Soviet version: 4/25-mm AA (II × 2)—4 RBU-1200 ASW RL (V × 4)—2/d.c. racks—mines
North Korean version: 1/85-mm DP—2/37-mm AA (I × 2)—4/14.5-mm mg (II × 2)
**Electron Equipt:** Radar: 1/Pot Head or Don-2—Sonar: 1/Tamir-11 (HF)
**M:** 3 Type 40D diesels; 3 props; 7,500 hp **Man:** 30–40 tot.

Remarks: Six transferred from U.S.S.R. in antisubmarine configuration 1957–61; remainder built in Korea for patrol purposes and in service by 1968.

◆ **8 Chinese Shantou (Swatow) class** (In serv. early 1960s)

**D:** 80 tons (fl) **S:** 28 kts **Dim:** 25.1 × 6.0 × 1.8
**A:** 4/37-mm AA (II × 2)—2/14.5-mm mg (I × 2)
**M:** 2 Type 3D12, 300-hp diesels; 2 M50-series, 1,200-hp diesels; 4 props

◆ **4 Chodo class** Bldr: North Korea (In serv. late 1950s)

**D:** 130 tons **S:** 24 kts **Dim:** 42.7 × 5.8 × 2.6
**A:** 1/76-mm DP—2/37-mm AA (I × 2)—4/25-mm AA (II × 2)
**Electron Equipt:** Radar: 1/Skin Head
**M:** 2 diesels; 2 props; 6,000 hp **Man:** 24 tot.

Remarks: Some have 3/37-mm AA, no 76-mm DP.

▲ **4 K-48 class** Bldr: North Korea (In serv. 1951–54)

**D:** 110 tons (fl) **S:** 24 kts **Dim:** 38.1 × 5.5 × 1.5
**A:** 1/76-mm DP—3/37-mm AA (I × 3)—4/14.5-mm AA (II × 2)
**Electron Equipt:** Radar: 1/Skin Head
**M:** 2 diesels; 2 props; 5,000 hp

Remarks: Appear to be Japanese seaplane support craft, left behind incomplete at the end of World War II and completed by North Korea.

Note: Twenty wooden-hulled Soviet-built M.O. IV-class patrol boats, built 1938–47 and transferred to North Korea in the 1950s, have been dropped from this edition as unlikely still to be operational.

TORPEDO BOATS

◆ **3 Soviet Shershen class**

**D:** 145 tons (170 fl) **S:** 45 kts **Dim:** 34.0 × 6.8 × 1.5
**A:** 4/30-mm AA (II × 2)—4/533-mm TT—2/d.c. racks (12 d.c.)
**Electron Equipt:** Radar: 1/Pot Drum, 1/Drum Tilt
IFF: 1/Square Head, 1/High Pole A
**M:** 3 M503A diesels; 3 props; 12,000 hp **Range:** 460/42; 850/30

KOREA-NORTH *(continued)*
TORPEDO BOATS *(continued)*

◆ **approx. 40 Soviet P 6/North Korean Sinpo class**

**D:** 55 tons (66.5 fl) **S:** 43 kts **Dim:** 25.3 × 6.1 × 1.7
**A:** 4/25-mm AA (I × 2)—2/533-mm TT—8/d.c. in tilt racks
**Electron Equipt:** Radar: 1/Skin Head or Pot Head
IFF: 1/Dead Duck, 1/High Pole
**M:** 4 M50F-4 diesels; 4 props; 4,800 hp **Range:** 450/30

REMARKS: Forty-five transferred by U.S.S.R. during early 1960s; wooden construction. A few similar Sinpo-class units were built in Korea during the early 1970s. Steel construction. Some lack torpedo tubes but have additional AA guns.

◆ **12 Iwon class** Bldr: North Korea (In serv. 1970s)

**D:** 25 tons (fl) **S:** 45 kts **Dim:** 19.2 × 3.7 × 1.5
**A:** 2/25-mm AA (II × 2)—2/533-mm TT **M:** 3 diesels; 3 props; 3,600 hp

◆ **6 An Ju class** Bldr: North Korea (In serv. 1970s)

**D:** 35 tons (fl) **S:** 50 kts **Dim:** 19.8 × 3.7 × 1.8
**A:** 2/25-mm AA (II × 2)—2/533-mm TT
**M:** 4 M50 diesels; 4 props; 4,800 hp **Man:** 20 tot.

◆ **74 Sin Hung class** Bldr: North Korea (In serv. 1970s)

**D:** 25 tons (fl) **S:** 40 kts **Dim:** 18.3 × 3.4 × 1.7
**A:** 4/14.5-mm (II × 2)—2/450-mm TT **M:** 2 diesels; 2 props; 2,400 hp

### AMPHIBIOUS CRAFT

◆ **4 Hantae-class medium landing ships** (In serv. 1980s)

REMARKS: Reportedly 50 m overall and capable of carrying three tanks.

◆ **100 Nampo-class assault landing craft** Bldr: North Korea

**D:** 82 tons (fl) **S:** 40 kts **Dim:** 27.7 × 6.1 × 1.8 **A:** 4/14.5-mm AA (II × 2)
**M:** 4 M50F-4 diesels; 4 props; 4,800 hp **Range:** 375/40 **Man:** 19 tot.
**Electron Equipt:** Radar: 1/Pot Head

REMARKS: Repeatedly 50 m overall and capable of carrying three tanks. commodations forward.

◆ **9 Hanchon-class utility landing craft** Bldr: North Korea

REMARKS: No reliable data available.

◆ **18 smaller landing craft, LCM type**

# KOREA, SOUTH

## Republic of Korea

PERSONNEL: Approximately 29,000 men, plus 20,000 Marines

MERCHANT MARINE (1986): 1,837 ships—7,183,617 grt (tankers: 95 ships—965,943 grt)

NAVAL AVIATION: About a dozen land-based U.S. S-2E Tracker aircraft remain employed for surveillance and ASW. Ten or more Alouette-III helicopters are available for use on destroyers. Ten Indonesian-built CN 235 twin-engined light transports may be acquired for coastal surveillance duties.

NOTE: Pendant numbers are subject to change at unspecified intervals. The numerals "0" and "4" are considered unlucky and are not used. Three "batteries" of shore-based Harpoon antiship missiles were ordered early 1987.

### SUBMARINES

REMARKS: A 175-ton submarine of local design was completed during 1983 at Hyundai Shipyard. No details are available. A program to construct four sea-going attack submarines of European design was officially announced as delayed for three years in late 1984; as many as a dozen had been contemplated. The first two would be built abroad. The West German IKL Type 1500 is reportedly preferred.

### DESTROYERS

◆ **0 (+1 + . . .) new design** Bldr: . . .

REMARKS: A new "3,000-ton" destroyer is to be built, employing Korean-built Marconi S-1810 search radar, Marconi S-1802 fire-control radars, the Ferranti WSA-423 combat data weapon-control system and Rademac electro-optical backup directors. The armament suite will include Breda twin 40-mm AA mountings, ordered late in 1986. A helicopter facility is planned.

◆ **5 ex-U.S. Gearing class, FRAM I**

| | Bldr | Laid down | L | In serv. |
|---|---|---|---|---|
| 919 TAEJON (ex-*New*, DD 818) | Consolidated Steel, Orange, Tex. | 14-4-45 | 18-8-45 | 5-4-46 |
| 921 KUANG JU (ex-*Richard E. Kraus*, DD 849) | Consolidated Steel, Orange, Tex. | 31-7-45 | 2-3-46 | 23-5-46 |
| 922 KANG WON (ex-*William R. Rush,* DD 714) | Federal SB, Newark, N.J. | 19-10-44 | 8-7-45 | 21-9-45 |
| 923 KYONG KI (ex-*Newman K. Perry*, DD 883) | Consolidated Steel, Orange, Tex. | 10-10-44 | 17-3-45 | 26-7-45 |
| 925 JEONG JU (ex-*Rogers*, DD 876 | Consolidated Steel, Orange, Tex. | 3-6-44 | 20-11-44 | 26-3-45 |

**Taejon (919)**—with 8 Harpoon, no ASROC L. & L. Van Ginderen, 11-86

**Jeong Ju (925)**—ASROC, no helicopter facilities L. & L. Van Ginderen, 11-86

**D:** 2,425 tons (3,500 fl) **S:** 30 kts
**Dim:** 119.03 (116.74 wl) × 12.52 × 4.45 (6.4 sonar)
**A:** 919, 921, 922: 8 Harpoon SSM (IV × 2)—4/127-mm DP (II × 2)—2/40-mm AA (II × 1)—2/20-mm gatling AA (I × 2)—6/324-mm Mk 32 ASW TT (III × 2)—1/Alouette-III ASW helo
923, 925: 4/127-mm DP (IV × 2)—2/40-mm AA (II × 1)—2/20-mm gatling AA (I × 2)—1/Mk 112 ASROC ASW RL (VIII × 1)—6/324-mm Mk 32 ASW TT
**Electron Equipt:** Radar: 1/SPS-10, 1/SPS-29 (919, 921: SPS-40), 1/Mk 25
Sonar: SQS-23
EW: WLR-1, ULQ-6, 2 chaff RL—TACAN: 919, 921, 922: SRN-15
**M:** 2 sets GT; 2 props; 60,000 hp **Electric:** 1,200 kw
**Boilers:** 4 Babcock & Wilcox; 39.8 kg/cm$^2$, 454°C **Fuel:** 640 tons
**Range:** 4,800/15; 2,400/25 **Man:** 274 tot.

REMARKS: 919, 921 were transferred 25-2-77; 922 on 1-7-79; 923 on 25-7-81; 925 on 11-8-81. Have one Mk 37 director, and 1 Mk 51 Mod. 2 for 40-mm; 40-mm AA added fwd. Korean-designed mountings for G.E. Vulcan gatling gun amidships on Harpoon ships, on former helicopter deck on ASROC ships. Harpoon added 1979 on ships without ASROC. ULQ-6 ECM equipment removed.

◆ **2 ex-U.S. Gearing class, FRAM II** Bldr: Bath Iron Works

| | Laid down | L | In serv. |
|---|---|---|---|
| 915 CHUNG BUK (ex-*Chevalier,* DD 805) | 12-6-44 | 29-10-44 | 8-9-44 |
| 916 JEONG BUK (ex-*Everett F. Larson,* DD 830) | 4-9-44 | 28-1-45 | 6-4-45 |

DESTROYERS *(continued)*

**Jeong Buk (916)** J.W. Goss, 11-81

**Chung Buk (915)** G. Gyssels, 11-81

**D:** 2,400 tons (3,500 fl) **S:** 30 kts **Dim:** 119.17 × 12.45 × 5.8
**A:** 8/Harpoon (IV × 2)—6/127-mm DP (II × 3)—2/20-mm gatling AA (I × 2)—2/12.7-mm mg (I × 2)—6/324-mm Mk 32 ASW TT (III × 2)—2/Mk 11 Hedgehogs—1/d.c. rack—1/Alouette-III helicopter
**Electron Equipt:** Radar: 1/SPS-10, 1/SPS-40, 1/Mk 25
Sonar: SQS-29 series—TACAN: SRN-15
EW: WLR-1, 2 chaff RL
**M:** 2 sets GT; 2 props; 60,000 hp **Electric:** 1,200 kw
**Boilers:** 4 Babcock & Wilcox; 39.8 kg/cm², 454°C **Fuel:** 640 tons
**Range:** 4,800/15; 2,400/25 **Man:** 14 officers, 260 men

REMARKS: Transferred on loan 5-7-72 and 30-10-72; sold outright 31-1-77. One Mk 37 director for 127-mm guns. Harpoon added 1979, flight deck widened and strengthened. ULQ-6 ECM equipment removed.

◆ **2 ex-U.S. Allen M. Sumner class, FRAM II**

| | Bldr | Laid down | L | In serv. |
|---|---|---|---|---|
| 917 DAE GU (ex-*Wallace L. Lind,* DD 703) | Federal SB, Kearny, N.J. | 19-9-43 | 14-6-44 | 8-9-44 |
| 918 INCHON (ex-*De Haven,* DD 727) | Bath Iron Works | 9-8-43 | 9-1-44 | 31-3-44 |

**D:** 2,350 tons (3,320 fl) **S:** 34 kts **Dim:** 114.8 × 12.4 × 5.2
**A:** 8/Harpoon SSM (IV × 2)—6/127-mm AA (II × 3)—4/40-mm AA (II × 2)—2/20-mm gatling AA (I × 2)—6/324-mm Mk 32 ASW TT (III × 2)—2/Mk 11 Hedgehogs—1/d.c. rack—1/Alouette-III helicopter
**Electron Equipt:** Radar: 1/SPS-10, 1/SPS-40 (918: SPS-29), 1/Mk 25
Sonar: 1/SQS-29 series, 1/SQA-10 VDS (917 only)
EW: WLR-1, 2 chaff RL
**M:** 2 sets G.E. GT; 2 props; 60,000 hp **Electric:** 1,200 kw
**Boilers:** 4 Babcock & Wilcox; 39.8 kg/cm², 454°C **Man:** 235 tot

REMARKS: Transferred 12-73. Harpoon added 1978–79; helicopter deck and hangar enlarged to accommodate Alouette-III, 1978.

NOTE: U.S. *Fletcher*-class destroyers *Chung Mu* (911, ex-*Erben,* DD 631) and *Pusan* (913, ex-*Hickox,* DD 673) decommissioned 1986.

## FRIGATES

◆ **3 (+2 + 8) Ulsan class**

| | Bldr | Laid down | L | In serv. |
|---|---|---|---|---|
| 951 ULSAN | Hyundai SY, Ulsan | 1-5-79 | 8-4-80 | 1-1-81 |
| 952 SEOUL | Korea SB, Pusan | 1982 | 24-4-84 | 18-12-84 |
| 955 MASAN | Korea Tacoma, Masan | ... | ... | 11-84 |
| ... N ....... | Daiwoo SY, Okpo | ... | ... | 1988 |
| ... N ....... | Daiwoo SY, Okpo | ... | ... | 1988 |

**Masan (955)** *Ships of the World,* 1985

**Ulsan (951)** Hyundai, 1981

**Seoul (952)** 1985

**D:** 1,600 tons (1,940 normal, 2,180 fl) **S:** 35 kts
**Dim:** 105.0 (98.0 pp) × 12.0 × 3.5
**A:** 8/Harpoon SSM (IV × 2)—2/76-mm OTO Melara DP—8/30-mm Emerlec AA (II × 4)—6/324-mm Mk 32 ASW TT (III × 2)—2/d.c. racks (6 d.c. each)
**Electron Equipt:** Radar: H.S.A. DA-05, 1/H.S.A. ZW-06, 1/H.S.A. WM-25
Sonar: 1/PHS-32—TACAN: SRN-15
EW: passive intercept, Mk 36 SRBOC (VI × 2)
**M:** CODOG: 2 G.E. LM-2500 gas turbines, 54,400 hp; 2 MTU 12V956 TB82 diesels, 7,200 hp; 2 CP props
**Range:** 900/35; 4,000/18 **Electric:** 1,600 kw **Man:** 25 officers, 120 men

REMARKS: Dutch electronic equipment, including 2 H.S.A. LIOD optronic standby gun directors. Three additional ordered 1981, and a fourth in 4-84. Later units may employ twin Breda 40-mm AA in lieu of the 30-mm mounts. Has stern-wedge hull form. The fourth and fifth units are to have Samsung-built Marconi 1810 radars, Ferranti WSA-423 combat data/control system, Marconi S-1802 tracker radars, and Rademac HK-409-029 electro-optical directors. The later ships may substitute twin Breda 40-mm AA mountings for some or all of the 30-mm mounts. Up to eight additional *Ulsan*-class frigates planned.

NOTE: The ROKN plans to construct a total of 16 to 19 modern light frigate/corvettes. Eight are to be equipped with Korean-made Marconi S-1810 search and ST-1802 fire-control radars, Ferranti WSA-423 combat data/control systems, Rademac electro-optical directors, and Breda twin 40-mm AA.

◆ **1 or more KCX . . . class** Bldr: . . .

**D:** 900 tons (1,140 fl) **S:** 31 kts
**Dim:** 81.0 × 10.4 × 2.88 (hull)
**A:** . . . SSM—1/76-mm OTO Melara Compact DP—2/40-mm AA (II × 1)—4/30-mm Emerlec AA (II × 2)—6/324-mm Mk 32 ASW TT—2/d.c. racks (6 d.c. each)
**Electron Equipt:** Radar: 1/SPS-64(V), 1/H.S.A. WM-28
Sonar: Edo 768—EW: . . .
**M:** CODOG: 1 LM-2500 gas turbine, 27,800 hp; 2 MTU 12V956 TB82 diesels, 6,260 hp; 2 CP props
**Range:** . . . **Endurance:** 21 days **Man:** . . .

**FRIGATES** *(continued)*

**HDC 1150** 1986

Remarks: Again, confusion as to numbers built and propulsion plant composition on this corvette design. The 40-mm twin AA is of World War II design and is located where the missile launchers are found in the longer light frigate design below; the mount is controlled by an electro-optical director or U.S. Mk 51 GFCS. Distinguished by narrower superstructure, lattice mast and less distance between mast and stack from the alternate design. Design appears to have been evolved from the South Korean Coast Guard HDP-1000 class.

◆ **10 (+1) An Yang Ho (KCX) class** Bldrs: (A) Korea Tacoma SB, Chinhae; (B) Hyundai SY, Ulsan; (C) Korea SB & Eng., Pusan; (D) Daewoo SY, Okpo

| | Bldr | Laid down | L | In serv. |
|---|---|---|---|---|
| . . . An Yang Po | D | 1981 | 1982 | 12-83 |
| 757 N . . . | B | 1981 | 15-5-83 | 30-11-83 |
| . . . Ma San Ho | C | 1981 | 1982 | 12-83 |
| . . . N . . . | D | . . . | 19-6-83 | 12-83 |
| . . . Po Hang | . . . | . . . | . . . | 18-12-84 |
| . . . Kunsan | . . . | . . . | . . . | 18-12-84 |
| . . . Kyong Nam | . . . | . . . | . . . | 5-85 |
| 7 . . N . . . | . . . | . . . | . . . | -85 |
| . . . N . . . | . . . | . . . | . . . | -86 |
| . . . N . . . | . . . | . . . | . . . | -86 |
| . . . N . . . | . . . | . . . | . . . | . . . |

**Number 757 with 2 Exocet** 1985

**D:** 950 tons (1,300 fl) **S:** 31 kts
**Dim:** 88.00 (83.47 wl) × 10.00 (9.80 wl) × 2.90 (hull)
**A:** 8/Harpoon (IV × 2) or 2/MM 38 Exocet SSM—1/76-mm OTO Melara Compact DP—4/30-mm Emerlec AA (II × 2)—6/324-mm Mk 32 ASW TT (III × 2)—d.c. racks (6 d.c. each)
**Electron Equipt:** Radar: 1/SPS-64(V) nav., 1 H.S.A. WM-28
Sonar: 1/PHS-32 or Edo 768—EW: 2 chaff RL
**M:** CODOG: 1 LM-2500 gas turbine, 27,200 hp; 2 MTU 12V956 TB82 diesels; 6,260 hp; 2 CP props
**Range:** 800/31 (turbine) 4,000/15 (diesel) **Electric:** 1,200 kw
**Man:** 8 officers,79 men

Remarks: Few reliable details released. First four have Harpoon SSM, later units have Exocet. Some may be all-diesel, with four 4,170-hp MTU diesels. Korea SB, Pusan, had delivered three by 5-85. First four had gas turbine rated at 27,200 hp, later units at 27,800. An additional increment of up to 10 may be ordered. Have also been referred to as the *Dong Hae* class, and one may be named *Su Yong.*

◆ **1 ex-U.S. Crosley-class former high-speed transport**

| | Bldr | Laid down | L | In serv. |
|---|---|---|---|---|
| 828 Che Ju (ex-*William M. Hobby,* APD 95) | Charleston Navy Yard, Charleston, S.C. | 15-11-43 | 11-2-44 | 4-4-45 |

**D:** 1,650 tons (2,130 fl) **S:** 23.6 kts **Dim:** 93.13 × 11.3 × 3.2
**A:** 2/127-mm DP (I × 2)—6/40-mm AA (II × 3)—6/12.7-mm mg (I × 6)—1 d.c. rack
**Electron Equipt:** Radar: 1/SPS-5, 1/SPS-6, 1/Mk 26—Sonar: QCU-2
**M:** 2 sets G.E. GT, turbo-electric drive; 2 props; 12,000 hp
**Boilers:** 2 Foster-Wheeler "D"-express; 30.6 kg/cm², 399°C
**Range:** 4,800/12; 2,300/22 **Man:** 200 tot.

Remarks: Transferred on loan 6-66, and 8-67; purchased outright 15-11-74. Second 127-mm gun added aft, as on Taiwanese sisters. Can still carry 160 troops; two LCVPs and two LCPLs stowed beneath quadrantal davits. One Mk 52 director for 127-mm gun; three Mk 51 Mod. 2 for 40-mm AA. Sisters *Kyong Nam* (821, ex-*Cavallaro,* APD 128) and *Ah San* (823, ex-*Harry L. Corl,* APD 108) stricken 1984. *Ung Po* (825, ex-*Julius A. Raven,* APD 110) reported stricken 1984 also. The similar *Charles Lawrence*-class frigate *Jon Nam* (827, ex-*Hayter,* APD 80) was stricken 1986–87.

## GUIDED-MISSILE PATROL BOATS

◆ **8 PSMM-5 class** Bldrs: PGM 352 to 355: Tacoma Boatbuilding Co.; others: Korea Tacoma, Chinhae

| | Laid down | In serv. |
|---|---|---|
| PGM 352 Paek Ku 52 | 1-75 | 14-3-75 |
| PGM 353 Paek Ku 53 | 2-75 | 14-3-75 |
| PGM 355 Paek Ku 55 | . . . | 1-2-76 |
| PGM 356 Paek Ku 56 | . . . | 1-2-76 |
| PGM 357 Paek Ku 57 | . . . | 1977 |
| PGM 358 Paek Ku 58 | . . . | 1977 |
| PGM 359 Paek Ku 59 | . . . | 1977 |
| PGM 361 Paek Ku 61 | . . . | 1978 |

**Paek Ku 61 (PGM 361)** *Ships of the World,* 1985

**Paek Ku 58 (PGM 358)**—with 4 Harpoon SSM 1985

**D:** 240 tons (268 fl) **S:** 40 kts **Dim:** 53.68 (50.30 pp) × 8.00 × 1.63
**A:** 4/Harpoon SSM (II × 2)—1/76-mm OTO Melara Compact DP—2/30-mm Emerlec AA (II × 1)—2/12.7-mm mg
**Electron Equipt:** Radar: 1/LN-66 HP, 1/SPG-50
**M:** 6 AVCO TF-35 gas turbines; 2 CP props; 16,800 hp
**Man:** 5 officers, 27 men

Remarks: Korean-built units have Westinghouse M-1200 fire-control systems, using inputs from the LN-66 HP radar and an optical director. Early ships have the U.S. Mk 63 GFCS. PGM 352–355 have 2 Standard ARM SSM launchers (each with one reload).

◆ **1 ex-U.S. Asheville class** Bldr: Tacoma Boat, Tacoma, Wash.

| | L | In serv. |
|---|---|---|
| PGM 351 Paek Ku 51 (ex-*Benicia,* PG 96) | 20-12-69 | 25-4-70 |

**D:** 225 tons (249 fl) **S:** 40 kts **Dim:** 50.14 × 7.28 × 2.9
**A:** 2/Standard ARM SSM box launchers—1/76.2-mm Mk 34 DP—1/40-mm AA—4/12.7-mm mg (II × 2)
**Electron Equipt:** Radar: 1/Raytheon 1645, 1/SPG-50
**M:** CODOG: 1 G.E. LM-1500-PE102 gas turbine, 12,500 hp; 2 Cummins VT12-875M diesels; 2 CP props; 1,450 hp
**Range:** 1,700/16; 390/35 **Man:** 29 tot.

## GUIDED-MISSILE PATROL BOATS *(continued)*

Remarks: Mk 63 radar GFCS for 76.2-mm Mk 34 gun. Transferred on loan 15-10-71. One reload missile carried for each box launcher.

◆ **2 "Wildcat" type** Bldr: Korea Tacoma SB, Chinhae (In serv. 1971–72)

PKM 271 Kilurki 71 PKM 272 Kilurki 72

**Kilurki 71 or 72** Korea Tacoma

**D:** 120 tons (140 fl) **S:** 34/35 kts **Dim:** 32.9 × 8.0 × 1.1
**A:** 2/MM 38 Exocet SSM (I × 2)—1/40-mm AA—3/12.7-mm mg—2/barrage RL (IV × 2)
**M:** PKM 271: 2 MTU MB518D diesels; 3 props; 9,960 hp
PKM 272: 3 MTU 16V538 TB90 diesels; 3 props; 10,800 hp
**Range:** 1,000/20 **Man:** 4 officers, 22 men

## PATROL BOATS

◆ **1 (+ . . .) . . . class** Bldr: Korea Tacoma SB (In serv. 4-8-84)

**D:** 150 tons **S:** 37 kts **Dim:** 37.00 × 6.25 × 1.68
**A:** . . . **Electron Equipt:** . . .
**M:** . . .

Remarks: No other details released. May be prototype for new series intended as anti-infiltration patrol boats. One report indicates 12 of this design delivered 1982–84.

◆ **32 "Sea Dolphin" type** Bldr: Korea Tacoma, Chinhae (In serv. 1970s)

PKM 211 Kilurki 11 to PKM 219 Kilurki 19
PKM 221 Kilurki 21 to PKM 229 Kilurki 29
PKM 231 Kilurki 31 to PKM 239 Kilurki 39
PKM 251 Kilurki 51 to PKM 259 Kilurki 59

**"Sea Dolphin" type** Korea Tacoma

**D:** 113 tons (144 fl) **S:** 34 kts
**Dim:** 33.10 (31.25 wl) × 6.92 × 1.75 (2.45 props)
**A:** 1/40-mm AA—2/30-mm Emerlec AA (II × 1)—2/20-mm AA (I × 2)—2/12.7-mm mg (I × 2)
**M:** 2 MTU 16V538 TB90 diesels; 2 props; 10,800 hp (9,000 sust.)
**Range:** 500/32; 1,000/20 **Fuel:** 15 tons **Man:** 5 officers, 24 men

Remarks: Gunboat version of the class above. In the above hull-number series, the "4" numbers have been omitted. Designed for 38 kts; can make 32 kts continuous. Also known commercially as the "Wildcat" class.

◆ **39 PK "Schoolboy" or "Sea Hawk" class** Bldr: Korea SB & Eng.

PK 151 to PK 189 Chebi 51 to Chebi 89

**D:** 70 tons (78 fl) **S:** 40 kts **Dim:** 25.7 × 5.4 × 1.2
**A:** 1/40-mm AA—1/20-mm AA—4/12.7-mm mg (II × 2)—2/7.62-mm mg (I × 2)
**M:** 2 MTU 16V538 TD90 diesels; 2 props; 5,200 hp **Range:** 500/20
**Man:** 25 tot.

**PK 153**—1/20-mm AA aft, 1/40-mm AA fwd. 1983

Remarks: Armament varies: recent units (and those refitted) have a Korean-designed 40-mm power-operated mount and three twin Korean-design 12.7-mm mg mounts (see photo of PK 153); early ships had a U.S. Mk 3 40-mm mount forward.

Note: Ex-U.S. Coast Guard "Cape"-class patrol boats PB 3, 5, 6, 8–12 stricken 1984.

## MINE WARFARE SHIPS

◆ **0 (+1 + . . .) SK5000-class minehunters** Bldr: Kangnam SB

**D:** . . . **S:** . . . **Dim:** . . . × . . . × . . .
**A:** . . . **Electron Equipt:** Radar: . . . —Sonar: Plessey 193M
**M:** . . . diesels; 2 Voith-Schneider cycloidal props; . . . hp

Remarks: Design based on Italian Intermarine *Lerici* design. First unit scheduled to deliver 12-86. Glass-reinforced plastic construction, with bow-thruster. Carries two Gaymarine Pluto mine-disposal vehicles and is to be equipped with Racal-Decca MAINS plotting gear. As many as 10 may ultimately be built.

◆ **5 U.S. MSC-289-class coastal minesweepers** Bldr: Peterson Bldrs., Sturgeon Bay, Wis.

| | In serv. |
|---|---|
| MSC 555 Nam Yang (ex-MSC 295) | 8-63 |
| MSC 556 Ha Dong (ex-MSC 296) | 11-63 |
| MSC 557 Sam Kok (ex-MSC 316) | 7-68 |
| MSC 558 Yong Dong (ex-MSC 320) | 2-10-75 |
| MSC 559 Ok Cheon (ex-MSC 321) | 2-10-75 |

**Sam Kok (MSC 557)**—old pendant number

**D:** 315 tons (380 fl) **S:** 14 kts **Dim:** 44.32 × 8.29 × 2.7
**A:** 2/20-mm AA (II × 1) **M:** 4 G.M. 6-71 diesels; 2 props; 1,020 hp
**Electric:** 1,260 kw **Fuel:** 33 tons **Man:** 40 tot.

Remarks: Wooden construction. Built under Military Aid Program. Gas-turbine sweep generator. Lower superstructure than on the MSC 268 class, below.

◆ **3 U.S. MSC 268-class coastal minesweepers** Bldr: Harbor Boat Bldg., Terminal Isl., Cal.

| | In serv. |
|---|---|
| MSC 551 Kum San (ex-MSC 284) | 6-59 |
| MSC 552 Ko Hung (ex-MSC 285) | 8-59 |
| MSC 553 Kum Kok (ex-MSC 286) | 10-59 |

MINE WARFARE SHIPS *(continued)*

**Kum San (MSC 551)**

**D:** 320 tons (370 fl) **S:** 14 kts **Dim:** 43.0 (41.5 pp) × 7.95 × 2.55
**A:** 2/20-mm AA (II × 2) **Electron Equipt:** Radar: Decca 45—Sonar: UQS-1
**M:** 2 G.M. 8-268A diesels; 2 props; 1,200 hp **Fuel:** 40 tons
**Range:** 2,500/16 **Man:** 40 tot.

REMARKS: Built under Military Aid Program. Wooden hulls.

### AMPHIBIOUS WARFARE SHIPS

◆ **8 ex-U.S. LST 1 and U.S. LST 542-class landing ships**

| | Bldr | L | In serv. |
|---|---|---|---|
| LST 671 UN BONG (ex-LST 1010) | Bethlehem, Fore River | 29-3-44 | 25-4-44 |
| LST 672 TUK BONG (ex-LST 227) | Chicago Bridge, Seneca, Ill. | 21-9-43 | 14-10-43 |
| LST 673 BI BONG (ex-*Berkshire County,* LST 218) | Chicago Bridge, Seneca, Ill. | 20-7-43 | 12-8-43 |
| LST 675 KAE BONG (ex-LST 288) | American Bridge, Pa. | 7-11-43 | 20-12-43 |
| LST 676 WEE BONG (ex-*Johnson County,* LST 849) | American Bridge, Pa. | 30-12-43 | 16-1-44 |
| LST 677 SU YONG (ex-*Kane County,* LST 853) | Chicago Bridge, Seneca, Ill. | 17-11-44 | 11-12-44 |
| LST 678 BUK HAN (ex-*Lynn County,* LST 900) | Dravo, Pittsburgh | 9-12-44 | 28-12-44 |
| LST 679 HWA SAN (ex-*Pender County,* LST 1080) | Bethlehem, Hingham, Mass. | 2-5-45 | 29-5-45 |

**D:** 1,653 tons (4,080 fl) **S:** 10 kts **Dim:** 100.04 × 15.24 × 4.30
**A:** 8/40-mm AA (II × 2, I × 4)—2/20-mm AA **Electric:** 300 kw
**M:** 2 G.M. 12-567A or 12-278A diesels; 2 props; 1,800 hp **Man:** 70 tot.

REMARKS: Transferred 1955–58; all purchased outright 15-11-74. LST 1 class had elevators from upper deck to tank deck; later ships had a ramp.

◆ **7 ex-U.S. LSM 1-class medium landing ships**

Bldr: Brown SB, Houston, Tex. (except: LSM 652: Federal SB, Newark, N.J.; LSM 661: Pullman Standard Car Co., Chicago, Ill.)

| | Laid down | L | In serv. |
|---|---|---|---|
| LSM 655 KO MUN (ex-LSM 30) | 7-5-44 | 28-5-44 | 1-7-44 |
| LSM 656 PI AN (ex-LSM 96) | 15-9-44 | 7-10-44 | 28-10-44 |
| LSM 657 WOL MI (ex-LSM 57) | 30-6-44 | 21-7-44 | 17-8-44 |
| LSM 658 KI RIN (ex-LSM 19) | 24-4-44 | 14-5-44 | 14-6-44 |
| LSM 659 NUNG RA (ex-LSM 84) | 22-8-44 | 15-9-44 | 7-10-44 |
| LSM 661 SIN MI (ex-LSM 316) | 6-4-44 | 18-6-44 | 21-7-44 |
| LSM 662 UL RUNG (ex-LSM 17) | 10-4-44 | 7-5-44 | 12-6-44 |

**D:** 520 tons (1,095 fl) **S:** 13 kts **Dim:** 62.0 × 10.52 × 2.53
**A:** 2/40-mm AA (II × 1)—4/20-mm AA (I × 4)
**Electric:** 240 kw **Fuel:** 160 tons
**M:** 2 Fairbanks-Morse 38D8$\frac{1}{8}$ × 10 diesels; 2 props; 2,880 hp **Man:** 75 tot.

REMARKS: Sisters *Tae Cho* (LSM 651, ex-U.S. LSM 546), *Tyo To* (LSM 652, ex-U.S. LSM 268), and *Ka Tok* (LSM 653, ex-U.S. LSM 462) stricken 1982. *Pung To* (ex-LSM 54), with minelaying capability, stricken 1984.

**Ko Mun (LSM 655)**—old number L. & L. Van Ginderen

◆ **6 U.S. LCU 1610-class utility landing craft** Bldr: So. Korea (In serv. 1979–81)

MULKAE 72–77

**D:** 190 tons (390 fl) **S:** 11 kts **Dim:** 41.07 × 9.07 × 2.08
**A:** 4/20-mm AA (II × 2)
**M:** 4 G.M. 6-71 diesels; 2 Kort-nozzle props; 1,200 hp
**Fuel:** 13 tons **Range:** 1,200/11 **Man:** 6 tot.

REMARKS: Cargo capacity: 143 tons; cargo deck 30.5 × 5.5. Copies of U.S. design with higher pilothouse; built with imported equipment.

◆ **1 LCU 501-class utility landing craft** Bldr: Bison SB, Buffalo, N.Y.

MULKAE 71 (ex-U.S. LCU 531) (L: 5-9-43)

**D:** 309 tons (fl) **S:** 10 kts **Dim:** 36.3 × 10.0 × 1.14 **A:** 2/20-mm AA (I × 2)
**M:** 3 Gray Marine 6-71 diesels; 2 props; 675 hp **Man:** 12 tot.

REMARKS: Transferred 1960.

◆ **10 ex-U.S. Army LCM(8)-class landing craft**

**D:** 95–115 tons (fl) **S:** 9–12 kts **Dim:** 22.7 × 6.4 × 1.4
**M:** 4 G.M. 6-71 diesels; 2 props; 600 hp

REMARKS: Transferred 9-78.

NOTE: South Korea also builds glass-reinforced plastic-hulled versions of the U.S. LCVP landing craft.

### AUXILIARIES

◆ **2 ex-U.S. Tonti-class gasoline tankers** Bldr: Todd SB, Houston, Tex.

| | L | In serv. |
|---|---|---|
| AO 55 N . . . . . . . (ex-*Rincon,* T-AOG 77, ex-*Tarland*) | 5-1-45 | 10-45 |
| AO 56 N . . . . . . . (ex-*Petaluma,* T-AOG 79, ex-*Raccoon Bend*) | 9-8-45 | 11-45 |

**D:** 2,100 tons (6,047 fl) **S:** 10 kts **Dim:** 99.1
**M:** 2 Nordberg diesels; 1 prop; 1,400 hp **Electric:** 515 kw
**Fuel:** 154 tons **Range:** 6,000/10 **Man:** 41 tot.

REMARKS: 3,160 grt/3,933 dwt. Cargo 31,284 bbl. light fuels (diesel, JP-5 gasoline). Acquired from Maritime Commission by U.S. Navy 1-7-50 and 7-9-50, respectively. Leased 21-2-82. Will probably be armed.

◆ **1 ex-Norwegian oiler** Bldr: Bergens Mekanske Verksteder, Norway (In serv. 1951)

AO 2 CHUN JI (ex-*Birk*)

**D:** 1,400 tons (4,160 fl) **S:** 12 kts **Dim:** 90.65 (84.0 pp) × 13.56 × 5.35
**A:** 1/40-mm AA—2/20-mm AA
**M:** 1 Sulzer 6 TD 48 diesel; 1 prop; 1,800 hp **Man:** 73 tot.

REMARKS: Bought in 1953. The *Puchon* of the same class was lost 5-71. Can replenish alongside while underway.

◆ **2 ex-U.S. 174-foot-class tankers**

| | Bldr | L | In serv. |
|---|---|---|---|
| YO 1 KU KYONG (ex-YO 118) | R.T.C. SB, Camden, N.J. | 6-5-44 | 8-8-44 |
| YO 6 N . . . . . . . (ex-YO 179) | Smith SY, Pensacola, Fla. | 24-11-44 | 26-5-45 |

**D:** 1,400 tons (fl) **S:** 7 kts **Dim:** 53.0 × 10.0 × 4.0
**M:** 1 Union diesel; 1 prop; 560 hp **Fuel:** 25 tons **Man:** 36 tot.

REMARKS: YO 1 transferred 1946, YO 6 in 9-71. Cargo: 900 tons.

◆ **1 ex-U.S. YO 55-class tanker** Bldr: R.T.C. SB, Camden, N.J.

| | Laid down | L | In serv. |
|---|---|---|---|
| HWA CHON (ex-*Derrick,* YO 59) | 15-6-42 | 21-11-42 | 2-2-43 |

**D:** 800 tons (2,700 fl) **S:** 10 kts **Dim:** 71.65 × 11.3 × 4.8
**M:** 2 Fairbanks-Morse 37E14-5 diesels; 2 props; 1,150 hp **Electric:** 160 kw
**Fuel:** 105 tons **Range:** 4,600/8 **Man:** 46 tot.

REMARKS: Transferred 4-55. Cargo: 1,600 tons.

NOTE: The last serving ex-U.S. Army FS 331-class small cargo ship, *Ma San* (AKL 909, ex-U.S. AKL 35, ex-*Lt. Thomas W. Weigle,* FS 383) was stricken during 1984.

**AUXILIARIES** *(continued)*

◆ **2 ex-U.S. Diver-class salvage ships** Bldr: Basalt Rock Co., Napa, Cal.

| | Laid down | L | In serv. |
|---|---|---|---|
| ARS 26 CHANG WON (ex-*Grasp,* ARS 24) | 27-4-43 | 31-7-43 | 22-8-44 |
| ARS 27 GUM I (ex-*Deliver,* ARS 23) | 2-4-43 | 25-9-43 | 18-7-44 |

**D:** 1,530 tons (1,970 fl) **S:** 14.8 kts **Dim:** 65.1 × 12.5 × 4.0
**A:** 2/20-mm AA **Electron Equipt:** Radar: 1/SPS-53
**M:** 4 Cooper-Bessemer GSB 8 diesels; electric drive; 2 props; 2,440 hp
**Electric:** 460 kw **Fuel:** 300 tons **Range:** 9,000/14; 20,000/7 **Man:** 83 tot.

REMARKS: ARS 5 transferred 31-3-78; ARS 6 on 15-8-79, both by sale. Equipped for salvage, diver support, and towing.

◆ **2 U.S. Sotoyomo-class auxiliary tugs**

| | Bldr | Laid down | L | In serv. |
|---|---|---|---|---|
| ATA 3 DO BANG (ex-*Pinola,* ATA 206) | Gulfport Boiler Wks, Port Arthur, Tex. | 26-10-44 | 14-12-44 | 10-2-45 |
| ATA 2 YONG MUN (ex-*Keosangua,* ATA 198) | Levingston SB, Orange, Tex. | 14-12-44 | 17-1-45 | 19-3-45 |

**D:** 835 tons (fl) **S:** 13 kts **Dim:** 43.6 (40.7 pp) × 10.3 × 4.0
**A:** 1/76-mm Mk 22 DP—4/20-mm AA (II × 2)
**M:** 2 G.M. 12-278A diesels, electric drive; 1 prop; 1,500 hp
**Electric:** 120 kw **Fuel:** 158 tons **Man:** 45 tot.

REMARKS: Transferred 2-62. ATA 3 is used in salvage work. Sister *Tan Yang* (ex-*Tillamook* ATA 192) operates in the Hydrographic Service. There are also about nine harbor tugs, including YTL 13 (ex-U.S.N. YTL 550), YTL 22 (ex-Army ST 2097), YTL 23 (ex-Army ST 2099), YTL 25 (ex-Army YT 2106), YTL 26 (ex-Army ST 2065), and YTL 30 (ex-Army ST 2101). All transferred 1968–72.

NOTE: There are also about 35 yard and service craft.

KOREAN HYDROGRAPHIC SERVICE
Subordinate to the Ministry of Transport.

◆ **2 ex-Belgian Herstal-class inshore minesweepers**

| | L |
|---|---|
| SURO 5 (ex-*Temse,* ex-MSI 470) | 6-8-56 |
| SURO 6 (ex-*Tournai,* ex-MSI 481) | 18-5-57 |

**D:** 160 tons (190 fl) **S:** 15 kts **Dim:** 34.5 × 6.6 × 2.1
**M:** 2 diesels; 2 props; 630 hp **Range:** 2,300/10 **Man:** 10 tot.

REMARKS: Built in Belgium with U.S. funds. Transferred 3-70. Wooden hulls.

◆ **1 U.S. Sotoyomo-class former auxiliary tug**

| | Bldr | Laid down | L | In serv. |
|---|---|---|---|---|
| TAN YANG (ex-*Tillamook,* ATA 192) | Levingston SB, Orange, Texas | 11-9-44 | 12-10-44 | 14-12-44 |

REMARKS: Data as for sisters in ROKN. Leased 7-1-71 and purchased outright 4-76.

◆ **1 ex-U.S. YMS-1-class minesweeper**

SURO 3 (ex-U.S. Coast Geodetic Survey *Hodgson*)

**D:** 289 tons (fl) **S:** 15 kts **Dim:** 44.6 × 8.1 × 3.0
**M:** 2 G.M. 8-268 diesels; 2 props; 1,000 hp

REMARKS: Converted post–World War II as a coastal survey ship. Wooden hull. Launched 1943, transferred 1968.

◆ **3 inshore survey craft**

SURO 7, SURO 8: 30 tons
SURO 2: 145 tons

COAST GUARD

The Republic of Korea Coast Guard operates about 70 seagoing patrol boats and several hundred small craft. There are about 12,000 personnel, most in shore billets.

◆ **1 HDP 1000-class patrol ship** Bldr: Korea SB & Eng., Pusan

**HDP 1000 class** Korea SB & Eng.

**D:** 1,200 tons (1,450 fl) **S:** 21.5 kts **Dim:** 80.50 × 8.90 × 3.15
**A:** 1/40-mm Mk 3 AA—4/20-mm AA (II × 2)
**Electron Equipt:** Radar: 2/navigational
**M:** 2 SEMT-Pielstick 12 PA6-280 diesels; 2 props; 9,600 hp
**Electric:** . . . **Range:** 7,000/18 **Man:** 11 officers, 58 men

REMARKS: A lower-powered and more lightly armed version of the *An Yang Ho*-class frigates built for the Navy. Passive-tank stabilization system. Engines built in Japan under license. Acts as Coast Guard flagship.

◆ **3 "Sea Whale"-class patrol boats**

| | Bldr | In serv. |
|---|---|---|
| 505 | Korea SB & Eng., Pusan | 3-80 |
| 5 . . . | Korea Tacoma SY, Chinhae | 5-79 |
| 5 . . . | Korea Tacoma SY, Chinhae | 7-82 |

**"Sea Whale/Sea Dragon" class** Korea Tacoma

**D:** 410 tons (580 fl) **S:** 24 kts **Dim:** 60.8 × 8.0 × 2.29
**A:** 1/40-mm AA—2/20-mm AA—2/7.62-mm mg (I × 2)
**M:** 2 MTU diesels; 2 props; 9,600 hp
**Range:** 1,500/25; 2,400/20 **Man:** 11 officers, 28 men

REMARKS: Intended for rescue and inspection duties. Flume-type passive tank roll stabilization.

◆ **22 "Sea Shark"-class patrol boats** Bldr: Hyundai SB and Korea Tacoma SB.

**"Sea Shark/Sea Wolf" class** Hyundai

**D:** 250 tons (280 fl) **S:** 28 kts **Dim:** 48.2 × 7.1 × 2.1 (2.5 over props)
**A:** 4/20-mm AA (II × 2 or II × 1, I × 2)—2/12.7-mm mg
**M:** 2 diesels; 2 props; 7,320 hp **Range:** 3,300/15 **Man:** 5 officers, 24 men

REMARKS: Some have a raised platform aft. Also offered as the "Sea Wolf" design by Korea Tacoma SB. Range also given as 2,000 n.m. at 17 kts.

◆ **18 "Sea Gull" class** Bldr: Korea SB & Eng.

**D:** 80 tons **S:** 30 kts **Dim:** 24.0 × 5.5 × . . . **A:** . . .
**M:** 2 diesels; 2 props; 3,920 hp **Range:** 950/20 **Man:** 18 tot.

◆ **. . . "Swallow" class, glass-reinforced plastic construction**

**D:** 32 tons (fl) **S:** 25 tons **Dim:** 20.0 × 4.7 × 1.3
**A:** 1/12.7-mm mg—1/7.62-mm mg **Range:** 500/20
**M:** 2 G.M. 12V71 TI diesels; 2 props; 1,060 hp **Man:** 8 tot.

**KOREA-SOUTH** *(continued)*
**COAST GUARD** *(continued)*

**Swallow class P-52** L. & L. Van Ginderen, 11-87

# KUWAIT

**State of Kuwait**

Personnel (1986): Approximately 1,100 tot.

Merchant Marine (1986): 239 ships—2,580,924 grt
(tankers: 26 ships—1,593,263 grt)

Naval Aviation: Six Aerospatiale AS.332F Super Puma helicopters armed with AM 39 Exocet missiles were ordered from France in 1983.

## GUIDED-MISSILE PATROL BOATS

◆ **2 FPB 57 class** Bldr: Lürssen, Bremen-Vegesack, West Germany

| | Laid down | L | In serv. |
|---|---|---|---|
| P 5702 Istiqlal | . . . | . . . | 8-83 |
| P 5704 Sabhan | . . . | . . . | 9-8-84 |

**Sabhan (P 5704)** French Navy, 7-84

**D:** 353 tons (398 fl) **S:** 36 kts **Dim:** 58.10 (54.40 wl) × 7.62 × 2.83
**A:** 4/MM 40 Exocet (II × 2)—1/76-mm OTO Melara DP—2/40-mm Breda AA (II × 1)—2/7.62-mm mg—mines
**Electron Equipt:** Radar: 1/Decca 1226C, 1/PEAB 9LV200 search, 1/9LV228 director, 1/Marconi S810
EW: MEL Matilda, 1/Dagaie decoy RL
**M:** 4 MTU 16V956 TB91 diesels; 4 props; 18,000 hp
**Electric:** 405 kVA **Range:** 700/35 **Man:** 4 officers, 35 men

Remarks: Ordered 1980. Function as leaders for the six TNC-45 class. Scheduled completion dates were 11-82 and 4-83. Marconi S810 search radar is in radome aft, Dagaie launcher and optical director for the 40-mm gun mount are amidships.

◆ **6 TNC-45 class** Bldr: Lürssen, Bremen-Vegesack, West Germany

| | L | In serv. | | L | In serv. |
|---|---|---|---|---|---|
| P 4501 Al Boom (ex-*Werjiya*) | 3-82 | 8-82 | P 4507 Al Saadi (ex-*Istiqlal*) | 12-82 | 9-8-84 |
| P 4503 Al Betteel (ex-*Mashuwah*) | 4-82 | 9-82 | P 4509 Al Ahmadi | . . . | 9-8-84 |
| P 4505 Al Sanbouk (ex-*Jalboot*) | . . . | 10-82 | P 4511 Al Istiqlal (ex-*Al Mubareki*) | . . . | 9-8-84 |

**Al Ahmadi (P 4509)** French Navy, 7-84

**Al Saadi (P 4507)**—with builder's number P. Voss, 10-83

**D:** 231 tons (259 fl) **S:** 41.5 kts **Dim:** 44.90 (42.30 wl) × 7.00 × 2.40
**A:** 4/MM 40 Exocet—1/76-mm OTO Melara DP—2/40-mm Breda AA (II × 1)—2/7.62-mm mg (I × 2)
**Electron Equipt:** Radar: 1/Decca 1226, 1/PEAB 9LV200 search, 1/PEAB 9LV200 director
EW: MEL Matilda intercept
**M:** 4 MTU 16V538 TB 92 diesels; 4 props; 15,600 hp (15,000 sust.)
**Electric:** 405 kw **Range:** 500/38.5; 1,500/16 **Man:** 5 officers, 27 men

Remarks: Ordered 1980. Carry 250 rounds 76-mm, 1,800 rounds 40-mm ammunition. Have CSEE Lynx optronic gun director for the 40-mm mount. Philips 9LV200 system for the 76-mm gun and missiles, and a flare rocket launcher amidships. First three accepted 26-4-84.

## PATROL CRAFT

◆ **5 "Sea Gull" class** Bldr: Korea SB & Eng., Okpo (In serv. 1985–86)

**D:** 80 tons **S:** 30 kts **Dim:** 24.0 × 5.5 × . . . **A:** . . .
**M:** 2 diesels; 2 props; 3,920 hp **Range:** 950/20 **Man:** 18 tot.

Remarks: Ordered 1985. Aluminum construction.

◆ **8 coastal patrol boats** Bldrs: Thornycroft, Woolston, first 2; Vosper Thornycroft, remainder

| | L | | L | | L | | L |
|---|---|---|---|---|---|---|---|
| Maymoon | 4-68 | Al Shurti | 1972 | Mashhoor | 1969 | Wathah | 1970 |
| Aman | 3-68 | Marzook | 1969 | Murshed | 1970 | Intisar | 1972 |

**D:** 40 tons **S:** 20 kts **Dim:** 27.78 × 4.73 × 1.38
**Electron Equipt:** Radar: Decca 202 **Man:** 5 officers, 7 men
**M:** 2 Rolls-Royce 8-cyl. diesels; 2 props; 1,340 hp **Range:** 700/15

◆ **5 56-foot boats** Bldr: Vosper Thornycroft Private, Ltd., Singapore

Dastoor Kasar Qahir Sagar Salam

**D:** 25 tons (fl) **S:** 29–30 kts **Dim:** 17.1 × 4.9 × . . .
**A:** 2/7.62-mm mg (I × 2) **M:** 2 MTU 6V331 diesels; 2 props; 1,350 hp
**Range:** 320/20 **Man:** 2 officers, 6 men

Remarks: Steel hull, aluminum superstructure. First two ordered 9-73, in service 6-74; others ordered 1978, in service 1979.

◆ **1 U.S. Cutlass class** Bldr: Halter Marine, New Orleans, La.

Dhaher (In serv. 6-8-79)

**D:** 34 tons (fl) **S:** 32 kts **Dim:** 19.66 × 5.18 × 1.12
**A:** 2/12.7-mm mg (I × 2) **Man:** 15 tot.
**M:** 2 MTU 8V 331 TB92 diesels; 2 props; 1,730 hp

PATROL CRAFT *(continued)*

◆ **14 36-foot boats** Bldr: Vosper Thornycroft Private, Ltd., Singapore

ANTAR AL SALMI II AL SEBBAH ISTIQLAL II
QARAH WARBAH—plus 8 unnamed

**Warbah** Vosper, 1972

**D:** 6.8 tons (fl) **S:** 22 kts **Dim:** 11.1 × 3.3 × 0.6 **Man:** 4 tot.
**A:** 4/7.62-mm mg (II × 2) **M:** 2 Sabre 210 diesels; 2 props; 420 hp

REMARKS: First four, in service 1972, and second four, in service 5-73, have no names. Wooden construction, nylon sheathed hulls.

◆ **27 Magnum Sedan class** Bldr: Magnum Marine, U.S.A.

**D:** . . . **S:** 60 kts **Dim:** 8.3 × 2.4 × 0.7 **Range:** 200/. . .
**M:** 2 Mercury Mercruiser inboard/outboard motors; 2 props; 660 hp

REMARKS: High-speed craft for inshore work. Three delivered 1977, one in 1978, three in 1979. Twenty more ordered 6-84. Glass-reinforced plastic construction.

◆ **1 46-foot craft** Bldr: Thornycroft Ltd., Singapore (In serv. 1-76)

MAHROOS

**D:** 21.5 tons (fl) **S:** 21.7 kts **Dim:** 14.1 × 4.5 × . . . **Man:** 1 officer, 4 men
**A:** 2/7.62-mm mg **M:** 2 Rolls-Royce C8M-410 diesels; 2 props; 780 hp

◆ **7 50-foot craft** Bldr: Thornycroft Ltd., Singapore (In serv. 1957–58)

MINE COUNTERMEASURES SHIPS

NOTE: Kuwait plans to add mine countermeasures units to its fleet and was holding discussions with Netherlands representatives during 11-84 over possibly ordering 4 units of the *Alkmaar* ("Tripartite") class. Discussions resumed, rather more in earnest, in 9-87.

AUXILIARIES

◆ **6 SR.N6 Mk 8 hovercraft** Bldr: British Hovercraft, Cowes, U.K.

**D:** 17 tons (fl) **S:** 50–55 kts **Dim:** 18.3 × 8.5 × . . .
**M:** 1 Rolls-Royce Gnome gas turbine; 1 airscrew, 1 lift fan; 1,060 hp
**Range:** 300 to 550 n.m./50–55 kts

REMARKS: Ordered 1981. Can carry two 450-liter fuel cells on deck to increase range. Primarily for logistics support.

◆ **4 Loadmaster Mk II logistics support landing craft** Bldr: Fairey Marine, Cowes, U.K. (In serv. 1984–85)

**Kuwaiti Loadmaster on trials** Fairey Marine, 1984

**D:** 175 tons light (350 normal/420 fl) **S:** 10.5 kts (10.0 sust.)
**Dim:** 33.00 (30.00 pp) × 10.20 × 1.75
**A:** none **Electron Equipt:** Radar: 1/Decca nav.
**M:** 2 Caterpillar 3412 DITA (V-12) diesels; 2 Kort-nozzle props; 1,214 hp (1,010 sust.)
**Range:** 1,000/10 **Electric:** 72 kw **Fuel:** 30 tons **Man:** 1 officer, 6 men

REMARKS: Ordered 1983. First pair completed 10-84. Cargo includes 150 tons on deck or 90 tons on deck and 60 tons liquid cargo. Can accommodate 2/60-ton tanks. Original design by Cheverton, taken over by Fairey in 1984.

◆ **3 logistics support landing craft** Bldr: Vosper Private, Ltd., Singapore (In serv. 1979–80)

AL JAHRA CERIFF HADIYA

**D:** 320 tons (fl) **S:** 9.5 kts **Dim:** 32.3 × 7.5 × 2.5
**M:** 2 Rolls-Royce C8M-410 diesels; 2 props; 750 hp **Range:** 1,500/9

REMARKS: Unusual in having landing ramp at stern. Have full forecastle bow, low fantail like oilfield supply boats. Cargo: 170 tons, 100 $m^2$ deck space. Carry 47 tons water ballast.

◆ **3 landing craft** Bldr: Vosper Thornycroft Private Ltd., Singapore

WAHEED (In serv. 5-71) REGGA (In serv. 5-71) FAREED (In serv. 11-75)

**D:** 88 tons (170 fl) **S:** 10 kts **Dim:** 27.0 × 6.9 × . . .
**M:** 2 Rolls-Royce C8M-410 diesels; 752 hp **Range:** 1,500/9 **Man:** 8 tot.

REMARKS: Carry 40 tons deck cargo, 24.4 $m^3$ cargo fuel, and 35.6 $m^3$ water.

◆ **2 fireboat tugs** Bldr: Fairey Marine, Cowes, U.K. (In serv. 11-6-84)

AL HANGAF AL MUTLAS

**D:** 67 tons (76 fl) **S:** 12 kts **Dim:** 21.00 (19.50 pp) × 5.90 × 2.15
**M:** 2 Caterpillar 3412 DITA (V-12) diesels; 2 props; 1,214 hp **Electric:** 72 kw

REMARKS: Ordered 1983. Carry 1,000 liters firefighting foam and have a 4,500 lit./min. firefighting monitor. Have 9.5-ton bollard pull. Can carry 50 deck passengers.

◆ **1 fireboat** Bldr: Vosper Thornycroft Private, Ltd., Singapore (In serv. 1978)

WAHEED

**D:** 112.6 grt **S:** 26.6 kts **Dim:** 26.2 × 5.8 × . . .
**M:** 2 diesels; 2 props; 2,200 hp **Man:** 16 tot.

◆ **6 utility launches** Bldr: Fairey Marine, Cowes, U.K. (In serv. 11-6-84)

**D:** 3.3 tons (fl) **S:** . . . **Dim:** 8.23 × 2.74 × 0.84
**M:** 1 or 2 Perkins 4.236 diesel(s); 1/2 props; 72/144 hp **Man:** 3 tot.

REMARKS: Four have 1 diesel, can carry 2 tons of cargo or 20 passengers. Two have 2 diesels, displace 3.8 tons, and can carry 1.5 tons cargo or 13 passengers. Glass-reinforced plastic construction. Ordered 1983.

CUSTOMS SERVICE

◆ **2 AZ 60 Sea Arrow class** Bldr: Azimut, Torino, Italy

JAMAREK I JAMAREK II (both in serv. 15-8-85)

**Jamarek I** Azimut, 1985

**D:** 26 tons (30 fl) **S:** 28 kts **Dim:** 18.60 (15.40 pp) × 5.10 × 0.93
**A:** 1/20-mm AA **Electron Equipt:** Radar: 1/Furuno . . . nav.
**M:** 2 M.A.N. D2842-LE diesels; 2 props; 1,520 hp
**Fuel:** 3.75 tons **Man:** 2 officers, 8 men

REMARKS: GRP construction. A similar AZ 66 design craft was delivered 15-1-86 to the Kuwaiti Environmental Protection Commission:

BEAH

**D:** 30 tons (3.5 fl) **S:** 27.6 kts **Dim:** 20.00 × 5.10 × 1.50
**Electron Equipt:** Radar: 1/Koden . . . nav.
**M:** 2 M.A.N. D2842-LE-12 diesels; 2 props; 1,560 hp

**KUWAIT** *(continued)*
**CUSTOMS SERVICE** *(continued)*

◆ **3 80-ft. U.S. Commercial Cruiser class** Bldr: Swiftships, Morgan City, La. (In serv. 15-12-83)

Sawahil 140 Sawahil 145 Sawahil 150

**D:** . . . **S:** . . . **Dim:** 24.4 × . . . × . . . **A:** . . . **M:** . . .

Remarks: Steel construction. Arrived in Kuwait for customs duties 4-84.

# LAOS

Personnel (1986): Approximately 1,700 total

◆ **46 river patrol craft**

Remarks: Reported by press to have been a gift of the U.S.S.R. in 1985. No other data available. There are probably other locally built craft in service.

# LEBANON

**Republic of Lebanon**

Personnel: Approximately 200 men

Merchant Marine (1986): 228 ships—484,624 grt
(tankers: 3 ships—14,087 grt)

### PATROL CRAFT

Note: Semi-independent Christian forces have operated five Dabur-class patrol craft, transferred by Israel in 1976; for characteristics, see Israel section.

◆ **2 Tracker Mk II class** Fairey Allday Marine, Hamble, U.K.

N . . . . . . . (In serv. 28-1-80) N . . . . . . . (In serv. 8-2-80)

**D:** 31.5 tons (fl) **S:** 29 kts **Dim:** 19.25 × 4.98 × 1.45 **A:** . . .
**M:** 2 G.M. 12V71 TI diesels; 2 props; 990 hp **Range:** 650/20 **Man:** 11 tot.

Remarks: Intended primarily for customs service. One under Christian Militia control since 1983.

◆ **6 Azteca class** Bldr: Crestitalia, Ameglia, La Spezia, Italy (In serv. 1980)

CF 1001 to CF 1006

**D:** 5.2 tons (fl) **S:** 24 **Dim:** 9.0 × 2.6 × 0.5
**M:** 2 diesels; 2 props; 320 hp **Range:** 240/. . .

Remarks: Glass-reinforced plastic construction, monohedron hull.

### AMPHIBIOUS SHIPS

◆ **2 French EDIC-III class** Bldr: SFCN, Villeneuve-la-Garenne

Sour (In serv. 1-85) Damour (L: 11-12-84)

**D:** 375 tons (712 fl) **S:** 10 kts
**Dim:** 59.00 (57.00 pp) × 11.90 × 1.67 (1.10 light)
**A:** 2/20-mm AA (I × 2)—1/81-mm mortar
**Electron Equipt:** Radar: 1/. . . nav.
**M:** 2 SACM MGO 175-V12-A diesels; 2 props; 1,040 hp
**Range:** 1,800/10 **Fuel:** 35 tons **Man:** 18 crew + 33 troops

Remarks: Ordered 30-7-83 as aid from the French government. *Sour* replaced an earlier EDIC (L 9096) of the same name and loaned 7-11-83. Can carry 11 trucks or 5 armored personnel carriers.

# LIBERIA

Personnel (1984): 445 total

Merchant Marine (1986): 1,568 ships—52,649,444 grt
(tankers: 423 ships—27,828,073 grt)

Naval Aviation: The one Cessna 337 operated by the Coast Guard for surveillance crashed on 30-1-87.

COAST GUARD

Note: The craft listed below are all in poor condition. Plans to acquire one 33.5-m and two 19.8-m patrol boats from the U.S. fell through in 1987. Liberia was reported negotiating with Greece for construction of two 23-m *Panagopoulos I*-class patrol boats in mid-1987.

### PATROL CRAFT

◆ **3 CG 27 class** Bldr: Karlskrona Varvet, Sweden (In serv. 27-9-80)

8801 Master Sergeant Samuel K. Doe (ex-*Nuah River*)
8802 Albert Porte (ex-. . .)
8803 General Thomas Quiwoukpa (ex-. . .)

**Master Sergeant Samuel K. Doe (8801)** 1980

**D:** 50 tons **S:** 25 kts **Dim:** 26.72 × 5.23 × 1.13
**A:** 1/12.7-mm mg—2/7.62-mm mg (I × 2)
**Electron Equipt:** Radar: 1/Decca 1226C
**M:** 2 MTU 8V331 TC82 diesels; 2 props; 1,866 hp
**Fuel:** 11 tons **Range:** 1,000/18 **Man:** 8 tot.

Remarks: Aluminum alloy construction. Names changed due to revolution; all originally named for rivers. Same design as Swedish Coast Guard TV 102.

◆ **2 U.S. 65-foot class** Bldr: Swiftships, Morgan City, La. (In serv. 22-7-76)

103 Cavilla 104 Mano

**D:** 38 tons (fl) **S:** 24 kts **Dim:** 19.8 × 5.8 × 0.8
**A:** 1/81-mm mortar combined with 12.7-mm mg—2/12.7-mm mg (I × 2)
**M:** 2 G.M. 12V71 TI diesels; 2 props; 1,920 hp
**Range:** 600/21.5 **Man:** 2 officers, 18 men

◆ **1 U.S. 42-foot class** Bldr: Swiftships, Morgan City, La. (In serv. 22-7-76)

101 St. Paul

**D:** 11 tons (12 fl) **S:** 20 kts **Dim:** 12.8 × 3.7 × 0.6
**A:** 2/12.7-mm mg (I × 2)
**M:** 2 G.M. 8V71 diesels; 2 props; 870 hp **Man:** 4 tot.

# LIBYA

**Socialist People's Libyan Arab Jamahiriya**

Personnel: Approximately 3,000 total

Merchant Marine (1986): 104 ships—825,231 grt
(tankers: 15 ships—708,030 grt)

Naval Aviation: About 18 Soviet-supplied Mi-14 Haze, 6 French-supplied Super Frélon (with AM 39 Exocet antiship missiles, L5 ASW torpedoes, and Sintra-Alcatel HS 73 dipping sonar), and 12 French Alouette-III helicopters are in service for naval use.

### SUBMARINES

Note: Two coastal submarines may have been ordered during 1982 in Yugoslavia, which has already delivered 6 *Mala*-class 2-man midget subs to Libya (2 in 1977 and 4 in 1981-82). Press reports of 1-87 indicate that two more Soviet-built submarines may be "leased."

◆ **6 Soviet Foxtrot class** Bldr: Sudomekh SY, Leningrad

311 Al Badr 312 Al Fateh 313 Al Ahad
314 Al Mitraqah 315 Al Khyber 316 Al Hunayn

**D:** 1,950/2,400 tons **S:** 18/16 kts **Dim:** 96.0 × 7.5 × 6.0
**A:** 10/533-mm TT (6 fwd, 4 aft)—22 torpedoes or 44 mines

SUBMARINES *(continued)*

**Electron Equipt:** Radar: Snoop Tray
Sonar: 1 med.-freq.; active, passive arrays
**M:** 3 diesels, electric motors; 3 props; 5,300 hp **Endurance:** 70 days
**Range:** 11,000/8 (snorkel) **Man:** 8 officers, 70 men

**Al Ahad (313)** 1978

REMARKS: One transferred in 12-76, two in 1978, fourth commissioned 30-3-81 at Tripoli, fifth delivered 2-82, and sixth in 3-83.

GUIDED-MISSILE FRIGATES

◆ **2 Soviet Koni class** Bldr: Zelenodolsk SY

212 AL HANI (In serv. 28-6-86) . . . AL GHARDABIA (In serv. 23-10-87)

**Al Hani** U.S. Navy, 6-86

**Al Hani (212)** U.S. Navy, 6-86

**D:** 1,440 tons (1,600 fl) **S:** 30 kts **Dim:** 96.40 × 12.55 × 3.48 (hull)
**A:** 4/SS-N-2C SSM (II × 2)—1/SA-N-4 SAM system (II × 1; 20 missiles)—4/76.2-mm DP (II × 2)—4/30-mm AA (II × 2)—1/RBU-6000 ASW RL(XII × 1)—4/400-mm ASW TT—mine rails
**Electron Equipt:** Radar: 1/Plank Shave, 1/Strut Curve, 1/Hawk Screech, 1/Pop Group, 1/Drum Tilt
Sonar: hull-mounted MF
EW: 2/Watch Dog intercept, 2 decoy RL(XVI × 2)
IFF: 2/Square Head interrogator, 1/Salt Pot transponder
**M:** CODAG: 1 19,000-hp gas turbine; 2 Type 68B, 8,000-hp diesels; 3 props; 35,000 hp
**Range:** 1,800/14 **Man:** approx. 130 total

REMARKS: First version of Koni (NATO "Koni-III") to have SSM and ASW torpedoes at the expense of one ASW RL. Second unit expected 1988. Plank Shave radar acts as surface search and acquisition for SS-N-2C missiles; Pop Group track-while-scan radar controls the SA-N-4 SAMs, Hawk Screech (with two pedestal target designators) handles the 76.2-mm guns, and Drum Tilt (again with two visual backup directors) serves the 30-mm guns.

◆ **1 Vosper Mk 7** Bldr: Vosper Thornycroft, Woolston, U.K.

| | Laid down | L | In serv. |
|---|---|---|---|
| F 211 DAT ASSAWARI | 27-9-68 | 9-69 | 1-2-73 |

**Dat Assawari (F 211)**—post-refit C. Martinelli, 5-84

**D:** 1,325 tons (1,650 fl) **S:** 37/17 kts **Dim:** 101.6 (94.5 pp) × 11.08 × 3.36
**A:** 4/Otomat Mk 2 SSM (I × 4)—1/114-mm Mk 8 DP—1/Albatros Mk 2 SAM syst. (IV × 1; Aspide missiles)—2/40-mm AA (I × 2)—2/35-mm Oerlikon AA (II × 1)—6/324-mm ILAS-3 ASW TT (III × 2)
**Electron Equipt:** Radar: 1/RAN-10S, 1/RAN-12, 1/navigational, 2/Orion RTN-10X
Sonar: 1/Diodon (TSM 2310)
EW: Decca RDS-1, Selenia INS-1 passive, U.K. FH-12 HFD/F
**M:** CODOG: 2 Rolls-Royce TM 2A Olympus gas turbines, 24,000 hp each; 2 Paxman Ventura diesels, 1,900 hp each; 2 CP props
**Fuel:** 300 tons **Range:** 1,000/36; 5,700/17 **Man:** 132 tot.

REMARKS: Began refitting in Italy, 1979; damaged by bomb 29-10-80. Ran trials in 3-83 and recommissioned 1-10-83, but did not return to Libya until 6-85. Sea Cat SAM and Limbo ASW mortar replaced by 4-cell Albatros launcher and ASW TT for A244 torpedoes. Received Selenia RAN-12L/X(IPN-10) combat data system. Otomat, new radars, sonar added. Has two NA-10 Mod. 2 gun/missile f.c.s.

CORVETTES

◆ **3 Soviet Nanuchka II class** Bldr: Petrovskiy SY, Leningrad

417 N . . . . . . . (ex-*Ain al Gazala*)
(In serv. 7-2-83)
418 N . . . . . . . (ex-*Ain Zaara*)
(In serv. 10-83)
419 N . . . . . . . (ex-*Ain Zaquit*)
(In serv. 8-85)

**Ex-Ain Al Gazala (417)** L. & L. Van Ginderen, 1986

**D:** 675 tons (fl) **S:** 32 kts **Dim:** 59.3 × 12.6 × 2.4
**A:** 4/SS-N-2c Styx SSM (II × 2)—1/SA-N-4 system (II × 1, 20 missiles)—2/57-mm DP (II × 2)
**Electron Equipt:** Radar: 1/Don-2, 1/Square Tie (in Band Stand radome), 1/Pop Group, 1/Muff Cob
EW: 1/Bell Tap passive array, 2/decoy RL (XVI × 2)
**M:** 3 Type M521 diesels; 3 props; 25,996 hp **Man:** 60 tot.
**Range:** 900/30; 2,500/12 (1 engine)

**CORVETTES** *(continued)*

REMARKS: Reason for slow delivery rate unknown. Considered to be poor sea boats by some customers, with unreliable propulsion plants (M507 is a double M503, 42-cylinder radial engine). Sister, *Tariq Ibn Ziyad* (ex-*Ain Mara,* 416) sunk 24-3-86 by U.S. aircraft.

◆ **4 Wadi M'ragh class** Bldr: CNR, Riva Trigoso, Italy

| | L | In serv. |
|---|---|---|
| 412 Assad Al Bihar (ex-*Wadi M'ragh*) | 29-4-77 | 14-9-77 |
| 413 Assad Al Tougour (ex-*Wadi Majer*) | 20-4-78 | 12-2-80 |
| 414 Assad Al Kalij (ex-*Wadi Mercit*) | 15-12-78 | 28-3-81 |
| 415 Assad Al Hudud (ex-*Wadi Megrawa*) | 21-6-79 | 28-3-81 |

**Assad Al Bihar (412)** CNR, 1979

**Assad Al Hudud (415)**—without Otomat missiles L. & L. Van Ginderen, 1986

**D:** 547 tons (630 fl) **S:** 34 kts **Dim:** 61.7 (57.8 pp) × 9.3 × 2.7
**A:** 4/Otomat Mk I SSM—1/76-mm OTO Melara DP—2/35-mm Oerlikon AA (II × 1)—6/324-mm ASW TT (III × 2)—16 mines
**Electron Equipt:** Radar: 1/RAN 11 L/X, 1/Decca TM 1226, 1/Orion RTN-10X
Sonar: Thomson-CSF Diodon
EW: Selenia 1NS-1 intercept
**M:** 4 MTU 16V956 TB91 diesels; 4 CP props; 16,400 hp **Electric:** 650 kw
**Fuel:** 126 tons **Range:** 1,400/33; 4,150/18 **Man:** 58 tot.

REMARKS: Ordered in 1974. Completion delayed by prolonged trials. Have fin stabilizers, automatic degaussing system, Selenia IPN-10 combat data system, 1/NA 10 Mod. 3 GFCS, with 2C03 optical backup director. Can maintain 31.5 kts sea speed. Names changed 1983. Poorly maintained. Missiles not usually mounted.

◆ **1 Vosper Mk 1B**

| | Bldr | L | In serv. |
|---|---|---|---|
| C 411 Tobruk | Vosper, Ltd., Portsmouth | 29-7-65 | 20-4-66 |

**Tobruk (C 411)** Shbldg. and Shipping Record, 1966

**D:** 440 tons (500 fl) **S:** 18 kts **Dim:** 53.95 (48.77 pp) × 8.68 × 4.0
**A:** 1/102-mm—4.40-mm AA (I × 4) **Range:** 2,900/14 **Man:** 5 officers, 58 men
**M:** 2 Paxman Ventura YJCM diesels; 2 props; 3,800 hp **Fuel:** 60 tons

REMARKS: Launched in 1965. Anti-rolling devices, air-conditioned living spaces. No ASW equipment. Can be used as a yacht. Low muzzle velocity, 102-mm gun has low-angle elevation only. Refitted and modernized at Taskizak Naval Shipyard, Turkey, during 1983-84. Has only a single navigational radar.

**GUIDED-MISSILE PATROL BOATS**

◆ **0 (+4) Type 400 class** Bldr: Kraljevica SY, Yugoslavia

**D:** 385 tons (525 fl) **S:** 34 kts **Dim:** 54.80 (51.88 pp) × 8.96 (8.16 wl) × 2.46
**A:** 4/SS-N-2C Styx (I × 4)—1/76-mm OTO Melara Compact DP—2/40-mm Breda Dardo AA (II × 1)—2/20-mm AA (I × 2)—2/7.62-mm mg (I × 2)
**Electron Equipt:** Radar: . . .
**M:** 4 MTU 20V538 TB92 diesels; 4 props; 1,400 hp
**Range:** . . . **Endurance:** 15 days **Man:** . . .

REMARKS: Ordered 12-84 or 1-85. Have chaff rocket launchers on the 76-mm gun mount. Draft given is at 455-ton normal displacement.

◆ **9 French Combattante-II class** Bldr: CMN, Cherbourg

| | Laid down | L | In serv. |
|---|---|---|---|
| 518 Sharara (ex-*Beir Grassa*) | 13-3-78 | 28-6-79 | 9-2-82 |
| 522 Shehab (ex-*Beir Gzir*) | 10-6-78 | 22-1-80 | 4-3-82 |
| 524 Wahg (ex-*Beir Gtifa*) | 30-1-79 | 20-5-80 | 29-5-82 |
| 528 Shouaiai (ex-*Beir Algandula*) | 12-9-79 | 14-1-81 | 2-11-82 |
| 532 Shoula (ex-*Beir Alkitat*) | 17-12-79 | 3-81 | 29-10-82 |
| 534 Shafak (ex-*Beir Alkirim*) | 11-3-80 | 23-6-81 | 17-12-82 |
| 536 Bark (ex-*Beir Alkardmen*) | 9-6-80 | 6-10-81 | 11-3-83 |
| 538 Rad (ex-*Beir Alkur*) | 20-10-80 | 30-11-81 | 19-5-83 |
| 542 Laheeb (ex-*Beir Alkuesat*) | 20-1-81 | 9-1-82 | 29-7-83 |

**Waheed (526)**—lost 24-3-86 Ceclant/Premar, 4-82

**D:** 258 tons (311 fl) **S:** 39 kts **Dim:** 49.0 (46.2 pp) × 7.1 × 2.4 (2.0 hull)
**A:** 4/Otomat SSM (II × 2)—1/76-mm OTO Melara DP—2/40-mm Breda/Bofors AA
**Electron Equipt:** Radar: 1/Triton search, 1/Castor tracking, 1/Vega II fire-control (all Thomson-CSF)
**M:** 4 MTU 20V538 TB91 diesels; 4 props; 18,000 hp **Range:** 1,600/15
**Man:** 8 officers, 19 men

REMARKS: Ordered 5-77. Delivery of first three embargoed 2-81 to 12-81. Names changed 1983. Delivery of final unit embargoed until 2-1-84. Sister *Waheed* (526, ex-*Beir Glulud*) sunk 24-3-86 by U.S. Navy aircraft; another may have been damaged.

◆ **12 Soviet Osa-II class**

| | | |
|---|---|---|
| 205 Al Katum | 209 Al Nabhar | 956 Al Zuara |
| 206 Al O'Wakh | 210 Al Fikar | . . . Al Mwash |
| 207 Al Rwae | 952 Al Safhaa | . . . Al Btar |
| 208 Al Baida | 954 Al Zakab | . . . Al Sidd |

NOTE: Hull numbers are in Arabic script to starboard, Western to port.

**Libyan Osa-II 517**—old number L. & L. Van Ginderen, 1986

## GUIDED-MISSILE PATROL BOATS *(continued)*

**D:** 210 tons (240 fl) **S:** 34 kts **Dim:** 38.6 × 7.6 × 2.0
**A:** 4/SS-N-2 Styx SSM (I × 4)—4/30-mm AA (II × 2)
**Electron Equipt:** Radar: 1/Square Tie, 1/Drum Tilt
IFF: 2/Square Head, 1/High Pole
**M:** 3 M504 diesels; 3 props; 15,000 hp **Range:** 500/34; 750/25 **Man:** 30 tot.

REMARKS: One transferred in 1976, four in 1977, one in 1978, three in 1979, one in 4-80, one in 5-80, and the twelfth in 7-80. Reportedly, the original order was reduced from twenty-four to twelve.

◆ **3 Sölöven class** Bldr: Vosper, Ltd, Portsmouth

| | L | In serv. | | L | In serv. |
|---|---|---|---|---|---|
| P 512 SUSA | 31-8-67 | 8-68 | P 514 SEBHA (ex-*Sokna*) | 29-2-68 | 1-69 |
| P 513 SIRTE | 10-1-68 | 4-68 | | | |

**Susa (P 512)**—firing a wire-guided missile Vosper, 1968

**D:** 95 tons (115 fl) **S:** 50 kts **Dim:** 30.38 (27.44 pp) × 7.3 × 2.15
**A:** 8/SS 12 SSM (II × 4)—2/40-mm AA (I × 2)
**M:** CODOG: 3 Bristol-Siddeley Proteus gas turbines; 3 props; 12,750 hp; 2 G.M. 6-71 cruising diesels; 190 hp
**Man:** 20 tot.

REMARKS: Modeled on the Danish *Sölöven* class. All-wood construction, nylon-sheathed hull. Missiles are wire-guided and are not very accurate, particularly at high speeds. Cruise diesels are on outboard propeller shafts. Refitted in Italy 1984-85, with new engines and new electronics.

## MINE WARFARE SHIPS

NOTE: Libya has laid several minefields, apparently employing the naval roll-on/roll-off cargo ship *El Timsah,* (burned out and lost, 1986) and her merchant sister *Ghat,* with mine rails on the vehicle deck for the purpose.

◆ **8 Soviet Natya-class fleet minesweepers**

| | |
|---|---|
| 111 AL I'SAR (ex-*Ras el Gelais*) | 119 AL . . . (ex-*Ras al Oula*) |
| 113 AL TAYYAR (ex-*Ras Hadad*) | 121 AL . . . (ex-*Ras al Dawar*) |
| 115 AL . . . (ex-*Ras al Hamman*) | 123 AL . . . (ex-*Ras Massad*) |
| 117 AL . . . (ex-*Ras al Falluga*) | 125 AL . . . (ex-*Ras al Hani*) |

**Ex-Ras al Oula (119)** P. Voss, 8-83

**Al I'sar (111)** L. &. L. Van Ginderen, 1986

**D:** 650 tons (750 fl) **S:** 18 kts **Dim:** 61.0 × 9.8 × 3.0
**A:** 4/30-mm AA (II × 2)—4/25-mm AA (II × 2)—2/RBU 1200 ASW RL (V × 2)—mines
**Electron Equipt:** Radar: 1/Don-2, 1/Drum Tilt
Sonar: . . .
IFF: 2/Square Head, 1/High Pole B
**M:** 2 diesels; 2 props; 5,000 hp **Range:** 1,600/16; 5,200/10 **Man:** 60 tot.

REMARKS: First pair delivered 3-81; second pair in 2-83; fifth on 3-9-83, the sixth during 2-84, the seventh on 20-1-85, and the last in 10-86. Like the six built for India, they lack the ramp at the stern found on Soviet units.

## AMPHIBIOUS WARFARE SHIPS

◆ **3 Soviet Polnocny-C-class landing ships** Bldr: Poland

112 IBN AL HADRAMI 116 IBN OMAYAR 118 IBN EL FARAT

**Ibn Omayar (116)**—in dry dock L. & L. Van Ginderen, 1986

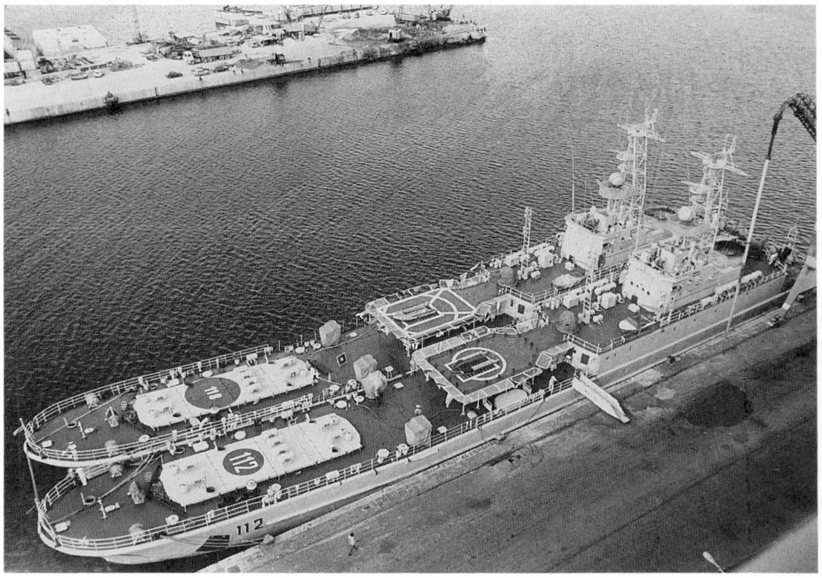
**Ibn al Hadrami (112) and Ibn el Farat (118)** L. Grazioli, 9-84

**D:** 1,150 tons (fl) **S:** 18 kts **Dim:** 81.3 × 10.1 × 2.1
**A:** 4/30-mm AA (II × 2)—2/122-mm artillery RL (XV × 2)
**Electron Equipt:** Radar: 1/Spin Trough, 1/Drum Tilt
**M:** 2 diesels; 2 props; 5,000 hp

REMARKS: One transferred in 12-77 and two in 6-79. Like the Iraqi examples of this Polish-built class of medium landing ships, these export versions have a raised helicopter deck forward of the superstructure. A fourth Libyan unit, the *Ibn al Qyis* (113), was lost on 14 or 15 September 1978 through fire at sea.

◆ **2 Ibn Ouf-class landing ships** Bldr: C.N.I.M., La Seyne

| | Laid down | L | In serv. |
|---|---|---|---|
| 132 IBN OUF | 1-4-76 | 22-10-76 | 11-3-77 |
| 134 IBN HARISSA | 18-4-77 | 18-10-77 | 10-3-78 |

## AMPHIBIOUS WARFARE SHIPS *(continued)*

**Ibn Harissa (134)** C. Martinelli, 1981

**D:** 2,800 tons (fl) **S:** 15 kts **Dim:** 100.0 × 15.65 × 2.6
**A:** 6/40-mm Breda AA (II × 3)—1/81-mm mortar
**M:** 2 SEMT-Pielstick diesels; 2 CP props; 5,340 hp
**Range:** 4,000/14 **Man:** 35 crew + 240 troops

Remarks: Cargo: 570 tons, including up to eleven tanks. Helicopter platform aft.

◆ **25 Turkish C 107-class large landing craft** Bldr: Taskizak SY, Istanbul, and Gölçük Naval SY

ex-Turk Ç 132 ex-Turk Ç 133
ex-Turk Ç 130 ex-Turk Ç 131 and 21 others

**D:** 280 tons (600 fl) **S:** 10 kts (8.5 loaded) **Dim:** 56.56 × 11.58 × 1.25
**A:** 2/20-mm AA (I × 2) **M:** 3 G.M. 6-71 TI diesels; 3 props; 900 hp
**Range:** 600/10; 1,100/8 **Man:** 15 tot.

Remarks: Cargo: five heavy tanks, up to 100 troops; up to 350 tons. Design follows World War II-era British LCT(4). Cargo deck 28.5 × 7.9 m. Ordered 7-12-79, with first two taken from among ships built for Turkish Navy and delivered 7-12-79. As many as 50 were to be acquired, with each Turkish yard building 25. Presumably M. Khadafi has designs on a near-neighbor's territory, as these ships are unsuitable for extended voyages. Sixteen were delivered by 4-81. Possible names: *Ras El Hilel, El Kobayat, Ibn al Idrissi, Ibn Marwan.*

## AUXILIARY SHIPS

◆ **1 support ship for small combatants**

| | Bldr | Laid down | L | In serv. |
|---|---|---|---|---|
| 711 Zeltin | Vosper Thornycroft, Woolston | 1967 | 29-2-68 | 23-1-69 |

**Zeltin (711)** 1968

**D:** 2,200 tons (2,470 fl) **S:** 15 kts **Dim:** 98.72 (91.44 wl) × 14.64 × 3.05
**A:** 2/40-mm AA (I × 2)
**M:** 2 Paxman Ventura 16 YSCM diesels; 2 props; 3,500 hp
**Electric:** 800 kw **Range:** 3,000/14 **Man:** 15 officers, 86 men

Remarks: The well deck, 41 × 12, can receive small craft that draw up to 2.3 m. Hydraulically controlled stern gate. A movable crane (3-ton loading capacity) is available for the well deck, and a 9-ton crane on the port side supports the workshops.

◆ **1 Yugoslav Spasilac-class submarine rescue ship** Bldr: Tito SY, Belgrade 722 Zlatica

**D:** 1,590 tons (fl) **S:** 13.4 kts **Dim:** 55.50 × 12.00 × 3.84 (4.34 props)
**A:** 4/14.5-mm mg (II × 2) **Electric:** 540 kVA
**M:** 2 diesels; 2 Kort-nozzle props; 4,340 hp **Range:** 4,000/13.4 **M:** 53 tot.

Remarks: Delivered to Tripoli late in 1982. Intended to support the six Foxtrot-class submarines. Has decompression chamber, extensive diving equipment, can lay a 4-point moor, and can tow. Carries 490 tons cargo fuel and up to 250 tons deck cargo. Can support divers to 300 m. Has a bow-thruster.

◆ **1 small transport**

El Fateh (ex-Panamanian *Mebo II*)

**D:** 640 grt **S:** 10.5 kts **Dim:** 44.00 × 8.90 × 3.20 **M:** 2 Sulzer diesels

Remarks: Acquired 1977.

◆ **3 harbor tugs** Bldr: Jonker & Stans SY, the Netherlands (In serv. 1980)

A 33 A 34 A 35

**D:** 150 grt **S:** . . . **Dim:** 26.60 × 7.90 × 2.48
**M:** 2 diesels; 2 Voith-Schneider vertical-cycloidal props; . . . hp

Remarks: Two 17.00 × 6.25 × 2.75 harbor tugs were delivered at the same time.

◆ **4 Ras El Helal-class tugs** Bldr: Mondego, Foz, Portugal

| | In serv. | | In serv. |
|---|---|---|---|
| Ras El Helal | 22-10-77 | Al Keriat | 17-2-78 |
| Al Shweiref | 17-2-78 | Al Tabkah | 29-7-78 |

**D:** 200 grt **S:** 14 kts **Dim:** 34.8 × 9.0 × 4.0 (moulded depth)
**M:** 2 diesels; 2 props; 2,300 hp

◆ **1 Soviet Yelva-class diving tender**

Al Manoud (ex-VM 917)

**D:** 295 tons (fl) **S:** 12.4 kts **Dim:** 40.9 × 8.0 × 2.1
**Electron Equipt:** Radar: 1/Spin Trough
**M:** 2 Type 3D12 A diesels; 2 props; 600 hp

Remarks: Transferred 19-12-77. Can support seven hard-hat divers working at 60 m and has a submersible decompression chamber.

◆ **1 floating dry dock** Bldr: Blohm & Voss, Hamburg (In serv. 1984)

**Capacity:** 3,200 tons **Dim:** 105.20 × 26.00 × 6.40

Remarks: Ordered 20-2-84, laid down 17-4-84.

◆ **1 Soviet Poluchat-I-class torpedo retriever**

**D:** 90 tons (fl) **S:** 18 kts **Dim:** 29.6 × 6.1 × 1.9 **A:** . . .
**M:** 2 props; 2,400 hp **Range:** 450/17; 900/10 **Man:** 20 tot.

Remarks: Delivered 20-5-85 under tow by Bulgarian tug *Neptun.*

CUSTOMS SERVICE

## PATROL BOATS AND CRAFT

◆ **6 Yugoslav PB 90 class** Bldr: Tito Brodotekhnika SY, Belgrade (In serv. 1985–86)

**D:** 90 tons (fl) **S:** 27 kts **Dim:** 30.3 × 5.9 × . . .
**A:** 1/40-mm Bofors AA—4/20-mm AA (IV × 1)
**Electron Equipt:** Radar: 1/Decca 1226
**M:** 3 MTU diesels; 3 props; 4,350 hp **Man:** 17 tot.

Remarks: Ordered 1984. May have a small, high-frequency sonar.

◆ **14 SAR 33-class patrol boats** Bldr: Taskizak SY, Turkey (In serv. 1982–84)

**D:** 150 tons (170 fl) **S:** 40 kts **Dim:** 34.5 × 8.60 × 1.85
**A:** 1/40-mm AA—2/12.7-mm mg (I × 2)
**M:** 3 SACM AGO V16CSHR diesels; 3 CP props; 12,000 hp
**Fuel:** 18 tons **Range:** 400/35; 1,000/. . . **Man:** 23 tot. **Electric:** 300 kw

Remarks: Ordered early 1980 to replace the earlier customs units in service. Wedge-shaped hull of remarkable steadiness at high speeds in heavy seas. Aluminum alloy construction. May be a lengthened variant, 37.5 m overall. Designed by Abeking & Rasmussen, West Germany. Half reportedly delivered by end of 1983.

◆ **2 patrol boats** Bldr: Müller, Hameln, West Germany (In serv. 1-78)

Jihad Salam

**D:** 120 tons (fl) **S:** 27 kts **Dim:** 37.0 × 6.2 × . . .
**A:** 4/30-mm Hispano-Suiza GCM AO2 AA
**M:** MTU diesels; . . . props; . . . hp **Range:** 1,100/27 **Man:** 21

Remarks: Ordered for Lebanon, but when that country could not pay, sold to Libya 1-78. Transferred to Palestine Liberation Organization control in 8-81 and kept in Syria.

◆ **4 Brooke type** Bldr: Brooke Marine, Lowestoft, U.K. (In serv. 1968–70)

PC 1 Zleitan (ex-*Garian*) PC 3 Merawa
PC 2 Khawlan PC 4 Sabratha

**D:** 100 tons (125 fl) **S:** 23.5 kts **Dim:** 36.58 × 7.16 × 1.75
**A:** 1/40-mm—1/20-mm AA
**M:** 2 Paxman Ventura 10 YJCM diesels; 2 props; 3,600 hp
**Range:** 1,800/13 **Man:** 22 tot.

Remarks: Have the same engines as the *Tobruk* and the *Zeltin.* At least one has a Soviet BM-21 multiple 122-mm rocket launcher (XX × 1) in place of the 20-mm AA gun. PC 1 renamed to commemorate former repair craft, 1982. Refitted at Taskizak Naval SY, Turkey, in 1983-84.

◆ **3 security craft** Bldr: Vosper Thornycroft, Portsmouth (In serv. 1967–69)

Benina Homs Misurata

**D:** 100 tons **S:** 18–20 kts **Dim:** 30.5 × 6.4 × 1.7 **A:** 1/20-mm AA
**M:** 3 Rolls-Royce diesels; 1,740 hp **Range:** 1,800/14 **Man:** 15 tot.

LIBYA *(continued)*
CUSTOMS SERVICE *(continued)*

Remarks: Used for customs and fishery protection. Sisters *Ar Rakib, Farwa,* and *Akrama* ceded to Malta, 1978.

Note: Upwards of 50 radio-controlled suicide boats of Swedish and Cyprian construction are said to be in service for coast defense. No details available, except that speeds of 30 knots are attainable.

# MADAGASCAR

**Democratic Republic of Madagascar/Malagasy Republic**

Personnel: Approximately 600 men, including a 120-man marine infantry company

Merchant Marine (1986): 71 ships—71,375 grt (tankers: 5 ships—8,863 grt)

## PATROL BOAT AND CRAFT

◆ **1 French PR 48-type coastal patrol boat** Bldr: SFCN, Villeneuve-la-Garenne

| | Laid down | L | In serv. |
|---|---|---|---|
| Malaika | 11-66 | 22-3-67 | 12-67 |

**D:** 235 tons (250 fl) **S:** 18.5 kts **Dim:** 47.5 (45.5 pp) × 7.1 × 2.25
**A:** 2/40-mm AA **M:** 2 MGO diesels; 2 props; 2,400 hp
**Range:** 2,000/15 **Man:** 3 officers, 22 men

Remarks: Sisters with more powerful propulsion plants in the Senegalese and Tunisian navies.

◆ **1 North Korean Nampo class** (In serv. 1979–80)

**D:** 70 tons (fl) **S:** 40 kts **Dim:** 27.7 × 6.1 × 1.8
**A:** 4/14.5-mm mg (II × 2)—1/75-mm recoilless rifle
**M:** 4 M50-series diesels; 4 props; 4,800 hp
**Range:** 375/40 **Man:** 19 tot.

Remarks: Unlike North Korean Navy version, has no bow ramp or troop accommodations, being intended for use strictly as patrol craft. Metal construction. Three sisters destroyed by typhoon during 4-84.

## AMPHIBIOUS WARFARE SHIPS

◆ **1 medium landing ship**

| | Bldr | Laid down | L | In serv. |
|---|---|---|---|---|
| Toky | Diego Suarez SY | 1972 | 1973 | 10-74 |

**Toky** French Navy, 1974

**D:** 810 tons (avg) **S:** 13 kts **Dim:** 66.37 (56.0 pp) × 12.5 × 1.9
**A:** 1/40-mm AA—2/20-mm AA—1/81-mm mortar **Man:** 27 tot.
**M:** 2 MGO diesels; 2 props; 2,400 hp **Electric:** 240 kw **Range:** 3,000/12

Remarks: Used as a transport and support ship. Transport capacity: 250 tons. Quarters for 30 passengers; 120 soldiers can be carried for short distances. Financed by the French government under the Military Cooperation Pact.

◆ **1 French EDIC-class tank landing craft** Bldr: CN Franco Belges (In serv. 1964)

Aina Vao Vao (ex-EDIC L9082)

**D:** 250 tons (670 fl) **S:** 8 kts **Dim:** 59.00 × 11.95 × 1.30 (1.62 max.)
**A:** 2/20-mm AA (I × 2)—1/81-mm mortar
**Electron Equipt:** Radar: 1/Decca 1226
**M:** 2 MGO diesels; 2 props; 1,000 hp **Range:** 1,800/8 **Man:** 17 tot.

Remarks: Transferred 27-9-85, having been laid up at Tahiti since stricken from French Navy in 1981. Can carry 11 trucks.

## TRADING SHIP

◆ **1 former trawler**

| | Bldr | L |
|---|---|---|
| Fanantenana (ex-*Richelieu*) | A.G. Weser, Bremen | 1959 |

**D:** 1,040 tons (1,200 fl) **S:** 12 kts
**Dim:** 62.0 (56 pp) × 9.15 × 4.52 **A:** 2/40-mm AA
**M:** 2 Deutz diesels ("father-son" system); 1 prop; 1,060 + 500 hp **Man:** . . .

Remarks: 691 grt. Bought and modified, 1966–67. Can carry 300 tons of freight and up to 120 military passengers.

MARITIME POLICE

◆ **5 coastal surveillance craft** Bldr: Bayerische Schiffbau, West Germany (In serv. 1962)

GC 1 Philiberi Isiranana
GC 2 Faheleovatena
GC 3 N . . . . . . .
GC 4 Fanrosoana
GC 5 Fahafahana

**D:** 46 tons **S:** 22 kts **Dim:** 24.0 × . . . × . . .
**A:** 1/40-mm AA **M:** 2 diesels; 2 props; . . . hp

# MALAWI

**Republic of Malawi**

Merchant Marine (1986): 2 ships—1,348 grt

POLICE

## PATROL CRAFT

◆ **1 for Lake Nyasa service** Bldr: SFCN, Villeneuve-la-Garenne, France (In serv. 17-12-84)

703 Chikala

**Chikala (703)** L. & L. Van Ginderen, 1984

**D:** 33 tons (36 fl) **S:** 22 kts **Dim:** 21.0 (18.5 wl) × 4.8 × 1.5
**A:** 1/20-mm GIAT F-2 AA **Electron Equipt:** Radar: 1/Decca . . . nav.
**M:** 2 Poyaud 520-V12-M2 diesels; 2 props; 1,400 hp
**Range:** 650/15 **Man:** 10 tot.

Remarks: Ordered 8-11-83. Delivered in sections 10-84 and assembled in Malawi.

◆ **1 Spear class** Bldr: Fairey Marine, Hamble, U.K. (In serv. 1976)

P 702

**D:** 4 tons (fl) **S:** 25 kts **Dim:** 9.1 × 2.8 × 0.8 **A:** 2/7.62-mm mg (I × 2)
**M:** 2 Perkins diesels; 2 props; 290 hp **Man:** 3 tot.

Remarks: There are also as many as three additional small patrol craft on Lake Nyasa.

# MALAYSIA

Note: Forces specifically assigned to the Malaysian state of Sabah are listed separately.

Personnel: Approximately 11,000 total, plus 900 reserves (with reserves to expand to about 7,000)

Merchant Marine (1986): 498 ships—1,743,629 grt (tankers: 73 ships—257,514 grt)

NAVAL AVIATION: A Naval Air Wing was to be established with 12 pilots in 5-86, to man helicopters yet to be acquired. Plans to acquire 6–8 ex-British Wasp light ASW helicopters were finalized in 1987. The Malaysian Air Force operates a Lockheed C-130H-MP Hercules on maritime patrol and SAR duties.

NOTE: In 1985 it was announced that submarines may be acquired.

## FRIGATES

◆ **2 new-construction Type 1500** Bldr: Howaldtswerke, Kiel

| | Laid down | L | In serv. |
|---|---|---|---|
| F 25 KASTURI | 31-1-83 | 14-5-83 | 15-8-84 |
| F 26 LEKIR | 31-1-83 | 14-5-83 | 15-8-84 |

**Kasturi (F 25)** Howaldtswerke, 1984

**Lekir (F 26)** P. Voss, 5-84

**D:** 1,690 tons (1,900 fl) **S:** 28 kts **Dim:** 97.3 (91.8 pp) × 11.3 × 3.5 (hull)
**A:** 4/MM 38 Exocet—1/100-mm Compact DP—1/57-mm Bofors DP—4/30-mm Emerlec AA (II × 2)—1/375-mm Bofors ASW RL (II × 1)—1/light helicopter.
**Electron Equipt:** Radar: 1/Decca 1226 nav., 1/H.S.A. DA .08, 1/H.S.A. WM-22
Sonar: Atlas ASO 84/5
EW: "Rapids" intercept, "Scimitar" jammer; 2 Dagaie RL
**M:** 4 MTU 20V 1163 TB92 diesels; 2 CP props; 21,460 hp **Fuel:** 200 tons
**Electric:** 1,392 kVA **Range:** 3,600/18; 7,000/14 **Man:** 128 tot.

REMARKS: Ordered 10-6-81. Acquisition of two more deferred. There is no hangar, only a deck for an as-yet-to-be-determined light helicopter. The 100-mm gun is of the new Creusot-Loire "Compact" model. Two H.S.A. LIOD optronic backup GFCS for the 100-mm and 57-mm guns. Both arrived in Malaysia 23-11-84. Can make 23 kts on 2 diesels. There are flare rocket launchers on the sides of the 57-mm mount. Four similar, but shorter and differently equipped, sisters built for Colombia.

◆ **1 "Yarrow frigate" class**

| | Bldr | Laid down | L | In serv. |
|---|---|---|---|---|
| F 24 RAHMAT (ex-*Hang Jebat*) | Yarrow, Scotstoun | 2-66 | 18-12-67 | 3-71 |

**D:** 1,290 tons (1,600 fl) **S:** 27 kts (16.5 on diesels alone)
**Dim:** 93.97 (pl. 44 pp) × 10.36 × 3.05
**A:** 1/114-mm Mk 6-mm DP—3/40-mm Bofors AA (I × 3)—1/Mk 10 Limbo ASW mortar (III × 1)
**Electron Equipt:** Radar: 1/Decca 626, 1/H.S.A. LW-02, 1/H.S.A. M-22
Sonar: 1/170B, 1/174—EW: UA-3 intercept, FH-4D/F
**M:** CODOG: 1 Rolls-Royce Olympus TM-1B gas turbine, 19,500 hp; 1 Crossley-Pielstick SPC2V diesel, 3,850 hp; 2 CP props; 22,000 hp
**Electric:** 2,000 kw **Range:** 1,000/27; 5,200/16.5 **Man:** 120 tot.

**Rahmat (F 24)** J. Bouvia, 1987

REMARKS: Ordered 11-2-66. M-22 fire-control radar atop the mast for the 114-mm gun. The ASW mortar is covered by a hatch that serves as a platform for a light helicopter. Sea Cat SAM system and radar director replaced by a 40-mm AA gun during 1981–82 refit. Plans to replace the 114-mm mount with a French 100-mm Compact were deferred. Both the 114-mm mount and the after 40-mm mount have U.K. 103-mm flare rocket launch rails on either side.

◆ **1 British built** Bldr: Yarrow, Scotstoun

| | Laid down | L | In serv. |
|---|---|---|---|
| F 76 HANG TUAH (ex-*Mermaid*) | 1965 | 29-12-66 | 16-5-73 |

**Hang Tuah (F 76)** G. Arra, 1980

**D:** 2,300 tons (2,520 fl) **S:** 24/23 kts **Dim:** 103.4 × 12.2 × 4.8
**A:** 2/102-mm Mk 19 DP—4/30-mm Emerlec AA (II × 2)—2/40-mm AA (I × 2)—1/Mk 10 Limbo ASW mortar (III × 1)
**Electron Equipt:** Radar: 1/Plessey AWS-1, 1/978
Sonar: 1/174, 1/170B
**M:** 8 16-cyl. Admiralty Standard Range-I diesels; 2 props; 14,400 hp
**Fuel:** 230 tons **Range:** 4,800/15 **Man:** 200–210 tot.

REMARKS: Ordered for Ghana in 1964. Because of the political situation, the ship was not delivered and at the end of 1971 was purchased by the British government. Transferred to Malaysia in 5-77. Has lead-computing STD Mk 1 sight for the Mk 19 twin 102-mm mount, and no fire-control radar. Helicopter pad.

## CORVETTES

◆ **2 (+1) offshore patrol vessels**

| | Bldr | L | In serv. |
|---|---|---|---|
| 160 MUSYTARI | Korea SB & Eng., Pusan | 20-7-84 | 1-4-85 |
| 161 MARIKH | Malaysian SY & Eng., Pasir Gudang | 21-1-85 | 9-4-87 |
| . . . N . . . . . . . | Malaysian SY & Eng., Pasir Gudang | . . . | . . . |

**Musytari (160)** G. Gyssels, 7-86

**D:** 1,000 tons (1,300 fl) **S:** 20 kts **Dim:** 75.0 × 10.8 × 3.7
**A:** 1/100-mm Compact DP—2/30-mm Emerlec AA (II × 1)
**Electron Equipt:** Radar: 1/Decca 1226, 1/DA-05, 1/9GA-600
**M:** 2 diesels; 2 props; 6,360 hp **Range:** 6,000/20 **Man:** 76 tot.

REMARKS: First two ordered 6-83. Intended to patrol the 200-n.m. economic zone. Third unit ordered 5-84. PEAB 9LV230 electro-optical control system for the 100-mm gun. Large helicopter deck aft, no hangar. Names mean "Jupiter" and "Mars."

## GUIDED-MISSILE PATROL BOATS

◆ **4 Spica-M class** Bldr: Karlskrona Varvet, Sweden

| | Laid down | L | In serv. |
|---|---|---|---|
| P 3511 HANDALAN | 24-5-77 | ... | 26-10-79 |
| P 3512 PERKASA | 27-6-77 | ... | 26-10-79 |
| P 3513 PENDIKAR | 15-7-77 | ... | 26-10-79 |
| P 3514 GEMPITA | 21-10-77 | ... | 26-10-79 |

**Pendikar (P 3513)** J. Bouvia, 1987

**D:** 240 tons (268 fl) **S:** 37.5 kts (34.5 sust.)
**Dim:** 43.62 (41.00 pp) × 7.0 × 2.4 (aft)
**A:** 4/MM 38 Exocet SSM (II × 2)—1/57-mm Bofors DP—1/40-mm Bofors AA
**Electron Equipt:** Radar: 1/Decca 1226, 1/Phillips 9LV200 Mk 2 system (1 tracker, 1/9GR600 search radar)
Sonar: Simrad SU—EW: MEL SUSIE-1
**M:** 3 MTU 16V538 TB91 diesels; 3 props; 10,800 hp **Fuel:** 80 tons
**Electric:** 400 kVA **Range:** 1,850/14 **Man:** 5 officers, 34 men

REMARKS: Ordered 13-8-76. Given the names of the four *Perkasa*-class torpedo/patrol boats that were stricken in 1977. Have 103-mm rocket flare launchers on the 57-mm mount and 57-mm RFL on the 40-mm mount. Can be equipped with ASW TT if required. Do *not* carry the Blowpipe SAM system offered with the original design.

◆ **4 French Combattante-II 4AL class** Bldr: CMN, Cherbourg

| | L | In serv. | | L | In serv. |
|---|---|---|---|---|---|
| P 3501 PERDANA | 31-5-72 | 31-12-72 | P 3503 GANAS | 26-10-72 | 28-2-73 |
| P 3502 SERANG | 22-12-71 | 31-2-73 | P 3504 GANYANG | 16-3-72 | 20-3-73 |

**Ganyang (P 3504)**—without missiles, 40-mm gun J. Jedrlinic, 1982

**D:** 234 tons (265 fl) **S:** 36.5 kts **Dim:** 47.0 × 7.1 × 2.5 (fl)
**A:** 2/MM 38 Exocet SSM (I × 2)—1/57-mm Bofors AA—1/40-mm Bofors AA
**Electron Equipt:** Radar: 1 Decca 1226, 1/Triton, 1/Pollux
**M:** 4 MTU MB 870 diesels; 4 props; 14,000 hp **Fuel:** 39 tons
**Range:** 800/25 **Man:** 5 officers, 30 men

REMARKS: Steel hulls. Superstructure in alloyed metal. Six 103-mm rocket flare launchers on the 57-mm mount, four 57-mm on the 40-mm mount. Thomson-CSF Vega fire-control system with Triton search radar. Pollux f.c. radar.

## PATROL BOATS

◆ **6 Jerong class** Bldr: Hong Leong-Lürssen, Butterworth, Malaysia

| | L | In serv. | | L | In serv. |
|---|---|---|---|---|---|
| P 3505 JERONG | 28-7-75 | 23-3-76 | P 3508 YU | 17-7-76 | 15-11-76 |
| P 3506 TUDAK | 16-3-76 | 16-6-76 | P 3509 BAUNG | 5-10-76 | 11-7-77 |
| P 3507 PAUS | 2-6-76 | 18-8-76 | P 3510 PARI | 1-77 | 23-3-77 |

**D:** 210 tons (255 fl) **S:** 34 kts **Dim:** 44.90 × 7.00 × 2.48 (props)
**A:** 1/57-mm Bofors AA—1/40-mm Bofors AA
**Electron Equipt:** Radar: 1/Decca 1226
**M:** 3 MTU MB 870 diesels; 3 props; 10,800 hp **Electric:** 384 kVA
**Range:** 700/31.5; 2,000/15 **Man:** 5 officers, 31 men

**Baung (P 3509)** J. Jedrlinic, 1981

REMARKS: Lürssen FPB 45 design. Rocket flare launchers are fitted on both gun mounts. C.S.E.E. Naja electro-optical GFCS. Fin stabilizers fitted.

◆ **20 103-foot Vosper type** Bldr: Vosper Ltd., Portsmouth

Ordered in 1965:

| | L | | L |
|---|---|---|---|
| P 34 KRIS | 11-3-66 | P 36 SUNDANG | 22-5-66 |
| P 37 BADEK | 8-5-66 | P 38 RENCHONG | 22-6-66 |
| P 39 TOMBAK | 20-6-66 | P 40 LEMBING | 22-8-66 |
| P 41 SERAMPANG | 15-9-66 | P 42 PANAH | 10-10-66 |
| P 43 KERAMBIT | 20-11-66 | P 44 BALADAU | 11-1-67 |
| P 45 KELEWANG | 31-1-67 | P 46 RENTAKA | 15-3-67 |
| P 47 SRI PERLIS | 26-5-67 | P 48 SRI JOHORE | 21-8-67 |

**Kelewang (P 45)**—with 2/40-mm AA G. Gyssels, 7-86

Ordered in March 1963:

| | L | | L |
|---|---|---|---|
| P 3144 SRI SABAH | 30-12-63 | P 3145 SRI SARAWAK | 20-1-64 |
| P 3146 SRI NEGRI SEMBILAN | 17-9-64 | | |

Ordered in September 1961:

| | L | | L |
|---|---|---|---|
| P 3139 SRI SELANGOR | 17-7-62 | P 3142 SRI KELANTAN | 8-1-63 |
| P 3143 SRI TRENGGANU | 12-12-62 | | |

**Sri Kelantan (P 3142)** J. Jedrlinic, 1983

**D:** 96 tons (109 fl) **S:** 27/23 kts **Dim:** 31.39 (28.95 pp) × 5.95 × 1.65
**A:** 1 or 2/40-mm AA (I × . . .)—2 mg **Electron Equipt:** Radar: 1/Decca 616
**M:** 2 Bristol-Siddeley or Maybach MD 655/18 diesels; 2 props; 3,550 hp
**Range:** 1,400/14 **Man:** 3 officers, 19–20 men

REMARKS: Welded hulls. Vosper anti-roll stabilizers. The Malaysian prototype was delivered in February 1963 and was soon followed by many others. The middle group have greater range: 1,660/14. The class prototype, the *Sri Kegah* (P 3138),

**PATROL BOATS** *(continued)*

and the *Sri Pahang* (P 3141) were stricken 1976; *Sri Perek* (P 3140) foundered 1-84. Bulwark configurations vary, while early units had hull portholes. Aft 40-mm gun removed in at least three. Seventeen of the survivors had been modernized by end-1984. Sister *Sri Melaka* (P 3147, 2nd group) is detached to Sabah (see later page).

## MINE WARFARE SHIPS

◆ **2 (+2) Italian Lerici-class minehunters** Bldr: Intermarine, La Spezia

| | L | In serv. |
|---|---|---|
| M 11 Mahamiru | 24-2-83 | 11-12-85 |
| M 12 Jerai | 8-12-83 | 11-12-85 |
| M 13 Ledang | 14-7-83 | 11-12-85 |
| M 14 Kinabulu | 19-3-83 | 11-12-85 |

**Mahamiru (M 11)** C. Martinelli, 8-85

**Jerai (M 12)** G. Arra, 7-85

**D:** 508 tons (540 fl) **S:** 16 kts **Dim:** 51.00 (46.50 pp) × 9.56 × 2.75
**A:** 1/40-mm AA
**Electron Equipt:** Radar: Decca 1226
Sonar: Thomson-CSF TSM 2022
**M:** 2 MTU 12V396 TC82 (DB512) diesels; 2 CP props; 2,394 hp—2/88-kw electric retractable auxiliary props
**Electric:** 1,000 kw (4 MTU V396 TC52 gen. sets) **Fuel:** 46 tons
**Range:** 1,400/14; 2,000/12 **Man:** 45 tot.

Remarks: Ordered 2-81. Intended for patrol duties also. Arrived in Malaysia 28-3-86. Glass-reinforced plastic construction. Have different main engine, armament, and sonar than Italian Navy sisters. Range at 12 kts can be extended to 4,000 n.m. by using the passive anti-rolling tanks to carry fuel. Have two PAP-104 remote-controlled minehunting devices, good in depths up to 300 m, and U.K. Oropesa Mk 4 mechanical sweep gear. Active tank stabilization, TSM 2060 autopilot, decompression chamber fitted.

## AMPHIBIOUS WARFARE CRAFT

Note: In addition to these small craft, the multipurpose ships of the *Sri Indera Sakti* class, the former U.S. Navy LSTs, and the miscellaneous utility landing craft listed under auxiliaries can be used for amphibious warfare purposes.

◆ **5 U.S. LCM(6)-class vehicle landing craft** Bldr: De Havilland Marine, Australia

LCM 1–5

**D:** 24 tons (56 fl) **S:** 10 kts **Dim:** 17.07 × 4.37 × 1.17
**M:** 2 diesels; 2 props; 330 hp **Range:** 130/10

Remarks: Transferred around 1970 from Australia. Cargo: 30 tons.

◆ **9 RCP-class personnel/vehicle landing craft** Bldr: Hong Leong-Lürssen SY, Butterworth, Malaysia (All in serv. 1974)

**RCP** J. Bouvia, 1987

**D:** 15 tons (30 fl) **S:** 17 kts **Dim:** 15.0 × 4.4 × . . .
**A:** 1/20-mm AA **M:** 2 diesels; 2 waterjets: . . . hp

Remarks: Cargo: 35 troops or one small vehicle.

◆ **15 LCP-class personnel landing craft** Bldr: De Havilland Marine, Australia

LCP 1–15

**D:** 19 tons (fl) **S:** 16 kts **Dim:** 14.6 × 4.3 × 1.0
**M:** 2 Cummins diesels; 2 props; 400 hp

Remarks: Transferred 1965–66. Essentially personnel launches, with pointed bows; have light armor over pilothouse amidships. There are also several De Havilland "Titan" Mk 3 12-meter landing craft in service.

Note: The Malaysian Army also operates small landing craft; including:

◆ **165 Damen 540 Class** Bldr: Damen, Gorinchem, Netherlands (65); Limbougan Timor, Kuala Trengganu (100) (In serv. 1986–87)

**D:** . . . **S:** 25–30 kts **Dim:** 5.4 × 1.83 × . . .
**M:** 1/40-hp outboard **Man:** 2 crew, 10 troops

Remarks: Ordered 10-85. About 250–300 other small river-crossing assault boats are available.

## HYDROGRAPHIC SHIP

◆ **1 seagoing oceanographic research and hydrographic survey ship**

| | Bldr | In serv. |
|---|---|---|
| A 152 Mutiara | Hong Leong-Lürssen, Butterworth, Malaysia | 18-11-77 |

**Mutiara (A 152)** G. Arra, 1980

**D:** 1,905 tons (fl) **S:** 16 kts **Dim:** 70.0 (64.0 pp) × 13.0 × 4.0
**A:** 2/20-mm AA (I × 2) **M:** 1 Deutz SBA-12M-528 diesel; 1 CP prop; 2,000 hp
**Range:** 4,500/16 **Man:** 13 officers, 143 men

Remarks: Ordered 1975. Carries six small survey launches and has a helicopter deck. White hull, buff stack.

## AUXILIARIES

◆ **2 multipurpose support ships**

| | Laid down | L | In serv. | Bldr |
|---|---|---|---|---|
| A 1503 Sri Indera Sakti | 15-2-80 | 1-7-80 | 24-10-80 | Bremer Vulcan |
| A 1504 Mahawangsa | . . . | . . . | 16-5-83 | Korea Tacoma, Masan |

**D:** 2,000 tons light (4,300 fl) **S:** 16.8 kts **Dim:** 100.00 (91.20 pp) × 15.00 × 4.75
**A:** 1 or 2/57-mm Bofors DP (I × 1 or 2)—2/20-mm AA (I × 2)
**M:** 2 Deutz-KHD SBV 6M540 diesels; 2 CP props; 5,986 hp
**Electric:** 1,200 kw **Endurance:** 60 days **Fuel:** 1,350 tons (max.)
**Range:** 14,000/15 **Man:** 14 officers, 126 men, 75 passengers

AUXILIARIES *(continued)*

**Sri Indera Sakti (A 1503)** LSPH E. Pitman, R.A.N., 11-84

**Mahawangsa (A 1504)** C. Martinelli, 3-86

Remarks: 1,800 dwt. A 1503 ordered 10-79, A 1504 in 2-81. Intended to perform a variety of tasks, such as: provide support (including up to 1,300 tons of fuel and 200 tons water) to deployed small combatants or mine-countermeasures ships; act as a flagship; perform as a vehicle and troop transport in amphibious operations; and act as a cadet training ship. There are 1,000 $m^3$ of cargo space for spare parts, and ten 20-ft standard cargo containers can be carried on deck amidships. Vehicle holds aft are reached by ramps on either side of the stern, which supports a helicopter deck; can carry 600 troops on the 680-$m^2$ vehicle deck. Extensive repair facilities and divers' support equipment are provided. Provisions spaces total 300 $m^2$, including 100 $m^3$ refrigerated stores. Bow-thruster fitted, as is a 16-ton crane amidships. Two CSEE Naja optical GFCS. A 1504 lacks a funnel, thus effectively doubling the size of the helo deck; she is configured to carry 410 tons of ammunition, has a higher, larger helicopter deck, and mounts a second 57-mm DP aft. A 1504 is 103.00 o.a., draws 5.00 m, displaces 5,000 tons (fl) and can reach 15.5 kts. Both can carry 17 tanks, while A 1504 can stow 11 3-ton trucks on deck beneath the helicopter platform.

◆ **2 utility landing craft/transports** Bldr: Penang SY, Pulau Jerejah

| | L | In serv. |
|---|---|---|
| A . . . Lang Siput | 1980 | 1980 |
| A . . . Lang Tiram | 25-9-80 | 21-10-80 |

**D:** 330 grt **S:** 9 kts **Dim:** 48.4 (45.0 pp) × 10.5 × . . .
**M:** 2 Caterpillar D3408 diesels; 2 props; 700 hp

◆ **2 Jernih-class utility landing craft/transports** Bldr: Brooke DY, Malaysia

A . . . Jernih (In serv. 1977) A . . . Terijah (In serv. 1978)

**D:** 290 (fl) **S:** 8 kts **Dim:** 38.0 (35.2 pp) × . . . × 1.4
**M:** 2 Caterpillar D343T diesels; 2 props; 730 hp

Remarks: Capacity: 170 tons of dry cargo or 240 tons of fresh water. Intended as supply craft for Sarawak.

◆ **1 Meleban-class utility landing craft** Bldr: Brooke DY, Malaysia

A . . . Meleban (L: 15-10-77)

**D:** . . . **S:** 8 kts **Dim:** 50.0 (43.5 pp) × . . . × 1.37
**M:** 2 Caterpillar D343T diesels; 2 props; 730 hp

◆ **1 small cargo ship** (In serv. 1977)

A 301 Enterprise

◆ **1 small tanker** (In serv. 1973)

A 8 Kepah (ex-*Asiatic Supplier*)—432 grt. Purchased 1980.

◆ **1 diving tender**

| | Bldr | L | In serv. |
|---|---|---|---|
| A 1109 Duyong | Kall Teck SY, Singapore | 18-8-70 | 5-1-71 |

**D:** 140 tons (fl) **S:** 10 kts **Dim:** 33.0 × 6.3 × 1.7
**A:** 1/20-AA **M:** 2 Cummins diesels; 2 props; 500 hp **Man:** 23 tot.

Remarks: Used as a support ship for divers. Originally configured as a torpedo retriever.

◆ **4 coastal tugs** Bldr: Penang SY, Pulau Jerejah

| | L | | L |
|---|---|---|---|
| Lang . . . | 5-81 | Lang Kangok | 1982 |
| Lang . . . | 1981 | Lang Hindek | 1982 |

**D:** . . . **S:** 12.5 kts **Dim:** 29.0 × 7.0 × 2.0
**M:** 2 Ruston Paxman diesels; 2 props; 1,800 hp

◆ **3 Tunda-class harbor tugs** Bldr: Ironwood SY, Malaysia (In serv. 1978–79)

A 1 Tunda 1 A 2 Tunda 2 A 3 Tunda 3

**D:** 150 tons **S:** . . . **Dim:** 26.0 × . . . × . . .
**M:** 1 Cummins diesel; 1 prop: . . . hp

◆ **1 salvage and fire-fighting tug** (In serv. 1976)

A 4 Penyu (ex-*Salvigilant*)—Purchased 1980; 398 grt.

◆ **2 salvage and fire-fighting tugs**

A 20 Badang I A 21 Badang II—400 grt

◆ **9 miscellaneous tugs**

A 6 Sotong (ex-*Asiatic Charm*)—233 grt, blt. 1976; purchased 1980

| | | |
|---|---|---|
| A 9 Siput | 1 10 Teritup | A 11 Belankas |
| A . . . Mangkasa | A . . . Selar | A . . . Tepuruk |
| A . . . Kempong | A . . . Patak | |

ROYAL MALAYSIAN MARINE POLICE

Note: Planned acquisitions include three 40-m patrol boats equipped with helicopter platforms and four 32-m patrol boats.

## PATROL BOATS

◆ **9 Brooke Marine 29-m design** Bldr: Penang SY, Pulau Jerejah (In serv. 1982–83)

PX 28 Sangitan 8 others (PX 29–36)

**Sangitan (PX 28)** Brooke Marine

**D:** 114 tons **S:** 36 kts **Dim:** 29.0 (26.5 pp) × 6.0 × 1.7
**A:** 2/20-mm AA (I × 2)—2/7.62-mm mg (I × 2)
**Electron Equipt:** Radar: 1/navigational
**M:** 2 Paxman Valenta 16 RP 200M diesels; 2 props; 8,000 hp
**Range:** 1,200/24 **Man:** 4 officers, 14 men

Remarks: Ordered 1980. Status of program unavailable. Originally reported as naval, but now stated to be Marine Police-subordinated. Design evolved from the PX 26 class. Carry 2,000 rds. 20-mm ammunition.

◆ **15 PZ class** Bldr: Hong Leong Lürssen, Butterworth, Malaysia (In serv. 1981–1983)

PZ 10 Lang Hitan 14 others (PZ 2–15)

**Lang Hitan (PZ 10)** R.A.N., 1982

**MALAYSIA** *(continued)*
**ROYAL MALAYSIAN MARINE POLICE** *(continued)*

**D:** 188 tons (205 fl) **S:** 34 kts **Dim:** 38.50 (36.00 wl) × 7.00 × 2.20
**A:** 1/40-mm AA—1/20-mm AA—2/7.62-mm mg
**M:** 2 MTU 20V538 TB92 diesels; 2 props; 9,000 hp **Electric:** 130 kVA
**Range:** 550/31.5; 1,100/16 **Man:** 3 officers, 24 men

REMARKS: Lürssen FPB 38 design. Have 2 rocket flare launchers, carry 1,000 rounds 40-mm, 2,000 rounds 20-mm. Ordered 1979; first delivered 8-81.

◆ **3 PX 26 class** Bldr: Hong Leong-Lürssen, Butterworth, Malaysia (In serv. 1973–74)

PX 25 N....... PX 26 SRI KUDAT PX 27 SRI TAWAU

**D:** 62.5 tons **S:** 25 kts **Dim:** 28.0 × 5.4 × 1.6
**A:** 2/20-mm AA (I × 2) **M:** 2 MTU MB820Db diesels; 2 props; 2,460 hp
**Range:** 1,050/15 **Man:** 19 tot.

◆ **6 improved PX class** Bldr: Vosper Thornycroft Pty, Singapore (In serv. 1973–74)

PX 19 ALOR STAR, PX 20 KOTA BAHRU, PX 21 KUALA TRENGGANU, PX 22 JOHORE BAHRU, PX 23 SRI MENANTI, PX 24 KUCHING

**Sri Menanti (PX 23)** Vosper, 1974

**D:** 92 tons (fl) **S:** 25 kts **Dim:** 27.3 × 5.8 × 1.5
**A:** 2/20-mm AA (I × 2) **M:** 2 MTU MB820Db diesels; 2 props; 2,460 hp
**Range:** 750/15 **Man:** 18 tot.

◆ **16 PX class** Bldr: Vosper Thornycroft Pty, Singapore, 1963–69

PX 1 MAHKOTA, PX 2 TEMENGGONG, PX 3 HULUBALANG, PX 4 MAHARAJESETIA, PX 5 MAHARAJELELA, PX 6 PAHLAWAN, PX 7 BENTARA, PX 8 PERWIRA, PX 9 PERTANDA, PX 10 SHAHBANDAR, PX 11 SANGSETIA, PX 12 LAKSAMANA, PX 13 PEKAN, PX 14 KELANG, PX 15 KUALA KANGSAR, PX 16 ARAU

**Shahbandar and Sangsetia (PX 10, PX 11)** 1975

**D:** 85 tons (fl) **S:** 25 kts **Dim:** 26.29 × 5.7 × 1.45 **A:** 2/20-mm AA (I × 2)
**M:** 2 Mercedes-Benz MB820Db diesels; 2 props; 2,460 hp
**Range:** 700/15 **Man:** 15 tot.

REMARKS: Sisters *Sri Gumantong* (PX 17) and *Sri Labuan* (PX 18) are operated by the Sabah government

NOTE: The Royal Malaysian Marine Police operate a large number of smaller patrol and support craft

MALAYSIAN CUSTOMS AND EXCISE SERVICE

**PATROL BOATS**

◆ **6 Vosper 103-ft design** Bldr: Malaysian SY & Eng. Co., Pasir Gudang

K 1 BAHTERA PERAK, K 2 BAHTERA BAYU, K 3 BAHTERA HIJAU, K 4 BAHTERA PULAI, K 5 BAHTERA JERAI, K 6 BAHTERA JUANG

**D:** 100 tons (143 fl) **S:** 27 kts **Dim:** 32.40 (29.50 pp) × 7.20 × 1.80
**A:** 1/20-mm AA—2/7.62-mm mg (I × 2)
**M:** Paxman Valenta 16RP200 diesels; 2 props; 4,000 hp; Cummins KTA-1550M cruise diesel; 1 prop; 575 hp
**Range:** 1,200/10; 2,000/8 **Fuel:** 36 tons **Man:** 26 tot.

REMARKS: Ordered built under license from Vosper Pty, Singapore. First two in service 1982; last delivered 30-3-84. Generally resemble Malaysian Navy units of this design. The Customs and Excise Service also operates a number of small craft, including 23 13.7-meter craft, 10 11.0-meter craft, and the 18.3-m *Kuala Bengkoka,* completed 3-12-76 by Mengsina, Singapore.

# MALDIVE ISLANDS

**Republic of the Maldives**

PERSONNEL: Approximately 150 total

MERCHANT MARINE (1986): 30 ships—84,808 grt (tankers: 3 ships—1,808 grt)

**PATROL BOATS AND CRAFT**

◆ **1 21-m Tracker** Bldr: Fairey Marine, Cowes, U.K. (In serv. 4-87)

**D:** 35 tons (fl) **S:** 25 kts **Dim:** 21.00 × 5.18 × 1.45
**A:** 1/20-mm AA—2/7.62-mm mg (I × 2)
**M:** 2 G.M. 12V71 TI diesels; 2 props; . . . hp
**Range:** 450/20 **Man:** 11 tot.

REMARKS: Ordered 6-85. Used for fisheries protection. GRP construction.

◆ **3 9-m craft** Bldr: Fairey Marine, Cowes, U.K. (Ordered 6-85)

◆ **1 ex-British RTTL Mk-2-class target-towing launch**

**D:** 34.6 tons (fl) **S:** 30 kts **Dim:** 20.7 × 5.8 × 1.8 **A:** mg
**M:** 2 Rolls-Royce Sea Griffon gasoline engines; 2 props; 1,100 hp **Man:** 9 tot.

REMARKS: Transferred in 1976 by the departing Royal Air Force.

◆ **1 ex-British 1300-class tender**

**D:** 28.3 tons **S:** 13 kts **Dim:** 19.2 × 4.9 × 1.5
**M:** 2 Rolls-Royce C6 diesels; 2 props; 190 hp **Man:** 5 tot.

REMARKS: Transferred by the departing Royal Air Force. Cargo: 5 tons.

◆ **3 ex-Taiwanese trawlers**

GAAFARU ISDU MULI MAGGUDU

REMARKS: Approximately 600 tons (fl); about 40-m overall. Fitted with 2/25-mm AA guns (II × 1) by the U.S.S.R. after confiscation for poaching in 1976.

◆ **4 ex-British 19.5-meter landing craft**

REMARKS: Transferred in 1976

◆ **1 customs launch** Bldr: Fairey Marine, U.K. 1975

# MALI

PERSONNEL: About 50 total

◆ **2 Yugoslav patrol boats for Niger River**

REMARKS: Transferred 1974 via Libya.

◆ **3 smaller river patrol craft**

# MALTA

**Republic of Malta**

MERCHANT MARINE (1986): 246 ships—2,014,947 grt (tankers: 12 ships—514,214 grt)

NAVAL AVIATION: Helicopter Flight: 1 AB-206, 4 AB-47G, 1 AB-204B

ARMED FORCES OF MALTA
MARITIME SQUADRON

## PATROL BOATS AND CRAFT

◆ **2 ex-Yugoslav Type 131 class** Bldr: Trogir SY (In serv. 1965–68)

P 38 President Tito (ex-*Durmitor,* 138)
P 39 Dom Mintoff (ex-*President Mintoff,* ex-*Cer,* 139)

**Dom Mintoff (P 39)** L. & L. Van Ginderen, 7-83

**D:** 85 tons light (120 fl) **S:** 22 kts **Dim:** 32.0 × 5.5 × 2.5
**A:** 6/20-mm Hispano-Suiza HS831 AA (III × 2)
**Electron Equipt:** Radar: 1/Kelvin-Hughes 14/9
**M:** 2 MTU 820Db diesels; 2 props; 1,800 hp

Remarks: Transferred 31-3-82.

◆ **2 ex-U.S. Swift-class PCF** Bldr: Sewart Seacraft, 1967

C 23 (ex- U.S. C 6823) C 24 (ex-U.S. C 6824)

**C 23** L. & L. Van Ginderen, 7-83

**D:** 22.5 tons (fl) **S:** 25 kts **Dim:** 15.6 × 4.12 × 1.5
**A:** 3/12.7-mm mg (II × 1 and 1 combined with 1/81-mm mortar)
**M:** 2 G.M. 12V71T diesels; 2 props; 960 hp
**Endurance:** 24–36 hours **Man:** 6–8 tot.

Remarks: Donated 1-71.

◆ **2 ex-Libyan customs patrol craft** Bldr: Thornycroft, Woolston

C 28 (ex-*Ar Rakib*) C 29 (ex-*Akrama*)

**C 28** L. & L. Van Ginderen, 11-87

**D:** 100 tons (fl) **S:** 18 kts **Dim:** 30.5 × 6.4 × 1.7 **A:** 1/20-mm AA
**M:** 3 Rolls-Royce diesels; 3 props; 1,740 hp **Range:** 1,800/14 **Man:** 15 tot.

Remarks: Transferred in 1978. C 30 (ex-*Farwa*) sank 1981.

◆ **2 British RAF RTTL Mk 2-class rescue launches**

C 68 (ex-2768) C 71 (ex-2771)

**C 68 and C 71** P. Voss, 10-82

**D:** 34.6 tons **S:** 30 kts **Dim:** 20.7 × 5.8 × 1.8
**M:** 2 Rolls-Royce Sea Griffon gasoline engines; 2 props; . . . hp **Man:** 9 tot.

Remarks: Transferred early 1970s; wooden construction.

◆ **2 ex-Libyan customs launches** Bldr: Mosir SY, Trogir, Yugoslavia, 1963

C 25 (ex-*Arraid*) C 26 (ex-. . .)

**C 25** P. Voss, 10-82

**D:** 86.2 tons (100 fl) **S:** 20 kts **Dim:** 35.0 × 5.0 × 1.7
**A:** 1/12.7-mm mg **M:** 2 MTU 12V493 diesels; 2 props; 1,800 hp
**Range:** 1,400/12 **Man:** 12 tot.

Remarks: Transferred 16-1-74.

◆ **1 ex-German customs launch**

C 27 (ex-*Brunsbuttel*) Bldr: Buschmann, Hamburg, 1953

**D:** 105 tons (fl) **S:** 16 kts **Dim:** 29.5 × 5.2 × 1.6 **A:** 1/12.7-mm mg
**M:** 2 MWM TRM 134S diesels; 2 props; . . . hp **Man:** 9 tot.

Remarks: Purchased in 1974.

◆ **2 small patrol craft** Bldr: Guy Coucher, France (In serv. 1979)

Aphrodite Kiklan

**D:** approx. 10 tons (fl) **S:** . . . **Dim:** . . . × . . . × . . .
**A:** 2/7.62-mm mg (I × 2) **Electron Equipt:** Radar: 1/Decca 110
**M:** 2 diesels; 2 props; . . . hp

◆ **1 British RAF 1300-series pinnace general-purpose tender**

C. . .

**M:** 2 Rolls-Royce C6 diesels; 2 props; 190 hp **Man:** 5 tot.

Remarks: Also transferred was an RAF 1600-series range safety craft; 12 tons, 13.1 × 4.0 × 1.2, 16 kts.

# MARSHALL ISLANDS

PERSONNEL: . . .

MERCHANT MARINE (1986): None registered

GOVERNMENT OF THE MARSHALL ISLANDS
MARITIME AUTHORITY

### PATROL BOATS

◆ **1 former oilfield supply boat** Bldr: . . .

IONMETO (ex-*Southern* . . .)

**Ionmeto** W. Donko, 7-87

**D:** approx. 110 tons (fl) **S:** . . . **Dim:** 30.5 × . . . × . . . **A:** . . .
**Electron Equipt:** Radar: 1/. . . nav. **M:** 2 . . . diesels; 2 props; . . . hp

REMARKS: Purchased in Gulf of Mexico area, 1987, and traveled to Marshall Islands under own power.

NOTE: Two former U.S. Navy YFU-type landing craft ferries transferred 1987 for inter-island service. See addenda.

# MAURITANIA

**Islamic Republic of Mauritania**

PERSONNEL: (1987): 320 tot.

MERCHANT MARINE (1986): 73 ships—22,752 grt

NAVAL AVIATION: Two Piper Cheyenne II, twin-turboprop aircraft were delivered 1981 for coastal surveillance duties. Capable of 7-hour patrols (1,525 n.m.), they have a belly-mounted Bendix RDR 1400 radar.

### PATROL BOATS AND CRAFT

◆ **1 French PATRA class** Bldr: C.N. Auroux, Arcachon

| | Laid down | L | In serv. |
|---|---|---|---|
| P 411 DIX JUILLET (ex-*Rapière,* P 674) | 15-2-81 | 3-6-81 | 1-11-81 |

**Dix Juillet (P 411)** C.N. Auroux, 1982

**D:** 115 tons (148 fl) **S:** 28 kts **Dim:** 40.70 (35.40 wl) × 5.90 × 1.55
**A:** 1/40-mm AA—1/20-mm AA—2/12.7-mm mg (I × 2)
**Electron Equipt:** Radar: 1/Decca 1226
**M:** 2 AGO 195 V12 CZSHR diesels; 2 CP props; 5,000 hp (4,400 sust.)
**Electric:** 120 kw **Range:** 750/20; 1,500/15 **Man:** 2 officers, 25 men

REMARKS: Built on speculation, acquired by French Navy, and then sold to Mauritania, commissioning 14-5-82. Reported to be in need of overhaul, 1987.

◆ **3 Spanish Barcelo class** Bldr: Bazán, San Fernando

| | In serv. | | In serv. | | In serv. |
|---|---|---|---|---|---|
| P 362 EL VIAZ | 12-79 | P 363 EL BEG | 5-79 | P 364 EL KENZ | 8-82 |

**D:** 134 tons (fl) **S:** 36.5 kts **Dim:** 36.2 × 5.8 × 1.75
**A:** 1/40-mm AA—2/20-mm **Electron Equipt:** Radar: 1/Raytheon 1620
**M:** 2 MTU MD 16V538 TB90 diesels; 6,000 hp **Electric:** 330 kVA
**Fuel:** 18 tons **Range:** 1,200/17 **Man:** 3 officers, 16 men

REMARKS: Delivery of the first two was greatly delayed when they collided on trials, 12-78. The third unit was ordered in 1979, with delivery delayed over financial problems. Have had engineering difficulties.

◆ **2 French 32-meter craft** Bldr: Chantiers Navals de l'Estérel, Cannes

P 321 TICHITT (In serv. 4-69) P 322 DAR EL BARKA (In serv. 9-69)

**Tichitt (P 321)** L'Estérel, 1969

**D:** 80 tons (fl) **S:** 28 kts **Dim:** 32.0 × 5.75 × 1.7
**A:** 1/20-mm—1/12.7-mm mg
**M:** 2 Mercedes-Benz MB820Db/h diesels; 2 props; 2,700 hp
**Fuel:** 15 tons **Range:** 1,500/15 **Man:** 17 tot.

◆ **2 French 18-meter class** Bldr: Chantiers Navals de l'Estérel, Cannes

IMAG'NI (In serv. 11-65) SLOUGHI (In serv. 5-68)

**D:** 20 tons (fl) **S:** 21 kts (22.7 on trials) **Dim:** 18.15 (17.03 pp) × 4.03 × 1.1
**A:** 1/12.7-mm mg **M:** 2 G.M. 6-71 diesels; 2 props; 512 hp
**Range:** 400/15 **Man:** 8 tot.

◆ **1 service launch** Bldr: ACM, . . . , France (In serv. 1980)

CHINGUETTI

**D:** 7 tons (fl) **S:** 20 kts **Dim:** 9.6 × 3.2 × 0.9
**M:** 2 Baudouin diesels; 2 props; . . . hp

REMARKS: In poor condition; may be stricken.

# MAURITIUS

MERCHANT MARINE (1986): 26 ships—151,978 grt

MAURITIUS POLICE

### PATROL BOATS

◆ **1 ex-Indian Ajay-class patrol boat** Bldr: Garden Reach DY, Calcutta, 1961

P 1 AMAR

**D:** 120 tons (160 fl) **S:** 18 kts **Dim:** 35.7 (33.52 pp) × 6.1 × 1.5
**A:** 1/40-mm AA **Electron Equipt:** Radar: 1/Kelvin-Hughes 14/9
**M:** 2 Paxman YHAXM diesels; 2 props; 1,000 hp; 1 Foden FD 6 cruise diesel; 100 hp
**Fuel:** 23 tons **Range:** 1,000/8; 500/12 **Man:** 20 tot.

REMARKS: Retained original name on transfer 4-74. Indian version of British "Ford"-class seaward defense boat.

NOTE: Two Soviet Zhuk-class patrol boats were to have been donated, as announced 11-82, but they never materialized. In 7-87, India agreed to donate 4 patrol boats.

**MAURITIUS** *(continued)*
**PATROL BOATS** *(continued)*

**Amar (P 1)** French Navy, 9-86

# MEXICO

## United Mexican States

Personnel (1986): 23,632 men, including 3,810 Marines

Merchant Marine (1986): 642 ships—1,520,246 grt

Naval Aviation: The Mexican Navy operates 10 Casa 212 coastal surveillance aircraft, 1 DNC Buffalo, 1 F-27, 1 DC-3 transport, and 35 light fixed-wing aircraft, including 1 Learjet 24D, 2 T-34 Mentor and 4 Beech F-33 Bonanza trainers. Helicopters include 12 MBB BO-105S, 4 Alouette-III, 5 Hughes 269 A, 4 Bell 47G/J, and 2 Bell HU-1H, plus 10 SA 315 Lama helicopters ordered in 1982 for search-and-rescue duties. Two locally designed Tonatiah trainers were completed in 1984 at Veracruz, with 5 more to come.

### DESTROYERS

◆ **2 ex-U.S. Gearing FRAM I class** Bldr: Bethlehem Steel, Staten Island

| | Laid down | L | In serv. |
|---|---|---|---|
| IE-03 Quetzalcoatl (ex-*Vogelgesang,* DD 862) | 3-8-44 | 15-1-45 | 28-4-45 |
| IE-04 Netzahualcoyotl (ex-*Steinaker,* DD 863) | 1-9-44 | 13-2-45 | 26-5-45 |

**D:** 2,448 tons light (3,528 fl) **S:** 30 kts
**Dim:** 119.03 × 12.52 × 4.45 (6.4 sonar)
**A:** 4/127-mm DP (II × 2)—1/ASROC ASW RL (VIII × 1)—6/324-mm Mk 32 ASW TT (III × 2)
**Electron Equipt:** Radar: 1/LN-66, 1/SPS-10, 1/SPS-40B (IE-04: SPS-29)
Sonar: SQS-23—EW: WLR-1
**M:** 2 sets G.E. GT; 2 props; 60,000 hp **Electric:** 1,200 kw
**Boilers:** 4 Babcock & Wilcox; 43.3 kg/cm$^2$, 454°C **Fuel:** 650 tons

Remarks: Transferred to Mexico 24-2-82 by sale, as intended replacements for the two *Fletcher*-class destroyers. Retained ASROC launcher, usually removed in recent USN transfers. Have unusual heat-suppressant stack caps.

◆ **1 ex-U.S. Fletcher class** Bldr: Consolidated Steel, Orange, Tex.

| | Laid down | L | In serv. |
|---|---|---|---|
| IE-02 Cuitlahuac (ex-*John Rodgers,* DD 574) | 25-7-41 | 7-5-42 | 25-1-43. |

**Cuitlahuac (IE-02)** 1983

**D:** 2,050 tons (2,850 fl) **S:** 30 kts **Dim:** 114.73 × 12.06 × 5.5
**A:** 5/127-mm Mk 30 DP (I × 5)—14/40-mm AA (IV × 2, II × 3)—5/533-mm TT (V × 1)
**Electron Equipt:** Radar: 1/Kelvin-Hughes 14/9, 1/Kelvin-Hughes 17/9, 1/Mk 12/22 f.c.
**M:** 2 sets G.E. GT; 2 props; 60,000 hp **Electric:** 590 kw
**Boilers:** 4 Babcock & Wilcox; 39.8 kg/cm$^2$, 454°C **Fuel:** 650 tons
**Range:** 4,400/15; 1,260/30 **Man:** 197 tot.

Remarks: Transferred 8-70. All ASW capability and obsolete U.S. electronics systems now deleted. Has one Mk 37 director for 127-mm guns; five Mk 51 Mod. 2 directors for 40-mm guns. Could make 35 kts when new. Sister *Cuauhtemoc* IE-01 (ex-*Harrison,* DD 573) discarded 1982.

### FRIGATES

◆ **1 ex-U.S. Charles Lawrence** (*) **and 3 Crosley class**

| | Bldr | Laid down | L | In serv. |
|---|---|---|---|---|
| IB-05 Tehuantepec (ex-*Joseph M. Auman,* APD 117, ex-DE 674) | Consolidated Steel, Orange, Tex. | 8-11-43 | 5-2-44 | 25-4-45 |
| IB-06 Usumacinta (ex-*Don O. Woods,* APD 118, ex-DE 721) | Consolidated Steel, Orange, Tex. | 1-12-43 | 19-2-44 | 28-5-45 |
| IB-07 Coahuila (ex-*Barber,* APD 57, ex-DE 161)* | Norfolk Navy Yd, Norfolk, Va. | 27-4-43 | 20-5-43 | 10-10-43 |
| IB-08 Chihuahua (ex-*Rednour,* APD 102, ex-DE 529) | Bethlehem SB, Hingham, Mass. | 30-12-43 | 12-2-44 | 30-12-44 |

**Coahuila (IB-07)** L. & L. Van Ginderen, 6-74

**D:** 1,450 tons (2,130 fl) **S:** 23 kts **Dim:** 93.26 × 11.28 × 3.83
**A:** 1/127-mm Mk 30 DP—6/40-mm AA (II × 3)—IB-07 also: 2/20-mm AA (I × 2)
**Electron Equipt:** Radar: 1/Kelvin-Hughes 14/9
**M:** 2 sets G.E. GT, turbo-electric drive; 2 props; 12,000 hp
**Boilers:** 2 "D"-Express; 30.6 kg/cm$^2$, 399°C
**Fuel:** 350 tons **Electric:** 680 kw **Range:** 5,000/15 **Man:** 204 tot.

Remarks: Former high-speed transports. IB-05 and IB-06 transferred 12-63; IB-07 and IB-08, 17-2-69. Used primarily as patrol ships; no longer carry the four landing craft that were once stowed amidships. Converted to APD while being built. IB-07, with a high bridge and lattice mast aft, is a member of the *Charles Lawrence* class; the others each have a low bridge and a tripod aft to support the 10-ton-capacity cargo boom. The 127-mm gun has no director, while there are three Mk 51 Mod. 2 directors for the 40-mm antiaircraft. Two others have been lost: *California* (B-3, ex-*Belet,* APD 109) went aground 16-1-72, and *Papaloapan* (B-4, ex-*Earhart,* APD 113) in 1976.

### CORVETTES

◆ **0 (+4) Aquila class**

| | Bldr | Laid down | L | In serv. |
|---|---|---|---|---|
| GH . . . N . . . . . . . | Salina Cruz NSY No. 8 | 6-86 | . . . | . . . |
| GH . . . N . . . . . . . | Tampico NSY No. 1 | 7-86 | . . . | . . . |
| GH . . . N . . . . . . . | Tampico NSY No. 1 | . . . | . . . | . . . |
| GH . . . N . . . . . . . | Salina Cruz NSY No. 8 | . . . | . . . | . . . |

**D:** 907 tons (1,175 fl) **S:** 22 kts **Dim:** 60.0 × 10.5 × . . .
**A:** 1/57-mm Bofors DP—1/40-mm Bofors AA—1/helicopter
**M:** 2 MTU 20V956 TB91 diesels; 2 props; 13,320 hp **Endurance:** 20 days
**Range:** 8,600/18 **Man:** 59 total—plus 16 passengers

**CORVETTES** *(continued)*

Remarks: A smaller variant of the Spanish-built Halcón design, with higher speed and heavier armament. Announced 23-6-83, plans called for construction of nine units at four naval shipyards, two each at Tampico and Salina Cruz. Reduced to four units in 10-84. Have smaller helicopter deck than Halcón class, less topweight, two (vice one) enginerooms. Originally planned as replacements for *Auk* and *Admirable* classes.

◆ **6 "Halcón" class** Bldr: Bazán, San Fernando, Cadiz, Spain

| | L | In serv. |
|---|---|---|
| GH-01 Cadete Virgilio Uribe | 13-12-81 | 10-9-82 |
| GH-02 Teniente José Azueta | 29-1-82 | 15-10-82 |
| GH-03 Capitan De Fragata Pedro Sainz De Barbranda | 26-2-82 | 3-83 |
| GH-04 Comodoro Carlos Castilio Breton | 12-11-81 | 9-6-82 |
| GH-05 ViceAlmirante Othón P. Blanco | 26-3-82 | 24-2-83 |
| GH-06 ContraAlmirante Angel Ortiz Monasterio | 23-4-82 | 24-3-83 |

**Teniente José Azueta (GH-02)** Bazán, 10-83

**D:** 767 tons (910 fl) **S:** 21 kts **Dim:** 67.00 (63.00 pp) × 10.50 × 3.08
**A:** 1/40-mm AA—1/BO-105S helicopter
**Electron Equipt:** Radar: 1/Decca AC 1226—TACAN: SRN-15
**M:** 2 MTU 20V956 TB91 diesels; 2 props; 13,320 hp
**Electric:** 710 kw **Range:** 5,000/18 **Man:** 10 officers, 42 men

Remarks: Ordered late 1980 for use in patrolling the 200-nautical-mile economic zone. Have been referred to as the "Puma" class. Generally identical to ships built for Argentina, but with more powerful engines and longer helicopter deck. Delivery of GH-04 delayed by accident; originally completed 23-10-82.

◆ **18 ex-U.S. Auk-class former fleet minesweepers**

| | Bldr | L |
|---|---|---|
| IG-01 Leandro Valle (ex-*Pioneer,* MSF 105)(1) | A | 26-7-42 |
| IG-02 Guillermo Prieto (ex-*Symbol,* MSF 123)(2) | B | 2-7-42 |
| IG-03 Mariano Escobedo (ex-*Champion,* MSF 314)(3) | C | 12-12-42 |
| IG-04 Ponciano Arriaga (ex-*Competent,* MSF 316)(3) | C | 9-1-43 |
| IG-05 Manuel Doblado (ex-*Defense,* MSF 317)(3) | C | 18-2-43 |
| IG-06 Sebastian Lerdo De Tejada (ex-*Devastator,* MSF 318)(3) | C | 19-4-43 |
| IG-07 Santos Degollado (ex-*Gladiator,* MSF 319)(3) | C | 7-5-43 |
| IG-08 Ignacio De La Llave (ex-*Spear,* MSF 322)(2) | D | 25-2-43 |
| IG-09 Juan N. Alvarez (ex-*Ardent,* MSF 340)(3) | C | 22-6-43 |
| IG-10 Melchior Ocampo (ex-*Roselle,* MSF 379)(4) | E | 29-8-45 |
| IG-11 Valentin G. Farias (ex-*Starling,* MSF 64)(5) | C | 15-2-42 |
| IG-12 Ignacio Altamirano (ex-*Sway,* MSF 120)(2) | F | 29-9-42 |
| IG-13 Francisco Zarco (ex-*Threat,* MSF 124)(2) | B | 15-8-42 |
| IG-14 Ignacio L. Vallarta (ex-*Velocity,* MSF 128)(2) | E | 19-4-42 |
| IG-15 Jésus G. Ortega (ex-*Chief,* MSF 315)(3) | C | 5-1-43 |
| IG-16 Gutierriez Zamora (ex-*Scoter,* MSF 381)(4) | E | 26-9-45 |
| IG-18 Juan Aldarma (ex-*Pilot,* MSF 104)(1) | A | 5-7-42 |
| IG-19 Hermenegildo Galeana (ex-*Sage,* MSF 111)(1) | G | 21-11-42 |

Bldrs: *A,* Pennsylvania Shipyard, Beaumont, Tex.; *B,* Savannah Machine & Foundry Co., Savannah, Ga.; *C,* General Engineering and Drydock Co., Alameda, Cal.; *D,* Associated Shipbuilders; *E,* Gulf Shipbuilding; *F,* J.H. Mathis, Camden, N.J.; *G,* Winslow Marine Railway and Shipbuilding, Seattle, Wash.

**D:** 890 tons (1,250 fl) **S:** 17/18 kts **Dim:** 67.4 (65.5 wl) × 9.8 × 3.28
**A:** 1/76.2-mm Mk 22 DP—4/40-mm AA (II × 2)
**Electron Equipt:** Radar: 1/SPS-5 or 1/Kelvin-Hughes 14/9, 1/SO-13
**M:** 2 diesels, electric drive (*see* Remarks); 2 props; 2,976, 3,118, or 3,532 hp
**Electric:** 300–360 kw **Fuel:** 216 tons **Man:** 9 officers, 96 men

Remarks: The numbers in parentheses after the ships' names refer to five different diesels used in propulsion plants: (1) Busch-Sulzer 539; (2) G.M. 12-278; (3) Baldwin VO-8; (4) G.M. 12-278A; (5) Alco 539. Diesels (1) and (5) produce 3,118 hp, (2) and (4) 3,532 hp, and (3) 2,976 hp.

All transferred in 1973. All minesweeping and ASW equipment removed. One other unit, *Mariano Metamoros* (ex-*Herald,* MSF 101), was converted for use as a surveying ship. Some have a small deckhouse between the stacks; some have no main deck bulwarks. New radars have been added to ships transferred without SPS-5.

**Ignacio L. Vallarta (IG-14)**—bulwarks amidships G. Arra, 1984

◆ **12 ex-U.S. Admirable-class former fleet minesweepers**

| | Bldrs | L |
|---|---|---|
| ID-01 DM 01 (ex-*Jubilant,* MSF 255) | American SB, Lorain, Oh. | 20-2-43 |
| ID-03 DM 03 (ex-*Execute,* MSF 232) | Puget Sound, Seattle, Wash. | 22-1-44 |
| ID-04 DM 04 (ex-*Specter,* MSF 306) | Associated Shipbldrs. | 15-2-44 |
| ID-05 DM 05 (ex-*Scuffle,* MSF 298) | Winslow, Seattle, Wash. | 8-8-43 |
| ID-11 DM 11 (ex-*Device,* MSF 220) | Tampa SB, Fla. | 21-5-44 |
| ID-12 DM 12 (ex-*Ransom,* MSF 283) | General Eng. & DD | 18-9-43 |
| ID-13 DM 13 (ex-*Knave,* MSF 256) | American SB, Lorain, Oh. | 13-3-43 |
| ID-14 DM 14 (ex-*Rebel,* MSF 284) | General Eng. & DD | 28-10-43 |
| ID-15 DM 15 (ex-*Crag,* MSF 214) | Tampa SB, Fla. | 21-3-43 |
| ID-17 DM 17 (ex-*Diploma,* MSF 221) | Tampa SB, Fla. | 21-5-44 |
| ID-18 DM 18 (ex-*Invade,* MSF 254) | Savannah Mach., Ga. | 6-2-44 |
| ID-19 DM 19 (ex-*Intrigue,* MSF 253) | Savannah Mach., Ga. | 8-4-44 |

**DM 19 (ID-19)**—and two sisters Dr. Y. Alloucherie, 7-87

**D:** 650 tons (945 fl) **S:** 15 kts **Dim:** 56.24 (54.86 wl) × 10.06 × 2.97
**A:** 1/76.2-mm Mk 22 DP—2/40-mm AA (I × 2)—6/20-mm AA (I × 6)
**M:** 2 Cooper-Bessemer GSB-8 diesels; 2 props; 1,710 hp
**Electric:** 240 or 280 kw **Fuel:** 138 tons **Man:** 9 officers, 86 men

Remarks: All minesweeping and ASW equipment deleted. Three more units were scrapped, and DM 20 was converted into a hydrographic survey ship. DM 04 was transferred 2-73; all others, 1-10-62. Stricken in 1986 were DM 02 (ID-02, ex-*Hilarity,* MSF 241), DM 06 (ID-06, ex-*Eager,* MSF 224), DM 10 (ID-10, ex-*Instill,* MSF 252) and DM 16 (ID-16, ex-*Dour,* MSF 223)

**PATROL BOATS**

◆ **31 (+4 or 5) Azteca class**

| | Bldr | In serv. |
|---|---|---|
| P-01 Andres Quintana Roo | Ailsa | 1-11-74 |
| P-02 Matias De Cordova | Scott | 22-10-74 |
| P-03 Miguel Ramos Arizpe | Ailsa | 23-12-74 |
| P-04 José Maria Izazago | Ailsa | 19-12-74 |
| P-05 Juan Bautista Morales | Scott | 19-12-74 |
| P-06 Ignacio Lopez Rayon | Ailsa | 19-12-74 |
| P-07 Manuel Crescencio Rejon | Ailsa | 4-7-75 |
| P-08 Antonio De La Fuente | Ailsa | 4-7-75 |

**PATROL BOATS** *(continued)*

| | | |
|---|---|---|
| P-09 Leon Guzman | Scott | 7-4-75 |
| P-10 Ignacio Ramirez | Ailsa | 17-7-75 |
| P-11 Ignacio Mariscal | Ailsa | 23-9-75 |
| P-12 Heriberto Jara Corona | Ailsa | 7-11-75 |
| P-13 José Maria Mata | Lamont | 13-10-75 |
| P-14 Felix Romero | Scott | 23-6-75 |
| P-15 Fernando Lizardi | Ailsa | 24-12-75 |
| P-16 Francisco J. Mujica | Ailsa | 21-11-75 |
| P-17 Pastor Rouaix José Maria | Scott | 7-11-75 |
| P-18 José Maria Del Castillo Velasco | Lamont | 14-1-75 |
| P-19 Luis Manuel Rojas | Lamont | 3-4-76 |
| P-20 José Natividad Macias | Lamont | 2-9-76 |
| P-21 Esteban Baca Calderon | Lamont | 18-6-76 |
| P-22 General Ignacio Zaragoza | Vera Cruz | 1-6-76 |
| P-23 Tamaulipas | Vera Cruz | 1978 |
| P-24 Yucatan | Vera Cruz | 1978 |
| P-25 Tabasco | Vera Cruz | 1-1-79 |
| P-26 Veracruz | Vera Cruz | 1-1-79 |
| P-27 Campeche | Vera Cruz | 1-1-79 |
| P-28 Puebla | Vera Cruz | 1-1-79 |
| P-29 Margarita Maza De Juarez | Salina Cruz | 1-79 |
| P-30 Leona Vicario | Salina Cruz | 1-79 |
| P-31 Josefa Ortiz De Dominguez | Salina Cruz | 1-79 |

**Heriberto Jara Corona (P-12)**—with 40-mm AA U.S. Navy, 7-76

**D:** 115 tons (165 fl) **S:** 23 kts **Dim:** 36.50 (30.94 pp) × 8.6 × 2.0
**A:** 1/7.62-mm mg (some have: 1/40-mm AA—1/20-mm AA)
**M:** 2 Ruston-Paxman Ventura 12-cyl. diesels; 7,200 hp **Electric:** 80 kw
**Range:** 2,500/12 **Man:** 2 officers, 22 men

Remarks: Original order for 21 placed 27-3-73 with Associated British Machine Tool Makers, Ltd., which subcontracted the actual construction and assisted with the construction of another 11 in Mexico. Four or 5 additional units reported ordered 23-6-83, but location and progress not announced. The 21 built in the U.K. are being rehabilitated in Mexico with British assistance for 10 more years' service.

**PATROL CRAFT**

◆ **10 Olmeca class** Bldr: Acapulco NSY, Mexico (In serv. 1979–84)

**D:** . . . **S:** 25 kts **Dim:** 15.0 × . . . × . . . **A:** 1/20-mm AA
**M:** 2 Cummins VT-series diesels; 800 hp **Man:** 7 tot.

Remarks: Glass-reinforced plastic construction. *Puebla,* the last of a first series, commissioned 22-2-83. Five additional ordered 23-6-83 and delivered by end 1984. Additional units planned.

◆ **4 Polimar class** Bldrs: Astilleros de Tampico (IF-01, IF-04); Iscacas SY, Guerrero (IF-02, IF-03)

| | L | | L |
|---|---|---|---|
| IF-01 Polimar 1 | 1962 | IF-03 Polimar 3 | 1966 |
| IF-02 Polimar 2 | 1966 | IF-04 Polimar 4 | 1968 |

**Polimar 1** 1962

**D:** 57 tons (fl) **S:** 16 kts **Dim:** 20.5 × 4.5 × 1.3
**A:** 2/13.2-mm mg (II × 1) **M:** 2 diesels; 2 props; 450 hp

◆ **2 Azueta class** Bldr: Astilleros de Tampico

IF-06 Azueta (L: 1959) IF-07 Villapando (L: 1960)

**D:** 80 tons (85 fl) **S:** 12 kts **Dim:** 26.0 × 4.9 × 2.1
**A:** 2/13.2-mm mg (II × 1) **M:** 2 Superior diesels; 2 props; 600 hp

**RIVER PATROL CRAFT**

◆ **6 AM-1 class** Bldrs: Astilleros de Tampico and Vera Cruz SY (L: 1960–62)

| | | |
|---|---|---|
| IF-14 AM 4 | IF-16 AM 6 | IF-18 AM 8 |
| IF-15 AM 5 | IF-17 AM 7 | IF-20 AM 10 |

**D:** 37 tons (fl) **S:** 6 kts **Dim:** 17.7 × 5.0 × . . . **A:** . . . **M:** diesels

Remarks: Sisters AM 1 to AM 3, and AM 9 stricken by 1986.

**AUXILIARIES**

**HYDROGRAPHIC SURVEY SHIPS**

◆ **1 ex-U.S. Robert D. Conrad-class oceanographic research ship**

| | Bldr | L | In serv. |
|---|---|---|---|
| H-05 Altair (ex-*James M. Gillis,* AGOR 4) | Christy Corp., Wisconsin | 19-5-62 | 5-11-62 |

**D:** 1,200 tons (1,380 fl) **S:** 13.5 kts **Dim:** 63.7 (58.30 pp) × 11.37 × 4.66
**Electron Equipt:** Radar: 1/Raytheon TM 1600/6X; 1/TM 1660/123
**M:** 2 Caterpillar D-378 diesels; electric drive; 1 prop; 2,000 hp—bow-thruster
**Electric:** 850 kw **Fuel:** 211 tons **Range:** 10,000/12
**Man:** 26 crew, 18 scientists

Remarks: Returned to U.S. Navy by University of Miami in 1980 and laid up, until leased to Mexico on 15-6-83; Mexico bore the expense of subsequent reactivation. The large stack contains a 620-hp gas-turbine generator set to drive the main shaft at speeds up to 6.5 kts for experiments requiring "quiet" sea conditions. Also has a retractable electric bow-thruster/propulsor, which can drive the ship to 4.5 kts. Refitted and recommissioned 27-11-84. 965 grt.

◆ **1 ex-U.S. Admirable-class former minesweeper** Bldr: Willamette Iron & Steel, Ore.

H-2 DM 20 (ex-*Oceanografico,* ex-DM 20, ex-*Harlequin,* MSF 365)

Remarks: Launched 3-6-44. Data as for corvettes, except for displacement, which is approximately 900 tons (full load); no armament. Converted 1976–78.

◆ **1 ex-U.S. Auk-class former minesweeper** Bldr: General Eng. & DD, Alameda, Cal.

| | Laid down | L | In serv. |
|---|---|---|---|
| H-1 Mariano Matamoros (ex-*Herald,* MSF 101) | 14-3-42 | 4-7-42 | 23-3-43 |

**Mariano Matamoros (H-1)** G. Arra, 1977

Remarks: Data generally as for corvette version. Has Busch-Sulzer BS539 diesels; 3,118 hp. No armament. Large deckhouse built around after stack with a portable facility for aerological balloon-launching atop it. Oceanographic crane at stern. Radars are one SPS-5 and one Kelvin-Hughes 14/9.

Note: H-1 or H-2 was to strike when H-05 became operational.

**REPAIR SHIP**

◆ **1 ex-U.S. Fabius-class former aircraft repair ship**

| | Bldr | L | In serv. |
|---|---|---|---|
| IA-05 General Vicente Guerrero (ex-*Megara,* ARVA 6, ex-LST 1095) | American Bridge, Pa. | 25-3-45 | 27-6-45 |

**D:** 4,100 tons (fl) **S:** 11.6 kts **Dim:** 100.0 (96.3 wl) × 15.24 × 3.4
**A:** 8/40-mm AA (IV × 2) **M:** 2 G.M. 12-567A diesels; 2 props; 1,700 hp
**Electric:** 520 kw **Fuel:** 474 tons **Range:** 10,000/10 **Man:** 250 tot.

Remarks: Transferred 1-10-73. Originally intended for repairing aircraft airframes. One 10-ton boom. Two Mk 51 Mod. 2 GFCS for the 40-mm AA.

**REPAIR SHIP** *(continued)*

**General Vicente Guerrero (IA-05)** L. & L. Van Ginderen, 7-84

## TRANSPORTS

◆ **2 Huasteco class**

| | Bldr | Laid down | L | In serv. |
|---|---|---|---|---|
| IA-21 Huasteco | Tampico NSY No. 1 | . . . | . . . | 1986 |
| IA-22 Zapoteco | Salina Cruz NSY No. 8 | . . . | . . . | 1986 |

**D:** . . . **S:** . . . **Dim:** . . . × . . . × . . . **M:** . . . **Range:** . . . **Man:** . . .

Remarks: Ordered 1984 as troop transports, vehicle carriers, transports for construction materials, food, and hospital equipment and to act as floating infirmaries and civil disaster relief ships to replace IA-01 and IA-02. First was to complete by end 1985.

◆ **2 U.S. LST 542-class former landing ships**

| | Bldr | L | In serv. |
|---|---|---|---|
| IA-01 Rio Panuco (ex-*Park Co.,* LST 1077) | Bethlehem Steel, Hingham, Mass. | 9-3-44 | 31-3-44 |
| IA-02 Manzanillo (ex-*Clearwater Co.,* LST 602) | Chicago Bridge & Iron, Seneca, Ill. | 18-4-45 | 8-5-45 |

**Rio Panuco (IA-01)** L. & L. Van Ginderen, 3-82

**D:** 1,625 tons (4,100 fl) **S:** 11.6 kts **Dim:** 100.0 × 96.3 × 15.24 × 3.4
**A:** 8/40-mm AA (II × 2, I × 4)—IA-02: none **Electric:** 300 kw
**Range:** 6,000/11 **Man:** 130 men, 170 troops/passengers

Remarks: Transferred 20-9-71 and 25-2-72. Intended as disaster relief ships. IA-02 had been used in Arctic Supply by the Military Sealift Command and has two cargo kingposts, no armament, and an ice-reinforced waterline forward. Were to have been stricken 1986.

Note: Transport *Zacatecas* (B-2) stricken 1986.

## TRAINING SHIPS

◆ **1 sail-training ship** Bldr: Ast. y Talleres Celaya, Bilbao, Spain

| | Laid down | L | In serv. |
|---|---|---|---|
| Cuauhtemoc | 27-4-81 | . . . | 11-12-82 |

**D:** 1,200 tons (fl) **S:** 15 kts **Dim:** 90.0 (67.0 pp) × 10.6 × 4.2
**M:** 1 G.M. 12V149 diesel; 1 prop; 750 hp **Man:** 90 tot.

Remarks: Ordered 1980.

◆ **1 ex-U.S. Edsall-class training frigate** Bldr: Brown SB, Houston, Tex.

| | Laid down | L | In serv. |
|---|---|---|---|
| IA-06 Manuel Azueta (ex-*Hurst,* DE 250) | 27-1-43 | 14-4-43 | 30-8-43 |

**D:** 1,200 tons (1,590 fl) **S:** 21 kts **Dim:** 93.26 × 11.15 × 3.73
**A:** 3/76.2-mm Mk 22 DP (I × 3)—8/40-mm AA (IV × 1, II × 2)
**Electron Equipt:** Radar: 1/Kelvin-Hughes 14/9, 1/Kelvin-Hughes 17/9, 1/Mk 26
**M:** 4 Fairbanks-Morse 38D$\frac{1}{8}$, 10-cyl. diesels; 2 props; 6,000 hp
**Electric:** 680 kw **Fuel:** 258 tons **Range:** 13,000/12
**Man:** 15 officers, 201 men

**Cuauhtemoc** P. Voss, 8-85

**Manuel Azueta (IA-06)** L. & L. Van Ginderen, 7-81

Remarks: Transferred 1-10-73. Former destroyer escort. Used as training ship for the Gulf Fleet. Has one Mk 52 radar fire-control director and one Mk 51 rangefinder for the 76.2-mm guns, and three Mk 51 Mod. 2 directors for the 40-mm AA.

◆ **1 former frigate** Bldr: Union Naval de Levante, Valencia, Spain

| | Laid down | L | In serv. |
|---|---|---|---|
| IB-01 Durango | 1934 | 28-6-35 | 1936 |

**D:** 1,600 tons (2,000 fl) **S:** 18 kts **Dim:** 78.2 × 11.2 × 3.1
**A:** 2/102-mm (I × 2)—2/57-mm (I × 2)—4/20-mm AA (II × 2)
**M:** 2 Enterprise DMR 38 diesels; electric drive; 2 props; 5,000 hp
**Fuel:** 140 tons **Range:** 3,000/12 **Man:** 24 officers, 125 men

Remarks: Originally built as an armed transport with accommodations for 20 officers, 450 men, and a number of horses. Steam-turbine propulsion plant replaced 1967. Immobile as a training hulk for new recruits, but in 1982 it was announced that she was to be rehabilitated for seagoing training and VIP cruising duties.

## TUGS

◆ **4 ex-U.S. Abnaki-class fleet tugs** Bldrs: IA-17, United Engineering, Alameda, Cal.; others, Charleston SB & DD, S.C.

| | Laid down | L | In serv. |
|---|---|---|---|
| IA-17 Otomi (ex-*Molala,* ATF 106) | 26-7-42 | 23-12-42 | 29-9-43 |
| IA-18 Seri (ex-*Hitichi,* ATF 103) | 24-8-43 | 29-1-44 | 27-5-44 |
| IA-19 Cora (ex-*Abnaki,* ATF 96) | 28-11-42 | 22-4-43 | 15-11-43 |
| IA-20 Yaqui (ex-*Cocopa,* ATF 101) | 23-5-43 | 5-10-43 | 25-3-44 |

**D:** 1,325 tons (1,675 fl) **S:** 16.5 kts **Dim:** 62.48 × 11.73 × 4.67
**A:** 1/76.2-mm DP **Electron Equipt:** Radar: 1/LN-66
**M:** 4 Busch-Sulzer BS539 diesels, electric drive; 1 prop; 3,000 hp
**Electric:** 400 kw **Fuel:** 304 tons **Range:** 7,000/15; 15,000/8 **Man:** 85 tot.

Remarks: IA-17 transferred 1-8-78, the others on 30-9-78. Unarmed on delivery. Used on patrol duties and as rescue tugs.

◆ **2 ex-U.S. Maritime Administration V-4 class** Bldr: Pendleton SY, New Orleans (In serv. 1943–44)

IA-12 R-2 (ex-*Montauk*) IA-13 R-3 (ex-*Point Vicente*)

**D:** 1,825 tons (fl) **S:** 14 kts **Dim:** 59.23 × 11.43 × 5.72
**A:** 1/76.2-mm Mk 22 DP—2/20-mm AA
**M:** 2 Enterprise diesels; 2 Kort-nozzle props; 2,250 hp **Fuel:** 566 tons
**Range:** 19,000/14 **Man:** 90 tot.

Remarks: Transferred 6-69. Sister R-4 lost in 1973; R-6 discarded in 1970. R-1 in 1978, and R-5 in 1979.

MEXICO *(continued)*

SERVICE CRAFT

◆ **2 ex-U.S. 174-foot-class harbor fuel lighters**

| | Bldr | L | In serv. |
|---|---|---|---|
| IA-03 Aguascalientes (ex-YOG 6) | J. H. Mathis, Camden, N.J. | 3-4-43 | 15-11-43 |
| IA-04 Tlaxcala (ex-YO 107) | G. Lawley, Neponset, Mass. | 3-11-43 | 27-11-43 |

**D:** 440 tons (1,480 fl) **S:** 8 kts **Dim:** 53.0 × 9.75 × 2.5
**A:** 1/20-mm AA **M:** 1 or 2 diesels; 1 prop; 500–600 hp
**Man:** 5 officers, 21 men

Remarks: Transferred 8-64. Cargo capacity: 980 tons (6,570 bbl).

◆ **2 yard tugs**

Pragmar Patron

Remarks: Bought in 1973.

◆ **1 ex-U.S. ARD-12-class floating dry dock**

| | Bldr | In serv. |
|---|---|---|
| N . . . . . . . (ex-ARD 15) | Pacific Bridge, Alameda, Cal. | 1-44 |

**Lift capacity:** 3,500 tons **Dim:** 149.87 × 24.69 × 1.73 (light)

Remarks: Transferred 4-71 on loan; purchased 1981.

◆ **2 ex-U.S. ARD-2-class floating dry docks** Bldr: Pacific Bridge, Alameda, Cal.

N . . . . . . . (ex-ARD 2) (In serv. 4-42) N . . . . . . . (ex-ARD 11) (In serv. 10-43)

**Lift capacity:** 3,500 tons **Dim:** 148.0 × 21.64 × 1.6 (light)

Remarks: Transferred 8-63 and 6-74.

◆ **1 ex-U.S. small auxiliary floating dry dock** Bldr: Doullut & Ewin, Mobile, Ala.

N . . . . . . . (ex-AFDL 28) (In serv. 8-44)

**Lift capacity:** 1,000 tons **Dim:** 60.96 × 19.51 × 1.04 (light)

Remarks: Transferred 1-73.

◆ **7 ex-U.S. floating cranes**

(ex-YD 156) (ex-YD 179) (ex-YD 183) (ex-YD 203)
(ex-YD 157) (ex-YD 180) (ex-YD 194)

Remarks: Transferred 1964–71; purchased 7-78 (except YD 179, 194).

◆ **1 ex-U.S. pile driver**

N . . . . . . . (ex-YPD 43)

Remarks: Leased 8-68.

◆ **1 pollution-clearance ship** Bldr: C. Lühring, Brake, West Germany

. . . N . . . (In serv. 1987)

**D:** . . . **S:** 10 kts **Dim:** 50.0 × 12.0 × 3.2
**M:** 2 diesels; 2 rudder-props; 1,600 hp—2 omnidirectional bow-thrusters; 400 hp
**Range:** . . . **Man:** 6 tot.

Remarks: Ordered 9-86 for delivery by end-1987. Enlarged version of *Bundesmarine's Bottsand,* with twin hulls hinged at the stern to open into a large vee-shape, sweeping a 45-m path, collecting oil spills at over 150 $m^3$/hr., traveling at 1 knot. Design known as THOR (Twin Hull Oil Recovery). Can also act as coastal tanker.

◆ **7 class I-D oil-spill recovery boats** Bldr: Marco, Seattle, Wash. (In serv. 1982)

**D:** . . . **S:** 15 kts **Dim:** 11.4 × 3.08 × . . .
**M:** 2 G.M. 4-53 diesels; 2 outdrives; 240 hp

Remarks: Use Marco Filterbelt recovery system; speed 2 kts when operating.

# MONTSERRAT

**Colony of Montserrat**

Merchant Marine (1986): 1 ship—711 grt

MONTSERRAT POLICE FORCE

PATROL CRAFT

◆ **1 glass-reinforced plastic-hulled** Bldr: Brooke Marine, Lowestoft, U.K.

Emerald Star (In serv. 1971)

**D:** 15 tons **S:** 22 kts **Dim:** 12.0 × . . . × . . .
**A:** 3/7.62-mm mg **Electron Equipt:** Radar: 1/Decca . . . nav.
**M:** 2 Perkins diesels; 2 props; 740 hp **Man:** 4 tot.

Remarks: Refitted and re-engined 1983.

# MOROCCO

**Kingdom of Morocco**

Personnel (1986): 6,500 men, including 150 officers, 1,000 senior petty officers, and 500 marines.

Merchant Marine (1986): 294 ships—416,482 grt (tankers: 4 ships—10,077 grt)

FRIGATE

◆ **1 Spanish Descubierta class** Bldr: Bazán, El Ferrol

| | Laid down | L | In serv. |
|---|---|---|---|
| 501 Lieutenant Colonel Errhamani | 20-3-79 | 26-2-82 | 28-3-83 |

**Lieutenant Colonel Errhamani (501)** P. Voss, 8-86

**D:** 1,270 tons (1,479 fl) **S:** 26 kts **Dim:** 88.88 (85.8 pp) × 10.4 × 3.25 (3.7 fl)
**A:** 1/Albatros SAM syst. (24 Aspide missiles)—1/76-mm OTO Melara DP—2/40-mm AA (I × 2)—1/375-mm Bofors ASW RL (II × 1, 24 rockets)—6/324-mm ASW TT (III × 2)
**Electron Equipt:** Radar: 1/DA-05, 1/ZW-06, 1/WM-25/41 (all H.S.A.)
Sonar: Raytheon DE 1160B
EW: ELT 715 intercept/jammer, 2/Dagaie decoy RL
**M:** 4 Bazán-MTU 16MA956 TB91 diesels; 2 CP props; 18,000 hp
**Electric:** 1,810 kw **Fuel:** 150 tons
**Range:** 4,000/18 (one engine) **Man:** 100 tot.

Remarks: Ordered 14-6-77. Carries 600 rds 76-mm. Has fin stabilizers. Planned four MM-38 Exocet missiles not mounted.

PATROL BOATS

◆ **1 (+1) Osprey 55 class** Bldr: Danyard AS, Fredrikshavn

P . . . N . . . (In serv. 11-87) P . . . N . . . (In serv. 1-88)

**D:** 420 tons (500 fl) **S:** 18 kts **Dim:** 55.00 (50.80) × 8.08 × 2.75
**A:** 1/40-mm AA—2/20-mm AA (I × 2) **Electron Equipt:** Radar: . . .
**M:** 2 M.A.N.-Burmeister & Wain Alpha 12V.23/30 DVO diesels; 2 props; 4,960 hp
**Range:** 4,500/16 **Fuel:** 125 tons **Electric:** 268 kw
**Man:** 15 tot., plus 16 passengers

Remarks: Ordered early 1986 for fisheries protection and search-and-rescue duties. Will have a helicopter pad. Similar ships in Danish, Burmese, and Senegalese service.

◆ **0 (+6) Vigilance class** Bldr: Bazán, Cadiz (In serv. 1988–89)

. . . N . . . . . . N . . .
. . . N . . . . . . N . . .
. . . N . . . . . . N . . .

**D:** 307 tons (425 fl) **S:** 22 kts **Dim:** 58.1 (54.4 pp) × 7.60 × 2.70
**A:** 1/40-mm Breda AA—2/20-mm AA (I × 2)
**Electron Equipt:** Radar: . . . **Endurance:** 10 days
**M:** 2 MTU 16V956 TB82 diesels; 2 props; 7,600 hp (sust.)
**Range:** 3,800/12 **Man:** 4 officers, 32 men, plus 15 passengers

Remarks: Three ordered 2-10-85, with option for three more. "Series P200/D" design, a reduced-power version of the *Lazaga* for 200-n.m. economic zone patrol.

## PATROL BOATS *(continued)*

◆ **4 Spanish Lazaga class** Bldr: Bazán, Cadiz

| | L | In serv. |
|---|---|---|
| 304 Commandant Al Khattabi | 21-7-80 | 3-6-81 |
| 305 Commandant Boutouba | . . . | 11-12-81 |
| 306 Commandant El Harti | . . . | 25-2-82 |
| 307 Commandant Azouggarh | . . . | 2-8-82 |

**Commandant Azouggarh (307)** L. & L. Van Ginderen, 12-82

**Commandant Al Khattabi (304) and a sister** L. & L. Van Ginderen, 1986

**D:** 303 tons (420 fl) **S:** 29.6 kts **Dim:** 57.40 (54.4 pp) × 7.60 × 2.70
**A:** 4/Exocet SSM—1/76-mm OTO Melara DP—1/40-mm AA—2/20-mm AA (I × 2)
**Electron Equipt:** Radar: 1/ZW-06, 1/H.S.A. WM-25
**M:** 2 Bazán-MTU MA16V956 TB91 diesels; 2 props; 7,780 hp
**Electric:** 405 kVA **Range:** 700/27; 3,000/15 **Man:** 41 tot.

Remarks: Ordered 14-6-77. Carry 300 rds 76-mm, 1,472 rds 40-mm, 3,000 rds 20-mm ammunition. Have added fuel capacity over Spanish Navy version. CSEE Naja optical director aft. Frequently carry only two MM 38.

◆ **2 French PR-72 type** Bldr: SFCN, Villeneuve-la-Garenne

| | L | In serv. | | L | In serv. |
|---|---|---|---|---|---|
| 302 Okba | 10-10-75 | 16-12-76 | 303 Triki | 2-2-76 | 2-77 |

**Triki (303)** G. Gyssels, 10-82

**D:** 370 tons (440 fl) **S:** 28 kts (at 413 tons) **Dim:** 57.0 (54.0 pp) × 7.6 × 2.5
**A:** 1/76-mm OTO Melara DP—1/40-mm Bofors AA
**M:** 4 SACM AGO 195V16 SZSHR diesels; 2 props; 11,040 hp
**Electric:** 360 kw **Range:** 2,500/16 **Man:** 5 officers, 48 men

Remarks: Ordered in 6-73. Have 2 CSEE optronic gun directors. 302 refitted 1985.

◆ **1 Al Bachir class** Bldr: Constr. Méc. de Normandie (CMN), Cherbourg

| | Laid down | L | In serv. |
|---|---|---|---|
| 22 Al Bachir | 6-65 | 25-2-67 | 4-67 |

**Al Bachir**—wearing old number

**D:** 124.5 tons (light) (153.5 fl) **S:** 25.5 kts **Dim:** 40.6 (38.0 pp) × 6.35 × 1.4
**A:** 2/40-mm—2 mg **M:** 2 SEMT-Pielstick 12 PA diesels; 2 props; 3,600 hp
**Fuel:** 21 tons **Range:** 2,000/15 **Man:** 3 officers, 20 men

◆ **1 French Fougueux class** Bldr: Constr. Méc. de Normandie, Cherbourg

| | Laid down | L | In serv. |
|---|---|---|---|
| 32 Lieutenant Riffi | 5-63 | 1-3-64 | 5-64 |

**D:** 311 tons (374 fl) **S:** 19 kts **Dim:** 52.95 (51.82 pp) × 7.04 × 2.01
**A:** 2/40-mm AA **M:** 2 SEMT-Pielstick diesels; 2 CP props; 3,600 hp
**Range:** 2,000/15; 3,000/12 **Man:** 4 officers, 55 men

Remarks: 1/76.2-mm gun and all ASW ordnance have been removed.

◆ **1 ex-French patrol boat** Bldr: Chantiers Navals de l'Estérel, Cannes

11 El Sabiq (ex-P 762, ex-VC 12) (L: 13-8-57)

**D:** 60 tons (80 fl) **S:** 28 kts **Dim:** 31.77 × 4.7 × 1.7 **Range:** 1,500/15
**A:** 2/20-mm AA **M:** 2 Mercedes-Benz diesels; 2 props; 2,700 hp **Man:** 17 tot.

Remarks: Transferred 15-11-60.

Note: French *Sirius*-class former minesweeper *Tawfic* (51, ex-*Aries,* M 758) stricken 1986.

## PATROL CRAFT

◆ **6 French P 92 type** Bldr: CMN, Cherbourg

| | L | In serv. | | L | In serv. |
|---|---|---|---|---|---|
| El Wacil | 12-6-75 | 9-10-75 | El Khafir | 21-1-76 | 16-4-76 |
| El Jail | 10-10-75 | 3-12-75 | El Haris | 31-3-76 | 30-6-76 |
| El Mikdam | 1-12-75 | 30-1-76 | Essahir | 2-6-76 | 16-7-76 |

**El Wacil** CMN, 1975

**D:** 89 tons **S:** 28 kts **Dim:** 32.0 × 5.35 × 1.7 (1.42 hull)
**A:** 2/20-mm AA (I × 2) **Electron Equipt:** Radar: 1/Decca
**M:** 2 MGO 12V BZSHR diesels; 2,700 hp **Range:** 1,200/15 **Man:** 12 tot.

Remarks: Contract, 2-74. Laminated-wood hull. Six additional sisters were reported ordered 6-85 for the Customs Service.

## AMPHIBIOUS WARFARE SHIPS

◆ **3 French Champlain-class medium landing ships** Bldr: Dubigeon, Normandy

| | In serv. |
|---|---|
| 402 Daoud Ben Aicha | 28-5-77 |
| 403 Ahmed Es Sakali | 9-77 |
| 404 Abou Abdallah El Ayachi | 12-78 |

**D:** 750 tons (1,305 fl) **S:** 16 kts **Dim:** 80.0 (68.0 pp) × 13.0 × 2.4 mean
**A:** 2/40-mm AA (I × 2)—2/14.5-mm mg (I × 2)—2/81-mm mortars (I × 2)
**Electron Equipt:** Radar: 1/Decca 1226
**M:** 2 SACM V-12 diesels; 2 CP props; 3,600 hp
**Range:** 4,500/13 **Man:** 30 officers, 54 men

**MOROCCO** *(continued)*
**AMPHIBIOUS WARFARE SHIPS** *(continued)*

**Ahmed Es Sakali (403)** French Navy, 1984

Remarks: Can carry 133 troops and about 12 vehicles. Helicopter platform aft. Cargo capacity: 330 tons beaching. Can also carry 208 tons potable water.

◆ **1 French EDIC-class utility landing craft** Bldr: C.N. Franco-Belges (In serv. 1965)

401 Lieutenant Malghagh

**Lieutenant Malghagh**—wearing old number 1977

**D:** 292 tons (642 fl) **S:** 8 kts **Dim:** 59.0 × 11.95 × 1.3 (1.62 fl)
**A:** 2/20-mm AA (I × 2)—1/120-mm mortar (fwd)
**M:** 2 MGO diesels; 2 props; 1,000 hp **Range:** 1,800/8 **Man:** 16 tot.

### AUXILIARIES

◆ **1 training ship**

Essaouira

**D:** 60 tons

Remarks: Yacht presented by Italy in 1967. Used for training watchstanders.

◆ **2 former Danish cargo ships** Bldr: Fredrikshavn Vaerft & Tørdok, Frederickshaven

| | In serv. |
|---|---|
| 405 El Aigh (ex-*Merc Caribe*) | 1972 |
| 406 Ad Dakhla (ex-*Anglian Merchant,* ex-*Merc Nordia*) | 1973 |

**El Aigh (405)** C. Martinelli, 8-85

**D:** Approx. 2,000 tons (fl) **S:** 12 kts **Dim:** 76.61 × 12.30 × 3.47
**A:** 2/14.5-mm mg (I × 2) **Electron Equipt:** Radar: 2/. . . nav.
**M:** Burmeister & Wain Alpha, 10-cyl. diesel; 1 prop; 1,250 hp
**Range:** . . . **Man:** . . .

Remarks: 499 grt/326 nrt/1,327 dwt. Ice-strengthened hulls with pronounced bulbous bow. Two holds. Four 5-ton cranes. Acquired to provide logistic support for operations along Saharan coast. Originally built for Per R. Henriksen P/R, Copenhagen. 405 bought 1981 by Moroccan Ministry of Travel and Commerce, then transferred to Navy. 406, sold to British interests 1978, acquired directly by Moroccan Navy in 1981.

◆ **2 yachts**

Akhir (In serv. 1982)
Sequet El Hamra

◆ **1 harbor launch** Bldr: ARCOR, La Teste, France

Al Makbas

**D:** 11 tons (fl) **S:** 17 kts **Dim:** 13.00 (11.30 pp) × 3.80 × 1.10
**M:** 1 Baudouin 12-F11-Sm diesel; 1 prop; 426 hp
**Range:** 400/. . . **Man:** 4 tot.

Remarks: Ordered 1-85. Glass-reinforced plastic construction.

CUSTOMS SERVICE

◆ **4 French P32-type patrol boats** Bldr: CMN, Cherbourg (In serv. 1986–87)

**D:** 89 tons **S:** 29 kts **Dim:** 32.00 (30.09 pp) × 5.35 × 1.42 (hull)
**A:** 2/20-mm AA **Electron Equipt:** Radar: 1/. . . **Range:** 1,200/12
**M:** 2 UNI UD 30V12 M5 diesels; 2 props; 2,700 hp **Man:** 12 tot.

Remarks: Ordered 6-85. Wooden construction. Six sisters in Navy. Keel for first laid down 4-86, second 30-6-86, third 1-12-86.

◆ **18 Arcor-45 patrol craft** Bldr: Arcor, CN d'Aquitane, La Teste, France (In serv. 1987–88)

**D:** 12.3 tons (15.1 fl) **S:** 33 kts **Dim:** 14.50 × 4.00 × 1.20
**A:** 2/12.7-mm mg (I × 2) **Electron Equipt:** Radar: 1/Furuno 701
**M:** 2 UNI UDV 8M5 diesels; 2 props; 1,120 hp **Range:** 300/20 **Man:** . . .

Remarks: Ordered 6-85. Glass-reinforced plastic construction.

◆ **18 patrol craft** Bldr: Ojedo & Aniceto, Aviles, Spain

Remarks: Ordered 7-11-85. No data available.

# MOZAMBIQUE

**People's Republic of Mozambique**

Personnel (1986): Approx. 700 total

Merchant Marine (1986): 104 ships—42,801 grt

### PATROL BOATS AND CRAFT

◆ **2 Soviet S.O.-1 class**

**D:** 190 tons (215 fl) **S:** 29 kts **Dim:** 42.0 × 6.1 × 1.9 (hull)
**A:** 4/25-mm AA (II × 2)—4/RBU-1200 ASW RL (V × 4)—2/d.c. racks (24 d.c.)—mines
**Electron Equipt:** Radar: 1/Pot Head—Sonar: 1/Tamir-11 (HF)
IFF: 1/Dead Duck interrogator, 1/High Pole A transponder
**M:** 3 Type 40D diesels; 3 props; 7,500 hp
**Range:** 340/28; 1,900/7 **Man:** 30 tot.

Remarks: Transferred 6-85. Built 1958–64 and hard-used, they are not likely to be of much combat value. Bad rollers and very noisy.

◆ **10 Indian-design** Bldr: Mazagon SY, Goa (In serv. 1984–85)

**D:** . . . **S:** 20 kts **Dim:** 18.0 × 5.0 × . . .
**A:** . . . **M:** 2 diesels; 2 props; 1,100 hp

Remarks: First four launched together 4-84. Can also be used for towing.

◆ **7 Soviet Zhuk class**

**D:** 60 tons (fl) **S:** 34 kts **Dim:** 24.0 × 5.0 × 1.8 (props)
**A:** 2 or 4/14.5-mm mg (II × 1 or 2) **Electron Equipt:** Radar: 1/Spin Trough
**M:** 2 M50 diesels; 2 props; 2,400 hp

Remarks: Transferred: 1 in 1979, 2 in 10-80, 2 in 10-81, and 2 in 1982.

◆ **1 Soviet Poluchat-1 class**

**D:** 90 tons (fl) **S:** 18 kts **Dim:** 29.6 × 6.1 × 1.9
**A:** 2/14.5-mm mg (II × 1) **M:** 2 M50 diesels; 2 props; 2,400 hp
**Range:** 450/17; 900/10 **Man:** 20 tot.

Remarks: Transferred 1977.

MOZAMBIQUE *(continued)*
PATROL BOATS AND CRAFT *(continued)*

◆ **2 Portuguese Jupiter class**

**D:** 32 tons (43.5 fl) **S:** 20 kts **Dim:** 21.5 × 5.0 × 1.3
**A:** 1/20-mm AA **M:** 2 Cummins diesels; 2 props; 1,270 hp **Man:** 8 tot.

REMARKS: Operate on Lake Malawi (Lake Nyasa).

◆ **2 Portuguese Bellatrix class**

N . . . . . . . (ex-*Sirius*) N . . . . . . . (ex-*Vega*)

**D:** 23 tons **S:** 15 kts **Dim:** 20.7 × 4.6 × 1.2
**A:** 1/20-mm AA **Man:** 7 tot.

REMARKS: Operate on Lake Malawi (Lake Nyasa).

MINE WARFARE CRAFT

◆ **2 Soviet Yevgenya class** Bldr: Sredniy Neva SY, Kolpino

PM 525 GRACIOSA PM . . . N . . .

**D:** 80 tons (90 fl) **S:** 11 kts **Dim:** 26.2 × 6.1 × 1.5
**A:** 2/25-mm AA (II × 2) **Electron Equipt:** Radar: 1/Spin Trough
**M:** 2 diesels; 2 props; 600 hp **Range:** 300/10 **Man:** 10 tot.

REMARKS: GRP construction. May have twin 14.5-mm mg vice twin 25-mm AA listed. Employs television minehunting system to locate mines in up to 30-m depths. Both arrived 6-9-85 as deck cargo.

AMPHIBIOUS WARFARE CRAFT

◆ **1 Portuguese Alfange-class landing craft**

N . . . . . . . (ex-*Cimitarra*)

**D:** 285 tons (635 fl) **S:** 10 kts **Dim:** 59.0 × 11.91 × 1.6
**A:** 2/20-mm AA (I × 2) **M:** 2 MTU MD225 diesels; 2 props; 1,000 hp
**Range:** 1,800/8 **Man:** 20 tot.

◆ **2 Portuguese LDM-100-class landing craft**

**D:** 50 tons (fl) **S:** 9 kts **Dim:** 15.25 × . . . × . . .
**M:** 2 G.M. diesels; 2 props; 450 hp

AUXILIARIES

◆ **2 small cargo lighters** Bldr: Mazagon SY, Goa, India

REMARKS: No details available; ordered 1983.

# NATO
## North Atlantic Treaty Organization

NOTE: The oceanographic research ship described below is the only vessel "owned" jointly by the NATO nations. There is, however, a NATO Standing Force of frigates and destroyers, which would be augmented in time of war by warships from the major signatory nations.

THE NATO FRIGATE PROGRAM

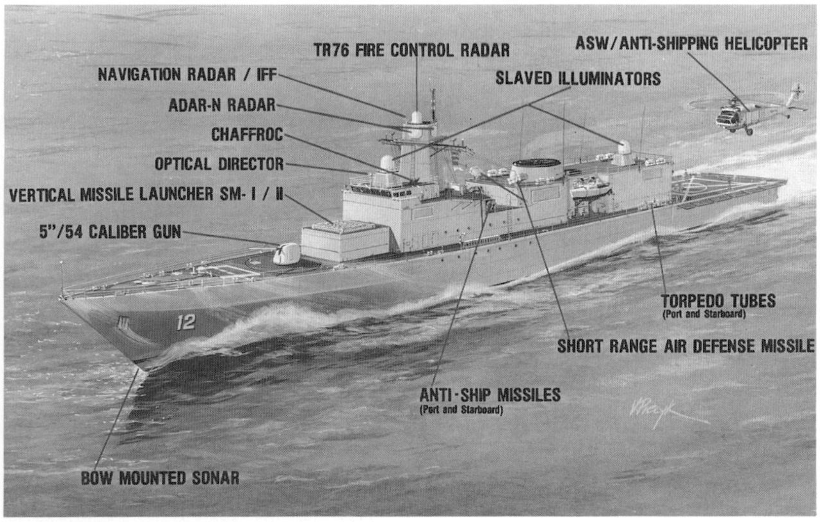


**RCA concept**—with fixed, phased-array radar V. Piecyk, 1985

NATO is jointly developing a standard frigate design for construction during the 1990s—the NFR 90 or "NATO Frigate Replacement 1990." Despite considerable expenditure of time and funds by the participants, however, there remains great lack of unanimity as to what the ship's function and characteristics should be. Most partner nations are developing parallel national frigate designs in the event that no common design can be agreed upon. The U.S. has made no commitment to build *any* ship and may view the project primarily as an opportunity for the sale of weapons and sensor systems. However, several European consortia have been formed to compete for the same systems. The resultant ship design may be as large as 6,000 tons (full load), placing it beyond the means of many of the partner nations, which are the United Kingdom, Spain, Canada, West Germany, France, the Netherlands, the United States, and Italy. The design is to carry the NATO Air-Defense Weapons System (NAWS), based on the Sea Sparrow. Below are illustrated some of the notional concepts of what an NFR-90 might look like. France and the U.K. did not sign the 3-year project-definition document on 21-10-87, although Britain may later.

◆ **0 (+1) oceanographic research ship**

| | Bldr | L | In serv. |
|---|---|---|---|
| ALLIANCE | Fincantieri, Muggiano | 9-7-86 | 1988 |

**RCA concept**—based on Dutch/German "Standard" frigate hull
V. Piecyk, 1985

**Blohm + Voss concept**—based on MEKO 360 design
Blohm + Voss/J. Sachse, 1986

**NFR 90**—variant with rotating phased-array radar 1986

NATO-NORTH ATLANTIC TREATY ORGANIZATION *(continued)*

**Alliance**—at launch C. Martinelli, 7-86

**Alliance**—fitting out A. Scrimali, 4-87

**D:** 2,466 tons (3,019 fl) **S:** 17 kts (16.3 sust.)
**Dim:** 93.00 (82.00 pp) × 15.20 × 5.10
**Electron Equipt:** Radar: 2/. . . nav.
Sonar: . . .
**M:** 2 GMT B.230-series diesels, AEG CC 3127 generators, electric drive: 2 AEG 1,470-kw motors; 2 props; 4,000 hp—side-thrusters fore and aft
**Range:** 8,000/12
**Man:** 10 officers, 20 men, 20 scientists
**Electric:** 1,850 kw (including 1/1,605-kw Kongsberg gas-turbine set)

REMARKS: 3,200 grt/533 dwt. Based at Naples and operated for the NATO ASW Research Center, La Spezia. Operated by U.K. Denholm Ship Management, Glasgow, with West German Naval Auxiliary Service officers and Italian non-rated personnel. Flies West German flag. Has 6,100 $m^2$ total working deck space, 400 $m^2$ lab space. Towing winch, 20-ton bollard pull, with 6,000 m of 50-mm cable. Also has 1,000-kg oceanographic crane with telescopic arm. Special attention paid to quieting. Has Flume-type passive tank stabilization. Replaces *Maria Paolina G,* a 2,800-grt stern-haul trawler chartered in 1964.

◆ **1 ex-U.S. Army T-boat, oceanographic tender** Bldr: Missouri Valley Steel

MANNING (ex-T-514) (In serv. 1953)

**D:** 96 tons (fl) **S:** 75 kts **Dim:** 20.0 × 5.4 × 2.1
**M:** Caterpillar D375 diesel; 325 hp
**Man:** 3 crew, 9 scientists **Range:** 400/7

REMARKS: Acquired 1955 by Columbia University, Crumb School of Mines; acquired by NATO 1964 and operated for NATO ASW Research Center, La Spezia.

# NETHERLANDS

## Kingdom of the Netherlands

PERSONNEL (1987): 16,880 (2,367 officers) including 2,800 Marines (203 officers), Naval Air Service, and 560 female personnel; 6,500 civilian employees

MERCHANT MARINE (1986): 1,324 ships—4,234,135 grt (tankers: 26 ships—666,813 grt)

NAVAL AVIATION: The Navy's aircraft are divided into four administrative groups: three maritime patrol squadrons at Valkenburg and one helicopter squadron at Dekoog. Principal types include (as of 7-87): 13 P-3C Orion; 2 F-27 Maritime; and 22 WG-13 Lynx helicopters.

The WG-13 Lynx are of the following subtypes: 6 UH-14A search-and-rescue, delivered in 1976; 9 SH-14B with dipping sonar; and 8 SH-14C.

Construction of 8 additional helicopters is planned for the 1990s. The SH-14B Lynx are to be upgraded to SH-14C standard with Rolls-Royce Gem 42 engines and French DUAV-4 dipping sonar; no ASQ-81 MAD gear for the SH-14Cs was ever acquired. Plans to lay up two P-3C abandoned. Six grounded BR-1050 Atlantic Mk 1 long-range patrol aircraft sold to French builder 1986.

WARSHIPS IN SERVICE, UNDER CONSTRUCTION, OR AUTHORIZED AS OF 1 JANUARY 1988

| | L | Tons (surfaced) | Main armament |
|---|---|---|---|
| ◆ **5 (+4) submarines** | | | |
| 0 (+4) ZEELEEUW | 1985–92 | 2,300 | 4/533-mm TT |
| 2 ZWAARDVIS | 1970–71 | 2,370 | 6/533-mm TT |
| 3 DOLFIJN/POTVIS | 1960–65 | 1,494 | 8/533-mm TT |
| ◆ **2 destroyers** | | | |
| | | Tons | |
| 2 TROMP | 1973–74 | 3,665 | 1/Standard, 8/Harpoon, and 1/Sea Sparrow systems, 2/120-mm DP, 6/ASW TT, 1/ASW helicopter |
| ◆ **14 (+8) frigates** | | | |
| 0 (+8) KAREL DOORMAN | 1988– | 2,800 | 4/Harpoon and 1/Sea Sparrow systems, 1/76-mm DP, 6/ASW TT, 1/helicopter |
| 2 JACOB VAN HEEMSKERCK | 1982–83 | 3,000 | 1/Standard, 8/Harpoon, 1/Sea Sparrow, 4/ASW TT |
| 10 KORTENAER | 1976–82 | 3,000 | 2/Harpoon and 1/Sea Sparrow systems, 1 or 2/76-mm DP, 4/ASW TT, 2/helicopters |
| 2 VAN SPEIJK | 1965–67 | 2,200 | 2/Harpoon, 2/Sea Cat systems, 1/76-mm DP, ASW weapons, 1/helicopter |
| ◆ **23 (+12) mine warfare ships** | | | |

WEAPONS AND SYSTEMS

### A. MISSILES

◆ *surface-to-air*

U.S./SM-1 MR Standard on the *Tromp*-class destroyers and on the two *Jacob Van Heemskerck*-class frigates

U.S. RIM-7M Sea Sparrow on the *Tromp*-class destroyers and *Jacob Van Heemskerck*- and *Kortenaer*-class frigates; British Sea Cat on the *Van Speijk*-class frigates

◆ *surface-to-surface*

U.S. Harpoon on the *Tromp, Van Heemskerck, Kortenaer, Karel Doorman,* and *Van Speijk* classes, and Sub-Harpoon on *Zeeleeuw*-class submarines.

### B. GUNS

120-mm twin-barreled automatic in the *Tromp*-class destroyers:
Weight: 65 tons
Arc of elevation: 10° to +85°
Muzzle velocity: 850 m/sec.
Direction rate: 25°/s in train, 40°/s in elevation
Rate of fire: 45 rounds/min/barrel
Maximum effective range in surface fire: 13,000 m
Maximum effective range in antiaircraft fire: 7,000 m

76-mm OTO Melara Compact on the *Kortenaer*- and *Van Speijk*-class frigates; to be upgraded to fire at 100 rpm

40-mm Bofors in single Bofors L70 mountings

30-mm SGE-30 "Goalkeeper," using the U.S. General Electric GAU-8A 30-mm gatling gun and EX-30 mounting co-mounted with an H.S.A. track-while-scan radar fire-control system. The latter uses independent I-band search/acquisition and

**GUNS** *(continued)*

I/K-band tracking radars. The 7-barreled gatling gun has a 4,200-rd/min. maximum rate of fire, 1,190 rds are carried on-mount. Muzzle velocity is 1,021 m/sec. Total weight, with ammunition, is 6,372 kg. The frigate *Callenburgh* is the first ship to carry "Goalkeeper." A total of 23 mounts had been ordered by 11-86.

20-mm Oerlikon AA in single World-War-II-era 70-cal. and modern 90-cal. 20 F-2 mountings

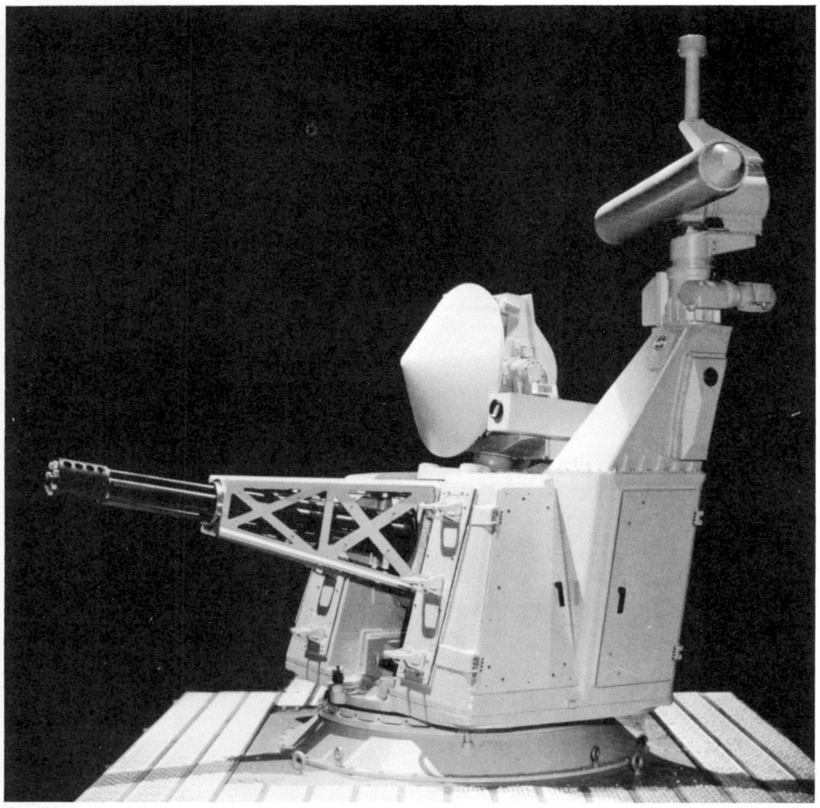

**Goalkeeper** Signaal-G.E.

### C. ANTISUBMARINE WEAPONS

U.S. Mk 44 and Mk 46 torpedoes on ships and aircraft

U.S. Mk 37 Mod. 2, NT-37C/D and Mk 48 torpedoes on submarines. Additional Mk 48 torpedoes were ordered in 1980. U.S. Honeywell NT-37E torpedoes (reworked Mk 37) have also been acquired.

### D. RADARS

All designed and manufactured by Hollandse Signaal Apparaaten (H.S.A.), a division of Phillips:

| Name | Type | Band |
|---|---|---|
| ZW-06 | Navigation/surface search | I |
| ZW-07 | Submarine, nav./surf. search | I |
| LW-02/03 | Long-range air-search | D |
| LW-04 | Long-range air-search | D |
| LW-08* | Long-range air-search | D |
| DA-05, 05A | Combined surveillance | F |
| DA-08 | Medium-range air-search | E/F |
| SPS-01 | 3-D air-search | F |
| WM-20/25 | Missile- and gunfire-control | K |
| M-44/45 | Missile- and gunfire-control | . . . |
| SMART† | 3-D air-search | F and C |
| STIR‡ | Missile- and gunfire-control | I/K (X + Ka) |
| LIROD-8 | radar, optronic weapon control | . . . |

* An extended-range version of LW-08 is under development.

† "Signaal Multi-beam Acquisition Radar for Targeting." For the *Jacob Van Heemskerck* class and possible refit to the *Tromp* class in place of SPS-01.

‡ U.S. design, built under license. STIR = "Separate Tracking and Illumination Radar"; has 1.8- and 2.9-m-dia. parabolic dish antennas and co-mounted t.v. camera.

### E. SONARS

CWE-610, LF, hull-mounted: On the *Tromp*-class destroyers, and *Van Speijk*-class frigates

SQR-18A: U.S. towed passive linear array on two *Van Speijk*-class frigates

SQR-19A: U.S. towed array, on *Witte de With* and *Karel Doorman* class

SQS-505, MF: license-built Canadian: On the *Kortenaer*-class frigates (PQS-36)

PHS-32, MF: Export sonar, hull-mounted or VDS

PHS-36, MF: On the *Jacob Van Heemskerck* and "M"-class frigates

Type 184, MF, hull-mounted: On the *Van Speijk*-class frigates

Octopus: Active/passive submarine array on *Walrus* class, derived from French Thomson-CSF "Eledone."

### F. ELECTRONIC WARFARE

In use are the "Scimitar" J-Band deception and jamming system, "RAPIDS" I 18-gHz passive intercept array, and "RAMSES" I/J-Band passive and deceptive repeater equipment. Chaff rocket launchers in use are the British-designed Knebworth/Corvus, 8-tubed, 76.2-mm launcher and the U.S. Mk 36 Super RBOC system with two Hycor 6-tubed Mk 136 launchers.

### G. DATA-PROCESSING

SEWACO (Sensoren Wapens Commando): built by Hollandse Signaal Apparaaten and centrally directed by a DAISY 1, 2, 3, 4, or 5 digital computer system. It exists in four versions (SEWACO I, II, III, and IV) tailored to the sensors and weapon systems of the ships that carry it.

SINBADS: Submarine tracking system. Can track 5 targets and engage 3 simultaneously.

The *Tromp* class, the *Jacob Van Heemskerck* class, and the *Karel Doorman* class have, or will have, LINK 11 data link.

## SUBMARINES

◆ **0 (+4 + 2) Zeeleeuw class** Bldr: Rotterdamse Droogdok Mij, Rotterdam

| | Laid down | L | Trials | In serv. |
|---|---|---|---|---|
| S 801 Walrus | 11-10-79 | 28-10-85* | 1990 | 1990 |
| S 803 Zeeleeuw | 24-9-81 | 20-6-87 | 1988 | 1989 |
| S 808 Dolfijn | 12-6-86 | . . . | 1991 | 1992 |
| S 810 Bruinvis | 1987 | . . . | 1992 | 1992–93 |
| S . . . N . . . | . . . | . . . | . . . | 1998 |
| S . . . N . . . | . . . | . . . | . . . | . . . |

* Returned to land for repairs 2-5-87

**Zeeleeuw (S 803)**—at launch R.Neth.N., 6-87

**D:** 1,900/2,450/2,800 tons **S:** 12/21 kts **Dim:** 67.73 × 8.40 × 7.0

**A:** 4/533-mm TT fwd. (20 Sub-Harpoon SSM/Mk 48 or NT.37C/D/E torpedoes/mines)

**Electron Equipt:** Radar: 1/ZW-07 (U.K. Decca Type 1001)
Sonar: Octopus active/passive, U.K. Type 2026 linear passive array

**M:** diesel-electric: 3 SEMT-Pielstick 12 PA4V 200, 2 Type 304 980-kw diesel generator groups; 1 Holec motor; 1 5-bladed prop; 3,950 surf./5,430 sub. hp (see Remarks)

**Fuel:** 310 tons **Range:** 10,000/9 (snorkel) **Man:** 7 officers, 43 men

Remarks: First two ordered 19-6-78 and 17-12-79. Second pair authorized 5-1-84. S 808 ordered 16-10-84, S 810 ordered 16-8-85. The intention is to construct six of these units. The final two will have new-design electric motors. Construction of first pair delayed by need to lengthen hull after keels laid, in order to accommodate diesel generator sets. Second pair will return to use of Brons-Werkspoor 0-RUB 215X12 diesels. Propulsion plant is on resilient mountings to reduce noise emissions. Each HOLEC a.c./d.c. generator has built-in rectifiers and produces 980 kw. There are three 140-cell batteries. Endurance is 60 days. Periscope depth: 18 m. Torpedo tubes are of the "water-slug" type, capable of launching at any operational depth. Hull construction is of MAREL steel, with single-hull midbody and double-hull ends; reserve bouyancy is 12%. Will have Gipsy data system, Sperry Mk 29 Mod. 2A inertial navigation system, NAVSAT receiver, and passive EW equipment.

*Walrus* severely damaged by fire 14-8-86, at which time it was thought she might have to be scrapped. Decision to repair made early 1987, adding over 30 percent to her overall cost. Delay in completion resulted in renaming class for first to be completed.

◆ **2 Zwaardvis class** Bldr: Rotterdamse Droogdok Mij, Rotterdam

| | Laid down | L | In serv. |
|---|---|---|---|
| S 806 Zwaardvis | 7-67 | 2-7-70 | 18-2-72 |
| S 807 Tijgerhaai | 7-67 | 25-5-71 | 20-10-72 |

**SUBMARINES** *(continued)*

**Zwaardvis (S 806)** L. & L. Van Ginderen, 6-87

**Tijgerhaai (S 807)** L. & L. Van Ginderen, 11-86

**D:** 2,350/2,408/2,640 tons **S:** 13/20 kts **Dim:** 66.92 × 8.40 × 7.10
**A:** 6/533-mm TT fwd (20 U.S. Mk 37, Mk 48, and NT-37C/D) torpedoes
**Electron Equipt:** Radar: 1/ZW-06
Sonar: . . .
**M:** diesel-electric: 3 sets Werkspoor RUB 215X12, 1,400-hp diesel generators, 920 kw each; 1 3,800-kw motor; 1 5-bladed prop; 5,100 hp
**Range:** 10,000/9 (snorkel) **Man:** 8 officers, 59 men

Remarks: Ordered 24-12-65 and 14-7-66. Based on the U.S. Navy's *Barbel* class, which has a teardrop hull. Use of Dutch equipment necessitated modifications to the original design. The H.S.A.-M8 Mod. 7 torpedo-firing system uses a digital computer that permits the simultaneous launching of two torpedoes, one of which may be wire-guided. For silent running, all noise-producing machinery is mounted on a false deck with spring suspension. Three 140-cell batteries. Mid-life refits planned for 1987–88 (S 806) and 1988–90 (S 807); will receive U.K. Type 2026 towed passive sonar arrays.

◆ **3 Dolfijn/Potvis class**

| | Bldr | Laid down | L | In serv. |
|---|---|---|---|---|
| S 804 Potvis | Wilton-Fijenoord | 17-9-62 | 12-1-65 | 2-11-65 |
| S 805 Tonijn | Wilton-Fijenoord | 26-11-62 | 14-6-65 | 24-2-66 |
| S 809 Zeehond | Rotterdam DDM | 30-12-54 | 20-2-60 | 16-3-61 |

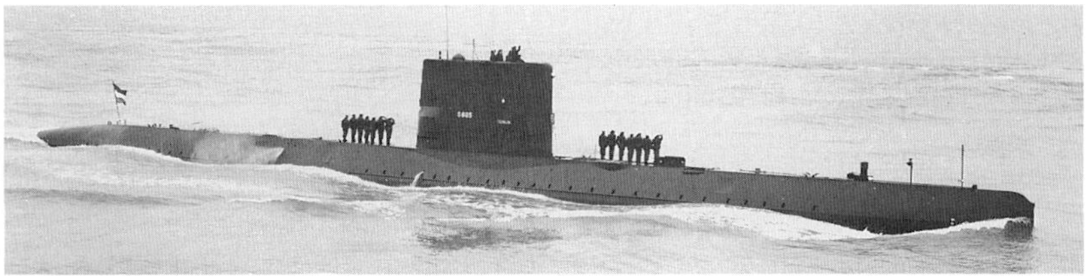

**Tonijn (S 805)** L. & L. Van Ginderen, 11-85

**Zeehond (S 809)** L. & L. Van Ginderen, 5-86

**D:** 1,140/1,510/1,830 tons **S:** 14.5/17 kts
**Dim:** 79.50 × 7.84 × 4.95—see Remarks
**A:** 8/533-mm TT (4 fwd, 4 aft) **Electron Equipt:** Radar: 1/ZW-06
**M:** diesel-electric: 2 SEMT-Pielstick 12 PA4V185 diesels, 1,550 hp each; 2/920-kw electric motors; 2 props; 4,400 hp—see Remarks
**Man:** 8 officers, 59 men

Remarks: S 804 and S 805 authorized in 1962, S 809 in 1949. S 809, 805: D: 1,509/1,831 tons; Dim: 78.25 × 7.80 × 4.95; 2 M.A.N. 12-V6V 22/30, 12-cylinder diesels, 1,400 hp each. The exterior hull has three parallel interior pressure cylinders, one of which is placed on top of a pair of slightly shorter ones. Diving depth: 300 m. Have two 168-cell batteries. The crew and the armament occupy the top cylinder, and the batteries and diesel engines are mounted in the other two. *Tonijn* received SEMT-Pielstick diesel generator sets during 1978; *Potvis* was given new engines in 1979. Sister *Dolfijn* (S 808) placed in reserve without refit or batteries during 1983 and was stricken 1-2-85 and sold for scrap 22-7-85. S 809 was to strike in 1986–87, S 804 in 1991, and S 805 in 1992, but S 809 extended to 1991 to replace damaged *Walrus*.

**GUIDED-MISSILE DESTROYERS**

◆ **2 Tromp class** Bldr: Kon. Mij. de Schelde, Flushing

| | Laid down | L | In serv. |
|---|---|---|---|
| F 801 Tromp | 4-8-71 | 4-6-73 | 3-10-75 |
| F 806 De Ruyter (ex-*Van Heemskerck*) | 22-12-71 | 9-3-74 | 3-6-76 |

**D:** 3,665 tons (4,308 fl) **S:** 28 kts (30 on trials)
**Dim:** 138.2 (131.0 pp) × 14.8 × 4.6 (6.6 max.)
**A:** 4/Harpoon missiles (II × 2)—1 Mk 13 missile launcher (I × 1, 40 SM-1 MR missiles)—1/NATO Sea Sparrow system (VII × 1, Mk 29, 16 missiles)—2/120-mm Bofors DP (II × 1)—6/324-mm Mk 32 ASW TT (III × 2)—1/Lynx ASW helicopter
**Electron Equipt:** Radar: 2/Decca 1226 nav., 1/SPS-01, 1/WM-25, 2/SPG-51C
Sonar: 1/EDO CWE-610, 1/162 (bottom search)
EW: Ramses active/passive array, Mk 36 SRBOC chaff syst. (VI × 4)
**M:** COGOG: 2 Rolls-Royce Olympus TM-3B gas turbines, 27,000 hp each; 2 Tyne RM-1C gas turbines, 4,100 hp each, for cruising (18 kts); 2 CP 4-bladed props; 54,000 hp
**Electric:** 4,000 kw **Fuel:** 600 tons **Range:** 5,000/18
**Man:** 34 officers, 271 men

**Tromp (F 801)** L. & L. Van Ginderen, 5-86

**De Ruyter (F 806)** L. & L. Van Ginderen, 8-87

GUIDED-MISSILE DESTROYERS *(continued)*

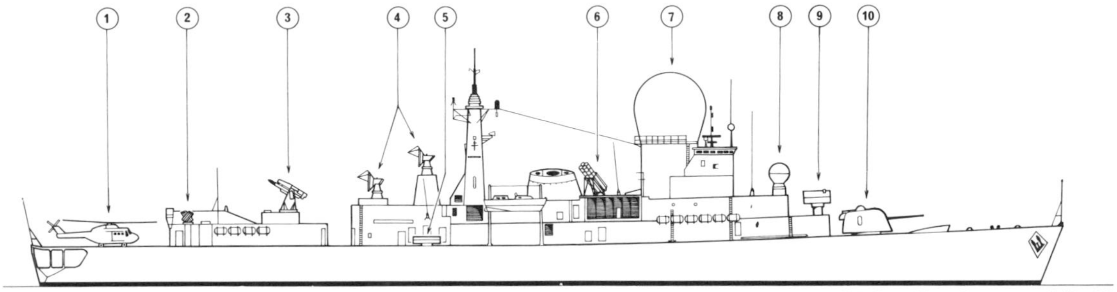


**Tromp** 1. Lynx helicopter 2. Mk 136 chaff RL 3. Mk 13 missile launcher 4. SPG-51C radars 5. Mk 32 torpedo tubes 6. Harpoon launchers 7. SPS-01 3-D radar 8. WM-25 fire-control radar 9. Sea Sparrow system 10. 120-mm gun mount

**Tromp (F 801)** R.Neth.N., 1987

REMARKS: Although the Dutch Navy designates them as frigates, these ships, by virtue of their armament and size, are more closely related to guided-missile destroyers. They have fin stabilizers, and are excellent sea boats. The 120-mm guns, modernized, come from the stricken destroyer *Gelderland.* Equipped with an admiral's cabin and command facilities, they can act as flagships. Berthing for enlisted men is in 6-, 9-, or 12-man compartments. The propulsion machinery is arranged in three compartments, forward to aft: 2 Olympus gas turbines, 2 generator sets, and the auxiliary boilers; 2 Tyne gas turbines; 2 generator sets. The 450-V, 3-phase, 60-Hz current is produced by four groups of 1,000-kw generators, each driven by a SMIT/Paxman Valenta RP 200, 12-cylinder diesel; two sets are sufficient for full combat power. There are three auxiliary boilers for heating. Fitted with Harpoon 1977/78; normally carry only 4 (II × 2), but can carry 8 (IV × 2). SEWACO-I data system. New plastic radomes for SPS-01 radar, 1980, called "Kojack." EW system updated 1984 on *Tromp* and LINK 11 data exchange system added; F 806 followed in 1985.

Both were to be given mid-life modernizations, but current plans are for F 801 to receive new radar in place of the large SPS-01 and to get the Goalkeeper CIWS. F 806 is to be given a refit and then placed in reserve in the early 1990s.

## GUIDED-MISSILE FRIGATES

◆ **0 (+8) Karel Doorman class** Bldr: de Schelde, Vlissingen

| | Laid down | L | In serv. |
|---|---|---|---|
| F 827 KAREL DOORMAN | 26-2-85 | 1988 | 1992 |
| F 828 WILLEM VAN DER ZAAN | 6-11-85 | . . . | 1992 |
| F 829 TJERK HIDDES | 28-10-86 | . . . | 1992 |
| F 830 VAN AMSTEL | 3-88 | . . . | 1993 |
| F 831 ABRAHAM VAN DER HULST | . . . | . . . | |
| F 832 VAN NES | . . . | . . . | |
| F 833 VAN GALEN | . . . | . . . | |
| F 834 VAN SPEIJK | . . . | . . . | |

**Karel Doorman (F 827)**—artist's rendering, old pendant number R.Neth.N., 1986

**D:** 2,800 tons light (3,320 fl) **S:** 29 kts (21 kts on diesels)
**Dim:** 122.25 (114.40 pp) × 14.40 (13.10 wl) × 4.30 (6.05 sonar)
**A:** 4/Harpoon SSM (II × 2)—VLS Sea Sparrow SAM syst. (16 missiles)—1/76-mm OTO Melara DP—1/30-mm Goalkeeper gatling CIWS—2/20-mm AA (I × 2)—4/324-mm ASW TT (II × 2, fixed)—1/Lynx helicopter
**Electron Equipt:** Radar: 1/Decca 1690/9, 1/DA-08, 1/LW-08, 1/STIR-18, 1/STIR-24, 1/Goalkeeper array
Sonar: PHS-36 (SQS-509) hull-mounted, SQR-19A TASS (provision for)
EW: Argo APECS-2 active/passive, Mk 36 SRBOC chaff RL (IV × 2)
**M:** CODOG: 2 Stork-Werkspoor 12 SWD 280 V-12 cruise diesels, 4,225 hp each; 2 Rolls-Royce SM-1A or C Spey gas turbines; 2 CP props; 37,540 hp (F 828, etc.: 48,972 hp)
**Electric:** 2,720 kw (4 × 650-kw diesel sets; 1 × 120-kw diesel set)
**Range:** 5,000/18 **Man:** 16 officers, 125 men

REMARKS: First four ordered 29-2-84, three years earlier than planned, to help ship-building industry; second group of four ordered 1-8-85; four more planned. Will nominally replace the scrapped *Roofdier* class, but are far more capable ships; indeed, they are little inferior to the larger *Kortenaers.* Intended for fisheries patrol and 200-nautical-mile economic zone patrol in peacetime. Accommodations for female crew members incorporated, plus bunks for 30 Marines. Endurance: 30 days.

Will have computer-controlled rudder stabilization system vice fins. Three rubber semi-rigid boats. DAISY VII/SEWACO VII data system with full LINK 10, 11, and 16 capability but delays in developing the combat system will keep first ship from being fully operational until 1992. F 827 will receive Spey SM-1A gas turbines operating at 14 MW each; the remainder will have the 18-MW RM-1C, to be back-fitted in F 827. The 76-mm gun will fire at up to 100 rpm. The second group may substitute the SMART-S 3-D radar for the DA-08 atop the foremast. Will have British SCOT SHF SATCOMM System.

The ships were originally to have been named *Groningen, Friesland, Utrecht, Noord Brabant, Limburg, Overijssel, Drenthe,* and *Gelderland.* Again changed mid-1987 to move *Van Speijk* from second to last.

◆ **2 Jacob Van Heemskerck class** Bldr: de Schelde, Vlissingen

| | Laid down | L | In serv. |
|---|---|---|---|
| F 812 JACOB VAN HEEMSKERCK (ex-*Pieter Floresz*) | 21-1-81 | 5-11-83 | 15-1-86 |
| F 813 WITTE DE WITH | 15-12-81 | 25-8-84 | 17-9-86 |

GUIDED-MISSILE FRIGATES *(continued)*

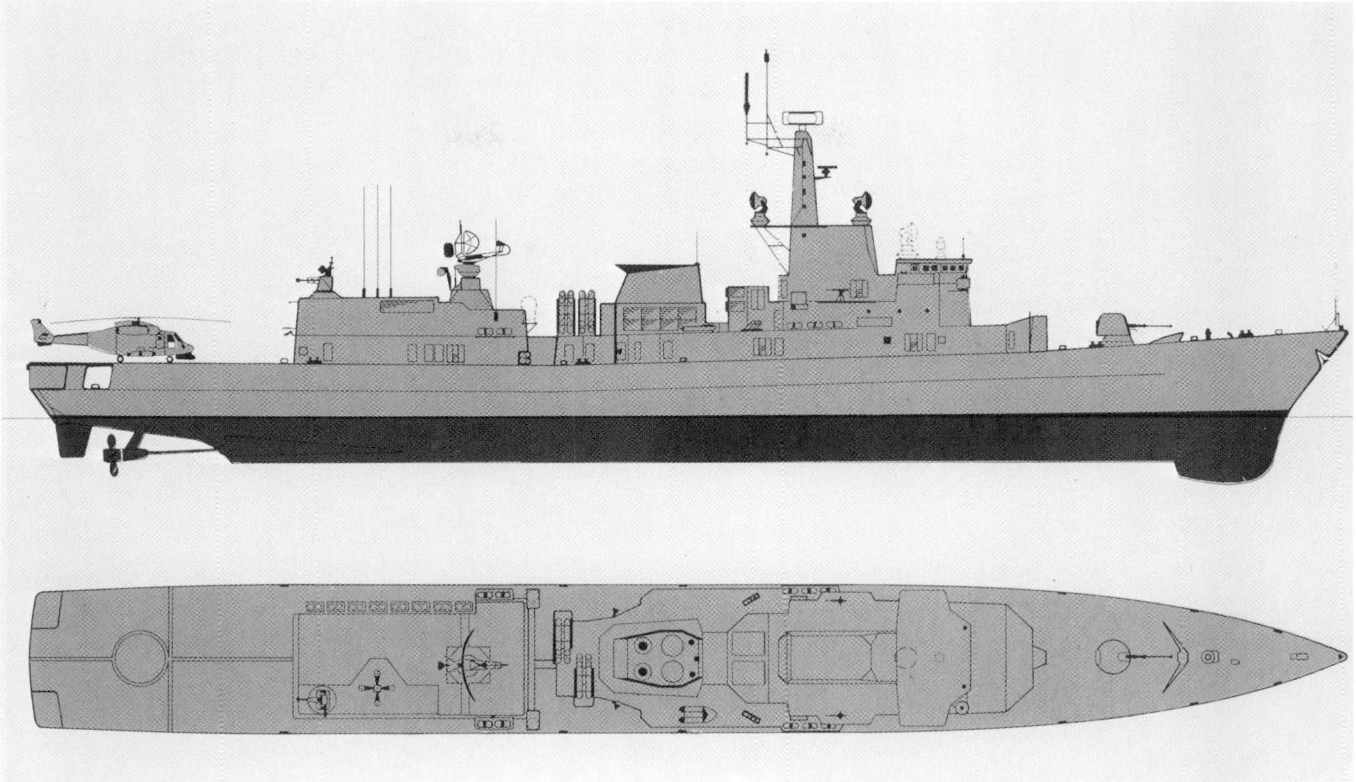

**Karel Doorman class** R.Neth.N., 1986

**Karel Doorman (F 827)**—model R.Neth.N., 1987

**Jacob Van Heemskerck (F 812)**—with Goalkeeper aft L. & L. Van Ginderen, 8-87

**Jacob Van Heemskerck (F 812)** R.Neth.N., 1986

**GUIDED-MISSILE FRIGATES** *(continued)*

**Witte De With (F 813)** L. & L. Van Ginderen, 9-86

**D:** 3,000 tons (3,750 fl) **S:** 30 kts (20 kts on cruise engines)
**Dim:** 130.20 (121.8 pp) × 14.40 × 4.23 (6.0 props)
**A:** 4 Harpoon SSM (II × 2)—1/Mk 13 Mod. 4 launcher (I × 1, 40 SM-1 MR Standard missiles)—1/Mk 29 launcher (VIII × 1, 24 Sea Sparrow missiles)—1/30-mm Goalkeeper gatling AA—4/324-mm ASW TT (II × 2, fixed)
**Electron Equipt:** Radar: 1/ZW-06, 1/DA-08, 1/LW-08, 1/STIR-18, 2/STIR-24, 1/Goalkeeper array
Sonar: PHS-36 (SQS-509)—provision for: SQR-19A towed array
EW: Ramses active/passive; Mk 36 Super RBOC chaff RL (VI × 2)
**M:** COGOG: 2 Rolls-Royce Olympus TM-3B gas turbines, 25,800 hp each; 2 Rolls-Royce Tyne RM-1C cruise gas turbines, 4,900 hp each; 2 LIPS CP props; 51,600 hp
**Electric:** . . . **Range:** 4,700/16 (on 1 Tyne turbine)
**Man:** 176 crew plus 20 flag staff

Remarks: Built as replacement hulls for the pair with the same pendant numbers (and original names) sold to Greece, but with the basic *Kortenaer* design modified to replace the helicopter facility with the U.S. Standard missile system. To act as flagships, permitting the Dutch Navy to operate four escort flotillas in wartime and obviating the need for the originally planned "13th *Kortenaer*." Have the SEWACO II data system and LINK 11 data-link capability. The DA-08 radar atop the foremast may later be replaced by H.S.A.'s new SMART (Signaal Multi-beam Acquisition Radar for Targeting), and the ships are to receive the U.S. SQR-19A TACTASS towed passive hydrophone array. Have the U.S. SLQ-25 Nixie torpedo decoy system.

◆ **10 Kortenaer class** Bldrs: F 823 and F 824: Wilton-Fijenoord; others: de Schelde

| | Laid down | L | In serv. |
|---|---|---|---|
| F 807 Kortenaer | 8-4-75 | 18-12-76 | 26-10-78 |
| F 808 Callenburgh | 30-6-75 | 12-3-77 | 26-7-79 |
| F 809 Van Kinsbergen | 2-9-76 | 16-4-77 | 24-4-80 |
| F 810 Banckert | 25-2-76 | 13-7-78 | 29-10-80 |
| F 811 Piet Heyn | 28-4-77 | 3-6-78 | 14-4-81 |
| F 816 Abraham Crijnssen | 25-10-78 | 16-5-81 | 26-1-83 |
| F 823 Philips Van Almonde | 1-10-77 | 11-8-79 | 2-12-81 |
| F 824 Bloys Van Treslong | 1-5-78 | 15-11-80 | 25-11-82 |
| F 825 Jan Van Brakel | 16-11-79 | 16-5-81 | 14-4-83 |
| F 826 Pieter Florisz (ex-*Willem Van Der Zaan*) | 15-1-80 | 8-5-82 | 1-10-83 |

**Callenburgh (F 808)**—with prototype Goalkeeper atop hangar R.Neth.N., 9-84

**Van Kinsbergen (F 809)** L. & L. Van Ginderen, 6-87

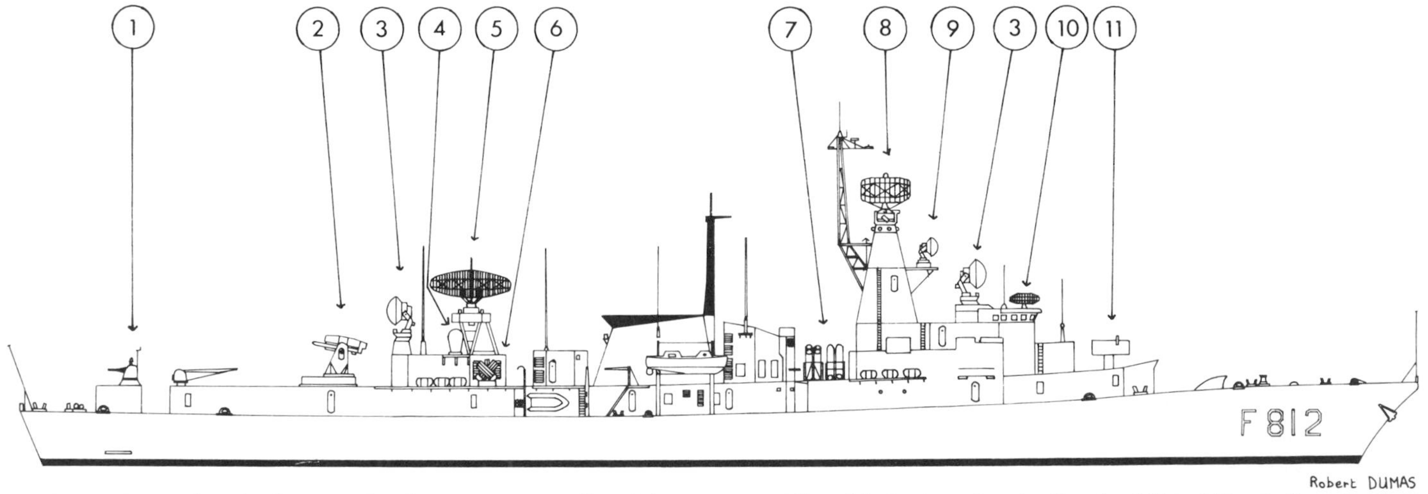


**Jacob Van Heemskerck class** 1. Goalkeeper 30-mm gatling AA system 2. Mk 13 Mod. 4 launcher for Standard SM-1 MR missiles 3. Modified STIR-24 missile fire-control radars for Standard 4. Satellite communications syst. antennas 5. LW-08 long-range air-search radar 6. U.S. Super RBOC chaff launchers (VI × 4) 7. Harpoon launch cells (IV × 2) 8. DA-08 9. STIR-18 fire-control radar for Sea Sparrow 10. ZW-06 navigational/surface-search radar 11. Mk 29 Sea Sparrow launcher (VIII × 1)

**GUIDED-MISSILE FRIGATES** *(continued)*

**Philips Van Almonde (F 823)** L. & L. Van Ginderen, 10-86

**Pieter Florisz (F 826)**—with Ramses EW arrays L. & L. Van Ginderen, 8-87

**Abraham Crijnssen (F 816)**—with portable EW hut on helo deck
L. & L. Van Ginderen, 10-86

**D:** 3,000 tons (3,786 fl) **S:** 30 kts (20, on 2 Tyne turbines)
**Dim:** 130.2 (121.8 pp) × 14.4 × 4.4 (6.0 props)
**A:** 4/Harpoon SSM (II × 2)—1/NATO Sea Sparrow system (VIII × 1, 24 missiles, Mk 29 launcher)—1/76-mm OTO Melara DP (I × 2)—1/40-mm Bofors AA—some: 2/20-mm AA (I × 2)—4/324-mm Mk 32 ASW TT (II × 2)—1 or 2/WG-13 Lynx ASW helicopters
**Electron Equipt:** Radar: 1/LW-08, 1/ZW-06, 1/WM-25, 1/STIR
Sonar: 1/SQS-505
EW: F 807–F 811: Sphinx passive system; later ships: Ramses active/passive system; all: 2/Knebworth/Corvus chaff RL (VIII × 2) or Mk 36 SRBOC (VI × 2)
**M:** COGOG: 2 Rolls-Royce Olympus TM-3B gas turbines, 25,800 hp each; 2 Rolls-Royce Tyne RM-1C cruise gas turbines, 4,900 hp each; 2 LIPS CP props; 51,600 hp
**Electric:** 3,000 kw **Range:** 4,700/16 (on 1 Tyne turbine)
**Man:** 18 officers, 182 men

Remarks: F 807 to F 810 ordered 31-8-74; F 811 to F 816 ordered 28-11-74; F 823–F 826 ordered 29-12-76. The original *Pieter Florisz* (F 812) and *Witte de With* (F 813) were sold to Greece in 1981. Initially, F 807 and F 808 had two 76-mm guns, replaced by a 40-mm mount in F 807 by 1982. All are scheduled to have the 40-mm AA replaced by a 30-mm Goalkeeper gatling AA gun system; F 808 received the prototype system in 9-84 (production versions will not have the raised platform below the Goalkeeper found on F 808). In peacetime, only one Lynx helicopter is carried. Normally, only two or four Harpoon SSM (II × 2) are carried, but up to 8 can be accommodated. All ships have the Sperry Mk 29 Mod. 1 inertial navigation system. Two 20-mm AA added atop the hangar, abreast the LW-08 radar on F 823, F 824 and others in 1986.

The engineering plant is distributed in four compartments, forward to aft: auxiliaries; Olympus gas turbines; Tyne gas turbines plus reduction gears; auxiliaries. The 450-volt, 3-phase, 60-Hertz electric current is supplied by four generators driven by four SEMT-Pielstick PA4, 750-kw diesels. There are two auxiliary boilers and two evaporators.

The hull is divided by fifteen watertight bulkheads. One pair of Denny-Brown, non-retracting fin stabilizers is fitted. Particular attention has been paid to habitability.

The Mk 36 Super RBOC chaff system (2, 6-tubed Mk 136 launchers) has replaced the original Knebworth/Corvus RL. All have the SEWACO-II data system. Two of these ten units may be offered up for sale, it was announced in mid-1985. F 826 first to backfit with Ramses (Reprogrammable Advanced Multimode Shipboard ECM system), in 1-86.

◆ **2 Van Speijk class**

| | Bldr | Laid down | L | In serv. |
|---|---|---|---|---|
| F 814 Isaac Sweers | Nederlandsche DSM | 6-5-65 | 10-3-67 | 15-5-68 |
| F 815 Evertsen | Kon. Mij. de Schelde | 6-7-65 | 18-6-66 | 21-12-67 |

**D:** 2,200 tons (2,835 fl) **S:** 28.5 kts
**Dim:** 113.42 (109.75 pp) × 12.48 × 4.57 (fl)
**A:** 2/Harpoon SSM (I × 2)—2/Sea Cat systems (IV × 2)—1/76-mm OTO Melara DP—6/324-mm Mk 32 ASW TT (III × 2)—1/Lynx ASW helicopter
**Electron Equipt:** Radar: 1/Decca TM 1229C, 1/DA-05/2, 1/LW-03, 2/M-44 (for Sea Cat), 1/M-45 (for 76-mm)
Sonar: 1/CWE-610, 1/PDE-700 (F 814, 815; SQR-18A also)
EW: passive intercept syst., UA-13 (F 814: FH-12) intercept array, 2/Mk 36 SRBOC (VI × 2)
**M:** 2 sets Werkspoor-English Electric double-reduction GT; 2 props; 30,000 hp
**Electric:** 1,900 kw **Boilers:** 2 Babcock & Wilcox; 38.7 kg/cm², 450°C
**Range:** 4,500/12 **Man:** 180 tot.

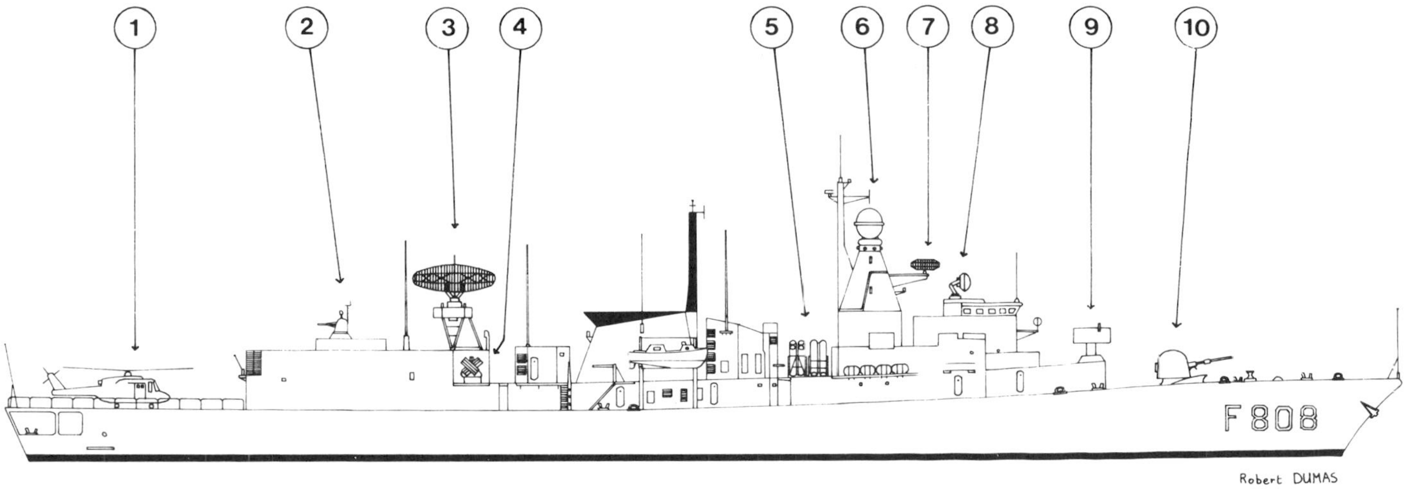


**Callenburgh** 1. Lynx helicopter 2. Goalkeeper 30-mm CIWS 3. LW-08 air-search radar 4. Mk 36 Super RBOC decoy RL (VI × 4) 5. Harpoon SSM (up to IV × 2) 6. WM-25 track-while-scan fire-control radar 7. ZW-06 navigational/surface-search radar 8. STIR-18 fire-control radar 9. Mk 29 Sea Sparrow SAM launcher (VIII × 1) 10. 76-mm OTO Melara Compact DP

FRIGATES *(continued)*

**Evertsen (F 815)** L. & L. Van Ginderen, 9-85

**Isaac Sweers (F 814)**—note towed array housing L. & L. Van Ginderen, 6-87

REMARKS: Originally similar in general to the British *Leander* class, but with broader bridge and *two* Sea Cat missile systems, each with a director. Major modernizations began 1977, during which the twin Mk 6, 114-mm gun mount was replaced by an OTO Melara 76-mm gun; the Limbo ASW mortar was deleted and two triple ASW TT added; the hangar was enlarged and made to telescope to accommodate the Lynx helicopter; positions for Harpoon SSM canisters (normally only two carried) were added; new radars, sonars, and the SEWACO-II data system were added; and the crew requirement was reduced from 247 to 180 total. Conversion dates: F 815: 18-7-79 to 26-11-82; and F 814: 1-7-80 to 28-10-83. New infrared signature suppression stack caps added. F 814 and F 815 received U.S. SQR-18A towed passive linear hydrophone array, and F 814 has SRBOC chaff RL. F 814 and F 815 are to be retained, due to their towed sonar installations; the others are available for sale.

Four sisters decommissioned for sale to Indonesia: *Van Speijk* (F 802) stricken 13-9-86, transferred 1-11-86; *Van Galen* (F 803) stricken 11-86 for transfer 2-11-87; *Tjerk Hiddes* (F 804) stricken 1-10-86 and transferred 13-10-86; *Van Nes* (F 805) decommissioned 11-86 for transfer in 2-88.

NOTE: All five *Balder*-class patrol boats have been removed from service except *Bulgia* (P 803), reassigned as a midshipman training craft (A 880) on 14-11-86. *Balder* (P 802) stricken 1-1-85, sold for scrap 6-6-85; *Freyr* (P 804) stricken 28-11-86 and transferred to youth group; *Hadda* (P 805) stricken 28-11-86 and retained as spares support for *Bulgia; Hefring* (P 806) stricken 1-1-85 and sold for scrap 6-6-85.

## MINE WARFARE SHIPS

◆ **0 (+10) New-construction deep-sea minesweeper/hunters** Bldr: . . .

| | Laid down | L | In serv. |
|---|---|---|---|
| M . . . N . . . | 1989 | . . . | 1993 |

**D:** . . . **S:** . . . **Dim:** . . . × . . . × . . . **A:** . . .
**Electron Equipt:** Radar: . . .
Sonar: . . .
**M:** . . . **Range:** . . . **Man:** . . .

REMARKS: Lineal replacements for the *Dokkum* class, intended to work out to the 100-meter curve. Fifteen originally planned; now plan 10, with six larger deep-sea minesweepers to deliver during late 1990s. First of new class expected to commence trials 1992, with seven operational by 1996. May use Norwegian air-cushion minehunter design.

◆ **13 (+2) Alkmaar ("Tripartite")-class minehunters** Bldr: Van der Giessen de Noord, Alblasserdam (*in reserve)

| | Ordered | Laid down | L | In serv. |
|---|---|---|---|---|
| M 850 ALKMAAR* | 26-7-77 | 30-1-79 | 18-5-82 | 28-5-83 |
| M 851 DELFZIJL* | 26-7-77 | 29-5-80 | 29-10-82 | 17-8-83 |
| M 852 DORDRECHT* | | 23-1-79 | 5-1-81 | 26-2-83 | 16-11-83 |
| M 853 HAARLEM | | 23-1-79 | 16-6-81 | 9-7-83 | 12-1-84 |
| M 854 HARLINGEN | | 31-3-81 | 30-11-81 | 9-7-83 | 12-4-84 |
| M 855 SCHEVENINGEN (ex-*Hellevoetsluis*) | 31-3-81 | 24-5-82 | 2-12-83 | 18-7-84 |
| M 856 MAASSLUIS | 16-12-81 | 7-11-82 | 5-5-84 | 12-12-84 |
| M 857 MAKKUM | 16-12-81 | 25-2-83 | 27-9-84 | 13-5-85 |
| M 858 MIDDELBURG | 21-7-82 | 11-7-83 | 23-2-85 | 10-12-86 |
| M 859 HELLEVOETSLUIS (ex-*Scheveningen*) | 21-7-82 | 12-12-83 | 18-7-85 | 10-12-86 |
| M 860 SCHIEDAM | 10-12-83 | 6-5-84 | 20-12-85 | 9-7-86 |
| M 861 URK | 10-12-83 | 30-9-84 | 2-5-86 | 10-12-86 |
| M 862 ZIERIKZEE (ex-*Veere*) | 3-7-84 | 28-2-85 | 4-10-86 | 7-5-87 |
| M 863 VLARDINGEN | 3-7-84 | 6-5-86 | 1-88 | 1988 |
| M 864 WILLEMSTAD | 3-7-84 | 3-10-86 | 6-88 | 1989 |

**Dordrecht (M 852)**—now in reserve M. Louagie, 3-87

**Makkum (M 857)** P. Voss, 11-86

**Zierikzee (M 862)** M. Louagie, 6-87

**D:** 510 tons (540 fl) **S:** 15 kts (7 kts hunting)
**Dim:** 51.6 (47.1 pp) × 8.96 × 2.45 (2.6 max.)
**A:** 1/20-mm 20F-2 AA—2/PAP-104 Mk IV remote-controlled minehunting devices
**Electron Equipt:** Radar: 1/Decca TM 1229C
Sonar: 1/DUBM-21B—1 EVEC 20 plot table, autopilot, Toran and Syledis radio navaids, Decca HiFix-6 precision navigation system

**MINE WARFARE SHIPS** *(continued)*

**M:** 1 Brons-Werkspoor A-RUB 215 × 12 diesel; 1 CP prop; 1,900 hp; 2/75-hp bow-thrusters; 2/120 hp ACEC active rudders
**Electric:** 880 kw **Range:** 3,500/10 **Man:** 34 tot.

REMARKS: Same design as "Tripartite" minehunters for France and Belgium. Hull made of a compound of glass and polyester resin. The 20-mm AA gun is not always aboard. These ships can also tow a mechanical drag sweep and carry OD-3 mechanical sweep gear. The DUBM-21A sonar can detect mines in waters up to 80-m depth, at slant ranges up to 500 m. Have 3 × 270-kw gas-turbine generator sets and one 160-kw diesel set. Active tank stabilization. The original *Vlaardingen* (M 863) and *Willemstad* (M 864) were sold to Indonesia while under construction in 1985 and were replaced with later units. M 858 and M 859 were to have been transferred to Egypt as *Mecca* and *Medina,* but the transaction was never completed. M 856 and M 859 deployed to the Persian Gulf in 9-87, with two 12.7-mm mg and portable U.S. Stinger missiles added; they may be sold to Kuwait on completion of their tours. M 850 to reserve 23-1-87, M 851 on 16-1-87, and M 852 on 21-6-87, the latter replaced by M 855, which had been undergoing extensive repairs after a grounding. The 20-mm AA is not normally aboard.

◆ **10 Dokkum class**

| | | | | |
|---|---|---|---|---|
| M 802 HOOGEZAND (ex-MSC 173) | Gusto/F.A. Smulders, Schiedam | 18-7-53 | 22-3-55 | 7-11-55 |
| M 809 NAALDWIJK (ex-MSC 175) | De Noord, Alblasserdam | 2-11-53 | 1-2-55 | 8-12-55 |
| M 810 ABCOUDE (ex-MSC 176) | Gusto/F.A. Smulders, Schiedam | 10-11-53 | 2-9-55 | 18-5-56 |
| M 812 DRACHTEN (ex-MSC 177) | Niestern SB, Hellevoetsluis | 9-12-53 | 24-3-55 | 27-1-56 |
| M 813 OMMEN (ex-MSC 178) | J. & K. Smits, Kinderdijk | 22-12-53 | 5-4-55 | 19-4-56 |
| M 815 GIETHOORN (ex-MSC 179) | L. Smit & Son, Kinderdijk | 22-12-53 | 30-3-55 | 29-3-56 |
| M 817 VENLO (ex-MSC 180) | Arnhemse SB, Arnhem | 10-2-54 | 21-5-55 | 26-4-56 |
| M 823 NAARDEN (ex-MSC 183) | Wilton-Fijenoord, Schiedam | 28-10-54 | 27-1-56 | 18-5-56 |
| M 827 HOOGEVEEN (ex-MSC 184) | De Noord, Alblasserdam | 1-2-55 | 8-5-56 | 6-11-56 |
| M 841 GEMERT (ex-MSC 187) | J. & K. Smits, Kinderdijk | 5-4-55 | 13-3-56 | 7-9-56 |

**Abcoude (M 810)** B. Prézelin, 6-87

**Naarden (M 823)** M. Louagie, 5-87

**D:** 373 tons (453 fl) **S:** 15 kts **Dim:** 46.62 × 8.75 × 2.28 **A:** 1/20-mm AA
**Electron Equipt:** Radar: 1/Decca TM 1229C
**M:** 2 Fijenoord-M.A.N. V 64 diesels; 2 props; 2,500 hp
**Range:** 2,500/10 **Man:** 38 tot.

REMARKS: Wooden construction units of same basic design as British "Ton" and French *Sirius* classes, funded by U.S. All units of the similar *Wildervank* class were disposed of by 1976. Four *Dokkums* converted to function as minehunters (with Plessey Type 193M sonar) during 1968–73 have recently been disposed of: *Dokkum* (M 801), placed in unmaintained reserve 4-83, was retrieved for use in oil fuel trials in 1984; *Drunen* (M 818) was stricken 19-4-84; *Staphorst* (M 828) was stricken 20-1-84; and *Veere* (M 842) was stricken 19-10-84. The original 2/40-mm "Boffin" AA mounts began to be replaced by a single 20-mm Oerlikon AA forward in all from 1982 on.

Of the three remaining units reconfigured as mine-disposal divers' tenders, *Rhenen* (M 844, ex-MSC 189) was stricken 1-1-84 and sold for scrap 12-3-86; *Roermond* (M 806, ex-MSC 174) was stricken 16-4-87; and *Woerden* (M 820, ex-MSC 182) was redesignated as a general-purpose auxiliary (A 882) for service in the Netherlands Antilles in 1986. *Sittard* (M 830) stricken 12-6-87. M 827, placed in reserve 5-11-82, was reactivated 1986. The surviving active units are expected to serve until the early 1990s.

## AMPHIBIOUS WARFARE SHIPS AND CRAFT

◆ **0 (+1) large landing ship**

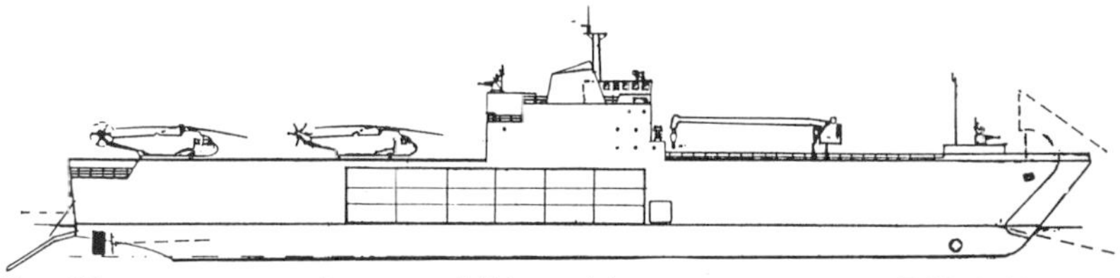
Possible appearance of new amphibious ship R.Neth.N., 1987

REMARKS: The 1987 Defense plan indicated that the 1993–97 construction program would include an 8,000-ton landing ship to transport 600 Marines. A true landing assault ship has been a long-term goal of the Royal Netherlands Marines, who must depend on the ships of other NATO nations to transport them.

◆ **6 LCA Mk 2 landing craft** Bldr: Naval Shipyard, Den Helder

| | |
|---|---|
| L 9530 (In serv. 10-10-84) | L 9533 (In serv. 13-12-85) |
| L 9531 (In serv. 20-12-84) | L 9534 (In serv. 13-12-85) |
| L 9532 (In serv. 4-7-85) | L 9535 (In serv. 5-1-87) |

**L 9530** L. & L. Van Ginderen, 9-85

**D:** 8.5 tons (13.6 fl) **S:** 11 kts **Dim:** 16.0 × 4.4 × 1.3
**A:** 1/7.62-mm mg **Electron Equipt:** Radar: 1/Decca 110
**M:** 1 DAF-Turbo diesel; 1 Schottel swivelling prop; 260 hp
**Range:** 220/11 **Man:** 3 crew + 25 troops

REMARKS: Glass-reinforced plastic construction, intended to replace the 10 LCA Mk 1 completed 1962–64. Were to have been 12, but only six have been ordered. Can carry a Land Rover truck or BV 202 tracked snow vehicle in place of the 25 troops.

◆ **6 LCA Mk 1 landing craft** Bldrs: L 9512, 9513: Naval SY, Den Helder; L 9514, 9515: A. La Comte, Jutphaas; others: Verolme, Heusden

L 9512 L 9513 L 9514 L 9515 L 9518 L 9520

**D:** 8.5 tons (13.6 fl) **S:** 11.6 kts **Dim:** 14.45 × 3.82 × 1.3
**A:** 1/7.62-mm mg **Man:** 3 tot., plus 25 troops
**M:** 1 Rolls-Royce diesel; 1 Schottel propeller; 200 hp

REMARKS: GRP construction. Sisters L 9510, L 9511, L 9517, and L 9522 stricken 1987.

## AMPHIBIOUS WARFARE SHIPS AND CRAFT *(continued)*

**L 9515** L. & L. Van Ginderen, 7-82

## HYDROGRAPHIC SHIPS

◆ **1 Tydeman class** Bldr: B.V. De Merwede, Hardinxveld-Giessendam

| | Laid down | L | In serv. |
|---|---|---|---|
| A 906 Tydeman | 29-4-75 | 18-12-75 | 10-11-76 |

**Tydeman (A 906)**—white hull, buff stack, orange boats L. & L. Van Ginderen, 3-85

**Tydeman (A 906)** P. Voss, 11-85

**D:** 3,000 tons (fl) **S:** 15 kts **Dim:** 90.15 × 14.43 × 4.75
**M:** 3 Stork-Werkspoor 8-FCHD-240 diesels, electric drive; 1 prop; 2,730 hp; 2 bow-thrusters; 1 active rudder
**Electric:** 1,400 kw **Range:** 10,300/13.5; 15,700/10.3
**Man:** 59 men, 15 civilians

Remarks: Assigned to civilian and military research. Hangar and flight deck for one small helicopter. Eight laboratories. Any two of the three main diesels power the propulsion motors, the other then provides ship's service power.

◆ **2 Blommendal class** Bldr: Boele S & M, Bolnes

| | Laid down | L | In serv. |
|---|---|---|---|
| A 904 Buyskes | 31-1-72 | 11-7-72 | 9-3-73 |
| A 905 Blommendal | 1-8-72 | 21-11-72 | 22-5-73 |

**D:** 867 tons (1,025 fl) **S:** 14 kts **Dim:** 58.80 × 11.13 × 3.70
**M:** 2 Paxman 742-hp 12 RPHCZ7 diesels, Smit electric drive; 1 prop; 1,100 hp
**Electric:** 745 kw **Range:** 7,000/10 **Man:** 43 tot.

Remarks: Carry two survey launches and two chain-clearance drag boats. Automated data-logging system. Used in wreck surveys; have sidescan sonar; wire-drag equipment.

**Buyskes (A 904)** L. & L. Van Ginderen, 11-86

## REPLENISHMENT SHIPS

Note: Construction of two replenishment oilers is planned, one to replace *Poolster* and the other to permit three task groups to operate independently.

◆ **1 improved Poolster class** Bldr: Verolme, Alblasserdam

| | Laid down | L | In serv. |
|---|---|---|---|
| A 832 Zuiderkruis | 16-7-73 | 15-10-74 | 27-6-75 |

**Zuiderkruis (A 832)** H. Ehlers, 2-87

**D:** 17,357 tons **S:** 21 kts **Dim:** 169.59 (157.00 pp) × 20.3 × 8.4 (max.)
**A:** 2/20-mm AA (I × 2), 1/d.c. rack (8 d.c.)
**Electron Equipt:** Radar: 2/Decca 1226
EW: passive syst., Mk 36 Super RBOC decoy RL (VI × 4)
**M:** 2 Werkspoor TM 410 16-cyl. diesels; 2 props; 21,000 hp **Electric:** 3,000 kw
**Man:** 17 officers, 26 petty officers, 130 men

Remarks: Cargo capacity: 9,000 tons fuel, 400 tons TR-5, 200 tons fresh water, spare parts, ammunition. Hangar for three Lynx helicopters. Can carry ASW torpedoes and other stores to support up to five ASW helicopters. Two fueling stations per side, amidships, and one sliding-stay, constant-tension, solid transfer station each side, forward.

◆ **1 Poolster class** Bldr: Rotterdamse Droogdok Mij, Rotterdam

| | Laid down | L | In serv. |
|---|---|---|---|
| A 835 Poolster | 18-9-62 | 16-10-63 | 10-9-64 |

**Poolster (A 835)** L. & L. Van Ginderen, 11-86

**D:** 16,836 tons (fl) **S:** 21 kts **Dim:** 168.41 (157.00 pp) × 20.33 × 8.24
**A:** 2/40-mm AA (I × 2)—1/d.c. rack (8 d.c.)
**Electron Equipt:** Radar: 1/Decca 1229, 1/Decca 2459
Sonar: 1/CWE-610
EW: passive syst., Mk 36 Super RBOC decoy RL (VI × 4)
**M:** 2 sets GT; 1 prop; 22,500 hp **Boilers:** 2
**Electric:** 2,100 kw **Man:** 200 tot.

**REPLENISHMENT SHIPS** *(continued)*

Remarks: Cargo capacity: 10,300 tons, including 8,000 tons of fuel. Hangar for three Lynx helicopters. Also a combat supply ship capable of participating effectively in antisubmarine warfare with a hunter/killer group, thanks to her ability to handle three Lynx ASW helicopters, if required. For short distances, she can carry 300 Marines as well as her own crew. Decca 2459 dual F/I-band radar replaced DA-01 radar 1983 for trials. A 835 will operate into the mid-1990s.

## TENDERS

◆ **1 new-construction torpedo-trials ship** Bldr: De Schelde, Vlissingen

| | Laid down | L | In serv. |
|---|---|---|---|
| A 900 Mercuur | 6-11-85 | 25-10-86 | 21-8-87 |

**Mercuur (A 900)** L. & L. Van Ginderen, 7-87

**D:** 1,200 tons (1,500 fl) **S:** 14 kts **Dim:** 64.85 × 12.00 × 4.30
**A:** 2/12.7-m mg (I × 2)—2/533-mm TT (underwater)—3/324-mm ASW TT (III × 1)—mines
**Electron Equipt:** Radar: . . .—Sonar: . . .
**M:** 2 Brons-M.A.N. diesel generator sets (650 kw each); electric drive; 2 props; . . . hp—bow-thruster
**Man:** 6 officers, 30 men + 3 trials personnel

Remarks: Ordered 13-6-84 to replace U.S. *Agile*-class former minesweeper of the same name as torpedo-trials ship. An ASW escort version of the design is offered commercially. Has a helicopter deck above the torpedo workshop.

Note: The U.S. *Agile*-class torpedo trials ship *Mercuur* (A 856, ex-*Onverschrokken*, M 886, ex-U.S. MSO 483) was decommissioned 12-2-87, but was to be retained for an unspecified period for trials with new minesweeping equipment. The smaller torpedo trials ship *Van Bochove* (A 923) was stricken 18-12-86.

◆ **1 Dokkum-class general-purpose tender, former minesweeper**

| | Bldr | Laid down | L | In serv. |
|---|---|---|---|---|
| A 882 Woerden, (ex-M 806, ex-MSC 174) | Haarlemse SB, Haarlem | 10-8-54 | 28-11-56 | 24-4-57 |

**D:** 373 tons (453 fl) **S:** 15 kts **Dim:** 46.62 × 8.75 × 2.28
**A:** none **Electron Equipt:** Radar: 1/Decca TM 1229C
**M:** 2 Fijenoord-M.A.N. V64 diesels; 2 props; 2,500 hp
**Range:** 2,500/10 **Man:** . . .

Remarks: Wooden construction. Redesignated as general-purpose tender for Netherlands Antilles Service in 1986, having earlier been converted as a mine countermeasures divers' support tender.

◆ **1 U.S. Agile-class mine-countermeasures support ship** Bldr: Astoria Marine, Astoria, Ore. (In reserve)

| | Laid down | L | In serv. |
|---|---|---|---|
| A 855 Onbevreesd (ex-M 885, ex-MSO 481) | 8-12-52 | 7-11-53 | 21-9-54 |

**Onbevreesd (A 855)** G. Gyssels, 1981

**D:** 735 tons (790 fl) **S:** 15.5 kts **Dim:** 52.7 × 10.75 × 3.7
**A:** 1/40-mm AA—2/d.c. racks
**Electron Equipt:** Radar: 1/Kelvin-Hughes 14/9—Sonar: QCU-2
**M:** 2 G.M. 8-278A diesels; 2 CP props; 1,600 hp **Electric:** 560 kw
**Fuel:** 47 tons **Range:** 3,000/10 **Man:** 67 tot.

Remarks: Former ocean minesweeper. Typed "escort ship" and intended to serve as flagship for a mine-countermeasures force and to lay mines in exercises. Sister *Onversaagd* was stricken in 31-7-79, and *Onvervaard* (A 858) and *Onverdroten* (A 859) were stricken 15-5-82 and returned to U.S. Navy control 8-7-83; scrapped 1-85. A 855 is in low-maintenance reserve.

## TUGS

◆ **2 (+2) Linge-class coastal tugs** Bldr: Delta SY, Sliedrecht (hulls for A 874, A 875 by Scheepswerf Bijlsmz B.V., Wartena)

| | Laid down | L | In serv. |
|---|---|---|---|
| A 874 Linge | 12-6-86 | 15-11-86 | 20-2-87 |
| A 875 Regge | 23-6-86 | 10-1-87 | 6-5-87 |
| A 876 Hunze | . . . | . . . | . . . |
| A 877 Rotte | . . . | . . . | . . . |

**Linge (A 874)** L. & L. Van Ginderen, 2-87

**D:** . . . **S:** 12.5 kts **Dim:** 27.45 (26.30 pp) × 8.30 × 3.80
**Electron Equipt:** Radar: 1/ . . . nav.
**M:** 2 Stork Werkspoor Type DRO 218 K diesels; 2 Kort-nozzle props; 1,632 hp
**Fuel:** 55 tons **Electric:** 192 kw **Man:** 7 tot.

Remarks: Other sources report hulls for first pair by Gruensscheepwerf, Leeuwarden.

◆ **2 Westgat-class coastal tugs** Bldr: Rijkswerf Willemsoord, Den Helder

| | Laid down | L | In serv. |
|---|---|---|---|
| A 872 Westgat | 3-4-67 | 22-8-67 | 10-1-68 |
| A 873 Wielingen | 28-8-67 | 6-1-68 | 31-5-68 |

**Westgat (A 872)** L. & L. Van Ginderen, 11-86

**D:** 206 tons (fl) **S:** 12 kts **Dim:** 27.18 × 6.97 × 2.34
**A:** none **Electron Equipt:** 1/Kelvin-Hughes 14/9
**M:** 1 Bolnes diesel; 1 prop; 720 hp **Man:** 9 tot.

TUGS *(continued)*

REMARKS: Will be replaced by new tugs *Hunze* and *Rotte,* above, on completion.

NOTE: The coastal tug *Wambrau* (A 871) was stricken 6-5-87 and sold 3-7-87.

## TRAINING SHIPS

◆ **1 Balder-class former patrol boat** Bldr: Rijkswerf Willemsoord, Den Helder

| | Laid down | L | In serv. |
|---|---|---|---|
| A 880 BULGIA (ex-P 803, ex-SC 1628) | 10-53 | 24-4-54 | 9-8-54 |

**Bulgia (A 880)** L. & L. Van Ginderen, 10-87

**D:** 150 tons (163 fl) **S:** 15.5 kts **Dim:** 36.35 (35.00 pp) × 6.21 × 1.80
**A:** none **Electron Equipt:** Radar: 1/. . . nav.
**M:** 2 Werkspoor RUB 1612 diesels; 2 props; 1,050 hp
**Range:** 1,000/13 **Electric:** 60 kw **Man:** . . .

REMARKS: Redesignated as navigational training craft for midshipmen 14-11-86. Sister *Hadda* (P 805) retained as source of space parts. Built with U.S. "Offshore Construction" funds. Carried 4/20-mm AA (I × 4) and 2 d.c. in drop racks when last used in patrol duties.

◆ **1 former pilot ship**

| | Bldr | Laid down | L | In serv. |
|---|---|---|---|---|
| A 903 ZEEFAKKEL | J. & K. Smit, Kinderjik | 28-11-49 | 21-7-50 | 16-3-51 |

**Zeefakkel (A 903)** G. Gyssels, 6-87

**D:** 303 tons (384 fl) **S:** 12 kts **Dim:** 45.38 × 7.5 × 2.2
**M:** 2 Smit-M.A.N. diesels; 2 props; 640 hp **Man:** 26 tot.

REMARKS: Used for seamanship training at Den Helder.

◆ **1 sail-training ketch**

| | Bldr | L | In serv. |
|---|---|---|---|
| Y 8050 URANIA (ex-*Tromp*) | Haarlemse Scheepsbouw Mij. | 1929 | 23-4-38 |

**D:** 76.4 tons (fl) **S:** 5 kts (10 under sail) **Dim:** 23.94 × 5.29 × 3.15
**M:** 1 Kromhout diesel; 1 prop; 65 hp (625-$m^2$ sail area) **Man:** 17 tot.

◆ **1 former Holland-class destroyer**

| | Bldr | Laid down | L | In serv. |
|---|---|---|---|---|
| D 811 GELDERLAND | Wilton-Fijenoord, Schiedam | 10-3-51 | 19-9-53 | 18-8-55 |

**D:** 2,215 tons (2,765 fl) **S:** 32 kts **Dim:** 111.3 × 11.33 × 3.88
**A:** none **M:** 2 sets Parsons GT; 2 props; 45,000 hp
**Electric:** 1,350 kw **Boilers:** 4 Babcock & Wilcox

**Urania (Y 8050)** L. & L. Van Ginderen, 8-86

**Gelderland (D 811)**—radar antennas remounted H. Ehlers, 9-85

REMARKS: Since 1973 used for technical training at Rotterdam and for accommodations. Does not get underway. Two twin 120-mm DP guns mounted on destroyers *Tromp* and *De Ruyter.*

NOTE: There are also 24 small sports and training sail yachts under naval control. Former *Dokkum*-class minesweeper *Grypskerk* (ex-M 826) donated to Sea Cadets in 1985.

## ACCOMMODATIONS SHIPS

◆ **1 non-self-propelled** Bldr: de Schelde, Vlissingen (In serv. 27-6-85)

A 887 THETIS

**Thetis (A 887)** L. & L. Van Ginderen, 3-85

**D:** 1,000 tons (fl) **Dim:** 68.47 (62.85 pp) × 12.82 × 1.60

REMARKS: Launched 1-83. Replaced former gunboat *Soemba* (A 891) as accommodations barge at Den Oever for use by diver and frogman trainees. Three floating fenders, delivered 1986, serve with A 887: Y 8611, Y 8612, Y 8613. The former cargo lighter *Tax* (Y 8500) is moored with *Thetis* to provide additional accommodations.

ACCOMMODATIONS SHIPS *(continued)*

**Tax (Y 8500)** L. & L. Van Ginderen, 10-81

◆ **1 non-self-propelled** Bldr: Voorwarts SY, Hoogezand

| | Laid down | L | In serv. |
|---|---|---|---|
| A 886 CORNELIUS DREBBEL | 18-5-70 | 19-11-70 | 30-11-71 |

**D:** 775 tons (fl) **Dim:** 63.22 × 11.82 × 1.1 **Man:** 201 tot.

REMARKS: Stationed at Rotterdam to serve ships in overhaul.

SERVICE CRAFT

◆ **5 steel workboats** Bldr: Deltawerf, Sliedrecht

Y 8055 SCHELDE (In serv. 12-2-87)
Y 8056 WIERBALG (In serv. 18-2-87)
Y 8057 MALZWIN (In serv. 24-12-86)
Y 8058 ZUIDWAL (In serv. 1-12-86)
Y 8059 WESTWAL (In serv. 29-12-86)

**Schelde (Y 8055)** H. Ehlers, 6-87

**D:** . . . **S:** . . . **Dim:** 10.80 × 3.76 × 1.60 **M:** DAF diesel; 1 prop; 115 hp

◆ **2 sludge barges** Bldr: Scheepswerf DeHoop B.V., Lobith

Y 8351 Y 8352 (Both in serv. 3-9-86)

**D:** . . . **Dim:** 25.25 × 6.24 × 3.30

◆ **1 fuel lighter** Bldr: H.H. Bodewes, Millingen (In serv. 1963)

Y 8536 PATRIA

**D:** 827 dwt **S:** . . . **Dim:** 61.6 × 8.1 × . . .
**M:** 1 Bolnes diesel; 1 prop; . . . hp **Man:** . . . tot.

REMARKS: Purchased 1978. Based at Den Helder.

◆ **6 fuel barges**

Y 8538 (In serv. 1955)
Y 8335 (In serv. 1952)
Y 8347 (In serv. 2-3-83)
Y 8348 (In serv. 20-7-83)
Y 8349 (In serv. 5-11-83)
Y 8350 (In serv. 5-11-83)

◆ **1 torpedo lighter:** Y 8512 (In serv. 1956)

◆ **1 small cargo lighter:** Y 8501 (In serv. 1951)

◆ **1 harbor launch:** Y 8011 (In serv. 1974)

**D:** . . . **Dim:** 11.38 × 3.54 × . . . **M:** 1 diesel; 60 hp

◆ **1 personnel launch:** Y 8217 (In serv. 1951–52)

REMARKS: U.S. Coast Guard 40-ft. utility boat design. Sisters Y 8216 and Y 8220 returned to U.S. control 13-2-87.

**Y 8512 torpedo lighter** L. & L. Van Ginderen, 8-83

◆ **2 steam supply craft:** Y 8122 (In serv. 1937), Y 8260 (In serv. 1940)

◆ **1 tank-cleaning boat:** Y 8262 (In serv. 1918)

◆ **1 hull-cleaning boat:** Y 8263 (In serv. 1967)

◆ **1 floating crane:** Y 8514 (In serv. 1974)

**Y 8514** L. & L. Van Ginderen, 4-82

◆ **1 wreck simulation craft:** Y 8690

◆ **1 target barge:** Y 8704 (acquired 5-86)

◆ **6 fast target craft** (In serv. 1982–83)

Y 8694 Y 8699–8703

◆ **14 dry-cargo barges** (In serv. 1900–1965): Y 8299, Y 8321, Y 8322, Y 8324, Y 8327, Y 8331, Y 8332, Y 8333, Y 8334, Y 8337, Y 8338, Y 8339, Y 8340, Y 8341,

◆ **10 mooring pontoons:** Y 8594, Y 8595 (In serv. 1956); Y 8606, Y 8607 (In serv. 3-2-81); Y 8604, Y 8605 (In serv. 14-10-83); Y 8614, Y 8615, Y 8616, Y 8617 (acquired 25-9-86)

## SERVICE CRAFT *(continued)*

◆ **13 miscellaneous barges:** Y 8600, Y 8601, Y 8602, Y 8603, Y 8711, Y 8713, Y 8714, Y 8590, Y 8592, Y 8579 (In serv. 30-5-86), Y 8580 (In serv. 18-12-85), Y 8551 (In serv. 2-4-86), Y 8552 (In serv. 28-5-86)

◆ **3 floating fenders for *Thetis* (A 887):** Y 8611, Y 8612, Y 8613 (In serv. 1986)

◆ **2 floating dry docks**

Y 8678 RW 22 (In serv. 1949) Y 8679 RW 60 (In serv. 1960)

Remarks: RW 22 is 40.0 × 9.0 × 3.8, with a 420-ton capacity. RW 60 is 40.0 × 10.6 × 4.0, with a 450-ton capacity. Both based at Willemsoord.

Note: Other service craft recently stricken include water tanker Y 8480 in 1987, communications tender *Dreg IV* (Y 8620) in 1987, electrical supply barge Y 8676 in 14-5-86, dry-cargo barges Y 8328 and 8330 on 22-5-86, pontoon barge Y 8716 on 19-4-86, dry-cargo barges Y 8325 and Y 8403 on 16-6-87 and 24-4-87, respectively.

◆ **1 Dokkum-class fuel-trials craft, former minehunter**

| | Bldr | Laid down | L | In serv. |
|---|---|---|---|---|
| Y 8001 Van Speijk (ex-*Dokkum*, M 801, ex-MSC 172) | Wilton Fijenoord, Schiedam | 15-6-53 | 12-10-54 | 26-7-55 |

**Van Speijk (Y 8001)**—note box beside stack H. Ehlers, 6-87

Remarks: Details generally as for minesweeper sisters; no armament. After having been placed in unmaintained reserve in 4-83, was reclaimed and adapted for testing fuels. Renamed 1-11-86 to keep tradition of a *Van Speijk* in R.Neth.N. service.

◆ **3 Berkel-class harbor tugs** Bldr: H.H. Bodewes, Millingen

| | Laid down | L | In serv. |
|---|---|---|---|
| Y 8037 Berkel | 27-4-56 | 29-9-56 | 27-12-57 |
| Y 8038 Dintel | 22-5-56 | 17-11-56 | 23-1-57 |
| Y 8040 IJssel | 17-9-56 | 19-1-57 | 20-3-57 |

**Dintel (Y 8038)** S. Terzibaschitsch, 6-86

**D:** 163.4 tons (fl) **S:** 10.6 kts **Dim:** 25.09 × 6.27 × 2.45
**M:** 1 Werkspoor diesel; 1 Kort-nozzle prop; 500 hp **Man:** 5 tot.

Remarks: Sister *Dommel* (Y 8039) stricken early 1987; other three were to follow by year's end.

◆ **2 Bambi-class harbor tugs** Bldr: Rijkswerf Willemsoord, Den Helder

Y 8016 Bambi (L: 12-5-53) Y 8017 Dombo (L: 25-5-57)

**Dombo (Y 8017)** H. Ehlers, 9-83

**D:** 43 tons (fl) **S:** . . . kts **Dim:** 16.58 × 4.63 × 1.9
**M:** 1 Bolnes diesel; 1 prop; 200 hp **Man:** 4 tot.

◆ **1 small harbor tug** Bldr: Foxhol (In serv. 1938)

Y 8028 (ex-A 868, ex-RS 28, ex-KM 15, ex-*Eems*)

**Y 8028** L. & L. Van Ginderen, 8-86

**D:** 70 tons (fl) **S:** . . . kts **Dim:** 19.5 × 5.1 × 2.3
**M:** 1 Bolnes diesel; 1 prop; 200 hp **Man:** 7 tot.

Note: Small tug Y 8014 (ex-A 857, ex-RS 17, ex-OZD 4, ex-*Jade*) stricken 28-7-87 and sold 22-9-87.

◆ **3 Triton-class diving tenders** Bldr: Rijkswerf Willemsoord, Den Helder

| | Laid down | L | In serv. |
|---|---|---|---|
| A 848 Triton (ex-Y 8125) | 3-2-64 | 27-2-64 | 5-8-64 |
| A 849 Nautilus (ex-Y 8126) | 17-3-64 | 1-5-64 | 20-4-65 |
| A 850 Hydra (ex-Y 8127) | 21-5-64 | 1-7-64 | 20-4-65 |

**Triton (A 848)** H. Ehlers, 8-85

**SERVICE CRAFT** *(continued)*

**D:** 69.3 tons (fl) **S:** 9 kts **Dim:** 23.28 × 5.15 × 1.35
**M:** 1 Volvo Penta diesel; 1 prop; 105 hp **Man:** 8 tot.

◆ **1 training tender for divers** Bldr: Rijkswerf Willemsoord, Den Helder

| | Laid down | L | In serv. |
| --- | --- | --- | --- |
| A 847 Argus (ex-Y 8124, ex-Y 8651, ex-A 950, ex-RD 10, ex-MOD IV, ex-D1) | 18-5-38 | 6-12-38 | 10-5-39 |

**D:** 44.5 tons (fl) **S:** 8 kts **Dim:** 23.0 × 4.68 × 1.05
**M:** 1 Kromhout diesel; 1 prop; 144 hp **Man:** 8 tot.

NETHERLANDS NATIONAL POLICE FORCE
(MINISTRY OF JUSTICE)

Note: This organization operates about 70 patrol craft, of which only the *De Ruiter* class, listed below, is considered seagoing. A number of other jurisdictions, including the Customs Service of the Ministry of Finance, the Rotterdam City Police, and the Department of Communications, also operate patrol craft. Some 20 marine service organizations are to be combined to form a single Coast Guard.

◆ **4 RP 16 class** Bldr: Schottel, Warmond

RP 16 (In serv. 1-84) RP 20 (In serv. 7-84) RP 63 (In serv. 10-84)
RP . . . (In serv. 1986)

**RP 16** L. & L. Van Ginderen, 6-84

**D:** 30 tons **S:** 19 kts **Dim:** 23.50 × 5.30 × 1.60
**Electron Equipt:** 1/Racal Decca . . . nav.
**M:** 3 M.A.N. D282-ME diesels; 3 props: 1,266 hp **Man:** 6 tot.

Remarks: Fourth unit ordered 1985.

◆ **8 15-meter class** Bldr: Schottel, Warmond

RP 59 (In serv. 1982) RP 63 (In serv. 1984) RP 69 (In serv. 4-2-83)
RP 70 (In serv. 12-84) RP . . . RP . . .
RP . . . RP . . .

**RP 59** L. & L. Van Ginderen, 1-87

**D:** 17.5 tons **S:** 17 kts **Dim:** 15.36 × 3.78 × 1.25
**M:** RP 69: 2 DAF DKA-1160M diesels; 2 props; 440 hp; others: 1 M.A.N. D2842-ME diesel; 1 prop; 422 hp
**Man:** 3 or 4 tot.

◆ **3 De Ruiter class** Bldr: Schottel, Warmond

RP 15 De Ruiter (In serv. 5-79) RP . . . N . . . . . . RP . . . N . . . . . .

**D:** 27 tons (fl) **S:** 18.5 kts **Dim:** 19.13 × 4.27 × 1.3
**M:** 2 12-cyl. diesels; 2 Schottel vertical cycloidal props; 680 hp **Man:** 3–4 tot.

Remarks: The second and third were ordered 6-80.

◆ **5 RP 17 class** Bldr: Le Comte, Vianen, 1974

RP 17 RP 26 RP . . . RP . . . RP. . .

**RP 17** L. & L. Van Ginderen, 6-84

**D:** 29 tons **S:** 15 kts **Dim:** 15.75 × 3.83 × 1.05
**M:** 1 MTU OM403 diesel; 1 Schottel vertical cycloidal prop; 250 hp

Note: Two 15-m, single-screw craft ordered 1985 from Schottel; no details available.

◆ **7 10.8-meter class** Bldr: Le Comte, Vianen, 1970

RP 40 RP 53 etc.

**D:** 8.5 tons **S:** 14.5 kts **Dim:** 10.8 × 3.22 × 1.2
**M:** 1 MTU OM346 diesel; 1 Schottel prop; 165 hp

◆ **RP 10** Bldr: Schuiten, Muiden, 1968

**RP 10** L. & L. Van Ginderen, 9-85

**D:** 70 tons (fl) **S:** 14 kts **Dim:** 23.0 × . . . × . . .
**M:** 1 Bolnes GDNL diesel; 600 hp

◆ **RP 3** Bldr: Koopman, Dordrecht, 1967

**D:** 60 tons (fl) **S:** 12.7 kts **Dim:** 22.0 × 5.3 × 1.5
**M:** 2 G.M. 12V71 diesels; 2 props; 670 hp

MINISTRY OF FINANCE
(CUSTOMS)

**PATROL BOATS AND CRAFT**

◆ **1 Stan Patrol 2600 class** Bldr: Damen SY, Gorinchem

Zeevalk (In serv. 1981)

**D:** 85 tons (96 fl) **S:** 25 kts **Dim:** 26.50 (24.27 pp) × 5.80 × 1.80
**Electron Equipt:** Radar: 1/. . . nav.
**M:** 2 MTU 12V396 TC83 diesels; 2 props; 2,966 hp
**Range:** 600/14 **Man:** 6 tot.

Remarks: Sisters in Hong Kong service.

**MINISTRY OF FINANCE** *(continued)*

**Zeevalk** L. & L. Van Ginderen, 1983

◆ **1 large patrol boat** Bldr: Schottel, Warmond

Dolfijn

**Dolfijn** L. & L. Van Ginderen, 9-85

Remarks: No details available. The Customs Service operates five large and 18 inland patrol craft altogether.

## MINISTRY OF TRANSPORT AND PUBLIC WORKS

Subordinated to this organization are over 320 ships and craft operated by three agencies: the Director General of Public Works, the Director General of Shipping and Maritime Affairs, and the Director General for Telecommunications.

### *DIRECTOR GENERAL OF PUBLIC WORKS*

In service in 1987 were five seagoing survey ships, five coastal survey craft, one large pollution-control ship, 48 survey and inspection launches, and nearly 200 riverine craft. Typical units are:

◆ **1 survey ship** Bldr: Damen SY, Vianen

Mitra (In serv. 2-7-82)

**Mitra** L. & L. Van Ginderen, 1984

**D:** 1,223 grt **S:** 12 kts **Dim:** 56.3 × 11.6 × . . .
**M:** 2 500-hp diesels, 1 297-hp diesel **Man:** 10 tot.

◆ **1 coastal survey ship**

Octans

**Octans** L. & L. Van Ginderen, 1981

Remarks: No data available.

◆ **1 pollution-control ship** Bldr: Boelwerf, Temse

Smal Agt (In serv. 1961)

**Smal Agt** L. & L. Van Ginderen, 9-84

**D:** 1,132 grt **S:** 10 kts **Dim:** 54.0 × 9.2 × 3.5
**M:** 2 diesels; . . . props; 600 hp **Man:** 10 tot.

Remarks: Former dump barge rebuilt 1976 by De Groot & Van Vliet for pollution-control duties.

### *DIRECTOR GENERAL OF SHIPPING AND MARITIME AFFAIRS*

The Pilot Service was under R. Neth. Navy control until 1981, and its seagoing pilot ships can be armed with 1/40-mm AA for patrol duties. In addition to the larger units described below, the Director General of Shipping and Maritime Affairs also operates five coastal buoy tenders, 29 patrol boats, and a number of small pilot craft. See 1980–81 edition for details of smaller units.

◆ **3 Mirfak-class pilot vessels** Bldr: A. Vuyk & Sons, Capelle-on-IJssel

| | Laid down | L | In serv. |
|---|---|---|---|
| Mirfak (ex-A830) | 22-7-76 | 4-12-76 | 9-5-77 |
| Menkar (ex-A829) | 17-12-76 | 28-5-77 | 9-12-77 |
| Markab (ex-A . . .) | . . . | . . . | 1978 |

**D:** 1,080 tons (fl) **S:** 13 kts **Dim:** 59.00 (56.33 pp) × 10.60 × 3.80
**A:** provision for 2/40-mm AA (I × 2) **Electron Equipt:** Radar: 2/. . . nav.
**M:** 3 Stork-Werkspoor DRO 216 K diesels, electric drive; 1 prop; 1,400 hp

Remarks: 864 grt/233 nrt. Helicopter deck aft

SHIPPING AND MARITIME AFFAIRS *(continued)*

**Mirfak** L. & L. Van Ginderen, 10-85

◆ **3 Altair-class pilot vessels** Bldr: C. Amels B.V., Makkum

| | Laid down | L | In serv. |
|---|---|---|---|
| ALTAIR (ex-A805) | 8-5-73 | 26-1-74 | 15-3-74 |
| FOMALHAUT (ex-A808) | 31-10-73 | 14-8-74 | 12-9-74 |
| SPICA (ex-A909) | 22-1-73 | 15-9-73 | 22-1-74 |

**Fomalhaut** L. & L. Van Ginderen, 9-84

**D:** 1,000 tons (fl) **S:** 13 kts **Dim:** 59.00 × 10.69 × 3.66
**A:** provision for 2/40-mm AA (I × 2) **Electron Equipt:** Radar: 2/. . . nav.
**M:** 2 Paxman RPHXZ 540-hp diesels, electric drive; 1 prop; 1,000 hp
**Man:** 44 tot.

REMARKS: Helicopter deck aft.

◆ **2 Capella-class pilot vessels**

| | Bldr | Laid down | L | In serv. |
|---|---|---|---|---|
| CAPELLA (ex-A809) | Boel S & M, Bolnes | 19-4-67 | 28-12-67 | 17-6-68 |
| WEGA (ex-A819) | A. Vuyk, Capelle | 2-10-67 | 14-3-68 | 23-7-68 |

**D:** 1,000 tons (fl) **S:** 13 kts **Dim:** 59.00 (53.95 pp) × 10.67 × 3.70
**A:** provision for 2/40-mm AA (I × 2) **Electron Equipt:** Radar: 2/. . . nav.
**M:** 3 Paxman RPHXZ diesels; electric drive; 1 prop; 1,200 hp

REMARKS: Helicopter deck aft.

**Wega** L. & L. Van Ginderen, 1984

**Pilot Boat No. 10** L. & L. Van Ginderen, 6-85

*DIRECTOR GENERAL FOR TELECOMMUNICATIONS*

Operates one cable layer and four riverine craft.

◆ **1 cable layer** Bldr: E.J. Smit & Sons

DIRECTEUR-GENERAAL BAST (In serv. 26-4-69)

**Directeur-Generaal Bast** L. & L. Van Ginderen, 1984

**D:** 1,075 grt **S:** 10.5 kts **Dim:** 55.0 × 9.4 × 4.5 (moulded depth)
**M:** 2 diesels; 1 prop; 700 hp

REMARKS: Cable laying and recovery via bow sheaves.

ROYAL NETHERLANDS ARMY

Operates two seagoing tank landing craft, three patrol boats, and a number of river assault boats.

◆ **2 RV 40-class tank landing craft**

| | Bldr | In serv. | | Bldr | In serv. |
|---|---|---|---|---|---|
| RV40 | Grave B.V. | 22-11-79 | RV . . . | Damen, Gorinchem | 11-85 |

**D:** 815 tons **S:** 9.4 kts **Dim:** 45.8 × 9.5 × 2.5
**M:** 2 diesels; 2 props; 654 hp **Man:** 4 tot.

◆ **58 Type ASA-540 river assault boats** Bldr: Damen, Gorinchem (In serv. 1980s)

**D:** 1.8 tons (fl) **S:** 25–30 kts **Dim:** 5.40 × 1.83 × 0.1
**M:** 1 25–40-hp diesel outboard **Man:** 4–8 tot.

REMARKS: Aluminum construction.

**River assault boat** Damen, 1987

NETHERLANDS *(continued)*
ROYAL NETHERLANDS ARMY *(continued)*

◆ **. . . Type 700 Bridge Support Boat** Bldr: Damen, Gorinchem

**Type 700 Bridge Support Boat** Damen, 4-86

**D:** 6 tons (fl) **S:** 8.6 kts **Dim:** 7.00 × 2.90 × 0.75
**M:** 1 Deutz BF 8L 513 diesel; 2 props; 250 hp

Remarks: Steel construction, intended to be carried by DAF YGZ 2300 trucks and used in assembling and positioning pontoon bridges. Has 2.6-ton bollard poll. Props are full-swiveling and ducted.

◆ **1 or more diving tenders** Bldr: . . .

RV 29 Torpedisten

**Torpedisten (RV 29)** L. & L. Van Ginderen, 4-86

**Army tug RV 1 towing river bridge pontoons** L. & L. Van Ginderen, 6-86

**RV 34**—Army freight lighter L. & L. Van Ginderen, 1979

**Army patrol craft RV 169** L. & L. Van Ginderen, 9-85

# NEW ZEALAND

**Dominion of New Zealand**

Personnel (1987): 365 officers, 2,272 enlisted (plus 1,200 reserves)

Merchant Marine (1986): 118 ships—314,206 grt
(tankers: 4 ships—73,496 grt)

Naval Aviation: Seven Wasp helicopters are available for the *Leander*-class frigates and the survey ship *Monowai;* the helicopters are flown by R.N.Z.N. crews but maintained by 6-man R.N.Z.A.F. detachments. Five Lockheed P-3B Orion patrol planes belong to No. 5 Squadron, Royal New Zealand Air Force; a sixth P-3B, ex-R.A.A.F., has not yet been updated. These were modernized by Boeing over a 41-month period commencing 7-80; the first was completed 2-83. A second round of modernizations is planned to bring the aircraft up to P-3C standard. Three Fokker F-27-100 Maritime, primarily for transport, also perform search-and-rescue duties. The R.N.Z.A.F.'s 22 A-4 Skyhawks have a maritime attack role.

## FRIGATES

◆ **0 (+4) new construction** Bldr: . . . , Australia

| | Laid down | L | In serv. |
|---|---|---|---|
| F . . . N . . . | . . . | . . . | . . . |
| F . . . N . . . | . . . | . . . | . . . |
| F . . . N . . . | . . . | . . . | . . . |
| F . . . N . . . | . . . | . . . | . . . |

**FRIGATES** *(continued)*

**D:** . . . **S:** 27+ kts **Dim:** . . . × . . . × . . .
**A:** point-defense system—1/76-mm DP—6/324-mm ASW TT (III × 2)—1/helicopter
**Electron Equipt:** Radar: 1/. . . nav., 1/3-D air-search, 2/f.c. for point-defense systems
Sonar: . . .
EW: . . .
**M:** . . . **Range:** 6,000/18

REMARKS: A cooperative program with Australia, as replacements for the existing four frigates. The first two to be delivered in the 1990s; the others at the end of the decade. As of 9-87, the "short list" of competing lines included the Blohm + Voss MEKO 200, Dutch *Karel Doorman* ("M"), and Y-ARD/Yarrow light frigate (a reduced variant of the U.K. Type 23). In the R.N.Z.N. the ships will not be called frigates, to avoid disturbing public sensibilities.

◆ **2 U.K. Broad-Beam Leander class**

| | Bldr | Laid down | L | In serv. |
|---|---|---|---|---|
| F 69 WELLINGTON (ex-*Bacchante*) | Vickers-Armstrong, Newcastle | 27-10-66 | 29-2-68 | 17-10-69 |
| F 421 CANTERBURY | Yarrow, Scotstoun | 12-4-69 | 6-5-70 | 22-10-71 |

**Wellington (F 69)** L. & L. Van Ginderen, 9-86

**Canterbury (F 421)** L. & L. Van Ginderen, 2-87

**D:** F 69: 2,500 tons std. (3,184 fl); F 421: 2,470 tons light (3,638 fl)
**S:** 28 kts (30 on trials) **Dim:** 113.38 (109.73 pp) × 13.12 × 5.49 (F 69)
**A:** 2/114-mm Mk 6 DP (II × 1)—1/Sea Cat GWS.22 syst. (IV × 1)—2/12.7-mm mg (I × 2)—6/324-mm ASW TT (III × 2)—1/Wasp HAS.1 helicopter
**Electron Equipt:** Radar: 1/1006, 1/965, 1/993, 1/RCA R76C5 for 114-mm guns, 1/904 for Sea Cat.
Sonar: 1/184M (F 69: Graseby G750), 1/162M
EW: UA-8/9 passive intercept, Type 668/669 jammer, FH-12 D/F, Mk 36 SRBOC decoy RL (VI × 2)
**M:** 2 sets White-English Electric GT; 2/5-bladed props; 30,000 hp
**Boilers:** 2 Babcock & Wilcox 3-drum; 38.7 kg/cm², 450°C Superheat
**Electric:** 2,500 kw **Fuel:** 500 tons (F 69: 720)
**Range:** 4,500/12 (F 69: 6,500/12) **Man:** 15 officers, 230 men

REMARKS: F 69 was purchased and commissioned in the New Zealand Navy on 4-10-82, proceeding to Auckland for a refit scheduled to end in 1-85, but delayed to 25-8-86. The ship's 20-mm AA and chaff RL were removed prior to transfer. The Type 199 VDS was removed and stored as a spare for *Southland*. The MRS.3 gunfire-control system was replaced by the RCA R76C5 system in F 69. F 69 also received a Marconi NTC-1 communications suite, Mk 32 ASW TT removed from *Taranaki* (F 148), and U.S. Mk 36 Super RBOC decoy RL. The Limbo ASW mortar was removed. F 69 was transferred with a Wasp helicopter aboard. F 421 began refit 11-87 with new electronics but did not receive additional fuel tankage. Contract let 10-87 to study life extension into 21st century.

◆ **1 U.K. Leander class**

| | Bldr | Laid down | L | In serv. |
|---|---|---|---|---|
| F 55 WAIKATO | Harland & Wolff | 10-1-65 | 18-2-65 | 16-9-66 |

**Waikato (F 55)** L. & L. Van Ginderen, 11-85

**D:** 2,489 tons (2,906 fl) **S:** 28 kts **Dim:** 113.38 (109.73 pp) × 12.50 × 5.49
**A:** 2/114-mm Mk 6 DP (II × 1)—1/Sea Cat MRS.22 syst. (IV × 1)—6/324-mm ASW TT (III × 2)—1/HAS.1 Wasp helicopter
**Electron Equipt:** Radar: 1/978, 1/965, 1/993, 1/903, 1/904
Sonar: 1/184, 1/162B
EW: UA-8/9 intercept, FH-12 HFD/F
**M:** 2 sets White-English Electric GT; 2 5-bladed props; 30,000 hp
**Electric:** 1,900 kw **Boilers:** 2 Babcock & Wilcox; 38.7 kg/cm², 450°C
**Range:** 4,100/12 **Fuel:** 460 tons **Man:** 16 officers, 227 men

REMARKS: Originally had a Mk 10 Limbo triple ASW mortar and no ASW TT; she was refitted in 1977, when the Type 170B sonar was also removed. Became training frigate when *Otago* was stricken. Refitted summer 1986 to 11-87.

◆ **1 ex-U.K. "Ikara Leander" class**

| | Bldr | Laid down | L | In serv. |
|---|---|---|---|---|
| F 104 SOUTHLAND (ex-*Dido*, ex-*Hastings*) | Yarrow, Scotstoun | 2-12-59 | 22-12-61 | 18-9-63 |

**Southland (F 104)** R.A.N., 9-86

**D:** 2,450 tons (2,860 fl) **S:** 28 kts **Dim:** 113.38 (109.73 pp) × 12.50 × 5.49
**A:** 2/40-mm AA (I × 2)—2/Sea Cat GWS.22 syst. (IV × 2)—1/Ikara ASW syst.—6/324-mm ASW TT (III × 2)—1/HAS.1 Was helicopter
**Electron Equipt:** Radar: 1/1006, 1/994, 1/904, 1/Ikara control
Sonar: 1/184, 1/170B, 1/199VDS
EW: Argo passive intercept; Type 668/669 jammer
**M:** 2 sets White–English Electric GT; 2/5-bladed props; 30,000 hp
**Boilers:** 2 Babcock & Wilcox 3-drum; 38.7 kg/cm², 450°C Superheat
**Electric:** 1,600 kw **Fuel:** 460 tons **Range:** approx. 4,100/12
**Man:** 19 officers, 238 men

REMARKS: Purchased and transferred to New Zealand in 18-7-83, with Wasp helicopter aboard. Commissioned 21-12-83 after refit in U.K., with Limbo ASW mortar deleted and ASW TT added, Argo EW gear installed and Type 993 radar updated to Type 994. The two Sea Cat short-range SAM launchers share a single radar director. Well equipped for ASW, but little capability for AAW or surface warfare.

**PATROL BOATS AND CRAFT**

◆ **4 Pukaki-class training patrol boats** Bldr: Brooke Marine, Lowestoft, U.K.

| | L | In serv. |
|---|---|---|
| P 3568 PUKAKI | 1-3-74 | 24-2-75 |
| P 3569 ROTOITI | 8-3-74 | 24-2-75 |
| P 3570 TAUPO | 25-7-74 | 29-7-75 |
| P 3571 HAWEA | 9-9-74 | 29-7-75 |

PATROL BOATS AND CRAFT *(continued)*

**Rotoiti (P 3569)**—with armament removed R.N.Z.N., 3-87

**D:** 107 tons (140 fl) **S:** 22 kts **Dim:** 32.6 × 6.1 × 1.7
**A:** removed (see Remarks) **Electron Equipt:** Radar: 1/Decca 916
**M:** 2 Ruston-Paxman 12 YCJM diesels; 2 props; 3,000 hp
**Range:** 2,500/12 **Man:** 3 officers, 18 men

REMARKS: Primarily used for training. Can be armed with 1/81-mm mortar 12.7-mm mg combination, 2/12.7-mm mg (I × 2), and 2/7.62-mm mg (I × 2).

◆ **4 Moa-class training/patrol craft** Bldr: Whangarei Engineering Co., Auckland

| | L | In serv. | | L | In serv. |
|---|---|---|---|---|---|
| P 3553 MOA | 16-7-83 | 19-2-84 | P 3555 WAKAKURA | 29-10-84 | 26-3-85 |
| P 3554 KIWI | 7-5-84 | 2-9-84 | P 3556 HINAU | 8-5-85 | 4-10-85 |

**Wakakura (P 3555)** L. & L. Van Ginderen, 5-86

**D:** 90 tons light (110.7 fl) **S:** 12 kts **Dim:** 26.82 (24.38 wl) × 6.10 × 2.18
**A:** removed **Electron Equipt:** Radar: 1/. . . nav.
**M:** 2 Cummins KT-1150M diesels; 2 props; 730 hp **Fuel:** 11 tons
**Range:** 1,000/12 **Man:** 2 officers, 10 men (18 accom.)

REMARKS: Ordered 11-2-82 to replace the remaining HDML-type patrol craft. Design derived from Australian 88-ft torpedo retriever; survey craft *Takapu* and *Tarapunga* and diving tender *Manawanui* are to same basic design. Can be fitted with 1/12.7-mm mg. Based as follows for naval reserve training: *Moa* at Dunedin, *Kiwi* at Lyttleton, *Wakakura* at Wellington, and *Hinau* at Auckland. Receiving side-scan sonars and enhanced navigation equipment to permit use as "Q-route" (cleared passage) mine survey boats and are planned to receive influence mine countermeasures gear at a later date.

NOTE: The last HDML-type training craft, *Kuparu* (P 3563) was to be discarded during 1987.

MINE COUNTERMEASURES SHIPS

REMARKS: The R.N.Z.N. has long-range plans to acquire mine countermeasures ships during the 1990s. As an interim solution, the six *Moa/Takapu*-class craft and the survey ship *Monowai* are being outfitted with a mine location capability.

AMPHIBIOUS WARFARE SHIPS

◆ **0 (+1) new construction or conversion** Bldr: . . . (In serv. 1990)

A . . . N . .

**D:** . . . **S:** 18+ kts **Dim:** 160.0 × . . . × 8.6
**A:** . . ./20-mm AA—2/medium helicopters **Electron Equipt:** Radar: . . .
**M:** diesel **Range:** 8,000/15 **Endurance:** 40 days or more
**Man:** 60 crew; 40 air, medical, and staff; 150 troops

REMARKS: Program announced 15-7-87 to provide vehicle and troop transport to carry one company of New Zealand Army troops and their equipment, or supplies for up to 1,000 troops. Will have vehicle loading ramp but not be capable of beaching. Landing craft to be carried as well as two UH-60 Blackhawk-sized helicopters. Alternative use is for disaster relief. Will be able to refuel ships alongside underway.

HYDROGRAPHIC SURVEY SHIPS

◆ **1 converted passenger-cargo ship** Bldr: Grangemouth DY (L: 4-60)

A 06 MONOWAI (ex-*Moana Roa*)

**Monowai (A 06)**—white hull, buff stack L. & L. Van Ginderen, 2-84

**D:** 4,027 tons (fl) **S:** 13.5 kts **Dim:** 90.33 (82.30 pp) × 14.02 × 5.21
**A:** 2/20-mm AA (I × 2) **Electron Equipt:** Radar: 2/. . . nav.
**M:** 2 Clark-Sulzer 7-cyl. diesels; 2 CP props; 3,640 hp (3,080 sust.)—bow-thruster
**Fuel:** 300 tons **Range:** 12,000/13 **Man:** 11 officers, 115 men

REMARKS: Taken over from the government-run commercial service in 1974 and converted at Scott-Lithgow, Greenock, Scotland, 9-77 to 4-10-77. Telescoping hangar fitted for one Wasp helicopter. Two 10.36-meter and one 8.84-meter survey craft carried, as well as one Rotork "Sea Truck" workboat. Decca HiFix positioning system and Omega radio navigational aids installed, as well as a navigational satellite receiver. One 4-ton crane. Side-scanning mapping sonar and other sophisticated survey equipment carried. Guns added 1980. Two "Phantom HDX" remote-operated submersibles purchased in the U.S. in 2-87 to permit the ship to operate in a mine-clearance role; clearance diver support gear also added by 4-87. Predecessor *Lachlan,* a former U.K. "River"-class frigate, is used as a barracks hulk.

◆ **2 inshore survey craft** Bldr: Whangarei Eng. Ltd., Auckland

| | L | In serv. | | L | In serv. |
|---|---|---|---|---|---|
| A 07 TAKAPU | 5-6-80 | 8-7-80 | A 08 TARAPUNGA | 5-11-79 | 9-4-80 |

**Tarapunga (A 08)**—white-painted L. & L. Van Ginderen, 6-86

**D:** 90 tons (112.6 fl) **S:** 12 kts **Dim:** 26.82 (24.38 wl) × 6.10 × 2.18
**M:** 2 Cummins KT-1150M diesels; 2 props; 730 hp **Fuel:** 11 tons
**Range:** 1,000/12 **Man:** 2 officer, 10 men

**HYDROGRAPHIC SURVEY SHIPS** *(continued)*

Remarks: Ordered 30-11-77. Similar to diving tender *Manawanui-* and *Moa*-class patrol boats. Have Magnavox MX 1102 NAVSAT receiver, E.G. and G. Mk 1B sidescan sonar, Decca Trisponder position fixing, and Atlas Deso 10 echo-sounder. Used in "Q-route" mine survey work: planned to receive influence mine countermeasures equipment.

**OCEANOGRAPHIC RESEARCH SHIP**

◆ **1 ex-U.S. Robert D. Conrad class** Bldr: Christy Corp., Sturgeon Bay, Wis.

| | Laid down | L | In serv. |
|---|---|---|---|
| A 02 Tui (ex-*Charles H. Davis,* T-AGOR 5) | 15-6-61 | 30-6-62 | 25-1-63 |

**Tui (A 02)**—white hull, buff stack L. & L. Van Ginderen, 3-86

**D:** 1,219 tons (1,402 fl) **S:** 12 kts **Dim:** 70.0 (63.7 pp) × 11.4 × 4.7 (6.3 max.)
**Electron Equipt:** Radar: 1/RCA CRM-N1A-75
**M:** 2 Caterpillar D-378 diesels, electric; 1 prop; 1,000 hp—175-hp bow-thruster
**Electric:** 850 kw **Fuel:** 211 tons **Range:** 12,000/12
**Man:** 8 officers, 16 men, 15 scientists

Remarks: Transferred on loan 28-7-70 and commissioned 11-9-70. Was used in acoustics research for the New Zealand Defense Scientific Establishment, which modified the ship so that it could be used to lay and tow hydrophone arrays. Has a 520-kw gas-turbine generator to drive the prop for quiet running.

**REPLENISHMENT SHIP**

◆ **1 small replenishment oiler** Bldr: Hyundai SY, Ulsan, S. Korea

| | Laid down | L | In serv. |
|---|---|---|---|
| A 11 Endeavour | 4-87 | 8-87 | 4-88 |

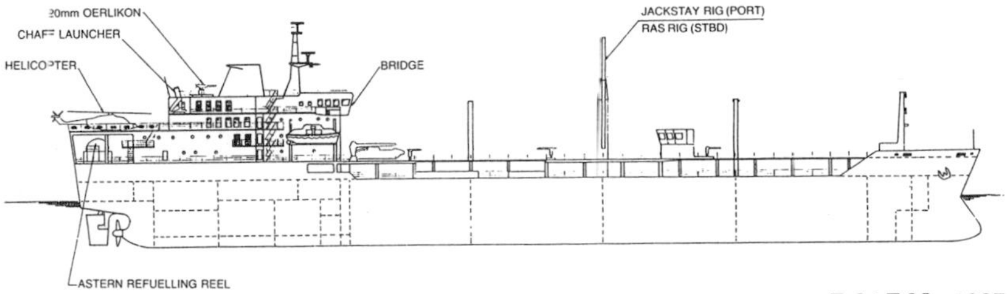


**Endeavour (A 11)** R.N.Z.N., 1987

**Endeavour (A 11)**—artist's rendering R.N.Z.N., 1987

**D:** 12,390 tons (fl) **S:** 14 kts **Dim:** 137.95 (128.00) × 18.40 × 7.30
**A:** 2/20-mm AA (I × 2)—not initially installed
**Electron Equipt:** Radar: 1/Decca-Racal RM-1290A/9; 1/Decca-Racal ARPA-1690S
EW: . . . passive; 2 chaff RL
**M:** 1 Hyundai-Burmeister & Wain 12V-32/36 diesel; 1 CP prop; 5,300 hp
**Electric:** 1,800 kw (3/600-kw alternators; 3/Daihatsu 6DL-20 diesels)
**Range:** 8,000/14 **Fuel:** 400 tons **Man:** 35 max. (25 normal)

Remarks: Ordered 28-7-86. Cargo: 7,600 tons fuel, 120 tons aviation fuel in five tanks. Deck storage for four 20-ft containers. One fueling station to starboard, one solid transfer station to port, plus over-the-stern fueling rig. Helicopter deck, but no hangar. Launch and completion dates delayed by shipyard labor and machinery problems; was to have delivered 20-1-88.

**SERVICE CRAFT**

◆ **1 harbor tug** Bldr: Price SY, Auckland (L: 1969)

A 10 Arataki (ex-*Aorangi*)

**Arataki (A 10)** R.N.Z.N., 11-84

**D:** 170 tons (264 fl) **S:** 12 kts **Dim:** 25.30 × 7.62 × 3.0
**M:** 1 Ruston 6ARM diesel; 1 prop; 1,100 hp

Remarks: Purchased 26-10-84 from Timaru Harbour Board to replace earlier tug *Arataki* and commissioned 16-11-84. Has 16-ton bollard pull.

◆ **1 diving tender**

| | Bldr | L | In serv. |
|---|---|---|---|
| Manawanui | Whangarei Eng. Ltd. | 8-12-78 | 28-5-79 |

**D:** 90 tons (110 fl) **S:** 12 kts **Dim:** 26.82 (24.38 wl) × 6.10 × 2.20
**M:** 2 Cummins KT 1150M diesels; 2 props; 730 hp
**Range:** 1,000/12 **Man:** 16 tot.

Remarks: Other than the addition of a davit at the stern and a free-standing tripod mast, resembles the *Takapu*-class inshore survey craft.

◆ **1 workboat** Bldr: Miller & Tunnage, Port Chalmers (In serv. 1976)

Meola

**D:** 6 tons **S:** 9 kts **Dim:** 13.1 × . . . × . . .
**M:** 1 4-cyl. Gardner diesel; . . . hp

Remarks: Transferred from Ministry of Public Works 1976. Used as diving tender and general tender to naval headquarters.

◆ **1 air-support training craft** Bldr: Naval DY, HMNZS *Philomel* (In serv. 4-84)

Matua

**D:** 8 tons **S:** 14 kts **Dim:** 12.0 × . . . × . . .
**M:** 2 Perkins diesels; 2 props; . . . hp **Range:** 200/14 **Man:** 2–4 tot.

Remarks: Used for parachute recovery, helo winch training, diver support, patrol, and rescue duties at Naval Air Support Unit, Hobsonville. Plywood hull. The same organization also operates two 12.2-m, 16-kt. crash boats and two 10-m, 8-kt. personnel launches.

NEW ZEALAND *(continued)*

DEPARTMENT OF SCIENTIFIC AND INDUSTRIAL RESEARCH

A non-naval New Zealand government agency headquartered at Wellington.

◆ **1 oceanographic research ship** Bldr: Seebeckwerft A.G. Weser, Bremerhaven

Rapuhia (ex-*Meteor*) (In serv. 1963)

**Rapuhia** P. Voss, 6-86

**Rapuhia** L. & L. Van Ginderen, 11-86

**D:** 2,800 tons **S:** 14 kts **Dim:** 82.1 (77.3 pp) × 13.5 × 5.2
**M:** diesel-electric; 3,765 hp **Man:** 52 crew + 24 scientists

Remarks: Elaborately equipped for oceanographic and hydrometeorological research. Acquired 12-85 and sailed for New Zealand 14-6-87, having travelled over 650,000 n.m. in West German service. Red hull, white upperworks.

# NICARAGUA

**Republic of Nicaragua**

Personnel (1987): Approximately 600 total

Merchant Marine (1986): 24 ships—22,930 grt
(tankers: 1 ship—687 grt)

MARINA DE GUERRA SANDINISTA

## PATROL CRAFT

◆ **2 North Korean Sin Hung class**

**D:** 25 tons **S:** 40 kts **Dim:** 18.3 × 3.4 × 1.7
**A:** 4/14.5-mm mg (II × 2) **M:** 2 M50-series diesels, 2 props; 2,400 hp

Remarks: Torpedo boats, with tubes deleted, delivered 10-83.

◆ **1 French 28.2-meter class** Bldr: C.N. de l'Estérel (In serv. 2-9-83)

GC 8 or 9 N . . . . . . .

**D:** 57 tons (fl) **S:** 24 kts **Dim:** 28.2 × 5.2 × 1.6
**A:** 2/20-mm AA (I × 2) **Range:** 800/15 **Man:** 12 tot.
**M:** 2 SACM AGO diesels; 2 props; 1,500 hp

Remarks: Two ordered 12-81 for Customs duties. Launched 6-9-83 and 26-5-83; delivered 24-6-83. Wooden construction. Sister *El Tayacan* lost 25-2-84 to a mine at El Bluff.

◆ **8 Soviet Zhuk class**

301–308

**D:** 60 tons (fl) **S:** 34 kts **Dim:** 24.0 × 5.0 × 1.8 (props)
**A:** 4/14.5-mm mg (II × 2) **Electron Equipt:** Radar: 1/Spin Trough
**M:** 2 M50 diesels; 2 props; 2,400 hp

Remarks: First unit transferred 4-82 from Algeria; second unit delivered 1984, via Cuba; additional units arrived 1986–87. Have side-by-side, enclosed machine gun mountings.

◆ **4 Israeli Dabur class** Bldr: Israeli Aircraft Industries (In serv. 5-78)

GC 10 GC 11 GC 12 GC 13

**D:** 25 tons (35 fl) **S:** 19.6 kts **Dim:** 19.79 × 5.40 × 1.75
**A:** 2/20-mm AA (I × 2) **M:** 2 G.M. 12V72 diesels; 2 props; 960 hp
**Electric:** 20 kw **Range:** 700/16 **Man:** 6 tot.

Remarks: One lost 4-85 to gunfire from Honduran units. Two larger *Dvora*-class patrol craft were also ordered from Israel, but their delivery was embargoed in 1979 at the request of the U.S. government.

◆ **6 U.S. Hatteras-class cabin cruisers** (In serv. 1972)

**D:** 10 tons (fl) **S:** 28 kts **Dim:** 11.6 × 4.1 × 0.9
**A:** 1/12.7-mm mg—1/7.62-mm mg **M:** 2 G.M. 8V53 diesels; 2 props; 560 hp

## MINE WARFARE CRAFT

◆ **2 Soviet Yevgenya-class inshore minesweepers** Bldr: Srednyy Neva SY, Kolpino

BM-503 BM-5 . . .

**D:** 80 tons (90 fl) **S:** 11 kts **Dim:** 26.2 × 6.1
**A:** 2/25-mm AA (II × 1) **Electron Equipt:** Radar: 1/Spin Trough
**M:** 2 diesels; 2 props; 600 hp **Range:** 300/10 **Man:** 10 tot.

Remarks: Delivered via Cuba in 10-84. Glass-reinforced plastic construction. Can hunt for mines via television system to 30-m depths.

◆ **4 Polish K-8-class minesweeping boats** Bldr: Polnocny SY, Gdansk (In serv. 1954–59)

**D:** 19.4 tons (26 fl) **S:** 12 kts **Dim:** 16.9 × 3.2 × 0.8
**A:** 1/14.5-mm mg (II × 1) **Range:** 300/9
**M:** 2 3D6 diesels; 2 props; 300 hp **Man:** 6 tot.

Remarks: Transferred 11-84. Wooden construction. Tow, but do not carry, wire sweeps.

## AMPHIBIOUS WARFARE CRAFT

◆ **2 tank landing lighters** Bldr: Damen, Gorinchem, Netherlands (In serv. 1985)

**D:** . . . **S:** 9 kts **Dim:** 45.8 × 9.5 × 2.5 **M:** 2 diesels; 2 props; 714 hp

Note: One U.S. LCM (6)-class landing craft (Transferred 6-70) may still be in use.

## SERVICE CRAFT

◆ **1 ex-U.S. Army 2001-design personnel transport** Bldr: Missouri Valley Steel, Ft. Leavenworth, Kansas (In serv. 1953)

GC-11 Carlina (ex-U.S. Army T-462)

**D:** 67 tons (96 fl) **S:** 7 kts **Dim:** 20.0 × 5.4 × 2.1 **A:** 1/12.7-mm mg
**Electric:** 5 kw **M:** 1 Caterpillar D375 diesel; 1 prop; 325 hp
**Range:** 400/7 **Fuel:** 3.7 tons **Man:** 7 crew + 24 passengers

Remarks: Transferred 9-75. Can carry 25 tons cargo in addition to passengers.

# NIGERIA

**Republic of Nigeria**

Personnel (1987): 550 officers, 4,500 men

Merchant Marine (1986): 206 ships—563,912 grt
(tankers: 15 ships—219,076 grt)

Naval Aviation: Three Lynx Mk 89 ASW helicopters with Gem 3, 1,128-hp turbines for use aboard N.N.S. *Aradu*. Two Fokker F 27 Maritime patrol aircraft were delivered 1983–84 for coastal surveillance.

## FRIGATES

◆ **1 MEKO 360-H class** Bldr: Blohm + Voss, Hamburg

| | Laid down | L | In serv. |
|---|---|---|---|
| F 89 Aradu (ex-*Republic*) | 2-5-79 | 25-1-80 | 22-2-82 |

**Aradu (F 89)** Ceclant/Premar II, 11-82

**Aradu (F 89)** H. Ehlers, 9-87

**D:** 3,680 tons (fl) **S:** 30.5 kts
**Dim:** 125.9 (119.0 pp) × 15.0 (14.0 wl) × 4.32 (5.8 props)
**A:** 8/Otomat Mk 1 SSM (I × 8)—1/127-mm OTO Melara DP—1/Albatros SAM syst., Mk 2 Mod. 9 (VIII × 1, 24 Aspide missiles)—8/40-mm Breda AA (II × 4)—6/324-mm ASW TT (III × 2, 18 torpedoes)—1/Lynx Mk 86 ASW helicopter
**Electron Equipt:** Radar: 1/Decca 1226, 1/Plessey AWS-5D, 1/H.S.A. WM-25, 1/H.S.A. STIR
Sonar: 1/H.S.A. PHS-32
EW: Decca RDL-2 intercept, RCM-2 jammer—2/SCLAR 105-mm chaff RL (XX × 2)
**M:** CODOG: 2 Rolls-Royce Olympus TM-3B gas turbines, 50,000 hp; 2 MTU 20V956 TB92 diesels, 11,070 hp; 2/5-bladed CP props
**Electric:** 4,120 kVA **Fuel:** 440 tons **Range:** 4,500/18
**Man:** 26 officers, 169 men, 35 cadets

Remarks: Ordered 3-11-77. Renamed 1-11-80. Arrived at Lagos 21-12-81. Similar ships (but with COGOG propulsion, two helicopters, and different electronics) built for Argentina. Makes use of modular containers for electronics and weapon systems. Carries 460 rounds of 127-mm ammunition, 10,752 rounds of 40-mm ammunition, and 120 chaff rounds for the Elsag/Breda chaff rocket launchers, H.S.A. Vesta ASW torpedo f.c.s. Name means "Thunder."

◆ **1 training frigate**

| | Bldr | Laid down | L | In serv. |
|---|---|---|---|---|
| F 87 Obuma (ex-*Nigeria*) | Wilton-Fijenoord, Netherlands | 4-64 | 9-65 | 9-66 |

**D:** 1,724 tons (2,000 fl) **S:** 25 kts **Dim:** 109.85 (104.0 pp) × 11.3 × 3.35
**A:** 1/76-mm OTO Melara DP—4/40-mm AA (I × 4)
**Electron Equipt:** Radar: 1/Plessey AWS-4 nav.
**M:** 4 M.A.N. VV24/30B diesels; 2 props; 16,000 hp
**Range:** 3,500/15
**Man:** 216 tot.

Remarks: Renamed 1981. Helicopter platform. Refit by Cammell Laird, 1970–71, and again at Schiedam, the Netherlands, in 1977. Only a simple lead-computing director is fitted for the 102-mm gun mount. Acts as training ship. Modernization, delayed since 1983, is to include replacing the 102-mm mount with an OTO Melara 76-mm Compact, an optronic f.c.s., and chaff RL. Former Squid ASW mortar and sonar sets deleted. To refit in Italy for 18 months, 1988–89.

**Obuma (F 87)** H. Ehlers, 6-83

## CORVETTES

◆ **2 Erin'mi class (Mk 9)** Bldr: Vosper Thornycroft, Portsmouth

| | Laid down | L | In serv. |
|---|---|---|---|
| F 83 Erin'mi | 14-10-75 | 20-1-77 | 29-1-80 |
| F 84 Enymiri | 11-2-77 | 9-2-78 | 2-5-80 |

**Enymiri (F 84)** H. Ehlers, 7-85

**Enymiri (F 84)** Vosper, 1980

**D:** 850 tons (fl) **S:** 27 kts **Dim:** 69.0 (64.0 pp) × 9.6 × 3.0 (3.6 max.)
**A:** 1/76-mm OTO Melara DP—1/Sea Cat system (III × 1; 15 missiles)—1/40-mm Bofors AA—2/20-mm AA (I × 2)—1/375-mm Bofors ASW RL (II × 1)
**Electron Equipt:** Radar: 1/Decca TM 1226, 1/AWS-2, 1/H.S.A. WM-24
Sonar: 1/Plessey PMS26—Decca intercept
EW: Decca "Cutlass" intercept
**M:** 4 MTU 20V956 TB92 diesels; 2 CP props; 20,512 hp
**Electric:** 889 kw **Endurance:** 10 days **Range:** 2,200/14 **Man:** 90 tot.

Remarks: Can sustain 20 kts on two diesels. Uses three MTU 6V51 diesel generator sets of 260 kw each and one 109-kw emergency generator. Carry 750 rounds 76-mm ammunition, 24 rounds. ASW rockets. Have 2/50-mm flare launchers. Funnel heightened on F 83 after initial trials. Both names are local words for "hippopotamus."

Note: The two *Dorina* (Vosper Mk 3)-class corvettes, *Dorina* (F 81) and *Otobo* (F 82), were stricken 4-87 after having been inoperative for several years following damage during fumigation and heavy cannibalization of useful materials. *Dorina* sank at her moorings in 1987 and was raised 18-5-87 and hulked. *Otobo* may be refitted as a pierside training hulk, although she is severely corroded.

## CORVETTES *(continued)*

### GUIDED-MISSILE PATROL BOATS

◆ **3 Combattante-IIIB class** Bldr: CMN, Cherbourg, France

| | Laid down | L | In serv. |
|---|---|---|---|
| P 181 Siri | 15-5-79 | 3-6-80 | 19-2-81 |
| P 182 Ayam | 7-9-79 | 10-11-80 | 11-6-81 |
| P 183 Ekun | 14-11-79 | 11-2-81 | 18-9-81 |

**Siri (P 181)** CMN, 1981

**Ekun (P 183)** H. Ehlers, 12-85

**D:** 376 tons light (430 fl) **S:** 37 kts
**Dim:** 56.0 (53.0 pp) × 8.16 (7.61 wl) × 2.15
**A:** 4/MM 38 Exocet SSM (II × 2)—1/76-mm OTO Melara DP—2/40-mm Breda AA (II × 1)—4/30-mm Emerlec AA (II × 2)
**Electron Equipt:** Radar: 1/Decca 1226, 1/Thomson-CSF Tritons, 1/Thomson-CSF Castor II
EW: Decca RDL intercept
**M:** 4 MTU 16V956 TB92 diesels; 4 props; 20,840 hp (17,320 sust.)
**Range:** 2,000/15 **Man:** 42 tot.

Remarks: Ordered 11-77. Remained at Cherbourg until 9-5-82 because of payment dispute. Official commissioning date was 6-2-82 for all. Thomson-CSF Vega gun and missile f.c.s., with 2 CSEE Panda optical directors also.

◆ **3 FPB 57 class** Bldr: Lürssen, Vegesack, West Germany

| | Laid down | L | In serv. |
|---|---|---|---|
| P 178 Ekpe | 17-2-79 | 17-12-79 | 8-80 |
| P 179 Damisa | 17-2-79 | 27-3-79 | 4-81 |
| P 180 Agu | 17-2-79 | 7-11-80 | 4-81 |

**Agu (P 180)** P. Voss, 8-81

**D:** 373 tons (436 fl) **S:** 35 kts **Dim:** 58.1 (54.4 wl) × 7.62 × 2.83 (props)
**A:** 4/Otomat Mk 1 (I × 4)—1/76-mm OTO Melara DP—2/40-mm Breda-Bofors (II × 1)—4/30-mm Emerlec AA (II × 2)
**Electron Equipt:** Radar: 1/Decca, TM 1226C, 1/H.S.A. WM-28
EW: Decca RDL intercept
**M:** 4 MTU 16V956 TB92 diesels; 4 props; 20,840 hp (17,320 sust.)
**Electric:** 405 kVA **Range:** 1,600/32; 3,000/16 **Man:** 40 tot.

**Agu (P 180)**—and a sister G. Koop, 11-83

**Ekpe (P 178)** P. Voss, 8-81

Remarks: Ordered late 1977. Sailed for Nigeria 21-8-81. Navigation systems include Decca Mk 21 "Navigator" NAVSAT receiver, Omega receiver, and Marconi "Lodestone" D/F. Made 42 kts on trials. Refitted by builders, 1983–84; P 180 badly damaged during 1984, losing 76-mm mount.

### PATROL BOATS

Note: See also Coast Guard section.

◆ **4 Makurdi class** Bldr: Brooke Marine Ltd., Lowestoft, U.K.

| | L | In serv. | | L | In serv. |
|---|---|---|---|---|---|
| P 167 Makurdi | 21-3-74 | 14-8-74 | P 171 Jebba | 1-12-76 | 29-4-77 |
| P 168 Hadejia | 25-5-74 | 14-8-74 | P 172 Oguta | 17-1-77 | 29-4-77 |

**Hadejia (P 168)**—as rearmed Brooke Marine, 1982

**D:** 115 tons (143 fl) **S:** 20.5 kts **Dim:** 32.6 × 6.1 × 3.5
**A:** 4/30-mm Emerlec AA (II × 2) **Electron Equipt:** Radar: 1/Decca 1226
**M:** 2 Ruston-Paxman YJCM diesels; 2 props; 3,000 hp **Fuel:** 18 tons
**Range:** 2,300/12 **Man:** 4 officers, 20 men

Remarks: First two refitted by builders, 1981–82, others refitted in Nigeria; rearmed, engines overhauled. Originally had 2/40-mm AA (I × 2).

◆ **4 Argundu class** Bldr: Abeking & Rasmussen, West Germany

| | L | In serv. | | L | In serv. |
|---|---|---|---|---|---|
| P 165 Argundu | 4-7-73 | 10-74 | P 169 Bras | 12-1-76 | 3-76 |
| P 166 Yola | 12-6-73 | 10-74 | P 170 Epe | 9-2-76 | 3-76 |

**D:** 90 tons **S:** 20 kts **Dim:** 32.0 (29.0 pp) × 6.0 × 1.7
**A:** 4/30-mm Emerlec AA (II × 2) **Electron Equipt:** Radar: 1/Decca 1229
**M:** 2 MTU diesels; 2 props; 2,070 hp **Range:** . . . **Man:** 25 tot.

Remarks: Refitted 1981–82 by builders; originally had 1/40-mm AA, 1/20-mm AA.

PATROL BOATS *(continued)*

**Yola (P 166) and Bras (P 169)**—as rearmed P. Voss, 3-82

## MINE COUNTERMEASURES SHIPS

◆ **2 Italian Lerici class** Bldr: Intermarine, Sarzana

| | Laid down | L | In serv. |
|---|---|---|---|
| M 371 Ohue | 6-84 | 22-11-85 | 28-5-87 |
| M 372 Maraba | 11-3-85 | 6-6-86 | 9-87 |

**Ohue (M 371)** M. Louagie, 7-87

**D:** 470 tons (550 fl) **S:** 15.5 kts **Dim:** 51.00 (46.50 pp) × 9.56 × 2.80
**A:** 2/30-mm Emerlec AA (II × 1)—2/20-mm AA(I × 2)
**Electron Equipt:** Radar: 1/3 ST7/DG—Sonar: Thomson-CSF TSM 1022
**M:** 2 MTU 8V396 TB83 diesels; 2 PG2000 waterjets; 2,840 hp
**Endurance:** 14 days **Electric:** 887 kVA **Range:** 2,500/12
**Man:** 3 officers, 17 men

Remarks: First ship ordered 9-4-83, second in 5-84, with option for two more. Glass-reinforced plastic construction throughout. Minehunting speed is 7 kts, using the two drop-down, rotating, shrouded thrusters. Range at 12 kts can be extended to 4,000 n.m. by using the passive roll stabilization tanks as fuel tanks. Can support 6–7 mine disposal divers. Carry two Gaymarine Pluto remote-controlled minehunting submersibles, Oropesa Mk 4 mechanical sweep gear, Thomson-CSF IBIS-V minehunting control system.

## AMPHIBIOUS WARFARE SHIPS

◆ **2 West German Type-502 landing ships** Bldr: Howaldtswerke, Hamburg

| | Laid down | L | In serv. |
|---|---|---|---|
| L 1312 Ambe | 3-3-78 | 7-7-78 | 11-5-79 |
| L 1313 Ofiom | 15-9-78 | 7-12-78 | 7-79 |

**D:** 1,190 tons light (1,470 normal, 1,750 fl) **S:** 17 kts
**Dim:** 86.9 (74.5 pp) × 14.0 × 2.30
**A:** 1/40-mm AA—2/20-mm AA (I × 2) **Electron Equipt:** Radar: 1/Decca 1226
**M:** 2 MTU 16V956 TB92 diesels; 4 props; 7,000 hp
**Electric:** 900 kw **Range:** 5,000/12
**Man:** 6 officers, 53 men, plus 540 troops (1,000 for short distances)

**Ambe (LST 1312) and Ofiom (L 1313)** H. Ehlers, 1-85

Remarks: Cargo: 400 tons vehicles plus troops (typically: 5/40-ton tanks or 7/18-ton tanks plus 4/45-ton trucks). Articulated bow ramp, short stern ramp for loading from a pier. Can fit an 81-mm mortar forward. Each engine drives two props.

◆ **2 Oton-class landing craft** Bldr: Scheepswerf Gravel/Akerboom, Leiden, the Netherlands

| | Laid down | L | In serv. |
|---|---|---|---|
| . . . Oton | 9-81 | 22-11-81 | 1982 |
| . . . Idah | 1-82 | 8-3-82 | 1982 |

**D:** approx. 320 tons (fl) **S:** 10.5 kts **Dim:** 35.0 (33.3 pp) × 8.0 × 1.50
**M:** 2 Kelvin TBS-08 diesels; 2 props; 1,000 hp

Remarks: 130 grt. Ordered 20-1-81. May in fact be commercial *vice* naval landing craft.

## HYDROGRAPHIC SHIPS

◆ **1 British Bulldog class** Bldr: Brooke Marine Ltd., Lowestoft, U.K.

| | Laid down | L | In serv. |
|---|---|---|---|
| A 498 Lana | 5-4-74 | 4-3-76 | 9-76 |

**Lana (A 498)** H. Ehlers, 12-85

**D:** 800 tons (1,100 fl) **S:** 15 kts **Dim:** 60.95 (57.8 pp) × 11.43 × 3.7
**A:** 2/20-mm AA (I × 2) **Electron Equipt:** Radar: 1/Decca 1226
**M:** 4 Lister-Blackstone ERS-8M diesels; 2 CP props; 2,000 hp
**Electric:** 880 kw **Range:** 4,000/12 **Man:** 38 tot.

◆ **1 coastal survey craft**

| | Bldr | L | In serv. |
|---|---|---|---|
| Murtula Muhamed | Akerboom, Leiden, Netherlands | 14-8-76 | 28-9-76 |

**D:** 13 tons **S:** 9 kts **Dim:** 11.75 × 3.5 × 1.0
**M:** 1 Perkins 6-354M diesel; 1 prop; 75 hp

## TRAINING SHIP

◆ **1 training ship** Bldr: Van Lent, Kaag, Netherlands (In serv. 10-5-75)

A 497 Ruwan Yaro (ex-*Ogina Bereton*)

**D:** 400 tons (fl) **S:** 17 kts **Dim:** 50.0 (44.2 pp) × 8.0 × 2.0
**A:** none **Electron Equipt:** Radar: 1/Decca TM 626
**M:** 2 Deutz SBA 12M528 diesels; 1 CP prop; 3,000 hp **Fuel:** 64 tons
**Range:** 3,000/15 **Man:** 31 + 11 in officers' training

Remarks: Purchased 1976. Originally a yacht, has a glass-reinforced plastic hull and a bow-thruster.

**TRAINING SHIP** *(continued)*

**Ruwan Yaro (A 497)** H. Ehlers, 12-83

**SERVICE CRAFT**

◆ **2 large harbor tugs** Bldr: SY de Wiel BV, Asperen, the Netherlands

A 499 Commander Apayi Joe (In serv. 9-83)
A 500 Commander Rudolf (In serv. 9-84)

**Commander Apayi Joe (A 499)**—with survey craft *Murtula Muhamed* H. Ehlers, 11-83

**D:** 310 tons (fl) **S:** 11 kts **Dim:** 23.17 × 7.19 × 2.91
**M:** 2 M.A.N. diesels; 2 props; 1,510 hp

Remarks: 130 grt.

◆ **1 harbor tug** Bldr: Oelkers, Hamburg (In serv. 19-5-73)

A 496 Ribadu

**D:** 147 grt **S:** 12 kts **Dim:** 28.5 × 7.2 × 3.7 **M:** 1 diesel; 1 prop; 800 hp

◆ **3 Dutch Sea Truck tenders** Bldr: Damen, Gorinchem (In serv. 10-85)

P 239 P 240 P 242

**P 242**—used for inshore survey H. Ehlers, 12-85

**D:** . . . tons **S:** 20 kts **Dim:** 14.50 × 4.40 × 0.85
**M:** 2 MTU diesels; 2 props, 1,200 hp **Man:** 8 tot.

Remarks: Aluminum construction, bow ramp. Can carry 1/7.62-mm mg. P. 242 used for inshore survey.

◆ **1 water lighter**

Water Barge One

**Water Barge One** H. Ehlers, 12-85

Note: There are also 44 service launches built by Fairey Marine, Hamble: 2/10 m, 22/7 m, 15/6.7 m, and 5/5.5 m. Four Cheverton 8.2-m launches are also in use. Eight Flight Refueling "Sea Flash" 8.5-m, radio-controlled target boats were delivered in 1987. Two 11.75-m torpedo retrievers were delivered by Crestitalia, Ameglia, in 1986. Damen SY, Gorinchem, delivered two 27-m fuel lighters and two small "Pushy-Cat 46" tugs early in 1986 for naval use.

NIGERIAN COAST GUARD

Note: The Coast Guard is under the operational control of the Navy, and naval personnel man its craft.

◆ **6 Type SM-5115 patrol craft** Bldr: Simonneau, Fontenay-le-Comte (In serv. 1986)

P 233–P 238

**D:** . . . **S:** 33 kts **Dim:** 15.80 × . . . × . . .
**A:** 2/7.62-mm mg (I × 2) **Electron Equipt:** Radar: 1/. . .
**M:** 2 MTU 6V396 TC82 diesels; 2 props; 1,200 hp

Remarks: Aluminum construction. First delivered 5-86, second in 6-86.

◆ **6 Stan Pat-1500 patrol craft** Bldr: Damen, Gorinchem

P 227–229 (In serv. 4-86) P 230–232 (In serv. 6-86)

**P 229** Damen, 2-86

**D:** 16 tons (fl) **S:** 32 kts **Dim:** 15.11 (13.57 wl) × 4.45 × 1.40 (0.75 mean hull)
**A:** 1/7.62-mm mg **Electron Equipt:** Radar: 1/Decca . . .
**M:** 2 MTU 6V331 TC82 diesels; 2 props; 2,250 hp **Fuel:** 2 $m^2$ **Man:** 6 tot.

## NIGERIAN COAST GUARD *(continued)*

◆ **4 65-ft Commercial Cruiser class** Bldr: Swiftships, Inc., Morgan City, La. (In serv. 24-2-86)

P 221 Iseyin P 223 Afikto
P 222 Eruwa P 224 Aba

**Aba (P 224)** Skeets Photo/Swiftships, 12-85

**D:** 36 tons (fl) **S:** 32 kts **Dim:** 19.96 × 5.59 × 1.52
**A:** . . . **Electron Equipt:** Radar: 1/Raytheon 1210
**M:** 2 MTU 8V396 TP93 diesels; 2 props; 2,176 hp (sust.)
**Range:** 500/18 **Electric:** 20 kw **Man:** 6 tot.

Remarks: Aluminum construction.

◆ **5 Millspeed P/20 class** Bldr: Van Mill Marine Service, Hardinxveld-Giessendam

P 215 (In serv. 11-9-85) P 217 (In serv. 14-12-85) P 219 (In serv. 17-1-86)
P 216 (In serv. 11-9-85) P 218 (In serv. 14-12-85)

**P 215** Van Mill, 1985

**D:** 45 tons (fl) **S:** 35+ kts **Dim:** 20.20 (18.00 wl) × 5.30 × 1.75
**A:** 1/20-mm Rheinmetall AA—2/7.62-mm mg (I × 2)
**Electron Equipt:** Radar: 1/Decca . . .
**M:** P 215, 216: 3 G.M. 12V71 TI diesels; 3 props; 2,100 hp
P 217–219: 2 MTU 6V331 TC82 diesels; 2 props; 2,250 hp
**Range:** 950/25; 1,200/11 **Man:** 2 officers, 10 men

Remarks: GRP construction. Sister P 220 presented to Equatorial Guinea, 27-6-86.

### PATROL CRAFT

◆ **14 Type Mk 2 AM patrol craft** Bldr: Intermarine, La Spezia

| | In serv. | | In serv. | | In. serv. |
|---|---|---|---|---|---|
| P 200 Abeokuta | 7-81 | P 205 Ikeja | 9-81 | P 210 Maidugiri | 4-82 |
| P 201 Akure | 7-81 | P 206 Iloren | 11-81 | P 211 Minna | 4-82 |
| P 202 Bauchi | 7-81 | P 207 Jos | 11-81 | P 212 Ouererri | 4-82 |
| P 203 Benin City | 7-81 | P 208 Kaduna | 11-81 | P 214 Sokoto | 4-82 |
| P 204 Enugu | 9-81 | P 209 Kano | 4-82 | | |

**Maidugiri (P 210)**—outboard *Ikeja* (P 205) H. Ehlers, 11-83

**D:** 20 tons (fl) **S:** 35 kts **Dim:** 18.2 (16.5 pp) × 5.0 × 0.85
**A:** 1/20-mm AA—2/7.62-mm mg (I × 2)
**M:** 2 MTU 8V331 TB91 diesels; 2 Castoldi waterjets; 2,700 hp
**Range:** 300/32 **Man:** 9 tot.

Remarks: Ordered 10-78. Glass-reinforced plastic construction. Sister *Port Harcourt* (P 213) lost 1984. Survivors refitted by builder, 1986.

◆ **1 "Tracker" class** Bldr: Fairey Marine, Hamble, U.K. (In serv. 2-78)

**D:** 31 tons (fl) **S:** 24 kts **Dim:** 19.3 × 5.0 × 1.5 **A:** 1/20-mm AA
**M:** 2 diesels; 2 props; 1,290 hp **Range:** 650/20 **Man:** 11 tot.

◆ **2 "Spear" class** Bldr: Fairey Marine, Hamble, U.K. (In serv. 1978)

**D:** 4.3 tons **S:** 25 kts **Dim:** 9.1 × 2.8 × 0.8

## MARINE POLICE

Note: For operations on the Niger River and Lake Chad. All craft built of glass-reinforced plastic. In addition to the craft listed below, in 4-82 it was announced that 4 13-m glass-reinforced plastic, 48 6.4-m aluminum, 34 5.5-m glass-reinforced plastic, and 30 4.9-m aluminum patrol craft and 3 4.9-m hovercraft were to be procured. Two patrol craft were ordered 5-84 from Fairey Allday Marine, U.K.

### PATROL AND SERVICE CRAFT

◆ **2 P 2000 class patrol craft** Bldr: Steelship, Truro, U.K. (In serv. 3-86?)

**D:** 45 tons (fl) **S:** 30 kts **Dim:** 21.80 (19.00 wl) × 5.80 × 1.50
**A:** . . . **Electron Equipt:** Radar: 1/. . .
**M:** 2 MTU 8V396 TB93 diesels; 2 props; 2,600 hp (2,176 sust.)

Remarks: Watercraft design, GRP construction. Ordered 25-1-85, but uncertain if delivered.

◆ **6 14 m** Bldr: Schottel, the Netherlands (In serv. 1982)

◆ **4 8 m** Bldr: Copeland, U.K. (In serv. 1982)

◆ **12 9.8 m** Bldr: Halmatic, Havant, U.K. (In serv. 1982–83)

**D:** 5.5 tons (6.5 fl) **S:** 25 kts **Dim:** 9.8 (8.8 wl) × 3.4 × 0.9
**M:** 2 Mermaid diesels; 2 props; 360 hp **Man:** 4–6 tot.

Remarks: Ordered 8-1-81. Glass-reinforced plastic construction.

◆ **10 Tiger-class air-cushion vehicles** Bldr: Air Vehicles, Cowes, U.K. (In serv.: 5 in 8-82; 5 in 1984–85)

**D:** 1 ton (fl) **S:** 34 kts **Dim:** 8.45 × 4.57 × 2.81 (high)
**A:** 1 diesel engine; 1 lift fan/1 prop; 200 hp **Man:** 12 tot.

◆ **2 Skima 12 hovercraft** Bldr: Pindair, U.K. (In serv. 1982)

◆ **13 Skua Q33 class** Bldr: Horne Bros., Fishbourne, U.K. (In serv. 1981–82)

**D:** 5 tons (fl) **S:** 30 kts **Dim:** 7.9 × 2.8 × 0.4
**M:** 2 Volvo Penta AQAD-40/280 diesels; 2 outdrive props; 310 hp
**Man:** 2–4 tot.

◆ **3 Q26-class landing craft** Bldr: Horne Bros., Fishbourne, U.K. (In serv. 1982)

**D:** 17 tons (fl) **S:** 35 kts **Dim:** 10.0 × 3.5 × 0.75
**A:** 2/7.62-mm mg (I × 2) **Man:** 2 crew, plus 24 police troops
**M:** 2 Sabre diesels; 2 props; 500 hp

◆ **1 P 1200 class** Bldr: Watercraft, Ltd., Shoreham, U.K. (In serv. 2-81)

**D:** 9.7 tons (fl) **S:** 27 kts **Dim:** 11.9 × 4.1 × 1.1
**M:** 2 G.M. 8V71 TI diesels; 2 props; 480 hp **Range:** 240/25

◆ **5 P 800 class** Bldr: Watercraft, Shoreham, U.K. (In serv. 12-80)

**D:** 3.2 tons (fl) **S:** 26 kts **Dim:** 8.0 × 2.6 × 0.8
**M:** 1 Volvo AQAD-40 outdrive diesel; 1 prop; 150 hp **Range:** 104/26

**NIGERIA** *(continued)*
**MARINE POLICE** *(continued)*

◆ **8 15-ton class** Bldr: Vosper Thornycroft (In serv. 1971–72)

**D:** 15 tons (fl) **S:** 19 kts **Dim:** 10.4 × 3.1 × 0.9
**M:** 2 Rolls-Royce diesels; 2 props; 290 hp

◆ **8 7-meter work boats** Bldr: Fairey Marine, Hamble, U.K. (In serv. 1982)

CUSTOMS SERVICE

◆ **1 patrol boat** Bldr: Chung Mu SY, Hong Kong

Yan-Yan (In serv. 14-9-83)

**D:** 100 tons (fl) **S:** 27.5 kts **Dim:** 34.0 (32.0 wl) × 6.0 × 1.34
**A:** . . . **M:** 2 MTU 12V396 TB93 diesels; 2 props; 3,560 hp
**Fuel:** 13 tons **Man:** 12 tot.

◆ **6 Watercraft 18-ton, 18-kt patrol craft** (In serv. 1982)

# NORWAY

## Kingdom of Norway

Personnel (1985): 8,750 men, 2,000 of whom are in the Coast Artillery

Merchant Marine (1986): 2,107 ships—9,294,630 grt
(tankers: 70 ships—3,201,801 grt)

Naval Aviation: The Norwegian Navy does not have an air arm, as such. However, two of the Air Force's formations are assigned to naval missions, usually reconnaissance and ASW patrol; a squadron of 10 Sea King Mk 43 and 20 UH-1D search-and-rescue helicopters; a group of 7 P-3B Orion patrol aircraft and 4 De Havilland Twin Otter utility aircraft. Two P-3C Orion ordered 9-6-87 to replace 5 oldest P-3B; to deliver 1989. In addition, 20 Bell UH-1D helicopters operate in the search-and-rescue role. The Coast Guard operates 6 WG-13 Lynx Mk 86 helicopters. The Penguin Mk 3 antiship missile is being acquired to permit Royal Norwegian Air Force F-16 fighters to attack ships.

**P-3B Orion**—Royal Norwegian Air Force Official

**Sea King Mk 43**—Royal Norwegian Air Force Official

WEAPONS AND SYSTEMS

The Norwegian Navy uses mostly British, American, and Swedish weapons and systems, but it has built two systems of its own, the Terne automatic ASW defense system and the Penguin surface-to-surface missile, which are described below. Submarines are equipped with Swedish T-61 (45 kts, 20,000 m) or American NT37C (20,000 m) and Mk 37 Mod. 2 wire-guided torpedoes. Norway has also developed its own radar and electro-optical gun and missile fire-control systems. Sonars are manufactured by the Simrad Co.

**Terne Mk III** (ASW)

Maximum range: 900 m. The entire system incorporates: search sonar, attack sonar ("Terne Mk 3" for range/depth determination), computer, and a sextuple launcher mount with a rapid-reloading system.

The sextuple launcher mount weighs a little less than 3 tons. Firing is done between 45° and 75° of elevation, the latter for minimum range. Six rounds are ripple-fired at a time. Reloading is done automatically in 40 seconds, as the carriage is returned to a vertical position, in which ready-service racks reload the launchers. The rocket is 1.97 m in length, 0.2 m in diameter, 120 kg in weight (warhead: 48 kg), and has a combination timed and proximity fuse. Employed on the *Oslo* and *Sleipner* classes.

**Penguin Mk 1** (antiship)

| | |
|---|---|
| Length: 2.95 m | Maximum range: 20,000 m |
| Wingspan: 1.42 m | Speed: Mach 0.7 |
| Diameter: 0.28 | Guidance: Infrared homing |
| Weight: 330 kg | |

The missile is protected by a fiberglass container that also serves as a launcher.

**Penguin Mk 2** (antiship)

| | |
|---|---|
| Length: 2.96 m | Maximum range: 27,000 m |
| Wingspan: 1.42 m | Speed: Mach 0.8 |
| Diameter: 0.28 m | Guidance: Infrared homing |
| Weight: 340 kg | Warhead: 120 kg Bullpup Mk 19 |

Note: A Mk 2 Mod. 7 helicopter-launched version is being developed for the U.S. Navy.

**Penguin Mk 3** (antiship, air-launched)

| | |
|---|---|
| Length: 3.20 m | Maximum range: 40,000+ m |
| Wingspan: 2.00 m | Speed: Mach 0.8 |
| Diameter: 0.28 m | Guidance: Infrared homing |
| Weight: 350 kg (400 with launcher) | Warhead: 120 kg |

Penguin Mk 3 can be launched at altitudes of 150 to 30,000 ft.

**76-mm Bofors gun**

Single-barrel automatic gun mounted on the *Storm*-class patrol boats. Not intended for AA. Also used by the Singapore Navy.

| | |
|---|---|
| Turret weight (no ammunition): 6.5 tons | Rate of fire: 30 rounds/min |
| | Cartridge weight: 11.3 kg |
| Length: 50 calibers | Shell weight: 5.9 kg |
| Muzzle velocity: 825 m/sec | Warhead weight: 0.54 kg |
| Rate of train: 25°/sec | Maximum range, surface mode: 8,000 m |
| Rate of elevation: 25°/sec | Arc of elevation: −10° to +30° |

**SUBMARINES**

◆ **0 (+6) Project 6071 (German Type 210)** Bldr: Thyssen Nordseewerke, Emden

| | Start | Laid down | L | In serv. |
|---|---|---|---|---|
| S 300 Ula | 6-85 | 29-1-87 | . . . | 1-2-89 |
| S 301 Utsira | 7-86 | . . . | . . . | 4-90 |
| S 302 Utstein | . . . | . . . | . . . | 10-90 |
| S 303 Utvaer | . . . | . . . | . . . | 4-91 |
| S 304 Uthaug | . . . | . . . | . . . | 10-91 |
| S 305 Uredd | . . . | . . . | . . . | 30-4-92 |

**Ula (S 300) model** IKL, 1986

**D.** 940 tons standard, 1,040 tons (surf.) (fl); 1,150 tons (sub.)
**S:** 11/23 kts **Dim:** 59.00 × 5.40 × 4.50
**A:** 8/533-mm TT (14 German Seeal 3, DM2A3 torpedoes)
**Electron Equipt:** Radar: . . .—Sonar: Krupp Atlas DBQS-21F (CSU-83); Thomson-CSF passive conformal arrays
**M:** 2 MTU 16V652 MB 1,260-bhp diesels, 2/870-kw, 3-phase NEBB generator sets, electric drive; 1 prop; 6,000 hp
**Range:** 5,000/8 (snorkel) **Endurance:** 40 days
**Fuel:** 100 tons **Man:** 18–20 tot.

Remarks: Six ordered 30-9-82, with option to order two more later dropped. Will have Kongsberg MSI-90U torpedo f.c.s. Diving depth: 250 m. Anker batteries, Zeiss periscopes. All but first to have pressure hulls built by Kvaerner Brug, Oslo.

**SUBMARINES** *(continued)*

◆ **11 German Type 207** Bldr: Rheinstahl-Nordseewerke, Emden

| | L | In serv. |
|---|---|---|
| S 301 Utsira | 11-3-65 | 1-7-65 |
| S 302 Utstein | 19-5-65 | 9-9-65 |
| S 305 Sklinna* | 21-1-66 | 17-8-66 |
| S 306 Skolpen* | 24-3-66 | 17-8-66 |
| S 308 Stord* | 2-9-66 | 9-2-67 |
| S 309 Svenner | 27-1-67 | 1-7-67 |
| S 315 Kaura | 16-10-64 | 5-2-65 |
| S 317 Kya* | 20-2-64 | 15-6-64 |
| S 318 Kobben* | 25-4-64 | 17-8-64 |
| S 319 Kunna* | 16-7-64 | 1-10-64 |
| S 316 Kinn (ex-*Ula*, S 300) | 19-12-64 | 7-5-65 |

* To be modernized

**Kya (S 317)** L. & L. Van Ginderen, 7-87

**D:** 370/482 tons **S:** 13.5/17 kts **Dim:** 45.41 (S 309: 46.41) × 4.6 × 3.80
**A:** 8/533-mm TT, fwd (8 Swedish Type 61 and U.S. NT 37C torpedoes)
**Electron Equipt:** Radar: 1/Thomson-CSF Calypso—Sonar: Krupp Atlas . . .
**M:** 2 Mercedes-Benz MB 820Db, 600-hp diesels, 2 405-kw generators, 1 1,100-kw motor; 1 prop (2.3-m diameter); 1,700 hp
**Man:** 17 tot.

Remarks: Based on the West German Type 205, but deeper-diving. MSI-700 torpedo fire-control. The *Svenner* is equipped for training, has a second periscope, and is one meter longer than the others. Diving depth: 190 m. Use MSI-70U torpedo fire-control system. Six are to be modernized, to complement the new Type 210 class; three others are to be transferred to Denmark. Sister *Kinn* (S 316) stricken 1982. *Stadt* (S 307), which was to have gone to Denmark, damaged in grounding spring 1987 and stricken; name of replacement not yet announced. S 316 renamed and renumbered 12-3-87; S 302 is to be renamed and renumbered *Stadt* (S 307) in 1989.

Units being modernized by Mjellum and Karlsen, near Bergen, getting Kongsberg MSI-90U torpedo f.c.s., new sonar and communications suites, Thorn-EMI D-3 data-distribution systems, and a propulsion-system overhaul. S 305 to deliver 4-88, followed by S 303 ex-*Utvaer* for Denmark, S 306, S 304, ex-*Uthaug* for Denmark, S 308, another for Denmark, S 317, S 318, and S 319—the last to complete 7-91.

**GUIDED-MISSILE FRIGATES**

◆ **5 Oslo class** Bldr: Marinens Hovedverft (Naval Dockyard), Horten

| | Laid down | L | In serv. |
|---|---|---|---|
| F 300 Oslo | 1963 | 17-1-64 | 29-1-66 |
| F 301 Bergen | 1963 | 23-8-65 | 15-5-67 |
| F 302 Trondheim | 1963 | 4-9-64 | 2-6-66 |
| F 303 Stavanger | 1964 | 4-2-66 | 1-12-67 |
| F 304 Narvik | 1964 | 8-1-65 | 30-11-66 |

**Oslo (F 300)** L. &. L. Van Ginderen, 6-87

**Bergen (F 301)** L. &. L. Van Ginderen, 9-86

**D:** 1,450 tons (1,850 fl) **S:** 25 kts **Dim:** 96.62 (93.87 pp) × 11.17 × 4.4
**A:** 6/Penguin SSM—1/NATO Sea Sparrow system (VIII × 1, 24 missiles)—4/76.2-mm DP (II × 2)—1/Terne-III ASW RL (VI × 1)—6/324-mm Mk 32 ASW TT (II × 2)—1/d.c. rack (6 d.c.)
**Electron Equipt:** Radar: 1/Decca TM 1226, 1/DRBV 22, 1/H.S.A. M 24, 1/U.S. Mk 91 Mod. 0
Sonar: 1/Terne Mk 3 attack, 1/SQS-36 or TSM 2633—
EW: . . .
**M:** 1 set Laval-Ljungstrom PN 20 GT; 1 prop; 20,000 hp
**Electric:** 1,100 kw **Boilers:** 2 Babcock & Wilcox; 42.18 kg/cm$^2$, 454°C
**Range:** 4,500/15 **Man:** 11 officers, 19 petty officers, 120 men

Remarks: Based on the U.S. *Dealey*-class destroyer escorts, but with higher free-board forward and many European subsystems. Rebuilt during the late 1970s with the Penguin antiship missile, NATO Sea Sparrow point-defense SAM, and ASW torpedo tubes. In the Sea Sparrow system, the Mk 91 radar director is on a pylon atop the missile-reload magazine; the launcher is a U.S. Mk 29. F 304 conducted trials during 1980 with the Raytheon C-LAS C-band acquisition radar and during 1985 mounted 2/20-mm Rheinmetall AA abaft the ASW TT.

All to be modernized, with Thomson-CSF TSM 2633 (Spherion) sonar in place of the U.S. AN/SQS-36, a VDS (requiring replacement of the aft 76.2-mm gun mount with a 40-mm AA mount), digital (*vice* analog) weapons-control systems, rocket decoy system added, and habitability improvements. F 302, first to modernize, fall 1985 to 5-87.

**CORVETTES**

◆ **2 Sleipner class** Bldr: Nylands Verksted, Oslo

| | L | In serv. | | L | In serv. |
|---|---|---|---|---|---|
| F 310 Sleipner | 9-11-63 | 29-4-65 | F 311 Aeger | 24-9-65 | 31-3-67 |

**Sleipner (F 310)** L. & L. Van Ginderen, 8-86

**D:** 600 tons (790 fl) **S:** 20+ kts **Dim:** 69.33 × 7.9 × 2.5
**A:** 1/76.2-mm Mk 34 DP—1/40-mm AA—1/Terne-III ASW RL (VI × 1)—6/324-mm Mk 32 ASW TT (III × 2)—1/d.c. rack (6 d.c.)
**Electron Equipt:** Radar: 1/Decca TM 1226, 1/Decca 202
Sonar: 1/Terne Mk 3 attack, 1/SQS-36
**M:** 4 Maybach diesels; 2 props; 9,000 hp **Man:** 61 tot.

Remarks: From the 1960 program. Now employed primarily for training. U.S. Mk 63 GFCS replaced by 2 Swedish TVT 300 optronic systems. The AN/SQS-36 sonar is to be replaced by a Thomson-CSF TSM2633 (Spherion) set. F 311 to reserve 10-1-83.

Note: The patrol vessel (former whaler) *Vadsø* (P 340) was sold commercial in 1985.

**GUIDED-MISSILE PATROL BOATS**

◆ **0 (+24) new construction** Bldr:

Remarks: A replacement class for the *Storm* and *Snögg* classes is in development. The *Storm*-class missile boat was fitted during 1987 with a prototype water jet propulsion system for the new boat, the first of which is to be completed in 1992.

**GUIDED-MISSILE PATROL BOATS** *(continued)*

◆ **14 Hauk class** Bldrs: (A) Bergens Mekaniske Verksteder; (B) Westamarin, Alta

| | Bldr | L | In serv. |
|---|---|---|---|
| P 986 Hauk | A | 2-77 | 17-8-78 |
| P 987 Ørn | A | 2-78 | 19-1-79 |
| P 988 Terne | A | 5-78 | 13-3-79 |
| P 989 Tjeld | A | 8-78 | 25-5-79 |
| P 990 Skarv | A | 10-78 | 17-7-79 |
| P 991 Teist | A | 6-12-78 | 11-9-79 |
| P 992 Jo | A | . . . | 1-11-79 |
| P 993 Lom | A | . . . | 15-1-80 |
| P 994 Stegg | A | . . . | 18-3-80 |
| P 995 Falk | A | . . . | 30-4-80 |
| P 996 Ravn | B | . . . | 20-5-80 |
| P 997 Gribb | B | . . . | 10-7-80 |
| P 998 Geir | B | . . . | 16-9-80 |
| P 999 Erle | B | . . . | 10-12-80 |

**Ørn (P 987)** L. & L. Van Ginderen, 6-86

**Erle (P 999)** G. Koop, 5-84

**D:** 130 tons (155 fl) **S:** 35 kts **Dim:** 36.53 × 6.3 × 1.65
**A:** 2–6/Penguin Mk II SSM (I × 6)—1/40-mm Bofors AA—1/20-mm Rheinmetall AA—2/533-mm TT for T-61 wire-guided torpedoes
**Electron Equipt:** Radar: 2/Decca TM 1226—Sonar: Simrad SQ3D/SF
**M:** 2 MTU 16V538 TB92 diesels; 2 props; 7,340 hp **Range:** 440/34
**Man:** 22 tot.

Remarks: MSI-80S fire-control system, developed by Kongsberg, uses two Decca radars plus a TVT-300 electro-optical tracker and an Ericssen laser range finder. Have 2/50-mm flare RL.

◆ **6 Snögg class** Bldr: Båtservice Verft, Mandal, 1970–71

| | | |
|---|---|---|
| P 980 Snögg (ex-*Lyr*) | P 982 Snarr | P 984 Kvik |
| P 981 Rapp | P 983 Rask | P 985 Kjapp |

**Snarr (P 982)**—2 Penguin Mk 1 aboard S. Terzibaschitsch, 6-86

**D:** 115 tons (140 fl) **S:** 36 kts **Dim:** 36.53 × 6.3 × 1.65
**A:** 2–4/Penguin Mk I SSM (I × 4)—1/40-mm AA—4/533-mm TT for T-61 wire-guided torpedoes—2/d.c. racks
**Electron Equipt:** Radar: 1/Decca TM 626, 1/PEAB TORI fire control
**M:** 2 MTU 16V538 TB92 diesels; 2 props; 7,200 hp
**Range:** 550/36 **Man:** 3 officers, 17 men

◆ **17 Storm class** Bldrs: P 963, P 966, P 969, P 972, P 975, and P 978: Westermöen, Mandal; others: Bergens MV

| | L | | L | | L |
|---|---|---|---|---|---|
| P 961 Blink | 28-6-65 | P 969 Steil | 20-9-66 | P 974 Brott | 27-1-67 |
| P 962 Glimt | 27-9-65 | P 970 Brann | 3-7-66 | P 975 Odd | 7-4-67 |
| P 963 Skjold | 17-2-66 | P 971 Tross | 29-9-66 | P 977 Brask | 27-5-67 |
| P 965 Kjekk | 27-1-66 | P 972 Hvass | 20-12-66 | P 978 Rokk | 1-6-67 |
| P 966 Djerv | 28-4-66 | P 973 Traust | 18-11-66 | P 979 Gnist | 15-8-67 |
| P 967 Skudd | 25-3-66 | | | | |
| P 968 Arg | 24-5-66 | | | | |

**Hvass (P 972)**—with 6 Penguin missiles aboard G. Koop, 5-84

**D:** 100 tons (125 fl) **S:** 37 kts **Dim:** 36.53 × 6.3 × 1.55
**A:** 4–6/Penguin Mk I SSM (I × 6)—1/76-mm—1/40-mm AA
**Electron Equipt:** Radar: 1/Decca TM 1226, 1/H.S.A. WM-26 fire-control
**M:** Mayback MB 872A diesels; 2 props; 7,200 hp **Range:** 550/36
**Man:** 4 officers, 9 petty officers, 13 men

Remarks: Backfitted with TVT-300 electro-optical tracker and laser range finder, in a tub abaft the radar mast. Diesels are essentially the same as those in the *Hauk* and *Snögg* classes above. Two d.c. racks can be carried in lieu of the after two Penguin containers. *Pil* (P 976) reported stricken 1982, while *Trygg* (P 964) was damaged beyond repair by grounding, 1983. The original *Storm,* launched 19-3-63, was stricken 1965 and replaced by a new unit, *Storm* (P 960), launched 28-11-68; that ship was stricken 1986 for use in waterjet propulsion trials.

**TORPEDOBOATS**

◆ **8 Tjeld class** Bldr: Båtservice, Mandal, Oslo

| | In serv. | | In serv. |
|---|---|---|---|
| P 343 Sel | 6-60 | P 380 Skrei | 1-66 |
| P 348 Hval | 6-61 | P 381 Hai | 7-64 |
| P 349 Laks | 6-61 | P 387 Lyr | 2-65 |
| P 357 Knurr | 12-61 | P 388 Delfin | 3-62 |

**Hai (P 381)** L. & L. Van Ginderen, 1982

**D:** 70 tons (82 fl) **S:** 45 kts (40 sust.) **Dim:** 24.50 × 7.50 × 1.95
**A:** 1/40-mm Bofors AA—1/20-mm Rheinmetall AA—4/533-mm TT (I × 4)
**Electron Equipt:** Radar: 1/Decca 707
**M:** 2 Napier Deltic T18-37 turbocharged diesels; 2 props; 6,280 hp
**Range:** 450/40; 600/25 **Fuel:** 10 tons **Man:** 4 officers, 14 men

**TORPEDOBOATS** *(continued)*

REMARKS: Survivors of a class of 15, with 22 others having been built for the U.S.A. 1963–68, six for Greece, and two for West Germany. All serve the Home Guard. Mahogany hull. Also known as the "Nasty" class, after the commercial prototype.

## MINE WARFARE SHIPS

◆ **2 Vidar-class minelayers** Bldr: Mjellem & Karlsen, Bergen

| | Laid down | L | In serv. |
|---|---|---|---|
| N 52 VIDAR | 1-3-76 | 18-3-77 | 21-10-77 |
| N 53 VALE | 1-2-76 | 5-8-77 | 10-2-78 |

**Vale (N 53)** G. Gyssels, 1984

**D:** 1,500 tons (1,722 fl) **S:** 15 kts **Dim:** 64.8 (60.0 pp) × 12.0 × 4.0
**A:** 2/40-mm AA (I × 2)—6/324-mm Mk 32 ASW TT (II × 2)—2/d.c. racks—320 mines
**Electron Equipt:** Radar: 2/Decca 1226—Sonar: Simrad SQ3D
**M:** 2 Wichmann 7AX diesels; 2 props; 4,200 hp **Electric:** 1,000 kw
**Fuel:** 247 tons **Man:** 50 tot.

REMARKS: Capable of serving as minelayers (mines carried on three decks, automatic hoist, three mine-laying rails), torpedo-recovery ships, personnel and cargo transports, fisheries-protection ships, and ASW escorts. Bow-thruster fitted.

◆ **1 inshore mine-planter**

| | Bldr | L |
|---|---|---|
| N 51 BORGEN | Marinens Hovedverft, Horten | 29-4-60 |

**D:** 282 tons (fl) **S:** 9 kts **Dim:** 31.28 × 8.0 × 3.35
**A:** 2/20-mm AA (I × 2)—2 mine rails
**M:** 2 G.M. 3-71 diesels; 2 Voith Schneider cycloidal props; 330 hp

REMARKS: Patterned on the Swedish MUL-12 class. Designed to "plant" controlled mines by crane.

◆ **0 (+10) new construction minehunter/minesweepers** Bldr: . . .

| | Laid down | L | In serv. |
|---|---|---|---|
| M . . . N . . . | 1989 | . . . | . . . |
| M . . . N . . . | . . . | . . . | . . . |
| M . . . N . . . | . . . | . . . | . . . |
| M . . . N . . . | . . . | . . . | . . . |

**New Air Cushion Vehicle mine countermeasures ship**—artist's impression R.Nor.N., 1987

**D:** 360 tons (500 fl) **S:** 20 kts (cruising)
**Dim:** 54.50 × 13.00 × 2.32 (0.84 on cushion) **A:** . . .
**Electron Equipt:** Radar: . . .—Sonar: . . .
**M:** 2 1,500-hp diesels for propulsion; 2 950-hp diesels for lift fans; 2 KaMeWa CP props; 3,000 hp
**Range:** . . ./. . . **Man:** . . .

REMARKS: Approved 3-8-87 by Ministry of Defense. Rigid sidewall air-cushion vehicle design like abortive U.S. *Cardinal* class. Six to be minesweepers, four to be minehunters. Last unit to deliver 1996.

◆ **8 U.S. Falcon-class minesweepers** Bldrs: M 332, M 334: Båtservice Verft, Mandal; M 316: Skåluren, Rosendal; M 331: Forenede Båtbyggeri, Risŏr; M 313, M 314, M 317: Hodgdon Bros., Gowdy & Stevens, Boothbay, Maine; M 312: C. Hiltebrant DD, Kingston, New York

| | In serv. | | In serv. |
|---|---|---|---|
| M 312 SIRA (ex-MSC 132) | 28-11-55 | M 317 GLOMMA (ex-*Bastogne*, ex-MSC 151) | 12-53 |
| M 313 TANA (ex-*Roeslaere*, ex-MSC 103) | 9-53 | M 331 TISTA | 27-4-55 |
| M 314 ALTA (ex-*Arlon*, ex-MSC 104) | 10-53 | M 332 KVINA | 12-7-55 |
| M 316 VOSSO | 16-3-55 | M 334 UTLA | 15-1-55 |

**Tana (M 313)**—minehunter, deckhouse aft L. & L. Van Ginderen, 1980

**Kvina (M 332)** G. Gyssels, 7-83

**D:** 300 tons (372 fl) **S:** 13 kts (8, sweeping) **Dim:** 43.0 × 7.95 × 2.55
**A:** 2/20-mm Rheinmetall AA (I × 2)
**Electron Equipt:** Radar: 1/Decca 202 or 1226
Sonar: 1/UQS-1 (M 313: 1/193 M)
**M:** 2 G.M. 8-268A diesels; 2 props; 1,200 hp **Fuel:** 40 tons
**Range:** 2,500/10 **Man:** 38 tot.

REMARKS: *Tana, Alta,* and *Glomma* were transferred by Belgium in 1966 in exchange for two ocean minesweepers, *Lagen* and *Namsen*. In 1977, *Tana* was converted to a prototype minehunter, with British Type 193M sonar, two PAP-104 remote-controlled minehunting devices, and divers' facilities in a large deckhouse aft. She was rearmed with 2/20-mm Rheinmetall AA guns (I × 2), now backfitted into the others. At the waterline, across the stern, she has a platform for diver recovery; this extends her overall length by more than one meter. Sisters *Sauda* (M 311, ex-MSC 102) and *Ogna* (M 315) stricken 1986.

## AMPHIBIOUS WARFARE SHIPS

◆ **5 Reinøysund-class utility landing craft** Bldr: Mjellem & Karlsen, Bergen (In serv. 1972–73)

L 4502 Reinøysund L 4504 Maursund L 4506 Borgsund
L 4503 Sørøysund L 4505 Rotsund

**D:** 596 tons (fl) **S:** 11 kts **Dim:** 51.4 × 10.3 × 1.85
**A:** 2/20-mm Rheinmetall (I × 2)—4/12.7-mm mg—rails for 120 mines
**M:** 2 MTU diesels; 2 props; 1,350 hp **Man:** 2 officers, 7 men

Remarks: Double-folding bow-ramp door. Cargo capacity: 5 Leopard tanks, 80–180 men. Similar to class below.

◆ **2 Kvalsund-class utility landing craft** Bldr: Mjellem & Karlsen, Bergen

L 4500 Kvalsund (In serv. 6-68) L 4501 Raftsund (In serv. 3-69)

**D:** 590 tons (fl) **S:** 11 kts **Dim:** 50.0 × 10.2 × 1.8
**A:** 2/20-mm Rheinmetall AA—rails for 120 mines
**M:** 2 MTU diesels; 2 props; 1,350 hp **Man:** 2 officers, 7 men

Remarks: Cargo capacity: 5 Leopard tanks, 80–180 men. Both subordinate to Home Guard, rather than Navy.

## AUXILIARY SHIPS

Note: The 14,989-grt auto/passenger ferry *Peter Wessel* was acquired 9-85 for conversion to a casualty evacuation ship with a medical staff of 450 and facilities for 800 seriously wounded and 1,200 lightly wounded troops. Subordination of the ship not reported. A second ship may also be obtained.

◆ **1 logistic-support ship** Bldr: Horten Verft, Horten

| | Laid down | L | In serv. |
|---|---|---|---|
| A 530 Horten | 28-1-77 | 12-8-77 | 9-6-78 |

**Horten (A 530)** G. Arra, 7-86

**D:** 2,500 tons (fl) **S:** 16.5 kts **Dim:** 87.0 (82.0 pp) × 13.7 × . . .
**A:** 2/40-mm AA (I × 2)—mines **Electron Equipt:** Radar: 3/Decca. . .
**M:** 2 Wichmann 7AX diesels; 2 props; 4,200 hp **Man:** 86 tot.

Remarks: Used to support submarines and small combatants. Can accommodate up to 190 additional personnel. Helicopter deck. Bow-thruster. Acted as Royal Yacht, 1985–86.

Note: The oceanographic research ship *H.U. Sverdrup* was stricken 1986.

◆ **1 royal yacht**

| | Bldr | L |
|---|---|---|
| A 533 Norge (ex-*Philante*) | Camper & Nicholson's Ltd., Gosport | 17-2-37 |

**Norge (A 533)** 1971

**D:** 1,686 tons **S:** 17 kts **Dim:** 76.27 × 8.53 × 4.65
**M:** 2 8-cyl. diesels; 2 props; 3,000 hp **Electric:** 300 kw
**Fuel:** 175 tons **Range:** 9,900/17

Remarks: Built as a yacht, then used by the Royal Navy as an ASW escort from 1940 to 1943, then as a training ship. Purchased by Norway in 1948. Displacement listed is in Thames Yacht Measurement. Can carry 50-passenger royal party. Severe fire 8-3-85, repaired by summer 1986.

## SERVICE CRAFT

◆ **1 torpedo-recovery and oil-spill cleanup ship** Bldr: Fjellstrand, Hardinger (In serv. 10-78)

VSD 1 Vernøy

**D:** 150 grt **S:** 12 kts **Dim:** 31.3 × 6.67 × 2.0
**M:** 2 MWM diesels; 2 Schottel props; . . . hp

◆ **8 Torpen-class support tenders**

| | Bldr | In serv. |
|---|---|---|
| VSD 4 Torpen | Båtservice, Mandal | 15-12-77 |
| ØSD 2 Wisting | Voldnes, Fosnavåg | 30-1-78 |
| TSD 5 Tautra | Båtservice, Mandal | 15-2-78 |
| NSD 35 Rotvaer | Båtservice, Mandal | 3-78 |
| RSD 23 Fjøløy | Voldnes, Fosnavåg | 4-78 |
| HSD 15 Krøttøy | Voldnes, Fosnavåg | 6-78 |
| TRSD 4 Karlsøy | P. Høivolds, Kristianstad | 7-78 |
| ROS 22 Kjeøy | . . . | . . . |

**Torpen (VSD 4)** L. & L. Van Ginderen, 11-87

**Kjeøy (ROS 22)** F. Jentsch, 1986

**D:** 215 tons (300 fl) **S:** 11 kts **Dim:** 29.0 × 6.4 × 2.57
**A:** 1/12.7-mm mg **M:** 1 MWM TBD 601-6K diesel; 1 CP prop; 530 hp
**Electron Equipt:** Radar: 1/Decca 1226
**Fuel:** 11 tons **Range:** 1,200/11 **Man:** 6 men + 100 passengers

## SERVICE CRAFT *(continued)*

Remarks: Basically similar craft tailored to a variety of duties, including logistics support, ammunition transport, personnel transport, and divers' support. Cargo: 100 tons.

◆ **2 navigational training craft** Bldr: Fjellstrand, Omastrand (In serv. 1-78)

P 358 Hessa (ex-*Hitra,* ex-*Kvarnen,* VSD 6) P 359 Vigra (ex-*Marsteinen,* VSD 2)

**Vigra (P 359)** Norwegian Navy, 1982

**D:** 40 tons **S:** 22 kts **Dim:** 23.2 × 5.0 × 1.1 **A:** 1/12.7-mm mg
**M:** 2 G.M. 12V71 diesels; 2 props; 1,800 hp **Man:** 5 men + 8 cadets

Remarks: Aluminum construction. For use at the Naval Academy. Renamed and renumbered 1981. P 358 renamed 5-87 to free name for craft below.

◆ **1 relic/training tender** Bldr: Fisher Boat Works, Detroit

| | Laid down | L | In serv. |
|---|---|---|---|
| P . . . Hitra (ex-U.S. SC 718) | 22-9-42 | 31-3-43 | 25-5-43 |

**D:** 95 tons light (148 fl) **S:** 21 kts (new)
**Dim:** 33.80 (32.77 wl) × 5.18 × 1.98 **A:** . . .
**M:** 2 diesels; 2 props; . . . hp **Fuel:** 16 tons **Man:** . . .

Remarks: Survivor of the ships and craft which served Free Norwegian naval forces during World War II. Reacquired 8-5-87 for restoration to operational service as cadet training craft and museum ship. Wooden construction. Originally armed with 1/40-mm AA, 3/20-mm AA, depth charges, and Mousetrap ASW RL. May have been re-engined during commercial career 1948–87.

◆ **2 tenders for combat divers** Bldr: Nielsen, Harstad (In serv. 1972)

A 531 Sarpen (ex-VDS 11, ex-SKV 11) A 532 Draug (ex-SKV 10)

**Sarpen (A 351)**—old number Norwegian Navy, 1981

**D:** 250 tons **S:** 12 kts **Dim:** 29.0 × 6.7 × 2.5 **M:** 1 diesel; 1 prop; 530 hp

Remarks: Renumbered 1982. Support frogmen.

◆ **1 harbor tug** Bldr: F. Schichau, Königsberg, Germany (In serv. 1938)

VSD 7 Samson

**D:** 303 grt **S:** 11 kts **Dim:** 38.7 × 8.0 × 3.25
**M:** 1 MWM diesel; 1 prop; 650 hp **Range:** 2,900/10

◆ **1 harbor tug** Bldr: Atlas Werke, Bremen, Germany (L: 6-2-39)

VSD 13 Ramnes (ex-German *Robbe*)

**D:** 101 grt **S:** 10 kts **Dim:** 24.0 × 5.70 × 2.45 **M:** 1 diesel; 250 hp

◆ **2 local patrol craft** Bldr: Fjellstrand Yacht, Omastrand

RSD 23 Tarva (In serv. 1-12-74) ØSD 1 Welding (In serv. 1-11-74)

**D:** 27.5 tons (fl) **S:** 15 kts **Dim:** 16.3 × 5.3 × 1.2
**A:** 1/12.7-mm mg **Electron Equipt:** Radar: 1/Decca. . .
**M:** 2 G.M. diesels; 2 props; 480 hp **Man:** 4 tot.

◆ **1 or more personnel launches**

SKO 122 Fuldin—No data available

Note: Other service craft, for which no data are available, include: SKV 20, *Gleodden; Varodden,* VSD 8; VSD 20; VSD 63; VSD 10, *Foracs; Petra;* SKØ 121; *Fjordbåt;* SKS 55; SSD 8; *Akerøy; Sigurd A.,* (RSD 21); VSD 3; *Torpedofisken; Arnøy; Folden;* NSD 33, NSD 81, NSD 84, and ØESD 66.

## COAST GUARD (KYSTVAKT)

The Norwegian Coast Guard was established in 1976 to perform fisheries-protection duties, patrol the waters in the vicinity of offshore oil rigs, and maintain surveillance over the 200-nautical-mile economic zone. The Coast Guard operates six WG-13 Lynx Mk 86 helicopters.

## PATROL SHIPS

◆ **3 Nordkapp (Type 320) class**

| | Bldr | L | In serv. |
|---|---|---|---|
| W 320 Nordkapp | Bergens Mek. Verk. | 14-5-80 | 25-4-81 |
| W 321 Senja | Horten Verft | 16-3-80 | 8-3-81 |
| W 322 Andennes | Haugesund Verk. | 21-3-81 | 30-1-82 |

**Andennes (W 322)** Norwegian Navy, 1984

**Nordkapp (W 320)** Norwegian Navy

**D:** 2,165 tons light (3,240 fl) **S:** 23 kts **Dim:** 105.00 (97.50 pp) × 13.85 × 4.55
**A:** 1/57-mm Bofors AA—4/20-mm Rheinmetall AA (I × 4)—6/324-mm Mk 32 ASW TT (III × 2)—1/d.c. rack (6 d.c.)—1/WG-13 Lynx helicopter
**Electron Equipt:** Radar: 2/Decca TM 1226, 1/Decca RM914, 1/Plessey AWS-4, 1/PEAB GLF 218 (9LV 200 Mk.2)
Sonar: 1/Simrad SS105
**M:** 4 Wichmann 9-AXAG diesels; 2 CP props; 14,400 hp **Electric:** 1,600 kw
**Fuel:** 350 tons **Range:** 7,500/15 **Man:** 42 crew + 6 helo crew (109 accomm.)

**NORWAY** *(continued)*
**COAST GUARD** *(continued)*

Remarks: Program delayed by design changes and lack of funding; four additional units deferred. W 322 and W 323 displace 2,854 tons full load and are not ice-strengthened, as is W 320, intended for service in arctic waters. In time of conflict, 6 Penguin II antiship missiles and chaff launchers are to be added. Fin stabilized. Carry three 300-$m^3$/hr. water cannon for firefighting and have meteorological reporting gear. The Kongsberg MSI-805 NAVKIS data system is fitted. Wartime crew: 75 total.

◆ **1 former purse-seiner** Bldr: Fredrikstad Mek. Verksted, Fredrikstad (In serv. 1956)

W 318 Garpeskjaer (ex-*Sun Tuna*, ex-*Tenor*, ex-*Star I*)

**D:** 1,122 grt **S:** . . . **Dim:** 66.54 × . . . × . . .
**A:** 1/40-mm AA **Electron Equipt:** Radar: 2/. . . nav.
**M:** 1 Alpha diesel; 1 prop; 4,240 hp **Man:** . . .

Remarks: Leased 1986 to replace *Grimsholm* (W 319). Built as a whaler, later converted as a purse-seiner.

◆ **1 former stern-haul purse-seiner** Bldr: Brødrene Lothes, Haugesund (In serv. 7-78)

W 317 Lafjord

**D:** 814 grt **S:** 14.6 kts **Dim:** 55.40 × 9.81 × 6.18
**A:** 1/40-mm AA **M:** 1 Wichmann 7-cyl. diesel; 1 prop; 2,100 hp
**Electric:** 419 kw **Fuel:** 220 tons **Range:** 7,700/14.6

Remarks: Chartered 1980. Side-thrusters fore and aft.

◆ **1 former stern-haul purse-seiner** Bldr: Smedvik, Tjørvåg (In serv. 4-78)

W 315 Nordsjøbas

**D:** 814 grt **S:** 13.5 kts **Dim:** 52.04 (44.75 pp) × 10.01 × 6.55
**A:** 1/40-mm AA **Electric:** 1,088 kw **Range:** 8,300/13.5
**M:** 1 MaK 6-cyl. diesel; 1 prop; 2,400 hp **Fuel:** 180 tons

Remarks: Chartered 1980. Side-thrusters fore and aft.

Note: Former purse-seiners chartered for Coast Guard service were returned to their owners in 1986–87: *Grimsholm* (W 319) in 11-85, *Sørfold* (W 312) in 1986, and *Møgsterfjord* (W 313) in 1987.

◆ **1 former purse-seiner** Bldr: Beliard, Crighton & Cie., France (In serv. 1955)

W 314 Stålbas (ex-*Trålbas*, ex-*Cdt. Charcot*, ex-*Jean Charcot*)

**D:** 498 grt **S:** . . . **Dim:** 58.76 × 9.41 × 4.51 **A:** 1/40-mm AA
**M:** 1 Klöckner-Humboldt-Deutz 8-cyl. diesel; 1 prop; 1,500 hp **Man:** . . .

Remarks: Side-thrusters fitted, fore and aft. Originally built as a trawler.

◆ **1 former purse-seiner** Bldr: . . .

W 313 Malene Østervold (ex-. . .)

**D:** . . . **S:** . . . **Dim:** . . . × . . . × . . .
**A:** . . . **Electron Equipt:** Radar: 2/. . . nav. **M:** . . .

Remarks: Leased 1987 to replace *Møgsterfjord* (W 313).

◆ **1 former whale catcher** Bldr: Fredrikstad MV (In serv. 1950)

W 316 Volstad Jr. (ex-XIV)

**Volstad Jr. (W 316)** 1982

**D:** 617 grt **S:** . . . **Dim:** 51.39 (45.32 pp) × 9.05 × 5.67 **A:** 1/40-mm AA
**M:** 2 Klöchner-Humboldt-Deutz NE-66 8-cyl. diesels; 1 CP prop; 1,200 hp
**Electric:** 224 kw **Man:** . . .

Remarks: Chartered from Einar Volstad Partrederi in 1977. Built as a side-haul trawler, converted to a whaler in 1966, and well deck filled in.

◆ **1 former naval fisheries-protection ship**

| | Bldr | L |
|---|---|---|
| W 300 Nornen | Mjellem & Karlsen, Bergen | 20-8-62 |

**Nornen (W 300)** 1978

**D:** 1,060 tons (fl) **S:** 17 kts **Dim:** 61.5 × 10.0 × 3.8
**A:** 1/76.2-mm Mk 26 DP **M:** 4 diesels; 1 prop; 3,700 hp **Man:** 32 tot.

Remarks: Considerably altered, 1976–77: bridge enlarged, stack heightened, mast moved aft, hull side openings plated up, two new radars added, gun enclosed.

◆ **2 former naval fisheries-protection ships**

| | Bldr | L |
|---|---|---|
| W 301 Farm (ex-A 532) | Ankerlokken Verft, Fredrikstad | 22-2-62 |
| W 302 Heimdal (ex-A 534) | Bolsones Verft, Molde | 7-3-62 |

**Farm (W 301)** Norwegian Navy, 1984

**D:** 600 grt **S:** 16.5 kts **Dim:** 54.28 (49.0 pp) × 8.2 × 3.2
**A:** 1/40-mm AA **M:** 2 Wichmann 9ACAT diesels; 2 CP props; 2,400 hp
**Electric:** 150 kVA **Man:** 29 tot.

Remarks: Modernized 1979 (W 301) and 1980 (W 302) with completely revised superstructure, new bridge resembling *Nornen*'s, new armament, and revised hull sides along the forecastle.

### HYDROGRAPHIC SURVEY SHIP

◆ **1 former Ministry of the Environment ship** Bldr: Mjellem & Karlsen, Bergen

Hydrograf (In serv. 12-67)

**D:** 302 grt **S:** 13 kts **Dim:** 38.95 (35.11 pp) × 7.83 × 2.94
**A:** 1/40-mm AA **M:** 1 Bergens Mek. Verk. 6-cyl. diesel; 1 prop; 780 hp
**Electric:** 100 kw **Fuel:** 38 tons **Range:** 3,900/13 **Man:** 3 officers, 15 men

Remarks: Now operated by the Coast Guard for the Ministry of the Environment. No pendant number. The Ministry of the Environment also operates 11 survey ships with its own personnel: *Lance* (960 tons, in serv. 1978); *Sjøvern* (215 tons, in serv. 1948); *Sjøfalk* (70 tons, in serv. 1937); *Sjøskvett* (80 tons, in serv. 1964); *Sjørokk* (75 tons, in serv. 1964); *Sjødrev* (80 tons, in serv. 1973); *Sjøtroll* (80 tons, in serv. 1976) and *Olijevern* 01–04 (200 tons, in serv. 1978).

# OMAN

**Sultanate of Oman**

Personnel (1987): 2,400 total

Merchant Marine (1986): 29 ships—14,793 grt (tankers: 2 ships—432 grt)

Naval Aviation: Two Dornier 228-100 for coastal surveillance

## GUIDED-MISSILE PATROL BOATS

◆ **3 (+1) "Province" class** Bldr: Vosper Thornycroft, Portchester, U.K.

| | Laid down | L | In serv. |
|---|---|---|---|
| B 10 DHOFAR | 39-9-80 | 14-10-81 | 7-8-82 |
| B 11 AL SHARQUIYAH | 10-81 | 2-12-82 | 5-12-83 |
| B 12 AL BAT'NAH | 9-12-81 | 11-82 | 18-1-84 |
| B . . . N . . . | . . . | 8-10-87 | 1988 |

**Dhofar (B 10)**—with AWS-4 radar, 6 SSM positions M. Louagie, 8-82

**Al Bat'nah (B 12)**—equipped for 8 Exocet Walles Foto, 3-84

**D:** 311 tons light (363 fl) **S:** 40 kts **Dim:** 56.7 (52.0 pp) × 8.2 × 2.1 (hull)
**A:** 6/MM 40 Exocet SSM (III × 2)—1/76-mm OTO Melara DP—2/40-mm Breda AA (II × 1)—2/12.7-mm mg (I × 2)
**Electron Equipt:** Radar: B 11: 1/Decca 1226, 1/Plessey AWS-4; others: 1/Decca TM 1226, 1/PEAB 9LV 300 syst.
EW: . . . intercept; 2 Wallops Barricade decoy RL (IX × 2)
**M:** 4 Paxman Valenta 18RP200 diesels; 4 props; 17,900 hp (15,000 sust.)—2/80-hp electric outdrives
**Electric:** 420 kw **Fuel:** 45.5 tons **Range:** 2,000/15
**Man:** 40, plus 19 trainees

REMARKS: B 10 ordered 1980; B 11, 12 in 1-81; fourth ordered 3-1-86. B 10 sailed for Oman 21-10-82. B 10 has the Sperry Sea Archer Mk 2 fire-control system, with two optical trackers. Complement includes trainees. B 9, B 10 have 8/MM 40 Exocet (IV × 2), PEAB 9LV 300 f.c.s. with I-band search radar and J-band radar/electro-optical fire-control director forward and a separate tv./IR director aft for the 40-mm AA.

NOTE: The 37.5-m missile boat *Al Mansur* (B 2) was stricken in 1986.

## PATROL BOATS

◆ **4 37.5-meter class** Bldr: Brooke Marine Ltd., Lowestoft, U.K.

| | In serv. |
|---|---|
| B 4 AL WAFI | 24-3-77 |
| B 5 AL FULK | 24-3-77 |
| B 6 AL AUL | 20-7-77 |
| B 7 AL JABBAR | 6-10-77 |

**D:** 153 tons (166 fl) **S:** 25 kts **Dim:** 37.50 × 6.86 × 1.78
**A:** 1/76-mm OTO Melara DP—1/20-mm AA—2/7.62-mm mg (I × 2)
**Electron Equipt:** Radar: 1/Decca 1226 or 1229
**M:** 2 Paxman Ventura 16 RP200 diesels; 2 props; 4,800 hp
**Range:** 3,250/12 **Man:** 3 officers, 24 men

**Al Fulk (B 5)** L. & L. Van Ginderen, 9-82

REMARKS: Carry 130 rounds 76-mm ammunition. Sperry Sea Archer fire-control system, with Lawrence Scott optical director.

## PATROL CRAFT

◆ **4 25-meter class** Bldr: Vosper Pty, Singapore (In serv. 15-3-81)

B 20 AL SEEB B 21 AL SHINAS B 22 AL SADAH B 23 AL KHASAB

**25-meter class**—on trials 1980

**D:** 75 tons (fl) **S:** 26 kts **Dim:** 25.0 (23.0 pp) × 5.8 × 1.5
**A:** 1/20-mm AA—2/7.62-mm mg (I × 2)
**M:** 2 MTU 12V331 TC92 diesels, plus 1 Cummins N855M diesel; 3 props; 3,072 hp + 197 hp
**Range:** 750/14; 2,300/8 **Man:** 13 tot.

REMARKS: Ordered 24-4-81. Craft completed 1980 on speculation by builder. Glass-reinforced plastic hulls. Have five spare berths. Max. speed on cruise diesel: 8 kts.

◆ **2 Tyler Vortex class** Bldr: Cheverton, Cowes (In serv. 1981)

QRB 1 QRB 2

**D:** 12 tons **S:** 30 kts **Dim:** 12.1 (11.5 pp) × 4.6 × . . .
**A:** . . . **M:** 2 Sabre 500 diesels; 2 props; 1,000 hp

REMARKS: Officially typed as "Quick-reaction Boats."

## AMPHIBIOUS WARFARE SHIPS AND CRAFT

◆ **1 troop and vehicle transport** Bldr: Bremer-Vulkan, Bremen-Vegesack, West Germany

| | L | In serv. |
|---|---|---|
| L 3 GHUBAT AL SALAMAH (ex-*Tulip*) | 29-8-86 | 5-87 |

**D:** 10,900 tons (fl) **S:** . . . **Dim:** . . . × . . . × . . .
**A:** . . . **Electron Equipt:** Radar: . . .
**M:** 2 diesels; 2 props; 16,800 hp **Range:** . . . **Man:** . . .

REMARKS: 8,000 grt (also reported as 10,900 grt). Described as a large ramp-equipped cargo transport with a helicopter deck.

◆ **1 new-construction landing ship** Bldr: Brooke Marine, Lowestoft, U.K.

| | Laid down | L | In serv. |
|---|---|---|---|
| L 2 NASR AL BAHR | . . . | 16-5-84 | 13-2-85 |

**D:** 2,200 tons (fl) **S:** 15.5 kts **Dim:** 93.00 (80.00 pp) × 15.50 × 2.3 (mean)
**A:** 4/40-mm Breda AA (II × 2)—2/20-mm AA (I × 2)
**Electron Equipt:** Radar: 1/Decca 1226, 1/Decca 1290
EW: . . . intercept; 2 Barricade RL (IX × 2)
**M:** 2 Paxman Valenta 18RP200CM diesels; 2 CP props; 7,800 hp
**Range:** 4,000/13 **Endurance:** 28 days (10 days with troops)
**Man:** 13 off., 16 chief petty officers, 52 men + troops: 13 officers, 16 noncommissioned officers, 211 enlisted

**Nasr Al Bahr (L 2)** Walles Foto, 3-85

## AMPHIBIOUS WARFARE SHIPS AND CRAFT *(continued)*

**Nasr Al Bahr (L 2)** Walles Foto, 2-85

REMARKS: Ordered 18-3-82. A refined version of the *Al Munassir* design. Two also built for Algeria. Vehicle deck 75 m × 7.4 m, with 30-m × 7-m cargo hatch; bow ramp 18 m long by 4.5 m wide; stern ramp: 5 m by 4 m. Intended to land 450 tons cargo or seven main battle tanks on a gradient of up to 1:40. Helicopter deck for one Sea King/Commando helicopter. Traveling 16-ton crane spans cargo deck forward. Max. cargo: 650 tons. One Philips PEAB and one CSEE Lynx electro-optical gunsight; 2,000 rds 40 mm, 2,450 rds 20 mm, 244 chaff rounds.

◆ **1 for logistic support**

| | Bldr | Laid down | L | In serv. |
|---|---|---|---|---|
| L 1 AL MUNASSIR | Brooke Marine, Lowestoft | 4-7-77 | 25-7-78 | 3-4-79 |

**Al Munassir (L 1)** French Navy, 5-81

**D:** 2,169 tons (fl) **S:** 12 kts **Dim:** 84.0 (81.25 pp) × 15.03 × 2.15 (max.)
**A:** 1/76-mm OTO Melara DP—2/20-mm AA (I × 2)
**Electron Equipt:** Radar: 1/Decca TM 1229
**M:** 2 Mirrlees-Blackstone ESL8MGR diesels; 2 CP props; 2,400 hp
**Range:** 2,500/12 **Man:** 9 officers, 38 men, 188 troops

REMARKS: Greatly modified version of British *Ardennes* class by same builder. Cargo: 550 tons of stores or 8 heavy tanks. Has bow doors and ramp for beaching. Large helicopter deck aft can accommodate Westland Sea King or Commando helicopters and is spanned by a 16-ton-capacity traveling crane. Unusually bluff-bowed hull form. Sperry Sea Archer optical fire-control director.

◆ **3 utility landing craft** Bldr: Vosper Pty, Singapore

| | Laid down | L | In serv. |
|---|---|---|---|
| C 8 SABA AL BAHR | . . . | 30-6-81 | 17-9-81 |
| C 9 AL DOGHAS | 9-7-82 | 12-11-82 | 10-1-83 |
| C 10 AL TEMSAH | 8-9-82 | 15-12-82 | 12-2-83 |

**D:** 230 tons (fl) **S:** 8 kts **Dim:** 30.0 (25.6 pp) × 8.0 × 1.2
**M:** 2 Caterpillar 3408 TA diesels; 2 props; 1,840 hp
**Range:** 1,800/8 **Man:** 11 tot.

REMARKS: C 8 ordered 24-4-81, C 9 and C 10 in 7-82. Cargo: 100 tons vehicles or stores, or 45 tons deck cargo plus 50 tons fresh water (plus 35 tons water ballast). C 9 and C 10 are 33 m o.a.

◆ **1 utility landing craft** Bldr: Lewis Offshore, Stornaway, Scotland (In serv. 1979)

C 7 AL NEEMRAN

**D:** 85 dwt **S:** 8 kts **Dim:** 25.5 × 7.4 × 1.8 **M:** 2 diesels; . . . hp

◆ **1 75-foot Loadmaster-class landing craft** Bldr: Cheverton, Cowes, U.K. (In serv. 1-75)

C 4 AL SANSOOR

**D:** 64 tons (130 fl) **S:** 8.75 kts **Dim:** 22.86 × 6.1 × 1.07 (max.)
**M:** 2 diesels; 2 props; 300 hp

REMARKS: Sister *Al Doghas* (C 5) stricken 1981. The larger *Al Dhaibah* (C 6) was stricken in 1982; the smaller *Sulhafa Al Bahr* has also been discarded.

## AUXILIARY SHIPS

◆ **1 training ship** Bldr: Brooke Marine, Lowestoft, U.K.

| | L | In serv. |
|---|---|---|
| A 1 AL MABRUKAH (ex-*Al Said*) | 7-4-70 | 1971 |

**Al Mabrukah (A 1)** Walles Foto, 4-84

**D:** 785 tons (930 fl) **S:** 17 kts **Dim:** 54.70 × 10.70 × 3.05
**A:** 1/40-mm AA—2/20-mm AA (I × 2)
**Electron Equipt:** Radar: 1/Decca TM 1226
EW: . . . intercept, 2 Barricade RL (IX × 2)
**M:** 2 Paxman Ventura 12YJCM diesels; 2 props; 3,350 hp
**Man:** 11 officers, 23 men, 37 passengers

REMARKS: Renamed and under conversion from royal yacht to fleet training ship at builders 1-83 to 4-84. Received new accommodations arrangements, communications suit, and armament; the helicopter deck was enlarged.

◆ **1 supply ship**

| | Bldr | L | In serv. |
|---|---|---|---|
| A 2 AL SULTANA | Conoship, Groningen, Netherlands | 18-5-75 | 4-6-75 |

**D:** 900 tons (1,380 dwt) **S:** 11 kts **Dim:** 65.4 × 10.7 × 4.2
**M:** 1 Mirrlees-Blackstone diesel; 1,150 hp

REMARKS: Traveling crane serves all holds. Replaced in training role by *Al Mabrukah.*

◆ **1 inshore survey craft** Bldr: Watercraft, U.K. (In serv. 4-81)

H 1 AL RAHMANYAI

**D:** 23.6 tons (fl) **S:** 13.5 kts **Dim:** 15.5 (14.0 pp) × 4.0 × 12.5
**Electron Equipt:** Radar: 1/Decca 101
**M:** 2 Volvo TMD 120A diesels; 2 props; 520 hp
**Electric:** 25 kVA **Range:** 500/12

REMARKS: Glass-reinforced plastic construction. Raytheon DE 719B and Kelvin-Hughes MS 48 echo-sounders, Decca DMU transponder and Sea Fix receiver, and Hewlett-Packard 9815A data storage computer fitted.

◆ **1 sail-training craft** Bldr: Hard & MacKenzie, Buckie, Scotland (In serv. . . .)

S 1 SHABAB OMAN (ex-*Youth of Oman,* ex-*Captain Scott*)

**Shahab Oman (S 1)** G. Arra, 7-86

**AUXILIARY SHIPS** *(continued)*

**D:** 386 tons **S:** . . . **Dim:** 44.0 × 8.5 × 4.6 **M:** 2 diesels; 1 prop; . . . hp
**Man:** 5 officers, 15 men + 3 officer/instructors, 24 trainees

REMARKS: Three-masted barkentine, purchased 1977 in U.K., for training Omani youth in seamanship.

◆ **10 miscellaneous workboats** Bldr: Cheverton, Cowes, U.K.

W 4,5, 7–11 WF 41–43 (In serv. 4-75)

**D:** 3.5 tons **S:** 25 kts **Dim:** 8.28 × 2.7 × 0.8 **M:** 2 diesels

◆ **1 or more Sea Flash radio-controlled target boats** Bldr: Flight Refuelling, U.K. (In serv. 1987)

ROYAL YACHT SQUADRON

◆ **1 royal yacht** Bldr: Picchiotti, Viareggio, Italy (In serv. 1982)

AL SAID

**D:** 3,250 tons (fl) **S:** 18 kts **Dim:** 106.0 × 17.0 × 5.0
**Electron Equipt:** 1/Decca TM 1226C, 1/Decca ACS 1230C
**M:** 2 GMT A420-6 diesels; 2 CP props; 8,400 hp
**Man:** 16 officers, 140 men

REMARKS: Replaced former *Al Said* (now training ship *Al Mabrukah*). Not considered to be a naval vessel, unlike her predecessor. Helicopter pad; bow-thruster.

ROYAL OMAN POLICE

AVIATION: Two Pilantus Porter light transports for search-and-rescue duties, delivered 4-84.

◆ **1 P 2000 class** Bldr: Watercraft Ltd., Shoreham, U.K.

DHEEB AL BAHAR 1 (In serv. 12-84)

**Dheeb Al Bahar** Watercraft, 9-84

**D:** 80 tons **S:** 38 kts **Dim:** 20.80 (18.00 pp) × 5.80 × 1.50
**A:** 1/20-mm AA—6/7.62-mm mg (I × 6)
**Electron Equipt:** Radar: 1/Furuno FR-701
**M:** 2 MTU 12V396 TB93 diesels; 2 props; 3,920 hp (3,260 sust.)
**Range:** 423/35; 660/22

REMARKS: Glass-reinforced plastic construction, with aluminum superstructure. Additional units may be procured.

◆ **2 P 1200 class** Bldr: Watercraft Ltd , Shoreham, U.K. (In serv. 9-84)

**D:** 10 tons **S:** 35 kts **Dim:** 11.90 (10.16 pp) × 4.08 × 1.06
**A:** 1/12.7-mm mg—6/7.62-mm mg (I × 6) **Electron Equipt:** Radar: 1/. . . nav.
**M:** 2 M.A.N. diesels; 2 props; 1,100 hp **Range:** 300/. . . **Man:** 8 tot.

REMARKS: Ordered 7-82. Glass-reinforced plastic construction.

**PATROL BOATS AND CRAFT**

◆ **1 . . . class** Bldr: . . . (In serv. 1982)

HARAS 9

**D:** 82 tons (fl) **S:** 25 kts **Dim:** 29.9 × 5.8 × 1.2
**A:** 2/20-mm AA **M:** 2 MTU 12V396 diesels; 2 props; . . . hp **Man:** 13 tot.

◆ **1 Type PT 1903 Mk III patrol craft** Bldr: Le Comte, Vianen, Netherlands

HARAS 8 (In serv. 8-81)

**D:** 30 tons (33 fl) **S:** 30 kts **Dim:** 19.27 × 4.95 × 1.25
**A:** 2/12.7-mm mg (I × 2) **Range:** 1,650/17; 2,300/12
**M:** 2 MTU 8V331 TC92 diesels; 2 props; 1,770 hp **Man:** 10 tot.

**Haras 8** Le Comte, 1981

◆ **2 CG 29 class** Bldr: Karlskrona, Sweden

HARAS 7 (In serv. 6-81) HARAS 10 (In serv. 14-4-82)

**Haras 7** P. Voss, 7-81

**D:** 82 tons (fl) **S:** 27 kts **Dim:** 28.9 × 5.4 × 1.3
**A:** 2/20-mm AA (I × 2) **Electron Equipt:** Radar: 1/Decca 1226C
**M:** 2 MTU 8V331 IC82 diesels; 2 props; 1,866 hp
**Range:** 600/15 **Man:** 13 tot.

REMARKS: Aluminum construction, enlarged version of design built for Liberia.

◆ **1 CG class** Bldr: Karlskrona, Sweden (In serv. 1980)

HARAS 6

**D:** 53 tons (fl) **S:** 25 kts **Dim:** 24.0 × 5.5 × 1.0
**A:** 1/20-mm AA **Man:** 11 tot. **M:** 2 MTU 12V331 diesels; 2 props; 2,800 hp

REMARKS: Glass-reinforced plastic construction.

◆ **5 Haras 1-class fiberglass-hulled** Bldr: Vosper, Singapore (In serv. 1–4: 22-12-75; 5: 11-78)

HARAS 1 HARAS 2 HARAS 3 HARAS 4 HARAS 5

**D:** 45 tons (fl) **S:** 24.5 kts **Dim:** 22.9 × 6.0 × 1.5
**A:** 1/20-mm AA **Electron Equipt:** Radar: 1/Decca 101
**M:** 2 Caterpillar D348 diesels; 2 props; 1,840 hp
**Range:** 600/20; 1,000/11 **Man:** 11 tot.

◆ **2 small patrol craft** Bldr: Watercraft, Shoreham (In serv. 1981)

ZARA 17 ZARA 18

**D:** 17.25 tons (fl) **S:** 22 kts **Dim:** 13.9 (12.6 wl) × 4.3 × 1.1
**M:** 2 Cummins VTA-903M diesels; 2 props; 700 hp
**A:** 1/7.62-mm mg **Range:** 700/20 **Man:** 6 tot.

**OMAN** *(continued)*
**PATROL BOATS AND CRAFT** *(continued)*

**Haras 1** 1980

◆ **2 landing craft** Bldr: Le Comte, Vianen, the Netherlands

Zara 20 (In serv. 1981) Zara 22 (In serv. 1982)

**D:** 11 tons (23 fl) **S:** 20 kts **Dim:** 18.0 × 3.0 × 0.5
**A:** 2/7.62-mm mg (I × 2) **Range:** . . . **Man:** 4 tot.
**M:** 2 Volvo Penta AQD 70/750 diesel outdrives; 540 hp

Remarks: *Zara 20* used as a fueling tender. *Zara 22* is 16.0 m o.a.

Note: Also in service are one 19-m and one 18-m tender, delivered by Le Comte, Vianen, the Netherlands, in 1983, along with a 16-m craft, and an 8.2-m workboat delivered by Cheverton, Cowes, U.K., in 1983. Two 8.5-m patrol craft, powered by 2/140-hp Evinrude outboards for 40 kts, were delivered in 1985 by Gulf Craft, Ajman, United Arab Emirates.

# PAKISTAN

## Islamic Republic of Pakistan

Personnel (1987): 1,200 officers, 9,800 men—plus 5,000 reservists

Merchant Marine (1986): 78 ships—434,079 grt (tankers: 1 ship—43,429 grt)

Naval Aviation: The naval arm consists of: 4 Bréguet BR1150 Atlantic Mk 1 patrol aircraft, 6 Sea King helicopters armed with AM-39 antiship missiles, 4 Alouette-III helicopters, 2 Cessna liaison aircraft, and 1 Fokker F-27 transport. The fourth Atlantic Mk 1 was purchased from the Netherlands 12-86.

### SUBMARINES

◆ **2 French Agosta class** Bldr: Dubigeon, Nantes

| | Laid down | L | In serv. |
|---|---|---|---|
| S 135 Hashmat (ex-*Astrant*) | 15-9-76 | 14-12-77 | 17-2-79 |
| S 136 Hurmat (ex-*Adventurous*) | . . . | 1-12-78 | 18-2-80 |

**Hurmat (S 136)** J.-C. Bellonne, 1980

**D:** 1,230/1,480/1,725 tons **S:** 12.5/20.5 kts **Dim:** 67.90 × 6.80 × 5.40
**A:** 4/550-mm TT, fwd (20 torpedoes and Sub-Harpoon SSM)
**Electron Equipt:** Radar: 1/DRUA-33
Sonar: DUUA-1D, DUUA-2A, DSUV-2H, DUUA-2B, DUUX-2A
EW: ARUR, ARUD
**M:** 2 SEMT-Pielstick A16 PA4 185 diesels, electric drive (1 3,500-kw motor); 1 prop; 4,600 hp; 1 23-hp cruise motor
**Fuel:** 200 tons **Range:** 7,900/10 (snorkel); 178/3.5 (submerged) **Man:** 55 tot.

Remarks: Originally ordered for South Africa, but sale canceled in 1977 by arms embargo and completion slowed. Sold to Pakistan in 11-78. Very quiet, highly automated submarines. Diving depth: 300 m. Battery capacity twice that of the *Daphné* class. Fitted for U.S. Sub-Harpoon antiship missiles in 1984–85.

◆ **4 French Daphné class**

| | Bldr | Laid down | L | In serv. |
|---|---|---|---|---|
| S 131 Hangor | Naval Arsenal, Brest | 1-12-67 | 30-6-69 | 12-1-70 |
| S 132 Shushuk | C.N. Ciotat, Le Trait | 1-12-67 | 30-7-69 | 12-1-70 |
| S 133 Mangro | C.N. Ciotat, Le Trait | 8-7-68 | 7-2-70 | 8-8-70 |
| S 134 Ghazi (ex-*Cachalote*) | Dubigeon, Normandy | 27-10-66 | 16-2-68 | 25-1-69 |

**Ghazi (S 134)** J.-C. Bellonne, 1977

**D:** 700 std./869 surf./1,043 sub. tons **S:** 13.5/16 kts **Dim:** 57.75 × 6.75 × 4.56
**A:** 12/550-mm TT (8 fwd, 4 aft, no reloads; Sub-Harpoon SSM)
**Electron Equipt:** Radar: DRUA 31
Sonar: DUUA–1 active, DSUV–1 passive
EW: ARUR, ARUD intercept
**M:** 2 SEMT-Pielstick 12PA4-135 450-kw diesel generator sets; 2 1,300-hp (1,000 sust.) electric motors; 2 props
**Range:** 4,300/7.5 (snorkel) **Man:** 5 officers, 45 men

Remarks: S 134 purchased in 12-75 from Portugal. S 131 sank the Indian frigate *Khukri* in 1971. Diving depth: 300 m.

◆ **2 SX-404-class midget submarines** Bldr: COSMOS, Livorno, Italy

**D:** 40/70 tons **S:** 11/6.5 kts **Dim:** 16.0 × 1.8 × . . .
**A:** 2/533-mm torpedoes in drop gear or 6–8 mines
**Range:** 1,200/11 surfaced, 60/6.5 submerged **Man:** 4 tot.

Remarks: Used for the transport of up to twelve raiders. Three discarded in 1982–83. A sixth sank 27-12-76 following an accident at sea. A number of 2-man Chariots from the same builder are also in service.

Note: Former ex-British "Modified *Dido*"-class cruiser *Jahangar* (C 85, ex-*Babur,* ex-HMS *Diadem*) has been an immobile training hulk and floating AA battery at Karachi since 1982.

### DESTROYERS

◆ **1 ex-U.K. County class** Bldr: Swan Hunter & Wigham Richardson, Wallsend-on-Tyne, U.K.

| | Laid down | L | In serv. |
|---|---|---|---|
| C 84 Babur (ex-*London,* D 16) | 26-2-60 | 7-12-61 | 4-11-63 |

**Babur (C 84)**—still with Sea Slug launcher L. & L. Van Ginderen, 6-82

**D:** 5,440 tons (6,200 fl) **S:** 32.5 kts (30 sust.)
**Dim:** 158.55 (153.90 pp) × 16.46 × 6.30 (max.)
**A:** 4/114-mm Mk 6 DP (II × 2)—2/Sea Cat GWS.22 systems (IV × 2)—1/20-mm Mk 15 CIWS gatling AA—2/20-mm AA (I × 2)—1/Alouette-III helicopter (non-ASW)
**Electron Equipt:** Radar: 1/978, 1/965, 1/992Q, 1/277, 1/903, 2/904
Sonar: 1/177, 1/174, 1/170B, 1/162
EW: UA-8, UA-9, 2/Knebworth/Corvus chaff RL (VIII × 2)
**M:** COSAG: 2 sets A.E.I. GT (15,000 hp each) and 4 G6 gas turbines (7,500 hp each); 2 props; 60,000 hp
**Boilers:** 2 Babcock & Wilcox; 43 kg/cm$^2$, 510°C superheat **Fuel:** 600 tons
**Electric:** 3,750 kw **Range:** 3,500/28 **Man:** up to 470 tot.

Remarks: Purchased from U.K. on 22-3-82 and commissioned 22-4-82. Considered to be a cruiser. Replaced the former *Babur* as training cruiser. The obsolete Sea Slug Mk 1 missile launcher, with its attendant Type 901 control radar, initially remained aboard but was inactivated and removed in 1984. The 114-mm guns are

**DESTROYERS** *(continued)*

controlled by a single MRS.3 director with Type 903 radar. The GWS.22 Sea Cat system has two directors with Type 904 radars. The portside-opening helicopter hangar is occupied by an Alouette-III helicopter for liaison and SAR duties; thus, despite having an extensive sonar suit, the ship has no ASW ordnance. The massive 80-m-long Sea Slug magazine may be converted into cadet berthing spaces, and the helicopter facility has been enlarged to handle a Sea King helicopter with SM-39 antiship missiles. U.S. Harpoon SSM are to be installed.

◆ **6 ex-U.S. Gearing class, FRAM-I** Bldrs: 165, 166: Federal SB & DD Co., Newark, N.J.; 167 and 169: Bethlehem, Staten Island; 168: Todd, Seattle; 170: Consolidated Steel

| | Laid down | L | In serv. |
|---|---|---|---|
| D 165 TARIQ (ex-*Wiltsie,* DD 716) | 13-3-45 | 31-8-45 | 12-1-46 |
| D 166 TAIMUR (ex-*Epperson,* DD 719) | 20-6-45 | 29-12-45 | 19-3-49 |
| D 167 TIPPU SULTAN (ex-*Damato,* DD 871) | 10-5-45 | 21-11-45 | 27-4-46 |
| D 168 TUGHRIL (ex-*Henderson,* DD 785) | 27-10-44 | 28-5-45 | 4-8-45 |
| D 169 ALAMGIR (ex-*Cone,* DD 866) | 30-11-44 | 10-5-45 | 18-8-45 |
| D 170 SHAH JAHAN (ex-*Harold J. Ellison,* DD 864) | 3-10-44 | 14-3-45 | 18-12-46 |

**Tippu Sultan (D 167)**—prior to refit G. Gyssels, 9-81

**D:** 2,425 tons (3,460 fl) **S:** 30 kts **Dim:** 119.0 × 12.45 × 5.8 (max.)
**A:** 4/127-mm DP (II × 2)—1/20-mm Mk 15 CIWS gatling AA—4/20-mm AA (II × 2)—1/ASROC Mk 116 ASW RL (VIII × 1; 17 missiles)—6/324-mm Mk 32 ASW TT (III × 2)
**Electron Equipt:** Radar: 1/Decca 1226, 1/SPS-10B, 1/SPS-40, 1/Mk 25
Sonar: SQS-23D
EW: WLR-1, 2/Plessey Shield chaff RL (VI × 2)
**M:** 2 sets G.E. GT; 2 props; 60,000 hp **Electric:** 1,300 kw
**Boilers:** 4 Babcock & Wilcox; 39.8 kg/cm², 454°C **Fuel:** 600 tons

REMARKS: First two sold to Pakistan 29-4-77, then extensively overhauled at Puget Sound Navy Yard, 165 being completed 2-6-78, and 166 on 16-2-78. Second pair transferred 30-9-80. D 169 purchased 1-10-82, D 170 on 1-10-83. All being refitted and modernized to above standard at Karachi. The helicopter facilities are not used. Sonars upgraded to solid-state electronics by Raytheon, U.S., four by 1985 and two subsequently. U.S. CIWS added 1986–87.

NOTE: The British "Battle"-class destroyer *Badr* was transferred to the new Maritime Security Agency on 1-1-87.

**FRIGATES**

◆ **0 (+3) new construction**

| | Bldr | Laid down | L | In serv. |
|---|---|---|---|---|
| F . . . N . . . | . . . | . . . | . . . | . . . |
| F . . . N . . . | . . . | . . . | . . . | . . . |
| F . . . N . . . | . . . | . . . | . . . | . . . |

**D:** . . . tons **S:** . . . **Dim:** . . . × . . . × . . . (mean hull) **A:** . . .
**Electron Equipt:** Radar: . . .
Sonar: . . .
EW: . . .
**M:** COCOG: . . . **Range:** . . . **Man:** . . .

REMARKS: Letter of intent for three U.K. Modified Type 21 signed 1985, but actual contracts were not let, and Pakistan is still investigating other possibilities. A 1987 plan to acquire the U.K. Type 23 (*Norfolk*)-class frigate *Argyll* while under construction and build one sister at Karachi and one in Scotland fell through in 9-87.

**GUIDED-MISSILE PATROL BOATS**

◆ **4 Chinese Huangfen (Soviet Osa-I) class**

P 1025 N . . . P 1026 N . . . P 1027 N . . . P 1028 N . . .

**D:** 186.5 tons normal (205 fl) **S:** 35 kts **Dim:** 38.75 × 7.60 × 1.70 (mean hull)
**A:** 4/HY-2 (CCS-N-1 Styx) SSM—4/25-mm AA (II × 2)
**Electron Equipt:** Radar: 1/Square Tie
**M:** 3 M503A diesels; 3 props; 12,000 hp **Range:** 800/30
**Electric:** 65 kw **Man:** 28 tot.

REMARKS: Arrived at Karachi 27-4-84 as deck cargo.

◆ **4 Chinese Hoku class**

P 1021 N . . . . . . . P 1022 N . . . . . . . P 1023 N . . . . . . . P 1024 N . . . . . . .

**(P 1024) Hoku-class** French Navy, 12-82

**D:** 68 tons (79 fl) **S:** 38 kts **Dim:** 27.0 × 6.3 × 1.30 mean (1.8 props)
**A:** 1/HY-2 (CSS-N-1 Styx) SSM (I × 2)—2/25-mm AA (II × 1)
**Electron Equipt:** Radar: 1/Pot Head **Electric:** 65 kw **Endurance:** 5 days
**M:** 4 M50F-4 diesels; 4 props; 4,800 hp **Range:** 520/26 **Man:** 20 tot.

REMARKS: Transferred: 2 in 11-81 and 2 in 2-82.

**PATROL BOATS**

◆ **4 Hainan class** Bldr: People's Republic of China

P 155 BALUCHISTAN P 159 SIND P 161 SARHAD P 197 PUNJAB

**Baluchistan (P 155)** 1978

**D:** 360 tons (400 fl) **S:** 30.5 kts **Dim:** 58.77 × 7.20 × 2.20 (mean hull)
**A:** 4/57-mm AA (II × 2)—4/25-mm AA (II × 2)—4/RBU-1200 ASW RL (V × 4)—2/d.c. throwers—2/d.c. racks—mines
**Electron Equipt:** Radar: 1/Pot Head—Sonar: HF, hull-mounted
**M:** 4 Type 9D diesels; 4 props; 8,800 hp **Range:** 1,000/10 **Man:** 60 tot.

REMARKS: First pair transferred in 1976, *Punjab* and *Sarhad* in 4-80.

◆ **8 Shanghai-II class** Bldr: People's Republic of China

P 140 LAHORE P 145 PISHIN P 154 BANNU
P 143 MARDAN P 147 SUKKUR P 156 KALAT
P 144 GILGIT P 149 BAHAWALPUR

**D:** 122.5 tons normal (134.8 fl) **S:** 28.5 kts **Dim:** 38.78 × 5.41 × 1.55 (hull)
**A:** 4/37-mm AA (II × 2)—4/25-mm AA (II × 2)—mines
**Electron Equipt:** Radar: 1/Pot Head
**M:** 2 M50F-4, 1,200-hp diesels, 2 12D6, 910-hp diesels; 4 props; 4,220 hp
**Electric:** 39 kw **Endurance:** 7 days **Range:** 750/16.5 **Man:** 36 tot.

PATROL BOATS *(continued)*

**Sukkur (P 147)** French Navy, 1980

REMARKS: Eight transferred in 1972, four in 1973. Very primitive ships. Sisters *Quetta* (P 141), *Bannu* (P 154), *Kalat* (P 156), and *Sahival* (P 160), officially in reserve since 1982, have been renovated and four were transferred to the Maritime Security Agency on 1-1-87: *Quetla* (P 141), *Sehwan* (P 148), *Larkana* (P 157), and *Sahiwel* (P 160).

## TORPEDO BOATS

◆ **4 Huchuan-class hydrofoils** Bldr: People's Republic of China

HDF 01 HDF 02 HDF 03 HDF 04

**HDF 03**—note small bow foil out of water below pendant number 1973

**D:** 39 tons (45 fl) **S:** 50 kts
**Dim:** 22.50 × 3.80 (6.26 over foils) × 1.15 (1.12 foilborne)
**A:** 4/14.5-mm AA (II × 2)—2/533-mm TT
**Electron Equipt:** Radar: 1/Skin Head **M:** 3 M50F diesels; 3 props; 3,600 hp
**Range:** 500/30 **Electric:** 5.6 kw **Man:** 11 tot.

REMARKS: Maintained in land storage to prevent corrosion. Cruising speed: 32 kts. Foils forward only; stern planes on surface.

## PATROL CRAFT

◆ **1 (+ . . .) "Swallow" class** Bldr: . . . , South Korea

P . . . (In serv. 3-86)

**D:** 32 tons (fl) **S:** 25 kts **Dim:** 20.0 × 4.7 × 1.3 **A:** . . .
**Range:** 500/20 **Man:** 8 tot. **M:** 2 G.M. 12V71 TI diesels; 2 props; 1,060 hp

REMARKS: GRP construction. First unit of a planned 12 delivered 3-86; further program developments uncertain. Probably used in Customs duties in peacetime.

◆ **2 U.S. patrol craft** Bldr: Uniflite, Bellingham, Wash. (In serv. 1983)

**D:** 10.0 tons (fl) **S:** 16 kts **Dim:** 12.19 × . . . × . . .
**A:** . . . **M:** 2 G.M. 6-71N diesels; 2 waterjets; 512 hp

◆ **2 U.S. PBR Mk III patrol craft** Bldr: Uniflite, Bellingham, Wash. (In serv. 1983)

**D:** 8.9 tons (fl) **S:** 30 kts **Dim:** 9.73 × 3.53 × 0.81
**A:** 3/12.7-mm mg (II × 1, I × 1)—1/60-mm mortar
**Electron Equipt:** Radar: 1/Raytheon 1900
**M:** 2 G.M. 6V53T diesels; 2 Jacuzzi waterjets; 550 hp
**Range:** 150/23 **Man:** 4 tot.

REMARKS: The above four glass-reinforced plastic construction craft were ordered 6-82, apparently for trials and comparison purposes.

◆ **18 MV55 class** Bldr: Crestitalia, Ameglia, Italy (In serv. 1979–80)

P 551–568

**D:** 22.8 tons (fl) **S:** 30 kts **Dim:** 16.5 × 5.2 × 0.88 **Man:** 5 tot.
**A:** 1/14.5-mm mg **M:** 2 V6 diesels; 2 props; 1,600 hp **Range:** 425/25

REMARKS: Glass-reinforced plastic construction. P 552 named *Shabaz,* P 553 named *Vaqar;* others presumably also named. These craft are used for Customs duties and are not under naval control in peacetime. Four sisters serve in the new Maritime Security Agency.

**Shabaz (P 552)** French Navy, 1983

## MINE WARFARE SHIPS

NOTE: In 4-84 it was announced that 4 minehunters were to be acquired; characteristics and dates not reported.

◆ **3 ex-U.S. Falcon-class coastal minesweepers**

| | Bldr | In serv. |
|---|---|---|
| M 160 MAHMOOD (ex-MSC 267) | Quincy Adams Yacht, Quincy, Mass. | 4-57 |
| M 164 MUJAHID (ex-MSC 261) | Hodgdon Bros., East Boothbay, Maine | 10-56 |
| M 165 MUKHTAR (ex-MSC 274) | Bellingham SY, Bellingham, Wash. | 7-59 |

**Mukhtar (M 165)** 1974

**D:** 320 tons (372 fl) **S:** 13 kts (8, sweeping) **Dim:** 43.0 × 7.95 × 2.55
**A:** 4/23-mm AA ZSU-23 (IV × 1)
**Electron Equipt:** Radar: 1/Decca 45
Sonar: UQS-1D
**M:** 2 G.M. 8-268A diesels; 2 props; 1,200 hp **Range:** 2,500/10 **Man:** 39 tot.

REMARKS: Wooden hulls. All built under the Military Assistance Program. *Munsif* (M 166, ex-MSC 273) stricken 1979; *Murabak* (ex-MSC 262) and MSC 289-class units *Momin* (ex-MSC 293) and *Moshal* (ex-MSC 294) stricken 1983.

## AUXILIARY SHIPS

◆ **1 oceanographic research ship**

| | Bldr | Laid down | L | In serv. |
|---|---|---|---|---|
| BEHR PAIMA | Ishikawajima Harima, Tokyo | 16-2-82 | . . . | 17-12-82 |

**D:** . . . **S:** 13.75 kts **Dim:** 61.0 × 11.8 × 3.7
**M:** 2 Daihatsu diesels; 2 props; 2,000 hp

REMARKS: Ordered 15-4-81. 1,183 grt.

NOTE: Ex-U.K. "River"-class frigate *Zulfiquar* (F 262), *ex-Dhanush,* ex-U.K. *Deveron,* used for many years as a hydrographic survey ship, and inshore survey craft *Jatli* were stricken 1983, with the former transferred to a civil agency for further service.

◆ **1 ex-U.S. T-2-class replenishment oiler** Bldr: Marinship Corp., Sausalito, Calif.

A 41 DACCA (ex-*Mission Santa Clara,* TAO 132) (In serv. 21-6-44)

**Dacca (A 41)**—with *Hangor* (S 131) alongside 1975

**AUXILIARY SHIPS** *(continued)*

**D:** 5,730 tons light (22,380 fl) **S:** 15 kts **Dim:** 159.56 × 20.73 × 9.4
**A:** 6/40-mm AA (I × 6) **Electron Equipt:** Radar: 1/RCA CRM-NIA-75
**M:** 1 set G.E. GT, electric drive; 1 prop; 10,000 hp **Electric:** 1,150 kw
**Boilers:** 2 Combustion Engineering "D"; 42 kg/cm², 440°C
**Fuel:** 1,300 tons **Man:** 15 officers, 145 men

REMARKS: Acquired by U.S. Navy 11-5-47. Loaned 17-1-63, after conversion to permit underway replenishment alongside, one station each side. Bought outright 31-5-74. Cargo: 15,300 tons.

◆ **1 ex-U.S. Cherokee-class ocean tug** Bldr: Commercial Iron Works, Portland, Ore.

| | Laid down | L | In serv. |
|---|---|---|---|
| A 42 MADADGAR (ex-*Yuma,* ATF 94) | 13-2-43 | 17-7-43 | 31-8-43 |

**Madadgar (A 42)**—note 20-mm AA before bridge J.-C. Bellonne, 1977

**D:** 1,325 tons (1,675 fl) **S:** 16.5 kts **Dim:** 62.48 (59.44 pp) × 11.73 × 4.67
**A:** 2/40-mm AA (I × 2)—1/20-mm AA **Electron Equipt:** Radar: 1/Decca 45
**M:** 4 G.M. 12-278 diesels, electric drive; 1 prop; 3,000 hp **Electric:** 260 kw
**Fuel:** 295 tons **Man:** 85 tot.

REMARKS: Employed as a salvage and rescue tug. Transferred 25-3-59.

◆ **1 large harbor tug** Bldr: Worst & Dutmer, Meppel, Netherlands (L: 29-11-55)

A 43 RUSTOM

**D:** 530 tons (fl) **S:** 9.5 kts **Dim:** 32.0 × 9.1 × 3.3
**M:** 1 Crossley diesel; 1 prop; 1,000 hp **Range:** 3,000/8 **Man:** 21 tot.

◆ **2 small harbor tugs** Bldr: Costaguta-Voltz, Italy (In serv. 9-58)

GAMA (ex-U.S. YTL 754) BHOLU (ex-U.S. YTL 755)

REMARKS: Built under the U.S. Offshore Procurement Program. 300 hp.

◆ **1 small pusher tug** Bldr: Naval DY, Karachi (In serv. 11-1-83)

GOGA

◆ **1 fuel lighter** Bldr: Karachi SY & Eng. Wks.

GWADAR (In serv. 1984)

**D:** 831 grt **S:** . . . **Dim:** 62.84 (57.92 pp) × 11.31 × 3.03
**M:** 1 Sulzer diesel; 1 prop; 550 hp

◆ **1 water tanker** Bldr: . . . , Trieste, Italy (In serv. 1957)

A 46 ZUM ZUM

**D:** 600 tons (1,225 fl) **S:** 8 kts **Dim:** 54.0 × 9.8 × 4.6
**A:** 2/20-mm AA (I × 2) **M:** 2 diesels; 2 props; 800 hp

◆ **2 logistics craft** Bldr: Le Comte, Vianen, Netherlands (In serv. 18-2-82)

**D:** 13 tons (fl) **S:** 21 kts **Dim:** 18.1 × 3.8 × 0.9
**M:** 2 Volvo Penta AQAD 40 diesels; 2 outdrives; 520 hp

REMARKS: Glass-reinforced plastic-hulled landing craft.

◆ **1 degaussing tender** Bldr: Karachi DY (In serv. 1979)

**D:** 260 tons (fl) **S:** 10 kts **Dim:** 35.22 (34.0 wl) × 7.00 × 2.4
**M:** 1 diesel; 1 prop; 375 hp **Man:** 5 tot.

REMARKS: Built with French technical assistance and very similar in design to French Navy's Y 732. Wooden hull.

◆ **1 floating dry dock** Bldr: Karachi DY (In serv. 1981)

N . . . **Lift capacity:** 2,000 tons

◆ **1 U.S. ARD-2-class floating dry dock** Bldr: Pacific Bridge, Alameda (In serv. 4-43)

PESHAWAR (ex-ARD 6)

**Dim:** 148.03 × 21.64 × 1.6 (light) **Lift capacity:** 3,500 tons

REMARKS: Transferred 6-61.

◆ **1 small floating dry dock** (In serv. 1974)

FC II **Lift capacity:** 1,200 tons

◆ **1 stationary training hulk, former cruiser**

| | Bldr | Laid down | L | In serv. |
|---|---|---|---|---|
| C 85 JAHANGIR (ex-*Babur,* ex-*Diadem*) | Hawthorn-Leslie, Hebburn-on-Tyne | 15-11-39 | 26-8-42 | 6-1-44 |

**D:** 5,900 tons (7,560 fl) **S:** . . . **Dim:** 165.05 (154.23 pp) × 15.70 × 5.70
**A:** 8/133.5-mm DP (II × 2)—12/40-mm AA (II × 3, I × 6)—6/533-mm TT (III × 2)—4/47-mm saluting battery (I × 4)
**Electron Equipt:** Radar: 1/. . . nav., 1/Marconi SNW-10, . . .
**Armor:** Belt: 52–76-mm; Deck: 52-mm; Turrets: 25-mm; Bridge: 25-mm
**M:** 4 sets Parsons GT; 4 props; 62,000 hp **Boilers:** 4 Admiralty 3-drum
**Range:** n.a. **Fuel:** 1,100 tons **Man:** . . .

REMARKS: Purchased 29-2-56; converted for training duties 1961. Unable to steam for many years. Renamed on purchase of new *Babur* (C 84, ex-*London,* D 18) in 3-82 and relegated to training hulk/relic status.

MARITIME SECURITY AGENCY

Established 1-1-87 to patrol the maritime exclusion zone. Aircraft are to be acquired. Personnel transferred from the Navy, to which the M.S.A. is subordinated. Ships and boats are painted white, with red and blue diagonal stripes and "MSA" on the side.

**DESTROYER**

◆ **1 ex-British Battle class**

| | Bldr | Laid down | L | In serv. |
|---|---|---|---|---|
| D 161 BADR (ex-*Gabbard*) | Swan Hunter | 2-2-44 | 16-3-45 | 10-12-46 |

**Badr (D 161)**—now painted white, with red and blue diagonal stripes 1974

**D:** 2,325 tons (3,360 fl) **S:** 31 kts **Dim:** 115.32 (108.2 pp) × 12.95 × 4.1
**A:** 4/114-mm DP (II × 2)—8/40-mm AA (I × 2, I × 4)—4/533-mm TT (IV × 1)—1/Mk 4 Squid ASW mortar (III × 1)
**Electron Equipt:** Radar: 1/975, 1/293Q, 1/Marconi SNW-10, 1/275
Sonar: 1/170, 1/174
**M:** 2 Parsons GT; 2 props; 50,000 hp **Boilers:** 2 Admiralty, three-drum
**Fuel:** 680 tons **Range:** 3,200/20 **Man:** 300 tot.

REMARKS: Transferred from U.K. 29-2-56. Sister ship *Khaibar* was sunk during the Indo-Pakistani conflict, 1971. Has one radar director for the 114-mm mounts and 2 STD.1 lead-computing directors for the twin 40-mm AA. Has HFD/F array amidships. Transferred to M.S.A. on 1-1-87.

**PATROL BOATS**

◆ **1 MV 70 class** Bldr: Crestitalia, Ameglia, Italy

P . . . N . . .

**D:** . . . **S:** . . . **Dim:** . . . × . . . × . . .
**A:** . . . **Electron Equipt:** Radar: . . . **M:** . . .

REMARKS: Ordered 1986.

◆ **2 MV 62 class** Bldr: Crestitalia, Ameglia, Italy

P . . . N . . . P . . . N . . .

**D:** . . . **S:** . . . **Dim:** 19.0 × . . . × . . .
**A:** . . . **Electron Equipt:** Radar: . . . **M:** . . . **Range:** . . .

REMARKS: Ordered 1986.

**PAKISTAN** *(continued)*
**MARITIME SECURITY AGENCY** *(continued)*

◆ **4 MV 55 class** Bldr: Crestitalia, Ameglia, Italy

P . . . N . . . P . . . N . . . P . . . N . . . P . . . N . . .

**D:** 22.8 tons (fl) **S:** 35 kts **Dim:** 16.5 × 5.2 × 0.88
**A:** 1/20-mm AA **Electron Equipt:** Radar: 1/. . .
**M:** 2 MTU diesels; 2 props; 2,200 hp **Range:** 425/25 **Man:** 5 tot.

Remarks: Ordered 1986. More powerful version of craft used for Customs duties.

◆ **4 Shanghai-II class** Bldr: . . . , China

P 141 Quetta P 159 Larkana
P 148 Sehwan P 160 Sahival

**D:** 122.5 tons (134.8 fl) **S:** 28.5 kts **Dim:** 38.78 × 5.41 × 1.55 (hull)
**A:** . . . **Electron Equipt:** Radar: . . .
**M:** 2 M50F-4, 1,200-hp diesels, 2 12D6, 910-hp diesels; 4 props; 4,220 hp
**Range:** 750/16.5 **Electric:** 39 kw **Man:** . . .

Remarks: Transferred to M.S.A. 1-1-87, P 141 and P 160 having been in reserve since 1982.

# PANAMA

**Republic of Panama**

Personnel (1987): Approx. 550 tot.

Merchant Marine (1986): 5,252 ships—41,305,009 grt (tankers: 407 ships—8,208,806 grt

Naval Aviation: There are no "naval" aircraft. The Air Force operates a number of aircraft with a secondary maritime patrol role, including 3 DHC Twin Otter, 3 Casa C-212, 2 Britten-Norman Islander, 2 Cessna U-17, and a Cessna 172. Helicopters include 8 Bell UH-1B, 9 UH-1H, and 4 UH-1N. Larger transports include an L-188 Electra, 4 C-47s, 1 Skyvan, and a Falcon 20 for VIP transport.

**Comandante Torrijas (GC 16)** Swiftships, 7-82

NATIONAL GUARD

## PATROL BOATS AND CRAFT

◆ **2 U.S. 65-ft class** Bldr: Swiftships, Morgan City, La. (In serv. 7-82)

GC 16 Comandante Torrijas GC 17 Presidente Porras

**D:** 31 tons (35 fl) **S:** 23 kts **Dim:** 19.81 (17.90 wl) × 5.64 × 1.83
**A:** 1/12.7-mm mg **Electron Equipt:** Radar: 1/Decca 110
**M:** 2 G.M. 12V71 TI N75 diesels; 2 props; 1,020 hp
**Electric:** 20 kw **Fuel:** 6 tons **Man:** 8 tot.

Remarks: Aluminum construction.

◆ **2 103-foot boats** Bldr: Vosper Thornycroft, Portsmouth, U.K. (In serv. 3-71)

GC 10 Panquiaco (L: 22-7-70) GC 11 Ligia Elena (L: 25-8-70)

**D:** 96 tons (123 fl) **S:** 24 kts **Dim:** 31.25 × 6.02 × 1.98
**A:** 2/20-mm AA (I × 2) **Electron Equipt:** Radar: 1/Decca 916
**M:** 2 Paxman Ventura 12-YJCM diesels; 2 props; 2,800 hp
**Electric:** 80 kVA **Man:** 23 tot.

Remarks: In poor condition.

◆ **2 ex-U.S. Coast Guard 40-foot Mk 1-class utility boats** (In serv. 1950)

GC 14 Marti GC 15 Jupiter

**D:** 13 tons (fl) **S:** 18 kts **Dim:** 12.3 × 3.4 × 1.0 **A:** 1/12.7-mm mg
**M:** 2 G.M. 6-71 diesels; 2 props; 300 hp **Range:** 160/8 **Man:** 4 tot.

Remarks: Transferred in 1962.

◆ **2 ex-U.S. 63-foot AVR class**

GC 12 Ayanasi GC 13 Zarti

**D:** 35 tons (fl) **S:** 22.5 kts **Dim:** 19.3 × 4.7 × 1.0
**A:** 2/12.7-mm mg (I × 2) **Electron Equipt:** Radar: 1/Raytheon 1500B
**M:** 2 G.M. 8V-71 diesels; 2 props; 900 hp **Man:** 8 tot.

Remarks: In service in 1943 and transferred 1965–66.

## AUXILIARY SHIPS AND CRAFT

◆ **1 ex-U.S. LSMR-class rocket-assault ship** Bldr: Brown SB Co., Houston

| | Laid down | L | In serv. |
|---|---|---|---|
| GC 10 Tiburon (ex-*Smokey Hill River,* LSMR 531) | 2-6-45 | 7-7-45 | 21-9-45 |

**D:** 2,084 tons (fl) **S:** 12 kts **Dim:** 62.87 × 10.52 × 2.18 **A:** none
**M:** 2 G.M. 16-278A diesels; 2 props; 2,800 hp **Electric:** 440 kw **Man:** . . .

Remarks: Purchased from a commercial source 14-3-75 and used for logistics-support duties. Has had bow doors added, although as completed she had none and had her well deck plated over. Cargo: approximately 400 tons.

◆ **2 logistics-support landing craft** Bldr: Ch. de la Manche, France (In serv. 1978)

GN . . . GN . . .

**D:** 60 tons (fl) **S:** 9 kts **Dim:** 12.6 × . . . × . . .
**M:** 2 SKL 8NVD26 diesels; 2 props; 400 hp

◆ **3 ex-U.S. Army LCM (8)-class landing craft**

GN 1 GN 2 GN 3

**D:** 115 tons (fl) **S:** 9 kts **Dim:** 22.7 × 6.4 × 1.4
**A:** none **M:** 4 G.M. 6-71 diesels; 2 props; 600 hp **Man:** 6 tot.

Remarks: Transferred 1972. Used for logistics-support duties. Two-level superstructure added aft.

◆ **1 ex-U.S. YF-852-class cargo lighter**

| | Bldr | Laid down | L | In serv. |
|---|---|---|---|---|
| N . . . (ex-YF 886) | Defoe SB, Bay City, Michigan | 13-4-45 | 25-5-45 | 4-8-45 |

**D:** 590 tons (fl) **S:** 11 kts **Dim:** 40.23 × 9.1 × 2.7
**M:** 2 G.M. 6-71 diesels; 2 props; 600 hp **Man:** 11 tot.

Remarks: Transferred 5-75. Cargo: 250 tons.

◆ **1 former shrimp boat,** used for logistics support

GN 8

**S:** 11 kts **Capacity:** 150 passengers

# PAPUA NEW GUINEA

Personnel (1987): approximately 400 total

Merchant Marine (1986): 88 ships—30,922 grt
(tankers: 5 ships—2,421 grt)

Naval Aviation: The Papua New Guinea Defense Force operates 6 Nomad N.22B light transports, 6 C-47, 1 Super King Air 200, and 1 Gulfstream II transports for coastal patrol and logistics duties.

## PATROL BOATS

◆ **2 (+2) ASI 315 class** Bldr: Australian SB Ind. (WA), Pty, Ltd., South Coogie

| | In serv. | | In serv. |
|---|---|---|---|
| P 01 Tarangau | 16-5-87 | P 03 Seeadler | 10-88 |
| P 02 Dreger | 31-10-87 | P 04 Lorengau | 6-89 |

**D:** 165 tons (fl) **S:** 21 kts (20 sust.)
**Dim:** 31.50 (28.60 wl) × 8.10 × 2.12 (1.80 hull)
**A:** 1/20-mm AA—2/12.7-mm mg (I × 2)

**PATROL BOATS** *(continued)*

**Electron Equipt:** Radar: 1/Furuno 1011 (I/J-band)
**M:** 2 Caterpillar 3516 diesels; 2 props; 2,820 hp (2,400 sust.)
**Range:** 2,500/12 **Fuel:** 27.9 tons **Endurance:** 8–10 days
**Electric:** 116 kw (2 × 50 kw; Caterpillar 3304 diesels; 1 × 16 kw)
**Man:** 3 officers, 14 men

**Tarangau (P 01)** POPH E. Pitman, R.A.N., 5-87

**Tarangau (P 01)** R.A.N., 5-87

REMARKS: First two ordered 19-3-85, other pair 3-10-85. Australian foreign aid program "Pacific Patrol Boat." Carry a 5-m aluminum boarding boat. Extensive navigational suite, including Furuno FSN-70 NAVSAT receiver, 525 HF/DF, 120 MH/HF/DF, FE-881 echo-sounder and DS-70 doppler log. Sisters in Fijian, Western Samoan, Vanuatu service.

◆ **4 ex-Australian Attack class**

| | Bldr | Laid down | L | In serv. |
|---|---|---|---|---|
| P 84 AITAPE | Walkers, Ltd., Maryborough | 11-66 | 6-7-67 | 13-11-67 |
| P 92 LADAVA | Walkers, Ltd., Maryborough | 2-68 | 11-5-68 | 21-10-68 |
| P 93 LAE | Walkers, Ltd., Maryborough | 5-67 | 5-10-67 | 3-4-68 |
| P 94 MADANG | Evans Deakin, Queensland | 3-68 | 10-8-68 | 29-11-68 |

**Aitape (P 84)** L. & L. Van Ginderen, 9-86

**D:** 146 tons (fl) **S:** 21–24 kts **Dim:** 32.76 (30.48 pp) × 6.2 × 1.9
**A:** 1/40-mm AA—2/7.62-mm mg (I × 2)
**Electron Equipt:** Radar: 1/Decca RM916
**M:** 2 Davey-Paxman Ventura 16-YJCM diesels; 3,500 hp
**Fuel:** 20 tons **Range:** 1,220/13 **Man:** 18 tot.

REMARKS: Transferred in 1975. *Samarai* (P 85) stricken 1981 for spares, and P 92 placed in reserve 1987.

**AMPHIBIOUS WARFARE SHIPS**

◆ **4 Burfoam-class utility landing craft** Bldr: Sing Koon Seng SY, Singapore

| | In serv. | | In serv. |
|---|---|---|---|
| BURFOAM | 21-7-81 | BURSEA | 6-4-82 |
| BURCREST | 8-9-81 | BURWAVE | 18-5-82 |

**D:** 200 tons light (725 fl) **S:** 9 kts **Dim:** 37.25 (33.50 pp) × 9.00 × . . .
**M:** 2 Deutz SBA-6M-816-1 LKR diesels; 2 props; 626 hp
**Range:** 1,870/9 **Fuel:** 160 tons **Man:** 18 tot.

REMARKS: 260 grt/350 dwt. Owned by government, employed in commercial and logistics service.

◆ **2 ex-Australian Balikpapan-class utility landing craft** Bldr: Walkers, Maryborough

31 SALAMAUA (In serv. 19-10-73) 32 BUNA (In serv. 7-12-73)

**Salamaua (31)** G. Gyssels, 1980

**D:** 310 tons (503 fl) **S:** 8 kts **Dim:** 44.5 × 12.2 × 1.9
**A:** 2/12.7-mm mg (I × 2) **M:** 3 G.M. 12V71 diesels; 3 props; 675 hp
**Range:** 1,300–2,280/10 depending on load **Man:** 2 officers, 11 men

REMARKS: In service in 1972 and transferred 1975. Cargo: 140–180 tons.

◆ **7 Kokuba-class personnel landing craft** Bldr: Australia (In serv. 1975)

KOKUBA KUTUBA KIAIPIT KANDEP
KUNIAWA KIUNGA KUKIPI

**D:** 12 tons (fl) **S:** 9 kts **Dim:** 12.0 × 4.0 × 1.0
**M:** 2 Gardner diesels; 2 props; 150 hp

**PAPUA NEW GUINEA** *(continued)*
**AMPHIBIOUS WARFARE SHIPS** *(continued)*

◆ **1 ex-Australian tug** Bldr: Perrin, Brisbane, 1972

HTS 503

**D:** 47.5 tons **S:** 9 kts **Dim:** 15.4 × 4.6 × . . .
**M:** 2 G.M. diesels; 2 props; 340 hp **Range:** 710/9 **Man:** 3 tot.

REMARKS: Transferred in 1974. Retained R.A.N. number.

# PARAGUAY

**Republic of Paraguay**

PERSONNEL (1987): 2,500 total, including 500 Marines and Coast Guard

MERCHANT MARINE (1986): 41 ships—43,298 grt
(tankers: 3 ships—2,935 grt)

NAVAL AVIATION: 4 H-13 Sioux helicopters, 2 SA-315B helicopters, 3 Cessna U-206, 1 Cessna 150M light utility aircraft.

## RIVER GUNBOATS

◆ **1 Brazilian Roraima class** Bldr: Ars. de Rio de Janeiro, Brazil

| | Laid down | L | In serv. |
|---|---|---|---|
| P. 2 ITAIPU | 3-3-83 | 16-3-84 | 2-4-85 |

**D:** 220 tons light (384 fl) **S:** 14.5 kts **Dim:** 46.3 (45.0 pp) × 8.45 × 1.42 (max.)
**A:** 1/40-mm—6/12.7-mm mg (II × 3)—2/81-mm mortar (I × 1)
**Electron Equipt:** Radar: 3/navigational **Range:** 4,500/11
**M:** 2 M.A.N. V6V 16/18 TL diesels; 2 props; 1,824 hp
**Endurance:** 30 days **Man:** 63 tot.

REMARKS: Order announced 11-4-83. Has small helicopter deck.

◆ **3 ex-Argentinian Bouchard-class former ocean minesweepers**

| | Bldr | L | In serv. |
|---|---|---|---|
| M. 1 NANAWA (ex-*Bouchard*) | Rio Santiago NY | 20-3-36 | 16-5-37 |
| M. 2 CAPITÁN MEZA (ex-*Seaver*) | Hansen & Puccini, San Fernando | 2-5-37 | 20-5-39 |
| M. 3 TENIENTE FARINA (ex-*Py*) | Rio Santiago NY | 31-3-38 | 1-7-38 |

**D:** 450 tons (650 fl) **S:** 16 kts **Dim:** 59.5 × 7.3 × 2.6
**A:** 4/40-mm AA (II × 2)—2/12.7-mm mg—mines
**M:** 2 M.A.N. diesels; 2 props; 2,000 hp **Range:** 3,000/12 **Man:** 70 tot.

REMARKS: Transferred: M. 1 donated 1-64, the other two purchased on 6-3-68.

◆ **2 Paraguay class** Bldr: Odero, Genoa (In serv. 5-31)

C. 1 PARAGUAY (ex-*Comodoro Meya*) C. 2 HUMAITÁ (ex-*Capitán Cabral*)

**Humaitá (C. 2)**—in floating dry dock DF.1 1970

**D:** 636 tons, 745 avg. (865 fl) **S:** 17.5 kts **Dim:** 70.15 × 10.7 × 1.65
**A:** 4/120-mm (II × 2)—3/76.2-mm AA (I × 3)—2/40-mm AA (I × 2)—6 mines
**M:** 2 sets Parsons GT; 2 props; 3,800 hp **Boilers:** 2
**Fuel:** 170 tons **Range:** 1,700/16 **Man:** 86 tot.

◆ **1 old former tug** Bldr: Werf Conrad, Haarlem (In serv. 1908)

A. 1 CAPITÁN CABRAL (ex-*Adolfo Riquelme*)

**D:** 206 tons (fl) **S:** 9 kts **Dim:** 30.5 × 7.0 × 2.9
**A:** 1/76.2-mm—2/37-mm **M:** reciprocating; 300 hp **Man:** 47 tot.

REMARKS: Wooden hull, used for riverine patrol on the Upper Paraña River.

## PATROL CRAFT

◆ **6 small craft** Bldr: Sewart Seacraft, Berwick, La.

P 101 P 102 P 103 P 104 P 105 P 106

**P 103** H. Ehlers, 1986

**D:** 15 tons (fl) **S:** 20 kts **Dim:** 13.1 × 3.9 × 0.9
**A:** 2/12.7-mm mg **M:** 2 G.M. 6-71 diesels; 2 props; 500 hp **Man:** 7 tot.

REMARKS: P 101 and P 102 in service in 12-67; P 103, P 104, and P 105, in 9-70; and P 106, in 3-71.

## AUXILIARY SHIPS

◆ **1 repair/headquarters ship** Bldr: Brown SB, Houston

| | Laid down | L | In serv. |
|---|---|---|---|
| BC. 1 BOQUERON (ex-*Teniente Pratt Gil,* PH. 1, ex-*Corrientes,* ex-LSM 86) | 22-8-44 | 15-9-44 | 13-10-44 |

**D:** 743 tons (1,095 fl) **S:** 12.6 kts **Dim:** 61.88 × 10.51 × 2.54
**A:** 2/40-mm AA (II × 1)
**M:** 2 Fairbanks-Morse $38D8\frac{1}{8}$ × 10 diesels; 2 props; 2,800 hp
**Electric:** 240 kw **Man:** . . .

REMARKS: An ex-U.S. LSM-1-class landing ship donated by Argentina on 13-1-72, after conversion to a command and repair ship. Well deck plated over to create a helicopter deck aft; superstructure enlarged and moved to the centerline. Renamed 1980.

◆ **1 cargo and training ship** Bldr: Thomás Ruiz de Velasco, Bilbao, Spain (In serv. 2-68)

GUARANI

**Guarani** L. & L. Van Ginderen, 10-83

**D:** 714 grt/1,047 dwt **S:** 12.2 kts **Dim:** 73.6 × 11.9 × 3.7
**M:** 1 diesel; 1 prop; 1,300 hp

REMARKS: Purchased to provide seagoing experience for naval cadets and to engage in commercial voyages to raise revenue for running the navy. Cargo: approximately 1,000 tons.

◆ **2 ex-U.S. LCU-501-class landing craft** (In serv. circa 1944–45)

BT. 1 (ex-YFB 82, ex-LCU . . .) BT. 2 (ex-YFB 86, ex-LCU . . .)

**D:** 143 tons (309 fl) **S:** 10 kts **Dim:** 36.3 × 9.8 × 1.2 (aft)
**M:** 3 Gray Marine 64YTL diesels; 3 props; 675 hp

REMARKS: Transferred in 6-70. Used for logistics duties. Cargo: 125 tons.

◆ **2 ex-U.S. 64-foot YTL-422-class tugs**

| | Bldr | Laid down | L | In serv. |
|---|---|---|---|---|
| R. 5 (ex-YTL 211) | Robert Jacob, Inc. | 26-12-41 | 20-6-42 | 21-8-42 |
| R. 6 (ex-YTL 567) | Gunderson Bros. | 5-3-45 | 17-8-45 | 30-10-45 |

**PARAGUAY** *(continued)*
**AUXILIARY SHIPS** *(continued)*

**D:** 84 tons **S:** 9 kts **Dim:** 20.2 × 5.5 × 2.4
**M:** 1 diesel; 300 hp **Man:** 5 tot.

REMARKS: Transferred in 3-67 and 4-74.

◆ **1 ex-U.S. floating dry dock** Bldr: Doullut & Ewin, Mobile, Ala. (In serv. 6-44)

N . . . (ex-AFDL 26)

**Dim:** 60.96 × 19.5 × 1.04 (light) **Lifting capacity:** 1,000 tons

REMARKS: Transferred in 3-65.

◆ **1 ex-U.S. floating workshop**

| | Bldr | Laid down | L | In serv. |
|---|---|---|---|---|
| N . . . (ex-YR 37) | Mare Island Naval SY | 14-12-41 | 12-1-42 | 15-5-42 |

**D:** 600 tons (fl) **Dim:** 45.72 × 10.36 × 1.8 **Electric:** 210 kw **Man:** 47 tot.

REMARKS: Transferred 3-65.

◆ **3 dredges**

D. 1 N . . . . . . . (In serv. 1907)—140 tons, 30 crew
D. 2 TENIENTE O. CARRERAS SAGUIER (In serv. 1957)—110 tons, 19 crew
RP. 1 N . . . . . . . (In serv. 1908)—107 tons, 29 crew

NOTE: Also believed in service are river transport *Presidente Stroessner* (T. 1, 150 tons, 10 kts, in serv. 1901), a 50-ton survey launch, buoy tender B. 1 (30 tons), and several small stores carriers.

# PERU

**Republic of Peru**

PERSONNEL (1987): 2,100 officers, 19,000 men, plus 3,500 officers and men of the Naval Infantry

MERCHANT MARINE (1986): 632 ships—754,179 grt (tankers: 14 ships—147,469 grt)

NAVAL AVIATION: The air arm consists of the following helicopters and fixed-wing aircraft: 9 AM 39 Exocet SSM-equipped SH-3D Sea King, 6 Agusta-Bell AB 212, 10 Bell 206 Jet Ranger, 6 Bell UH-1, and 2 Alouette-III helicopters; 2 Fokker F-27 Maritime, 9 Grumman S-2 Tracker ASW aircraft, 2 DHC-6 Twin Otter floatplanes, 2 C-47 transports, 1 Piper Aztec liaison aircraft, and 6 Beech T-34C trainers.

WARSHIPS IN SERVICE AND UNDER CONSTRUCTION
AS OF 1 JANUARY 1986

| | L | Tons (surfaced) | Main armament |
|---|---|---|---|
| ◆ **12 submarines** | | | |
| 6 TYPE 209 | 1973–1981 | 980–1,000 | 8/533-mm TT |
| 4 DOS DE MAYO | 1953–57 | 825 | 6/533-mm TT, 1/127-mm DP (on two units) |
| 2 GUPPY-IA | 1944 | 1,830 | 10/533-mm TT |
| ◆ **2 cruisers** | | (Std) | |
| 1 ALMIRANTE GRAU | 1950 | 9,850 | 4/152-mm DP, 6/57-mm AA, 4/40-mm AA, 3 helicopters |
| 1 ex-Dutch | 1944 | 9,529 | 8/152-mm DP, 8/57-mm AA |
| ◆ **6 destroyers** | | | |
| 6 FRIESLAND | 1954–56 | 2,496 | 4/20-mm DP, 4/40-mm AA |
| ◆ **3 (+1) guided-missile frigates** | | | |
| 3 (+1) LUPO | 1976–83 | 2,208 | 8/Otomat, 1/Albatros SAM system, 1/127-mm DP |
| ◆ **6 guided-missile corvettes** | | | |
| 6 PR 72 | 1978–79 | 560 | 4/MM 38 Exocet, 1/76-mm DP, 2/40-mm AA |

## SUBMARINES

◆ **6 German Type 209** Bldr: Howaldtswerke, Kiel

| | L | In serv. |
|---|---|---|
| S 31 CASMA | 31-8-79 | 19-12-80 |
| S 32 ANTOFAGASTA | 19-12-79 | 14-3-80 |
| S 33 PISAGUA (ex-*Blume*) | 19-5-81 | 8-4-82 |
| S 34 CHIPANA (ex-*Pisagua*) | 7-8-81 | 12-7-83 |
| S 35 ISLAY | 11-10-73 | 23-1-75 |
| S 36 ARICA | 5-4-74 | 4-4-75 |

**Pisagua (S 33)**—bulged sonar bow Skyfotos, 9-83

**Islay (P 35)**—low bow L. & L. Van Ginderen, 9-83

**D:** 980/1,230 tons **S:** 21 kts for 5 minutes, submerged, 12 snorkel, 11 surf.
**Dim:** 54.40 × 6.20 × 5.50
**A:** 8/533-mm TT—(14 total SST-4 and NT37C torpedoes)
**Electron Equipt:** Radar: 1/Calypso
Sonar: S 31, 32: Krupp-Atlas CSU 3-Z active, PRS 3-4 passive; others: Krupp-Atlas CSU-83
**M:** 4 MTU Type 12V493 TY60 diesels, each linked to a 450-kw AEG generator, 1 Siemens electric motor; 1 prop; 5,000 hp
**Range:** 230/8; 400/4 (sub.) **Endurance:** 40 days
**Fuel:** 63 tons **Man:** 5 officers, 26 men

REMARKS: S 31 and S 32 were ordered 12-8-76, and two more in 3-77. S 33 and later are 56.1 m overall, 1,185 tons surfaced/1,290 tons submerged. S 31, 32 use H.S.A. Mk 8 Mod. 24 f.c.s.; others use H.S.A. SINBADS f.c.s. S 33 delivery delayed by collision 2-4-82. S 35 and S 36 have DUUX-2CN sonar equipment. Italian SEPA Mk 3 torpedo fire-control equipment and Whitehead A-184 wire-guided torpedoes ordered 6-86.

◆ **4 Dos de Mayo class** Bldr: General Dynamics, Groton, Conn.

| | Laid down | L | In serv. |
|---|---|---|---|
| S 41 DOS DE MAYO (ex-*Lobo*) | 12-5-52 | 6-2-54 | 14-6-54 |
| S 42 ABTAO (ex-*Tiburon*) | 12-5-52 | 27-10-53 | 20-2-54 |
| S 43 ANGAMOS (ex-*Atun*) | 27-10-55 | 5-2-57 | 1-7-57 |
| S 44 IQUIQUE (ex-*Merlin*) | 27-10-55 | 5-2-57 | 1-10-57 |

**Angamos (S 43)**—now has bow sonar dome

**D:** 825/1,400 tons **S:** 16/10 kts **Dim:** 74.1 × 6.7 × 4.2
**A:** S 41, S 42: 1/127-mm DP—all: 6/533-mm TT (4 fwd, 2 aft)
**Electron Equipt:** Radar: 1/SS-2A—Sonar: BQR-3, BQA-1A, Thomson-CSF Eledone
**M:** 2 G.M. 12-278A diesels, 2 electric motors; 2 props; 2,400 hp
**Fuel:** 45 tons **Range:** 5,000/10 (snorkel) **Man:** 40 tot.

REMARKS: Patterned after the U.S. *Marlin* class of 1941. These were the last U.S. submarines to be built for a foreign customer. S 41 and S 42 were refitted in 1965, S 43 and S 44 in 1968. The 127-mm gun carried by S 41 and S 42 is a 25-caliber U.S. "Wet" model and is mounted abaft the sail. New batteries 1981.

◆ **2 ex-U.S. Guppy-IA class** Bldr: Portsmouth Naval SY, New Hampshire

| | Laid down | L | In serv. |
|---|---|---|---|
| S 49 PEDRERA (ex-*Sea Poacher*, SS 406) | 23-2-44 | 20-5-44 | 31-7-44 |
| S 50 PACOCHA (ex-*Atule*, SS 403) | 2-12-43 | 6-3-44 | 21-6-44 |

**SUBMARINES** *(continued)*

**Peruvian submarines in silhouette**—from background to foreground: *Dos de Mayo* or *Abtao* (S 41 or 42) with deck gun and bow dome; a Guppy-1A; and a Type 209 U.S. Navy, 1982

**D:** 1,830/2,440 tons **S:** 17/15 kts **Dim:** 93.57 × 8.23 × 5.18
**A:** 10/533-mm TT (6 fwd, 4 aft)
**Electron Equipt:** Radar: 1/SS-2A—Sonar: BQS-4, BQR-2B
**M:** 4 Fairbanks-Morse $38D8\frac{1}{8}$ diesels, 2 electric motors; 2 props; 4,610 hp
**Fuel:** 330 tons **Range:** 10,000/10 **Man:** 82 tot.

Remarks: Purchased in 7-74. Both were converted to Guppy-IA configuration during 1951. They can maintain 15 kts for half an hour while submerged, 3 kts for thirty-six hours. Snorkel speed is 7.5 kts. A third submarine of this class, ex-*Tench* (SS-417), was towed out in 11-76 for cannibalization.

**CRUISERS**

◆ **1 ex-Dutch guided-missile cruiser** Bldr: Rotterdamse Droogdok Mij. Rotterdam

| | Laid down | L | In serv. |
|---|---|---|---|
| 81 Almirante Grau (ex-*Aguirre*, 84, ex-*De Zeven Provincien*, ex-*Eendracht*, ex-*Kijkduin*) | 19-5-49 | 22-8-50 | 17-12-53 |

**Almirante Grau (81)**—with old number 1978

**Almirante Grau (81)**—with old number 1981

**D:** 9,850 tons (12,250 fl) **S:** 32 kts **Dim:** 185.7 (182.4 pp) × 17.25 × 6.7
**A:** 4/152-mm DP (II × 2)—6/57-mm AA (II × 3)—4/40-mm AA (I × 4)—2/d.c. racks (8 d.c.)—3 SH-3D Sea King helicopters
**Electron Equipt:** Radar: 2/Decca. . . , 1/LW-02, 1/SGR-103, 1/DA-02, 1/ZW-03, 1/M 25, 2/M 45
Sonar: CWC-10N
**M:** 2 sets Parsons GT; 2 props; 79,000 hp
**Boilers:** 4 Yarrow-Werkspoor, three-drum
**Armor:** Belt: 76–102-mm; decks (2): 20–25-mm
**Electric:** 4,000 kw **Range:** 6,000/17 **Man:** 856 tot.

Remarks: Purchased in 8-76. The Terrier missile system was replaced by a hangar (20.4 × 16.5) and a helicopter platform (35.0 × 17.0) at Rotterdam. Recommissioned on 31-10-77. The helicopters carry French AM 39 Exocet antiship missiles. The hangar roof is also a helicopter platform. Carries 1,620 rounds 152-mm, 6,400 rds 57-mm, 8,000 rds 40-mm ammunition.

◆ **1 ex-Dutch cruiser** Bldr: Wilton-Fijenoord, Schiedam

| | Laid down | L | In serv. |
|---|---|---|---|
| N . . . (ex-*Almirante Grau*, ex-*de Ruyter*, ex-*de Zeven Provincien*) | 5-9-39 | 24-12-44 | 18-11-53 |

**"Proyecto 01" during conversion** L. & L. Van Ginderen, 4-87

**D:** 9,529 tons (11,850 fl) **S:** 32 kts **Dim:** 187.32 (182.4 pp) × 17.25 × 6.7
**A:** 8/MM 38 Exocet (I × 8)—8/152-mm 53-cal. Bofors DP (II × 4)— . . ./40-mm AA (I × . . .)—. . .
**Electron Equipt:** Radar: 1/ZW-06, 1/DA-08, 1/LW-08, 1/WM-25, 1/STIR-24, 2/LIROD
Sonar: . . .
EW: . . . intercept, . . . jammer, 1/Sagaie decoy RL, 2/Dagaie decoy RL
**M:** 2 sets Parsons GT; 2 props; 85,000 hp
**Boilers:** 4 Yarrow-Werkspoor, three-drum
**Armor:** Belt: 76–102-mm; decks (2): 20–25-mm **Electric:** 4,000 kw
**Range:** 2,100/32; 6,900/12 **Man:** 49 officers, 904 men

Remarks: Purchased 7-3-73, commissioning 23-5-73. Planned refitting at Amsterdamse Droogdok Maatschappij 26-3-85 to 1987; delayed by shipyard bankruptcy and Peruvian payment difficulties. Four twin Bofors 57-mm AA removed prior to arrival in Netherlands. Received new H.S.A. radars and fire-control systems. Carries 3,250 rds, 152-mm, 16,000 rds 40-mm ammunition. Name *Almirante Grau* conferred on sister after decommissioning for conversion; new name may be *Aguirre*.

**DESTROYERS**

◆ **6 ex-Dutch Friesland class**

| | Bldr | Laid down | L | In serv. |
|---|---|---|---|---|
| 70 Colonel Bolognesi (ex-*Overijssel*, D 815) | Wilton-Fijenoord, Schiedam | 15-10-53 | 8-7-56 | 4-10-57 |
| 71 Castilla (ex-*Utrecht*, D 817) | Kon. Mij. De Schelde, Vlissingen | 15-2-54 | 2-6-56 | 1-10-57 |
| 76 Capitán Quiñones (ex-*Limburg*, D 814) | Kon. Mij. De Schelde, Vlissingen | 28-11-53 | 5-9-55 | 31-10-56 |
| 77 Villar (ex-*Amsterdam*, D 819) | Nederlandse Dok, Amsterdam | 26-3-55 | 25-8-56 | 10-8-58 |
| 78 Galvez (ex-*Groningen*, D 813) | Nederlandse Dok, Amsterdam | 4-2-52 | 9-1-54 | 19-9-56 |
| 79 Diez Canseco (ex-*Rotterdam*, D 818) | Rotterdamse DDM, Rotterdam | 7-4-54 | 26-1-56 | 28-2-57 |

**Colonel Bolognesi (70)** L. & L. Van Ginderen, 7-82

**DESTROYERS** *(continued)*

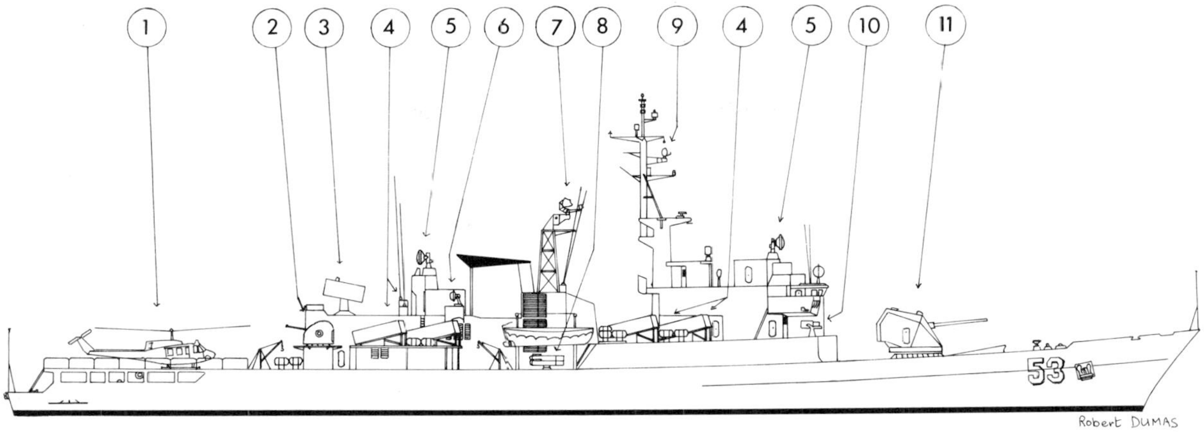


**Montero** 1. AB 212 helicopter 2. 40-mm Dardo AA mounts (II × 2) abreast fixed hangar 3. Albatros launcher for Aspide missiles (VIII × 1) 4. Otomat antiship missiles 5. RTN-30X/RTN-10X missile and gun f.c. radars 6. RTN-20X radar f.c.s. for 40-mm Dardo system 7. RAN-10S search radar 8. ILAS-3 ASW TT (III × 2) 9. RAN-11 L/X radar 10. Breda SCLAR multipurpose rocket launchers (XX × 2) 11. OTO Melara 127-mm/54-cal. gun

**D:** 2,496 tons (3,100 fl) **S:** 36 kts **Dim:** 116.0 (112.8 pp) × 11.77 × 5.2
**A:** 4/120-mm DP (II × 2)—4/40-mm AA (I × 4)—2/375-mm Bofors ASW RL (IV × 2)—1/d.c. rack (8 d.c.)
**Electron Equipt:** Radar: 1/Decca 1229, 1/LW-02, 1/DA-01, 1/ZW-06, 1/M 45
Sonar: 1/CWE-10N, 1/PAE 1N
**M:** 2 sets G.E. GT; 2 props; 60,000 hp
**Boilers:** 4 Babcock & Wilcox; 39.8 kg/cm², 454°C **Electric:** 1,350 kw
**Range:** 920/36; 3,300/22; 4,000/15 **Man:** 284 tot.

REMARKS: 77 transferred 19-5-80; 76 transferred 27-6-80; 78 purchased 27-8-80 and transferred 2-2-81; 79 transferred 11-7-81; 70 purchased 14-6-82. Two forward 40-mm AA removed 1965, fire control for remaining 40-mm AA removed 1977–78. Same propulsion plant as U.S. *Gearing* class. Have one 103-mm rocket flare launcher with 100 rds. Carry 1,300 rds 120-mm, 4,300 rds 40-mm, and 98 rds 375-mm ASW ammunition. Sister *Guise* (72, ex-*Drenthe,* D 816) purchased 11-7-81, stricken 8-85. Two of the ships are in reserve.

## GUIDED-MISSILE FRIGATES

◆ **3 (+1) Italian Lupo type**

| | Bldr | Laid down | L | In serv. |
|---|---|---|---|---|
| 51 MELITON CARVAJAL | CNR, Riva Trigoso | 8-10-74 | 17-11-76 | 5-2-79 |
| 52 MANUEL VILLAVICENCIO | CNR, Riva Trigoso | 6-10-76 | 7-2-78 | 25-6-79 |
| 53 MONTERO | CNTR, Callao | 1977 | 8-10-82 | 25-7-84 |
| 54 MARIATEGUI | CNTR, Callao | 1977 | 8-10-84 | . . . |

**Meliton Carvajal (51)** R.Neth.N., 1983

**Montero (53)** U.S. Navy, 1984

**D:** 2,208 tons (2,500 fl) **S:** 32 kts **Dim:** 108.4 (106.0 pp) × 11.28 × 3.66
**A:** 8/Otomat Mk 2 (I × 8)—1/127-mm OTO Melara DP—1/Albatros SAM system (VIII × 1)—4/40-mm Breda Dardo AA (II × 2)—6/324-mm Mk 32 ASW TT (III × 2)—1/AB-212 ASW helicopter
**Electron Equipt:** Radar: 1/3RM20, 1/RAN-10S air search, 1/RAN-11LX surface search, 1/RTN-10X, 2/RTN-20X, 1/RTN-30X
Sonar: Edo 610E
EW: passive intercept, 2/SCLAR chaff RL (XX × 2)
**M:** CODOG: 2 Fiat-G.E. LM-2500 gas turbines, 25,000 hp each; 2 GMT A230-20M diesels, 3,900 hp each; 2 CP props
**Electric:** 3,120 kw **Range:** 900/35; 3,450/20.5 (diesel)
**Man:** 20 officers, 165 men

REMARKS: Italian technicians assisted in the building of Nos. 53 and 54 at Callao. Differ from the Italian Navy's version in having a fixed (vice telescoping) hangar and a step down to the hull at the stern; the Dardo 40-mm mounts are one deck higher, and the SAM fire-control system differs. Selenia IPN-IC data system fitted. There are no reloads for the Albatros system, which uses Aspide missiles. The helicopter provides over-the-horizon targetting and mid-course guidance for the Otomat missiles.

## GUIDED-MISSILE CORVETTES

◆ **6 French PR-72-560 class**

| | Bldr | L | In serv. |
|---|---|---|---|
| P 101 VELARDE | Lorient DY | 16-9-78 | 25-7-80 |
| P 102 SANTILLANA | SFCN | 11-9-79 | 25-7-80 |
| P 103 DE LOS HEROES | Lorient DY | 20-5-79 | 17-11-80 |
| P 104 HERRERA | SFCN | 16-2-79 | 26-2-81 |
| P 105 LARREA | Lorient DY | 20-5-79 | 16-6-81 |
| P 106 SANCHEZ CARRION | SFCN | 28-6-79 | 14-9-81 |

**GUIDED-MISSILE CORVETTES** *(continued)*

**Herrera (P 104)**—old number SFCN, 1981

**D:** 470 tons light (560 normal, 610 fl) **S:** 37 kts (34 sust.)
**Dim:** 64.0 (59.0 pp) × 8.35 × 2.6
**A:** 4/MM 38 Exocet SSM (II × 2)—1/76-mm OTO Melara DP—2/40-mm Breda-Bofors AA (II × 1)
**Electron Equipt:** Radar: 1/Decca 1226, 1/Thomson-CSF THD 1040 Triton, 1/Castor III fire control
**M:** 4 SACM AGO 240, V-16 diesels; 4 props; 22,000 hp **Electric:** 560 kw
**Range:** 1,200/30; 2,500/16 **Man:** 36 tot.

REMARKS: These ships, designed by SFCN Villeneuve-la-Garonne, have been given the names of the Vosper patrol boats that were transferred to the Coast Guard. Vega weapons control system, with backup optical gun director.

**RIVER GUNBOATS**

◆ **1 Marañon class** Bldr: John I. Thornycroft, Woolston, U.K.

| | Laid down | L | In serv. |
|---|---|---|---|
| 13 MARAÑON | 4-50 | 23-4-51 | 7-51 |
| 14 UCAYALI | 4-50 | 7-3-51 | 7-51 |

**Marañon (13)** 1975

**D:** 350 tons (365 fl) **S:** 12 kts **Dim:** 47.22 × 9.75 × 1.22
**A:** 2/76.2-mm DP (I × 2)—4/20-mm (II × 2) **Man:** 4 officers, 36 men
**M:** 2 British Polar 441 diesels; 2 props; 800 hp **Range:** 5,000/10

REMARKS: Based at Iquitos and in service on the Upper Amazon. Superstructure of aluminum alloy.

◆ **2 Amazonas class** Bldr: Electric Boat Co., Groton, Conn. (In serv. 1934)

11 AMAZONAS 12 LORETO

**Loreto (12)** 1975

**D:** 250 tons **S:** 15 kts **Dim:** 46.7 × 6.7 × 1.2
**A:** 2/76.2-mm DP (I × 2)—2/40-mm AA (I × 2)—2/20-mm AA (I × 2)
**M:** 2 diesels; 2 props; 750 hp **Range:** 4,000/10 **Man:** 5 officers, 20 men

REMARKS: Based at Iquitos on Upper Amazon.

NOTE: Old river gunboat *America* (15), reported nonoperational 1981, may be retained as a hulk or relic. The former U.S. *Cannon*-class frigate *Castilla* (ex-*Bangust,* DE 739) is hulked at Iquitos on the upper Amazon as headquarters and training ship for the Amazon Flotilla.

**PATROL CRAFT**

◆ **3 P-33 class** Bldr: American Shipbldg. & Designs, Miami, Fla. (In serv. 1982)

P-33 (In serv. 15-9-82) P-34 (In serv. 20-11-82) P-35 (In serv. 4-2-83)

**P-33** Am. Shipbldg., 1982

**D:** 4.8 tons (fl) **S:** 27 kts **Dim:** 10.06 (9.19 pp) × 3.35 × 0.76
**A:** 1 or 2/12.7-mm mg (I × 1 or 2)
**Electron Equipt:** Radar: 1/Raytheon 2800 **Range:** 450/27
**M:** 2 Perkins ST-6-354-4M diesels; 2 props; 480 hp

REMARKS: Glass-reinforced plastic construction with Kevlar armor.

**AMPHIBIOUS WARFARE SHIPS**

◆ **4 ex-U.S. Terrebonne Parish-class tank landing ships**

| | Bldr: | L | In serv. |
|---|---|---|---|
| DT 141 PAITA (ex-*Walworth County,* LST 1164) | Ingalls SB, Pascagoula | 18-5-53 | 26-10-53 |
| DT 142 PISCO (ex-*Waldo County,* LST 1163) | Ingalls SB, Pascagoula | 17-3-53 | 17-9-53 |
| DT 143 CALLAO (ex-*Washoe County,* LST 1165) | Ingalls SB, Pascagoula | 14-7-53 | 30-11-53 |
| DT 144 ETEN (ex-*Traverse County,* LST 1160) | Bath Iron Wks, Bath, Me. | 3-10-53 | 19-12-53 |

**D:** 2,590 tons (6,225 fl) **S:** 13 kts **Dim:** 117.35 × 16.76 × 3.7 mean (5.18 max.)
**A:** none **Electron Equipt:** Radar: 1/. . . nav.
**M:** 4 G.M. 15-278A diesels; 2 CP props; 6,000 hp **Electric:** 600 kw
**Range:** 6,000/9 **Fuel:** 1,060 tons **Man:** . . .

REMARKS: Leased from U.S. for five years on 7-8-84; reactivated from Maritime Administration reserve by Todd SY, San Francisco, Cal., and delivered mid-10-84. Having been in Military Sealift Command Service from 1972 until deactivated, they were unarmed at time of transfer; formerly carried 6/76.2-mm DP (II × 3), with 2 Mk 63 GFCS; were to receive some 40-mm AA after arrival in Peru. Have accommodation for 395 troops, bow ramp. Cargo: approx. 2,200 tons. All officially recommissioned 4-3-85.

**HYDROGRAPHIC SURVEY SHIPS**

◆ **1 oceanographic research and survey ship** Bldr: SIMA, Callao

| | Laid down | L | In serv. |
|---|---|---|---|
| HUMBOLDT | 3-1-77 | 13-10-78 | 1980 |

**D:** 1,200 tons (1,980 fl) **S:** 14 kts **Dim:** 76.0 × 12.0 × 4.4
**M:** 2 diesels; 2 props; 3,000 hp **Man:** 48 tot.

◆ **1 ex-U.S. Sotoyomo-class former tug** Bldr: Levingston SB, Orange, Tex.

| | Laid down | L | In serv. |
|---|---|---|---|
| 136 UNANUE (ex-*Wateree,* ATA 174) | 5-10-43 | 18-11-43 | 20-7-44 |

**D:** 534 tons (835 fl) **S:** 13 kts **Dim:** 43.59 × 10.31 × 4.01
**M:** 2 G.M. 12-278A diesels, electric drive; 1 prop; 1,500 hp **Electric:** 120 kw

REMARKS: Sold to Peru in 11-61. Refitted 1985 with reinforced bow, improved heating, for possible antarctic expedition 1985–86.

◆ **2 Dutch Van Straelen-class inshore survey ships, former inshore minesweepers** Bldr: De Vries-Leutsch, Amsterdam

| | Laid down | L | In serv. |
|---|---|---|---|
| EH . . . ICARO (ex-*Van Hamel,* M 871) | 27-4-59 | 28-5-60 | 14-10-60 |
| EH . . . MELO (ex-*Van der Wel,* M 878) | 30-5-60 | 3-5-61 | 6-10-61 |

## HYDROGRAPHIC SURVEY SHIPS *(continued)*

**D:** 151 tons (171 fl) **S:** 13 kts **Dim:** 33.08 (30.30 wl) × 6.88 × 1.80
**Electron Equipt:** Radar: 1/. . . nav.
**M:** 2 Werkspoor diesels; 2 props; 1,100 hp

REMARKS: Purchased 23-2-84 for conversion in Peru to inshore survey duties. May have received Interplot 200 survey system and new engines: 2 G.M. 16V92N diesels; 1,400 hp; wooden construction.

◆ **1 inshore survey craft** Bldr: SIMA, Chimbote (In serv. 1982)

EH 174

**D:** 49 tons **S:** 13 kts **Dim:** 19.8 × 5.2 × 0.9
**M:** diesels **Man:** 3 crew, plus 2 scientists

REMARKS: Has a side-looking sonar for bottom mapping to 1,200-m depths. Former patrol boat, transferred from Coast Guard.

◆ **1 "Anchova"-class former patrol boat** Bldr: MacLaren, Niteroi, Brazil (In serv. 1981)

STIGLICH (ex-*Rio Chillón*)

**D:** 45 tons (fl) **S:** 25 kts **Dim:** 18.60 × 5.35 × 1.65
**M:** 2 G.M. 12V71 TI diesels; 2 props; 1,800 hp

REMARKS: Transferred from Coast Guard for inshore survey duties. Wooden construction.

◆ **1 river research craft** (In serv. 5-76)

EH 173 **Dim:** 23.5 × . . . × . . . **Man:** 16 tot.

REMARKS: Operated on the Amazon by the navy for the Oceanographic Institute.

## REPLENISHMENT OILERS

◆ **1 former commercial tanker** Bldr: C.N. de la Ciotat (In serv. 1976)

ATP 150 BAYOVAR (ex-*Loreto II*, ex-*St. Vincent*)

**D:** 15,175 tons light (107,320 fl) **S:** 16 kts
**Dim:** 250.53 (239.55 pp) × 35.56 × 14.57
**M:** 1 Sulzer 7RND90 diesel; 1 prop; 20,300 hp **Range:** . . . **Man:** . . .

REMARKS: 44,489 grt/92,145 dwt. Acquired by navy 1986 for commercial revenue service.

◆ **1 Talara class** Bldr: SIMA, Callao

| | Laid down | L | In serv. |
|---|---|---|---|
| ATP 152 TALARA | 1975 | 9-7-76 | 3-77 |

**D:** 30,000 tons (fl) **S:** 16.25 kts **Dim:** 171.18 (161.55 pp) × 25.38 × 9.53
**M:** 1 Burmeister & Wain 6K 47EF diesel; 1 prop; 11,600 hp
**Electric:** 1,890 kw

REMARKS: 16,633 grt, 25,648 dwt. Cargo: 35,642 $m^3$. Sisters *Trompeteros* and *Bayovar* (transferred 1979) are operated by Petroperu, the state fuel monopoly, which transferred this ship to the navy upon completion. One underway fueling station per side.

◆ **1 Parinas class** Bldr: SIMA, Callao

| | L | In serv. |
|---|---|---|
| ATP 156 PIMENTAL | 5-4-68 | 27-6-69 |

**D:** 13,600 tons (fl) **S:** 14.25 kts **Dim:** 134.19 (124.82 pp) × 18.98 × 7.27
**M:** 1 Burmeister & Wain 7-cyl. diesel; 1 prop; 4,900 hp **Electric:** 464 kw
**Fuel:** 610 tons

REMARKS: 7,121 grt, 10,140 dwt. Cargo: 13,851 $m^3$. Normally used by Petroperu for commercial purposes, but has naval crew and can refuel ships from one rig on either beam. Sister *Parinas* (ATP 155) stricken 1986.

◆ **2 Sechura class** Bldr: SIMA, Callao

| | Laid down | L | In serv. |
|---|---|---|---|
| ATP 158 ZORRITOS | 8-10-55 | 8-10-58 | 1959 |
| ATP 159 LOBITOS | 1964 | 5-65 | 1966 |

**Zorritos (ATP 158)** H. Ehlers, 9-85

**D:** 8,700 tons (fl) **S:** 12 kts **Dim:** 116.82 (109.73 pp) × 15.91 × 6.63
**M:** 1 Burmeister & Wain 562-VTF-115 diesel; 1 prop; 2,400 hp
**Electric:** 750 kw **Fuel:** 549 tons

REMARKS: 4,297 grt, 5,732 dwt. Cargo: 7,488 $m^3$. Sister *Sechura*, built in England 1952–55 and fully equipped for underway replenishment, was stricken in 1968. Nos. 158 and 159 are used for commercial cargoes for Petroperu, but have one fueling station on either beam. Navy crews.

## CARGO SHIPS

◆ **1 Ilo-class transport** Bldr: SIMA, Callao

ATA 131 ILO

**Ilo (ATA 131)** B. Risseeuw, 7-86

**D:** 18,400 tons (fl) **S:** 15.6 kts **Dim:** 153.85 (144.53 pp) × 20.4 × 9.2
**M:** 1 B & W 6K 47EF diesel; 1 prop; 11,600 hp **Electric:** 1,140 kw

REMARKS: In service 15-12-71. Cargo: 13,000 tons. Sister *Rimac* is in commercial service for the state shipping company. *Ilo* is also used to carry commercial cargo. Navy crew.

◆ **1 ex-U.S. Bellatrix-class attack cargo ship** Bldr: Tampa SB, Tampa, Fla.

| | L | In serv. |
|---|---|---|
| ATA 130 INDEPENDENCIA (ex-*Bellatrix*, AKA 3, ex-*Raven*, AK 20) | 16-4-41 | 16-2-42 |

**Independencia (ATA 130)** J.-C. Bellonne, 2-87

**D:** 6,200 tons (14,225 fl) **S:** 15 kts **Dim:** 140.0 × 19.2 × 7.95
**A:** 1/127-mm DP—4/76.2-mm 50-cal. DP (I × 4)—10/20-mm AA (I × 10)
**Electron Equipt:** Radar: 1/SPS-6, 1/Decca . . . , 1/Mk 26
**M:** 1 Nordberg TSM diesel; 1 prop; 6,000 hp **Range:** 18,000/14
**Man:** 19 officers, 220 men

REMARKS: Former U.S. C2-T-class cargo ship. Transferred under MAP in 20-7-63. Used for training midshipmen as well as for carrying military and commercial cargo (4,500 tons). Has one Mk 52 radar gunfire-control system and three Mk 51 gunfire-control systems. Normally carries two LCVP.

## HOSPITAL SHIPS

◆ **3 Morona class** Bldr: SIMA, Iquitos, 1976–77

ABH 302 MORONA ABH . . . N . . . . . . . ABH . . . N . . . . . . .

**D:** 150 tons (fl) **S:** 12 kts **Dim:** 30.0 × 6.0 × 0.6 **M:** diesels; . . . hp

REMARKS: Serve on the upper Amazon River.

## TUGS

◆ **1 ex-U.S. Cherokee-class ocean tug** Bldr: Cramp SB, Philadelphia, Pa.

| | Laid down | L | In serv. |
|---|---|---|---|
| ARB 123 GUARDIAN RIOS (ex-*Pinto*, ATF 90) | 10-8-42 | 5-1-43 | 1-4-43 |

**TUGS** *(continued)*

**D:** 1,235 tons (1,675 fl) **S:** 16.5 kts **Dim:** 62.48 × 11.73 × 4.67
**M:** 4 G.M. 12-278 diesels, electric drive; 1 prop; 3,000 hp **Electric:** 260 kw
**Man:** 85 tot.

Remarks: Transferred in 12-60. Unarmed. Used for salvage and rescue.

### SERVICE CRAFT

◆ **2 Selendon-class harbor tugs** Bldr: Ruhrorter, Duisburg, W. Germany (In serv. 1967)

ARB 128 Olaya ARB 129 Selendon

**D:** 80 grt **S:** 10 kts **Dim:** 61.3 × 20.3 × 2.3 **M:** 1 diesel; 1 prop; 600 hp

◆ **1 ex-U.S. medium harbor tug** Bldr: Ira S. Bushey, Brooklyn, NY (In serv. 1939)

ARB 124 Franco (ex-*Tigre,* ex-*Menewa,* YTM 2, ex-YN 34, ex-*Consultor*)

**D:** 192 tons (fl) **S:** 9 kts **Dim:** 27.73 × 7.01 × 3.35
**M:** 1 diesel; 1 prop; 805 hp

Remarks: Purchased 1940 by U.S. Navy for use as a net tender. Transferred in 14-3-47. Has push-bar built across bows for handling barges. Operates in the Upper Amazon Flotilla.

◆ **3 small harbor tugs**

ARB 120 Mejia ARB 121 Huerta ARB 126 Duenas

Remarks: No data available.

◆ **2 ex-U.S. 174-foot-class yard oilers**

| | Bldr | Laid down | L | In serv. |
|---|---|---|---|---|
| ACP 118 Noguera (ex-YO 221) | Jeffersonville Boat & Mach., Ind. | 15-1-45 | 22-5-45 | 31-8-45 |
| ACP 111 Colayeras (ex-YO 171) | RTC Shbldg., Camden, N.J. | 18-3-44 | 20-7-44 | 15-11-44 |

**D:** 1,400 tons (fl) **S:** 10 kts **Dim:** 53.04 × 9.75 × 4.0
**M:** 2 diesels; 2 prop; 540 hp **Range:** 2,000/8 **Man:** 20 tot.

Remarks: Ex-YO 221 transferred in 2-75; ex-YO 171 purchased 26-1-81. Cargo: approximately 900 tons (6,570 barrels).

◆ **2 ex-U.S. 174-foot water tankers**

| | Bldr | Laid down | L | In serv. |
|---|---|---|---|---|
| ACA 110 Mantilla (ex-YW 122) | Henry C. Grebe, Chicago, Ill. | 29-6-45 | 22-9-45 | 17-11-45 |
| ACA . . . Gauden (ex-YW 128) | Leatham D. Smith, Wisc. | 9-4-45 | 22-5-45 | 28-7-45 |

**D:** 440 tons (1,390 fl) **S:** 7 kts **Dim:** 53.04 × 9.75 × 4.0
**M:** 1 G.M. diesel; 1 prop; 640 hp **Fuel:** 25 tons **Man:** 23 tot.

Remarks: No. 110 transferred in 3-63; ex-YW 128 purchased 26-1-81. Cargo: 930 tons.

◆ **2 river-service water tankers**

ABA 332 **D:** 330 tons Bldr: SIMA, Iquitos (In serv. 1972)
ABA 330 Barge with 800-ton capacity Built: 1972

◆ **1 torpedo retriever** Bldr: Lürssen, Vegesack, W. Germany

ART 322 San Lorenzo (In serv. 1-12-81)

**San Lorenzo (ART 322)** P. Voss, 9-81

**D:** 51.5 tons (65.5 fl) **S:** 19 kts **Dim:** 25.35 (23.47 pp) × 5.62 × 1.68
**M:** 2 MTU 8V396 TC 82 diesels; 2 props; 1,590 hp **Range:** 500/15
**Fuel:** 14 tons **Man:** 9 tot.

Remarks: Can stow 4 long or 8 short torpedoes on ramp aft.

◆ **1 floating dry dock** Bldr: West Germany (In serv. 1979)

AFD 109

**Dim:** 195.0 × 42.0 × . . . **Lift capacity:** 15,000 tons

Remarks: Ordered 13-2-78; first unit lost en route Peru, 1978. Lift capacity can be increased to 18,000 tons by use of extension sections, bringing total length to 225 meters. A new 4,500-ton capacity dock is being built by SIMA, Callao, for use there; design by Senermar, Spain.

◆ **1 ex-U.S. ARD 2-class floating dry dock** Bldr: Pacific Bridge, Alameda, Cal.

AFD 112 (WY 20, ex-ARD 8) (In serv. 8-43)

**Dim:** 148.03 × 21.64 × 1.6 (light) **Lift capacity:** 3,500 tons

Remarks: In service in 1943. Transferred in 2-61; purchased outright 1981.

◆ **1 ex-U.S. AFDL 7-class floating dry dock** Bldr: Foundation Co., Kearny, N.J.

AFD 111 (ex-WY 19, ex-AFDL 33) (In serv. 10-44)

**Dim:** 87.78 × 19.51 × 0.99 (light) **Lift capacity:** 1,900 tons

Remarks: In service in 10-44. Transferred in 7-59.

◆ **1 small floating dry dock** Bldr: Thornycroft, Southampton (In serv. 1951)

AFD 108

**Dim:** 59.13 × 18.7 × . . . **Lift capacity:** 600 tons

Remarks: Serves the Amazon Flotilla.

◆ **1 ex-U.S. YR 24-class floating workshop** Bldr: DeKom SB, Brooklyn, NY

| | Laid down | L | In serv. |
|---|---|---|---|
| ATR 105 (ex-YR 59) | 3-11-43 | 22-4-44 | 24-8-44 |

**D:** 520 tons (770 fl) **Dim:** 45.72 × 10.36 × 1.8 **Electric:** 220 kw
**Fuel:** 75 tons **Man:** 47 tot.

Remarks: Transferred 8-8-61.

◆ **1 floating crane**

AGF 101 **Capacity:** 120 tons

Remarks: Serves at Callao.

## COAST GUARD

The Peruvian Coast Guard was established in 1975 and is intended to patrol to the extent of the 200-nautical-mile economic zone.

### PATROL BOATS AND CRAFT

◆ **6 Rio Cañete class** Bldr: SIMA, Chimbote (PC 248: SIMA, Callao)

| | In serv. | | In serv. |
|---|---|---|---|
| PC 243 Rio Nepeña | 1-12-81 | PC 246 Rio Huarmey | 1982 |
| PC 244 Rio Tambo | 1982 | PC 247 Rio Zaña | 12-2-85 |
| PC 245 Rio Ocoña | 1982 | PC 248 Rio Cañete (ex-8234) | 31-3-76 |

**Rio Ocoña (PC 245)**—*Rio Tambo* (PC 244) in background U.S. Navy, 1984

**D:** 296 tons (fl) **S:** 22 kts **Dim:** 50.98 (49.1 pp) × 7.4 × 1.7
**A:** 1/40-mm AA—1/20-mm AA
**M:** 4 Bazán/MTU V8V 16/18 TLS diesels; 2 props; 5,640 hp **Electric:** 170 kw
**Endurance:** 20 days **Range:** 3,000/17 **Man:** 4 officers, 26 men

Remarks: PC 248 (ex-234), launched 8-10-74 as prototype, has 4 MTU diesels and a 21-kt max. speed. All but PC 248 have steel hulls, aluminum superstructure.

◆ **2 ex-U.S. PGM 71 class**

| | Bldr | In serv. |
|---|---|---|
| PC 222 Rio Sama (ex-PGM 78) | Peterson, Sturgeon Bay, Wisc. | 9-66 |
| PC 223 Rio Chira (ex-PGM 11) | SIMA, Callao | 6-72 |

**D:** 130 tons (145 fl) **S:** 17 kts **Dim:** 30.8 (30.2 wl) × 6.4 × 1.85
**A:** 1/40-mm AA—4/20-mm AA (II × 2)—2/12.7-mm mg (I × 2)
**Electron Equipt:** Radar: 1/Raytheon 1500 Pathfinder
**M:** 8 G.M. 6-71 diesels; 2 props; 2,200 hp **Range:** 1,000/12 **Man:** 27 tot.

Remarks: Transferred to the Coast Guard in 1975. *Rio Chira* was built with U.S. aid and equipment.

**PERU** *(continued)*
**COAST GUARD** *(continued)*

◆ **3 110-foot class** Bldr: Vosper, Portsmouth

| | L | | L |
|---|---|---|---|
| PC 225 Rio Pativilca (ex-*Herrera*) | 26-10-64 | PC 229 Rio Vitor (ex-*Velarde*) | 10-7-64 |
| PC 227 Rio Locumba (ex-*Sanchez Carrion*) | 18-2-65 | | |

**D:** 100 tons (130 fl) **S:** 30 kts **Dim:** 33.4 (31.46 wl) × 6.4 × 1.7
**A:** 2/20-mm AA **Electron Equipt:** Radar: 1/Decca TM 707
**M:** 2 Napier Deltic T38-37 diesels; 2 props; 6,280 hp
**Range:** 1,100/15 **Man:** 4 officers, 27 men

Remarks: All delivered under own power by 10-65. Never fully equipped with armament, although fittings for four 533-mm torpedo tubes were installed in the decks. Air-conditioned. Steel hull, aluminum-alloy superstructure. Transferred to the Coast Guard in 1975 and renamed, their old names going to a new class of naval guided-missile corvettes. Sisters *Rio Ica* (228, ex-*Sautillana*) stricken 1982, *Rio Huaora* (PC 226, ex-*Larrea*) in 1983, and *Rio Chicama* (P 224, ex-*de los Heroes*) in 1986.

◆ **6 "Anchova" class** Bldr: MacLaren, Niteroi, Brazil (In serv. 1981–82)

PP 230 La Punta — PP 233 Rio Majes — PP 235 Rio Viru
PP 232 Rio Santa — PP 234 Rio Reque — PP 236 Rio Lurin

**D:** 43 tons (fl) **S:** 25 kts **Dim:** 18.6 × 5.35 × 1.65
**A:** 2/20-mm AA **M:** 2 G.M. 12V71 TI diesels; 2 props; 1,800 hp

Remarks: Wooden construction. Chile also operates units of this class. Sister *Rio Chillon* (PP 231) transferred to navy as an inshore survey craft.

◆ **3 Rio Zarumilla class** Bldr: Korody Marine, Viareggio, Italy (In serv. 5-9-60)

PC 240 Rio Zarumilla — PC 241 Rio Tumbes — PC 242 Rio Piura

**D:** 37 tons (fl) **S:** 18 kts **Dim:** 20.0 × 5.2 × 1.1 **Range:** 1,000/14
**A:** 2/40-mm AA (I × 2) **M:** 2 G.M. 8V71 diesels; 2 props; 1,200 hp

◆ **2 Rio Ramis class**—on Lake Titicaca

PL 290 Rio Ramis — PL 291 Rio Ilave

**D:** 12–14 tons (fl) **S:** . . . **Dim:** . . . × . . . × . . .
**A:** 1/12.7-mm mg **M:** . . . **Man:** 4 tot.

◆ **3 patrol craft**—on Bolivian border

Rio Manu — Rio Inambari — Rio Tambopata

◆ **1 small patrol craft:** Rio Lagato

# PHILIPPINES

Personnel (1987): 14,700 navy, plus 9,250 Marines

Merchant Marine (1986): 1,131 ships—6,922,499 grt
(tankers: 74 ships—646,614 grt)

Naval Aviation: Ten Philippine-built Britten-Norman BN-2 Defender light maritime patrol aircraft and 10 MBB BO-105 helicopters are in service or on order. The Air Force purchased 3 Fokker F-27 Maritime patrol aircraft in 1981.

Note: Most ships and craft in poor condition, with future plans in abeyance due to lack of funds.

## FRIGATES

◆ **1 ex-U.S. Savage class**

| | Bldr | Laid down | L | In serv. |
|---|---|---|---|---|
| PS 4 Rajah Lakandula (ex-*Tran Hung Dao*, ex-*Camp*, DER 251) | Brown SB, Houston | 27-1-43 | 16-4-43 | 16-9-45 |

**D:** 1,590 tons (1,850 fl) **S:** 19 kts **Dim:** 93.27 × 11.15 × 4.27
**A:** 2/76.2-mm DP Mk 34 (I × 2)—2/40-mm AA (II × 1)—4/20-mm AA (II × 2)—1/81-mm mortar combined with 1/12.7-mm mg—2/12.7-mm mg—6/324-mm Mk 32 ASW TT (III × 2)
**Electron Equipt:** Radar: 1/SPS-10, 1/SPS-28, 1/Mk 34
Sonar: SQS-31
**M:** 4 Fairbanks-Morse 38D$\frac{1}{8}$ × 10 diesels; 2 props; 6,080 hp
**Electric:** 580 kw **Fuel:** 300 tons **Range:** 11,500/11 **Man:** 150 tot.

Remarks: Transferred to Vietnam 6-1-71; to the Philippines, 5-4-75. Converted to radar picket in the late 1950s, but most electronic warfare gear and ASW ordnance was removed in 1971. Has one Mk 63 and one Mk 51 gunfire-control system.

Note: The four U.S. *Barnegat*-class frigates, former seaplane tenders, were to have been modernized and equipped with Harpoon missiles. Instead, all were de-

**Rajah Lakandula (PS 4)**—twin 40-mm AA now fwd of bridge 1977

commissioned 6-85: *Andres Bonifacio* (PS 7, ex-*Ly Thoung Kiet*, ex-*Chincoteague*, WHEC 375, ex-AVP 24), *Gregorio de Pilar* (PS 8, ex-*Ngo Kuyen*, ex-*McCulloch*, WHEC 386, ex-*Wachapreague*, AGP-8, ex-AVP 56), *Diego Silang* (ex-*Tran Quang Khai*, ex-*Bering Strait*, WHEC 382, ex-AVP 34), and *Francisco Dagahoy* (ex-*Tran Binh Trong*, ex-*Castle Rock*, WHEC 383, ex-AVP 35).

◆ **2 ex-U.S. Cannon class** Bldr: Federal SB & DD Co., Newark, N.J.

| | Laid down | L | In serv. |
|---|---|---|---|
| PF 5 Datu Sikatuna (ex-*Asahi*, ex-*Amick*, DE 168) | 30-11-42 | 27-5-43 | 26-7-43 |
| PF 6 Rajah Humabon (ex-*Hatsuhi*, ex-*Atherton*, DE 169) | 14-1-43 | 27-5-43 | 29-8-43 |

**D:** 1,240 tons (1,620 fl) **S:** 20 kts **Dim:** 93.27 (91.44 wl) × 11.15 × 3.56 (hull)
**A:** 3/76-mm DP (I × 3)—6/40-mm AA (II × 3)—12/20-mm AA (II × 6)—2/12.7-mm mg (I × 2)—6/Mk 6 d.c. projectors—1/Hedgehog—1/d.c. rack
**Electron Equipt:** Radar: 1/navigational, 1/Mk 26
Sonar: SQS-17B
**M:** 4 G.M. 16-278A diesels, electric drive; 2 props; 6,000 hp
**Electric:** 680 kw **Fuel:** 260 tons **Range:** 11,600/11 **Man:** 165 tot.

Remarks: Transferred to Japan on 14-6-55 and stricken 6-75, reverting to U.S. ownership; they were sold to the Philippines 23-12-78 but remained laid up in Japan until towed to South Korea for overhaul in 1979. Both recommissioned 27-2-80. Have one Mk 52 radar GFCS and one Mk 41 range finder for 76.2-mm gun control, plus three Mk 51 Mod. 2 GFCS for the 40-mm guns. Sister *Datu Kalantiaw* (PS 76, ex-*Booth*, DE 170) was grounded in a typhoon 21-9-81 and capsized.

## CORVETTES

◆ **2 ex-U.S. Auk-class former minesweepers**

| | Bldr | Laid down | L | In serv. |
|---|---|---|---|---|
| PS 69 Rizal (ex-*Murrelet*, MSF 372) | Savannah Mach. & Foundry, Ga. | 24-8-44 | 29-12-44 | 21-8-45 |
| PS 70 Quezon (ex-*Vigilance*, MSE 324) | Associated SB, Seattle, Wash. | 28-11-42 | 5-4-43 | 28-2-44 |

**Rizal (PS 69)**—prior to addition of helicopter deck L. & L. Van Ginderen, 5-65

**D:** 890 tons (1,250 fl) **S:** 18 kts **Dim:** 67.39 (65.53 wl) × 9.8 × 3.28
**A:** 1/76.2-mm DP—4/40-mm AA (II × 2)—4/20-mm AA (II × 2)—3/324-mm Mk 32 ASW TT (III × 2)—1/Hedgehog—2/Mk 6 d.c. throwers—2/d.c. racks
**Electron Equipt:** Radar: 1/SPS-5C
Sonar: SQS-17B
**M:** 2 G.M. 12-278 (PS 70: 12-278A) diesels, electric drive; 2 props; 3,532 hp
**Electric:** 360 kw **Fuel:** 216 tons **Man:** 100 tot.

## CORVETTES *(continued)*

Remarks: PS 69 transferred 18-6-65, PS 70 on 19-8-67. A small raised helicopter deck has replaced the after 76.2-mm gun.

◆ **7 ex-U.S. PCE 827 and PCER 848 classes**

| | Bldr | Laid down | L | In serv. |
|---|---|---|---|---|
| PS 19 Miguel Malvar (ex-*Ngoc Hoi,* ex-*Brattleboro,* EPCER 852) | A | 28-10-43 | 1-3-44 | 26-5-44 |
| PS 22 Sultan Kudarat (ex-*Dong Da II,* ex-*Crestview,* PCE 895) | B | 2-12-42 | 18-5-43 | 30-10-44 |
| PS 23 Datu Marikudo (ex-*Van Kiep II,* ex-*Amherst,* PCER 853) | A | 16-11-43 | 18-3-44 | 16-6-44 |
| PS 28 Cebu (ex-PCE 881) | C | 11-8-43 | 10-11-43 | 31-7-44 |
| PS 29 Negros Occidental (ex-PCE 885) | C | 25-2-44 | 20-6-44 | 30-4-45 |
| PS 31 Pangasinan (ex-PCE 891) | B | 28-10-42 | 24-4-43 | 15-6-44 |
| PS 32 Iloilo (ex-PCE 897) | B | 16-12-42 | 3-8-43 | 6-1-45 |

Bldrs: *A*: Pullman Standard Car Co., Chicago; *B*: Willamette Iron & Steel Corp., Portland, Ore.; *C*: Albina Eng. & Machine Works, Portland, Ore.

**D:** 903 tons (fl) **S:** 15 kts **Dim:** 56.24 (54.86 wl) × 10.08 × 2.87
**A:** PS 19–23: 1/76.2-mm DP—2/40-mm AA (I × 2)—4/20-mm AA (I × 4)—1/81-mm mortar
PS 28–32: 1/76.2-mm DP—6/40-mm AA (II × 3)—4/20-mm AA (I × 4)
**Electron Equipt:** Radar: 1/RCA CR 104A
**M:** 2 G.M. 12-278A diesels; 2 props; 2,000 hp (PS 19, 28, 31: 2 G.M. 12-567A diesels; 2 props; 1,800 hp)
**Electric:** 240–280 kw **Fuel:** 125 tons **Range:** 9,000/10 **Man:** 100 tot

Remarks: PS 28 through PS 32 were transferred 7-48; a fifth, *Leyte* (PS 30, ex-PCE 885), was lost by grounding in 1979. PS 19 through 23 were transferred to South Vietnam on 11-7-66, 29-11-61, and 6-70, and escaped Vietnam in 5-75; they were sold to the Philippines 11-75 (PS 23: 5-4-76). All ASW equipment is now deleted from all units. Ex-PCER and EPCER built with longer forecastles as rescue ships. All generally resemble *Magat Salamat,* below.

◆ **1 ex-U.S. Admirable-class former minesweeper** Bldr: Winslow Marine Railway, Seattle, Wash.

| | Laid down | L | In serv. |
|---|---|---|---|
| PS 20 Magat Salamat (ex-*Chi Lang II,* ex-*Gayety,* MSF 239) | 14-11-43 | 19-3-44 | 23-9-45 |

**Magat Salamat (PS 20)** 1977

**D:** 650 tons light (905 fl) **S:** 14 kts **Dim:** 56.24 (54.86 wl) × 10.06 × 2.75
**A:** 1/76.2-mm DP—2/40-mm (I × 2)—8/20-mm AA (II × 4)
**Electron Equipt:** Radar: 1/RCA CR 104A **Electric:** 280 kw **Fuel:** 140 tons
**M:** 2 Cooper-Bessemer GSB-8 diesels; 2 props; 1,710 hp

Remarks: Transferred to Vietnam and escaped to the Philippines 4-75. Acquired by the latter in 11-75.

## PATROL BOATS

◆ **0 (+1) "Guided Missile Boat"** Bldr: Cavite NSY

PM 140 General Amilio Aguinaldo (L: 23-6-84)

**D:** . . . **S:** 22 kts **Dim:** 45.0 × . . . × . . . **A:** . . . **M:** . . .

Remarks: No work done since launch. No engines or weapons installed. Was to have carried 4 SSM.

◆ **4 Katapangan class**

| | Bldr: | In serv. |
|---|---|---|
| P 101 Kagitingan | W. Müller, Hameln, West Germ. | 9-2-79 |
| P 102 Bagong Lakas | W. Müller, Hameln, West Germ. | 9-2-79 |
| P 103 Katapangan | Cavite NSY | 1982 |
| P 104 Bagong Silang | Cavite NSY | 1982 |

**D:** 132 tons (150 fl) **S:** 16 kts **Dim:** 37.0 × 6.2 × 1.7
**A:** 2/30-mm AA Emerlec (II × 1)—2/12.7-mm mg (I × 2)
**M:** 2 MTU MB 820 Db1 diesels; 2 props; 2,050 hp

Remarks: Designed in West Germany. Prototype delivered for trials 11-10-78. Program to build more at Boseco, Bekan, abandoned due to poor performance; intended to reach 28 kts, but obviously underpowered. All in reserve, inoperable.

◆ **1 ex-U.S. PGM 71 class** Bldr: Peterson Builders, Sturgeon Bay, Wis.

PG 60 Basilan (ex-*Hon Troc,* ex-PGM 83)

**D:** 130 tons (145 fl) **S:** 17 kts **Dim:** 30.8 (30.2 wl) × 6.4 × 1.85
**A:** 1/40-mm AA—4/20-mm AA (II × 2)—4/12.7-mm mg (III × 2)
**Electron Equipt:** Radar: 1/Raytheon 1500B
**M:** 8 G.M. 6-71 diesels; 2 props; 2,200 hp **Range:** 1,000/12 **Man:** 27 tot.

Remarks: In service 4-67. Escaped from Vietnam 4-75, the only one of her class to do so out of 20 transferred; acquired officially by the Philippines 12-76.

◆ **4 ex-U.S. PGM 39 class** Bldr: Tacoma Boat, Tacoma, Wash.

| | In serv. |
|---|---|
| PG 61 Agusan (ex-PGM 39) | 3-60 |
| PG 62 Catanduanes (ex-PGM 40) | 3-60 |
| PG 63 Romblon (ex-PGM 41) | 3-60 |
| PG 64 Palawan (ex-PGM 42) | 6-60 |

**D:** 122 tons **S:** 17 kts **Dim:** 30.6 × 6.4 × 2.1 (props)
**A:** 2/20-mm AA (I × 2) **Electron Equipt:** Radar: 1/Raytheon 1500
**M:** 2 MTU MB 820 diesels; 2 props; 1,900 hp **Man:** 15 tot.

◆ **2 ex-U.S. PC 461-class former submarine chasers**

| | Bldr | Laid down | L | In serv. |
|---|---|---|---|---|
| PS 29 Negros Oriental ex-E 312, ex-*L'Inconstant,* ex-PC 1171) | L.D. Smith, Sturgeon Bay, Wis. | 12-3-43 | 15-5-43 | 24-9-43 |
| PS 80 Nueva Viscaya (ex-USAF *Altus,* ex-PC 568) | Brown SB, Houston, Tex. | 15-9-41 | 25-4-42 | 13-7-42 |

**D:** 280 tons (450 fl) **S:** 18 kts **Dim:** 52.93 × 7.01 × 2.31 (hull)
**A:** 1/76.2-mm DP— 1/40-mm AA—3 or 5/20-mm AA (I × 3 or 5)
**M:** 2 G.M. 16-278A diesels; 2 props; 2,880 hp
**Electric:** 120 kw **Fuel:** 62 tons **Man:** 70 tot.

Remarks: PS 29 escaped from Cambodia to the Philippines and was acquired by the latter in 1976; she had previously been transferred to France in 1951, then to Cambodia in 1956. PS 80 served the U.S. Air Force 1963–68, transferring to the Philippines in 3-68. Both originally had different diesels, but now have been standardized.

## AMPHIBIOUS WARFARE SHIPS

◆ **21 ex-U.S. LST 1 and LST 542-class landing ships**

| | Bldr | In serv. |
|---|---|---|
| LT 54 Agusan del Sur (ex-*Nha Trang,* ex-*Jerome Cty.,* LST 848) | A | 20-1-45 |
| LT 87 Cotabato del Sur (ex-*Thi Nai,* ex-*Cayuga Cty.,* LST 529) | D | 29-2-44 |
| LT 93 Mindoro Occidental (ex-T-LST 222) | B | 10-9-43 |
| LT 94 Surigao del Norte (ex-T-LST 488) | E | 24-5-43 |
| LT 95 Surigao del Sur (ex-T-LST 546) | C | 27-3-44 |
| LT 96 Maquindanao (ex-*Caddo Parrish,* LST 515) | B | 28-1-44 |
| LT 97 Cagayan (ex-*Hickman Cty.,* LST 825) | C | 8-12-44 |
| LT 98 Ilocos Norte (ex-*Madera Cty.,* LST 905) | F | 20-1-45 |
| LT 500 Tarlac (ex-T-LST 47) | F | 8-11-43 |
| LT 501 Laguna (ex-T-LST 230) | B | 3-11-43 |
| LT 502 Samar Oriental (ex-T-LST 287) | A | 15-12-43 |
| LT 503 Lanao del Sur (ex-T-LST 491) | C | 3-12-43 |
| LT 504 Lanao del Norte (ex-T-LST 566) | C | 29-5-44 |
| LT 505 Leyte del Sur (ex-T-LST 607) | B | 24-4-44 |
| LT 506 Davao Oriental (ex-*Oosumi,* ex-*Daggett Cty.,* LST 689) | D | 2-5-44 |
| LT 507 Benguet (ex-*Davies Cty.,* T-LST 692) | D | 10-5-44 |
| LT 508 Aurora (ex-*Harris Cty.,* T-LST 822) | C | 23-11-44 |
| LT 509 Cavite (ex-*Shimokita,* ex-*Hillsdale Cty.,* LST 835) | A | 20-11-44 |
| LT 510 Samar del Norte (ex-*Shiretoko,* ex-*Nansemond Cty.,* LST 1064) | G | 12-3-45 |
| LT 511 Cotabato del Norte (ex-*Orleans Parrish,* T-LST 1069, ex-MCS 6, ex-LST 1069) | G | 31-3-45 |
| LT 512 Tawi-Tawi (ex-T-LST 1072) | G | 12-4-45 |

Bldrs: *A,* American Bridge, Ambridge, Pa.; *B,* Chicago Bridge & Iron Co., Seneca, Ill.; *C,* Missouri Valley Bridge & Iron Co., Evansville, Ind.; *D,* Jeffersonville Boat and Machinery Co., Jeffersonville, Ind.; *E,* Kaiser Co., Richmond, Cal.; *F,* Dravo Corp., Pittsburgh, Pa.; *G,* Bethlehem Steel, Hingham, Mass.

**Surigao del Sur (LT 95)** G. Arra

## AMPHIBIOUS WARFARE SHIPS (continued)

**D:** 1,620 tons (4,080 fl) **S:** 11 kts **Dim:** 99.98 (96.32 wl) × 15.24 × 4.29
**A:** 7–8/40-mm AA (II × 1 or 2, I × 4-6)—2–4/20-mm AA (ex-T-LST: 6/20-mm AA)
**M:** 2 G.M. 12-567A diesels (LT 510, 511, 512: 2 G.M. 12-278A); 2 props; 1,700 hp
**Electric:** 300 kw **Fuel:** 570 tons **Man:** 60–100 tot.

Remarks: LT 54 and LT 87 escaped from Vietnam (to which they had been transferred in 4-70 and 12-63, respectively) in 4-75; they were officially transferred to the Philippines on 17-11-75. LT 86 and LT 97 were transferred in 11-69. LT 93, LT 94, and LT 95 were transferred unarmed in 7-72 but may since have received guns. LT 500–LT 505, LT 507, LT 508, LT 511, and LT 512 were purchased in 1976, having previously been stricken by the U.S.N. and laid up in Japan. LT 506, LT 509, and LT 510 had been transferred to Japan 4-61 and stricken in 1975; they were purchased in 1978. All the LT 500 series were refitted and thoroughly overhauled in Japan, recommissioning in 1978–79. Armament: Some ex-T-LSTs carry only four 20-mm AA (I × 4), while others received a single 40-mm forward after transfer, plus several 20-mm AA. LT 87 has four sets of Welin davits for LCVP landing craft, the others only two; some ex-T-LSTs do not carry LCVPs. All reportedly in poor condition.

◆ **4 ex-U.S. LSM 1-class landing ships**

| | Bldr | L | In serv. |
|---|---|---|---|
| LP 41 Isabela (ex-LSM 463) | Brown SB, Houston | 3-2-45 | 7-3-45 |
| LP 65 Batanes (ex-*Huong Giang*, ex-*Oceanside*, ex-LSM 175) | Charleston Naval SY | 3-8-44 | 25-9-44 |
| LP 66 Western Samar (ex-*Hat Giang*, ex-9011, ex-LSM 335) | Pullman, Chicago | 10-11-44 | 9-12-44 |
| LP 68 Mindoro Oriental (ex-LSM 320) | Pullman, Chicago | 20-7-44 | 19-8-44 |

**D:** 513 tons (1,095 fl) **S:** 12 kts **Dim:** 62.03 (59.89 wl) × 10.52 × 2.54
**A:** 2/40-mm AA (II × 1)—4/20-mm AA (I × 4)
**M:** 2 G.M. 16-278A (LP 41: Fairbanks-Morse 38D8$\frac{1}{8}$ × 10) diesels; 2 props; 2,800 hp
**Electric:** 240 kw **Fuel:** 165 tons **Range:** 5,000/7 **Man:** 39 tot.

Remarks: LP 41 transferred 3-61, LP 68 in 4-62. LP 65 and LP 66 escaped from Vietnam (to which they had been transferred in 8-61 and 10-55, respectively, LP 65 having served in the French Navy from 1-54 to 10-55) in 4-75 and were officially transferred on 17-11-75. LP 66 was equipped with hospital facilities in a deckhouse filling much of her tank deck while in Vietnamese service, but retained guns. Ex-*Han Giang*, ex-LSM 110, which also escaped, was transferred also on 17-11-75, but was used for cannibalization.

◆ **3 ex-U.S. LSSL 1-class gunfire-support landing ships**

Bldr: Lawley & Sons, Neponset, Mass. (LS 49: Albina Eng. & Mach., Portland, Ore.)

| | L | In serv. |
|---|---|---|
| LF 48 Camarines Sur (ex-*Nguyen Duc Bong*, ex-LSSL 129) | 13-12-44 | 31-12-44 |
| LF 49 Sulu (ex-*Nguyen Ngoc Long*, ex-LSSL 96) | 6-1-45 | 24-1-45 |
| LF 50 La Union (ex-*Doan Ngoc Tang*, ex-*Hallebarde*, ex-LSSL 9) | 17-8-44 | 6-9-44 |

**D:** 250 tons (387 fl) **S:** 14.4 kts **Dim:** 48.15 × 7.21 × 1.73
**A:** 1/76-mm DP—4/20-mm AA (II × 2)—4/12.7-mm mg (I × 4)
**M:** 8 G.M. 6-71 diesels; 2 CP props; 1,320 hp
**Electric:** 120 kw **Fuel:** 84 tons **Range:** 5,000/12

Remarks: These are ex-Vietnamese ships (transferred 1965–66) that took refuge in the Philippines and were acquired by the latter 17-11-75. LF 50 had earlier served in the French (1951–55) and Japanese (1956–64) navies. Four additional ex-Japanese sisters were to have been transferred in 1978, but the sale was canceled.

◆ **3 ex-U.S. LCU 1466-class utility landing craft** Bldr: Japan (In serv. 3-55)

L . . . N . . . . . . . (ex-LCU 2002, ex-LCU 1603)
L . . . N . . . . . . . (ex-LCU 2003, ex-LCU 1604)
L . . . N . . . . . . . (ex-LCU 2005, ex-LCU 1606)

**D:** 180 tons (347 fl) **S:** 8 kts **Dim:** 35.05 × 10.36 × 1.6 (aft)
**A:** 2/20-mm AA (I × 2) **M:** 3 G.M. Gray Marine 64YTL diesels; 3 props; 675 hp
**Cargo capacity:** 167 tons **Man:** 6 men plus 8 troops

Remarks: Built in Japan under the Offshore Procurement Plan; in service 3-55, stricken 1975. Purchased 17-11-75 while laid up, then refitted and recommissioned in 1979.

◆ **9 U.S. LCM(8)-class landing craft**

LCM 257 LCM 258 LCM 260–LCM 266

**D:** 118 tons (fl) **S:** 9 kts **Dim:** 22.43 × 6.42 × 1.4 (aft)
**M:** 4 G.M. 6-71 diesels; 2 props; 600 hp **Cargo capacity:** 54 tons

Remarks: Transferred 19-3-75. The similar *Bagong Filipino* (TK 81) and *Dakila* (TK 82), built in the Philippines, have been stricken.

◆ **75 ex-U.S. LCM(6)-class landing craft** (Transferred 1955–75)

**D:** 56 tons (fl) **S:** 10 kts **Dim:** 17.1 × 4.4 × 1.2 (aft)
**M:** 2 G.M. Gray Marine 64HN9 diesels; 2 props; 330 hp
**Cargo capacity:** 30 tons

◆ **1 (+ . . .) Imelda-class LCVP** Bldr: Navy Yd, Cavite (In serv. 7-85)

**D:** 8 tons **S:** 13 kts **Dim:** 11.0 × 3.6 × 0.76
**M:** 1 G.M. 6-71 diesel; 1 prop; 225 hp

Remarks: Glass-reinforced plastic trimaran prototype.

◆ **10 U.S. "Mini-ATC" class** Bldr: Tacoma BY, Tacoma, Washington (In serv. 1978)

ex-U.S.N. AT 781, 782, 787–7814

**D:** 9.3 tons light (13 fl) **S:** 28.5 kts **Dim:** 10.97 × 3.89 × 0.30
**A:** up to 4/12.7-mm mg (I × 4)—1/40-mm Mk 19 grenade launcher—1/160-mm M60 mortar
**M:** 2 G.M. 8V53N diesels; 2 Jacuzzi 14Y waterjets; 566 hp
**Range:** 37/28 **Man:** 2 crew + 15 troops

Remarks: Aluminum construction. Rectangular planform. Can carry small radar. Very quiet in operation.

## AUXILIARY SHIPS

### YACHT

◆ **1 presidential yacht** Bldr: Vosper, Singapore (In serv. 12-77)

TP 77 Ang Pinuno

**D:** 150 tons **S:** 28.5 kts **Dim:** 37.9 × 7.2 × 3.8 **Range:** . . . **Man:** . . .
**A:** none **M:** 3 MTU 12V538 TB91 diesels; 3 props; 7,500 hp

Remarks: Used as a "command ship" for the president. White-painted. Sister *Bataan* is used as a search-and-rescue ship by the Coast Guard.

Note: The former presidential yacht *Ang Pangulo* (ex-*The President*, ex-*Roxas*, ex-*Lapu-Lapu*) was placed up for sale on 23-4-86 and was at Hong Kong, awaiting a buyer in 1987.

### TENDERS

◆ **3 ex-U.S. Achelous-class repair ships** Bldr: Chicago Bridge & Iron Co., Seneca, Ill. (AR 67: Bethlehem Steel, Hingham, Mass.)

| | L | In serv. |
|---|---|---|
| AR 517 Yakal (ex-*Satyr*, ARL 23, ex-LST 852) | 13-11-44 | 24-11-44 |
| AR 67 Kamagong (ex-*Aklan*, ex-*Romulus*, ARL 22, ex-LST 926) | 15-11-44 | 9-12-44 |
| AR 88 Narra (ex-*Krishna*, ARL 38, ex-LST 1149) | 25-5-45 | 3-12-45 |

**D:** 3,960 tons (fl) **S:** 11.6 kts **Dim:** 99.98 (96.32 wl) × 15.24 × 3.71
**A:** 8/40-mm AA (IV × 2)
**M:** 2 G.M. 12-567A diesels; (AR 67: G.M. 12-278A); 2 props; 1,800 hp
**Electric:** 420 kw **Fuel:** 620 tons **Man:** 250 tot.

Remarks: AR 517, transferred 24-1-77. AR 67 was transferred in 11-61 and AR 88 on 31-10-71. All have a 60-ton capacity A-frame lift boom to port and one 10-ton derrick and one 20-ton derrick.

◆ **2 ex-U.S. LST 542-class small craft tenders**

| | Bldr | In serv. |
|---|---|---|
| AL 57 Sierra Madre (ex-*Dumagat*, ex-*My Tho*, ex-*Harnett County*, AGP 821, ex-LST 821) | Missouri Valley B & I, Evansville, Ind. | 14-11-44 |
| AE 516 Apayao (ex-*Can Tho*, ex-*Garrett County*, AGP 786, ex-LST 786) | Dravo Corp., Pittsburgh, Pa. | 28-8-44 |

**D:** 1,620 tons (4,080 fl) **S:** 11.6 kts
**Dim:** 99.98 (96.32 wl) × 15.24 × 4.29 (max.)
**A:** 8/40-mm AA (II × 2, I × 4)—4/20-mm AA (II × 2)
**M:** 2 G.M. 12-567A diesels; 2 props; 1,700 hp **Electric:** 500 kw
**Fuel:** 370 tons **Range:** 19,000/10 **Man:** 160 tot.

Remarks: Converted in the mid-1960s to act as tenders to riverine-warfare craft. Retain bow doors, but much of the tank deck is filled with repair ships and bins for spare parts. Helicopter deck amidships, tripod masts, 10-ton derrick, and enlarged hatch. Transferred to South Vietnam 10-70 and 4-71; both escaped 4-75 and purchased outright on 13-9-77. Different hull numbers (and change of letter-designator and name to AL 57 from AE 57) may indicate new roles.

### CARGO TRANSPORTS

◆ **1 ex-U.S. Alamosa class** Bldr: Froemming Bros. Inc., Milwaukee, Wis.

TK 90 Mactan (ex-*Kukui*, WAK 186, ex-*Colquitt*, AK 174)

**D:** 4,900 tons (7,450 fl) **S:** 12 kts
**Dim:** 103.18 (97.54 wl) × 15.24 × 6.43
**A:** 2/20-mm AA **M:** 1 Nordberg TSM6 diesel; 1 prop; 1,750 hp
**Electric:** 500 kw **Fuel:** 350 tons **Man:** 85 tot.

Remarks: In service 22-9-45; 6,071 dwt. Built for U.S. Maritime Commission, taken over by the navy upon completion, then transferred to the U.S. Coast Guard 24-9-45. First platform deck in cargo-hold area converted to personnel accommodations. Transferred to the Philippines 1-3-72 and used as a military transport, supply ship, and lighthouse tender. Purchased outright 1-8-80.

**CARGO TRANSPORTS** *(continued)*

**Mactan (TK 90)**—with LCM(6) on deck R.A.N., 6-82

◆ **3 ex-U.S. Army FS 381 class** Bldr: Ingalls, Pascagoula, Miss. (In serv. 1943–44)

TK 79 Limasawa (ex-*Nettle,* WAK 129, ex-FS 169)
AS 59 Badjao (ex-*Miho,* ex-FS 524)
AS 71 Mangyan (ex-*Nasami,* ex-FS 408)

**D:** 473 tons light (950 fl) **S:** 13 kts **Dim:** 53.8 (50.27 pp) × 9.75 × 3.05
**A:** 2/20-mm AA (I × 2) **M:** 2 G.M. 6-278A diesels; 2 props; 1,000 hp
**Electric:** 225 kw **Cargo capacity:** 345 tons
**Fuel:** 67 tons **Range:** 4,150/10; 3,700/11 **Man:** . . .

Remarks: *Limasawa* was loaned in 1-68 and purchased outright 31-8-78. The other two were purchased 24-9-76 after having served in the Japanese Navy, one as an inshore minesweeper depot ship and one as a mine-countermeasures support ship; they were to be refitted and were recommissioned during 1979. All were to serve as buoy tenders and lighthouse supply ships.

◆ **2 ex-U.S. Army FS 330 class** Bldr: Higgins, Inc., New Orleans (In serv. 1943–44)

TK 45 Lauis Ledge (ex-FS 185) TK 46 Cape Bojeador (ex-FS 203)

**Cape Bojeador (TK 46)**—in Coast Guard colors G. Arra, 1977

**D:** 420 tons light (742 fl) **S:** 10 kts
**Dim:** 51.77 (48.77 pp) × 9.75 × 2.43 **A:** 2/20-mm AA (I × 2)
**M:** 4 Buda-Lanova 6 DHMR-1879 diesels; 2 props; 680 hp
**Electric:** 225 kw **Fuel:** 18 tons **Range:** 1,370/10 **Man:** . . .

Remarks: TK 45 transferred 11-47; TK 46 transferred 2-50. Can carry up to 50 tons of fuel for a range of 3,830/10. Used as navigational buoy tenders and lighthouse supply ships. Cargo capacity: 150 tons.

◆ **1 ex-Australian motor stores lighter** Bldr: Australia (In serv. 1944)

TK . . . Pearl Bank (ex-U.S. Army LO 4, ex-. . .)

**D:** 140 tons light (345 fl) **S:** 8 kts **Dim:** 37.26 × 7.47 × 2.07
**A:** 2/20-mm AA **M:** 2 Fairbanks-Morse 35F8$\frac{3}{4}$ diesels; 2 props; 240 hp
**Fuel:** 20 tons **Range:** 2,000/6 **Man:** 35 tot.

Remarks: Transferred 1947. Used as a navigational buoy tender and lighthouse supply ship. Cargo capacity: 170 tons

◆ **1 ex-U.S. Admirable-class minesweeper** Bldr: Gulf SB Corp., Madisonville, La.

| | Laid down | L | In serv. |
|---|---|---|---|
| TK 21 Mount Samat (ex-*Pagasa,* ex-*Santa Maria,* ex-*Quest,* MSF 281) | 24-11-43 | 16-3-44 | 25-10-44 |

**Mount Samat (TK 21)** G. Arra, 1977

**D:** 650 tons (945 fl) **S:** 14.8 kts **Dim:** 58.0 (54.86 wl) × 10.06 × 2.97
**A:** 2/20-mm AA **M:** 2 Cooper-Bessemer GSB-8 diesels; 2 props; 1,710 hp
**Electric:** 280 kw **Fuel:** 138 tons **Man:** 60 tot.

Remarks: Transferred 2-7-48 and then converted to presidential yacht with considerable additions to superstructure and increased rake to bow. Now primarily used as a lighthouse supply ship. Has 2 navigational radars.

◆ **1 ex-U.S. Coast Guard Balsam-class buoy tender** Bldr: Marine Iron & SB Corp., Duluth, Minn. (In serv. 2-5-44)

TK 89 Kalinga (ex-*Redbud,* WAGL 398, ex-T-AKL 398, ex-AG 398)

**Kalinga (TK 89)**—in Coast Guard colors 1977

**D:** 935 tons (1,020 fl) **S:** 13 kts **Dim:** 54.86 × 11.28 × 3.96 **A:** 1/20-mm AA
**M:** 2 Cooper-Bessemer GSD-8 diesels; electric drive; 1 prop; 1,200 hp
**Range:** 3,500/7.5 **Man:** 50 tot.

Remarks: Built for U.S. Coast Guard, transferred to the U.S. Navy on 25-3-49 as AG 398, to Military Sealift Command on 10-49 as T-AKL 398, and returned 20-11-70 to the U.S. Coast Guard. Transferred to the Philippines 1-3-72. Has helicopter platform and ice-breaking bow—the latter a useful feature in Philippine waters.

**SERVICE CRAFT**

◆ **2 ex-U.S. 174-foot YO and YOG-class small tankers** Bldr: R.T.C. SB, Camden, N.J. (YO 78: Puget Sound Naval SY, Washington)

| | Laid down | L | In serv. |
|---|---|---|---|
| YO 43 Lake Naujan (ex-YO 173) | 17-5-44 | 30-9-44 | 22-1-45 |
| YO 78 Lake Buhi (ex-YOG 73) | 15-12-43 | 23-2-44 | 28-11-44 |

**Lake Naujan (YO 43)** G. Arra, 1977

**SERVICE CRAFT** *(continued)*

**D:** 445 tons light (1,420 fl) **S:** 8 kts **Dim:** 53.04 × 10.01 × 4.27
**A:** 1/20-mm AA **Fuel:** 25 tons **Man:** 23 tot.
**M:** 2 Union diesels; 2 props; 560 hp (YO 78: 2 G.M. 8-278A diesels; 2 props; 640 hp)

REMARKS: YO 43 was transferred in 7-48, and YO 78 (formerly used as a gasoline tanker) in 7-67. Ex-U.S. YOG 33 and YOG 80, which escaped from Vietnam, were used for cannibalization spares. Cargo capacity: 985 tons. Sister *Lake Mainit* (YO 35) stricken 1979.

◆ **3 ex-U.S. 174-foot YW-class water tankers** Bldr. L.D. Smith SB, Sturgeon Bay, Wis. (YW 33: Marine Iron & SB Co., Duluth, Minn.)

| | Laid down | L | In serv. |
|---|---|---|---|
| YW 33 LAKE BOLUAN (ex-YW 111) | 30-9-44 | 16-12-44 | 1-8-45 |
| YW 34 LAKE PAOAY (ex-YW 130) | 14-5-45 | 24-6-45 | 28-8-45 |
| YW 42 LAKE LANAO (ex-YW 125) | 18-12-44 | 7-4-45 | 16-6-45 |

**D:** 440 tons light (1,390 fl) **S:** 8 kts **Dim:** 53.04 × 10.01 × 4.0
**A:** 2/20-mm AA (I × 2) **M:** 2 G.M. 8-278A diesels; 2 props; 640 hp
**Electric:** 80 kw **Fuel:** 25 tons **Man:** 23 tot.

REMARKS: YW 33 and YW 34 transferred on 16-7-75 and YW 42 in 7-78. Cargo capacity: 930 tons.

◆ **1 ex-U.S. Army tug**

YQ 58 TIBOLI (ex-LT 1976)

REMARKS: Transferred, 3-76.

◆ **5 ex-U.S. YTL 442 class** Bldr: Everett-Pacific Co., Everett, Wash. (YQ 222: Winslow Marine Railway & SB, Winslow, Wash.)

YQ 222 IGOROT (ex-YTL 572) YQ 226 TASADAY (ex-YTL 425)
YQ 223 TAGBANUA (ex-YTL 429) YQ 271 AFNO RIVER (ex-YAS 3, ex-YTL 750)
YQ 225 ILONGOT (ex-YTL 427)

**D:** 70 tons (80 fl) **S:** 9 kts **Dim:** 20.17 × 5.18 × 1.5
**M:** 1 Hamilton 685A diesel; 300 hp

REMARKS: Built 1944–45. Transferred 7-48, 5-63, 12-69, 8-71, and 11-75—the last from Japan, which had received her from the U.S. in 1-55. The ex-Japanese craft was overhauled and arrived in the Philippines during 1979, sister ex-YAS 4 (ex-YTL 748) having been lost overboard en route.

◆ **1 ex-U.S. AFDL** Bldr: V.P. Loftis, Wilmington, N.C. (In serv. 11-44)

YD 205 (ex-AFDL 44, ex-ARDC 11)

**Lift Capacity:** 2,800 tons **Dim:** 118.6 × 25.6 × 3.1 (light)

REMARKS: Transferred, 9-69. Purchased outright 1-8-80.

◆ **3 ex-U.S. AFDL 1 class**

| | Bldr | In serv. | Transferred |
|---|---|---|---|
| YD 200 (ex-AFDL 24) | Doullet & Ewin, Mobile, Ala. | 1-44 | 7-48 |
| YD 204 (ex-AFDL 20) | G.D. Auchter, Jacksonville, Fla. | 6-44 | 10-61 |
| YD . . . (ex-AFDL 10) | Chicago Bridge & Iron | 12-43 | 12-78 |

**Lift Capacity:** 1,000 tons **Dim:** 60.96 × 19.51 × 1.04 (light)

REMARKS: YD 200 transferred 7-48, YD 204 loaned 10-61, purchased 1-8-80; ex-AFDL 10 loaned 12-78.

◆ **2 ex-U.S. Army**

| | L | Transferred |
|---|---|---|
| YD 201 (ex-AFDL 3681) | 1943 | 5-52 |
| YD 203 (ex-AFDL 3682) | 1943 | 8-55 |

**Lift Capacity:** 150 tons **Dim:** 30.63 × 15.83 × 1.0 (light)

◆ **1 ex-U.S. floating crane**

| | In serv. | Transferred |
|---|---|---|
| YU 206 (ex-YD 163) | 12-5-46 | 1-71 |

**D:** 650 tons (fl) **Dim:** 36.58 × 13.72 × 2.13 **Lift Capacity:** 30 tons

◆ **1 ex-U.S. floating crane**

| | In serv. | Transferred |
|---|---|---|
| YU 207 (ex-YD 191) | 3-52 | 8-71 |

**D:** 920 tons (fl) **Dim:** 36.58 × 18.24 × 2.13 **Lift Capacity:** 60 tons

◆ **1 ex-U.S. Army 230 class**

| | L | Transferred |
|---|---|---|
| YD 202 (ex-BCL 1791) | 1943 | 7-49 |

**D:** 2,100 tons (fl) **Dim:** 64.0 × 12.5 × 3.4 **A:** 2/20-mm AA

◆ **1 ex-U.S. YCV 3-class former aircraft transport lighter** Bldr: Pearl Harbor Naval SY (In serv. 25-11-43)

YB 206 (ex-YCV 7)

**Dim:** 33.53 × 9.14 × . . . **Cargo Capacity:** 250 tons

REMARKS: Transferred, 5-63

◆ **2 ex-U.S. Navy barges**

| | Transferred |
|---|---|
| YC 227 (ex-YC 1402) | 8-59 |
| YC 301 (ex-YC 1403) | 8-71 |

**Dim:** 24.38 × 8.73 × 1.22

## COAST GUARD

PERSONNEL (1983): 300 officers, 1,700 enlisted men

The size of the Philippine Coast Guard has fluctuated widely since its establishment in the early 1970s. At one time it had responsibility for maintaining navigational aids and included many of the tenders now returned to the navy. The majority of the patrol craft operated by the Coast Guard have been back under naval control since 1977, leaving only a few small craft and the larger ships described below still under Coast Guard control. In 1982, most small patrol craft in Philippine military service appeared to be under Coast Guard subordination. Up to 60 new patrol craft are planned, but funds are lacking.

### PATROL BOATS

◆ **1 Bessang Pass-class search-and-rescue boat** Bldr: Sumidagawa, Tokyo, Japan (In serv. 1976–77)

SAR 100 TIRAD PASS

**Bessang Pass (SAR 99)**—since lost G. Arra, 1977

**D:** 275 tons (fl) **S:** 30 kts **Dim:** 44.0 × 7.4 × 1.5
**A:** none **M:** 2 diesels; 2 props; . . . hp **Man:** 32 tot.

REMARKS: Sister *Bessang Pass* (SAR 99) ran aground and was lost 9-83. Similar craft constructed for Indian Coast Guard.

◆ **1 search-and-rescue boat** Bldr: Vosper, Singapore (In serv. 12-75)

SAR 77 BATAAN

**Bataan (SAR 77)** G. Gyssels, 1986

**D:** 150 tons **S:** 28 kts **Dim:** 37.9 × 7.2 × 3.8
**M:** 3 MTU 12V538 TB91 diesels; 3 props; 7,500 hp

REMARKS: Externally identical to presidential yacht *Ang Pinuno* (TP 77), and apparently intended more for pleasure than rescue duties.

### PATROL CRAFT

◆ **1 (+3) Mk II design** Bldr: Cavite Navy Yd. (In serv. 7-85)

**D:** 24.6 tons (fl) **S:** 36 kts **Dim:** 16.7 × 5.0 × 1.3
**A:** . . . **Electric Equipt:** Radar: 1/. . . nav.
**M:** 2 MTU 8V396 TB93 diesels; 2 props; 2,400 hp

REMARKS: Improved version of following class; glass-reinforced plastic hull. Were to have been 55 built under 18-6-82 order, but by 1986 only 4 hulls were ready.

**PATROL CRAFT** *(continued)*

◆ **10 fiberglass-hulled** Bldr: Marcelo Fiberglass Corp., Manila

PSB 411 through PSB 435 (In serv. 1975–76)

**PSB 431** R.A.N., 6-82

**D:** 15 tons (21.75 fl) **S:** 20 kts **Dim:** 14.07 × 4.32 × 1.04 (1.48 props)
**A:** 3/12.7-mm mg (II × 1, I × 1) **Electron Equipt:** Radar: 1/LN-66
**M:** 2 MTU 8V-331 TC80 diesels; 2 props; 1,800 hp
**Electric:** 7.5 kVA **Range:** 200/36 **Man:** 6 tot.

Remarks: Eighty were ordered 8-75, but of 25 hulls completed during 1975, 15 were destroyed by fire, and the program was terminated. Twin machine-gun mount is recessed into the forecastle. Later examples employ Cummins diesels; craft originally intended to achieve 46 kts(!).

◆ **6 Australian fiberglass-hulled** Bldr: De Havilland Marine, Sydney

PC 326–331 (In serv. 20-11-74 to 8-2-75)

**D:** 16.5 tons (fl) **S:** 25 kts **Dim:** 14.0 × 4.6 × 1.0 **A:** 2/12.7-mm mg
**M:** 2 Caterpillar D348 diesels; 2 props; 740 hp **Range:** 500/12 **Man:** 8 tot.

◆ **20 U.S. Swift Mk III class** Bldr: Sewart Seacraft, Morgan City, La. and Peterson Bldrs, Sturgeon Bay, Wisc. (last four)

PCF 333 through PCF 352

**PCF 352** G. Gyssels, 1986

**D:** 28 tons (36.7 fl) **S:** 30 kts **Dim:** 19.78 × 5.5 × 1.8
**A:** 2/12.7-mm mg (I × 2)—2/7.6-mm mg (I × 2)
**Electron Equipt:** Radar: 1/LN-66
**M:** 3 G.M. 8V71 TI diesels; 3 props; 1,950 hp **Range:** 500/30 **Man:** 8 tot.

Remarks: Aluminum construction. Pilothouse offset to starboard. In service 1972–76.

◆ **3 Abra class**

| | Bldr | In serv. |
|---|---|---|
| FB 83 Abra | Vosper, Singapore | 8-1-70 |
| FB 84 Bukindon | Cavite NY | 1971 |
| FB 85 Tablas | Cavite NY | 1975 |

**D:** 40 tons **S:** 25 kts **Dim:** 26.7 × 5.8 × 1.5
**A:** 2/20-mm AA **M:** 2 MTU diesels; 2 props; 2,400 hp **Man:** 3 officers, 12 men

Remarks: Wooden hulls, aluminum superstructure. Construction financed by Australia. FB 85 disarmed in 1980.

◆ **12 U.S. Swift Mk I and II class** Bldr: Sewart, Berwick, La.

PCF 300 PCF 301 PCF 306 PCF 307 PCF 309–316

**PCF 308**—Swift Mk II type (stricken 1979) G. Arra, 1977

**D:** 17.5 tons (22.1 fl) **S:** 24 kts **Dim:** 15.66 × 4.55 × 1.8 (props)
**A:** 2/12.7-mm mg (II × 1) **Electron Equipt:** Radar: 1/Raytheon 1500B
**M:** 2 G.M. 12V71 N diesels; 2 props; 850 hp **Electric:** 6 kw
**Range:** 400/22 **Man:** 6 tot.

Remarks: In service 1966–70. PCF 300 and PCF 301, transferred 1966, are Swift Mk I class, 15.3 m overall and with flush-decked hulls. All-aluminum construction. PCF 303, PCF 324, PCF 325, and PCF 317 (the last of ferro-concrete construction and used as a yacht) were discarded in 1976; PCF 304, PCF 305, and one other were written off in 1976, and PCF 308 was discarded 1979.

## COAST AND GEODETIC SURVEY

The ships listed below are subordinate to the Ministry of Defense and are used for hydrographic survey.

◆ **1 survey ship** Bldr: Ishikawajima Harima, Tokyo

Explorer (In serv. 9-2-84)

**D:** 500 grt **S:** 12 kts **Dim:** 54.50 × 9.40 × 3.80
**M:** 2 diesels; 2 props; 1,200 hp

◆ **1 survey ship** Bldr: Walkers, Maryborough, Australia (In serv. 1969)

Atyimba

**Atyimba** L. & L. Van Ginderen, 1981

**D:** 611 tons (686 fl) **S:** 11 kts **Dim:** 49.08 (44.3 pp) × 10.14 × 2.74
**M:** Mirrlees-Blackstone 6-cyl. diesels; 1,620 hp
**Electric:** 175 kw **Range:** 5,000/8 **Man:** 54 tot.

◆ **2 Arinya-class coastal survey ships** Bldr: Walkers, Maryborough, Australia

Arinya (L: 1962) Alunya (L: 1964)

**D:** 245 tons (fl) **S:** 10 kts **Dim:** 30.64 (27.44 pp) × 6.76 × 2.43
**M:** 2 G.M. 6-71 diesels; 2 props; 336 hp **Man:** 6 officers, 27 men

◆ **1 ex-U.S. Coast & Geodetic Survey ship** Bldr. Lake Washington SY, Houghton, Wash.

| | Laid down | In serv. |
|---|---|---|
| Pathfinder (ex-*Pathfinder,* OSS 30, ex-AGS 1) | 3-8-42 | 31-8-43 |

**D:** 2,175 tons (fl) **S:** 14 kts **Dim:** 69.9 (63.8 wl) × 11.89 × 4.88
**M:** 2 sets GT; 2 props; 2,000 hp **Electric:** 145 kw
**Boilers:** 2 Babcock & Wilcox, 22 kg/cm$^2$, 330°C
**Fuel:** 340 tons **Man:** 150 tot.

Remarks: Served in the U.S. Navy during World War II, transferred to the Philippines in the mid-1970s.

# POLAND

**Polish People's Republic**

Personnel (1987): 21,800 total, including 4,100 coast defense personnel

Merchant Marine (1986): 749 ships—3,457,242 grt (tankers: 20 ships, 289,888 grt)

Naval Aviation: About 54 Mig-17 Fresco fighters and about 12 Mi 14 Haze A ASW, 3 Mi-14 Haze SAR, 10 Mi-2 Hoplite, and 5 Mi-8 Hip helicopters, and 7 An-2 Colt transports used for maritime surveillance

## SUBMARINES

◆ **2 (+ . . .) Soviet Kilo class** Bldr: Admiralty/Sudomekh SY, Leningrad

291 Orzel (In serv. 21-6-86) 292 Kondor (In serv. 7-87)

**Orzel (291)** M.O.D. Bonn, 1986

**D:** 2,300 tons surf./2,900 sub. **S:** 16 kts surf./20 kts sub.
**Dim:** 73.0 × 9.9 × 6.5
**A:** 6/533-mm TT (fwd.; 12 tot. torpedoes, or 24 mines)
**Electron Equipt:** Radar: 1/Snoop Tray
Sonar: passive array, LF active
**M:** diesel electric: 2 diesel generators, 1 motor; 16-bladed prop; . . . hp
**Man:** approx. 60 tot.

Remarks: Will probably continue to replace the Whiskey class on a one-for-one basis. Names taken from two stricken submarines of the Whiskey class below.

◆ **2 Soviet Whiskey class** Bldr: . . .

293 Sokol 295 Bielik

**D:** 1,050 tons surf./1,350 sub. **S:** 17/13.5 kts **Dim:** 76.0 × 6.3 × 4.8
**A:** 6/533-mm TT (4 fwd. 2 aft., 14 tot. torpedoes or 28 mines)
**Electron Equipt:** Radar: 1/Snoop Plate
Sonar: passive array, Tamir-5 MF active
**M:** diesel-electric: 2 Type 37D, 2,000-hp diesels, 2 motors; 2 props; 2,000 hp
**Range:** 6,000/5 snorkel **Endurance:** 40 days **Man:** 50 tot.

Remarks: Transferred 1962–65. Sister *Orzel* (292) stricken 30-12-83, *Kondor* (294) stricken 10-85.

Note: The Soviet SAM Kotlin-class guided-missile destroyer *Warszawa* (ex-*Spravedlivyy*) was stricken 31-1-86.

## FRIGATES

◆ **1 (+ . . .) Kaszub class** Bldr: Gdansk SY

. . . Kaszub (In serv. 6-1-87)

**D:** approx. 1,200 tons **S:** . . . **Dim:** 81.0 × 10.0 × 3.0
**A:** 1/SA-N-4 SAM syst. (II × 1; 20 Gecko missiles)—2/57-mm DP (II × 1)—4/ . . . ASW TT (II × 2)—2/RBU 6000 ASW RL (XII × 2)
**Electron Equipt:** . . . **M:** CODAG?

Remarks: NATO temporary nickname: "Balcom 6." First seagoing surface combatant built in Poland since before World War II. Series expected to produce four units.

## GUIDED-MISSILE PATROL BOATS

◆ **4 (+ . . .) Soviet Tarantul I class** Bldr: Sredniy Neva SY, Kolpino

434 Gornik (In serv. 30-12-83) 435 Hutnik (In serv. 31-3-84)
436 Stoczniowiec (In serv. 1-85) 437 N . . . (In serv. 1987)

**D:** 385 tons (455 fl) **S:** 40 kts **Dim:** 56.10 × 10.2 × 2.20 (3.50 props)
**A:** 4/SS-N-2C SSM (II × 2)—1/76.2-mm DP—1/SA-N-5 point-defense SAM syst. (IV × 1)—2/30-mm gatling AA (I × 2)
**Electron Equipt:** Radar: 1/Krivach nav., 1/Plank Shave, 1/Bass Tilt
IFF: 1/Square Head, 1/Salt Pot transponder
**M:** COGOG: 2NK-12MV, 12,000-hp gas turbines: 2 4,000-hp cruise gas turbines; 2 props: 24,000 hp max.
**Range:** 2,300/. . . (1 cruise turbine) **Man:** 38 tot.

**Gornik (434)** Polish Navy, 1984

Remarks: Beam is 10.5 m across missile sponsons. Unlike Soviet Navy version, have no EW gear.

◆ **12 Osa-I class**

422–433

**Polish Navy Osa-I 424** 1980

**D:** 175 tons (209 fl) **S:** 36 kts **Dim:** 38.6 × 7.6 × 1.8
**A:** 4/SS-N-2A Styx SSM (I × 4)—4/30-mm AA (II × 2)
**Electron Equipt:** Radar: 1/Square Tie, 1/Drum Tilt
IFF: 2 Square Head, 1/High Pole B
**M:** 3 M503A diesels; 3 props, 12,000 hp **Range:** 500/34; 750/25 **Man:** 30 tot.

Remarks: Built in the U.S.S.R. during the early 1960s, transferred 1966–1967. Three names are known: *Darlowo* (430), *Ustka,* and *Szczecin.* Sister *Gdynia* (421) stricken 1986. The others should be discarded shortly.

Note: The remaining Wisla-class torpedo boats were stricken, 1984–86, after brief and apparently unsuccessful careers.

## PATROL BOATS

◆ **8 Modified Obluze class** Bldr: Oksywie SY, 1970–72

| | |
|---|---|
| 351 Grozny | 355 Zwinny |
| 352 Wytrwaly | 356 Zreczny |
| 353 Zawziety | 357 Nieugiety |
| 354 Zwrotny | 358 Czujny |

**Zawziety (353)** 1975

PATROL BOATS *(continued)*

**D:** 210 tons (240 fl) **S:** 24 kts **Dim:** 41.0 (39.5 pp) × 6.0 × 2.0 (hull)
**A:** 4/30-mm AA (II × 2)—4/d.c. racks (2 topside; 2 through stern)
**Electron Equipt:** Radar: 1/RN-231, 1/Drum Tilt
Sonar: 1/Tamir-11—IFF: 2/Square Head, 1/High Pole
**M:** 2 Type 40D diesels: 2 props: 5,000 hp **Electric:** 150 kw
**Fuel:** 25 tons **Man:** 40 tot.

REMARKS: Similar to larger group in the Polish Border Guard that do *not* have Drum Tilt fire-control radars.

## MINE WARFARE SHIPS

◆ **12 Krogulec-class minesweepers** Bldr: Stocznia Gdynska, Gdynia, 1963–67

| | | |
|---|---|---|
| 613 ORLIK | 617 CZAJDA | 621 KANIA |
| 614 KROGULEC | 618 ALBATROS | 622 JASKOLKA |
| 615 JASTRZAB | 619 PELIKAN | 623 ZURAW |
| 616 KORMORAN | 620 TUKAN | 624 CZAPLA |

**Krogulec class**—with six 25-mm AA Polish Navy

**Krogulec class**—with four 23-mm AA aft 1978

**D:** 450 tons (484 fl) **S:** 18 kts **Dim:** 60.0 (58.0 pp) × 7.6 × 2.3
**A:** 6/25-mm AA (II × 3)—2/d.c. racks—mines
**M:** 2 Fiat A-230S diesels; 2 props; 3,740 hp **Range:** 3,200/12
**Electron Equipt:** Radar: 1/RN-231 **Fuel:** 55 tons
**Man:** 6 officers, 24 men

REMARKS: Some of these ships have four 23-mm rapid-fire AA (II × 2) mounted aft in place of the original four 25-mm AA.

◆ **12 Soviet T-43-class minesweepers** Bldr: Stocznia Gdynska, Gdynia, 1957–62

| | | | | | |
|---|---|---|---|---|---|
| 601 ZUBR | 603 LOZ | 605 BIZON | 607 ROZMAK | 609 FOKA | 611 RYS |
| 602 TUR | 604 DZIK | 606 BOBR | 608 DELFIN | 610 MORS | 612 ZBIK |

**D:** 520 tons (590 fl) **S:** 14 kts **Dim:** 60.0 × 8.6 × 2.3 (3.5 sonar)
**A:** 4/37-mm AA (II × 2)—4/25-mm AA (II × 2)—4/14.5-mm mg (II × 2)—2/d.c. projectors—mines
**Electron Equipt:** Radar: 1/RN-231—Sonar: 1/Tamir-11
IFF: 1/Square Head, 1/High Pole A
**M:** 2 Type 9D diesels; 2 props; 2,200 hp **Electric:** 550 kw
**Fuel:** 70 tons **Range:** 3,200/10 **Man:** 7 officers, 33 men

**Foka (609)**—long-hulled version 1978

**Zubr (601)**—short-hulled version Polish Navy

REMARKS: *Zubr, Tur, Loz,* and *Dzik,* built in the U.S.S.R., are 2 meters shorter and displace 569 tons (fl); they have 8/14.5-mm mg, but no 25-mm AA. *Tur* has been converted into a radar picket, losing the after twin 37-mm AA and all sweep capability in favor of a quadripod mast to support a large radar antenna.

◆ **6 (+ . . .) Notek-class coastal minesweepers** Bldr: Gdynia NSY

| | | |
|---|---|---|
| 630 GARDNO (In serv. 2-82) | 631 GOPLO (In serv. 31-3-84) | 632 N . . . (In serv. 1985) |
| 633 N . . . (In serv. . . .) | 634 N . . . (In serv. . . .) | 635 N . . . (In serv. 1987) |

**Gardno (630)** Polish Navy, 10-84

**D:** 250 tons (fl) **S:** 12 kts **Dim:** 38.5 × 8.3 × 1.9
**A:** 2/23-mm ZU-23/2 AA (II × 2)
**Electron Equipt:** Radar: 1/RN-231
IFF: High Pole B transponder
**M:** 2 diesels; 2 props; . . . hp

REMARKS: Glass-reinforced plastic construction. First unit launched 16-4-81.

◆ **2 (+ . . .) Leniwka-class minesweeping boats**

625 626

**D:** . . . **S:** . . . **Dim:** . . . × . . . × . . . **A:** . . . **M:** . . .

REMARKS: No details available; first reported 1985. One source indicates craft are converted trawlers.

NOTE: The 23 K8-class minesweeping boats delivered 1953 are believed to have been discarded 1984–86.

## AMPHIBIOUS WARFARE SHIPS

◆ **1 Soviet Polnocny-C-class landing ship** Bldr: Polnocny SY, Gdansk (In serv. 1971)

811 GRUNWALD

**D:** 1,150 tons (fl) **S:** 18 kts **Dim:** 81.3 × 10.1 × 2.1
**A:** 4/30-mm AA (II × 2)—2/140-mm RL (XVIII × 2)
**Electron Equipt:** Radar: 1/Drum Tilt, 1/Don 2
IFF: 1/Square Head, 1/High Pole A
**M:** 2 Type 40D diesels; 2 props; 5,000 hp **Range:** 900/17

◆ **22 Polnocny-A* and -B-class landing ships** Bldr: Polnocny SY, Gdansk (In serv. 1964–70)

| | | |
|---|---|---|
| 801 LENINO | 809 N . . . | 894* N . . . |
| 802 STUDZIANKO | 810 BALAS | 895* N . . . |
| 803 SIEKERKI | 888* N . . . | 896* N . . . |
| 804 BRDA | 889* N . . . | 897* N . . . |
| 805 POLICHNO | 890* BUDYSZYN | 898* WARTA |
| 806 RABLOW | 891* N . . . | 899* N . . . |
| 807 JANOW | 892* N . . . | |
| 808 NARWIK | 893* N . . . | |

**Polish Navy Polnocny-A (896)** L. & L. Van Ginderen, 1987

**Polish Navy Polnocny-B Lenino (801)** L. & L. Van Ginderen, 1987

**D:** A: 770 tons (fl); B: 740 tons (800 fl) **S:** 19 kts
**Dim:** 73.0 (B: 74.0) × 8.6 × 1.9 **A:** 4/30-mm AA—2/140-mm RL (XVIII × 2)
**Electron Equipt:** Radar: 1/RN-231, 1/Drum Tilt
IFF: 1/Square Head, 1/High Pole A
**M:** 2 Type 40D diesels; 2 props; 5,000 hp
**Fuel:** 36 tons **Range:** 900/18 **Man:** 35 tot.

REMARKS: The 12 Polnocny-A have blunt, convex bow form; the ten "B" versions introduced a raked, flared bow to improve seaworthiness. Unlike Soviet Navy units, Polish Polnocnys have a standard armament suit. Cargo: 180 tons vehicles, 130 troops. 801–810 and 890 are Type A; 888, 889, 891–899 are Type B. At least one Type A has a high bridge and low-mounted Drum Tilt radar like the "B" version. Some now receiving 2–4 SA-N-5 launchers (IV × 2 or 4), as on Soviet units of the class.

◆ **4 Marabut-class landing craft** (In serv. 1975)

872 873 874 875

**D:** 60 tons (fl) **S:** 15 kts **Dim:** 21.0 × 4.2 × 1.0
**A:** 1/14.5-mm mg **M:** 2 diesels; 2 props; . . . hp

REMARKS: Glass-reinforced plastic construction. One report indicates these craft were discarded in 1986.

**Marabut class (872)**

◆ **15 Eichstaden-class personnel landing craft** (In serv. early 1960s)

857–871

**Eichstaden class (866)** Polish Navy, 1983

**D:** 25 tons (fl) **S:** 18 kts **Dim:** 16.6 × 4.0 × 1.7
**A:** small arms **M:** 2 3D6 diesels; 2 props; 300 hp **Man:** 3 tot.

REMARKS: Cargo: 20 troops. Pointed bow, troops exiting cargo compartment via ramps on sides.

## HYDROGRAPHIC SHIPS

◆ **2 modified Fenik class** Bldr: Polnocny SY, Gdansk (In serv. 2-83)

265 HEWELIUSZ 266 ARCTOWSKI

**Arctowski (266)** M.O.D., Bonn, 1984

**D:** 1,112 tons (fl) **S:** 12 kts **Dim:** 61.30 × 10.80 × 3.27 **Electric:** 675 kVA
**Electron Equipt:** Radar: 1/RN-231 **Range:** 3,000/10 **Man:** 24 tot.
**M:** 2 Cegielski-Sulzer 6 AL 25/30 diesels; 2 CP props; 1,920 hp; 2 150-kw electric auxiliary drive motors

REMARKS: 751 grt, 250 dwt. Able to link via chain drag for clearance surveys. Have a bow-thruster, 4 precision echo-sounders. Compared to Soviet sisters, have forecastle extended nearly to stern, no buoy-handling capability. Civilian sisters *Planeta* (launched 21-5-82) and *Zodiak* (launched 28-8-82) are subordinated to the Maritime Agency, Szczecin. Also sisters in Soviet and East German navies.

◆ **1 Soviet Moma class** Bldr: Polnocny SY, Gdansk (In serv. 1973)

KOPERNIK

**D:** 1,260 tons (1,540 fl) **S:** 17 kts **Dim:** 73.3 × 10.8 × 3.8
**Electron Equipt:** Radar: 2/RN-231
**M:** 2 Zgoda-Sulzer 6TD48 diesels; 2 CP props; 3,600 hp
**Endurance:** 35 days **Range:** 8,700/11 **Man:** 56 tot.

HYDROGRAPHIC SHIPS *(continued)*

**Kopernik**—with seismic survey gear streamed 1978

Remarks: Sisters in Bulgarian and Yugoslav navies. *Piast*-class salvage ships and *Wodnik*-class training ships are very similar. Two others, the *Nawigator* and *Hydrograf* serve as intelligence collectors. The *Kopernik* has 35 $m^2$ of laboratory deck area and has been modified for use in seismic survey and oil exploration work. Forward crane removed 1983.

## AUXILIARY SHIPS

◆ **3 Moskit-class coastal oilers** Bldr: Poland (In serv. 1971–72)

Z 3 Krab Z 8 Medusa Z 9 Ukrain

**Medusa (Z 8)** 1973

**D:** 1,200 tons (fl) **S:** 10 kts **Dim:** 57.7 (54.0 pp) × 9.5 × 3.4
**A:** 4/25-mm AA (II × 2) **Electron Equipt:** Radar: 1/RN-231
**M:** 2 Cegielski-Sulzer diesels; 2 CP props; 850 hp **Man:** 12 tot.

Remarks: Cargo: 800 tons. Guns occasionally removed.

◆ **3 Type 5-class coastal oilers** (In serv. early 1960s)

Z 5 Z 6 Z 7

**D:** 625 tons (fl) **S:** 9 kts **Dim:** 44.2 × 6.5 × 3.0
**M:** 1 diesel; 1 prop; 300 hp **Range:** 1,200/9 **Man:** 16 tot.

Remarks: Cargo: 280 tons. Can carry 2/25-mm AA (II × 1).

◆ **2 Piast-class salvage ships** Bldr: Polnocny SY, Gdansk

281 Piast (In serv. 30-11-74) 282 Lech (In serv. 1975)

**Piast (281)** R.Neth.N., 1982

**D:** 1,560 tons (1,732 fl) **S:** 16.5 kts **Dim:** 72.6 (67.2 pp) × 12.0 × 4.0
**Electron Equipt:** Radar: 2/RN-231
**M:** 2 Cegielski-Sulzer 6TD48 diesels; 2 CP props; 3,600 hp **Range:** 3,000/12

Remarks: Variation of *Moma* design for salvage and rescue duties. Equipped to mount eight 25-mm AA in wartime (II × 4). Carry submarine rescue bell to port, can tow, and have extensive pump and fire-fighting facilities. Sister *Otto von Güricke* is in the East German Navy.

◆ **2 Gniewko-class salvage tugs** Bldr: . . .

R11 Gniewko (In serv. 29-8-81) R12 Bolko (In serv. . . .)

**D:** . . . **S:** . . . **Dim:** . . . × . . . × . . . **M:** . . .

Remarks: No data available. May be civil.

◆ **3 Mrovka-class degaussing/deperming tenders** (In serv. 1970–71)

SD-11 Wrona SD-12 N . . . . . . . SD-13 N . . . . . . .

**SD-12** 1980

**D:** 550 tons (fl) **S:** 9 kts **Dim:** 44.6 × 8.2 × 3.0
**M:** 1 diesel; 1 prop; 300 hp **Man:** 20 tot.

Remarks: Provision for 2/25-mm AA (II × 2) on forecastle.

◆ **1 icebreaker** Bldr: P.K. Harris & Sons, Appledore, U.K.

Perkun (In serv. 1963)

**D:** . . . **S:** 10 kts **Dim:** 56.5 × 14.0 × . . .
**M:** 4 920-hp diesel generators, 4 motors; 2 props; 3,000 hp **Man:** . . .

Remarks: 1,152 grt. Civilian-subordinated harbor icebreaker; manned by the Polish Navy.

## INTELLIGENCE COLLECTORS

◆ **2 modified Moma class** Bldr: Polnocny SY, Gdansk (In serv. 1975–76)

262 Nawigator 263 Hydrograf

**Hydrograf (263)** R.Neth.N., 1986

Remarks: Data as for hydrographic ship *Kopernik* above. Crane removed, superstructure lengthened, lattice mainmast as on *Piast* class, two large radomes. Euphemistically described as "navigational training ships." Provision for mounting 8/25-mm AA (II × 4), 2 fwd., 2 aft.

## TRAINING SHIPS

◆ **2 Wodnik class** Bldr: Polnocny SY, Gdansk

251 Wodnik (L: 29-11-75; in serv. 27-5-76) 252 Gryf (L: 13-3-76)

**D:** 1,800 tons (fl) **S:** 16.8 kts **Dim:** 72.0 × 12.0 × 4.2
**A:** 4/30-mm AA (II × 2)—4/23-mm AA (II × 2)
**Electron Equipt:** Radar: 2/RN-231, 1/Drum Tilt
**M:** 2 Cegielski-Sulzer 6TD48 diesels; 2 CP props; 3,600 hp
**Range:** 7,500/11 **Man:** 60 men + 13 instructors and 87 cadets

**Wodnik (251)** Skyfotos, 3-86

Remarks: Nearly identical to the East German Navy's *Wilhelm Pieck* and similar to the *Luga* and *Oka* in the Soviet Navy. Developed from the *Moma* design. Have latest navigational systems from the West and the U.S.S.R. Twin 23-mm substituted for twin 25-mm mounts in 1986.

◆ **4 Bryza class** Bldr: Wisla SY

| | In serv. | | In serv. |
|---|---|---|---|
| K 18 Bryza | 1965 | 712 Kadet | 19-7-75 |
| 711 Podchorazy | 30-11-74 | 713 Elew | 8-4-76 |

**Podchorazy (711)** 1976

**D:** 147 tons (fl) **S:** 10 kts **Dim:** 26.8 × 6.8 × 1.8
**Electron Equipt:** Radar: 2/RN-231 **M:** 2 Wola diesels; 2 props; 300 hp
**Electric:** 84 kw **Range:** 1,100/10 **Man:** 11 men, 36 midshipmen

Remarks: *Bryza,* with a less elaborate superstructure, displaces 167 tons (fl). This class also widely employed by Soviet naval schools and Merchant Marine schools for navigation and seamanship training. 711 serves at the Heroes of the Westerplatte Naval School and was launched 6-4-74.

◆ **1 sail-training craft** Bldr: Gdynia SY (In serv. 11-8-82)

Iskra II

**D:** 341 tons **S:** . . . **Dim:** . . . × . . . × . . .
**M:** 1 diesel; 1 prop; . . . ; ketch-rigged

Remarks: Can accommodate 40 cadets. The much larger sail-training ship *Dar Mlodziezy,* also completed in 1982, is civilian-subordinated. The old naval sail-training ship *Iskra,* renamed *Iotka,* survives as a youth training craft.

## MISCELLANEOUS SERVICE CRAFT

◆ **2 Pajak-class torpedo retrievers** Bldr: Gdynia SY (In serv. 1971)

K 8 Kormoran I K 11 Kormoran II

**D:** 130 tons (fl) **S:** 21 kts **Dim:** 38.0 × 6.0 × 1.6 **Man:** 18 tot.
**A:** 2/25-mm AA (II × 1) **M:** 2 M50F-4 diesels; 2 props; 2,400 hp

◆ **4 East German FLB-class fireboats** Bldr: Schiffswerft Berlin (In serv. 1961)

Strazak N . . . N . . . N . . .

**D:** 124 tons (fl) **S:** 12 kts **Dim:** 32.3 (29.3 pp) × 5.9 × 1.6
**M:** 2 Buckau-Wolff 6 NVD 26A diesels; 1 prop; 540 hp **Man:** 13 tot.

Remarks: Have three fire monitors. Also known as the Ibis class.

◆ **2 (+ . . .) Bucha-class harbor tugs** (In serv. 1981– . . .)

H 4 H 7

**D:** 310 tons (fl) **S:** 11 kts **Dim:** 26.3 (25.4 pp) × 7.0 × 3.0
**Electron Equipt:** Radar: 1/SRN-206 **Electric:** 76 kw
**M:** 1 Cegielski-Sulzer 6AL 20/24H diesel; 1 CP prop; 760 hp
**Fuel:** 20 tons
**Man:** 7 tot.

Remarks: Class also built for civil use. Bollard pull: 10 tons

◆ **3 Motyl-class tugs** Bldr: Polnocny SY, Gdansk (In serv. 1962–66)

H 12 H 19 H 20

**Motyl-class tug H 20** 1974

**D:** 500 tons (fl) **S:** 12.8 kts **Dim:** 31.8 (28.6 pp) × 8.7 × 3.5
**M:** 1 Zgoda-Sulzer 5TD48 diesel; 1 prop; 1,500 hp
**Electric:** 150 kw **Fuel:** 20 tons **Range:** 2,000/12.8
**Man:** 20 tot.

◆ **7 Goliat-class harbor tugs** Bldr: Gdynia SY (In serv. early 1960s)

H 5 H 13–18

**D:** 150 tons (fl) **S:** 12 kts **Dim:** 21.4 × 6.1 × 2.6 **Man:** 5 tot.
**M:** 1 Buckau-Wolff 8 NVD 36 diesel; 1 prop; 300 hp **Range:** 300/9

◆ **2–4 K-15-class mooring buoy tenders (In serv. 1962)**

**D:** 40 tons (fl) **S:** 9.6 kts **Dim:** 17.8 (15.2 pp) × 4.2 × 1.5
**M:** 1 Wola diesel; 1 prop; 150 hp
**Man:** 5 tot.

◆ **6 R 34-class mooring buoy tenders**

**D:** 58.5 tons (64.5 fl) **S:** 11 kts **Dim:** 16.8 × 5.5 × 2.4
**M:** 1 Wola diesel; 1 prop; 300 hp

◆ **1 research submersible** Bldr: Paris Commune SY (In serv. 1982)

Geonur II

**D:** 34 tons (67 submerged fl) **S:** . . . **Dim:** 9.5 × 4.4 × 3.5 (height)

Remarks: Operated jointly by the navy and the Institute of Baltic Geodesy. Diving depth: 150 m.

BORDER GUARD (WOP)

## PATROL BOATS

◆ **5 Obluze class** Bldr: Oksywie SY (In serv. 1965–68)

321–325

**D:** 150 tons (fl) **S:** 24 kts **Dim:** 41.0 × 6.0 × 2.1
**A:** 4/30-mm AA (II × 2)—4 d.c. racks (2 internal)
**Electron Equipt:** Radar: 1/RN-231
Sonar: Tamir-11
IFF: 1/Square Head, 1/High Pole A
**M:** 2 Type 40D diesels; 2 props; 5,000 hp

**POLAND** *(continued)*
**PATROL BOATS** *(continued)*

**Polish Border Guard Obluze**—old number

REMARKS: Two (including 324) have no 30-mm AA mount aft. Five additional units with Drum Tilt fire-control radars for the 30-mm AA serve in the Polish Navy.

NOTE: The nine similar Gdansk-class patrol boats were stricken 1986–87.

### PATROL CRAFT

◆ **16 Pilica class** Bldr: Poland (In serv. 1973–. . .)

KP 161 to KP 177 series

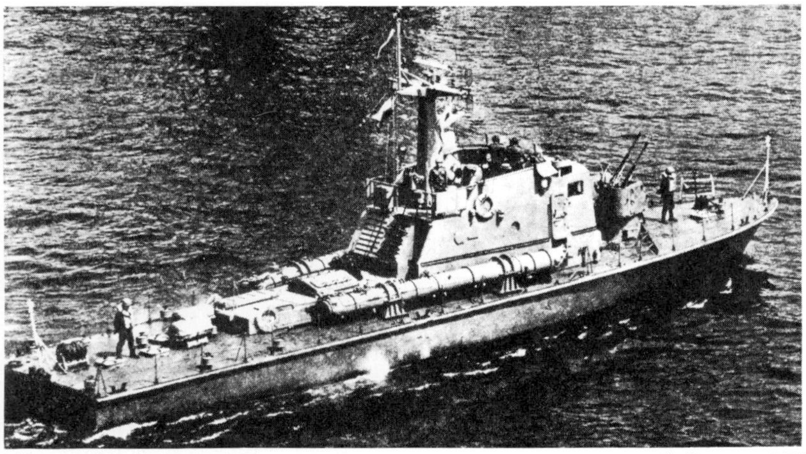

**Pilica**—with 2/533-mm TT S. Breyer, 1979

**D:** 100 tons (fl) **S:** 24 kts **Dim:** 29.2 × 6.0 × 1.4
**A:** 2/25-mm AA (II × 1)—2/533-mm TT
**Electron Equipt:** Radar: 1/RN-231 IFF: 1/High Pole A
**M:** 3 M50F-4 diesels; 3 props; 3,600 hp **Man:** 15 hp

REMARKS: All but the first three have had two 533-mm torpedo tubes added

◆ **12 Wisloka class** Bldr: Poland (In serv. early 1970s)

KP 141–152

**Wisloka class** S. Breyer, 1979

**D:** 45 tons (fl) **S:** 14 kts **Dim:** 22.8 × 5.0 × 1.1
**A:** 2/14.5-mm mg (II × 1) **Electron Equipt:** Radar: 1/navigational
**M:** 2 diesels; 2 props; 600 hp **Man:** 10 tot.

◆ **21 K-15-class harbor craft** Bldr: Poland (In serv. early 1960s)

KP 108–128

**D:** 40 tons **S:** 10 kts **Dim:** 17.8 × 4.2 × 1.5
**A:** small arms **M:** 1 diesel; 1 prop; 300 hp **Man:** 5 tot.

REMARKS: May have been discarded.

# PORTUGAL

**Portuguese Republic**

PERSONNEL (1987): 14,800, including 2,470 Marines

MERCHANT MARINE (1986): 355 ships—1,114,444 grt
(tankers: 14 ships—533,351 grt)

NAVAL AVIATION: There is no aviation arm *per se,* but eight Air Force Casa 212 Aviocar light transports (four with photo equipment) are equipped for maritime reconnaissance duties. Six ex-Australian P-3B Orions, refurbished by Lockheed, purchased 1985; the first was delivered 7-87, after modernization by OGMA, to the 601st Squadron at Montijo.

### SUBMARINES

◆ **3 Daphné class** Bldr: Dubigeon, Normandy

| | Laid down | L | In serv. |
|---|---|---|---|
| S 163 ALBACORA | 6-9-65 | 15-10-66 | 1-10-67 |
| S 164 BARRACUDA | 19-10-65 | 24-4-67 | 4-5-68 |
| S 166 DELFIM | 14-5-67 | 23-9-68 | 1-10-69 |

**Albacora (S 163)** G. Gyssels, 10-84

**D:** 869 surf. f.l./1,043 sub. tons **S:** 13.5/16 kts **Dim:** 57.75 × 6.76 × 4.56
**A:** 12/550-mm TT (8 fwd, 4 aft, no reloads)
**Electron Equipt:** Radar: 1/DRUA-31—EW: ARUR, ARUD
Sonar: DUUA-1 active, DSUV passive
**M:** diesel-electric propulsion: SEMT-Pielstick 12PA1 diesels (450 kw); 2 props; 1,200 hp
**Range:** 4,300/7.5 snorkel **Man:** 5 officers, 45 men

REMARKS: See remarks on the *Daphné* class in the French section. Sister *Cachalote* (S 165) was purchased by the Pakistani Navy in 1975. Modernization of the sonar suite is planned.

### FRIGATES

◆ **0 (+3) MEKO 200 class**

| | Bldr: | Laid down | L | In serv. |
|---|---|---|---|---|
| F . . . VASCO DA GAMA | Blohm + Voss, Hamburg | 8-88 | 6-89 | 11-90 |
| F . . . ALVARES CABRAL | Howaldtswerke, Kiel | 2-89 | 12-89 | 5-91 |
| F . . . CORTE REAL | Howaldtswerke, Kiel | 8-89 | 6-90 | 11-91 |

**D:** 2,900 tons (3,180 fl) **S:** 31.75 kts (20 kts on diesel)
**Dim:** 117.50 (109.50 pp) × 14.80 (13.80 wl) × 5.97 (4.10 hull)
**A:** 8/Harpoon SSM (IV × 2)—1/Mk 29 SAM launcher (VIII × 1, 8 NATO Sea Sparrow missiles)—1/100-mm Creusot-Loire Compact DP—1/20-mm Mk 15 CIWS gatling AA—6/324-mm Mk 32 ASW TT (III × 2)—2/helicopters
**Electron Equipt:** Radar: 1/Kelvin-Hughes 1007 nav., 1/H.S.A. MW-08 air/surf. search, 1/H.S.A. DA-08 early warning, 2/STIR f.c.
Sonar: Westinghouse SQS-510
EW: APECS II/AR-700 suite, Mk 36 Super RBOC decoy RL (VI × 2), SLQ-25 Nixie torpedo decoy
**M:** CODOG: 2 MTU 12V1163 TB83 diesels (4,420 hp each), 2 G.E. LM-2500-30 gas turbines (30,000 hp each); 2 CP props; 8,840/60,000 hp
**Electric:** 2,480 kw (4 × 620-kw diesel sets) **Fuel:** 300 tons
**Range:** 900/31.75; 4,100/18 (2 diesels) **Man:** 167–175 tot.

REMARKS: Ordered 25-7-86. Financed by U.S., Canada, West Germany, Norway, and the Netherlands. Will have H.S.A. SEWACO (Sensor Weapon, Control & Command System), STACOS tactical command system, and Vespa data link transponder. MW-08 is a short-range 3-D radar. Helicopter type to be carried not yet decided.

**FRIGATES** *(continued)*

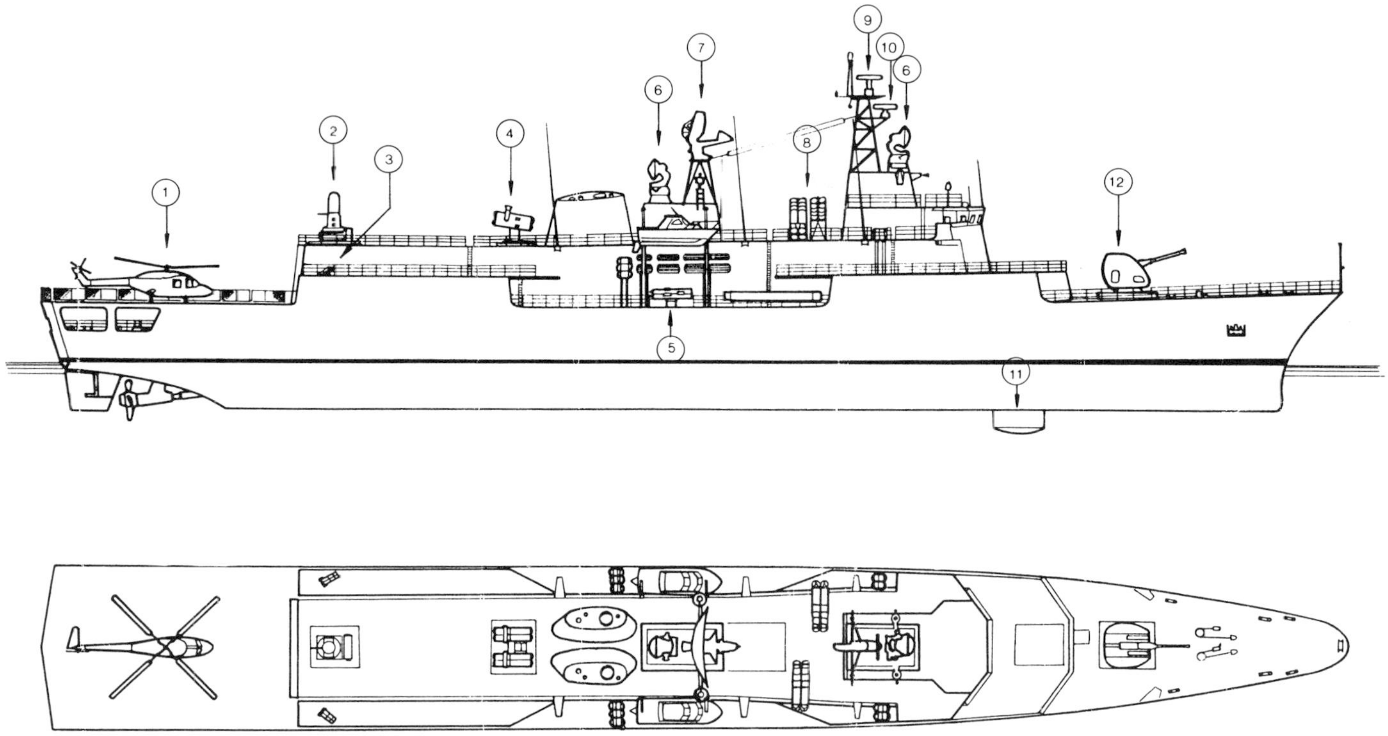


**Vasco da Gama** Portuguese Navy, 12-86
1. ASW helicopter 2. Mk 15 CIWS gatling AA 3. Super RBOC decoy RL 4. Sea Sparrow 5. Mk 32 ASW TT 6. STIR f.c. radar 7. DA-08 early warning 8. Harpoon SSM 9. MW-08 air/surf.-search radar 10. 1007 nav. radar 11. AN/SQS 510 sonar 12. Creusot-Loire 100-mm Compact DP

◆ **4 Baptiste de Andrade class** Bldr: Bazán, Spain

| | Laid down | L | In serv. |
|---|---|---|---|
| F 486 Baptiste de Andrade | 1972 | 3-73 | 19-11-74 |
| F 487 João Roby | 1972 | 3-6-73 | 18-3-75 |
| F 488 Afonso Cerqueira | 1973 | 6-10-73 | 26-6-75 |
| F 489 Oliveira E. Carmo | 1973 | 2-74 | 2-76 |

**Afonso Cerqueira (F 488)** L. & L. Van Ginderen, 2-87

**Afonso Cerqueira (F 488)** Portuguese Navy, 1987

**Oliveira E. Carmo (F 489)** P. Voss, 6-83

**D:** 1,252 tons (1,348 fl) **S:** 21 kts **Dim:** 84.59 (81.0 pp) × 10.3 × 3.3
**A:** 1/100-mm DP, French Model 1968—2/40-mm AA (I × 2)—6/324-mm Mk 32 ASW TT (III × 2)—1/d.c. rack
**Electron Equipt:** Radar: 1/Decca TM626, 1/Plessey AWS-2, 1/Thomson-CSF Pollux
Sonar: Diodon
**M:** 2 OEW-Pielstick 12PC2V400 diesels; 2 props; 10,560 hp
**Electric:** 1,110 kVA **Range:** 5,900/18 **Man:** 113 tot.

Remarks: Developed version of the *João Coutinho* class with more modern weapons and electronics. Helicopter platform. Vega GFCS with CSEE Panda optical backup director for 100-mm gun, 2 directors for 40-mm.

◆ **6 João Coutinho class** Bldrs: F 475 to F 477: Blohm + Voss, Germany; F 484 to F 471: Bazán, Spain

| | Laid down | L | In serv. |
|---|---|---|---|
| F 475 João Coutinho | 9-68 | 2-5-69 | 7-3-70 |
| F 476 Jacinto Candido | 4-68 | 16-6-69 | 10-6-70 |
| F 477 General Pereira D'eca | 10-68 | 26-7-69 | 10-10-70 |
| F 484 Augusto Castilho | 8-68 | 5-7-69 | 14-11-70 |
| F 485 Honorio Barreto | 7-68 | 11-4-70 | 15-4-71 |
| F 471 Antonio Enes | 4-68 | 1-8-69 | 18-6-71 |

FRIGATES *(continued)*

**João Coutinho (F 475)** Portuguese Navy

**João Coutinho (F 475)** L. & L. Van Ginderen, 5-87

**D:** 1,252 tons (1,401 fl) **S:** 24.4 kts **Dim:** 84.59 (81.0 pp) × 10.30 × 3.30
**A:** 2/76.2-mm Mk 33 DP (II × 1)—2/40-mm AA (II × 1)—Mk 10 Hedgehog—2/Mk 6 d.c. projectors—2/Mk 9 d.c. racks
**Electron Equipt:** Radar: 1/Decca TM 626, 1/MLA-1B, 1/SPG-34
Sonar: 1/QCU-2
**M:** 2 OEW-Pielstick 12PC2V280 diesels; 2 props; 10,560 hp
**Electric:** 900 kw **Range:** 5,900/8 **Man:** 9 officers, 84 men

Remarks: Can carry 34 Marines. Have Mk 63 Mod. 21 GFCS for the 76.2-mm mount, Mk 51 Mod. 2 GFCS for the 40-mm. Modernization planned. Carry 1,200 rounds 76.2-mm, 240 Hedgehog projectiles, and up to 84 d.c. Surpassed 22 kts on trials; F 475 made 25 kts. Modernization with SSM and short-range SAM planned.

◆ **4 French Commandant Rivière class** Bldr: A.C. de Bretagne, Nantes

| | Laid down | L | In serv. |
|---|---|---|---|
| F 480 Comandante João Belo | 6-9-65 | 22-3-66 | 1-7-67 |
| F 481 Comandante Hermegildo Capelo | 13-5-66 | 29-11-66 | 26-4-68 |
| F 482 Comandante Roberto Ivens | 13-12-66 | 11-8-67 | 23-11-68 |
| F 483 Comandante Sacadura Cabral | 18-8-67 | 15-3-68 | 25-11-69 |

**Comandante Hermegildo Capelo (F 481)** L. & L. Van Ginderen, 6-87

**Comandante João Belo (F 480)** Portuguese Navy, 1987

**Comandante João Belo (F 480)** P. Voss, 6-85

**D:** 1,760 tons (2,250 fl) **S:** 25 kts (26.6 max.)
**Dim:** 103.0 (98.0 pp) × 11.5 × 3.8
**A:** 3/100-mm DP, Model 1953 (I × 3)—2/40-mm AA (I × 2)—1/305-mm ASW mortar (IV × 1)—6/550-mm ASW TT (III × 2)
**Electron Equipt:** Radar: 1/Decca RM 316, 1/DRBV-22A, 1/DRBV-50, 1/DRBC-31D
Sonar: 1/DUBA-3, 1/SQS-17A—EW: ARBR-10
**M:** 4 SEMT-Pielstick diesels; 2 props; 16,000 hp **Electric:** 1,280 kw
**Range:** 2,300/25; 4,500/15 **Man:** 214 tot.

Remarks: See remarks on *Commandant Rivière* class in French section. Modernization deferred, but will receive new sonars and EW gear in near future. Two were to have had aft 100-mm mounts replaced by a helicopter deck and hangar; the other two by SSM.

◆ **3 U.S. Dealey class** Bldrs: F 472 and F 473: Est. Nav. Lisnave, Lisbon; F 474: Est. Nav. de Viana do Castelo

| | Laid down | L | In serv. |
|---|---|---|---|
| F 472 Almirante Pereira da Silva | 14-6-62 | 2-12-63 | 20-12-66 |
| F 473 Almirante Gago Coutinho | 2-12-63 | 13-8-65 | 29-11-67 |
| F 474 Almirante Magalhaes Correa | 30-8-63 | 26-4-65 | 4-11-68 |

**Almirante Magalhaes Correa (F 474)** G. Gyssels, 8-82

**Almirante Magalhaes Correa (F 474)** Portuguese Navy, 1987

**D:** 1,450 tons (1,950 fl) **S:** 26 kts **Dim:** 95.86 (93.88 wl) × 11.18 × 4.04 (hull)
**A:** 4/76.2-mm DP (II × 2)—2/375-mm Bofors ASW RL (IV × 2)—6/324-mm Mk 32 ASW TT (III × 2)
**Electron Equipt:** Radar: 1/Decca RM 316P, 1/978, 1/MLA-1B, 2/Mk 34
Sonar: SQS-30/31/32, DUBA-3A, 1/SQA-10 (VDS)
EW: WLR-1
**M:** 1 set GT; 1 prop; 20,000 hp **Electric:** 700 kw
**Boilers:** 2 Foster-Wheeler, 42 kg/cm$^2$, 510°C **Fuel:** 360 tons
**Range:** 1,600/25; 4,400/11 **Man:** 11 officers, 154 men

Remarks: Funded as U.S. DE 1039, DE 1042, and DE 1046, respectively. Two Mk 63 gunfire-control systems. Search sonars are SQS-30, SQS-31, and SQS-32, respectively, to avoid frequency interference. Two are to be converted to perform 200-n.m. economic zone patrol and search-and-rescue duties.

## PATROL BOATS

◆ **10 Cacine class** (Launch dates in parentheses)

| | | |
|---|---|---|
| P 1140 Cacine (1968) | P 1144 Quanza (30-5-69) | P 1160 Limpopo (9-4-73) |
| P 1141 Cunene (1968) | P 1145 Geba (21-5-69) | P 1161 Save (24-10-72) |
| P 1142 Mandovi (1968) | P 1146 Zaire (28-11-70) | |
| P 1143 Rovuma (1968) | P 1147 Zambeze (1971) | |

Bldrs: P 1140 to 1143: Arsenal do Alfeite; others: Est. Nav. do Mondego

**Cacine (P 1140)** Portuguese Navy, 1987

**D:** 292 tons (310 fl) **S:** 20 kts **Dim:** 44.0 × 7.67 × 2.2
**A:** 2/40-mm AA (I × 2)—1/20-mm AA—2/d.c. racks
**Electron Equipt:** Radar: 1/975 **M:** 2 Maybach 12V538 diesels; 2 props; 4,400 hp
**Range:** 4,400/12 **Man:** 3 officers, 30 men

◆ **4 São Roque-class former minesweepers** Bldr: Estaleiros Navais da C.U.F., Lisbon

| | In serv. | | In serv. |
|---|---|---|---|
| M 401 São Roque | 6-6-56 | M 403 Lagoa | 10-8-56 |
| M 402 Ribeira Grande | 8-2-57 | M 404 Rosario | 8-2-56 |

**São Roque (M 401)** L. & L. Van Ginderen, 1983

**D:** 394 tons (452 fl) **S:** 15 kts **Dim:** 46.33 (42.69 pp) × 8.75 × 2.5
**A:** 1/20-mm AA **M:** 2 Mirrlees JVSS-12 diesels; 2 props; 2,500 hp
**Fuel:** 45 tons **Range:** 2,300/13; 3,000/8 **Man:** 4 officers, 43 men

Remarks: All portable sweep gear off-loaded; now used as patrol vessels. Ordered early in 1954 and all launched in 1955. M 401 and M 403 built with U.S. "Offshore" funds as MSC 241 and MSC 242. Similar in appearance to the British "Ton" class. Wooden hulls, fin stabilizers. One 40-mm AA removed in 1972.

## PATROL CRAFT

◆ **4 glass-reinforced plastic hulled** Bldr: Cheverton, Cowes, U.K.

| | |
|---|---|
| UAM 612 Bonanca | UAM 605 Mareta |
| UAM 613 Mar Chao | UAM 602 Surriada |

**D:** 9 tons (fl) **S:** 20 kts **Dim:** 12.0 × 3.6 × 1.0
**A:** small arms **Electron Equipt:** Radar: 1/Decca 110
**M:** 2 Volvo Penta TAMD 66B outdrive diesels; 2 props; 426 hp
**Man:** 4 tot.

Remarks: First pair delivered 5-82, others in 7-82. Intended to patrol on the Tagus in the Lisbon area. Have service craft pendant numbers.

◆ **6 Albatroz class** Bldr: Arsenal do Alfeite (In serv. 1974–75)

| | | |
|---|---|---|
| P 1162 Albatroz | P 1164 Andorhina | P 1166 Condor |
| P 1163 Acor | P 1165 Aguia | P 1167 Cisne |

**D:** 45 tons (fl) **S:** 20 kts **Dim:** 23.6 (21.88 pp) × 5.25 × 1.6
**A:** 1/20-mm AA—2/12.7-mm mg (I × 2)
**Electron Equipt:** Radar: 1/Kelvin-Hughes 14/9
**M:** 2 Cummins diesels; 2 props; 1,100 hp **Range:** 450/18; 2,500/12
**Man:** 8 tot.

**Bonanca (UAM 612)** H. Ehlers, 11-86

**Condor (P 1166)** L. & L. Van Ginderen, 1981

◆ **1 Dom Aleixo class** Bldr: San Jacintho Aveiro (L: 12-67)

P 1148 Dom Aleixo

**Dom Aleixo (P 1148)**

**D:** 62.6 tons (67.7 fl) **S:** 16 tons **Dim:** 25.0 × 5.2 × 1.6
**A:** 1/20-mm **Electron Equipt:** Radar: Decca RM 316P
**M:** 2 Cummins diesels; 2 props; 1,600 hp **Man:** 2 officers, 8 men

Remarks: Sister *Dom Jeremias* (A 5202, ex-P 1149) is used as an inshore survey craft.

◆ **3 harbor patrol craft**

UAM 611 Bolina

**D:** . . . **S:** . . . **Dim:** 12.0 × 3.6 × 1.0
**M:** 2 Rolls-Royce Sabre 212 diesels; 2 props; 424 hp

UAM 608 Maresia

**D:** . . . **S:** . . . **Dim:** 12.0 × 2.7 × 1.8
**M:** 2 Rolls-Royce Sabre 212 diesels; 2 props; 424 hp

UAM 631 Levante

**D:** . . . **S:** . . . **Dim:** 12.0 × 3.8 × . . .
**M:** 2 Volvo Penta diesels; 2 props; 520 hp

◆ **1 river patrol craft**

P 360 Atria

Remarks: No data available. Operates on Rio Minho.

## AMPHIBIOUS WARFARE CRAFT

◆ **3 Bombarda-class landing craft** Bldr: Mondego SY

LDG 201 Bombarda (In serv. 1969) LDG 202 Alabarda (In serv. 1971)
LDG 203 Bacamarte (In serv. 12-85)

**AMPHIBIOUS WARFARE CRAFT** *(continued)*

**Bombarda (LDG 201)** 1983

**D:** 285 tons (635 fl) **S:** 11 kts **Dim:** 59.0 (52.88 pp) × 11.91 × 1.6
**M:** 2 MTU MD 225 diesels; 2 props; 1,000 hp **Range:** 1,800/8
**Man:** 2 officers, 18 men

◆ **6 LDM 400-class landing craft** (In serv. 1967)

| | | |
|---|---|---|
| LDM 406 | LDM 420 | LDM 422 |
| LDM 418 | LDM 421 | LDM 423 |

**LDM 421** H. Ehlers, 11-86

**D:** 56 tons (fl) **S:** 9 kts **Dim:** 17.0 × 5.0 × 1.2
**A:** 1/20-mm **M:** 2 Cummins diesels; 2 props; 450 hp

Remarks: Resemble British LCM(7) class. LDM 424 stricken 1982.

◆ **3 LDM 100-class landing craft** Bldr: Mondego SY (In serv. 1965)

LDM 119 LDM 120 LDM 121

**D:** 50 tons (fl) **S:** 9 kts **Dim:** 15.25 × 4.37 × 1.17
**M:** 2 G.M. 6-71 diesels; 2 props; 450 hp **Range:** 130/9

Remarks: U.S. LCM(6) class.

**HYDROGRAPHIC SHIPS**

◆ **1 (+1) Andromeda class** Bldr: Alfeite Navy Yard

| | Laid down | L | In serv. |
|---|---|---|---|
| A 5203 Andromeda | . . . | 12-12-85 | 1-7-87 |
| A 5205 Auriga | 6-84 | . . . | 1988 |

**Andromeda (A 5203)**—fitting out H. Ehlers, 12-86

**D:** . . . **S:** 12 kts **Dim:** 31.50 (28.00 pp) × 7.74 × 2.50
**A:** none **Electron Equipt:** Radar: 1/Racal-Decca RM 914C
**M:** 1 MTU 12V396 TC 82 diesel; 1 prop; 1,030 hp
**Electric:** 160 kw (1 × 100 diesel set, 1 × 60-kw shaft generator)
**Range:** 1,100/12 **Fuel:** 35.5 tons **Man:** 17 tot.

Remarks: Intended to replace the U.K. "Bay"-class survey ship *Alfonso de Albuquerque* (A 526), stricken 1983. Also used for oceanographic research.

◆ **1 ex-U.S. Kellar class** Bldr: Marietta SB Co., Pt. Pleasant, W. Va.

| | Laid down | L | In serv. |
|---|---|---|---|
| A 527 Almeida Carvalho (ex-*Kellar,* T-AGS 25) | 20-11-62 | 30-7-64 | 31-1-69 |

**Almeida Carvalho (A 527)** L. & L. Van Ginderen, 1983

**D:** 1,297 tons (fl) **S:** 13.5 kts **Dim:** 63.50 (58.00 pp) × 11.90 × 4.32
**Electron Equipt:** 1/RCA CRM-N2A-30, 1/Decca TM 829
**M:** 2 Caterpillar D-378 diesels, electric drive; 1 prop; 1,000 hp
**Fuel:** 211 tons **Man:** 5 officers, 25 men

Remarks: Transferred on loan 21-1-72. Similar to U.S. *Robert D. Conrad*-class T AGOR. Sister *S.P. Lee* is operated by the United States Geological Survey.

◆ **1 inshore survey craft** Bldr: San Jacintho Aveiro (L: 12-67)

A 5202 Dom Jeremias (ex-P 1149)

**Dom Jeremias (A 5202)** H. Ehlers, 12-86

Remarks: Data as for patrol craft sister *Dom Aleixo.* Retains the 20-mm AA gun.

◆ **2 Coral-class inshore survey/lighthouse tenders** Bldr: . . . (In serv. . . .)

UAM 801 Coral UAM 802 Hidra

**Coral (UAM 801)**—outboard *Hidra* (UAM 802) H. Ehlers, 11-86

**HYDROGRAPHIC SHIPS** *(continued)*

REMARKS: GRP construction. No data available

◆ **2 inshore survey/lighthouse tenders, former fishing boats**

UAM 803 ACTINIA    UAM 804 SICANDRA

Portuguese Navy inshore survey and lighthouse tenders, *Coral* (UAM 801), *Hidra* (UAM 802), *Actinia* (UAM 803), and *Sicandra* (UAM 804). The latter pair are dissimilar, wooden-hulled former fishing boats. Pendant numbers are in yardcraft series    H. Ehlers, 11-86

**AUXILIARY SHIPS**

◆ **1 logistic support ship**    Bldr: Howaldtswerke, Kiel (In serv. 1962)

A 5208 SÃO MIGUEL (ex-*Cabo Verde*, ex-*Sirefjell*)

**São Miguel (A 5208)**    H. Ehlers, 2-87

**D:** 7,510 tons (fl) **S:** 14.5 kts **Dim:** 108.80 (97.90 pp) × 15.59 × 7.54
**A:** none **Electron Equipt:** Radar: 1/Kelvin Hughes KH1600, 1/Kelvin Hughes 18/12
**M:** 1 M.A.N. K62 60/105C, 6-cyl. diesel; 1 prop; 4,050 hp
**Electric:** 492 kw **Fuel:** 267 tons **Man:** 5 officers, 25 men

REMARKS: 2,690 grt/3,875 dwt. Cargo ship purchased 8-10-85 for Azores service. Blue hull, white upperworks. Three holds with after hold refrigerated. One 25-ton, six 5-ton, and six 3-ton derricks. A helicopter platform may be added later.

◆ **1 replenishment oiler**    Bldr: Est. Nav. de Viana do Castelo

| | L | In serv. |
|---|---|---|
| A 5206 SÃO GABRIEL | 1961 | 3-63 |

**São Gabriel (A 5206)**    H. Ehlers, 2-87

**D:** 9,000 tons (14,200 fl) **S:** 17 kts **Dim:** 146.0 (138.0 pp) × 18.22 × 8.0
**Electron Equipt:** Radar: 1/Decca RM 1226C, 1/Decca RMS 1230C, 1/SPS-6C
**M:** 1 set Pamtreda GT; 1 prop; 9,500 hp **Boilers:** 2
**Range:** 6,000/15 **Man:** 9 officers, 93 men

REMARKS: 9,854 grt/9,000 dwt. Two liquid- and one solid-store replenishment stations per side. Helicopter platform aft. Former oiler *Sam Bras* is now an accommodations hulk.

◆ **1 lighthouse tender and tug**

| | Laid down | L | In serv. |
|---|---|---|---|
| A 54 SCHULTZ XAVIER | 2-70 | 1972 | 14-7-72 |

**Schultz Xavier (A 54)**    J.-C. Bellonne, 1973

**D:** 900 tons **S:** 14 kts **Dim:** 56.1 × 10.0 × 3.8
**M:** 2 diesels; 1 prop; 2,400 hp **Range:** 3,000/12.5
**Man:** 4 officers, 50 men

◆ **1 sail-training ship**    Bldr. Blohm + Voss, Hamburg

| | L | In serv. |
|---|---|---|
| A 520 SAGRES II (ex-*Guanabara*, ex-*Albert Leo Schlageter*) | 30-10-37 | 1-2-38 |

**Sagres II (A 520)**    G. Gyssels, 7-85

**D:** 1,725 tons (1,784 fl) **S:** 10.5 kts (18 sail)
**Dim:** 90.0 (75.90 hull, 70.4 pp) × 11.9 × 5.2
**M:** 2 M.A.N. diesels; 1 prop; 750 hp
**Range:** 5,450/7.5 (power) **Man:** 10 officers, 143 men

REMARKS: Acquired by U.S. Navy as reparations, 1945; sold to Brazil in 1948 and to Portugal in 1972, commissioning on 2-2-72. Sail area: 2,355 m$^2$. Sisters are U.S. Coast Guard *Eagle* and Soviet *Tovarisch*.

◆ **1 sail-training sloop** (In serv. . . .)

A 5201 VEGA (ex-*Arreda*)

**D:** 60 tons **S:** . . . **Dim:** 19.8 × 4.3 × 2.5

◆ **1 sail-training yacht** (In serv. . . .)

A 5204 POLAR (ex-*Anne Linde*)

**D:** 70 tons **S:** . . . **Dim:** 22.9 × 4.9 × 2.5

REMARKS: Acquired in trade for large sail-training ship *Sagres* I, now a museum ship at Hamburg.

PORTUGAL *(continued)*

## SERVICE CRAFT

◆ **1 U.S. 174-foot-class yard oiler** Bldr: Brunswick Marine, Georgia

| | Laid down | L | In serv. |
|---|---|---|---|
| UAM 303 OEIRAS (ex-BC-3, ex-YO 194) | 14-5-45 | 25-8-45 | 30-1-46 |

**Oeiras (UAM 303)**—in light condition (old number) L. & L. Van Ginderen, 1983

**D:** 440 tons light (1,390 fl) **S:** 11 kts **Dim:** 53.04 × 9.75 × 3.96
**M:** 1 G.M. diesel; 1 prop; 800 hp **Electric:** 120 kw
**Fuel:** 25 tons **Man:** 23 tot.

REMARKS: Transferred in 4-62. Cargo: 924 tons.

◆ **2 small yard oilers**

UAM 301 ODELEITE UAM 302 ODIVELAS

REMARKS: Cargo: 674 tons; no other data available.

◆ **1 river navigational buoy tender** Bldr: San Jacintho Aveiro

UAM 675 GUIA (In serv. . . .)

**Guia (UAM 675)** H. Ehlers, 8-86

**D:** 70 tons **S:** 8.5 kts **Dim:** 22.0 × 7.9 × 2.2
**M:** 1 Deutz SBA 6M 816U diesel; 1 Schottel prop; 350 hp—1 Harbor Master 50 F76 maneuvering unit (3.5 kts)

REMARKS: Catamaran hull.

◆ **1 ex-U.S. Army harbor tug**

UAM 614 NISA (ex-RB 2, ex-ST 1996)

REMARKS: Transferred 2-3-62 from U.S. Navy, Sister RB 1 stricken 1984.

◆ **1 yacht/tender** Bldr: Halmatic, U.K. (In serv. 10-84)

UAM 901 ALVA

**D:** 6.5 tons (fl) **S:** 20 kts **Dim:** 10.62 (9.37 wl) × 3.50 × 0.84
**M:** 2 Volvo TAMD 60C diesels; 2 props; 420 hp

REMARKS: Glass-reinforced plastic construction. Used as C-in-C's yacht. Carries 12 passengers.

◆ **10 miscellaneous harbor launches**

| | | |
|---|---|---|
| UAM 854 BARROCAS | UAM 907 COURA | UAM 910 TAMEGA |
| UAM 905 CAIA | UAM 908 PAIVA | UAM 911 TUA |
| UAM 906 CORGO | UAM 909 SORRAIA | UAM 912 VASCÃO |
| | | UAM 913 ZEZERE |

**Zezere (UAM 913)**—ferry H. Ehlers, 2-87

**Vascão (UAM 912)**—ferry H. Ehlers, 2-87

REMARKS: Majority intended to ferry personnel in Lisbon area. UAM 854 is a berthing boat; UAM 905 and 906 are admirals' barges.

# QATAR

**State of Qatar**

PERSONNEL (1987): 700 total

MERCHANT MARINE (1986): 55 ships—306,673 grt
(tankers: 5 ships—112,197 grt)

AVIATION: Six Agusta-built SH-3D Sea King helicopters are in service for search-and-rescue duties

## GUIDED-MISSILE PATROL BOATS

◆ **3 French Combattante-III class** Bldr: CMN, Cherbourg

| | Laid down | L | In serv. |
|---|---|---|---|
| Q 01 DAMSAH | 6-5-81 | 17-6-82 | 10-11-82 |
| Q 02 AL GHARIYAH | 26-8-81 | 23-9-82 | 10-2-83 |
| Q 03 RBIGAH | 27-10-81 | 22-12-82 | 11-5-83 |

**Rbigah (Q 03)** G. Gyssels, 6-83

GUIDED-MISSILE PATROL BOATS *(continued)*

**Damsah (Q 01)** CMN, 1982

**D:** 395 tons (430 fl) **S:** 38.5 kts
**Dim:** 56.0 (53.0 pp) × 8.16 × 2.15 hull (2.5 max.)
**A:** 8/MM 40 Exocet SSM—1/76-mm OTO Melara DP—2/40-mm Breda AA (II × 1)—4/30-mm Emerlec AA (II × 2)
**Electron Equipt:** Radar: 1/Decca 1226, 1/Thomson-CSF Pollux, 1/Thomson-CSF Castor,
EW: . . . passive, Dagaie chaff RL
**M:** 4 MTU 20V538 TB93 diesels; 4 props; 19,300 hp **Range:** 2,000/15

Remarks: Ordered 10-80. Very similar in appearance and equipment to the three Nigerian units of the class. Two CSEE Panda optical gun directors, with Vega weapons-control system.

## PATROL BOATS AND CRAFT

◆ **6 103-foot boats** Bldr: Vosper Thornycroft, Portchester

| | In serv. | | In serv. |
|---|---|---|---|
| Q 11 Barzan | 13-1-75 | Q 14 Al Wussail | 28-10-75 |
| Q 12 Hwar | 30-4-75 | Q 15 Fateh Al Khatab | 22-1-76 |
| Q 13 That Assuari | 3-10-75 | Q 16 Tariq | 1-3-76 |

**Fateh Al Khatab (Q 15)** L. & L. Van Ginderen, 1976

**D:** 120 tons **S:** 27 kts **Dim:** 32.4 (31.1 pp) × 6.3 × 1.6
**A:** 2/20-mm AA (I × 2)
**M:** 2 Paxman Valenta 16RP200 diesels; 2 props; 6,250 hp **Man:** 25 tot.

Remarks: Originally had a twin 30-mm AA forward, replaced by single 20-mm AA.

◆ **6 Polycat 1450 class** Bldr: Damen, Gorinchem, Netherlands (In serv. 1984)

Q 31 Q 32 Q 33 Q 34 Q 35 Q 36

**Q 32 and a sister** L. & L. Van Ginderen, 1984

**D:** 18 tons (fl) **S:** 26 kts **Dim:** 14.5 × 4.7 × 1.5
**A:** 1/20-mm AA **Electron Equipt:** Radar: 1/Decca . . . nav.
**M:** 2 G.M. 12V71 TI diesels; 2 props; 1,300 hp **Range:** 650/20 **Man:** 11 tot.

Remarks: Ordered 2-83. Glass-reinforced plastic construction.

◆ **7 P 1200 class** Bldr: Watercraft, Shoreham, U.K. (In serv. 1980)

**D:** 12.7 tons (fl) **S:** 29 kts **Dim:** 11.9 × 4.1 × 1.1 **A:** 2/7.62-mm mg (I × 2)
**M:** 2 Wizeman-Mercedes WM400 diesels; 2 props; 660 hp **Man:** 4 tot.

◆ **2 45-foot craft** Bldr: Vosper/Keith Nelson

**D:** 13 tons **S:** 26 kts **Dim:** 13.5 × 3.8 × 1.1
**A:** 1/12.7-mm mg—2/7.62-mm mg (I × 2)
**M:** 2 Caterpillar diesels; 2 props; 800 hp **Man:** 6 tot.

Remarks: Third unit purchased converted to a pilot boat.

◆ **25 Spear-class craft Mk I and Mk II** Bldr: Fairey Marine, Hamble, U.K. (In serv. 1974–77)

Q 71–Q 95

QATAR *(continued)*
PATROL BOATS AND CRAFT *(continued)*

**D:** 4.3 tons **S:** 26 kts **Dim:** 9.1 × 2.8 × 0.8
**A:** 3/7.62-mm mg (I × 3) **M:** 2 diesels; 2 props; 290 hp **Man:** 4 tot.

REMARKS: First seven delivered 19-6-74 to 2-75; five more ordered 12-75; three more delivered 30-6-75 to 14-7-75. Ten more delivered 4-77.

◆ **2 Interceptor class** Bldr: Fairey Marine, Hamble, U.K. (In serv. 28-11-75)

**D:** 1.25 tons **S:** 35 kts **Dim:** 7.9 × 2.4 × 0.9
**M:** 2 Johnson outboards; 270 hp **Range:** 150/30 **Man:** 3 crew + 10 troops

◆ **1 Bulldog-class workboat** Bldr: Fairey Allday Marine (In serv. 1979)

# ROMANIA

**Socialist Republic of Romania**

PERSONNEL (1984): 7,700 men, 600 of whom are in the Border Guard and 100 in aviation

MERCHANT MARINE (1986): 426 ships—3,233,906 grt
(tankers: 12 ships—383,720 grt)

NAVAL AVIATION: Six Soviet Mi-14 Haze A land-based ASW helicopters and several Alouette-III helicopters are in service.

## SUBMARINES

◆ **1 (+ . . .) Soviet Kilo class** Bldr: Admiralty-Sudomekh SY, Leningrad

**D:** 2,300 tons surf./2,900 sub. **S:** 16 kts surf./20 kts sub.
**Dim:** 73.0 × 9.9 × 6.5 **A:** 6/533-mm TT (fwd., 12 tot. torpedoes or 24 mines)
**Electron Equipt:** Radar: 1/Snoop Tray
Sonar: passive array, LF active
**M:** diesel-electric: 2 diesel generator sets; 1/6-bladed prop; . . . hp
**Range:** . . . **Man:** 60 tot.

REMARKS: Transferred 12-86, possibly from Gorkiy SY construction, rather than Admiralty-Sudomekh. Additional units likely to be transferred.

## DESTROYERS

◆ **1 Muntenia class** Bldr: Mangalia SY No. 2

MUNTENIA (In serv. 8-85)

**Muntenia**—fitting out Agerpress, 1985

**D:** approx. 6,000 tons (fl) **S:** 28 kts **Dim:** 145.0 × 16.0 × . . .
**A:** 8/SS-N-2C SSM (II × 4)—1/SA-N-4 SAM system (II × 1, 20 Gecko missiles)—4/76.2-mm DP (II × 2)—8/30-mm AA (II × 4)—. . ./533-mm ASW TT—2/Alouette-III helicopters
**Electron Equipt:** Radar: 1/. . . nav., 1/Strut Curve, 1/Pop Group, 1/Owl Screech, 1/Muff Cob
Sonar: . . .—EW: . . .
**M:** 4 gas turbines; 2 props; 96,000 hp **Range:** . . . **Man:** . . .

REMARKS: Reportedly laid down in 1981 and launched by 1983. Also serves as naval cadet training ship. May have only one twin 76.2-mm DP, and presence of SA-N-4 SAM system is uncertain.

## FRIGATES

◆ **4 Tetal class** Bldr: Mangalia SY No. 2

260 N . . . . . . . (In serv. 1983)
261 N . . . . . . . (In serv. 1983)
262 N . . . . . . . (In serv. 1985)
263 N . . . . . . . (In serv. . . .)

**Tetal 261**—with a second unit at left 1986

**D:** 1,800 tons (fl) **S:** . . . **Dim:** 93.0 × 11.5 × 3.0
**A:** 4/76.2-mm DP (II × 2)—4/30-mm AA (II × 2)—4/14.5-mm mg (II × 2)—2/RBU-2500 ASW RL (XVI × 2)—4/533-mm ASW TT (II × 2)—1/helicopter (platform only)
**Electron Equipt:** Radar: 1/. . . nav., 1/Strut Curve, 1/Drum Tilt
Sonar: . . .
EW: 2 Watch Dog intercept
**M:** diesels; 2 props; . . . hp **Range:** . . . **Man:** . . .

REMARKS: "Tetal" is the NATO code name for this class. There is a helicopter platform. First unit laid down 1980. Program slowed by economic problems.

## CORVETTES

◆ **3 ex-Soviet Poti class**

V 31 V 32 V 33

**V 32 and V 33**—alongside Cosar-class minelayer 274 1982

**D:** 400 tons (fl) **S:** 38 kts **Dim:** 59.4 × 7.9 × 2.0 (mean)
**A:** 2/57-mm AA (II × 1)—2/RBU-2500 ASW RL—2/533-mm ASW TT (I × 2)
**Electron Equipt:** Radar: 1/Don 2, 1/Strut Curve, 1/Muff Cob
IFF: 1/High Pole B—EW: 2/Watch Dog
Sonar: med.-frequency hull-mounted
**M:** CODAG: 2 M503A diesels (4,000 hp each); 2 GT (20,000 hp each); 2 props
**Range:** 500/37; 4,500/10 **Man:** 50 tot.

REMARKS: Transferred 1970. Have simpler systems than the Soviet units: 533-mm vice 400-mm torpedo tubes. RBU-2500 vice RBU-6000 rocket launchers, etc. Gas turbines force air into tubes abaft the propellers, in a kind of "waterjet" system. The "V" in the pendant number stands for *Vanatore* (chaser).

◆ **4 Democratia-class ex-minesweepers (German M-40 class)**
Bldr: Galati SY (In serv. 1951)

DB 13 DEMOCRATIA DB 15 DESROBIREA
DB 14 DESCATUSARIA DB 16 DREPTATEA

CORVETTES *(continued)*

**Dreptatea (DB 16) and Desrobirea (DB 15)**—with Cosar-class minelayer 271 1982

**D:** 643 tons (775 fl) **S:** 17 kts **Dim:** 62.3 × 8.5 × 2.6
**A:** 5/37-mm AA (II × 2, I × 1)—4/14.5-mm mg (II × 2)—2/RBU-1200 ASW RL (V × 2)—mines
**Electron Equipt:** Radar: 1/Don-2—Sonar: . . .—IFF: High Pole A
**M:** 2 diesels; 2 props; 12,400 hp
**Fuel:** 152 tons **Range:** 4,000/10 **Man:** 80 tot.

REMARKS: Begun for German Navy as coal burners, launched postwar. Converted to burn fuel oil on completion. Recently modernized with new superstructures, diesel engines in place of the original reciprocating steam plant; minesweeping gear deleted, ASW ordnance updated.

## GUIDED-MISSILE PATROL BOATS

◆ **6 ex-Soviet Osa-I class**

194 195 196 197 198 199

**Romanian Osa-I 196** 1974

**D:** 175 tons (209 fl) **S:** 36 kts **Dim:** 38.6 × 7.6 × 1.8
**A:** 4/SS-N-2-missile launchers—4/30-mm AA (II × 2)
**Electron Equipt:** Radar: 1/Square Tie, 1/Drum Tilt
IFF: 2/Square Head, 1/High Pole B
**M:** 3 M503A diesels; 3 props; 12,000 hp **Range:** 500/34; 750/25 **Man:** 30 tot.

REMARKS: Transferred after 1960.

## PATROL BOATS

◆ **21 Shanghai-II class** Bldr: Mangalia SY, Romania (In serv. 1973–. . .)

VS 41 to VS 44 VP 20 to VP 35, VP 38

**Shanghai-IIs VP 27, 28, 31, and 30 with a service craft** 1982

**D:** 123 tons (135 fl) **S:** 28.5 kts **Dim:** 38.78 × 5.41 × 1.55
**A:** VS 41 series: 1/37-mm AA—2/14.5-mm mg (II × 1)—2/RBU-1200 ASW RL (V × 2)—VP 20 series: 4/14.5-mm mg (II × 2)
**Electron Equipt:** Radar: 1/Pot Head
**M:** 2 M50F-4, 4,200-hp diesels, 2 12D6, 910-hp diesels; 4 props; 4,220 hp
**Range:** 750/16.5 **Electric:** 39 kw **Endurance:** 7 days **Man:** 36 tot.

REMARKS: Units with VP pendants serve the Border Guard; two with only two 14.5-mm machine guns and a large deckhouse aft, serve as search-and-rescue boats. VS = *Vanatore de Submarin* (submarine chaser); VP = *Vedette Patrolare* (patrol boat).

◆ **3 ex-Soviet Kronshtadt class** Bldr: U.S.S.R. (In serv. early 1950s)

V 1 V 2 V 3

**D:** 300 tons (330 fl) **S:** 18 kts **Dim:** 52.1 × 6.5 × 2.2
**A:** 1/85-mm DP—2/37-mm AA **M:** 3 Type 9D diesels; 3 props; 3,330 hp
**Fuel:** 20 tons **Range:** 3,500/14 **Man:** 40 tot.

## TORPEDO BOATS

◆ **12 (+. . .) Epitrop class** Bldr: Romania (In serv. 1979–. . .)

201–212

**Epitrop class** 1982

**D:** 215 tons (fl) **S:** 36 kts **Dim:** 38.6 × 7.6 × 1.8
**A:** 4/30-mm AA (II × 2)—4/533-mm TT (I × 4)
**Electron Equipt:** Radar: 1/Pot Drum, 1/Drum Tilt—IFF: 1/High Pole A
**M:** 3 M503A diesels; 3 props; 12,000 hp
**Range:** 500/35; 750/20 **Man:** 28 tot.

REMARKS: Design based on Osa class; "Epitrop" is the NATO nickname for the class.

◆ **23 Huchwan-class hydrofoils** Bldr: Dobreta SY, Turnu (1973–. . .)

VT 51 to VT 73

**Romanian Huchwan VT 53** 1974

**D:** 39 tons (45 fl) **S:** 50 kts **Dim:** 22.50 × 6.26 (3.80 deck) × 1.15 (1.11 foiling)
**A:** 4/14.5-mm AA (II × 2)—2/533-mm TT **Man:** 11 tot.
**Electron Equipt:** 1/Type 756—IFF: 1/High Pole B
**M:** 3 M50 diesels; 3 props; 3,600 hp **Range:** 500/30 **Electric:** 5.6 kw

REMARKS: Three built in China, remainder in Romania. Two, named *Jupiter* and *Marte,* have had the torpedo tubes and hydrofoils removed and are used as search-and-rescue craft. VT = *Vedette Torpedinare* (torpedo boat).

## MINE WARFARE SHIPS

◆ **2 Cosar-class minelayers** Bldr: Romania (In serv. 1980–82)

271 N. . . . . . . 274 N. . . . . . .

MINE WARFARE SHIPS *(continued)*

**Cosar 274** 1986

**D:** 1,500 tons (fl) **S:** . . . **Dim:** 79.0 × 10.6 × . . .
**A:** 1/57-mm AA—4/30-mm AA (II × 2)—4/14.5-mm mg (II × 2)—2/RBU-1200 ASW RL (V × 2)—mines
**Electron Equipt:** Radar: 1/navigational, 1 Strut Curve, 1/Muff Cob, 1/Drum Tilt
Sonar: . . .
**M:** diesels; 2 props; . . . hp

REMARKS: "Cosar" is the NATO nickname. Shares the same hull as the oceanographic research ship *Grigore Antipa* and the rescue tug *Emil Racovita.*

◆ **12 ex-Soviet T-301-class minesweepers**

DR 6–9, DR 17–20, DR 26–29

**D:** 145.8 tons (160 fl) **S:** 12.5 kts **Dim:** 38.0 × 5.1 × 1.6
**A:** 1/45-mm AA—4/12.7-mm mg (II × 2)—mines
**M:** 3 6-cyl. diesels; 3 props; 1,440 hp
**Fuel:** 20 tons **Range:** 2,500/8 **Man:** 32 tot.

REMARKS: Transferred 1956–60. Gradually being disposed of; most probably in reserve or inoperable.

AUXILIARY SHIPS

◆ **1 oceanographic research ship** Bldr: Romania

GRIGORE ANTIPA (In serv. 1980)

**D:** 1,500 tons (fl) **S:** . . . **Dim:** 79.0 × 10.6 × . . .
**M:** diesels; 2 props; . . . hp

REMARKS: Same hull and propulsion system as Cosar-class minelayers above. Carries a small research submersible.

◆ **2 Croitor-class small combatant tenders** Bldr: Romania (In serv. 1980)

281 N . . . . . . . 283 N . . . . . . .

**D:** 3,500 tons (fl) **S:** . . . kts **Dim:** 110.0 × . . . × . . .
**A:** 2/57-mm AA (II × 1—2/SA-N-5 SAM syst (IV × 2)—4/30-mm AK-230 AA (II × 2)—4/14.5-mm mg (II × 2)—2/RBU-1200 ASW RL (V × 2)
**Electron Equipt:** Radar: 1/. . . nav., 1/Strut Curve, 1/Muff Cob, 1/Drum Tilt
Sonar: . . .—IFF: 1 High Pole A
**M:** diesels; 2 props; . . . hp

**Croitor-class No. 281** 1982

**Croitor 283**—composite photo 1982

REMARKS: "Croitor" is the NATO nickname. Resembles a smaller edition of the Soviet "Don" class. Helicopter hangar and flight deck aft. Crane forward of bridge tends magazine for torpedoes and missiles. SA-N-5 rack-launchers mounted atop hangar, with ready-service lockers for 8 missiles.

◆ **3 coastal tankers** (In serv. 1971–73)

TM 530 TM . . . TM . . .

**D:** 1,300 tons (fl) **S:** 10 kts **Dim:** 60.0 × 9.2 × 4.1
**A:** 1/37-mm AA—2/12.7-mm mg (I × 2) **M:** 1 diesel; 1 prop; 600 hp

◆ **1 seagoing rescue tug** Bldr: Romania (In serv. 1984)

EMIL RACOVITA

REMARKS: Same hull and propulsion as the Cosar-class minelayers and the oceanographic research ship *Grigore Antipa.*

◆ **2 Soviet Roslavl-class ocean tugs** Bldr: Galati SY (In serv. 1953–54)

RM 101 VITEAZUL RM . . . VOINICUL

**D:** 750 tons (fl) **S:** 11 kts **Dim:** 44.5 × 9.5 × 3.5
**M:** diesel-electric; 2 props; 1,200 hp **Man:** 28 tot.

REMARKS: RM = *Remorcher de Mare* (seagoing tug).

◆ **1 sail-training ship** Bldr: Blohm + Voss, Hamburg

| | Laid down | L | In serv. |
|---|---|---|---|
| MIRCEA | 30-4-38 | 22-9-38 | 29-3-39 |

**Mircea** French Navy, 1980

**D:** 1,630 tons (fl) **S:** 6 kts (10 sail) **Dim:** 81.78 (73.5 hull) × 12.5 × 5.2
**M:** 1 M.A.N. diesel; 500 hp **Sail area:** 1,750 $m^2$
**Man:** 20 men + 120 cadets

REMARKS: Refitted in Germany, 1966–67.

NOTE: The training ship *Neptun* serves the Merchant Marine, not the Navy.

**ROMANIA** *(continued)*
**AUXILIARY SHIPS** *(continued)*

◆ **2 ex-French Friponne-class former minesweepers** Bldrs: Lorient and Brest Dockyards (In serv. 1916–17)

ND 112 CONSTANTA (ex-*Ghiculescu, ex-Impatiente*)
ND 113 STIHI (ex-*Mignonne*)

**Constanta (ND 112)**—white-painted, behind yard oiler 131 1982

**D:** 330 tons (443 fl) **S:** 12 kts **Dim:** 60.9 × 7.0 × 2.5
**S:** 1/37-mm AA—4/14.5-mm AA (II × 2)—2/RBU-1200 ASW RL (V × 2)
**Electron Equipt:** Radar: 2/. . . nav.—Sonar: HF, hull-mounted
IFF: 1/High Pole A
**M:** 2 Sulzer diesels; 2 props; 900 hp
**Fuel:** 30 tons **Range:** 3,000/10 **Man:** 50 tot.

REMARKS: ND 113 used as a headquarters ship, ND 112 as survey ship. Recently modernized with streamlined superstructures, new armament, etc. Sister *Dumitrescu* (ND 111, ex-*Friponne*) has been stricken.

**YARDCRAFT**

◆ **10 miscellaneous service boats**

| | | | | |
|---|---|---|---|---|
| SRS 571 | SRS 572 | SRS 573 | SRS 577 | SRS 675: harbor tugs |
| MM 131 | MM 132 | MM 133 | MM 136 | MM 137: fuel lighters |

◆ **4 diving tenders**

◆ **3 accommodations barges**

OLTUL IALOMITA SIRETUL

◆ **6 small floating workshops**

◆ **3 fireboats**

AUTOMATICE ELECTRONICA ENERGERICA

**D:** 160 tons (fl) **S:** 12 kts **Dim:** 38.0 × 5.5 × 1.4
**M:** 2 diesels; 2 props; . . . hp

DANUBE FLOTILLA

◆ **1 (+. . .) Brutar-class monitor** Bldr: . . . (In serv. 1982)

**D:** 350–400 tons (fl) **S:** . . . **Dim:** 43.0 × 8.0 × 1.5
**A:** 1/100-mm tank gun—4/14.5-mm mg (II × 2)—1/22-mm BM-21 RL (XVIII × 1)—mines
**M:** diesels; . . . props; . . . hp

REMARKS: "Brutar" is the NATO nickname. Very low-lying craft, armored tank turret and machine-gun turrets.

◆ **18 monitors** Bldr: Dulcea SY (In serv. 1973–76)

VB 76 to VB 93

**D:** 85 tons **S:** 17 kts **Dim:** 32.0 × 4.8 × 0.9
**A:** 1/85-mm—4/14.5-mm AA (II × 2)—2/81-mm mortars (I × 2)
**M:** 2 diesels; 2 props; 1,200 hp **Man:** 25 tot.

REMARKS: VB = *Vedeta Blindata* (Armored Boat)

◆ **8 VG-class patrol craft** Bldr: Galati (In serv. 1954)

VG 10–VG 17

**VG class, VG 11** 1971

**D:** 40 tons (fl) **S:** 18 kts **Dim:** 16.0 × 4.4 × 1.2
**A:** 1/20-mm AA—1/7.9-mm mg
**M:** 2 3D12 diesels; 2 props; 600 hp **Man:** 10 men

◆ **20 river minesweepers** Bldr: Turnu-Severin SY (In serv. 1975–. . .)

VD 141–VD 160

**D:** 65 tons (fl) **S:** 18 kts **Dim:** 26.0 × 4.0 × 0.8
**A:** 4/14.5-mm mg (II × 2)—mines **M:** 2 M50 diesels; 2 props; 1,200 hp

REMARKS: Replaced the now-discarded Polish TR-40 class.

◆ **9 SM 165-class patrol/utility craft**

SM 161–SM 169

**D:** 22 tons **S:** 12 kts **Dim:** 12.2 × 3.0 × 0.9

◆ **5 SD 200-class patrol/utility boats**

SD 270 SD 274 SD 275 SD 277 SD 278

◆ **1 headquarters ship**

REPUBLICA

REMARKS: A very old side-wheel paddle boat of about 300 tons (fl).

# SABAH

**State of Sabah** (semi-autonomous Malaysian state)

**PATROL BOATS**

◆ **2 55-foot boats** Bldr: Cheverton, Isle of Wight, U.K. (In serv. 2-75)

SRI SEMPORNA SRI BANGJI

**D:** 50 tons (fl) **S:** 20 kts **Dim:** 16.8 × 4.6 × 0.9 **A:** 1/12.7-mm mg
**M:** 2 diesels; 2 props; 1,200 hp **Range:** 300/15 **Man:** 11 tot.

◆ **2 91-foot boats** Bldr: Vosper Thornycroft, Singapore

PX 17 SRI GUMANGTONG (In serv. 8-4-70) PX 18 SRI LABUAN (In serv. 6-4-70)

**D:** 85 tons (fl) **S:** 29 kts **Dim:** 26.29 × 5.7 × 1.45
**A:** 2/20-mm AA **M:** 2 Mercedes-Benz MB820Db diesels; 2 props; 2,790 hp
**Range:** 700/15 **Man:** 15 tot.

REMARKS: On detachment from the Royal Malaysian Marine Police.

◆ **1 patrol boat** Bldr: Mengsina Ltd., Singapore (In serv. 3-12-76)

KUALA BENGKOKA

**D:** . . . **S:** . . . **Dim:** 18.3 × . . . × . . . **A:** . . . **M:** diesels

◆ **1 103-foot class** Bldr: Vosper Ltd., Portsmouth, U.K.

P 3147 SRI MELAKA (L: 25-2-64)

**D:** 96 tons (109 fl) **S:** 23 kts **Dim:** 31.39 (28.95 pp) × 5.95 × 1.65
**A:** 2/40-mm AA (I × 2)—2/7.62-mm mg (I × 2)
**Electron Equipt:** Radar: 1/Decca 1226
**M:** 2 Mayback MD 655/18 diesels; 2 props; 3,550 hp
**Range:** 1,660/14 **Man:** 3 officers, 19 men

REMARKS: On detachment from Royal Malaysian Navy. Has fin stabilizers.

**MISCELLANEOUS UNITS**

◆ **1 yacht** Bldr: Vosper Thornycroft, Singapore (In serv. 11-7-71)

PUTRI SABAH

**D:** 117 tons **S:** 22 kts **Dim:** 27.3 × 9.5 × 1.65
**M:** 1 diesel; 1 prop; . . . hp **Man:** 22 tot.

◆ **1 utility landing craft** Bldr: Chung Wah SY, Hong Kong (In serv. 28-1-78)

GAYA II

**D:** 220 grt **S:** 8 kts **Dim:** . . . × . . . × . . .
**M:** 2 Caterpillar D3406TA diesels; 2 props; 275 hp

# ST. KITTS

**State of Saint Christopher-Nevis**

NOTE: Achieved full independence 8-83; the formerly associated island of Anguilla remains a British dependent.

MERCHANT MARINE (1986): 1 ship—256 grt

ST. KITTS *(continued)*

POLICE FORCE

### PATROL BOAT

◆ **1 U.S. 110-ft. Commercial Cruiser design** Bldr: Swiftships Inc., Morgan City, Louisiana

C-253 STALWART (In serv. 7-85)

**Stalwart (C-253)** Swiftships, 7-85

**D:** 99.8 tons (fl) **S:** 24 kts (22 cruise) **Dim:** 33.53 × 7.62 × 2.13
**A:** 2/12.7-mm mg (I × 2)—2/7.62-mm mg (I × 2)
**Electron Equipt:** Radar: 1/. . . nav.
**M:** 4 G.M. 12V71 TI diesels; 4 props; 2,400 hp
**Range:** 1,800/15 **Fuel:** 31,608 liters **Man:** . . .

REMARKS: Aluminum construction. Acquired with U.S. financial assistance.

### PATROL CRAFT

◆ **1 Spear-class patrol craft** Bldr: Fairey Marine, U.K. (In serv. 10-9-74)

RANGER I

**D:** 4.3 tons (fl) **S:** 30 kts **Dim:** 9.1 × 2.8 × 0.8 **A:** 2/7.62-mm mg (I × 2)
**M:** 2 Ford Mermaid diesels; 2 props; 360 hp **Man:** 2 tot.

◆ **1 8.2-m patrol craft** Bldr: Buhlers Yachts, Ltd.

RANGER II

**D:** 6 tons (fl) **S:** 19 kts **Dim:** 8.20 × 2.95 × 0.90
**M:** 1 Perkins T6.3544 diesel; 1 prop; 200 hp **Man:** 2 tot. **Range:** 105/19

REMARKS: Sister to craft in St. Lucia and St. Vincent service.

# ST. LUCIA

**State of Saint Lucia**

MERCHANT MARINE (1986): 8 ships—2,766 grt

COAST GUARD

### PATROL CRAFT

◆ **1 U.S. 65-ft. Commercial Cruiser design** Bldr: Swiftships, Inc., Morgan City, Louisiana

P-02 DEFENDER (In serv. 3-5-84)

**Defender (P-02)** Swiftships, 5-84

**D:** 35 tons (fl) **S:** 23 kts **Dim:** 19.96 × 5.59 × 1.52
**A:** small arms **Electron Equipt:** Radar: 1/Raytheon 1210
**M:** 2 G.M. 12V71 TI diesels; 2 props; 1,350 hp **Electric:** 20 kw
**Range:** 500/18 **Man:** 6 tot.

REMARKS: Aluminum construction. Ordered 9-11-83 with U.S. financial aid. Blue hull, white superstructure.

CUSTOMS SERVICE

◆ **1 small craft** Bldr: Buhlers Yachts, Ltd. (In serv. 11-81)

VIGILANT

**D:** 6 tons (fl) **S:** 19 kts **Dim:** 8.20 × 2.95 × 0.90
**M:** 1 Perkins T6.3544 diesel; 1 prop; 200 hp **Range:** 105/19

REMARKS: Sister *Helen II* is operated by the police; delivered 31-5-83. Sisters in St. Kitts and St. Vincent service.

# ST. VINCENT

**State of Saint Vincent and the Grenadines**

MERCHANT MARINE (1986): 103 ships—509,878 grt
(tanker: 1 ship—79,746 grt)

MARINE WING, POLICE FORCE

### PATROL BOATS AND CRAFT

◆ **1 120-ft. Commercial Cruiser class** Bldr: Swiftships, Inc., Morgan City, La.

SVG 08 CAPTAIN MULVAC (L: 6-6-86; in serv. 1-6-87)

**Captain Mulvac (SVG 08)** Swiftships, 1987

**D:** 101 tons light (. . . fl) **S:** 21 kts **Dim:** 36.56 × 7.62 × 2.10
**A:** 2/12.7-mm mg (I × 2)—2/7.62-mm mg (I × 2)
**Electron Equipt:** Radar: 1/Raytheon 1010
**M:** 4 G.M. 12V71 TI diesels; 4 props; 2,700 hp
**Range:** 1,800/15 **Man:** 4 officers, 10 men

REMARKS: Ordered 8-86, with U.S. financial aid. Aluminum construction.

◆ **1 patrol craft** Bldr: Vosper Thornycroft, Portchester (In serv. 23-2-81)

SVG 05 GEORGE MCINTOSH

**D:** 70 tons (fl) **S:** 24.5 kts **Dim:** 22.86 × 7.43 × 1.64
**A:** 1/20-mm AA **M:** 2 Caterpillar 12V D348 TA diesels; 2 props; 1,840 hp
**Electric:** 24 kw **Range:** 600/21; 1,000/11 **Man:** 3 officers, 8 men

**George McIntosh (SVG 05)** L. & L. Van Ginderen, 3-84

**ST. VINCENT** *(continued)*
**PATROL BOATS AND CRAFT** *(continued)*

REMARKS: Glass-reinforced Nelson-design, plastic hull.

◆ **2 8.2-m patrol craft** Bldr: Buhlers Yachts, Ltd.

SVG 06 LARKAI SVG 07 BRIGHTON

**Brighton (SVG 07)** L. & L. Van Ginderen, 3-84

**D:** 6 tons (fl) **S:** 19 kts **Dim:** 8.20 × 2.95 × 0.90
**M:** 1 Perkins T6.3544 diesel; 1 prop; 200 hp **Range:** 105/19

REMARKS: Sisters in St. Kitts and St. Lucia service.

# SAUDI ARABIA

## Kingdom of Saudi Arabia

PERSONNEL (1987): 4,500 total

MERCHANT MARINE (1986): 380 ships—2,978,016 grt
(tankers: 90 ships—1,587,969 grt)

NAVAL AVIATION: The Saudi Navy has received 24 helicopters from S.N.I.A.S., France: 20 SA-365 F/AS Dauphin 2 for ship- and shore-based ASW and ship attack, and 4 SA-365N Dauphin 2 configured for search-and-rescue duties, with the Omera DRB 32 search radar. The first production SA-365 F/AS flew 2-7-82. First six production units delivered 8-85 (4 SAR, 2 attack); six more delivered by end-85, last 12 by mid-1986. One SA-365F lost 17-6-86.

Saudi Arabia, in conjunction with Bahrain, Qatar, Kuwait, Oman, and the U.A.E., is studying purchase of 10–12 new P-3C Orion long-range patrol aircraft for Persian Gulf service; six would be owned by Saudi Arabia.

**SA-365 F/AS Dauphin production version**—launching AS 15 missile
S.N.I.A.S., 1982

SA-365 Dauphin 2 helicopter:
Rotor diameter: 13.29 m; fuselage length: 11.41 m; height: 4 m; weight: light: 1,850 kg/max.: 3,900 kg; propulsion: 2 Turbomeca "Arriel" 1C turbines, 710 hp each.
Performance:
Speed: 130 kts max.
Radius of action—100 nautical miles with 4/AS 15; 140 nautical miles with 2/AS 15
Endurance—2 hours with 4/AS 15; 3 hours with 2/AS 15
Armament: 2 or 4 Aerospatiale AS 15 antiship missiles or 2 Mk 36 ASW torpedoes.
The AS 15 missile has a range of 15 km, weighs 96 kg, and is 2.16 m long. The helicopter will carry an "Agrion-15" frequency-agile, pulse-doppler radar to provide missile targeting and to permit the helicopter to provide mid-course guidance update information to the ship-launched Otomat Mk 2 ("Erato") missiles.
Otomat Mk 2 Erato antiship missile:
Length: 4.66 m; range: 90 nautical miles; diameter: 0.40 m (0.46 m rear); weight: 780 kg (210 kg warhead); propulsion: Turbomeca "Arbizon" turbojet, 2 rocket boosters.

### SUBMARINES

◆ **0 (+6 or 8) diesel-electric** Bldr: . . .

REMARKS: Saudi Arabia has announced plans to purchase 6 to 8 submarines, with initial bids requested by 12-86. Designs being considered are the Dutch *Walrus/Zeeleeuw* class, the Vickers Type 2400, the West German IKL 2000, Swedish Kockums Type 471, a French design, and an Italian design. The winner had not been announced as of 10-87.

### GUIDED-MISSILE FRIGATES

◆ **0 (+2) new construction**

REMARKS: Planned for acquisition are two larger guided-missile frigates. France has offered the F4000 design, with the U.S. Standard SM1 missile (Mk 13 launcher) and Otomat antiship missiles. The U.S. has offered the *Oliver Hazard Perry* (FFG 7) class. No progress in this program, due to lack of funds.

◆ **4 Al Madinah class**

| | Bldr | Laid down | L | In serv. |
|---|---|---|---|---|
| 702 AL MADINAH | Arsenal de Lorient | 15-10-81 | 23-4-83 | 4-1-85 |
| 704 HOFOUF | CNIM, La Seyne | 14-6-82 | 24-6-83 | 31-10-85 |
| 706 ABHA | CNIM, La Seyne | 7-12-82 | 23-12-83 | 4-4-86 |
| 708 TAIF | CNIM, La Seyne | 1-3-83 | 25-5-84 | 29-8-86 |

**D:** 2,000 tons (2,250 normal, 2,610 fl) **S:** 30 kts
**Dim:** 115.00 (106.50 pp) × 12.50 wl × 3.40 (4.65 over sonar)
**A:** 8/Otomat Mk 2 "Erato" SSM (IV × 2)—1/Crotale EDIR SAM syst. (VIII × 1; 26 total missiles)—1/100-mm Compact DP—4/40-mm Breda AA (II × 2)—4 tubes for F17P wire-guided torpedoes—1/Dauphin 2 ASW/antiship helicopter
**Electron Equipt:** Radar: 2/Decca TM 1226, 1/Sea Tiger (DRBV 15), 1/Castor IIC, 1/DRBC-32E (on Crotale launcher); 1/helo control

**Hofouf (704)** G. Gyssels, 6-85

**Taif (708)** Pradignac & Leo, 11-86

### GUIDED-MISSILE FRIGATES *(continued)*

Sonar: Thomson-CSF TSM 2630 (Diodon) hull-mounted, TSM 2630 (Sorel) VDS
EW: Thomson-CSF DR 4000S intercept syst., Janet jammer, Telegon VI D/F, 2/Dagaie decoy RL

**M:** 4 SEMT-Pielstick 16 PA 6 BTC diesels/2 props; 32,500 hp
**Fuel:** 370 tons **Range:** 6,500/18; 8,000/15 **Endurance:** 30 days
**Electric:** 2,560 kw (4 × 480-kw diesel sets; 2 × 320 kw diesel sets)
**Man:** 15 officers, 50 petty officers, 114 men

**Al Madinah (702)** DCAN, 3-4-84

**Abha (706)** G. Gyssels, 11-85

Remarks: Ordered 10-80 as part of the "Sawari" program, under which France replaced the U.S. Navy as principal naval equipment supplier. Very complex ships, with much new, untried equipment. Have Thomson-CSF TAVITAC computer data system, with 2 Type 15M 125F computers, 6 display consoles, E7000 tactical table; similar to French Navy's SENIT-VI. Retractable fin stabilizers fitted. Alcatel Type DLA torpedo f.c.s. 702 arrived 7-85 in Saudi Arabia, 708 on 17-1-87 with the final Dauphin 2 helicopter.

Sorel is a VDS version of the Diodon sonar; both operate at 11, 12, or 13 kHz. There are 4 generator sets of 480 kw and 2 of 320 kw each. Carry 500 rds 100-mm ammunition, 6,300 rds 40-mm. There are two CSEE optical gun directors. There are 13 main watertight bulkheads to the hull.

### GUIDED-MISSILE CORVETTES

◆ **4 U.S. PCG class** Bldr: Tacoma Boatbuilding, Tacoma, Wash.

| | Laid down | L | In serv. |
|---|---|---|---|
| 612 Badr (ex-PCG 1) | 30-5-79 | 26-1-80 | 28-9-81 |
| 614 Al-Yarmook (ex-PCG 2) | 13-12-79 | 13-5-80 | 10-5-82 |
| 616 Hitteen (ex-PCG 3) | 19-5-80 | 5-9-80 | 12-10-82 |
| 618 Tabuk (ex-PCG 4) | 22-9-80 | 18-6-81 | 10-1-83 |

**D:** 903 tons (1,038 fl) **S:** 30 kts gas turbine, 21 kts diesels
**Dim:** 74.68 × 9.60 × 2.59
**A:** 8/Harpoon SSM (IV × 2)—1/76-mm U.S. Mk 75 DP—1/20-mm Vulcan/Phalanx AA—2/20-mm AA (I × 2)—1/81-mm mortar—2/40-mm Mk 19 grenade launchers—6/Mk 32 ASW TT (III × 2)
**Electron Equipt:** Radar: 1/SPS-55, 1/SPS-40B, 1/Mk 92 fire-control system
Sonar: SQS-56
EW: SLQ-32 (V)1, Mk 36 SRBOC chaff RL (VI × 2)
**M:** CODOG: 1 G.E. LM-2500 gas turbine (23,000 hp); 2 MTU 12V652 TB91 diesels (3,058 hp tot.); 2 CP props
**Electric:** 1,200 kw **Man:** 7 officers, 51 men

**Badr (612)** G. Arra, 1982

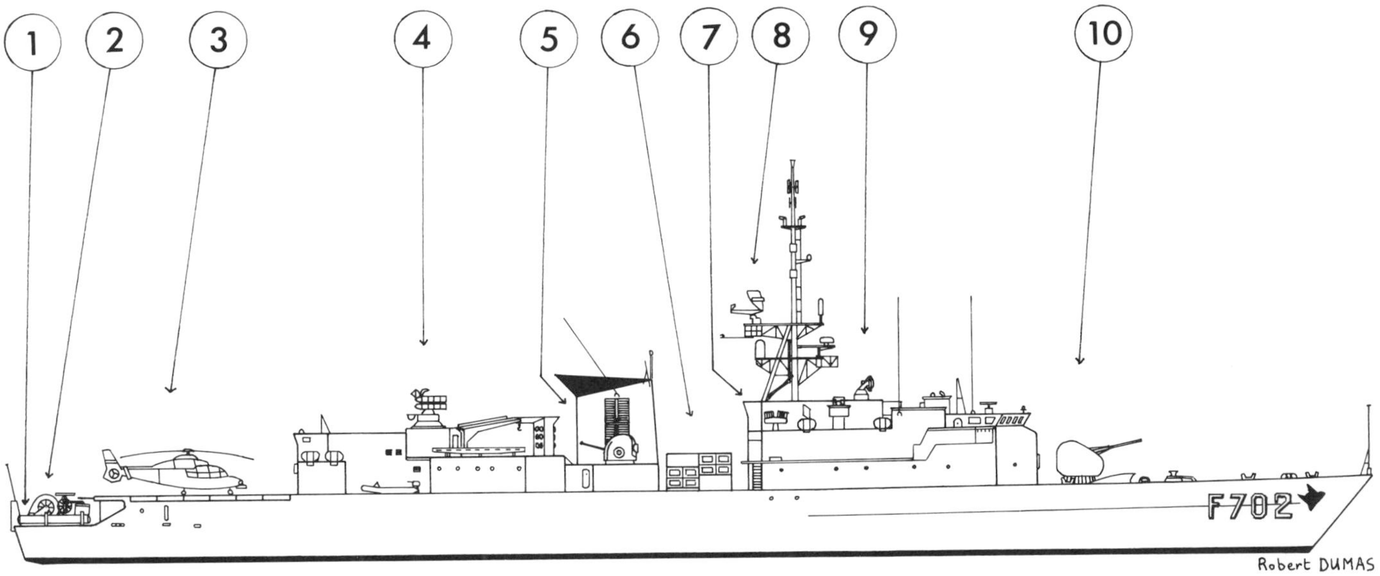


**Al Madinah (702)** 1. torpedo tubes 2. Sorel variable-depth sonar 3. Dauphin 2 helicopter 4. Crotale EDIR SAM launcher 5. twin 40-mm Breda AA 6. Otomat SSM launchers 7. Dagaie decoy RL 8. Sea Tiger search radar 9. Castor IIC f.c. radar director 10. 100-mm Compact DP gun

## GUIDED-MISSILE CORVETTES *(continued)*

**Tabuk (618)** G. Arra, 1983

REMARKS: Ordered 30-8-77. Have fin stabilizers. Program completed well behind schedule, with the ships considerably overweight. Have one Mk 24 optical target designator, Mk 309 ASW f.c.s.

## GUIDED-MISSILE PATROL BOATS

◆ **9 U.S. PGG class** Bldr: Peterson Builders, Sturgeon Bay, Wisc.

| | Laid down | L | In serv. |
|---|---|---|---|
| 511 AS-SIDDIQ (ex-PGG 1) | 30-9-78 | 22-9-79 | 15-12-80 |
| 513 AL-FAROUQ (ex-PGG 2) | 12-3-79 | 17-5-80 | 22-6-81 |
| 515 ABDUL-AZIZ (ex-PGG 3) | 19-10-79 | 23-8-80 | 3-9-81 |
| 517 FAISAL (ex-PGG 4) | 4-3-80 | 15-11-80 | 23-11-81 |
| 519 KHALID (ex-PGG 5) | 27-6-80 | 28-3-81 | 11-1-82 |
| 521 AMR (ex-PGG 6) | 21-10-80 | 13-6-81 | 21-6-82 |
| 523 TARIQ (ex-PGG 7) | 10-2-81 | 23-9-81 | 16-8-82 |
| 525 OQBAH (ex-PGG 8) | 8-5-81 | 12-12-81 | 18-10-82 |
| 527 ABU OBAIDAH (ex-PGG 9) | 4-9-81 | 3-4-82 | 6-12-82 |

**Amr (521)** G. Arra, 1983

**Abu Obaidah (527)** L. & L. Van Ginderen, 11-82

**D:** 425 tons (495 fl) **S:** 34 kts gas turbine, 16 kts diesels
**Dim:** 58.02 × 8.08 × 1.95
**A:** 4/Harpoon (II × 2)—1/76-mm U.S. Mk 75 DP—1/20-mm Vulcan/Phalanx AA—2/20-mm AA (I × 2)—1/81-mm mortar—2/40-mm Mk 19 grenade launchers
**Electron Equipt:** Radar: 1/SPS-55, 1/Mk 92 fire-control system
EW: SLQ-32 (V)1, Mk 36 SRBOC chaff RL (VI × 2)
**M:** CODOG: 1 G.E. gas turbine (23,000 hp); 2 MTU 12V652 TB91 diesels (3,058 hp tot.); 2 CP props
**Electric:** 800 kw **Range:** 600/30; 2,900/14 **Man:** 5 officers, 33 men

REMARKS: Ordered 16-2-77. Fin stabilizers fitted. Delivered behind schedule and considerably over designed displacement. Have one Mk 24 optical target designation transmitter.

## TORPEDO BOATS

◆ **3 German Jaguar class (Type 141)** Bldr: Lürssen, Vegesack (In serv. 1969)

DAMMAM KHABAR MACCAH

**Khabar** 1975

**D:** 170 tons (210 fl) **S:** 40 kts **Dim:** 42.62 × 7.10 × 2.39
**A:** 2/40-mm AA (I × 2)—4/533-mm TT
**M:** 4 Maybach 16-cyl. diesels; 4 props; 12,000 hp **Range:** 500/39; 1,000/32
**Man:** 3 officers, 33 men

REMARKS: Refitted 1976 by builders; possibly no longer operable.

## MINE WARFARE SHIPS

◆ **4 U.S. MSC 322 class** Bldr: Peterson Builders, Sturgeon Bay, Wisc.

| | Laid down | L | In serv. |
|---|---|---|---|
| 412 ADDIRIYAH (ex-MSC 322) | 12-5-76 | 20-12-76 | 6-7-78 |
| 414 AL-QUYSUMAH (ex-MSC 323) | 24-8-76 | 26-5-77 | 15-8-78 |
| 416 AL-WADEEAH (ex-MSC 324) | 28-12-76 | 6-9-77 | 7-9-78 |
| 418 SAFWA (ex-MSC 325) | 5-3-77 | 7-12-77 | 20-10-78 |

**Safwa (418)** L. & L. Van Ginderen, 1984

**D:** 320 tons (407 fl) **S:** 14 kts **Dim:** 46.63 × 8.29 × 4.06 max.
**A:** 2/20-mm AA Mk 67 (II × 1)
**Electron Equipt:** Radar: SPS-55—Sonar: SQQ-14
**M:** 2 Waukesha E1616 diesels; 2 props; 1,200 hp
**Electric:** 2,150 kw **Man:** 4 officers, 35 men

REMARKS: Ordered 30-9-75. Longer than standard U.S. export coastal minesweepers. Wooden construction. Have a 1,750-kw sweep current generator. Used primarily as patrol boats.

## AMPHIBIOUS WARFARE CRAFT

◆ **4 U.S. LCU 1646 class** Bldr: Newport SY, Rhode Island (In serv. 1976)

212 AL-QIAQ (ex-SA 310) 216 AL-ULA (ex-SA 312)
214 AS-SULAYEL (ex-SA 311) 218 AFIF (ex-SA 313)

**D:** 173 tons (403 fl) **S:** 11 kts **Dim:** 41.07 × 9.07 × 2.08
**A:** 2/20-mm AA (I × 2) **Electron Equipt:** Radar: 1/LN-66
**M:** 4 G.M. 6-71 diesels; 2 Kort-nozzle props; 900 hp **Cargo:** 168 tons
**Electric:** 80 kw **Range:** 1,200/10 **Man:** 2 officers, 12 men, 20 passengers

◆ **4 landing craft (LCM)** Bldr: Schlichting Werft, Travemünde, West Germany (In serv. 1982)

201–204

## AMPHIBIOUS WARFARE CRAFT *(continued)*

**D:** 26 tons (light) **S:** . . . **Dim:** 16.5 × 4.0 × . . .
**M:** 2 diesels; 2 props; . . . hp

◆ **8 U.S. LCM(6)-class landing craft** (4 in serv. 7-77, 4 in serv. 7-80)

**D:** 24 tons (57.5 fl) **S:** 13 kts **Dim:** 17.07 × 4.37 × 1.14
**A:** 2/40-mm Mk 19 grenade launchers
**M:** 2 G.M. 6V71 diesels; 2 props; 450 hp
**Range:** 130/9 (loaded) **Man:** 5 tot.

Remarks: Cargo: 30 tons or 80 troops. Cargo well: 11.9 × 3.7.

## AUXILIARIES

◆ **2 underway replenishment oilers** Bldr: CN la Ciotat, Marseilles

| | Laid down | L | In serv. |
|---|---|---|---|
| 902 Boraida | 13-4-82 | 22-1-83 | 29-2-84 |
| 904 Yunbou | 9-10-83 | 20-10-84 | 29-8-85 |

**Yunbou (904)** DCN, 1985

**Boraida (902)** L. & L. Van Ginderen, 8-84

**D:** 10,500 tons (trials) **S:** 20.5 kts **Dim:** 135.0 × 18.7 × 7.0
**A:** 4/40-mm AA (II × 2)—2/Dauphin 2 helicopters
**Electron Equipt:** Radar: 2/. . . nav.
**M:** 2 SEMT-Pielstick 14 PC 2.5V400 diesels; 2 CP props; 13,200 hp
**Electric:** 3,440 kw **Range:** 7,000/17 **Man:** 140 tot. + 55 cadets

Remarks: Ordered 10-80 as part of the "Sawari" program. Design a reduced version of the French *Durance* class. To act as training ships as well as replenishment vessels. Cargo includes 4,350 tons diesel fuel; 350 tons aviation fuel; 140 tons potable water; 100 tons provisions; 100 tons munitions; and 70 tons spares. One replenishment station per side, plus over-the-stern refueling. Can transfer 1.7-ton solid loads. Have electrical, mechanical, and metal workshops. Endurance: 30 days. Two CSEE Naja directors for the 40-mm AA. The helicopters will be supplied with ASW and antiship weapons. 902 left 3-8-84 for Saudi Arabia.

◆ **1 Jetfoil-type hydrofoil royal yacht** Bldr: Boeing, Seattle (In serv. 8-85)

N . . .

**D:** 115 tons (fl) **S:** 46 kts
**Dim:** 27.4 (foils down) × 9.1 × 1.9 hull (5.2 foils down at rest/2.0 foiling)
**A:** 2/20-mm G.E. Sea Vulcan gatling AA (I × 2), with 2 Stinger missiles co-mounted
**Electron Equipt:** Radar: 1/. . . nav.
**M:** 2 Allison 501-KF20A gas turbines; 2 Rocketdyne R-20 waterjet pumps; 9,000 hp (7,560 sust.)—2 G.M. 8V92 TI diesels; 2 props; 900 hp for hullborne cruise
**Range:** 890/40; 1,500/15 (hullborne) **Fuel:** 33 tons **Man:** . . .

Remarks: Aluminum construction. Subcontracted to Boeing by Lockheed. Has a Kollmorgen HSV-20NCS electro-optical GFCS with Mk 35 Mod. L3 electro-optical sight for the gun mounts. Acts as tender for the larger yachts.

◆ **1 royal yacht** Bldr: Helsingor Vaerft, Denmark (In serv. 12-83)

Abdul Aziz

**D:** approx. 5,200 tons (fl) **S:** 22 kts **Dim:** 147.00 (126.00 pp) × 18.00 × 4.90
**M:** 2 Lindholmen-Pielstick 12 PC 2-5V400 diesels; 2 props; 15,600 hp
**Fuel:** 640 tons **Man:** 65 crew, plus 4 royalty, plus 60 passengers

**Abdul Aziz**—white with blue funnels Walles Foto. 5-84

Remarks: Delivered by builders 4-83 to Vosper Shiprepairers, Southampton, for final fitting out and ran post-outfitting trials 15-5-84. Stern ramp leading to vehicle garage. Swimming pool. Helicopter hangar forward. Perhaps the nicest touch: a retractable figurehead, with closure doors in the stem. Presumably supplements the *Al Riyadh,* below.

◆ **1 royal yacht** Bldr: C. Van Lent & Sons, Kaag, Netherlands (In serv. 1-78)

Al Riyadh

**D:** 670 tons (fl) **S:** 20 kts **Dim:** 64.64 (59.22 pp) × 9.7 × 3.0
**A:** none **Electron Equipt:** Radar: 1/Decca RM 916
**M:** 2 MTU 16V956 diesels; 2 props; 5,720 hp **Electric:** 370 kw
**Range:** 1,750/18 **Man:** 16 tot.

Remarks: Fin stabilizers and Schottel bow-thruster fitted.

◆ **1 salvage tug** Bldr: Hayashikane, Shimonoseki (In serv. 1978)

13 Jeddah

**D:** 350 tons **S:** 12 kts **Dim:** 34.4 × . . . × . . . **M:** 2 diesels; 800 hp

◆ **2 U.S. YTB 760-class tugs** (In serv. 15-10-75)

EN 111 Tuwaig (ex-YTB 837) EN 112 Dareen (ex-YTB 838)

**D:** 291 tons (316 fl) **S:** 12 kts **Dim:** 33.22 × 9.30 × 4.14
**A:** 2/20-mm AA (I × 2) **Electron Equipt:** Radar: 1/LN-66
**M:** 2 diesels; 1 prop; 2,000 hp **Electric:** 120 kw
**Range:** 2,000/10 **Man:** 4 officers, 8 men

Remarks: 25-ton bollard pull. Intended for target towing, firefighting, torpedo recovery, and local patrol duties.

Note: Eleven more tugs in the *Radhwa*-series are government-owned, but not naval.

COAST GUARD

## PATROL BOATS

◆ **0 (+4) shallow-draft** Bldr: Blohm + Voss, Hamburg (In serv. 1989)

**D:** 210 tons (fl) **S:** 30 kts **Dim:** 38.9 (36.0 pp) × 8.0 × 1.7
**A:** 2/20-mm AA (I × 2)—2/12.7-mm mg **Electron Equipt:** Radar: . . .
**M:** 3 MTU diesels; . . . **Range:** . . . **Man:** 20 tot.

Remarks: Ordered 9-86 for delivery during 1987. No further data available.

◆ **2 (+14) 26-meter patrol boats** Bldr: Abeking & Rasmussen, Lemwerder, West Germany

| | Laid down | L | In serv. |
|---|---|---|---|
| Al Yarmouk | 1-3-86 | 3-87 | 4-87 |
| N . . . | 1-3-86 | 3-87 | 4-87 |

**Al Yarmouk** J. Bouvia, 1987

**SAUDI ARABIA** *(continued)*
**COAST GUARD** *(continued)*

**D:** 80 tons **S:** 40 kts **Dim:** 26.20(23.00 pp) × 5.80 × . . .
**A:** 1/20-mm AA—2/12.7-mm mg (I × 2) **Electron Equipt:** Radar: 1/. . . nav.
**M:** 216V396 TB94 MTU diesels; 2 props; 6,340 hp **Range:** . . . **Man:** . . .

Remarks: Ordered 11-8-85. Steel construction. Up to 14 more may be ordered.

◆ **1 U.S. Coast Guard Cape class**

Riyadh

**D:** 102 tons (fl) **S:** 18 kts **Dim:** 28.95 × 5.8 × 1.55
**A:** 1/40-mm AA **M:** 4 Cummins VT-12-M-700 diesels; 2 props; 2,324 hp
**Electric:** 40 kw **Range:** 1,500/12 **Man:** 15 tot.

Remarks: Transferred in 1969.

### PATROL CRAFT

◆ **25 Scorpion class** Bldrs: 20 units: Bayerische Schiffsbau, Erlenbach; 5 units: Arminias Werft, Bodenwerder, West Germany (In serv. 1979, except last 10: 28-2-81)

139–164

**143** P. Voss, 5-82

**D:** 33 tons (fl) **S:** 25 kts **Dim:** 17.14 (15.6 pp) × 4.98 × 1.40
**A:** 2/7.62-mm mg **Electron Equipt:** Radar: 1/Decca RM 914
**M:** 2 G.M. 12V71 TI diesels; 2 props; 1,300 hp (1,050 sust.)
**Range:** 200/20 **Man:** 7 tot.

◆ **12 Rapier class** Bldr: Halter Marine, New Orleans, La. (In serv. 1976–77)

127–138

**Rapier class** Halter Marine, 1976

**D:** 26 tons (fl) **S:** 28 kts **Dim:** 15.24 × 4.57 × 1.35
**A:** 2/7.62-mm mg (I × 2) **M:** 1 G.M. 12V71 TI diesels; 2 props; 1,300 hp
**Electric:** 20 kw **Man:** 1 officer, 8 men

◆ **43 C-80 class** Bldr: Northshore Yacht Yard, U.K. (In serv. 1975–77)

**D:** 2.8 tons (fl) **S:** 20 kts **Dim:** 8.9 × 2.9 × 0.6 **A:** 1/7.62-mm mg
**M:** 1 Caterpillar diesel; Castoldi water jet; 210 hp **Man:** 3 tot.

◆ **10 Huntress class** Bldr: Fairey Marine, Hamble, U.K. (In serv. 1976)

**D:** 4 tons (fl) . . . **S:** 20 kts **Dim:** 7.1 × 2.7 × 0.8
**A:** 1/7.62-mm mg **M:** 1 diesel; 180 hp **Range:** 150/20 **Man:** 4 tot.

◆ **8 SRN.6 Mod. 8 hovercraft** Bldr: British Hovercraft, Cowes (In serv.: 6 in 1981, 2 in 1-82)

**D:** 17 tons (fl) **S:** 50–55 kts **Dim:** 18.3 × 8.5 × . . .
**A:** small arms **Electron Equipt:** Radar: 1/Decca . . .
**M:** 1 Rolls-Royce Gnome gas turbine; 1 lift fan, 1 airscrew; 1,060 hp

Remarks: Payload: 6 tons. Endurance: 6 to 11 hours. Carry 1,200 liters fuel internally, plus two 450-lit. deck tanks.

◆ **16 SRN.6-class hovercraft** Bldr: British Hovercraft, 1970 and 1981

**D:** 10 tons **S:** 58 kts **Dim:** 14.8 × 7.7 × 4.8 (high) **A:** 1/7.62-mm mg
**M:** 1 Rolls-Royce Gnome gas turbine; 900 hp

◆ **8 harbor patrol craft** Bldr: Yokohama Yacht, Japan, 1972

**Two Saudi Coast Guard SRN.6 Mod. 8** British Hovercraft, 1981

**D:** . . . **S:** 20 kts **Dim:** 10.5 × 3.0 × . . . **M:** 2 diesels; 2 props; 280 hp

Note: There are also several hundred small boats: 200 of 5.1-m length with 40-hp engines and 100 of 4.2-m length with a 20-hp engine.

### AUXILIARIES AND SERVICE CRAFT

◆ **1 training ship** Bldr: Bayerische Schiffsbau, Erlenbach, West Germany (In serv. 12-77)

Tebuk

**D:** 600 tons (750 fl) **S:** 20 kts **Dim:** 60.0 (55.5 pp) × 10.0 × 2.50
**Electron Equipt:** Radar: 1/Decca TM 1226
**M:** 2 MTU 16V538 TB81 diesels; 2 props; 5,260 hp (4,800 sust.)
**Range:** 2,400/18; 3,900/12 **Electric:** 1,040 kVA
**Man:** 24 crew, plus 36 trainees

◆ **3 small fuel lighters**—27 m overall

Al Forat Dajlah N . . . . . . .

◆ **2 yachts**

Al Deriyah Promineut

◆ **5 barges**

◆ **4 motor dhows**

# SENEGAL

**Republic of Senegal**

(Note: The "confederation" with The Gambia does not affect military forces.)

Personnel (1987): 650 men

Merchant Marine (1986): 148 ships—50,429 grt
(tankers: 2 ships—1,422 grt)

Naval Aviation: One Canadian de Havilland DHC-6-300M Twin Otter for maritime patrol.

### PATROL BOATS

◆ **1 Osprey 55 design** Bldr: Danyard A/S, Fredrikshavn, Denmark

| | Laid down | L | In serv. |
|---|---|---|---|
| P . . . Fouta | . . . | . . . | 1-6-87 |

**D:** 500 tons (fl) **S:** 20.2 kts; 19 sust.
**Dim:** 54.75 (50.83 pp) × 10.30 (9.15 wl) × 2.55 **A:** 2/20-mm AA (I × 2)
**Electron Equipt:** Radar: 1/Furuno FR-1411, 1/Furuno FR-1221
**Electric:** 424 kVA
**M:** 2 M.A.N. 12V.23/30-DVO diesels; 2 CP props; 4,960 hp
**Range:** 4,500/16 **Fuel:** 95 tons **Man:** 4 officers, 34 men, 8 trainees

**PATROL BOATS** *(continued)*

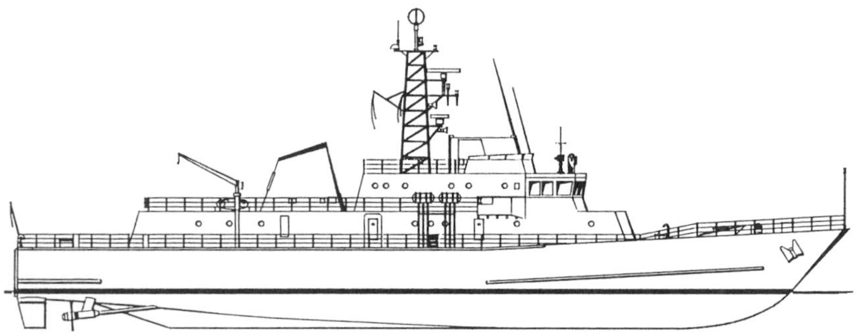

**Fouta** Danyard, 1987

Remarks: Ordered early 1986. Giles Thornycroft "short, fat ship" hull. Near-sisters in Danish, Moroccan, and Burmese service. Used for 200-n.m. economic zone and fisheries patrol, and financed by the Ministry of Equipment, rather than the navy. Armed after delivery. No helicopter facility. Berths for 20 rescued personnel. A stern docking well holds a 6.5-m Watercraft RI-22 inspection/rescue boat.

◆ **1 French PR 72 MS class** Bldr: SFCN, Villeneuve-la-Garenne

| | Laid down | L | In serv. |
|---|---|---|---|
| P 773 N'Jambuur | 5-80 | 23-12-80 | 9-81 |

**N'jambuur** (P 773) SFCN, 1981

**D:** 381 tons light (451 fl) **S:** 30 kts **Dim:** 58.70 (54.0 pp) × 8.22 × 2.18
**A:** 2/76-mm OTO Melara Compact (I × 2)—2/20-mm Type F2 AA (I × 2)
**Electron Equipt:** Radar: 1/Decca 1226
**M:** 4 AGO 195V16 RVR diesels; 4 props; 12,800 hp
**Range:** 2,500/16 **Man:** 39 tot. plus 7 passengers

Remarks: Can be equipped later with 4/Exocet SSM. Two CSEE Naja optical GFCS.

◆ **3 PR-48 class** Bldr: SFCN, Villeneuve-la-Garenne

| | Laid down | L | In serv. |
|---|---|---|---|
| Saint Louis | 20-4-70 | 5-8-70 | 1-3-71 |
| Popenguine | 12-73 | 22-3-74 | 10-8-74 |
| Podor | 12-75 | 20-7-76 | 13-7-77 |

**Saint Louis** 1971

**D:** 240 tons (avg.) **S:** 23 kts **Dim:** 47.5 (45.5 pp) × 7.1 × 2.5
**A:** 2/40-mm AA (I × 2)—2/7.62-mm mg (I × 2)
**Electron Equipt:** Radar: 1/Decca 1226
**M:** 2 AGO V12 CZSHR diesels; 2 props; 6,240 hp
**Range:** 2,000/16 **Man:** 3 officers, 22 men

**PATROL CRAFT**

◆ **3 "Interceptor" class** Bldr: Turbec Ltd., St. Catharines, Canada

Senegal II Siné Saloum II Casamance II

**Casamance II** L. & L. Van Ginderen

**D:** 52 tons (62 fl) **S:** 32 kts **Dim:** 26.5 × 5.81 × . . .
**A:** 2/20-mm AA (I × 2) **Electron Equipt:** Radar: 1/LN-66
**M:** 2 diesels; 2 props; 2,700 hp

Remarks: In service 2-79, 7-79, and 10-79, respectively. Used for fisheries protection patrol.

**AMPHIBIOUS WARFARE SHIPS**

◆ **1 French EDIC 700-class tank landing craft** Bldr: SFCN, Villeneuve-la-Garenne

| | Laid down | L | In serv. |
|---|---|---|---|
| 841 Karabene | 23-4-85 | 6-3-86 | 23-6-86 |

**D:** 410 tons light (730 fl) **S:** 12 kts
**Dim:** 59.00 (52.90 pp) × 11.90 × 1.69 (max.)
**A:** 2/20-mm AA (I × 2)—1/81-mm mortar
**Electron Equipt:** Radar: 1/Decca 1226
**M:** 2 UNI UD30.V12 diesels; 2 props; 1,400 hp (1,040 sust.)
**Range:** 1,800/8 **Man:** 18 tot.

Remarks: Ordered 3-6-85 to replace sister *Faleme* (ex-EDIC 9095), on loan from France since 7-1-74. Cargo: 340 tons, carried in 28.50 × 8.0 vehicle well: eleven trucks or five light tanks. Arrived in Senegal 8-86. A reported second new unit, "*Damour,*" does not seem to exist.

◆ **2 ex-U.S. LCM(6)-class landing craft**

Djomboss Douloulou

**D:** 26 tons (52 fl) **S:** 10 kts **Dim:** 17.1 × 4.4 × 1.2
**M:** 2 Gray Marine 64 HN9 diesels; 2 props; 330 hp

Remarks: Transferred in 7-68.

**AUXILIARY SHIPS**

◆ **1 training ship**

Crame Jean (ex-*Raymond Sarr*)

**D:** 18 tons

Remarks: A former fishing vessel, acquired 1978.

◆ **1 tug**

Ibis

**D:** 200 tons (fl) **S:** 9 kts **Dim:** 18.4 × 5.7 × 2.5
**M:** 1 Poyaud diesel; 250 hp **Range:** 1,700/9

Remarks: On loan from the French Navy.

CUSTOMS

**PATROL CRAFT**

◆ **3 Type DS 01** Bldr: Celayo, Bilbao, Spain (In serv. 1-82)

**D:** 26 tons (fl) **S:** 20 kts **Dim:** 16.0 (13.3 pp) × 4.8 × 1.6
**A:** 1/12.7-mm mg **Electron Equipt:** Radar: 1/Decca 110
**M:** 2 G.M. 5V71 TI diesels; 2 props; 870 hp **Man:** 8 tot.

**SENEGAL** *(continued)*
**CUSTOMS** *(continued)*

◆ **4 harbor craft** Bldr: ARESA, Arenys de Mar, Spain (In serv. 1979)

**D:** 3.5 tons (fl) **S:** 18 kts **Dim:** 8.5 × . . . × . . .

◆ **3 Lance class** Bldr: Fairey Marine, Hamble, U.K. (In serv. 1974–77)

Djibeill Djilor Gorée

**D:** 15.7 tons **S:** 24 kts
**Dim:** 14.8 × 4.7 × 1.3 **A:** 2/7.62-mm mg (I × 2)
**M:** 2 G.M. 8V71 TI diesels; 2 props; 850 hp **Man:** 7 tot.

◆ **7 45-foot class** Bldr: Vosper Thornycroft

**D:** 10 tons (fl) **S:** 25 kts **Dim:** 13.7 × 4.0 × 1.1
**A:** 1/12.7-mm mg—2/7.62-mm mg (I × 2)
**M:** 2 diesels; 2 props; 920 hp **Man:** 6 tot.

Remarks: Five sisters discarded.

◆ **2 Huntress class** Bldr: Fairey Marine, Hamble, U.K. (In serv. 1974)

**D:** 4 tons (fl) **S:** 20 kts **Dim:** 7.1 × 2.7 × 0.8
**A:** 1/7.62-mm mg **M:** 1 diesel; 180 hp **Man:** 2 tot.

# SEYCHELLES

## Republic of Seychelles

Personnel (1987): Approx 200 tot.

Merchant Marine (1986): 7 ships—3,813 grt

Naval Aviation: 1 Britten-Norman BN-42 B/T Maritime Defender for surveillance ordered 1983. Libya donated 2 Super Rallye light planes in 1980, and India delivered 2 Chetak (Alouette-III) helicopters in 6-82.

### PATROL BOATS AND CRAFT

◆ **1 Soviet Turya-class semi-hydrofoil**

**D:** 215 tons (250 fl) **S:** 40 kts
**Dim:** 39.0 × 7.6 (12.5 over foils) × 2.0 (4.0 over foils)
**A:** 2/57-mm DP (II × 1)—2/25-mm AA (II × 1)
**Electron Equipt:** Radar: 1/Pot Drum, 1/Muff Cob f.c.
IFF: High Pole B transponder, Square Head interrogator
**M:** 3 Type M504 diesels; 3 props; 15,000 hp
**Range:** 400/38; 650/25 **Man:** 24 tot.

Remarks: Delivered 21-6-86 without the standard 4/533-mm TT and sonar installation.

◆ **1 FPB 42 class** Bldr: C.N. Picchiotti, Viareggio, Italy (In serv. 10-1-83)

605 Andromanche

**Andromanche (605)** C. Martinelli, 9-86

**D:** 240 tons (268 fl) **S:** 28 kts **Dim:** 41.80 × 8.00 × 2.50 (props; 1.70 hull)
**A:** 1/20-mm AA—2/7.62-mm mg (I × 2)
**Electron Equipt:** Radar: 2/Furuno. . .
**M:** 2 Paxman Valenta 16 RP200 CM diesels; 2 props; 6,800 hp (5,700 sust.)
**Range:** 3,000/16 **Man:** 22 tot.

Remarks: Ordered 8-10-81. Also used as a personnel transport. Refitted 1985–86 in Italy.

◆ **1 ex-French Sirius-class former minesweeper** Bldr: Seine Maritime (L: 13-6-56)

P . . . Topaz (ex-*Croix du Sud,* P 658)

**D:** 400 tons (440 fl) **S:** 15 kts **Dim:** 46.4 (42.7 pp) × 8.55 × 2.5
**A:** 1/40-mm AA—1/20-mm AA
**M:** 2 SEMT-Pielstick diesels; 2 props; 2,000 hp
**Fuel:** 48 tons **Range:** 3,000/10 **Man:** 2 officers, 35 men

Remarks: Transferred 1979. Minesweeping gear removed.

◆ **2 Soviet Zhuk class**

Constant (In serv. 17-10-81) Fortune (In serv. 6-11-82)

**Constant and Fortune**—outboard *Topaz* French Navy, 8-85

**D:** 60 tons (fl) **S:** 34 kts **Dim:** 24.0 × 5.0 × 1.8 (props)
**A:** 4/14.5-mm mg (II × 2) **Electron Equipt:** Radar: 1/Spin Trough
**M:** 2 M50F-4 diesels; 2 props; 2,400 hp

◆ **1 glass-reinforced plastic-hulled** Bldr: Tyler, U.K. (In serv. 4-80)

Junon

**D:** 40 tons **S:** 26 kts **Dim:** 18.3 × . . . × . . .
**M:** 2 G.M. diesels; 2 props; 1,040 hp **Range:** 1,000/22

### AUXILIARY SHIP

◆ **1 medium landing ship** Bldr: A.C. de la Perrière, France

| | Laid down | L | In serv. |
|---|---|---|---|
| 5 Juin | 7-4-78 | 19-9-78 | 11-1-79 |

**D:** 350 tons (855 fl) **S:** 9 kts **Dim:** 58.2 × 11.37 × 1.9
**M:** 2 Poyaud A12 150M diesels; 2 props; 880 hp **Range:** 2,000/9

Remarks: Owned by the government but operated in local commercial service. Bow ramp. Cargo: 272 tons.

# SIERRA LEONE

**Republic of Sierra Leone**

Personnel (1985): 45 men

Merchant Marine (1986): 29 ships—6,979 grt

### PATROL BOATS

Note: The U.S.A. has offered to donate a refitted 32.0-m patrol boat, armed with 2/12.7-mm and 2/7.62-mm mg in single mountings. Negotiations were in progress during 1987.

◆ **2 Chinese Shanghai-II Class (In serv. 3-87)**

Moa Maimbana

**D:** 122.5 tons (134.8 fl) **S:** 28.5 kts **Dim:** 38.78 × 5.41 × 1.49 hull
**A:** 4/37-mm AA (II × 2)—4/25-mm (II × 2)
**Electron Equipt:** Radar: 1/Pot Head **Endurance:** 7 days
**M:** 2 M50F-4, 1,200-hp diesels, and 2 Type 12 D6,910-hp diesels; 4 props; 4,220 hp
**Range:** 750/16.5 **Electric:** 39 kw **Mau:** 36 tot.

Remarks: Delivered as replacements for three sisters transferred 1976 and no longer in service.

Note: The Fairey Tracker Mk II-class patrol craft *President Saika Stevens* had been discarded by 1-87; she was delivered in 1982.

### SERVICE CRAFT

◆ **3 small landing craft** Bldr: Shikoku DY (first two), and Kegoya SY, Japan (L: 2 to 3-80)

Pompoli Gulama Kallondo

Remarks: No characteristics available.

◆ **1 Soviet PO-2-class launch**

**D:** 50 tons **S:** 9 kts **Dim:** 21.0 × 4.5 × . . .
**M:** 1 Type 3D6 diesel; 1 prop; 150 hp

Remarks: Delivered 1980; may be out of service.

# SINGAPORE

**Republic of Singapore**

Personnel (1987): Approximately 4,500 men

Merchant Marine (1986): 716 ships—6,267,627 grt
(tankers: 121 ships—1,604,411 grt)

Naval Aviation: The Singapore Air Force 125 Squadron received the first 5 of a programmed 22 AS-332M Super Puma helicopters, equipped for ASW; the last was to be delivered by end 1987. The Air Force also operates 4 E-2C Hawkeye radar surveillance aircraft and some 50 A-4 Skyhawk fighter-bombers capable of maritime strike. Eight F-16A/B fighters will be delivered in 1988.

### GUIDED-MISSILE PATROL BOATS

◆ **0 (+6) MGB 62 class** Bldr: first unit: Lürssen, Vegesack; others: Singapore SB & Eng., Jurong

| | L | In serv. |
|---|---|---|
| P . . . N . . . | . . . | 7-88 |
| P . . . N . . . | . . . | . . . |
| P . . . N . . . | . . . | . . . |
| P . . . N . . . | . . . | . . . |
| P . . . N . . . | . . . | . . . |
| P . . . N . . . | . . . | . . . |

**D:** 600 tons (fl) **S:** 34 kts **Dim:** 62.95 (59.90 pp) × 9.30 × 2.60
**A:** 8/Harpoon SSM (IV × 2)—1/76-mm OTO Melara Super Rapid DP—1/20-mm Mk 15 CIWS Phalanx gatling AA—6/324-mm ILAS-3 ASW TT (III × 2; 6 A244 torpedoes)
**Electron Equipt:** Radar: 1/nav., . . .
Sonar: EDO 780 VDS
EW: . . .
**M:** 4 MTU 20V538 TB93 diesels; 4 props; 18,740 hp
**Range:** 700/34; 4,000/16 **Electric:** 408 kw **Man:** 34 tot.

**MGB 62 class**—artist's rendering Singapore SB & Eng.

Remarks: Same hull as pair for Bahrain, but without helicopter facilities. Intended to receive a SAM system, possibly French modular Crotale (IV × 1), Israeli Barak, or U.K. Sea Wolf. First unit ordered 6-86.

◆ **6 FPB 45 class**

| | In serv. | | In serv. |
|---|---|---|---|
| P 76 Sea Wolf | 1972 | P 79 Sea Tiger | 1974 |
| P 77 Sea Lion | 1972 | P 80 Sea Hawk | 1975 |
| P 78 Sea Dragon | 1974 | P 81 Sea Scorpion | 1975 |

**Sea Scorpion (P 81)** L. & L. Van Ginderen, 3-84

Bldrs: P 76, P 77: Lürssen, Vegesack; others: Singapore SB & Eng., Jurong

**D:** 225 tons (252 fl) **S:** 38 kts **Dim:** 44.90 (42.30 wl) × 7.00 × 2.48
**A:** 5 Gabriel I missiles (III × 1, I × 2)—1/57-mm AA—1/40-mm AA
**Electron Equipt:** Radar: 1/Decca TM 626, 1/H.S.A. WM-28
**M:** 4 MTU 16V538 diesels; 4 props; 14,400 hp **Range:** 2,000/15 **Man:** 40 tot.

Remarks: Ordered in 1970. Frequently seen without missiles. Two multiple 57-mm flare launchers on 57-mm mount. Carry 504 rounds 57-mm, 1,008 rounds 40-mm. Intercept equipment on tripod topmast added 1980–81. These craft are to transfer to a new Naval Reserve force on completion of the MGB 62 class and may be rearmed with Harpoon SSM.

### PATROL BOATS

◆ **3 110-foot, "Type A"**

| | Bldr | L | In serv. |
|---|---|---|---|
| P 69 Independence | Vosper Thornycroft, Portsmouth | 15-7-69 | 8-7-70 |
| P 70 Freedom | Vosper Thornycroft, Singapore | 18-11-69 | 11-1-71 |
| P 72 Justice | Vosper Thornycroft, Singapore | 20-6-70 | 23-4-71 |

**Freedom (P 70)** J. Jedrlinic, 1987

**PATROL BOATS** *(continued)*

**D:** 100 tons (130 fl) **S:** 30 kts **Dim:** 33.4 (31.46 pp) × 6.4 × 1.71
**A:** 1/40-mm Bofors AA—1/20-mm Oerlikon AA
**Electron Equipt:** Radar: 1/Decca TM 626
**M:** 2 MTU 16V538 diesels; 2 props; 7,200 hp
**Electric:** 100 kw **Range:** 1,100/15 **Man:** 3 officers, 16 men

REMARKS: Ordered 21-5-68. Two 50-mm flare RL on 40-mm shield sides.

◆ **3 110-foot, "Type B"**

| | Bldr | L | In serv. |
|---|---|---|---|
| P 71 SOVEREIGNTY | Vosper Thornycroft, Portsmouth | 25-11-69 | 2-71 |
| P 73 DARING | Vosper Thornycroft, Singapore | 1970 | 18-9-71 |
| P 74 DAUNTLESS | Vosper Thornycroft, Singapore | 6-5-71 | 7-71 |

**Dauntless (P 74)** L. & L. Van Ginderen, 3-83

**D:** 100 tons (130 fl) **S:** 32 kts **Dim:** 33.4 × 6.4 × 1.71
**A:** 1/76.2-mm Bofors—1/20-mm Oerlikon AA
**Electron Equipt:** Radar: 1/Decca TM 626, 1/H.S.A. M-26
**M:** 2 MTU 16V538 diesels; 2 props; 7,200 hp
**Range:** 1,000/15 **Man:** 3 officers, 16 men

REMARKS: Gun and fire-control system as on the Norwegian *Storm* class. The 76.2-mm is for surface fire only.

◆ **1 British Ford class**

| | Bldr | L | In serv. |
|---|---|---|---|
| P 48 PANGLIMA | United Engineers, Singapore | 14-1-56 | 5-56 |

**Panglima (P 48)** J. Bouvia, 1987

**D:** 119 tons (131 fl) **S:** 14 kts **Dim:** 35.76 × 6.1 × 1.68
**A:** 1/20-mm AA—2/7.62-mm mg (I × 2)
**Electron Equipt:** Radar: 2/. . . nav.
**M:** 2 Paxman 12YHAXM diesels; 2 props; 1,000 hp
**Fuel:** 15 tons **Man:** 15 tot.

REMARKS: Transferred by Malaysia in 1967 and used for training. 1/40-mm AA removed.

◆ **1 ex-French craft** Bldr: Deggendorfer Werft, West Germany (In serv. 1955)

P 75 ENDEAVOR

**D:** 184 tons (fl) **S:** 20 kts **Dim:** 40.9 × 7.6 × 2.4 **Range:** 800/8
**A:** 2/20-mm AA (I × 2) **M:** 2 Maybach diesels; 2 props; 2,000 hp **Man:** 24 tot.

REMARKS: Purchased on 30-9-70. Low freeboard. Used for training and as a diving tender.

**PATROL CRAFT**

◆ **12 "Swift" class** Bldr: Singapore SB & Eng., Jurong (In serv. 20-10-81)

| | | |
|---|---|---|
| P 10 SWIFT ARCHER | P 14 SWIFT WARRIOR | P 18 SWIFT CHALLENGER |
| P 11 SWIFT WARLORD | P 15 SWIFT SWORDSMAN | P 19 SWIFT CAVALIER |
| P 12 SWIFT LANCER | P 16 SWIFT COMBATANT | P 20 SWIFT CENTURION |
| P 13 SWIFT KNIGHT | P 17 SWIFT CONQUEROR | P 21 SWIFT CHIEFTAIN |

**Swift Cavalier (P 19)** L. & L. Van Ginderen, 3-84

**D:** 45.7 tons (fl) **S:** 33 kts (31 sust.)
**Dim:** 22.7 (20.0 pp) × 6.2 × 1.6 (3.0 props)
**A:** 1/20-mm AA—2/7.62-mm mg (I × 2)
**Electron Equipt:** Radar: 1/Decca 1226
**Electric:** 2 generators **M:** 2 Deutz SBA-16M816 diesel; 2 props; 2,660 hp
**Fuel:** 8.6 tons **Range:** 550/20; 900/10 **Man:** 3 officers, 9 men

REMARKS: All commissioned same date; first unit launched 8-6-80. Design based on Australian de Havilland "Capricornica" design. Provision for installing 2 Gabriel SSM. Aluminum contruction. Carry 2 tons fresh water.

**MINE WARFARE SHIPS**

◆ **2 ex-U.S. Redwing-class minesweepers** Bldrs: M 101: Tampa Marine, Tampa, Florida; M 102: Bellingham SY, Bellingham, Washington

| | Laid down | L | In serv. |
|---|---|---|---|
| M 101 JUPITER (ex-*Thrasher*, MSC 203) | 1-4-54 | 6-10-54 | 16-8-55 |
| M 102 MERCURY (ex-*Whippoorwill*, MSC 207) | 7-1-54 | 13-8-54 | 20-10-55 |

**D:** 300 tons (372 fl) **S:** 13 kts **Dim:** 43.0 × 7.95 × 2.55
**A:** 1/20-mm **Electron Equipt:** Radar: 1/SPS-5—Sonar: UQS-1D
**M:** 2 G.M. 8-268A diesels; 2 props; 1,200 hp **Fuel:** 40 tons
**Range:** 2,500/10 **Man:** 39 tot.

REMARKS: Purchased on 5-12-75. M 101 re-armed with new Oerlikon 20-mm AA, 1980; M 102 is unarmed. There are plans to replace these ships with new construction.

**AMPHIBIOUS WARFARE SHIPS**

◆ **5 ex-U.S. LST 542 class**

| | Laid down | L | In serv. |
|---|---|---|---|
| L 201 ENDURANCE (ex-*Holmes County*, LST 836) | 11-9-44 | 29-10-44 | 25-11-44 |
| L 202 EXCELLENCE (ex-T-LST 629) | 13-4-44 | 8-7-44 | 28-7-44 |
| L 203 INTREPID (ex-T-LST 579) | 4-5-44 | 22-6-44 | 21-7-44 |
| L 204 RESOLUTION (ex-T-LST 649) | 19-7-44 | 6-10-44 | 26-10-44 |
| L 205 PERSISTENCE (ex-T-LST 614) | 28-1-44 | 6-5-44 | 22-5-44 |

Bldrs: L 201: American Bridge, Pa.; L 202, L 204, L 205, L 206: Chicago Bridge & Iron, Seneca, Ill.; L 203: Missouri Valley Bridge & Iron, Evansville, Ind.

**Resolution (L 204)** L. & L. Van Ginderen, 11-85

**AMPHIBIOUS WARFARE SHIPS** *(continued)*

**Endurance (L 201)** L. & L. Van Ginderen, 3-83

**D:** 1,653 tons, light (4,080 fl) **S:** 11.6 kts **Dim:** 99.98 (96.32 pp) × 15.24 × 4.29
**A:** L 201: 5/40-mm AA (I × 5)—others: 1/40-mm AA—all: 2 or more/7.62-mm mg
**Electron Equipt:** Radar: 1/Decca 626, 1/. . . **Electric:** 300 kw
**Range:** 19,000/9 **M:** 2 G.M. 12-567A diesels; 2 props; 1,800 hp **Man:** 120 tot.

Remarks: Originally numbered A 81 to A 85, L 201 loaned 1-7-71 and purchased 5-12-75; chartered in 1976 for commercial service at which time guns were removed. Others purchased 4-6-76. L 202 has a helicopter deck aft, projecting well beyond the stern. L 204 to 205 in reserve until 1980 when refitting began. Three more ex-Military Sealift Command T-LSTs (ex-T-LST 117, ex-T-LST 276, and ex-*Chase County,* T-LST 532) were purchased 4-6-76 but later sold commercially. Sister *Perseverance* (L 206, ex-T-LST 623) is in reserve for spare parts. L 201 and L 205 have new aft superstructures.

◆ **4 RPL 60-class utility landing craft**

| | Bldr | Laid down | L | In serv. |
|---|---|---|---|---|
| RPL 60 | North SY, Singapore | . . . | 11-85 | 1986 |
| RPL 61 | North SY, Singapore | . . . | 11-85 | 1986 |
| RPL 62 | Singapore SY & Eng. | 5-85 | 10-85 | 2-11-85 |
| RPL 63 | Singapore SY & Eng. | 5-85 | 10-85 | 2-11-85 |

**RPL 60** L. & L. Van Ginderen, 3-87

**D:** 151 tons **S:** 10 kts **Dim:** 36.0 (33.0 pp) × 8.5 × 2.5
**A:** none **Electron Equipt:** Radar: 1/. . . **M:** 2 Deutz diesels; 2 props; 860 hp

Remarks: Differ in detail, by builder. Can carry 450 standing troops or two AMX 13 tanks. Painted green. Ordered 28-2-85.

◆ **4 Ayer Chawan-class landing craft** Bldr: Vosper Thornycroft, Singapore (In serv. 1968–69)

RPL 54 Ayer Chawan RPL 56 N . . . . . . .
RPL 55 Ayer Merban RPL 57 N . . . . . . .

**D:** 150 tons (fl) **S:** 10 kts **Dim:** 27.0 × 6.9 × 1.3
**M:** 2 diesels; 2 props; 650 hp

◆ **2 Brani-class landing craft** Bldr: Australia (In serv. 1955–56)

RPL 41 Brani RPL 42 Berlayer

**D:** 56 tons (fl) **S:** 9 kts **Dim:** 17.0 × 4.3 × 1.4 **M:** 2 diesels; 2 props; 460 hp

◆ **2 ALC-1800-class personnel tenders** Bldr: Le Comte, Vianen, the Netherlands (L: 16-10-85; In serv. 1-11-85)

FL 1 FL 2

Remarks: No data available. Ordered 10-4-85 and laid down 12-6-85 and 4-7-85, respectively.

Note: In 5-81 it was announced that a small tanker powered by 2 MWM TBP-6K diesels (2,060 hp) was to be acquired.

MARINE POLICE

**PATROL CRAFT**

◆ **11 PT 1 class** Bldr: Singapore SB & Eng., Jurong

| | Laid down | L | In serv. | | Laid down | L | In serv. |
|---|---|---|---|---|---|---|---|
| PT 1 | 21-7-83 | 19-12-83 | 14-1-84 | PT 7 | 11-10-83 | 30-5-84 | 19-6-84 |
| PT 2 | 25-7-83 | 6-1-84 | 17-2-84 | PT 8 | 14-10-83 | 16-6-84 | 5-7-84 |
| PT 3 | 28-7-83 | 16-1-84 | 13-3-84 | PT 9 | 21-12-83 | 4-7-84 | 1-8-84 |
| PT 4 | 1-8-83 | 23-3-84 | 6-4-84 | PT 10 | 6-1-84 | 23-7-84 | 24-8-84 |
| PT 5 | 15-9-83 | 23-4-84 | 15-5-84 | PT 11 | 19-1-84 | 10-8-84 | 5-9-84 |
| PT 6 | 30-9-83 | 14-5-84 | 1-6-84 | | | | |

**PT 2** L. & L. Van Ginderen, 7-85

**D:** 20 tons **S:** 30 kts **Dim:** 14.54 × 4.23 × 1.20 (props)
**A:** 1/7.62-mm mg **Electron Equipt:** Radar: 1/Decca . . . nav.
**M:** 2 M.A.N. D2542 MLE diesels; 2 props; 1,076 hp **Man:** 7 tot.
**Range:** 310/22 **Fuel:** 2,600 liters.

Remarks: Aluminum construction. Four sisters built for Singapore Customs (CE.5–CE.8, delivered 6-2-87) and 7 built for Brunei.

◆ **24 PX 10 class** Bldr: Sembawang SY (In serv. 1981)

PX 10–33

**PX 12** J. Bouvia, 1987

**D:** . . . **S:** 32 kts **Dim:** 11.2 × . . . × . . . **M:** 2 MTU diesels; 2 props; 770 hp

◆ **20 PC 32 class** Bldr: Vosper Thornycroft, Singapore (In serv. 1978–79)

PC 32 to PC 51

**PC 35** J. Bouvia, 1987

**SINGAPORE** *(continued)*
**MARINE POLICE** *(continued)*

**D:** 2 tons (fl) **S:** 35 kts **Dim:** 6.5 × 2.5 × 0.46 **A:** small arms
**M:** 2 Johnson outboards; 280 hp **Man:** 4 tot.

# SOLOMON ISLANDS

MERCHANT MARINE (1986): 27 ships—6,022 grt

ROYAL SOLOMON ISLANDS POLICE FORCE

### PATROL BOATS AND CRAFT

◆ **0 (+1) ASI 315 design** Bldr: Australian SB Ind. (WA), Pty., Ltd., South Coogie, Western Australia

N. . . (In serv. 6-88)

**D:** 165 tons (fl) **S:** 21 kts **Dim:** 31.50 (28.60 wl) × 8.10 × 2.12
**A:** small arms **Electron Equipt:** Radar: 1/Furuno 1011
**M:** 2 Caterpillar 3516 diesels; 2 props; 2,820 hp **Endurance:** 10 days
**Range:** 2,500/12 **Fuel:** 27.9 tons **Electric:** 116 kw
**Man:** 3 officers, 14 men

REMARKS: "Pacific Patrol Boat" design winner for Australian foreign aid program. Ordered 3-10-85. A second may be ordered later. Sisters in Papua New Guinea, Vanuatu, Fiji, Western Samoa service.

◆ **1 P-150 class** Bldr: Australian Marine Services Assoc., North Fremantle

02 SAVO (ex-*Pioneer*) (In serv. 1984)

**Savo (02)** L. & L. Van Ginderen, 7-85

**D:** . . . **S:** 26 kts **Dim:** 25.0 × . . . × . . . **A:** . . .
**Electron Equipt:** 1/. . . nav. **Range:** 520/20; 1,100/12
**M:** 2 Caterpillar 3412 V-12 diesels; 2 props, 1,500 hp

REMARKS: Glass-reinforced plastic demonstration patrol boat purchased 1984 after Pacific sales tour. Used for fisheries patrol.

◆ **1 Carpentaria class** Bldr: De Havilland Marine, Homebush Bay, Australia

01 TULAGI (In serv. 30-3-79)

**Tulagi (01)** L. & L. Van Ginderen, 1984

**D:** 27 tons (fl) **S:** 27 kts **Dim:** 16.0 × 5.0 × 1.2 **Man:** 8 tot.
**A:** 2/7.62-mm mg (I × 2) **Electron Equipt:** Radar: 1/Decca 110
**M:** 2 G.M. 12V71 TI diesels; 2 props; 1,120 hp **Range:** 700/22

REMARKS: Operated by the Government Marine Division for search-and-rescue duties.

### SERVICE CRAFT

◆ **3 27-m landing craft** Bldr: Carpenter Boatyard, Suva (ordered 1980)

LIGOMO III (L: 24-2-81) ULUSAGHE (L: 26-3-81) N . . . . . . . (L: . . .)

**D:** 195 grt/105 dwt **S:** 9 kts **Dim:** 27.0 × . . . × . . .
**M:** 2 diesels; 2 props; . . . hp

◆ **2 140-grt oceanographic research craft** Bldr: Murakima (L: 10-8-81)

SOLOMON ATU SOLOMON KARIQUA

# SOMALIA

## Somali Democratic Republic

PERSONNEL (1987): 600 total

MERCHANT MARINE (1986): 26 ships—15,719 grt

NOTE: Virtually all craft are in very poor condition.

### GUIDED-MISSILE PATROL BOATS

◆ **2 ex-Soviet Osa-II class** (transferred 12-75)

**Osa-II class**—under tow to Somalia 1976

**D:** 205 tons (240 fl) **S:** 35 kts **Dim:** 38.6 × 7.6 × 2.0
**A:** 4/SS-N-2 Styx SSM—4/30-mm AA (II × 2)
**Electron Equipt:** Radar: 2/Square Tie, 1/Drum Tilt
IFF: 2 Square Head, 1/High Pole B
**M:** 3 M504 diesels; 3 props; 15,000 hp **Range:** 500/34; 750/25 **Man:** 30 tot.

### TORPEDO BOATS

◆ **4 Soviet Mol class**

**Somali Mol class**—without torpedo tubes 1976

**Somali Mol class**—with torpedo tubes 1976

**SOMALIA** *(continued)*
**TORPEDO BOATS** *(continued)*

**D:** 170 tons (205 fl) **S:** 38 kts **Dim:** 39.0 × 7.6 × 1.7
**A:** 4/30-mm AA (II × 2)—4/533-mm TT (I × 4)
**Electron Equipt:** Radar: 1/Pot Head, 1/Drum Tilt
IFF: 1/Square Head, 1/High Pole B
**M:** 3 M504 diesels; 3 props; 15,000 hp **Range:** 450/34; 700/20 **Man:** 25 tot.

REMARKS: New units transferred in 1976. Two did not have torpedo tubes. Boats with tubes are approximately 215 tons (fl), 36 kts max.

### PATROL BOATS

◆ **1 U.S. 105-ft Commercial Cruiser class** Bldr: Swiftships, Inc., Morgan City, La. (In serv. 4-77)

**D:** 118 tons (fl) **S:** 32 kts **Dim:** 31.73 × 7.10 × 2.16
**A:** 4/30-mm Emerlec AA (II × 2) **Electron Equipt:** Radar: Decca RM 916
**M:** 2 MTU MB16V538 TB 90 diesels; 2 props; 7,000 hp
**Range:** 1,200/18 **Man:** 21 tot.

REMARKS: Former Ethiopian P-202, which defected in 1984. Aluminum construction. Armament may have been altered post-1984. Plans to acquire a second unit of this class in 1987 from the U.S. were deferred for lack of funds.

◆ **5 ex-Soviet Poluchat-I class** (transferred 1968–69)

**D:** 80 tons (90 fl) **S:** 18 kts **Dim:** 29.86 × 5.8 × 1.5
**A:** 2/14.5-mm AA (II × 1) **M:** 2 M50 diesels; 2 props; 2,400 hp
**Electron Equipt:** Radar: 1/Spin Trough
**Range:** 450/17; 900/10 **Man:** 20 tot.

### AMPHIBIOUS WARFARE SHIPS

◆ **1 ex-Soviet Polnocny-A-class landing ship** (transferred 12-76)

**D:** 770 tons (fl) **S:** 19 kts **Dim:** 73.0 × 8.6 × 1.9
**A:** 2/25-mm AA (II × 1)—2/140-mm RL (XVII × 2)
**Electron Equipt:** Radar: 1/Don-2 **Range:** 900/18; 1,500/14
**M:** 2 diesels; 2 props; 4,000 hp **Cargo:** 180 tons **Man:** 35 tot.

◆ **4 ex-Soviet T-4-class landing craft** (transferred 1968–69)

**D:** 70 tons (fl) **S:** 10 kts **Dim:** 19.0 × 4.3 × 1.0
**M:** 2 diesels; 2 props; 600 hp **Man:** 5 tot.

# SOUTH AFRICA

**Republic of South Africa**

PERSONNEL (1987): 7,483, including 695 officers, 5,228 enlisted, and 1,560 conscripts

MERCHANT MARINE (1986): 271 ships—599,509 grt
(tankers: 4 ships—38,990 grt)

NAVAL AVIATION: An Air Force detachment is available to the Navy. 18 Piaggio P166 Albatross aircraft are used for patrol, and 9 Wasp helicopters are available to be embarked on the ships. Air Force Super Frélon helicopters now can operate from the replenishment ship *Tafelberg*. With the striking of the Shackleton long-range maritime patrol aircraft in 1984 and the arms embargo preventing replacements, two C-47 transports equipped with radars have been pressed into service. Two SafAir L-100 Hercules have been chartered for search-and-rescue and pollution-control duties.

### SUBMARINES

◆ **3 French Daphné class** Bldr: Dubigeon, Nantes

| | Laid down | L | In serv. |
|---|---|---|---|
| S 97 MARIA VAN RIEBEECK | 14-3-68 | 18-3-69 | 22-6-70 |
| S 98 EMILY HOBHOUSE | 18-11-68 | 24-10-69 | 25-1-71 |
| S 99 JOHANNA VAN DER MERWE | 24-4-69 | 21-7-70 | 21-7-71 |

**Maria Van Riebeeck (S 97)** L. & L. Van Ginderen, 10-87

**D:** 869 surf./1,043 sub. tons **S:** 13/15.5 kts **Dim:** 57.75 × 6.75 × 4.5
**A:** 12/550-mm TT (8 fwd, 4 aft—no reloads)
**Electron Equipt:** Radar: DRUA-31—Sonar: DUUA-1 active, . . . passive
**M:** SEMT-Pielstick 12PA4-135 diesels, 2 450-kw generator sets, electric drive; 2 props; 2,600 hp
**Range:** 4,300/7.5 (snorkel) **Man:** 6 officers, 41 men

REMARKS: See French *Daphné* class. Were modernized with new sonar and combat data systems by Trivetts-UEC, Durban, 1985–86. Two embargoed *Agosta*-class submarines ordered from France in 1975 were sold by France to Pakistan.

NOTE: There continue to be plans to build submarines in South Africa, and plans for an IKL design were reportedly acquired from West Germany's Howaldtswerke in mid-1986.

### FRIGATES

NOTE: Plans to construct a new 1,400–1,500-ton-frigate design in South Africa have been held in abeyance, due to the embargo on arms-related imports.

◆ **1 British Whitby class**

| | Bldr | Laid down | L | In serv |
|---|---|---|---|---|
| F 145 PRESIDENT PRETORIUS | Yarrow, Scotstoun | 21-11-60 | 28-9-62 | 4-3-64 |

**President Pretorius (F 145)** L. & L. Van Ginderen, 8-85

**President Pretorius (F 145)**—note stern extension L. & L. Van Ginderen, 8-85

**D:** 2,250 tons (2,800 fl) **S:** 29 kts **Dim:** 114.00 (100.73 pp) × 12.5 × 5.2 (fl)
**A:** 2/114-mm Mk 6 DP (II × 1)—2/40-mm AA (I × 2)—6/324-mm Mk 32 ASW TT (III × 2)—1/Mk 10 Limbo mortar (III × 1)—1/Wasp helicopter (Mk 44 torpedoes)
**Electron Equipt:** Radar: 1 U.K. Type 293M, 1/Thomson-CSF Jupiter, 1/Elsag NA 9C fire-control
Sonar: 1/177, 1/174—EW: UA-8, UA-9 intercept, FH-12 D/F
**M:** 2 double-reduction GT; 2 props; 30,000 hp **Electric:** 1,140 kw
**Boilers:** 2 Babcock & Wilcox; 38.7 kg/cm$^2$, 454°C **Fuel:** 370 tons
**Range:** 2,100/26; 4,500/12 **Man:** 13 officers, 190 men

REMARKS: Modernized at Simonstown, 1971–77. Placed in "operational reserve" in 1986. Jupiter is an export version of the French Navy DRBV-23, L-band radar. Sisters *President Steyn* (F 147) to reserve 1981, with the hulk being retained for possible future reconstruction and reactivation. *President Kruger* (F 146) lost in collision with oiler *Tafelberg* 18-2-82.

### GUIDED-MISSILE PATROL BOATS

◆ **9 Israeli Reshev ("Minister") class**

| | Bldr | L | In serv. |
|---|---|---|---|
| P 1561 JAN SMUTS | Israeli SY, Haifa | 2-77 | 9-77 |
| P 1562 P.W. BOTHA | Israeli SY, Haifa | 9-77 | 12-77 |
| P 1563 FREDERICK CRESWELL | Israeli SY, Haifa | 1-78 | 6-78 |
| P 1564 JIM FOUCHE | Sundock Austral, Durban | 9-78 | 12-78 |
| P 1565 FRANZ FRASMUS | Sundock Austral, Durban | 3-79 | 7-79 |
| P 1566 OSWALD PIROW | Sundock Austral, Durban | 9-79 | 4-3-80 |
| P 1567 HENDRIK MENTZ | Sundock Austral, Durban | 26-3-82 | 11-2-83 |
| P 1568 KOBIE COETZEE | Sundock Austral, Durban | 3-9-82 | 11-2-83 |
| P 1569 MAGNUS MALAN | Sundock Austral, Durban | 27-3-86 | 4-7-86 |

**D:** 415 tons (450 fl) **S:** 32 kts **Dim:** 58.1 × 7.6 × 2.4
**A:** 6/Skorpioen SSM (I × 6)—2/76-mm OTO Melara DP (I × 2)—2/20-mm AA (I × 2)—4/12.7-mm mg (II × 2)

GUIDED-MISSILE PATROL BOATS (*continued*)

**Electron Equipt:** Radar: 1/Thomson-CSF THD-1040 Neptune, 1/Selenia RTN-10X Orion
EW: Elta MN-53 passive intercept, 4 chaff RL
**M:** 4 MTU 16V956 diesels; 4 props; 14,000 hp
**Range:** 1,500/30; 5,000/15 **Man:** 6 officers, 41 men

REMARKS: First six ordered 1974. The second six were ordered 15-11-77. Carry 500 rds 76-mm ammunition. Skorpioen is a license-built version of the Israeli Gabriel II antiship missile. All named for former Ministers of Defense. The name *Frank Chappel* has also been reported. P 1561 recommissioned 3-11-85, P 1502 on 4-7-86, both from reserve, where they had reposed since about 1982. P 1569 originally launched 25-11-82, then placed in reserve.

NOTE: The single-unit patrol boat P 1558 and the five British "Ford"-class Seaward Defense Boats were stricken 1987: *Gelderland* (P 3105, ex-*Brayford*), *Nautilus* (P 3120, ex-*Glassford*), *Rijger* (P 3125), *Haerlem* (P 3126), and *Oosterland* (P 3127); *Haerlem* had served for many years as an inshore survey craft.

**South African Reshev**—note spherical EW radomes L. & L. Van Ginderen, 8-85

**South African Reshev** S.A.N., 1984

## PATROL CRAFT

◆ **24 Namicurra class** Bldr: . . . , South Africa (In serv. 1980–81)

Y 1051–Y 1074

**Namicurra class** S.A.N., 1984

**D:** 5 tons (fl) **S:** 30 kts **Dim:** 9.0 × . . . × . . .
**A:** 1/12.7-mm mg—2/7.62-mm mg **M:** 2 diesels **Man:** 4 tot.

REMARKS: Radar-equipped, glass-reinforced, plastic-hulled harbor craft, which can be land-transported on trailers.

## MINE WARFARE SHIPS

◆ **3 British "Ton"-class minesweepers and 1 minehunter***

| | Bldr | L |
|---|---|---|
| M 1210 KIMBERLEY (ex-*Stratton*)* | Dorset Yacht | 29-7-57 |
| M 1214 WALVISBAAI (ex-*Packington*) | Harland & Wolff, Belfast | 3-7-58 |
| M 1215 EAST LONDON (ex-*Chilton*) | Cook, Welton & Gemmell | 15-7-57 |
| M 1498 WINDHOEK | Thornycroft, Woolston | 28-6-57 |

**Johannesburg (M 1207)**—now stricken L. & L. Van Ginderen, 8-85

**D:** 370 tons (425 fl) **S:** 15 kts (cruising) **Dim:** 46.33 (42.68 pp) × 8.76 × 2.5
**A:** 1/40-mm AA—1/20-mm AA
**Electron Equipt:** Radar: 1/978 (*1/1006)—Sonar: (*only): 1/193M
**M:** 2 Paxman Deltic 18A-7A; 2 props; 3,000 hp **Fuel:** 45 tons
**Range:** 2,300/13; 3,000/8 **Man:** 27 tot. (*36)

REMARKS: M 1210, converted as minehunter, with Type 193M minehunting sonar, Type 1006 radar, two PAP-104 remote-controlled minehunting devices, and mine-disposal diver facilities. All now have enclosed bridges and tripod masts. Single 80-cal 20-mm AA has replaced the twin 70-cal. mount aft.

M 1214 had been redesignated a patrol boat in 1977–78, retaining most sweep gear as P 1559; she was redesignated a minesweeper in the early 1980s. Six sisters stricken 1987: minesweepers *Johannesburg* (M 1207, ex-*Castleton*) and *Durban* (M 1499), minehunters *Port Elizabeth* (M 1212, ex-*Dumbleton*) and *Mosselbaai* (M 1213, ex-*Oakington*), and patrol boats *Pretoria* (P 1556, ex-*Dunkerton*) and *Kaapstad* (P 1557, ex-*Hazelton*).

## AUXILIARY SHIPS

◆ **1 British Hecla-class hydrographic ship**

| | Bldr | Laid down | L | In serv. |
|---|---|---|---|---|
| A 324 PROTEA | Yarrow, Scotstoun | 20-7-70 | 14-7-71 | 23-5-72 |

**Protea (A 324)**—white hull, buff stack L. & L. Van Ginderen, 4-87

**D:** 2,750 tons (fl) **S:** 15.5 kts **Dim:** 71.6 × 14.9 × 4.6
**A:** 2/20-mm AA (I × 2)
**Electron Equipt:** Radar: 1/1006
EW: see Remarks.
**M:** 4 Paxman Ventura diesels; 1 CP prop; 4,800 hp
**Fuel:** 500 tons **Range:** 12,000/11 **Man:** 123 tot.

REMARKS: Ordered 7-11-69. Hull reinforced for navigating in ice. Bow-thruster and anti-roll tanks fitted. Helicopter hangar and flight deck for one Wasp. Has been equipped for electronic surveillance duties.

◆ **0 (+1) new fleet replenishment ship** Bldr: Sandock Austral, Durban

| | Laid down | L | In serv. |
|---|---|---|---|
| A 301 DRAKENSBERG | 8-84 | 24-4-86 | 11-11-87 |

**D:** 6,000 tons light (12,500 fl) **S:** 20+ kts **Dim:** 157.0 × 20.0 × 7.5
**A:** 4/20-mm AA (I × 4)—2 Puma helicopters (S.A.A.F.)
**Electron Equipt:** Radar: 1/. . . nav.
**M:** 2 diesels; 1 CP prop; 16,320 hp **Man:** 10 officers, 86 men

**AUXILIARY SHIPS** *(continued)*

**Drakensberg (A 301)** S.A.N., 11-87

REMARKS: Ordered 22-9-84. Was to complete 6-87. Can carry 5,500 tons cargo fuel, 750 tons dry stores. Hangar can accommodate 2 Super Frélon helicopters. One dual refueling/solid transfer station on each beam and capable of over-the-stern refueling. Helicopter decks fore and aft. Three-month endurance. Equipped with bow-thruster.

◆ **1 fleet replenishment ship** Bldr: Nakskovs Skibsvaert, Denmark (L: 20-6-58)

A 243 TAFELBERG (ex-Danish tanker *Annam*)

**Tafelberg (A 243)** S.A.N., 1985

**Tafelberg (A 243)** L. & L. Van Ginderen, 7-86

**D:** approx. 27,000 tons (fl) **S:** 15 kts **Dim:** 170.6 × 21.9 × 9.2
**A:** 2/40-mm AA (I × 2)—2/20-mm AA (I × 2) **Electron Equipt:** 2/. . . nav.
**M:** 1 Burmeister & Wain diesel; 1 prop; 8,420 hp **Man:** 100 tot.

REMARKS: 12,499 grt/18,980 dwt (prior to 1984). Purchased and refitted in Durban, 1965–67. Two refueling stations and one solid-stores transfer station per side. Modernized 1983 to 16-7-84, with flight deck amidships, a hangar for two Super Frélon helicopters for search-and-rescue duties, and a hospital facility; one refueling station per side deleted. Can carry four Namicurra-class patrol craft. Temporarily laid up 1986 for lack of funds.

NOTE: Net and mooring buoy tender *Somerset* (P 285) was stricken 1987 after 45 years' service.

◆ **1 torpedo-recovery and diver-training ship** Bldr: Dorman Long, Durban

P 3148 FLEUR (In serv. 3-12-69)

**Fleur (P 3148)** S.A.N., 1984

**D:** 220 tons (257 fl) **S:** 14 kts **Dim:** 35.0 × 7.5 × 3.4
**M:** 2 Paxman-Ventura diesels; 2 props; 1,400 hp **Man:** 4 officers, 18 men

REMARKS: Ramp at stern for torpedo recovery. Divers' decompression chamber. Refitted by 1981 with fantail area enlarged, new stacks.

◆ **1 training craft** Bldr: Fred Nicholls, Durban (In serv. 1964)

NAVIGATOR

**D:** 75 tons (fl) **S:** 9.5 kts **Dim:** 19.2 × 6.0 × . . .
**M:** 2 Foden FD-6 diesels; 2 props; 200 hp

REMARKS: Wooden-hulled fishing-cutter type. Serves as tender at Naval College, Gordon's Bay.

◆ **1 seagoing tug**

| | Bldr | L | In serv. |
|---|---|---|---|
| DE MIST | Dorman Long, Durban | 21-12-78 | 12-78 |

**D:** 275 grt **S:** 12.5 kts **Dim:** 34.3 (32.3 pp) × 7.8 × 3.4
**M:** 2 Mirrlees-Blackstone ESL-8-MGR diesels; 2 props; 2,440 hp

◆ **1 large harbor tug**

| | Bldr | L | In serv. |
|---|---|---|---|
| DE NEYS | Globe Engineering, Capetown | 7-69 | 23-7-69 |

**De Neys** S.A.N., 1978

**D:** 282 tons (fl) **S:** 11.5 kts **Dim:** 28.6 (27.0 wl) × 8.1 × 3.6
**M:** 2 Lister-Blackstone ERS-8-M diesels; 2 Voith-Schneider vertical cycloidal props; 1,268 hp
**Man:** 10 tot.

REMARKS: 14-ton max. bollard pull.

◆ **1 large harbor tug** Bldr: Globe Engineering, Capetown

DE NOORDE (L: 12-61)

**D:** 170 grt **S:** 9 kts **Dim:** 34.2 × 8.2 × . . .
**M:** 2 Lister-Blackstone ERS-8-M diesels; 2 Voith-Schneider vertical cycloidal props; 1,268 hp

SOUTH AFRICA *(continued)*
AUXILIARY SHIPS *(continued)*

**De Noorde** S.A.N., 1978

◆ **1 catamaran trials craft** (In serv. 4-80)

Shirley T.

Remarks: A 10.8-m prototype for a 50-m fast combatant design concept.

**AIR SEA RESCUE BOATS**

◆ **2 Fairey Tracker class** Bldr: Groves & Gutteridge, Cowes, U.K. (In serv. 1973)

P 1554 P 1555

**D:** 31 tons (fl) **S:** 29 kts **Dim:** 19.25 × 4.98 × 1.45
**M:** 2 G.M. 12V71 diesels; 2 props; 1,120 hp **Range:** 650/20 **Man:** 11 tot.

◆ **2 German-built** Bldr: Krogerwerft, Rendsburg (In serv. 1961–62)

P 1551 P 1552

**P 1551**—now has smaller radar S.A.N., 1978

**D:** 67 tons (73 fl) **S:** 30 kts **Dim:** 28.8 (27.9 pp) × 5.0 × 1.6
**A:** 1/12.7-mm mg **Electron Equipt:** Radar: 1/. . . nav.
**M:** 2 Maybach 12-cyl. diesels; 2 props; 3,000 hp **Range:** 600/25 **Man:** 8 tot.

DEPARTMENT OF TRANSPORT

◆ **1 antarctic survey and supply ship**

| | Bldr | Laid down | L | In serv. |
|---|---|---|---|---|
| Agulhas | Mitsubishi, Shimonoseki | 14-6-77 | 30-9-77 | 31-1-78 |

**Agulhas** L. & L. Van Ginderen, 1-86

**D:** 3,035 dwt **S:** 14 kts **Dim:** 109.2 (100.0 pp) × 18.0 × 5.8
**M:** 2 Mirrlees-Blackstone K-6 Major diesels; 1 prop; 6,000 hp
**Range:** 8,200/14 **Man:** 40 crew + 92 scientists/passengers

Remarks: Manned by the South African Navy. Twin helicopter hangar. Red hull, white upperworks.

# SPAIN

**Spanish State**

Personnel (1987): 64,700 including 12,196 Naval Infantry, with 696 officers, and 11,500 enlisted; about 9,000 civilians

Merchant Marine (1986): 2,397 ships—5,422,002 grt
(tankers: 68 ships—2,350,291 grt)

Warships In Service Or Under Construction
As Of 1 January 1988

| | L | Tons | Main armament |
|---|---|---|---|
| ◆ **1 (+1) aircraft carrier** | | | |
| 1 Principe De Asturias | 1982 | 15,150 | 4/20-mm, 18–22 aircraft |
| 1 Independence | 1943 | 13,000 | 22/40-mm, 12 aircraft |
| ◆ **8 submarines** | | Tons (surfaced) | |
| 4 Agosta | 1981–84 | 1,490 | 4/550-mm TT |
| 4 Daphné | 1972–74 | 870 | 12/550-mm TT |
| ◆ **8 destroyers** | | Tons | |
| 1 Roger De Lauria | 1968 | 3,012 | 6/127-mm DP, ASW weapons |
| 5 Gearing FRAM-I | 1945 | 2,425 | 4/127-mm, 1/ASROC system |
| 2 Fletcher | 1942–44 | 2,080 | 4 or 5/127-mm, 0 or 6/76.2-mm, ASW weapons |
| ◆ **12 (+3) frigates** | | | |
| 1 (+3) Oliver Hazard Perry | 1984–89 | 2,769 | 1/76-mm, 1 Standard SAM system, 2 helicopters |
| 6 Descubierta | 1975–79 | 1,270 | 1/76-mm, 1/Sea Sparrow |
| 5 Baléares | 1970–72 | 3,015 | 1/127-mm, 1/ASROC system, 1/Standard system, ASW weapons |
| ◆ **4 corvettes** | | | |
| 4 Atrevida | 1955–56 | 977 | 1/76.2-mm DP, 3/40-mm, ASW weapons |

Naval Aviation: Five single-seat AV-8A and two two-seat TAV-8A were delivered in 1976 for service in the *Dedalo;* subsequently, two of the aircraft, named Matador in Spanish service, have been lost. Five more AV-8A were ordered for delivery in 1980–81. In 1987, 8 AV-8A and the 2 TAV-8A were in service, and 12 EAV-8B were ordered in 1986, with the first three delivered 6-10-87.

The *Arma Aerea de la Armada* also operates 11 Augusta-Bell 212 (with SS-12 missiles), 10 Bell 47G, 15 Sikorsky SH-3D/G Sea King (with AS-12 missiles), and 11 Hughes 369-HM (500M) Cayuse helicopters plus 2 Cessna Citations, 2 Piper Comanche, and 2 Piper Twin Comanche liaison aircraft. Six U.S. SH-60B Seahawk LAMPS III helicopters were ordered 1983; 12 more may be ordered later. The first of four of the Sea Kings to be provided Searchwater air/surface-search radar was redelivered 9-87.

**The first EAV-8B Harrier II** McDonnell Douglas, 8-87

The search-and-rescue service (*Servicio de Busqueda y Salvamento*) received 3 Fokker F-27 SAR aircraft in 1979 for coastal surveillance; they carry Litton APS-504V radar. Ten AS.332F Super Puma helicopters for rescue duties and 2 as VIP transports were delivered 21-1-84.

The Spanish Air Force performs a maritime surveillance role, using six Lockheed P-3A and four P-3C Orion. Twelve Casa C-212 Aerocar with APS-128 radars are used for search-and-rescue work.

WEAPONS AND SYSTEMS

Except for naval guns, which are domestically designed and manufactured, most of the weapon systems in use are of American or French make. Twenty-five U.S. Harpoon missiles were ordered 1985 for delivery 1987–90; 55 Harpoons had been delivered earlier. However, an antiaircraft/antimissile point-defense system of Spanish origin is in development. Called Meroka, it consists of two rows of six 20-mm Oerlikon guns, whose characteristics are:

Length: 120 calibers — Round weight: 320 gr. all-up
Muzzle velocity: 1,200 m/sec — Projectile weight: 102 gr.
Maximum rate of fire: 9,000 rds/min (per mount)
Maximum effective range: 2,000 m

Meroka uses a Lockheed Electronics AN/PVS-2 Sharpshooter x-band monopulse radar on the mount, with target designation via the RAN-12L/X search radar and a Selenia PDS-10 TDS console. Current models carry 720 rds on-mount; later versions will have 2,160 rds. Twenty or more systems are to be procured.

## AIRCRAFT CARRIERS

◆ **1 new construction**

| | Bldr | Laid down | L | In serv. |
|---|---|---|---|---|
| R 11 Principe De Asturias (ex-*Canarias,* ex-*Almirante Carrero Blanco*) | Bazán, el Ferrol | 8-10-79 | 22-5-82 | 2-89 |

**Principe de Asturias (R 11)** — Fermin Gallego Serra, 11-87

**D:** 16,200 tons (fl) **S:** 26.27 kts **Dim:** 195.1 (187.5 pp) × 24.4 (30.0 flight deck) × 6.7
**A:** 4/Meroka 20-mm gun systems (XII × 4)—20 aircraft (6–8 EAV-8B and 12–14 SH-60B, SH-3D/G, and AB-212)
**Electron Equipt:** Radar: 1/SPS-55, 1/SPS-52C, 1/SPN-35A air control, 4/PVS-2 f.c.
TACAN: URN-25
EW: Nettunel intercept, Mk 36 Mod. 2 SRBOC decoy RL (VI × 4)
**M:** 2 G.E. LM-2500 gas turbines; 1 prop; 46,400 hp (plus 2/800-hp retractable Pleuger auxiliary props, electric drive)
**Electric:** 7,500 kw **Range:** 6,500/20
**Man:** 774 total; 88–94 officers, 145–153 senior petty officers, 539–542 men

Remarks: Ordered 29-6-77. Design is essentially that of the final version of the U.S. Navy's Sea Control Ship concept, with a 12-degree ski-jump bow added. The flight deck is 175.3 × 29 m and is served by two elevators, one at the extreme aft end. Takeoff pattern angled to starboard. There are 3 Allison 501-K17 gas turbine-driven 2,500-kw generators. Has two pair Denny-Brown fin stabilizers. LINK 11 and LINK 14 data link and U.S. Fleet SATCOMM installed. SPS-52C is to be replaced by SPS-52D later. Has U.S. Prairie/Masker bubbler noise suppression system, SLQ-25 Nixie towed torpedo decoy. Now planned to be fully operational in 2-89. Began sea trials 11-87.

◆ **1 ex-U.S. Independence-class light aircraft carrier** — Bldr: New York SB

| | Laid down | L | In serv. |
|---|---|---|---|
| R 01 Dedalo (ex-*Cabot,* AVT 3, ex-CVL 28, ex-*Wilmington,* CL 79) | 16-3-42 | 4-4-43 | 24-7-43 |

**D:** 13,000 tons (16,416 fl) **S:** 31 kts (trials)
**Dim:** 188.35 (182.9 wl) × 21.87 (hull) 31.7 (flight deck) × 7.2 (8.1 max.)
**A:** 22/40-mm AA (IV × 1, II × 9)—4/AV-8A—4/SH-3D/G—4/AB-212
**Electron Equipt:** Radar: 1/SPS-10, 1/SPS-40A, 1/SPS-8, 1/SPS-6C, 4/Mk 34 fire-control
TACAN: SRN-15A—EW: WLR-1 intercept
**M:** 4 sets GT; 4 props; 100,000 hp
**Boilers:** 4 Babcock & Wilcox; 39.8 kg/cm$^2$, 454°C **Electric:** 2,400 kw
**Fuel:** 1,800 tons **Armor:** Partial belt: 37–127 mm **Range:** 7,200/15
**Man:** 51 officers, 1,049 men

Remarks: Ended service in the U.S. Navy as an aviation transport (AVT 3). Transferred on five-year loan on 30-8-67 and purchased in 12-73. Redesignated from PH (portahelicópteros) to PA (portaaviones) on 28-9-76, when AV-8A V/STOL fighters were added to her complement. The flight deck is 166.1 × 32.9 m (max.). Two elevators. Four Mk 63 radar gunfire-control systems and seven Mk 51 Mod. 2, optical gunfire control installed. Did not receive SPS-52B radar in place of SPS-8 height-

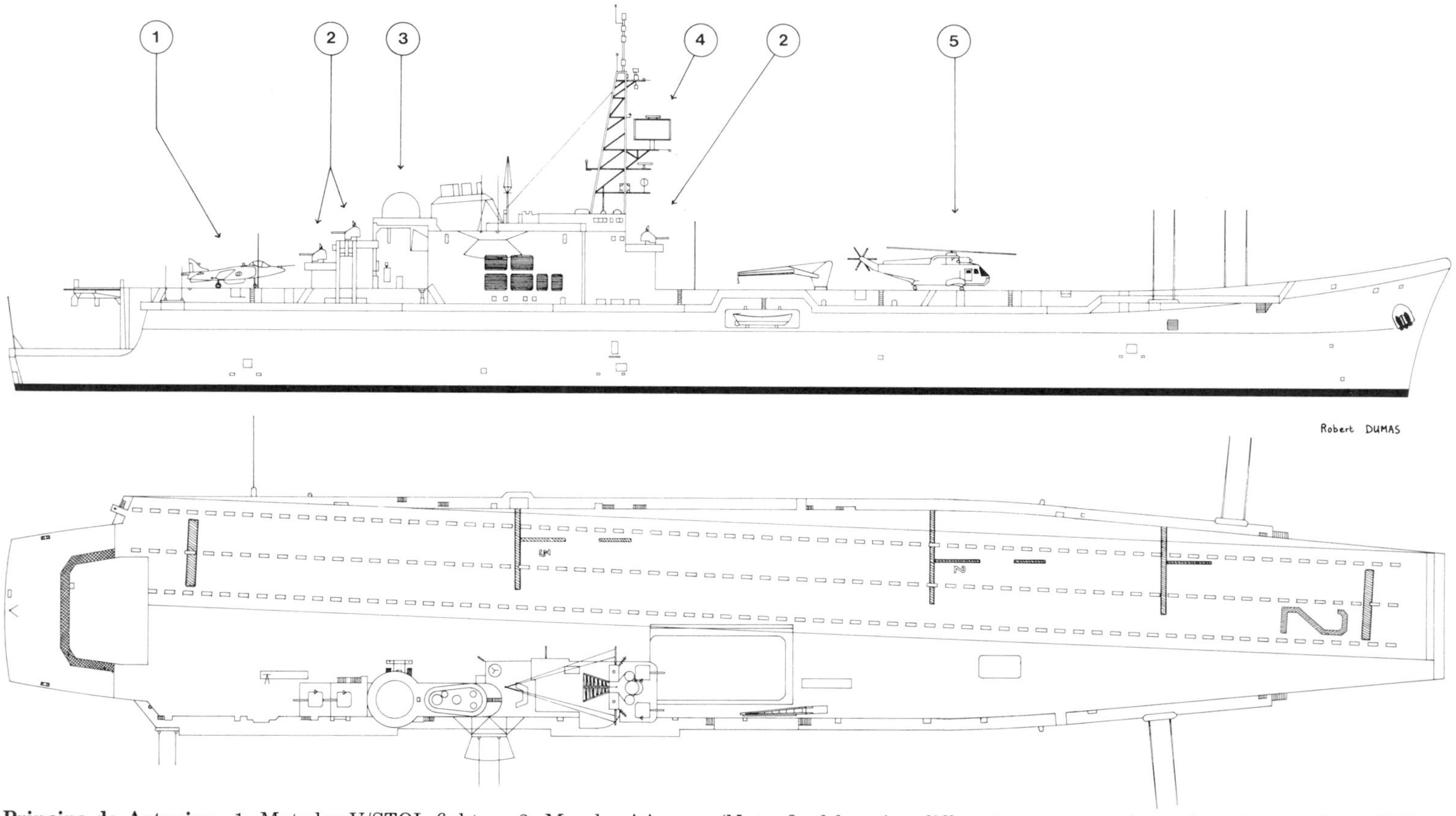


**Principe de Asturias** 1. Matador V/STOL fighter 2. Meroka AA guns (Note: final location differs: 2 mounts are located on the stern) 3. SPN-35 air-control radar 4. SPS-52 3-D radar 5. Sea King helicopter

## AIRCRAFT CARRIERS *(continued)*

finder as planned. Forward quad 40-mm AA now removed. She is supposed to be given the Meroka point-defense gun system and will probably be retained even after the completion of *Principe de Asturias.*

**Dedalo (R 01)** J.-C. Bellonne, 1987

**Dedalo (R 01)** J.-C. Bellonne, 1987

## SUBMARINES

◆ **0 (+4) "Submarino Biparto" (S 80) program** Bldr: Bazán, Cartagena

| | Laid down | L | In serv. |
|---|---|---|---|
| S . . . N . . . | . . . | . . . | 1992 |
| S . . . N . . . | . . . | . . . | . . . |
| S . . . N . . . | . . . | . . . | . . . |
| S . . . N . . . | . . . | . . . | . . . |

**D:** 2,410 tons (sub.) **S:** 12 kts surf./25 kts sub **Dim:** 76.0 × 7.8 × . . .
**A:** 4 or 6/533-mm bow TT (20 tot. F 17 Mod. 2 torpedoes and sub-Harpoon or SM 39 Exocet SSM)
**Electron Equipt:** Radar: . . .
Sonar: . . .
**M:** diesel-electric: . . . **Range:** 10,500/. . .
**Endurance:** 70 days **Fuel:** 210 tons **Man:** 35 tot.

Remarks: Intended to replace *Daphné* class. Cooperative design effort between Bazán and DCN/Dubigeon, France. Diving depth: 300 m. None yet ordered as of 10-87.

◆ **4 Agosta (S 70) class** Bldr: Bazán, Cartagena

| | Laid down | L | In serv. |
|---|---|---|---|
| S 71 Galerna | 5-9-77 | 5-12-81 | 17-1-83 |
| S 72 Sciroco | 1978 | 13-11-82 | 5-12-83 |
| S 73 Mistral | 30-5-80 | 14-11-83 | 5-6-85 |
| S 74 Tramontana | 18-12-81 | 30-11-84 | 27-1-86 |

**D:** 1,230/1,490/1,750 tons **S:** 12 kts (surf.)/20.5 kts (sub.)
**Dim:** 67.90 × 6.8 × 5.4
**A:** 4/550-mm bow TT (rapid reload—20 F 17, E 18, and L 5 torpedoes)
**Electron Equipt:** Radar: 1/DRUA-33
Sonar: DUUA-2A, DUUA-2B active, DSUV-22 passive, Elédone intercept, S 71, 72: DUUX-2A ranging—S 73, 74: DUUX-5
**M:** 2 SEMT-Pielstick 16 PA4 185 diesel generator sets, 850 kw each; 4,600-hp main engine; 1/23-kw cruising engine; 1 prop
**Fuel:** 185 tons **Range:** 17.5/1 hr. (sub.); 8,500/9 (snorkel)
**Man:** 8 officers, 53 men **Endurance:** 45 days

**Tramontana (S 74)** L. & L. Van Ginderen, 4-86

Remarks: See also *Agosta* class in section on France. As with the *Daphné* class, built with French technical assistance. Agreement signed 6-2-74; first two ordered 9-5-75, second pair 29-6-77. Can dive to 300 m. S 71 refitted 12-86 to 12-87. S 72 in collision with destroyer *Valdes,* 10-85; repaired.

◆ **4 French Daphné (S 60) class** Bldr: Bazán, Cartagena

| | Laid down | L | In serv. |
|---|---|---|---|
| S 61 Delfin | 13-8-68 | 25-3-72 | 3-5-73 |
| S 62 Tonina | 1969 | 3-10-72 | 10-7-73 |
| S 63 Marsopa | 19-3-71 | 15-3-74 | 12-4-75 |
| S 64 Narval | 1972 | 14-12-74 | 22-11-75 |

**Narval (S 64)**—with original bow sonar dome L. & L. Van Ginderen, 10-84

**Delfin (S 61)**—in refit, with new sonar dome L. & L. Van Ginderen, 10-84

**D:** 865/1,042 tons **S:** 12.5/15.5 kts **Dim:** 57.78 × 6.75 × 4.60
**A:** 12/550-mm TT (8 fwd, 4 aft)—no reloads
**Electron Equipt:** Radar: 1/DRUA-31 or -33A (with ESM)
Sonar: DUUA-2A and DUUA-1D active, DSUV-22 passive (see Remarks)
**M:** 2 SEMT-Pielstick PA1 450-kw diesel generators; 2 props; 2,000 hp
**Man:** 6 officers, 41 men

Remarks: Built with French technical assistance; agreement made on 16-7-66. Beginning with S 61, refitting at Cartagena with DUUA-2A forward (retain DUUA-1D aft), DSUV-22 passive sonar and updated torpedo fire-control system; modified units have large bow sonar dome, like French Navy *Daphnés.* S 61–63 have been completed.

## DESTROYERS

Note: There are tentative plans to construct two destroyers, possibly of the U.S. *Spruance* class.

◆ **1 Roger de Lauria class** Bldr: Bazán, el Ferrol, Cartagena

| | Laid down | L | Relaunch | In serv. |
|---|---|---|---|---|
| D 43 Marques De La Ensenada | 4-9-51 | 15-7-59 | 22-2-68 | 10-9-70 |

**DESTROYERS** *(continued)*

**Marques de la Ensenada (D 43)** L. & L. Van Ginderen, 1980

**D:** 3,012 tons (3,785 fl) **S:** 28 kts (31.5 on trials)
**Dim:** 116.68 (110.8 pp) × 12.5 × 6.5 (max.)
**A:** 6/127-mm DP (II × 3)—6/324-mm Mk 32 ASW TT (III × 2)—2/533-mm fixed Mk 25 ASW TT for Mk 37 torpedoes
**Electron Equipt:** Radar: 1/Decca RM 426, 1/SPS-10B, 1/SPS-40, 1 Mk 25, 1/Mk 35
Sonar: 1/SQS-32, 1/SQA-10 VDS—EW: WLR-1
**M:** 2 sets Rateau-Bretagne GT; 2 props; 60,000 hp **Electric:** 1,900 kw
**Boilers:** 3 three-drum; 35 kg/cm², 375°C **Fuel:** 673 tons
**Range:** 4,500/15 **Man:** 20 officers, 235 men

REMARKS: Widened and lengthened during reconstruction after original launching in order to eliminate defects found in the *Oquendo* prototype; completion consequently delayed. U.S. semiautomatic, 38-caliber guns, 1 Mk 37 and 1 Mk 56 radar gun-control system. *Oquendo* was stricken on 2-11-78. Helicopters not currently carried. May receive Meroka 20-mm AA gun system. Badly damaged by a terrorist bomb 2-10-81; repaired at considerable expense, in part by cannibalizing sister *Roger de Lauria* (D 42), which was stricken 15-1-82. Despite being plagued with continued boiler problems, is not scheduled for disposal until the 1990s.

◆ **5 ex-U.S. Gearing FRAM-I class**

| | Bldr | Laid down | L | In serv. |
|---|---|---|---|---|
| D 61 CHURRUCA (ex-*Eugene A. Greene,* DD 711) | Federal SB, Newark | 17-8-44 | 18-3-45 | 8-6-45 |
| D 62 GRAVINA (ex-*Furse,* DD 882) | Consolidated, Orange, Tex. | 23-9-44 | 9-3-45 | 10-7-45 |
| D 63 MENDEZ NUÑEZ (ex-*O'Hare,* DD 889) | Consolidated, Orange, Tex. | 27-1-45 | 22-6-45 | 29-11-45 |
| D 64 LANGARA (ex-*Leary,* DD 879) | Consolidated, Orange, Tex. | 11-8-44 | 20-1-45 | 7-5-45 |
| D 65 BLAS DE LEZO (ex-*Noa,* DD 841) | Bath Iron Works | 26-3-45 | 30-7-45 | 2-11-45 |

**Langara (D 64)** L. & L. Van Ginderen, 1-87

**Mendez Nuñez (D 63)** J.-C. Bellonne, 1987

**D:** 2,425 tons light (3,520 fl) **S:** 31 kts
**Dim:** 119.02 × 12.45 × 6.4 (sonar) 4.45 (hull)
**A:** 4/127-mm 38-cal. (II × 2)—1/ASROC Mk 116 ASW RL (VIII × 1; 17 missiles)—6/324-mm Mk 32 ASW TT (III × 2)
**Electron Equipt:** Radar: 1/SPS-10, 1/SPS-29: (D 61, D 62: SPS-40), 1/Mk 25
Sonar: 1/SQS-23—TACAN: D 65 only: SRN-15
EW: WLR-1, ULQ-6 (not in D 64)
**M:** GT; 2 props; 60,000 hp **Electric:** 1,100 kw
**Boilers:** 4 Babcock & Wilcox; 39.8 kg/cm²; 454°C
**Fuel:** 650 tons **Range:** 2,400/25; 4,800/15 **Man:** 17 officers, 257 men

REMARKS: D 61 and D 62 were loaned on 31-8-72, and D 63 to D 65 on 31-10-73. All purchased outright on 17-4-78. D 65 has both her 127-mm mounts forward and no ASROC. Mk 37 fire-control system for guns, Mk 114 ASW f.c.s. Carried Hughes 369 manned helicopter in place of original drones; all but D 65 no longer do so. Scheduled for disposal beginning 1988–89.

◆ **2 ex-U.S. Fletcher class**

| | Bldr | Laid down | L | In serv. |
|---|---|---|---|---|
| D 24 ALCALA GALIANO (ex-*Jarvis,* DD 799) | Todd, Seattle, Wash. | 7-6-43 | 14-2-44 | 3-6-44 |
| D 25 JORGE JUAN (ex-*McGowan,* DD 678) | Federal SB, Kearny, N.J. | 30-6-43 | 14-11-43 | 20-12-43 |

**D:** 2,850 tons (3,050 fl) **S:** 30–32 kts **Dim:** 114.85 × 12.03 × 5.5
**A:** 4/127-mm DP (I × 4)—6/76.2-mm AA (II × 3)—6/324-mm Mk 32 ASW TT (III × 2)—2/Mk 11 Hedgehogs—4/Mk 6 d.c. mortars (I × 4)—1/d.c. rack
**Electron Equipt:** Radar: 1/SPS-10, 1SPS-6C, 2/Mk 25, 1/Mk 35, 2/Mk 34
Sonar: SQS-29 series
EW: D 24: BLR-1
**M:** 2 sets G.E. GT; 2 props; 60,000 hp
**Electric:** 580 kw **Boilers:** 4 Babcock & Wilcox; 39.8 kg/cm², 454°C
**Fuel:** 650 tons **Range:** 1,250/32; 4,400/15 **Man:** 17 officers, 273 men

REMARKS: D 24 transferred on 3-11-60, and D 25 on 1-12-60. Have one Mk 37 gunfire-control system, one Mk 56, two Mk 63 gunfire-control systems, and Mk 5 torpedo director. These very outdated ships were scheduled to be retired by 1985, but are now being extended. Sister *Lepanto* (D 21, ex-*Capps,* DD 550) stricken 12-85, *Almirante Ferrandiz* (D 22, ex-*David W. Taylor,* DD 551) in 10-86, and *Almirante Valdes* (D 23, ex-*Converse,* DD 509) in 1987.

**GUIDED-MISSILE FRIGATES**

◆ **1 (+3 + 1) U.S. Oliver Hazard Perry class** Bldr: Bazán, El Ferrol

| | Laid down | L | In serv. |
|---|---|---|---|
| F 81 SANTA MARIA (ex-*Navarra*) | 22-5-82 | 24-11-84 | 12-10-86 |
| F 82 VICTORIA (ex-*Murcia*) | 11-83 | 23-7-86 | -88 |
| F 83 NUMANCIA (ex-*Léon*) | 8-1-86 | 29-1-87 | . . . |
| F 84 PRINCESA SOFIA (ex-*América*) | 9-87 | . . . | . . . |
| F 85 N . . . | . . . | . . . | . . . |

**D:** 2,851 tons light (3,740 fl) **S:** 30 kts max.
**Dim:** 138.80 (125.90 wl) × 13.72 × 4.52 (8.60 sonar dome)
**A:** 1/Mk 13 Mod. 4 missile launcher (8 Harpoon SSM and 32 Standard SM-1 MR SAM)—1/76-mm OTO Melara Compact DP (U.S. Mk 75)—1/20-mm Meroka Mod. 2 AA system—6/324-mm Mk 32 Mod. 5 ASW TT (III × 2)—2/SH-60B Seahawk LAMPS-III ASW helos
**Electron Equipt:** Radar: 1/Raytheon SPS-64(V), 1/SPS-49, 1/RAN-12 L/X, 1/Mk 92, 1/STIR, 1/PVS-2
Sonar: 1/Raytheon 1164B hull-mounted, SQR-19 TASS
EW: Elettronica Nettunel active/passive system, Mk 36 Super RBOC decoy RL (VI × 2)
TACAN: URN-25

**GUIDED-MISSILE FRIGATES** *(continued)*

**M:** 2 Fiat-G.E. LM-2500 gas turbines; 1 CP prop; 41,000 hp (2/350-hp electric auxiliary propulsion motors)
**Range:** 5,000/18 **Fuel:** 587 tons
**Electric:** 4,000 kw (4 × 1,000-kw Kato-Allison 114-DOOL diesel sets)
**Man:** 13 officers, 188 men

**Santa Maria (F 81)** Spanish Navy, 10-86

**Santa Maria (F 81)**—on trials—inset shows Meroka CIWS Bazán, 10-86

**Santa Maria (F 81)**—at launch Bazán, 11-84

Remarks: Although first three officially ordered on 29-6-77, little progress was made until 1981 on construction, the new carrier *Principe de Asturias* taking precedence. Fourth unit ordered mid-1986, with a fifth planned. All have the longer hull used in U.S. FFG 36–61. Similar to latest U.S. version except for close-defense AA gun system, different radar and EW suite, and lack of SATCOMM gear. Sonar essentially the same as the U.S. Navy's SQS-56. Have RAST helicopter deck-handling system to handle SH-60B LAMPS-III helicopters; F 83 and later will get SSQ-28 LAMPS-III data link. Final full-load displacement may top 3,900 tons, as in U.S. units. Have NATO LINK-11 data link equipment, Prairie-Masker bubble noise reduction system, and SLQ-25 Nixie torpedo decoys.

◆ **6 Descubierta class**

| | Bldr | Laid down | L | In serv. |
|---|---|---|---|---|
| F 31 Descubierta | Bazán, Cartagena | 16-11-74 | 8-7-75 | 18-11-78 |
| F 32 Diana | Bazán, Cartagena | 18-7-75 | 26-1-76 | 30-6-79 |
| F 33 Infanta Elena | Bazán, Cartagena | 26-1-76 | 14-9-76 | 12-4-80 |
| F 34 Infanta Cristina | Bazán, Cartagena | 14-9-76 | 19-4-77 | 24-11-80 |
| F 35 Cazadora | Bazán, el Ferrol | 14-12-77 | 17-10-78 | 20-7-81 |
| F 36 Vencedora | Bazán, el Ferrol | 1-5-78 | 27-4-79 | 27-3-82 |

**Infanta Cristina (F 34)** French Navy, 7-86

**Diana (F 32)** L. Grazioli, 3-87

**Diana (F 32)** J.-C. Bellonne, 3-87

**D:** 1,363 tons (1,575 fl) **S:** 26 kts **Dim:** 88.88 (85.8 pp) × 10.4 × 3.9
**A:** 1/Sea Sparrow SAM system (VIII × 1; 24 missiles)—1/76-mm OTO Melara—2/40-mm AA (I × 2)—1/375-mm Bofors ASW RL (II × 1)—6/324-mm Mk 32 ASW TT (III × 2)
**Electron Equipt:** Radar: 1/H.S.A. ZW-06/2, 1/H.S.A. DA-05/2, 1/H.S.A. WM-25 fire-control
Sonar: Raytheon 1160B
EW: Elettronica Beta passive system
**M:** 4 MTU-Bazán 16MA956 TB91 diesels; 2 CP props; 18,000 hp
**Electric:** 1,810 kw **Fuel:** 250 tons **Range:** 6,100/18
**Man:** 10 officers, 106 men

### GUIDED-MISSILE FRIGATES *(continued)*

REMARKS: Design evolved from the Portuguese Navy's *João Coutinho* class, built by same yard. The first four were ordered on 7-12-73, the others on 25-5-76. Intended to receive 8 Harpoon SSM (IV × 2) between bridge superstructure and Y-shaped stacks, aimed athwartships. All are scheduled to get 1/20-mm Meroka in place of upper 40-mm, and two chaff launchers. Plans call for backfitting Raytheon Type 1167 VDS. Have fin stabilization, plus U.S. Prairie-Masker bubble system to reduce radiated noise below the waterline. Can accommodate thirty troops. Carry 600 rounds 76-mm gun ammunition. Have SEWACO weapons-control system. Eight improved units with gas-turbine propulsion were to follow; they have been delayed in programming. Sisters *Centinella* (F 37) and *Serviola* (F 38) were sold to Egypt in 1982, prior to completion; another sister has been built for Morocco.

◆ **5 Baleares class** Bldr: Bazán, El Ferrol

| | Laid down | L | In serv. |
|---|---|---|---|
| F 71 BALEARES | 31-10-68 | 20-8-70 | 24-9-73 |
| F 72 ANDALUCIA | 2-7-69 | 30-3-71 | 23-5-74 |
| F 73 CATALUÑA | 20-8-70 | 3-11-71 | 16-1-75 |
| F 74 ASTURIAS | 30-3-71 | 13-5-72 | 2-12-75 |
| F 75 ESTREMADURA | 3-11-71 | 21-11-72 | 10-11-76 |

**Asturias (F 74)** J.-C. Bellonne, 1987

**Cataluña (F 73)** French Navy, 1986

**Estremadura (F 75)** L. & L. Van Ginderen, 11-87

**D:** 3,015 tons (4,177 fl) **S:** 27/28 kts
**Dim:** 133.59 (126.5 pp) × 14.33 × 4.6 (7.01 over sonar)
**A:** 4/Harpoon SSM (II × 2)—1/Mk 22 guided-missile launcher (16 Standard SM-1 MR)—1/127-mm Mk 42 DP—1/ASROC Mk 116 ASW RL (VIII × 1, plus reloads)—4/324-mm Mk 32 fixed ASW TT (I × 4)—2/fixed Mk 25 ASW TT for Mk 37 torpedoes
**Electron Equipt:** Radar: 1/Decca 1226, 1/SPS-10, 1/SPS-52A, 1/SPG-51C, 1/SPG-53B—TACAN: SRN-15A
Sonar: 1/SQS-23 (hull), 1/SQS-35V (VDS)
EW: Elsa Mk 1000 passive system—TACAN: SRN-15A
**M:** 1 set Westinghouse GT; 1 prop; 35,000 hp **Electric:** 3,000 kw
**Boilers:** 2 Combustion-Engineering; 84 kg/cm², 510°C
**Fuel:** 750 tons **Man:** 15 officers, 241 men

REMARKS: Built with American aid (agreement of 31-5-66) as U.S. DEG 7 to DEG 11. The Mk 74 missile fire-control system can use both the Mk 73 director (with SPG-51C radar) and Mk 68 director (with SPG-53B) to control two Standard missiles; the Mk 68 is also used to control the 127-mm gun. The ships have the Mk 114 digital ASW computer to control ASROC and ASW-torpedo firing. Forty-one ASW torpedoes of the Mk 44/46 and Mk 37 wire-guided types can be accommodated. The Mk 32 torpedo tubes are built into the port and starboard sides of the after superstructure and are oriented to a 45-degree angle outboard of the centerline. The two Mk 25 tubes are built into the stern, facing aft. Can accommodate 8 Harpoon SSM (IV × 2), but normally carry only four. The Meroka 20-mm AA gun system to be installed on the stern. Fifteen Harpoon missiles were ordered for these ships in 1982. The TRITAN-1 combat data system is being installed during modernizations, along with the Elsag Mk 1000 EW system, NATO LINK 11 data link, U.S. NTDS, an updated missile fire-control system with Mk 152 digital fire-control computer, and U.S. SRN-15A TACAN. F 72 began modernization in 1985, F 73 late in 1986. F 75 received some of the new equipment in a refit completed in 1983.

### CORVETTES

◆ **4 Atrevida class**

| | Bldr | Laid down | L | In serv. |
|---|---|---|---|---|
| P 61 ATREVIDA | Bazán, Cartegena | 26-6-50 | 2-12-52 | 25-4-53 |
| P 62 PRINCESA | Bazán, Cartegena | 18-3-53 | 31-3-55 | 2-10-59 |
| P 64 NAUTILUS | Bazán, Cádiz | 27-7-53 | 10-9-56 | 10-12-59 |
| P 65 VILLA DE BILBAO | Bazán, Cádiz | 18-3-53 | 19-2-58 | 2-9-60 |

**Nautilus (P 64)**—"A" now deleted L. & L. Van Ginderen, 10-84

**D:** 977 tons (1,136 fl) **S:** 16–17 kts
**Dim:** 75.5 (68.0 pp) × 10.2 × 2.64 (4.08 max.)
**A:** 1/76.2-mm U.S. Mk 26 DP—3/40-mm AA (I × 3)
**Electron Equipt:** Radar: 1/SPS-5B, 1/Decca . . .
**M:** 2 Sulzer diesels; 2 props; 3,000 hp
**Fuel:** 100 tons **Range:** 8,000/10
**Man:** 9 officers, 123 men

REMARKS: Tandem machinery arrangement. Electronic equipment and weapons modernized with U.S. aid. Can carry twenty mines. *Diana* (P 63) stricken in 1972. P 61 and P 65 were to be stricken in 1979, but all have been refitted and are now employed in patrolling between Gibraltar and the Canaries. ASW ordnance and sonar removed 1980 when redesignated PA, *Patrullero de Altura.* Have a single lead-computing director for the 40-mm AA; 76.2-mm mount has a rangefinder only. Planned for disposal by 1991. Redesignated *Patrullero* in 1986.

### PATROL BOATS

◆ **6 Lazaga class** Bldr: P 01: Lürssen, Vegesack; others: Bazán, La Carraca, Cádiz

| | L | In serv. | | L | In serv. |
|---|---|---|---|---|---|
| P 01 LAZAGA | 30-9-74 | 14-6-75 | P 04 VILLAMIL | 15-5-75 | 26-4-77 |
| P 02 ALSEDO | 8-1-75 | 28-2-77 | P 05 BONIFAZ | 15-5-75 | 11-7-77 |
| P 03 CADARSO | 8-1-75 | 10-7-76 | P 06 RECALDE | 16-10-75 | 15-12-77 |

**PATROL BOATS** *(continued)*

**Villamil (P 04)**—before redesignation L. & L. Van Ginderen, 11-85

**D:** 275 tons (397 fl) **S:** 29.7 kts **Dim:** 57.4 (54.4 pp) × 7.60 × 2.70
**A:** 1/76-mm OTO Melara DP—1/40-mm Breda-Bofors AA—2/20-mm AA (I × 2)
**Electron Equipt:** Radar: 1/Raytheon 1620/6, 1/H.S.A. M 22
**M:** 2 MTU MA-16V956 TB91 diesels; 2 props; 7,780 hp **Electric:** 405 kVA
**Fuel:** 112 tons **Range:** 2,260/27; 4,200/17 **Man:** 4 officers, 35 men

REMARKS: P 01 and P 03 were commissioned with a U.S. Mk 22, 76-mm instead of an OTO Melara 76-mm. Space reserved for addition of six 324-mm Mk 32 ASW torpedo tubes and a small, high-frequency sonar. Carry 300 rounds of 76-mm, 1,472 rounds of 40-mm, and 3,000 rounds of 20-mm. Redesignated PC = *Patrulleros Cañaneros* in 1980, and plain *Patrulleros* in 1986. P 03 conducted Meroka sea trials in 1984, with the 12-barreled 20-mm gun in place of the 76-mm mount.

◆ **6 Barcelo class** Bldrs: P 11 Lürssen; others: Bazán, La Carraca, Cádiz

| | L | In serv. | | L | In serv. |
|---|---|---|---|---|---|
| P 11 BARCELO | 6-10-75 | 26-3-76 | P 14 ORDONEZ | 10-9-76 | 7-6-77 |
| P 12 LAYA | 16-12-75 | 23-12-76 | P 15 ACEVEDO | 10-9-76 | 14-7-77 |
| P 13 JAVIER QUIROGA | 16-12-75 | 1-4-77 | P 16 CANDIDO PEREZ | 3-3-77 | 25-11-77 |

**Ordonez (P 14)**—before redesignation L. & L. Van Ginderen, 9-86

**D:** 110 tons (134 fl) **S:** 36.5 kts **Dim:** 36.2 (43.2 pp) × 5.8 × 1.75 (2.15 props)
**A:** 1/40-mm Bofors AA—1/20-mm AA—2/12.7-mm mg (I × 2)
**Electron Equipt:** Radar: 1/Raytheon 1620/6
**M:** 2 MTU 16V538 TB90 diesels; 2 props; 7,320 hp (6,120 sust.)
**Electric:** 220 kVA **Fuel:** 18 tons **Range:** 600/33.5; 1,200/16
**Man:** 3 officers, 16 men

REMARKS: Lürssen FPB 36 design. Carry 750 rounds 40-mm, 2,500 rounds 20-mm ammunition. Redesignated *Patrulleros* from *Patrulleros Cañaneros* in late 1986.

## FISHERIES PATROL BOATS

NOTE: The following units were designated PVZ—*Patrulleros de Vigilancia de Zona* in 9-80 and are operated by the Navy in behalf of the Ministry of Commerce for 200-nautical-mile economic zone patrol. All were redesignated plain *Patrulleros* in late 1986.

◆ **10 Anaga class** Bldr: Bazán, San Fernando, Cádiz

| | L | In serv. | | L | In serv. |
|---|---|---|---|---|---|
| P 21 ANAGA | 14-2-80 | 30-1-81 | P 26 MEDAS | 15-12-80 | 16-10-81 |
| P 22 TAGOMAGO | 14-2-80 | 30-1-81 | P 27 IZARO | 15-12-80 | 9-12-81 |
| P 23 MAROLA | ... | 4-6-81 | P 28 TABARACA | 15-12-80 | 30-12-81 |
| P 24 MOURO | ... | 14-7-81 | P 29 DEVA | 24-11-81 | 3-6-82 |
| P 25 GROSA | 15-12-80 | 15-9-81 | P 30 BERGANTIN | 24-11-81 | 30-7-82 |

**D:** 296 tons (350 fl) **S:** 20 kts **Dim:** 44.4 (40.0 pp) × 6.6 × 2.6
**A:** 1/76.2-mm U.S. Mk 22 DP—1/20-mm AA—2/12.7-mm mg (I × 2)
**Electron Equipt:** Radar: 1/Decca 1226 navigational **Man:** 25 tot.
**M:** 1 Bazán/MTU 16V956 diesel; 1 prop; 4,800 hp **Range:** 4,000/15

REMARKS: Ordered 22-7-78. P 21 laid down 4-79. P 30 originally numbered PVZ 210.

**Tabaraca (P 28)** B. Prézelin, 8-86

◆ **4 Conejera class** Bldr: Bazán, San Fernando, Cádiz

| | L | In serv. |
|---|---|---|
| P 31 CONEJERA (ex-LVE 1) | 9-81 | 31-12-81 |
| P 32 DRAGONERA (ex-LVE 2) | 9-81 | 31-12-81 |
| P 33 ESPALMADOR (ex-LVE 3) | 11-1-82 | 10-5-82 |
| P 34 ALCANADA (ex-LVE 4) | 10-2-82 | 10-5-82 |

**Conejera (P 31)** L. & L. Van Ginderen, 10-84

**D:** 85 tons (fl) **S:** 25 kts **Dim:** 32.15 (30.0 pp) × 5.30 × 1.42
**A:** 1/20-mm AA—1/12.7-mm mg **Electron Equipt:** Radar: 1/. . . nav.
**M:** 2 Bazán/M.A.N. V8V16/18TLS diesels; 2 props; 2,800 hp
**Range:** 1,200/15 **Man:** 12 tot.

REMARKS: Ordered 1978; first two laid down 20-12-79. Aluminum construction. A planned further six were not built.

◆ **3 U.S. Adjutant-class former minesweepers**

| | Bldr | L | In serv. |
|---|---|---|---|
| P 51 NALON (ex-M 21, ex-MSC 139) | South Coast Co., Newport Beach, Cal. | 22-11-52 | 16-2-54 |
| P 52 ULLA (ex-M 24, ex-MSC 265) | Adams Yacht, Quincy, Mass. | 28-1-56 | 24-7-58 |
| P 54 TURIA (ex-M 27, ex-MSC 130) | Hiltebrand DD, Kingston, N.Y. | 14-7-54 | 1-6-55 |

**Ulla (P 52)** L. & L. Van Ginderen, 1986

REMARKS: Redesignated 9-80; all portable minesweeping gear removed. Data as for sisters retained as minesweepers. Two others redesignated PVZ have been returned to mine-warfare duties: *Miño* (PVZ 53/M 25) and *Sil* (PVZ 55/M 29).

**FISHERIES PATROL BOATS** *(continued)*

◆ **1 small patrol boat** Bldr: Viudes SY, Barcelona

P 81 Toralla (In serv. 4-87)

**D:** 56 tons (78 fl) **S:** 20 kts **Dim:** 28.5 × 6.5 × 1.8
**A:** 1/12.7-mm mg **Electron Equipt:** Radar: 1/Decca RM 1070, 1/Decca 270
**M:** 2 Bazán-MTU 369TB93-series diesels; 2 props; 1,305 hp
**Range:** 1,000/12 **Man:** 14 tot.

Remarks: Used for fishery-protection duties.

◆ **1 former trawler** Bldr: Juliana, Gijón (In serv. 1948)

P 20 Salvora (ex-PVZ 11, ex-W 32, ex-*Virgen de la Almudena,* ex-*Mendi Eder*)

**D:** 274 tons (fl) **S:** 11 kts **Dim:** 32.58 × 6.22 × 3.77
**A:** 1/20-mm AA **M:** 1 Sulzer diesel; 1 prop; 400 hp
**Electron Equipt:** Radar: 1/Furuno . . . **Fuel:** 25 tons **Man:** 31 tot.

Remarks: Purchased 25-9-54.

**PATROL CRAFT**

◆ **23 P 101 class** Bldr: Aresa, Arenys del Mar, Barcelona (In serv. 1978–82)

P 101–123 (ex-PVC 11–19, 110–123)

**P 117**—old number L. & L. Van Ginderen, 8-86

**D:** 16.9 tons (21.7 fl) **S:** 26 kts **Dim:** 15.90 (13.7 pp) × 4.36 × 1.33
**A:** 1/12.7-mm mg **Electron Equipt:** Radar: 1/Decca 110
**M:** 2 Baudouin DNP-8 MIR diesels; 2 props; 768 hp **Electric:** 12 kVA
**Fuel:** 2.2 tons **Range:** 430/18 **Man:** 2 officers, 4–5 men

Remarks: Originally LVC 1–LVC 23. Glass-reinforced plastic construction. P 121–123 have supercharged engines producing 1,024 hp and were completed 1981–82.

◆ **1 former customs patrol craft** Bldr: . . . (In serv. . . .)

P 126 (ex-PVC 41, ex-*Roquero*)

**D:** 34 tons (fl) **S:** 14 kts **Dim:** 14.5 × 3.5 × . . .
**A:** . . . **M:** 2 G.M. diesels; 2 props; 292 hp **Man:** 9 tot.

Remarks: Transferred 1983. Wooden construction.

◆ **1 small patrol craft** Bldr: Aresa del Mar, Barcelona

P 125 (ex-PVC 31, ex-V 34) (L: 2-1-75)

**D:** 14 tons (16.4 fl) **S:** 24 kts **Dim:** 15.7 × 3.9 × 0.7
**A:** 1/12.7-mm mg **Electron Equipt:** Radar: 1/Decca 110 nav.
**M:** 2 Cummins 8TV-370-M diesels; 2 props; 740 hp
**Range:** 500/20 **Man:** 7

Remarks: Was prototype for PVI 11 design; wooden construction.

◆ **1 glass-reinforced plastic patrol craft** Bldr: Viudes, Barcelona

P 124 (ex-PVC 21, ex-V 33) (L: 24-3-77)

**D:** 20.3 tons (25 fl) **S:** 27 kts **Dim:** 16.06 × 4.30 × 0.97
**A:** 1/12.7-mm mg **Electron Equipt:** Radar: 1/Decca 110
**M:** 2 M.A.N. D-2542-MTE diesels; 2 props; 1,100 hp
**Range:** 700/18 **Man:** 9 tot.

◆ **27 P 202 class** Bldr: Rodman, Vigo (In serv. 1978–80)

P 202–210, 212–218, 220–230 (ex-PVI 11–18, 110–130)

**D:** 3 tons (4.2 fl) **S:** 18 kts **Dim:** 9.0 × 3.1 × 0.8
**Range:** 120/18 **Man:** 6 tot. **A:** 1/7.62-mm mg
**M:** 2 Volvo inboard/outboard diesels; 2 props; 240 hp

Remarks: Formerly LVI 1–20, redesignated 9-80. Ten units stationed at northern ports have Decca 060 radar. PVI = *Patrullero de Vigilancia Interior;* redesignated again 1986. PVI 19 lost early 1980s, PVI 11 stricken 1986.

**P 217**—old number L. & L. Van Ginderen, 1986

◆ **5 P 231 class** Bldr: Bazán, La Carraca, Cádiz (In serv. 1963–64)

P 231–235 (ex-PVI 21–25)

**P 234**—old number P. Voss, 5-82

**D:** 17.2 tons (25 fl) **S:** 13 kts **Dim:** 14.04 × 4.57 × 1.0
**A:** 2/7.62-mm mg (II × 1)
**M:** 2 Gray Marine 64HN9 diesels; 2 props; 450 hp **Man:** 8 tot.

Remarks: Copy of U.S. "45-foot picket boat." Formerly LPI 1–5. No radar.

◆ **3 U.S. Coast Guard 83-foot craft** Bldr: Bazán, Cádiz

P 311 (ex-PAS 11, in serv. 24-3-65) P 313 (ex-PAS 13, in serv. 13-9-65)
P 312 (ex-PAS 12, in serv. 21-4-65)

**P 311**—old number 1969

**D:** 49 tons (63 fl) **S:** 15 kts **Dim:** 25.4 (23.8 pp) × 4.9 × 2.0
**A:** 1/20-mm AA—2/7.62-mm mg—2 Mk 20 Mousetrap ASW RL (IV × 2)
**Electron Equipt:** Radar: 1/Decca . . .—Sonar: QCU or QHB
**M:** 2 diesels; 2 props; 800 hp **Man:** 15 tot.

Remarks: Wooden hull. Based on U.S.C.G. WPB design. PAS = *Patrullero de Antisubmarino.*

◆ **1 river patrol boat** Bldr: Bazán, La Carraca, Cádiz (In serv. 11-1-63)

P 201 Cabo Fradera (ex-PVI 01, ex-V 22)

**D:** 28 tons **S:** 10 kts **Dim:** 17.80 × 4.20 × 0.82 **A:** 2/mg **M:** diesel; 280 hp

Remarks: For use on the Miño River, as are the two following craft.

◆ **1 small river patrol craft** Bldr: Cartagena SY (L: 5-5-69)

P 236 (ex-PVI 31, ex-V5)

**D:** 3.1 tons (5 fl) **S:** 7.5 kts **Dim:** 8.3 × 2.7 × 0.8
**M:** . . . diesel; . . . props; . . . hp **Man:** 7 tot.

**PATROL CRAFT** *(continued)*

◆ **1 small river patrol craft** Bldr: Luarca SY (In serv. 10-8-52)

P 237 (ex-PVI 32, ex-V6)

**D:** 4.5 tons **S:** 7 kts **Dim:** 8.3 × 3.0 × 1.25 **M:** . . . **Man:** 4 tot.

**MINE WARFARE SHIPS**

◆ **0 (+12) Cazador program minehunter minesweepers** Bldr: . . .

**D:** approx. 600 tons (fl) **S:** 20 kts **Dim:** . . . × . . . × . . .
**A:** . . . **Electron Equipt:** Radar: . . .—Sonar: . . .
**M:** 2 diesels; 2 vertical cycloidal props; . . . hp **Range:** 3,000/. . .

REMARKS: "Cazador" is the program name for a proposed Spanish design; the Italian *Lerici* class is also being considered. Four will be configured as minehunters, the rest as minesweepers, to replace the present 12 U.S.-built mine countermeasures ships.

◆ **4 ex-U.S. Aggressive-class minesweepers**

| | Bldr | L | In serv. |
|---|---|---|---|
| M 41 GUADALETE (ex-PVZ 41, ex-M 41, ex-*Dynamic,* MSO 432) | Colbert Boatworks, Stockton, Cal. | 17-12-52 | 15-12-53 |
| M 42 GUADALMEDINA (ex-*Pivot,* MSO 463) | Wilmington Boatworks, Wilmington, Cal. | 9-1-54 | 12-7-54 |
| M 43 GUADALQUIVIR (ex-*Persistent,* MSO 491) | Tacoma Boat, Tacoma, Wash. | 23-4-55 | 3-2-56 |
| M 44 GUADIANA (ex-*Vigor,* MSO 473) | Burgess Boat, Manitowoc, Wisc. | 24-6-53 | 8-11-54 |

**Guadalquivir (M 43)** L. & L. Van Ginderen, 5-87

**D:** 665 tons (780 fl) **S:** 14 kts **Dim:** 52.75 × 10.70 × 3.88 (4.2 max.)
**A:** 1/20-mm AA—2/12.7-mm mg (I × 2)
**Electron Equipt:** Radar: 1/SPS-5C, 1/Decca TM 626
Sonar: SQQ-14
**M:** 4 Packard diesels; 2 CP props; 2,280 hp
**Range:** 2,000/12; 3,000/10 **Man:** 6 officers, 65 men

REMARKS: Modernized 1969–70. Loaned 1-7-71, except M 44 on 4-4-72. All purchased in 8-74. Equipped for mechanical, magnetic, and acoustic sweeping. *Guadelete* (M 41, ex-MSO 432) redesignated PVZ 41 in 9-80, redesignated M 41 late 1981. M 44, equipped as a flagship, has no 20-mm AA.

◆ **8 ex-U.S. Adjutant, MSC 268*, and Redwing†-class minesweepers**

| | Bldr | L | In serv. |
|---|---|---|---|
| M 21 JUCAR (ex-M 23, ex-MSC 220) | Bellingham SY, Bellingham, Wash. | 24-1-55 | 22-6-56 |
| M 22 EBRO (ex-M 26, ex-MSC 269)* | Bellingham SY, Bellingham, Wash. | 8-11-57 | 19-12-58 |
| M 23 DUERO (ex-M 28, ex-*Spoonbill,* MSC 202)† | Tampa Marine, Tampa, Fla. | 3-8-54 | 16-6-59 |
| M 24 TAJO (ex-M 30, ex-MSC 287)* | Tampa Marine, Tampa, Fla. | 1-5-56 | 9-7-59 |
| M 25 GENIL (ex-M 31, ex-MSC 279)* | Tacoma Boat, Tacoma, Wash. | 8-8-58 | 11-9-59 |
| M 26 ODIEL (ex-M 32, ex-MSC 288)* | Tampa, Marine, Tampa, Fla. | 3-9-58 | 9-10-59 |
| M 27 SIL (ex-PVZ 55, ex-M 29, ex-*Redwing,* MSC 200)† | Tampa Marine, Tampa, Fla. | 29-4-54 | 16-6-59 |
| M 28 MIÑO (ex-PVZ 53, ex-M 25, ex-MSC 266) | Adams Yacht, Quincy, Mass. | 14-4-56 | 25-10-56 |

**Duero (M 23)**—Redwing class L. & L. Van Ginderen, 7-86

**Jucar (M 21)**—Adjutant class Spanish Navy, 1984

**Odiel (M 26)**—MSC 268 class Spanish Navy, 1984

**D:** 355 tons (384 fl) **S:** 12 kts **Dim:** 43.0 (41.5 pp) × 7.95 × 2.55
**A:** 2/20-mm AA (II × 1) **M:** 2 G.M. 8-268A diesels; 2 props; 1,200 hp
**Electron Equipt:** Radar: 1/Decca TM 626 or RM 914—Sonar: UQS-1D
**Fuel:** 40 tons **Range:** 2,500/10 **Man:** 2 officers, 35 men

REMARKS: Originally a group of twelve, transferred under MAP: two in 1954, one in 1955, three in 1956, one in 1958, two in 1959, and three in 1960. *Llobregat* (M 22, ex-MSC 143) was stricken on 4-7-79 after a fire. M 21 and M 23 have a mast well astern of the stack; the others have only a small davit beside the stack. MSC 268-class ships were 43.9 m overall by 8.51 max. beam and had 4 G.M. 6-71 diesels; 2 props; 900 hp. Five sisters were redesignated PVZ in 9-80 and had portable sweep gear removed; two were redesignated minesweepers in 1984: M 27 and M 28.

**AMPHIBIOUS WARFARE SHIPS**

◆ **2 ex-U.S. Paul Revere-class transports** Bldr: New York SB Corp., Camden, N.J.

| | L | In serv. |
|---|---|---|
| L 21 CASTILLA (ex-*Paul Revere,* LPA 248, ex-*Diamond Mariner*) | 13-2-54 | 3-9-58 |
| L 22 ARAGÓN (ex-*Francis Marion,* LPA 249, ex-*Prairie Mariner*) | 11-4-53 | 6-7-61 |

**AMPHIBIOUS WARFARE SHIPS** *(continued)*

**Castilla (L 21)** Spanish Navy, 1984

**D:** 10,704 light (16,838 fl) **S:** 22.5 kts
**Dim:** 171.80 (160.94 pp) × 23.24 × 7.32 **A:** 8/76.2-mm Mk 33 DP (II × 4)
**Electron Equipt:** Radar: 1/LN-66, 1/SPS-10, 1/SPS-12 (L 22: SPS-40)
EW: WLR-1, ULQ-6
**M:** 1 set G.E. GT; 1 prop; 22,000 hp **Electric:** 2,400 kw
**Boilers:** 2 Combustion-Eng. (L 22: Foster-Wheeler); 42.3 kg/cm$^2$, 467°C
**Range:** 10,000/22; 17,000/14
**Man:** 28 officers, 424 men + troops: 96 officers, 1,561 men

REMARKS: Mariner-class C4-S-1A merchant ships converted to troop transports. L 21 by Todd Shipyard, San Diego, and L 22 by Bethlehem Steel, Baltimore. Can carry seven LCM(6) and sixteen LCVP. Four Mk 63 gunfire-control systems removed between 1977 and 1978, but intercept and jamming equipment retained. In recent years had served the Naval Reserve Force. Were sold to Spain: L 21 on 17-1-80, and L 22 on 11-7-80. TACAN now removed from L 21.

◆ **1 ex-U.S. Cabildo-class landing ship, dock** Bldr: Philadelphia Navy Yard

| | Laid down | L | In serv. |
|---|---|---|---|
| L 31 GALICIA (ex-*San Marcos,* LSD 25) | 1-9-44 | 10-1-45 | 15-4-45 |

**Galicia (L 31)**—with old number French Navy, 3-78

**D:** 4,790 tons (9,375 fl) **S:** 15 kts **Dim:** 139.52 × 21.9 × 5.49 max.
**A:** 12/40-mm AA (IV × 2, II × 2)
**Electron Equipt:** Radar: 1/Decca TM 626, 1/SPS-10
**M:** 2 sets GT; 2 props; 7,000 hp **Boilers:** 2 two-drum, 17.6 kg/cm$^2$
**Range:** 8,000/15 **Man:** 18 officers, 283 men + 137 troops

REMARKS: Loaned 1-7-71 and sold outright 8-74. Well deck is 103.0 × 13.3 m. Platform for three helicopters. Can carry eighteen LCMs with one LCVP nested in each in the well. Cargo capacity: 1,347 tons. Four Mk 51, Mod. 2, lead-computing GFCS (no radar).

◆ **3 ex-U.S. Terrebonne Parish-class tank landing ships** Bldrs: L 11 and L 13: Bath Iron Works; L 12: Christy Corp., Sturgeon Bay, Wisc.

| | L | In serv. |
|---|---|---|
| L 11 VELASCO (ex-*Terrebonne Parish,* LST 1156) | 9-8-52 | 21-11-52 |
| L 12 MARTIN ALVAREZ (ex-*Wexford County,* LST 1168) | . . . | 15-6-54 |
| L 13 CONDE DEL VENADITO (ex-*Tom Green County,* LST 1159) | 10-7-53 | 12-9-53 |

**Martin Alvarez (L 12)** L. & L. Van Ginderen, 4-87

**Conde del Venadito (L 13)** L. Grazioli, 3-87

**D:** 2,590 tons (6,225 fl) **S:** 13 kts **Dim:** 117.35 × 16.7 × 3.7
**A:** 6/76.2-mm Mk 33 AA (II × 3)
**Electron Equipt:** Radar: 1/Decca TM 626, 1/Decca 1229, 2/Mk 34
**M:** 4 G.M. 16-278A diesels; 2 props; 6,000 hp **Electric:** 600 kw
**Fuel:** 1,060 tons **Range:** 6,000/9 **Man:** 115 tot.

REMARKS: L 11 and L 12 transferred on 29-10-71, and L 13 on 5-1-72. All purchased outright on 1-11-76. Accommodations for 395 troops. Cargo: 2,200 tons. Carry two LCVP to starboard and one LCPL to port. Two Mk 63 radar GFCS.

◆ **3 "Pelicano"-class utility landing craft** Bldr: Bazán, La Carraca, Cádiz

| | L | In serv. | | L | In serv. |
|---|---|---|---|---|---|
| A 06 (ex-LCT 6) | 10-11-65 | 6-12-66 | A 08 (ex-LCT 8) | 10-11-66 | 30-12-66 |
| A 07 (ex-LCT 7) | 10-2-66 | 30-12-66 | | | |

**A 06**—old number L. & L. Van Ginderen, 8-85

**D:** 279 tons (710 fl) **S:** 9.5 kts **Dim:** 59.00 (52.9 pp) × 11.90 × 1.86
**A:** 1/20-mm AA—2/12.7-mm mg (I × 2)
**Electron Equipt:** Radar: 1/Decca 404
**M:** 2 Bazán-M.A.N. R6V16/18 TLS diesels; 2 props; 1,060 hp
**Electric:** 25 kw **Range:** 1,500/9.5 **Man:** 17 crew + 35 troops

REMARKS: In service in 12-66. Cargo: 300 tons. Formerly BDK 6–8. Design based on the French EDIC type. Redesignated as logistics support craft in 1986.

NOTE: Utility landing craft LCT 4 and LCT 5 stricken 9-5-85.

◆ **2 ex-U.S. LCU 1466-class utility landing craft** Bldr: Kingston Dry Dock Const. Co., Kingston, N.Y. (L: 4-55)

L 71 (ex-LCU 11, ex-LCU 1471) L 72 (ex-LCU 12, ex-LCU 1491)

**D:** 180 tons (347 fl) **S:** 8 kts **Dim:** 35.05 × 10.36 × 1.6
**A:** 2/20-mm AA **M:** 3 Gray Marine 64YTL diesels; 3 props; 675 hp
**Man:** 6 crew + 8 troops

REMARKS: Transferred in 6-72. Cargo: 160 tons. Formerly LCU 1, 2.

◆ **1 experimental air-cushion vehicle landing craft** Bldr: Chaconsa, Murcia

VCA 36 (In serv. 1985)

## AMPHIBIOUS WARFARE SHIPS *(continued)*

**D:** 22 tons (40 fl) **S:** 60 kts (50 cruise) **Dim:** 25.17 × 11.04 × 9.50 (high)
**A:** none **Electron Equipt:** . . .
**M:** 2 Avco-Lycoming gas turbines; 2 airscrew props, 5,000 hp
**Range:** 150/50 **Electric:** 30 kVA **Man:** 3 crew + 70 troops

REMARKS: Ordered 12-82 for the Marine Infantry, who also operate the 400-kg, 6-m, 40-kt trials hovercraft *Furtivo*. VCA 36 will be able to transport 14 tons of cargo or 3 Land Rover trucks, plus 70 troops. There are two centrifugal lift fans. The Navy also operates Chaconsa's VCA-3 hovercraft, a 4-ton test craft completed 1978. Cargo compartment: 18.65 × 2.60 m. Powered by two 220-hp Dodge gasoline engines.

◆ **8 (+ . . .) new-construction landing craft** Bldr: Bazán, San Fernando

LCM 601 (In serv. 28-12-84) LCM 603–608 (In serv. 1985–86)
LCM 602 (In serv. 1-2-85)

REMARKS: No data available.

◆ **6 U.S. LCM(8)-class landing craft** Bldr: Oxnard Boat, Cal. (In serv. 1975)

L 81–86 (ex-LCM 81–86)

**L 81**—with old number 1975

**D:** 115 tons (fl) **S:** 10 kts **Dim:** 22.7 × 6.55 × 1.83 (aft)
**M:** 4 G.M. 6-71 diesels; 2 props; 600 hp **Man:** 5 tot.

REMARKS: Transferred 7-75 to 9-75. Formerly E 81–86.

◆ **6 ex-U.S. LCM(6)-class landing craft** Bldr: Lukens Steel, Pa.

LCM 61 through LCM 66

**D:** 24 tons (57 fl) **S:** 10.2 kts **Dim:** 17.07 × 4.37 × 1.52
**M:** 2 Gray Marine 64HN9 diesels; 2 props; 330 hp

REMARKS: Transferred on 23-12-74. Cargo: 30 tons

◆ **7 ex-U.S. LCM(3)-class landing craft**

**D:** 20 tons (50 fl) **S:** 10.2 kts **Dim:** 15.24 × 4.37 × 1.17
**M:** 2 Gray Marine 64HN9 diesels; 2 props; 330 hp

REMARKS: Transferred in 12-57. Cargo: 25 tons.

◆ **4 LCVP Mk 7 personnel landing craft** Bldr: Ast. y Talleres Ferrolanos S.A. (In serv. 1987)

**D:** 11.77 tons (fl) **S:** . . . **Dim:** . . . × . . . × . . . **M:** . . .

REMARKS: First two delivered 2-87, third in 3-87.

NOTE: The surviving 11 (of 16 delivered) U.S. LCP(L)-type landing craft have been redesignated as service craft, Y572–584.

◆ **49 ex-U.S. LCVP**

**D:** 13 tons (fl) **S:** 5 kts **Dim:** 11.0 × 3.2 × 1.1 (aft)
**M:** 1 Gray Marine 64HN9 diesel; 1 prop; 225 hp

NOTE: Above totals reflect landing craft on hand before the transfer of LPA 248 and LPA 249, which retained their nine LCM(6) and eleven LCVP each. Most LCP(L) and LCVP are aboard larger ships.

## AUXILIARY SHIPS

◆ **0 (+1) SWATH prototype** Bldr: Bazán, . . .

| | Laid down | L | In serv. |
|---|---|---|---|
| . . . N . . . | 1985 | . . . | . . . |

**D:** . . . **S:** . . . **Dim:** 50.0 × 20.0 × 5.0 **A:** . . . **M:** . . . ; 2 props; . . . hp

REMARKS: SWATH = Small Waterplane Twin Hull, a type of catamaran. Program announced for experimental prototype, financed half by Bazán and half by the Commission on Scientific Research of the Ministry of Education.

◆ **0 (+1) antarctic oceanographic ship** Bldr: . . .

**D:** 2,600 tons (light) **S:** 15 kts **Dim:** 67.00 (pp) × 14.00 × 4.80
**M:** 3,600-bhp diesel generator plant, electric drive; 1 prop; 2,700 hp (bow- and stern-thrusters)

REMARKS: Icebreaker bow for antarctic duties. Helicopter deck, but no hangar. Endurance of 100 days. Diver-support to 200 m. Total 330 m² laboratory space. To be paid for by Min. Foreign Affairs; operated by Navy—if built. Still in planning 1987.

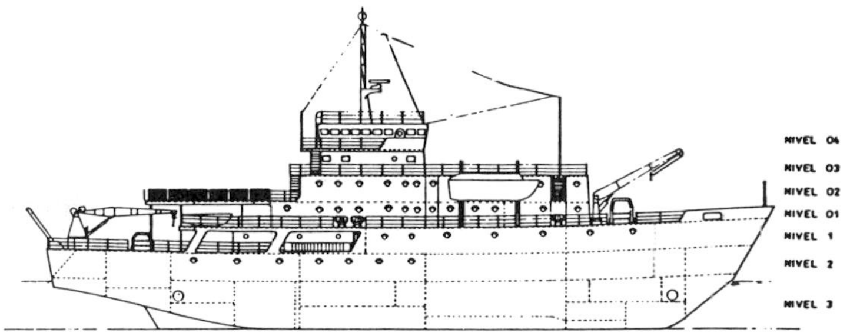


**Proposed oceanographic ship** Bazán, 1985

◆ **4 Castor-class survey ships** Bldr: Bazán, La Carraca, Cádiz

| | L | In serv. | | L | In serv. |
|---|---|---|---|---|---|
| A 21 CASTOR | 5-11-64 | 1-12-66 | A 23 ANTARES | 5-3-73 | 21-11-74 |
| A 22 POLLUX | 5-11-64 | 15-12-66 | A 24 RIGEL | 5-3-73 | 21-11-74 |

**Castor (A 21)** H. Ehlers, 10-86

**D:** 354.5 tons (383.4 fl) **S:** 11.5 kts **Dim:** 38.36 (33.8 pp) × 7.60 × 3.10
**Electron Equipt:** Radar: 1/Raytheon 1620
**M:** 1 Echevarria-B & W Alpha 408-26VO diesel; 1 prop; 800 hp
**Fuel:** 22.5 tons **Range:** 3,000/11.5 **Man:** 38 tot.

REMARKS: Produced in pairs, the later units having full main-deck bulwarks. A 21 and A 22 have one Sulzer diesel, one prop, and 720 hp. Have Raydist navigation system, Omega receivers, three echo-sounders, and a Hewlett-Packard 2100A computer. Redesignated A 21–24 from AH 21–24 in 1986.

◆ **2 Malaspina-class hydrographic ships** Bldr: Bazán, La Carraca, Cádiz

| | L | In serv. | | L | In serv. |
|---|---|---|---|---|---|
| A 31 MALASPINA | 14-8-73 | 21-2-75 | A 32 TOFIÑO | 22-12-73 | 23-4-75 |

**Tofiño (A 32)** L. & L. Van Ginderen, 7-87

**D:** 820 tons (1,090 fl) **S:** 15 kts **Dim:** 57.7 (51.4 pp) × 11.7 × 3.64
**A:** 2/20-mm AA **Electron Equipt:** Radar: 1/Raytheon 1620
**M:** 2 San Carlos-MWM TbRHS-345-6I diesels; 2 CP props; 2,700 hp
**Electric:** 780 kVA **Range:** 3,140/14.5; 4,000/12 **Man:** 63 tot.

**AUXILIARY SHIPS** *(continued)*

Remarks: Have Magnavox satellite navigation system, Omega, Raydist, three echo-sounders, side-scanning mapping sonar Mk 8, and a Hewlett-Packard 2100AC computer. Formerly AH 31, 32, redesignated 1986.

◆ **1 supply ship, ex-merchant refrigerated cargo ship** Bldr: Eriksbergs M/V AB, Göteborg, Sweden (In serv. 5-53)

A 01 Contramaestre Casado (ex-*Thanasis K.*, ex-*Fortuna Reefer*, ex-*Bonzo*, ex-*Bajamar*, ex-*Leeward Islands*)

**Contramaestre Casado (A 01)**—old number French Navy, 3-84

**D:** approx. 5,300 tons (fl) **S:** 16 kts **Dim:** 104.20 (96.12 pp) × 14.36 × 6.11
**A:** none **Electron Equipt:** Radar: 1/Decca 626, 1/Decca TM 1226
**M:** 1 Eriksberg 7-cyl. heavy-oil diesel; 1 prop; 3,600 hp
**Range:** 18,600/16 **Fuel:** 727 tons **Electric:** 660 kw **Man:** 72 tot.

Remarks: 2,272 grt/2,743 dwt refrigerated cargo ship acquired to supply the Canary Islands, commissioned 15-12-82. Four cargo holds. Two 5-ton derricks. Helicopter platform at stern.

◆ **0 (+1) planned new-construction oiler** Bldr: Bazán, . . .

A 21 N . . .

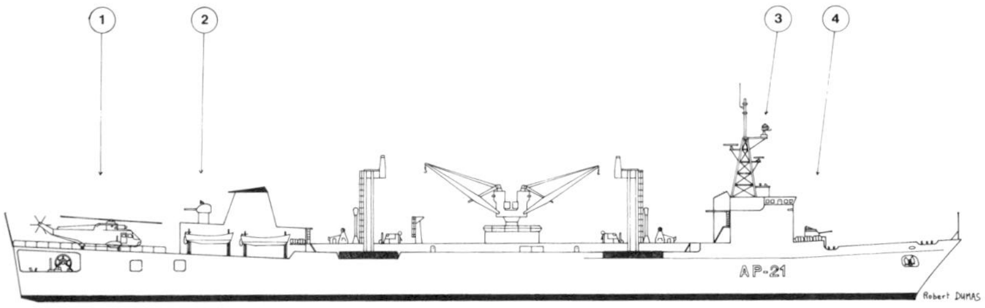


**A 21 design concept** R. Dumas, 1986
1. Sea King helicopter 2. Meroka 12-barreled 20-mm AA system 3. Combined air/surf.-search radar 4. 40-mm AA

**D:** 13,500 tons (fl) **S:** 20 kts **Dim:** 145.0 × 20.0 × 8.0
**A:** 1/40-mm AA—1/20-mm Meroka AA **Electron Equipt:** . . .
**M:** 1 or 2 Bazán SEMT-Pielstick high-speed diesels; . . . prop; . . . hp
**Range:** 4,000/20 **Man:** 15 officers, 85 men

Remarks: A Bazán (not naval) project to replace *Teide*. Would carry 7,000 tons cargo fuel, provisions, ammunition, spares, etc. to service a carrier and a 3- to 5-frigate task force. Flight deck for one Sea King aft. Two replenishment stations per side, plus astern refueling. Not yet ordered.

◆ **1 oiler** Bldr: Bazán, Cartagena

| | Laid down | L | In serv. |
|---|---|---|---|
| A 11 Teide | 11-11-54 | 20-6-55 | 20-10-56 |

**Teide (A 11)**

**D:** 2,750 tons (8,030 fl) **S:** 13.5 kts **Dim:** 117.5 × 14.85 × 7.73
**A:** none **Electron Equipt:** Radar: 1/Decca TM 626
**M:** 2 diesels; 1 prop; 3,360 hp **Man:** 98 tot.

Remarks: Fitted for underway refueling, one station each side; can transfer 300 tons/hr. Formerly AP 01, BP 11. Cargo: 5,350 $m^3$. Normally on charter to state-owned CEPSA oil company for Spain–Canaries service.

◆ **1 netlayer**

| | Bldr | L | In serv. |
|---|---|---|---|
| A 13 Cyclope (ex-AC 01, ex-CR 1, ex-G 6) | Penhoët-Loire, Gran-Querilly | 29-9-54 | 29-7-55 |

**Cyclope (A 13)**

**D:** 770 tons (831 fl) **S:** 12 kts **Dim:** 50.45 (44.5 pp) × 10.37 × 3.20
**A:** 1/40-mm AA—4/20-mm AA (I × 4)
**Electron Equipt:** Radar: 1/Decca TM 626
**M:** diesel-electric propulsion, 2 SEMT-Pielstick PA 1-series diesels, 2/600 generators; 2 prop; 1,600 hp
**Range:** 5,200/12 **Electric:** 120 kw **Man:** 40 tot.

Remarks: Same characteristics as the French *Scarabée*. Transferred in 1955 under the U.S. Military Aid Program. Named 1982. Refitted 1984; stricken 1987.

◆ **1 submarine rescue, salvage ship, and diving tender** Bldr: Bazán, La Carraca, Cádiz (In serv. 8-8-64)

A 12 Poseidón (ex-AS 01, ex-BS 1, ex-RA 6)

**Poseidón (A 12)**—old number L. & L. Van Ginderen, 1-85

**D:** 951 tons (1,107 fl) **S:** 15 kts **Dim:** 55.90 (49.80 pp) × 10.00 × 4.80
**A:** 4/20-mm AA (II × 2) **Electron Equipt:** Radar: 1/Decca TM 626
**M:** 2 Sulzer diesels; 1 CP prop; 3,200 hp **Range:** 4,640/14 **Man:** 60 tot.

Remarks: Near sister to AR 45. Can support a frogman group and has a 300-meter-depth rescue bell. Equipped for fire-fighting, towing, and has salvage pumps.

◆ **2 former commercial oilfield support tugs** Bldr: Astilleros Atlantico, Santander (In serv. 1978)

A 51 Mahón (ex-*Circos*) A 52 Las Palmas (ex-*Somiedo*)

**D:** . . . **S:** 14 kts **Dim:** 41.0 × 11.6 × 5.5
**A:** 2/12.7-mm mg (I × 2) **Electron Equipt:** Radar: 2/Decca . . .
**M:** 2 AESA-Sulzer 16 ASV 25/30 diesels; 2 props; 7,744 hp
**Range:** . . . **Man:** . . .

Remarks: 700 dwt. Purchased from Compañía Hispano Americana de Offshore SA and commissioned 30-7-81. Redesignated from AR 51 and 52 in 1986.

**AUXILIARY SHIPS** *(continued)*

**Las Palmas (A 52)** P. Voss, 5-82

◆ **2 Cádiz-class ocean tugs** Bldr: Bazán, La Carraca, Cádiz

| | L | In serv. |
|---|---|---|
| A 42 CADIZ (ex-AR 42, ex-AR 44, ex-R 4) | 20-7-62 | 25-3-64 |
| A 43 FERROL (ex-AR 43, ex-AR 45, ex-R 5) | 14-9-62 | 11-4-64 |

**Ferrol (A 43)**—old number P. Voss, 5-82

**D:** 951 tons (1,069 fl) **S:** 15 kts **Dim:** 55.9 (49.8 pp) × 10.0 × 4.0
**A:** 4/20-mm AA (II × 2) **Electron Equipt:** Radar: 1/Decca TM 626
**M:** 2 Sulzer diesels; 1 CP prop; 3,200 hp **Range:** 4,640/14 **Man:** 49 tot.

REMARKS: Improved version of AR 41 design, similar to A 12. Can carry and lay twenty-four mines.

◆ **1 seagoing tug** Bldr: Bazán, Cartagena (In serv. 9-7-55)

A 41 CARTAGENA (ex-AR 41, ex-*Valen*)

**Cartagena (A 41)**—old number L. & L. Van Ginderen, 10-84

**D:** 757 tons (1,039 fl) **S:** 15 kts **Dim:** 56.1 × 10.1 × 3.9
**A:** 2/20-mm AA (I × 2)—up to 24 mines **Electron Equipt:** 2/Decca RM . . .
**M:** 2 Bazán-Sulzer diesels; 1 CP prop; 3,200 hp
**Range:** 5,500/15 **Man:** 49 tot.

◆ **1 royal yacht**

| | Bldr | L | In serv. |
|---|---|---|---|
| A 91 AZOR (ex-A 11, ex-W 01) | Bazán, el Ferrol | 9-6-49 | 21-7-49 |

**Azor (A 91)** L. & L. Van Ginderen, 1-81

**D:** 442 tons (486 fl) **S:** 13.3 kts **Dim:** 46.65 × 7.70 × 3.81
**Electron Equipt:** Radar: 1/Decca TM 626 **M:** 2 diesels; 2 props; 1,200 hp
**Range:** 4,000/13 **Man:** 47 tot.

◆ **1 sail-training ship** Bldr: Ast. Echevarrieta, Cádiz

| | Laid down | L | In serv. |
|---|---|---|---|
| A 71 JUAN SEBASTIAN DE ELCANO | 24-11-25 | 5-3-27 | 17-8-28 |

**Juan Sebastian de Elcano (A 71)** C. Martinelli, 1-86

**D:** 3,420 tons (3,754 fl) **S:** 10 kts **Dim:** 94.11 × 13.6 × 6.95
**Electron Equipt:** Radar: 2/Decca TM 626 **M:** 1 Sulzer diesel; 1 prop; 1,500 hp
**Fuel:** 230 tons **Range:** 13,000/8 **Man:** 224 men, 80 cadets

REMARKS: Four-masted schooner, 2,467-$m^2$ sail area. Carries two 37-mm saluting cannon. Renumbered from A 01 in 1986, but number is not borne. Also in use is the 10-m, two-masted *Galatea* (in serv. 1941), purchased 1970.

## SERVICE CRAFT

NOTE: The diverse descriptive pendant numbers formerly assigned these units were consolidated in 1986 into NATO-like "A" and "Y" numbers.

◆ **5 navigational training tenders** (In serv. 1982)

A 81 GUARDIAMARINA BARRUTIA
A 82 GUARDIAMARINA SALAS
A 83 GUARDIAMARINA GODINEZ
A 84 GUARDIAMARINA RULL
A 85 GUARDIAMARINA CHEREGUINI

**D:** 90 tons (fl) **S:** 12.5 kts **Dim:** 21.89 × 5.10 × 1.52
**A:** none **Electron Equipt:** Radar: 1/Halcon 948
**M:** 2 MTU diesels; 2 props; 800 hp **Range:** 1,000/. . .
**Man:** . . . crew + 1 instructor and 12–21 cadets

REMARKS: A 81 in service 14-9-82; A 84, 85 delivered 6-84. Tenders to the Naval School. Have Magnavox NAVSAT receiver, Decca 21 Navigator. Formerly numbered YE 01–05 and AI 01–05.

SERVICE CRAFT *(continued)*

**Guardiamarina Salas (A 82)**—old number   Spanish Navy, 1984

◆ **1 sail-training schooner** (In serv. 1-4-81)

A 21 AROSA

◆ **1 yard oiler**   Bldr: Bazán, San Fernando (In serv. 1980)

Y 231 (ex-YPF 21, ex-PP 6) (In serv. 1980)

**D:** 523 grt **S:** 10.8 kts **Dim:** 34.0 × 7.0 × 3.0
**M:** 1 diesel; 1 prop; 600 hp **Cargo:** 300 tons

◆ **1 yard oiler**   Bldr: Bazán, San Fernando (In serv. 1980)

Y 232 (ex-YPF 31, ex-PP 23)

**D:** 830 grt **S:** 10.7 kts **Dim:** 42.8 × 8.4 × 3.1
**M:** 1 diesel; 1 prop; 600 hp **Cargo:** . . . tons

◆ **3 YPF 3-class yard oilers**   Bldr: Bazán Cartagena (In serv. 1956–60)

Y 233 (ex-YPF-51, ex-YPF 3, ex-PP 3)   Y 235 (ex-YPF 53, ex-YPF 5, ex-PP 5)
Y 234 (ex-YPF 52, ex-YPF 4, ex-PP 4)

**D:** 510 grt **S:** 10 kts **Dim:** 37.0 × 6.8 × 3.0 **M:** 1 diesel; 1 prop; . . . hp

◆ **1 diesel-fuel lighter**   Bldr: Bazán, Cartagena (In serv. 1981)

Y 254 (ex-YPG 41)

**D:** 214 grt **S:** 10.7 kts **Dim:** 24.0 × 5.5 × 2.2
**M:** 1/M.A.N. diesel; 1 prop; 400 hp **Cargo:** 100 tons

◆ **1 diesel-fuel lighter**   Bldr: Bazán, Cádiz (In serv. 1980)

Y 255 (ex-YPG 51)

**D:** 520 grt **S:** . . . **Dim:** 34.0 × 7.0 × 2.9
**M:** 1 diesel; prop; . . . hp **Cargo:** . . .

◆ **3 YPG 21-class diesel-fuel lighters**   Bldr: Bazán, Cádiz

Y 252 (ex-YPG 21, in serv. 1963)   Y 253 (ex-YPG 23, in serv. 1965)
Y 237 (ex-YPG 22, in serv. 1965)

**D:** 337 grt **S:** 10.7 kts **Dim:** 34.3 × 6.2 × 2.3
**M:** 1 diesel; 1 prop; 220 hp **Cargo:** 100 tons

◆ **2 YPG 01 class**   Bldr: Bazán, El Ferrol

Y 251 (ex-YPG 11, ex-YPG 01) (In serv. 1956)
Y 236 (ex-YPG 13, ex-YPG 03) (In serv. 1959)

**D:** 200 grt **S:** 10 kts **Dim:** 34.0 × 6.0 × 2.7
**M:** 1 diesel; 1 prop; . . . hp **Cargo:** 193 tons

REMARKS: Formerly numbered in the PB series. Sister YPG 02 stricken 1982.

◆ **1 large water tanker**   Bldr: Bazán, San Fernando (In serv. 16-10-81)

A 66 CONDESTABLE ZARAGOZA (ex-AA 41, ex-AA 32, ex-A 32)

**Condestable Zaragoza (A 66)**—old number   Spanish Navy, 1984

**D:** 895 tons (fl) **S:** 10.8 kts **Dim:** 48.8 (42.85 pp) × 8.40 × 3.35
**M:** 1 diesel; 1 prop; 700 hp **Cargo:** 600 tons

◆ **1 large water tanker**   Bldr: Bazán, San Fernando (In serv. 1981)

A 65 MARINERO JARANA (ex-AA 31, ex-A 31)

**D:** 535 tons (fl) **S:** 10.8 kts **Dim:** 34.0 × 7.0 × 3.03
**M:** 1 diesel; 1 prop; 600 hp **Cargo:** 300 tons

◆ **3 A-7-class large water tankers**   Bldr: Bazán, La Carraca (all in serv. 6-62)

A 62 MAQUINISTA MACIÁS (ex-AA 21, ex-A 9; L: 25-10-58)
A 63 TORPEDISTA HERNANDEZ (ex-AA 22, ex-A 10; L: 10-10-58)
A 64 FOGONERA BAÑOBRE (ex-AA 23, ex-A 11; L: 5-3-62)

**Torpedista Hernandez (A 63)**—old number   Spanish Navy, 1984

**D:** 610 tons (fl) (ex-A-7, A-8: 706 fl) **S:** 9 kts **Dim:** 44.8 × 7.6 × 3.0
**M:** 1 diesel; 1 prop; 700 hp **Range:** 1,000/9 **Man:** 16 tot.

REMARKS: Cargo: 300 tons. Named 1982.

◆ **1 large water tanker**   Bldr: Bazán, La Carraca (In serv. 1-4-51)

A 61 CONTREMAESTRE CASTELLO (ex-AA 06, ex-A 6)

**D:** 1,860 tons (fl) **S:** 8 kts **Dim:** 64.05 × 9.60 × 4.80 **M:** diesel

NOTE: Water tankers AA 17 and AA 02 stricken 14-7-82 and 2-8-82, respectively.

◆ **3 small water tankers**   Bldr: Bazán, Cádiz (In serv. 1965)

Y 271 (ex-YA 01, ex-AB 1)   Y 273 (ex-YA 03, ex-AB 3)
Y 272 (ex-YA 02, ex-AB 2)

**D:** 337 grt **S:** 10.7 kts **Dim:** 34.3 × 6.2 × 2.5
**M:** 1 diesel; 1 prop; 220 hp **Cargo:** 100 tons

◆ **2 fuel oil barges** (In serv. . . .)

Y 201 (ex-YPFN 11)   Y 202 (ex-YPFN 31)

◆ **1 diesel fuel barge** (In serv. . . .)

Y 211 (ex-YPGN 01)

◆ **1 gate craft** (In serv. 1959–60)

Y 611 (ex-YBPN 01, ex-YPB 01)

**D:** 140 tons (fl) **Dim:** 22.3 × 8.7 × 0.8 **M:** non-self-propelled

REMARKS: Sisters YPB 02, 03 discarded.

◆ **4 netlaying barges** (In serv. 1959–60)

Y 361 (ex-YDS 01)   Y 363 (ex-YDS 04)
Y 362 (ex-YDS 02)   Y 364 (ex-YDS 05)

**D:** 140 tons **Dim:** 22.3 × 8.7 × 0.8 **M:** non-self-propelled

REMARKS: Sister YDS 03 stricken 1984. Originally PR 1, 2, 4, 5

◆ **1 harbor-defense support tug** (In serv. 1960)

Y 364 (ex-YDS 15)

**D:** . . . **S:** . . . **Dim:** 28.0 × 8.5 × 0.7 **M:** 1 diesel; 1 prop; . . . hp

REMARKS: Handle the former YPB-series gate craft and former YDS-series netlaying barges. Sisters YDS 13, 14 stricken 1984, YDS 11, 12, 21, 22 by 1986.

◆ **2 large torpedo retrievers**   Bldr: Bazán, . . . (In serv. 1961–63)

Y 372 (ex-YTM 13)   Y 373 (ex-YTM 14)

**D:** 178 tons (190 fl) **S:** 7 kts **Dim:** 30.9 × 6.6 × 1.4
**A:** 50 mines **M:** 1 diesel; . . . hp

**SERVICE CRAFT** *(continued)*

◆ **1 small torpedo retriever** Bldr: Bazán, . . . (In serv. 1963)

Y 374 (ex-YTM 21)

**D:** 98 tons **S:** 7 kts **Dim:** 33.4 × 6.2 × 1.3
**A:** 79 mines **M:** diesels; . . . hp

◆ **2 large diving tenders** Bldr: Bazán, Cartagena

Y 562 Nereida (ex-YBZ 11, in serv: . . .)
Y 563 Proserpina (ex-YBZ 12, in serv. 13-4-81)

**D:** 103.5 tons (fl) **S:** 9 kts **Dim:** 21.5 × 5.9 × . . .
**M:** 1 diesel; 1 prop; 200 hp

◆ **1 small diving tender** Bldr: . . . (In serv. 9-9-82)

Y 579 (ex-YBZ 61)

**D:** 8 tons **S:** 12 kts **Dim:** 11.0 × 4.0 × 0.8 **M:** diesels; waterjets

◆ **2 small diving tenders** Bldr: Ferrolanos, La Grana

Y . . . (ex-YBZ 83, in serv. 30-6-86) Y . . . (ex-YBZ 84, in serv. 11-6-86)

Remarks: No data available.

◆ **1 small diving tender** (In serv. 15-6-83)

Y 580 (ex-YBZ 71)

**D:** 13.7 tons **S:** 7 kts **Dim:** 10.9 × 3.8 × 0.8 **M:** 1 diesel; 70 hp

◆ **1 non-self-propelled diving platform**

Y 565 (ex-YBZN 31)

◆ **2 coastal tugs** Bldr: Bazán, El Ferrol

Y 116 (ex-YRR 21, ex-YRR 71) (In serv. 10-4-81)
Y 117 (ex-YRR 22, ex-YRR 72) (In serv. 1-6-81)

**D:** 422 tons (fl) **S:** 12.4 kts **Dim:** 28.0 × 8.0 × 3.8
**M:** 1 diesel; 1 prop; 1,500 hp

◆ **3 YRR 53-class coastal tugs** Bldr: Bazán, Cartagena (In serv. 1967)

Y 113 (ex-YRR 14, ex-YRR 53, ex-RR 53) Y 115 (ex-YRR 16, ex-YRR 56, ex-RR 56)
Y 114 (ex-YRR 15, ex-YRR 54, ex-RR 54)

**D:** 227 tons (320 fl) **S:** 12 kts **Dim:** 27.8 × 7.0 × 2.6
**M:** 1 diesel; 1 prop; 1,400 hp **Man:** 13 tot.

◆ **2 YRR 50-class coastal tugs** Bldr: Bazán, Cartagena (In serv. 1963)

Y 111 (ex-YRR 11, ex-YRR 31, ex-RR 50) Y 112 (ex-YRR 13, ex-YRR 33, ex-RR 52)

**D:** 205 tons (300 fl) **S:** 10 kts **Dim:** 27.8 × 7.0 × 2.5
**M:** 1 diesel; 1 prop; 800 hp **Man:** 13 tot.

◆ **2 large harbor tugs** Bldr: Bazán, Cartagena (In serv. 1981)

Y 141 (ex-YRP 11) Y 142 (ex-YRP 12)

**D:** 229 tons (fl) **S:** 11 kts **Dim:** 28.0 × 7.5 × 3.4 **M:** 1 diesel; 1 prop; 950 hp

◆ **1 large harbor tug** Bldr: S. España d. C.N. Cádiz (In serv. 1965)

Y 146 (ex-YRP 61)

**D:** 173 tons (fl) **S:** 10 kts **Dim:** 23.3 × 6.0 × 2.9 **M:** 1 diesel; 825 hp

Remarks: Entered naval service 27-10-83.

◆ **1 medium harbor tug** (In serv. 27-12-61)

Y 143 (ex-YRP 41, ex-RP 40)

**D:** 150 tons (fl) **S:** 9 kts **Dim:** 21.3 × 5.9 × . . . **M:** 1 diesel; 1 prop; 600 hp

Remarks: In service in 12-61. Former U.S. Army tug.

◆ **1 small harbor tug** Bldr: Bazán, San Fernando

Y 147 (In serv. 4-87)

**D:** 87 tons (fl) **S:** . . . **Dim:** 16.5 × . . . × . . . **M:** . . .

Remarks: Ordered 18-12-85; launched 3-87.

◆ **11 YRP 01-class small harbor tugs** (In serv. 1965–67)

Y 131–141 (ex-YRP 01–09, 011, 012)

**D:** 65 tons (fl) **S:** . . . **Dim:** 13.5 × 4.7 × . . . **M:** 1 diesel; 1 prop; 200 hp

Remarks: Sister YRP 010 stricken 1984.

◆ **3 submarine-support push tugs**

Y 171 (ex-YRS 01, in serv. 3-11-82) Y 173 (ex-YRS 03, in serv. 6-85)
Y 172 (ex-YRS 02, in serv. 5-85)

**D:** 10.5 tons (fl) (Y 172, 173: 9.8 tons) **S:** 11 kts
**Dim:** 8.3 (Y 172, 173: 9.5) × . . . × . . .
**M:** 2 diesels; 2 waterjets; 440 hp

◆ **1 suction dredge** Bldr: IHC, the Netherlands

Y 441 (ex-YDR 11, in serv. 2-12-81)

**D:** 150 tons (fl) **S:** . . . **Dim:** 25.2 × 5.8 × 1.0 **M:** 1 diesel; 530 hp

◆ **5 personnel launches** Bldr: Rodman, Vigo (In serv. 1980–81)

Y 531–535 (ex-QF 01–05)

**Y 535** L. & L. Van Ginderen, 10-86

**D:** 3 tons (4.2 fl) **S:** 18 kts **Dim:** 9.0 × 3.1 × 0.8
**M:** 2 Volvo-Penta inboard/outboard diesels; 2 props; 240 hp
**Range:** 120/18

Remarks: GRP construction. Similar to patrol craft P202–230.

◆ **5 miscellaneous personnel launches**

Y 538 (ex-QF 31, ex-V 31) Y 539 (ex-QF 32, ex-V 32)
Y 537 (ex-LVC 79, ex-*Cynosure*) Y 540 (ex-. . .)
Y 536 (ex-. . .)

Remarks: Former small patrol craft and yachts. Y 536 is 21.1 tons, 12.8 × 3.5 m and can make 12 kts.

◆ **13 U.S. LCP(L)-class former personnel landing craft** (In serv. 1943–44)

Y 572–Y 584

**D:** 10.2 tons (fl) **S:** 19 kts **Dim:** 10.91 × 3.42 × 1.07
**M:** 1 G.M. 8V71N diesel; 1 prop; 350 hp

Remarks: Transferred 10-58 and in 1971. Wooden construction. Redesignated as service craft in 1986.

◆ **18 miscellaneous personnel launches**

Y 501–Y 518

Remarks: Six different designs, from 2.9 to 17.5 tons (fl). Four ordered 11-6-86 from Ferrolanos, La Grana, as YQP 16–19.

◆ **1 barracks barge** Bldr: Pullman Std. Car Co., Chicago, Ill.

Y 601 (ex-YFCN 01, ex-LSM 329, 331, or 343) (In serv. 1944)

**D:** 1,095 tons (fl) **Dim:** 62.03 (59.89 wl) × 10.52 × 2.54

Remarks: Former medium landing ship, transferred 5-60. Hulked and employed as an accommodations ship.

◆ **1 large floating crane** (In serv. 1929)

Y 381 Sanson (ex-YGR 11)

**D:** 589 tons (fl) **Dim:** 31.2 × 16.5 × 3.2 **Capacity:** 100 tons

◆ **3 miscellaneous floating cranes**

Y 382 (ex-YGR 21, in serv. 1954) Y 384 (ex-YGR 23, in serv. 1954)
Y 383 (ex-YGR 22, in serv. 1954)

**D:** 470–490 tons (fl) **Dim:** 22.5 × 14.0 × 3.0 **Capacity:** 30 tons

◆ **2 miscellaneous floating cranes**

Y 385 (ex-YGR 31, in serv. 1954) Y 386 (ex-YGR 33, in serv. 1953)

**D:** 272 tons **Dim:** 19.0 × 11.7 × 2.4 **Capacity:** 15 tons

◆ **37 miscellaneous barges**

Y 301–305, 307–323, 331, 332, 341–346, 351–354, 365, 411, 412

Remarks: Formerly barges, fuel barges, water barges, pontoons, etc. with YGC, YGG, YGP, YGT-series pendant numbers. Y 365 is a pontoon barge ordered 30-12-85 and launched 25-9-86 at the Cartagena Naval Dockyard.

CUSTOMS SERVICE
*(Servicio Especial de Vigilancia Fiscal)*

Note: All carry "Aduanes" (customs) on hull sides.

SPAIN *(continued)*

## CUSTOMS PATROL CRAFT

◆ **7 waterjet-powered** Bldr: Rodman, Vigo (In serv. 1986)

**D:** 13 tons (15 fl) **S:** 55 kts **Dim:** 14.00 (11.55 pp) × 3.80 × 0.70
**A:** small arms **Electron Equipt:** Radar: 1/. . . nav.
**M:** 2 MWM Deutz TBD-234-V12 diesels; 2 Riva Calzoni IRC 41.DL waterjets; 2,000 hp
**Range:** 300/. . . **Man:** 3–4 tot.

Remarks: GRP construction. A 9-m prototype was also built.

◆ **1 wooden, 32-meter class** Bldr: Chantiers Navals de l'Estérel, Cannes

Aguila (In serv. 1974)

**Aguila** L. & L. Van Ginderen, 1981

**D:** 80 tons (fl) **S:** 30 kts **Dim:** 32.0 × 5.8 × 1.6
**A:** 1/20-mm AA **Electron Equipt:** Radar: 1/Decca 926
**M:** 2 MTU 820Db diesels; 2,750 hp **Man:** 16 tot.

◆ **4 Aguilucho class** Bldr: J. Roberto Rodriguez, Vigo

Aguilucho (In serv. 1974) Gavilan-I (In serv. 1976) Gavilan-II (In serv. 1976) Gavilan-III (In serv. 8-7-82)

**Aguilucho** L. & L. Van Ginderen, 5-86

**D:** 45 tons (fl) **S:** 30 kts **Dim:** 26.1 × 5.1 × 1.3
**A:** 1/20-mm AA **M:** 2 MTU 820Db diesels; 2 props; 2,750 hp
**Range:** 750/30 **Man:** 14 tot.

Remarks: *Aguilucho* is 26.1 m o.a., Gavilan-III is 32.0 m.

◆ **3 Albatros class** Bldr: CMN, Cherbourg (In serv. 1968)

Albatros-I Albatros-II Albatros-III

**D:** 82 tons (fl) **S:** 28 kts **Dim:** 31.8 × 4.7 × 1.7
**A:** 1/20-mm AA **M:** 2 MTU 820Db diesels; 2 props; 2,750 hp **Man:** 15 tot.

◆ **5 22-meter patrol craft**

Alca Gerifalte Halcon-II Milano Nebli-II

**S:** 17 kts (*Alca:* 10, *Gerifalte:* 12, *Halcon-II:* 32 kts)

◆ **1 16.5-meter patrol craft:** Colimbo **S:** 20 kts

◆ **13 LVR-class patrol craft:** LVR 1 to LVR 13

**Dim:** 11.4 × . . . × . . . **S:** 14 kts

# SRI LANKA

**Republic of Sri Lanka**

Personnel (1987): 4,805 men, including 328 officers; plus 540 tot. Volunteer Naval Force, including 18 officers; 49 naval reservists, including 7 officers

Merchant Marine (1986): 91 ships—622,226 grt (tankers: 10 ships—139,870 grt)

Naval Aviation: One Beech Super King Air was acquired 1986 by the Air Force for maritime surveillance.

## PATROL BOATS

◆ **. . . class** Bldr: China

Remarks: Four (or five?) patrol boats were ordered 1-85 for delivery late 1985. Class not reported; may be additional units of the Shanghai-II class (see below).

◆ **2 (+3) large patrol boats** Bldr: Colombo DY

| | Laid down | L | In serv. |
|---|---|---|---|
| P 601 Jayesagara | 5-82 | 26-5-83 | 9-12-83 |
| P 602 Sagarawardene | 7-82 | 20-11-83 | 4-6-84 |
| P 603 N . . . | . . . | . . . | . . . |
| P 604 N . . . | . . . | . . . | . . . |
| P 605 N . . . | . . . | . . . | . . . |

**D:** 330 tons (fl) **S:** 15 kts **Dim:** 39.80 × 7.00 × 2.20
**A:** 2/25-mm AA (II × 1) **M:** 2 M.A.N. 8L 20/27 diesels; 2 props; 2,040 hp
**Electric:** 220 kw **Man:** 40 tot. **Range:** 3,000/11

Remarks: First two ordered 31-12-81; three more authorized 8-84. Intended as "offshore patrol boats." P 603–605 do not appear to have commenced construction.

◆ **6 Chinese Shanghai-II class**

P 3140 Suraya P 3141 Weeraya P 3144 Balawitha P 3145 Jagatha P 3146 Rakshaka P 3147 Ranakami

**Weeraya (P 3141)**—as rearmed J. Bouvia, 1987

**D:** 122.5 tons (135 fl) **S:** 28.5 kts **Dim:** 38.78 × 5.41 × 1.55
**A:** 2/37-mm AA (II × 1)—2/25-mm AA (II × 1)—4/14.5-mm mg (II × 2)
**Electron Equipt:** 1/Decca TM 1226
**M:** 2 M50F-4 1,200-hp diesels; 2 12D6, 910-hp diesels; 4 props; 4,220 hp
**Range:** 750/16.5 **Electric:** 39 kw **Endurance:** 7 days **Man:** 36 tot.

Remarks: First five transferred in February 1972 and in 1975; *Jagatha* and *Pakshaka* transferred 1980, commissioning 30-11-80. Sister *Daksaya* stricken 1983. Originally armed with 4/37-mm AA (II × 2) and 4/25-mm AA (II × 2) and equipped with Pot Head radars. P 3141 refitted and rearmed 1985.

## PATROL CRAFT

◆ **. . . (+ . . .) S. Korean-built** Bldr: Samsung Ind.

**D:** . . . **S:** . . . **Dim:** 23.0 × . . . × . . . **A:** . . .
**Electron Equipt:** Radar: . . . **M:** 2 MTU diesels; 2 props; . . . hp

**SRI LANKA** *(continued)*
**PATROL CRAFT** *(continued)*

REMARKS: A "repeat order" for craft of this type was placed in 10-86. No further data available.

◆ **11 Cougar Cat 900 patrol craft** Bldr: Cougar Marine, Netley, U.K. (in serv. 1984–85)

**Cougar Cat 900 prototype**—production version has the gun forward
Cougar Marine

**D:** 4.5 tons (fl) **S:** 40–42 kts **Dim:** 10.40 × 2.89 × 0.78 (0.48 at speed)
**A:** 1/20-mm AA or several mg **Range:** 150/32 **Man:** 3–8 tot.
**M:** 2 Volvo Penta AQAD41 diesels; 2 Type 290P outdrives; 400 hp

REMARKS: First unit, purchased 1984 for evaluation in operations from mother ships, was 9.20 m o.a. Glass-reinforced plastic construction. Ten more ordered 1-85 and delivered by 10-85.

◆ **6 (+8) Dvora class** Bldr: Israeli Aircraft Ind., Bir Shiva (In serv. 1985)

**D:** 47 tons (fl) **S:** 36 kts **Dim:** 21.62 × 5.49 × 0.94 (1.82 props)
**A:** 2/20-mm AA (I × 2)—2/12.7-mm mg (I × 2)
**Electron Equip:** Radar: 1/Decca 926 **Range:** 700/32 **Electric:** 30 kw
**M:** 2 MTU 12V331 TC81 diesels; 2 props; 2,720 hp **Man:** 8–10 tot.

REMARKS: Ordered late 1984. Aluminum construction. Eight more, of "Super Dvora" version, ordered 10-86.

◆ **5 P 445 class** Bldr: Colombo DY

| | L | In serv. | | L | In serv. |
|---|---|---|---|---|---|
| P 445 | . . . | 20-9-82 | P 448 | 27-8-82 | 1982 |
| P 446 | . . . | 17-9-82 | P 449 | 20-9-82 | 1982 |
| P 447 | 15-6-82 | 1982 | | | |

**D:** 40 tons (44 fl) **S:** 22 kts **Dim:** 20.0 (18.3 pp) × 5.1 × 1.3
**A:** 2/12.7-mm mg (I × 2) **Electron Equipt:** Radar: 1/Decca . . .
**M:** 2 DDA-G.M. 12V71 TI diesels; 2 props; 1,300 hp
**Fuel:** 10 tons **Range:** 1,600/14 **Man:** 10 tot.

REMARKS: Improved version of the *Pradeepa* class. Steel construction. Provision for mounting 1/20-mm AA. More may be built.

◆ **4 P 201 class** Bldr: Colombo DY (In serv. 1981–82)

P 201 P 202 P 203 P 205

**D:** 15 tons (22 fl) **S:** 20 kts **Dim:** 13.73 × 3.63 × 0.90
**A:** 1/12.7-mm mg **Range:** 450/14 **Man:** 1 officer, 5 men
**M:** 2 G.M. 8V71 TI diesels; 2 props; 800 hp **Fuel:** 2.5 tons **Electric:** 1 kw

REMARKS: Also employed for customs inspection.

◆ **6 Pradeepa class** Bldr: Colombo DY (In serv. 1980–81)

P 431 PRADEEPA P 432 P 433 P 434 P 435 P 436

**D:** 40 tons (44 fl) **S:** 19 kts **Dim:** 19.5 × 4.9 × 1.1 **A:** 2/20-mm AA (I × 2)
**M:** 2 G.M. 8V71 TI diesels; 2 props; 800 hp **Range:** 1,200/14 **Man:** 10 tot.

◆ **5 Belikawa class** Bldr: Cheverton, Cowes, U.K.

P 421 BELIKAWA P 423 KORAWAKKA P 425 TARAWA
P 422 DIYAKAWA P 424 SERUWA

**D:** 22 tons (fl) **S:** 23.6 kts **Dim:** 17.0 × 4.5 × 1.2
**A:** 3/7.62-mm mg **M:** 2 G.M. 8V71 TI diesels; 2 props; 800 hp
**Range:** 790/18, 1,000/12.2 **Man:** 7 tot.

REMARKS: In service between 4-77 and 10-77. GRP construction. Originally intended for customs duties but used as patrol craft. The names may have been deleted.

### COMMAND MOTHER SHIPS

◆ **3 former "Deckship" container carriers** Bldr: Chung Wah SB & Eng. Co., Ltd., Hong Kong (L: 1976–77; in serv. 9-8-84)

P 714 ABHEETHA (ex-*Carinia*) P 715 EDITHARA (ex-*Francisca*)
P 716 WICKRAMA (ex-*Delicia*)

**D:** approx. 2,700 tons **S:** 11 kts
**Dim:** 76.66 (71.17 pp) × 17.07 × 3.81 (normal)
**A:** . . . **Electron Equipment:** Radar: 1/. . . nav.
**M:** 2 Deutz SBA 12M528 diesels; 2 CP props; 3,000 hp
**Range:** 5,000/11 **Electric:** 315 kw **Fuel:** 202 tons

REMARKS: Former 1,550-grt/4,318-dwt container carriers with no below-decks cargo capacity and a 30-ton traveling crane. Had a stern ramp to weather deck for vehicle cargo. Purchased 6-84 for use as mother ships for small patrol craft.

◆ **3 former general-cargo ships** Bldr: DeWeal SY, Zaltbommel, IJssel SY, Gorinchem; and de Biesbosch, Dordrecht, the Netherlands (L: 1959)

A 24 MAHWELI (ex-. . .) A 25 LANKA (ex-. . .) A 26 KANTHI (ex-. . .)

**D:** . . . **S:** 13.75 kts **Dim:** 99.45 × 15.65 × 6.84
**A:** . . . **Electron Equipt:** Radar: . . .
**M:** 1 Werkspoor diesel; 1 prop; 3,600 hp **Electric:** 450 kw (3 × 150 kw)
**Range:** 14,600/. . . **Man:** 37 tot. **Fuel:** 448 tons

REMARKS: Former M/V *Kota Ria, ex-Tjitaram* (purchased 6-10-84); *Kota Rukun,* ex-*Mercury Cove,* ex-*Tijmanuc* (purchased 17-9-84); and one other, of 3,276–3,314 grt/4,360 dwt. Intended to act as mother ships for small patrol craft. Typed "Surveillance Command Tenders," vice "Surveillance Command Ships" for trio above. Placed in service 19-10-84.

### SERVICE CRAFT

◆ **2 utility landing craft** Bldr: Vosper PTY, Singapore (In serv. 1-86)

A 537 A 538

**D:** 200 tons (fl) **S:** 8 kts **Dim:** 30.00 × 8.00 × 1.50
**A:** 1/20-mm AA **Electron Equipt:** 1/. . . nav.
**M:** 2 Caterpillar 3408 TA diesels; 2 props; 762 hp
**Range:** 1,800/8 **Man:** 2 officers, 10 men

◆ **2 catamaran personnel transports** Bldr: International Catamarans, Hobart, Tasmania (In serv. 1983)

A 540 (ex-*Offshore Pioneer*) A 541 (ex-*Offshore Pride*)

**A 540 during conversion** 1986

**D:** 153.2 tons (fl) **S:** 32 kts **Dim:** 30.00 × 11.20 × 2.34
**A:** 1/20-mm AA **Electron Equipt:** Radar: 1/. . . nav.
**M:** 2 MTU diesels; 2 props; . . . hp

REMARKS: 169 grt. Cargo: 60 tons. Acquired 1-86 and converted by Sing Koon Seng SY, Singapore, when they were lengthened 5 m and had additional superstructure added. Originally built as oilfield supply boats.

◆ **1 coastal tanker:** MAHEWELI

◆ **1 fuel lighter:** MADERA OYA

NOTE: Training for the Sri Lankan Navy is carried out aboard the commercial cargo ship LANKA KANTHI, operated by the Sri Lanka Shipping Corporation. The lighthouse and navigational tender A 501 was stricken 1986.

# SUDAN

## Democratic Republic of the Sudan

PERSONNEL (1987): 650 men

MERCHANT MARINE (1986): 23 ships—96,134 grt

AVIATION: Two CASA Aviocar C-212-200 were ordered 6-84 for Maritime Patrol duties.

NOTE: Due to operating conditions and the withdrawal of traditional sources of aid, the material condition of the units of the Sudanese fleet is rapidly declining. A number of patrol craft are no longer operable, and all auxiliaries have been discarded.

**SUDAN** *(continued)*

### PATROL BOATS

◆ **3 ex-Iranian** Bldr: Abeking & Rasmussen, West Germany (In serv. 1970)

SHEKAN (ex-*Gohar*) KADER (ex-*Shahpar*) KARARI (ex-*Shakram*)

**D:** 80 tons (fl) **S:** 28 kts **Dim:** 22.9 × 5.0 × 1.8
**A:** 3/20-mm AA (I × 3) **Electron Equipt:** Radar: 1/Decca 202
**M:** 2 MTU diesels; 2 props; 2,200 hp **Range:** 1,220/21 **Man:** 3 officers, 16 men

REMARKS: Built for the Iranian Navy, transferred to the Iranian Coast Guard in 1975 and to Sudan the same year. In very poor condition.

NOTE: The four *El Gihad*-class patrol boats, built in Yugoslavia in 1961–62, were out of service by 1987. Two 31.7-m Commercial Cruiser patrol boats and a 50-m patrol boat were to have been made available in 1986–87 by the U.S., but funding was not available. A 1984 plan to build two "Cormoran" missile boats in Spain also fell through.

### PATROL CRAFT

◆ **4 ex-Iranian 40-foot class** Bldr: Sewart, Morgan City, La. (In serv. 1970)

**D:** 10 tons (fl) **S:** 39 kts **Dim:** 12.2 × 3.4 × 1.1
**A:** 1/12.7-mm mg **M:** 2 G.M. 6-71 diesels; 2 props; 600 hp

REMARKS: Transferred from the Iranian Coast Guard in 1975. Used for training. One being re-engined, 1984–85. Others inoperable, but could be repaired.

# SURINAM

**Republic of Surinam**

PERSONNEL (1987): 160 total.

MERCHANT MARINE (1986): 25 ships—12,655 grt (tankers: 1 ship—208 grt)

NAVAL AVIATION: The Air Force uses four Britten-Norman BN-42 B/T Maritime Defender aircraft for coastal patrol.

### PATROL BOATS AND CRAFT

◆ **3 32-meter** Bldr: De Vries, Aalsmeer, Netherlands

S 401 (In serv. 6-11-76) S 402 (In serv. 3-5-77) S 403 (In serv. 1-11-77)

**S 403** 1980

**D:** 127 tons (140 fl) **S:** 17.5 kts **Dim:** 32.0 × 6.5 × 1.7
**A:** 2/40-mm AA (I × 2)—2/7.62-mm mg (I × 2)
**Electron Equipt:** Radar: 1/Decca 110
**M:** 2 Paxman 12 YHCM diesels; 2 props; 2,110 hp
**Range:** 1,200/13.5 **Man:** 15 tot.

◆ **3 22-meter** Bldr: Schottel, Warmond, the Netherlands

C 301 (In serv. 2-76) C 302 (In serv. 2-76) C 303 (In serv. 11-76)

**D:** 65 tons (70 fl) **S:** 13.5 kts **Dim:** 22.0 × 4.7 × . . .
**A:** 1/12.7-mm mg—2/7.62-mm mg (I × 2)
**Electron Equipt:** Radar: 1/Decca 110
**M:** 2 Dorman 8JT diesels; 2 props; 560 hp **Range:** 650/13.5 **Man:** 8 tot.

◆ **3 12.6-meter river patrol craft** Bldr: Schottel, Warmond, the Netherlands (In serv. 1975)

RP 201 BAHADOER RP 202 FAJABLOW RP 203 KORANGON

**D:** 15 tons (20 fl) **S:** 14 kts **Dim:** 12.6 × 3.8 × 1.1 **A:** 1/12.7-mm mg
**M:** 1 Dorman 8JT diesel; 280 hp **Range:** 350/10 **Man:** 4 tot.

◆ **1 10-meter river patrol craft** Bldr: Schottel, Warmond, the Netherlands (In serv. 8-75)

**D:** 10 tons **S:** 14 kts **Dim:** 10.0 × . . . × . . .
**A:** . . . **M:** 1 Dorman 8JT diesel; 280 hp

# SWEDEN

**Kingdom of Sweden**

PERSONNEL (1987): 3,500 men of the regular Navy, including officers, petty officers, enlisted men, and civilians with permanent status, plus 6,200 national service men available for immediate service and 3,500 reserves. Additionally, some 8,000 conscripts receive annual naval training.

The Coastal Artillery has 3,900 personnel (2,800 conscripts). Its five regiments operate 75-, 120- and 152-mm fixed coast defense gun batteries, 40-mm AA guns, 120-mm mortars, and Carl Gustav anti-tank missiles. The Bofors 120-mm Karin towed gun, and RBS-15 and RBS-17 missiles are being introduced into service.

MERCHANT MARINE (1986): 660 ships—2,516,614 grt
(tankers: 62 ships—459,025 grt)

NAVAL AVIATION: 350 men. 26 helicopters: 9 Agusta Bell 206-A JetRanger (HKP-6), and 17 Vertol 107 (3 HKP-4B for minesweeping and 14 HKP-4C for rescue and ASW, with 6 depth charges or up to 4 Type 422 torpedoes, DUAV-4 dipping sonar). Seven of the 14 HKP-4C were transferred from the Air Force in 1984–86. A Cessna 404 Titan with a prototype side-looking radar (SLAR) was delivered 6-83. Of three CASA C-212-200 Aviocar light transports ordered 16-12-85, 2 are for the Coast Guard, and one for the Navy as a TP-89 maritime surveillance aircraft. A Fairchild Metro-III light transport with an Ericsson side-looking radar in a 10.7-m radome began trials in 1987 for Swedish Air Force use in maritime surveillance. The HKP-4-series helicopters are being re-engined with Rolls-Royce Gnome H1400-1 engines ordered 8-86. The five Alouette-II helicopters were discarded in 9-85.

**HKP-4 (Vertol 107)** Royal Swedish Navy

**HKP-6 (Agusta Bell 206-A)** Royal Swedish Navy

WEAPONS AND SYSTEMS

Most of the electronic equipment in use in the Swedish Navy is of Dutch design (for example, LW-03 air-search radars, H.S.A. fire-control radars), locally manufactured or of wholly Swedish design and construction.

## WEAPONS AND SYSTEMS *(continued)*

### A. Missiles

◆ The U.S. Laser-Hellfire missile is to be procured as the RBS-17 for coastal defense service between 1989–95; 25 battalions with RBS-17 are to be formed to replace 32 battalions with French wire-guided SS-11 missiles. The first 700 RBS-17 missiles were ordered 6-87.

Length: 1.625 m
Weight: 48 kg (71 with launcher) Range: 5+ km

◆ The Saab RB-08A, a surface-to-surface missile based on the CT-30 of the S.N.I.A.S., is in use in the coastal defense batteries.

Length: 5.7 m Wingspan: 3.6 m
Diameter: 0.65 m Weight: 9,000 kg
Max range: 70 nautical miles

◆ The infrared homing Norwegian Penguin Mk 2 missile is in use on board the *Hugin*-class patrol boats, where it is called the RB-12. It has a 120-kg warhead.

Length: 3.0 m Weight: 340 kg
Diameter: 280 mm Speed: Mach 0.7
Wingspan: 1.4 m Max. range: 30 km at an altitude of 60–100 m

◆ The Saab RBS-15 became operational in 1985. The missile has a solid rocket booster and a turbojet sustainer. A sea-skimmer, it has a terminal-homing guidance system. The RBS-15F version will be launched from Air Force Viggen jet fighters, and a vertical submerged-launched RBS-17 version may be developed for the *Västergötland*-class submarines.

Length: 4.350 m Weight: 598 kg (770 kg with booster)
Diameter: 0.500 m Speed: Mach 0.8
Wingspan: 0.85 m (folded) Range: 80–100 km at an altitude of 10–20 m
1.4 (extended)

◆ The RBS-70 shoulder-launched SAM entered development in 1983 as a weapon for surface combatants in a version known as the RBS-70 SLM. Range of the IR-homing missile is 5 km, to be extended to 6 km with the Mk II version in the late 1980s. The weapon is also being offered as an add-on to the H.S.A.-Philips LIOD optronic director, with 4 launch tubes co-mounted.

Length: 1.735 m Range: 5–6 km
Weight: 25 kg Altitude: 3 km
Diameter: 152 mm Launcher weight: 150 kg (loaded)

### B. Guns

The Swedish Bofors firm furnishes the guns, the principal ones being:

◆ **57-mm single-barrel automatic SAK 57 Mk 1**

Installed on the *Hugin*-class missile boats, the *Spica* and *Spica-II* torpedo boats

Mount weight (without ammunition): 6 tons Elevation: −10°/+75°
Train speed: 55°/sec Max. rate of fire: 200 rounds/min
Elevation speed: 20°/sec

◆ **57-mm single-barrel automatic SAK 57 Mk 2**

Entered service aboard *Stockholm* in 1985. Trials with the weapon took place 1981–82 on the *Hugin*-class missile boat *Mjölner*. Also purchased by Canada.

Mount weight: 6 tons Max. rate of fire: 220 rounds/min
Train speed: 55°/sec Shell weight: AA: 5.8 kg (projectile: 2.4 kg)
Elevation: −10°/+85° Surface fire: 6.8 kg
Muzzle velocity: 1,020 m/sec. Range: 14,000 m max. horizontal

Will carry 120 rounds ready service within the low, streamlined gunhouse, automatically loading clips of 20 rounds each.

◆ **40-mm single-barrel semi-automatic L70**

World-standard weapon, by Bofors. Mk 2 proximity fuze now offered. A new mounting, the 3.7-ton "Trinity" with 1.025 m/sec muzzle velocity, a 4-km range, and a 330-rpm firing rate; fitted with an integral radar, the "Trinity" fires a 1.1-kg 3-P (Programmed Proximity Prefragmented) round.

### C. Torpedoes—FFV Ordnance, Motala

The wire-guided Type 61 is used for anti-surface duties from surface ships and submarines. The weapon entered service in 1977, and is now delivered in the Type 613 version, with a wakeless hydrogen peroxide engine.

Length: 7,025 mm Weight: 1,765 kg Range: 30,000 m
Diameter: 533.4 mm Warhead: 240 kg

The Type 617 is a 6.98-m-long export version weighing 1,850 kg and having a 20,000-m range.

The Type 42 torpedo is wire-guided and has acoustic homing, for use by submarines, surface ships, and aircraft against submarines. It was developed from the similar Type 41, which is still in service. The current Type 422 entered Swedish service in 1983; a reduced-charge warhead is available for peacetime use against intruders. A Type 431, improved ASW torpedo was to enter service in 1987.

Data for the Type 422 include;

Length: 2,600 mm (2,440 mm without wire-guidance attachment)
Diameter: 400 mm Warhead: 50 kg
Weight: 298 kg Range: 20,000 m (10,000 at high speed)

### D. ASW Weapons

The Malin.small depth charge and Elma harassment device are being procured for helicopter and surface-ship use. Elma is a rocket launcher firing 100-mm-dia. charges to ranges of 250–300 m in patterns of 9, 18, 27, or 36 grenades when installed in the normal 4-unit suit. Each grenade weighs 4.2 kg and has a shaped-charge warhead. A shallow-water (10-m minimum) version entered service in 1986, followed by chaff and IR decoy rounds.

The Bofors 375-mm ASW rocket launcher, no longer in Swedish Navy service, is widely used in foreign navies in 2-, 4-, or 6-tubed versions. Two types of rockets are furnished: the Erika, with ranges from 600–1,600 m and the Nelli, with ranges from 1,600–3,600 m. The SR-375 twin-tubed launcher has a 24-round auto-loading magazine.

### E. Sensors

The Ericsson Sea Giraffe series C-band radars are offered for export in various models and provide for air and surface search via two separate channels. The digital, pulse-compression radar is offered at 15–60-kw power with differing antenna gains.

Seven sets of U.S. Klein sidescan high-frequency sonars were purchased in 1984 to assist in locating intruding submarines.

## SUBMARINES

◆ **0 (+5) Type 90 Project** (Type A-19)

Remarks: The UB 90 is scheduled to replace the *Sjöormen* class, with the first to complete in 1995. Few details made public yet, but will probably incorporate Sterling-cycle external-combustion engines in the generator sets and otherwise be similar to the Type A-17.

◆ **0 (+4) Västergötland class** (Type A-17) Bldrs: Kockums, Malmö, and Karlskrona

| | | Laid down | L | In serv. |
|---|---|---|---|---|
| Vgd | Västergötland | 10-1-83 | 17-9-86 | 3-87 (trials) |
| Hgd | Hälsingland | 1-1-84 | 31-8-87 | 1988 |
| Söd | Södermanland | . . . | 1988 | 1989 |
| Ögd | Östergötland | . . . | 1989 | 1990 |

**D:** 990 tons light, 1,070 surfaced (1,140 sub.) **S:** 12 kts surf./20 kts sub.
**Dim:** 48.50 × 6.06 × 6.10 (surf.)
**A:** 6/533-mm TT (12 Type 613 torpedoes or mines)—4/400-mm TT (6 Type 422 or 431 torpedoes)—all bow
**Electron Equipt:** Radar: 1/Terma . . .—Sonar: DBQS-21 (CSU-83)
EW: Argo intercept
**M:** 2 Hedemora V12A/15-Ub, 1,080-hp diesels; 2 Jeumont-Schneider 760-kw generators; 1 ASEA electric motor; 1/5-bladed prop; 1,800 shp
**Man:** 17 tot.

Remarks: Design by Kockums under 17-4-78 contract. Ships ordered 8-12-81, with Kockums building the mid-bodies and Karlskrona building the bows and sterns. May later be equipped with four vertical tubes for RBS-17 antiship missiles (a submerged-launch version of the RBS-15) in the sail. The torpedo tubes are arranged with the row of six 533-mm tubes above the four short 400-mm tubes, with

**Västergötland—at launch** Kockums, 9-86

SUBMARINES *(continued)*

separate reload magazine compartments. Very low reserve buoyancy—7%. Bow planes on sail, cruciform stern controls surfaces. Three spare berths for trainees. Two Tudor 84-cell lead-acid batteries. Two main watertight compartments. Two Barr & Stroud periscopes. Will use Ericsson IPS-17 combat data/fire-control system.

**Västergötland**—at launch Kockums, 9-86

### ◆ 3 Näcken (Type A-14) class

| | | Bldr | Laid down | L | In serv. |
|---|---|---|---|---|---|
| Näk | Näcken | Kockums, Malmö | 11-72 | 17-4-78 | 25-4-80 |
| Naj | Najad | Karlskrona | 9-73 | 6-12-78 | 5-12-80 |
| Nep | Neptun | Kockums, Malmö | 3-74 | 13-8-79 | 26-6-81 |

**Najad (Naj)**—with snorkel intake raised G. Davies, Maritime Photographic, 10-86

**Najad (Naj)** L. & L. Van Ginderen, 10-86

**D:** 1,030 surf. (fl)/1,125 tons **S:** 20/20 kts **Dim:** 49.5 × 6.1 × 4.1
**A:** 6/533-mm TT (8 Type 61B or 613 torpedoes or mines)—2/400-mm TT (4 Type 422 or 431 torpedoes)
**Electron Equipt:** Radar: 1/Terma . . .
Sonar: DBSQS-21 (CSU-83)
EW: Argo intercept
**M:** diesel-electric: 1 MTU 16V652 MB, 1,800-hp diesel; 1 Jeumont-Schneider generator; 1 5-bladed prop; 1,500 hp
**Electric:** 150 kw (Scania diesel) **Man:** 5 officers, 14 men

Remarks: Ordered at the end of 1972. The 168-cell Tudor electric battery installation is mounted on shock absorbers. Two Kollmorgen periscopes. An Ericsson IDPS central data system furnishes, in addition to tactical information, data on the main engines; it uses 2 Censor 932 computers. Able to lay mines. Stern planes are x-configuration; bow planes on the sail. *Näcken* and *Neptun* were launched by cranes. Diving depth: 300 m (500-m collapse). Kockums is developing a "mine-girdle" removable minelaying magazine for this and other Swedish submarine classes. One of these submarines was being lengthened by 6 m in 1987 by Kockums to accommodate a United Sterling A-275 engine system to give a 3-week submerged endurance. The system employs liquid oxygen.

### ◆ 5 Sjöormen (Type A-11B) class

| | | Bldr | Laid down | L | In serv. |
|---|---|---|---|---|---|
| Sor | Sjöormen | Kockums, Malmö | 1965 | 25-1-67 | 31-7-67 |
| Sle | Sjölejonet | Kockums, Malmö | 1966 | 29-6-67 | 16-12-68 |
| Shu | Sjöhunden | Kockums, Malmö | 1966 | 21-3-68 | 25-6-69 |
| Sbj | Sjöbjörnen | Karlskrona | 1967 | 6-8-68 | 28-2-69 |
| Shä | Sjöhästen | Karlskrona | 1966 | 9-1-68 | 15-9-69 |

**Sjöormen (Sor)** L. & L. Van Ginderen, 10-86

**Sjöormen (Sor)** L. & L. Van Ginderen, 10-86

**D:** 1,130/1,400 tons **S:** 15/20 kts **Dim:** 50.5 × 6.1 × 5.1
**A:** 4/533-mm TT (8 Type 61B torpedoes or mines)—2/400-mm TT (4 Type 427 ASW torpedoes)
**M:** diesel-electric: 4 Hedemora-Pielstick V12A2 diesel generator groups, 2,100 hp; 1 ASEA electric motor; 1 5-bladed prop; 1,500 hp
**Endurance:** 21 days **Man:** 7 officers, 11 men

Remarks: Maximum diving depth 150 meters. Four battery compartments. Stern planes are x-configuration; bow planes on the sail. One unit given turbocharged (vice supercharged) diesels, 1982. Modernized 1984–85 with Ericsson IBS-A17 combat data/fire control system, Krupp-Atlas CSU-3-2 sonar suites. Two are to receive mid-life modernizations under FY 87-91 planning.

### ◆ 4 Draken (A-11) class

| | | Bldr | Laid down | L | In serv. |
|---|---|---|---|---|---|
| Del | Delfinen | Karlskrona | 1959 | 7-3-61 | 7-6-62 |
| Nor | Nordkaparen | Kockums, Malmö | 1959 | 8-3-60 | 4-4-62 |
| Spr | Springaren | Kockums, Malmö | 1960 | 21-8-61 | 7-11-62 |
| Vgn | Vargen | Kockums, Malmö | 1958 | 20-5-60 | 15-11-61 |

**D:** 770/835 surf./1,110 tons sub. **S:** 17/20 kts **Dim:** 69.0 × 5.1 × 5.0
**A:** 4/533-mm TT fwd—12 full-sized torpedoes (see Remarks)
**M:** diesel-electric: 2 Hedemora-Pielstick 16V-12 PA diesels, 1,660 bhp; 2 electric motors; 1 prop; 1,500 hp
**Man:** 36 tot.

## SUBMARINES *(continued)*

**Delfinen (Del)**—with Alvsborg (M 02) beyond L. & L. Van Ginderen, 3-82

REMARKS: Snorkel-equipped; 1 periscope. Sisters *Draken* and *Gripen* stricken 1-7-81; the survivors have been modernized. A-17 type will replace them in 1988–90. Two or three Type 427 torpedoes can fit in each tube, via adapters, using swim-out launching. *Springaren* in reserve.

◆ **1 two-man midget submarine** Bldr: Yugoslavia (In serv. 1-85)

R 2 STOR KLAS

**D:** 1.4 tons **S:** 4.4 kts **Dim:** 4.9 × 1.4 × . . .
**A:** 24-kg total limpet mines **M:** electric motor; 6 hp **Range:** 18/4.4; 23/1.7

REMARKS: Aluminum and Plexiglas hull. Diving depth: 60 m max. Also purchased was a 2-man chariot, R 1, *Lille Klas,* with a range of 8 n.m. at 2.5 kts; the device is 3.7 m long and weighs 145 kg without riders. Both craft are intended to assist in the search for submarine intruders and to act as training targets.

◆ **1 URF-class salvage and rescue submersible** Bldr: Kockums, Malmö (L: 8-78)

URF 1

**D:** 50 tons (surfaced) **S:** 3 kts **Dim:** 13.5 × 4.3 × 2.9

REMARKS: Has a depth capability of 460 meters and can accommodate up to 25 persons rescued from a bottomed submarine. Based at the Naval Diving Center, Berga. Can be towed at up to 10 kts to the scene of an accident. Lock-out capability to support two divers to 300 meters. Pressure hull of HY 130 steel; collapse depth 900 meters. Two projected sisters not built.

## GUIDED-MISSILE PATROL BOATS

◆ **0 (+4 + 2) Göteborg class (KKV-90 design)** Bldr: Karlskronavarvet

| | Laid down | L | In serv. |
|---|---|---|---|
| K 13 GÖTEBORG | 10-2-86 | . . . | 1990 |
| K 14 GÄVLE | . . . | . . . | . . . |
| K 15 KALMAR | . . . | . . . | . . . |
| K 16 SUNDSVALL | . . . | . . . | . . . |
| K 17 HELSINGBORG | . . . | . . . | . . . |
| K 18 HÄRNÖSAND | . . . | . . . | . . . |

**D:** 380 tons (425 fl) **S:** 32 kts **Dim:** 57.0 (50.0 wl) × 8.0 (7.3 wl) × 1.93
**A:** 8/RBS-15 SSM (II × 4)—1/57-mm Bofors SAK57 Mk 2 DP—1/40-mm Bofors Trinity AA—4/400-mm ASW TT (Type 431 torpedoes)—4/Elma ASW RL (IX × 4)—mines

**Göteborg class**—artist's impression K. Netzlev/Karlskrona, 1987

**Electron Equipt:** Radar: 1/Terma PN-612 nav., 1/Sea Giraffe 150 HC, 2/9GR-440 f.c.
Sonar: Simrad SS 304 Spira, Thomson-CSF TSM 2643 Salmon VDS (dismountable)
EW: Argo CAROL intercept/deception syst., IR detector, Peab 9CM-300 decoy RL (XXXII × 2)
**M:** 3 MTU 16V396 TB94 diesels; 3 KaMeWa 80-S62/6 waterjets; 8,640 hp (6,390 sust.)
**Range:** . . . **Electric:** 855 kVA (3 × 285 kVA diesel sets)
**Man:** 7 officers, 36 men

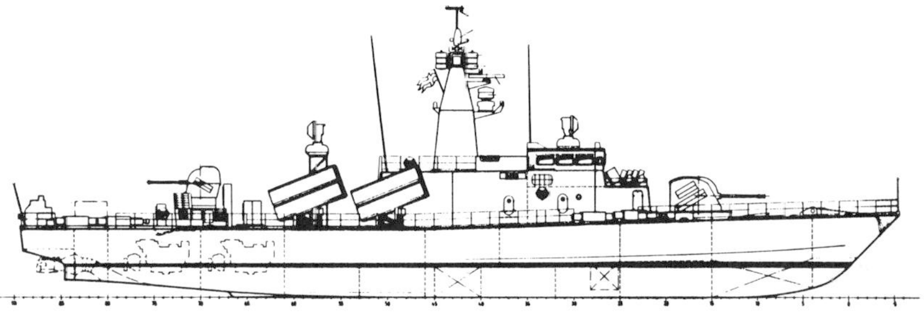

**Göteborg class** Karlskrona, 1984

REMARKS: First four ordered 1-12-85; others may be requested later in 1980s; considered to be "corvettes." An expanded version of the *Stockholm* design, intended to replace the remaining Spica-I missile boats. The Phillips 9LV 450 gunfire control system will use the ARTE-726E gun-control system, RCI-400 missile fire-control, TORPE torpedo-control, 9AU-300 ASW fire-control and 9CM-300 EW-control systems. The two 9LV 200 Mk 3 optronic directors have co-mounted 9GR-400 radars. The four fixed ASW TT are mounted on the starboard side, two firing aft, two forward, for wire-guided Type 431 ASW torpedoes. Steel hull, aluminum superstructures. Infrared, radar, and noise signature suppression measures incorporated. K 17 and K 18 may not be built, as entire program is under criticism from the Minister of Defense.

◆ **2 Stockholm class (Spica III/YA-81 design)** Bldr: Karlskronavarvet

| | Laid down | L | In serv. |
|---|---|---|---|
| K 11 STOCKHOLM | 1-8-82 | 24-8-84 | 1-3-85 |
| K 12 MALMÖ | 14-3-83 | 21-3-85 | 10-5-85 |

**Malmö (K 12)**—with standard 57-mm gun during trials Swedish Navy, 1985

**Stockholm (K 11)**—launching RBS-15 missile Swedish Navy, 1986

**D:** 290 tons (320 fl) **S:** 32 kts (20 kts on diesels)
**Dim:** 50.5 (46.6 wl) × 7.5 (6.8 wl) × 2.0 (hull)
**A:** 6–8 RBS-15 SSM (II × 4 or II × 2, I × 1)—1/57-mm Bofors SAK 57 Mk 2 DP—1/40 mm AA—2/533-mm TT—4 Elma ASW RL (IV × 4)—mines

GUIDED-MISSILE PATROL BOATS *(continued)*

**Stockholm (K 11)**—with 533-mm TT flanking the prototype SAK 57 Mk 2 gun mount forward — Karlskronavarvet, 1985

**Electron Equipt:** Radar: 1/. . . nav., 1/Ericsson Sea Giraffe 50HC, 1/PEAB 9LV 200 Mk 2
Sonar: Simrad SS 304 Spira; Thomson-CSF TSM 2642 Salmon VDS (dismountable)
EW: Saab-Scania EWS-905 intercept; 2 PEAB Philax decoy RL (XXXII × 2)

**M:** CODAG 1 Allison 570KF, 7,170-hp (6,000 sust.) gas turbine; 2 MTU 16V396 TB93 diesels (2,095 hp each); 3 CP props; 11,360 hp

**Electric:** 648 kw **Range:** . . . **Man:** 4.3 tot.

REMARKS: Considered to be "corvettes." Armament suit interchangeable, the RBS-15 missiles being replaceable by 2 more torpedo tubes, 4 400-mm ASW torpedo tubes, and/or mine rails. Have the Ericsson MARIL weapons-control system, with an SRA Censor 932E computer. A 6-cell 57-mm rocket flare launcher is mounted before the bridge. The 9LV300 gunfire-control system incorporates a 9LV200 radar director forward and a 9LV100 optronic director on the aft face of the main mast. During 1986–87 K 11 conducted trials with the Plessey COMTASS towed linear sonar array.

◆ **17 Hugin class** Bldrs: Bergens Mekanske Verksted, Norway (P 154–158 subcontracted to Westermoen, Mandal, Norway)

| | L | In serv. | | L | In serv. |
|---|---|---|---|---|---|
| P 150 Jägeren | . . . | 8-6-72 | P 159 Kaparen | 8-8-79 | 7-8-80 |
| P 151 Hugin | 3-6-77 | 3-7-78 | P 160 Väktaren | 12-12-79 | 19-9-80 |
| P 152 Munin | 3-10-77 | 3-7-78 | P 161 Snapphanen | 18-3-80 | 14-1-81 |
| P 153 Magne | 9-1-78 | 12-10-78 | P 162 Spejaren | 13-5-80 | 21-3-81 |
| P 154 Mode | 8-8-78 | 12-1-79 | P 163 Styrbjörn | 8-80 | 26-10-81 |
| P 155 Vale | 3-10-78 | 26-4-79 | P 164 Starkodder | 1-81 | 24-8-81 |
| P 156 Vidar | 6-3-79 | 10-8-79 | P 165 Tordön | 3-2-81 | 26-10-81 |
| P 157 Mjölner | 12-6-79 | 24-10-79 | P 166 Tirfing | 17-9-81 | 21-1-82 |
| P 158 Mysing | 18-9-79 | 14-2-80 | | | |

**Tordön (P 165)**—with 2 Penguin Mk 2, Elma ASW RL, new EW gear — H. Ehlers, 8-86

**Hugin (P 151)**—no missiles, 6 mines — L. & L. Van Ginderen, 10-84

**D:** 120 tons (150 fl) **S:** 35 kts **Dim:** 36.53 (33.6 pp) × 6.20 × 1.60

**A:** 2–6 Penguin Mk 32 (I × 6)—1/57-mm Bofors SAK 57 Mk 1 DP—24 mines or 2/d.c. racks in lieu of missiles—4 Elma ASW RL (IX × 4)

**Electron Equipt:** Radar: 1/Scanter 009, 1/PEAB 9LV200 Mk 2 system
Sonar: 1/Simrad SQ3D/SF
EW: Saab-Scania EWS-905

**M:** 2 MTU 20V672 TB90 diesels; 2 props; 7,200 hp

**Electric:** 200 kVA **Range:** 550/35 **Man:** 3 officers, 19 men

REMARKS: Can carry 6 Norwegian Penguin Mk 2 (Swedish RB-12) SSM (I × 6), but normally mount only two. P 150 briefly carried 6 Penguin Mk 1. Prototype *Jägaren,* renumbered from P 151, had new engines; those in the others came from discarded *Plejad*-class torpedo boats. Carry 103-mm rocket flare launchers on either side of the 57-mm gun mount. The PEAB 9LV200 Mk 2 fire-control system employs separate search and tracking radars. P 157 carried the prototype SAK 57 Mk 2 57-mm DP gun, but mounted within the original high gunhouse. Saab-Scania EWS-905 "Doughnut" passive intercept EW systems have been added, with the toroidal radome mounted just below the search antenna for the 9LV200 system.

◆ **12 Spica-II class** Bldr: Karlskronavarvet and Götaverken

| | L | In serv. | | L | In serv. |
|---|---|---|---|---|---|
| R 131 Nörrkoping | 16-11-72 | 5-11-73 | R 137 Umea | 13-1-75 | 15-5-75 |
| R 132 Nynäshamn | 24-4-73 | 8-9-73 | R 138 Pitea | 12-5-73 | 13-9-75 |
| R 133 Nortälje | 18-9-73 | 1-8-74 | R 139 Lulea | 19-8-75 | 28-11-75 |
| R 134 Varberg | 2-2-74 | 13-6-74 | R 140 Halmstad | 28-11-75 | 9-4-76 |
| R 135 Västeras | 15-5-74 | 25-10-74 | R 141 Strömstad | 26-4-76 | 13-9-76 |
| R 136 Västervik | 2-9-74 | 15-1-75 | R 142 Ystad | 3-9-76 | 10-12-76 |

**D:** 190 tons (230 fl) **S:** 40.5 kts **Dim:** 43.6 × 7.1 × 1.6 (2.4 props)

**A:** 2/RBS-15 SSM—1/57-mm Bofors SAK-57 Mk 1 DP—2/533-mm TT—4/Elma ASW RL (IX × 4)

**Electron Equipt:** Radar: 1/Scanter 009, 1/Sea Giraffe 50HC, 1/PEAB 9LV200 Mk 1
EW: Saab-Scania EWS-905

**M:** 3 Rolls-Royce Proteus gas turbines; 3 props; 12,900 hp

**Man:** 7 officers, 20 men

GUIDED-MISSILE PATROL BOATS *(continued)*

**Strömstad (R 141)**—with 2 RBS-15, 2 TT H. Ehlers, 8-86

**Umea (R 137)**—with 2 RBS-15, 2 TT, 4 Elma RL L. & L. Van Ginderen, 8-85

Remarks: All reequipped for the Saab RBS-15 cruise missile during 1982–85. Two missiles are normally carried, and up to six 533-mm torpedo tubes for wire-guided Type 61 torpedoes. The fire-control system is an analog version of the digital system used in the *Hugin* class. The gas turbines exhaust through the transom to provide residual thrust. Mines can be substituted for the missiles and the torpedo tubes, the forward-most of which must be swung out several degrees before firing. The MARIS 880 (SRA) weapons-control system permits over-the-horizon targeting data to be received from a helicopter. All have 6 rails for 103-mm rocket radar flares on the 57-mm gun mount.

## TORPEDO BOATS

◆ **4 Spica class** (In serv. 1966–68) Bldrs: T 121, 123: Götaverken; others: Karlskronavarvet

| | L | | L |
|---|---|---|---|
| T 121 Spica | 26-4-66 | T 125 Vega | 7-6-67 |
| T 123 Capella | 26-4-66 | T 126 Virgo | 7-6-67 |

**Sirius (T 122)**—since stricken Royal Swedish Navy, 1981

**D:** 190 tons (235 fl) **S:** 40 kts
**Dim:** 42.5 × 7.3 × 1.6 (2.6 props)
**A:** 1/57-mm Bofors SAK 57 Mk 1 DP—6/533-mm TT
**Electron Equipt:** Radar: 1/Scanter 009, 1/H.S.A. M22
**M:** 3 Bristol-Siddeley Proteus 1274 gas turbines; 3 KaMeWa CP props; 12,720 hp
**Electric:** 120 kw
**Man:** 7 officers, 21 men

Remarks: Carry four 103-mm (I × 4) and six 57-mm (VI × 1) rocket flare launchers. Mines can be substituted for the torpedo tubes, the forwardmost of which must be swung out several degrees before firing. There are two Rover IS90 gas-turbine generators. No longer scheduled to receive RBS-15 missiles. Sisters *Sirius* (T 122) and *Castor* (T 124) stricken 1-7-85. Two in reserve as of 1987.

## PATROL BOATS

◆ **3 Dalerö class** Bldr: Djupviks Varvet, Rönnäng

V 09 Dalerö (In serv. 21-9-84) V 10 Sandhamn (In serv. 5-12-84)
V 11 Osthammar (In serv. 1-3-85)

**Dalerö (V 09)** Djupviks, 1984

**D:** 50 tons (fl) **S:** 30 kts **Dim:** 23.40 × 5.10 × 1.05
**A:** 1/40-mm AA—2/7.62-mm mg (I × 2)—mines
**Electron Equipt:** Radar: 1/Terma TM 610
**M:** 2 MTU 8V396 TB83 diesels; 3 props; 2,100 hp
**Electric:** 60 kw **Man:** 3 officers, 4 men + 3 passengers

Remarks: Ordered 28-2-83 in lieu of further torpedo-boat-to-patrol-boat conversions.

◆ **8 Skanör class** Bldr: V 01–V 04: Kockums, Malmö; others: Naval Dockyard, Stockholm (In serv. 1956–59)

| | Conv. | | Conv. |
|---|---|---|---|
| V 01 Skanör (ex-T 42) | 12-76 | V 05 Öregrund (ex-T 47) | 1-2-83 |
| V 02 Smyge (ex-T 43) | 1977 | V 06 Slite (ex-T 48) | 15-4-83 |
| V 03 Arild (ex-T 45) | 1977 | V 07 Marstrand (ex-T 50) | 16-5-83 |
| V 04 Viken (ex-T 44) | 1977 | V 08 Lysekil (ex-T 52) | 13-6-83 |

**Marstrand (V 07)**—with mines aft L. & L. Van Ginderen, 5-87

**D:** 40 tons (44.5 fl) **S:** 27 kts **Dim:** 23.0 × 5.9 × 1.2 (1.4 props)
**A:** 1/40-mm AA—mines **Electron Equipt:** Radar: 1/Scanter 009
**M:** 2 MTU 8V396 TB83 diesels; 2 props; 2,100 hp **Man:** 7 tot.

Remarks: First four converted at Karlskrona 1976–77 for service as surveillance boats; original three gasoline engines replaced for safety and economy. The second batch converted 1981–83 by Djupviks Varvet, with V 05 recommissioning 14-1-83, V 06 on 15-4-83, V 07 on 16-5-83, and V 08 on 13-6-83. Have one six-railed 57-mm rocket flare launcher on the bow. Conversion of four more canceled in favor of building the three *Dalerö*-class patrol boats.

◆ **4 Hanö-class former minesweepers** Bldr: Karlskrona (All in serv. 1954)

V 52 Tärnö (ex-M 52) V 54 Sturkö (ex-M 54)
V 53 Tjurkö (ex-M 53) V 55 Ornö (ex-M 56)

PATROL BOATS (*continued*)

**Tärnö (V 52)** L. & L. Van Ginderen, 9-85

**D:** 270 tons **S:** 14.5 kts **Dim:** 42.0 (40.0 pp) × 7.0 × 2.7
**A:** 2/40-mm AA (I × 2) **Electron Equipt:** Radar: 1/Scanter 009
**M:** 2 Nohab diesels; 2 props; 910 hp **Man:** 25 tot.

REMARKS: In service since 1954. Redesignated as patrol craft on 1-1-79. Have steel hulls. Renumbered with V-series pendants on 1-1-79. Each has one six-railed 57-mm rocket flare launcher. Two sisters, *Hanö* (V 51) and *Utö* (V 56), stricken 1980.

MINE WARFARE SHIPS

◆ **1 fleet minelaying/training ship** Bldr: Karlskrona

| | Laid down | L | In serv. |
|---|---|---|---|
| M 04 CARLSKRONA (ex-*Karlskrona*) | 1980 | 28-5-80 | 19-3-82 |

**Carlskrona (M 04)** L. & L. Van Ginderen, 2-87

**D:** 3,130 tons (3,300 fl) **S:** 20 kts **Dim:** 105.70 (97.50 pp) × 15.2 × 4.00
**A:** 2/57-mm Bofors Mk 1 DP (I × 2)—2/40-mm Bofors AA (I × 2)—105 mines
**Electron Equipt:** Radar: 1/Scanter 009, 1/Raytheon . . . , 1/Sea Giraffe HC50, 2/PEAB 9LV200 Mk 2 (9LV400 system)
Sonar: Simrad SQ3D/SF—EW: . . .
**M:** 4 Nohab-Polar F212-D825, 12-cyl. diesels; 2 CP props; 10,560 hp
**Electric:** 2,570 kVA **Man:** 118 crew + 136 cadets, 46 instructors

REMARKS: Ordered 25-11-77 to replace cadet training ship *Alvsnabben,* which, in the event, expired before her completion. Intended to act as a mine countermeasures ship support tender and submarine torpedo hard target in peacetime, when not conducting the annual Cadet Training Cruise. Hull reinforced below waterline to permit exercise torpedo hits; there are 14 watertight compartments. A bow-thruster is fitted. Has two complete combat information centers (CIC), one duplicating that of a *Hugin* and one duplicating a *Spica-II.* Extensive navigational systems, including Decca Navigator and Omega receivers. Raised helicopter deck above fantail. Name changed to honor the Swedish king. There are 2 lead-computing optical directors to control the 40-mm AA, and 2 radar/optronic 9LV200 Mk 2 directors for the 57-mm guns.

◆ **2 Älvsborg-class minelayers** Bldr: Karlskrona

| | Laid down | L | In serv. |
|---|---|---|---|
| M 02 ÄLVSBORG | 11-68 | 11-11-69 | 10-4-71 |
| M 03 VIBORG | 16-10-73 | 22-1-75 | 6-2-76 |

**Viborg (M 03)** L. & L. Van Ginderen, 8-85

**Älvsborg (M 02)** L. & L. Van Ginderen, 10-86

**D:** 2,660 tons (fl) (M 03: 2,450 fl) **S:** 16 kts **Dim:** 92.4 (83.3 pp) × 14.7 × 4.0
**A:** 3/40-mm AA (I × 3)—300 mines **Electric:** 1,200 kw
**Electron Equipt:** Radar: 1/Scanter 009, 1/Raytheon . . . , 1/H.S.A. M22 f.c.—EW . . .
**M:** 2 Nohab-Polar 12-cyl. diesels; 1 CP prop; 4,200 hp **Man:** 97 tot.

REMARKS: M 02 is used as a submarine tender in peacetime and has accommodations for 205 submarine crew members. M 03 is equipped as Flagship, Coastal Fleet, and has accommodations for 158 flag staff. Each has a helicopter deck. Radar suit expanded 1977–78. An intercept array is mounted on the mast just forward of the stack.

◆ **4 (+2) Landsort (M80)-class coastal minesweeper/hunters** Bldr: Karlskronavarvet

| | Laid down | L | In serv. |
|---|---|---|---|
| M 71 LANDSORT | 5-10-81 | 22-11-82 | 19-3-84 |
| M 72 ARHOLMA | 13-2-82 | 10-10-84 | 23-11-84 |
| M 73 KOSTER | 1-9-84 | 16-1-86 | 30-5-86 |
| M 74 KULLEN | 1-1-85 | 15-8-86 | . . .-87 |
| M 75 VINGA | 27-4-86 | . . .-87 | . . .-88 |
| M 76 VEN | 15-5-87 | . . .-88 | . . .-88 |

**Landsort (M 71)** L. & L. Van Ginderen, 6-87

MINE WARFARE SHIPS *(continued)*

**Kullen (M 74)** L. & L. Van Ginderen, 4-87

**D:** 310 tons (360 fl) **S:** 15 kts **Dim:** 47.50 (45.00 pp) × 9.60 × 2.30
**A:** 1/40-mm AA—4/Elma ASW RL (IX × 4)—mines
**Electron Equipt:** Radar: 1/. . . nav.
Sonar: Thomson-CSF TSM 2022
**M:** 4 Saab-Scania DSI-14 diesels; 2 Voith-Schneider vertical cycloidal props; 1,440 hp
**Electric:** 585 kVA **Range:** 2,000/12 **Man:** 7 officers, 32 men

REMARKS: Glass-reinforced plastic construction, based on Swedish Coast Guard's TV 171. First pair ordered 25-2-81. Next four ordered 31-1-84; two more planned for 1987–88. PEAB 9LV100 optronic director for the gun. Y-shaped portable mine-rail arrangement, with single laying-point. Computerized integrated navigational/mine system and gun-control system by Philips Elektronikindustier AB (PEAB) in conjunction with Decca-Racal. Carry 2 SUTEC Uven remote-controlled mine-disposal vehicles, as well as controlling three SAM, glass-reinforced plastic, self-propelled magnetic/acoustic catamaran minesweeping devices.

◆ **5 radio-controlled mine countermeasures craft** Bldr: Karlskronavarvet

SAM 01 (In serv. 29-3-83)
SAM 02 (In serv. 29-3-83)
SAM 03 (In serv. 26-5-83)
SAM 04 (In serv. 26-5-83)
SAM 05 (In serv. 17-6-83)

**SAM 05** Karlskronavarvet, 1983

**D:** 15 tons **S:** 8 kts **Dim:** 18.0 × 6.0 × 0.7 (1.6 prop)
**M:** 1 Volvo-Penta TAMD 70D diesel; 2 Schottel shrouded props; 210 hp
**Range:** 330/7

REMARKS: The catamarans also automatically lay swept-channel danbuoy markers. An eventual total of 20 SAMs is planned.

◆ **7 Arkö-class coastal minesweepers** Bldrs: Odd numbers—Karlskrona; even numbers—Hälsingborg

| | L | In serv. |
|---|---|---|
| M 57 Arkö | 21-1-57 | 1958 |
| M 58 Spårö | 1957 | 1958 |
| M 61 Styrsö | 1961 | 1962 |
| M 62 Skaftö | 1961 | 1962 |
| M 64 Hasslö | 1962 | 1962 |
| M 67 Nåmdö | 1964 | 1964 |
| M 68 Blidö | 1964 | 1964 |

**D:** 285 tons (300 fl) **S:** 14.5 kts **Dim:** 44.4 × 7.5 × 2.5 (3.0 prop)
**A:** 1/40-mm AA **M:** 2 MTU 12V493 diesels; 2 props; 1,000 hp **Man:** 25 tot.

REMARKS: Wooden-hulled construction. M 61 through M 68 have a curved rubbing-strake line along the hull side; in earlier ships there are two strakes, paralleling the hull sheer. Have one six-railed 57-mm rocket flare launcher. Sisters *Karlsö* (M 59), *Iggö* (M 60) and *Aspö* (M 63) stricken 1984, *Vinö* (M 65) and *Vallö* (M 66) in 1985.

**Skaftö**—curved strake variant L. & L. Van Ginderen, 8-87

**Arkö (M 57)**—straight strake variant G. Gyssels, 4-87

◆ **3 Gåssten-class inshore minesweepers**

| | Bldr | L | In serv. |
|---|---|---|---|
| M 31 Gåssten | Knippla SY | 11-72 | 16-11-73 |
| M 32 Norsten | Hellevikstrands SY | 4-73 | 12-10-73 |
| M 33 Viksten | Karlskrona | 18-4-74 | 1-7-74 |

**Norsten (M 32)**—wooden hull L. & L. Van Ginderen, 9-85

**Viksten (M 33)**—GRP hull L. & L. Van Ginderen, 5-83

MINE WARFARE SHIPS *(continued)*

**D:** 120 tons (M 33: 130 tons) **S:** 11 kts **Dim:** 23.0 (M 33: 25.3) × 6.6 × 3.7
**A:** 1/20-mm AA **M:** 1 diesel; 1 prop; 460 hp

REMARKS: The hull of M 33 is made of glass-reinforced plastic; she was intended to serve as the prototype for a new class of 300-ton, 43-meter coastal minesweepers, which were not built. The other two are built of wood. A 20-mm AA gun has replaced the 40-mm/60-cal. originally carried.

◆ **7 Hisingen-class inshore minesweepers**

| | L | | L |
|---|---|---|---|
| M 43 HISINGEN | 1960 | M 47 GILLÖGA | 1964 |
| M 44 BLACKAN | 1960 | M 48 RÖDLÖGA | 1964 |
| M 45 DÄMMAN | 1960 | M 49 SVARTLÖGA | 1964 |
| M 46 GALTEN | 1960 | | |

**Hisingen (M 43)**—with new deckhouse amidships L. & L. Van Ginderen, 6-87

**D:** 140 tons **S:** 9 kts **Dim:** 22.0 × 6.4 × 1.4
**A:** 1/20-mm AA **M:** 1 diesel; 1 prop; 380 hp

REMARKS: Wooden-hulled fishing boats. M 47 through M 49 have higher bridges and bluffer bow lines. A 20-mm AA has replaced the original 40-mm/60-cal. AA in all. All received new deckhouse amidships in 1987.

◆ **6 M 15-class inshore minesweepers** (All L: 1941)

M 21 through M 26

**M 22**—note sweep gear and gun deleted, new pole mast atop pilothouse
L. & L. Van Ginderen, 8-85

**D:** 70 tons **S:** 12–13 kts **Dim:** 27.7 × 5.05 × 1.4 (2.0 props)
**A:** 1/20-mm AA **M:** diesels; 1 prop; 320–430 hp **Man:** 10 tot.

REMARKS: Wooden hulls. M 21, M 22, M 25 are used as tenders for mine-clearance divers. Sisters M 15 and M 16 were stricken during 1984.

◆ **4 minesweeping boats** (In serv. 1955–56)

SVK 11 (ex-Tv 226) SVK 12 (ex-Tv 228) SVK 13 SVK 14

**D:** 12 tons **S:** 20 kts **Dim:** 14.0 × 3.4 × 1.2
**A:** 1/20-mm AA **M:** 1 Volvo Penta diesel; 1 prop; . . . hp

REMARKS: Used for Naval Reserve training. Reclassified from patrol craft in 1983.

AUXILIARIES

◆ **1 intelligence collection ship** Bldr: Karlskronavarvet

| | Laid down | L | In serv. |
|---|---|---|---|
| A 201 ORION | 23-4-82 | 30-11-83 | 7-6-84 |

**Orion (A 201)** Karlskrona, 1984

**D:** 1,400 tons (fl) **S:** 15 kts **Dim:** 61.3 × 11.0 × 4.2
**A:** none **Electron Equipt:** Radar: 1/. . . nav.—EW: . . .
**M:** 2 Hedemora V8A/135 diesels; 1 CP prop; 1,840 hp **Man:** 35 tot.

REMARKS: Ordered 25-6-81. To last 30 years. Signal collection antennas beneath a large glass-reinforced plastic radome atop full length of the superstructure. In collision with Soviet minesweeper, 26-10-85.

◆ **1 coastal tanker** Bldr: D. W. Kremer Sohn, Elmshorn, West Germany (In serv. 1965)

A 228 BRANNAREN (ex-*Indio*)

**Brannaren (A 228)** Royal Swedish Navy, 1972

**D:** 857 tons (fl) **S:** 11 kts **Dim:** 61.71 (56.76 pp) × 8.6 × 3.57
**M:** 1 MAK 6 Mu 51 diesel; 1 prop; 800 hp

REMARKS: Eight cargo tanks totaling 1,170 $m^3$. Purchased in 1972.

◆ **1 submarine rescue and salvage ship** Bldr: . . .

| | L | In serv. |
|---|---|---|
| A 211 BELOS | 15-11-61 | 29-5-63 |

**Belos (A 211)** H. Ehlers, 9-83

**AUXILIARIES** *(continued)*

**D:** 965 tons (fl) **S:** 13 kts **Dim:** 62.3 × 11.2 × 4.0
**M:** 2 diesels; 2 props; 1,200 hp

Remarks: Well-equipped for underwater search: decompression chamber, active rudder, underwater television, and a small helicopter deck. Modernized in 1979–80 to support the URF submarine-rescue submersible.

## SERVICE CRAFT

◆ **1 harbor tanker** Bldr: Asiverken, Åmål (In serv. 4-59)

A 229 Eldaren (ex-*Brotank*)

**D:** 231 grt/320 dwt **S:** 8 kts **Dim:** 37.22 (34.14 pp) × 6.53 × 2.95
**M:** 2 Volvo Penta 6-cyl. diesels; 1 CP prop; 420 hp

Remarks: Purchased 5-81 from commercial service.

◆ **1 water tanker** (L: 1959)

A 217 Fryken

**D:** 307 tons **S:** 10 kts **Dim:** 34.4 (32.0 pp) × 6.1 × 2.9
**M:** 1 diesel; 1 prop; 370 hp

Note: Water tanker *Unden* (A 216) stricken 1983, and provisions lighter *Freja* (A 221) stricken 1984.

◆ **1 torpedo- and missile-recovery craft** Bldr: Lundervarv-Ooverkstads AB, Kramfors

| | L | In serv. |
|---|---|---|
| A 248 Pingvinen | 26-9-73 | 3-75 |

Pingvinen (A 248) — H. Ehlers, 8-86

**D:** 191 tons **S:** 13 kts **Dim:** 33.0 × 6.1 × 1.8
**M:** 2 MTU 12V493 diesels; 2 props; 1,040 hp

Remarks: Similar to A 247 but has superstructure aft, 2 articulated cranes, and bow bulwarks.

◆ **1 torpedo- and missile-recovery craft** (L: 9-63)

A 247 Pelikanen

Pelikanen (A 247) — G. Gyssels, 9-85

**D:** 130 tons **S:** 15 kts **Dim:** 33.0 × 5.8 × 1.8
**M:** 2 MTU 12V493 diesels; 2 props; 1,040 hp

◆ **1 torpedo-recovery craft** (L: 1951)

A 246 Hägern

Hägern (A 246) — H. Ehlers, 9-83

**D:** 50 tons **S:** 10 kts **Dim:** 29.0 × 5.4 × 1.6 **M:** 2 diesels; 2 props; 480 hp

◆ **1 trials craft** (L: 1969)

A 241 Urd (ex-*Capella*)

**D:** 63 tons (90 fl) **S:** 8 kts **Dim:** 27.0 × 5.6 × 2.8 **M:** 2 diesels; 200 hp

Remarks: Acquired 1970.

◆ **2 mine transport lighters**

| | L | | L |
|---|---|---|---|
| A 236 Fällaren | 1941 | A 237 Minören | 1940 |

**D:** 165 tons **S:** 9 kts **Dim:** 31.5 × 6.1 × 2.1 **M:** 2 diesels; 1 prop; 240 hp

◆ **1 laundry ship** (L: 1961)

A 256 Sigrun

Sigrun (A 256) — Royal Swedish Navy, 1974

**D:** 250 tons **S:** 11 kts **Dim:** 32.0 × 6.8 × 3.6 **M:** 1 diesel; 1 prop; 320 hp

Remarks: Probably the world's only camouflaged floating laundry, and certainly the fastest.

◆ **1 M 15-class general-purpose tender, former minesweeper** (L: 1941)

A 242 Skuld (ex-M 20)

Skuld (A 242) — L. & L. Van Ginderen, 7-86

**D:** 70 tons (fl) **S:** 13 kts **Dim:** 26.0 × 5.0 × 1.4
**M:** 2 diesels; 2 props; 410 hp

**SERVICE CRAFT** *(continued)*

Remarks: Wooden-hulled craft used for mine warfare trials; new deckhouse added abaft original pilothouse. Sisters *Lommen* (A 231, ex-M 17) and *Spoven* (A 232, ex-M 18) stricken 1984.

◆ **2 stores lighters**

A 341 ATB 1 A 342 ATB 2

**ATB 1 (A 341)** L. & L. Van Ginderen, 8-86

**D:** 240 tons (fl) **S:** 10 kts **Dim:** 30.4 × 6.0 × 2.0
**A:** mines **Electron Equipt:** Radar: 1/Terma . . . nav.
**M:** 1 diesel; 1 prop; . . . hp **Man:** 4 tot.

Remarks: 70 grt. Cargo capacity: 100 tons.

◆ **2 sail-training schooners**

S 01 Gladan (L: 1947) S 02 Falken (L: 1948)

**Falken (S 02)** Royal Swedish Navy, 1986

**D:** 220 tons **S:** . . . kts **Dim:** 42.5 (28.3 pp) × 7.27 × 4.2
**M:** 1 diesel auxiliary; 1 prop; 50 hp; sail area: 512 $m^2$

◆ **2 diving tenders** Bldr: Storebro Bruks AB (In serv. 1980)

**D:** . . . tons **S:** 24 kts **Dim:** 10.35 × 3.30 × 1.0
**Electron Equipt:** Radar: 1/Decca 091
**M:** 2 Volvo Penta TAMD 60C diesels; 2 props; 370 hp

Remarks: Fold-down door at stern. 1.7-ton useful load.

◆ **2 range safety boats** Bldr: Storebro Bruks AB (In serv. 1980)

Remarks: Data as for diving tender version above.

◆ **3 personnel launches** Bldr: Storebro Bruks AB (In serv. 1980)

**D:** 5.5 tons (fl) **S:** 24 kts **Dim:** 9.30 × 3.30 × 1.0
**M:** 2 Volvo Penta TAMD 60C diesels; 2 props; 370 hp

Remarks: Builder's Type 31 design; glass-reinforced plastic construction. Can carry 25 men or 6 stretchers. Can reach 27 kts in light condition.

**TUGS**

◆ **2 Herkules-class icebreaking tugs**

A 323 Herkules (L: 1969) A 324 Hera (L: 1971)

**D:** 127 tons **S:** 11.5 kts **Dim:** 21.4 × 6.9 × 3.7 **M:** diesels; 615 hp

◆ **2 Achilles-class icebreaking tugs** (L: 1962, 1963)

A 251 Achilles A 252 Ajax

**Ajax (A 252)** L. & L. Van Ginderen, 8-85

**D:** 450 tons **S:** 12 kts **Dim:** 35.5 (33.15 pp) × 9.5 × 3.9
**M:** diesels; 1,650 hp **Electron Equipt:** Radar: 1 or 2/Decca 1226C

◆ **3 Hermes-class icebreaking tugs** (L: 1953–57)

A 253 Hermes A 321 Hector A 322 Heros

**D:** 185 tons **S:** 11 kts **Dim:** 24.5 (23.0 pp) × 6.8 × 3.6 **M:** diesel; 600 hp

◆ **5 small harbor tugs/tenders** Bldr: Lundevarv (In serv. 1978–79)

A 751–755

**D:** 42 tons (fl) **S:** 9.5 kts **Dim:** 15.5 × 5.0 × 2.7 **M:** 1 diesel

Remarks: Can break thin ice. Carry 40 passengers.

◆ **3 miscellaneous small tugs**

A 326 Hebe (In serv. 1969)—34 tons (fl), 9 kts
A 327 Passop (In serv. 1957)—25 tons (fl), 9 kts
A 330 Atlas (In serv. 1975)—35 tons (fl), 9 kts

**Atlas (A 330)**—a small push-tug with vertical cycloidal propellers
L. & L. Van Ginderen, 1986

MINISTRY OF TRANSPORT

## ICEBREAKERS

NOTE: All Swedish icebreakers are owned by the Ministry of Transport, but are manned and administered by the Swedish Navy. In 1984, it was decided to permanently arm all seagoing icebreakers.

◆ **0 (+2) new construction** Bldr: Götaverken, Arendel

| | Laid down | L | In serv. |
|---|---|---|---|
| ODEN | 5-87 | ... | 10-88 |
| THULE | ... | ... | ... |

**D:** 10,300 tons (fl) **S:** ... kts **Dim:** ... × ... × ...
**A:** 4/40-mm AA (I × 4)—mines **Electron Equipt:** Radar: ...
**M:** diesel-electric; ... Kort-nozzle props; 25,000 hp **Range:** ... **Man:** ...

REMARKS: Ordered 1-87 as replacements for *Oden* and *Thule*. To be capable of breaking a 29.5-m swath through ice.

◆ **3 Finnish Urho class** Bldr: Wärtsilä, Helsinki, Finland

| | Laid down | L | In serv. |
|---|---|---|---|
| ATLE | 10-5-73 | 27-11-73 | 21-10-74 |
| FREJ | ... | 3-6-74 | 30-9-75 |
| YMER | 12-2-76 | 3-9-76 | 26-10-77 |

**Frej** L. & L. Van Ginderen, 8-85

**D:** 7,800 tons **S:** 19 kts **Dim:** 104.6 (99.0 pp) × 23.8 × 7.8
**A:** 4/40-mm AA (I × 4)—3 mine rails
**M:** 5 Wärtsilä-Pielstick 5,000-bhp diesels; diesel-electric drive; 4 props; 22,000 hp
**Man:** 16 officers, 38 men

REMARKS: Two props forward, two aft. Helicopter platform. All personnel live and normally work above the main deck. Given permanent gun armament, mine rails, and fuel facilities for helicopters: *Frej* in 10-83, others in 1984. Guns mounted atop hangar and forward of pilothouse.

◆ **1 Ale class** Bldr: Wärtsilä, Helsinki, Finland

| | L | In serv. |
|---|---|---|
| ALE | 1-6-73 | 12-12-73 |

**Ale** L. & L. Van Ginderen, 8-82

**D:** 1,488 tons **S:** 14 kts **Dim:** 46.0 × 13.0 × 5.0
**M:** diesels; 2 props; 4,750 hp **Man:** 21 tot.

REMARKS: Built for service on Lake Vänern in central Sweden, also used for surveying in summer.

◆ **1 modified Tor class** Bldr: Wärtsilä, Helsinki, Finland

| | L | In serv. |
|---|---|---|
| NJORD | 2-10-68 | 10-69 |

**Njord** L. & L. Van Ginderen, 2-85

**D:** 5,150 tons (5,686 fl) **S:** 18 kts **Dim:** 86.45 (79.45 pp) × 21.18 × 6.9
**A:** 3/40-mm AA (I × 3)
**M:** diesel-electric propulsion: 4 Sulzer 9MH-51 diesels; Stromberg electric motors, 2 fwd (3,400 kw each), 2 aft (2,200 kw each); 4 props; 13,620 hp

REMARKS: Three directors installed for the 40-mm AA guns.

◆ **1 Tor class** Bldr: Wärtsilä, Turku, Finland

| | L | In serv. |
|---|---|---|
| TOR | 25-5-63 | 31-1-64 |

**Tor** Wärtsilä

**D:** 4,980 tons (5,290 fl) **S:** 18 kts **Dim:** 84.4 × 20.42 × 6.2
**A:** 3/40-mm AA (I × 3)
**M:** diesel-electric propulsion, 4 Sulzer 9MH-51 diesels; 4 props; 11,200 hp
Same motors as the *Njord*.

REMARKS: The Finnish *Tarmo* is similar. Two propellers fwd, two aft.

◆ **1 Oden class** Bldr: Sandviken, Helsinki, Finland

| | L | In serv. |
|---|---|---|
| ODEN | 16-10-56 | 1958 |

**Oden** L. & L. Van Ginderen, 3-86

## ICEBREAKERS *(continued)*

**D:** 4,950 tons (3,370 light) **S:** 17 kts **Dim:** 83.35 (78 pp) × 19.4 × 6.9
**M:** diesel-electric; 4 props (2 fwd, 2 aft); 10,500 hp
**Fuel:** 740 tons **Man:** 75 tot.

REMARKS: Very similar to the Finnish *Voima* and the three Soviet *Kapitan Belousov* class. Can be armed with 4/40-mm AA (I × 4). Refitted 1984–85.

◆ **2 Thule class** Bldr: Karlskrona

| | L | In serv. |
|---|---|---|
| THULE | 10-51 | 1953 |

**Thule** G. Gyssels, 9-85

**D:** 2,280 tons (fl) **S:** 14 kts **Dim:** 57.00 × 16.07 × 5.90
**M:** 3 diesels, electric drive; 3 props (1 fwd); 4,800 hp **Man:** 43 tot.

REMARKS: A 1980 plan to convert this ship to act as a mine countermeasures support ship was apparently canceled.

◆ **1 harbor icebreaker/navigational aids tender** Bldr: Åsiverken AB

BALTICA (In serv. 1982)

**D:** 1,238 tons (fl) **S:** 15 kts **Dim:** 54.9 (50.0 pp) × 12.0 × 3.7 (mean)
**Electron Equipt:** Radar: 1/Decca "Arpa," 1/Decca "Clearscan"
**M:** 2 Hedemora V16A/12 diesels; 1 CP prop; 3,520 hp
**Electric:** 1,375 kVA **Fuel:** 140 tons **Man:** 12 tot.

REMARKS: 857 grt/252 nrt. Two 300-hp tunnel side-thrusters. Twelve-ton electrohydraulic crane serving combination buoy hold/workshop. Can tow at 50-ton bollard pull. Capable of operating in light ice conditions. Civilian-manned.

## HYDROGRAPHIC SHIPS

NOTE: Swedish hydrographic ships are operated by the Navy, but are owned by the Ministry of Transport. The icebreaker *Ale* also performs survey tasks.

◆ **1 new-construction survey ship** Bldr: Oskarshamns SY

NILS STRÖMKRONA (In serv. 28-6-85)

**D:** 175 tons **S:** 12 kts **Dim:** 29.0 × 10.0 × 1.6
**M:** 4 Saab Scania diesels; 2 props; 1,732 hp **Man:** 14 tot.

REMARKS: Built to replace 1894-vintage unit with the same name. Catamaran hull.

◆ **1 seagoing survey ship** Bldr: Falkenbergs Varvet

| | Laid down | L | In serv. |
|---|---|---|---|
| JOHAN NORDENANKAR | 1977 | 1-11-79 | 1-7-80 |

**D:** 2,000 tons (fl) **S:** 15 kts **Dim:** 73.0 (64.0 pp) × 14.0 × 3.8
**Electron Equipt:** Radar: 1/Raytheon Raycas, 1/Decca . . .
**M:** 2 Hedemora V16A/12 diesels; 2 KaMeWa CP props; 3,520 hp
**Electric:** 2,246 kVA **Man:** 66 tot.

REMARKS: Acts as mother ship for nine small survey craft that act in teams. Data collected by the launches are telemetered to the ship and collected via the Krupp-Atlas computer. There are three sets of davits per side, with 3 additional boats in an internal hangar. Ship very maneuverable, with 700-hp drop-down bow-thruster, which can also drive the ship at 4.5 kts, and a Becker KSV flap-rudder; turning radius 150 m. Navigation equipment includes Decca Navigator, Magnavox NAVSAT receiver, Decca Sea Fix, Syledis Ranger, Syledis Miniranger, and 8 echo-sounders. Passive tank stabilization. Helo platform aft. Hull red, superstructure white.

◆ **1 seagoing survey ship** (L: 14-1-66)

JOHAAN MÅNSSON

**D:** 977 tons (1,030 fl) **S:** 15 kts **Dim:** 56.0 × 11.0 × 2.6
**M:** Nohab-Polar diesel; 3,300 hp **Man:** 85 tot.

REMARKS: Survey boats are stowed in a hangar aft and launched/recovered via a ramp.

**Johaan Månsson** Royal Swedish Navy, 1975

◆ **1 coastal survey boat** Bldr: Djupviks, Rönnäng (In serv. 10-82)

JACOB HÄGG

**D:** 130 tons (fl) **S:** 16.5 kts **Dim:** 36.50 × 7.50 × 1.65
**M:** 4 Saab-Scania DSI-14 diesels; 2 props; 1,684 hp (1,300 sust.)

REMARKS: Aluminum construction. The same builder also delivered a 42-ton, 400-hp hydrographic survey launch in 1953. The former "lead boats" No. 1 and No. 94 were named *Sirius* and *Kompass* in 1982, respectively, and now operate independently.

◆ **1 coastal survey boat** (In serv. 1968)

ANDERS BURE (ex-*Rali*)

**D:** 54 tons **S:** 15 kts **Dim:** 24.6 × 5.9 × 2.0
**M:** 2 diesels; 2 props; . . . hp **Man:** 11 tot.

REMARKS: Former yacht bought in 1971.

### COASTAL ARTILLERY SERVICE

The Coastal Artillery Service has 3,900 active personnel (2,800 conscripts) and 3,000 reservists. In addition to the craft described below it operates 75-mm, 120-mm, and 152-mm coast defense artillery, 40-mm AA guns, 120-mm mortars, and Carl Gustav anti-armor missiles. The *Kustartilleriet* is receiving 120-mm Bofors Karin mobile artillery, RBS-15, and RBS-17 antiship missiles. Organized into 5 regiments and subordinated to the Navy, the Coast Artillery also has a 265-man ranger battalion.

## PATROL CRAFT

◆ **1 antisubmarine patrol boat** Bldr: Wico Oy, Helsinki (In serv. 6-87)

**D:** . . . **S:** . . . **Dim:** . . . × . . . × . . . **A:** 6 ASW rockets **M:** . . .

REMARKS: Prototype ordered 1987 as a transport for "submarine mobile surveillance systems." "Rockets" may mean depth charges. Craft also described as a tender.

◆ **17 61 class**

61 to 77

**72** H. Ehlers, 6-85

**D:** 28 tons (30 fl) **S:** 19 kts **Dim:** 21.1 × 4.6 × 1.3
**A:** 1/20-mm AA **M:** 2 diesels; 2 props; . . . hp
**Electron Equipt:** Radar: 1/Decca RM914C

REMARKS: Built in two series, nos. 61 to 70 in 1960–61 and nos. 71 to 77 in 1966–67.

## MINELAYERS

◆ **1 (+9) MUL 20 class** Bldr: Åsiverken, Araal

| | L | In serv. |
|---|---|---|
| MUL 20 FURUSUND | 16-12-82 | 10-10-83 |

**D:** 225 tons (245 fl) **S:** 11 kts **Dim:** 32.4 (30.0 pp) × 8.4 × 1.8
**A:** 1/20-mm AA—2/7.62-mm mg (I × 1)—24 tons mines
**Electron Equipt:** Radar: 1/Decca RM 1226C

**MINELAYERS** *(continued)*

**M:** 2 Saab-Scania GASI-14 diesels (335 hp each), ASEA 300 kVA electric drive; 2 props; 420 hp + 1/125-hp maneuvering prop
**Man:** 24 tot. (10 peacetime) **Electric:** 73 kw

**Furusund (MUL 20)** Royal Swedish Navy, 1984

Remarks: MUL 20 ordered 23-6-81. An ultimate total of ten is planned.

◆ **8 MUL 12-class mine planters** (In serv. 1952–56)

MUL 12 Arkosund
MUL 13 Kalmarsund
MUL 14 Arnösund
MUL 15 Grundsund
MUL 16 Färösund
MUL 17 Skramsösund
MUL 18 Öresund
MUL 19 Bårösund

**Öresund (MUL 18)** H. Ehlers, 6-85

**D:** 245 tons **S:** 10.5 kts **Dim:** 31.18 (29.0 pp) × 7.62 × 3.1
**A:** 1/40-mm AA—. . . mines **Electron Equipt:** Radar: 1/Decca RM 1226C
**M:** 2 Nohab diesels; 2 props; 460 hp

Remarks: Launched 1952–56. These craft are used for placing and maintaining controlled mine fields. Given names 1985–86.

◆ **1 coastal mine planter** (L: 1946)

MUL 11

**MUL 11** L. & L. Van Ginderen, 10-82

**D:** 200 tons **S:** 10 kts **Dim:** 30.1 (27.0 pp) × 7.21 × 3.65
**A:** 2/20-mm (I × 2)—mines **M:** 2 Atlas diesels; 1 prop; 300 hp

◆ **42 501-class minelaying launches** (L: 1969–71)

501 through 542

**502** Royal Swedish Navy, 1981

**D:** 14 tons (fl) **S:** 14 kts **Dim:** 14.6 × 4.2 × 0.9 **A:** 12 mines
**Electron Equipt:** Radar: 1/Decca RM 914C **M:** diesels **Man:** 7 tot.

Note: The 80 201-series personnel landing craft can also be fitted to lay mines.

◆ **6 small minelaying craft** Bldr: Marinvarvet, Fårösund

1879–1881 (In serv. 4-7-83) 1882–1884 (In serv. 23-1-84)

Remarks: Displace 2.5 tons; no other data available. Ordered 27-11-82.

**LANDING CRAFT**

◆ **3 Grim-class utility landing craft** Bldr: Åsiverken

Bore Grim Heimdal

**Bore** Royal Swedish Navy, 1969

**D:** 340 tons (fl) **S:** 12 kts **Dim:** 36.0 × 8.5 × 2.6
**A:** none **M:** 2 diesels; 2 props; 800 hp

Remarks: *Grim* was launched in 1962, *Bore* and *Heimdal* in 1967. Car ferry design; bow hinges upward to permit extending ramp. Can be adapted to lay mines.

◆ **2 Sleipner-class utility landing craft**

Skagul (L: 1960) Sleipner (L: 1959)

**D:** 335 tons **S:** 10 kts **Dim:** 35.0 × 8.5 × 2.9
**A:** none **M:** 2 diesels; 2 props; 640 hp

Remarks: Similar to the *Grim* class. Can be adapted to lay mines.

◆ **4 Ane-class utility landing craft** (L: 1943–45)

324 Ane 325 Balder 326 Loke 327 Ring

**D:** 135 tons **S:** 8.5 kts **Dim:** 28.0 × 8.0 × 1.8
**A:** 1/20-mm AA **M:** 2 diesels

Remarks: Equipped with a bow ramp. Can be adapted to lay mines.

LANDING CRAFT *(continued)*

**Loke** L. & L. Van Ginderen, 7-87

◆ **13 vehicle landing craft** Bldr: Djupviks, Tjörn; Oskarhamms; Marinvarvet, Fårösund

601, 603, 607–610, 651–657

**Donso (653)** L. & L. Van Ginderen, 8-87

**D:** 20 tons (53 fl) **S:** 8–10 kts **Dim:** 21.0 (20.0 pp) × 7.2 × 0.7
**A:** none **Electron Equipt:** Radar: 1/Decca RM 914C
**M:** 2 Saab-Scania DSI-11/40-M20 diesels; 2 Schottel props; 340 hp
**Cargo:** 25 tons deck cargo or 30 tons liquid **Man:** . . .

Remarks: The prototype was delivered in 1978: classified as "support boats." No. 603 delivered 2-4-84 by Marinvarvet; Nos. 604, 605 delivered 1-10-84 by Djupviks. No. 607 in service 1-9-86; 608 on 22-9-86, 609 on 12-3-87, 610 on 27-4-86. Are apparently being given names.

◆ **0 (+1) S-90-class prototype** Bldr: Djupviks, Tjörn

**D:** . . . **S:** . . . **Dim:** 23.0 × . . . × . . . **A:** . . . **M:** . . .

Remarks: Ordered 1987. Another attempt at a replacement design for the 201 class. To carry 40 troops.

◆ **1 (+ . . .) M 85-class large personnel landing craft** Bldr: Marinvarvet, Fårösund

81 (In serv. 31-7-85)

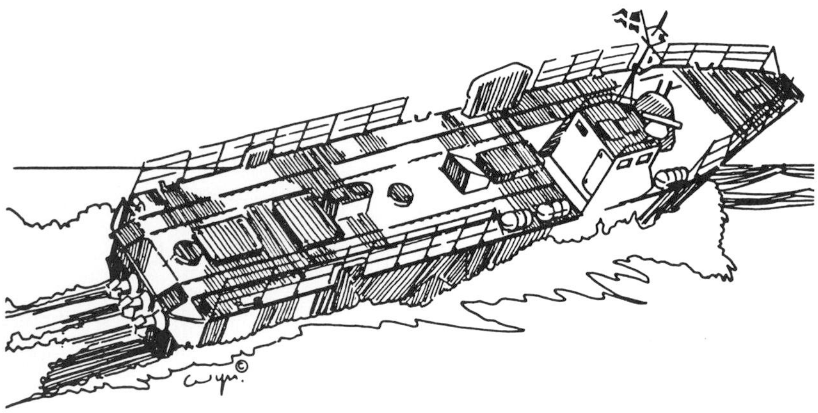

**M 85 design** 1984

**D:** 55 tons (65 fl) **S:** 20 kts **Dim:** 28.40 (24.00 pp) × 5.60 × 0.80
**A:** 2 or 3/7.62-mm mg (I × 2 or 3)—mines
**Electron Equipt:** Radar: 1/. . . nav.
**M:** 3 Saab-Scania DSI-14 diesels; 3 waterjets; 1,350 hp
**Man:** 4 crew + 45 troops

Remarks: Enclosed troop compartment, ramps on either side of bow. Aluminum prototype replacement design for 201 series. Ordered 27-7-84; laid down 5-12-84. As many as 140 may be built.

◆ **80 201-series large personnel landing craft**

Bldrs: Lundevarv Verkstads and Marinteknik, Oregrund (In serv. 1957–77)

201 through 208; 210 through 276; 280 through 284

**259** L. & L. Van Ginderen, 5-87

**281**—with mine rails L. & L. Van Ginderen, 5-81

**D:** 31 tons (fl) **S:** 17 kts **Dim:** 21.4 × 4.2 × 1.3
**A:** 2 or 3/6.5-mm mg (II × 1, I × 1)—mines
**Electron Equipt:** Radar: 1/Decca RM 914C
**M:** 3 Saab-Scania 6 DS 11 diesels; 3 props; 705 hp **Man:** 5 crew, 40 troops

Remarks: 266 through 269 have Volvo Penta diesels. Early units were 20 meters overall and had three 200-hp diesels. Patrol-boat-like bow opens to permit extension of ramp from troop compartment below decks. Twin machine gun to port, plus single mount aft in some. Mine rails can be laid from the pilothouse over the stern. 210 was re-engined 1984 by Djupviks with 2 Saab-Scania DSI-14 diesels; 2 steerable hydraulic drives; 950 hp; pilot program for a class-wide rehabilitation. 209 was stricken in 1984.

◆ **1 DVA.115-class inspection boat** Bldr: Djupviks, Tjörn/Rönnäng

344 (L: 1-7-86; in serv. 1-11-86)

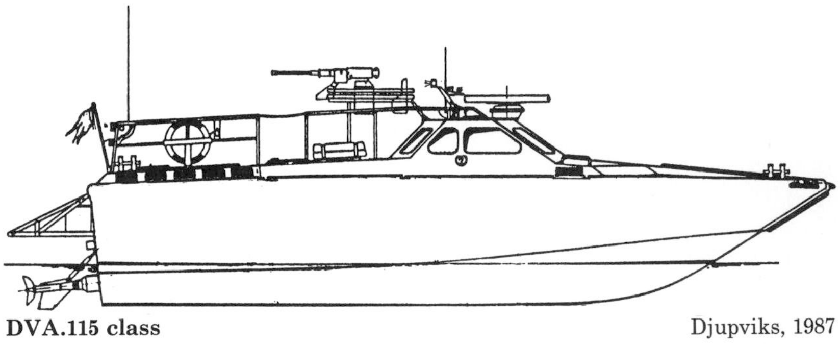

**DVA.115 class** Djupviks, 1987

**D:** . . . **S:** 40 kts (35.4 sust.) **Dim:** 11.64 × 3.80 × 0.63
**A:** 1/12.7-mm mg **Electron Equipt:** Radar: 1/. . . nav.
**M:** 2 Volvo Penta TAMD 71 outdrive diesels; 2 props; 700 hp
**Range:** 180/35.4 **Man:** 3 crew + 7 to 9 troops

Remarks: GRP construction. Ordered 1-4-86. Also referred to as 90-m class by builder. Has bow ramp atop Vee-form hull. Payload: 3 tons. Up to 150 additional may be procured.

**LANDING CRAFT** *(continued)*

◆ **25 (+ . . .) personnel landing craft**

| | L | | | |
|---|---|---|---|---|
| 370 . . . | 1981 | **D:** . . . tons | **S:** . . . kts | **M:** 560 hp |
| 337 through 354 | 1970–73 | **D:** 6 tons | **S:** 21 kts | **M:** 225 hp |
| 332 through 336 | 1967 | **D:** 5.4 tons | **S:** 25 kts | **M:** 225 hp |
| 331 | 1965 | **D:** 6 tons | **S:** 20 kts | |

**333 (332 series)** L. & L. Van Ginderen

**348 (337 series)** L. & L. Van Ginderen, 8-82

Remarks: The prototype of a new series, number 370, was delivered 2-9-81; the craft is powered by two Volvo Penta TAMD 70 diesels. 301 through 330 stricken 1984.

◆ **20 support tenders** Bldr: Djupviks, Tjörn (In serv. 1982–85)

701–705; 751–756, . . .

**703** H. Ehlers, 4-85

**D:** 42 tons **S:** 9.5 kts **Dim:** 15.5 × 5.0 × 2.7 **M:** 1 diesel; 1 prop; . . . hp

Remarks: Can be used to transport cargo, personnel, to plant mines, or as tugs. Bulwarks at bow open to permit debarking personnel over a beach.

◆ **12 (+ . . .) support tenders**

401–412 (+ . . . ?)

**404** L. & L. Van Ginderen, 7-86

Remarks: Wooden-hulled utility tenders. Number in service not available. Powered by a single diesel; have a Decca RM914C radar.

## COAST GUARD

The Swedish Coast Guard, organized in 1638, is primarily concerned with rescue and customs services and with anti-pollution patrol and cleanup. In addition to some 130 boats and craft, it also operates 2 Cessna F337G patrol aircraft with side-looking radar (SLAR), one Cessna 402C, and a chartered helicopter. Two CASA C-212-200 Aviocar light transports were ordered 16-12-85 and delivered 20-8-86 with side-looking radar. Four BO-105 helicopters ordered 1985. All boat pendants are prefixed "Tv"—*Tullverket* (Central Customs Office). The Coast Guard is organized into four Regions, with a total of 15 Districts; each District has 2 to 4 stations. All units are painted white and have a narrow red diagonal stripe on each side of the hull. None are armed.

**PATROL BOATS AND CRAFT**

Note: A 600-ton patrol boat is in the planning stages.

◆ **2 Tv 171 class** Bldr: Karlskrona

| | L | In serv. |
|---|---|---|
| Tv 171 | 11-79 | 3-9-80 |
| Tv 172 | 13-9-80 | 10-81 |

**Tv 172** H. Ehlers, 4-85

**D:** 375 tons (fl) **S:** 20 kts **Dim:** 49.90 (46.00 pp) × 8.52 × 2.40
**Electron Equipt:** Radar: 2/Decca navigational—Sonar: Simrad Subsea
**M:** 2 Hedemora V16A/15 diesels; 2 KaMeWa CP props; 4,480 hp
**Electric:** 340 kVA **Range:** 500/20; 3,000/12 **Man:** 14 tot.

Remarks: Class "A" cutters. Tv 171 lengthened by 6 m in 1981; Tv 172 longer as completed. Helicopter platform, bow-thruster. Glass-reinforced plastic sandwich hull construction, originally developed for the not-built M 70-class naval minesweeper. Fire monitor can be replaced by a 40-mm gun, and mine rails can be fitted.

◆ **5 Tv 103 class** Bldr: Djupviks, Tjörn (In serv. 1969–73)

Tv 101 Tv 102 Tv 103 Tv 104 Tv 105

**D:** 53 tons (fl) **S:** 22 kts **Dim:** 26.72 × 5.23 × 1.13
**M:** 2 MTU 8V331 TC82 diesels; 2 props; 1,866 hp **Electric:** 60 kVA
**Fuel:** 11 tons **Range:** 1,000/15 **Man:** 6 tot.

PATROL BOATS AND CRAFT *(continued)*

**Tv 102** L. & L. Van Ginderen, 8-86

REMARKS: Class "A" cutters. Aluminum construction. Tv 101: **D:** 50 tons (fl); **Dim:** 24.9 × 5.0 × . . . ; pilothouse farther forward than in others. Three sisters in Liberian Coast Guard.

◆ **8 Tv 271-class** (In serv. 1974–77)

Tv 271 through Tv 278

**Tv 275** L. & L. Van Ginderen, 10-86

**D:** 20 tons (fl) **S:** 20 kts **Dim:** 19.0 × 4.2 × 1.4
**M:** 2 Volvo Penta TAMD 120A diesels; 2 props; 700 hp
**Electric:** 46.5 kw **Man:** 5 tot.

REMARKS: Aluminum construction. Tv 271, 272: 18.7 × 4.0 × 1.4. Class "B" cutters.

◆ **1 Tv 116-class steel-hulled** (In serv. 1935)

Tv 116

**D:** 36 tons (fl) **S:** . . . **Dim:** 24.4 × 4.2 × . . . **M:** diesels

**Tv 116** H. Ehlers, 4-85

◆ **7 (+ . . .) Tv 281 class** Bldr: Djupviks, Tjörn/Rönnäng

Tv 281
Tv 282 (In serv. . . .)
Tv 283 (In serv. 1979–80)
Tv 284 (In serv. 30-1-84)
Tv 285 (In serv. 2-5-84)
Tv 286 (In serv. 21-8-86)
Tv 287 (In serv. 12-2-87)

**Tv 284** H. Ehlers, 4-85

**D:** 37 tons (42 fl) **S:** 30+ kts **Dim:** 21.0 × 5.0 × . . . **Man:** 5 tot.
**M:** 2 Cummins diesels; 2 props; 2,100 hp **Electron Equipt:** 2/Decca . . . nav.

REMARKS: Class "B" cutters. Additional units planned. Aluminum construction. Tv 286, 287 ordered 1-9-85. Tv 286 launched 14-6-86, Tv 287 on 25-1-87.

◆ **21 Tv 236-class aluminum-hulled class "D" cutters** (In serv. 1961–72)

Tv 236 through Tv 238, Tv 240 through Tv 250, Tv 255 through Tv 261

**D:** 17 tons **S:** . . . **Dim:** 16.2 × 3.7 × . . .

**Tv 250**—with enclosed pilothouse L. & L. Van Ginderen, 8-86

**Tv 256** H. Ehlers, 4-85

**PATROL BOATS AND CRAFT** *(continued)*

REMARKS: Tv 250 has an enlarged pilothouse and no open bridge. Tv 238 has tripod mast on forecastle.

◆ **1 Tv 234-class aluminum-hulled, Class "B"** (In serv. 1960)

Tv 234

**D:** 15 tons (fl) **S:** . . . **Dim:** 15.2 × 3.6 × . . .

◆ **4 Tv 251-class aluminum-hulled, Class "B"** (In serv. 1958–61)

Tv 251 Tv 252 Tv 253 Tv 254

**D:** 12 tons (fl) **S:** . . . **Dim:** 15.0 × 3.7 × . . .

◆ **3 Tv 220-class**

Tv 220 (In serv. 1954) Tv 230 (In serv. 1957) Tv 232 (In serv. 1957)

**D:** 12 tons (fl) **S:** 20 kts **Dim:** 14.0 × 3.4 × . . .
**M:** 1 Volvo Penta diesel; . . . hp

◆ **26 miscellaneous speedboats** (In serv. 1962–79)

Tv 314, 315, 317, 318, 341, 350, 356, 360, 363, 365, 366, 368, 369, 371–374, 381–385, 388–391

◆ **6 inflatable boats** (In serv. 1971–75)

Tv 602, 661–665

◆ **5 iceboats** (In serv. 1965–72)

Tv 801, Tv 804–807—**Dim:** 5.0 × 2.0

**POLLUTION-CONTROL SHIPS AND CRAFT**

NOTE: Class A anti-pollution units are described as "Depôt Ships"; Class B are "Sea Trucks"; Class C are "Base Ships"; and Class D are catamarans.

◆ **1 Class A** Bldr: Lunde, Ramvik

Tv 06 (L: 24-3-85)

**D:** 450 tons (fl) **S:** 15 kts **Dim:** 37.35 (33.70 pp) × 8.80 × . . .
**M:** 2 Cummins KTA-2300M diesels; 2 rudder props; 2,100 hp
**Fuel:** 30.5 tons **Man:** 6 tot.

REMARKS: Similar to Tv 04 design; ordered 12-84. Also reported as "Tv 010."

◆ **2 Class A** Bldr: Lunde, Ramvik

Tv 04 (In serv. 1980)

**Tv 04** H. Ehlers, 4-85

**D:** 450 tons (fl) **S:** 12 kts **Dim:** 35.5 × 8.0 × 3.0
**M:** 2 diesels; 2 props; 1,200 hp **Electric:** 224 kVA **Man:** 10 tot.

REMARKS: Helipad on fantail, 200-hp bow-thruster, 30-kt workboat, 80-m$^3$ oil-containment tanks, 500-m containment boom stowage, oil-spill skimming equipment, firefighting gear.

◆ **3 Class A**

| | In serv. | D: | Dim: |
|---|---|---|---|
| Tv 01 | 1971 | 190 tons (fl) | 26.0 × 6.7 × . . . |
| Tv 02 MÅKLAPPAN | 1973 | 260 tons (fl) | 33.0 × 7.2 × . . . |
| Tv 03 | 1973 | 300 tons (fl) | 34.0 × 6.6 × . . . |

◆ **2 Tv 050 class, Class B** Bldr: Lunde, Ramvik

Tv 050 (In serv. 20-9-83) Tv 051 (In serv. 6-83)

**D:** 340 tons (fl) **S:** . . . **Dim:** 32.6 × 8.5 × . . . **M:** diesels

REMARKS: Enlarged version of Tv 045 class.

◆ **5 Class B** Bldr: Lunde, Ramvik (In serv. 1980–83)

Tv 045 Tv 046 Tv 047 Tv 048 Tv 049

**Måklappan (Tv 02)**—the only named Coast Guard unit H. Ehlers, 4-85

**Tv 03** L. & L. Van Ginderen, 4-83

**Tv 051** L. & L. Van Ginderen, 7-87

**Tv 046** H. Ehlers, 4-85

## POLLUTION-CONTROL SHIPS AND CRAFT *(continued)*

**D:** 133 tons (230 fl) **S:** 11 kts **Dim:** 28.9 (24.80 pp) × 6.5 × 1.9
**Fuel:** 18 tons **M:** 2 Saab-Scania DST-11 diesels; 2 props; 540 hp
**Electric:** 300 kw **Man:** 4 tot.

REMARKS: Resemble landing craft, with bow ramp. 110-$m^3$ tanks for recovered oil. Hydraulic thrusters fore and aft. Stowage for 800-m oil-spill-containment booms. Endless belt-type oil-recovery device.

◆ **3 Tv 041 class, Class B oil-spill-combating boats** (In serv. 1972)

Tv 041 Tv 042 Tv 043

**Tv 042** H. Ehlers, 4-85

**D:** 70 tons (fl) **S:** . . . **Dim:** 18.4 × 5.4 × . . .

◆ **2 miscellaneous Class B oil-spill-combating boats**

| | In serv. | D: | Dim: |
|---|---|---|---|
| Tv 044 | 1976 | 100 tons (fl) | 25.0 × 6.0 |
| Tv 059 | 1974 | 22 tons (fl) | |

◆ **3 Tv 011 class, Class C**

Tv 011 (In serv. 1974) Tv 012 (In serv. 1970) Tv 014 (In serv. 1971)

**Tv 012** L. & L. Van Ginderen, 11-82

**D:** 50 tons (fl) **S:** . . . **Dim:** 25.0 × 5.1 × . . .

REMARKS: Wooden construction.

◆ **1 Tv 015 class, Class C** (In serv. 1971)

Tv 015

**D:** 140 tons (fl) **S:** . . . **Dim:** 23.0 × 5.5 × . . .

◆ **1 Class D1 catamaran** Bldr: Djupvik, Tjörn (In serv. 8-6-82)

Tv 020

**Tv 020** L. & L. Van Ginderen, 8-86

**D:** 60 tons (fl) **S:** 27 kts **Dim:** 27.6 × 9.2 × 1.5
**M:** 2 MTU J2V396 TB82 diesels; 2 props; 2,600 hp

REMARKS: Drum-type skimmer mounted forward between the hulls can recover up to 40 tons/hr., or a belt-type cleaner can recover 10–20 tons/hr. Design is Norway's Westermoen 88.

◆ **3 miscellaneous Class D2 catamarans**

| | In serv. | D: | Dim: |
|---|---|---|---|
| Tv 021 | 1973 | 30 tons (fl) | 14.0 × 7.0 |
| Tv 022 | 1973 | 30 tons (fl) | 14.0 × 7.0 |
| Tv 023 | 1975 | 30 tons (fl) | 16.5 × 7.5 |

**Tv 023**—catamaran oil-spill boat H. Ehlers, 4-85

**Tv 022** H. Ehlers, 4-85

**SWEDEN** *(continued)*
**POLLUTION-CONTROL SHIPS AND CRAFT** *(continued)*

◆ **5 Class E shore-cleaning boats** (In serv. 1979–1982)

Tv 0701 Tv 0702 Tv 0703 Tv 0704 Tv 0705

**Tv 0705**—shore-cleaning boat (with sister) H. Ehlers, 4-85

**D:** 9 tons **S:** . . . **Dim:** 9.0 × 3.1 × . . .

◆ **6 miscellaneous Class G oil barges**

| | In serv. | D: | Dim: |
|---|---|---|---|
| Tv 061 | 1974 | 300 tons (fl) | 28.8 × 6.3 × . . . |
| Tv 062 | 1975 | 140 tons (fl) | 12.0 × 6.0 × . . . |
| Tv 063 | 1974 | 250 tons (fl) | 28.8 × 6.3 × . . . |
| Tv 064 | 1981 | . . . | . . . |
| Tv 065 | . . . | . . . | . . . |
| Tv 068 | 1979 | 400 tons (fl) | 30.6 × 6.8 × . . . |
| Tv 069 | 1980 | 360 tons (fl) | 30.6 × 6.7 × . . . |

**Tv 061**—oil barge H. Ehlers, 4-85

Remarks: Tv 065 is a car ferry at Göteborg

◆ **4 Class H small craft** (In serv. 1973–75)

Tv 031–Tv 034

**D:** 6 tons (fl) **S:** . . . **Dim:** 7.5 × 2.5 × . . .

◆ **1 Class J seasled** (In serv. 1979): Tv 036—**Dim:** 11.8 × 4.6

◆ **20 miscellaneous Class K workboats** (In serv. 1971–82)

Tv 080–Tv 099

**D:** 0.8 to 1.0 tons (fl) **S:** . . . **Dim:** 5.8 to 6.5 × 2.4 to 2.7 × . . .

# SWITZERLAND

## Swiss Confederation

Merchant Marine (1986): 34 ships—346,220 grt (1 tanker—799 grt)

SWISS ARMY

### PATROL CRAFT

◆ **11 Patrouillenboat 80 class** Bldr: Müller AG, Spiez (In serv. 1981–84)

Antares, Aquarius, Castor, Mars, Orion, Perseus, Pollux, Saturn, Sirius, Venus, Uranus

**P 80 class** Swiss Army

**D:** 5.9 tons (fl) **S:** 35 kts **Dim:** 10.7 × 3.3 × 0.9 (0.6 hull)
**A:** 2/12.7-mm M3 mg (I × 2) **Man:** 6 tot.
**M:** 2 Volvo Penta AQ 260A gasoline engines; 2 props; 560 hp

Remarks: Glass-reinforced plastic construction, wooden superstructure. Replaced a group of wooden-hulled craft built in 1942. Employed on Lakes Constance, Leman, and Majeur.

# SYRIA

## Syrian Arab Republic

Personnel (1987): approximately 2,500 total, plus 2,500 reserves

Merchant Marine (1986): 57 ships—63,142 grt

Naval Aviation: Helicopters: 3 Kamov Ka-25 Hormone-A ASW and 20 Mi-14 Haze-A ASW

Note: Coast-defense batteries of SSC-1b Shaddock and SSC-3 Styx missiles have been transferred from the U.S.S.R. They are mounted on vehicles.

### SUBMARINES

◆ **3 Soviet Romeo class** Bldr: Baltic SY, Leningrad (In serv. 1957–60)

**Syrian Romeo** L. & L. Van Ginderen, 11-86

**D:** 1,350 tons surfaced/1,700 tons submerged **S:** 15.5/13 kts
**Dim:** 77.0 × 6.7 × 4.9 **A:** 8/533-mm TT (6 fwd, 2 aft; 14 torpedoes or 28 mines)
**Electron Equipt:** Radar: 1/Snoop Plate
Sonar: MF active, passive
EW: Stop Light intercept
**M:** 2 Type 37D diesels (2,000 hp each), 2 electric motors; 2 props; 2,700 hp
**Range:** 7,000/5 snorkel **Endurance:** 45 days **Man:** 56 tot.

Remarks: First pair transferred 11-85, with the third arriving 12-86. Also transferred was a Whiskey-class submarine converted as a battery-charging hulk to support these ships.

### FRIGATES

◆ **2 ex-Soviet Petya class**

12 N . . . . . . . 14 N . . . . . . .

**D:** 950 tons (1,150 fl) **S:** 29 kts **Dim:** 81.8 (78.00 pp) × 9.2 × 2.97 (mean hull)
**A:** 4/76.2-mm DP (II × 2)—4/RBU-2500 ASW RL (XVI × 4)—3/533-mm TT (III × 1)—2/d.c. racks—mines
**Electron Equipt:** 1/Don-2, 1/Strut Curve, 1/Hawk Screech
IFF: 2/Square Head, 1/High Pole B
Sonar: Hull-mounted HF

**FRIGATES** *(continued)*

**M:** CODAG: 2 gas turbines (15,000 hp each); 1 Type 61V3 diesel (6,000 hp); 3 props; 36,000 hp
**Range:** 450/29; 4,800/10 **Man:** 8 officers, 84 men

**Syrian Petya No. 14** 6th F., French Navy, 10-83

Remarks: Transferred: 1975. Standard export version, with triple 533-mm TT substituted for Soviet Navy quintuple 400-mm mount.

## CORVETTE

◆ **1 Soviet Natya class**

**Syria's Natya (transfer No. 642)** 21st F., French Navy, 1-85

**D:** 650 tons (750 fl) **S:** 18 kts **Dim:** 61.0 × 9.8 × 3.0
**A:** 4/30-mm AK-230 AA (II × 2)—4/25-mm AA (II × 2)
**Electron Equipt:** Radar: 1/Spin Trough nav., 1/Drum Tilt f.c.
IFF: 2/Square Head interrogators, 1/High Pole A transponder
**M:** 2 diesels; 2 props; 5,000 hp **Range:** 1,800/16; 5,200/10 **Man:** 60 tot.

Remarks: Transferred 26-1-85. Not equipped with any of the normal Natya-class seagoing minesweeper mine countermeasures equipment, winches, cranes, etc., nor does she have the standard 2/RBU-1200 ASW rocket launchers or mine rails.

## GUIDED-MISSILE PATROL BOATS

◆ **12 ex-Soviet Osa-II class**

**Syrian Osa-II** 6th F., French Navy, 10-83

**D:** 215 tons (240 fl) **S:** 35 kts **Dim:** 38.6 × 7.6 × 2.0
**A:** 4/SS-N-2B Styx SSM (I × 4)—4/30-mm AA (II × 2)
**Electron Equipt:** Radar: 1/Square Tie, 1/Drum Tilt
IFF: 2/Square Head, 1/High Pole B
**M:** 3 M504 diesels; 3 props; 15,000 hp **Range:** 500/34; 750/25
**Man:** 28–30 tot.

Remarks: Two transferred 1978, four in 1979, two in 1982, two in 5-84, two in 1985. The pair delivered in 1984 were each equipped with one 16-tubed decoy RL.

◆ **6 ex-Soviet Osa-I class**

**Syrian Osa-I** 6th F., French Navy, 10-83

**D:** 175 tons (209 fl) **S:** 36 kts **Dim:** 38.6 × 7.6 × 1.8
**A:** 4/SS-N-2 Styx (I × 4)
**Electron Equipt:** Radar: 1/Square Tie, 1/Drum Tilt
IFF: 2/Square Head, 1/High Pole B
**M:** 3 M503A diesels; 3 props; 12,000 hp **Range:** 500/34 **Man:** 28–30 tot.

Remarks: Transferred 1966; two others were sunk during the Arab-Israeli War, October 1973.

## PATROL CRAFT

◆ **9 Soviet Zhuk class**

**D:** 48 tons (60 fl) **S:** 34 kts **Dim:** 24.0 × 5.0 × 1.2 (1.8 props)
**A:** 4/14.5-mm mg (II × 2)
**Electron Equipt:** Radar: 1/Spin Trough
IFF: 1/High Pole A
**M:** 2 M50F-4 diesels; 2 props; 2,400 hp **Fuel:** 10 tons
**Range:** 700/28; 1,100/15 **Man:** 12 tot.

Remarks: Three delivered 12-83, 3 in 12-84, three in 1-85.

## MINE WARFARE UNITS

◆ **1 Soviet T-43-class fleet minesweeper**

504 Yarmouk

**D:** 500 tons (570 fl) **S:** 14 kts **Dim:** 58.0 × 8.6 × 2.3 (hull)
**A:** 4/37-mm AA (II × 2)—8/12.7-mm mg (II × 4)—2/d.c. mortars—mines
**Electron Equipt:** Radar: 1/Ball End **M:** 2 Type 9D diesels; 2 props; 2,200 hp
**Fuel:** 70 tons **Range:** 2,000/14; 3,200/10 **Man:** 75 tot.

Remarks: Transferred 1962; one sister lost in the October 1973 war.

◆ **1 Soviet Sonya-class coastal minesweeper** Bldr: Petrozavodsk SY

**D:** 380 tons (450 fl) **S:** 15 kts **Dim:** 48.8 × 8.8 × 2.1
**A:** 2/30-mm AA (II × 1)—2/25-mm AA (II × 1)
**Electron Equipt:** Radar: 1/Spin Trough
Sonar: . . .
IFF: 1/High Pole B transponder, 2/Square Head
**M:** 2 diesels; 2 props; 2,400 hp **Range:** 1,600/14; 3,000/10 **Man:** 40 tot.

Remarks: Wooden construction, with hull sheathed in GRP. Arrived in Syria 1-86.

◆ **2 ex-Soviet Vanya-class coastal minesweepers**

**D:** 210 tons (250 fl) **S:** 16 kts **Dim:** 40.2 × 7.9 × 1.7
**A:** 2/30-mm AA (II × 1)—mines **Electron Equipt:** Radar: 1/Don-2
**M:** 2 diesels; 2 props; 2,200 hp **Range:** 1,400/14; 2,400/10 **Man:** 30 tot.

Remarks: Transferred 12-72. Wooden construction; glass-reinforced plastic-sheathed hull.

◆ **5 Soviet Yevgenya-class inshore minesweepers** Bldr: Sredniy Neva SY, Kolpino

**D:** 80 tons (90 fl) **S:** 11 kts **Dim:** 26.2 × 6.1 × 1.5
**A:** 2/14.5-mm mg (II × 1) **M:** 2 diesels; 2 props; 600 hp
**Electron Equipt:** Radar: 1/Spin Trough—IFF: 1/High Pole B
**Range:** 300/10 **Man:** 10 tot.

Remarks: Glass-reinforced plastic construction. Use television minehunting system to 30-m depths. First unit transferred 1978, second in 1981, the third and fourth arrived on 15-2-85, and the fifth on 19-1-86.

**SYRIA** *(continued)*

**AMPHIBIOUS WARFARE SHIPS**

◆ **3 Soviet Polnocny-B-class medium landing ships**

**D:** 800 tons (fl) **S:** 18 kts **Dim:** 74.0 × 8.6 × 2.0
**A:** 4/30-mm AK-230 AA (II × 2)—2/140-mm barrage RL (XVIII × 2)
**Electron Equipt:** Radar: 1/Spin Trough, 1/Drum Tilt
IFF: 1/Square Head, 1/High Pole B
**M:** 2 diesels; 2 props; 5,000 hp **Range:** 900/18; 1,500/14
**Man:** 40 crew + 100 troops

REMARKS: Transferred from U.S.S.R. 15-1-84, two in 2-85. Cargo: about 180 tons. May also have 2 or 4/SA-N-5 point-defense SAM stations (IV × 2 or 4).

**AUXILIARIES AND SERVICE CRAFT**

◆ **1 training ship/tender** Bldr: Gdansk SY, Poland

N . . . (L: 8-2-87; in serv. end-1987)

**D:** 3,500 tons (fl) **S:** . . . **Dim:** 105.00 × 17.20 × 4.00 **A:** . . .
**Electron Equipt:** Radar: . . . **M:** 2 diesels; 2 props; . . . hp

REMARKS: Ordered at the beginning of 1984. Combination repair ship and training ship.

◆ **1 Soviet Sekstan-class degaussing tender** (In serv. 1949–55)

**D:** 400 tons (fl) **S:** 11 kts **Dim:** 41.0 × 9.3 × 4.2
**M:** 1 diesel; 1 prop; 400 hp **Range:** 1,200/10.5 **Man:** 24 tot.

REMARKS: Transferred 12-83. Wooden construction.

◆ **1 Soviet Nyryat-1-class diving tender**

**D:** 120 tons (fl) **S:** 12 kts **Dim:** 29.0 × 5.0 × 1.7
**Electron Equipt:** Radar: 1/Spin Trough **M:** 1 diesel; 1 prop; 450 hp
**Range:** 1,600/10 **Man:** 15 tot.

◆ **3 survey launches** Bldr: ARCOR, La Teste, France (In serv. 1985)

**D:** . . . **S:** 25 kts **Dim:** 9.80 (8.50 pp) × 3.40 × 0.90
**M:** 2 Volvo Penta AQAD-40 diesels; 310 hp **Range:** 300/. . . **Man:** 4 tot.

REMARKS: Ordered 12-84. Glass-reinforced plastic construction.

◆ **1 ex-Soviet Whiskey-class battery-charging barge**

**D:** approx. 1,100 tons (fl) **Dim:** 76.0 × 6.3 × 4.8
**Electric:** approx. 2,800 kw (2 Type 37D, 2,000-hp diesels)

REMARKS: Former submarine, with tubes sealed, propellers removed, etc., used in support of the Romeo-class submarines. Transferred by 11-86.

# TAIWAN

## Republic of China

PERSONNEL (1985): 38,000 total Navy, plus 39,000 Marines; 45,000 naval reservists, 35,000 Marine reservists

MERCHANT MARINE (1986): 587 ships—4,272,795 grt
(tankers: 18 ships—581,173 grt)

**R.O.C.N. S-2E prior to modernization** *Defense Technology,* 1985

**R.O.C.N. Hughes-500 MD/ASW helicopter** *Defense Technology,* 1985

NAVAL AVIATION: Thirty-two S-2E/G. Twelve Hughes-500 MD/ASW helicopters with ASQ-81 (V) 2 magnetic anomaly detection (MAD) gear were ordered during 1979 for use from destroyers. The Marines have several light observation aircraft and helicopters. The S-2G are being modernized with two Garrett TPE 331-4/15, 1,645-hp turbine engines to give 270-kt maximum speed at 5,000 ft; the updates, performed by Grumman, include a new sonobuoy processor, MAD gear, FLIR, a new radar (APS-128 or APS-504), and new navigational and communications gear. The prototype conversions delivered 4-87, with series deliveries beginning in 1988. The Sikorsky S-70 helicopter is being built in an ASW version under license.

WARSHIPS IN SERVICE OR UNDER CONSTRUCTION
AS OF 1 JANUARY 1988

| | L | Tons (Surfaced) | Main Armament |
|---|---|---|---|
| ◆ **4 submarines** | | | |
| 2 HAI LUNG | 1986 | 2,300 | 6/533-mm TT |
| 2 GUPPY II | 1944–45 | 1,870 | 10/533-mm TT |
| ◆ **26 destroyers** | | Tons | |
| 12 GEARING FRAM-I | 1945–46 | 2,425 | 4/127-mm, 0–4/40-mm, ASW weapons |
| 2 GEARING FRAM-II | 1945 | 2,425 | 4–6/127-mm, 4–8/40-mm, ASW weapons |
| 2 ALLEN M. SUMNER FRAM-II | 1944 | 2,350 | 4 or 6/127-mm, SSM, ASW weapons |
| 6 ALLEN M. SUMNER | 1943–44 | 2,200 | 4 or 6/127-mm, SSM, ASW weapons |
| 4 FLETCHER | 1942–43 | 1,680 | 4–5/127-mm, Sea Chaparral SAM, ASW weapons |
| ◆ **10 (+6) frigates** | | | |
| 0 (+6) new design | . . . | 2,800 | . . . |
| 1 RUDDEROW | 1943 | 1,450 | 2/127-mm, 4/40-mm, ASW weapons |
| 9 CROSLEY/CHARLES LAWRENCE | 1943–45 | 1,680 | 2/127-mm, 6/40-mm, ASW weapons |
| ◆ **3 corvettes** | | | |
| 3 AUK | 1942–45 | 890 | 2/76.2-mm, 4/40-mm, ASW weapons |

◆ **52 guided-missile patrol boats**

◆ **13 minesweepers**

◆ **50 amphibious ships and craft**

NOTE: Almost all ships, weapons, and electronics systems currently in use originated in the United States, the principal exception being the Hsiung Feng antiship missile, a copy of the Israeli Aviation Industries' Gabriel II, and a 16-tubed 127-mm decoy rocket launcher of Taiwanese design. Ten U.S. Honeywell H 930 Mod. 1 weapons-control systems have been installed in destroyers. Although nearly all ships are ex-U.S. Navy units dating to World War II, maintenance has been superb, and many subsystems have been renewed and updated. Destroyer gunfire-control systems have been upgraded by U.S. contractors Hull numbers are periodically altered and now are not usually worn. The latest known numbers are given, but ships are listed in alphabetical order. A longer-range version of Hsiung Feng is under development.

WARSHIPS IN SERVICE OR UNDER CONSTRUCTION *(continued)*

**Taiwanese Sea Chaparral SAM launcher** R.O.C.N., 1987

**Gearing-class destroyer launching a Hsiung Feng SSM** *Defense Technology,* 1986

**SUBMARINES**

◆ **2 modified Dutch Zwaardvis class** Bldr: Wilton Fijenoord, Schiedam

| | Laid down | L | In serv. |
|---|---|---|---|
| ... Hai Lung | 12-82 | 4-10-86 | 28-10-87 |
| ... Hai Hu | ... | 20-12-86 | 16-12-87 |

**D:** 2,300 tons surf./2,600 sub. **S:** 11 kts **Dim:** 66.92 × 8.40 × 6.70
**A:** 6/533-mm TT fwd (28 U.S. Mk 37 torpedoes)
**Electron Equipt:** Radar: 1/Decca . . .—EW: H.S.A. RAPIDS
Sonar: H.S.A. SIASS integrated system
**M:** 3 Brons/Stork-Werkspoor 12 ORUB 215 diesels (1,350 hp each); 2/922-kw generator groups, 1 3,800-kw motor; 1 5-bladed prop; 5,100 hp
**Fuel:** 310 tons **Range:** 10,000/9 (surf.) **Man:** 8 officers, 59 men

**Hai Lung**—on trials L. & L. Van Ginderen, 4-87

**Hai Hu** L. & L. Van Ginderen, 12-87

Remarks: Ordered late 1980, over mainland China's protests. Design also referred to as "Sea Dragon" class, as names mean "Sea Dragon" and "Sea Tiger," respectively. The first submarine left the Netherlands for Taiwan as deck cargo on a heavy-lift ship on 28 October 1987. Highly automated design. SINBADS-M, 8-target track data system, Sperry Mk 29 Mod. 2A inertial navigation system. Two 196-cell batteries. Torpedoes are ex-Dutch Navy. Program delayed by shipyard financial problems. Request for 2 more (and option for 5th and 6th) turned down by Dutch government in 1984, due to Chinese pressure.

◆ **2 ex-U.S. Guppy II class**

| | Bldr | Laid down | L | In serv. |
|---|---|---|---|---|
| 736 Hai Shih (ex-*Cutlass,* SS 478) | Portsmouth, NSY | 22-7-44 | 5-11-44 | 17-3-45 |
| 794 Hai Pao (ex-*Tusk,* SS 426) | Cramp SB, Philadelphia | 23-8-43 | 8-7-45 | 11-4-46 |

**Hai Pao (794) or Hai Shih (736)** *Defense Technology,* 1986

**D:** 1,517/1,870/2,440 tons **S:** 18/16 kts **Dim:** 93.57 × 8.33 × 5.18
**A:** 10/533-mm TT (6 fwd, 4 aft, 22 torpedoes)
**Electron Equipt:** Radar: 1/SS-2
Sonar: BQR-2B, BQS-4C, DUUG-1B
**M:** diesel-electric propulsion: 4 Fairbanks-Morse 38D8$\frac{1}{8}$ diesels; 2 electric motors; 4,610/5,200 hp
**Range:** 10,000/10 surfaced **Man:** 11 officers, 70 men

Remarks: Transferred 12-4-73 and 18-10-73, for ASW training. Four 126-cell batteries. Source of torpedoes uncertain: may use old Japanese or U.S. Mk 14 World War II-era straight-runners, U.S. Mk 37 or NT-37C homing torpedoes, or U.K. Mk 24 Tigerfish; tubes were welded shut at time of delivery.

**DESTROYERS**

◆ **12 ex-U.S. Gearing FRAM-I class**

| | Bldr | Laid down | L | In serv. |
|---|---|---|---|---|
| 912 Chao Yang (ex-*Hammer,* DD 718) | Federal SB Newark, N.J. | 5-4-45 | 24-11-45 | 11-7-46 |
| 928 Cheng Hua (ex-*Hollister,* D 788) | Todd Pacific SY, Seattle | 18-1-45 | 9-10-45 | 29-3-46 |
| 921 Chien Yang (ex-*James E. Kyes,* DD 787) | Todd Pacific SY, Seattle | 27-12-44 | 4-8-45 | 8-2-46 |
| 978 Han Yang (ex-*Herbert J. Thomas,* DD 833) | Bath Iron Wks | 30-10-44 | 25-3-45 | 29-5-45 |

**DESTROYERS** *(continued)*

| | | | | |
|---|---|---|---|---|
| 915 Kai Yang ex-*Richard B. Anderson,* DD 786 | Todd Pacific SY, Seattle | 1-12-44 | 7-7-45 | 26-10-45 |
| 981 Lai Yang (ex-*Leonard F. Mason,* DD 852) | Bethlehem Steel, Quincy | 8-6-45 | 4-1-46 | 28-6-46 |
| 928 Lao Yang (ex-*Shelton,* DD 790) | Todd Pacific SY, Seattle | 31-5-45 | 8-3-46 | 21-6-46 |
| 938 Liao Yang (ex-*Hanson,* DD 832) | Bath Iron Wks | 7-10-44 | 11-3-45 | 11-5-45 |
| 926 Shao Yang (ex-*Hawkins,* DD 873) | Consolidated Steel, Orange, Tex. | 14-5-44 | 7-10-44 | 10-2-45 |
| 932 Shen Yang (ex-*Power,* DD 839) | Bath Iron Wks | 26-2-45 | 30-6-45 | 13-9-45 |
| 925 Te Yang (ex-*Sarsfield,* DD 837) | Bath Iron Wks | 15-1-45 | 27-5-45 | 31-7-45 |
| 927 Yung Yang (ex-*Johnston,* DD 821) | Consolidated Steel, Orange, Tex. | 6-5-45 | 19-10-45 | 10-10-46 |

**Chao Yang or Lai Yang**—as modified with Honeywell H 930 Mod. 1 fire-control system. Argos 680 EW array, 5 Hsiung Feng SSM (triple, trainable mount in place of aft 127-mm mount), 76-mm OTO Melara Compact forward, Sea Chaparral at stern, 2/40-mm AA (I × 2) flanking aft stack, and SRN-15A TACAN.

**Unmodified Gearing FRAM-I** R.O.C.N., 1987

**Chien Yang wearing 912**—note TACAN atop aft mast, chaff RL abaft second stack L. & L. Van Ginderen, 7-85

**D:** 2,425 tons (3,465–3,540 fl) **S:** 32 kts
**Dim:** 119.03 (116.74 wl) × 12.52 × 4.61 (6.5 over sonar)
**A:** modernized units: 5 Hsiung Feng SSM (III × 1, I × 2)—1/Sea Chaparral SAM syst. (IV × 1)—2/127-mm DP (II × 2)—1/76-mm OTO Melara DP—2/40-mm AA (I × 2)—1/ASROC ASW RL (VIII × 1)—1/Hughes-500 MD helo; others: 4/127-mm DP (II × 2)—*Han Yang, Kai Yang:* 4/40-mm AA (II × 2); *Chao Yang* and *Yung Yang:* 2/40-mm AA (I × 2)—all: 4 to 6/12.7-mm mg—1/ASROC ASW RL (VIII × 1) (not in *Han Yang, Kai Yang, Chao Yang,* or *Yung Yang*)—6/324-mm Mk 32 ASW TT (III × 2)—1/Hughes-500 MD ASW helo—see Remarks

**Electron Equipt:** Radar: 1/SPS-10 or SPS-58, 1/SPS-29 (*Chien Yang, Te Yang, Shao Yang, Cheng Hua:* SPS-40), 1/Mk 25 or 2/R.C.A. HR-76 C5
Sonar: SQS-23—TACAN: SRN-15
EW: Argo 680/681 or WLR-1, ULQ-6 in some, 4/chaff RL (XVI × 4)
**M:** 2 sets G.E. GT; 2 props; 60,000 hp **Electric:** 1,200 kw
**Boilers:** 4 Babcock & Wilcox; 43.3 kg/cm², 454°C
**Fuel:** 720 tons **Range:** 1,500/31; 5,800/12 **Man:** 275 tot.

Remarks: *Chien Yang, Lao Yang,* and *Liao Yang* transferred 18-4-73; *Han Yang,* 6-5-74; *Kai Yang,* 10-6-77; *Te Yang, Shen Yang,* 1-10-77; *Lai Yang,* 10-3-78. A ninth unit, *Chao Yang* (ex-*Rowan,* DD 782) was lost 22-8-77 while on tow to Taiwan. Ex-DD 718 and 821 purchased (without ASROC) 27-2-81; ex-DD 788 purchased 3-4-83, ex-DD 873 purchased 17-4-83. *Kai Yang* and *Lao Yang* both have 127-mm twin mounts forward and the Mk 32 ASW torpedo tubes abreast the after stack. *Han Yang* has extra superstructure, as she was converted for NBC-warfare defense trials 1963–64; she has an extra gas-turbine generator to run additional air-conditioning systems. She had no ASROC on transfer and has received two twin 40-mm antiaircraft guns, each with a Mk 51 Mod. 2 director in the ASROC location.

As part of a phased modernization program, at least three of these ships have received the Honeywell H 930 weapons-control system, which employs two radome-mounted R.C.A. HR-76 C5 fire-control radars (the original Mk 37 f.c.s. director is retained, with its Mk 25 radar deleted and its optics replaced by a Kollmorgen Mk 35 optical periscopic sight), a triple, trainable Hsiung Feng SSM launcher substituted for the aft twin 127-mm mount, single fixed SSM launchers atop the hangar, a Chaparral quadruple SAM launcher situated on the fantail, an OTO Melara 76-mm Compact DP gun placed between the ASW TT before the bridge, the Argo 680 ESM system substituted for the original WLR-1/ULQ-6 combination, substitution of the Westinghouse SPS-58 for SPS-10 (same antenna), and refurbishment of other systems. One ship was modified with Israeli assistance (probably *Kai Yang*) with an enlarged twin hangar for S-70 helos and flight deck, a twin 40-mm AA and Mk 51 Mod. 2 lead-computing director atop the hangar, Hsiung Feng SSM, and Israeli radars (Elta EL-1040 in place of SPS-10, and RTN-10X added). Seven to ten of this class are planned to receive U.S. Standard SM-1 MR Mod. 6 SAM missiles (using box launchers or replacing the helo facility with a U.S. Mk 13, 40-missile launcher complex), H.S.A. DA-08 radars in place of the SPS-29 or 40, a STIR SAM control radar, and Westinghouse W 160 f.c. radars (where HR-76 is not already fitted).

◆ **2 ex-U.S. Gearing FRAM-II class**

| | Bldr | Laid down | L | In serv. |
|---|---|---|---|---|
| 911 Dang Yang (ex-*Lloyd Thomas,* DD 764) | Bethlehem Steel, San Francisco | 26-3-44 | 5-10-45 | 21-3-47 |
| 907 Fu Yang (ex-*Ernest G. Small,* DD 838) | Bath Iron Works | 30-1-45 | 14-6-45 | 21-8-45 |

**Fu Yang (907)**—as modernized R.O.C.N., 1987

**D:** 2,425 tons (3,477 fl) **S:** 32 kts
**Dim:** 119.03 (116.74 wl) × 12.52 × 4.61 (6.54 over sonar)
**A:** 907: 5/Hsiung Feng SSM (III × 1, I × 2)—1/Chaparral SAM syst. (IV × 1, 16 RIM-72C missiles)—4/127-mm DP (II × 2)—1/76-mm OTO Melara DP—2/40-mm AA (I × 2)—2/Mk 11 Hedgehog—6/324-mm Mk 32 ASW TT (III × 2)—1/d.c. rack
911: 3/Hsiung Feng SSM (III × 1)—4/127-mm DP (II × 2)—2/40-mm AA (I × 2)—6/324-mm Mk 32 ASW TT (III × 2)—1/Hughes-500 ASW helicopter
**Electron Equipt:** Radar: 907: 1/SPS-58, 1/SPS-37, 2/RCA HR-76 C5
EW: Argo AR 680/681
911: 1/Elta EL-1040, 1/SPS-6B, 1/RTN-10X
EW: WLR-1, WLR-3, ULQ-6, 4/127-mm decoy RL (XVI × 4)
Sonar: SQS-23 series (hull)
**M:** 2 sets G.E. GT; 2 props; 60,000 hp **Electric:** 1,200 kw
**Boilers:** 4 Babcock & Wilcox; 43.3 kg/cm², 454°C
**Fuel:** 720 tons **Range:** 1,600/31; 6,100/12 **Man:** 275 tot.

Remarks: *Dang Yang,* completed as an ASW destroyer (DDE), finished FRAM-I modernization in 11-61 and was transferred to Taiwan on 12-10-72. *Fu Yang,* transferred in 2-71, completed FRAM-II modernization as a radar picket destroyer in

**DESTROYERS** *(continued)*

8-61; her SPS-30 height-finder was removed before transfer. *Fu Yung* acts as fleet flagship and has been modernized with the Honeywell H 930 Mod. 1 weapons-control system, with two R.C.A. HR-76 C5 f.c. radars, five Hsiung Feng SSM, an OTO Melara 76-mm DP, a Chaparral point-defense SAM system, the Mk 37 director converted to carry a Kollmorgen Mk 35 periscopic sight, SPS-58 substituted for SPS-10, and new EW equipment. *Dang Yang* was modernized with Israeli assistance, receiving an Israeli-made official Galileo optronic GFCS in place of the Mk 37, a Selenia RTN-10X radar on the reinforced mainmast (for SSM control), and the Elta EL-1040 radar in place of the SPS-10.

◆ **2 ex-U.S. Allen M. Sumner FRAM-II class**

| | Bldr | Laid down | L | In serv. |
|---|---|---|---|---|
| 949 Lo Yang (ex-*Taussig,* DD 746) | Bethlehem Steel, Staten I. | 30-8-43 | 25-1-44 | 20-5-44 |
| 954 Nan Yang (ex-*John W. Thomason,* DD 760) | Bethlehem Steel, San Francisco | 21-11-43 | 30-9-44 | 11-10-45 |

**Lo Yang or Nan Yang** R.O.C.N., 1987

**D:** 2,350 tons (3,220 fl) **S:** 33 kts **Range:** 1,000/32 **Man:** 275 tot.
**Dim:** 114.63 (112.52 wl) × 12.52 × 4.4 (5.9 over sonar)
**A:** 5/Hsiung Feng SSM (III × 1, I × 2)—1/Sea Chaparral point-defense SAM system (IV × 1; 16 RIM-72C missiles)—2/127-mm DP (II × 1)—1/76-mm OTO Melara Compact DP—2/40-mm Bofors AA (I × 2)—2/Mk 11 Hedgehog ASW mortars (XXIV × 2)—6/324-mm Mk 32 ASW TT (III × 2)—1/Hughes-500-MD helicopter
**Electron Equipt:** Radar: 1/SPS-58, 1/SPS-29, 2 R.C.A. HR-76 C5
Sonar: SQS-29 series
EW: Argo AR 680/681, 4 chaff RL—TACAN: SRN-15
**M:** 2 sets GT: 2 props; 60,000 hp **Electric:** 1,200 kw
**Boilers:** 4 Babcock & Wilcox; 43.3 kg/cm², 454°C **Fuel:** 500 tons

Remarks: Both transferred on 6-5-74, having completed FRAM-II modernization in 9-62 and 1-60, respectively. Rebuilt by mid-1985 with "B" 127-mm mount replaced by 76-mm gun, aft 127-mm mount by triple, trainable SSM launcher. The manned Sea Chaparral launcher is at the extreme stern. The Honeywell H930 weapons-control system is supported by two Westinghouse radars mounted on new lattice masts: the old Mk 37 GFCS director is retained without its Mk 25 radar, but with a Kollmorgen Mk 35 electro-optical system added.

◆ **6 ex-U.S. Allen M. Sumner class**

| | Bldr | Laid down | L | In serv. |
|---|---|---|---|---|
| 976 Heng Yang (ex-*Samuel N. Moore,* DD 747) | Bethlehem Steel, Staten Isl. | 30-9-43 | 23-2-44 | 24-6-44 |
| 986 Hsiang Yang (ex-*Brush,* DD 745) | Bethlehem Steel, Staten Isl. | 30-7-43 | 28-12-43 | 17-4-44 |
| 988 Hua Yang (ex-*Bristol,* DD 857) | Bethlehem Steel, San Pedro | 5-5-44 | 29-10-44 | 17-3-45 |
| 972 Huei Yang (ex-*English,* DD 696) | Federal SB, Kearny, N.J. | 19-10-43 | 27-2-44 | 4-5-44 |
| . . . Po Yang (ex-*Maddox,* DD 731) | Bath Iron Works | 28-10-43 | 19-3-44 | 2-6-44 |
| 944 Yuen Yang (ex-*Haynsworth,* DD 700) | Federal SB, Kearny, N.J. | 16-12-43 | 15-4-44 | 22-6-44 |

**Po Yang or Huei Yang**—with lattice masts *Defense Technology,* 1986

**Allen M. Sumner class**—with two triple Hsiung Feng SSM, Sea Chaparral on the fantail R.O.C.N., 1987

**Allen M. Sumner class launching Sea Chaparral point-defense SAM** R.O.C.N., 1986

**D:** 2,200 tons (3,300 fl) **S:** 33 kts **Dim:** 114.63 (112.52 wl) × 12.52 × 4.4 (5.9 over sonar)
**A:** 5 or 6/Hsiung Feng SSM (III × 2 *or* III × 1, I × 2)—1/Sea Chaparral SAM system (IV × 1, 16 RIM-72C missiles)—4/127-mm DP (II × 2)—4/40-mm AA (II × 2)—6/324-mm Mk 32 ASW TT (III × 2)—2/Mk 11 Hedgehog ASW mortars (XXIV × 2)—1/d.c. rack (9 d.c.)—*Po Yang, Huei Yang* also: 1/76-mm OTO Melara Compact DP
**Electron Equipt:** Radar: 1/SPS-10 or SPS-58, 1/SPS-6C (*Po Yang:* SPS-40), 2/R.C.A. HR-76 C5 f.c. *or* 1/Mk 25 and 1/Orion RTN-10X
Sonar: SQS-29 series
EW: Argo AR-680/681 or BLR-1, 4 decoy RL (XVI × 4)
**M:** 2 sets GT; 2 props; 60,000 hp **Electric:** 1,000 kw
**Boilers:** 4 Babcock & Wilcox; 43.3 kg/cm², 454°C
**Fuel:** 500 tons **Range:** 1,000/32; 4,400/11 **Man:** 275 tot.

Remarks: *Heng Yang* transferred in 2-70; *Hsiang Yang* and *Hua Yang* on 9-12-69; *Huei Yang* in 9-70; *Po Yang* on 6-7-72; *Yuen Yang* on 12-5-70. All were unmodified units of the class. *Hsiang Yang* had four 76.2-mm DP before Hsiung Feng conversion. The 40-mm antiaircraft guns had them added in Taiwan; each mount has one associated Mk 51 Mod. 2 GFCS. *Hsiung Yang, Hua Yang, Yuen Yang,* and *Heng Yang* were equipped, with Israeli assistance, to launch the Hsiung Feng SSM through the addition of an Orion RTN-10X f.c. radar on a platform on the tripod mast; they retain the U.S. Mk 37 GFCS with Mk 25 radar to control the 127-mm guns. *Huei Yang* and *Po Yang* have received a more recent update, with Honeywell H 930 weapons-control system, two R.C.A. HR-76 C5 f.c. radars, the Mk 37 director converted to accommodate the Kollmorgen Mk 35 periscopic sight, Argo EW gear, and an OTO Melara 76-mm Compact DP mounted forward.

◆ **4 ex-U.S. Fletcher class** Bldrs: *An Yang:* Bethlehem Steel, Staten Island; others: Bethlehem, San Francisco

| | Laid down | L | In serv. |
|---|---|---|---|
| 997 An Yang (ex-*Kimberly,* DD 521) | 27-7-42 | 4-2-43 | 24-5-43 |
| 947 Chiang Yang (ex-*Mullany,* DD 528) | 15-1-42 | 12-10-42 | 23-4-43 |
| 934 Kun Yang (ex-*Yarnell,* DD 541) | 5-12-42 | 25-7-43 | 30-12-43 |
| 908 Kwei Yang (ex-*Twining,* DD 540) | 21-11-42 | 11-7-43 | 1-2-44 |

**Modernized Fletcher with 3/127-mm DP, no 76-mm DP**
*Defense Technology,* 1986

**DESTROYERS** *(continued)*

**Kwei Yang (908)**—with 76-mm DP forward *Defense Technology,* 1985

**D:** 2,100 tons (3.036 fl) **S:** 35 kts **Range:** 860/35; 4,700/13 **Man:** 275 tot.
**Dim:** 114.65 (112.52 wl) × 11.99 × 4.39 (5.38 over sonar)
**A:** 3/Hsiung Feng SSM (III × 1)—1/Sea Chaparral SAM system (IV × 1, 16 RIM-72C missiles)—3/127-mm DP (I × 3) *or* 2/127-mm DP (I × 2) and 1/76-mm OTO Melara Compact DP—2/40-mm AA (I × 2)—6/324-mm Mk 32 ASW TT (III × 2)—2/Mk 11 Hedgehog ASW mortars (XXIV × 2)—1/d.c. rack (9 d.c.)—1/mine rail
**Electron Equipt:** Radar: 1/SPS-10 or SPS-58, 1/SPS-66, 2/R.C.A. R-76 C5
Sonar: DD 934, 997: SQS-50; DD 947: SQS-40, DD 956: SQS-41
EW: Argo AR 680/681, 4/chaff RL (XVI × 4)
**M:** 2 sets GT; 2 props; 60,000 hp **Electric:** 880 kw
**Boilers:** 4 Babcock & Wilcox; 43.3 kg/cm$^2$, 454°C **Fuel:** 512 tons

Remarks: *An Yang* transferred in 6-67; *Chiang Yang* in 10-71; *Kun Yang* in 6-68; *Kwei Yang* in 10-71. Sea Chaparral is a manned mounting for launching Redeye, heat-seeking, short-range SAMs; it replaced a twin 40-mm antiaircraft mount. SQS-50 is an updated SQS-4; SQS-40 and -41 are updated versions of the SQS-29 and -30. At least two have been modernized with the Honeywell H 930 weapons-control system, two R.C.A. HR-76 C5 f.c. radars, the Mk 37 f.c.s. converted with the Kollmorgen Mk 35 periscopic sight and, on *Kwei Yang,* the superfiring 127-mm DP forward replaced by a 76-mm mount. *Kun Yang* and one other *may* retain the original tripod mast and U.S. Mk 37 f.c.s. with Mk 25 radar. *All* now apparently carry one mine rail to port on the main deck.

## GUIDED-MISSILE FRIGATES

◆ **0 (+6 + 6) modified U.S. Oliver Hazard Perry class** Bldr: China Shipbuilding, Kaohsiung

| | Laid down | L | In serv. |
|---|---|---|---|
| . . . N . . . | . . . | . . . | . . . |
| . . . N . . . | . . . | . . . | . . . |
| . . . N . . . | . . . | . . . | . . . |
| . . . N . . . | . . . | . . . | . . . |
| . . . N . . . | . . . | . . . | . . . |
| . . . N . . . | . . . | . . . | . . . |

**D:** approx. 2,800 tons light (3,700 fl) **S:** 29 kts
**Dim:** 135.64 (125.90 wl) × 13.72 × 5.70 (prop)
**A:** 6/Hsiung Feng II SSM (I × 6)—1/Mk 13 Mod. 4 launcher (40 Standard SM-1 MR Mod. 6 SAM)—1/127-mm Mk 45 or 76-mm Mk 75 DP—1/20-mm Mk 15 CIWS gatling AA—6/324-mm Mk 32 ASW TT (III × 2)—1/375-mm Bofors ASW RL (IV × 1)—2/Sikorsky S-70 helicopters
**Electron Equipt:** Radar: 1/. . . nav., 1/. . . early warning, 2/. . . f.c.
Sonar: . . .
EW: . . .
**M:** 2 G.E. LM-2500 gas turbines; 1 CP prop; 41,000 hp—2 drop-down electric propulsors; 700 hp
**Electric:** 3,000 kw **Fuel:** 587 tons + 64 tons helicopter fuel
**Range:** 4,200/20; 5,000/18 **Man:** . . .

Remarks: Program announced 6-87 for a more heavily armed version of the U.S. FFG 7 class, using the original "short" hull (which precludes installation of a towed passive hydrophone array like SQR-19). A U.S. technical partner, either Bath Iron Works or Todd, is to be selected. The first of six authorized will probably not complete before the mid-1990s; an additional six are planned to complete replacement of the current World War II-era U.S.-built destroyers and frigates.

## FRIGATES

◆ **1 ex-U.S. Rudderow class** Bldr: Bethlehem Steel, Hingham, Mass.

| | Laid down | L | In serv. |
|---|---|---|---|
| 959 Tai Yuan (ex-*Riley,* DE 579) | 20-10-43 | 29-12-43 | 13-3-44 |

**D:** 1,450 tons (1,950 fl) **S:** 24 kts **Dim:** 93.27 × 11.24 × 3.43 (4.3 over sonar)
**A:** 2/12.7-mm DP (I × 2)—4/40-mm AA (I × 2)—4/20-mm AA(I × 4)—1/Mk 11 Hedgehog—6/324-mm Mk 32 ASW TT (III × 2)—2/Mk 9 d.c. racks—mines
**Electron Equipt:** Radar: 1/SPS-5, 1/SPS-6, 1/Mk 26 fire-control
Sonar: . . .
**M:** 2 sets G.E. turbo-electric drive; 2 props: 12,000 hp **Electric:** 1,140 kw
**Boilers:** 2 Foster-Wheeler D-type; 31.7 kg/cm$^2$, 399°C
**Fuel:** 354 tons **Range:** 1,100/24; 5,000/12 **Man:** 200 tot.

Remarks: Transferred, after modernization, on 10-7-69; purchased outright in 3-74. Has one Mk 52 radar GFCS and two Mk 51 Mod. 2 GFCS. Minelaying capability added in Taiwan.

◆ **9 former high-speed transports**

**6 ex-U.S. Crosley class**

| | Bldr | Laid down | L | In serv. |
|---|---|---|---|---|
| 838 Fu Shan (ex-*Truxtun,* APD 98, ex-DE 282) | Charleston NY, Charleston, S.C. | 13-12-43 | 9-3-44 | 3-7-44 |
| 854 Hua Shan (ex-*Donald W. Wolf,* APD 129, ex-DE 713) | Defoe SB, Bay City, Mich. | 17-4-44 | 22-7-44 | 13-4-45 |
| 893 Shou Shan (ex-*Kline,* APD 120, ex-DE 687) | Bethlehem Steel, Quincy, Mass. | 27-5-44 | 27-6-44 | 18-10-44 |
| 878 Tai Shan (ex-*Register,* APD 92, ex-DE 233) | Charleston NY, Charleston, S.C. | 27-10-43 | 20-1-44 | 11-1-45 |
| 615 Tien Shan (ex-*Kleinsmith,* APD 134, ex-DE 718) | Defoe SB, Bay City, Mich. | 30-8-44 | 27-1-45 | 12-6-45 |
| 826 Yu Shan (ex-*Kinzer,* APD 91, ex-DE 232) | Charleston NY, Charleston, S.C. | 9-9-43 | 9-12-43 | 1-11-44 |

**Fu Shan (838)**—wearing old number *Ships of the World,* 1975

**Crosley-class unit with Sea Chaparral** R.O.C.N., 1987

**3 ex-U.S. Charles Lawrence class**

| | Bldr | Laid down | L | In serv. |
|---|---|---|---|---|
| 845 Chung Shan (ex-*Blessman,* APD 48, ex-DE 69) | Bethlehem Steel, Hingham, Mass. | 23-3-43 | 19-6-43 | 19-9-43 |
| 821 Lu Shan (ex-*Bull,* APD 78, ex-DE 693) | Defoe SB, Bay City | 14-12-42 | 25-3-43 | 12-8-43 |
| 834 Wen Shan (ex-*Gantner,* APD 42, ex-DE 60) | Bethlehem Steel, Hingham, Mass. | 21-12-42 | 17-4-43 | 23-7-43 |

**D:** 1,680 tons (2,150 fl) **S:** 22 kts **Dim:** 93.27 × 11.24 × 3.96 (hull)
**A:** 2/127-mm DP (I × 2)—6/40-mm AA (II × 3)—4/20-mm AA (I × 4)—2/Mk 9 d.c. racks—*see also* Remarks
**Electron Equipt:** Radar: 1/SPS-5, 1/Decca 707; some: 1/Mk 26
Sonar: . . .
**M:** 2 sets G.E. turbo-electric drive; 2 props; 12,000 hp **Electric:** 1,140 kw
**Boilers:** 2 Babcock & Wilcox, Foster-Wheeler, or Combustion Engineering; 31.7 kg/cm$^2$, 399°C
**Fuel:** 346 tons **Range:** 1,800/22; 5,000/13 **Man:** 200 crew + 160 troops

FRIGATES *(continued)*

REMARKS: *Yu Shan* transferred in 4-62; *Hua Shan* in 5-65; *Fu Shan* and *Shou Shan* in 3-66; *Wen Shan* in 5-66; *Lu Shan* in 8-66; *Tai Shan* in 10-66; *Tien Shan* in 6-67, and *Chung Shan* in 8-67. All were sold outright except *Tien Shan* which, because she was on loan, was not modified by the addition of a second 127-mm mount aft until after her purchase in 1974; the others all received the second gun in lieu of a cargo hold and derrick, beginning about 1970. ASW armaments vary, with *Fu Shan* having two Mk 11 Hedgehogs on her main deck forward and several (but not all) carrying six 324-mm Mk 32 ASW torpedo tubes (III × 2); all have two Mk 9 depth-charge racks, and *Hua Shan* had four *twin* 20-mm antiaircraft guns. Most have only a Mk 51 rangefinder for 127-mm fire-control forward and a Mk 51 optical gunfire-control system aft, plus three Mk 51 Mod. 2 GFCS for the 40-mm antiaircraft guns. In some, Welin davits are retained amidships, but only two (vice the original four) landing craft are carried, to save topweight. The former *Crosley*-class ships have low navigating bridges, the other ships have high ones. At least one has been modernized with a Sea Chaparral point-defense SAM system (16 RIM-72C missiles) aft but with no upgrade to other weaponry or sensors. Sisters *Heng Shan* (ex-*Raymond W. Herndon*, APD 121) and *Lung Shan* (ex-*Schmitt*, APD 76) were stricken in 1976, and *Kang Shan* (ex-*George W. Ingram*, APD 43) was stricken in 1978.

## CORVETTES

◆ **3 ex-U.S. Auk-class former minesweepers**

| | Laid down | L | In serv. |
|---|---|---|---|
| 867 PING JIN (ex-*Steady*, MSF 118) | 17-11-41 | 6-6-42 | 16-11-42 |
| 884 WU SHENG (ex-*Redstart*, MSF 378) | 14-6-44 | 18-10-45 | 4-4-45 |
| 896 CHU YUNG (ex-*Waxwing*, MSF 389) | 24-5-44 | 10-3-45 | 6-8-45 |

Bldrs: *Wu Sheng:* Savannah Machine & Foundry, Ga; others: American SB, Cleveland, Ohio

**D:** 890 tons (1,250 fl) **S:** 18 kts **Dim:** 67.39 (65.53 pp) × 9.8 × 3.3
**A:** 2/76.2-mm DP (I × 2)—4/40-mm AA (II × 2)—4/20-mm AA (II × 2)—1/Mk 11 Hedgehog—3/324-mm Mk 32 ASW TT (III × 1)—2/Mk 9 d.c. racks
**Electron Equipt:** Radar: 1/SPS-5
Sonar: SQS-17
**M:** 2 G.M. 12-278A diesels; 2 props; 3,532 hp
**Electric:** 360 kw **Fuel:** 216 tons **Man:** 80 tot.

REMARKS: After conversion to corvettes, transferred as follows: *Chu Yung* in 11-65, *Ping Jin* in 3-68, and *Wu Sheng* in 7-65. *Chu Yung* was fitted with mine rails in 1975.

## GUIDED-MISSILE PATROL BOATS

NOTE: Negotiations in 1984 to purchase former U.S. Navy *Asheville*-class patrol boats *Asheville* (PG 84), *Marathon* (PG 89), and *Ready* (PG 87) from the Massachusetts Maritime Academy fell through, but decommissioned sisters *Gallup* (PG 85) and Canon (PG 90) may still be transferred from the U.S. government; permission requested from Congress 7-4-86.

◆ **50 Hai Ou class** Bldr: China SB, Kaohsiung (In serv. 1980–84)

**D:** 47 tons (fl) **S:** 36 kts **Dim:** 21.62 × 5.49 × 0.94 (1.82 props)
**A:** 2/Hsiung Feng SSM (I × 2)—2/12.7-mm mg (I × 2) **Electric:** 30 kw
**Electron Equipt:** Radar: 1/LN-66 nav., 1/R.C.A. CS/SPG-24 **Man:** 10–12 tot.
**M:** 2 MTU 12V331 TC81 diesels; 2 props; 2,720 hp **Range:** 700/32

REMARKS: Design evidently based closely on the Israeli Dvora class; name means "Seagull." Have Kollmorgen Mk 35 optical sight, four AV-2 chaff RL (I × 4). The fire-control radar is a variant of the HR-76 C2 used on destroyers. Early units had a pylon mast and the missile launchers situated near the stern; late units (the majority) have a lattice mast and the missile launchers located closer to amidships, with an unoccupied mounting ring for a 20-mm AA near the stern.

**Hai Ou-class FAB-24** R.O.C.N., 1987

**Hai Ou class** *Defense Technology*, 1986

◆ **2 Lung Chiang class**

| | Bldr | In serv. |
|---|---|---|
| 581 LUNG CHIANG | Tacoma Boatbldg, Tacoma, Wash. | 15-5-78 |
| 583 SUIKIANG | China SB, Kaohsiung | 1982 |

**Lung Chiang on trials** Tacoma, 1978

**D:** 218 tons (250 fl) **S:** 40 kts **Dim:** 50.14 (46.94 pp) × 7.60 × 2.26
**A:** 4/Hsiung Feng SSM—1/76-mm OTO Melara DP—2/30-mm Emerlec AA (II × 1)—2/12.7-mm mg (I × 2)
**Electron Equipt:** Radar: 1 navigational, 1/RAN-11L/X (NA 10 system) (583: see Remarks)—EW: 4 AV-2 chaff RL (I × 4)
**M:** CODOG: 3 G.M. 12V149 TI diesels (3,600 hp), 3 AVCO-Lycoming TF-40A gas turbines; 3 CP props; 15,000 hp
**Range:** 700/40 (gas turbines), 1,900/30 (3 diesels); 2,700/12 (1 diesel)
**Man:** 5 officers, 30 men

REMARKS: Design is a variation of Tacoma Boatbuilding (U.S.) PSMM Mk-5 design. Prototype built in U.S. with follow-on unit to be built in Taiwan. Second unit is of revised design, with the R.C.A. HR-76 C5 fire-control radar and fin stabilizers; a planned six additional were cancelled.

## PATROL CRAFT

◆ **1 (+5) Taiwanese-built** Bldr: . . .

**D:** . . . **S:** 32 kts **Dim:** 12.8 × . . . × . . .
**A:** 1/12.7-mm mg **Electron Equipt:** Radar: 1/. . . nav.
**M:** 2 G.M. diesels; 2 Arneson surface-piercing outdrives; 1,300 hp
**Range:** 400/. . .

REMARKS: GRP construction, C. Raymond Hunt design. Program reported 1987.

**Prototype 21-m patrol craft** Vosper, 1986

**PATROL CRAFT** *(continued)*

◆ **1 (+6) Vosper design** Bldr: prototype: Vosper Pty, Singapore

**D:** . . . **S:** 40+ kts **Dim:** 21.00 (16.60 wl) × 4.80 × 1.00
**A:** 1/20-mm AA—2/7.62-mm mg **Electron Equipt:** Radar: 1/Decca 170
**M:** 2 G.M.-Stewart & Stevenson 16V92 TMAB diesels; 2 Arneson ASD 14 surface-piercing outdrives; 2,700 hp
**Range:** 400/. . . **Electric:** 18 kw **Man:** . . .

REMARKS: Aluminum construction. Program delayed by 1986–87 insolvency of the now-reorganized Vosper Pty; series craft to be built in Taiwan. Up to 24 planned.

◆ **1 prototype** Bldr: . . . (In serv. 1987)

**D:** . . . **S:** 40 kts **Dim:** 26.2 × . . . × . . .
**A:** 1/20-mm AA
**M:** 3 Isotta Fraschini diesels; 3 Castoldi waterjets; 3,000 hp

REMARKS: No further details available; may be of GRP construction.

◆ **10 or more aluminum-hulled** Bldr: China SB, Kaohsiung

**D:** 12 tons **S:** 25 kts **Dim:** 15.0 × . . . × . . .
**A:** 1/40-mm AA **M:** 2 diesels; waterjet drive

REMARKS: Date from 1971. There are believed to be a number of other small patrol craft of Taiwanese construction, for which no details are available.

**MINE WARFARE SHIPS**

NOTE: New mine countermeasures ships are badly needed to replace the following ships, which have considerably deteriorated. Negotiations with Van der Giessen de Noord in the Netherlands during 1983–84 for six *Alkmaar* ("Tripartite")-class minehunters fell through. 1986 reports indicate the possible ordering of two minehunters of the same type ordered by Thailand from Lürssen, Vegesack, West Germany; the ships would have a Krupp-Atlas sonar and carry Gaymarine "Pluto" minehunting, remote-controlled submersibles.

◆ **13 ex-U.S. and ex-Belgian Adjutant, MSC 268*, and MSC 289† classes of coastal minesweepers**

| | Bldr | In serv. |
|---|---|---|
| 449 YUNG AN (ex-MSC 123) | . . . | 6-55 |
| 441 YUNG CHEN (ex-*Maaseick*, ex-MSC 78) | Adams Yacht, Quincy, Mass. | 7-53 |
| 497 YUNG CHI (ex-*Charleroi*, ex-MSC 152) | Hodgdon Bros., Me. | 2-54 |
| 432 YUNG CHING (ex-*Eakloo*, ex-MSC 101) | Hodgdon Bros., Me. | 5-53 |
| 423 YUNG CHOU (ex-MSC 278)* | Tacoma Boat, Wash. | 7-59 |
| 482 YUNG FU (ex-*Diest*, ex-*Macaw*, ex-MSC 77) | Adams Yacht, Quincy, Mass. | 5-53 |
| 488 YUNG HSIN (ex-MSC 302)† | Dorchester Bldrs., N.J. | 3-65 |
| 485 YUNG JEN (ex-*St. Nicholas*, ex-MSC 64) | H. B. Nevins, N.Y. | 2-54 |
| 457 YUNG JU (ex-MSC 300)† | Tacoma Boat, Wash. | 3-65 |
| 469 YUNG LO (ex-MSC 306)† | Dorchester Bldrs., N.J. | 4-66 |
| 479 YUNG NIEN (ex-MSC 277)* | Tacoma Boat, Wash. | 5-59 |
| 476 YUNG SHAN (ex-*Lier*, ex-MSC 63) | H. B. Nevins, N.Y. | 7-53 |
| 462 YUNG SUI (ex-*Diksmude*, ex-MSC 65) | H. B. Nevins, N.Y. | 2-54 |

**Yung Chi**—Adjutant class, ex-Belgian, wearing old number 1970

**Yung Chou**—MSC 268 class, wearing old number 1970

**Yung Lo**—MSC 289 class, wearing old number 1970

**D:** 320 tons (378 fl) **S:** 12.5 kts **Dim:** 43.0 (41.5 wl) × 7.95 × 2.55
**A:** 2/20-mm AA (II × 1)
**Electron Equipt:** Radar: 1/Decca 45 or 707
Sonar: UQS-1D
**M:** 2 G.M. 8-268A diesels; 2 props; 1,200 hp (MSC 268 class; 4 G.M. 6-71 diesels; 2 props; 890 hp)
**Fuel:** 40 tons **Range:** 2,500/12 **Man:** 40 tot.

REMARKS: Wooden hulls. All transferred on completion except ex-Belgian ships, transferred in 11-69. Have a variety of configurations, the ex-MSC 258 having a different propulsion scheme and the ex-MSC 289 class having a lower bridge and taller stack. Sister *Yung Ping* (ex-MSC 140) stricken 1982; several others soon to follow.

◆ **1 ex-U.S. minesweeping boat**

MSB 12 (ex-U.S. Navy MSB 4, ex-U.S. Army . . .)

**D:** 39 tons (fl) **S:** 12 kts **Dim:** 17.5 × 4.6 × 1.25
**M:** 2 Packard diesels; 2 props; 600 hp **Man:** 6 tot.

REMARKS: Built in 1945 and transferred in 12-61. Wooden hull. Sister to South Korean MSB 1.

◆ **8 ex-U.S. minesweeping launches**

| | | | |
|---|---|---|---|
| MSML 1 | MSML 3 | MSML 5 | MSML 6 |
| MSML 7 | MSML 8 | MSML 11 | MSML 12 |

**D:** 24 tons (fl) **S:** 8 kts **Dim:** 15.29 × 3.96 × 1.31
**M:** 1 diesel; 1 prop; 60 hp **Range:** 800/8 **Man:** 4 tot.

REMARKS: Built between 1943 and 1945, and converted from personnel launches before transfer in 3-61. Wooden hulls.

**AMPHIBIOUS WARFARE SHIPS**

◆ **1 command ship** Bldr: Dravo Corp., Neville I., Pittsburgh, Pa.

| | L | In serv. |
|---|---|---|
| 219 KAO HSIUNG (ex-*Chung Hai*, LST 229, ex-*Dukes County*, LST 735) | 11-3-44 | 26-4-44 |

**Kao Hsiung (219)**—wearing old number 1968

**D:** 1,650 tons (4,080 fl) **S:** 11 kts **Dim:** 99.98 × 15.24 × 3.4
**A:** 8/40-mm AA (II × 2, I × 4)—4/20-mm AA (II × 2)
**Electron Equipt:** Radar: 1/SPS-10, 1/SPS-12
**M:** 2 G.M. 12-567A diesels; 2 props; 1,700 hp **Range:** 15,000/9

REMARKS: Transferred in 5-57, converted to command ship in 1964, with additional communications gear and radars. Retains bow doors.

◆ **1 ex-U.S. Cabildo-class dock landing ship** Bldr: Gulf SB, Chickasaw, Ala.

| | Laid down | L | In serv. |
|---|---|---|---|
| 618 CHEN HAI (ex-*Fort Marion*, LSD 22) | 15-9-44 | 22-5-45 | 29-1-46 |

**AMPHIBIOUS WARFARE SHIPS** *(continued)*

**D:** 4,790 tons (9,375 fl) **S:** 15.6 kts **Dim:** 139.52 (138.38 wl) × 22.0 × 5.49
**A:** 12/40-mm AA (IV × 2, II × 2) **Electron Equipt:** Radar: 1/LN-66, 1/SPS-5
**M:** 2 sets GT; 2 props; 9,000 hp **Boilers:** 2; 30.6 kg/cm$^2$, 393°C
**Fuel:** 1,758 tons **Range:** 8,000/15 **Man:** 326 crew + several hundred troops

Remarks: Transferred by sale on 15-4-77, having been stricken from the U.S. Navy in 10-74. Modernized under FRAM-II program 12-59 to 4-60. Helicopter platform over 119.5 × 13.4-meter docking well, which can accommodate three LCUs, eighteen LCMs, or thirty-two amphibious armored troop carriers.

◆ **21 ex-U.S. LST 1 and LST 542-class tank landing ships**

| | Bldr | In serv. |
|---|---|---|
| 224 Chung Cheng (ex-*Lafayette County,* LST 859) | Chicago B & I, Seneca, Ill. | 29-12-44 |
| 206 Chung Chi (ex-LST 1017) | Bethlehem, Fore River, Mass. | 12-4-44 |
| 225 Chung Chiang (ex-*San Bernardino County,* LST 1110) | Missouri Valley B & I, Evansville, Ind. | 7-3-45 |
| 205 Chung Chien (ex-LST 716) | Jeffersonville B & M, Ind. | 18-8-44 |
| 226 Chung Chih (ex-*Sagadohoc County,* LST 1091) | American Br., Ambridge, Pa. | 6-4-45 |
| 221 Chung Chuan (ex-LST 1030) | Boston Navy Yd. | 19-7-44 |
| 223 Chung Fu (ex-*Iron County,* LST 840) | American Br., Ambridge, Pa. | 11-12-44 |
| 201 Chung Hai (ex-LST 755) | American Br., Ambridge, Pa. | 29-7-44 |
| 204 Chung Hsing (ex-LST 557) | Missouri Valley B & I, Evansville, Ind. | 5-5-44 |
| 216 Chung Kuang (ex-LST 503) | Jeffersonville B & M, Ind. | 14-12-43 |
| 209 Chung Lien (ex-LST 1050) | Dravo, Pittsburgh, Pa. | 3-4-45 |
| 227 Chung Ming (ex-*Sweetwater County,* LST 1152) | Dravo, Pittsburgh, Pa. | 13-4-45 |
| 230 Chung Pang (ex-LST 578) | Missouri Valley B & I, Evansville, Ind. | 15-7-44 |
| 222 Chung Sheng (ex-LST(H) 1033) | Chicago B & I, Seneca, Ill. | . . .-4-44 |
| 228 Chung Shu (ex-LST 520) | Chicago B & I, Seneca, Ill. | 28-2-44 |
| 208 Chung Shun (ex-LST 732) | Dravo, Pittsburgh, Pa. | 10-4-44 |
| 217 Chung Suo (ex-*Bradley County,* LST 400) | Newport News SB & DD, Va. | 7-1-43 |
| 203 Chung Ting (ex-LST 537) | Missouri Valley B & I, Evansville, Ind. | 9-2-44 |
| 229 Chung Wan (ex-LST 535) | Missouri Valley B & I, Evansville, Ind. | 4-2-44 |
| 231 Chung Yeh (ex-*Sublette County,* LST 1144) | Chicago B & I, Seneca, Ill. | 28-5-45 |
| 210 Chung Yung (ex-LST 574) | Missouri Valley B & I, Evansville, Ind. | 26-6-44 |

**Chung Kuang** 1969

**D:** 1,653 tons (4,080 fl) **S:** 11.6 kts **Dim:** 99.98 × 15.24 × 3.4
**A:** several: 2/76.2-mm DP (I × 2)—6–8/40-mm AA (II × 2, or I × 2 or 4)—4–8/20-mm AA
**M:** 2 G.M. 12-567A diesels; 2 props; 1,700 hp **Electric:** 300 kw
**Fuel:** 569 tons **Range:** 15,000/9 **Man:** 100-125 tot.

Remarks: Six transferred in 1946, two in 1947, *Chung Shu* in 1948, seven in 1958, *Chung Yun* in 1959, *Chung Kuang* in 1960, *Chung Yeh* in 1961, and two subsequently. All extensively rebuilt during the late 1960s, in many cases becoming almost new ships; re-engined at the same time. Most have four pairs of Welin davits, while *Chung Chih, Chung Yung, Chung Sheng,* and *Chung Shu* have six, and *Chung Chien* has two; each pair of davits handles one LCVP. Five or more have two 76.2-mm guns. *Chung Chih* (ex-216, ex-LST 279) was stricken in 1978. Have reportedly reverted to hull numbers worn in 1960s.

◆ **4 ex-U.S. LSM 1-class medium landing ships**

| | Bldr | In serv. |
|---|---|---|
| 637 Mei Lo (ex-LSM 362) | Brown SB, Houston, Tex. | 11-1-45 |
| 659 Mei Ping (ex-LSM 471) | Brown SB, Houston, Tex. | 23-2-45 |
| 694 Mei Sung (ex-LSM 457) | Western Pipe & Steel, San Pedro, Cal. | 28-3-45 |
| 649 Mei Tseng (ex-LSM 431) | Dravo, Wilmington, Del. | 25-2-45 |

**Mei Tseng (649)**—wearing old number 1969

**D:** 1,095 tons (fl) **S:** 12.5 kts **Dim:** 62.03 (59.89 wl) × 10.52 × 2.54 (max.)
**A:** 2/40-mm AA—4 or 8/20-mm AA (I or II × 4)—4/12.7-mm mg (I × 4)
**M:** *Mei Lo, Mei Ping:* 2 Fairbanks-Morse 38D8$\frac{1}{8}$ × 10 (others: 2 G.M. 16-278A) diesels; 2 props; 2,800 hp
**Electric:** 240 kw **Fuel:** 161 tons **Man:** 60 tot.

Remarks: *Mei Sung* and *Mei Tseng* transferred in 1946, *Mei Ping* in 11-56, and *Mei Lo* in 5-62.

◆ **6 ex-U.S. LCU 1466-class utility landing craft** Bldr: Ishikawajima, Harima, Japan

| | |
|---|---|
| 488 Ho Shan (ex-LCU 1596) | 491 Ho Meng (ex-LCU 1599) |
| 489 Ho Chuan (ex-LCU 1597) | 492 Ho Mou (ex-LCU 1600) |
| 490 Ho Seng (ex-LCU 1598) | 493 Ho Shou (ex-LCU 1601) |

**Ho Mou**—wearing old number 1955

**D:** 347 tons (fl) **S:** 8 kts **Dim:** 35.08 × 10.36 × 1.6 (max.)
**A:** 4/20-mm AA (II × 2)
**M:** 3 Gray Marine 64/65YTL diesels; 3 props; 675 hp
**Fuel:** 11 tons **Range:** 1,200/6 **Man:** 14 tot.

Remarks: Built under Offshore Procurement Program. In service in 3-55. Cargo: 167 tons.

◆ **16 ex-U.S. LCU 501 (LCT(6))-class utility landing craft**

| | In serv. | | In serv. |
|---|---|---|---|
| 485 Ho Chang (ex-LCU 512) | 7-9-43 | 404 Ho Deng (ex-LCU 1367) | 12-10-44 |
| 406 Ho Chao (ex-LCU 1429) | 8-12-44 | 405 Ho Feng (ex-LCU 1397) | 26-10-44 |
| 486 Ho Cheng (ex-LCU 1145) | 11-5-44 | 402 Ho Huei (ex-LCU 1218) | 25-8-44 |
| 401 Ho Chi (ex-LCU 1212) | 16-8-44 | 481 Ho Shun (ex-LCU 1225) | 4-9-44 |
| SB1 Ho Chie (ex-LCU 700) | 18-4-44 | 407 Ho Teng (ex-LCU 1452) | 20-10-44 |
| 496 Ho Chien (ex-LCU 1278) | 22-7-44 | 482 Ho Tsung (ex-LCU 1213) | 17-8-44 |
| 494 Ho Chun (ex-LCU 892) | 27-7-44 | 403 Ho Yao (ex-LCU 1244) | 22-9-44 |
| 484 Ho Chung (ex-LCU 849) | 7-8-44 | 495 Ho Yung (ex-LCU 1271) | 19-8-44 |

**D:** 143 tons (309 fl) **S:** 10 kts **Dim:** 36.3 (32.0 wl) × 9.96 × 1.14
**A:** 2/20-mm AA (I × 2)—2/12.7-mm mg
**M:** 3 G.M. 6-71 diesels; 3 props; 675 hp **Electric:** 20 kw **Man:** 10 tot.

Remarks: Six transferred between 1946 and 1948, the others between 1958 and 1959. *Ho Chie* evidently serves in an auxiliary role.

◆ **several hundred U.S. LCM(3)- and LCM(6)-class landing craft**

Bldrs: U.S. and Taiwan

**D:** 62 tons (fl) **S:** 9 kts **Dim:** 17.07 × 4.37 × 1.07
**A:** 1/20-mm AA or 12.7-mm mg in some
**M:** 2 Gray Marine 64HN9 diesels; 2 props; 450 hp **Range:** 130/9 **Man:** 9 tot.

Remarks: LCM(3) are 56 tons (fl), 15.38 m overall. Cargo: LCM(3): 30 tons, LCM(6): 34 tons.

◆ **about 100 U.S. LCVP class**

**D:** 13 tons (fl) **S:** 9 kts **Dim:** 10.9 × 3.21 × 1.04
**A:** 2/7.62-mm mg (I × 2) **M:** 1 Gray Marine 64HN9 diesel; 225 hp
**Range:** 110/9 **Man:** 3 tot.

Remarks: Most attached to LSTs and former APDs. Wooden construction. Cargo: 36 troops or 4 tons.

## HYDROGRAPHIC SHIPS

◆ **1 modified stern trawler** Bldr: Flekkefjord, . . . (In serv. . . .)

. . . Bien Dou

**D:** 1,050 grt **S:** 14.2 kts **Dim:** 50.0 × 10.3 × . . .
**M:** 1 diesel; 1 prop; 1,680 hp **Man:** 34 tot.

Remarks: Converted and placed in service 20-6-85 in support of civilian and naval oceanographic research tasks.

◆ **1 ex-U.S. C1-M-AV1-class former transport** Bldr: Walter Butler SY, Duluth, Minn.

398 Chiu Hua (ex-*Sgt. George D. Keathley,* T-AGS 35, ex-T-APC 117, ex-*Acorn Knot*)

**Chiu Hua**—wearing old number 1972

**D:** 4,100 tons (6,090 fl) **S:** 11.5 kts **Dim:** 103.18 (97.54 wl) × 15.24 × 5.33
**A:** 1/40-mm AA—2/20-mm AA (I × 2)
**M:** 1 Nordberg TSM6 diesel; 1 prop; 1,750 hp **Man:** 72 tot.

Remarks: Completed in 1945 as a Maritime Commission cargo ship and taken over by the U.S. Army as a personnel transport. Transferred to the U.S. Navy in 1950 and converted for hydrographic-survey duties in 1966–67. Loaned to Taiwan on 29-3-72 and extended on 19-5-76; purchased outright 1981.

◆ **1 ex-U.S. Sotoyomo-class former auxiliary tug** Bldr: Gulfport Boiler & Welding Works, Port Arthur, Tex.

| | Laid down | L | In serv. |
|---|---|---|---|
| 563 Chiu Lien (ex-*Geronimo,* ATA 207) | 10-11-44 | 4-1-45 | 1-3-45 |

**Chiu Lien (563)** 1969

**D:** 835 tons (fl) **S:** 13 kts **Dim:** 43.59 (40.74 wl) × 10.31 × 4.01
**A:** 1/20-mm AA **M:** 2 G.M. 12-278A diesels, electric drive; 1 prop; 1,500 hp
**Electric:** 120 kw **Fuel:** 158 tons **Man:** 45 tot.

Remarks: Transferred in 2-69. Operated for the Institute of Oceanology and equipped with various oceanographic winches and laboratories.

◆ **1 ex-U.S. LSIL 351-class former landing craft** Bldr: Albina Eng. & Mach. Works, Portland, Ore.

| | Laid down | L | In serv. |
|---|---|---|---|
| 466 Lien Chang (ex-LSIL 1017) | 31-1-44 | 14-3-44 | 12-4-44 |

**D:** 387 tons (fl) **S:** 14.4 kts **Dim:** 48.46 (46.63 wl) × 7.21 × 1.73
**A:** 1/40-mm AA—4/20-mm AA (I × 4) **M:** 8 G.M. 6-71 diesels; 2 props; 2,320 hp
**Fuel:** 113 tons **Man:** 40 tot.

Remarks: Transferred in 5-58. Retains LSIL appearance.

## AUXILIARY SHIPS

◆ **1 offshore-island support tanker**

| | Bldr | In serv. |
|---|---|---|
| 512 Wan Shou | Ujina SB, Hiroshima, Japan | 1-11-69 |

**Wan Shou (512)** 1970

**D:** 1,049 tons light (4,150 fl) **S:** 13 kts **Dim:** 86.5 × 16.5 × 5.5
**A:** 2/40-mm AA (I × 2)—2/20-mm AA (I × 2)
**M:** 1 diesel; 1 prop; 2,100 hp **Fuel:** 230 tons **Man:** 70 tot.

Remarks: No underway-replenishment capability. Cargo: 2,600 tons.

◆ **3 ex-U.S. Patapsco-class support tankers** Bldr: Cargill Inc., Savage, Minn.

| | Laid down | L | In serv. |
|---|---|---|---|
| . . . Chang Pei (ex-*Pecatonica,* AOG 57) | 6-12-44 | 17-3-45 | 28-11-45 |
| . . . Hsin Lung (ex-*Elkhorn,* AOG 7) | 7-9-42 | 15-5-43 | 12-2-44 |
| 515 Lung Chuan (ex-*Endeavor,* ex-*Namakagon,* AOG 53) | 1-8-44 | 4-11-44 | 10-5-45 |

**Lung Chuan (515)**—no armament L. & L. Van Ginderen, 1979

**D:** 1,850 tons light (4,335 fl) **S:** 14 kts **Dim:** 94.72 (89.0 wl) × 14.78 × 4.78
**A:** 2/76.2-mm DP (I × 2)—4/20-mm AA (I × 4)
**M:** 2 G.M. 16-278A diesels; 2 props; 3,300 hp **Electric:** 460 kw
**Fuel:** 295 tons **Range:** 6,670/10 **Man:** 124 tot.

Remarks: Former gasoline tankers. Cargo: 2,040 tons. *Chang Pei* transferred on 24-4-61, *Hsin Lung* on 1-7-72, and *Lung Chuan* on 29-6-71 after serving in the New Zealand Navy as Antarctic supply ship since 5-10-62. All used for supplying offshore islands. All purchased outright 19-5-76.

◆ **1 large transport** Bldr: Tsoying Naval SY

525 Wu Kang (In serv. 2-85)

**Wu Kang (525)** *Defense Technology*

**D:** 3,040 tons (fl) **S:** . . . **Dim:** 101.0 × 17.0 × . . .
**A:** 2/40-mm AA (I × 2) **Electron Equipt:** Radar: 1/. . . nav.
**M:** 2 diesels; 2 props; . . . hp—bow-thruster

Remarks: Roll-on/Roll-off vehicle and passenger ferry to serve Quemoy and Matsu garrisons. Stern truncated to fit small berthing area. Can carry over 600 passengers.

AUXILIARY SHIPS *(continued)*

◆ **1 transport** Bldr: China SB, Keelung

523 Yuen Feng (In serv. 1983)

**D:** . . . **S:** . . . **Dim:** 110.0 × . . . × . . .
**A:** 2/20-mm AA **M:** 1 diesel; . . . hp

Remarks: Passenger-cargo ship with accommodations for 500 troops.

◆ **1 transport**

| | Bldr | L | In serv. |
|---|---|---|---|
| 522 Ling Yuen | China SB, Keelung | 27-1-75 | 15-8-75 |

**D:** 4,000 tons (fl) **S:** . . . **Dim:** 100.2 × 14.6 × 5.0
**A:** 2/20-mm AA (I × 2)—2/12.7-mm mg (I × 2)
**M:** 1 6-cylinder diesel; 1 prop; . . . hp **Man:** 55 tot.

Remarks: 2,510 dwt/3,040 grt. Can carry 500 troops.

◆ **1 ex-U.S. Achelous-class transport** Bldr: Kaiser Co., Vancouver, Wash.

| | Laid down | L | In serv. |
|---|---|---|---|
| 520 Wu Tai (ex-*Sung Shan,* ex-*Agenor,* ARL 3, ex-LST 490) | 24-1-43 | 3-4-43 | 20-8-43 |

**D:** 4,100 tons (fl) **S:** 11.6 kts **Dim:** 99.98 × 15.24 × 3.4
**A:** 8/40-mm AA (IV × 2) **M:** 2 G.M. 12-567A diesels; 2 props; 1,800 hp
**Electric:** 500 kw **Man:** 100 men + 600 troops

Remarks: Converted to a repair ship while building. Transferred to France in 1951, then to Taiwan on 15-9-57. Converted to transport, 1973–74.

◆ **1 ex-U.S. Army 427-class small transport** Bldr: Higgins, New Orleans, La. (In serv. 21-12-44)

359 Yung Kang (ex-*Mark,* AKL 12, ex-AG 143, ex-Army FS 214)

**Yung Kang (359)**—wearing old number 1971

**D:** 693 tons (899 fl) **S:** 12 kts **Dim:** 54.86 (52.37 wl) × 9.75 × 3.05
**A:** 2/20-mm AA (I × 2) **M:** 2 G.M. 6-278A diesels; 2 props; 1,000 hp
**Electric:** 225 kw **Fuel:** 100 tons **Range:** 4,000/11 **Man:** 37 tot.

Remarks: Built as an aircraft maintenance ship for the U.S. Army Air Forces. Transferred to the U.S. Navy on 30-9-47 and to Taiwan on 1-6-71. Sold outright on 19-5-76. Now has intelligence-gathering equipment.

◆ **1 ex-U.S. Amphion-class repair ship** Bldr: Tampa SB, Tampa, Fla.

| | Laid down | L | In serv. |
|---|---|---|---|
| 521 Yu Tai (ex-*Cadmus,* AR 14) | 30-10-44 | 5-8-45 | 23-4-46 |

**Yu Tai (521)**—with MARISAT SATCOMM radome L. & L. Van Ginderen, 7-85

**D:** 7,826 tons light (14,490 fl) **S:** 16.5 kts
**Dim:** 149.96 (141.73 pp) × 21.18 × 8.38 **Electron Equipt:** Radar: 1/SPS-5
**A:** 1/127-mm DP—6/40-mm AA (II × 3)
**M:** 1 set Westinghouse GT; 2 props; 8,500 hp **Electric:** 3,600 kw
**Boilers:** 2 Foster-Wheeler D-type; 30.6 kg/cm², 399°C **Fuel:** 2,430 tons
**Man:** 920 tot.

Remarks: Transferred on 15-1-74.

◆ **1 ex-U.S. Diver-class salvage ship** Bldr: Basalt Rock Co., Napa, Cal.

| | Laid down | L | In serv. |
|---|---|---|---|
| 324 Tai Hu (ex-*Grapple,* ARS 7) | 8-9-42 | 31-12-42 | 16-12-43 |

**D:** 1,530 tons (1,900 fl) **S:** 14.8 kts **Dim:** 65.08 (63.09 wl) × 11.89 × 4.29
**A:** 2/20-mm AA (I × 2) **Electron Equipt:** Radar: 1/SPS-53
**M:** 4 Cooper-Bessemer GSB-8 diesels, electric drive; 2 props; 3,060 hp
**Electric:** 460 kw **Fuel:** 283 tons **Range:** 9,000/14; 20,000/7 **Man:** 85 tot.

Remarks: Transferred on 1-12-77.

◆ **4 ex-U.S. Cherokee-, Abnaki-* and Achomawi-† class fleet tugs**

Bldrs: *Ta Tung, Ta Wan:* United Eng., Alameda, Cal.; others: Charleston SB & DD, Charleston, S.C.

| | Laid down | L | In serv. |
|---|---|---|---|
| 542 Ta Han (ex-*Tawakoni,* ATF 114)* | 19-5-43 | 28-10-43 | 15-9-44 |
| 548 Ta Tung (ex-*Chickasaw,* ATF 83) | 14-2-42 | 23-7-42 | 4-2-43 |
| 550 Ta Wan (ex-*Apache,* ATF 67) | 8-11-44 | 8-5-45 | 12-12-45 |
| 551 N . . . . . . . (ex-*Shakori,* ATF 162) | 9-5-45 | 9-8-45 | 20-12-45 |

**D:** 1,235 tons (1,675 fl) **S:** 15 kts **Dim:** 62.48 (59.44 wl) × 11.73 × 4.67
**A:** 1/76.2-mm DP—2/12.7-mm mg
**M:** 4 G.M. 12-278 diesels, electric drive; 1 prop; 3,000 hp **Electric:** 260–400 kw
**Fuel:** 295 tons **Range:** 6,500/16; 15,000/8 **Man:** 85 tot.

Remarks: *Ta Tung* transferred 1-66 (sold on 19-5-75), *Ta Wan* on 30-6-74, *Ta Han* on 1-6-78, and ex-ATF 162 on 29-8-80. *Ta Han* has Busch-Sulzer BS-539 diesels and only a small exhaust pipe, and ex-ATF 162 has G.M. 12-278A diesels.

◆ **3 ex-U.S. Sotoyomo-class ocean tugs** Bldr: Levingston SB, Orange, Tex.

| | Laid down | L | In serv. |
|---|---|---|---|
| 357 Ta Sueh (ex-*Tonkawa,* ATA 176) | 30-1-44 | 1-3-44 | 19-8-44 |
| 367 Ta Teng (ex-*Cahokia,* ATA 186) | 16-8-44 | 18-9-44 | 24-11-44 |
| 395 Ta Peng (ex-*Mahopac,* ATA 196) | 24-11-44 | 21-12-44 | 6-3-45 |

**D:** 435 tons (835 fl) **S:** 13 kts **Dim:** 43.59 (40.74 wl) × 10.31 × 4.01
**A:** 1/76.2-mm DP—2/20-mm AA (I × 2)
**M:** 2 G.M. 12-278A diesels, electric drive; 1 prop; 1,500 hp
**Electric:** 120 kw **Fuel:** 158 tons **Man:** 45 tons

Remarks: *Ta Peng* transferred on 1-7-71, *Ta Sueh* in 4-62, and *Ta Teng* on 29-3-72 after serving the U.S. Air Force since 1971. Sister *Chiu Lien* is an oceanographic research ship.

SERVICE CRAFT

◆ **1 ex-U.S. 174-foot yard oiler** Bldr: Manitowoc SB, Manitowoc, Wisc.

| | Laid down | L | In serv. |
|---|---|---|---|
| 504 Szu Ming (ex-YO 198) | 10-2-45 | 21-4-45 | 14-7-45 |

**D:** 650 tons (1,595 fl) **S:** 10.5 kts **Dim:** 53.04 × 9.75 × 4.10
**A:** 1/40-mm AA—5/20-mm AA (I × 5)
**M:** 1 Union diesel; 1 prop; 560 hp **Man:** 65 tot.

Remarks: Transferred in 12-49. In reserve.

◆ **6 ex-U.S. Navy YTL 422-class small harbor tugs**

| | | |
|---|---|---|
| YTL 8 (ex-ST-2002) | YTL 10 (ex-ST-2008) | YTL 12 (ex-YTL 584) |
| YTL 9 (ex-ST-2004) | YTL 11 (ex-YTL 454) | YTL 14 (ex-YTL 585) |

**D:** 70 tons (80 fl) **S:** 8 kts **Dim:** 20.3 × 5.18 × 2.4
**M:** 1 diesel; 1 prop; 375 hp

Remarks: YTL 8 to YTL 10 transferred in 3-62, YTL 11 in 8-63, YTL 12 and YTL 14 in 7-64. First three are former U.S. Army units, built during World War II.

◆ **1 ex-U.S. ARD 12-class floating dry dock** Bldr: Pacific Bridge, Alameda, Cal.

Fo Wu 6 (ex-*Windsor,* ARD 22)

**Dim:** 149.86 × 24.69 × 1.73 (light) **Capacity:** 3,500 tons

Remarks: In service 4-44, transferred on 19-5-76; purchased 1981.

◆ **1 ex-U.S. ARD 2-class floating dry dock** Bldr: Pacific Bridge, Alameda, Cal.

Fo Wu 5 (ex-ARD 9)

**Dim:** 148.03 × 21.64 × 1.75 (light) **Capacity:** 3,500 tons

Remarks: In service 9-43, transferred on 12-1-77; purchased outright 1981.

◆ **2 ex-U.S. floating dry docks** Bldr: V.P. Loftis, Wilmington, N.C.

Hay Tan (ex-AFDL 36) Han Jih (ex-AFDL 34)

**Dim:** 73.15 × 19.69 × 1.3 (light) **Capacity:** 1,000 tons

Remarks: In service 5- and 6-44, transferred in 3-47 and 7-59.

◆ **1 ex-U.S. floating dry dock**

Kim Men (ex-AFDL 5)

**Dim:** 60.96 × 19.5 × 1.04 **Capacity:** 1,000 tons

Remarks: Built in 1944, transferred in 1-48.

TAIWAN *(continued)*

CUSTOMS SERVICE

Subordinate to the Ministry of Finance in peacetime and to the Navy in time of war.

**PATROL SHIPS**

◆ **0 (+2) patrol vessels** Bldr: Wilton-Fijenoord, Schiedam

| | Laid down | L | In serv. |
|---|---|---|---|
| . . . Hsing | . . . | . . . | 1988 |
| . . . Hsing | . . . | . . . | 1988 |

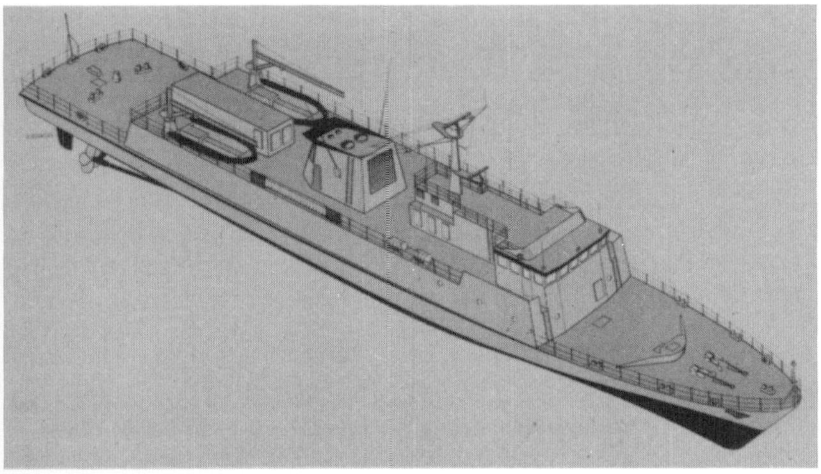

**New patrol vessel** Wilton-Fijenoord, 1986

**D:** 700 tons (850 fl) **S:** . . . **Dim:** 65.00 × 9.60 × . . .
**A:** . . . **Electron Equipt:** Radar: 2/. . . nav.
**M:** 2 diesels; 2 props; . . . hp **Range:** . . . **Man:** . . .

Remarks: Ordered 4-86. Will replace the two U.S. *Admirable*-class patrol ships.

◆ **3 (+. . .) Taiwan-built** Bldr: China SB, Keelung

. . . Hsing (In serv. 1983) . . . Hsing (In serv. 11-86)
Chin Hsing (In serv. 23-5-85)

**D:** 578 grt **S:** . . . **Dim:** 75.00 × . . . × . . .
**A:** 1/40-mm AA—1/20-mm AA **M:** 2 diesels; 2 props; . . . hp

Remarks: A flush-decked design resembling South Korean Coast Guard "Sea Whale" design, but somewhat smaller. Replace three U.S. PC 461-class patrol ships. *Chin Hsing* launched 26-12-84.

◆ **2 ex-U.S. Admirable-class former minesweepers**

| | Bldr | L | In serv. |
|---|---|---|---|
| Hung Hsing (ex-*Embattle,* MSF 226) | American SB, Lorain, O. | 17-9-44 | 25-4-45 |
| N . . . . . . . (ex-*Improve,* MSF 247) | Savannah Mach., Ga. | 26-9-43 | 29-2-44 |

**D:** 945 tons (fl) **S:** 14.8 kts **Dim:** 56.24 × 10.06 × 2.97
**A:** 2/20-mm AA **M:** 2 Cooper-Bessemer GSB-8 diesels; 2 props; 1,710 hp

Remarks: Transferred to Taiwan in late 1940s and handed over to the Customs Service in early 1970s. Used in lighthouse supply duties.

**PATROL CRAFT**

◆ **3 Swedish-built** Bldr: Boghammar, Stockholm (In serv. 1979)

**D:** 5.5 tons (fl) **S:** 50 kts
**Dim:** 11.30 × 2.30 × 0.90 **A:** small arms
**M:** 2 Volvo Penta TAMD-70E diesels; 2 outdrive props; 600 hp
**Range:** 500/40 **Man:** 3–5 tot.

Remarks: Aluminum construction. Sisters to craft used by Iranian Revolutionary Guards.

◆ **3 aluminum-hulled** Bldr: China SB, Kohsiung

Hai Ping (In serv. 28-2-79) Hai An (In serv. 18-3-79)
Hai Cheng (In serv. 1979)

**D:** . . . **S:** . . . **Dim:** 26.0 × 5.6 × 2.7
**A:** . . . **M:** 2 MTU 8V331 TC81 diesels; 2 props; . . . hp

◆ **2 aluminum-hulled** Bldr: Halter Marine, New Orleans (In serv. 1977)

**D:** 70 tons **S:** . . . **Dim:** 23.77 × . . . × . . . **A:** . . .
**M:** 2 G.M. diesels; 2 props; . . . hp

# TANZANIA

**United Republic of Tanzania**

Personnel (1987): Approximately 700 men

Merchant Marine (1986): 41 ships—50,726 grt
(5 tankers—3,682 grt)

**PATROL BOATS**

◆ **4 modified North Korean Nampo class**

**D:** 82 tons (fl) **S:** 40 kts **Dim:** 27.7 × 6.1 × 1.8
**A:** 4/14.5-mm mg (II × 2) **Electron Equipt:** Radar: 1/Pot Head
**M:** 4 M50F diesels; 4 props; 4,800 hp **Range:** 375/40 **Man:** 19 tot.

Remarks: Transferred 1979–81; lack the bow ramp employed on the landing craft version used by North Korea.

◆ **7 Chinese Shanghai-II class**

JW 9861 through JW 9867

**Two Tanzanian Shanghai-II**—with survey craft *Utafiti* and patrol craft *Rafiki* and *Uhuru* in background A. Zioko, 10-84

**D:** 122.5 tons (135 fl) **S:** 28.5 kts **Dim:** 38.78 × 5.41 × 1.55
**A:** 4/37-mm AA (II × 2)—4/25-mm AA (II × 2)
**Electron Equipt:** Radar: 1/Pot Head
**M:** 2 M50F-4, 1,200-hp diesels; 2 12D6, 910-hp diesels; 4 props; 4,220 hp
**Electric:** 39 kw **Endurance:** 7 days **Range:** 750/16.5 **Man:** 36 tot.

Remarks: Transferred 1970–71.

**TORPEDO BOATS**

◆ **4 Chinese Huchuan class** Bldr: Hudung SY, Shanghai

JW 9841 through JW 9844

**JW 9842** 1976

**D:** 39 tons (45 fl) **S:** 50 kts **Dim:** 22.50 × 3.80 × 1.146
**A:** 4/14.5-mm mg (II × 2)—2/533-mm TT (I × 2)
**Electron Equipt:** Radar: 1/Skin Head **Electric:** 5.6 kw
**M:** 3 M50 diesels; 3 props; 3,600 hp **Range:** 500/30 **Man:** 11 tot.

Remarks: Transferred 1975. Unlike Chinese Navy Huchuans, these craft have no hydrofoils. Gun mounts are fore and aft, while on most units of this class both mounts are aft.

**COASTAL PATROL CRAFT**

◆ **1 or more "Seneca" class** Bldr: Crestitalia, Ameglia (In serv. . . .)

**D:** 8 tons (fl) **S:** 23 kts **Dim:** 11.10 × . . . × . . .
**A:** . . . **M:** 2 G.M. diesels; 2 Castoldi waterjets; 864 hp

Remarks: GRP construction, delivered post-1980.

TANZANIA *(continued)*
COASTAL PATROL CRAFT *(continued)*

◆ **2 East German Schwalbe-class former inshore minesweepers**

ARAKA SALAAM

**D:** 70 tons (fl) **S:** 14 kts **Dim:** 26.0 × 4.5 × 1.4
**A:** 2/25-mm AA (II × 2) **M:** 2 diesels; 2 props; 600 hp

REMARKS: Transferred in 1-66 and 1-67. Minesweeping gear removed. No radar.

◆ **4 Chinese Yu Lin-class craft**

**D:** 9.8 tons (fl) **S:** 25 kts **Dim:** 13.0 × 2.9 × 1.1
**A:** 2/12.7-mm mg (I × 2) **M:** 1 diesel; 1 prop; 300 hp

REMARKS: Transferred by the Chinese People's Republic in 11-66. These craft operate on Lake Victoria.

◆ **2 aluminum-hulled craft** Bldr: Bayerische Schiffsbau, West Germany, 1967

RAFIKI UHURU

**D:** 40 tons (fl) **S:** 14 kts **Dim:** 24.0 × 5.0 × 1.3
**A:** 1/40-mm AA—2/mg **M:** 2 Caterpillar diesels; 2 props . . . hp

NOTE: The 3 ex-East German, ex-Soviet P-6-class converted torpedo boats and the one ex-Soviet Poluchat-I-class armed torpedo retriever were discarded by 1984.

MISCELLANEOUS UNITS

◆ **1 coastal survey craft** Bldr: Bayerische Schiffsbau, West Germany (In serv. 1979)

UTAFITI

**D:** 33 tons (fl) **S:** 14 kts **Dim:** 19.05 × . . . × 1.0
**Electron Equipt:** Radar: 1/Decca 060
**M:** 2 Caterpillar diesels; 2 props; 456 hp **Range:** 250/12 **Man:** 6 tot.

REMARKS: Has Atlas DESO 10 echo-sounder. Steel hull, aluminum superstructure.

◆ **2 ex-Chinese Yu Chai-class landing craft for logistics duties** (In serv. 1967–68)

**D:** 70 tons (fl) **S:** 10 kts **Dim:** 20.0 × 4.3 × 1.0
**M:** 2 Type 12V150 diesels; 2 props; 600 hp

# THAILAND

**Kingdom of Thailand**

PERSONNEL (1987): Navy: 21,200 total (including 900 in Naval Air Arm)
Marines: 1,000 officers, 19,000 enlisted

MERCHANT MARINE (1986): 243 ships—533,138 grt
(tankers: 60 ships—59,315 grt)

NAVAL AVIATION: Available are: 8 Grumman S-2F land-based ASW aircraft; 2 Fokker F-27-400M and 3 Fokker F-27-200 Maritime, 10 Nomad Searchmaster, and 2 Cessna T-337 Skymaster for maritime surveillance; 2 CL-215 and 2 HU-16 amphibians; 20 C-46 and C-47 transports; 10 Cessna 0-1 Bird Dog observation aircraft; 14 U-17 Skywagon utility aircraft, 2 Lake L-A4 Skimmer training amphibians; and 5 Bell 214 ST, 3 Bell UH-1H, and 10 Bell 212 helicopters. Fourteen Marconi Stingray ASW torpedoes were ordered 9-84 for the F-27 Maritime and for the new U.S.-built corvettes. The F-27 aircraft are equipped to launch U.S. Harpoon missiles. Seven more Bell 214 ST helos to deliver by end 1988. Ten MM 38 Exocet SSM coast defense batteries ordered 1986.

## SUBMARINES

NOTE: The Thai Navy had planned to order three submarines during 1985. Negotiations have been under way since 1983 with a number of submarine builders, with China (Romeo class), Italy, and West Germany as the leading contenders.

## FRIGATES

◆ **1 "Yarrow frigate" class** Bldr: Yarrow, Scotstoun, Glasgow, Scotland

| | Laid down | L | In serv. |
|---|---|---|---|
| 7 MAKUT RAJAKUMARN | 11-1-70 | 18-11-71 | 7-5-73 |

**D:** 1,650 tons (1,900 fl) **S:** 26 kts (gas turbines)/18 kts (diesel)
**Dim:** 97.56 (92.99 pp) × 10.97 × 5.5 (over sonar)
**A:** 2/114-mm DP Mk 8—2/40-mm AA (I × 2)—6/324-mm STW-1 ASW TT (III × 2)—2/d.c. projectors, 1/d.c. rack
**Electron Equipt:** Radar: 1/Decca 626, 1/H.S.A. DA-05, 1/H.S.A. WM-22
Sonar: Krupp-Atlas DSQS-21B
**M:** CODOG: 1 Rolls-Royce Olympus TBM 3B gas turbine (23,125 hp), 1 Crossley-Pielstick 12 PC2 diesel; 2 CP props; 6,000 hp
**Electric:** 2,200 kw **Range:** 1,000/25; 4,000/18 **Man:** 16 officers, 124 men

**Makut Rajakumarn (7)**—prior to modernization R.A.N., 1981

REMARKS: Similar to the Malaysian *Rahmat* but longer and more heavily armed. Highly automated. The WM-22 track-while-scan radar controls the 114-mm guns. Modernized 1985–86: new sonar, air-search radar; Sea Cat missile launcher and director deleted, Limbo ASW mortar replaced by ASW TT (with U.K. Stingray torpedoes). Plans call for further modernization, with aft 114-mm gun replaced by U.S. Harpoon missiles and either a Mk 29 launcher for Sea Sparrow short-range SAMs or a Mk 15 20-mm Phalanx gatling CIWS.

◆ **2 ex-U.S. PF 103 class**

| | Bldr | Laid down | L | In serv. |
|---|---|---|---|---|
| 5 TAPI (ex-PF 107) | American SB, Toledo, Oh. | 1-4-70 | 17-10-70 | 1-11-71 |
| 6 KHIRIRAT (ex-PF 108) | Norfolk SB & DD, Va. | 18-2-72 | 2-6-73 | 10-8-74 |

**Tapi (5)** U.S. Navy, 8-86

**Tapi (5)** U.S. Navy, 8-86

**D:** 864 tons light (1,143 fl) **S:** 20 kts **Dim:** 84.04 × 10.06 × 3.05 (4.27 sonar)
**A:** 1/76-mm OTO Melara Compact DP—1/40-mm AA—2/20-mm AA (I × 2)—2/12.7-mm mg (I × 2)—6/324-mm Mk 32 ASW TT (III × 2)—1/Mk 9 d.c. rack
**Electron Equipt:** Radar: 1/Raytheon navigational, 1/SPS-6, 1/H.S.A. WM-25
Sonar: 1/SQS-17A
**M:** 2 Fairbanks-Morse 38D8$\frac{1}{8}$-10 diesels; 2 props; 5,300 hp **Electric:** 750 kw
**Fuel:** 110 tons **Range:** 2,400/18 **Man:** 16 officers, 124 men

REMARKS: Ordered 27-6-69 and 25-6-71, respectively. Patterned after the Italian-built *Pattimura* class for Indonesia; four sisters built for the Iranian Navy. *Tapi* completed modernization in 1983 with the OTO Melara gun replacing the for-

**FRIGATES** *(continued)*

ward U.S. 76.2-mm mount, a Bofors 40-mm on a raised bandstand replacing the aft 76.2-mm mount, 2 single 20-mm AA replacing the original twin 40-mm mount, and an H.S.A. WM-25 track-while-scan radar director being mounted above the bridge; a Hedgehog ASW mortar was removed. *Khirirat* in modernization 1985–86.

◆ **1 ex-U.S. Cannon class** Bldr: Western Pipe and Steel, Los Angeles

| | Laid down | L | In serv. |
|---|---|---|---|
| 3 Pin Klao (ex-*Hemminger,* DE 746) | 8-5-43 | 27-12-43 | 30-5-44 |

**Pin Klao (3)** U.S. Navy, 8-86

**D:** 1,240 tons light (1,940 fl) **S:** 20 kts
**Dim:** 93.27 (91.44 wl) × 11.15 × 4.3 (sonar)
**A:** 3/76.2-mm DP Mk 22 (I × 3)—6/40-mm AA (II × 3)—2/12.7-mm mg (I × 2)—1/Mk 10 Hedgehog—6,324-mm Mk 32 ASW TT (III × 2)—8/Mk 6 d.c. projectors (3 Mk 9 d.c. each)—2/Mk 9 d.c. racks (7 Mk 9 d.c. each)
**Electron Equipt:** Radar: 1/Decca . . . , 1/SPS-21, 1/SPS-6C, 1/Mk 26, 1/Mk 34
Sonar: SQS-11
EW: WLR-1
**M:** 2 G.M. 16-278A diesels, electric drive; 2 props; 6,000 hp **Electric:** 680 kw
**Fuel:** 260 tons **Range:** 11,500/11 **Man:** 14 officers, 178 men

Remarks: Transferred 7-59; sold outright 6-6-75, at which time the ship underwent extensive overhaul in Guam. Has Mk 52 radar GFCS for 76.2-mm guns, one Mk 63 radar GFCS and two Mk 51 Mod. 2 optical GFCS for the 40-mm guns. To replace *Maeklong* as cadet training ship. WLR-1 EW equipment removed.

◆ **2 ex-U.S. Tacoma class** Bldr: Consolidated Steel, Los Angeles

| | Laid down | L | In serv. |
|---|---|---|---|
| 1 Tahchin (ex-*Glendale,* PF 36) | 6-4-43 | 28-5-43 | 1-10-43 |
| 2 Prasae (ex-*Gallup,* PF 47) | 18-8-43 | 17-9-43 | 29-2-44 |

**Prasae (2)** U.S. Navy, 8-86

**D:** 1,430 tons (2,100 fl) **S:** 19 kts **Dim:** 92.63 (87.02 pp) × 11.43 × 4.17 (hull)
**A:** 3/76.2-mm DP (I × 3)—2/40-mm AA (I × 2)—9/20-mm AA (I × 9)—1/Mk 10 Hedgehog—2/324-mm fixed Mk 32 ASW TT (I × 2)—8/Mk 6 d.c. projectors—2/Mk 9 d.c. racks
**Electron Equipt:** Radar: 1/. . . nav., 1/SPS-6C—Sonar: SQS-17B
**M:** 2 sets triple-expansion steam; 2 props; 5,500 hp
**Boilers:** 2, 3-drum Express; 16.9 kg/cm² **Fuel:** 685 tons
**Range:** 5,600/16; 7,800/12 **Man:** 13 officers, 201 men

Remarks: Transferred 29-10-57. Both refitted at Guam in the early 1970s. Last active examples of a class that once numbered 100 ships. Were to be stricken with full operational capability of the *Ratanakosin*-class corvettes. Both used primarily for training.

**CORVETTES**

◆ **0 (+3) new construction**

| | Bldr | Laid down | L | In serv. |
|---|---|---|---|---|
| 3 N . . . | Italthai, Bangkok | . . . | . . . | . . . |
| 4 N . . . | Italthai, Bangkok | . . . | . . . | . . . |
| 5 N . . . | Royal Thai DY, Bangkok | . . . | . . . | . . . |

**D:** 450 tons (550 fl) **S:** 38 kts **Dim:** 56.50 (52.00 wl) × 9.00 × 2.25
**A:** 1/57-mm Bofors SAK-57 Mk 2 DP—2/40-mm Breda AA (II × 2)—2/12.7-mm mg (I × 2)—6/324-mm ASW TT (III × 2)—2/d.c. mortars—1/d.c. rack—mines
**Electron Equipt:** Radar: 1/. . . nav., 1/. . . air/surf.-search, 1/. . . f.c.
Sonar: . . .
EW: . . .
**M:** 4 Paxman Valenta 18RP200 diesels; 4 CP props; 17,900 hp (15,000 sust.)
**Range:** 2,500/15 **Fuel:** . . . **Man:** 10 officers, 47 men

Remarks: Ordered 10-87 as a variant of the Vosper Thornycroft "Vita" 56-m fast strike craft design. Five more may be ordered later. Can be equipped with a variable-depth sonar. The main gun may, in fact, be an OTO Melara 76-mm Compact or Super-Rapid, and there is space for later installation of SSM.

◆ **2 PFMM Mk 16 class** Bldr: Tacoma Boatbldg., Tacoma, Wash.

| | Laid down | L | In serv. |
|---|---|---|---|
| 1 Ratanakosin | 6-2-84 | 11-3-86 | 26-9-86 |
| 2 Sukhothai | 26-3-84 | 20-7-86 | 19-2-87 |

**Sukhothai (2)** G. Arra, 11-86

**Sukhothai (2)** V. Baca, 2-87

**Ratanakosin (1)** Tacoma Boat, 9-86

**CORVETTES** *(continued)*

**D:** 840 tons normal (960 fl) **S:** 26 kts **Dim:** 76.82 × 9.55 × 2.44
**A:** 8/Harpoon SSM (IV × 2)—1/Albatros SAM system (VIII × 1, . . . Aspide missiles)—1/76-mm OTO Melara DP—2/40-mm Breda AA (II × 1)—2/20-mm AA (I × 2)—6/324-mm Mk 32 ASW TT (III × 2)
**Electron Equipt:** Radar: 1/Decca 1226, 1/ZW-06 nav., 1/H.S.A. DA-05, 1/H.S.A. WM-25, 1/H.S.A. LIROD-8
Sonar: Krupp-Atlas DSQS-21B
EW: Elettronica Newton intercept; 1/Dagaie chaff RL
**M:** 2 MTU 20V1163 TB83 diesels; 2 props; 16,000 hp (14,730 sust.)
**Man:** 15 officers, 72 enlisted

REMARKS: Ordered 9-5-83. Enlarged version of Saudi Arabian PCG class. Have H.S.A. Mini-SADOC weapons control. A Dutch Goalkeeper 30-mm CIWS may be installed later. Plans to build a third ship in Thailand canceled.

**GUIDED-MISSILE PATROL BOATS**

◆ **3 Ratcharit class** Bldr: Breda, Venice, Italy

| | L | In serv. |
|---|---|---|
| 4 RATCHARIT | 30-7-78 | 10-8-79 |
| 5 WITTHAYAKOM | 2-9-78 | 12-11-79 |
| 6 UDOMET | 28-9-78 | 21-2-80 |

**Ratcharit (4)** U.S. Navy, 5-80

**D:** 235 tons light (270 fl) **S:** 36 kts **Dim:** 49.8 (47.25 pp) × 7.5 × 1.68
**A:** 4/MM 38 Exocet (II × 2)—1/76-mm OTO Melara DP—1/40-mm Breda AA
**Electron Equipt:** Radar: 1/navigational, 1/H.S.A. M-25
**M:** 3 MTU MD20 V538 TB91 diesels; 3 CP props; 13,500 hp
**Electric:** 440 kw **Range:** 650/36; 2,000/15 **Man:** 7 officers, 38 men

REMARKS: Ordered 23-7-76. Can make 30 kts on two engines.

◆ **3 Prabrarapak class** Bldr: Singapore SB & Eng. Co., Jurong, Singapore

| | L | In serv. |
|---|---|---|
| 1 PRABRARAPAK | 29-7-75 | 28-7-76 |
| 2 HANHAK SATTRU | 28-10-75 | 6-11-76 |
| 3 SUPHAIRIN | 20-2-76 | 1-2-77 |

**Hanhak Sattru (2)** G. Arra, 1981

**D:** 224 tons (260 fl) **S:** 41 kts **Dim:** 44.9 × 7.0 × 2.1 (2.46 props)
**A:** 5/Gabriel-I (III × 1, I × 2)—1/57-mm Bofors AA—1/40-mm Bofors AA—2/12.7-mm mg (I × 2)
**Electron Equipt:** Radar: 1/Decca TM 626, 1/H.S.A. WM-28
EW: passive intercept system
**M:** 4 MTU 16V538 TB92 diesels; 4 props; 14,000 hp **Electric:** 405 kVA
**Range:** 500/38.5; 1,500/16 **Man:** 40 tot.

REMARKS: Similar to the Singapore Navy's Lürssen-designed boats; built under license. 103-mm rocket flare launch rails are mounted on the 57-mm mount.

**PATROL BOATS**

◆ **6 PSMM Mk 5 class** Bldr: Italthai SY, Samutprakarn

| | Laid down | L | In serv. |
|---|---|---|---|
| 4 SATTAHIP | 15-1-82 | 27-7-83 | 16-9-83 |
| 5 KLONGYAI | . . . | 9-3-84 | 5-84 |
| 6 TAKBAI | . . . | 25-5-84 | 7-84 |
| 7 KATANG | . . . | 26-10-84 | 14-10-85 |
| 8 THEPA | . . . | 1985 | 17-4-86 |
| 9 THAI MUANG | . . . | 12-85 | 17-4-86 |

**D:** 270 tons (300 fl) **S:** 22 kts **Dim:** 50.14 (47.22 wl) × 7.30 × 1.58 (1.80 props)
**A:** 1/76.2-mm U.S. Mk 26 DP—1/40-mm AA—2/20-mm AA (I × 2)—2/12.7-mm mg (I × 2)
**Electron Equipt:** Radar: 1/. . . nav.
**M:** 2 MTU 16V538 TB91 diesels; 2 props; 6,840 hp
**Electric:** 420 kw **Fuel:** 80 tons **Range:** 2,500/15 **Man:** 56 tot.

REMARKS: First four ordered 9-9-81, others on 27-12-83 and 31-8-84. NA 18 GFCS.

◆ **3 MV 400th design** Bldr: Breda, Puerto Marghera, Venice, Italy

| | Laid down | L | In serv. |
|---|---|---|---|
| 1 CHONBURI | 15-8-81 | 7-6-82 | 22-2-83 |
| 2 SONGKHLA | 15-9-81 | 6-9-82 | 12-83 |
| 3 PHUKET | 15-12-81 | 3-2-83 | 5-84 |

**Phuket (3)** U.S. Navy, 8-86

**Songkhla (2)** *Ships of the World,* 1983

**D:** 400 tons (450 fl) **S:** 30 kts **Dim:** 60.40 (57.50 pp) × 8.80 × 1.95
**A:** 2/76-mm OTO Melara DP (I × 2)—2/40-mm Breda AA (II × 1)
**Electron Equipt:** Radar: 1/H.S.A. ZW-06, 1/H.S.A. WM-22/61, 1/H.S.A. LIROD-8
EW: passive intercept, 4/Breda chaff RL (VI × 4)
**M:** 2 MTU 20V538 TB92 diesels; 3 CP props; 15,000 hp (12,600 sust.)
**Electric:** 800 kw **Range:** 900/29; 2,500/18 **Man:** 7 officers, 38 men

REMARKS: Ordered 11-79, originally for delivery in 1982, but this slipped considerably. First unit delivered 29-11-82 by shipyard. Able to accommodate antiship missiles, but none were to be installed at delivery. Steel hull, aluminum-alloy superstructure. Have LIROD-8 radar optronic GFCS to back up the WM-22/61 system.

◆ **7 (+ . . .) T 93 class** Bldr: Royal Thai Naval Dockyard, Bangkok

| | | |
|---|---|---|
| T 93 (L: 1973) | T 94 (In serv. 16-9-81) | T 95 (In serv. 1981) |
| T 96 (In serv. 1982) | T 97 (In serv. 16-9-83) | T 98 (In serv. 1984) |
| | | T 99 (In serv. 5-87) |

**D:** 117 tons (125 fl) **S:** 25 kts **Dim:** 34.00 (32.00 wl) × 5.70 × 1.40 (1.65 props)
**A:** 2/40-mm 60-cal. AA (I × 2)—2/12.7-mm mg (I × 2)
**Electron Equipt:** Radar: 1/Decca . . .
**M:** 2 MTU 12V538 TB81 diesels; 2 props; 3,300 hp **Man:** 16 tot.

## PATROL BOATS *(continued)*

**T 95** 1983

Remarks: Revised version of T 91 design. T 99 has 20-mm aft, vice 40-mm. Receiving Sea Archer Mk 5A optronic directors.

◆ **2 T 91 class** Bldr: Royal Thai Naval Dockyard, Bangkok

T 91 (L: 1965) T 92 (L: 1973)

**T 92** G. Arra, 1976

**D:** 87.5 tons **S:** 25 kts **Dim:** 31.8 × 5.36 × 1.5
**A:** 2/40-mm AA (I × 2)—2/12.7-mm mg (I × 2)
**Electron Equipt:** Radar: 1/Decca . . .
**M:** 2 MTU diesels; 2 props; 3,300 hp **Range:** 770/21 **Man:** 21 tot.

Remarks: T 91 has a longer superstructure and no spray strakes on the hull sides forward, and only one 40-mm AA gun. In refit 1984–85.

◆ **10 ex-U.S. PGM 71 class** Bldr: Peterson Builders, Sturgeon Bay, Wis.

| | L | In serv. | | L | In serv. |
|---|---|---|---|---|---|
| T 11 (ex-PGM 71) | 22-5-65 | 1-2-66 | T 16 (ex-PGM 115) | 24-4-69 | 12-2-70 |
| T 12 (ex-PGM 79) | 18-12-65 | 1967 | T 17 (ex-PGM 116) | 3-6-69 | 12-2-70 |
| T 13 (ex-PGM 107) | 13-4-67 | 28-8-67 | T 18 (ex-PGM 117) | 24-6-69 | 12-2-70 |
| T 14 (ex-PGM 113) | 3-6-69 | 18-8-69 | T 19 (ex-PGM 123) | 4-5-70 | 25-12-70 |
| T 15 (ex-PGM 114) | 24-6-69 | 18-8-69 | T 20 (ex-PGM 124) | 22-6-70 | 10-70 |

**T 11** G. Arra, 1980

**D:** 130 tons (144 fl) **S:** 17 kts **Dim:** 30.81 × 6.45 × 2.3
**A:** 1/40-mm AA—4/20-mm AA (II × 2)
**Electron Equipt:** Radar: 1/Decca . . .
**M:** 8 G.M. 6-71 diesels; 2 props; 2,040 hp **Range:** 1,000/12 **Man:** 30 tot.

Remarks: On some the twin 20-mm on the fantail is replaced by an 81-mm mortar/12.7-mm mg combination.

Note: The three ex-U.S.C.G. Cape-class patrol boats, T 81, T 82, and T 84, were stricken 10-87.

◆ **5 ex-U.S. PC 461 class**

| | Bldr | L | In serv. |
|---|---|---|---|
| 1 Sarasin (ex-PC 495) | Dravo, Pittsburgh | 30-12-41 | 23-4-42 |
| 4 Phali (ex-PC 1185) | Gibbs, Jacksonville, Fla. | 27-8-43 | 24-4-44 |
| 5 Sukrip (ex-PC 1218) | Luders, Stamford, Conn. | 24-10-43 | 29-5-44 |
| 6 Tongpliu (ex-PC 616) | G. Lawley, Neponset, Mass. | 4-7-42 | 19-8-42 |
| 7 Liulom (ex-PC 1253) | Brown, Houston, Tex. | 14-10-42 | 1-4-43 |

**Tongpliu (6)**—outboard the now-stricken *Thayanchon*

**D:** 280 tons (450 fl) **S:** 19 kts **Dim:** 52.93 × 7.01 × 2.31 (3.31 over sonar)
**A:** 1/75.2-mm DP—1/40-mm AA—5/20-mm AA (I × 5)—2/324-mm Mk 32 fixed ASW TT (I × 2)—2/Mk 6 d.c. projectors—2 d.c. racks
**Electron Equipt:** Radar: 1/Decca . . .—Sonar: QCU-2
**M:** 2 Hoover, Owens, & Rentschler RB-99DA diesels; 2 props; 2,560 hp
**Electric:** 120 kw **Fuel:** 60 tons **Range:** 6,000/10 **Man:** 62–71 tot.

Remarks: In poor condition. Transferred 1947–52. *Sarasin* does not have the two fixed ASW torpedo tubes. *Tongpliu* and *Liulom* have two Fairbanks-Morse 38D8$\frac{1}{8}$ diesels; 2,880 hp. Sister *Thayanchon* (2, ex-PC 575) stricken 1982; *Longlom* (8, ex-PC 570) in 1984; the others are overdue to follow. *Sarasin* and *Phali* are in reserve.

## PATROL CRAFT

◆ **1 Hysucat 18 class** Bldr: Tecnautic, Prapradaeng, Bangkok

T 231 (L: 21-9-86, in serv.:—see Remarks)

**T 231** Tecnautic, 1986

**D:** 32 tons (39 fl) **S:** 36 kts **Dim:** 18.25 × 6.57 × 1.61 (props)
**A:** 1/20-mm G.E. Vulcan 20 gatling AA
**Electron Equipt:** Radar: 1/. . . nav.
**M:** 2 M.W.M. TBD 234 V-12 diesels; 2 props; 1,640 hp
**Range:** 500/36 **Man:** 2 officers, 8 men

Remarks: Ordered 23-9-85 after trials with a 6.5-m, 85-hp prototype. Deep-vee catamaran hull built of Kevlar, with Airex expanded foam core. Trials not successful (failed to make designed speed) and plans to build 12 more apparently canceled. Design assisted by Lürssen, Vegesack. T 231 has not been accepted for Thai Navy service. Hysucat = Hydrofoil-Supported Catamaran. Has Kollmorgen-G.E. SV-20NCS fire-control system with Mk 35 Mod. L3 periscopic gunsight.

## PATROL CRAFT *(continued)*

◆ **16 (+ . . .) T 213 class** Bldr: Ital Thai Development Co., Bangkok

| | In serv. | | In serv. |
|---|---|---|---|
| T 213 | 29-8-80 | T 221 | 16-9-81 |
| T 214 | 29-8-80 | T 222 | 16-9-81 |
| T 215 | 29-8-80 | T 223 | 16-9-81 |
| T 216 | 26-3-81 | T 224 | 19-11-81 |
| T 217 | 26-3-81 | T 225 | 28-3-84 |
| T 218 | 26-3-81 | T 226 | 28-3-84 |
| T 219 | 16-9-81 | T 227 | 1984 |
| T 220 | 16-9-81 | T 228 | 1984 |

**T 216**—alongside T 92 1981

**D:** 34 tons (fl) **S:** 22 kts (18 sust.) **Dim:** 19.8 × 5.3 × 1.5
**A:** 1/20-mm AA—1/12.7-mm mg—1/81-mm mortar
**Electron Equipt:** Radar: 1/Decca 110
**M:** 2 MTU diesels; 2 props; 1,300 hp **Man:** 1 officer, 7 men

Remarks: Aluminum construction. Intended for fisheries protection duties. A T 229 and T 230 have been reported; thus construction may be continuing.

◆ **12 ex-U.S. Swift Mk II-class inshore patrol craft** Bldr: Swiftships, Morgan City, La.

T 27 through T 35 T 210 through T 212

**D:** 22.5 tons (fl) **S:** 25 kts **Dim:** 15.64 × 4.14 × 1.06
**A:** 3/12.7-mm mg (II × 1, and 1 combined with an 81-mm mortar)
**Electron Equipt:** Radar: 1/Raytheon 1500B **Range:** 400/24
**M:** 2 G.M. 12V71 N diesels; 2 props; 860 hp **Man:** 1 officer, 7 men

Remarks: Transferred 1968–75, with some units possibly being of the larger Mk 3 variety: 37 tons fl, 19.78 × 5.50 × 1.80. First two ordered 31-12-67.

◆ **37 ex-U.S. PBR Mk II river patrol boats**

**D:** 8 tons (fl) **S:** 24 kts **Dim:** 9.73 × 3.53 × 0.6
**A:** 3/12.7-mm mg (II × 1, I × 1)—1/60-mm mortar
**M:** 2 Detroit 6V53 N diesels; 2 Jacuzzi waterjets; 430 hp
**Range:** 150/23 **Man:** 4 tot.

Remarks: Transferred: 20 in 1966–67; 10 in 1972; 7 in 1973. Employed on upper Mekong River.

◆ **3 ex-U.S. 36-foot RPC class**

T 21 T 22 T 23

**D:** 10.4 tons (13 fl) **S:** 14 kts **Dim:** 10.9 × 3.15 × 1.0
**A:** 4/12.7-mm mg (II × 2)—2/7.62-mm mg (I × 2)
**M:** 2 Gray Marine 64 HN9 diesels; 2 props; 450 hp **Man:** 6 tot.

Remarks: Transferred 3-67. Survivors of six. Unsuccessful design, supplanted by PBR in the U.S. Navy. Employed on upper Mekong River.

## MINE WARFARE SHIPS

◆ **1 mine countermeasures support ship**

| | Bldr | L | In serv. |
|---|---|---|---|
| 1 Thalang | Bangkok Naval DY | . . . | 4-8-80 |

**D:** 1,000 tons (fl) **S:** 12 kts **Dim:** 55.7 × 10.0 × 3.1
**A:** 1/40-mm AA—2/20-mm AA (I × 2)—2/12.7-mm mg (I × 2)—mines
**Electron Equipt:** Radar: 1/Decca TM 1226
**M:** 2 MTU diesels; 2 props; 1,310 hp **Man:** 77 tot.

Remarks: Replaces *Rang Kwien* (11), stricken 1979. Designed by Ferostaal, Essen, Germany. Has two 3-ton cranes and carries four sets of spare mine countermeasures equipment for transfer to minesweepers.

◆ **2 M 48-class mine hunter/sweepers** Bldr: Lürssen, Vegesack, West Germany

2 Bangrachan (In serv. 10-87) 3 Nhongsarhai (In serv. 1-88)

**Bangrachan (2)**—prior to launch P. Voss, 11-86

**D:** 460 tons (fl) **S:** 18 kts (sust.) **Dim:** 49.10 (45.70 pp) × 9.30 × 2.50
**A:** 1/40-mm AA—2/20-mm AA (I × 2)—mine rails
**Electron Equipt:** Radar: 1/Decca 1229
Sonar: Krupp-Atlas DSQS-11
**M:** 2 MTU 16V396 TB83-DB51L diesels; 2 CP props; 4,000 hp—auxiliary diesel low-speed (7-kt) propulsion and 2 Becker active rudders
**Range:** 4,500/11 **Electric:** 620 kw **Man:** 39 tot.

Remarks: First ordered 31-8-84, second 5-8-85 with option for two more. Composite hull construction: non-magnetic metal framing with wooden skin. Krupp-Atlas MWS-80R mine countermeasures system. Carry two Gaymarine Pluto remote-controlled minehunting/disposal submersibles, plus mechanical, magnetic, and acoustic sweep gear. Use a removeable generator module when sweeping.

◆ **4 ex-U.S. MSC 289-class minesweepers** (3 in reserve)

| | Bldr | In serv. |
|---|---|---|
| 5 Ladya (ex-MSC 297) | Peterson, Sturgeon Bay, Wis. | 14-12-63 |
| 6 Bangkeo (ex-MSC 303) | Dorchester SB, Camden, N.J. | 9-7-65 |
| 7 Tadindeng (ex-MSC 301) | Tacoma Boat, Wash. | 23-8-65 |
| 8 Don Chedi (ex-MSC 313) | Peterson, Sturgeon Bay, Wis. | 17-9-65 |

**Bangkeo (6)** 1967

**D:** 330 tons (362 fl) **S:** 13 kts **Dim:** 44.32 × 8.29 × 2.6
**A:** 2/20-mm AA (II × 1)
**Electron Equipt:** Radar: 1/Decca 707—Sonar: UQS-1D
**D:** 4 G.M. 6-71 diesels; 2 props; 1,000 hp (880 sust.)
**Range:** 2,500/10 **Man:** 7 officers, 36 men

Remarks: Transferred on completion. Wooden construction. Are to be re-engined; 5, 6, and 7 are in reserve, with inoperable propulsion plants.

◆ **5 ex-U.S. 50-foot motor-launch minesweepers**

MLMS 6 to MLMS 10

**D:** 21 tons (fl) **S:** 8 kts **Dim:** 15.29 × 4.01 × 1.31 **A:** 1/7.62-mm mg
**M:** 1 Navy DB diesel; 1 prop; 50 hp **Range:** 150/8 **Man:** 6 tot.

Remarks: Transferred 1963–64. Wooden-hulled former personnel launches, converted before transfer.

Note: Replacement inshore minesweepers are in planning.

## AMPHIBIOUS WARFARE SHIPS

◆ **0 (+2) PS 700** Bldr: Italthai SY, Samatprakarn, Bangkok

| | Laid down | L | In serv. |
|---|---|---|---|
| 6 Sichang | . . . | 14-4-87 | 1988 |
| 7 N . . . | 1987 | . . . | . . . |

## AMPHIBIOUS WARFARE SHIPS *(continued)*

**D:** 3,540 tons (4,235 fl) **S:** 16 kts **Dim:** 103.00 (91.65 pp) × 15.65 × 3.52
**A:** 4/40-mm Breda AA (II × 2) **Electron Equipt:** Radar: . . .
**M:** 2 MTU 20V1163 TB62 diesels; 2 CP props; 9,600 hp
**Range:** 4,000/14; 7,000/12 **Man:** 38 crew + 343 troops

Remarks: License-built French Normed design, built with technical assistance from Korea Tacoma SY. 2,045 dwt. Cargo: 850 tons. (Up to 13 50-ton tanks, 6 2-ton trucks.) Beaching draft 2.88 m at 1,162 dwt. Use Sea Archer Mk 1A Mod. 1 optronic (low-light t.v., laser, IR) f.c.s. for 40-mm. Helicopter deck aft, 17-m bow ramp. Program well behind schedule. Two more planned.

◆ **4 ex-U.S. LST 542-class tank-landing ships**

| | Bldr | L | In serv. |
|---|---|---|---|
| 2 Chang (ex-*Lincoln Cty.*, LST 898) | Dravo, Pittsburgh | 25-11-44 | 29-12-44 |
| 3 Pangan (ex-*Stark Cty.*, LST 1134) | Chicago Br. & Iron, Ind. | 16-3-45 | 7-4-45 |
| 4 Lanta (ex-*Stone Cty.*, LST 1141) | Chicago Br. & Iron, Ind. | 18-4-45 | 9-5-45 |
| 5 Prathong (ex-*Dodge Cty.*, LST 722) | Jeffersonville Br. & Mach. Co., Ind. | 21-8-44 | 13-9-44 |

**Chang (2)** U.S. Navy, 8-86

**Prathong (5)** U.S. Navy, 8-86

**D:** 1,625 tons (4,080 fl) **S:** 11 kts **Dim:** 99.98 × 15.24 × 4.36
**A:** 8/40-mm AA (II × 2, I × 4)—2 also: 2/20-mm AA (I × 2)—all: 4/12.7-mm mg (I × 4)
**Electron Equipt:** Radar: 1/Decca 1229
**M:** 2 G.M. 12-567A diesels; 2 props; 1,700 hp **Electric:** 300 kw
**Range:** 15,000/9 **Fuel:** 569 tons **Man:** 80 crew + 348 troops

Remarks: The *Chang* was transferred in 8-62, the *Pangan* in 5-66, the *Lanta* on 12-3-70, and the *Prathong* on 17-12-75. The *Chang* has a reinforced bow and waterline, originally intended for arctic navigation. Sister *Anthong* (1, ex-U.S. LST 924) discarded. Cargo: 1,230 tons maximum/815 tons beaching. Two Mk 51 Mod. 2 lead-computing directors for twin 40-mm AA.

◆ **3 ex-U.S. LSM 1-class medium landing ships** Bldrs: Pullman Standard Car Mfg. Co., Chicago (3: Brown SB, Houston, Tex.)

| | Laid down | L | In serv. |
|---|---|---|---|
| 1 Kut (ex-LSM 338) | 17-8-44 | 5-12-44 | 10-1-45 |
| 2 Phai (ex-LSM 333) | 13-7-44 | 27-10-44 | 25-11-44 |
| 3 Kram (ex-LSM 469) | 27-1-45 | 17-2-45 | 17-3-45 |

**Kut (1)** G. Arra, 1980

**D:** 743 tons (1,095 fl) **S:** 12.5 kts **Dim:** 62.03 × 10.52 × 2.54
**A:** 2/40-mm AA (II × 1)—4/20-mm AA (I × 4)
**Electron Equipt:** Radar: 1/Raytheon 1500B Pathfinder (3: 1/SPS-5)
**M:** 2 Fairbanks-Morse 38D8⅛ diesels; 2 props; 2,800 hp
**Range:** 2,500/12 **Man:** 6 officers, 85 men, +50 troops

Remarks: The *Kut* and *Phai* were transferred in 10-46, the *Kram* on 25-5-62. Have a Mk 51 Mod. 2 optical lead-computing director for the 40-mm mount. Cargo: 452 tons.

◆ **1 ex-U.S. LCI(M) 351-class infantry-landing ship** Bldr: Commercial Iron Works, Portland, Ore.

| | Laid down | L | In serv. |
|---|---|---|---|
| 2 Satakut (ex-LSIM 739) | 30-1-44 | 27-2-44 | 6-3-44 |

**Satakut (2)** G. Arra, 1980

**D:** 231 tons (381 fl) **S:** 14 kts **Dim:** 48.46 × 7.21 × 1.73
**A:** 1/40-mm AA—4/20-mm AA (I × 4)
**Electron Equipt:** Radar: 1/Raytheon 1500B
**M:** 8 G.M. 6-71 diesels; 2 CP props; 1,320 hp **Range:** 5,600/12.5
**Electric:** 40 kw **Fuel:** 113 tons **Man:** 7 officers, 42 men, +76 troops

Remarks: Originally one of 60 LCIL (later LSIL) converted to carry three 107-mm chemical mortars, removed before transfer in 5-47. Now used as personnel landing craft. Sister *Prab* (ex-LCI(M) 739) exists as a hulk. Cargo: 101 tons.

## AMPHIBIOUS WARFARE SHIPS *(continued)*

◆ **1 ex-U.S. LSSL 1-class support landing craft** Bldr: Commercial Iron Works, Portland, Ore.

| | Laid down | L | In serv. |
|---|---|---|---|
| 3 NAKHA (ex-*Himiwari,* ex-LSSL 102) | 13-1-45 | 3-2-45 | 17-2-45 |

**D:** 233 tons (387 fl) **S:** 14 kts **Dim:** 48.16 × 10.52 × 2.54
**A:** 1/76.2-mm DP Mk 22—4/40-mm AA (II × 2)—4/20-mm AA (I × 4)—4/12.7-mm mg (I × 4)—4/81-mm mortars (I × 4)
**Electron Equipt:** Radar: 1/Raytheon 1500B Pathfinder **Man:** 60 tot.
**M:** 8 G.M. 6-71 diesels; 2 CP props; 1,320 hp **Electric:** 120 kw **Fuel:** 84 tons

REMARKS: Transferred to Japan in 7-59 and to Thailand in 10-66 on return to U.S. control. Used mainly as a tender to small patrol craft.

◆ **5 Thong Kaeo-class utility landing craft** Bldr: Bangkok Naval DY

7 THONG KAEO (In serv. 23-12-82)
8 THONGLANG (In serv. 19-4-83)
9 WANG NOK (In serv. 16-9-83)
10 WANG NAI (In serv. 11-11-83)
11 N . . . (In serv. 1986)

**Thonglang (8)** U.S. Navy, 8-86

**D:** 193 tons (396 fl) **S:** 10 kts **Dim:** 41.0 × 9.0 × 2.1
**A:** 2/20-mm AA (I × 2) **Electron Equipt:** Radar: 1/ . . . nav.
**M:** 2 G.M. 16V71N diesels; 2 props; 1,400 hp **Range:** 1,200/10
**Man:** 3 officers, 29 men

REMARKS: Based on U.S. LCU 1626 class. First four ordered 1980, fifth ordered 1984. Cargo: 143 tons, with 30.5 × 5.5-m vehicle deck.

◆ **5 ex-U.S. LCU 501-class utility landing craft**

| | Bldr | L | In serv. |
|---|---|---|---|
| 1 MATAPHON (ex-LCU 1260) | Quincy Barge, Ill. | 29-7-44 | 8-9-44 |
| 2 RAWI (ex-LCU 800) | Mt. Vernon Br. Co., Oh. | 14-6-44 | 16-6-44 |
| 3 ADANG (ex-LCU 861) | Darby, Kansas City, Kans. | 15-2-44 | 22-2-44 |
| 4 PHE TRA (ex-LCU 1089) | Quincy Barge, Ill. | 10-5-44 | 10-6-44 |
| 6 TALIBONG (ex-LCU 753) | Quincy Barge, Ill. | 30-3-44 | 10-5-44 |

**D:** 134 tons (309 fl) **S:** 10 kts **Dim:** 36.3 × 9.96 × 1.14
**A:** 4/20-mm AA (II × 2) **M:** 3 G.M. 6-71 diesels; 3 props; 675 hp
**Fuel:** 10.5 tons **Range:** 1,200/7 **Man:** 13 tot.

REMARKS: Transferred 10-46 to 11-47. Used as logistics transports on the Chao Phraya river. Cargo: 150 tons. Sister *Kolum* (5, ex-LCU 904) stricken 1984.

◆ **24 ex-U.S. LCM(6)-class landing craft**

L 14–16; L 61–68; L 71–78; L 81–82; L 85–87

**D:** 24 tons (56 fl) **S:** 9 kts **Dim:** 17.11 × 4.27 × 1.17
**M:** 2 Gray Marine 64 HN 9 diesels; 2 props; 330 hp **Range:** 130/9 **Man:** 5 tot.

REMARKS: Transferred 2-65 to 4-69. Cargo capacity: 34 tons.

◆ **12 ex-U.S. LCVP-class landing craft**

L 51–59; L 510–512

**D:** 12 tons (fl) **S:** 9 kts **Dim:** 10.9 × 3.21 × 1.04
**M:** 1 Gray Marine 64 HN 9 diesel; 1 prop; 225 hp
**Range:** 110/9 **Cargo capacity:** 39 troops

REMARKS: Transferred 3-63. Eight LCVPs are carried aboard the four Thai LSTs.

◆ **3 armored personnel transports** Bldr: Bangkok Dock Co., Ltd. (In serv. 1984)

L 41 L 42 L 43

**D:** . . . **S:** 25 kts **Dim:** 12.0 × . . . × . . .
**M:** 2 Ford Sabre diesels; 2 props; . . . hp

◆ **1 personnel landing craft** Bldr: Royal Thai Naval Dockyard, Bangkok (In serv. 11-68)

**D:** 10 tons (fl) **S:** 25 kts **Dim:** 12.0 × 3.0 × 1.0
**M:** 2 Chrysler diesels; 2 Castoldi model 6 waterjets; . . . hp
**Cargo capacity:** 35 troops

REMARKS: Built with U.S. aid. Glass-reinforced plastic construction. Additional units may have been constructed.

## HYDROGRAPHIC SHIPS

◆ **1 oceanographic and survey ship** Bldr: Bangkok Navy DY

| | Laid down | L | In serv. |
|---|---|---|---|
| . . . SUK | 27-8-79 | 16-9-81 | 3-9-82 |

**D:** 1,400 tons (1,526 fl) **S:** 15 kts **Dim:** 62.9 × 11.0 × 4.1
**A:** 2/20-mm AA (I × 2)—2/7.62-mm mg (I × 2)
**M:** 2 MTU diesels; 2 props; 2,400 hp **Man:** 58 tot.

◆ **1 navigational buoy tender** Bldr: Royal Thai Naval DY, Bangkok (In serv. 18-1-79)

. . . SURIYA

**D:** 690 tons light (960 fl) **S:** 12 kts **Dim:** 54.2 (47.3 pp) × 10.0 × 3.0
**A:** 2/20-mm AA (I × 2) **M:** 2 MTU diesels; 1 prop; 1,310 hp
**Electric:** 300 kw **Range:** 3,000/12 **Man:** 14 officers, 46 men

REMARKS: One 10-ton crane. Cargo capacity: 270 tons.

◆ **1 oceanographic ship** Bldr: C. Melchers, Bremen, W. Germany

| | Laid down | L | In serv. |
|---|---|---|---|
| 11 CHANDHARA | 27-9-60 | 17-12-60 | 1961 |

**Chandhara (11)** 1966

**D:** 870 tons (997 fl) **S:** 13 kts **Dim:** 70.0 (61.0 pp) × 10.5 × 3.0
**A:** 1/40-mm AA—1/20-mm AA **M:** 2 Deutz diesels; 2 props; 1,000 hp
**Range:** 10,000/12 **Man:** 72 tot.

REMARKS: Built as a training ship.

◆ **2 inshore survey craft** Bldr: Lürssen, Vegesack, West Germany, 1956

**D:** 96 tons (fl) **S:** 12 kts **Dim:** 29.0 × 5.5 × 1.5
**M:** 2 diesels; 2 props; . . . hp **Man:** 8 tot.

## AUXILIARIES

◆ **1 small underway-replenishment oiler**

| | Bldr | L | In serv. |
|---|---|---|---|
| 2 CHULA | Singapore SY & Eng. | 24-9-80 | 1981 |

**D:** 2,000 tons (fl) **S:** 14 kts **Dim:** 67.0 × 9.5 × 4.35 **Man:** 7 officers, 32 men
**A:** 2/20-mm AA (I × 2) **M:** 2 MTU 12V396 TC62 diesels; 2 props; 2,400 hp

REMARKS: 960 dwt. Cargo: 800 tons, transferred by means of an electrohydraulic boom supporting the hose.

## TRAINING SHIPS

◆ **1 ex-British Algerine-class former fleet minesweeper** Bldr: Redfern Const. Co., Toronto, Canada

| | Laid down | L | In serv. |
|---|---|---|---|
| 1 PHOSAMTON (ex-*Minstrel*) | 27-6-44 | 5-10-44 | 9-6-45 |

**Phosamton (1)** 1981

**TRAINING SHIPS** *(continued)*

**D:** 1,010 tons (1,300 fl) **S:** 16 kts **Dim:** 68.58 × 10.82 × 3.28
**A:** 1/102-mm DP—1/40-mm AA—6/20-mm AA (II × 2, I × 2)
**Electron Equipt:** Radar: 1/Raytheon 1500B Pathfinder, 1/. . . nav.
**M:** 2 sets triple-expansion steam; 2 props; 2,400 hp
**Boilers:** 2, 3-drum
**Fuel:** 235 tons **Range:** 10,000/10 **Man:** 103 tot.

REMARKS: Transferred 4-47. Mechanical minesweeping equipment removed, replaced by a deckhouse to increase accommodations.

◆ **1 Tachin-class former frigate** Bldr: Uraga Dockyard, Japan

| | Laid down | L | In serv. |
|---|---|---|---|
| 3 MAEKLONG | 24-7-36 | 27-11-36 | 6-37 |

**Maeklong (3)** R.A.N., 3-82

**D:** 1,400 tons (2,000 fl) **S:** 14 kts **Dim:** 112.5 × 10.5 × 3.2
**A:** 4/76.2-mm U.S. Mk 22 DP (I × 4)—3/40-mm AA (I × 3)—3/20-mm AA (I × 3)—mines
**M:** 2 sets triple-expansion reciprocating steam; 2 props; 2,500 hp
**Boilers:** 2, watertube **Fuel:** 487 tons **Range:** 8,000/12 **Man:** 155 tot.

REMARKS: Sister *Tachin* bombed in 1945 and discarded circa 1950. Formerly carried four 102-mm guns (replaced in 1974) and four 450-mm torpedo tubes (II × 2).

**SERVICE CRAFT**

◆ **1 Samed-class harbor oiler** Bldr: Royal Thai Navy DY, Bangkok

YO 11 SAMED (In serv. 15-12-70)

**Samed (11)**—while fitting out 1967

**D:** 306 tons (485 fl) **S:** 9 kts **Dim:** 39.0 (36.6 pp) × 6.1 × 2.8
**A:** 2/20-mm AA (I × 2) **M:** 1 diesel; 500 hp **Cargo:** 210 tons

◆ **1 Proet-class harbor oiler** Bldr: Royal Thai Navy DY, Bangkok

YO 9 PROET (In serv. 16-1-70)

**D:** 360 tons (465 fl) **S:** 9 kts **Dim:** 37.4 (pp) × 6.0 × 2.7
**A:** 2/20-mm AA (I × 2) **M:** 1 diesel; 500 hp

◆ **1 provisions transport** Bldr: Rusnes Mek. Verksted, Arandal, Norway

AF 7 KLED KEO (ex-*Norfrost,* in serv. 1948)

**Kled Keo (AF 7)** 1967

**D:** 382 tons (450 fl) **S:** 12 kts **Dim:** 46.0 × 7.6 × 4.3
**A:** 3/20-mm AA (I × 3) **M:** 1 diesel; 600 hp **Man:** 54 tot.

REMARKS: Refrigerated cargo ship. Acquired in 1967 from Byelland & Co., Stavanger.

◆ **1 Charn-class water tanker** Bldr: Bangkok Naval DY

YW 8 CHUANG (L: 14-1-65)

**D:** 355 tons (485 fl) **S:** 11 kts **Dim:** 42.0 × 7.5 × 3.1
**A:** 1/20-mm AA **M:** 1 G.M. diesel; 500 hp **Man:** 29 tot.

REMARKS: Near-sister *Charn* stricken during 1984.

◆ **2 Rang-class coastal tugs** Bldr: Singapore SB & Eng. (In serv. 9-80)

6 RANG (L: 12-6-80) 5 RIN (L: 14-6-80)

**D:** 250 tons (300 fl) **S:** 12 kts **Dim:** 32.3 × 9.0 × . . .
**M:** 1 MWM TBD 441V/12K diesel; 1 prop; 2,100 hp
**Electric:** 233 kw **Range:** 1,000/10 **Man:** 16 tot.

REMARKS: Bollard pull: 22 tons. Have 2 firefighting monitors.

◆ **2 ex-Canadian small harbor tugs** Bldr: Central Bridge Co., Trenton, Ontario (In serv. 1943–44)

YTL 2 KLUENG BADEN YTL 3 MARIN VICHAI

**D:** 63 grt **S:** 8 kts **Dim:** 19.8 × 5.0 × 1.8 **M:** 1 diesel; 240 hp

REMARKS: Acquired in 1953.

ROYAL THAI MARINE POLICE

This organization performs duties analogous to those of a coast guard and operates a large number of patrol boats and craft. A number of the newer and larger units are listed below.

**PATROL BOATS AND CRAFT**

◆ **3 27-meter class** Bldr: Tecnautic, Bangkok (In serv. 1984–. . .)

810–812

**27-meter class** U.S. Navy, 8-86

**D:** . . . **S:** 27 kts **Dim:** 27.00 × 5.85 × . . .
**A:** 1/20-mm AA—2/7.62-mm mg (I × 2)
**M:** 3 Isotta-Fraschini diesels; 3 Castoldi 07 waterjets; 2,500 hp

◆ **17 18-meter class** Bldr: Tecnautic, Bangkok (In serv. 1983–19-2-86)

608–624

**D:** . . . **S:** 26 kts **Dim:** 18.00 × 4.45 × . . .
**A:** 1/12.7-mm mg
**M:** 2 Isotta-Fraschini diesels; 2 Castoldi 07 waterjets; 1,260 hp

◆ **4 11.5-meter class** Bldr: Tecnautic, Bangkok (In serv. 1984–85)

**D:** . . . **S:** . . . **Dim:** 11.50 × . . . × . . . **A:** . . . **M:** 1 diesel; 250 hp

◆ **8 aluminum-hulled** Bldr: Captain Co., Thailand (In serv. 1978)

**D:** 18 tons (fl) **S:** 22 kts **Dim:** 16.5 × 3.8 × . . .
**A:** 2/12.7-mm mg **M:** 2 Cummins diesels; 400 hp

◆ **3 U.S. Cutlass class** Bldr: Halter Marine, New Orleans, La. (In serv. 1978)

807 PHRA ONG CHAO KHAMROP 808 PICHARN PHOLAKIT 809 RAM INTHRA

**D:** 34 tons (fl) **S:** 25 kts **Dim:** 19.66 × 5.18 × 1.12
**A:** 2/12.7-mm mg (I × 2) **M:** 2 G.M. 12V71 TI diesels; 2 props; 960 hp
**Fuel:** 2.7 tons **Man:** 15 tot.

**THAILAND** *(continued)*
**PATROL BOATS AND CRAFT** *(continued)*

**Phra Ong Chao Khamrop and sisters**—with old numbers Halter, 1978

◆ **1 seagoing patrol boat** Bldr: Yokohama Yacht, Japan (In serv. 1975)

1802 Damrong Rachanuphat (ex-112)

**D:** 200 grt **S:** 32 kts **Dim:** 37.0 × 6.5 × . . .
**A:** 1/76.2-mm DP—2/20-mm AA **M:** 4 diesels; 2 props; 2,200 hp

◆ **2 seagoing patrol boats**

1801 N . . . . . . . 1803 N . . . . . . .

**1803** 1983

**D:** approx. 400 tons (fl) **A:** 1/40-mm AA—2/20-mm AA **M:** diesel-powered

Note: There are a number of other craft, mostly armed with either one 20-mm antiaircraft or two 12.7-mm machine guns. Most craft are Japanese built.

CUSTOMS SERVICE

Like the Royal Thai Marine Police, the Thai Customs Service operates a fleet of patrol craft, including:

◆ **1 Customs 1201 class** Bldr: . . . , Japan

Customs 1201

**Customs 1201** U.S. Navy, 8-86

**D:** . . . **S:** . . . **Dim:** 37.0 × 6.8 × 1.5
**A:** small arms **Electron Equipt:** Radar: 1/ . . . nav.
**M:** 4 diesels; 2 props; . . . hp **Man:** 4 officers, 12 men

◆ **5 GRP-hulled** Bldr: . . .

Customs 508–512

**D:** . . . **S:** . . . **Dim:** 16.8 × 4.0 × 1.0
**A:** small arms **M:** 2 diesels; 2 props; . . . hp

Remarks: The smaller *Customs 501–507* are also in service.

# TOGO

**Republic of Togo**

Personnel (1986): 108 men

Merchant Marine (1986): 11 ships—54,882 grt (1 tanker—434 grt)

## PATROL BOATS

◆ **2 wooden-hulled** Bldr: C.N. de l'Estérel, Cannes, France

Kara (L: 18-5-76) Mono (L: 1976)

**Mono** French Navy, 12-82

**D:** 80 tons (fl) **S:** 30 kts **Dim:** 32.0 × 5.8 × 1.5
**A:** 1/40-mm AA—1/20-mm AA **Electron Equipt:** Radar: 1/Decca 916
**M:** 2 MTU 12V493 diesels; 2,700 hp **Range:** 1,500/15
**Man:** 1 officer, 17 men

# TONGA

**Kingdom of Tonga**

Merchant Marine (1986): 19 ships—16,349 grt

MARITIME DEFENSE DIVISION
TONGAN DEFENSE SERVICE

## PATROL CRAFT

Note: Plans to acquire two Australian "Pacific Patrol Boat," AST 315-class patrol boats under Australian foreign aid did not reach fruition.

◆ **2 fiberglass-hulled** Bldr: Brooke Marine, Lowestoft, U.K.

P 101 Ngahau Koula (In serv. 10-3-73) P 102 Ngahau Siliva (In. serv. 10-5-74)

**D:** 15 tons (fl) **S:** 21 kts **Dim:** 13.7 × 4.0 × 1.2
**A:** 2/12.7-mm mg (I × 2) **Electron Equipt:** Radar: 1/Koden MD306
**M:** 2 Cummins KT2300M diesels; 2 props; 700 hp **Range:** 800/21 **Man:** 7 tot.

## AUXILIARIES

◆ **1 Australian-built U.S. LCM(8)-class landing craft** Bldr: North Queensland Eng., Cairns

Late (ex-Australian Army 1057)

**D:** 34 tons light (116 fl) **S:** 12 kts **Dim:** 22.70 × 6.41 × 1.37
**M:** 2 G.M. 12V71 diesels; 2 props; 600 hp **Range:** 140/9
**Electron Equipt:** Radar: 1/Koden MD305

Remarks: Transferred to Tongo 1-9-82. Cargo: 55 tons. Has been fitted with a pilothouse and navigational radar.

◆ **2 Sea Truck utility craft** Bldr: Rotork, U.K.

Fangailifuka (In serv. 29-9-83) 'Ald-i-talau (In serv. 25-3-85)

**D:** 5.4 tons (fl) **S:** 25 kts **Dim:** 12.7 × 2.3 × 0.60
**Electron Equipt:** Radar: 1/Decca 060
**M:** 2 Volvo Penta AQAD 40 diesels; 2 outdrives; 560 hp
**Range:** 85/. . . **Man:** 3 tot.

Remarks: GRP construction, bow-ramp. First is builder's model PBF 512, second is an LSC 512.

◆ **1 royal yacht**

Titilupe

Remarks: 10.4-m glass-reinforced plastic craft capable of 8 kts.; also used in patrol work.

# TRINIDAD AND TOBAGO

**Republic of Trinidad and Tobago**

PERSONNEL (1987): 45 officers, 596 men

MERCHANT MARINE (1986): 51 ships—19,381 grt

NAVAL AVIATION: The Coast Guard operates one Twin Beech maritime surveillance aircraft and one Cessna light aircraft. The Air Division of the National Security Forces operates 2 SA.341G Gazelle and 2 Sikorsky S-76 helicopters for surveillance and rescue service.

COAST GUARD

### PATROL BOATS AND CRAFT

◆ **2 CG 40 class** Bldr: Karlskrona, Sweden (Both in serv. 6-6-80)

CG 5 BARRACUDA CG6 CASCADURA

**Barracuda (CG 5)** L. & L. Van Ginderen, 1-84

**D:** 210 tons (fl) **S:** 32 kts **Dim:** 40.6 × 6.7 × 1.7
**A:** 1/40-mm Bofors AA—1/20-mm AA
**Electron Equipt:** Radar: 1/Decca TM 1226
**M:** 2 Paxman Valenta 16RP200 diesels; 2 props; 8,000 hp
**Range:** 2,200/15 **Man:** 22 tot. (plus 9 spare berths)

REMARKS: Ordered 8-78. Have an optronic GFCS for the 40-mm AA; rescue dinghy carried on stern. 27 kts sustained speed. Have HF and VHF D/F gear.

◆ **2 103-foot** Bldr: Vosper, Portsmouth

| | L | In. serv. |
|---|---|---|
| CG 3 CHAGUARAMAS | 29-3-71 | 18-2-72 |
| CG 4 BUCCO REEF | 1971 | 18-3-72 |

**Bucco Reef (CG 4)** Trinidad & Tobago CG, 1982

**D:** 96–100 tons (123–125 fl) **S:** 23 kts **Dim:** 31.29 (28.95 pp) × 5.94 × 1.68
**A:** 1/20-mm AA **M:** 2 Paxman 12 YJCM Ventura diesels; 2 props; 2,900 hp
**Fuel:** 18 tons **Range:** 2,000/13 **Man:** 3 officers, 16 men

REMARKS: Air-conditioned and have roll-damping fins. Near-sisters *Trinity* (CG 1) and *Courland Bay* (CG 2) stricken 1986.

◆ **4 Wasp 17-m-class patrol craft** Bldr: W.A. Souter & Sons, Cowes, U.K. (In serv. 27-8-82)

CG 27 PLYMOUTH CG 28 CARONI CG 29 GALEOTA CG 30 MORUGA

**Galeota (CG 29)** L. & L. Van Ginderen, 1-84

**D:** 19.25 tons (fl) **S:** 28 kts (25 sust.) **Dim:** 16.76 (13.90 wl) × 4.20 × 1.40
**A:** 2/7.62-mm mg (I × 2) **Electron Equipt:** Radar: 1/Decca 150
**M:** 2 Stevenson-G.M. 8V92 MTI diesels; 2 props; 1,300 hp
**Range:** 500/18 **Man:** 2 officers, 4–6 men

REMARKS: Glass-reinforced plastic construction. Ordered 8-81.

◆ **2 coastal patrol craft** Bldr: Tugs & Lighters, Ltd., Port-of-Spain

CG 01 NAPARIMA (In serv. 15-8-76) CG 25 EL TUCUCHE (In serv. 1977)

**D:** 20 tons **S:** 20 kts **Dim:** 16.4 × 5.2 × 2.6
**M:** 2 G.M. 6V71 diesels; 2 props; 460 hp **Man:** 6 tot.

REMARKS: Craft dissimilar in appearance. CG 25 is 16.7 m o.a.

◆ **1 fiberglass patrol launch** Bldr: Trinidad (In serv. . . .)

CG 9 FORT CHACON

**D:** . . . **S:** 27 kts **Dim:** 7.0 × . . . × . . .
**M:** 1 Caterpillar diesel; . . . hp

NOTE: Sail-training ketch *Hummingbird II* stricken 1986.

MARINE POLICE

### PATROL CRAFT

◆ **2 Wasp 20-m class** Bldr: W.A. Souter & Sons, Cowes (In serv. 11-82)

N . . . . . . . N . . . . . . .

**D:** 32 tons (fl) **S:** 36 kts (30 sust.) **Dim:** 20.0 × 5.0 × 1.5
**A:** 2/7.62-mm mg (I × 2) **Electron Equipt:** Radar: 1/Decca 150
**M:** 2 G.M. 16V92 TI diesels; 2 props; 2,400 hp
**Range:** 300/30 **Man:** 2 officers, 4 men

REMARKS: Aluminum hulls. Ordered 30-9-81.

◆ **1 fiberglass-hulled** Bldr: Watercraft, Shoreham, U.K. (In serv. 1980)

SEA DRAGON

**D:** 14.9 tons (fl) **S:** 23.5 kts **Dim:** 13.7 × 4.1 × 1.2
**A:** 2/7.62-mm mg (I × 2) **Electron Equipt:** Radar: 1/Decca 110
**M:** 2 G.M. 8V92 diesels; 2 props; 700 hp **Range:** 360/20 **Man:** 4 tot.

◆ **2 Sword class** Bldr: Fairey Marine Hamble, U.K.

SEA SPRAY (In serv. 1-78) FOX (In serv. 12-78)

**D:** 15.2 tons (fl) **S:** 28 kts **Dim:** 13.7 × 4.1 × 1.32
**A:** 1/7.62-mm mg **M:** 2 G.M. 8V71 TI diesels; 2 props; 850 hp
**Range:** 500/. . . **Man:** 6 tot.

# TUNISIA

**Republic of Tunisia**

PERSONNEL (1987): approx. 2,600 men

MERCHANT MARINE (1986): 71 ships—285,735 grt (tankers: 3 ships—131,836 grt)

## FRIGATE

◆ **1 ex-U.S. Savage-class former radar picket** Bldr: Consolidated Steel, Orange, Tex.

| | Laid down | L | In serv. |
|---|---|---|---|
| E7 President Bourguiba (ex-*Thomas J. Gary,* DER 326, ex-DE 326) | 15-6-43 | 21-8-43 | 27-11-43 |

**President Bourguiba (E 7)** G. Gyssels, 7-86

**D:** 1,590 tons (1,850 fl) **S:** 19 kts **Dim:** 93.27 (91.5 pp) × 11.22 × 4.27
**A:** 2/76.2-mm DP (I × 2)—2/20-mm AA (I × 2)—6/324-mm ASW TT (III × 2)
**Electron Equipt:** Radar: 1/. . . nav., 1/SPS-10, 1/SPS-29, 1/Mk 34
Sonar: SQS-29 series
**M:** 4 Fairbanks-Morse 38D8$\frac{1}{8}$ × 10 diesels; 2 props; 6,080 hp
**Fuel:** 310 tons **Electric:** 580 kw **Range:** 11,500/11 **Man:** 160–170 tot.

Remarks: Modified as a radar picket ship in 1957, transferred on 27-10-73. SPS-8 height-finding radar, TACAN, EW, Hedgehog removed about 1968. Has one Mk 63 radar GFCS and one Mk 51 Mod. 2 GFCS for 76.2-mm guns.

## GUIDED-MISSILE PATROL BOATS

◆ **3 Combattante-III class** Bldr: CMN, Cherbourg

| | Laid down | L | In serv. |
|---|---|---|---|
| P 501 La Galite | 26-5-82 | 16-6-83 | 27-2-85 |
| P 502 Tunis | 28-9-82 | 27-10-83 | 28-3-85 |
| P 503 Carthage | 6-1-83 | 24-1-84 | 29-4-85 |

**La Galite (P 501)** CMN, 1985

**D:** 395 tons (425 fl) **S:** 38.5 kts
**Dim:** 56.80 (53.00 pp) × 8.16 × 2.15 (2.50 props)
**A:** 8/MM 40 Exocet SSM (IV × 2)—1/76-mm OTO Melara DP—2/40-mm Breda AA (II × 2)—4/30-mm Oerlikon AA (II × 2)
**Electron Equipt:** Radar: 1/Castor IIB, 1/Triton S
EW: . . . passive, 1/Dagaie chaff RL
**M:** 4 MTU 20V538 TB93 diesels; 4 props; 19,300 hp **Electric:** 405 kVA
**Range:** 700/33; 2,800/10 **Man:** 35 tot.

Remarks: Ordered 27-6-81. Have Thomson-CSF Vega II control system for missiles, 76-mm and 40-mm guns; two CSEE Naja optronic directors for the 30-mm AA; CSEE Sylosat navigational system.

## PATROL BOATS AND CRAFT

◆ **3 French P 48 class** Bldr: SFCN, Villeneuve-la-Garenne

| | L | In serv. |
|---|---|---|
| P 301 Bizerte | 20-11-69 | 10-7-70 |
| P 302 Horria (ex-*Liberty*) | 19-2-70 | 10-70 |
| P 304 Monastir | 25-6-74 | 25-3-75 |

**Horria (P 302)** L. & L. Van Ginderen, 1982

**D:** 250 tons (fl) **S:** 22 kts **Dim:** 48.0 (45.5 pp) × 7.1 × 2.25
**A:** 2/40-mm AA (I × 2)—2/20-mm AA (I × 2)—8/SS-12 wire-guided missiles (IV × 2)
**Electron Equipt:** Radar: 1/Decca TM 1226 (DRBN-31)
**M:** 2 MGO MB-839 Db diesels; 2 props; 4,000 hp **Range:** 2,000/16
**Man:** 4 officers, 30 men

Remarks: P 301 lacks the 20-mm AA.

◆ **1 French Le Fougueux class** Bldr: Dubigeon, Nantes (In serv. 12-3-57)

P 303 Sakiet Sidi Youssef (ex-UW 12, ex-PC 1618)

**Sakiet Sidi Youssef (P 303)** French Navy, 7-80

**D:** 325 tons (402 fl) **S:** 18.7 kts **Dim:** 53.1 × 6.4 × 2.1 (3.0 max.)
**A:** 1/40-mm AA—2/20-mm AA (I × 2)—2/Mk Mousetrap ASW RL—2/Mk 9 d.c. racks
**Electron Equipt:** Radar: 1/Decca 1226 (DRBN-31)—Sonar: DUBA-2
**M:** 4 SEMT-Pielstick 14 PA17V diesels; 2 CP props; 3,240 hp **Electric:** 60 kw
**Fuel:** 45 tons **Range:** 3,300/15; 6,350/12 **Man:** 4 officers, 42 men

Remarks: Begun as P 7 for the French Navy, using U.S. Offshore funds. Transferred to West Germany and used as a training ship at the Underwater Weapons School. Purchased by Tunisia on 16-6-70. Four depth-charge projectors and Hedgehog removed mid-1970s.

◆ **2 ex-U.S. Adjutant-class former coastal minesweepers**

| | Bldr | In serv. |
|---|---|---|
| P . . . Hannibal (ex-*Coquelicot,* ex-MSC 48) | Steven Bros., Cal. | 10-53 |
| P . . . Sousse (ex-*Marjolaine,* ex-MSC 66) | Harbor Boat, Cal. | 4-53 |

**Hannibal** J.-C. Bellonne, 1973

**D:** 300 tons (372 fl) **S:** 13 kts **Dim:** 43.0 (41.5 pp) × 7.95 × 2.55
**A:** 2/20-mm AA (II × 1) **Electron Equipt:** Radar: 1/DRBN-31
**M:** 2 G.M. 8-268A diesels; 2 props; 1,200 hp
**Fuel:** 40 tons **Range:** 2,500/10 . **Man:** 3 officers, 35 men

Remarks: Loaned in 1973 and 1977. Minesweeping gear removed. Used in fisheries-protection duties.

◆ **2 103-foot class** Bldr: Vosper Thornycroft, Portchester, U.K.

| | L | In serv. |
|---|---|---|
| P 205 Tazarka | 19-7-76 | 27-10-77 |
| P 206 Menzel Bourguiba | 19-7-76 | 27-10-77 |

TUNISIA *(continued)*
**PATROL BOATS AND CRAFT** *(continued)*

**D:** 100 tons (125 fl) **S:** 27 kts **Dim:** 31.29 (28.95 pp) × 6.02 × 1.98
**A:** 2/20-mm AA (I × 2) **Electron Equipt:** Radar: 1/Decca 916
**M:** 2 MTU diesels; 2 props; 4,000 hp **Range:** 1,500/14 **Man:** 24 tot.

◆ **2 Chinese Shanghai-II class** (In serv. 2-5-77)

P 305 GAFSA  P 306 AMILCAR

**Gafsa (P 305)** 1978

**D:** 122.5 tons (135 fl) **S:** 28.5 kts **Dim:** 38.78 × 5.41 × 1.55
**A:** 4/37-mm AA (II × 2)—4/25-mm AA (II × 2)
**Electron Equipt:** Radar: 1/. . . nav.
**M:** 4 MTU 8V331 TC92 diesels; 4 props; 4,260 hp (3,540 sust.)
**Range:** 800/17 **Man:** 38 tot.

REMARKS: Re-engined and refitted at Socomena SY, Bizerte, completing 12-84.

◆ **4 French 32-meter class** Bldr: CN de l'Estérel, Cannes

| | In serv. | | In serv. |
|---|---|---|---|
| P 201 ISTIKLAL (ex-French VC 11) | 1957 | P 203 AL JALA | 11-63 |
| P 202 JOUMHOURIA | 1-61 | P 204 REMADA | 7-67 |

**Istiklal (P 201)** 1970

**D:** 60 tons (82 fl) **S:** 28 kts **Dim:** 31.45 × 5.75 × 1.7
**A:** 2/20-mm AA (I × 2) **Electron Equipt:** Radar: 1/Decca 1226
**M:** 2 MTU 12V493 diesels; 2 props; 2,700 hp
**Range:** 1,400/15 **Man:** 3 officers, 14 men

REMARKS: Wooden construction. P 201 was launched on 25-5-57 and transferred in 3-59.

◆ **6 French 25-meter class** Bldr: CN de l'Estérel, Cannes (In serv. 1961–63)

V 101 through V 106

**V 101** L. & L. Van Ginderen, 1984

**D:** 38–39 tons **S:** 23 kts **Dim:** 25.0 × 4.75 × 1.25 **Man:** 10 tot.
**A:** 1/20-mm AA **M:** 2 G.M. 12V71 TI diesels; 2 props; 940 hp **Range:** 900/16
**Electron Equipt:** Radar: 1/Decca 1226

REMARKS: V 107 and V 108 were transferred to the Fisheries Administration, disarmed, in 1971, as *Sabeq el Bahr* (T 2) and *Jaouel el Bahr* (T 3).

**AUXILIARY SHIPS**

◆ **1 ex-U.S. Sotoyomo-class oceangoing tug** Bldr: Gulfport Boilers & Welding Works, Port Arthur, Tex.

| | Laid down | L | In serv. |
|---|---|---|---|
| . . . RAS ADAR (ex-*Zeeland*, ex-*Pan America*, ex-*Ocean Pride*, ex-*Oriana*, ex-BAT 1) | 16-3-42 | 15-8-42 | 13-12-42 |

**D:** 570 tons (835 fl) **S:** 13 kts **Dim:** 43.59 (41.0 pp) × 10.31 × 4.01
**A:** none **M:** 2 G.M. 12-278A diesels, electric drive; 1 prop; 1,500 hp
**Electric:** 90 kw **Fuel:** 171 tons **Man:** 45 tot.

REMARKS: Built under Lend-Lease, transferred to Great Britain on 22-12-42. Returned and sold commercially in 1946. Purchased for Tunisia from Dutch company in late 1960s. BAT-series had larger superstructure than standard *Sotoyomo* class and were considered to be ocean rescue tugs.

◆ **1 diving tender** (In serv. 1948)

KERKENNAH

**D:** 653 grt **S:** 10 kts **Dim:** 53.95 × 9.75 × 2.75
**M:** diesel-electric; . . . props; . . . hp **Man:** 4 officers, 20 men, 4 civilians

CUSTOMS

◆ **1 (+9) Tunisian-built** Bldr: Socomena, Bizerte

ASSAD LBN FOURAT (L: 25-2-86; in serv. 2-3-86)

**D:** 32 tons (fl) **S:** 28 kts **Dim:** 20.5 × 4.7 × 1.3
**A:** 1/12.7-mm mg—2/7.62-mm mg **Man:** 8 tot.
**M:** 2 diesels; 2 props; 1,000 hp **Range:** 500/20

REMARKS: GRP construction, built with South Korean assistance. Nine more planned; program status uncertain.

◆ **4 GRP construction** Bldr: Aresa, Arenys del Mar, Barcelona (In serv: 2 in 1981, 2 in 1983)

**D:** . . . **S:** . . . **Dim:** 23.0 × . . . × . . .
**A:** . . . **M:** . . .

# TURKEY

## Republic of Turkey

PERSONNEL (1987): 49,000 naval; 4,000 Marines; 70,000 naval reserve

MERCHANT MARINE (1986): 825 ships—3,423,745 grt
(tankers: 77 ships—1,029,048 grt)

NAVAL AVIATION: The naval air arm, organized in 1972, consists of 8 S-2A and 18 S-2E Tracker ASW airplanes, 3 AB-204 helicopters, and 9 AB-212 helicopters.

WARSHIPS IN SERVICE, AUTHORIZED, OR UNDER CONSTRUCTION
AS OF 1 JANUARY 1988

| | L | Tons (surfaced) | Main armament |
|---|---|---|---|
| ◆ **14 (+4) submarines** | | | |
| 5 (+4) TYPE 209 | 1974–81 | 990 | 8/533-mm TT |
| 2 TANG | 1951 | 2,100 | 8/533-mm TT |
| 2 Guppy III | 1945 | 1,975 | 10/533-mm TT |
| 5 Guppy II-A | 1944 | 1,848 | 10/533-mm TT |
| ◆ **12 destroyers** | | Tons | |
| 2 CARPENTER | 1945–46 | 2,425 | 2/127-mm 1/ASROC, 6/ASW TT |
| 7 GEARING FRAM-I | 1944–46 | 2,425 | 4/127-mm, 1/ASROC, 6/ASW TT |
| 1 GEARING FRAM-II | 1945 | 2,390 | 4/127-mm, 2/35-mm AA, 1/Hedgehog, 6/ASW TT |
| 1 ALLEN M. SUMNER FRAM-II | 1944 | 2,200 | 6/127-mm 6/ASW TT |
| 1 ROBERT H. SMITH | 1944 | 2,250 | 6/127-mm, 2/76.2-mm, mines |
| ◆ **5 (+3) frigates** | | | |
| 1 (+3) MEKO 200 | 1985–88 | 2,000 | 8/Harpoon SSM, Albatros SAM, 1/127-mm DP, ASW weapons |
| 2 BERK | 1971–72 | 1,450 | 4/76.2-mm, 6/ASW TT |
| 2 KÖLN | 1959 | 2,425 | 2/100-mm, ASW weapons, mines |

◆ **46 patrol and torpedo boats**

◆ **49 mine warfare ships and craft**

◆ **71 (+. . .) seagoing landing ships and craft**

## WEAPONS AND SYSTEMS

Most weapons and systems are furnished by the U.S.A., some by West Germany. For characteristics, see the sections on the U.S.A. and Germany, Federal Republic. Twelve Harpoon SSM were ordered in 1981 to supplement existing stocks; Norwegian Penguin Mk 1 missiles are also used. British Sea Skua antiship missiles have been purchased for use by AB-212 helicopters.

*Sea Guard Close-In Weapons System*—Contraves

This point-defense system employs three Sea Zenith quadruple 25-mm AA with a combined rate of fire of 3,200 rounds per minute. With a practical range of about 2,000 m, the mountings can depress to −15 deg. and elevate to +127 deg., with extremely rapid elevation and traversing. In the MEKO-200 class, the three mounts are controlled by two Siemens Albis radar-electro-optical directors.

**Sea Zenith and Sea Sparrow on Turgut (F 240)** S. Terzibaschitsch, 6-87

## SUBMARINES

◆ **0 (+ . . .) 1,400 ton** Bldr: Gölcük NSY

Remarks: Tenders placed Europe-wide in mid-1987 for a licensed design of about 1,400 tons submerged displacement to succeed the Type 209 class in production.

◆ **5 (+4) German Type 209** Bldrs: S 347, S 348, S 349; Howaldtswerke, Kiel; S 350 and later: Gölcük NSY

| | Laid down | L | In serv. |
|---|---|---|---|
| S 347 Atilay | 1-12-72 | 23-10-74 | 23-7-75 |
| S 348 Saldiray | 2-1-73 | 14-2-75 | 21-10-75 |
| S 349 Batiray | 11-6-75 | 24-10-77 | 20-7-78 |
| S 350 Yildiray | 1-5-76 | 20-7-77 | 20-7-81 |
| S 351 Doganay | 21-3-80 | 16-11-83 | 16-11-84 |
| S 352 Titiray | 9-3-81 | -85 | -88 |
| S 353 Dolunay | . . . | 31-3-88 | 31-3-89 |
| S 354 N . . . | . . . | . . . | . . . |
| S . . . N . . . | . . . | . . . | . . . |

**Atilay (S 347)**—note lower casing forward H. Ehlers, 10-86

**Yildiray (S 350)**—with *Ikinci Inönü* (S 333), *Canakkale* (S 341), *Atilay* (S 347), and *Birinci Inönü* (S 346) beyond H. Ehlers, 3-84

**D:** 990 tons std./1,180 tons surf./1,290 sub. **S:** 11/22 kts
**Dim:** 56.10 × 6.20 × 5.50 **A:** 8/533-mm TT fwd (14 torpedoes)
**Electron Equipt:** Radar: . . .
Sonar: Krupp-Atlas CSU-3 suite: AN526 passive/AN407AS active, DUUX-2 telephone
**M:** 4 MTU 12V493 TY60 diesels (600 hp each); 4/405-kw generator sets; 1 Siemens electric motor, 5,000 hp
**Fuel:** 100 tons **Range:** 7,800/8 surf.; 400/4 sub.
**Man:** 6 officers, 27 men

Remarks: First two have H.S.A. M8 torpedo-fire control, others have SINBADS. Two periscopes. A total of 12 were planned, with 9 to be built in Turkey, but a larger design is now being sought.

◆ **2 ex-U.S. Tang class** Bldr: Portsmouth Naval SY, N.H.

| | Laid down | L | In serv. |
|---|---|---|---|
| S 342 Hizir Reis (ex-*Gudgeon,* SSAG 567) | 20-5-50 | 11-6-52 | 21-11-52 |
| S 343 Piri Reis (ex-*Tang,* SS 563) | 18-4-49 | 19-6-51 | 25-10-52 |

**Hizir Reis (S 342)** G. Valentini, 4-87

**D:** 1,975/2,600 tons **S:** 15.5/16 kts **Dim:** 87.5 × 8.3 × 5.7
**A:** 8/533-mm TT (6 fwd, 2 short aft)
**Electron Equipt:** Radar: 1/BPS-12, 1/ST-3
Sonar: BQS-4, BQG-4 (PUFFS)
**M:** 3 Fairbanks-Morse 38D8$\frac{1}{8}$ × 10 diesels; 2 Westinghouse motors; 2 props; 5,600 hp
**Range:** 7,600/15; 17/9 submerged **Man:** 11 officers, 75 men

Remarks: S 343 leased for five years 8-2-80, ex-SSAG 567 leased 30-9-83. Have Mk 106, Mod. 18, torpedo FCS. Aft tubes can fire Mk 37 torpedoes only.

◆ **2 ex-U.S. Guppy III class** Bldr: Electric Boat Co., Groton, Conn.

| | Laid down | L | In serv. |
|---|---|---|---|
| S 333 Ikinci Inönü (ex-*Corporal,* SS 346) | 27-4-44 | 1-4-45 | 8-8-45 |
| S 341 Canakkale (ex-*Cobbler,* SS 344) | 3-4-44 | 1-4-45 | 9-11-45 |

**Ikinci Inönü (S 333)** H. Ehlers, 12-86

**D:** 1,975/2,450 tons **S:** 17.2/14.5 kts **Dim:** 99.52 × 8.23 × 5.18
**A:** 10/533-mm TT (6 fwd, 4 aft)—24 torpedoes
**Electron Equipt:** Radar: 1/SS-2A—Sonar: BQG-4 (PUFFS), BQR-2B
**M:** 4 G.M. 16-278A diesels (1,625 hp each), diesel-electric drive; 2 props; 6,500/5,200 hp
**Range:** 10,000–12,000/10; 95/5 (sub.) **Man:** 8 officers, 78 men

Remarks: Transferred on 21-11-73. Lengthened by 3.6 meters in 1962 at Philadelphia (S 341) and Charleston (S 333). Two 126-cell batteries. Direct drive on surface.

◆ **5 ex-U.S. Guppy II-A** Bldrs: S 345: Electric Boat Co., Groton, Gonn.; others: Portsmouth NSY

| | Laid down | L | In serv. |
|---|---|---|---|
| S 335 Burak Reis (ex-*Sea Fox,* SS 402) | 2-11-43 | 28-3-44 | 13-6-44 |
| S 336 Murat Reis (ex-*Razorback,* SS 394) | 9-9-43 | 27-1-44 | 3-4-44 |
| S 338 Uluç Ali Reis (ex-*Thornback,* SS 418) | 5-4-44 | 7-7-44 | 13-10-44 |
| S 340 Çerbe (ex-*Trutta,* SS 421) | 22-5-44 | 18-8-44 | 16-11-44 |
| S 346 Birinci Inönü (ex-*Threadfin,* SS 410) | 18-3-44 | 26-6-44 | 30-8-44 |

**SUBMARINES** *(continued)*

**Murat Reis (S 336)** H. Ehlers, 10-85

**Çerbe (S 340)**—showing "stepped" sail H. Ehlers, 10-85

**D:** 1,525/1,848/2,440 tons **S:** 17.4/14 kts, 9.4 snorkel
**Dim:** 93.36 × 8.32 × 5.04
**A:** 10/533-mm TT (6 fwd, 4 aft)—24 torpedoes or 40 mines
**Electron Equipt:** Radar: 1/SS-2A
Sonar: BQR-2B, BQS-4
**M:** 3 Fairbanks-Morse $38D8\frac{1}{8}$ × 10 (S 345: G.M. 16/278A) diesels, electric drive; 2 props; 3,430/5,200 hp
**Fuel:** 330 tons **Range:** 10,000/10; 95/5 (sub.) **Man:** 8–9 officers, 76 men

Remarks: S 335 was transferred in 12-70, S 336 in 11-70, S 338 on 24-8-73, S 340 in 6-72, and S 346 on 15-8-73. S 336 and S 338 were at one time while in U.S. service equipped as "hard" targets for ASW training. S 340 is the only operational ex-USN Guppy to retain the original stepped sail. Sisters *Oruç Reis* (S 337, ex-*Pomfret,* SS 391) and *Prevece* (S 345, ex-*Entemedor,* SS 340) stricken 1987.

Note: The ex-U.S. Guppy I-A submarine *Dumlupinar* (S 339, ex-*Caiman,* SS 323) stricken in 1987.

**DESTROYERS**

◆ **2 ex-U.S. Carpenter class**

| | Bldr | Laid down | L | In serv. |
|---|---|---|---|---|
| D 346 Alcitepe (ex-*Robert A. Owens,* DD 827) | Bath Iron Works, Bath, Maine | 29-10-45 | 15-7-46 | 5-11-49 |
| D 347 Anitepe (ex-*Gemlik,* ex-*Anitepe,* ex-*Carpenter,* DD 825) | Consolidated Steel, Orange, Tex. | 30-7-45 | 30-12-45 | 15-12-49 |

**Alcitepe (D 346)** H. Ehlers, 6-86

**Anitepe (D 347)** C. Martinelli, 11-86

**D:** 2,425 tons (3,540 fl) **S:** 34 kts
**Dim:** 119.03 × 12.52 × 4.61 (6.4 over sonar)
**A:** 2/127-mm DP (II × 1)—2/76.2-mm Mk 3 DP (II × 1)—2/35-mm Oerlikon AA (II × 1)—1/ASROC ASW RL (VIII × 1, 6 reloads)—6/324-mm Mk 32 ASW TT (III × 2)—1/d.c. rack (9 d.c.)
**Electron Equipt:** Radar: 1/. . . nav., 2/SPS-10, 1/SPS-40, 1/Mk 35
Sonar: SQS-23—EW: WLR-1, ULQ-6
**M:** 2 sets G.E. GT; 2 props; 60,000 hp **Electric:** 1,200 kw
**Boilers:** 4 Babcock & Wilcox; 43.3 $kg/cm^2$, 454°C **Fuel:** 720 tons
**Range:** 1,500/31; 5,800/12 **Man:** 14 officers, 260 men

Remarks: D 347 purchased 20-2-81, ex-DD 827 purchased 16-2-82. Name for D 347 changed two weeks after transfer. Variant of the *Gearing* design, originally optimized for ASW. Completed FRAM-I modernizations 1962, retaining high bridges. Have Mk 56 radar GFCS, tripod mast aft, larger hangar superstructure than *Gearing* FRAM-I. Twin 76.2-mm placed on fantail, twin 35-mm forward after transfer. GFCS for the 35-mm mount not identified; the 76.2-mm is locally controlled.

◆ **7 ex-U.S. Gearing FRAM-I class**

| | Bldr | Laid down | L | In serv. |
|---|---|---|---|---|
| D 345 Yucetepe (ex-*Orleck,* DD 886) | Consolidated Steel, Orange, Tex. | 18-11-44 | 12-5-45 | 15-9-45 |
| D 348 Savastepe (ex-*Meredith,* DD 890) | Consolidated Steel, Orange, Tex. | 27-1-45 | 28-6-45 | 31-12-45 |
| D 349 Kiliç Ali Paşa (ex-*Robert H. McCard,* DD 822) | Consolidated Steel, Orange, Tex. | 26-1-45 | 9-11-45 | 26-10-46 |
| D 350 Piyale Paşa (ex-*Fiske,* DD 842) | Bath Iron Wks., Bath, Maine | 9-4-45 | 8-9-45 | 28-11-45 |
| D 351 M Fevzi Cakmak (ex-*Charles H. Roan,* DD 853) | Bethlehem Steel, Quincy, Mass. | 27-9-45 | 15-3-46 | 12-9-46 |
| D 352 Gayret (ex-*Eversole,* DD 789) | Todd SY, Seattle, Wash. | 28-2-45 | 8-1-46 | 10-7-46 |
| D 353 Adatepe (ex-*Forrest Royal,* DD 872) | Bethlehem, Staten Isl., N.Y. | 6-6-45 | 17-1-46 | 28-6-46 |

**D:** 2,425 tons (3,600 fl) **S:** 32 kts
**Dim:** 119.03 × 12.49 × 4.56 (6.4 over sonar)
**A:** D 351, 352 only: 8/Harpoon SSM (IV × 2)—all: 4/127-mm 38 cal. AA (II × 2)—2/40-mm AA (I × 2) (not in D 345, 348–350)—2/35-mm Oerlikon AA (II × 1)—6/324-mm Mk 32 ASW TT (III × 2)—1/ASROC ASW RL (VIII × 1)—1/Mk 9 d.c. rack (9 d.c.)

**Savastepe (D 348)**—both 127-mm mounts fwd, chaff RL atop pilothouse and hangar L. & L. Van Ginderen, 11-85

**Piyale Paşa (D 350)**—prior to installation of Harpoon SSM on helicopter deck C. Martinelli, 10-84

**DESTROYERS** *(continued)*

**Electron Equipt:** Radar: 1/. . . nav., 1/SPS-10, 1/SPS-40 (D 345, 348–50: SPS-29), 1/Mk 25 (D 345, 351–353: 1/. . . also)
Sonar: SQS-23
EW: WLR-1, WLR-3, ULQ-6 (not in D 348), 2 or 4/chaff RL (XX × 2 or 4)
**M:** 2 sets GT; 2 props; 60,000 hp **Electric:** 1,200 kw
**Boilers:** 4 Foster-Wheeler and/or Babcock & Wilcox, 43.3 kg/cm², 454°C
**Fuel:** 720 tons **Range:** 2,400/25; 4,800/15 **Man:** 14 officers, 260 men

**Adatepe (D 353)**—twin 35-mm mount aft, twin 40-mm fwd H. Ehlers, 4-84

**Yucetepe (D 345),** new EW radome on foremast L. Grazioli, 11-87

Remarks: D 351 was transferred on 29-9-73, D 352 on 11-7-73, and D 353 on 27-3-71. All received a twin 40-mm mount just before the bridge (with Mk 51 Mod. 2, optical director) and a twin 35-mm antiaircraft gun on the former DASH drone helicopter deck in the mid-1970s. D 351 has four Babcock & Wilcox boilers, while the other pair have two Babcock & Wilcox and two Foster-Wheeler boilers. All have chaff RL atop former hangar, two saluting guns fwd. GFCS include Mk 37 for 127-mm DP, 1 Mk 51 Mod. 2 for the 40-mm mount, and a radar GFCS (antenna atop after mast). D 348 was purchased 20-3-80 for cannibalization, but was instead refurbished and recommissioned 20-7-81; she has both 127-mm mounts fwd, the twin 35-mm AA on the fantail, no 40-mm AA, and retains the helo deck as does D 345. D 349 and D 350 were leased for 5 years 5-6-80 and formally recommissioned 30-7-81. Because of their status they were not drastically altered, although one depth-charge rack, the twin 35-mm AA, and chaff RL were added. D 345 purchased 1-10-82, recommissioning 29-3-83; 40-mm AA not added as of late 1987. *McKean* (DD 784), previously damaged in a collision, transferred 1982 for cannibalization. D 351 and D 352 received Harpoon missiles in 1986, mounted on the former helicopter deck, forward of the 35-mm AA mount. Four are to be modernized with vertical-launch Sea Sparrow SAM and two H.S.A. STIR-24 radar directors.

◆ **1 ex-U.S. Gearing FRAM-II class** Bldr: Bethlehem Steel, San Pedro, Cal.

| | Laid down | L | In serv. |
|---|---|---|---|
| D 354 Kocatepe (ex-*Norris,* DD 859) | 29-8-44 | 25-2-45 | 9-6-45 |

**Kocatepe (D 354)** H. Ehlers, 4-86

**D:** 2,390 tons (3,480 fl) **S:** 32 kts **Dim:** 119.03 × 12.49 × 4.6 (6.54 over sonar)
**A:** 4/127-mm DP (II × 2)—2/35-mm AA (II × 1)—4/40-mm AA (II × 2)—1/Mk 15 trainable Hedgehog—6/324-mm Mk 32 ASW TT (III × 2)—1/Mk 9 d.c. rack
**Electron Equipt:** Radar: 1/. . . nav., 1/SPS-10, 1/SPS-40, 1/Mk 25, 1/. . . f.c.
Sonar: 1/SQS-23
EW: WLR-1, 4 chaff RL (XX × 4)
**M:** 2 sets GT; 2 props; 60,000 hp **Electric:** 1,200 kw
**Boilers:** 4 Babcock & Wilcox; 43.3 kg/cm², 454°C
**Fuel:** 720 tons **Range:** 2,400/25; 4,800/15 **Man:** 14 officers, 260 men

Remarks: A previous *Kocatepe* (ex-*Harwood,* DD 861) was lost on 21-7-74 when mistakenly bombed by the Turkish Air Force. She was replaced by the *Norris* (DD 859), which had been transferred on 7-7-74 for cannibalization spares. Two single 40-mm AA were mounted on former DASH drone helicopter deck in 1974 and two twin 40-mm AA (with two Mk 51 Mod. 2 directors) added on upper deck between stacks in 1977. Has one Mk 37 radar GFCS.

D 354 had a twin Oerlikon 35-mm AA substituted for the two single 40-mm aft and SPS-40 in place of SPS-6D radar in 1980. Sister *Tinaztepe* (D 355) badly damaged in collision 2-5-84 and laid up, awaiting possible restoration.

◆ **1 ex-U.S. Allen M. Sumner FRAM-II class** Bldr: Federal SB, Kearny, N.J.

| | Laid down | L | In serv. |
|---|---|---|---|
| D 356 Zafer (ex-*Hugh Purvis,* DD 709) | 23-5-44 | 17-12-44 | 1-3-45 |

**Zafer (D 356)** H. Ehlers, 3-84

**D:** 2,200 tons (3,300 fl) **S:** 33 kts
**Dim:** 114.76 × 12.49 × 4.39 (5.79 over sonar)
**A:** 6/127-mm DP (II × 3)—4/40-mm AA (II × 2)—2/35-mm Oerlikon (II × 1)—2/Mk 11 Hedgehogs—6/324-mm Mk 32 ASW TT—1/Mk 9 d.c. rack
**Electron Equipt:** Radar: 1/. . . nav., 1/SPS-10, 1/SPS-29, 1/Mk 25
Sonar: SQS-29 series
EW: WLR-1, ULQ-6, 4/chaff RL (XX × 4)
**M:** GT; 2 props; 60,000 hp **Electric:** 1,200 kw
**Boilers:** 4 Babcock & Wilcox; 43.3 kg/cm², 454°C
**Fuel:** 650 tons **Range:** 800/32; 4,300/11 **Man:** 15 officers, 260 men

Remarks: Transferred on 15-2-72. In 1977 two twin 40-mm AA with two Mk 52 Mod. 2, optical GFCS for the twin mounts were added amidships; also has Mk 37 radar GFCS for 127-mm DP. Twin 35-mm AA replaced 2 single 40-mm AA on former helicopter flight deck in 1979.

◆ **1 ex-U.S. Robert H. Smith-class destroyer minelayer** Bldr: Bethlehem Steel, San Pedro, Cal.

| | Laid down | L | In serv. |
|---|---|---|---|
| DM 357 Muavenet (ex-*Gwin,* MMD 33, ex-DD 772) | 31-10-43 | 9-4-44 | 30-9-44 |

**Muavenet (DM 357)** H. Ehlers, 10-84

**D:** 2,250 tons (3,375 fl) **S:** 34 kts **Dim:** 114.76 × 12.49 × 4.4 (hull)
**A:** 6/127-mm DP (II × 3)—2/76.2-mm Mk 33 DP (II × 1)—12/40-mm AA (IV × 2; II × 2)—6/324-mm Mk 32 ASW TT (III × 2)—1/Mk 11 Hedgehog ASW mortars (XXIV × 2)—1/Mk 9 d.c. rack (9 d.c.)
**Electron Equipt:** Radar: 1. . . nav., 1/SPS-10, 1/SPS-40, 1/Mk 25 f.c., 1/SPG-34 f.c.
Sonar: . . .
EW: WLR-1 intercept, 4 decoy RL (XX × 4)

**DESTROYERS** *(continued)*

**M:** 2 sets GT; 2 props; 60,000 hp **Electric:** 900 kw
**Boilers:** 4 Babcock & Wilcox; 43.3 kg/cm$^2$, 454°C
**Fuel:** 494 tons **Range:** 4,600/15 **Man:** 274 tot.

Remarks: Transferred on 22-10-71 after reactivation and modernization. Fire control includes 1 Mk 37 radar GFCS for 127-mm guns, Mk 63 radar GFCS for the 76.2-mm mount, and two Mk 51 Mod. 2, optical GFCS for 40-mm AA. Mine rails on either side of main deck of what is basically an *Allen M. Sumner*-class destroyer. Survivor of a U.S. Navy class of twelve. Modernized with new radars and armament 1982–83, SPS-40 replacing SPS-6, a twin 76.2-mm mount replacing the after quadruple 40-mm mount, etc.

Note: The two ex-U.S. *Fletcher*-class destroyers *Istanbul* (D 340, ex-*Clarence K. Bronson,* DD 668) and *Izmir* (D 341, ex-*Van Valkenburgh,* DD 656) were stricken in 1987.

**FRIGATES**

◆ **1 (+3) MEKO 200-class guided-missile frigates**

| | Bldr | Laid down | L | In serv. |
|---|---|---|---|---|
| F 240 Yavuz | Blohm + Voss, Hamburg | 31-5-85 | 7-11-85 | 17-7-87 |
| F 241 Turgut | Howaldtswerke, Kiel | 20-9-85 | 30-5-86 | 2-88 |
| F 242 Fatih | Gölçük NSY | 11-85 | 24-4-87 | 9-88 |
| F 243 Yildirim | Gölçük NSY | 8-87 | . . . | 6-89 |

**D:** 2,700 tons (3,000 fl) **S:** 27 kts (18 cruise)
**Dim:** 110.50 (102.20 pp) × 13.25 × 3.94 (mean hull)
**A:** 8/Harpoon SSM (IV × 2)—1/Mk 29 SAM launcher (VIII × 1, Sea Sparrow missiles)—1/127-mm Mk 45 Mod. 1 DP—12/25-mm AA (IV × 3, Sea Zenith)—6/324-mm Mk 32 Mod. 5 ASW TT (III × 2)—1/AB-212 helicopter with Sea Skua missiles and Sea Spray radar
**Electron Equipt:** Radar: 1/nav., 1/Plessey Dolphin, 1/H.S.A. DA-08, 1/WM-25, 1/STIR, 2/Albis f.c.
Sonar: SQS-56 hull-mounted—TACAN: H.S.A. Vesta
EW: . . . passive, Super RBOC decoy RL (VI × 2)

**Yavuz (F 240)** L. & L. Van Ginderen, 7-87

**Yavuz (F 240)** H. Ehlers, 9-87

**M:** 4 MTU 20V1163 TB93 diesels; 2 CP props; 22,536 hp
**Range:** 4,000/20 **Fuel:** 380 tons **Electric:** 1,440 kw
**Man:** 24 officers, 114 petty officers, 42 non-rated men

**Yavuz (F 240)** H. Ehlers, 9-87

Remarks: Ordered 4-83, with Blohm + Voss supplying technical assistance in constructing two in Turkey. The Contraves quadruple 25-mm Sea Guard AA gun system replaced the earlier-proposed single U.S. Vulcan-Phalanx AA. Have the H.S.A. SEWACO data system. Later pair may receive vertical-launch Sea Sparrow SAM. All have U.S. SLQ-25 Nixie torpedo decoy. Fin stabilizers. Albis, by Siemens, is a radar-optronic f.c. director for the Sea Zenith guns. Up to eight additional ships of this class are planned.

◆ **2 Berk class** Bldr: Gölçük Naval SY

| | Laid down | L | In serv. |
|---|---|---|---|
| D 358 Berk | 9-3-67 | 25-6-71 | 12-7-72 |
| D 359 Peyk | 18-1-68 | 7-6-72 | 24-7-75 |

**Peyk (D 359)** L. & L. Van Ginderen, 9-83

**D:** 1,450 tons (1,950 fl) **S:** 25 kts **Dim:** 95.15 × 11.82 × 4.4 (5.5 over sonar)
**A:** 4/76.2-mm DP (II × 2)—2/Mk 11 Hedgehog ASW mortar (XXIV × 2)—6/324-mm Mk 32 ASW TT (III × 2)—1/Mk 9 d.c. rack
**Electron Equipt:** Radar: 1/. . . nav., 1/SPS-10, 1/SPS-40, 2/SPG-34
Sonar: 1/SQS-11—EW: WLR-1
**M:** 4 Fiat-Tosi 16 cyl., 800-rpm, Type 3-016-RSS diesels; 1 prop; 24,000 hp

Remarks: Based on the U.S. *Claud Jones* class, but more heavily armed. Can carry an AB-212 helicopter but have no hangar. Two Mk 63 GFCS, with the SPG-34 radars mounted on the gun mounts.

◆ **2 ex-German Köln (Type 120) class** Bldr: H.C. Stülcken, Hamburg

| | Laid down | L | In serv. |
|---|---|---|---|
| D 360 Gelibolu (ex-*Gazi Osman Paşa,* ex-*Karlsruhe,* F 223) | 15-12-58 | 24-10-59 | 15-12-62 |
| D 361 Gemlik (ex-*Emden,* F 221) | 15-4-58 | 21-3-59 | 24-10-61 |

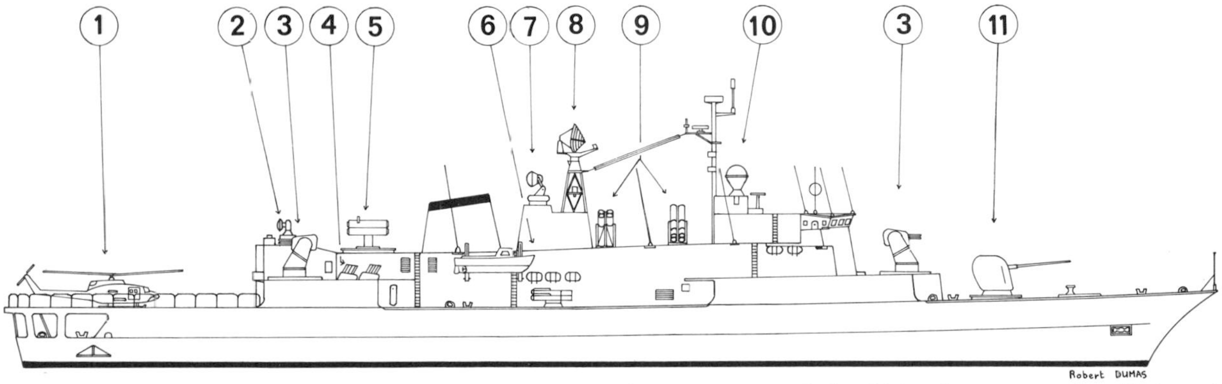


**Yavuz (F 240)** 1. AB-212 helicopter 2. Siemens optronic director (a second should be shown atop the pilothouse) 3. Sea Zenith AA 4. decoy RL 5. Mk 29 launcher for Sea Sparrow 6. Mk 32 ASW TT 7. STIR radar f.c. director 8. DA-08 air-search radar 9. Harpoon missiles 10. WM-25 track-while-scan radar f.c.s. 11. 127-mm DP

FRIGATES *(continued)*

**Gemlik (D 361)** H. Ehlers, 9-84

**Gelibolu (D 360)** H. Ehlers, 4-84

**D:** 2,425 tons (2,970 fl) **S:** 30 kts (20 on diesels)
**Dim:** 109.83 (105.00 pp) × 10.50 × 4.61
**A:** 2/100-mm Mod. 1953 DP (I × 2)—6/40-mm AA (II × 2, I × 2)—2/375-mm Bofors ASW RL (IV × 2)—4/533-mm ASW TT (I × 4)—2/d.c. racks (12 d.c.)—up to 82 mines
**Electron Equipt:** Radar: 1/Kelvin-Hughes 14/9, 1/DA-08, 1/SGR-103, 2/M 44, 1/M 45
Sonar: 1 PAE CWE hull-mounted
EW: . . . intercept, 2 decoy RL (XX × 2)
**M:** CODAG: 4 M.A.N. 16-cyl., 3,000-hp diesels, 2 Brown-Boveri 13,000-hp gas turbines; 2 CP props; 38,000 hp
**Electric:** 2,700 kw **Fuel:** 361 tons **Range:** 900/30; 2,900/22
**Man:** 17 officers, 193 men (in German service)

REMARKS: D 360 transferred 28-3-83 at Gölçük. Ex-*Emden* transferred late 1983. Made 33 kts on original trials. Carry 72 rockets for the ASW RL.

## GUIDED-MISSILE PATROL BOATS

◆ **6 (+4) German FPB 57 class**

Bldrs: P 340: Lürssen, Vegesack, W. Germany; others: Taskizak NDY, Istanbul

| | Laid down | L | In serv. |
|---|---|---|---|
| P 340 Dogan | 2-6-75 | 16-6-76 | 15-6-77 |
| P 341 Marti | 1-7-75 | 30-6-77 | 27-7-78 |
| P 342 Tayfun | 1-12-75 | 19-7-79 | 1980 |
| P 343 Volkan | . . . | 11-8-80 | 1981 |
| P 344 Rüzgar (ex-*Gurbet*) | 30-7-81 | . . . | 1983 |
| P 345 Poyraz | . . . | 17-12-84 | 1985 |
| P 346 Gurbet | . . . | 24-7-87 | . . . |
| P 347 N . . . | . . . | . . . | . . . |
| P 348 N . . . | . . . | . . . | . . . |
| P 349 N . . . | . . . | . . . | . . . |

**Tayfun (P 342)** H. Ehlers, 10-85

**Marti (P 341)** L. & L. Van Ginderen, 5-87

**D:** 353 tons (398 fl) **S:** 36.5 kts **Dim:** 58.1 (54.4 pp) × 7.62 × 2.83
**A:** 8/Harpoon SSM (IV × 2)—1/76-mm OTO Melara Compact DP—2/35-mm Oerlikon AA (II × 1)—2/7.62-mm mg (I × 2)
**Electron Equipt:** Radar: 1/Decca 1226, 1/H.S.A. WM-28-41
EW: SUSIE-1 intercept, 2 decoy RL (XX × 2)
**M:** 4 MTU 16V956 TB91 diesels; 4 props; 18,000 hp (16,000 sust.)
**Electric:** 405 kVA **Range:** 700/35; 1,600/32.5; 3,300/16
**Man:** 5 officers, 33 men

REMARKS: The 76-mm mount has a local control cupola. Carry 300 rounds 76-mm, 2,750 rounds 35-mm. Steel hulls, aluminum superstructures. Plan continued construction at rate of one per year, for a total of ten. Usually carry only 4 Harpoon.

◆ **8 Kartal-class guided-missile and torpedo boats** Bldr: Lürssen, Vegesack (In serv. 1967–71)

| | | |
|---|---|---|
| P 321 Denizkusu | P 324 Kartal | P 328 Simsek |
| P 322 Atmaca | P 326 Pelikan | P 329 Karsiga |
| P 323 Sahin | P 327 Albatros | |

**Sahin (P 323)** L. & L. Van Ginderen, 11-83

**Sahin (P 323)** H. Ehlers, 5-84

**D:** 184 tons (210 fl) **S:** 42 kts **Dim:** 42.8 × 7.14 × 2.21
**A:** 2/40-mm AA (I × 2)—2/Penguin Mk 1 SSM—2/533-mm TT (4 torpedoes)
**Electron Equipt:** Radar: 1/Decca 1226
**M:** 4 MTU 16V538 diesels; 4 props; 12,000 hp
**Range:** 500/39; 1,000/32 **Man:** 39 tot.

REMARKS: Similar to the German *Jaguar* class. Wooden planking; steel and light-metal keel and frames; light-metal superstructure. Can be fitted as fast gunboats or mine layers (four mines). All now carry two Penguin IR-homing antiship missiles. Sister *Melten* cut in two by Soviet naval training ship *Khasan* 25-9-85.

## TORPEDO BOATS

◆ **4 ex-German Jaguar class (Type 140)**

Bldrs: P 336: Krögerwerft, Rendsburg; others: Lürssen, Vegesack

| | L | | L |
|---|---|---|---|
| P 331 Tufan (ex-*Storch*) | 16-11-59 | P 335 Kalkan (ex-*Löwe*) | 8-11-58 |
| P 333 Mizrak (ex-*Häher*) | 9-1-60 | P 336 Karayel (ex-*Tiger*) | 21-4-58 |

**D:** 184 tons (210 fl) **S:** 42 kts **Dim:** 42.62 × 7.1 × 2.21 (props)
**A:** 2/40-mm AA (I × 2)—4/533-mm TT or 2/TT and mines
**M:** 4 MTU 16V538 diesels; 4 props; 12,000 hp
**Range:** 500/39; 1,000/32 **Man:** 39 tot.

TORPEDO BOATS *(continued)*

**Kalkan (P 335)** L. & L. Van Ginderen, 5-87

**Mizrak (P 333)** H. Ehlers, 5-86

REMARKS: Transferred 1975–76. The *Alk, Iltis,* and *Reiher* were transferred at the same time to be cannibalized for the maintenance of the seven in service. Similar to *Kartal* class but shorter deckhouse with stepped face. Sisters *Firtina* (P 330, ex-*Pelikan*), *Kiliç* (P 332, ex-*Pinguin*), and *Yildiz* (P 334, ex-*Wolf*) stricken 8-6-82. The others have been refitted. Two reload torpedoes carried, for forward tubes.

NOTE: Six former West German *Zobel*-class torpedo boats purchased in 1984 have not been placed in service and may be being retained for spares. Characteristics in 1986–87 edition.

PATROL BOATS AND CRAFT

◆ **1 German PB 57 class** Bldr: Taskizak Naval DY, Istanbul (In serv. 30-7-76)

P 140 GIRNE

**Girne (P 140)** H. Ehlers, 3-83

**D:** 341 tons (399 fl) **S:** 29.5 kts **Dim:** 58.1 (54.4 pp) × 7.6 × 2.8
**A:** 2/40-mm AA (I × 2)—2/12.7-mm mg (I × 2)—4/Mk 20 Mousetrap ASW RL—2/d.c. projectors—2/d.c. racks
**Electron Equipt:** Radar: 2/navigational
**M:** 2 MTU 16V956 TB91 diesels; 2 props; 9,000 hp **Electric:** 405 kVA
**Range:** 2,200/28; 4,200/16 **Man:** 3 officers, 27 men

REMARKS: Same basic design as the Spanish *Lazaga*-class patrol boats, but with lighter armament. Design by Lürssen. Construction program canceled after one unit. One CSEE Naja optronic GFCS. Single 40-mm Bofors replaced twin 40-mm aft by 1982.

◆ **1 ex-U.S. Asheville class** Bldr: Peterson Builders, Sturgeon Bay, Wisc.

| | L | In serv. |
|---|---|---|
| P 339 BORA (ex-*Surprise,* PG 97) | 15-11-68 | 24-9-69 |

**D:** 225 tons (240 fl) **S:** 40 kts (16 on diesels)
**Dim:** 50.14 (46.94 pp) × 7.28 × 2.9
**A:** 1/76.2-mm Mk 34 DP—1/40-mm AA—4/12.7-mm mg (II × 2)
**Electron Equipt:** Radar: 1/SPS-53, 1/SPG-50
**M:** CODAG: 1 LM 1500 Mk 7 gas turbine (12,500 hp); 2 Cummins 875V12 diesels (1,450 hp); 2 props
**Fuel:** 50 tons **Range:** 325/35; 1,700/16 **Man:** 25 tot.

**Bora (P 339)** H. Ehlers, 5-83

REMARKS: Leased on 28-2-73. Mk 63 radar GFCS, with SPG-50 on 76.2-mm gun mount. Sister *Yildirim* (P 338, ex-*Defiance,* PG 95) lost through explosion 11-4-85 near Lesbos.

◆ **12 AB 25 class** Bldrs: Gölçük Naval SY (In serv. 1967–70)

| | | |
|---|---|---|
| P 1225 AB 25 | P 1229 AB 29 | P 1233 AB 33 |
| P 1226 AB 26 | P 1230 AB 30 | P 1234 AB 34 |
| P 1227 AB 27 | P 1231 AB 31 | P 1235 AB 35 |
| P 1228 AB 28 | P 1232 AB 32 | P 1236 AB 36 |

**AB 27 (P 1227)** L. & L. Van Ginderen, 5-87

**D:** 150 tons (170 fl) **S:** 22 kts **Dim:** 40.24 × 6.4 × 1.65
**A:** 1/40-mm AA—1/20-mm AA—2/12.7-mm mg (I × 2)—2/Mk 20 Mousetrap ASW RL (IV × 2)—4/d.c. release racks
**Electron Equipt:** Radar: 1/. . . nav.—Sonar: . . .
**M:** SACM-AGO V16CSHR diesels; 2 props; 4,800 hp; 2 cruise diesels; 300 hp

REMARKS: Fourteen others are assigned to the Marine Police. Built with French assistance. AB 35 and 36, delivered two years later than others, have a lower hull knuckle forward and bow bulwarks.

◆ **4 ex-U.S. PGM 71 motor gunboats** Bldr: Peterson Builders, Sturgeon Bay, Wisc.

| | L | In serv. |
|---|---|---|
| P 1221 AB 21 (ex-PGM 104) | 4-5-67 | 8-67 |
| P 1222 AB 22 (ex-PGM 105) | 25-5-67 | 9-67 |
| P 1223 AB 23 (ex-PGM 106) | 7-7-67 | 10-67 |
| P 1224 AB 24 (ex-PGM 108) | 14-9-67 | 5-68 |

**AB 22 (P 1222)** 1982

**D:** 104 tons (144 fl) **S:** 17 kts **Dim:** 30.81 × 6.45 × 1.83
**A:** 1/40-mm AA—4/20-mm AA (II × 2)—2/Mk 22 double Mousetrap ASW RL—2/d.c. racks (4 d.c.)
**Electron Equipt:** Radar: 1/Raytheon 1500B—Sonar: SQS-17A
**M:** 8 G.M. 6-71 diesels; 2 props; 2,040 hp **Electric:** 30 kw
**Fuel:** 16 tons **Range:** 1,000/12 **Man:** 30 tot.

REMARKS: Two single 12.7-mm mg have been removed. First three handed over 12-67.

## PATROL BOATS AND CRAFT *(continued)*

◆ **6 ex-U.S. PC 1638-class antisubmarine patrol boats** Bldrs: P 116; Gölçük Naval SY; others: Gunderson Bros., Portland, Ore.

| | L | In serv. |
|---|---|---|
| P 111 Sultan Hisar (ex-PC 1638) | 1964 | 5-64 |
| P 112 Demirhisar (ex-PC 1639) | 9-7-64 | 22-4-65 |
| P 113 Yarhisar (ex-PC 1640) | 14-5-64 | 9-64 |
| P 114 Akhisar (ex-PC 1641) | 14-5-64 | 3-12-64 |
| P 115 Sivrihisar (ex-PC 1642) | 5-11-64 | 6-65 |
| P 116 Kochisar (ex-PC 1643) | 12-64 | 7-65 |

**Kochisar (P 116)** H. Ehlers, 4-83

**D:** 325 tons (477 fl) **S:** 19 kts **Dim:** 52.9 × 7.0 × 3.1 (hull)
**A:** 1/40-mm AA—4/20-mm AA (II × 2)—1/Mk 15 trainable Hedgehog ASW mortar (XXIV × 1)—4/Mk 6 d.c. projectors—1/Mk 9 d.c. rack (9 d.c.)
**Electron Equipt:** Radar: 1/Decca 707—Sonar: SQS-17A
**M:** 2 Alco 169 × $10\frac{1}{2}$ T diesels; 2 props; 4,800 hp
**Fuel:** 60 tons **Range:** 5,000/10 **Man:** 5 officers, 60 men

Remarks: Based on the PC 471 class of World War II.

◆ **4 ex-U.S. Coast Guard 83-foot class** Bldr: U.S.C.G. Yard, Curtis Bay, Md.

P 1209 LS 9 P 1210 LS 10 P 1211 LS 11 P 1212 LS 12

**LS 12 (P 1212)** H. Ehlers, 5-82

**D:** 63 tons **S:** 18 kts **Dim:** 25.3 × 4.25 × 1.55
**A:** 1/20-mm AA—2/Mk 20 Mousetrap ASW RL (IV × 2)
**Electron Equipt:** Radar: 1/SO-2—Sonar: QBE-3
**M:** 4 G.M. 6-71 diesels; 2 props; 900 hp **Man:** 15 tot.

Remarks: Transferred on 25-6-53. Former Turkish hull numbers P 339, P 308, P 309, and P 310. Wooden hulls.

## MINE WARFARE SHIPS

Note: The destroyer *Muavenet* (D 357) is also a minelayer when required, and the ex-German *Köln*-class frigates have mine rails.

◆ **1 Danish Falster-class minelayer** Bldr: Frederikshaven Naval DY, Denmark

| | Laid down | L | In serv. |
|---|---|---|---|
| N 110 Nusret (ex-N 108, ex-MMC 16) | 1962 | 1964 | 16-9-64 |

**D:** 1,880 tons **S:** 16.5 kts **Dim:** 77.0 (72.5 pp) × 12.8 × 3.4
**A:** 4/76.2-mm AA Mk 33 (II × 2)—400 mines
**Electron Equipt:** Radar: 1/navigational, 1/RAN 7S, 2/SPG-34
**M:** 2 G.M. 16-567D3 diesels; 2 CP props; 4,800 hp
**Fuel:** 130 tons **Man:** 130 tot.

Remarks: Paid for by the U.S.A. Two Mk 63 radar GFCS systems.

**Nusret (N 110)**—wearing old number

◆ **2 Saruçabey-class minelayer/landing ships** Bldr: Taskizak NSY, Istanbul

| | Laid down | L | In serv. |
|---|---|---|---|
| $N^{L}$ 123 Saruçabey (ex-*Karaçebey*) | 25-7-80 | 30-7-81 | 26-7-84 |
| $N^{L}$ 124 Karamürselbey | 26-7-83 | 26-7-84 | 27-7-85 |

**Saruçabey ($N^{L}$ 123)** H. Ehlers, 7-84

**D:** 2,600 tons (fl) **S:** 14 kts **Dim:** 92.0 × 14.0 × . . .
**A:** 3/40-mm AA (I × 3)—4/20-mm AA (II × 2)—150 mines
**M:** 3 diesels; 3 props; 4,320 hp

Remarks: Enlarged version of *Çakabey,* with raised forecastle and larger superstructure, helicopter deck aft. Two LCVP stowed on deck amidships, handled by large articulated crane. Unusual in having two disembarkation ports on each side at tank-deck level. Can carry 11 tanks, 12 trucks, and 600 troops. Minelaying ports in stern. Three more may be built.

◆ **1 Çakabey-class minelayer/landing ship** Bldr: Taskizak NSY, Istanbul

| | Laid down | L | In serv. |
|---|---|---|---|
| $N^{L}$ 122 Çakabey (ex-L 405) | . . . | 3-6-77 | 25-7-80 |

**Çakabey ($N^{L}$ 122)** H. Ehlers, 4-84

**D:** 1,600 tons **S:** 14 kts **Dim:** 77.3 (74.3 pp) × 12.0 × 2.3
**A:** 4/40-mm AA (II × 2)—8/20-mm AA (II × 4)—150 mines
**M:** 3 diesels; 3 props; 4,500 hp

Remarks: Redesignated as a minelayer/landing ship in 1980. Originally planned as a class of four. As a landing ship, $N^{L}$ 112 can carry 400 troops, 9 U.S. M-48 tanks, and 10 jeeps. Carries two LCVP in davits. Deck cleared forward as a helicopter platform. Two disembarkation ports on each side, at tank deck level.

◆ **2 ex-German, ex-U.S. LST 542-class minelayer/tank landing ships**

Bldrs: $N^{L}$ 120: Missouri Valley Bridge & Iron, Evansville, Ind.; $N^{L}$ 121: American Bridge Co., Ambridge, Pa.

| | Laid down | L | In serv. |
|---|---|---|---|
| $N^{L}$ 120 Bayraktar (ex-L 403, ex-*Bottrop,* ex-*Saline County,* LST 1101) | 22-11-44 | 3-1-45 | 26-1-45 |
| $N^{L}$ 121 Sancaktar (ex-*Bochum,* ex-*Rice County,* LST 1089) | 20-12-44 | 17-2-45 | 14-3-45 |

**D:** 3,640 tons (4,140 fl) **S:** 11 kts **Dim:** 101.37 × 15.28 × 3.98 (max.)
**A:** 6/40-mm AA (II × 2, I × 2)—mines **Electric:** 860 kw **Range:** 15,000/9
**Electron Equipt:** Radar: 1/Kelvin-Hughes 14/9
**M:** 2 G.M. 16-567A diesels; 2 props; 1,700 hp **Man:** 60 tot.

MINE WARFARE SHIPS *(continued)*

**Bayraktar (N$^L$ 120)** 1983

REMARKS: N$^L$ 120 was transferred to West Germany on 6-2-64 and to Turkey on 13-12-72; N$^L$ 121 to West Germany on 23-1-64 and to Turkey on 12-12-72. Converted to minelayers while in German service. Six rails on the upper deck, tapering to two at the stern, have been removed, but there remain four rails below decks, exiting through a broadened stern. Four two-ton mine-handling cranes added. Bow doors retained. Redesignated as amphibious ships 1974–75, but again placed in mine warfare category 1980.

◆ **4 minelayers** Bldr: Brown SB, Houston, Tex.

| | Laid down | L | In serv. |
|---|---|---|---|
| N 101 MORDOGAN (ex-MMC 11, ex-LSM 484) | 17-2-45 | 10-3-45 | 15-4-45 |
| N 102 MERIC (ex-MMC 12, ex-LSM 481) | 17-2-45 | 10-3-45 | 8-4-45 |
| N 104 MERSIN (ex-*Vale,* ex-MMC 13, ex-LSM 492) | 28-5-44 | 22-6-44 | 4-8-44 |
| N 105 MUREFTE (ex-*Vidar,* ex-MMC 14, ex-MSC 493) | 10-3-45 | 30-3-45 | 4-5-45 |

**Meric (N 102)** L. & L. Van Ginderen, 6-82

**D:** 743 tons (1,100 fl) **S:** 12.5 kts **Dim:** 62.0 × 10.52 × 2.54
**A:** 6/40-mm AA (II × 3)—5/20-mm AA (I × 5)—400 mines
**Electron Equipt:** Radar: 2/navigational
**M:** 2 G.M. 16-278A diesels; 2 props; 2,800 hp
**Fuel:** 60 tons **Range:** 2,500/12 **Man:** 70 tot.

REMARKS: Ex-U.S. LSM 1-class medium landing ships. In 10-52 after conversion, the first three were transferred to Turkey, the other two to Norway; the latter were returned to U.S. control in 1960, then reassigned to Turkey. Four booms, two forward, two aft, for the loading of mines. Two minelaying rails. Originally had four twin 40-mm AA and six 20-mm AA. N 104 has two Fairbanks-Morse 38D8$\frac{1}{8}$ × 10 diesels. *Marmaris* (N 103, ex-MMC 10, ex-LSM 490) stricken in 1987.

◆ **1 mine-planter** Bldr: Higgins, New Orleans, La. (L: 1958)

N 115 MEHMETCIK (ex-YMP 3)

**Mehmetcik (N 115)** H. Ehlers, 6-83

**D:** 540 tons (fl) **S:** 10 kts **Dim:** 39.62 × 10.67 × 3.05
**A:** . . . mines **Electron Equipt:** Radar: 1/Decca . . .
**M:** 2 G.M. 6-71 diesels; 2 props; 600 hp **Man:** 22 tot.

REMARKS: Paid for by the U.S. Military Aid Program. Used to place controlled minefields. The 40-mm AA formerly carried has been removed. Tends controlled minefields.

◆ **6 ex-German French Mercure-class coastal minesweepers** Bldr: Amiot (CMN), Cherbourg

| | Laid down | L | In serv. |
|---|---|---|---|
| M 520 KARAMÜRSEL (ex-*Wörms*) | 19-3-58 | 30-1-60 | 30-4-60 |
| M 521 KEREMPE (ex-*Detmold*) | 19-2-58 | 17-11-59 | 20-2-60 |
| M 522 KILIMLI (ex-*Siegen*) | 18-4-58 | 29-3-60 | 9-7-60 |
| M 523 KOZLU (ex-*Hameln*) | 20-1-58 | 20-8-59 | 15-10-59 |
| M 524 KUSADASI (ex-*Vegesack*) | 20-12-57 | 21-5-59 | 19-9-59 |
| M 525 KEMER (ex-*Passau*) | 19-5-58 | 25-6-60 | 15-10-60 |

**Kerempe (M 521)** H. Ehlers, 10-86

**D:** 366 tons (383 fl) **S:** 14.5 kts **Dim:** 44.62 (42.5 pp) × 8.41 × 2.55
**A:** 2/20-mm AA (II × 1) **Electric:** 520 kw
**Electron Equipt:** Radar: 1/Decca 707
**M:** Mercedes-Benz MB-820 Db diesels; 2 CP props; 4,000 hp **Man:** 40 tot.

REMARKS: These ships were built for the German Navy, placed in reserve in 1963, and stricken on 31-12-73. Transferred to Turkey between 6-75 and 10-75, except M 525, in 1979. French sister *Mercure* now a fisheries-protection ship. Wooden construction.

◆ **12 ex-U.S. Adjutant-, MSC 268(*)-, and MSC 289(†)-class coastal minesweepers** Bldrs: M 507: Hiltebrant DD, Kingston, N.Y.; M 508: Stephen Bros.; M 509: South Coast Co., Newport Beach, Cal.; M 510 to M 513: Bellingham SY, Bellingham, Wash.; M 514, M 515; Dorchester Builders, Dorchester, N.J.; M 516 to M 518: Peterson Builders, Sturgeon Bay, Wisc.

| | L | In serv. |
|---|---|---|
| M 507 SEYMEN (ex-*De Panne,* ex-MSC 131) | . . . | 28-10-55 |
| M 508 SELÇUK (ex-*Pavot,* ex-MSC 124) | . . . | 6-54 |
| M 509 SEYHAN (ex-*Renoncule,* (ex-MSC 142) | . . . | 8-54 |
| M 510 SAMSUN (ex-MSC 268)* | 6-9-57 | 30-9-58 |
| M 511 SINOP (ex-MSC 270)* | 4-1-58 | 2-59 |
| M 512 SÜRMENE (ex-MSC 271)* | 1958 | 27-3-59 |
| M 513 SEDDUL BAHR (ex-MSC 272)* | 1958 | 5-59 |
| M 514 SILIFKE (ex-MSC 304)† | 21-11-64 | 9-65 |
| M 515 SAROS (ex-MSC 305)† | 1-5-65 | 2-66 |
| M 516 SIGAÇIK (ex-MSC 311)† | 12-6-64 | 6-65 |
| M 517 SAPANCA (ex-MSC 312)† | 14-9-64 | 26-7-65 |
| M 518 SARIYER (ex-MSC 315)† | 21-4-66 | 8-9-67 |

**D:** 300 tons (392 fl) **S:** 14 kts **Dim:** 43.0 (41.5 pp) × 7.95 × 2.55
**A:** 2/20-mm AA (II × 1) **M:** 2 G.M. 8/268A diesels; 2 props; 1,200 hp
**Electron Equipt:** Radar: 1/Decca 45 or 707—Sonar: UQS-1D
**Range:** 2,500/10 **Man:** 4 officers, 34 men

**Seyhan (M 509)**—Adjutant class H. Ehlers, 10-85

MINE WARFARE SHIPS *(continued)*

**Sinop (M 511)**—MSC 268 class H. Ehlers, 12-86

**Sigaçik (M 516)**—MSC 289 class H. Ehlers, 9-86

Remarks: M 507 was returned to the U.S.A. by Belgium in 1970, and M 508 and M 509 were returned by France on 23-3-70, then transferred to Turkey. The MSC 268 class have 4 G.M. 6-71 diesels; 2 props; 880 hp. The MSC 289 class have lower superstructure, taller stacks, and 2 Waukesha L-1616 diesels of 600 hp each; **Dim:** 44.32 × 8.29 × 2.55.

◆ **4 ex-Canadian Bay-class coastal minesweepers** Bldr: Davie SB, Lauzon, Quebec

| | L | | L |
|---|---|---|---|
| M 530 Trabzon (ex-*Gaspé*) | 20-5-53 | M 532 Tirebolu (ex-*Comax*) | 24-4-52 |
| M 531 Terme (ex-*Trinity*) | 31-7-53 | M 533 Tekirdag (ex-*Ungava*) | 12-11-51 |

**Tekirdag (M 533)** H. Ehlers, 12-86

**D:** 390 tons (412 fl) **S:** 16 kts **Dim:** 50.0 (46.05 pp) × 9.21 × 2.8
**A:** 1/40-mm AA—2/12.7-mm mg (I × 2)
**Electron Equipt:** Radar: 1/Sperry Mk 2
**M:** 2 G.M. 12-278A diesels; 2 props; 2,400 hp **Range:** 4,000/10 **Man:** 44 tot.
**Electric:** 940-kw sweep/plus 690-kw ship's service **Fuel:** 52 tons

Remarks: Transferred under U.S. Military Aid Program on 19-5-58. Wood-planked skin on steel frame. M 533 has been equipped with an EW intercept antenna array and 2/12.7-mm mg far forward on the forecastle. The 40-mm mount is a World War II-era U.K. "Boffin."

◆ **4 ex-U.S. Cape-class inshore minesweepers** Bldr: Peterson Builders, Sturgeon Bay, Wisc.

| | L | In serv. |
|---|---|---|
| M 500 Foca (ex-MSI 15) | 23-8-66 | 8-67 |
| M 501 Fethiye (ex-MSI 16) | 7-12-66 | 9-67 |
| M 502 Fatsa (ex-MSI 17) | 11-4-67 | 10-67 |
| M 503 Finike (ex-MSI 18) | 11-67 | 12-67 |

**Fatsa (M 502)** H. Ehlers, 9-86

**D:** 203 tons (239 fl) **S:** 12.5 kts **Dim:** 34.06 × 7.14 × 2.4
**A:** 1/12.7-mm mg **M:** 4 G.M. 6-71 diesels; 2 props; 960 hp
**Electron Equipt:** Radar: 1/SPS-21 **Electric:** 120 kw **Fuel:** 20 tons
**Range:** 1,000/9 **Man:** 20 tot.

Remarks: Transferred on completion. Wooden construction.

◆ **2 ex-U.S. 64-foot distribution-box minefield tenders**

Y 1148 Samandira L 1 Y 1149 Samandira L 2

**D:** 72 tons (fl) **S:** 9.5 kts **Dim:** 19.58 × 5.72 × 1.83
**A:** 1 Gray Marine 64HN9 diesel; 1 prop; 225 hp **Man:** 6 tot.

Remarks: Transferred in 1959.

◆ **9 mine-disposal diving tenders** Bldr: U.K. (In serv. 1942)

| | | |
|---|---|---|
| P 311 Dalgiç 1 (ex-MTB 1) | P 314 MTB 4 | P 317 MTB 7 |
| P 312 Dalgiç 2 (ex-MTB 2) | P 315 MTB 5 | P 318 MTB 8 |
| P 313 MTB 3 | P 316 MTB 6 | P 319 MTB 9 |

**Dalgiç 2 (P 312)** H. Ehlers, 7-84

**D:** 70 tons **S:** 20 kts **Dim:** 21.8 × 4.2 × 2.6
**M:** 2 diesels; 2,000 hp **A:** 1/12.7-mm mg or 20-mm AA in some

Remarks: First two redesignated diver support boats in 1983.

**AMPHIBIOUS WARFARE SHIPS AND CRAFT**

Note: The *Çakabey* ($\text{N}^{\text{L}}$ 112), *Bayraktar* ($\text{N}^{\text{L}}$ 120), and *Sancaktar* ($\text{N}^{\text{L}}$ 121), formerly listed as landing ships, are now listed as minelayers; they can still be employed in amphibious landings, as can the new *Saruçabey* ($\text{N}^{\text{L}}$ 123) class.

◆ **2 ex-U.S. Terrebonne Parish-class tank landing ships** Bldr: Christy Corp., Sturgeon Bay, Wisc.

| | L | In serv. |
|---|---|---|
| L 401 Ertugrul (ex-*Windham County,* LST 1170) | 22-5-54 | 15-12-54 |
| L 402 Serdar (ex-*Westchester County,* LST 1167) | 18-4-53 | 10-3-54 |

**D:** 2,590 tons (5,786 fl) **S:** 15 kts **Dim:** 117.35 (112.77 pp) × 17.06 × 5.18
**A:** 6/76.2-mm DP (II × 3) **Electron Equipt:** Radar: 1/SPS-21, 2/Mk 34
**M:** 4 G.M. 16-268A diesels; 2 CP props; 6,000 hp **Electric:** 600 kw
**Fuel:** 874 tons **Man:** 116 crew + 395 troops

Remarks: L 401 transferred in 6-73 and L 402 in 8-74. Cargo: 2,200 tons. Can carry four LCVPs in Welin davits. Two Mk 63 radar GFCS.

## AMPHIBIOUS WARFARE SHIPS AND CRAFT *(continued)*

**Serdar (L 402)** H. Ehlers, 10-85

◆ **35 (+3 + . . .) Ç 107-class utility landing craft** (In serv. 1966–. . .)

Bldrs: Ç 107 through Ç 138: Gölçük Naval SY; Ç 139–144: Taskizak NDY

Ç 107 through Ç 130; Ç 134; Ç 135; Ç 137–141; Ç 142–144 (L: 25-7-85); Ç 145 (L: 24-7-87)

**Ç 109**—short-hulled version H. Ehlers, 6-84

**Ç 141**—long-hulled version H. Ehlers, 6-86

**D:** 280 tons light (600 fl) **S:** 8.5 kts (loaded)
**Dim:** 56.56 (Ç 139-on: 60.16) × 11.58 × 1.25 (aft)
**A:** 2/20-mm AA (I × 2)—2/12.7-mm mg (I × 2)
**M:** 3 G.M. 6-71 diesels; 3 props; 900 hp (675 sust.)
**Range:** 600/10 (light); 1,100/8

REMARKS: Continuing construction program, design based on British LCT(4) design. Also being built for Libya, which received Ç 133 and Ç 134 from Turkish inventory in 12-79, and Ç 131–Ç 133 in 1983. Ç 137 and Ç 138 were launched 21-3-80 and commissioned 20-7-81; Ç 139 through Ç 141 were launched at Taskizak during Aug.-Sept. 1984. Can carry 100 troops and five M-48 tanks. Superstructure configurations vary: Ç 121 and later have mg platform atop pilothouse. Ç 136 lost in storm 30-1-85. Ç 139 and later have higher sides to the tank deck and are 3.6 m longer.

◆ **14 utility landing craft** Bldr: Taskizak, Istanbul, 1965–66

Ç 205 through Ç 218

**Ç 212, outboard Ç 206 and Ç 211** H. Ehlers, 6-86

**D:** 320 tons (405 fl) **S:** 10 kts **Dim:** 44.3 (40.8 wl) × 8.8 × 1.7
**A:** 2/20-mm AA (I × 2) **M:** 2 G.M. 6-71 diesels; 2 props; 600 hp (450 sust.)

NOTE: The last U.S. LCU 501-class utility landing craft, Ç 204, was stricken during 1986.

◆ **20 U.S. LCM(8)-class landing craft** Bldr: Taskizak NDY, Istanbul (In serv. 1965–66)

Ç 301 through Ç 320

**Ç 308** H. Ehlers, 9-84

**D:** 56 tons (113 fl) **S:** 9 kts **Dim:** 22.43 × 6.42 × 1.6
**A:** 2/12.7-mm mg (I × 2) **M:** 4 G.M. 6-71 diesels; 2 props; 660 hp **Man:** 5 tot.

## HYDROGRAPHIC SHIPS

◆ **1 oceanographic research and hydrographic survey ship** Bldr: Gölçük NSY (L: 17-11-83; in serv. 7-84)

A 594 ÇUBUKLU (ex-Y 1251)

**Çubuklu (A 594)** H. Ehlers, 8-87

**D:** 512 tons (600 fl) **S:** 11 kts **Dim:** 40.40 (36.40 wl) × 9.60 × 3.20
**A:** 2/20-mm AA (I × 2) **Electron Equipt:** Radar: 1/. . . nav.
**M:** 1 MWM diesel; 1 CP prop; 1,004 hp (820 sust.) **Man:** 39 tot.

## HYDROGRAPHIC SHIPS *(continued)*

Remarks: Carries one survey launch to port. Forecastle side plating extends to abaft boat installation on port side.

Note: British *Catherine*-class survey ship *Çandarli* (A 593, ex-*Frolic*) stricken 1986.

◆ **2 ex-U.S. 52-foot inshore-survey craft** (In serv. 1966)

Y 1221 Mesaha 1   Y 1222 Mesaha 2

**Mesaha 2 (Y 1222)** L. & L. Van Ginderen, 5-87

**D:** 31.7 tons (37.6 fl) **S:** 10 kts **Dim:** 15.9 × 4.45 × 1.3
**M:** 2 G.M. 6-71 diesels; 2 props; 330 hp **Range:** 600/10 **Man:** 10 tot.

## AUXILIARY SHIPS

◆ **1 replenishment oiler** Bldr: Gölçük Naval SY, Istanbul (L: 16-11-83)

A 580 Akar (L: 16-11-83; in serv. 24-4-87)

**D:** approx. 20,000 tons (fl) **S:** 15 kts **Dim:** 145.1 × 22.8 × . . .
**A:** 2/76.2-mm DP (II × 1)—2/40-mm AA (I × 2)
**M:** 1 diesel; 1 prop; 6,500 hp **Man:** 329 tot.

Remarks: 15,000 dwt. Underway replenishment capability. Construction suspended for several years after launching. Has U.S. Mk 63 GFCS (with SPG-34 radar) for the twin U.S. Mk 34 76.2-mm gun mount. A sister may be built.

◆ **1 new-construction transport oiler**

| | Bldr | L | In serv. |
|---|---|---|---|
| A 570 Taskizak | Taskizak NDY | 28-7-83 | 1-8-84 |

**Taskizak (A 570)**—fitting out H. Ehlers, 5-84

**D:** 1,440 tons (fl) **S:** 13 kts **Dim:** 64.6 × 9.4 × 3.5
**A:** 1/40-mm AA—2/20-mm AA (I × 2)
**M:** 1 diesel; 1 prop; 1,400 hp **Man:** 57 tot. **Cargo:** 1,000 dwt

◆ **1 Turkish-designed replenishment oiler** Bldr: Taskizak NDY, Istanbul (L: 7-69)

A 573 Binbaşi Saadettin Gürçan

**Binbaşi Saadettin Gürçan (A 573)** H. Ehlers, 1-85

**D:** 1,505 tons (4,680 fl) **S:** 16 kts **Dim:** 89.7 × 11.8 × 5.4
**A:** 1/40-mm AA—2/20-mm AA (I × 2)
**M:** 4 G.M. 16-567A diesels, electric drive; 2 props; 4,400 hp

Remarks: One liquid-replenishment station on each side. Primarily a tanker.

◆ **1 Turkish-designed transport oiler** Bldr: Gölçük NSY, 1964

A 572 Albay Hakki Burak

**Albay Hakki Burak (A 572)** L. & L. Van Ginderen, 8-86

**D:** 1,800 tons (3,740 fl) **S:** 16 kts **Dim:** 83.73 × 12.25 × 5.49
**A:** 2/40-mm AA (I × 2) **Electron Equipt:** Radar: 1/Decca 707
**M:** 4 G.M. 16-567A diesels, electric drive; 2 props; 4,400 hp **Man:** 88 tot.

Remarks: One liquid-replenishment station on each side. Primarily a transport tanker.

◆ **1 ex-West German Bodensee-class transport oiler** Bldr: Lindenau-Werft, Kiel

| | Laid down | L | In serv. |
|---|---|---|---|
| A 575 Inebolu (ex-*Bodensee,* ex-*Unkas*) | 24-8-55 | 19-11-55 | 11-2-56 |

**Inebolu (A 575)** H. Ehlers, 5-86

**D:** 1,237 tons (1,840 fl) **S:** 13.5 kts **Dim:** 67.1 (61.2 pp) × 9.84 × 4.27
**A:** 2/20-mm AA **Electron Equipt:** Radar: 1/Kelvin-Hughes 14/9
**M:** 1 MAK 6-cyl. diesel; 1 prop; 1,050 hp **Electric:** 238 kVA
**Range:** 6,240/12 **Man:** 21 tot.

Remarks: Former merchant tanker acquired on 26-3-59 for the West German Navy; transferred to Turkey on 25-8-77. Cargo: 1,231 tons. One replenishment station.

◆ **1 Turkish-designed transport oiler** Bldr: Taskizak NDY, Istanbul

A 571 Yuzbasi Tolünay (ex-*Taskizak*)

**Yuzbasi Tolünay (A 571)**—with *Pinar*-class water tender Y 1216 alongside H. Ehlers, 3-84

**AUXILIARY SHIPS** *(continued)*

**D:** 2,500 tons (3,500 fl) **S:** 14 kts **Dim:** 79.0 × 12.4 × 5.9
**A:** 2/40-mm AA (I × 2)
**M:** 2 Atlas-Polar diesels; 2 props; 1,900 hp

REMARKS: Launched on 22-8-50. Has one alongside replenishment station and can replenish over the stern.

NOTE: U.S. *Mettawee*-class oiler *Akpinar* (A 574, ex-*Chiwaukum,* AOG 26) stricken 1986.

◆ **2 ex-German Rhein-class tenders**

| | Bldr | L | In serv. |
|---|---|---|---|
| A 577 SOKULLU MEHMET PAŞA (ex-*Isar,* A 54) | Blohm + Voss, Hamburg | 14-7-62 | 25-1-64 |
| A 579 CEZAYIRLI GAZI HASAN PAŞA (ex-*Ruhr,* A 64) | Schlieker, Hamburg | 18-8-60 | 2-5-64 |

**Sokullu Mehmet Paşa (A 577)** L. & L. Van Ginderen, 8-86

**Cezayirli Gazi Hasan Paşa (A 579)** L. & L. Van Ginderen, 5-87

**D:** A 579: 2,370 tons (2,740 fl); A 577: 2,330 tons (2,930 fl)
**S:** 20 kts (22 trials)
**Dim:** A 579: 98.18 (92.80 pp) × 11.80 × 3.90
A 577: 98.80 (92.80 pp) × 11.80 × 3.95
**A:** 2/100-mm Mod. 1953 DP (I × 2)—4/40-mm AA (I × 4)—70 mines
**Electron Equipt:** Radar: 1/. . . nav., 1/SGR-105, 1/SGR-103, 2/M 45
**M:** 6 Maybach (A 577: Mercedes-Benz 839Db) diesels (A 577: electric drive); 2 props; 11,400 hp (A 577: 11,000)
**Electric:** 2,250 hp **Fuel:** 334 tons **Range:** 2,500/16
**Man:** 98 tot. (accommodations for 40 officers, 170 men)

REMARKS: A 579, transferred on 15-11-76, was built as a Type 401 small combatant tender, but was employed as a training ship in the West German Navy; she continues in this latter role in the Turkish Navy. A 577, transferred on 30-9-82, is configured as a Type 402 mine countermeasures support ship and had been in reserve since 1968. A 579 has CP props. Both have 2 M4 directors for the 100-mm guns.

◆ **2 tenders, ex-West German Angeln-class cargo ships** Bldr: Ateliers et Chantiers de Bretagne, Nantes, France

| | Laid down | L | In serv. |
|---|---|---|---|
| A 586 ÜLKÜ (ex-*Angeln,* ex-*Borée*) | 17-5-54 | 9-10-54 | 20-1-55 |
| A 588 UMURBEY (ex-*Dithmarschen,* ex-*Hebé*) | 20-10-54 | 7-5-55 | 17-11-55 |

**D:** 2,998 tons (4,089 fl) **S:** 19 kts **Dim:** 90.53 (84.5 pp) × 13.32 × 6.2
**A:** 2/20-mm AA (I × 2) **M:** 2 SEMT-Pielstick 6-cyl. diesels; 1 prop; 3,000 hp
**Electric:** 335 kw **Range:** 3,660/15 **Man:** 57 tot.

**Umurbey (A 588)** H. Ehlers, 5-86

REMARKS: Former French cargo ships acquired for the West German Navy on 27-11-59 and 19-12-59, respectively. A 586 was transferred to Turkey on 28-3-72 and A 588 on 6-10-76. A 586 is used as a patrol-boat tender and A 588 as a submarine tender. A 588's displacement is 3,098 tons (4,189 fl). Cargo: A 586, 2,665 tons; A 588, 2,670 tons. Six 2.5-ton derricks, three holds.

◆ **1 ex-U.S. Portunus-class patrol-boat tender** Bldr: Bethlehem Steel, Hingham, Mass.

| | Laid down | L | In serv. |
|---|---|---|---|
| A 581 ONARAN (ex-*Alecto,* AGP 14, ex-LST 977) | 12-12-44 | 15-1-45 | 8-2-45 |

**Onaran (A 581)** G. Arra, 1971

**D:** 4,100 tons (fl) **S:** 11.6 kts **Dim:** 99.98 × 15.24 × 3.4
**A:** 8/40-mm AA (IV × 2)—8/20-mm AA (I × 8)
**Electron Equipt:** Radar: 1/SPS-5
**M:** 2 G.M. 12-278A diesels; 2 props; 1,800 hp **Electric:** 500 kw
**Fuel:** 590 tons **Range:** 9,000/9 **Man:** 291 tot.

REMARKS: Transferred in 11-52. Retains bow doors. Superstructure enlarged after transfer.

◆ **1 ex-U.S. Achelous-class submarine tender** Bldr: Bethlehem Steel, Hingham, Mass.

| | Laid down | L | In serv. |
|---|---|---|---|
| A 582 BAŞARAN (ex-*Patroclus,* ARL 19, ex-LST 955) | 22-9-44 | 22-10-44 | 13-11-44 |

**Başaran (A 582)** H. Ehlers, 4-86

REMARKS: Former landing-craft repair ship. Data as for *Onaran,* above, except: **Electric:** 420 kw; **Fuel:** 621 tons. Has less superstructure than *Onaran.*

◆ **1 ex-U.S. Dixie-class destroyer tender** Bldr: Tampa SB, Tampa, Fla.

| | Laid down | L | In serv. |
|---|---|---|---|
| A 576 DERYA (ex-*Piedmont,* AD 17) | 1-12-41 | 7-12-42 | 5-1-44 |

**D:** 9,450 tons light (17,190 fl) **S:** 18 kts **Dim:** 161.70 × 22.33 × 7.80
**A:** 5/20-mm AA (I × 5) **Electron Equipt:** Radar: 1/LN-66, 1/SPS-10
**M:** 2 sets GT; 2 props; 11,000 hp **Electric:** 3,600 kw
**Fuel:** 3,680 tons **Range:** 12,200/12 **Man:** approx. 1,200 tot.

**AUXILIARY SHIPS** *(continued)*

**Derya (A 576)** H. Ehlers, 3-84

REMARKS: Transferred by sale 18-10-82 and recommissioned 29-3-83. Modernized early 1960s under FRAM program to serve as repair tender to missile-equipped ships. Extensive workshops, spares capacity. Two 20-ton cranes. Small helicopter deck.

NOTE: U.S. *Aegir*-class submarine tender *Donatan* (A 583, ex-*Anthedon,* AS 24) stricken 1985. Submarine tender *Erkin* (A 590, ex-*Ege*) suffered engineroom fire in 1986, scrapped in Spain 12-86, having only been in Turkish Navy service since 1983.

◆ **1 ex-U.S. AN 103-class net tender** Bldr: Krögerwerft, Rendsburg, West Germany

| | Laid down | L | In serv. |
|---|---|---|---|
| P 305 AG 5 (ex-AN 104) | 1960 | 20-10-60 | 25-2-61 |

**AG 5 (P 305)** L. & L. Van Ginderen, 5-87

**D:** 680 tons (975 fl) **S:** 12.8 kts **Dim:** 52.50 (48.5 hull; 44.6 pp) × 10.6 × 3.70
**A:** 1/40-mm AA—3/20-mm AA (I × 3) **Electron Equipt:** Radar: 1/Decca . . .
**M:** 1 M.A.N. G7V 40/60 diesel; 1 prop; 1,470 hp
**Range:** 6,500/10.8 **Fuel:** 134 tons **Man:** 5 officers, 45 men

REMARKS: Sister to the net layer *Thetis* in the Greek Navy. Built with U.S. Offshore Procurement funds. Carries 1,600 rds 40-mm, 25,200 rds 20-mm ammunition.

◆ **1 ex-U.S. AN 93-class net tender** Bldr: Bethlehem Steel, Staten Island, N.Y.

| | L | In serv. |
|---|---|---|
| P 306 AG 6 (ex-*Cerberus,* ex-AN 93) | 5-52 | 10-11-52 |

**AG 6 (P 306)** H. Ehlers, 5-84

**D:** 780 tons (902 fl) **S:** 12.8 kts **Dim:** 50.29 (44.5 pp) × 10.20 × 3.2
**A:** 1/76.2-mm DP—4/20-mm AA (I × 4)
**M:** 2 G.M. 8-268A diesels, electric drive; 1 prop; 1,500 hp
**Range:** 5,200/12 **Man:** 48 tot.

REMARKS: Prototype of a class also built in France and Italy. Transferred to the Netherlands in 12-52 and returned 17-9-70; transferred to Turkey the same day.

◆ **1 ex-U.S. Aloe-class net tender** Bldr: Marietta Mfg. Co., Pt. Pleasant, W. Va.

| | Laid down | L | In serv. |
|---|---|---|---|
| P 304 AG 4 (ex-*Larch,* AN 21, ex-YN 16) | 18-10-40 | 2-7-41 | 13-12-41 |

**AG 4 (P 304)** L. & L. Van Ginderen, 6-82

**D:** 560 tons (805 fl) **S:** 12.5 kts **Dim:** 49.73 (44.5 wl) × 9.3 × 3.56
**A:** 1/76.2-mm DP—4/20-mm AA (I × 4)
**M:** 2 Alco 538-6 diesels, electric drive; 1 prop; 620 hp
**Electric:** 120 kw **Fuel:** 80 tons **Man:** 48 tot.

REMARKS: Transferred in 5-46.

◆ **1 ex-British "Bar"-class net tender** Bldr: Blyth DD & SB Co., U.K.

| | Laid down | L | In serv. |
|---|---|---|---|
| P 301 AG 1 (ex-*Barbarian*) | 10-6-37 | 21-10-37 | 16-4-38 |

**D:** 750 tons (1,000 fl) **S:** 11.7 kts **Dim:** 52.96 × 9.8 × 4.62
**A:** 1/76.2-mm DP **M:** 2 diesels; 1 prop: . . . hp
**Range:** 3,100/10 **Man:** 32 tot. **Fuel:** 214 tons

REMARKS: Transferred in 1947. Sisters *AG 2* (ex-*Barbette*) and *AG 3* (ex-*Barfair*) were stricken in 1975. Original reciprocating steam propulsion plant replaced by diesels in the 1960s.

◆ **1 ex-U.S. Bluebird-class submarine-rescue ship** Bldr: Charleston SB & DD Co., Charleston, S.C.

| | Laid down | L | In serv. |
|---|---|---|---|
| A 584 KURTARAN (ex-*Bluebird,* ASR 19, ex-*Yurok,* ATF 164) | 23-6-45 | 15-2-46 | 28-5-46 |

**Kurtaran (A 584)** H. Ehlers, 5-82

**D:** 1,294 tons (1,760 fl) **S:** 16 kts **Dim:** 62.48 (59.44) × 12.19 × 4.88
**A:** 1/76.2-mm DP **M:** 4 G.M. 12-278A diesels, electric drive; 1 prop; 3,000 hp
**Electric:** 600 kw **Fuel:** 300 tons **Man:** 100 tot.

REMARKS: Begun as an *Achomawi*-class fleet tug, but altered while under construction, wooden fenders adding .5 meter to the beam. Carries McCann rescue diving bell and four marker buoys. Transferred on 15-8-50.

◆ **1 ex-U.S. Chanticleer-class submarine-rescue ship** Bldr: Moore SB & DD Co., Oakland, Cal.

| | Laid down | L | In serv. |
|---|---|---|---|
| A 585 AKIN (ex-*Greenlet,* ASR 10) | 15-10-41 | 12-7-42 | 29-5-43 |

**D:** 1,770 tons (2,321 fl) **S:** 15 kts **Dim:** 76.61 (73.15 pp) × 12.8 × 4.52
**A:** 1/40-mm AA—4/20-mm AA (II × 2) **Electron Equipt:** Radar: 1/Decca . . .
**M:** 4 Alco 539 diesels, electric drive; 1 prop; 3,000 hp
**Electric:** 460 kw **Fuel:** 235 tons **Man:** 85 tot.

REMARKS: Loaned on 12-6-70 and purchased outright on 15-2-73. Carries McCann rescue diving bell and four marker buoys.

AUXILIARY SHIPS *(continued)*

**Akin (A 585)** H. Ehlers, 4-86

◆ **1 ex-U.S. Diver-class salvage ship** Bldr: Basalt Rock Co., Napa, Cal.

| | Laid down | L | In serv. |
|---|---|---|---|
| A 589 IŞIN (ex-*Safeguard,* ARS 25) | 5-6-43 | 20-11-43 | 31-10-44 |

**Işin (A 589)** H. Ehlers, 5-83

**D:** 1,480 tons (1,970 fl) **S:** 14.8 kts **Dim:** 65.08 (63.09 pp) × 12.5 × 4.0
**A:** 2/20-mm AA (I × 2) **Electric:** 460 kw **Fuel:** 300 tons **Man:** 97 tot.
**M:** 4 Cooper-Bessemer GSB-8 diesels, electric drive; 2 props; 3,000 hp

REMARKS: Purchased on 28-9-79. Wooden fenders add .6 meter to beam.

NOTE: The training ship *Savarona* (A 578, ev-*Gunes Dil*), badly damaged by fire in 1979, was stricken in 1987.

◆ **1 ex-U.S. Cherokee-class fleet tug** Bldr: United Eng. Co., Alameda, Cal.

| | Laid down | L | In serv. |
|---|---|---|---|
| A 587 GAZAL (ex-*Sioux,* ATF 75) | 14-2-42 | 27-5-42 | 6-12-42 |

**Gazal (A 587)** L. & L. Van Ginderen, 8-86

**D:** 1,235 tons (1,675 fl) **S:** 16.5 kts **Dim:** 62.48 (59.44 pp) × 11.73 × 4.67
**A:** 1/76.2-mm DP—2/20-mm AA (I × 2) **Electric:** 260 kw **Fuel:** 300 tons
**M:** 4 G.M. 12-278 diesels, electric drive; 1 prop; 3,000 hp **Man:** 85 tot.

REMARKS: Transferred on 30-10-72 and purchased outright on 15-8-73. Can be used for salvage. Similar to submarine rescue ship *Kurtaran* (A 584).

◆ **3 small yard oilers** Bldr: Taskizak NDY, Istanbul (In serv. 1970s)

Y 1231 H 500 Y 1232 H 501 Y 1233 H 503

**D:** 300 tons **S:** 11 kts **Dim:** 33.6 × 8.5 × 1.8
**M:** 1 G.M. 6-71 diesel; 1 prop; 225 hp **Cargo:** 150 tons

◆ **1 small water tanker** Bldr: Gölçük Naval DY (L: 1979)

Y 1240

**D:** 850 tons (fl) **S:** 10 kts **Dim:** 51.8 (46.8 pp) × 8.1 × . . .
**M:** 1 diesel; 1 prop; 480 hp **Cargo:** 530 dwt

◆ **2 Van-class water tankers** Bldr: Gölçük NSY, 1969–70

Y 1208 VAN Y 1209 ULABAT

**Ulabat (Y 1209)** H. Ehlers, 5-86

**D:** 900 tons (1,250 fl) **S:** 10 kts **Dim:** 53.1 × 9.0 × 3.0
**A:** 1/20-mm AA **M:** 1 diesel; 1 prop; 650 hp **Cargo:** 700 tons
**Electron Equipt:** Radar: 1/Decca 707

◆ **1 ex-German FW 1-class water tanker** Bldr: Schichau, Bremerhaven

| | Laid down | L | In serv. |
|---|---|---|---|
| Y 1217 SÖGÜT (ex-FW 2) | 5-4-63 | 3-9-63 | 4-1-64 |

**Sögüt (Y 1217)** H. Ehlers, 11-85

**D:** 598 tons (647 fl) **S:** 9.5 kts **Dim:** 44.03 (41.4 pp) × 7.8 × 2.63
**M:** 1 MWM 12-cyl. diesel; 1 prop; 230 hp **Electric:** 130 kVA
**Fuel:** 15 tons **Range:** 2,150/9 **Man:** 12 tot.

REMARKS: Transferred on 3-12-75. Cargo: 343 tons of fresh water.

◆ **4 Pinar-3-class small water tenders** Bldr: Taskizak NDY, Istanbul

Y 1213 PINAR 3 Y 1214 PINAR 4 Y 1215 PINAR 5 Y 1216 PINAR 6

**Pinar 4 (Y 1214)** H. Ehlers, 4-86

AUXILIARY SHIPS *(continued)*

**D:** 300 tons **S:** 11 kts **Dim:** 33.6 × 8.5 × 1.8
**M:** 1 G.M. 6-71 diesel; 1 prop; 225 hp **Cargo:** 150 tons

◆ **1 small water tanker** Bldr: Gölçük NDY (In serv. 1958)

Y 1212 PINAR 2

**Pinar 2 (Y 1212)** H. Ehlers, 6-86

**D:** 1,300 tons (fl) **S:** 10 kts **Dim:** 51.0 × 8.5 × . . .
**A:** none **M:** 1 diesel; 1 prop; . . . hp **Man:** 11 tot.

◆ **1 small water tanker** Bldr: Meentzer SY, Neth. (In serv. 1938)

Y 1211 PINAR 1 (ex-*Istanbul*)

**Pinar 1 (Y 1211)** H. Ehlers, 4-80

**D:** 490 tons (fl) **S:** . . . **Dim:** . . . × . . . × . . . **M:** 1 diesel; 240 hp

◆ **1 small water tanker**

Y 1210 MEHMET KAPTAN

REMARKS: No data available.

◆ **4 Kanarya-class cargo lighters** Bldr: Taskizak NDY, Istanbul (In serv. 1972–74)

Y 1155 KANARYA Y 1156 SARKÖY Y 1157 KARADENIZ ERIGLI Y 1165 ECEABAT

**Sarköy (Y 1156)** H. Ehlers, 5-84

**D:** 823 tons (fl) **S:** 10 kts **Dim:** 50.7 (47.4 pp) × 8.0 × . . .
**A:** 1/20-mm AA **M:** 1 diesel; 1 prop; 1,440 hp

REMARKS: 500 dwt. Moulded depth: 3.6 m.

◆ **13 Salopa-class stores lighters**

Y 1031–1043 SALOPA 1–13

REMARKS: No data available.

**Salopa 2 (Y 1032)** H. Ehlers, 7-84

◆ **6 Layter-class lighters**

Y 1011–1016 LAYTER 1–6

**Layter 2 (Y 1012)** H. Ehlers, 4-86

◆ **7 pontoon barges**

Y 1061–1067 PANTON 1–7

NOTE: Transport ferries *Kilya* (Y 1166) and *Tuzla* (Y 1168) were stricken 1987, along with the smaller ferry *Gonca* (Y 1099).

◆ **3 personnel ferries**

Y 1096 IŞÇI TASITI 1 Y 1097 IŞÇI TASITI 2 Y 1110 IŞÇI TASITI 3

◆ **2 Cephane-class ammunition lighters**

Y 1195 CEPHANE 2 Y 1197 CEPHANE 3

REMARKS: Sister *Cephane* 1 (Y 1194) stricken 1987.

◆ **1 small ammunition lighter**

Y 1196 BEKIRDERE

◆ **7 small danbuoy layers**

Y 1141–1147 SAMANDIRA MOTORU 1–7

◆ **1 training craft, tender to Naval Academy**

Y 1100 TOROS

**Toros (Y 1100)** H. Ehlers, 12-79

REMARKS: Small coastal passenger-cargo type. No data available.

◆ **1 training craft, former minelayer** Bldr: Gölçük NSY (In serv. 1938)

Y 1101 ATAK

**D:** 350 tons (500 fl) **S:** 13 kts **Dim:** 44.0 × 7.4 × 3.6
**M:** 1 Atlas-Polar diesel; 1 prop; 1,025 hp

REMARKS: Tender to Naval Academy.

AUXILIARY SHIPS *(continued)*

**Atak (Y 1101)** H. Ehlers, 5-82

◆ **3 ex-U.S. non-self-propelled gate craft** Bldr: Weaver SY, Orange, Texas (In serv. 1960–61)

Y 1201 (ex-YNG 45) Y 1202 (ex-YNG 46) Y 1203 (ex-YNG 47)

**D:** 325 tons (fl) **Dim:** 33.5 × 10.4 × 1.5

◆ **2 ex-U.S. APL 41-class barracks barges**

| | Bldr | L |
|---|---|---|
| Y 1204 Naşit Öngeren (ex-APL 47) | Puget Sound Bridge & Dredge, Seattle, Wash. | 5-1-45 |
| Y 1205 Binbaşi Metin Sülüs (ex-APL 53) | Tampa SB, Tampa, Fla. | 3-3-45 |

**D:** 2,660 tons (fl) **Dim:** 79.6 × 14.99 × 2.59
**Electric:** 300 kw **Man:** 650 tot.

Remarks: Y 1204 was leased in 10-72, Y 1205 in 12-74. Non-self propelled. Lease extended 1982.

◆ **2 Öncü-class coastal tugs** Bldr: Gölçük NSY (In serv. 1953)

Y 1120 Öncü Y 1124 Önder

**Öncü (Y 1120)** L. & L. Van Ginderen, 1980

**D:** 500 tons **S:** 12 kts **Dim:** 40.0 × 9.1 × 4.0
**A:** 2/20-mm AA (I × 2) **M:** diesel; 1 prop; . . . hp

Note: A new tug, Y 1123, was completed at Taskizak 25-7-85, no data available.

◆ **1 coastal tug**

Y 1122 Kuvvet (In serv. 2-62)

**D:** 390 tons **S:** . . . **Dim:** 32.1 × 7.9 × 3.6

Remarks: Built in Turkey with U.S. Grant Aid funds.

◆ **1 ex-U.S. Army 320-design small harbor tug**

Y 1134 Ersen Bayrak

**D:** 30 tons **S:** 9 kts **Dim:** 13.8 × 3.9 × 1.6 **M:** 1 diesel; 1 prop; 175 hp

Remarks: Transferred in 6-71.

◆ **2 Turkish-designed harbor tugs** Bldr: Denizcilik, Bancusi (In serv. 1976)

Y 1130 Güven Y 1132 Atil

**D:** 300 grt **S:** . . . **Dim:** 32.8 × 8.9 × . . . **M:** diesels; 250 hp

Remarks: Sister *Doğanarslan* (Y 1133) stricken 1984.

◆ **3 ex-U.S. small harbor tugs**

Y 1117 Sonduren (ex-YTL 751) Y 1229 Kudret (ex-YTL . . .)
Y 1121 Yedekci (ex-YTL 155)

**Kudret (Y 1229)**—alongside APL 41-class barracks barge H. Ehlers, 5-81

**D:** 100 tons (120 fl) **S:** 12 kts **Dim:** 21.34 × 5.89 × 2.21
**M:** 1 Atlas diesel; 1 prop; 500 hp **Fuel:** 18 tons

Remarks: Transferred in 5-54 and 11-57.

◆ **18 push tugs** (do not have Y-pendants)

Katir 1–18

Note: The last ex-U.S. *Balao*-class submarine used as a battery-charging craft, *Ceryan Bolu IV* (ex-*Preveze,* ex-*Guitarro* (SS 363)), was scrapped 12-86 in Spain.

◆ **4 miscellaneous torpedo retrievers**

Y1051 Torpito Tender 1 Y1102 Ikmal
Y1052 Takip Y1125 Darica

Remarks: Y1125, launched 27-7-87 at Taskizak NDY, is described as a tug-torpedo retriever.

◆ **1 ex-U.S. floating crane** Bldr: Odenback SB, Rochester, N.Y. (In serv. 14-8-51)

Y 1023 Algarna III (ex-YD 185)

**D:** 1,200 tons (fl) **Dim:** 36.6 × 13.7 × 2.7

Remarks: Transferred in 9-63.

◆ **3 miscellaneous floating cranes**—no data available, except Y 1022: 600-ton lift

Y 1021 Algarna I Y 1022 Levent Y 1024 Turgut Alp

◆ **1 dredge**

Y 1029 Tarak—D: 200 tons

◆ **26 miscellaneous service launches**—no data available

Y 1181 through Y 1193, Y 1198, Y 1199 Mavna 1 through Mavna 15

**Mavna 10 (Y 1190)** H. Ehlers, 5-84

◆ **1 ex-U.S. ARD-12-class floating dry dock** Bldr: Pacific Bridge, Alameda, Cal.

Y 1087 (ex-ARD-12) (In serv. 10-43)

**Dim:** 149.86 × 24.69 × 1.73 (light) **Lift capacity:** 3,500 tons

Remarks: Launched in 1943 and loaned in 11-71.

## AUXILIARY SHIPS *(continued)*

◆ **6 miscellaneous floating dry docks**

| | |
|---|---|
| Y 1081 (16,000-ton capacity) | Y 1084 (4,500-ton capacity) |
| Y 1082 (12,000-ton capacity) | Y 1085 (400-ton capacity) |
| Y 1083 (2,500-ton capacity) | Y 1086 (3,000-ton capacity) |

Remarks: Y 1083 was built in Turkey in 1958 with U.S. funds; **Dim:** 116.5 × 26.4 × 9.0 max. These docks are named in sequence *Havuz I* to *Havuz VI*. A new 3-section floating dry dock was completed late in 1980.

◆ **4 miscellaneous officers' yachts**

Acar Halas Ersan Gül

**Acar** H. Ehlers, 7-83

Remarks: Assigned pendant numbers between Y 1088–1092, but do not bear them.

MINISTRY OF THE INTERIOR
COAST GUARD
*(SAHIL GÜVENLIK)*

Personnel (1985): approx. 1,000 total, headed by a Turkish Navy rear admiral

## PATROL BOATS

◆ **0 (+10) 200T class** Bldr: Taskizak NDY, Istanbul

SG 75–84 (In serv. 1988–. . .)

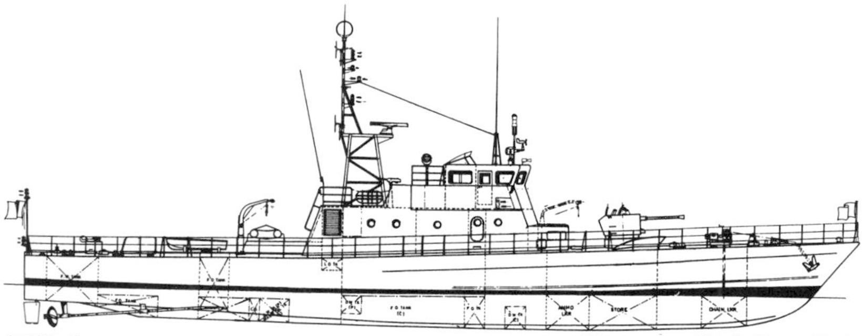

**200T class** Singapore SB & Eng., Ltd.

**D:** 200 tons (fl) **S:** 26 kts **Dim:** 44.90 (42.30 pp) × 7.00 × 2.59
**A:** 1/40-mm AA—2/7.62-mm mg (II × 1)
**Electron Equipt:** Radar: 1/Decca . . .
**M:** 2 MTU 12V538 TB82 diesels; 2 props; 4,430 hp
**Range:** 2,400/14 **Fuel:** 30 tons **Endurance:** 7 days
**Electric:** 260 kw (2 × 100 kw; 1 × 60 kw) **Man:** 5 officers, 27 men

Remarks: Successor construction to SG 71 class. License-built from Singapore Shipbuilding and Eng., Ltd., to a design by Lürssen, Vegesack. Sisters to Indian Coast Guard *Tara Bai,* etc. Ordered 1986. May have more powerful engines than listed, as one source gives design speed as 34 kts.

◆ **4 SG 71 class** Bldr: Taskizak NDY

| | |
|---|---|
| SG 71 (In serv.: 25-7-85) | SG 73 (L: . . .) |
| SG 72 (L: 25-7-85) | SG 74 (L: 24-7-87) |

**D:** 210 tons (fl) **S:** 40 kts (35 sust.)
**Dim:** 36.60 × 8.60 × 1.90 (3.20 moulded depth)
**A:** 1/40-mm AA—2/7.62-mm mg (I × 2)
**Electron Equipt:** Radar: 1/Decca . . .
**M:** 3 SACM (UNI) AGO V16 CSHR diesels; 3 CP props; 12,000 hp
**Range:** 450/35; 1,000/. . . **Man:** 24 tot.

Remarks: Lengthened version of SAR-33 class, with longer superstructure.

◆ **10 SAR-33 class** Bldrs: J 61: Abeking & Rasmussen, Lemwerder, West Germany; others: Taskizak NDY, Istanbul (In serv. 1978–84)

SG 61–SG 70 (ex-J 61–J 69)

**SG 65** A. Scrimali, 1986

**D:** 150 tons (170 fl) **S:** 40 kts **Dim:** 33.00 (29.50 wl) × 8.60 × 1.85
**A:** 1/40-mm AA—2/76.2-mm mg (I × 2)
**Electron Equipt:** Radar: 1/Decca . . .
**M:** 3 SACM-AGO V16CSHR diesels; 3 CP props; 12,000 hp
**Electric:** 300 kw **Fuel:** 18 tons **Range:** 450/35; 1,000/. . . **Man:** 23 tot.

Remarks: SG 61 was launched on 12-12-77 and SG 62 in 7-78; SG 65 through SG 67 in service 30-7-81. Wedge-shaped hull design of remarkable seaworthiness and steadiness at high speeds in heavy weather. Turkey also built fourteen units of this class for Libya. The same design can accommodate guns of up to 76-mm bore, missiles, and a propulsion plant of up to twice the power of the above. The 40-mm AA is in a Mk 3 mount.

◆ **14 AB 25 class** Bldr: Taskizak NDY, Istanbul, 1972–78

SG 21–34

**SG 33** A. Scrimali, 1986

**D:** 170 tons (fl) **S:** 22 kts **Dim:** 40.24 × 6.4 × 1.65
**A:** 2/40-mm AA (I × 2)—2/12.7-mm mg (I × 2)
**M:** 2 SACM-AGO V16 CSHR diesels; 2 props; 4,800 hp; 2 cruise diesels; 300 hp

Remarks: Twelve sisters are operated by the Turkish Navy. Some have one 40-mm AA aft and one 20-mm AA forward. Built with French assistance.

◆ **8 German KW 15 class** Bldr: Schweers, Bardenfleth, West Germany, 1961–62

SG 12–SG 16 SG 18–SG 20

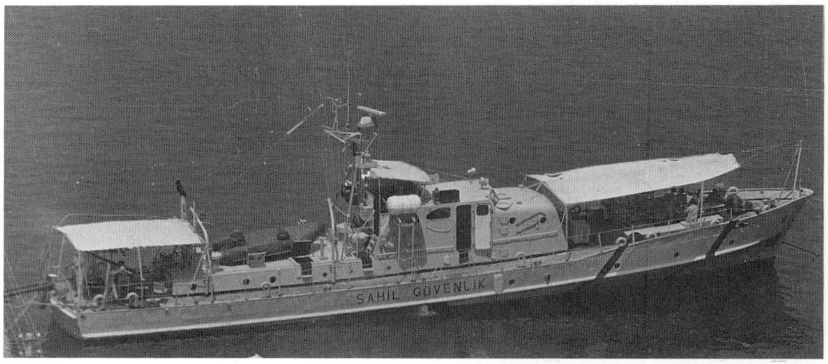

**SG 16** H. Ehlers, 7-86

**TURKEY** *(continued)*
**PATROL BOATS** *(continued)*

**D:** 59.5 tons (69.6 fl) **S:** 25 kts **Dim:** 28.9 × 4.7 × 1.42
**A:** 1/40-mm AA—2/20-mm (I × 2)
**M:** 2 MTU 12-cyl. diesels; 2 props; 2,000 hp
**Fuel:** 8 tons
**Range:** 1,500/19
**Man:** 15 tot.

◆ **10 ex-U.S. 45-ft Picket Boat class**

SG 41–50

**SG 44** H. Ehlers, 6-86

**D:** 15 tons (fl) **S:** 18 kts **Dim:** 13.94 × 4.17 × 1.10
**A:** 2/7.62-mm mg (II × 1)
**M:** 2 Gray Marine 64 HN 9 diesels; 2 props; 450 hp
**Range:** 200/18
**Man:** 5 tot.

REMARKS: Wooden-hulled. Transferred during the 1950s.

◆ **2 miscellaneous small transports**

SG 101 SG 104

**SG 104** H. Ehlers, 4-84

REMARKS: SG 104 built 1978, Hasköy SY, Istanbul. SG 101 is smaller and older.

◆ **4 miscellaneous launches**

SG 51–54

◆ **1 utility craft**

SG 102

◆ **1 dispatch boat**

SG 103

**SG 103** H. Ehlers, 10-85

# TURKS AND CAICOS

**BRITISH PROTECTORATE**

POLICE

## PATROL CRAFT

◆ **1 Dagger class** Bldr: Fairey Marine, Cowes (In serv. 6-86)

**Turks & Caicos Dagger** Fairey, 6-86

**D:** 12 tons (fl) **S:** 24 kts **Dim:** 12.2 × . . . × . . .
**A:** small arms
**Electron Equipt:** Radar: 1/Decca . . .
**M:** 2 Perkins T.6354.4 diesels; 2 props; 440 hp
**Man:** 6 tot.

REMARKS: GRP construction. Based at Grand Turk.

# TUVALU

## PATROL BOATS

◆ **0 (+1) ASI 315 Class** Bldr: Australian SB Ind. (WA), PTY, South Coogie, W. Australia (In serv. 2-91)

**D:** 165 tons (fl) **S:** 21 kts **Dim:** 31.50 (28.60 wl) × 8.10 × 2.12
**A:** small arms **Electron Equipt:** Radar: 1/Furuno 1011
**M:** 2 Caterpillar 3516 diesels; 2 props; 2,820 hp (2,400 sust.)
**Electric:** 116 kw (2 × 50 kw; 1 × 16 kw) **Endurance:** 8–10 days
**Range:** 2,500/12 **Fuel:** 27.9 tons **Man:** 3 officers, 14 men

REMARKS: Under consideration 1987 as part of the Australian foreign aid "Pacific Patrol Boat" program. Would be thirteenth unit in series. Extensive navigational, communications, and direction-finding equipment suite is standard.

# U.S.S.R.

## Union of Soviet Socialist Republics

PERSONNEL (1987): 465,000 total men and women, including 83,700 officers, 37,200 career enlisted petty officers, and 344,100 men and women conscripts. These personnel are apportioned: 189,000 seagoing, 84,200 assigned to the Ministry of Defense and other central command staff organizations, 137,800 shore establishment (including roughly 15,000 Naval Infantry), and 54,000 to Naval Aviation. Some 6,000 naval personnel are assigned to the KGB-subordinated Maritime Border Guard, including seagoing and shore personnel. Of some 100,000 civilian employees, 30,000 serve in seagoing positions, chiefly in the Naval Auxiliary Service. The period of service for naval conscripts is three years.

MERCHANT MARINE (1986): 6,726 ships—24,560,888 grt
(tankers: 412 ships—4,086,850 grt)

DISPOSITION OF THE SOVIET FLEET ON 1-10-87
(Submarines and major surface combatants)

| | Northern | Baltic | Black Sea | Pacific | Total |
|---|---|---|---|---|---|
| Strategic Subs: | | | | | |
| a) nuclear: | | | | | |
| Typhoon, Delta-I, -II, -III, -IV, Yankee-I, -II, Hotel-III | 35 | | | 25 | 60 |
| b) conventional: | | | | | |
| Golf-II, -III | 1 | 6 | | 7 | 14 |
| Cruise-Missile Subs: | | | | | |
| a) nuclear: | | | | | |
| Oscar, Papa, Charlie-I, -II, Echo-II, Yankee | 26 | | | 23 | 49 |
| b) conventional: | | | | | |
| Juliett | 6 | 3 | 2 | 3 | 14 |
| Torpedo Submarines: | | | | | |
| a) nuclear: | | | | | |
| Akula, Mike, Sierra, Alfa, Victor-I, -II, -III, November, Yankee conv., Echo | 51 | | | 28 | 79 |
| b) conventional: | | | | | |
| Kilo, Tango, Foxtrot, Zulu, Romeo, Whiskey | 40 | 31 | 27 | 37 | 135 |
| Aviation Ships: Kiev, Moskva | | | 3 | 2 | 5 |
| Guided-Missile Cruisers: Kirov, Kara, Kresta-I, -II, Kynda, Slava | 9 | 2 | 6 | 12 | 29 |
| Gun-cruisers: Sverdlov, Mod. Sverdlov (some reserve) | 2 | 2 | 3 | 4 | 11 |
| Guided-Missile Frigates and Destroyers: Udaloy, Sovremennyy, Mod. Kashin, Kashin, Provornyy, Krivak-I, -II, -III, Kanin, SAM Kotlin, Kildin, Mod. Kildin (some reserve) | 18 | 11 | 13 | 12 | 54 |
| Gun Destroyers: Mod. Kotlin, Kotlin, Mod. Skoryy, Skoryy (some reserve) | 3 | 5 | 9 | 9 | 26 |
| Frigates: Krivak-I, -II, -III | 8 | 8 | 8 | 13 | 37 |
| Small Frigates: Koni, Riga, Grisha-I, -II, -III, -IV, -V, Petya-I, -II, -III, Mirka-I, -II, Parchim | 46 | 30 | 41 | 43 | 160 |

WARSHIPS IN SERVICE OR UNDER CONSTRUCTION AS OF 1 JANUARY 1988
(*Note:* Many of the older units are in reserve, but the numbers are not available; thus, this table differs from others in the book, which list only *active* units.)

**◆ 3 (+3) V/STOL carriers**

| | L | Tons | Main armament |
|---|---|---|---|
| 0 (+2) LEONID BREZHNEV | 1985– | 65,000 (?) | 60 aircraft . . . |
| 3 (+1) KIEV | 1972–82 | 36,000 | Missile launchers, guns, helicopters, VTOL aircraft |

**◆ 429 (+ . . .) submarines** Tons (surfaced)

*77 (+ . . .) ballistic-missile* (62 nuclear):

| | | Tons (surfaced) | |
|---|---|---|---|
| 5 (+2 or 3) TYPHOON (nuclear) | 1980– . . . | 18,500 | 20/SS-N-20, . . ./TT |
| 4 (+ . . .) DELTA-IV (nuclear) | 1984– . . . | 10,800 | 16/SS-N-23, 6/TT |
| 14 DELTA-III (nuclear) | 1975– | 10,600 | 16/SS-N-18, 6/TT |
| 4 DELTA-II (nuclear) | 1975 | 10,550 | 16/SS-N-8, 6/TT |
| 18 DELTA-I (nuclear) | 1972–75 | 9,000 | 12/SS-N-8, 6/TT |
| 1 YANKEE-II (nuclear) | 1967? | 7,900 | 16/SS-N-6, 6/TT |
| 16 YANKEE-I (nuclear) | 1967–74 | 7,900 | 16/SS-N-6, 6/TT |
| 1 HOTEL-III (nuclear) | 1965 | 5,500 | 3/SS-N-8, 8/TT |
| 1 GOLF-III (diesel) | 1958–61 | 2,900 | 3/SS-N-8, 10/TT |
| 13 GOLF-II (diesel) | 1958–61 | 2,900 | 3/SS-N-5, 10/TT |

*61 (+ . . .) cruise-missile attack* (48 nuclear):

| | | | |
|---|---|---|---|
| 4 (+ . . .) OSCAR (nuclear) | 1980– | 11,500 | 24/SS-N-19, 8/TT |
| 1 PAPA (nuclear) | 1970 | 6,400 | 10/SS-N-9, 8/TT |
| 6 CHARLIE-II (nuclear) | 1973– | 4,300 | 8/SS-N-7 or 9, 6/TT |
| 9 CHARLIE-I (nuclear) | 1968–72 | 4,000 | 8/SS-N-7, 6/TT |
| 1 YANKEE (nuclear) | . . . | . . . | 12/SS-N-24, 6/TT |
| 26 ECHO-II (nuclear) | 1960–68 | 5,000 | 8/SS-N-3 or SS-N-12, 10/TT |
| 14 JULIETT (diesel) | 1961–68 | 3,000 | 4/SS-N-23, 10/TT |

*202 (+ . . .) attack:* (72 nuclear)

| | | | |
|---|---|---|---|
| 2 (+ . . .) AKULA (nuclear) | 1984– | 7,500 | 6/TT |
| 2 (+ . . .) SIERRA (nuclear) | 1983– | 6,000 | 6/TT |
| 1 MIKE (nuclear) | 1983 | 4,400 | 6/TT |
| 6 ALFA (nuclear) | 1972–81 | 2,800 | 6/TT |
| 21 (+ . . .) VICTOR-III (nuclear) | 1978– . . . | 4,900 | 6/TT |
| 7 VICTOR-II (nuclear) | 1972–77 | 4,500 | 6/TT |
| 16 VICTOR-I (nuclear) | 1967–74 | 4,300 | 6/TT |
| 2 (+14) YANKEE (nuclear) | 1967–74 | 7,900 | 6/TT |
| 3 ECHO (nuclear) | 1960–68 | 4,500 | 10/TT |
| 12 NOVEMBER (nuclear) | 1958–62 | 4,500 | 12/TT |
| 1 (+ . . .) BELUGA (diesel) | 1986 | 2,000 | . . . |
| 14 (+ . . .) KILO (diesel) | 1980– | 2,500 | 6/TT |
| 22 TANGO (diesel) | 1972–82 | 3,000 | 10/TT |
| 45 FOXTROT (diesel) | 1957–74 | 1,950 | 10/TT |
| 48 WHISKEY (diesel) | 1949–57 | 1,050 | 6/TT |

*17 auxiliary submarines:*

| | | | |
|---|---|---|---|
| 1 UNIFORM (nuclear) | 1982 | . . . | . . . |
| 1 X RAY | 1983 | . . . | . . . |
| 2 INDIA (diesel) | 1978–79 | 3,900 | . . . |
| 4 BRAVO (diesel) | 1968–72 | 2,400 | 6/TT |
| 1 LIMA (diesel) | 1979 | 2,000 | . . . |
| 1 MOD. ECHO (nuclear) | 1960–68 | 5,000 | 10/TT |
| 3 ZULU-IV (diesel) | 1952–57 | 1,900 | 10/TT |
| 1 HOTEL (nuclear) | 1954–61 | 5,000 | 10/TT |
| 3 MOD. GOLF (diesel) | 1958–61 | 2,300 | 10/TT |

**◆ 42 (+3) cruisers**

*2 helicopter:*

| | | | |
|---|---|---|---|
| 2 MOSKVA | 1964–66 | 14,500 | 2/SA-N-3, 1/SUW-N-1, 14 helicopters* |

*28 (+3) guided-missile:*

| | | | |
|---|---|---|---|
| 2 (+2) KIROV (nuclear) | 1977–81 | 24,000 | 20/SS-N-19, 2/SS-N-14, 12/SA-N-6, 2/SA-N-4, 2/100-mm DP, 10/TT, 3/helos |
| 2 (+1) SLAVA | 1979– | 10,000 | 16/SS-N-12, . . ./SA-N-6, 2/SA-N-4, 2/130-mm* |
| 6 KARA | 1971–78 | 8,200 | 8/SS-N-14, 2/SA-N-3, 4/SA-N-4, 4/76.2-mm DP, 10/TT, 1 helo |
| 10 KRESTA-II | 1967–76 | 6,200 | 8/SS-N-14, 2/SA-N-3, 4/57-mm, 10/TT, 1/helo* |
| 4 KRESTA-I | 1965–66 | 6,200 | 4/SS-N-3, 2/SA-N-1, 4/57-mm, 10/TT, 1/helo* |
| 4 KYNDA | 1961–65 | 4,400 | 8/SS-N-3, 1/SA-N-1, 4/76.2-mm DP, 6/TT* |

*11 conventional (some in reserve):*

| | | | |
|---|---|---|---|
| 2 MOD. SVERDLOV | 1950–54 | 12,900 | 1/SA-N-4, 6 or 9/152-mm, 12/100-mm DP |
| 9 SVERDLOV | 1950–60 | 12,900 | 12/152-mm, 12/100-mm DP |

**◆ 69 (+ . . .) destroyers**

*52 guided-missile:*

| | | | |
|---|---|---|---|
| 8 (+2 . . .) UDALOY | 1978– | 6,700 | 8/SS-N-14, 8/SA-N-9, 2/100-mm DP, 4/30-mm AA, 8/533-mm TT, 2/helos, mines* |

**WARSHIPS** *(continued)*

| | L | Tons | Main armament |
|---|---|---|---|
| 7 (+2 . . .) SOVREMENNYY | 1978– | 6,700 | 8/SS-N-22, 2/SA-N-7, 4/130-mm DP, 4/30-mm AA, 4/533-mm TT, 1/helo, mines* |
| 6 MOD. KASHIN | 1963–72 | 3,950 | 4/SS-N-2C, 2/SA-N-1, 4/76.2-mm DP, 5/TT* |
| 12 KASHIN | 1963–72 | 3,750 | 2/SA-N-1, 4/76.2-mm DP, 5/TT* |
| 8 KANIN | 1958–60 | 3,700 | 1/SA-N-1, 8/57-mm, 10/TT* |
| 3 MOD. KILDIN | 1958 | 2,800 | 4/SS-N-2C, 4/76.2-mm DP, 16/45- or 57-mm AA, 4/TT* |
| 8 SAM KOTLIN | 1955–57 | 2,700 | 1/SA-N-1, 2/130-mm DP, 12/45-mm AA, 5/TT* |
| *17 conventional (some in reserve):* | | | |
| 17 KOTLIN AND MOD. KOTLIN | 1954–57 | 2,600 | 4/130-mm DP, 16/45-mm AA, 4 or 8/25-mm AA, 5 or 10/TT* |
| ◆ **198 (+ . . .) frigates** (some in reserve) | | | |
| 4 (+. . .) KRIVAK-III | 1983– | 3,000 | 1/SA-N-4, 1/100-mm, 8 TT*, helo |
| 32 KRIVAK-I, -II | 1970– | 3,100 | 4/SS-N-14, 2/SA-N-4, 2/100-mm or 4/76.2-mm DP, 8/TT* |
| 5 (+7) PARCHIM | 1986–. . . | 800 | 1/76.2, 4/TT* |
| 1 KONI | 1978 | 1,600 | 1/SA-N-4, 4/76.2-mm DP* |
| 7 (+. . .) GRISHA-V | 1984 | 950 | 1/SA-N-4, 1/76.2-mm DP, 4/TT* |
| 31 GRISHA-III | 1975–84 | 950 | 1/SA-N-4, 2/57-mm DP, 4/TT* |
| 12 GRISHA-II | 1974–76 | 950 | 4/57-mm DP, 4/TT* |
| 15 GRISHA-I | 1967–73 | 950 | 1/SA-N-4, 2/57-mm DP, 4/TT* |
| 18 PETYA-II | 1964–69 | 950 | 4/76.2-mm DP, 10/TT* |
| 7 PETYA-I | 1960–63 | 950 | 2 or 4/76.2-mm DP, 5/TT* |
| 11 MOD. PETYA-I | 1960–63 | 950 | 4/76.2-mm DP, 5/TT* |
| 1 MOD. PETYA-II | 1964–69 | 950 | 4/76.2-mm DP, 5/TT* |
| 18 MIRKA-I, II | 1964–66 | 950 | 4/76.2-mm DP, 5 or 10/TT* |
| 36 RIGA | 1951–56 | 1,260 | 3/100-mm DP, 2 or 3/TT* |
| ◆ **176 (+ . . .) corvettes** (some in reserve) | | | |
| 20 (+. . .) TARANTUL-I, -II, -III | 1979– | 480 | 4/SS-N-2C, 1/76.2-mm DP |
| 27 (+. . .) NANUCHKA-I, -III | 1969– | 770 | 6/SS-N-9, 1/SA-N-4, 1/76.2 DP or 2/57-mm AA |
| 22 (+. . .) PAUK | 1979– | 480 | 1/76.2-mm DP, 4/TT* |
| 57 POTI | 1960–67 | 500 | 2/57-mm DP, 2-4/TT* |
| 6 IVAN SUSANIN | 1975–81 | 3,400 | 2/76.2-mm DP |
| 1 PURGA | 1955 | 4,500 | 4/100-mm DP |
| 13 SORUM | 1974–. . . | 1,210 | 4/30-mm AA |
| 19 T-58 | 1956–61 | 725 | 4/57-mm DP* |
| 11 T-43 | 1947–57 | 500 | 4/37-mm AA* |

* Indicates additional ASW weapons

◆ **126 guided-missile and torpedo units**

◆ **over 251 patrol boats and craft**

◆ **over 300 mine warfare ships and craft**

◆ **75 amphibious warfare ships**

A note to ship class names: The class names used herein are for the most part those used by NATO. Until 1973, Soviet combatants usually did not display names, and thus NATO had devised a series of nicknames based on Russian words (combatants: geographical place names beginning with "K"; small combatants: insects; mine warfare types: diminutives of personal names; amphibious warfare types: reptiles; auxiliaries: rivers). Subsequently, the policy has been to use the actual name of the first ship of a class, as in the West. Often that name is not immediately available, and thus a three-part *interim* nickname is applied. The first syllable denotes the *fleet area* where the class was first identified (BAL = Baltic, BLK = Black Sea, etc), the second syllable indicates the *type* of ship (COM = combatant, SUB = submarine, AUX = auxiliary, etc.), and the third syllable is a roman numeral indicating the order of discovery within a category. Thus, "BAL-COM-III" would be the third new major combatant discovered under construction in the Baltic. As actual names are learned, they replace the temporary nickname. The Soviet Navy itself uses a series of Project Numbers to identify its ships, as in the West German Navy; these are generally not available.

The Soviet Navy has a number of unique ship-type classifications; these are translated, where applicable, in the individual class entries.

## WEAPONS AND SYSTEMS

NOTE: All weapon and sensor designations that follow are those assigned by NATO, except where indicated; the Soviet designations are generally unavailable.

### A. MISSILES

◆ **Ballistic Missiles**

NOTE: All have liquid-fuel propulsion, except the SS-N-17 and SS-N-20, which have solid-fuel propulsion.

**SS-N-5** Serb (Soviet R5) (1963)

Range: 900 nautical miles. Single nuclear warhead of about 800 kilotons. Can be launched while submerged. Range has been increased from its original 700 nautical miles. Obsolescent but still significant, due to basing of 6 Golf-II in the Baltic and 7 in the Western Pacific. CEP (Circular Error Probable): 3,000 m

weight: 16,500 kg — range: 900 nm
length: 13 m — guidance: inertial
diameter: 1.2 m

**SS-N-6** (1968)

Range: Initially, 1,300 nautical miles. Nuclear warhead of about 1 megaton in Mod. 1, 2; Mod. 3 has two re-entry vehicles. Fitted in Yankee-I-class nuclear submarines. Can be launched while submerged. 1,850-m CEP.

weight: 18,900 kg — range: Mod. 1—1,300 n.m. (one warhead)
length: 10 m — Mod. 2—1,600 n.m. (one warhead)
diameter: 1.8 m — Mod. 3—1,600 n.m. (two warheads)
guidance: inertial

**SS-N-8** Sawfly (1973/77)

Single nuclear warhead of about 1.5 megatons. Fitted in Delta-I and -II nuclear submarines and in the Golf-III experimental submarine. 1,500-m CEP.

weight: 30,000 kg — range: Mod. 1—4,240 n.m. (one 1.2-megaton warhead)
length: 13 m — Mod. 2—4,950 n.m. (two 800-kiloton warheads)
diameter: . . . — guidance: inertial

**SS-N-17** Snipe (1977)

Single 1-megaton nuclear warhead. First Soviet ballistic missile with solid-fuel propulsion. Aboard the one Yankee-II-class submarine. One 800-kiloton or two 500-kiloton warheads.

weight: . . . — range: 2,000 n.m.
length: 10.6 m — guidance: inertial

**SS-N-18** Stingray (Soviet RSM 50) (1978)

Two-stage missile employed on Delta-III class. Three versions: Mod. 1 with three 200-kiloton (KT) re-entry vehicles (RV), Mod. 2 with one 450-KT RV, and Mod. 3 with 7 Multiple Independent Re-entry Vehicles of 200 KT. CEP estimated at 1,100 m.

weight: 34,000 kg — range: Mod. 1—3,530 n.m.
length: 13.6 m — Mod. 2—4,350 n.m.
guidance: inertial — Mod. 3—3,530 n.m.

**SS-N-20** Sturgeon (Soviet RSM 52) (1983)

Three-stage weapon with 6–9 100-KT multiple independent re-entry vehicle (MIRV) payload. Range over 4,000 nautical miles. Used by the Typhoon class. CEP estimated at 600 m.

weight: 60,000 kg — range: 4,300 n.m.
length: . . . — guidance: inertial

**SS-N-23** Skiff (1985)

Three-stage weapon with 7 multiple-independent re-entry-vehicle (MIRV) payload. Range about 5,000 n.m. Used by Delta-IV class. Weight: Approx. 40,000 kg.

◆ **Surface-to-Surface Cruise Missiles**

NOTE: Liquid-fuel propulsion, except for SS-N-7 and 9, which have solid-propellant engines.

**SS-N-2 A and B** Styx (1958/1964)

Maximum range: 25 nautical miles. Practical range: 16 nautical miles. Liquid-propulsion rocket with solid booster. I-band active radar guidance in targeting, with infrared or radar homing in the most recent version, SS-N-2B. Altitude can be preset at 100, 150, 200, 250, or 300 m. 500-kg conventional warhead. Installed in Osa-I and Osa-II guided-missile boats. The SS-N-2B has folding wings.

**SS-N-2C** (formerly SS-N-11) (1967)

Maximum range: 45 nautical miles. Weight: 2,500 kg; length: 5.8 m; span: 2.8 m. Radar or infrared terminal-homing versions. 500-kg warhead. In order to employ fully the over-the-horizon maximum range of the SS-N-2C, it is necessary to have a forward observer. The SS-N-2C is carried by the destroyers of the Modified Kashin and Modified Kildin classes, by the Tarantul guided-missile corvettes, and by the exported Nanuchka-II-class guided-missile corvettes. Widely exported. Length: 6.5 m.

**SS-N-3** Shaddock (A: 1962; B: 1962, C: 1960)

Produced in three versions: SS-N-3A for launch by submarines (Juliett and Echo-II classes), with inertial guidance, mid-course correction, and active radar terminal homing; SS-N-3B for Kynda- and Kresta-I-class cruisers, with similar guidance; and SS-N-3C with inertial-only guidance, possibly still in use from submarines. SS-N-3 is a variant of the SS-C-1 coast-defense missile.

weight: 5,400 kg — span: 5 m
warhead: 1,000 kg — range: SS-N-3A/B: 250 n.m.
length: 10.2 m (SS-N-3C: 111.8 m) — SS-N-3C: 400 n.m.

**SS-N-7** Siren (1970)

Maximum range: 35 nautical miles. Conventional warhead. Launched while submerged. Charlie-I-class nuclear-powered attack submarines have eight per ship. 500-kg conventional or nuclear warhead. Weight: 2,900 kg; Length: 7 m.

**WEAPONS AND SYSTEMS** *(continued)*

**SS-N-9** (1969)

Inertial guidance, and active radar homing to the target. 500-kg conventional or nuclear warhead. Installed in Nanuchka-I- and -III-class guided-missile corvettes and the Sarancha-class hydrofoil. A submerged-launch version is available for the Charlie-I- and II- and Papa-class submarines. Weight: 3,300 kg; Length: 8.8 m.

**SS-N-12** Sandbox (1973)

Maximum range: 300 nautical miles. 1,000-kg conventional or nuclear warhead. Replacing the SS-N-3 on Echo-II-class submarines and is aboard the *Kiev* class and *Slava*-class cruisers.

**SS-N-19** (1971)

Maximum range: 300 nautical miles. Conventional or nuclear warhead. Evidently has improved performance characteristics over the SS-N-12 and is carried by the *Kirov*-class cruisers and the Oscar-class nuclear-powered submarine (from which it is submerged-launched).

**SS-N-21** (1986?)

A torpedo-tube-launched weapon similar in concept to the U.S. Tomahawk. Submerged-launched intended for submarines, but also developed for surface (SSC-4) and air launch (AS 15 Kent) as well. Range estimated at 1,600 n.m. Speed: Mach 0.7. Probably has a nuclear warhead.

**SS-N-22** (1981)

A Mach 2.5 successor to the SS-N-9, but not, to date, used by submarines. Reportedly flies at "sea-skimming" altitudes to a range of 55–68 n.m. Carried by the *Sovremennyy*-class destroyers and Tarantul-III-class missile boats. Active radar homing.

**SS-NX-24** (1988?)

New, large cruise missile. Used in single Yankee conversion and probably intended for a new class. May be a strategic, vice antiship, weapon. Range: circa 2,200 n.m.

◆ **Surface-to-Air Missiles**

**SA-N-1** Goa (1961)

Twin-launcher. Range: 20,000 m, interception altitude: 300 to 50,000 feet. Guidance: radar/command. Conventional warhead, 60 kg. Fitted on Kynda and Kresta-I cruisers, as well as on Kashin, Kanin, and Kotlin destroyers. Also has a surface-to-surface capability. Uses Peel Group radar directors. Weight: 400 kg. Sixteen per magazine.

**SA-N-3** Goblet (1967)

Twin launcher. Range: 30,000 m, interception altitude: 300 to 80,000 feet. Guidance: radar/command via Head Lights-series radar director. Conventional warhead, 60 kg. Fitted on Kresta-II and Kara cruisers as well as the *Moskva*-class helicopter cruisers. An improved version has a range of 55,000 m and is on the *Kiev*. Goblet has an anti-surface target capability. Weight: 550 kg. Mach 2.5.

**SA-N-4** Gecko (1969)

Twin launcher, retracting into a cylindrical magazine holding 20 missiles on 4 rings of 5. Range: 9,000 m, interception altitude: 30 to 10,000 feet. Guidance: radar/command via Pop Group radar director. Conventional warhead. Fitted in Kara and *Kirov* cruisers, two *Sverdlov* cruisers, Krivak guided-missile frigates, Grisha- and Nanuchka-class corvettes, the Sarancha hydrofoil, the landing ship *Ivan Rogov,* and the replenishment ship *Berezina*. Can be used against surface targets. Weight: 190 kg. Launcher designation: ZIF-122.

**SA-N-5** Grail (1974)

Naval version of SA-7 Grail. Fitted on Pauk- and Tarantul-class corvettes, some Osa-class guided-missile patrol boats, landing ships, some minesweepers, and many auxiliaries. Employs either a 4-missile launch rack with operator, or is shoulder-launched, singly. IR-homing, visually aimed. 4.4-km range, 7,800-ft altitude. Weighs 15 kg with launch tube.

**SA-N-6** Grumble (1981)

A navalized version of the land-based SA-10. Range 80,000 m or greater, altitudes to 90,000 ft. Employs vertical launch from 8-missile rotating magazines and reportedly uses track-via-missile guidance via the Top Dome radar system. Carried by the *Kirov* and *Slava*-class cruisers. Probably also has an antiship capability.

**SA-N-7** Gadfly (1981)

A navalized version of the land-based SA-11, employing single-armed launchers. Twenty missiles per magazine. Mach 3 weapon with 28,000-m range (3,000 minimum) and usable against targets from 100- to 46,000-ft. altitude. Operational on the *Sovremennyy*-class destroyers and the trials destroyer *Provornyy*. Guidance via Front Dome radar tracker/illuminators. Probably has an antiship capability.

**SA-N-8** Gremlin (1986?)

A navalized version of the SA-14, the successor to the SA-7 Grail. Uses the same 4-position manned launcher or shoulder launcher. Head-on targeting capability and, possibly, greater range than SA-N-5, from which it is virtually indistinguishable while in the launch tube.

**SA-N-9**

A new vertically launched, short-range system, probably intended as a successor to SA-N-4. To be carried in groups of 8 in 2-m-diameter launch cylinders aboard the *Udaloy*-class destroyers, and to be fitted in cruiser *Frunze,* carrier *Novorossiysk* and other new construction. Range estimated at 15–16 km and altitude at 40–60,000 ft. Uses Cross Sword radar directors.

◆ **Air-to-Surface Missiles** (naval use only)

**AS 2** Kipper (1961)

Range: 100 nautical miles. Turbojet propulsion. Inertial guidance or automatic pilot with radar homing head. 1,000-kg conventional or nuclear warhead. Launched from Badger-C and -G aircraft. Weight: 4,200 kg.

**AS 4** Kitchen (Soviet *Burya*) (1967)

Range: 170 nautical miles. 1,000-kg conventional or nuclear warhead. Inertial guidance with radar-terminal homing. Mach 3.5. In service on Backfire-B and Blinder-B aircraft. Weight: 6,500 kg.

**AS 5** Kelt (1965)

Range: 100 nautical miles. Liquid-fueled rocket propulsion. Inertial or autopilot guidance with J-band radar terminal homing. Conventional and nuclear warheads. In service on Badger-C and -G aircraft. Weight: 4,700 kg.

**AS 6** Kingfish (1970)

Range: 150–250 nautical miles. Mach 2.5–3.5. 500-kg conventional or nuclear warhead. In service on Badger-C and -G aircraft, two on each. Weight: 4,900 kg.

**AS 7** Kerry (Soviet *Grom*) (late 1970s)

Range: 6 nautical miles. Mach 1. Tactical weapon. Solid-fuel propulsion. Pencil-beam radar terminal homing. 100-kg conventional warhead. Used on Forger aircraft.

**AS 9** Kyle (late 1970s)

Range: 60 nautical miles. Anti-radar missile. Turbojet propulsion; Mach 3.0. Passive homing on electromagnetic radiation. 150-kg conventional warhead. In use on Badger, Backfire, and Fitter-C and Fitter-D aircraft.

**AS 10** Karen (1980)

Range: 6 nautical miles. Mach 1.0. Solid propulsion. Electro-optical guidance. Conventional warhead of 100 kg. Carried by Fitter-D.

**AS 15** Kent (1986)

Air-launched version of the SS-N-21. Strategic weapon carried by Soviet Air Force Bear-H and Blackjack bombers.

NOTE: The AS 12 Kegler, AS 13, and AS 14 Kedge are tactical missiles used by land-based aircraft.

**B. GUNS**

**152-mm dual-purpose**

Fitted in triple turrets on *Sverdlov*-class cruisers. Individual barrels can be loaded and elevated separately. Limited AA capability, using barrage fire.

barrel length: 57 calibers
muzzle velocity: 915 m/sec
altitude arc: −5° to +50°
maximum rate of fire: 4 to 5 rds/min/barrel
maximum range: 27,000 m
effective range: 18,000 m
projectile weight: 50 kg
fire control: optical directors with two 8-m base range finders and associated Top Bow ranging radars, or local control using 8-m base range finders in each turret and Egg Cup ranging radars atop upper turrets.

**130-mm twin, new model dual-purpose**

Fully automatic, for surface and aerial targets. Fitted on *Sovremennyy*-class destroyers, *Slava*-class cruisers, and *Frunze*. May be mechanically triaxially stabilized. Water-cooled.

barrel length: 70 calibers
muzzle velocity: . . .
arc of elevation: −15° to +85°
max. rate of fire: 65 rds/min per mount
max. range: approx. 28,000 m
fire-control: Kite Screech radar director or local control by on-mount operator

**130-mm twin dual-purpose**

Semi-automatic. Fitted on Kotlin and SAM Kotlin destroyers. Mechanically triaxially stabilized. Twin mount with electric or hydraulic-electric pointing system.

barrel length: 58 calibers
muzzle velocity: 900 m/sec
arc of elevation: −5° to +80°
maximum rate of fire: 10 rounds/min/barrel
maximum range, surface target: 28,000 m
effective range, surface target: 16,000 to 18,000 m
maximum vertical range: 13,000 m
projectile weight: 27 kg
fire control: stabilized Wasp Head director, with Sun Visor tracking radar. Egg Cup ranging radar on most mounts.

**130-mm twin dual-purpose**

Semi-automatic type fitted on *Skoryy*-class destroyers. Obsolescent.

barrel length: 50 calibers
muzzle velocity: 875 m/sec
arc of elevation: −5° to +45°
maximum rate of fire: 10 rounds/min/barrel
maximum range: 24,000 m
effective range: 14,000 to 15,000 m
projectile weight: 27 kg

**WEAPONS AND SYSTEMS** *(continued)*

fire control: Four Eyes optical director and associated Top Bow or Post Lamp radars.

**100-mm twin dual-purpose**

Mechanically triaxially stabilized mounts installed on *Sverdlov*-class cruisers.

barrel length: 50 calibers
weight: approx. 40 tons
muzzle velocity: 900 m/sec
effective range, surface target: 10,000 to 12,000 m
maximum range, AA fire: 15,000 m
maximum range, surface target: 20,000 m
effective range, AA fire: 8,000 to 9,000 m
projectile weight: 16 kg
arc of elevation: −15° to 85°
maximum rate of fire: 15 rounds/min/barrel
fire control: Round Top stabilized director with Sun Visor tracking radar and/or associated Top Bow or Post Lamp radars: Egg Cup ranging radar on each mount (being removed) for local surface control.

**100-mm automatic dual-purpose**

A single-barreled, water-cooled gun in an enclosed mounting found on the cruiser *Kirov, Udaloy*-class destroyers, and Krivak-II- and -III-class frigates.

rate of fire: 80 rounds/min
maximum theoretical range: 15,000 m
maximum effective range: 8,000 m
fire control: Kite Screech radar director or local, on-mount control

**100-mm single dual-purpose**

Gun mount with a shield. Installed on Riga frigates, and Don-class submarine tenders. Obsolescent.

barrel length: 56 calibers
muzzle velocity: 850 m/sec
arc of elevation: −5° to +40°
projectile weight: 13.5 kg
maximum rate of fire: 15 rounds/min
maximum range: 16,000 m
effective range: 10,000 m
fire control: stabilized Wasp Head director fitted with Sun Visor radar

**85-mm AA**

Twin-barreled gun mount on unmodified *Skoryy* destroyers. Obsolescent.

barrel length: 50 calibers
muzzle velocity: 850 m/sec
arc of elevation: −5° to +70°
maximum rate of fire: 10 rounds/min/barrel
maximum range, surface target: 15,000 m
effective range, surface target: 8,000 to 9,000 m
practical maximum range, AA fire: 6,000 m
fire control: Cylinder Head optical director (no radar)

**76.2-mm twin dual-purpose**

Installed on Kara and Kynda cruisers, Kashin destroyers and Krivak-I, Koni, Petya, and Mirka frigates, *Smol'nyy*-class training ships, and *Ivan Susanin*-class icebreakers.

barrel length: 60 calibers
muzzle velocity: 900 m/sec
maximum rate of fire: 45 rounds/min/barrel
arc of elevation: +80°
maximum range, AA fire: 10,000 m
effective range, AA fire: 6,000 to 7,000 m
projectile weight: 16 kg
fire control: Owl Screech or Hawk Screech radar director

**76.2-mm single automatic dual-purpose**

Fully automatic, with on-mount crew. Carried by Grisha-V light frigates, Nanuchka-III, Pauk, and Tarantul-class corvettes, Matka-class guided-missile hydrofoils, and the Slepen-class patrol boat.

rate of fire: 120 rounds/min
theoretical maximum range against surface target: 14,000 m
practical range against aerial target: 6,000 to 7,000 m
fire control: Bass Tilt radar director or local, on-mount control

**57-mm twin automatic dual-purpose** (Soviet ZIF-72)

This equipment, which is entirely automatic from the ammunition-handling room to the gun mount, is installed on *Moskva,* Kresta-I and Kresta-II cruisers, Poti and Grisha corvettes, Nanuchka-I guided-missile corvettes, Turya torpedo boats, Ropucha LSTs, Ugra submarine tenders, and the replenishment ship *Berezina.* Now removed from *Boris Chilikin* replenishment ships and *Manych*-class water tankers. Water-cooling system.

barrel length: 70 calibers
maximum rate of fire: 120 rounds/min/barrel
maximum effective vertical range: 5,000 to 6,000 m
fire control: Muff Cob or Bass Tilt radar directors

**57-mm dual-purpose**

Single-barrel gun mount (Mod. *Skoryy* destroyers and some Sasha minesweepers), twin-barrel (several classes), and quadruple on Kanin and Kildin destroyers; in the latter case the guns are mounted in superimposed pairs. Has surface-fire capability.

barrel length: 70 calibers
muzzle velocity: 900 to 1,000 m/sec
arc of elevation: 0° to +90°
maximum rate of fire: 150 rounds/min/gun
effective vertical range: 4,500 m
fire control: Hawk Screech or Muff Cob radar directors

**Twin 57-mm ZIF-72 DP mounts on oiler Berezina**

**Twin 76.2-mm DP mounts on a Krivak-I**

**Quadruple SS-N-3b trainable launcher on a Kynda**

**Inclined, below-decks SS-N-19 launchers on Kirov**

**SS-N-3b/c Styx launcher on an Osa-II**

**SS-N-3b/c Styx launcher on a Mod. Kildin**

**Quadruple SS-N-22 launchers on Sovremennyy**

**Quadruple, trainable SS-N-14 launchers on Krivak-I and -II**

**WEAPONS AND SYSTEMS** *(continued)*

**Twin, elevatable SS-N-12 launchers on a Kiev-class carrier**

**Twin, fixed-elevation SS-N-12 launchers on Slava**

**Twin 130-mm DP mount on a Sovremennyy (SA-N-7 at left)**

**SS-N-2b/c Styx launchers on a Tarantul-II**

**SUW-N-1 launcher and missile on Moskva**

**RBU-1000 ASW rocket launcher on Sovremennyy**

**Raised SA-N-4 launcher on a Krivak (RBU-6000 ASW RL at left)**

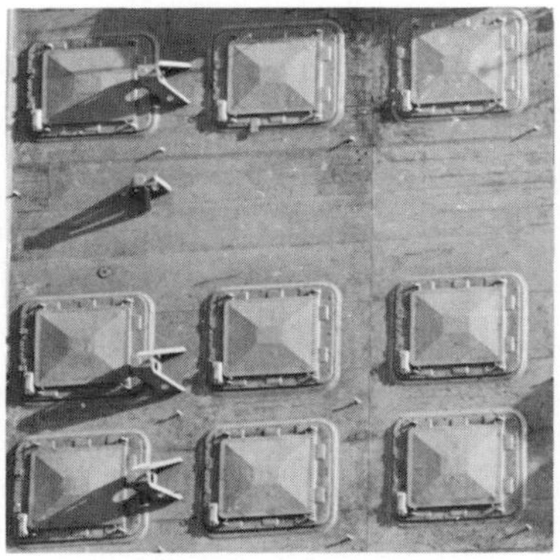

**SA-N-6 vertical-launch hatch covers on Kirov**

Vertical view of the amidships portion of Slava, showing the SA-N-6 installation, flanked by two twin-barreled chaff RL. The stack uptakes reveal the ship to have a combined gas turbine/gas turbine propulsion plant, with two cruise and four boost gas turbines.

WEAPONS AND SYSTEMS *(continued)*

**Twin, reloading SS-N-14 launcher on Kirov (SA-N-6 launchers at top)**

**Quadruple, fixed SS-N-14 launchers on Udaloy**

**RBU-6000 ASW rocket launchers on a Krivak**

**SA-N-3 launcher with Goblet missile on Moskva**

**Rotating SA-N-6 vertical launchers on Slava** (8 launchers/64 missiles)

**SA-N-7 single-arm launcher on Sovremennyy** (20 missiles per launcher)

**Forward four SA-N-9 vertical-launch positions on Udaloy** (8 missiles per launcher)

**Top Pair back-to-back early-warning/3-D antennas on Slava**

**Top Steer back-to-back early-warning/3-D antennas on Sovremennyy** (with three Palm Frond surface-search antennas and two Front Dome missile directors)

**Top Steer/Top Plate on Osmotritel'nyy**

**Front Door on the forward side of Slava's tower mast**

**Big Net early-warning radar antenna on a Kashin**

**Top Sail (right) and Head Net-C antennas on a Kresta-II**

**Strut Pair search antenna on Udaloy** (with three Palm Frond surface-search antennas)

**Top Plate on Admiral Zakharov** (above Round House TACAN antennas)

**Eye Bowl SS-N-14/missile-control radar directors on a Krivak**

WEAPONS AND SYSTEMS *(continued)*

**Kiev** 1. Top Sail 3-D radar 2. Top Knot TACAN radome with High Pole-B IFF transponder atop 3. Top Steer 3-D radar 4. Rum Tub ESM antennas 5. Bell Bash jammer antennas 6. Bell Thump jammer radome 7. Tee Plinth electro-optical device with conical Pert Spring radome just below it 8. Side Globe EW radomes

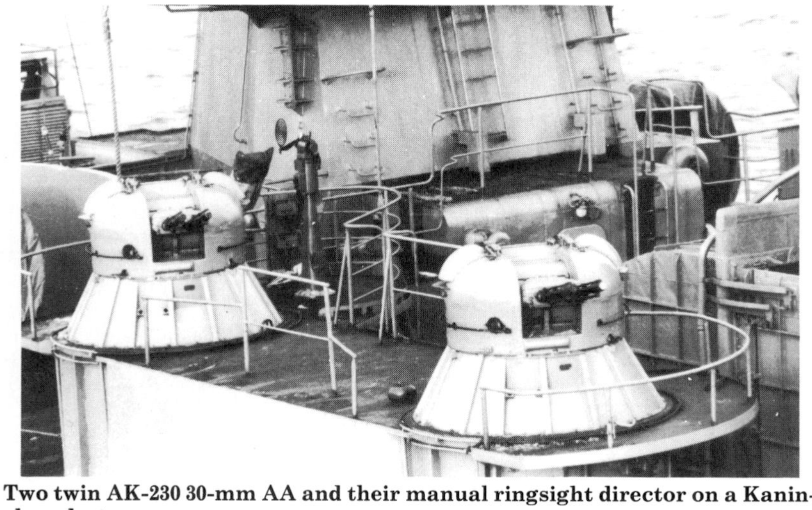

**Two twin AK-230 30-mm AA and their manual ringsight director on a Kanin-class destroyer**

**Pop Group SA-N-4 radar director on a Krivak**

**Peel Group radar director for SA-N-1, on a Kashin**

**Front Dome SA-N-7 radar director on Sovremennyy**

**Top Dome SA-N-6 radar director on Kirov**

**Cross Sword guidance radar on Admiral Spiridonov**

**76-mm DP gun on a Nanuchka-III corvette**

WEAPONS AND SYSTEMS *(continued)*

**Kite Screech gun director on Sovremennyy**

**SS-N-3 cruise-missile tubes in elevated, firing position on a Kresta-I missile cruiser. (Note electro-optical devices on bridge wings.)** U.S. Navy

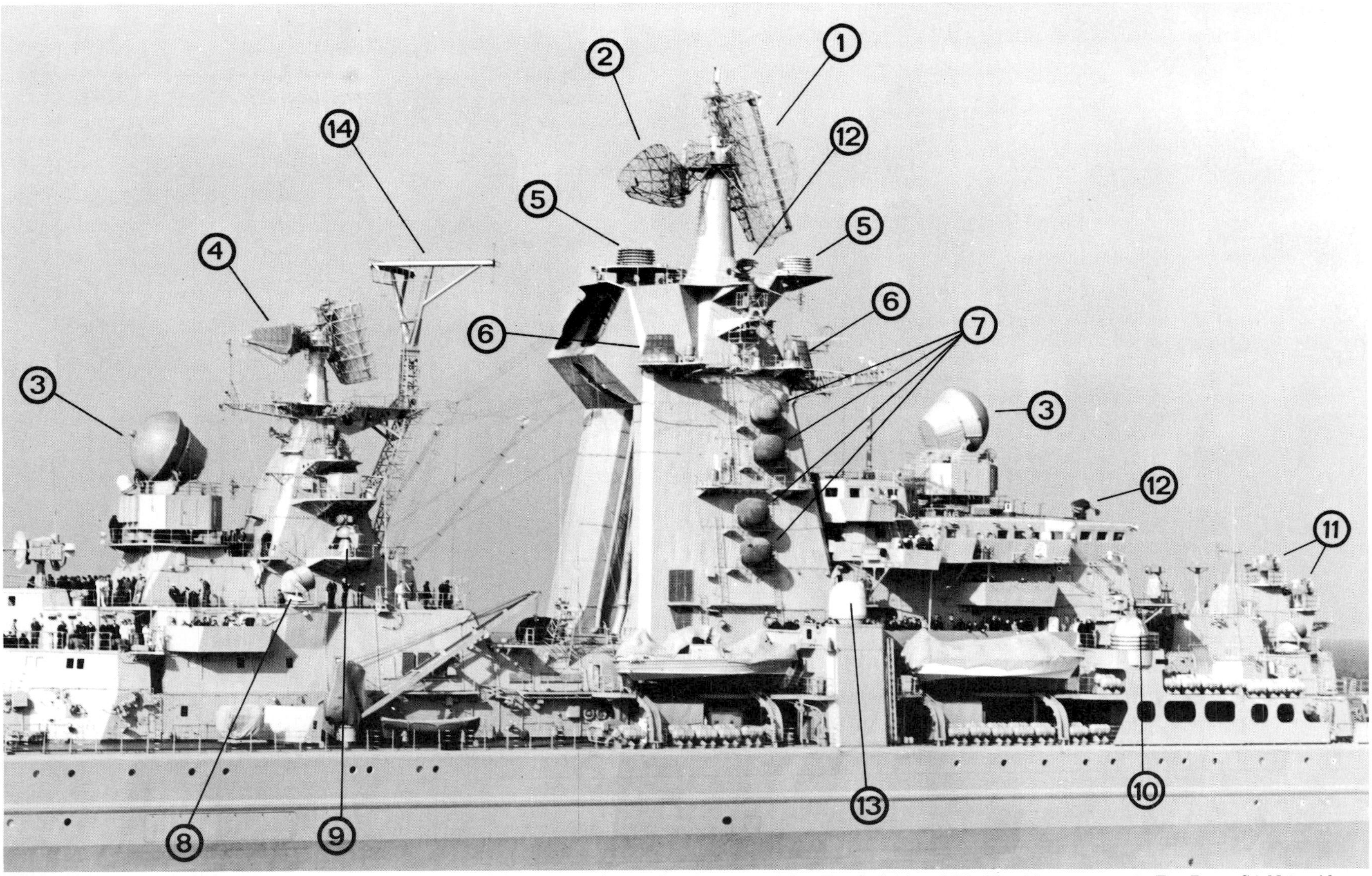


**Electronic antennas on the Kirov** 1. and 2. Top Pair 3-D long-range air-search radar, comprising Top Sail (1) and Big Net (2) antennas 3. Top Dome SA-N-6 guidance radar 4. Top Steer 3-D air-search radar 5. Round House helicopter-control/TACAN arrays 6. Rum Tub EW radomes 7. Side Globe EW radomes 8. Bass Tilt 30-mm gatling gun-control radar 9. Tin Man stabilized t.v./IR tracker 10. Bob Tail (in aluminized rubber protective cover) radionavigation sextant (with Pop Group radar for SA-N-4 SAM system just above) 11. Eye Bowl control radars for SS-N-14 ASW cruise missiles 12. Palm Frond surface-search radar 13. Punch Bow satellite communications antenna radome 14. Vee Tube-C long-range HF communications antenna array

**WEAPONS AND SYSTEMS** *(continued)*

A vertical view of the forward missile area on the *Kiev*-class *Novorossiysk,* showing the reloading tray arrangements of the 8 SS-N-3 SSM tubes and the blanking plate over where the circular SA-N-4 SAM magazine had been in her earlier sisters. The SUW-N-1 launcher, forward twin 76-mm DP gun mount, and forward SA-N-3 launcher are also visible. French Navy, 1983

Towed variable-depth sonar partially deployed from a Krivak-class frigate; the equipment has, in this instance, suffered a casualty to the hoist system.

Helicopter-type dipping sonar being deployed from a Mirka-II-class frigate. Note the circular covers over gas-turbine exhausts and the towed torpedo decoys on deck.

**45-mm AA**

Quadruple-barreled installations in SAM Kotlin, Kotlin, and one Mod. Kildin destroyers; single on some Sasha minesweepers. The quadruple-mounted guns are arranged in two superimposed pairs. Obsolescent.

barrel length: 85 calibers
muzzle velocity: 900 m/sec
arc of elevation: 0° to +90°
rate of fire: 300 rounds/min/mount
effective maximum vertical range: 4,000 m
fire control: Hawk Screech radar director (local in Sasha)

**37-mm Model 39 AA**

Installed in twin-barreled mounts in *Sverdlov* cruisers, *Skoryy* destroyers, Riga frigates, and T-43-class minesweepers. Obsolescent.

barrel length: 60 calibers
muzzle velocity: 900 m/sec
arc of elevation: 0° to +80°?
maximum rate of fire: 160 rounds/min/gun
fire control: on-mount lead-computing sights

**30-mm gatling gun AA**

This gun is in service on *Kiev*-class carriers, Kara and Kresta-II cruisers, and several other classes. It is installed in mounts similar to those of the 30-mm AA double-barreled automatic guns, and is designed to fire a great number of rounds at an extremely high rate in order to intercept a cruise missile at a relatively short distance. It has six 30-mm barrels. The often-used designation "ADMG-630" is a NATO nickname, not the Soviet name, which is probably AK-630.

minimum rate of fire: 3,000 rounds/min/mount
fire control: Bass Tilt radar director or remote visual director

**30-mm twin automatic AA**

Installed in a light mount on several classes of ships—cruisers, destroyers, guided-missile boats, supply ships, etc. Widely exported. Soviet designation: AK-230.

barrel length: 60 calibers
muzzle velocity: 1,000 m/sec
maximum rate of fire: 1,050 rounds/min/barrel
effective maximum range, AA fire: 2,500 to 3,000 m
fire control: Drum Tilt radar director or remote optical director.

**25-mm twin AA**

Found on many ships and made up of two superimposed guns.

barrel length: 60 calibers
muzzle velocity: 900 m/sec
maximum rate of fire: 150–200 rounds/min/barrel
fire control: on-mount ring sights

## C. ANTISUBMARINE WEAPONS

### ◆ missiles

**SUW-N-1 system** (1967)

Rocket-propelled weapon, installed in *Kiev*-class carriers and *Moskva*-class helicopter cruisers. Maximum range: 16 miles. Nuclear warhead. Unguided solid-fuel rocket based on land-based FROG-7 artillery rocket and often referred to as FRAS-1. There may be a variant with a homing torpedo payload.

**SS-N-14** Silex (1974)

A weapon conceptually resembling the Australian Ikara, using a solid-propelled aerodynamic cruise missile that drops a parachute-retarded homing torpedo. Maximum range: 30 nautical miles (4 nautical miles minimum). Carried by *Kirov,* Kara- and Kresta-class cruisers, and Krivak-I- and Krivak-II-class frigates. Can also be used against surface ships. Controlled by Head Lights or Eye Bowl radar directors.

**SS-N-15** (1972)

ASW missile similar to the U.S. Navy's SUBROC. Maximum range: 21.6 nautical miles. Nuclear warhead. Submerged-launched from submarine torpedo tubes. Carried by Victor I, II, and III, Alfa-, Mike-, Akula-, and Sierra-class nuclear-powered attack submarines. Also usable against surface targets. Uses a 533-mm torpedo tube.

**SS-N-16** (circa 1980)

Derived from the SS-N-15 system but using a homing torpedo payload in lieu of the nuclear depth bomb. Maximum range: 54 nautical miles. Would also be useful against surface targets. Probably requires the large-diameter 650-mm torpedo tube.

### ◆ rockets

NOTE: RBU = *Raketnaya Bombometnaya Ustanovka* (Rocket Depth-charge Launcher)

**RBU-6000** (Soviet designation)

Formerly MBU-2500 A. Made up of twelve barrels, approximately 1.600 m in length, arranged in a horseshoe and fired in paired sequence. Vertical automatic loading system, barrel by barrel. Can be trained and elevated. Range: 6,000 m. Installed in *Kiev*-class carriers, *Slava, Kirov, Moskva,* Kynda, Kresta-I, and Kresta-II cruisers, *Udaloy,* Kashin, and Kanin guided-missile destroyers, Krivak frigates, the smaller Mirka and Petya frigates, and the Poti and Grisha corvettes.

**RBU-2500** (Soviet designation)

Made up of two horizontal rows of eight barrels each, approximately 1.600 m in length, which can be trained and elevated. Manual reloading. Range: 2,500 m. 21-kg warhead. Carried by Kildin and Mod. Kildin, one SAM Kotlin, most Mod. Kotlin, and all Mod. *Skoryy* destroyers, Riga frigates, Petya-I frigates, and *Smol'nyy* training ships.

**RBU-1200** (Soviet designation)

Made up of two horizontal rows of short, superimposed barrels, three on two. Tube diameter: 0.250 m; length: 1.400 m; the 70-kg (34-kg warhead) rocket is somewhat shorter. Range: 1,200 m. Tubes elevate but are fixed in train. Installed in T 58- and Pauk-class corvettes, S.O.-1 patrol boats, and Natya-class minesweepers.

**RBU-1000** (Soviet designation)

Made up of six barrels arranged in two vertical rows of three and fired in order, with vertical automatic loading. Trainable. Tube diameter: approx. 0.300 m. Length: approx. 1.800 m. Range: 1,000 m. 90-kg rocket with 55-kg warhead. Installed in Kara, Kresta-I, and Kresta-II cruisers, *Sovremennyy* and Kashin destroyers, and the replenishment ship *Berezina.*

**RBU-600** (Soviet designation)

Made up of six barrels, 0.300 m in diameter and 1.500 in length, superimposed in two rows and fired simultaneously. Trainable. Range: 600 m. 90-kg rocket with 55-kg warhead. Used only in Mod. Kotlin destroyers.

### ◆ torpedoes

The Soviet Navy uses 533-mm anti-surface and ASW torpedoes, and short 400-mm ASW homing torpedoes. A larger, probable 650-mm-diameter weapon with a range of around 54 n.m. at 30 kts and about 22 n.m. at 45 kts is also reported to have entered service for submarines, using a wake-homing sensor. Nuclear warheads are apparently widely deployed, especially in submarines, as witness their presence

**WEAPONS AND SYSTEMS** *(continued)*

aboard the Whiskey-class submarine that ran aground near Karlskrona Naval Base in Sweden 10-81.

### ◆ Mines

The Soviet Union has a vast inventory of air-, surface-, and submarine-launched mines, using mechanical (contact), acoustic, magnetic, and, possibly, pressure fuzing. Specific details are unavailable for modern systems.

## D. RADARS

NOTE: Designations are NATO code names.

### ◆ Navigation

The most widely used are the I-band Neptune, Ball End, various Don types, and Spin Trough. Don-Kay was placed on most large ships in the 1970s, until it was succeeded by the I-band Palm Frond. Kivach 3 is used on recent small combatants.

### ◆ Surface-Search

Most common on small surface combatants are Square Tie (also used for cruise-missile target-designation), Pot Head, and Pot Drum. Submarines carry Snoop Tray, Snoop Slab, Snoop Plate, or Snoop Pair, the latter two operating in the H/I-band.

### ◆ Long-Range Air-Search

**Cross Bird,** still carried by some *Skoryy*-class destroyers. Copy of British World War II Type 291 gear—Soviet name: Gius-2. (P-band, 225–390 mHz).

**Head Net-A** (C-band, 500–1,000 mHz)

**Head Net-B,** consisting of 2 Head Net-A antennas, mounted back-to-back in a horizontal plane (found only on Desna-class missile range ships).

**Head Net-C,** consisting of 2 Head Net-A antennas, mounted back-to-back, one in a horizontal plane, the other inclined. Widely used on cruisers and destroyers.

The Head Net-series radars use a band that gives a 60- to 70-mile detection range on an attack bomber flying at high altitude.

**Big Net,** a large C-band radar fitted on Kresta-I and a few *Sverdlov* cruisers, and some Kashin destroyers. Its detection range on an aircraft is probably over 100 miles.

**Slim Net** (E-band), early-model radar fitted on some cruisers and destroyers.

**Top Trough** (C-band), on some *Sverdlov* cruisers.

**Knife Rest** A/B (A-band, 0–250 mHz), antenna resembles a large television antenna.

**Strut Curve** (F-band, 3–4 mHz), mounted on the Petya and Mirka frigates and Poti and Grisha corvettes.

**Strut Pair** (F-band), mounted on *Udaloy* class and one Mod. Kildin destroyer. Employs pulse-compression. Antenna essentially two Strut Curve reflectors back-to-back.

**Plank Shave** (. . . band) on Tarantul-class corvettes. An apparent successor to Square Tie.

**Peel Cone,** air/surface-search combined radar used on Pauk-class ASW corvettes.

**High Sieve.** Carried by some *Sverdlov* cruisers and *Skoryy* destroyers.

**Top Pair** (C/F-band), three-dimensional; a Top Sail and a Big Net antenna mounted back-to-back; used on *Kirov.*

**Top Plate** Back-to-back, identical phased-array 3-dimensional radar antenna on *Udaloy*-class destroyers *Marshal Vasilevskiy, Admiral Zakharov,* and later.

**Top Plate/Top Steer,** Back-to-back, 3-dimensional radar antenna using one Top Steer and one Top Plate antenna; on *Sovremennyy*-class destroyer *Osmotritel'nyy* and later.

**Top Sail** (C-band), three-dimensional radar installed in *Kiev, Moskva,* Kresta-II, and Kara cruisers.

**Top Steer** (F-band), three-dimensional radar found with Top Sail on *Kiev.* Possibly for air-controlling.

### ◆ Missile Tracking and Control

**Trap Door,** in a retractable mount. Used for SS-N-12 on *Kiev*-class carriers, where it is mounted at the extreme bow; the similar Front Door/Front Piece is used on Echo-II and Juliett submarines and *Slava* cruisers for SS-N-3 and SS-N-12.

**Peel Group,** mounted on Kynda and Kresta-I cruisers as well as Kashin, Kanin, and SAM Kotlin destroyers. Consists of a tracking radar for high altitudes (I-band) and a missile-guidance radar at lower altitudes (E-band). The assembly is made up of two groups of large and small reflectors, in both horizontal and vertical position, with parabolic design. Maximum range approximately 30 to 40 miles. Used for guidance of the Goa missile in the SA-N-1 system.

**Head Lights** (F-, G-, H-, and D-bands), mounted on *Kiev* carriers and *Moskva,* Kresta-II and Kara cruisers. Similar to the Peel Group with an assembly of tracking radar for the target and guidance radar for the missile. Used for guidance for the Goblet missile of the SA-N-3 system and for the surface-to-underwater missiles of the SS-N-14 system. In several versions, designated "A," "B," and "C."

**Scoop Pair** (E-band), guidance radar for the Shaddock missile of the SS-N-3 system on board Kynda and Kresta-I cruisers.

**Pop Group** (F-, H-, and I-bands), missile guidance for the SA-N-4 system.

**Cross Sword** (. . .-band), missile guidance for the SA-N-9 SAM system. Incorporates both detection/tracker radar and illuminator/tracker antennas. Probably has electro-optical backup. Now on some *Udaloy* class and will be on all SA-N-9 ships eventually.

**Eye Bowl** (F-band), smaller version of Head Lights, installed in the cruiser *Kirov, Udaloy* destroyers, and Krivak frigates; missile-guidance radar for the SS-N-14 system.

**Fan Song E,** installed in the *Dzerzhinskiy;* used with the Guideline missile of the SA-N-2 system.

**Top Dome,** associated with the SA-N-6 vertically launched SAM system in the cruiser *Kirov.* Employs a 4-m-diameter hemispheric radome, fixed in elevation, but mechanically steerable in azimuth. Three smaller dielectric radomes are mounted on the face of its mounting pedestal, and there is also a smaller hemispheric radome below it. Apparently can track multiple targets.

**Front Dome,** tracker-illuminator associated with the SA-N-7 SAM system in the *Sovremennyy*-class destroyers (with six) and the trials Kashin, *Provornyy* (with eight). Resembles the gun fire-control radar Bass Tilt and is very compact.

### ◆ Data Link

**Plinth Net,** a large parabolic mesh antenna found only in the Kresta-I- and Kynda-class cruisers and apparently associated with the SS-N-3 antiship missile.

**Band Stand,** on *Sovremennyy* destroyers, Tarantul-II, and Nanuchka corvettes, and the Sarancha hydrofoil, possibly for missile-tracking and control. In large radome.

NOTE: The Soviet Navy also employs numerous other data link systems, for which details are unavailable.

### ◆ Gun Fire-Control

**Half Bow** }
**Post Lamp** } (I-band), mounted on older destroyers: also for torpedo fire control.

**Top Bow,** 152-mm gun.

**Sun Visor,** 130-mm, 100-mm DP guns; mounted on Round Top or Wasp Head directors.

**Hawk Screech,** 45-mm and 76.2-mm AA guns; always found in conjunction with back-up optical directors.

**Owl Screech,** 76.2-mm DP; improved version of Hawk Screech.

**Kite Screech,** 100-mm and new 130-mm twin DP.

**Muff Cob** (H-band), for 57-mm AA twin automatic guns. Has t.v. camera attachment.

**Egg Cup** (E-band), installed in turrets for 152-mm, old twin 130-mm, and old twin 100-mm AA guns

**Drum Tilt** (H- and I-bands), installed on Osa missile boats and other ships fitted with 30-mm twin-barrel AA.

**Bass Tilt** (H-band), used with gatling gun fitted in *Kiev* carriers, Kara and Kresta-II cruisers, and Mod. Kildin destroyers, as well as in Grisha-III corvettes, where it also controls the twin 57-mm, and on Nanuchka-III corvettes and Matka guided-missile hydrofoils, where it also controls the 76.2-mm gun.

## E. SONARS

Until the late 1950s, the Soviet Navy showed little interest in antisubmarine warfare or, of course, submarine detection. Most of its ships were equipped with high-frequency sonar (Tamir 11, Pegas, Herkules). New or modernized ships appear to have much-improved sensors.

**Medium-frequency hull sonar,** on Kresta-II cruisers, Kanin destroyers, Krivak frigates, and Grisha corvettes.

**Medium-frequency, towed, variable-depth sonar,** on *Kiev* carriers, *Moskva* and Kara cruisers, Mod. Kashin destroyers, and Krivak frigates.

**Low-frequency hull sonar,** on *Kiev* carriers and *Moskva* cruisers, the cruiser *Kirov,* and *Udaloy* destroyers. A low-frequency variable-depth sonar is used on the *Kirov* and *Udaloy* classes.

**Helicopter dipping sonar,** on Mirka frigates, Stenka and Pchela patrol boats, Turya torpedo boats and others. Most diesel submarines still have old equipment (active-passive Herkules, passive Feniks), but nuclear submarines have modern low-frequency sonar and extensive passive hydrophone arrays.

The Soviets are interested in surface-ship-towed passive sonar arrays. There are a number of prototype arrays on surface ships that may be for towed linear hydrophone arrays, and the teardrop-shaped domes on the upper rudder assemblies of Victor-III-class, Akula- and Sierra-class submarines may house a towed array, while the Delta-IV and Oscar classes may deploy arrays from a tube at the top of the rudder (these could, however, merely be towed communications wire housings).

## F. ELECTRONIC WARFARE

The increasing number of radomes of every description that can be seen on Soviet ships, especially on the newest and most important types (helicopter and guided-missile cruisers, for example) is an indication of the attention the Soviet Navy gives to electronic warfare. NATO code names for the antenna arrays for intercept or for jamming radars include: Side Globe, Top Hat A and B, Bell Clout, Bell Shroud, Bell Squat, Cage Pot, Wine Flask, Watch Dog, and Rum Tub. Submarines employ antennas nicknamed Stoplight, Brick Pulp, Brick Spit, Park Lamp, etc.

Many of the more modern ships are equipped with twin-tubed chaff rocket launchers (*Kiev, Moskva,* Kresta-I and -II, Kara, *Berezina*) or 16-tubed fixed chaff rocket launchers (Mod. Kashin, Krivak-I and -II, Tarantul, Pauk, Nanuchka, Matka, etc).

IFF (Identification Friend or Foe) is taken care of by High Pole A and B transponders and by Square Head or other interrogators. The newer Salt Pot A transponders are slowly replacing High Pole A and B. The modern radars have integral IFF interrogation. TACAN systems included the large Top Knot spherical array

## WEAPONS AND SYSTEMS *(continued)*

on the *Kiev*-class carriers, and the various forms of the paired cylindrical Round House array on the *Kirov, Udaloy,* and other classes.

### G. COMMUNICATIONS

All Soviet warships are equipped to transmit and receive MF through VHF communications, while submarines have a VLF capability (using towed buoy antennas), and UHF equipment is coming into wider use in surface ships. VHF antennas in use include: Cage Bare, Cage Cone, Cage Stalk, and the older Straight Key. Major warships usually have a Pop Art VHF antenna. Long-range HF communications are handled via the "Vee" series antennas Vee Cone, Vee Tube, or Vee Bars. Fixed arrangements 9 m long with two identical conical components mounted at 70 deg. to each other in the horizontal plane are termed Vee Cone. Vee Tube uses tubular, 8.6-m-long components at 90-deg. separation, and Vee Bars is the nickname for an open-framework arrangement on the *Kiev* class. Submarines rely on VLF, and an ELF station is building. Some Bear aircraft are equipped with a strategic submarine communications system analogous to the U.S. TACAMO.

### H. SATELLITES

The Soviets use an ocean surveillance satellite system whose data is transmitted either to ground stations or directly to ships equipped with the SS-N-12 and SS-N-19 cruise-missile systems. The receiving antenna is mounted in a large cylindrical radome termed Punch Bowl. The cruisers *Zhdanov* and *Admiral Senyavin* have two 4.5-m-diameter Big Ball radomes, associated with the Molniya and Raduga satellite communications systems, although many other ships can apparently receive transmissions from communications and navigational satellites.

### I. INFRARED AND ELECTRO-OPTICAL SYSTEMS

**Squeeze Box,** installed in *Sovremennyy*-class destroyers and in amphibious ships with 140-mm artillery rocket launchers. Believed to incorporate t.v., laser range finder, and infrared sensors and used in gun and rocket fire control.

**Tee Plinth,** television system installed in large ships in the 1960s and 1970s. Replaced in newer ships by:

**Tin Man,** which may incorporate a laser range finder also.

**Cod Eye,** in large submarines, is probably a radiometric or optical sextant device for precise navigation.

NOTE: Also in use are smaller, fixed television cameras (Tilt Pot) and periscopic devices mounted atop pilothouses to permit operations in bw/cw warfare conditions and poor weather.

## V/STOL CARRIERS

### ◆ 0 (+2 + 2) Leonid Brezhnev class    Bldr: Black Sea SY, Nikolayev

| | Laid down | L | In serv. |
|---|---|---|---|
| LEONID BREZHNEV | 1-83 | 12-85 | 1990 |
| N . . . | 10-12-85 | . . . | . . . |

**D:** approx 65,000 tons (fl) **S:** . . . **Dim:** 300.0 + × . . . × . . .
**A:** est. antiship missile system—est. 18–20 SA-N-9 SAM launch groups (144–160 missiles)— . . ./30-mm gatling AA—approx. 60 aircraft (see Remarks)

Cartoon of Leonid Brezhnev    *Soviet Military Power,* D.O.D., 1987

**Electron Equipt:** Radar: 3 or 4/. . . nav., 1/Top Plate (?), 4/. . . planar arrays, . . ./Cross Sword
Sonar: . . .—TACAN: . . .—EW: . . .
**M:** est. CONAS (Combined Nuclear and Steam Turbine); 2 or 4 reactors, 4 GT; 4 props; 300,000 hp
**Range:** effectively unlimited **Man:** . . .

REMARKS: Has a ski-jump bow, indicating probable use of V/STOL aircraft such as the Yak-38 Forger or a successor, as well as an angled deck, indicating an eventual intention to operate higher-performance, fixed-wing aircraft such as the Su-27 Flanker or MiG-29 Fulcrum. Although a land-based prototype carrier flight deck has been built at Saki and reportedly is intended to test steam catapults and wire arrester gear systems, the first ship (whose name was revealed by the U.S. Navy's Chief of Naval Operations in 2-87) will probably not have the catapults and, possibly, not the arrester gear. The Su-25 Frogfoot ground attack is another candidate for this ship, if a specialized naval aircraft is not developed. There are reported to be two deck-edge elevators to starboard.

The estimated nuclear and conventional steam-turbine propulsion system is essentially a double-*Kirov* plant. It has not yet been proven that nuclear power is, in fact, incorporated.

Unlike Western carriers, *Leonid Brezhnev* is likely to be equipped with both offensive and defensive missiles and, possibly, self-defense ASW ordnance. The "billboard" radar arrays will probably be the same as those carried on the modified *Kiev*-class carrier *Baku.*

The features thus far revealed about the *Leonid Brezhnev* indicate that it is *not* a U.S. Navy-style power projection ship but is, rather, a more elaborate version of the *Kiev* class intended to operate in a sea-control role. The U.S. Navy continues to believe that the Soviets will eventually evolve a conventional carrier design, possibly derived from the *Brezhnev,* and that the two *Brezhnev*s and two more similar carriers will be in operation by 2000.

### ◆ 0 (+1) Modified Kiev class    Bldr: Black Sea SY, Nikolayev

| | Laid down | L | In serv. |
|---|---|---|---|
| BAKU | 1978 | 3-82 | 1988 |

**D:** 36,000 tons (43,000 fl) **S:** 32 kts
**Dim:** 274.0 (249.5 wl) × 51.0 max. (32.7 wl) × 8.5 (10.0 max.)
**A:** 12/SS-N-12 (II × 6, . . . Sandbox missiles)—2/SA-N-3 SAM systems (II × 2, 72 Goblet missiles)— . . ./SA-N-9 SAM systems (VIII × . . . , . . . missiles)—DP guns—8/30-mm gatling AA (I × 8)— . . .
**Electron Equipt:** Radar: 1/Top Plate, 4/fixed planar arrays, 2/Head Lights, . . ./Cross Sword
Sonar: 1/low-freq., hull-mounted, 1 MF VDS
EW: . . .
**M:** 4 sets GT; 4 props; 200,000 hp **Boilers:** 8, turbopressurized
**Range:** 4,000/30;13,500/18 **Fuel:** 7,000 tons **Man:** approx. 1,200 tot.

REMARKS: The installation and testing of the U.S.S.R.'s first fixed planar array radar system may be one of the causes for the lengthy fitting out period for this ship, which otherwise could have been expected to be operational in 1986. Given the greater number of launchers reported, there may not be reload SS-N-12 Sandbox missiles.

### ◆ 3 Kiev class

| | Bldr | Laid down | L | In serv. |
|---|---|---|---|---|
| KIEV | Black Sea SY, Nikolayev | 9-70 | 31-12-72 | 5-75 |
| MINSK | Black Sea SY, Nikolayev | 12-72 | 5-75 | 2-78 |
| NOVOROSSIYSK | Black Sea SY, Nikolayev | 10-75 | 12-78 | 9-82 |

**D:** 36,000 tons (43,000 fl) **S:** 32 kts
**Dim:** 273.0 (249.5 wl) × 51.0 (32.70 wl) × 8.5 (10.0 max.)
**A:** 8/SS-N-12 (II × 4, 16 Sandbox missiles)—2/SA-N-3 systems (II × 2; 72 Goblet missiles)—2/SA-N-4 systems (II × 2, 40 Gecko missiles—not in *Novorossiysk*—4/76.2-mm DP (II × 2)—8/30-mm gatling AA (I × 8)—10/533-mm TT (V × 2)—1/SUW-N-1 ASW RL (II × 1)—2 RBU-6000 ASW RL (XII × 2)—14–17/Hormone-A or Helix-A and Hormone-B or Helix-C helicopters—12–13/Forger A/B VTOL aircraft—*Novorossiysk:* 12/SA-N-9 SAM silos (VIII × 12, 96 missiles, not yet fitted)
**Electron Equipt:** Radar: 1/Don Kay, 2/Don-2, 1/Top Sail, 1/Top Steer, 2/Head Lights, 2/Pop Group, 2/Owl Screech, 4/Bass Tilt, 1/Trap Door (*Novorossiysk:* 3 Palm Frond vice Don Kay, Don-2, no Pop Group, plus 2/Strut Pair)
Sonar: 1/low-freq., hull-mounted; 1/med.-freq., towed VDS
EW: 8/Side Globe (not in *Novorossiysk*), 4/Top Hat A, 4/Top Hat B, 4/Rum Tub, 2/Bell Clout—2/chaff RL (II × 2)
**M:** 4 sets GT; 4 props; 200,000 hp **Boilers:** 8, turbopressurized
**Fuel:** 7,000 tons **Range:** 4,000/30; 13,500/18 **Man:** approx 1,200 tot.

REMARKS: *General:* The Soviet Navy's designation for the *Kiev* class is *Bolshoy Protolovadochnyy Kreyser* (Large Antisubmarine Cruiser), although the *Minsk* was referred to briefly as a *Taktycheskoye Avionosnyy Kreyser* (Tactical Aircraft-Carrying Cruiser) on her initial deployment. The ships have capabilities for ASW, sea-control, and sea-denial missions. The hull is unusual in having a counter stern that sweeps up several meters above the waterline before meeting the transom. The variable-depth sonar is deployed through doors on the centerline of the transom stern; the black-painted, ribbed recess to port of the VDS housing is a spray deflector to prevent spray from entering air intakes of Forger V/STOL aircraft while landing. For their size and function, the ships carry very small crews. The

V/STOL CARRIERS *(continued)*

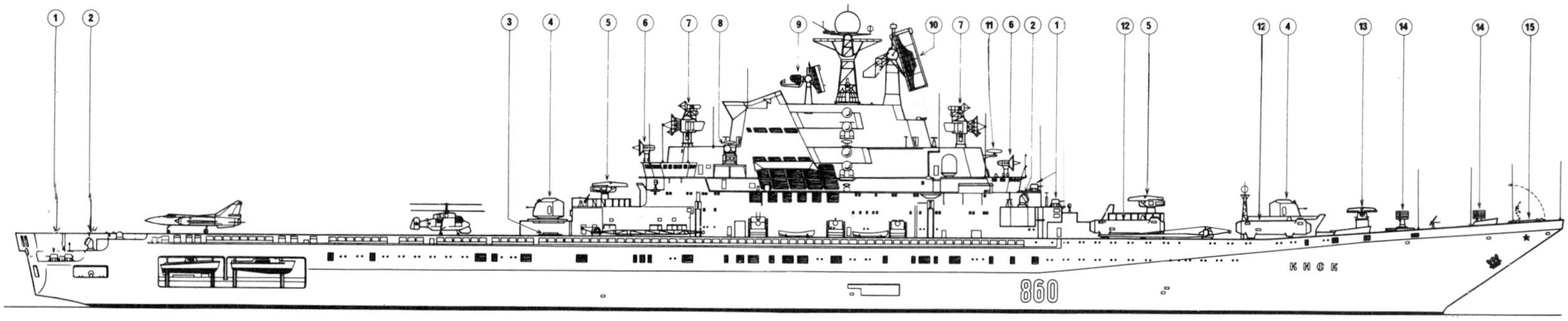

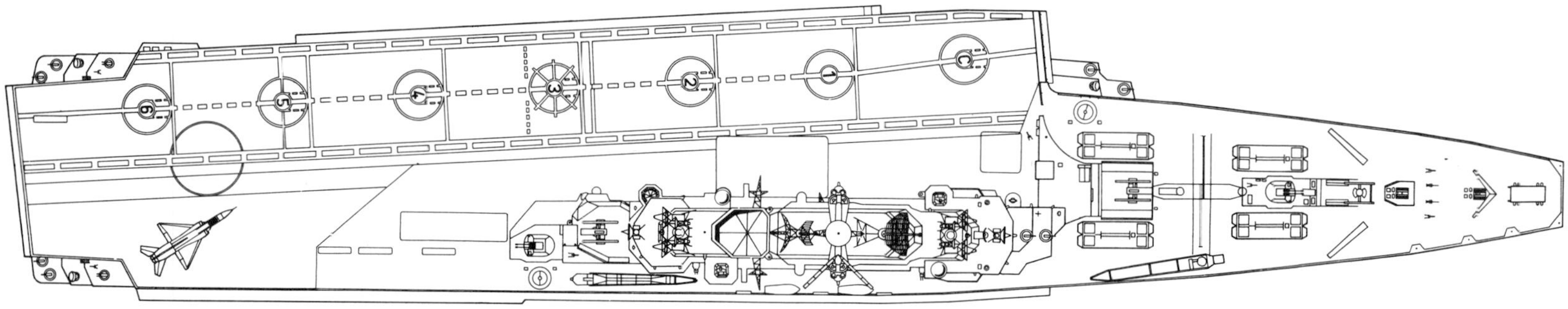

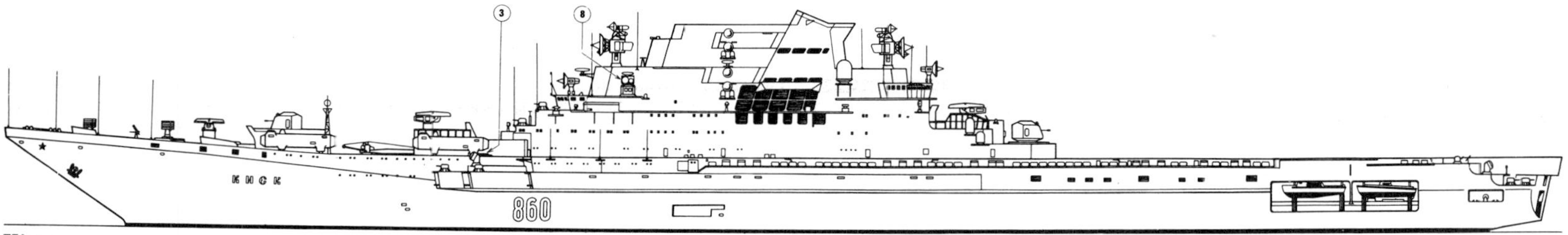

**Kiev** H. Simoni

1. 30-mm gatling guns 2. Bass Tilt radar 3. SA-N-4 launcher 4. twin 76.2-mm DP mount 5. SA-N-3 launcher 6. Owl Screech radar 7. Head Lights radar 8. Pop Group radar 9. Top Steer radar 10. Top Sail radar 11. Don-2 radar 12. twin launchers for SS-N-12 system 13. SUW-N-1 launcher 14. RBU-6000 15. Trap Door radar (*Note:* Plan view shows flight configuration as completed in 1976; the angled-deck centerline stripe is now straight at its forward end, and the after two ammunition elevators have been combined into a single 12.5-m-long lift.)

displacement is still uncertain, with U.S. sources quoting a draft of 8.3 m and a full-load of only 37,100 tons.

*Minsk* was refitted in 1981-82 at Vladivostok with an extended port forward sponson supporting the 30-mm gatling guns, a rounded leading edge to the flight deck, and a number of blast deflector or wind deflection plates erected on the forecastle abaft the SS-N-12 launchers; all these changes should improve air flow over the flight deck (which has been given an additional V/STOL landing spot) and should prevent sea damage to the guns. The third unit, *Novorossiysk,* has the deflectors and rounded deck edge, but retains the original sponson configuration. *Kiev* entered the Black Sea in 1982 to undergo her first major overhaul and emerged in 1985 with fewer alterations than expected, although air-flow baffles had been added. These ships are hampered by their low freeboard and have a noticeable squat at the stern when moving at higher speeds. There is an enormous bow bulge to accommodate the hull-mounted sonar transducer.

*Novorossiysk* lacks the SA-N-4 SAM system, instead having blanking plates over what will eventually be SA-N-9 vertical-launch installations abaft the island and forward to port; there are empty Cross Sword director platforms on the superstructure. The ship showed a number of electronics array differences from the first two, including the elimination of the 8-radome Side Globe array and the substitution of six new t.v./electro-optical devices ("Tin Man") for the Tee Plinth devices formerly used.

The ships have a retractable, spherical Bob Tail radio sextant antenna abaft the stack; all have microwave aircraft landing systems. The Vee Bars long-range HF communications antenna is fitted, as are satellite communications equipments (2 Punch Bowl antennas) and a very extensive VLF through UHF communications suite.

*Aviation installations:* The flight deck portion of the upper deck is angled about 4.5° to port of the centerline axis of the ship and is about 185 m long by 20 m wide. To protect against the hot exhaust of the Forger vertical take-off and landing aircraft, it is partially covered with a mosaic of refractory tiles. There are two elevators to the hangar deck; one (19.20 m × 10.35 m) beside the stack; the other (18.50 m × 4.70 m) abaft the island. Four small ammunition elevators are connected by an on-deck rail system. Both *Kiev* and *Novorossiysk* have deployed with the new Helix-A (Ka-27) ASW helicopter.

*Armament:* The SS-N-12 missiles are launched from four twin, non-trainable elevating tubes. In order to use the full over-the-horizon range of the missiles, a forward-located, target-designation observer platform has to be used. On the *Kiev,* that requirement is met by the Hormone-B, which carries a long-range radar giving a range of 100 nautical miles with the helicopter at an altitude of 4,000 feet. The ship can also use target information relayed by satellite, using the two receiving antennas in the Punch Bowl radomes. There are eight missiles in the launch tubes, plus sixteen reloads raised from a below-decks magazine by a centerline elevator between the launch-tube sets and aligned with the launchers for loanding by a traversing system.

**Kiev** R. Neth. Navy, 1987

**V/STOL CARRIERS** *(continued)*

**Kiev** French Navy, 1-87

**Kiev** French Navy, 1985

**Novorossiysk**—note absence of SA-N-4 launchers and Side Globe antennas PH1 Loveall, USN, 11-85

**Novorossiysk**—showing the "black hole" exhaust spray deflector to port of the VDS door in the transom stern and the current arrangement of the flight-deck markings French Navy, 5-83

**Minsk**—with the forward port sponson and flight-deck forward edge rearranged to improve air flow, blast shields added abaft SS-N-12 launchers J.M.S.D.F., 1986

## V/STOL CARRIERS *(continued)*

**Novorossiysk**—refueling from a *Boris Chilikin*-class oiler
JO2 V. Everts, USN, 1986

**Novorossiysk**—showing wind-baffle arrangement to port of SS-N-12 installation
French Navy, 5-83

**Minsk** J.M.S.D.F., 1984

## HELICOPTER CRUISERS

◆ **2 Moskva class**

| | Bldr | Laid down | L | In serv. |
|---|---|---|---|---|
| MOSKVA | Black Sea SY, Nikolayev | 1962 | 1964 | 7-67 |
| LENINGRAD | Black Sea SY, Nikolayev | 1964 | 1966 | 1968 |

**Moskva** French Navy, 5-82

**Leningrad** VP-26, U.S. Navy, 5-84

**Leningrad** U.S. Navy, 5-84

**HELICOPTER CRUISERS** *(continued)*

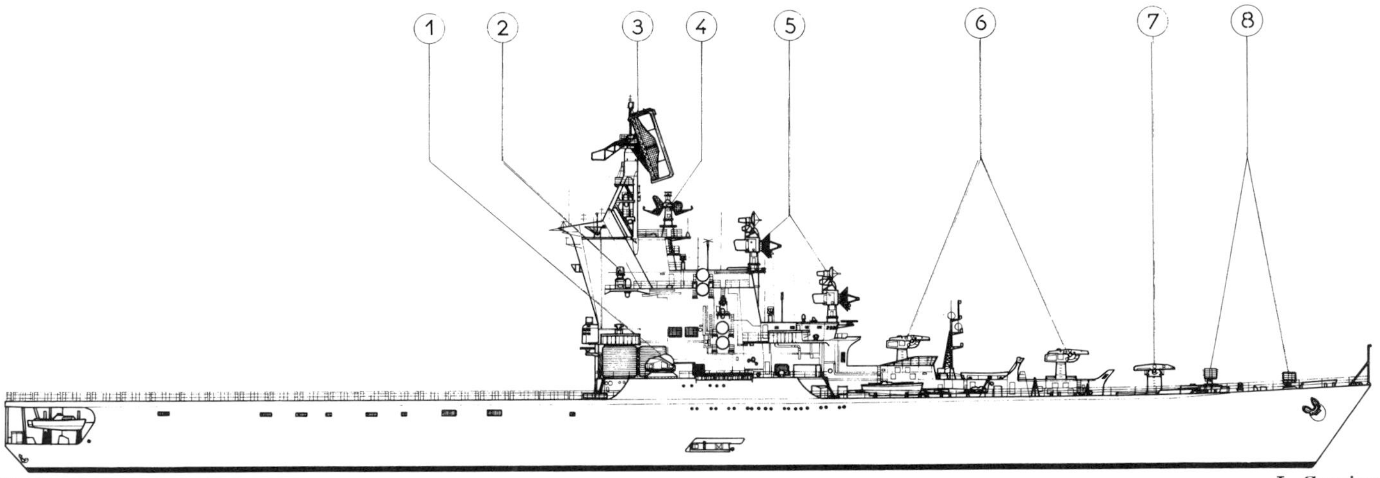


**Moskva** L. Gassier

1. twin 57-mm DP mount 2. Muff Cob radar/t.v. gun director 3. Top Sail 3-D radar antenna 4. Head Net-C air-search radar antenna 5. Head Lights missile fire-control radars 6. SA-N-3 launchers 7. SUW-N-1 ASW rocket launcher 8. RBU-6000 ASW rocket launchers

**D:** 15,500 tons (19,200 fl) **S:** 30 kts
**Dim:** 190.0 (179.0 wl) × 34.1 (flight deck), 26.0 (wl) × 7.6 (8.5 max.)
**A:** 2/SA-N-3 systems (II × 2; 44 Goblet missiles)—4/57-mm DP (II × 2)—1/SUW-N-1 ASW RL (II × 1)—2/RBU-6000 ASW RL (XII × 2)—14 Hormone-A/B/C helicopters
**Electron Equipt:** Radar: 3/Don-2, 1/Top Sail, 1/Head Net-C, 2/Head Lights, 2/Muff Cob
Sonar: 1/LF hull-mounted, 1/MF VDS
EW: 8/Side Globe, 2/Top Hat, 8/misc. Bell-series, 2/chaff RL (II × 2)
**M:** 2 sets GT; 2 props; 100,000 hp **Boilers:** 4, turbopressurized
**Range:** 4,500/29; 14,000/12 **Man:** 850 tot.

REMARKS: Soviet type designation: *Protivolodochnyy Kreyser* (Antisubmarine cruiser). Flight deck 86 × 34 m. Two elevators to hangar aft, plus small hangar for two helicopters at forward end of flight deck, between the stack uptakes. The *Moskva* was modified for a time to permit the testing of Yak-38 Forger-A aircraft which were to go aboard the *Kiev* carriers. Both ships had their ten 533-mm ASW TT removed and the side embrasures plated in during the mid-1970s. Sonar dome is retractable within hull. Fin stabilizers fitted. Have carried Haze-type mine countermeasures helicopters, but cannot hangar them. Carry two Tee Plinth electro-optical surveillance devices. Hulls trim down about 1 m by the bow, and they are poor sea-boats.

## NAVAL AVIATION

Naval aviation, which dates from 1919, is an integral part of the Soviet Navy in which approximately 70,000 men are involved, but its organization and ranks are the same as those of the air forces. Aircraft are part of the four naval fleets (Northern, Baltic, Black Sea, and Pacific) and are under the direct control of the commanders of those fleets. The air arm has some 1,570 aircraft, including:

505 Tactical:
370 strike bombers: 130 Backfire-B, -C, 210 Badger-C, -G, 30 Blinder-A
135 fighters/fighter-bombers: 60 Forger-A, 75 Fitter-C
240 Tactical Support:
65 tankers: Badger-A
175 reconnaissance & electronic warfare: 15 Bear-D, 80 Badger-D, -E, -F, -H, -K, -J, 20 Blinder, 25 An-12, 35 misc. (Fencer-E, Coot, etc.)
550 Antisubmarine Warfare:
205 fixed wing: 65 Bear-F, 50 May, 90 Mail
345 helicopters: 190 Hormone-A, 105 Haze-A, 50 Helix-A
Utility:
410 miscellaneous training, transports, utility helicopters, etc.

Operational first-line aircraft are divided into the four fleets as follows:

| | Northern | Baltic | Black Sea | Pacific | Total |
|---|---|---|---|---|---|
| Reconnaissance | 45 | 10 | 15 | 45 | 115 |
| Electronic warfare | 15 | 20 | 15 | 30 | 80 |
| Bombers | 60 | 75 | 80 | 115 | 330 |
| Attack fighters | 25 | 35 | 0 | 80 | 140 |
| Refueling | 20 | 15 | 10 | 20 | 65 |
| ASW (fixed wing) | 80 | 20 | 25 | 80 | 205 |
| Helicopters (all types) | 125 | 50 | 105 | 160 | 440 |

COMBAT AIRCRAFT

| NATO code name and builder | Mission | Year put in serv. | Max. weight | Wing-span | Length | Engine | Speed max. cruising | Operational radius[1] | Armament | Fitted with | Remarks |
|---|---|---|---|---|---|---|---|---|---|---|---|
| ◆ **FIXED-WING** | | | | | | | | | | | |
| **Backfire-B, -C** **Tu-22M** (Tupolev) | Reconnaissance and ship attack | 1975 | 121.5 t | 34.45 m (26.2 m fully swept) | 40.2 m | 2 Kuznetsov NK-144 turbojets of 24,000-kg thrust each | Mach 2.2 at 50,000 ft; Mach 1.3 at 3,000 ft | Supersonic: 3,485/2.250 km with/without refueling Subsonic: 6,300/5,320 km with/without refueling | 2/23-mm cannon, 12,000 kg of bombs (nuclear or conventional), on external racks, 2 AS-4, AS-6, or AS-9; mines | 1 Down Beat navigation and bombing radar; 1 optical bomb sight; 1 Fan Tail tail radar; IFF | The naval version of Backfire has ECM and ECCM equipment. Has variable-geometry, swept wing. Backfire-C has a different air intake configuration, more powerful engines. Naval units carry no refueling probes. |
| **Blinder-A, -C, -D** **Tu-22** (Tupolev) | A: gravity bomber C: photo reconn D: trainer | 1963 | 85 t | 28.8 m | 41.7 m | 2 Kolesov RD-7 turbojets, 20,000-kg thrust each (14,000-kg thrust without using after burners) | Mach 1.5 at 36,000 ft | Supersonic speeds: 1,000 km without refueling; 1,600 km with refueling Subsonic speeds: 1,500 km without refueling, 2,000 km with refueling | 1/23-mm cannon, 5,000-kg bombs or 1 AS-4 Kitchen | 1 Down Beat navigation radar; 1 Bee Hind tail radar; IFF; 7 cameras | The "C" version is especially configured for maritime reconnaissance. The "D" version is a trainer. Not a very successful design; few in service. |
| **Bear-C, -D** **Tu-95** **Bear-F** **Tu-142** (Tupolev) | Reconnaissance and electronic warfare | 1955 | 160 t (F: 171 t) | 48.5 m (F: 51.1) | 47.5 m (F: 49.5) | 4 Kuznetsov NK-12MV turboprops of 15,000 hp each; 4 bladed, contrarotating props | 500 kts at 25,000 ft 440 kts at sea level | 8,000 km without refueling; 9,500 km with refueling | Up to 7/23-mm cannon plus 8,000 kg of torpedoes; bombs in Bear-F | Big Bulge A (F: Wet Eye), tail radar; well-equipped with electronic countermeasures | Bear-F (Tu-142), the ASW version, has sonobuoys, depth charges, and torpedoes; the newest now have a MAD boom. |

## COMBAT AIRCRAFT *(continued)*

COMBAT AIRCRAFT *(Cont.)*

| NATO code name and builder | Mission | Year put in serv. | Max. weight | Wing-span | Length | Engine | Speed max. cruising | Operational radius[1] | Armament | Fitted with | Remarks |
|---|---|---|---|---|---|---|---|---|---|---|---|
| **Badger-A Tu-16** (Tupolev) | Aerial refueling | 1954 | 77 t | 34.5 m | 36.5 m | 2 AM-3 M turbojets, 9,550-kg thrust each | 540 kts at 22,000 ft<br>445 kts at sea level | 4,800 km | 7/23-mm cannon; up to 3,800 kg bombs | 1 navigation and bombing radar; 1 tail radar; some electronic warfare equipment. | Wing-tip hose dispensers for refueling; retains a second ary bombing capability |
| **Badger-C Tu-16** (Tupolev) | Ship attack | 1960 | 77 t | 34.5 m | 36.5 m | 2 AM-3 M turbojets, 9,550-kg thrust each | 540 kts at 22,000 ft<br>445 kts at sea level | 3,200 km without refueling | 6/23-mm cannon, 1 AS-2 Kipper or 2 AS-6 Kingfish | 1 Puff Ball navigation and bombing radar; 1 doppler radar; 1 Bee Hind tail radar. | |
| **Badger-G Tu-16** (Tupolev) | Ship attack | 1965 | 77 t | 34.5 m | 36.5 m | 2 AM-3 M turbojets, 9,550-kg thrust each | 540 kts at 22,000 ft<br>445 kts at sea level | 3,200 km without refueling | 8/23-mm cannon, 2 AS-5 Kelt or 2 AS-6 Kingfish | 1 Short Horn navigation and bombing radar; 1 Doppler radar; 1 Bee Hind tail radar. | |
| **Badger-D, -E, -F, -J Tu-16** (Tupolev) | Reconnaissance and electronic warfare | . . . | 77 t | 34.5 m | 36.5 m | 2 AM-3 M turbojets, 9,550-kg thrust each | 540 kts at 22,000 ft<br>445 kts at sea level | 3,200 km without refueling | 6–7/23-mm cannon | 1 Puff Ball navigation and bombing radar; electronic warfare equipment; 1 tail radar. | Different versions for ELINT, photo reconnaissance, etc. |
| **Forger-A/B Yak-38** (Yakolev) | A: Ship attack, day interceptor<br>B: 2-seat trainer | 1976 | 9.9 t | 7 m | 15 m (B: 17.7 m) | 1/7,650-kg thrust main engine; 2/3,600-kg lift engines | Mach 1.1 at 36,000 ft | 125 nautical miles low-low-low; 240 n.m. low-high-low | 16 or 32 rockets, 2/23-mm cannon, 2/AS-7 or AS-10 missiles, or 1,000 kg bombs | Passive warning system; inertial navigation. No radar. | Forger-B, the two-seat training version, is also carried aboard ship. A-version can also carry 2 AA-8 air-to-air missiles. Originally vertical takeoff only, now V/STOL. |
| **Fitter-C, -D Su-20** (Sukhoi) | Ship attack | 1976 | 17 t | 14 m (10.5 m swept) | 17.6 m | 1/Lyulka, AL-21F, 11,000-kg thrust turbojet | Mach 1.8 at 50,000 ft | 220 nautical miles low-low-low; 435 n.m. high-low-high | 32/57-mm rockets, 2/30-mm cannon, 3,500 kg bombs, nuclear or conventional | Ranging radar; tail warning radar; laser range finder; automatic control | Used by Naval Air Force in Baltic area. Can also carry AA-2 Atoll or AA-8 Aphid air-air or AS-7 or AS-10 air-ground missiles |
| **May Il-38** (Ilyushin) | ASW | 1969 | 68 t | 37.4 m | 36.9 m | 4 turboprops, 5,200 hp each | 380 kts at 30,000 ft<br>315 kts at sea level | 3,000 km; endurance: 12 hours | 7,000 kg of bombs, depth charges, torpedoes | Radar, MAD[2], sonobuoys | Il-18 Coot ELINT and ECM aircraft use the same basic airframe; 12-hour endurance. |
| **Mail Be-12** (Beriev) | ASW | 1967 | 30 t | 29.7 m | 30.2 m | 2 AL-20D turboprops, 4,190 hp each | 310 kts at 30,000 ft<br>240 kts at sea level | 1,300 km | Bombs, charges, mines | Radar, MAD[2], sonobuoys | Amphibian, but used primarily from land |
| ◆ **HELICOPTERS** | | | | | | | | | | | |
| **Haze-A, -B Mi-14** (Mil) | A: ASW, B: Mine countermeasures | 1976 | 12 t | rotor diam. 21.3 m | 24 m (18.2 fuselage | 2 Isotov TV 3 117A turboshafts, 2,200 hp each | 140 kts<br>122 kts | 305 km; endurance: 2.5 hours | Depth bombs or torpedoes: 2,000 kg total | Dipping sonar, towed MAD[2] pod | Land-based; rotors do not fold. Crew of four. B-version tows hydrofoil sled. |
| **Hormone-A, -B, -C Ka-25** (Kamov) | A: ASW<br>B: Targeting<br>C: Utility | 1967 | 7.3 t | rotor diam. 16 m | 10 m | 2 GTD 3 F turboshafts, 905 hp each | 120 kts<br>105 kts | 250 km; endurance: 1.5 to 2 hours | Depth charges or torpedoes: 1,000 kg total | Sonobuoys and dipping sonar | Carried on board *Kiev*, *Moskva*, Kara, and Kresta classes. The B version has a Video Data Link system. C version in various utility configurations, including reconn. |
| **Helix-A, -B, -D Ka-27** (Kamov) | A: ASW<br>B: Troop-carrying<br>D: Search-and-rescue | 1980 | 12.6 t | rotor diam. 15.90 m | 11.30 m (12.25 folded) | 2 Glushevkov TV3 117V turboshafts; 4,450 hp | 140 kts<br>124 kts (with 5,000-kg payload) | 400 km; endurance: 2 to 2.5 hours | Depth charges or 2 torpedoes | Sonobuoys and dipping sonar, possible MAD | Civil version, Ka-32 (Helix-C) has lifted 5,000 kg. Helix-B for use on *Ivan Rogov*. |
| **Hip-C Mi-8** (Mil) | Transport | 1967 | 12 t | rotor diam. 21.0 m | 18.3 m | 2 Isetov TV-2-117A turboshafts, 1,500 hp each | 125 kts<br>100 kts | 220 km | 12 troops, or 4,000 kg cargo | | Land-based. Some used for aerial minesweeping. |

1. The operational radius is roughly 60% of the radius given by one-half of the range
2. MAD = Magnetic Detection

**Backfire-B (Tu-22M) naval bomber** U.S.D.O.D., 1987

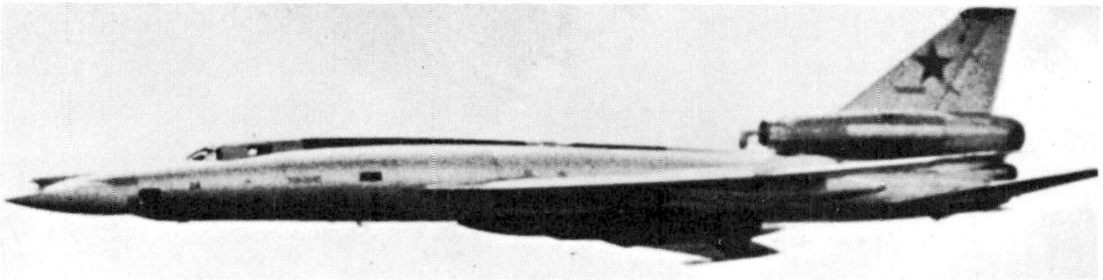

**Blinder-A (Tupolev Tu-22)** U.S. Navy

COMBAT AIRCRAFT *(continued)*

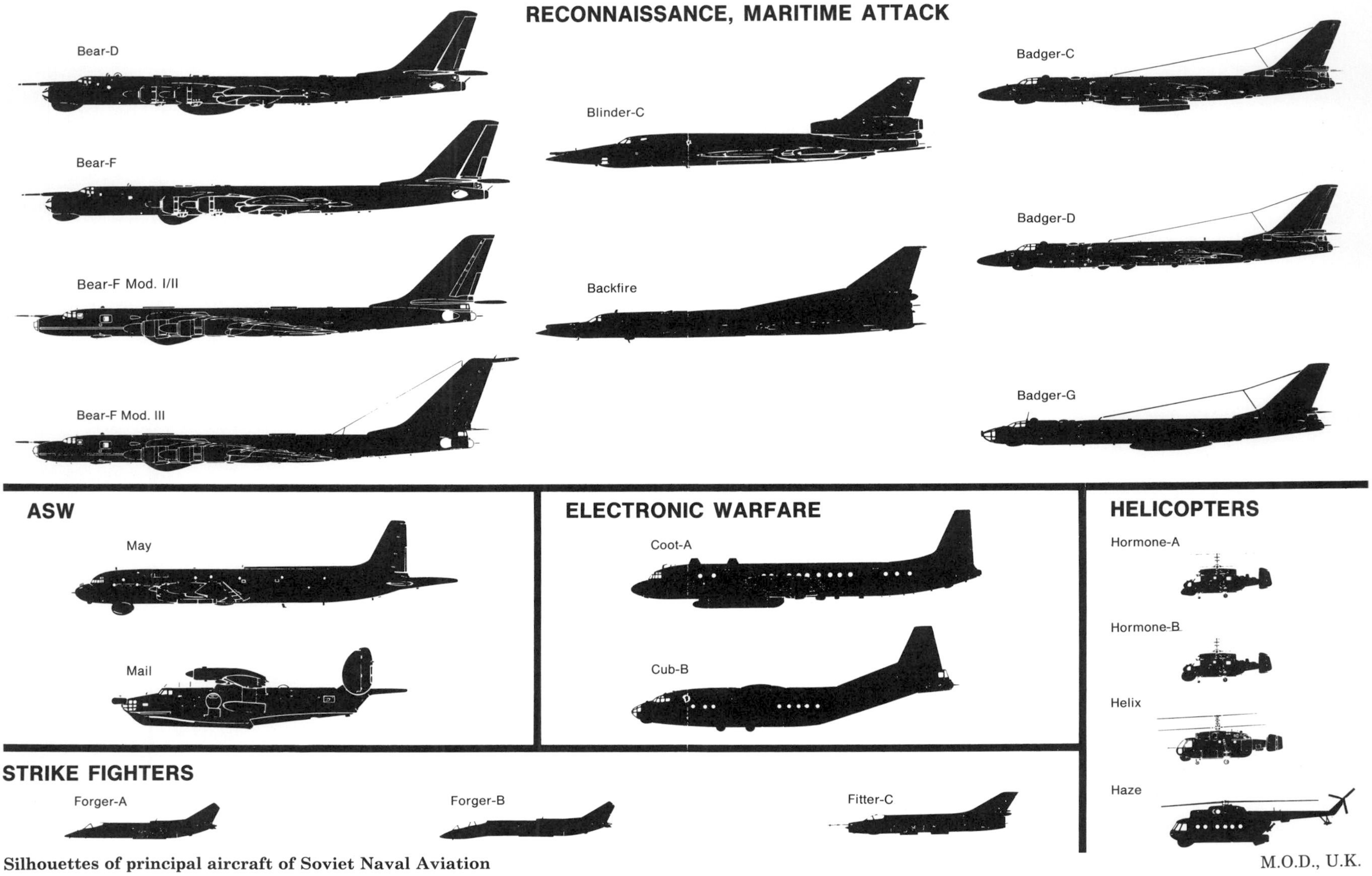


**Silhouettes of principal aircraft of Soviet Naval Aviation** M.O.D., U.K.

**Bear-D (Tu-95)**—reconnaissance, with U.S. Navy F-14A of VF-102
Lt. D. Parsons, USN, 9-85

**Bear-D (Tu-95)**—reconnaissance U.S. Navy, 9-82

**COMBAT AIRCRAFT** *(continued)*

**Bear-F (Tu-142) long-range ASW aircraft** U.S. Navy, 4-86

**Badger-A (Tu-16)**—tanker, with wingtip drogue system 1972

**Badger-C (Tu-16)**—missile carrier French Navy, 5-82

**Badger-E (Tu-16)**—ELINT U.S. Navy, 1985

**Forger-A (Yak-38)**—showing flow fences added atop the fuselage 1981

**Badger-D (Tu-16)**—ship attack French Navy, 5-86

**Forger-B (Yak-38) two-seat training VTOL aircraft** 1981

**May (Il-38)**—ASW aircraft U.S. Navy, 1986

**May (Il-38)**—ASW aircraft U.S. Navy, 5-83

COMBAT AIRCRAFT *(continued)*

**Coot-A (Il-18) intelligence collector** 1983

**Mail (Be-12)**—ASW amphibian, MAD boom protruding aft French Navy, 1986

**Haze-A (Mi-14) land-based ASW helicopter** PH2 P. Soutar, USN, 9-83

**Hormone-A (Ka-25) ASW helicopter** PH2 P. Soutar, USN, 9-83

**Hormone-B (Ka-25) targeting helicopter** U.S. Navy, 1986

**Hormone-C utility helicopter in SAR configuration** French Navy, 1981

**Hip-C (Mi-8) utility helicopter** 1981

**Helix-A (Ka-27) ASW helicopter** 1987

COMBAT AIRCRAFT *(continued)*

**Helix-B (Ka-27)**—assault helicopter on *Ivan Rogov*—note rocket pod 1987

**Helix-D (Ka-27) search-and-rescue helicopter** French Navy, 1987

## SUBMARINES

NOTE: Nuclear-powered submarines are built or modernized in the Severodvinsk (formerly, Molotovsk) Naval Shipyard on the White Sea, near Arkhangelsk; at Komsomolsk-on-Amur in the Far East; in the Gorkiy Shipyard on the Volga; and at the United Admiralty Shipyard in Leningrad (comprising the former Sudomekh and Admiralty Shipyards).

Most modern Soviet submarines have an anechoic hull coating that absorbs the echoes of sonars and thus reduces the intensity of reflected echoes. Reports of exotic propulsion systems, such as magnetohydrodynamic drive, electromagnetic drive, or the use of compliant coatings to improve boundary layer flow, although discussed in the popular press, apparently have yet to find use on an actual operational Soviet submarine class.

### BALLISTIC-MISSILE SUBMARINES (NUCLEAR-POWERED)

(Soviet Type: PLARB—*Podvodnaya Lodka Atomnaya Raketnaya Ballisticheskaya* = Nuclear-powered Ballistic Missile Submarine.)

**◆4 (+ · · ·) Delta-IV class** Bldr: Severodvinsk SY (In serv. 1985–. . .)

**D:** 10,800 tons (surf.)/13,500 tons (sub.) **S:** 24 kts (sub.)
**Dim:** 164.0 × 12.0 × 8.7
**A:** 16/SS-NX-23 ballistic missiles—6/533 or 650-mm TT (bow)
**Electron Equipt:** Radar: 1/Snoop Tray—Sonar: LF passive/active—EW: . . .
**M:** 2 nuclear reactors, steam turbines; 2/7-bladed props; 50,000 hp
**Man:** . . .

**Helix-A (Ka-27)**—with dipping sonar deployed U.S. Navy, 1986

**Delta-IV class** R. Nor. A.F., 1985

**BALLISTIC-MISSILE SUBMARINES (NUCLEAR)** *(continued)*

**Delta-IV class** R. Nor. A.F., 1985

Remarks: First unit launched 2-84, operational by 1985. A further elongation of the early-1960s Yankee design and apparently externally similar to Delta-III. Believed capable of operating under the ice pack. Distinguishable from Delta-III by possible towed antenna tube atop rudder and camera housing at aft end of turtledeck. Has Pert Spring SATCOMM antenna, as well as Cod Eye radiometric sextant and Park Lamp D/F loop.

◆ **5 (+2 or 3) Typhoon class** Bldr: Severodvinsk SY (In serv. 1983–. . .)

**D:** 18,500 tons surf. (25,000 sub.) **S:** 25 kts (sub.)
**Dim:** 171.0 × 24.0 × 12.5 (approx.)
**A:** 20/SS-N-20 ballistic missiles—est. 6/533-mm or 650-mm TT (torpedoes, SS-N-15/16) **Man:** 150 tot.
**Electron Equipt:** Radar: 1/Snoop Pair—Sonar: LF active/passive
**M:** 2/330–360 MW pressurized-water nuclear reactors; 2/7-bladed props, . . . hp

Remarks: World's largest submarines. Eight total units expected. Evidently intended to operate beneath the Arctic ice pack, breaking through to launch. The first Typhoon launched two missiles within 15 sec. in 10-82. Design incorporates two parallel pressure hulls within the outer hull, with the massive sail being an additional pressure vessel. Forward location of the missile tubes is unique. Propulsion plant probably generates over 100,000 hp.

The first, laid down in 1975, was launched in 9-80, commenced trials 6-81, and entered service 1983. The second launched 9-82, commenced trials 6-83, and entered service in 1984. The third was launched 12-83 and began trials at the beginning of 1985. The fourth was launched at the end of 1984, and the fifth at the end of 1986. All are based at a facility on the Kola Peninsula about 200 km east of Murmansk.

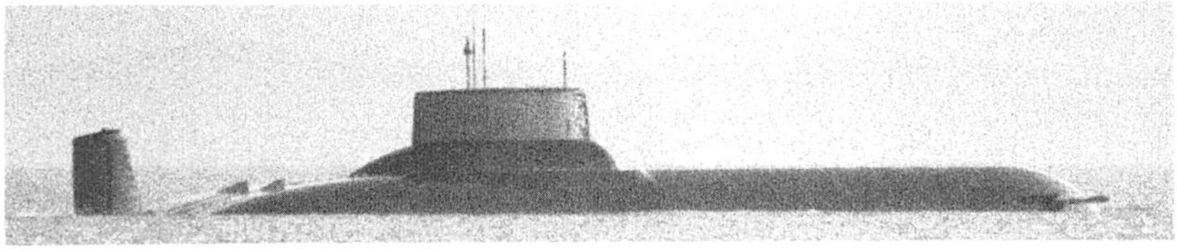

**Typhoon class**

**Typhoon class** M.O.D., U.K., 1984

**Typhoon class**—pyramidal structures abaft probable communications-buoy hatches abaft sail probably house t.v. cameras
U.S.D.O.D., *Soviet Military Power,* 1987

◆ **14 Delta-III class** Bldr: Severodvinsk SY (In serv. 1975–82)

**Delta-III class** U.S. Navy, 1987

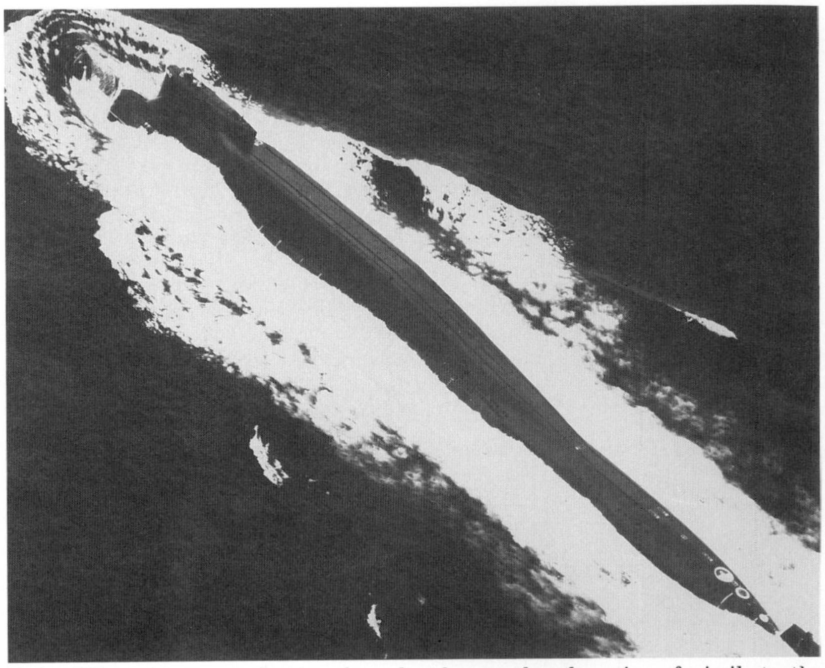

**Delta-III**—note communications-buoy hatches on sloped portion of missile turtledeck U.S. Navy, 1986

**BALLISTIC-MISSILE SUBMARINES (NUCLEAR)** *(continued)*

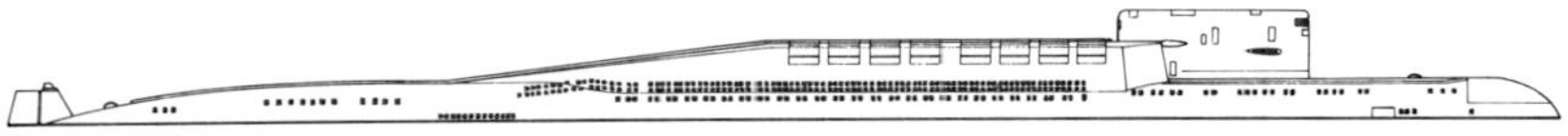

**Delta-III**

**D:** 10,600/13,250 tons **S:** 24 kts (sub.) **Dim:** 152.0 × 12.0 × 8.6
**A:** 16/SS-N-18—6/533-mm TT fwd. (18 torpedoes) **Man:** 120 tot.
**Electron Equipt:** Radar: 1/Snoop Tray
Sonar: 1/LF active, passive array
**M:** 2 nuclear reactors, steam turbines; 2/5-bladed props; 50,000 hp

Remarks: Two went into service in 1975, four in 1976, two in 1977, two in 1978, and three in 1979–81; the 13th was launched 3-4-81, the 14th in 12-81. Has higher "turtle-deck" than Delta-II to accommodate the longer SS-N-18 tubes. Have towed VLF communications buoys and Pert Spring SATCOMM antenna. One is named *60 Let Velikyo Oktyabr*.

◆ **4 Delta-II class** Bldr: Severodvinsk (In serv. 1974–75)

**Delta-II** R. Nor. A.F., 1982

**Delta-II** U.S. Navy, 1985

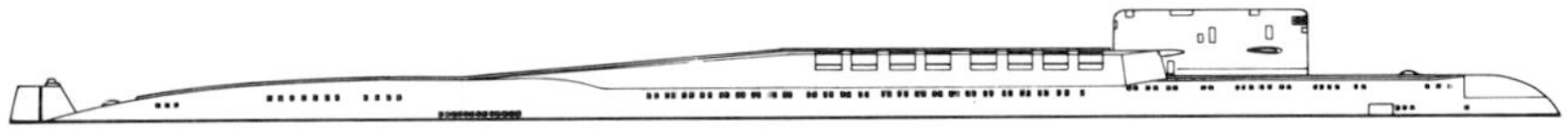

**Delta-II**

**D:** 10,550/13,250 tons **S:** 24 kts (sub.) **Dim:** 155.5 × 12.0 × 8.6
**A:** 16/SS-N-8—6/533-mm TT fwd. (18 torpedoes) **Man:** 120 tot.
**Electron Equipt:** Radar: 1/Snoop Tray—Sonar: LF active, passive array
**M:** 2 pressurized-water nuclear reactors, steam turbines; 2/5-bladed props; 50,000 hp

Remarks: Lengthened version of Delta-I, so as to carry four more SS-N-8.

◆ **18 Delta-I class** Bldrs: Severodvinsk and Komsomolsk (In serv. 1973–76)

**Delta-I class**—note stepped casing abaft missile tube area U.S. Navy, 1979

**Delta-I class**

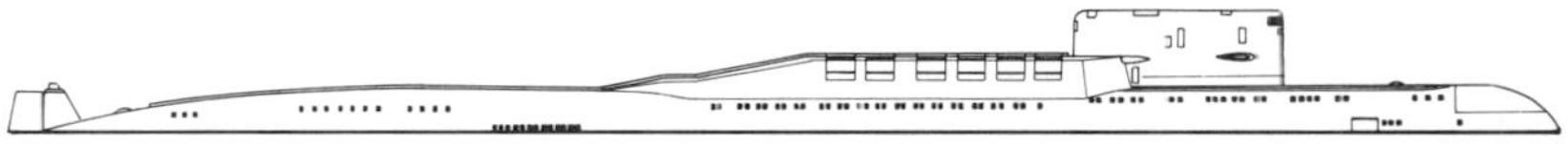

**Delta-I**

**D:** 9,000/11,750 tons **S:** 25 kts **Dim:** 140.0 × 12.0 × 8.6
**A:** 12/SS-N-8—6/533-mm TT fwd. (18 torpedoes)
**Electron Equipt:** Radar: 1 Snoop Tray
Sonar: 1/LF active, passive arrays
**M:** 2 pressurized-water nuclear reactors, steam turbines; 2/5-bladed props; 50,000 hp
**Man:** 120 tot.

Remarks: One entered service in 1972, four in 1973, six in 1974, two in 1975, two in 1976, and three in 1977. Distinguished from later, longer Delta-II and -III by stepped turtleneck abaft sail. All have Pert Spring SATCOMM antennas.

◆ **1 Yankee-II class** Bldr: Severodvinsk SY (In serv. 1978?)

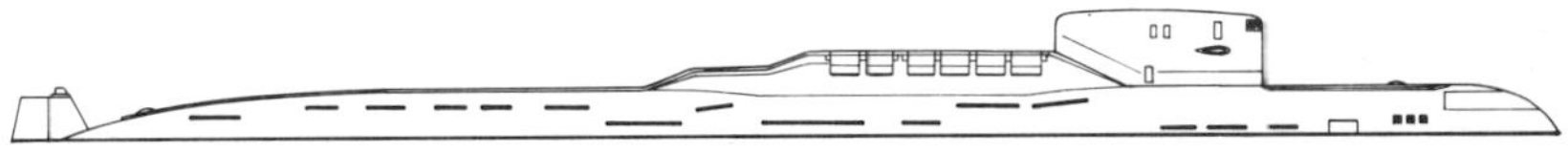

**Yankee-II**

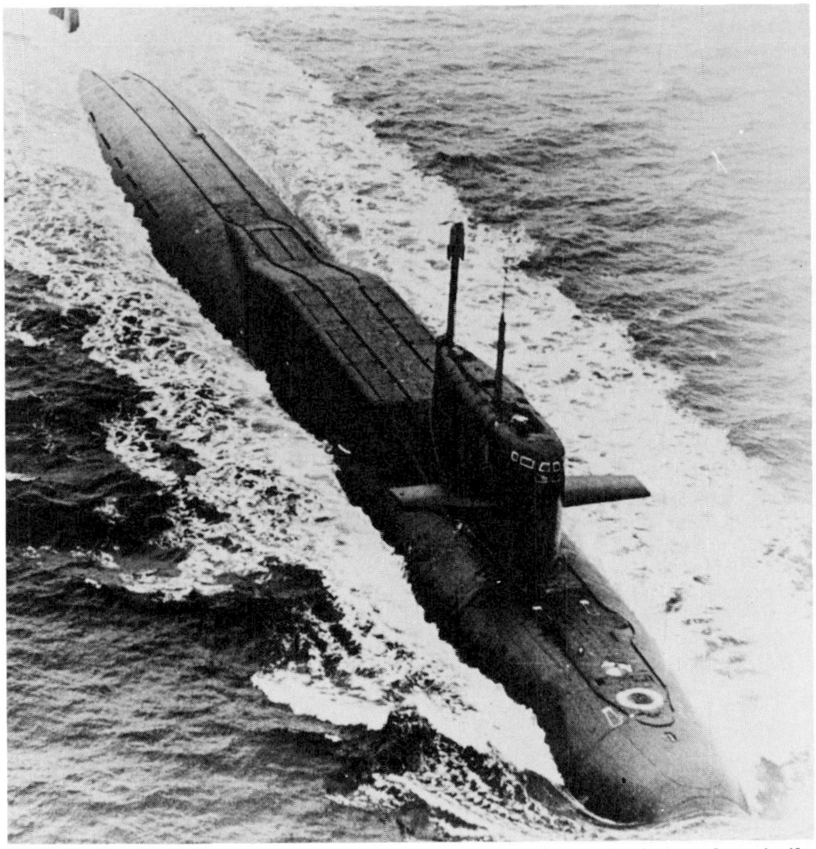

**Yankee-II**—distinguishable from Delta-I by sloping forward edge to the missile-tube casing hump 1982

**D:** 7,900 tons surf. (10,000 sub.) **S:** 27 kts (sub.)
**Dim:** 130.0 × 12.0 × 8.6 **Man:** 120 tot.
**A:** 12/SS-N-17 solid-fueled SLBM—6/533-mm TT (18 torp.)
**Electron Equipt:** Radar: 1/Snoop Tray—EW: Brick Group
Sonar: low-frequency active/passive
**M:** 2 pressurized-water nuclear reactors; 2/5-bladed props; 50,000 hp

Remarks: Converted/completed as trials ship for the SS-N-17, which did not enter large-scale production. Nonetheless, the submarine is retained as a first-line unit.

◆ **16 Yankee-I class** Bldrs: Severodvinsk SY and Komsomolsk SY (In serv. 1967–74)

**BALLISTIC-MISSILE SUBMARINES (NUCLEAR)** *(continued)*

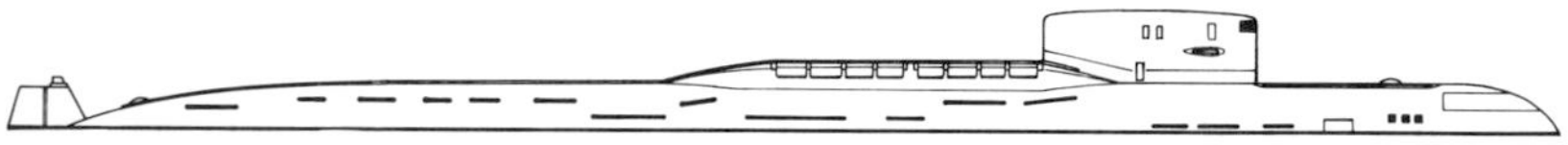

**Yankee-I**

**Yankee-I**—with angled forward edge to sail, ESM, D/F, and comms. masts extended, bare metal sonar window U.S. Navy

**Yankee class**—with painted sonar window, straight forward edge to sail 1982

**The Yankee-I that was lost after a missile-fuel explosion** U.S. Navy, 10-86

**D:** 7,900/9,600 tons **S:** 27 kts **Dim:** 130.0 × 12.0 × 8.6
**A:** Yankee-I: 16/SS-N-6—6/533-mm TT (18 torpedoes)
Yankee-II: 12/SS-N-17—6/533-mm TT (18 torpedoes)
**Electron Equipt:** Radar: 1/Snoop Tray—EW: Brick Group
Sonar: 1/LF active, passive arrays
**M:** 2 pressurized-water nuclear reactors, steam turbines; 2/5-bladed props; 50,000 hp
**Man:** 120 tot.

REMARKS: In one unit, nicknamed "Yankee-II," SS-N-6 has been replaced by SS-N-17 with twelve tubes. A total of 34 were completed: two in 1967, four in 1968, six in 1969, eight in 1970, six in 1971, five in 1972, two in 1973, and one in 1974. To date, 16 have had their missile tubes deactivated, in compliance with the U.S.-Soviet SALT agreements; these "de-fanged" Yankees are listed under attack submarines, except for one that has been converted to carry cruise missiles and up to three serving as attack submarines. One Yankee-I was lost at sea east of Bermuda on 6-10-86 after a fire and explosion in the missile bay area. Yankees are equipped with the Cod Eye radiometric sextant and have a towed VLF buoy antenna and the Pert Spring SATCOMM antenna.

◆ **1 Hotel-III class** Bldr: Severodvinsk (In serv. 1963)

**D:** 5,500/6,400 tons **S:** 20/25 kts **Dim:** 130.0 × 9.0 × 7.0
**A:** 2/SS-N-8—6/533-mm TT—2/400-mm TT
**Electron Equipt:** Radar: 1/Snoop Tray—EW: Stop Light
Sonar: 1/MF active, passive arrays
**M:** 2 nuclear reactors, steam turbines; 2/6-bladed props; 30,000 hp
**Man:** 80 tot.

REMARKS: Used as trial ship for SS-N-8 missiles. Lengthened during conversion. Has the Cod Eye radiometric sextant. No longer first-line equipment.

NOTE: All Hotel-II-class nuclear-powered ballistic-missile submarines are believed to have had their SS-N-5 ballistic-missile systems disabled in compliance with SALT requirements. One has been converted as a communications unit, and the others may reappear as attack submarines, although they are quite obsolescent.

**BALLISTIC-MISSILE SUBMARINES (DIESEL-POWERED)**

(Soviet Type: PLRB = *Podvodnaya Lodka Raketnaya Ballisticheskaya* = Ballistic-Missile Submarine)

◆ **1 Golf-III class** Bldr: Severodvinsk SY (In serv. 1958–61)

**Golf-III** U.S. Navy

**D:** 2,900/3,300 tons **S:** 12 kts (sub.) **Dim:** 110.0 × 8.5 × 6.6
**A:** 6/SS-N-8—10/533-mm TT (6 fwd, 4 aft)
**Electron Equipt:** Radar: 1/Snoop Tray—Sonar: 1/MF, passive array
**M:** 3 diesels; 2,000 hp each, electric drive; 3 props; 5,300 hp (sub.)
**Endurance:** 70 days **Range:** 9,000/5 **Man:** 87 tot.

REMARKS: Converted for trials purposes, early 1970s.

◆ **13 Golf-II class** Bldr: Severodvinsk (In serv. 1958–61)

**Golf-II**—with VLF comms.-buoy housing near stern (smoke from sail evidently part of a damage-control/salvage exercise) *Ships of the World,* 11-84

**Golf-II class**—communications-buoy housing abaft sail 1976

**D:** 2,300/2,700 tons **S:** 12 kts (sub.) **Dim:** 100.0 × 8.5 × 6.6
**A:** 3/SS-N-5—10/533-mm TT (6 fwd, 4 aft)
**M:** diesel-electric drive, 3/2,000-hp diesels; 3 props; 5,300 hp (sub.)
**Endurance:** 70 days **Range:** 9,000/5 **Man:** 80 tot.

REMARKS: These submarines continue to be active. Six of them have been stationed in the Baltic, with the rest in the Far East. The range of the SS-N-5 has been extended from the original 700 nautical miles to 900. All Golf-IIs are conversions from Golf-I. The few remaining unconverted Golf-I-class submarines have been scrapped or converted to other functions.

NOTE: The Golf-V trials submarine, converted with a single SLBM tube (probably for SS-N-20) for trials purposes, is believed to have been discarded, as has the single Golf-IV, converted for SS-N-6 trials with six tubes.

## CRUISE-MISSILE ATTACK SUBMARINES (NUCLEAR-POWERED)

(Soviet Type: PLARK—*Podvodnaya Lodka Atomnaya Reketnaya Krylataya* = Nuclear-Powered Cruise-Missile Submarine)

◆ **4 (+. . .) Oscar class** Bldr: Severodvinsk SY (In serv. 1982–. . .)

**Second Oscar-class unit**—note missile-tube doors abreast sail
R. Nor. A.F., 1984

**First Oscar-class unit**—note buoy housing abaft sail M.O.D., U.K.

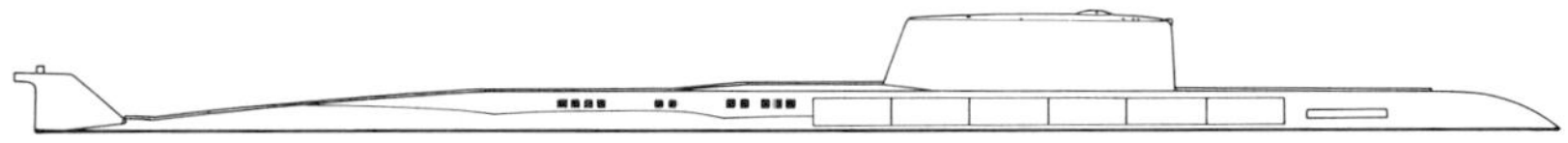

**Oscar class** (second unit)

**First Oscar**—note large number of missing anechoic tiles and the enormous girth of the missile bay area abreast sail. One periscope, Pert Spring SATCOMM antenna and H/F radio mast raised M.O.D., U.K.

**First Oscar**—note split rudder U.S. D.O.D., *Soviet Military Power,* 1987

**D:** 11,500/14,500 tons (#3 and later 13,000/16,000) **S:** 33 kts (sub.)
**Dim:** 146.0 (#3 and later: 156.0) × 18.0 × 10.0
**A:** 24/SS-N-19 SSM—6/533- or 650-mm TT fwd (24 SS-N-15/16; torpedoes)
**Electron Equipt:** Radar: 1/Snoop Tray—Sonar: 1/LF active, 1/MF active, passive arrays
**M:** 2 pressurized-water nuclear reactors, steam turbines; 2/7-bladed props; 90,000 hp
**Man:** . . .

Remarks: The first was launched in 4-80, the second in 12-82; the third entered service in 1984 and the fourth was launched in the spring of 1986. The missile tubes are mounted in two rows of twelve, abreast the sail, fixed in elevation at about 40°, with doors opening through the outer hull, as on the Papa and Charlie-I and -II classes. The missiles are launched while the submarine is submerged, presumably using targeting data from a forward observer or from satellite targeting. Six outer hatch doors each cover two tubes. The tubes provide a 3.5-m stand-off between the outer hull and the pressure hull. A towed antenna is dispensed from a tube at the top of the rudder on the second and later units. The third and later are lengthened 10.0 m abaft the sail. All carry the Punch Bowl antenna to receive satellite targeting data and the Pert Spring SATCOMM antenna. As many as ten may be built.

◆ **1 Papa class** Bldr: Gorkiy SY (In serv. 1970)

**Papa class** S. Breyer collection

**Papa class**—note 4 TT, reload hatch, missile-tube covers visible
M.O.D., U.K., 1981

**D:** 6,400/8,000 tons **S:** 39 kts **Dim:** 109.0 × 12.2 × 9.5
**A:** 10/SS-N-9—6/533-mm TT fwd (torpedoes and SS-N-15 missiles)
**Electron Equipt:** Radar: 1/Snoop Tray—Sonar: LF active/passive
**M:** 2 pressurized-water nuclear reactors, steam turbines; 2/5-bladed props; 60,000–75,000 hp
**Man:** 85 tot.

Remarks: May have been a concept prototype. Launched 1968. Missiles launched from submerged condition, apparently against acoustically located targets. Has had two lengthy overhauls and very little active service. May have a titanium

**CRUISE-MISSILE ATTACK SUBMARINES (NUCLEAR)** *(continued)*

pressure hull. Has Pert Spring SATCOMM antenna. Large sonar array in leading edge of sail.

◆ **6 Charlie-II class** Bldr: Gorkiy SY (In serv. 1973–1982)

**Charlie-II class** U.S. Navy

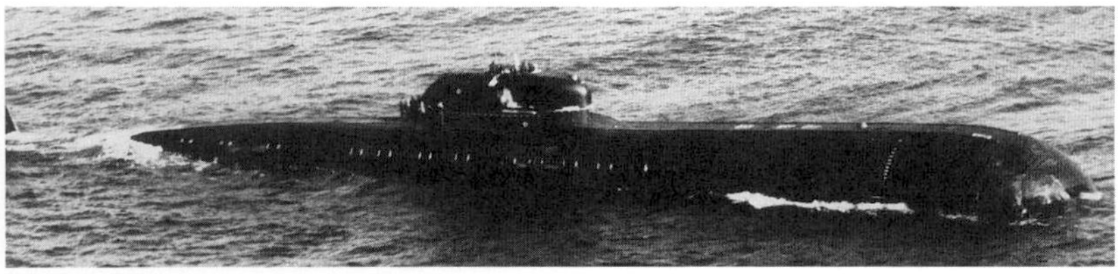

**Charlie-II class**—note "collar" at base of sail U.S. Navy, 12-80

**D:** 4,300/5,500 tons **S:** 24 kts (sub.) **Dim:** 103.0 × 10.0 × 8.0
**A:** 8/SS-N-9—6/533-mm TT fwd. (12 SS-N-15, torpedoes)
**Electron Equipt:** Radar: 1/Snoop Tray—EW: 1/Brick Spit, 1/Brick Pulp
Sonar: 1/LF active, passive arrays
**M:** 1 pressurized-water nuclear reactor, steam turbines; 1/5-bladed prop; 30,000 hp
**Man:** 85 tot.

Remarks: All in Northern Fleet. One in service in each of the years 1973, 1974, 1977, 1979, 1980/81, and 1982. The additional 9-m length over the Charlie-I comes between the missile tubes and the sail. Have VLF comms-bucy housing abaft the sail.

◆ **9 Charlie-I class** Bldr: Gorkiy SY (In serv. 1968–72)

**Charlie-I class**—note "collar" added at base of sail 1982

**Charlie-I class** 2-84

**D:** 4,000/5,000 tons **S:** 24 kts (sub.) **Dim:** 94.0 × 10.0 × 8.0
**A:** 8/SS-N-7—6/533-mm TT fwd. (12 SS-N-15, torpedoes)
**Electron Equipt:** Radar: 1/Snoop Tray—EW: 1/Brick Spit, 1/Brick Pulp
Sonar: 1/LF active, passive arrays
**M:** 1 nuclear reactor, steam turbines; 1/5-bladed prop; 15,000 hp
**Man:** 100 tot.

Remarks: In service at the rate of about two a year between 1968 and 1973. "Collar" structures being added at the forward base of the sail, apparently to smooth water flow. Diving depth: 400 m normal/600 m max. One sank 6-83 in the Pacific; subsequently raised, but probably not returned to service. One loaned to India 5-1-88.

◆ **1 Yankee-class conversion**

**Yankee cruise-missile submarine**—artist's concept
U.S.D.O.D., *Soviet Military Power,* 1987

**D:** 13,650 tons (sub.) **S:** 23 kts (sub.) **Dim:** 153.0 × 15.0–16.0 × 9.0
**A:** 12/SS-N-24 SSM—6/533-mm TT (fwd)
**Electron Equipt:** Radar: . . .—Sonar: . . .
**M:** 2 nuclear reactors, steam turbines; 2/5-bladed props; 50,000 hp

Remarks: Converted from a Yankee-I that had her SS-N-6 ballistic-missile system deleted in compliance with SALT. Relaunched 12-82, and apparently operational as trials submarine for the SS-NX-24 cruise-missile system by 1985. Addition of cruise missiles apparently greatly added to the ship's beam, reducing speed and maneuverability.

Note: See addenda for another Yankee cruise-missile conversion variant.

◆ **26 Echo-II class** Bldr: Severodvinsk and Komsomolsk (In serv. 1960–67)

**Echo-II with two of the four pairs of SS-N-3 missile tubes elevated**
U.S. Navy

## CRUISE-MISSILE ATTACK SUBMARINES (NUCLEAR) *(continued)*

**Echo-II class** U.S. Navy, 1985

**Echo-II class** French Navy, 1-80

**Echo-II with SS-N-12**—note Front Door/Front Piece antenna deployed at forward end of sail, bulge on sail side, and relocated hinge bulge at forward end of the second missile-tube pair 1980

**D:** 5,000/6,000 tons **S:** 20/23 kts **Dim:** 115.0 × 9.0 × 7.5
**A:** 8/SS-N-3A or SS-N-12—6/533-mm TT (fwd)—4/400-mm TT (aft)
**Electron Equipt:** Radar: 1/Snoop Tray, 1/Front Piece, 1/Front Door
Sonar: 1/LF active, passive arrays, including Feniks.
**M:** 2 nuclear reactors, steam turbines; 2/4-bladed props; 30,000 hp
**Man:** 90 tot.

Remarks: Approximately six to date have been modified to launch SS-N-12; they have a bulge on either side of the sail and a bulge at the forward ends of the missile tubes abreast the sail and have been equipped with the Punch Bowl satellite targeting reception antenna. The Echo-II must be surfaced to launch, the tubes elevating in pairs to fire. The forward part of the sail rotates 180° to expose the Front Door/Front Piece guidance radar. One Echo-II may be named *Dekabrist*. One unit has been converted to an auxiliary function, and two others have apparently been retired.

## CRUISE-MISSILE ATTACK SUBMARINES (DIESEL-POWERED)

(Soviet Type: PLRK = *Podvodnaya Lodka Raketnaya Krylataya* = Cruise-Missile Submarine)

◆ **14 Juliett class** Bldr: Gorkiy SY (In serv. 1961–63)

**D:** 3,000/3,750 tons **S:** 16/13 kts **Dim:** 90.0 × 10.0 × 7.0
**A:** 4/SS-N-3A—6/533-mm TT (fwd)—4/400-mm TT (aft)
**Electron Equipt:** Radar: 1/Snoop Slab, 1/Front Piece, 1/Front Door
Sonar: 1/MF active, passive arrays—EW: 1/Stop Light
**M:** 2 diesels, electric drive; 2 props; 5,000 hp
**Range:** 9,000/7 (snorkel) **Man:** 80 tot.

**Juliett class**—after pair SS-N-3A tubes raised U.S. Navy, 3-87

**Juliett class** Skyfotos, 5-83

Remarks: Missiles are in paired tubes, elevating to fire, as on the Echo-II class. Since 1981, six have been based in the Baltic. One has been equipped with SS-N-12 missiles and the Punch Bowl satellite targeting reception antenna. Two have been discarded.

## ATTACK SUBMARINES (NUCLEAR-POWERED)

(Soviet Type: PLA—*Podvodnaya Lodka Atomnaya* = Nuclear-Powered Submarine)

◆ **2 (+ . . .) Akula class** Bldr: Komsomolsk SY, Komsomolsk-na-Amur

**Akula class** U.S Navy, 1986

**Akula class** U.S.D.O.D., *Soviet Military Power,* 1987

**D:** 7,500/10,000 tons **S:** 35 kts **Dim:** 113.0 × 13.0 × 10.0
**A:** 6/650 or 533-mm TT (SS-N-15, -16, and -21 missiles, torpedoes)
**Electron Equipt:** Radar: Snoop Pair
Sonar: LF active/passive, passive array towed LF linear hydrophone array
EW: Amber Light, Stop Light, Park Lamp D/F
**M:** 2 pressurized-water nuclear reactors, steam turbines; 1/7-bladed prop; . . . hp
**Man:** . . .

Remarks: First unit launched 7-84; the second ran trials during 1987. Differs from Sierra in having a longer, more streamlined sail. Broader hull than preceding Victor series indicates probable use of "rafted" (sound-isolated) propulsion plant to greatly reduce radiated noise. *Akula* means "shark" in Russian; the NATO nickname was chosen because all the letters of the phonetic alphabet have been used to name recent classes. Steel hull. U.S. D.O.D. reports overall length at 107.0 m. Have Pert Spring SATCOMM antenna. A third was launched in 1987.

◆ **2 (+ . . .) Sierra class** Bldr: Gorkiy SY

**Sierra class** R. Nor. A.F., 1984

**ATTACK SUBMARINES (NUCLEAR)** *(continued)*

**Sierra class** R. Nor. A.F., 1984

**Sierra class**—note raised Snoop Pair radar with EW antennas surrounding base, periscope and Pert Spring SATCOMM antenna also extended R. Nor. A.F., 1984

**Sierra class** R. Nor. A.F., 1984

**D:** 6,000/7,550 tons **S:** 34–36 kts **Dim:** 107.0 × 12.0 × . . .
**A:** 4/650-mm TT—2/533-mm TT (SS-N-15/16/21 missiles/torpedoes)
**Electron Equipt:** Radar: 1/Snoop Pair
Sonar: LF suite, towed passive hydrophone array
EW: . . .
**M:** 2 pressurized-water reactors; 1/7-bladed prop; . . . hp **Man:** . . .

Remarks: First unit launched 7-83 at Gorkiy and transferred via river/canal system to Severodvinsk for completion. Second reported on trials 1987. Differs from Akula in having a blunter, shorter sail and in lacking a towed communications buoy housing abaft the sail; probably has the same propulsion plant, optimized for radiated noise reduction. May have a titanium hull; if so, this is a successor to the Alfa, while the Akula may be considered as a successor to the Victor-III.

◆ **1 Mike class** Bldr: Severodvinsk SY (In serv. 1986)

**Mike class** R. Nor. A.F., 1986

**Mike class**—note bulge above bow plane housing near bow R. Nor. A.F., 1986

**D:** 4,400/6,400 tons **S:** 36 kts **Dim:** 110.0 × 11.0 × 9.0
**A:** 6/650- or 533-mm TT (SS-N-15/16/21 missiles, torpedoes)
**Electron Equipt:** Radar: Snoop Head—EW: Bald Head
Sonar: LF active/passive
**M:** 2 liquid-metal reactors; 1/7-bladed prop; approx. 60,000 hp **Man:** . . .

**ATTACK SUBMARINES (NUCLEAR)** *(continued)*

Remarks: First unit launched 6-83. Hull built of titanium, and reactor may employ liquid metal coolant, as in the Alfa-class. Lacks the towed antenna housing atop the rudder of the Akula, Sierra, and Victor-III classes. Believed to be an experimental design, with no second unit expected. Probable titanium pressure hull, giving 700 m+ operating depth.

◆ **6 Alfa class** Bldr: Admiralty (Sudomekh) SY, Leningrad, and Severodvinsk SY (In serv. 1979–83)

**Alfa-class SSN**—note smooth blending of sail to hull U.S. Navy, 1983

**Alfa class** R. Nor. A.F.

**D:** 2,900/3,680 tons **S:** 43–45 kts (sub.) **Dim:** 81.4 × 9.5 × 7.0
**A:** 6/533-mm TT (with SS-N-15 missiles, torpedoes)
**Electron Equipt:** Radar: 1/Snoop Tray—EW: 1/Brick Pulp, 1/Brick Spit, 1/Park Lamp D/F
Sonar: 1/LF active, passive arrays
**M:** 2 liquid-metal nuclear reactors, steam turbines; 1/5-bladed prop; 45,000 hp
**Man:** 45 tot.

Remarks: The prototype, completed 1972, was scrapped about 1974, but the class later entered production as the world's fastest and deepest-diving (over 700 m) combatant submarine. The pressure hull is constructed of titanium, and the ships are highly automated. High speeds are achieved through use of a very "dense" propulsion plant, with safety and accessibility standards much less than those of the West. The reactors use a lead-bismuth mixture as coolant. The second entered active service in 1979.

◆ **21 (+...) Victor-III class** Bldrs: Admiralty SY, Leningrad, and Komsomolsk SY (In serv. 1978, 1983, 1985–...)

**D:** 4,900/6,000 tons **S:** 29 kts (sub.) **Dim:** 106.0 × 10.0 × 7.0
**A:** 4/650-mm TT—2/533-mm TT (SS-N-15 and/or SS-N-16 missiles, torpedoes)
**Electron Equipt:** Radar: 1/Snoop Tray—Sonar: 1/LF active, passive arrays
**M:** 2 pressurized-water reactors, steam turbines; 1/tandem 8-bladed prop; 30,000 hp (plus 2 small props for maneuvering)
**Man:** 85 tot.

Remarks: Further lengthened over basic Victor-I; distinguished by large teardrop-shaped pod atop vertical stabilizer. At least one unit has a 10-m fairing on deck forward of the sail. Most employ an unusual 8-bladed propeller, consisting of two tandem 4-bladed props oriented 22.5-deg. apart and co-rotating; others have a standard 7-bladed prop. Have Pert Spring SATCOMM antenna.

**Victor-III**—showing tandem 8-bladed propeller U.S. Navy, 1983

**Victor-III** French Navy, 1986

**Victor-III** French Navy, 1986

**Victor-III** French Navy, 1983

**Victor-III** M.O.D., U.K., 7-86

ATTACK SUBMARINES (NUCLEAR) *(continued)*

After apparently coming to a close in 1982–83, production resumed with the launch of a 21st unit at Admiralty Shipyard, Leningrad, in 7-85 and a probable 22nd in the spring of 1987. The continued program may be for force-level maintenance, in view of the slow production of the newer and quieter Akula and Sierra-class submarines, or it may be for export, with India the likely recipient.

◆ **7 Victor-II class** Bldr: Admiralty SY, Leningrad (In serv. 1972–78)

**Victor-II class** French Navy, 1986

**Victor-II class**—sail detail, Park Lamp D/F antenna raised U.S. Navy, 2-86

**D:** 4,500/5,900 tons **S:** 30 kts **Dim:** 102.0 × 10.0 × 7.0
**A:** 4/650-mm TT—2/533-mm TT (SS-N-15 and/or SS-N-16 missiles, torpedoes)
**Electron Equipt:** Radar: Snoop Tray—Sonar: LF active/passive
EW: Brick Pulp, Brick Spit, Park Lamp D/F
**M:** 2 nuclear reactors, steam turbines; 1/5-bladed prop (plus 2 small props for maneuvering); 30,000 hp
**Man:** 80 tot.

Remarks: One went into service in each of the years 1972, 1974, and 1975, two in 1976, and one each in 1977 and 1978. Longer than Victor-I, without pronounced hump on forward casing. Have a VLF comms-buoy housing within the casing abaft the sail. Some may have 8-bladed propellers as per the Victor-III class.

◆ **16 Victor-I class** Bldr: Admiralty SY, Leningrad (In serv. 1968–75)

50 Let SSR 15 others

**Victor-I class**—with collision-damaged bow U.S. Navy, 1986

**Victor-I class** U.S. Navy, 1984

**D:** 4,300/5,100 tons **S:** 30 kts **Dim:** 95.0 × 10.0 × 7.0
**A:** 6/533-mm TT (SS-N-15 missiles, torpedoes)
**Electron Equipt:** Radar: 1/Snoop Tray—EW: 1/Brick Pulp, 1/Brick Spit, 1/Park Lamp D/F
Sonar: 1/LF active/passive arrays
**M:** 2 pressurized-water nuclear reactors, steam turbines; 1/5-bladed prop; 30,000 hp (2 small, 2-bladed props for slow speeds)
**Man:** 80 tot.

Remarks: Completed two per year between 1968 and 1975. Diving depth: 600 m max. operating.

**Victor-I class** French Navy, 1984

**ATTACK SUBMARINES (NUCLEAR)** *(continued)*

◆ **2 (+14) Yankee class** Bldr: Severodvinsk SY and Komsomolsk SY (In serv. 1967–1974)

**D:** 7,900/10,000 tons **S:** 27 kts **Dim:** 130.0 × 12.0 × 9.0
**A:** 6/533-mm TT (bow)
**Electron Equipt:** Radar: 1/Snoop Tray
Sonar: LF suite, passive arrays
**M:** 2 pressurized-water reactors, steam turbines; 2/5-bladed props; 45,000 hp
**Man:** 80 tot.

Remarks: These are former ballistic-missile submarines that have had their 16 SS-N-6 tubes disabled in compliance with the U.S.-Soviet SALT agreements. As more Delta-II and Typhoon ballistic-missile submarines are built, more Yankees will receive similar treatment in order to keep the number of submarine-launched ballistic-missile tubes at no more than 950. It is believed that, as the Yankees are relatively new, the Soviet Navy is probably adapting them for some other purpose, probably as attack submarines, or, possibly, as minelayers. The first unit completed alteration and reactivated 1984. Of two operational in 1987, the U.S. D.O.D.'s *Soviet Military Power* reports only one is configured as an attack submarine, leaving the other as a possible cruise missile (SS-NX-21?) conversion. See addenda for photo. Due to length of time out of service, it is likely that not all laid-up Yankees will be converted to new configurations.

◆ **3 Echo class** Bldr: Komsomolsk (In serv. 1960–62)

**Echo class** U.S. Navy, 1975

**Echo class**—with periscope, Stop Light EW, D/F loop, etc. raised 1978

**D:** 4,600/5,400 tons **S:** 20/25 kts **Dim:** 114.0 × 9.0 × 6.5
**A:** 6/533-mm TT (fwd)—4/400-mm TT (aft)
**Electron Equipt:** Radar: 1/Snoop Tray—Sonar: 1/MF.
**M:** 2 nuclear reactors, steam turbines; 2/5-bladed props; 25,000 hp
**Man:** 75 tot.

Remarks: Former cruise-missile submarines that carried six SS-N-3C. Converted circa 1970–75. One involved in a casualty 20-8-80, had to be towed to Vladivostok; several men died; that unit and one other have apparently been discarded: The sonar suite appears to duplicate that of the Foxtrot class. Survivors of marginal utility. All in Pacific Fleet.

◆ **12 November class** Bldr: Severodvinsk SY (In serv. 1958–62)

Leninskiy Komsomol Leninets 10 others

**D:** 4,500/5,300 tons **S:** 30 kts (sub.) **Dim:** 110.0 × 9.0 × 7.7
**A:** 8/533-mm TT (fwd)—4/400-mm TT (aft)—32 torpedoes or mines
**Electron Equipt:** Radar: 1/Snoop Tray
Sonar: 1/MF active, passive arrays
**M:** 2 nuclear reactors, steam turbines; 2 (4- or 6-bladed) props; 30,000 hp
**Man:** 80 tot.

Remarks: First unit completed 8-58. One of this class was lost off Cape Finisterre in 4-70. Another was apparently scrapped 1982–83. *Leninskiy Komsomol,* the U.S.S.R.'s first nuclear-powered ship, was commissioned 4-8-58; she later made the Soviet Navy's first trip to the North Pole. Obsolescent, but remains in service, probably on training and local defense duties.

**November class**

## ATTACK SUBMARINES (DIESEL-POWERED)

(Soviet Type: PL—*Podvodnaya Lodka* = Submarine)

◆ **1 Beluga class** Bldr: United Admiralty (Sudomelch) SY, Leningrad (In serv. 1987)

**D:** 2,000 tons (surf)/. . . (sub.) **S:** . . .
**Dim:** . . . × . . . × . . . **A:** . . .
**Electron Equipt:** Radar: . . .
Sonar: . . .—EW: . . .
**M:** diesel-electric: . . . **Man:** . . .

Remarks: Experimental submarine. Hull form reported to be like that of the Alfa.

◆ **14 (+ . . .) Kilo class** Bldr: Komsomolsk-na-Amur SY and Gorkiy SY (In serv. 1982–. . .)

**Kilo class**—note bow and sail sonar arrays French Navy, 6-86

**Kilo class**—EW mast and periscope raised French Navy, 1986

**ATTACK SUBMARINES (DIESEL)** *(continued)*

**Kilo class** U.S. Navy, 1986

**D:** 2,300/2,900 tons **S:** 12/20 kts **Dim:** 73.0 × 9.9 × 6.5
**A:** 6/533-mm TT (12 torpedoes)
**Electron Equipt:** Radar: 1/Snoop Tray—Sonar: LF suite
**M:** 2 diesels, electric drive; 1/6-bladed prop; . . . hp **Man:** approx. 60 tot.

Remarks: Function uncertain; may be intended to replace Whiskey/Romeo-class submarines in the "medium-range" category or Foxtrot, as a "long-range" boat. First unit launched 9-80, entering service 4-82. The second launched 8-81. Production now seems to be 2 or 3 per year, with some being for export. Reported to have some form of surface-to-air missile system in the sail. Also built at Leningrad's United Admiralty Shipyard for Soviet clients; some Gorkiy production may also be for export. To date Algeria (2), India (5), Romania (1 or 2), and Poland (4) have ordered the Kilo, with Cuba and Libya also likely to receive units. Number listed here as serving with Soviet Navy may be high, with possibly as few as 8 to 10 retained for domestic use.

◆ **22 Tango Class** Bldr: Gorkiy SY (In serv. 1972–82)

**Tango class** U.S. Navy, 1-85

**Tango class** U.S. Navy, 10-86

**Tango class** French Navy, 6-84

**Tango class** U.S. Navy, 2-86

**D:** 3,100/3,900 tons **S:** 20/16 kts **Dim:** 91.5 × 9.0 × 7.0
**A:** 10/533-mm TT (6 fwd, 4 aft, SS-N-15 missiles, torpedoes)
**Electron Equipt:** Radar: 1/Snoop Tray—EW: 1/Brick Pulp, 1/Brick Spit, D/F
Sonar: 1/LF active/passive
**M:** 3 diesels, electric motors; 3 props; 6,000 hp **Man:** 72 tot.

Remarks: Two entered in 1972, and roughly two per year were built. Hull sheathed in sonar-absorbent rubber compound. Have significantly greater battery capacity than the Foxtrot class. Other sources give as few as 18 or 19 completed.

◆ **45 Foxtrot class** Bldr: Admiralty/Sudomekh SY, Severodvinsk SY (In serv. 1957–68)

| | |
|---|---|
| Bryanskiy Komsomolets | Ul'yanovskiy Komsomolets |
| Chelyabinskiy Komsomolets | Vladimirskiy Komsomolets |
| Komsomolets Kazakhstana | Yaroslavskiy Komsomolets |
| Kuibishevskiy Komsomolets | 37 others |
| Magnitogorskiy Komsomolets | |

**Foxtrot class**—early limber-hole pattern, with folding HF whip raised 1982

**Foxtrot class**—later limber-hole pattern U.S. Navy, 2-87

## ATTACK SUBMARINES (DIESEL) *(continued)*

**Foxtrot class**—late-construction limber-hole pattern U.S. Navy, 1-79

**Whiskey class** G. Gyssels, 11-87

**Globus**—a Foxtrot on an oceanographic research cruise
LSPH S. Given, R.A.N., 1981

**D:** 1,950/2,400 tons **S:** 16/15.5 kts **Dim:** 91.5 × 7.5 × 6.0
**A:** 10/533-mm TT (6 fwd, 4 aft)—22 torpedoes or 44 mines
**Electron Equipt:** Radar: 1/Snoop Tray—EW: 1/Stop Light
Sonar: 1/MF active, passive arrays
**M:** 3 diesels of 2,000 hp, electric motors; 3 props; 5,300 hp (sub.)
**Endurance:** 70 days **Range:** 11,000/8 (snorkel), 350/2 (sub.)
**Man:** 8 officers, 70 men

Remarks: Foxtrot is a "long-range" submarine, and the design is a development of that of the Zulu class, with a large bow passive sonar array and a more streamlined sail. When used in oceanographic research service, Foxtrots are given temporary astronomical names; to date *Sirius, Saturn, Yupiter, Regul,* and *Globus* have been applied. Between 1967 and 1983, 17 were built for export at Leningrad: eight to India, six to Libya, and three to Cuba. Several Soviet Navy units have been lost. Early units are obsolescent, based on planned 27-year service life for this class, and at least 15 had been discarded or lost by 1987.

Note: Of the six Romeo-class attack submarines listed in the last edition, two were transferred to Bulgaria in 1985–86, and three went to Syria in 1985–86; it is unlikely that the sixth remains in use. The three Golf-class submarines converted as communications ships are now listed with the auxiliary submarines, as are the surviving Zulu-class submarines.

◆ **48 Whiskey class** Bldrs: Baltic SY, Leningrad; Marti SY, Nikolayev; Gorkiy SY; Komsomolsk-na-Amur SY (In serv. 1949–57)

**D:** 1,050/1,350 tons **S:** 17/13.5 kts **Dim:** 76.0 × 6.3 × 4.8
**A:** 6/533-mm TT (4 fwd, 2 aft)—12 torpedoes or 24 mines
**Electron Equipt:** Radar: 1/Snoop Plate—EW: Stop Light, D/F loop
Sonar: 1/Tamir 5 MF active; small passive array
**M:** 2 Type 37D, 2,000-hp diesels, electric motors; 2 props; 2,500 hp (sub.)
**Endurance:** 40–45 days **Range:** 6,000/5 (snorkel) **Man:** 50 tot.

Remarks: Built in prefabricated sections, these strong, uncomplicated boats have proven quite satisfactory. Approximately 236 were built in the U.S.S.R., with China also having built the design. Despite the age and total obsolescence, a number remain active. Considered to be "medium-range" submarines. Twelve were converted to cruise-missile boats. Four were modified as radar-picket submarines. Some have been transferred to Bulgaria, Egypt, Poland, Albania, China, and Indonesia. One active Baltic Fleet boat is named *Pskovskiy Komsomolets.*

**Whiskey class** G. Gyssels, 11-87

**Whiskey class** 1977

**Whiskey class** U.S. Navy, 11-84

## AUXILIARY SUBMARINES (NUCLEAR-POWERED)

◆ **1 X ray class** Bldr: United Admiralty (Sudomekh) SY, Leningrad (In serv. 1983)

**D:** . . . **S:** . . . **Dim:** . . . × . . . × . . .
**A:** probably none **Electron Equipt:** . . .
**M:** 1 nuclear reactor; . . . **Man:** . . .

Remarks: Reportedly analogous to the U.S. Navy's NR-1 and intended for oceanographic research purposes.

◆ **1 Uniform class** Bldr: United Admiralty (Sudomekh) SY, Leningrad (L: 6-82)

**D:** 2,000 tons (sub.) **S:** . . . **Dim:** . . . × . . . × . . .
**A:** . . . **M:** nuclear reactor; . . . prop; . . . hp **Man:** . . .

Remarks: Apparently intended for research or special operations. The first Soviet single-hulled nuclear-powered submarine.

**AUXILIARY SUBMARINES (NUCLEAR)** *(continued)*

◆ **1 converted Echo-II class**

Remarks: One Echo-II-class nuclear-powered cruise-missile submarine has been modified for an unknown research purpose. The eight tubes for SS-N-3A missiles have apparently been removed. May be intended for special operations with *Spetsnaz* sabotage swimmers. General data listed earlier otherwise apply.

◆ **1 converted Hotel-II class** (In serv. circa 1959–62)

**D:** approx. 4,500 tons (surf.)/5,500 tons (sub.) **S:** 20/25 kts
**Dim:** 116.0 × 9.0 × 7.0 **Man:** . . .
**A:** 6/533-mm TT fwd.—4/400-mm TT aft
**Electron Equipt:** Radar: . . .—EW: . . .
Sonar: MF active/passive
**M:** 2 pressurized-water nuclear reactors, steam turbines; 2/6-bladed props; 30,000 hp

Remarks: Three SS-N-5 ballistic-missile tubes removed, sail shortened. Transformed into a communications relay/command submarine during the early 1980s, apparently similar to the three Golf-class conversions for that purpose. Four other Hotel-IIs, retired as part of the SALT-I disarmament agreement, may yet receive similar conversions.

**AUXILIARY SUBMARINES (DIESEL-POWERED)**

◆ **1 Lima-class research submarine** Bldr: Admiralty SY, Leningrad (In serv. 1978)

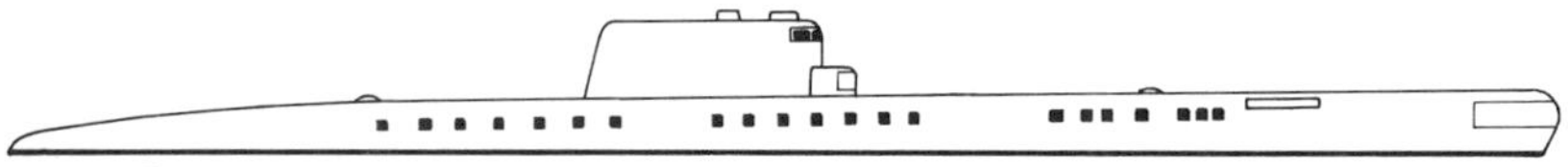

**Lima class**

**D:** 2,000/2,400 tons **S:** . . . **Dim:** 86.0 × 9.5 × 7.4
**A:** none **M:** diesels, electric drive; . . . props; . . . hp **Man:** . . .

Remarks: Function not available. Sail, set well aft on unusually bulky hull, has forward extension housing an active sonar transducer and has fixed radar mast.

◆ **2 India-class salvage submarines** Bldr: Komsomolsk-na-Amur SY (In serv. 1979–80)

**D:** 3,900/4,800 tons **S:** 15/15
**Dim:** 106.0 × 10.0 × . . . **A:** probably none
**Electron Equipt:** Radar: . . .—Sonar: 1/MF; passive arrays
**M:** . . . diesels, electric motors; 2 props; . . . hp **Man:** . . .

**The Pacific Fleet India** J.M.S.D.F., 1987

**The Northern Fleet India**—with two salvage submersibles in their docking wells U.S. Navy, 1982

**The Pacific Fleet India** U.S. Navy, 1987

Remarks: Originally carried two 11-m salvage/submarine-rescue submersibles in wells on after casing; the Pacific Fleet unit had been re-equipped with 12.1-m craft by 1987. Hull designed for surface cruising. May not have armament, considering function and the narrow hull configuration forward. One unit remains in Pacific, the other transited the Arctic to the Northern Fleet, 1980.

◆ **4 Bravo-class target-training submarines** Bldr: Komsomolsk SY, Komsomolsk-na-Amur (In serv. 1968–70)

**Bravo class** 1975

**Bravo class** U.S. Navy, 1979

**D:** 2,400/2,900 tons **S:** 14/16 kts **Dim:** 70.1 × 9.8 × 7.3
**A:** 6/533-mm TT (fwd)
**Electron Equipt:** Radar: 1/Snoop Tray—Sonar: 1 passive array—EW: . . .
**M:** diesel-electric drive; 1 prop; 4,500 hp **Man:** 65 tot.

Remarks: Configured as "hard" targets for torpedo-firing training, they may also have a training role and, if indeed armed, could be used as attack subs in wartime. Given bow shape and low location of sonar window, may actually not be armed.

◆ **3 Modified Golf class**

**Modified Golf class** *Ships of the World,* 5-84

### AUXILIARY SUBMARINES (DIESEL) *(continued)*

**D:** 2,300/2,700 tons **S:** 12 kts (sub.) **Dim:** 100.0 × 8.5 × 6.6
**A:** 10/533-mm TT (6 fwd, 4 aft)
**Electron Equipt:** Radar: 1/Snoop Tray—EW: 1/Stop Light
Sonar: 1/MF active; passive arrays
**M:** 3 diesels of 2,000 hp, electric motors; 3 props; 5,300 hp (sub.)
**Endurance:** 70 days **Range:** 9,500/5 (snorkel) **Man:** 80 tot.

REMARKS: Three missile tubes removed. Apparently converted in 1978 as submersible command ships. Structure aft supports folding whip antennas; there are similar whips on either side of the sail. Sail extension houses VLF buoy antenna. A Hotel nuclear-powered ballistic-missile submarine has received a similar conversion.

◆ **3 Zulu-IV class** Bldr: Sudomekh SY, Leningrad (In serv. 1952–57)

**Zulu-IV class** U.S. Navy, 8-84

**D:** 1,900/2,350 tons **S:** 18/16 kts **Dim:** 90.0 × 7.5 × 6.0
**A:** 10/533-mm TT (6 fwd, 4 aft)—22 torpedoes or 44 mines
**Electron Equipt:** Radar: 1/Snoop Plate
Sonar: 1/MF; small passive array
**M:** 3 Type 37D diesels of 2,000 hp, electric drive; 3 props; 5,300 hp (sub.)
**Endurance:** 70 days **Range:** 9,500/8 (snorkel) **Man:** 70 tot.

REMARKS: Between 1956 and 1957, several (since scrapped) were converted as Zulu-V ballistic-missile submarines, the world's first of their type; each had two tubes for surface launch of SS-N-4. Twenty other Zulu-IVs have been scrapped. Earlier configurations (Zulu-I to Zulu-III) had deck guns, AA guns in the sail, and no snorkel; all later updated to Zulu-IV standard. Two have served in "oceanographic research" roles as *Vega* and *Lira*.

### MINIATURE SUBMARINES (SUBMERSIBLES)

The Soviet Navy possesses a number of small submersibles for clandestine operations by *Spetsnaz* forces. Some are probably similar to the salvage submersibles carried by the India class. Many other small submersibles, Soviet and foreign-built, are used for military and civilian research purposes.

### GUIDED-MISSILE CRUISERS (NUCLEAR-POWERED)

◆ **2 (+2) Kirov class** Bldr: Baltic SY, Leningrad

| | Laid down | L | In serv. |
|---|---|---|---|
| KIROV | 1973 | 12-77 | 9-80 |
| FRUNZE | 1-78 | 23-5-81 | 8-84 |
| KALININ | . . . | 4-86 | 1989 |
| N . . . | 4-86 | 1989 | . . . |

**D:** 24,000 tons (28,000 fl) **S:** 32 kts
**Dim:** 248.0 (230.0 wl) × 28.0 (24.0 wl) × 8.8 (10.5 max.)
**A:** *Kirov:* 20/SS-N-19 SSM (20 inclined tubes)—12/SA-N-6 vertical SAM launchers (96 Grumble missiles)—2/SA-N-4 SAM syst. (II × 2, 40 Gecko missiles)—2/100-mm DP (I × 2)—8/30-mm gatling AA (I × 8)—1/SS-N-14 ASW cruise-missile launcher (II × 1, 14–16 missiles)—10/533-mm TT (V × 2)—1/RBU-6000 ASW RL (XII × 1)—2/RBU-1000 ASW RL (VI × 2)—3/Hormone-A and/or -B helicopters or Helix-A.
*Frunze:* 20/SS-N-19 SSM (20 inclined tubes)—12/SA-N-6 vertical SAM launchers (96 Grumble missiles)—16/SA-N-9 vertical SAM launchers, not yet operational (128 missiles)—2/SA-N-4 SAM syst. (II × 2, 40 Gecko missiles)—2/130-mm DP (II × 1)—8/30-mm gatling AA (I × 8)—10/533-mm TT (V × 2)—1/RBU-6000 ASW RL (XII × 1)—2/RBU-1000 ASW RL (VI × 2)—2/Helix-A and 1/Hormone-B helicopters
**Electron Equipt:** *Kirov:* Radar: 3/Palm Frond, 1/Top Pair, 1/Top Steer, 2/Top Dome, 2/Pop Group, 2/Eye Bowl, 1/Kite Screech, 4/Base Tilt, 1/Fly Screen landing aid
IFF: 1/Salt Pot transponder—E/O: 4/Tin Man
Sonar: 1/LF bow-mounted, 1/LF VDS
EW: 8/Side Globe, 4/Rum Tub, 10/Bell-series, 2/chaff RL (II × 2)
TACAN: 2/Round House
SATCOMM: 2/Punch Bowl
*Frunze:* Radar: 3/Palm Frond, 1/Top Steer, 2/Top Dome, 2/locations for future SA-N-9 f.c., 2/Pop Group, 1/Kite Screech, 4/Bass Tilt, 1/Fly Screen
IFF: . . .—E/O: 4/Tin Man
Sonar: as for *Kirov*
EW: 8/Wine Flask, 10/Bell-series, 2/chaff RL (II × 2)
TACAN: 2/Round House
SATCOMM: 2/Low Ball, 2/Punch Bowl
**Man:** CONAS: 2 nuclear reactors + 2 oil-fired boilers, steam turbines; 2 props; 150,000 hp
**Range:** effectively unlimited **Fuel:** 2,500 tons **Man:** approx. 800 tot.

REMARKS:
1. *General:* The *Kirov* class are the world's largest "cruisers" and might best be termed "battlecruisers." The Soviet type-designation applied has been merely RKR—*Raketnyy Kreyser* (Missile Cruiser). The ship is capable of independent operations, due to the virtual autonomy conveyed by the nuclear propulsion

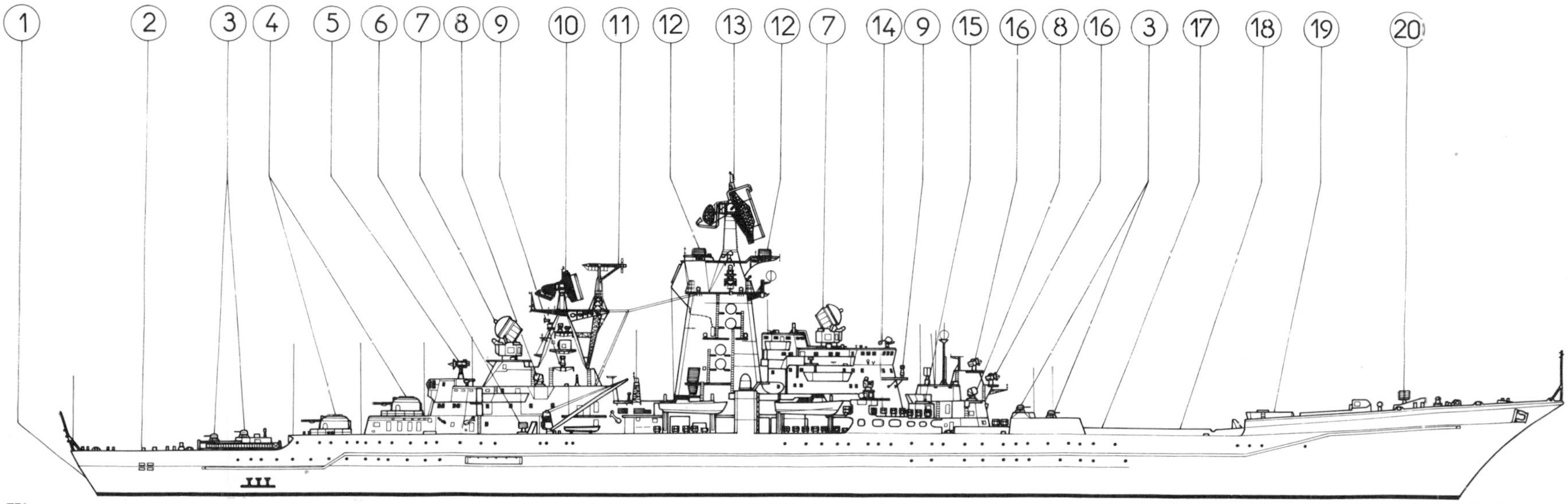


**Kirov** L. Gassier
1. variable-depth sonar 2. helicopter pad 3. 30-mm gatling AA guns 4. 100-mm DP gun mounts 5. Kite Screech radar director for 100-mm guns 6. RBU-1000 ASW RL 7. Top Dome radar director for SA-N-6 8. Bass Tilt radar director for 30-mm AA 9. Tin Man optronic device 10. Top Steer radar 11. Vee Tube HF comms. antenna 12. Round House TACAN 13. Top Pair 3-D early-warning radar antenna 14. Palm Frond navigational radar 15. SA-N-4 SAM launcher 16. Eye Bowl radar director for SS-N-14 17. SS-N-19 cruise-missile launchers 18. SA-N-6 vertical SAM launch silos 19. twin SS-N-14 ASW/SSM launcher 20. RBU-6000 ASW RL

GUIDED-MISSILE CRUISERS (NUCLEAR) *(continued)*

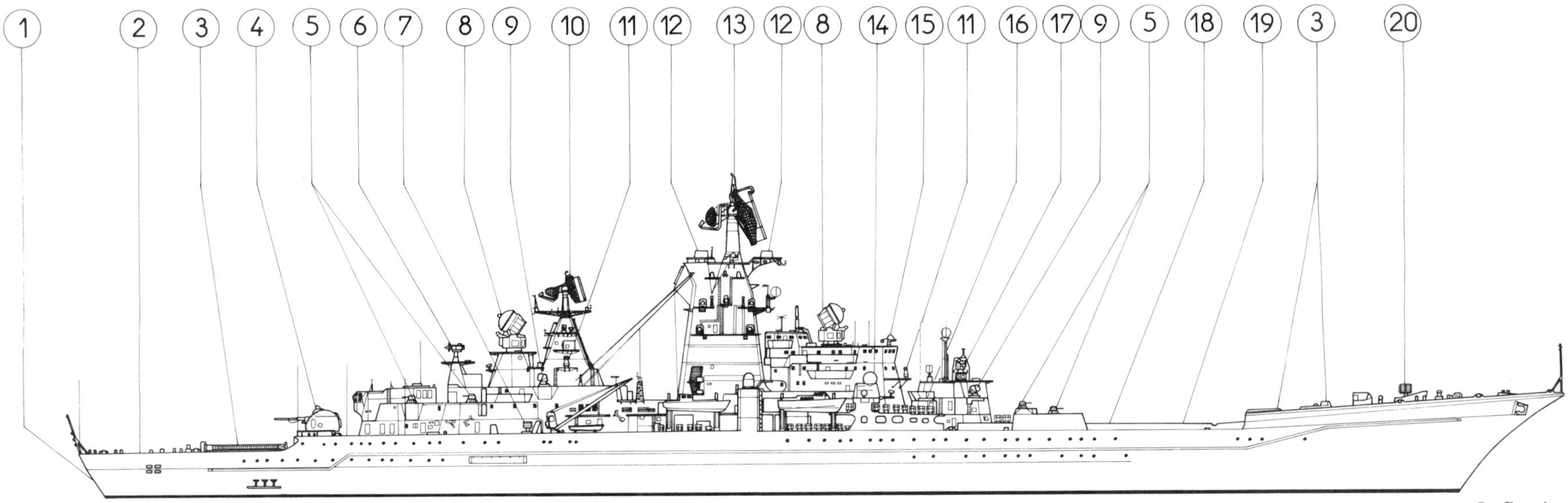


**Frunze** L. Gassier

1. variable-depth sonar 2. helicopter pad 3. SA-N-9 vertical-launch SAM silos 4. twin 130-mm DP gun mount 5. 30-mm gatling AA 6. Kite Screech radar director for 130-mm guns 7. RBU-1000 ASW RL 8. Top Dome radar director for SA-N-6 9. Bass Tilt radar director for 30-mm AA 10. Top Steer radar antenna 11. Tin Man optronic device 12. Round House TACAN 13. Top Pair 3-D early-warning radar antenna 14. Big Ball SATCOMM antenna radome 15. Palm Frond navigational radar 16. SA-N-4 SAM launcher 17. Pop Group track-while-scan radar director for SA-N-4 18. SS-N-19 cruise-missile launchers 19. SA-N-6 vertical SAM launch silos 20. RBU-6000 ASW RL

**Kirov** French Navy, 1984

**Kirov** French Navy, 1984

**Kirov**—showing VDS door in stern U.S. Navy, 1984

**GUIDED-MISSILE CRUISERS (NUCLEAR)** *(continued)*

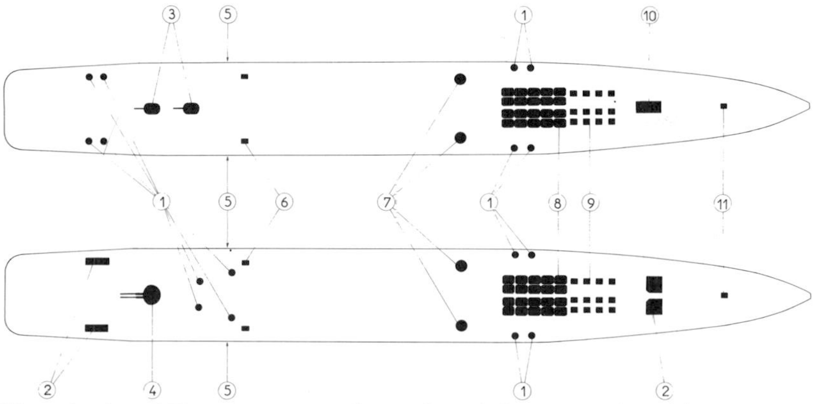


**Kirov (top) and Frunze compared** 1. 6-barreled 30-mm gatling AA 2. SA-N-9 silos (8 missiles each) 3. 100-mm single-mount DP 4. 130-mm twin-mount DP 5. quintuple torpedo tubes 6. RBU-1000 ASW RL (6-tubed) 7. SA-N-4 twin SAM launchers (20 missiles each) 8. SS-N-19 inclined cruise-missile launch-tube hatches 9. SA-N-6 vertical-launch SAM hatches (8 missiles to each position) 10. twin SS-N-14 ASW missile launcher 11. RBU-6000 ASW RL (12-tubed)

**Frunze**—showing twin 130-mm gun aft U.S. Navy, 1986

**Frunze** PHC(NAC) J. Kristoffersen, USN, 11-85

**Frunze** J.M.S.D.F., 1986

system, but it would also make an ideal escort for the forthcoming nuclear-powered carrier. The *Kirov* and *Frunze* differ considerably in armament and sensors, and *Kalinin,* laid down some years later, may differ further still. *Frunze* deployed to the Pacific in 9-10-85, while *Kirov* is in the Northern Fleet. A fourth has been laid down.

2. *Hull:* On *Kirov* the high forecastle shelters the reloadable SS-N-14 ASW cruise-missile launcher within a redoubt or cul-de-sac. A long, raised strake down either side of the hull acts as an external hull stiffener, as on smaller Soviet warships. The helicopter hangar is beneath the forward portion of the fantail, with an elevator delivering the aircraft to the flight deck. The steeply raked stern has a 9-m broad centerline recess for the VDS installation, whose door when closed is raked forward past the vertical. The screws appear to be mounted unusually far forward. Two solid-stores replenishment stations are fitted: one amidships to port, and one folding station forward to port, abreast the SA-N-6 system; both employ the sliding-stay, constant-tension concept. Oil and water replenishments are handled at stations on either beam abreast the Kite Screech radar. *Frunze*'s forward transfer gear is considerably more compact.
3. *Propulsion:* The two circular reactor access hatches can be seen amidships, just abaft the enormous twin exhaust uptakes for the unusual CONAS (Combined Nuclear and Steam) propulsion system. The oil-fired boilers provide steam to completely separate turbines, which are geared to the same drive shafts as the nuclear-supplied turbines. One stack probably serves the oil-fired boilers, while the other serves to ventilate the reactor spaces. Speed on reactors alone (90,000 hp) would be about 24 kts.
4. *Armament:* The launch tubes for the 20 SS-N-19 antiship missiles are buried within the hull at a fixed angle of 40–45-degree elevation, in four rows of five, forward of the superstructure. Before these are the 12 vertical launchers for SA-N-6; each has a door, beneath which is a rotating magazine containing 8 missiles. Targeting data, for the SS-N-19, with its 300-nautical-mile maximum range, can come either from a Hormone-B helicopter embarked on the ship, or from satellites, via the Punch Bowl satellite communications antennas on either side of the ship. In *Kirov* only, the SS-N-14 ASW cruise-missile system is the first *reloadable* installation in a Soviet ship, employing a magazine forward of the launcher, buried within the forecastle. The gatling guns are paired and located so as to cover all four quadrants; each pair is served by a Bass Tilt radar director and a manned, optical backup director. *Frunze* has a single twin 130-mm gun mount in place of the two 100-mm mounts and lacks the SS-N-14 system; instead, eight SA-N-9 launchers will be buried in the forecastle, while eight more are to be located in place of the after 30-mm gatling guns, four per side (the gatling guns are mounted on the aft superstructure). The two Cross Sword directors for SA-N-9 were yet to be mounted by 1986 and are intended to be positioned abaft the Kite Screech aft and between the two Pop Group directors forward; the SA-N-4 installation may be a temporary stopgap.
5. *Electronic equipment:* As might be expected, the communications antenna array is extensive and diverse and includes satellite communications equipment and long-range HF gear. There are four stabilized Tin Man electro-optical sensors,

### GUIDED-MISSILE CRUISERS (NUCLEAR) *(continued)*

covering all four quadrants, as well as smaller remote t.v. cameras. Two Bob Tail radiometric sextant antennas are housed in spherical enclosures. A Fly Screen microwave landing approach radar is mounted on a starboard platform on the after tower mast. The VDS employs a lens-shaped "fish" about 4 m in diameter to house the transducer and has a twin boom-mounted empennage with horizontal and vertical control surfaces. In addition to a low-frequency bow-mounted sonar, there is probably a medium-frequency set for fire-control purposes (including depth determination) for the RBU-series rocket launchers. *Frunze* lacks the large Vee Tube HF communications antenna but has port-and-starboard Low Ball SATCOMM antenna radomes; she has a newer model EW suite also. (The devices listed here as Wine Flask have also been referred to as "Modified Football"; they appear to be combined receiver/jammers.)

### GUIDED-MISSILE CRUISERS

◆ **2 (+1) Slava class** Bldr: 61 Kommuna SY, Nikolayev

| | Laid down | L | In serv. |
|---|---|---|---|
| Slava ("Glory") | 1976 | 1979 | 1982 |
| Marshal Ustinov | 1978 | 1981 | 1986 |
| N. . . . . . . | 1979 | 1983 | 1988 |

**D:** 10,000 tons (12,500 fl) **S:** 32 kts
**Dim:** 186.0 × 20.3 × 8.0 (mean hull)
**A:** 16/SS-N-12 SSM (II × 8)—8/SA-N-6 vertical-launch SAM groups (VIII × 8, 64 Grumble missiles)—2/SA-N-4 SAM syst. (II × 2, 40 Gecko missiles)—2/130-mm 70-cal. DP (II × 1)—6/30-mm gatling AA (I × 6)—10/533-mm TT (V × 2)—2/RBU-6000 ASW RL (XII × 2)—1/Hormone-B helicopter

**Slava** French Navy, 1986

**Marshal Ustinov** French Navy, 1987

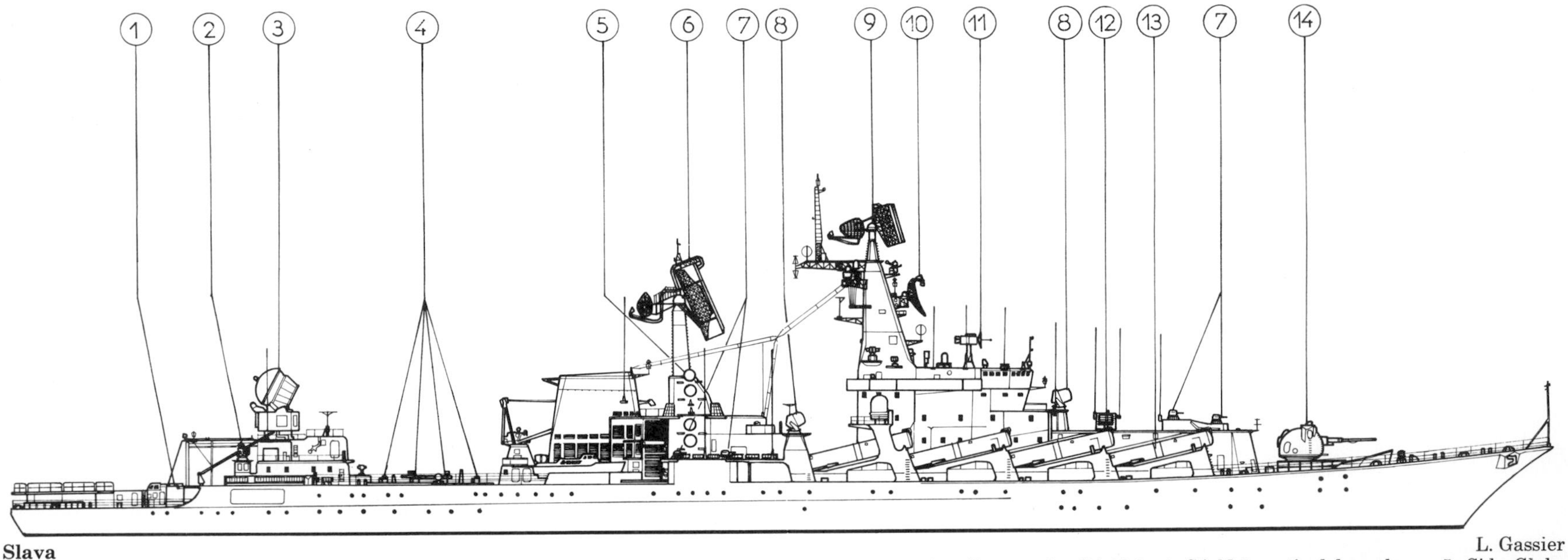


**Slava** L. Gassier
1. SA-N-4 launchers port and starboard 2. Pop Group radar director for SA-N-4 3. Top Dome radar director for SA-N-6 4. SA-N-6 vertical launchers 5. Side Globe electronic-warfare antennas 6. Top Pair 3-D early-warning radar 7. 30-mm gatling AA 8. Bass Tilt radar directors for 30-mm AA 9. Top Steer 3-D air-search radar 10. Front Door/Front Piece tracking radar for SS-N-12 11. Kite Screech fire-control radar for 130-mm DP 12. RBU-6000 ASW RL 13. SS-N-12 antiship missile tubes 14. twin 130-mm DP gun mount

GUIDED-MISSILE CRUISERS *(continued)*

**Marshal Ustinov** French Navy, 1987

**Slava** CDR S. Lyle/LCDR F. Gordon, USN, 9-84

**Slava** U.S.D.O.D., 1983

**Electron Equipt:** Radar: 3/Palm Frond, 1/Top Pair, 1/Top Steer, 1/Top Dome, 2/Pop Group, 1/Kite Screech, 3/Bass Tilt, 1/Front Door-Front Piece
EW: 8/Slide Globe, 4/Rum Tub, numerous Bell-series, 2/Chaff RL (II × 2)
Sonar: LF hull-mounted, MF VDS—E/O: 2/Tee Plinth

**M:** COGOG: 4 boost gas turbines, 30,000 hp each; 2 cruise gas turbines, 12,000 hp each; 2 props; 120,000 hp

**Man:** 720 tot. **Range:** 2,000/30; 8,800/15

**Electric:** 4 gas-turbine sets; 6,000 kw

Remarks: *Slava* first deployed from the Black Sea on 15-9-83. Unusual in having considerable equipment that is not the latest of its type in Soviet service, including the main battery, SS-N-12 missile system. There are two Punch Bowl targeting satellite data receivers. Typed *Raketnyy Kreyser* (Missile Cruiser) by the Soviet Navy. Fitted as flagships. *Slava* is attached to the Black Sea Fleet. At least four will probably be built.

Only one Top Dome director is fitted for the SA-N-6 system, limiting its flexibility. The torpedo tubes are mounted behind shutters in the ship's sides, near the stern. Initially referred to by the NATO code name "Blk-Com-1" and later, briefly, as the "Krasina" class. The hangar floor is one-half-deck below the flight deck, which is reached via an inclined ramp, the helicopter being maneuvered by a chain-haul system. Each of the paired stack uptakes incorporates one cruise-turbine exhaust, two boost-turbine exhausts, and two gas-turbine generator exhausts.

**Slava**—showing hangar open, crane raised French Navy, 10-83

GUIDED-MISSILE CRUISERS *(continued)*

◆ **1 Modified Kara class** Bldr: Black Sea SY, Nikolayev

| | Laid down | L | In serv. |
|---|---|---|---|
| Azov | 1972 | 1974 | 1977 |

**Azov** French Navy, 1986

**Azov**—note Top Dome aft French Navy, 1986

**Azov** French Navy, 1986

**D:** 8,200 tons (9,700 fl) **S:** 34 kts **Dim:** 173.0 × 18.6 × 6.7 (mean hull)
**A:** 8/SS-N-14 Silex ASW/antiship (IV × 2)—4/SA-N-6 vertical SAM launchers (VIII × 4, 32 Grumble missiles)—1/SA-N-3 SAM system (II × 1, 22 Goblet missiles)—2/SA-N-4 SAM systems (II × 2, 40 Gecko missiles)—4/76.2-mm DP (II × 2)—4/30-mm gatling AA (I × 4)—4/533-mm TT (II × 2)—2/RBU-6000 ASW RL (XII × 2)—2/RBU-1000 ASW RL (VI × 2)—1/Ka-25 Hormone-A ASW helicopter
**Electron Equipt:** Radar: 1/Don-2, 2/Don Kay, 1/Top Sail, 1/Head Net-C, 1/Top Dome, 2/Head Lights-C, 2/Pop Group, 2/Owl Screech, 2/Bass Tilt
Sonar: 1/LF hull-mounted, 1/MF VDS
EW: 8/Side Globe, 2/Bell Clout, 2/Bell Slam, 2/Bell Tap, 2/chaff RL (II × 2)
**M:** 4 gas turbines; 2 props; 120,000 hp
**Range:** 3,000/32; 8,000/15 **Man:** 43 officers, 330 men

Remarks: The fourth hull in the Kara series, *Azov* was modified as trials ship for the SA-N-6 vertical-launch SAM system and only made her first (and only, to date) deployment from the Black Sea in mid-1986. The SA-N-6 installation replaces the after SA-N-3 launcher, magazine, and associated Head Lights-C guidance radar. Because of restricted space, it was possible to fit only two twin torpedo tubes instead of the normal quintuple mounts.

◆ **6 Kara class** Bldr: 61 Kommuna SY, Nikolayev

| | Laid down | L | In serv. |
|---|---|---|---|
| Nikolayev | 1969 | 1971 | 1973 |
| Ochakov | 1970 | 1972 | 1975 |
| Kerch | 1971 | 1973 | 1976 |
| Petropavlovsk | 1973 | 1975 | 1978 |
| Tashkent | 1975 | 1976 | 1979 |
| Tallin | 1976 | 1977 | 1980 |

**Ochakov** AO1 Boddie, USN, 10-86

**Petropavlovsk**—with higher hangar, small Round House TACAN radome, and no RBU-1000 U.S. Navy, 3-82

**Tashkent**—with Hormone-A on deck U.S. Navy, 1987

**Nikolayev** U.S. Navy, 1986

**GUIDED-MISSILE CRUISERS** *(continued)*

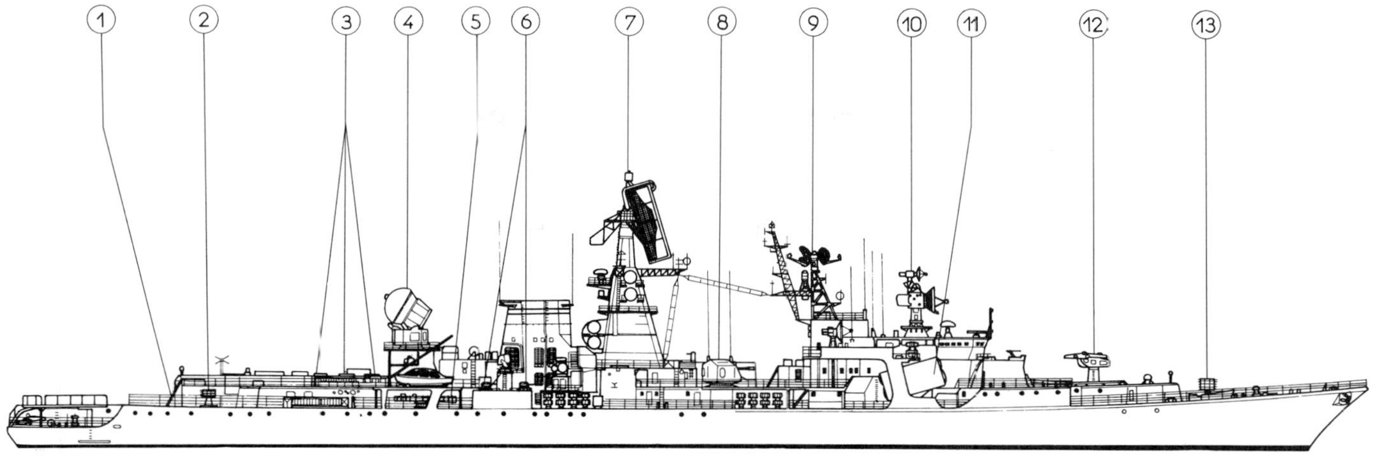

**Azov** L. Gassier
1. helicopter hangar 2. RBU-1000 ASW RL (VI × 2) 3. SA-N-6 vertical-launch SAM silo area 4. Top Dome guidance radar 5. 533-mm torpedo tubes (II × 2) 6. 30-mm 6-barreled gatling AA 7. Top Sail 3-D air-search radar 8. 76.2-mm DP (II × 2) 9. Head Net-C air/surface-search radar 10. Head Lights-C guidance radar 11. SS-N-14 antisubmarine/antiship missile launchers (IV × 2) 12. SA-N-3 SAM launcher 13. RBU-6000 ASW RL (XII × 2)

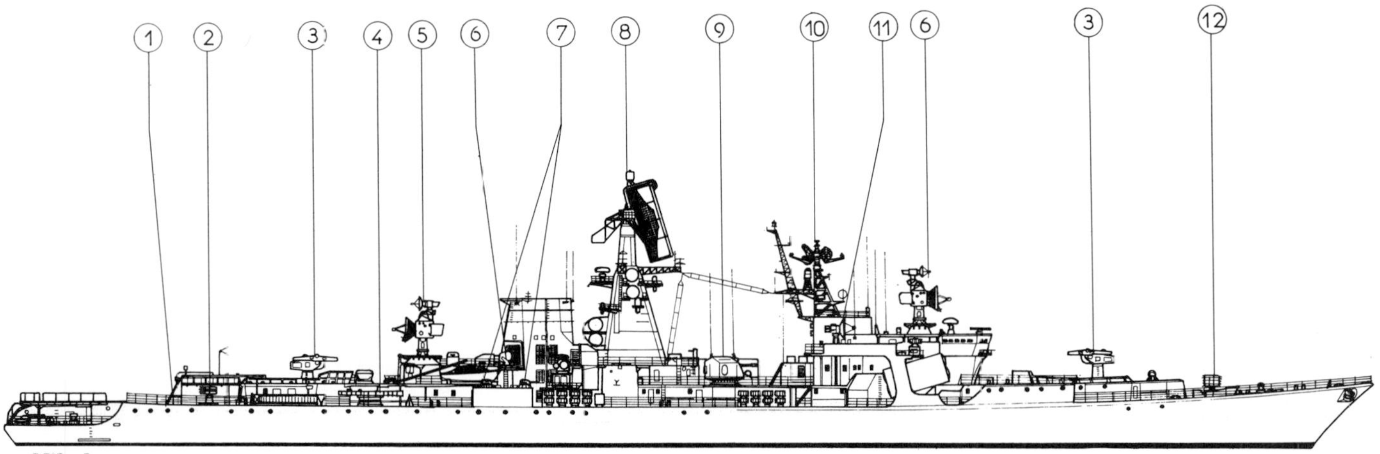

**Nikolayev** L. Gassier
1. helicopter hangar 2. RBU-1000 ASW RL (VI × 2) 3. SA-N-3 SAM launcher 4. 533-mm TT (V × 2) 5 and 6. Head Lights-C guidance radars 7. 30-mm 6-barreled gatling AA (I × 4) 8. Top Sail 3-D air-search radar 9. 76.2-mm DP (II × 2) 10. Head Net-C air/surface-search radar 11. Owl Screech gun-control radar (2) 12. RBU-6000 ASW RL (XII × 2)

**D:** 8,200 tons (9,700 fl) **S:** 34 kts **Dim:** 173.0 × 18.6 × 6.7
**A:** 8/SS-N-14 (IV × 2, 8 Silex missiles)—2/SA-N-3 systems (II × 2, 44 Goblet missiles)—4/SA-N-4 (II × 2, 40 Gecko missiles)—4/76.2-mm DP (II × 2)—4/30-mm gatling AA (I × 4)—10/533-mm TT (V × 2)—2/RBU-6000 ASW RL (XII × 2)—2/RBU-1000 ASW RL (VI × 2)—1/Hormone-A helicopter—see Remarks
**Electron Equipt:** Radar: 1/Don-2 or Palm Frond, 2/Don-Kay, 1/Top Sail, 1/Head Net-C, 2/Head Lights, 2/Pop Group, 2/Owl Screech, 2/Bass Tilt
Sonar: 1/LF hull-mounted, 1/MF VDS
EW: 8/Side Globe, 2/Bell Clout, 2/Bell Slam, 2/Bell Tap (or 4/Rum Tub), 2/chaff RL (II × 2)
IFF: 1/Salt Pot transponder (interrogation by search radars)
**M:** 4 gas turbines; 2 props; 120,000 hp
**Range:** 3,000/32; 8,000/15 **Man:** 30 officers, 490 men

Remarks: Soviet type designation: *Bol'shoy Protivolodochnyy Korabl'* (Large Antisubmarine Ship), a type considered to be more in the destroyer than the cruiser category. *Petropavlovsk* has two cylindrical Round House TACAN abreast the helicopter hangar, which is higher than on the other ships; she has no RBU-1000 rocket launchers. She and the *Tashkent* joined the Pacific Fleet in 1979, with *Ochakov* following later. The others are in the Black Sea Fleet. *Ochakov* was in collision with the Kashin-class destroyer *Strogiy* in 10-86. The last three built have incomplete EW suites, having been equipped to take 4 Rum Tub, as on *Petropavlovsk* and *Kerch*. *Nikolayev* is unique in having Square Head IFF interrogators on either side of the stack. SA-N-3, SA-N-4, and SS-N-14 can also be used against surface targets. As in the Kresta-II class, the helicopter hangar is at main-deck level, the helicopter being raised to flight-deck level by means of an inclined elevator.

◆ **10 Kresta-II class** Bldr: Zhdanov SY, Leningrad

| | L | In serv. | | L | In serv. |
|---|---|---|---|---|---|
| Kronshtadt | 1967 | 12-69 | Admiral Oktyabr'skiy | 1971 | 11-73 |
| Admiral Isakov | 1968 | 9-70 | Admiral Isachenkov | 1972 | 9-74 |
| Admiral Nakhimov | 1969 | 8-71 | Marshal Timoshenko | 1973 | 9-75 |
| Admiral Makarov | 1970 | 8-72 | Vasily Chapaev | 1975 | 10-76 |
| Marshal Voroshilov | 1970 | 5-73 | Admiral Yumashev | 1976 | 1-78 |

**Admiral Makarov** U.S. Navy

**GUIDED-MISSILE CRUISERS** *(continued)*

**Admiral Isachenkov** *Ships of the World,* 1984

**D:** 6,200 tons (7,700 fl) **S:** 34 kts **Dim:** 158.5 × 17.1 × 6.3 (6.0 hull)
**A:** 8/SS-N-14 (IV × 2, 8 Silex missiles)—2/SA-N-3 systems (II × 2, 44 Goblet missiles)—4/57-mm DP (II × 2)—4/30-mm gatling AA (I × 4)—2/RBU-6000 ASW RL (XII × 2)—2/RBU-1000 ASW RL (VI × 2)—10/533-mm TT (V × 2)—1/Hormone-A helicopter
**Electron Equipt:** Radar: 1/Don-2, 2/Don-Kay, 1/Top Sail, 1/Head Net-C, 2/Head Lights-C, 2/Muff Cob, 2/Bass Tilt (not in all)
Sonar: 1/MF hull-mounted—E/O:2/Tee Plinth
EW: 8/Side Globe, 1/Bell Clout, 2/Bell Slam, 2/Bell Tap, 2/chaff RL (II × 2)
IFF: 1/High Pole B, 1/High Pole A (interrogation by search radars)
**M:** 2 sets GT: 2 props; 100,000 hp **Boilers:** 4, turbopressurized
**Fuel:** 1,100 tons **Range:** 2,400/32; 10,500/14 **Man:** 380 tot.

Remarks: Soviet type designation: BPK—*Bol'shoy Protivolodochnyy Korabl'* (Large Antisubmarine Ship). The first four units do not have Bass Tilt and must control their 30-mm AA with lead-computing optical directors only. *Kronshtadt* has earlier versions of the Head Lights control radar for SA-N-3 and SS-N-14. The three final units have larger forward superstructure, the area between the tower foremast and the bridge being filled in by a two-level deckhouse. *Admiral Makarov* has prototype solid-stores equipment to port and prototype underway refueling equipment to starboard. SA-N-3 and SS-N-14 can also be used against surface targets. Have fin stabilizers. The helicopter hangar is one deck lower than the flight deck and is reached by means of an inclined elevator, as on the Kara class.

**Admiral Nakhimov**—without Bass Tilt radar directors U.S. Navy, 5-83

**Marshal Timoshenko**—note enlarged superstructure between bridge and tower mast, Bass Tilt radar directors on bridge wings above SS-N-14 launchers U.S. Navy, 1982

GUIDED-MISSILE CRUISERS *(continued)*

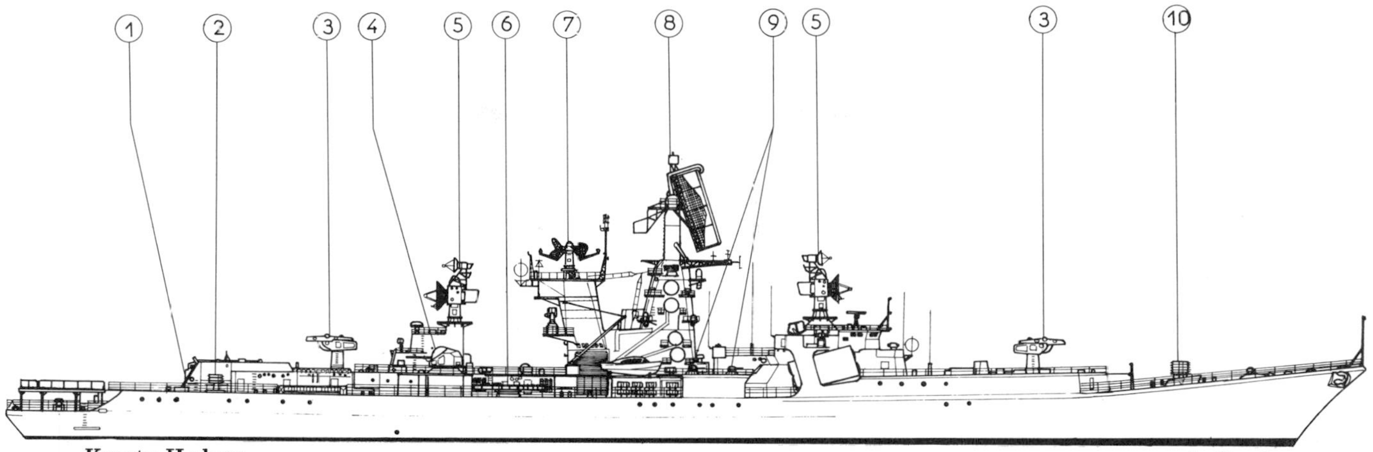


**Kresta-II class** L. Gassier

1. helicopter hangar 2. RBU-1000 ASW RL (VI × 2) 3. SA-N-3 SAM launcher (II × 2) 4. 57-mm DP (II × 2) 5. Head Lights-C missile-guidance radars 6. 533-mm TT (V × 2) 7. Head Net-C air/surface-search radar 8. Top Sail 3-D air-search radar 9. 30-mm 6-barreled gatling AA 10. RBU-6000 ASW RL (XII × 2) (*Note:* Drawing applies to *Marshal Voroshilov, Admiral Oktyabr'skiy,* and *Admiral Isachenkov.*)

◆ **4 Kresta-I class** Bldr: Zhdanov SY, Leningrad

| | L | In serv. | | L | In serv. |
|---|---|---|---|---|---|
| Admiral Zozulya | 10-65 | 3-67 | Vitse-Admiral Drozd | 1-67 | 8-68 |
| Vladivostok | 8-66 | 1-68 | Sevastopol | 6-67 | 7-69 |

**Vitse-Admiral Drozd**—detail of enlarged superstructure
23 F., French Navy, 2-85

**D:** 6,150 tons (7,500 fl) **S:** 34 kts **Dim:** 155.5 (148.5 wl) × 17.1 × 6.0 (6.7 max.)

**A:** 4/SS-N-3B Shaddock SSM (II × 2)—2/SA-N-1 systems (II × 2, 32 Goa missiles)—4/57-mm DP (II × 2)—2/RBU-6000 ASW RL (XI × 2)—2/RBU-1000 ASW RL (VI × 2)—10/533-mm TT (V × 2)—1/Hormone-B helicopter—*Vitse-Admiral Drozd* also: 4/30-mm gatling AA (I × 4)

**Electron Equipt:** Radar: 2/Don-2 or 1/Don-2 and 1/Don-Kay (except *Adm. Zozulya:* 2/Palm Frond, 1/Don Kay), 1/Big Net, 1/Head Net-C, 1/Scoop Pair, 2/Peel Group, 2/Muff Cob—*Vitse-Admiral Drozd* also: 2/Bass Tilt
Sonar: 1/MF, hull-mounted—E/O: 2/Tee Plinth
EW: 8/Side Globe, 1/Bell Clout, 2/Bell Slam, 2/Bell Tap, 2/Bell . . . , 2/chaff RL (II × 2)
IFF: 2/High Pole-B or Salt Pot transponders

**M:** 2 sets GT; 2 props; 100,000 hp **Boilers:** 4, turbopressurized

**Fuel:** 1,150 tons **Range:** 1,600/34; 7,000/14 **Man:** 380 tot.

**Vitse-Admiral Drozd**—with gatling AA guns, Bass Tilt fire-control radars, and enlarged superstructure U.S. Navy, 3-86

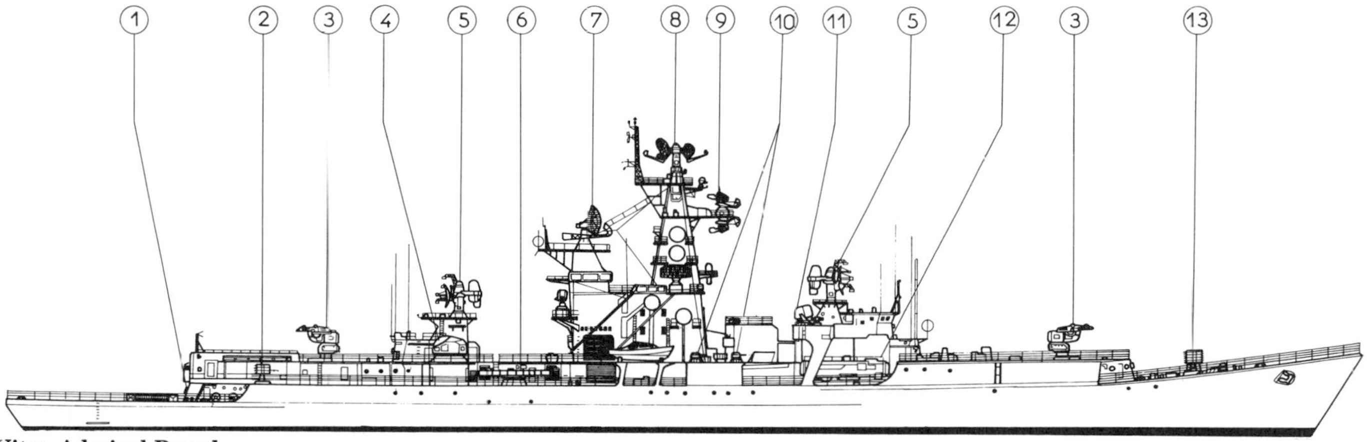


**Vitse-Admiral Drozd**

1. helicopter hangar 2. RBU-1000 ASW RL (VI × 2) 3. SA-N-1 SAM launchers (II × 2) 4. 57-mm DP (II × 2) 5. Peel Group guidance radars for SA-N-1 6. 533-mm TT (V × 2) 7. Big Net air-search radar 8. Head Net-C air/surface-search radar 9. Scoop Pair guidance radar for SS-N-3B 10. 30-mm 6-barreled gatling AA (I × 4) 11. Bass Tilt f.c. radar for 30-mm AA 12. SS-N-3B Shaddock SSM launchers (II × 2) 13. RBU-6000 ASW RL (XII × 2) (*Note: Sevastopol* similar, but lacks 30-mm AA and Bass Tilt.)

**GUIDED-MISSILE CRUISERS** *(continued)*

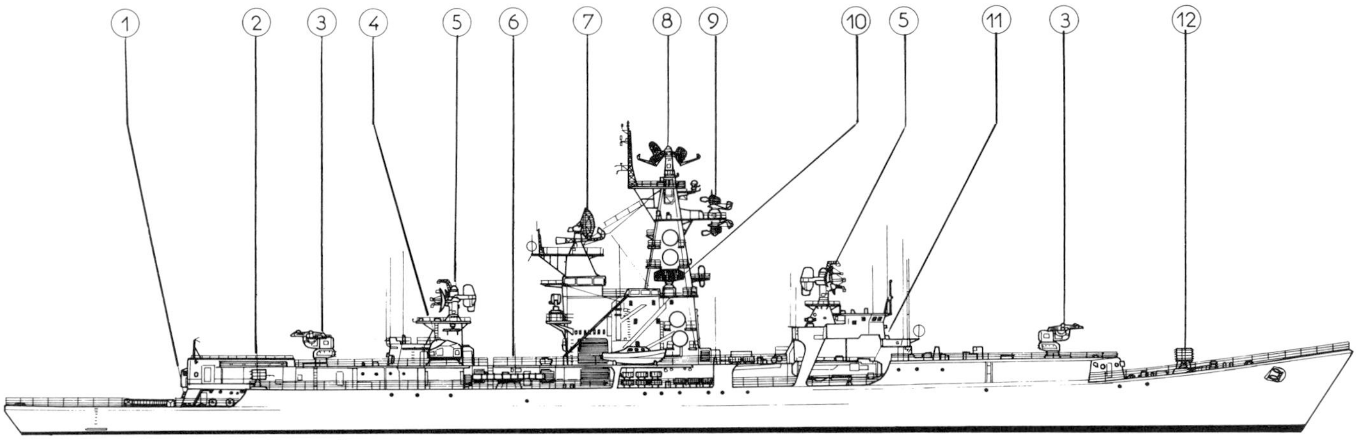


**Admiral Zozulya and Vladivostok**
1. helicopter hangar 2. RBU-1000 ASW RL (VI × 2) 3. SA-N-1 SAM launchers (II × 2) 4. 57-mm DP (II × 2) 5. Peel Group guidance radars for SA-N-1 6. 533-mm TT (V × 2) 7. Big Net air-search radar 8. Head Net-C air/surface-search radar 9. Scoop Pair guidance radar for SS-N-3B 10. Plinth Net data-link antennas for SS-N-3B 11. SS-N-3B Shaddock SSM launchers (II × 2) 12. RBU-6000 ASW RL (XII × 2)

**Vladivostok** J.M.S.D.F., 3-87

Remarks: Soviet type designation: RKR—*Raketnyy Kreyser* (Missile Cruiser). Based on the Kynda class, but has a better-balanced mixture of weapons. The surface-to-surface launchers, fitted on each side of the superstructure forward under the bridge wings, are elevated to fire, but cannot be trained. No SS-N-3 missile reloads. Installation of gatling guns abaft the Shaddock launchers and construction of a new deckhouse between the gatling guns altered the silhouette of the *Vitse-Admiral Drozd* in 1976 (see photos). *Sevastopol* received the new deckhouse, but not the gatling guns or radar, in 1980. All have 2 Plinth Net missile data link antennas.

◆ **4 Kynda class** Bldr: Zhdanov SY, Leningrad

| | Laid down | L | In serv. |
|---|---|---|---|
| Groznyy ("Terrible") | 6-59 | 4-61 | 6-62 |
| Admiral Fokin | 8-60 | 5-62 | 8-63 |
| Admiral Golovko | 12-60 | 1962 | 7-64 |
| Varyag | 9-61 | 6-63 | 2-65 |

**D:** 4,600 tons (5,700 fl) **S:** 34 kts
**Dim:** 141.7 (134.0 pp) × 15.8 (15.4 wl) × 5.4 (hull: 6.1 max.)

**A:** 8/SS-N-3B (IV × 2, 16 Shaddock missiles)—1 SA-N-1/SAM system (II × 1, 16 Goa missiles)—4/76.2-mm DP (II × 2)—2/RBU-6000 ASW RL (XII × 2)—6/533-mm TT (III × 2)—*Varyag* and *Groznyy* also: 4/30-mm gatling AA
**Electron Equipt:** Radar: 2/Don-2 (*Varyag:* 3), 2/Head Net-A or -C, 2/Scoop Pair, 1/Peel Group, 1/Owl Screech—*Varyag* and *Groznyy* also: 2/Bass Tilt
Sonar: 1/HF, hull-mounted
EW: 2/Guard Dog, 1/Bell Clout, 1/Bell Slam, 1/Bell Tap, 4/Top Hat (varies)
IFF: 2/High Pole B
**M:** 2 sets GT: 2 props; 10,000 hp **Boilers:** 4, turbopressurized
**Range:** 2,000/32; 7,000/14 **Man:** 375 tot.

**Groznyy**—modernized like *Varyag,* but retaining 2 Head Net-A! Has 45-mm saluting cannon mounted atop deckhouse amidships French Navy, 12-85

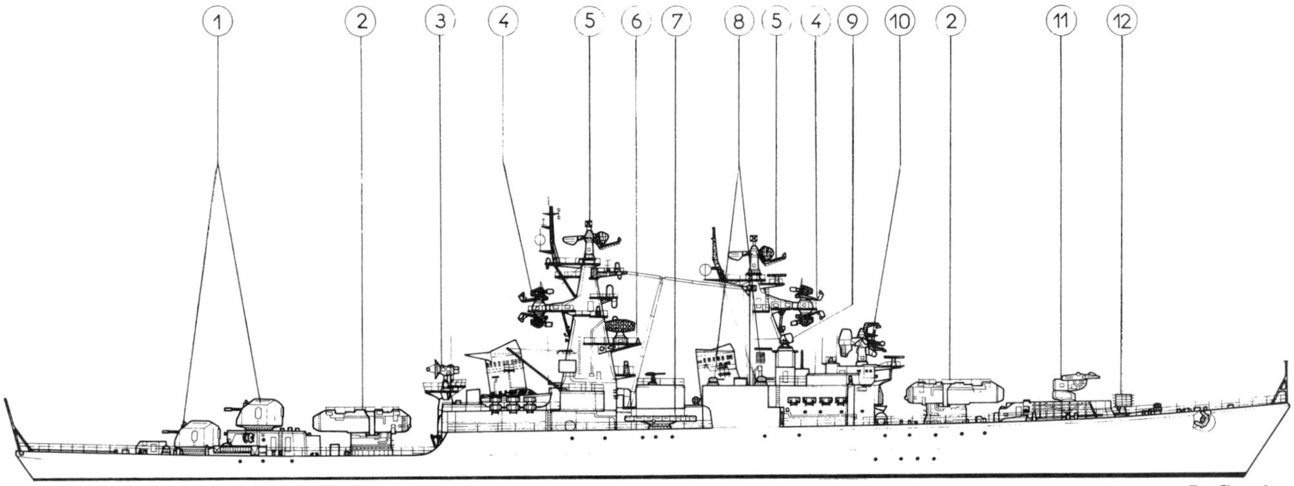


**Groznyy** L. Gassier
1. twin 76.2-mm DP 2. quadruple SS-N-3B launcher (reloads in adjacent deckhouses) 3. Owl Screech radar director for 76.2-mm DP 4. Scoop Pair radars for SS-N-3B 5. Head Net-A air-search radars 6. Plinth Net antennas 7. triple 533-mm TT 8. 30-mm gatling AA 9. Bass Tilt radar directors for 30-mm AA 10. Peel Group radar director for SA-N-1 11. twin SA-N-1 SAM launcher 12. RBU-6000 ASW RL (*Note: Varyag* similar, but with Head Net-C, no Plinth Net.)

**GUIDED-MISSILE CRUISERS** *(continued)*

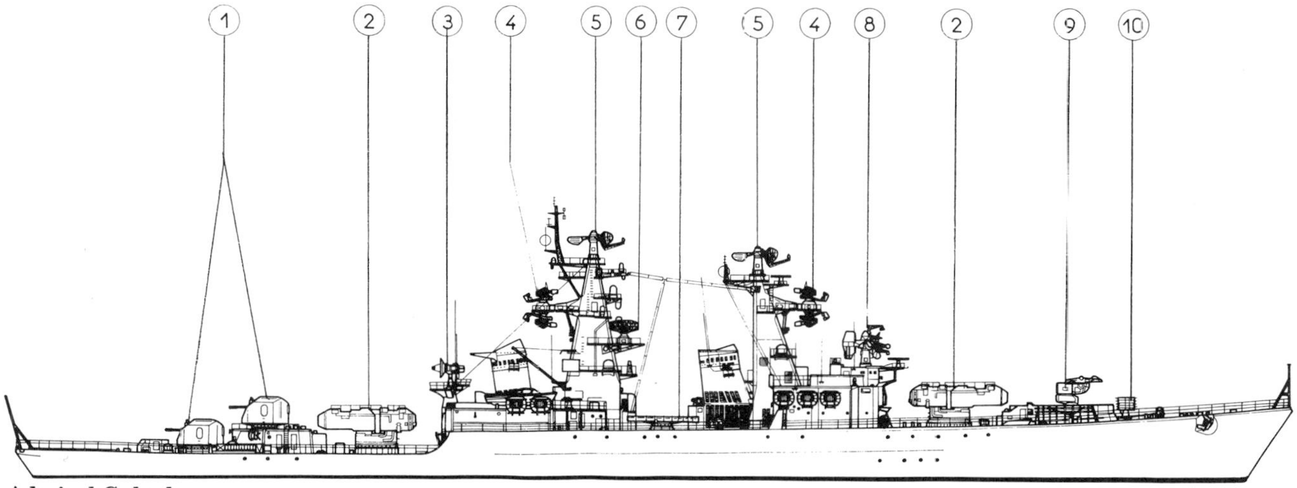


**Admiral Golovko** L. Gassier

1. twin 76.2-mm DP mounts 2. quadruple SS-N-3B launcher 3. Owl Screech radar director for 76.2-mm DP 4. Scoop Pair radars for SS-N-3B 5. Head Net-A air-search radar antennas 6. Plinth Net antennas 7. triple 533-mm TT 8. Peel Group radar director for SA-N-1 9. twin SA-N-1 launcher 10. RBU-6000 ASW RL (*Note: Admiral Fokin* similar, but Head Net-C on after mast.)

**Admiral Fokin**—with Head Net-A, 1 Head Net-C, 2 Plinth Net J.M.S.D.F., 6-81

**Varyag**—as modernized, with 4 gatling AA guns and 2 Bass Tilt added, 2 Head Net-C substituted for Head Net-A, and superstructure added between the torpedo-tube mounts; still without Plinth Net 1981

## GUIDED-MISSILE CRUISERS *(continued)*

**Groznyy** French Navy, 12-85

Remarks: Soviet type designation: RKR—*Raketnyy Kreyser* (Missile Cruiser). Eight Shaddock missiles are loaded in the trainable and elevatable quadruple tubes; reloading from the handling rooms requires some time. *Admiral Fokin* now has one Head Net-A, one Head Net-C, and two Plinth Net; *Groznyy* received two Plinth Net around 1973. *Varyag* received 2 Head Net-C, 2 Plinth Net, 2 Bass Tilt and 4/30-mm gatling AA in 1981, and *Groznyy* received the same treatment during 1980–82. All have a seldom-used helicopter pad on the stern. The two Plinth Net data-link antennas for the SS-N-3B missiles are carried. *Groznyy* joined the Baltic Fleet in 1982. *Admiral Golovko* is in the Black Sea Fleet, and the other two are in the Pacific.

## COMMAND CRUISERS

◆ **2 Modified Sverdlov class**

| | Bldr | Laid down | L | In serv. |
|---|---|---|---|---|
| Admiral Senyavin | Severodvinsk SY | 5-51 | 9-52 | 7-54 |
| Zhdanov | Baltic SY, Leningrad | 10-49 | 12-50 | 1-52 |

For characteristics of hull and machinery, see *Sverdlov*-class light cruisers

**A:** 6 (*Admiral Senyavin*) or 9/152-mm (III × 2, or 3)—12/100-mm DP (II × 6)—1/SA-N-4 system (II × 1; 40 Gecko missiles)—16/37-mm AA—8 (*Zhdanov*) or 16/30-mm AK-230 AA (II × 4 or 8)

**Zhdanov**—with triple 152-mm mount aft French Navy, 5-83

**Electron Equipt:** Radar: 2/Top Bow, 1/Top Trough, 2/Sun Visor, 6/Egg Cup, 1/Pop Group—*Zhdanov:* 2/Drum Tilt—*Admiral Senyavin* also: 4/Drum Tilt
EW: none

Remarks: Soviet type designation: KU—*Korabl' Upravleniy* (Command Ship). Both completed modernization in 1972. Excellent long-range communications, including a Vee Cone HF antenna, which can be seen on the after tripod mast, and two Big Ball SATCOMM antenna radomes. The 30-mm guns are divided on each side of the forward stack and, on the *Admiral Senyavin*, on each side of the after deckhouse as well; her two after turrets have been replaced by a hangar and platform for one Hormone helicopter. Both ships have had their mine rails removed. Big Ball satellite communications antennas were added to both in 1979–81. *Zhdanov* is in the Black Sea Fleet, *Adm. Senyavin* in the Pacific.

**Zhdanov** U.S. Navy, 7-83

## LIGHT CRUISERS

◆ **9 Sverdlov class** Bldrs: A: Baltic SY, Leningrad; B: Marti SY, Nikolayev; C: Severodvinsk SY

| | Bldr | Laid down | L | In serv. | Fleet |
|---|---|---|---|---|---|
| Admiral Lazarev* | A | 5-50 | 10-51 | 11-52 | Pac. |
| Admiral Ushakov | A | 7-50 | 5-52 | 8-53 | Blk. |
| Alexandr Nevskiy | B | 3-50 | 6-51 | 1952 | Nor. |
| Alexandr Suvorov* | B | 10-50 | 6-52 | 1953 | Pac. |
| Dmitriy Pozharskiy* | A | 9-51 | 4-53 | 1953 | Pac. |
| Mikhail Kutuzov | B | 1950 | 5-54 | 1955 | Blk. |
| Murmansk | C | 1952 | 1955 | 1955 | Nor. |
| Oktyabrskaya Revolutsiya (ex-*Molotovsk*) | C | 1951 | 1954 | 9-54 | Bal. |
| Sverdlov* | A | 7-49 | 7-50 | 1951 | Bal. |

* In Reserve

**Admiral Senyavin** J.M.S.D.F., 1983

LIGHT CRUISERS *(continued)*

**Alexandr Suvorov**—modernized, Strut Curve atop foremast French Navy, 3-81

**Admiral Ushakov**—modernized version with 16/30-mm AA, 4 Drum Tilt, Knife Rest aft A01 Mears, USN, 11-81

**Dmitriy Pozharskiy**—note enlarged deckhouse below pilothouse, Big Net air-search radar on after mast-supported deckhouse 1975

**D:** 12,900 tons (17,200 fl) **S:** 32 kts **Dim:** 210.0 (199.95 pp) × 21.6 × 7.2
**A:** 12/152-mm (III × 4)—12/100-mm DP (II × 6)—32/37-mm AA (II × 16)—140 mines—*Oktyabrskaya Revolutsiya, Admiral Ushakov, Alexandr Suvorov:* 16/30-mm AA (II × 8) also
**Electron Equipt:** Radar: 1/Neptune or Don-2, 1/Low Sieve or High Sieve, 1/Big Net or Top Trough, 1/Slim Net, 2/Top Bow, 2/Sun Visor, 8/Egg Cup—Knife Rest in some—ships with 30-mm AA: 4/Drum Tilt also
EW: 2/Watch Dog—IFF: 1/High Pole
**Armor:** 152-mm turret; 76–100-mm; deck: 25–50 and 50–75-mm; 100-mm; gun shields: 25-mm
**M:** 2 sets GT; 2 props; 110,000 hp **Boilers:** 6/3-drum; 26 kg/cm$^2$, 350°C
**Fuel:** 3,800 tons **Electric:** 3,500 kw
**Range:** 2,400/32; 10,000/13.5 **Man:** 70 officers, 940 men

REMARKS: Soviet type designation: KR—*Kreyser* (Cruiser). Based on the preceding *Chapayev*-class design, but with armor added. Twenty-four were planned, fourteen put in service between 1951 and 1956; others were laid down, but construction was suspended in 1956 and canceled in 1960. Slight differences in profile, the merging of the forward stack with the bridge structure being noticeable. *Admiral Nakhimov* was scrapped in 1961; *Ordzhonikidze* was transferred to Indonesia in 1962 and has since been scrapped. By 1961 *Dzerzhinskiy* (discarded 1979) had been converted to a guided-missile cruiser: two others, *Zhdanov* and *Admiral Senyavin,* completed conversion to command cruisers in 1972. In 1977 *Oktyabrskaya Revolutsiya* completed overhaul, during which eight twin 30-mm AA and four Drum Tilt radars were added, the Egg Cup radars were removed from her 100-mm mounts, and her bridge was enlarged. Radar suits vary widely. In 1979 the *Admiral Ushakov* and *Alexandr Suvorov* appeared with similar alterations; all three ships have had four of their twin 37-mm AA removed. At least four are now in reserve, and the ships (which give the Soviet Navy a powerful naval gunfire support capability) are increasingly obsolescent.

**Alexandr Nevskiy** U.S. Navy, 9-83

## GUIDED-MISSILE DESTROYERS

### ◆ 8 (+2 + . . .) Udaloy class

| | Bldr | Laid down | L | In serv. |
|---|---|---|---|---|
| UDALOY ("Daring") | Kaliningrad SY | 1978 | 1980 | 1981 |
| VITSE-ADMIRAL KULAKOV | Zhdanov SY, Leningrad | 1978 | 1982 | 4-82 |
| MARSHAL VASIL'YEVSKIY | Kaliningrad SY | 1979 | 1981 | 1983 |
| ADMIRAL ZAKHAROV | Zhdanov SY, Leningrad | 1979 | 4-82 | 1984 |
| ADMIRAL SPIRIDONOV | Kaliningrad SY | 1981 | 1983 | 1985 |
| ADMIRAL TRIBUTS | Zhdanov SY, Leningrad | 1982 | 1984 | 1986 |
| MARSHAL SHAPOSHNIKOV | Zhdanov SY, Leningrad | 1983 | 1985 | 1986 |
| SIMFEROPOL | Kaliningrad SY | 1983 | 1986 | 1987 |
| N . . . | Kaliningrad SY | 1984 | 1987 | . . . |
| N . . . | Zhdanov SY, Leningrad | 1985 | 1987 | . . . |

**D:** 6,500 tons (7,900 fl) **S:** 35 kts
**Dim:** 163.5 (150.0 wl) × 19.3 (17.8 wl) × 6.2 (7.5 max.)
**A:** 8/SS-N-14 Silex SSM (IV × 2)—8/SA-N-9 vertical SAM launchers (VIII × 8, 64 missiles; see Remarks)—2/100-mm DP (I × 2)—4/30-mm gatling AA (I × 4)—2/RBU-6000 ASW RL (XII × 2)—8/533-mm TT (IV × 2)—mines—2/Helix-A ASW helicopters
**Electron Equipt:** Radar: 3/Palm Frond; *Udaloy, V. Adm. Kulakov:* 2/Strut Pair; others: 1/Top Plate; all: 2/Eye Bowl, 1/Kite Screech, 1/Cross Sword (late units), 2/Bass Tilt, 1/Fly Screen helo landing control
Sonar: 1/LF bow-mounted, 1/LF VDS
EW: 2/Bell Shroud, 2/Bell Squat, 2/chaff RL (II × 2)
TACAN: 2/Round House—IFF: 1/Salt Pot-B, 1/Salt Pot-C
**M:** 4 gas turbines; 2 4-bladed, fixed-pitch props; 120,000 hp
**Electric:** . . . **Range:** 2,000/32; 5,000/20 **Man:** approx. 300 tot.

REMARKS: Formerly carried NATO nickname BAL-COM-3. Soviet type designation BPK—*Bol'shoy Protivolodochniy Korabl'* (Large Antisubmarine Ship), as the design is obviously primarily intended for ASW. Provision was made for installation of the SA-N-9 vertically launched SAM system: four on the raised portion of the forecastle, two more disposed athwartships in the small deckhouse between the torpedo tubes, and two arranged fore and aft in the deckhouse between the RBU-6000 ASW RL mounts. Each rotating cylinder can hold 8 missiles, for a total of 64. *Admiral Zakharov* was the first ship to actually have the operational SA-N-9 system (a short-range successor to SA-N-4) installed, with two Cross Sword-equipped radar directors mounted in mid-1984 (one later removed). Subsequent ships, have had only one of the two Cross Sword positions occupied, and the first three ships have not been backfitted. This is the first BPK design to carry two ASW helicopters. The two hangars are side by side and use inclined elevator ramps to raise the aircraft to the flight deck; the hangar roofs slide forward in two segmented sections to clear the rotors. From the third unit on, the helicopter deck is wider, extending to the sides of the ship. Two Round House TACAN radomes are mounted on yards on the after mast, while the Fly Screen microwave landing-control radar is beside the starboard hangar. The EW suite is incomplete, with several empty platforms on the after mast. The sonar suite duplicates that of the nuclear-powered cruiser *Kirov. Marshall Vasil'yevskiy* began

**Vitse-Admiral Kulakov**—with Helix-A on deck U.S. Navy, 1-84

**Udaloy**—detail showing 100-mm mounts at left, fixed-elevation SS-N-14 mounts (with 45-mm saluting cannon inboard), blank platform atop pilothouse for Cross Sword SAM system radar director, and electronics arrays. First two ships have 2 Strut Pair vice 1 Top Plate in later units. R. Neth. Navy, 6-84

**Admiral Spiridonov** French Navy, 1985

**Marshal Vasil'yevskiy**—first *Udaloy* with the Top Plate radar in place of two Strut Pair U.S. Navy, 11-86

**GUIDED-MISSILE DESTROYERS** *(continued)*

trials 7-83 with the Top Plate antenna atop the after mast and the forward position empty; the earlier ships lack a height-finding capability. The two twin-barreled chaff RL are located near the bow. *Adm. Spiridonov* to Pacific, 12-85. On *Adm. Tributs* and *Simferopol* the Cross Sword is forward, vice aft. A total of 12 to 14 *Udaloy*-class BPKs are expected to be built.

**Admiral Spiridonov**—Cross Sword aft J.M.S.D.F., 1-86

**Marshal Shaposhnikov** M.O.D., Bonn, 11-86

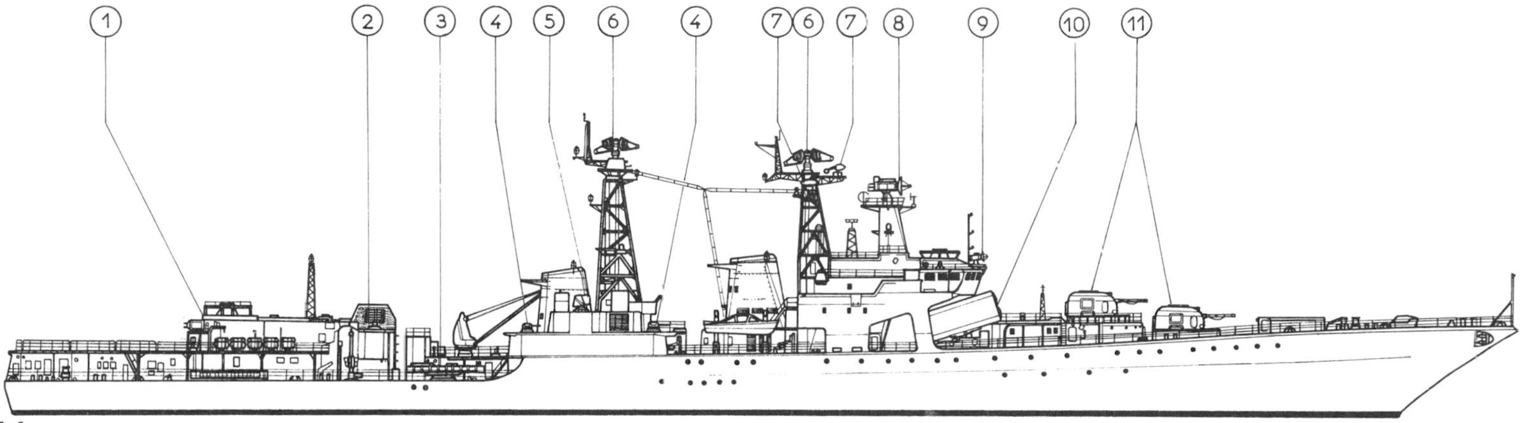


**Udaloy** L. Gassier

1. helicopter hangar (2 Helix-A) 2. RBU-6000 ASW RL 3. 533-mm ASW TT (IV × 2) 4. 30-mm gatling AA 5. Bass Tilt control radar for 30-mm AA 6. Strut Pair air/surface-search radars 7. Palm Frond navigational/surface-search radars 8. Kite Screech radar gunfire-control director (100-mm guns) 9. Eye Bowl radar directors (SS-N-14 missiles) 10. SS-N-14 missiles (IV × 2) 11. 100-mm DP guns (*Note:* The SA-N-9 launch groups are located: 2 between the RBU-6000 RL, 2 in the small deckhouse abaft the stores crane, and 4 within the forecastle, forward of the 100-mm gun mounts.)

**Vitse-Admiral Kulakov** U.S. Navy, 1-84

**GUIDED-MISSILE DESTROYERS** *(continued)*

◆ **7 (+2 + . . .) Sovremennyy class** Bldr: Zhdanov SY, Leningrad

| | Laid down | L | In serv. |
|---|---|---|---|
| Sovremennyy ("Modern") | 1976 | 11-78 | 1981 |
| Otchayannyy ("Merciless") | 1977 | 8-80 | 1982 |
| Otlichnyy ("Perfect") | 1978 | 1981 | 1983 |
| Osmotritel'nyy ("Circumspect") | 1979 | 6-83 | 1984 |
| Bezuprechnyy ("Irreproachable") | 1980 | 1983 | 7-85 |
| Boyevoy ("Militant") | 1981 | 1984 | 1987 |
| Stoykiy ("Steadfast") | 1982 | 1985 | 1987 |
| N . . . | 1983 | 1986 | 1988 |
| N . . . | 1984 | 1987 | 1989 |

**Osmotritel'nyy**—with Top Steer/Top Plate radar M.O.D., Bonn, 7-84

**Otlichnyy** French Navy, 7-86

**Bezuprechnyy**—with combined Top Plate/Top Steer air-search radar antenna
PH1 (SW) J. Hilton, USN, 9-86

**Boyevoy**—with two 45-mm saluting cannon between forward SA-N-7 launcher and 130-mm gun mount, Top Plate air-search radar G. Davies, Maritime Photographic, 9-87

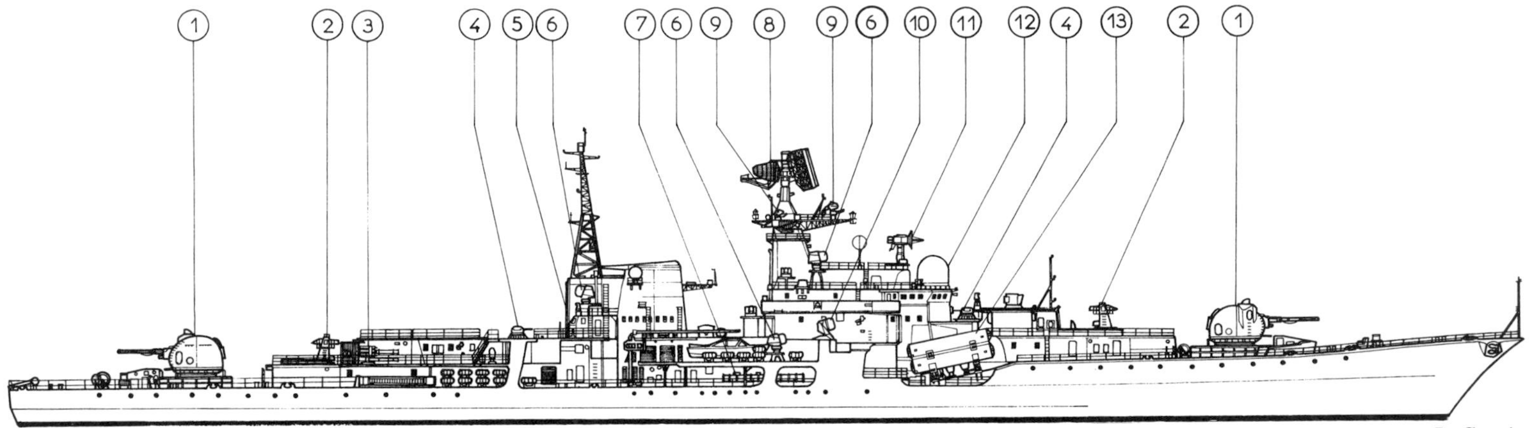


**Sovremennyy** L. Gassier

1. 130-mm dual-purpose guns (II × 2) 2. SA-N-7 SAM launcher (I × 2) 3. RBU-1000 4. 30-mm gatling AA guns 5. telescoping helicopter hangar (shown in retracted position) 6. Front Dome radar directors for the SA-N-7 system 7. 533-mm TT (II × 2) 8. Top Steer 3-D air-search radar 9. Palm Frond navigational/surface-search radars 10. Bass Tilt radar directors for the 30-mm gatling AA 11. Kite Screech radar director for the 130-mm guns 12. Band Stand radome (SS-N-22 SSM-associated) 13. SS-N-22 SSM (IV × 2)

**GUIDED-MISSILE DESTROYERS** *(continued)*

**D:** 6,300 tons (7,850 fl) **S:** 34 kts
**Dim:** 156.0 (145.0 wl) × 17.5 (16.5 wl) × 6.2 (7.0 max.)
**A:** 8/SS-N-22 SSM (IV × 2)—2/SA-N-7 SAM systems (I × 2, 40 missiles)—4/130-mm DP (II × 2)—4/30-mm gatling AA (I × 4)—4/533-mm TT (II × 2)—2/RBU-1000 ASW RL (VI × 2)—mines—1/Hormone-B helicopter
**Electron Equipt:** Radar: 3/Palm Frond, 1 Top Steer (*Osmotritel'nyy, Bezuprechnyy:* Top Steer/Top Plate combined; *Boyevoy* and later: Top Plate), 6/Front Dome, 1/Kite Screech, 2/Bass Tilt
Sonar: 1/MF hull-mounted—1/Squeeze Box
EW: 2/Bell Shroud, 2/Bell Squat, 4/. . . , 2/chaff RL (II × 2)
**M:** 2 sets GT; 2/4-bladed props; 100,000 hp **Boilers:** 4, turbo-pressurized, 500°C
**Range:** 2,400/32; 10,500/14 **Man:** 380 tot.

REMARKS: Design derived from the Kresta-I and -II series built at the same shipyard; uses same hull form and propulsion. Formerly called the BAL-COM-2 class by NATO. The class is primarily intended for surface warfare tasks, including antiship, shore bombardment, and antiair defense; the ASW capability is primarily for self-defense. The SS-N-22 antiship missile system is probably capable of ranges of not more than 120 nautical miles, as there are no satellite receiving radomes of the Punch Bowl type; the Hormone-B helicopter can provide targeting data for the missiles, and the ships also have the large Band Stand radome associated with missile targeting for the SS-N-9 in the Nanuchka class. There are also two small spherical Light Bulb radomes on the sides of the stack that might be missile-associated. The chaff launchers are at the extreme stern. The 130-mm guns are of a new, fully automatic, water-cooled model, capable of AA or surface fire. The helicopter hangar is partially telescoping, extending aft from the stack structure, and the helicopter facilities are less elaborate than in other contemporary Soviet classes, with no support for ASW helicopter provided. Squeeze Box is believed to be an optronic gunfire control director combining a laser rangefinder, low light-level television, and infrared devices. *Sovremennyy* had 4 Wine Glass EW antennas, but the positions have remained empty on succeeding ships.

◆ **1 Kashin, converted for missile trials** Bldr: Zhdanov SY, Leningrad (In serv. 1964)

PROVORNYY ("Ferocious")

**D:** 3,750 tons (4,750 fl) **S:** 38 kts **Dim:** 144.0 × 15.8 × 4.8 (hull)
**A:** 1/SA-N-7 SAM syst. (I × 1, 20 missiles)—4/76.2-mm DP (II × 2)—5/533-mm TT (V × 1)—2/RBU-6000 (XII × 2)—2/RBU-1000 (VI × 2)—mines
**Electron Equipt:** Radar: 1/Don-2, 2/Don-Kay, 1/Top Steer, 1/Head Net-C, 2/Owl Screech, 8/Front Dome
Sonar: 1/MF, hull-mounted
EW: no intercept arrays, 4/chaff RL (XVI × 4)
**M:** 4 gas turbines; 2 props; 96,000 hp
**Range:** 1,500/35; 4,000/20 **Man:** 300 tot.

**Provornyy**—SA-N-7 launcher aft, swathed in canvas U.S. Navy, 9-81

REMARKS: Converted during the mid-1970s at a Black Sea shipyard as trials ship for the SA-N-7 SAM system. Both SA-N-1 SAM systems were removed and the superstructure reconfigured as on the Modified Kashin class. An SA-N-7 single-armed launcher was emplaced aft, while provision was made for two more to be added forward. No EW equipment (other than chaff launchers) is installed, but provision has been made for adding 2 Bell Shroud and 2 Bell Squat. With eight SAM directors, the ship has an unusual antiaircraft capability. *Provornyy* has made only one deployment from the Black Sea since conversion.

◆ **6 Modified Kashin class**

| | Bldr | In serv. | Conv. |
|---|---|---|---|
| OGNEVOY ("Curtain of Fire") | Zhdanov SY, Leningrad | 8-64 | 2-73 |
| SLAVNYY ("Glorious") | Zhdanov SY, Leningrad | 6-66 | 9-75 |
| STROYNYY ("Harmonious") | 61 Kommuna, Nikolayev | 1966 | 1980 |
| SMYSHLENNYY ("Clever") | 61 Kommuna, Nikolayev | 1968 | 1974 |
| SMEL'YY ("Daring") | 61 Kommuna, Nikolayev | 1970 | 1974 |
| SDERZHANNYY ("Cautious") | 61 Kommuna, Nikolayev | 1973 | . . . |

**Provornyy**—showing empty SA-N-7 positions forward U.S. Navy, 9-81

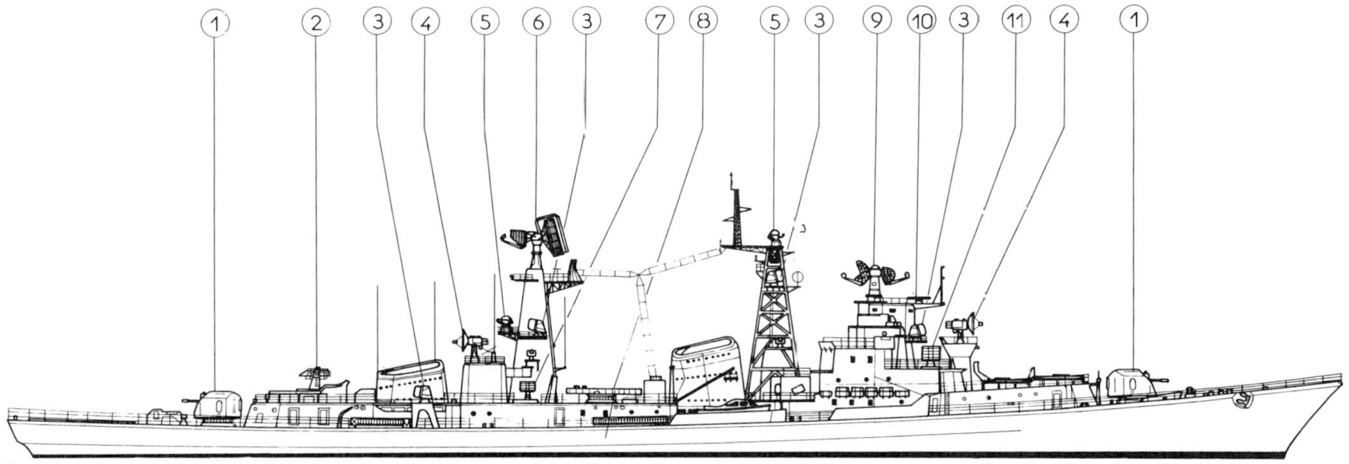

**Provornyy** L. Gassier
1. 76.2-mm DP (II × 2) 2. SA-N-7 Gadfly SAM launcher 3. Front Dome guidance radars for SA-N-7 4. Owl Screech gunfire-control 5. Don-Kay navigational radar 6. Top Steer 3-D air/surface-search radar 7. RBU-1000 ASW RL (IV × 2) 8. 533-mm TT (V × 1) 9. Head Net-C air-search radar 10. Don-2 navigational radar 11. RBU-6000 ASW RL (XII × 2)

**GUIDED-MISSILE DESTROYERS** *(continued)*

**Slavnyy** U.S. Navy, 9-85

**Sderzhannyy** U.S. Navy, 7-83

**Ognevoy**—reequipped with standard search radar fit French Navy, 2-84

**Stroynyy** French Navy, 7-84

**D:** 3,950 tons (4,950 fl) **S:** 35 kts **Dim:** 146.0 × 15.8 × 4.8 (hull)
**A:** 4/SS-N-2C (I × 4)—2/SA-N-1 SAM syst. (II × 2, 32 Goa missiles)—4/76.2-mm DP (II × 2)—4/30-mm gatling AA (I × 4)—5/533-mm TT (V × I)—2/RBU-6000 ASW RL (XII × 2)
**Electron Equipt:** Radar: 2/Don-Kay, 1/Head Net-C, 1/Big Net, 2/Peel Group, 2/Owl Screech, 2/Bass Tilt
Sonar: 1/MF, hull-mounted, 1/MF VDS—E/O: 2/Tee Plinth, 4/Tilt Pot
EW: 2/Bell Squat, 2/Bell Shroud, 4/chaff RL (XVI × 4)
IFF: 1/Salt Pot transponder
**M:** 4 gas turbines, 2 props; 96,000 hp
**Range:** 1,000/35; 4,500/18; 7,000/12 **Man:** 280 tot.

Remarks: Soviet type designation: BPK—*Bol'shoy Protivolodochniy Korabl'* (Large Antisubmarine Ship), having briefly been listed as "Large Missile Ships." Conversions completed from 1973 onward, with *Sderzhannyy* having probably been built to the new configuration. Hull lengthened by 2 meters, helicopter platform raised above new VDS installation, gatling guns added in place of 2 RBU-1000, new EW gear (not yet fully fitted in all) and radars; *Ognevoy,* the first converted, initially retained original two Head Net-A air-search radars, but now has the standard fit.

◆ **12 Kashin class** Bldrs: *Obraztsovyy, Odarennyy, Steregushchiy:* Zhdanov, Leningrad; others: 61 Kommuna SY, Nikolayev

| | In serv. | | In serv. |
|---|---|---|---|
| Komsomolets Ukrainyy | 2-62 | Reshitelnyy ("Decisive") | 1-68 |
| Soobrazitel'nyy ("Bright") | 9-63 | Strogiy ("Severe") | 8-68 |
| Obraztsovyy ("Exemplary") | 7-65 | Smetlivyy ("Intelligent") | 9-69 |
| Odarennyy ("Gifted") | 9-65 | Krasnyy Krym ("Red Crimea") | 9-70 |
| Steregushchiy ("Protective") | 10-66 | Sposobnyy ("Capable") | 8-71 |
| Krasnyy Kavkaz ("Red Kavkaz") | 1967 | Skoryy ("Swift") | 8-72 |

**Komsomolets Ukrainyy**—2 Head Net-A U.S. Navy, 6-83

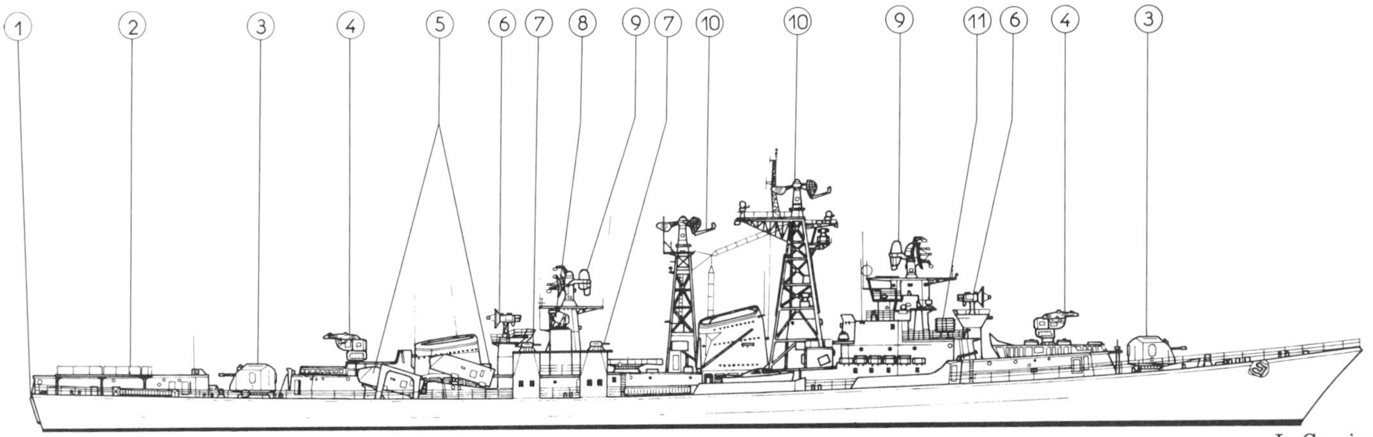

**Modified Kashin** L. Gassier

1. variable-depth sonar housing 2. helicopter platform 3. 76.2-mm DP (II × 2) 4. SA-N-1 Goa SAM launchers (II × 2) 5. SS-N-2C SSM (I × 4) 6. Owl Screech gun-control radars 7. 30-mm 6-barreled gatling AA (I × 4) 8. Bass Tilt control radars for 30-mm AA 9. Peel Group guidance radars for SA-N-1 10. locations for Head Net-C (forward) and Big Net (aft) air-search radars (incorrectly shown as 2 Head Net-A—the original fit on *Ognevoy*)

**GUIDED-MISSILE DESTROYERS** *(continued)*

**Strogiy**—after collision with *Ochakov;* note Head Net-C/Big Net radar fit
U.S. Navy, 10-86

**Obraztsovyy**—with unique extra EW suite, 2 Head Net-A Skyfotos, 6-84

**Odarennyy**—a Pacific Fleet Kashin, with 2 Head Net-C, 3 Don-2
PH2 P. Soutar, USN, 9-83

**Krasnyy Kavkaz** **U.S. Navy, 11-85**

**Sposobnyy** French Navy, 3-85

**D:** 3,750 tons (4,750 fl) **S:** 36 kts **Dim:** 144.0 × 15.8 × 4.8 hull (6.00 max.)
**A:** 2/SA-N-1 SAM syst. (II × 2, 32 Goa missiles)—4/76.2-mm DP (II × 2)—2/RBU-6000 ASW RL (XII × 2)—2/RBU-1000 ASW RL (VI × 2)—5/533-mm TT (V × I)—mines
**Electron Equipt:** Radar: 2-3/Don-2 or 2/Don-Kay, or 2/Palm Frond; 2/Head Net-A or 1/Head Net-C and 1/Big Net, (*Odarennyy, Soobrazitel'nny:* 2/Head Net-C), 2/Peel Group, 2/Owl Screech—IFF: 2/High Pole B or Salt Pot
Sonar: 1/MF, hull-mounted—EW: 2/Watch Dog
E/O: 2/Tee Plinth, 4/Tilt Pot
**M:** 4 gas turbines; 2 props; 96,000 hp **Range:** 1,500/36; 4,000/20
**Man:** 280 tot.

Remarks: Soviet type designation: *Bol'shoy Protivolodochnyy Korabl'* (Large Antisubmarine Ship). One of this class, the *Otvazhnyy,* was sunk 31-8-74 following an explosion; six others have been converted to Modified Kashin configuration, and *Provornyy* was converted as SA-N-7 SAM trials ship. All have a helicopter pad on the fantail. The earlier ships carried 2 Head Net-A air-search radars, replaced

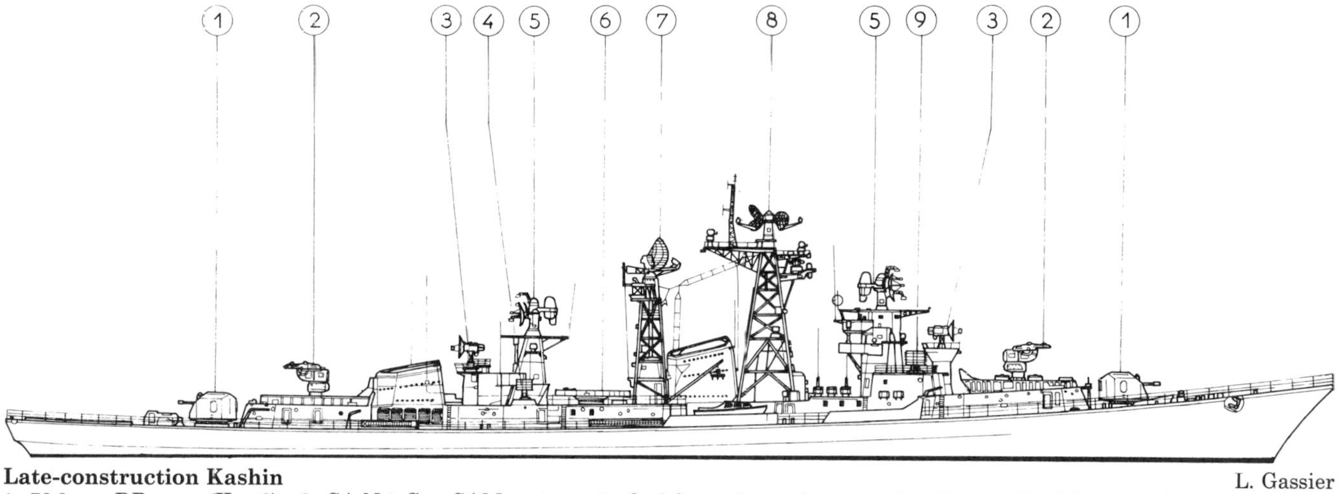


**Late-construction Kashin** L. Gassier
1. 76.2-mm DP guns (II × 2) 2. SA-N-1 Goa SAM system 3. Owl Screech gunfire-control radar 4. Peel Group guidance radars for SA-N-1 5. RBU-1000 ASW RL (VI × 2) 6. 533-mm TT (V × 1) 7. Big Net air-search radar 8. Head Net-C air/surface-search radar 9. RBU-6000 ASW RL (XII × 2)

**GUIDED-MISSILE DESTROYERS** *(continued)*

by two Head Net-C in two ships. *Obraztsovyy* and *Soobrazitel'nyy* have additional Guard Dog EW radomes. The majority are in the Black Sea Fleet.

◆ **8 Kanin class**

| | Bldr | In serv. |
|---|---|---|
| Gremyashchiy ("Thunderous") | Zhdanov SY, Leningrad | 1959 |
| Zhguchiy ("Ardent") | Zhdanov SY, Leningrad | 1960 |
| Gordyy ("Proud") | 61 Kommuna SY, Nikolayev | 1960 |
| Upornyy ("Persistent") | Komsomolsk SY | 1960 |
| Derzkiy ("Audacious") | Zhdanov SY, Leningrad | 1961 |
| Zorkiy ("Vigilant") | Zhdanov SY, Leningrad | 1961 |
| Boykiy ("Valiant") | 61 Kommuna SY, Nikolayev | 1961 |
| Gnevnyy ("Angry") | 61 Kommuna SY, Nikolayev | 1961 |

**Gremyashchiy** U.S. Navy, 3-82

**Unidentified Kanin**—with Palm Frond navigational radars French Navy, 5-86

**Zhguchiy** French Navy, 1977

**D:** 3,660 tons (4,650 fl) **S:** 34 kts
**Dim:** 140.5 (130.5 wl) × 14.6 (14.2 wl) × 4.9 hull (5.8 max.)
**A:** 1/SA-N-1 system (II × 1, 16 Goa missiles)—8/57-mm AA (IV × 2)—8/30-mm AA (II × 4)—3/RBU-6000 ASW RL (XII × 3)—10/533-mm TT (V × 2)
**Electron Equipt:** Radar: 2/Don-Kay or Palm Frond, 1/Head Net-C, 1/Peel Group, 1/Hawk Screech, 2/Drum Tilt—IFF: 1/High Pole B or Salt Pot
Sonar: 1/Herkules MF, hull-mounted—EW: 4/Top Hat, 2/Bell-series
**M:** 2 sets GT; 2 props; 72,000 hp **Boilers:** 4; 64 kg/cm$^2$, 510°C
**Range:** 1,000/30; 4,500/18 **Man:** 300 tot.

Remarks: Soviet type designation: BPK—*Bol'shoy Protivolodochnyy Korabl'* (Large Antisubmarine Ship). Helicopter platform, but no hangar. Converted from Krupnyy class SS-N-1-equipped "Missile Ships" at Zhdanov SY, Leningrad, except for *Gnevnyy* and *Gordyy*, at Vladivostok in the Far East, 1968–77; bows lengthened to incorporate a bow-mounted sonar, and superstructures substantially reconfigured.

◆ **3 Modified Kildin class**

| | Bldr | In serv. |
|---|---|---|
| Bedovyy ("Daredevilish") | 61 Kommuna SY, Nikolayev | 1958 |
| Neulovimyy ("Elusive") | Zhdanov SY, Leningrad | 1958 |
| Prozorlivyy ("Sagacious") | Zhdanov SY, Leningrad | 1959 |

**D:** 3,000 tons (3,950 fl) **S:** 34 kts **Dim:** 126.5 × 12.9 × 4.7 (5.7 sonar)
**A:** 4/SS-N-2C (I × 4)—4/76.2-mm DP (II × 2)—16/57-mm AA (IV × 4) [except *Bedovyy:* 16/45-mm AA (IV × 4)]—2/RBU-2500 ASW RL (XVL × 2)—4/533-mm TT (II × 2)
**Electron Equipt:** Radar: 2/Don-2, 1/Head Net-C (*Bedovyy:* Strut Pair), 1/Owl Screech, 2/Hawk Screech
Sonar: 1/HF, hull-mounted (Herkules or Pegas)
EW: 2/Watch Dog—IFF: 1/High Pole B or Salt Pot
**M:** 2 sets GT; 2 props; 72,000 hp **Boilers:** 4; 64 kg/cm$^2$, 510°C
**Electric:** 1,400 kw **Range:** 1,000/32; 3,600/18; 4,700/11 **Man:** 300 tot.

Remarks: Soviet type designation: BRK—*Bol'shoy Raketnyy Korabl'* (Large Missile Ship). The *Bedovyy* has broader stacks than her sisters and has Strut Pair radar in place of Head Net-C. Conversions from Kildin configuration completed at

**Bedovyy**—with Strut Pair radar, large "Kotlin" stacks U.S. Navy, 8-84

**Neulovimyy**—small stacks, Head Net-C French Navy, 6-86

GUIDED-MISSILE DESTROYERS *(continued)*

Nikolayev, 1973–75. *Prozorlivyy,* launched 30-7-57, is in the Baltic Fleet; the others are in the Black Sea Fleet. Unconverted sister *Neuderzhimyy,* in the Pacific Fleet, has not been sighted in over a decade and has probably been stricken.

**Prozorlivyy**—small stacks, Head Net-C 1982

◆ **8 SAM Kotlin class** Bldr: Zhdanov SY, Leningrad; (except *Bravyy:* 61 Kommuna SY, Nikolayev; *Vozbuzhdennyy:* Komsomol'sk SY)

| | In serv. | Conv. |
|---|---|---|
| Skromnyy ("Modest") | 1955 | 1969 |
| Nesokrushimyy ("Invincible") | 1956 | 1967 |
| Nakhodchivyy ("Ingenious") | 1957 | 1968 |
| Vozbuzhdennyy ("Excited") | 1957 | 1970 |
| Skrytnyy ("Mysterious") | 1957 | 1971 |
| Nastoychivyy ("Persistent") | 1958 | 1970 |
| Soznatel'nyy ("Conscientious") | 1958 | 1972 |
| Bravyy ("Gallant") | 1961 | . . . |

**Bravyy**—conversion prototype, with 12/45-mm AA, Head Net-A, RBU-2500
U.S. Navy, 2-75

**Nakhodchivyy**—no 30-mm AA U.S. Navy, 5-83

**Soznatel'nyy** French Navy, 1-85

**D:** 2,850 tons (3,950 fl) **S:** 34 kts **Dim:** 126.5 × 12.9 × 4.7 hull (5.7 max.)
**A:** *Bravyy:* 1/SA-N-1 system (II × 1, 16 Goa missiles)—2/130-mm DP (II × 1)—12/45-mm AA (IV × 3)—5/533-mm TT (V × 1)—2/RBU-2500 ASW RL (XVI × 2)
Others: 1/SA-N-1 system (II × 1, 16 Goa missiles)—2/130-mm DP (II × 1)—4/45-mm AA (IV × 1)—8/30-mm AA (II × 4; not in 3 units)—5/533-mm TT (V × 1)—2/RBU-6000 ASW RL (XII × 2) (*Skromnyy* has RBU-2500, see Remarks)
**Electron Equipt:** Radar: 1 or 2/Don-2, 1/Head Net-C, 1/Peel Group, 1/Sun Visor, 1/Hawk Screech, 1/Egg Cup, 2/Drum Tilt (not in 4)
Sonar: 1/HF (Herkules or Pegas)
EW: 2/Watch Dog—IFF: 1/High Pole B or Salt Pot
**M:** 2 sets GT; 2 props; 72,000 hp **Boilers:** 4; 64 kg/cm², 510°C
**Electric:** 1,400 kw **Range:** 1,000/34; 3,600/18; 4,700/11 **Man:** 300 tot.

Remarks: Soviet type designation: EM—*Eskhadrennyy Minonosets* (Destroyer). *Nesokrushimyy, Skrytnyy, Soznatel'nyy,* and *Vozbuzhdennyy* have eight 30-mm AA (II × 4) in addition to the above, with two Drum Tilt fire-control radars. *Nastoychivyy* has no Egg Cup radar. *Bravyy* has Head Net-A, two extra quadruple 45-mm AA mounts and, as does *Skromnyy,* RBU-2500 vice RBU-6000. *Bravyy,* which was completed as the SA-N-1 trials ship, was further modified in the mid-1960s with 2 additional 45-mm AA mounts and TT added. Sister *Spravedlivyy* was transferred to Poland in 1970 and scrapped in 1986.

**Vozbuzhdennyy**—with 8/30-mm AA, Head Net-C, RBU-6000 U.S. Navy, 7-84

## DESTROYERS

◆ **17 Kotlin and Modified Kotlin classes** Bldrs: A: Zhdanov SY, Leningrad; B: 61 Kommuna SY, Nikolayev; C: Komsomol'sk-na-Amur

*11 Modified Kotlin Class:*

| | Bldr | In serv. |
|---|---|---|
| Svedushchiy ("Experienced") | A | 1956 |
| Moskovskiy Komsomolets (ex-*Smyshlennyy*) | A | 1956 |
| Burlivyy ("Turbulent") | B | 1956 |
| Byvalyy ("Veteran") | B | 1956 |
| Vdokhnovennyy ("Inspired") | C | 1956 |
| Vyzyvayushchiy ("Defiant") | C | 1956 |
| Blestyashchiy ("Magnificent") | B | 1957 |
| Blagorodnyy ("Noble") | B | 1957 |
| Plamennyy ("Fiery") | B | 1958 |
| Naporistyy ("Assertive") | B | 1958 |
| Vyderzhannyy ("Steadfast") | C | 1958 |

*6 Kotlin Class:*

| | | |
|---|---|---|
| Speshnyy ("Urgent") | A | 1955 |
| Spokoynyy ("Tranquil") | A | 1956 |
| Svetlyy ("Luminous") | A | 1957 |
| Veskiy ("Imposing") | C | 1957 |
| Vliyatelnyy ("Influential") | C | 1958 |
| Dalnyvostochnyy Komsomolets (ex-*Vozmushchyennyy*) | C | 1958 |

**D:** 2,825 tons (3,750 fl) **S:** 36 kts **Dim:** 126.5 × 12.9 × 4.6 (5.6 sonar)
**A:** Kotlin: 4/130-mm DP (II × 2)—16/45-mm AA (IV × 4)—4/25-mm AA (II × 2)—10/533-mm TT (V × 2)—6/BMB-2 d.c. projectors—2/d.c. racks—70 mines; Mod. Kotlin: 4/130-mm DP (II × 2)—16/45-mm AA (IV × 4)—8/25-mm AA (II × 4)—5/533-mm TT (V × 1)—2/RBU-2500 ASW RL (XVI × 2)—2/RBU-600 ASW RL (VI × 2)—70 mines
**Electron Equipt:** Radar: 1/Neptune or 1 or 2/Don-2, 1/Slim Net, 1/Sun Visor, 2/Hawk Screech, 2/Egg Cup, 1/Post Lamp or Top Bow
Sonar: 1/MF (Herkules)
EW: 2/Watch Dog—IFF: 1/High Pole, 2/Square Head
**M:** 2 sets GT; 2 props; 72,000 hp
**Boilers:** 4; 64 kg/cm$^2$, 510°C
**Electric:** 1,400 kw
**Range:** 1,000/34; 3,600/18, 4,700/11
**Man:** 36 officers, 300 men

**Moskovskiy Komsomolets**—Modified Kotlin with RBU-6000, towed array, no RBU-600 8-80

**Svetlyy**—only Kotlin with a helo deck 1977

**Mod. Kotlin with only 4/25-mm AA (II × 2)** U.S. Navy, 6-82

**Vdokhnovennyy**—Modified Kotlin with 8/25-mm AA (II × 4) abreast aft stack 4-79

Remarks: Soviet type designation: EM—*Eskhadrennyy Minonosets* (Destroyer). Eleven were modified between 1960 and 1965, receiving two RBU-2500 forward and two RBU-600 in place of their depth-charge equipment, the after bank of five 533-mm TT being removed. Later, most of these ships got eight 25-mm AA (II × 4). The *Moskovskiy Komsomolets* got RBU-6000 forward, nothing aft; in 1978 she received a variable-depth sonar on her stern. Most of those that were not modified received four 25-mm AA (II × 2). *Svetlyy* has a helicopter platform in place of depth-charge gear and thus has no ASW armament. Helicopter decks were removed from the other two ships that had them. Many have had their Egg Cup radars removed. Only about 10 total of both types are active.

◆ **9 Skoryy and Modified Skoryy class** (In serv. 1949–53)—in reserve

Bldrs: Molotovsk (now Severodvinsk) SY; Zhdanov SY, Leningrad; 61 Kommuna SY, Nikolayev; Komsomol'sk SY, Komsomol'sk-na-Amur

**D:** 2,600 tons (3,130 fl) **S:** 34 kts **Dim:** 121.2 (116.5 pp) × 12.0 × 4.5 (hull)
**A:** Standard: 4/130-mm DP (II × 2)—2/85-mm AA (II × 1)—7 or 8/37-mm AA (I × 7 or II × 4)—4 or 6/25-mm AA (II × 2 or 3—not in 7/37-mm ships)—10/533-mm TT (V × 2)—2/d.c. projectors—2/d.c. racks—50 mines
Modified: 4/130-mm DP (II × 2)—5/57-mm AA (I × 5)—2/RBU-2500 ASW RL (XVI × 2)—5/533-mm TT (V × 1)—50 mines
**Electron Equipt:** Radar: Standard: 1/High Sieve, 1/Top Bow or Half Bow or Post Lamp, 1/Cross Bird, 1 or 2/Don-2
Modified: 1/Slim Net, 1/Top Bow, 1 or 2/Don-2, 2/Hawk Screech
Sonar: 1/HF (Tamir-5 or Pegas)
EW: 2 Watch Dog—IFF: 2/Square Head, 1/High Pole A
**M:** 2 sets GT; 2 props; 60,000 hp **Boilers:** 4; 27 kg/cm$^2$, 367°C
**Electric:** 475 kw **Fuel:** 786 tons **Range:** 850/30; 3,000/18
**Man:** 18 officers, 200 men

Remarks: Soviet type designation: EM—*Eskhadrennyy Minonosets* (Destroyer). Survivors of seventy-two built, derived from prewar *Ognevoy* design. Six early-construction units were modernized around 1960 to *Modified Skoryy* configuration, with improved AAW and ASW equipment and enhanced EW suits. Only those with eight 37-mm AA have been given two or three twin 25-mm AA. Several *Skoryy* class were transferred to Egypt, Poland, and Indonesia. Now of little value, and all believed to be in reserve, with a few periodically activated only for local training duties.

**Buynyy**—Skoryy class with seven 37-mm AA, no 25-mm AA 7-79

**Modified Skoryy class**

DESTROYERS *(continued)*

**Solidnyy**—with 8/37-mm (II × 4), 6/25-mm AA (II × 3) U.S. Navy, 10-80

## FRIGATES

◆ **4 (+ . . .) Krivak-III class** Bldr: Kamysh Burun SY, Kerch'

MENZHINSKIY (In serv. 8-84)
IMENI XXVII SYEZDA K.P.S.S. (In serv. 2-87)
DZERZHINSKIY (In serv. 8-85)
N . . . (In serv. 1987)

**D:** 3,780 tons (fl) **S:** 30 kts (29 sust.)
**Dim:** 125.0 (116.9 pp) × 14.1 (13.2 wl) × 4.8
**A:** 1/SA-N-4 syst. (II × 1, 40 Gecko missiles)—1/100-mm automatic DP—2/30-mm gatling AA (I × 2)—2/RBU-6000 ASW RL (XII × 2)—8/533-mm TT (IV × 2)—1/Ka-27 Helix helicopter—mines

**Electron Equipt:** Radar: 1/Palm Frond, 1/Don-Kay, 1/Spin Trough, 1/Head Net-C (3rd ship: Top Plate), 1/Pop Group, 1/Kite Screech, 1/Bass Tilt
Sonar: MF hull-mounted, MF VDS
EW: 2/Bell Shroud, 2/Bell Squat, 4/decoy RL (XVI × 4)
IFF: 1/Salt Pot transponder, 1/High Pole B transponder

**M:** COGOG: 2 cruise gas turbines of 12,100 hp each/2 high-speed gas turbines of 24,300 hp each; 2 props; 48,600 hp max.
**Range:** 700/30; 3,900/20; 4,500/16 **Man:** 200 tot.

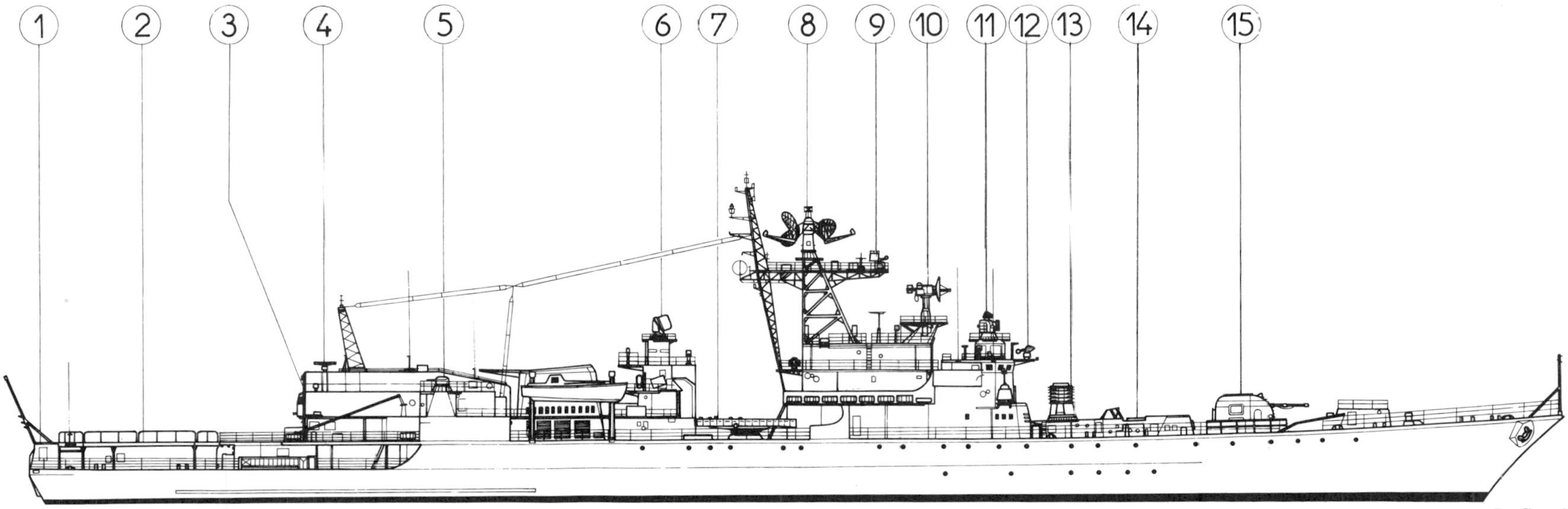


**Krivak-III** L. Gassier
1. variable-depth sonar housing 2. helicopter deck 3. helicopter hangar 4. Spin Trough radar for helicopter control 5. 30-mm gatling AA 6. Bass Tilt radar director for 30-mm AA 7. quadruple 533-mm TT 8. Head Net-C air-search radar 9. Don-Kay nav. radar 10. Kite Screech radar director for 100-mm gun 11. Pop Group track-while-scan radar for SA-N-4 12. Palm Frond nav. radar 13. RBU-6000 ASW RL 14. twin SA-N-4 launcher 15. 100-mm DP

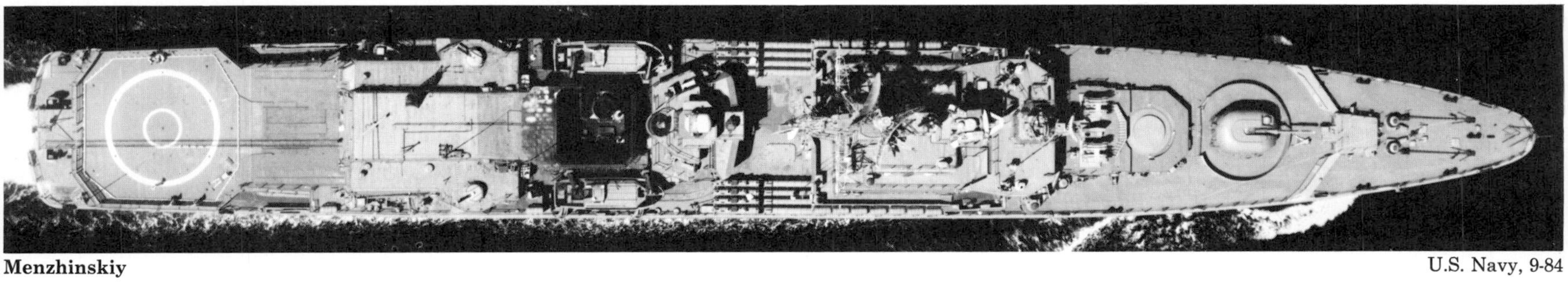

**Menzhinskiy** U.S. Navy, 9-84

**FRIGATES** *(continued)*

**Dzerzhinskiy** J.M.S.D.F., 1986

**Imeni XXVII Syezda K.P.S.S.** J.M.S.D.F., 3-87

**Menzhinskiy** U.S. Navy, 9-84

REMARKS: Revised version of basic Krivak design for KGB Maritime Border Guard service. Typed PSKR—*Pogranichnyy Storozhevoy Korabl'* (Border Patrol Ship). First two named for prominent KGB "heroes." *Menzhinskiy* deployed from the Black Sea 7-9-84, bound for the Pacific, and *Dzerzhinskiy* followed a year later. The name for the third unit means "In honor of the 27th anniversary of the Communist Party of the Soviet Union." More probably are building, although the basic design is essentially nearly 20 years old.

The addition of a helicopter facility (with simple deck-transit system) and helicopter weapons reload magazines cost two gun mounts and one SA-N-4 positions aft, while the Krivak-I/II SS-N-14 dual-purpose missile system was replaced by a 100-mm gun, more useful for the mission of these ships. Two 6-barreled gatling guns were added to improve close-in defense. Sensors are not the latest available. *Imeni XXVII Syezda* K.P.S.S substituted Top Plate for the Head Net-C air/surface-search radar. These ships have a significantly greater displacement than earlier Krivak variants. The Spin Trough radar is mounted atop the helicopter hangar.

◆ **11 Krivak-II class** Bldr: Kaliningrad SY

| | In serv. | | In serv. |
|---|---|---|---|
| REZVYY ("Lively") | 1975 | GROMKIY ("Thunderous") | 1979 |
| REZKIY ("Brusque") | 1976 | GORDELIVYY ("Trustworthy") | 1979 |
| RAZITEL'NYY ("Wrathful") | 1977 | R'YANYY ("Spirited") | 1980 |
| GROZYASHCHIY ("Dissuasive") | 1977 | REVNOSTNYY ("Roaring") | 1980 |
| NEUKROTIMYY ("Indomitable") | 1978 | PYTLIVYY ("Curious") | 1982 |
| BESSMENNYY ("Irremoveable") | 1978 | | |

**Razitel'nyy** 22 F., French Navy, 3-85

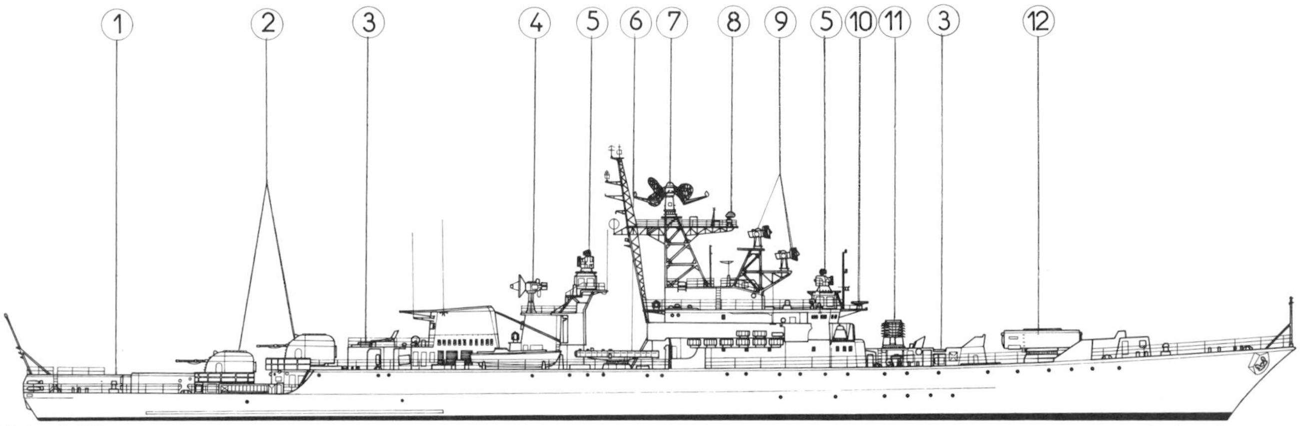


**Krivak-II** L. Gassier, 1985
1. variable-depth sonar housing 2. single 10-mm DP mounts 3. twin SA-N-4 launcher 4. Kite Screech radar director for 10-mm guns 5. Pop Group track-while-scan radar director for SA-N-4 6. quadruple 533-mm TT 7. Head Net-C air-search radar 8. Don-Kay or Palm Frond nav. radar 9. Eye Bowl radar directors for SS-N-14 10. Spin Trough nav. radar 11. RBU-6000 ASW RL 12. quadruple SS-N-14 launcher

**FRIGATES** *(continued)*

**Razitel'nyy**—Don-2 and Palm Frond navigational radars U.S. Navy, 1-85

**Pytlivyy** U.S. Navy, 10-86

**Gromkiy** U.S. Navy, 10-83

**D:** 3,100 tons (3,600 fl) **S:** 30.6 kts
**Dim:** 125.0 (116.9 wl) × 14.1 (13.2 wl) × 4.6 (hull)
**A:** 4/SS-N-14 Silex SSM (IV × 1)—2/SA-N-4 systems (II × 2, 40 Gecko missiles)—2/100-mm DP (I × 2)—2/RBU-6000 ASW RL (XII × 2)—8/533-mm TT (IV × 2)—mines
**Electron Equipt:** Radar: 1/Palm Frond or Don-Kay, 1/Spin Trough or Don-2, 1/Head Net-C, 2/Eye Bowl, 1/Kite Screech, 2 Pop Group
Sonar: 1/MF hull-mounted, 1/MF VDS
EW: 2/Bell Shroud, 2/Bell Squat, 4/decoy RL (XVI × 4)
IFF: 1/High Pole B or Salt Pot transponder
**M:** COGOG: 2 cruise gas turbines of 12,100 hp each and 2 high-speed gas turbines of 24,300 hp each; 2 props; 48,600 hp max.
**Range:** 700/30; 3,900/20; 4,500/16 **Man:** 200 tot.

REMARKS: Soviet type designation: SKR—*Storozhevoy Korabl'* (Patrol Ship), formerly BPK—Large Antisubmarine Ship. The VDS housing at the stern is somewhat larger than on the Krivak-Is, but the principal difference is substitution of two single 100-mm for the two twin 76.2-mm guns. The chaff/decoy rocket launchers were moved from the stern to the 01 level, abreast the aft SA-N-4 launcher. *Revnostnyy* has four 4-tubed decoy RL mounted between the torpedo tubes, in addition to her normal chaff RL system.

◆ **21 Krivak-I class** Bldrs: A: Zhdanov SY, Leningrad; B: Kaliningrad SY; C: Kamysh-Burun SY, Kerch'

| | Bldr | In serv. |
|---|---|---|
| Bditel'nyy ("Vigilant") | B | 1970 |
| Dostoynyy ("Dignified") | C | 1971 |
| Bodryy ("Brave") | B | 1971 |
| Svirepyy ("Ferocious") | B | 1971 |
| Sil'nyy ("Powerful") | B | 1972 |
| Doblestnyy ("Valorous") | C | 1972 |
| Storozhevoy ("Guarding") | B | 1973 |
| Razumnyy ("Sensible") | B | 1973 |
| Razyashchiy ("Perceptive") | B | 1974 |
| Druzhnyy ("Amicable") | A | 1975 |
| Deyatel'nyy ("Active") | C | 1975 |
| Zharkyy ("Passionate") | B | 1975 |
| Retivyy ("Zealous") | A | 1976 |
| Leningradskiy Komsomolets | A | 1976 |
| Letuchiy ("Flying") | A | 1977 |
| Bezzavetnyy ("Conscientious") | C | 1978 |
| Pylkiy ("Ardent") | A | 1979 |
| Zadornyy ("Provocative") | A | 1979 |
| Bezukoriznennyy ("Irreproachable") | C | 1980 |
| Ladnyy ("Friendly") | C | 1980 |
| Poryvistyy ("Impetuous") | C | 1982 |

**D:** 3,575 tons (fl) **S:** 30.6 kts
**Dim:** 125.0 (116.9 wl) × 14.1 (13.2 wl) × 4.5 (hull)
**A:** 4/SS-N-14 Silex SSM (IV × 1)—2/SA-N-4 systems (II × 2, 40 Gecko missiles)—4/76.2-mm DP (II × 2)—2/RBU-6000 ASW RL (XII × 2)—8/533-mm TT (IV × 2)—mines
**Electron Equipt:** Radar: 1/Don-2 or Spin Trough, 1/Don-Kay or Palm Frond, 1/Head Net-C, 2/Eye Bowl, 1/Owl Screech, 2/Pop Group
Sonar: 1/MF hull-mounted, 1/MF VDS
EW: 2/Bell Shroud, 2/Bell Squat, 4/chaff launchers (XVI × 4)
IFF: High Pole B or Salt Pot
**M:** COGOG: 2 cruise gas turbines of 12,100 hp each and 2 boost gas turbines of 24,300 hp each; 2 props; 48,600 hp max.
**Range:** 700/30; 3,900/20; 4,500/16
**Man:** 200 tot.

**Druzhnyy**—with SIGINT van abaft stack U.S. Navy, 9-86

**FRIGATES** *(continued)*

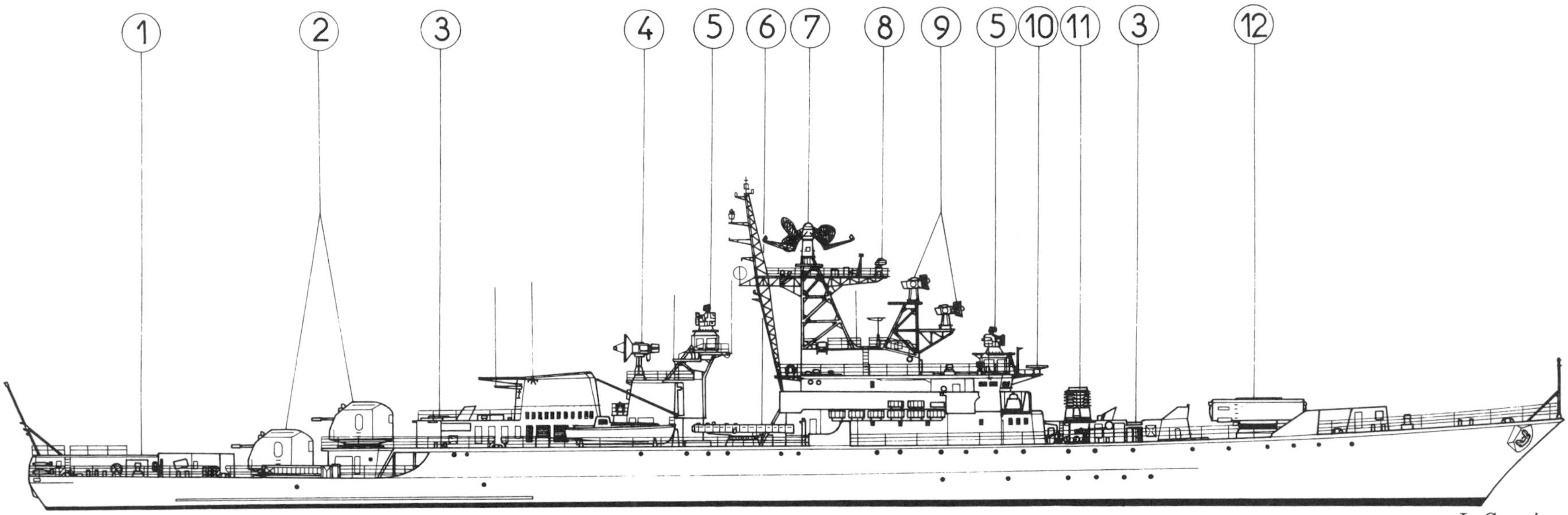


**Krivak-I** L. Grassier

1. variable-depth sonar housing 2. twin 76.2-mm DP 3. twin SA-N-4 launcher 4. Owl Screech radar director for 76.2-mm DP 5. Pop Group track-while-scan radar directors for SA-N-4 6. quadruple 533-mm TT 7. Head Net-C air-search radar 8. Don-Kay or Palm Frond nav. radar 9. Eye Bowl radar directors for SS-N-14 10. Spin Trough nav. radar 11. RBU-6000 ASW RL 12. quadruple SS-N-14 launcher

**Pilkiy**—note bow sonar dome, visible beneath the water's surface U.S. Navy, 7-84

**Unidentified Krivak-I** R. Neth. N., 1987

**Ladnyy**—with enlarged VDS housing U.S. Navy, 1986

Remarks: Soviet type designation: SKR—*Storozhevoy Korabl'* (Patrol Ship). In 1978 Krivak-I and Krivak-II classes were rerated from BPK (*Bol'shoy Protivolodochnyy Korabl'*—large ASW ship) to SKR (*Storozhevoy Korabl'*—patrol ship), a demotion prompted perhaps by their limited endurance at high speeds, speed, and size. Not all units have the EW gear. *Bodryy* has been equipped with ten 10-tubed chaff RL, *replacing* the original four 16-tubed. *Bditel'nyy* and *Ladnyy* have had their VDS housings enlarged, and the chaff RL relocated as on the Krivak-II class.

◆ **1 Koni class** Bldr: Zelenodolsk SY (In serv. circa 1978)

Timofey Ul'yantsev

**D:** 1,440 tons (1,600 fl) **S:** 30 kts
**Dim:** 96.40 × 12.55 × 3.48 hull (4.9 max.)
**A:** 1/SA-N-4 SAM syst. (II × 1, 20 Gecko missiles)—4/76.2-mm DP (II × 2)—4/30-mm AK-230 AA—2/RBU-6000 ASW RL (XII × 2)—2/d.c. racks—20 mines
**Electron Equipt:** Radar: 1/Don-2, 1/Strut Curve, 1/Pop Group, 1/Hawk Screech, 1/Drum Tilt
Sonar: 1/MF hull-mounted
EW: 2/Watch Dog—IFF: 1/High Pole B
**M:** CODAG: 1 gas turbine of 19,000 hp, 2 Type 68B diesels of 8,000 hp; 3 props; 35,000 hp
**Range:** 1,800/14
**Man:** 110 tot.

Remarks: One unit of this export SKR—*Storozhevoy Korabl'* (Patrol Ship) design, reportedly with the listed name, has been retained in the Black Sea Fleet for training foreign crews. Only about one Koni per year has been built—all for export—although the design would seem to have been a natural successor for the Riga class. Have a large teardrop-shaped sonar dome. The d.c. racks are bolted to the mine rails. Centerline shaft, powered by the diesel, has controllable-pitch prop. Fin stabilizers. Units have been exported to Libya, East Germany, Cuba, Algeria, and Yugoslavia; recent ships have had a continuous after deckhouse and 2 chaff RL (XVI × 2) added.

**FRIGATES** *(continued)*

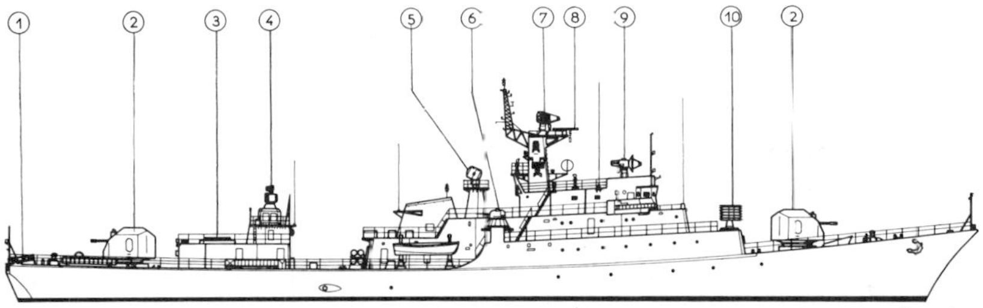


**Koni class** L. Gassier
1. depth-charge racks 2. twin 76.2-mm DP guns 3. twin SA-N-4 SAM launcher 4. Pop Group radar director for SA-N-4 5. Drum Tilt radar director for 30-mm AA 6. twin 30-mm AA 7. Strut Curve surface/air-search radar 8. Don-2 nav. radar 9. Hawk Screech radar director for 76.2-mm guns 10. RBU-6000 ASW RL (*Note:* This drawing represents an early-construction Koni with separate deckhouse aft; the Soviet Navy's unit should be very similar.)

◆ **36 Riga class** Bldrs: Yantar SY, Kaliningrad; Khabarovsk SY, Marti SY, Nikolayev (In serv. 1952–58)

Known names:

Astrakhan'skiy Komsomolets
Arkhangel'skiy Komsomolets
Bars ("Snow Leopard")
Barsuk ("Badger")
Bobr ("Beaver")
Buyvol ("Buffalo")
Byk ("Bull")
Gepard ("Cheetah")
Giena ("Hyena")
Komsomolets Astrakhanskiy
Komsomolets Litviy
Krasnogarskiy Komsomolets
Kunitsa ("Martin")
Leopard ("Leopard")
Lev ("Lion")
Lisa ("Fox")
Medved' ("Bear")
Pantera ("Panther")
Rys ("...")
Rosomakha ("Wolverine")
Shakal ("Jackal")
Sovetskiy Azerbaydzhan
Sovetskiy Dagestan
Sovetskiy Turkmenistan
Straus ("Ostrich")
Tigr ("Tiger")
Tuman ("...")
Volk ("Wolf")
Voron ("Raven")
Yaguar ("Jaguar")
6 others

**D:** 1,186 tons (1,415 fl) **S:** 28 kts
**Dim:** 91.58 (88.00 wl) × 10.20 × 3.15 hull (4.40 max.)
**A:** 3/100-mm Mod. B-34 DP (I × 3)—4/37-mm AA (II × 2)—4/25-mm AA (II × 2)—2 or 3/533-mm ASW TT (II or III × 1)—2/RBU-2500 ASW RL (XVI × 2)—2/d.c. racks—mines (2 rails, 80 total)
**Electron Equipt:** Radar: 1/Neptune or Don-2, 1/Slim Net, 1/Sun Visor B
Sonar: 1/HF Pegas 2-M
EW: 2/Watch Dog
IFF: 1/High Pole, 2/Square Head
**M:** 2 sets GT; 2 props; 20,000 hp **Boilers:** 2; 27 kg/cm², 360°C
**Fuel:** 230 tons **Electric:** 450 kw
**Range:** 550/28; 2,000/13 **Man:** 16 officers, 154 men

**Riga class** PH2 P. Soutar, USN, 9-83

**Riga class**—with 2-level deckhouse in place of TT, no 25-mm AA
L. & L. Van Ginderen, 10-85

**Riga class** J.M.S.D.F., 1983

Remarks: Soviet type designation: SKR—*Storozhevoy Korabl'* (Patrol Ship). One ship has a Hawk Screech radar director forward and the main gun director aft. Transfers to other countries include Indonesia, Finland, Bulgaria, China, and East Germany. Not all active units have had the two twin 25-mm AA added abreast the stack. Twelve watertight compartments. A dozen have been discarded by the Soviet Navy, and some of the surviving 36 are probably in reserve.

**LIGHT FRIGATES**

◆ **5 (+7) Parchim-II class** Bldr: Peenewerft, Wolgast (In serv. 1986–...)

**Parchim-II No. 1** M.O.D., Bonn, 5-87

**Parchim-II No. 2** M.O.D., Bonn, 5-87

**D:** 800 tons (950 fl) **S:** 28 kts **Dim:** 72.5 × 9.4 × 3.0 hull (4.1 max.)
**A:** 1/76.2-mm DP—1/30-mm gatling AA—2/SA-N-5/8 SAM syst. (IV × 2, ... Grail or Gremlin missiles)—4/533-mm TT (II × 2)—2/RBU-6000 ASW RL (XII × 2)—2/d.c. racks—mines
**Electron Equipt:** Radar: 1/... nav., 1/... air/surf-search (in radome), 1/Bass Tilt
Sonar: MF hull-mounted, HF dipping
EW: 2 Watch Dog, 2 chaff RL (XVI × 2)
IFF: 1/High Pole A, 1/High Pole B transponders
**M:** 3 Type M504 diesels; 3 props; 14,250 hp **Man:** 60 tot.
**Range:** ...

Remarks: An improved version of the East German Navy's Parchim, with later armament and a new radar, apparently mounted in the same radome as is used on the Pavornik-class air-cushion vehicle. As this design is inferior in all respects to the current-production, Soviet-built Grisha-V, its acquisition may be a form of aid to the East German shipbuilding industry. The dipping sonar deploys through a door on the starboard side of the main deck superstructure. The d.c. racks exit through ports in the stern. A dozen are projected, with five completed during 1986–87. Probably will replace Baltic-area Petya- and Mirka-class ships.

◆ **7 (+ ...) Grisha-V class** Bldr: Leninskaya Kuznitsa SY, Kiev; Khabarovsk SY; Kamysh Burun SY, Kerch'; Zelenodolsk SY (In serv. 1985–...)

**LIGHT FRIGATES** *(continued)*

**Grisha-V class**—KGB unit French Navy, 5-86

**D:** 860 tons (1,150 fl) **S:** 31 kts **Dim:** 71.6 (66.9 wl) × 9.8 × 3.6 hull
**A:** 1/SA-N-4 SAM system (II × 1, 20 Gecko missiles)—1/76.2-mm, DP—1/30-mm gatling AA—2/SA-N-5/8 SAM positions (I × 2, . . . Grail or Gremlin, shoulder-launched)—4/533-mm TT (II × 2)—1/RBU-6000 ASW RL (XII × 1)—2/d.c. racks (6 d.c. each) or mines
**Electron Equipt:** Radar: 1/Don-2, 1/Strut Pair, 1/Pop Group, 1/Bass Tilt
Sonar: MF hull-mounted, HF/MF dipping
EW: 2/Watch Dog, 2/chaff RL (XVI × 2)
IFF: 1/Square Head interrogator, 1/High Pole A, 1/High Pole B transponders
**M:** CODAG: 1/19,000-hp gas turbine, 2 twin Type M504 diesels; 3 props; 39,000 hp
**Range:** 450/30; 4,000/18 **Man:** 60 tot.

Remarks: The latest production variant of the basic Grisha substitutes the Strut Pair radar for Strut Curve and a 76.2-mm gun for the twin 57-mm mount, with one RBU-6000 ASW RL removed as weight compensation (the surviving mount is carried in the port position). Two launch positions for shoulder-fired point-defense SAMS have been added at the break of the 01 level superstructure, just forward of the stack. The torpedo tubes have been modified to launch wire-guided torpedoes. The dipping sonar is housed in the after superstructure, lowering through the hull between the starboard and centerline propeller shafts. Some of these ships are KGB Border Guard subordinated.

**Detail of Grisha-V**—showing lengthened torpedo tubes for wire-guidance and shoulder-fired SAM launch positions just forward of the stack
French Navy, 5-86

Note: The lack of a NATO "Grisha-IV" designation may indicate that the nickname was assigned to an experimental variant of the Grisha, or to a sub-variant of the Grisha-III.

◆ **31 Grisha-III class** Bldr: Zelenodolsk SY; Leniskaya Kuznitsa SY, Kiev; Kamysh Burun SY, Kerch'; Komsomolsk SY (In serv. 1975–85)

| | |
|---|---|
| Komsomolets Gruzin | Orlovskiy Komsomolets |
| Komsomolets Bashkirin | Smelyy 27 others |

**Grisha-III class** J.M.S.D.F., 5-87

**Smelyy**—a KGB Border Guard Grisha-III with boat to port beside stack
U.S. Navy, 1986

**D:** 860 tons (1,150 fl) **S:** 31 kts **Dim:** 71.6 (66.9 wl) × 9.8 × 3.6 hull
**A:** 1/SA-N-4 syst. (II × 1, 20 Gecko missiles)—2/57-mm DP (II × 1)—1/30-mm gatling AA—2/RBU-6000 ASW RL (XII × 2)—4/533-mm TT (II × 2)—2/d.c. racks (12 d.c.) or mines
**Electron Equipt:** Radar: 1/Don-2, 1/Strut Curve, 1/Pop Group, 1/Bass Tilt
Sonar: MF hull-mounted, HF/MF dipping
EW: 2 Watch Dog
IFF: 1 High Pole A, 1 High Pole B transponders
**M:** CODAG: 1/19,000 hp gas turbine, 2 twin Type M504 diesels; 3 props; 39,000 hp
**Range:** 450/30; 4,000/18 **Man:** 60 tot.

**LIGHT FRIGATES** *(continued)*

**Grisha-III class**—topmast askew U.S. Navy, 7-84

Remarks: Soviet type designation: MPK—*Malyy Protivolodochnyy Korabl'* (Small Antisubmarine Ship). Bass Tilt, which is atop a small deckhouse to port on the aft superstructure, has been substituted for Muff Cob radar fire control, while a gatling gun has been mounted in the space occupied by Muff Cob in the Grisha-I and -II. Depth-charge racks can be mounted on the aft end of the mine rails. Several Pacific Fleet units serve the KGB Maritime Border Guard; at least one, *Smelyy*, has had an extra boat added to port of the stack, stowed on an 01-level platform. Some may have 2 SA-N-5/8 SAM launch positions, as on Grisha-V.

◆ **12 Grisha-II class** Bldrs: Zelenodolsk SY (In serv. 1974–. . .)

| | | | | |
|---|---|---|---|---|
| Ametist | Izumrud | Provornyy | Saffir | 4 others |
| Brilliant | Predanyy | Rubin | Zhemchug | |

**Zhemchug**—Grisha-II class, 57-mm guns fore and aft 1983

**Provornyy** U.S. Navy, 3-83

**D:** 850 tons (1,100 fl) **S:** 30–31 kts **Dim:** 71.6 (66.9 wl) × 9.8 × 3.5 hull
**A:** 4/57-mm DP (II × 2)—2/RBU-6000 ASW RL (XIII × 2)—4/533-mm TT (II × 2)—2/d.c. racks (12 d.c.) or mines
**Electron Equipt:** Radar: 1/Don-2, 1/Strut Curve, 1/Muff Cob
Sonar: MF hull-mounted, HF/MF dipping
EW: 2/Watch Dog
IFF: 1/High Pole B
**M:** CODAG: 1/15,000- or 19,000-hp gas turbine, 2 twin M503 or twin M504 diesels; 3 props; 31,000 or 39,000 hp (see Remarks)
**Range:** 450/30; 4,000/18 **Man:** 60 tot

Remarks: Soviet type designation: PSKR—*Pogranichniy Storozhevoy Korabl'* (Border Patrol Ship). Manned by the KGB Maritime Border Guard. A second twin 57-mm was substituted for SA-N-4 forward, and the Pop Group missile-control radar was not installed. At least one Black Sea Fleet unit has had a boat added to port of the stack, stowed on a new 01-level platform; the after twin 57-mm DP was removed as weight compensation on that unit. Early units probably had the lower horsepower plant, with recent construction employing the Grisha-III plant.

◆ **15 Grisha-I class** Bldrs: Zelenodolsk SY; Leninskaya Kuznitsa SY, Kiev; Kamysh Burun SY, Kerch'; Khabarovsk SY (In serv. 1968–74)

**D:** 850 tons (1,100 fl) **S:** 30 kts **Dim:** 71.6 (66.9 wl) × 9.8 × 3.5 hull
**A:** 1/SA-N-4 syst. (II × 1, 20 Gecko missiles)—2/57-mm DP (II × 1)—2/RBU-6000 ASW RL (XII × 2)—4/533-mm TT (II × 2)—2/d.c. racks (12 d.c.) or mines
**Electron Equipt:** Radar: 1/Don-2, 1/Strut Curve, 1/Pop Group, 1/Muff Cob
Sonar: 1/MF hull-mounted, 1/HF dipping
EW: 2/Watch Dog—IFF: 1/High Pole B, 1/High Pole A
**M:** CODAG: 2/twin M503 diesels; 1/15,000-hp gas turbine; 3 props; 31,000 hp
**Range:** 450/30; 4,000/18 **Man:** 60 tot.

**Unique Grisha-I**—probably the first unit, with rubbing strake fore and aft of anchor pocket, Square Head IFF interrogator aft U.S. Navy, 2-80

**Grisha-I class**—using smoke generator U.S. Navy, 2-86

**LIGHT FRIGATES** *(continued)*

Remarks: More specialized for ASW than the earlier Petya and Mirka "patrol ships." Russian type designation: MPK—*Malyy Protivolodochnyy Korabl'* (Small Antisubmarine Ship). A plate has been added forward of the Muff Cobb fire-control radar to protect personnel on the bridge from its radiation. The dipping sonar is housed beneath a hump to starboard on the after deckhouse, evidently deploying through the hull bottom between the starboard and centerline propeller shafts. Some Grisha-Is are subordinated to the KGB Maritime Border Guard.

**Grisha-I class**—with enlarged stack casing French Navy, 1982

**Grisha-I**—with standard stack casing U.S. Navy, 2-80

◆ **1 Modified Petya-II class**

**Modified Petya-II class** U.S. Navy, 4-86

**A:** 4/76.2-mm DP—2/RBU-6000 ASW RL (XII × 2)—5/400-mm ASW TT (V × 1)—mines

Remarks: Conversion in 1978 similar to Modified Petya-I, but new VDS deckhouse at stern does not extend to the sides of the ship, which permits retention of mine rails. One quintuple ASW torpedo-tube mounting and the d.c. racks have been removed. Apparently experimental, as only one was converted.

◆ **11 Modified Petya-I class** Bldrs: Kaliningrad SY, Komsomol'sk SY (In serv. 1961–64)

**A:** Standard version (see Remarks): 4/76.2-mm DP (II × 2)—2/RBU-2500 ASW RL—5/400-mm ASW TT (V × 1)—1/d.c. rack
Others: 2/76.2-mm DP (II × 1), 2/RBU-2500 ASW RL (XVI × 2)

**Modified Petya-I class**—small deckhouse at stern 1980

**Modified Petya-I class**—standard version with Strut Curve radar U.S. Navy, 8-83

**Modified Petya-I**—standard configuration with Slim Net radar L. & L. Van Ginderen, 9-83

**Petya-I modified for possible towed-array research** U.S. Navy, 2-86

Remarks: Conversions began in 1973. Petya-I class altered by the addition of a medium-frequency towed sonar in a new raised stern deckhouse. The designation "Modified Petya-I" is also applied to several trials units, one with a very large VDS exposed at the stern (no raised stern); another with a deckhouse abaft the stack and a complex towing array, reels, and winch on her stern; still another with a small, boxlike deckhouse containing a towed sensor at the extreme stern. At least one "standard" Mod. Petya-I has Strut Cuve via Slim Net air-search radar. Some have 2 Don-2 navigational radars.

◆ **2 Petya-III class** (In serv. . . .)

**A:** 4/76.2-mm DP (II × 2)—3/533-mm TT (III × 1)— 4/RBU-2500 ASW RL (XVI × 4)—2/d.c. racks—mines

Remarks: Other details as for Petya-I and -II class. These are export versions of the Petya, which for some reason were never delivered. Probably have Strut Curve air-search radars. Units with this configuration have been exported to Ethiopia, India, Syria, and Vietnam.

**LIGHT FRIGATES** *(continued)*

◆ **18 Petya-II class** Bldrs: Kaliningrad SY, Khabarovsk SY (1964–69)

◆ **7 Petya-I class** Bldrs: Kaliningrad SY; Khabarovsk SY (In serv. 1961–64)

**D:** 950 tons (1,150 fl) **S:** 30 kts **Dim:** 81.8 (78.0 pp) × 9.2 × 2.8 (hull)

**A:** Petya-I: 4/76.2-mm DP (II × 2)—4/RBU-2500 ASW RL (XVI × 4)—5/400-mm ASW TT (V × 1)—2/d.c. racks—mines
Petya-II: 4/76.2-mm DP (II × 2)—2/RBU-6000 ASW RL (XII × 2)—10/400-mm ASW TT (V × 2)—2/d.c. racks—mines

**Electron Equipt:** Radar: 1/Don-2, 1/Slim Net or Strut Curve, 1/Hawk Screech
Sonar: 1/HF hull-mounted, 1/HF helo dipping sonar (on some)
EW: 2/Watch Dog—IFF: 1/High Pole B

Petya-II

**M:** CODAG: 2/15,000-hp gas turbines + 1/6,000-hp Type 61V-3 diesel; 3 props; 36,000 hp

**Range:** 450/29 (diesel + gas turbine); 1,800/16 (diesel) **Man:** 8 officers, 84 men

**Petya-I** U.S. Navy, 12-82

Remarks: Soviet type designation: SKR—*Storozhevoy Korabl'* (Patrol Ship). Most carry helicopter dipping sonars in temporary installations amidships. Petya-I has two Square Head IFF interrogators. The diesel drives the centerline CP prop and can drive the ships at up to 16 kts. Two small electro-hydraulic maneuvering propellers are mounted at the extreme stern and can produce 3 kts. The teardrop-shaped sonar dome adds 1.5 m to the navigational draft. Some Petya-Is have Slim Net search radars; all Petya-IIs and other Petya-Is have Strut Curve. One Black Sea Fleet Petya-I or -II carried a twin SUW-N-1 ASW RL on the bow in place of the gun mount in 1976. The eldest of these ships have now served over 25 years, and some are probably in reserve. Six standard Petya-IIs were transferred to Ethiopia and Vietnam during 1983–84.

◆ **9 Mirka-II class** Bldr: Kaliningrad SY (In serv. 1965–66)

Gangutets Ivan Sladkov 60 Let Komsomola Belorussiy 6 others

**Mirka-II**—4/RBU-6000, 5/400-mm TT, Slim Net U.S. Navy, 1986

**Petya-II** U.S. Navy, 8-83

**LIGHT FRIGATES** *(continued)*

**Mirka-II** U.S. Navy, 1986

◆ **9 Mirka-I class** Bldr: Kaliningrad SY (In serv. 1964–65)

**Mirka-I class** French Navy, 1986

**Mirka-I class**—with 2 Don-2 radars G. Koop, 1986

**D:** 950 tons (1,150 fl) **S:** 34 kts **Dim:** 82.4 × 9.2 × 2.9 (hull)
**A:** Mirka-I: 4/76.2-mm DP (II × 2)—4/RBU-6000 ASW RL (XII × 4)—5/400-mm ASW TT (V × I)—1/d.c. rack
Mirka-II: 4/76.2-mm DP (II × 2)—2/RBU-6000 ASW RL (XII × 2)—10/400-mm ASW TT (V × 2)
**Electron Equipt:** Radar: 1 or 2/Don-2, 1/Slim Net or Strut Curve, 1/Hawk Screech
Sonar: HF hull-mounted—Mirka-II also: dipping (aft)
EW: 2/Watch Dog—IFF: 1/High Pole B, 2/Square Head
**M:** CODAG: 2/15,000-hp gas turbines + 2/6,000-hp diesels; 2 props in pump-jet tunnels
**Range:** 500/30 (gas turbine); 4,800/10 (1 diesel) **Man:** 8 officers, 84 men

Remarks: Soviet type designation: SKR—*Storozhevoy Korabl'* (Patrol Ship). Propulsion system similar in concept to that of the Poti class, using gas turbines to power compressors the inject air into tunnels beneath the ship to produce a jet effect; the diesel-driver propellers are also within the tunnels, while the gas turbine exhaust residual thrust contributes to the overall power. All Mirka-Is have Slim Net, while a few late Mirka-IIs have Strut Curve. All Mirka-IIs have been modernized with a dipping sonar in place of the internal depth-charge rack on the port side of the stern. Most actiue ships have 2 Don-2 navigational radars. Some units of both versions are believed to be in reserve.

**GUIDED-MISSILE CORVETTES**

Note: A new class of missile corvette intended for the Soviet Navy is reportedly under construction in Szczecin, Poland. No details are available.

◆ **2 or more (+ . . .) Tarantul-III class** Bldr: Petrovskiy SY, Leningrad; Sredniy Neva SY, Kolpino; . . . SY (Pacific area)

**Tarantul-III** M.O.D., Bonn, 1987

**D:** 480 tons (540 fl) **S:** 36 kts **Dim:** 56.5 (52.5 wl) × 10.5 (9.4 wl) × 2.5 hull
**A:** 4/SS-N-22 SSM (II × 2)—1/76.2-mm DP—1/SA-N-5/8 SAM syst. (IV × 1, 16 Grail/Gremlin missiles)—2/30-mm gatling AA (I × 2)
**Electron Equipt:** Radar: 1/Kivach-3, 1/Band Stand, 1/Bass Tilt
EW: 4/. . . intercept, 2/chaff RL (XVI × 2)
IFF: 1 or 2/Square Head, 1/High Pole B transponder
**M:** CODOG: 2 NK-12M gas turbines (12,100 hp each), 1 Type M504 diesel (5,000 hp); 2 props; 24,200 hp
**Range:** 400/36; . . . **Fuel:** 50 tons **Man:** 40 tot.

Remarks: Although a prototype Tarantul appeared in the early 1980s configured with four SS-N-22 supersonic, sea-skimming missiles, not until 1987 was what appears to be a production version sighted. The propulsion system also differs from that of earlier Tarantuls. A Light Bulb probable missile data link antenna radome is located atop a vertical lattice mast. Band Stand apparently provides targeting and guidance for the SS-N-22 SSM. There is a back-up lead-computing optical director aft for the six-barreled 30-mm gatling guns.

◆ **16 (+ . . .) Tarantul-II class** Bldr: Sredniy Neva SY, Kolpino; Petrovskiy SY, Leningrad; . . . (Pacific Area) (In serv. 1981–1986)

**Tarantul-II**—Band Stand atop bridge, Light Bulb atop raked mast 1981

**Tarantul-II class** M.O.D., Bonn, 1982

**D:** 480 tons (540 fl) **S:** 36 kts **Dim:** 56.5 (52.5 wl) × 10.5 (9.4 wl) × 2.5 hull
**A:** 4/SS-N-2C SSM (II × 2)—1/76.2-mm DP—1/SA-N-5/8 SAM syst. (IV × 1, 16–20 Grail/Gremlin missiles)—2/30-mm gatling AA (I × 2)
**Electron Equipt:** Radar: 1/Kivach-3 nav., 1/Band Stand, 1/Bass Tilt
EW: . . .—IFF: 1/Square Head, 1/High Pole B

GUIDED-MISSILE CORVETTES *(continued)*

**M:** COGOG: 2 cruise gas turbines (est. 3,000 hp each), 2 high-speed gas turbines, Type NK-12M (12,100 hp each); 2 props; 24,200 hp
**Range:** 400/36; 2,000/20 **Fuel:** 50 tons **Man:** 40 tot.

REMARKS: The initial large-scale production variant of the Tarantul design for the Soviet Navy. The cruise gas turbines exhaust through a stack, while the high-speed turbines exhaust through the transom stern, adding their residual thrust to the propulsive power. A Light Bulb probable missile data link antenna has been added at the masthead, while Band Stand appears to act as missile target acquisition and guidance radar. There are four unoccupied positions for EW antennas.

◆ **2 Tarantul-I class** Bldr: Petrovskiy SY, Leningrad (In serv. 1979–80)

**Tarantul-I class**—upper missile-tube doors open M.O.D., Bonn, 1982

**Tarantul-I-class prototype** 1979

**D:** 480 tons (540 fl) **S:** 36 kts **Dim:** 56.5 (52.5 wl) × 10.5 (9.4 wl) × 2.50
**A:** 4/SS-N-2C (II × 2)—1/76.2-mm DP—1/SA-N-5/8 system (IV × 1, 16–20 Grail/Gremlin missiles)—2/30-mm gatling AA (VI × 2)
**Electron Equipt:** Radar: 1/Kivach-3, 1/Bass Tilt, 1/Plank Shave targeting
EW: 4/passive arrays, 2/chaff RL (XVI × 2)
IFF: 1/High Pole, 1/Square Head
**M:** COGOG: 2 NK-12M gas turbines (12,000 hp each), 2 cruise gas turbines (est. 3,000 hp each); 2 props; 6,000–8,000 hp
**Range:** 400/36; 2,000/20 **Fuel:** 50 tons **Man:** 40 tot.

REMARKS: Probably typed *Raketnyy Kater* (Missile Boat). Two prototype Tarantul-I retained for trials; others, all for export, have been built at Volodarskiy SY, Rybinsk. Minor differences in cruise gas-turbine stack configuration.

◆ **10 Nanuchka-III class** Bldr: Petrovskiy SY, Leningrad, and Ulis SY, Vladivostok (In serv. 1977–1984)

BURAN TUCHA SMERCH 7 others

**D:** 685 tons (fl) **S:** 32 kts **Dim:** 60.3 × 12.2 × 2.4 (3.1 max.)
**A:** 6/SS-N-9 SSM (III × 2)—1/SA-N-4 system (II × 1, Gecko 20 missiles)—1/76.2-mm DP—1/30-mm gatling AA (VI × 1)
**Electron Equipt:** Radar: 1/Peel Pair, 1/Band Stand, 1/Bass Tilt
EW: 4/passive arrays, 2/chaff RL (XVI × 2)
IFF: 1/High Pole, 1/Square Head
**M:** 3 M517 diesels; 3 props; 30,000 hp **Man:** 60 tot.
**Range:** 900/30; 2,500/12 (1 engine)

**Nanuchka-III class**—30-mm gatling gun, 76.2-mm DP aft G. Gyssels, 11-87

**Nanuchka-III class**—Band Stand on higher pilothouse than Nanuchka-I U.S. Navy, 5-84

REMARKS: Soviet type designation: MRK—*Malyy Raketnyy Korabl'* (Small Missile Ship). The single 76.2-mm DP was substituted for the twin 57-mm AA aft, the gatling gun is in the position occupied by Muff Cob in the Nanuchka-I, and Bass Tilt is situated atop a new deckhouse abaft the mast. The pilothouse is higher and the superstructure is enlarged. The 30-mm gatling gun is off centerline, to starboard. Two Fish Bowl radomes on the mast are believed to house SS-N-9 missile data-link antennas.

◆ **17 Nanuchka-I class** Bldr: Petrovskiy SY, Leningrad (In serv. 1969–76)

| | | | | | |
|---|---|---|---|---|---|
| GRAD | MOLNIYA | RADUGA | SHTORM | TSIKLON | ZYB' |
| METEL' | MUSSON | SHKVAL | TAYFUN | ZARNITSA | 6 others |

**Nanuchka-I class**—late version, note EW devices atop mast on shielded platform U.S. Navy, 5-84

**Nanuchka-I class**—early version with free-standing missile blast shields French Navy, 1982

**D:** 675 tons (fl) **S:** 32 kts **Dim:** 60.3 × 12.2 × 2.4 (3.1 max.)
**A:** 6/SS-N-9 SSM (II × 3)—1/SA-N-4 system (II × 1, 20 Gecko missiles)—2/57-mm DP (II × 1)
**Electron Equipt:** Radar: 1/Peel Pair, 1/Pop Group, 1/Muff Cob, 1/Band Stand
EW: 4/passive arrays, 2/chaff RL (XVI × 2)
IFF: 1/High Pole, 1/Square Head
**M:** 3 M517 diesels; 3 props; 30,000 hp
**Range:** 900/30; 2,500/12 (1 engine) **Man:** 60 tot.

REMARKS: Soviet type designation: MRK—*Malyy Raketnyy Korabl'* (Small Missile Ship). Named for meteorological phenomena; some of the names above may apply to the Nanuchka-III version. These are reported to be poor sea boats with very unreliable engines. Early units have separate blast shields abaft the SS-N-9 launchers; they have smaller engine air intakes and may employ paired M503 diesels for 24,000 hp total, 30 kts max. Band Stand is associated with target designation for the SS-N-9 missiles. New EW antennas are being added near the top of the mast. The similar Nanuchka-II for export has 4 SS-N-2C missiles.

## CORVETTES

◆ **22 (+ . . .) Pauk class** Bldr: . . . (In serv. 1980– . . .)

| | |
|---|---|
| Komsomolets Bashkiriy | Kiyevskiy Komsomolets |
| Komsomolets Gruzin | Odesskiy Komsomolets |
| Komsomolets Moldaviy | 17 others |

**Pauk class**—high bridge version M.O.D., Bonn, 1986

**Pauk class**—KGB unit with low pilothouse U.S. Navy, 1985

**Pauk class** L. &. L. Van Ginderen, 8-85

**D:** 480 tons (580 fl) **S:** 32 kts **Dim:** 58.5 (52.5 wl) × 9.8 (9.4 wl) × 2.5 hull
**A:** 1/76.2-mm DP—1/SA-N-5/8 SAM syst. (IV × 1, 16–20 Grail/Gremlin missiles)—1/30-mm gatling AA—2/RBU-1200 ASW RL (V × 2)—4/400-mm ASW TT (I × 4)—2/d.c. racks (12 d.c.)
**Electron Equipt:** Radar: 1/Spin Trough, 1/air-surface search, 1/Bass Tilt
Sonar: MF hull-mounted, MF dipping, HF dipping
IFF: 2/Square Head, 1/High Pole B
EW: . . . passive arrays; 2/chaff RL (XVI × 2)
**M:** 2 M517 diesels; 2 props; 20,000 hp **Man:** 40 tot.
**Range:** 2,000/20 **Fuel:** 50 tons

Remarks: Built in the Baltic and Pacific areas. Some are operated by the KGB Maritime Border Guard. This class uses same hull as Tarantul-class missile corvette but has ASW armament vice SS-N-2C and an all-diesel propulsion plant vice Tarantul's COGOG/CODOG system. A large housing for a dipping sonar system projects 2 m out from the stern. A new variant noted in 1982 in the Baltic has the pilothouse one half-deck higher. Platforms on the mast are intended to carry EW arrays, while there is a backup optical director for the single gatling AA gun; Bass Tilt can control both the 76.2-mm and 30-mm guns. The main engines are probably the same twin diesels as used in the Nanuchka class. Probable Soviet designation MPK—*Malyy Protivolodochnyy Korabl'* (Small Antisubmarine Ship), and apparently intended to replace the Poti class. A helicopter-type dipping sonar installation, housed in a cabinet on the starboard side near the stern, has been added, possibly indicating that the larger dipping sonar is not fully effective.

◆ **57 Poti class** Bldrs: Zelenodolsk SY, poss. others (In serv. 1961–67)

**D:** 400 tons (fl) **S:** 38 kts **Dim:** 59.4 × 7.9 × 2.0 (hull)
**A:** 2/57-mm DP (II × 1)—2/RBU-6000 ASW RL (XII × 2)—2 or 4/400-mm TT (I × 2 or 4)
**Electron Equipt:** Radar: 1/Don-2, 1/Strut Curve, 1/Muff Cob
Sonar: 1/HF hull-mounted, 1/Hormone dipping
EW: 2/Watch Dog—IFF: 1/High Pole B
**M:** CODAG: 2 M503A diesels (8,000 hp) + 2 gas turbines (40,000 hp); 2 props
**Range:** 500/37; 4,500/10 (1 diesel) **Man:** 40 tot.

Remarks: Soviet type designation: MPK—*Malyy Protivolodochnyy Korabl'* (Small Antisubmarine Ship). Several have old-type open 57-mm AA mounts and two RBU-2500. This class has been exported to Romania and Bulgaria. The two propellers are mounted in thrust tubes of the same length as the poop, which contains the two turbines; the jets exhaust through ports in the stern and also power air compressors that exhaust into the propeller tubes, producing a thrust-jet effect. Slowly being stricken, as Pauk class enters service.

**Poti class** L. &. L. Van Ginderen, 1984

**Poti class** G. Koop, 1986

◆ **6 Ivan Susanin-class patrol icebreakers** Bldr: Admiralty SY, Leningrad (In serv. 1975–81)

| | | |
|---|---|---|
| Aysberg | Imeni XXV Syezda K.P.S.S. | Neva |
| Dunay | Imeni XXVI Syezda K.P.S.S. | Volga |

**Imeni XXV Syezda K.P.S.S.** U.S. Navy, 9-85

**Imeni XXV Syezda K.P.S.S.** U.S. Navy, 9-85

**CORVETTES** *(continued)*

**D:** 3,400 tons (fl) **S:** 14.5 kts **Dim:** 70.0 (62.0 pp) × 18.3 × 6.5
**A:** 2/76.2-mm DP (II × 1)—2/30-mm gatling AA (I × 2)
**Electron Equipt:** Radar: 2/Don-Kay, 1/Strut Curve, 1/Owl Screech
AFF: 1/High Pole B
**M:** 3 Type 13D100 diesels, electric drive; 2 props; 5,400 hp **Fuel:** 550 tons
**Electric:** 1,000 kw **Range:** 5,500/12.5; 13,000/9.4 **Man:** 140 tot.

Remarks: Operated by the KGB Maritime Border Guard in the Pacific area. KGB Type designator: *Pogranichnyy Storozhevoy Korabl'* (Border Patrol Ship). Two sisters, disarmed and painted with black hull and white superstructure, serve as naval auxiliaries: *Ivan Susanin* and *Ruslan.* Have a helicopter deck aft, but no hangar. The gatling AA guns have only lead-computing ringsight directors; Bass Tilt radar directors are not fitted. The Owl Screech radar director controls the 76.2-mm DP mount. *Dunay* and *Neva* also have two positions for hand-launching SA-N-5/8 Grail/Gremlin missiles.

◆ **1 Purga-class patrol icebreaker** Bldr: . . . SY, Leningrad

Purga (In serv. 1955)

**Purga** 1983

**D:** 4,500 tons (fl) **S:** 18 kts **Dim:** 97.5 × 15.2 × 6.4
**A:** 4/100-mm DP (I × 4)—mines
**Electronic Equipt:** Radar: 2/Don-2, 1/High Sieve, 1/Strut Curve, 1/Sun Visor-B
EW: 2/Watch Dog—IFF: 2/High Pole
**M:** 4 diesels, electric drive; 2 props; 8,000 hp **Man:** 250 tot.

Remarks: Operated by the KGB Maritime Border Guard in the Pacific. Laid down prior to World War II and launched circa 1952. Has a Wasp Head stabilized optical GFCS, with Sun Visor radar. Formerly also carried 8/37-mm AA (II × 4). Riveted construction. Name duplicates that of a Soviet Navy-subordinated auxiliary icebreaker.

◆ **13 Sorum-class armed tugs** Bldr: Yaroslavl SY (In serv. 1974–. . .)

| | | | |
|---|---|---|---|
| Amur | Kaluga | Primorsk | Yan Berzin' |
| Bug | Kamchatka | Primorye | Zabaykalye |
| Brest | Kareliya | Sakhalin | |
| Chukotka | Ladoga | | |

**Sakhalin** 1975

**D:** 1,210 tons (1,656 fl) **S:** 14 kts **Dim:** 58.3 × 12.6 × 4.6
**A:** 4/30-mm AK-230 AA (II × 2)
**Electron Equipt:** Radar: 2/Don-2—IFF: 1/High Pole B
**M:** 2 Type 5-2D42 diesels, electric drive; 1 prop; 1,500 hp
**Fuel:** 322 tons **Range:** 6,720/13 **Man:** 35 tot.

Remarks: Armed units of a standard naval/commercial seagoing tug, used by KGB Maritime Border Guard for patrol duties. Typed PSKR—*Pogranichnyy Storozhevoy Korabl'* (Border Patrol Ship).

Note: Several Okhtenskiy-class seagoing tugs have also been employed by the KGB Maritime Border Guard, armed with a twin 57-mm gun mount. See later page, under tug version, for details.

◆ **16 T-58-class ex-minesweepers** (In serv. 1957–61)

| | |
|---|---|
| Irkutskiy Komsomolets | Primorskiy Komsomolets |
| Kaliningradskiy Komsomolets | Sovetskiy Pogranichnik |
| Komsomolets Latviy | Starshiy Leytenant Vladimirov |
| Malakhit | 8 others |
| P. Vinogradev | |

**T-58 class** U.S. Navy, 4-83

**T-58 class** U.S. Navy, 11-84

**D:** 725 tons (860 fl) **S:** 18 kts **Dim:** 70.0 × 9.1 × 2.5
**A:** 4/57-mm AA (II × 2)—2/RBU-1200 ASW RL (V × 2)—2/d.c. racks—mines
**Electron Equipt:** Radar: 1/Spin Trough, 1/Don-2, 1/Muff Cob
Sonar: 1/HF hull-mounted
EW: 2/Watch Dog—IFF: 2/Square Head, 1/High Pole A
**M:** 2 diesels; 2 props; 4,000 hp **Range:** 2,500/13.5 **Man:** 60 tot.

Remarks: Reclassified SKR—*Storozhevoy Korabl'* (Patrol Ship) in 1978 and portable minesweeping gear offloaded. Some are operated by the KGB Maritime Border Guard as PSKR—*Pogranichnyy Storozhevoy Korabl'* (Border Patrol Ship). Most are in the Pacific Fleet. One has been transferred to Guinea, one to Yemen, and three others have been converted as radar pickets, with a Big Net radar aft. (See below.)

◆ **3 T-58-class radar pickets, former minesweepers** (In serv. 1957–61)

**D:** 760 tons (880 fl) **S:** 17 kts **Dim:** 70.0 × 9.1 × 2.5
**A:** 2/57-mm AA (II × 1)—4/30-mm AA (II × 2)—2/SA-N-5 syst. (IV × 2, 16 SA-7 Grail missiles)—2/d.c. racks
**Electron Equipt:** Radar: 1/Spin Trough, 1/Strut Curve, 1/Big Net, 1/Muff Cob
Sonar: HF hull-mounted—EW: . . .
**M:** 2 diesels; 2 props; 4,000 hp **Range:** 2,500/13.5 **Man:** 100 tot.

**T-58-class radar picket**—former minesweeper U.S. Navy, 1981

**CORVETTES** *(continued)*

**T-58-class radar picket** M.O.D., Bonn, 1981

Remarks: First unit conversion completed 1979 at Izhora SY, Leningrad, second in 1981, the third around 1983–84. Considering the small number converted, the age of the hulls, and the pace of the program, these ships are probably intended for a specialized range security role, rather than as classical "radar pickets." Naval-operated.

◆ **11 T-43 class ex-minesweepers** (In serv. 1947–57)

**T-43-class Border Patrol Ship**—60-meter version 1981

Remarks: Data as for minesweeper version on later page. Portable minesweeping gear deleted (winch and crane retained). Reclassified during 1970s when transferred to the KGB Maritime Border Guard as PKSR—*Pogranichnyy Storozhevoy Korabl'* (Border Patrol Ship). Operate in the Pacific area. A few have 2/45-mm AA vice 4/37-mm AA.

## GUIDED-MISSILE PATROL BOATS

◆ **1 (+ . . .) Wing-In-Ground Effect craft** Bldr: . . . (In serv. 1986–87)

Remarks: The U.S. Dept. of Defense publication *Soviet Military Power 1987* reports the existence of a Soviet wing-in-ground effect (WIG) craft larger than the Orlan-class amphibious WIG and equipped with six antiship cruise missiles. No further details available.

◆ **17 Matka-class semi-hydrofoils** Bldr: Izhora SY, Kolpino (In serv. 1978–81)

**D:** 225 tons (260 fl) **S:** 36 kts **Dim:** 40.0 × 12.0 (7.6 hull) × 2.1 (hull; 3.2 foils)
**A:** 2/SS-N-2C SSM (I × 2)—1/76.2-mm DP—1/30-mm gatling AA
**Electron Equipt:** Radar: 1/Cheese Cake, 1/Plank Shave, 1/Bass Tilt
EW: 2/chaff launchers (XVI × 2)
IFF: 1/High Pole B, 1/Square Head
**M:** 3 M504 diesels; 3 props; 15,000 hp **Range:** 400/36; 650/25 **Man:** 30 tot.

**Matka class at speed, on foils, with Plank Shave targeting radar**

**Matka class, hull-borne**—note low freeboard 1979

Remarks: Essentially a missile-armed version of the Turya-class hydrofoil torpedo boat, with larger superstructure, 76.2-mm gun forward, and missiles and gatling gun aft. Construction proceeded very slowly. Uses Plank Shave targeting radar, larger than Square Tie. Appears to be overloaded, and construction ceased in favor of the Tarantul-series.

◆ **1 Sarancha class** Bldr: Petrovskiy SY, Leningrad (In serv. 1977)

**Sarancha class**—note two steps to bottom of hydroplane hull

**D:** 320 tons (fl) **S:** 58 kts
**Dim:** 53.6 (50.6 foils down hull) × 31.3 (11.0 hull) × 7.3 (2.6 hull)
**A:** 4/SS-N-9 SSM (II × 2)—1/SA-N-4 syst. (II × 1, 20 Gecko missiles)—1/30-mm gatling AA (VI × 1)
**Electron Equipt:** Radar: 1/Band Stand, 1/Pop Group, 1/Bass Tilt
IFF: 1/Square Head, 1/High Pole B
**M:** 2 gas turbines; 4 props; 30,000 hp

Remarks: Too large and complex to be a successor to the Osa class. Essentially a reduced, high-speed Nanuchka. Folding-foil hydrofoil system, with 2 propellers on each of two pods on the after foils. Stepped hydroplane hull bottom. Not a success.

◆ **30 Osa-II class** (In serv. 1966–70)

| | |
|---|---|
| Amurskiy Komsomolets | Kirovskiy Komsomolets |
| Brestskiy Komsomolets | Michurinskiy Komsomolets |
| Kaliningradskiy Komsomolets | Tambovskiy Komsomolets |
| | 24 others |

**D:** 215 tons (245 fl) **S:** 35 kts **Dim:** 38.6 × 7.6 × 2.0
**A:** 4/SS-N-2B/C Styx SSM (I × 4)—4/30-mm AA (II × 2)
**Electron Equipt:** Radar: 1/Square Tie, 1/Drum Tilt
IFF: 1/High Pole B, 2/Square Head
**M:** 3 M504 diesels; 3 props; 15,000 hp **Range:** 500/34; 750/25 **Man:** 30 tot.

**Osa-II class** 1978

GUIDED-MISSILE PATROL BOATS *(continued)*

**Osa-II class** U.S. Navy, 1986

REMARKS: Soviet type designation: RKA—*Raketnyy Kater* (Missile Cutter). Some units have been given SA-N-5/8 systems aft, with the quadruple, manned launcher and one 4-missile reload locker. Widely exported during 1970–present, primarily using new-built units. Some reports indicate that they are mediocre sea boats and that the engines are very temperamental. Numbers beginning to decline, through foreign transfer and attrition.

◆ **48 Osa-I class** Bldrs: Various (In serv. 1959–66)

KOMSOMOLETS TATARIY KRONSHTADTSKIY KOMSOMOLETS 46 others

**Osa-I class**—rib-sided SS-N-2 launchers 1974

**Osa-I class**—quadruple SA-N-5 launcher abaft Drum Tilt, smooth-sided launchers U.S. Navy, 5-84

**D:** 185 tons (215 fl) **S:** 36 kts **Dim:** 38.6 × 7.6 × 1.8
**A:** 4/SS-N-2 Styx SSM (I × 4)—4/30-mm AA (II × 2)—1/SA-N-5/8 SAM syst. (IV × 1, 4 Grail/Gremlin missiles) in some
**Electron Equipt:** Radar: 1/Square Tie, 1/Drum Tilt
IFF: 1/High Pole B, 2/Square Head
**M:** 3 M503A diesels; 3 props; 12,000 hp
**Range:** 500/34; 750/25 **Man:** 30 tot

REMARKS: Originally built by Petrovskiy SY, Leningrad, but other yards were also involved in the program. Soviet type designation: RKA—*Raketnyy Kater* (Missile Cutter). These small craft can launch their missiles in a Force-4 sea (2-m waves). Many of them have been transferred to other navies. Some have been built as, or converted to, targets. Stenka, Matka, Turya, and Mol (an export torpedo boat, see Somalia) all use Osa hulls and propulsion plants. Diminishing in numbers, as some are nearly 30 years old.

PATROL BOATS

◆ **4 (+ . . .) Muravey-class hydrofoils** Bldr: (In serv. 1982– . . .)

**D:** 200 tons (230 fl) **S:** . . . **Dim:** 38.6 × 7.6 × . . .
**A:** 1/76.2-mm DP—1/30-mm gatling AA—4/400-mm ASW TT
**Electron Equipt:** Radar: . . .
Sonar: . . .
**M:** . . . **Range:** . . . **Man:** . . .

REMARKS: First reported 1983. No further data available. May be KGB Maritime Border Guard-subordinated.

◆ **1 Babochka class** Bldr: . . . (In serv. 1978)

**Babochka class** 1978

**D:** 400 tons (fl) **S:** 45 kts **Dim:** 50.0 × 13.0 (8.5 hull) × . . .
**A:** 8/400-mm ASW TT (IV × 2)—2/30-mm gatling AA (VI × 2)
**Electron Equipt:** Radar: 1/Don-2, 1/Peel Cone, 1/Bass Tilt
**M:** CODOG: 2 cruise diesels, 3 gas turbines; 3 props; 30,000 hp (max.)

REMARKS: A prototype ASW hydrofoil with fixed, fully submerged foils fore and aft. The torpedo tubes are mounted, two on two, on either side of the forecastle between the forward gatling gun and the superstructure.

◆ **1 Slepen class** Bldr: Petrovskiy SY, Leningrad (In serv. circa 1969)

**D:** 205 tons (230 fl) **S:** 36 kts **Dim:** 38.6 × 7.6 × 1.9
**A:** 1/76.2-mm DP—1/30-mm gatling gun
**Electron Equipt:** Radar: 1/Don-2, 1/Bass Tilt
EW: 2/passive arrays, 2/chaff RL (XVI × 2)
IFF: 1/High Pole B, 2/Square Head
**M:** 3 M504 diesels; 3 props; 15,000 hp **Range:** 500/34; 750/25 **Man:** 30 tot.

REMARKS: Trials craft for systems for small combatants. Twin 57-mm AA replaced by single 76.2-mm DP forward in 1975. Resembles a Matka but does not have missiles or hydrofoils.

◆ **115 (+ . . .) Stenka class** Bldrs: Petrovskiy SY, Leningrad; . . . (In serv. 1967– . . .)

**Stenka class**—with Peel Cone navigational radar U.S. Navy, 11-84

**Stenka**—with Pot Drum nav. radar L. & L. Van Ginderen, 9-83

**PATROL BOATS** *(continued)*

**D:** 170 tons (210 fl) **S:** 36 kts **Dim:** 39.5 × 7.6 × 1.8
**A:** 4/30-mm AA (II × 2)—4/400-mm ASW TT—2/d.c. racks (12 d.c.)
**Electron Equipt:** Radar: 1 Pot Drum or Peel Cone, 1/Drum Tilt
Sonar: 1/Hormone-helicopter, dipping
IFF: 1/High Pole B, 2/Square Head
**M:** 3 M503A diesels; 3 props; 12,000 hp **Range:** 550/34; 750/25 **Man:** 22 tot.

Remarks: Soviet type designation: PSKR—*Pogranichnyy Storozhevoy Korabl'* (Border Patrol Ship). Recent units have a new navigational radar vice Pot Drum. Manned by the Maritime Border Guard of the KGB. Construction has continued for over 20 years, although at a low rate in recent years. Recent units have a new navigational radar.

**HYDROFOIL TORPEDO BOATS**

◆ **30 Turya class** Bldr: Ulis SY, Vladivostok; Srednyy Neva SY, Kolpino (In serv. 1974–79)

**Turya class at speed, bow raised on foil**

**Turya class at low speed, in displacement condition** G. Koop, 1984

**D:** 215 tons (250 fl) **S:** 35 kts
**Dim:** 39.0 × 7.6 (12.5 over foils) × 2.0 (4.0 over foils)
**A:** 2/57-mm AA aft (II × 1)—2/25-mm AA (II × 1)—4/533-mm TT (I × 4)
**Electron Equipt:** Radar: 1/Pot Drum, 1/Muff Cob
Sonar: 1/Hormone-helicopter, dipping
IFF: 1/High Pole B, 1/Square Head
**M:** 3 M504 diesels; 3 props; 15,000 hp **Range:** 400/36; 650/25 **Man:** 24 tot.

Remarks: Fixed hydrofoils forward only; stern planes on water surface. Has Osa-II hull and propulsion. The dipping sonar is housed in a sponson over the starboard quarter. Nine of this class, without dipping sonar, have been delivered to Cuba since 1-79, and others have been exported to Vietnam, Kampuchea, and the Seychelles.

**PATROL CRAFT**

◆ **30 or more Zhuk class** Bldr: . . . (In serv. 1975– . . .)

**Zhuk class**—export version (for the Seychelles), with 4/14.5-mm mg (II × 2) French Navy, 1983

**D:** 48 tons (60 fl) **S:** 34 kts **Dim:** 24.0 × 5.0 × 1.2 (1.8 props)
**A:** 2/14.5-mm mg (II × 1) **Electron Equipt:** Radar: 1/Spin Trough
**M:** 2 M50F-4 diesels; 2 props; 2,400 hp **Fuel:** 10 tons
**Range:** 700/28; 1,100/15 **Man:** 12 tot.

Remarks: Probably manned by the KGB Border Guard. A large number have been exported, armed with a side-by-side turreted gun mount, as shown in the photo; Soviet units have one (or occasionally two) over-and-under gun mounts.

**RIVERINE CRAFT**

Note: The U.S.S.R. maintains a number of river gunboats on the Lower Danube, on the Amur and Ussuri river systems in the Far East, and possibly elsewhere. In addition to gunboats, the riverine forces have a few support craft, including the administrative craft SSV-10 (ex-PS 10) on the Danube (360 tons, 49 m overall).

**SSV-10 (former number)**—flagship of the Danube Flotilla, with two 45-mm saluting cannon abreast stack 1972

◆ **15 (+ . . .) Yaz-class monitors** Bldr: . . . (In serv. 1981– . . .)

Khabarovskiy Komsomolets 14+ others

**Yaz class**

**D:** approx. 400 tons (fl) **S:** 14–16 kts **Dim:** 60.0 × . . . × . . .
**A:** 2/115-mm tank guns (I × 2)—2/30-mm gatling AA (I × 2)—4/14.5-mm mg (II × 2)
**Electron Equipt:** Radar: 1/Spin Trough or Kivach, 1/Bass Tilt
**M:** diesels; 2 props; . . . hp **Man:** . . .

Remarks: Low-freeboard monitors for the Amur River Flotilla. Also reported in service are several Pivyaka-class river monitors and several Vosh class; no data available.

◆ **85 Shmel-class patrol gunboats** Bldr: . . . (In serv. 1967–74)

**Shmel class**—RL, armored 25-mm mount aft 4-80

**D:** 60 tons (fl) **S:** 22 kts **Dim:** 28.3 × 4.6 × 0.9
**A:** 1/76.2-mm, 48 cal., fwd in a tank turret—2/25-mm AA (II × 1) aft—5/7.62-mm mg (I × 5)—1/122-mm RL (XVIII × 1)—mines
**M:** 2 M50F-4 diesels; 2 props; 2,400 hp **Range:** 240/20; 600/10 **Man:** 15 tot.

**RIVERINE CRAFT** *(continued)*

REMARKS: Soviet type designation: AKA—*Artilleriyskiy Kater* (Artillery Cutter). Not all these craft have a rocket launcher. An earlier version has a twin machine-gun mount aft that resembles a tank turret. One 7.62-mm is mounted coaxially with the 85-mm gun; the others fire through slits in the sides of the open-topped redoubt forward of the artillery RL. Four transferred to Kampuchea, 1984–85. Many are maintained in reserve.

## MINE WARFARE SHIPS

NOTE: Four or more Polnocny-class landing craft have been converted as assault minesweepers, carrying two radio-controlled boats to tow line-charge, inshore-obstacle-clearance systems into place. The ships remain capable of landing vehicles and are listed with the amphibious ships.

◆ **3 Alesha-class minelayers** Bldr: . . . (In serv. 1967–69)

PRIPET' VYCHEGDA N . . .

**Vychegda**—the first Alesha 1969

**Vychegda** J.M.S.D.F., 10-85

**D:** 2,900 tons (3,500 fl) **S:** 17 kts **Dim:** 97.0 × 14.0 × 5.4
**A:** 4/57-mm (IV × 1)—300 mines
**Electron Equipt:** Radar: 1/Don-2, 1/Strut Curve, 1/Muff Cob
IFF: 1/High Pole B
**M:** 4 diesels; 2 props; 8,000 hp **Range:** 4,000/16; 8,500/8 **Man:** 190 tot.

REMARKS: Can also be used as netlayers, minesweeper tenders, and command ships. The second and third ships had two king posts and booms vice the forward crane.

◆ **1 Natya-II-class fleet minesweeper** Bldr: Sredniy Neva SY, Kolpino (In serv. 1982)

**Natya-II class**—deckhouse on stern, no 25-mm AA or ASW RL French Navy, 7-85

◆ **34 Natya-I-class fleet minesweepers** Bldr: Various (In serv. 1970–1982)

| | | |
|---|---|---|
| ADMIRAL PERSHIN | MASHINIST | SNAYPER |
| ARTILLERIST | MINER | SVYAZIST |
| DIZELIST | MOTORIST | TURBINIST |
| DMITRIY LYSOV | PULEMETCHIK | VSEVOLOD VISHNEVSKIY |
| ELEKTRIK | RADIST | ZARYAD |
| KONTRADMIRAL HOROSHKIN | RULEVOY | ZENITCHIK |
| KURSKIY KOMSOMOLETS (ex-*Navodchik*) | SIGNAL'SHCHIK | 14 others |

**D:** 650 tons (750 fl) **S:** 17 kts **Dim:** 61.0 (57.6 wl) × 9.6 × 2.8
**A:** 4/30-mm AA (II × 2)—4/25-mm AA (II × 2)—most: 2/SA-N-5/8 SAM syst. (IV × 2, 16 Grail/Gremlin missiles)—2/RBU-1200 ASW RL (V × 2)—mines
**Electron Equipt:** Radar: 1/Don-2, 1/Drum Tilt—Sonar: 1/HF
IFF: 1/High Pole B, 2/Square Head
**M:** 2 diesels; 2 props; 5,000 hp **Range:** 1,800/16; 5,200/10 **Man:** 60 tot.

REMARKS: Soviet type designation: MT—*Morskoy Tral'shchik* (Seagoing Minesweeper). Equipped to serve as ASW escorts. Early units have rigid davits aft; on later units they are articulated. Stem cut back sharply below waterline, as

**Natya class**—early unit with gooseneck sweep-gear davits, and 2 SA-N-5/8 SAM launchers abaft stack French Navy, 10-84

**MINE WARFARE SHIPS** *(continued)*

in T-43 and Yurka classes. Aluminum alloy hull. One, designated Natya-II and completed 1982, has a long deckhouse aft, no 25-mm AA or RBU-2500, but does have 2/SA-N-5/8 shoulder-launch positions. Two SA-N-5/8 quadruple launchers have been added to a number of units of the class, just abaft the lattice mast. Some also have an extra navigational radar atop the pilothouse. Current production is for export, with one unit delivered to Syria with no ASW ordnance or minesweeping gear in 1985 as a training ship. Eight have been built for India and eight for Libya.

**Natya-I class**—with articulated sweep-gear davits U.S. Navy, 7-83

◆ **41 Yurka-class fleet minesweepers** Bldr: Ust Izhora SY, Kolpino; Kamysh-Burun SY, Kerch'; etc. (In serv. 1962–69)

| | |
|---|---|
| Gafel' | Yevgeniy Nikonov |
| Semen Roshal' | 38 others |

**Yurka class**

**Yurka**—with two SA-N-5/8 launchers, two Don-2 radars 9-83

**D:** 400 tons (460 fl) **S:** 16 kts **Dim:** 52.0 × 9.3 × 2.0
**A:** 4/30-mm AA (II × 2)—20 mines
**Electron Equipt:** Radar: 1 or 2 Don-2, 1/Drum Tilt
Sonar: Tamir-11 H/F hull-mounted
IFF: 1/High Pole B, 2–3/Square Head
**M:** 2 diesels; 2 props; 4,000 hp **Range:** 2,000/14; 3,200/10 **Man:** 45–50 tot.

Remarks: Soviet type designation: MT—*Morskoy Tral'shchik* (Seagoing Minesweeper). Aluminum-alloy hull. Four transferred to Egypt in 1969, one to Vietnam in 1979. Several have received two SA-N-5/8 SAM systems (IV × 2, 16 Grail/Gremlin missiles).

◆ **38 T-43-class fleet minesweepers** Bldr: Ust Izhora SY, Kolpino; Kamysh-Burun SY, Kerch'; etc. (In serv. 1947–57)

| | |
|---|---|
| Ivan Fioletov | Nikolay Markin |
| Kontradmiral Yurokovskiy | Sakhalinskiy Komsomolets |
| Komsomolets Kalmykiy | Stephan Saumyan |
| Lamine Sadjikaba | 30 others |
| Mezhadiy Azizbakov | |

**T-43 class**—long-hull version 1975

**T-43 class**—short-hull version 1978

**D:** 500 tons (590 fl) **S:** 14 kts **Dim:** 60.0 × 8.6 × 2.3
**A:** 4/37-mm AA (II × 2)—0 or 4/25-mm AA (II × 2)—2/d.c. projectors—mines
**Electron Equipt:** Radar: 1/Don-2 or Spin Trough, 1/Ball End
Sonar: 1/Tamir-11 H/F
IFF: 1/Square Head, 1/High Pole A
**M:** 2 Type 9D diesels; 2 props; 2,200 hp **Electric:** 550 kw
**Fuel:** 70 tons **Range:** 3,200/10 **Man:** 65 tot.

Remarks: Soviet type designation: MT—*Morskoy Tral'shchik* (Seagoing Minesweeper). Many of the T-43 class have been transferred to Poland, Egypt, Algeria, China, etc. The version armed with four 25-mm AA amidships is 60 m long and displaces 590 tons (fl); early units were 58.0 m long, had less hull flare at the stern, and displaced 569 tons (fl). Also built on the T-43 hull were radar pickets, noise-measurement ships, diving tenders, and trials ships. Well over 200 were built. Rapidly being disposed of, with many or most of the survivors probably in reserve. Eleven are operated by the KGB Border Guard as patrol ships, with sweep gear removed (see under Corvettes).

◆ **56 (+ . . .) Sonya-class coastal minesweepers** Bldr: Petrozavodsk SY; Ulis SY, Vladivostok (In serv. 1973– . . .)

| | | |
|---|---|---|
| Kolomenskiy Komsomolets | Orenburgskiy Komsomolets | 52 others |
| Komsomolets Kirgiziy | Sevastopol'skiy Komsomolets (ex-*Komsomol'skiy Telegraf*) | |

**D:** 350 tons (400 fl) **S:** 15 kts **Dim:** 48.5 × 7.3 × 1.9
**A:** 2/30-mm AA (II × 1)—2/25-mm AA (II × 1)

**MINE WARFARE SHIPS** *(continued)*

**Electron Equipt:** Radar: 1/Spin Trough
IFF: 1/High Pole B, 2/Square Head
**M:** 2 diesels; 2 props; 2,400 hp **Range:** 1,600/14; 3,000/10 **Man:** 40 tot.

REMARKS: Soviet type designation: BT—*Basovyy Tral'shchik* (Base Minesweeper). Wooden hull with plastic sheathing. Two transferred to Cuba, 1980, and two in 1985; others have gone to Bulgaria and Syria. Several have received one SA-N-5/8 SAM quadruple launcher system, abaft the boat, to starboard.

**Sonya class** U.S. Navy, 11-84

**Sonya class** 1976

◆ **2 Zhenya-class coastal minesweepers** Bldr: . . . (In serv. 1967–1972)

**Zhenya class** 1974

**D:** 220 tons (300 fl) **S:** 16 kts **Dim:** 42.4 × 7.9 × 1.8
**A:** 2/30-mm AA (II × 1) **Electron Equipt:** Radar: 1/Spin Trough
**M:** 2 diesels; 1 prop; 2,400 hp **Range:** 1,400/14 **Man:** 40 tot.

REMARKS: Soviet type designation: BT—*Basovyy Tral'shchik* (Base Minesweeper). Glass-reinforced plastic hull. Apparently not successful, as the similar, but larger, wooden-hulled Sonya class went into production instead.

◆ **68 Vanya-class coastal minesweepers** Bldr: . . . (In serv. 1961–73)

**D:** 200 tons (245 fl) **S:** 14 kts **Dim:** 39.9 × 7.5 × 1.8
**A:** 2/30-mm AA (II × 1)
**Electron Equipt:** Radar: 1/Don-2
IFF: 1/High Pole B, 1/Dead Duck
**M:** 1 diesel; 1 prop; 2,200 hp **Range:** 1,400/14; 2,400/10 **Man:** 30 tot.

**Vanya class** J.M.S.D.F., 1984

REMARKS: Soviet type designation: BT—*Basovyy Tral'shchik* (Base Minesweeper). Wooden construction. At least one was built or has been converted to a minehunter, armed with two 25-mm AA (II × 1)—more accurate than 30-mm for mine-disposal—and with one Don-Kay in place of Don-2; has two boats in davits on the fantail. The last three built, classed Vanya-II, are one meter longer, have a larger diesel exhaust pipe amidships, and have heavier davits at the stern. A few have been exported.

◆ **1 (+ . . .) Pelikan-class air-cushion vehicles**

REMARKS: Reported operational in 1986 and to have been built in the "Black Sea area." No other data available.

◆ **46 Yevgenya-class inshore minesweepers** Bldr: Sredniy Neva SY, Kolpino (In serv. 1970–76)

**Yevgenya class** M.O.D., Bonn, 1982

**D:** 80 tons (90 fl) **S:** 11 kts **Dim:** 26.2 × 6.1 × 1.5
**A:** 2/14.5-mm mg (II × 1) **M:** 2 diesels; 2 props; 600 hp
**Electron Equipt:** Radar: 1/Spin Trough—IFF: 1/High Pole B
**Range:** 300/10 **Man:** 10 tot. (plus 2 or 3 mine-clearance divers)

REMARKS: Glass-reinforced plastic hull. Production since 1976 has all been for export. Some foreign ships have two 25-mm AA (II × 1). Employs a television mine-hunting system that dispenses marker buoys to permit later disposal of mines useful to 30-m depths.

◆ **2 Andryusha-class special minesweepers** Bldr: . . . (In serv. 1975–76)

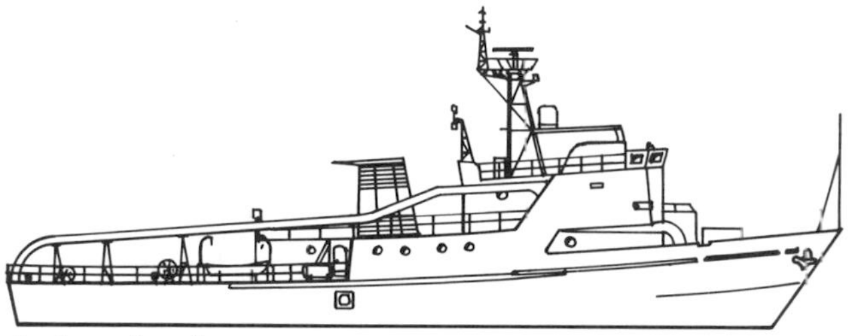
**Andryusha class**

**D:** 320 tons (360 fl) **S:** 15 kts **Dim:** 47.8 × 8.5 × 3.0 **A:** none
**Electron Equipt:** Radar: 1/Spin Trough—IFF: 1/High Pole B
**M:** 2 diesels; 2 props; 2,200 hp **Man:** 40 tot.

REMARKS: Wooden or plastic hulls. Large cable ducts running down both sides indicate probable role in sweeping magnetic mines. Prominent stack for gas-turbine generator; diesel engines exhaust through hull sides. No armament.

MINE WARFARE SHIPS *(continued)*

◆ **4 Olya-class minesweeping boats** Bldr: . . . (In serv. 1976)

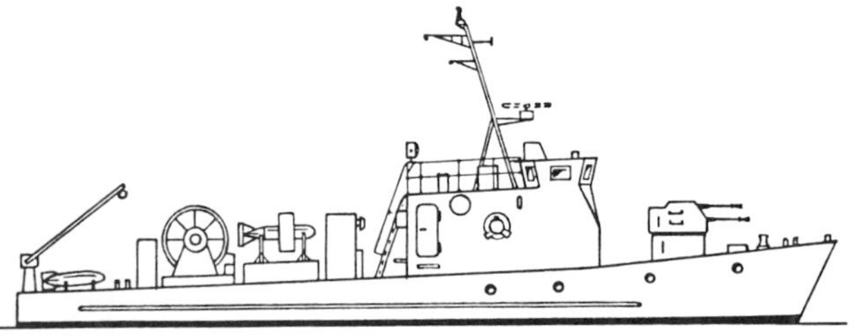

**Olya class**

**D:** 44 tons (50 fl) **S:** 18 kts **Dim:** 24.6 × 4.2 × 1.0
**A:** 2/25-mm AA **Electron Equipt:** Radar: 1/Spin Trough
**M:** 2 diesels; 2 props; 600 hp **Range:** 500/10 **Man:** 15 tot.

REMARKS: Found only in Baltic Fleet area. Apparently unsuccessful.

◆ **11 Ilyusha-class minesweeping drones** (In serv. 1970–. . .)

**Ilyusha class** 1977

**D:** 80 tons (85 fl) **S:** 12 kts **Dim:** 26.2 × 5.8 × 1.5 **A:** none
**Electron Equipt:** Radar: 1/Spin Trough—IFF: 1/High Pole B
**M:** 1 diesel; 450 hp **Man:** 10 tot.

REMARKS: Apparently radio-controlled while operating, but can be manned for transit. Stream sweep arrays through five chocks over stern; may be line-charge mine-disposal deploying systems.

◆ **26 K-8-class minesweeping boats** Bldr: Polnocny SY, Gdansk, Poland (In serv. 1954–59)

**K-8 class**

**D:** 19.4 tons (26 fl) **S:** 12 kts **Dim:** 16.9 × 3.2 × 0.8
**A:** 2/14.5-mm mg (II × 1) **Electron Equipt:** none **Electric:** 80 kw
**M:** 2 3D6 diesels; 2 props; 300 hp **Range:** 300/9 **Man:** 6 tot.

REMARKS: Wooden construction. Tow, but do not carry, wire sweep or self-powered solenoid arrays. Long overdue for replacement. Most probably in reserve.

◆ **25 Polish TR-40-class river minesweepers** Bldr: . . . SY, Poland (1950s)

**D:** 46 tons (49 fl) **S:** 18 kts **Dim:** 27.70 × 4.10 × 0.60
**A:** 2/25-mm AA (II × 1)—2/14.5-mm mg (II × 1)—mines
**Electron Equipt:** Radar: none—IFF: 1/High Pole A
**M:** 2 diesels; 2 props; 600 hp **Man:** 16 tot.

REMARKS: Wooden construction. Overdue for replacement. Most probably in reserve.

◆ **1 or more Baltika-class auxiliary minesweepers** Bldr: Leninskaya Kuznitsa SY, Kiev (In serv. 1978–. . .)

**D:** 210 tons (fl) **S:** 9.5 kts **Dim:** 25.50 (22.00 pp) × 6.80 × 2.45
**A:** 1/14.5-mm mg **Electron Equipt:** Radar: 1/navigational
**Range:** 1,350/9.5 **M:** 1 ChISP 18/22 diesel; 1 CP prop; 300 hp
**Electric:** 25 kw **Man:** 5–10

REMARKS: 108 grt/145 nrt. A small stern-haul purse-seiner fishing boat acquired circa 1980–81, apparently for testing the feasibility for rapid conversion of the several hundred civil craft of this class to simple wire-sweep minesweepers in time of war.

◆ **several dozen non-self-propelled mine countermeasures craft**

**Towed mine countermeasures craft** 1977

**D:** approx. 25 tons (fl) **Dim:** 12.0 × 4.0 × 1.5

REMARKS: Apparently a towed equivalent to the Ilyusha class, with an internal cable reel and winch to deploy magnetic sweep arrays or explosive line-charge arrays. Helicopters tow a modified "Volga"-class sports hydrofoil, equipped with noise and electric field generators.

AMPHIBIOUS WARFARE SHIPS

◆ **2 Ivan Rogov-class landing ships** Bldr: Kaliningrad SY

| | L | In serv. |
|---|---|---|
| IVAN ROGOV | 1976 | 1978 |
| ALEKSANDR NIKOLAYEV | . . . | 11-82 |

**D:** 11,000 tons (13,000 fl) **S:** 23 kts **Dim:** 158.0 × 24.0 × 8.2
**A:** 1/SA-N-4 SAM syst. (II × 1, 20 Gecko missiles)—2/76.2-mm DP (II × 1)—2/SA-N-5/8 SAM syst. (IV × 2; 16–20 Grail/Gremlin missiles)—4/30-mm gatling AA (VI × 4)—1/122-mm automatic bombardment RL (XL × 1) for BM-21 rockets—4/Helix-B helicopters—3/Lebed air-cushion landing craft or 6 Ondatra-class LCM.
**Electron Equipt:** Radar: 2/Don-Kay (*A. Nikolayev:* 2/Palm Frond), 1/Head Net-C, 1/Owl Screech, 1/Pop Group, 2/Bass Tilt
EW: 2 (*A. Nikolayev:* 3)/Bell Shroud, 2/Bell Squat
IFF: 1/High Pole B, 1/Salt Pot B—E/O: 1/Squeeze Box
**M:** 2 gas turbines; 2 props; 50,000 hp
**Range:** 8,000/20; 12,500/14 **Man:** 200 crew + 550 troops

REMARKS: Soviet type designation: BDK—*Bol'shoy Desantnyy Korabl'* (Large Landing Ship). The second unit apparently suffered construction delays.

**Ivan Rogov** French Navy, 11-86

**AMPHIBIOUS WARFARE SHIPS** *(continued)*

Equipped with bow doors and articulating ramp leading to a vehicle cargo deck in the forward part of the hull, while a stern door provides access to a floodable docking well intended to accommodate up to 3 Lebed air-cushion landing craft or 6 Ondatra-class landing craft. The massive superstructure incorporates a helicopter hangar, with a steep ramp leading downward to a helicopter pad on the foredeck, and doors aft leading to a second helicopter platform over the stern. There are also hydraulically raised ramps leading from the upper deck forward of the superstructure to both the bow doors and the docking well. Capable of transporting an entire naval infantry battalion and its vehicles, including 10 tanks, 30 armored personnel carriers, and trucks. The ability to use helicopters, to beach, and to deploy air-cushion vehicles gives a versatility unmatched by any other amphibious-warfare ship; this is combined with an organic shore fire-bombardment capability and very extensive command, control, and surveillance facilities. The hull has a pronounced bulb projecting forward below the waterline. During 1982–83, both were in the Baltic, with *A. Nikolayev* deploying to the Pacific late 1983 and *Ivan Rogov* late in 1986. Both now carry Helix-B assault helicopters in place of Hormone-C, and *Rogov* has been backfitted with the SA-N-5/8 point-defense SAM system.

**Ivan Rogov** Skyfotos, 11-86

◆ **22 (+ . . .) Ropucha-class tank landing ships** Bldr: Polnocny SY, Gdansk, Poland (In serv. 1975–78, 1982–. . .)

Aleksandr Shabalin 21 others

**D:** 2,600 tons (3,600 fl) **S:** 18 kts **Dim:** 113.0 × 14.0 × 2.9 (aft)/2.0 (fwd)
**A:** 4/57-mm AA (II × 2)—some: 4/SA-N-5/8 syst. (IV × 4; 32 Grail/Gremlin missiles)—5 also: 2/122-mm bombardment RL (XL × 2)
**Electron Equipt:** Radar: 2/Don-2, 1/Strut Curve, 1/Muff Cob
IFF: 1/High Pole B
**M:** 2 diesels; 2 props; 10,000 hp **Range:** 3,500/16
**Man:** 70 crew + 230 troops

Remarks: Soviet type designation: BDK—*Bol'shoy Desantnyy Korabl'* (Large Landing Ship). Bow and stern doors permit roll-on/roll-off loading. Cargo capacity: 450 tons; usable deck space: 600 m$^2$. The later units have angled hances to the corners of the main-deck superstructure and reinforcing gussets around the forward 57-mm AA platform. Several have received 4/SA-N-5/8 quadruple launchers for point-defense SAMs. Although the entire class was intended to receive two barrage rocket launchers on the forecastle, only the five most recently completed actually carry the weapons. Although equipped to receive the accompanying Squeeze Box electro-optical rangefinder/director, none of the ships yet has it. One unit was transferred to the People's Democratic Republic of Yemen in 1979. A second series of ten identical in nearly all respects to later units of the first, was completed in 1982–87, with a 23rd under construction.

**Ropucha class**—with two 122-mm RL forward Skyfotos, 3-86

**Aleksandr Nikolayev**—vehicles on forward helicopter deck *Ships of the World,* 1-85

**AMPHIBIOUS WARFARE SHIPS** *(continued)*

**Ropucha class**—late version, with curved hances to first superstructure deck; note saluting cannon on deck, abaft empty rocket launcher pedestals
24 F., French Navy, 7-84

**Ropucha class**—BM-21 rocket launcher-equipped unit Skyfotos, 3-86

◆ **14 Alligator-class tank landing ships** Bldr: Kaliningrad SY (In serv. 1964–77)

| | | |
|---|---|---|
| Aleksandr Tortsev* | Krymskiy Komsomolets* | Sergei Lazo |
| Donetskiy Shakhter* | Nikolay Fil'chenkov* | Tomskiy Komsomolets |
| Ilya Azarov* | Nikolay Vilkov* | Voronezhskiy Komsomolets |
| Komsomolets Kareliyy | Nikolay Obyekov | 50 Let Shefstva V.L.K.S.M.* |
| Krasnaya Presnya* | Petr Il'ichyev* | |

**Alligator class**—late unit with 122-mm rocket launcher forward, 3/SA-N-5 launchers French Navy, 4-83

**Komsomolets Kareliyy**—early unit with 2/14.5-mm mg (I × 2) abaft stack, no SA-N-5/8 French Navy, 2-86

**Voronezhskiy Komsomolets**—early unit with two quadruple SA-N-5/8 SAM launchers added U.S. Navy, 2-84

**Soviet 140-mm barrage rocket launcher**—with two clusters of 20 rocket tubes loaded; empty tubes are discarded and two new sets automatically reloaded from below after firing. The rockets carry a 19.2-kg fragmentation warhead and have a range of 20 km. 1981

**AMPHIBIOUS WARFARE SHIPS** *(continued)*

**D:** 3,400 tons (4,700 fl) **S:** 18 kts **Dim:** 112.8 × 15.3 × 4.4 (aft)
**A:** 2/57-mm AA (II × 1—*N. Fil'chenkov, N. Vilkov* also: 4/25-mm AA (II × 2)—starred units: 1/BM-21, 122-mm RL (XL × 1)
**Electron Equipt:** Radar: 2/Don-2 and/or Spin Trough
IFF: 1/High Pole B—E/O: starred units: 1/Squeeze Box
**M:** 2 diesels; 8,000 hp **Range:** 9,000/16; 14,000/10
**Man:** 75 crew + 300 troops

REMARKS: Soviet type designation: BDK—*Bol'shoy Desantnyy Korabl'* (Large Landing Ship). The design evolved continually during the time these ships were built. They have ramps fore and aft. Their hoisting equipment varies (one or two 5-ton cranes, one 15-ton crane), as does their armament: later ships also have a BM-21, 40-tubed, 140-mm rocket launcher forward for shore bombardment, the last two have four 25-mm AA (II × 2) aft, and some are equipped with 3/SA-N-5/8 launchers for Grail or Gremlin point-defense SAMs (IV × 3). Cargo capacity is about 600 tons for beaching, twice that in freighting service; can carry about two dozen tanks, plus lighter vehicles on upper decks.

◆ **37 Polnocny-class medium landing ships** Bldr: Polnocny SY, Gdansk, Poland (In serv. 1961–73)

**5 A version:**

**Polnocny-A**—with original low bridge; troughs down sides of hull, davits for line-charge towing boats are mounted before the bridge on this ship 1977

**Polnocny-A**—with four SA-N-5 quadruple launchers 1977

**D:** 770 tons (fl) **S:** 19 kts **Dim:** 73.0 × 8.6 × 1.9 (aft)
**A:** 2/14.5-mm mg (II × 1) or 2/30-mm AA (II × 1) or none—2/140-mm barrage RL (XVIII × 2)—0–2 or 4/SA-N-5/8 systems (IV × 0, 2, 4; up to 32 Grail or Gremlin missiles)
**Electron Equipt:** Radar: 1/Spin Trough
IFF: 1/High Pole A; some: 1/Square Head
**M:** 2 diesels; 2 props; 5,000 hp **Range:** 900/18; 1,500/14 **Man:** 35 tot.

**23 B version:**

**Polnocny-B**—with high stack and 30-mm AA aft, 4/SA-N-5/8 launchers 1977

**Polnocny-B class**—with 4/SA-N-5/8 systems, no 30-mm aft U.S. Navy, 8-83

**Polnocny-B**—with side troughs for line charges and two chutes at the stern for launching the tow boats; unit also has four SA-N-5/8 launchers J.M.S.D.F., 8-84

**D:** 800 tons (fl) **S:** 18 kts **Dim:** 74.0 × 8.6 × 2.0
**A:** 2 or 4/30-mm AA—2/140-mm barrage RL (XVIII × 2)—4/SA-N-5/8 systems (IV × 4; 32 Grail or Gremlin missiles)
**Electron Equipt:** Radar: 1/Spin Trough, 1/Drum Tilt
IFF: 1/Square Head, 1/High Pole B
**M:** 2 diesels; 2 props; 5,000 hp **Range:** 900/18; 1,500/14
**Man:** 40 crew + 100 troops

**9 C version:**

**Polnocny-C**—longer hull and superstructure French Navy, 10-83

**D:** 1,150 tons (fl) **S:** 18 kts **Dim:** 81.3 × 10.1 × 2.1
**A:** 4/30-mm AA (II × 2)—2/140-mm barrage RL (XVIII × 2)—4/SA-N-5/8 systems (IV × 2, 32 Grail or Gremlin missiles)
**Electron Equipt:** Radar: 1/Spin Trough, 1/Drum Tilt
IFF: 1/Square Head, 1/High Pole B
**M:** 2 diesels; 2 props; 5,000 hp **Range:** 1,800/18; 3,000/14
**Man:** 40 crew, plus 180 troops

REMARKS: Soviet type designation: SDK—*Srednyy Desantnyy Korabl'* (Medium Landing Ship). Most have now been equipped with two or four point-defense SAM systems. The Polnocny-Bs that have 30-mm aft have heightened stacks. This class delivered to India, Iraq, Indonesia, Egypt, Angola, etc. Cargo: about 180 tons in A and B, 250 tons in C. "Trough unit" Polnocny-A and -B are line-charge layers for beach-defense minefield clearance; they carry two small remote-controlled motor boats to tow the line charges. "A" version has convex bow form; "B" has concave bow-flare; "C" is longer and has additional accommodations. Numbers of "A"-version declining through strikings, while "B"'s continue to be transferred to Soviet clients. Only export-version Type C have helicopter decks.

**AMPHIBIOUS LANDING CRAFT**

◆ **16 Vydra-class utility landing craft** Bldr: U.S.S.R. (In serv. 1967–69)

**Vydra class**

**AMPHIBIOUS LANDING CRAFT** *(continued)*

**D:** 425 tons (600 fl) **S:** 12 kts **Dim:** 54.9 × 7.6 × 2.0 **A:** none
**Electron Equipt:** Radar: 1/Spin Trough
IFF: 1/High Pole
**M:** 2 diesels; 2 props; 800 hp **Range:** 1,900/11.9; 2,700/10
**Man:** 20 crew, plus 100 troops

◆ **2 (+ . . .) Pomornik class** Bldr: Dekabristov SY, Leningrad (In serv. 1986– . . .)

**Pomornik class** M.O.D., Bonn, 11-86

**Pomornik class** M.O.D., Bonn, 11-86

**Pomornik class** M.O.D., Bonn, 11-86

**D:** 360 tons (fl) **S:** 55 kts **Dim:** 59.0 × 21.0 × 12.0 high
**A:** 2/SA-N-5/8 SAM syst. (IV × 2, 16 Grail or Gremlin missiles)—2/30-mm gatling AA
**Electron Equipt:** Radar: 1/. . . nav., 1/. . . surface-search, 1/Bass Tilt
IFF: 2/. . . transponders—E/O: 1/Mod. Squeeze Box
**M:** 5 NK-12 gas turbines (12,100 hp each; 2 to power lift fans); 3 ducted airscrew propellers, 4 lift fans; 36,300 hp
**Range:** . . . **Man:** 40 crew + 220 troops

REMARKS: Largest air-cushion warships in the world. Believed capable of carrying 4 PT-76 amphibious tanks or similar-sized armored personnel carriers plus a detachment of infantry. Has small bow and stern ramps. Too large for shipboard transportation, Pomornik is intended for short-range independent assault operations. A third was under construction during 1987. Three of the gas-turbine engines are mounted on pylons and drive airscrew propellers; they are equipped with exhaust thrust diverters to enhance mobility. The lift-fan gas turbines are mounted near the stern in the wing compartments and exhaust through the stern. The modified Squeeze Box electro-optical device has no weather cover, as in other installations; there is also a television camera mounted just below the pilothouse. The navigational radar is mounted within a lozenge-shaped radome and the probable surface/air-search radar within a radome identical to that on the Parchim-II-class light frigate. Liferafts are carried for only 40 personnel.

◆ **2 or more Orlan-class wing-in-ground effect craft**

**Orlan class**—artist's rendering U.S.D.O.D., *Soviet Military Power*

**D:** . . . **S:** 140–160 kt **Dim:** . . . × . . . × . . .
**A:** . . . **Electron Equipt:** Radar: . . .
**M:** 1/turboprop sustainer, 2 turbofan lift/thrust engines; . . . hp
**Range:** approx. 900/120 **Man:** . . .

REMARKS: Wing-in-ground (WIG) effect craft take advantage of cushions of air generated by blowing beneath a broad-chord wing at low altitude. The Orlan appears to be configured for amphibious assault, with a flying-boat hull, and an overall length of about 60 m. The nose probably opens to one side to permit troop and vehicle egress. The pylon-mounted navigational radar appears to be the same as the set on the Pomornik ACV. The Soviets are also reported by the U.S. D.O.D. to be experimenting with an antiship missile-equipped WIG.

◆ **3 (+ . . .) Tsaplya-class air-cushion landing craft** Bldr: . . . (In serv. 1982– . . .)

**D:** 90 tons (fl) **S:** . . . **Dim:** . . . × . . . × . . .
**A:** . . . **M:** . . .

REMARKS: Class reportedly can carry one amphibious tank plus 80 troops, or 160 troops, or 25 tons of stores. Appears to be a Lebed successor.

◆ **2 (+ . . .) Utenok-class air-cushion vehicles** Bldr: Yuznaya Tochka SY, Feodosiya (In serv. 1982– . . .)

**D:** . . . **S:** . . . **Dim:** 26.3 × 13.0 × . . .
**A:** 4/30-mm AA (II × 2) **M:** . . .

REMARKS: Can carry one 45-ton T-72/T-80 tank.

◆ **20 Lebed-class surface-effects landing craft** Bldr: . . .

**Lebed class** M.O.D., Bonn, 1982

**Lebed class**

**AMPHIBIOUS LANDING CRAFT** *(continued)*

**D:** 85 tons (fl) **S:** 70 kts **Dim:** 24.8 × 10.8 × . . .
**A:** 2/14.5-mm mg (II × 1) **M:** 3 gas turbines; 2 props **Range:** 100/65; 250/60

Remarks: Broad bow ramp, ducted props, control cab to starboard, gun mount atop. Can carry one or two PT-76 light tanks or 120 troops or about 45 tons of cargo.

◆ **20 Aist-class surface-effects landing craft** Bldr: Dekabristov SY, Leningrad (In serv. 1971–1986)

**Aist class**—on cushion 1978

**Aist class**—at rest M.O.D., Bonn

**D:** 220 tons (fl) **S:** 45 kts **Dim:** 47.8 × 17.5 × . . .
**A:** 4/30-mm AA (II × 2)
**Electron Equipt:** Radar: 1/Spin Trough, 1/Drum Tilt
IFF: 1/High Pole B, 1/Square Head
**M:** 2 gas turbines; 4 props; 2 lift fans **Range:** 100/45; 208/40

Remarks: Can carry four PT-76 light tanks or one medium tank and 220 troops. Recent units carry 2/SA-N-5/8 SAM syst. (IV × 2) and chaff RL (XVI × 2).

◆ **30 Gus-class surface-effects landing craft** Bldr: Dekabristov SY, Leningrad (In serv. 1970–74)

**Gus class** 1970

**D:** 27.2 tons (fl) **S:** 57.5 kts **Dim:** 21.3 × 7.1 × 0.2 (at rest)
**A:** none **M:** 3 gas turbines; 2 props; 1 lift fan; 2,340 hp
**Range:** 185/50; 200/43

Remarks: Can carry twenty-four troops. A training version with two pilot positions is also in service.

◆ **16 Ondatra-class landing craft** (In serv. 1978–79)

**D:** 90 tons (140 fl) **S:** 10 kts **Dim:** 24.2 × 5.0 × 1.5
**A:** none **M:** 2 diesels; 2 props; 600 hp **Man:** 4 tot.

Remarks: Apparently intended as successor to the T-4 class. One carried by *Ivan Rogov* as a tug for Lebed-class air-cushion vehicles. In lieu of Lebed, *Rogov* can carry 6 Ondatra. Cargo well is 15 m × 3.8 m.

**Ondatra class**

◆ . . . **T-4-class landing craft** (In serv. 1954–74)

**T-4 class**—later, deep-bowed version

**D:** 70 tons (fl) **S:** 10 kts **Dim:** 19.0 × 4.3 × 1.0
**M:** 2 diesels; 2 props; 600 hp **Man:** 5 tot.

Remarks: Built in two versions; later variant with deeper bow could accommodate a medium tank.

## NAVAL AUXILIARIES

### SUBMARINE TENDERS

◆ **6 Ugra-class command tenders** Bldr: Black Sea SY, Nikolayev (In serv. 1963–72)

| | | |
|---|---|---|
| Ivan Kolyshkin | Ivan Vakhrameev | Volga |
| Ivan Kucherenko | Tobol | N . . . |

**Ivan Kolyshkin**—helicopter hangar aft 1978

**The unnamed Ugra**—with 2/SA-N-5/8 launchers French Navy, 1-83

**SUBMARINE TENDERS** *(continued)*

**D:** 6,750 tons (9,600 fl) **S:** 17 kts **Dim:** 145.0 × 17.7 × 6.4
**A:** 8/75-mm AA (II × 4)—most: 2/SA-N-5/8 SAM syst. (IV × 2, 16 Grail or Gremlin missiles)
**Electron Equipt:** Radar: 1–3 Don-2, 1/Strut Curve, 2/Muff Cob
EW: 4/Watch Dog
IFF: 1/High Pole B, 1/High Pole A, 2/Square Head
**M:** 4 diesels; 2 props; 8,000 hp **Range:** 21,000/10 **Man:** 450 tot.

REMARKS: Soviet type designation: PB—*Plavuchaya Baza* (Floating Base). One modified version was built for India, as *Amba*. The *Ivan Kolyshkin* has a tall helicopter hangar. *Ivan Kucherenko* and *Volga* have a Vee Cone HF communications antenna. Can support eight to twelve submarines at sea with supplies, fuel, provisions, water, and spare torpedoes and can offer repair services. This class and the Don class are frequently used as flagships. One 10-ton and two 6-ton cranes are fitted. Sisters *Gangut* and *Borodino* are configured as training ships for naval officer cadets and do not serve submarines—see Training Ships.

◆ **6 Don-class command tenders** Bldr: Black Sea SY, Nikolayev (In serv. 1958–61)

| | | |
|---|---|---|
| DMITRIY GALKIN | KAMCHATSKIY KOMSOMOLETS | MAGOMED GADZIEV |
| FYODOR VIDYAEV | MAGADANSKIY KOMSOMOLETS | VIKTOR KOTEL'NIKOV |

**D:** 6,730 tons (9,000 fl) **S:** 17 kts **Dim:** 140.0 × 17.7 × 6.4
**A:** 4/100-mm AA (I × 4)—4/57-mm AA (II × 2)—see Remarks

**Fyodor Vidyaev**—Vee Cone communications antenna aft, 8/25-mm AA; Echo-II alongside French Navy, 1981

**Magadanskiy Komsomolets**—no 100-mm guns, large helo deck J.M.S.D.F., 4-83

**Dmitriy Galkin**—Vee Cone aft, lattice foremast, no 25-mm AA French Navy, 3-86

**Electron Equipt:** Radar: 1 or 2/Don-2, 1/Slim Net, 1/Sun Visor, 2/Hawk Screech—see Remarks
EW: 2/Watch Dog
IFF: 1/High Pole B, 2/Square Head
**M:** 4 diesels; 2 props; 8,000 hp
**Range:** 21,000/10 **Man:** 450 tot.

**Viktor Kotel'nikov**—helicopter platform aft, 2/100-mm guns forward, Big Ball SATCOMM radomes French Navy, 5-84

REMARKS: Soviet type designation: PB—*Plavuchaya Baza* (Floating Base). Can serve as logistic support for a flotilla of eight to twelve submarines. *Viktor Kotel'nikov's* after 100-mm mounts were replaced by a helicopter platform, while the *Magadanskiy Komsomolets* has always had a very large helicopter platform aft and has never carried any 100-mm guns. *Fyodor Vidyaev* has eight 25-mm (II × 4) also, but no Hawk Screech; she and *Dmitriy Galkin* have been fitted with a Vee Cone antenna for long-range communications. A bow lift-hook of 100-ton capacity is fitted, as are one 10-ton, two 5-ton, and two 1-ton cranes. All are used as flagships. One other unit was transferred to Indonesia.

NOTE: The six *Atrek*-class small submarine tenders completed 1955–57 are believed to have either been scrapped or hulked as accommodations vessels.

**MISSILE TRANSPORTS**

◆ **1 Aleksandr Brykin class** Bldr: United Admiralty SY, Leningrad (In serv. 1987)

ALEKSANDR BRYKIN

**Aleksandr Brykin** 333 Squ. R. Nor. A.F., 1987

**D:** 17,000 tons (fl) **S:** . . . **Dim:** 160.0 (147.0 wl) × 24.0 × 8.8
**A:** 4/30-mm gatling AA (I × 4)
**Electron Equipt:** Radar: 1 or 2/. . . nav., 2/Bass Tilt
**M:** diesel-electric; 1 prop; . . . hp—bow-thruster
**Range:** . . . **Man:** . . .

REMARKS: Intended to transport SS-N-20 missiles for the Typhoon class, and, possibly, SS-N-23 for the Delta-IV. Missiles are stowed vertically in a large "barn" served by a 75-ton crane. There are also two 5–10-ton cranes amidships. In Northern Fleet.

◆ **3 Amga class** Bldr: Krasnoye Sormovo SY, Gorkiy

AMGA (In serv. 1973) VETLUGA (In serv. 1976) DAUGAVA (In serv. 1981)

**D:** 4,500 tons (5,500 fl) **S:** 12 kts **Dim:** 102.0 × 17.7 × 4.4 (see Remarks)
**A:** 4/25-mm AA (II × 2)
**Electron Equipt:** Radar: 1/Don-2—IFF: 1/High Pole B
**M:** 2 diesels; 2 props; 4,000 hp
**Range:** 4,500/12

REMARKS: One 55-ton crane with a reach of 34 meters. Have ice-reinforced hulls. Intended to transport ballistic missiles for strategic submarines. The *Vetluga* is 6 m longer than her sister, and *Daugava* is 113.0 m long, displacing 6,200 tons (fl), and has a different crane, with solid sides. *Vetluga* and *Daugava* are in the Pacific Fleet.

MISSILE TRANSPORTS *(continued)*

**Vetluga** J.M.S.D.F., 1976

**Daugava** J.M.S.D.F., 1981

◆ **7 Lama class** Bldr: Black Sea SY, Nikolayev (In serv. 1963–79)

| | | | |
|---|---|---|---|
| General Ryabakov | PB-868 | PM-946 | |
| Voronezh (PM 872) | PM-150 | PM-938 | PM-. . . |

**D:** 4,500 tons (fl) **S:** 14 kts **Dim:** 112.8 × 14.9 × 4.4
**A:** 4 or 8/57-mm DP (IV × 1 or 2, or II × 2)—2 or 4/SA-N-5/8 SAM syst. (IV × 4, 16 or 32 Grail or Gremlin missiles)—*Voronezh* & one other also: 4/25-mm AA (II × 2)
**Electron Equipt:** Radar: 1/Don-2, 1/Slim Net or Strut Curve, 1 or 2/Hawk Screech or 2/Muff Cob
IFF: 1/High Pole B, 2/Square Head
**M:** 2 diesels; 1 prop; 4,000 hp **Man:** 240 tot. (420 in missile boat tenders)

Remarks: PM—*Plavuchaya Masterskaya* (Floating Workshop) and PB—*Plavuchaya Baza* (Floating Base). Vary greatly in equipment. Intended to transport cruise missiles for submarines and surface units. *Voronezh* (PM-872) and one other have larger missile-stowage areas and smaller cranes, and carry open 57-mm DP (II × 1; one only on *Voronezh*), and four 25-mm AA (II × 2), but have no fire-control radar. These serve Nanuchka-class corvettes and Osa-class patrol boats. Two 20-ton (10-ton on missile-boat tenders) precision cranes. *General Ryabakov,* completed 1979, has an enclosed, automatic 57-mm AA mount and four SA-N-5/8 systems. Two based in the Arctic, three (including *General Ryabakov, Voronezh,* and the other SS-N-2-series missile tender) are in the Black Sea Fleet, and two (including PM-150) are in the Pacific Fleet.

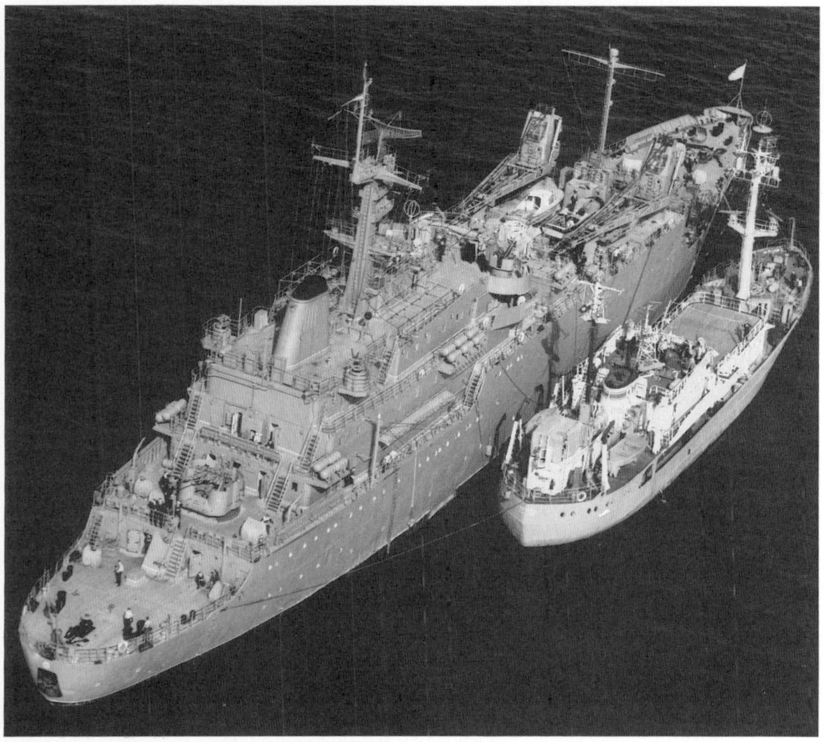

**One of two SS-N-2-series missile carriers in the Lama class**—with Mayak-class intelligence collector GS 239 alongside U.S. Navy, 1986

**PM-150**—with twin 57-mm DP forward, 2/SA-N-5 launchers abreast stack

◆ **1 converted Yuniy Partizan-class cargo ship** Bldr: Turnu-Severin or Oltenitza SY, Romania (In serv. 1974–78)

Vitse-Admiral Fomin (ex-*Pinega*)

**D:** 3,800 tons (fl) **S:** 12.9 kts **Dim:** 88.75 (80.25 pp) × 12.8 × 4.6
**A:** 4/14.5-mm mg (II × 2)
**Electron Equipt:** Radar: 1/Don-2—IFF: 1/High Pole A
**M:** 1 Sulzer-Zgoda 8 TAD 36 diesel; 1 prop; 2,080 hp
**Range:** 4,000/12 **Fuel:** 125 tons
**Electric:** 306 kw **Man:** . . .

Remarks: Former naval cargo ship of 2,079 grt/2,150 dwt, one of 24 sisters (20 civilian) originally intended as container vessels. Reappeared 1-86 with forecastle deck extended past forward hold, sides raised by two decks abreast number three hold, and a single electrohydraulic crane having replaced the original king posts and three 10-ton booms.

◆ **2 Modified Andizhan class** Bldr: Neptunwerft, Rostock, East Germany (In serv. 1960–61)

Venta Vilyuy

**Vilyuy** French Navy. 5-86

**D:** 6,740 tons (fl) **S:** 13.5 kts **Dim:** 104.0 × 14.4 × 6.6
**A:** none **Man:** 60 tot.
**Electron Equipt:** Radar: 2/Don-2—IFF: 1/High Pole B, 1/Square Head
**M:** 1 diesel; 1 prop; 1 ,890 hp
**Range:** 6,000/13.5

Remarks: Converted from cargo ships during the 1970s. Large crane forward, two small cranes and a helicopter deck aft. Forward holds can accommodate ten SS-N-9 missiles and twenty SA-N-1 or SA-N-3. Helicopter pad aft used mostly for volleyball.

◆ **2 MP 6 class** Bldr: Hungary (In serv. 1959–60)

Bureya Khoper

**D:** 2,100 tons (fl) **S:** 10.5 kts **Dim:** 74.7 (70.1 pp) × 11.3 × 4.4
**Electron Equipt:** Radar: 1/Don-2 **Range:** 3,300/9
**M:** 2 Buchau-Wolff 6 NVD 48 diesels; 1 prop; 800 hp **Man:** 40 tot.

Remarks: Former medium landing ships, resembling engines-aft coastal freighters. Bow doors welded shut circa 1960, when they were adapted as cargo vessels. Subsequently modified to transport SS-N-5 ballistic missiles. *Khoper* in the Northern Fleet and *Bureya* in the Pacific.

MISSILE TRANSPORTS *(continued)*

**General Ryabakov, Lama class**—with Oskol-class repair ship PM-24 alongside. *Ryabakov* has four quadruple SA-N-5/8 launchers aft and a twin automatic 57-mm mount forward U.S. Navy, 1984

**Bureya**—long forward hatch to missile hold 1982

◆ **2 Melitopol class** Bldr: . . . , U.S.S.R. (In serv. 1952–55)

INDIRKA FORT SHEVERENKO

**D:** 1,200 tons (fl) **S:** 11.3 kts **Dim:** 57.6 × 9.0 × 4.3
**Electron Equipt:** Radar: 1/Don-2 **Range:** 2,500/10.5
**M:** 1 Type 6DR 30/40 diesel; 1 prop; 600 hp

REMARKS: Converted late 1970s from small, engines-aft coastal cargo vessels. Have one long hold. All cargo-handling gear removed. In Baltic Fleet. Three sisters serve as survey vessels.

NOTE: Muna-class small ammunition transports are described on a later page.

## REPAIR SHIPS

◆ **2 Malina class** Bldr: Black Sea SY, Nikolayev

PM-63 (In serv. 1984) PM-74 (In serv. 1985)

**PM-74** U.S. Navy, 1985

**PM-74** J.M.S.D.F., 1985

**PM-63** U.S. Navy, 10-84

**D:** 12,000 tons (fl) **S:** 12 kts **Dim:** 140.0 (126 wl) × 22.0 × 5.0 **A:** none
**Electron Equipt:** Radar: 2/Palm Frond—IFF: 1/High Pole B transponder
**M:** 4 gas diesels; 1 prop; 8,000 hp **Man:** 380 tot.

REMARKS: PM—*Plavuchaya Masterskaya* (Floating Workshop). Second unit began trials in the spring of 1985. Unusual hull form with no curved surfaces, indicates not intended to move very often. Intended to serve nuclear-powered submarines, as evidenced by the mooring pockets along the hull sides and the two large, specialized reactor recoring cranes. PM-74 to Pacific Fleet, late 1985.

◆ **25 Amur class** Bldr: A. Warski SY, Szczecin, Poland (In serv. 1968–78, 1981–83)

| | | | | |
|---|---|---|---|---|
| PM-5 | PM-37 | PM-59 | PM-82 | PM-140 |
| PM-9 | PM-40 | PM-64 | PM-94 | PM-156 |
| PM-10 | PM-49 | PM-73 | PM-129 | PM-161 |
| PM-15 | PM-52 | PM-75 | PM-138 | PM-163 |
| PM-34 | PM-56 | PM-81 | PM-139 | PM-164 |

REPAIR SHIPS *(continued)*

PM-82 U.S. Navy, 2-84

**PM-5**—with long deckhouse on forecastle, first of the second-series Amur-class repair ships U.S. Navy, 2-83

**PM-9** 16 F., French Navy, 11-86

**D:** 4,000 tons (5,490 fl) **S:** 12 kts **Dim:** 121.7 × 17.0 × 5.1 **A:** none
**Electron Equipt:** Radar: 1/Don-2
IFF: 1/High Pole B
**M:** 2 diesels; 1 prop; 4,000 hp **Range:** 13,200/8
**Man:** 210 tot., plus up to 210 passengers (PM-5 and later: 300 total)

REMARKS: PM—*Plavuchaya Masterskaya* (Floating Workshop). Enlarged version of the Oskol class. Two 5-ton cranes. Construction resumed 1980–82, with PM-5 of the new series having a long deckhouse in the forecastle. Early units do not have the passenger facilities. Serve surface ships and submarines with basic repair facilities and spare parts. PM-59, the first in a third series of these ships ordered in 1-85, appeared in 1987, with more, presumably, to follow.

◆ **12 Oskol class** Bldr: A. Warski SY, Szczecin, Poland (In serv. 1964–67)

| | | | | | |
|---|---|---|---|---|---|
| PM-2 | PM-21 | PM-26 | PM-51 | PM-68 | PM-148 |
| PM-20 | PM-24 | PM-28 | PM-62 | PM-146 | PM-477 |

**D:** 2,500 tons (3,000 fl) **S:** 12 kts **Dim:** 91.4 × 12.2 × 4.0
**Electron Equipt:** Radar: 1 or 2/Don-2—IFF: 1/High Pole A
**M:** 2 diesels; 1 prop; 4,000 hp **Range:** 9,000/8 **Man:** 60 tot.

**PM-26** 22 F., French Navy, 10-86

**PM-24**—4/25-mm AA aft, with a Tango-class submarine alongside showing the small size of the repair ship U.S. Navy, 5-86

**PM-146**—flush-decked Oskol class 1970

REMARKS: PM—*Plavuchaya Masterskaya* (Floating Workshop). Most have a well deck forward of the bridge. PM-24 has four 25-mm AA (II × 2); a twin 57-mm gun mount forward was removed between 1980 and 1984. All have one or two 3.4-ton cranes.

◆ **5 Dnepr class** Bldr: Black Sea SY, Nikolayev (In serv. 1960–64)

| | | | | |
|---|---|---|---|---|
| PM-17 | PM-22 | PM-30 | PM-130 | PM-135 |

**D:** 4,500 tons (5,300 fl) **S:** 11 kts **Dim:** 113.3 (100.0 pp) × 16.5 × 4.4
**Electron Equipt:** Radar: 1/Don or Don-2—IFF: 1/High Pole A
**M:** 1 diesel; 2,000 hp **Range:** 6,000/8.3 **Man:** 420 tot.

**REPAIR SHIPS** *(continued)*

**PM-17** 1960

Remarks: PM—*Plavuchaya Masterskaya* (Floating Workshop). Have one 150-ton bow hoist, one king post, and one crane. Equipment varies from ship to ship. PM-130 and -135, the last two units (Modified Dnepr class) are flush-decked. Intended to serve submarines. Can be armed with 2/57-mm AA (II × 1). Not seen since initial delivery voyages.

**GENERATOR SHIPS**

◆ **4 Tomba class** Bldr: A. Warski SY, Szczecin, Poland (In serv. 1974–76)

ENS-244 ENS-254 ENS-348 ENS-357

**A Tomba on trials** 11-74

**D:** 4,400 tons (5,800 fl) **S:** 12 kts **Dim:** 107.0 × 17.0 × 5.0 **A:** none
**Electron Equipt:** Radar: 1/Don-2—IFF: 1/High Pole B
**M:** 1 diesel; 1 prop; 4,500 hp **Range:** 7,000/12 **Man:** 50 tot.

Remarks: ENS—*Elektrostantsiye Nativatel'noye Sudno* (Electric Power Station and Steam-Source Ship). Two stacks and a "mack" on the forecastle, all containing diesel-engine exhausts, while the stack amidships also has the uptake from a large boiler. Two 3.5-ton cranes.

**SUBMARINE RESCUE SHIPS**

◆ **1 (+1) El'brus class** Bldr: 61 Kommuna SY, Nikolayev

| | L | In serv. | | L | In serv. |
|---|---|---|---|---|---|
| El'brus | 1977 | 1981 | N . . . | 1984 | 1988 |

**El'brus** French Navy, 5-84

**D:** 20,000 tons (fl) **S:** 17 kts **Dim:** 175.0 × 25.0 × 7.5
**A:** provision for 4/30-mm gatling AA (I × 4) or 8/30-mm AA (II × 4)
**Electron Equipt:** Radar: 1/Don-2, 2/Don Kay—IFF: 2/Salt Pot-C
**M:** 4 diesels; 2 props; . . . hp **Range:** . . . **Man:** 420 tot.

Remarks: Icebreaking hull indicates probable association with the Typhoon program, but first unit is still attached to the Black Sea Fleet. Large hangar aft of stack holds two or four salvage-and-rescue submersibles, which are moved forward on rails for launching by extendable overhead gantry cranes on either side. Hangar for one Hormone or Helix helicopter, with hangar door dropping to form a ramp leading to the helicopter flight deck. Can lay and retrieve a four-point moor. The 3-ton crane on port quarter has very long folding arm. Has submersible decompression and observation chambers, firefighting equipment. Far and away the world's largest and most elaborate submarine salvage-and-rescue ship. *El'brus* made one brief deployment in 12-81 to 1-82 and then returned to the Black Sea, not emerging again until 5-84. Second unit reported building 3-83. Program may not be entirely successful.

◆ **1 Nepa class** Bldr: Black Sea SY, Nikolayev (In serv. 1970)

Karpaty

**Karpaty** 1971

**D:** 9,800 tons (fl) **S:** 16 kts **Dim:** 129.5 × 19.2 × 6.4 **A:** none
**Electron Equipt:** Radar: 2/Don-2—IFF: 1/High Pole B
**M:** 2–4 diesels; 2 props; 8,000 hp **Range:** 8,000/14 **Man:** 270 tot.

Remarks: Has a 600-ton lift hook supported by horns extending over the stern, two others beneath the hull. Very large all-purpose salvage ship with submarine-rescue equipment, including several rescue bells and observation chambers.

◆ **8 Prut class** Bldr: Nosenko/Black Sea SY, Nikolayev (In serv. 1960–68)

| | | | |
|---|---|---|---|
| Altay | Vladimir Trefolev | SS-21 | SS-26 |
| Beshtau | Zhiguli | SS-23 | SS-83 |

**D:** 2,800 tons (3,300 fl) **S:** 20 kts **Dim:** 90.2 × 14.3 × 5.5
**Electron Equipt:** Radar: 1–2/Don-2 and/or Don
**M:** 4 diesels; 2 props; 8,000 hp **Range:** 10,000/16 **Man:** 120 tot.

**El'brus** U.S. Navy, 1-82

**SUBMARINE RESCUE SHIPS** *(continued)*

**Zhiguli**—tripod foremast, mooring buoys in chutes 1980

**SS-26**—quadripod foremast, horizontally stowed mooring buoys
French Navy, 5-83

REMARKS: SS—*Spasitel'noye Sudno* (Rescue Ship). One derrick, two or three special carriers for rescue chambers, submersible decompression chamber for divers, and salvage observation bells. Four anchor buoys are stowed on inclined racks on the after deck. One unit was armed for a while with four 57-mm AA (IV × 1) controlled by a Muff Cob radar director, long since removed. SS-21, SS-26, SS-83, *Beshtau,* and *Vladimir Trefolev* have quadripod foremasts, smaller mooring buoys; others have tripod foremasts. Sister SS-44 lost during early 1970s.

◆ **11 Modified T-58-class minesweepers** Bldr: . . . (In serv. late 1950s)

| | | | | | |
|---|---|---|---|---|---|
| KAZBEK | VALDAY | ZANGEZUR | SS-35 | SS-47 | SS-51 |
| KHIBINY | POLKOVO | SS-30 | SS-40 | SS-50 | |

**SS-40** 1978

**D:** 815 tons (930 fl) **S:** 17 kts **Dim:** 71.7 × 9.6 × 2.7
**Electron Equipt:** Radar: 1/Don-2, 1/Spin Trough or Don or Don-2
Sonar: 1/Tamir—IFF: 1/High Pole A
**M:** 2 diesels; 2 props; 4,000 hp **Range:** 2,500/12 **Man:** 60 tot.

REMARKS: SS—*Spasitel'noye Sudno* (Rescue Ship). Altered while under construction. Lift rig overhanging the stern to handle divers' gear and submersible decompression chamber. Rescue diving chamber to port, amidships. Can be armed with one 37-mm AA. Sister *Gidrolog* served as an intelligence collector until struck, early 1980s. Another was transferred to India.

**FLEET REPLENISHMENT SHIPS**

◆ **2 Kaliningrad class** Bldr: Rauma-Repola, Finland

VYAZ'MA (ex-*Katun*) (In serv. 5-83) ARGUN (ex-*Kallavere*) (In serv. 7-83)

**Argun**—fueling a Krivak-II moored alongside
LT Weaver/LCDR Fenzl, VF-111, U.S. Navy, 5-83

**Vyaz'ma** U.S. Navy, 10-83

**D:** 8,700 tons (fl) **S:** 14 kts **Dim:** 115.5 (112.0 pp) × 17.0 × 6.5
**A:** none **M:** Radar: 1/Okean A, 1/Okean B
**M:** 1 Russkiy/Burmeister & Wain 5 DKRP 50/110-2 diesel; 1 prop; 3,850 hp
**Electric:** 805 kw **Range:** 5,000/14 **Man:** 32 tot.

REMARKS: 4,821 grt/5,873 dwt. Last two built of a class that had over two dozen units delivered to the U.S.S.R. Ministry of Fisheries from 1979 to 1982. Originally completed 12-82 and 11-82, respectively. Three liquid replenishment stations (one each side, plus astern); no underway solids replenishment. Carry 5,750 $m^3$ (5,350 tons) liquid cargo in 10 tanks, 80 $m^3$ dry cargo. Two cargo pumps have combined 400 $m^3$/hr capacity. Have a 1,600-ton water ballast capacity.

◆ **1 Berezina class** Bldr: 62 Kommuna SY, Nikolayev (In serv. 1978)

BEREZINA

**D:** 36,000 tons (fl) **S:** 22 kts **Dim:** 212.0 × 26.0 × 10.0
**A:** 1/SA-N-4 system (II × 1,20 Gecko missiles)—4/57-mm DP (II × 2)—4/30-mm gatling AA (VI × 4)—2/RBU-1000 ASW RL (VI × 2)—2/Hormone helicopters
**Electron Equipt:** Radar: 1/Don-2, 2/Don-Kay, 1/Strut Curve, 1/Pop Group, 1/Muff Cob, 2/Bass Tilt
Sonar: . . .—IFF: 1/High Pole
EW: 2/chaff RL (II × 2)
**M:** 2 diesels; 2 props; 54,000 hp **Range:** 12,000/18 **Man:** 600 tot.

REMARKS: Soviet type designation: VTR—*Voyenyy Transport* (Military Transport). The largest multipurpose underway replenishment ship yet built for the Soviets and the only one currently to be armed. Can refuel over the stern and from single constant-tension stations on either side, amidships. Solid replenishment is by two sliding-stay, constant-tension transfer rigs on either side. Vertical replenishment is by two specially configured Hormone helicopters hangared in the after superstructure. There are four 10-ton stores-handling cranes to supply ships moored alongside. Cargo: approx. 16,000 tons of fuel oil and diesel fuel, 500 tons fresh water, and 2,000–3,000 tons of provisions, munitions, and combat spares. The very

**Berezina** 10-81

**FLEET REPLENISHMENT SHIPS** *(continued)*

large crew may be accounted for, in part, by a capability to transport spare crews for submarines, for which mooring pockets are provided along the ship's side. No additional units are expected. *Berezina* was involved in a serious collision in the Sea of Marmara on 15-5-86.

**Berezina** U.S. Navy, 1979

◆ **6 Boris Chilikin class** Bldr: Baltic SY, Leningrad (In serv. 1971–78)

| | | |
|---|---|---|
| Boris Butoma | Dnestr | Ivan Bubnov |
| Boris Chilikin | Genrikh Gasanov | Vladimir Kolyachitskiy |

**Dnestr** U.S. Navy, 12-84

**Genrikh Gasanov** U.S. Navy, 8-83

**Boris Butoma**—refueling *Novorossiysk* from two stations U.S. Navy, 2-84

**D:** 8,700 tons light (24,500 fl) **S:** 17 kts
**Dim:** 162.3 × 21.4 × 11.5 **A:** removed
**Electron Equipt:** Radar: 2/Don-Kay—IFF: 1/High Pole B
**M:** 1 diesel; 9,600 hp **Range:** 10,000/16.6

Remarks: Soviet type designation: VTR—*Voyenyy Tanker* (Military Tanker). Naval version of the merchant *Velikiy Oktyabr* class. 16,300 dwt. Equipment varies: early units had solid-stores, constant tension-rigs on both sides forward; later units, only to starboard, with liquids to port. All have port and starboard liquid-replenishment stations amidships and can replenish liquids over the stern. Cargo: 13,500 tons liquiid (fuel oil, diesel, water); 400 tons ammunition; 400 tons provisions; 400 tons stores. The *Ivan Bubnov* and *Genrikh Gasanov* were completed in merchant colors, without guns, Strut Curve, or Muff Cob; that equipment has now been removed from the other ships, although several retained their gun houses for a short period.

◆ **4 Dubna class** Bldr: Rauma-Repola, Rauma, Finland

| | In serv. | | In serv. |
|---|---|---|---|
| Dubna | 1974 | Pechenga | 1978 |
| Irkut | 1975 | Sventa | 1979 |

**Dubna** U.S. Navy, 7-86

**Dubna**—replenishing intelligence collector *Seliger* (SSV-514) U.S. Navy, 7-86

**D:** 4,300 tons light (11,100 fl) **S:** 16 kts **Dim:** 130.1 (126.3 pp) × 20.0 × 7.2
**A:** none **Electron Equipt:** Radar: 2/Don-2
**M:** 1 Russkiy 8DRPH 23/230, 8-cyl. diesel; 1 prop; 6,000 hp
**Electric:** 1,485 kVA **Fuel:** 1,056 m³ **Range:** 8,000/15 **Man:** 60 tot.

Remarks: Soviet type designation: VTR—*Voyenyy Tanker* (Military Tanker). 6,022 grt/6,500 dwt. Cargo: 4,364 m³ heavy fuel oil; 2,646 m³ diesel fuel; 140 m³ cargo water; 537 m³ refrigerated provisions; 810 m³ dry stores. Twenty-seven cargo tanks. Can transfer one-ton loads from constant-tension stations forward. Liquid replenishment from one station on port and starboard, amidships, and over the stern. Additional berths for "turnover crews." Original commercial Okean-series radars replaced.

◆ **5 Altay class** Bldr: Rauma-Repola, Rauma, Finland (In serv. 1969–73)

Ilim Izhora Kola Yegorlik Yel'nya

**Izhora** J.M.S.D.F., 1984

FLEET REPLENISHMENT SHIPS *(continued)*

**D:** 2,183 light (2,228 fl) **S:** 14.2 kts **Dim:** 106.0 (97.0 pp) × 15.0 × 6.7
**Electron Equipt:** Radar: 2/Don-2—IFF: 1/High Pole A
**M:** 1 Valmet-Burmeister & Wain BM-550 VTBN-110 diesel; 3,250 hp (2,900 sust.)
**Electric:** 650 kw **Range:** 8,600/12 **Man:** 60 tot.

REMARKS: 3,670 grt/5,045 dwt. All have had an underway replenishment. A-frame king post added forward since 1975, permitting them to refuel one ship at a time on either beam. Also able to replenish over stern. Differ in details, heights of masts, etc. More than two dozen sisters in the Soviet merchant marine.

◆ **1 Sofia class** Bldr: U.S.S.R. (In serv. 1969)

AKHTUBA (ex-*Khanoi*)

**Akhtuba** 1976

**D:** 62,600 tons (fl) **S:** 17 kts **Dim:** 230.6 × 31.0 × 11.8
**M:** 1 steam turbine; 1 prop; 19,000 hp **Boilers:** 2
**Range:** 20,900/17 **Man:** 70 tot.

REMARKS: 32,840 grt/49,385 dwt. Largest ship in the Soviet Navy. Carries 44,500 tons of liquid cargo. Can refuel over the stern only; primarily used to refuel other tankers.

◆ **3 Olekhma and Pevek class** Bldr: Rauma-Repola, Rauma, Finland

OLEKHMA IMAN ZOLOTOI ROG

**Olekhma**—modified for underway replenishment U.S. Navy, 9-85

**Iman**—unmodified U.S. Navy, 2-86

**D:** 6,700 tons (fl) **S:** 14 kts **Dim:** 105.0 × 14.8 × 6.8
**Electron Equipt:** Radar: 1/Don-2 **M:** 1 Burmeister & Wain diesel; 2,900 hp
**Range:** 7,900/13.6 **Man:** 40 tot.

REMARKS: *Zolotoi Rog* belongs to the *Pevek* class. All built in the mid-1960s. 3,300 grt/4,400 dwt. *Olekhma* was modernized in 1978 with A-frame abaft the bridge to permit underway fueling of one ship at a time on either beam. The other two have not been similarly upgraded. Predecessor to the *Altay* design, but with conventional "three-island" tanker layout. The *Zolotoi Rog* differs only slightly. All can refuel over the stern.

◆ **6 Uda class** Bldr: Vyborg SY (In serv. 1962–64)

DUNAY KOIDA LENA SHEKSNA TEREK VISHERA

**D:** 7,100 tons (fl) **S:** 17 kts **Dim:** 122.0 × 15.8 × 6.3 **A:** removed
**Electron Equipt:** Radar: 1/Don, 1/Don-2 (or 2/Don-2)
IFF: High Pole A
**M:** 2 diesels; 2 props; 8,000 hp **Range:** 4,000/17 **Man:** 85 tot.

REMARKS: Soviet type designation: VTR—*Voyenyy Tanker* (Military Tanker). Equipped to carry eight 57-mm AA (IV × 2), *Dunay, Vishera, Sheksna,* and *Lena*

**Sheksna**—with two refueling positions amidships French Navy, 5-84

**Koida**—still with only one bipod refueling king post U.S. Navy, 2-84

have been equipped with a second A-frame king post for liquid replenishment, amidships. Three transferred to Indonesia during the early 1960s.

◆ **3 Kazbek class** Bldr: Admiralty SY, Leningrad, or Kherson SY

ALATYR' DESNA VOLKHOV

**Volkhov** U.S. Navy, 8-86

**D:** 16,250 tons (fl) **S:** 14 kts **Dim:** 145.5 × 19.24 × 8.5 **A:** none
**Electron Equipt:** Radar: 2/Don-2—IFF: 1/High Pole A
**M:** 2 Russkiy Dizel diesels; 2 props; 4,000 hp **Range:** 18,000/14 **Man:** 46 tot.

REMARKS: Soviet type designation: VTR—*Voyenyy Tanker* (Military Tanker). Built in the mid-1950s. 8,230 grt/11,800 dwt. Carry 11,600 tons of fuel. The three naval units can be distinguished from their civilian sisters because they have two tall king posts and an A-frame king post to support fueling hoses before the bridge, and working decks were added over the cargo decks before and abaft the bridge. Merchant units of this class are among those most frequently used to support naval forces.

◆ **1 ex-German, ex-Dutch** Bldr: C. van der Giessen, Krimpen, Netherlands

POLYARNIK (ex-*Kärnten,* ex-*Tankboot-I*)

**Polyarnik** 1975

**D:** 12,500 tons (fl) **S:** 17.1 kts **Dim:** 132.1 (125.0 pp) × 16.15 × 7.6
**M:** 2 Werkspoor 8-cyl. diesels; 2 props; 7,000 hp **Man:** 57 tot.

REMARKS: Launched 3-5-41. War reparations 30-12-45. Oldest replenishment oiler in any navy. 5,709 grt/6,640 dwt. Liquid cargo 5,600 tons; solid stores and provisions. In the Pacific Fleet. Due to great age, may have been discarded.

## OILERS

NOTE: Eleven 2,500-deadweight-ton tankers were ordered for the Soviet Navy from Finland's Laivateollisuus Shipyard on 7-1-87. Some or all of these may be intended for the Soviet Navy, which has a large number of elderly small fuel carriers needing replacement.

◆ **2 Baskunchak class** Bldr: Kamysh-Burun SY, Kerch' (In serv. 1964–68)

IVAN GOLUBETS UKHTA

**OILERS** *(continued)*

**D:** 2,940 tons (fl) **S:** 13.2 kts **Dim:** 83.6 (74.0 pp) × 12.0 × 4.9
**Electron Equipt:** Radar: 1/Don-2 **M:** 1 Type 8DR 43/61 W diesel; 2,220 hp
**Electric:** 325 kw **Fuel:** 124 tons **Range:** 5,000/12.6 **Man:** 30 tot.

Remarks: 1,768 grt/1,660 dwt. Cargo: 1,490 tons (9,993 bbl.) Subordinated to the KGB Maritime Border Guard, in the Pacific area. One sister, *Usedom,* in East German Navy; others in Soviet merchant marine.

◆ **4 Konda class** Bldr: Sweden (In serv. mid 1950s)

Konda Rossoch' Soyana Yakhroma

**Yakhroma** French Navy, 1981

**D:** 1,980 tons (fl) **S:** 12 kts **Dim:** 69.0 × 10.0 × 4.3
**Electron Equipt:** Radar: 1-2/Don-2 and/or Spin Trough
**M:** 1 diesel; 1,600 hp **Range:** 2,470/10 **Man:** 26 tot.

Remarks: 1,117 grt/1,265 dwt. Can refuel over the stern.

◆ **3 Nercha class** Bldr: Crichton-Vulcan or Valmet, Abo, Finland (In serv. 1952–55)

Klyaz'ma Narva Nercha

**Nercha** 1967

**D:** 1,800 tons (fl) **S:** 11.3 kts **Dim:** 63.5 × 10.0 × 4.5
**Electron Equipt:** Radar: 1/Don **M:** 1 diesel; 1,000 hp
**Range:** 2,000/10 **Man:** 25 tot.

Remarks: 1,081 grt/1,127 dwt. Can refuel over the stern.

◆ **13 Khobi class** Bldr: Zhdanov SY (In serv. early 1950s)

| | | | | |
|---|---|---|---|---|
| Cheremshan | Indiga | Khobi | Lovat' | Metan |
| Orsha | Sasha | Seima | Shelon' | Sos'va |
| Sysola | Tartu | Tunguska | | |

**Lovat'** 1978

**D:** 1,525 tons (fl) **S:** 12 kts **Dim:** 62.0 × 10.0 × 4.4
**Electron Equipt:** Radar: 1/Don-2, 1/Spin Trough—IFF: High Pole A
**M:** 2 diesels; 2 props; 1,600 hp **Man:** 29 tot.

Remarks: 795 grt/834–915 dwt. Refuel over bows while being towed by receiving ship. *Linda* and one other went to Albania in 1959; others to Indonesia. At least four have been stricken: *Alazan, Baymak, Goryn,* and *Titan.*

◆ **2 ex-German Dora class** Bldr: D. W. Kremer Sohn, Elmshorn (In serv. 1941–43)

Izhma (ex-. . .) Iskra (ex-. . .)

**D:** 973 tons (fl) **S:** 12 kts **Dim:** 61.0 (56.5 pp) × 9.0 × 2.75
**A:** none **Electron Equipt:** Radar: . . .
**M:** 2 M.W.M. 6-cyl. diesels; 2 props; 900 hp **Fuel:** 17.5 tons
**Range:** 1,200/12 **Man:** 26 tot.

Remarks: Two of a group of four Luftwaffe aviation-fuel tankers—*Dora, Else, Grete,* and *Hanna*—all of which passed into British hands in 5-45 and went to the U.S.S.R. in 1946. The others may also remain in service. 638 grt. Cargo: 331 tons.

Note: The World War II-era former German tanker *Feolent* is believed to have been stricken.

**WATER TANKERS**

◆ **2 Manych class** Bldr: Vyborg SY

Manych (In serv. 1971) Tagil (In serv. 1977)

**Manych** U.S. Navy, 1982

**Tagil** 1983

**D:** 7,800 tons (fl) **S:** 18 kts **Dim:** 115.8 × 15.8 × 6.7
**A:** removed **Electron Equipt:** Radar: 2/Don-Kay; *Manych* also: 2/Muff Cob
**M:** 2 diesels; 2 props; 9,000 hp **Range:** 11,500/12 **Man:** 90 tot.

Remarks: Originally intended to be small replenishment oilers to carry fuel and solid stores for submarines. Reported in the Soviet press as unsuccessful. *Manych* was assigned as a water tender to support the Mediterranean Squadron. Her four 57-mm guns were removed in 1975. *Tagil* was completed without armament.

◆ **14 Voda class** Bldr: . . . (In serv. 1950s)

| | | | | |
|---|---|---|---|---|
| Abakan | MVT-9 | MVT-17 | MVT-21 | MVT-138 |
| Sura | MVT-10 | MVT-18 | MVT-24 | MVT-428 |
| MVT-6 | MVT-16 | MVT-20 | MVT-134 | |

**Abakan** U.S. Navy, 2-84

**D:** 2,100 tons (3,100 fl) **S:** 12 kts **Dim:** 81.5 × 11.5 × 4.3
**Electron Equipt:** Radar: 1/Don-2
**M:** 2 diesels; 2 props; 1,600 hp **Range:** 3,000/10 **Man:** 40 tot.

Remarks: MVT-*Morskoy Vodnyy Tanker* (Seagoing Water Tanker). Several have no working deck over the cargo tank area.

## SPECIAL-LIQUIDS TANKERS

◆ **1 (+. . .) Belyanka class** Bldr: . . . (In serv. 1987)

AMUR

**D:** 6,000 tons (fl) **S:** 12 kts **Dim:** . . . × . . . × . . .
**A:** none **Electron Equipt:** Radar: . . . **M:** . . .
**Range:** . . ./. . . **Man:** . . .

REMARKS: Prototype of a new design believed intended to replace the Vala-class radioactive-liquid-waste tankers.

◆ **1 Ural class** Bldr: Dalzavod SY, Vladivostok (In serv. 1969)

URAL

**Ural** 1969

**D:** 2,600 tons (fl) **S:** 12 kts **Dim:** 90.0 × 10.0 × 3.7
**Electron Equipt:** Radar: 1/Spin Trough **M:** 2 diesels; 1 prop; 1,200 hp

REMARKS: Transports liquid nuclear waste. High freeboard, superstructure aft, traveling crane.

◆ **6 Luza class** Bldr: Sredniy Neva SY, Kolpino (In serv. 1960s)

| | | |
|---|---|---|
| ALAMBAY | BARGUZIN | KANA |
| ARAGVY | DON | SELENGA |

**Barguzin** 1982

**D:** 1,900 tons (fl) **S:** 12 kts **Dim:** 62.5 × 10.7 × 4.3
**Electron Equipt:** Radar: 1/Don-2 **M:** 1 diesel; 1,000 hp **Range:** 2,000/11

REMARKS: Carry volatile liquids, probably missile fuel. Three sisters have been stricken: *Oka, Sasima,* and *Yenisey.*

◆ **5 Vala class** (In service: early 1960s)

TNT-11 TNT-12 TNT-19 TNT-25 TNT-29

**TNT-12**—Vala class

**D:** 3,100 tons (fl) **S:** 14 kts **Dim:** 76.2 × 12.5 × 5.0
**M:** 1 diesel; 1,000 hp **Range:** 2,000/11

REMARKS: Carry waste liquids from nuclear-propulsion plants. Some carry 2/12.7-mm mg (II × 1).

## TRANSPORT

◆ **1 Mikhail Kalinin class** Bldr: Mathias Thesen Werft, Wismar, East Germany (In serv. 1963)

KUBAN (ex-*Nadezhda Krupskaya*)

**Kuban** French Navy, 5-83

**D:** 6,400 tons (fl) **S:** 18 kts **Dim:** 122.2 × 16.0 × 5.1
**A:** none **Electron Equipt:** Radar: 2/Don-2, 1/Spin Trough
**M:** 2 M.A.N. 6-cyl. diesels; 2 props; 8,000 hp **Range:** 8,100/17

REMARKS: Former passenger-cargo ship used to rotate crews on ships in the Mediterranean Squadron. 5,260 grt/1,354 dwt. Can carry 340 passengers, 1,000 tons of dry cargo.

## CARGO SHIPS

NOTE: Cargo ships are usually referred to as VTR—*Voyenyy Transport* (Military Transport).

◆ **10 Neon Antonov class** Bldr: . . . (In serv. 1978–. . .)

| | | |
|---|---|---|
| IRBIT | MIKHAIL KONOVALOV | NIKOLAY STARSHINKOV |
| IVAN ASDNEV | NEON ANTONOV | SERGEY SUDYESKIY |
| IVAN LEDNEV | NIKOLAY SIPYAGIN | 2 others |

**Mikhail Konovalov** 5-83

**D:** 5,200 tons (fl) **S:** 16 kts **Dim:** 95.1 × 14.7 × 6.5
**Electron Equipt:** Radar: 2/Palm Frond—IFF: 1/High Pole B
**A:** none (see Remarks) **M:** 1 diesel; 1 prop; . . . hp

REMARKS: Specialized supply ships for remote garrisons of the KGB Maritime Border Guard in the Pacific area. Carry one or two small landing craft aft. Position for a twin 30-mm AA on the forecastle, two twin 14.5-mm machine guns amidships, and two SA-7 Grail launching positions. *Irbit* is naval-subordinated.

◆ **1 Amguema class** Bldr: U.S.S.R. (In serv. 1975)

YAUZA

**D:** 15,100 tons (fl) **S:** 15 kts **Dim:** 133.1 × 18.9 × 9.1
**Electron Equipt:** Radar: 2/Don-2—IFF: 1/High Pole A
**M:** 4 1,800-hp diesels, electric drive; 1 prop; 7,200 hp **Range:** 10,000/15

**Yauza** 1976

**CARGO SHIPS** *(continued)*

Remarks: 7,900 grt/9,045 dwt. Icebreaking passenger-cargo ship. Cargo: 6,600 tons. Numerous merchant sisters. Two 60-ton, two 10-ton, and six 5-ton cranes.

◆ **3 Yuniy Partizan class** Bldr: Turnu-Severin SY and Oltenitza SY, Romania (In serv. 1975–78)

Pechora Turgay Ufa

**Turgay** 11-80

**D:** 3,947 tons (fl) **S:** 12.9 kts **Dim:** 88.75 (80.25 pp) × 12.8 × 5.2 **A:** none
**Electron Equipt:** Radar: 1/Don-2—IFF: 1/High Pole A **Electric:** 306 kw
**M:** 1 Zgoda-Sulzer 8 TAD 36 diesel; 1 prop; 2,080 hp **Range:** 4,000/12
**Fuel:** 125 tons **Man:** 25 tot.

Remarks: 2,079 grt/2,150 dwt. Small container ships. Three 10-ton cranes, one of which can be rigged to lift 28 tons. Cargo: 3,200 $m^3$. Originally intended to be able to carry 58 standard cargo containers. Twenty sisters are civilian. Sister *Pinega* converted to a missile transport and renamed *Vitse-Admiral Fomin.*

◆ **8 Vytegrales class** Bldr: Zhdanov SY, Leningrad (In serv. 1963–66)

| | |
|---|---|
| Apsheron (ex-*Tosnales*) | Donbass (ex-*Kirishi*) |
| Baskunchak (ex-*Vostok-4*) | Sevan (ex-*Vyborgles*) |
| Dauriya (ex-*Suzdal*) | Taman' (ex-*Vostok-3*) |
| Dikson (ex-*Vagales*) | Yamal (ex-*Svirles*) |

**Taman'**—with Hormone helicopter on deck U.S. Navy, 2-86

**Sevan** 1979

**D:** 9,650 tons (fl) **S:** 16 kts **Dim:** 121.9 × 16.7 × 7.3 **A:** none
**Electron Equipt:** Radar: 2/Don-2—IFF: 1/High Pole B **Range:** 7,380/14.5
**M:** 1 Burmeister & Wain 950 VTBF 110 diesel; 1 prop; 5,200 hp **Man:** 90 tot.

Remarks: Originally built as merchant timber-carriers, then converted as space-event support ships by the addition of more communications facilities and a helicopter platform over the stern—consequently losing access to the after hold. They can carry one Hormone helicopter but have no hangar. Now used as fleet supply ships and, occasionally, as flagships. *Donbass* has a Big Net air-search radar. A deckhouse over hold number three forward of the superstructure in *Dikson, Taman, Dauriya,* and *Baskunchak.* Seven sisters were converted to serve the Academy of Sciences as satellite-tracking ships.

◆ **2 Leninskiy Komsomol class** Bldr: Kherson SY (In serv. 1959–68)

Kolkhida (ex-. . .) Samara (ex-. . .)

**D:** approx. 22,000 tons (fl) **S:** 19 kts **Dim:** 169.9 × 21.8 × 9.7
**Electron Equipt:** Radar: 2/. . . nav.
**M:** 2 sets GT; 1 prop; 13,500 hp **Boilers:** 2 **Range:** . . .

Remarks: Approximately 11,200 grt/16,230 dwt. Transferred to naval service early 1980s. Six holds totaling 19,800 $m^3$ to 25,460 $m^3$. *Kolkhida* has two 60-ton booms and twelve 5-ton electric cranes; *Samara* may have two 60-ton booms, four 10-ton booms, and 16 5-ton booms. Twenty-five ships of this class were built for the Soviet merchant marine.

◆ **9 Keyla class** Bldr: Hungary (In serv. 1960–66)

| | | | | |
|---|---|---|---|---|
| Mezen' | Ponoy | Teriberka | Unzha | Yeruslan |
| Onega | Ritsa | Tuloma | Ussuri | |

**Mezen'** U.S. Navy, 2-84

**D:** 832 tons light (2,042 fl) **S:** 12 kts **Dim:** 78.5 (71.4 pp) × 10.5 × 4.6
**A:** none **Electron Equipt:** Radar: 1/Don-2 or Spin Trough
**Electric:** 300 kw **M:** 1 Lang 8LD315RF diesel; 1 prop; 1,000 hp
**Range:** 4,200/10.7 **Man:** 26 tot. **Fuel:** 72 tons

Remarks: 1,296 grt/1,280 dwt. Carry 1,100 tons of cargo. One 10-ton, six 2.5-ton cranes. *Ritsa* has a deckhouse over her after hatch and numerous communications antennas, and may collect intelligence.

◆ **3 MP-6-class former landing ships** Bldr: Hungary (In serv. 1959–60)

Bira Irgiz Vologdya

**Bira** 1975

**D:** 2,000 tons (fl) **S:** 12 kts **Dim:** 74.7 (70.1 pp) × 11.3 × 4.4
**M:** 2 Buchau-Wolff 6NVD48 diesels; 1 prop; 800 hp **Range:** 3,000/9

Remarks: Unsuccessful as landing ships, bow doors welded closed. Sisters *Bureya* and *Khoper* serve as missile transports. *Vologdya* has one crane serving all three hatches: the other two have six 2.5-ton cranes.

◆ **2 Andizhan class** Bldr: Neptunwerft, Rostock, East Germany (In serv. 1959–60)

Onda Poset

**D:** 6,739 tons (fl) **S:** 13.5 kts **Dim:** 104.2 (95.8 pp) × 14.4 × 6.6
**A:** none **Electron Equipt:** Radar: 1/Don-2 **Range:** 6,000/13.5
**M:** 2 Gorlitzer-Sulzer 8SV55 MA diesels; 1 prop; 2,500 hp
**Electric:** 550 kw **Fuel:** 238 tons diesel/150 tons heavy oil **Man:** 43 tot.

**CARGO SHIPS** *(continued)*

**Onda** 5-83

REMARKS: 3,368 grt/4,324 dwt. Cargo: 3,954 tons. Sister *Yemetsk* stricken. Two naval sisters are now missile transports; other sisters are in the merchant service. *Poset* entered naval service around 1978, *Onda* in 1980–81. Have one 40-ton, one 18-ton, and eight 3-ton cranes.

◆ **1 Kolomna class** Bldr: Neptunwerft, Rostock (In serv. 1952–54)

SVANETIYA

**Svanetiya** 1976

**D:** 6,700 tons (fl) **S:** 13 kts **Dim:** 102.3 (95.8 pp) × 14.4 × 6.6
**Electron Equipt:** Radar: 1/Don-2, 1/Neptune
IFF: 1/High Pole A
**M:** reciprocating steam plus GT; 1 prop; 2,450 hp
**Boilers:** 2 watertube; 16 kg/cm$^2$, 320°C **Fuel:** 580 tons **Electric:** 300 kw
**Range:** 6,890/13 **Man:** 44 tot.

REMARKS: 3,758 grt/4,355 dwt. Cargo: 3,634 tons. One 35-ton, one 15-ton, and eight 3-ton cranes. Four cargo holds. Coal-burner. *Svanetiya* supports research work. Six sisters serve as *Atrek*-class submarine tenders. Sisters *Kuznetsk, Krasnoarmeysk,* and *Megra* discarded.

◆ **3 Telnovsk class** Bldr: Ganz SY, Budapest, Hungary (In serv. 1949–57)

BUREVESTNIK LAG MANOMETR

**D:** 1,900 tons (fl) **S:** 11 kts **Dim:** 70.2 (64.6 pp) × 10.1 × 4.2
**M:** 2 Buchau-Wolff 8NVD48 diesels; 800 hp **Range:** 3,300/9.7
**Man:** 40 tot. **Fuel:** 85 tons

REMARKS: 1,194 grt/1,133 dwt. Several others serve as survey ships. Two 10-ton and four 2-ton cranes, three holds.

NOTE: The remaining Khabarovsk-class small cargo ships, the *Chulym*-class cargo ship *Severodonetsk,* and the *Donbass*-class cargo ship *Svir* have been deleted here due to age and lack of sightings.

**PROVISION SHIPS**

◆ **8 Mayak class** Bldr: Dnepr SY, Kiev (In serv. 1971–76)

| | | | |
|---|---|---|---|
| BUZULUK | LAMA | NEMAN | ULMA |
| ISHIM | MIUS | RIONI | VYTEGRA |

**D:** 1,050 tons (fl) **S:** 11 kts **Dim:** 54.3 × 9.3 × 3.6
**A:** none **Electron Equipt:** Radar: 1/Spin Trough
**M:** 1 diesel; 800 hp **Range:** 9,400/11 **Man:** 29 tot.

**Neman** 1982

REMARKS: 690 grt. Former trawlers. Refrigerated fish holds are used to carry provisions. *Lama* has two lifeboats and lacks bulwarks around the stern. Other naval sisters operate as intelligence-collectors and ASW training ships.

**AMMUNITION SHIPS**

◆ **10 Muna class** Bldr: Nakhodka SY (In serv. 1960s)

| | | | | |
|---|---|---|---|---|
| VTR-81 | VTR-82 | VTR-83 | VTR-84 | VTR-85 |
| VTR-91 | VTR-92 | VTR-93 | VTR-94 | VTR-148 |

**Muna-class VTR-91**—munitions transport version 1982

**Muna class**—torpedo transport version 1982

**D:** 680 tons (fl) **S:** 11 kts **Dim:** 51.0 × 8.5 × 2.7
**Electron Equipt:** Radar: 1-2/Spin Trough—IFF: 1/High Pole A
**M:** 1 diesel; 600 hp **Man:** 40 tot.

REMARKS: When deployed, carry VTR—*Voyenyy Transport* (Military Transport) numbers, but in home waters are listed as MBSS—*Morskaya Barzha Samokhodnaya Sukhogruznaya* (Seagoing Self-Propelled Dry-Cargo Lighter). Specialized transports for torpedoes, surface-to-air missiles, and other munitions; cargo hatch arrangements differ, depending on function.

**MOORING TENDERS**

◆ **10 Sura class** Bldr: Neptunwerft, Rostock, East Germany (In serv. 1965–72, 1976–78)

| | | | | |
|---|---|---|---|---|
| KIL-1 | KIL-21 | KIL-23 | KIL-29 | KIL-32 |
| KIL-2 | KIL-22 | KIL-27 | KIL-31 | KIL-33 |

**KIL-2** L. &. L. Van Ginderen, 11-86

MOORING TENDERS *(continued)*

**KIL-27**—note twin hatches amidships U.S. Navy, 1-87

**D:** 2,370 tons (3,150 fl) **S:** 13 kts **Dim:** 87.0 (68.0 pp) × 14.8 × 5.0
**A:** none **Electron Equipt:** Radar: 2/Don-2
**M:** 4 diesels, electric drive; 2 props; 2,240 hp **Range:** 4,000/10

Remarks: KIL—*Kilektor* (Mooring Tender). 2,366 grt. 890 tons of cargo in hold amidships. Stern rig, which can lift 60 tons, is used for buoy-handling and salvage. Can also carry several hundred tons of cargo fuel. One has been used to transport two Gus-class amphibious air-cushion personnel landing craft. Mooring buoys are stowed amidships and moved aft for handling by the stern gallows rig via a chain-haul system. The diesel propulsion generator plant is forward.

◆ **10 Neptun class** Bldr: Neptunwerft, Rostock, East Germany (In serv. 1957–60)

| | | | | |
|---|---|---|---|---|
| KIL-3 | KIL-6 | KIL-12 | KIL-15 | KIL-17 |
| KIL-5 | KIL-9 | KIL-14 | KIL-16 | KIL-18 |

**Neptun class**

**D:** 700 tons (1,240 fl) **S:** 12 kts **Dim:** 57.3 (46.5 pp) × 11.4 × 3.4
**M:** 2 triple-expansion; 1,000 hp **Range:** 1,000/11
**Boilers:** 2 **Man:** 41 tot.

Remarks: KIL—*Kilektor* (Mooring Tender). Most burn coal. 80-ton bow lift for buoy-handling and salvage. Four units deleted 1983; no recent sightings.

## CABLE LAYERS

◆ **2 Biriusa class** Bldr: Wärtsilä, Turku, Finland

| | L | In serv. | | L | In serv. |
|---|---|---|---|---|---|
| Biriusa | 29-11-85 | 4-7-86 | Kem' | 23-11-85 | 23-10-86 |

**D:** 2,370 tons (fl) **S:** 11.8 kts **Dim:** 86.10 (78.70 pp) × 12.60 × 3.10
**Electron Equipt:** Radar: 1/. . . nav.
**M:** diesel-electric: 2 Wärtsilä Vasa 8R22 diesels; 2 shrouded Schottel props; 1,700 hp
**Man:** . . .

Remarks: Lengthened version of *Emba* class, with more powerful engines, carrying twice as much cable (600 tons) and equipped with a gantry over the bow cable. Ordered 1-85. Propellers swivel through 360 degrees. Have a bow-thruster. Both in Pacific Fleet.

◆ **3 Emba class** Bldr: Wärtsilä SY, Turku, Finland

Emba (In serv. 5-80) Nepryadva (L: 24-4-81) Setun (L: 29-4-81)

**D:** 2,050 tons (fl) **S:** 11.8 kts **Dim:** 75.90 (68.50 pp) × 12.60 × 3.10
**Electron Equipt:** Radar: 1/. . . nav.
**M:** diesel-electric: 2 Wärtsilä Vasa 6R22 diesels; 2 shrouded Schottel props; 1,360 hp
**Man:** 38 tot.

Remarks: 1,900 grt. Cargo: 300 tons cable. Intended for use in shallow coastal areas, rivers, and harbors. Intended to replace the discarded Kalar class. Have a bow-thruster.

**Setun** Wärtsilä, 4-81

◆ **8 Klazma class** Bldr: Wärtsilä SY, Turku, Finland (In serv. 1962–78)

| | In serv. | | In serv. | | In serv. | | In serv. |
|---|---|---|---|---|---|---|---|
| Donets | 1963 | Inguri | 1978 | Tavda | 1977 | Yana | 1963 |
| Ingul | 1962 | Katun' | 1974 | Tsna | 1968 | Zeya | 1970 |

**Ingul**—early unit VF-111, U.S. Navy, 1985

**Tavda**—late unit 1979

**D:** 6,920 tons (fl) **S:** 14 kts **Dim:** 130.4 (120.0 pp) × 16.0 × 5.75
**Electron Equipt:** Radar: 2/Don-2
**M:** 5 1,000-hp Wärtsilä 624TS diesels, electric drive; 2 props; 4,400 hp
**Fuel:** 250 tons **Range:** 12,000/14 **Man:** 110 tot.

Remarks: 5,760 grt/3,750 dwt. *Ingul* and *Yana,* the first built, have four 2,436-hp diesels, a longer forecastle, and are 5,645 grt/3,400 dwt (6,810 tons fl). All have ice-strengthened hulls. In the later units, the diesel engines drive five 680-kw generators, which provide power for propulsion and for all auxiliary functions. Soviet type designation: KS—*Kabel'noye Sudno* (Cable Ship). All cable machinery built by Submarine Cables, Ltd., Great Britain. *Katun'* carries 1,850 $m^3$ of cable and displaces 7,885 tons (fl), drawing 5.76 m; she capsized while fitting out. The others have 3 cable tanks totaling 1,600 $m^3$. *Ingul* refitted in Japan 1978, receiving new Dowty paired-wheel cable gear. All have a 500-hp active rudder and a bow-thruster.

Note: With the arrival in the Far East of the new small cable layers *Birinsa* and *Kem',* the *Telnovsk*-class cable layer KS-7 is believed to have been stricken.

## FLEET TUGS

◆ **2 Neftegaz-class oilfield tug/supply vessels** Bldr: A. Warski SY, Szczecin, Poland

Aleksey Kortunov (10-83) Ilga (In serv. 4-11-83)

**D:** 2,800 tons (fl) **S:** 15 kts **Dim:** 81.5 (71.5 pp) × 16.3 (15.0 wl) × 5.4
**A:** none **Electron Equipt:** 2/. . . nav.
**M:** 2 Sulzer-Zgoda diesels; 2 CP props; 7,200 hp
**Range:** . . . **Fuel:** 533 tons **Man:** 25

Remarks: 2,372 grt/1,396 dwt. Two of a class of 33 oilfield supply tugs ordered in 1982, the third and fourth to be delivered. Cargo: up to 600 tons dry cargo on

**FLEET TUGS** *(continued)*

deck plus 1,000 $m^3$ liquid cargo. Can act as a tug and has four fire-fighting water monitors. Has a bow-thruster. Broad, level fantail and round-down stern would permit the ship to be rapidly adapted for minelaying.

**Neftegaz-27**—a civilian sister 1984

◆ **10 Goryn class** Bldr: Rauma-Repola, Finland (In serv. 1977–78, 1982–83)

MB-105 (Baykalsk) MB-18 (Berezinsk) MB-119 (Bilbino)
MB-30 MB-31 MB-32 MB-35 MB-36 MB-38 MB-61

**MB-36**—second series French Navy, 1983

**MB-105**—which initially bore the name *Baykalsk* 9-83

**D:** 2,240 tons (2,600 fl) **S:** 13.5 kts **Dim:** 63.5 × 14.3 × 5.1
**Electron Equipt:** Radar: 2/Don-2
**M:** 1 Russkiy Type 67N diesel; 3,500 hp **Range:** . . . **Man:** 40 tot.

Remarks: Soviet type designation: MB—*Morskoy Buksir* (Seagoing Tug). 1,600 grt. 35-ton pull. For ocean towing, salvage, and fire-fighting. Sister *Bolshevetsk* lost 2-79 off Japan. Later units have a Type 671 diesel and produce 43 tons bollard pull. Second series of ten began with MB-30, launched 15-12-81 and ended with MB-108, delivered 9-83. Four others have been redesignated as rescue tugs—SB—*Spastel'noye Buksir*: SB-365 (ex-MB-29), SB-522 (ex-MB-62), SB-523 (ex-MB-64), and SB-524 (ex-MB-108). The two series can be distinguished visually by the overlapping rubbing strakes at the forecastle break in the early units and the sloping connecting strake in late units.

◆ **12 (+ . . .) Sorum class** Bldr: Yaroslavl SY, U.S.S.R. (In serv. 1974–. . .)

| | | | |
|---|---|---|---|
| MB-6 | MB-28 | MB-115 | MB-236 |
| MB-25 | MB-58 | MB-119 | MB-304 |
| MB-26 | MB-112 | MB-148 | MB-307 |

**D:** 1,210 tons (1,656 fl) **S:** 14 kts **Dim:** 58.3 × 12.6 × 4.6
**A:** named units only: 4/30-mm AA (II × 2)
**Electron Equipt:** Radar: 2/Don-2—IFF: 1/High Pole B
**M:** 2 Type 5-2D42 diesels, electric drive; 1 prop; 1,500 hp
**Fuel:** 322 tons **Range:** 6,720/13 **Man:** 35 tot.

Remarks: MB means *Morskoy Buksir* (Seagoing Tug). A modified version with larger superstructure and an A-frame king post aft is used by the Ministry of Fisheries as a rescue tug, prominently displaying *Spastel'* (Rescue) on the black hull sides; named the *Almaz*-class, it includes *Almaz, Kapitan Beklemishev,* and *Ametist.* Twelve armed versions of the design serve the KGB Maritime Border Guard as patrol ships; see under corvettes on an earlier page.

**MB-25**—a Soviet Navy Sorum 1983

◆ **48 Okhtenskiy class** Bldr: Petrozavod SY, Leningrad (In serv. 1958–early 1960s)

**MB-175**—Okhtenskiy class J.M.S.D.F., 1985

**SB-5**—a rescue tug Okhtenskiy

**D:** 663 tons light (926 fl) **S:** 13.3 kts
**Dim:** 47.3 (43.0 pp) × 10.3 × 5.5 **Electric:** 340 kw
**Electron Equipt:** Radar: 1–2/Don-2 or Spin Trough—IFF: 1/High Pole A
**M:** diesel-electric: 2 Type D5D50 diesels; 1 prop; 1,500 hp
**Range:** 7,800/7 **Fuel:** 197 tons **Man:** 30 tot.

Remarks: Several have two 57-mm AA (II × 1) and are operated by the KGB Maritime Border Guard for use as patrol ships. Units with names are civilian; naval units have MB—*Morskoy Buksir* (Seagoing Tug) or SB—*Spastel'noye Buksir* (Rescue Tug) hull numbers; the latter carry an "unsinkable" lifeboat or divers' workboat to port and are submarine-associated. A total of 63 were built, Soviet name: *Goliat* class. Bollard pull: 27 tons initial/17 sustained.

◆ **10 Roslavl class** Bldr: Riga SY and Repair, and Vano Sturua SY (In serv. 1950s)

MB-69 MB-94 MB-134 MB-143 MB-145 MB-146 MB-147
3 others

**D:** 750 tons (fl) **S:** 11 kts **Dim:** 44.5 × 9.5 × 3.5
**Electron Equipt:** Radar: 1/Don-2 **M:** diesel-electric; 2 props; 1,200 hp
**Range:** 6,000/11 **Man:** 28 tot.

Remarks: All have MB pendants—*Morskoy Buksir* (Seagoing Tug). Distinguished from the Okhtenskiy class by a shorter forecastle, small pilothouse, and single pole mast. Beginning to be discarded. At least one sister (SB-43) operates as a rescue tug.

FLEET TUGS *(continued)*

**MB-94**—Roslavl class L. & L. Van Ginderen, 1987

## SALVAGE AND RESCUE SHIPS

◆ **4 Pionier Moskvyy-class salvage ships** Bldr: Vyborg SY

MIKHAIL RUDNITSKIY (In serv. 1979) GIORGIY KOZ'MIN (In serv. 1980)
GIORGIY TITOV (In serv. 1983) SAYANY (In serv. 1984)

**Sayany**—with longer forecastle and poop, additional deckhouse U.S. Navy, 11-86

**Mikhail Rudnitskiy** U.S. Navy, 12-85

**D:** 10,000 tons (fl) **S:** 15.4 kts **Dim:** 130.3 (119.0 pp) × 17.3 × 6.93
**A:** none **Electron Equipt:** Radar: 2/Don-2 **Man:** 120 tot.
**M:** 1 5DKRN 62/140-3 diesel; 1 prop; 6,100 hp **Electric:** 1,500 kw

REMARKS: Modification of a standard merchant timber-carrier/container-ship design, retaining two holds. The after hold has two superstructure levels built over it, and the small hold forward has been plated over. Retains two 40-ton and two 20-ton booms and has had heavy-cable fairleads cut in the bulwarks fore and aft and a number of boat booms added to starboard. *Titov* has a larger superstructure built over number three hold than do the first two. *Sayany,* painted in white and gray, has had the forecastle and poop decks extended, the deckhouse amidships one deck higher, and a two-level deckhouse over the forward hold area: she appears intended for some research role. Equipped with bow- and stern-thrusters and can be attached to a four-point salvage moor. First three carry the ensign of the Naval Salvage and Rescue Service and are named for important developers of research/salvage submersibles. Operate one salvage submersible, stowed in hold number two.

◆ **0 (+2) . . . class salvage tugs** Bldr: Hollming SY, Rauma, Finland

N . . . N . . . .

**D:** approx 8,000 tons (fl) **S:** 18 kts **Dim:** 98.00 × 19.50 × 7.10
**Electron Equipt:** Radar: . . . **M:** 4 diesels; 2 CP props; 24,480 hp
**Range:** . . . **Man:** 51 crew, 20 passengers

REMARKS: Ordered 29-8-86. Will be world's most powerful rescue tugs. Will have helicopter platform; Two 150-ton salvage winches, one 60-ton towing winch, two 30-ton, and two 10-ton winches. Two 8-ton and one 3-ton cranes. Will be able to support two divers working at up to 60 m.

◆ **4 Sliva-class salvage tugs** Bldr: Rauma-Repola Uusikaupunki SY, Finland

| | Laid down | L | In serv. |
|---|---|---|---|
| SB-406 | . . . | 6-7-83 | 20-2-84 |
| SB-408 | . . . | 28-10-83 | 5-6-84 |
| SB-921 | 17-8-84 | 28-12-84 | 5-7-85 |
| SB-922 | 31-8-84 | 3-5-85 | 20-12-85 |

**SB-406**—exercising fire monitors Rauma-Repola, 1984

**SB-408** Rauma-Repola, 1984

**D:** 3,400 tons (fl) **S:** 16 kts **Dim:** 69.20 (60.10 pp) × 15.40 × 5.10
**Electron Equipt:** Radar: 2/. . . nav.
**M:** 2 SEMT-Pielstick/Russkiy Dizel 6PC 2.5 L400 (TS HN40/46) diesels; 2 CP props; 7,800 hp—bow-thruster
**Man:** 43 crew + 10 salvage party

REMARKS: 2,050 grt/810 dwt. Ice-reinforced hull. Able to support divers to 60 m. Have four water monitors. One 60- and one 30-ton winch. Unique 350-m floating power cable to support vessels in distress. 5-ton electrohydraulic crane. Second pair ordered 4-84.

◆ **4 Goryn-class rescue tugs** Bldr: Rauma-Repola, Finland (In serv. 1982–83)

SB-236 (ex-MB-29) SB-365 (ex-MB-62) SB-523 (ex-MB-64) SB-524 (ex-MB-108)

REMARKS: Data as for tug sisters on earlier page. SB—*Spastel'noye Buksir* (Rescue Tug). Change in designation appears to have been administrative only; no change to characteristics. Several Okhtenskiy class and at least one Roslavl class (SB-46) are also designated as rescue tugs.

◆ **3 Ingul-class salvage tugs** Bldr: United Admiralty SY, Leningrad

PAMIR (In serv. 1975) MASHUK (In serv. 1972) ALATAU (In serv. 1984)

**Alatau** U.S. Navy, 2-86

## SALVAGE AND RESCUE SHIPS *(continued)*

**D:** 3,200 tons (4,050 fl) **S:** 20 kts **Dim:** 92.8 × 15.4 × 5.8
**Electron Equipt:** Radar: 2/Don-2
IFF: 1/High Pole B, 1/Square Head
**M:** 2 type 58D-4R diesels; 2 props; 9,000 hp
**Range:** 9,000/18.7 **Man:** 120 tot.

REMARKS: Two sisters, *Yaguar* and *Bars*, in the merchant marine, have 35-man crews, plus bunks for 50 rescued personnel. Very powerful tugs with constant-tension highline personnel rescue system, salvage pumps, fire-fighting equipment, and complete diving gear, capable of supporting divers to 60-m depths. Have a 94-ton bollard-pull. Large bulbous bow.

◆ **2 Pamir class** Bldr: Gävle, Sweden (In serv. 1958)

AGATAN ALDAN

**Aldan** French Navy, 1-83

**D:** 1,443 tons (2,240 fl) **S:** 17.5 kts **Dim:** 78.0 × 12.8 × 4.0
**Electron Equipt:** Radar: 2/Don-2
**M:** 2 M.A.N. G10V 40/60 diesels; 2 CP props; 4,200 hp
**Range:** 15,200/17.5; 21,800/12

REMARKS: 1,443 grt. One 10-ton and two 1.5-ton booms. Carry fixed fire pumps with 2,600 tons/hour capacity and portable pumps with 1,650 tons/hour capacity. Can support divers to a depth of 90 m, and have decompression chambers and powerful air compressors. Two sisters, the *Gidrograf* and *Peleng*, are intelligence collectors. *Agatan* refitted 1981 in Sweden.

◆ **2 Orel class** Bldr: Valmet SY, Turku, Finland

SB 38 SB 43

**SB 43**—Orel class J.M.S.D.F., 1985

**D:** 1,200 tons (1,760 fl) **S:** 15 kts **Dim:** 61.3 × 11.9 × 4.5
**Electron Equipt:** Radar: 1/Don or Don-2 **Man:** 37 tot.
**M:** 1 M.A.N. G5Z52/70 diesel; 1,700 hp **Range:** 13,000/13.5

REMARKS: SB—*Spastel'noye Buksir* (Rescue Tug). Built in the late 1950s. Several civilian sisters, including the *Stremitel'nyy* and *Strogyy*, serve the fishing fleet.

## SEAGOING FIRE BOATS

NOTE: The large (approx. 3,000 tons fl) Polish-built fire-fighting tugs of the *Vikhr* series are not naval-subordinated. The 13th ship of the class, *Vikhr-13,* was launched 25-11-86 at Stocznia Polnocna, Gdansk.

◆ **11 Katun class** Bldr: U.S.S.R. (In serv. 1970–1981)

| | | | |
|---|---|---|---|
| PZHS-64 | PZHS-96 | PZHS-98 | PZHS-123 |
| PZHS-124 | PZHS-209 | PZHS-282 | PZHS-. . . |
| PZHS-. . . | PZHS-. . . | PZHS-. . . | |

**Katun class**

**D:** 1,016 tons (fl) **S:** 17 kts **Dim:** 62.6 × 10.2 × 3.6
**Electron Equipt:** Radar: 1/Don-2—IFF: 1/High Pole B
**M:** 2 40DM diesels; 2 props; 4,000 hp **Range:** 2,200/16 **Man:** 32 tot.

REMARKS: Originally PDS—*Pozharno-Degazatsionnoye Sudno* (Fire-Fighting and Decontamination Ship); this designation later revised to PZHS—*Pozharnoye Sudno* (Fire-Fighting Ship). Extensive fire-fighting gear, including extendable boom. Powerful pumps. There are several civilian sisters, including the *General Gamidov*. PZHS-64, completed 1981, is approx. 3 m longer and has an extra level to the superstructure; designated "Katun II" by NATO.

NOTE: See also harbor fireboat entries on page 672.

## HOSPITAL SHIPS

◆ **2 Ob' class** Bldr: A Warski SY, Szczecin, Poland

OB' (In serv. 1980) YENESEY (In serv. 1981)

**Yenesey** French Navy, 3-85

**Ob'** U.S. Navy, 12-81

**D:** 11,000 tons (fl) **S:** 20 kts **Dim:** 154.0 (142.0 pp) × 20.5 × 5.2
**Electron Equipt:** Radar: 3/Don-2 **M:** 2 diesels; 2 props; . . . hp
**Man:** 80 crew + 200 medical personnel

REMARKS: Have civilian crews but carry uniformed naval medical personnel. Have 100 beds, 7 operating rooms. The hangar aft can accommodate a Hormone-C utility helicopter. Bow-thrusters fitted. Intended to "provide medical and recreational facilities." There are a physical therapy facility, 2 gymnasiums, 2 pools, a library, and a 100-seat auditorium.

◆ **20 ambulance craft** Bldr: Wisla SY, Poland (In serv. 1978–81)

**D:** 240 tons (fl) **S:** 11.5 kts **Dim:** 32.7 × 7.4 × 2.0
**Electron Equipt:** Radar: 1/Mius navigational
**M:** 2 diesels; 2 props; 570 hp **Man:** 17 tot.

REMARKS: Pendant numbers in the SK-600 (SK—*Sanitarnyy Kater* = Clinic Cutter) series. White-painted.

## INTELLIGENCE COLLECTORS (AGI)

Note: Many of the Soviet ships of this type, often designated ELINT (electronic intelligence) or SIGINT (signal intelligence) collectors, look like trawlers; others, such as the *Primor'ye* and the Bal'zam class are obviously configured for their roles. No pretense is made that the AGIs are anything but intelligence collectors, which detect and analyze radioelectric and electromagnetic signals. Some of them patrol offshore from the home ports of ballistic-missile submarines, others follow Western fleets. Most now have pendant numbers in the *Sudno Svyazyy* (communications vessel) series, and names have mostly been deleted. A few are still in the once widely used GS—*Gidrograficheskoye Sudno* (hydrographic vessel) series.

◆ **1 (+ . . .) Bambuk class** Bldr: . . .

Kamchatka (In serv. 12-87)

**D:** 5,500 tons (fl) **S:** . . . **Dim:** 100.0 × 18.0 × 6.0
**A:** 2/30-mm gatling AA (I × 2)—2/SA-N-5/8 SAM systems (IV × 2, . . . SA-7 or SA-14 missiles)
**Electron Equipt:** Radar: . . .—EW: . . . **M:** . . . **Range:** . . .

Remarks: *Kamchatka*'s first deployment as a Pacific Fleet unit began 12-87. Has a helicopter deck and an extremely tall, four-sided pylon mast. Few collection antennas evident.

◆ **3 (+ 1 + . . .) Vishnaya class** Bldr: Stocznia Polnocna SY, Gdansk

SSV-520 (In serv. 1985) SSV-535 (In serv. 1987)
SSV-. . . (In serv. 1987) SSV-. . . (In serv. 1988)

**SSV-520** R. Neth. N., 9-86

**SSV-520** U.S. Navy, 9-86

**D:** 2,500 tons (fl) **S:** 18 kts **Dim:** 91.50 × 14.50 × 4.0
**A:** 2/30-mm gatling AA (I × 2)—2/SA-N-5/8 SAM systems (IV × 2, . . . Grail and Gremlin missiles)
**Electron Equipt:** Radar: 2/Nayada nav.
EW: See Remarks
**M:** 2 diesels; 2 props; . . . hp **Range:** . . . **Man:** 160 tot.

Remarks: SSV-520 on first deployment lacked an extensive intelligence collection antenna suite, other than MF, HF, and VHF D/F gear. Two large circular radome foundations indicate planned later installation of satellite communications antennas like those on the Bal'zam class, of which they appear to be a reduced edition, possibly intended to replace the *Nikolay Zubov* and *Pamir* classes. There are two lead-computing directors for the 30-mm, six-barreled gatling AA guns mounted forward. The point-defense SAM launchers are aft. SSV-520 first deployed in 9-86, SSV-535 in 2-87.

◆ **Al'pinist class** Bldr: Yaroslavl SY, U.S.S.R. (In serv. 1981–82)

GS-7 GS-8 GS-19 GS-39

**GS-19**—Al'pinist class U.S. Navy, 1986

**GS-19**—with ELINT "huts" atop pilothouse and fore and aft of the after mast 7-84

**D:** 1,202 tons (fl) **S:** 13 kts **Dim:** 53.7 (46.2 pp) × 10.5 × 4.3
**Electron Equipt:** Radar: 1/Don-2
**M:** 1 Type 8NVD48-2U diesel; 1 CP prop; 1,320 hp
**Fuel:** 162 tons **Electric:** 450 kw **Range:** 7,600/13 **Man:** approx. 50 tot.

Remarks: Selected from a class of several hundred 322-dwt stern-haul trawlers, modified as intelligence collectors, although there are few identifiable intercept antennas. The 218-m³ former fish hold may provide electronics and/or additional accommodations spaces. Have a bow-thruster. The Soviet Navy also uses an Al'pinist in an experimental role (OS-104, see later page), and several are used in oceanographic research.

◆ **3 Bal'zam class** Bldr: Kaliningrad SY (In serv. 1980–83)

SSV-80 (In serv. 1983) SSV-493 (In serv. 1982) SSV-516 (In serv. 1980)

**SSV-516** U.S. Navy, 10-86

**SSV-493** U.S. Navy, 9-83

**INTELLIGENCE COLLECTORS (AGI)** *(continued)*

**D:** 5,400 tons (fl) **S:** 22 kts **Dim:** 105.5 × 15.5 × 5.8
**A:** 1/30-mm gatling AA—2/SA-N-5/8 syst. (IV × 2, 16 Grail or Gremlin missiles)
**Electron Equipt:** Radar: 2/Don-Kay
**M:** 2 diesels; 2 props; 9,000 hp **Man:** 220 tot.

REMARKS: SSV—*Sudno Svyazyy* (Communications Vessel). Built-for-the-purpose intelligence-collection-and-processing ships, wholly military in concept. The two spherical radomes probably house satellite transmitting and receiving antennas. There are numerous intercept and direction-finding antenna arrays. Equipped to refuel under way and to transfer solid cargo and personnel via constant-tension rigs on either side of the after mast. There is only a remote "Kolonka" pedestal director for the gatling gun, no radar GFCS. SSV-516 operates in the Atlantic, the other two in the Pacific.

◆ **6 Primor'ye class** Bldr: . . . SY, U.S.S.R. (In serv. . . .)

| | | |
|---|---|---|
| SSV-591 (ex-*Kavkaz*) | SSV-465 (ex-*Primor'ye*) | SSV-502 (ex-*Zakarpat'ye*) |
| SSV-590 (ex-*Krym*) | SSV-464 (ex-*Zabaykal'ye*) | SSV-501 (ex-*Zaporozh'ye*) |

**D:** 2,600 tons (3,700 fl) **S:** 13 kts **Dim:** 84.7 × 14.0 × 5.5
**Electron Equipt:** Radar: 2/Don-Kay **A:** . . ./Grail/Gremlin SAM
**M:** 2 diesels; 1 prop; 2,000 hp **Range:** 12,000/13; 18,000/12 **Man:** 120 tot.

**SSV-591**—without forward stump mast U.S. Navy, 8-84

**SSV-502**—with new "Christmas tree" intercept array mast amidships U.S. Navy, 3-86

**SSV-590**—with rounded radome forward French Navy, 8-86

**SSV-464**—with dish antenna aft U.S.D.O.D. *Soviet Military Power,* 1987

REMARKS: Although these ships resemble small passenger liners, they are in fact modified versions of *Mayakovskiy*-class stern-haul factory trawlers. All given SSV—*Sudno Svyazyy* (Communications Vessel) pendants, and names obliterated, 1979–81. Carry hand-held Grail/Gremlin SAMs. SSV-465 has had the aft king posts and booms removed; SSV-590, -591 have lost the forward stump masts, and SSV-590 has a rounded radome in place of the original angular structure forward. SSV-464 has had the aft rectangular radome replaced by a deckhouse surmounted by a parabolic dish antenna.

◆ **9 Moma class** Bldr: Stocznia Polnocna, Gdansk, Poland (In serv. 1968–74)

| | | |
|---|---|---|
| EKVATOR | SSV-472 (ex-*Il'men*) | SSV-509 (ex-*Pelorus*) |
| KIL'DIN | SSV-501 (ex-*Vega*) | SSV-512 (ex-*Arkhipelag*) |
| YUPITER | SSV-506 (ex-*Nakhodka*) | SSV-514 (ex-*Seliger*) |

**Yupiter**—with 9-m-long by 4-m-high radome aft U.S. Navy, 7-86

**SSV-514**—modernized unit with deckhouse forward, log-periodic antennas atop bridge and aft U.S. Navy, 6-86

**Ekvator**—with 3 ELINT "huts" aft, crane retained forward U.S. Navy, 2-84

**INTELLIGENCE COLLECTORS (AGI)** *(continued)*

**D:** 1,260 tons (1,540 fl) **S:** 17 kts **Dim:** 73.3 × 10.8 × 3.8
**A:** 2/SA-N-5/8 SAM systems (IV × 2, 16 Grail or Gremlin missiles) in most
**Electron Equipt:** Radar: 2/Don-2 **Range:** 8,000/11 **Man:** 80–120 tot.
**M:** 2 Zgoda-Sulzer 6TD48 diesels; 2 CP props; 3,600 hp

REMARKS: Ex-survey ships/buoy tenders. *Yupiter,* SSV-472, SSV-509, and SSV-512 have new superstructures in the area forward of the bridge and new masts. The others are much less modified, most having only a few canvas-covered antennas atop the bridge and "vans" for support equipment. SSV-472 carried a submarine EW intercept antenna atop her bridge in 1983–1986.

◆ **8 Mayak class** Bldr: . . . (In serv. 1967–70)

| | | | |
|---|---|---|---|
| ANEROYD | KHERSONES | KURSOGRAF | GS-239 |
| GIRORULEVOY (ex-GS-536) | KURS | LADOGA | GS-242 |

**Girorulevoy**—circular radome atop bridge, poop extended U.S. Navy, 1986

**Kursograf**—with two twin 14.5-mm mg atop long deckhouse in waist U.S. Navy, 8-86

**Khersones**—short poop-deck extension in waist, with SA-7 positions atop Skyfotos, 11-84

**GS-242**—submarine Stop Light intercept array atop stack French Navy, 7-86

**D:** 1,050 tons (fl) **S:** 11 kts **Dim:** 54.2 × 9.3 × 3.6
**Electron Equipt:** Radar: 1–2/Don-2 and/or Spin Trough
**M:** 1 8NVD48 diesel; 800 hp **Range:** 9,400/11 **Man:** 40 tot.

REMARKS: GS—*Gidrograficheskoye Sudno* (Hydrographic Survey Ship), an interesting euphemism. These ships vary greatly in appearance and equipment carried. Most carry hand-held Grail or Gremlin missiles launched from two railed positions fitted either at the bow and stern or atop the deckhouse amidships. *Ladoga* carried 4/14.5-mm mg (II × 2) in 1980, since removed, but added to *Kursograf.* GS-239 has a tall deckhouse at the extreme stern.

◆ **3 Nikolay Zubov class** Bldr: A. Warski SY, Szczecin, Poland (In serv. 1963–68)

SSV-503 (ex-*Khariton Laptev*)
SSV-469 (ex-*Semyen Chelyushkin*)
SSV-468 (ex-*Gavril Sarychev*)

**SSV-469** L. & L. Van Ginderen, 1-87

**SSV-468** U.S. Navy, 11-85

**D:** 2,200 tons (3,100 fl) **S:** 16.5 kts **Dim:** 90.0 × 13.0 × 4.7
**Electron Equipt:** Radar: 2/Don-2—IFF: 1/High Pole B
**M:** 2 Zgoda 8TD48 diesels; 2 props; 4,800 hp
**Range:** 11,000/14 **Man:** 80–100 tot.

REMARKS: Ex-oceanographic ships. Similar to oceanographic sisters, but have a collection of antenna arrays. SSV-468 has been extensively reconstructed: her forecastle has been extended to her stern, and an extra deck has been added to her superstructure. All have three launch positions for Grail or Gremlin missiles. SSV-469 formerly carried a Strut Curve radar. SSV-468 and 469 operate in the Pacific.

◆ **2 Pamir class** Bldr: Gävle, Sweden (In serv. 1958)

SSV-480 (ex-*Gidrograf*) SSV-477 (ex-*Peleng,* ex-*Pamir*)

### INTELLIGENCE COLLECTORS (AGI) *(continued)*

**Gidrograf (SSV-480)** French Navy, 10-82

**D:** 1,443 tons (2,300 fl) **S:** 17.5 kts **Dim:** 78.0 × 12.8 × 4.0
**Electron Equipt:** Radar: 2/Don-2
**M:** 2 M.A.N. G10V 40/60 diesels; 2 CP props; 4,200 hp
**Range:** 15,200/17.5; 21,000/12 **Man:** 120 tot.

REMARKS: Ex-rescue tugs. Both heavily modified: extra deckhouse levels, extended forecastle, numerous collection antenna arrays, etc. Their extremely long endurance makes them invaluable in the Pacific and Indian oceans. Sisters *Agatan* and *Aldan* are salvage ships. Redesignated SSV—*Sudno Svyazyy* (Communications Vessel) in 1979-80. Have three launch positions for Grail or Gremlin missiles.

◆ **4 Mirnyy class** Bldr: 61 Kommuna SY, Nikolayev (In serv. circa 1962–64)

BAKAN LOTSMAN VAL VERTIKAL

**Bakan** French Navy, 6-86

**D:** 850 tons (1,300 fl) **S:** 17.5 kts **Dim:** 63.6 × 9.5 × 4.5
**A:** 2/SA-N-5/8 SAM positions (I × 2, 16 Grail or Gremlin missiles)
**Electron Equipt:** Radar: 2/Don-2 **Man:** 60 tot.
**M:** 4 6-cyl. diesels, electric drive; 1 prop; 4,000 hp **Range:** 18,700/11

REMARKS: Ex-whalers. Differ in detail. Very low freeboard amidships. All received new deckhouse forward during 1970s. All in Black Sea Fleet, operating mainly in the Mediterranean.

◆ **15 Okean trawler class** Bldr: East Germany (In serv. 1962–67)

| | | | |
|---|---|---|---|
| ALIDADA | DEFLEKTOR | LINZA | TEODOLIT |
| AMPERMETR | EKHOLOT | LOTLIN' (GS-319) | TRAVERS |
| BAROGRAF | GIDROFON | REDUKTOR | ZOND |
| BAROMETR | KRENOMETR | REPITER | |

**D:** 700 tons (fl) **S:** 11 kts **Dim:** 50.8 × 8.9 × 3.7
**A:** *Barograf:* 4/14.5-mm mg (II × 2)—all: 2/SA-N-5/8 SAM positions (I × 2, 16 Grail or Gremlin missiles)
**Electron Equipt:** Radar: 1–2/Don-2 **M:** 1 diesel; 540 hp
**Range:** 7,900/11 **Man:** 60 tot.

REMARKS: Ex-trawlers. Appearances vary greatly, many having had their poop deck extended well forward of the bridge superstructure and their port sides plated in. Some have not been sighted in many years, and may have been discarded.

NOTE: The Keyla class cargo ship *Ritsa* may also be an intelligence collector.

**Lotlin'**—poop deck extended French Navy, 10-82

**Teodolit**—original, short-poop configuration French Navy, 9-83

### OCEANOGRAPHIC-RESEARCH SHIPS

NOTE: The only units included here are those known to be subordinate to the Soviet Navy. There are in addition nearly 300 research ships under the control of civilian agencies, primarily the Ministry of Science and the Ministry of Fisheries. Some of the civilian ships may from time to time perform research in support of military aims, but their purpose is primarily peaceful. All naval units are painted white.

◆ **18 Yug class** Bldr: Polnocny SY, Gdansk, Poland (In serv. 5-78 to 6-9-83)

| | | |
|---|---|---|
| BRIZ | MARSHAL GELOVANI | STRELETS |
| DONUZLAY | NIKOLAY MATUSEVICH | STVOR |
| GALS | PEGAS | TAYGA |
| GIDROLOG | PERSEY | VIZIR |
| GORIZONT | PLUTON | YUG |
| MANGYSHLAK | SENEZH | ZODIAK |

**D:** 2,500 tons (fl) **S:** 15.6 kts **Dim:** 82.50 (75.80 pp) × 13.50 × 3.97
**Electron Equipt:** Radar: 2/Don-2—IFF: 1/High Pole B
**M:** 2 Zgoda-Sulzer 8TD48 diesels; 2 CP props; 4,400 hp (3,600 sust.)
**Electric:** 1,920 kVA **Fuel:** 343 tons **Endurance:** 40 days
**Range:** 9,000/12 **Man:** 8 officers, 38 men, 20 scientists

REMARKS: Deck reinforcements for six 25-mm AA (II × 3). Two 100-kw electric motors for slow-speed operations; 300-hp bow-thruster. Quadrantial davit over stern ramp, with 4-ton lift. Two 5-ton booms and several oceanographic davits. Two Type 727 fiberglass-hulled survey launches. Have 3 echo-sounders, 6 laboratories. Intended to perform all forms of oceanographic research and hydrographic survey duties. *Zodiak* fitted about 1985 with large gantry at stern to handle a towed object and main deck superstructure extended.

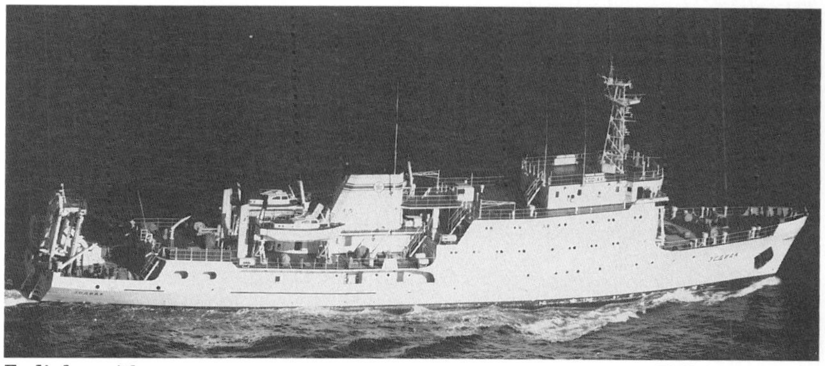

**Zodiak**—with gantry at stern U.S. Navy, 11-86

**OCEANOGRAPHIC-RESEARCH SHIPS** *(continued)*

**Vizir** U.S. Navy, 1986

◆ **6 Akademik Krylov class** Bldr: A. Warski SY, Szczecin, Poland (In serv. 1974–79)

| | | |
|---|---|---|
| Admiral Vladimirskiy | Ivan Kruzenshtern | Leonid Sobelyev |
| Akademik Krylov | Leonid Demin | Mikhail Krupskiy |

**Ivan Kruzenshtern**—blunt stern U.S. Navy, 2-86

**Admiral Vladimirskiy**—blunt stern, Post Lamp radars
L. & L. Van Ginderen, 2-83

**Mikhail Krupskiy**—cropped stern, large radome amidships U.S. Navy, 1985

**D:** 6,600 tons (9,100 fl) **S:** 20.4 kts **Dim:** 147.0 × 18.6 × 6.3
**Electron Equipt:** Radar: 3/Don-2—IFF: 1/High Pole B
**M:** 4 diesels; 2 props; 16,000 hp **Endurance:** 90 days
**Range:** 23,000/15.4 **Man:** 90 tot.

Remarks: The largest ships of their type in any navy. Equipped with helicopter hangar and flight deck, two survey launches, and twenty-six laboratories totaling 900 m$^2$. The *Leonid Demin* and *Mikhail Krupskiy* were delivered in 1978 and 1979, respectively, and, because they have pointed sterns, are about 2.5 m longer, as is *Leonid Sobelyev. Admiral Vladimirskiy* carries 2 Post Lamp gun/torpedo fire-control radars, one atop the forward superstructure and one on the foremast—both offset to starboard. *Akademik Krylov* has a small hemispherical radome before the stack, while *Mikhail Krupskiy* has a large, spherical dome in the same position.

◆ **1 Vladimir Kavrayskiy class** Bldr: Admiralty SY, Leningrad (In serv. 1973)

Vladimir Kavrayskiy

**Vladimir Kavrayskiy** 1974

**D:** 3,900 tons (fl) **S:** 15.4 kts **Dim:** 70.0 × 18.0 × 6.4
**M:** 3 Type 13D100 diesels, electric drive; 2 props; 4,800 hp
**Endurance:** 60 days **Range:** 13,900/9.4

Remarks: Greatly modified version of the *Dobrynya Nikitich* icebreaker class for arctic research. Has helicopter deck but no hangar, a survey launch, nine laboratories, totaling 180 m$^2$, one 8-ton crane, two 3-ton booms, and a hold capacity of 200 m$^3$. The *Otto Schmidt,* completed in 1979 and subordinate to the Academy of Sciences, differs in appearance but is of similar design. The civilian research icebreakers *Georgiy Sedov* and *Petr Pakhtusov,* also subordinated to the Academy of Science, are units of the *Dobrynya Nikitich* class with very few external alterations.

◆ **4 Abkhaziya class** Bldr: Mathias Thiesen Werft, Wismar, East Germany (In serv. 1971–73)

| | | | |
|---|---|---|---|
| Abkhaziya | Adzhariya | Bashkiriya | Moldaviya |

**Abkhaziya**—home-ported at Vladivostok U.S. Navy, 7-84

**Moldaviya** U.S. Navy, 2-86

**D:** 5,460 tons (7,500 fl) **S:** 21 kts **Dim:** 124.7 × 17.0 × 6.4
**Electron Equipt:** Radar: 3/Don-2
**M:** 2 M.A.N. K6Z 57/80 diesels; 2 props; 8,000 hp
**Endurance:** 60 days **Range:** 20,000/16 **Man:** 85 tot.

Remarks: Military version of the Academy of Science's *Akademik Kurchatov* class, with helicopter deck, telescoping hangar, Vee Cone communications antenna, stern-mounted A-frame lift gear, two survey launches, and twenty-seven laboratories totaling 460 m$^2$.

## OCEANOGRAPHIC-RESEARCH SHIPS *(continued)*

◆ **8 Nikolay Zubov class** Bldr: A. Warski SY, Szczecin, Poland (In serv. 1963–68)

| | |
|---|---|
| Aleksey Chirikov | Fyodor Litke |
| Andrey Vil'kitskiy | Nikolay Zubov |
| Boris Davydov | Semen Dezhnev |
| Faddey Bellingsgauzen | Vasiliy Golovnin |

**Semen Dezhnev**—survey launches deleted U.S. Navy, 7-83

**Faddey Bellingsgauzen**—late unit with large platform aft L. & L. Van Ginderen, 2-83

**Vasiliy Golovnin** G. Gyssels, 1987

**D:** 2,200 tons (3,020 fl) **S:** 16.5 kts **Dim:** 90.0 × 13.0 × 4.7
**Electron Equipt:** Radar: 2/Don-2—IFF: 1/High Pole
**M:** 2 Zgoda-Sulzer 8TD48 diesels; 2 props; 4,800 hp
**Endurance:** 60 days **Range:** 11,000/14 **Man:** 50 tot.

Remarks: Considerable variation from ship to ship. Can carry four survey launches, but usually have only two. Nine laboratories, totalling 120 m$^2$. Two 7-ton and two 5-ton booms, nine .5–1.2-ton oceanographic-equipment davits, 600 m$^3$ capacity total in two holds. The after platform, *not* for helicopters, is larger in the later ships. Three others serve as intelligence collectors.

◆ **1 Nevel'skoy class** Bldr: . . . SY, Nikolayev (In serv. 1962)

Nevel'skoy

**Nevel'skoy** 1983

**D:** 2,350 tons (fl) **S:** 17 kts **Dim:** 83.8 × 15.2 × 3.8 **Man:** 45 tot.
**Electron Equipt:** Radar: 2/Don-2 **M:** 2 diesels; 2 props; 4,000 hp
**Range:** 10,000/11

Remarks: The only naval oceanographic research ship, other than the *Vladimir Kavrayskiy,* built in the Soviet Union; apparently the prototype for the *Nikolay Zubov* design. In the Pacific Fleet.

◆ **3 Polyus class** Bldr: Neptunwerft, Rostock, East Germany (In serv. 1962–64)

Baykal Balkhash Polyus

**Balkhash** U.S. Navy, 11-86

**Polyus** U.S. Navy, 7-86

**D:** 4,560 tons (6,900 fl) **S:** 14.2 kts **Dim:** 111.6 × 14.4 × 6.3
**Electron Equipt:** Radar: 2/Don-2 (*Balkhash:* 2/Palm Frond)
**M:** 4 diesels, electric drive; 2 props; 4,000 hp
**Endurance:** 75 days **Range:** 25,000/12.3

Remarks: Seventeen laboratories, totaling 290 m$^2$. *Polyus* has less-extensive superstructure, different mast arrangement. *Balkhash* has a large oceanographic-equipment gantry at the stern and a small "hangar" for towed objects.

## HYDROGRAPHIC-SURVEY SHIPS

Note: Ships of the Finik, Moma, Biya, Kamenka, and Samara classes are used as hydrographic-survey ships and as navigation tenders, handling buoys, marking channels, etc. They set and retrieve the 2,000 buoys and 4,000 spar buoys that are taken up for the winter months. Most can carry from two to six navigation buoys. In addition, they are equipped to take basic oceanographic and meteorological samplings. The Soviet Navy's Hydrographic Service has the task not only of surveying Soviet and overseas waters, but of maintaining no less than 600 lighthouses, 150 noise beacons, and 8,000 navigation buoys.

**HYDROGRAPHIC-SURVEY SHIPS** *(continued)*

◆ **2 Vinograd class** Bldr: Rauma-Repola SY, Savonlinna, Finland

GS-525 (In serv. 12-11-85) GS-526 (In serv. 17-12-85)

**GS-525** Rauma-Repola, 1985

**D:** 450 tons (fl) **S:** 10 kts **Dim:** 32.30 (28.60 pp) × 9.60 × 2.60
**Electron Equipt:** Radar: . . .—EW: . . .
**M:** 2 Baykal 300 diesels; 2 props; 598 hp **Man:** . . .

REMARKS: Although these small ships have been listed by NATO as intelligence collectors, it is obvious from their equipment and appearance that they perform the survey mission for which they were built.

◆ **24 Finik class** Bldr: Stocznia Polnocna Gdansk, Poland (In serv. 1979–81)

| | | | | | |
|---|---|---|---|---|---|
| GS-44 | GS-87 | GS-278 | GS-301 | GS-398 | GS-402 |
| GS-47 | GS-260 | GS-280 | GS-388 | GS-399 | GS-403 |
| GS-84 | GS-270 | GS-296 | GS-392 | GS-400 | GS-404 |
| GS-86 | GS-272 | GS-297 | GS-397 | GS-401 | GS-405 |

**GS-401** 25 F., French Navy, 1984

**D:** 1,200 tons (fl) **S:** 13 kts **Dim:** 61.30 × 11.80 (10.80 wl) × 3.27
**Electron Equipt:** Radar: 2/Don-2—IFF: 1/High Pole B
**M:** 2 Cegielski-Sulzer diesels; 2 CP props; 1,920 hp (plus two 75-kw electric motors for quiet, 6-kt operations)
**Electric:** 675 kVA **Endurance:** 15 days **Range:** 3,000/13
**Man:** 5 officers, 23 men

REMARKS: GS—*Gidrograficheskoye Sudno* (Hydrographic Vessel). Intended for navigational buoy-tending and survey, for which 4 echo-sounders are fitted. Up to 3 fiberglass 3-dwt utility landing craft can be stowed on the buoy working deck, beneath the 7-ton crane. Bow-thruster of 130 kw fitted. Have hydrological, hydrographic, and cartographic facilities. Also, one built for East Germany and four for Poland (two civilian).

◆ **19 Moma class** Bldr: Stocznia Polnocna, Gdansk, Poland (In serv. 1967–74)

| | | | |
|---|---|---|---|
| Al'tayr | Artika | Kril'on | Rybachiy (ex-*Odograf*) |
| Anadyr' | Askol'd | Liman | Sever |
| Andromeda | Cheleken | Mars | Taymyr |
| Antares | El'ton | Morzhovets | Zapolar'ye |
| Antartika | Kolguev | Okean | |

**Liman** Skyfotos, 3-86

**Kolguev**—with boats disembarked; note auxiliary stack between davits U.S. Navy, 8-83

**Rybachiy**—armed unit, with deckhouse filling well deck U.S. Navy, 9-83

**D:** 1,260 tons (1,540 fl) **S:** 17 kts **Dim:** 73.3 × 10.8 × 3.8
**Electron Equipt:** Radar: 2/Don-2—IFF: 1/High Pole A
**M:** 2 Zgoda-Sulzer 6TD48 diesels; 2 CP props; 3,600 hp
**Endurance:** 35 days **Range:** 8,700/11 **Man:** 56 tot.

REMARKS: Carry one survey launch and a 7-ton crane, and have four laboratories, totaling 35 $m^2$. The *Rybachiy* (ex *Odograf*) has a deckhouse in place of the crane and may be involved in oceanographic research; the ship is armed with 4/12.7-mm mg (II × 2) forward and 2/SA-N-5 18 systems (IV × 2; 16 Grail or Gremlin missiles) aft. Sisters in Polish, Bulgarian, and Yugoslav navies. Nine more serve as intelligence collectors.

◆ **14 Biya class** Bldr: Stocznia Polnocna, Gdansk, Poland (In serv. 1972–76)

| | | | | | | |
|---|---|---|---|---|---|---|
| GS-182 | GS-193 | GS-198 | GS-204 | GS-208 | GS-214 | GS-271 |
| GS-192 | GS-194 | GS-202 | GS-206 | GS-210 | GS-269 | GS-273 |

**D:** 750 tons (fl) **S:** 13 kts **Dim:** 55.0 × 9.2 × 2.6
**Electron Equipt:** Radar: 1/Don-2 **M:** 2 diesels; 2 CP props; 1,200 hp
**Endurance:** 15 days **Range:** 4,700/11 **Man:** 25 tot.

REMARKS: GS—*Gidrograficheskoye Sudno* (Hydrographic Survey Ship). Similar to Kamenka class, but have longer superstructure and less buoy-handling space; one survey launch; one 5-ton crane. Laboratory space: 15 $m^2$. One unit transferred to Guinea-Bissau, one (GC-186) to Cuba in 1980 and one to Cape Verde in 1980.

**HYDROGRAPHIC-SURVEY SHIPS** *(continued)*

**GS-186**—under tow to Cuba; note crane at forecastle break 1980

◆ **11 Kamenka class** Bldr: Stocznia Polnocna, Gdansk, Poland (In serv. 1968–72)

| | | |
|---|---|---|
| GS-66 | GS-103 | GS-203 |
| GS-74 | GS-107 | GS-207 |
| GS-78 | GS-108 (ex-*Vernier*) | GS-211 |
| GS-82 | GS-113 (ex-*Bel'bek*) | |

**Kamenka class**—note crane in center of working deck U.S. Navy, 1985

**D:** 703 tons (fl) **S:** 13.7 kts **Dim:** 53.5 × 9.1 × 2.6
**Electron Equipt:** Radar: 1/Don-2 **M:** 2 diesels; 2 props; 2 CP props; 1,765 hp
**Range:** 4,000/10 **Man:** 40 tot.

Remarks: GS—*Gidrograficheskoye Sudno* (Hydrographic Survey Ship). Similar to Biya class, but have more facilities for stowing and handling buoys. No survey launch. One 5-ton crane. One sister in the East German Navy.

◆ **15 Samara class** Bldr: Stocznia Polnocnia, Gdansk, Poland (In serv. 1962–64)

| | | | |
|---|---|---|---|
| Azimut | Gorizont | Rumb (GS-118) | Vostok |
| Deviator | Gradus | Tropik | GS-275 (ex-*Yug*) |
| Gigrometr | Kompas | Tura (ex-*Globus*) | Zenit |
| Glubometr | Pamyat' Merkuriya | Vaygach | |

**D:** 1,050 tons (1,276 fl) **S:** 15.5 kts **Dim:** 590.0 × 10.4 × 3.8
**Electron Equipt:** Radar: 2/Don-2
**M:** 2 Zgoda 5TD48 diesels; 2 CP props; 3,000 hp **Endurance:** 25 days
**Range:** 6,200/11 **Man:** 45 tot. (*Tura:* 140 tot.)

Remarks: Have one survey launch and 15 m$^2$ of laboratory space. The *Tura* (ex-*Globus*) had her forecastle extended to her superstructure in 1978 and her 7-ton crane removed; able to accommodate 120 personnel, she is used for training. *Deviator* served briefly as an intelligence collector. *Vaygach* has a large deckhouse surrounding the base of the buoy crane.

Note: Due to age and lack of recent sightings, the four survey ships of the Telnovsk class have been deleted: *Aytodor, Sirena, Sviyaga,* and *Ulyana Gromova.*

**Gigrometr** U.S. Navy, 9-86

**Kompas** French Navy, 3-84

**Tura**—buoy-handling crane removed, forecastle extended 1978

◆ **3 Melitopol class** Bldr: U.S.S.R. (In serv. 1952–55)

Mayak Niviler Prizma

**D:** 1,200 tons (fl) **S:** 11.3 kts **Dim:** 57.6 × 9.0 × 4.3 **Range:** 2,500/10.5
**Electron Equipt:** Radar: 1/Don **M:** 1 Type 6DR30/40 diesel; 600 hp

Remarks: Converted small, two-hatch cargo ships with few modifications; 673 grt/776 dwt. Carry one survey launch on deck.

◆ **several GPB-480-class inshore-survey craft** Bldr: U.S.S.R. (In serv. 1960s)

GPB-480, GPB-767, etc.

**GPB-767**—GPB-480 class French Navy, 8-79

**D:** 120 tons (fl) **S:** 12 kts **Dim:** 29.0 × 5.0 × 1.7
**Electron Equipt:** Radar: 1/Spin Trough **M:** 1 diesel; 450 hp
**Endurance:** 10 days **Range:** 1,600/10 **Man:** 15 tot.

Remarks: GPB—*Gidrograficheskoye Pribezhnyy Bot* (Coastal Hydrographic Survey Boat). VM on the diving-tender version stands for *Vodolaznyy Morskoy* (Seagoing Diving Tender). Same hull and propulsion as the Nyryat-I-class diving tenders. The charthouse/laboratory is 6 m$^2$, and there are two 1.5-ton derricks. The smaller GPB-710 class is carried aboard the larger survey and oceanographic ships listed above.
**D:** 7 tons (fl) **S:** 10 kts for 150 nautical miles **Dim:** 11.0 × 3.0 × 0.7.

**MISSILE-RANGE INSTRUMENTATION SHIPS**

◆ **1 nuclear-powered** Bldr: Baltic SY, Leningrad

| | Laid down | L | In serv. |
|---|---|---|---|
| SSV-33 | 5-81 | 5-83 | 1987 |

## MISSILE-RANGE INSTRUMENTATION SHIPS *(continued)*

**D:** 36,000 tons (fl) **S:** 30 kts **Dim:** 265.0 × 30.0 × 9.0
**A:** 2/76.2-mm DP (I × 2)—4/30-mm gatling AA (I × 4)
**Electron Equipt:** . . .
**M:** CONAS: 2 pressurized-water reactors; 2 props; 150,000 hp

REMARKS: Believed to be either a range-instrumentation ship or space event support ship or, as with *Marshal Nedelin,* both; also usable as a command ship. See addenda.

◆ **1 Marshal Nedelin class** Bldr: United Admiralty SY, Leningrad

MARSHAL NEDELIN (In serv. 1984)

**Marshal Nedelin**—note 2 covered theodolite tracking camera positions forward French Navy, 1985

**Marshal Nedelin** U.S. Navy, 1986

**D:** 24,000 tons (fl) **S:** 20 kts **Dim:** 213.0 × 27.1 × 7.7
**Electron Equipt:** Radar: 3/Palm Frond, 1/Strut Pair, 1/Fly Screen (helo control), 1/End Tray (balloon tracking)
IFF: 2/Salt Pot, 1/High Pole transponders
TACAN: 2/Round House
**M:** 2 gas turbines; 2 props; 54,000 hp **Range:** . . . **Man:** 200 tot.

REMARKS: Possibly intended to begin replacement of the aged *Desna-* and *Sibir'*-class range-tracking ships, but equipped also to serve in a space-tracking and communications role. Tracking antennas include 1/Quad Leaf, 3/Quad Wedge, 4/Quad Rods, and 6/telemetry reception arrays. A large Ship Globe radome conceals a satellite communications antenna. Twin hangars accommodate 2/Ka-27 Helix utility helicopters. Hull has a bulbous bow form. Foundations for 6/30-mm gatling AA and 3/Bass Tilt radar directors are present. Has a swimming pool just abaft the stack. Operates in the Pacific Fleet. A second unit will probably be built.

◆ **2 Desna class** Bldr: Warnow Werft, Warnemünde (In serv. 1963)

CHAZHMA (ex-*Dangera*) CHUMIKAN (ex-*Dolgeschtchel'ye*)

**Chumikan** U.S. Navy, 1980

**D:** 14,065 tons (fl) **S:** 15 kts **Dim:** 139.9 × 18.0 × 7.9
**Electron Equipt:** Radar: 2/Don-2, 1/Head Net-B, 1/Ship Globe (tracking)
EW: 2/Watch Dog
**M:** 1 M.A.N. diesel; 1 prop; 5,400 hp **Range:** 9,000/13 **Man:** 240 tot.

REMARKS: Heavily modified cargo ships. Tracking radar in large dome atop the bridge, with three tracking directors mounted forward. Hormone helicopter with hangar aft. Vee Cone communications antennas atop the stack. Based in the Pacific. Only ships with Head Net-B radar (both reflectors in the same plane).

◆ **4 Sibir' class** Bldr: A. Warski SY, Szczecin, Poland (In serv. 1958)

CHUKOTKA SAKHALIN SIBIR' SPASSK (ex-*Suchan*)

**Chukotka**—note different superstructure, Big Net radar U.S. Navy, 1986

**Sibir'**—with Head Net-C, Hormone-C helo on deck U.S. Navy, 1986

**D:** 7,800 tons (fl) **S:** 12 kts **Dim:** 108.2 × 14.6 × 7.2
**Electron Equipt:** Radar: 2/Don-2, 1/Head Net-C (*Chukotka:* Big Net): two tracking sets
**M:** triple-expansion; 1 prop; 2,300 hp **Range:** 11,800/12
**Man:** 240 tot. **Boilers:** 2

REMARKS: Converted (circa 1960) Donbass-class cargo ships. Originally, only *Chukotka* was flush-decked; the others had a well deck forward. Now all are flush-decked. All carry one Hormone-C helicopter, but have no hangar. All are in the Pacific Fleet. All now carry two tracking radars forward, plus two Quad Rods telemetry trackers; *Sakhalin, Spassk,* and *Chukotka* also have an optical tracking device on the forecastle. All carry a swimming pool to starboard, forward.

## SHIP SIGNATURE-MEASUREMENT SHIPS

◆ **8 or more Onega class** Bldr: . . . (In serv. 1973–. . .)

GKS-52 GKS-224 SFP-95 SFP-340
GKS-83 GKS-286 SFP-283 SFP-511

**GKS-52**

**SFP-511** M.O.D., Bonn, 5-87

## SHIP SIGNATURE-MEASUREMENT SHIPS *(continued)*

**SFP-340** U.S. Navy, 1986

**D:** 1,925 tons (fl) **S:** 16 kts **Dim:** 81.0 × 11.0 × 4.2
**Electron Equipt:** Radar: 1/Don-2
**M:** 2 diesels; 1 or 2 props; 8,000 hp **Man:** 120 tot.

REMARKS: GKS—*Gidroakusticheskoye Kontrol'noye Sudno* (Hydroacoustic Monitoring Ship)—indicates that these ships are successors to the T-43-class noise-monitoring ships. SFP—*Sudno Fizicheskiy Poley* (Physical Fields Measuring Vessel)—indicates different mission and sensors. SFP-ships have the helicopter platform farther forward, abutting the stack and have lattice vice pylon masts.

◆ **17 Modified T-43 class** Bldr: Various (In serv. mid-1950s)

| | | | | | |
|---|---|---|---|---|---|
| GKS-11 | GKS-14 | GKS-17 | GKS-20 | GKS-23 | GKS-42 |
| GKS-12 | GKS-15 | GKS-18 | GKS-21 | GKS-24 | GKS-45 |
| GKS-13 | GKS-16 | GKS-19 | GKS-22 | GKS-26 | |

**GKS-15**

**D:** 500 tons (570 fl) **S:** 14 kts **Dim:** 58.0 × 8.6 × 2.3
**Electron Equipt:** Radar: 1/Neptune or Spin Trough
IFF: 1/High Pole
**M:** 2 Type 9D diesels; 2 props; 2,200 hp **Man:** 77 tot.

REMARKS: GKS—*Gidroakusticheskoye Kontrol'noye Sudno* (Hydroacoustic Monitoring Ship)—indicates that these ships measure the radiated noise of other ships, including submarines, by laying hydrophone arrays via the numerous small davits they carry aft. One 37-mm AA gun can be installed on the forecastle. At least two (GKS-25, -46) have been stricken.

## DEGAUSSING/DEPERMING SHIPS

◆ **4 (+ . . .) Bereza class** Bldr: . . . SY, Poland (In serv. 1985– . . .)

SR-28 SR-479 SR-541 SR-548

**D:** 2,700 tons (fl) **S:** 15 kts **Dim:** 84.00 (75.80 pp) × 13.50 × 4.0
**Electron Equipt:** Radar: 1/Kivach—IFF: 1/High Pole B
**M:** 2 Zgoda-Sulzer 8TD48 diesels; 2 CP props; 4,400 hp (3,600 sust.)
**Electric:** . . . **Range:** . . . **Man:** 60 tot.

REMARKS: SR—*Sudno Razmagnichivanya* (Deperming Vessel). Design appears to be based on that of the *Yug*-class oceanographic ship, with the forecastle raised one deck higher. A large crane is fitted aft to handle deperming cables.

**SR-541** French Navy, 11-86

**SR-548** G. Koop, 1986

◆ **9 (+ . . .) Pelym class** Bldr: . . . (In serv. 1971– . . .)

SR-191 SR-203 SR-222 SR-241 SR-407 SR-409 3 others

**SR-191**—late unit with tripod aft 9-83

**SR-222**—early unit J.M.S.D.F., 6-85

**D:** 1,300 tons (fl) **S:** 16 kts **Dim:** 65.5 × 11.6 × 3.4
**Electron Equipt:** Radar: 1/Don-2 **M:** 2 diesels; 2 props; . . . hp
**Range:** 4,500/12 **Man:** 40 tot.

## DEGAUSSING/DEPERMING SHIPS *(continued)*

Remarks: Numbers in the SR—*Sudno Razmagnichivanya* (Deperming Vessel) series. Apparently intended to replace the aged Sekstan and Korall classes. One transferred to Cuba. Late units have a tripod mast aft to support radio antenna wires; early ships had an aerial spreader on the stack.

Note: The remaining Sekstan- and Korall-class deperming ships are believed to have been replaced by new Pelym- and Bereza-class units.

## ICEBREAKERS

Note: The Soviet Union has far and away the largest and most powerful icebreaker fleet in the world. Its civilian component includes the atomic-powered *Arktika* class, the most powerful of all. The two types, patrol and support, that the navy operates are both based on the same civilian design and are among the very few conventionally driven icebreakers in Soviet service to be designed and built in the U.S.S.R. All other Soviet icebreakers now in service were built in Finland.

◆ **2 Ivan Susanin-class support icebreakers** Bldr: Admiralty SY, Leningrad

Ivan Susanin (In serv. 1974) Ruslan (In serv. 1981)

**Ivan Susanin** 1983

**D:** 3,400 tons (fl) **S:** 14.5 kts **Dim:** 70.0 (62.0 pp) × 18.3 × 6.5
**Electron Equipt:** Radar: 2/Don-Kay—IFF: 1/High Pole B
**M:** 3 Type 13D100 diesels, electric drive; 2 props; 5,400 hp **Electric:** 1,000 kw
**Fuel:** 550 tons **Range:** 5,500/12.5; 13,000/9.4 **Man:** 140 tot.

Remarks: Based on the *Dobrynya Nikitich* and *Vladimir Kavrayskiy* design. Sisters *Aysberg, Dunay, Imeni XXV Syezda K.P.S.S.,* and *Imeni XXVI Syezda K.P.S.S.* are armed and are operated by the KGB Maritime Border Guard as PSKR—*Pogranichnyy Storozhevoy Korabl'* (Border Patrol Ship). Helicopter deck aft, but no hangar. Both had their guns and Owl Screech and Strut Curve radars removed, were repainted black and white, and are operated as naval icebreakers.

◆ **7 Dobrynya Nikitich-class support icebreakers** Bldr: Admiralty SY, Leningrad (In serv. 1959–74)

| | | | |
|---|---|---|---|
| Buran | Il'ya Muromets | Purga | Vyuga |
| Dobrynya Nikitich | Peresvet | Sadko | |

**Sadko** U.S. Navy, 9-85

**D:** 2,940 tons (fl) **S:** 14.5 kts **Dim:** 67.7 × 18.3 × 6.1
**Electron Equipt:** Radar: 1–2/Don-2—IFF: 1/High Pole
**M:** 3 13D100 diesels, electric drive; 3 props (1 fwd); 5,400 hp
**Range:** 5,500/12; 13,000/9.4 **Man:** 80 tot.

Remarks: More than twenty of this class were built, the remainder being civilian. *Peresvet, Purga, Sadko,* and *Vyuga* were armed with 2/57-mm AA (II × 1) and 2/25-mm AA (II × 1), now removed. Resemble the *Ivan Susanin* class, but have much less superstructure and an open fantail rigged for ocean towing. Later units do not have a bow propeller but have the same horsepower. The name *Purga* is also carried by a KGB Maritime Border Guard patrol icebreaker.

## TRAINING SHIPS

◆ **3 Smol'nyy class** Bldr: A. Warski SY, Szczecin, Poland (In serv. 1976–78)

Khasan Perekop Smol'nyy

**Smol'nyy** Skyfotos, 8-86

**Perekop** Skyfotos, 7-86

**D:** 8,500 tons (fl) **S:** 20 kts **Dim:** 138.0 × 18.0 × 6.2
**A:** 4/76.2-mm DP (II × 2)—4/30-mm AA (II × 2)—RBU-2500 ASW RL (XII × 2)
**Electron Equipt:** Radar: 1/Don-Kay, 2/Don-2, 1/Spin Trough, 1/Head Net-C, 1/Owl Screech, 1/Drum Tilt
Sonar: MF, hull-mounted
EW: 2/Watch Dog—IFF: 1/Salt Pot
**M:** 4 diesels; 2 props; 16,000 hp
**Range:** 12,000/15 **Man:** 210 crew + 270 cadets

Remarks: Built to relieve the *Sverdlov*-class cruisers that were formerly used for cadet training. Carry six rowboats aft for exercising the cadets. Similar navigational training facilities to the Ugra-class training ships.

◆ **2 Ugra class** Bldr: Nikolayev (In serv. 1970–71)

Borodino Gangut

**Gangut** French Navy, 1982

## TRAINING SHIPS *(continued)*

**D:** 6,900 tons (9,650 fl) **S:** 17 kts **Dim:** 145.0 × 17.7 × 6.4
**A:** 8/57-mm AA (II × 4)
**Electron Equipt:** Radar: 4/Don-2, 1/Strut Curve, 2/Muff Cob—Sonar: . . .
EW: 4/Watch Dog—IFF: 1/High Pole B
**M:** 4 diesels; 2 props; 8,000 hp
**Range:** 21,000/10 **Man:** 300 crew + 400 cadets

Remarks: Soviet type designation: *Uchebnoye Sudo* (Training Ship). Similar to the submarine-tender version, but have accommodations and training facilities in place of workshops, magazines, storerooms, etc. Enlarged after deckhouse incorporates navigation-training space, including numerous duplicate navigator's positions. No helicopter facilities.

◆ **2 Modified Wodnik class** Bldr: Poland (In serv. 1977)

Oka Luga

**Oka** 1977

**D:** 1,500 tons (1,800 fl) **S:** 15 kts **Dim:** 72.0 × 12.0 × 4.0
**Electron Equipt:** Radar: 3/Don-2
**M:** 2 Zgoda-Sulzer 6TD48 diesels; 2 CP props; 3,600 hp
**Range:** 7,500/11 **Man:** 58 men + 90 cadets

Remarks: Used for navigation training. Similar to Polish and East German units of the Wodnik class, but have slightly larger superstructures, pilothouse one deck higher, and are not armed. Based on the Moma design. Both in Baltic Fleet.

◆ **2 or more Mayak class** Bldr: . . . (In serv. 1967–1974)

**Mayak-class ASW training ship** U.S. Navy, 6-86

**D:** 1,050 tons (fl) **S:** 11 kts **Dim:** 54.2 (50.4 pp) × 9.3 × 3.6
**A:** 2/25-mm AA (II × 1)—4/RBU-1200 ASW RL (V × 4)—4/400-mm ASW TT (fixed)—2/d.c. racks (6 d.c. each)
**Electron Equipt:** Radar: 1/Spin Trough—Sonar: HF, hull mounted
**M:** 1 Karl Liebnecht 8NVD48 diesel; 1 prop; 800 hp
**Range:** 9,400/11 **Man:** 60 tot., including students

Remarks: Late-production Mayak hull with basic ASW armament and sensors, apparently converted to provide basic ASW orientation or coastal ASW flotilla proficiency training. ASW RL mounted on forecastle, torpedo tubes in the waist area, depth-charge racks at the stern. The fish-hold area is used for accommodations. Due to low speed, would have little wartime utility.

## YACHT

◆ **1 ex-German** Bldr: H. Stülcken Sohn, Hamburg

| | Laid down | L | In serv. |
|---|---|---|---|
| Angara (ex-*Hela*) | 1937 | 28-12-39 | 16-10-40 |

**D:** 2,113 tons (2,520 fl) **S:** 21 kts (19.3 sust.)
**Dim:** 99.8 (92.5 wl) × 12.3 × 4.05 max.
**Electron Equipt:** Radar: . . .
**M:** 4 M.A.N. Type W9Vu 40/46 diesels; 2 props; 8,360 hp
**Range:** 2,000/15 **Fuel:** 224 tons **Man:** 224 tot.

Remarks: Built as a fleet tender (i.e., yacht) for the German Navy; acquired 1946 as reparations by the U.S.S.R. Refitted in Greece 1983. Little change from original appearance. Used as yacht for C-in-C. Soviet Fleet and for commander, Black Sea Fleet.

Note: Each fleet commander also has a high-speed yacht of about 80-ton displacement.

## TRIALS SHIPS AND CRAFT

◆ **1 or more Al'pinist class** Bldr: Yaroslavl SY (In serv. . . .)

OS-104

**OS-104** J.M.S.D.F., 1985

**D:** 1,200 tons (fl) **S:** 13 kts **Dim:** 53.7 (46.2 pp) × 10.5 × 4.3
**Electron Equipt:** Radar: 1/Don-2, 1/. . . nav.
**M:** 1 Type 8NVD48-2U diesel; 1 CP prop; 1,320 hp
**Fuel:** 162 tons **Electric:** 450 kw **Range:** 7,600/13 **Man:** . . .

Remarks: Modification of a 322-dwt stern-haul trawler. Gallows crane at stern resembles those used to handle submersible decompression chambers on T-58-class submarine-rescue ships. Forecastle has been extended aft and supports 2-level deckhouse on starboard side. OS-104 is in the Pacific Fleet.

◆ **5 Potok class** Bldr: . . . (In serv. 1978–. . .)

OS-100 OS-138 OS-145 OS-225 OS-. . .

**D:** 750 tons (860 fl) **S:** 17 kts **Dim:** 71.0 × 9.1 × 2.5
**A:** 1/533-mm TT, 1/400-mm TT **Electron Equipt:** Radar: 1/Don-2
**M:** 2 diesels; 2 props; 4,000 hp **Range:** 5,000/12 **Man:** 40 tot.

Remarks: OS—*Opitnoye Sudno* (Experimental Vessel). The design closely resembles the T-58 class, but the forecastle extends well aft. The trainable torpedo tubes are on the bow. A large crane aft is presumably used for retrieval. These ships are probably replacements for modified T-43-class minesweepers, which had been used in torpedo trials since the 1950s.

**OS-225**

**TRIALS SHIPS AND CRAFT** *(continued)*

**Potok class**—with missile launcher on deckhouse at stern 1986

◆ **1 or 2 Daldyn class**

**Daldyn class** 1976

**D:** 360 tons (fl) **S:** 9 kts **Dim:** 31.7 × 7.2 × 2.8
**Electron Equipt:** Radar: 1/Spin Trough
**M:** 1 Type 8NVD 36U diesel; 1 prop; 305 hp **Man:** 15 tot.

Remarks: Modified Kareliya-class purse-seiner, possibly for use in mine countermeasures trials.

◆ **1 Polnocny-B-class former landing ship** Bldr: Stocznia Polnocna, Gdansk, Poland (In serv. 1961–64)

OS-246

**OS-246** U.S. Navy, 1985

**D:** 800 tons (fl) **S:** 19 kts **Dim:** 74.0 × 8.6 × 1.9 **A:** none
**Electron Equipt:** Radar: 1/Don-2
IFF: 1/High Pole A
**M:** 2 diesels; 2 props; 5,000 hp **Range:** 900/18; 1,500/14 **Man:** 60 tot.

Remarks: Converted for unidentified trials purposes. King post and boom fitted to port.

◆ **several T-43-class former minesweepers**

**T-43-class trials tender** 1976

Remarks: Data as for minesweeper version. Some are disarmed former long-hulled minesweepers, while four or more 58-m versions were built as torpedo trials ships.

Note: There are probably a number of additional ships of various classes with OS—*Opitnoye Sudno* (Experimental Vessel)—pendants, either built for the purpose or former combatants or auxiliaries adapted for specific trials duties. The largest was OS-24, the former heavy cruiser *Voroshilov,* since scrapped.

**TARGET SERVICE CRAFT**

◆ **9 Osa-class target-control boats**

**Osa target controller** 1974

Remarks: Have Osa hull and propulsion. Used to operate craft shown below by remote control. Carry Square Tie and a High Pole B IFF transponder. Communications antennas have been enhanced to provide for radio-control.

◆ **8 Modified Osa-class missile targets**

Remarks: KTs—*Kontrol'naya Tsel'* (Controlled Target). Have Osa hull and propulsion. Crew departs when ship is in operation. Equipped with radar corner reflectors to strengthen target and two heat-generator chimneys to attract infrared homing missiles.

◆ **14 or more Shelon-class torpedo retrievers** Bldr: . . . (In serv. 1978– . . .)

**D:** 270 tons (fl) **S:** 24 kts **Dim:** 41.0 × 6.0 × . . .
**Electron Equipt:** Radar: 1/Spin Trough
Sonar: 1/helicopter dipping-type
IFF: 1/High Pole B
**M:** 2 M504 diesels; 2 props; 10,000 hp **Man:** 40 tot.

Remarks: High-speed hull with a covered torpedo-recovery ramp aft. May be replacing the Poluchat-I class.

A new variant of the Shelon-class torpedo-retriever design was sighted during 1983 while under tow from the Black Sea to Vladivostok. Unlike earlier units it does not have a slope to the weapons recovery area of the after portion of the deckhouse; it has no hatch in the deckhouse roof and no recovery hatch through

TARGET SERVICE CRAFT *(continued)*

the transom stern. The function of the craft, which has a crew of about 30, is unknown.

**KTs-897, Osa target**—with nets strung between the masts 8-80

**Shelon class** L. & L. Van Ginderen, 6-85

**Shelon variant**—no dipping sonar or recovery ramp 1983

◆ **up to 40 Poluchat-I-class torpedo-retrievers**

**Poluchat-I-class torpedo retriever** 1982

**D:** 90 tons (fl) **S:** 18 kts **Dim:** 29.6 × 6.1 × 1.9
**A:** 2/14.5-mm AA (II × 1) in some
**Electron Equipt:** Radar: 1/Spin Trough—IFF: 1/High Pole A
**M:** 2 M50 diesels; 2 props; 2,400 hp **Range:** 450/17; 900/10 **Man:** 20 tot.

REMARKS: Carry numbers in the TL—*Torpedolov* (Torpedo-Retriever) series. Built in the 1950s. Recovery ramp aft. Some configured as patrol boats. Many exported abroad. See photo in section on Patrol Craft.

TARGET BARGES

**Soviet Navy built-for-the-purpose 107-m target barge**—with numerous corner reflectors to enhance radar return U.S. Navy, 7-84

**107-m target barge**—with two heat-generator arrays to attract IR homing missiles G. Koop, 1985

**Soviet Navy 64-meter catamaran gunnery target barge** G. Koop, 1985

DIVING TENDERS

◆ **8 or more Yelva class** (In serv. 1973–. . .)

**VM-268, Yelva class** G. Koop, 1985

**D:** 295 tons (fl) **S:** 12.4 kts **Dim:** 40.9 (37.0 pp) × 8.0 × 2.1
**Electron Equipt:** Radar: 1/Spin Trough **Electric:** 200 kw
**M:** 2 Type 3D12A diesels; 2 props; 600 hp **Man:** 30 tot.

**DIVING TENDERS** *(continued)*

REMARKS: Can support 7 divers at once to 60 m. Have a compression chamber; some (but not all) also have a submersible decompression chamber. Replaced T-43 minesweepers built for the role. Several exported. Soviet class name: *Krab-M.*

◆ **several Nyryat-1 class** (In serv. late 1950s–mid 1960s)

**D:** 120 tons (fl) **S:** 12 kts **Dim:** 29.0 × 5.0 × 1.7
**Electron Equipt:** Radar: 1/Spin Trough
**M:** 1 diesel; 1 prop; 450 hp **Endurance:** 10 days
**Range:** 1,600/10 **Man:** 15 tot.

REMARKS: Carry VM—*Vodolaznyy Morskoy* (Seagoing Diving Tender)—pendants. Same hull used for GPB-480-class inshore survey craft. Many exported.

◆ **several Nyryat-2 class** (In serv. 1950s)

**PO-2 class**—Nyryat-2 class similar 1975

**D:** 50 tons (fl) **S:** 9 kts **Dim:** 21.0 × 4.5 × . . .
**Electron Equipt:** Radar: 1/Spin Trough
**M:** 1 Type 3D6 diesel; 1 prop; 150 hp **Man:** 10 tot.

REMARKS: Uses same hull as PO-2-class utility launch; distinguishable by bulwarks to hull at bow and stern. Hundreds of PO-2 hulls were built; many were exported.

**FIREBOATS**

◆ . . . **PZhK-415-class fireboats** Bldr: . . . U.S.S.R. (In serv. 1984–. . .)

**D:** 320 tons (fl) **S:** 12.5 kts **Dim:** 36.53 × 7.80 × 2.20
**M:** 2 Type ZKD 12N-520 diesels; 2 CP props; 1,040 hp
**Range:** 450/12.5 **Electric:** 400 kw **Man:** 20 tot.

REMARKS: Four firefighting water monitors, two with 220 $m^3$/hr capacity and two of 500 $m^3$/hr, driven by two 750 $m^3$/hr diesel-powered pumps. Foam and Freon extinguishing systems. Water curtain to protect boat. Can also be used for towing.

◆ . . . **Pozharney-I-class fireboats** (In serv. 1950s)

**D:** 180 tons (fl) **S:** 17 kts **Dim:** 35.0 × 6.2 × 2.0
**M:** 2 Type M50-F1 diesels; 2 props; 1,800 hp

**HARBOR TUGS**

◆ . . . **Stividor class** Bldr: . . .

**RB-325** U.S. Navy, 2-87

**D:** 340 tons (fl) **S:** 12 kts **Dim:** 30.0 × 8.3 × 3.2
**M:** 2 diesels; 2 Kort-nozzle props; 1,200 hp

REMARKS: Successor design to *Prometey* class; probably also built at Petrozavod SY, Leningrad. Has 2 firefighting monitors.

◆ . . . **Prometey-class large harbor tugs** Bldr: Petrozavod SY, Leningrad

**Prometey-class RB-202** 1980

**D:** 319 tons (fl) **S:** 12 kts **Dim:** 29.8 (28.2 pp) × 8.3 × 3.2
**M:** 2 Type 6D30/50-4 diesels; 2 Kort-nozzle props; 1,200 hp
**Electron Equipt:** Radar: 1/Spin Trough
**Electric:** 50 kw **Range:** 1,800/12 **Fuel:** 30 tons **Man:** 3–5 tot.

REMARKS: Built 1970s–80s at Leningrad and Gorokhovets SY; some exported. Also in civil use. Have 14-ton bollard pull, ice-strengthened hull. Over 100 built since 1971.

◆ **26 Sidehole-II-class harbor tugs** Bldr: Petrozavod SY, Leningrad (In serv. 1970s)

**D:** 197 tons (fl) **S:** 10 kts **Dim:** 24.2 × 7.0 × 3.4
**Electron Equipt:** Radar: 1/Spin Trough
**M:** 2 Type 6 CHN25/34 diesels; 2 vertical cycloidal props; 900 hp

REMARKS: Soviet class name: *Peredovik.* Also in civil use. Bollard pull: 10.5 tons. Naval units have RB—*Rednyy Buksir* (Roadstead Tug) pendants.

◆ **30 Sidehole-I-class harbor tugs** (In serv. 1960s)

**D:** 183 tons (fl) **S:** 9 kts **Dim:** 24.4 × 7.0 × 3.3
**Electron Equipt:** Radar: 1/Spin Trough
**M:** 2 Type 6 CH25/34 diesels; 2 vertical cycloidal props; 600 hp

◆ . . . **Tugur-class harbor tugs** Bldr: Finland (In serv. 1950s)

**D:** 300 tons (fl) **S:** 12 kts **Dim:** 30.7 × 7.7 × 2.3
**M:** 1 set reciprocating steam; 1 prop; 500 hp **Boilers:** 2

REMARKS: Originally considered to be seagoing tugs; have MB pendants. Coal-fueled. 214 built.

**FUEL-OIL LIGHTERS**

◆ . . . **Toplivo-2 class** Bldr: U.S.S.R. and Egypt (In serv. 1958–1975)

**D:** 466 tons (1,180 tons fl) **S:** 10 kts **Dim:** 54.26 (49.40 pp) × 7.40 × 3.10
**Electron Equipt:** Radar: 1/Spin Trough
**M:** 1 Russkiy Dizel 6 DR30/50-5-2 diesel; 1 prop; 600 hp
**Electric:** 250 kw **Fuel:** 19 tons **Range:** 1,500/10 **Man:** 24 tot.

REMARKS: 308 grt/508 dwt. Four cargo tanks, totaling 606 $m^3$. Built in several versions including fuel-oil lighter, water lighter, and diesel-fuel lighter. Final series built at Alexandria, Egypt, with deliveries terminated by Soviet expulsion. Fully seagoing if required.

◆ . . . **Toplivo-3 class** (In serv. 1950s)

**D:** 1,300 tons (fl) **S:** 9 kts **Dim:** 53.0 × 10.0 × 3.0
**M:** 1 diesel; 1 prop; 300 hp

REMARKS: Low freeboard, low superstructure harbor craft. There are probably a number of the smaller (450-ton fl) Toplivo-1-class harbor fuel lighters remaining also.

**ACCOMMODATIONS BARGES**

◆ . . . **Bolva series** Bldr: Valmet Oy, Helsinki, Finland

**Myass**—Bolva-III class Valmet, 1978

## ACCOMMODATIONS BARGES *(continued)*

**D:** 6,500 tons (fl) **Dim:** 110.9 × 13.8 × 2.8 **Man:** 374–394 total berthing

REMARKS: First series of 8 Bolva-I built 1960–63, second series of 21 Bolva-II built 1963–72, with hangar-like auditorium built atop superstructure aft. Bolva-III built 1971–. . . , with 34 completed to date, 3 more ordered 1983. Many went to civilian service.

◆ . . . **Vyn-class** (In serv. 1960s)

**D:** 3,000 tons (fl) **Dim:** 92.0 × 13.4 × 4.6 **Man:** approx. 200

REMARKS: Converted from cargo barges built in Finland in the late 1940s–early 1950s. One was based in Somalia during the mid-1970s. Apparently support submarines, as there is a torpedo-loading hatch. Pendant numbers in the PKZ—*Plavuchiya Kazarma* (Floating Barracks) series.

## MISCELLANEOUS SERVICE CRAFT

◆ **1 (+ . . .) nuclear support barge** Bldr: Rauma-Repola, Savonlinna, Finland

ROSTA-1 (In serv. 9-86)

**D:** 1,700 tons (fl) **Dim:** 63.00 × 12.00 × 2.30

REMARKS: Launched 21-3-86. Intended to provide radiation hazard disposal, decontamination, laboratory services, and refit assistance to nuclear-powered ships at Murmansk. There are large numbers of other classes of service barges.

◆ **1 historical relic, former armored cruiser**

| | Bldr | Laid down | L | In serv. |
|---|---|---|---|---|
| AVRORA | New Admiralty SY, Petrograd | 6-97 | 5-00 | 1903 |

**Avrora** C.P. Lemieux

**D:** 6,732 tons normal (7,271 fl) **S:** 19 kts
**Dim:** 126.83 (123.47 wl) × 16.63 × 7.30 max.
**A:** 14/130-mm low-angle (I × 14)—5/45-mm AA (I × 5)
**M:** 3 sets vertical triple-expansion; 3 props; 13,000 ihp
**Boilers:** 20 Belleville-Dolgolenko
**Range:** 1,200/18; 1,778/10 **Fuel:** 800 tons coal (732 normal)
**Electric:** 3 generators **Man:** 129 officers, 318 men

REMARKS: Famous as the ship that fired the signal starting the Bolshevik Revolution, on 25-10-17. Used for training between World Wars I and II; damaged during WWII. A museum since 1948, with over 19 million visitors to date. Underwent massive restoration at Zhdanov SY, Leningrad, essentially receiving a new hull 32-mm plating intended to last for several centuries; refloated early 1987 and rededicated 25-10-87. Data above pertain to the ship in 1917.

## CIVILIAN SPACE-EVENT SUPPORT SHIPS

NOTE: The ships listed below are subordinated to the Academy of Sciences and are primarily intended to provide communications relay services with manned satellites. The large satellite support/tracking ship *Marshal Nedelin,* completed 1983, is a naval unit. The eight naval-subordinated *Vytegrales*-class ships are also used in space-event work, as have been several naval Moma- and Samara-class survey ship/buoy tenders.

◆ **4 Kosmonavt Pavel Belyayev class** Bldr: Zhdanov SY, Leningrad

| | In serv. | Conv. |
|---|---|---|
| KOSMONAVT GEORGIY DOBROVOLSKIY (ex-*Semyon Kosinov*) | 1968 | 1978 |
| KOSMONAVT PAVEL BELYAYEV (ex-*Vytegrales*) | 1963 | 1977 |
| KOSMONAVT VIKTOR PATSEYEV (ex-*Nazar Gubin*) | 1968 | 1978 |
| KOSMONAVT VLADILAV VOLKOV (ex-*Yeniseiles*) | 1964 | 1977 |

**D:** 9,000 tons (fl) **S:** 16 kts **Dim:** 121.8 (113.0 pp) × 16.7 × 7.3
**Electron Equipt:** Radar: 1/Don-2, 1/Okean, 1/Mod. Kite Screech
**M:** 1 Bryansk-Burmeister & Wain 950 VTBF 110 diesel; 1 prop; 5,200 hp
**Fuel:** 350 tons **Range:** 7,400/15 **Man:** 90 tot.

**Kosmonavt Viktor Patseyev** L. & L. Van Ginderen, 8-87

**Kosmonavt Pavel Belyayev** L. & L. Van Ginderen, 4-87

REMARKS: 4,482 grt/2,010 dwt. Like the less-elaborately altered *Borovichi* group, these are conversions from *Vytegrales*-class timber carriers, performed at the building yard. Named for cosmonauts killed on missions. Have large, stabilized Quad Spring communications array amidships and three smaller satellite communications arrays. Based in the Baltic.

◆ **1 Kosmonavt Yuriy Gagarin class** Bldr: Baltic SY, Leningrad

KOSMONAVT YURIY GAGARIN (In serv. 12-71)

**Kosmonavt Yuriy Gagarin** L. & L. Van Ginderen, 8-87

**Kosmonavt Yuriy Gagarin** L. & L. Van Ginderen, 8-87

**D:** 53,500 tons (fl) **S:** 18 kts **Dim:** 231.7 (213.9 pp) × 31.1 × 10.0
**Electron Equipt:** Radar: 1/Don-Kay, 1/Okean
**M:** 1 set GT, electric drive; 1 prop; 19,000 hp **Boilers:** 2
**Range:** 24,000/17.7 **Man:** 160 crew + 180 scientists-technicians

REMARKS: 32,291 grt/31,300 dwt. A *Sofiya*-class tanker hull adapted prior to construction. Has two 27-m-diameter Ship Shell and two 12.5-m diameter Ship Bowl stabilized communications dishes, 2 Vee Tube HF, and four Quad Ring arrays. Bow- and stern-thrusters. Three swimming pools, 300-seat theater; gymnasium. Endurance: 120 days. Home port: Odessa.

## CIVILIAN SPACE-EVENT SUPPORT SHIPS *(continued)*

◆ **1 Akademik Sergey Korolev** (In serv. 1970)

**Akademik Sergey Korolev** L. & L. Van Ginderen, 8-86

**D:** 21,465 tons (fl) **S:** 17 kts **Dim:** 181.9 (167.9 pp) × 25.0 × 7.9
**Electron Equipt:** Radar: 1/Okean, 1/Don-2
**M:** 1 Bryansk-Burmeister & Wain diesel; 1 prop; 12,000 hp
**Range:** 22,500/17 **Man:** 188 crew + 170 scientists-technicians

REMARKS: 17,114 grt/7,067 dwt. Has 80 "laboratories." Space communications antennas include 2 Ship Bowl and 1 Ship Globe and 4 Quad Ring.

◆ **1 Kosmonavt Vladimir Komarov class** Bldr: Kherson SY

KOSMONAVT VLADIMIR KOMAROV (ex-*Genichevsk*) (In serv. 1966)

**Kosmonavt Vladimir Komarov** 1984

**D:** 17,500 tons (fl) **S:** 17.5 kts **Dim:** 155.7 (146.4 pp) × 22.3 × 8.6
**Electron Equipt:** Radar: 2/Don-Kay
**M:** 1 Bryansk-Burmeister & Wain diesel; 1 prop; 9,000 hp
**Fuel:** 1,656 tons **Range:** 16,700/17.5 **Man:** 254 tot.

REMARKS: 13,935 grt/7,065 dwt. Converted from a *Poltava*-class bulk carrier at Baltic Shipyard, Leningrad, completing in 7-67. Hull amidships replaced by a broader section giving a distinct discontinuity to the lines fore and aft. Space communications antennas include two Ship Globe and 1 Ship Wheel, 2 Quad Ring, and 1 larger multiple yagi array. Two Vee-Cone HF antennas are carried at the mastheads. Based at Odessa.

◆ **4 Borovichi class** Bldr: Zhdanov SY, Leningrad, & Vyborg SY (In serv. 1965–66)

BOROVICHI (ex-*Svirles*) KEGOSTROV (ex-*Taymyr*) MORZHOVETS NEVEL

**D:** 7,600 tons (fl) **S:** 15.4 kts **Dim:** 121.9 (113.0 pp) × 16.7 × 4.7
**Electron Equipt:** Radar: 2/Don-2
**M:** 1 Bryansk-Burmeister & Wain 950 VTBF 110 diesel; 1 prop; 5,200 hp
**Fuel:** 325 tons **Range:** 7,400/15 **Man:** 78 tot.

**Kegostrov** L. & L. Van Ginderen, 1-86

**Morzhovets** 6-84

REMARKS: 5,277 grt/1,834 dwt. Space communications antennas include 1 Quint Ring and 4 Quad Ring yagi arrays, and a Vee Cone HF antenna is carried aft. Home-ported in the Baltic. Retain forward cargo hold. Converted 1967 at Zhdanov SY, Leningrad, from *Vytegrales*-class timber carriers.

## CIVILIAN SCIENTIFIC RESEARCH SHIPS

The ships listed below are subordinated to a variety of scientific organizations. Many perform military-related research. Major fisheries research ships are presented, but a large number of smaller trawlers of the *Mayak* and similar classes are omitted for reasons of space. Foxtrot-class diesel-powered submarines have also supported civilian research in recent years. Ships are presented in reverse order of class introduction.

◆ **0 (+2) . . . class** Bldr: Rauma-Repola, Savonlinna

| | Laid down | L | In serv. |
|---|---|---|---|
| N . . . | . . . | 11-4-87 | . . . |
| N . . . | . . . | 24-8-87 | . . . |

**D:** . . . **S:** 11 kts **Dim:** 49.80 (46.40 pp) × 10.50 × 2.00
**Electron Equipt:** Radar: . . .—Sonar: . . .
**M:** 2 diesels, electric drive; 2 rudder-props; 1,114 hp
**Fuel:** 95 tons **Man:** 30 tot.

REMARKS: 920 grt. Ordered 28-2-85. For hydrographic research.

◆ **2 new construction** Bldr: Hollming, Rauma, Finland

| | Laid down | L | In serv. |
|---|---|---|---|
| AKADEMIK SERGEI VAVILOV | 18-8-86 | 16-12-86 | 1988 |
| AKADEMIK PETR LEBEDEV | . . . | . . . | 1989 |

**Akademik Sergei Vavilov**—artist's impression MacGregor-Navire, 1987

**D:** 6,600 tons **S:** 15 kts **Dim:** 117.10 × 18.20 × 5.90
**Electron Equipt:** . . .
**M:** 2 SEMT-Pielstick/Russkiy Dizel 6PC2.5 L400 diesels; 2 CP props; 6,800 hp
**Range:** 20,000/15 **Man:** 128 tot.

REMARKS: Ordered 13-5-85. Intended for ocean floor sampling and physical oceanography. One 12-ton A-frame gantry aft, 5 oceanographic cranes to starboard.

## CIVILIAN SCIENTIFIC RESEARCH SHIPS *(continued)*

◆ **1 Antarctic research ship** Bldr: Rauma-Repola, Savonlinna

| | Laid down | L | In serv. |
|---|---|---|---|
| Akademik Fedorov | 29-8-86 | 27-2-87 | 8-87 |

**Akademik Fedorov** Rauma-Repola, 1987

**D:** 16,200 tons (fl) **S:** 16 kts **Dim:** 139.3 × 23.5 × 8.5
**Electron Equipt:** Radar: 2/. . . nav.
**M:** 2 Wärtsilä Vasa R32, 6-cyl. 11,222-hp diesels, electric drive; 1 prop; 16,000 hp—1,700-hp bow-thruster
**Range:** 20,000/16 **Endurance:** 80 days
**Man:** 90 crew + 160 scientists/passengers

Remarks: 7,600 dwt. Operated for the Arctic and Antarctic Institute. Intended as replacement for *Mikhail Somov* as Antarctic expedition and supply ship. Ordered 12-85. Can operate in up to 1.8-m-thick ice. Helicopter deck, with hangar for one Mi-8. Two 50-ton and two 10-ton cranes. Carries one ramped landing craft. Commenced initial Antarctic cruise 12-87.

◆ **5 (+2) Vadim Popov class** Bldr: Laivateollisuus SY, Turku

| | Laid down | L | In serv. |
|---|---|---|---|
| Vadim Popov | 15-10-85 | 3-86 | 6-10-86 |
| Viktor Buynitskiy | 21-11-85 | 15-4-86 | 30-11-86 |
| Pavel Gordienko | 14-2-86 | 25-6-86 | 2-87 |
| Vasiliy Lominadze | 15-4-86 | 31-10-86 | 5-5-87 |
| N . . . | 25-6-86 | 17-3-87 | 10-87 |
| N . . . | 8-86 | 5-87 | 1988 |
| N . . . | 10-86 | 7-87 | 1988 |

**D:** approx. 960 tons (fl) **S:** 12 kts **Dim:** 49.90 (44.50 pp) × 10.00 × 3.50
**Electron Equipt:** Radar: 2/. . . nav.
**M:** 1 Wärtsilä Vasa 824-TS diesel; 1 prop; 1,340 hp
**Range:** . . . **Electric:** 500 kw (2 × 250-kw diesel sets) **Man:** 35 tot.

Remarks: 886 grt. First four ordered 1-9-85, others on 16-5-86. Intended for hydrometeorological reporting and for supply of remote weather stations in the Far East. Carry a small beachable cargo launch forward, atop cargo hold.

**Vadim Popov** French Navy, 1986

**Pavel Gordienko** L. & L. Van Ginderen, 4-87

◆ **2 (+3) Iskatel' 2 class** Bldr: Stocznia Wisla, Gdansk

| | L | In serv. |
|---|---|---|
| Iskatel' 2 | 16-12-85 | 11-86 |
| Iskatel' 3 | 16-12-86 | 12-87 |
| Iskatel' 4 | . . . | . . . |
| Iskatel' 5 | . . . | . . . |
| Iskatel' 6 | . . . | . . . |

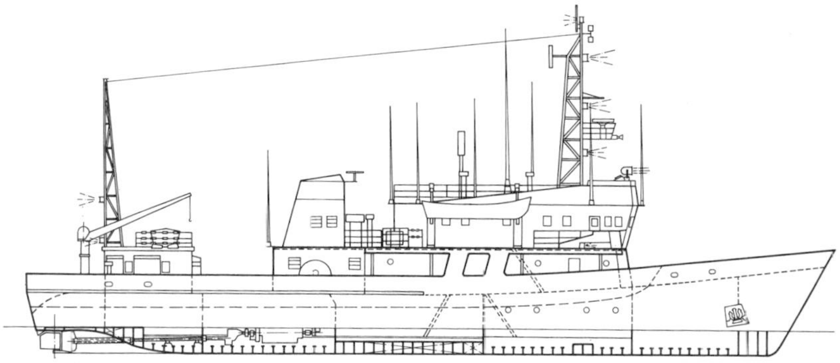

**Iskatel' 2**

**D:** 742 tons (fl) **S:** 11.9 kts **Dim:** 49.30 (44.50 pp) × 18.20 × 1.52
**Electron Equipt:** Radar: 1/. . . nav.
**M:** 2 Cegielski-Sulzer 6 AL 20/24 diesels; 2 CP Kort-nozzle props; 1,140 hp (sust.)
**Range:** . . ./. . . **Endurance:** 10 days **Fuel:** 53.6 m³
**Electric:** 600 kVA **Man:** 15 crew + 10 scientists

Remarks: 600 grt. Catamaran design, using Polish *Nadezhnyy*-class trawler hull. Intended for seismological/geophysical research in shallow water in the Barents, Kara, and Baltic seas and the sea of Okhotsk, as part of the "Shel'f" program for offshore oil exploration. Aluminum alloy deckhouse. Equipped with both towed hydrophone array, with a capacity of 3,200 m of 51-mm array cable, and a pneumatic pulsator array.

◆ **1 modified Akademik Aleksey Krylov class** Bldr: Okean SY, Nikolayev

Akademik Nikolay Andreyev (In serv. 10-86)

**D:** 11,600 tons (fl) **S:** 15 kts **Dim:** 142.7 (128.0 pp) × 17.5 × 7.2
**Electron Equipt:** Radar: 1/Palm Frond, 1/Okean-A, 1/Okean-B
**M:** 2 Type 58D-6R diesels; 2 CP props; 9,000 hp **Range:** . . ./. . .
**Electric:** . . . **Man:** . . .

Remarks: An enlarged, lengthened version of *Akademik Aleksey Krylov*, with a pronounced bulbous bow and facilities to starboard for handling two large submersible devices. Home-ported at Sevastopol.

**Akademik Nikolay Andreyev** U.S. Navy, 11-86

**CIVILIAN SCIENTIFIC RESEARCH SHIPS** *(continued)*

**Akademik Nikolay Andreyev** U.S. Navy, 11-86

◆ **2 Bavenit class** Bldr: Hollming, Rauma, Finland

| | Laid down | L | In serv. |
|---|---|---|---|
| Bavenit | 1-2-85 | . . . | 20-5-86 |
| Bakerit | 8-5-85 | 17-1-86 | 17-12-86 |

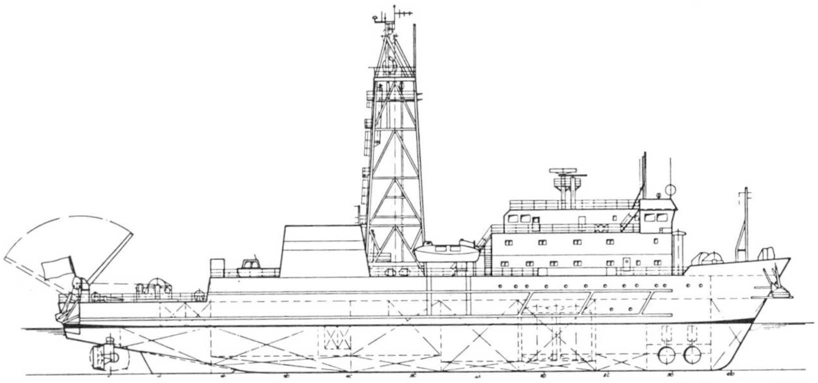

**Bavenit** Hollming, 1984

**D:** 5,300 tons **S:** 12.75 kts **Dim:** 85.80 (75.40 pp) × 16.80 × 5.60
**Electron Equipt:** . . .
**M:** 4 Russkiy Dizel EG-74/2 (1,700 hp) diesels, electric drive; 2 Aquamaster rudder-props, 6,000 hp
**Range:** 8,000/12 **Man:** 65 tot. **Endurance:** 56 days

Remarks: 2,000 dwt. Ordered 13-4-84 for the Arctic Complex Marine Geology Expedition of the Ministry of the Oil and Gas Industry. Able to drill to 200-m depths in waters up to 300 m deep, using a 35-m derrick drill support amidships. A-frame trawl gantry at the stern. Ice-reinforced hulls. Two 1,360-hp bow-thrusters plus the two U.S.-supplied Aquamaster, 360-deg.-pivoting props give a dynamic position-keeping capability.

◆ **4 (+5) Type B-93 geophysical research ships** Bldr: A. Warski SY, Szczecin, Poland

| | L | In serv. |
|---|---|---|
| Akademik Fersman | 24-1-85 | 5-86 |
| Akademik Shatskiy | 19-7-85 | 1986 |
| Akademik Seiskly | 14-12-85 | 1986 |
| Akademik Lazarev | 1986 | 1986 |
| Akademik Gubin | 24-3-87 | 1988 |
| Akademik Nalivkin | 4-87 | 1988 |
| Akademik Nametkin | 12-7-87 | . . . |
| N . . . | . . . | . . . |
| N . . . | . . . | . . . |

**Akademik Shatskiy** M.O.D., Bonn, 1986

**D:** approx. 3,300 tons (fl) **S:** 14.5 kts **Dim:** 81.85 (73.50 pp) × 14.80 × 5.00
**Electron Equipt:** Radar: 2/. . . nav.—Sonar: 6-km-long seismic array
**M:** 1 Zgoda-Sulzer 6 ZL 40/48 diesel; 1 Kort-nozzle CP prop; 4,200 hp
**Range:** 12,000/14.5 **Man:** 31 crew, 29 scientists
**Fuel:** 700 m$^3$ heavy oil, 170 m$^3$ diesel
**Electric:** 2,760 kVA (1 × 1500-kVA shaft alternator, 2 × 630-kw diesel sets)

Remarks: 1,000 dwt. A series of ships to support the "Shel'f" research program to search for offshore gas and oil deposits. Ice-strengthened hulls, stern ramp for towing seismic array. Bow-thruster. Geophysical, gravimetric, and chemical laboratories. JMR-4A NAVSAT receiver, Krupp-Atlas DESO-20 echo-sounder, Syledis radiogeodetic receiver, EC-1010 computer.

◆ **1 research training ship** Bldr: . . .

Gidrobiolog (In serv. 1985)

**D:** 168 tons (fl) **S:** 9 kts **Dim:** 26.7 × 6.1 × 2.7
**M:** 1 diesel; 1 prop; 200 hp

Remarks: Built for the Moscow State University as a training ship in physical and biological oceanography.

◆ **1 Pulkovskiy Meridian class** Bldr: Chernomorskiy SY, Nikolayev

Akademik Aleksandr Karpenskiy (In serv. 1984)

**Akademik Aleksandr Karpenskiy** L. & L. Van Ginderen, 6-86

**D:** 5,620 tons (fl) **S:** 17 kts **Dim:** 103.10 (94.00 pp) × 16.00 × 5.90
**Electron Equipt:** Radar: 1/Don-2, 1/Okean
**M:** 2 Zgoda-Sulzer 6L52511PV diesels; 1 CP prop; 6,900 hp
**Range:** 7,000/14.5 **Electric:** 450 kw **Man:** approx. 90 tot.
**Fuel:** 1,150 tons **Endurance:** 60 days

Remarks: One of a class of two dozen or more stern-haul factory trawlers built since 1974 adopted for fisheries-related oceanographic research.

◆ **6 Akademik Boris Petrov class** Bldr: Hollming, Rauma, Finland

| | Laid down | L | In serv. |
|---|---|---|---|
| Akademik Boris Petrov | 7-4-83 | 7-7-83 | 29-6-84 |
| Akademik M.A. Lavrent'yev | 18-8-83 | 28-10-83 | 12-10-84 |
| Akademik Nikolai Strakhov | 9-11-83 | 3-2-84 | 14-5-85 |
| Akademik Oparin | . . . | 1-2-85 | 29-11-85 |
| Akademik N . . . | . . . | . . . | . . . |
| Akademik N . . . | . . . | . . . | . . . |

**D:** 2,550 tons (fl) **S:** 15.5 kts **Dim:** 75.45 (68.00 pp) × 14.70 × 4.70
**Electron Equipt:** Radar: 1/Okean, 1/. . . nav.
**M:** 2 SEMT-Pielstick/Russkiy Dizel 6PC 2.5 L400 diesels; 1 CP prop; 3,500 hp
**Range:** 15,000/14.75 **Man:** 74 tot.

Remarks: First three ordered 17-6-82 for the Academy of Sciences Vernadskiy Institute for Geochemistry and Analytical Chemistry. Second trio ordered 28-6-84.

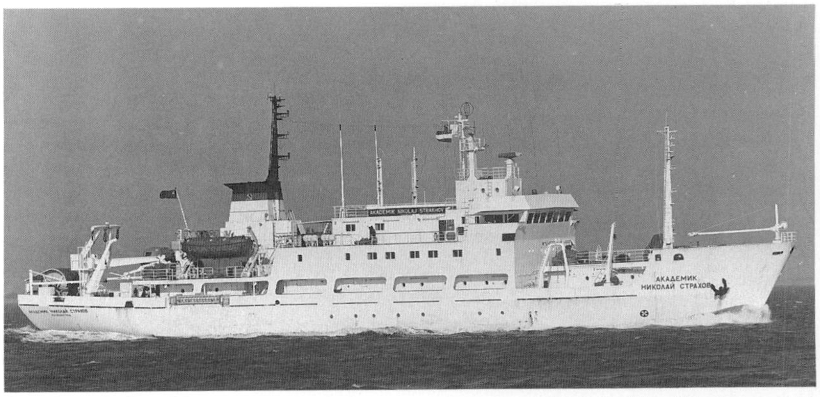

**Akademik Strakhov** L. & L. Van Ginderen, 2-86

**CIVILIAN SCIENTIFIC RESEARCH SHIPS** *(continued)*

**Akademik M.A. Lavrent'yev** L. & L. Van Ginderen, 3-86

Intended to conduct geophysical and hydrophysical research worldwide. Bow-thruster; bulbous forefoot to bow. Carry MARISAT SATCOMM system. Ships are assymetric, with portside plated in, starboard open along main deck for working equipment. Carry large seismic cable reel at stern.

◆ **1 geological research catamaran** Bldr: . . . SY, Vladivostok (In serv. 10-83)

GEOLOG PRIMOR'YE

**D:** 791 tons (fl) **S:** 9 kts **Dim:** 85.8 (75.3 pp) × 18.2 × 5.6
**M:** 2 diesels; 2 props; 1,200 hp—2/1,150-hp bow-thrusters

REMARKS: Intended for mineral resources research. Able to 4-point moor.

◆ **11 (+3) Akademik Shuleykin class** Bldr: Laivateollisuus, Turku, Finland

| | In serv. | | In serv. |
|---|---|---|---|
| AKADEMIK SHULEYKIN | 1982 | GEOLOG DMITRIY NALYVKIN | 14-2-85 |
| PROFESSOR PAVEL MOLCHANOV | 1982 | AKADEMIK ALEKSANDR SIDORENKO | 18-6-85 |
| AKADEMIK SHOKALSKIY | 1982 | ARNOL'D VEYMER | 1986 |
| PROFESSOR KHROMOV | 1983 | N . . . | . . . |
| PROFESSOR MUL'TANOVSKIY | 7-83 | N . . . | . . . |
| AKADEMIK GAMBURTSEV | 20-12-83 | N . . . | . . . |
| AKADEMIK GOLITSYN | 22-2-84 | | |
| PROFESSOR POLSHAOV | 7-4-84 | | |

**D:** 2,140 tons (fl) **S:** 14 kts **Dim:** 71.6 (64.3 pp) × 12.8 × 4.8
**Electron Equipt:** Radar: 1/Okean M, 1/Okean B
**M:** 2 Gor'kiy Type G-74 diesels; 2 CP props; 3,120 hp **Electric:** 600 kVA
**Range:** 14,000/12 **Man:** 38 crew + 38 scientists **Endurance:** 50 days

**Akademik Shokalskiy**—first group French Navy, 1-83

**Geolog Dmitriy Nalyvkin**—second group, with deckhouse aft and open waist abaft stack L. & L. Van Ginderen, 1-87

**Arnol'd Veymer**—third group, open stern, with large crane Laivateollisuus, 1986

REMARKS: 1,800 grt/620 dwt. Academy of Sciences hydrometeorological reporting ships, equipped for cold-weather operations. Home ports: *Shuleykin* at Leningrad, *Shokalskiy* and *Khromov* at Vladivostok, *Molchanov* at Murmansk, and *Mul'tanovskiy* at Leningrad. Second five ordered 1982 for the Ministry of Geology for seismic survey duties; they are of 1,650 grt/600 dwt, draw 4.50 m, and can carry a submersible robot. Third group of four ordered 1-85; first launched 14-2-86. All have a 200-hp bow-thruster.

◆ **1 Akademik Aleksey Krylov class** Bldr: Okean SY, Nikolayev

AKADEMIK ALEKSEY KRYLOV (In serv. 1981)

**Akademik Aleksey Krylov** U.S. Navy, 9-83

**D:** 9,920 tons (fl) **S:** 16 kts **Dim:** 124.7 (110.0 pp) × 17.5 × 7.2
**Electron Equipt:** Radar: 1/Okean A, 1/Okean B, 1 Palm Frond
**M:** 2 Type 58D-6R diesels; 2 CP props; 9,000 hp **Range:** 10,000/16
**Electric:** 3,600 kw **Man:** 117 crew, 32 scientists

REMARKS: 6,358 grt/1,930 dwt. Supports a 13.4-m submersible, hangared amidships, with a large door and internal handling gantry to port. The submersible weighs 10 tons and can dive to 1,500 m. The ship has bow- and stern-thrusters, with a "Zaliv" automated control system. Home-ported at Sevastopol. Lengthened, modified half-sister *Akademik Nikolay Andreyev,* completed 1986, is described on page 675.

◆ **5 modified Al'pinist class** Bldr: Yaroslavl' SY

RIFT (In serv. 1982) GIDROBIOLOG (In serv. 1983) GIDRONAVT (In serv. 1983)
DIORAT (In serv. 1983) DIABAZ (In serv. 1983)

**Rift**—with Pisces submersible U.S. Navy, 9-82

**D:** 1,185 tons (fl) **S:** 12 kts **Dim:** 53.7 × 10.5 × 4.4
**Electron Equipt:** Radar: 1/Spin Trough
**M:** 1 Type 8NVD48-2U diesel; 1 CP prop; 1,320 hp
**Electric:** 778 kw **Range:** 6,900/12 **Man:** 26 crew + 11 scientists

REMARKS: Al'pinist stern-haul trawlers modified while under construction to carry and support a manned submersible beneath a traveling double gantry crane amidships. Employed on oceanography, hydrology, and marine ecology research by the Ministry of Fisheries. Equipped with bow- and stern-thrusters. In late 1983 *Rift,* designed for the Tinro-2 submersible, was carrying the *Argus* submersible

## CIVILIAN SCIENTIFIC RESEARCH SHIPS *(continued)*

and a *Zvuk*-4M towed drone submersible. *Diorat* and *Diabaz* are used for geophysical research and have a 15-m drill tower for the 9-ton ZIF-1200 drill in place of the submersible facility.

◆ **3 Vityaz' class** Bldr: Adolf Warski SY, Szczecin, Poland

Vityaz' (In serv. 1981) Akademik A. Nesmeyanov (In serv. 1982)
Akademik Alexandr Vinogradov (In serv. 1983)

**Vityaz'** French Navy, 1984

**Akademik A. Nesmeyanov** U.S. Navy, 7-83

**D:** 5,700 tons (fl) **S:** 16 kts **Dim:** 110.90 (100.00 pp) × 16.60 × 5.70
**Electron Equipt:** Radar: 2/Don-2, 1/Okean
**M:** 2 Zgoda-Sulzer 6ZL140/48 diesels; 2 CP props; 6,400 hp
**Endurance:** 60 days **Electric:** 925 kVA **Range:** 16,000/16
**Man:** 61 crew + 65 scientists

Remarks: 4,940 grt/1,810 dwt. Operated by the Academy of Sciences for seabed research, exploring for exploitable natural materials to 10,000-m depths. Haye 25 laboratories. Carry the *Argus* submersibles: 8 tons, 600-m diving depth, 3-kt. max. speed, crew of 3, with an 8-hour powered endurance. *Vityaz'* also carries a submersible decompression chamber for 3 divers. Cargo holds total 477 m$^3$ capacity. *Vityaz'* home-ported at Novorossiysk, *Nesmeyanov* at Vladivostok.

◆ **1 Akademik Keldysh class** Bldr: Hollming SY, Rauma, Finland

Akademik Mstislav Keldysh (In serv. 12-80)

**D:** 5,500 (fl) **S:** 16 kts **Dim:** 122.2 × 17.8 × 5.4
**M:** 4 Wärtsilä Vasa 824TS diesels; 2 props; 5,840 hp
**Range:** 20,000/165 **Man:** 50 crew + 80 scientists

Remarks: 5,500 grt/1,500 dwt. Operated by the Academy of Sciences for general-purpose oceanography. Has 17 internal laboratories and can carry 4 containerized laboratories. Home-ported at Kaliningrad. Carries two *Pisces*-class research submersibles, capable of descending to 2,000 m with a crew of three. Passive tank anti-rolling system. Bow-thruster and a 360-deg.-rotatable Aquamaster stern propulser.

**Akademik Mstislav Keldysh** L. & L. Van Ginderen, 3-84

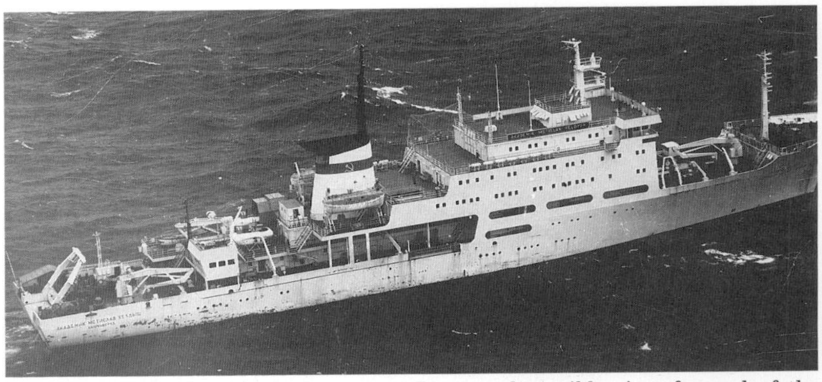

**Akademik Mstislav Keldysh**—note 2 Pisces submersibles just forward of the crane-control station, aft U.S. Navy, 9-86

**Akademik Mstislav Keldysh** French Navy, 3-87

◆ **1 modified Dobrynya Nikitich class** Bldr: Admiralty SY, Leningrad

Otto Schmidt (In serv. 17-7-79)

**Otto Schmidt** U.S. Navy, 1-87

**D:** 2,528 tons (3,600 fl) **S:** 14.8 kts **Dim:** 73.0 (62.0 pp) × 18.0 × 6.6
**Electron Equipt:** Radar: 1/Okean, 1/Don-2
**M:** 3 Type 13D100 diesels, electric drive; 2 props; 5,440 hp
**Electric:** 1,875 kw **Range:** 11,000/14 **Man:** 32 crew + 20 scientists

Remarks: 2,828 grt/1,095 dwt. Operated by the Arctic/Antarctic Scientific Research Institute. Can break 60-cm ice at 2-kt speeds; 50 days endurance. Has 14 laboratories. The naval research icebreaker *Vladimir Kavrayskiy* has the same hull

**CIVILIAN SCIENTIFIC RESEARCH SHIPS** *(continued)*

and propulsion, while two standard units of the *Dobrynya Nikitich* class, *Petr Pakhtusov* and *Georgiy Sedov,* are also employed on research tasks as needed. Endurance: 60 days. Had made 25 expeditions by 1986. Home-ported at Murmansk.

◆ **1 sea-mining research ship** Bldr: . . . , U.S.S.R.

SHEL'F 1 (In serv. 1976)

**D:** . . . **S:** 16.5 kts **Dim:** 62.6 × 10.5 × 3.1
**M:** 2 12-cyl. diesels; 2 props; . . . hp **Range:** . . . **Man:** . . .

REMARKS: 669 grt/193 dwt. Built to test ocean-shelf mining techniques to 100-m depths. Has a 5-ton crane.

◆ **1 Antarctic research and supply ship** Bldr: Kherson SY

MIKHAIL SOMOV (In serv. 1975)

**Mikhail Somov** L. & L. Van Ginderen, 8-86

**D:** 5,000 tons (14,000 fl) **S:** 20 kts **Dim:** 133.1 (123.3 pp) × 18.8 × 9.2
**Electron Equipt:** Radar: 2/Don-2
**M:** 2 diesels, electric drive; 2 props; 7,150 hp
**Range:** 10,000/16.4 **Man:** 100 tot.

REMARKS: 7,714 grt/8,445 dwt. Operated by the Arctic and Antarctic Institute. Essentially an *Amguema*-class icebreaking passenger/cargo ship intended for annual resupply duties to Soviet research stations in the Antarctic. Commercial sisters, including *Kapitan Myshevskiy* in 1983, are also used for Antarctic resupply. *Somov* replaced as principal Antarctic expedition ship by *Akademik Fedorov* in 1987.

◆ **18 Valerian Uryvayev class** Bldr: Khabarovsk SY

| | In serv. | | In serv. |
|---|---|---|---|
| CHAYVO | 1982 | POISK | 1974 |
| ELM | 1982 | PROFESSOR FEDYNSKIY | 1982 |
| DALNIYE ZELENTSY* | 1978 | RUDOLF SAMOYLOVICH* | 1977 |
| GEOFIZIKH | 1983 | VALERIAN URYVAYEV* | 1974 |
| ISKATEL' | 1977 | VEKTOR | 1980 |
| ISSLEDOVATEL' | 1977 | VSEVLOD BEREZKIN* | 1975 |
| LEV TITOV* | 1980 | VULKANOLOG | 1976 |
| MODUL | 1981 | VYACHESLAV FROLOV* | 1979 |
| MORSKOY GEOFIZIK | 1975 | YAKOV GAKKEL* | 1975 |

**D:** 1,050 tons (fl) **S:** 11 kts **Dim:** 54.8 × 9.5 × 4.2
**Electron Equipt:** Radar: 1/Don-2, 1/Okean, 1/End Shield (on 7)
**M:** 1 Karl Liebnecht diesel; 1 CP prop; 880 hp **Electric:** 450 kw
**Range:** 10,000/11 **Man:** 40 crew + 12 scientists

**Geofizikh**—pole mast aft, large winch on stern French Navy, 2-84

**Valerian Uryvayev**—hydromet version, king posts at stern G. Gyssels, 6-86

**Professor Fedynskiy**—king posts abaft stack U.S. Navy, 1986

**Modul**—pole mast, no boats amidships, air-sampling module on stern U.S. Navy, 12-85

REMARKS: 697 grt/350 dwt average. Variously subordinated; those operated for the Institute of Hydrometeorology(*) are equipped to mount an End Shield radiosonde balloon-tracking radar. Others operate for the Arctic and Antarctic Institute or the Academy of Sciences. Have 8 laboratories. Some have twin king posts at the stern, others a single mast aft, and still others have twin king posts just abaft the stack. Home-ported: *Berezkin, Zelentsy* at Murmansk; *Titov, Samoylovich* in the Baltic; *Issledovatel', Modul, Vektor, Gakkel* in the Black Sea; *Elm* in the Caspian; remainder in the Far East.

◆ **3 modified Passat-class weather-reporting ships** Bldr: Adolf Warski SY, Szczecin, Poland (In serv. 1971)

ERNST KRENKEL' (ex-*Vikhr*) VIKTOR BUGAYEV (ex-*Poriv*)
GEORGIY USHAKOV (ex-*Schkval*)

**D:** 4,200 tons (fl) **S:** 16 kts **Dim:** 100.1 (88.4 pp) × 14.8 × 5.1
**Electron Equipt:** Radar: 2/Don-2, 1/End Tray
**M:** 2 Cegielski-Sulzer diesels; 2 CP props; 4,800 hp
**Electric:** 1,089 kw **Fuel:** 652 tons
**Range:** 15,000/16 **Man:** 110 crew + 63 scientists

REMARKS: 3,311 grt/1,450 dwt. Improved version of the Passat-class hydrometeorological reporting ships. Facilities for launching and tracking radiosonde balloons and rockets. All home-ported in the Black Sea, at Odessa.

## CIVILIAN SCIENTIFIC RESEARCH SHIPS *(continued)*

**Ernst Krenkel'** L. & L. Van Ginderen, 10-86

**Viktor Bugayev** L. & L. Van Ginderen, 12-87

◆ **1 shipbuilding techniques trials ship** Bldr: Black Sea SY, Nikolayev

IZUMRUD (In serv. 1970)

**Izumrud** L. & L. Van Ginderen, 1986

**D:** 5,170 tons (fl) **S:** 14 kts **Dim:** 99.4 (90.0 pp) × 14.0 × 5.4
**Electron Equipt:** Radar: 1/Don-2, 1/Okean, 1/Low Sieve
**M:** 4 diesels, electric drive; 1 prop; 4,000 hp
**Range:** . . . **Man:** 110 crew + 40 scientists

REMARKS: 3,862 grt/2,640 dwt. A modified version of the *Tavriya*-class passenger/cargo ship, built for the Ministry of Shipbuilding for trials with structural concepts, coatings, navigational and communications systems. Portions of the superstructure are made from glass-reinforced plastic. Home-ported at Odessa.

◆ **19 Dmitriy Ovtsyn class** Bldr: Laivateollisuus SY, Abo, Finland

| | In serv. | | In serv. |
|---|---|---|---|
| DMITRIY LAPTEV | 1970 | PROFESSOR BOGOROV* | 1976 |
| DMITRIY OVTSYN | 1970 | PROFESSOR KURENTSOV* | 1976 |
| DMITRIY STERLEGOV | 1971 | PROFESSOR SHTOKMAN* | 1979 |
| EDUARD TOLL | 1972 | PROFESSOR VODYANITSKIY* | 1976 |
| FEDOR MATISEN* | 1976 | SERGEY KRAVKOV | 1974 |
| GEORGIY MAKSOMOV* | 1977 | STEPAN MALYGIN | 1970 |
| IVAN KIREYEV* | 1977 | VALERIAN ALBANOV | 1972 |
| NIKOLAY KOLOMEYTSEV | 1972 | VLADIMIR SUKHOTSKIY | 1974 |
| NIKOLAY YEVGENOV | 1974 | YAKOV SMIRNITSKIY* | 1977 |
| PAVEL BASHMAKOV* | 1977 | | |

**Professor Shtokman**—seismic research French Navy, 1-87

**Nikolay Kolomeytsev** L. & L. Van Ginderen, 12-86

**D:** 1,600 tons (fl) **S:** 14 kts **Dim:** 68.7 (60.0 pp) × 11.9 × 4.1
**Electron Equipt:** Radar: varies: 2/Don-2, or 1/Okean, or 1/Don, 1/Don-2
**M:** 1 Humboldt-Klockner-Deutz diesel; 1 CP prop; 2,200 hp
**Fuel:** 180 tons **Electric:** 595 kw **Range:** 9,700/13.5 **Man:** 42 tot.

REMARKS: 1,134 grt/295 dwt. Ships delivered 1976 and later(*) are considered a second series, but are very similar. Fourteen are subordinated to the Ministry of the Maritime Fleet for hydrographic survey and seismic survey duties, the remainder to the Academy of Sciences or to the Hydrometeorological Institute (units with "Professor" names). *Bogorov* built at Turku.

◆ **23 Agat class** Bldr: . . . (In serv. 1969–79)

| | | | |
|---|---|---|---|
| AGAT | GIDROLOG | MONATSIT | TANTAL |
| AKVANAVT | GRANAT | MORION | TOPAZ |
| BERILL | ILMENIT | PLUTON | TSIRKON |
| BOREY | KARTESH | RADON | URAN |
| BRIG | KVARTS | RUTIL | YANTAR |
| GEOTERMIK | METAN | SHELF | |

**Shelf** L. & L. Van Ginderen, 9-83

**D:** 350 tons (fl) **S:** 9.5 kts **Dim:** 34.0 × 7.1 × 2.6
**Electron Equipt:** Radar: 1/navigational
**M:** 1 Karl Liebnecht 8-cyl. diesel; 1 prop; 300 hp
**Electric:** 411 kw **Range:** 1,600/9 **Man:** . . .

REMARKS: 166 grt/35 dwt. A general-purpose oceanographic tender version of the *Manevrennyy*-class seiner fishing boat. Endurance: 7 days. Subordination about equally divided between the Ministry of Geology, Academy of Sciences, and the Hydrometeorological Institute.

**CIVILIAN SCIENTIFIC RESEARCH SHIPS** *(continued)*

◆ **12 Atlantik-I* and -II-class fisheries research ships** Bldr: Volkswerft, Stralsund, East Germany (In serv. 1968–72)

| | | |
|---|---|---|
| Alba* | Gerakl' | Professor Sergey Dorofeyev |
| Artemida | Kamenskoye | Professor Mesyatsev |
| Evrika | Milogradvo | Shanta |
| Fiolent | Professor | Zond |

**Professor Sergey Dorofeyev** L. & L. Van Ginderen, 5-87

**D:** 2,240 tons (3,360 fl) **S:** 13.7 kts **Dim:** 82.2 (73.0 pp) × 13.6 × 5.0
**Electron Equipt:** Radar: 2/Don-2
**M:** 2 Karl Liebnecht diesels; 2 CP prop; 2,350 hp
**Electric:** 1,660 kw **Fuel:** 600 tons **Range:** . . . **Man:** 85 tot.

Remarks: Average 2,242 grt/1,025 dwt. Stern-haul factory trawlers adapted for fisheries-related oceanographic research; subordinated to the Ministry of Fisheries. Have a 75-hp bow-thruster.

◆ **6 Passat-class hydrometeorological reporting ships** Bldr: Adolf Warski SY, Szczecin, Poland

| | In serv. | | In serv. | | In serv. |
|---|---|---|---|---|---|
| Musson | 1968 | Volna | 1968 | Priboy | 1969 |
| Passat | 1968 | Okean | 1969 | Priliv | 1970 |

**Volna**—a bit worse for wear L. & L. Van Ginderen, 1987

**Priboy**—Vee Cone HF antenna atop foremast L. & L. Van Ginderen, 1984

**D:** 4,145 tons (fl) **S:** 16 kts **Dim:** 96.9 (88.4 pp) × 13.8 × 5.3
**Electron Equipt:** Radar: 2/Don-2, 1/End Tray (radiosonde tracker)
**M:** 2 Cegielski-Sulzer 8TD48 diesels; 2 CP props; 4,800 hp
**Electric:** 800 kw **Range:** . . .
**Man:** 50–55 crew + 50–60 scientists and technicians

Remarks: 3,284 grt/1,170 dwt. B-88 design, with 23 laboratory spaces. Have End Tray radiosonde tracking antenna aft and can launch weather ballons and atmospheric probe rockets. 45-day endurance. Subordinated to the Hydrometeorological Institute. Home-ported: Vladivostok, except *Musson, Passat:* Odessa; *Priliv:* Baltic. Vee-series HF antenna atop foremast on *Priboy, Priliv,* and *Okean.*

◆ **1 Sever class** Bldr: Black Sea SY, Nikolayev

Sever (In serv. 1967)

**Sever** 1982

**D:** 1,780 tons (2,530 fl) **S:** 13.1 kts **Dim:** 71.0 (64.0 pp) × 13.1 × 5.0
**Electron Equipt:** Radar: 1/Don-2
**M:** 3 diesels, electric drive; 1 CP prop; 3,000 hp
**Fuel:** 350 tons **Range:** 11,000/13 **Man:** 51 tot.

Remarks: 1,940 grt/706 dwt. Operated by the Ministry of Geophysics in geological oceanography studies. Was originally the prototype for a class of stern-haul trawlers, but no others were built. Endurance: 50 days. Operates in the Black Sea.

◆ **1 modified Nereida class** Bldr: Khabarovsk SY

Akademik Petrovskiy (ex-*Moskovskiy Universitet*) (In serv. 1966)

**Akademik Petrovskiy** U.S. Navy, 7-81

**D:** 922 tons (fl) **S:** 11 kts **Dim:** 54.1 (52.8) × 9.3 × 3.7
**Electron Equipt:** Radar: 1/Don-2, 1/Spin Trough
**M:** 1 diesel; 1 CP prop; 780 hp
**Range:** 10,000/11 **Man:** 41 crew + 10 scientists

Remarks: 577 grt/277 dwt. Operated by Moscow State University for studies in oceanology, hydrobiology, ichthyology, and seismology. Modernized and renamed 1970. Large numbers of this class (unmodified) and the very similar Mayak class perform fisheries research duties.

◆ **7 Akademik Kurchatov class** Bldr: Mathias Thiesen Werft, Wismar, East Germany (In serv. 1966–68)

| | |
|---|---|
| Akademik Kurchatov | Dmitriy Mendeleyev |
| Akademik Korolev | Professor Vize |
| Akademik Shirshov | Professor Zubov |
| Akademik Vernadskiy | |

**D:** 6,986 tons (fl) **S:** 18.3 kts **Dim:** 124.2 (110.0 pp) × 17.0 × 6.1
**Electron Equipt:** Radar (standard): 2/Don or Don-2, 1 or 2/tracking radars
**M:** 2 Halberstadt-M.A.N. 6KZ 57/60 diesels; 2 props; 8,000 hp
**Fuel:** 1,415 tons **Electric:** 1,840 kw **Range:** 20,000/18
**Man:** 80 crew + 74 scientists & technicians

Remarks: 5,460 grt/1,986 dwt. Vary considerably in equipment. *Kurchatov, Vernadskiy,* and *Mendeleyev* subordinate to the Academy of Sciences, the others to the Hydrometeorological Institute. The weather ships originally had radiosonde balloon- and rocket-launching facilities. End Tray tracking radar, and two theodolite trackers, one of which was a converted naval Wasp Head director (*Shirshov* has two side-by-side tracking radars in radomes amidships and a new type

## CIVILIAN SCIENTIFIC RESEARCH SHIPS *(continued)*

of tracking radar aft, while *Korolev* has had the twin radars, and occasionally the radomes, removed). The other three have a large crane aft for handling oceanographic gear and small submersibles; they also carry one End Tray. The weather ships also have Vee Bars HF antennas atop the foremast. *Korolev* and *Mendeleyev* have an Okean-series navigational radar in lieu of one Don-2. All have two 190-hp bow-thrusters, and a 300-hp Pleuger active rudder. Unlike their naval half-sisters of the *Abkhaziya* class, these ships have *no* helicopter facilities. Most now have a MARISAT SATCOMM receiver. Home ports: *Korolev, Mendeleyev,* and *Shirshov* at Vladivostok, *Vernadskiy* in the Black Sea, and the others in the Baltic.

**Akademik Shirshov**—note twin radomes amidships, elaborate tracking-radar antenna aft — L. & L. Van Ginderen, 1983

**Professor Vize**—hydrometeorological reporting ship with Vee Bars HF antenna atop foremast — P. Voss, 10-86

**Akademik Kurchatov**—scientific unit; note stack cap — L. & L. Van Ginderen, 9-86

◆ **4 Tropik A class** Bldr: V.E.B. Volkswerft, Stralsund, East Germany

| | In serv. | | In serv. |
|---|---|---|---|
| Kallisto | 1964 | Pegas | 1963 |
| Nauka | 1966 | Raduga | 1966 |

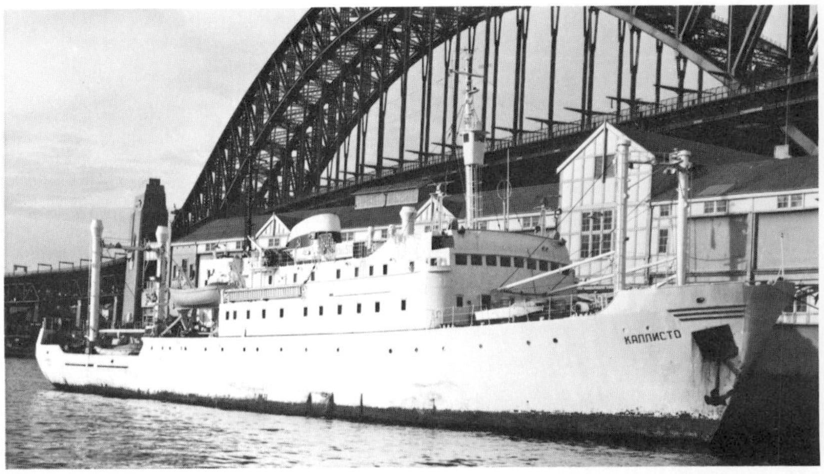

**Kallisto** — L. & L. Van Ginderen, 3-83

**D:** approx. 3,000 tons (fl) **S:** 12.5 kts **Dim:** 79.8 (71.0 pp) × 13.2 × 5.2
**Electron Equipt:** Radar: 2/Don-2
**M:** 2 Karl Liebnecht 8-cyl. diesels; 1 prop; 1,680 hp
**Electric:** 1,080 kw **Fuel:** 400 tons **Range:** . . .
**Man:** 42 crew + 29 scientists

Remarks: 2,435 grt/988 dwt. Former stern-haul factory trawlers. Approximately 70 sisters operate as fishing boats. *Pegas* operates for the Academy of Sciences, *Kallisto* for the Oceanographic Science Research Institute, and the other two for the Ministry of Fisheries.

◆ **3 modified Bologoe-class trawlers** Bldr: Leninskaya Kuznitsa SY, Kiev (In serv. 1963)

Akademik A. Kovalevskiy — Akademik Archangel'skiy — Yuriy Godin

**Akademik A. Kovalevskiy** — L. & L. Van Ginderen, 1985

**D:** 580 tons (fl) **S:** 10 kts **Dim:** 43.6 × 7.6 × 3.0
**Electron Equipt:** Radar: 1/Spin Trough
**M:** 1 Karl Liebnecht diesel; 1 prop; 450 hp
**Range:** . . . **Man:** 35 crew + 13 scientists

Remarks: 416 grt/142 dwt. Greatly modified versions of a standard side-trawler design. *Ak. Archangel'skiy* and *Godin* perform seismic and geophysical studies in the Black Sea and Mediterranean under the Ministry of Geology and Geophysics Institute, respectively. The less-modified *Ak. A. Kovalevskiy* performs general oceanography in the same area.

◆ **1 small research ship** (In serv. 1962)

Professor Kolesnikov

**Professor Kolesnikov** — French Navy, 1984

**D:** . . . **S:** . . . **Dim:** . . . × . . . × . . . **M:** . . .

## CIVILIAN SCIENTIFIC RESEARCH SHIPS *(continued)*

◆ **1 ex-passenger ship** (In serv. 1961)

AYU-DAG

**Ayu-Dag** L. & L. Van Ginderen, 6-83

**D:** approx. 1,000 tons (fl) **S:** 13 kts **Dim:** 63.8 × 9.3 × 3.0
**M:** diesels; 2 props; . . . hp

REMARKS: 1,002 grt. Subordinated to the Academy of Sciences of the Estonian S.S.R. Very little scientific equipment carried.

◆ **1 ex-Norwegian seismic research ship** Bldr: A.M. Liasen SY, Alesund

SHEL'F II (ex-*Longva*) (In serv. 1962)

**D:** approx. 1,400 tons (fl) **S:** 13 kts **Dim:** 63.0 (57.9 pp) × 10.0 × 4.2
**Electron Equipt:** Radar: 3/navigational
**M:** 1 Klockner-Humboldt-Deutz diesel; 1 prop; 1,500 hp
**Electric:** 360 kw **Fuel:** 249 tons **Range:** . . . **Man:** 52 tot.

REMARKS: 793 grt. Purchased 1977 for oil exploration. Very elaborately equipped, including data-storage computers. Has passive tank stabilization, bow-thruster.

NOTE: The two converted *Fryazino*-class acoustic research ships, *Petr Lebedev* and *Sergey Vavilov*, have been deleted from this edition, since their names have been assigned to new vessels. The converted tug *Vladimir Obruchev* has been deleted due to age and lack of sightings.

◆ **11 Mayakovskiy class** Bldr: Black Sea (Nosenko) SY, Nikolayev

| | In serv. | | In serv. |
|---|---|---|---|
| A.I. VOYEYKOV | 1959 | ODISSEY | 1970 |
| AKADEMIK BERG | 1963 | PERSEY-III | 1968 |
| AKADEMIK KNIPOVICH | 1964 | POSEIDON | 1971 |
| ARGUS | 1969 | PROFESSOR DERYUGIN | 1967 |
| EKVATOR | 1968 | SKIF | 1969 |
| IKHTIANDER | 1973 | | |

**A.I. Voyeykov**—hydrometeorological ship L. & L. Van Ginderen, 1-87

**D:** approx. 3,600 tons (fl) **S:** 13 kts **Dim:** 84.7 (78.1 pp) × 14.0 × 5.7
**Electron Equipt:** Radar: 2/Don-2
**M:** 2 Russkiy Dizel diesels; 1 CP prop; 2,000 hp
**Electric:** 800 kw **Range:** 18,000/12 **Man:** 53 crew + 37 scientists

REMARKS: Average 3,220 grt/1,287 dwt. Stern-haul fish-factory trawlers adapted for research purposes. *Voyeykov,* with stern ramp plated up, operates for the Hydrometeorological Institute and has an End Tray radiosonde tracking radar. The remainder support fisheries research for the Ministry of Fisheries. *Odissey* and *Ikhtiander* have a large internal hangar opening through the port side of the hull to launch a *Sever-II* or *Tinro-2* research submersible. *Deryugin, Persey-III, Argus,* and *Poseidon* carry a *Sever-I* submersible, launched via crane. *Skif* and *Ekvator* are essentially unmodified from the fishing-boat version. The six *Primorye*-class intelligence collection ships were built on the same hull.

◆ **1 Mikhail Lomonosov class** Bldr: Neptunwerft, Rostock, East Germany

MIKHAIL LOMONOSOV (In serv. 1957)

**Mikhail Lomonosov** L. & L. Van Ginderen, 9-86

**D:** 5,960 tons (fl) **S:** 13.6 kts **Dim:** 102.4 (95.5 pp) × 14.4 × 6.0
**Electron Equipt:** Radar: 2/Don-2
**M:** 1 set reciprocating steam with turbine booster; 1 prop; 2,450 hp
**Electric:** 746 kw **Fuel:** 780 tons **Boilers:** 2
**Range:** 11,000/13.6 **Man:** 80 crew + 55 scientists

REMARKS: 3,898 grt/2,254 dwt. Altered while under construction as a *Kolomna*-class cargo ship. Operated by the Academy of Sciences, Ukrainian Institute of Oceanology. Has 16 laboratories. Home-ported at Sevastopol'.

◆ **2 Korall class** Bldr: Laivateollisuus SY, Turku, Finland

POLYARNYY ODISSEY (In serv. 1950) ZARYA (In serv. 9-52)

**Zarya** L. & L. Van Ginderen, 10-87

**D:** approx. 600 tons (fl) **S:** 8 kts **Dim:** 52.5 (42.5 pp) × 9.0 × 3.1
**Electron Equipt:** Radar: 1/Spin Trough
**M:** 1 Halberstadt 6NVD36 diesel; 1 prop; 300 hp
**Range:** 4,000/8 **Man:** 35 crew + 10 scientists

REMARKS: 333 grt/78 dwt. Among the last survivors of a large class of wooden-hulled sealer schooners built as war reparations. *Zarya* has been made as completely non-magnetic as is possible and is used in gravimetric and ocean-current research by the Academy of Sciences. Home-ported at Murmansk. Refitted 1984–85. *Polyarnyy Odissey* operates for the Northern Branch of the Geographical Society of the U.S.S.R.

## CIVILIAN ICEBREAKERS

NOTE: Because of their importance to the Soviet Navy in keeping Arctic sea lanes open, the Ministry of the Merchant Marine's icebreakers are listed here. There is little doubt that they would come under naval jurisdiction in wartime, and, in fact, the nuclear-powered icebreaker *Leonid Brezhnev* (ex-*Arktika*) was heavily armed during initial sea trials. Naval-subordinated icebreakers are listed in the Soviet Navy section.

## NUCLEAR-POWERED ICEBREAKERS

◆ **0 (+2) Taymyr class** Bldr: Wärtsilä, Helsinki/Baltic SY, Leningrad

TAYMYR (In serv. 1989) VAYGACH (In serv. 1990)

**Taymyr**—artist's rendering Wärtsilä, 1984

**D:** 20,480 tons (23,460 fl) **S:** 20.5 kts
**Dim:** 140.2 (136.00 pp) × 30.00 (28.60 wl) × 8.05
**Electron Equipt:** Radar: 4/. . . nav.
**M:** 2 pressurized-water reactors, steam turbines, electric drive; 3 props; 52,000 hp
**Electric:** 11,400 kw (5/2,000-kw turboalternators, 1/1,000-kw diesel set, 2/200-kw diesel sets)
**Man:** 142 crew + helicopter crew and medical personnel

REMARKS: Ordered 1984 for shallow-water work in Arctic estuaries. Reactors to be installed at Leningrad after delivery in 1987 and 1988 from Finland. Will be able to break 1.77-m-thick ice continuously at 2 kts. *Taymyr* launched 4-87. Originally to have had 74,800 hp and be capable of breaking 2-m ice.

◆ **3 (+2) Arktika class** Bldr: Baltic SY, Leningrad

| | Laid down | L | In serv. |
|---|---|---|---|
| ARKTIKA (ex-*Leonid Brezhnev*, ex-*Arktika*) | 1971 | 12-72 | 12-74 |
| SIBIR' | 1973 | 2-76 | 1977 |
| ROSSIYA | . . . | 11-83 | 11-85 |
| LEONID BREZHNEV | 11-83 | 25-9-86 | 1988 |
| OKTYABRSKAYA REVOLUTSIYA | 31-10-86 | . . . | 1990 |

**D:** 19,300 tons light (23,460 fl) **S:** 21 kts (15 kts service)
**Dim:** 148.0 (136.0 pp) × 30.0 × 11.0
**Electron Equipt:** Radar: 1/Okean, 1/Don-2, 1/Head Net C (*Rossiya:* Top Plate)
**M:** 2 pressurized-water reactors, turbogenerators, electric drive; 3 props; 75,000 hp
**Electric:** 11,400 kw **Man:** 148 crew + 35 passengers

REMARKS: 18,172 grt/4,096 dwt. *Arktika,* renamed 1982, was armed during her trials period with 8/76.2-mm DP (II × 4, controlled by 2/Hawk Screech radar GFCS) and 8/30-mm AA (II × 4, controlled by 2/Drum Tilt radar GFCS) and had an air-search radar; these were removed before the ship left the Baltic. *Rossiya* and subsequent units are equipped to accommodate a single 76-mm automatic DP gun

**Rossiya**—with 76-mm gun and Bass Tilt director forward 1985

**Sibir'** *Ships of the World,* 1984

and Bass Tilt radar GFCS forward. Propulsion power is distributed 37,500 hp on the centerline shaft and 18,750 hp on each of the outboard shafts. Each shaft is driven by two 8,800-kw a.c./8,100-kw d.c. motors. *Rossiya* and the fourth unit have heated waterline ice-strakes and improved, corrosion-resistant hull-steel alloys. *Rossiya* began dock trials 8-85 and has five 2,000-kw primary generators, one 1,000-kw emergency generator, and two 2,000-kw "emergency electrical aggregates." She has a later air-search radar and was stated to be 150.0 overall and to have a 10.3-m draft. All have seven watertight compartments. Cinema, library, "nature hall," and 7.5 × 3.0-m pool fitted. There is a hangar and flight deck for two Helix-C (Ka-32) ice-reconnaissance helicopters. *Arktika* traveled to the North Pole in 8-87, the first surface ship to do so. *Arktika* renamed *Brezhnev* after his death, restored to original name, 1985, when the fourth unit was named *Brezhnev.*

◆ **1 Lenin class** Bldr: Admiralty SY, Leningrad

LENIN (In serv. 20-12-59)

**Lenin** Sovfoto

**D:** 15,940 tons light (19,240 fl) **S:** 19.7 kts (18 kts service)
**Dim:** 134.0 (124.0 pp) × 26.8 × 10.5
**M:** 2/4-loop pressurized-water reactors, 4/8,200-kw turbogenerators, electric drive; 3/4-bladed props; 39,800 hp
**Electric:** . . . **Man:** 218 tot.

REMARKS: 14,067 grt/3,849 dwt. The world's first nuclear-powered surface ship. *Lenin* was out of service for many years in the late 1960s and re-emerged with a new reactor plant having only two reactors vice the original three. Helicopter deck and hangar.

## SEAGOING ICEBREAKERS

◆ **4 Kapitan Sorokin class** Bldr: Wärtsilä, Helsinki

KAPITAN SOROKIN (In serv. 1977) KAPITAN DRANITSYN (In serv. 1980)
KAPITAN NIKOLAYEV (In serv. 1978) KAPITAN KHLEBNIKOV (In serv. 1981)

**D:** 10,440 tons light (14,655 fl) **S:** 19 kts (16 kts service)
**Dim:** 131.9 (122.5 pp) × 26.5 × 8.5
**M:** 6 Wärtsilä-Sulzer 9ZL 40/48 diesel generator sets, electric drive; 3 props; 22,300 hp
**Electric:** 4,900 kw **Fuel:** 3,666 tons **Range:** 10,700/16
**Man:** 11 officers, 65 crew

**SEAGOING ICEBREAKERS** *(continued)*

**Kapitan Nikolayev** Wärtsilä, 1983

Remarks: 10,609 grt/4,225 dwt. Equipped with the Wärtsilä bubbler system to keep the hull bottom ice-free. Helicopter pad, no hangar. All personnel accommodated in the superstructure. Considered to be "shallow-draft" ships. Equipped to perform salvage and towing operations.

◆ **3 Yermak class** Bldr: Wärtsilä, Helsinki

Yermak (In serv. 4-7-74) Krasin (In serv. 2-76)
Admiral Makarov (In serv. 6-75)

**Admiral Makarov** Wärtsilä, 1975

**D:** 13,280 tons light (20,241 fl) **S:** 19.5 kts
**Dim:** 135.8 (130.0 pp) × 26.0 × 11.0
**M:** 9 Wärtsilä-Sulzer 12 ZN 40/48-3,050 diesel generator sets, electric drive; 3/4-bladed props; 36,500 hp
**Electric:** see Remarks **Fuel:** 5,750 tons **Range:** 29,300/14
**Man:** 146 tot.

Remarks: 12/231 grt/7,441 dwt. The U.S.S.R.'s most powerful conventional icebreakers. Can break 6-m ice or maintain 2 kts through 1.8-m ice. Have Wärtsilä bubbler system, helicopter pad. Electrical power taken from propulsion generators. *Krasin* refitted 1-84 to 3-84 by Böttcher and Gröning, Hamburg; re-engined.

◆ **5 Moskva class** Bldr: Wärtsilä, Helsinki

Moskva (In serv. 1960) Murmansk (In serv. 1968)
Leningrad (In serv. 1962) Vladivostok (In serv. 1969)
Kiev (In serv. 1966)

**D:** 13,290 tons (15,360 fl) **S:** 18.3 kts **Dim:** 122.1 (112.4 pp) × 24.5 × 10.5
**M:** 8 Wärtsilä-Sulzer 9MH51, 2,160-kw diesel generator sets, electric drive; 3/4-bladed props; 26,300 hp
**Fuel:** 5,200 tons **Range:** 20,000/14
**Man:** 116 tot.

Remarks: 9,427 grt/4,221 dwt. Have heeling tanks, capable of shifting 480 tons of water in two minutes. Can carry two ice-reconnaissance helicopters. 60-ton bollard pull towing capacity. *Leningrad* was overhauled at Yokohama in 1969–70 and re-engined.

**Kiev** Wärtsilä

**MEDIUM ICEBREAKERS**

◆ **1 modified Mudyug class** Bldr: Wärtsilä, Helsinki

Mudyug (In serv. 29-10-82)

**Mudyug** Thyssen, 10-86

**D:** 7,775 tons (fl) **S:** 17.45 kts **Dim:** 111.00 (88.80 pp) × 22.20 × 6.50
**Electron Equipt:** Radar: 1/Don-2, 1/Okean
**M:** 4 Wärtsilä Vasa 8R32 heavy-oil diesels; 2 KaMeWa CP props; 12,405 hp
**Electric:** 2,530 kw **Range:** . . . **Fuel:** 690 m$^3$
**Man:** 34 tot. (43 accommodations)

Remarks: 5,342 grt. Modified at Thyssen Nordseewerke, Emden, 28-7-86 to 29-10-86 with new 1,150-ton Thyssen/WAAS flat-form bow and Jastran water hull-lubrication and thruster system. Icebreaking capability improved to .9 m from .5 m, with 50 percent power saving in ice. Full tankage also increased. Highly successful trials, spring 1987, may result in further conversions.

◆ **2 Mudyug class** Bldr: Wärtsilä, Helsinki

Magadan (In serv. 12-82) Dikson (In serv. 17-3-83)

**Mudyug**—as built L. & L. Van Ginderen, 7-83

**D:** 5,560 tons light (6,210 fl) **S:** 17.45 kts (16.5 sust.)
**Dim:** 8/92.00 (88.49 hull, 78.50 wl) × 20.92 (20.00 wl) × 6.50
**M:** 4 Wärtsilä Vasa 8R32 heavy-oil diesels; 2 CP props; 12,405 hp (9,500 in ice)
**Electric:** 2,530 kw **Range:** 15,000/16.5 **Man:** 34 tot.
**Fuel:** 1,902 tons heavy oil, 388 tons diesel

Remarks: Approx. 4,400 grt. Have Wärtsilä air-bubbler system. Intended for use in the Barents, Baltic, and Sea of Okhotsk. Have 917-ton bollard pull. Unusual in not employing electric drive. Have three 800-kw ship's service generators. Can break .5-m ice.

## MEDIUM ICEBREAKERS *(continued)*

### ◆ 14 Dobrynya Nikitich class   Bldr: Admiralty SY, Leningrad

| | In serv. | | In serv. |
|---|---|---|---|
| Vasiliy Pronchishchev | 1961 | Semen Chelyushkin | 1965 |
| Afanasiy Nikitin | 1962 | Yuriy Lisyanskiy | 1965 |
| Khariton Laptev | 1962 | Petr Pakhtusov | 1966 |
| Vasiliy Poyarkov | 1963 | Georgiy Sedov | 1967 |
| Yerofey Khabarov | 1963 | Fedor Litke | 1970 |
| Ivan Kruzhenshtern | 1964 | Ivan Moskvitin | 1971 |
| Vladimir Rusanov | 1964 | Semen Dezhnev | 1971 |

**Yuriy Lisyanskiy** L. & L. Van Ginderen, 7-84

**D:** 2,675–2,940 tons (fl) **S:** 14.5 kts (12.0 service)
**Dim:** 67.7 (62.0 pp) × 18.3 × 6.1 **Electron Equipt:** Radar: 1 or 2/Don-2
**M:** 3 Type 13D100 diesel generator sets; 3/3-bladed props (1 fwd); 5,400 hp
**Fuel:** 600 tons **Range:** 5,500/12 **Man:** 39 tot.

Remarks: 2,305 grt/1,092 dwt typical. Seven sisters, several of which are armed, serve the Soviet Navy. *Petr Pakhtusov* and *Georgiy Sedov* have been employed on occasional scientific voyages by the Academy of Sciences. The specially built research icebreakers *Otto Schmidt* (civilian) and *Vladimir Kavrayskiy* (naval) are variants of this design, as are the *Ivan Susanin*-class patrol icebreakers. Ships of this class are often used as ocean tugs in summer months.

### ◆ 3 Kapitan Belousov class   Bldr: Wärtsilä, Helsinki

Kapitan Belousov (In serv. 1954)
Kapitan Voronin (In serv. 1955)
Kapitan Melekhov (In serv. 1956)

**Kapitan Belousov**

**D:** 5,360 tons (fl) **S:** 16.5 kts **Dim:** 83.20 (77.10 pp) × 19.40 × 7.0
**M:** 6 Wärtsilä diesel generator sets, electric drive; 4 props (2 fwd); 10,600 hp
**Fuel:** 1,025 tons **Range:** 10,000/14.8 **Man:** 120 tot.

Remarks: 3,377 to 3,710 grt/1,308 to 1,423 dwt. The U.S.S.R.'s first post-W.W. II icebreakers; primarily for harbor and thin-ice work, hence forward-mounted pair of propellers. Can break 1–2-m ice.

## RIVER ICEBREAKERS

### ◆ 9 Kapitan Yevdokimov class   Bldr: Wärtsilä, Helsinki

Kapitan Yevdokimov (In serv. 31-3-83)
Kapitan Babichev (In serv. 30-6-83)
Kapitan Borodkin (In serv. 13-11-83)
Kapitan Chudinov (In serv. 9-9-83)
Kapitan Evdokimov (In serv. 1983)
Avraamiy Zavenyagin (In serv. 12-4-84)
Kapitan Metsayk (In serv. 8-84)
Kapitan Demidov (In serv. 22-11-84)
Kapitan Moshkin (In serv. 14-5-86)

**Kapitan Evdokimov** Wärtsilä, 1984

**D:** 2,200 tons (fl) **S:** 13.5 kts (12 kts service) **Dim:** 76.5 (. . . pp) × 16.6 × 2.5
**M:** 4 Wärtsilä Vasa 12V22B, 1,640-hp diesel generator sets, electric drive; 4 props (2 fwd); 5,170 hp
**Man:** 25 tot.

Remarks: 1,500 grt. Remarkably shallow draft. Intended to clear Arctic rivers. Equipped with Wärtsilä bubbler system and a sewage-treatment plant. Ninth ordered 27-6-84 and launched 12-7-85.

### ◆ 6 Kapitan Chechkin class   Bldr: Wärtsilä, Helsinki

| | In serv. | | In serv. |
|---|---|---|---|
| Kapitan Bukayev | 1978 | Kapitan Krutov | 1978 |
| Kapitan Chadayev | 1978 | Kapitan Plakhin | 1977 |
| Kapitan Chechkin | 1977 | Kapitan Zarubin | 1978 |

**Kapitan Krutov** Wärtsilä, 1978

**D:** 2,240 tons (fl) **S:** 14 kts **Dim:** 77.6 (73.9 pp) × 16.3 × 3.3
**M:** 3 Wärtsilä diesels, electric drive; 3 props; 6,300 hp
**Electric:** 330 kw **Range:** . . . **Man:** 28 tot.

Remarks: Approx. 1,600 grt. Capable of breaking 1-meter-thick ice; have air-bubbler system. Service speed 10 kts.

### ◆ 3 Kapitan M. Izmaylov class   Bldr: Wärtsilä, Helsinki (In serv. 1976)

Kapitan A. Radzhabov
Kapitan Kosolabov
Kapitan M. Izmaylov

**Kapitan A. Radzhabov** L. & L. Van Ginderen, 7-86

**U.S.S.R.** *(continued)*
**RIVER ICEBREAKERS** *(continued)*

**D:** 2,048 tons (fl) **S:** 14 kts **Dim:** 56.3 (52.2 pp) × 16.3 × 4.2
**M:** 4 Wärtsilä Vasa 824TS diesels, 2/4-bladed props; 5,330 hp
**Fuel:** 380 tons **Range:** 5,000/14 **Man:** 24 tot.

REMARKS: 1,362 grt/354 dwt. Endurance: 15 days.

# UNITED ARAB EMIRATES

PERSONNEL (1985): 80 officers, 1,120 men

MERCHANT MARINE (1986): 220 ships—653,525 grt (32 tankers—371,684 grt)

NAVAL AVIATION: Two Britten-Norman BN-2 Islander Maritime Defender ordered 1982 for patrol duties. Abu Dhabi ordered 8 AS-332 Super Puma helicopters with AS 39 Exocet antiship missiles in 1983.

NOTE: Primarily incorporating the former Defense Force Sea Wing of the Abu Dhabi National Defense Force, the UAE Navy was formed on 1 February 1978 as part of the federated forces of Abu Dhabi, Ajman, Dubai, Fujairah, Ras al Khaimah, Sharjah, and Umm al Qaiwan. The merchant marines of these states are also combined into a single administrative unit. Several of these nation states, including Abu Dhabi and Dubai, also operate separate Customs Services with patrol craft.

### GUIDED-MISSILE CORVETTES

◆ **0 (+2) Type 62** Bldr: Lürssen, Vegesack

P 6201 N . . . (In serv. . . .) P 6202 N . . . (In serv. . . .)

**62-meter missile boat for U.A.E.**—builder's model Lürssen, 1987

**D:** 630 tons (fl) **S:** 34.7 kts (32.25 sust.) **Dim:** 62.95 (59.90 pp) × 9.30 × 2.60
**A:** 8/MM 40 Exocet SSM (IV × 2)—1/Crotale SAM system (VIII × 1, . . . missiles)—1/76-mm OTO Melara "Super Rapid" DP—1/30-mm Goalkeeper CIWS
**Electron Equipt:** Radar: . . .
EW: . . .
**M:** 4 MTU . . . diesels; 4 props; 19,600 hp
**Range:** 4,000/16 **Electric:** 408 kw **Man:** 40 tot.
**Fuel:** 120 tons

REMARKS: Ordered mid-1987. Same basic design built for Bahrain.

### GUIDED-MISSILE PATROL BOATS

◆ **6 TNC-45-class guided-missile boats** Bldr: Lürssen, Vegesack

| | In serv. | | In serv. |
|---|---|---|---|
| P 4501 BANIYAS | 11-80 | P 4504 SHAHEEN | 4-81 |
| P 4502 MARBAN | 11-80 | P 4505 SAQAR | 6-81 |
| P 4503 RODQUM | 4-81 | P 4506 TARIF | 6-81 |

**D:** 231 tons (259 fl) **S:** 41.5 kts **Dim:** 44.9 (42.3 pp) × 7.0 × 2.46 (prop)
**A:** 4/MM 40 Exocet (II × 2)—1/76-mm OTO Melara DP—2/40-mm Breda AA (II × 1)—2/76.2-mm mg (I × 2)
**Electron Equipt:** Radar: 1/Decca TM 1226, 1/PEAB 9LV 200 Mk 2 system
EW: Decca Cutlass RDL-2 passive, 1 Dagaie chaff RL
**M:** 4 MTU 16V538 TB92 diesels; 4 props; 15,600 hp (13,000 sust.)
**Electric:** 405 kVA **Range:** 500/38.5; 1,600/16 **Man:** 5 officers, 27 men

**Rodqum (P 4503)** French Navy, 1986

REMARKS: The radar director is equipped with low light-level t.v. and an infrared tracker and has an associated search radar atop the mast. There is a CSEE Panda optical director for the 40-mm mount. Carry 350 rds 76-mm, 1,800 rds 40-mm, and 6,000 rds mg ammunition.

### PATROL BOATS AND CRAFT

◆ **6 110-foot class** Bldr: Vosper Thornycroft, Portsmouth, U.K.

| | L | | L |
|---|---|---|---|
| P 1101 ARDHANA | 7-3-75 | P 1104 AL GHULIAN | 16-9-75 |
| P 1102 ZURARA | 13-6-75 | P 1105 RADOOM | 15-12-75 |
| P 1103 MURBAN | 15-9-75 | P 1106 GHANADHAH | 1-3-76 |

**Ardhana (P 1101)** French Navy, 1986

**D:** 110 tons (140 fl) **S:** 29 kts **Dim:** 33.5 (31.5 pp) × 6.4 × 1.7
**A:** 2/30-mm BMARC/Oerlikon A32 AA (II × 1)—1/20-mm AA
**Electron Equipt:** Radar: 1/Decca TM 1226
**M:** 2 Ruston-Paxman Valenta RP200M diesels; 2 props; 5,400 hp
**Range:** 1,800/14 **Man:** 26 tot.

◆ **3 Kawkab-class patrol craft** Bldr: Keith Nelson, Bembridge, U.K.

P 561 KAWKAB (In serv. 7-3-69) P 562 THOABAN (In serv. 7-3-69)
P 563 BANIYAS (In serv. 27-12-69)

**Kawkab (P 561)** Vosper, 1960

**PATROL BOATS AND CRAFT** *(continued)*

**D:** 25 tons (32 fl) **S:** 17.52 (15.84 pp) × 4.72 × 1.37
**A:** 2/20-mm AA (I × 2) **Electron Equipt:** Radar: 1/Decca RM 916
**M:** 2 Caterpillar diesels; 2 props; 750 hp **Endurance:** 7 days
**Electric:** 24 kw **Man:** 2 officers, 9 men

REMARKS: Fiberglass hull. Used for coastal patrol, hydrographic surveys, and surveillance of petroleum leases. Designed by Keith Nelson, a division of Vosper. Freshwater evaporator provides 900 liters daily.

◆ **3 fast patrol craft** Bldr: Boghammar, Stockholm (In serv. 1986)

**D:** 5.5 tons (fl) **S:** 50 kts **Dim:** 13.00 × 2.66 × 0.90
**M:** 2 Volvo Penta TAMD-70E diesels; 2 outdrive props; 600 hp
**Range:** 500/35 **Man:** 3–5 tot.

REMARKS: Purchased by Abu Dhabi specifically for the defense of the Sultan's palace.

**SERVICE CRAFT**

◆ **1 repair tender** Bldr: Singapore Slipway (In serv. 6-83)

BARRACUDA

**D:** . . . **S:** . . . **Dim:** 58.0 × . . . × . . .
**M:** 2 Ruston-Paxman RKCM diesels; 2 props; 6,000 hp

◆ **2 workboats** Bldr: Cheverton, Cowes, U.K. (In serv. 1975)

A 271 A 272

**D:** 3.3 tons **S:** 8 kts **Dim:** 8.2 × 2.7 × 0.8
**M:** 1 Lister-Blackstone RMW3 diesel; 150 hp

REMARKS: Glass-reinforced plastic construction.

◆ **2 diving tenders** Bldr: Crestitalia, Ameglia, La Spezia

**D:** 97 tons (fl) **S:** 25 kts **Dim:** 30.0 × 6.9 × 1.2
**Electron Equipt:** Radar: 1/. . . nav.
**M:** 2 Isotta Fraschini: ID36 S12V diesels; 2 props; 3,040 hp **Range:** 500/25

REMARKS: Lengthened version of the *Mario Marino*-class built for the Italian Navy. Ordered 12-85. GRP construction. Intended to support combat swimmers, as well as providing diving support services. Decompression chamber.

◆ **2 utility landing craft** Bldr: Siong Huat SY, Singapore

GHAGA II (In serv. 8-4-87) AL FEY (In serv. 5-87)

REMARKS: *Ghaga II* is 40 m o.a.; *Al Fey* is 50 m. No other details available; may be commercial craft.

COAST GUARD

REMARKS: The Coast Guard operates under the Ministry of the Interior.

**PATROL CRAFT**

◆ **4 Type 23GC class** Bldr: Baglietto SY (In serv. 1986–87)

**23GC class for U.A.E. Coast Guard** Baglietto, 7-87

**D:** 40 tons light/44.50 standard (48 fl) **S:** 41.8 kts (38 sust.)
**Dim:** 23.00 (20.00 wl) × 5.50 × 1.17 **A:** 1/20-mm AA—2/7.62-mm mg (I × 2)
**Electron Equipt:** Radar: 1/. . . nav.
**M:** 2 MTU 12V396 TB93 diesels; 2 props; 3,560 hp (2,960 sust.)
**Range:** 700/20 **Fuel:** 7,500 liters **Endurance:** 4 days
**Electric:** 64 kVA **Man:** 9 tot.

REMARKS: Design derived from Italian Customs *Meattini* class. Aluminum-magnesium alloy hull and superstructure. First unit, paid for by Dubai, delivered 3-86. Second, paid for Abu Dhabi, delivered 5-86. Third and fourth, paid for by Dubai, delivered 14-7-87 and 9-87.

◆ **9 45-ft Mk-II class** Bldr: Watercraft, Ltd., U.K. (In serv. 1982–83)

**D:** 10 tons (fl) **S:** 26 kts **Dim:** 13.90 × 4.26 × 1.14
**A:** 1/7.62-mm mg **Electron Equipt:** Radar: . . .
**M:** 2 M.A.N. D2542 MLE diesels; 2 props; 1,300 hp
**Man:** 5 tot.

REMARKS: Glass-reinforced plastic construction. Ordered 2-82.

◆ **17 P 1200 class** Bldr: Watercraft, Ltd., U.K. (In serv. 1979–81)

**D:** 10 tons (fl) **S:** 29 kts **Dim:** 11.90 (10.16 wl) × 4.08 × 1.06
**A:** 2/7.62-mm mg (I × 2) **M:** 2 MTU diesels; 2 props; 800 hp
**Range:** 300/20 **Man:** 4 tot.

REMARKS: Glass-reinforced plastic hulls. First ten delivered 1979–80; seven more ordered, 1980.

◆ **6 Dhafeer-class patrol craft** Bldr: Keith Nelson, Bembridge, U.K.

| | L | In serv. | | L | In serv. |
|---|---|---|---|---|---|
| P 401 DHAFEER | 2-68 | 1-7-68 | P 404 DURGHAM | 9-68 | 7-6-69 |
| P 402 GHADUNFAR | 5-68 | 1-7-68 | P 405 TIMSAH | 9-68 | 7-6-69 |
| P 403 HAZZA | 5-68 | 1-7-68 | P 406 MURAYJIB | 2-70 | 7-7-70 |

**Dhafeer class** J. Bouvia, 1987

**D:** 10 tons **S:** 19 kts **Dim:** 12.5 × 3.65 × 1.1
**A:** 2/7.62-mm mg (I × 2) **M:** 2 Cummins diesels; 2 props; 370 hp
**Range:** 15/18; 350/15 **Man:** 1 officer, 5 men

REMARKS: Subordinate to Marine Police. Fiberglass hull.

◆ **6 Spear-class police patrol craft** Bldr: Fairey Marine, Hamble, U.K.

**D:** 10 tons **S:** 26 kts **Dim:** 9.1 × 2.75 × 0.84 **A:** 2/12.7-mm mg
**M:** 2 Perkins T 6-354 diesels; 2 props; 580 hp **Man:** 3 tot.

REMARKS: In service in 8-74, 9-74, and 1-75. Fiberglass hull.

CUSTOMS SERVICES

NOTE: Several of the component states of the United Arab Emirates operate their own Customs Service patrol craft. Dubai (listed elsewhere) has two U.S. Swiftships 19.8-m Commercial Cruisers, while Sharjah received from Halter Marine, Moss Point, Mississippi, in 1987 two patrol boats:

**D:** . . . **S:** 24 kts **Dim:** 23.77 × 5.64 × 1.42
**M:** 2 G.M. 12 V71 TI diesels; 2 props; 1,350 hp

REMARKS: Modified oilfield crew boat design.

◆ **5 P-77A Customs patrol craft** Bldr: Camcraft, New Orleans, La. (In serv. 9-75)

No. 21 through No. 25

**D:** 70 tons (fl) **S:** 25 kts **Dim:** 23.4 × 5.5 × 1.5 **A:** 2/20-mm AA (I × 2)
**M:** 2 G.M. 12V71T diesels; 2 props; 1,400 hp **Range:** 750/25

◆ **2 50-foot Customs patrol craft** Bldr: Cheverton, Cowes, U.K. (In serv. 2-75)

AL SHAHEEN AL AQAB

**D:** 20 tons **S:** 23 kts **Dim:** 15.2 × 4.3 × 1.4 **A:** 1/7.62-mm mg
**M:** 2 G.M. diesels; 2 props; 850 hp **Range:** 1,000/20 **Man:** 8 tot.

# U.S.A.

PERSONNEL (10-87): Navy: 592,700 active (73,627 officers, 514,548 enlisted, 4,525 midshipmen); Marines: 199,600 active (20,280 officers, 179,320 enlisted).

In addition, there were 128,010 paid billet Naval Reservists, 21,476 TAR active Naval Reservists, and 42,800 paid Marine Corps Reservists. About 353,000 civil service civilians serve the Navy and Marine Corps. For FY 88, the Navy was authorized 593,200 active/152,600 paid reserve billets, the Marine Corps 199,600 active/43,600 paid reserve. About 54,600 women in the Navy, 5,000 on ships.

MERCHANT MARINE (1986): 6,496 ships—19,900,843 grt
(tankers: 259 ships—7,001,599 grt)

## NAVAL PROGRAM

The table lists new construction programs for fiscal years 1986 through 1992. The annual five-year program has fluctuated drastically for many years and, because of changing political pressures, cannot be relied on as an accurate projection of what will actually be proposed, let alone authorized and appropriated by the Congress. It is nonetheless given here as the best available forecast; it will probably be reduced. In FY 88, partial 2-year authorization began, but funding remains annual.

SHIPBUILDING PROGRAM 1986–92

| | Authorized | | | | Proposed | | |
|---|---|---|---|---|---|---|---|
| New construction: | FY 86 | FY 87 | FY 88 | FY 89 | FY 90 | FY 91 | FY 92 |
| SSBN, *Ohio* | 1 | 1 | 1 | 1 | 1 | 1 | 1 |
| SSN, *Los Angeles* | 4 | 4 | 3 | 2 | 2 | 2 | 1 |
| SSN, *Seawolf* | — | — | — | 1 | — | 2 | 2 |
| CVN, *T. Roosevelt* | — | — | 2 | — | 2 | — | — |
| CG, *Ticonderoga* | 3 | 3 | 5 | — | — | — | — |
| DDG, *Arleigh Burke* | — | 2 | — | 3 | 5 | 6 | 6 |
| MCM, *Avenger* | 2 | 3 | — | — | — | — | — |
| MHC | 1 | — | — | 2 | 3 | 3 | 4 |
| LHD, *Wasp* | 1 | — | 1 | 1 | — | 1 | — |
| LSD, LSD 49 | — | — | 1 | — | 1 | 1 | 2 |
| LSD, *Whidbey Isl.* | 2 | — | — | — | — | — | — |
| PCM Patrol Craft | — | — | — | — | 1 | — | 4 |
| T-AO, *H.S. Kaiser* | 2 | 2 | 2 | 2 | 2 | 1 | — |
| T-AGOS, T-AGOS 19 | — | 1 | 2 | 3 | 3 | 2 | — |
| T-AGOS, *Stalwart* | 2 | 2 | — | — | — | — | — |
| AE, AE 36 | — | — | — | — | — | 1 | 1 |
| AOE, *Supply* | — | 1 | — | 1 | — | 2 | — |
| AGOR, AGOR 23 | — | 1 | — | — | — | — | — |
| T-AGOR, T-AGOR 24 | — | — | — | 1 | — | — | — |
| AGOR, AGOR 25 | — | — | — | — | 1 | — | — |
| T-AGS, *Maury* | — | — | — | — | — | 1 | — |
| T-AGS, T-AGS 43 | — | — | — | — | 1 | 2 | — |
| LCAC | 12 | — | — | 9 | 9 | 9 | 9 |
| Major Conversions/ SLEP/Reactivations: | | | | | | | |
| CV SLEP | — | — | — | — | — | 1 | — |
| BB, *Iowa* | 1 | — | — | — | — | — | — |
| AO-177 Jumbo | — | — | 1 | 2 | 2 | — | — |
| T-ACS conv. | 3 | 2 | 2 | — | — | — | — |
| T-AGS conv. | — | 2 | — | — | — | — | — |

* Authorization granted in FY 88 bill; one DDG 51 in FY 89 may be a CG 47, if insufficient funds are appropriated in FY 88 for all five.

## MARINE CORPS

Created in 1775, the Marine Corps has three missions:

—to seize and/or defend advanced bases as needed for the operations of the fleet
—to furnish security detachments on board ships and at land bases
—to carry out any other operations that the president of the United States may assign.

The third mission permits the corps to be used in operations that are not purely naval (e.g., Belleau Wood in 1918 and Vietnam in the 1960s and 1970s).

Its total strength of about 199,600 men and women forms three Marine Expeditionary Force (MEF) divisions (one stationed in Okinawa/Japan, two in the United States), each of 32,600 men, and three air wings, organized under two Fleet Marine Forces (FMF). These last also maintain heavy support elements for the divisions. A fourth division-wing team constitutes a reserve cadre. Each MEF has 70 tanks, 280 aircraft, 340 helicopters, and 100 artillery batteries attached.

The Marine Corps has approximately 400 fighter and attack aircraft (A-4M, A-6, AV-8A/C, F-4), 600 assault and utility helicopters, more than 500 tanks, and some 450 amphibious landing vehicles.

The major operational unit is the Marine Expeditionary Force (MEF), which consists of one division, one air wing, and Fleet Marine Forces augmentation, for a total of about 58,000 Marines, plus about 26,300 naval personnel aboard ships, etc.

Amphibious ships currently in service do not permit the rapid overseas deployment of MEFs, but only of two Marine Expeditionary Brigades (MEB). A MEB consists of one Regimental Landing Team, a strong unit with two or more battalion landing teams of about 822 men each; one mixed air group of 110 fighter/attack fixed-wing aircraft and 120 helicopters, 15 tanks and 30 artillery batteries, and some augmentation from the Fleet Marine Force, for a total of about 15,500 men. The smallest assault unit is the Marine Expeditionary Unit (MEU), with a landing team, air squadrons, and support personnel, totaling 2,500, and has 5 tanks, 6 aircraft, 30 helicopters, and 5 artillery batteries.

## SPECIAL FORCES

Consisting of 1,700 men in 1985, the 6 SEAL Teams were divided into 41 platoons. By 1990 the force is to grow to 2,700 men in 7 teams/70 platoons, all capable of aerial or seaborne insertion.

## THE NAVAL RESERVE FORCE

Naval Reserve Force ships have cadre crews of regular naval personnel, with reserve augmentation personnel constituting up to two-thirds of the total crew assigned. As of 1-1-88, the Force included: 1 destroyer, 20 frigates, 18 ocean minesweepers, 2 tank landing ships, 4 Special Boat Units, 16 Mobile Inshore Undersea Warfare Units, 17 Mobile Construction Battalions, and 6 Cargo-Handling Battalions. Naval Reserve Force Air Wings consist of 51 aircraft squadrons: 4 fighter, 6 attack, 2 light photographic, 2 carrier air early warning, 2 tactical electronic warfare, 2 aerial refueling, 13 patrol squadrons (organized into 2 patrol wings), 1 helicopter wing (4 ASW squadrons, 1 combat support squadron, and 2 light attack squadrons), 1 tactical support wing (with 11 logistical support squadrons), and 2 fleet composite squadrons. Also incorporated in the Naval Reserve program are 2,100 other units supporting 35 programs to augment Regular Navy staffs in wartime.

## THE MILITARY SEALIFT COMMAND

The Military Sealift Command (MSC) operates or charters ships in support of the United States Navy. Headed by an active-duty U.S. Navy flag officer, its ships are manned primarily by civilians, either civil service or contract employees. The ships of the MSC are listed in a separate section, after naval units.

WARSHIPS IN ACTIVE SERVICE, UNDER CONSTRUCTION, OR APPROPRIATED AS OF 1 JANUARY 1988

| | L | Std. Tons | Main armament |
|---|---|---|---|
| **◆ 15 (+4) attack carriers** | | | |
| 1 (+4) THEODORE ROOSEVELT (CVN) | 1984–. . . | 82,000 | 88–90 aircraft, 3/Sea Sparrow |
| 3 NIMITZ (CVN) | 1972–80 | 81,600 | 88–90 aircraft, 3/Sea Sparrow |
| 1 ENTERPRISE (CVN) | 1960 | 75,700 | 88–90 aircraft, 2/Sea Sparrow |
| 1 JOHN F. KENNEDY (CV) | 1967 | 61,000 | 88–90 aircraft, 3/Sea Sparrow |
| 3 KITTY HAWK (CV) | 1960–64 | 60,100 | 88 aircraft, 2-3/Sea Sparrow |
| 4 FORRESTAL (CV) | 1954–58 | 59,600 | 88 aircraft, 2/Sea Sparrow |
| 2 MIDWAY (CV) | 1945–46 | 56,000 | 65 aircraft, 0 or 2/Sea Sparrow |
| **◆ 12 (+3) amphibious assault helicopter carriers** | | | |
| 0 (+3) WASP (LHD) | 1987–. . . | 28,000 | 2/Sea Sparrow, up to 42 a/c |
| 5 TARAWA (LHA) | 1972–78 | 28,000 | 3/127-mm DP, 2/Sea Sparrow, 19 or 30 helicopters |
| 7 IWO JIMA (LPH) | 1960–69 | 17,000 | 4/76.2-mm, 2/Sea Sparrow, 28 helicopters |
| **◆ 36 (+7) nuclear-powered ballistic-missile submarines** | | | |
| | | (surfaced) | |
| 8 (+7) OHIO (SSBN) | 1979–. . . | 15,750 | 24/Trident, 4/TT |
| 28 LAFAYETTE (SSBN) | 1962–66 | 7,250 | 16/Poseidon or Trident, 4/TT |
| **◆ 94 (+22) nuclear-powered attack submarines** | | | |
| 37 (+22) LOS ANGELES | 1973–. . . | 6,000 | 4/TT |
| 1 GLENARD P. LIPSCOMB | 1973 | 5,813 | 4/TT |
| 37 STURGEON | 1966–74 | 3,640 | 4/TT |
| 1 NARWHAL | 1967 | 4,550 | 4/TT |
| 13 PERMIT | 1961–66 | 3,526 | 4/TT |
| 2 ETHAN ALLEN | 1960–62 | 6,300 | 4/TT |
| 3 SKIPJACK | 1958–60 | 3,075 | 6/TT |
| **◆ 4 diesel/electric-powered attack submarines** | | | |
| 3 BARBEL | 1958–59 | 2,146 | 6/TT |
| 1 DARTER | 1956 | 1,720 | 8/TT |

**WARSHIPS IN ACTIVE SERVICE** *(continued)*

◆ **3 (+1) battleships**

| | | | |
|---|---|---|---|
| 3 (+1) Iowa | 1942–44 | 46,100 | 32 Tomahawk, 16 Harpoon, 9/406-mm, 12/127-mm DP, 4/20-mm Vulcan/Phalanx AA, 3 helicopters |

◆ **36 (+18) cruisers**

| | | | |
|---|---|---|---|
| *9 nuclear-powered:* | | Tons | |
| 4 Virginia (CGN) | 1974–78 | 10,400 | 2/missile launchers, 8/Tomahawk, 8/Harpoon, 2/127-mm DP, 6/ASW TT |
| 2 California (CGN) | 1971–72 | 10,400 | 2/missile launchers, 8/Harpoon, 2/127-mm DP, ASROC, 4/ASW TT |
| 1 Truxtun (CGN) | 1964 | 8,600 | 1/missile launcher, 8/Harpoon, 1/127-mm DP, 4/ASW TT |
| 1 Bainbridge (CGN) | 1961 | 8,600 | 2/missile launchers, 8/Harpoon, ASROC, 6/ASW TT |
| 1 Long Beach (CGN) | 1959 | 15,500 | 2/missile launchers, 8/Tomahawk, 8/Harpoon, ASROC, 6/ASW TT |
| *27 (+18) conventional:* | | | |
| 9 (+18) Ticonderoga | 1981–. . . | 7,400 | 2/missile launchers, 8/Harpoon, 2/127-mm DP, 6/ASW TT, 1/helicopter |
| 9 Belknap (CG) | 1963–65 | 6,570 | 1/missile launcher, 8/Harpoon, 1/127-mm DP, 6/ASW TT, 1/helicopter |
| 9 Leahy (CG) | 1961–63 | 6,070 | 2/missile launchers, 8/Harpoon, ASROC, 6/ASW TT |

◆ **69 (+3) destroyers**

| | | | |
|---|---|---|---|
| 0 (+3) Arleigh Burke | 1989–. . . | 6,600 | 2/VLS missile groups, 8/Harpoon, 1/127-mm DP, 6/ASW TT |
| 4 Kidd | 1979–80 | 8,140 | 2/missile launchers, 2/127-mm DP, 6/ASW TT, 1/helicopter |
| 31 Spruance | 1973–81 | 5,830 | 1/Sea Sparrow, 8/Harpoon, 2/127-mm DP, ASROC, 6/ASW TT, 1/helicopter |
| 23 Charles F. Adams | 1959–63 | 3,370 | 1/missile launcher, Harpoon, 2/127-mm DP, ASROC, 6/ASW TT |
| 10 Coontz | 1958–60 | 4,700 | 1/missile launcher, 8/Harpoon, 1/127-mm DP, ASROC, 6/ASW TT |
| 1 Forrest Sherman | 1958 | 2,780 | 3/127-mm DP, 6/ASW TT |

◆ **115 (+1) frigates**

| | | | |
|---|---|---|---|
| 50 (+1) Oliver Hazard Perry | 1976–88 | 2,997 | 1/missile launcher, Harpoon, 1/76-mm, 6/ASW TT, 1/helicopter |
| 46 Knox | 1966–73 | 3,011 | 0 or 1/Sea Sparrow, Harpoon, 1/127-mm DP, ASROC, 4/ASW TT, 1/helicopter |
| 6 Brooke | 1963–66 | 2,643 | 1/missile launcher, 1/127-mm DP, ASROC, 6/ASW TT, 1/helicopter |
| 10 Garcia | 1963–65 | 2,624 | 2/127-mm DP, ASROC, 6/ASW TT, 1/helicopter |
| 1 Glover | 1965 | 2,650 | 1/127-mm DP, ASROC, 6/ASW TT |
| 2 Bronstein | 1962 | 2,360 | 2/76.2-mm DP, ASROC, 6/ASW TT |

◆ **6 guided-missile patrol hydrofoils**

◆ **23 (+9) mine countermeasures ships**

◆ **45 (+6) amphibious warfare ships (plus helicopter carriers above)**

## WEAPONS AND SYSTEMS

### A. MISSILES

◆ **fleet ballistic missiles**

**Poseidon C-3 (UGM 73A)**—Lockheed

Length: 10.4 m
Diameter: 1.8 m
Weight: 29.48 tons at launch
Propulsion: solid propellant, two stages
Guidance: inertial
Range: 2,500 or 3,200 nautical miles
Warhead: 14 warheads with independent and controllable trajectory, each of 50 kt (MIRV) to 2,500 nautical miles or 10 of 50 kt to 3,200 nautical miles. Some warheads have been "uploaded" to increase destructive force.

**Trident-1 C-4 (UGM-96A)**—Lockheed

Operational in 1978. Designed for the *Ohio*-class SSBNs, which carry 24, and for 12 *Lafayette* and *Benjamin Franklin* SSBNs, which carry 16. The first eight *Ohio*-class SSBNs will slowly convert to the later D-5, from 1-91 to 1999. Seventy-two procured FY 83, 52 approved FY 84, the final year of production requests. Total procurement of 818 Trident of all kinds planned.

Length: 10.4 m
Weight: 31.75 tons at launch
Propulsion: solid propellant, three stages
Guidance: inertial
Range: 4,350 nautical miles
Warhead: 8 MIRV of 100 kt, Mk 4

The Mk 500 Evader MARV (Maneuverable Re-entry Vehicle) with six 100-kt warheads was developed by Lockheed, with procurement commencing in 1980.

**Trident-2 D-5**—Lockheed

In development for deployment in the late 1980s in the Pacific Fleet, and 1992 in the Atlantic. First ship to carry will be SSBN 734. First 21 authorized under FY 87, 66 under FY 88 and FY 89.

Length: 13.9 m
Weight: 57.15 tons at launch
Propulsion: solid propellant, three stages
Range: 6,000 nautical miles with 122-m circular point of error (CEP)
Warhead: 14 MIRV of 150 kt each or 7 MARV (Maneuverable Re-entry Vehicles) of 300 kt each. Initially will use same Mk 12A re-entry vehicles as the land-based Minuteman III and Peacemaker (MX), with 475-kt W87 warheads.

◆ **surface-to-surface missiles**

**Tomahawk (BGM-109)**—General Dynamics and McDonnell Douglas

Two versions are in service, strategic and tactical. Planned procurement is for 3,994 total missiles, with 2,600 potential launchers: submarines (using torpedo tubes or special vertical launch tubes), surface ships (using 4-missile armored box launchers or vertical launch cells), and aircraft. Fifty-one procured FY 83, 124 approved FY 84, 180 in FY 85, 249 in FY 86, 324 in FY 87; 475 in FY 88, 510 under FY 89.

Length: 6.17 m
Diameter: 0.52 m
Weight: 1,542 kg at launch (1,816 kg encapsulated for submarine launch)
Propulsion: solid booster, F-107 turbojet sustainer
*Strategic version:* 1,400 nautical miles range, operating at an altitude between 15 and 100 meters, at a speed of Mach 0.7. For launching from submarines, the weapon will be fired from torpedo tubes in a special container, jettisoned on leaving the water. Nuclear or conventional warhead. Guidance: TAINS (Tercom-

MISSILES *(continued)*

Aided Inertial Navigation System) using preprogrammed data plus TERCOM (Terrain Contour Matching). By 30-9-86, there were 14 surface ships and 30 attack submarines equipped for Tomahawk.

*Tactical version:* 250 nautical miles range, thus requiring an external means of target designation. Warhead weight up to 454 kg, conventional. Guidance: inertial, with active radar and anti-radiation homing.

| Tomahawk variant designations are: | | Navy procurement goal: |
|---|---|---|
| BGM-109A: | land-attack, nuclear warhead | 758 |
| BGM-109B: | antiship | 593 |
| BGM-109C: | land-attack, conventional | 2,643* |
| BGM-109D: | land-attack, bomblets | 0 |
| BGM-109E: | antiship | 0 |
| BGM-109F: | land-attack, anti-airfield | 560 |
| BGM-109G: | ground-launched, nuclear (GLCM) | 0 |
| AGM-109C: | MRASM proposal, terrain follower | 0 |
| AGM-109I: | MRASM proposal, infrared seeker | 0 |
| AGM-109H: | MRASM proposal, bomblets | 0 |

* 1,486 Block IIA with Bullpup warheads, 1,157 Block IIB with bomblet payloads. There are also sub-variants for ship or submarine launch.

**Harpoon (RGM-84A/D)**—McDonnell Douglas

An all-weather cruise missile that can be launched by aircraft, surface ships, or submarines. A total of 281 surface ships and submarines are programmed to receive it. Navy goal is 4,103 of all types; 4,800 had been ordered for U.S. and foreign customers by end-1986; over 4,000 had been delivered. Under FY 82, 240 were procured, with 221 approved under FY 83, 315 in FY 84, 354 in FY 85, 395 in FY 86, 96 in FY 87, 124 in FY 88, and 138 in FY 89.

Length: 4.628 m ship-launched/3.848 m air-launched
Diameter: 0.343 m—Wingspan: 0.914 m
Weight: 681 kg from canister, 680 kg from SAM launcher or 653 kg from ASROC launcher (with booster)
Propulsion: CAE-JA02 turbojet, with a rocket booster added to the ship- and submarine-launched versions
Speed: Mach 0.85
Guidance: inertial, then active homing on J band in the final trajectory
Range: "over 60" nautical miles
Warhead: 227 kg

**AGM-84** is the 526-kg, air-dropped version, which does not require a solid rocket booster, and **UGM-84** is the submarine version. The submarine version is shrouded and is launched from the torpedo tubes while submerged. In order to reach the maximum range, it is necessary to use targeting systems external to the launching unit—helicopters, for example. The AGM-84 will be carried by A-6E, P-3B, P-3C, and Air Force B-52 (12 each) aircraft. The U.S. Air Force acquired 85 undelivered Iranian AGM-84 in 8-84. Beginning with FY 88 procurement, will have "Dash-4" seeker and improved guidance.

◆ **surface-to-air missiles** (*Note:* Standard and Sea Sparrow can also be used against surface ships)

**Standard SM-1 MR (RIM-66B)**—General Dynamics

Single-stage missile, replaced Tartar.

Length: 4.47 m — Guidance: semi-active homing
Diameter: 0.34 m — Range: 25 nautical miles, 150–60,000 ft
Weight: 625 kg

System comprises Mk 11 twin launcher or Mk 13 single launcher with a vertical ready-service magazine containing 40 missiles (on the FFG 1 class: Mk 22 with 16 missiles), a computer, an air-search radar, a three-dimensional SPS-39, SPS-48, or SPS-52 radar, and SPG-51 guidance radars. A series of missiles of approximately the same size as the first RIM-24 Mod. 0 (U.S. military designation) but with constantly improved propulsion, miniaturization of components, and improved missile flight profile. Acceptance trials with the Block 6 variant (digital computer, monopulse radar) were carried out 3-83. 650 approved under FY 83, when procurement ended.

**Standard SM-2 MR (RIM-66C)**—General Dynamics and Raytheon

Single-stage missile. Initial procurement of 30 in FY 80. 150 approved under FY 83, 846 in FY 86, 844 in FY 87, 1,310 in FY 88; 1,635 requested FY 89.

Length: 4.70 m
Diameter: 0.34 m
Weight: 706 kg (Block II missiles)
Guidance: semi-active homing, with mid-course guidance capability, inertial reference, and improved ECCM
Range: more than 25 nautical miles

FY 88 and later missiles are Block III, with improved low-altitude fuze. A Block 4 version with new booster for vertical launch, better ECCM and a digital autopilot is to enter service in 1989, built by Raytheon (220) and General Dynamics (60).

**Standard SM-1 ER (RIM-67)**—General Dynamics

Two-stage missile that replaced the Terrier family. "Block II" series (1,095 ordered under FY 82, 375 under FY 83) to get increased intercept altitude, greater warhead lethality, and improved jam resistance. No longer being procured.

Length: 7.98 m
Diameter: 0.34 m (booster diameter: 0.46 m)
Weight: 1,306 kg
Guidance: semi-active homing
Range: 30–40 nautical miles

**Standard SM-2 ER (RIM-67B)**—General Dynamics and Raytheon

Two-stage missile to replace Talos. Will be employed in ships with Mk 10 or Mk 26 launch systems, and later in vertical launchers. A nuclear warhead option is under development. Initial procurement of 55 in FY 80. 470 authorized under FY 86, 350 in FY 87, none in FY 88, 89. Force goal is 13,560.

Length: 7.98 m
Diameter: 0.34 m (booster diameter: 0.46 m)
Weight: 1,442 kg
Guidance: semi-active homing, with mid-course guidance capability, inertial reference, and improved ECCM
Range: 75–90 nautical miles

NOTE: A number of the superannuated RIM-2 Terrier missiles with nuclear warheads will be retained in inventory until a nuclear warhead SM-2 Standard is available. Under FY 84, funds were appropriated for 1,190 Standard missiles of all types, with 1,380 under FY 85 and 1,316 in FY 86.

**Sea Sparrow (RIM-7)**—Raytheon

Known at first as BPDMS (Basic Point Defense Missile System). The 50 initial installations employed RIM-7E-5 fixed-fin missiles launched from the eight-celled Mk 25 launcher and controlled by the Mk 115 radar-equipped fire-control system. These are being replaced by the Mk 15 Vulcan/Phalanx 20-mm gatling gun system, beginning in 1982. A lightweight launcher, Mk 29, employing eight RIM-7F folding-fin missiles and the Mk 91 radar fire-control system, is now in use. In Europe this later system, IPDMS (Independent Point Defense Missile System), is also known as NATO Sea Sparrow and was first tested in the *Downes* (FF 1070). The RIM-7M version now being procured uses a blast-fragmentation warhead vice the earlier RIM-7H's expanding rod variety and has a monopulse radar; 1,593 were ordered in FY 82–83. 314 RIM-7M authorized under FY 85. Subsequent totals have been combined with air-launched AIM-7F/M, page 693.

Length: 3.657 m — Weight: 204 kg
Diameter: 0.20 m — Range: 8 nautical miles

**RAM (Rolling Airframe Missile) (XRIM-116A)**—General Dynamics

A point-defense system intended to replace or supplement Sea Sparrow, becoming operational in 1992. Uses a 127-mm missile that employs slow spinning for stability (hence the name). Guidance is by dual-mode anti-radiation and/or infrared proportional navigation homing, and either a Mk 31 21-missile launcher or modified Mk 29 Sea Sparrow-type launchers may be used as the launcher. The 21-missile launcher uses the Phalanx mounting, while the version for use in the Mk 29 launcher would put 5 missiles into each of two cells of the 8-celled launcher. A 2,950-kg, 8-round launcher is under development. The missile homes on active radiation from the target until it picks up an infrared target signature and employs the current Stinger seeker in conjunction with Sidewinder fuzes, warheads, and rocket motors. The 21-missile launch installation weighs 4,977 kg above deck, 800 kg below. Target designation will be by the Mk 23 TAS system in U.S. Navy ships. Being developed under a 7-76 agreement by the U.S., Denmark, and West Germany, with introduction into U.S. Navy service planned for late 1980s. First 30 built under FY 85. The U.S. Navy plans to acquire 4,600 total. The 21-cell launcher will be installed on 2 LCC, 5 LHA and 7 LPH. The Sea Sparrow cell conversion version will go on CV/CVN, LHD 1 class, AORs, and the DD 963 class.

Under FY 86, 117 initial production missiles were authorized for the U.S. Navy, with another 130–150 to be built for West Germany, which will produce the missiles itself by the RAM System GmbH consortium (Messerschmidt, AEG-Telefunken, RTG). 240 authorized 1988, 260 in FY 89.

Length: 2.794 m — Weight: 70.9 kg
Diameter: 127 mm — Speed: Mach 2+

**Stinger (FM-92A)**—General Dynamics and Raytheon

The Marine Corps employs the shoulder-launched infrared-homing with troops, and the Navy uses it for shipboard defense. Under FY 84, 1,205 Stingers were authorized for procurement, with 2,360 authorized in FY 85, 3,439 in FY 86, and 536 for the Navy in FY 87. The Navy authorized 425, the Marines 3,067 in FY 88. 3,115 for Marines, 0 for Navy requested FY 89.

Length: 1.52 m — Warhead: 3 kg (proximity fuze)
Diameter: 0.07 m — Speed: Mach 2.0
Weight: 15.1 kg

**Hawk (MIM-23B)**—Raytheon

A readily deployable point-defense SAM used by the Marine Corps in its latest Improved Hawk ("I-Hawk") version for airfield and strong-point defense. 525 I-Hawks were authorized under FY 88, 526 in FY 89.

◆ **antisubmarine warfare missiles**

**ASROC (RUR-5A)**—Honeywell

A solid-fuel rocket used with a parachute-retarded Mk 46 torpedo. Range is regulated by the combustion time of the rocket motor. Rocket-torpedo separation is

**MISSILES** *(continued)*

timed. The Mk 112 launcher carries eight rockets that can be trained together and elevated in pairs. Fire control is made up of a computer linked with an SQS-23, SQS-26, or SQS-53 sonar.

| | |
|---|---|
| Length: 4.42 m | Range: 9,200 m |
| Diameter: 0.324 m | Warhead: Mk 46 Mod. 1 torpedo or Mk |
| Weight: 454 kg | 17 nuclear depth bomb |

On *Knox*-class frigates the ASROC launcher was modified to permit the launching of Standard SSM missiles (later, Harpoon) in place of two ASW weapons. On older installations, loading is slow because the rockets have to be manually transferred from the magazines. However, on later *Brooke*- and *Garcia*-class and all *Knox*-class frigates, a hoist transfers the rocket from a magazine below the bridge for semi-automatic loading, while in the *Spruance* class the missiles are reloaded vertically. Some 12,000 ASROC rounds were procured between 1960 and 1970, when production ceased.

ASROC is launched from the Mk 10 missile launchers in the CG 26 and CGN 35 classes and from the Mk 26 launchers in the CGN 38 and CG 47 classes. A vertical-launch ASROC is under development for use with Mk 41 launchers in CG 52 and later *Ticonderoga*-class cruisers and in DDG 51-class destroyers. With booster attached, the weapon will be 5.08 m long, 0.358 m in diameter, and will weigh about 750 kg. Built by Goodyear and Martin Marietta, vertical-launch ASROC has suffered program delays and was expected to enter service late in 1989, but Congress authorized no procurement under FY 88 and 340 for FY 89 were deferred to FY 90.

**SUBROC (UUM-44A-2)**

Introduced in 1962 as a submarine torpedo-tube-launched ASW weapon with a nuclear depth-bomb payload, SUBROC was to be phased out because of the age of its solid-fueled rocket motors and because its analog fire-control system was incompatible with the Mk 117 Mod. 3 digital fire-control systems installed or backfitted in U.S. Navy submarines. However, in 1983, Congress authorized funds to alter the fire-control systems.

| | |
|---|---|
| Length: 6.40 m | Guidance: inertial |
| Diameter: 0.533 m | |
| Weight: 1,816 kg | Propulsion: two-stage solid-fuel rocket |

**SOW (Sea Lance)**

A replacement for SUBROC, designated the ASW SOW (Stand-Off Weapon), was canceled in 1981 in favor of an abortive program to produce a *single* weapon to replace both SUBROC and ASROC. That having predictably proven impracticable, the programs were again separated in 1982. The new SOW will be launched from SSN 688-class submarines operating at down to 80 percent of their test depths. Plans call for acquisition of 2,400 weapons, with either nuclear or conventional warheads, and with operational deliveries commencing about 1992; program delayed FY 89.

| | |
|---|---|
| Length: 6.25 m | Range: 106 nautical miles |
| Diameter: 0.533 m | Guidance: inertial in flight |
| Weight: 1,406 kg | |

◆ **air-to-surface missiles**

**AIWS (AGM-. . .)**

A developmental concept for a 7- to 15-n.m. "fire-and-forget" ground-attack weapon to replace Skipper, Walleye, Paveway, and Laser Maverick and enter service circa 2000. Program decision point is 1992. May weigh up to 1,000 kg, with either a 444- or 888-kg explosive or cluster bomb payload. Television, infrared, and fiber-optic guidance all being considered.

**SLAM (AGM-84 SLAM)**—McDonnell Douglas

The SLAM (Stand-off Land Attack Missile) is under development. Only 290 total are planned. Using the Harpoon missile propulsion section and warhead, it has the infrared Maverick missile seeker, incorporates the Global Positioning System, and uses the Walleye missile's data link. For use on F/A-18 and A-6E aircraft. Trials began 1987, with the initial 19 trials missiles requested under FY 87. Four could be carried by either A-6E or F/A-18 aircraft.

| | |
|---|---|
| Length: 4.50 m | Weight: 537.4 kg |
| Diameter: 0.343 m | Propulsion: CAE-JA02 turbojet |
| Speed: Mach 0.85 | Warhead: 227 kg |

**Penguin Mk 2 Mod. 7 (AGM-. . .)**—Norsk Forsvarsteknologie/Grumman

Initially tested for the U.S. Navy in 1982–83 as a surfaced-launched weapon, Penguin is being developed for firing by SH-60B LAMPS-III helicopters. Range is being extended, the wings are being made foldable, and the infrared homing seeker is being improved. Only 272 are planned for procurement, to be carried aboard 35 FFG 7 frigates and 20 DD 963 destroyers. About 130 helicopters will be modified to carry the missile. The first 64 will be requested under FY 89.

| | |
|---|---|
| Weight: 1,202 kg | Warhead: Bullpup Mk 19 |
| Range: 15+ n.m. | |

Other data approximately as for the Norwegian Navy version.

**Skipper (AGM-123A)**—Aerojet General, Emerson Electric, and Texas Instruments

Skipper is essentially a Mk 83 Mod. 5, 1,000-lb bomb, equipped with a Paveway II infrared seeker and guidance head and a Shrike (AGM-45) solid rocket motor. Developed by the Naval Weapons Station, China Lake, Cal., it offers a very low unit price ($20,000/weapon) and reasonable accuracy. Some 2,500 were acquired during FY 84. 1,520 each year have been authorized through FY 88. Program halted FY 89.

| | | |
|---|---|---|
| Length: 4.33 m | Span: 0.914 m | Range: . . . |
| Diameter: 0.356 m | Weight: 581.8 kg | |

**Maverick (AGM-65E and AGM-65F)**—Hughes

Developed from the Air Force AGM-65D, the AGM-65E is a laser-designated, air-launched missile for the Marine Corps, while the AGM-65F version for the Navy will use infrared homing. Both have the same 136-kg penetrator, blast-fragment warhead. For use by A-7 and F/A-18 aircraft and, later, the A-6E. Rapid escalation of price initially forced scaling back of procurement; 90 were procured under FY 83 and 165 were bought under FY 84. In FY 85 600 were authorized, while under FY 86, 1,500 AGM-65E and 195 AGM-65F were authorized. In FY 87 0 laser and 248 IR variants were purchased. In FY 88 1,300 laser/425 IR, and for FY 89 0 laser and 731 of the IR variant.

| | |
|---|---|
| Length: 2.49 m | Propulsion: solid-fuel rocket |
| Diameter: 0.305 m | Range: 50 nautical miles |
| Weight: E: 208.8 kg; F: 307 kg | Span: 0.72 m |

**Standard-ARM (AGM-78)**—General Dynamics

Air-launched version of Standard that homes on electromagnetic radiation. More versatile than Shrike. No longer in production.

| | |
|---|---|
| Length: 4.57 m | Warhead: 97.6 kg |
| Range: 35 nautical miles | Weight: 624.2 kg |

**Shrike (AGM-45)**—Texas Instruments

An anti-radar missile. No longer in production.

| | |
|---|---|
| Length: 3.048 m | Propulsion: solid-propellant rocket motor |
| Diameter: 0.2 m | Range: 12,000 to 16,000 m |
| Weight: 117 kg | Speed: Mach 2 |
| | Wingspan: 0.914 m |

**Walleye I and II (AGM-62)**—Martin-Marietta/Hughes

Glide bomb guided by television. Uses Mk 82 or Paveway II bomb. No longer produced.

| | |
|---|---|
| Length: I: 3.5 m; II: 4.0 m | Range: I: 16 nautical miles; II: 35 nautical miles |
| Diameter: 0.325 m | |
| Weight: I: 511 kg; II: 1,090 kg | Warhead: conventional—I: 373 kg; II: 908 kg |
| | Wingspan: 1.16 m |

**Harpoon (AGM-84)**

See under surface-to-surface missiles.

**HARM (AGM-88A)**—Texas Instruments and Ford Instrument

HARM (High-Speed Anti-Radiation Missile) will be employed by A-7E, A-6E, F/A-18, and U.S. Air Force F-4E Wild Weasel aircraft to suppress or destroy ground defenses. Replacing the obsolescent Shrike. Ford Instrument is developing a "low-cost seeker" variant, with the first 6 delivered 1987 for evaluation. Production of 5,000 was scheduled to start in 1982, with 160 authorized in FY 83, 381 in FY 84, 813 in FY 85, 904 in FY 86, 988 in FY 87, 766 in FY 88. The 2,000th was delivered 29-6-87. 1,307 requested under FY 89. Plan 200 in FY 90, 400 in FY 91.

| | |
|---|---|
| Length: 4.17 m | Propulsion: solid-propellant, low-smoke rocket |
| Diameter: 0.253 m | Guidance: homes on electromagnetic radiation |
| Weight: 360 kg | Range: . . . |
| Span: 1.13 m | Speed: Mach 2.0+ |

**Tacit Rainbow (AGM-136A)**—Northrop

In development as a supplement to HARM, Tacit Rainbow is intended to be a long-endurance, "lingering" weapon that would attack electronic emitters. The weapon uses the 2.54-m-long jet-engined-powered airframe of the BQM-136 target drone and will be carried by Navy A-6 and Air Force B-52 bombers.

**Sidearm (AGM-122A)**—Motorola

A low-cost radiation-seeking conversion of early AIM-9C missiles for use by Marine Corps helicopters. Data generally as for AIM-9 series. Conversion of 885 authorized in FY 86, 256 in FY 87, 276 in FY 88, 0 in FY 89.

**TOW-2 (MGM-71)**—Hughes

Wire-guided, helicopter- or ground-launched anti-tank weapon that uses optical sight and tube launcher. TOW = Tube-launched, Optically tracked, Wire-guided. 400,000 TOW built since 1970 for all customers. TOW-2A detonates reactive armor, then penetrates; 16,000 in service by 4-88. 2,200 approved under FY 84, 4,782 ITOW-2 under FY 86, 2,575 under FY 87, 2,680 in FY 88, 2,585 in FY 89.

| | |
|---|---|
| Length: 1.174 m | Span: 1.14 m |
| Weight: 18.9 kg | Propulsion: solid-propellant rocket |
| Diameter: 0.152 m | Warhead: 3.6-kg hollow, shaped-charged |
| | Range: 2.3 nautical miles at Mach 1.0 |

ITOW (Improved TOW) weighs 19.1 kg, ITOW-2 weighs 21.5 kg.

NOTE: The Marine Corps uses TOW from AH-1T helicopters and from land, with each division now programmed to have 144 launchers.

**Hellfire (AGM-114A)**—Rockwell, Martin-Marietta

A lightweight anti-tank missile replacing the M82 LAW. First 219 authorized

**MISSILES** *(continued)*

under FY 84, 438 in FY 85, 1,304 in FY 86, none in FY 87, 1,393 in FY 88, 200 requested FY 89.

Length: 1.727 m or 1.778 m (imaging IR version) Range: 5 km+
Diameter: 0.1778 m (span: 0.3262 m) Speed: Mach 1.0+
Weight: 45.7 to 47.88 kg (71 kg in container)

Hellfire has three variants: Laser-designated, RF/IR (Radio-Frequency Infrared), and IRIS (Imaging Infrared). Also in use is the Dragon, made by McDonnell Douglas.

◆ **air-to-air missiles**

**Sparrow-III (AIM-7F, M)**—Raytheon

The AIM-7F entered service in 1976 with a continuous-rod warhead. AIM-7M, the current version, entered service in 1983 with a blast/fragmentation warhead, active fuze, and improved seeker. In FY 85, 936 were authorized for procurement; 1,948 in both air and surfaced launch authorized under FY 86, 1,716 in FY 87, 600 in FY 88.

Length: 3.65 m Guidance: semi-active homing
Diameter: 0.203 m Speed: Mach 2.5
Weight: 232 kg Range: 26,000 m
Propulsion: solid-fuel rocket Warhead: 27 kg, proximity fuze

**Sidewinder (AIM-9H, L, M)**—Raytheon and Ford Instrument

Over 110,000 Sidewinder missiles have been built. The AIM-9L version uses an active optical fuze and has a guidance system permitting all-angle attacks. The AIM-9M version supplanted the -9L in production in 1981 and has improved capabilities against countermeasures and against targets seen against warm backgrounds. Only 500 AIM-9 L/M were authorized under FY 83, 350 under FY 84, none in FY 85, 1,850 (for all services) under FY 86, 391 in FY 87, 288 in FY 88, 0 in FY 89.

Length: 2.90 m Propulsion: solid-fueled rocket
Diameter: 0.127 m Guidance: infrared homing
Wingspan: 0.61 m Speed: Mach 2 5
Weight: 84.4 kg Range: 12 nautical miles

**Phoenix (AIM-54A, C)**—Hughes

AIM-54A ceased production in 1980 after only 2,500 had been built for the U.S. and, unfortunately, Iran. The first 30 pilot-production AIM-54C were delivered 10-81, with 60 more to follow. Scheduled to enter service 1983–84. Only 90 procured under FY 83, rising to 265 under FY 84; in FY 85 only 265 were authorized, with 265 again in FY 86, 205 in FY 87, 350 in FY 88, and 560 in FY 89.

Length: 3.96 m Weight: 453 kg
Diameter: 0.380 m Propulsion: solid-fueled rocket
Wingspan: 0.914 m Range: about 120 km
Warhead: 60.3 kg (continuous rod)

**AMRAAM (AIM-120A)**—Hughes and Raytheon

AMRAAM (Advanced Medium-Range Air-to-Air Missile) is intended to replace the AIM-7F Sparrow. In development; first firings in 1985. The AIM-120B will have infrared homing added, and the AIM-120C will have improved aerodynamic performance. 90 developmental missiles requested under FY 86 for Navy and Air Force. First 50 production missiles requested for FY 89. Navy goal is 7,249 total.

Length: 3.65 m Warhead: 22.7 kg
Diameter: 0.178 m Range: over 74 km
Weight: 151.5 kg
Guidance: inertial mid-course, active terminal homing

## B. GUNS

**406-mm, Model 1936**

Fitted in 1,700-ton triple turrets in *Iowa*-class battleships. Requires a crew of 77 men per mount, plus 30–36 men in the magazine. In 1981, 15,500 high-capacity, 3,200 armor-piercing, and 2,300 B, L, & P rounds were available, with 12,500 full-service and 12,600 reduced-charge sets remaining. Armor-piercing rounds can penetrate 9 m of reinforced concrete. Reworked powder has produced very high accuracy. A new round with doubled range is to enter service in 1992.

Length: 50 calibers
Muzzle velocity: armor-piercing: 739 m/sec.; high-cap: 902 m/sec.
Rate of fire: 2 rounds/minute/barrel
Maximum range: armor-piercing shell: 36,700 m; high-capacity shell: 38,000 m
Weight of projectile: armor-piercing shell: 1,226 kg; high-capacity shell: 863 kg
Cartridge bags: 6 per charge, 50-kg or 24-kg reduced-charge
Fire control: Mk 38 director with Mk 13 radar

**203-mm Mk 16 Mod. 0**

Automatic weapon fitted in 451-ton triple turrets on *Des Moines*-class cruisers.

Length: 55 calibers
Muzzle velocity: 900 m/second
Arc of elevation: −5° to +41°
Rate of fire: 10 rounds/min/barrel
Maximum range: armor-piercing shell: 27,500 m; high-capacity shell: 28,670 m
Weight of projectile: armor-piercing shell: 152 kg; high-capacity shell: 113 kg
Fire control: Mk 54 director with Mk 13 radar

**127-mm, twin barrel, Mk 12 Mod. 1**

Semiautomatic, dual-purpose gun fitted in the Mk 32 series mounts of the *Iowa*-class battleships and *Des Moines*-class cruisers. 720,000 rounds of 127-mm ammunition for these and the single "5-inch/38" mounts below remained available in 1981.

Length: 38 calibers
Muzzle velocity: 792 m/sec
Elevation: −15° to +85°
Rate of fire: 18 rounds/minute/barrel with a well-trained crew
Maximum range on a surface target: 16,500 m
Maximum effective range on a ship target: 12,000 to 13,000 m
Maximum range in antiaircraft fire: 11,400 m
Maximum effective range in antiaircraft fire: 8,000 m
Weight of projectile: 25 kg
Fire control: Mk 37 director with Mk 25 radar; Mk 56 director with Mk 35 radar in a few ships

**127-mm, Mk 30**

Single mounting, weighing 20.4 tons, enclosed Mk 30 series mountings on FFG 1, FF 1040, and CGN 9 classes. Other data as for twin mounting.

**127-mm, Mk 42**

Single-barrel, dual-purpose gun fitted on ships built in the 1950s and 1960s. Most mounts converted to Mk 42 Mod. 10 configuration. An SAL (Semi-Active Laser-guided projectile) named Deadeye is being developed for these and the Mk 45 gun. Trials at sea of the Martin-Marietta Deadeye round commenced in *Briscoe* (DD 977) in 1981. The round is 1.548 m long, weighs 47.17 kg. 300 rounds are to deliver 1989, and procurement of 15,100 was planned, but program again canceled FY 89.

Length: 54 calibers Rate of elevation: 80°/second
Muzzle velocity: 810 m/second Rate of fire: 20 rounds/minute
Mount weight: 65.8 tons; Mod. 10: 63.9 tons Weight of projectile: 32 kg
Arc of elevation: −5° to +80° Range: 23,700 m horizontal/14,840 vertical
Rate of train: 50°/second
Fire control: Mk 68 system with SPG-53 radar in most ships
Personnel: 13 men, with 2 in mount

Loading entirely automatic from two ammunition drums in the handling room up to the loading tray by means of a rotating hoist. Each drum contains twenty rounds. The rate of fire can be maintained for only one minute, inasmuch as it is necessary to reload the drums. Firing rate reduced from original 40 rds/min for safety.

**127-mm Mk 45**—Northern Ordnance/FMC

Single-barrel mount fitted on *Ticonderoga*-, *California*-, and *Virginia*-class cruisers, *Spruance*-, *Kidd*-, and *Arleigh Burke*-class destroyers, and *Tarawa*-class amphibious assault ships. The Mod. 1 version permits rapid switching from one type of ammunition to another. A laser-guided projectile is in development; see above.

Length: 54 calibers
Muzzle velocity: 810 m/second
Mount weight: 21.7 tons
Arc of elevation: −5° to +65°
Rate of fire: 16 to 20 rounds/minute
Range: 23,700 m horizontal/14,840 vertical
Fire control: Mk 86 GFCS with SPQ-9 search radar: SPG-60 tracking radar
Personnel: none on mount; 6 in handling room to reload ammunition drums

**76.2-mm, Mk 22**

Automatic dual-purpose gun in single (Mk 34) or twin (Mk 33) mounts, Mk 27 twin mounts in CA 134 and CA 139. Thoroughly obsolescent.

Length: 50 calibers
Mount weight: 15 tons. Mk 33 open mount
Weight of projectile: 3.2 kg
Rate of fire: 45 rounds/minute/barrel
Maximum range: 12,840 m horizontal/8,950 vertical
Fire control: Mk 56 system with Mk 35 radar or none in active ships

**76.2-mm, Mk 21**

Obsolescent. Single-fire, dual-purpose gun on two auxiliaries and some Coast Guard ships. Mk 26 mount.

Length: 50 calibers
Mount weight: 4.2 tons
Weight of projectile: 3.2 kg
Rate of fire: 20 rounds/minute
Maximum range: 12,840 horizontal/8,950 vertical
Fire control: ring sight only

**76-mm, Mk 75**—Northern Ordnance/FMC and OTO Melara

Single-barrel, license-built version of OTO Melara Compact, tested in the frigate *Talbot* and used in PHM and FFG 7 classes and Coast Guard *Bear*-class cutters; to backfit in Coast Guard ships. 1985 order to OTO Melara vice U.S. licensee, Northern Ordnance.

Length: 62 calibers
Mount weight: 6.2 tons
Weight of projectile: 6.4 kg
Rate of fire: 85 rounds/minute

**GUNS** *(continued)*

Maximum range: 19,200 m horizontal/11,900 m vertical
Fire control: Mk 92 radar system
Personnel: 4 below decks

**40-mm, Mk 19 Mod. 3**—Socko Corp.

Strickly speaking not a gun, but rather a lightweight rapid-fire grenade launcher in portable tripod-legged mountings. Found aboard auxiliaries and Coast Guard ships. Being procured at 25 per year.

Range: 2,195 m; rate of fire: 300 rds/min

**25-mm Mk 88 (M 242 Bushmaster)**—Hughes Helicopter

A "chain gun," using linked Oerlikon M790 ammunition. For use on Mk-III patrol boats and later LSD 42-class landing ships. In FY 86, 29 were authorized; 25 in FY 87, 22 in FY 88; 57 requested FY 89.

| | |
|---|---|
| Length: 2.74 m overall | Rate of fire: single-shot, 100, or 200 r.p.m |
| Weight: 109 kg (gun) | Fire control: ring sight |

**20-mm, Mk 16 Mod. 5**

Single-barrel Mk 67 or Mk 68 mounting in small combatants, amphibious ships, and auxiliaries.

| | |
|---|---|
| Length: 80 calibers | Maximum range: 3,000 m horizontal |
| Mount weight: . . . | Fire control: ring sights on mount |
| Rate of fire: 800 rds/min | Weight of projectile: 0.34 kg |

NOTE: The 30-mm Mauser 30 F in DS 30 F and Breda 30-mm Compact were to be given comparison trials in 1987–88. The General Electric Sea Vulcan 25, 25-mm naval gatling gun conducted successful trials early in 1987.

**20-mm Mk 10**

Single-barrel, license-built Oerlikon mounting in minesweepers and auxiliaries.

Length: 70 calibers
Mount weight: 318–500 kg
Rate of fire: 450 rounds/minute
Maximum range: 4,390 m horizontal/3,050 m vertical
Fire control: ring sights on mount

**20-mm, Mk 15 Mod. 0 Block 0 and 1 CIWS (Close-In Weapon System)**—General Dynamics (G. E. gun), and General Electric

Vulcan/Phalanx "Close-in" system designed to destroy missiles. It consists of a multibarrel, M61A1 20-mm gun with a very high rate of fire, which is co-mounted with two radars, one of which follows the target and the other the projectile stream. A computer furnishes necessary corrections for train and elevation so that the two radar targets coincide, bringing heavy fire to bear on the target. 676 units programmed to be fitted to U.S. ships. Only 989 rds in Block 0 magazine. The first production unit completed 9-8-79 and was installed, with two others, in *America* (CV 66) on 17-4-80. An improved "Block 1" version with more rounds on mount and a higher rate of fire will enter service in late 1988—five years late. Block 0 mounts upgrading to Block 1, 45 in FY 88, 59 in FY 89. Uses Mk 149 rounds with depleted uranium sub-caliber penetrators, although tungsten rounds are furnished for export. Later versions may use a 4-barreled GAU-10, 30-mm gatling gun or a 5- or 7-barreled 25-mm gatling gun. Five Mk 15 Mod. 1 authorized under FY 88 and FY 89.

Mount weight: 5.4 tons
Rate of fire: 3,000 rounds/minute
Maximum range: 1,486 m horizontal

## C. TORPEDOES

### ◆ submarine torpedoes

**Low Cost Torpedo**—Whitehead Motofides, Italy

A trials program begun in 1986 for a low-cost anti-surface ship torpedo with goal of one-tenth Mk 48 ADCAP cost, to have a range of 3 n.m. at 35 kts. Development contract won 13-2-87 by Whitehead, with variant of its A-184 wire-guided torpedo, but the Secretary of the Navy was attempting to end the program late in 1987. 34 trials torpedoes authorized under FY 86. Navy had hoped to buy 2,000 between FY 88–94. Not in FY 89 budget; program essentially ended.

**Mk 48 Mod. 1, Mod. 3, and Mod. 4 and ADCAP**—Gould and Hughes Helicopter

Entered service 1972. Can be launched from a submarine against a surface target or a submarine. No surface ships are currently equipped to launch Mk 48, although that capability was originally intended. A total of 3,059 Mk 48s were procured through 1980, plus 56 for Australia and 92 for the Netherlands; 144 additional for the U.S. Navy were appropriated under FY 80 and again in FY 81 through FY 84. FY 85 was the last year of production, with 108 authorized.

| | |
|---|---|
| Length: 5.84 m | Speed: 55 kts |
| Diameter: 0.533 m | Propulsion: 500 hp Otto-cycle swashplate engine |
| Weight: 633 kg | Depth: up to 760 m |

Can be launched with its own active-passive or acoustic homing system or with a wire-guidance system. High speed (40 knots) and long run duration (50,000 m). An improvement program, ADCAP (Added Capability) is being instituted, with the first twenty-two conversion kits requested under FY 80. The first "Near-Term Update" Mk 48 Mod. 4 torpedo was delivered 12-80. ADCAP will enter service in 1989, with the first 30 having been authorized under FY 85 and 123 authorized under FY 86, 50 in FY 87, 100 in FY 88, 261 in FY 89. Technical evaluation began 8-86, suffered initial setbacks. Westinghouse bought Mk 48 rights from Gould, 1-88.

### ◆ surface-launched torpedoes

**Mk 46 Mod. 1, 2, and 5**—Honeywell

ASW torpedo using liquid fuel (Otto fuel), and twin, counter-rotating props. Entered service 1963. Active-passive guidance. Launched from Mk 32 ASW torpedo tubes or as payload for the ASROC ASW missile system.

| | |
|---|---|
| Length: 2.60 m (4.50 with ASROC booster) | Weight: 232.4 kg |
| Diameter: 0.324 m | Warhead: 45.4 kg HE |

The Mk 46 Mod. 1 and Mod. 2 are being upgraded to Mod. 6 NEARTIP (Near-Term Improvement Program) status with improved acoustic homing system and countermeasures resistance. Under FY 80, 576 conversion kits were requested, and 1,128 more were requested under FY 82; ultimately, some 2,700 torpedoes will be updated. The Mk 46 Mod. 4 is the payload for the Captor mine. 570 *new* Mk 46 Mod. 5 torpedoes were ordered from Honeywell in 1980, 440 under FY 83, and 1,200 under FY 84, 1,565 authorized FY 85, and 500 in FY 86.

**Mk 50 ALWT**—Honeywell (second-source for FY 90)

The ALWT (Advanced Lightweight Torpedo) is being developed as a replacement for the Mk 46 series and will be supplied in surface-launched and air-droppable configurations. It will be roughly the same weight as the Mk 46 and of the same dimensions, but will be deeper-diving (over 600 m), faster (over 40 knots), and have better homing and counter-countermeasures capabilities. Due to continuing program delays, will not be operational before the early 1990s. Weight: 362 kg; length: 2.93 m. Under FY 87, 39 were authorized; 16 under FY 88, and 140 for FY 89.

**NT-37E**—Honeywell

Remanufactured and greatly improved Mk 37 homing torpedoes available for export, but not used by U.S. Navy. Propelled by a 90-hp Otto-fuel motor. The last U.S. Navy Mk 37 torpedo was retired 30-9-86.

| | |
|---|---|
| Length: 3,467 m | Speed: 35 kts |
| Diameter: 0.483 m | Range: 18,000 m |
| Weight: . . . | Warhead: 148 kg HE |

### ◆ aircraft torpedoes

**Mk 46 Mod. 0**

Similar to the surface-launched weapon, but equipped with a retarding parachute, solid vice liquid propellant, and does not have a straight run-out before commencing helical search. Will be replaced by the ALWT.

## D. MINES

**Mk 52 Mod. 1, 2, 3, 5, 6**

Air-dropped. All 2.75 m long by 338-mm diameter (830 mm over fins). All carry 270-kg HBX explosive. Mod. 1 is an acoustic mine, weight: 542.5 kg. Mod. 2 is a magnetic influence version, weight: 568 kg. Mod. 3 is a dual-pressure/magnetic influence version, weight: 572.5 kg. Mod. 5 is an acoustic/magnetic influence version, weight: 570.7 kg. Mod. 6 is a pressure/acoustic/magnetic influence version, weight: 546 kg. All are bottom mines for depths of up to 47 m (Mod. 2: 183 m) and can be carried by U.S.A.F. B-52D and H bombers as well as Navy aircraft.

**Mk 53**

A 225-kg mine-sweep rig obstruction weapon used to protect minefields from mine-countermeasures efforts.

**Mk 55 Mod. 2, 3, 5, 6, 7**

Air-dropped bottom mines. All 2.89 kg long by .592-m diameter (1.03 m over fins) and carry 577-kg HBX-1 explosive. Versions: Mod. 2: magnetic influence, weight: 989 kg; Mod. 3: pressure/magnetic influence, weight: 994 kg; Mod. 5: acoustic/magnetic influence, weight: 994 kg; Mod. 6: pressure/acoustic/magnetic, weight: 997 kg; Mod. 7: dual-channel magnetic influence, weight: 996 kg. All can be laid in 46-m-deep water, except Mod. 2, 7: 183 m. Can also be laid by surface ships, using portable rails.

**Mk 56 Mod. 0**

Aircraft-dropped moored mine. 996 kg. 3.51 m long by 592-mm diameter (1.06 over fins). Total-field magnetic influence exploder. Carries 577-kg HBX-3 explosive. Depth: 350 m.

**Mk 57 Mod. 0**

Submarine-laid version of Mk 56 moored mine. 1,012 kg, 3.07 long by 510-mm diameter. Carries 935-kg HBX-3 explosive. Depth: 250 m.

**Mk 60 CAPTOR (enCAPsulated TORpedo)**

Submarine-laid or aircraft-dropped. Uses Mk 46 Mod. 4 acoustic-homing torpedo payload. Primarily ASW in function. 908 kg, 3.66 m long by 324-mm diameter. 44.5-kg warhead. Development began 1961. 260 requested under FY 80 in first major operational buy, with 500 approved under FY 83, 300 under FY 84, 300 under FY 85, and 150 (unrequested) under FY 86. Mod. 1 conversion kit gives improved target detection: 3.35 m long, 932 kg. All have 300-m mooring capability.

**Mk 62 DST-36 Quickstrike series (Mods. 0–5)**

Aircraft-dropped bottom mine. Converted from 500-lb (227-kg) Mk 82 standard aircraft bomb. Magnetic. 87-kg H-6 explosive charge. Over 4,000 procured.

MINES *(continued)*

**Mk 63 DST-40 Quickstrike series (Mods. 0–5)**

Aircraft-dropped bottom mine. Converted from 1,000-lb (454-kg) Mk 83 standard aircraft bomb. Magnetic.

**Mk 64 DST-41 Quickstrike series (Mods. 0–5)**

Aircraft-dropped bottom mine. Converted from 2,000-lb (908-kg) Mk 84 bomb. Magnetic or magnetic/seismic influence. 3.83 m long.

**Mk 65 Quickstrike**

Submarine-launched, 3.25 m long. 1,000 on order 1985.

**Mk 66**

A practice version of CAPTOR.

**Mk 67 SLMM** (Submarine-Launched Mobile Mine)

Converted Mk 37 Mod. 0 torpedo. 754 kg, 4.09 m long by 483-mm diameter. Bottom mine. Production version not yet in service.

**NGM-Hammerhead**—Goodyear/Marconi

A joint U.S.-U.K. development of a 533-mm torpedo tube/air-drop launchable weapon for production in the mid-1990s. Will be a mobile, homing weapon for deep-water use. NGM = New Generation Mine.

Minelaying: no surface ships are capable of minelaying. Naval aircraft of the S-3, P-3, A-6, and A-7 types are capable of laying mines, as are some 80 operational Air Force B-52D bombers. Theoretically, any U.S. Navy submarine can lay mines from its torpedo tubes, except early units of the SSN 688 class.

## E. RADARS

Radars for active ships are:

### ◆ surface-search and navigation

**SPS-10:** C-band, Mods. B through F in service. Primary surface-search set before the introduction of SPS-55. Being replaced by SPS-67.

**SPS-53:** X-band. Navigational set for large ships and for MSOs, auxiliaries, and Coast Guard ships.

**SPS-55:** X-band, slotted waveguide antenna. On *Spruance*-class destroyers and FFG 7 frigates, etc.

**SPS-59:** Official designation for the LN-66 navigational radar.

**SPS-63:** X-band. U.S. version of the Italian 3RM-20N for use on the *Pegasus*-class hydrofoils.

**SPS-64:** X-band. Used by USCG in several versions and being introduced into the USN for auxiliaries and minesweepers, etc., in the SPS-64(V)9 version. Raytheon. Range: About 48 n.m.; can automatically track 20 targets.

**SPS-67:** C-band. A solid-state replacement for the SPS-10, using same antenna. Also has an ultra-short pulse mode for navigation. First used on refitted *Long Beach* (CGN 9) in 1982. Being processed in large numbers.

Also in use are the small navigational radar sets LN-66, SPS-51, SPS-57, SPS-59, SPS-60, SPS-64, and SPS-66, all X-band and most using slotted-waveguide antennas.

**BPS-4, 11, 14, 15:** X-band. Submarine search, navigational, and fire-control radars. Mounted on telescoping masts.

### ◆ two-dimensional air-search

**SPS-6C:** L-band (1250–1350 MHz). Obsolescent; used only on *Thomaston* (LSD 28) class.

**SPS-29:** P-band (200 MHz). On some of the older DDGs and DDs. Same antenna as SPS-37 and SPS-43A.

**SPS-37:** P-band (200 MHz). On some CVs, CGs, and DDGs. SPS-37A uses 12.6-m long SPS-43A antenna. Pulse-compression version of SPS-29.

**SPS-40:** B-band (400 MHz). The most widely used air-search radar. Range against medium bombers: 150–180 miles. Earlier "A" models being modernized to SPS-40D. P-band pulse-compression. In FY 87, 37 were converting with solid-state transmitters.

**SPS-43:** SPS-43A with 12.6-m antenna. Being replaced in aircraft carriers by SPS-49; SPS-43 with small antenna on missile cruisers, also being replaced by SPS-49.

**SPS-49:** Aboard FFG 7 class and others, replacing SPS-37, -43, etc. S-band (851–942 MHz).

**SPS-58/62/65:** L(D)-band, pulse-doppler. Combined air surface-search radar, SPS-62 and -65 use modified SPS-10 antenna; used for low-altitude defense. Some 51 sets procured. Used in carriers; being replaced by Mk 23 TAS. SPS-62 and -65 also operate in C-band as surface-search radars, using dual-feed antennas.

### ◆ three-dimensional air-search

**SPS-39:** S-band. Mod. A uses same antenna as SPS-52. In some DDGs: E-band. SPS-52 is a version developed to interface directly with the NTDS data system.

**SPS-48A:** Mounted on CG classes. Frequency-scanning system.

**SPS-48C, E:** Electronic frequency scanning in elevation, improved SPS-48A. E version has doubled power, armored antenna, reduced side-lobe level, adaptive energy beam management, solid-state transmitter.

**SPS-52C:** S-band improvements on SPS-39. Electronic frequency scanning in elevation.

**SPY-1A:** S-band. Aegis system. Obtaining a directional effect by dipole radiation to secure an electronic sweep, it has four fixed aerials that provide instant 360° coverage. Long-range air-search, target-tracking, and missile-guidance. SPY-1B, with reduced side lobes to enter service 1988; SPY-1C developed for possible use on carriers; lighter-weight SPY-1D in development for DDG 51 program.

**TPS-71 (XNI):** Relocatable Over-the-Horizon Radar (ROTHR). Land-based radar to track air and surface targets. Initial procurements at one per year under FY 88 and FY 89. Enormously powerful, extremely low frequency.

### ◆ fire-control

**Mk 13:** 3-cm wavelength. Ranging set for Mk 38 director on *Iowa*-class battleships and for Mk 34 director on CA 134 and CA 139.

**Mk 25:** X-band. Mounted on Mk 37 GFCS directors on CA, BB. Dish antenna.

**Mk 35:** 3-cm wavelength. Mounted on Mk 56 GFCS director for 127-mm and 76.2-mm guns. On older FFGs and FFs. Removed from auxiliaries. Dish antenna.

**Mk 91:** Technically, the fire-control *system* for the Sea Sparrow SAM system, used with the Mk 29 lightweight launcher. Either one (Mod. 0) or two (Mod. 1) radar directors per launcher. Uses Mk 57 Mod. 2 radar.

**Mk 92/94:** U.S. Navy adaptation of Dutch H.S.A. (Hollandse Signaal Apparaaten) WM-20 series track-while-scan gun/missile fire-control system. Used in FFG 7, PHM 1, and the Coast Guard's new WMEC classes. Antennas mounted in egg-shaped radome. Combined with STIR (modified SPG-60) antenna in FFG 7 class. Improvement program in FFG 7 to end Phase I in 1984. Phase II CORT will further update system; 6 authorized FY 88.

**Mk 115:** Technically the fire-control *system* for Sea Sparrow when launched from the Mk 25 heavy launcher. Older than Mk 91 and being phased out.

**SPQ-9:** X-band, track-while-scan special surface search and weapons control for use with Mk 86 GFCS. Antenna mounted in spherical radome. Range: 36 km.

**SPG-51B, C, D:** Standard MR illuminator-tracker; used with Mk 74 missile fire-control system.

**SPG-53:** Mounted on Mk 68 GFCS director on CG, DDG, and DD with 127-mm Mk 42 guns.

**SPG-55A, B:** Standard ER illuminator-tracker; used with Mk 76 missile fire-control system.

**SPG-60:** Standard MR X-band, 4-horn monopulse, pulse-doppler illuminator-tracker with Mk 74 missile fire-control system in later CGN classes; also illuminates for guns in conjunction with Mk 86 GFCS. STIR version, used on FFG 7 class, is modified for use with Mk 92 Mod. 2 missile/gun control system. STIR = Separate Tracking & Illumination Radar. Can track Mach 3.0 targets to 183 km. Has a co-mounted t.v. tracker.

**SPG-62:** Standard SM-2 illuminator; used with Aegis system in CG 47 class. Slaved to SPY-1 radar.

**TAS/Mk 23:** D-band. Technically a Target Acquisition System, employing a rapidly rotating, stabilized linear-array antenna in conjunction with a UYK-20 computer to counter high- and low-angle aircraft and cruise-missile attacks. Range 20 n.m. on small missiles to 90 n.m. on aircraft. Mod. 0 on *Downes* (FF 1070) in 1975, Mod. 1 being added to *Spruance* (DD 963) class, Mod. 2 (with UYA-4 console) on *Sacramento* class, beginning with AOE 3 in 4-80. Can track 54 targets simultaneously.

### ◆ carrier-controlled approach systems

**SPN-6:** Formerly installed on aircraft carriers but now limited to AVT 16 and some LPH. Antenna in large radome.

**SPN-10:** Aircraft landing aid, incorporating a radar set to determine aircraft position relative to the carrier. Antennas are two small conical dishes; SPN-10 remained on 5 ships in 1985 as the radar associated with the ACLS (Automatic Carrier Landing System) and CCA (Carrier-Controlled Approach) systems. Being replaced by SPN-42, which is less bulky. Other carrier aircraft landing aid/radar systems include SPN-41, SPN-43, and SPN-44. SPN-46 is to be added beginning in 1986 for use with Automatic Carrier Landing System; made by Varian, operates at 32.9–33.5 gHz.

## F. COUNTERMEASURES SYSTEMS

### ◆ electronic systems, surface ships and submarines

**BLQ-3–5, 8:** Acoustic jamming system for submarines.

**BLR-1–10, 13–15:** Radar warning systems for submarines; BLR-14 also launches countermeasures.

**SLA-12:** Passive D/F and EW receiver used in conjunction with ULQ-6, SLQ-22/23/24. Fixed and trainable antenna arrays.

**COUNTERMEASURES SYSTEMS** *(continued)*

**SLA-15:** Trainable tracker array for ULQ-6.

**SLQ-17:** Jammer array for carriers; creates false target. Unsatisfactory; to be replaced by SLQ-32(V)3.

**SLQ-26:** Deceptive jammer used in conjunction with SLD-1A microwave D/F set. Antenna array resembles ULQ-6 series.

**SLQ-29:** The combined WLR-8/SLQ-17 package.

**SLQ-32(V)1:** Radar warning (H-, I-, J-bands) for auxiliaries and amphibious ships; most to be upgraded to (V)2.

**SLQ-32(V)2:** Radar warning (B–J bands) for newer destroyers and frigates; replaces WLR-1 where fitted.

**SLQ-32(V)3:** Radar warning (B–J bands) *and* jamming/spoofing (H–J bands) for cruisers, DDG 37 class, and major amphibious ships.

**SLQ-33:** A ship-towed acoustic deception device.

**SLQ-34:** An intelligence collective system, "Classic Outboard", with SRD-19 and SLR-16.

**SLQ-36:** Towed torpedo detection and spoofing; in development.

**SLQ-48:** Mine countermeasures system, using Honeywell MNS submersible; i.e., *not* an EW system.

**SLQ-49:** air- or surface-launched inflatable decoy, "Rubber Duck." U.S. version of U.K. DLF.

**SLQ-650:** EW system using SLQ-640 intercept and SLQ-630 jammer.

**SLR-16:** HF SIGINT receiver set using SRD-19 antenna arrays.

**SLR-24:** On-board torpedo detection processor.

**SLR-600:** EW intercept system for small ships (2–20 gHz).

**SLR-610:** Another small-ship EW intercept system (6.5–22 gHz).

**SLR-640:** Improved SLR-610.

**SLT-5, 8:** Communications jammers.

**SRD-19:** "Classic Outboard" LF/MF/VHF shipboard SIGINT exploitation system using 24 small deck-edge antennas, whip antennas, and a masthead Adcock-type VHF D/F array; often used in conjunction with SLR-16.

**URD-9(V):** Radar D/F (225–400 MHz).

**URD-27:** Broadcast frequency D/F device for SIGINT (250 MHz–18 gHz).

**ULQ-6:** Deception repeater/jammer in cruisers, destroyers—being replaced by SLQ-32(V)3 in high-value ships.

**WLR-1:** Radar warning array in older ships. Being updated to WLR-1H (0.55–20 gHz).

**WLR-3:** Radar warning and signal collection—also in some submarines.

**WLR-8:** Radar warning system for the SSN 688 class, (V)4 (0.5–18 gHz) version in one carrier, (V)5 in SSBNs. Uses WLR-1 antenna suite on surface ships.

**WLR-9:** Sonar detection system.

**WLR-10:** Radar warning receiver.

**WLR-11A:** Radar warning/SIGINT system. 7–18 gHz. Uses WLR-1's antenna suite.

◆ **physical countermeasures systems**

**T-Mk 6 Fanfare:** Mechanical towed anti-torpedo noisemaker—obsolescent.

**SLQ-25 Nixie:** Towed torpedo countermeasure/noisemaker, to replace T-Mk 6; 180 sets procured.

**Chaffroc:** Two-celled (8-rocket) launcher for modified Zuni chaff-deploying rockets; obsolescent.

**Mk 30:** Submarine target simulator. Torpedo-sized.

**Mk 33 RBOC:** Rapid-Blooming Overboard Chaff launcher; replaced by Mk 36.

**Mk 36 SRBOC:** Super-RBOC—Mod. 1 with two 6-tubed mortars for ships under 140 m; Mod. 2 with four 6-tubed mortars for ships over 140 m. All use Mk 182 chaff-dispensing cartridges, which climb to 244 m. "Torch" infrared decoy being developed for use with Mk 36 SRBOC, and the NATO Sea Gnat rocket chaff dispenser may be adopted.

**Mk 70 MOSS:** Mobile Submarine Simulator—small torpedo-like device for launch by *Ohio*-class SSBNs.

**G. SONARS**

◆ **on surface ships**

**SQQ-14:** High-frequency, minehunting, and classification set in retractable-transducer array on MSOs. A towed version, SQQ-35, is in development. Search mode 80 kHz; 350 kHz classification.

**SQQ-23:** PAIR (Performance and Integration Refit). Modified SQS-23 using two transducer domes (except in CGN 9 and CG 16 classes: one dome); also in 4 DDG 2, 2 DDG 37 class.

**SQQ-28:** LAMPS-III helicopter data-link processing system.

**SQQ-30:** Minehunting sonar developed by General Electric for use on mine countermeasures ships; used only on MCM 1–8, MSH 1.

**SQQ-32:** Raytheon/Thomson-CSF sonar to replace SQQ-30 in later units of the MCM 1 class and for the MSH 1 class. Separate detection and classification transducers lowered through well and towed well below the hull. Uses two UYK-44 computers.

**SQQ-89:** Suite integrating the SQR-19 towed array, SQS-53B hull-mounted sonar, Mk 116 Underwater Fire Control System, LAMPS-III helicopter, SQQ-28 processor, and UYQ-28 SIMAS (Sonar In-Situ Mode Assessment System) for CG 56 and later, for DDG 51, FFG 7 class. Trials in DD 980 late 1985.

**SQR-15:** Developmental passive towed array, in some DD 963-class destroyers.

**SQR-17:** Passive classification device for processing data transmitted to CG 26, DD 963, F 1040, 1052, and FFG 7-class ships via LAMPS-I helicopters from various sonobuoys. Uses SKR-4 link receiver, AKT-22 link, ARR-75 sonobuoy receiver, UYS-1 processor. To develop for torpedo warning.

**SQR-18A:** TACTAS (Tactical Towed Acoustic Sensor). For use on FF 1052 class equipped with SQS-35 VDS; array attaches to VDS towed body. Normal cable length is 1,706 m; towed at depths up to 366 m; array is 82.6-mm diameter, 222.5 m long. Latest version, SQR-18(V)1 with 730-m cable is aboard 35 FF 1052-class ships; uses 8 modular hydrophone sections. SQR-18A(V)2 uses SQR-19 towing rig for the non-VDS-equipped units of the FF 1052 class and has 1,524-m tow cable.

**SQR-19:** Improved TACTAS for use on CG 47, DD 963, and FFG 7 classes; to be deployed through port in stern. 1,707-m cable. Has 16 acoustic reception modules in array: 8 VLF, 4 LF, 2 MF, 2 HF. UYQ-21 display.

**SQS-23:** Bow- or hull-mounted low-frequency, active-passive. In CV 66, CGN 25, some CG, older DDG, and DD 931 classes.

**SQS-26:** Bow-mounted, low-frequency set, in various versions. In older CGN, CG 26, FFG 1, FF 1037, FF 1040, FF 1052, and FF 1098 classes.

**SQS-35:** Independent, variable-depth, towed, active-passive. In some DD 931 class, most FF 1052 class.

**SQS-38:** Hull-mounted SQS-35 for USCG cutters.

**SQS-53:** SQS-26 with digital computer interface, for use with Mk 116 UWFCS (Underwater Fire Control System) on DD 963, DDG 993, CG 47 classes. The digital SQS-53B (General Electric/Hughes) has multiple target tracking and classification aids, weapons checkout routines, UYK-44 imbedded computers, UYQ-21 display, UYS-1 signal processor, a 60-percent reduction in required manning, 2,000-hour mean time between failures, and a 30-minute mean time to repair. SQS-53C, with improved active performance, simultaneous active/passive modes, more power, greater bandwidth, UYH-1 mass memory, faster reaction time, etc., is in advanced development.

**SQS-56:** Raytheon 1160B commercial active-passive, hull-mounted, medium-frequency set; used on FFG 7 class.

**SQS-58:** Raytheon. In development. No data available.

**UQQ-2 SURTASS:** SURveillance Towed-Array Sonar System, for use in the *Stalwart* (T-AGOS 1) class. Trials 1,830-m passive hydrophone array at about 3 knots.

◆ **on submarines**

**BQQ-4:** PUFFS (Passive Underwater Fire Control). Three-fin arrays, on SSN 597 and SS 576.

**BQQ-2:** Active-passive system on SSN 594 class, SSN 597, SSN 637 class, SSN 671, SSN 685. Incorporates BQR-7 conformal hydrophone array and BQS-6 spherical hydrophone array. Being upgraded to BQQ-5 in most ships.

**BQQ-5:** Active-passive system on the SSN 688 class; being backfitted in SSN 594 and SSN 637 classes. Incorporates BQS-11, -12, or -13 spherical bow hydrophone array. BQQ-5C has expanded DIFAR reception. BQQ-5D, with long-aperture, thin-line array, operational 1988.

**BQQ-6:** Passive-only version of the BBQ-5 system, for SSBN 626 class; has 944 hydrophone transducers mounted on a sphere.

**BQQ-9:** Towed array signal processing system for BQR-15; Rockwell. TASPE (Towed Array Signal Processing Equipment) for *Ohio* class.

**BQR-15:** Towed, passive array for SSN 608, SSBN 616 classes. Incorporates BQR-23 signal processor.

**BQR-19:** Active, short-range, navigational set for SSBNs. Raytheon.

**BQR-21:** DIMUS (Digital Multi-Beam Steering). Passive array for old SSBNs, SSNs.

**BQR-23:** STASS (Submarine Towed Array Sonar System). Used with BQR-25 in SSN 688, SSBN 726 classes. Current version: BQR-23A.

**BQR-24:** Raytheon; processor, used with BQR-21.

**BQR-25:** See BQR-23.

**BQS-4:** Active/passive set in older SSN, SS.

SONARS *(continued)*

**BQS-14, 20:** Under-ice and mine-avoidance, high-frequency set, mostly on later SSNs. Part of the BQQ-2, -5, -6 systems.

**BQS-13:** Raytheon. Active set.

**BQS-15:** Under-ice set tailored to the requirements of the SSN 688 class.

**BSY-1:** "Basic" version is suite for later SSN 688-class SSNs. To use UYS-1 signal processor, USH-26 signal recorder, UYK-20A data processor. Passive arrays plus SADS (Submarine Active Detection Sonar) and towed passive array. BSY-2 for Seawolf class.

◆ **on helicopters**

**AQS-13:** Dipping sonar used on SH-3 Sea King series.

**AQS-14:** Mine countermeasures set used by MH/CH-53D helicopters.

◆ **Sonobuoys**

A wide variety are in use, including those listed below, which are current production:

| | Production | | |
|---|---|---|---|
| | FY 87 | FY 88 | FY 89 request |
| SSQ-36 bathythermograph | 31,600 | 28,231 | 30,173 |
| SSQ-53 DIFAR | 235,802 | 150,816 | 108,666 |
| SSQ-57 Special-Purpose | 11,935 | 11,947 | 11,564 |
| SSQ-62 DICASS | 20,900 | 12,229 | 15,026 |
| SSQ-77 VLAD | 98,812 | 51,663 | 32,644 |
| SSQ-86 DLC | — | — | — |
| "Low-Cost Sonobuoy" | — | — | (310,000 deferred) |

## H. ELECTRO-OPTICAL SYSTEMS

The U.S. Navy lags Europe and the U.S.S.R. in the development of electro-optical (television, low-light television, laser, infrared) devices for widespread use on ships. In development are:

**SAR-8:** Joint U.S.-Canadian (General Electric, Spar) detection and tracking infrared system. Large, heavy antenna.

**Seafire:** The multi-mode fire-control system for the "Deadeye" guided 127-mm projectile. Development has halted several times because of rising costs.

## I. PROCESSING OF TACTICAL DATA

The NTDS (Naval Tactical Data System) uses digital calculators (AN/UYK-20 and AN/UYK-7) to give an overall picture of a tactical situation—air, surface, and underwater—and enables the commander to employ the means necessary to oppose the enemy. Excellent automatic data transmission systems (Link-11 and Link-14) permit the exchange of tactical information with similarly equipped ships and aircraft carrying the ATDS (P-3C Orion and S-3A Viking) and amphibious landing forces equipped with NTDS.

NTU—New Threat Upgrade

Improved weapons control and command system to upgrade Standard SM-2 MR/ER ships. Trials in DDG 42. Uses SPS-48E 3-D radar, SPS-49(V)2 2-D air search, the SYS-2 IADT (Integrated Automatic Target Detection and Tracking) computerized action information system, Mk 14 Weapons Direction System, and Standard SM-2 ER/MR Block 2 missiles. To be installed in 31 or more ships, per the following schedule:

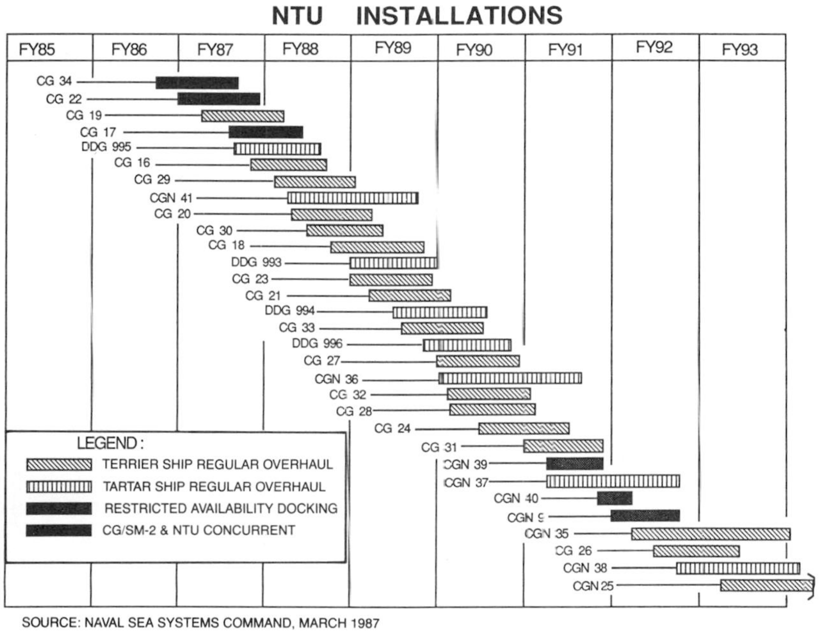


SOURCE: NAVAL SEA SYSTEMS COMMAND, MARCH 1987

Nearly all ships are equipped to receive SATCOMM (Satellite Communications) messages, while most can send ultra-high-frequency messages via satellite, and 31 can send super-high-frequency messages. The Tactical Flag Command Center (TFCC) is being backfitted into 13 CV/CVN, 2 LCC, and 5 CG. It employs USQ-81(V) computer-generated displays in an integrated 6.2-m × 6.2-m display space. T-AGOS sonar surveillance ships used the AN/WSC-6 VHF SATCOMM system.

## NUCLEAR-POWERED AIRCRAFT CARRIERS

◆ **1 (+4) improved Nimitz class** Bldr: Newport News SB & DD

| | Program | Laid down | L | In serv. |
|---|---|---|---|---|
| CVN 71 Theodore Roosevelt | FY 80 | 31-10-81 | 27-10-84 | 25-10-86 |
| CVN 72 Abraham Lincoln | FY 83 | 3-11-84 | 13-2-88 | 12-89 |
| CVN 73 George Washington | FY 83 | 25-8-86 | 9-89 | 12-91 |
| CVN 74 N . . . | FY 88 | . . . | 1993 | 1996 |
| CVN 75 N . . . | FY 88 | . . . | 1995 | 1997 |

**Theodore Roosevelt (CVN 71)** J. Baldwin/Newport News, 10-86

**Theodore Roosevelt (CVN 71)** C. Castle, 2-87

**Theodore Roosevelt (CVN 71)**—island G. Arra, 9-86

NUCLEAR-POWERED AIRCRAFT CARRIERS *(continued)*

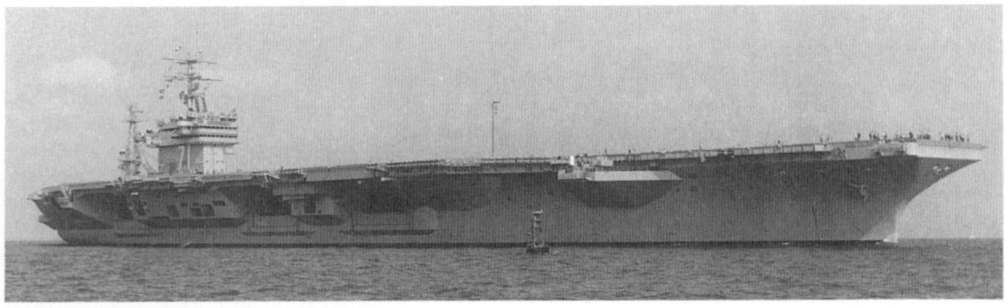

**Theodore Roosevelt (CVN 71)** G. Arra, 9-86

**Theodore Roosevelt (CVN 71)** Newport News, 10-86

**D:** 73,973 tons light (96,300–96,836 fl) **S:** 30+ kts
**Dim:** 332.85 (317.0 pp) × 40.85 (flight deck: 78.33) × 11.71
**A:** 3/Mk 29 launchers (VIII × 3) for Sea Sparrow—4/20-mm Mk 15 CIWS gatling AA—86 aircraft, including 20 F-14, 18 F/A-18, 5 EA-6B, 20 A-6E, 5 E-2C, 10 S-3A, and 8 SH-3D
**Electron Equipt:** Radar: 1/LN-66 nav., SPS-64 nav., 1/SPS-67(V), 1/SPS-48E, 1/SPS-49, 1/SPS-65, 1/SPN-46, 1/SPN-43A, 1/SPN-44, SPN-45, 3/Mk 91 Mod. 1 (6 directors)
EW: WLR-8, SLQ-17, Mk 36 SRBOC chaff RL (VI × 4)
TACAN: URN-25
**M:** 2 G.E. A4W/A1G pressurized-water reactors (42.3 kg/cm$^2$), 4 sets GT; 4 props; 280,000 hp
**Electric:** 64,000-kw + 8,000-kw emergency power from 4 diesel sets
**Man:** 6,286 tot. (203 officers, 3,205 men crew + 366 officers, 2,512 men air wing).

REMARKS CVN 71 authorized under FY 80; had been repeatedly delayed in favor of conventionally powered designs of inferior capabilities. Won out over both a Carter administration-sponsored 62,427-ton (fl) paper CVV design and a compromise 82,561-ton repeat *John F. Kennedy* (CV 67) design. CVN 72 and 73 built in same graving dock, requiring the latter to be made watertight during launch of CVN 72. CVN 73 may be named *John C. Stennis* at the desire of Congress.

The hangar has 7.6-m clear height. The angled deck is 237.7 m long and is equipped with four arrester wires and a Mk 7 Mod. 3 barrier, as well as four C 13 Mod. 1 catapults (92.1 m long), and four elevators (21.3 × 1.58 m, 47-ton capacity). An aviation payload of some 14,909 tons is carried, and the aviation ordnance magazines hold 1,954 tons. Aviation fuel capacity is about 9,000 tons. Kevlar armor is fitted over vital spaces, and hull-protection arrangements have been improved. Other data under the *Nimitz* class will generally apply. CVN 72 and 73 will have new, lower-pressure catapults and SPN-46 landing aids.

◆ **3 Nimitz class (SCB 102 Type)** Bldr: Newport News SB & DD

| | Program | Laid down | L | In serv. |
|---|---|---|---|---|
| CVN 68 NIMITZ | FY 67 | 22-6-68 | 13-5-72 | 3-5-75 |
| CVN 69 DWIGHT D. EISENHOWER | FY 70 | 15-8-70 | 11-10-75 | 18-10-77 |
| CVN 70 CARL VINSON | FY 74 | 11-10-75 | 15-3-80 | 13-3-82 |

**D:** 72,798–72,916 tons light; 81,600 standard (93,300–93,900 fl) **S:** 30+ kts
**Dim:** 327.0 (over catapult bridle retrieval horns: 332.8, pp: 317.0) × 40.85 (flight deck: 77.11, max.: 89.4) × 11.3
**A:** 86 airplanes and helicopters: 20 F-14, 18 F/A-18, 5 EA-6B, 20 A-6E, 5 E-2C, 10 S-3A, 8 SH-3D—3/Mk 29 launchers (VIII × 3) for Sea Sparrow—3 (CVN 70: 4)/20-mm Mk 15 CIWS
**Electron Equipt:** Radar: 1/SPS-64, 1/SPS-67, 1/SPS-49, 1/SPS-48B, 1/SPN-41, 2/SPN-42 or 46, 1/SPN-43A, 1/SPN-44, 3/Mk 115 (6 directors), 1/Mk 23 TAS
EW: WLR-1H, WLR-8, SLQ-17, Mk 36 SRBOC chaff (VI × 4)
TACAN: URN-25
**M:** 2 G.E. A4W/A1G pressurized-water reactors, 4 sets GT; 4 props; 280,000 hp
**Electric:** 64,000-kw + 8,000-kw emergency power from 4 diesel sets
**Man:** 6,286 tot. (569 officers, 3,091 crew, plus aviation personnel: 304 officers, 2,322 men)

REMARKS: CV 69 in Atlantic, CV 68 and 70 in Pacific. Carry 90% more aviation fuel and 50% more ammunition than the *Forrestal* class. ASCAC (Anti-submarine Classification and Analysis Center) permits instant sharing of target data between the carrier, its ASW aircraft, and escorting ships. *Nimitz* in refit 6-83 to 9-84; *Eisenhower* in refit 28-10-85 to 13-4-87.

**Dwight D. Eisenhower (CVN 69)**—post-overhaul W. Donko, 7-87

**Carl Vinson (CVN 70)** L. & L. Van Ginderen, 1-87

**Nimitz (CVN 68)**—note enlarged CIWS sponson Skyfotos, 9-86

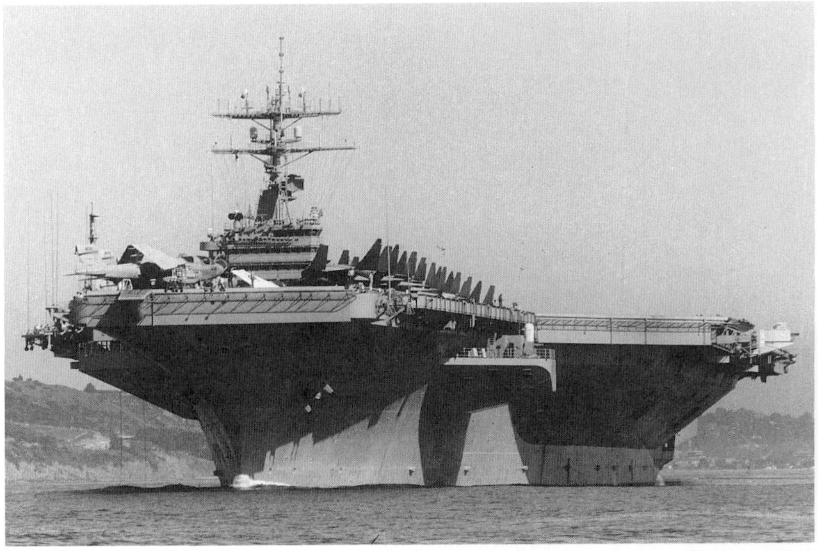

**Carl Vinson (CVN 70)**—one bow catapult horn G. Arra, 1986

NUCLEAR-POWERED AIRCRAFT CARRIERS *(continued)*

**Nimitz (CVN 68)** French Navy, 1987

**Nimitz (CVN 68)** G. Arra, 9-86

**Electronics:** SPS-49 replaced SPS-43A in CVN 68 and CVN 70 in 1983, and in CVN 69 in 1986. Carry OE-82 satellite communications antennas and have full NTDS installations. The Mk 23 TAS was added to improve defense against low-fliers and cruise missiles.

**Armament:** *Carl Vinson* completed with three Mk 29 launchers (VIII × 3) for Sea Sparrow, six directors for the missile (3 Mk 91 Mod. 1 FCS), and four Mk 15 CIWS (Vulcan/Phalanx) gatling AA guns. The others have been similarly refitted, but have only three Vulcan/Phalanx. All Mk 15 CIWS now protected by "maintenance enclosures."

**Armor:** Decks and hull are of extra-strong, high-tensile steel to limit the impact of semi-armor-piercing bombs. Apart from the longitudinal bulkheads, there are twenty-three watertight transverse bulkheads (more than 2,000 compartments) and ten firewall bulkheads. Foam devices for firefighting are very well developed, and pumping equipment is excellent, a 15° list being correctable in 20 minutes. Thirty damage-control teams are available at all times. *Nimitz*-class ships can withstand three times the severe pounding taken by the *Essex*-class aircraft carriers in 1944–45, and they can take impacts and shock waves in the same proportion. They are being equipped with Kevlar armor over vital spaces during refits.

**Machinery:** The cores of these ships are expected to last 13 years (CVN 70: 15) in normal usage, for a cruising distance of 800,000 to 1,000,000 miles. The evaporators can produce 1,520 tons of fresh water per day.

**Aircraft-handling installations:** There are four side elevators: two forward, one aft of the island to starboard, and one on the stern to port. There are also four C13 Mod. 1 steam catapults, 94.5 m long. CVN 69 and 70 have only the forward starboard bridle retrieval horn, because most aircraft in service do not require the bridle for launching. The 15,134 m$^3$ total aviation magazine spaces can hold 1,954 tons of aviation ordnance, and the total aviation-associated payload is on the order of 15,000 tons. The hangar is 7.8 meters high and can accommodate only 35–40% of the aircraft aboard. The angled part of the flight deck is 237.7 meters long and has four Mk 14 arrester wires and a barrier to halt aircraft (to be changed to 3 wires, 1 net). Sufficient aviation fuel for 16 days' operations is carried. CVN 69 has the prototype AVCARS (Augmented Visual Carrier Aircraft Recovery System); the production version entered service 1984.

◆ **1 Enterprise class (SCB 160 type)**

| | Bldr | Laid down | L | In serv. |
|---|---|---|---|---|
| CVN 65 Enterprise | Newport News SB & DD | 4-2-58 | 24-9-60 | 25-11-61 |

Authorized: FY 58

**D:** 74,730 tons light (92,200 fl) **S:** 33 kts
**Dim:** 335.75 (over catapult bridle horn: 342.3, wl: 317.0) × 40.54 (flight deck: 78.4) × 11.9
**A:** 86 airplanes and helicopters: 20 F-14, 20 F/A-18, 5 EA-6B, 20 A-6E, 5 E-2C, 10 S-3A, 6 SH-3A—2/Mk 29 launchers (VIII × 2) for Sea Sparrow—3/20-mm Mk 15 CIWS gatling AA (I × 3)
**Electron Equipt:** Radar: 1/SPS-64, 1/SPS-65, 1/SPS-48C, 1/SPS-49, 1/SPN-41, 2/SPN-42, 1/SPN-35A, 1/SPN-44, 2/Mk 91 Mod. 1 (4 directors)
EW: WLR-1H, WLR-8, WLR-11, SLQ-17(V)4, Mk 36 SRBOC chaff RL (VI × 4)
TACAN: URN-25
**M:** 8 Westinghouse A2W reactors, supplying 32 Foster-Wheeler heat exchangers; 4 sets Westinghouse GT; 4 props; 280,000 hp
**Electric:** 40,000 kw + 8,000 kw emergency
**Man:** 462 officers, 5,102 men (including 304/2,323 aviation personnel)

Remarks: In Atlantic Fleet, 1988. Began what was to have been a two-year overhaul at Puget Sound NSY 15-1-79, during which the radar and other electronics

**Enterprise (CVN 65)** G. Gyssels, 6-86

**Enterprise (CVN 65)** W. Donko, 7-87

NUCLEAR-POWERED AIRCRAFT CARRIERS *(continued)*

**Enterprise (CVN 65)**—rebuilt island, port side, with SPS-49 and SPS-48C radars atop superstructure, SPS-65 and SPN-35A on mast W. Donko, 7-87

**Enterprise (CVN 65)** Pradignac & Leo, 9-86

suites were extensively renovated; completed 11-81. The SPS-32 and SPS-33 "billboard" radar arrays were removed, as was the "beehive" dome atop the blockhouse superstructure. A new mast, resembling that on the *Nimitz*, was installed atop the superstructure. SPS-48C and SPS-49 are mounted atop the island. There are four C13 Mod. 1 steam catapults and four elevators—one on the port side of the angled deck, three to starboard—two of which are forward of and one abaft the island. Elevators are steel and alloy and weigh 105 tons; 26 m long, 16 m wide, lift 45 tons. The hangar is 7.62 m high and the flight deck is more than 20,000 m$^2$. Carries half again as much aviation fuel as the *Forrestal* class (8,500 tons), which permits 12 days of intensive aerial operations without replenishment. Carries fuel oil to replenish other ships. Has NTDS and ASCAC (Antisubmarine Classification and Analysis Center) and will receive TFCC (Tactical Flag Communications Center). A third Mk 29 Sea Sparrow SAM launcher and the Mk 23 TAS radar are to be added during the next major overhaul. In refit at Newport News through 9-88.

## CONVENTIONAL AIRCRAFT CARRIERS

### ◆ 1 John F. Kennedy class (SCB 127C type) Bldr: Newport News SB & DD

| | Program | Laid down | L | In serv. |
|---|---|---|---|---|
| CV 67 John F. Kennedy | FY 63 | 22-10-64 | 27-5-67 | 7-9-68 |

**John F. Kennedy (CV 67)** G. Arra, 3-87

**John F. Kennedy (CV 67)** G. Arra, 3-87

**John F. Kennedy (CV 67)** Pradignac & Leo, 9-86

**D:** 60,660 tons light (32,400 fl) **S:** 32 kts
**Dim:** 320.34 (301.8 wl) × 39.17 (flight deck: 81.38, max. 82.30) × 11.20
**A:** 78 aircraft: 24 F-14, 24 A-6E, 4 KA-6D, 5 EA-6B, 5 E-2C, 10 S-3A, 6 SH-3H—3/Mk 29 launchers (VIII × 3) for Sea Sparrow—3/20-mm Mk 15 CIWS (I × 3)
**Electron Equipt:** Radar: 1/SPS-64, 1/SPS-67, 1/SPS-49, 1/SPS-48C, 1/SPN-35, 1/SPN-41, 1/SPN-43A, 1/SPN-44, 2/SPN-46, 3/Mk 91 Mod.1 (6 directors), 1 Mk 23 TAS
EW: WLR-1, WLR-3, WLR-11, SLQ-26, SLQ-17, Mk 36 SRBOC RL (VI × 4)
TACAN: URN-25
**M:** 4 sets G.E. GT; 4 props; 280,000 hp
**Boilers:** 8 Foster-Wheeler; 83.4 kg/cm$^2$, 520°C **Electric:** 17,000 kw
**Man:** 535 officers, 5,224 men (including aviation personnel)

Remarks: Operates in the Atlantic Fleet. Four side elevators, three to starboard (two forward of and one abaft the island) and one on the port quarter. Completely automatic landing system, permitting all-weather operation. Four arrester wires and a barrier on the 227-m angled flight deck. Three 90-m C13 and one 94.5-m C13-1 catapults. Has PLAT, which facilitates the control of launching and recovery operations. Stack angled to starboard. The 11,808-m$^2$ aviation-ordnance magazine can accommodate 1,250 tons of ammunition. Carries 5,919 tons of aviation fuel. Equipped to carry SQS-23 sonar in bow dome, but it was not installed. SPS-49 replaced SPS-43A in 1979–80, and SPS-58 was deleted. Obsolescent Chaffroc chaff RL replaced with Mk 36 SRBOC (VI × 4), during 10-84 to 10-85 refit, when two additional Mk 15 CIWS and the Mk 23 TAS radar were also added. To receive major SLEP overhaul 1-99 to 2-02.

### ◆ 3 Kitty Hawk class (SCB 127A and SCB 127B types)

| | Bldr | Laid down | L | In serv. |
|---|---|---|---|---|
| CV 63 Kitty Hawk | New York SB | 27-12-56 | 21-5-60 | 29-4-61 |
| CV 64 Constellation | Brooklyn NSY | 14-9-57 | 8-10-60 | 27-10-61 |
| CV 66 America | Newport News SB | 9-1-61 | 1-2-64 | 23-1-65 |

Authorized: CV 63 in FY 56, CV 64 in FY 57, CV in FY 61

CONVENTIONAL AIRCRAFT CARRIERS *(continued)*

**Constellation (CV 64)** V. Baca, 2-87

**America (CV 66)** G. Arra, 9-86

**Kitty Hawk (CV 63)** J. Kürsener, 10-86

**Constellation (CV 64)** G. Arra, 3-86

**Constellation (CV 64)**—visible on deck are 13 F-14A, 19 F/A-18, 10 A-6E, 3 EA-6B, 1 EA-3, 8 S-3A, 1 C-2, 3 SH-3G, and 1 CH-46 LSPH W. McBride, R.A.N., 9-87

**Kitty Hawk (CV 63)** G. Arra, 1986

## CONVENTIONAL AIRCRAFT CARRIERS *(continued)*

**D:** 60,100 tons (81,800 fl; CV 66: 79,400) **S:** 33 kts
**Dim:** 318.8 (CV 66: 319.25) (301.76 pp) × 39.62 (flight deck: 76.81) × 11.4 (CV 66: 11.3)
**A:** 88 aircraft: 24 F-14, 12 A-6E, 24 A-7E, 4 KA-6D, 4 EA-6B, 10 S-3A, 4 E-2C, 6 SH-3H—3/Mk 29 launchers (VIII × 3) for Sea Sparrow—3/20-mm Mk 15 CIWS gatling AA (I × 3)
**Electron Equipt:** Radar: 1/SPS-64, 1/SPS-10F or SPS-67, 1/SPS-48C, 1/SPS-49, 1/SPN-35, 1/SPN-41, 2/SPN-42, 1/SPN-43A, 2 or 3/Mk 91 Mod. 1 (4 or 6 directors)
EW: SLQ-29 (WLR-8 + SLQ-17); WLR-1H, WLR-11, Mk 36 SRBOC RL (VI × 4)
TACAN: URN-25
**M:** 4 sets Westinghouse GT; 4 props; 280,000 hp **Fuel:** 7,800 tons
**Boilers:** 8 Foster-Wheeler, 83.4 kg/cm², 520°C **Range:** 4,000/30; 8,000/20
**Man:** approx. 5,400: 137 officers, 2,765 men + air wing: 290 officers, 2,200 men
**Electric:** 15,000 kw (CV 66: 18,000 kw)

REMARKS: These ships are a great improvement over the *Forrestal* class, on which they are based, and have one significant difference: three elevators on the starboard side, two forward of and one abaft the island, and one to port, abaft the angled flight deck. Aircraft can be landed and catapulted simultaneously, a difficult operation on the earlier ships. Four C13 steam catapults, except on CV 66, on which one is of the longer C13-1 type. Carry 5,882 tons of aviation fuel. CV 66 was the first ship to receive the Mk 15 CIWS, in 4-80. CV 64 retained two Mk 10 twin launchers for Terrier HT missiles and two SPQ-55B radar directors until 12-82 to 2-84 refit at Bremerton. CV 66 was the first to have a special integrated CIC and airborne ASW control center (ASCAC). CV 66 had an SQS-23 bow sonar until 1981. CV 63 entered SLEP (Service Life Extension Program) 1-88 to emerge in 2-91 with new catapult rotary engines, Mk 7 Mod. 3 arrester gear (3 wires), SPN-46 landing-aid radar, SPS-48E and SPS-49(V) upgrade air-search radars, updated NTDS (Naval Tactical Data System), a torpedo decoy system, the WQN-1 "channel-finder" sonar, upgraded EW equipment, and the Mk 23 TAS low-altitude radar added. CV 64 is to undergo a similar SLEP from 10-90 to 11-93. CV 66 is not scheduled for SLEP until 4-96 to 5-99, but will receive Mk 23 TAS during regular overhaul in the late 1980s.

Air groups being modified, with 18 F/A-18 replacing the 24 A-7E, the number of F-14 being reduced to 20. CV 63 and CV 64 are in the Pacific, CV 66 in the Atlantic Fleet.

### ◆ 4 Forrestal class (CV 59: SCB 80 type; CV 60 to CV 62: SCB 80M type)

| | Bldr | Laid down | L | In serv. |
|---|---|---|---|---|
| CV 59 FORRESTAL | Newport News SB & DD | 14-7-52 | 11-12-54 | 1-10-55 |
| CV 60 SARATOGA | Brooklyn NSY | 16-12-52 | 8-10-55 | 14-4-56 |
| CV 61 RANGER | Newport News SB & DD | 2-8-54 | 29-9-56 | 10-8-57 |
| CV 62 INDEPENDENCE | Brooklyn NSY | 1-7-55 | 6-6-58 | 10-1-59 |

Authorized: CV 59 in FY 52, CV 60 in FY 53, CV 61 in FY 54, CV 62 in FY 55

**D:** approx. 60,000 tons light (CV 59: 79,000; CV 60: 81,300; CV 61:80,900; CV 62: 81,600 fl)
**S:** 33 kts
**Dim:** CV 59: 331.0; CV 60: 324.0; CV 61: 326.4; CV 62: 326.1 (319.13 flight deck, 301.8 wl) × 39.63 (CV 59, 60: 76.3; CV 61, 62: 82.3 max.) × 11.3
**A:** 86 aircraft: 20 F-14, 20 F/A-18, 16 A-6E, 4 KA-6D, 5 EA-6B, 10 S-3A, 5 E-2C, 6 SH-3H—2 Mk 29 (CV 60, 62: 3) launchers (VIII × 2 or 3) for Sea Sparrow—3/20-mm Mk 15 CIWS gatling AA (I × 3)

**Ranger (CV 61)**—with Mk 23 TAS on mast G. Arra, 2-87

**Ranger (CV 61)**—note large sponsons forward G. Arra, 1-86

**Electron Equipt:** Radar: 1/SPS-64, 1/SPS-67, 1/SPS-49, 1/SPS-48C, 1/SPN-35, 1/SPN-41, 2/SPN-42, 1/SPN-43A, 2 or 3/Mk 91 Mod. 1 (4 or 6 directors); 1/Mk 23 TAS
EW: WLR-1, WLR-3, WLR-11, SLQ-26, Mk 36 SRBOC chaff RL (VI × 4)
TACAN: URN-25
**M:** 4 sets G.E. or Westinghouse GT; 4 props; CV 59: 260,000 hp, others: 280,000 hp
**Boilers:** 8 Babcock & Wilcox; CV 59: 41.7 kg/cm², other: 83.4 kg/cm². 520°C
**Fuel:** 7,800 tons **Range:** 4,000/30; 8,000/20
**Man:** approx. 4,940: 138–163 officers, 2,713–2,880 enlisted + air wing: 290 officers, 3,100 enlisted

REMARKS: CV 61 in Pacific Fleet, others in the Atlantic. Hangar is 7.6 m high and 234–240 m long. Four side elevators (15.95 × 18.9). Deck angled at 8°. Armored

**Forrestal (CV 59)** Pradignac & Leo, 11-86

**Forrestal (CV 59)**—island, starboard side Pradignac & Leo, 11-86

## CONVENTIONAL AIRCRAFT CARRIERS *(continued)*

**Saratoga (CV 60)** PH3 L. Hilley, USN, 4-84

flight deck. Four-cable arresting gear. CV 59 and CV 60 have two Mk-C7 (75 m) and two Mk-C11 (65 m) steam catapults; the others have four Mk-C7. Carry 5,880 tons of aviation fuel. CV 59 has three rudders and four propellers, the two outboard being five-bladed, the two inboard, four-bladed. Deck protection and internal compartmentation are extensive (1,200 watertight compartments). Two longitudinal bulkheads are fitted from keel to waterline from stem to stern; there are transverse bulkheads about every 10 meters. Air groups evolving as F/A-18 replaced A-7E; formerly ships carried 24 F-14, 12 A-6E, 24 A-7E. CV 61 carries: 24 F-14, 28 A-6E/KA-6D, 10 S-3A, 6 SH-3H, 5 E-2C, and 5 EA-6B.

**Forrestal (CV 59)** L. & L. Van Ginderen, 9-87

**Forrestal (CV 59)** L. & L. Van Ginderen, 9-87

**Saratoga (CV 60)**—post-SLEP modernization U.S. Navy, 1984

**CONVENTIONAL AIRCRAFT CARRIERS** *(continued)*

CV 60 received first SLEP (Service Life Extension Program) modernization, beginning 1-10-80 at Philadelphia Navy Yard, completing 2-83 (but boiler defects kept her inoperative until 18-11-83). CV 59 SLEP from 21-3-83 to 20-5-85; CV 62 18-4-85 to 2-88. *Ranger* not scheduled for SLEP until 7-93 to 8-96, but did get extensive overhaul at Puget Sound NSY 5-84 to 6-85, when improved evaporators, Halon and aqueous film firefighting systems, Mk 23 TAS, and 3 Mk 15 CIWS were added. All will ultimately be armed with three Mk 29 Sea Sparrow launchers, each with two directors, three Mk 15 CIWS Vulcan/Phalanx gatling guns, and the Mk 23 TAS low-altitude radar. All catapults will be replaced with longer and more powerful C13s. The ships will get Kevlar armor, improved data systems, the Tactical Flag Command Center, and more habitability. All originally carried eight 127-mm/54, Mk 42 guns. CV 61 relinquished her last two guns in 1977, later than her sisters did, and retains her forward gun sponsons. Stacks raised 3 m in CV 59 and 62.

◆ **2 Midway class** Bldr: Newport News SB & DD

| | Laid down | L | In serv. |
|---|---|---|---|
| CV 41 Midway | 27-10-43 | 20-3-45 | 10-9-45 |
| CV 43 Coral Sea | 10-7-44 | 2-4-46 | 1-10-47 |

**D:** CV 41: 56,400 tons light (67,500 fl)—CV 43: 48,300 tons (65,400 fl)
**S:** 32 kts
**Dim:** CV 41: 306.78 (274.32 wl) × 55.78 (42.90 wl) × 10.46
CV 43: 306.00 (274.32 wl) × 47.55 (36.38 wl) × 10.70
**A:** CV 41: 36 F/A-18, 14/A-6E and KA-6D, 4/EA-6B, 6/SH-3H—2/Mk 25 BPDMS launchers (VIII × 2 for Sea Sparrow)—2/20-mm Mk 15 CIWS (I × 2)
CV 43: 40 F/A-18, 12/A-6E, 5/KA-6D, 7 SH-3H, 4 E-2C—3/20-mm Mk 15 CIWS (I × 3)
**Electron Equipt:** Radar: CV 41: 1/SPS-64, 1/SPS-65, 1/SPS-49, 1/SPS-48C, 2/SPN-42, 1/SPN-44, 2/Mk 115
CV 43: 1/SPS-64, 1/SPS-67, 1/SPS-49, 1/SPS-48C, 1/SPN-41, 2/SPN-42, 1/SPN-43A

**Midway (CV 41)** R. Gillett, 6-87

**Midway (CV 41)** L. & L. Van Ginderen, 6-87

**Coral Sea (CV 43)** G. Arra, 3-87

EW: WLR-1, WLR-10, WLR-11; CV 41: SLQ-17; CV 43: ULQ-6; both: Mk 36 SRBOC chaff RL (VI × 4)
TACAN: URN-25
**M:** 4 sets Westinghouse GT; 4 props; 212,000 hp **Electric:** 11,700 kw
**Boilers:** 12 Babcock & Wilcox; 41.7 kg/cm², 454°C
**Man:** CV 41: 402 officers, 4,278 enlisted (including aviation personnel)
CV 43: 2,605 crew + 1,464 aviation personnel.

**Midway (CV 41)** L. & L. Van Ginderen, 6-87

**Coral Sea (CV 43)** L. & L. Van Ginderen, 2-86

Remarks: CV 43 transferred to the East Coast 1983 and was modernized at Norfolk for service up to 1992. Reentered service 29-1-85, but was damaged in collision 11-4-85, losing 11 m of the bow; repaired by 7-85. CV 41, home-ported at Yokosuka, Japan, since 10-73, had 183-m-long by 3-m-wide bulges added during her 1-4-86 to 28-11-86 refit to reduce draft and hangar deck wetness. Unfortunately, the bulges caused the roll period to decrease to 9 sec and increased flight deck wetness. After operating with a reduced air wing during 1987, CV 41 is having a "slot" cut into the bulges by Sumitomo Heavy Industries to restore her original waterline beam while retaining most of the added buoyancy. Sister *Franklin D. Roosevelt* (CV 42) was stricken on 1-10-72. Machinery and ships' bottoms very similar to the *Iowa*-class battleships.

Two side-elevators to starboard, one forward of and one abaft the island; one side elevator to port abaft the angled flight deck. CV 41 has a considerably larger flight deck than does CV 43. CV 41 has two C13 steam catapults (both forward) and three arrester wires on the angled deck. CV 43 retains three C11-1 steam catapults. The hangar is 211.1 m long by 25.9 m wide.

**Earlier Refits:** From 1954 to 1963, the ships underwent several overhauls: angled flight deck installed; flight deck lengthened; hydraulic catapults replaced with steam ones; side armor removed and "bulges" added. Reinforced arresting gear and barriers installed; centerline elevators replaced with side ones; aviation fuel capacity increased. In October 1967 CV 41 began another major overhaul and returned to service in 1-70. Her angled flight deck was extended to port; her three elevators were enlarged; her forward port elevator was moved aft; her catapults were replaced by more powerful ones; and all her electronic equipment was replaced. In 1979–80, during short overhauls at Yokosuka, CV 41's radar suit was updated and the Tactical Flag Command Center was added. CV 43 was overhauled 11-78 to 10-79 at Puget Sound NSY, where her catapults were brought up to C13 capability.

**RESERVE AIRCRAFT CARRIERS**

◆ **4 Essex,* and Hancock† class** (all in reserve)

| | Bldr | Laid down | L | In serv. |
|---|---|---|---|---|
| CVS 12 Hornet* | Newport News SB | 3-8-42 | 29-8-43 | 29-11-43 |
| CVS 20 Bennington* | New York NSY | 15-12-42 | 26-2-44 | 6-8-44 |
| CVA 31 Bon Homme Richard† | New York NSY | 1-2-43 | 29-4-44 | 26-11-44 |
| CV 34 Oriskany† | New York NSY | 1-5-44 | 13-10-45 | 25-9-50 |

**D:** approx. 33,000 tons (40,600 to 41,900 fl) **S:** 30+ kts
**Dim:** 274.01 (CVS 38: 270.97) (249.9 wl) × 31.39 (CV 34: 32.46) (flight deck: approx. 58.5 × 9.45)
**A:** 4/127-mm DP (I × 4), except CV 34: 2/127-mm DP (I × 2)

**RESERVE AIRCRAFT CARRIERS** *(continued)*

**Electron Equipt:** Radar: 1/SPS-10, 1/SPS-30, 1/SPS-43A (CVS 11, CV 34: SPS-37), 1/SPN-10, 1/SPN-43, 1–2/Mk 25, 0–4 Mk 35
Sonar: CVS only: SQS-23 (bow-mounted)
TACAN: SRN-6 or URN-20

**M:** Westinghouse GT; 4 props; 150,000 hp
**Boilers:** 8 Babcock & Wilcox; 41.7 kg/cm$^2$, 454°C **Electric:** 7,000 kw
**Fuel:** 6,750 tons **Range:** 18,000/12 **Man:** none

**Bennington (CVS 20)**—Essex class U.S. Navy, 1967

**Oriskany (CV 34)**—in reserve at Bremerton G. Arra, 10-85

Remarks: All in Category "C" reserve, all berthed at Bremerton, Washington. CV 34 was placed in reserve on 30-9-76; recommissioning (to cost approx. $510 million), to take 28–34 months, proposed by Reagan Administration for FY 82 but was turned down by Congress. *Lexington* (formerly CVT 16) was redesignated AVT 16 on 1-7-78 and is used for training in deck landing; see entry in auxiliary section. CVS 12 was decommissioned on 26-6-70, CVS 20 on 15-1-70, and CVA 31 on 2-7-71. CVS 12 and CVS 20 retain their Mk-H8 hydraulic catapults; the others have C8 steam catapults. All have three elevators: one on the centerline between the catapults, one at the forward end of the angled deck, and one (vertically stowable) to starboard, abaft the island. Four arrester wires. CV 34 has two Mk 37 gun directors. The others have one Mk 37 and two or three Mk 56 directors.

## NAVAL AND MARINE CORPS AVIATION

Aviation is an integral part of the U.S. Navy and Marine Corps. In FY 88 there were 5,109 aircraft assigned to naval aviation, of which 1,364 were operated by the Marine Corps. In 1987, the principal combat aircraft included:
428+ F-14A Tomcat interceptors
375+ F/A-18A/B Hornet fighter-bombers
340+ A-6E Intruder attack bombers
65 KA-6D aerial refuelers
80+ EA-6A Prowler electronics warfare
20 EA-6B Prowler electronics warfare
162 S-3A Viking ASW (shipboard)
500+ P-3A/B/C Orion maritime patrol and ASW (land-based)
30+ EP-3A/B/E Orion ELINT
48 EA-3 Skywarrior ELINT
120+ SH-3-series Sea King ASW helo
100+ SH-2F LAMPS-I Sea Sprite ASW helo
85+ SH-60B LAMPS-III Seahawk ASW helo
80 CH-53A heavy-lift helo
20 RH-53D minesweeping helo
300+ CH-46 troop/utility helo

In 1988, there will be 14 active Carrier Air Wings and two deployable Reserve Carrier Air Wings for duty aboard carriers. Two types of air wing composition are in use: the "Traditional Navy Wing" with 24 F-14A, 24 F/A-18, 10 A-6E, 4 KA-6D, 4 EA-6B, 4 E-2C, 10 S-3A, and 6 SH-3H; and the "Notional Navy Air Wing," with 20 F-14A, 20 F/A-18, 20 A-6E, 5 EA-6B, 10 S-3A, 5 E-2C, and 6 SH-3H. CV 41 and CV 43 carry non-standard air wings. Air Wing 10 to deactivate end-FY 88.

The U.S. Air Force has programmed conversion of two 15-aircraft B-52G squadrons (one for each coast) for sea-control duties. The B-52G will carry up to 12 Harpoon missiles externally and 8 internally and will have a 2,000-n.m. combat radius with 2 hrs on station.

Air squadrons are designated alphanumerically, the letter prefixes for the principal squadron types being ("X" denotes various models in aircraft type listings):

Navy:

| | |
|---|---|
| HC | Helicopter Combat Support (CH-46) |
| HCS | Helicopter Combat Support (HH-60H) |
| HM | Helicopter Mine Countermeasures (RH-53D, MH-53E) |
| HS | Helicopter Antisubmarine (SH-3) |
| HSL | Light Helicopter Antisubmarine (SH-2, SH-60B) |
| HT | Helicopter Training (TH-57X, UH-1E, TH-1L) |
| VAL | Light Attack (A-7) |
| VA | Attack (A-6, KA-6) |
| VAQ | Tactical Electronic Warfare (EA-6B) |
| VAW | Carrier Airborne Early Warning (E-2C) |
| VC | Fleet Composite (utility aircraft) |
| VF | Fighter (F-4, F-14, F/A-18) |
| VP | Patrol (P-3) |
| VQ | Fleet Air Reconnaissance (EP-3, EA-3B), also: Communications Support (EC-130) |
| VR | Fleet Logistics Support (C-9, C-130, C-131, etc.) |
| VRC | Fleet Logistics Support-COD (Carrier Onboard Delivery) (C-1A, C-2A) |
| VS | Air Antisubmarine (S-3A) |
| VT | Training (TA-4J, T-2C, T-39D, T-44A) |
| VX | Air Test and Evaluation |
| VXE | Antarctic Development (LC-130F, UH-1) |
| VXN | Oceanographic Development (RP-3A/D) |

Marine Corps:

| | |
|---|---|
| HMA | Marine Attack Helicopter (AH-1) |
| HMH | Marine Heavy Helicopter (CH-53) |
| HML | Marine Light Helicopter (UH-1) |
| HMM | Marine Medium Helicopter (CH-46) |
| VMA | Marine Attack (A-4, A-6E, AV-8B) |
| VMAQ | Marine Electronic Warfare (EA-6B) |
| VMFA | Marine Fighter-Attack (F-4, F/A-18) |
| VMFP | Marine Photo Reconnaissance (RF-4B) |
| VMGR | Marine Refueler-Transport (KC-130F) |
| VMO | Marine Observation (OV-10) |

### ◆ Marine Corps Aviation

The Marines operate a considerable air force, with all aircraft procured and "owned" by the Navy. U.S.M.C. aircraft are intended to operate principally from amphibious-warfare ships, but squadrons of attack, reconnaissance, and electronic-warfare aircraft frequently operate from carriers as well. In 1987, 7,150 officers and 32,350 enlisted men served Marine Corps Aviation.

Marine Corps combat aviation is organized into three active wings and one reserve wing, with each active wing nominally including: 48 F/A-18, 20 A-6E, 40 AV-8B, 9 TA-4 or OA-4, 8 RF-4B (to be replaced by F/A-18C/DR), 8 EA-6B, 12 KC-130 aerial refuelers, 48 CH-53, 60 CH-46, 24 AH-1T/W, 24 UH-1, and 12 OV-10. In addition, there are 4 Training Squadrons for fixed-wing aircraft, 3 for helicopters, and one Base and Command Support Squadron with about 36 fixed-wing aircraft and helicopters.

NAVY AIRCRAFT PROCUREMENT PLAN

| | FY 86 | FY 87 | FY 88 | FY 89 | FY 90 | FY 91 | FY 92 |
|---|---|---|---|---|---|---|---|
| A-6E/F Intruder | 11 | 11 | — | — | — | — | — |
| EA-6B Prowler | 12 | 12 | 12 | 9 | 9 | 9 | 9 |
| F-14A/D Tomcat | 18 | 15 | 12 | 12 | 12 | 30 | 42 |
| F/A-18A/D Hornet | 84 | 84 | 84 | 72 | 72 | 72 | 72 |
| AV-8B Harrier | 46 | 42 | 24 | 24 | 24 | 24 | — |
| AH-1W SeaCobra | 22 | 22 | 34 | — | — | — | — |
| SH-2F Seasprite | 6 | 6 | — | — | — | — | — |
| CH-53E Super Stallion | 4 | 4 | 6 | 10 | — | — | — |
| MH-53E Sea Dragon | 10 | 10 | 8 | 4 | — | — | — |
| SH-60B Seahawk | 18 | 11 | 6 | 6 | 6 | 12 | 12 |
| SH-60F Ocean Hawk | — | 7 | 18 | 18 | 18 | 12 | 12 |
| HH-60A | 4 | — | 9 | — | — | — | — |
| P-4/LRAACA | — | — | — | — | 2 | | 18 |
| MV-22A Osprey | — | — | — | — | 12 | 45 | 61 |
| E-2C Hawkeye | 6 | 6 | 6 | 6 | 6 | 6 | 6 |
| C-2A Greyhound | 8 | 9 | — | — | — | — | — |
| T-34C Mentor | 38 | — | — | — | — | — | — |
| T-44A King Air | — | — | — | — | 15 | — | — |
| T-45A Goshawk | — | — | 12 | 24 | 24 | 48 | 48 |
| E-6A Hermes | 2 | 3 | 3 | 7 | — | — | — |
| KC-130T Hercules | 2 | 2 | 2 | — | — | — | — |
| F-16N Fighting Falcon | 12 | — | — | — | — | — | — |
| F-21 Kfir (lease) | 26 | — | — | — | — | — | — |

Note: Represents aircraft authorized through FY 89 (with FY 89 subject to change), plus Navy plan for FY 90-92 as presented to Congress 2-88 (modified to show direction by Congress under FY 88). Twelve A-6F *appropriated* for in FY 88 budget but not *authorized;* A-6F canceled, to be replaced by A-6G upgrades: 10 in FY 88, 15 in FY 90, 24 in FY 91, 92.

## NAVAL AND MARINE CORPS AVIATION *(continued)*

### ◆ Aircraft Losses

Operational loss rates remain high, largely because of the intense tempo of U.S. Navy flight operations. In 1982, 88 aircraft were lost, while in 1983, 87 were lost. In 1984 the number lost fell to 69, and in 1986, 71 were lost: 10 F-14A, 2 F/A-18, 5 F-4, 6 A-6E, 3 EA-6B, 9 A-7, 9 A-4, 3 AV-8B, 2 S-3A, 2 T-2, 3 T-34B/C, 4 H-1, 2 SH-2, 4 H-3, 5 H-46, 2 H-53E, and 2 SH-60B. Aircraft losses for FY 87 totaled only 50 and included 10 A-6E, 8 F/A-18, and 7 F-14A.

### ◆ Aircraft Designations

Besides the name given to an aircraft—Phantom, Intruder, Orion, etc.—each type is designated by a group of letters and figures divided by a hyphen and made up in the following manner:

1. The letter immediately preceding the hyphen indicates the principal mission:

| | |
|---|---|
| A—attack | P—patrol |
| B—bomber | S—antisubmarine |
| C—cargo/transport | T—training |
| E—airborne early warning | U—utility |
| F—fighter | V—VTOL/STOL, vertical or short takeoff and landing |
| K—tanker, inflight refueling | X—research |
| O—observation | |

2. The figure that comes immediately after the hyphen is the design sequence number. When a letter follows this figure, its position in the alphabet indicates that the aircraft is the first, second, third, etc., modification to the original design.

Example: A-4E = an attack aircraft, the fourth attack plane design, the fifth modification.

3. When an aircraft is assigned to duty that is not its principal mission, a second letter precedes the letter of that mission (see para. 1 above):

| | |
|---|---|
| A—attack | M—missile carrier or mine countermeasures |
| C—cargo/transport | Q—drone aircraft |
| D—direction or control of drones, aircraft, or missiles | R—reconnaissance |
| | S—antisubmarine |
| E—special electronic installation | T—trainer |
| H—search and rescue | U—utility, general service |
| K—tanker, inflight, refueling | V—staff |
| L—cold weather; for arctic regions | W—weather, meteorology |

4. A third prefixed letter in front of an aircraft's designation means:

| | |
|---|---|
| G—permanently grounded | X—experimental |
| J—temporary special test | Y—prototype |
| N—permanent special test | Z—planning |

CURRENT U.S. NAVY, MARINE CORPS AIRCRAFT DESIGNATIONS

### ◆ Attack

A-3 SKYWARRIOR:

| | |
|---|---|
| EA-3B | ECM mission equipment |
| KA-3B | Tanker |
| ERA-3B | FEW support group configuration |
| TA-3B | Bombardier/navigator training version |
| VA-3B | High-speed personnel transport |

A-4 SKYHAWK:

| | |
|---|---|
| A-4E | J-52, basic attack |
| A-4F | A-4E with improved systems |
| EA-4F | ECM version of TA-4F |
| TA-4F | Two-place training version |
| TA-4J | Advanced training version of TA-4F |
| A-4M | Uprated engine and improved system |
| OA-4M | TA-4F modified to TACA configuration |

A-6 INTRUDER:

| | |
|---|---|
| EA-6A | ECM mission equipment |
| EA-6B | ECM mission |
| KA-6D | A-6A configured as tanker |
| A-6E | A-6A with improved systems |
| A-6F | New engines, avionics |
| A-6G | Upgraded A-6E |

A-7 CORSAIR II:

| | |
|---|---|
| A-7B | A-7A with improved engine |
| A-7C | Advanced weapon delivery system |
| TA-7C | A-7B/C modified to two-place trainer |
| A-7E | A-7B with TF-41 and improved weapons systems |

F/A-18 HORNET:

| | |
|---|---|
| F/A-18A | First-line fighter/attack aircraft |
| TF/A-18A | Two-place trainer version |
| F/A-18C | upgraded F/A-18A, AMRAAM-capable |
| F/A-18D | Two-seat attack, for USMC |

AV-8 HARRIER:

| | |
|---|---|
| TAV-8B | Two-seat trainer |
| AV-8B | Major redesign, improved capability |
| AV-8C | AV-8A reworked, modernized |

### ◆ Fighters

F-4 PHANTOM:

| | |
|---|---|
| QF-4B | F-4B target drone |
| RF-4B | Photoreconnaissance |
| F-4J | Improved systems and engines |
| EF-4J | EW version |
| F-4S | F-4J modified for extended life |

F-5 TIGER II:

| | |
|---|---|
| F-5E | Adversary aircraft |
| F-5F | Two-place version |

F-8 CRUSADER:

| | |
|---|---|
| RF-8G | Photoreconnaissance |

F-14 TOMCAT:

| | |
|---|---|
| F-14A | Front-line fighter aircraft, TF-30 |
| F-14A Plus | Re-engined F-14A |
| F-14D | Improved systems |

F-16 FIGHTING FALCON:

| | |
|---|---|
| F-16N | Adversary aircraft |

F-21 KFIR:

| | |
|---|---|
| F-21A | Adversary aircraft |

### ◆ Utility

OV-10 BRONCO:

| | |
|---|---|
| OV-10A | COIN/LARA twin turboprop |
| OV-10D | Night gunship |

### ◆ Patrol

P-3 ORION:

| | |
|---|---|
| P-3A | Land-based ASW, T56-A-10W engine |
| EP-3A | Electronic reconnaissance configuration |
| RP-3A | Special T&E and ocean research |
| VP-3A | Personnel transport |
| P-3B | P-3A with T56-A-14 engines |
| EP-3B | Electronic reconnaissance |
| P-3C | Improved avionics systems |
| RP-3D | Configured for Project Magnet |
| EP-3E | Electronic reconnaissance |
| P-3G | Proposed update |

### ◆ Cargo Transport

C-1 TRADER:

| | |
|---|---|
| C-1A | COD transport, twin engines, piston R-1820s |

C-2 GREYHOUND:

| | |
|---|---|
| C-2A | Carrier logistics |

C-9 SKYTRAIN II:

| | |
|---|---|
| C-9B | Commercial DC-9 |

C-12 SUPER KING AIR:

| | |
|---|---|
| UC-12B | Passenger logistics |

C-130 HERCULES:

| | |
|---|---|
| C-130F | Turboprop logistics transport |
| KC-130F | Tactical tanker/cargo transport |
| LC-130F | Polar use, ski/wheel gear |
| EC-130G | TACAMO |
| EC-130Q | Improved TACAMO |
| KC-130R | Improved tanker |
| LC-130R | Improved polar version |
| KC-130T | Improved avionics, tanker capabilities |

C-131 SAMARITAN:

| | |
|---|---|
| C-131F | Convair 340 cargo version |
| C-131G | Convair 440 cargo version |
| C-131H | Modified turboprop |

### ◆ Antisubmarine Warfare

S-3 VIKING:

| | |
|---|---|
| S-3A | Carrier-based ASW aircraft |
| US-3A | Utility version |
| S-3B | Improved avionics |
| ES-3A | EW conversion |

### ◆ Airborne Early Warning

E-2 HAWKEYE:

| | |
|---|---|
| E-2B | AEW aircraft, carrier-based (inactive) |
| E-2C | Improved system |

**NAVAL AND MARINE CORPS AVIATION** *(continued)*

◆ **Trainers**

| | |
|---|---|
| T-2 BUCKEYE: | |
| T-2B | Two-engine jet trainer, J60 engines |
| T-2C | J85 engines |
| C-4 ACADEME/GULFSTREAM: | |
| TC-4C | Bombardier/navigator trainer, prop |
| T-34 MENTOR: | |
| T-34B | Primary trainer, single-engine, piston 0-470-4 engine |
| T-34C | Improved systems, PT6A-25 turboprop |
| T-39 SABRELINER: | |
| T-39D | Pilot/NFO trainer, jet |
| CT-39E | Rapid response airlift |
| CT-39G | Modified CT-39E, lengthened fuselage |
| T-44 KING AIR: | |
| T-44A | Advanced multiengine trainer |
| T-45 GOSHAWK: | |
| T-45A | Advanced jet trainer |

◆ **Tilt-Wing Aircraft (JVX)**

| | |
|---|---|
| V-22 OSPREY: | |
| MV-22A | Marine Corps Transport |
| SV-22 | Proposed ASW version |

◆ **Airborne Mine Countermeasures**

| | |
|---|---|
| H-53 SEA STALLION/SUPER STALLION: | |
| RH-53D | Sea Stallion, twin-engine, AMCM, logistics (see Helicopters) |
| MH-53E | Sea Dragon, three-engines, AMCM version of the CH-53E |

◆ **Helicopters**

| | |
|---|---|
| UH-1 IROQUOIS/HUEY: | |
| UH-1E | Single rotor, T53-L-11 engine |
| HH-1K | T53-L-13 engine, similar to UH-1E, orange paint |
| TH-1L | Trainer, UH-1E armor/armament deleted, T53-L-13 engine |
| UH-1L | Utility, UH-1E, T53-L-13 engine |
| UH-1M | T53-L-13 engine |
| UH-1N | Special transport, twin-engine T400-CP-400 |
| VH-1N | Executive version |
| AH-1 SEACOBRA: | |
| AH-1G | Attack version, T53-L-13 engine |
| AH-1J | USMC avionics, T400-CP-400 engine |
| AH-1T | Modified AH-1J, T400-WV-402 engine |
| AH-1W | Two T-700-GE-401 engines |
| H-2 SEASPRITE: | |
| SH-2F | LAMPS MK 1 sea-based ASW |
| H-3 SEA KING: | |
| HH-3A | Search and rescue, T58-GE-8 engines |
| SH-3A | Sea-based ASW, amphibious, twin-engine |
| UH-3A | Utility |
| VH-3A | Executive transport |
| SH-3D | SH-3A with T58-GE-10 engines |
| VH-3D | Executive transport |
| SH-3G | Improved SH-3A, sea-based ASW and logistics |
| SH-3H | SH-3G for sea-based ASW/ASMD, T58-GE-10 engines |
| H-46 SEA KNIGHT: | |
| HH-46A | CH/UH-46A with improved systems |
| UH-46A | Utility version |
| CH-46D | Improved T58-GE-10 engines |
| UH-46D | Utility version, T58-GE-10 engines |
| CH-46E | Improved T58-GE-16 engines |
| CH-46F | CH-46D with instrument panel changes |
| H-53 SEA STALLION: | |
| CH-53A | Two-engine assault helicopter, T64-GE-6B engines |
| CH-53D | Improved T64-GE-413 engines |
| RH-53D | AMCM |
| H-53E SUPER STALLION: | |
| CH-53E | Three-engines |
| MH-53E | AMCM version of CH-53E, larger fuel tanks |

**First production F/A-18C strike fighter** McDonnell Douglas, 9-87

| | |
|---|---|
| H-57 SEA RANGER: | |
| TH-57A | Trainer |
| TH-57C | Advanced Instrument Trainer |
| SH-60 SEAHAWK: | |
| SH-60B | Sea-based LAMPS MK III ASW |
| SH-60F | Carrier-based, dipping-sonar |
| UH-60A | Combat SAR |
| VH-60A | VIP transport |

**The 500th production F/A-18 Hornet** McDonnell Douglas, 5-87

**F-14A Tomcat, all-weather fighter** U.S. Navy, 9-83

**F-4S**—U.S. Marines McDonnell Douglas, 1-82

**A-6E Intruder heavy attack aircraft**—with Tacit Rainbow AGM-136A ARM for trials D.O.D., 1987

**A-6F Intruder**—first prototype of a canceled program Grumman, 8-87

**NAVAL AND MARINE CORPS AVIATION** *(continued)*

**AV-8B Harrier attack aircraft (Marine Corps), night-attack-capable prototype** McDonnell Douglas, 7-87

**TAV-8B Harrier 2-seat trainer, first production aircraft** McDonnell Douglas, 7-87

**A-4F Skyhawk attack aircraft of VT-43** S. Terzibaschitsch, 4-84

**EA-3B Skywarrior** LCDR D. Parsons, USN, 4-86

**A-7E Corsair light attack aircraft** U.S. Navy, 1982

**P-3C Orion patrol aircraft** PHC J. Kristoffersen, USN, 11-85

**P-3C Update III prototype** Lockheed, 1-87

**C-2A Greyhound COD (Carrier Onboard Delivery) aircraft** L. & L. Van Ginderen, 12-86

**S-3A Viking ASW aircraft** French Navy, 1981

**OV-10D**—with new engines and FLIR Rockwell, 1986

**NAVAL AND MARINE CORPS AVIATION** *(continued)*

**SH-3H Sea King ASW helicopter** L. & L. Van Ginderen, 1-87

**VH-3D Sea King VIP transport of HMX-1** U.S. Navy

**SH-2F Seasprite LAMPS-I ASW helicopter**—in new low-visibility paint U.S. Navy, 1987

**CH-46E Sea Knight transport helicopter, U.S.M.C.** F. Jentsch, 7-87

**SH-60B Seahawk LAMPS-III ASW helicopter of HSL-41** Sikorsky, 1987

**SH-60F Ocean Hawk prototype** Sikorsky, 1987

**EA-6B Prowler electronics warfare aircraft**—with HARM missile Texas Instruments, 1986

**E-2C Hawkeye early-warning aircraft** Grumman, 1976

**MV-22A Osprey**—artist's rendering Bell-Boeing, 1987

## NAVAL AND MARINE CORPS AVIATION *(continued)*

**AH-1T SeaCobra**—with Sidearm trials missile, U.S.M.C. S. Wyatt, USN, 10-81

**AH-1W SeaCobra** Bell/Textron, 1986

### PRINCIPAL COMBAT AIRCRAFT

| Class, builder | Mission | Wingspan in m | Length in m | Height in m | Weight in kg | Engine | Max speed Mach/knots | Ceiling in feet | 1) Ferry range (nautical miles) 2) Combat radius (nautical miles) 3) Range (hours) |
|---|---|---|---|---|---|---|---|---|---|
| **SHIP-BASED FIXED WING:** | | | | | | | | | |
| **F/A-18A/B/C/D Hornet** (McDonnell Douglas) | Multirole fighter (Navy/U.S.M.C.) | 11.43 | 17.07 | 4.67 | 10,437 (empty) 32,150 (max.) | 2 G.E. F404-GE-400 6,800-kg thrust each | M 1.8 | 49,400 | 1,600<br>450 with 1,814 kg payload<br>3 |

Armament: 5,900 kg of conventional or nuclear bombs; 2/Sidewinder; 4/Sparrow-III; 1/20-mm M61A1 cannon. APG-65 radar; FLIR pod to add. Harpoon-capable.

REMARKS: Uses a microprocessor to control the various weapons. The two-seat TF/A-18B is also being built at about 5/yr. Procurement of at least 1,377 planned. First U.S.M.C. squadron operational 7-1-83; first U.S.N. squadron 10-83; first of 10 planned Naval Reserve squadrons in 1984. First upgraded F-14C flight 15-9-86; C and 2-seat D will have AMRAAM and IR Maverick compatibility, plus ALQ-165 ASPJ EW gear. D for U.S.M.C. will receive reconnaissance pod and are intended for all-weather attack capability from 1989-on. U.S.M.C. to receive F/A-18D "Plus" in trade for A-6Es, plans five 12-plane F/A-18D and 12 12-plane F/A-18C squadrons. 500th F/A-18 delivered 15-5-87; Navy had 375 in 21 squadrons as of 5-87. Aircraft has had rear fuselage cracking and engine turbine blade problems.

| Class, builder | Mission | Wingspan in m | Length in m | Height in m | Weight in kg | Engine | Max speed Mach/knots | Ceiling in feet | Range |
|---|---|---|---|---|---|---|---|---|---|
| **F-14A/A-Plus/D Tomcat** (Grumman) | Two-man all-weather fighter with variable-geometry wing | 19.53/ 11.63 | 18.85 | 4.88 | 28,236 (18,186 empty) (F-14D): 32,865 (max.) | 2 P&W TF30-P-414A 9,480-kg thrust each, with afterburners A-Plus, D: 2 G.E. F110-GE -400, 12,698 kg thrust each | M 2.34 | 60,000 | 2,000<br>500<br>2.50 to 3 |

Armament: 1/20-mm M61A1 Vulcan gun; 2/Phoenix, 2/Sidewinder, and 2/Sparrow missiles or 3,856 kg of Sparrow and Sidewinder missiles. AWG-9 radar. Three in each squadron fitted for TARPS photo-reconnaissance pod.

REMARKS: 428 in service 1-1-86; Max. landing speed: 120 knots. The F-14D, using the Hughes APG-71 radar, and other avionics improvements, supplanted the F-14A in production under FY 1988. Thirty-eight F-14A-Plus with new engine but old avionics are being procured, and 32 earlier F-14A will be re-engined. First 18 new A-Plus ordered under FY 86, 15 in FY 87, 5 in FY 88. First 7F-14D of a planned 127 authorized FY 88, for delivery FY 90 (had originally planned 304 F-14D).

| Class, builder | Mission | Wingspan in m | Length in m | Height in m | Weight in kg | Engine | Max speed Mach/knots | Ceiling in feet | Range |
|---|---|---|---|---|---|---|---|---|---|
| **F-4J/S, RF-4B Phantom** (McDonnell Douglas) | All-weather fighter (Navy) reconnaissance (Marine Corps) | 11.71 | 17.75 | 4.96 | 24,767 (12,700 empty) | 2 G.E. J79-GE-8-10B 8,120-kg thrust each, with afterburners (RF-4B: F-4J,N: J79-GE-8) | M 2.2 | 51,800–55,000 | 2,300<br>900<br>2.25 |

Armament: 4/Sparrow-III and 4/Sidewinder missiles (standard weapons) or 6/Sparrow III or 7,258 kg of missiles, rockets, or bombs: 18/340-kg, 15/309-kg, 11/454-kg bombs; 7/smoke bombs; 11/napalm bombs; 15/air-to-surface rocket pods.

REMARKS: Remaining 1987: 24 F-4J, 223 F-4S, 28 RF-4B (reconnaissance). Max. landing speed: 140 knots. Marine-operated RF-4B has G.E. J79-GE-10B smokeless engines. Four Reserve squadrons fly F-4S, 3 U.S.M.C. fly RF-4B.

| Class, builder | Mission | Wingspan in m | Length in m | Height in m | Weight in kg | Engine | Max speed Mach/knots | Ceiling in feet | Range |
|---|---|---|---|---|---|---|---|---|---|
| **A-4E,F Skyhawk** (McDonnell Douglas) | Attack (Navy Reserve and Marine Corps) | 8.38 | 12.50 | 4.57 | 10,904 (4,747 empty) | 1 P&W J52-P-408A 5,080-kg thrust | 504 kts (sea level) 537 kts (10,000 ft) | 33,250 | 2,055<br>150 at 396 kts<br>2.12 |

Armament: 2/20-mm Mk 12 guns; 2,950 kg (12 MU 81) bombs, rockets. U.S.M.C. aircraft equipped with Maverick missiles.

REMARKS: In 1-87 54 A-4E, 42 A-4F, and 279 2-seat T-A4J remained in service. Nonfolding wings. Several versions: A-4E & M remain in 4 active Marine squadrons, but Navy use is by Reserves and in support duties. Final units built 1979, after 25 years' production. A-4M has large hump on spine for electronics. About 260 two-seat TA-4F and J trainers also in use, as well as several dozen specialized aircraft.

| Class, builder | Mission | Wingspan in m | Length in m | Height in m | Weight in kg | Engine | Max speed Mach/knots | Ceiling in feet | Range |
|---|---|---|---|---|---|---|---|---|---|
| **A-6E/KA-6D Intruder** (Grumman) | All-weather attack (Navy and Marine Corps) | 16.15 | 16.67 | 4.92 | 27,392 (11,627 empty) | 2 P&W J52-P8A/8B 4,218-kg thrust each | 594 kts | 52,700 | 2,400<br>320 at 400 kt<br>. . . |

Armament: 18,000 pounds of conventional or nuclear bombs, rockets, etc. Examples of ordnance: 46/250-pound, 30/450-pound, 15/900-pound, 4/2,000-pound bombs; 13 pods with 247 rockets; 52/Zuni rockets; 4/Sidewinder or 4/Bullpup missiles. Now equipped for Harpoon, HARM, Maverick, Sidewinder, and Walleye. APQ-156 radar.

REMARKS: Approx. 340 A-6E in service in 4-87. KA-6D tanker versions, conversions of A-6A/E, carry 30,000 lb fuel for transfer; 65 now operational. All A-6E have TRAM (Target Recognition-Attack Multisensor). As of 8-86, 177 new A-6E had been delivered, plus 228 earlier A-6 updated to E-variant. Sixteen Navy squadrons, 5 U.S.M.C.,

## NAVAL AND MARINE CORPS AVIATION *(continued)*

### PRINCIPAL COMBAT AIRCRAFT *(continued)*

the latter to transfer to Navy. Five FY 84/85 airframes for A-6F program. Planned 150 A-6F, but Congress rejected FY 88. Would have had 2 T404-G.E.-400D engines for Mach 0.84 and 38,740-ft max. altitude, 27,553 kg max. t.o. weight, 600+ n.m. combat radius, new avionics, more hard-points, Sidewinder, HARM, and AMRAAM capability, and new synthetic aperture radar. 120 A-6E being re-winged by Boeing. Last new A-6E to deliver 8-89. Wholly new replacement to be developed. In lieu of A-6F, Navy plans to update 167 A-6E to A-6G, with J52-P-408 engines: 10 under FY 88, 15 in FY 90, 24/yr. thereafter.

| Class, builder | Mission | Wingspan in m | Length in m | Height in m | Weight in kg | Engine | Max speed Mach/knots | Ceiling in feet | 1) Ferry range (nautical miles) 2) Combat radius (nautical miles) 3) Range (hours) |
|---|---|---|---|---|---|---|---|---|---|
| **A-7E Corsair-II** (Ling-Temco-Vought) | Attack | 11.80 | 14.06 | 4.90 | 17,278 (8,973 empty) | 1 Allison TF41-A-2 6,800-kg thrust | 553 kts (sea level) | 33,500 | 2,800<br>425 at 460 kt.<br>2.25 |

Armament: 1/20-mm M61A1 Vulcan gun; up to 6,800 kg bombs, rockets, or missiles, according to the mission and the target distance. Examples of weapons: 24/113-kg Mk 81 bombs; 4/Zuni rockets; 28/2.75-inch rockets; 1/Shrike missile, and 1/Walleye guided bomb; 12/Snakeye bombs; 2/Shrike missiles; 2/907-kg bombs. Normally carry two Sidewinder AAM for defense. Have APQ-126 attack radar. APR-43 warning syst. (to be replaced by ALR-45F).

REMARKS: 285 of all variants active 1-87. A-7E is now used for operational training; earlier A-7E with P&W TF30-P-408 engines are used by the Reserves. 81 TA-7C two-seat trainers converted from single-seat B&C models, with 43 getting TF-41 engines in place of TF30-P-408; ETA-7C electronics aircraft are also being re-engined 1985–86. A-7E getting capability to launch HARM missiles, plus FLIR sensor being added.

| Class, builder | Mission | Wingspan in m | Length in m | Height in m | Weight in kg | Engine | Max speed Mach/knots | Ceiling in feet | 1) Ferry range 2) Combat radius 3) Range (hours) |
|---|---|---|---|---|---|---|---|---|---|
| **AV-8B Harrier** (McDonnell Douglas) | Attack (Marine Corps) | 9.22 | 14.10 | 3.53 | VTOL: 8,720<br>STOL: 13,492 | 1 Rolls-Royce Pegasus F402-RR-406 9,751-kg thrust | 650 kts; 585 kts at sea level (Mach 0.91/0.86) | 50,000 | 2,460<br>VTOL:100+ STOL: 300<br>1 |

Armament: 2/30-mm guns; 2/Sidewinder AAM, and 14/227-kg or 6/454-kg bombs or 4/Maverick ASM. No radar.

REMARKS: Acquisition plan reduced to 184 tot. aircraft (15 being 2-seat TAV-8B); 86 were flying by 7-87. First AV-8B squadron operational 6/85, with first of four AV-8B developmental aircraft flying 10-81. First T-AV-8B two-seater flew 7-87. First night-attack-capable variant, with FLIR, flew 6-87. All AV-8A and AV-8C retired by 1-87.

| Class, builder | Mission | Wingspan in m | Length in m | Height in m | Weight in kg | Engine | Max speed Mach/knots | Ceiling in feet | 1) Ferry range 2) Combat radius 3) Range (hours) |
|---|---|---|---|---|---|---|---|---|---|
| **S-3A Viking** (Lockheed) | ASW | 20.93 | 16.26 | 6.94 | 23,853 (12,160 empty) | 2 G.E. TF34-GE-400 4,210-kg thrust each | Max: 450 kts<br>Cruise: 350 kts<br>Patrol: 210 kts | 40,000 | 3,000<br>1,150<br>9 |

Armament: 60/sonobuoys, 4/Mk 32 bombs; 4/Mk 57 depth charges; 4/Mk 53 depth charges or 4/Mk 53 mines or 4/Mk 46 torpedoes. APS-116 radar. ASQ-81(V)1 magnetic anomaly detector (MAD).

REMARKS: Fitted with a Univac AYK-10 digital computer to apply the information from the sensors on board. Four-man crew. 187 built; conversions include six US-3A COD aircraft for Indian Ocean deployments and one KS-3A serial refueler. Some 140 of the 160 S-3A survivors were to be updated to S-3B, at the rate of 3/month, beginning 4/87. Will receive WSIP (Weapon & Sensor Improvement Program) with APS-137(V)1 synthetic aperture radar, Harpoon launch capability, new Auxiliary Power Unit (APU), ALE-40 ECM dispenser. Program currently behind schedule, however, and 144 of 164 surviving S-3A are to convert. Sixteen designated for conversion to ES-3A ELINT aircraft to replace overaged EA-3Bs, but Congress did not authorize under FY 88 as requested, leaving major gap in future Navy capability. First series S-3B conversion kit delivered 9-87.

| Class, builder | Mission | Wingspan in m | Length in m | Height in m | Weight in kg | Engine | Max speed Mach/knots | Ceiling in feet | 1) Ferry range 2) Combat radius 3) Range (hours) |
|---|---|---|---|---|---|---|---|---|---|
| **E-2C Hawkeye** (Grumman) | Airborne early warning and air control | 24.58 | 17.56 | 5.59 | 23,810 (17.091 empty) | 1 Allison T56-A-425 turboprops, 4,591 shp each | 315 kts (270 kts, cruise) | 30,800 | 1,525<br>. . .<br>6 |

REMARKS: APS-125 radar in 7.32-m circular, rotating radome. ESM-equipped. Five-man crew. By 1-1-87 a total of 92 E-2C were available, 6/yr built. Can track 600+ air and surface targets in a 250 n.m. radius and control 25 simultaneous intercepts; to be improved by TRAC-A (Total Radiation Aperture Control Antenna) radar to reduce side-lobes. First reserve squadron received in 1984. Beginning with FY 86, uprated T56-A-427 engines are used, increasing power 24% and cutting fuel consumption 12%. Eighty E-2C to be re-winged, at 16 per year. Last E-2B retired by 1-87.

| Class, builder | Mission | Wingspan in m | Length in m | Height in m | Weight in kg | Engine | Max speed Mach/knots | Ceiling in feet | 1) Ferry range 2) Combat radius 3) Range (hours) |
|---|---|---|---|---|---|---|---|---|---|
| **EA-6B Prowler** (Grumman) | Electronics warfare | 16.15 | 18.11 | 4.95 | 27,392 (12,185 empty) | 2 P&W J52-P-408, 5,080-kg thrust each (late units; J52-P-409, 5,442 kg each) | 520 kts (410 kts, cruise) | 34,400 | 2,400<br>710<br>. . . |

REMARKS: ECM version of A-6 Intruder; four-man crew. APS-130 radar. Five ALQ-99F jammer rods beneath wings and fuselage. 76 in service 1-1-86; 15 operated by U.S.M.C. Two-seat Naval Reserve and Marine Corps Reserve EA-6A Intruders carry five ALQ-31B jammar pods and can alternatively be used as an attack aircraft, with up to 8,160 kg of ordnance; 27 were built, of which 21 remain. Both aircraft are distinguished from the standard A-6E by a large, streamlined electronics-equipment pod atop the vertical stabilizer. See also remarks under A-6E. HARM anti-radiation missile capability being added to EA-6B.

| Class, builder | Mission | Wingspan in m | Length in m | Height in m | Weight in kg | Engine | Max speed Mach/knots | Ceiling in feet | 1) Ferry range 2) Combat radius 3) Range (hours) |
|---|---|---|---|---|---|---|---|---|---|
| **EA-3B Skywarrior** (McDonnell Douglas) | Electronics warfare | 22.11 | 23.28 | 6.94 | 35,380 (18,685 empty) | 2 P&W J57-P-10 5,625-kg thrust each | 556 kts (400 kts, cruise) | 41,300 | 5,000<br>1,100<br>6 |

REMARKS: Badly need replacement. RA-3B and ERA-3B are used for reconnaissance. There is also one VA-3B transport. 49 of all variants left in mid-1987, of 283 built, first flying 1952. Only 10 EA-3B left; carrier flight banned 11-87 due to lack of experienced pilots.

| Class, builder | Mission | Wingspan in m | Length in m | Height in m | Weight in kg | Engine | Max speed Mach/knots | Ceiling in feet | 1) Ferry range 2) Combat radius 3) Range (hours) |
|---|---|---|---|---|---|---|---|---|---|
| **P-3C Orion** (Lockheed) | Maritime patrol and ASW | 30.37 (P-3C Update IV and P-3B: 31-13) | 35.61 | 10.28 | 62,994 (27,892 empty) | 4 Allison T56-A-14 turboprops, 4,910 hp each | 405 kts (209 kts patrol) | 34,000 | 4,500<br>2,380 patrol<br>14.5 |

Armament: 6/908-kg mines; 2/Mk 101 nuclear depth charges; 4/Mk 46 torpedoes; 87/sonobuoys, 4/Harpoon antiship missiles, etc. Weapons vary. Can carry a total of 7,700 kg of disposable ordnance and sensors. APS-115 radar. ASQ-81(V)1 magnetic anomaly detector (MAD), ASQ-114 digital computer, P-3C has AAS-36 FLIR gear. 63 to receive 4 Harpoon stations under FY 83 budget.

REMARKS: In service 1-1-85: 151 P-3A flown by Reserves, 124 P-3B (Reserves plus 3 active squadrons), 233 P-3C (19 squadrons), 12 EP-3. Crews of up to 15 men. The P-3C is fitted with an A-NEW central operations module built around the ASQ-114 miniaturized computer and with an Air Tactical Data System. ASQ-10 magnetic anomaly detector (MAD), APS-115 radar, electronics countermeasures carried. EP-3B/E are for electronics warfare, RP-3A/D are for research, and WP-3D perform weather reconnaissance. P-3Cs are expected to last 28 years each. Total built for U.S.N. through 1985: 157 P-3A, 124 P-3B, 233 P-3C, 1 RP-3D, 2 WP-3D. Over 30 converted to EP-3A/B/E. RP-3A, VP-3A and CP-3A. Also over 70 to date for overseas customers. FY 84 aircraft are Update III, with new sonobuoy communications. Adapative-Controlled Phased Array antennas; Update IV will have new wingtip EW antennas. (ALR-77). First Update IV conversions: 18 under FY 86. Boeing to perform Update IV conversion to up to 120–140 P-3Cs, with series deliveries beginning 1988. Last 7 new P-3C authorized FY 87. To follow either with P-3G, an up-dated P-3 airframe with Update IV avionics, longer weapons bay for Harpoon ASM, and Allison 501-H80C engines or "P-4," a version of the McDonnell Douglas MD-80 or Boeing 757 as the LRAACA (Long-Range Air ASW Capable Aircraft). Two P-3C began conversion 1986 to EP-3C with option for 10 more; equipment cannibalized from earlier EP-3A/B

| Class, builder | Mission | Wingspan in m | Length in m | Height in m | Weight in kg | Engine | Max speed Mach/knots | Ceiling in feet | 1) Ferry range 2) Combat radius 3) Range (hours) |
|---|---|---|---|---|---|---|---|---|---|
| **E-6A Hermes** (Boeing) | Strategic comms. | 45.6 | 46.61 | . . . | 155,100 (78,365 empty) | 4 SNECMA-G.E. (FM-56) | 530 kts (455 kts cruise) | 40,000 (cruise) | . . .<br>6,350<br>15.4 w.o. refueling<br>28.9 one refuel |

REMARKS: Fifteen submarine airborne VLF communications relay aircraft for SSBNs. Prototype flew 1-6-87. Uses 707-320B airframe. Nuclear-hardened against electromagnetics, thermal blast, gamma and neutron radiation. Ten crew, plus 8 relief crew.

**NAVAL AND MARINE CORPS AVIATION** *(continued)*

## PRINCIPAL COMBAT AIRCRAFT *(continued)*

| Class, builder | Mission | Wingspan in m | Length in m | Height in m | Weight in kg | Engine | Max speed Mach/knots | Ceiling in feet | 1) Ferry range (nautical miles) 2) Combat radius (nautical miles) 3) Range (hours) |
|---|---|---|---|---|---|---|---|---|---|
| **C-1A Trader** (Grumman) | Carrier Onboard Delivery (COD) | 21.23 | 22.80 | 4.98 | 12,247 | 2 Wright R1820–82 piston; 1,525 hp each | 242 kts | 22,000 | 965 at 145 kts<br>. . .<br>. . . |

REMARKS: Despite advanced obsolescence, retained until more C-2A can be built. Cargo version of out-of-service S-2 Tracker ASW aircraft. Two-man crew plus 9 passengers. Cargo capacity: 1,589 kg. Fewer than 30 remain.

| Class, builder | Mission | Wingspan in m | Length in m | Height in m | Weight in kg | Engine | Max speed Mach/knots | Ceiling in feet | 1) Ferry range (nautical miles) 2) Combat radius (nautical miles) 3) Range (hours) |
|---|---|---|---|---|---|---|---|---|---|
| **C-2A Greyhound** (Grumman) | Carrier Onboard Delivery (COD) | 24.57 | 17.27 | 4.85 | 24,668 (14,175 empty) | 2 Allison T56-A-8A turboshaft; 4,050 shp each | old: 296 kts<br>new: 343 kts (257 kts, cruise) | 28,800 (33,800 new units) | 1,490 at 260 kt |

REMARKS: Variant of E-2 Hawkeye with large-diameter fuselage. Twelve of the original series remain, with 39 more delivering 8/yr 1985–89. Three-man crew plus 32 passengers or 20 litter patients or 3,724 kg cargo. Stern ramp for loading, provision for aerial refueling. New aircraft use T-56-A-425 engines. Payload: 5,535 kg.

| Class, builder | Mission | Wingspan in m | Length in m | Height in m | Weight in kg | Engine | Max speed Mach/knots | Ceiling in feet | 1) Ferry range (nautical miles) 2) Combat radius (nautical miles) 3) Range (hours) |
|---|---|---|---|---|---|---|---|---|---|
| **MV-22A Osprey** (Boeing-Bell) | Troop-carrier (Marines) | 14.17 (11.58 rotor dia.) | 17.32 | 6.14 (5.28 folded) | 24,943 (max.) | 2 Allison 501-M80C turboshaft; 6,150 shp each | 380 kts (cruise) | 32,000 | 1,200 range (1,814 kg cargo)<br>2,100 max. |

REMARKS: To enter service 1991 with Marines, 1992 with Navy. U.S.M.C. plans 552 aircraft, Navy about 50 HV-22A for SAR duties. To carry 24 troops 200 n.m. at 3,000 ft. Up to 4,535-kg external load. SAR version is to rescue 4 persons at up to 460-n.m. radius. Planned 12.7-mm nose gun deleted. First flight planned for 1988. APQ-168 radar. To replace the S-3A/B an SV-22 variant has been proposed, using a modified fuselage with same avionics as P-3C, 60 sonobuoys, and ASW ordnance, plus new engines. Some 300 would be required, with first flight in 1992 and service introduction in 1996.

**HELICOPTERS:**

| Class, builder | Mission | Diameter (rotor) | Length (overall) | Height in m | Weight in kg | Engine | Max speed in/knots | Ceiling in feet | 1) Mission range (nautical miles) 2) Ferry range (nautical miles) 3) Endurance (hours) |
|---|---|---|---|---|---|---|---|---|---|
| **SH-3D/G/H Sea King** (Sikorsky) | ASW | 18.9 | 22.16 (16.70, fuselage) | 5.13 | 9,300 (5,302 empty | 2 G.E. T58-GE-10 turboshaft, 1,400 shp each | 144 (118 cruise) | 10,800 | 625<br>. . .<br>4.50 |

Armament: Two Mk 46 torpedoes, sonobuoys.

REMARKS: Four-man crew. On CV aircraft carriers or land-based; can be carried on *Spruance*-class DD. SH-3H is a multipurpose version of the SH-3G utility model. Fitted with AQS-13 dipping sonar. AQS-81(V)2 MAD. SH-3G models updating to SH-3H standard, carry APS-24 radar. Planned to replace with SH-60F. Eleven U.S.M.C.VH-3A/D serve the Presidential Flight, and there are also several UH-3A in service. 119 SH-3H were in service as of 1987; 26 SH-3D more were to convert to "H" model.

| Class, builder | Mission | Diameter (rotor) | Length (overall) | Height in m | Weight in kg | Engine | Max speed in/knots | Ceiling in feet | 1) Mission range (nautical miles) 2) Ferry range (nautical miles) 3) Endurance (hours) |
|---|---|---|---|---|---|---|---|---|---|
| **SH-2F Seasprite LAMPS-I** (Kaman) | ASW | 13.42 | 16.04 (11.69 fuselage) | 4.73 | 5,806 (3,154 empty) | 2 G.E. T58-GE-8F turboshaft, 1,350 hp each | 143 (130 cruise) | 22,500 | 445<br>. . .<br>2.50 |

Armament: 15/DIFAR and DICASS sonobuoys, 2/Mk 46 ASW torpedoes, 8 smoke markers. ASQ-81(V)2 MAD (Magnetic Anomaly Detector), LN-66 radar, ALR-66 ESM, ARR-75 sonobuoy dispenser fitted.

REMARKS: Found on FF, DD, and CG types. 106 in service 1-1-86. Until 1983, all were conversions of UH-2 Sea Sprite utility helicopters. Reintroduced into production, with 42 new aircraft approved in FY 83 to FY 87 to serve in ASW ships not getting SH-60B. First *new* SH-2F delivered 12-8-83. 24 older SH-2F to Reserve squadrons to replace SH-3D. Contract placed 6-87 to upgrade 6 to SH-2G with T700 engines, digital database, new acoustic processor, tactical navigation system, data link, and 99-channel sonobuoy receiver, for delivery beginning 1990; prototype flew 4-85.

| Class, builder | Mission | Diameter (rotor) | Length (overall) | Height in m | Weight in kg | Engine | Max speed in/knots | Ceiling in feet | 1) Mission range (nautical miles) 2) Ferry range (nautical miles) 3) Endurance (hours) |
|---|---|---|---|---|---|---|---|---|---|
| **SH-60B Seahawk LAMPS-III SH-60F Ocean Hawk** (Sikorsky) | ASW | 16.36 | 19.76 (15.24, fuselage) | 5.23 | B: 9,435<br>F: 9,925 | 2 G.E. T700-GE-401 turboshaft, 1,723 max. hp each (1,543-hp cont.) | 150 kts (130 cruise) | . . . | 150<br>. . .<br>1.3<br>4.5 |

Armament: 25/sonobuoys; 2/Mk 46 ASW torpedoes.

REMARKS: 204 SH-60B sought, 93 of which to be in service by 10-88. 203 planned, for use on 53 ships. APS-124 radar. ASQ-811(V)2 MAD, 25 SSQ-53 DIFAR, and SSQ-60 DICASS active sonobuoys, UYS-1 computer, ALQ-142 ESM, LINK 11. Highly automated; all sensors display on ship that controls the helicopter. Congress required 9 HH-60H version for combat search and rescue in FY 85-86 for delivery in 1989. Nine VH-60 in FY 86 for Presidential Flight. 85 SH-60B in service by 4-87. SH-60F is intended to replace the SH-3 series and differs primarily from the SH-60B in having a Bendix AQS-13F dipping sonar and deleting the APS-124 radar. SH-60F prototype flew 19-3-87; 175 total planned. SH-60B airframe tested with 2,100-hp Rolls-Royce Turbomeca RTM 322 turboshaft for possible series conversions, 1988.

| Class, builder | Mission | Diameter (rotor) | Length (overall) | Height in m | Weight in kg | Engine | Max speed in/knots | Ceiling in feet | 1) Mission range (nautical miles) 2) Ferry range (nautical miles) 3) Endurance (hours) |
|---|---|---|---|---|---|---|---|---|---|
| **CH-46 HH-46A, D, E Sea Knight** (Boeing Vertol) | Troop-carrying assault (Marine Corps) | 15.56 | 25.72 (13.67 fuselage) | 5.08 | 10,438 (5,947 empty) | 2 G.E. T58-GE-10 turboshaft, 1,450 shp each<br>CH-46E: 2 G.E. T58-GE-10, 1,870 shp each | 144 | 14,000 | 206<br>774<br>. . . |

REMARKS: Can carry 18 fully equipped troops. The cargo version (HH-46A) is Navy-subordinated and is usually assigned to vertical-replenishment duties in modern underway replenishment ships. Can carry 1,360 kg of cargo internally or 4,536 kg in a sling beneath. CH-46E is updated (1977) version with automatic navigation system and armored seats; all earlier CH-46D will be modernized. Glass-reinforced plastic rotors being substituted and infrared jamming equipment being added. Over 300 in service, all models. U.S.M.C. reorganized from 13 squadrons of 18 CH-46E to 15 squadrons of 12 helos each in 1985.

| Class, builder | Mission | Diameter (rotor) | Length (overall) | Height in m | Weight in kg | Engine | Max speed in/knots | Ceiling in feet | 1) Mission range (nautical miles) 2) Ferry range (nautical miles) 3) Endurance (hours) |
|---|---|---|---|---|---|---|---|---|---|
| **CH-53 A, D, RH-53D Sea Stallion** (Sikorsky) | Navy RH-53D: Minesweeping<br>Marine Corps CH-53A, D: Assault transport | 22.04 | 26.92 (20.48, fuselage) | 7.59 | 19,050 (10,718 empty) | 2 G.E. T64-GE-413 turboshaft, 2,925 hp each | 170 (150 cruise) | 21,000 | 540<br>886<br>3.50 |

REMARKS: 81 CH-53A/D left in 1-87. CH-53A and D can carry 38 fully equipped troops or 24 occupied stretchers with 4 hospital corpsmen or 4 tons of freight (2 Hawk missiles, for example). The RH-53D version is equipped for serial minesweeping and has T64-GE-415 engines, 2/12.7-mm machine guns, and points for towing Mk 103 cutters, Mk 104 magnetic minesweeping arrays, Mk 105 hydrofoil sled, MK 106 acoustic sweep array, SPU-1 shallow-water rig, and AQS-14 minehunting sonar; 22 RH-53D remained by 1987; 16 U.S.M.C. CH-53 have provision for mine countermeasures towing.

| Class, builder | Mission | Diameter (rotor) | Length (overall) | Height in m | Weight in kg | Engine | Max speed in/knots | Ceiling in feet | 1) Mission range (nautical miles) 2) Ferry range (nautical miles) 3) Endurance (hours) |
|---|---|---|---|---|---|---|---|---|---|
| **CH-53E Super Stallion MH-53E Sea Dragon** (Sikorsky) | Troop-carrying assault (Marines)<br>Heavy lift (Navy) | 24.08 | 30.18 (22.35 fuselage; 18.44 folded) | 8.64 | 33,339 (15,071 empty)<br>MH: 16,482 empty | 3 G.E. T64-GE-416 turboshaft; 4,380 max. shp each (3,695 shp cont.) | 170 (150 cruise) | 18,500 | 230 with 8,630 kg; 50 with 14,500 kg cargo;<br>1,000<br>. . . |

## NAVAL AND MARINE CORPS AVIATION *(continued)*

### PRINCIPAL COMBAT AIRCRAFT *(continued)*

REMARKS: CH-53E can carry 56 troops or 14,512 kg cargo. Three-man crew. Seven-bladed main rotor. 35th CH-53E rebuilt under FY 80 budget as MH-53E minesweeper prototype, delivered 1983. First MH-53E requested under FY 84. Navy use for CH-53E is for cargo, aircraft-recovery, and heavy lift. 93 CH-53E delivered by 4-87. Plan total of 194 CH-53E/32 MH-53E, but production FY 86-89 mostly MH-version. MH-53 has enlarged side sponsons holding 4,478 lbs fuel and has a cable winch with 137-m cable, exerting a 13.6-ton pull; tows the ALQ-166 mine countermeasures sled, day or night. First production MH-53E delivered 26-6-86.

| Class, builder | Mission | Diameter (rotor) | Length (overall) | Height in m | Weight in kg | Engine | Max speed in knots | Ceiling in feet | 1) Mission range (nautical miles) 2) Ferry range (nautical miles) 3) Endurance (hours) |
|---|---|---|---|---|---|---|---|---|---|
| **UH-1E/N Iroquois** (Bell) | Assault (Marine Corps) | 14.70 | 17.47 (12.93, fuselage) | 4.39 | 4,763 (2,517 empty) | 2 Pratt & Whitney PT6 turboshaft, 900 shp each | 110 | 15,000 | 250 / . . . / 2 |

Armament: 2/7.62-mm machine guns and rockets.

REMARKS: Can carry 16 troops. UH-1N replaced earlier UH-1E, which had 1 Lycoming T53 turboshaft of 1,100 shp. Navy uses UH-1E and TH-1L for utility and training duties.

| Class, builder | Mission | Diameter (rotor) | Length (overall) | Height in m | Weight in kg | Engine | Max speed in knots | Ceiling in feet | 1) Mission range 2) Ferry range 3) Endurance |
|---|---|---|---|---|---|---|---|---|---|
| **AH-1J, T, W SeaCobra** (Bell) | Attack (Marine Corps) | 13.42 | 16.27 (13.60, fuselage) | 4.17 | 4,536 (3,000 empty) | 2 Pratt & Whitney T400-WV-402 turboshaft; W: 2 T700-G.E.-401, 1,690 shp each) 1,025 shp each | 180 | 10,500 | 360 / . . . / 2 |

Armament: 1/20-mm XM-197 gatling gun, plus 76/2.75-in rockets or 2/7.62-mm minigun, Hellfire and Sidearm missiles (AH-1T also: TOW anti-tank missiles).

REMARKS: AH-1W Super Cobra in production. T-700 engine, 1,700-kg (vice 680-kg) payload, 120 kts at 6,349 kg gross with 8 Hellfire or TOW missiles, 27 2.75-in or 165-in Zuni rockets, or 2 GPU-2A, 20-mm gunpods; 2 Sidewinder AAM. Plan to update 37 earlier AH-1T with same engines. First AH-1W delivered 3-86

Also in service with Navy and Marine Corps aviation are 13 F-5E/F and 20 OA-4M aircraft for "Top Gun" training to simulate Soviet aircraft, about 38 OV-10D twin-engine observation/attack aircraft for the Marines (all OV-10A converting to OV-10D under FY 83, with engine upgrade, laser designator), 27 C-9B transports (military DC-9) for the Marines and Naval Reserve, C-130 Hercules (in C-130, LC-130 arctic, DC-130 drone control, and EC-130 TACAMO communications, and U.S.M.C. KC-130T refueler versions), C-131F, G, and H Samaritan transports, T-2C Buckeye jet trainers, T-34B/C student trainers, T-38A Talon jet test-pilot trainers, T-39D Sabreliner flight-officer trainers (and CT-39E/G light transport versions), T-44A Pegasus twin-engine trainers, and TH-57A/B helicopter trainers. Nineteen T-34C, ordered 5-87 for delivery 6-89 to 4-90, follow 334 delivered earlier; all have 400 hp for 213-kt max. speed. For helicopter training, 104 TH-57B and C were ordered during 1983, followed by 36 TH-57B in 1986. Two C-20A transports were acquired 1987.

Two EC-130Q TACAMO aircraft delivered 1984 (with the USC-13(V) trailing wire communications system) were the last of their type, with production planned to switch to the E-6A.

The T-45 Goshawk (British Aviation Hawk variant) series of trainers from McDonnell Douglas was planned to include 54 T-45B land-only and 253 F-45A carrier-capable aircraft; first T-45B flight 1987, first T-45A a year later. Congress canceled T-45B in late 1983. In the interim, 15 stored T-2B Buckeye jet trainers were reactivated in 1982. 302 T-45A are planned.

Fifteen Cessna Citation II corporate jets were leased 5-83 as the T-47A for flight-officer navigational training, with initial deliveries late in 1984; Emerson APQ-159 radar added. For adversary training, Congress authorized 4 new aircraft in FY 84, 8 in FY 85, and 12 in FY 86; these will be a stripped version of the Air Force Fighting Falcon, as the F-16N. The 26 F-16N use the G.E. F110 engine; the last four will be 2-seat TF-16N, and all 26 will be in service at VF-126 Miramar and VF-45 Key West by 4-88. As an interim measure, 12 Israeli early model Kfir fighters were leased for 3 years as F-21As, arriving beginning in 4-85; a second squadron of 13 was leased 1986 for Marine adversary training.

The Navy ordered its first lighter-than-air aircraft on 5-6-87 from Westinghouse-Airship Industries, for delivery in 10-90 as part of a 60-month evaluation of the use of airships as a fleet radar support vehicle. Ultimately, 40–50 airships may be built. The airship will have 21,650-hp Isotta-Fraschini diesels and one G.E. CT-7 turbo shaft for propulsion and have an endurance of 47 hours at 50 kts or 55 hrs at 40 kts, with a maximum ferry range of 3,500 n.m. Some 129 m overall, it will have a crew of 12 to 15 and carry an APS-139 radar. The airship program was terminated under FY 89.

The Navy is acquiring several types of remotely piloted vehicles, including the Israeli AII Pioneer, with a 185-km radius, 6-hr endurance, and a 45-kg payload, for weapons spotting and reconnaissance; plan 43 "systems" with 344 total drones. The Northrop NV-144, with a 950-n.m. range and 136-kg payload, is being developed; it is a variant of the jet-powered BQM-126 target drone.

**T-34C Mentor trainer** Beech Aircraft

**EC-130G Hercules TACAMO communications aircraft** PH2 W. Harvey, USN, 1977

**T-44A King Air trainer** Beech Aircraft

**E-6A Hermes TACAMO** Boeing, 1987

**NAVAL AND MARINE CORPS AVIATION** *(continued)*

**KC-130T Hercules of the U.S.M.C.** Sikorsky, 1987

**T-45A Goshawk trainer**—artist's rendering
R.G. Smith/McDonnell Douglas, 1987

**T-2C Buckeye advanced trainer** PHCS L. Ramage, USN, 8-78

**CH-53E Super Stallion** Sikorsky, 1987

**RH-53D Sea Stallion minesweeper** PH2 Hicks, USN, 8-87

**MH-53E Sea Dragon minesweeper** Sikorsky, 1987

**UH-1E Iroquois of the U.S.M.C.** U.S. Navy, 1987

NAVAL AND MARINE CORPS AVIATION *(continued)*

**F-21A Kfir adversary trainer** U.S. Navy, 10-85

## NUCLEAR-POWERED BALLISTIC-MISSILE SUBMARINES

◆ **8 (+7 + 5) Ohio class (SCB 304 design)** Bldr: General Dynamics, Groton, Conn. (SSBN 726–739)

| | Program | Laid down | L | In serv. |
|---|---|---|---|---|
| SSBN 726 Ohio | FY 74 | 10-4-76 | 7-4-79 | 11-11-81 |
| SSBN 727 Michigan | FY 75 | 4-4-77 | 26-4-80 | 11-9-82 |
| SSBN 728 Florida | FY 75 | 9-6-77 | 14-11-81 | 8-6-83 |
| SSBN 729 Georgia | FY 76 | 7-4-79 | 6-11-82 | 11-2-84 |
| SSBN 730 Henry M. Jackson (ex-*Rhode Island*) | FY 77 | 19-1-81 | 15-10-83 | 6-10-84 |
| SSBN 731 Alabama | FY 78 | 27-8-81 | 19-5-84 | 20-5-85 |
| SSBN 732 Alaska | FY 78 | 9-3-83 | 12-1-85 | 25-1-86 |
| SSBN 733 Nevada | FY 80 | 8-8-83 | 14-9-85 | 16-8-86 |
| SSBN 734 Tennessee | FY 81 | ... | 13-12-86 | 1-89 |
| SSBN 735 Pennsylvania | FY 83 | ... | 23-4-88 | 8-89 |
| SSBN 736 West Virginia | FY 84 | ... | 1-89 | 4-90 |
| SSBN 737 Kentucky | FY 85 | ... | ... | 12-90 |
| SSBN 738 Maryland | FY 86 | ... | ... | 12-91 |
| SSBN 739 Nebraska | FY 87 | ... | ... | 12-92 |
| SSBN 740 N....... | FY 88 | ... | ... | 12-93 |
| SSBN 741 N....... | FY 89 | ... | ... | 12-94 |
| SSBN 742 N....... | FY 90 | ... | ... | 12-95 |
| SSBN 743 N....... | FY 91 | ... | ... | 12-96 |
| SSBN 744 N....... | FY 92 | ... | ... | 12-97 |
| SSBN 745 N....... | FY 93 | ... | ... | 12-98 |

**Henry M. Jackson (SSBN 730)** G. Arra, 1986

**Florida (SSBN 728)** Gen. Dynamics, 6-83

**D:** 16,764/18,750 tons **S:** 20+ kts (sub.) **Dim:** 170.69 × 12.80 × 11.13 (surf.)
**A:** 24/Trident C-4 (SSBN 734 on: D-5) missiles—4/533-mm Mk 68 TT
**Electron Equipt:** Radar: BPS-15A—EW: WLR-8(V)5
Sonar: BQQ-6, BQS-13, BQS-15, BQR-15, BQR-19, BQQ-9 TASPE
**M:** 1 G.E. S8G natural-circulation pressurized-water reactor; turboreduction drive; 1 prop; 60,000 hp
**Endurance:** 70 days **Man:** 15 officers, 142 men (2 crews)

**Alabama (SSBN 731)** Gen. Dynamics, 5-85

Remarks: SSBN 726 ran first trials 17-6-81 and was delivered 3 years late. Program now on schedule. The availability of this class as a whole is to be 66 percent, using a planned schedule of 70-day patrols, followed by 25-day refit periods, and with a 12-month overhaul every nine years. Each ship has two crews. None ordered under FY 79 because of program delays and cost overruns. Ordering of SSBN 734 was deferred to 7-1-82 due to contract disputes between the Navy and General Dynamics. SSBN 738 was ordered 7-3-86. SSBN 739 offered to Newport News as well as General Dynamics, awarded to the latter 5-1-88. Name of SSBN 730 changed 27-9-83.

Able to submerge to 300 meters. Carry two Mk 2 SINS (Ship's Inertial Navigational System) and have navigational satellite receivers. Mk 98 digital computer missile-fire-control system and Mk 118 torpedo-fire-control system are installed. SSBN 734 and later will have Trident D-5 as built. All have 1 Kollmorgen Type 152 and 1 Type 82 periscopes. The reactor plant reportedly does not generate the full rated horsepower in service. Four countermeasures launchers per side are located in the casing below the sail. Announced late 1987 that later units may receive improved BSY-1 or BSY-2 sonar suites.

SSBN 726 made her first operational deployment 1-10-82 to 10-12-82, having fired her first missile on 17-1-82. The first eight are based at Bangor, Washington; later units are to base at King's Bay Georgia. SSBN 732 began sea trials 18-9-85 and SSBN 733 on 28-5-86.

◆ **28 Lafayette class (SCB 216 and SCB 216A types)**

| | Bldr | Laid down | L | In serv. |
|---|---|---|---|---|
| SSBN 616 Lafayette | Gen. Dynamics | 17-1-61 | 8-5-62 | 23-4-63 |
| SSBN 617 Alexander Hamilton | Gen. Dynamics | 26-6-61 | 18-8-62 | 27-6-63 |
| SSBN 619 Andrew Jackson | Mare Island NSY | 26-4-61 | 15-9-62 | 3-7-63 |
| SSBN 620 John Adams | Portsmouth NSY | 19-5-61 | 12-1-63 | 12-5-64 |
| SSBN 622 James Monroe | Newport News | 31-7-61 | 4-8-62 | 7-12-63 |
| SSBN 624 Woodrow Wilson | Mare Island NSY | 13-9-61 | 22-2-63 | 27-12-63 |
| SSBN 625 Henry Clay | Newport News | 23-10-61 | 30-11-62 | 20-2-64 |
| SSBN 626 Daniel Webster | Gen. Dynamics | 23-12-61 | 27-4-63 | 9-4-64 |
| SSBN 627 James Madison* | Newport News | 5-3-62 | 15-3-63 | 28-7-64 |
| SSBN 628 Tecumseh | Gen. Dynamics | 1-6-62 | 22-6-63 | 29-5-64 |
| SSBN 629 Daniel Boone* | Mare Island NSY | 6-2-62 | 22-6-63 | 23-4-64 |
| SSBN 630 John C. Calhoun* | Newport News | 4-6-62 | 22-6-63 | 15-9-64 |
| SSBN 631 Ulysses S. Grant | Gen. Dynamics | 18-8-62 | 2-11-63 | 17-7-64 |
| SSBN 632 Von Steuben* | Newport News | 4-9-62 | 18-10-63 | 30-9-64 |
| SSBN 633 Casimir Pulaski* | Gen. Dynamics | 12-1-63 | 1-2-64 | 14-8-64 |
| SSBN 634 Stonewall Jackson* | Mare Island NSY | 4-7-62 | 30-11-63 | 26-8-64 |
| SSBN 640 Benjamin Franklin* | Gen. Dynamics | 25-5-63 | 5-12-64 | 22-10-65 |
| SSBN 641 Simon Bolivar* | Newport News | 17-4-63 | 22-8-64 | 29-10-65 |
| SSBN 642 Kamehameha | Mare Island NSY | 2-5-63 | 16-1-65 | 10-12-65 |
| SSBN 643 George Bancroft* | Gen. Dynamics | 24-8-63 | 20-3-65 | 22-1-66 |
| SSBN 644 Lewis and Clark | Newport News | 29-7-63 | 21-11-64 | 22-12-65 |
| SSBN 645 James K. Polk | Gen. Dynamics | 23-11-63 | 22-5-65 | 16-4-66 |
| SSBN 654 George C. Marshall | Newport News | 2-3-64 | 21-5-65 | 29-4-66 |
| SSBN 655 Henry L. Stimson* | Gen. Dynamics | 4-4-64 | 13-11-65 | 20-8-66 |
| SSBN 656 George Washington Carver | Newport News | 24-8-64 | 14-8-65 | 15-6-66 |
| SSBN 657 Francis Scott Key* | Gen. Dynamics | 5-12-64 | 23-4-66 | 3-12-66 |
| SSBN 658 Mariano G. Vallejo* | Mare Island NSY | 7-7-64 | 23-10-65 | 16-12-66 |
| SSBN 659 Will Rogers | Gen. Dynamics | 20-3-65 | 21-7-66 | 1-4-67 |

Authorized: SSBN 616 to SSBN 626 in FY 61, SBN 627 to SSBN 636 in FY 62, SSBN 640 to SSBN 645 in FY 63, and SSBN 654 to SSBN 659 in FY 64

## NUCLEAR-POWERED BALLISTIC-MISSILE SUBMARINES *(continued)*

**D:** 7,350/8,250 tons **S:** 15/25 kts **Dim:** 129.54 × 10.05 × 9.0
**A:** 16/Poseidon or Trident-1 missiles—4/533-mm TT (fwd)
**Electron Equipt:** Radar: BPS-11A or BPS-15
Sonar: BQR-7, BQR-15, BQR-19, BQR-21, BQS-4
**M:** 1 Westinghouse SW5 pressurized-water reactor; 1/7-bladed prop; 15,000 hp
**Endurance:** 68 days **Man:** 13–14 officers, 129–133 men

**Lewis and Clark (SSBN 644)** L. Grazioli, 12-87

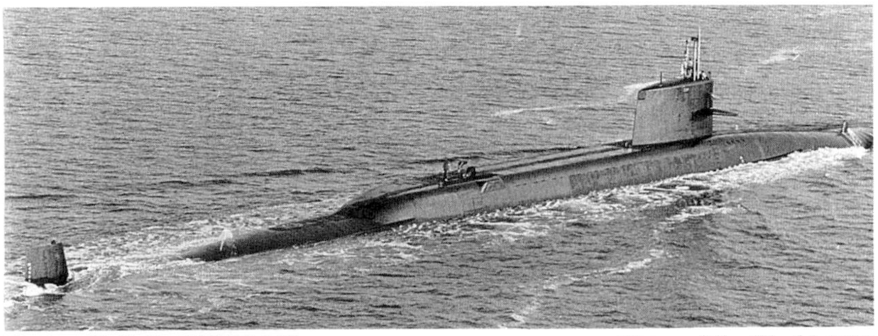

**James K. Polk (SSBN 645)** *Ships of the World,* 1986

**Stonewall Jackson (SSBN 634)** *Ships of the World,* 1986

Remarks: The 12 units marked with an asterisk received Trident-1 missiles by 12-82. SSBN 640 and following units have quieter propulsion machinery and are officially designated the *Benjamin Franklin* class. Three Mk 2 SINS were installed during conversion. Also carry a portable, commercial navigational radar for surfaced operations. All now have eight countermeasures launch tubes in the casing, abreast the sail, four per side. Submersion depth for all is more than 300 meters. Mk 88 missile-fire-control system and Mk 113 torpedo-fire-control system fitted. Conversion of both classes from Polaris A-3 to Poseidon missiles was completed between 1970 and 1977. Funds were requested each year thereafter through FY 82. SSBN 657 commenced the first Trident-1 operational patrol on 20-10-79. All Trident-1 (C-4) units are to be home-ported at King's Bay, Georgia, and all ships in both classes belong to the Atlantic Fleet. They operate on a schedule of 68-day patrols, followed by 32-day refit periods; every six years a 16-month yard period is requested, giving an overall force availability of 55 percent. Each ship has two crews. SSBN 641 and two others are now on a nine-year operational/overhaul cycle. *Sam Rayburn* (SSBN 635) began deactivation of her missile system 16-9-85, preparatory to striking 9-86; she is being converted to an immobile engineering training craft, the ARTB (Auxiliary Reactor Training Barge). *Nathan Hale* (SSBN 623) and *Nathanael Greene* (SSBN 636) were deactivated 5-86 as SALT II compensation when *Nevada* (SSBN 733) began sea trials. SSBN 623 formally decommissioned 3-11-86 and SSBN 636 (substituted for SSBN 619, as a result of grounding damage 13-3-86) on 15-12-86; both will be scrapped. Two more to decommission 1988-89 as compensation for SSBN 784. SSBN 658 completed the 2,500th SSBN patrol on 4-4-87. SSBN 617 and 642 operated with single crews beginning 1986.

## NUCLEAR-POWERED ATTACK SUBMARINES

◆ **0 (+0 + 1 + 27) Seawolf ("SSN 21") class**

| | Bldr | Laid down | L | In serv. |
|---|---|---|---|---|
| SSN . . . Seawolf | . . . | . . . | . . . | 1994 |

Planned: 1 in FY 89, 2 in FY 91, 2 in FY 92

**Seawolf submerged**—artist's rendering W. Lupien/U.S. Navy, 1985

**Seawolf surfaced in an icepack**—artist's impression W. Lupien/U.S. Navy, 1985

**D:** 9,150 tons (sub.) **S:** 35 kts (sub.) **Dim:** 106.68 × 12.19 × 10.94
**A:** 8/TT (about 50 Sea Lance, Tomahawk, Harpoon missiles, Mk 48 ADCAP torpedoes, mines)
**Electron Equipt:** Radar: . . . —EW: WLQ-4(V)1
Sonar: BSY-2(V) suite, wide-aperture passive array
**M:** 1 G.E. S6W pressurized-water reactor, . . . drive; 1 prop; 60,000 hp
**Man:** approx. 12 officers, 118 enlisted

Remarks: First unit requested under FY 89. General Dynamics and Newport News SB & DD competing for initial unit. Will offer significant improvements in speed, quietness, weapons load, sonar processing, etc., over *Los Angeles* class, to continue U.S. lead over Soviet submarine technology, being able to travel at up to 20 kts while silent.

## NUCLEAR-POWERED ATTACK SUBMARINES *(continued)*

Submarine will have smaller length-to-beam ratio to improve maneuverability. Retractable bow planes and six stern fins will be carried. A small wedge at the base of the forward edge of the sail will improve hydrodynamic flow. Propeller will be of pump-jet design. Planned to carry 12 Tomahawk missiles.

### ◆ 37 (+22 + 7) Los Angeles class (SCB 303 type)

| | Bldr | Laid down | L | In serv. |
|---|---|---|---|---|
| SSN 688 Los Angeles | Newport News | 8-1-72 | 6-4-74 | 13-11-76 |
| SSN 689 Baton Rouge | Newport News | 18-11-72 | 18-4-75 | 25-6-77 |
| SSN 690 Philadelphia | Gen. Dynamics | 12-8-72 | 19-10-74 | 25-6-77 |
| SSN 691 Memphis | Newport News | 23-6-73 | 3-4-76 | 17-12-77 |
| SSN 692 Omaha | Gen. Dynamics | 27-1-73 | 21-2-76 | 11-3-78 |
| SSN 693 Cincinnati | Newport News | 6-4-74 | 19-2-76 | 10-6-78 |
| SSN 694 Groton | Gen. Dynamics | 3-8-73 | 9-10-76 | 8-7-78 |
| SSN 695 Birmingham | Newport News | 26-4-75 | 15-10-77 | 20-12-78 |
| SSN 696 New York City | Gen. Dynamics | 15-12-73 | 18-6-77 | 10-3-79 |
| SSN 697 Indianapolis | Gen. Dynamics | 19-10-74 | 30-7-77 | 5-1-80 |
| SSN 698 Bremerton | Gen. Dynamics | 8-5-76 | 22-7-78 | 28-3-81 |
| SSN 699 Jacksonville | Gen. Dynamics | 21-2-76 | 18-11-78 | 16-5-81 |
| SSN 700 Dallas | Gen. Dynamics | 9-10-76 | 28-4-79 | 18-7-81 |
| SSN 701 La Jolla | Gen. Dynamics | 16-10-76 | 11-8-79 | 24-10-81 |
| SSN 702 Phoenix | Gen. Dynamics | 30-7-77 | 18-12-79 | 19-12-81 |
| SSN 703 Boston | Gen. Dynamics | 11-8-78 | 19-4-80 | 30-1-82 |
| SSN 704 Baltimore | Gen. Dynamics | 21-5-79 | 18-12-80 | 24-7-82 |
| SSN 705 City of Corpus Christi | Gen. Dynamics | 4-9-79 | 25-4-81 | 8-1-83 |
| SSN 706 Albuquerque | Gen. Dynamics | 27-12-79 | 13-3-82 | 21-5-83 |
| SSN 707 Portsmouth | Gen. Dynamics | 8-5-80 | 18-9-82 | 1-10-83 |
| SSN 708 Minneapolis-Saint Paul | Gen. Dynamics | 20-1-81 | 19-3-83 | 10-3-84 |
| SSN 709 Hyman G. Rickover | Gen. Dynamics | 23-7-81 | 27-8-83 | 21-7-84 |
| SSN 710 Augusta | Gen. Dynamics | 1-4-82 | 21-1-84 | 19-1-85 |
| SSN 711 San Francisco | Newport News | 26-5-77 | 27-10-79 | 24-4-81 |
| SSN 712 Atlanta | Newport News | 17-8-78 | 16-8-80 | 6-3-82 |
| SSN 713 Houston | Newport News | 29-1-79 | 21-3-81 | 25-9-82 |
| SSN 714 Norfolk | Newport News | 1-8-79 | 31-10-81 | 21-5-83 |
| SSN 715 Buffalo | Newport News | 25-1-80 | 8-5-82 | 5-11-83 |
| SSN 716 Salt Lake City | Newport News | 26-8-80 | 16-10-82 | 12-5-84 |
| SSN 717 Olympia | Newport News | 31-3-81 | 30-4-83 | 17-11-84 |
| SSN 718 Honolulu | Newport News | 10-11-81 | 24-9-83 | 6-7-85 |
| SSN 719 Providence | Gen. Dynamics | 30-9-82 | 4-8-84 | 27-7-85 |
| SSN 720 Pittsburgh | Gen. Dynamics | 15-4-83 | 8-12-84 | 23-11-85 |
| SSN 721 Chicago | Newport News | 5-1-83 | 13-10-84 | 27-9-86 |
| SSN 722 Key West | Newport News | 6-7-83 | 20-7-85 | 12-9-87 |
| SSN 723 Oklahoma City | Newport News | 4-1-84 | 2-11-85 | 6-88 |
| SSN 724 Louisville | Gen. Dynamics | 16-9-84 | 14-12-85 | 8-11-86 |
| SSN 725 Helena | Gen. Dynamics | 28-3-85 | 28-6-86 | 11-7-87 |
| SSN 750 Newport News | Newport News | 3-3-84 | 15-3-86 | 9-88 |
| SSN 751 San Juan | Gen. Dynamics | 16-8-85 | 6-12-86 | 7-88 |
| SSN 752 Pasadena | Gen. Dynamics | 20-12-85 | 12-9-87 | 11-88 |
| SSN 753 Albany | Newport News | 22-4-85 | 12-6-87 | 11-89 |
| SSN 754 Topeka | Gen. Dynamics | 4-5-86 | 23-1-88 | 1989 |
| SSN 755 Miami | Gen. Dynamics | 24-10-86 | 30-7-88 | 1989 |
| SSN 756 Scranton | Newport News | 5-5-86 | 11-88 | 7-90 |
| SSN 757 Alexandria | Gen. Dynamics | 3-87 | 2-89 | 7-89 |
| SSN 758 Asheville | Newport News | 14-1-87 | 5-89 | 11-90 |
| SSN 759 Jefferson City | Newport News | 1987 | . . . | 3-91 |
| SSN 760 Annapolis | Gen. Dynamics | 1-88 | . . . | 2-90 |
| SSN 761 Springfield | Gen. Dynamics | 4-88 | . . . | 6-90 |
| SSN 762 Columbus | Gen. Dynamics | 8-89 | . . . | 10-90 |
| SSN 763 Santa Fe | Gen. Dynamics | . . . | . . . | 2-91 |
| SSN 764 N . . . . . . . | Newport News | . . . | . . . | 2-91 |
| SSN 765 N . . . . . . . | Newport News | . . . | . . . | 5-91 |
| SSN 766 N . . . . . . . | Newport News | . . . | . . . | 8-91 |
| SSN 767 N . . . . . . . | Newport News | . . . | . . . | 11-91 |
| SSN 768 N . . . . . . . | . . . | . . . | . . . | . . . |
| SSN 769 N . . . . . . . | . . . | . . . | . . . | . . . |
| SSN 770 N . . . . . . . | . . . | . . . | . . . | . . . |
| SSN 771 N . . . . . . . | . . . | . . . | . . . | . . . |
| SSN 772 N . . . . . . . | . . . | . . . | . . . | . . . |

**Minneapolis-Saint Paul (SSN 708)** L. & L. Van Ginderen, 8-86

**Providence (SSN 719)**—with Tomahawk VLS hatches open U.S. Navy, 1986

**La Jolla (SSN 701)** G. Arra, 4-86

**Pittsburgh (SSN 720)** G. Arra, 9-86

Authorized: SSN 688 to SSN 690 in FY 70, SSN 691 to SSN 694 in FY 71, SSN 695 to SSN 700 in FY 72, SSN 701 to SSN 705 in FY 73, SSN 706 to SSN 710 in FY 74, SSN 711 to SSN 713 in FY 75, SSN 714 to SSN 715 in FY 76, SSN 716 to SSN 718 in FY 77, SSN 719 in FY 78, SSN 720 in FY 79, SSN 721 to SSN 722 in FY 80, SSN 723 to SSN 724 in FY 81, SSN 725 and 750 in FY 82, SSN 751 to SSN 752 in FY 83, SSN 753 to SSN 755 in FY 84, SSN 756 to SSN 759 in FY 85, SSN 760 to SSN 763 in FY 86. Requested: SSN 764 to SSN 767 in FY 87, SSN 768 to 770 in FY 88. Planned: 2 in FY 89, 2 in FY 90, 2 in FY 91, 1 in FY 92.

**D:** 6,080/6,927 tons **S:** 30+ kts. (sub.) **Dim:** 109.73 × 10.06 × 9.75
**A:** SSN 719 and later: 12/vertical tubes for Tomahawk—all: 4/533-mm TT Mk 67 (amidships) for Tomahawk, Harpoon, Mk 48 torpedoes, etc. (22 reloads)—SSN 756 and later: mining capability
**Electron Equipt:** Radar: 1/BPS-15A
EW: BRD-7 direction finder, WLR-8(V)2, WLR-12
Sonar: 1/BQQ-5A(V)1 or BQQ-5D, BQS-15, BQR-15 (SSN 751 on: BSY-1)
**M:** G.E. S6G pressurized-water reactor, 2 GT; 1/7-bladed prop; 35,000 hp
**Man:** 12 officers, 115 to 127 men (berths for 95 total)

Remarks: SSN 719 and later are receiving twelve vertical-launch tubes for Tomahawk cruise missiles, located between the forward end of the pressure hull and the spherical array for the BQQ-5 bow sonar; SSN 751 and later have bow-mounted vice sail-mounted diving planes and will have the first-generation BSY-1 (formerly SUBACS-Submarine Advanced Combat System) integrated sonar/weapons-control suite from I.B.M.; development problems have slowed delivery of SSN 751-on and 751 through 755 will have to be backfitted with their UYK-43 computers after completion. SSN 751 and later are described as "arctic-capable." All carry

NUCLEAR-POWERED ATTACK SUBMARINES *(continued)*

a UYK-7 general-purpose computer and have WSC-3 satellite comms. gear. One Mk 2 optical and one Sperry Mk 18 multifunction periscope fitted. Mk 113 Mod. 10 torpedo-fire-control in SSN 688 to SSN 699, Mk 117 in later units to be backfitted in all. Under FY 83, the Mk 117 f.c.s. is being modified to permit launching SUBROC missiles. Will carry Sea Lance missiles (ASW SOW) when available in the early 1990s. Harpoon began to be carried in 1978. SSN 688–718 carry 8 Tomahawk cruise missiles, later units will have 20. Maximum diving depth is 450 m. Described as the finest ASW platforms now afloat. Bow is of fiberglass as a streamlined cover over the spherical BQQ-5-A(V)1 sonar array. There are two SINS, to be replaced by the ESGN (Electrically Suspended Gyro Navigator). All have one Fairbanks-Morse $38D8\frac{1}{8}$ diesel generator set and batteries for emergency propulsion. The BLD-1 electromagnetic interferometer is being added, beginning 1985. The reactor core is expected to last 10–13 years between refuelings. SSN 694 traveled around the world submerged 4-4-80 to 8-10-80. SSN 701 was the first of the class to be equipped to launch Tomahawk missiles from the torpedo tubes, in 1983; SSN 712 first *operational* sub with Tomahawk, 30-11-83.

**◆ 1 Glenard P. Lipscomb class**

| | Bldr | Laid down | L | In serv. |
|---|---|---|---|---|
| SSN 685 GLENARD P. LIPSCOMB | Gen. Dynamics | 5-6-71 | 4-8-73 | 21-12-74 |

Authorized: FY 68

**Glenard P. Lipscomb (SSN 685)** G. Arra, 1987

**D:** 5,813 standard/6,480 tons (sub.) **S:** 25 kts **Dim:** 111.3 × 9.7 × 8.8
**A:** 4/533-mm TT (amidships) **Man:** 14 officers, 115 men
**Electron Equipt:** Radar: BPS-15—Sonar: BQQ-5, BQS-14—EW: WLQ-4
**M:** 1 Westinghouse S5WA, natural-circulation reactor, G.E. turboelectric drive; 1 prop; . . . hp

REMARKS: This TEDS (Turbo-Electric Drive Submarine) was an effort to make an exceptionally quiet submarine at the expense of some speed. Most other equipment is similar to the *Sturgeon* class. During 3-81 to 7-82 overhaul, was equipped to launch Harpoon, with BQQ-5 vice BQQ-2 sonar, and Mk 117 torpedo-fire-control vice Mk 113 Mod. 8; problems with the turbogenerator system kept the ship in the yard into early 1985. Will carry up to 8 Tomahawk cruise missiles and 4 Sub-Harpoon.

**◆ 1 Narwhal class (SCB 245)**

| | Bldr | Laid down | L | In serv. |
|---|---|---|---|---|
| SSN 671 NARWHAL | Gen. Dynamics | 17-1-66 | 9-9-67 | 12-7-69 |

Authorized: FY 64

**Narwhal (SSN 671)**—with R.N. tug *Powerful* (A 223) L. & L. Van Ginderen, 3-87

**Narwhal (SSN 671)** L. & L. Van Ginderen, 3-87

**D:** 5,284/5,830 tons **S:** 20/25 kts **Dim:** 96.0 × 11.5 × 7.9
**A:** 4/533-mm TT (amidships, for Mk 48 torp., Harpoon, up to 8 Tomahawk)
**Electron Equipt:** Radar: BPS-14—EW: WLQ-4 suite
Sonar: BQQ-5 BQS-8
**M:** 1 G.E. S5G reactor, 2 GT; 1 prop; 17,000 hp **Man:** 12 officers, 108 men

REMARKS: Prototype seagoing reactor designed to study the cooling of the S5G reactor by natural circulation, thus eliminating circulation pumps and their noise. In most other respects, essentially a lengthened *Sturgeon*. Original BQQ-2 sonar suit and Mk 113 Mod. 6 fire-control system replaced by Mk 117 f.c.s. and BQQ-5. Towed array housing is on starboard side of hull.

**◆ 37 Sturgeon class (SCB 188A and SCB 188M types)**

| | Bldr | Laid down | L | In serv. |
|---|---|---|---|---|
| SSN 637 STURGEON | Gen. Dynamics | 10-8-63 | 26-2-66 | 3-3-67 |
| SSN 638 WHALE | Gen. Dynamics | 27-5-64 | 14-10-66 | 12-10-68 |
| SSN 639 TAUTOG | Ingalls SB | 27-1-64 | 15-4-67 | 17-8-68 |
| SSN 646 GRAYLING | Portsmouth NSY | 12-5-64 | 22-6-67 | 11-10-69 |
| SSN 647 POGY | New York SB | 4-5-64 | 3-6-67 | 15-5-71 |
| SSN 648 ASPRO | Ingalls SB | 23-11-64 | 29-11-67 | 20-2-69 |
| SSN 649 SUNFISH | Gen. Dynamics | 15-1-65 | 14-10-66 | 15-3-69 |
| SSN 650 PARGO | Gen. Dynamics | 3-6-64 | 17-9-66 | 1-5-68 |
| SSN 651 QUEENFISH | Newport News | 11-5-64 | 25-2-66 | 6-12-66 |
| SSN 652 PUFFER | Ingalls SB | 8-2-65 | 30-3-68 | 9-8-69 |
| SSN 653 RAY | Newport News | 1-4-65 | 21-6-66 | 12-4-67 |
| SSN 660 SANDLANCE | Portsmouth NSY | 15-1-65 | 11-11-69 | 25-9-71 |
| SSN 661 LAPON | Newport News | 26-7-65 | 16-12-66 | 14-12-67 |
| SSN 662 GURNARD | Mare Island NSY | 22-12-64 | 20-5-67 | 6-12-68 |
| SSN 663 HAMMERHEAD | Newport News | 29-11-65 | 14-4-67 | 28-6-68 |
| SSN 664 SEA DEVIL | Newport News | 12-4-66 | 5-10-67 | 30-1-69 |
| SSN 665 GUITARRO | Mare Island NSY | 9-12-65 | 27-7-68 | 9-9-72 |
| SSN 666 HAWKBILL | Mare Island NSY | 12-9-66 | 12-4-69 | 4-2-71 |
| SSN 667 BERGALL | Gen. Dynamics | 16-4-66 | 17-2-68 | 13-3-69 |
| SSN 668 SPADEFISH | Newport News | 21-12-66 | 15-5-68 | 14-8-69 |
| SSN 669 SEAHORSE | Gen. Dynamics | 13-8-66 | 15-6-68 | 19-9-69 |
| SSN 670 FINBACK | Newport News | 26-6-67 | 7-12-68 | 4-2-70 |
| SSN 672 PINTADO | Mare Island NSY | 27-10-67 | 16-8-69 | 11-9-71 |
| SSN 673 FLYING FISH | Gen. Dynamics | 30-6-67 | 17-5-69 | 29-4-70 |
| SSN 674 TREPANG | Gen. Dynamics | 28-10-67 | 27-9-69 | 14-8-70 |
| SSN 675 BLUEFISH | Gen. Dynamics | 13-3-68 | 10-1-70 | 8-1-71 |
| SSN 676 BILLFISH | Gen. Dynamics | 20-9-68 | 1-5-70 | 12-3-71 |
| SSN 677 DRUM | Mare Island NSY | 20-8-68 | 23-5-70 | 15-4-72 |
| SSN 678 ARCHERFISH | Gen. Dynamics | 19-6-69 | 16-1-71 | 24-12-71 |
| SSN 679 SILVERSIDES | Gen. Dynamics | 13-12-69 | 4-6-71 | 5-5-72 |
| SSN 680 WILLIAM H. BATES (ex-*Redfish*) | Ingalls SB | 4-8-69 | 12-71 | 5-5-73 |
| SSN 681 BATFISH | Gen. Dynamics | 9-2-70 | 9-10-71 | 1-9-72 |
| SSN 682 TUNNY | Ingalls SB | 22-5-70 | 10-6-72 | 26-1-74 |
| SSN 683 PARCHE | Ingalls SB | 10-12-70 | 12-72 | 17-8-74 |
| SSN 684 CAVALLA | Gen. Dynamics | 4-6-70 | 19-2-72 | 9-2-73 |
| SSN 686 MENDEL RIVERS | Newport News | 26-6-71 | 2-6-73 | 1-2-75 |
| SSN 687 RICHARD B. RUSSELL | Newport News | 19-10-71 | 12-1-74 | 16-8-75 |

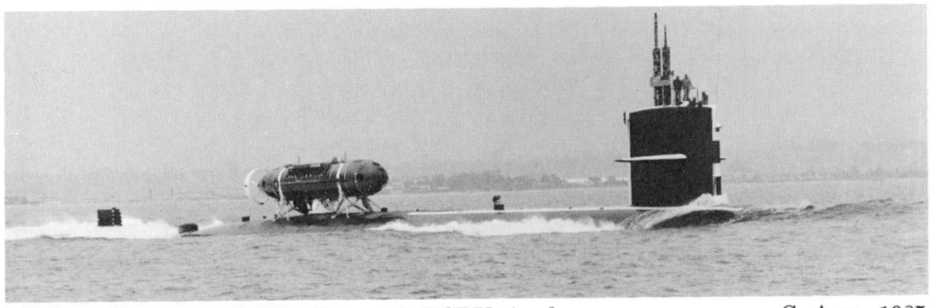

**William H. Bates (SSN 680)**—with DSRV *Avalon* G. Arra, 1985

**Sea Devil (SSN 664)** G. Arra, 9-86

**NUCLEAR-POWERED ATTACK SUBMARINES** *(continued)*

Authorized: SSN 637 to SSN 639 in FY 62, SSN 646 to SSN 653 in FY 63, SSN 660 to SSN 664 in FY 64, SSN 665 to SSN 670 in FY 65, SSN 672 to SSN 677 in FY 66, SSN 678 to SSN 682 in FY 67, SSN 683 and SSN 684 in FY 68, SSN 686 and SSN 687 in FY 69.

**Richard B. Russell (SSN 687)**—with large sonar domes abaft sail and near stern
G. Arra, 9-86

**Lapon (SSN 661)**—note towed array housing down port side
L. & L. Van Ginderen, 3-87

**Silversides (SSN 679)** L. & L. Van Ginderen, 10-87

**Silversides (SSN 679)**—with aftward sail extension for "Bustle" communications system L. & L. Van Ginderen, 5-84

**D:** 4,250/4,780 tons (SSN 678 and later, plus modernized units: 4,460/4,960)
**S:** 15/30 kts **Man:** 12 officers, 95 men
**Dim:** 89.0 (SSN 678 and later and 19 refitted units: 92.1) × 9.65 × 8.8
**A:** 4/533-mm TT (amidships for 15/Mk 48 torpedoes, 4/Harpoon, and 4/SUBROC—up to 8 Tomahawk in lieu of other weapons)
**Electron Equipt:** Radar: 1/BPS-14 or 15—EW: WLQ-4 suite
Sonar: BQQ-2 (with BQS-6 active/BQR-7 passive) or BQQ-5, BQS-8, SSN 637 to SSN 664: BQS-12; others: BQS-13; all: BQR-15 towed array
**M:** 1 Westinghouse S5W2 pressurized-water reactor, 2 G.E. or de Laval GT; 1 prop; 20,000 hp

Remarks: The construction contract of SSN 647 with New York Shipbuilding, Camden, N.J., was canceled in 4-6-67, and completion of the ship was given to Ingalls, Pascagoula, Miss. on 5-12-67. Completion of SSN 665 was delayed twenty-eight months after ship sank while fitting out. The Mk 113 torpedo-fire-control system is being replaced by Mk 117 to permit Harpoon launching. SSN 678 and later units (SCB 188M) were lengthened to permit installation of BQQ-5 sonar suit. Diving planes are 11.6 ft wide. Maximum depth is about 400 m. The 70-megawatt S5W reactor plant operates at 160 kg/cm$^2$, has two primary steam loops and two steam generators to supply steam to the two steam turbines. Original core life was 5,000 hours. SSN 666, SSN 672, and others have been modified to carry a DSRV (salvage submarine), which can be launched and recovered while submerged. The after hatch is so constructed that people can be transferred between the two ships while submerged. Since 1978, SSN 679 and 687 have an aftward extension to the lower portion of the sail to accommodate a towed communications array. Class expected to serve 30 years each. SSN 665 conducted the initial Tomahawk missile trials. SSN 680 has a low, forward extension to the sail. Will be receiving ESGN (Electronically Suspended Gyro Navigator) in lieu of SINS. SSN 680 has the protruding sonar dome for BQR-26 at the upper, forward edge of the sail. SSN 684 modified 8-82 to 16-12-82 to accommodate Dry Deck Shelter (as on SSN 609, 611) for swimmer support; SSN 678, 679, 680, 682, and 686 were to be similarly altered FY 88-91. Three to receive anechoic hull coatings under FY 88.

◆ **13 Permit class (SSN 594 to SSN 612 and SSN 621 are SCB 188 type, SN 613 to SSN 615 are SCB 188M type)**

| | Bldr | Laid down | L | In serv. |
|---|---|---|---|---|
| SSN 594 Permit | Mare Island NSY | 16-7-59 | 1-7-61 | 29-5-62 |
| SSN 595 Plunger | Mare Island NSY | 2-3-60 | 9-12-61 | 21-11-62 |
| SSN 596 Barb (ex-*Pollack*) | Ingalls SB | 9-11-59 | 12-2-62 | 24-8-63 |
| SSN 603 Pollack (ex-*Barb*) | New York SB | 14-3-60 | 17-3-62 | 26-5-64 |
| SSN 604 Haddo | New York SB | 9-9-60 | 18-8-62 | 16-12-64 |
| SSN 605 Jack | Portsmouth NSY | 16-9-60 | 24-4-63 | 31-3-67 |
| SSN 606 Tinosa | Portsmouth NSY | 24-11-59 | 9-12-61 | 17-10-64 |
| SSN 607 Dace | Ingalls SB | 6-6-60 | 18-8-62 | 4-4-64 |
| SSN 612 Guardfish | New York SB | 28-2-61 | 15-5-65 | 20-12-66 |
| SSN 613 Flasher | Gen. Dynamics | 14-4-61 | 22-6-63 | 22-7-66 |
| SSN 614 Greenling | Gen. Dynamics | 15-8-61 | 4-4-64 | 3-11-67 |
| SSN 615 Gato | Gen. Dynamics | 15-12-61 | 14-5-64 | 25-1-68 |
| SSN 621 Haddock | Ingalls SB | 24-4-61 | 21-5-66 | 22-12-67 |

Authorized: SSN 594 to SSN 596 in FY 58, SSN 603 to SSN 607 in FY 59, SSN 612 to SSN 615 in FY 60, SSN 621 in FY 61

SSN 594 to SSN 604, SSN 606 to SSN 612, and SSN 621:

**D:** 3,780/4,465 tons **Dim:** 84.88 × 9.65 × 8.80

SSN 605:

**D:** 4,000/4,467 tons **Dim:** 90.65 × 9.65 × 8.80

SSN 613 to SSN 615:

**D:** 4,250/4,770 tons **Dim:** 89.1 × 9.65 × 8.80
**S:** 15/30 kts **A:** 4/533-mm TT (amidships) **Man:** 13 officers, 114 men
**Electron Equipt:** Radar: BPS-15,BPS-5 or 9—EW: WLR-1
Sonar: BQQ-3 (BQS-11 active/BQR-7 passive), BQS-14, BQR-15
**M:** 1 Westinghouse S5W reactor; 2 G.E. or de Laval GT; 1 prop; 15,000 hp

**Haddo (SSN 604)**—low sail variant G. Arra, 2-86

**Greenling (SSN 614)**—large sail variant L. & L. Van Ginderen, 4-86

## NUCLEAR-POWERED ATTACK SUBMARINES *(continued)*

**Barb (SSN 596)** G. Arra, 6-86

REMARKS: Sister *Thresher* (SSN 593) was lost 10-4-63. SSN 605 has contrarotating props with a contrarotating turbine and no reduction gearing. SSN 613 to SSN 615 have longer and taller sails (6.1 m long vice 4.2 or 4.6 in other ships), heavier machinery, and had safety features built in that were later backfitted in the others. The BQR-7 spherical array is in the bow, necessitating placement of the tubes abreast the sail. These ships are fitted to carry Harpoon, and received Mk 117 torpedo-fire-control systems in place of Mk 113. SSN 594 conducted Harpoon trials during 1976. All are scheduled to receive the BQQ-5 sonar suite during refits. SSN 621 ran trials in 7-79 for the Sperry PASRAN (passive-ranging) sonar system, which is similar to the exported "Micro Puffs" concept, but with an array of six larger hydrophones. SSN 607 to deactivate beginning 27-2-88.

### ◆ 2 Ethan Allen class (SCB 180 type) former ballistic-missile submarines

| | Bldr | Laid down | L | In serv. |
|---|---|---|---|---|
| SSN 609 SAM HOUSTON | Newport News | 28-12-59 | 2-2-61 | 6-3-62 |
| SSN 611 JOHN MARSHALL | Newport News | 4-4-60 | 15-7-61 | 21-5-62 |

Authorized: FY 59

**John Marshall (SSN 611)**—with Dry Deck Shelter aboard L. & L. Van Ginderen, 5-87

**John Marshall (SSN 611)**—note fittings atop former missile bay to accept two Dry Deck Shelters Pradignac & Leo, 2-87

**D:** 6,930/7,880 tons **S:** 15/20 kts **Dim:** 124.96 × 10.05 × 9.0
**A:** 4/533-mm TT (fwd; 8 total torpedoes)—up to 67 swimmers
**Electron Equipt:** Radar: BPS-9—Sonar: BQR-7, BQR-15, BQR-19, BQS-4
**M:** 1 Westinghouse SW5 pressurized-water reactor, GT; 1/7-bladed prop; 15,000 hp
**Man:** 13 officers, 111 men

REMARKS: Survivors of a class of five: first U.S. submarines designed from the outset to launch ballistic missiles. Retained Polaris A-3 missiles until redesignated SSN: SSBN 609 on 10-11-80; SSBN 611 on 1-5-81 at conclusion of final Polaris cruises. Modified by 1984 for further service as SSNs. Beginning with SSN 608 in 1-82 and followed by SSN 609 and 610 in FY 83 and the others in FY 84, cement ballast filled the 16 missile tubes, one of the two Mk 2 Mod. 3 SINS (Ship's Inertial Navigation Systems) was removed, and the Mk 84 missile-control system was depleted. Formerly had two complete crews; complement reduced as SSNs. Deeper-diving (300 m+) than SSN 598 class. Converted beginning 10-84 to carry up to 67 SEAL swimmers at Puget Sound Naval SY in two removable Dry Deck Shelters, although only one was available until 5-88. Each DDS holds one swimmer-delivery vehicle, a decompression chamber, and an access section permitting entry while the submarine is submerged.

Sisters *Ethan Allen* (SSN 608) deactivated 30-9-82 and decommissioned 31-3-83; *Thomas A. Edison* (SSN 610) deactivated 30-9-83 for decommissioning 15-1-84, *Thomas Jefferson* (SSN 618) deactivated beginning 1-6-84 for decommissioning 24-1-85—all three were stricken 30-4-86.

NOTE: The two remaining *George Washington*-class SSNs (ex-SSBN) were decommissioned to storage for ultimate scrapping: *George Washington* (SSB 598) on 24-1-85 and *Patrick Henry* (SSN 599) on 3-2-85; both stricken 30-4-86. *Tullibee* (SSN 597), inactive since early 1986, decommissioned 1-12-87 for eventual scrapping. The one-of-a-kind nuclear-powered submarines *Halibut* (SSN 587, ex-SSGN 587) and *Triton* (SSN 586, ex-SSGN 586), in reserve since 30-6-76 and 3-5-69, respectively, were stricken 30-4-86.

### ◆ 3 Skipjack class (SCB 154 type)

| | Bldr | Laid down | L | In serv. |
|---|---|---|---|---|
| SSN 585 SKIPJACK | Gen. Dynamics | 29-5-56 | 26-5-58 | 15-4-59 |
| SSN 590 SCULPIN | Ingalls | 3-2-58 | 31-3-60 | 1-6-61 |
| SSN 591 SHARK | Newport News SB | 24-2-56 | 16-3-60 | 9-2-61 |

Authorized: SSN 585 in FY 56, SSN 558 and SSN 590 to SSN 592 in FY 57

**Sculpin (SSN 590)**

**D:** 3,080/3,500 tons **S:** 15/30 kts **Dim:** 76.8 × 9.75 × 8.5
**A:** 6/533-mm TT (fwd) **Man:** 9 officers, 85 men
**Electron Equipt:** Radar: BPS-12—Sonar: Modified BQS-4, BQR-2, SQS-49
**M:** 1 Westinghouse S5W reactor; SSN 585: 2 Westinghouse GT, others: 2 G.E. G.T.; 1 prop; 15,000 hp

REMARKS: The reactor compartment takes up 6.10 m. Between the reactor and the propeller, all engine fittings are duplicated (two heat exchangers, two pressurized-water coolers; two groups of turbines, two groups of turbo generators). In case of emergency, submerged propulsion can take over by means of two electric motors linked directly on the propeller shaft and feeding off two electric batteries or two small diesel generators. Better hull form than later SSNs. Still considered first-line submarines. Mk 101 Mod. 17 torpedo-fire-control system. Sister *Scame* (SSN 588), and possibly others, had a removable towed hydrophone array, with the towline externally coiled on the sail extension. Sister *Scorpion* (SSN 589) disappeared in the Atlantic about 27-5-68. *Scamp* (SSN 588) deactivated 9-7-87 for striking/decommissioning 4-88; *Snook* (SSN 592) deactivated 15-5-86, decommissioned 8-10-86, and was stricken 15-12-86, having "steamed" over 675,000 n.m. during her 25-year career.

NOTE: Of the earlier *Skate*-class nuclear-powered submarines, *Seadragon* (SSN 584) began deactivation 30-9-83, decommissioned 12-6-84, and was stricken 30-4-86; *Skate* (SSN 578) deactivated late 1985, decommissioned 12-9-86, and was stricken 12-9-86. *Sargo* (SSN 583) began deactivation 2-10-86 and was decommissioned 6-5-87 for later striking. *Swordfish* (SSN 579) deactivated 17-8-87 for decommissioning 15-5-88 and later disposal. The single-unit *Seawolf* (SSN 575) began deactivation 30-6-86 and decommissioned 30-3-87 for disposal. *Nautilus* (SSN 571), the world's first nuclear-powered ship, was deactivated 30-9-79 and decommissioned 3-3-80; since 6-7-85 she has been on exhibit at Groton, Connecticut.

## CONVENTIONAL SUBMARINES

### ◆ 3 Barbel class (SCB 150 type)

| | Bldr | Laid down | L | In serv. |
|---|---|---|---|---|
| SS 580 BARBEL | Portsmouth NSY | 18-5-56 | 19-7-58 | 17-1-59 |
| SS 581 BLUEBACK | Ingalls | 15-4-57 | 16-5-59 | 15-10-59 |
| SS 582 BONEFISH | New York SB | 3-6-57 | 22-11-58 | 9-7-59 |

Authorized: FY 56

**CONVENTIONAL SUBMARINES** *(continued)*

**Blueback (SS 581)** G. Arra, 8-86

**Blueback (SS 581)** G. Arra, 1985

**D:** 1,740/2,146/2,640 tons **S:** 12/25 kts **Dim:** 66.75 × 8.84 × 8.50
**A:** 6/533-mm TT (fwd, Mk 48 torpedoes)
**Electron Equipt:** Radar: BPS-12—Sonar: BQR-2, SQS-49
EW: WLR-1
**M:** 3 1,600-hp Fairbanks-Morse 38D8$\frac{1}{8}$ × 10 diesels, 2 Westinghouse electric motors; 1 prop; 3,150 hp
**Man:** 8 officers, 77 men

Remarks: Teardrop hull design. Diving planes were moved to the sail structure in 1961–62. Dutch *Zwaardvis* class based on this design. Mk 101 Mod. 20 torpedo-fire-control system. Last conventional submarines built for the U.S. Navy. SS 582 transferred to the Atlantic Fleet in 1982, the only U.S. Navy diesel-powered submarine in that area.

**◆ 1 Darter class (SCB 116 type)**

| | Bldr | Laid down | L | In serv. |
|---|---|---|---|---|
| SS 576 Darter | Electric Boat Co. | 10-11-54 | 28-5-56 | 26-10-56 |

Authorized: FY 54

**Darter (SS 576)** L. & L. Van Ginderen, 1986

**D:** 1,590/1,975/2,250 tons **S:** 16/20 tons **Dim:** 81.68 × 8.23 × 5.8
**A:** 8/533-mm TT (6 fwd for Mk 48 torpedoes, 2 aft no longer used)
**Electron Equipt:** Radar: 1/BPS-12—EW: WLR-1
Sonar: BQS-4, BQG-4 (PUFFS), BQR-4
**M:** 3 Fairbanks-Morse 38D8$\frac{1}{8}$ × 10 diesels, 2 Westinghouse motors; 2 props; 3,200 hp
**Man:** 8 officers, 85 men

Remarks: Very similar to the ultimate configuration of the *Tang* class. Mk 106 Mod. 11 torpedo-fire-control system. Home-ported at Sasebo, Japan, in 3-79. To have been stricken in 9-79, but has been retained in service. Collided with merchant ship 18-6-85 but not badly damaged. Near-sister *Kusseh* (ex-*Trout*, SS 566) of the similar *Tang* class, transferred to Iran 19-12-79 and later abandoned, remains in storage in good condition at Philadelphia Naval SY; sister *Wahoo* (ex-SS 565), stricken 27-6-80, was towed away for scrap 4-85.

Note: The research submarine *Dolphin* (AGSS 555) is described later, with auxiliary ships.

**MIDGET SUBMARINES**

Some 15 miniature Swimmer-Delivery Vehicle (SDV) submersibles are used by Navy SEAL special forces. The smallest are modified Mk 37 torpedoes and the largest, which can be accommodated in the new Dry Deck Shelters carried by SSNs, can carry six swimmers, as well as mines and other weapons. A new type of Autonomous Underwater Vehicle (AUV) is being developed for submarine decoy, ASW, and mine-countermeasure purposes. The Martin Marietta-proposed version would be 9.14 m long and 1.37 m in diameter. Under the proposed program, 78 would be acquired as decoys for SSBNs, 204 for carriage by SSNs, and 97 for use by surface ships.

**BATTLESHIPS**

**◆ 4 Iowa class**

| | Bldr | Laid down | L | In serv. | Recomm. |
|---|---|---|---|---|---|
| BB 61 Iowa | New York NSY | 27-6-40 | 27-8-42 | 22-2-43 | 28-4-84 |
| BB 62 New Jersey | Philadelphia NSY | 16-9-40 | 7-12-42 | 23-5-43 | 28-12-82 |
| BB 63 Missouri | New York NSY | 6-1-41 | 29-1-44 | 11-6-44 | 10-5-86 |
| BB 64 Wisconsin | Philadelphia NSY | 25-1-41 | 7-12-43 | 16-4-44 | 22-10-88 |

**D:** 46,177 tons light (57,353 fl) **S:** 33+kts (30.5 sust.)
**Dim:** 270.43 (262.13 pp) × 32.97 × 11.58
**A:** 32/Tomahawk (IV × 8)—16 Harpoon (IV × 4)—9/406-mm (III × 3)—12/127-mm DP (II × 6)—4/20-mm Mk 15 CIWS gatling AA (I × 4)

**Iowa (BB 61)**—with drone-control radome atop aft stack G. Arra, 1987

**New Jersey (BB 62)** R.A.N., 1986

**Iowa (BB 61)** PHC (SW) J. Hilton, USN, 1-87

**BATTLESHIPS** *(continued)*

**Electron Equipt:** Radar: 1/LN-66, 1/SPS-67, (BB 62: SPS-10F), 1/SPS-49, 2/Mk 13, 4/Mk 25
TACAN: URN-25
EW: SLQ-32(V)3, Mk 36 SRBOC chaff RL (VI × 8)
**M:** 4 sets G.E. GT; 4 props; 212,000 hp **Electric:** 10,500 kw
**Boilers:** 8 Babcock & Wilcox; 44.6 kg/cm², 454°C **Fuel:** 8,800 tons
**Armor:** Belt: 307 mm, tapering to 41 mm (343 mm abreast prop shafts)
Main turrets: 432-mm face/184-mm top/305-mm back
Barbettes: 295 mm max.
Decks: 3 armored (152-mm second deck)
Conning tower: 440 mm (184-mm top)
**Range:** 5,000/30; 14,800/20
**Man:** 65 officers, 1,415 men, plus 2 Marine officers, 38 men

Remarks: BB 62, reactivated 6-4-68 for Vietnam service and decommissioned again 17-12-69, was towed from the Bremerton, Washington, mothball facility on 27-7-81, arriving 8-8-81 at Long Beach Naval Shipyard. Congress voted $326 mil. under FY 82 to modernize the ship with new radars and gear, Tomahawk and Harpoon cruise missiles, upgraded communications gear (including the WSC-3 SATCOMM system), seven new 125-ton/hr. air-conditioning plants, provision for Link-11 data link (but not NTDS), and conversion of the boilers to burn distillate fuel (which cut endurance by approx. 10 percent). Further major modifications ("Phase II") are no longer planned. Funds were authorized in FY 82 for work on BB 61 at Avondale SY, New Orleans, and Ingalls, Pascagoula. BB 63, towed to Long Beach Naval SY, began reactivation 1-10-84. Funds to reactivate BB 64 were authorized under FY 86, with work to take place 10-86 to 8-88 at Ingalls, Pascagoula. These ships act in autonomous battle groups, augmenting carrier forces on carrying out independent assignments. BB 61 in Atlantic Fleet, BB 62, 63 in Pacific.

The helicopter facilities include increased parking area to accommodate up to four helicopters, but there is no hangar; some maintenance facilities, a control cab, fuel tankage, and a glide-path indicator were added. The Tomahawk missiles are in eight elevating armored box launchers, while the Harpoons are placed abreast the after stack in the standard fixed 4-missile canister arrangement. BB

**Missouri (BB 63)** LSPH W. McBride, R.A.N., 12-87

**Iowa (BB 61)** L. & L. Van Ginderen, 9-86

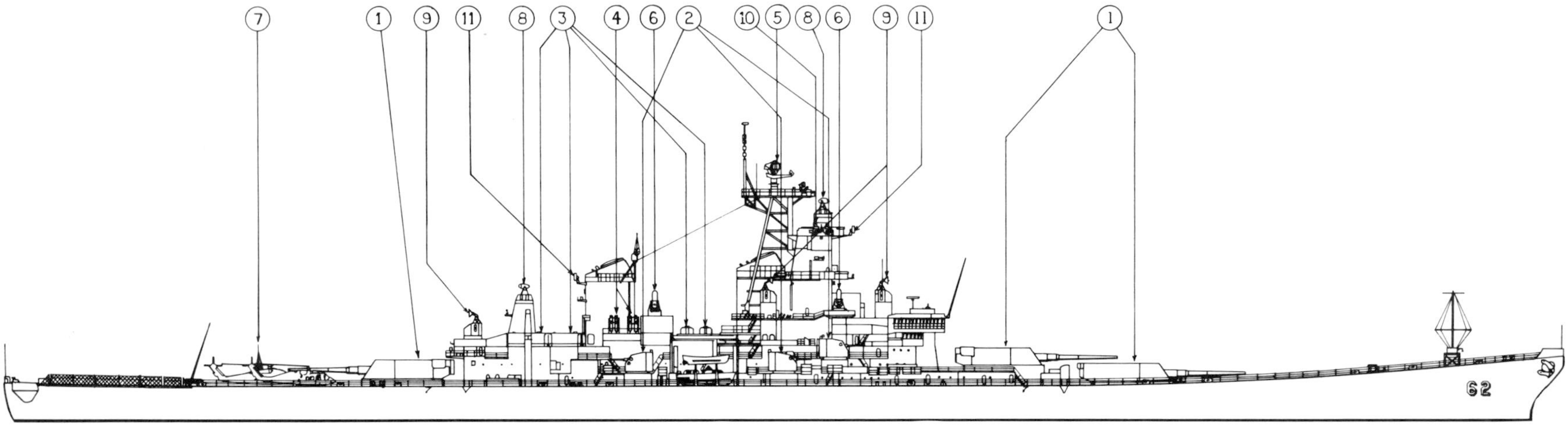

**New Jersey (BB 62)** A.D. Baker III
1. 406-mm triple turret 2. 127-mm twin DP 3. Tomahawk box-launcher (IV × 8) 4. Harpoon canister launcher (IV × 4) 5. SPS-49 radar 6. Mk 15 20-mm gatling CIWS 7. helicopter parking area 8. Mk 38 GFCS (with Mk 13 radar) 9. Mk 37 GFCS (with Mk 25 radar) 10. SLQ-32 EW gear 11. OE-82 SATCOMM antennas

**Missouri (BB 63)**—MARISAT commercial SATCOMM radome amidships LSPH E. Pitman, R.A.N., 10-86

**BATTLESHIPS** *(continued)*

62 successfully launched her first land-attack Tomahawk on 10-5-83 and deployed with eight aboard in 6-83. All have SLQ-25 Nixie torpedo decoys.

The 406-mm guns are controlled by two Mk 38 radar (Mk 13) GFCS and one Mk 40 director, while four Mk 37 GFCS (with Mk 25 radar) will be retained for the 127-mm guns. BB 62's six Mk 56 AA GFCS were replaced by the Vulcan/Phalanx (Mk 15 CIWS) gatling guns and 8 Super RBOC chaff launchers. While in reserve, BB 61 retained 6 Mk 56 and 2 Mk 63 GFCS, and BB 63 had 6 Mk 57 and 2 Mk 63 GFCS; BB 64 had all light AA GFCS removed when decommissioned in 1958. As activated, have WRN-5A NAVSAT, Omega, and other modern navigational systems. BB 61 deployed 1-87 with five AAI/Mazlat Pioneer surveillance drones and a control system with antenna mounted in a geodesic radome atop the after stack; the drones were launched and recovered from the helo deck, using a net landing system. Although initially unsuccessful, drones for artillery spotting are to be fitted to all four.

**NUCLEAR-POWERED GUIDED-MISSILE CRUISERS**

◆ **4 Virginia class**

| | Bldr | Laid down | L | In serv. |
|---|---|---|---|---|
| CGN 38 Virginia | Newport News SB | 19-8-72 | 14-12-74 | 11-9-76 |
| CGN 39 Texas | Newport News SB | 18-8-73 | 9-8-75 | 10-9-77 |
| CGN 40 Mississippi | Newport News SB | 22-2-75 | 31-7-76 | 5-8-78 |
| CGN 41 Arkansas | Newport News SB | 17-1-77 | 21-10-78 | 18-10-80 |

Authorized: CGN 38 in FY 70, CGN 39 in FY 71, CGN 40 in FY 72, and CGN 41 in FY 75

**Arkansas (CGN 41)**—showing loss of helo facility Pradignac & Leo, 9-86

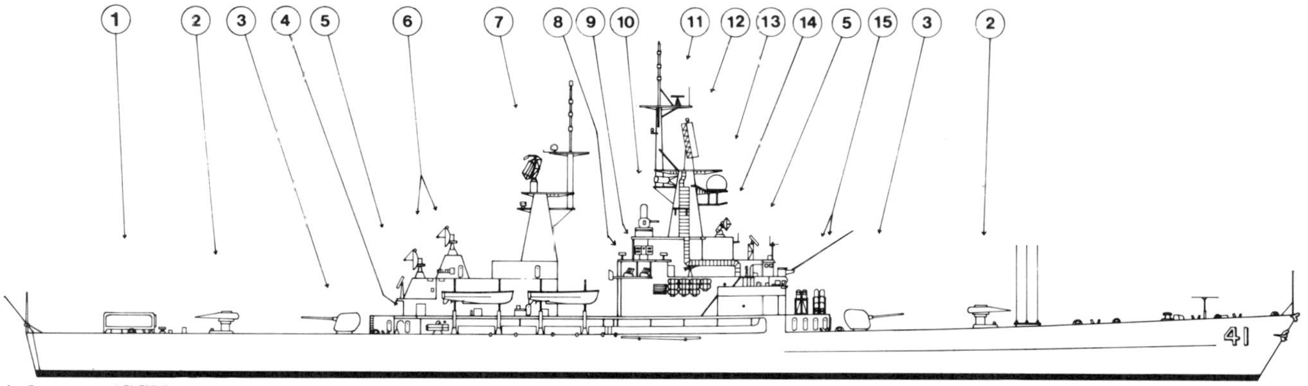


**Arkansas (CGN 41)** R. Dumas

1. Tomahawk Armored Box Launchers (IV × 2) 2. Mk 26 guided-missile launcher 3. 127-mm Mk 45 gun 4. Mk 32 ASW TT (III × 2) 5. OE-82 SATCOMM antennas 6. SPG-51D radar missile directors 7. SPS-40B radar 8. Mk 36 SRBOC RL (VI × 4 Mk 137 launchers) 9. SLQ-32(V)3 EW antennas 10. 20-mm Mk 15 CIWS 11. SPS-55 radar 12. SPS-48B 3-D air-search radar 13. SPQ-9A gun-control radar 14. SPG-60D missile/gun-control radar 15. Harpoon antiship missiles (IV × 2)

**Arkansas (CGN 41)**—with Tomahawk armored box-launchers aft, but still without Mk 15 CIWS Pradignac & Leo, 9-86

**NUCLEAR-POWERED GUIDED-MISSILE CRUISERS** *(continued)*

**D:** 10,400 tons light (11,300 fl) **S:** 30+ kts
**Dim:** 177.3 × 19.2 × 9.6 (sonar; 7.4 hull)
**A:** 8/Tomahawk SSM (IV × 2)—8/Harpoon SSM (IV × 2)—2/Mk 26 launchers (II × 2; 68 total Standard SM-2 MR block 1 surface-to-air and ASROC ASW missiles)—2/127-mm Mk 45 DP (I × 2)—2/20-mm Mk 15 CIWS gatling AA (I × 2)—4/12.7-mm mg (I × 4)—6/324-mm Mk 32 ASW TT (III × 2, Mk 46 torpedoes)
**Electron Equipt:** Radar: 1/LN-66, 1/SPS-55, 1/SPS-40B, 1/SPS-48A, 2/SPG-51D, 1/SPQ-9A, 1/SPG-60D
Sonar: 1/SQS-53A—TACAN: URN-25
EW: SLQ-32(V)3, (CGN 38: SLQ-34 also), Mk 36 SRBOC chaff RL (VI × 4)
**M:** 2 G.E. D2G reactors; 2 props; 70,000 hp
**Man:** 38–45 officers, 520–579 men

**Virginia (CGN 38)**—with SM-2 missile capability, Mk 15 CIWS, and Tomahawk
G. Arra, 4-86

**Virginia (CGN 38)** G. Arra, 4-86

Remarks: These ships are expected to operate for 10 years on one nuclear fueling. The original Standard SM-1 MR antiaircraft missiles, stowed vertically, have been replaced by SM-2 MR, and the ships are intended to receive the "New Threat Upgrade" combat system improvements. All now carry eight Tomahawk cruise missiles in two armored box-launchers in place of the original helicopter facility at the stern (which had a below-decks hangar). CGN 40 and 41 have SPS-48C vice 48A. All have WSC-3 SATCOMM and NTDS data system. The missile fire-control system is Mk 74; ASW fire control is Mk 116; and the GFCS is Mk 86 Mod. 5. SQS-53A sonar is a greatly improved version of SQS-26. Kevlar plastic armor has been added over vital topside and magazine spaces during sequential overhauls scheduled from FY 82 to FY 86. Mk 16 CIWS added on an 05-level platform, with the SLQ-32(V)3 arrays being moved down to the platform originally intended for the guns; this prevents electronic interference. CGN 38 and 40 in Atlantic Fleet, CGN 39, 41 in Pacific.

◆ **2 California class (SCB 241.65 type)**

| | Bldr | Laid down | L | In serv. |
|---|---|---|---|---|
| CGN 36 California | Newport News SB | 23-1-70 | 22-9-71 | 16-2-74 |
| CGN 37 South Carolina | Newport News SB | 1-12-70 | 1-7-72 | 25-1-75 |

Authorized: CGN 36 in FY 67, CGN 37 in FY 68

**D:** 9,676 tons light (10,530 fl) **S:** 30+ kts
**Dim:** 181.66 × 18.6 × 9.6 (sonar: 7.4 hull) **Man:** 70–44 officers, 555–559 men
**A:** 4/Harpoon SSM (IV × 1)—2/Mk 13 launchers (I × 2; 80 Standard SM-1 MR missiles)—2/127-mm Mk 45 DP (I × 2)—2/20-mm Mk 15 CIWS AA (I × 2)—4/12.7-mm mg (I × 4)—1/Mk 116 ASROC ASW RL (VIII × 1)—4/324-mm Mk 32 ASW TT (II × 2)
**Electron Equipt:** Radar: 1/LN-66, 1/SPS-10, 1/SPS-40B, 1/SPS-48C, 4/SPG-51D, 1/SPQ-9A, 1/SPG-60
Sonar: 1/SQS-26CX—TACAN: URN-25
EW: SLQ-32(V)3, SLQ-34, Mk 36 SRBOC chaff RL (VI × 4)
**M:** 2 G.E. D2G pressurized-water reactors, 2 GT; 2 props; 70,000 hp

Remarks: Each Mk 13 launcher magazine holds 40 vertically stowed missiles, and the ASROC system includes automatic reloading from a magazine on deck, forward of the launcher. Both will eventually get Tomahawk in two 4-missile box launchers. They have no helicopter hangar. Weapons are controlled by the Mk 11 Mod. 3 direction system, handling two Mk 74 Mod. 2 missile fire-control

**California (CGN 36)** G. Arra, 7-86

**California (CGN 36)**—amidships detail G. Arra, 7-86

**South Carolina (CGN 37)** F. Jentsch, 10-86

NUCLEAR-POWERED GUIDED-MISSILE CRUISERS *(continued)*

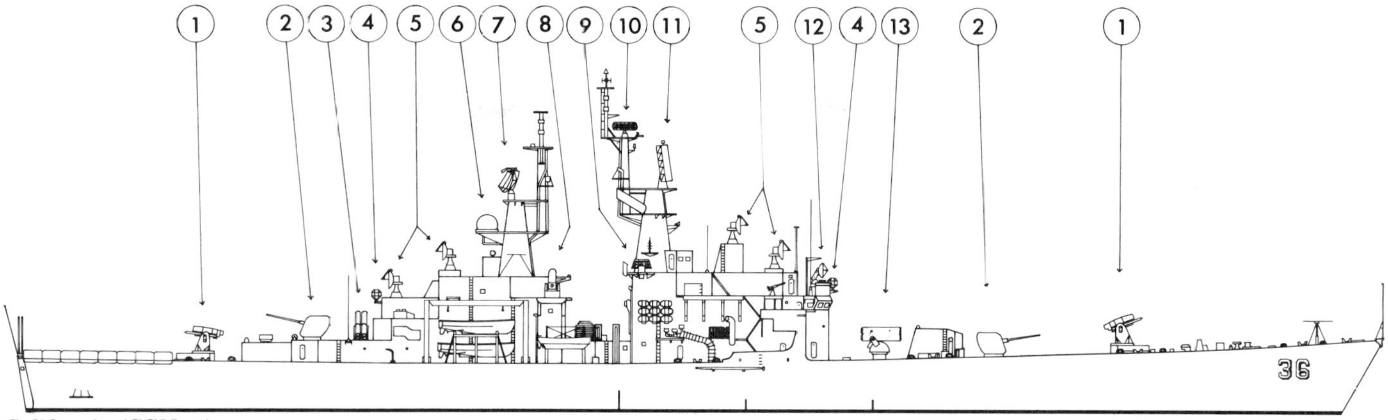


**California (CGN 36)** Robert Dumas
1. Mk 13 Standard SM-1 MR SAM launchers 2. 127-mm Mk 45 DP 3. Harpoon SSM canister launchers (IV × 1) 4. UHF satellite communications antennas 5. SPG-51D radar directors 6. SPQ-9A gun f.c. radar 7. SPS-40 air-search radar 8. 20-mm Mk 15 CIWS gatling AA 9. SLQ-32(V)3 EW antenna 10. SPS-10 surface-search radar 11. SPS-48C 3-D air-search radar antenna 12. SPG-60D gun f.c. radar director 13. ASROC ASW RL

**California (CGN 36)**—note Harpoon launchers just forward of aft 127-mm gun
G. Arra, 7-86

systems and Mk 86 Mod. 3 gunfire-control system. ASW fire is controlled by a Mk 114 system. Both have WSC-3 SATCOMM and NTDS data system. Kevlar plastic armor added over vital spaces. Eventually, SPS-67 will replace SPS-10, and SPS-49 the SPS-40B. Both will receive the NTU (New Threat Upgrade) modernization. There was space for only one quadruple Harpoon SSM installation, launching broadside to port. Helicopter deck, but no hangar. CGN 36 in Atlantic Fleet, CGN 37 in Pacific.

◆ **1 Truxtun class (SCB 222 type)**

| | Bldr | Program | Laid down | L | In serv. |
|---|---|---|---|---|---|
| CGN 35 Truxtun | New York SB, Camden, N.J. | FY 62 | 17-6-63 | 19-12-64 | 27-5-67 |

**Truxtun (CGN 35)** LSPH E. Pitman, R.A.N., 7-86

**Truxtun (CGN 35)** G. Arra, 1986

**D:** 8,000 tons light (8,800 fl) **S:** 30+ kts
**Dim:** 171.91 × 17.67 × 9.5 (sonar, 7.3 hull)
**A:** 8/Harpoon (IV × 2)—1/Mk 10 launcher (II × 1, for 40 Standard SM-2 ER Block 1 and 20 ASROC missiles)—1/127-mm Mk 42, 54-cal. DP—2/20-mm Mk 15 CIWS AA (I × 2)—4/12.7-mm mg (I × 4)—4/324-mm Mk 32 ASW TT (II × 2)—1/SH-2F LAMPS-I ASW helicopter
**Electron Equipt:** Radar: 1/LN-66, 1/SPS-67, 1/SPS-40D, 1/SPS-48C, 1/SPG-53F, 2/SPG-55C
Sonar: 1/SQS-26AXR—TACAN: URN-25
EW: WLR-1, SLQ-32(V)3, SLQ-34, Mk 36 SRBOC chaff RL (VI × 4)
**M:** 2 G.E. D2G pressurized-water reactors, 2 sets GT; 2 props; 70,000 hp
**Electric:** 14,500 kw **Man:** 39 officers, 552 men

Remarks: During 4-10-82 to 4-84 received two Vulcan/Phalanx Mk 15 CIWS 20-mm AA, new TACAN, and EW suite. Eight Harpoon SSM (IV × 2) replaced 2/76.2-mm DP in 1980. Two Mk 25 torpedo tubes at stern removed. Eventually will receive the NTU (New Threat Upgrade) modernization. The magazine has 3/20-missile horizontal drums. Has flag accommodations for six officers and twelve enlisted in addition to crew. Mk 76 Mod. 6 missile-control system. Mk 68 fire-control system for the 127-mm gun. Has Mk 14 weapon-direction system, WSC-3 SATCOMM, and NTDS data system. Mk 114 ASW fire-control system. The fixed Mk 32 ASW TT are mounted within the superstructure. Has SLQ-25 Nixie torpedo decoys. In Pacific Fleet.

◆ **1 Bainbridge class**

| | Bldr | Program | Laid down | L | In serv. |
|---|---|---|---|---|---|
| CGN 25 Bainbridge | Bethlehem Steel, Quincy | FY 59 | 5-59 | 15-4-61 | 6-10-62 |

**NUCLEAR-POWERED GUIDED-MISSILE CRUISERS** *(continued)*

**D:** 8,000 tons light (9,100 fl) **S:** 30+ kts
**Dim:** 172.21 (167.65 wl) × 17.57 × 9.5 (sonar, 7.3 hull) **Electric:** 14,500 kw
**A:** 8/Harpoon SSM (IV × 2)—4/Mk 10 launchers (II × 2; 80 Standard SM-2 ER missiles)—2/20-mm Mk 15 CIWS gatling AA (I × 2)—4/12.7-mm mg (I × 4)—1/Mk 116/ASROC ASW RL (VIII × 1)—6/324-mm Mk 32 ASW TT (III × 2)
**Electron Equipt:** Radar: 1/LN-66, 1/SPS-67, 1/SPS-48C, 1/SPS-49, 4/SPG-55C
Sonar: 1/SQQ-23—TACAN: URN-25
EW: WLR-1, SLQ-32(V)3, Mk 36 SRBOC (VI × 6)
**M:** 2 G.E. D2G reactors, 2 GT; 2 props; 70,000 hp **Man:** 42 officers, 516 men

**Bainbridge (CGN 25)** G. Gyssels, 6-87

**Bainbridge (CGN 25)** L. & L. Van Ginderen, 6-87

**Bainbridge (CGN 25)** Pradignac & Leo, 10-86

Remarks: In refit-modernization at Puget Sound NSY from 30-6-74 to 24-9-76 to improve AAW; refit completed at San Diego in 4-77. Obsolete 76.2-mm DP removed, temporarily replaced by two 20-mm AA, 1978-79. Two quadruple Harpoon canister launch groups replaced the 20-mm AA during 1979, those to port firing forward and those to starboard firing aft. Large deckhouse added aft to house NTDS data system. Two Mk 15 Vulcan/Phalanx 20-mm AA added during 10-83 to 4-85 refit; SPS-37 replaced by SPS-49, SLQ-32(V)3 ECM/ESM and Mk 36 RBOC chaff-flare system added and missile system updated to launch Standard SM-2 ER. Helicopter platform but no hangar. Mk 111 ASW fire-control system, two Mk 76 missile fire-control systems. Mk 14 weapon-direction system. Has flag accommodations for 6 officers, 12 men. In Atlantic Fleet since 8-85.

◆ **1 Long Beach class (SCB 169 type)**

| | Bldr | Program | Laid down | L | In serv. |
|---|---|---|---|---|---|
| CGN 9 Long Beach | Bethlehem Steel, (Quincy) | FY 57 | 2-12-57 | 14-7-59 | 9-9-61 |

**Long Beach (CGN 9)**—with foretopmast folded to port V. Baca, 2-87

**Long Beach (CGN 9)** G. Arra, 1986

**D:** 15,100 tons light (17,100 fl) **S:** 30.5 kts
**Dim:** 219.75 × 22.35 × 9.45 (over sonar)
**A:** 8/Tomahawk SSM (IV × 2)—8/Harpoon SSM (IV × 2)—1/Mk 10 Mod. 0 and 1/Mk 10 Mod. 1 launcher (II × 2, 120 Standard SM-2 ER missiles)—2/127-mm 38-cal. DP (I × 2)—2/20-mm Mk 15 CIWS AA (I × 2)—1/Mk 116 ASROC ASW RL (VIII × 1)—6/324-mm ASW TT (III × 2)
**Electron Equipt:** Radar: 1/LN-66, 1/SPS-67, 1/SPS-48C, 1/SPS-49, 4/SPG-55D, 2/Mk 35
Sonar: SQQ-23 PAIR (single-dome)—TACAN: URN-25
EW: SLQ-32(V)3, SLQ-34, Mk 36 SRBOC chaff RL (VI × 4)
**M:** 2 Westinghouse C1W pressurized-water reactors, 8 Foster-Wheeler heat exchangers, 2 sets G.E. GT; 2 props; 80,000 hp
**Electric:** 17,000 kw
**Man:** 65 officers, 893 men, + 1 Marine officer, 44 enlisted Marines

Remarks: The first U.S. surface ship to have nuclear propulsion. Original number was CLGN 160, then CGN 160. Originally intended to carry Regulus-II cruise missiles and eight Polaris ballistic missiles. Under FY 77, Congress appropriated long-lead funds to equip the ship with Aegis radar/fire-control system, since it is planned to operate the ship into the twenty-first century; the radical modernization plans were, however, canceled in 12-76.

*Long Beach* entered Puget Sound NSY 6-10-80 for a less-extensive two-year modernization period. The Mk 12 launch system aft for Talos missiles (deactivated in 1978) was stripped out in 1979, and the pedestals on the after superstructure that formerly supported SPG-49B Talos missile-direction radars carry the two Mk 15 CIWS (Vulcan/Phalanx) gatling AA guns. Harpoon canister clusters, arranged to fire athwartships, were situated abaft the superstructure, which is surmounted by a tall lattice mast to support the antenna for the SPS-49 air-search radar. The "billboard" fixed-array antennas on the blockhouse-style forward superstructure were removed, and the forward superstructure received 44-mm aluminum armor. Radar foundations and waveguides also were armored. SPS-48C replaced SPS-12 on the foremast. The obsolescent Mk 30, 127-mm, dual-purpose guns and their two equally aged Mk 56 directors (Mk 35 radars) were retained, as were the original ASW weapons and the forward missile-launching arrangements. No helicopter hangar was provided, only a pad on the stern. The Mk 10 Mod. 0 launcher for Standard missiles has two magazine drums, each holding 20 missiles; the Mk 10 Mod. 1 in the upper position has four magazine drums. Standard SM-2 ER has been substituted for SM-1 ER. The *Long Beach* will continue to have

## NUCLEAR-POWERED GUIDED-MISSILE CRUISERS *(continued)*

flagship facilities (10 officers, 58 men), and extensive satellite-communications facilities are provided. The Tactical Flag Command Center (TFCC) will be added at her next overhaul, as will additional protective armor. Armored box-launchers for Tomahawk SSM replaced the Harpoon SSMs in 1985; the Harpoon canister launchers were relocated atop the after superstructure.

## GUIDED-MISSILE CRUISERS

◆ **9 (+ 18) Ticonderoga class (*Atlantic Fleet, †Pacific Fleet)**

| | Bldr | Laid down | L | In serv. |
|---|---|---|---|---|
| CG 47 Ticonderoga* | Ingalls, Pascagoula | 21-1-80 | 25-4-81 | 22-1-83 |
| CG 48 Yorktown* | Ingalls, Pascagoula | 19-10-81 | 17-1-83 | 4-7-84 |
| CG 49 Vincennes† | Ingalls, Pascagoula | 20-10-82 | 14-1-84 | 6-7-85 |
| CG 50 Valley Forge† | Ingalls, Pascagoula | 14-4-83 | 23-6-84 | 18-1-86 |
| CG 51 Thomas S. Gates† | Bath Iron Works | 31-8-84 | 14-12-85 | 22-8-87 |
| CG 52 Bunker Hill† | Ingalls, Pascagoula | 11-1-84 | 11-3-85 | 20-9-86 |
| CG 53 Mobile Bay* | Ingalls, Pascagoula | 6-6-84 | 22-8-85 | 21-2-87 |
| CG 54 Antietam* | Ingalls, Pascagoula | 15-11-84 | 14-2-86 | 6-6-87 |
| CG 55 Leyte Gulf* | Ingalls, Pascagoula | 18-3-85 | 20-6-86 | 26-9-87 |
| CG 56 San Jacinto | Ingalls, Pascagoula | 22-7-85 | 14-11-86 | 23-1-88 |
| CG 57 Lake Champlain | Ingalls, Pascagoula | 3-3-86 | 3-4-87 | 8-88 |
| CG 58 Philippine Sea | Bath Iron Works | 8-5-86 | 25-4-87 | 2-89 |
| CG 59 Princeton | Ingalls, Pascagoula | 15-10-86 | 26-9-87 | 2-89 |
| CG 60 Normandy | Bath Iron Works | 7-4-87 | 19-3-88 | 9-89 |
| CG 61 Monterey | Bath Iron Works | 8-87 | 10-88 | 12-89 |
| CG 62 Chancellorsville | Ingalls, Pascagoula | 22-6-87 | 6-88 | 10-89 |
| CG 63 Cowpens | Bath Iron Works | 12-87 | 3-89 | 4-90 |
| CG 64 Gettysburg | Bath Iron Works | ... | 7-89 | 11-90 |
| CG 65 Shiloh | Ingalls, Pascagoula | ... | ... | 5-90 |
| CG 66 Chosin | Ingalls, Pascagoula | 6-89 | 7-90 | 10-90 |
| CG 67 Hue City | Bath Iron Works | ... | ... | 1-92 |
| CG 68 Anzio | Ingalls, Pascagoula | 12-89 | 1-91 | 4-92 |
| CG 69 N....... | Ingalls, Pascagoula | ... | ... | 9-92 |
| CG 70 N....... | Bath Iron Works | ... | ... | 12-92 |
| CG 71 N....... | Ingalls, Pascagoula | ... | ... | 3-93 |
| CG 72 N....... | Ingalls, Pascagoula | ... | ... | 6-93 |
| CG 73 N....... | Ingalls, Pascagoula | ... | ... | 1-94 |

Authorized: CG 47 in FY 78, CG 48 in FY 80, CG 49, 50 in FY 81, CG 51–53 in FY 82, CG 54–56 in FY 83, CG 57–59 in FY 84, CG 60–62 in FY 85, CG 63–65 in FY 86; CG 66–68 in FY 87, CG 69–73 in FY 88

**D:** CG 47, 48: 7,019 tons light (9,589 fl); CG 49, 50: 7,014 light (9,407 fl); CG 52 and later: 9,466 fl
**S:** 30+ kts **Dim:** 172.5 (162.4 wl) × 16.76 × 6.52 (9.57 over sonar)

**Leyte Gulf (CG 55)**—on sea trials R. Elias, Ingalls SB, 7-87

**A:** CG 47–51: 2/Mk 26 Mod. 1 launchers (II × 2; 68 Standard SM-2 MR and 20 ASROC)—8/Harpoon SSM (IV × 2)—2/127-mm Mk 45 DP (I × 2)—2/20-mm Mk 15 CIWS AA (I × 2)—4/12.7-mm mg (I × 4)—6/324-mm Mk 32 ASW TT (III × 2)—1 or 2/SH-60B LAMPS-III ASW helicopters (CG 47, 48: SH-2F LAMPS-I)
CG 52–73: 2/Mk 41 Mod. 0 vertical launch groups (122 missiles: Standard SM-2 MR Block 2 or 4, Tomahawk, and ASROC, when available —2/127-mm Mk 45 Mod. 1 DP (I × 2)—2/20-mm Mk 15 CIWS AA (I × 2)—6/324-mm Mk 32 Mod. 14 ASW TT (III × 2)—1 or 2/SH-60B LAMPS-III ASW helicopters
**Electron Equipt:** Radar: 1/SPS-53 (CG 49–73: SPS-64), 1/SPS-55, 1/SPS-49(V)6, 1/SPY-1A (CG 59–73: SPY-1B), 4/SPG-62, 1/SPQ-9A
Sonar: CG 47–55: SQS-53A (CG 54, 55: SQR-19 also); CG 56–73: SQQ-89 (SQS-53B, SQR-19)
TACAN: URN-25—IFF: UPX-29 interrogator
EW: SLQ-32(V)3, Mk 36 SRBOC chaff RL (VI × 4)
**M:** 4.G.E. LM-2500 gas turbines; 2/5-bladed CP props; 86,000 hp (80,000 normal)
**Electric:** 7,500 kw **Fuel:** 2,000 tons **Range:** 6,000/20
**Man:** 33 officers, 327 men (CG 54: 37 officers, 372 men)

**Ticonderoga (CG 47)** Pradignac & Leo, 7-86

**Ticonderoga (CG 47)** Pradignac & Leo, 7-86

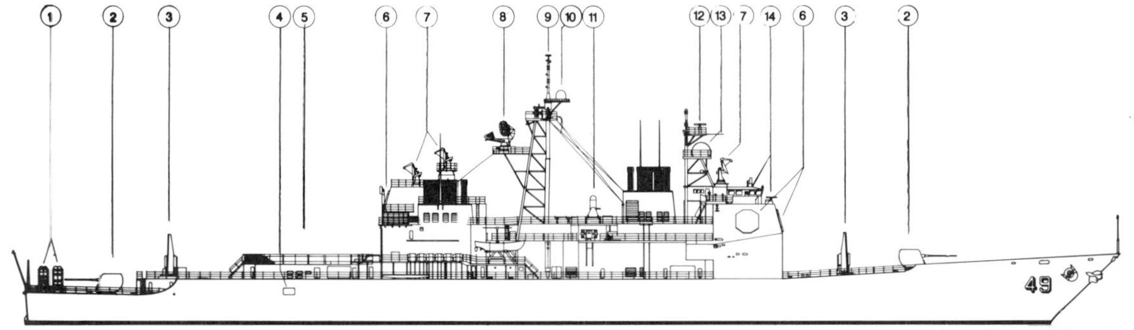

**Vincennes (CG 49)** A.D. Baker III, 1-86
1. Harpoon SSM 2. 127-mm Mk 45 DP 3. Mk 26 GMLS 4. Mk 32 ASW TT (behind shutters) 5. helicopter deck 6. AN/SPY-1A radar 7. AN/SPG-62 illuminator 8. AN/SPS-49(V)6 radar 9. AN/URN-25 TACAN 10. AN/SQQ-28 LAMPS antenna 11. 20-mm Mk 15 CIWS 12. AN/SPS-55 radar 13. AN/SPQ-9 radar director 14. AN/SPS-64 radar

**GUIDED-MISSILE CRUISERS** *(continued)*

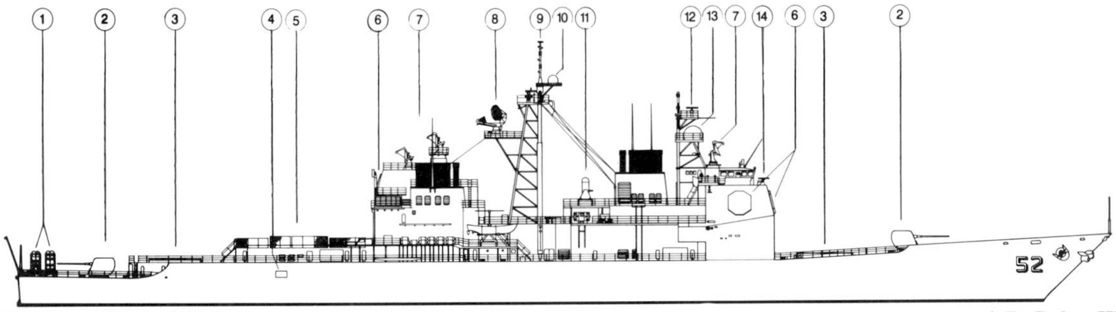


**Bunker Hill (CG 52)** A.D. Baker III

1. Harpoon SSM 2. 127-mm Mk 45 DP 3. Mk 41 Mod. 0 vertical launch 4. Mk 32 ASW TT (behind shutters) 5. Helicopter deck 6. AN/SPY-1A radar 7. AN/SPG-62 illuminator 8. AN/SPS-49(V)6 radar 9. AN/URN-25 TACAN 10. AN/SQQ-28 LAMPS antenna 11. 20-mm Mk 15 CIWS 12. AN/SPS-55 radar 13. AN/SPQ-9 radar director 14. AN/SPS-64 radar

**San Jacinto (CG 56)** R. Elias, Ingalls SB, 1987

**Antietam (CG 54)** R. Elias, Ingalls SB, 1987

**Yorktown (CG 48)** L. & L. Van Ginderen, 7-86

**Valley Forge (CG 50)** LSPH W. McBride, R.A.N., 9-87

GUIDED-MISSILE CRUISERS *(continued)*

**Bunker Hill (CG 52)**—with *Preble,* DDG 46 R. Elias, Ingalls SB, 9-86

**Bunker Hill (CG 52)** LSPH W. McBride, R.A.N., 12-87

**Valley Forge (CG 50)** G. Arra, 3-86

REMARKS: Greatly revised version of the *Spruance*-class destroyer, using same hull and propulsion but incorporating the Aegis Mk 7 weapon system (SPY-1A phased-array radar, four missile illuminator radars, Mk 26 missile-launch system, etc.). Designation changed from DDG to CG in late 1979. A total of 27 to be built. Named for battles and campaigns, except for CG 51, named for a former Secretary of Defense and of the Navy.

The last five were to have been authorized 2 each in FY 88 and FY 89, and the last in FY 90. Instead, Congress authorized a "buy-out" of this class under FY 88, denying a request for 3 DDG 51. However, sufficient *funds* were authorized only for CG 69–72, with CG 73 possibly slipping to FY 89 for funding. CG 60–62 ordered 26-11-84, CG 63 and 64 on 9-1-86, CG 65 on 8-1-86, CG 66–68 on 16-4-87, and CG 69–73 on 25-2-88.

Each Mk 26 Mod. 1 missile-launcher magazine holds 44 missiles, the forward magazine holding the 20 ASROC. The Mk 86 fire-control system for the 127-mm guns provides no AA capability in this class, as no SPG-60 radar is carried. The R.C.A.-built Aegis Mk 7 Mod. 2 system, which uses 12 UYK-7 and 1 UYK-20 computers, uses the four fixed faces of the SPY-1A radar to detect and track up to several hundred targets simultaneously; the four illuminators are slaved to the system and can, through time-share switching, serve more than a dozen missiles in the air at once; the Mk 99 missile fire-control *system* uses 4 Mk 80 *illuminator-directors* with SPG-62 *radars.* The UPX-29 IFF circular antenna array is carried on the mainmast. The Harpoon missiles are in an exposed position at the extreme stern. Bow bulwarks were required to keep decks dry, as draft was increased about one meter over that of the original *Spruance* design. No fin stabilization is fitted. CG 48's keel was "laid" at Yorktown, Virginia, by President Reagan as part of the ceremonies commemorating the defeat of the British there in 1781; actual structural work commenced 12-81 at Pascagoula, Mississippi.

Modifications to accept newly developed equipments are to be phased in, with the Ingalls yard intended to receive the building contract for the first ship of each new block:

Block 0: CG 47, 48: Basic Aegis Mk 7 system, with SPY-1A, Weapons Control System Mk 1, Standard SM-2 MR Block 1 missiles, the Mk 116 Mod. 4 ASW fire-control system, and the SH-2F LAMPS-I ASW helicopter.

Block 1: CG 49–51: The RAST haul-down and deck-maneuvering system is added for SH-60B LAMPS-III helicopters, Standard SM-2 MR Block 2 missiles are carried, Aegis has improved data displays, and the EW suit is enhanced. Both masts tripods vice quadripods.

Block 2: CG 52–55: The Mk 40 Mod. 0 vertical-launch system is substituted for the Mk 26 twin-armed launchers, vertical-launch Tomahawk capability is added, as is an improved LINK 11 data-link system. As vertical-launch ASROC will not be ready in time, these ships will not receive a launch capability until early 1990s refits. Congress mandated the omission of SPS-49 radars and the SQQ-28 LAMPS-III data link in CG 54–56, but gave permission in 5-84 to add the equipment. CG 54 and 55 have stand-alone SQR-19 linear towed passive sonar arrays and SQS-53A.

Block 3: CG 56 introduces the SQQ-89 (V)3 integrated ASW suite, with SQQ-53B hull-mounted sonar, SQR-19 towed array, and the Mk 116 Mod. 6 ASW fire-control system.

Block 4: CG 59 and later: The lighter SPY-1B radar, with improved radiating characteristics, is substituted for SPY-1A, and new computers (UYK-44) will be employed, along with improved displays.

There have been a number of ill-informed criticisms of this class, which is nonetheless *the* most capable AAW platform in any navy, as well as being among the most effective ASW platforms and, with the addition of vertical-launch Tomahawk, a strategic threat as well. The ships are not unstable, although quite cramped, and have sufficient stability margin to operate at up to 10,200 tons full load. CG 47 and 48 carry a small amount of lead ballast, but later units do not. All carry up to 36 Mk 46 ASW torpedoes.

◆ **9 Belknap class (SCB 212 type) (*Atlantic Fleet; others in Pacific)**

| | Bldr | Laid down | L | In serv. |
|---|---|---|---|---|
| CG 26 BELKNAP* | Bath Iron Works | 5-2-62 | 20-7-63 | 7-11-64 |
| CG 27 JOSEPHUS DANIELS* | Bath Iron Works | 23-4-62 | 2-12-63 | 8-5-65 |
| CG 28 WAINWRIGHT* | Bath Iron Works | 2-7-62 | 25-4-64 | 8-1-66 |
| CG 29 JOUETT | Puget Sound NSY | 25-9-62 | 30-6-64 | 3-12-66 |

**GUIDED-MISSILE CRUISERS** *(continued)*

**Josephus Daniels (CG 27)** G. Arra, 9-86

**Sterett (CG 31)** L. & L. Van Ginderen, 6-87

**Belknap (CG 26)**—6th Fleet flagship, with enlarged superstructure, SHF SATCOMM, no hangar Pradignac & Leo, 9-86

**Belknap (CG 26)** H. Ehlers, 6-87

| | | | | |
|---|---|---|---|---|
| CG 30 Horne | San Francisco NSY | 12-9-62 | 30-10-64 | 15-4-67 |
| CG 31 Sterett | Puget Sound NSY | 25-9-62 | 30-6-64 | 8-4-67 |
| CG 32 William H. Standley | Bath Iron Works | 29-7-63 | 19-12-64 | 9-7-66 |
| CG 33 Fox | Todd SY, San Pedro | 15-1-63 | 21-11-64 | 28-5-66 |
| CG 34 Biddle* | Bath Iron Works | 9-12-63 | 2-7-65 | 21-1-67 |

Authorized: Three in FY 61 and six in FY 62

**D:** 5,340 light/6,570 std. tons (8,065 fl; CG 26: 8,575) **S:** 33 kts
**Dim:** 166.72 × 16.76 × 5.9 (8.8 over sonar)
**A:** 8/Harpoon SSM (IV × 2)—1/Mk 10 Mod. 7 launcher (II × 1, 40 Standard SM-2 ER and 20 ASROC missiles)—1/127-mm Mk 42 DP (aft)—2/20-mm Mk 15 CIWS AA (I × 2)—4/12.7-mm mg (I × 4)—6/324-mm Mk 32 ASW TT (III × 2; 18 Mk 46 torpedoes)—1/SH-2F LAMPS-I helicopter (not in CG 26)
**Electron Equipt:** Radar: 1/LN-66, 1/SPS-10F or SPS-67, 1/SPS-49(V)3 (except CG 31–34: SPS-40), 1/SPS-48C, 2/SPG-55D, 1/SPG-53A
Sonar: 1/SQS-26BX (CG 26: SQS-53A)
TACAN: URN-25
EW: SLQ-32(V)3, SLQ-34 (not in CG 26, 30, 31), Mk 36 SRBOC chaff RL (VI × 4)
**M:** 2 sets GT; 2/6-bladed props; 85,000 hp
**Boilers:** CG 24, CG 28, CG 32, CG 34: 4 Foster-Wheeler; others: 4 Combustion Engineering; 84 kg/cm$^2$, 520°C
**Electric:** 6,800 kw **Range:** 2,500/30; 8,000/14
**Man:** 31 officers, 461 men + flag group: 6 officers, 12 enlisted (CG 26: plus 30 officers, 81 enlisted in flag group)

**Horne (CG 30)** LSPH W. McBride, R.A.N., 2-88

**William H. Standley (CG 32)** V. Baca, 12-87

Remarks: Formerly typed DLG; classified CG on 1-7-75. CG 26, severely damaged in collision with CV 67 in Mediterranean in 22-11-75, was out of commission for repairs at Philadelphia until 10-5-80. She had her 76.2-mm guns replaced by 8 Harpoon SSM, received SPS-48C and SPS-49 radar, SM-2 ER missiles, the SLQ-25 Nixie towed torpedo decoy system, improved electronics (including NTDS Mod. 4) and communications gear, and SQS-53A sonar and is now officially considered to be a separate class. In a further refit, from 6-85 to 7-86, the ship was equipped as 6th Fleet Flagship, with enhanced communications and staff accommodations at the expense of the helicopter hanger: included were the WSC-6 SHF SATCOMM antennas, a new 2-level deckhouse before the bridge, and the conversion of the hangar to additional accommodations. CG 31 was the first to lose her 76.2-mm, in 1976, to make way for eight Harpoon ASM (IV × 2), now also carried by the others (firing forward to port, aft to starboard). CG 28 has been used as trials ship for SM-2 ER, now carried by all units of the class. The 127-mm gun is controlled by a Mk 68 radar GFCS. Mk 114 (CG 26: Mk 116) ASW fire-control system, one Mk 11 (CG 26: Mk 14) weapon-direction system, and two Mk 76 Mod. 9 missile fire-control systems. These ships will not receive the SH-60B LAMPS-III ASW

GUIDED-MISSILE CRUISERS *(continued)*

helicopter. CG 26, 28, 30, and 31 received the Tactical Flag Command Center in 1983-85. All will eventually have the SPS-10F replaced by SPS-67, and the SPS-48 updated to SPS-48E; the SYS-2 weapon-control system will be added. Several have enhanced electronics warfare suites, with additional equipment over the SLQ-32(V)3 fit. All are scheduled to receive the NTU (New Threat Upgrade) modernization, with Weapons Direction System Mk 14 and missile tracking set SYR-1 during refits from 1986 to the early 1990s; CG34, in refit 7-86 to 7-87, was first ship to receive the production version of NTU.

**Wainwright (CG 28)** R. Parkinson, 10-86

◆ **9 Leahy class (SCB 172 type)** (*Atlantic Fleet; others Pacific Fleet)

| | Bldr | Laid down | L | In serv. |
|---|---|---|---|---|
| CG 16 Leahy | Bath Iron Works | 3-12-59 | 1-7-61 | 4-8-62 |
| CG 17 Harry E. Yarnell* | Bath Iron Works | 31-5-60 | 9-12-61 | 2-2-63 |
| CG 18 Worden | Bath Iron Works | 19-9-60 | 2-6-62 | 3-8-63 |
| CG 19 Dale* | New York SB | 6-9-60 | 28-7-62 | 23-11-63 |
| CG 20 Richmond K. Turner* | New York SB | 9-1-61 | 6-4-63 | 13-6-64 |
| CG 21 Gridley | Puget Sound SB & DD Co. | 15-7-60 | 31-7-61 | 25-5-63 |
| CG 22 England* | Todd SY, Los Angeles | 4-10-60 | 6-3-62 | 7-12-63 |
| CG 23 Halsey | San Francisco NSY | 26-8-60 | 15-1-62 | 20-7-63 |
| CG 24 Reeves | Puget Sound NSY | 1-7-60 | 12-5-62 | 15-5-64 |

Authorized: 3 in FY 58, 6 in FY 59

**Worden (CG 18)** L. & L. Van Ginderen, 7-87

**Leahy (CG 16)** L. & L. Van Ginderen, 1-87

**Harry E. Yarnell (CG 17)** G. Arra, 1-87

**Worden (CG 18)** G. Arra, 7-86

**Gridley (CG 21)**—enlarged superstructure amidships G. Arra, 8-86

**D:** 6,070 tons (8,200 fl) **S:** 33 kts **Dim:** 162.46 × 16.15 × 5.9 (7.9 over sonar)
**A:** 8/Harpoon SSM (IV × 2)—2/Mk 10 launchers (II × 2, 80 Standard SM-2 ER missiles)—2/20-mm Mk 15 CIWS AA (I × 2)—4/12.7-mm mg (I × 4)—1/Mk 116/ASROC ASW RL (VIII × 2)—6/324-mm Mk 32 ASW TT (III × 2)
**Electron Equipt:** Radar: 1/LN-66, 1/SPS-10F or SPS-67, 1/SPS-49(V)3, 1/SPS-48A, 4/SPG-55C
Sonar: SQS-23 (CG 17: SQQ-23B PAIR, single-dome)
TACAN: SRN-6 or URN-25
EW: SLQ-32(V)3, Mk 36 SRBOC chaff RL (VI × 4) (CG 21, 23, 24: WLR-1, WLR-3 also)
**M:** CG 16 to CG 19: 2 sets G.E. GT, CG 20 to CG 22: 2 sets de Laval GT, CG 23 and CG 24: 2 sets Allis Chalmers GT; 2/5-bladed props; 85,000 hp
**Boilers:** CG 16 to CG 20: 4 Babcock & Wilcox; others: 4 Combustion Engineering; 84 kg/cm², 520°C
**Electric:** 6,800 kw **Fuel:** 1,800 tons **Range:** 2,500/30; 8,000/14
**Man:** 27–31 officers, 366–376 men + flag group: 6 officers, 12 men

Remarks: These are former DLGs, classified CG on 1-7-75. During overhauls 1967–72, the *Leahy*-class ships received an advanced version of the Mk 76 missile fire-control system, permitting firing of Standard SM-1 ER missiles. CG 16 was the first to complete this overhaul and returned to active service on 17-8-68. All had received SM-2 ER missile capability by 1985. The four 76.2-mm (II × 2) guns have

GUIDED-MISSILE CRUISERS *(continued)*

**Dale (CG 19)** Pradignac & Leo, 6-86

been removed from all, and their gun tubs are used as locations for Harpoon missile launchers. Like CGN 25, these ships are, unfortunately, completely devoid of larger gun armament. There are no reloads for the ASROC system. CG 19 received SPS-49 in place of SPS-43 in 1976; the others were similarly re-equipped, and all now have the SLQ-32(V)3 EW system, with CG 21 and CG 24 also retaining the older WLR-1 and WLR-3 equipment, updated. Mk 76 missile fire-control system, with 4 SPG-55B radar trackers/illuminators. Mk 114 ASW fire control, Mk 14 weapon-control system. All have NTDS data system and WSC-3 SATCOMM equipment. CG 22 received NTU (New Threat Upgrade) modernization during refit 10-86 to 10-87; CG 20 began NTU refit late in 1987.

## HEAVY CRUISERS

◆ **2 Des Moines class**—In reserve

| | Bldr | Laid down | L | In serv. |
|---|---|---|---|---|
| CA 134 Des Moines | Bethlehem, Fore River | 28-5-45 | 27-9-46 | 16-11-48 |
| CA 139 Salem | Bethlehem, Fore River | 4-7-45 | 25-3-47 | 14-5-49 |

The stricken *Newport News* (ex-CA 148) moored outboard *Des Moines* (CA 134) and *Salem* (CA 139) at Philadelphia Naval Shipyard A.D. Baker, 8-84

**D:** 17,225 tons (21,470 fl) **S:** 32 kts **Dim:** 218.42 (213.36 wl) × 22.96 × 7.5
**A:** 9/203-mm (III × 3)—12/127-mm DP (II × 6)—20–22/76.2-mm DP (II × 10 or 11)
**Electron Equipt:** Radar: 1/SG-6, 1/SPS-8, 1/SPS-6C (CA 139: SPS-12), 2/Mk 13, 4/Mk 25, 4/Mk 35 (CA 139: 2/Mk 34 also)
TACAN: URN-6
**M:** 4 sets GT; 4 props; 120,000 hp **Electric:** 7,700 kw
**Boilers:** 4 Babcock & Wilcox; 43.9 kg/cm$^2$, 454°C
**Armor:** Belt: 102–152-mm; Upper deck: 25-mm; Lower deck: 85-mm; Turrets: 203-mm face, 95-mm sides, 102-mm roof; Barbettes: 160-mm; Conning Tower: 102–160-mm; Steering Room: 96–160-mm
**Fuel:** 2,600 tons **Range:** 8,000/15 **Man:** 105 officers, 1,745 men (wartime)

Remarks: CA 139 to reserve on 30-1-59, CA 134 on 14-7-61, both at Philadelphia. Sister *Newport News* (CA 148), in reserve since 27-6-75, was stricken on 30-6-78 but remained at Philadelphia; offered for museum use 1987. CA 134 has ten twin 76.2-mm Mk 34 DP mounts, her sister has eleven. Each has two Mk 54 directors (with Mk 13 radar) for the 203-mm guns, four Mk 37 fire-control systems for the 127-mm guns, and four Mk 56 and Mk 63 fire-control systems for the 76.2-mm guns. Magazines can carry 1,350 rounds 203-mm, 6,060 rounds 127-mm, 12,000 rounds 76.2-mm. All radar antennas have been removed for storage. To be retained for possible reactivation as naval gunfire-support ships; are in excellent condition but have badly outdated electronics.

## GUIDED-MISSILE DESTROYERS

◆ **0 (+3 + 26) Arleigh Burke class**

| | Bldr | Laid down | L | In serv. |
|---|---|---|---|---|
| DDG 51 Arleigh Burke | Bath Iron Works | 3-4-88 | 21-8-89 | 8-90 |
| DDG 52 Barry (ex-*John Barry*) | Ingalls, Pascagoula | 9-89 | 7-90 | 10-91 |
| DDG 53 John Paul Jones | Bath Iron Works | ... | ... | 5-92 |
| DDG 54 Curtis Wilbur | ... | ... | ... | ... |
| DDG 55 N... | ... | ... | ... | ... |
| DDG 56 N... | ... | ... | ... | ... |
| DDG 57 N... | ... | ... | ... | ... |

Authorized: DDG 51 in FY 85, DDG 52, 53 in FY 87; DDG 54–56 in FY 89. Plan in FY 90, 6/yr FY 91 onward

**GUIDED-MISSILE DESTROYERS** *(continued)*

**Arleigh Burke (DDG 51)**—1987 concept Gibbs & Cox, 1987

**Arleigh Burke (DDG 51)**—original mast V. Piecyk/R.C.A., 11-84

**D:** 6,624 tons light (8,315 fl) **S:** 30+ kts
**Dim:** 153.77 (142.03 wl) × 20.40 (18.0 wl) × 6.09 (9.32 over sonar)
**A:** 2 Mk 41 Mod. 0 vertical-launch groups (1/64-cell, 1/32-cell; 90 Standard SM-2 MR Block 4, ASROC and Tomahawk missiles)—8/Harpoon SSM (IV × 2)—1/127-mm Mk 45 Mod. 1 DP—2/20-mm Mk 15 CIWS AA (I × 2)—6/324-mm Mk 32 ASW TT (III × 2)

**Electron Equipt:** Radar: 1/SPS-64, 1/SPS-67, 1/SPY-1D, 3/SPG-62
Sonar: SQQ-89(V)4 suite: SQS-53C, SQR-19 towed array
EW: SLQ-32(V)2, Mk 36 SRBOC chaff RL (VI × 4)
TACAN: URN-25—IFF: UPX-29
**M:** 4 G.E. LM-2500-30 gas turbines; 2/5-bladed CP props; 100,000 hp
**Electric:** 7,500 kw **Fuel:** . . .
**Range:** 4,400/20 **Man:** 303 tot. (26 officers, 315 men)

**Arleigh Burke (DDG 51)**—artist's rendering—note new raked tripod mast, vice original lattice tripod Gibbs & Cox, 1987

Remarks: This design, overly long in development, is intended to provide a general-purpose destroyer capable of carrying out its assignments in the threat environment of the 1990s and beyond. The ships will have steel superstructures and the first comprehensive CBR protection system in a U.S. Navy ship. Over 130 tons of armor will be used for vital spaces. Congress has forced development of the RACER (Rankine-Cycle Energy Recovery) system, to provide cruising power by using the waste heat from one of the gas turbines to generate about 8,000 propulsion horsepower; it will not be incorporated until at least the 10th ship and may not be used at all. With or without RACER, the ships will have considerably reduced endurance as compared to other recent U.S.N. destroyers. The hull form is unusually broad in relation to length; fin stabilizers are not planned.

The flight deck will accept the SH-60B/F Seahawk helicopter, and the SQQ-28 LAMPS-III data-link/control system will be installed. DDG 52 and later will have helicopter haul-down system, plus helicopter refueling/rearming facilities, which will add 58 tons to the full-load displacement. DDG 61–68 are to have improved fire control, Standard missiles, NTDS Mod. 5, improved displays, and later communications. The SLQ-25 Nixie towed torpedo decoy system will be carried.

The Aegis SPY-1D will have all four faces mounted on the forward superstructure; the system will employ 5 UYK-43B computers, and the Combat Information Center will be below the main deck. The gun will be controlled by the Mk 160 Mod. 4 GFCS (which uses radar input data from the SPS-67 or SPY-1D); the

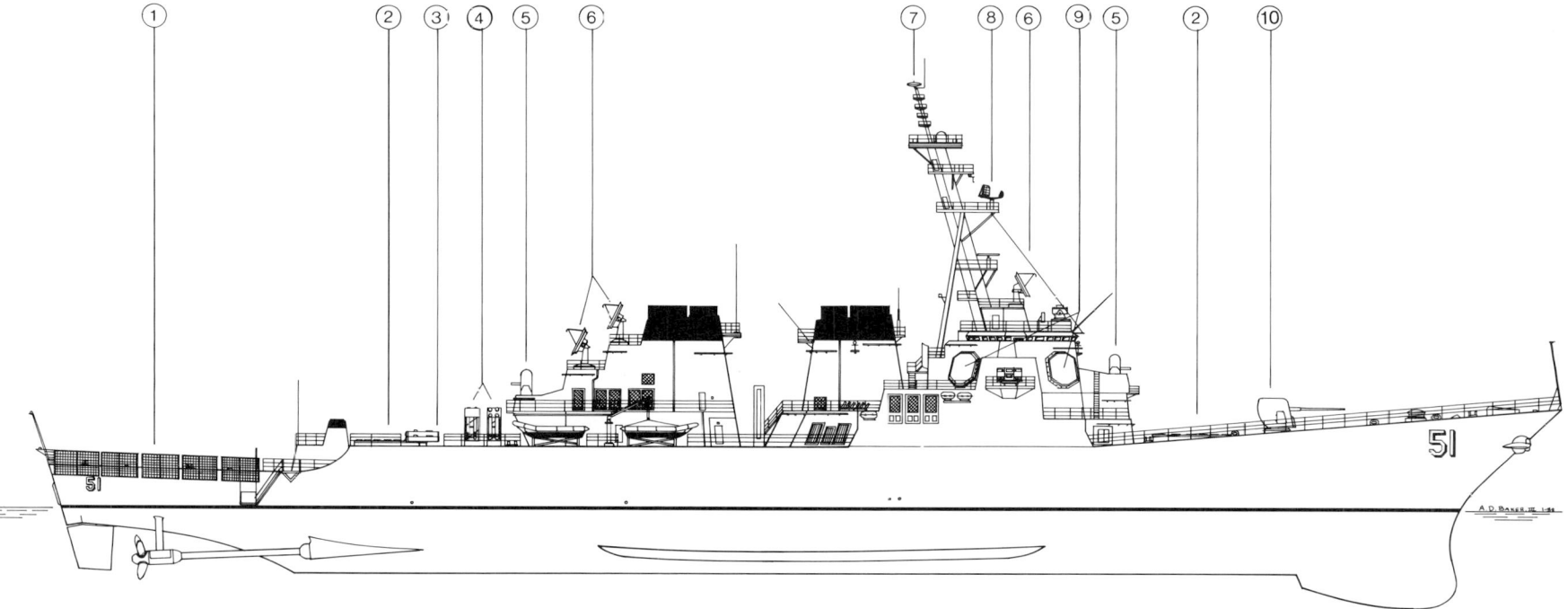

**Arleigh Burke (DDG 51)** A.D. Baker III
1. helicopter deck 2. Mk 41 vertical-launch missile system (VLS) 3. Mk 32 triple ASW TT. 4. Harpoon SSM 5. Mk 15 CIWS 20-mm AA 6. SPG-62 radars for Mk 99 illuminator system 7. URN-25 TACAN 8. SPS-67 radar (SPS-64 below) 9. SPY-1D radar 10. 127-mm Mk 45 DP

## GUIDED-MISSILE DESTROYERS *(continued)*

planned Mk 121 Mod. 0 Seafire t.v./laser/infrared director has been canceled but may be replaced by a less-costly system. The gun will have no AA capability and will be furnished with a probable 600 rounds of ammunition. The Standard SM-2 MR Block 2 missiles will be controlled by the Aegis system, using the three Mk 80 illuminators for terminal designation only. The Mk 116 Mod. 7 ASW f.c.s. will be carried. WSC-3 satellite communications and Links 11 and 14 will be fitted. The SQQ-89(V)4 ASW suite includes the SQS-53C bow-mounted sonar, SQR-19 towed passive sonar array, SQQ-28 helicopter data link, SIMAS, and the Mk 116 Mod. 7 weapon-control system. Name for DDG 52 changed 1-2-88.

DDG 54 named in expectation of approval under FY 87, but Congress gave Navy only two ships. None approved FY 88 in favor of CG 47-class buy-out. Five authorized 1987 by Congress for FY 89, with proviso that one may be deferred in favor of the 5th FY 88 CG 47. Program well behind by late 1987, with launch of DDG 51 delayed one year, delivery by 10 months. DDG 51 ordered 2-4-85, DDG 52 on 26-5-87, DDG 53 8-87. Congress required a third yard to participate in FY 89. Only three requested for FY 89 in 2-88.

◆ **4 Kidd class** Bldr: Ingalls, Pascagoula (*Atlantic Fleet; others: Pacific)

| | Laid down | L | In serv. |
|---|---|---|---|
| DDG 993 KIDD (ex-*Kouroush*)* | 26-6-78 | 11-8-79 | 27-6-81 |
| DDG 994 CALLAGHAN (ex-*Daryush*) | 23-10-78 | 1-12-79 | 29-8-81 |
| DDG 995 SCOTT (ex-*Nader*)* | 12-2-79 | 1-3-80 | 24-10-81 |
| DDG 996 CHANDLER (ex-*Andushirvan*) | 7-5-79 | 24-5-80 | 13-3-82 |

Authorized: FY 79 Supplemental

**Scott (DDG 995)** G. Arra, 6-86

**Kidd (DDG 993)**—in light gray paint Pradignac & Leo, 11-87

**Callaghan (DDG 994)** F. Jentsch, 7-87

**Chandler (DDG 996)** G. Arra, 2-86

**D:** 6,950 tons light (9,574 fl) **S:** 30+ kts
**Dim:** 171.7 (161.23 wl) × 16.76 × 7.01 (10.06 over sonar)
**A:** 1/Mk 26 Mod. 3 and 1/Mk 26 Mod. 4 launcher (II × 2, 52 Standard SM-1 [DDG 995: SM-2] MR and 16 ASROC missiles)—8/Harpoon SSM (IV × 2)—2/127-mm Mk 45 DP (I × 2)—2/20-mm Mk 15 CIWS AA (I × 2)—4/12.7-mm mg (I × 4)—6/324-mm Mk 32 ASW TT (III × 2; 24 torpedoes)—1/SH-2F LAMPS-I ASW helicopter
**Electron Equipt:** Radar: 1/SPS-64(4), 1/SPS-55, 1/SPS-48C, 2/SPG-51D, 1/SPG-60, 1/SPQ-9A
Sonar: SQS-53A—TACAN: URN-25
EW: SLQ-32(V)2, Mk 36 SRBOC chaff RL (VI × 4)
**M:** 4 G.E. LM-2500 gas turbines; 2/5-bladed CP props; 86,000 hp
**Electric:** 6,000 kw **Range:** 3,300/30; 6,000/20 **Man:** 32 officers, 332 men

REMARKS: The original order for these superb ships placed with the U.S. Navy by Iran in 1974 was for six; two were canceled before the order to Ingalls Shipbuilding for the remaining four was issued on 23-3-78. DDG 993 and DDG 994 were

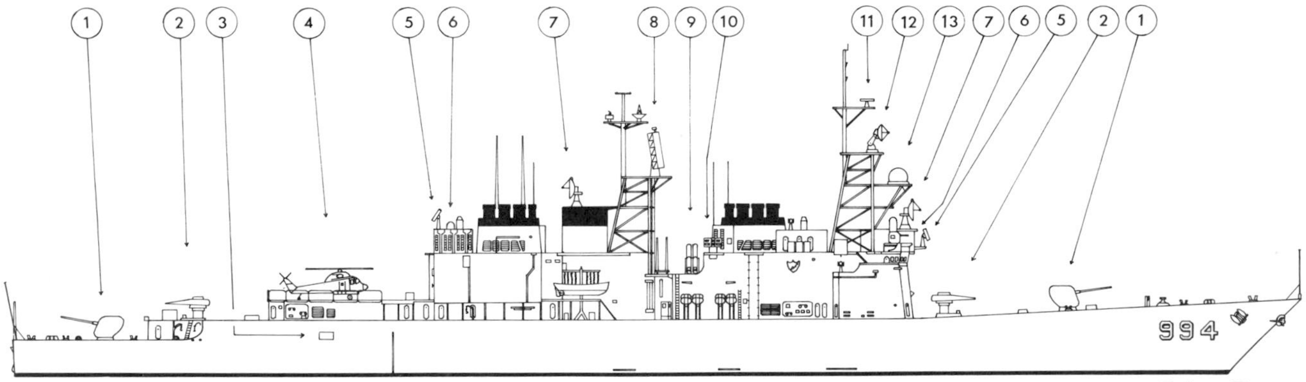

**Kidd (DDG 993)** Robert Dumas
1. 127-mm Mk 45 DP gun 2. Mk 26 guided-missile launcher 3. ports for Mk 32 ASW TT (III × 2) 4. SH-2F helicopter 5. OE-82 UHF SATCOMM antennas 6. Mk 15 CIWS 7. SPG-51D missile-control radar 8. SPS-48C 3-D radar 9. Harpoon SSM (IV × 2) 10. SLQ-32(V)2 array 11. SPS-55 radar 12. SPG-60 radar gun director 13. SPQ-9A radar gun director

## GUIDED-MISSILE DESTROYERS *(continued)*

canceled by the new Iranian government on 31-3-79, and the other pair shortly thereafter. Their completion for the U.S. Navy was authorized by the U.S. Congress under a Fiscal 1979 Supplementary Appropriation Act. Acquired 25-7-79, at approximately $510 million each, they represented a considerable bargain. The hull numbers do not fit in U.S.N. hull-numbering sequence for guided-missile destroyers.

The capability to control Standard SM-2 MR missiles is being backfitted, with DDG 995 to complete 3-88 and DDG 993 to begin conversion early 1988. The ships are planned to receive the NTU (New Threat Upgrade) modernization. Two Mk 74 missile fire-control systems (with SPG-55D radar tracker/illuminators) are carried, as well as the Mk 86 Mod. 5 gunfire-control system, which uses the SPQ-9A radar for surface fire and the SPG-60 for AA (the latter can also be used as a missile illuminator). The ASROC missiles are carried in the larger Mk 26 Mod. 1 missile-launch system's magazine, which is aft; the Mk 116 underwater battery fire-control system is carried. SLQ-25 Nixie towed anti-torpedo decoys are fitted; the ships were not intended to have the SQR-19A TACTASS towed passive sonar array, but it may be backfitted later. During post-commissioning yard periods, URN-25 TACAN replaced URN-20, Harpoon was added amidships, and two Vulcan/Phalanx Mk 15 CIWS were installed.

These ships were given better air-intake filter systems than the U.S. *Spruance* class has, in order to handle the dust and sand prevailing in Iranian operating areas. They also have greater air-conditioning capacity. These features make them invaluable for duties in the Indian Ocean. The Iranian Navy planned to type them as cruisers. Full-load displacement has grown by over 1,000 tons above the original plan, partly as a result of additional Kevlar and aluminum-alloy armor being added. DDG 993 was painted very pale gray for Persian Gulf service in 1987.

◆ **23 Charles F. Adams class (SCB 155 type)** (*Atlantic Fleet, †modified ships)

| | Bldr | Laid down | L | In serv. |
|---|---|---|---|---|
| DDG 2 Charles F. Adams* | Bath Iron Works | 16-6-58 | 8-9-59 | 10-9-60 |
| DDG 3 John King* | Bath Iron Works | 25-8-58 | 30-1-60 | 4-2-61 |
| DDG 4 Lawrence* | New York SB | 27-10-58 | 27-2-60 | 6-1-62 |
| DDG 5 Claude V. Ricketts (ex-*Biddle*)* | New York SB | 18-5-59 | 16-4-60 | 5-5-62 |
| DDG 6 Barney* | New York SB | 18-8-59 | 10-12-60 | 11-8-62 |
| DDG 7 Henry B. Wilson | Defoe SB | 28-2-58 | 22-4-59 | 17-12-60 |
| DDG 8 Lynde McCormick | Defoe SB | 4-4-58 | 9-9-60 | 3-6-61 |
| DDG 9 Towers | Todd, Seattle | 1-4-58 | 23-4-59 | 24-6-61 |
| DDG 10 Sampson* | Bath Iron Works | 2-3-59 | 9-9-60 | 24-6-61 |
| DDG 11 Sellers* | Bath Iron Works | 3-8-59 | 9-9-60 | 28-10-61 |
| DDG 12 Robison | Defoe SB | 23-4-59 | 27-4-60 | 9-12-61 |
| DDG 13 Hoel | Defoe SB | 1-6-59 | 4-8-60 | 16-6-62 |
| DDG 14 Buchanan | Todd, Seattle | 23-4-59 | 11-5-60 | 7-2-62 |
| DDG 15 Berkeley | New York SB | 1-6-60 | 29-7-61 | 15-12-62 |
| DDG 16 Joseph Strauss | New York SB | 27-12-60 | 9-12-61 | 20-4-63 |
| DDG 17 Conyngham* | New York SB | 1-5-61 | 19-5-62 | 13-7-63 |
| DDG 18 Semmes* | Avondale SY | 18-8-60 | 20-5-61 | 10-12-62 |
| DDG 19 Tattnall† | Avondale SY | 14-11-60 | 26-8-61 | 13-4-63 |
| DDG 20 Goldsborough† | Puget Sound SB & DD | 3-1-61 | 15-12-61 | 9-11-63 |
| DDG 21 Cochrane | Puget Sound SB & DD | 31-7-61 | 18-7-62 | 21-3-64 |
| DDG 22 Benjamin Stoddert† | Puget Sound SB & DD | 11-6-62 | 8-1-63 | 12-9-64 |
| DDG 23 Richard E. Byrd* | Todd, Seattle | 12-4-61 | 6-2-62 | 7-3-64 |
| DDG 24 Waddell | Todd, Seattle | 6-2-62 | 26-2-63 | 28-8-64 |

Authorized: 8 in FY 57, 5 in FY 58, 5 in FY 59, 3 in FY 60, and 2 in FY 61

**D:** 3,570 tons light (4,825 fl) **S:** 31.5 kts
**Dim:** 133.19 (128.0 wl) × 14.32 × 6.1 (8.3 over sonar)
**A:** 1/Mk 11 twin missile launcher or, beginning with DDG 15, 1/Mk 13 single launcher (4–6 Harpoon and 34–36 Standard SM-1 MR missiles)—2/127-mm Mk 42 DP (I × 2)—4/12.7 mm mg (I × 4)—1/Mk 116 ASROC ASW RL (VIII × 1; 8 or 12 missiles)—6/324-mm Mk 32 ASW TT (III × 2)
**Electron Equipt:** Radar: 1/SPS-10F, 1/SPS-40B/D, 1/SPS-52B, 2/SPG-51C, 1/SPG-53A (DDG 19, 20, 22: 1/LN-66, 1/SPS-10D, 1/SPS-40D, 1/SPS-52C, 1/SPQ-9A, 2/SPG-51D, 1/SPG-60)
Sonar: SQQ-23A or 1/SQS-23A (hull-mounted in DDG 2 to DDG 19: bow-mounted in DDG 20 to DDG 24)
EW: SLQ-32(V)2, SLQ-20, Mk 36 SRBOC (VI × 4)
TACAN: URN-25
**M:** 2 sets GT; 2 props; 70,000 hp
**Electric:** 2,200 kw (DDG 19, 20, 22; 3,000 kw)
**Boilers:** 4; 84 kg/cm², 520°C
**Fuel:** 900 tons
**Range:** 1,600/30; 6,000/14
**Man:** 20–24 officers, 319–330 men

Remarks: Sisters DDG 25, DDG 26, and DDG 27, built at the Defoe Shipbuilding Company, Bay City, Michigan, were ordered by Australia; DDG 28, DDG 29, and DDG 30 were built at Bath Iron Works for the West German Navy. DDG 2–9 authorized as DD 952–959; reclassified as DDG on 26-6-57. Ships with bow-mounted sonars have stem-mounted anchors. Many have been backfitted with an ASROC

**Goldsborough (DDG 20)**—modernized, with Mk 86 GFCS and other new electronics, but with no ASROC reload magazine G. Arra, 7-86

**Hoel (DDG 13)**—Mk 11 launcher, SPS-40 radar, SLQ-32(V)2, *and* WLR-1 EW LSPH W. McBride, R.A.N., 12-87

**Benjamin Stoddert (DDG 22)**—modernized unit, with Mk 86 GFCS G. Arra, 7-86

**Lawrence (DDG 4)**—early version, with twin Mk 11 launcher G. Arra, 9-86

GUIDED-MISSILE DESTROYERS *(continued)*

**Richard E. Byrd (DDG 23)**—with unidentified towed device at stern; note bow anchor, enlarged forward deckhouse at 02 level G. Arra, 1986

**Conyngham (DDG 17)**—with ASROC reload magazine to starboard G. Arra, 4-86

ASW missile reload magazine (with 4 missiles) beside the forward stack, to starboard. It was planned to give these ships a badly needed modernization, beginning with DDG 3 under FY 80. Costs rose enormously, and the program was cut to ten, permitting them to operate for another fifteen to twenty years. Congressional reluctance to spend $221 million per ship (then equal to the cost of a new FFG 7-class frigate) forced cancellation of even the reduced program. Congress was considering early decommissioning of several of this class as of 12-87.

The full modernization program was finally cut to only three ships: DDG 19, 20, and 22. DDG 19 underwent conversion 31-8-81 to 28-11-82 at Philadelphia; DDG 20 and 22 converted at Pearl Harbor 4-83 to 7-84 and 4-84 to 8-85. Changes include: replacement of the Mk 68 GFCS with Mk 86 Mod. 8 (with 1/SPQ-9A and 1/SPG-60 radar); SLQ-32(V)2, SLQ-20, and Mk 36 SRBOC replacing the original suite; the original missile f.c.s. replaced by Mk 74 Mod. 4, with the Weapons Direction System Mk 13 Mod. 4 replacing the original Mk 4; the addition of the SYS-1 data system with UYA-4 NTDS; upgrading the search radar suite to: 1/LN-66, 1/SPS-10D, 1/SPS-40D, and SPS-52C; improving the communications suite; and increasing the output of the four generator sets to 750 kw each. The ships can direct 3 Standard missiles simultaneously, using the SPG-60 and the two SPG-51D tracker/illuminators.

The non-conversion ships are also being upgraded during regular overhauls: SPS-40 has replaced the SPS-37 originally fitted to the first 13 ships; SLQ-32(V)2 replaced the WLR-1F and ULQ-6B suite, and Mk 36 SRBOC chaff launchers have been added; URN-25 lightweight TACAN is replacing SRN-6; the Mk 68 GFCS is receiving a digital computer system in DDG 4–6, 8–12, 15, 18, and 21; SPS-39A radars have been replaced by SPS-52B in nearly all, and other improvements are being made to the communications suites. Only four ships have the SQQ-23 sonar. DDG 9, 13, 15, 16, and 21 have *both* SLQ-32 and WLR-11 EW equipment.

In ships with Mk 11 launchers, 4 Harpoons are carried; in Mk 13-equipped ships, 6 are carried. Several carry one or more small navigational radars.

◆ **10 Coontz class (SCB 142/149 type)** (all Atlantic Fleet)

| | Bldr | Laid down | L | In serv. |
|---|---|---|---|---|
| DDG 37 Farragut (ex-DLG 6) | Bethlehem Steel (Quincy) | 3-6-57 | 18-7-58 | 12-10-60 |
| DDG 38 Luce (ex-DLG 7) | Bethlehem Steel (Quincy) | 1-10-57 | 11-12-58 | 20-5-61 |
| DDG 39 Macdonough (ex-DLG 8) | Bethlehem Steel (Quincy) | 15-4-58 | 9-7-59 | 4-11-61 |
| DDG 40 Coontz (ex-DLG 9) | Puget Sound NSY | 1-3-57 | 6-12-58 | 15-7-60 |
| DDG 41 King (ex-DLG 10) | Puget Sound NSY | 1-3-57 | 6-12-58 | 17-11-60 |
| DDG 42 Mahan (ex-DLG 11) | San Francisco NSY | 31-7-57 | 7-10-59 | 25-8-60 |
| DDG 43 Dahlgren (ex-DLG 12) | Philadelphia NSY | 1-3-58 | 16-3-60 | 8-4-61 |
| DDG 44 William V. Pratt (ex-DLG 13) | Philadelphia NSY | 1-3-58 | 16-3-60 | 4-11-61 |
| DDG 45 Dewey (ex-DLG 14) | Bath Iron Works | 10-8-57 | 30-11-58 | 7-12-59 |
| DDG 46 Preble (ex-DLG 15) | Bath Iron Works | 16-12-57 | 23-5-59 | 9-5-60 |

Authorized: DDG 37 to 42 in FY 57, DDG 43 to 46 in FY 57

**Mahan (DDG 42)**—New Threat Upgrade trials ship, with SPS-48E radar, SM-2 ER missiles, etc. G. Arra, 8-84

**Preble (DDG 46)** C.O., DDG 46, 1986

**King (DDG 41)** G. Gyssels, 9-87

**D:** 4,700 tons (5,960–6,150 fl) **S:** 34 kts **Dim:** 156.21 × 16.0 × 7.6 (max.)
**A:** 8/Harpoon SSM (IV × 2)—1/Mk 10 Mod. 0 twin launcher (II × 1, 40 Standard SM-1 ER or SM-2 ER missiles)—1/127-mm Mk 42 automatic DP—4/12.7-mm mg (I × 4)—1/ASROC ASW RL (VIII × 1)—6/324-mm ASW TT (III × 2)
**Electron Equipt:** Radar: 1/SPS-53 or Raytheon 2900, 1/SPS-10B, 1/SPS-49, 1/SPS-48C (48E in DDG 42), 2/SPG-55B, 1/SPG-53A
Sonar: SQS-23 PAIR
TACAN: SRN-6 (DDG 37, 41, 42; URN-25)
EW: SLQ-32(V)3, Mk 36 SRBOC (VI × 4)

## GUIDED-MISSILE DESTROYERS *(continued)*

**M:** DDG 37 to 39, DDG 45: 2 sets de Laval GT; others: 2 sets Allis-Chalmers GT; 2 props; 85,000 hp
**Boilers:** 4 Foster-Wheeler (Babcock & Wilcox in DDG 40 to DDG 46); 84 kg/cm$^2$, 520°C
**Electric:** 4,000 kw **Fuel:** 900 tons **Range:** 1,500/30; 6,000/14
**Man:** 21 officers, 356 men + flag group: 7 officers, 12 men

**King (DDG 41)** L. & L. Van Ginderen, 9-87

**Farragut (DDG 37)**—with ASROC reload facility G. Arra, 9-86

Remarks: These are the only *destroyers* with Standard SM-1 ER. Reclassified DDG from DLG 6 to DLG 15 in 1975. All modernized between 1970 and 1977 with Standard SM-1 ER missiles, NTDS (fitted earlier in DDG 40, DDG 41), SPS-48 radar, etc.; four 76.2-mm DP (II × 2) removed and Harpoon launchers installed in their former locations (firing forward to port, aft to starboard). DDG 37, the first to be modernized, received an ASROC reload magazine forward of the bridge and a taller after mast; to save weight and cost, the others were not similarly equipped. Missile fire control is Mk 76. A Mk 68 fire-control system is carried for the 127-mm gun. DDG 40 carried two Vulcan gatling guns (*not* Phalanx) in 1975. DDG 41 conducted Mk 15 CIWS Vulcan/Phalanx 20-mm gatling AA sea trials in 1973–74, before she was modernized; however, the ships will not receive two Vulcan/Phalanx, due to their age, space, and weight problems. Mk 111 Mod. 8 ASW fire-control systems and satellite-communications antenna systems in all units. The SQQ-23A PAIR sonar installed uses two separate domes. Helicopter landing pad on stern. The SPS-49 2-D air-search radar had replaced SPS-37 and the SLQ-32(V)3 EW system had replaced WLR-1, WLR-11, and ULQ-6B in all by 1982.

DDG 42 is trials ship for the NTU (New Threat Upgrade) refit, with the SPS-48E 3-D radar, SPS-49(V)5 2-D radar, the SYS-2 IADT (Integrated Automatic Target Detection and Tracking) computerized action information system, Weapons Direction System Mk 14, and Standard SM-2 ER Block 2 missiles. The full suite will not be backfitted to the others, but they are receiving SM-2 Block 2 capability, with DDG 37 and 43 equipped by 1987.

Note: Of the four *Decatur*-class guided-missile destroyers, *Parsons* (DDG 33, ex-DD 949), decommissioned 19-11-82, was stricken 15-5-84 and *John Paul Jones* (DDG 32, ex-DD 932), decommissioned 15-12-82, was stricken 30-4-86. Ex-*Decatur* (DDG 31, ex-DD 936), decommissioned 30-6-83 (and name officially deleted 24-3-86), and *Somers* (DDG 34, ex-DD 947), decommissioned 19-11-82, remained on the Navy List at the end of 1987, awaiting striking and cannibalization.

## DESTROYERS

◆ **31 Spruance class (SCN 275 type)** Bldr: Ingalls SB, Pascagoula, Miss. (Litton Industries) (*Atlantic Fleet; others in Pacific Fleet)

| | Laid down | L | In serv. |
|---|---|---|---|
| DD 963 Spruance* | 17-11-72 | 10-11-73 | 20-9-75 |
| DD 964 Paul F. Foster | 6-2-73 | 23-2-74 | 21-2-76 |
| DD 965 Kinkaid | 19-4-73 | 25-5-74 | 10-7-76 |
| DD 966 Hewitt | 23-7-73 | 24-8-74 | 25-9-76 |
| DD 967 Elliot | 15-10-73 | 19-12-74 | 22-1-76 |
| DD 968 Arthur W. Radford* | 14-1-74 | 1-3-75 | 16-4-77 |
| DD 969 Peterson* | 29-4-74 | 21-6-75 | 9-7-77 |
| DD 970 Caron* | 1-7-74 | 24-6-75 | 1-10-77 |
| DD 971 David R. Ray | 23-9-74 | 23-8-75 | 19-11-77 |
| DD 972 Oldendorf | 27-12-74 | 21-10-75 | 4-3-78 |
| DD 973 John Young | 17-2-75 | 7-2-76 | 20-5-78 |
| DD 974 Comte De Grasse* | 4-4-75 | 26-3-76 | 5-8-78 |
| DD 975 O'Brien | 9-5-75 | 8-7-76 | 3-12-77 |
| DD 976 Merrill | 16-6-75 | 1-9-76 | 11-3-78 |
| DD 977 Briscoe* | 21-7-75 | 15-12-76 | 3-6-78 |
| DD 978 Stump* | 25-8-75 | 29-1-77 | 19-8-78 |
| DD 979 Conolly* | 29-9-75 | 19-2-77 | 14-10-78 |
| DD 980 Moosbrugger* | 3-11-75 | 23-7-77 | 16-12-78 |
| DD 981 John Hancock* | 16-1-76 | 29-10-77 | 10-3-79 |
| DD 982 Nicholson* | 20-2-76 | 11-11-77 | 12-5-79 |
| DD 983 John Rodgers* | 12-8-76 | 25-2-78 | 14-7-79 |
| DD 984 Leftwich | 12-11-76 | 8-4-78 | 25-8-79 |
| DD 985 Cushing | 2-2-77 | 17-6-78 | 22-9-79 |
| DD 986 Harry W. Hill | 1-4-77 | 10-8-78 | 10-11-79 |
| DD 987 O'Bannon* | 24-6-77 | 25-9-78 | 1-12-79 |
| DD 988 Thorn* | 29-8-77 | 22-11-78 | 12-1-80 |
| DD 989 Deyo* | 14-10-77 | 20-1-79 | 22-3-80 |
| DD 990 Ingersoll | 5-12-77 | 10-3-79 | 12-4-80 |
| DD 991 Fife | 6-3-78 | 1-5-79 | 31-5-80 |
| DD 992 Fletcher | 24-4-78 | 16-6-79 | 12-7-80 |
| DD 997 Hayler* | 20-10-80 | 2-3-82 | 5-3-83 |

Authorized: D 963–965 in FY 70, DD 966–971 in FY 71, DD 972–978 in FY 72, DD 979–985 in FY 74, DD 986–992 in FY 75, DD 997 in FY 78

**Comte de Grasse (DD 974)**—Tomahawk box-launchers G. Arra, 6-86

**Elliot (DD 967)** L. & L. Van Ginderen, 6-87

**Deyo (DD 989)**—with SH-60F helicopter, Tomahawk box-launchers G. Davies/Maritime Photographic, 4-87

**DESTROYERS** *(continued)*

**Paul F. Foster (DD 964)**—with SH-2F on deck R.A.N., 9-86

**O'Brien (DD 975)**—with WLR-1 EW gear L. Akin, 10-86

**D:** 5,916 tons light (8,040 fl) **S:** 32.5 kts
**Dim:** 171.68 (o.a.) (161.25 pp) × 16.76 × 5.79 (8.84 over sonar)
**A:** DD 974, 976, 979, 983, 984, 989: 8/Tomahawk SSM (IV × 2)—DD 963, 964, 967, 968, 990, 991, 992, and ultimately all but box-launcher ships: 1/Mk 41 VLS group (61 Tomahawk and, when available, vertical-launch ASROC)—1/Mk 29 launcher (VIII × 1, 24 Sea Sparrow)—2/127-mm Mk 45 DP (I × 2)—2/20-mm Mk 15 CIWS (I × 2)—4/12.7-mm mg (I × 4)—1/Mk 112 ASROC ASW RL (VIII × 1, 24 missiles—removed from VLS ships)—6/324-mm Mk 32 Mod. 5 ASW TT (III × 2, 18 Mk 46 torpedoes)—1/SH-2F LAMPS-I or SH-60B LAMPS-III ASW helicopter
**Electron Equipt:** Radar: 1/SPS-53 or LN-66, 1/SPS-55, 1/SPS-40 B/C/D (DD 997: SPS-49), 1/SPQ-9A, 1/SPG-60, 1/Mk 91 1 Mk 23 TAS Mod. 0, 1/Mk 23 TAS
Sonar: 1/SQS-53A (DD 963, 965, 980, 990: SQQ-89 (V); DD 978: SQS-53C)
TACAN: URN-25
EW: SLQ-32(V)2, Mk 36 SRBOC chaff RL (VI × 4); DD 971, 975: WLR-1 also; DD 963, 969, 970, 972, 983, 985, 988, 989: SLQ-34 also

**M:** 4 G.E. LM-2500 gas turbines; 2 CP props; 86,000 hp (80,000 sust.)
**Electric:** 6,000 kw **Fuel:** 1,650 tons
**Range:** 3,300/30; 6,000/20; 8,000/17 **Man:** 19 officers, 315 men

**Hayler (DD 997)**—only DD 963 with SPS-49 radar; also note SQR-15 TASS array on fantail, to port of 127-mm gun L. & L. Van Ginderen, 10-87

**Briscoe (DD 977)** L. & L. Van Ginderen, 5-86

**John Young (DD 973)** G. Arra, 8-86

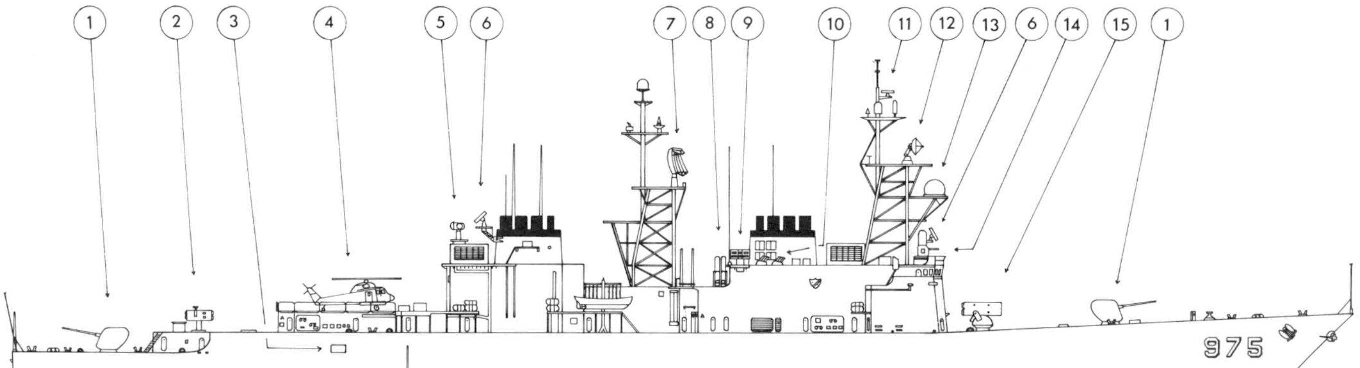


**O'Brien (DD 975)** Robert Dumas
1. 127-mm Mk 45 DP 2. octuple Mk 29 Sea Sparrow launcher 3. shutters over triple Mk 32 ASW TT 4. SH-2F LAMPS-I helicopter 5. radar director for Mk 91 Mod. 0 Sea Sparrow 6. OE-82 UHF SATCOMM antenna 7. SPS-40 air-search radar 8. quadruple Harpoon canister launcher mounting 9. SLQ-32(V)2 EW array 10. Mk 137 launchers for Mk 36 Super RBOC decoy system 11. SPS-55 surface-search radar 12. SPG-60 radar gun director 13. SPQ-9A radar gun director radome 14. Mk 15 CIWS 20-mm gatling AA 15. Mk 112 ASROC ASW missile launcher

**DESTROYERS** *(continued)*

**Leftwich (DD 984)**—with two quadruple Tomahawk ABL flanking the ASROC, but still lacking Mk 23 TAS on the after mast LSPH W. McBride, R.A.N., 12-87

**Spruance (DD 963)**—post-VLS conversion, with 61 vertical-launch missile cells forward R. Elias, Ingalls SB, 1987

**DESTROYERS** *(continued)*

REMARKS: Largest post–World War II U.S. destroyer program, and the first non-SAM destroyers ordered since the 1950s. DD 997 intended by Congress to be of an "air-capable" design, with enlarged hangar for 4 ASW helicopters, but costs rose to the point that the ship was ordered 29-9-79 as a nearly standard version of the class. The basic *Spruance* hull and propulsion plant have also served as the basis for the *Kidd* (DDG 993) and *Ticonderoga* (CG 47, ex-DDG 47) designs. DD 981 carries her name across the stern in script, duplicating the signature of the first signer of the Declaration of Independence. Displacements have risen considerably as equipment has been added; they were originally intended to displace under 7,000 tons full load. Limiting displacement is 8,800 tons.

The propulsion machinery is very quiet. Prairie-Masker bubbler systems are installed to enhance quietness. On each of the two shafts, two General Electric LM-2500 gas turbines are coupled to a reduction gear. Each shaft turns a controllable-pitch propeller (5.1 m in diameter, 168 rpm at 30 knots). Electric power is furnished by three Allison 501-K17 gas turbines, each powering one 2,000-kw alternator and mounted in separate compartments. Full speed can be reached from 12 knots in only 53 seconds. All propulsion machinery is under the control of a single operator in a central control station (CCS). 30 knots was considerably exceeded on trials. Endurance can be extended greatly by using one engine on one shaft for cruising. The plant has been very successful, except for the exhaust-gas auxiliary boilers. The mean time between overhauls for the LM-2500 gas turbines has been extended to 9,000 hours. DD 997 has the Litton automated engine control system prototype for the DDG 51 class.

The hull form was designed to minimize rolling and pitching; there are no fin stabilizers. Habitability received particular attention, living spaces being divided by bulkheads and intended for no more than six men each, with a recreational area and good sanitary facilities. The crew is small for a ship the size of the *Spruance* class, because all the machinery and systems have advanced automation. Originally operated with 232 enlisted but now have up to 315.

ASW is handled by a Mk 116 fire-control system. The Mk 32 torpedo tubes are standard triple trainable mountings, fired through doors in the ships' sides. The Mk 91 Mod. 0 fire-control system for Sea Sparrow uses a single radar director; RAM missiles will be installed, 4 each in two cells, in the early 1990s. The Mk 86 Mod. 3 fire-control system for the 127-mm guns uses the SPG-60 radar for AA and the SPQ-9A for surface fire. Magazines hold 1,200 rounds 127-mm. The ASROC reload missiles are stowed vertically, directly beneath the launcher. Kevlar plastic armor is to be added inside vital spaces, beginning with four ships under FY 81; the entire class was to be equipped by 1986. Nine ships (including DD 976 in FY 83, DD 974, 979, 983 in FY 84, DD 984, 985, 989 in FY 85) received 8 Tomahawk cruise missiles (IV × 2); box-launcher firing trials were carried out on DD 976 in 1-81 and later, while first operational installation was in DD 974 in late 1984. Under FY 86 DD 963 and 990 received Mk 41 Mod. 0 vertical-launch groups in place of the ASROC launcher; the 61-cell group will hold up to 45 Tomahawk and, later, 16 vertical-launch ASROC missiles. At some future date it may be possible to launch Standard SM-2 MR missiles as well, with the missiles to be controlled by an accompanying Aegis-equipped ship. DD 966, 967, and 968 received the vertical launch group in 1986–87. DD 977 has had the GFCS modified to Mk 86 Mod. 10 (with a UYK-7 computer in place of the Mk 152 computer, Mk 113 display consoles, new fuze-setters, etc.) to conduct trials with semi-active laser-guided projectiles. DD 976 was also used in 1981 for trials with the General Electric EX-83, 30-mm gatling gun system, which uses a GAU-8 heavy gun and was to carry out trials with an extended-range version of Sea Sparrow. Planned backfitting of the Mk 71, 203-mm gun in the forward position was canceled in 1978 when development of that excellent weapon was unfortunately canceled. DD 971 carries a prototype EX-41 RAM point-defense missile launcher on the starboard quarter and also has the prototype USC-38(V) EHF SATCOMM installation ("FLTSAT-7").

All ships of the class are scheduled to receive the Hughes Mk 23 TAS (Target Acquisition System), which uses a high-r.p.m. radar mounted on an aft-projecting platform on the mainmast to detect low-flying, high-speed missiles and aircraft. The SPS-55 surface-search radar has been moved to a new, higher platform on the foremast. DD 980 commenced trials fall 1985 with the integrated SQQ-89 sonar system, incorporating the SQS-53B active bow sonar and the SQR-19 TACTASS array. All will eventually have the SQQ-89(V)1 system, with SQS-53C sonar, SQR-19 towed array, SQQ-28 helicopter ASW data link, Mk 116 Mod. 5 ASW f.c.s. and SIMAS processing. DD 966 carried the SQR-15 TASS on a WestPac tour during 1985. All have the SLQ-25 Nixie torpedo decoy system. Early units were given the WLR-1 EW system as an interim installation until SLQ-32(V)2 was available; at least two ships (DD 971, 975) now have *both*. In 1987, it was announced that the EW suite would be upgraded to SLQ-32(V)3 in all. DD 974 carries the prototype SSQ-74 ICADS (Integrated Cover and Deception System). RAST deck-haul systems are being added (beginning with DD 989 in 4-85) to permit handling the SH-60B LAMPS-III ASW helicopter; SQQ-28 data link equipment is also being added. SH-60B helicopters will also carry Penguin antiship missiles. Half the class had received TAS by late 1985. DD 976 has WSN-5 SINS.

**John Rodgers (DD 983)**—with Tomahawk armored box-launchers
Pradignac & Leo, 1986

### ◆ 11 Forrest Sherman and Hull classes (SCB 240 type)

NOTE: All in reserve, except DD 946, in Atlantic Fleet (NRF)

**6 ASW refits (1967–71) (SCB 221 modernization)**

| | Bldr | Laid down | L | In serv. |
|---|---|---|---|---|
| DD 937 DAVIS | Bethlehem, Quincy | 1-2-55 | 28-3-56 | 28-2-57 |
| DD 940 MANLEY | Bath Iron Works | 10-2-55 | 12-4-56 | 1-2-57 |
| DD 941 DUPONT | Bath Iron Works | 11-5-55 | 8-9-56 | 1-7-57 |
| DD 943 BLANDY | Bethlehem, Quincy | 29-12-55 | 19-12-56 | 8-11-57 |
| DD 948 MORTON | Ingalls, Pascagoula | 4-3-57 | 23-5-58 | 26-5-59 |
| DD 950 RICHARD S. EDWARDS | Puget Sound SB & DD | 20-12-56 | 21-9-57 | 5-2-59 |

**5 unmodified:**

| | Bldr | Laid down | L | In serv. |
|---|---|---|---|---|
| DD 931 FORREST SHERMAN | Boston NSY | 27-10-53 | 5-2-55 | 9-11-55 |
| DD 942 BIGELOW | Bath Iron Works | 6-7-55 | 2-2-57 | 8-11-57 |
| DD 944 MULLINIX | Bethlehem, Quincy | 5-4-56 | 18-3-57 | 7-3-58 |
| DD 946 EDSON | Bath Iron Works | 3-12-56 | 1-1-58 | 7-11-58 |
| DD 951 TURNER JOY | Puget Sound SB & DD | 30-9-57 | 5-5-58 | 3-8-59 |

Authorized: DD 931 in FY 55, DD 937 in FY 54, DD 940–944 in FY 55, others in FY 56

**D:** 2,780–2,850 tons (4,050–4,090 fl) **S:** 32.5 kts
**Dim:** 127.51 (DD 945 to DD 951: 127.4) × 13.7 × 6.1
**A:** ASW refits: 2/127-mm Mk 42 DP (I × 2)—1/Mk 116 ASROC ASW RL (VIII × 1)—6/324-mm Mk 32 ASW TT (III × 2)
Others: 3/127-mm Mk 42 DP (I × 3)—6/324-mm Mk 32 ASW TT (III × 2)

**Edson (DD 946)**—the only active unit G. Arra, 3-87

**Mullinix (DD 944)**—unmodified, outboard the ASW conversion *Dupont* (DD 941) at Philadelphia NSY A.D. Baker, 8-84

**DESTROYERS** *(continued)*

**Electron Equipt:** Radar: 1/SPS-10, 1/SPS-40 (DD 937, DD 942, DD 946, DD 951: SPS-29), 1/SPG-53A, 1/Mk 35
Sonar: SQS-23D; ASW refits: SQS-35 VDS also
EW: WLR-1, WLR-3, ULQ-6
TACAN: DD 946, 951: SRN-6
**M:** 2 sets G.E. (DD 931, Westinghouse) GT; 2 props; 70,000 hp
**Boilers:** DD 937, DD 943, DD 944, DD 948: 4 Foster-Wheeler; others: 4 Babcock & Wilcox; 84 kg/cm², 520°C
**Fuel:** 750 tons **Range:** 4,500/20
**Man:** ASW refits: 19 officers, 287 men; others: 13 officers, 275 men

**Richard S. Edwards (DD 950)**—ASW version G. Gyssels, 9-81

**Turner Joy (DD 951)**—unmodified, while active L. & L. Van Ginderen, 1980

Remarks: All in reserve, except DD 946, assigned to the Naval Reserve Force for reserve training and as a training ship for the Officer Candidate School, Newport. Being retained as potential gunfire-support ships. From DD 937 on, the bows are somewhat higher than DD 931 and DD 933, while DD 945 and later were considered a separate class by reason of their different bow design. Four of the same series were rebuilt as DDGs. There are two radar gunfire-control systems, Mk 68 forward and Mk 56 aft (positions reversed in DD 931 and DD 944). ASW refits have Mk 114 ASW fire-control systems, the others Mk 105. All Hedgehog and depth charges removed in early 1970s. Originally had four 76.2-mm DP (II × 2), but they were removed from all by 1978. There is an ASROC reload magazine just forward of the launcher on the ASW conversion units. Unlikely to see further service, as they were not overhauled prior to decommissioning.

Decommissioned to reserve: DD 931, DD 942, and DD 943 on 5-11-82; DD 948 and DD 951 on 22-11-82; DD 950 on 15-12-82; DD 937 on 20-12-82; DD 940 and DD 941 on 11-3-83; and DD 944 on 11-8-83. Ex-*Barry* (DD 933), decommissioned 5-11-82 and struck 31-1-83, has been on exhibition at the Washington, D.C., Navy Yard since 2-2-84. Sister *Jonas Ingram* (DD 938), decommissioned 4-3-83 and stricken 15-6-83, was stripped of armament and radars for use as engineering equipment test hulk at Philadelphia NSY; *Hull* (DD 945), decommissioned 11-7-83, was stricken 15-10-83 for eventual use as a target.

## NAVAL RESERVE FORCE FRIGATES

Twenty-six *Oliver Hazard Perry-* and *Knox*-class frigates are programmed for the Naval Reserve Force, transferring from the active fleet between 1982 and 1990. In addition, three Reserve Force Squadrons of SH-2F LAMPS-I helicopters have been formed to supply aircraft for the ships. The dates of transfer to the Naval Reserve Force are:

| | | | |
|---|---|---|---|
| Miller (FF 1091) | 15-1-82 | Sides (FFG 14) | 16-8-86 |
| Lang (FF 1060) | 15-1-82 | Estocin (FFG 15) | 9-86 |
| Gray (FF 1054) | 15-7-82 | John A. Moore (FFG 19) | 30-1-87 |
| Valdez (FF 1096) | 14-8-82 | Antrim (FFG 20) | 30-1-87 |
| Blakeley (FF 1072) | 11-6-83 | Lewis B. Puller (FFG 23) | 13-6-87 |
| Patterson (FF 1061) | 15-6-83 | Roark (FF 1053) | 30-6-87 |
| Duncan (FFG 10) | 13-1-84 | Flatley (FFG 21) | 11-87 |
| Oliver Hazard Perry (FFG 7) | 31-5-84 | Tisdale (FFG 27) | 1-88 |
| Clifton Sprague (FFG 16) | 31-8-84 | Fahrion (FFG 22) | 1-88 |
| Wadsworth (FFG 9) | 30-6-85 | Copeland (FFG 25) | 1-88 |
| Clark (FFG 11) | 30-9-85 | Meyerkord (FF 1058) | 1-88 |
| George Philip (FFG 12) | 18-1-86 | Jack Williams (FFG 24) | 1990 |
| Samuel Eliot Morison (FFG 13) | 30-6-86 | Gallery (FFG 27) | 1990 |

## GUIDED-MISSILE FRIGATES

◆ **50 (+1) Oliver Hazard Perry class (SCN 207/2081 type)**
(*Atlantic Fleet; others in Pacific; †NRF)

| | Bldr | Laid down | L | In serv. |
|---|---|---|---|---|
| FFG 7 Oliver Hazard Perry*† | Bath Iron Works | 6-12-75 | 9-25-76 | 17-12-77 |
| FFG 8 McInerney* | Bath Iron Works | 16-1-78 | 4-11-78 | 15-12-79 |
| FFG 9 Wadsworth† | Todd, San Pedro | 13-7-77 | 29-7-78 | 28-2-80 |
| FFG 10 Duncan† | Todd, Seattle | 29-4-77 | 1-3-78 | 24-5-80 |
| FFG 11 Clark*† | Bath Iron Works | 17-7-78 | 24-3-79 | 17-5-80 |
| FFG 12 George Philip† | Todd, San Pedro | 14-12-77 | 16-12-78 | 15-11-80 |
| FFG 13 Samuel Eliot Morison*† | Bath Iron Works | 4-12-78 | 14-7-79 | 11-10-80 |
| FFG 14 Sides† | Todd, San Pedro | 7-8-78 | 19-5-79 | 30-5-81 |
| FFG 15 Estocin*† | Bath Iron Works | 2-4-79 | 3-11-79 | 10-1-81 |
| FFG 16 Clifton Sprague*† | Bath Iron Works | 30-7-79 | 16-2-80 | 21-3-81 |
| FFG 19 John A. Moore† | Todd, San Pedro | 19-12-78 | 20-10-79 | 14-11-81 |
| FFG 20 Antrim*† | Todd, Seattle | 21-6-78 | 27-3-79 | 26-9-81 |
| FFG 21 Flatley*† | Bath Iron Works | 13-11-79 | 15-5-80 | 20-6-81 |
| FFG 22 Fahrion*† | Todd, Seattle | 1-12-78 | 24-8-79 | 16-1-82 |
| FFG 23 Lewis B. Puller† | Todd, San Pedro | 23-5-79 | 15-3-80 | 17-4-82 |
| FFG 24 Jack Williams* | Bath Iron Works | 25-2-80 | 30-8-80 | 19-9-81 |
| FFG 25 Copeland† | Todd, San Pedro | 24-10-79 | 26-7-80 | 7-8-82 |
| FFG 26 Gallery* | Bath Iron Works | 17-5-80 | 20-12-80 | 5-12-81 |
| FFG 27 Mahlon S. Tisdale† | Todd, San Pedro | 19-3-80 | 7-2-81 | 13-11-82 |
| FFG 28 Boone* | Todd, Seattle | 27-3-79 | 16-1-80 | 15-5-82 |
| FFG 29 Stephen W. Groves* | Bath Iron Works | 16-9-80 | 4-4-81 | 17-4-82 |
| FFG 30 Reid | Todd, San Pedro | 8-10-80 | 27-6-81 | 19-2-83 |
| FFG 31 Stark* | Todd, Seattle | 24-8-79 | 30-5-80 | 23-10-82 |
| FFG 32 John L. Hall* | Bath Iron Works | 5-1-81 | 24-7-81 | 26-6-82 |
| FFG 33 Jarrett | Todd, San Pedro | 11-2-81 | 17-10-81 | 2-7-83 |
| FFG 34 Aubrey Fitch* | Bath Iron Works | 10-4-81 | 17-10-81 | 9-10-82 |
| FFG 36 Underwood* | Bath Iron Works | 3-8-81 | 6-2-82 | 29-1-83 |
| FFG 37 Crommelin | Todd, Seattle | 30-5-80 | 1-7-81 | 18-6-83 |
| FFG 38 Curts | Todd, San Pedro | 1-7-81 | 6-3-82 | 8-10-83 |
| FFG 39 Doyle* | Bath Iron Works | 16-11-81 | 22-5-82 | 21-5-83 |
| FFG 40 Halyburton* | Todd, Seattle | 26-9-80 | 13-10-81 | 7-1-84 |
| FFG 41 McClusky | Todd, San Pedro | 21-10-81 | 18-9-82 | 10-12-83 |
| FFG 42 Klakring* | Bath Iron Works | 19-2-82 | 18-9-82 | 20-8-83 |
| FFG 43 Thach | Todd, San Pedro | 6-2-82 | 18-12-82 | 17-3-84 |
| FFG 45 De Wert* | Bath Iron Works | 14-6-82 | 18-12-82 | 19-11-83 |
| FFG 46 Rentz | Todd, San Pedro | 18-9-82 | 16-7-83 | 30-6-84 |
| FFG 47 Nicholas* | Bath Iron Works | 27-9-82 | 23-4-83 | 10-3-84 |
| FFG 48 Vandegrift | Todd, Seattle | 13-10-81 | 15-10-82 | 24-11-84 |
| FFG 49 Robert G. Bradley* | Bath Iron Works | 28-12-82 | 13-8-83 | 11-8-84 |
| FFG 50 Taylor* | Bath Iron Works | 5-5-83 | 5-11-83 | 1-12-84 |
| FFG 51 Gary | Todd, San Pedro | 18-12-82 | 19-11-83 | 17-11-84 |
| FFG 52 Carr* | Todd, Seattle | 26-3-82 | 26-2-83 | 27-7-85 |
| FFG 53 Hawes* | Bath Iron Works | 22-8-83 | 17-2-84 | 9-2-85 |
| FFG 54 Ford | Todd, San Pedro | 16-7-83 | 23-6-84 | 29-6-85 |
| FFG 55 Elrod* | Bath Iron Works | 14-11-83 | 12-5-84 | 6-7-85 |
| FFG 56 Simpson* | Bath Iron Works | 27-2-84 | 31-8-84 | 9-11-85 |
| FFG 57 Reuben James | Todd, San Pedro | 10-9-83 | 8-2-85 | 22-3-86 |
| FFG 58 Samuel B. Roberts* | Bath Iron Works | 21-5-84 | 8-12-84 | 12-4-86 |
| FFG 59 Kauffman* | Bath Iron Works | 8-4-85 | 29-3-86 | 28-2-87 |
| FFG 60 Rodney M. Davis* | Todd, San Pedro | 8-2-85 | 11-1-86 | 9-5-87 |
| FFG 61 Ingraham | Todd, San Pedro | 30-3-87 | 6-88 | 6-89 |

Authorized: FFG 7 in FY 73, FFG 8–10 in FY 75, FFG 11–16 in FY 76, FFG 19–26 in FY 77, FFG 27–34 in FY 78, FFG 36–43 in FY 79, FFG 45–49 in FY 80, FFG 50–55 in FY 81, FFG 56–58 in FY 82, FFG 59, 60 in FY 83, FFG 61 in FY 84

**Antrim (FFG 20)**—NRF ship with CIWS L. & L. Van Ginderen, 6-87

**GUIDED-MISSILE FRIGATES** *(continued)*

**Samuel B. Roberts (FFG 58)** Bath Iron Wks./R. Farr, 4-86

**McCluskey (FFG 41)** L. & L. Van Ginderen, 1-87

**D:** 2,769 tons light (3,658 fl); FFG 8, 36–61: 3,010–3,210 tons light (3,900–4,100 fl)
**S:** 29 kts (30.6 trials)
**Dim:** 135.64; FFG 8, 36–58: 138.80 (125.9 wl) × 13.72 × 5.7 (8.6 max.)
**A:** 1/Mk 13 Mod. 4 launcher (4 Harpoon and 36 Standard SM-1 MR missiles)—1/76-mm Mk 75 DP—1/20-mm Mk 15 CIWS—6/324-mm ASW TT (III × 2)—1/SH-2F LAMPS-I (FFG 8, 36–61: 1 or 2/SH-60B LAMPS-III) ASW helicopters

**Electron Equipt:** Radar: 1/SPS-55, 1/SPS-49(V)2 (FFG 61: (V)5), 1/Mk 92 Mod. 4 (FFG 61: Mod. 6), 1/STIR (SPG-60 Mod.)
Sonar: 1/SQS-56 (FFG 38, 48, 55, 56, 60, others: SQQ-89(V)2 with SQR-19 TASS)—TACAN: URN-25
EW: SLQ-32(V)2, Mk 36 SRBOC chaff RL (VI × 2)
**M:** 2 G.E. LM-2500 gas turbines; 1 5.5-m diameter CP, 5-bladed prop; 41,000 hp (40,000 sust.)—2 drop-down propulsors; 720 hp
**Electric:** 3,000 kw **Fuel:** 587 tons + 64 tons helicopter fuel
**Range:** 4,200/20; 5,000/18
**Man:** 17–20 officers, 15 chief petty officers, 183–190 men

**Vandegrift (FFG 48)** G. Arra, 2-86

**Underwood (FFG 36)** L. & L. Van Ginderen, 7-87

**Curts (FFG 38)**—as class trials ship for SQQ-89(V)2 ASW suite; note deployment point for SQR-19 towed array to port of name at stern D. Moore, 4-86

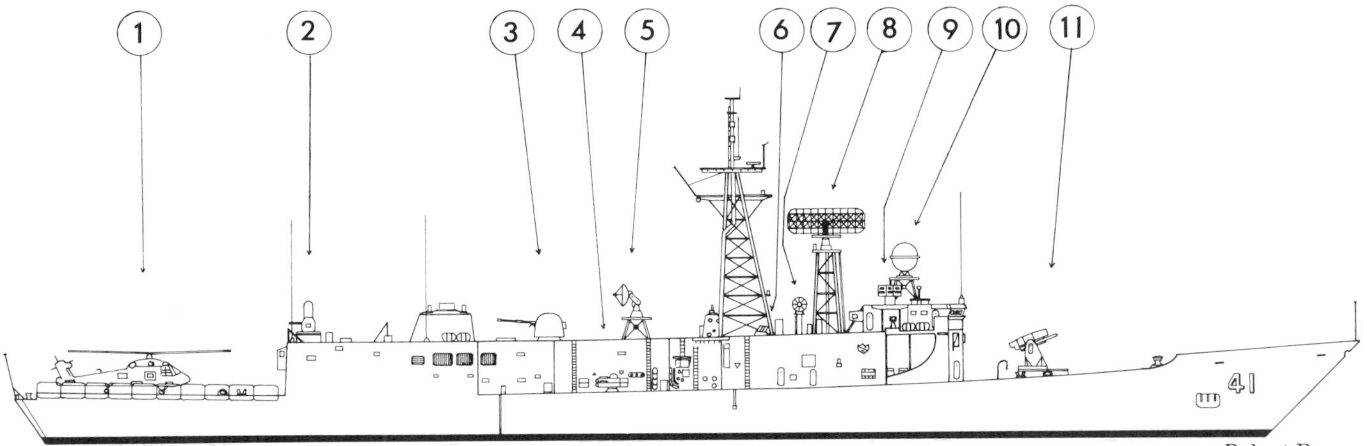


**McCluskey (FFG 41)** Robert Dumas
1. SH-2F LAMPS-I helicopter 2. Mk 15 CIWS 3. 76-mm Mk 75 DP 4. Mk 32 triple ASW TT 5. STIR f.c. radar 6. Mk 137 RL for Mk 36 SRBOC system 7. OE-82 UHF SATCOMM antennas 8. SPS-49 air-search radar 9. SLQ-32 EW array 10. Mk 92 f.c.s. radome 11. Mk 13 launcher

GUIDED-MISSILE FRIGATES *(continued)*

**Robert G. Bradley (FFG 49)**—Mk 15 CIWS, long stern, no RAST
G. Arra, 1984

**Rodney M. Davis (FFG 60)** F. Jentsch, 7-87

**Taylor (FFG 50)** L. & L. Van Ginderen, 6-87

REMARKS: Although these ships were intended to operate the LAMPS-III ASW helicopter, FFG 7–35 (less FFG 8) lack the equipment necessary to handle them and will retain LAMPS-I. Beginning with the FY 79 ships (FFG 36 and later), helicopter support equipment is aboard on completion: fin stabilizers, RAST (Recovery Assistance, Securing, and Traversing System, not fitted as completed until FFG 50), and other systems. The RAST system permits helicopter launch and recovery with the ship rolling through 28 degrees and pitching 5 degrees. The equipment was first installed in *McInerney* (FFG 8), which was reconstructed, completing 12-2-81 at Bath Iron Works, to act as LAMPS-III/SH-60B Seahawk helicopter trials ship; the stern was lengthened by 2.2 m (the extension being slightly lower than the flight deck, to accommodate mooring equipment) by changing the rake of the stern. FFG 26 conducted fin stabilizer trials in 1982. These ships were supposed to have received SQR-19 TACTASS equipment, beginning with FFG 36, and SQR-18A to be backfitted in earlier units; however, delays in development left *none* of the ships with the gear into 1985. FFG 38 began SQQ-89(V)2 integrated ASW suite trials with SQR-19 in 1986. The Navy now plans *all* ships in class to have SQR-19. Displacements have steadily increased, to the detriment of stability. FFG 59 was delivered at 4,100 tons full load, although the class was designed for 3,600 tons and only 39 tons growth margin! The Mk 15 CIWS (Close-In Weapon System) 20-mm Vulcan/Phalanx was to be backfitted into all by 1988.

FFG 38 and 27 have Mk 15 Mod. 1 CIWS. Two Mk 24 optical target designators (mounted in tubs atop the pilothouse) were not fitted to the ships as completed until FFG 27 and have been backfitted in the earlier ships. FFG 7 was originally numbered PF 109. Speed on one turbine is 25 knots; the auxiliary power system uses two retractable pods located well forward and can drive the ships at up to 6 knots. The Mk 92 Mod. 4 fire-control system controls missile and 76-mm gunfire; it uses a STIR (modified SPG-60) antenna and a U.S.-built version of the Hollandse Signaal Apparaaten WM-28 radar forward, and can track four separate targets. The Mk 92 system is programmed for three stages of improvement; the first, given trials in FFG 29 in 1983, was to be backfitted to all by 10-84 as the "Near-Term Improvement," along with Standard SM-1 MR Block 6 missiles. Phase two (Mk 92 CORT) began trials in FFG 15 in 5-86. Six additional CORT upgrades funded FY 88. The Mk 75 gun is a license-built version of the OTO Melara Compact. A Mk 13 weapons-direction system is fitted. The only ship-launched ASW ordnance is the Mk 46 torpedoes in the two triple torpedo tubes. These ships are particularly well protected against splinter and fragmentation damage, with 19-mm aluminum-alloy armor over magazine spaces, 16-mm steel over the main engine-control room, and 19-mm Kevlar plastic armor over vital electronics and command spaces.

Original complement was planned at 17 officers, 167 men, which was found to be too many officers but far too few enlisted men to run and maintain the ships. Therefore, FFG 19 and up are fitted with 30 additional enlisted bunks, with the others backfitted. NRF ships have about 76 Naval Reservists in their complements.

FFG 17, 18, 35, and 44 of this class were built by Todd, Seattle, for Australia, which is building two more in-country. Spain is building five. FFG 31 was hit 17-5-87 by two Exocet missiles (one did not explode) and survived; repairs underway until 8-88 at Ingalls, Pascagoula.

The Navy had hoped to phase out construction of this class with the FY 83 ships, FFG 59 and 60, but Congress authorized (but did not fully fund) FFG 61 in FY 84; FFG 61 was initially mandated to have the as yet unbuilt and untested Sperry Phase-III update to the Mk 92 f.c.s., adding four fixed phased-array radar panels (two facing the after quadrants on a mast platform and two covering the forward quadrants atop the bridge). Instead, the ship will have the "Phase-II" Mk 92 Mod. 6 f.c.s. with SYS-2(V)2 automatic tracking system and SPS-49(V)5 digital search radar; FFG 61 ordered 28-11-84.

Conversion to launch SM-2 MR SAMs canceled.

Already possessing a "surplus" of frigates, the U.S. Navy has no immediate plans for new construction in this category.

◆ **6 Brooke class (SCR 199B type)** (*Atlantic Fleet)

| | Bldr | Laid down | L | In serv. |
|---|---|---|---|---|
| FFG 1 BROOKE | Lockheed, Seattle | 10-12-62 | 19-7-63 | 12-3-66 |
| FFG 2 RAMSEY | Lockheed, Seattle | 4-2-63 | 15-10-63 | 3-6-67 |
| FFG 3 SCHOFIELD | Lockheed, Seattle | 15-4-63 | 7-12-63 | 11-5-68 |
| FFG 4 TALBOT* | Bath Iron Works | 4-5-64 | 6-1-66 | 2-4-67 |
| FFG 5 RICHARD L. PAGE* | Bath Iron Works | 4-1-65 | 4-4-66 | 5-8-67 |
| FFG 6 JULIUS A. FURER* | Bath Iron Works | 12-7-65 | 22-7-66 | 11-11-67 |

Authorized: FFG 1–3 in FY 62, FFG 4–6 in FY 63

**D:** 2,643 tons (3,600 fl) **S:** 27.2 kts
**Dim:** 126.33 (121.9 wl) × 13.47 × 7.9 (over sonar)
**A:** 1/Mk 22 launcher (I × 1, 16 Standard SM-1 MR missiles)—1/127-mm 38-cal. DP—1/Mk 116 ASROC ASW RL (VIII × 1; FFG 4–6: 8 reloads)—6/324-mm Mk 32 ASW TT (III × 2)—1/SH-2F LAMPS-I ASW helicopter
**Electron Equipt:** Radar: 1/LN-66, 1/SPS-10F, 1/SPS-52B, 1/SPG-51C, 1/Mk 35
Sonar: 1/SQS-26AX or BX—TACAN: SRN-15
EW: SLQ-32(V)2, Mk 36 SRBOC chaff RL (VI × 2)
**M:** 1 set Westinghouse (FFG 4 to FFG 6: G.E.) GT; 1 prop; 35,000 hp
**Boilers:** 2 Foster-Wheeler; 84 kg/cm², 510°C **Electric:** 2,000 kw
**Fuel:** 600 tons **Range:** 4,000/20 **Man:** 16 officers, 250 men

REMARKS: Differ from the *Garcia* class in having their aft 127-mm gun replaced by a missile launcher. Excellent sea-keeping qualities. Anti-rolling stabilizers. The hangar, which was enlarged for the SH-2 LAMPS-I helicopter, is telescoping, as

**Schofield (FFG 3)**—no ASROC reloads G. Arra, 2-87

**GUIDED-MISSILE FRIGATES** *(continued)*

on the *Knox* class. FFG 4 through FFG 6 have an ASROC reload magazine with 8 missiles. FFG 4 was used as an experimental ship for the weapons and systems of the *Oliver Hazard Perry* (FFG 7), but was restored to standard configuration. A Mk 56 Mod. 43 radar gunfire-control system is carried, while the missile system is Mk 74 Mod. 6; Mk 4 Mod. 2 weapons-direction system is fitted, as is the Mk 114 ASW control system. These ships are not scheduled to receive Harpoon SSM or the Mk 15 CIWS 20-mm gatling gun, but now have the SLQ-32(V)2 intercept array in place of the original WLR-1, WLR-3, and ULQ-6 suite. FFG 6 has SQS-26AXR sonar. Do not have SLQ-25 Nixie torpedo decoys. Three to reserve FY 88, three in FY 89.

**Richard L. Page (FFG 5)**—ASROC reload version G. Arra, 1987

**Ramsey (FFG 2)** L. & L. Van Ginderen, 3-87

**FRIGATES**

◆ **46 Knox class (SCN 199C, 200, and 200-65 types)**
(*Atlantic Fleet; †Naval Reserve Force)

| | Bldr | Laid down | L | In serv. |
|---|---|---|---|---|
| FF 1052 Knox | Todd, Seattle | 5-10-65 | 19-11-66 | 12-4-69 |
| FF 1053 Roark† | Todd, Seattle | 2-2-66 | 24-4-67 | 22-11-69 |
| FF 1054 Gray | Todd, Seattle | 19-11-66 | 3-10-67 | 4-4-70 |
| FF 1055 Hepburn† | Todd, San Pedro | 1-6-66 | 25-3-67 | 3-7-69 |
| FF 1056 Connole* | Avondale SY | 23-3-67 | 20-7-68 | 30-8-69 |
| FF 1057 Rathburne | Lockheed, Seattle | 8-1-68 | 2-5-69 | 16-5-70 |
| FF 1058 Meyerkord† | Todd, San Pedro | 1-9-66 | 15-7-67 | 28-11-69 |
| FF 1059 W. S. Sims* | Avondale SY | 10-4-67 | 4-1-69 | 3-1-70 |
| FF 1060 Lang† | Todd, San Pedro | 25-3-67 | 17-2-68 | 28-3-70 |
| FF 1061 Patterson*† | Avondale SY | 12-10-67 | 3-5-69 | 14-3-70 |
| FF 1062 Whipple | Todd, Seattle | 24-4-67 | 12-4-68 | 22-8-70 |
| FF 1063 Reasoner | Lockheed, Seattle | 6-1-69 | 1-8-70 | 31-1-71 |
| FF 1064 Lockwood | Todd, Seattle | 3-11-67 | 5-9-68 | 5-12-70 |
| FF 1065 Stein | Lockheed, Seattle | 1-6-70 | 19-12-70 | 8-1-72 |
| FF 1066 Marvin Shields | Todd, Seattle | 12-4-68 | 23-10-69 | 10-4-71 |
| FF 1067 Francis Hammond | Todd, San Pedro | 15-7-67 | 11-5-68 | 25-7-70 |
| FF 1068 Vreeland* | Avondale SY | 20-3-68 | 14-6-69 | 13-6-70 |
| FF 1069 Bagley | Lockheed, Seattle | 22-9-70 | 24-4-71 | 6-5-72 |
| FF 1070 Downes | Todd, Seattle | 5-9-68 | 13-12-69 | 28-8-71 |
| FF 1071 Badger | Todd, San Pedro | 17-2-68 | 7-12-68 | 1-12-70 |
| FF 1072 Blakely*† | Avondale SY | 3-6-68 | 23-8-69 | 18-7-70 |
| FF 1073 Robert E. Peary (ex-*Conolly*) | Lockheed, Seattle | 20-12-70 | 23-6-71 | 23-9-72 |
| FF 1074 Harold E. Holt | Todd, San Pedro | 11-5-68 | 3-5-69 | 26-3-71 |
| FF 1075 Trippe* | Avondale SY | 29-7-68 | 1-11-69 | 19-9-70 |
| FF 1076 Fanning | Todd, San Pedro | 7-12-68 | 24-1-70 | 23-7-71 |
| FF 1077 Ouellet | Avondale SY | 15-1-69 | 17-1-70 | 12-12-70 |
| FF 1078 Joseph Hewes* | Avondale SY | 15-5-69 | 7-3-70 | 24-4-71 |
| FF 1079 Bowen* | Avondale SY | 11-7-69 | 2-5-70 | 22-5-71 |
| FF 1080 Paul* | Avondale SY | 12-9-69 | 20-6-70 | 14-8-71 |
| FF 1081 Aylwin* | Avondale SY | 13-11-69 | 29-8-70 | 18-9-71 |
| FF 1082 Elmer Montgomery* | Avondale SY | 23-1-70 | 21-11-70 | 30-10-71 |
| FF 1083 Cook | Avondale SY | 20-3-70 | 23-1-71 | 18-12-71 |
| FF 1084 McCandless* | Avondale SY | 4-6-70 | 20-3-71 | 18-3-72 |
| FF 1085 Donald B. Beary | Avondale SY | 24-7-70 | 22-5-71 | 22-7-72 |
| FF 1086 Brewton | Avondale SY | 2-10-70 | 24-7-71 | 8-7-72 |
| FF 1087 Kirk | Avondale SY | 4-12-70 | 25-9-71 | 9-9-72 |
| FF 1088 Barbey | Avondale SY | 5-2-71 | 4-12-71 | 11-11-72 |
| FF 1089 Jesse L. Brown* | Avondale SY | 8-4-71 | 18-3-72 | 17-2-73 |
| FF 1090 Ainsworth* | Avondale SY | 11-6-71 | 15-4-72 | 31-3-73 |
| FF 1091 Miller*† | Avondale SY | 6-8-71 | 3-6-72 | 30-6-73 |
| FF 1092 Thomas C. Hart* | Avondale SY | 8-10-71 | 12-8-72 | 28-7-73 |
| FF 1093 Capodanno* | Avondale SY | 12-10-71 | 21-10-72 | 17-11-73 |
| FF 1094 Pharris* | Avondale SY | 11-2-72 | 16-12-72 | 26-1-74 |
| FF 1095 Truett* | Avondale SY | 27-4-72 | 3-2-73 | 1-6-74 |
| FF 1096 Valdez*† | Avondale SY | 30-6-72 | 24-3-73 | 27-7-74 |
| FF 1097 Moinester* | Avondale SY | 25-8-72 | 12-7-73 | 2-11-74 |

Authorized: 10 in FY 64, 16 in FY 65, 10 in FY 66, 10 in FY 67

**Downes (FF 1070)**—Mk 15 CIWS aft, WLR-1 and SLQ-32 EW gear G. Arra, 6-86

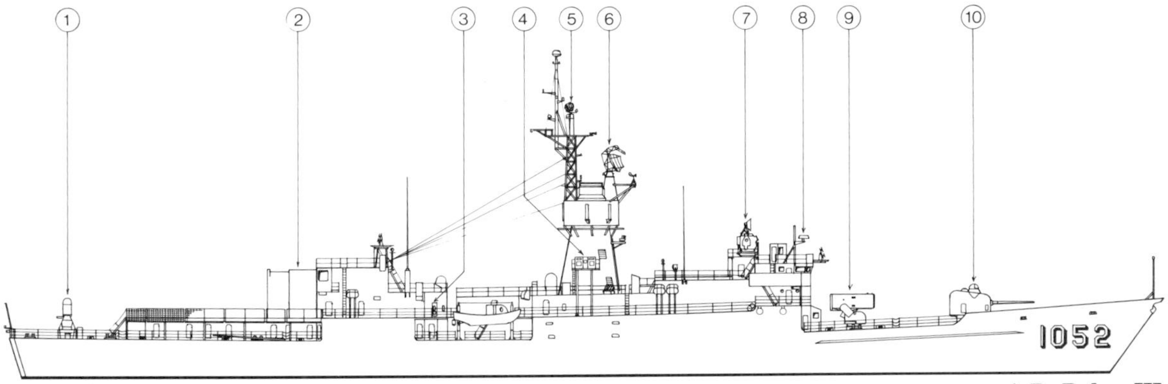


**Knox (FF 1052)** **A.D. Baker III**
1. Mk 15 CIWS (20-mm Vulcan/Phalanx) 2. telescoping hangar for LAMPS-I helicopter 3. Mk 32 ASW TT (II × 2) 4. SLQ-32(V)2 EW 5. SPS-10 surface-search radar 6. SPS-40 air-search radar 7. Mk 68 GFCS 8. navigational radar 9. Mk 116 ASROC ASW RL (VIII × 1) 10. 127-mm 54-cal. Mk 42 DP gun

**FRIGATES** *(continued)*

**Rathburne (FF 1057)**—no bow bulwarks L. & L. Van Ginderen, 6-86

**McCandless (FF 1084)**—with Mk 15 CIWS aft, bow bulwarks G. Arra, 8-86

**Badger (FF 1071)**—still with BPDMS Mk 25 SAM launcher aft G. Arra, 7-86

**D:** 3,075 tons light (4,260 fl) **S:** 27+ kts
**Dim:** 134.0 (126.5 wl) × 14.33 × 4.60 (7.55 over sonar)—see Remarks
**A:** 4/Harpoon SSM (using Mk 116 ASROC launcher system)—1/127-mm Mk 42 DP—1/20-mm Mk 15 CIWS—1/Mk 116 ASROC system (VIII × 1)—4/324-mm Mk 32 fixed ASW TT—1/SH-2F LAMPS-I ASW helicopter
**Electron Equipt:** Radar: 1/LN-66 or SPS-53, 1/SPS-10 or SPS-67, 1/SPS-40B, 1/SPG-53
Sonar: 1/SQS-26CX, SQS-35(V) VDS (except FF 1053 to FF 1055, FF 1057 to FF 1062, FF 1072, FF 1077), SQR-18A(V)1 TACTASS on VDS ships, SQR-18A(V)2 on others
EW: SLQ-32(V)1 or 32(V)2, Mk 36 SRBOC chaff RL (VI × 2)
TACAN: SRN-15
**M:** 1 set Westinghouse GT; 1 prop; 35,000 hp **Electric:** 3,000 kw
**Boilers:** 2 Babcock & Wilcox or Foster-Wheeler; 84 kg/cm$^2$, 510°C
**Fuel:** 750 tons **Range:** 4,300/20 **Man:** 17–20 officers, 255–265 men

**W. S. Sims (FF 1059)** L. & L. Van Ginderen, 9-86

**Meyercord (FF 1058)** G. Arra, 8-86

**Bagley (FF 1069)**—Mk 15 CIWS aft, hangar extended Pradignac & Leo, 10-86

**Moinester (FF 1097)**—long spray strake G. Gyssels, 10-86

**FRIGATES** *(continued)*

Remarks: An additional ten ships of the FY 68 program (FF 1098 to FF 1107) were canceled. Bow bulwarks and a spray strake are being added forward to reduce deck wetness, a problem in this class; the addition added 9.1 tons and extended the overall length from the original 133.59 m. By 1-1-85, all but 18 had been altered, and by 1-87 at least 5 of those had received the bulwarks. The spray strake was longer in the earlier conversions. The ASROC system has an automatic reloading magazine beneath the bridge; it is also used to stow Harpoon missiles, which are launched from the port pair of eight launcher cells (FF 1091 first to receive Harpoon, 1976). FF 1084 to FF 1097 never received a Mk 25 BPDMS (Basic Point Defense Missile System) launcher for Sea Sparrow. FF 1070 was used as NATO Sea Sparrow trials ship; she carried a Mk 29 NATO Sea Sparrow launcher and the two-director Mk 91 Mod. 1 fire-control system, later reduced to one director (Mk 91 Mod. 0 system); FF 1070 also carried the Hughes Mk 23 Mod. 0 TAS (Target Acquisition System) in place of the SPS-40 radar; these systems were removed during her 1983 refit. The ASW torpedo tubes are fixed, in the forward end of the hangar superstructure, aimed outboard at an angle of 45°. The Mk 25 BPDMS launcher for Sea Sparrow has been replaced by a 20-mm Mk 15 CIWS, Vulcan/Phalanx gatling AA system, beginning with FF 1087 in 1982. Beginning with twelve ships under FY 80, the SQS-35 towed VDS transducer body and hoist was modified to permit towing the SQR-18A TACTASS. Non-VDS ships to get SQR-18A(V)2 TACTASS; trials in FF 1077, 1983. FF 1088 had a controllable-pitch prop. All carry a Mk 68 gunfire-control system with SPG-53A, D, or F radar. SPS-67 radar will replace SPS-10 later in the 1980s; a few had their SPS-10 sets replaced by SPS-58. SLQ-32(V)1 (later upgraded to (V)2) replaced WLR-1C as the EW suite; some (FF 1064, 1067, 1070, 1087, etc.) have *both*. A few ships have navigational radars and all have two OE-82 satellite-communications antennas for the WSC-3 system. Ships with Sea Sparrow had a single Mk 115 missile fire-control system (Mk 71 director). All have Mk 114 ASW fire-control system. FF 1078 to FF 1097 have a TEAM (SM-5) computer system for the continual monitoring of the ship's electronic equipment. Anti-rolling fin stabilizers fitted in all. Prairie-Masker bubbler system fitted to hulls and propellers to reduce radiated noise. All are receiving the ASW TDS (ASW Tactical Data System) beginning FY 83. Seven serve the Naval Reserve Force, with one more to follow; see the names and dates on page 741.

**◆ 1 former experimental escort ship (SCB 198 type)**

| | Bldr | Laid down | L | In serv. |
|---|---|---|---|---|
| FF 1098 Glover (ex-AGFF 1, ex-AGDE 1, ex-AG 163) | Bath Iron Works | 29-7-63 | 17-4-65 | 13-11-65 |

Authorized: FY 61

**Glover (FF 1098)**—note Great Lakes rubbing strakes retained
L. & L. Van Ginderen, 6-87

**Glover (FF 1098)**—note sliding hatch for VDS deployment
Louagie & Plokker, 6-87

**D:** 2,700 tons (3,630 fl) **S:** 27 kts
**Dim:** 126.33 (121.9 wl) × 13.47 × 7.9 (over sonar)
**A:** 1/127-mm 38-cal. DP—1/Mk 116 ASROC ASW RL (VIII × 1)—6/324-mm Mk 32 ASW TT (III × 2)
**Electron Equipt:** Radar: 1/SPS-10, 1/SPS-40, 1/Mk 35
Sonar: SQS-26AXR, SQS-35 VDS
EW: WLR-1, ULQ-6, 2/Mk 33 RBOC chaff (VI × 2)
**M:** 1 set Westinghouse GT; 1 prop; 35,000 hp **Electric:** 2,000 kw
**Boilers:** 2 Foster-Wheeler; 83.4 kg/cm², 510°C **Man:** 15 officers, 218 men
**Range:** 4,000/20 **Fuel:** 600 tons

Remarks: Redesignated from AGFF on 1-10-79 because she now conducts operational cruises. "FF 1098" was previously used for a later-canceled *Knox*-class frigate. Basically a *Garcia*-class ship with identical hull form, but with a pump-jet propeller and the after 127-mm gun omitted to provide laboratories and accommodations for civilian technicians (no longer carried). Extreme stern raised during installations of SQS-35 VDS. No ASROC reload magazine. In Atlantic Fleet.

**◆ 10 Garcia class (SCB 199A type)** (*Atlantic Fleet)

| | Bldr | Laid down | L | In serv. |
|---|---|---|---|---|
| FF 1040 Garcia* | Bethlehem, San Francisco | 16-10-62 | 31-10-63 | 21-12-64 |
| FF 1041 Bradley | Bethlehem, San Francisco | 17-1-63 | 26-3-64 | 15-5-65 |
| FF 1043 Edward McDonnell* | Avondale SY | 1-4-63 | 15-2-64 | 15-2-65 |
| FF 1044 Brumby* | Avondale SY | 1-8-63 | 6-6-64 | 5-8-65 |
| FF 1045 Davidson | Avondale SY | 20-9-63 | 3-10-64 | 7-12-65 |
| FF 1047 Voge* | Defoe SB, Michigan | 21-11-63 | 4-2-65 | 25-11-66 |
| FF 1048 Sample | Lockheed, Seattle | 19-7-63 | 28-4-64 | 23-3-68 |
| FF 1049 Koelsh* | Defoe SB, Michigan | 19-2-64 | 8-6-65 | 10-6-67 |
| FF 1050 Albert David | Lockheed, Seattle | 29-4-64 | 19-12-64 | 19-10-68 |
| FF 1051 O'Callahan | Defoe SB, Michigan | 19-2-64 | 20-10-65 | 13-7-68 |

Authorized: 2 in FY 61, 3 in FY 62, 5 in FY 63

**D:** 2,624 tons (3,400–3,560 fl) **S:** 27 kts
**Dim:** 126.33 (121.9 wl) × 13.47 × 7.9 (over sonar)
**A:** 2/127-mm 38-cal. DP (I × 2)—1/ASROC ASW RL (VIII × 1; 8 reloads—see Remarks)—6/324-mm Mk 32 ASW TT (III × 2)—1/SH-2F LAMPS-I ASW helicopter (except FF 1040, 1043, 1048, 1050)
**Electron Equipt:** Radar: 1/LN-66, 1/SPS-10, 1/SPS-40, 1/Mk 35
Sonar: FF 1040–1045: SQS-26BX; others: SQS-26AXR; FF 1040, 1043 also: SQR-15 TACTASS
EW: WLR-1, WLR-3, ULQ-6, 2/Mk 33 RBOC (VI × 2)
TACAN: SRN-15 in LAMPS-I ships
**M:** 1 set G.E. GT; 1 prop; 35,000 **Electric:** 2,000 kw
**Boilers:** 2 Foster-Wheeler; 83.4 kg/cm², 510°C **Range:** 4,000/20
**Fuel:** 600 tons **Man:** 18 officers, 250 men

**Davidson (FF 1045)**—no ASROC reload magazine G. Arra, 7-86

**Sample (FF 1048)**—no helicopter hangar or towed array G. Arra, 7-86

**FRIGATES** *(continued)*

**Albert David (FF 1050)**—ASROC reloads, but no LAMPS capability or SRN-15 TACAN G. Arra, 6-86

**O'Callahan (FF 1051)**—ASROC reload and LAMPS-I hangar G. Arra, 8-86

Remarks: Anti-rolling stabilizers fitted. FF 1047 and FF 1049 have a special ASW NTDS. The boilers are vertical and have turbopressurized combustion. Hangar enlarged 14.6 × 5.4 m for SH-2F LAMPS-I helicopter, 1972–75, except for FF 1048 and FF 1050, which carried the SQR-15 towed passive linear hydrophone array on their sterns until 1982; FF 1040 and 1043, which have the enlarged hangar, carry SQR-15 *instead* of helicopters. Gunfire control is by a Mk 56 radar director, and the Mk 114 ASW fire-control system is installed. FF 1047 and later have an ASROC reload magazine beneath the bridge. Twin Mk 25 torpedo tubes at the stern were removed from the ships that had them. FF 1041 carried Mk 25 Sea Sparrow launcher in 1967–68 for trials. Although these are relatively recent ships, there are no plans to modernize their obsolescent gun systems or to add Harpoon or modern EW gear. Five to reserve FY 88, five in FY 89.

◆ **2 Bronstein class (SCB 199 type)** (*Atlantic Fleet)

| | Bldr | Laid down | L | In serv. |
|---|---|---|---|---|
| FF 1037 Bronstein | Avondale SY | 16-5-61 | 31-5-62 | 16-6-63 |
| FF 1038 McCloy* | Avondale SY | 15-9-61 | 9-6-62 | 21-10-63 |

**McCloy (FF 1038)** L. & L. Van Ginderen, 6-87

**Bronstein (FF 1037)** L. & L. Van Ginderen, 3-84

**D:** 2,360 tons (2,650 fl) **S:** 24 kts **Dim:** 113.23 (106.68 wl) × 12.34 × 7.0
**A:** 2/76.2-mm Mk 33 (II × 1)—1/Mk 116 ASROC ASW RL (VIII × 1)—6/324-mm Mk 32 ASW TT (III × 2)
**Electron Equipt:** Radar: 1/LN-66, 1/SPS-10, 1/SPS-40, 1/Mk 35
Sonar: 1/SQS-26AXR, 1/SQR-15 TASS (not in FF 1037)
EW: WLR-1, WLR-3, ULQ-6, 2/Mk 33 RBOC RL (VI × 2)
**M:** 1 set de Laval GT; 1 prop; 20,000 hp **Fuel:** 480 tons
**Boilers:** 2 Foster-Wheeler; 42.2 kg/cm$^2$, 440°C **Man:** 13 officers, 197 men

Remarks: Only remaining U.S. frigates with 76.2-mm guns, controlled by a Mk 56 radar director. Single 76.2-mm aft replaced by SQR-15 TASS towed passive hydrophone array sonar. Have Mk 114 Mod. 7 ASW fire-control system. No ASROC reload magazine. TASS towed array gear removed from FF 1037 circa 1981; port boat and davits removed from both.

## GUIDED-MISSILE PATROL BOATS

Note: In December of 1987, the Secretary of the Navy canceled the proposed PCM program for five missile patrol boats for Caribbean service. The first would have been ordered under FY 90 and the other four under FY 92. Still listed as a program, FY 88.

◆ **6 PHM (Patrol Hydrofoil Missile) class (SCB 602 type)** (all Atlantic Fleet)

| | Bldr | Laid down | L | In serv. |
|---|---|---|---|---|
| PHM 1 Pegasus (ex-*Delphinus*) | Boeing, Seattle | 10-5-73 | 9-11-74 | 9-7-77 |
| PHM 2 Hercules | Boeing, Seattle | 12-9-80 | 13-4-82 | 12-3-83 |
| PHM 3 Taurus | Boeing, Seattle | 30-1-79 | 8-5-81 | 7-10-81 |
| PHM 4 Aquila | Boeing, Seattle | 10-7-79 | 16-9-81 | 19-12-81 |
| PHM 5 Aries | Boeing, Seattle | 7-1-80 | 11-81 | 18-9-82 |
| PHM 6 Gemini | Boeing, Seattle | 13-5-80 | 17-2-82 | 12-3-83 |

Authorized: 2 in FY 73, 4 in FY 75

**D:** 198 tons light (241 fl, except PHM 1: 235 fl) **S:** 50 kts (11 on diesel)
**Dim:** 40.5 (44.7 with foils retracted; 36.00 wl) × 8.6 (14.5 over aft foils) × 7.1 (1.9 with foils retracted)/2.7 foilborne
**A:** 8 Harpoon SSM (IV × 2)—1/76-mm Mk 75 DP (OTO Melara Compact)
**Electron Equipt:** Radar: 1/SPS-64(V)1, 1/Mk 92 Mod. 1 fire-control system
EW: SLQ-650, Mk 34 RBOC chaff RL (VI × 2) (PHM 1: ALR-66, 2 Rospatch LADS RL (IX × 2)

**Aquila (PHM 4)**—navigational radar now on mast U.S. Navy, 9-83

**GUIDED-MISSILE PATROL BOATS** *(continued)*

**M:** CODOG: 1 G.E. LM-2500 PB 102 gas turbine; 1 Aerojet AJW-18800-1 water jet; 16,000–19,416 hp; 2 MTU 8V331 TC81, 815-hp diesels; 2 Aerojet AJW-800-1 water jets; 1,340 hp
**Electric:** 405 kVA **Range:** 600/40; 1,200+/11
**Fuel:** 50 tons **Man:** 4 officers, 17 men

**Pegasus (PHM 1)**—with foils raised G. Arra, 6-86

**Pegasus (PHM 1)** G. Arra, 6-86

REMARKS: PHM 2 originally authorized under FY 73 using R & D funds and laid down on 30-5-74; her construction was suspended in 8-75, when 40.9 percent complete, but a new hull was laid down 12-9-80 with FY 76 funds. Originally projected as a class of thirty, also to be built by or for other NATO nations, but the additional cost over that of conventional missile craft with similar capabilities was prohibitive, and the U.S. Navy's interest in the type waned. PHM 1 began her protracted trials on 2-25-75. PHM 2 through PHM 6 were canceled on 6-4-77, then reinstated on 14-8-77 at the insistence of Congress, the contract going to Boeing on 20-10-77. PHM 1's gas turbine develops 16,000 hp; on the others 19,416 hp is possible, with the water jet pumping some 341,000 liters/min. at full speed; 55 kts was achieved on trials. Two AIResearch ME 831-800 gas turbines power the two generators. The Mk 92 Mod. 1 fire-control system is an Americanized version of the Hollandse Signaal Apparaaten WM-28 system. PHM 1 has the earlier Mk 94 Mod. 1 variant. The SPS-63, an Americanized version of the Italian SMA 3TM 20-H radar, was replaced by Raytheon SPS-64(V)1 in 1985–86, when the radar antenna was moved onto a mast platform. It was planned at one time to carry eight reload Harpoons, for a total of sixteen. Magazine capacity 400 rds 76-mm. PHM 6 didn't receive her armament or Mk 92 f.c.s. until 9-83. These craft are extraordinarily steady weapons platforms. All have the SSQ-87(V) collision-avoidance and tracking system. Based at Key West, Florida, as PHM Squadron 2; they are supported by 7 officers and 181 men, working from 73 mobile vans.

NOTE: Approval to strike the last 2 of 17 *Asheville*-class gunboats, *Gallup* (PG 85) and *Canon* (PG 90), was granted 12-84; both had been stricken 31-1-77 but restored to the Navy List 17-7-81 and are stored at Bremerton. Sisters *Beacon* (PG 99) and *Green Bay* (PG 101), stricken 1-4-77, remain in storage at Little Creek, Va., for possible foreign sale.

## PATROL CRAFT

◆ **3 Sea Spectre PB Mk-IV Class** Bldr: Atlantic Marine, Ft. George Island, Fla.

| | Laid down | L | In serv. |
|---|---|---|---|
| 68PB851 | 24-12-84 | 23-9-85 | 2-1-86 |
| 68PB852 | 25-3-85 | 11-11-85 | 2-1-86 |
| 68PB853 | 17-6-85 | 31-12-85 | 15-2-86 |

**68PB851**—on trials, with 20-mm fore and aft U.S. Navy, 1-86

**68PB851** U.S. Navy, 1-86

**D:** 42.25 tons (fl) **S:** 30 kts **Dim:** 20.85 × 5.50 × 1.07 (hull)
**A:** 1/25-mm Mk 88—1/20-mm AA—1/81-mm mortar/12.7-mm mg—2/40-mm Mk 19 grenade launchers
**Electron Equipt:** Radar: 1/. . . navigational
**M:** 3 G.M. 12V71 TI diesels; 3 props; 1,950 hp
**Range:** . . ./. . . **Man:** 5 tot.

REMARKS: Approved FY 85 for Canal Zone service. Essentially a lengthened version of the PB Mk-III below. Aluminum construction. A 25-mm Bushmaster gun replaced one 20-mm gun in 1987.

◆ **17 Sea Spectre PB Mk-III class** Bldr: Peterson Bldrs. (In serv. 1975–79)
65PB731–738 65PB751–755 65PB775–778

**D:** 28 tons (36.7 fl) **S:** 30 kts (now less) **Dim:** 19.78 × 5.50 × 1.80 (props)
**A:** 1/40-mm AA or 1–2/25-mm Mk 88 AA or 20-mm (I × 1 or 2)—2/12.7-mm mg (I × 2)—2/7.62-mm mg (I × 2)—1/81- or 60-mm mortar (see Remarks)
**Electron Equipt:** Radar: 1 or 2/. . . nav.
**M:** 3 G.M. 8V71 TI diesels; 3 props; 1,800 hp
**Endurance:** 3 days **Range:** 450/26; 2,000/. . . **Man:** 1 officer, 8 men

**PB Mk-III class (65PB751)** G. Arra, 5-86

PATROL CRAFT *(continued)*

PB Mk-III capturing Iranian minelayer, 22-9-87, with 40-mm AA fwd (no reload drum), 1/20-mm AA aft, 1/12.7-mm mg, 2/7.62-mm mg, 1/40-mm Mk 19 grenade launcher, 1/60-mm mortar, and miscellaneous small arms; note two radar sets, smoke generator aft U.S. D.O.D.

REMARKS: Thirteen operate with active fleet Special Boat Units, 4 with Naval Reservists. Winner in competition with Mk-I. Sisters were built for Iran and the Philippines. One was used as trials craft for Norwegian Penguin Mk II missiles in 1981–82, with four missiles mounted on the stern. The 40-mm weapon is in a special stabilized Mk 3 Mod. 9 mounting with a removable reload magazine. Armament is interchangeable. Additional personnel carried where full suite is installed. Six sent to Persian Gulf, 9-87. Eight built under FY 73, 10 under FY 75, 3 under FY 77; several since transferred abroad. Have trouble making speed.

◆ **2 PB Mk-I class** Bldr: Sewart Seacraft, Berwick, La. (In serv. 1972)

**PB Mk-I class**—disarmed as a pilot boat G. Arra, 1985

**D:** 27 tons (36.3 fl) **S:** 20 kts **Dim:** 19.78 × 5.25 × 1.37
**A:** provision for 2/12.7-mm mg (II × 1)
**M:** 2 G.M. 12V71 diesels; 2 props; 1,200 hp
**Range:** 30/26 **Man:** 2 officers, 6 men

REMARKS: Originally carried 2/20-mm AA (I × 2), 4/12.7-mm mg, 1/81-mm mortar/12.7-mm mg combination.

◆ **2 PCF Mk-II class** Bldr: Swiftships, Morgan City, La. (In serv. 1967–68)

◆ **3 PCF Mk-I** Bldr: Swiftships (In serv. 7-65 to 7-66)

**PCF Mk-I class (PCF 67)**

**D:** 17.5 tons (22.5 fl) **S:** 22 kts **Dim:** 15.3 (Mk-II: 15.66) × 4.55 × 1.1
**A:** 1/81-mm mortar/12.7-mm mg combination—2/12.7-mm mg (II × 1)
**Electron Equipt:** Radar: 1/Raytheon 1500B or Decca 202 **Range:** 400/22
**Man:** 6 tot. **M:** 2 G.M. 12V71 TI diesels; 2 props; 850 hp **Electric:** 6 kw

REMARKS: Survivors of 104 Mk-I and 14 Mk-II built for the U.S. Navy. Aluminum alloy construction. Used for Naval Reserve training by Special Boat Unit SBU 22 at New Orleans. Mk-II added a low forecastle.

RIVERINE WARFARE CRAFT

◆ **32 PBR (Patrol Boat, Riverine) Mk-II** Bldr: Uniflite, Bellingham, Wash. (In serv. 12-81 to 8-83)

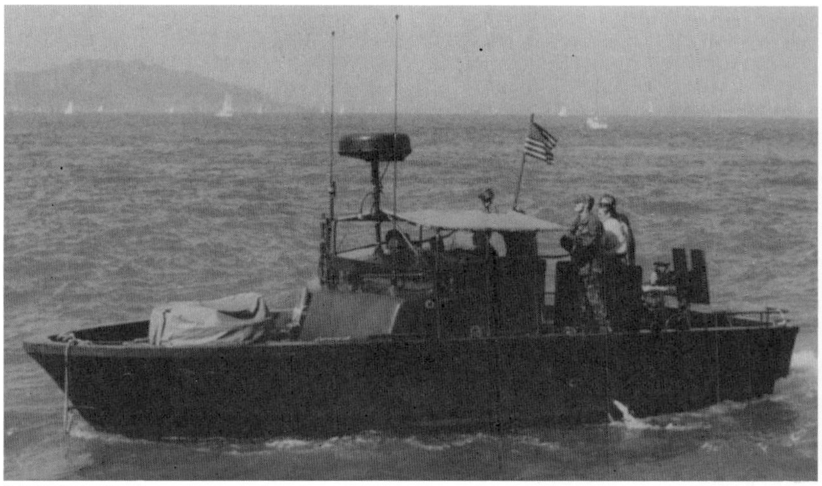

**PBR Mk-II class** G. Arra, 1986

**D:** 8.9 tons (fl) **S:** 24 kts **Dim:** 9.73 × 3.53 × 0.81
**A:** 3/12.7-mm mg (II × 1, I × 1)—1/60-mm mortar
**Electron Equipt:** Radar: 1/Raytheon 1900
**M:** 2 G.M. 6V53N diesels; 2 Jacuzzi water jets; 430 hp
**Range:** 150/23 **Man:** 4 tot.

REMARKS: Fiberglass hull, plastic armor. Used for Naval Reserve training by Special Boat Units. Some recent export versions of this class have G.M. 6V53T engines, for 550 hp and speeds of 30 kts. Three delivered 1982 had G.M. 4-53N diesels.

HARBOR PATROL CRAFT

◆ **0 (+50) Harbor Security Boats** Bldr: Peterson Bldrs., Sturgeon Bay, Wisc.

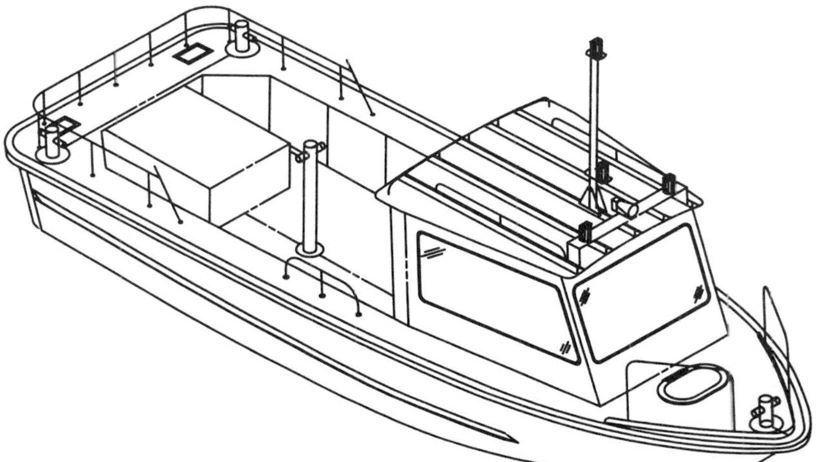

**Harbor Security Boat** Peterson, 7-87

**D:** . . . **S:** . . . **Dim:** 7.32 × . . . × . . .
**A:** 1/12.7-mm or 7.62-mm mg **Electron Equipt:** Radar: none
**M:** 2 diesel outdrives; . . . hp **Man:** 3 tot.

REMARKS: Ordered 29-7-87 for delivery during 1988–89. Aluminum construction. No fixed armament, but post-mountings will be provided fore and aft. Intended to counter terrorist threat; for use in sheltered waters.

◆ **4 Raider-class Port Security Boats** Bldr: NAPCO International, North Miami, Fla. (In serv. 1986)

**D:** . . . **S:** 40 kts **Dim:** 6.0 × . . . × . . .
**A:** 2/12.7-mm M2 mg (I × 2)
**Electron Equipt:** Radar: none **Man:** 3 tot.
**M:** 2 gasoline outboards; 280 hp **Range:** 200/. . .

**HARBOR PATROL CRAFT** *(continued)*

Remarks: GRP construction. Acquired for counter-terrorist work.

Note: The Navy has also purchased a number of MonArk, Monticello, Arkansas-built 33-ft (10.05-m) utility boats for range safety and patrol duties, including 33 UB 841 through 33 UB 846, delivered 14-10-86 to 6-87 for use at Point Mugu. They are powered by twin Volvo Penta AQAD outdrive diesels. Also from MonArk, delivered 28-1-87, were two 30-ft (9.14-m) patrol craft.

## MINE WARFARE SHIPS

Note: In addition to the ships and craft listed below, there are also 22 RH-53D mine-sweeping helicopters in service, and 16 Marine Corps CH-53D that can be used to tow sweep gear; 56 MH-53E minesweeping helicopters are programmed. Except for MSO 443, MSO 448, MSO 490, and MCM 1, all minesweepers are assigned to the Naval Reserve Force.

◆ **0 (+1 + 16) coastal minehunters**

| | Bldr | Laid down | L | In serv. |
|---|---|---|---|---|
| MHC 51 N . . . | Intermarine/Hercules, Savannah, Ga. | 5-88 | . . . | 4-91 |
| MHC 52 N . . . | . . . | . . . | . . . | . . . |
| MHC 53 N . . . | . . . | . . . | . . . | . . . |
| MHC 54 N . . . | . . . | . . . | . . . | . . . |

Authorized: MHC 51 under FY 86 (see Remarks); MHC 52–53 in FY 89; plan 3/year FY 90, 91, 4 in FY 92.

**MHC 51** Intermarine, 1987

**D:** 785 tons (fl) **S:** 14 kts **Dim:** 57.30 × 10.97 × 2.80
**A:** 1 or 2/12.7-mm mg (I × 1 or 2)
**Electron Equipt:** Radar: 1/SPS-64(V)9
Sonar: SQQ-32
**M:** 2 Isotta-Fraschini ID 36 SS 6V-AM diesels; Voith-Schneider vertical cycloidal props; 1,160 hp—2/180-hp hydraulic motors for quiet running—1/180-hp bow-thruster
**Range:** . . ./. . . **Electric:** . . . **Man:** 4 officers, 41 men
**Endurance:** 5 days

Remarks: Ordered 20-2-87 as a replacement for the abortive *Cardinal* (MSH 1)-class air-cushion vehicle minehunter, using $5 million in remaining FY 84 funds plus FY 86 funds originally authorized for the MSH 1 program. First unit building at leased former Sayler Marine boatyard at Savannah, as a cooperative venture between Italy's Intermarine and the U.S. Hercules Powder Co., of Wilmington, Delaware. Congress has stipulated that a second yard must be brought into the program for the FY 89 and later ships.

GRP construction, with the design based on the Italian Navy *Lerici*-class hull. In addition to minehunting capability (using the Honeywell SLQ-48 Mine Neutralization System remote-controlled submersible), the ships will also carry mechanical minesweeping equipment. After a one-year shakedown with regular Navy crews, each ship will be passed to the Naval Reserve Force.

Note: The *Cardinal* (MSH 1)-class air-cushion minehunter program was canceled 24-11-86 after all work had been halted 25-8-86 at Bell-Halter Shipyard, New Orleans, with the prototype only 16% completed. The test vehicle for the hull had failed its shock trials, and the craft was becoming greatly overweight. MSH 2–5 had already been authorized and appropriated for by Congress, and saved funds are being devoted to the replacement MHC 51 program.

◆ **1 (+ 10) MCM 1-class oceangoing minesweeper/minehunters** (*Atlantic Fleet)

| | Bldr | Laid down | L | In serv. |
|---|---|---|---|---|
| MCM 1 Avenger* | Peterson Bldrs. | 3-6-83 | 15-6-85 | 12-9-87 |
| MCM 2 Defender | Marinette Marine | 1-12-83 | 4-4-87 | 9-88 |
| MCM 3 Sentry | Peterson Bldrs. | 8-10-84 | 20-9-86 | 8-88 |
| MCM 4 Champion | Marinette Marine | 28-6-84 | 2-4-88 | 12-88 |
| MCM 5 Guardian | Peterson Bldrs. | 8-5-85 | 20-6-87 | 6-89 |
| MCM 6 Devastator | Peterson Bldrs. | 9-2-87 | 7-5-88 | 8-89 |
| MCM 7 Patriot | Marinette Marine | 31-3-87 | 11-88 | 10-89 |
| MCM 8 Scout | Peterson Bldrs. | 8-6-87 | 9-88 | 6-90 |
| MCM 9 N . . . . . . . | . . . | . . . | . . . | . . . |
| MCM 10 N . . . . . . . | . . . | . . . | . . . | . . . |
| MCM 11 N . . . . . . . | . . . | . . . | . . . | . . . |

Authorized: MCM 1 in FY 82, MCM 2 in FY 83, MCM 3–MCM 5 in FY 84, MCM 6–9 in FY 85, MCM 10–11 in FY 86

**Avenger (MCM 1)** Peterson, 12-86

**Avenger (MCM 1)** Peterson, 12-86

**AN/SLQ-48 Mine Neutralization System** Honeywell, 1987

MINE WARFARE SHIPS *(continued)*

**D:** 1,145 tons light (1,262 fl—see Remarks) **S:** 14 kts
**Dim:** 68.37 (64.80 wl) × 11.86 × 3.42 (hull) **A:** 2/12.7-mm M2 mg (I × 2)
**Electron Equipt:** Radar: 1/SPS-55
Sonar: SQQ-30 (MCM 6 and later: SQQ-32), WQN-1 channel finder
**M:** MCM 1 and 2: 4 Waukesha L-1616 diesels; 2 CP props; 2,280 hp—MCM 3–8: 4 Isotta-Fraschini ID 36 SS 6V-AM diesels; 2 CP props; 2,600 hp—all: 2/200 hp Hansome low-speed motors geared to props, 1/350-hp Omnithruster at bow
**Range:** . . ./. . . **Man:** 6 officers, 5 chief petty off., 70 men
**Electric:** 1,125 kw (3 L-1616 or ID 36 SS 6V-AM diesels)

Remarks: To be operated by the Naval Reserve Force. First unit was ordered 29-6-82. Wooden-hulled, with fiberglass superstructure. Able to sweep deep-moored mines to 180 m as well as sweep magnetic and acoustic mines. The Mk 116 Mod. 0 Mine Neutralization System (MNS) includes two Honeywell SLQ-48 MNS, a remote-controlled mine-hunting and destruction device 3.8 m long by .9 m high, weighing 1,136 kg; powered by two 15-hp hydraulic motors for 6-kt speeds, it will have 1,524 m of control cable. Also aboard are the SLQ-37(V)2 magnetic/acoustic sweep array, Type 0 Size 1 mechanical sweep gear, and two semi-rigid boats for mine-disposal divers. Carry the SSN-2(V) precision navigation system and/or the Decca-Racal Hyper-Fix precision radio navaid system. MCM 2 to displace 1,312 tons (fl).

The wooden hull employs four glued layers of 127-mm planking over 254-mm × 457-mm frames spaced at 1.07-m intervals. All structural members are built up from thinner materials, using phenol/resorcinal glue. The hull had to be lengthened by about 1.8 m after construction had begun, due to stability problems. The first unit was also delayed by design problems and the discovery that the main engines rotated opposite to the gear boxes.

This program has been fraught with major delays and cost increases. Contracts to build the FY 85 quartet had not been let by 3-86, and Congress cut the 4 requested for FY 86 authorization to 2. Congress also stipulated that MCM 10 and later must have U.S.-made diesels. Three requested under FY 88 were denied because program was over a year behind schedule; dropped from FY 89–93 program but to be reconsidered FY 90.

◆ **2 Acme-class oceangoing minesweepers**

Bldr: Frank L. Sample, Jr., Boothbay Harbor, Maine

| | Laid down | L | In serv. |
|---|---|---|---|
| MSO 509 Adroit | 18-11-54 | 20-8-55 | 4-3-57 |
| MSO 511 Affray | 24-8-55 | 18-12-56 | 8-8-58 |

**Adroit (MSO 509)** G. Arra, 4-86

**D:** 682 tons light (818 fl) **S:** 14 kts
**Dim:** 52.73 × 10.97 × 4.3 **A:** 2/12.7-mm mg (I × 2)
**Electron Equipt:** Radar: 1/SPS-53L or E—Sonar: SQQ-14
**M:** 4 Packard 1D-1700 diesels; 2 CP props; 2,280 hp **Fuel:** 47 tons
**Range:** 3,000/10 **Man:** 8 officers, 37 men + 4 officers, 38 men (Reserves)

Remarks: Similar to the *Aggressive* class below, but slightly larger and originally equipped as Mine Division flagships. Not modernized. In Naval Reserve Force, in Atlantic Fleet.

◆ **19 Aggressive-class oceangoing minesweepers** (*Atlantic Fleet)

| | Bldr | Laid down | L | In serv. |
|---|---|---|---|---|
| MSO 427 Constant | Fulton SY, Antioch, Cal. | 16-8-51 | 14-2-53 | 8-9-54 |
| MSO 433 Engage* | Colberg Boat Wks | 7-11-51 | 18-6-53 | 29-6-54 |
| MSO 437 Enhance | Martinolich SB, S. Diego | 12-7-52 | 11-10-52 | 16-4-55 |
| MSO 438 Esteem | Martinolich SB, S. Diego | 1-9-52 | 20-12-52 | 10-9-55 |
| MSO 439 Excel | Higgins, New Orleans | 4-2-53 | 25-9-53 | 24-2-55 |
| MSO 440 Exploit* | Higgins, New Orleans | 28-12-51 | 10-4-53 | 31-3-54 |
| MSO 441 Exultant* | Higgins, New Orleans | 22-5-52 | 6-6-53 | 22-6-54 |
| MSO 442 Fearless* | Higgins, New Orleans | 23-7-52 | 17-7-53 | 22-9-54 |
| MSO 443 Fidelity* | Higgins, New Orleans | 15-12-52 | 21-8-53 | 19-1-55 |
| MSO 446 Fortify* | Seattle, SB & DD | 30-11-51 | 14-2-53 | 16-7-54 |
| MSO 448 Illusive* | Martinolich SB, S. Diego | 23-10-51 | 12-7-52 | 14-11-53 |
| MSO 449 Impervious* | Martinolich SB, S. Diego | 18-11-51 | 29-8-52 | 15-7-54 |
| MSO 455 Implicit | Wilmington Boat Wks. | 29-10-51 | 1-8-53 | 10-3-54 |
| MSO 456 Inflict | Wilmington Boat Wks. | 29-10-51 | 6-10-53 | 11-5-54 |
| MSO 464 Pluck | Wilmington Boat Wks. | 31-3-52 | 6-2-54 | 11-8-54 |
| MSO 488 Conquest | J.M. Martinac, Tacoma | 26-3-53 | 20-5-54 | 20-7-55 |
| MSO 489 Gallant | J.M. Martinac, Tacoma | 21-5-53 | 4-6-54 | 14-9-55 |
| MSO 490 Leader* | J.M. Martinac, Tacoma | 22-9-53 | 15-9-54 | 16-11-55 |
| MSO 492 Pledge | J.M. Martinac, Tacoma | 24-6-54 | 20-7-55 | 20-4-56 |

**Fearless (MSO 442)** G. Arra, 4-86

**Exploit (MSO 440)** G. Arra, 8-86

**D:** 716 tons light (853 fl) **S:** 14 kts **Dim:** 52.42 × 10.97 × 4.2
**A:** 2/12.7-mm mg (I × 2) **Range:** 2,400/10
**Electron Equipt:** Radar: SPS-53E or L—Sonar: SQQ-14
**M:** 4 Waukesha L-1616 diesels; 2 CP props; 2,400 hp **Fuel:** 48 tons
**Man:** 8 officers, 70–75 men (Naval Reserve Force ships: 3 officers, 36 men + 3 officers and 44 men Reserves)

Remarks: Wooden construction; nonmagnetic, stainless-steel machinery. Except for MSO 443, MSO 448, and MSO 490, which are employed in experimental mine-warfare-related duties, all are operated for the Naval Reserve Force. Ninety-three of the MSO 421 to MSO 508 classes were built; many transferred abroad. Hoist machinery for the SQQ-14 minehunting sonar occupies the position of the former 40-mm AA gun. Twelve of the *Aggressive* class were re-engined with Waukesha diesels; the remainder (MSO 427, 439, 440, 455, 464, 489, and 492) retained Packard 1D1700 diesels, totaling 2,280 hp; those ships displace 684 tons light, 762 full load. *All* the survivors were given very thorough rehabilitations during the early to mid-1970s, receiving semi-enclosed bridges, enlarged superstructures abaft the bridge, SQQ-14 minehunting sonars, new communications gear, and upgraded accommodations. The SPS-53 radars are to be replaced by SPS-64(V)9. MSO 437, 439, 442, to Persian Gulf 1987, with Super Sea Rover commercial remote-control submersibles. MSO 488 in collision 10-9-87; MSO 449 grounded 5 days, 5-87.

In 1975 MSO 440 was equipped with the prototype SSN-2 precise-navigation system for the new MCM class, and in 1980 MSO 443 conducted trials with the prototype SQQ-30 sonar being developed for the MCM 1 class. Disposals of these old ships delayed by late delivery of MCM 1 class and MSH 1 class cancellation.

MINESWEEPING BOATS

◆ **1 MSB 29 class** Bldr: Trumpy, Annapolis (In serv. 1954)

**MINESWEEPING BOATS** *(continued)*

**MSB 29** U.S. Navy, 1986

**D:** 80 tons (fl) **S:** 12 kts **Dim:** 25.0 × 5.8 × 1.7 **A:** 1/12.7-mm mg
**Electron Equipt:** Radar: 1/Raytheon 1900—Sonar: Mk 24 Mod. 0 Hydroscan
**M:** 2 Packard 2D850 diesels; 2 props; 600 hp **Man:** 2 officers, 9 men

REMARKS: Enlarged MSB 5; only one built. Based at Charleston, S. Carolina.

◆ **6 MSB 5 class**

MSB 15, MSB 16, MSB 25, MSB 28, MSB 41, MSB 51

**MSB 16** G. Arra, 1984

**D:** 30 tons light (44 fl) **S:** 12 kts
**Dim:** 17.45 × 4.83 × 1.2 **A:** 1/12.7-mm mg
**Electron Equipt:** Radar: 1/Raytheon 1900—Sonar: Mk 24 Mod. 0 Hydroscan
**M:** 2 Packard 2D850 diesels; 2 props; 600 hp **Man:** 6 tot.

REMARKS: Survivors of a class of 47 built between 1952 and 1956. Wooden hulls; nonmagnetic machinery. Two Garrett diesel sweep generator sets, except MSB 25: 2 Boeing 502 gas-turbine sets. All based at Charleston. Former MSB 7, 13, 17, 35, and 50 were rerated as training craft for the Surface Warface Officers' School, San Diego. Four to Persian Gulf, 9-87. No plans exist to replace these useful craft, which can be transported in LSD well-decks or as deck cargo.

◆ **2 (+15) COOP (Craft of Opportunity Program) conversions from wooden-hulled training craft**

| | Bldr | L | In serv. | To COOP |
|---|---|---|---|---|
| CT-4 (ex-YP 659) | Stephens Bros., Stockton, Cal. | 3-58 | 7-58 | 9-85 |
| CT-5 (ex-YP 660) | Stephens Bros., Stockton, Cal. | 3-58 | 8-58 | 11-85 |

**D:** 60 tons (fl) **S:** 13.3 kts **Dim:** 24.51 × 5.72 × 1.60
**Electron Equipt:** Radar: 1/Raytheon 1220—Sonar: Mk 24 Mod. 0 Hydroscan towed side-scan array
**M:** 4 G.M. 6-71 diesels; 2 props; 590 hp **Man:** 9 tot.

REMARKS: CT stands for COOP Trainer. Conversions from YP 654–675 series wooden-hulled training craft built for the Naval Academy, Annapolis, and the Naval Officer Candidate School, Newport, Rhode Island: first two in 1985. The after deckhouse is to be removed, handling gear for a towed precision side-scan sonar added at the stern, and ballast added. Each will have four rotating, 9-man Naval Reserve Force crews, the idea being that three crews will take over previously designated civilian craft in wartime. All will operate on the U.S. East and Gulf coasts. CT-4 at King's Bay, Ga., and CT-5 at Savannah.

This program has experienced major delays because of low priorities, program indecision, and political difficulties over potential home-porting. Planned for conversion are ex-YP 654, 658, 659, 661–666, 668, 670–675, and two others; all await conversion and assignment. Program was to complete by 1988, now delayed into 1990.

**CT-4** G. Arra, 1986

◆ **4 COOP conversions from miscellaneous craft**

| | Home port |
|---|---|
| CT-3 (ex-*Scheherezade*) | Charleston, South Carolina |
| CT-20 (ex-*Sirod*) | Seattle, Washington |
| CT-21 (ex-*Cheyenne*) | Astoria, Oregon |
| CT-22 (ex-*Widgeon*) | Long Beach, California |

**CT-3** U.S. Navy, 1985

REMARKS: Conversion from commercial fishing craft. CT-3, placed in service 28-6-85, is a former shrimp boat 30.8 m o.a. used for COOP trials. Some 66 additional legitimate commercial craft are to be identified for wartime use by the Naval Reserve crews of these units. In peacetime, the 9-man crews will conduct detailed bottom obstacle surveys using Mk 24 Mod. 0 Hydroscan towed sidescan sonars, commercial ROVs, and net trawl gear. The COOP prototype, MSSB 1 (ex-*Robin Gail* II), has been discarded. CT-1 (ex-*Ida Green*) was returned to her owners 10-86, and CT-2 (ex-*Tiki*) was replaced by CT-22.

**MINELAYING CRAFT**

◆ **1 LCU 1610-class exercise minelayer** Bldr: Marinette Marine, Marinette, Wisc.

LCU 1641 (In serv. 1967)

**D:** 190 tons light **S:** 11 kts
**Dim:** 41.07 × 9.07 × 2.08 **A:** 1 mine rail
**Electron Equipt:** Radar: 1/LN-66
**M:** 4 G.M. 6–71 diesels; 2 Kort-nozzle props; 1,200 hp
**Range:** 1,200/11 **Fuel:** 13 tons **Man:** 6 tot.

REMARKS: Standard utility landing craft fitted with one mine rail over stern, derrick to port, and raised, enclosed pilothouse. Based at Charleston, South Carolina.

**MINELAYING CRAFT** *(continued)*

**LCU 1641** G. Arra, 1984

## AMPHIBIOUS WARFARE SHIPS

### ◆ 2 Blue Ridge-class amphibious command ships (SCN 400-65 type)

| | Bldr | Laid down | L | In serv. |
|---|---|---|---|---|
| LCC 19 Blue Ridge | Philadelphia NSY | 27-2-67 | 4-1-69 | 14-11-70 |
| LCC 20 Mount Whitney | Newport News SB & DD | 8-1-69 | 8-1-70 | 16-1-71 |

Authorized: FY 65 and FY 66

**Blue Ridge (LCC 19)** R.A.N., 9-86

**Blue Ridge (LCC 19)**—with Mk 15 CIWS fore and aft G. Arra, 11-86

**D:** 19,290 tons (fl) **S:** 21.5 kts
**Dim:** 193.98 (176.8 wl) × 32.9 (25.0 wl) × 7.5 (8.8 max.)
**A:** 4/76.2-mm DP (II × 2)—2/Mk 25 BPDMS for Sea Sparrow (VIII × 2)—2/20-mm Mk 15 CIWS (I × 2)
**Electron Equipt:** Radar: 1/LN-66, 1/SPS-65, 1/SPS-48, 1/SPS-40, 2/Mk 115
EW: SLQ-32(V)3, Mk 36 SRBOC chaff RL (VI × 4)
TACAN: URN-25
**M:** 1 set G.E. GT; 1 prop; 22,000 hp **Fuel:** 2,800 tons
**Boilers:** 2 Foster-Wheeler; 42.3 kg/cm², 467°C **Range:** 13,000/16
**Man:** LCC 19: 38 officers, 761 men + 170 flag staff; LCC 20: 50 officers, 727 men + 193 flag staff

Remarks: LCC 19 is the flagship of the Seventh Fleet; LCC 20 is the flagship of the Second Fleet. These ships have a good cruising speed (20 knots) and excellent satellite communications and analysis systems: ACIS (Amphibious Command Information System); NIPS (Naval Intelligence Processing System); NTDS, and photographic laboratories and document-publication facilities. Three LCP, two LCVP landing craft, and one 10-m personnel launch are carried in Welin davits. No helicopter hangar, but they do have a landing pad at the stern. Same machinery and basic hull form as the *Iwo Jima*-class LPH. Air-conditioned; fin stabilizers. Two Mk 56 fire-control systems for the 76.2-mm guns deleted in 1978; two Mk 115 fire-control systems for Sea Sparrow retained. Kevlar plastic armor to be added, as will be the Tactical Flag Command Center. LCC 19 received Mk 15 CIWS in 1985 and LCC 20 in 1987, with stern sponson and bow bulwarks lengthening the ships some 5 m overall. Satellite communications antennas on after mast differ.

### ◆ 0 (+3 + 8) Wasp-class helicopter/dock landing ships

| | Bldr | Laid down | L | In serv. |
|---|---|---|---|---|
| LHD 1 Wasp | Ingalls, Pascagoula | 30-5-85 | 4-8-87 | 31-3-89 |
| LHD 2 Essex | Ingalls, Pascagoula | ... | ... | 4-92 |
| LHD 3 Kearsarge | Ingalls, Pascagoula | ... | ... | 1993 |
| LHD 4 N... | Ingalls, Pascagoula | ... | ... | ... |

Authorized: LHD 1 in FY 84, LHD 2 in FY 86, LHD 3 in FY 88, LHD 4 in FY 89; programmed: LHD 5 in FY 91

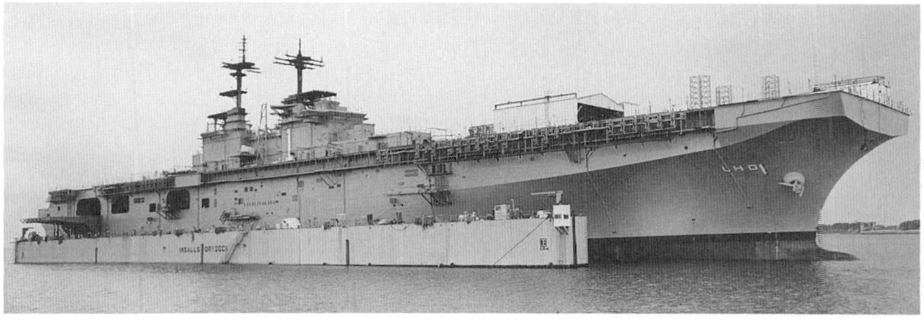

**Wasp (LHD 1)**—at launch, 4-8-87 Ingalls

**Wasp (LHD 1)**—note stern door to well-deck Ingalls, 7-87

**Wasp (LHD 1)**—note bulbous bow Ingalls, 9-87

**AMPHIBIOUS WARFARE SHIPS** *(continued)*

**D:** 28,233 tons light (40,532 fl) **S:** 24 kts
**Dim:** 257.30 (237.14 wl) × 42.67 (32.31 wl) × 8.13
**A:** Assault mode: 30–32/CH-46 (or fewer CH-53) helicopters and 6/AV-8B Harriers; carrier mode: 20/AV-8B Harriers and 4–6/SH-60B ASW helicopters—2/Mod. Mk 29 launchers (XVI × 2; 6 Sea Sparrow, 10 RAM each)—3/20-mm Mk 15 CIWS AA (I × 3)—8/12.7-mm mg (I × 8)
**Electron Equipt:** Radar: 1/SPS-64(V)9, 1/SPS-67, 1/SPS-49(V)5, 1/SPS-52C (LHD2 and later: SPS-48E) 1/Mk 23 TAS, 2/Mk 57 Mod. 2 (on Mk 91 f.c.s.), 1/SPN-35A, 1/SPN-43B
EW: SLQ-32(V)3, Mk 36 SRBOC (VI × 4 or 8)
**M:** 2 sets GT: 2 props; 77,000 hp (70,000 sust.)
**Fuel:** 6,200 tons, plus 1,232 tons aircraft fuel
**Boilers:** 2; 49.3 kg/cm$^2$, 482°C **Electric:** 16,500 kw **Range:** 9,500/20
**Man:** 98 officers, 61 chief petty officers, 921 men, plus 1,873 troops (+200 additional emergency troops accom.)

Remarks: Design based on that of the LHA 1 class, but intended to be convertible from an assault ship to an ASW ship with Harrier V/STOL fighters for ground assault. Because of the desire to maximize the number of deck spots, no ski-jump V/STOL ramp will be fitted. Differences from the LHA 1 include: use of an LSD/LPD-type lowering stern gate, vice the sectional, rising gate of the LHA; provision for three LCAC in a single-bay, narrower docking well (which can alternatively hold up to 12 LCM(6)); using larger 34-ton elevators, with the stern elevator relocated to starboard; internal stowage for ship's boats; a bulbous forefoot to the bow; a squared-off flight deck forward (made possible by the omission of the 127-mm guns); using HY 100 steel to construct the stronger flight deck; additional cargo elevators (6 total: 7.6 × 3.6 m); a lower, narrower, and longer island; provision of 3 hospitals, totaling 600 beds; a narrower vehicle ramp to the flight deck; and better ballistic protection. They will have 2,127 m$^2$ of vehicle parking space and 3,087 m$^3$ of dry cargo space. Some 1,232 tons of JP-5 aviation fuel and about 50 tons of vehicle fuel will be carried. The SYS-2(V)3 data system will control defensive weapons. Marconi ICS.3 integrated communications system. Can take on up to 15,000 tons ballast to launch landing craft. Over 1,500 compartments. LHD 1 ordered 28-2-84, LHD 2 on 11-9-85, LHD 3 on 24-11-87; LHD 4 to order 12-88, as third unit in a 3-ship option.

◆ **5 Tarawa-class amphibious assault ships (SCB 410 type)** Bldr: Ingalls SB, Pascagoula, Miss. (*Atlantic Fleet)

| | Laid down | L | In serv. |
|---|---|---|---|
| LHA 1 Tarawa | 15-11-71 | 1-12-73 | 29-5-76 |
| LHA 2 Saipan* | 21-7-72 | 18-7-74 | 15-10-77 |
| LHA 3 Belleau Wood (ex-*Philippine Sea*) | 5-3-73 | 11-4-77 | 23-9-78 |
| LHA 4 Nassau (ex-*Leyte Gulf*)* | 13-8-73 | 21-1-78 | 28-7-79 |
| LHA 5 Peleliu (ex-*Da Nang*, ex-*Khe Sanh*) | 12-11-76 | 25-11-78 | 3-5-80 |

Authorized: 1 in FY 69, 2 in FY 70, 2 in FY 71

**Saipan (LHA 2)**—with Mk 15 CIWS on deckhouse in place of forward Sea Sparrow launcher L. & L. Van Ginderen, 10-86

**Nassau (LHA 4)**—with Mk 15 CIWS on port quarter L. Grazioli, 11-87

**Peleliu (LHA 5)** PH2 G. Leech, USN, 6-84

**Belleau Wood (LHA 3)**—no Mk 15 CIWS; aircraft on deck include 4 AV-8B, 2 CH-53, 7 CH-46, 1 AH-1 L. & L. Van Ginderen, 6-87

**Belleau Wood (LHA 3)** L. & L. Van Ginderen, 6-87

**D:** 25,120 tons light (39,400 fl) **S:** 24 kts
**Dim:** 254.20 (237.14 pp) × 40.23 (32.31 wl) × 7.92
**A:** 2/127-mm 54-cal. Mk 45 DP (I × 2)—2/20-mm Mk 15 CIWS (I × 2)—6/20-mm Mk 67 AA (I × 6)—typical: 16/CH-46, 6/CH-53, and 4/UH-1 helicopters (maximum: 38 CH-46 equivalents)—see Remarks
**Electron Equipt:** Radar: 1/SPS-53, 1/SPS-10F, 1/SPS-40B, 1/SPS-52B, 1/SPN-35, 1/SPG-60, 1/SPQ-9A,
EW: SLQ-32(V)3, 4/Mk 36 SRBOC chaff (VI × 4)
TACAN: URN-25
**M:** 2 sets Westinghouse GT; 2 props; 77,000 hp (70,000 sust.); 900-hp bow-thruster
**Electric:** 14,600 kw (4 × 2,500 kw, 2 × 2,000 kw, 4 × 150 kw)
**Boilers:** 2 Combustion Engineering V2M-VS; 49.3 kg/cm$^2$, 482°C
**Fuel:** 5,900 tons **Range:** 10,000/20
**Man:** 58 officers, 882 men + 1,924 troops

Remarks: The LHA is a multipurpose assault transport, a combination of LPH and LPD. It has the general profile of an aircraft carrier, with its superstructure to starboard, flight deck, helicopter elevators to port (folding) and aft, and an 80 × 23.4-m well deck for landing craft (up to four LCU 1610 class). Two LCM(6) and two LCP are stowed on deck. Vehicle stowage garage forward of docking well totals 3,134 m$^2$, and the palletized cargo holds total 3,311 m$^3$. Carry approx. 1,200 tons JP-5 fuel for helicopters. The boilers are the largest ever installed in a U.S. Navy ship; the propulsion plant is highly automated. Communications systems include satellite antennas and a large, long-range, high-frequency, log-periodic array. LHA-4 carried 20 AV-8A Harrier V/STOL attack fighters as well as transport helicopters during a 1981 exercise. Very complete 300-bed hospital and mortuary facilities are fitted. All troops have bunks. Completely air-conditioned. Four additional units were canceled in 1971. The 127-mm guns are aboard primarily to provide shore fire support, but can also be used for AA; they are

**AMPHIBIOUS WARFARE SHIPS** *(continued)*

controlled by a Mk 86 Mod. 4 fire-control system with SPQ-9A radar for surface fire, SPG-60 for AA, and two unmanned electro-optical backup directors. As completed, carried 2 Mk 25 BPDMS launchers for Sea Sparrow SAMs, controlled by 2 Mk 71 directors with Mk 115 radars, and three 127-mm DP. Ultimate configuration (LHA 2, 4 already so equipped) calls for retention of port and starboard 127-mm mounts forward, replacement of the BPDMS by Mk 15 CIWS gatling guns, and use of the starboard aft 127-mm position for a control antenna for drone reconnaissance aircraft (trials held on LHA 2 late in 1986). LHA 3 was still in original configuration as of mid-1987. Planned addition of bulbous bow canceled. All have had original WLR-1 EW suite replaced by SLQ-32(V)3 and URN-20 TACAN replaced by URN-25. LHA 5 renamed 15-2-78.

**AMPHIBIOUS ASSAULT HELICOPTER CARRIERS**

◆ **7 Iwo Jima class (SCB 157, LPH 12: SCB 401-66)** (*Atlantic Fleet)

| | Bldr | Laid down | L | In serv. |
|---|---|---|---|---|
| LPH 2 Iwo Jima* | Puget Sound NSY | 2-4-59 | 17-9-60 | 26-8-61 |
| LPH 3 Okinawa | Philadelphia NSY | 1-4-60 | 14-8-61 | 14-4-62 |
| LPH 7 Guadalcanal | Philadelphia NSY | 1-9-61 | 16-3-63 | 20-7-63 |
| LPH 9 Guam* | Philadelphia NSY | 15-11-62 | 22-8-64 | 16-1-65 |
| LPH 10 Tripoli | Ingalls, Pascagoula | 15-6-64 | 31-7-65 | 6-8-66 |
| LPH 11 New Orleans | Philadelphia NSY | 1-3-66 | 3-2-68 | 16-11-68 |
| LPH 12 Inchon* | Ingalls, Pascagoula | 8-4-68 | 24-5-69 | 20-6-70 |

Authorized: 1 each year in FY 58, 59, 60, 62, 63, 65, 66

**D:** 11,000 tons light (17,515–18,300 fl) **S:** 23 kts
**Dim:** 183.6 (169.5 wl) × 31.7 (25.5 wl) × 7.9 (hull)
**A:** 4/76.2-mm DP (II × 2)—2/Mk 25 Sea Sparrow launchers (VIII × 2)—2/20-mm Mk 15 CIWS (I × 2)—4, 6, or 8/12.7-mm mg(I)—20–24/CH-46 helicopters—4/CH-53 heavy helicopters—4/UH-1 utility or AH-1 attack helicopters—see Remarks

**Inchon (LPH 12)**—only unit with LCVP in davits G. Arra, 6-86

**Inchon (LPH 12)**—with 2 OV-10A Broncos forward, port elevator stowed R. Parkinson, 10-86

**Okinawa (LPH 3)**—with CIWS in lieu of both Sea Sparrow launchers, stbd. elevator stowed G. Arra, 3-86

**Electron Equipt:** Radar: 1/LN-66, 1/SPS-10, 1/SPS-40, 1/SPN-35, SPN-43, 2/Mk 115 (not in LPH 3)
EW: SLQ-32(V)3, Mk 36 SRBOC chaff RL (VI × 4)
TACAN: URN-25
**M:** 1 set GT; 1 prop; 23,000 hp **Electric:** 6,500 kw
**Boilers:** 2 Combustion Engineering (LPH 9: Babcock & Wilcox); 42.3 kg/cm², 467°C
**Man:** 47 officers, 638 men + 190 Marine officers, 1,900 troops

**Guadalcanal (LPH 7)**—in the Persian Gulf, with 6 RH-53E embarked for mine countermeasures duties PH2 Hicks, USN, 8-87

**Tripoli (LPH 10)** LSPH W. McBride, R.A.N., 9-87

Remarks: The ships can also act as carriers for RH-53/MH-53E minesweeping helicopters or for AV-8B Harriers. One folding side elevator forward, to port; one to starboard, aft of the island; 70-m hangar. Excellent medical facilities (300 beds). LPH 9 has an ASCAC (Air-Surface Classification and Analysis Center). LPH 12, to a slightly different design, carries two LCVP in davits.

Two Mk 15 CIWS gatling AA have been added to all; in LPH 3 only, they *replace* the obsolescent Mk 25 BPDMS Sea Sparrow launchers, retained in the others. Sea Sparrows are controlled by two Mk 71 directors with Mk 115 radars. All now have SLQ-32(V)3 EW in place of the WLR-1 suite, and URN-25 has replaced SRN-6. LPH 12 was last to receive the SPN-35 aircraft control radar.

**AMPHIBIOUS TRANSPORTS, DOCK**

◆ **11 Austin class (SCB 187B type)** (*Atlantic Fleet)

| | Bldr | Laid down | L | In serv. |
|---|---|---|---|---|
| LPD 4 Austin* | New York NSY | 4-2-63 | 27-6-64 | 6-2-65 |
| LPD 5 Ogden | New York NSY | 4-2-63 | 27-6-64 | 19-6-65 |
| LPD 6 Duluth | New York NSY | 18-12-63 | 14-8-65 | 18-12-65 |
| LPD 7 Cleveland | Ingalls, Pascagoula | 30-11-64 | 7-5-66 | 21-4-67 |
| LPD 8 Dubuque | Ingalls, Pascagoula | 25-1-65 | 6-8-66 | 1-9-67 |
| LPD 9 Denver | Lockheed SB, Seattle | 7-2-64 | 23-1-65 | 26-10-68 |
| LPD 10 Juneau | Lockheed SB, Seattle | 23-1-65 | 12-2-66 | 12-7-69 |
| LPD 12 Shreveport* | Lockheed SB, Seattle | 27-12-65 | 25-10-66 | 12-2-70 |
| LPD 13 Nashville* | Lockheed SB, Seattle | 14-3-66 | 7-10-67 | 14-2-70 |
| LPD 14 Trenton* | Lockheed SB, Seattle | 8-8-66 | 3-8-68 | 6-3-71 |
| LPD 15 Ponce* | Lockheed SB, Seattle | 31-10-66 | 20-5-70 | 10-7-71 |

Authorized: 3 in FY 62, 4 in FY 63, 3 in FY 64, 2 in FY 65

**D:** 11,050 tons (16,550–17,595 fl) **S:** 21 kts
**Dim:** 173.4 × 25.6 (hull) × 7.0–7.2
**A:** 4/76.2-mm DP (II × 2)—LPD 4, 12–15 also: 2/20-mm Mk 15 CIWS (I × 2)
**Electron Equipt:** Radar: 1/LN-66, 1/SPS-10, 1/SPS-40
EW: SLQ-32(V)1; all: Mk 36 SRBOC chaff RL (VI × 4)
TACAN: URN-25
**M:** 2 sets de Laval GT; 2 props; 24,000 hp **Range:** 7,700/20
**Boilers:** 2 Foster-Wheeler (LPD 5, LPD 12: Babcock & Wilcox), 42.3 kg/cm², 467°C
**M:** 24 officers, 373 men (+90 staff in LPD 7 to LPD 13) + 930 troops (840 in LPD 7 to LPD 13)

**AMPHIBIOUS TRANSPORTS, DOCK** *(continued)*

**Shreveport (LPD 12)**—flagship, with 2 Mk 15 CIWS G. Arra, 1987

**Nashville (LPD 13)**—flagship version, with 2 Mk 15 CIWS, ballasted down aft G. Arra, 8-86

**Duluth (LPD 6)**—non-flagship version, still without CIWS LSPH W. McBride, R.A.N., 9-87

**Austin (LPD 4)**—no telescoping hangar R. Parkinson, 10-86

REMARKS: Lengthened version of the *Raleigh* class. Combination LSD and assault transports; well deck 120 × 15.24; helicopter platform. Either 1 LCU and 3 LCM(6) or 9 LCM(6) or 4 LCM(8) or 28 LVT can be carried in the well deck. Six cranes, one 8.15-ton elevator, two forklifts. Up to six CH-46 helicopters can be carried for brief periods, but the small, telescoping hangar can accommodate only one utility helicopter; no hangar in LPD 4. LPD 7 to LPD 13 are fitted for flagship duty and have one additional superstructure deck. All have lost their one Mk 56 and two Mk 63 gunfire control, leaving the 76.2-mm guns locally controlled. Two twin 76.2-mm DP removed 1977-78 (port fwd, stbd aft). Four Mk 36 SRBOC chaff launchers and the SLQ-32(V)1 EW system have been added, and URN-25 TACAN has replaced SRN-6 in all. Sister *Coronado* (LPD 11) redesignated AGF 11, 1-10-80. These ships were programmed to receive a SLEP (Service Life Extension Program) modernization to extend their service lives by 10–15 years, but this was canceled by Congress. Will still receive SPS-67 in place of SPS-10, new pumps and compressors, and increased vehicle and cargo space. All Atlantic Fleet units have Mk 15 CIWS gatling AA, but no PacFlt ship had it as of 10-87.

**Trenton (LPD 14)** G. Arra, 3-87

◆ **2 Raleigh class** (*Atlantic Fleet)

| | Bldr | Laid down | L | In serv. |
|---|---|---|---|---|
| LPD 1 RALEIGH* | New York NSY | 23-6-60 | 17-3-62 | 8-9-62 |
| LPD 2 VANCOUVER | New York NSY | 19-11-60 | 15-9-62 | 11-5-63 |

Authorized: FY 59 and FY 60

**Raleigh (LPD 1)**—with CIWS L. & L. Van Ginderen, 10-86

**Raleigh (LPD 1)** G. Gyssels, 10-86

**D:** 8,276 tons light (14,650 fl) **S:** 21 kts
**Dim:** 159.0 (152.4 wl) × 25.60 (hull) × 6.7
**A:** 6/76.2-mm DP (II × 3)—LPD 1: 2/20-mm Mk 15 CIWS (I × 2)
**Electron Equipt:** Radar: 1/LN-66, 1/SPS-10, 1/SPS-40—TACAN: URN-25
EW: SLQ-32(V)1, Mk 36 SRBOC chaff RL (VI × 4)
**M:** 2 de Laval GT; 2 props; 24,000 hp **Electric:** 3,600 kw
**Boilers:** 2 Babcock & Wilcox; 40.8 kg/cm$^2$, 467°C
**Range:** 9,600/16; 16,500/10
**Man:** LPD 1: 24 officers, 396 men + 930 troops (LPD 2: 26 officers, 405 men + 930 troops)

REMARKS: Sister *La Salle* (LPD 3), modified as flagship for CoMideastFor in the Indian Ocean and reclassified AGF 3 on 1-7-72. Docking well, 51.2 × 15.2 m, is shorter than on *Austin* class. Emphasis in LPD is on personnel capacity, in LSD on dock capacity; the flight deck, which forms the top of the well deck, can handle

## AMPHIBIOUS TRANSPORTS, DOCK *(continued)*

up to six CH-46 helicopters; there is no hangar. The port, fwd twin 76.2-mm gun mount and all fire-control systems were removed 1977–78. These ships are not planned to receive SLEP modernization.

## DOCK LANDING SHIPS

### ◆ 0 (+1 + 5) Harpers Ferry class

| | Bldr | Laid down | L | In serv. |
|---|---|---|---|---|
| LSD 49 Harpers Ferry | . . . | 1989 | | 1992–93 |

Authorized: LSD 49 in FY 88; 1 in FY 90, 1 in FY 91, 2 in FY 92

**D:** 16,695 tons (fl) **S:** 22 kts **Dim:** 185.80 (176.80 wl) × 25.60 × 6.03
**A:** 2/20-mm Mk 15 CIWS AA (I × 2)—2/25-mm Mk 88 AA (I × 2)—8/12.7-mm mg (I × 8)
**Electron Equipt:** Radar: 1/. . . nav., 1/SPS-67, 1/SPS-49
EW: SLQ(V)2, Mk 36 SRBOC (VI × 4)—TACAN: URN-25
**M:** 4 Colt-Pielstick 16 PC2.5V400 diesels; 2 CP props; 41,600 hp (33,600 sust.)
**Electric:** . . . **Man:** . . . approx. 410 crew + 504 troops
**Range:** approx. 8,000/20 **Fuel:** 2,000 tons

Remarks: Officially referred to as the "LSD 41 CV (Cargo Variant)" class. Originally requested FY 88, withdrawn because of late design changes (which may enlarge ship over figures given above) and then approved by Congress with Navy concurrence. Was to have been a relatively simple modification of LSD 41 design with increased cargo capacity at the expense of a shorter well deck able to accommodate only 2 LCAC, leaving space for 2 LCAC or 10 LCM (6). Cargo space: 1,208 $m^2$ vehicle parking, 1,133 $m^3$ cargo volume.

### ◆ 3 (+5) Whidbey Island class (*Atlantic Fleet)

| | Bldr | Laid down | L | In serv. |
|---|---|---|---|---|
| LSD 41 Whidbey Island* | Lockheed, Seattle | 4-8-81 | 10-6-83 | 9-2-85 |
| LSD 42 Germantown | Lockheed, Seattle | 5-8-82 | 29-6-84 | 8-2-86 |
| LSD 43 Fort McHenry | Lockheed, Seattle | 10-6-83 | 1-2-86 | 8-8-87 |
| LSD 44 Gunston Hall | Avondale SY | 26-5-86 | 27-6-87 | 8-88 |
| LSD 45 Comstock | Avondale SY | 27-10-86 | 16-1-88 | 11-88 |
| LSD 46 Tortuga | Avondale SY | 23-3-87 | 11-6-88 | 4-89 |
| LSD 47 Rushmore | Avondale SY | 9-11-87 | 11-88 | 11-89 |
| LSD 48 Ashland | Avondale SY | 4-4-88 | 5-89 | 5-90 |

Authorized: LSD 41 in FY 81, LSD 42 in FY 82, LSD 43 in FY 83, LSD 44 in FY 84, LSD 45, 46 in FY 85, LSD 47, 48 in FY 86.

**D:** 11,854 tons (15,745 fl) **S:** 22 kts **Dim:** 185.80(176.80 wl) × 25.60 × 5.97
**A:** 2/20-mm Mk 15 CIWS AA (I × 2)—2/20-mm Mk 67 AA (I × 2)—8/12.7-mm mg (I × 8)
**Electron Equipt:** Radar: 1/LN-66, 1/SPS-67, 1/SPS-49—TACAN: URN-25
EW: SLQ-32(V)1, Mk 36 SRBOC chaff RL (VI × 4)
**M:** 4 Colt-Pielstick 16 PC2.5V400 diesels; 2 CP props; 41,600 hp (33,600 sust.)
**Electric:** 9,200 kw **Fuel:** 2,000 tons **Range:** approx. 8,000/20
**Man:** 22 officers, 390 men + 504 troops (including 166 staff)

**Germantown (LSD 42)** LSPH W. McBride, R.A.N., 9-87

**Fort McHenry (LSD 43)** U.S. Navy, 4-87

**Germantown (LSD 42)** Lockheed SB, 10-85

**Whidbey Island (LSD 41)** R. Parkinson, 10-86

**Germantown (LSD 42)** G. Arra, 1986

Remarks: The design was originally to have been a near-repeat of the LSD 36 class, but a requirement to be able to hold four LCAC (Air-Cushion Landing Craft) in the docking well, which measures 134.0 × 15.24 m clear, necessitated the change. The helicopter deck is raised above the docking well (which can also hold 21 LCM(6) or 3 LCU or 64 LVTP) in order to provide all-around ventilation for the gas turbine-engined LCACs. There are two landing spots for up to CH-53-sized helicopters but no hangar facilities. Forward of the docking well is 1,214 $m^2$ of vehicle parking space and 149 $m^3$ of palletized cargo. Carry 90 tons JP-5 fuel for helicopters. Carry one LCM(6), two LCPL Mk-II, and one LCVP on deck, handled by one 20-ton and one 60-ton crane. The FY 85 and later ships will have the Mk 88 Mod. 0 Bushmaster 25-mm gun in place of the 20-mm Mk 67 AA. LSD 44–48 to have a collective BW/CW protection system. All have Inogen Leading Mark optical guidance system for LCAC entry to well deck.

### ◆ 5 Anchorage class (SCN 404-65 and 66 types) (*Atlantic Fleet)

| | Bldr | Laid down | L | In serv. |
|---|---|---|---|---|
| LSD 36 Anchorage | Ingalls, Pascagoula | 13-3-67 | 5-5-68 | 15-3-69 |
| LSD 37 Portland* | Gen'l Dynamics, Quincy | 21-9-67 | 20-12-69 | 3-10-70 |
| LSD 38 Pensacola* | Gen'l Dynamics, Quincy | 12-3-69 | 11-7-70 | 27-3-71 |
| LSD 39 Mount Vernon | Gen'l Dynamics, Quincy | 29-1-70 | 17-4-71 | 13-5-72 |
| LSD 40 Fort Fisher | Gen'l Dynamics, Quincy | 15-7-70 | 22-4-72 | 12-9-72 |

Authorized: 1 in FY 65, 3 in FY 66, 1 in FY 67

**DOCK LANDING SHIPS** *(continued)*

**Portland (LSD 37)**—open 76.2-mm gun mounts, SLQ-32, 2 CIWS
L. Grazioli, 7-86

**Portland (LSD 37)**—note stern gate L. & L. Van Ginderen, 7-86

**Anchorage (LSD 36)**—enclosed gun mounts, no CIWS G. Arra, 7-86

**D:** 8,600 tons light (14,000 fl) **S:** 22 kts
**Dim:** 168.66 (162.8 wl) × 25.9 × 5.6 (6.1 max.)
**A:** 6/76.2-mm DP (II × 3)—LSD 37, 38 also: 2/20-mm Mk 15 CIWS (I × 2)
**Electron Equipt:** Radar: 1/LN-66, 1/SPS-10, 1/SPS-40
EW: SLQ-32(V)1, Mk 36 SRBOC chaff RL (VI × 4)
**M:** 2 sets de Laval GT; 2 props; 24,000 hp
**Boilers:** 2 Foster-Wheeler (LSD 36: Combustion Eng.); 42.3 kg/cm$^2$, 467°C
**Fuel:** 2,750 tons **Man:** 18 officers, 340 men + 338 troops

REMARKS: Carry assault landing craft in the well deck (113.28 × 15.24); can accommodate 3 LCU or 15 LCM(6) or 8 LCM(8) or 50 LVT. One or two LCM(6) stowed on deck, handled by the two 50-ton cranes. Have 1,115 m$^2$ of vehicle parking space forward of the docking well. The helicopter deck is removable; 90 tons JP-5 fuel carried for helicopters. The starboard forward twin 76.2-mm removed. CIWS only on Atlantic Fleet units to date. Mk 56 and Mk 63 directors removed in 1977.

◆ **8 Thomaston class (SCB 75 type)** (*Atlantic Fleet) Bldr: Ingalls, Pascagoula, Miss.

| | Laid down | L | In serv. | To Reserve |
|---|---|---|---|---|
| LSD 28 THOMASTON | 3-3-53 | 9-2-54 | 17-9-54 | 5-9-84 |
| LSD 29 PLYMOUTH ROCK | 5-5-53 | 7-5-54 | 29-11-54 | 30-9-83 |
| LSD 30 FORT SNELLING | 17-8-53 | 16-7-54 | 24-1-55 | 28-9-84 |
| LSD 31 POINT DEFIANCE | 23-11-53 | 28-9-54 | 31-3-55 | 30-9-83 |
| LSD 32 SPIEGEL GROVE* | 7-9-54 | 10-11-55 | 8-6-56 | . . . |
| LSD 33 ALAMO | 11-10-54 | 20-1-56 | 24-8-56 | . . . |
| LSD 34 HERMITAGE* | 11-4-55 | 12-6-56 | 14-12-56 | . . . |
| LSD 35 MONTICELLO | 6-6-55 | 10-8-56 | 29-3-57 | 1-10-85 |

Authorized: 4 in FY 52, 2 in FY 54, 2 in FY 55

**Hermitage (LSD 34)**—with Mk 15 CIWS port and starboard G. Arra, 8-86

**Alamo (LSD 33)** G. Arra, 1984

**D:** 6,880 tons (12,150 fl) **S:** 22.5 kts **Dim:** 155.45 × 25.6 × 5.4 (5.8 max.)
**A:** 6/76.2-mm DP (II × 3)—LSD 34 also: 2/20-mm Mk 15 CIWS (I × 2)
**Electron Equipt:** Radar: 1/LN-66, 1/SPS-10, 1/SPS-6
**M:** 2 sets G.E. GT; 2 props; 24,000 hp **Range:** 5,300/22.5; 10,000/20; 13,000/10
**Boilers:** 2 Babcock & Wilcox, 40.8 kg/cm$^2$ pressure
**Fuel:** 1,390 tons **Man:** 18 officers, 325 men + 318 troops

REMARKS: Portable helicopter platform. Can carry 3 LCU, 18 LCM(6), or 9 LCM(8) in 119.2 × 14.6 well deck, with 975 m$^2$ of vehicle parking space forward of the docking well. Two 50-ton cranes. Originally had 16 76.2-mm DP (II × 8). Now have one mount forward to starboard, and two amidships. Two Mk 56 and Mk 63 gunfire-control systems removed in 1977. Last active U.S. ships with SPS-6 air-search radar. Being decommissioned to reserve for retention for possible emergency mobilization; LSD 32 extended in active service two years, was to have decommissioned 30-9-87.

**TANK LANDING SHIPS**

◆ **20 Newport class (SCN 405-66 type)** (*Atlantic Fleet, †Naval Reserve Force)
Bldrs: LST 1179: Philadelphia NSY; others: National Steel SB, San Diego

| | Laid down | L | In serv. |
|---|---|---|---|
| LST 1179 NEWPORT* | 1-11-66 | 3-2-68 | 7-6-69 |
| LST 1180 MANITOWOC* | 1-2-67 | 4-6-69 | 24-1-70 |
| LST 1181 SUMTER* | 14-11-67 | 13-12-69 | 20-6-70 |
| LST 1182 FRESNO | 16-12-67 | 28-9-68 | 22-11-69 |
| LST 1183 PEORIA | 22-2-68 | 23-11-68 | 21-2-70 |
| LST 1184 FREDERICK | 13-4-68 | 8-3-69 | 11-4-70 |
| LST 1185 SCHENECTADY | 2-8-68 | 24-5-69 | 13-6-70 |
| LST 1186 CAYUGA | 28-9-68 | 12-7-69 | 8-8-70 |
| LST 1187 TUSCALOOSA | 23-11-68 | 6-9-69 | 24-10-70 |
| LST 1188 SAGINAW* | 24-5-69 | 7-2-70 | 23-1-71 |
| LST 1189 SAN BERNARDINO | 12-7-69 | 28-3-70 | 27-3-71 |

TANK LANDING SHIPS *(continued)*

| | | | |
|---|---|---|---|
| LST 1190 BOULDER† | 6-9-69 | 22-5-70 | 4-6-71 |
| LST 1191 RACINE† | 13-12-69 | 15-8-70 | 9-7-71 |
| LST 1192 SPARTANBURG COUNTY* | 7-2-70 | 11-11-70 | 1-9-71 |
| LST 1193 FAIRFAX COUNTY* | 28-3-70 | 19-12-70 | 16-10-71 |
| LST 1194 LA MOURE COUNTY* | 22-5-70 | 13-2-71 | 18-12-71 |
| LST 1195 BARBOUR COUNTY | 15-8-70 | 15-5-71 | 12-2-72 |
| LST 1196 HARLAN COUNTY* | 7-11-70 | 24-7-71 | 8-4-72 |
| LST 1197 BARNSTABLE COUNTY* | 19-12-70 | 2-10-71 | 27-5-72 |
| LST 1198 BRISTOL COUNTY | 13-2-71 | 4-12-71 | 5-8-72 |

Authorized: 1 in FY 65, 8 in FY 66, 11 in FY 67

**Saginaw (LST 1188)**—with CIWS atop pilothouse G. Arra, 6-86

**Sumter (LST 1181)**—with four pontoons aft L. & L. Van Ginderen, 10-86

**Boulder (LST 1190)**—Naval Reserve Force R. Parkinson, 10-86

**Frederick (LST 1184)**—with four pontoons, no CIWS LSPH W. McBride, R.A.N., 4-87

**D:** 4,793 tons light (8,450 fl) **S:** 22 kts (20 sust.)
**Dim:** 159.2 (171.3 over horns) × 21.18 × 5.3 (aft) × 1.80 (fwd)
**A:** 4/76.2-mm DP (II × 2)—Atlantic Fleet units also: 1/20-mm Mk 15 CIWS—all: 2 or 4/12.7-mm mg (I × 2 or 4)
**Electron Equipt:** Radar: 1/LN-66, 1/SPS-10—see Remarks
**M:** 6 Alco 16-251 (LST 1179 to LST 1181: G.M. 16-645-E5) diesels; 2 CP props; 16,500 hp
**Fuel:** 1,750 tons **Man:** 12 officers, 174 men + 20/411 troops

REMARKS: Seven more planned under FY 71 were canceled. LST 1190 transferred to the Naval Reserve Force 1-12-80 and LST 1191 on 15-1-81. Can carry 500 tons of cargo on 1,765 $m^2$ of deck space, and up to 431 troops (386 normal). A side-thruster propeller forward helps when marrying to a causeway. There is a 34-m, mobile aluminum ramp forward, which is linked to the tank deck by a second ramp. These ramps can carry 75 tons. Aft is a helicopter platform and a stern door for loading and unloading vehicles. Four pontoon causeway sections can be carried on the hull sides. Mk 63 radar gunfire-control systems removed 1977-78. SLQ-32(V)1 and chaff RL are *not* planned. LST 1179 has *two* navigational radars. Atlantic Fleet ships have 1 Mk 15 CIWS 20-mm gatling AA atop pilothouse in an interim installation; still plan to carry 2 CIWS and delete 76.2-mm guns on all. LST 1184 home-ported at Sasebo, Japan.

NOTE: Three surviving *DeSoto County* tank landing ships have been in the National Defense Reserve Fleet since 1972: *Suffolk County* (LST 1173), *Wood County* (LST 1178), and *Lorain County* (LST 1177); they are *not* Navy property. Two *Terrebonne Parish*-class tank landing ships also remain in the Maritime Administration's National Defense Reserve Fleet: *Tioga County* (LST 1158) and *Wahkiakum County* (LST 1162), while four sisters were leased to Peru on 7-8-84: *Traverse County* (LST 1160), *Waldo County* (LST 1163), *Washoe County* (LST 1164), and *Walworth County* (LST 1165). The five NDRF ships are subject to Navy recall, but this is unlikely, due to their age and condition.

## AMPHIBIOUS CARGO SHIPS

◆ **5 Charleston class (SCB 403 Design)** (*Atlantic Fleet)

| | Bldr | Laid down | L | In serv. |
|---|---|---|---|---|
| LKA 113 CHARLESTON* | Newport News | 5-12-66 | 2-12-67 | 14-12-68 |
| LKA 114 DURHAM | Newport News | 10-7-67 | 29-3-68 | 24-5-69 |
| LKA 115 MOBILE | Newport News | 15-1-68 | 19-10-68 | 29-9-69 |
| LKA 116 ST. LOUIS | Newport News | 3-4-68 | 4-1-69 | 22-11-69 |
| LKA 117 EL PASO* | Newport News | 22-10-68 | 17-5-69 | 17-1-70 |

Authorized: 4 in FY 65, 1 in FY 66

**El Paso (LKA 117)**—with two CIWS R. Parkinson, 10-86

**El Paso (LKA 117)** G. Arra, 8-86

**Durham (LKA 114)** LSPH W. McBride, R.A.N., 3-87

**AMPHIBIOUS CARGO SHIPS** *(continued)*

**D:** 10,000 tons (18,600 fl) **S:** 20 kts
**Dim:** 175.6 (167.6 wl) × 18.9 × 8.5 (max.)
**A:** 6/76.2-mm DP (II × 3) (LKA 113, 117: 4/76.2-mm DP (II × 2)—2/20-mm Mk 15 CIWS (I × 2))
**Electron Equipt:** Radar: 1/LN-66, 1/SPS-10
EW: SLQ-32(V)1, Mk 36 SRBOC chaff RL (VI × 2)
**M:** 1 set Westinghouse GT; 1 prop; 22,000 hp
**Boilers:** 2 Combustion Engineering; 42.2 kg/cm², 443°C
**Fuel:** 2,400 tons **Man:** 25 officers, 366 men + 15 officers, 211 troops

REMARKS: All but LKA 116 transferred to the Naval Reserve Force, LKA 113 on 21-11-79, LKA 114 on 1-10-79, LKA 115 on 1-9-80, and LKA 117 on 1-3-81. Returned to Regular Navy: LKA 113 on 13-2-83, LKA 114 on 1-10-82, LKA 115 on 1-7-83 and LKA 117 on 1-10-82. Air-conditioned. Machinery control is automatic. Helicopter platform. Fittings include two 70-ton heavy-lift booms, two 40-ton booms, and eight 15-ton booms. Normally carry four LSM(8), five LCM(6), two LCVP, and two LCP. Two Mk 56 radar gunfire-control systems and one twin 76.2-mm gun mount removed 1977–78. The Atlantic Fleet pair have Mk 15 CIWS on the forecastle to port and atop the superstructure to starboard (the latter replacing a twin 76.2-mm mount).

NOTE: The *Mariner*-class amphibious cargo ship *Tulare* (LKA 112) was stricken on 1-8-81 and is retained in the National Defense Reserve Fleet by the Maritime Administration.

## UTILITY LANDING CRAFT

NOTE: A new "LCX" design to replace the rapidly aging LCUs is in development. The initial construction contract, however, is not expected until 10-93, with two prototypes to deliver 1995–96. The craft may either be conventional, a hybrid hydrofoil type, or an air-cushion vehicle larger than the LCAC.

◆ **37 LCU 1610 class (SCB 149, 149B, and 406 types)** Bldrs: See Remarks (In serv. 6-59 to 12-71, except LCU 1680: 11-10-87, and LCU 1681: 12-11-87)

| | |
|---|---|
| LCU 1616 | LCU 1629 to 1635 |
| LCU 1617 | LCU 1643 to 1646 |
| LCU 1619 | LCU 1648 to 1666 |
| LCU 1624 | LCU 1680 |
| LCU 1627 | LCU 1681 |

**D:** 190 tons (390 fl)(LCU 1680, 81: 404 tons fl) **S:** 11 kts
**Dim:** 41.07 × 9.07 × 2.08 **A:** 2/12.7-mm mg (I × 2)
**Electron Equipt:** Radar: 1/LN-66 or SPS-53 navigational
**M:** 4 G.M. 6-71 diesels; 2 Kort-nozzle props; 1,200 hp
(LCU 1680, 81: 2 G.M. 12V71 TI diesels; 2 Kort-nozzle props; 1,700 hp)
**Fuel:** 13 tons **Range:** 1,200/11
**Man:** 6 men + 8 troops (1680, 81: 2 officers, 12 men)

**LCU 1664**—with two M-109A2 self-propelled howitzers aboard
PHC E. Bailey, USN, 6-87

**LCU 1645**—12.7-mm mg abaft conning position G. Arra, 8-86

**LCU 1681** Moss Point, 11-87

REMARKS: LCU 1616–1619, LCU 1623, LCU 1624 delivered 6-59 to 9-60 by Gunderson Bros., Portland, Oregon; LCU 1621, 1626, 1629, and 1630 delivered 6-60 to 1968 by Southern Shipbuilding, Slidell, La.; LCU 1627, 1628, 1631–1635 built by General Ship & Eng. Wks., East Boston, Mass.; LCU 1643–1645 delivered 8-67 to 1969 by Marinette Marine, Marinette, Wisc.; LCU 1646–1666 delivered 1969–70 by Defoe SB, Bay City, Wisc.; LCU 1667–1670 built by General Ship & Eng. Wks.; LCU 1680, 81 ordered 10-85 from Moss Point Marine, Escatawpa, Miss., for delivery 9-86 to Naval Reserve Force units; both laid down 2-4-86, but not delivered until late 1987. The similar, aluminum-hulled LCU 1637 is now a seagoing training device at Roosevelt Roads, Puerto Rico. Missing numbers have either been redesigned as yard craft (YFU—see later pages) or transferred to the U.S. Army (LCU 1667–1679). Cargo capacity is 143 tons; cargo space, 30.5 × 5.5 m. Usually unarmed: Minor differences as construction progressed: five others serve as workboats: LCU 1613, 1614, 1637, 1641, 1647: Three have been designated as ASDV (Auxiliary Swimmer Delivery Vehicle). Twelve of these extremely useful craft are being rehabilitated, beginning with 2 under FY 87; the others will be discarded by the mid-1990s.

## MINOR LANDING CRAFT

◆ **12 (+21 + 57) LCAC class**

| | Bldr | Laid down | L | In serv. |
|---|---|---|---|---|
| LCAC 1 | Textron, New Orleans | . . . | 2-5-84 | 24-12-84 |
| LCAC 2 | Textron, New Orleans | . . . | . . . | 22-2-86 |
| LCAC 3 | Textron, New Orleans | . . . | 31-5-85 | 9-6-86 |
| LCAC 4 | Textron, New Orleans | . . . | 20-12-85 | 17-8-86 |
| LCAC 5 | Textron, New Orleans | . . . | 13-8-86 | -86 |
| LCAC 6 | Textron, New Orleans | . . . | 26-9-86 | 1-12-86 |
| LCAC 7 | Textron, New Orleans | . . . | 8-12-86 | 18-3-87 |
| LCAC 8 | Textron, New Orleans | 9-11-84 | . . . | 10-2-87 |
| LCAC 9 | Textron, New Orleans | 29-3-85 | 3-4-87 | 3-87 |
| LCAC 10 | Textron, New Orleans | 17-6-85 | 5-6-87 | -87 |
| LCAC 11 | Textron, New Orleans | 3-10-85 | . . . | -87 |
| LCAC 12 | Textron, New Orleans | . . . | . . . | 23-12-87 |
| LCAC 13 | Lockheed, Gulfport | 5-12-86 | . . . | 1988 |
| LCAC 14 | Lockheed, Gulfport | 21-1-87 | . . . | 1988 |
| LCAC 15 | Textron, New Orleans | . . . | . . . | 11-88 |
| LCAC 16 | Lockheed, Gulfport | . . . | . . . | 1989 |
| LCAC 17 | Textron, New Orleans | . . . | . . . | . . . |
| LCAC 18 | Lockheed, Gulfport | . . . | . . . | . . . |
| LCAC 19 | Textron, New Orleans | . . . | . . . | . . . |
| LCAC 20 | Textron, New Orleans | . . . | . . . | . . . |
| LCAC 21 | Lockheed, Gulfport | 17-11-86 | . . . | . . . |
| LCAC 22 | Textron, New Orleans | . . . | . . . | . . . |
| LCAC 23 | Textron, New Orleans | . . . | . . . | . . . |
| LCAC 24 | Textron, New Orleans | . . . | . . . | . . . |
| LCAC 25 | Textron, New Orleans | . . . | . . . | . . . |
| LCAC 26 | Textron, New Orleans | . . . | . . . | 1991 |
| LCAC 27 | Lockheed, Gulfport | . . . | . . . | 1992 |
| LCAC 28 | Textron, New Orleans | . . . | . . . | 1992 |
| LCAC 29 | Textron, New Orleans | . . . | . . . | 1992 |
| LCAC 30 | Textron, New Orleans | . . . | . . . | 1992 |
| LCAC 31 | Lockheed, Gulfport | . . . | . . . | 1993 |
| LCAC 32 | Lockheed, Gulfport | . . . | . . . | 1993 |
| LCAC 33 | Lockheed, Gulfport | . . . | . . . | 1993 |

Authorized: 3 in FY 82, 3 in FY 83, 6 in FY 84, 9 in FY 85, 12 in FY 86
Programmed: 9 each in FY 89-94

**D:** 88 tons light (200 fl) **S:** 54 kts (40 when loaded)
**Dim:** 26.8 (24.7 hull) × 14.3 (13.4 hull) × 0.87 (at rest)
**A:** none **Electron Equipt:** Radar: 1/navigational
**M:** 4 Avco TF40B gas turbines (2 for lift); 2 shrouded airscrews; 12,444 hp
**Fuel:** 6.2 tons **Range:** 223/48; 200/40 (loaded) **Man:** 4 crew + 24 troops

REMARKS: Design derived from that of the JEFF-B prototype. Original program for 101 or more has been cut to 90 total. Cargo capacity: 60 tons normal/75 overload.

**MINOR LANDING CRAFT** *(continued)*

**LCAC 12** Bell Textron, 12-87

**LCAC 9** Bell Textron, 3-87

**LCAC 3** Bell Textron, 6-86

To be carried by the LSD 41, LPD 17, LHD 1, and LHA 1 classes. Bow ramp is 8.8 m wide, stern ramp 4.6 m. The deck has 168-m$^2$ parking area. First unit launched 2-5-84 and placed in service 24-12-84; second unit launched 18-1-85 and delivered 19-7-85. First 12 by Bell-Halter, numbers 13, 14 ordered 10-85 from Lockheed, with orders for 7 other FY 85 units delayed. Prototype has experienced numerous design and reliability problems. LCAC 1–6 operate as ACU 5 from Camp Pendleton, Cal., LCAC 7–12 as ACU 4 from Little Creek, Va. LCAC 15, 17, 19, 20, 22–26 ordered 1-7-87, LCAC 27–33 ordered 7-87. Congress directed that one FY 88 LCAC be configured for Arctic duties. Lockheed sold its Gulfport facility to Avondale SY in 1-88.

◆ **23 (+15) LCM(8) Mk 4 class** (In serv. 1967–79; 1985–88)

◆ **54 LCM(8) Mk 3 class** (In serv. 1953–55)

◆ **25 LCM(8) Mk 2 class** (In serv. 1967–69)

**LCM(8) Mk 2 class** L. & L. Van Ginderen, 10-86

**D:** 34 tons light (121 fl) **S:** 12 kts **Dim:** 22.43 × 6.40 × 1.40 (aft)
**M:** 4 G.M. 6-71 diesels; 2 props; 590 hp **Range:** 150/12

Remarks: Began building in 1969. Aluminum version of LCM(8) Mk 1. Cargo: 58 tons. Some have two G.M. 12V71 diesels. Ten were to be built under FY 82 for use aboard the new T-AKX maritime prepositioning ships; canceled. Eight were ordered from Marine Power Co., Seattle, under FY 83; 10 authorized (some for T-AKX) under FY 84; 3 authorized under FY 85. Four ordered 10-85 from Twin City shipyards. Some 34 of the steel-hulled Mk 3 class are to be rehabilitated under FY 92 and 93, and 20 new aluminum-hulled versions are planned for FY 90/91. Totals above may not be entirely accurate, as some were to be transferred to the Philippines in 1987.

◆ **6 LCM(8) Mk 1 class** (In serv. 1954)

**LCM(8) Mod. 1 class of ACU 2** L. & L. Van Ginderen, 3-82

**D:** 56 tons light (116 fl) **S:** 9 kts **Dim:** 22.43 × 6.42 × 1.57
**M:** 4 G.M. 6-71 diesels; 2 props; 620 hp **Range:** 140/9

Remarks: Built between 1949 and 1976. Cargo: 54 tons. U.S. Army also uses large numbers of this type.

◆ **approx. 106 LCM(6) class**

**LCM(6)**—rigged as push tug and beach retrieval craft L. & L. Van Ginderen, 7-85

**Standard LCM(6)**—attached to Naval Air Base, San Diego W. Donko, 7-84

**D:** 24 tons (56 fl) **S:** 10 kts **Dim:** 17.07 × 4.37 × 1.17 (aft)
**M:** 2 Gray Marine 64HN9 (G.M. V71 on Mk 3) diesels; 2 props; 330 hp
**Range:** 130/10

Remarks: Designed during World War II and built between 1952 and 1980. Many used in utility roles. Cargo: 30 tons. Two new examples requested under FY 85 for delivery 1-86. Majority (67) in service are Mk 3, delivered 1977–80; another 36 are Mk 2, delivered 1960–71.

**MINOR LANDING CRAFT** *(continued)*

◆ **136 LCVP Mk 7 class** (In serv. 1966–69)

**LCVP stowed below an LCPL on LST 1197** S. Terzibaschitsch, 11-86

**D:** 13 tons (fl) **S:** 9 kts **Dim:** 10.90 × 3.21 × 1.04 (aft)
**M:** 1 Gray Marine 64HN9 diesel; 225 hp **Range:** 110/9

REMARKS: Glass-reinforced plastic hulls. Can carry 36 troops or 3.5 tons cargo.

◆ **214 LCPL Mk 12 class**

**LCPL Mk 12 class** G. Arra, 7-86

**D:** 13 tons (fl) **S:** 19 kts **Dim:** 10.98 × 3.97 × 1.13
**Electron Equipt:** Radar: 1/LN-66 **M:** 1 G.M. 8V71 TI diesel; 350–425 hp
**Range:** 150/. . . **Man:** 3 crew + 17 passengers

REMARKS: Plastic construction. For use as control craft. Carried aboard LHA, LPD, LSD, LST classes, etc. Total includes 75 LCP(L) Mk 12 ordered from Watercraft America, Edgewater, Fla., in 30-6-83, with 23 more on option; first delivered 8-84 and last by 9-85. Earlier Mk 12 delivered 9-81 to 4-84. In FY 85, 48 more planned for ordering, plus 50 in FY 86 and 16 in FY 87-88, for an eventual total of 214.

◆ **2 amphibious warfare warping tugs** Bldr: Campbell Machine Wks., San Diego, Cal. (In serv. 4-70)

LWT 1 LWT 2

**D:** 61 tons light **S:** 9 kts **Dim:** 25.9 × 6.7 × 2.1
**M:** 2 G.M. 8V71 diesels; 2 steerable props; 420 hp **Man:** 6 tot.

REMARKS: Aluminum construction, intended for handling causeway sections and ship-to-beach fuel lines. Series production not pursued.

◆ **5 powered causeway section side-loadable warping tugs**

SLWT 1–5 (In serv. 1969)

**SLWT-series warping tug** G. Arra, 7-86

**D:** 81.5 tons (light) **S:** 9.5 kts **Dim:** 27.61 × 6.48 × 0.81
**M:** 2 G.M. 8V71 TI diesels; 2 Peerless centrifugal waterjet pumps; 850 hp

REMARKS: Essentially standard Navy "lighter pontoon" barges with a built-in waterjet propulsion section. Intended for vehicle or container offloading for larger ships and for deploying the Amphibious Assault Fuel Supply Facility to a beachhead.

◆ **0 (+37) powered causeway pontoons** Bldr: Wedtech, Bronx, N.Y., and Otonagon, Mich.

**Self-propelled causeway section** W. Donko, 7-87

REMARKS: 37 powered and 51 "dumb" causeway sections were ordered 6-86, but the program has been mired in legal scandals. The Navy has a number of earlier causeway pontoons, which can be propelled by portable diesel engines.

◆ **1 HAVIC commercial prototype** Bldr: CACI, Inc.—Federal/Progressive Metals, Galveston, Tex.

**HAVIC** CACI, 1987

**D:** 13.8 tons (29.7 fl) **S:** 27 kts (20 loaded) **Dim:** 13.77 × . . . × . . .
**M:** 3 Cummins VT-903-M diesels; 3 Roper waterjets; . . . hp
**Range:** 80/20 (loaded) **Man:** 1 tot.

REMARKS: Private proposal evaluated 1987 by Navy and Marine Corps as high-speed, planing-hulled craft to land U.S.M.C. Light Armored Vehicles (LAV). HAVIC = High-speed Assault Vessel and Interdiction Craft. Aluminum construction. *Not* Navy-owned, and no acquisition program yet announced.

**SPECIAL WARFARE CRAFT**

NOTE: The ill-fated SWCM—Special Warfare Craft, Medium—program was canceled by the Secretary of the Navy. The prototype, ordered 10-5-84, was never completed, and the Navy placed the incomplete hull in storage 7-1-87, after work had ceased by the builder, R.M.I., Inc., in summer 1986. Congress had funded a new SWCM prototype under FY 87, to be powered by 2 MTU diesels and displace 132 tons full load, but no contracts were let. The SWCM (originally typed PBM—Patrol Boat, Medium), was to have been a rigid-sidewall air-cushion vehicle to deliver SEAL special forces and could accommodate two swimmer delivery sub-

**SPECIAL WARFARE CRAFT** *(continued)*

mersibles in a floodable well aft. A new, more austere SEAL support craft will presumably be developed.

◆ **24 SWCL "Seafox" class** Bldr: Uniflite, Bellingham, Wash.

36PB801-807 (In serv. 1980–81) 36PB811 (In serv. 1981) 36PB821-8216 (In serv. 1983–84)

**Seafox** G. Arra, 3-85

**D:** 11.3 tons (fl) **S:** 30+ kts **Dim:** 11.0 × 3.0 × 0.84
**A:** 2/12.7-mm mg (I × 2)—2/7.62-mm mg (I × 2)
**Electron Equipt:** Radar: 1/LN-66
**M:** 2 G.M. 6V-92 TA diesels; 2 props; 930 hp **Man:** 3 tot.

Remarks: Glass-reinforced plastic construction. SWCL = Special Warfare Craft, Light. Intended for use by SEAL team commandos; can stow a rubber raft. Have secure voice communications gear, IFF, night-vision equipment, and an echo-sounder. Prototype delivered 11-77 and stricken 2-84. Seven built under FY 80, one under FY 81, and 16 under FY 82. Also built for foreign transfer.

◆ **22 Mini-ATC class** Bldr: Sewart Seacraft, Berwick, La. (In serv. 1972–73)

**Mini-ATC** G. Arra, 1986

**D:** 9.3 tons light (13 fl) **S:** 28.5 kts **Dim:** 10.97 × 3.89 × 0.30
**A:** up to 4/12.7-mm mg (I × 4)—1/40-mm Mk 19 grenade launcher—1/M60 mortar
**M:** 2 G.M. 8V53N diesels; 2 Jacuzzi 14YJ waterjets; 566 hp
**Range:** 37/28 **Man:** 2 crew + 15 troops

Remarks: Aluminum construction. Rectangular planform; bow ramp. Seven weapon-mounting positions. Can carry an LN-66 radar. Very quiet in operation. All operated by Naval Reserve Force Special Boat Units.

◆ **3 Auxiliary Swimmer Delivery Vehicles** Bldr: Southern SB, Slidell, La. (In serv. 1960–68)

ASDV 1 (ex-LCU 1621) ASDV 2 (ex-LCU 1623) ASDV 3 (ex-LCU 1628)

**D:** approx. 210 tons (390 fl) **S:** 11 kts **Dim:** 41.07 × 9.07 × 2.08 (max.)
**Electron Equipt:** 1/LN-66 or SPS-53
**M:** 4 G.M. 6-71 diesels; 2 Kort-nozzle (vertical cycloidal on ASDV 1) props; 1,200 hp
**Range:** 1,200/11 **Fuel:** 13 tons **Man:** 10–14 tot.

Remarks: Assigned to Special Boat Unit 12. Converted to train combat swimmers and to handle and service their equipment. Have a decompression chamber, large crane on port quarter.

**ASDV 3** G. Arra, 3-86

**ASDV 1** G. Arra, 1984

Note: SEAL teams also operate 4-man Mk-7, 6-man Mk-8, and 2-man Mk-9 swimmer delivery submersibles.

**AUXILIARY SHIPS**

Note: This section includes only ships that are subordinate to the U.S. Navy proper. Ships assigned to the civilian-manned Military Sealift Command are listed separately in a following section. Below, ships are listed alphabetically by their U.S. Navy type designation, i.e., AD, AF, AG, etc.

◆ **6 Samuel Gompers-class destroyer tenders (SCB 244 and 700 type)**
Bldrs: AD 37 and AD 38, Puget Sound NSY; AD 41 to AD 44, National Steel, San Diego (*Atlantic Fleet)

| | Laid down | L | In serv. |
|---|---|---|---|
| AD 37 Samuel Gompers | 9-7-64 | 14-5-66 | 1-7-67 |
| AD 38 Puget Sound* | 15-2-65 | 16-9-66 | 27-4-68 |
| AD 41 Yellowstone* | 27-6-77 | 27-1-79 | 28-6-80 |
| AD 42 Acadia | 14-2-78 | 28-7-79 | 6-6-81 |
| AD 43 Cape Cod | 27-1-79 | 2-8-80 | 17-4-82 |
| AD 44 Shenandoah* | 2-8-80 | 6-2-82 | 17-12-83 |

Authorized: 1 in FY 64, 1 in FY 65, 1 in FY 75, 1 in FY 76, 1 in FY 77, 1 in FY 79

**Puget Sound (AD 38)** C. Valentini, 1-87

AUXILIARY SHIPS *(continued)*

**Acadia (AD 42)** L. & L. Van Ginderen, 5-85

**Cape Cod (AD 43)** G. Arra, 2-86

**Shenandoah (AD 44)** L. & L. Van Ginderen, 10-85

**D:** AD 37, 38: 13,600 tons light (20,500 fl); AD 41–44: 13,318 tons light (20,224 fl)
**S:** 20 kts **Dim:** 196.29 × 25.91 × 6.86
**A:** AD 37, 38: 4/20-mm AA (I × 4); others: 2/20-mm AA (I × 2); all: 2/40-mm Mk 19 grenade launchers
**Electron Equipt:** Radar: 1/LN-66, 1/SPS-10—TACAN: AD 38, 41: URN-25
**M:** 1 set de Laval GT; 1 prop; 20,000 hp **Electric:** 12,000 kw
**Boilers:** 2 Combustion Engineering; 43.6 kg/cm$^2$, 462°C
**Man:** AD 37, 38: 43 officers, 1,233 men; AD 41–44; 87 officers, 1,508 men

Remarks: Similar to *L. Y. Spear*-class submarine tenders; AD 41 and later considered a separate class (SCB 700 type) and have facilities to carry and overhaul LM-2500 gas turbines, being tailored to support DD 963, DDG 993, and FFG 7-class ships. All have helo deck aft, no hangar (except AD 38). Maintenance ships for guided-missile cruisers and destroyers. Two 30-ton cranes; two 3.5-ton traveling cranes. Excellent workshops for electronic equipment and surface-to-air missiles. Carry 60,000 different types of repair parts in 65 storerooms totaling 1,795 m$^3$. Originally planned to carry Sea Sparrow in AD 41 and later. One 127-mm DP removed from AD 38 in 1979. AD 38 became 6th Fleet flagship in 7-80, having received an extra mast to support a special SATCOMM antenna (all have the standard WSC-3 SATCOMM installation, with two OE-82 drum-shaped antennas); relieved by *Coronado* (AGF 11) in 4-10-85.

◆ **1 Klondike-class destroyer tender—in reserve**

| | Bldr | Laid down | L | In serv. |
|---|---|---|---|---|
| AD 24 Everglades | Los Angeles SB | 26-6-44 | 28-1-45 | 25-5-51 |

**Everglades (AD 24)**—in reserve A.D. Baker, 8-84

**D:** 8,165 tons (14,700 fl) **S:** 18 kts **Dim:** 149.96 (141.73 pp) × 21.25 × 8.3
**A:** none **Electron Equipt:** Radar: 1/SPS-10
**M:** 1 set Westinghouse GT; 1 prop; 8,500 hp **Electric:** 3,600 kw
**Boilers:** 2 Foster-Wheeler; 30.6 kg/cm$^2$, 393°C
**Fuel:** 2,415 tons **Man:** 800–918 tot.

Remarks: In reserve, used as an accommodations ship at Philadelphia. Built on C-3 cargo hull. Helicopter deck; hangar for DASH.

◆ **3 Dixie-class destroyer tenders** (*Atlantic Fleet)

| | Bldr | Laid down | L | In serv. |
|---|---|---|---|---|
| AD 15 Prairie | New York SB | 7-12-38 | 9-12-39 | 5-8-40 |
| AD 18 Sierra* | Tampa SB | 31-12-41 | 23-2-43 | 20-3-44 |
| AD 19 Yosemite | Tampa SB | 19-1-42 | 16-5-43 | 25-3-44 |

**D:** 9,450 tons (17,190 fl) **S:** 18 kts **Dim:** 161.7 × 22.33 × 7.8
**A:** 4/20-mm AA (I × 4) **Electron Equipt:** Radar: 1/LN-66, 1/SPS-10
**M:** 2 sets Allis-Chalmers (AD 15: Parsons) GT; 2 props; 11,000 hp
**Electric:** 4,100 kw **Boilers:** 4 Babcock & Wilcox; 28.4 kg/cm$^2$, 382°C
**Fuel:** 3,680 tons **Range:** 12,200/12 **Man:** 37 officers, 893 men

**Prairie (AD 15)** G. Arra, 6-86

**Yosemite (AD 19)** L. & L. Van Ginderen, 1986

**AUXILIARY SHIPS** *(continued)*

Remarks: The design of these support ships goes back to pre-1939 programs. Modernized under the FRAM program from 1959 to 1963 to serve as maintenance vessels for guided-missile ships, they have workshops, space parts for missiles, and two 20-ton rotating cranes. Helicopter deck. 127-mm guns removed 1974–75. Sisters *Dixie* (AD 14) struck 15-6-82 for scrap, *Piedmont* (AD 17) struck 30-9-82; sold to Turkey 18-10-82.

◆ **0 (+0 + 5) new-construction ammunition ships**

| | Bldr | Laid down | L | In serv. |
|---|---|---|---|---|
| AE 36 N....... | ... | ... | ... | ... |

Programmed: 1 in FY 91, 1 in FY 92, 2 in FY 93, 1 in FY 94

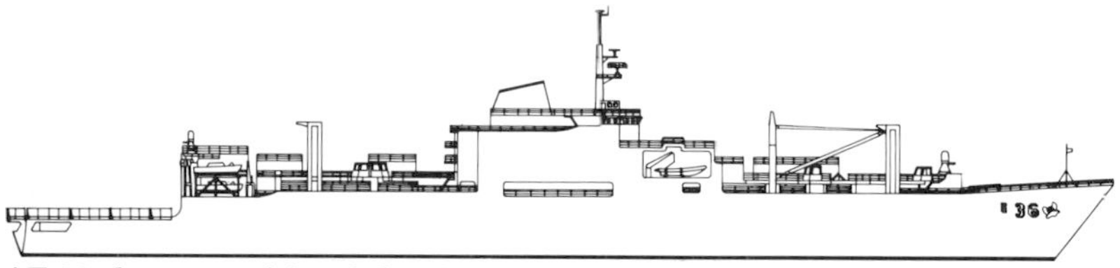

**AE 36 class**—provisional sketch A.D. Baker III, 1985

**D:** 22,790 tons (fl) **S:** 20 kts **Dim:** 175.9 × 26.8 × 8.5
**A:** 2/20-mm Mk 15 CIWS AA (I × 2)—2/25-mm Mk 88 AA (I × 2)—1 or 2/UH-46 helicopters
**Electron Equipt:** Radar: 1/SPS-64(V)9, 1/SPS-67—TACAN: URN-25
EW: SLQ-32(V)1, Mk 36 SRBOC (VI × 2)
**M:** 1 or 2 G.E. LM-2500 gas turbines or diesels; 1 CP prop; 25,000 hp
**Man:** 30 officers, 420 men **Range:** 10,000/20

Remarks: Intended to replace AE 21–25. Construction authorization requests delayed from FY 86 by fiscal constraints. Will carry 6,000 tons ammunition and other cargo and will have a helicopter hangar and flight deck.

◆ **7 Kilauea-class ammunition ships (SCB 703 type)** (*Atlantic Fleet)

| | Bldr | Laid down | L | In serv. |
|---|---|---|---|---|
| AE 27 Butte* | Gen. Dynamics | 21-7-66 | 9-8-67 | 14-12-68 |
| AE 28 Santa Barbara* | Bethlehem, Sparrows Pt | 20-12-66 | 23-1-68 | 11-7-70 |
| AE 29 Mount Hood | Bethlehem, Sparrows Pt | 8-5-67 | 17-7-68 | 1-5-71 |
| AE 32 Flint | Ingalls, Pascagoula | 4-8-69 | 9-11-70 | 20-11-71 |
| AE 33 Shasta | Ingalls, Pascagoula | 10-11-69 | 3-4-71 | 26-2-72 |
| AE 34 Mount Baker* | Ingalls, Pascagoula | 10-5-70 | 23-10-71 | 22-7-72 |
| AE 35 Kiska | Ingalls, Pascagoula | 4-8-71 | 11-3-72 | 16-12-72 |

Authorized: 2 in FY 65, 2 in FY 66, 2 in FY 67, 2 in FY 68

**D:** 9,338 tons light (19,937 fl) **S:** 22 kts **Dim:** 171.9 × 24.7 × 8.5
**A:** 4/76.2-mm DP (II × 2)—AE 33, 35: 2/20-mm Mk 15 CIWS AA (I × 2)—all: 2/UH-46 helicopters
**Electron Equipt:** Radar: 1/LN-66, 1/SPS-10—TACAN: URN-25
EW: SLQ-32(V)1, Mk 36 SRBOC chaff RL (VI × 2)
**M:** 1 set G.E. GT; 1 prop; 22,000 hp **Electric:** 5,500 kw
**Boilers:** 3 Foster-Wheeler; 42.3 kg/cm², 467°C **Man:** 28 officers, 373 men
**Range:** 10,000/20; 18,000/11

**Flint (AE 32)**—both 76.2-mm mounts forward L. & L. Van Ginderen, 1-87

**Kiska (AE 35)**—with Mk 15 CIWS to port fwd. and to starboard amidships, UH-46 helicopter aft G. Arra, 8-86

**Santa Barbara (AE 28)** P. Voss, 3-84

Remarks: Sister *Kilauea* (AE 26) disarmed and transferred to Military Sealift Command 1-10-80. Sophisticated FAST rapid-replenishment system. Twin hangar and flight deck aft. Two twin 76.2-mm mounts and both Mk 56 directors removed. Mk 36 SRBOC chaff-flare launchers to be added to all. AE 32 and later have a larger bulbous forefoot to the bow. Carry cargo fuel for transfer, as well as ammunition. Several solid transfer rigs deactivated to reduce crew size.

◆ **3 Nitro-class ammunition ships (SCB 114A type)** Bldr: Bethlehem Steel Corp., Sparrows Point, Md. (*Atlantic Fleet)

| | Laid down | L | In serv. |
|---|---|---|---|
| AE 23 Nitro* | 20-5-57 | 26-6-58 | 1-5-59 |
| AE 24 Pyro | 21-10-57 | 5-11-58 | 24-7-59 |
| AE 25 Haleakala | 10-3-58 | 17-2-59 | 3-11-59 |

**Nitro (AE 23)**—open gun mounts L. & L. Van Ginderen, 9-86

**Nitro (AE 23)** Skyfotos, 9-86

**D:** 13,990 tons (17,450 fl) **S:** 20 kts **Dim:** 156.1 × 22.0 × 8.8
**A:** 4/76.2-mm DP (II × 2)—4/12.7-mm mg (I × 4)
**Electron Equipt:** Radar: 1/LN-66, 1/SPS-10
**M:** 1 set Bethlehem GT; 1 prop; 16,000 hp **Range:** 10,000/20; 12,000/15
**Boilers:** 2 Combustion Eng.; 43.9 kg/cm², 454°C **Man:** 17 officers, 312 men

Remarks: All had landing platforms for cargo helicopters added aft during the 1960s. Mk 63 gun directors removed, 1977–78. SPS-6 radar removed. AE 24 transferred to Naval Reserve Force 1-9-80 but returned to regular Navy 1-1-82. AE 24 and 25 have enclosed gun houses. Planned to receive SLQ-32(V)1 and Mk 36 SRBOC EW equipment, but had not by 1987. AE 24 has enclosed gun houses.

◆ **2 Suribachi-class ammunition ships (SCB 114 type)** Bldr: Bethlehem Steel Corp., Sparrows Point, Md. (*Atlantic Fleet)

| | Laid down | L | In serv. |
|---|---|---|---|
| AE 21 Suribachi* | 16-5-55 | 3-5-56 | 30-3-57 |
| AE 22 Mauna Kea | 31-1-55 | 2-11-55 | 17-11-56 |

AUXILIARY SHIPS *(continued)*

**Mauna Kea (AE 22)**—note gun arrangement on forecastle
L. & L. Van Ginderen, 10-84

**Mauna Kea (AE 22)** V. Baca, 3-85

**D:** 14,000 tons (17,000 fl) **S:** 21 kts **Dim:** 156.1 × 22.0 × 8.8
**A:** 4/76.2-mm DP (II × 2)
**Electron Equipt:** Radar: 1/LN-66, SPS-10
EW: AE 21: SLQ-32(V)1, Mk 36 SRBOC chaff RL (VI × 2)
**M:** 1 set GT; 1 prop; 16,000 hp **Boilers:** 2 Combustion Eng.; 42.2 kg/cm², 440°C
**Electric:** 12,550 kw **Man:** 17 officers, 312 men **Range:** 10,000/20, 12,000/15

REMARKS: SPS-6 radar removed. Gun mounts superfiring, whereas AE 23 to AE 25 have them side by side. Mk 63 gunfire-control systems removed, 1977–78. AE 22 conducted minelaying trials with Mk 55 aircraft mines laid from portable rails during 1983.

◆ **7 Mars-class combat stores ships (SCB 208 type)** Bldr: National Steel & SB Co., San Diego (*Atlantic Fleet)

| | Laid down | L | In serv. |
|---|---|---|---|
| AFS 1 MARS | 5-5-62 | 15-6-63 | 21-12-63 |
| AFS 2 SYLVANIA* | 18-8-62 | 10-8-63 | 11-7-64 |
| AFS 3 NIAGARA FALLS | 22-5-65 | 25-3-66 | 29-4-67 |
| AFS 4 WHITE PLAINS | 2-10-65 | 23-7-66 | 23-11-68 |
| AFS 5 CONCORD* | 26-3-66 | 17-12-66 | 27-11-68 |
| AFS 6 SAN DIEGO* | 11-3-67 | 13-4-68 | 24-5-69 |
| AFS 7 SAN JOSE | 8-3-69 | 13-12-69 | 23-10-70 |

Authorized: 1 in FY 61, 1 in FY 62, 1 in FY 64, 2 in FY 65, 1 in FY 66, 1 in FY 67

**D:** 9,200 tons light (16,070 fl) **S:** 20 kts **Dim:** 177.08 (161.54 pp) × 24.08 × 7.32
**A:** 4/76.2-mm DP (II × 2)—AFS 4: 2/20-mm Mk 15 CIWS (I × 2)—all: 2/UH-46 helicopters
**Electron Equipt:** Radar: 1/LN-66, 1/SPS-10—TACAN: URN-25
**M:** 1 set de Laval (AFS 6: Westinghouse) GT; 1 prop; 22,000 hp
**Boilers:** 3 Babcock & Wilcox; 40.8 kg/cm², 440°C **Man:** 45 officers, 441 men
**Range:** 10,000/20; 18,000/11 **Electric:** 4,800 kw

**San Diego (AFS 6)** G. Arra, 8-86

**White Plains (AFS 4)**—with Mk 15 CIWS abreast stack
LSPH E. Pitman, R.A.N., 7-85

**Niagara Falls (AFS 3)** LSPH W. McBride, R.A.N., 9-87

REMARKS: Helicopter platform and hangar. Four M-shaped cargo masts with constant-tension equipment; transfer from the supply ship to the receiving ship takes 90 seconds. Five holds (1 and 5 for spare parts, 3 and 4 for provisions, 2 for aviation parts) have only two hatches. Eleven hoists, which raise up to 5.5 tons, link the decks; several others feed into the helicopter area. Ten loading areas (five on each side) and palletized cargo help in the control of replenishment. There are four refrigerated compartments, and three for the storage of dried provisions. Some 25,000 types of spare parts are divided between 40,000 bins and racks and are accounted for by five data-processing machines. 16,597 m³ total stores volume. Quarters air-conditioned. Draw 2.7 m more aft than forward. One boiler always in reserve. SPS-40 radar, Mk 56 fire-control directors and two twin 76.2-mm mounts amidships removed. Remaining twin gun mounts on the forecastle are enclosed. Have yet to receive planned SLQ-32(V)1 EW suite, and few had received the planned 2 CIWS. URN-25 TACAN has replaced SRN-6.

NOTE: Three ex-Royal Fleet Auxiliaries of the "Ness" class are operated by the Military Sealift Command as T-AFS 8, 9, and 10 and are described on page 790.

◆ **1 former salvage ship** Bldr: Sun SB & Dry Dock, Chester, Pa.

| | Laid down | L | In serv. |
|---|---|---|---|
| AG 193 GLOMAR EXPLORER (ex-*Hughes Glomar Explorer*) | . . . | 14-11-72 | 7-73 |

**D:** 63,300 tons (fl) **S:** 10.8 kts **Dim:** 188.6 (169.8 pp) × 35.3 × 14.3
**M:** 5 Nordberg 16-cyl. diesels; 6 G.E. electric motors, 2 props; 13,200 hp—6 side-thrusters
**Man:** 178 tot.

**AG 193**—as *Hughes Glomar Explorer* U.S. Navy

**AUXILIARY SHIPS** *(continued)*

REMARKS: 27,445 grt/37,705 dwt. Built for the Central Intelligence Agency for the sole purpose of recovering a sunken Soviet Golf-class ballistic-missile submarine; given the "cover" role as a deep-sea mining ship (for which she was also usable) by the titular owners, the Summa Corporation. Transferred to Navy ownership 30-9-76 and laid up at Suisun Bay, California, under Maritime Administration control on 17-1-77; she was chartered in June 1978 for thirteen months by Global Marine Corporation for deep-water mineral exploration. In late 1979 it was announced that she would be placed at the disposal of the National Science Foundation and would embark on a ten-year research program as a deep-sea drilling ship for the Ocean Marine Drilling Program. When conversion was completed, the ship would have been able to drill to depths of 6,100 meters beneath the sea floor while operating in 4,000–5,500 meters of water. The project was unfortunately not funded, and AG 193 was returned to the Navy 25-4-80 and transferred to the Maritime Administration for layup at Suisun Bay, California. The ship's associated support barge, HMB-1, was reacquired from the Environmental Protection Agency in 10-82 and laid up.

NOTE: Navigational trials ship *Compass Island* (AG 153), laid up in the National Defense Reserve Fleet at James River, Virginia, was stricken from the Navy List 31-1-86. Auxiliary Deep-Submergence support ship *Point Loma* (AGDS 2, ex-*Point Barrow*, T-AKD 1) was transferred to the Military Sealift Command on 1-10-86 and is described in the Military Sealift Command Section.

◆ **1 Austin-class miscellaneous command ship, ex-amphibious transport, dock**

| | Bldr | Laid down | L | In serv. |
|---|---|---|---|---|
| AGF 11 CORONADO (ex-LPD 11) | Lockheed SB, Seattle | 3-5-65 | 30-7-66 | 23-5-70 |

**Coronado (AGF 11)** G. Arra, 2-87

**Coronado (AGF 11)**—CH-46 helicopter on deck G. Arra, 2-87

**D:** 11,050 tons (17,000 fl) **S:** 21 kts **Dim:** 173.4 × 25.6 (hull) × 7.2
**A:** 4/76.2-mm DP (II × 2)—2/20-mm Mk 15 CIWS (I × 2)—2/12.7-mm mg (I × 2)
**Electron Equipt:** Radar: 1/LN-66, 1/SPS-10, 1/SPS-40—TACAN: URN-25
EW: SLQ-32(V)2, WLR-1H, Mk 36 SRBOC chaff RL (VI × 2)
**M:** 2 sets de Laval GT; 2 props; 24,000 hp
**Boilers:** 2 Foster-Wheeler; 42.3 kg/cm², 467°C **Range:** 7,700/20
**Man:** 27 officers, 446 men + staff: 120 officers, 47 men

REMARKS: Redesignated AGF on 1-10-80, initially only as a temporary relief for *La Salle* (AGF 3), but now retained in a command ship role. Communications enhanced over that of rest of class, but otherwise not as extensively altered as AGF 3. Replaced *Puget Sound* (AD 38) as flagship, Sixth Fleet, 8-85 to 6-86. Transferred to Pacific Fleet and became Flagship, 3rd Fleet, on 26-11-86. Has WSC-6 SATCOMM system antenna on lattice mast to starboard (raised early 1987) and a one-deck-high sponson built out to port forward of the stack. Retains telescoping hangar (22.9 m extended by 6.3) and docking well.

◆ **1 Raleigh-class auxiliary command ship**

| | Bldr | Laid down | L | In serv. |
|---|---|---|---|---|
| AGF 3 LA SALLE (ex-LPD 3) | New York NSY | 2-4-62 | 3-8-63 | 22-2-64 |

Authorized: FY 61

**La Salle (AGF 3)**—white-painted G. Arra, 1983

**La Salle (AGF 3)** Lt. T. Walczyk, USN, 1986

**D:** 8,040 tons light (14,650 fl) **S:** 21 kts **Dim:** 158.4 (155.4 wl) × 25.6 × 6.4
**A:** 4/76.2-mm DP (II × 2)—2/20-mm Mk 15 CIWS gatling AA (I × 2)
**Electron Equipt:** Radar: 1/LN-66, 1/SPS-10, 1/SPS-40—TACAN: URN-25
EW: SLQ-32(V)2, WLR-1, Mk 36 SRBOC chaff RL (VI × 4)
**M:** 2 sets de Laval GT; 2 props; 24,000 hp **Range:** 9,600/16; 16,500/10
**Boilers:** 2 Babcock & Wilcox; 42.2 kg/cm², 467°C **Electric:** 3,600 kw
**Man:** 23 officers, 464 men + flag staff: 4 officers, 40 men

REMARKS: Ex-landing platform, dock (LPD). Since redesignated 1-7-72, employed as flagship of Commander, Middle East Force. Painted white. Well deck used for ship's boats. Helicopter hangar (14.5 × 5.9 m) built on flight deck, to port, with shelter for ceremonial activities to starboard. One Mk 56 and two Mk 63 gunfire-control systems removed 1977–78; lost one gun mount but gained two 20-mm Mk 15 CIWS during major overhaul commencing 27-1-81; resumed flagship duty 13-3-83. A large parabolic dish SATCOMM antenna is mounted on the first mast platform, and a radome for the WSC-6 SATCOMM system is mounted to port, forward of the hangar.

◆ **1 Dolphin class (SCB 207 type) research submarine**

| | Bldr | Laid down | L | In serv. |
|---|---|---|---|---|
| AGSS 555 DOLPHIN | Portsmouth NSY | 9-11-62 | 8-6-68 | 17-8-69 |

Authorized: FY 61

**Dolphin (AGSS 555)** G. Arra, 3-85

**D:** 860/950 tons **S:** 7.5/10 or 15 (see Remarks) **Dim:** 50.29 × 5.92 × 4.9
**Electron Equipt:** Sonar: BQS-15, bow passive array, towed array, BQR-2
**M:** diesel-electric, 2 G.M. 12V71 diesels; 1 prop; 1,650 hp
**Endurance:** 14 days (12 hours sub.) **Man:** 3 officers, 26 men, 5 scientists

## AUXILIARY SHIPS *(continued)*

Remarks: The pressure hull is a perfect cylinder, 5.49 m in diameter, strongly braced and closed at the forward and after ends by two hemispheric bulkheads. Used for deep-diving tests as well as acoustic and oceanographic experiments. Single torpedo tube removed in 1970. Scientific payload of 12 tons. Using two 165 cell, 250-volt, lead-acid batteries, 10 knots can be reached when submerged; when silver-zinc batteries are substituted, the speed is 15 knots. Very quiet machinery. Has four mini-computers for scientific data processing. Several scientific, passive multihydrophone arrays are fitted at the bow, and acoustic arrays can be towed at up to 4,000 feet behind the craft. Most support is shore-based. Home-ported at San Diego. Has a portable SPS-53 radar for surface navigation.

Note: Hospital ship *Sanctuary* (AH 17), in reserve since 28-3-74 and transferred to Maritime Administration custody on 23-8-78, was stricken from the Navy list on 31-1-86. Hospital ships *Mercy* (T-AH 19) and *Comfort* (T-AH 20) are described in the Military Sealift Command section.

◆ **5 Cimarron-class oilers (SCB 379 type)** (*Atlantic Fleet)

| | Bldr | Laid down | L | In serv. |
|---|---|---|---|---|
| AO 177 Cimarron | Avondale SY | 18-5-78 | 28-4-79 | 10-1-81 |
| AO 178 Monongahela* | Avondale SY | 15-8-78 | 4-8-79 | 5-9-81 |
| AO 179 Merrimack* | Avondale SY | 16-7-79 | 17-5-80 | 14-11-81 |
| AO 180 Willamette | Avondale SY | 4-8-80 | 18-7-81 | 18-12-82 |
| AO 186 Platte* | Avondale SY | 2-2-81 | 30-1-82 | 16-4-83 |

**Cimarron (AO 177)** LSPH W. McBride, R.A.N., 2-88

**Willamette (AO 180)**—with 2 CIWS, electronics van on helicopter deck G. Arra, 7-86

**Platte (AO 186)**—with 2 Mk 15 CIWS S. Terzibaschitsch, 7-86

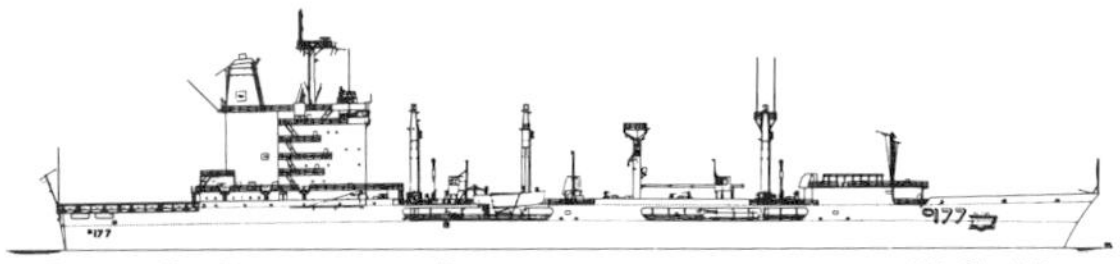
**AO 177 before stretch** U.S. Navy

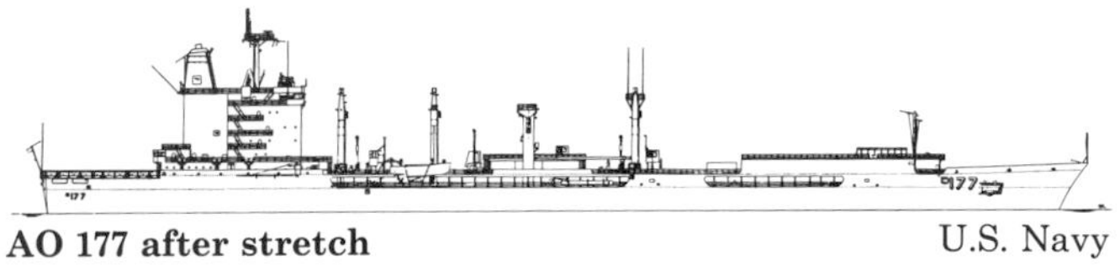
**AO 177 after stretch** U.S. Navy

**D:** 27,500 tons (fl) **S:** 20 kts
**Dim:** 180.29 (167.64 pp) × 25.33 × 10.16 (11.35 prop)
**A:** AO 180, 186: 2/20-mm Mk 15 CIWS (I × 2)
**Electron Equipt:** Radar: 1/LN-66, 1/SPS-55 (AO 180, 186: SPS-10B)
**M:** 1 set GT; 1 prop; 24,000 hp **Electric:** 8,250 kw
**Boilers:** 2 Combustion Engineering; 42.25 kg/cm², 454°C
**Man:** 11 officers, 124 men (225 tot. accommodations)

Remarks: Carry 72,000 barrels fuel oil, 48,000 barrels JP-5 gas-turbine fuel, and can replenish ships while making 15 knots. Also carry 98 m³ dry stores and 3 refrigerated stores containers. There is a helicopter platform aft. Four constant-tension replenishment stations to port, three to starboard. Able to transfer 408,000 liters of fuel oil and 245,000 liters JP-5 per hour. No additional units planned; subsequent oilers will be under Military Sealift Command control. Although these are high-value targets, no chaff or SLQ-32 systems are installed.

These ships are scheduled to be lengthened; one under FY 88, and 2 each in FY 89 and 90. Subsequent to "jumboizing," they will displace 37,866 tons (fl) on a draft of 10.16 m, and length will be 215.95 m overall. Speed will drop to 19.4 kts. Cargo capacity will be 183,000 barrels fuel oil/JP-5, 401 m³ feedwater, 397 m³ potable water, 205 m³ dry stores, and 8 refrigerated stores containers. Accommodations will be increased to 235, Mk 15 CIWS will be added to AO 177–179; SLQ-32(V)1 and Mk 36 SRBOC EW equipment will be added, as will SLQ-25 Nixie towed torpedo decoys. A new-design propeller and rudder will be fitted, and underway transfer capability will be enhanced.

◆ **3 Ashtabula-class oilers (SCB 244 jumbo type)—1 in reserve**
Bldr: Bethlehem Steel, Sparrows Point, Md. (*Atlantic Fleet; †reserve)

| | L | In serv. |
|---|---|---|
| AO 51 Ashtabula† | 22-5-43 | 7-8-43 |
| AO 98 Caloosahatchee* | 6-7-45 | 10-10-45 |
| AO 99 Canisteo* | 2-6-45 | 3-12-45 |

**Canisteo (AO 99)** G. Arra, 8-86

**Caloosahatchee (AO 98)**—in light condition W. Donko, 7-85

**D:** 36,500 tons (fl) **S:** 18 kts **Dim:** 196.3 × 22.9 × 9.6
**A:** 2/76.2-mm Mk 26 DP (I × 2)
**Electron Equipt:** Radar: 1/Raytheon 1650/6x, 1/SPS-10
**M:** 1 set GT; 2 props; 13,500 hp **Range:** 16,000/11
**Boilers:** 4 Foster-Wheeler "K"; 31.7 kg/cm², 399°C **Man:** 20 officers, 350 men

Remarks: Lengthened 27 m by insertion of new mid-body during 1960s. Two 76.2-mm removed, 1977–78, along with one Mk 52 and two Mk 51 GFCS. Carry 143,000 barrels of fuel, 175 tons of ammunition, and 100 tons of provisions. No helicopter deck. Last World War II-built oilers in regular naval service; both in Atlantic. AO 51 decommissioned 30-9-82 to National Defense Reserve Fleet. Attempts to decommission AO 98 and 99 in FY 88 by Congress were defeated; nonetheless, they are very old and hard-worked ships and will soon be replaced by Military Sealift Command *Henry J. Kaiser*-class oilers.

◆ **0 (+0 + 4) new-construction fast combat support ships**
Bldr: National Steel, San Diego

| | Laid down | L | In serv. |
|---|---|---|---|
| AOE 6 Supply | 11-88 | 7-90 | 4-91 |
| AOE 7 N . . . . . . . | . . . | . . . | . . . |
| AOE 8 N . . . . . . . | . . . | . . . | . . . |
| AOE 9 N . . . . . . . | . . . | . . . | . . . |

Authorized: AOE 6 in FY 87; planned: AOE 7 in FY 89, AOE 8 and 9 in FY 91

**D:** 19,700 tons light (48,800 fl) **S:** 26 kts **Dim:** 230.10 × 32.61 × 11.89
**A:** 1/Mk 29 launcher (XVI × 1, Sea Sparrow and RAM missiles)—2/20-mm Mk 15 CIWS (I × 2)—2/25-mm Mk 88 AA (I × 2)—3 helicopters

**AUXILIARY SHIPS** *(continued)*

**Electron Equipt:** Radar: 1/SPS-64(V)9, 1/SPS-67, 1/Mk 23 TAS, 1/Mk 91 f.c.s. (2 directors)
EW: SLQ-32(V)3, Mk 36 SRBOC chaff RL (VI × 4)
TACAN: URN-25
**M:** 4 G.E. LM-2500 gas turbines; 2/6-bladed props; 100,000 hp
**Range:** . . . **Man:** 35 officers, 625 men (accommodations)
**Electric:** 12,500 kw (5 Caterpillar 3608 diesel-driven sets)

**AOE 6**—artist's concept T. Freeman/U.S. Navy, 1985

REMARKS: Modified versions of the AOE 1 class with better protective systems. Cargo: 156,000 bbl liquid, plus 2,450 tons dry stores (including 1,800 tons ammunition and 400 tons refrigerated provisions). AOE 6 ordered 23-1-87, with option to build AOE 7–9. Will have Franca-Tosi-type clutch/gearbox, fixed-pitch props.

◆ **4 Sacramento-class fast combat support ships (SCB 196 type)** (*Atlantic Fleet)

| | Bldr | Laid down | L | In serv. |
|---|---|---|---|---|
| AOE 1 SACRAMENTO | Puget Sound NSY | 30-6-61 | 14-9-63 | 14-3-64 |
| AOE 2 CAMDEN | New York SB | 17-2-64 | 29-5-65 | 1-4-67 |
| AOE 3 SEATTLE* | Puget Sound NSY | 1-10-65 | 2-3-68 | 5-4-69 |
| AOE 4 DETROIT* | Puget Sound NSY | 29-11-66 | 21-6-69 | 28-3-70 |

Authorized: 1 in FY 61, 1 in FY 63, 1 in FY 65, 1 in FY 66

**D:** 18,700 tons light (53,600 fl) **S:** 26 kts **Dim:** 241.4 (215.8 pp) × 32.9 × 11.6
**A:** 1/Mk 29 launcher for Sea Sparrow (VIII × 1)—2/20-mm Mk 15 CIWS (I × 2)—4/12.7-mm mg (I × 4)—2/UH-46 helicopters.

**Sacramento (AOE 1)**—with SPS-40 and WLR-1 EW suite G. Gyssels, 7-86

**Seattle (AOE 3)**—with Mk 23 TAS on foremast, SLQ-32 EW G. Arra, 6-86

**Electron Equipt:** Radar: 1/SPS-53, 1/SPS-10 (AOE 1 and 2: 1/SPS-40 also), 1/Mk 91 Mod. 1, AOE 3: Mk 23 TAS
EW: AOE 1, 2, 4: WLR-1, WLR-3; AOE 3: SLQ-32(V)3, Mk 36 SRBOC chaff RL (III × 4)
TACAN: SRN-6 (AOE 3, 4: URN-25)
**M:** G.E. GT; 2 props; 100,000 hp
**Boilers:** 4 Combustion Engineering, 42.2 kg/cm², 480°C
**Range:** 6,000/26; 10,000/17 **Man:** 33 officers, 567 men

**Detroit (AOE 4)**—no SPS-40 or Mk 23 L. & L. Van Ginderen, 9-86

REMARKS: Sea Sparrow launcher and Mk 91 Mod. 1 control system with two directors replaced two twin 76.2-mm DP forward; two Mk 56 GFCS removed. The two remaining 76.2-mm gun mounts aft replaced by two 20-mm Mk 15 CIWS Vulcan/Phalanx. The SLQ-32(V)3 ECM will replace WLR-1, and Mk 36 SRBOC chaff rocket system is being added. AOE 3 was the first to get the Mk 23 TAS Mod. 2 (Target Acquisition System), which in these ships will be a stand-alone system employing the UYA-4 computer. Carry 177,000 barrels fuel plus 2,150 tons ammunition, 750 tons provisions. Helicopter hangar and flight deck for 2–3 UH-46 Sea Knight vertical-replenishment helicopters. Turbines in AOE 1 and AOE 2 are from battleship *Kentucky* (BB 66). A fifth unit was canceled. AOR 2 is testing the "standard Navy UNREP" suite, with new winches, rams, ram-tensioners, and control booths.

◆ **7 Wichita-class replenishment oilers (SCB 707 type)** Bldr: General Dynamics, Quincy, Mass. (*Atlantic Fleet)

| | Laid down | L | In serv. |
|---|---|---|---|
| AOR 1 WICHITA | 18-6-66 | 18-3-68 | 7-6-69 |
| AOR 2 MILWAUKEE* | 29-11-66 | 17-1-69 | 1-11-69 |
| AOR 3 KANSAS CITY | 20-4-68 | 28-6-69 | 6-6-70 |
| AOR 4 SAVANNAH* | 22-1-69 | 25-4-70 | 5-12-70 |
| AOR 5 WABASH | 21-1-70 | 6-2-71 | 20-11-71 |
| AOR 6 KALAMAZOO* | 28-10-70 | 11-11-72 | 11-8-73 |
| AOR 7 ROANOKE | 19-1-74 | 7-12-74 | 30-10-76 |

Authorized: 2 in FY 65, 2 in FY 66, 2 in FY 67, 1 in FY 72

**Milwaukee (AOR 2)**—Sea Sparrow and CIWS L. & L. Van Ginderen, 10-87

**Kalamazoo (AOR 6)**—with Mk 23 TAS and SLQ-32(V)3 Skyfotos, 9-86

AUXILIARY SHIPS *(continued)*

**Roanoke (AOR 7)** L. & L. Van Ginderen, 1-87

**Kansas City (AOR 3)**—Mk 15 CIWS added, SRN-15 TACAN atop foremast LSPH W. McBride, R.A.N., 12-87

**D:** 13,000 tons light (41,350 fl) **S:** 20 kts **Dim:** 200.9 × 29.3 × 10.1
**A:** AOR 1: unarmed—AOR 2–7: 1/Mk 29 launcher (VIII × 1)—2/Mk 15 CIWS gatling AA (I × 2)—AOR 2 also: 2/20-mm AA (I × 2)
**Electron Equipt:** Radar: 1/LN-66 or SPS-53, 1/SPS-10; Sea Sparrow ships: 2/Mk 91 Mod. 1 (2 directors)—AOR 6 also: Mk 23 TAS
EW: Mk 36 SRBOC chaff RL (VI × 4)—AOR 4–6 also: SLQ-32(V)3
TACAN: URN-25 (AOR 2, 3, 7: SRN-15)
**M:** G.E. GT; 2 props; 32,000 shp
**Boilers:** 3 Foster-Wheeler; 43.3 kg/cm², 454°C **Electric:** 8,000 kw
**Range:** 6,500/20; 10,000/17 **Man:** 20 officers, 363-420 men

Remarks: Carry 175,000 barrels fuel (90,000 distillate fuel), 600 tons ammunition, 575 tons provisions. All except AOR 7 originally had no hangars flanking stack and had 4/76.2-mm DP. Several carried interim armaments of 2 or 4 single 20-mm AA after hangars were added. SLQ-32(V)3 will be added to all. As with AOE 1 class, they are eventually to get the Mk 23 Mod. 2 TAS (Target Acquisition System) radar with associated UYA-4 computerized data system; AOR 6 had it by 7-86. The two Mk 76 radar directors for the Mk 91 Mod. 1 missile fire-control system are mounted atop tall lattice towers just forward of the stack. There are four stations for liquid transfer and two for solid transfer to port, three liquid and two solid to starboard; all have constant-tension devices. AOR 2 used in minelaying trials 1983, using Mk 55 mines and portable rails.

◆ **4 Vulcan-class repair ships** (*Atlantic Fleet, †in reserve)

| | Bldr | Laid down | L | In serv. |
|---|---|---|---|---|
| AR 5 Vulcan* | New York SB, Camden | 26-12-39 | 14-12-40 | 16-6-41 |
| AR 6 Ajax† | Los Angeles SB & DD | 7-5-41 | 22-8-42 | 30-10-43 |
| AR 7 Hector† | Los Angeles SB & DD | 28-7-41 | 11-11-42 | 7-2-44 |
| AR 8 Jason | Los Angeles SB & DD | 9-3-42 | 3-4-43 | 19-6-44 |

**Vulcan (AR 5)** Pradignac & Leo, 9-86

**Jason (AR 8)** G. Arra, 1987

**D:** 9,325 tons (16,245 fl) **S:** 19.2 kts **Dim:** 161.37 (158.5 pp) × 22.35 × 7.11
**A:** 4/20-mm AA (I × 4)
**Electron Equipt:** Radar: 1/LN-66 or CRP 1500, 1/SPS-10
**M:** 2 sets GT; 2 props; 11,535 hp **Electric:** 4,500 kw
**Boilers:** 4 Babcock & Wilcox; 28.2 kg/cm², 382°C
**Fuel:** 3,800 tons **Range:** 18,000/12 **Man:** 41 officers, 979 men

Remarks: Very elaborately equipped repair facilities. Two 10-ton cranes fitted. Four 127-mm DP (I × 4) removed from all. *Jason,* typed ARH 1 (heavy hull-repair ship), was redesignated as AR 8 in 1957. AR 8 badly damaged in collision with AO 186, 2-86, but repaired by 6-86. Pacific Fleet units AR 6 and AR 7 to reserve 31-12-86 and 31-3-87, respectively.

◆ **1 Achelous-class small repair ship** Bldr: Bethlehem Steel, Hingham, Mass.

| | Laid down | L | In serv. | Recomm. |
|---|---|---|---|---|
| ARL 24 Sphinx (ex-LST 963) | 20-10-44 | 18-11-44 | 12-12-44 | 26-7-85 |

**Sphinx (ARL 24)** U.S. Navy, 7-85

**D:** 3,960 tons (fl) **S:** 11.6 kts **Dim:** 99.98 (96.32 wl) × 15.24 × 3.71
**A:** 8/40-mm Mk 2 AA (IV × 2)—4/Stinger SAM launch positions—6/12.7-mm mg (I × 6)
**Electron Equipt:** Radar: 1/SPS-10—TACAN: URN-25
EW: intercept and D/F arrays
**M:** 2 G.M. 12-278A diesels; 2 props; 1,800 hp **Electric:** 520 kw
**Fuel:** 620 tons **Man:** 11 officers, 180 men

Remarks: Recommissioned after extensive alterations 9-84 to 7-85 at Puget Sound NSY that took over three times the period required to build her during World War II. Equipped for duties off Central America, with new communications and intercept arrays, helicopter deck amidships. Has two obsolete Mk 51 Mod. 2 lead-computing optical directors for the antiquated 40-mm gun mounts. Retains a 25-ton boom forward and carries two LCVP in Welin davits abreast enlarged after superstructure. Sister *Indra* (ARL 37, ex-LST 1147) was stricken 1-12-77 but has since been retained at Norfolk as an accommodations hulk. ARL 24 is attached to the Atlantic Fleet.

◆ **4 (+1) ARS 50-class salvage ships** Bldr: Peterson Bldrs., Sturgeon Bay, Wisc. (*Atlantic Fleet)

| | Laid down | L | In serv. |
|---|---|---|---|
| ARS 50 Safeguard | 8-11-82 | 12-11-83 | 17-8-85 |
| ARS 51 Grasp* | 30-3-83 | 21-4-84 | 14-12-85 |
| ARS 52 Salvor | 16-9-83 | 28-7-84 | 14-6-86 |
| ARS 53 Grapple* | 25-4-84 | 8-12-84 | 15-11-86 |

Authorized: 1 in FY 81, 2 in FY 82, 1 in FY 83; planned: 1 in FY 90

**D:** 2,725 tons light (3,193 fl) **S:** 13.5 kts **Dim:** 77.72 (73.15 wl) × 15.54 × 4.72
**A:** 2/12.7-mm mg (I × 2) **Electron Equipt:** Radar: 1/SPS-64(V)
**M:** 4 Caterpillar diesels, geared drive; 2 CP Kort-nozzle props; 4,800 hp (4,200 sust)
**Electric:** 2,250 kw (3 Caterpillar diesel sets) **Range:** 8,000/12
**Man:** 6 officers, 85 enlisted

AUXILIARY SHIPS *(continued)*

**Safeguard (ARS 50)**—on trials U.S. Navy, 5-85

**Grasp (ARS 51)** U.S. Navy, 8-85

**Grapple (ARS 53)** G. Arra, 1987

REMARKS: First unit ordered 1981, with option for four more from same shipyard; fifth ship deleted from program by Congress. Design developed from ARS 38. Have 54-ton open-ocean bollard pull and, using beach extraction gear, are able to exert 360-ton pull. Have 500-hp bow-thruster. 40-ton boom aft, 7.5-ton forward. Able to dead-lift 150 tons over bow or stern. Cargo hold 596 m$^3$. Two 914-m-long, 57-mm towing hawsers; able to tow a CVN at 5 kts. Have Mk 12 diving system; able to support hard-hat divers to 58 m and SCUBA divers; decompression chamber fitted. Up to 25 percent of crew may be women; 12 extra berths to be fitted. Four foam fire-fighting monitors. One additional unit of this class is planned, under FY 91.

◆ **7 Diver- and Bolster-class salvage ships** Bldr: Basalt Rock Co., Napa, Calif. (*Atlantic Fleet, †Naval Reserve Force)

| | Laid down | L | In serv. |
|---|---|---|---|
| ARS 8 PRESERVER*† | 26-10-42 | 1-4-43 | 11-1-44 |
| ARS 38 BOLSTER† | 20-7-44 | 23-12-44 | 1-5-45 |
| ARS 39 CONSERVER* | 10-8-44 | 27-1-45 | 9-6-45 |
| ARS 40 HOIST*† | 13-9-44 | 31-3-45 | 21-7-45 |
| ARS 41 OPPORTUNE* | 13-9-44 | 31-3-45 | 5-10-45 |
| ARS 42 RECLAIMER† | 11-11-44 | 25-6-45 | 20-12-45 |
| ARS 43 RECOVERY* | 6-1-45 | 4-8-45 | 15-5-46 |

**Recovery (ARS 43)** G. Gyssels, 6-86

**Hoist (ARS 40)**—2 OE-82 SATCOMM antennas above pilothouse G. Arra, 4-86

**D:** 1,530 tons (1,970 ft), ARS 38 to ARS 43: 2,045 (fl) **S:** 14.8 kts
**Dim:** 65.1 × 12.5 (ARS 38 to ARS 43: 13.4) × 4.0
**A:** 2/20-mm AA (I × 2)—2/12.7-mm mg (I × 2)
**Electron Equipt:** Radar: 1/SPS-53 (ARS 40, 41, 43: SPS-10), ARS-43: 1/Raytheon 3400 also
**M:** 4 Cooper-Bessemer GSB-8 or Caterpillar D399 diesels, electric drive; 2 props; 3,060 hp (2,440 sust.)
**Electric:** 460 kw **Fuel:** 300 tons **Range:** 9,000/14; 20,000/7
**Man:** 6 officers, 77 men (ARS 30–43: 7 officers, 98 men)

REMARKS: Equipped for diver support, salvage, and towing. ARS 38, ARS 39, and ARS 42 re-engined with Caterpillar diesels. ARS 8 transferred to Naval Reserve Force 1-11-79, ARS 38 on 30-6-83, and ARS 70 and 72 in 9-86. ARS 8 and 39 decommissioned 30-9-83 but were recommissioned 26-9-87 for salvage and patrol duties in the Caribbean area. *Escape* (ARS 6) reactivated from Maritime Administration reserve and transferred to Coast Guard 4-12-80. *Clamp* (ARS 33) stricken 1963 to MARAD reserve fleet; reacquired 1973, but not reactivated and again stricken. *Curb* (ARS 21) and *Gear* (AR 34) stricken and sold 30-4-81.

◆ **5 L. Y. Spear-class submarine tenders (SCB 702 and 737 types)** (*Atlantic Fleet)

| | Bldr | Laid down | L | In serv. |
|---|---|---|---|---|
| AS 36 L. Y. SPEAR* | Gen. Dynamics, Quincy | 5-5-66 | 7-9-67 | 28-2-70 |
| AS 37 DIXON | Gen. Dynamics, Quincy | 7-9-67 | 20-6-70 | 7-8-71 |
| AS 39 EMORY S. LAND* | Lockheed SB, Seattle | 2-3-76 | 4-5-77 | 7-7-79 |
| AS 40 FRANK CABLE* | Lockheed SB, Seattle | 2-3-76 | 14-1-78 | 5-2-80 |
| AS 41 MCKEE | Lockheed SB, Seattle | 14-1-78 | 16-2-80 | 15-8-81 |

Authorized: 1 in FY 65, 1 in FY 66, 1 in FY 72, 1 in FY 73, 1 in FY 77

**D:** AS 36, 37: 12,770 tons light (23,493 fl); AS 39–41: 13,842 tons light (22,650 fl)
**S:** 20 kts (18 sust.) **Dim:** 196.29 × 25.91 × 7.77 **A:** 4/20-mm AA (I × 4)
**Electron Equipt:** Radar: 1/. . . nav., 1/SPS-10
**M:** 1 set de Laval GT; 1 prop; 20,000 hp **Electric:** 11,000 kw
**Boilers:** 2 Combustion Engineering; 43.6 kg/cm$^2$, 462°C
**Man:** AS 36 and AS 37: 52 officers, 480 men (accommodations: 1,080 tot)
AS 39 to AS 41: 53 officers, 567 men + flag staff: 25 officers, 44 men

**AUXILIARY SHIPS** *(continued)*

**Dixon (AS 37)** L. & L. Van Ginderen, 10-84

**Frank Cable (AS 40)** G. Arra, 1984

**L.Y. Spear (AS 36)** S. Terzibaschitsch, 7-86

REMARKS: Provide support to up to 12 submarines with up to 4 alongside at once. AS 39 to AS 41 having been specifically tailored to the needs of the *Los Angeles* class. One 30-ton crane and two 5-ton traveling cranes. Have a total of 53 specialized repair shops. Medical facilities include operating room, 23-bed ward, and dental clinic. AS 39 and later also carry 2/40-mm Mk 19 grenade launchers. Helicopter deck, but no hangar. AS 37 equipped to support Tomahawk cruise missiles. AS 36 and AS 37 have General Electric turbines and Foster-Wheeler boilers. No longer planned to fit Vulcan/Phalanx or Sea Sparrow in later ships. Two 127-mm DP (I × 2) removed from AS 36 and AS 37. AS 38 (FY 69) canceled 27-3-69. No other submarine tenders currently programmed.

◆ **2 Simon Lake-class submarine tenders (SCB 238 type)** (*Atlantic Fleet)

| | Bldr | Laid down | L | In serv. |
|---|---|---|---|---|
| AS 33 SIMON LAKE* | Puget Sound NSY | 7-1-63 | 8-2-64 | 7-11-64 |
| AS 34 CANOPUS* | Ingalls, Pascagoula | 2-3-64 | 12-2-65 | 4-11-65 |

Authorized: 1 in FY 63, 1 in FY 64

**D:** 12,000 tons (AS 33: 19,934 fl, AS 34: 21,089 fl) **S:** 18 kts
**Dim:** 196.2 × 25.9 × 8.7 **A:** 4/76.2-mm DP (II × 2)
**Electron Equipt:** Radar: 1/LN-66, 1/SPS-10
**M:** de Laval GT; 1 prop; 20,000 hp **Electric:** 11,000 kw
**Boilers:** 2 Combustion Engineering; 43.6 kg/cm², 462°C **Range:** 7,600/18
**Man:** AS 33: 58 officers, 857 men; AS 34: 56 officers, 604 men (accommodations: 1,266 tot.)

**Simon Lake (AS 33)** G. Arra, 8-85

REMARKS: Specifically equipped to support nuclear-powered, ballistic-missile submarines, with 16 missiles stowed vertically amidships. Converted to carry Poseidon missiles, 1969–71. Both are to serve Trident-equipped SSBNs; AS 33 converted under FY 78, and AS 34 converted 1984–85 and has been given new cranes. Sister AS 35 canceled on 3-12-64. Two 30-ton cranes and four 5-ton traveling cranes. Helicopter deck aft, but no hangar. Two Mk 63 fire-control systems for guns removed.

◆ **2 Hunley-class submarine tenders (SCB 194 type)** (*Atlantic Fleet)

| | Bldr | Laid down | L | In serv. |
|---|---|---|---|---|
| AS 31 HUNLEY* | Newport News SB | 28-11-60 | 28-9-61 | 16-6-62 |
| AS 32 HOLLAND* | Ingalls, Pascagoula | 5-3-62 | 19-1-63 | 7-9-63 |

Authorized: 1 in FY 60, 1 in FY 62

**Hunley (AS 31)** L. & L. Van Ginderen, 5-82

**Hunley (AS 31)** F. Jentsch, 8-87

**D:** 11,000 tons light (19,819 fl) **S:** 19 kts **Dim:** 182.6 × 25.3 × 7.4
**A:** 4/20-mm AA (I × 4) **Electron Equipt:** Radar: 1/LN-66, 1/SPS-10
**M:** 10 Fairbanks-Morse 38D$\frac{1}{8}$ diesels, electric drive; 1 prop; 15,000 hp
**Electric:** 12,000 kw **Range:** 10,000/12
**Man:** AS 31: 54 officers, 558 men; AS 32: 55 officers, 604 men (accommodations: 1,266 tot.)

REMARKS: Intended to support SSBNs; converted to carry Poseidon missiles, 1973–75. Air-conditioned. Helicopter platform. Original 32.5-ton rotating hammerhead gantry crane removed around 1970 and replaced by two 30-ton cranes.

**AUXILIARY SHIPS** *(continued)*

◆ **1 Proteus-class submarine tender (SCB 190 conversion type)** Bldr: Moore SB & DD, Oakland, Cal.

| | Laid down | L | In serv. | Conv. |
|---|---|---|---|---|
| AS 19 Proteus | 15-9-41 | 12-11-42 | 31-1-44 | 8-7-60 |

**Proteus (AS 19)** LSPH E. Pitman, R.A.N., 9-84

**D:** 14,195 tons (20,295 fl) **S:** 15.4 kts **Dim:** 175.1 (171.9 wl) × 27.3 × 8.4
**A:** 4/20-mm AA (I × 4) **Electron Equipt:** Radar: 1/LN-66, 1/SPS-10
**M:** 8 G.M. 16-248 diesels, electric drive; 2 props; 11,520 hp
**Electric:** 5,000 kw **Range:** 26,000/10
**Man:** 53 officers, 624 men (accommodations: 1,176 tot.)

Remarks: Lengthened 13.4 m, 1959–60, as the first SSBN tender, carrying Polaris missiles in the new section, handled by an extendable gantry crane. Superstructure enlarged over that of former sisters in the *Fulton* class. Served the *George Washington* and *Ethan Allen* class SSBNs in the Pacific; often stationed at Diego Garcia since 1981 as a general-purpose tender; home-ported at Guam.

◆ **2 Fulton-class submarine tenders** (*Atlantic Fleet)

| | Bldr | Laid down | L | In serv. |
|---|---|---|---|---|
| AS 11 Fulton* | Mare Island NSY | 19-7-39 | 27-12-40 | 12-9-41 |
| AS 18 Orion* | Moore SB, Oakland | 31-7-41 | 14-10-42 | 30-9-43 |

**D:** 9,734 tons (18,000 fl) **S:** 15.4 kts **Dim:** 161.4 × 22.3 × 7.8
**A:** 4/20-mm AA (I × 4) **Electron Equipt:** Radar: 1/LN-66, 1/SPS-10
**M:** 8 G.M. 16-248 diesels, electric drive; 2 props; 11,200 hp **Electric:** 2,300 kw
**Range:** 32,000/15 **Fuel:** 3,760 tons
**Man:** AS 11: 53 officers, 522 men; AS 18: 56 officers, 690 men (accommodations: 1,274 tot.)

**Orion (AS 18)**—with new cranes L. & L. Van Ginderen, 10-86

**Fulton (AS 11)**—note gun tub at bow Skyfotos, 4-85

Remarks: All received FRAM-II modernization and can support nuclear submarines. Foundry can cast pieces up to 250 kg. Two 20-ton rotating cranes are fitted. Sperry (AS 12) decommissioned and stricken 30-9-82; *Bushnell* (AS 15) stricken 15-11-80 and sunk 3-6-83 as a torpedo target; *Howard W. Gilmore* (AS 16) decommissioned 30-9-80 and struck 1-12-80; *Nereus* (AS 17), decommissioned and stricken 27-10-71, remains as a hulk at Bremerton.

◆ **2 Pigeon-class submarine-rescue ships (SCB 721 type)** Bldr: Alabama DD & SB, Mobile (*Atlantic Fleet)

| | Laid down | L | In serv. |
|---|---|---|---|
| ASR 21 Pigeon | 17-7-68 | 13-8-69 | 28-4-73 |
| ASR 22 Ortolan* | 22-8-68 | 10-9-69 | 14-7-73 |

Authorized: 1 in FY 67, 1 in FY 68

**Pigeon (ASR 21)** G. Arra, 3-86

**Ortolan (ASR 22)** G. Arra, 1984

**D:** 3,411 tons (4,570 fl) **S:** 15 kts **Dim:** 76.5 × 26.2 × 6.5
**A:** 2/20-mm AA (I × 2) **Electron Equipt:** Radar: 1/SPS-53, 1/. . . nav.
**M:** 4 Alco high-speed diesels; 2 props; 6,000 hp **Range:** 8,500/13
**Man:** 10 officers, 186 men + DSRV crew: 4 officers, 20 men **Range:** 8,500/13

Remarks: The catamaran hulls (7.92-m beam) are separated by 10.36 m. Diving bells and other salvage equipment are lowered between the two hulls by a moving crane. The ships can carry two small DSRV (Deep Submergence Rescue Vehicle) submarines, but the only two DSRV built are land-stored in fly-away status. Excellent lowering and handling equipment for up to 60 tons; divers to 260 m. Carry Mk 2 Mod. 1 saturation diving gear. Helicopter platform aft spans both hulls. Not considered to be successful ships, being overly complex and difficult to maneuver. ASR 21 has an LN-66 navigational radar, ASR 22 a Raytheon set.

◆ **4 Chanticleer-class submarine-rescue ships** Bldr: Savannah Machine Foundry (ASR 9: Moore SB & DD, Oakland) (*Atlantic Fleet)

| | Laid down | L | In serv. |
|---|---|---|---|
| ASR 9 Florikan | 30-9-41 | 14-6-42 | 5-4-43 |
| ASR 13 Kittiwake* | 5-1-45 | 10-7-45 | 18-7-46 |
| ASR 14 Petrel* | 26-2-45 | 29-9-45 | 24-9-46 |
| ASR 15 Sunbird* | 2-4-45 | 3-4-46 | 28-1-47 |

**AUXILIARY SHIPS** *(continued)*

**Kittiwake (ASR 13)** L. & L. Van Ginderen, 8-84

**Florikan (ASR 9)**—SATCOMM antennas flanking foremast G. Arra, 5-85

**D:** 1,670 tons (2,015 fl) **S:** 14.9 kts **Dim:** 76.7 × 13.4 × 4.9
**A:** 2/20-mm AA (I × 2) **Electron Equipt:** Radar: 1/SPS-53
**M:** 4 G.M. 12-278A diesels, electric drive; 1 prop; 3,000 hp
**Electric:** 460 kw **Man:** 7 officers, 96 men **Fuel:** 350 tons

Remarks: Carry a McCann rescue bell aft. All equipped for helium/oxygen diving. ASR 9 has Alco Model 539 diesels. All have sonar and underwater communications equipment. No plans to replace these elderly units before mid-1990s.

◆ **5 Abnaki and Achomawi-class fleet ocean tugs—all in reserve**

| | Bldr | L | In serv. | To reserve |
|---|---|---|---|---|
| ATF 105 Moctobi | Charleston SB & DD | 25-3-44 | 25-7-44 | 30-9-85 |
| ATF 110 Quapaw | United Eng., Alameda | 15-5-43 | 6-5-44 | 30-8-85 |
| ATF 113 Takelma | United Eng., Alameda | 18-9-43 | 3-8-44 | 30-9-83 |
| ATF 159 Paiute | Charleston SB & DD | 4-6-45 | 27-8-45 | 23-8-85 |
| ATF 160 Papago | Charleston SB & DD | 21-6-45 | 3-10-45 | 28-6-85 |

**D:** 1,235 tons (1,640 fl) **S:** 16.2 kts **Dim:** 62.48 (59.44 pp) × 11.73 × 4.67
**A:** none **M:** 4 Caterpillar D399 diesels, electric drive; 1 prop; 3,000 hp
**Electron Equipt:** Radar: 1/SPS-53, 1/SPS-64(V)9
**Electric:** 400 kw **Range:** 6,500/16; 15,000/8
**Man:** 8 officers, 85 men

Remarks: All now in National Defense Reserve Fleet, on Navy List. Developed from pre–World War II *Apache* class. ATF 105, ATF 110, and ATF 113 originally had four Busch-Sulzer BS-539 diesels and a small-diameter funnel; the others had G.M. 12-278A diesels and a large funnel. Have a 150-ton pull capability to salvage beached vessels, carry 640-m 53-mm steel towing cable, plus 730-m nylon towing line. Five sisters serve in the U.S. Coast Guard, and the class can be found in many of the world's navies. ATF 159 and 160 scheduled to reactivate about 5-88 for Caribbean area patrol duties.

Two sisters survive in the National Defense Reserve Fleet: *Atakapa* (ATF 149) and *Mosopelea* (ATF 158), both of the *Achomawi* class. *Seneca* (ATF 91), reacquired 21-11-85 from the NDRF, is an immobile engineering trials craft at Annapolis, Md., and *Tenino* (ATF 115) is used as a salvage training hulk. Permission to scrap *Chippewa* (ATF 69), *Hopi* (ATF 71), *Moreno* (ATF 87), *Narragansett* (ATF 88), and *Achomawi* (ATF 148) was granted on 31-1-86.

**Moctobi (ATF 105)** PHC Ahlgrim, USN, 4-83

Note: The four surviving units of the *Sotoyomo*-class auxiliary ocean tugs, *Tunica* (ATA 179), *Accokeek* (ATA 181), *Navigator* (ATA 203), and *Keywadin* (ATA 213) are used as salvage training hulks.

◆ **3 Edenton-class salvage-and-rescue ships** Bldr: Brooke Marine, Lowestoft, U.K. (*Atlantic Fleet)

Authorized: 1 in FY 66; 2 in FY 67

| | Laid down | L | In serv. |
|---|---|---|---|
| ATS 1 Edenton* | 1-4-67 | 15-5-68 | 23-1-71 |
| ATS 2 Beaufort | 19-2-68 | 20-12-68 | 22-1-72 |
| ATS 3 Brunswick | 5-6-68 | 14-11-69 | 19-12-72 |

**Edenton (ATS 1)** L. & L. Van Ginderen, 6-85

**Beaufort (ATS 2)** L. & L. Van Ginderen, 1-87

**AUXILIARY SHIPS** *(continued)*

**D:** 2,650 tons (3,200 fl) **S:** 16 kts **Dim:** 88.0 (80.5 pp) × 15.25 × 4.6
**A:** 2/20-mm AA (I × 2) **Electron Equipt:** Radar: 1/SPS-53, 1/SPS-64(V)9
**M:** 4 Paxman 12 YLCM (900 rpm) diesels; 2 Escher-Wyss CP props; 6,000 hp
**Electric:** 1,200 kw **Range:** 10,000/13 **Man:** 7 officers, 106 men

Remarks: ATS 4 (FY 72) and ATS 5 (FY 73) canceled in favor of *Powhatan*-class T-ATF. Can tow ships up to AOE 1-class size. 272-ton dead lift over the bow. 20-ton crane aft; 10-ton boom forward, Can conduct dives to 260 m. Powerful pumps and complete fire-fighting equipment. Equipped with bow-thruster.

Note: Guided-missile trials ship *Norton Sound* (AVM 1, ex-AV 11) was decommissioned and stricken on 11-12-86, without replacement.

◆ **1 Intrepid-class auxiliary-training aircraft carrier**

| | Bldr | Laid down | L | In serv. |
|---|---|---|---|---|
| AVT 16 Lexington | Bethlehem, Quincy | 16-7-41 | 25-9-42 | 17-2-43 |

**Lexington (AVT 16)**—with SPS-40 replacing SPS-12 G. Arra, 1987

**D:** approx. 33,000 tons (42,550 fl) **S:** 30+ kts
**Dim:** 270.97 (249.94 wl) × 31.39 (58.5 flight deck) × 9.4
**A:** removed (no aircraft permanently assigned)
**Electron Equipt:** Radar: 1/SPS-64(V)9, 1/SPS-10, 1/SPS-40, 1/SPN-35, 1/SPN-43—TACAN: URN-25
**M:** 4 sets Westinghouse GT; 4 props; 150,000 hp
**Boilers:** 8 Babcock & Wilcox; 41.7 kg/cm$^2$, 454°C **Electric:** 7,000 kw
**Fuel:** 6,750 tons **Range:** 18,000/12 **Man:** 74 officers, 1,382 men

Remarks: Employed in deck-landing training at Pensacola, Fla. Was to have been stricken in FY 80 and replaced by the *Coral Sea* (CV 43), but has been extended in service through FY 91. On 29-12-68 her number changed from CVS 16 to CVT 16: changed to AVT 16 on 15-7-78. Has two Type C11 Mod. 1 steam catapults, two elevators (one centerline forward and one to starboard, abaft the island), and four Mk 7 arrester wires. A third elevator, at the forward end of the angled deck, has been deactivated. Flight deck composed of 76-mm-thick Douglas fir planking. All guns and fire-control equipment removed. Completed major overhaul 5-80; received a 12-month overhaul beginning 10-84, during which the SPS-12 air-search radar was replaced by SPS-40.

**UNCLASSIFIED MISCELLANEOUS SHIPS**

◆ **1 Trident missile-firing-simulator barge** Bldr: . . . (In serv. . . .)

IX 516 (ex-barge *Matthew*)

Remarks: Conversion contract to McDermott Inc., Morgan City, La., for missile-launch training-simulation barge for service at the Trident facility at King's Bay, Georgia.

◆ **1 BH 110-class Rigid Sidewall Surface Effect Trials craft**

| | Bldr | L | In serv. |
|---|---|---|---|
| IX 515 (ex-SES-200, ex-USCG *Dorado*, WSES 1) | Bell-Halter, New Orleans | 12-78 | 2-79 |

**D:** 128 tons light (205 fl) **S:** 32 kts
**Dim:** 48.49 × 11.89 × 2.83 at rest/1.68 on cushion
**Electron Equipt:** Radar: 2/Decca navigational
**M:** 2 G.M. 16V149 TI diesels for propulsion; 2 CP props; 3,200 hp, 4 G.M. 8V92 TI diesels for lift; 4/1.07-m dia. centrifugal fans; 1,980 hp
**Electric:** 140 kw **Range:** 300–500/35 on cushion; 3,700/23
**Man:** 1 officer, 14 men, 3 civilian technicians **Fuel:** 59.6 tons

**IX 515** L. & L. Van Ginderen, 1-86

Remarks: Designed by Bell Aerospace-Textron and built by Halter Marine in a jointly financed effort. Leased 1-80 for one month by U.S. Coast Guard and then again for a longer trials period in 1981, commencing with a six-month joint USN/USCG operational evaluation from Key West. On 29-9-82 the ship came under U.S. Navy control and had accommodations for 14 additional personnel added. Placed in service 24-9-82. Functions by trapping a fan-generated air bubble between the rigid sidewalls and rubber seals at bow and stern. Assigned to David Taylor Naval Ship Research and Development Center. Conducted trials for U.S. Coast Guard late 1984. Two more lift fans added 1984. Unofficially named *Jaeger* for European tour 1985–86. Conducted trials with G.E. EX-25, 25-mm gatling gun and various f.c.s., spring 1987. Redesignated IX 515 on 11-5-87.

◆ **1 YFU 71-class helicopter training craft** Bldr: Pacific Coast Eng. Co., Alameda, Cal. (In serv. 1968)

IX 514 (ex-YFU 79)

**IX 514** U.S. Navy

**D:** 220 tons (380 fl) **S:** 8 kts **Dim:** 38.1 × 10.97 × 2.30
**Electron Equipt:** Radar: 1/Decca . . . navigational
**M:** 4 G.M. 6-71 diesels; 2 props: 1,000 hp **Man:** . . .

Remarks: Redesignated 31-3-86 and completed conversion 28-4-86 to serve as helicopter landing platform training craft at Pensacola, Fla. Bow ramp welded closed, new superstructure with rudimentary flight-control station and flight deck added. Originally a sister to IX 506, below.

◆ **0 (+1) electric radiation trials barge** Bldr: Eastern Marine, Panama City, Fla.

IX 513 (In serv. . . .)

**D:** approx. 4,400 tons (fl) **Dim:** 36.57 × 27.43 × 4.57
**Electric:** . . . kw (2 diesel sets)

Remarks: Ordered 1986 in support of EMPRESS-II electric pulse protection trials to be conducted in the lower Chesapeake Bay. Would have 45.7-m-high tower supporting 57.53-m-diameter ring pulse transmission antenna. Program stalled by bankruptcy of builder in 2-87 and environmental impact concerns by Congress and the state of Maryland. Future uncertain.

◆ **1 Trident missile-firing-simulator barge** Bldr: . . .

IX 512 SUPLS II (ex-U.S. Army BD 6651, in serv. 1954)

**D:** approx. 1,000 tons (fl) **Dim:** 43.28 × 17.68 × 1.55
**A:** 1/Trident D-5 launch tube

**IX 512** G. Arra, 3-86

## UNCLASSIFIED MISCELLANEOUS SHIPS *(continued)*

Remarks: Former U.S. Army design 413D floating crane. Acquired 1-9-83 and converted by Westinghouse Marine Division for San Clemente, Cal., test facility as SUPLS II (Simulated Underwater Partial Launch System) in support of the Trident-II D-5 SLBM program. Retains the original 52-ton crane and performs submerged launch and post-launch activities.

Note: IX 511 (ex-LST 399) was stricken 15-6-85 for use as a target.

◆ **1 explosives damage-control barge** Bldr: Norfolk NSY (In serv. 1942)

IX 509 (ex-*Underwater Test Barge No. 1,* ex-YC . . .)

**IX 509** W. Donko, 7-84

**D:** 3,000 tons (fl) **Dim:** 56.1 × . . . × 3.7

Remarks: Operated for the Naval Ships Research and Development Center. Reclassified IX 509 on 1-12-79. Has a 60-ton crane.

◆ **1 satellite navigation systems trials craft**

IX 508 (ex-LCU 1618) Bldr: Gunderson Bros., Portland, Ore. (In serv. 1959)

**IX 508** G. Arra, 3-86

**D:** 190 tons (390 fl) **S:** 11 kts **Dim:** 41.07 × 9.07 (hull) × 2.08
**M:** 4 G.M. 6-71 diesels; 2 Kort-nozzle props; 1,200 hp
**Fuel:** 13 tons **Range:** 1,200/11 **Man:** . . .

Remarks: Adapted 1978 for Naval Ocean Systems Center, San Diego, to conduct trials with NAVSTAR global positioning system. Reclassified IX from LCU 1-12-79.

◆ **2 Admiral W.S. Benson-class barracks ships** Bldr: Bethlehem Steel, Alameda, Cal.

| | L | In serv. |
|---|---|---|
| IX 507 General Hugh J. Gaffey (ex T-AP 121, ex-*Admiral W.L. Capps,* AP 121) | . . . | 18-9-44 |
| IX 510 (ex-*General William O. Darby,* T-AP 127, ex-*Admiral W.S. Sims,* AP 127) | 4-6-45 | 27-9-45 |

**D:** 12,657 tons light (22,574 fl) **S:** 19 kts
**Dim:** 185.6 (174.65 pp) × 23.01 × 8.05
**M:** 2 sets G.E. GT, electric drive; 2 props; 18,000 hp **Electric:** 2,875 kw
**Boilers:** 4 Combustion Engineering "D," 42.3 kg/cm², 449°C
**Fuel:** 4,037 tons **Man:** Berthing for 499 officers, 1,577 men

Remarks: Former troop transports transferred to the Army in 1946, reacquired by the Navy on 1-3-50 for MSC (then MSTS). IX 507 stricken on 9-1-69 and transferred to Maritime Commission Reserve Fleet. Partially reactivated and redesignated IX 507 on 1-11-78 for service at Bremerton NSY, Washington, as berthing ship for crew of CVN 65, then undergoing overhaul; was towed to Yokosuka 11-85, but returned to Puget Sound NSY in 1987. IX 510 reclassified 10-81 and towed from James River, Virginia, to Norfolk Naval Shipyard; placed in service 1-7-82. Propulsion plants not reactivated. Name officially deleted from IX 510 on 6-7-76, but ship still bears it!

**General Hugh J. Gaffey (IX 507)** L. & L. Van Ginderen, 12-86

◆ **1 YFU 71-class trials tender** Bldr: Pacific Coast Eng. Co., Alameda, Cal.

IX 506 (ex-YFU 82) (In serv. 10-68)

**IX 506** G. Arra, 1-85

**D:** 220 tons (380 fl) **S:** 8 kts **Dim:** 38.1 × 10.97 × 2.29 **Electric:** 120 kw
**A:** 3/324-mm Mk 32 ASW TT (III × 1) **Electron Equipt:** Radar: 2/nav.
**M:** 4 G.M. 6-71 diesels; 2 props; 1,000 hp **Man:** 2 officers, 10 men

Remarks: Ex-harbor utility craft. Reclassified on 1-4-78 for service with Naval Ocean Systems Center, San Diego, to replace IX 505 (ex-YTM 759). Barge YFNX 36 is used as a work platform with this unit. IX 506 has an extra generator set beneath the forecastle, atop which is mounted the ASW TT mount.

◆ **3 Benewah-class barracks ships** Bldr: Boston NSY

| | Laid down | L | In serv. |
|---|---|---|---|
| IX 502 Mercer (ex-APB 39) | 25-8-44 | 17-11-44 | 19-9-45 |
| IX 503 Nueces (ex-APB 40) | 2-1-45 | 6-5-45 | 30-11-45 |
| IX 504 Echols (ex-APB 37) | 6-45 | 30-7-45 | 1-1-47 |

**Mercer (IX 502)** W. Donko, 7-85

**D:** 2,189 tons light (3,640 fl) **S:** 10 kts **Dim:** 100.0 × 15.2 × 3.4
**M:** 2 G.M. 12-267 ATL diesels; 2 props; 1,600 hp **Electric:** 500 kw
**Man:** (when operational): 13 officers, 180 men + 26 officers, 1,200 troops

Remarks: IX 502 and IX 503 recommissioned 1968 for service in Vietnam, placed back in reserve 1969-71; activated again in 1-11-75 as barracks ships on West Coast. IX 504, in reserve since completion in 1947, activated 1-2-76 as a barracks ship for *Ohio*-class SSBN crews at General Dynamics, Groton. Propulsion plants inactivated. Eight 40-mm AA (IV × 2) retained on IX 503, removed on others Names restored to all in 1986.

## UNCLASSIFIED MISCELLANEOUS SHIPS *(continued)*

◆ **1 barracks ship (ex-LSMR)** Bldr: Brown SB, Houston

| | Laid down | L | In serv. |
|---|---|---|---|
| IX 501 Elk River (ex-LSMR 501) | 24-3-45 | 21-4-45 | 27-5-45 |

**Elk River (IX 501)**—gantry crane now deleted G. Arra, 1983

**D:** 1,280 tons (fl) **S:** 11 kts **Dim:** 70.0 × 15.2 × 2.8
**Electron Equipt:** Radar: 1/LN-66 **Electric:** 440 kw
**M:** 2 G.M. 16-278A diesels; 2 props; 2,880 hp **Man:** 25 men + 20 technicians

Remarks: Former fire-support rocket ship converted 1967–68 at Avondale Shipyards, Westwego, Louisiana, to act as support ship at the San Clemente Island Range for the Navy deep-submergence diving program. 2.4-m bulges were added to her hull sides and a center well cut for lowering equipment through the hull. The well was straddled by a 65-ton traveling gantry crane. Thrusters added to allow accurate dynamic mooring. Tests diving procedures, equipment, and small diving vehicles. In 10-86, the crane was removed, and IX 501 was relegated to serve as a barracks hulk.

◆ **1 sonar test barge**

IX 310 (no name)

Remarks: Actually, two barges (built in 1917!) moored in Lake Seneca, New York; subordinated to the Naval Underwater Sound Laboratory, Newport, Rhode Island. In service 1-4-71. IX 309, *Monob One,* is now numbered YAG 61.

◆ **1 U.S. Army FS 381-class torpedo-trials ship**

| | Bldr | In serv. |
|---|---|---|
| IX 308 New Bedford (ex-AKL 17, ex-FS 289) | Wheeler SB, Brooklyn, NY | 3-45 |

**D:** 526 tons light (940 fl) **S:** 13 kts **Dim:** 54.10 (50.29 wl) × 9.75 × 3.05
**A:** 1/533-mm TT—3/324-mm Mk 32 ASW TT (III × 1)
**M:** 2 G.M. 6-278A diesels; 2 props; 1,000 hp
**Electric:** 225 kw **Fuel:** 67 tons **Range:** 3,200/11 **Man:** 24 accomm.

Remarks: Operated by the Coast Guard for the Army during World War II; transferred to the Navy as a cargo ship on 1-3-50. Converted as a torpedo-trials ship in 1963. Operated by the Naval Torpedo Station, Keyport, Washington. Carries the CURV remote-controlled underwater recovery vehicle. To be replaced by new YTT 9-class torpedo trials ship.

◆ **1 U.S. Army FS 330DC-class torpedo-trials ship**

| | Bldr | In serv. |
|---|---|---|
| IX 306 (ex-FS 221) | Higgins Industries, New Orleans | 1-45 |

**D:** 460 tons (960 fl) **S:** 12 kts **Dim:** 54.81 × 9.75 × 4.32
**A:** 1/533-mm TT—3/324-mm Mk 32 ASW TT (III × 1)
**M:** 2 Enterprise diesels; 2 props; 800 hp **Electric:** 225 kw **Fuel:** 62 tons

Remarks: Employed by the Army as a cargo ship until transferred to the Navy on 1-1-69 as a torpedo- and general-experimentation trials ship for the Naval Underwater Weapons Research and Engineering Center, Newport, R.I., at the Atlantic Underwater Test and Evaluation Center (AUTEC) at Andros Island in the Bahamas. Naval and R.C.A. civilian crew. Painted white with blue bow; torpedo-tube exits on starboard bow.

◆ **1 ocean construction platform** Bldr: Missouri Valley Br. & Iron, Ind.

| | Laid down | L | In serv. |
|---|---|---|---|
| Seacon (ex-YFNB 33) | 16-1-45 | 22-3-45 | 25-10-45 |

**D:** 2,780 tons (fl) **S:** 7 kts **Dim:** 79.25 × 14.63 × 2.9
**M:** 1 G.M. 12-71 diesel, 2 G.M. 6-71 diesels; 3 Voith-Schneider 14E/87 vertical cycloidal props; 1,020 hp
**Electric:** 575 kw **Man:** 50 tot.

Remarks: A large covered barge belonging to the Navy and formerly used by NASA for transporting rockets, the *Seacon* was converted 1974–76 by Norfolk SB & Dry Dock Co. to serve as a seagoing work ship for the Navy Ocean Engineering and Construction Project Office. Intended to be towed at up to 11 knots to work locations and then to use own propulsion for precision maneuvering. Can be used to lay cable, can moor in 200-m water, and has open work deck 40 × 14 aft. Unique in having no ship or yard-craft number. Operated from San Diego during 1987.

**Seacon** A. Grobmeier, 10-87

◆ **1 sail frigate relic** Bldr: Hart's SY, Boston, Mass.

Constitution (ex-IX 21) (L: 21-10-1797)

**Constitution** U.S. Navy, 7-86

**D:** 2,200 tons **S:** 13 kts (sail) **Dim:** 62.18 (53.34 hull) × 13.26 × 6.86
**A:** 32/24 pdr.—26/32-pdr carronade—2/24-pdr bow-chasers
**Man:** 2 officers, 47 men (orig.: 450 tot., incl. 55 Marines and 30 "boys")

Remarks: Remains in commission. Wooden construction. First went to sea 22-7-1798. Three masts: 28.7, 31.7, and 24.7 m high. Sail area: 3,968 m$^3$. Remains docked at former Boston Navy Yard except for once-yearly "turnaround" to prevent warpage. Designated IX 21 from 8-12-41 to 1-9-75, and briefly bore name *Old Constitution* from 1917 to 1925.

## EXPERIMENTAL CRAFT

◆ **1 space-vechicle booster recovery ship** Bldr: Bishop Marine Service (In serv. 1966)

RSB 1 (ex-*A.B. Wood II*)

**RSB 1** U.S. Navy

## EXPERIMENTAL CRAFT *(continued)*

**D:** 291 tons (fl) **S:** 13 kts **Dim:** 47.85 × 10.97 × 3.35
**M:** 2 diesels; 2 props; 1,530 hp **Man:** 5 (civilians)

Remarks: Operated by civilian contractor for Naval Surface Warfare Center, Fort Lauderdale, Fla. Used to recover space-vehicle boosters. Has a bow-thruster and a 35-ton telescoping crane.

### ◆ 1 propulsion trials craft

Jupiter II

**Jupiter II** U.S. Navy, 9-80

Remarks: Jupiter II is a 19.8-m workboat operated by the Naval Ships Research and Development Center, Annapolis, Md. On 23-9-80 the gas-turbine-powered craft began trials with a 300-kw superconducting electric propulsion motor, producing 6–7 kt speeds. A 2,250-kw, 3,000-hp superconducting motor was substituted late in 1981.

### ◆ 1 SWATH (Small Waterplane Area, Twin-Hull) prototype

SSP 1 Kaimalino Bldr: U.S. Coast Guard, Curtis Bay, Md. (L: 7-3-73)

**Kaimalino (SSP 1)** U.S. Navy, 1980

**D:** 228 tons (fl) **S:** 22 kts **Dim:** 26.92 × 12.99 × 4.65
**Electron Equipt:** Radar: 1/LN-66 (SPS-59)
**M:** CODOG 2 G.E. T64-6B gas turbines, chain drive; 2 CP props; 5,000 hp—or: 2 G.M. 6-71 diesels, 2 hydraulic motors; 160 hp
**Electric:** 78 kw **Range:** 450/17; 1,500/5 **Man:** 15 max.

Remarks: Catamaran hull with cigar-shaped flotation pontoons. Helicopter deck. Operated by the Naval Ocean Systems Center, Hawaii Laboratory. The SWATH concept shows great promise as an economical, high-performance/high endurance ASW ship, but has been hampered in its development by a lack of funding. *Kaimalino* has been used in torpedo-firing trials and as a weapons-recovery craft. Planned stretch to 600 tons (fl) not carried out, due to costs, although material was assembled 1982 for the conversion.

### ◆ 2 Asheville-class engineering-trials ships Bldr: Tacoma Boat

| | In serv. |
|---|---|
| Athena I (ex-*Chehalis,* PG 94) | 11-8-69 |
| Athena II (ex-*Grand Rapids,* PG 98) | 9-5-70 |

**D:** 225 tons (250 fl) **S:** 40 kts **Dim:** 50.14 × 7.28 × 2.9
**M:** CODOG: 1 G.E. 7LM-1500-PE 102 LM-1500 gas turbine (12,500 hp), 2 Cummins VT12-875M diesels (1,400 hp); 2 CP props
**Electric:** 200 kw **Fuel:** 50 tons **Range:** 325/37; 2,400/14

Remarks: These craft are regarded as equipment, and therefore do not have USN hull numbers. Operate from Panama City, Florida, for the Naval Ships Research and Development Center, Carderock, Md. Have civilian crews and are disarmed. *Athena I* reclassified as "floating equipment" on 21-8-75, *Athena II* on 1-10-77. Have a 10-ton instrumentation payload. Both can carry a 14.9-$m^2$, portable, glass-reinforced plastic laboratory on the stern, and *Athena I* has a permanent 18.6-$m^2$ lab added forward. *Douglas* (PG 100) was to have been converted to *Athena III* in FY 83; lack of funds canceled project and ship discarded 12-84, with *Deer Island* (YAG 62) acquired in her place.

**Athena I (foreground) and Athena II**—yellow hulls, white superstructure
David Taylor Model Basin, 1980

### ◆ 1 hydrofoil research craft Bldr: Boeing/Martinac, Tacoma, Washington

| | Laid down | L | In serv. |
|---|---|---|---|
| High Point (ex-PCH 1) | 27-2-61 | 17-8-62 | 15-8-63 |

**High Point (PHC 1)**—ashore, auxiliary propeller lowered W. Donko, 7-83

**D:** 93 tons light (120 fl) **S:** 48 kts
**Dim:** 35.28 × 9.75 (10.16 max.) × 1.98 (5.18, foils extended)
**M:** 2 Bristol-Siddeley/Rolls-Royce Proteus gas turbines; 4 props (paired, counter-rotating); 6,200 hp—1 G.M. 12V71 diesel; 1 prop; 600 hp for hull-borne drive (12 kts)
**Man:** 6 tot. (civilians) **Range:** 500/45; 2,000/12 (hull-borne)
**Electric:** 85 kw

Remarks: Officially stricken 30-9-79, but retained as "floating equipment" for experimental purposes at Bremerton, Wash., until deactivated 1-12-84. Foils retract vertically: single forward set is steerable, while after pair each have a nacelle with a propeller at each end. Originally had SQS-33XN1 retractable sonar, and later tested various towed sonars, including the Canadian Westinghouse HS-1001 and the BQ5-15 towed submarine sonar in 1985, and EW gear, including AN/ALR-66(V)2 in 1984. Has one Solar 40-kw gas-turbine generator and one G.M. 4071 diesel set. Initial gun armament was as single 12.7-mm mg. Forward foil spans 6.10 m, aft is 9.60. 1,635 foil-borne hours by 1985. A 40-mm AA and 4/324-mm Mk 32 ASW TT (I × 4, fixed) have been removed. Used for high-speed Harpoon SSM launch trials in 1973–74. On loan to Boeing since 23-1-85.

## DEEP-SUBMERGENCE RESEARCH CRAFT

### ◆ 1 nuclear research submarine for deep diving

| | Bldr | Laid down | L | In serv. |
|---|---|---|---|---|
| NR-1 | General Dynamics, Groton | 10-6-67 | 25-1-69 | 27-10-69 |

Authorized: FY 66

**DEEP-SUBMERGENCE RESEARCH CRAFT** *(continued)*

**NR-1** U.S. Navy

**D:** 372 tons surfaced/700 submerged **S:** 4.6/3.6 kts **Dim:** 41.78 × 3.81 × 4.57
**M:** 1 pressurized-water reactor, turboelectric drive; 2 props
**Man:** 2 officers, 3 men, 2 scientists

REMARKS: Project approved 18-4-65. Fitted for all oceanographic missions, military and civilian, and for bottom salvage. Thick cylindrical hull. Wheels for moving on ocean bottom. A very successful vehicle, but cost three times the original estimate. No periscope, uses television cameras. Four ducted maneuvering thrusters. Can dive to over 800 m. Operated by Submarine Squadron 17, Bangor, Washington, since 1-84.

◆ **2 DSRV class** Bldr: Lockheed Missile & Space Co., Sunnyvale, Calif.

| | In serv. | Accepted |
|---|---|---|
| DSRV 1 MYSTIC | 6-8-71 | 4-11-77 |
| DSRV 2 AVALON | 28-7-72 | 1-1-78 |

**Avalon (DSRV 2)**—Deep Submergence Rescue Vehicle, aboard *William H. Bates* (SSN 680) G. Arra, 1985

**D:** 30.5 tons (37 sub.) **S:** 4.5 kts **Dim:** 15.0 × 2.5 × 3.28 (high)
**M:** 1 electric motor; 1 shrouded-pivoting prop; 15 hp
**Man:** 4 tot. + 24 rescued men

REMARKS: The DSRVs are intended to: operate at a maximum depth of 1,500 m; stand pressure equal to 2,750 m; dive and rise at 30 m a minute; make a maximum speed of 5 knots while submerged; remain submerged for 30 hours at 3 knots; maintain station in a 1-knot current; and operate all machinery even while submerged at a 45° angle. DSRVs can bring to the surface as many as 24 men at one time. Motor, powered by a silver-zinc battery, turns a regular propulsion propeller and two thrusters, one forward and one aft, which can be positioned to permit a close approach to a sunken object. Their size and weight were determined by the possible need to airlift them in an Air Force Starlifter (Lockheed C-141A) cargo plane. Additional equipment, especially a truck transport for the DSRV, would be carried in a second Starlifter. In addition, SSNs have received the equipment necessary to fasten a DSRV to their decks and carry it at 15 knots. The SSN will serve as a base for the DSRV while it awaits the arrival of a *Pigeon*-class rescue ship (ASR). Hull consists of two HY-140 steel spheres surrounded by a fiberglass outer hull. One received a potassium superoxide ($KO_2$) breathing system in 1982, providing 480 man hours submerged endurance. A cost overrun of nearly 1,500 percent prevented the procurement of any more DSRVs. Twelve were originally planned. Names were assigned in 1977.

◆ **2 Turtle class** Bldr: General Dynamics, Groton, Conn.

DSV 3 TURTLE (ex-*Autec-I*) DSV 4 SEA CLIFF (ex-*Autec-II*)

**D:** 21 tons (*Sea Cliff:* 29) **S:** 2 kts
**Dim:** 7.9 (*Sea Cliff:* 9.4) × 2.4 (3.7 over thrusters)
**M:** 1 electric motor; 1 prop; 2 thrusters **Man:** 2 men + 1 scientist
**Endurance:** 16 hrs.

REMARKS: Launched on 11-12-68. Could originally descend to 1,980 m. Spherical pressure hull of HY-100 steel. The *Turtle* was modified in 1979 to descend to 3,660 meters, and the *Sea Cliff* received a titanium pressure sphere in 1981–84, permitting 6,100-m descents. Air transportable. Fitted with external manipulator arms. Eight hours' endurance at 1 knot. Operated by Submarine Development Group 1, San Diego. *Sea Cliff* dove to 6,096 m on 10-3-85, supported by *Point Loma* (AGDS 2). *Turtle* had a serious fire 17-8-84 and was still in repair at end-1985. Support craft R.V. *Lulu* discarded 1986; support craft *Laney Chouset* chartered 1987 as tender to DSV 3 and 4.

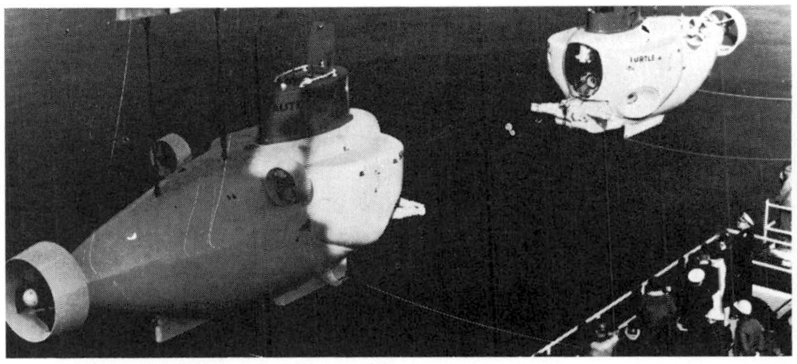

**Sea Cliff and Turtle**—at "launch" 1968

◆ **1 Alvin class** Bldr: General Mills, Minneapolis, Minn. (In serv. 1965)

DSV 2 ALVIN

**D:** 16 tons **S:** 2 kts **Dim:** 6.9 × 2.4 × . . .
**M:** electric motors; 1 prop; 2 thrusters **Man:** 1 man + 2 scientists

REMARKS: Operated by civilian Woods Hole Oceanographic Institute on contract to the Navy. Sank on 16-10-68, but raised, repaired, and returned to service in 11-72. Single titanium pressure sphere permits descents to 4,000 m. Supported by the Woods Hole Institute research ship *Atlantis II*. *Trieste II* (DSV 1) was stricken 1-4-85. *Nemo* (DSV 5) is a remote-controlled vehicle, now on display at the Naval Ocean Science Center, San Diego.

**SERVICE CRAFT**

NOTE: The force still consists largely of craft built during World War II. *The units marked with an asterisk are non-self-propelled.*

◆ **1 former West German floating dry dock*** Bldr: Seebeckwerft AG, Bremerhaven

AFDB 8 MACHINIST (In serv. 1981)

**Machinist (AFDB 8)**—with *Knox* (FF 1052) aboard PHC C. King, USN, 1987

**Dim:** 251.46 (285.31 on blocks) × 53.54 (42.77 between wingwalls) × 10.0 over blocks (flooded)
**Lift Capacity:** 39,300 tons

REMARKS: Purchased from builder 5-8-85 and towed to the Philippines for service at Subic Bay, arriving 7-86. Has two 7.5-ton traveling cranes. Replaced *Artisan* (AFDB 1).

◆ **3 AFDB large auxiliary floating dry docks***

| | Bldr | In serv. | Capacity (tons) |
|---|---|---|---|
| AFDB 2 | Mare Island NY | 4-44 | 30,000 |
| AFDB 4 | Mare Island NY | 8-44 | 55,000 |
| AFDB 7 LOS ALAMOS | Mare Island NY | 3-45 | 31,000 |

**Dim:** AFDB 2: 143.9 × 73.2 (36.4 clear width) × 2.7 (23.8 sub.)
AFDB 4: 251.5 × 73.2 (36.4 clear width) × 2.6 (20.5 sub.)
AFDB 7: 108.0 × 73.2 (36.4 clear width) × 2.6 (20.5 sub.)
**Man:** AFDB 7: 5 officers, 192 men; AFDB 2: . . .

REMARKS: AFDB 2 was originally a 10-section, 90,000-ton-capacity dock. Sections C, D, H, and I of AFDB 2 are active at Subic Bay, with the remainder in reserve at Pearl Harbor. The others were originally all 7-section docks. AFDB 4 is in reserve at Bremerton, while sections C, E, and G of ADFB 7 are active at Holy Loch, Scotland, in support of SSBNs; sections A and B are in reserve; placed in NDRF, James River, 20-5-86. *Artisan* (AFDB 1) was placed on sale in 1983. AFDB 3, long in reserve, was transferred to the state of Maine in 1982 for use by Bath Iron Works at Portland; AFDB 5 was transferred to the city of Port Arthur, Texas, in 1984 and leased to Todd Shipyards.

**SERVICE CRAFT** *(continued)*

**◆ 3 AFDL small auxiliary floating docks***

| | Bldr | In serv. | Capacity (tons) |
|---|---|---|---|
| AFDL 6 Dynamic | Chicago Bridge & Iron | 3-44 | 1,000 |
| AFDL 23 Adept | G.D. Auchter | 12-44 | 1,900 |
| AFDL 25 Undaunted | Doullut, Ewin | 2-44 | 1,000 |

**Dynamic (AFDL 6)** G. Arra, 8-86

Remarks: All one-piece docks. *Diligence* (AFDL 48), built of concrete, and the only postwar unit, was commercially leased 23-3-80. *Reliance* (AFDL 47) had been reacquired 18-1-81 from Maritime Commission reserve, but was returned 12-8-81. Two additional units (AFDL 21, 40) are leased to commercial shipbuilders and ship repairers; AFDL 37, 38, and 45, long on lease, were sold outright 1-10-81; AFDL 8 was stricken 1-12-81 and sunk as a fishing reef; AFDL 2 was stricken 15-11-81, AFDL 9 was stricken 15-7-82, AFDL 19 and 41 sold 4-83, *Endeavor* (AFDL 1) stricken 1986; AFDL 16, on commercial lease, returned and stricken 15-8-86; AFDL 14 stricken 1-10-83, AFDL 15 on 18-12-83, AFDL 22 (captured by Vietnam 30-4-75) stricken 30-7-85, AFDL 29 on 15-7-85. AFDL 25 reacquired 6-84 at end of commercial lease, refitted, and towed to Guantánamo Bay 9-84 to replace *Endeavor* (AFDL 1). AFDL 6 and 25 are 61.0 m by 19.5 m; AFDL 23 is 87.8 × 19.5 m. AFDL 6 has an assigned crew: 1 officer, 23 men.

**◆ 6 AFDM medium auxiliary floating dry docks*** Bldr: Everett Pacific (AFDM 8: Chicago Bridge & Iron, AFDM 14: Pollock-Stockton SB, Cal.)

| | In serv. |
|---|---|
| AFDM 5 Resourceful (ex-YFD 21) | 2-43 |
| AFDM 6 Competent (ex-YFD 62) | 6-44 |
| AFDM 7 Sustain (ex-YFD 63) | 1-45 |
| AFDM 8 Richland (ex-YFD 64) | 12-44 |
| AFDM 10 Resolute (ex-YFD 67) | 1945 |
| AFDM 14 Steadfast (ex-YFD 71) | 7-45 |

**Resourceful (AFDM 5)** PHC C. King, USN, 5-87

**Dim:** 189.6 × 37.8 (28.3 clear width) × 1.9 (16.1 sub);
AFDM 14: 182.3 × 36.0 (26.5 clear width) × 1.1 (18.9 max.)
**Man:** 4–6 officers, 139–157 men

Remarks: All active and of 18,000-ton capacity except AFDM 14: 14,000 tons. AFDM 14 reclassified 1-2-83. AFDM 3 and 9 are on commercial lease; AFDM 2 returned from lease and transferred to MARAD or lay-up 2-6-86, and AFDM 1 returned and stricken for scrap 1-9-86. AFDM 7 refitted 1987 to 2-88. Built in three sections, with 26.5-m end sections bolted to mid-section.

**◆ 17 APL barracks craft***

APL 2, 4, 5, 15, 18, 19, 29, 31, 32, 34, 42, 43, 45, 50, 54, 57, 58

**APL 45** F. Zeitlhofer, 7-85

Remarks: Built 1944–45. All active. 2,600 tons (fl), 79.6 × 15.0 × 2.6. Can accommodate 6 officers and 680 men. Have 300-kw generator capacity.

**◆ 2 ARD 4- and 12-class auxiliary repair dry docks*** Bldr: Pacific Bridge, Alameda, Cal.

ARD 5 Waterford (In serv. 6-42) ARD 30 San Onofre (In serv. 8-44)

**San Onofre (ARD 30)**—*Dixon* (AS 37) in background L. & L. Van Ginderen, 5-82

**Dim:** ARD 5: 148.1 × 21.6 (14.9 clear width) × 1.6 (9.9 sub.)
ARD 30: 149.9 × 24.7 (18.0 clear width) × 1.7 (10.0 sub.)
**Man:** ARD 5: 6 officers, 125 men; ARD 30: 5 officers, 105 men

Remarks: Both active, 3,500-ton capacity. Sister *West Milton* (ARD 7) to Maritime Commission for lay-up 16-7-81. Three remain in use as ARDMs as well; see below.

**◆ 2 Shippingport-class submarine support docks***

| | Bldr | In serv. |
|---|---|---|
| ARDM 4 Shippingport | Bethlehem Steel, Sparrows Pt., Md. | 1-79 |
| ARDM 5 Arco | Todd Pacific, Seattle | 27-2-86 |

**Arco (ARDM 5)** V. Baca, 2-87

**Capacity:** 7,800 tons (8,400 emergency)
**Dim:** 150.0 × 29.3 (29.3 clear width) × 16.6 (max.)
**Man:** 5–6 officers, 125 enlisted

Remarks: Intended to support *Los Angeles*-class submarines. First floating dry docks built for U.S. Navy since World War II. Length of blocks: 118 m. 20.7 m clear height inside. Require shore support. Have 2/25-ton cranes. ARDM = Medium Support Dock. ARDM 5 ordered 13-10-82, laid down 25-7-83, launched 14-12-84. Have accommodations for 12. ARDM 4 at New London, ARDM 5 at San Diego.

**◆ 3 ARD 12-class submarine support docks*** Bldr: Pacific Bridge, Alameda, Cal.

| | In serv. |
|---|---|
| ARDM 1 Oak Ridge (ex-ARD 19) | 3-44 |
| ARDM 2 Alamagordo (ex-ARD 26) | 6-44 |
| ARDM 3 Endurance (ex-ARD 18) | 2-44 |

**SERVICE CRAFT** *(continued)*

**Oak Ridge (ARDM 1)**—with APL 31 to port and YFND 36 to starboard
PH 1 H. Dement, USN, 7-77

**Alamagordo (ARDM 2)** JO1 J. Cabot, USN, 3-81

**Dim:** 156.25 (ARDM 1, 2: 163.4) × 24.7 (13.0 clear width) × 2.2 (13.1 sub.)
**Man:** 5 officers, 174 enlisted **Capacity:** 8,000 tons

Remarks: Lengthened and capacity increased from 3,500 tons to serve as submarine repair docks. One end is closed, to permit towing. ARDM 1 at Kings Bay, Ga., ARDM 2 and 3 at Charleston, S.C.,

Note: Other Navy-owned floating dry docks include YFD 54 and 68–70, on commerical lease, and YFD 83, on loan to the U.S. Coast Guard since 1-47.

◆ **1 YAG miscellaneous auxiliary yard craft** Bldr: Halter Marine, New Orleans, La.

YAG 62 Deer Island

**D:** approx. 400 tons (fl) **S:** 10.5 kts **Dim:** 36.58 × 8.53 × 2.13
**M:** 2 diesels; 2 props; . . . hp **Electron Equipt:** Radar: 2/. . . nav.
**Range:** 6,200/10.5 **Man:** 20 crew and scientists

**Deer Island (YAG 62)** MAR, Inc., 1983

Remarks: 172 grt/117 nrt, former oilfield supply tug placed on Navy List 15-3-83 and operated for David Taylor Naval Ship Research and Development Center from Port Everglades, Fla., by MAR Inc. in support of sound-quieting trials.

◆ **1 YAG miscellaneous auxiliary yard craft** Bldr: Zenith Dredge Co., Duluth, Minn.

| | Laid down | L | In serv. |
|---|---|---|---|
| YAG 61 Monob One (ex-IX 309, ex-YW 87) | 1-12-42 | 3-4-43 | 11-11-43 |

**Monob One (YAG 61)**—yellow hull, masts, white superstructure
U.S. Navy, 1986

**D:** 1,390 tons (fl) **S:** 11 kts **Dim:** 58.5 × 10.1 × 4.8
**M:** 1 Caterpillar D 398 diesel; 1 Harbormaster swivelling prop; 850 hp
**Range:** 2,500/9 **Man:** . . .

Remarks: Redesignated from IX 309 on 1-7-70. Former water lighter modified in 1959 to support the ballistic-missile submarine silencing program. Based at Port Canaveral, Fla., and operated by the David Taylor Naval Ships Research and Development Center, Carderock, Md., Acoustic Trials Detachment. Has four laboratories, totaling 279 m$^2$. Stern extended to house new engine. To be replaced in 1990 by *Hayes* (T-AG 195, ex-T-AGOR 16).

◆ **252 (+13) YC open lighters*** (In serv. 1915–1989)

YC 306–1602

**YC 1596**—of the new YC 1554 class Moss Point, 3-87

Remarks: Built 1915–83. Five are in reserve. YC 1517 to YC 1522 built 1976–77, YC 1523–1527 built 1978–79, YC 1528–1551 built 1979–83. Three authorized under FY 82 budget. Current design is YC 1554 class, of which six were authorized FY 83, 14 authorized FY 84, 11 in FY 85, 2 in FY 86, and 13 in FY 88. Moss Point Marine, Escatawpa, Miss., delivered YC 1572–1602 from 27-2-85 to 23-4-87: 250 tons light (660 fl), 33.53 × 9.75 × 1.98 (max.). Ex-YD 89 reclassified YC 1553 on 1-6-83; YFN 1214 reclassified YC 1552 on 15-3-83; YC 1530 reclassified a camel, 1-6-84; YC 1546 reclassified floating equipment 6-84. YFN 1178 reclassified YC 1615 on 31-10-86. YC 1583 and 1586 converted 4-86 as cable-reel support barges for the T-AGOS program. YC 1572 and 1573 to MARAD 27-2-85 for lay-up but reacquired 21-5-85. Recent strikes: YC 1497 on 1-2-84; YC 852 on 1-4-84; YC 764 on 1-5-84; YC 1545 on 15-8-86; YC 1544 on 16-1-87; YC 972 in 1987.

◆ **1 YCF car float***

YCF 16 (In serv. 25-1-42)

Remarks: 45.72 × 10.21; used to transport railroad cars. Active.

◆ **4 (+3) YCV aircraft transportation lighters***

| | | |
|---|---|---|
| YCV 8 (In serv. 4-3-44) | YCV 11 (In serv. 6-10-44) | YCV 17 (In serv. 7-89) |
| YCV 10 (In serv. 21-8-44) | YCV 16 (In serv. 29-8-45) | YCV 18 (In serv. . . .) |
| | | YCV 19 (In serv. . . .) |

Remarks: 2,480 tons (fl); 28.96 × 9.14; 80-ton capacity. All active. YCV 17–19 approved FY 88 to replace earlier units.

◆ **51 (+16) YD floating cranes*** (some are self-propelled)

**SERVICE CRAFT** *(continued)*

**YD 200** G. Arra, 4-86

Remarks: Built 1913–70s. All active. YD 171, ex-German, has largest capacity: 350 tons: refitted 1984–85, built 1941 by Demag, Bremerhaven (62.5 × 33.5 × 114.0 high, uses 3,560 m wire rope!). Most U.S. Navy YD are rectangular barges. Typical data: 1,630 tons (fl), 42.7 × 21.3, 90–100 tons capacity. One new YD authorized FY 82, 3 in FY 83, 5 in FY 84, 3 under FY 85, 2 in FY 86, and 3 in FY 87. 1,650 tons (fl); 54.4 × 24.4 × 2.0. Program stalled by builder's bankruptcy, 2-87. Recent strikes include YD 77 and 170 in 1-4-84, YD 238 on 15-10-83, YD 216 on 1-12-83, YD 240 to Army 12-8-86, YD 149, 154, 181, 189, 231, 241 stricken 15-1-85; all but YD 189 were in reserve. YD 88 stricken 1-9-85. YD 145 stricken 15-1-86.

◆ **3 YDT diving tenders**

YDT 14 Phoebus (ex-YF 294), YDT 15 Suitland (ex-YF 336): 600 tons, 40.4 × 9.1, 1 Union diesel: 600 hp (In serv. 10-12-42 and 16-6-43, respectively)
YDT 16* Tom O'Malley (ex-YFNB 43): 2,000 tons (fl), 79.6 × 14.6 (non-self-propelled)

◆ **2 YF covered lighters, YF 852 class**

| | Bldr | L | In serv. |
|---|---|---|---|
| YF 866 Kodiak | Missouri Valley Bridge & Iron | 26-10-45 | 17-11-45 |
| YF 885 Keyport | Defoe SB | 19-5-45 | 4-8-45 |

**D:** 300 tons light (505 fl) **S:** 10 kts **Dim:** 40.5 × 9.1 × 2.7
**M:** 2 G.M. diesels; 2 props; 1,000 hp **Electric:** 120 kw **Fuel:** 40 tons

Remarks: YF 885 active at Torpedo Testing Station, Keyport, Washington, with 3/324-mm Mk 32 ASW TT; has "Omnithruster" bow-thruster. YF 866 in reserve. Sister YF 862 stricken from reserve 15-2-85.

◆ **6 YFB ferryboats**

YFB 83 Wa'a Hele Honua Bldr: John H. Mathis Co., Camden, N.J. (In serv. 4-49)

**D:** 500 tons (fl) **S:** 8.5 kts **Dim:** 49.4 × 17.7
**M:** 2 diesels **Cargo:** 500 passengers, 38 vehicles

YFB 87 Moku Holo Hele Bldr: Western Boat (In serv. 5-70)

**D:** 773 tons (fl) **Dim:** 54.9 × 18 **Man:** 2 G.M. diesels

YFB 88 to YFB 91 (ex-LCU 1646, ex-LCU 1638 to LCU 1640)

**YFB 90** L. & L. Van Ginderen, 10-81

**D:** 390 tons (fl) **S:** 10 kts **Dim:** 41.0 × 9.0
**M:** 4 G.M. diesels; 2 props; 1,200 hp **Man:** 6 tot.

Remarks: Built 1965–69. Modified 1969–70. All active. YFB 83 name means "A canoe that travels on land"; YFB 87 name means "Ship that goes back and forth"; both at Pearl Harbor.

◆ **155 (+8) YFN covered lighters***

YFN 862–1264

**YFN 968** L. & L. Van Ginderen, 10-86

Remarks: Built 1940–84. 153 active. Majority are 685 tons (fl), 33.5 × 9.8. Large rectangular deckhouse. Nine YFN 1254 class authorized under FY 81 (11 actually built), 6 (3 ordered) under FY 85, 2 under FY 86: 260 tons light (660 fl); 33.53 × 9.75 × 2.23 m; have a small deckhouse; were to be delivered 4-86 to 10-86; ordered 30-7-85, but only 3 had been completed when builder went bankrupt 2-87. Recent strikes include: YFN 1187 and 1190 on 25-9-83, YFN 371 on 15-3-83, YFN 906 on 1-10-83, YFN 1188 and 1190 on 15-9-83, YFN 650 on 15-1-86, and YFN 815 on 30-6-87. YFN 1178 reclassified YC 1615 on 31-10-86.

◆ **13 YFNB large covered lighters***

YFNB 5, 8, 25, 30, 31, 32, 34, 36, 37, 39, 41, 42, 47 (ex-YRR 9)

**YFNB 24**—now stricken 1969

Remarks: Built 1945. All active. All 831 tons light (2,780 fl), 79.2 × 14.6 × 2.9. YFNB 47 reclassified 11-83. YFNB 4, on loan to Maritime Administration since 1980, transferred permanently 1-6-85 and stricken 1-7-85. See also aerial photo of YFNB 36 on pg. 781.

◆ **2 YFND dry-dock companion craft***

YFND 5 (ex-YFN 268; in serv. 3-2-41) YFND 29 (ex-YFN 974; in serv. 28-8-45)

Remarks: 590 tons (fl), 33.53 × 9.75, converted YFN. YFND 5 in reserve.

◆ **13 YFNX special-purpose lighters***

| | In serv. | | In serv. |
|---|---|---|---|
| YFNX 4 | 1942 | YFNX 25 (ex-YFN 1224) | 1965 |
| YFNX 7 | 1942 | YFNX 26 (ex-YFN 1225) | 1965 |
| YFNX 15 (ex-YNG 22) | 1942 | Sea Turtle (YFNX 30, ex-YFN 1186) | 1952 |
| YFNX 20 | 1952 | | |
| YFNX 22 | 1941 | YFNX 31 (ex-YFN 1249) | 1970 |
| YFNX 23 (ex-YFN 289) | 1941 | YFNX-32 (ex-YRBM 7) | 1961 |
| YFNX 24 (ex-YFN 1215) | 1965 | YFNX 37 (ex-YFN 1192) | 1952 |

Remarks: All active except YFNX 7. Most converted YFN. Delivered 1942–70. YFNX 30 (200 tons light; 34.0 × 10.0 × 1.7 m) at Naval Ocean Science Center, San Diego, supports the remote-controlled submersible CURV II. YFNX 4–24 are 33.5 m × 10.0 × 1.7 m; YFNX 25, 26 are 38.4 × 10.0. Several have maneuvering

SERVICE CRAFT *(continued)*

**Sea Turtle (YFNX 30)**—submersible support craft G. Arra, 8-86

propulsion systems, including YFNX 30. YFNX 15 is a former "gate craft" (non-self-propelled net tender).

◆ **YFP floating power barges***

YFP 3 (ex-YC 1114) YFP 11 (ex-YFN 1207) YFP 12 (ex-YFN 1216)

REMARKS: 33.5 × 9.7-m. YFP 12 in reserve. Completed: YFD 3 in 4-45, other two in 1965.

YFP 14 INDUCTANCE (ex-Army BD 6235)

REMARKS: Built 1943–45. Transferred 1-10-77. Former floating crane (43.28 × 17.68 × . . .).

NOTE: Refrigerated cargo lighter YFR 888 stricken 15-2-85.

◆ **4 YFRN refrigerated cargo lighters***

YFRN 385 (ex-YF 385) YFRN 412 (ex-YF 412) YFRN 997 (ex-YF 997)
YFRN 1235 (ex-U.S. Army BR 6435)

REMARKS: Built 1943–45. All in reserve. Most 45.7 × 10.4. Sisters YFRN 1256 and 1257 stricken 7-3-84.

◆ **3 YFRT covered lighter range tenders**

| | Bldr | Laid down | L | In serv. |
|---|---|---|---|---|
| YFRT 287 | Norfolk NSY | 2-41 | 5-41 | 7-41 |
| YFRT 451 SPRIT | Basalt Rock Co., Napa, Cal. | 2-44 | 7-44 | 10-44 |
| YFRT 520 POTENTIAL | Erie Concrete & Steel, Erie, Pa. | 10-42 | 3-43 | 8-43 |

**D:** 300 tons light (650 fl) **S:** 9.5 kts **Dim:** 40.5 × 9.1 × 2.7
**A:** 3/324-mm Mk 32 ASW TT
**M:** 2 Caterpillar D 379 diesels; 2 props; 1,000 hp **Electric:** 180 kw

REMARKS: Torpedo trials craft. YFRT 287 built as such, rest converted from YFR. Sister YFRT 418 stricken 2-84, and YFRT 523 on 3-4-86. To be replaced by new-construction YTT.

◆ **8 YFU harbor utility craft:**

—2 LCU 1466 class Bldr: Defoe SB, Bay City, Mich.

YFU 50 (ex-LCU 1486) (In serv. 1955)
YFU 94 (ex-LCU 1488) (In serv. 1955)

**D:** 180 tons (347 fl) **S:** 8 kts **Dim:** 35.08 × 10.36 × 1.6
**M:** 3 Gray Marine 64YTL diesels; 3 props; 675 hp
**Range:** 1,200/6 **Fuel:** 11 tons **Electric:** 40 kw **Man:** . . .

REMARKS: In reserve. Can carry 167 tons cargo.

—1 LCU 1608 class Bldr: Defoe SB, Bay City, Mich.

YFU 91 (ex-LCU 1608) (In serv. 1957)

**D:** 351 tons (fl) **S:** 8 kts **Dim:** 35.11 × 10.36 × 1.52 (aft)
**M:** 3 Gray Marine 64 HN12 diesels; 3 Kort-nozzle props; 675 hp (495 hp sust.)
**Range:** 1,200/6 **Fuel:** 11.7 tons **Man:** . . .

REMARKS: Converted landing craft. Cargo: 183 tons. Active.

**YFU 91**—landing craft with sides cut down, superstructure raised and relocated
L. & L. Van Ginderen, 1981

—1YFU 71 class Bldr: Pacific Coast Eng. Co., Alameda, Cal.

YFU 81 (In serv. 1968)

**D:** 220 tons (380 tons fl) **S:** 8 kts **Dim:** 38.10 × 10.97 × 2.29
**M:** 4 G.M. 6-71 diesels; 2 Kort-nozzle props; 1,000 hp **Electric:** 120 kw
**Range:** . . . **Man:** . . .

REMARKS: Active. Built as a YFU, last of 12 sisters intended for Vietnam service. Engines and superstructure centerline aft. Bow ramp. Sister to IX 506 (ex-YFU 82) and IX 514 (ex-YFU 79). Sisters YFU 74 and 75 transferred to MARAD for lay-up 18-12-84, reacquired 3-6-86, and then stricken 30-9-86. YFU 71, 72, 76 and 77 to Department of the Interior 1-12-84; two of these were transferred to the Marshall Islands in 1987.

—4 LCU 1610 class Bldr: Defoe SB, Bay City, Mich.

YFU 83 YFU 100 (ex-LCU 1610)
YFU 97 (ex-LCU 1611) YFU 102 (ex-LCU 1642)

**YFU 100**—in near-standard LCU configuration R. Scheina, 7-84

**D:** 190 tons (390 fl) **S:** 11 kts **Dim:** 41.07 × 9.07 × 2.08
**M:** 4 G.M. 6-71 diesels; 2 Kort-nozzle props; 1,200 hp
**Range:** 1,200/11 **Fuel:** 13 tons **Man:** 6 tot.

REMARKS: All active. LCU 83 built as utility craft, but to standard LCU configuration; others redesignated. Cargo capacity: 143 tons in 30.5 × 5.5-m cargo deck. Retain bow ramp.

◆ **3 YGN garbage lighters***

YGN 80, 81, 83 Bldr: Zidel, Portland, Ore. (In serv. 1970–71)

REMARKS: All active. 309 tons light (855 fl), 37.8 × 10.7 rectangular barges. Have hopper-type bottoms to permit dumping at sea. YGN 70 and 82, redesignated as "equipment" 1-84, remain available also.

◆ **2 YHLC salvage lift craft, heavy*** Bldr: A.G. Weser, Seebeck, Bremerhaven (In serv. 1951)

YHLC 1 CRILLEY YHLC 2 CRANDALL

**Crilley (YHLC 1)**—outboard *Crandall* (YHLC 2), in reserve J. Jedrlinic, 1980

**SERVICE CRAFT** *(continued)*

Remarks: Ex-*Hiev* and ex-*Griep* purchased 19-12-66 from Germany for Vietnam War duties. Renamed 14-9-67. In the James River Maritime Commission reserve fleet since 9-76, but remain Navy property.

◆ **4 (+1) YM dredge**

YM 17 (In serv. 1934) YM 33 (In serv. 1970) YM 39 (In serv . . .)
YM 32 (In serv. 1969) YM 35 (In serv. 1970)

Remarks: Characteristics vary. YM 32 and YM 33 in reserve. YM 17 displaces 500 tons. YM 33, 35 are only 13.1 m and 21.3 m overall, respectively. YM 38 stricken 31-1-87. One new dredge authorized under FY 88.

◆ **2 YNG gate craft***

YNG 11 YNF 17

Remarks: Built 1941 to tend harbor-defense nets. **D:** 225 tons (fl); **Dim:** 33.5 × 10.5.

◆ **1 YO 46-class fuel-oil lighter**—in reserve Bldr: Lake Superior SB, Superior, Wisc.

YO 47 Casing Head (In serv. 11-42)

**D:** 950 tons (2,660 fl) **S:** 10 kts **Dim:** 71.6 × 11.3 × 4.6 **Cargo:** 1,350 tons
**M:** 2 Enterprise diesels; 820 hp. **Electric:** 280 kw **Man:** 34 tot.

◆ **9 YO 43† and YO 65 class** Bldr: Jeffersonville Boat & Machine Co., Jeffersonville, Ind. (except: YO 129: Smith SY, Pensacola, Fla.; YO 203: Manitowoc SB, Manitowoc, Wisc.; YO 241: John H. Mathis, Camden, N.J.)

| | In serv. | | In serv. | | In serv. |
|---|---|---|---|---|---|
| YO 129 | 4-44 | YO 224 | 10-45 | YO 241† (ex-YOG 5) | 10-43 |
| YO 203 | 8-45 | YO 225 | 10-45 | | |
| YO 220 | 8-45 | YO 228 | 11-45 | | |
| YO 223 | 9-45 | YO 230 | 12-45 | | |

**YO 223**—with LN-66 radar V. Baca, 3-87

**YO 203**—at light load S. Kürsener, 11-87

**D:** 440 tons light (1,390 fl) **S:** 9 kts **Dim:** 53.04 × 9.75 × 3.96
**M:** 1 G.M. (see Remarks) diesel; 1 prop, 640 hp **Electric:** 80 kw

Remarks: YO 228 and YO 241 are in reserve. Cargo is 900 tons/6,570 bbl. YO 129 has a Union diesel, 560 hp; YO 241 has a Fairbanks-Morse diesel, 480 hp. Sisters YO 106 stricken 12-83, YO 200 and 202 stricken 7-83, YO 264 stricken 15-11-85. Same basic design as 53.04-m YOG and YW.

◆ **1 YO 153 class** Bldr: Ira S. Bushey, Brooklyn, N.Y.—In reserve

YO 153 (In serv. 7-43)

**YO 153**—in reserve at Philadelphia, with 5 reserve YO/YOG/YW A.D. Baker, 8-84

**D:** 370 tons light (1,095 fl) **S:** 10 kts **Dim:** 47.63 × 9.32 × 3.66
**M:** 1 Fairbanks-Morse diesel; 1 prop; 525 hp **Electric:** 39 kw

Remarks: Cargo: 660 tons/6,071 bbl.

◆ **6 YOG . . . gasoline lighters** Bldrs: RTC SB, Camden, N.J. (except: YOG 78, 79: Puget Sound NSY; YOG 68: George Lawley & Sons, Neponset, Mass.)

YOG 58, YOG 68, YOG 78, YOG 88, YOG 93, YOG 196 (ex-YO 196) (In serv. 1945–46)

**YOG 88**—at light load; no radar G. Arra, 7-86

**D:** 440 tons light (1,390 fl) **Dim:** 53.04 × 9.75 × 3.96
**M:** 1 G.M. diesel; 1 prop; 640 hp **Electric:** 80 kw

Remarks: Three in reserve. Carry about 950 tons aviation fuel. YOG 58 has a Union diesel. YOG 67, captured by Vietnam 30-4-75, not officially stricken until 30-7-85. YOG 79 stricken 1987.

◆ **12 YOGN gasoline barges***

YOGN 8, 9, 10, 26, 110, 111, 113, 114, 115, 123, 124, 125

Remarks: Built 1943–71. All active. Carry aviation fuel. All 1,270–1,360 tons (fl), approx. 50 × 10.7 m. YOGN 122 stricken 24-4-86.

◆ **46 (+3) YON fuel-oil barges**

Remarks: Most built 1942–76. 46 active. Typical unit: 1,445 tons (fl); 50.3 × 12.0 × 2.7. YON 305, 306 built under FY 80. YON 255 and later (30 units) were built 1964–76. Five are ex-U.S. Army, including YON 305, 306, transferred 7-79. YON 235 is ex-YW 73. Can carry a variety of fuels. Three YON 307 approved under FY 87: 1,600 tons (fl); 56.0 × 10.7 × 3.0. YON 239 stricken 15-6-83. YON 268 (ex-U.S. Army, transferred 1967) stricken 21-7-86.

◆ **13 YOS oil-storage barges***

YOS 8, 10–12, 15–17, 20, 21, 24, 28 (ex-YC 707), 33 (ex-YSR 46), 34

Remarks: Built 1944–65. All active. Ten: 100 tons light; 24.4 × 10.4; others: 140 tons light; 33.5 × 10.4. YOS 34 (ex-Army OB61-2) acquired 1-9-79. Two new YOS requested under FY 87: 725 tons (fl).

**SERVICE CRAFT** *(continued)*

◆ **20 (+7) YP 676-class patrol craft/training tenders** Bldrs: YP676–682: Peterson Bldrs., Sturgeon Bay, Wisc.; others: Marinette SB, Marinette, Wisc.

| | Laid down | L | In serv. | | Laid down | L | In serv. |
|---|---|---|---|---|---|---|---|
| YP 676 | 7-4-83 | 9-4-84 | 14-11-84 | YP 690 | 18-8-86 | . . . | -87 |
| YP 677 | 10-10-83 | 23-6-84 | 5-12-84 | YP 691 | 28-10-86 | . . . | -87 |
| YP 678 | 15-12-83 | 3-11-84 | 13-5-85 | YP 692 | 10-12-86 | . . . | 27-7-87 |
| YP 679 | 18-4-84 | 11-12-84 | 6-6-85 | YP 693 | 26-1-87 | 14-8-87 | 10-87 |
| YP 680 | 2-7-84 | 23-3-85 | 8-8-85 | YP 694 | 20-2-87 | . . . | -87 |
| YP 681 | 29-10-84 | 1-6-85 | 30-9-85 | YP 695 | . . . | . . . | 10-87 |
| YP 682 | 7-1-85 | 3-8-85 | 18-11-85 | YP 696 | . . . | . . . | . . . |
| YP 683 | 23-7-85 | 19-6-86 | 13-10-86 | YP 697 | . . . | . . . | . . . |
| YP 684 | 29-8-85 | 14-8-86 | 10-12-86 | YP 698 | . . . | . . . | . . . |
| YP 685 | 8-10-85 | 25-9-86 | 23-11-86 | YP 699 | 9-7-87 | . . . | . . . |
| YP 686 | 23-1-86 | 25-10-86 | 1-87 | YP 700 | . . . | . . . | . . . |
| YP 687 | 27-2-86 | 3-87 | -87 | YP 701 | . . . | . . . | . . . |
| YP 688 | 7-4-86 | 4-87 | -87 | YP 702 | . . . | . . . | 6-88 |
| YP 689 | 15-7-86 | . . . | -87 | | | | |

**YP 683** Marinette, 7-86

**YP 680** L. & L. Van Ginderen, 6-87

**D:** 167–172.4 tons (fl) **S:** 12 kts **Dim:** 32.92 (30.99 pp) × 7.39 × 1.83
**Electric Equipt:** Radar: 1/SPS-64(V)9 nav.
**M:** 2 G.M. 12V71N diesels; 2 props; 874 hp **Electric:** 100 kw
**Man:** 2 officers, 4 men, 24 midshipmen (30 berths) **Range:** 1500/12

Remarks: Wooden construction boats to replace YP 654 class. Aluminum superstructure. YP 676 ordered 15-10-82; YP 677–682 ordered 25-5-83; YP 683–695 ordered 12-6-84; YP 696–702 on 13-9-85. Made up to 13.3 kts on trials. Have NAVSAT and Loran C receivers. YP 676, 678, 680, 682 to Naval Academy; YP 677, 679 to Officer Candidate School, Newport, R.I. YP 686 equipped for oceanographic research. Congress directed that YP 702 be completed as a prototype inshore minehunter under FY 88, a conversion neither required nor desired by the Navy.

◆ **17 YP patrol craft** (In serv. 2-58 to 11-79) Bldrs: YP 654–663, 666: Stephens Bros., Stockton, Cal; YP 664, 665: Elizabeth City SY, Elizabeth City, N.C.; others: Peterson Bldrs., Sturgeon Bay, Wisc.

YP 654, 657, 662–666, 668–675

**YP 671** G. Arra, 7-86

**D:** 57–60 tons (68–71 fl) **S:** 12.6–13.3 kts **Dim:** 24.51 × 5.72 × 1.6
**M:** 2 G.M. 6-71 diesels; 2 props; 590 hp **Electric:** 20–30 kw
**Range:** 400/12 **Man:** 2 officers, 8 men, 24 midshipmen
**Electron Equipt:** Radar: Raytheon 1220

Remarks: Wooden construction. Seven were used for navigation and maneuvering training at Naval Academy, Annapolis, and rest at Naval Officer Candidate School, Newport. Not armed. Some (including YP 673) had 2 G.M. 12V71N diesels, 680 hp. Sisters YP 659 and YP 660 were transferred to the COOP minehunting program in 9-85 and 11-85. Fifteen others are to become COOP craft under FY 86–88. YP 655, 656, and 667 were retyped as "boats" during 8-85 and transferred to the Surface Warfare Officers' School, San Diego. The others remain awaiting redesignation as COOP craft. YP 658, at Surface Warfare Officers School, Coronado, is named *Perseverance.*

◆ **4 YPD floating pile drivers***

YPD 37, 41, 45 (ex-YC 1498), 46 (ex-YFNB 35)

Remarks: Built 1943–65. One is in reserve. Most built on standard 24.4 × 10.4 barge hulls, except YPD 46: 79.6 × 14.6; 2,700 tons (fl). YPD 42 stricken 9-6-83.

◆ **27 YR floating workshops***

YR 25–27, 29, 36, 44, 46, 50, 60–65, 68, 70, 73, 76–78, 83 (ex-YRL 5), 84–89

**YR 26** 1969

Remarks: Built 1941–45. Twenty-one active. Most 520 tons light (770 fl); 46.6 × 10.7 × 1.8. Differ in equipment. YR 24 (captured by Vietnam 30-4-75) stricken 30-7-85. YR 89 reclassified from YRR 4 (ex-YFN 685) 15-8-86. YR 9 stripped and transferred to U.S. Army 31-1-87.

◆ **5 YRB repair and berthing barges***

YRB 1 (ex-YFN 258), 2, 22 (ex-YC 1079), 25 (ex-YFN 298), 29 (ex-YRST 5)

Remarks: All 33.5 × 9.1. Built 1940–45. Support submarines.

◆ **38 YRBM repair, berthing, and messing barges***

YRBM 1–6, 8, 9, 11–15, 20, 23–46

Remarks: Built 1955–83. All active; support submarines and ships in overhaul. Marinette SB constructed YRBM 31 to YRBM 46 during 1979–83: 688 tons; 44.5 × 14.0 × 1.3; accommodations for 26 officers, 231 men. Have office, workshop, eating, and recreation spaces, 96-seat training theater, galley, etc. YRBM 23–30, also by Marinette (In serv. 8-70 to 6-71) of similar dimensions, but 585 tons (fl). YRBM 20 is 2,700 tons, 79.6 × 14.6; remainder are approx. 310 tons (fl), 33.5 × 10.4.

**SERVICE CRAFT** *(continued)*

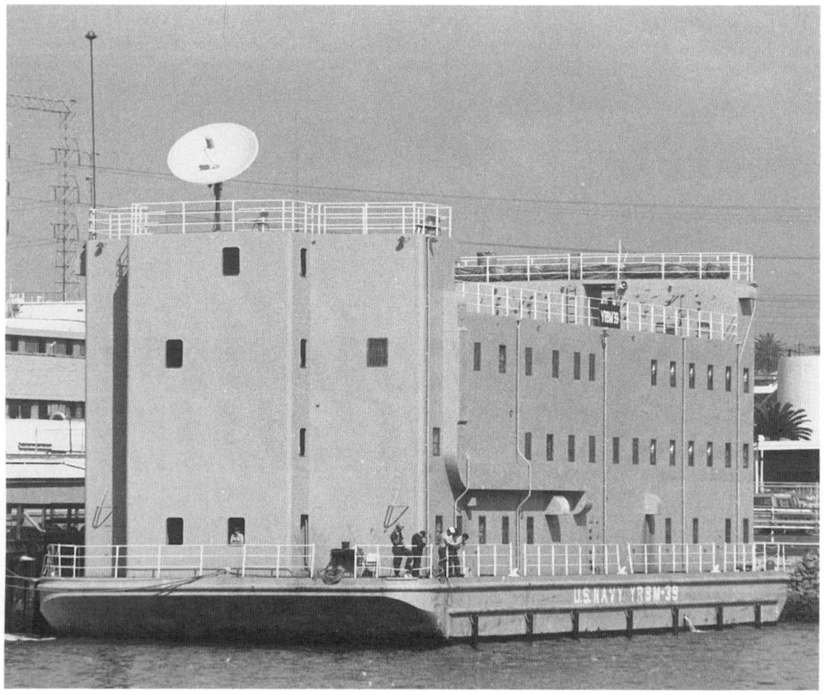

**YRBM 39** V. Baca, 2-87

**YRBM 15** W. Donko, 7-84

◆ **4 YRDH floating dry-dock workshops, hull***

YRDH 1 (ex-YR 55), 2 (ex-YR 56), 6, 7 (In serv. 1943–44)

Remarks: YRDH 6 active. 770 tons (fl), 46.6 × 10.7 × 1.8.

◆ **4 YRDM floating dry-dock workshops, machinery***

YRDM 1 (ex-YR 52), 2 (ex-YR 53), 5, 7 (In serv. 1943–44)

Remarks: YRDM 5 active. 770 tons (fl), 46.6 × 10.7 × 1.8.

◆ **11 YRR radiological repair barges***

| | | |
|---|---|---|
| YRR 1 (ex-YR 49) | YRR 5 (ex-YRDM 8) | YRR 11 (ex-YRDH 3) |
| YRR 2 (ex-YR 74) | YRR 6 (ex-YR 39) | YRR 12 (ex-YRDH 4) |
| YRR 3 (ex-YFN 333) | YRR 7 (ex-YR 31) | YRR 13 (ex-YRDM 3) |
| | YRR 10 (ex-YR 79) | YRR 14 (ex-YRDM 4) |

Remarks: In serv. 1937–45; all active. All converted from other barge-hulled functions: 770 tons (fl), 46.6 × 10.7 × 1.8. Sister YRR 9 reclassified YFND 47 in 11-83; YRR 4 became YR 89 on 15-8-86.

◆ **3 YRST salvage-craft tender***

YRST 1 (ex-YDT 11) YRST 2 (ex-YDT 12) YRST 6 (ex-YFNX 10)

Remarks: In serv. 1945; all active. YRST 3 and YRST 5 stricken 15-4-84. YRST 1, 2 are 2,700 tons (fl), 79.6 × 14.6; YRST 6 is 670 tons (fl), 33.5 × 10.7. All are rectangular barges.

◆ **4 YSD seaplane wrecking derricks**

| | Bldr | In serv. |
|---|---|---|
| YSD 39 | Norfolk Navy Yard | 1943 |
| YSD 53 | Gulfport Boiler Welding, Port Arthur, Texas | 1943 |
| YSD 63 | Sonle Steel, San Francisco | 1944 |
| YSD 74 | Pearl Harbor Navy Yard | 1943 |

**YSD 53**—with decompression chamber on deck M. Curtin, 11-85

**D:** 240 tons (276 fl) **S:** 6 kts **Dim:** 31.70 × 9.50 × 1.20
**M:** 2 Superior diesels; 2 props; 320 hp

Remarks: All active. Employed as 10-ton capacity, self-propelled cranes. Known as "Mary Anns." Sister YSD 15 stricken 1-4-84; YSD 77 stricken 15-11-85. YSD 53 is used as a diving tender, with FADS-2 (Fly-Away Diving System, Mk 2) at Norfolk.

◆ **20 YSR sludge-removal barges***

Remarks: Built 1932-46. Eighteen active. Most either 24.4 × 9.8 or 33.5 × 10.4. YSR 39 stricken 8-85, YSR 17 stricken late 1985; both to other U.S. government agencies.

◆ **81 YTB large harbor tugs (SCB 147/147A type)** Bldrs: YTB 752, 753: Christy Corp., Sturgeon Bay, Wisc.; YTB 756–759, 763–766, 799–802: Southern SB Corp., Slidell, La.; YTB 760–761: Jakobson SY, Oyster Bay, New York; YTB 762: Commercial Iron Wks., Portland, Ore.; YTB 767–771: Mobile Ship Repair, Mobile, Ala.; YTB 774–798, 816–836: Marinette Marine Corp., Marinette, Wisc.; YTB 803–815: Peterson Bldrs, Sturgeon Bay, Wisc.

| | | |
|---|---|---|
| YTB 752 Edenshaw | YTB 783 Redwing | YTB 810 Anoka |
| YTB 753 Marin | YTB 784 Kalispell | YTB 811 Houma |
| YTB 756 Pontiac | YTB 785 Winnemucca | YTB 812 Accomac |
| YTB 757 Oshkosh | YTB 786 Tonkawa | YTB 813 Poughkeepsie |
| YTB 758 Paducah | YTB 787 Kittanning | YTB 814 Waxahatchie |
| YTB 759 Bogalusa | YTB 788 Wapato | YTB 815 Neodesha |
| YTB 760 Natick | YTB 789 Tomahawk | YTB 816 Campti |
| YTB 761 Ottumwa | YTB 790 Menominee | YTB 817 Hyannis |
| YTB 762 Tuscumbia | YTB 791 Marinette | YTB 818 Mecosta |
| YTB 763 Muskegon | YTB 792 Antigo | YTB 819 Iuka |
| YTB 764 Mishawaka | YTB 793 Piqua | YTB 820 Wanamassa |
| YTB 765 Okmulgee | YTB 794 Mandan | YTB 821 Tontogany |
| YTB 766 Wapakoneta | YTB 795 Ketchikan | YTB 822 Pawhuska |
| YTB 767 Apalachicola | YTB 796 Saco | YTB 823 Canonchet |
| YTB 768 Arcata | YTB 797 Tamaqua | YTB 824 Santaquin |
| YTB 769 Chesaning | YTB 798 Opelika | YTB 825 Wathena |
| YTB 770 Dahlonega | YTB 799 Natchitoches | YTB 826 Washtuena |
| YTB 771 Keokuk | YTB 800 Eufaula | YTB 827 Chetek |
| YTB 774 Nashua | YTB 801 Palatka | YTB 828 Catahecassa |
| YTB 775 Wauwatosa | YTB 802 Cheraw | YTB 829 Metacom |
| YTB 776 Weehawken | YTB 803 Nanticoke | YTB 830 Pushmataha |
| YTB 777 Nogales | YTB 804 Ahoskie | YTB 831 Dekanawida |
| YTB 778 Apopka | YTB 805 Ocala | YTB 832 Petalesharo |
| YTB 779 Manhattan | YTB 806 Tuskegee | YTB 833 Shabonee |
| YTB 780 Saugus | YTB 807 Massapequa | YTB 834 Newagen |
| YTB 781 Niantic | YTB 808 Wenatchee | YTB 835 Skenandoa |
| YTB 782 Manistee | YTB 809 Agawan | YTB 836 Pokagon |

**D:** 286 tons (356 fl) **S:** 12.5 kts **Dim:** 33.05 × 9.3 × 4.14
**M:** 1 Fairbanks-Morse $38D8\frac{1}{8}$ × 12 diesel; 1 prop; 2,000 hp
**Electric:** 120 kw **Fuel:** . . . **Range:** 2,000/12 **Man:** 12 tot.

**Campti (YTB 816)** L. & L. Van Ginderen, 5-87

## SERVICE CRAFT *(continued)*

**Anoka (YTB 810)** L. & L. Van Ginderen, 2-87

REMARKS: Built 1959–70. YTB 752 to YTB 759 have a less-streamlined superstructure, and are considered a separate class (SCB 147 type); YTB 752, 753 have Alco diesels. All active. Minor differences in displacement between units by different builders. All have a small commercial navigational radar. Three also built for Saudi Arabia.

NOTE: Planned procurement of 28 YTB 839 tugs of 3,000–4,000 hp was canceled 1984 in favor of contracting for tug services from private industry. The result will be lower overall costs and a diminished requirement for military personnel. Nearly all surviving active YTL- and YTM-type tugs were stricken during 1985–87 (dates below) as a result of the same decision.

### ◆ 1 YTL 422-class small harbor tug Bldr: Robert Jacob, City Isl., N.Y.

YTL 602 (In serv. 10-45)

**D:** 70 tons (80 fl) **S:** 8 kts **Dim:** 20.1 × 5.5 × 2.4
**M:** 1 Hoover, Owens, Rentschler diesel; 375 hp **Man:** 4 tot.

REMARKS: Survivor of several hundred YTL 422 class; many still in foreign navies. A few others remain in Navy use, retyped as craft. Sisters YTL 588 stricken 15-12-85, YTL 422, 438, 439, 583 stricken 15-2-85; YTL 434 stricken 30-9-85 and transferred to MARAD for further use. YTL 591 stricken 31-7-85.

NOTE: Of the YTM medium harbor tugs listed in the previous edition, all have been stricken for disposal or permanent transfer to other government agencies: on 9-6-86, *Mascoutah* (YTM 760) and *Menasha* (YTM 761) were transferred to MARAD for use at Beaumont, Texas. On 15-5-86, the following reserve tugs were stricken: *Nepanet* (YTM 189), *Pawtucket* (YTM 359), *Chepanoc* (YTM 381), *Coatopa* (YTM 382), *Cochali* (YTM 383), *Hiawatha* (YTM 265), Red Cloud (YTM 268), *Sassaba* (YTM 364), *Kittaton* (YTM 406), *Natahki* (YTM 398), *Nadli* (YTM 534), *Takos* (YTM 546), *Hackensack* (YTM 750), the unnamed YTM 748, and *Apohola* (YTM 768). Of the others *Hiamonee* (YTM 776) was stricken 30-11-86; *Yatanocas* (YTM 544), *Accohanoc* (YTM 545), and *Migadan* (YTM 549) were stricken 28-2-87 (the first two for transfer to MARAD and the latter as a target). Of the tugs listed as stricken in the last edition, *Secota* (YTM 415), although stricken 30-9-85, was kept in use at Wake Island and was lost 23-6-86 in collision with *Georgia* (SSBN 729). In addition, *Wahpeton* (YTM 527) should have been reported as stricken 31-12-85.

NOTE: A large number of converted LCM(6) landing craft have been converted for use as push-tugs for local use, in place of YTLs.

### ◆ 0 (+2 + 2) torpedo trials ships Bldrs: McDermott, Morgan City, La.

| | Laid down | L | In serv. |
|---|---|---|---|
| YTT 9 N... | 8-88 | ... | 7-90 |
| YTT 10 N... | 11-88 | ... | 7-90 |

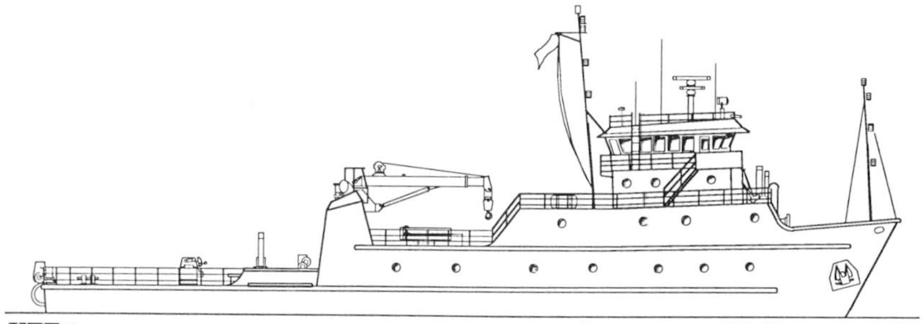

**YTT 9** McDermott, 1987

**D:** 1,000 tons light (1,200 fl) **S:** 11 kts sust.
**Dim:** 56.85 (53.83 pp) × 12.19 × 3.20
**A:** 2/533-mm TT (submerged)—3/324-mm Mk 32 Mod. 5 ASW TT
**Electron Equipt:** Radar: 1/... nav.
**M:** 1 Cummins KTA-50m diesel; 1 prop; 1,280 hp—
2 electric Z-drive thrusters, 300 hp each
**Range:** 1,800/11 **Endurance:** 12 days
**Electric:** 1,185 kw (3 × 395-kw, Cummins VTA-28 GS/G.C. sets)
**Man:** 24 tot. crew + 12 civilian technicians

REMARKS: Intended to replace IX 306 and YFRT currently used for torpedo trials. First unit was in FY 86 Budget as a YFRT but was rejected by Congress; both in FY 87. Will have crane to recover torpedoes and to handle sensor arrays and recovery equipment. Will have batteries to permit quiet operations. Will test Mk 48 ADCAP, Mk 46 and Mk 50 ASW torpedoes. Both ordered 8-87; additional units planned.

### ◆ 6 YW water barges

| | Bldr | L | In serv. |
|---|---|---|---|
| YW 83 | John H. Mathis, Camden, N.J. | 7-43 | 3-44 |
| YW 86 | Zenith Dredge Co., Duluth, Minn. | 4-43 | 8-43 |
| YW 98 | George Lawley & Son, Neponset, Mass. | 9-45 | 11-45 |
| YW 101 | Mare Island NSY, Cal. | 5-44 | 12-44 |
| YW 126 | Leatham D. Smith, Sturgeon Bay, Wisc. | 1945 | 1945 |
| YW 127 | Leatham D. Smith, Sturgeon Bay, Wisc. | 5-45 | 7-45 |

**D:** 1,282 tons (fl) **S:** 8 kts **Dim:** 53.0 × 9.7 × 4.6 **Man:** 22 tot.
**M:** 1 G.M. 8-2784 (YW 86: Fairbanks-Morse) diesel: 1 prop; 560 hp

REMARKS: Cargo: 930 tons water. YW 127 active; others in reserve. Same basic design as YO and YOG classes. Sister YW 123 stricken 15-2-84 but remains in use for anti-terrorist training under the name *Vigilant;* refurbished late 1985, but engine remains inoperative. YW 108 stricken 15-10-85 (to Kings Pt. Maritime Academy). YW 113 stricken 5-85 and used as a target.

### ◆ 6 YWN water barges*

YWN 70, 71, 78, 79, 82, 156

REMARKS: Built 1944–45. All but YWN 79 active; 220 tons light (1,270 fl); 50.3 × 10.7 × 2.4. YWN 147 stricken 19-7-85.

## SMALL CRAFT

In addition to the above yard and service craft, all of which have hull numbers and are carried on the Navy List, there are over 3,000 craft carried as "floating equipment." These range in size from the Naval Academy's rowing shells through the 2,780-ton *Seacon* described earlier and include all ships' boats and independent landing craft. Most of the more significant units are identified by a numbering system that begins with digits signifying the craft's length to the nearest foot, followed by an alphabetical designator indicating the craft's type, two digits indicating the fiscal year in which the craft was authorized, and subsequent digits indicating *which* craft of that year, i.e., "65PB778" is the eighth 65-ft patrol boat built under FY 77. *Unofficial* names and hull numbers are in widespread use.

Below are described some of the more significant and/or recent independent craft operated by the U.S. Navy.

### ◆ 10 821-class torpedo retrievers

| | | | Laid down | L | In serv. |
|---|---|---|---|---|---|
| TWR 821 | SWAMP FOX | (120 TR 821) | ... | 17-10-84 | 4-11-85 |
| TWR 822 | N... | (120 TR 822) | 7-4-84 | 18-10-84 | 20-11-85 |
| TWR 823 | N... | (120 TR 823) | 22-8-84 | 4-5-85 | 6-12-85 |
| TWR 824 | N... | (120 TR 824) | 21-9-84 | 10-6-85 | 6-12-85 |
| TWR 825 | N... | (120 TR 825) | 18-2-85 | 8-8-85 | 6-12-85 |
| TWR 831 | N... | (120 TR 831) | 29-3-85 | 4-9-85 | 3-7-86 |
| TWR 832 | N... | (120 TR 832) | 10-5-85 | 22-3-86 | 3-7-86 |
| TWR 833 | N... | (120 TR 833) | 28-5-85 | 4-4-86 | 3-7-86 |
| TWR 841 | N... | (120 TR 841) | 2-8-85 | 15-8-86 | 18-10-86 |
| TWR 842 | N... | (120 TR 842) | 23-8-85 | 22-9-86 | 24-12-86 |

**D:** 174 tons (213 fl) **S:** 16 kts **Dim:** 36.58 × 7.62 × 3.65 **Range:** 1,700/16
**Electron Equipt:** Radar: 1/LN-66
**M:** 2 Caterpillar D 3512 diesels; 2 props; 2,350 hp **Man:** 1 officer, 14 men
**Electric:** 128 kw **Fuel:** 28 tons **Endurance:** 7 days

**TWR 823** G. Arra, 6-86

**SMALL CRAFT** *(continued)*

**TWR 841**—white-painted for the AUTEC range  Marinette, 10-86

REMARKS: First five ordered 8-7-83 for delivery 15-12-84 to 15-3-85; three more ordered 10-83, all for delivery 7-85; two ordered 2-85 for delivery 6-86. However, program was behind schedule, and first not accepted until 11-85; four more accepted 12-85. Stern ramp and electro-hydraulic crane aft. Can carry 14 Mk 48 torpedoes. Have 43.7 tons permanent ballast! Congress halted further procurement, 1985. Eight operate on West Coast; 2 (painted white) at AUTEC range in the Bahamas.

◆ **7 modified patrol-boat-design torpedo retrievers**  Bldr: Peterson Bldrs., Sturgeon Bay, Wisc. (In serv. 1969–70)

| | | |
|---|---|---|
| TWR 1 DIAMOND | TWR 5 HARRIER | TWR 771 PHOENIX |
| TWR 2 N . . . | TWR 6 FERRET | . . . . . . N . . . |
| TWR 3 CONDOR | | |

**Diamond (TWR 1)**  L. & L. Van Ginderen, 11-86

**D:** 110 tons light (162 fl) **S:** 17 kts **Dim:** 31.09 × 6.40 × 2.36
**Electron Equipt:** Radar: 1/LN-66 **Electric:** 60 kw (2 × 30 kw)
**M:** 4 G.M. 12V-149 diesels; 2 props; 2,000 hp **Range:** 1,920/10
**Man:** 1 officer, 13 men **Fuel:** 27 tons

REMARKS: Design based on PGM 59-class patrol boat. Ramp at stern. Stowage for 17 tons of recovered ordnance. Maximum displacement without torpedoes is 149 tons.

◆ **2 85-ft torpedo retrievers**  Bldr: Tacoma Boat, Tacoma, Wa. (In serv. 1976?)

TWR 7 CHAPARRAL  271 N . . .

**271**  N. Polmar, 1986

**D:** . . . **S:** 18 kts **Dim:** 25.9 × . . . × . . .
**Electron Equipt:** Radar: 1/LN-66
**M:** 4 G.M. diesels; 2 props; . . . hp **Man:** . . .

REMARKS: Aluminum construction. Characteristics unknown. TWR 7 is at San Diego.

◆ **6 65-ft torpedo retrievers**  Bldr: . . . 65TR 671–676 (In serv. 10-67 to 7-68)

**TR 4 at work, a 65-ft craft**  G. Arra, 7-86

**D:** 34.8 tons (35.2 fl) **S:** 18.7 kts **Dim:** 22.17 × 5.18 × 1.68
**Electron Equipt:** Radar: 1/. . .
**M:** 2 G.M. 12V71 diesels; 2 props; 1,008 hp (800 sust.)
**Range:** 280/18 **Electric:** 10 kw **Man:** 6 tot.

REMARKS: Aluminum construction. Can recover up to 5 tons of weapons (3 torpedoes). Also in use are near-sisters 65AR 681 and 682, completed in 11-69 and 12-69, respectively, as general utility craft.

◆ **up to 17 72-ft Mk 2 torpedo retrievers**  Bldr: . . . (In serv. 1950s)

**72-ft torpedo retriever Mk 2**  G. Arra, 10-85

**D:** 53 tons (fl) **S:** 18 kts **Dim:** 22.17 × 5.18 × 1.68
**M:** 2 diesels; 2 props; 1,000 hp **Range:** 450/18 **Man:** 6 tot.

REMARKS: Wooden construction. Can carry up to 10.8 tons of weapons retrieved via a stern ramp. Obsolescent; were to be replaced by new Marinette-built units. Craft in photo above modified to a non-torpedo retrieval role.

◆ **1 drone retriever**  Bldr: Electric Boat, Groton (L: 7-8-50)

DR 1 RETRIEVER (ex-*Guardian*, ex-PT 809)

**D:** 125 tons (fl) **S:** 22 kts **Dim:** 30.02 × 7.92 × 2.13
**Electron Equipt:** Radar: 1/Raytheon . . .
**M:** 4 G.M. diesels; 4 props; 2,400 hp **Man:** 1 officer, 17 men

**SMALL CRAFT** *(continued)*

**Retriever (DR 1)** G. Arra, 4-86

REMARKS: Survivor of four prototype torpedoboats, later named *Guardian* as Secret Service chase boat for presidential yacht *Sequoia*. Used at Little Creek, Va., since 12-74 as a drone target-control and recovery craft. Aluminum construction.

◆ **1 95-ft. pilot boat** Bldr: U.S. Coast Guard Yard, Curtis Bay, Md. (In serv. 1955–56)

VANGUARD (ex-*Cape Hedge,* WPB 95311)

**D:** 87 tons (106 fl) **S:** 18 kts **Dim:** 28.96 × 6.1 × 1.55
**Electron Equipt:** Radar: 1/SPS-64(V)1 **Electric:** 40 kw
**M:** 4 Cummins VT-12-M-700 diesels; 2 props; 2,324 hp
**Range:** 570/20; 1,300/9

REMARKS: Former U.S. Coast Guard "Cape"-class cutter stricken 7-1-87 and transferred to the U.S. Navy for use as a pilot boat at San Diego. The Navy operates other craft in pilotage duties, including a Patrol Boat Mk I at Charleston, S.C.

NOTE: Former maneuvering training craft *Knowledge* (UB 761), *Confidence* (UB 762), *Diligence* (UB 763), *Perseverance* (UB 764), and the unnamed UB 765, all formerly employed at the Surface Warfare Officers School, Coronado, were stricken late 1987 as YP 654-class training boats began arriving to replace them; UB 761–765 were formerly MSB 7, 13, 17, 35, and 50.

◆ **8 (+28) Navy-44-class sail-training cutters** Bldr: Tillotson-Pearson, Inc., Warren, R.I. (In serv. 1987–89)

NA-1 AUDACIOUS
NA-2 COURAGEOUS
NA-3 INVINCIBLE
NA-4 VALIANT
NA-5 ACTIVE
NA-6 ALERT
NA-7 DAUNTLESS
NA-8 FEARLESS

**D:** 12.7 tons (fl) **S:** . . . **Dim:** 13.41 × 3.78 × 2.21
**M:** 1 auxiliary diesel; 33 hp **Man:** 10 midshipmen

REMARKS: First 8 ordered 3-87, with options for 20 more. First 11 funded under FY 87; 12 each planned under FY 88 and 89, but Congress denied funds. NA-1 delivered 21-5-87 for extensive trials; NA-2—8 delivered spring 1988. GRP construction. Intended to replace Naval Academy's 12 Luders yawls and 18 miscellaneous donated craft used for midshipman training; the older boats in good condition are to be sent to universities with Naval Reserve Officer Training Centers. Designed by McCurdy and Rhodes, Inc. Sail-training craft *Rattlesnake, Severn,* and *Shenandoah* were stricken for public sale 19-5-86.

◆ **102 50-ft workboats** Bldr: 52 by Marinette, Marinette, Wisc. (In serv. 1984 to 16-12-85) and 50 by Oregon Iron Works, Clackamas, Or. (all in serv. by 15-7-88)

50WB841–8428 50WB851–8524 50WB861–8650

**D:** . . . **S:** . . . **Dim:** 15.24 × 4.37 × 1.07
**M:** 2 G.M. 8V71 diesels; 2 props; . . . hp

REMARKS: Used for general-purpose workboats and as push tugs. Steel construction. First 28 ordered 2-84, 24 more in 11-84 from Marinette; 50 ordered 12-9-86 from Oregon Iron Works.

NOTE: As a measure of the number of small craft in U.S. Navy service, the following were on order as of 1-1-87 (not including craft described elsewhere in this volume or foreign sale units): 24 5.49-m target boats, 85 5.49-m utility boat/boom tenders, 80 5.49-m utility boats, 12 6.69-m utility boats, 7 12.19-m Mk 5 personnel boats, 92 4.27-m punts, 41 7.32-m explosive ordnance disposal boats, 68 7.92-m Mk 4 and Mk 6 personnel boats, 2 9.1-m range-control boats, 6 10.06-m utility boats, 145 combat raider craft, 83 7.92-m motor whaleboats, 25 17.07-m target boats, 17 10.06-m Mk 5 personnel boats, 22 12.19-m Mk 4 personnel boats, 14 12.19-m utility boats, and 19 15.24-m utility boats. Under FY 87, 150 4.27-m punts, 30 5.49-m utility boats, 20 to 25 6.71-m utility boats, 15 7.92-m motor whaleboats, 11 9.75-m personnel boats, and 10 10.06-m utility boats were planned for construction. In FY 88, some 280 craft were approved, and 101 were requested under FY 89.

**50-ft workboat being readied for shipment, pilothouse stowed in well**
Marinette, 2-85

**An earlier 50-ft workboat, with decked-over well; YD 73 in background**
W. Donko, 7-87

**DS 1**—a divers' support boat converted from an LCM(8) landing craft—typical of the landing craft used in a variety of support roles G. Arra, 6-86

SMALL CRAFT *(continued)*

**SWOB-049**—alongside DDG 8, a necessary craft used for the disposal of human waste W. Donko, 7-87

◆ **0 (+1) presidential yacht** Bldr: Mathias Yacht & SB Co., Camden, NJ

SEQUOIA (ex-AG 23) (L: 1925)

**Sequoia** L. & L. Van Ginderen, 7-86

**D:** 105 tons (fl) **S:** 12 kts **Dim:** 31.70 (30.18 pp) × 5.54 × 1.37
**M:** 2 diesels; 2 props; 400 hp

REMARKS: Wooden-hulled craft purchased from private owner as presidential yacht on 31-3-31. Served as Secretary of the Navy's yacht 3-36 to 1969 when again used as presidential yacht until sold during Carter Administration, 1977. Received refit and re-engined 1986 in preparation for donation to Navy after 1988 presidential election by private foundation.

MILITARY SEALIFT COMMAND

This organization was founded 1-10-49 as the Military Sea Transportation Service, and given its current name on 1-8-70. It is headed by a flag officer of the U.S. Navy. Its ships, most of which are not armed, are considered to be noncommissioned, and are manned by civilians (either government civil servants or contract personnel). The prefix "T" is appended to the hull numbers of MSC ships.

In the following pages the government-owned units are listed and described in alphabetical order by ship type. Then MSC chartered ships are described, in particular the ships of the Forward Deployment Logistics Force, the Near-Term Prepositioning Force, and, finally, the other ships on charter for cargo, tanker, scientific support, and fleet services duties.

MSC ships are painted gray (AGOR/AGS: white) and have blue and gold-yellow stack bands. Fleet support replenishment ships operated by MSC began to carry their hull numbers during late 1979; other MSC ships do *not* display hull numbers.

## AMMUNITION SHIP (T-AE)

◆ **1 Kilauea class**

| | Bldr | Laid down | L | In serv. |
|---|---|---|---|---|
| T-AE 26 KILAUEA | Gen. Dynamics, Quincy | 10-3-66 | 9-8-67 | 10-8-68 |

**D:** 17,937 tons (fl) **S:** 20 kts **Dim:** 171.9 × 24.7 × 8.5 **A:** 2/12.7-mm mg
**Electron Equipt:** Radar: 1/navigational, 1/SPS-10—TACAN: URN-25
**M:** 1 set G.E. GT; 1 prop; 22,000 hp **Man:** 121 MSC crew, 67 Navy
**Boilers:** 3 Foster-Wheeler; 42.3 kg/cm², 467°C **Fuel:** 2,612 tons

**Kilauea (T-AE 26)** M.S.C., 1986

REMARKS: 8,593 dwt. Transferred to MSC 1-10-80; six sisters remain in regular Navy. Can carry about 6,500 tons of munitions and has a hangar and flight deck for two UH-46 replenishment helicopters. Can also refuel ships, using forward, starboard station. Navy personnel perform ammunition handling and operate the communications and helicopter. Superstructure filled in on starboard side to increase accommodations space. Unusual in being armed; operates in the Pacific.

## STORES SHIPS (T-AF)

◆ **1 Rigel class**

| | Bldr | L | In serv. |
|---|---|---|---|
| T-AF 58 RIGEL | Ingalls, Pascagoula | 15-3-55 | 2-9-55 |

**Rigel (T-AF 58)** Skyfotos, 1986

**D:** 9,696 tons light (15,540 fl) **S:** 20 kts **Dim:** 153.0 × 22.0 × 8.8
**Electron Equipt:** Radar: 1/SPS-10, 1/Raytheon 1650/CX
**M:** 1 set G.E. GT; 1 prop; 16,000 hp
**Boilers:** 2 Combustion Engineering; 42.2 kg/cm², 440°C
**Range:** 10,000/21; 15,000/15 **Man:** 16 officers, 97 men MSC, +67 Navy

REMARKS: 10,781 grt/8,112 dwt. Twelve 10-ton booms. Cargo: 5,975 m³ dry, 5,400 m³ refrigerated. Transferred to MSC 23-6-75 and disarmed. Provides fleet support. Satellite communications equipment carried. Operates in Atlantic.

## COMBAT STORES SHIPS (T-AFS)

◆ **3 British Lyness-class combat stores ships** Bldrs: Swan Hunter & Wigham Richardson, Wallsend-on-Tyne, U.K.

| | Laid down | L | In serv. |
|---|---|---|---|
| T-AFS 8 SIRIUS (ex-*Lyness*) | 4-65 | 7-4-66 | 22-12-66 |
| T-AFS 9 SPICA (ex-*Tarbatness*) | 4-66 | 22-2-67 | 10-8-67 |
| T-AFS 10 SATURN (ex-*Stromness*) | 10-65 | 16-9-66 | 21-3-67 |

**D:** 9,010 tons light (16,792 fl) **S:** 19 kts
**Dim:** 159.52 (149.35 pp) × 22.0 × 7.77
**Electron Equipt:** Radar: 2/. . . nav.
TACAN: URN-25
**M:** 1 Sulzer 8RD76 diesel; 1 prop; 12,700 hp **Electric:** 3,575 kw
**Fuel:** 1,310 tons heavy oil, 264 tons diesel
**Range:** 11,000/19; 27,500/12 **Man:** 130 MSC, 45 Navy

REMARKS: T-AFS 8 was leased from Great Britain on 17-1-81 for one year for use in the Mediterranean and was to be purchased outright 1-3-82; T-AFS 9, which had been in reserve at Gibraltar, was leased 30-9-81 and was purchased 30-9-82. An agreement to purchase T-AFS 10 was made on 27-1-83, and the ship arrived at Bayonne, New Jersey, 4-83 awaiting purchase under the FY 84 budget, 13-12-83;

## COMBAT STORES SHIPS (T-AFS) *(continued)*

**Sirius (T-AFS 8)**—with hangar L. & L. Van Ginderen, 11-86

**Spica (T-AFS 9)** L. & L. Van Ginderen, 6-87

T-AFS 10 was modernized under FY 85 with improved helicopter facilities, improved communications, five STREAM transfer stations, an automated data facility, and conversion to use U.S. Navy fuel. T-AFS 8 completed a similar upgrading 1-10-83 and T-AFS 9 by 1986; all three can accommodate 2 UH-46 helicopters. 12,358 grt/4,744 nrt. Helicopter deck aft 33.5 × 18.3. Have four holds, with 15 levels, 8 stores elevators. Total cargo volume: 12,234 m³ (8,313 m³ dry stores, 3,921 m³ refrigerated/frozen). Cranes: 1/25-ton, 2/12.5-ton, 1/12-ton, and 2/5-ton. Carry 40,000 different repair parts and can support 15,000 men at sea for one month. Accommodations for 193 total. Very successful, comfortable ships—a useful bargain.

## MISCELLANEOUS RESEARCH SHIPS (T-AG)

◆ **1 sound trials ship (SCB 726 type)** Bldr: Todd SY, Seattle

| | Laid down | L | In serv. |
|---|---|---|---|
| T-AG 195 HAYES (ex-T-AGOR 16) | 12-11-69 | 2-7-70 | 21-7-71 |

**Hayes (T-AG 195)**—before conversion L. & L. Van Ginderen, 6-83

**D:** 4,037 tons (fl) **S:** 12 kts **Dim:** 75.10 (67.06 pp) × 22.86 × 6.70
**Electron Equipt:** Radar: 1/Raytheon TM 1650/6X, 1/Raytheon TM 1660/12S
Sonar: TUMS towed sound-measurement array
**M:** 3 Caterpillar 3516 diesels, electric drive; 2 props; . . . hp
**Endurance:** 30 days **Range:** 6,000/12
**Man:** 10 officers, 26 men, MSC crew + 29 technicians

REMARKS: Catamaran, with each hull of 7.3 m. Being converted 8-7-87 to 18-1-90 by Tacoma Boat, Tacoma, Wash., as sound trials vessel under FY 86 Budget to replace *Monob One* (YAG 61). Will transport, deploy, and retrieve acoustic arrays in support of the Submarine Noise Reduction Program. Has 371.6 m² laboratory space. Will be re-engined, with original 4 high-speed diesels driving controllable-pitch props being replaced by a diesel-electric plant. New propulsion plant will be suspended in a vibration-damping compartment above deck, along with 2 Caterpillar 3412 diesel generator sets. Will tow TUMS noise-monitoring gear. Had been laid up since 1982 at Bayonne, N.J., and was transferred from the Oceanographer of the Navy to the David Taylor Naval Ships Research and Development Center's control in 1983 awaiting the FY 86 conversion. Was not a success as a research platform, suffering from excessive pitching.

◆ **1 Vanguard class** Bldr: Marine Ship Corp., Sausalito, Cal.

| | L | In serv. |
|---|---|---|
| T-AG 194 VANGUARD (ex-T-AGM 19, ex-*Muscle Shoals*, ex-*Mission San Fernando*, T-AO 122) | 23-11-43 | 21-10-47 |

**Vanguard (T-AG 194)** L. & L. Van Ginderen, 2-84

**D:** 21,478 tons (fl) **S:** 16 kts **Dim:** 181.4 × 22.9 × 7.6
**Electron Equipt:** Radar: 1/Raytheon 1650/9X, 1/Raytheon 1660/12S
**M:** 1 set G.E. GT, electric drive; 1 prop; 8,700 hp
**Boilers:** 2 Babcock & Wilcox "D"; 42.3 kg/cm², 440°C
**Range:** 27,000/16 **Fuel:** 3,995 tons **Man:** 19 officers/179 men

REMARKS: 16,060 grt/16,255 dwt.; *Vanguard* was converted 1964–66 from a T2-SE-A2-type tanker to a tracking and communications ship to support NASA manned space flights. Reclassified 30-9-80 as T-AG 194 while under conversion to replace *Compass Island* (AG 153) as ballistic-missile submarine navigational system trials ship for the Navy Strategic Systems Project Office. Conversion commenced 1-4-80 at Todd Shipyard, San Pedro, Cal. Appearance similar to *Redstone* (T-AGM 20) but without tracking radars. Has a MARISAT satellite communications facility. Trials with a ring-laser gyro for navigation began 4-85.

## DEEP SUBMERGENCE SUPPORT SHIP (T-AGDS)

◆ **1 auxiliary deep-submergence support ship** Bldr: Maryland SB & DD

| | L | In serv. |
|---|---|---|
| T-AGDS 2 POINT LOMA (ex-*Point Barrow*, T-AKD 1) | 25-5-57 | 28-2-58 |

**Point Loma (T-AGDS 2)**—note radomes near bow G. Arra, 4-86

**D:** 8,000 tons light (12,430 fl) **S:** 12 kts **Dim:** 150.0 (144.8 pp) × 22.6 × 5.8
**Electron Equipt:** Radar: 1/SPS-53, 1/SPS-10
**M:** 2 sets Westinghouse GT; 2 props; 3,000 hp—2/omnithrusters; 6,000 hp
**Boilers:** 2 Foster-Wheeler; 32 kg/cm², 400°C
**Range:** 8,800/10 **Man:** 44 MSC

REMARKS: Maritime Commission S2-ST-23A design. Built for Arctic supply and configured like a landing ship, dock (LSD). Served in MSC until 28-9-72, when placed in reserve. Transferred to the Navy on 28-2-74, renamed, renumbered, and reactivated as a tender for deep-submergence vehicles, recommissioning 30-4-75. Operates from San Diego. Four "GolfBall" spherical antennas on white-painted deckhouses on bow. Carries 275 tons of gasoline as flotation liquid for submersibles. Two cranes. Second stack added for diesel-generator exhausts. Transferred to MSC 1-10-86.

NOTE: Commercial M/V *Laney Chouset* chartered 1987 as tender to submersibles *Turtle* (DSV 3) and *Sea Cliff* (DSV 4) to replace R/V *Lulu*.

## RANGE INSTRUMENTATION SHIPS (T-AGM)

◆ **1 Mariner class**

| | Bldr | L | In serv. |
|---|---|---|---|
| T-AGM 23 OBSERVATION ISLAND (ex-AG 154, ex-YAG 53, ex-*Empire State Mariner*) | New York SB, Camden, N.J. | 15-8-53 | 5-12-53 |

**Observation Island (T-AGM 23)** L. & L. Van Ginderen, 1-87

**D:** 16,076 tons (fl) **S:** 20 kts **Dim:** 171.6 × 23.27 × 9.1
**Electron Equipt:** Radar: 1/Raytheon 1650/9X, 1/Raytheon 1660/12S, 1/SPQ-11
**M:** 1 set G.E. GT; 1 prop; 22,000 hp—2/WP 1700 omnithrusters; 6,000 hp
**Boilers:** 2 Combustion Engineering, 42.3 kg/cm$^2$, 467°C
**Fuel:** 2,652 tons **Range:** 17,000/13 **Man:** 78 civilians + 60–65 technicians

REMARKS: Former ballistic-missile trials ship. Acquired by the Navy on 10-9-56; used for Polaris and Poseidon missile trials until placed in reserve on 29-9-72. Reclassified T-AGM 23 on 1-5-79. Converted between 7-79 and 4-81 to carry Cobra Judy (SPQ-11) missile-tracking, phased-array radar aft. Two large parabolic collection antennas in geodesic radomes atop bridge. Operated for the U.S. Air Force in the Pacific. Painted white. Refitted 10-84 to 3-85 by Northwest Marine, Portland, Ore., with a new foremast, heightened stacks, 3 new turbogenerator sets, new deckhouses, 2 new evaporators, and upgraded electronics (including adding an X-band tracking radar abaft the stack).

◆ **1 converted Haskell-class attack transport** Bldr: Permanente Metals, Richmond, Cal.

| | L | In serv. |
|---|---|---|
| T-AGM 22 RANGE SENTINEL (ex-*Sherburne,* APA 205) | 10-7-44 | 20-9-44 |

**Range Sentinel (T-AGM 22)** N. Friedman, 7-86

**Range Sentinel (T-AGM 22)** M.S.C., 1983

**D:** 11,860 tons (fl) **S:** 15.5 kts **Dim:** 138.7 × 18.9 × 8.8
**Electron Equipt:** Radar: 1/Raytheon TM 1650/9X, 1/Raytheon TM 1660/12S, 1/SPQ-7, 3/other tracking
**M:** 1 set Westinghouse GT; 1 prop; 8,500 hp
**Boilers:** 2 Combustion Engineering, 37 kg/cm$^2$, 399°C **Fuel:** 1,197 tons
**Range:** 10,000/15.5 **Man:** 14 officers, 54 men, 27 technicians

REMARKS: 8,306 grt/5,301 dwt. Converted between 10-69 and 14-10-71 as support ship for the Poseidon (and later, Trident) program. Reclassified T-AGM 22 on 14-10-71. VC2-S-AP 5 Victory-type hull and propulsion. Operates from Port Canaveral, Florida, for the Atlantic Test Range.

◆ **1 Vanguard class** Bldr: Marine Ship, Sausalito, Cal.

| | In serv. |
|---|---|
| T-AGM 20 REDSTONE (ex-*Johnstown,* ex-*Mission de Pala,* AO 114) | 22-4-44 |

**Redstone (T-AGM 20)**—note radiosonde balloon hangar aft F. Jentsch, 7-86

**D:** 16,800 tons light (24,700 fl) **S:** 16 kts **Dim:** 181.4 × 22.9 × 7.6
**Electron Equipt:** Radar: 1/Raytheon 1650/9X, 1/Raytheon 1660/12S
**M:** 1 set G.E. GT, electric drive; 1 prop; 8,700 hp
**Boilers:** 2 Babcock & Wilcox "D," 42.3 kg/cm$^2$, 440°C **Fuel:** 3,995 tons
**Range:** 27,000/16 **Man:** 19 officers, 71 men, 108 technicians

REMARKS: 16,060 grt/16,255 dwt. Former T2-SE-A2-type tanker converted 1964–66 to serve as tracking and communications ship for NASA manned space flights; 22 meters added amidships. Sister *Mercury* (T-AGM 21) stricken in 1969 after very little use, and sister *Vanguard* (T-AGM 19) redesignated T-AG in 1980. Two tracking radars, two large communications dish antennas, now all mounted in geodesic plastic radomes. Operates in Atlantic.

NOTE: *General H. H. Arnold* (T-AGM 9) was stricken and placed in the Maritime Commission National Defense Reserve Fleet on 23-2-82 and sold for scrap 25-10-82. Sister *General Hoyt S. Vandenberg* (T-AGM 10) was transferred to the MARAD NDRF on 8-2-83 and remains in storage in the James River in Virginia.

## OCEANOGRAPHIC RESEARCH SHIPS (T-AGOR)

NOTE: *All* naval-owned oceanographic research ships are listed here, for convenience sake; those without "T" before their hull numbers are operated by private organizations, generally on naval-related research programs.

◆ **0 (+2) SWATH oceanographic research ships**

| | Bldr | Laid down | L | In serv. |
|---|---|---|---|---|
| AGOR 24 N . . . | . . . | . . . | . . . | . . . |
| AGOR 25 N . . . | . . . | . . . | . . . | . . . |

**D:** approx. 5,000 tons (fl) **S:** 15 kts (cruise) **Dim:** . . . × . . . × . . .
**Electron Equipt:** Radar: . . .
**M:** diesel-electric; 2 props; . . . hp
**Range:** 8,000/15 **Endurance:** 50–60 days
**Man:** . . . crew, 30 scientists (+10 in portable van)

REMARKS: Authorization programmed to be requested under FY 90. May be a variant of the T-AGOS 19 design now under construction. SWATH = Small Waterplane Area, Twin Hull; the concept provides considerable seakeeping improvement over monohulls in heavy sea conditions; will be able to maintain heading at 6–10 kts in Sea State 6.

◆ **0 (+1) UNOLS oceanographic research ship**

| | Bldr | Laid down | L | In serv. |
|---|---|---|---|---|
| AGOR 23 N . . . | . . . | . . . | . . . | 1991 |

**D:** . . . **S:** . . . **Dim:** . . . × . . . × . . .
**Electron Equipt:** Radar: . . .—Sonar: . . .
**M:** . . . **Range:** 8,000/12–15 **Man:** . . .

REMARKS: Intended to begin replacement of the early 1960s-built, Navy-owned, university-operated oceanographic research ships, AGOR 23 is to be requested under FY 89. UNOLS = University-National Oceanographic System. Expected to be 60–84 m overall, the ship will be a conventional monohull, built to commercial standards.

The UNOLS program foresees the construction of two new general-purpose research ships (AGOR 23 class), a new maritime geology and geophysics research ship, and a polar research ship, as well as rehabilitation of *Knorr* (AGOR 14) and *Melville* (AGOR 15) by 1999, along with construction of a series of at least 2 coastal research ships and 3 intermediate-sized research ships. Four oceanographic research ships are planned for FY 91, to follow the SWATH units included under FY 90. Bids for design and construction due 2-88. Will replace AGOR 9, *Thomas G. Thompson,* at the University of Washington.

**OCEANOGRAPHIC RESEARCH SHIPS (T-AGOR)** *(continued)*

◆ **2 Gyre class (SCB 734 type)** Bldr: Halter Marine, New Orleans

| | Laid down | L | In serv. |
|---|---|---|---|
| AGOR 21 GYRE | 9-10-72 | 25-5-73 | 14-11-73 |
| AGOR 22 MOANA WAVE | 9-10-72 | 18-6-73 | 16-1-74 |

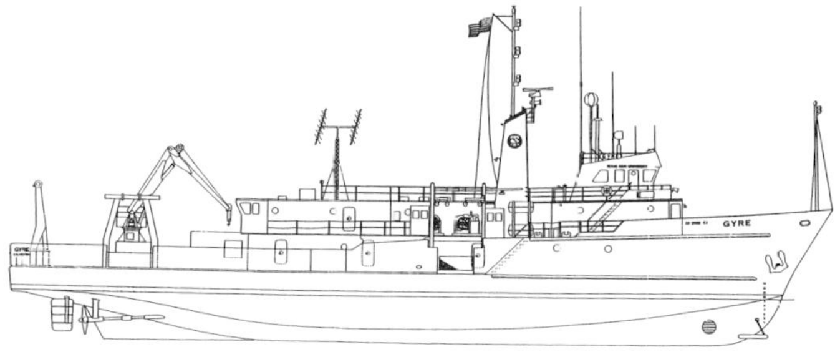

**Gyre (AGOR 21)** U.S. Navy

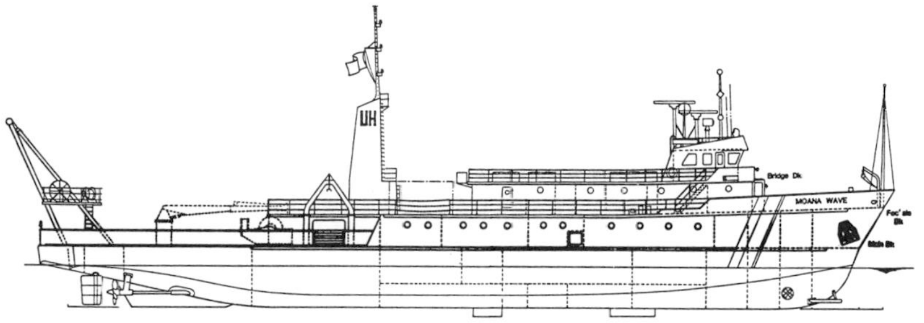

**Moana Wave (AGOR 22)** U.S. Navy

**D:** AGOR 21: 946 tons light (1,190 fl); AGOR 22: . . . tons light (1,853 fl)
**S:** 11.8 (AGOR 22: 11.5) kts
**Dim:** 53.14 (AGOR 22: 64.92) × 11.05 × 3.05 (AGOR 22: 4.57 max.)
**Electron Equipt:** Radar: 1/. . . nav. **Endurance:** 40 days (AGOR 22: 50)
**M:** 2 Caterpillar diesels; 2 CP props; 1,700 hp—170-hp bow-thruster
**Range:** 8,000/9.5 (AGOR 22: 12,000/10) **Fuel:** 290 tons (AGOR 22: 418 tons)
**Man:** 5 officers, 5 men, 19 scientists (AGOR 22: 4 officers, 9 men, 19 scientists)

REMARKS: 294–298 grt. On completion, assigned to Texas A&M University and University of Hawaii, respectively. Modified oil-field supply ships using modular equipment vans on long, open fantail. AGOR 22 conducted trials 1979–84 with the satellite communications and towed passive sonar equipment for the T-AGOS program, under contract to the Naval Electronics Command (NAVELEX); the SATCOMM antenna was mounted on a platform between the ship's paired stacks. In 1984–85, the ship was lengthened by Halter Marine at New Orleans, and given a lengthened permanent deckhouse laboratory aft, plus facilities for two portable lab modules. AGOR 21 has an HY 600A computer, AGOR 22 a Nova 1220.

◆ **2 Melville class (SCB 710 type)** Bldr: Defoe SB, Bay City, Mich.

| | Laid down | L | In serv. |
|---|---|---|---|
| AGOR 14 MELVILLE | 12-7-67 | 10-7-68 | 27-8-69 |
| AGOR 15 KNORR | 9-8-67 | 21-8-68 | 14-1-70 |

**Melville (AGOR 14)**—blue hull, white superstructure U.S. Navy, 1969

**D:** 2,075 tons fl (AGOR 15: 1,915) **S:** 12.5 kts
**Dim:** 74.7 (67.0 pp) × 14.1 × 4.87
**M:** 2 Enterprise diesels; 2 Voith-Schneider cycloidal props; 2,500 hp
**Fuel:** 342 tons **Range:** 9,000/11; 10,000/10
**Man:** 9 officers, 16 men, 29 researchers (39 with vans)
**Endurance:** 35–40 days

REMARKS: 1,806 grt. Operated for the Office of Naval Research, AGOR 14 by Scripps Institute, AGOR 15 by Woods Hole Oceanographic Institution. One vertical cycloidal propeller forward, larger unit aft; intended for precise maneuvering but, because mechanical rather than electric drive was used, have proven troublesome. AGOR 19 and AGOR 20 of this class were therefore canceled. AGOR 15 located the wreck of RMS *Titanic* on 1-9-85, using a new remote-controlled submersible. AGOR 14 has 2 VAX-730 computers.

◆ **6 Robert D. Conrad class (SCB 185 and 710* types)**

| | Bldr | L | In serv. |
|---|---|---|---|
| AGOR 3 ROBERT D. CONRAD | Gibbs, Jacksonville | 26-5-62 | 29-11-62 |
| T-AGOR 7 LYNCH | Marinette, Wisc. | 17-3-65 | 22-10-65 |
| AGOR 9 THOMAS G. THOMPSON | Marinette, Wisc. | 18-7-64 | 4-9-65 |
| AGOR 10 THOMAS WASHINGTON | Marinette, Wisc. | 1-8-64 | 17-9-65 |
| T-AGOR 12 DE STEIGUER* | N.W. Marine, Portland | 3-6-66 | 28-2-69 |
| T-AGOR 13 BARTLETT* | N.W. Marine, Portland | 24-3-66 | 15-4-69 |

**Lynch (T-AGOR 7)**—tripod foremast L. & L. Van Ginderen, 8-84

**Thomas G. Thompson (AGOR 9)** G. Arra, 4-86

**De Steiguer (T-AGOR 12)** G. Arra, 3-86

**D:** 1,088 tons light (see Remarks) **S:** 13.5 kts
**Dim:** 63.7 (59.7 pp) × 11.4 × 4.9 (6.3 m max.) over sonar domes
**Electron Equipt:** Radar: MSC units: 1/Raytheon 1650/SX, 1/Raytheon 1660/12S
**M:** 2 Caterpillar D-378 (T-AGOR 7–13: Cummins) diesels, electric drive; 1 prop; 1,000 hp—T-AGOR 7: 3T800 TD Omnithruster, 600 hp; T-AGOR 12, 13: JT700 Omnithruster, 350 hp
**Electric:** 850 kw **Fuel:** 211 tons **Endurance:** 45 days
**Range:** varies: 9,000/12; 8,500/9.5 typical
**Man:** 11 officers, 17 men, 22 researchers

## OCEANOGRAPHIC RESEARCH SHIPS (T-AGOR) *(continued)*

Remarks: Navy units operated by Lavinos Shipping Co., Philadelphia, under contract to MSC. Others assigned as follows: AGOR 3: Lamont-Doherty Geological Observatory, Palisades, N.Y.; AGOR 9: University of Washington, Seattle; AGOR 10: Scripps Institute of Oceanography, La Jolla, Cal. Displacements vary: AGOR 3: 1,428 tons fl; AGOR 7: 1,643 fl; AGOR 9: 1,400 tons fl; AGOR 12 and 13: 1,643 tons fl. AGOR 9 and 10 have much longer forecastles than the others. Near-sister *S.P. Lee* (ex-T-AG 192, ex-T-AGS 31) has been on loan to the Pacific Branch, U.S. Geological Survey since 27-2-1974; near-sister *Keller* (T-AGS 25) transferred to Portugal 21-7-72. *Sands* (T-AGOR 6) on loan to Brazil since 1-7-74; *Charles H. Davis* (T-AGOR 5) on loan to New Zealand since 28-7-70; *James M. Gillis* (AGOR 4) loaned to Mexico 15-6-83.

Large stack contains 620-hp gas-turbine generator set used to drive main shaft at speed up to 6.5 kts for experiments requiring "quiet" conditions. Also have retractable electric bow-thruster/propulsor, which provides up to 4.5 kts. AGOR 3 has a wide aperture array, multi-channel seismic system. AGOR 10 carries the Sea Beam bottom contour mapping system. AGOR 3, 9, and 10 were modernized 1981–84 with new oceanographic winches and cables to work to 4,000–5,000-m depths; they are to be replaced by AGOR 23 and later ships. AGOR 10's hull is painted blue.

◆ **2 Eltanin class** Bldr: Avondale Marine, New Orleans, La.

| | L | In serv. |
|---|---|---|
| AGOR 8 Eltanin (ex-*Islas Orcadas,* Q9, ex-*Eltanin,* T-AGOR 8) | 16-1-57 | 7-3-58 |
| T-AGOR 11 Mizar (ex-T-AK 272) | 7-10-57 | 7-3-58 |

**Mizar (T-AGOR 11)**—new superstructure amidships, foremast struck G. Arra, 1982

**D:** 2,040 tons light (3,750 fl) **S:** 13 kts **Dim:** 81.1 × 15.8 × 6.9
**Electron Equipt:** Radar: T-AGOR 11: Raytheon TM 1650/6X, 1/Raytheon TM 1660/12S
**M:** 4 Alco diesels, Westinghouse motors; 2 props; 3,200 hp
**Fuel:** 675 tons **Range:** 14,000/12 **Man:** 11 officers, 30 men, 15 technicians

Remarks: 2,486 grt/1,850 dwt. Former sisters to *Mirfak* (T-AK 271). Reclassified AGOR on 15-4-64. T-AGOR 11 operates for the Naval Electronics Command, having been transferred to MSC 23-8-62. Icebreaker hull; covered well on centerline for lowering equipment. AGOR 8 loaned to Argentina in 12-73 as *Islas Orcadas,* returned 1-8-79 and laid up at Norfolk Virginia.

◆ **1 oceanographic research barge** Bldr: Gunderson Bros., Portland, Or.

Flip (In serv. 6-8-62)

**D:** 700 tons (fl) **S:** 2–3 kts **Dim:** 109.73 × 8.53 × 3.81
**M:** 1/60-hp thruster **Man:** . . .

Remarks: Operated for and by the Scripps Institute of Oceanography of California, although Navy-owned. Designed to be towed into position and then "flipped" (hence name) upright to provide vertical enclosed column for water-property research; essentially a long cylinder with a ship-type bow at one end for towing.

◆ **1 oceanographic support craft** Bldr: Equitable Equipment Co., New Orleans, La. (In serv. 1965)

Erline (ex-M/V *Orrin*)

**D:** 96 tons (120 fl) **S:** . . . **Dim:** 32.00 × 6.31 × 1.80
**M:** 2 diesels; 2 props; . . . hp **Range:** 1,200/10

Remarks: Former offshore crew boat acquired 1967 and currently operated by the Naval Underwater Systems Center at Tudor Hill, Bermuda. Also Navy-owned, on loan, is the 19.8-m *Edgerton,* operated by the Massachusetts Institute of Technology.

## OCEAN SURVEILLANCE SHIPS (T-AGOS)

◆ **0 (+1 + 8) SWATH T-AGOS** Bldr: McDermott, Inc., Morgan City, La. (first 4)

| | Laid down | L | In serv. |
|---|---|---|---|
| T-AGOS 19 Victorious | 29-2-88 | 1-89 | 10-89 |
| T-AGOS 20 N . . . . . . . | . . . | . . . | . . . |
| T-AGOS 21 N . . . . . . . | . . . | . . . | . . . |
| T-AGOS 22 N . . . . . . . | . . . | . . . | . . . |

Authorized: T-AGOS 19 in FY 87, T-AGOS 20–22 in FY 89. Programmed: 3 in FY 90, 2 in FY 91.

**Victorious (T-AGOS 19)**—artist's rendering T. Freeman/U.S.N., 1987

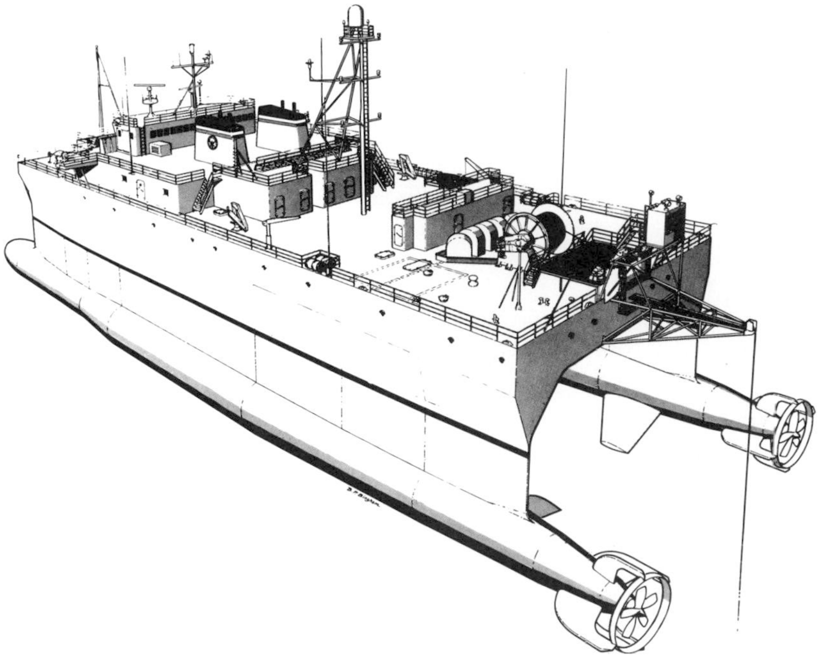

**T-AGOS 19**—showing underwater configuration B. Bingham, U.S.N., 1987

**D:** 2,608 tons light (3,370 fl) **S:** 9.6 kts (sustained)
**Dim:** 70.70 × 28.65 × 7.54
**Electron Equipt:** Radar: 2/. . . nav.
Sonar: UQQ-2 SURTASS
**M:** 4 Caterpillar-Kato D-398B 835-kw diesel generator sets (2 for ship's service); 2 750 v.d.c. inductance motors; 2 props; 1,600 hp—2 600-hp Omnithrusters
**Range:** 3,000/9.6 plus . . . /3
**Electric:** 1,970 kw (2 × 835-kw main generators, 1 × 300-kw emergency)
**Man:** 8 officers, 13 men, 12 technicians **Endurance:** 90 days

Remarks: First ship ordered 31-10-86, with option for three more. Will carry same sensor payload as *Stalwart* class, including WSC-6 satellite communications data link. Will be able to maintain heading in Sea State 6 and be survivable in Sea State 9. SWATH (Small Waterplane Twin-Hull) hull form, with two submerged pontoons for buoyancy. Horizontal fins between hulls control pitching. Should be remarkably stable ships, able to operate in higher latitudes in winter than *Stalwart* class.

◆ **10 (+8) Stalwart class** Bldr: T-AGOS 1–12: Tacoma Boat, Tacoma, Wash.; 13–18: Halter Marine, Moss Point, Miss.

| | Laid down | L | In serv. |
|---|---|---|---|
| T-AGOS 1 Stalwart | 3-11-82 | 11-7-83 | 9-4-84 |
| T-AGOS 2 Contender | 1-10-82 | 20-12-83 | 29-7-84 |
| T-AGOS 3 Vindicator | 14-4-83 | 1-6-84 | 21-11-84 |
| T-AGOS 4 Triumph | 3-1-84 | 7-9-84 | 19-2-85 |
| T-AGOS 5 Assurance | 31-5-84 | 12-1-85 | 1-5-85 |
| T-AGOS 6 Persistent | 22-10-84 | 6-4-85 | 14-8-85 |
| T-AGOS 7 Indomitable | 26-1-85 | 16-7-85 | 1-12-85 |
| T-AGOS 8 Prevail | 13-3-85 | 7-12-85 | 5-3-86 |

### OCEAN SURVEILLANCE SHIPS (T-AGOS) *(continued)*

| | | | |
|---|---|---|---|
| T-AGOS 9 Assertive | 30-7-85 | 20-6-86 | 12-9-86 |
| T-AGOS 10 Invincible | 8-11-85 | 1-11-86 | 26-1-87 |
| T-AGOS 11 Audacious (ex-*Dauntless*) | . . . | 10-88 | 6-89 |
| T-AGOS 12 Bold (ex-*Vigorous*) | . . . | 2-89 | 9-89 |
| T-AGOS 13 Adventurous | 19-12-85 | 23-9-87 | 6-88 |
| T-AGOS 14 Worthy | 3-4-86 | 6-2-88 | 1988 |
| T-AGOS 15 Titan | 23-9-87 | 6-88 | 1989 |
| T-AGOS 16 Capable | 17-10-87 | 1-89 | 1989 |
| T-AGOS 17 Intrepid | . . . | 5-89 | 11-89 |
| T-AGOS 18 Relentless | . . . | . . . | 3-90 |

Authorized: T-AGOS 1 and 2 in FY 79, T-AGOS 3 in FY 80, T-AGOS 4–8 in FY 81, T-AGOS 9–12 in FY 82, T-AGOS 13, 14 in FY 85, T-AGOS 15, 16 in FY 86, T-AGOS 17, 18 in FY 87

**Prevail (T-AGOS 8)** G. Arra, 9-86

**Indomitable (T-AGOS 7)** W. Donko, 7-86

**Vindicator (T-AGOS 3)** L. & L. Van Ginderen, 9-87

**D:** 1,600 tons light (2,285 fl) **S:** 11 kts **Dim:** 68.28 (62.1 wl) × 13.10 × 4.57
**Electron Equipt:** Radar: 2/navigational—Sonar: UQQ-2 SURTASS
**M:** 4 Caterpillar-Kato D-398B 800-hp diesels, G.E. electric drive; 2/4-bladed props; 2,200 hp (1,600 hp sust.)—550-hp bow-thruster
**Fuel:** 834 tons **Range:** 3,000/11 plus 6,480/3 **Endurance:** 98 days
**Man:** 8 officers, 11 men contract crew, 7 RCA technicians
**Electric:** 1,500 kVA from main generators, plus 250-kw emergency set.

Remarks: 1,584 grt/786 dwt. The first three T-AGOS were contracted for 26-9-80. AN/UQQ-2 SURTASS (SURveillance Towed Array Sensor) is an 1,829-m linear, hydrophone array deployed over the ship's stern in a flexible, neutrally buoyant cable; the output from the SURTASS will be instantaneously relayed to shore monitoring stations via WSC-6 satellite communications, and the on-board technicians are primarily for maintenance and backup. Main-engine motor/generator sets also supply ship's-service power: Flat chine hull form without bilge keels; have passive tank roll stabilization. Intended to conduct 60–90-day patrols and to be at sea 292 days per year. T-AGOS 13 and later have 3 more berths and more space per man; T-AGOS 13, 14 ordered 4-6-85, with option to build through T-AGOS 18; T-AGOS 15–18 ordered 30-6-86. T-AGOS 13, christened 17-10-87 by Mrs. A.D. Baker III, had been launched earlier.

First 12 to be operated under 1-2-85 contract with Sea Mobility Div., Falcon Contractors; contract duration 4 years, 8 months, with six each to base at Pearl Harbor and Little Creek, Va. Technicians supplied by RCA on contract. Tacoma Boat's bankruptcy caused halt on work on T-AGOS 11, 12; rebid 1987, with new delivery dates.

### SURVEYING SHIPS (T-AGS)

◆ **0 (+1) ice-capable ocean survey ship**

| | Bldr | Laid down | L | In serv. |
|---|---|---|---|---|
| T-AGS . . . N . . . | . . . | . . . | . . . | . . . |

Planned: 1 for FY 91

Remarks: Planned for Arctic research, in conjunction with the National Science Foundation. Will presumably have an icebreaker hull.

◆ **0 (+1) SWATH ocean survey ship**

| | Bldr | Laid down | L | In serv. |
|---|---|---|---|---|
| T-AGS . . . N . . . | . . . | . . . | . . . | . . . |

Planned: 1 in FY 89

**D:** approx. 5,000 tons (fl) **S:** 15 kts (cruise) **Dim:** . . . × . . . × . . .
**Electron Equipt:** Radar: . . .
**M:** diesel-electric; 2 props; . . . hp **Man:** . . .
**Range:** 8,000/15 **Endurance:** 50–60 days

Remarks: Would employ same hull and propulsion plant as the SWATH AGOR planned for FY 89. Will be a commercial design.

◆ **0 (+3) Maury class**

| | Bldr | Laid down | L | In serv. |
|---|---|---|---|---|
| T-AGS 39 Maury | Bethlehem, Sparrows Pt. | 29-7-86 | 4-9-87 | 8-88 |
| T-AGS 40 Tanner | Bethlehem, Sparrows Pt. | 29-9-86 | 5-88 | 2-89 |
| T-AGS . . . N . . . | . . . | . . . | . . . | . . . |

**Maury (T-AGS 39)**—artist's impression T. Freeman/U.S.N., 1986

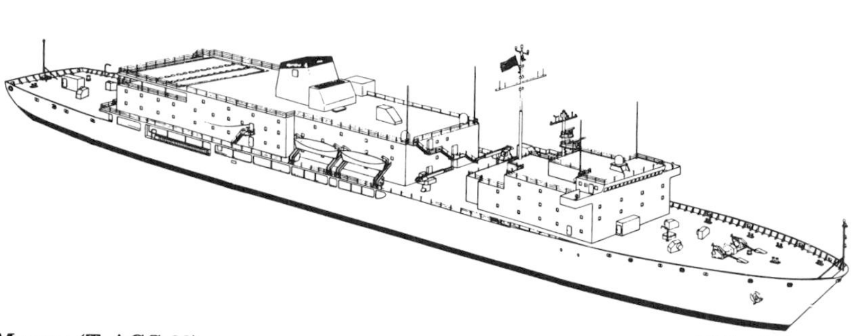

**Maury (T-AGS 39)** U.S. Navy, 6-85

**SURVEYING SHIPS (T-AGS)** *(continued)*

**D:** 8,810 tons light (15,821 fl) **S:** 21 kts
**Dim:** 152.35 (140.84 pp; 145.09 wl) × 21.95 × 9.30
**Electron Equipt:** Radar: 2/. . . nav.—Sonar: SQN-17
**M:** 2 Transamerica Delaval R5-V16 Enterprise diesels; 1 CP prop; 25,000 hp
**Range:** 17,800/20 **Fuel:** 3,200 tons **Endurance:** 34 days
**Electric:** 2,550 kw (3 diesel sets)
**Man:** 56 MSC crew; 3 naval officers, 29 naval men, 20 scientists

Remarks: Ordered 28-6-85 under FY 85 funding. Third unit programmed for FY 91 to replace T-AGS 38, but may be of modified design. Replaced a program to convert two C3-S-33a cargo ships (*Lake* and *Scan*) from the Navy/MARAD Ready Reserve Force. Intended as replacements for *Bowditch* (T-AGS 21) and *Dutton* (T-AGS 22) in support of SSBN operations through sea-floor charting and gravimetric mapping. Hull volume largely voids except for engineering spaces. Will carry up to 7,339 tons of water ballast. Ships delayed in launch by about a year, due to engine installation problems. SQN-17 BOTOSS (BOttom TOpography Survey System) maps to depths of 7,300 m. Also have 2 BQN-3 narrow-beam mapping sonars, doppler sonar, expendable bathythermograph, velocimeter, "MiniSINS" inertial navigation, Mk 29 gyro. Equipment on both removed from T-AGS 21 and 22.

◆ **1 converted cargo ship (C4-SA type)** Bldr: National Steel, San Diego, Cal.

| | L | In serv. |
|---|---|---|
| T-AGS 38 H.H. Hess (ex-*Canada Mail*) | 3-65 | 16-1-78 |

**H.H. Hess (T-AGS 38)** L. & L. Van Ginderen, 8-86

**D:** 13,525 tons light (21,255 fl) **S:** 21 kts
**Dim:** 171.8 (160.93 pp) × 23.16 × 9.6
**Electron Equipt:** Radar: 1/Raytheon TM 1650/6X, 1/Raytheon TM 1660/12S
**M:** 1 set G.E. GT; 1 prop; 19,250 hp **Electric:** 1,400 kw
**Boilers:** 2 Foster-Wheeler; 43.3 kg/cm$^2$, 457°C
**Fuel:** 3,178 tons **Range:** 23,140/20 **Man:** 30 MSC crew, 74 Navy

Remarks: Mariner-type passenger-cargo ship acquired from the Maritime Administration on 17-7-75 for conversion to replace the *Michelson* (T-AGS 23) in the SSBN navigational support program. Retains original six cargo holds, but most cargo booms removed. Converted at National Steel and SB, San Diego, 3-77 to 1-78. Operated by Lavino Shipping under contract to MSC.

◆ **2 Chauvenet class (SCB 723 type)** Bldr: Upper Clyde SB, Glasgow, U.K.

| | Laid down | L | In serv. |
|---|---|---|---|
| T-AGS 29 Chauvenet | 24-5-67 | 13-5-68 | 13-11-70 |
| T-AGS 32 Harkness | 30-6-67 | 12-6-68 | 29-1-71 |

**Harkness (T-AGS 32)** G. Arra, 1983

**D:** 3,540 tons (4,830 fl) **S:** 15 kts **Dim:** 119.8 (101.8 pp) × 16.5 × 5.1
**Electron Equipt:** Radar: 1/Raytheon TM 1650/6X, 1/Raytheon TM 1660/12S
**M:** 2 Alco diesels, Westinghouse motor; 1 CP prop; 3,600 hp
**Electric:** 1,500 kw **Endurance:** 90 days
**Fuel:** 824 tons **Range:** 9,300/14; 15,000/12
**Man:** MSC: 13 officers, 56 men + Navy: 6 officers, 49 men + 12 civilian scientists

Remarks: 2,890 grt/1,030 dwt. Very complete navigation and communications systems. Can carry four small survey launches; hangar (13.9 × 3.7 m) and flight deck for two helicopters. Operated for the Oceanographer of the Navy; 61–76 naval personnel aboard in 1985. Both operate in the Pacific.

◆ **4 Silas Bent class (SCB 226, 725*, and 728† types)** (‡Atlantic)

| | Bldr | L | In serv. |
|---|---|---|---|
| T-AGS 26 Silas Bent‡ | American SB, Lorain | 16-5-64 | 23-7-65 |
| T-AGS 27 Kane‡ | Christy, Sturgeon Bay | 20-11-65 | 19-5-67 |
| T-AGS 33 Wilkes*‡ | Defoe, Bay City, Mich. | 31-7-69 | 28-6-71 |
| T-AGS 34 Wyman† | Defoe, Bay City, Mich. | 30-10-69 | 3-11-71 |

**Kane (T-AGS 27)** G. Arra, 8-86

**D:** 1,900 to 2,166 tons (2,550 to 2,827 fl) **S:** 15 kts
**Dim:** 86.9 (80.8 pp) × 14.6 × 4.6
**Electron Equipt:** Radar: 1/Raytheon RM 1650/9X, 1/Raytheon TM 1660/12S
**M:** 2 Alco diesels, Westinghouse or G.E. motor; 1 CP prop; 3,600 hp (plus 350-hp bow-thruster)
**Electric:** 960 kw **Fuel:** 461 tons **Range:** 5,800–6,300/14.5; 8,000/13
**Man:** 12 officers, 35 men, 30 scientists

Remarks: Operated for Oceanographer of the Navy. T-AGS 34, used in support of the strategic-missile programs, is equipped with the Sperry SQN-17 BOTOSS (BOttom TOpography Survey System) for mapping depths to 7,300 m; the system consists of two planar transducer arrays and an HP 2100 computer, which averages the results of four separate passes through an area. Have MARISAT satellite communications equipment. Planned to convert T-AGS 34 to an AGOR under FY 92. Full load displacements vary: T-AGS 26: 2,743 tons; T-AGS 27: 2,827; T-AGS 33: 2,565; T-AGS 34: 2,550 tons.

◆ **1 Bowditch class** Bldr: Oregon SB, Portland, South Coast Co.

| | L | Conv. |
|---|---|---|
| T-AGS 22 Dutton (ex-*Tuskegee Victory*) | 8-5-45 | 30-9-48 |

**Bowditch (T-AGS 21)**—now stricken L. & L. Van Ginderen, 6-84

**D:** 4,700 tons light (13,050 fl) **S:** 16.5 kts
**Dim:** 138.76 (133.05 pp) × 18.98 × 7.62
**Electron Equipt:** Radar: 1/Raytheon TM 1650/9X, 1/Raytheon TM 1660/12S
**M:** 1 set GT; 1 prop; 8,500 hp
**Boilers:** 2 Combustion Engineering; 37 kg/cm$^2$, 399°C
**Electric:** 1,260 kw **Fuel:** 2,824 tons
**Range:** 17,000/16 **Man:** 14 officers, 47 men, 15 scientists

Remarks: 7,783 grt/8,350 dwt. Victory-class cargo ship converted to support the SSBN program. Used for sea-floor charting and magnetic mapping. Sister *Michelson* (T-AGS 23) stricken in 1975. *Bowditch* (T-AGS 21) suffered a major engineering casualty in 1-87 and was laid up at New Orleans until stricken 1-88; her survey

**SURVEYING SHIPS (T-AGS)** *(continued)*

equipment was removed and mounted in the National Oceanic and Atmospheric Administration ship *Discoverer,* which replaced her during 1987. T-AGS 22's equipment and T-AGS 21's gear will be transferred to the new T-AGS 39 and 40 during 1988, and T-AGS 22 will be stricken (see *Maury*-class entry for equipment listing).

**COASTAL SURVEY SHIPS (T-AGSC)**

◆ **0 (+2 + 3) coastal survey ships**

| | Bldr | Laid down | L | In serv. |
|---|---|---|---|---|
| T-AGSC N . . . | . . . | . . . | . . . | . . . |
| T-AGSC N . . . | . . . | . . . | . . . | . . . |

Authorized: 2 in FY 87; programmed: 1 in FY 90, 2 in FY 91

**D:** . . . **S:** . . . **Dim:** . . . × . . . × . . .
**Electron Equipt:** Radar: . . .
**M:** . . .
**Range:** . . ./. . . **Man:** . . .

**Remarks:** Incorrectly referred to as the "T-AGSC 51 class" in congressional documents. First two were *not* requested by Navy under FY 87 but were provided by Congress, which desired that they would be conversions from fishing boats. Navy, to obtain uniformity with planned T-AGSC to be built in the 1990s, hopes to build new ships. Design and characteristics to be determined by successful bidder, to be announced mid-1988. Will replace *Silas Bent* class.

**HOSPITAL SHIPS (T-AH)**

◆ **2 converted San Clemente-class merchant tankers** Bldr: National Steel, San Diego, Cal.

| | L | Conv. start | In serv. |
|---|---|---|---|
| T-AH 19 Mercy (ex-*Worth*) | 1976 | 20-7-84 | 28-2-87 |
| T-AH 20 Comfort (ex-*Rose City*) | 1976 | 2-4-85 | 1-12-87 |

**D:** 24,752 tons light (69,360 fl) **S:** 17.5 kts (sust.)
**Dim:** 272.49 (260.61 pp) × 32.23 × 9.98
**Electron Equipt:** Radar: 1/. . . nav., 1/SPS-67—TACAN: URN-25
**M:** 1 set steam turbines; 1 prop; 24,500 hp
**Boilers:** 2/. . . **Fuel:** 5,747 tons **Range:** 13,420/17.5
**Man:** 14 officers, 154 men MSC, 1,207 Navy staff + 1,000 patients
**Electric:** 9,250 kw (3 × 2,000-kw diesel, 1 × 1,500 kw diesel, 1 × 1,000-kw turbogenerator, 1 × 750-kw emergency diesel

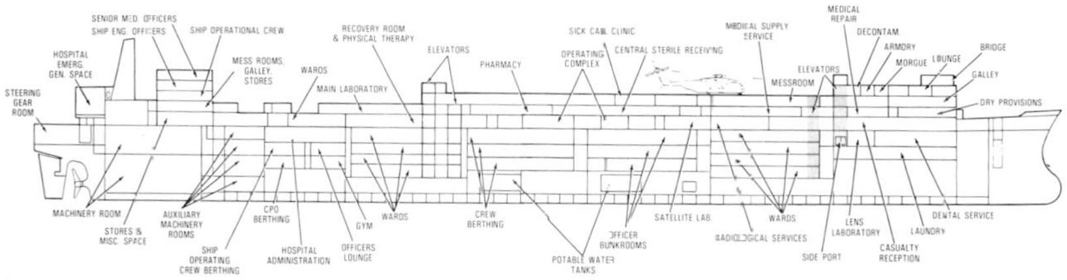

**Mercy (T-AH 19)**—internal arrangements U.S. Navy

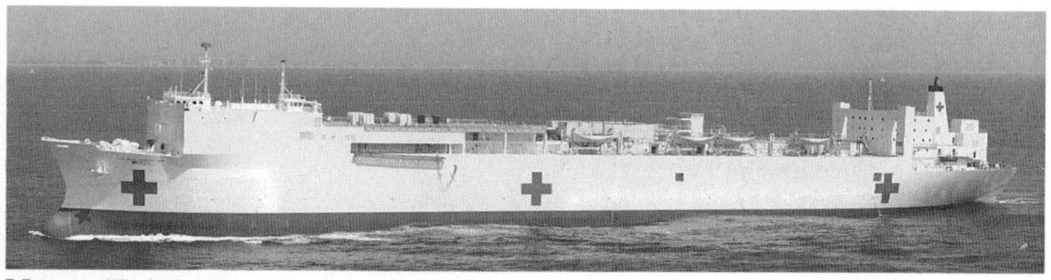
**Mercy (T-AH 19)**—on trials K. Lee/Nat'l Steel, 4-86

**Mercy (T-AH 19)** U.S. Navy, 5-87

**Comfort (T-AH 20)**—fitting out U.S. Navy, 10-87

**Remarks:** Builder contracted 29-6-83 to convert Apex Marine's tanker *Worth* to a hospital ship with FY 83 funds; T-AH 20's conversion ordered from same yard 16-12-83 with FY 84 funds. Were originally 44,875 grt/91,849 dwt.

The entire midships area has been altered to provide a large helicopter deck, accommodations, and boat stowage. Have 12 operating rooms, 4 X-ray rooms, an 80-bed intensive-care unit, a burn-care facility, a 50-bed reception/triage area, and 1,000 ward beds. Of the 1,508 accommodations for naval personnel, there will be 259 officers, 31 chief petty officers, and 530 enlisted, augmented in emergencies by 372 naval medical support personnel; also aboard will be 14 communications specialists. One is kept on each U.S. coast, on 5-days' steaming notice, and they will be used about 7 days per year on exercises. In port, they are maintained by the MSC crew and a small civilian contract crew, totaling 68 per ship. Freshwater tankage for 1,525 tons will be carried, plus two 278-ton/day distilling plants. Much of the displacement is sea-water ballast.

**CARGO SHIPS (T-AK)**

◆ **1 Northern Light class (C2-S-33a type)** Bldr: Sun SB & DD Co., Chester, Pa.

| | In serv. | In USN |
|---|---|---|
| T-AK 286 Vega (ex-*Bay,* ex-*Mormacbay*) | 14-10-60 | 15-10-81 |

**Vega (T-AK 286)** G. Arra, 8-85

**D:** 16,363 tons (fl) **S:** 19 kts **Dim:** 148.15 (139.59 pp) × 20.72 × 8.68
**Electron Equipt:** Radar: 1/Raytheon TM 1650/6X, 1/Raytheon TM 1660/12S
**M:** 1 set G.E. GT; 1 prop; 11,000 hp (15,700 emergency) **Electric:** 1,275 kw
**Boilers:** 2 Combustion Engineering; 43.3 kg/cm², 457°C
**Fuel:** 3,056 tons **Range:** 14,000/18 **Man:** 68 MSC crew plus 7 naval

**Remarks:** T-AK 286 (originally to have been renamed *King's Bay*) acquired 29-4-81 and placed on the Navy List on 15-10-81, reactivated 18-3-83 after being converted to transport 16 Trident ballistic missiles in vertical cells in place of No. 3 hold. Former 9,260-grt/12,500-dwt cargo ship acquired from Maritime Administration's National Defense Reserve Fleet.

Sisters *Northern Light* (T-AK 284, ex-*Cove,* ex-*Mormaccove*) and *Southern Cross* (T-AK 285, ex-*Trade,* ex-*Mormactrade*) were deactivated 26-4-84 and 13-9-84, respectively, and transferred to the Maritime Administration-administered Ready Reserve Force, although remaining as Navy property. Both were configured as general cargo ships. Funds were requested in FY 85 to convert sister *Cape* as a ballistic-missile transport (T-AK 295) but were denied by Congress; *Cape* and sisters *Lake* and *Scan* (which were to have been converted as survey ships T-AGS 39 and 40) are also in the Ready Reserve Force. (*Cape* as *Cape Catawba*).

CARGO SHIPS (T-AK) *(continued)*

◆ **2 Norwalk class**
Bldr: Oregon SB, Portland (T-AK 281: Permanente, Richmond, Calif.)

| | L | Conv. |
|---|---|---|
| T-AK 280 FURMAN (ex-*Furman Victory*) | 18-5-45 | 7-10-64 |
| T-AK 282 MARSHFIELD (ex-*Marshfield Victory*) | 15-5-44 | 28-5-70 |

**Marshfield (T-AK 282)** G. Arra, 1984

**D:** 6,700 tons light (11,150 fl) **S:** 16.5 kts
**Dim:** 138.76 (133.05 pp) × 18.90 × 7.32
**Electron Equipt:** Radar: 1/Raytheon TM 1650/6X, 1/Raytheon 1660/12S
**M:** 1 set GT; 1 prop; 8,500 hp **Boilers:** 2; 37 kg/cm$^2$, 399°C
**Fuel:** 2,824 tons **Range:** 20,000/16.5
**Man:** T-AK 280: 35 tot. MSC; T-AK 282: 14 officers, 57 men MSC, plus 7 Navy

REMARKS: 7,491 grt/9,649 dwt. In T-AK 282, hold No. 3 accommodates 16 vertically stowed Poseidon or Polaris SLBMs to support SSBN activities. Has MARISAT SATCOMM system. Carries torpedoes, submarine spares, etc.; also carries 18,000 barrels cargo fuel (7,566 bbl diesel/10,434 bbl fuel oil). 40-ton cargo booms. Small Navy security detachment aboard. T-AK 280, originally converted like T-AK 282, was to have been stricken 20-9-81, but was instead reserved for conversion to a cable transporter for the Naval Electronics Command. Contracted to Atlantic Drydock Co., Jacksonville, Fla., on 17-11-82, the ship had all winches and cargo booms removed, as well as the refrigeration equipment deleted; completed 20-4-83, she now requires a crew of only 35. T-AK 280 was laid up 10-86 at Beaumont, Texas, with the intent to reactivate her in 10-88.

Sister *Norwalk* (T-AK 279) was stricken 1-8-79 and *Victoria* (T-AK 281) was transferred to the Maritime Commission for long-term lay-up on 18-1-84; stricken 31-3-86.

◆ **1 Eltanin-class Arctic service**—in reserve

| | Bldr | L | In serv. |
|---|---|---|---|
| T-AK 271 MIRFAK | Avondale Marine, New Orleans, La. | 5-8-57 | 30-12-57 |

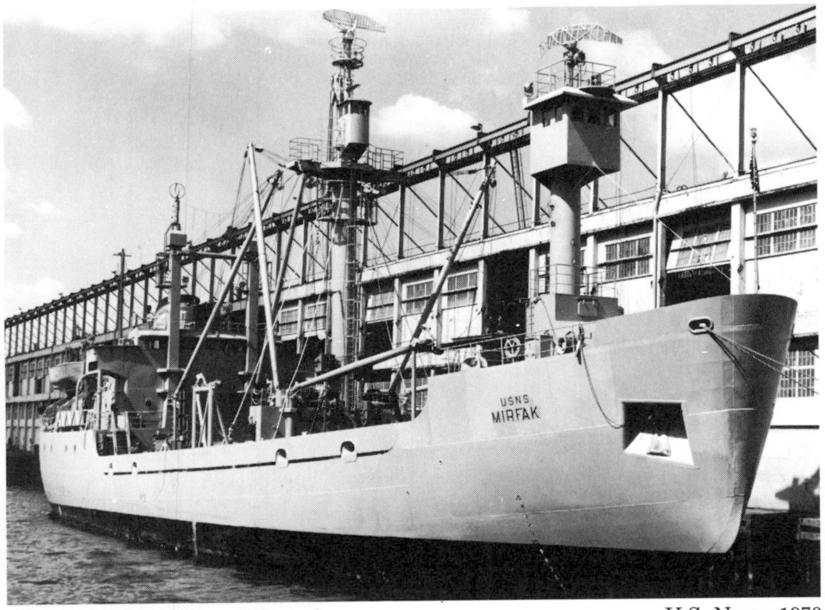


**Mirfak (T-AK 271)**—while active U.S. Navy, 1970

**D:** 2,022 tons light (4,800 fl) **S:** 13 kts **Dim:** 81.1 × 15.8 × 7.0
**Electron Equipt:** Radar: 1/Raytheon TM 1650/6X, 1/Raytheon TM 1660/12S
**M:** 4 Alco diesels, Westinghouse electric drive; 2 props; 3,200 hp (2,700 hp sust.)
**Fuel:** 612 tons **Range:** 14,000/13 **Man:** 48 tot.

REMARKS: 2,486 grt/1,850 dwt. Maritime Administration C1-ME2-13a type, intended for Arctic operations and having an icebreaker hull form. Cargo: 2,634 m$^3$ dry/ 227 m$^3$ refrigerated. Deactivated 11-12-79 and transferred to the Maritime Administration; remains Navy property and is laid up in the James River, in Virginia. Sisters *Eltanin* (AGOR 8, ex-AK 270) and *Mizar* (T-AGOR 11) were converted to serve as oceanographic research ships.

VEHICLE CARGO SHIPS (T-AKR)

◆ **8 SL-7-class container cargo ships**

| | Bldr | In serv. | In Navy | AKR conv. |
|---|---|---|---|---|
| T-AKR 287 ALGOL (ex-*Sea-Land Exchange*) | Rotterdamse DDM, Rotterdam | 7-5-73 | 13-10-81 | 22-6-84 |
| T-AKR 288 BELLATRIX (ex-*Sea-Land Trade*) | Rheinstahl Nord-seewerke, Emden | 6-4-73 | 13-10-81 | 10-9-84 |
| T-AKR 289 DENEBOLA (ex-*Sea-Land Resource*) | Rotterdamse DDM, Rotterdam | 4-12-73 | 27-10-81 | 10-10-85 |
| T-AKR 290 POLLUX (ex-*Sea-Land Market*) | A.G. Weser, Bremen | 20-9-73 | 16-11-81 | 27-3-86 |
| T-AKR 291 ALTAIR (ex-*Sea-Land Finance*) | Rheinstahl Nord-seewerke, Emden | 17-9-73 | 5-1-82 | 13-11-85 |
| T-AKR 292 REGULUS (ex-*Sea-Land Commerce*) | A.G. Weser, Bremen | 30-3-73 | 27-10-81 | 28-8-85 |
| T-AKR 293 CAPELLA (ex-*Sea-Land McLean*) | Rotterdamse DDM, Rotterdam | 4-10-72 | 16-4-82 | 30-6-84 |
| T-AKR 294 ANTARES (ex-*Sea-Land Galloway*) | A.G. Weser, Bremen | 27-9-72 | 16-4-82 | 12-7-84 |

**Antares (T-AKR 294)** L. & L. Van Ginderen, 1-86

**Altair (T-AKR 291)** G. Arra, 1987

**Algol (T-AKR 287)** Skyfotos, 1-86

**D:** 29,692 tons light (55,355 fl) **S:** 33 kts (27 sust.)
**Dim:** 288.38 (268.37 pp) × 32.16 × 11.18
**M:** 2 sets G.E. MST-19 GT; 2 props; 120,000 hp **Electric:** 8,000 kw
**Boilers:** 2 Foster-Wheeler; 61.6 kg/cm$^2$, 507°C **Fuel:** 8,500 tons
**Range:** 12,200/27 **Man:** 62 max. (45 normal crew)

REMARKS: 48,525 grt/24,270 dwt (varies). Six acquired under FY 81 and two under FY 82, with the original intent of extensively converting them to serve as T-AKR,

**VEHICLE CARGO SHIPS (T-AKR)** *(continued)*

"Roll-on/Roll-off" vehicle cargo ships for the Rapid Deployment Force. Instead, under FY 82 Congress mandated that four be given a "partial" Ro/Ro conversion and the other four be given only a "mini-modification." This has since been changed to give all the same modification, T-AKR 287, 288, 293, and 294 under FY 82 and the others under FY 84. The conversions were performed by: T-AKR 287, 288, 292: National Steel, San Diego; T-AKR 289 and 293: Pennsylvania SB, Chester, Pa.; and the others by Avondale SY, Westwego, La.; the latter have an additional hinged internal ramp. The ships were given T-AK hull numbers when purchased; these were changed to T-AKR without changing the actual numbers assigned, AKR 287 on 19-6-84, AKR 288 on 10-9-84, AKR 293 and 294 on 30-6-84, rest on 1-11-83.

The ships were originally tailored to transport up to 1,086 nonstandard *35-ft.* containers (standard cargo containers are either 20 or 40 feet in length); 4,000 containers were purchased along with the first six ships. These ships proved expensive to operate for the former merchant owner, and their sophisticated propulsion plants have not been overly reliable. Made 35 kts on trials in light condition, 33 kts at 32,600 tons. Fuel tankage includes 5,384 tons fuel oil, 3,116 tons diesel. Also carry 569 tons potable water and 4,893 tons permanent ballast water. Have 2 × 3,000-kw, 1 × 1,500-kw, and 1 × 500-kw diesel generators. Up to 9,484 tons of salt-water ballast can be carried.

Three are maintained crewed, ready for sea on each coast, with the other two to be placed on 5 days' notice in the Ready Reserve Force. Conversion entailed filling in the amidships portion to produce a multi-deck vehicle cargo area and helicopter hangar totaling 12,170 $m^2$ on 5 decks (can accommodate up to 120 UH-1 helicopters or 183 M-1 tanks). This is topped by a flight deck of 3,252 $m^2$ with a twin 35-ton crane plumbing two hatches interrupting the forward half. The stern provides 1,719 $m^2$ of vehicle parking, as well as cargo space for 8 "Sea Shed" containerized vehicle stowage or 44 or 46/20-ft. containers; it is served by a twin 50-ton crane. There are vehicle access ramps amidships, port and starboard. Operated on contract by original owners, SeaLand Service, Inc.

◆ **1 Maine (C7-S-95a-type) class** Bldr: Bath Iron Wks., Me.

| | L | In serv. |
|---|---|---|
| T-AKR 10 Mercury (ex-*Illinois*) | 7-76 | 1977 |

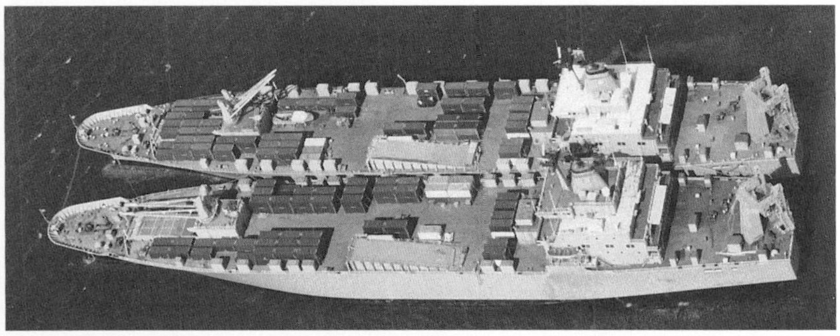

**Mercury (T-AKR 10)**—and the now-stricken *Jupiter* (T-AKR 11) at Diego Garcia R. Smith, 1983

**D:** 14,222 tons light (33,765 fl) **S:** 23 kts (sust.)
**Dim:** 208.71 (195.07 pp) × 31.09 × 9.78
**Electron Equipt:** Radar: 1/Raytheon TM 1650/6X, 1/Raytheon TM 1660/12S
**M:** 2 sets G.E. GT; 2 props; 37,000 hp **Electric:** 4,000 kw
**Boilers:** 2 Babcock & Wilcox; 77.5 kg/$cm^2$ **Fuel:** 3,394 tons
**Range:** 10,000/23 **Man:** 41 tot. MSC

Remarks: 13,156 grt/19,172 dwt. T-AKR 10 long-term chartered from Lykes Brothers 14-4-80. MSC contract crew, as part of the Near-Term Prepositioning Force at Diego Garcia. Capable of carrying container, as well as vehicle, cargo and can land helicopters amidships on upper deck; can also transport 728 tons liquid cargo. Two 15-ton cranes (paired) forward. A 7.3-m-wide by 24.4-m stern ramp is fitted, and there are two side-loading doors also. Total bale cargo volume is 56,640 $m^3$; vehicle cargo deck space is 16,258 $m^2$. Plans to acquire two more ships of this class and to enlarge and modify T-AKR 10 were abandoned. Sister *Jupiter* (T-AKR 11), ex-*Lipscomb Lykes*, ex-*Arizona*), chartered 7-5-80, was stricken by the Navy on 24-4-86, acquired by the Maritime Administration, and became part of Ready Reserve Force on 2-5-86. Sister *Cape Isabel* (ex-*Charles Lykes*, ex-*Nevada*) became part of the RRF on 23-5-86.

Note: *Meteor* (T-AKR 9) was deactivated and placed in the Ready Reserve Force in 9-85. The similar *Comet* (T-AKR 7) was transferred to the Maritime Commission Ready Reserve Force 3-85; both remain Navy property.

**REPLENISHMENT OILERS**

◆ **4 (+9 + 5) Henry J. Kaiser class** Bldr: A: Avondale SY, Westwego, La.; B: PennShip, Chester, Pa.

| | Bldr | Budget | Laid down | L | In serv. |
|---|---|---|---|---|---|
| T-AO 187 Henry J. Kaiser | A | FY 82 | 22-8-84 | 5-10-85 | 19-12-86 |
| T-AO 188 Joshua Humphreys | A | FY 83 | 17-12-84 | 22-2-86 | 3-4-87 |
| T-AO 189 John Lenthall | A | FY 84 | 15-7-85 | 9-8-86 | 5-6-87 |
| T-AO 190 Andrew J. Higgins | A | FY 84 | 21-11-85 | 17-1-87 | 22-10-87 |
| T-AO 191 Benjamin Isherwood | B | FY 85 | 14-7-86 | 6-88 | 1989 |
| T-AO 192 Henry Eckford | B | FY 85 | 22-1-87 | 1-89 | 1990 |
| T-AO 193 Walter S. Diehl | A | FY 85 | 7-8-86 | 10-10-87 | 8-88 |
| T-AO 194 John Ericsson | B | FY 86 | 15-9-87 | ... | 1990 |
| T-AO 195 Leroy Grumman | A | FY 86 | 1-87 | 8-88 | 5-89 |
| T-AO 196 Kanawha | B | FY 87 | ... | ... | 6-91 |
| T-AO 197 Pecos | A | FY 87 | ... | 3-89 | 12-89 |
| T-AO 198 N....... | ... | FY 88 | ... | ... | ... |
| T-AO 199 N....... | ... | FY 88 | ... | ... | ... |
| T-AO 200 N....... | ... | FY 89 | ... | ... | ... |
| T-AO 201 N....... | ... | FY 90 | ... | ... | ... |
| T-AO 202 N....... | ... | FY 90 | ... | ... | ... |
| T-AO 203 N....... | ... | FY 91 | ... | ... | ... |
| T-AO 204 N....... | ... | FY 91 | ... | ... | ... |

**Henry J. Kaiser (T-AO 187)** Avondale, 1986

**John Lenthall (T-AO 189)** U.S. Navy, 5-87

**Joshua Humphreys (T-AO 188)** U.S. Navy, 2-87

**REPLENISHMENT OILERS** *(continued)*

**Joshua Humphreys (T-AO 188)** U.S. Navy, 2-87

**D:** 9,500 tons light (40,700 fl) **S:** 20 kts (sust.)
**Dim:** 206.50 (198.10 pp) × 29.72 × 10.67
**A:** provision for 2/20-mm Mk 15 CIWS (I × 2)
**Electron Equipt:** Radar: 2/navigational **Electric:** 10,600 kw
**M:** 2 Colt-Pielstick 10 PC4.2V diesels; 2 CP props; 32,540 hp
**Range:** 6,000/20 **Man:** 95 MSC crew, plus 21 Navy (137 berths)

REMARKS: 26,500 dwt. Cargo: 180,000 bbl liquid (86,400 bbl fuel oil; 54,000 bbl JP-5; 39,600 convertible; plus 327 tons feedwater, 390 tons potable water), plus dry cargo and eight 20-ft provisions containers. Initially intended to be an MSC variant of the *Cimarron* class, designed to merchant standards, but the design has since grown. Equipped for underway replenishment of liquids and solids. Helicopter deck aft, no hangar. Design contract to George Sharp, Inc., 11-7-80. A total of 18 to replace all earlier MSC-manned replenishment oilers, is planned, but building program has been scaled back from 4/yr to 2/yr. Five alongside fueling stations (3 to port), 1 solid transfer station per side. The engines for the first two were built by Alsthom in France. Have a CGEE-Alsthom integrated auxiliary electric drive system for low speeds, driving either or both props. Will have the SLQ-25 Nixie anti-torpedo system but no EW gear. T-AO 191, 192 ordered 6-5-85; T-AO 193 on 28-6-85; T-AO 194, 195 in 2-86; T-AO 196, 197 on 12-2-87.

◆ **6 Neosho class (SCB 82 type)**
Bldr: New York SB, Camden, N.J. (T-AO 143: Bethlehem, Quincy, Mass.)

| | L | In serv. | To MSC |
|---|---|---|---|
| T-AO 143 NEOSHO | 10-11-53 | 24-9-54 | 25-5-78 |
| T-AO 144 MISSISSINEWA | 12-6-54 | 18-1-55 | 15-11-76 |
| T-AO 145 HASSAYAMPA | 12-9-54 | 19-4-55 | 17-8-78 |
| T-AO 146 KAWISHIWI | 11-12-54 | 6-7-55 | 1-10-79 |
| T-AO 147 TRUCKEE | 10-3-55 | 23-11-55 | 30-1-80 |
| T-AO 148 PONCHATOULA | 9-7-55 | 12-1-56 | 5-9-80 |

**D:** 19,533 tons light (36,840 fl) **S:** 20 kts
**Dim:** 199.65 (195.07 wl) × 26.21 × 10.67
**Electron Equipt:** Radar: 1/SPS-10, 1/Raytheon TM 1650/6X or 12X
**M:** 2 sets G.E. GT; 2 props; 28,000 hp **Electric:** 1,500 kw
**Boilers:** 2 Babcock & Wilcox; 42.2 kg/cm², 357°C
**Fuel:** 5,000 tons **Man:** 21 officers, 105 men MSC + 21 Navy

**Kawishiwi (T-AO 146)** G. Arra, 1-86

**Truckee (T-AO 147)**—helo deck aft G. Arra, 9-86

**Ponchatoula (T-AO 148)**—no helo deck L. & L. Van Ginderen, 12-86

REMARKS: 19,553 grt/36,840 dwt. Carry 180,000 bbl. liquid cargo (approx. 23,600 tons). Helicopter platform aft in all but T-AO 145, 146, and 148. Operated by MSC as underway-replenishment ships for Navy. Transferred to MSC as a cost-saving measure (Navy crew was 360 total). Masting and superstructures differ in detail, with T-AO 144 having an extra flying bridge level.

◆ **5 Mispillion class (jumboized T3-S2-A3 type)** Bldr: Sun SB, Chester, Pa.

| | L | In serv. | To MSC |
|---|---|---|---|
| T-AO 105 MISPILLION | 10-8-45 | 29-12-45 | 26-7-73 |
| T-AO 106 NAVASOTA | 30-8-45 | 27-2-46 | 13-8-75 |
| T-AO 107 PASSUMPSIC | 31-10-45 | 1-4-46 | 24-7-73 |
| T-AO 108 PAWCATUCK | 19-2-46 | 10-5-46 | 15-7-75 |
| T-AO 109 WACCAMAW | 30-3-46 | 25-6-46 | 24-2-75 |

**Mispillion (T-AO 105)** L. & L. Van Ginderen, 1-87

**Passumpsic (T-AO 107)** LSPH W. McBride, R.A.N., 9-87

**Pawcatuck (T-AO 108)** L. Grazioli, 11-86

**D:** 9,486 tons light (35,090 fl) **S:** 16 kts **Dim:** 196.9 × 22.9 × 10.8
**Electron Equipt:** Radar: 1/SPS-10, 1/Raytheon TM 1650/6X
**M:** 2 sets Westinghouse GT; 2 props; 13,500 hp
**Boilers:** 4 Babcock & Wilcox; 32.7 kg/cm², 393°C **Fuel:** 2,205 tons
**Man:** 23 officers, 85 men MSC, plus 21 Navy (1 officer, 20 men)

REMARKS: 19,294 grt/23,250 dwt. Cargo: 107,000 bbl fuel oil, diesel, etc., plus dry cargo. Fleet support units transferred from the Navy and intended for underway replenishment. Had four single 76.2-mm guns, but now disarmed. Helicopter deck forward. Replenishment station forward of bridge removed around 1980. All lengthened 28.3 m during the mid-1960s. T-AO 105 scheduled to be deactivated FY 81, but was retained in active service. T-AO 108, 109 in Atlantic; rest in Pacific.

## REPLENISHMENT OILERS *(continued)*

◆ **2 Cimarron class (T3-S2-A1 type)** Bldr: Bethlehem, Sparrows Point, Md. —in reserve.

| | L | In serv. | To MSC |
|---|---|---|---|
| T-AO 57 Marias | 21-12-43 | 12-2-44 | 2-10-73 |
| T-AO 62 Taluga | 10-7-44 | 25-8-44 | 4-5-72 |

**Marias (T-AO 57)** 1975

**D:** 24,450 tons (fl) **S:** 18 kts **Dim:** 168.56 × 22.86 × 10.1
**Electron Equipt:** Radar: 1/SPS-10, 1/Raytheon 1650/9X
**M:** 2 sets GT; 2 props; 13,500 hp **Electric:** 950 kw
**Range:** 10,000/18; 14,000/10 **Boilers:** 4 Foster-Wheeler; 31.7 kg/cm², 399°C
**Range:** 10,000/15 **Fuel:** 2,205 tons
**Man:** 20 officers, 85 men MSC, plus 16 Navy

Remarks: 12,000 grt/18,400 dwt. Cargo: 87,000 bbl fuel oil, diesel, etc. Fleet support ships intended for underway replenishment. Deactivated and placed in National Defense Reserve Fleet (on Navy List), T-AO 57 on 22-11-82 and T-AO 62 on 21-11-83.

## TRANSPORT OILERS (T-AOT)

◆ **9 Sealift class** Bldrs: First four: Todd, Los Angeles; others: Bath Iron Works

| | L | In serv. |
|---|---|---|
| T-AOT 168 Sealift Pacific | 13-10-73 | 14-8-74 |
| T-AOT 169 Sealift Arabian Sea | 26-1-74 | 6-5-75 |
| T-AOT 170 Sealift China Sea | 20-4-74 | 9-5-75 |
| T-AOT 171 Sealift Indian Ocean | 27-7-74 | 29-8-74 |
| T-AOT 172 Sealift Atlantic | 26-1-74 | 26-8-74 |
| T-AOT 173 Sealift Mediterranean | 9-3-74 | 6-11-74 |
| T-AOT 174 Sealift Caribbean | 8-6-74 | 10-2-75 |
| T-AOT 175 Sealift Arctic | 31-8-74 | 22-5-75 |
| T-AOT 176 Sealift Antarctic | 26-10-74 | 1-8-75 |

**D:** 33,000 tons (fl) **S:** 16 kts **Dim:** 178.92 (170.80 pp) × 25.61 × 10.50
**Electron Equipt:** Radar: 1/Raytheon TM 1650/6X, 1/Raytheon TM 1645
**M:** 2 Colt-Pielstick, 14PC-2V400 14-cyl., 520-rpm diesels; 1 CP prop; 14,000 hp
**Electric:** 2,600 kw **Fuel:** 3,440 tons **Range:** 12,000/16
**Man:** 9 officers, 17 men, 2 cadets (contract crew)

**Sealift Caribbean (T-AOT 174)**—light load L. & L. Van Ginderen, 3-86

**Sealift Antarctic (T-AO 176)**—MARISAT radome atop bridge L. & L. Van Ginderen, 1-87

Remarks: 17,157 grt/27,217 dwt (vary slightly). All now used in freighting service. Cargo: 225,154 barrels fuel oil, diesel, etc. Equipped with bow-thruster. MSC chartered these ships for twenty years and has a commercial contractor operating them; current owner is the Irving Trust Co., New York. All redesignated T-AOT on 30-9-78. A five-year operating contract for these ships was signed with Marine Transport Lines, Secaucus, N.J., in 3-85.

Note: *American Explorer* (T-AOT 165), deactivated 4-4-84, was transferred to the MARAD Ready Reserve Force on 27-6-84.

◆ **2 Maumee class (T5-S-12A type)**—in reserve

| | Bldr | Laid down | L | In serv. |
|---|---|---|---|---|
| T-AOT 149 Maumee | Ingalls SB | 8-3-55 | 16-2-56 | 12-12-56 |
| T-AOT 152 Yukon | Ingalls SB | 16-5-55 | 16-3-56 | 17-5-57 |

**Yukon (T-AOT 152)** L. & L. Van Ginderen, 6-83

**D:** 32,000 tons (fl) **S:** 18 kts **Dim:** 189.0 × 25.5 × 9.8
**Electron Equipt:** Radar: 1/Raytheon TM 1650/6X, 1/Raytheon TM 1660/12S
**M:** 1 set GT; 1 prop; 20,460 hp **Boilers:** 2 Combustion Engineering
**Fuel:** 4,321 tons **Range:** 18,000/18 **Man:** 11 officers, 20 men MSC

Remarks: 15,626 grt/26,943 dwt. Cargo: 187,000 bbl fuel oil, diesel, etc., plus 878 m³ dry cargo. T-AOT 149 has ice-reinforced bow. Sister *Potomac* (T-AO 150, later T-AOT 181) rebuilt to different design. All retyped T-AOT on 30-9-78. Sister *Shoshone* (T-AOT 151) was placed in the MARAD-administered Ready Reserve Force in 6-84, still under Navy ownership. T-AOT 149 deactivated 2-10-85, to RRF 15-10-85; T-AOT 152 deactivated 20-10-85, to RRF 20-10-85. Both "demoted" to National Defense Reserve Fleet 2-4-87, still on Navy List.

◆ **1 Mission class (T2-SE-A2 type)** Bldr: Marineship, Sausalito, Calif.—in reserve

| | Laid down | L | In serv. |
|---|---|---|---|
| T-AOT 134 Mission Santa Ynez | 9-9-43 | 19-12-43 | 13-3-44 |

**D:** 5,730 tons light (22,380 fl) **S:** 16.5 kts **Dim:** 159.7 (153.3 pp) × 20.7 × 9.4
**M:** 1 set G.E. GT, electric drive; 1 prop; 10,000 hp **Electric:** 1,120 kw
**Boilers:** 2 Babcock & Wilcox; 42.2 kg/cm², 441°C
**Fuel:** 1,375 tons **Range:** 13,000/14.5 **Man:** 52 tot.

Remarks: 10,461 grt/17,056 dwt. Acquired by the Navy on 22-10-47. Cargo: 16,500 tons liquid (approx. 134,000 bbl). In National Defense Reserve Fleet at Suisun Bay, Cal., since 6-3-75. Retyped T-AOT on 30-9-78.

◆ **1 Suamico class (T2-SE-A1 type)** Bldr: Sun SB & DD, Chester, Pa.—in reserve

| | Laid down | L | In serv. |
|---|---|---|---|
| T-AOT 75 Saugatuck (ex-*Newton*) | 16-9-41 | 7-7-42 | 19-2-43 |

**D:** 5,782 tons light (21,880 fl) **S:** 15 kts **Dim:** 159.7 (153.3 pp) × 20.7 × 9.4
**M:** 1 set G.E. GT, electric drive; 1 prop; 8,250 hp (T-AOT 67 and T-AOT 75: 1 set Westinghouse GT, electric drive; 1 prop; 6,600 hp)
**Electric:** 1,100–1,160 kw **Boilers:** 2 Babcock & Wilcox; 42.2 kg/cm², 441°C
**Fuel:** 1,375 tons **Range:** 13,000/14.5 **Man:** 43 tot.

Remarks: 10,296 grt/16,500 dwt. Sisters *Tallulah* (T-AOT 50, ex-*Valley Forge*), *Cache* (T-AOT 67, ex-*Stillwater*), *Millicoma* (T-AOT 73, ex-*Conestoga*, ex-*King's Mountain*), and *Schuylkill* (T-AOT 76, ex-*Louisburg*) were approved for disposal in 31-1-86. Taken over by the Navy while under construction and completed as a fleet oiler. Transferred to MSTS (later MSC) in 1949 and operated with civilian crews until placed in the Maritime Administration's National Defense Reserve Fleet between 1972 and 1975. Cargo: 141,000 bbl. Reclassified T-AOT on 30-9-78.

## TRANSPORTS

Note: The transports listed below are maintained in the Maritime Administration's National Defense Reserve Fleet, but remain the Navy's property, earmarked for the MSC, should the requirement arise. Most were placed in reserve in 1969 and 1970. Of the three *Barrett*-class transports, *Barrett* (AP 196) has been on loan to the New York State Maritime Academy since 5-9-73 and is to be replaced under FY 88 funding, *Geiger* (AP 197), on loan to the Massachusetts Maritime Academy in 12-2-80, was damaged by fire in 1981 and was returned to the Maritime Commission for disposal, and was replaced by *Santa Mercedes* (now *Patriot State*) and *Upshur* (T-AP 198) serves the Maine Maritime Academy as *State of Maine*.

**TRANSPORTS** *(continued)*

◆ **3 Admiral class (P2-S2-R1 type)** Bldr: Bethlehem, Alameda, Cal.—in reserve

| | L | In serv. |
|---|---|---|
| AP 122 General Alexander M. Patch (ex-*Admiral R.E. Coontz*) | 22-4-44 | 21-11-44 |
| AP 123 General Simon B. Buckner (ex-*Admiral E.W. Eberle*) | 14-6-44 | 24-1-45 |
| AP 126 General Maurice Rose (ex-*Admiral Hugh Rodman*) | 25-2-45 | 10-7-45 |

**General Maurice Rose (AP 126)**—in the James River L. & L. Van Ginderen, 9-87

**D:** 12,657 tons light (22,574 fl) **S:** 19 kts
**Dim:** 185.6 (174.65 wl) × 23.01 × 8.07 **Fuel:** 3,877 tons **Range:** 15,000/19
**M:** 2 sets G.E. GT, electric drive; 2 props; 18,000 hp **Electric:** 2,000 kw
**Boilers:** 4 Combustion Engineering "D", 42.2 kg/cm$^2$, 449°C **Man:** 319 tot.

Remarks: 16,039 grt/9,944 dwt. In reserve in the James River, in MARAD custody. All operated by the Army Transportation Service until 1-3-50, when transferred to MSTS (later MSC). Active into the late 1960s. Can carry 1,757 troops, 2,889 m$^3$ dry cargo. *Hugh J. Gaffey* (T-AP 121) redesignated IX 507 on 1-11-78 and used as a barracks ship. *General William O. Darby* (AP 127) reactivated as barracks ship (IX 510) in 10-81 (see pg. 776). *General Nelson M. Walker* (AP 125) donated 25-1-81 to Life International for conversion as a civilian hospital ship. All could originally carry 5,100 troops. Two others, *General John Pope* (ex-AP 110) and *General Edwin Patrick* (ex-AP 124) are Maritime Administration property, stored at Suisun Bay, Cal.

Note: Of the two P2-S2-R2 transports remaining on the Navy List in 1986, *General W. H. Gordon* (AP 117) and *General William Weigel* (AP 119) were stricken 31-3-86 and scrapped in Taiwan in 1987, along with *General W. A. Mann* (ex-AP 112), stricken earlier. Sisters *Gen. D. I. Sultan* (ex-AP 120), *Gen. William Mitchell* (ex-AP 114), and *Gen. J. C. Breckenridge* (ex-AP 176) were released in 6-86 for scrapping by MARAD.

**CABLE SHIPS (T-ARC)**

◆ **1 Zeus class** Bldr: National Steel, San Diego, Calif.

| | Laid down | L | In serv. |
|---|---|---|---|
| T-ARC 7 Zeus | 1-6-81 | 9-10-82 | 19-3-84 |

Authorized: FY 79

**Zeus (T-ARC 7)**—on trials L. & L. Van Ginderen, 7-85

**D:** 8,297 tons light (14,225 fl) **S:** 15.8 kts **Dim:** 153.2 (138.4 pp) × 22.3 × 7.3
**Electron Equipt:** Radar: 2/navigational
**M:** 5 G.M. EMD 20-cyl., 3,600-hp diesels, electric drive; 2 CP props; 12,500 hp
**Range:** 10,000/15 **Fuel:** 1,816 tons **Electric:** 3,500 kw
**Man:** 88 MSC crew, 8 Navy, 32 civilian technicians, 38 spare berths

Remarks: 3,750 dwt. Ordered 17-8-79 to replace T-ARC. Plans to request a second have been canceled. Has passive tank roll stabilization, two 1,200-hp funnel bow-thrusters forward and two aft. Cable capacity is 1,170 m$^3$ coiled (about 590 n.m.) plus 1,004 m$^3$ spare capacity (506 n.m.), and up to 3,117 tons of cable repeaters can be stowed. Able to conduct acoustic, hydrographic, and bathymetric surveys. The five main engines also provide for the ship's-service generators; there is also a 500-kw emergency generator. Painted white. Operation to be contracted out during 1988.

◆ **2 Neptune class (S3-S2-BP1 type)** Bldr: Pusey & Jones, Wilmington, Del.

| | L | In serv. |
|---|---|---|
| T-ARC 2 Neptune (ex-*Wm. H.G. Bullard*) | 1945 | 1-6-53 |
| T-ARC 6 Albert J. Meyer | 1945 | 13-5-63 |

**Albert J. Meyer (T-ARC 6)**—note heavy bow sheaves and OE-82 SATCOMM antennas L. & L. Van Ginderen, 10-85

**Neptune (T-ARC 2)** G. Arra, 10-85

**D:** 5,818 tons light (8,510 fl; T-ARC 2: 8,625 fl) **S:** 13 kts
**Dim:** 112.8 (98.1 pp) × 14.3 × 7.6
**Electron Equipt:** Radar: 1/Raytheon TM 1650/6X, 1/Raytheon TM 1660/12S
**M:** 4 G.E. diesels, electric drive; 2 props; 4,000 hp
**Fuel:** 980 tons (T-ARC 6: 1,129 tons) **Range:** 10,000/13
**Man:** 16 officers, 58 men MSC, 18 technicians

Remarks: T-ARC 2: 3,929 grt/2,000 dwt; T-ARC 6: 4,012 grt/4,332 dwt. Differ in detail, with T-ARC 6 being flush-decked. T-ARC 2 was in Army reserve from 1946–52, then in U.S. Navy, and was transferred to MSC 8-11-73. T-ARC 6 transferred from Army on 18-9-63. Both have been extensively modernized, including the replacement of the original Skinner Uniflow reciprocating steam plants with diesel-electric machinery: T-ARC 2 from 2-80 to 10-82 and T-ARC 6 from 3-78 to 5-80. Both have a 1,000-hp tunnel thruster forward. Cable capacity is nominally 1,240 m$^3$ (about 625 nautical miles), and they can carry 2,020 tons of cable repeaters. T-ARC 2 had a helicopter deck; removed during modernization. T-ARC 2 to be contractor-operated by end 1988.

**FLEET TUGS**

◆ **7 Powhatan class** Bldr: Marinette Marine, Wisc.

| | Laid down | L | In serv. |
|---|---|---|---|
| T-ATF 166 Powhatan | 30-9-76 | 24-6-78 | 15-6-79 |
| T-ATF 167 Narragansett | 5-5-77 | 28-11-78 | 9-1-79 |
| T-ATF 168 Catawba | 14-12-77 | 12-5-79 | 28-5-80 |
| T-ATF 169 Navajo | 14-12-77 | 20-12-79 | 13-6-80 |
| T-ATF 170 Mohawk | 22-3-79 | 5-4-80 | 16-10-80 |
| T-ATF 171 Sioux | 22-3-79 | 30-10-80 | 12-5-81 |
| T-ATF 172 Apache | 22-3-79 | 20-12-80 | 30-7-81 |

Authorized: 1 in FY 75, 3 in FY 76, 3 in FY 78

**FLEET TUGS** *(continued)*

**Navajo (T-ATF 169)**—note bow anchor slot V. Baca, 7-87

**Powhatan (T-ATF 166)** G. Arra, 4-86

**D:** 2,000 tons (2,260 fl) **S:** 15 kts **Dim:** 73.2 (68.88 pp) × 12.8 × 4.6
**Electron Equipt:** Radar: 1/Raytheon TM 1660/12S, 1/SPS-53
**M:** 2 G.M. EMD 20-645X7 diesels, electric drive; 2 Kort-nozzle props; 4,500 hp (3,600 sust.)
**Electric:** 1,200 kw **Fuel:** 600 tons **Range:** 10,000/13
**Man:** 6 officers, 14 men + Navy communications team

Remarks: Modified oilfield-supply-boat design built to merchant marine specifications. If required, could mount two 20-mm AA (I × 2) and two 12.7-mm machine guns (I × 2). Five were requested under FY 78, three approved. Have a 300-hp bow-thruster and one 10-ton electrohydraulic crane. Can carry the Mk 1 Mod. 1, 90-ton deep-diving support module on the stern and can support a 20-man Navy salvage team. Have a 60-ton bollard-pull capacity. Foam fire-fighting equipment. Hull has unusual double-chine configuration. Electrohydraulic 10-ton crane. Operation to be contracted out for all, between 7- and 12-88.

Note: Former Military Sealift Command *Achomawi*-class tugs *Atakapa* (T-ATF 149) and *Mosopelea* (T-ATF 158), stricken from the Navy List, remain in the Maritime Administration National Defense Reserve Fleet.

## MILITARY SEALIFT COMMAND CHARTERED FLEET

The following section describes those MSC-controlled ships on long-term charter, beginning with the 13 units intended for the Afloat Prepositioning Force (formerly the Rapid Deployment Logistics Force).

### MARITIME PREPOSITIONING SHIPS

◆ **5 2nd Lt John P. Bobo class** Bldr: General Dynamics, Quincy

| | Laid down | L | In serv. |
|---|---|---|---|
| 2nd Lt John P. Bobo | 1-7-83 | 19-1-85 | 14-2-85 |
| Pfc Dewayne F. Williams | 1-9-83 | 18-5-85 | 6-6-85 |
| 1st Lt Baldomero Lopez | 23-3-84 | 26-10-85 | 21-11-85 |
| 1st Lt Jack Lummus | 22-6-84 | 22-2-86 | 6-3-86 |
| Sgt William R. Button | 22-8-84 | 17-5-86 | 22-5-86 |

**1st Lt Baldomero Lopez** G. Arra, 8-86

**2nd Lt John P. Bobo** Gen. Dynamics, 2-85

**Pfc Dewayne Williams** G. Arra, 9-86

**D:** 22,700 tons light (40,846 fl) **S:** 18.8 kts (trials); 17.7 kts sustained
**Dim:** 205.18 (187.32 pp/199.00 wl) × 32.16 × 8.99
**Electron Equipt:** Radar: 2/navigational
**M:** 2 Stork Werkspoor 18TM410V diesels; 1 prop; 26,400 hp—1,000-hp bow-thruster
**Electric:** 7,850 kw **Range:** 11,107/17.7 **Fuel:** 3,080 tons
**Man:** 30 contractor crew, 7 MSC crew, 7 Navy, 25 maintenance crew + 102 troops

Remarks: 44,543 grt/26,523 dwt (22,454 cargo dwt)/14,461 nrt. Maritime Administration C8-M-MA134j design. First two contracted for on 17-8-82, others on 14-1-83. Intended to transport material needed for $\frac{1}{4}$ of one Marine Expeditionary Brigade. In addition to listed personnel, have 102 temporary berths. Cargo capacity includes up to 522 standard 20-ft vans (350 for ammunition, 110 general stores, 30 with fuel drums, and 32 refrigerated), plus 14,000 m$^2$ of roll-on/roll-off vehicle capacity to carry up to 1,400 vehicles. A Navire stern slewing ramp provides access to the six vehicle decks and can either discharge 60-ton vehicles to a pier or amphibious vehicles of up to 23 tons directly into the water; the stern door is 11 × 4.55 m. The upper deck can stow 2 LCM(8) landing craft, 6 unpowered causeway sections, 4 powered causeway sections, a warping tug, 4 pipe trailers, and 16 hose reels. The ships carry 5,764.6 m$^3$ (1,523,000 gallons) of transferable

**MARITIME PREPOSITIONING SHIPS** *(continued)*

bulk fuel, plus 2,039 55-gallon drums and can also transport 307 $m^3$ of potable water. Five 39-ton pedestal cranes are fitted, with two sets being paired, and there is a large helicopter deck at the stern. Unloading rates: all vehicles and $\frac{1}{6}$ cargo at a pier in 12 hrs; all cargo at a pier in 3 days; all cargo while moored out in 5 days; there is a 4-point mooring system. Operated on expected 25-year charter by American Overseas Marine. *Bobo* is in MPS Squadron One in the Atlantic; rest formed MPS Squadron 3 in 10-86, operating near Guam.

◆ **5 Cpl Louis J. Hauge, Jr., class** Bldr: Odense SY, Lindo, Denmark

| | In serv. | Acq. | Conv. by | In serv. |
|---|---|---|---|---|
| Cpl Louis J. Hauge, Jr. (ex-*Estelle Maersk*) | 10-79 | 3-1-84 | Bethlehem SY, Baltimore, Md. | 7-9-84 |
| Pfc William B. Baugh (ex-*Eleo Maersk*) | 4-79 | 17-1-83 | Bethlehem SY, Beaumont, Tx. | 30-10-84 |
| Pfc James Anderson, Jr. (ex-*Emma Maersk*) | 7-79 | 31-10-83 | Bethlehem SY, Baltimore, Md. | 26-3-85 |
| 1st Lt Alex Bonnyman (ex-*Emelie Maersk*) | 1-80 | 30-1-84 | Bethlehem SY, Beaumont, Tx. | 26-9-85 |
| Pvt Harry Fisher (ex-*Evelyn Maersk*) | 4-80 | 2-4-83 | Bethlehem SY, Baltimore, Md. | 12-9-85 |

**Cpl Louis J. Hauge, Jr.** Bethlehem Steel, 1985

**Pfc James Anderson, Jr.** L. & L. Van Ginderen, 10-85

**1st Lt Alex Bonnyman**—note offset ramp and fueling hose reel at the stern L. & L. Van Ginderen, 7-87

**D:** 28,249 tons light (46,484 fl) **S:** 18.5 kts (17.2 sust.)
**Dim:** 230.25 (215.00 pp) × 27.48 × 10.02
**Electron Equipt:** Radar: 2/navigational **Fuel:** 3,228 tons
**M:** 1 Sulzer 7RND 76M, 7-cyl. diesel; 1 prop; 16,800 hp
**Electric:** 4,250 kw **Range:** 10,800/17.2
**Man:** 20 contractor and 7 MSC crew, 30 maintenance crew + 80 troops

Remarks: Operated by Maersk Lines on long-term charter. Carry $\frac{1}{5}$ of the vehicles, equipment, and supplies to outfit a Marine Expeditionary Brigade. Transport up to 413 containers (280 ammunition, 86 general cargo, 23 drummed fuel, 24 refrigerated), plus providing 11,369 $m^2$ vehicle cargo space. There are 4/30-ton and 2/36-ton pedestal cranes, side-loading vehicle ports amidships, and a Navire slewing ramp has been added aft, beneath a helicopter deck. There are 8 cargo hatches, and three vehicle parking decks. Liquid cargo includes 4,920 $m^3$ transferable vehicle fuel, 504 $m^3$ potable water, and 2,252 $m^3$ of lube oil. There is a bow-thruster. First 3 ordered 17-8-82, others on 14-1-83. All five are part of Maritime Prepositioning Ship Squadron 2, operating in the Indian Ocean, with *Bonnyman,* as flagship, carrying 8 Navy communications teams. *Bonnyman* originally to be named *1st Lt. Alexander Bonnyman, Jr.;* changed 4-3-86.

◆ **3 Sgt Matej Kocak class** Bldr: Sun Shpbldg., Chester, Pa.

| | In serv. | Converted by | In serv. |
|---|---|---|---|
| Sgt Matej Kocak (ex-*John D. Waterman*) | 14-3-81 | National Steel, San Diego | 5-10-84 |
| Pfc Eugene A. Obregon (ex-*Thomas Heywood*) | 11-82 | National Steel, San Diego | 15-1-85 |
| Maj Stephen W. Pless (ex-*Charles Carroll*) | 3-83 | National Steel, San Diego | 1-5-85 |

**Sgt Matej Kocak**—note traveling container crane M.S.C., 10-84

**Pfc Eugene A. Obregon** G. Arra, 8-86

**Maj Stephen W. Pless**—with 20-ft containers forward, pontoon sections and an LCM(8) on deck amidships G. Arra, 7-86

**D:** 15,000 tons light (38,500 fl) **S:** 20.9 kts
**Dim:** 250.24 (234.85 pp) × 32.16 × 10.06
**Electron Equipt:** Radar: 2/navigational
**M:** 2 sets G.E. GT; 1/6-bladed prop; 32,000 hp **Boilers:** 2; . . .
**Fuel:** 3,450 tons (+300 tons diesel) **Range:** 13,000/20.9
**Man:** 85 crew, 7 MSC crew, 8 Navy, 25 maintenance crew

Remarks: 25,426 grt/22,910 dwt. First two contracted for on 17-8-82, third on 14-1-83, all with Waterman Steamship Co. as operator. Intended to transport $\frac{1}{4}$ of the vehicles, fuel, supplies, and provisions to support a Marine Expeditionary Battalion. Will carry 213 ammunition containers, 150 "Lo/Lo" containers, 10 general cargo containers, 32 drummed fuel containers, and 32 refrigerated containers, plus a large number of vehicles and cargo fuel and water. Lengthened 39.8 m during conversion, and helicopter deck and ramp added. Have paired 50-ton and paired 35-ton portal cranes and retain a traveling container gantry forward. Owned by various investment consortia. All operated from U.S. East Coast in MPS Squadron 1.

## GENERAL CARGO SHIPS

◆ **1 Maritime Administration C1-M-122a type** Bldr: . . .

RAINBOW HOPE (ex-*Amazonia*) (In serv. 1980)

**D:** **S:** 13.7 kts **Dim:** 89.9 × 13.7 × 4.6 **Man:** 5 off., 6 unlicensed
**Electron Equipt:** Radar: . . . **M:** 1 diesel; 1 prop; . . . hp **Range:** 6,000/13.7

REMARKS: 1,000 grt/2,062 dwt. Cargo: 2,945 m³ bale (680 m³ refrigerated).

◆ **1 oilfield supply ship** Bldr: Moss Point Marine, Escatawpa, Miss.

NICOR CLIPPER (In serv. 1983)

**D:** . . . **S:** 10 kts **Dim:** 77.42 × 13.42 × 3.98
**M:** 2 G.M. EMD 12-cyl. diesels; 2 props; . . . hp—bow-thruster
**Range:** . . . **Electric:** 300 kw **Man:** . . .

REMARKS: 425 grt/1,200 dwt. Chartered 6-5-87 for 17 months, with two 17-month extension options, to carry cargo in the Caribbean Sea area.

◆ **1 Antarctic support ship** Bldr: Howaldtswerke, Kiel, West Germany (In serv. 1-80)

GREEN WAVE (ex-*Woerman Mira*, ex-*Sloman Mira*)

**D:** . . . **S:** 17 kts **Dim:** 154.5 × 21.3 × 7.6 **Man:** 9 officers, 12 unlicensed
**M:** diesels **Range:** 11,000/17 **Fuel:** 7,725 tons

REMARKS: 9,521 grt/12,487 dwt. Chartered 8-84 for 4 to 5 years from Central Gulf Lines to act as Antarctic supply ship in place of *Southern Cross* (T-AK 285). Has ice-strengthened hull, long hatches for container or break-bulk cargo. Six 25-ton cranes, four of which can be ganged to lift up to 80 tons from holds 3 and 4.

◆ **1 C5-78 type combination cargo ship** Bldr: Ingalls SY, Pascagoula

| | In serv. | Chartered | To |
|---|---|---|---|
| ROVER (ex-*American Rover*, ex-*Defiance*, ex-*Mormacsea*) | 4-69 | 6-3-82 | 6-3-87 |

**D:** 27,980 tons (fl) **S:** 23.6 kts **Dim:** 183.33 (170.69 pp) × 27.43 × 10.39
**Electron Equipt:** Radar: 2/navigational **Man:** 11 off., 23 unlicensed
**M:** 2 sets G.E. GT; 1 prop; 30,000 hp **Boilers:** 2 Combustion Eng.; 74 kg/cm²
**Fuel:** 2,790 tons **Electric:** 3,000 kw **Range:** 12,000/23.6

REMARKS: 11,757 grt/15,694 dwt. Chartered from Central Gulf Lines for general cargo carrying. Cargo: 70 standard containers, plus 33,814 m³ dry cargo volume. Stern door for vehicle cargo, seven hatches. Sister *Rapid* off-charter 12-85, to RRF 9-12-87 as *Cape Nome* (see photo in Ready Reserve Force section).

◆ **1 Maritime Administration C4-S-69 type** Bldr: Avondale SY, Westwego, La.

| | In serv. | Chartered | To |
|---|---|---|---|
| AMERICAN TROJAN (ex-*Montana*) | 1-69 | 23-12-81 | 23-12-86 |

**American Spitfire, sister to American Trojan** M.S.C., 1982

**D:** 21,617 tons (fl) **S:** 23 kts **Dim:** 176.48 (165.96 pp) × 24.99 × 9.78
**M:** 2 sets G.E. GT; 1 prop; 24,000 hp **Boilers:** 2 Babcock & Wilcox
**Electric:** 2,000 kw **Fuel:** 2,658 tons **Range:** 12,000/23
**Man:** 10 officers, 19 unlicensed

REMARKS: 13,053 grt/13,074 dwt. Cargo: 21,665 m³ bale dry cargo/1,133 m³ refrigerated. Can carry standard shipping containers and can also accommodate 7,000 bbl liquid cargo. Seven cargo holds. Cranes: one 70-ton, eight 20-ton, eight 10-ton, eight 5-ton. Chartered from Central Gulf Lines and used as an equipment prepositioning ship at Diego Garcia. Gray-painted, MARISAT terminals added, extra cargo containers even-stacked on superstructure. Sister *American Spitfire* off-charter 12-85, and *American Titan* in 9-86.

◆ **3 Maritime Administration C4-S-66 type** Bldr: Avondale SY, Westwego, La.

| | In serv. | Chartered | To |
|---|---|---|---|
| ELIZABETH LYKES | 1-66 | 23-5-83 | 23-5-88 |
| LETITIA LYKES | 1-68 | 23-5-83 | 23-5-88 |
| LOUISE LYKES | 1965 | 23-5-84 | 23-5-88 |

**D:** 21,840 tons (fl) **S:** 20 kts **Dim:** 164.59 (156.94 pp) × 23.16 × 9.96
**Electron Equipt:** Radar: 1/navigational **Electric:** 1,500 kw
**M:** 2 sets de Laval or Westinghouse GT; 1 prop; 15,500 hp
**Boilers:** 2 Foster-Wheeler; 49 kg/cm² **Fuel:** 2,753 tons **Range:** 12,000/20
**Man:** 12 officers, 26 unlicensed

REMARKS: 10,723 grt/14,662 dwt. Chartered from Lykes Brothers Lines. First two used as equipment prepositioning ships, *Louise Lykes* in cargo carrying. Cargo: 21,240 m³ bale, plus 4,000 bbl liquid. Six hatches; one 80-ton Stülcken boom, 20 smaller capacity. *Letitia Lykes* carries the 1,000-bed "Navy Rapidly Deployable Medical Facility," replacing the Army portable medical facility carried by *Gulf Trader* at Diego Garcia on 30-6-83. Thirteen near-sister ships are in the Ready Reserve Force.

◆ **2 Maritime Administration C4-S-64 class** Bldr: Bethlehem Steel, Sparrows Point, Maryland

SANTA ADELA (ex-*Delta Africa*, ex-*Prudential Oceanjet*) (In serv. 1-66)
SANTA JUANA (ex-*Delta America*, ex-*Prudential Sealift*) (In serv. 1-66)

**D:** . . . **S:** 20.8 kts **Dim:** 165.8 × 22.9 × 9.8 **Man:** 12 officers, 17 unlicensed
**M:** GT; 1 prop; . . . hp **Range:** 7,000/20 **Fuel:** 2,354 tons

REMARKS: 11,039 grt/13,695 dwt. Chartered 1984 from Vessel Charters, Inc., and Prudential Lines. Have 19,400 m³ dry cargo capacity plus 481 m³ refrigerated cargo and 9,000 bbl liquid cargo. *Santa Adela* used in general cargo work; *Santa Juana* supports Diego Garcia.

◆ **1 Maritime Administration C4-S-582 type** Bldr: Ingalls SB, Pascagoula

| | In serv. | Chartered | To |
|---|---|---|---|
| DAWN (ex-*African Dawn*) | 6-63 | 3-5-80 | 3-5-88 |

**Dawn** L. & L. Van Ginderen, 9-84

**D:** 17,379 tons (fl) **S:** 20 kts **Dim:** 174.35 (164.90 pp) × 22.86 × 9.40
**Electron Equipt:** Radar: . . . **Man:** 10 officers, 23 unlicensed
**M:** 2 sets G.E. GT; 1 prop; 18,150 hp **Boilers:** 2 Foster-Wheeler; 49 kg/cm²
**Electric:** 1,800 kw **Fuel:** 3,353 tons **Range:** 17,000/20

REMARKS: 11,309 grt/12,728 dwt. Chartered from Central Gulf Lines; extended 5-84. Cargo: 17,841 m³ dry bale cargo, plus 821 m³ refrigerated and 8,000 bbl liquid cargo.

NOTE: General-cargo ship *President Adams* was returned to her owners in 1987.

## FLOAT-ON/FLOAT-OFF CARGO SHIP

◆ **1 converted tanker** Bldr: Eriksbergs Mek. Verkstads, Gothenburg, Sweden (In serv. 17-9-75)

AMERICAN CORMORANT (ex-*Ferncarrier*, ex-*Kollbris*)

**American Cormorant**—with Army equipment American Automar, 1985

### FLOAT-ON/FLOAT-OFF CARGO SHIPS *(continued)*

**D:** 69,555 tons (fl) **S:** 15 kts
**Dim:** 225.06 (213.90 pp) × 41.15 × 10.49 (19.81 flooded)
**M:** 1 Eriksberg/Burmeister & Wain 10K84EF 10-cyl., 114-rpm diesel; 1 prop; 25,000 hp (19,900 under owner's restrictions)—1,500-hp thrusters fore and aft
**Fuel:** 3,464 tons **Range:** 23,700/13 **Electric:** 3,360 kw
**Endurance:** 76 days **Man:** 19 tot.

REMARKS: 10,195 grt/47,230 dwt. Former 135,900-dwt tanker converted to a heavy-lift float-on/float-off cargo ship in 1982. Capacity: 45,000 tons on the 120-m × 42-m, 4,870-m$^2$ midbody cargo deck created by removing the upper portions of the cargo tanks and reducing original length by 55 m. Can also be used to transport 10,000 bbl liquid cargo. Has been at Diego Garcia since 1985 with 7,000 tons of U.S. Army floating equipment: 2 BD-series floating cranes, 4 LCU 1466 and 10 LCM(8) landing craft, 4 32.6-m tugs, and 2 LASH barges; stowed atop these are 4 cranes, 9 fork-lifts, and various cargo-handing gear. Can also stow 25 40-ft containers (15 refrigerated) on fantail. Takes 4 hours to ballast/deballast to load. Owned by American Automar and operated by Pacific Gulf Marine. Chartered 10-85 for 18 mos. to test "flo/flo" utility for Military Sealift Command missions; renewed 1987.

### VEHICLE CARGO SHIP

◆ **1 Finneagle class** Bldr: Kockums, Mälmo, Sweden

| | In serv. | Chartered | To |
|---|---|---|---|
| AMERICAN EAGLE (ex-*Zenit Eagle*, ex-*Finneagle*) | 20-2-81 | 22-8-83 | . . . |

**American Eagle** L. & L. Van Ginderen, 10-86

**D:** . . . **S:** 19.5 kts **Dim:** 194.00 (180.80 pp) × 28.00 × 9.00
**Electron Equipt:** Radar: 2/navigational **Man:** 8 officers, 12 unlicensed
**M:** 2 Cegielski-Sulzer 6RND68M diesels; 1 prop; 21,500 hp
**Electric:** . . . **Fuel:** 2,823 tons **Range:** 16,000/19

REMARKS: 15,700 grt/20,404 dwt. Chartered for U.S.—Europe service. Owned by American Automar; operated by Pacific Gulf Marine, Inc. Versatile design capable of transporting up to 1,040 standard 20-ft cargo vans or vehicles, with 10,500 m$^3$ parking space for the latter. Has two side-by-side slewing stern ramps, two bow-thrusters. Can carry up to 8,500 tons salt-water ballast.

NOTE: Vehicle cargo ships ("Ro/Ro") *Lyra* and *Cygnus* were returned to their owner, Lykes Brothers, on 30-9-86. *Admiral Wm. M. Callaghan* was transferred to the Maritime Administration and joined the Ready Reserve Force on 31-5-87.

### CARGO BARGE CARRIERS

◆ **2 Maritime Administration C9-S-81d Type** Bldr: Avondale SY, Westwego, La.

| | In serv. | Chartered |
|---|---|---|
| GREEN ISLAND (ex-*George Wythe*, ex-*Green Island*) | 2-75 | 17-9-82 |
| GREEN VALLEY (ex-*Button Gwinnett*, ex-*Green Valley*) | 1-74 | 2-84 |

**Green Valley** L. & L. Van Ginderen, 1985

**D:** 62,314 tons (fl) **S:** 22 kts **Dim:** 272.29 (243.03 pp) × 30.48 × 12.44
**Electron Equipt:** Radar: 2/navigational
**M:** 2 sets de Laval GT; 1 prop; 32,000 hp **Electric:** 4,000 kw
**Boilers:** 2 Combustion Eng.; 75.7 kg/cm$^2$ **Fuel:** 5,800 tons
**Range:** 15,000/22 **Man:** 27 tot

REMARKS: 32,278 grt/46,152 dwt. Chartered from Central Gulf Lines as prepositioning ships at Diego Garcia. Unlike many LASH ships, do not have a separate, self-loading container-handling capability. Can carry 89 standard LASH barges, loaded and unloaded by a 455-ton-capacity traveling crane. Carry a small tug to move the barges.

◆ **2 Maritime Administration C8-S-81b-type lighter carriers**

Bldr: Avondale SY, Westwego, La.

| | In serv. | Chartered | To |
|---|---|---|---|
| AUSTRAL RAINBOW (ex-*American Veteran*, ex-*Austral Moon*, ex-*Australian Bear*, ex-*Philippine Bear*) | 1-73 | 12-4-84 | 29-10-88 |
| GREEN HARBOUR (ex-*Austral Rainbow*, ex-*China Bear*) | 5-72 | 27-10-81 | . . . |

**Austral Rainbow (as American Veteran)** L. & L. Van Ginderen, 3-86

**D:** 44,606 tons (fl) **S:** 22.5 kts **Dim:** 249.94 (220.68 pp) × 30.48 × 12.43
**M:** 2 sets de Laval GT; 1 prop; 32,000 hp **Boilers:** 2 Babcock & Wilcox
**Electric:** 4,500 kw **Fuel:** 5,500 tons (10,427 max.) **Range:** 13,000/22.5
**Man:** 12 officers, 21 unlicensed

REMARKS: 26,456 grt/29,820 dwt. Converted from cargo-barge-only carriers to container or barge carriers by owners, prior to lease. Can carry up to 71 cargo barges or 840 (*Green Harbour:* 1,004) standard cargo containers, handled by a 30-ton traveling crane. The traveling barge crane can lift 446 tons. Also have two 5-ton cranes. Both are carrying palletized munitions, the largest such explosive cargo ever carried by individual ships. Have 1 2,500-and 1 2,000-kw diesel generator sets. *Austral Rainbow* owned and operated by Farrell Lines; *Green Harbour* by Central Gulf Lines. Both act as prepositioning ships at Diego Garcia.

### TANKERS

◆ **5 Paul Buck (T-5) class** Bldr: American SB, Tampa, Fla.

| | Laid down | L | In serv. |
|---|---|---|---|
| PAUL BUCK (ex-*Ocean Champion*) | 28-10-84 | 1-6-85 | 11-9-85 |
| GUS W. DARNELL (ex-*Ocean Freedom*) | 25-11-84 | 10-8-85 | 11-9-85 |
| SAMUEL L. COBB (ex-*Ocean Triumph*) | 17-4-85 | 2-11-85 | 15-11-85 |
| RICHARD G. MATTHIESON (ex-*Ocean Spirit*) | 13-8-85 | 15-2-86 | 18-2-86 |
| LAWRENCE H. GIANELLA (ex-*Ocean Star*) | 2-12-85 | 19-4-86 | 22-4-86 |

**D:** 9,000 tons light (39,624 fl) **S:** 16 kts
**Dim:** 187.45 (179.07 pp) × 27.43 × 10.36
**Electron Equipt:** Radar: 1/. . . nav. **Electric:** 3,400 kw
**M:** 1 Mitsubishi- or Ishikawajima-Sulzer 5RTA-76 diesel; 1 prop; 15,300 hp
**Range:** 12,000/16 **Fuel:** 1,675 tons **Man:** 9 officers, 15 unlicensed

**Gus W. Darnell** American SB, 9-85

TANKERS *(continued)*

**Lawrence H. Gianella**—with platforms added for later installation of UNREP gear American SB, 4-86

REMARKS: 19,037 grt/30,150 dwt. First two contracted for on 30-9-82, and other three ordered 24-4-83. Some sections of the ships built at Nashville, Tenn., for later joining to the main body, and the forebodies were subcontracted to Avondale SY. Ice-strengthened hulls. Engines in first two built by Mitsubishi; others by Ishikawajima-Harima Heavy Industries. Cargo: 238,400 bbl (last two: 239,500 bbl). Chartered for five years. The last two were completed with the capability to add rapidly an underway replenishment station on each beam, as well as an astern refueling capability. All have 3 Caterpillar 3/50 diesel generator sets, plus a Nishishiba shaft generator and a G.M. emergency diesel generator. Can make 16 kts at 75 percent full power. Can carry up to 14,675 bbl liquid ballast. Owned by Bank America Leasing Corp., Baltimore Capital Reserve, Inc., Pacatine Hills, Inc., and, last two, Bank America Leasing Corp., respectively, and operated in freighting service by Ocean Ships (*Paul Buck:* Ocean Carriers).

◆ **2 Falcon Leader class** Bldr: Bath Iron Works

| | Laid down | L | In serv. |
|---|---|---|---|
| FALCON LEADER | 7-6-82 | 26-2-83 | 19-9-83 |
| FALCON CHAMPION | . . . | 10-9-83 | 19-1-84 |

**Falcon Leader** M. Oehler, 1987

**D:** 42,369 tons (fl) **S:** 16 kts **Dim:** 203.0 (194.8 pp) × 25.6 × 10.97
**M:** 2 de Laval Enterprise RV16 diesels; 1 prop; 14,720 hp (11,500 sust.)
**Fuel:** 3,321 tons **Range:** 27,000/16 **Man:** 9 officers, 13 unlicensed

REMARKS: 17,735 grt/33,870 dwt. Maritime Administration T6-M-136A design. Ordered 19-1-81 for Falcon Sea Transport Co. for 5-year charter to MSC, with option for 5 years more; operated by Seahawk Management. Cargo: 225,100 bbl. *Falcon Leader* was chartered 20-2-85 and is stationed at Diego Garcia as a prepositioned fuel ship. *Falcon Champion* is used as a shuttle tanker in the Mediterranean. Both supported Arabian Sea operations during 1987. Can fuel astern, using 230-m of 152-mm hose and have two alongside positions for fueling on each beam. Have segregated ballast system and inert gas plant.

◆ **4 Maritime Administration T6-M-982 type** Bldr: Todd SY, San Pedro, Cal.

COURIER (ex-*Zapata Courier*) (In serv. 1-77)
PATRIOT (ex-*Zapata Patriot*) (In serv. 1976)
RANGER (ex-*Zapata Ranger*) (In serv. 1-76)
ROVER (ex-*Zapata Rover*) (In serv. 1-77)

**D:** 44,150 tons (fl) **S:** 16 kts **Dim:** 216.7 × 25.6 × 11.3
**M:** 2 Fairbanks-Morse diesels; 1 prop; 14,000 hp **Range:** 12,000/16
**Fuel:** 3,416 tons

**Rover** L. & L. Van Ginderen, 10-83

REMARKS: 21,572 grt/35,100 dwt. Cargo: 308,000 bbl. Chartered from Ogden Transport and operated by Ocean Ships in shuttle-tanker and freighting service. *Patriot* (owned by O.M.I.) chartered 1986.

◆ **3 Overseas class** Bldr: Bethlehem Steel, Sparrows Point, Md.

| | In serv. | Chartered | To |
|---|---|---|---|
| OVERSEAS ALICE | 1-68 | 8-82 | 2-91 |
| OVERSEAS VALDEZ (ex-*Overseas Audrey*) | 1-68 | 8-82 | 2-91 |
| OVERSEAS VIVIAN | 1-69 | 8-82 | 2-91 |

**Overseas Vivian** L. & L. Van Ginderen, 1983

**D:** 46,273 tons (fl) **S:** 16.25 kts **Dim:** 201.23 (192.03 pp) × 27.49 × 11.17
**M:** 2 sets G.E. GT; 1 prop; 15,000 hp **Boilers:** 2 . . .
**Electric:** 1,200 kw **Fuel:** 2,845 tons **Range:** 13,000/16
**Man:** 9 officers, 16 unlicensed

REMARKS: 20,879 grt/38,421 dwt. Cargo: 336,000 bbl. Have 25 cargo tanks. Chartered from Overseas Tankships Corporation and operated by Maritime Overseas Corp. Charter rerenewed for 54 months, 8-87. All used as prepositioning ships at Diego Garcia.

◆ **1 coastal tanker** Bldr: Fosen Mek. Verksteder, Fevag, Norway

BRAVADO (In serv. 1-77)

**D:** 4,430 tons (fl) **S:** 12.5 kts **Dim:** 92.7 × 14.6 × 6.7
**M:** 1 diesel; 1 prop; 2,800 hp **Range:** 6,000/12 **Fuel:** 250 tons
**Man:** 7 officers, 4 unlicensed

REMARKS: 2,110 grt/4,330 dwt. Cargo: 28,000 bbl. Chartered from Sealift, Inc., and operated by Ocean Carriers in the Western Pacific in place of three MSC-owned T-AOG since 1984. Also on charter for the same purpose in the Pacific area are the combination articulated tug/barges *Susan Hannah* (ex-*Kings Challenger*), *Barge Hanna 4002,* and *Seneca/Barge 255.*

NOTE: Tankers *Knight* and *Texas Trader* went off charter in 1986. The Military Sealift Command also spot-charters tankers and colliers for Department of Defense cargo and in support of the Strategic Petroleum Reserve. In 12-87, one bulk carrier, *Star of Texas,* was on charter. Tankers on voyage charter included U.S.-flag ships *Mormacsun, Texaco California,* and *Solar* and foreign-flag ships *Texaco Oslo, United Peace, Seki Oak,* and *Spica.* Strategic Petroleum Reserve voyage charters included U.S.-flag ships *Chesapeake Trader* and *Potomac Trader* and foreign-flag tankers *Jaguar* and *Houston Accord.* Needless to say, this list changes constantly.

## READY RESERVE FORCE

The Ready Reserve Force (RRF) is a group of vessels maintained within the National Defense Reserve Fleet (NDRF) by the Maritime Administration (MARAD) in 5- 10- or 20-day readiness status. RRF ships are activated by a Navy (Military Sealift Command) request to MARAD. Selected ships are exercised periodically. Acquisition and maintenance of the RRF ships are funded by the Navy, which retains ownership of former naval units included in the fleet. As of 1-1-88 there were 90 ships in the RRF, most of them maintained at NDRF anchorages at Beaumont, Texas, Suisun Bay, California, and in the James River, Virginia; another 16 ships were in preparation for RRF entry during 1988. In addition to these ships, there are approximately 130 units in the NDRF that could be activated given longer notice. The RRF is scheduled to grow to 120 ships by 1992.

Before inclusion in the Ready Reserve Fleet, ships are upgraded as to their navigation, safety, and communications systems (including provision of a MARISAT SATCOMM facility) and repainted gray, with red, white, and blue stack striping. Certain sealift enhancement features, as specified by the Military Sealift Command, are added during the overhauls or during later maintenance overhauls; these include such items as provision to carry "Seashed" or "Flatrack" large-capacity

**READY RESERVE FORCE** *(continued)*

containers, helicopter decks, refueling-at-sea gear, and extra tie-downs. This increasingly large fleet is intended to compensate for the decline of the U.S.-flag merchant marine as a wartime strategic sealift asset; how to crew the RRF ships and the increasing age of the ships, however, has not been fully addressed. The RRF was created in 1976. All funding for the RRF to transfer to MARAD under FY 89.

## TROOPSHIP

◆ **1 Maritime Administration S5-S-MA49C type**

| | Bldr | Laid down | L | In serv. | In RRF |
|---|---|---|---|---|---|
| PATRIOT STATE (ex-*Santa Mercedes*) | Bethlehem SY, Sparrows Pt. | 29-10-62 | 30-7-63 | 7-4-64 | 4-3-86 |

**Patriot State** L. & L. Van Ginderen, 6-86

**D:** approx. 20,500 tons (fl) **S:** 20 kts **Dim:** 166.12 (155.00 pp) × 24.13 × 8.87
**Electron Equipt:** Radar: 2/Raytheon nav. **Man:** 11 officers, 22 unlicensed
**M:** 2 sets G.E. GT; 2 props; 19,800 hp **Boilers:** 2/. . . **Range:** 7,000/20
**Fuel:** 2,120 tons **Electric:** 2,250 (3 × 750-kw turbogenerators)

REMARKS: 11,188 grt/9,376 dwt. Former passenger/cargo liner employed by Massachusetts Maritime Academy as training ship. *Patriot State* is fully active and, when not on training cruises, is at her home port of Buzzard's Bay. Can carry 175 20-ft containers and up to 598 passengers (normally 121 cadets). Has 5 holds, 13 hatches. 4 × 20-ton, 2 × 6-ton, and 2 × 5-ton cargo derricks.

## ROLL-ON/ROLL-OFF CARGO SHIPS

◆ **3 former Barber Line Ro/Ro vehicle cargo ships**

| | Bldr | In serv. | In RRF |
|---|---|---|---|
| CAPE HENRY (ex-*Barber Priam*) | Mitsubishi, Nagasaki | 1979 | 1987 |
| CAPE HORN (ex-*Barber Tonsberg*) | Kaldenes M/V A/S, Tonsberg | 1979 | 10-12-86 |
| CAPE HUDSON (ex-*Barber Tiaf*) | Tangen Vaerft, Kragero | 1979 | 30-10-86 |

**Cape Henry** L. & L. Van Ginderen, 10-86

**D:** approx. 47,200 tons (fl) **S:** 21 kts **Dim:** 228.50 (211.50 pp) × 32.26 × 10.80
**M:** 1 Mitsubishi-Sulzer diesel; 1 prop; 30,150 hp **Range:** 25,000/21
**Fuel:** 4,154 tons **Man:** 9 officers, 18 unlicensed

REMARKS: Vary slightly in design: *Cape Henry* is 21,747 grt, *Cape Horn* 22,090, and *Cape Hudson* is 21,976 grt. All purchased 1-6-86 and overhauled at Norfolk SB & DD before entering RRF. *Cape Horn* is at San Francisco, other two in the James River. Data above are for *Cape Henry;* others have 1 Burmeister & Wain diesel; 30,700 hp. All have 1 40-ton crane; can also carry 1,607 to 1,629 20-ft containers.

◆ **3 Maritime Administration C7-S-95a type** Bldr: Bath Iron Works, Bath, Me.

| | L | In serv. | In RRF |
|---|---|---|---|
| CAPE INSCRIPTION (ex-*Tyson Lykes,* ex-*Maine*) | 24-5-75 | 27-5-76 | 5-86 |
| CAPE ISABEL (ex-*Charles Lykes,* ex-*Nevada*) | 15-5-76 | 1977 | 23-5-86 |
| JUPITER (ex-T-AKR 11, ex-*Lipscomb Lykes,* ex-*Arizona*) | 1-11-75 | 14-5-76 | 2-5-86 |

**D:** 14,222 tons light (33,765 fl) **S:** 23 kts
**Dim:** 208.71 (195.07 pp) × 31.09 × 9.78
**M:** 2 sets G.E. GT; 2 props; 37,000 hp **Electric:** 4,000 kw
**Boilers:** 2 Babcock & Wilcox; 77.5 kg/cm$^2$ **Fuel:** 3,394 tons
**Range:** 10,000/23 **Man:** 12 officers, 24 unlicensed

**Jupiter** M.S.C., 1982

REMARKS: 13,156 grt/19,172 dwt. Can carry containers as well as vehicles and 728 tons liquid. Cargo capacity is 56,640 m$^3$ bale, with 16,258 m$^2$ vehicle cargo space. Two side doors, plus 7.3-m-wide by 24.4-m-long stern ramp. Sister *Mercury* (T-AKR 10) remains active in MSC service. *Cape Isabel* at Portland, Oregon; *Cape Inscription* at New Orleans; *Jupiter* at Tacoma, Wash.

◆ **5 former Barber Line Ro-Ro vehicle cargo ships**

| | Bldr | In serv. | In RRF |
|---|---|---|---|
| CAPE DECISION (ex-*Tombarra*) | Eriksberg M/V, Lindholmen, Sweden | 30-8-73 | 15-10-85 |
| CAPE DIAMOND (ex-*Tricolor*) | Ch. de France, Dunkerque | 9-72 | 15-10-85 |
| CAPE DOMINGO (ex-*Tarago*) | Ch. de France, Dunkerque | 1-73 | 30-10-85 |
| CAPE DOUGLAS (ex-*Lalandia*) | Eriksberg M/V, Lindholmen, Sweden | 22-2-73 | 15-11-85 |
| CAPE DUCATO (ex-*Barranduna*) | Eriksberg M/V, Lindholmen, Sweden | 9-72 | 5-12-85 |

**Cape Douglas**—activated for exercise G. Davies, Maritime Photographic, 8-87

**Cape Domingo** G. Arra, 7-86

**D:** 35,173 tons (fl) **S:** 22 kts **Dim:** 207.40 (193.24 pp) × 29.57 × 9.59
**Electron Equipt:** 2/Raytheon nav. **Man:** 9 officers, 18 unlicensed
**M:** French-built: 3 Ch. d'Atlantique-Pielstick diesels; 1 CP prop; 28,890 hp
Swedish-built: 3 Lindholmen-Pielstick 18 PC2V diesels; 1 CP prop; 27,000 hp (22,860 sust.)—1,500-hp bow-thruster, 1,000-hp stern-thruster in all
**Range:** 26,000/20.6 **Fuel:** 3,529–3,658 tons heavy oil, 240 diesel
**Electric:** 6,384 kw (2 × 2,200-kw, 2 × 992-kw diesel sets)

REMARKS: Tonnages vary: 23,972–24,437 grt/21,299–21,398 dwt. Five-deck vehicle cargo ships purchased 1-85 and "reflagged" (safety features brought into line with U.S. Coast Guard standards) by Bethlehem SY, Sparrows Point, Maryland. Have 65-ton-capacity stern ramp. Can carry 1,327 20-ft containers and have 52,863 m$^3$ bale capacity internal, including 1,784 m$^3$ refrigerated. Stored at Baltimore, Md., New York City, James River, and Suisun Bay.

◆ **1 (+1) former Great Lakes newsprint/vehicle carriers** Bldr: Port Weller Dry Dock, St. Catharines, Ontario

| | In serv. | In RRF |
|---|---|---|
| CAPE LAMBERT (ex-*Federal Lakes,* ex-*Avon Forest*) | 1973 | 7-12-87 |
| CAPE LOBOS (ex-*Federal Seaway,* ex-. . .) | 1972 | 14-3-88 |

**ROLL-ON/ROLL-OFF CARGO SHIPS** *(continued)*

**D:** . . . **S:** 19 kts **Dim:** 207.88 (189.44 pp) × 22.92 × 9.30
**M:** 2 Crossley-Pielstick 18-cyl. diesels; 2 props; 18,000 hp
**Range:** 6,000/17.5 **Fuel:** 1,207 tons heavy oil, 217 tons diesel
**Electric:** 2,700 kw (3 × 900-kw diesel sets) **Man:** 10 officers, 17 unlicensed

Remarks: 15,005 grt/16,382 dwt. Ice-strengthened hull with side doors and two vehicle ramps. Cargo capacity 35,428 $m^3$ bale, 17,094 $m^2$ vehicle parking. Purchased 5-6-87 for $14.5 million each from Fed Nav (U.S.A.), but permission to retain *Cape Lobos* in commercial service into 1988 later granted. Both assigned to James River on 5-day readiness.

◆ **1 commercial roll-on/roll-off vehicle cargo ship** Bldr: Eriksberg M/V, Lindholmen, Sweden

| | In serv. | In RRF |
|---|---|---|
| Cape Edmont (ex-*Parralla*) | 1972 | 10-4-87 |

**D:** approx. 32,000 tons (fl) **S:** 19 kts **Dim:** 199.00 (183.70 pp) × 28.65 × 9.40
**M:** 3 diesels; 1 prop; 25,920 hp
**Range:** 17,000/19 **Fuel:** 3,369 tons **Man:** 32 tot.

Remarks: 13,355 grt/20,224 dwt. Stored at Portland, Oregon. Has 1 stern ramp, container capacity: 309 TEU above decks, 903 below; 10,649 $m^2$ vehicle space.

◆ **1 Admiral Wm. M. Callaghan class** Bldr: Sun SB & DD Co., Chester, Pa.

| | L | In serv. | In RRF |
|---|---|---|---|
| Admiral Wm. M. Callaghan | 17-10-67 | 12-67 | 31-5-87 |

**Adm Wm. M. Callaghan** L. & L. Van Ginderen, 1-86

**D:** 26,573 tons (fl) **S:** 26 kts **Dim:** 211.61 (193.12 pp) × 28.00 × 8.86
**Electron Equipt:** Radar: 1/navigational
**M:** 2 G.E. LM-2500 gas turbines; 2 props; 40,000 hp **Electric:** 1,500 kw
**Fuel:** 4,421 tons **Range:** 6,000/25 **Man:** 10 officers, 18 unlicensed

Remarks: 24,471 grt/13,500 dwt. Built for U.S. Navy service, as the earliest example of the current "Build-and-Charter" concept; owned by Sunexport Holdings. Original Pratt & Whitney FT-4 gas turbines replaced 12-77 by LM-2500 engines; used as trials ship for LM-2500 engine life extension and fuel economy improvements. Has stern ramp and four side-loading ports for up to 750 vehicles, on 15,607 $m^2$ of parking area. Unusual for a "Ro/Ro" in having full set of cargo booms: 2 of 120 tons capacity and 12 of 5–10 tons; flush hatches permit access to 38,515 $m^3$ of cargo space. To Ready Reserve Force 31-5-87, at expiration of nearly 20 years on Navy charter. Stored at James River, Va.

◆ **1 Meteor class (C4-ST-67a type)** Bldr: Puget Sound Bridge & DD

| | Laid down | L | In serv. | In RRF |
|---|---|---|---|---|
| Meteor (T-AKR 9, ex-*Sea Lift,* ex-LSV 9) | 19-5-64 | 18-4-64 | 25-5-67 | 31-10-85 |

**Meteor** L. & L. Van Ginderen, 1984

**D:** 9,154 tons light (21,480 fl) **S:** 22 kts **Dim:** 164.7 × 25.5 × 8.8
**Electron Equipt:** Radar: 1/Raytheon TM 1650/6X, 1/Raytheon TM 1660/12S
**M:** 1 set GT; 2 props; 19,400 hp **Boilers:** 2; 52.8 kg/$cm^2$, 471°C
**Range:** 10,000/20 **Man:** 56 tot. MSC

Remarks: 16,467 grt/12,326 dwt. Cargo: 10,200 tons: 26,819 $m^3$ vehicle parking volume (7,896 $m^2$ deck space). Stern and four side ramps for Ro/Ro loading/unloading. Can carry 12 passengers. Authorized as T-AK 278, completed as T-LSV 9, retyped T-AKR 14-8-69. Renamed 12-9-75. Assigned to Rapid Deployment Force 4-80–6-81. Placed in Ready Reserve Force 30-10-85, at San Pedro, Cal.

◆ **1 Maritime Administration C3-ST-14A type**

| | Bldr | Laid down | L | In serv. |
|---|---|---|---|---|
| Comet (T-AKR 7) | Sun SB & DD, Chester, Pa. | 15-5-56 | 31-7-57 | 27-1-58 |

**Comet (T-AKR 7)** L. & L. Van Ginderen, 9-82

**D:** 8,175 tons light (18,286 fl) **S:** 18 kts **Dim:** 152.1 × 23.8 × 8.9
**Electron Equipt:** Radar: 1/Raytheon TM 1650/6X, 1/Raytheon TM 1660/12S
**M:** 1 set G.E. GT; 1 props; 13,200 hp **Fuel:** 2,423 tons **Range:** 12,000/18
**Boilers:** 2 Babcock & Wilcox; 43.3 kg/$cm^2$, 454°C
**Man:** 11 officers, 33 unlicensed

Remarks: 13,792 grt/10,111 dwt. Cargo: 7,350 tons: more than 700 military vehicles in holds totaling 19,370 $m^3$ volume (7,525 $m^2$ deck space). Side and stern ramps. Denny-Brown fin stabilizers. Authorized as T-AK 269, changed to T-LSV 7 on 1-6-63, then to T-AKR 7 on 1-1-69. Remains Navy property; placed in the Maritime Administration RRF in 15-3-85, having been out of service since 22-4-84. Stored at Portland, Oregon.

## AIRCRAFT MAINTENANCE SHIPS

◆ **2 converted Maritime Administration C5-S-78a, "Seabridge" type**
Bldr: Ingalls SB, Pascagoula, Miss.

| | In serv. | Converted |
|---|---|---|
| T-AVB 3 Wright (ex-*Young America,* ex-*Mormacsun*) | 1970 | 14-12-84 to 14-5-86 |
| T-AVB 4 Curtiss (ex-*Great Republic,* ex-*Mormacsky*) | 1969 | 17-12-85 to 18-8-87 |

**Wright (T-AVB 3)** U.S. Navy, 5-86

**Curtiss (T-AVB 4)** U.S. Navy, 8-87

**AIRCRAFT MAINTENANCE SHIPS** *(continued)*

**D:** 12,409 tons light (27,580 fl) **S:** 23.6 kts
**Dim:** 183.49 (170.69 pp) × 27.43 × 10.36 **Electron Equipt:** 2/. . . nav.
**M:** 2 sets G.E. GT; 1 prop; 30,000 hp **Boilers:** 2 Combustion Engineering
**Electric:** 3,000 kw (2 × 1,500 kw) **Range:** 9,000/23
**Fuel:** 2,781 tons + 839 tons diesel **Man:** 11 off., 22 unlicensed + 300 Marines

REMARKS: 23,255 grt/13,651 dwt. Roll-on/Roll-off vehicle cargo and container carriers converted by Todd SY, Galveston, Texas, to transport the men and equipment vans of a Marine Intermediate Maintenance Activity in support of aircraft deployed ashore. Additional accommodations built on aft and helicopter deck added over former forward hold. Still able to carry 664 standard 20-ft containers and 14,000 bbl liquid cargo. Intended to revert to cargo-carrying role after delivering the aviation support personnel and equipment. Maintained in the RRF (but not strictly part of it), being broken out for exercises. T-AVB 3 at Philadelphia, T-AVB 4 at . . . . Cargo capacity: 34,903 $m^3$ grain/31,824 $m^3$ bale, including 170-$m^3$ refrigerated. Can carry 332 40-ft containers or 654 20-ft containers, 352 vehicles. Has stern ramp and two side doors aft for vehicles. Ten 30-ton, one 70-ton cargo derricks. Six holds, but forward two can only be unloaded by off-ship cranes.

**AUXILIARY CRANE SHIPS (T-ACS)**

◆ **0 (+2) converted Maritime Administration C6-S-60b type** Bldr: Ingalls SB, Pascagoula, Miss.

| | Laid down | L | In serv. | In RRF |
|---|---|---|---|---|
| T-ACS 9 N . . . (ex-*American Altair*, ex-*Mormacaltair*) | 2-12-63 | 20-8-64 | 23-6-65 | 15-9-89 |
| T-ACS 10 N . . . (ex-*American Draco*, ex-*Mormacdraco*) | 19-4-64 | 14-1-65 | 28-5-65 | 15-11-89 |

**D:** 16,600 tons light **S:** 21 kts **Dim:** 202.98 (193.55 pp) × 22.92 × 9.63
**M:** 2 sets G.E. GT; 1 prop; 19,000 hp **Boilers:** 2; . . .
**Range:** 17,000/20 **Fuel:** 4,083 tons **Electric:** 1,500 kw **Man:** . . .

REMARKS: 14,001-grt/12,763-dwt containerships prior to conversion; could carry 649 20-ft containers. Will resemble *Keystone State* as crane ships, with three pair 30-ton capacity, 36.9-m-reach electrohydraulic cranes mounted to starboard. Conversion authorized FY 88; conversion contract to be let circa 9-88.

◆ **0 (+2) converted Maritime Administration C6-S-1qc type** Bldr: Todd SY, San Pedro, Cal.

| | Laid down | L | In serv. | In RRF |
|---|---|---|---|---|
| T-ACS 7 DIAMOND STATE (ex-*President Truman*, ex-*Japan Mail*) | 22-11-60 | 8-8-61 | 14-4-62 | 15-11-88 |
| T-ACS 8 EQUALITY STATE (ex-*American Builder*, ex-*Philippine Mail*, ex-*Santa Rosa*, ex-*President Roosevelt*, ex-*Washington Mail*) | 12-5-61 | 6-1-62 | 25-7-62 | 15-2-89 |

**D:** 16,600 tons light **S:** 20 kts **Dim:** 203.61 (192.95 pp) × 23.22 × 10.16
**Electron Equipt:** Radar: 2/ . . . nav. **M:** 2 sets G.E. GT; 1 prop; 22,000 hp
**Boilers:** 2; . . . **Range:** 14,000/20 **Fuel:** 3,124 tons
**Electric:** 2,275 kw **Man:** . . .

REMARKS: 16,518 grt/19,871 dwt prior to conversion under FY 86, which was contracted with American SB, Tampa, Florida, 14-9-87 to commence 1-88. Will resemble *Keystone State* on completion, with three pair 30-ton, 36.9-m-reach electrohydraulic cranes mounted to starboard. Were containerships with 625 20-ft container capacity prior to conversion. Planned conversion of sister *American Banker* (ex-*Santa Paula*, ex-*President Eisenhower*) and one other ship under FY 89 as T-ACS 11 and 12 canceled 11-87.

◆ **1 (+2) converted Maritime Administration C5-S-73b type** Bldr: Bath Iron Works, Bath, Maine

| | In serv. | Converted |
|---|---|---|
| T-ACS 4 GOPHER STATE (ex-*Export Leader*) | 1969 | 21-10-86 to 24-10-87 |
| T-ACS 5 FLICKERTAIL STATE (ex-*Lightning*) | 1970 | 18-12-86 to 15-2-88 |
| T-ACS 6 CORNHUSKER STATE (ex-*Staghound*) | 1969 | 3-87 to 16-3-88 |

**D:** 15,060 tons light (25,000 fl) **S:** 20 kts (sust.)
**Dim:** 185.93 (177.35) × 27.77 × 9.14
**Electron Equipt:** Radar: 2/. . . nav.
**M:** 2 sets GT; 1 prop; 17,500 hp **Boilers:** 2, . . .
**Range:** 9,340/20 **Fuel:** 3,450 tons **Electric:** . . .
**Man:** . . .

REMARKS: 17,902 grt as built. T-ACS 3 had been used in ARAPAHO portable helicopter facility trials 20-9-82 to 27-10-82. All three acquired 11-8-86 from MARAD for conversion. Two pair 30-ton capacity/36.9-m-reach electrohydraulic cranes mounted on starboard side. Additional generators placed in former after hold. Equipped to stow sea shed and standard cargo containers. Can carry 3 LCM (8) landing craft and 2 side-loading warping tugs (self-propelled pontoons) and pontoon sections on deck. Bow-thruster added. Converted by Norshipco, Norfolk. T-ACS 3 at Cheatham Annex, Va., for training.

**Gopher State (T-ACS 4)** U.S. Navy, 10-87

**Gopher State (T-ACS 4)** U.S. Navy, 10-87

◆ **3 Maritime Administration C6-S-1qd class** Bldr: National Steel, San Diego, Cal.

| | L | In serv. | Conversion to T-ACS |
|---|---|---|---|
| T-ACS 1 KEYSTONE STATE (ex-*President Harrison*) | 2-10-65 | 1-66 | 21-3-83 to 7-5-84 |
| T-ACS 2 GEM STATE (ex-*President Monroe*) | 22-5-65 | 1965 | 26-9-84 to 31-10-85 |
| T-ACS 3 GRAND CANYON STATE (ex-*President Polk*) | 23-1-65 | 1966 | 28-10-85 to 27-10-87 |

**Keystone State (T-ACS 1)** M.S.C., 6-84

**D:** 28,660 tons (fl) **S:** 20 kts **Dim:** 203.82 (192.95 pp) × 23.22 × 10.06
**Electron Equipt:** Radar: 2/. . . nav. **Electric:** 4,780 kw
**M:** 2 sets G.E. GT; 1 prop; 19,250 hp **Boilers:** 2; . . .
**Range:** 13,000/20 **Fuel:** 3,450 tons **Man:** 14 officers, 50 unlicensed

REMARKS: 17,128 grt/13,600 dwt. Cargo: 303 20-ft containers. "T-ACS" is an authorization number and not an official U.S. Navy hull number designation. Conversion of T-ACS 1 by Bay SB, Sturgeon Bay, Wisc., took place under FY 83 funding; ordered 18-3-83. T-ACS 2 (FY 84) converted by Continental Marine, San Francisco. T-ACS 3 under FY 85 converted by Dillingham, San Francisco. All in Ready Reserve Force, T-ACS 1 in James River, T-ACS 2 at Tacoma, Wash., and T-ACS 3 at Portland, Oregon.

The original cargo-handling gear was replaced by three sets of twin 30-ton cranes mounted on the starboard side. The T-ACS is expected to unload its own container cargo and then unload containers from non-self-sustaining container carriers at the rate of about 300 containers per day; the cranes have a 33-m reach.

AUXILIARY CRANE SHIPS (T-ACS) *(continued)*

Additional generator capacity (3,280 kw) was added. In wartime, or during peacetime exercises, the ships will operate under MSC control, with contractor crews.

## CARGO BARGE CARRIERS

◆ **3 "Sea Bee"-type, Maritime Administration C8-S-82 type** Bldr: General Dynamics, Quincy, Mass.

| | In serv. | In RRF |
|---|---|---|
| CAPE MAY (ex-*Almeria Lykes*) | 1972 | 21-7-86 |
| CAPE MENDOCINO (ex-*Doctor Lykes*) | 1972 | 15-10-86 |
| CAPE MOHICAN (ex-*Tillie Lykes*) | 1973 | 22-8-86 |

**D:** 18,880 tons light (57,290 fl) **S:** 20 kts
**Dim:** 266.39 (219.92 pp) × 32.31 × 11.93
**Electron Equipt:** Radar: 2/. . . nav. **Man:** 12 officers, 26 unlicensed
**M:** 2 sets G.E. GT; 1 prop; 36,000 hp **Boilers:** 2; . . .
**Range:** 16,000/20 **Fuel:** 6,346–6,448 tons
**Electric:** 4,000 kw (2 × 2,000-kw turbogenerators)

REMARKS: 21,667 grt/38,410 dwt. All purchased 1-86 and stored at New Orleans after refits for RRF service. "Sea-Bee" design intended to carry 38 cargo barges totaling 41,476 m³ bale capacity and placed in the water via a 2,000-ton-capacity elevator at the stern. Can also accommodate 4,000 bbl (*Cape Mohican:* 11,000 bbl) liquid cargo and 797 tons water. Have 797-ton-capacity passive anti-rolling tanks.

◆ **2 (+2) Maritime Administration C9-S-81d type** Bldr: Avondale SY, Westwego, La.

| | In serv. | In RRF |
|---|---|---|
| CAPE FAREWELL (ex-*Delta Mar*) | 1973 | 2-4-87 |
| CAPE FLATTERY (ex-*Delta Norte*) | 1973 | 5-6-87 |
| CAPE . . . . . . (ex-*Edward Rutledge*) | . . . | . . . |
| CAPE . . . . . . (ex-*Benjamin Harrison*) | . . . | . . . |

**D:** 63,314 tons (fl) **S:** 22 kts **Dim:** 272.30 (243.03) × 30.56 × 12.44
**Electron Equipt:** Radar: 2/. . . nav.
**M:** 2 sets de Laval GT; 1 prop; 32,000 hp **Fuel:** 6,016 tons
**Boilers:** 2 Combustion Engineering; 75.7 kg/cm²
**Range:** 15,000/22 **Electric:** 4,000 kw (2 × 2,000-kw turbogenerators)
**Man:** 12 officers, 20 unlicensed

REMARKS: 29,508 grt/41,363 dwt. First two purchased 1-86, along with *Delta Sud,* which was to have become *Cape Fear* but suffered severe machinery damage during RRF overhaul and will probably be scrapped. Have 510-ton traveling crane to handle 85 cargo lighters and 72 20-ft containers, 74 lighters and 288 20-ft containers, or 1,728 20-ft containers alone. Also have one 30-ton crane and one 5-ton crane. Second pair acquired by MARAD 1987 for later upgrading for RRF but are currently in the National Defense Reserve Fleet at Beaumont, Texas. *Cape Farewell* and *Cape Flattery* are stored at Mobile, Ala. For appearance, see sisters listed under Military Sealift Command section.

◆ **2 Maritime Administration C8-S-81b-type lighter carriers** Bldr: Avondale SY, Westwego, La.

| | In serv. | In RRF |
|---|---|---|
| AUSTRAL LIGHTNING (ex-*Lash España*) | 4-71 | 30-9-85 |
| CAPE FLORIDA (ex-*Delta Caribe,* ex-*Lash Turkey*) | 1971 | 13-2-87 |

**Austral Lightning** F. Jentsch, 8-87

**D:** 44,606 tons (fl) **S:** 22.5 kts **Dim:** 249.94 (220.68 pp) × 30.48 × 10.70
**M:** 1 set de Laval GT; 1 prop; 32,000 hp **Boilers:** 2 Babcock & Wilcox
**Electric:** 4,500 kw **Fuel:** 5,500 tons (10,427 max.) **Range:** 13,000/22.5
**Man:** 12 officers, 20 unlicensed

REMARKS: *Austral Lightning:* 26,456 grt/29,820 dwt. *Cape Florida:* 26,406 grt/29,820 dwt. LASH-ships, converted from cargo barge-only carriers to container or barge carriers. Can carry up to 71 cargo barges or 840 standard cargo containers, handled by a 30-ton traveling crane. The traveling barge crane can lift 446 tons. Also have two 5-ton cranes. *Austral Lightning* formerly chartered for the Near-Term Prepositioning Force, until 1-4-85. *Cape Florida* stored at Mobile, Ala.; *Austral Lightning* at San Francisco.

## GENERAL CARGO SHIPS

◆ **1 Maritime Administration C5-78 combination cargo ship** Bldr: Ingalls SY, Pascagoula, Miss.

| | In serv. | In RRF |
|---|---|---|
| CAPE NOME (ex-*Rapid,* ex-*American Rapid,* ex-*Red Jacket,* ex-*Mormacstar*) | 9-69 | 9-12-87 |

**Cape Nome (as Rapid)** L. & L. Van Ginderen, 9-85

**D:** 27,980 tons (fl) **S:** 23.6 kts **Dim:** 183.33 (170.69 pp) × 27.43 × 10.39
**Electron Equipt:** Radar: 2/. . . navigational
**M:** 2 sets G.E. GT; 1 prop; 30,000 hp **Man:** 11 officers, 23 unlicensed
**Boilers:** 2 Combustion Engineering; 74 kg/cm²
**Range:** 12,000/23.6 **Fuel:** 2,790 tons **Electric:** 3,000 kw

REMARKS: 11,757 grt/15,964 dwt. Cargo: 70 20-ft containers, plus 33,814 m³ dry cargo volume. Stern door for vehicle cargo, seven cargo holds. Off-charter to MSC from Central Gulf Lines 12-85; to MARAD 6-87. Sister *Rover* is on charter to MSC.

◆ **0 (+3) Maritime Administration C5-S-75a type** Bldr: Newport News SB & DD (In serv. 1968)

| | In RRF |
|---|---|
| CAPE GREIG (ex-*President Taylor,* ex-*Korean Mail*) | 15-3-88 |
| CAPE GIBSON (ex-*President Jackson,* ex-*Indian Mail*) | 15-3-88 |
| CAPE GIRARDEAU (ex-*President Adams,* ex-*Alaskan Mail*) | 15-3-88 |

**D:** . . . **S:** 21 kts **Dim:** 184.41 (177.55 pp) × 25.05 × 9.50 (10.68 max.)
**Electron Equipt:** Radar: 2/. . . nav.
**M:** 2 sets G.E. GT; 1 prop; 24,000 hp—bow-thruster
**Boilers:** 2; . . . **Fuel:** 3,702 tons **Man:** 47 tot.
**Range:** 14,000/20.8 **Electric:** 2,500 kw (2 × 1,250 kw)

REMARKS: 15,949 grt/22,208 (*Cape Gibson:* 22,216; *Cape Girardeau:* 22,273) dwt. Self-sustaining container/break-bulk ships with six holds. Cargo: 409 20-ft containers/28,830 m³ bale dry cargo (623 m³ refrigerated), 17,000 bbl liquid, and 22 passengers. Have one 70-ton, twenty 20-ton, and four 15-ton-capacity cargo derricks. Purchased from American President Lines 5-6-87 for $5M each. To be stored at Suisun Bay.

◆ **0 (+2) Maritime Administration C4-S-64a type** Bldr: Sun Ship, Chester, Pa.

| | Laid down | L | In serv. | In RRF |
|---|---|---|---|---|
| CAPE GASPÉ (ex-*American Moon,* ex-*Mormacmoon,* ex-*Austral Pilot,* ex-*American Rover*) | 15-5-63 | 7-7-64 | 15-1-65 | . . . |
| CAPE GEORGIA (ex-*Mormacdawn,* ex-*Austral Patriot,* ex-*American Resolute*) | 3-6-64 | 15-4-65 | 16-9-65 | . . . |

**D:** . . . **S:** 21 kts **Dim:** 165.82 (154.90) × 22.92 × 9.74
**M:** 2 sets G.E. GT; 1 prop; 18,750 hp **Boilers:** 2; . . .
**Range:** . . . **Fuel:** 3,479 tons **Electric:** 2,500 kw **Man:** 12 off., 26 unlic.

REMARKS: 7,509 grt/11,202 (13,477 max.) dwt. Six cargo holds capable of transporting up to 119 20-ft containers. Have one 40-ton, fourteen 15-ton, six 10-ton, and two 5-ton cargo derricks. Selected 1986 for upgrading from National Defense Reserve Fleet but not funded under FY 87.

◆ **0 (+2 + 1) Maritime Administration C4-S-1u type** Bldrs: A: National Steel, San Diego; B: Newport News SB & DD

| | Bldr: | Laid down | L | In serv. | In RRF |
|---|---|---|---|---|---|
| CAPE JOHNSON (ex-*Mormacsaga,* ex-*M.M. Dant*) | A | 17-8-61 | 5-5-62 | 26-11-62 | 25-2-88 |
| CAPE JUBY (ex-*Mormacsea,* ex-*Hawaii*) | B | 31-7-61 | 9-2-62 | 16-8-62 | 29-2-88 |
| CAPE JUNCTION (ex-*Mormactide,* ex-*Oregon*) | B | 1-3-61 | 16-9-61 | 19-4-62 | . . . |

**D:** . . . **S:** 20 kts **Dim:** 172.22 (161.09 pp) × 23.22 × 9.63
**M:** 2 sets G.E. GT; 1 prop; 17,500 hp **Boilers:** 2; . . .
**Range:** . . . **Fuel:** 3,538 tons **Electric:** 1,500 kw **Man:** 14 off., 30 unlic.

REMARKS: 9,298 grt/12,691 dwt. Selected 1986 from ships turned in to the Maritime Administration and stored in the NDRF. Six holds. Can carry up to 200 20-ft containers. Have one 60-ton, ten 20-ton, two 10-ton, and ten 5-ton cargo derricks. First two refitted for RRF service under FY 87 for storage in the James River. The other two had not been funded as of 1-88.

◆ **3 Maritime Administration C3-S-76a type** Bldr: Ingalls SB, Pascagoula, Miss. (In serv. 1968)

DEL MONTE (ex-*Delta Brazil*) DEL VALLE (ex-*Delta Uruguay*)
DEL VIENTO (ex-*Delta Mexico*)

GENERAL CARGO SHIPS *(continued)*

**D:** 19,285 tons (fl) **S:** 18.6 kts **Dim:** 159.1 × 21.3 × 9.4
**M:** 2 sets G.E. GT; 1 prop; 11,700 hp **Boilers:** 2 Babcock & Wilcox
**Range:** 15,000/18.6 **Fuel:** 2,175 tons **Man:** 9 officers, 18 unlicensed

REMARKS: 10,396 grt/13,039 dwt. Cargo: 17,077 m³ bale dry cargo, 1,246 m³ refrigerated cargo, 11,000 bbl liquid. Six holds. One 75-ton boom, . . . smaller. All laid up at Beaumont, Texas.

◆ **6 Maritime Administration C4-S-65a class** Bldr: Sun SB & DD, Chester, Pa.

| | In serv. |
|---|---|
| SANTA BARBARA (ex-*Delta Bolivia,* ex-*Santa Barbara*) | 1967 |
| SANTA CLARA (ex-*Delta Colombia,* ex-*Santa Clara*) | 1966 |
| SANTA CRUZ (ex-*Delta Ecuador,* ex-*Santa Cruz*) | 1966 |
| SANTA ELENA (ex-*Delta Panama,* ex-*Santa Elena*) | 1967 |
| SANTA ISABEL (ex-*Delta Peru,* ex-*Santa Isabel*) | 1967 |
| SANTA LUCIA (ex-*Delta Venezuela,* ex-*Santa Lucia*) | 1966 |

**D:** 19,793 tons (fl) **S:** 20 kts **Dim:** 170.7 × 24.7 × 9.1
**M:** 2 sets Westinghouse GT; 1 prop; 14,000 hp **Boilers:** 2 Babcock & Wilcox
**Range:** 12,000/20 **Fuel:** 2,287 tons **Man:** 12 officers, 25–27 unlicensed

REMARKS: 9,322 grt (*S. Cruz, S. Lucia:* 9,313)/12,472–12,693 dwt. Cargo: 20,872 m³ bale dry cargo, plus 7,000 bbl liquid. Can carry 12 passengers. *Santa Isabel* has a 150-ton heavy-lift boom; the others have a 70-ton boom. Seven holds. All laid up in the James River, Virginia.

◆ **5 Maritime Administration C4-S-66a type** Bldr: Avondale SY, Westwego, La.

| | L | In serv. | In RRF |
|---|---|---|---|
| CAPE BLANCO (ex-*Mason Lykes*) | 10-7-65 | 9-66 | 9-7-85 |
| CAPE BON (ex-*Velma Lykes*) | 16-7-65 | 1-67 | 26-6-85 |
| CAPE BORDA (ex-*Howell Lykes*) | 16-4-66 | 1-67 | 25-4-85 |
| CAPE BOVER (ex-*Frederick Lykes*) | 12-2-66 | 1-67 | 1-4-85 |
| CAPE BRETON (ex-*Dolly Turman*) | 4-6-66 | 5-67 | 11-10-85 |

**Cape Blanco (as Mason Lykes)** G. Arra, 6-84

**D:** 21,840 tons (fl) **S:** 20 kts **Dim:** 164.59 (156.94 pp) × 23.16 × 9.96
**Electron Equipt:** Radar: 1/nav. **Electric:** 1,500 kw
**M:** 2 sets de Laval or Westinghouse GT; 1 prop; 15,500 hp
**Boilers:** 2 Foster-Wheeler; 49 km/cm² **Fuel:** 2,753 tons **Range:** 12,000/20
**Man:** 12 officers, 26 unlicensed

REMARKS: 10,723 grt/14,662 dwt. Break-bulk ships purchased from Lykes Brothers Lines for $21,250,000 in 1-85. Cargo: 21,240 m³ bale plus 4,000 bbl liquid. Six hatches; one 80-ton heavy-lift boom, 20 smaller. All stored on West Coast.

◆ **5 Maritime Administration C3-S-37d type** Bldr: Avondale SY, Westwego, La.

| | L | | L |
|---|---|---|---|
| GULF BANKER | 5-10-63 | GULF SHIPPER | 15-2-64 |
| GULF FARMER | 3-8-63 | GULF TRADER | 28-12-63 |
| GULF MERCHANT | 16-5-64 | | |

**Gulf Trader**—while active L. & L. Van Ginderen, . . .

**D:** . . . **S:** 18 kts **Dim:** 150.78 (143.26 pp) × 21.09 × 9.17
**Electron Equipt:** Radar: 2/. . . nav.
**M:** 2 sets Westinghouse (*Banker, Farmer:* G.E.) GT; 1 prop; 11,000 hp
**Boilers:** 2; . . . **Electric:** 1,200 kw (2 × 600-kw turbogenerators)
**Range:** 15,000/18 **Fuel:** 1,978 tons **Man:** 13 officers, 32 unlicensed

REMARKS: First two: 8,970 grt/11,367 dwt; others: 8,988 grt/11,368 dwt. Can carry 41 20-ft containers in addition to dry cargo. Have five holds. One 66-ton, two 15-ton, two 10-ton, and ten 5-ton cargo derricks. Can carry 12 passengers and 6,000 bbl liquid cargo. All stored at Beaumont, Texas.

◆ **5 Maritime Administration C4-S-58a class** Bldr: Ingalls, Pascagoula, Miss.

| | L |
|---|---|
| CAPE ANN (ex-*Meteor,* ex-*African Meteor*) | 12-5-62 |
| CAPE ALEXANDER (ex-*Mercury,* ex-*African Mercury*) | 7-7-62 |
| CAPE ARCHWAY (ex-*Neptune,* ex-*African Neptune*) | 15-9-62 |
| CAPE ALAVA (ex-*Comet,* ex-*African Comet*) | 24-3-62 |
| CAPE AVINOF (ex-*Sun,* ex-*African Sun*) | 8-12-62 |

**Cape Alava** W. Donko, 7-85

**D:** 18,560 tons (fl) **S:** 20 kts **Dim:** 174.35 (164.90 pp) × 22.92 × 9.40
**M:** 2 sets G.E. GT; 1 prop; 18,150 hp **Boilers:** 2; . . . **Range:** 17,000/20
**Fuel:** 3,407 tons **Electric:** 1,800 kw (3 × 600 kw) **Man:** 11 off., 28 unlic.

REMARKS: 11,309 grt/12,932 dwt. Cargo: 19,385 m³ grain/19,022 m³ bale in seven holds. Booms: 1/60-ton, 6/10-ton, 14/5-ton. *Cape Avinoff* and *Cape Ann* received helicopter decks and other sealift enhancement features during overhauls ending 15-3-88 and 27-2-88, respectively. Assigned to Quonset Point, Rhode Island, Jacksonville, Fla., Baltimore, Md., James River, and Quonset Point, respectively, for storage.

◆ **8 Maritime Administration C3-S-37c type** Bldr: Avondale, Westwego, La.

| | L |
|---|---|
| CAPE CANAVERAL (ex-*Allison Lykes*) | 11-5-63 |
| CAPE CANSO (ex-*Aimee Lykes*) | 13-10-62 |
| CAPE CARTHAGE (ex-*Margaret Lykes*) | 9-3-63 |
| CAPE CATOCHE (ex-*Christopher Lykes*) | 22-12-62 |
| CAPE CHALMERS (ex-*Adabelle Lykes*) | 6-12-62 |
| CAPE CHARLES (ex-*Charlotte Lykes*) | 16-5-63 |
| CAPE CLEAR (ex-*Mayo Lykes*) | 14-8-63 |
| CAPE COD (ex-*Sheldon Lykes*) | 11-7-62 |

**Cape Canso** W. Donko, 7-87

GENERAL CARGO SHIPS *(continued)*

**D:** 18,560 tons (fl) **S:** 18.0 kts **Dim:** 150.8 × 21.0 × 9.75
**Electron Equipt:** Radar: 1/. . . nav.
**M:** 2 sets GT; 1 prop; 11,000 hp **Boilers:** 2/. . .
**Range:** 17,000/18 **Fuel:** 2,827 tons **Man:** 11 officers, 23–29 unlicensed

REMARKS: 9,296 grt/12,684 dwt. Cargo: 16,000 m³ dry bale, plus 8,000 bbl liquid. Five cargo holds; 1/60-ton boom, 20 others. Stored at Portland, Me., Norfolk, Va., Melville, R.I., Providence, R.I., and, last four, Beaumont, Texas, respectively.

◆ **3 Maritime Administration C4-S-57a type** Bldr: Bethlehem SY, Quincy, Mass.

| | L |
|---|---|
| PIONEER COMMANDER (ex-*American Commander*) | 20-12-62 |
| PIONEER CONTRACTOR (ex-*American Contractor*) | 22-3-63 |
| PIONEER CRUSADER (ex-*American Crusader*) | 30-7-63 |

**D:** 21,053 tons (fl) **S:** 21.0 kts **Dim:** 171.0 × 22.9 × 9.8
**M:** 2 sets Bethlehem GT; 1 prop; 19,500 hp **Boilers:** 2 Foster-Wheeler
**Range:** 12,000/21 **Fuel:** 2,538 tons **Man:** 13 officers, 30 unlicensed

REMARKS: 11,164 grt/13,535 dwt (varies slightly). Cargo: 18,210 m³ bale dry cargo, 1,246 m³ refrigerated, 8,000 bbl liquid. Six holds. One 70-ton boom, . . . smaller. All stored at Beaumont, Texas.

◆ **1 Maritime Administration C4-S-1u type** Bldr: National Steel, San Diego

SANTA ANA (ex-*C.E. Dant*) (L: 18-8-62)

**D:** 22,629 tons (fl) **S:** 20.0 kts **Dim:** 172.2 × 23.2 × 9.8
**M:** 2 sets GT; 1 prop; 19,200 hp **Boilers:** 2; . . .
**Range:** 14,000/20 **Fuel:** 3,266 tons **Man:** 14 officers, 27 unlicensed

REMARKS: 12,724 grt/14,376 dwt. Cargo: 19,059 m³ bale dry cargo, 1,104 m³ refrigerated, 17,000 bbl liquid; can also carry 12 passengers. Has 6 holds; one 60-ton boom, . . . smaller. Stored at Beaumont, Texas.

◆ **1 Maritime Administration C4-S-1u type** Bldr: Newport News SB & DD

CALIFORNIA (ex-*Santa Rita,* ex-*California*) (L: 28-7-61)

**California** L. & L. Van Ginderen, 5-87

**D:** 22,629 tons (fl) **S:** 20.0 kts **Dim:** 172.2 × 23.2 × 9.8
**M:** 2 sets GT; 1 prop; 19,200 hp **Boilers:** 2 Foster-Wheeler
**Range:** 14,000/20 **Fuel:** 3,266 tons **Man:** 12 officers, 31 unlicensed

REMARKS: 12,693 grt/14,349 dwt. Cargo: 19,059 m³ bale dry cargo; 1,104 m³ refrigerated cargo; 17,000 bbl liquid; 12 passengers. Six holds; 1/60-ton boom; several smaller. Stored at Naval Supply Center, Oakland, Cal.

◆ **3 Maritime Administration C3-S-46a type**

| | Bldr | L |
|---|---|---|
| BANNER (ex-*Export Banner*) | National Steel, San Diego | 17-12-60 |
| BUYER (ex-*Export Buyer*) | National Steel, San Diego | 1960 |
| COURIER (ex-*Export Courier*) | Sun Ship, Chester, Pa. | 5-4-62 |

**Banner** W. Donko, 7-87

**D:** 19,400 tons (fl) **S:** 18.5 kts **Dim:** 150.26 (143.26 pp) × 22.25 × 9.32
**Electron Equipt:** Radar: 2/. . . nav.
**M:** 2 sets G.E. GT; 1 prop; 13,750 hp **Boilers:** 2 Babcock & Wilcox; 53 kg/cm²
**Range:** 13,000/18.5 (*Courier:* 9,000) **Man:** 12 officers, 27 unlicensed
**Fuel:** 3,280 tons (*Courier:* 1,333 tons) **Electric:** 1,400 kw

REMARKS: *Banner:* 10,659 grt/12,629 dwt; *Courier:* 11,000 grt/12,705 dwt; *Buyer:* 10,659 grt/12,529 dwt. Cargo: *Banner:* 18,776 m³ bale dry cargo, 708 m³ refrigerated, 12,000 bbl liquid; *Courier:* 20,277 m³ bale dry cargo; 12,000 bbl liquid. Six holds; one 60-ton boom, 18 smaller, plus 2 cranes. *Courier* altered to carry containers. In James River, Virginia, with non-RRF sisters *Builder* and *Commerce. Buyer,* at Beaumont, Texas, joined RRF 1987.

◆ **6 Maritime Administration C3-S-33a type** Bldr: Sun SB & DD Co., Chester, Pa., and Todd SY, San Pedro, Cal.

| | L | In serv. | In RRF |
|---|---|---|---|
| CAPE CATAWBA (ex-*Cape,* ex-*Mormaccape*) | . . . | 1961 | 1987 |
| LAKE (ex-*Mormaclake*) | 5-1-61 | 1961 | 1985 |
| NORTHERN LIGHT (T-AK 285, ex-*Cove,* ex-*Mormaccove*) | 14-10-60 | 29-6-61 | 22-7-85 |
| PRIDE (ex-*Mormacpride*) | 1-2-60 | 1960 | 1985 |
| SCAN (ex-*Mormacscan*) | 21-3-61 | 1961 | 1985 |
| SOUTHERN CROSS (T-AK 286, ex-*Trade,* ex-*Mormactrade*) | 23-1-62 | 1962 | 30-9-85 |

**Southern Cross (as T-AK 286)** G. Gyssels, 6-83

**Lake (with Scan beyond)** A.D. Baker, 8-84

**D:** 18,365 tons (fl) **S:** 19 kts **Dim:** 148.15 (139.59 pp) × 20.72 × 8.68
**Electron Equipt:** Radar: ex-T-AK: 1/Raytheon TM 1650/6X, 1/Raytheon TM 1650/12S; others: 1/. . . nav.
**M:** 1 set G.E. GT; 1 prop; 12,100 hp (15,700 emergency/11,000 normal)
**Boilers:** 2 Combustion Engineering; 43.3 kg/cm², 457°C
**Fuel:** 2,556 (T-AK: 3,064; *C. Catawba:* 5,461) **Range:** 14,000/18
**Electric:** 1,275 kw **Man:** 11 officers, 30 unlicensed + 12 passengers

REMARKS: 9,260 grt/12,500 dwt. Cargo: 16,992 m³ bale dry cargo and 1,333 m³ refrigerated cargo, 20,000 bbl liquid cargo. Have 5 holds, plus 10 deep tanks for liquids. One 75-ton, 8/10-ton, and 10/5-ton cargo booms. Accommodations for 12 passengers. *Lake* and *Scan,* stored at Philadelphia NSY with *Pride* and *Southern Cross,* were to have been converted into survey ships T-AGS 39 and 40; *Northern Light* was acquired for the U.S. Navy Military Sealift Command 22-4-80 and laid up 22-10-84, while *Southern Cross,* acquired 30-4-80 for MSC and placed out of service on 13-9-84, refitted for the RRF beginning 2-85. *Cape Catawba,* renamed 1987 on joining RRF, is at Beaumont, Texas; *Northern Light* is at Portland, Ore.

◆ **4 Maritime Administration C3-S-38a type** Bldr: National Steel, San Diego (*Adventurer:* New York Ship, Camden, N.J.)

| | L |
|---|---|
| ADVENTURER (ex-*Export Adventurer*) | 9-7-60 |
| AGENT (ex-*Export Agent*) | 30-1-60 |
| AIDE (ex-*Export Aide*) | 4-6-60 |
| AMBASSADOR (ex-*Export Ambassador*) | 23-4-60 |

**D:** 17,570 tons (fl) **S:** 18.5 kts **Dim:** 150.27 × 22.25 × 8.53
**Electron Equipt:** Radar: 1/. . . nav.
**M:** 1 set G.E. GT; 1 prop; 13,000 hp **Boilers:** 2 Babcock & Wilcox
**Range:** 13,000/18.5 **Fuel:** 2,230 tons **Man:** 10 officers, 23 unlicensed

GENERAL CARGO SHIPS *(continued)*

**Agent** S. Terzibaschitsch, 7-86

REMARKS: 7,848 grt/10,986–11,089 dwt. Cargo: 16,284 m$^3$ bale dry plus 9,000 bbl liquid. Can carry 12 passengers. Have 5 holds. All stored in the James River, Virginia.

◆ **2 Maritime Administration VC2-S-APS "Victory" type** Bldr: California SB Corp., Los Angeles, Cal.

| | In serv. |
|---|---|
| AMERICAN VICTORY (ex-*Carthage,* AG 185, ex-*American Victory*) | 6-45 |
| HATTIESBURG VICTORY | 9-45 |

**Brigham Victory**—a typical NDRF "Victory Ship" L. & L. Van Ginderen, 6-82

**D:** 15,200 tons (fl) **S:** 16.5 kts **Dim:** 138.76 (133.50 pp) × 18.90 × 8.53
**Electron Equipt:** Radar: 2/. . . nav.
**M:** 1 set Allis-Chalmers GT; 1 prop; 6,600 hp **Electric:** . . .
**Boilers:** 2 Henry Vogt (*Hattiesburg V.:* Springfield); 37 kg/cm$^2$, 399°C
**Range:** 24,000/16.5 **Fuel:** 2,881 tons **Man:** 11 officers, 28 unlicensed

REMARKS: 7,637 grt/10,681 dwt. Cargo: 12,829 m$^3$ bale dry cargo. Five holds; one 50-ton boom, 14/5-ton booms. *American Victory* is stored in the James River, *Hattiesburg Victory* at Beaumont, Texas. Sister *Catawba Victory,* used 1984-85 in trials to determine feasibility of upgrading other "Victory" ships, was returned to the NDRF in 5-87. Some 95 other ships remain in the National Defense Reserve Fleet, 35 in the James River, 16 at Beaumont, and 44 at Suisun Bay, as of 1-88, but they are being disposed of rapidly.

◆ **2 Seatrain-type former T2-SE-A2 tankers** Bldr: Marinship Corp., Sausalito, Cal.

| | In serv. |
|---|---|
| MAINE (ex-*Seatrain Maine,* ex-*Tomahawk*) | 4-44 |
| WASHINGTON (ex-*Seatrain Washington,* ex-*Mission San Diego*) | 4-44 |

**Washington** M.S.C., 1980

**D:** 21,177 (*Washington:* 21,240) tons (fl) **S:** 16.5 kts
**Dim:** 170.66 (164.3 pp) × 20.70 × 8.22
**M:** 1 set G.E. GT, electric drive; 1 prop; 10,000 hp **Electric:** 1,120 kw
**Boilers:** 2 Babcock & Wilcox; 42.2 kg/cm$^2$, 441°C
**Range:** 12,000/16 **Fuel:** 2,438 tons **Man:** 9 officers, 18 unlicensed

REMARKS: *Maine:* 8,025 grt/12,249 dwt; *Washington:* 8,039 grt/12,292 dwt. Converted to carry containers, railway cars, and vehicles by Maryland SB & DD, Baltimore, for Hudson Waterways Corp. 1966–67, using portions of various tankers plus a new mid-body; ex-original names above are those of the propulsion sections. Can also carry aircraft. *Maine* at James River, *Washington* at Beaumont. Sisters *Ohio* (returned to NDRF from RRF 30-11-85), *Florida,* and *Puerto Rico* are in the National Defense Reserve Fleet, but not in RRF.

NOTE: Of the other general-cargo RRF ships listed in the previous edition but deleted here, *President* was returned to the NDRF on 2-5-86 and *Cracker State Mariner* on 1-11-85.

◆ **1 Falcon-class commercial tanker** Bldr: Ingalls SY, Pascagoula, Miss.

| | L | In serv. | In RRF |
|---|---|---|---|
| MISSION CAPISTRANO (ex-*Falcon Lady,* ex-*Colombia,* T-AOT 182, ex-*Falcon Lady*) | 12-9-70 | 11-3-71 | 15-1-88 |

**Falcon Duchess (as Neches, T-AOT 183)**—sister to *Mission Capistrano*
L. & L. Van Ginderen, 11-82

**D:** 45,877 tons (fl) **S:** 16.5 kts **Dim:** 204.93 (194.47 pp) × 27.18 × 11.04
**M:** 2 Crossley-Pielstick 16 PC-2V400 diesels; 1 prop; 16,000 hp
**Range:** 16,000/16.5 **Fuel:** 2,272 tons heavy oil
**Electric:** 1,000 kw (2 × 500-kw diesel sets) **Man:** 9 officers, 14 unlicensed

REMARKS: 20,751 grt/37,874 dwt. Cargo: 303,000 bbl (49,213 m$^3$) in 18 tanks. Served on charter to U.S. Navy from 1974 to 1985. Purchased 5-6-87 from Falcon Carriers for $10.9M.

◆ **1 former commercial tanker** Bldr: Bethlehem SY, Sparrows Point, Md. (In serv. . . .)

MISSION BUENAVENTURA (ex-*Spirit of Liberty*)

**D:** approx. 46,000 tons (fl) **S:** 16.5 kts **Dim:** 201.23 (192.03) × 27.49 × 11.67
**M:** 2 sets G.E. GT; 1 prop; 15,000 hp **Boilers:** 2 . . . **Range:** 12,000/16.5
**Fuel:** 2,869 tons **Electric:** 2,000 kw **Man:** 9 officers, 17 unlicensed

REMARKS: 20,947 grt/38,851 dwt. Cargo: 326,000 bbl (53,186 m$^3$) in 16 tanks. Purchased 5-6-87 from Keystone Shipping for $9.0M and delivered to RRF 7-12-87. Stored at Beaumont, Texas.

◆ **1 former commercial tanker** Bldr: . . .

| | In serv. | In RRF |
|---|---|---|
| MISSION . . . (ex-*American Osprey*) | 1958 | 10-87 |

**D:** . . . **S:** 17 kts **Dim:** 201.5 × 27.4 × 11.0
**M:** 2 sets GT; 1 prop; . . . hp **Boilers:** . . .
**Range:** 14,000/17 **Fuel:** 2,871 tons **Man:** 11 officers, 26 unlicensed

REMARKS: 20,143 grt/34,723 dwt. Cargo: 268,000 bbl. Taken from the National Defense Reserve Fleet and contract to Alabama Drydock 30-10-87 for 120-day conversion for installation of a barge skid launching system, 4-point mooring system, and hydraulic-powered reels for 6,400 m of 152-mm fuel piping to act as an offshore fuel transfer point to serve beachheads. The system is essentially the same as that mounted on *Potomac.* To be stored at Beaumont, Texas.

◆ **1 Potomac class** Bldr: Ingalls SB, Pascagoula, Miss.

| | Laid down | In serv. |
|---|---|---|
| POTOMAC (T-AOT 181, ex-*Shenandoah,* ex-*Potomac,* T-AO 150) | 9-6-55 | 1-57/14-12-64 |

**Potomac (T-AOT 181)**—with MARISAT radome J. Jedrlinic, 12-79

## GENERAL CARGO SHIPS *(continued)*

**D:** 35,000 tons (fl) **S:** 18 kts **Dim:** 189.0 × 25.5 × 10.4
**Electron Equipt:** Radar: 1/Raytheon RM 1650/6X, 1/Raytheon 1660/12S
**M:** 1 set GT; 1 prop; 20,460 hp **Boilers:** 2
**Fuel:** 4,321 tons **Range:** 18,000/18 **Man:** 11 officers, 19 unlicensed

Remarks: 15,739 grt/26,040 dwt. Carries 200,000 bbl fuel plus 878 $m^3$ dry cargo. Originally belonging to the *Maumee* class, she was heavily damaged in 1961; only her stern was salvaged. Rebuilt by Sun SB & DD, Chester, Pa., and operated on charter to MSC as the *Shenandoah* from 1964 until purchased on 12-1-76. Reclassified T-AOT on 30-9-78. Placed in RRF at Suisun Bay on 5-3-84. Briefly used for trials with the prototype "Product Transfer System," a 4-mile floating offshore pipeline for bringing fuels to a beachhead, from 5-4-85 to 29-4-86. Now stored at Beaumont, Texas.

◆ **1 American Explorer class (T5-S-RM2A type)** Bldr: Ingalls SB, Pascagoula, Miss.

| | Laid down | L | In serv. |
|---|---|---|---|
| American Explorer (T-AOT 165) | 9-7-57 | 11-5-58 | 27-10-59 |

**American Explorer (T-AOT 165)** L. & L. Van Ginderen, 4-81

**D:** 8,400 tons light (31,300 fl) **S:** 20 kts **Dim:** 187.5 × 24.4 × 9.8
**Electron Equipt:** Radar: 1/Raytheon TM 1650/6X, 1/Raytheon TM 1660/12S
**M:** 1 set GT; 1 prop; 22,000 hp **Boilers:** 2 Babcock & Wilcox
**Fuel:** 3,482 tons **Range:** 14,000/20 **Man:** 11 officers, 21 unlicensed

Remarks: 14,984 grt/22,908 dwt. Cargo: 174,000 bbl fuel oil, diesel, etc., plus 878 $m^3$ dry cargo. Operated by commercial firm. Retyped TAO on 30-9-78. Deactivated to RRF 6-84 at Beaumont, Texas.

◆ **1 Maumee class (Maritime Administration T5-S-12a type)**

| | Bldr | Laid down | L | In serv. |
|---|---|---|---|---|
| Shoshone (T-AOT 151) | Sun SB, Chester, Pa. | 15-8-85 | 17-7-57 | 15-4-57 |

**D:** 32,000 tons (fl) **S:** 18 kts **Dim:** 189.0 × 25.5 × 9.8
**Electron Equipt:** Radar: 1/Raytheon TM 1650/6X, 1/Raytheon TM 1660/12S
**M:** 1 set GT; 1 prop; 20,460 hp **Boilers:** 2 Combustion Engineering
**Fuel:** 4,321 tons **Range:** 18,000/18 **Man:** 11 officers, 19 unlicensed

Remarks: 15,626 grt/26,943 dwt. Cargo: 187,000 bbl fuel oil, diesel, etc., plus 878 $m^3$ dry cargo. T-AOT 149 has ice-reinforced bow. Sister *Potomac* (T-AO 150, now T-AOT 181) rebuilt to different design. All retyped T-AOT on 30-9-78. Attached to the Near-Term Rapid Deployment Force on 30-9-83, but deactivated to the RRF at Suisun Bay 6-84. Sisters *Maumee* (T-AOT 149) and *Yukon* (T-AOT 152) were added to the RRF on 15-10-85 and 20-10-85, respectively, but both were "demoted" to the National Defense Reserve Fleet on 2-4-87, still under Navy ownership.

Note: Tanker *Chancellorsville* returned to NDRF 6-1-86.

## GASOLINE TANKERS

◆ **2 Alatna class (T1-MET-24a type)** Bldr: Bethlehem Steel, Staten I., N.Y.

| | L | In serv. | In RRF |
|---|---|---|---|
| Alatna (T-AOG 81) | 6-9-56 | 7-57 | 1985 |
| Chattahoochee (T-AOG 82) | 4-12-56 | 22-10-57 | 1985 |

**D:** 5,720 tons (fl) **S:** 12 kts **Dim:** 92.0 × 18.6 × 7.0
**M:** 4 Alco diesels, Westinghouse electric motors; 2 props; 4,000 hp
**Fuel:** 535 tons **Range:** 5,760/10 **Man:** 9 officers, 15 unlicensed

Remarks: 3,459 grt/4,933 dwt. Icebreaker-type hulls; originally intended as Arctic/Antarctic support ships. Cargo: 30,000 bbls light petroleum products. Both placed in the Maritime Administration's reserve fleet on 8-8-72; reacquired 10-5-79 and 24-5-79, respectively; reactivation began 28-11-79 at National Steel, San Diego. Returned to service to replace T-AOG 77 and T-AOG 79, T-AOG 81 on 3-2-82 and T-AOG 82 on 11-1-82. Received new diesel engines. Laid up 22-1-85 in Japan as part of the RRF when replaced by chartered tug/barge combinations.

◆ **1 Tonti class (T1-M-BT2 type)** Bldr: Todd SY, Houston, Texas

| | Laid down | L | In serv. |
|---|---|---|---|
| Nodaway (T-AOG 78, ex-*Tarcoola*) | 19-2-42 | 15-5-45 | 11-9-50 |

**D:** 2,060 tons light (5,984 fl) **S:** 10 kts **Dim:** 99.1 × 14.7 × 5.9
**Electron Equipt:** Radar: 1/Raytheon 1660, 1/R.C.A. CRM-N1C-75
**M:** 2 Nordberg diesels; 1 prop; 1,400 hp **Electric:** 515 kw
**Fuel:** 154 tons **Range:** 5,500/10 **Man:** 9 officers, 15 unlicensed

Remarks: 3,160 grt/3,933 dwt. Cargo: 31,284 bbl light fuels (diesel, JP-5, gasoline). Laid up 22-7-84 at Pearl Harbor, transferred to RRF on 30-9-85.

**Chattahoochee (T-AOG 82)** L. & L. Van Ginderen, 12-83

# UNITED STATES COAST GUARD

Personnel (1-88): 39,000 active duty officers and enlisted, plus 5,793 civilians, 14,000 Reserves, and about 40,000 Coast Guard Auxiliary

## GENERAL

The Revenue Marine, which was created in 1790, became the Coast Guard on 28 January 1915 by act of Congress. Until 1 April 1967 the Coast Guard was part of the Department of the Treasury; at that time it was transferred to the Department of Transportation. The act that created the service calls for it to operate in time of crisis under the control of the Navy. The principal responsibilities of the Coast Guard are:

—preparation and training for combat in cooperation with the Navy;
—enforcement of the laws of the sea and the policing of navigation;
—control of territorial waters, suppression of smuggling, and policing and assisting the fishing industry;
—surveillance of the coasts and protection of access to ports and bases;
—search and rescue at sea, including transocean air routes;
—manning and maintaining aids to navigation: lighthouses, beacons, buoys, and Loran stations (46,000 in all);
—control of piloting and the investigation of accidents at sea;
—control of the safety and seaworthiness aspects of shipbuilding;
—international ice patrols (keeping track of drifting icebergs);
—protection of offshore oil installations;
—pollution control and protection of the environment;
—meteorologic, oceanographic, and hydrographic surveying.

## ORGANIZATION

The Coast Guard is divided into two main components, one for the Pacific and one for the Atlantic. The Coast Guard is further divided into Coast Guard Districts in order to fulfill its responsibilities along the U.S. coastline (more than 10,000 nautical miles, not including Hawaii).

A four-star admiral heads the Coast Guard. He is appointed for four years and is assisted by a general staff. The commandant reports to the Secretary of Transportation and not the Joint Chiefs of Staff.

Coast Guard patrol ships have their names preceded by USCGC (United States Coast Guard Cutter). Cutters and patrol craft are white, icebreakers have red hulls, buoy tenders, black. All ships and craft carry a diagonal red stripe and the USCG shield on the hull.

## AVIATION

As of 9-87, the Coast Guard had the following aircraft:

| | |
|---|---|
| 26 | HC-130H Hercules long-range search-and-rescue aircraft (21 in service) |
| 41 | HU-25A Guardian patrol aircraft (32 in service) |
| 2 | E-2C Hawkeye radar surveillance aircraft |
| 1 | VC-4A Gulfstream-I transport |
| 1 | VC-11A Gulfstream-II transport |
| 50 | HH-65A Dolphin rescue helicopters (42 in service) |
| 65 | HH-52A Sea Guard rescue helicopters (38 in service) |
| 36 | HH-3F Pelican rescue helicopters (30 in service) |

In 6-79, ninety Aérospatiale SA-366N SRR (Short-Range Recovery) helicopters were ordered from France under the USCG designation HH-65A Dolphin to replace the HH-52A helicopters. The first HH-65A Dolphin was to deliver in 9-82, with all 90 to be in service by early 1986, but the first was not accepted until 19-11-84, and sub-

**AVIATION** *(continued)*

PRINCIPAL U.S. COAST GUARD AIRCRAFT

| Class, builder | Mission | Wingspan in m | Length in m | Height in m | Weight in kg | Engines | Max. speed | Ceiling in feet | Radius (nautical miles) |
|---|---|---|---|---|---|---|---|---|---|
| **FIXED-WING** | | | | | | | | | |
| HC-130 B/E/H[1] Hercules (Lockheed) | SAR/cargo/personnel transport (Dates apply to HC-130H) | 40.42 | 29.80 | 11.66 | 33,397 empty, 49,780 loaded, 70,300 max. | 4 Allison T 56-A-15 turboprops; 4,508 shp (4,061 sust.) each | 302 kts (287 cruise) | 25,000 | 3,734 ferry, 2,517 with max. payload at 5,000 ft. |
| HU-25[2] Guardian (Dassault/ Grumman) | SAR | 16.30 | 17.15 | 5.32 | 8,618 empty 9,476 loaded; 14,515 max. | 2 Garrett AiResearch ATF3-6-2C turbofans; 2,512 kg thrust each | 461 kts (40,000 ft); 150 kts (search) | 40,000 | 2.250 SAR |
| **HELICOPTERS:** | Mission | Rotor di-ameter (m) | Length overall (m) | Height in m | Weight in kg | Engines | Max. speed | Ceiling in feet | |
| HH-60J (Sikorsky) | SAR | 16.36 | 19.76 (15.24 fuselage) | 5.23 | 9,435 | 2 G.E. T700-GE-401 turboshafts; 1,723 max. hp each (1,543 cont.) | 150 kts max. 140 kts cruise | . . . | 700 3.5 hrs (300 n.m. radius with 1 hr on station) |
| HH-3F Pelican (Sikorsky) | SAR/transport | 18.90 | 22.25 | 5.51 | 10,000 max. | 2 G.E. T58-GE-5 turboshafts; 1,500 shp each | 141 kts (109 cruise) | 11,400 | 400 |
| HH-52A Sea Guard (Sikorsky) | SAR | 16.17 | 13.87 | 4.88 | 2,306 empty; 3,674 max. | 1 G.E. T58-GE-8B turboshaft; 1,250 shp | 95 kts (85 cruise) | 11,200 | 475 ferry, 150 SAR radius |
| HH-65A Dolphin (Aérospatiale) | SAR | 11.94 | 11.43 | 3.99 | 1,900 empty; 3,992 max. | 2 Avco Lycoming LTS 101-750A-1[3] turboshafts; 680 hp each (646 sust.) | 165 kts (145 cruise; 128 SAR) | 7,150 | 400 ferry (3.8 hr mission) |

[1] Five HC-130H delivered 1984 with T56-A-7 engines; 4 delivered 1985 with T56-A-15 turboprops and provision for APS-137 radar.
[2] Trials 1983–84 with Aerojet General "Aireye" Surveillance System: APA-131 Side-looking radar (SLAR), Low-light tv (LLTV), RS-18C infrared/ultraviolet linescanner, KS-87B camera. All have APS-127 radar. A conversion program to substitute APG-66 radars for drug-interdiction duties to 8 HU-25 began 1-4-87.
[3] Later units may receive uprated LTS 101-750A-3 engines.

sequent deliveries have continued behind schedule. A total of 65 HU-25 Guardians are on order.

Two ex-USN E-2C aircraft were transferred in 1987 for drug-interdiction duties; 2 more went to the Customs Service. Under FY 86, 3 more HC-130H were approved by Congress, with 2 more approved under FY 87; 16 of the HC-130 aircraft are to receive APS-137 radars to improve their surveillance capabilities; 30 will eventually be so equipped.

The first 2 of a planned 32 HH-60J Seahawk helicopters, essentially similar to the HH-60H rescue version, were authorized under FY 86; 2 more were authorized under FY 87, and 15 were approved under FY 88 to begin replacement of the HH-3F Pelicans delivered 1969–73. The HH-60Js will begin delivery in 11-90.

After working with various prototype systems during 1986–87, the Coast Guard ordered three aerostat balloon radar systems for use in drug interdiction from R.C.A. on 9-9-87. The Eaton radar-equipped balloon, filled with helium, will operate at about a 2,500-ft altitude, tethered to one of three leased mother ships converted from an offshore supply vessel. The aerostat balloons are of about 1,506-m$^3$ capacity.

A program to develop manned non-rigid dirigibles for the Coast Guard has been deferred for lack of funds.

**Prototype radar aerostat and tender Atlantic Sentry** R.C.A., 1987

**HU-25A Guardian**—with prototype "Air Eye" surveillance system Aerojet General, 1983

**USCG HC-130H-7 Hercules** Lockheed

**USCG HH-52A Sea Guard** U.S.C.G.

AVIATION *(continued)*

**HH-65A Dolphin** V. Baca, 2-87

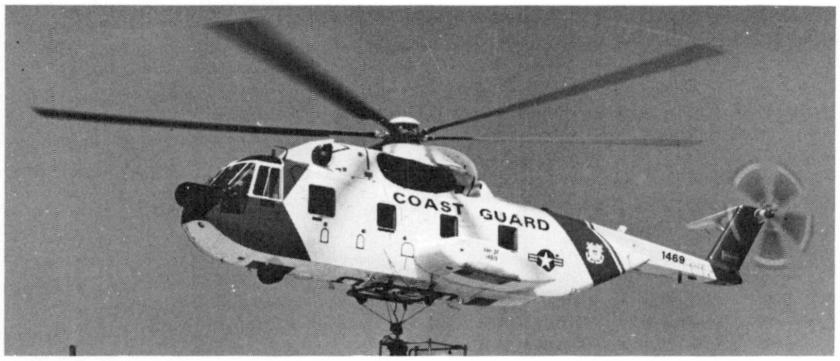


**USCG HH-3F Pelican** U.S.C.G.

## HIGH-ENDURANCE CUTTERS

◆ **12 Hamilton class (378-ft class)** Bldr: Avondale SY, Westwego, La.

| | Laid down | L | In serv. | Modernize |
|---|---|---|---|---|
| WHEC 715 Hamilton | 1-65 | 18-12-65 | 20-2-67 | 1986 to 10-88 |
| WHEC 716 Dallas | 7-2-66 | 1-10-66 | 1-10-67 | 1-88 to 4-89 |
| WHEC 717 Mellon | 25-7-66 | 11-2-67 | 22-12-67 | 3-88 to 9-88 |
| WHEC 718 Chase | 15-10-66 | 20-5-67 | 1-3-68 | . . . to 12-89 |
| WHEC 719 Boutwell | 12-12-66 | 17-6-67 | 14-6-68 | . . . to 11-89 |
| WHEC 720 Sherman | 13-2-67 | 23-9-67 | 23-8-68 | 14-5-86 to 1-89 |
| WHEC 721 Gallatin | 17-4-67 | 18-11-67 | 20-12-68 | . . . to 1-90 |
| WHEC 722 Morgenthau | 17-7-67 | 10-2-68 | 14-2-69 | . . . to 4-90 |
| WHEC 723 Rush | 23-10-67 | 16-11-68 | 3-7-69 | . . . to 6-89 |
| WHEC 724 Munro | 18-2-70 | 5-12-70 | 10-9-71 | . . . to 6-89 |
| WHEC 725 Jarvis | 9-9-70 | 24-4-71 | 30-12-71 | . . . to 9-90 |
| WHEC 726 Midgett | 5-4-71 | 4-9-71 | 17-3-72 | . . . to 2-91 |

**D:** 2,716 tons (3,050 fl) **S:** 29 kts (28.4 post-modernization)
**Dim:** 115.37 (106.68 pp) × 13.06 × 4.27 (6.2 over sonar)
**A:** 1/127-mm 38-cal. DP—2/20-mm AA (I × 2)—4/12.7-mm mg (I × 4)—2/40-mm Mk 64 grenade launchers (I × 2)—6/324-mm Mk 32 Mod. 5 ASW TT (III × 2)
**Electron Equipt:** Radar: 2/SPS-64(V)6 navigational surface-search, 1/SPS 29D air-search, 1/Mk 35
Sonar: SQS-38—EW: WLR-1C, WLR-3
**M:** CODOG: 2 Fairbanks-Morse 38TD8⅛, 12-cyl. diesels, 3,500 hp each; 2 Pratt & Whitney FT4-A6 gas turbines, 18,000 hp each; 2 CP props; 36,000 hp—350-hp retractable bow propeller
**Electric:** 1,500 kw **Fuel:** 800 tons
**Range:** 2,400/29; 9,600/19 (gas turbines); 14,000/11 (diesel)
**Endurance:** 45 days **Man:** 15 officers, 140 men (169 tot. post-modernization)

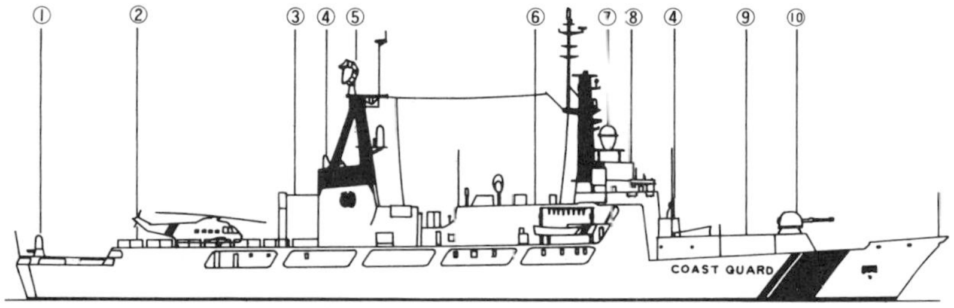


**Hamilton class as modernized** *Ships of the World*
1. Mk 15 CIWS location 2. LAMPS-I ASW helicopter capability
3. telescoping hangar 4. OE-82C antenna for WSC-3 SATCOMM
5. SPS-40B air-search radar 6. Mk 36 SRBOC decoy RL
7. Mk 92 Mod. 1 radar f.c.s. 8. enlarged deckhouse above bridge
9. extended main deck superstructure 10. Mk 75 76-mm DP

**Morgenthau (WHEC 722)** G. Arra, 7-86

**Gallatin (WHEC 721)** G. Arra, 7-86

**Boutwell (WHEC 719)** L. & L. Van Ginderen, 1986

Remarks: Helicopter platform, 26.82 × 12.2. Living spaces air-conditioned. Laboratories for weather and oceanographic research. Welded hull; aluminum superstructure. Named after early Secretaries of the Treasury and Coast Guard heroes. Thirty-six planned, only twelve built. Mk 56 radar gunfire-control director and Mk 309 ASW fire-control system installed. For FY 85 through FY 88, modernizations will include: replacing the 127-mm gun and Mk 56 gunfire-control system with a 76-mm Mk 75 (OTO Melara Compact) gun and Mk 92 Mod. 1 radar gunfire-control system, replacing the SPS-29D radar with SPS-40B, replacing the WLR-1 EW system with SLQ-32 and the Mk 36 SRBOC chaff system, and adding satellite communications gear; provision will be made to carry the LAMPS-I ASW helicopter and one 20-mm Mk 15 CIWS gatling AA gun. Other modifications include: Mk 32 Mod. 7 ASW TT, SQR-17A(V)1 sonobuoy signal analyzer, Mk 36 Mod. 1 SRBOC decoy RL, RAYCAS (Raytheon Collision-Avoidance System), an HP-9020 computer, SLQ-25 Nixie acoustic torpedo decoys, new secure communications gear, and telescoping hangars. The program is about one year behind schedule. Eight are to be modified by Todd SY, Seattle, and WHEC 715, 716, 718, and 721 by Bath Iron Works, Maine. The grenade launchers have replaced the 81-mm mortars formerly carried. The helicopter hangars had been blanked off. SQS-38 is a hull-mounted version of the Navy's SQS-35 variable-depth sonar. WHEC 716–723 have synchronizing clutches; the final three have synchro-self-shifting (SSS) clutches. WHEC 717, 722, and 725 have rudder roll-stabilization systems.

### HIGH-ENDURANCE CUTTERS *(continued)*

◆ **1 Secretary class (327-ft class)**

| | Bldr | Laid down | L | In serv. |
|---|---|---|---|---|
| WHEC 35 INGHAM | Philadelphia NSY | 1-5-35 | 3-6-36 | 6-11-36 |

**Ingham (WHEC 35)** G. Arra, 9-86

**D:** 2,397 tons (2,656 fl) **S:** 19.8 kts **Dim:** 99.67 (93.88 wl) × 12.55 × 4.57
**A:** 1/127-mm 38-cal. DP—2/12.7-mm mg (I × 2)—2/40-mm Mk 64 grenade launchers (I × 2)
**Electron Equipt:** Radar: 1/SPS-64(V)1, 1/SPS-64(V)6
**M:** 2 sets Westinghouse GT; 2 props; 6,200 hp
**Boilers:** 2 Babcock & Wilcox; 28.2 kg/cm$^2$ **Fuel:** 572 tons
**Range:** 4,000/19.8; 8,000/10.5 **Man:** 13 officers, 124 men

REMARKS: Despite great age, a comfortable and highly reliable ship. All gunfire-control and ASW equipment removed, and SPS-29D air-search radars removed 1981–82. Sister *Spencer* (WHEC 36) was sold 1982; *Campbell* (WHEC 32) stricken 1-4-82; *Bibb* (WHEC 31) stricken 30-7-85; *Duane* (WHEC 33) stricken 1-8-85; *Ingham* (WHEC 35) was scheduled to strike 12-85, but will remain in service into 1989. *Taney* struck 7-12-86 after over 50 years' service; now on display at Baltimore.

◆ **1 Casco class (311-ft class)** Bldr: Associated SB, Seattle

| | Laid down | L | In serv. |
|---|---|---|---|
| WHEC 379 UNIMAK (ex-WTR, ex-WHEC, ex-AVP 31) | 12-2-42 | 27-5-43 | 31-12-43 |

**Unimak (WHEC 379)** L. & L. Van Ginderen, 6-81

**D:** 1,766 tons (2,505 fl) **S:** 17 kts **Dim:** 94.7 (91.5 pp) × 12.52 × 3.65
**A:** 1/127-mm 38-cal. DP—4/12.7-mm mg (I × 4)—2/40-mm Mk 64 grenade launchers (I × 2)
**Electron Equipt:** Radar: 1/SPS-64(V)1, 1/SPS-64(V)6
**M:** 4 Fairbanks-Morse 38D8$\frac{1}{8}$ diesels; 2 props; 6,080 hp **Electric:** 600 kw
**Fuel:** 400 tons **Range:** 8,000/17; 22,000/11 **Man:** 12 officers, 77 men

REMARKS: The last of a series of small seaplane tenders (AVP), eighteen of which were transferred to the Coast Guard, 1946–49; seven were given to South Vietnam beginning in 1970, and eight have been taken out of service since 1968. WHEC 379 was a training ship from 11-69 until placed in reserve on 30-5-75. She was recommissioned on 15-8-77 for patrol duties in the 200-nautical-mile economic zone. Gunfire-control and ASW systems have been removed. Planned to strike 1989. Based at New Bedford, Mass.

### MEDIUM-ENDURANCE CUTTERS

◆ **8 (+5) Bear class (270-ft class)** Bldr: WMEC 901–904: Tacoma Boatbuilding, Tacoma, Wash.; WMEC 905–913: Robert E. Direcktor, Middletown, R.I.

| | Laid down | L | In serv. |
|---|---|---|---|
| WMEC 901 BEAR | 23-8-79 | 25-9-80 | 4-2-83 |
| WMEC 902 TAMPA | 2-4-80 | 19-3-81 | 16-3-84 |
| WMEC 903 HARRIET LANE | 15-10-80 | 6-2-82 | 20-9-84 |
| WMEC 904 NORTHLAND | 9-4-81 | 7-5-82 | 17-12-84 |
| WMEC 905 SPENCER (ex-*Seneca*) | 26-6-82 | 16-6-84 | 28-6-86 |
| WMEC 906 SENECA (ex-*Pickering*) | 16-9-82 | 16-6-84 | 9-5-87 |
| WMEC 907 ESCANABA | 1-4-83 | 24-8-85 | 30-8-87 |
| WMEC 908 TAHOMA (ex-*Legare*) | 28-6-83 | 24-8-85 | 12-8-87 |
| WMEC 909 CAMPBELL (ex-*Argus*) | 10-8-84 | 30-8-86 | 1-88 |
| WMEC 910 THETIS (ex-*Tahoma*) | 24-8-84 | 30-8-86 | 5-88 |
| WMEC 911 FORWARD (ex-*Erie*) | 11-6-86 | 22-8-87 | 9-88 |
| WMEC 912 LEGARE (ex-*McCulloch*) | 11-6-86 | 22-8-87 | 1-89 |
| WMEC 913 MOHAWK (ex-*Ewing*) | 18-6-87 | . . . | 5-89 |

Authorized: 2 in FY 77, 2 in FY 78, 2 in FY 79, 3 in FY 80, 1 in FY 81, 3 in FY 82.

**Tahoma (WMEC 908)**—hangar retracted R. B. Direcktor, 8-87

**Seneca (WMEC 906)** G. Arra, 5-87

**Escanaba (WMEC 907)**—with hangar extended L. & L. Van Ginderen, 8-87

**D:** 1,200 tons light (1,780 fl) **S:** 19.5 kts **Dim:** 82.3 (77.7 wl) × 11.58 × 4.11
**A:** 1/76-mm Mk 75 DP—2/12.7-mm mg (I × 2)—2/40-mm Mk 19 grenade launchers (I × 2)—1/HH-52A or HH-65A helicopter
**Electron Equipt:** Radar: 1/SPS-64(V)1, 1/SPS-64(V)6, 1/Mk 92 Mod. 1 fire-control
Sonar: Provision for SQR-19A TASS
EW: SLQ-32(V)1, Mk 36 SRBOC chaff RL (VI × 2)
TACAN: URN-25
**M:** 2 Alco Model 251, 18-cyl. diesels; 2 CP props; 7,000 hp
**Electric:** 1,350 kw **Range:** 3,850/19.5, 6,370/15; 10,250/12
**Man:** 11 officers, 89 men **Endurance:** 14 days

REMARKS: Names have been altered since original listing. Program has suffered numerous delays; first ship was to have completed 31-12-80; In service dates given for last six are deliveries, and WMEC 913 will not actually enter active service until 5-90—over three years late. WMEC 905–913 originally ordered from Tacoma in 8-80, but lawsuit caused reassignment to R.E. Direcktor, 17-1-81. Intended to be able to act as ASW escorts in wartime. No hull-mounted sonar or on-board

**MEDIUM-ENDURANCE CUTTERS** *(continued)*

ASW weapons. Space and weight reserved for Mk 15 CIWS 20-mm gatling AA gun and two quadruple Harpoon missile-launch canisters. Satellite-communications system will be carried. Can carry van-mounted towed passive sonar array on fantail. Telescoping hangar, provision for fin stabilization. Have six light weapons mountings capable of accepting 12.7-mm mg or 40-mm Mk 19 grenade launchers. Reportedly overloaded and very uncomfortable ships in a seaway; 76-mm gun raised .76 m to reduce damage. Have accommodations for up to 17 officers, 123 men.

Congress provided $20M in FY 88 to equip one ship for ASW, with SQR-18A TASS, SQR-17A sonobuoy analyzer, APR-78 sonobuoy receiver, SKR-4 helicopter data link receiver; this will make the ship compatible with the U.S. Navy's LAMPS-III system. The "COMDAC" computerized control system on this class has given considerable difficulty.

◆ **16 Reliance class (210-ft A* and 210-ft B class)**

Bldrs: 1. Todd Shipyards—2. Christy Corp., Sturgeon Bay, Wis.—3. Coast Guard SY, Curtis Bay, Md.—4. American SB, Lorain, Ohio.

| | Bldr | L | In serv. | Modernized |
|---|---|---|---|---|
| WMEC 615 RELIANCE* | 1 | 25-5-63 | 20-6-24 | 6-4-87 to 4-8-88 |
| WMEC 616 DILIGENCE* | 1 | 20-7-63 | 26-8-64 | 5-7-88 to 2-3-90 |
| WMEC 617 VIGILANT* | 1 | 24-12-63 | 3-10-64 | 1-2-88 to 6-8-89 |
| WMEC 618 ACTIVE* | 2 | 31-7-65 | 17-9-66 | 1-10-84 to 12-2-87 |
| WMEC 619 CONFIDENCE* | 3 | 8-5-65 | 19-2-66 | 18-10-86 to 3-3-88 |
| WMEC 620 RESOLUTE | 3 | 30-4-66 | 8-12-66 | 2-4-90 to 17-12-90 |
| WMEC 621 VALIANT | 4 | 14-1-67 | 28-10-67 | 1-12-87 to 15-8-88 |
| WMEC 622 COURAGEOUS | 4 | 18-5-67 | 10-4-68 | 2-3-87 to 17-12-87 |
| WMEC 623 STEADFAST | 4 | 24-6-67 | 25-9-68 | 1-4-88 to 15-12-88 |
| WMEC 624 DAUNTLESS | 4 | 21-10-67 | 10-6-68 | 1-8-89 to 16-4-90 |
| WMEC 625 VENTUROUS | 4 | 11-11-67 | 16-8-68 | 1-12-88 to 15-8-89 |
| WMEC 626 DEPENDABLE | 4 | 16-3-68 | 27-11-68 | 3-8-87 to 18-4-88 |
| WMEC 627 VIGOROUS | 4 | 4-5-68 | 2-5-69 | 4-12-89 to 20-8-90 |
| WMEC 628 DURABLE | 3 | 29-4-67 | 8-12-67 | 1-10-86 to 17-8-87 |
| WMEC 629 DECISIVE | 3 | 14-12-67 | 23-8-68 | 1-8-88 to 17-4-89 |
| WMEC 630 ALERT | 3 | 19-10-68 | 4-8-69 | 3-4-89 to 18-12-89 |

**D:** 759 tons (930 fl) **S:** 18 kts **Dim:** 64.16 (60.96 pp) × 10.36 × 3.2
**A:** 1/76.2-mm Mk 22 DP—2 or 4/12.7-mm mg (I × 2 or 4)—2/40-mm Mk 64 grenade launchers (I × 2)—1/HH-52A or HH-65A helicopter
**Electron Equipt:** Radar: 2/SPS-64(V)1 **Endurance:** 21 days (Mod. 30 days)
**M:** 2 Alco 251B 16-cyl. diesels; 2 CP props; 5,000 hp
**Electric:** 500 kw **Range:** 2,700/18; 6,100/14 (*2,200/18; 5,000/15)
**Man:** 8 officers, 54 men (accommodations: 12 officers, 70 men)

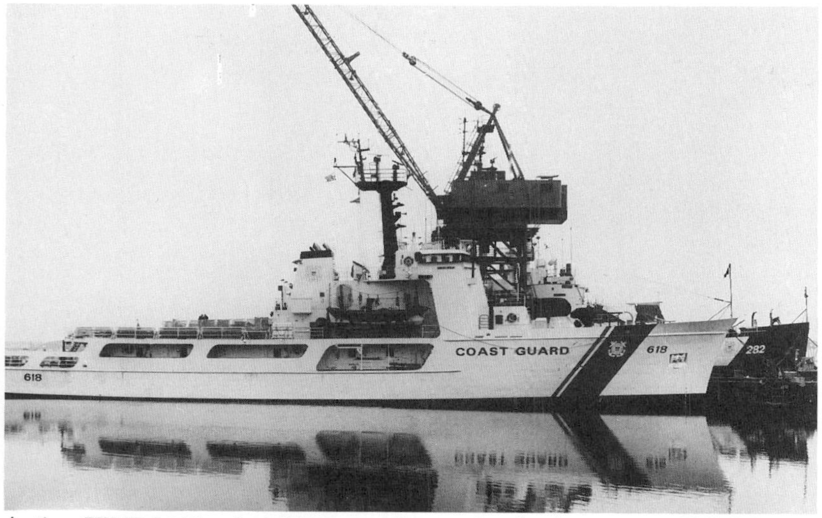


**Active (WMEC 618)**—first ship to complete modernization U.S.C.G., 2-87

**Alert (WMEC 630)**—original profile G. Arra, 10-86

**Venturous (WMEC 625)** G. Arra, 4-86

REMARKS: No hangar. Designed to operate up to 500 miles off the coast. High superstructure permits 360-degree visibility. Can tow a 10,000-ton ship. Air-conditioned.

WMEC 615–WMEC 619 originally had CODAG propulsion, with two 1,500-hp Cooper-Bessemer FVBM12-T diesels and two Solar Saturn T-100s gas turbines providing an additional 2,000 hp; the turbines have been removed. These five ships are being re-engined and otherwise updated by the U.S. Coast Guard Yard, Curtis Bay, with Alco 251B engines like their sisters. The remaining ships are being refitted by Colonna's SY, Norfolk, beginning with WMEC 628 in 10-86 (see schedule in ship listing); the ships receive a new stack, enlarged superstructure, greater fire-fighting capability, but the helo deck is reduced in size, and topweight is reduced. Crews are to be enlarged to 86 total, provisions capacities enlarged, and exhausts are to be rearranged; displacements will rise to over 1,300 tons on completion.

◆ **3 Diver class (213-ft class)** Bldr: Basalt Rock Co., Napa, Calif.

| | Laid down | L | In serv. |
|---|---|---|---|
| WMEC 6 ESCAPE (ex-ARS 6) | 24-8-42 | 22-11-42 | 20-11-43 |
| WMEC 167 ACUSHNET (ex-WAGO 167, ex-WAT 167, ex-*Shackle,* ARS 9) | 26-10-42 | 1-4-43 | 5-2-44 |
| WMEC 168 YOCONA (ex-WAT 168, ex-*Seize,* ARS 26) | 28-9-43 | 8-4-44 | 3-11-44 |

**Acushnet (WMEC 167)** G. Arra, 1987

**Escape (WMEC 6)** G. Arra, 8-85

**MEDIUM-ENDURANCE CUTTERS** *(continued)*

**D:** 1,246 tons (1,745 fl) **S:** 15.5 kts **Dim:** 65.08 (63.09 wl) × 12.5 × 4.57
**A:** none **Electron Equipt:** Radar: 2/SPS-64(V)1 **Electric:** 460 kw
**M:** 4 Cooper-Bessemer GSB-8 diesels, electric drive; 2 props; 3,000 hp
**Fuel:** 300 tons **Range:** 9,000/15.5; 20,000/7 **Man:** 7 officers, 65 men

Remarks: Former salvage ships; WMEC 167, 168 taken over from the Navy in 1946. WMEC 167 served as WAGO 167 from 1968 to 1978, then retyped WMEC. WMEC 6, reactivated from reserve and transferred on loan from U.S. Navy 4-12-80, has a mainmast. Maximum sustained speed is 13 kts. Plan to strike 1990.

◆ **1 Storis class (230-ft class)** Bldr: Toledo SB, Toledo, Ohio

| | Laid down | L | In serv. |
|---|---|---|---|
| WMEC 38 Storis (ex-Eskimo) | 14-7-41 | 4-4-42 | 30-9-42 |

**Storis (WMEC 38)** 1971

**D:** 1,296 tons light (1,916 fl) **S:** 14 kts **Dim:** 70.1 × 13.1 × 4.6
**A:** 1/76.2-mm Mk 22 DP—4/12.7-mm mg (I × 4)
**Electron Equipt:** Radar: 2/SPS-64
**M:** 3 Fairbanks-Morse $38D8\frac{1}{8}$ diesels, electric drive; 1 prop; 1,800 hp
**Fuel:** 330 tons **Range:** 12,000/14; 22,000/8 **Man:** 10 officers, 96 men

Remarks: Rated as WAG until 1966, and WAGB until 1-7-72, when she was retyped WMEC. Resembles a *Balsam*-class buoy tender, but is larger. Has an icebreaker hull, but is no longer considered capable of acting as such. Based at Kodiak, Alaska.

◆ **5 Cherokee and Achomawi* class (205-ft class)**

| | Bldr | Laid down | L | In serv. |
|---|---|---|---|---|
| WMEC 76 Ute (ex-T-ATF 76) | United Eng., Alameda | 27-2-42 | 24-6-42 | 31-12-42 |
| WMEC 85 Lipan (ex-T-ATF 85) | United Eng., Alameda | 30-5-42 | 17-9-42 | 29-4-43 |
| WMEC 153 Chilula* (ex-ATF 153) | Charleston SB | 13-7-44 | 1-12-44 | 5-4-45 |
| WMEC 165 Cherokee (ex-ATF 66) | Bethlehem, Staten I. | 23-12-38 | 10-11-39 | 26-4-40 |
| WMEC 166 Tamaroa (ex-*Zuni,* ATF 95) | Commercial Iron Works, Portland, Oregon | 8-3-43 | 13-7-43 | 9-10-43 |

**D:** 1,217 tons (1,731 fl) **S:** 16.2 kts **Dim:** 62.48 (59.44 pp) × 11.73 × 5.18
**A:** 1/76.2-mm Mk 22 DP **Electron Equipt:** Radar: 2/SPS-64
**M:** 4 G.M. 12-278 diesels, electric drive; 1 prop; 3,000 hp **Electric:** 260 kw
**Fuel:** 315 tons **Range:** 6,500/16.2; 15,000/8 **Man:** 6 officers, 65 men

Remarks: WMEC 165 and WMEC 166 were the first and last of their numerous group to be built; WMEC 153 is one of a later version that has similar appearance, but her diesels are G.M. 12-278A. WMEC 153, 165, and 166 are former U.S. Navy fleet tugs loaned to the Coast Guard in 1946 and transferred outright on 1-6-69; WMEC 76 and 85 were transferred on 30-9-80 and then towed from San Francisco to Curtis Bay, Md., for refits; they have no 76.2-mm guns. WMEC 153, 165, and 166 planned to strike, 1988–89.

**Chilula (WMEC 153)** G. Arra, 3-86

**Cherokee (WMEC 165)** G. Arra, 8-80

◆ **3 Balsam-class (180-ft.) former seagoing buoy tenders** Bldr: Marine Iron & SB, Duluth, Minn.

| | Laid down | L | In serv. |
|---|---|---|---|
| WMEC 292 Clover (ex-WLB 292) | 3-12-41 | 25-4-42 | 8-11-42 |
| WMEC 295 Evergreen (ex-WAGO 295, ex-WLB 295) | 15-4-42 | 3-7-42 | 30-4-43 |
| WMEC 300 Citrus (ex-WLB 300) | 29-4-42 | 15-8-42 | 30-5-43 |

**D:** 935 tons (1,025 fl) **S:** 13 kts **Dim:** 54.9 × 11.3 × 4.0
**A:** 2/12.7-mm mg (I × 2)—2/40-mm Mk 19 grenade launcher (I × 2)
**Electron Equipt:** Radar: 2/SPS-64(V)1
**M:** 2 diesels, electric drive; 1 prop; 1,000 hp **Electric:** 400 kw

**Evergreen (WMEC 295)** S. Terzibaschitsch, 7-86

**Citrus (WMEC 300)** G. Arra, 8-86

**MEDIUM-ENDURANCE CUTTERS** *(continued)*

**Range:** WMEC 292,295: 4,600/12.8; 14,000/7.4; WMEC 300: 7,600/12.9; 16,000/7.4
**Fuel:** . . . **Man:** 7 officers, 45 men

REMARKS: WMEC 292 reclassified 6-79 to replace *Comanche* (WMEC 202), and WMEC 300 reclassified 2-80 to replace *Modoc* (WMEC 194). WMEC 300, stationed at Coos Bay, Oregon, has had her hull strengthened for icebreaking. WMEC 292 based at Eureka, Cal. WMEC 295, converted as an oceanographic research ship and redesignated WAGO 295 in 2-73, was redesignated WMEC 295 on 1-5-83 and has a bow-thruster.

## ICEBREAKERS

◆ **0 (+2) new construction polar icebreakers** Bldr: . . .

| | Laid down | L | In serv. |
|---|---|---|---|
| WAGB 12 N . . . | 1-90 | . . . | 1992 |
| WAGB 13 N . . . | . . . | . . . | 3-94 |

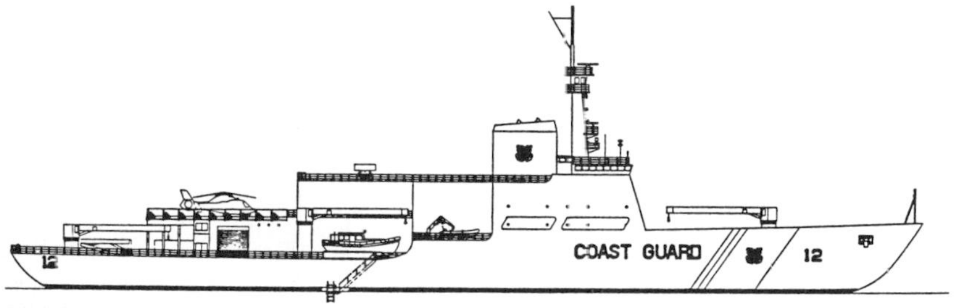


**WAGB 12** U.S.C.G., 1987

**D:** 17,000 tons (fl) **S:** 12.5 kts (cruise)
**Dim:** 140.21 (122.23 wl) × 28.96 (26.82 wl) × 9.45
**A:** 2/12.7-mm mg (I × 2)—2/. . . helicopters
**Electron Equipt:** Radar: . . .
**M:** diesel-electric: 4 medium-speed diesels; 2 props; 30,000 hp
**Range:** 34,500/12.5 **Endurance:** 180 days **Fuels:** . . .
**Man:** 17 officers, 108 enlisted, plus 30 scientists

REMARKS: To replace the overaged "Wind"-class pair. Will be capable of breaking 1.4-m ice at 3 kts or 2.4-m ice by backing and ramming. Will have five laboratories, totaling 377 m$^2$. U.S.C.G. had sought to build or lease foreign, but Congress decreed that these must be U.S.-built ships.

◆ **2 Polar Star class (399-ft class)** Bldr: Lockheed SB, Seattle

| | Laid down | L | In serv. |
|---|---|---|---|
| WAGB 10 POLAR STAR | 15-5-72 | 17-11-73 | 19-1-76 |
| WAGB 11 POLAR SEA | 27-11-73 | 24-6-75 | 23-2-78 |

**Polar Star (WAGB 10)** G. Gyssels, 3-86

**Polar Star (WAGB 10)** G. Arra, 11-85

**D:** 10,863 tons (13,623 fl) **S:** 18 kts **Dim:** 121.91 (102.78 pp) × 25.45 × 1.14
**Electron Equipt:** Radar: 2/SPS-64—TACAN: SRN-15
**M:** CODAG: 6 Alco 16V251 diesels, 3,000 hp each; 3 Pratt & Whitney FT-4A12 gas turbines, 25,000 hp each, down-rated; electric drive; 3 CP props; 66,000 hp
**Fuel:** 3,555 tons **Range:** 16,000/18; 28,275/13
**Man:** 13 officers, 125 men, 10 scientists, 14 helicopter detachment

REMARKS: Carry two HH-52A helicopters, painted red. Can break 2-meter ice at 3 knots, 6.4-meter ice maximum. Propulsion plant completely cross-connected and automatic. Two 15-ton cranes. Four 20-mm AA (I × 4) and two 40-mm Mk 64 grenade launchers (I × 2) can be installed. Both homeported at Seattle.

◆ **2 Wind class (269-ft class)** Bldr: Western Pipe & Steel, San Pedro, Calif.

| | Laid down | L | In serv. |
|---|---|---|---|
| WAGB 281 WESTWIND (ex-AGB 6, ex-*Severniy Polyus*) | 24-8-42 | 31-3-43 | 18-9-44 |
| WAGB 282 NORTHWIND | 10-7-44 | 22-2-45 | 28-7-45 |

**Northwind (WAGB 282)** H. Serig, 7-84

**D:** 3,502 tons (6,260 fl) **S:** 16 kts **Dim:** 81.99 (76.2 pp) × 19.36 × 8.84
**Electron Equipt:** Radar: 2/SPS-64
**M:** 4 Enterprise diesels, electric drive; 2 props; 10,000 hp **Fuel:** 2,200 tons
**Electric:** 400 kw **Range:** 16,000/16; 38,000/10
**Man:** 14 officers, 100 men, 14 scientists

REMARKS: Can make way in 2.7-m ice. Double hull entirely welded. Telescoping hangar for one HH-52A helicopter. Both reengined 1973–75. Two 12.5-ton cranes. WAGB 281 was in the Soviet Navy from 31-3-45 to 6-12-51. Can break 1-m ice at 3 kts, 3.3-m ice by ramming. WAGB 281, damaged badly by ice in 1984, was repaired 1986–87 and is based at Wilmington, North Carolina, until decommissioned 1-11-88. WAGB 282 is based at Mobile, Ala., and will be decommissioned in early 1988. Both are long overdue for replacement.

NOTE: *Glacier* (WAGB 4) was stricken 7-6-87 for disposal due to her poor condition and the high estimated cost of repairs.

◆ **1 Mackinaw class (290-ft class)** Bldr: Toledo SB, Toledo, Ohio

| | Laid down | L | In serv. |
|---|---|---|---|
| WAGB 83 MACKINAW (ex-*Manitowoc*) | 20-3-43 | 4-3-44 | 20-12-44 |

**D:** 3,049 tons (5,252 fl) **S:** 18.7 kts **Dim:** 88.39 × 22.66 × 5.79
**Electron Equipt:** Radar: 2/SPS-64 **Electric:** 1,260 kw
**M:** 4 Fairbanks-Morse 38D8$\frac{1}{8}$ diesels, electric drive; 3 props (2 aft, 1 fwd); 10,000 hp
**Range:** 10,000/18.7; 41,000/9 **Man:** 10 officers, 97 men

**Mackinaw (WAGB 83)** U.S.C.G., 1985

**ICEBREAKERS** *(continued)*

Remarks: Built for use on the Great Lakes. Helicopter platform. Fitted with two 12-ton cranes. Can break 1.2-m solid ice. Overhauled 1982 at Bay SB, Sturgeon Bay, Wisc.; cranes aft removed and some fuel tankage converted to ballast tanks. Based at Cheboygan, Wisconsin. Placed in caretaker status in the spring of 1988.

## PATROL BOATS

◆ **0 (+2 + 34) "Heritage" class** Bldr: . . .

| | Laid down | L | In serv. |
|---|---|---|---|
| WPB . . . N . . . | 1-10-90 | . . . | 1-10-91 |
| WPB . . . N . . . | . . . | . . . | . . . |

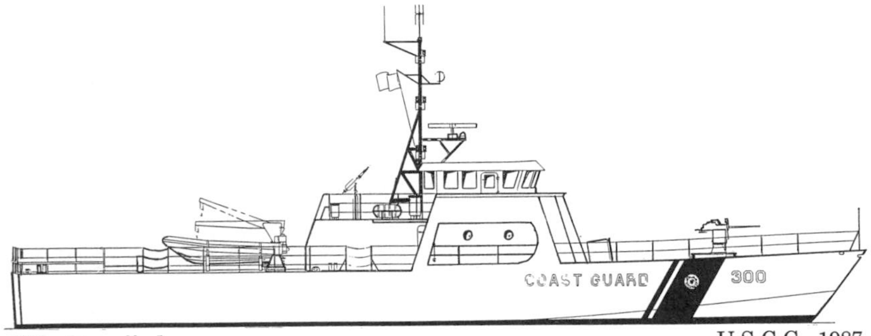


**"Heritage" class** U.S.C.G., 1987

**D:** 140 tons (160 fl) **S:** 30 + kts **Dim:** 36.56 × 6.85 × 2.53
**A:** 1/20-mm AA—2/12.7-mm mg (I × 2)
**Electron Equipt:** Radar: 1/SPS-64(V)1 **M:** 2 diesels; 2 props; . . . hp
**Electric:** 160 kw **Range:** 720/30; 1,152/12
**Fuel:** . . . **Endurance:** 5 days **Man:** 2 officers, 14 men

Remarks: Intend to order first two 1-7-89 as prototypes for series production to begin 12-92. Plan 36 total to replace older 83-ft patrol boats. Will have "deep-vee" hull form and are expected to last 25 years.

Note: The 42.4-m SWATH WPB described in the previous edition was not proceeded with, but the Coast Guard still envisions construction of as many as 23 SWATH patrol boats during the 1990s.

◆ **16 (+21) "Island" (110-ft) class** Bldr: Bollinger Machine Ship & SY, Lockport, Louisiana

| | L | In serv. |
|---|---|---|
| WPB 1301 Farallon | 27-8-85 | 21-2-86 |
| WPB 1302 Manitou | 9-10-85 | 28-2-86 |
| WPB 1303 Matagorda | 15-12-85 | 25-4-86 |
| WPB 1304 Maui | 13-1-86 | 9-5-86 |
| WPB 1305 Monhegan | 15-2-86 | 16-6-86 |
| WPB 1306 Nunivak | 15-3-86 | 4-7-86 |
| WPB 1307 Ocracoke | 12-4-86 | 4-8-86 |
| WPB 1308 Vashon | 10-5-86 | 15-8-86 |
| WPB 1309 Aquidneck | 14-6-86 | 26-9-86 |
| WPB 1310 Mustang | 11-7-86 | 29-8-86 |
| WPB 1311 Naushon | 22-8-86 | 3-10-86 |
| WPB 1312 Sanibel | 3-10-86 | 14-11-86 |
| WPB 1313 Edisto | 21-11-86 | 7-1-87 |
| WPB 1314 Sapelo | 8-1-87 | 24-2-87 |
| WPB 1315 Matinicus | 26-2-87 | 16-4-87 |
| WPB 1316 Nantucket | 17-4-87 | 4-6-87 |
| WPB 1317 Attu | . . . | 2-88 |
| WPB 1318 Baranof | . . . | . . . |
| WPB 1319 Chandeleur | . . . | . . . |
| WPB 1320 Chincoteague | . . . | . . . |
| WPB 1321 Cushing | . . . | . . . |
| WPB 1322 Cuttyhunk | . . . | . . . |
| WPB 1323 Drummond | . . . | . . . |
| WPB 1324 Largo | . . . | . . . |
| WPB 1325 Metomkin | . . . | . . . |
| WPB 1326 Monomoy | . . . | . . . |
| WPB 1327 Orcas | . . . | . . . |
| WPB 1328 Padre | . . . | . . . |
| WPB 1329 Sitkinak | . . . | . . . |
| WPB 1330 Tybee | . . . | . . . |
| WPB 1331 Washington | . . . | . . . |
| WPB 1332 Wrangell | . . . | . . . |
| WPB 1333 Adak | . . . | . . . |
| WPB 1334 Liberty | . . . | . . . |
| WPB 1335 Anacapa | . . . | . . . |
| WPB 1336 Kiska | . . . | . . . |
| WPB 1337 Assateague | . . . | . . . |

**Aquidneck (WPB 1309)** G. Arra, 9-86

**Matinicus (WPB 1315)** U.S.C.G., 4-87

**D:** 117 tons light (165 fl) **S:** 29.7 kts **Dim:** 33.53 × 6.40 × 2.23
**A:** 1/20-mm AA—2/40-mm Mk 19 grenade launchers—2/12.7-mm mg (I × 2)
**Electron Equipt:** Radar: 1/SPS-64(V)1 **Endurance:** 5 days
**M:** 2 Alco-Paxman Valenta 16 RP200 CM diesels; 2 props; 5,820 hp
**Electric:** 198 kw
**Range:** 1,853 n.m. (26 kts × 24 hrs + 13.1 kts × 96 hrs); 3,380/8
**Man:** 2 officers, 2 CPO, 12 men

Remarks: Fifteen ordered 8-84; 16th ordered 3-5-85 in place of earlier winner Marine Power & Equipment, Seattle, Washington, whose contract was successfully contested by Bollinger. Modified Vosper-Thornycroft design, with increased tophamper. Steel hull, aluminum deck and superstructure. Fin stabilizers fitted. Carry Loran-C and Omega receivers, IFF transponder, and SQN-18 echo-sounder. Engines governor-limited to 2,880 hp each from nominal max. 4,000 hp. First delivered 23-8-85 for trials; others were to follow at 45-day intervals.

Sixteen more ordered 11-2-87 under Congressional Coast Defense Augmentation; five more ordered 24-2-87 under Drug Omnibus Act of 1987. These 21 later units are to be delivered at 35-day intervals and will have minor improvements, including heavier bow plating and a better anchor. High minimum speed of 9 kts makes these craft difficult to use in towing small craft in distress. Have 3-ton payload margin. Expected to last only 15 years.

◆ **3 Bell 110 surface-effect patrol boats** Bldr: Bell-Halter, Inc., New Orleans

WSES 2 Sea Hawk (In serv. 16-10-82) WSES 3 Petrel (In serv. 18-6-83)
WSES 3 Shearwater (In serv. 16-10-82)

**D:** 110 tons (160 fl) **S:** 35 kts (designed; now make about 30 kts)
**Dim:** 33.53 × 11.89 × 2.36 at rest/1.37 on cushion **Man:** 2 officers, 16 men
**A:** 2/12.7-mm mg (I × 2) **Electron Equipt:** Radar: 2/Decca 914
**M:** 2 G.M. 16V149 TI diesels for propulsion; 2 CP props; 3,600 hp;
2 G.M. 8V92 TI diesels for lift; 2 centrifugal lift fans; 990 hp
**Electric:** 60 kw **Range:** 1,000/30; 1,500/23 on cushion

Remarks: Ordered 6-82 after the very successful trials with *Dorado* (WSES 1), now in U.S. Navy service. Rigid sidewall design, with rubber seal bags fore and aft. Aluminum construction. Based at Key West on anti-drug patrol and intercept duties. Extra equipment had greatly lowered performance to 18 kts max., vibration problems caused redesign of skirt vents, and speed has now been restored.

**PATROL BOATS** *(continued)*

**Sea Hawk (WSES 2) and Shearwater (WSES 3)** Bell Aerospace, 10-82

**PATROL CRAFT**

◆ **17 95-ft Cape class** Bldr: Coast Guard Yard, Curtis Bay, Maryland

| | In serv. | Modernized | Disposal |
|---|---|---|---|
| WPB 95302 Cape Higgon | 14-10-53 | 13-2-81 | 1990 |
| WPB 95303 Cape Upright | 2-7-53 | 20-11-77 | 1989 |
| WPB 95304 Cape Gull | 8-6-53 | 18-9-78 | 13-5-88 |
| WPB 95305 Cape Hatteras | 28-7-53 | 7-11-80 | 1990 |
| WPB 95306 Cape George | 10-8-53 | 21-5-81 | 1990 |
| WPB 95307 Cape Current | 24-8-53 | 3-10-78 | 1989 |
| WPB 95309 Cape Carter | 7-12-53 | 7-5-83 | 1992 |
| WPB 95312 Cape Knox | 13-5-55 | 13-7-79 | 1989 |
| WPB 95313 Cape Morgan | 5-7-55 | 21-4-80 | 1990 |
| WPB 95316 Cape Fox | 22-8-55 | 8-9-80 | 1990 |
| WPB 95319 Cape Romain | 11-10-55 | no | 1989 |
| WPB 95321 Cape Cross | 20-8-58 | 16-4-82 | 1992 |
| WPB 95322 Cape Horn | 3-9-58 | 21-1-83 | 1992 |
| WPB 95324 Cape Shoalwater | 17-10-58 | 13-7-79 | 1989 |
| WPB 95326 Cape Corwin | 14-11-58 | 15-10-82 | 1991 |
| WPB 95328 Cape Henlopen | 5-12-58 | 15-1-82 | 1990 |
| WPB 95332 Cape York | 6-9-59 | 15-7-81 | 1990 |

**Cape Corwin (WPB 95326)** U.S.C.G., 1983

**D:** 87–90 tons (106 fl) **S:** 24 kts (20 limit) **Dim:** 28.96 × 6.1 × 1.55
**A:** 2/12.7-mm mg (I × 2)—2/40-mm Mk 64 grenade launchers (I × 2)
**Electron Equipt:** Radar: 1/SPS-64(V)1 **Electric:** 60 kw
**M:** 2 G.M. 16V149 TI diesels; 2 props; 2,470 hp **Endurance:** 5 days
**Range:** 556/23; 1,900/11.5 (WPB 95319; 571/20; 1,347/9)

Remarks: Two transferred to Haiti (1956), two to Ethiopia (1958), four to Thailand, and one to Saudi Arabia. Nine were given to South Korea (1969–70). Several others have been scrapped. Sister *Cape Coral* (WPB 95301) stricken 6-6-83, *Cape Strait* (WPB 95308) in 1-83, *Cape Newhagen* (WPB 95318) in 9-82, *Cape Fairweather* (WPB 95314) 4-3-85, *Cape Jellison* (WPB 95317) on 12-12-86, *Cape Hedge* (WPB 95311—to U.S. Navy as pilot boat *Vanguard*) on 7-1-87. *Cape Starr* (WPB 95320) on 16-1-87, *Cape Small* (WPB 95300) on 13-4-87, and *Cape Wash* (WPB 95310) on 1-6-87. All survivors except WPB 95319 have been re-engined, completing as per the dates on the ship list; the original 4 Cummins VT-12-M-700 diesels produced 18 kts from 2,324 hp. The new plant cannot be run at full power without straining the hull.

◆ **53 83-ft Point class** Bldr: Coast Guard Yard, Curtis Bay, Md. (except WPB 82345 to WPB 83249: J. Martinac SB, Tacoma, Wash.)

| | In serv. |
|---|---|
| WPB 82302 Point Hope | 5-10-60 |
| WPB 82311 Point Verde | 15-3-61 |
| WPB 82312 Point Swift | 22-3-61 |
| WPB 82314 Point Thatcher | 13-9-61 |
| WPB 82354 Point Evans | 10-1-67 |
| WPB 82355 Point Hannon | 23-1-67 |
| WPB 82356 Point Francis | 3-2-67 |
| WPB 82357 Point Huron | 17-2-67 |
| WPB 82318 Point Herron | 14-6-61 |
| WPB 82332 Point Roberts | 6-6-62 |
| WPB 82333 Point Highland | 27-6-62 |
| WPB 82334 Point Ledge | 18-7-62 |
| WPB 82335 Point Countess | 8-8-62 |
| WPB 82336 Point Glass | 29-8-62 |
| WPB 82337 Point Divide | 19-9-62 |
| WPB 82338 Point Bridge | 10-10-62 |
| WPB 82339 Point Chico | 29-10-62 |
| WPB 82340 Point Batan | 21-11-62 |
| WPB 82341 Point Lookout | 12-12-62 |
| WPB 82342 Point Baker | 30-10-63 |
| WPB 82343 Point Wells | 20-11-63 |
| WPB 82344 Point Estero | 11-12-66 |
| WPB 82345 Point Judith | 26-7-66 |
| WPB 82346 Point Arena | 26-8-66 |
| WPB 82347 Point Bonita | 12-9-66 |
| WPB 82348 Point Barrow | 4-10-66 |
| WPB 82349 Point Spencer | 25-10-66 |
| WPB 82350 Point Franklin | 14-11-66 |
| WPB 82351 Point Bennett | 19-12-66 |
| WPB 82352 Point Sal | 5-12-66 |
| WPB 82353 Point Monroe | 27-12-66 |
| WPB 82358 Point Stuart | 17-3-67 |
| WPB 82359 Point Steele | 26-4-67 |
| WPB 82360 Point Winslow | 3-3-67 |
| WPB 82361 Point Charles | 15-5-67 |
| WPB 82362 Point Brown | 30-3-67 |
| WPB 82363 Point Nowell | 1-6-67 |
| WPB 82364 Point Whitehorn | 13-7-67 |
| WPB 82365 Point Turner | 14-4-67 |
| WPB 82366 Point Lobos | 29-5-67 |
| WPB 82367 Point Knoll | 27-6-67 |
| WPB 82368 Point Warde | 14-8-67 |
| WPB 82369 Point Heyer | 3-8-67 |
| WPB 82370 Point Richmond | 25-8-67 |
| WPB 82371 Point Barnes | 21-4-70 |
| WPB 82372 Point Brower | 21-4-70 |
| WPB 82373 Point Camden | 4-5-70 |
| WPB 82374 Point Carrew | 18-5-70 |
| WPB 82375 Point Doran | 1-6-70 |
| WPB 82376 Point Harris | 22-6-70 |
| WPB 82377 Point Hobart | 13-7-70 |
| WPB 82378 Point Jackson | 3-8-70 |
| WPB 82379 Point Martin | 20-8-70 |

**Point Arena (WPB 82346)** G. Arra, 7-86

**Point Evans (WPB 82354)** V. Baca, 4-87

**D:** 64 tons (66–69 fl) **S:** 23.7 kts (see Remarks) **Dim:** 25.3 × 5.23 × 1.95
**A:** 2/12.7-mm mg (I × 2)—2/40-mm Mk 64 grenade launchers (I × 2)
**Electron Equipt:** Radar: 1/SPS-64(V)1
**M:** 2 Cummins VT-12-M diesels; 2 props; 1,600 hp **Fuel:** 5.7 tons
**Range:** 490/23.7; 1,500/8 **Man:** 1 officer, 7 men

Remarks: Hull in mild steel. High-speed diesels controlled from the bridge. The heavier WPB 82371 and later make 22.6 knots, and have a range of 320/22.6; 1,200/8. WPB 82314 had two gas turbines with 1,000 hp (27-knot potential) and controllable-pitch propellers, but was re-equipped with diesels. Well-equipped for salvage and towing. Beginning in 6-65, 26 others were sent to Vietnam; transferred 1969–70. To be discarded 1992–98. First four are "Group A": 67 tons fl.

**PATROL CRAFT** *(continued)*

WPB 82371–82379 (less WPB 82374) have a range of 320/22.6 or 1,200/8 and displace 69 tons (fl).

**TRAINING CUTTER**

◆ **1 Horst Wessel class** Bldr: Blohm + Voss, Hamburg, Germany

| | L | In U.S.C.G. |
|---|---|---|
| WIX 327 Eagle (ex-*Horst Wessel*) | 13-6-36 | 15-5-46 |

**Eagle (WIX 327)** 1977

**D:** 1,519 tons light (1,816 fl) **S:** 17 kts (10 under power)
**Dim:** 89.92 (70.41 wl) × 11.92 × 5.18 **Electron Equipt:** Radar: 1/SPS-64(V)1
**M:** 1 Caterpillar D-399, V-16 diesel; 1 prop; 1,000 hp (10 kts); 1,983 $m^2$ sail area
**Electric:** 450 kw **Range:** 5,450/7.5 (diesel)
**Man:** 19 officers, 46 men, 175 cadets and instructors **Fuel:** 79 tons

Remarks: Training ship at the Coast Guard Academy, New London. Sisters operate in the Portuguese Navy and Soviet merchant marine. Re-engined and extensively overhauled at the U.S. Coast Guard Yard, Curtis Bay. Has 344 tons fixed ballast.

Note: Four small training tenders, T1 through T4, are used at the Coast Guard Academy for navigational and maneuvering training

**BUOY TENDERS, SEAGOING**

Note: A new class of buoy tenders to replace the elderly and hard-worked *Balsam* class is being planned. Some 28 ships would be built, beginning in the early 1990s.

◆ **30 Balsam class** Bldrs: WLB 297: U.S. Coast Guard Yard, Curtis, Bay, Md.; others: A: Marine Iron SB Co.; B: Duluth Iron & SB Co.; C: Zenith Dredge Co.—all of Duluth, Minn.

| | Bldr | Laid down | L | In serv. | SLEP |
|---|---|---|---|---|---|
| WLB 277 Cowslip‡ | A | 16-9-41 | 11-4-42 | 17-10-42 | 1-83 to 7-84 |
| WLB 290 Gentian* | B | 3-10-41 | 23-5-42 | 3-11-43 | 11-79 to 8-83 |
| WLB 291 Laurel* | B | 17-4-42 | 4-8-42 | 24-11-42 | 7-86 to 11-89 |
| WLB 296 Sorrel* | B | 26-5-42 | 28-9-42 | 15-4-43 | 10-79 to 1-83 |
| WLB 297 Ironwood‡ | | 2-11-42 | 16-3-43 | 4-8-43 | |
| WLB 301 Conifer* | A | 6-7-42 | 3-11-42 | 1-7-43 | 8-83 to 1-86 |
| WLB 302 Madrona* | B | 6-7-42 | 11-11-42 | 30-5-43 | 4-84 to 7-89 |
| WLB 305 Mesquite‡ | A | 20-8-42 | 14-11-42 | 27-8-43 | |
| WLB 306 Buttonwood* | A | 5-10-42 | 30-11-42 | 24-9-43 | 3-91 to 10-92 |
| WLB 307 Planetree* | A | 4-12-42 | 20-3-43 | 4-11-43 | 3-93 to 3-94 |
| WLB 308 Papaw* | A | 16-11-42 | 19-2-43 | 12-10-43 | 7-89 to 11-90 |
| WLB 309 Sweetgum* | A | 21-2-43 | 15-4-43 | 20-11-43 | 11-89 to 3-91 |
| WLB 388 Basswood† | A | 21-3-43 | 20-5-43 | 12-1-44 | |
| WLB 389 Bittersweet‡ | B | 16-9-43 | 11-11-43 | 11-5-44 | |
| WLB 390 Blackhaw* | A | 16-4-43 | 18-6-43 | 17-2-44 | 10-92 to 10-93 |
| WLB 392 Bramble‡ | B | 2-8-43 | 23-10-43 | 22-4-44 | |
| WLB 393 Firebrush | B | 12-11-43 | 3-2-44 | 20-7-44 | |
| WLB 394 Hornbeam‡ | A | 19-6-43 | 14-8-43 | 14-4-44 | |
| WLB 395 Iris† | B | 10-12-43 | 18-5-43 | 11-8-44 | |
| WLB 396 Mallow* | B | 10-10-43 | 9-12-43 | 6-6-44 | 10-93 to 10-94 |
| WLB 397 Mariposa‡ | B | 25-10-43 | 14-1-44 | 1-7-44 | |
| WLB 399 Sagebrush* | B | 15-7-43 | 30-9-43 | 1-4-44 | 11-90 to 3-92 |
| WLB 400 Salvia* | B | 24-6-43 | 15-9-43 | 19-2-44 | 3-92 to 3-93 |
| WLB 401 Sassafras | A | 16-8-43 | 5-10-43 | 23-5-44 | |
| WLB 402 Sedge‡ | A | 6-10-43 | 27-11-43 | 5-7-44 | |
| WLB 403 Spar‡ | A | 13-9-43 | 2-11-43 | 12-6-44 | |
| WLB 404 Sundew‡ | A | 29-11-43 | 8-2-44 | 24-8-44 | |
| WLB 405 Sweetbrier‡ | A | 3-11-43 | 30-12-43 | 26-7-44 | |
| WLB 406 Acacia (ex-*Thistle*)‡ | B | 16-1-44 | 7-4-44 | 1-9-44 | |
| WLB 407 Woodrush‡ | B | 4-2-44 | 28-4-44 | 22-9-44 | |

* has received Service Life Extension overhaul
† has received austere renovation
‡ has received major renovation

**Cowslip (WLB 277)** G. Arra, 4-86

**Blackhaw (WLB 390)**—working buoys L. Akin, 10-84

**Conifer (WLB 301)**—post-SLEP, with new hull plating, new double topping lift buoy-handling gear, rigid inflatable in place of port boat, with hydraulic crane V. Baca, 4-87

**D:** 935 tons (1,025 fl) **S:** 12.8–13 kts **Dim:** 54.9 × 11.3 × 4.0
**A:** WLB 297, 389, 401, 402, 405: 2/20-mm AA (I × 2)
**Electron Equipt:** Radar: 1/SPS-64(V)1
**M:** 2 diesels, electric drive; 1 prop; WLB 277 to WLB 302: 1,000 hp; WLB 297, WLB 305 to WLB 407: 1,200 hp. WLB 404: 1,800 hp (see Remarks)
**Range:** Most: 4,600/12–18: 14,000/7.4; WLB 297, WLB 306 to WLB 308, WLB 388, WLB 390, WLB 396, WLB 401: 8,000/12; 23,500/7.5; WLB 305, WLB 392, WLB 406, WLB 407: 10,500/13; 31,000/7.5
**Fuel:** varies **Man:** 7 officers, 45 men **Electric:** 400 kw

Remarks: *Evergreen* (WLB 295) converted to oceanographic research ship and now used as a patrol ship. WLB 296, WLB 390, WLB 392, WLB 402, WLB 403, and

**BUOY TENDERS, SEAGOING** *(continued)*

WLB 404 have strengthened hulls for icebreaking, but all have icebreaker hull form. All have 20-ton derrick. Ships in SLEP (Service Life Extension Program) have rebuilt G.E. EMD 8-645E6A engines and propulsion motors, improved habitability, hydraulic cargo-handling gear, and bow-thrusters; 14 were to receive SLEP (see table), but the total may reduce to nine, due to fiscal constraints. *Blackthorn* (WLB 391) rammed and sunk 28-1-80, replaced by *Cowslip* (WLB 277), which was previously stricken 23-3-73, sold 1976, repurchased 19-1-81, and recommissioned 9-11-81. *Clover* (WLB 292) redesignated WMEC in 2-80, *Citrus* (WLB 300) redesignated WMEC in 6-79. WLB 404 has a maximum speed of 15 knots. Modernized ships have greater endurance. WLB 388 may decommission 1988. WLB 297, 307, 396, 402, 405, and 407 have long-range communications suites. WLB 365, 392, 397, 404, and 406 operate on the Great Lakes.

**BUOY TENDERS, COASTAL**

◆ **5 Red class (157-ft class)** Bldr: Coast Guard Yard, Curtis Bay, Md.

WLM 685 Red Wood
WLM 686 Red Beech
WLM 687 Red Birch
WLM 688 Red Cedar
WLM 689 Red Oak

**Red Oak (WLM 689)** L. & L. Van Ginderen, 8-87

**D:** 471 tons (512 fl) **S:** 12 kts **Dim:** 47.9 × 10.1 × 1.9
**M:** 2 diesels; 2 CP props; 1,800 hp **Range:** 2,248/12.8; 3,055/11.6
**Man:** 4 officers, 27 men

Remarks: WLM 685 and WLM 686 completed in 1964, WLM 687 in 1965, WLM 688 in 1970, and WLM 689 in 12-71. Can break light ice. Have 10-ton derrick and a bow-thruster. All operate on U.S. East Coast.

◆ **6 White class (133-ft class)**

WLM 540 White Sumac
WLM 543 White Holly
WLM 544 White Sage
WLM 545 White Heath
WLM 546 White Lupine
WLM 547 White Pine

**White Sage (WLM 544)** 1976

**D:** 435 tons (600 fl) **S:** 9.8 kts **Dim:** 40.5 × 9.4 × 2.7
**M:** 2 Union diesels; 2 props; 600 hp **Range:** 2,100/9.8; 4,500/5.1
**Electric:** 90 kw **Fuel:** 40 tons **Man:** 1 officer, 20 men

Remarks: WLM 540 completed in 1943, WLM 542 and WLM 543 in 1944; others in 1942. Former U.S. Navy YF (covered lighter, self-propelled). One 10-ton boom. Sister *White Bush* (WLM 542) stricken 16-9-85. All operate on U.S. East Coast.

◆ **1 Hollyhock class (175-ft class)** Bldr: Moore DD Co., Oakland, Cal.

WLM 212 Fir (In serv. 1-10-40)

**D:** 828 tons (989 fl) **S:** 12 kts **Dim:** 53.4 × 10.4 × 3.7
**M:** 2 diesels; 2 props; 1,350 hp **Electron Equipt:** Radar: 1/SPS-64(V)1
**Range:** 5,650/12; 8,675/7.5 **Man:** 5 officers, 35 men

**Fir (WLM 212)** 1974

Remarks: Redesignated from WLB to WLM on 1-1-65. Has a 20-ton boom. Sisters *Hollyhock* (WLM 220) and *Walnut* (WLM 252) stricken 31-3-82 and 15-6-82, respectively, with the latter having been transferred to Honduras. WLM 212 is based at Seattle.

**BUOY TENDERS, INLAND**

◆ **1 Tern (80-ft class)**

| | Bldr | Laid down | L | In serv. |
|---|---|---|---|---|
| 80801 Tern | U.S.C.G. Yard, Curtis Bay | 3-68 | 7-2-69 | 5-69 |

**Tern (80801)** U.S.C.G., 5-69

**D:** 135 tons (168 normal fl) **S:** 10 kts **Dim:** 24.6 × 7.0 × 1.45
**Electron Equipt:** Radar: 1/. . . navigational
**M:** 2 diesels; 2 right-angle hydraulic drive props; 470 hp—1/125-hp, 360-degree rotating bow-thruster
**Fuel:** 53 tons

Remarks: Can carry and lay buoys of up to 35 tons weight. Considered a "boat," hence no WLI number. Was prototype for an unbuilt class.

◆ **1 Buckthorn class** (In serv. 1963)

WLI 642 Buckthorn

**Buckthorn (WLI 642)** U.S.C.G., 1970

BUOY TENDERS, INLAND *(continued)*

**D:** 200 tons (fl) **S:** 11.9 kts **Dim:** 30.5 × 7.3 × 1.2
**M:** 2 diesels; 2 props; 600 hp **Range:** 1,300/11.9; 2,000/7.3
**Man:** 1 officer, 13 men

REMARKS: Bow rectangular at main deck. Has one 5-ton boom. Based on the Great Lakes.

◆ **2 Bayberry class (65-ft class)** (In serv. 1954)

WLI 65400 BAYBERRY WLI 65401 ELDERBERRY

**Bayberry (WLI 65400)** U.S.C.G., 1979

**D:** 68 tons (fl) **S:** 11.3 kts **Dim:** 19.8 × 5.2 × 1.2
**M:** 2 diesels; 2 props; 400 hp **Range:** 800/11.3; 1,700/6 **Man:** 5 tot.

REMARKS: Based at Seattle, Wash., and Petersburg, Alaska, respectively.

◆ **2 Blackberry class (65300 class)** (In serv. 1946)

WLI 65303 BLACKBERRY WLI 65304 CHOKEBERRY

**D:** 68 tons (fl) **S:** 9 kts **Dim:** 19.8 × 5.2 × 1.2
**M:** 1 diesel; 1 prop; 220 hp **Range:** 700/9; 1,500/5 **Man:** 5 tot.

REMARKS: Both operate on U.S. East Coast.

◆ **1 Cosmos class (100-ft class)** Bldr: Burchfield Boiler Co., Tacoma, Wash.

| | Laid down | L | In serv. |
|---|---|---|---|
| WLI 313 BLUEBELL | 20-3-44 | 28-9-44 | 24-3-45 |

**D:** 178 tons (fl) **S:** 10.5 kts **Dim:** 30.5 × 7.3 × 1.5
**M:** 2 diesels; 2 props; 600 hp **Range:** 1,400/10.5; 2,700/7

REMARKS: Four sisters retyped WLIC on 1-10-79. WLI 313 based at Portland, Ore.

BUOY TENDERS, RIVER

◆ **0 (+1 + 3) new-construction 75 ft. (F-class)** Bldr: Avondale SY, Louisana

REMARKS: One new unit requested under FY 86 Budget to act as push-tug for an aids-to-navigation barge on the Arkansas River. Ordered 1-88 to replace *Lantana* (WLR 80310) and *Dogwood* (WLR 259). Three more are to be requested, the last to deliver 10-89, all for service on western rivers.

◆ **9 Gasconade class (75-ft class)**

| | In serv. | | In serv. |
|---|---|---|---|
| WLR 75401 GASCONADE | 1964 | WLR 75406 KICKAPOO | 1969 |
| WLR 75402 MUSKINGUM | 1965 | WLR 75407 KANAWHA | 1969 |
| WLR 75403 WYACONDA | 1965 | WLR 75408 PATOKA | 1970 |
| WLR 75404 CHIPPEWA | 1965 | WLR 75409 CHENA | 1970 |
| WLR 75405 CHEYENNE | 1966 | | |

**D:** 141 tons (fl) **S:** 7.6-8.7 kts **Dim:** 22.9 × 6.7 × 1.2
**M:** 2 diesels; 2 props; 600 hp **Range:** 1,600/7.6; 3,100/6.5 **Man:** 12 tot.

REMARKS: Flat-ended, barge-like hulls. WLR 75405 has an associated buoy push-barge, and a slightly larger crew. One 1-ton crane. All operate on the Mississippi River and its tributaries.

◆ **6 Ouachita class (65-ft class)**

WLR 65501 OUACHITA WLR 65503 OBION WLR 65505 OSAGE
WLR 65502 CIMARRON WLR 65504 SCIOTO WLR 65506 SANGAMON

**D:** 130–143 tons (fl) **S:** 10 kts **Dim:** 20.1 × 6.4 × 1.5
**M:** 2 diesels; 2 props; 600 hp **Range:** 1,700/10.5; 3,500/6 **Man:** 10 tot.

REMARKS: WLR 65501 and WLR 65502 completed in 1960, others in 1962. WLR 65504 has an associated push-type buoy barge with a 3-ton crane, and a larger crew. All have a 3-ton crane aboard. Operate on the Mississippi River and its tributaries.

**Gasconade (WLR 75401)**—with CGB 90008, a 27.4-m buoy barge U.S.C.G., 6-83

**Ouachita (WLR 65501)**—with CGB 90009, a 27.4-m buoy barge U.S.C.G., 12-83

◆ **1 Sumac class (115-ft class)** Bldr: Peterson & Haecker, Blair, Nebraska

WLR 311 SUMAC (In serv. 11-11-44)

**Sumac (WLR 311)**—with work barge U.S.C.G., 3-85

**D:** 404 tons (478 fl) **S:** 10.6 kts **Dim:** 35.1 × 9.1 × 1.8
**M:** 3 Fairbanks-Morse diesels; 3 props; 2,250 hp
**Range:** 5,000/10.6; 11,600/5 **Man:** 1 officer, 22 men

REMARKS: Based at St. Louis, Missouri.

◆ **1 Lantana class (80-ft class)** Bldr: Peterson & Haecker, Blair, Nebraska

WLR 80310 LANTANA (In serv. 6-11-43)

**D:** 235 tons (fl) **S:** 10 kts **Dim:** 24.3 × 9.1 × 1.8
**M:** 3 diesels; 3 props; 945 hp **Range:** 5,000/10 **Man:** 1 officer, 19 men

REMARKS: Based at Natchez, Mississippi. To strike 1989.

◆ **1 Dogwood class (114-ft class)** Bldr: Dubuque Boat & Boiler Wks., Iowa

WLR 259 DOGWOOD (In serv. 17-9-41)

**D:** 230 tons (310 fl) **S:** 11 kts **Dim:** 34.8 × 7.9 × 1.2
**M:** 2 diesels; 2 props; 800 hp
**Range:** 1,300/11; 2,800/5.5 **Man:** 1 officer, 20 men

REMARKS: Based at Pine Bluff, Arkansas. To strike 1989.

NOTE: Construction of a total of eleven 39.6-m work barges to work with the River Buoy Tenders is planned. Three have been completed in a construction program that began in 10-83; the last is planned for completion by 4-89.

CONSTRUCTION TENDERS, INLAND

◆ **4 Pamlico class (160-ft class)** Bldr: Coast Guard Yard, Curtis Bay, Md. (all in serv. 1976)

WLIC 800 PAMLICO WLIC 803 KENNEBEC
WLIC 801 HUDSON WLIC 804 SAGINAW

## CONSTRUCTION TENDERS, INLAND *(continued)*

**Pamlico (WLIC 800)** U.S.C.G., 1976

**D:** 413 tons (459 fl) **S:** 11.5 kts **Dim:** 49.1 × 9.1 × 1.2
**Electron Equipt:** Radar: 1/Raytheon 1900
**M:** 2 Cummins D379, 8-cyl. diesels; 2 props; 1,000 hp
**Range:** 1,400/11; 2,200/6.5 **Man:** 1 officer, 13 men

REMARKS: Design combines capabilities of the *Anvil* class and their associated equipment barges. One 9-ton crane.

◆ **9 Anvil class (75-ft class)** (In serv. 1962–65)

| | | |
|---|---|---|
| WLIC 75301 ANVIL | WLIC 75305 VISE | WLIC 75309 HATCHET |
| WLIC 75302 HAMMER | WLIC 75306 CLAMP | WLIC 75310 AXE |
| WLIC 75303 SLEDGE | WLIC 75307 WEDGE | |
| WLIC 75304 MALLET | | |

**D:** 145 tons (fl) **S:** 9.1 kts **Dim:** 22.9 × 6.7 × 1.2
**M:** 2 diesels; 2 props; 600 hp **Man:** 0 or 1 officer, 9 men

REMARKS: All except *Anvil* and *Mallet* have an associated push-type barge with a 9-ton crane. WLIC 75306 to WLIC 75310 are 23.2 m overall and can make 9.4 knots. Sister *Spike* (WLIC 75308) and associated barge stricken 30-5-86. Ranges vary: WLIC 75301 and 75302: 1,300/9; 2,400/5; WLIC 75303–75305: 1,000/9; 2,200/5; others: 1,050/9; 2,500/5.

◆ **3 Cosmos class (100-ft class)** Bldr: Dubuque Boat & Boiler, Dubuque, Iowa

| | L | In serv. |
|---|---|---|
| WLIC 298 RAMBLER | 6-5-43 | 26-5-43 |
| WLIC 315 SMILAX | 18-8-44 | 1-11-44 |
| WLIC 316 PRIMROSE | 18-8-44 | 23-10-44 |

**Primrose (WLIC 316)**—with non-standard pile driver U.S.C.G., 5-81

**D:** 178 tons (fl) **S:** 10.5 kts **Dim:** 30.5 × 7.3 × 1.5
**Electron Equipt:** Radar: 1/Raytheon 1900 **M:** 2 diesels; 2 props; 600 hp
**Range:** 1,400/10.5; 2,700/7 **Man:** 1 officer, 14 men

REMARKS: Reclassifed from WLI on 1-10-79. Sister *Bluebell* remains typed WLI (WLI 313). WLIC 298 has an associated construction barge, while WLIC 316 has a pile driver on her bow. All have a 5-ton crane. Sister *Cosmos* (WLIC 293) stricken 1985.

## ICEBREAKING TUGS

◆ **8 (+1) Katmai Bay class (140-ft class)** Bldr: Tacoma Boatbuilding, Tacoma, Wash., except WTGB 107: Bay City Marine, Tacoma, Wash., WTGB 108, 109: Bay City Marine, National City, Cal.

| | Laid down | L | In serv. |
|---|---|---|---|
| WTGB 101 KATMAI BAY | 7-11-77 | 8-4-78 | 8-1-79 |
| WTGB 102 BRISTOL BAY | 13-2-78 | 22-7-78 | 5-4-79 |
| WTGB 103 MOBILE BAY | 13-2-78 | 11-11-78 | 6-5-79 |
| WTGB 104 BISCAYNE BAY | 29-8-78 | 3-2-79 | 8-12-79 |
| WTGB 105 NEAH BAY | 6-8-79 | ... | 18-8-80 |
| WTGB 106 MORRO BAY | 6-8-79 | ... | 25-1-80 |
| WTGB 107 PENOBSCOT BAY | 1-7-83 | 27-7-84 | 2-1-85 |
| WTGB 108 THUNDER BAY | 20-7-84 | 15-8-85 | 4-11-85 |
| WTGB 109 STURGEON BAY | 7-86 | 12-9-87 | 4-88 |

**Penobscot Bay (WTGB 107)** L. & L. Van Ginderen, 7-87

**Morro Bay (WTGB 106)**—white hull as training ship
L. & L. Van Ginderen 11-86

**D:** 662 tons (fl) **S:** 14.7 kts **Dim:** 42.67 (39.62 pp) × 11.43 × 3.66
**Electron Equipt:** Radar: 1/SPS-64(V)1
**M:** 2 Fairbanks-Morse $38D8\frac{1}{8}$ diesels, Westinghouse electric drive; 1 prop; 2,500 hp
**Electric:** 250 kw (2 × 125 kw) **Range:** 1,800/14.7; 4,000/12
**Fuel:** 71 tons **Man:** 3 officers, 14 men

REMARKS: Displace 673 tons in fresh water. Reclassified from WYTM on 5-2-79. WTGB 101–105 operate on the Great Lakes, the others on the U.S. East Coast. Can break 51-mm ice. Have portable bubble-generator system housed in a removable deckhouse on the fantail. Two fire-fighting monitors atop the pilothouse, which provides near 360-degree viewing. One 2-ton crane handles a 4.9-m plastic workboat. Initially intended to replace the older WYTMs in service. WTGB 109 ordered 11-2-86, using Navy funds; at least one more was planned, to be named *Curtis Bay*, but funds will not be available.

WTGB 102 operates with a 45.72 × 18.29 × 3.05 former jackup barge converted 11-84 by Bay SB, Sturgeon Bay, Wisc., for a 2-year experimental program on the Great Lakes. A 300-hp Schottel vertical cycloidal bow-thruster prop, powered by a G.M. 8V92 diesel was added to the barge, as was a 10-ton 21.3-m extendable boom, to permit the craft to act as an aids-to-navigation tender. WTGB 106 acts as enlisted training ship in the summer, at Yorktown, Va.

### HARBOR TUGS, MEDIUM

◆ **1 110-ft class** Bldr: Ira S. Bushey, Brooklyn, N.Y.

WYTM 93 Raritan (In serv. 11-4-39)

**D:** 370 tons (384 fl) **S:** 11.2 kts **Dim:** 33.54 × 8.29 × 3.51
**Electron Equipt:** Radar: 1/SPS-64(V)1 or Raytheon 1900
**M:** 2 G.M. or Ingersoll-Rand 8-cyl. diesels, electric drive; 1 prop; 1,000 hp
**Range:** 1,845/11.2; 4,000/8 **Man:** 1 officer, 19 men

Remarks: Sisters *Arundel* (WYTM 90) stricken 30-4-82; *Yankton* (WYTM 72) and *Mahoning* (WYTM 91) stricken 10-84; *Sauk* (WYTM 99) stricken 1-4-85; *Apalachee* (WYTM 71) stricken 4-11-85; *Mohican* (WYTM 73) stricken 26-6-86; *Chinook* (WYTM 96) stricken 1-7-86; *Snohomish* (WYTM 98) stricken 4-4-86; *Manitou* (WYTM 60) stricken . . . - . . . -86. WYTM 93 to strike by 4-88. Two 33.5-m replacements planned.

### HARBOR TUGS, SMALL

◆ **14 65-ft class** (In serv. 1961–67)

| | | |
|---|---|---|
| WYTL 65601 Capstan | WYTL 65606 Catenary | WYTL 65611 Line |
| WYTL 65602 Chock | WYTL 65607 Bridle | WYTL 65612 Wire |
| WYTL 65603 Swivel | WYTL 65608 Pendant | WYTL 65614 Bollard |
| WYTL 65604 Tackle | WYTL 65609 Shackle | WYTL 65615 Cleat |
| WYTL 65605 Towline | WYTL 65610 Hawser | |

**Catenary (WYTL 65606)** L. & L. Van Ginderen, 11-86

**D:** 72 tons (fl) **S:** 9.8 (first 6: 10.5) **Dim:** 19.8 × 5.8 × 2.1
**Electron Equipt:** Radar: 1/Raytheon 1900 **M:** 1 diesel; 1 prop; 400 hp
**Range:** 850/9.8; 2,700/5.8 (WYTL 65601 to WYTL 65606: 3,600/6.8, 8,900/10.5)
**Man:** 10 tot.

Remarks: Sister *Bitt* (WYTL 65613) stricken 10-4-82. All serve on U.S. East Coast.

### FERRIES

Note: The following four ships are not commissioned cutters of the U.S. Coast Guard, but are under Coast Guard control. Their status is "in service" and they are civilian-manned. They operate from Governors Island in New York Harbor.

◆ **2 ex-U.S. Army ferries** Bldr: John H. Mathis, Camden, N.J.

Lt Samuel S. Coursen (In serv. 1956) Pvt Nicholas Minue (In serv. 1956)

**Lt Samuel S. Coursen** U.S.C.G., 1974

**D:** 869 tons **S:** 12 kts **Dim:** 54.9 × 18.9 × 3.0
**M:** diesel-electric drive; 2 props; 1,000 hp

Remarks: Former U.S. Army ferries FB 812 and FB 813.

◆ **1 former Puget Sound ferry** Bldr: Moore DD, Oakland, Cal.

Governor (ex-*Kulshan*, ex-*Crown City*) (In serv. 1952)

**Governor** U.S.C.G., 2-85

**D:** 1,600 tons (fl) **S:** 12 kts **Dim:** 73.97 × 19.96 × 4.27
**M:** 2 diesels, electric drive; 2 props; . . . hp

Remarks: Originally built for U.S. Navy use at San Diego, then sold to Washington State. Acquired 1982 and refitted at U.S.C.G. Yard, Curtis Bay, into early 1985 for use at Governors Island. Can carry 55 automobiles and 150 passengers.

◆ **1 former New York City ferry** Bldr: . . .

The Tides (In serv. 1946)

**The Tides** G. Arra, 7-86

**D:** 774 tons (fl) **S:** 12 kts **Dim:** 56.4 × 16.8 × 2.7
**M:** diesel-electric drive; 2 props; 1,350 hp

### FLOATING DRY DOCK

◆ **1 U.S. Navy dock, on loan** Bldr: Foundation Co. (In serv. 12-43)

YFD 83 (ex-AFDL 31)

**Lift capacity:** 1,000 tons **Dim:** 60.96 × 19.51 × 1.04 (light)

Remarks: Steel dock used at U.S.C.G. Yard, Curtis Bay, Maryland, since completion and officially loaned 1-47. Length over blocks is 56.4 m, clear width is 13.7 m, maximum draft over blocks is 4.4 m, and maximum draft flooded is 8.2 m.

### SMALL CRAFT

The U.S. Coast Guard operates some 2,000 small craft, including over 1,000 under 7.62 m long classified as UTL (Utility Boat, Light). No central registry of their numbers is maintained, their administration being the responsibility of the stations to which they are attached. All carry five-digit serial numbers, the first two digits of which denote the craft's length in feet. Many are to be laid up or discarded under FY 88 budget cuts.

### PATROL CRAFT/UTILITY BOATS

◆ **4 fast coastal interceptors** Bldr: Tempest Marine, North Miami Beach, Florida

| | |
|---|---|
| 43501 (In serv. 1-4-87) | 43503 (In serv. 7-87) |
| 43502 (In serv. 6-87) | 43504 (In serv. 11-8-87) |

PATROL CRAFT/UTILITY BOATS *(continued)*

**43501** PA3 D. Vogeley, U.S.C.G., 4-87

**D:** 7 tons **S:** 40+ kts **Dim:** 13.41 × 2.90 × 0.97
**A:** small arms **Electron Equipt:** Radar: 1/Raytheon 1900
**M:** 2 Caterpillar 3208 TA diesels; 2 props; 750 hp
**Range:** . . . **Man:** 4 to 6 tot.

Remarks: Adaptation of commercial "Riviera"-class "cigarette boat" with diesel vice usual gasoline engines. Operate from Miami in drug interdiction duties. GRP construction hull with 25-deg. V-bottom hull. Additional units may be ordered. An unspecified number of seized and donated craft of this general type are also used by the U.S.C.G. in the "drug war."

◆ **207 41-ft utility boats** Bldr: U.S.C.G. Yard, Curtis Bay, Md. (In serv. 1973–83)

**41373** V. Baca, 1-87

**D:** 12.8 tons (fl) **S:** 22–26 kts **Dim:** 12.40 × 4.11 × 1.22
**Electron Equipt:** Radar: 1/Raytheon 1900 **Man:** 4–6 tot.
**M:** 2 Cummins V903M or VT903M diesels; 2 props; 560 or 640 hp

Remarks: Prototype delivered 1971; between 1973–1982 some 206 more followed. Aluminum construction. Hull numbers start with 41300. 43400 has special vanes on the propeller shafts, adding 2.5 kts speed; will be backfitted to others.

◆ **365 32-ft ports and waterways boats**

**D:** 8.6 tons (fl) **S:** 25 kts **Dim:** 10.16 × 3.58 × 0.86
**Electron Equipt:** Radar: 1/Raytheon 1900
**M:** 2 Caterpillar 3208 diesels; 2 props; 406 hp

Remarks: GRP construction; built late 1970s to replace 30-ft Mk-III class. Have a 90-hp G.M. 3-53 diesel to drive a 500 gallon/min. fire pump.

◆ **22 31-ft port security boats** Bldr: U.S.C.G. Yard, Curtis Bay, Md. (In serv. 1960s, 1970s)

31001–31022

Remarks: No data available. GRP construction.

**32338**—32-ft ports and waterways boat L. & L. Van Ginderen, 8-87

**31019**—31-ft port security boat W. Donko, 7-86

◆ **. . . 30-ft utility boat Mk III** (In serv. 1950s)

**D:** 6 tons (fl) **S:** 25 kts **Dim:** 9.14 × 2.31 × 0.86
**Electron Equipt:** Radar: 1/Raytheon 1900
**M:** 1 Cummins VT8-370M or VT6-250M diesel; 1 prop; 260 or 280 hp

Remarks: Most replaced by 32-ft Ports and Waterways Boat class. GRP construction.

**30430**—30-ft utility boat L. & L. Van Ginderen, 5-83

◆ **1 Lake Champlain patrol craft** Bldr: MonArk Boat, Monticello, Arkansas (In serv. 1987)

**D:** . . . **S:** 38 kts **Dim:** 8.53 × 4.0 × . . .
**Electron Equipt:** Radar: 1/Furuno . . . **Man:** 2–3 tot
**M:** 2 Volvo AQAD 41/290 outdrive diesels; 2 props; 400 hp

PATROL CRAFT/UTILITY BOATS *(continued)*

**Lake Champlain patrol craft** MonArk, 1987

REMARKS: Aluminum construction. Based at Burlington, Vermont. Used in SAR duties.

◆ **. . . miscellaneous utility and patrol craft**

A 20-ft outdrive-powered, glass-reinforced, plastic-hulled local patrol craft, Number 201511 is a standard Penn Van pleasure craft adapted for Coast Guard requirements A.D. Baker, 7-76

## NAVIGATIONAL AID CRAFT

◆ **1 cable repair craft, former LCM(6)**

560500

**560500** U.S.C.G., 6-86

**D:** 50 tons (fl) **S:** 10 kts **Dim:** 17.07 × 4.37 × 1.17
**Electron Equipt:** 1/. . . nav. **Range:** 130/10
**M:** 2 G.M. 6-71 diesels; 2 props; 330 hp

REMARKS: Conversion from U.S. Navy landing craft completed 6-86 at U.S.C.G. Yard, Curtis Bay, Md., for service at South Portland, Maine, as a telephone and power cable layer. New pilothouse added, bow altered.

◆ **20 55-ft-class aids-to-navigation boats**

**D:** 28.8 tons (fl) **S:** 22 kts **Dim:** 17.68 × 5.18 × 1.52
**M:** 2 G.M. 12 V71 TI diesels; 2 props; 1,080 hp

REMARKS: Aluminum construction.

◆ **9 46-ft stern-loading buoy boats** (In serv. 1968–69)

46301–46309

**46309** G. Arra, 7-86

REMARKS: No data available. Have Raytheon 1900 radar. Pilothouse configurations vary.

◆ **. . . 45-ft-class aids-to-navigation boats**

Powered by a single G.M. 6-71 diesel, the 45-ft buoy-tender class handles small navigational buoys with a hydraulically powered quadrantial derrick over the bow. Number 45312 has a Raytheon 1900 radar C. Dragonette, 1980

◆ **50 (+ . . .) 21-ft aids-to-navigation boats** Bldr: MonArk, Monticello, Ark. (In serv. 1981–. . .)

**21-ft aids-to-navigation boat** MonArk, 1985

**D:** 1.59 tons light (3.17 fl) **S:** 30 kts **Dim:** 6.50 × 2.44 × 0.36 (hull)
**M:** 1 gasoline engine; 1 prop; 228 hp

REMARKS: Aluminum construction, design based on builder's 21-V, deep-Vee hull design. Can be mounted on a trailer for land transport.

◆ **1 46-ft oil-spill clearance boat** Bldr: U.S.C.G. Yard, Curtis Bay (In serv. 1982)

NAVIGATIONAL AID CRAFT *(continued)*

**Zero Relative Velocity Skimmer** U.S.C.G., 1982

REMARKS: Catamaran hull with rotary belt/wringer oil-spill cleanup system. Prototype. Aluminum construction.

## LIFEBOATS

◆ **0 (+105) 47-ft lifeboats** Bldr: . . . (In serv. 3-89 to 1996)

47301–47405

**D:** 17.9 tons (fl) **S:** 25 kts **Dim:** 14.33 × 4.27 × 1.22
**Electron Equipt:** Radar: 1/. . . nav. **Man:** 4 tot.
**M:** 2 diesels; 2 props; . . . hp **Range:** 200/25; 208/10

REMARKS: Intended to replace the 44-ft class and to provide significantly greater speed of reaction. Prototype to order 3-88 for delivery 3-89, followed by order for five service trial units in 10-89 for delivery by 10-90; the remaining boats would be ordered 9-91 for delivery by 12-96. May reach 26.4 kts max.

◆ **104 44-ft motor lifeboat class** Bldr: U.S.C.G. Yard, Curtis Bay, Md. (In serv. 31-3-61 to 8-5-73)

44300 series

**44-ft motor lifeboat 44350** R. Scheina, 8-84

**D:** 14.9 tons light (17.7 fl) **S:** 15 kts (11.8 sust.) **Dim:** 13.44 × 3.87 × 1.19
**Electron Equipt:** Radar: 1/. . . nav. **Man:** 4 tot.
**M:** 2 G.M. 6-71 diesels; 2 props; 372 hp **Range:** 185/11.8; 200/10
**Fuel:** 1.2 tons

REMARKS: "Unsinkable" design, built during the 1960s. Also built for Canadian Coast Guard, under license. 44300 used for training at Motor Lifeboat School, along with 44301, 44304, 44369, and 44381. The rest are on independent detachments. To be disposed of by 1998.

◆ **4 52-ft motor lifeboats** Bldr: U.S.C.G. Yard, Curtis Bay, Md.,

52312 (In serv. 29-11-56) 52314 (In serv. 1-4-61)
52313 (In serv. 11-10-60) 52315 (In serv. 11-10-61)

REMARKS: No data available. All in service on Pacific Northwest coast. The 36-ft Motor Lifeboat 36535, last of her type, is on museum display.

◆ **19 30-ft surf rescue boats** Bldr: U.S.C.G. Yard, Curtis Bay, Md. (In serv. 1979–83)

30201 series

**30-ft surf rescue boat 30607** F. Jentsch, 8-87

**D:** 4.6 tons (fl) **S:** 28 kts **Dim:** 9.25 × 2.84 × 1.09
**M:** 1 G.M. 6V92T diesel; 1 prop; 375 hp

◆ **206 25-ft 8-in surf boats** Bldr: U.S.C.G. Yard, Curtis Bay, Md. (In serv. 1969–83)

25-ft motor surfboat 253308, with 30-ft motor surfboat 30618. The 26-ft MSB (SV) is a modified version of the standard 25-ft motor whaleboat. GRP construction
V. Baca, 4-86

NOTE: In addition to the craft listed above, the U.S. Coast Guard completed the following GRP-construction small craft between the late 1960s and 1983: 41 25-ft 8-in (7.82 m) cargo boats (similar to the surf boat of the same length), four 17-ft motor launches, and 28 "Fast Delivery Sled" aircraft-deployed oil-spill cleanup craft.

## NATIONAL OCEANIC AND ATMOSPHERIC ADMINISTRATION
## U.S. DEPARTMENT OF COMMERCE

PERSONNEL: 350 commissioned officers, approx. 2,250 civilians

NOAA operates a fleet of 23 research ships divided into the two categories of Research and Survey. Headquartered in Rockville, Maryland, and commanded by a rear admiral, it has its major maritime facilities at the Atlantic Marine Center in Norfolk, Virginia, and the Pacific Marine Center in Seattle, Washington.

Hulls and superstructures are white, masts and stacks buff. Hull numbers appear on either side (preceded by "R" for research or "S" for Survey) above the letters "NOAA." The front digit in the 3-digit hull number is the NOAA class (i.e., size) number for the ship, determined from the gross tonnage and horsepower. The ships are described below in descending size order.

## OCEANOGRAPHIC RESEARCH SHIPS

◆ **2 Oceanographer class** Bldr: Aerojet-General SY, Jacksonville, Fla.

| | L | In serv. | Base |
|---|---|---|---|
| R 101 OCEANOGRAPHER | 18-4-64 | 13-7-66 | Seattle |
| R 102 DISCOVERER | 29-10-64 | 29-4-67 | Seattle |

**D:** 4,033 tons (fl) **S:** 15 kts (sust.) **Dim:** 92.4 × 15.8 × 6.0
**M:** 2 Westinghouse 1,150 diesel generator sets, 2 Westinghouse motors; 2/4-bladed props; 5,000 hp
**Range:** 12,250/15 **Fuel:** 937 tons **Electric:** 1,200 kw **Endurance:** 34 days
**Man:** R 101: 14 NOAA officers; 6 licensed officers; 57 crew, 30 scientists
R 102: 13 NOAA officers, 6 licensed officers, 60 crew, 24 scientists

OCEANOGRAPHIC RESEARCH SHIPS *(continued)*

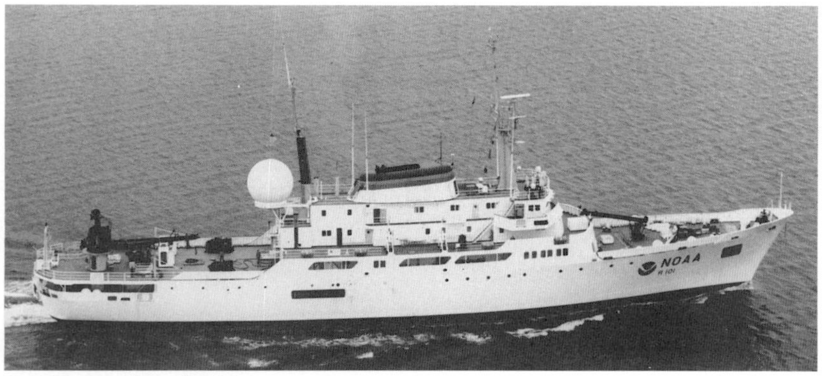

**Oceanographer (R 101)** NOAA, 1987

**Discoverer (R 102)** NOAA, 1987

REMARKS: 3,701 grt/1,095 nrt. Maritime Administration S2-MET-MA62a design. Both carry PDP 11/34 data-processing computers. R 101 has a large weather radar aft; both have two navigational radars. Laboratories include chemistry, wet and dry oceanographic meteorological, gravimetric, and photographic. A computerized data recording and processing system is installed. There are several precision oceanographic winches. A 400-hp bow-thruster is fitted. R 102 received the Sea-beam, 12-kHz multi-beam bathymetric mapping sonar, Inmarsat SATCOMM system for dataline transmission, and the TI-410 Global Position Indicator in 1985; she has an underwater observation chamber. In 1987, R 102 was employed by the U.S. Navy as a replacement for *Bowditch* (T-AGS 21); she was equipped with T-AGS 21's two BQN-3 narrow-beam mapping sonars, doppler sonar, and navigational equipment. R 101, in reserve in 7-81, reactivated 8-4-86 after refit with Alden weatherfax, Sperry Mk 37 gyro, a new Raytheon X-band Pathfinder radar, Inmarsat, MX1102 Global Positioning System, a new Salinometer, a Shipboard Environmental Acquisition System (SEAS) with expendable bathythermograph gear, a new meteorological station, and a doppler current profiling system.

◆ **1 Researcher class** Bldr: American Shpbldg., Toledo, Ohio

| | Launched | In serv. | Base |
|---|---|---|---|
| R 103 MALCOLM BALDRIDGE (ex-*Researcher*) | 5-10-68 | 8-10-70 | Miami |

**Malcolm Baldridge (R 103)** NOAA, 1987

**D:** 2,963 tons (fl) **S:** 12.5 kts (sust.) **Dim:** 84.8 × 15.5 × 5.6
**M:** 2 Alco diesels; 2 CP props; 3,200 hp **Endurance:** 36 days
**Range:** 10,800/12.5 **Fuel:** 568 tons **Electric:** 1,500 kw
**Man:** 13 NOAA officers, 5 licensed officers, 50 crew, 14 scientists

REMARKS: 2,802 grt/946 nrt. Maritime Administration S2-MT-MA7a design. Bow dome for sonars and echo-sounders, five laboratories, 5 oceanographic winches. PDP 11/34 computerized data system. Has a 450-hp Pleuger retractable bow-thruster. Receiving Inmarsat and Global Position Indicator, Seabeam multi-beam mapping sonar in 1986. Carries seismic profile compressors. Helicopter deck aft removed, replaced by quadrantial gallows for towed equipment. Renamed 5-3-88.

◆ **1 Miller Freeman class** Bldr: American Shipbldg., Lorain, Ohio

| | L | In serv. | Base |
|---|---|---|---|
| R 223 MILLER FREEMAN | 1967 | 1974 | Seattle |

**Miller Freeman (R 223)** NOAA, 1987

**D:** 1,920 tons (fl) **S:** 14 kts (sust.) **Dim:** 66.0 × 12.5 × 6.1
**M:** 1 G.M. diesel; 1 CP prop; 2,200 hp **Electric:** 700 kw
**Range:** 13,800/14 **Fuel:** 450 tons **Endurance:** 41 days
**Man:** 7 NOAA officers, 4 licensed officers, 30 crew, 11 scientists

REMARKS: 1,515 grt/680 nrt. Conducts fisheries and living marine resources research. Chemical, wet oceanographic, fish processing, utility labs. Fish-finder sonars, several echo-sounders. Lowerable stabilization centerboard increases draft to 9.3 m. Has a stern trawl ramp and net-handling gallows. 400-hp Schottel lowerable bow-thruster.

◆ **1 Oregon II class** Bldr: Ingalls SB, Pascagoula, Miss.

| | L | In serv. | Base |
|---|---|---|---|
| R 332 OREGON II | 2-67 | 8-67 | Pascagoula |

**Oregon II (R 332)** NOAA, 1987

**D:** 952 tons **S:** 12 kts (sust.) **Dim:** 51.8 × 10.4 × 4.3
**M:** 2 Fairbanks-Morse diesels; 1 CP prop; 1,600 hp
**Range:** 9,500/12 **Fuel:** 255 tons **Electric:** 400 kw
**Man:** 6 licensed officers, 10 crew, 6 scientists **Endurance:** 33 days

REMARKS: 703 grt/228 nrt. Conducts fisheries and living marine resource research in the Gulf of Mexico, Caribbean, South Atlantic, and southeast U.S. Atlantic Coast. Has 2 trawls, 1 hydrographic and 1 bathythermographic winches, five laboratories.

◆ **1 Albatross IV class** Bldr: Southern SB, Slidell, Louisiana

| | L | In serv. | Base |
|---|---|---|---|
| R 342 ALBATROSS IV | 4-62 | 5-63 | Woods Hole, Mass. |

**D:** 1,089 tons (fl) **S:** 12 kts (sust.) **Dim:** 57.0 × 10.0 × 4.9
**M:** 2 Caterpillar diesels; 1 Kort-nozzle CP prop; 1,130 hp
**Range:** 4,300/12 **Fuel:** 150 tons **Electric:** 450 kw
**Man:** 7 NOAA officers, 15 crew, 15 scientists **Endurance:** 15 days

REMARKS: 931 grt/300 nrt. Conducts fisheries and living marine resources research off the U.S. northeastern Atlantic coast. Has wet and dry oceanographic, photographic, biological, plankton, and electronics laboratories, four scientific winches, vertical fish-finding sonar, and deep- and shallow-water echo-sounders. There is a 125-hp bow-thruster.

OCEANOGRAPHIC RESEARCH SHIPS *(continued)*

**Albatross IV (R 342)** NOAA, 1987

◆ **1 Townsend Cromwell class** Bldr: J. Ray McDermott Co., Morgan City, La.

| | L | In serv. | Base |
|---|---|---|---|
| R 443 Townsend Cromwell | 7-62 | 7-63 | Honolulu |

**Townsend Cromwell (R 443)** NOAA, 1987

**D:** 652 tons (fl) **S:** 11.5 kts (sust.) **Dim:** 49.7 × 10.0 × 3.9
**M:** 2 White-Superior diesels; 2 CP props; 800 hp **Electric:** 350 kw
**Range:** 8,300/11.5 **Fuel:** 132 tons **Endurance:** 30 days
**Man:** 4 NOAA officers, 3 licensed officers, 10 crew, 9 scientists

Remarks: 564 grt/384 nrt. Conducts fisheries and living marine resources research off the Hawaiian Islands and in the central Pacific. Has a single oceanographic laboratory and an underwater bow observation chamber. Taken over by NOAA 6-75.

◆ **1 David Starr Jordan class** Bldr: Christy Corp., Sturgeon Bay, Wisc.

| | L | In serv. | Base |
|---|---|---|---|
| R 444 David Starr Jordan | 12-64 | 1-66 | San Diego, Cal. |

**David Starr Jordan (R 444)** NOAA, 1987

**D:** 993 tons (fl) **S:** 11.5 kts (sust.) **Dim:** 52.1 × 11.2 × 3.8 (4.8 over sonar)
**M:** 2 White-Superior diesels; 2 CP props; 1,086 hp
**Electric:** 400 kw **Fuel:** 180 tons **Range:** 8,560/11.5
**Man:** 6 licensed officers, 10 crew, 13 scientists **Endurance:** 31 days

Remarks: 873 grt/262 nrt. Conducts fisheries and living marine resources research off U.S., Central, and South American Pacific coasts. Physical and biological oceanography, chemical and photographic labs. Has a retractable fish-finding sonar, a vertical fish-finder, and several echo-sounders. Schottel retractable bow-thruster of 200 hp. Has an underwater observation chamber at the bow.

◆ **1 Delaware II class** Bldr: South Portland Engineering Corp., South Portland, Maine

| | L | In serv. | Base |
|---|---|---|---|
| R 445 Delaware II | 12-67 | 10-68 | Woods Hole, Mass. |

**Delaware II** NOAA, 1987

**D:** 758 tons (fl) **S:** 11.5 kts (sust.) **Dim:** 47.2 × 9.2 × 4.5
**M:** 1 G.M. diesel; 1 prop; 1,230 hp **Electric:** 300 kw
**Fuel:** 132 tons **Range:** 6,600/11.5
**Man:** 6 licensed officers, 9 crew, 9 scientists

Remarks: 483 grt/231 nrt. Conducts fisheries and living marine resources research off U.S. Atlantic coast. Two oceanographic labs, fish-finding sonars, stern net ramp. Endurance: 24 days.

◆ **1 Chapman class** Bldr: Bender SB & Repair Co., Washington

| | L | In serv. | Base |
|---|---|---|---|
| R 446 Chapman | 12-79 | 7-80 | Pascagoula, Miss. |

**Chapman (R 446)** NOAA, 1987

**D:** 520 tons (fl) **S:** 11 kts (sust.) **Dim:** 38.7 × 9.1 × 4.3
**M:** 1 Caterpillar D 399 diesel; 1 CP prop; 1,250 hp **Electric:** 420 kw
**Fuel:** 126 tons **Range:** 6,000/11
**Man:** 3 NOAA officers, 1 licensed officer, 7 crew, 6 scientists

Remarks: 427 grt/290 nrt. Conducts fisheries and living marine resources research off the coasts of the Pacific Northwest and Alaska. Has a fish-processing and a dry laboratory. Stern-haul trawler with a 150-hp Omnithruster bow-mounted waterjet. Laid up 1984 to 1-86; refitted 7-86 to 9-86.

◆ **1 John N. Cobb class** Bldr: Western Boatbldg., Tacoma, Wash.

| | L | In serv. | Base |
|---|---|---|---|
| R 552 John N. Cobb | 1-50 | 2-50 | Seattle |

**D:** 250 tons (fl) **S:** 9.3 kts (sust.) **Dim:** 28.3 × 7.9 × 3.3 **Electric:** 60 kw
**M:** 1 Fairbanks-Morse diesel; 1 prop; 325 hp **Endurance:** 13 days
**Range:** 2,900/9.3 **Fuel:** 25 tons **Man:** 4 licensed officers, 4 crew, 4 scientists

## OCEANOGRAPHIC RESEARCH SHIPS *(continued)*

**John N. Cobb (R 552)** NOAA, 1987

REMARKS: 185 grt/78 nrt. Conducts fisheries and living marine resources research off southeastern Alaska and the U.S. Pacific Northwest. Has a single laboratory. Endurance: 13 days.

◆ **1 Murre II class** Bldr: U.S. Army

| | L | In serv. | Base |
|---|---|---|---|
| R 663 MURRE II | 1943 | ... | Juneau, Alaska |

**Murre II (R 663)** NOAA

**D:** 295 tons (fl) **S:** 8 kts **Dim:** 26.1 × 8.2 × 2.3 **Electric:** 32 kw
**M:** 2 Caterpillar diesels; 2 props; 330 hp **Endurance:** 8 days
**Fuel:** 15 tons **Range:** 1,500/8 **Man:** 2 licensed officers, 1 crew, 5 scientists

REMARKS: 189 grt/95 nrt. Conducts fisheries research and cargo shipment duties in southeastern Alaskan waters. Former wooden-hulled Army powered barge. One chemical and one biological laboratory. Has a 2-ton cargo boom for deck cargo.

## SURVEY SHIPS

◆ **1 Surveyor class** Bldr: National Steel & SB, San Diego, Cal.

| | L | In serv. | Base |
|---|---|---|---|
| S 132 SURVEYOR | 25-4-59 | 30-4-60 | Seattle |

**Surveyor (S 132)** NOAA, 1987

**D:** 3,440 tons (fl) **S:** 15 kts (sust.) **Dim:** 89.0 × 14.0 × 5.9
**M:** 2 sets de Laval GT; 1 prop; 3,200 hp **Electric:** 800 kw
**Boilers:** 2 Combustion Engineering; 32.7 kg/cm$^2$, 385°C
**Fuel:** 785 tons **Range:** 13,680 n.m./15 **Endurance:** 38 days
**Man:** 12 NOAA officers, 6 licensed officers, 58 crew, 16 scientists

REMARKS: 2,653 grt/682 nrt. Maritime Administration S2-S-RM 28a design. Has PDP 11/34 data-processing computer, seismic reflection profile compressors, wet and dry oceanography, gravimetric, and photographic laboratories, extensive navigational equipment, deep and shallow echo-sounders, stabilized mapping sonar system, Hydroplot data-processing system, seismic reflection profile compressors, and a small helicopter platform. Carries 3/11-m wooden survey launches, an ex-U.S. Navy LCVP, and 2/7.9-m motor whaleboats. Has a 200-hp electric auxiliary propulsion motor aft. Received Seabeam 12-kHz, 9,000-m multi-beam mapping sonar in 1985.

◆ **3 Mt. Mitchell class** Bldr: Aerojet-General SY, Jacksonville, Fla.

| | L | In serv. | Base |
|---|---|---|---|
| S 220 FAIRWEATHER | 15-3-67 | 2-10-68 | Seattle |
| S 221 RAINIER | 15-3-67 | 2-10-68 | Seattle |
| S 222 MT. MITCHELL | 29-11-66 | 23-3-68 | Norfolk |

**Mt. Mitchell (S 222)** NOAA, 1987

**D:** 1,800 tons (fl) **S:** 13 kts **Dim:** 70.4 × 12.8 × 4.2
**M:** 2 G.M. diesels; 2 CP props; 2,400 hp **Electric:** 600 kw
**Fuel:** 353 tons **Range:** 7,000/13 **Endurance:** 22 days
**Man:** 12 NOAA officers, 5 licensed officers, 52 crew, 4 scientists

**SURVEY SHIPS** *(continued)*

REMARKS: 1,591 grt/578 nrt. Maritime Administration S1-MT-72a design. Have an oceanographic laboratory, Hydroplot data-processing system (also carried in two of the 3 or 4 8.8-m survey boats aboard), several echo-sounders, and an oceanographic winch. In addition to the survey launches, carry 2 motor whaleboats and 3 Boston Whaler utility boats. Have a 200-hp bow-thruster.

◆ **2 Peirce class** Bldr: Marietta Mfg. Co., Pt. Pleasant, West Va.

| | L | In serv. | Base |
|---|---|---|---|
| S 328 PEIRCE | 15-10-62 | 6-5-63 | Norfolk (laid up) |
| S 329 WHITING | 20-11-62 | 8-7-63 | Norfolk |

**Whiting (S 329)** NOAA, 1987

**D:** 907 tons (fl) **S:** 12 kts (sust.) **Dim:** 49.7 × 10.1 × 3.4
**M:** 2 G.M. diesels; 2 CP props; 1,600 hp **Electric:** 440 kw
**Fuel:** 138 tons **Range:** 5,700/12 **Endurance:** 20 days
**Man:** 8 NOAA officers, 3 licensed officers, 30 crew, 2 scientists

REMARKS: 696 grt/151 nrt. Maritime Administration S1-MT-59a design. Have the Hydroplot data system to record hydrographic data; also fitted to the two 8.8-m survey launches. Have deep, shallow, and hydrographic survey echo-sounders. Work on the U.S. Atlantic Coast, Gulf of Mexico, and U.S. Caribbean possessions; *Peirce* also operates in the Great Lakes. S 328 laid up 1987.

◆ **2 McArthur class** Bldr: Norfolk SB & DD, Norfolk, Va.

| | L | In serv. | Base |
|---|---|---|---|
| S 330 MCARTHUR | 15-11-65 | 15-12-66 | Seattle |
| S 331 DAVIDSON | 7-5-66 | 10-3-67 | Seattle |

**McArthur (S 330)** NOAA, 1985

**D:** 995 tons (fl) **S:** 12 kts (sust.) **Dim:** 53.3 × 11.6 × 3.7
**Endurance:** 17 days **M:** 2 G.M. diesels; 2 CP props; 1,600 hp
**Electric:** 440 kw **Fuel:** 186 tons **Range:** 6,000/12
**Man:** 8 NOAA officers, 3 licensed officers, 27 crew, 2 scientists

REMARKS: 854 grt/207 nrt. Maritime Administration S1-MT-70a design. S 330 primarily performs seawater circulatory studies, and S 331 performs hydrographic surveys; both operate off the U.S. Pacific Coast, and in Alaskan coastal waters. S 331 has the Hydroplot data-recording system, while S 330 uses the same system's PDP 11/34 computer to record current data. S 331 has the Bathymetric Swath Survey System, a stabilized, 22-beam 600-m deep mapping sonar.

◆ **1 Ferrell class** Bldr: Zigler SY, Jennings, La.

| | L | In serv. | Base |
|---|---|---|---|
| S 492 FERRELL | 4-4-68 | 4-6-68 | Norfolk |

**Ferrell (S 492)** NOAA, 1985

**D:** 360 tons (fl) **S:** 10 kts (sust.) **Dim:** 40.5 × 9.8 × 2.5
**M:** 2 Caterpillar diesels; 2 props; 750 hp **Electric:** 300 kw
**Fuel:** 46 tons **Range:** 2,200/10 **Endurance:** 9 days
**Man:** 5 NOAA officers, 2 licensed officers, 12 crew

REMARKS: 349 grt/86 nrt. Maritime Administration S1-MT-MA83a design. Has a PDP 11/34 data-processing computer. Conducts coastal and estuarine seawater circulation studies off the U.S. East Coast and Gulf of Mexico. Has an electronics laboratory and a small oceanographic laboratory, and carries an 8.5-m workboat. Has a 100-hp bow-thruster. Computerized data-recording system.

◆ **2 Rude class** Bldr: Jakobson SY, Oyster Bay, N.Y.

| | L | In serv. | Base |
|---|---|---|---|
| S 590 RUDE | 17-8-66 | 3-67 | Norfolk |
| S 591 HECK | 1-11-66 | 3-67 | Norfolk |

**Heck (S 591)** NOAA, 1985

**D:** 220 tons (fl) **S:** 10 kts (sust.) **Dim:** 27.4 × 6.7 × 2.2
**M:** 2 Cummins diesels; 2 Kort-nozzle props; 800 hp **Electric:** 120 kw
**Fuel:** 12 tons **Range:** 800/10 **Endurance:** 3 days
**Man:** 3 NOAA officers, 1 licensed officer, 7 crew

REMARKS: 150 grt/42 nrt. Work together in making wire drag surveys off U.S. Atlantic and Gulf coasts. Have side-scan sonars and computerized data storage. Equipped with two 70-hp hydraulic auxiliary drives.

NOTE: U.S. Navy sludge-removal barge YSR 29 was transferred to NOAA 8-85 for use as an underwater habitat support barge. Completed 12-45, the craft displaces 160 tons light (360 fl) and measures 24.4 × 9.8. It will be equipped with a centerline "moon pool."

## U.S. ARMY

The U.S. Army's fleet is divided into units (primarily survey craft, dredges, and construction craft) operated by the Corps of Engineers, and landing craft and logistics support craft operated by the Corps of Transportation. Some 1,065 6-ton, 8-m bridging boats for use by combat troops have been delivered or are on order to a design by Fairey; most recent order was for 225 on 26-2-87 to American Development, Charleston, S.C. Principal Corps of Transportation units are listed below.

U.S. ARMY *(continued)*

Most U.S. Army ships and craft are classed by design number. They carry alphanumeric serials in the following categories:

| | |
|---|---|
| BC | Barge, dry cargo, non-self-propelled |
| BCDX | Conversion kit, barge, deck enclosure |
| BD | Crane, floating |
| BDL | Lighter, beach discharge |
| BG | Barge, liquid cargo, non-self-propelled |
| BK | Barge, dry cargo, non-self-propelled, knock-down |
| BPL | Pier, barge-type, self-elevating |
| BR | Barge, refrigerated, non-self-propelled |
| FMS | Repair shop, floating, marine repair, non-self-propelled |
| FS | Freight and supply vessel, over 140-ft (42.67 m) o.a. |
| FSR | Refrigerated cargo vessel, self-propelled, all sizes |
| J | Work and inspection boat, under 50 ft (15.24 m) o.a. |
| LARC | Lighter, amphibious, resupply, cargo |
| LCM | Landing Craft, Mechanized |
| LCU | Landing Craft, Utility |
| LCV | Landing Craft, Vehicle |
| LT | Tug, large, 100 ft (30.48 m) and over |
| Q | Work and Inspection boat, large, over 50 ft (15.24 m) |
| ST | Tug, Small, under 100 ft. (30.48 m) |
| T | Freight and supply vessel, small, under 100 ft (3.48 m) |
| Y | Liquid cargo vessel, self-propelled, all sizes |

## VEHICLE LANDING SHIPS

◆ **1 (+3) Gen. Frank S. Besson-class vehicle landing ships** Bldr: Moss Point Marine, Escatawpa, Miss.

| | L | In serv. |
|---|---|---|
| LSV 1 Gen. Frank S. Besson, Jr. | 30-6-87 | 25-11-87 |
| LSV 2 Cw3 Harold C. Clinger | 16-9-87 | 20-2-88 |
| LSV 3 Gen. Brehon B. Somervell | 18-11-87 | 2-4-88 |
| LSV 4 Lt. Gen. William B. Bunker | 11-1-88 | 18-5-88 |

**Gen. Frank S. Besson, Jr. (LSV 1)** J. Sims/Moss Pt., 12-87

**D:** 1,612 tons light (4,199 tons fl) **S:** 11.25 kts
**Dim:** 83.14 (78.03 pp) × 18.28 (18.16 wl) × 3.66 (max.)
**A:** none **Electron Equipt:** Radar: 1 SPS-64(V)2, 1/SPS-64(V) . . .
**M:** 2 G.M. EMD 16-645-E2 diesels; 2 props; 3,900 hp
**Range:** 5,500/11 **Endurance:** 30 days **Fuel:** 477 tons
**Electric:** 500 kw (2 × 250-kw diesel sets)
**Man:** 6 officers, 24 men

Remarks: Ordered 19-9-86. Design based on Australian roll-on/roll-off, beachable cargo ship *Frances Bay,* designed by Burness, Corlett, Ltd. Built to commercial specifications. Intended to transport 1,500 to 2,000 tons of vehicles. Carry up to 122 tons potable water. Bow and stern ramps of 8.23-m width. LSV 1 laid down 11-86. All use rebuilt engines.

◆ **1 Design 5002 beach discharge lighter (medium landing ship)**

| | Bldr | L | In serv. |
|---|---|---|---|
| Lt. Col. John U.D. Page | National Steel, San Diego, Cal. | 28-9-57 | 11-58 |

**Lt. Col. John U.D. Page** W. Donko, 7.86

**D:** 1,548 tons light (4,126 fl) **S:** 10 kts **Dim:** 103.09 × 19.83 × 4.17 (max.)
**M:** 2 Fairbanks-Morse diesels; 2 vertical cycloidal props; 2,400 hp
**Electric:** 525 kw **Range:** 7,776/9 **Man:** 49 crew + 200 passengers

Remarks: A large, open-deck vehicle ferry, intended to mate with U.S. Navy's vehicle cargo ship *Comet* (T-AKR 7). Only one built of a projected large class. Cargo: 600 tons landing, 2,200 tons max. 1,395 m$^2$ deck space. Beaching displacement is 2,340 tons. Based at Oahu, Hawaii.

## UTILITY LANDING CRAFT

◆ **1 (+14 + 25) 2000 Design utility landing craft** Bldr: Lockheed SB, Savannah Div., Savannah, Ga.

| | Laid down | L | In serv. |
|---|---|---|---|
| LCU 159 Runnymede | 8-12-86 | 9-87 | 18-12-87 |
| LCU 160 Kenesaw Mountain | 22-5-87 | 6-10-87 | 18-3-88 |
| LCU 161 Macon | 22-7-87 | . . . | 20-5-88 |
| LCU 162 Aldie | 9-11-87 | . . . | 22-7-88 |
| LCU 163 Brandy Station | 1-2-88 | . . . | 9-9-88 |
| LCU 164 Bristoe Station | 1-4-88 | . . . | 21-10-88 |
| LCU 165 Broad Run | 5-7-88 | . . . | 20-11-88 |
| LCU 166 Buena Vista | . . . | . . . | 12-88 |
| LCU 167 Calabozo | . . . | . . . | 27-2-89 |
| LCU 168 Cedar Run | . . . | . . . | 30-4-89 |
| LCU 169 Chickahominy | . . . | . . . | 28-7-89 |
| LCU 170 Chickasaw Bayou | . . . | . . . | -- |
| LCU 171 Churubusco | . . . | . . . | 27-9-89 |
| LCU 172 Coamo | . . . | . . . | 27-10-89 |
| LCU 173 Contreres | . . . | . . . | 27-11-89 |

**D:** 599 tons light (1,029 fl) **S:** 11.5 kts
**Dim:** 53.03 (47.55 pp) × 12.80 × 1.43 (2.60 max. loaded)
**A:** none **Electron Equipt:** Radar: 1/SPS-64(V)2, 1/SPS-64(V) . . .
**M:** 2 Cummins KTA-50M diesels, 2 Kort-nozzle props; 2,500 hp—1/100-hp bow-thruster
**Range:** 4,500/11.5 (light) **Fuel:** 282 tons **Endurance:** 18 days
**Electric:** 555 kw (2 × 250 kw, 1 × 55 kw) **Man:** 2 officers, 11 men

Remarks: First seven ordered 11-6-86 in four-year program; six more were to order in 1987, five in 1988, and seven in 1989, with option for five more each year if budget permitted. Can carry up to 350 tons beaching cargo. Vehicle/cargo container deck totals 2,560 sq ft. Beaching draft forward is 1.22 m. There is a 50-ton-capacity kedging winch. Intended to replace the LCU 1466 class. Six approved FY 88; plan 12 in FY 89.

◆ **13 U.S. Navy LCU 1646-class utility landing craft** (In serv. 1976–78) Bldr: General Ship & Eng. Works, . . .

| | |
|---|---|
| LCU 1667 Manassas | LCU 1674 St. Mihel |
| LCU 1668 Belleau Wood | LCU 1675 Commando |
| LCU 1669 Marseilles | LCU 1676 Birmingham |
| LCU 1670 San Isidro | LCU 1677 Brandywine |
| LCU 1671 Catawba Ford | LCU 1678 Naha |
| LCU 1672 Bushmaster | LCU 1679 Chateau Thierry |
| LCU 1673 Double Eagle | |

**Chateau Thierry (LCU 1679)** G. Arra, 1987

**St. Mihel (LCU 1674)** L. & L. Van Ginderen, 8-87

**D:** 190 tons (390 fl) **S:** 11 kts (max.) **Dim:** 41.07 × 9.07 × 2.08 (max.)
**M:** 4 G.M. 6-71 diesels; 2 Kort-nozzle props; 1,200 hp
**Range:** 1,200/11 (light) **Fuel:** 13 tons **Man:** 6 tot.

## UTILITY LANDING CRAFT *(continued)*

**Remarks:** Retain former U.S. Navy hull numbers. Cargo: 143 tons in 30.5 × 5.5-m deck with ramps at both ends. Have small navigational radar.

◆ **43 U.S. Navy LCU 1466-class utility landing craft** (In serv. 1954)

**Tunisia (LCU 1586)**—with amphibian LARC LX 6 aboard
L. & L. Van Ginderen, 11-86

**Atlanta (LCU 1510)** L. & L. Van Ginderen, 5-87

**D:** 180 tons light (347 fl) **S:** 8 kts **Dim:** 35.08 × 10.36 × 1.6 (aft)
**M:** 3 Gray Marine 64 YTL diesels; 3 props; 675 hp **Electric:** 40 kw
**Fuel:** 11 tons **Range:** 1,200/6 (700/7 loaded) **Man:** 11 tot.

**Remarks:** Despite age, in good condition, with some kept in land storage. Some 35 are to be rehabilitated for further service. Names known are: *Antietam* (LCU 1509), *Atlanta* (LCU 1510), *Neptune* (LCU 1511), *Roi-Namur* (LCU 1521), *Hollandia* (LCU 1525), *Leyte* (LCU 1526), *Guadalcanal* (LCU 1527), *Saipan* (LCU 1534), *Solomon Islands* (LCU 1547), *Guam* (LCU 1549), *Rhineland* (LCU 1560), *Inchon* (LCU 1562), *Chattanooga* (LCU 1583), *Tunisia* (LCU 1586), and *Chickamauga* (LCU 1586). Cargo: 150 tons or 300 troops on 15.8 × 9.0 deck, with 4.3-m-wide bow ramp.

## MECHANIZED LANDING CRAFT

◆ **about 120 U.S. Navy LCM(8)-class landing craft** (In serv. 1954–72)

**D:** 58.8 tons light (116 fl) **S:** 9.2 kts (loaded)
**Dim:** 22.40 × 6.42 × 1.40 (mean) **M:** 2 G.M. 6-71 diesels; 2 props; 600 hp
**Range:** 150/9.2 (loaded) **Fuel:** 2.4 tons **Man:** 2–4 tot.

**Remarks:** Data apply to final 39 built, delivered late 1960s–1972. Earlier Army LCM(8)s were rated at 57.8 tons light/111.4 full load. Late version carries up to 57.4 tons cargo, earlier: 53.5. About 30 are crewed by Army reserves, 37 by National Guard forces, and 30 are in land storage.

## AIR-CUSHION LANDING CRAFT

◆ **0 (+ . . .) LAMP-H concept** Bldr: Textron Marine Systs., New Orleans

**D:** 86.9 tons light (177.6 fl/186.7 overload) **S:** 45 kts light/13.9 loaded
**Dim:** 24.33 (21.34 hull) × 17.97 (15.09 hull) × 8.46 high (less mast)
**M:** 2 AVCD TF40B gas turbines; 2 airscrew props/2 centrifugal lift fans; 7,840 hp
**Endurance:** 10 hrs. **Fuel:** 30 tons **Man:** 4 crew, 2 passengers

**Remarks:** Contract late 1987 for design and prototype construction to perform Logistics-Over-The-Shore (LOTS) duties to service Military Sea-lift Command resupply ships. Can be deck-carried on merchant-type ships. Cargo: 89 long tons. Aluminum hull atop a 1.52-m-deep air cushion. Loading/unloading ramp is at stern, 5.5 m wide.

◆ **30 LACV-30 class** Bldr: Textron Marine, New Orleans (In serv. 1976–87)

**D:** . . . **S:** 40 kts **Dim:** 23.29 × 11.20 × 17.63 (high, on cushion)
**M:** 2 Pratt & Whitney ST6T gas turbines; 2/2.74-m-dia. airscrew propellers; 2/21.3-m-dia. centrifugal lift fans.
**Endurance:** 8–10 hours **Man:** . . .

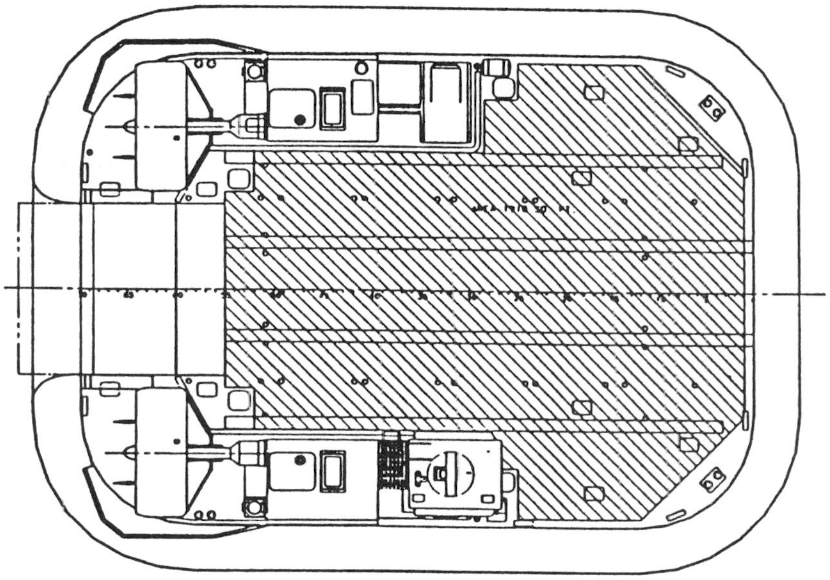

ARRANGEMENT

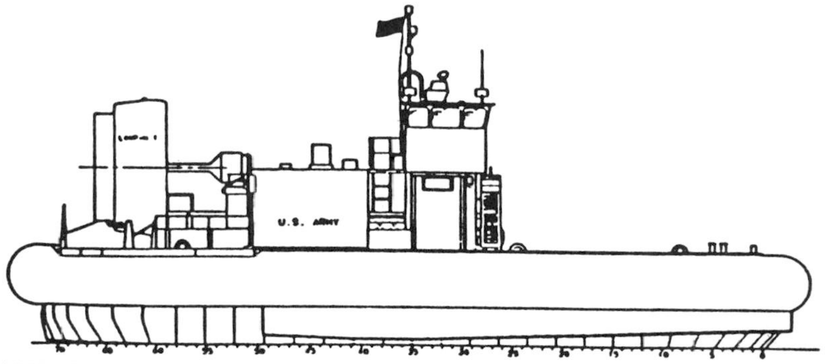

**LAMP-H** Textron, 1987

**LACV-30 at rest** W. Donko, 7-86

**Remarks:** Cargo: 35 tons max., two 20-ft containers at 35 kts. Cargo deck 15.54 × 9.75. Can be broken down for transport aboard trailers, railcars, aircraft, or ships. Intended for Logistics-Over-The-Shore (LOTS) support duties.

## AMPHIBIOUS VEHICLES

◆ **65 LARC XV Design 8004** Bldr: . . .

**D:** 20.8 tons light (35.7 fl) **S:** 8.25 kts water/29.5 mph land
**Dim:** 13.72 × 4.42 × 4.75 (high) **M:** 2 diesels; 1 prop; 600 hp
**Range:** 45/8.25 water; 300/29.5 mph land

**Remarks:** Four-wheeled vehicle with 15-ton payload, unloading ramp.

◆ **30 LARC LX Design 2303** Bldr: . . .

**D:** 88 tons light (about 190 fl) **S:** 6.5 kts max./15.2 mph on land
**Dim:** 19.07 × 8.10 × 5.92 **M:** 4 diesels; 2 props; 660 hp
**Range:** 75/6 (60-ton load) **Man:** . . .

**Remarks:** Four-wheeled vehicle with 100-ton maximum/60-ton normal payload. Cargo well 12.9 × 4.1, with full-width bow ramp.

◆ **25 LARC V Design 8005** Bldr: . . .

**D:** 8.9 tons light (13.4 fl) **S:** 8.7 kts/30 mph on land
**Dim:** 10.67 × 3.05 × 3.10 **M:** 1 diesel; 1 prop; 300 hp
**Range:** 40/8.7 loaded **Man:** . . .

**Remarks:** Four-wheeled vehicle with 5-ton payload, bow unloading ramp.

## AUXILIARIES

◆ **1 Design 7014 tanker** Bldr: . . . (In serv. 1950s)

**D:** 1,068 tons light (2,038 fl) **S:** 12.7 kts (10 loaded)
**Dim:** 67.91 (64.01 pp) × 11.79 × 4.74 (max. aft)
**M:** 2 diesels; 2 props; 1,440 hp **Fuel:** 152 tons
**Range:** 8,000/12.7 light; 6,300/10 loaded
**Man:** 32 tot. accommodations **Electric:** 260 kw

Remarks: Cargo: 1,500 tons in nine tanks (11,103 bbl gasoline). Two 1-ton hose-handling cranes. Can be grounded in tidal basins.

◆ **1 Design 7015 refrigerated cargo ship** Bldr: . . . (In serv. 1950s)

N . . .

**D:** 975 tons light (2,935 fl) **S:** 12.6 kts (10 loaded)
**Dim:** 67.91 (64.01 pp) × 11.79 × 5.18 (max.) **M:** 2 diesels; 2 props: 1,440 hp
**Fuel:** 152 tons **Range:** 8,000/12.6 light; 6,300/10 loaded
**Man:** 32 tot. accommodations **Electric:** 380 kw

Remarks: Cargo: 1,532 $m^3$ in three holds. Two 5-ton level luffing cranes.

◆ **1 Design 7013 cargo ship** Bldr: . . . (In serv. 1950s)

Virginia (ex-FS 790)

**Virginia** L. & L. Van Ginderen, 6-83

**D:** 1,068 tons light (2,038 fl) **S:** 13.8 kts (12 loaded)
**Dim:** 67.91 (64.01 pp) × 11.79 × 4.34 (max. aft)
**M:** 2 diesels; 2 props; 1,440 hp **Fuel:** 140 tons
**Range:** 7,500/13.8 light; 6,300/12 loaded
**Man:** 32 tot. accommodations **Electric:** 260 kw

Remarks: Cargo: 1,597 $m^3$ bale in three holds; two 5-ton level luffing cranes. Based at Ft. Eustis, Va., for training.

◆ **1 Maritime Commission C1-M-AV1 cargo ship** Bldr: Consolidated Steel, Wilmington, Cal. (L: 6-45)

Gen. William J. Sutton (ex-*Hickory Knoll*)

**D:** 7,435 tons (fl) **S:** 11 kts **Dim:** 103.18 (97.54 pp) × 15.24 × 5.49
**M:** 1 Nordberg TSM 6 diesel; prop; 1,750 hp
**Range:** 14,500/11 **Man:** 35 tot.

Remarks: 3,805 grt/5,032 dwt. Three cargo holds. One of 236 built; served United Kingdom on completion to 1947. Used at Fort Eustis, Va., in cargo-handling training and generally immobile.

◆ **1 Design 381 cargo ship** Bldr: J.H. Mathis, Camden, N.J. (In serv. 1944)

FS 313 Betsy Ross

**Betsy Ross (FS 313)** L. & L. Van Ginderen, 3-85

**D:** 465 tons light (935 fl) **S:** 11 kts **Dim:** 54.10 × 9.75 × 3.05 (max.)
**M:** 2 G.M. 6-278A diesels; 2 props; 1,000 hp **Man:** . . .
**Range:** 3,200/11 **Fuel:** 55 tons **Electric:** 225 kw

Remarks: Last U.S. Army survivor of a once numerous type. Cargo capacity: 608 $m^3$ in two holds. Two 5-ton cargo derricks.

## TUGS

◆ **2 (+6 + . . .) new-construction large tugs** Bldr: Robert E. Direcktor, Middletown, R.I.

**D:** . . . **S:** 12 kts **Dim:** 39.0 × . . . × . . . **M:** 2 diesels; 2 props; . . . hp
**Range:** 5,000/12 **Man:** . . .

Remarks: First two ordered 5-1-88, with option for 8 more under FY 87 funding; The first is to deliver 7-89. Congress rejected 2 more under FY 88 and directed the Army to study having its tug needs taken care of by the Military Sealift Command.

◆ **25 Design 3006 large harbor tugs** Bldr: . . . (In serv. 1950s)

**D:** 295 tons light (390 fl) **S:** 12.75 kts **Dim:** 32.61 × 8.08 × 3.71 (max.)
**M:** 1 Fairbanks-Morse diesel; 1 prop; 1,200 hp **Fuel:** 54 tons
**Range:** 3,323/12 light **Man:** 16 tot. **Electric:** 80 kw

Remarks: Bollard pull: 12 tons. Built in two series: LT 1936 through 1977 and LT 2202, and LT 2075 through LT 2096, of which 30 survive. Four tugs of this class can be seen aboard *American Cormorant* on pg. 805.

◆ **28 Design 3004 medium harbor tugs** Bldr: . . . (In serv. circa 1954)

**D:** 100 tons light (122 fl) **S:** 12 kts **Dim:** 21.31 × 5.94 × 2.50
**M:** 1 diesel; 1 prop; 600 hp **Fuel:** 15 tons **Range:** 3,500/12 **Man:** 6 tot.

Remarks: Many in land storage, including several in the U.K.

**ST-2199 of the Design 3004 class** L. & L. Van Ginderen, 4-86

U.S.A. *(continued)*

## SERVICE CRAFT

◆ **10 (+1) troop transport catamarans** Bldr: Nichols Bros., Whidbey Island, Wash.

FB-816 Jera (In serv. 2-88)

**D:** 63.7 tons (fl) **S:** 25 kts **Dim:** 23.00 × 8.68 × . . .
**M:** 2 G.M. 16V92 TA diesels; 1,920 hp **Electric:** 80 kw

Remarks: Intended to carry 75 passengers at Kwajalein. Second unit on option.

◆ **26 floating cranes** in two types:

—Design 264B floating cranes Bldr: . . . (In serv. 1950s)

**D:** 1,630 tons (fl) **Dim:** 42.67 × 21.34 × 1.91
**Electric:** 250 kw **Fuel:** 40 tons

Remarks: Crane capacity is 89 tons at 24.4-m radius, 75 tons at 31.8-m radius; auxiliary hook can lift 15 tons at 37.3 m.

—Design 413D floating cranes Bldr: . . . (In serv. 1950s)

**BD-6076, 60-ton Design 413D crane** L. & L. Van Ginderen, 12-86

**D:** 1,000 tons (fl) **Dim:** 43.28 × 17.68 × 1.04 (1.55 max.)
**Electric:** 155 kw **Fuel:** 4 tons

Remarks: Crane capacity: 60 tons at 22.2-m radius; auxiliary hook can lift 15 tons at 30.5 m.

◆ **4 Design 7011 floating machine shops** Bldr: . . .

FMS 786 Athena FMS 788 Ares FMS 789 Vulcan FMS . . . N . . .

**Athena**—Design 7011 L. & L. Van Ginderen, 1-87

**D:** 1,160 tons light (1,525 fl) **Dim:** 64.14 × 12.19 × 2.36 (max.)
**Electric:** 400 kw (4 × 100-kw) **Fuel:** 140 tons **Man:** 30 tot.

Remarks: Modified from Design 7016 refrigerated stores barges (which they outwardly resemble). Have 8.9-ton crane amidships. Workshops include: battery, blacksmith, carpentry, electrical, engine, fuel injector, machine, paint, pipefitting, electronic, refrigeration, sheet metal, shipfitting, and welding.

◆ **3 Design 7016 refrigerated stores barges** Bldr: . . .

**D:** 1,100 tons light (2,250 fl) **Dim:** 64.14 × 12.19 × 2.62
**Electric:** 360 kw (3 × 100 kw, 1 × 60 kw) **Fuel:** 129 tons **Man:** 28 tot.

Remarks: Cargo capacity: 1,316 $m^3$ provisions in seven holds. Resemble Design 7011 repair barges, except for smaller 1-ton crane and no forward deckhouse atop two-level storehouse.

◆ **174 barges:**

Note: Included in the total are 14 liquid cargo barges ordered in 1986 from AK-Wa, Inc., Tacoma, Wash., for delivery by 10-86.

—Design 229 harbor and inland waterways barge

**D:** 116.8 tons light (591.8 fl) **Dim:** 33.53 × 9.14 × 2.13 max.

—Design 231A ocean-towing barge

Three Design 231A barges, one with a "Conversion Kit, barge, Deck Enclosure, Design 7006" portable deckhouse M. Louagie, 8-86

**D:** 175 tons light (760 fl) **Dim:** 36.58 × 10.06 × 2.44

—Design 7005 deck-cargo barge

**D:** 120 tons light (690 fl) **Dim:** 33.53 × 9.75 × 2.34 (max.) **Cargo:** 570 tons

—Design 7010 refrigerated-cargo barge

**D:** 225 tons (546 fl) **Dim:** 36.58 × 10.06 × 1.77
**Cargo:** 395 $m^3$ refrigerated stores **Electric:** 120 kw

Note: Also in inventory are 20 Delong floating piers, all of which are due for replacement. 14 new ordered.

### U.S. AIR FORCE

The U.S. Air Force operates a number of small craft for search-and-rescue and training duties. The newest of these are:

◆ **9 Parasail training craft** Bldr: MonArk, Monticello, Arkansas (In serv. 29-7-86 to 6-4-87)

PR-40-8601 through PR-40-8609

**PR-40-8601** MonArk, 8-86

**D:** . . . **S:** 28 kts **Dim:** 12.57 × . . . × . . .
**M:** 2 G.M. 8V71 TI diesels; 2 props; 870 hp

Remarks: For use in parachute training by 3616th Combat Crew Training Squadron, Homestead AFB, Fla. Tow parasails. Aluminum construction.

Note: For the U.S.A.F., the Navy ordered two 33.53 "missile retrievers" from Swiftships, Morgan City, La., on 13-3-87; No details available.

# URUGUAY

**Eastern Republic of Uruguay**

Personnel (8-87): 3,942 total, including about 500 Marines

Merchant Marine (1986): 89 ships—149,811 grt
(tankers: 6 ships—76,378 grt)

Naval Aviation: Fixed-wing assets include 3 S-2G Tracker ASW patrol aircraft delivered 1982–83, 9 T-28 Fennec light attack aircraft, 3 Beech TC-45H utility trainer/light transports, a Beech King Air 200 Maritime Patrol aircraft, and 3 Beech T-34C-1 turbo-trainers. Helicopters include 1 Bell 222, 2 Bell 476,

**NAVAL AVIATION** *(continued)*

and 2 Sikorsky SH-34C. The Air Force operates one Embraer EMB 110B Bandeirante for photo duties and 4 Casa 212 Aviocar transports (one for coast patrol).

NOTE: The former letter designations in the alphanumeric hull numbers listed below were deleted by 1985.

## FRIGATES

◆ **1 ex-U.S. Dealey class** Bldr: Bath Iron Works, Me.

| | Laid down | L | In serv. |
|---|---|---|---|
| 3 18 DE JULIO (ex-*Dealey,* DE 1006) | 15-10-52 | 8-11-53 | 3-6-54 |

**18 de Julio (3)**—old hull pendant L. & L. Van Ginderen, 1975

**D:** 1,450 tons (1,914 fl) **S:** 25 kts **Dim:** 95.86 × 11.2 × 4.04 (5.27 over sonar)
**A:** 4/76.2-mm DP (II × 2)—6/324-mm Mk 32 ASW TT—1/d.c. rack
**Electron Equipt:** Radar: 2/. . . nav., 1/SPS-6E, 2/SPG-34
Sonar: 1/SQS-29 series—EW: WLR-1
**M:** 1 set de Laval GT; 1 prop; 20,000 hp
**Boilers:** 2 Foster-Wheeler "D"; 42-kg/cm², 510°C
**Fuel:** 360 tons **Range:** 4,400/11 **Man:** 11 officers, 150 men

REMARKS: First and least-modified of her class and also the last survivor. Two Mk 63 GFCS. New superstructure added abreast the stack. Purchased on 28-7-72. Refitted 1979–80 in Brazil, original SPS-5D surface-search radar replaced by two commercial navigational radars.

◆ **2 ex-U.S. Cannon class** Bldr: Federal SB & DD, Newark, N.J.

| | Laid down | L | In serv. |
|---|---|---|---|
| 1 URUGUAY (ex-*Baron,* DE 166) | 30-11-42 | 9-5-43 | 5-7-43 |
| 2 ARTIGAS (ex-*Bronstein,* DE 189) | 26-8-43 | 14-11-43 | 13-12-43 |

**Uruguay (1)** *Ships of the World,* 1985

**D:** 1,240 tons light (1,900 fl) **S:** 19 kts **Dim:** 93.27 × 11.15 × 3.56 (hull)
**A:** 3/76.2-mm DP (I × 3)—2/40-mm AA (II × 1)—3/20-mm AA (I × 3)—1/Mk 11 Hedgehog
**Electron Equipt:** Radar: 1/SPS-5, 1/SPS-6C (not in 1), 1/navigational
Sonar: SQS-4 series
**M:** 4 G.M. 16-278A diesels, electric drive; 2 props; 6,000 hp
**Electric:** 680 kw **Fuel:** 315 tons **Range:** 8,300/14 **Man:** 160 tot.

REMARKS: 1 was transferred in 5-52 and 2 in 3-52. Modernized in late 1960s with new radars. No radar fire control, but do have Mk 51 range-finder for 76.2-mm guns and Mk 51 Mod. 2 lead-computing director for 40-mm AA. 1 does not have stub mainmast and has had the SPS-6C radar removed. Both have had single 20-mm AA added. Depth-charge equipment had been removed by 1985, and both are in marginal operating condition.

## CORVETTE

◆ **1 ex-U.S. Auk-class former minesweeper**

Bldr: Defoe Boiler & Machine Works, Bay City, Mich.

| | Laid down | L | In serv. |
|---|---|---|---|
| 4 COMANDANTE PEDRO CAMPBELL (ex-MS 31, ex-*Chickadee,* MSF 59) | 21-8-41 | 20-7-42 | 9-11-42 |

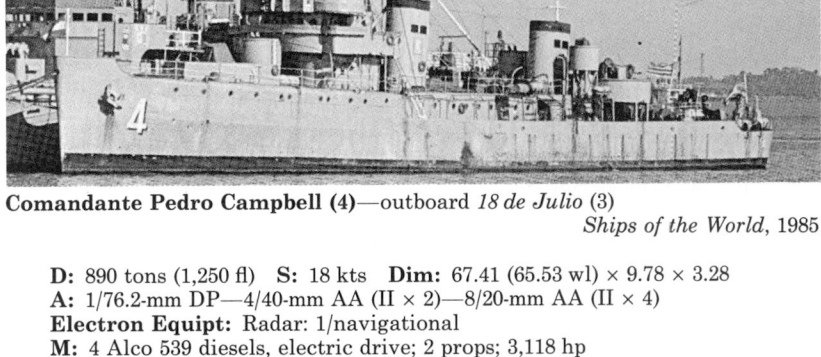

**Comandante Pedro Campbell (4)**—outboard *18 de Julio* (3) *Ships of the World,* 1985

**D:** 890 tons (1,250 fl) **S:** 18 kts **Dim:** 67.41 (65.53 wl) × 9.78 × 3.28
**A:** 1/76.2-mm DP—4/40-mm AA (II × 2)—8/20-mm AA (II × 4)
**Electron Equipt:** Radar: 1/navigational
**M:** 4 Alco 539 diesels, electric drive; 2 props; 3,118 hp
**Electric:** 300 kw **Man:** 105 tot.

REMARKS: Transferred on 18-8-66 and purchased on 18-8-76. All minesweeping equipment removed; has no ASW capability. Minesweeping winch used for towing.

## PATROL BOATS

◆ **3 French Vigilante class** Bldr: CMN, Cherbourg

| | Laid down | L | In serv. |
|---|---|---|---|
| 5 15 DE NOVIEMBRE | 6-12-79 | 16-10-80 | 25-3-81 |
| 6 25 DE AGOSTO | 6-2-80 | 11-12-80 | 25-3-81 |
| 7 COMODORO COE | 16-5-80 | 27-1-81 | 25-3-81 |

**15 de Noviembre (5)**—on trials CMN, 1981

**D:** 166 tons (190 fl) **S:** 28 kts
**Dim:** 41.15 (28.00 pp) × 6.80 × 2.5 (1.50 hull) **A:** 1/40-mm AA
**Electron Equipt:** Radar: 1/Decca TM 1226C, 1/Decca 1229
**M:** 2 MTU 12V538 TB91 diesels; 2 props; 5,400 hp
**Range:** 2,400/15 **Man:** 5 officers, 22 men

REMARKS: Ordered 1978. CSEE Panda optronic GFCS for the 40-mm gun, which has a fiberglass cover to the mount. All commissioned day of departure under own power to Uruguay from Cherbourg. Twin 20-mm AA planned aft, not mounted.

## PATROL CRAFT

◆ **1 U.S. 85-foot Commercial Cruiser** Bldr: Sewart Seacraft, Morgan City, La.

PR 12 PAYSANDU (L: 11-68)

**D:** 43.5 tons (54 fl) **S:** 22 kts **Dim:** 25.91 × 5.69 × 2.1
**A:** 3/12.7-mm mg (I × 3) **Electron Equipt:** Radar: 1/Raytheon 1500B
**M:** 2 G.M. 16V71N diesels; 2 props; 1,400 hp **Electric:** 40 kw
**Range:** 800/21 **Man:** 8 tot.

REMARKS: Built under U.S. Military Assistance Program. Aluminum construction.

◆ **1 ex-German FL-9 class** Bldr: Krögerwerft, Rendsburg (In serv. 1955)

PR 11 CARMELO

**D:** 67 tons (73 fl) **S:** 30 kts **Dim:** 28.8 (27.9 pp) × 5.0 × 1.6
**A:** 1/20-mm AA **Electron Equipt:** Radar: 1/Decca 12
**M:** 2 Maybach 12-cyl. diesels; 2 props; 3,000 hp **Range:** 600/25 **Man:** 8 tot.

## PATROL CRAFT *(continued)*

REMARKS: One of five sisters built as air-sea-rescue craft for the British Royal Air Force. Taken over by Uruguayan Navy in 1964. Wooden construction.

NOTE: Patrol craft *Colonia* (PR 10) was stricken 1986.

## MINE COUNTERMEASURES SHIP

◆ **1 ex-U.S. Adjutant-class** Bldr: National Steel SB, San Diego, Cal.

| | In serv. |
|---|---|
| 13 RIO NEGRO (ex-MS 32, ex-*Marguerite,* ex-MSC 94) | 3-54 |

**Rio Negro (13)**—old number

**D:** 300 tons (372 fl) **S:** 13 kts
**Dim:** 43.0 (41.5 pp) × 7.95 × 2.95 **A:** 2/20-mm AA (II × 1)
**Electron Equipt:** Radar: 1/DRBN-31—Sonar: UQS-1D
**M:** 2 G.M. 8-268A diesels; 2 props; 1,200 hp
**Range:** 2,500/10 **Man:** 38 tot.

REMARKS: On completion, transferred to France, then to Uruguay on 10-11-69. Wooden construction. Minesweeping equipment, including sweep winch and cable drum, replaced by 1986; had been removed.

## AMPHIBIOUS WARFARE CRAFT

◆ **3 LD 43-class landing craft** Bldr: Dieque Nacional, Montevideo

LD 43 (In serv. 26-7-78) LD 46 (In serv. 1979) LD 47 (In serv. 1981)

**D:** 31.4 tons (fl) **S:** 9 kts **Dim:** 14.1 × 3.50 × 0.80
**M:** 2 G.M. 6-71 diesels; 2 props; 272 hp **Range:** 580/9

REMARKS: Up to four more may have been completed 1979–81. Can carry five tons cargo.

◆ **1 LD 45-class personnel landing craft** Bldr: Mapell S.A., Paysandu

LD 45

**D:** 15 tons **S:** 8 kts **Dim:** 10.85 × 3.50 × 0.70
**M:** 1 G.M. 6V71 diesel; 1 prop; 140 hp

REMARKS: LD 45 laidown 12-79. Referred to as Type 5-06.

◆ **1 small landing craft** Bldr: Mapell S.A., Paysandu (In serv. . . .)

LD 42

**D:** 12 tons **S:** 6 kts **Dim:** 12.0 × 3.4 × 1.1
**M:** 2 British G.M. Bedford 330 diesels; 2 props; 192 hp

◆ **2 U.S. LCM(6)-class landing craft**

LD 40 LD 41

**D:** 24 tons (57 fl) **S:** 10 kts **Dim:** 17.07 × 4.37 × 1.17
**M:** 2 Gray Marine 64HN9 diesels; 2 props; 450 hp **Range:** 130/9

REMARKS: LD 40 and LD 41 were leased in 10-72; lease extended 1982. Cargo: 30 tons.

## HYDROGRAPHIC SHIPS

◆ **1 Paysandu-class former patrol boat** Bldr: CNR, Ancona

14 SALTO (ex-GS 24) (L: 11-8-35)

**D:** 150 tons (180 fl) **S:** 17 kts **Dim:** 42.1 × 5.8 × 1.58
**M:** 2 Krupp-Germania diesels; 2 props; 1,000 hp
**Range:** 4,000/10 **Man:** 26 tot.

REMARKS: Survivor of a class of three, placed on present duties as a survey craft and navigational-buoy tender in 1972.

## AUXILIARY SHIPS

NOTE: 19,656-grt tanker *Presidente Rivera* (28) was sold 1-86. Plans called for acquisition of a replacement, the 42,235-grt/87,325-dwt *Viking Harrier* (Norwegian registry) which was to enter the Uruguayan Navy early in 1988.

◆ **1 supertanker** Bldr: Kawasaki, Kobe, Japan, 1975

27 JUAN A. LAVALLEJA (ex-*Solfonn*)

**D:** 145,000 tons (fl) **S:** 15.5 kts **Dim:** 273.0 × 44.1 × 15.7
**M:** 2 sets GT; 1 prop; 24,500 hp **Boilers:** 2 **Man:** 40 tot.

REMARKS: 131,633 dwt, 68,931 grt. Literally, the world's largest naval ship, by a wide margin. Laid up by Norwegian owner on 13-10-75, when she was completed. Purchased by Uruguay on 24-5-77 for use by ANCAP, the state petroleum monopoly, in commercial service with a naval crew. No underway replenishment capability. Grounded 28-12-80 off Arzew, Algeria; refloated 17-2-81 and repaired in France. Now has black hull, white superstructure and has no hull number printed on.

◆ **1 transport, former merchant cargo ship**

| | Bldr | In serv. |
|---|---|---|
| 29 PRESIDENTE ORIBE (ex-Danish *Cathrina,* ex-*Golf Princess,* ex-*Cathrina*) | Frederikshavn, Denmark | 1966 |

**D:** 1,153 tons **S:** 10 kts **Dim:** 54.2 × 9.6 × 3.3
**M:** 1 Burmeister & Wain diesel; 1 prop; 520 hp

REMARKS: Ran aground while in merchant service 11-78 and salvaged by Uruguayan Navy; purchased from British insurance company and commissioned 19-8-80.

◆ **1 ex-U.S. Cohoes-class salvage ship** Bldr: Commercial Ironworks, Portland, Ore.

| | Laid down | L | In serv. |
|---|---|---|---|
| AM 25 HURACÁN (ex-*Nahant,* AN 83, ex-YN 102) | 31-3-45 | 30-6-45 | 24-8-45 |

**Huracán (AM 25)** L. & L. Van Ginderen, 1969

**D:** 650 tons (855 fl) **S:** 12.3 kts **Dim:** 51.36 (44.5 pp) × 10.31 × 3.3
**A:** removed **Electron Equipt:** Radar: 1/SPS-5
**M:** 2 Busch-Sulzer BS539 diesels, electric drive; 1 prop; 1,200 hp **Man:** 48 tot.

REMARKS: Former netlayer. Transferred in 12-68. A decompression chamber for divers is carried.

◆ **0 (+1) new-construction buoy tender** Bldr: Dieque Nacional, Montevideo

N . . . (In serv. . . .)

**D:** 290 tons (fl) **S:** 11 kts **Dim:** 35.0 × 10.0 × 2.8
**M:** 2 G.M. 12V71 TA diesels; 2 props; 860 hp **Man:** 15 tot.

REMARKS: Being built with assistance from Damen SY, Hardinxveld, the Netherlands. Large electrohydraulic articulated crane forward.

◆ **1 miscellaneous service tender** Bldr: . . . , Glasgow, Scotland

AM 26 VANGUARDIA (ex-*Balizador*) (In serv. 1908)

**D:** 95 tons **S:** 12 kts **Dim:** approx. 32.0 × . . . × . . .
**M:** 1 set triple-expansion reciprocating steam; 1 prop; 200 hp

REMARKS: Employed on hydrographic survey duties; white hull, buff upper works.

NOTE: A craft named *Oyarvide* is also in naval service, function and characteristics not available. A 21-m tender, 71 (ex-PS 1), is used as a tug.

◆ **1 sail-training ship**

| | Bldr | In serv. |
|---|---|---|
| 20 CAPITAN MIRANDA (ex-GS 20) | Soc. Española de Construcción Naval, Matagorda, Cádiz, Spain | 1930 |

**URUGUAY** *(continued)*
**AUXILIARY SHIPS** *(continued)*

**Capitan Miranda (20)**—number not borne R.A.N., 1-88

**D:** 516 tons (550 fl) **S:** 11 kts **Dim:** 54.6 (61.0 bowsprit/45.0 pp) × 8.4 × 3.2
**Electron Equipt:** Radar: 1/Decca TM 1226C
**M:** 1 M.A.N. diesel; 1 prop; 500 hp **Fuel:** 45 tons **Man:** 49 tot.

REMARKS: Originally built as a hydrographic survey ship. Refitted and rigged as a three-masted schooner for cadet training, recommissioning 1978.

COAST GUARD
(PREFECTURA MARITIMA)

The Uruguayan Coast Guard has 100 officers and about 1,900 enlisted men. Primarily intended for a shore-based coast watch and port police function, it does operate three 21-m patrol boats, three 9-m patrol craft, and a number of outboard-motor-powered semi-inflatable rubber boats; all have pendant numbers beginning with PM, PS, etc.

# VANUATU

PERSONNEL: . . .

MERCHANT MARINE: (1986): 47 ships—164,953 grt

## PATROL BOATS

◆ **1 Australian ASI 315 class** Bldr: Australian SB Industries, South Coogie, Western Australia

TUKORO (In serv. 13-6-87)

**Tukoro** L. & L. Van Ginderen, 5-87

**D:** 165 tons (fl) **S:** 20 kts **Dim:** 31.50 (28.60 wl) × 8.10 × 2.12 (1.80 hull)
**A:** none **Electron Equipt:** Radar: 1/Furuno 1011
**M:** 2 Caterpillar 3516 diesels; 2 props; 2,820 hp (2,400 sust.) **Electric:** 100 kw
**Range:** 2,500/12 **Fuel:** 27.9 tons **Man:** 3 officers, 14 men
**Endurance:** 8–10 days

REMARKS: Provided by Australian foreign aid. Sisters being built for other Southwest Pacific nations. A second unit is planned. See Papua New Guinea entry for additional data.

◆ **1 patrol boat, former yacht**

MALA (In serv. . . .)

**Mala** L. & L. Van Ginderen, 5-85

REMARKS: No data available.

# VENEZUELA

**Republic of Venezuela**

PERSONNEL: (1987): 10,000 men, including 4,500 Marines

MERCHANT MARINE (1986): 279 ships—998,296 grt
(tankers: 22 ships—458,900 grt)

NAVAL AVIATION: The small naval aviation component operates 4 Casa 212A Aviocar, one de Havilland Dash-7, one transport, 2 Beech King Air 98 light, and one Turbo Commander transports, one Cessna 337 liaison aircraft, and twelve Agusta-Bell AB-212 helicopters.

The newly established Coast Guard operates four HU-16A Albatross amphibians for maritime surveillance, as well as four Casa C-212 series 200 light transports with radars for coastal surveillance; 4 more are planned, as are 4 Sikorsky S-61 helicopters for rescue duties.

## SUBMARINES

NOTE: Venezuela is considering acquiring two more submarines, either repeat Type 209-class or Argentine-built TR-1700-class units. The U.S. Guppy-II-class submarine *Picua* (S-22, ex-*Grenadier,* SS 525) is used for pierside training.

◆ **2 German Type 209** Bldr: Howaldtswerke, Kiel

| | Laid down | L | In serv. |
|---|---|---|---|
| S-31 SABALO | 2-5-73 | 1-17-75 | 6-8-76 |
| S-32 CARITE | 1-8-73 | 6-11-75 | 11-3-77 |

**Sabalo (S-31)** Venezuelan Navy, 1987

**D:** 990/1,290 tons **S:** 11/22 kts **Dim:** 56.10 × 6.20 × 5.50
**A:** 8/533-mm TT—14 U.S. Mk 37 and West German SST-4 torpedoes
**M:** diesel-electric propulsion: 4 MTU Type 12V492 Tb90, 600-hp diesels; 4/405-kw generators; Siemens electric motor; 5,000 hp
**Electron Equipt:** Radar: Calypso—Sonar: CSU-3 series suite
**Fuel:** 100 tons **Range:** 7,800/8 surf.; 400/4 sub. **Man:** 5 officers, 26 men

REMARKS: Ordered 1971: S-31 damaged by fire in 1979, overhauled at Kiel. A planned second pair were not ordered. S-32 refitted by builder 1984. Have H.S.A. Mk 8 Mod. 24 fire-control system.

## GUIDED-MISSILE FRIGATES

◆ **6 Italian Lupo class** Bldr: CNR, Riva Trigoso and Ancona(*), Italy

| | Laid down | L | In serv. |
|---|---|---|---|
| F-21 Mariscal Sucre | 4-10-77 | 28-9-78 | 14-7-80 |
| F-22 Almirante Brion | 26-1-78 | 22-2-79 | 7-3-81 |
| F-23 General Urdaneta* | 23-1-78 | 23-3-79 | 8-8-81 |
| F-24 General Soublette | 26-8-78 | 4-1-80 | 4-12-81 |
| F-25 General Salom* | 7-11-78 | 13-1-80 | 3-4-82 |
| F-26 Almirante José M. Garcia (ex-*General José Felix Ribas*) | 21-8-79 | 4-10-80 | 30-7-82 |

**General Soublette (F-24)**—launching an Otomat SSM Venezuelan Navy, 1987

**General Urdaneta (F-23)**—AB 212 helo on deck R. Scheina, 7-84

**General Soublette (F-24)** C. Martinelli, 12-82

**D:** 2,213 tons (2,525 fl) **S:** 35 kts (20.5 on diesels)
**Dim:** 112.8 (106.0 pp) × 11.98 × 3.84 (hull)
**A:** 8/Otomat Mk II SSM (I × 8)—1/Albatros SAM system (VIII × 1, 8 Aspide missiles)—1/127-mm OTO Melara DP—4/40-mm Breda Dardo AA (II × 2)—6/324-mm Mk 32 ASW TT (III × 2, for A244 torpedoes)—1/AB-212 ASW helicopter
**Electron Equipt:** Radar: 1/3RM-20 navigational, 1/RAN-11/X air and surface search, 1/RAN-10S air search, 2/Orion RTN-10X, 2/Orion RTN-20X—TACAN: SRN-15A
Sonar: Edo 610E
EW: Lambda-F, 2/SCLAR chaff RL (XX × 2)
**M:** CODOG: 2 Fiat G.E. LM-2500 gas turbines, 25,000 hp each; 2 GMT A230-2M diesels, 3,900 hp each; 2 CP props
**Electric:** 3,120 kw **Range:** 900/35; 1,050/31.7; 5,500/16 **Man:** 185 tot.

Remarks: Ordered 24-10-75. Fin stabilizers fitted. Gun (127-mm) and missile fire control by two Elsag NA-10 Mod. 0 systems. The Albatros system uses Aspide missiles, a re-engineered version of NATO Sea Sparrow. Each twin 40-mm Dardo system antiaircraft mount has an associated RTN-20X radar director. All weapons controlled by a Selenia IPN-10 computerized data system. Fixed, nontelescopic hangar. Near-sisters in the Iraqi, Italian, and Peruvian navies.

## PATROL BOATS

◆ **0 (+2) Cormoran class** Bldr: Bazán, San Fernando, Spain

| | Laid down | L | In serv. |
|---|---|---|---|
| P-53 N....... | ... | 15-10-85 | ... |
| P-54 N....... | ... | ... | ... |

**P-53 on trials**—weapons and sensors added by retoucher Bazán, 1987

**D:** 300 tons light (374 fl) **S:** 36 kts **Dim:** 56.50 × 7.54 × 1.87
**A:** ...
**Electron Equipt:** Radar: ...—EW: ...
**M:** 3 Bazán-MTV 16V956 TB91 diesels; 3 props (centerline prop CP); 11,250 hp
**Range:** 2,000/15 **Electric:** 405 kVA **Man:** 5 officers, 27 men

Remarks: Begun and launched on speculation by builder. Reported purchased 2-87 by Venezuela, *but not confirmed.* Steel construction. Weapon suite offered by Bazán: 4/Otomat or MM-40 Exocet (II × 2), 1/76-mm OTO Melara Compact DP, 1/40-mm AA, 2/12.7-mm mg; sensor and weapon-control suite would include an H.S.A. WM-25 system, 2 Lirod directors, and a surface-search/navigational radar.

◆ **6 Constitución class** Bldr: Vosper Thornycroft, Portsmouth, U.K.

| | Laid down | L | In serv. |
|---|---|---|---|
| P-11 Constitución | 1-73 | 1-6-73 | 16-8-74 |
| P-12 Federación | 8-73 | 26-2-74 | 25-3-75 |
| P-13 Independencia | 2-73 | 24-7-73 | 20-9-74 |
| P-14 Libertad | 9-73 | 5-3-74 | 12-6-75 |
| P-15 Patria | 3-73 | 27-9-73 | 9-1-75 |
| P-16 Victoria | 3-73 | 3-9-74 | 22-9-75 |

**Federación (P-12)**—missile version

**Constitución (P-11)**—76-mm gun version Venezuelan Navy, 1987

### PATROL BOATS *(continued)*

**D:** 150 tons (170 fl) **S:** 31 kts **Dim:** 36.88 (33.53 wl) × 7.16 × 1.73
**A:** P-11, P-13, P-15: 1/76-mm OTO Melara Compact
P-12, P-14, P-16: 2/Otomat Mk I SSM (I × 2)—1/40-mm AA
**Electron Equipt:** 1/SPQ-2D; P-11, P-13, P-15: 1/Orion RTN-10X also
**M:** 2 MTU MD 16V538 TB90 diesels; 1 prop; 7,080 max. hp/5,900 sust. hp
**Electric:** 250 kw **Range:** 1,350/16 **Man:** 3 officers, 14 men

REMARKS: Ordered 4-72. All equipped with Vosper fin stabilizers. New hull numbers assigned 1978. Maximum sustained speed is 27 knots. NA-10 Mod. 1 GFCS in 76-mm-gun-equipped boats. Transferred from the Navy, 1983.

NOTE: There are apparently a number of river patrol boats subordinated to the River Command, cif. the photo of *Margarita* (T-43) showing such a craft (PF-21) alongside. The only available name is *Caripito* (PF-43). Four National Guard U.S.-built 42-ft patrol craft were transferred to the River Command in 1986.

◆ **4 tank landing ships** Bldr: Korea-Tacoma SY, Masan, S. Korea

| | L | In serv. |
|---|---|---|
| T-61 CAPAÑA | 25-3-83 | 21-6-84 |
| T-62 ESEQUIBO | 25-3-83 | 21-6-84 |
| T-63 GOAJIRA | . . . | 11-84 |
| T-64 LOS LLANOS | . . . | 11-84 |

**Capaña (T-61)**—without armament 7-85

**Esequibo (T-62)**—without armament Venezuelan Navy, 1985

**D:** 1,800 tons light (3,770 fl) **S:** 15 kts **Dim:** 104.0 × 15.4 × 3.0 (4.2 max.)
**A:** 3/40-mm AA (I × 3)—2/20-mm AA (I × 2)
**Electron Equipt:** Radar: . . .
**M:** 2 diesels; 2 props; 5,600 hp **Electric:** 750 kw
**Range:** 7,500/13 **Man:** 13 officers, 104 men + troops: 10 officers, 192 men

REMARKS: Ordered 8-82. Cargo: 1,800 tons maximum, 690 tons beaching load. Improved version of U.S. WW II-era LST. Have an elevator to the upper deck and a 50-ton tank turntable on the tank deck. Sisters in the Indonesian Navy. T-61, 62 arrived 10-84 in Venezuela, T-63 in 12-84, and T-64 early in 1985; all delivered without armament. Have a helicopter deck aft.

◆ **1 ex-U.S. Terrebonne Parish-class landing ship**
Bldr: Ingalls, Pascagoula

| | Laid down | L | In serv. |
|---|---|---|---|
| T-51 AMAZONAS (ex-*Vernon County,* LST 1161) | 14-4-52 | 1952 | 1954 |

**Amazonas (T-51)** 1977

**D:** 2,590 tons (5,786 fl) **S:** 13 kts **Dim:** 117.35 × 16.76 × 5.18
**A:** 6/76.2-mm DP (II × 3) **Electric:** 600 kw
**Electron Equipt:** 1/Decca navigational, 1/SPS-21, 2/SPG-34
**M:** 4 G.M. 16-278A diesels; 2 CP props; 6,000 hp **Man:** 116 tot.
**Range:** 6,000/9 **Fuel:** 1,060 tons

REMARKS: Loaned 29-6-73, purchased outright 30-12-77. Cargo: 2,200 tons vehicles and stores, 395 troops. Two Mk 63 radar GFCS. Normally carries 2 LCVPs. Went aground 6-8-80 at St. Lucia in a hurricane but was salvaged. To be refitted.

◆ **2 utility landing craft** Bldr: Swiftships, Morgan City, La. (In serv. 1984)

T-43 MARGARITA (ex-T71, in serv. 20-1-84) T-72 LA ORCHILA (In serv. 11-5-84)

**Margarita (T-43)**—old number, with unidentified river patrol PF-21 alongside Venezuelan Navy, 1986

**D:** 428 tons (fl) **S:** 13 kts **Dim:** 39.62 × 10.97 × 1.30
**A:** 2/12.7-mm mg (I × 2) **Electron Equipt:** Radar: 1/. . . nav.
**M:** 2 G.M. Detroit Diesel 16V149 N diesels; 2 props; 1,800 hp
**Range:** 2,500/10 **Fuel:** 64 tons **Man:** 4 officers, 17 men

REMARKS: Aluminum construction. Cargo: vehicles, supplies, up to 108 tons fuel and 149 tons water. Bow ramp, 15-ton crane on bow. Carry 156 tons ballast. Intended for coastal and riverine use. T-43 transferred to River Command in 1986, under Marine Corps control

◆ **12 U.S. LCVP-class landing craft** Bldr: Dianca, Puerto Cabello, 1976–77

**D:** 12 tons (fl) **S:** 9 kts **Dim:** 10.9 × 3.2 × 1.0
**M:** 1 diesel; 1 prop; 225 hp **Range:** 110/9

REMARKS: Follow design of U.S.-built LCVP. Several other LCVP and LCPL transferred with U.S. Navy ships probably also survive.

### AUXILIARY SHIPS

◆ **2 Gabriela-class survey craft**

Bldr: Abeking & Rasmussen, Lemwerder, West Germany

| | Laid down | L | In serv. |
|---|---|---|---|
| LH-11 GABRIELA | 10-3-73 | 29-11-73 | 5-2-74 |
| LH-12 LELY | 28-5-73 | 12-12-73 | 7-2-74 |

**D:** 90 tons (fl) **S:** 20 kts **Dim:** 27.0 × 5.6 × 1.5
**M:** 2 MTU diesels; 2 props; 2,300 hp **Man:** 16 tot.

REMARKS: Civilian-manned. Transferred to Navy in 1986 from civilian agency.

◆ **1 transport, former merchant ship** Bldr: Drammen SY, Drammen, Norway (In serv. 1972)

T-44 PUERTO CABELLO (ex-*Sierra Nevada,* ex-*Ragni Berg,* ex-*Golar Ragni,* ex-*Kongsfjell*)

**Puerto Cabello (T-44)** C. Martinelli, 2-87

**D:** approx. 13,000 tons (fl) **S:** 22.5 kts
**Dim:** 140.62 (131.88 pp) × 18.04 × 9.04 **A:** none
**Electron Equipt:** Radar: 2/. . . nav. **M:** 1 Sulzer diesel; 1 prop; 13,200 hp

REMARKS: 6,682-grt/9,218-dwt former refrigerated cargo ship with 10,280 $m^3$ refrigerated cargo capacity in four holds. Acquired for Venezuelan Navy and commissioned 22-5-84. Replaced transport *Las Aves* (T-11), stricken 1983.

◆ **1 Maracaibo-class transport** Bldr: Canadian Vickers, Montreal (In serv. 1953)

T-42 VALENCIA (ex-*Ciudad de Valencia*)

**D:** approx. 8,100 tons (fl) **S:** 15 kts **Dim:** 128.15 × 16.76 × 6.78
**M:** 1 Nordberg diesel; 1 prop; 4,275 hp **Man:** 7 officers, 50 men

**AUXILIARY SHIPS** *(continued)*

Remarks: 4,297 grt/5,885 dwt. Transferred from State Shipping Co. in 1977. Five cargo holds. Additional superstructure added on stern to increase accommodations. Refitted 1982 at Port Everglades, Florida.

◆ **1 sail-training ship** Bldr: Ast. Celeya, Bilbao, Spain

| | Laid down | L | In serv. |
|---|---|---|---|
| Simón Bolívar | 5-6-79 | 21-9-79 | 14-8-80 |

**Simón Bolívar** Venezuelan Navy, 7-86

**D:** 1,260 tons (fl) **S:** 10.5 kts **Dim:** 82.42 (58.5 pp) × 10.6 × 4.2
**M:** 1 G.M. 12V149 diesel; 1 prop; 750 hp
**Man:** 17 officers, 75 men, 18 instructors, 84 cadets

Remarks: 934 grt. Sister to Ecuadorian *Guayas.* Three-masted bark; sail area: 1,650 m². Ordered 7-78.

**SERVICE CRAFT**

◆ **1 large harbor tug** Bldr: Dianca, Puerto Cabello, 1978

C-142

**D:** . . . **S:** . . . **Dim:** . . . × . . . × . . .
**M:** 2 Werkspoor diesels; 2 props; 1,600 hp

Remarks: Ordered 1973. Used for Navy by Dianca SY. Three sisters operated by Ministry of Communications: C-139, C-140, C-141.

Note: Tug *Fernando Gomez* (R-11) has been transferred to the Coast Guard.

◆ **1 River tug** Bldr: . . .

R-. . . Cardones (In serv. 1-86)

Remarks: No data available.

◆**1 ex-U.S. floating repair barge** Bldr: Mare Isl. NSY, Cal. (L: 30-5-43)

. . . (ex-YR 48)

**D:** 520 tons (770 fl) **Dim:** 46.6 × 13.1 × 2.1
**Electric:** 220 kw **Fuel:** 75 tons **Man:** 46 tot.

Remarks: Leased 7-61; purchased outright 30-12-77.

◆ **1 floating dry dock** Bldr: Conrad SY, Morgan City, La.

GS-01 Rio Manzanare (In serv. 7-86)

Remarks: Lift capacity 1,829 tons.

◆ **1 floating crane—Capacity:** 40 tons

◆ **1 small service craft** Bldr: Ast. Lago Maracaibo (In serv. 5-80)

ANGU-01

◆ **3 service launches** Bldr: American SB & Design, Miami, Fla.

MTC-6 (In serv. 31-10-83) MTC-7 (In serv. 15-12-83) MTC-8 (In serv. 26-2-84)

**D:** 4 8 tons (fl) **S:** 32 kts **Dim:** 10.06 (9.19 pp) × 3.35 × 0.76
**M:** 2 G.M. diesels; 2 props; 550 hp **Range:** 450/. . .

Remarks: Glass-reinforced plastic construction.

VENEZUELAN COAST GUARD

The Venezuelan Coast Guard was established in 8-82 to patrol the 200-nautical-mile economic zone. Initially operating only four Cessna 210 light aircraft, it has now received a number of former Venezuelan Navy vessels, as well as four CASA Aviocar maritime-patrol-configured light transports, four former naval HU-16 Albatross amphibians, and six former naval S-2E Tracker aircraft (the latter discarded 2-85). The Coast Guard is headquartered at Puerto Cabello under the Ministry of the Navy and is commanded by a navy rear admiral.

**FRIGATES**

◆ **2 Almirante Clemente class** Bldr: Ansaldo, Livorno

| | Laid down | L | In serv. |
|---|---|---|---|
| GC-11 Almirante Clemente (ex-F-12) | 5-5-54 | 12-12-54 | 1956 |
| GC-12 General José Trinidad Moran (ex-F-22) | 5-5-54 | 12-12-54 | 1956 |

**Almirante Clemente (GC-11)**—old number French Navy, 12-85

**Almirante Clemente (GC-11)** Venezuelan Navy, 3-86

**D:** 1,300 tons (1,500 fl) **S:** 22 kts **Dim:** 97.6 × 10.84 × 2.6
**A:** 2/76-mm OTO Melara DP (I × 2)—2/40-mm AA (II × 2)—6/324-mm ILAS-3 ASW TT (III × 2)
**Electron Equipt:** Radar: 1/Decca 1226, 1/Plessey AWS-2, 1/Orion RTN-10X
Sonar: Plessey MS-26
**M:** 2 G.M.T. 16-645E7CA diesels; 2 props; 6,000 hp **Range:** . . .
**Fuel:** 350 tons **Man:** 12 officers, 150 men

Remarks: Survivors of a class of six: *General José de Austria* stricken 1976, *General José Garcia* stricken 1977, and *General Juan José Flores* and *Almirante Brion* stricken 1978. Both were extensively refitted by Cammell Laird, Birkenhead, from 1968 to 1975–76 (much delay caused by financial and labor problems). New radars, sonar, and armament fitted, with OTO Melara Compact mounts replacing the original four 102-mm dual-purpose (II × 2). Have NA-10 GFCS for the 76-mm guns and a lead-computing sight for the 40-mm AA mount. When new, could make 32 knots. Very lightly built, with much use of aluminum alloy. Denny-Brown fin stabilizers. Being re-engined by C.N.R., Genoa, Italy, with diesels 10-84 to 24-7-85 and transferred to the new Coast Guard in 3-86.

**PATROL BOATS**

◆ **2 ex-U.S. Achomawi-class fleet tugs** Bldr: Charleston SB & DD, S.C.

| | Laid down | L | In serv. |
|---|---|---|---|
| R-21 Felipe Larrazabel (ex-*Utina,* ATF 163) | 6-6-45 | 31-8-45 | 30-1-46 |
| R-23 Miguel Rodriguez (ex-*Salinin,* ATF 161) | 13-4-45 | 20-7-45 | 11-9-45 |

**D:** 1,235 tons (1,675 fl) **S:** 16.5 kts **Dim:** 62.48 (59.44) × 11.74 × 4.67
**A:** R-21 only: 1/76.2-mm DP **Electron Equipt:** Radar: 1/SPS-53
**M:** 4 G.M. 16-278A diesels, electric drive; 1 prop; 3,000 hp
**Electric:** 400 kw **Fuel:** 300 tons **Range:** 7,000/15 **Man:** 85 tot.

Remarks: R-21 loaned 3-9-71; purchased outright 30-12-77. R-23 purchased 1-9-78. Sister *Antonio Picardi* (R-22, ex-*Nipmuc,* AFT 157), ran aground and was lost 12-4-82, R-21 and R-23 transferred to Coast Guard in 1983, where they are used in patrol duties.

Note: Former trawler LG-12 was commissioned for Coast Guard use as a patrol boat in early 1984; no data available. A widely reported order for five Picchiotti of Italy 41.8-m patrol boats has not yet materialized.

PATROL BOATS (*continued*)

**Miguel Rodriguez (R-23)** L. & L. Van Ginderen, 5-81

AUXILIARIES

◆ **1 ex-U.S. Cohoes-class survey ship** Bldr: Commercial Iron Works, Portland, Ore.

| | Laid down | L | In serv. |
|---|---|---|---|
| H-11 Puerto Santo (ex-*Marietta,* AN 82, ex-YN 101) | 17-2-45 | 27-4-45 | 25-6-45 |

**D:** 650 tons (855 fl) **S:** 12 kts **Dim:** 48.2 (44.5 wl) × 10.3 × 3.6
**A:** 3/20-mm AA
**M:** 2 Busch-Sulzer BS 539 diesels, electric drive; 1 prop; 1,500 hp
**Electric:** 240 kw **Fuel:** 110 tons **Man:** 46 tot.

Remarks: Ex-net tender. Transferred 1-61 under Military Aid Program; purchased outright 30-12-77. Converted for use as a hydrographic survey ship in 1962 by U.S. Coast Guard Yard, Curtis Bay, Md. Original bow horns removed, reducing overall length from 51.4 meters. Retains 12-ton boom forward. Bridge superstructure raised one deck. Transferred to Coast Guard 1986. A replacement, to be named *Francisco de Miranda,* entered the planning stage in 5-84.

◆ **1 ex-U.S. medium harbor tug** Bldr: Ramsey & Sons, New Orleans, La.

R-11 Fernando Gomez (ex-*Dudley,* YTM 744)

**D:** 161 tons **S:** 15 kts **Dim:** 24.5 × 5.8 × 2.4 **A:** 2/12.7-mm mg (I × 2)
**M:** 1 Clark 6-cyl. diesel; 1 prop; 380 hp **Man:** 10 tot.

Remarks: Built 1938. Acquired by U.S. Navy 1-42; sold to Venezuela 1-47. Transferred to Coast Guard 1986.

NATIONAL GUARD

PATROL CRAFT

◆ **12 42-ft design** Bldr: MonArk Workboats, Monticello, Ark., U.S.A.

| | In serv. | | In serv. |
|---|---|---|---|
| B-8421 Rio Arauca II | 2-7-84 | B-8427 Rio Sarare | 4-9-84 |
| B-8422 Rio Catatumbo II | 2-7-84 | B-8428 Rio Uribante | 4-9-84 |
| B-8423 Rio Apure II | 1-8-84 | B-8429 Rio Cinaruco | 1-11-84 |
| B-8424 Rio Nearo II | 1-8-84 | B-8430 Rio Icabara | 1-11-84 |
| B-8425 Rio Meta II | 30-8-84 | B-8431 Rio Guarico II | -84 |
| B-8426 Rio Portuguesa II | 30-8-84 | B-8432 Rio Yaracuy | -84 |

**D:** 15 tons (fl) **S:** 28 kts **Dim:** 13.03 (12.55 pp) × 4.47 × 1.17
**A:** 3/12.7-mm mg **Electron Equipt:** Radar: 1/Raytheon 1900
**M:** 2 G.M. Detroit Diesel 8V92 T diesels; 2 props; 1,100 hp
**Range:** 600/. . . **Electric:** 10.5 kw **Man:** 4 tot.

Remarks: Aluminum construction. For river and lake patrol. Replace 12 French-built craft delivered 1970–77. Four of the craft were transferred to the Navy's River Command in 1986.

◆ **10 21-ft design** Bldr: MonArk Workboats, Monticello, Ark., U.S.A.

| | | |
|---|---|---|
| A-6901 Lago 1 | A-7918 Rio Cabriales | A-7921 Rio Tuy |
| A-6902 Lago 2 | A-7919 Rio Chama | A-7929 Rio Manati |
| A-6903 Lago 3 | A-7920 Rio Caribe | A-8223 Rio Goaigoaza |
| A-6904 Lago 4 | | |

**D:** 1.25 tons (fl) **S:** 30 kts **Dim:** 6.02 × 2.36 × 0.33 **A:** 1/12.7-mm mg
**Man:** 4 tot. **M:** 2 Evinrude gasoline outboard motors; 230 hp

**Rio Catatumbo II (B-8422)** MonArk, 7-84

**21-ft design**—outboard motors not fitted MonArk, 1984

Remarks: Aluminum construction. For river and lake patrol. Equipped with push-knees to act as pusher tugs.

◆ **15 18-ft chase-boat design** Bldr: MonArk Workboats, Monticello, Ark., U.S.A. (In serv. 11-1-85)

**18-ft chase boat** MonArk, 1985

**D:** 0.5 tons (fl) **S:** 30 kts **Dim:** 5.48 × 2.08 × 0.15 **A:** 1/12.7-mm mg
**Man:** 4 tot. **M:** 1 Evinrude gasoline outboard motor; 140 hp

Remarks: Aluminum construction.

◆ **12 U.S. design** Bldr: Robert E. Direcktor SY, Mamaroneck, N.Y.

| | |
|---|---|
| A-8201 Punta Peret | A-8207 Punta Ballena |
| A-8202 Punta Mulato | A-8208 Punta Macuro |
| A-8203 Punta Barima | A-8209 Punta Mariusa |
| A-8204 Punta Mosquito | A-8210 Punta Moron |
| A-8205 Punta Playa | A-8211 Punta Macoya |
| A-8206 Punta Mulatos | A-8212 Punta Cardon |

**D:** approx. 50 tons (fl) **S:** 28.5 kts **Dim:** 23.44 × 4.88 × . . .
**A:** . . . **Electron Equipt:** Radar: 1/Furuno . . . **Electric:** 60 kw
**M:** 2 G.M. 12V92M TI diesels; 2 props; 1,950 hp **Range:** 1,100/22
**Man:** 10 tot.

Remarks: First six ordered 1980, delivered 8-82; second six ordered 1982 and delivered by 10-84. Aluminum construction. Of the first increment, three have a small helicopter platform aft, and three have ramps for landing small vehicles.

**VENEZUELA** *(continued)*
**PATROL CRAFT** *(continued)*

**"Punta" class**—ramp stern version F. Nakajima/Direcktor SY, 1984

◆ **26 28.3-mm class** Bldrs: *units: INMA, La Spezia, Italy; others: Dianca, Puerto Cabello (In serv. 1974–78)

| | | |
|---|---|---|
| A-7414 Rio Oronoco* | A-7423 Rio Torres* | A-7432 Rio Neveri |
| A-7415 Rio Cuyuni | A-7424 Rio Escalante* | A-7433 Rio Caroni |
| A-7416 Rio Ventuari* | A-7425 Rio Capanaparo | A-7434 Rio Guanare |
| A-7417 Rio Caparo* | A-7426 Rio Yuruari | A-7435 Rio Guainia |
| A-7418 Rio Tucuyo* | A-7427 Rio Caura | A-7436 Rio Guaicaipuro |
| A-7419 Rio Venamo* | A-7428 Rio Motatan | A-7437 Rio Tamanaco |
| A-7420 Rio Limon* | A-7429 Rio Grita | A-7438 Rio Manaure |
| A-7421 Rio San Juan* | A-7430 Rio Yuruan | A-7439 Rio Ara |
| A-7422 Rio Turbio* | A-7431 Rio Bocono | |

**D:** 43 (*48) tons (fl) **S:** 30–31 kts **Dim:** 23.8 × 4.8 × 1.5
**A:** 1/12.7-mm mg **Electron Equipt:** Radar: 1/Furuno FR 711 or FR 24
**M:** Italian-built: 2 MTU 12V493 TY diesels; 2 props; 2,200 hp
Venezuelan-built: 2 G.M. 12V92 TI diesels; 2 props; 2,000 hp
**Range:** 500 to 1,000/. . . **Man:** 8 to 12 tot.

Remarks: Wooden construction.

◆ **2 Venezuelan design** Bldr: . . . (In serv. . . .)

A-7404 Rio Altagracia A-7405 Rio Manzanare

**D:** . . . **S:** 12 kts **Dim:** 15.0 × 3.8 × 1.9
**A:** . . . **Electron Equipt:** Radar: 1/Furuno FR 10
**M:** 1 diesel; . . . hp **Range:** 140/12 **Man:** 6 tot.

◆ **17 U.S. Enforcer class** Bldr: Bertram Yacht, Miami, Fla.

Remarks: Four of the 11.6-m version delivered 1978, ten more in 1980. One 14.0-m version and two 13.4-m version delivered 1980. All have outdrive motors and glass-reinforced plastic hulls. **A:** small arms.

Note: The National Guard is also acquiring numbers of 11.6-m "Batalla del Lago" and 8.5-m "General José Antonio Piez"-class glass-reinforced plastic-hulled patrol craft built in Venezuela by Yamaha Fibra, C.A. Numbers built and characteristics are unavailable.

# VIETNAM

**Socialist Republic of Vietnam**

Personnel (1987): Approx. 6,000 total

Merchant Marine (1986): 150 ships—338,668 grt
(tankers: 6 ships—26,087 grt)

Note: The following listings include ships known to have been in North Vietnamese service in 1975, those units left behind in South Vietnam that did not escape the communist victory, and a number of ships known to have been turned over to Vietnam by the Soviet Union since 1975. The operability of much of the former U.S. equipment is questionable, but several of the larger units have been seen at sea. New ship names are not known.

Naval Aviation: Three Soviet Beriev Be-12 Mail antisubmarine patrol amphibians were delivered in 1981 for coastal surveillance duties, and there may be up to 10 Mi-4 helicopters.

## FRIGATES

◆ **5 ex-Soviet Petya-II and -III class**

HQ 08 HQ 09 HQ . . . HQ . . . HQ . . .

**Petya-III of the Vietnamese Navy** U.S. Navy, 1982

**D:** 950 tons (1,150 fl) **S:** 30 kts **Dim:** 82.3 × 9.1 × 3.2
**A:** 4/76.2-mm DP (II × 2)—3/533-mm TT (III × 2)—4/RBU-2500 ASW RL (XVI × 4)—2/d.c. racks—mines
**Electron Equipt:** Radar: 1/Don-2, 1/Strut Curve, 1/Hawk Screech
Sonar: 1/high frequency—EW: 2/Watch Dog
**M:** CODAG: 2 gas turbines, 15,000 hp each; 1 diesel, 6,000 hp; 3 props
**Range:** 4,000/10 (diesel); 500/30 (CODAG) **Man:** 80–90 tot.

Remarks: Of the same export version as has been transferred to India and Syria ("Petya-III"). Two transferred 12-78, two transferred 1-83, one transferred 12-84; the last three had 2/RBU-6000 ASW RL and 5/400-mm ASW TT (V × 1).

◆ **1 ex-U.S. Savage-class former radar picket** Bldr: Consolidated Steel Corp., Orange, Texas

| | Laid down | L | In serv. |
|---|---|---|---|
| HQ 03 Dai Ky (ex-*Tran Khan Du*, ex-*Forster*, DER 334) | 31-8-43 | 13-11-43 | 25-1-44 |

**D:** 1,590 (1,850 fl) **S:** 20 kts **Dim:** 93.3 (91.4 wl) × 11.2 × 4.3 (hull)
**A:** 2/76.2-mm DP (I × 2)—1/81-mm mortar—2/127-mm mg (I × 2)
**Electron Equipt:** Radar: 1/SPS-10, 1/SPS-29, 1/SPG-34
Sonar: SQS-29 series
**M:** 4 Fairbanks-Morse $38D8\frac{1}{8}$ diesels; 2 props; 6,000 hp **Electric:** 580 kw
**Fuel:** 310 tons **Range:** 10,000/15 **Man:** approx. 170 tot.

Remarks: Transferred to South Vietnam 25-9-71. Was in overhaul at Saigon in 1975 and has been reactivated by the new government. Mk 63 radar GFCS forward, Mk 51 Mod. 2 optical GFCS aft. Additional AA guns probably added.

◆ **1 ex-U.S. Barnegat class** Bldr: Lake Washington SY, Houghton, Wash.

| | Laid down | L | In serv. |
|---|---|---|---|
| HQ 06 N . . . . . . . (ex-*Tham Ngu Lao*, ex-U.S.C.G. *Absecon*, WHEC 374, ex-AVP 23) | 23-7-41 | 8-3-42 | 28-1-43 |

**D:** 1,766 tons (2,800 fl) **S:** 18 kts **Dim:** 94.7 (91.4 wl) × 12.5 × 4.1
**A:** 1/27-mm 38-cal. DP—2/81-mm mortars (I × 2)
**Electron Equipt:** Radar: 1/SPS-21, 1/SPS-29, 1/Mk 26
**M:** 4 Fairbanks-Morse $38D8\frac{1}{8}$ diesels; 2 props; 6,080 hp **Electric:** 600 kw
**Fuel:** 26 tons **Range:** 20,000/10 **Man:** approx. 200 tot.

Remarks: Transferred to South Vietnam in 1971, having served in the U.S. Coast Guard since 1948. Believed to have been made operational by Vietnam. Has probably had 37-mm AA added to armament and reportedly has been equipped with 2 SS-N-2A Styx missiles removed from a stricken Komar-class unit.

## CORVETTES

◆ **2 ex-U.S. Admirable-class former fleet minesweepers**

| | Bldr | Laid down | L | In. serv. |
|---|---|---|---|---|
| HQ . . . (ex-*Ky Hoa*, ex-*Sentry*, MSF 299) | Winslow Marine Railway, Winslow, Wash. | 16-5-43 | 15-8-43 | 30-5-44 |
| HQ-07 (ex-*Ha Hoi*, ex-*Prowess*, IX 305, ex-MSF 280) | Gulf SB, Chickasaw, La. | 15-9-43 | 17-2-44 | 27-9-44 |

**D:** 650 tons (945 fl) **S:** 14.8 kts **Dim:** 56.2 (54.9 wl) × 10.1 × 3.0
**A:** 2/57-mm AA (II × 1)—2/37-mm AA (I × 2)—6/23-mm AA (II × 3)
**Electron Equipt:** Radar: 1/SPS-53
**M:** 2 Cooper-Bessemer GSB-8 diesels; 1,710 hp **Electric:** 280 kw
**Man:** Approx. 80 tot.

Remarks: Transferred to South Vietnam 8-62 and 6-70, respectively. All minesweeping gear removed before transfer, and antisubmarine warfare gear removed during overhauls in early 1970s. At least one, now numbered HQ 07, is operational, rearmed with Soviet or Chinese weapons.

## GUIDED-MISSILE PATROL BOATS

◆ **8 Soviet Osa-II class**

**D:** 215 tons (245 fl) **S:** 35 kts **Dim:** 38.6 × 7.6 × 2.0
**A:** 4/SS-N-2B Styx (I × 4)—4/30-mm AA (II × 2)
**Electron Equipt:** Radar: 1/Square Tie, 1/Drum Tilt
IFF: 2/Square Head, 1/High Pole B

**GUIDED-MISSILE PATROL BOATS** *(continued)*

**M:** 3 M504 diesels; 3 props; 15,000 hp
**Range:** 500/34; 750/25 **Man:** 30 tot.

Remarks: Transferred: 2 in 10-79, 2 in 9-80, 2 in 11-80, and 2 in 2-81.

**TORPEDO BOATS**

◆ **16 Soviet Shershen class**

**Shershen, with torpedo tubes, under tow to Vietnam** U.S. Navy, 9-79

**D:** 145 tons (170 fl) **S:** 45 kts **Dim:** 34.0 × 6.8 × 1.5
**A:** 4/30-mm AA (II × 2)—4/533-mm TT—2/d.c. racks (12 d.c.)
**Electron Equipt:** Radar: 1/Pot Drum, 1/Drum Tilt—IFF: 1/High Pole A, 1–2/Square Head
**M:** 3 M503A diesels; 2 props; 12,000 hp **Range:** 460/42; 850/30 **Man:** 19 tot.

Remarks: Transferred: 2 (without torpedo tubes) on 16-4-79, 2 on 12-9-79, 2 in 8-80, 2 in 10-80, 2 in 1981, and 4 in 6-83.

**PATROL BOATS**

◆ **5 Soviet Turya-class semi-hydrofoils** Bldr: Ulis SY, Vladivostok

**D:** 210 tons (245 fl) **S:** 40 kts
**Dim:** 39.0 × 7.6 (12.5 over foils) × 2.0 (4.0 over foils)
**A:** 2/57-mm DP aft (II × 1)—2/25-mm AA fwd (II × 1)
**Electron Equipt:** Radar: 1/Pot Drum, A/Muff Cob
IFF: 1/High Pole B, 1/Square Head
**M:** 3 M504 diesels; 3 props; 15,000 hp **Range:** 400/38; 650/25 **Man:** 24 tot.

Remarks: One transferred 5-84, the second in 11-84, and 2 in 1986. Had no torpedo tubes or the standard helicopter-type dipping sonar.

◆ **11 Soviet Zhuk class**

**D:** 48 tons (60 fl) **S:** 34 kts **Dim:** 24.0 × 5.0 × 1.2
**A:** 4/14.5-mm AA (II × 2) **Electron Equipt:** Radar: 1/Spin Trough
**M:** 2 M50F diesels; 2 props; 2,400 hp **Range:** 700/28; 1,100/15 **Man:** 12 tot.

Remarks: Transferred: three in 1978, three in 11-80, one in 11-81, one in 5-85, and three in 1986.

◆ **up to 17 PGM 59 and PGM 71 class** Bldrs: ex-PGM 59 to ex-PGM 63: J. M. Martinac SB, Seattle, Wash.; ex-PGM 64 to ex-PGM 69: Marinette Marine, Marinette, Wisc.; others: Peterson Bldrs., Sturgeon Bay, Wisc. (In serv. 1963–67)

ex-HQ 600 ex-Phu Du (ex-PGM 64)
ex-HQ 601 ex-Tien Moi (ex-PGM 65)
ex-HQ 602 ex-Minh Hoa (ex-PGM 66)
ex-HQ 603 ex-Kien Vang (ex-PGM 67)
ex-HQ 606 ex-May Rut (ex-PGM 59)
ex-HQ 607 ex-Nam Du (ex-PGM 61)
ex-HQ 608 ex-Hoa Lu (ex-PGM 62)
ex-HQ 609 ex-To Yen (ex-PGM 63)
ex-HQ 610 ex-Dinh Hai (ex-PGM 69)
ex-HQ 611 ex-Truong Sa (ex-PGM 70)
ex-HQ 612 ex-Thai Binh (ex-PGM 72)
ex-HQ 613 ex-Thi Tu (ex-PGM 73)
ex-HQ 614 ex-Song Tu (ex-PGM 74)
ex-HQ 615 ex-Tat Sa (ex-PGM 80)
ex-HQ 616 ex-Hoang Sa (ex-PGM 82)
ex-HQ 617 ex-Phu Qui (ex-PGM 81)
ex-HQ 619 ex-Tho Chau (ex-PGM 91)

**D:** 102 tons light (142 fl) **S:** 17 kts **Dim:** 30.81 × 6.45 × 2.3
**A:** 1/40-mm AA—4/20-mm AA (II × 2)—4/12.7-mm mg (II × 2)

**ex-Dinh Hai (HQ 610)** 1967

**M:** ex-PGM 59 to ex-PGM 70: 2 Mercedes Benz MB 820 Db diesels; 2 props; 1,900 hp
ex-PGM 71 to ex-PGM 91: 2 G.M. 6-71 diesels; 2 props; 2,040 hp
**Electric:** 30 kw **Fuel:** 16 tons **Range:** 1,000/17 **Man:** 30 tot.

◆ **8 ex-Soviet S.O.-I class**

**D:** 190 tons (215 fl) **S:** 28 kts **Dim:** 42.0 × 6.1 × 1.9
**A:** 4/25-mm AA (II × 2)—4/RBU-1200 ASW RL (V × 4)—2/d.c. racks (24 d.c.)—mines
**Electron Equipt:** Radar: 1/Pot Head—Sonar: 1/high frequency
**M:** 3 Type 40D diesels; 3 props; 7,500 hp **Range:** 1,100/13 **Man:** 30 tot.

Remarks: Transferred: 2 in 3-80, 2 in 9-80, 2 in 5-81, and 2 in 9-83. An earlier increment transferred in 1960–66 have all been discarded.

◆ **8 ex-Chinese Shanghai-II class**

**D:** 122.5 tons normal (134.8 fl) **S:** 28.5 kts **Dim:** 38.78 × 5.41 × 1.55 hull
**A:** 4/37-mm AA (II × 2)—4/25-mm AA (II × 2)
**Electron Equipt:** Radar: Skin Head
**M:** 2 M50F-4, 1,200-hp diesels, 2 12D6, 900-hp diesels; 4 props; 4,220 hp
**Range:** 750/16.5 **Electric:** 39 kw **Endurance:** 7 days **Man:** 36 tot.

Remarks: Transferred: four in 1966 and four in 1968. Probably in very poor condition.

◆ **up to 26 ex-U.S. Coast Guard Point class** Bldr: Coast Guard Yard, Curtis Bay, Md. (In serv. late 1950s)

ex-HQ 700 ex-Le Phuoc Dui (ex-*Pt. Garnet,* WPB 82310)
ex-HQ 701 ex-Le Van Nga (ex-*Pt. League,* WPB 82304)
ex-HQ 702 ex-Huynh Van Cu (ex-*Pt. Clear,* WPB 82315)
ex-HQ 703 ex-Nguyen Dao (ex-*Pt. Gammon,* WPB 82328)
ex-HQ 704 ex-Dao Thuc (ex-*Pt. Comfort,* WPB 82317)
ex-HQ 705 ex-Le Ngoc Than (ex-*Pt. Ellis,* WPB 82330)
ex-HQ 706 ex-Nguyen Ngoc Thach (ex-*Pt. Slocum,* WPB 82313)
ex-HQ 707 ex-Dang Van Hoanh (ex-*Pt. Hudson,* WPB 82322)
ex-HQ 708 ex-Le Dinh Hung (ex-*Pt. White,* WPB 82308)
ex-HQ 709 ex-Thuong Tien (ex-*Pt. Dume,* WPB 82325)
ex-HQ 710 ex-Pham Ngoc Chau (ex-*Pt. Arden,* WPB 82309)
ex-HQ 711 ex-Dao Van Dang (ex-*Pt. Glover,* WPB 82307)
ex-HQ 712 ex-Le Ngoc An (ex-*Pt. Jefferson,* WPB 82306)
ex-HQ 713 ex-Huynh Van Ngan (ex-*Pt. Kennedy,* WPB 82320)
ex-HQ 714 ex-Tran Lo (ex-*Pt. Young,* WPB 82303)
ex-HQ 715 ex-Bui Vet Thanh (ex-*Pt. Partridge,* WPB 82305)
ex-HQ 716 ex-Nguyen An (ex-*Pt. Caution,* WPB 82301)
ex-HQ 717 ex-Nguyen Han (ex-*Pt. Welcome,* WPB 82329)
ex-HQ 718 ex-Ngo Van Quyen (ex-*Pt. Banks,* WPB 82327)
ex-HQ 719 ex-Van Dien (ex-*Pt. Lomas,* WPB 82321)
ex-HQ 720 ex-Ho Dang La (ex-*Pt. Grace,* WPB 82323)
ex-HQ 721 ex-Dam Thoaj (ex-*Pt. Mast,* WPB 82316)
ex-HQ 722 ex-Huynh Bo (ex-*Pt. Grey,* WPB 82324)
ex-HQ 723 ex-Nguyen Kim Hung (ex-*Pt. Orient,* WPB 82319)
ex-HQ 724 ex-Ho Duy (ex-*Pt. Cypress,* WPB 82326)
ex-HQ 725 ex-Troung Ba (ex-*Pt. Maromec,* WPB 82331)

**ex-Ngo Van Quyen (HQ 718)** 1969

**D:** 64 tons (67 fl) **S:** 23.7 kts **Dim:** 25.3 × 5.23 × 1.95
**A:** 1/81-mm mortar combined with 12.7-mm mg—4/12.7-mm mg (I × 4)
**M:** 2 Cummins VT-12-M-700 diesels; 2 props; 1,600 hp
**Fuel:** 5.7 tons **Range:** 460/23.7; 1,400/8 **Man:** 12 tot.

Remarks: Had been operating in Vietnamese waters with U.S. Coast Guard crews when transferred to South Vietnam in 1969–70. Probably rearmed, if operational.

**PATROL CRAFT**

◆ **2 ex-Soviet PO 2 class**

**D:** 50 tons (fl) **S:** 9 kts **Dim:** 21.0 × 4.5 × . . .
**A:** 1/12.7-mm mg **M:** 1 diesel; 1 prop; 150 hp

Remarks: Transferred 2-80. Utility craft also usable as a tug or, with appropriate equipment, a diving tender.

PATROL CRAFT *(continued)*

◆ **2 ex-East German Bremse class**

**D:** 25 tons **S:** 14 kts **Dim:** 23.0 × 5.0 × 1.1
**A:** . . . **M:** 2 diesels; 2 props; 600 hp

REMARKS: Transferred late 1970s. Intended for patrol in sheltered waters and inland waterways.

◆ **up to 107 ex-U.S. Swift Mk-I and Mk-II class** Bldr: Swiftships Inc., Morgan City, La. (In serv. 1968–70)

**D:** 19 tons (fl—Mk-II: 19.2) **S:** 25 kts
**Dim:** Mk-I: 15.28 × 3.99 × 1.07; Mk-II: 15.64 × 4.14 × 1.07
**A:** 1/81-mm mortar combined with 12.7-mm mg—2/12.7-mm mg (II × 1)
**M:** 2 G.M. 12V71N diesels; 2 props; 860 hp **Range:** 400/24 **Man:** 6 tot.

REMARKS: Transferred on completion. Most believed still serviceable. Most (approx. 90) were of the Mk-I variety, without forecastle.

RIVERINE WARFARE CRAFT

◆ **up to 9 ex-U.S. CCB (command and control boat) class** (In serv. 1969–70)

**CCB class** 1967

**D:** 160 tons light (75.5 fl) **S:** 8.5 kts **Dim:** 18.29 × 5.33 × 1.0
**A:** 1/20-mm AA—1/12.7-mm mg—2/7.62-mm mg (I × 2)—1/60-mm mortar
**M:** 2 Gray Marine 64HN9 diesels; 2 props; 450 hp
**Range:** 160/8 **Man:** 11 tot.

REMARKS: Equipped with communications facility in well, occupied by 105-mm mortar in otherwise similar LCM monitor class. Can tow disabled craft. Some had three 20-mm AA (I × 3) with an ASPB-type turret forward.

◆ **up to 60 ex-U.S. ASPB (assault support patrol boat) class** (In serv. 1969–70)

**D:** 30 tons light (38 fl) **S:** 14 kts **Dim:** 15.3 × 5.32 × 1.22
**A:** 2/20-mm AA (I × 2)—2/76.2-mm mg (I × 2)—2/40-mm grenade launchers
**M:** 2 G.M. 12V71N diesels; 2 props; 1,050 hp **Range:** 200/10 **Man:** 5 tot.

REMARKS: Two armored turrets with interchangeable armaments of one 20-mm AA, two 12.7-mm mg, or two 40-mm grenade launchers (or a combination thereof). A few had an 81-mm mortar aft in an open well.

◆ **up to 42 ex-U.S. Monitor Mk-V class** (In serv. 1969–70)

**Monitor Mk-V class** 1967

**D:** 60.3 tons light (75.5 fl) **S:** 8.5 kts **Dim:** 18.29 × 5.33 × 1.0
**A:** 2/20-mm AA (I × 2)—2/12.7-mm mg (I × 2)—4/7.62-mm mg—1/81-mm mortar
**M:** 2 Gray Marine 64HN9 diesels; 2 props; 450 hp
**Range:** 160/8 **Man:** 11 tot.

REMARKS: Originally built as monitors, rather than converted as the class below. A few had a turret-mounted 105-mm howitzer in place of the bow 20-mm turret and 81-mm mortar in well. All had screen and "venetian-blind-like" bar armor to break up projectiles. Towing rig on stern of most.

◆ **up to 22 ex-U.S. converted LCM(6) monitors**

**D:** 75 tons (fl) **S:** 8 kts **Dim:** 18.29 × 5.2 × 1.0
**A:** 1/40-mm AA (in some)—1/20-mm AA—2/12.7-mm mg (I × 2)—1/81-mm mortar (or 2 M10-8 flame throwers)
**M:** 2 Gray Marine 64HN9 diesels; 2 props; 450 hp **Man:** 10 tot.

REMARKS: Converted from LCM(6)-class landing craft. Transferred 1964–67.

◆ **up to 60 ex-U.S. ATC (armored troop carriers) class**

**ATC class**—note bar armor 1967

**D:** 55.8 tons light (70 fl) **S:** 8.5 kts **Dim:** 17.09 × 5.33 × 3.0
**A:** 1/20-mm AA—2/12.7 mm mg (I × 2)—2-6/7.62-mm mg (I × 2-6)—2/40-mm grenade launchers (I × 2)
**M:** 2 Gray Marine 64HN9 diesels; 2 props; 450 hp **Man:** 7 tot.

REMARKS: Transferred 1969. Converted LCM(6)-class landing craft. Can carry up to 40 troops. Bow ramp. Bar armor on hull and superstructure, bullet-proof awning over troop space. A few had a small helicopter platform in place of awning. Others were configured for refueling with 4,500-liter tank in the cargo well. Four CSB (combat salvage boat) versions of the LCM(6) design were also left in Vietnam, having been transferred 1969–70.

◆ **up to 293 ex-U.S. PBR (patrol boat, riverine) Mk-II class** Bldr: Uniflite, Bellingham, Wash. (In serv. 1968–70)

**D:** 6.7 tons light (8 fl) **S:** 24 kts **Dim:** 9.73 × 3.53 × 0.6
**A:** 3/12.7-mm mg (II × 1, I × 1)—1/60-mm mortar
**M:** 2 G.M. 6V53N diesels; 2 Jacuzzi waterjets; 430 hp
**Range:** 150/23 **Man:** 4 tot.

MINE WARFARE SHIPS AND CRAFT

◆ **1 ex-Soviet Yurka-class fleet minesweeper**

**D:** 400 tons (460 fl) **S:** 18 kts **Dim:** 52.0 × 9.3 × 2.0
**Electron Equipt:** Radar: 1/Don-2, 1/Drum Tilt
IFF: 3/Square Head, 1/High Pole B
**M:** 2 diesels; 2 props; 4,000 hp **Man:** 45 tot.

REMARKS: Transferred 12-79. Aluminum alloy hull.

◆ **1 Sonya-class coastal minesweeper** Bldr: Petrozavodsk SY

**D:** 350 tons (400 fl) **S:** 15 kts **Dim:** 48.5 × 7.3 × 1.9
**A:** 2/30-mm AA (II × 1)—2/25-mm AA (II × 1)
**Electron Equipt:** Radar: 1/Spin Trough
IFF: 1/High Pole B, 2/Square Head
**M:** 2 diesels; 2 props; 2,400 hp **Range:** 1,600/14; 3,000/10 **Man:** 40 tot.

REMARKS: One delivered 1987.

◆ **2 Soviet Yevgenya-class inshore minesweepers** Bldr: Sredniy Neva SY, Kolpino

**D:** 80 tons (90 fl) **S:** 11 kts **Dim:** 26.2 × 6.1 × 1.5
**A:** 2/14.5-mm mg (II × 1) **Electron Equipt:** Radar: 1/Spin Trough
**M:** 2 diesels; 2 props; 660 hp **Range:** 300/10 **Man:** 10 tot.

REMARKS: Delivered to Cam Ranh Bay 11-84. Glass-reinforced plastic hull. Employ a television minehunting system that dispenses marker buoys to permit later disposal of the mines; useful to 30-m depths.

◆ **5 ex-Soviet K-8-class minesweeping boats**

**D:** 26 tons (fl) **S:** 12 kts **Dim:** 16.9 × 3.2 × 0.8
**A:** 2/14.5-mm mg (II × 1) **M:** 2 6D12 diesels; 2 props; 300 hp **Man:** 6 tot.

REMARKS: Transferred 10-80. Wooden construction; built in Poland in the late-1950s. No radar.

◆ **up to 8 ex-U.S. MSB-5-class minesweeping boats** (In serv. 1952–56)

**D:** 30 tons (42 fl) **S:** 12 kts **Dim:** 17.45 × 4.83 × 1.32
**A:** several 12.7-mm mg **M:** 2 Packard 2D850 diesels; 2 props; 600 hp
**Fuel:** 15.8 tons **Man:** 6 tot.

MINE WARFARE SHIPS AND CRAFT *(continued)*

REMARKS: Transferred 1970. Wooden construction. Two sweep-current generators; capable of sweeping magnetic, contact, and acoustic mines.

◆ **up to 8 ex-U.S. MSR (minesweeper, riverine) class** (In serv. 1970)

**D:** 30 tons light (38 fl) **S:** 14 kts **Dim:** 15.3 × 5.32 × 1.22
**A:** 2/12.7-mm mg (II × 1)—1/7.62-mm mg—1/60-mm mortar
**M:** 2 G.M. 12V71N diesels; 2 props; 1,050 hp **Range:** 200/10 **Man:** 5 tot.

REMARKS: A minesweeping version of the ASPB class. Some were equipped with a pipe frame projecting ahead of the craft to explode contact mines. Others had four 88.9-mm rocket launch tubes mounted on the twin machine-gun turret on the bow. One or two 40-mm grenade launchers could also be carried.

◆ **up to 8 ex-U.S. MSM (minesweeping monitor) river minesweepers**

**D:** 70 tons (fl) **S:** 8.5 kts **Dim:** 17.09 × 5.33 × 3.1
**A:** 2/20-mm AA (I × 2)—1/12.7-mm mg—2/40-mm grenade launchers
**M:** 2 G.M. 64HN9 diesels; 2 props; 450 hp **Man:** 5 tot.

REMARKS: Converted LCM(6)-class landing craft, transferred in 1970. Not all had the 20-mm AA. Bar armor fitted to sides. Retained bow ramp. Could sweep mechanical and acoustic mines.

AMPHIBIOUS WARFARE SHIPS

◆ **3 ex-Soviet Polnocny-B medium landing ships** Bldr: Polnocny SY, Gdansk, Poland

**D:** 770 tons (fl) **S:** 18 kts **Dim:** 72.5 × 8.4 × 1.8
**A:** 2 or 4/30-mm AA (I or II × 2)—2/140-mm barrage RL (XVIII × 2)
**Electron Equipt:** Radar: 1/Spin Trough, 1/Drum Tilt
**M:** 2 40D diesels; 2 props; 5,000 hp

REMARKS: Transferred: 1 in 5-79, 1 in 11-79, and 1 in 2-80.

◆ **3 ex-U.S. LST 1- and LST 542-class tank landing ships**

| | Bldr | Laid down | L | In serv. |
|---|---|---|---|---|
| ex-HQ 501 ex-DA NANG (ex-*Maricopa County,* LST 938) | Bethlehem, Hingham, Mass. | 12-7-44 | 15-8-44 | 9-9-44 |
| ex-HQ 503 ex-VUNG TAU (ex-*Coconino County,* LST 603) | Chicago B & I, Seneca, Ill. | 10-12-43 | 15-4-44 | 15-5-44 |
| ex-HQ 504 ex-QUI NHON (ex-*Bullock County,* LST 509) | Jeffersonville B & M, Ind. | 7-10-43 | 23-11-43 | 8-1-44 |

**D:** 1,623 tons light (4,080 fl) **S:** 11.6 kts **Dim:** 99.98 × 15.24 × 4.29
**Electron Equipt:** Radar: 1/SPS-53
**M:** 2 G.M. 12-567A (ex-HQ 501: G.M. 12-278A) diesels; 2 props; 1,700 hp
**Electric:** 300 kw **Fuel:** 590 tons **Range:** 6,000/9 (loaded)
**Man:** approx. 100 tot.

REMARKS: Transferred to South Vietnam 7-62, 7-69, and 4-70, respectively. All believed to be operational; probably rearmed with Soviet-supplied weapons. Two ex-U.S. LSTs were transferred to Vietnam by China, configured as fuel tankers.

◆ **3 ex-U.S. LSM 1-class medium landing ships**

| | Bldr | Laid down | L | In serv. |
|---|---|---|---|---|
| ex-HQ 403 ex-NINH GIANG (ex-LSM 85) | Brown SB, Houston | 22-8-44 | 15-9-44 | 12-10-44 |
| ex-HQ 405 ex-TIEN GIANG (ex-LSM 313) | Pullman Car, Chicago | 16-3-44 | 24-5-44 | 25-6-44 |
| ex-HQ 406 ex-HAU GIANG (ex-LSM 276) | Federal SB, Newark, N.J. | 11-8-44 | 20-9-44 | 16-10-44 |

**D:** 520 tons light (1,095 fl) **S:** 12.5 kts **Dim:** 62.03 × 10.52 × 2.54
**A:** 2/40-mm AA (II × 1)—4 or 5/20-mm AA (I × 4 or 5)—4/12.7-mm mg (I × 4)
**M:** 2 Fairbanks-Morse $38D8\frac{1}{8}$ diesels (ex-HQ 406: G.M. 278A); 2 props; 2,880 hp
**Fuel:** 160 tons **Range:** 4,900/12 **Man:** approx. 70 tot.

REMARKS: Transferred to South Vietnam 10-55 (after service in French Navy), 10-56, 6-62, and 3-63, respectively. Ex-HQ 401 (ex-*Han Giang,* ex-LSM 110), listed in previous editions, in fact escaped to the Philippines 30-4-75 and was sold by the U.S. to the Philippines 17-11-75 for cannibalization spares.

◆ **up to 14 ex-U.S. LCU 1466-class utility landing craft**

| | | |
|---|---|---|
| ex-LCU 1475 | ex-LCU 1485 | ex-LCU 1502 |
| ex-LCU 1479 | ex-LCU 1493 | ex-LCU 1594 |
| ex-LCU 1480 | ex-LCU 1494 | ex-LCU 1595 |
| ex-LCU 1481 | ex-LCU 1498 | ex-YFU 90 (ex-LCU 1582) |
| ex-LCU 1484 | ex-LCU 1501 | |

**D:** 367 tons (fl) **S:** 8 kts **Dim:** 35.14 × 10.36 × 1.5
**A:** 4/20-mm AA (II × 2) **M:** 3 Gray Marine 64YTL diesels; 3 props; 675 hp
**Fuel:** 11 tons **Range:** 1,200/6 **Man:** 14 tot.

REMARKS: Transferred 1954–70 (ex-YFU 90 in 7-71). Cargo: 167 tons.

◆ **1 ex-U.S. LCU 501 (LCT(6))-class utility landing aircraft** Bldr: Bison SB, Buffalo, N.Y.

ex-LCU 1221 (L: 27-8-44)

**D:** 143 tons light (309 fl) **S:** 8 kts **Dim:** 36.42 × 9.75 × 1.3
**A:** 4/20-mm AA (II × 2) **M:** 3 Gray Marine 64HN9 diesels; 3 props; 675 hp
**Fuel:** 11 tons **Range:** 1,200/7 **Man:** 13 tot.

REMARKS: Transferred to South Vietnam 11-55. Cargo: 150 tons. Three half-sisters converted as salvage lift craft were also left behind in 1975; ex-YLLC 1 (ex-LCU 1348), ex-YLLC 3 (ex-YFU 33, ex-LCU 1195), and ex-YLLC 5 (ex-YFU 2, ex-LCU 529).

NOTE: Eighty-four U.S. LCM(6), 38 LCM(8), 40 LCVP, and several LCP-type landing craft were also abandoned; many have probably been returned to service.

◆ **12 or more ex-Soviet T4-class landing craft**

**D:** 35 tons (93 fl) **S:** 10 kts **Dim:** 19.9 × 5.6 × 1.4
**M:** 2 3D6 diesels; 2 props; 600 hp **Range:** 6,500/10

REMARKS: Transferred 1979 and later.

AUXILIARIES AND SERVICE CRAFT

◆ **1 ex-Soviet Kamenka-class hydrographic survey ship/buoy tender**

Bldr: Polnocny SY, Gdansk, Poland

**D:** 703 tons (fl) **S:** 13.7 kts **Dim:** 53.5 × 9.1 × 2.6
**Electron Equipt:** Radar: 1/Don-2
**M:** 2 diesels; 2 CP props; 1,765 hp **Range:** 4,000/10

REMARKS: Transferred 12-79. One 5-ton buoy crane.

◆ **3 ex-U.S. 174-foot-class gasoline tankers** Bldr: George Lawley & Sons, Neponset, Mass. (ex-YOG 56: R.T.C. SB, Camden, N.J.)

| | Laid down | L | In serv. |
|---|---|---|---|
| ex-HQ 472 (ex-YOG 67) | 26-1-45 | 17-3-45 | 4-5-45 |
| ex-HQ 473 (ex-YOG 71) | 11-6-45 | 24-7-45 | 27-8-45 |
| ex-HQ 475 (ex-YOG 56) | 17-5-44 | 30-9-44 | 19-2-45 |

**D:** 440 tons light (1,390 fl) **S:** 11 kts **Dim:** 53.04 (51.2 pp) × 9.75 × 3.94
**A:** 2/20-mm AA (I × 2)
**M:** 1 G.M. diesel (ex-YOG 56: Union diesel); 1 prop; 640 hp (ex-YOG 56: 540 hp)
**Electric:** 80 kw **Fuel** 25 tons **Cargo:** 860 tons **Man:** 23 tot.

REMARKS: Transferred to South Vietnam in 7-67, 3-70, and 6-72, respectively. Employed in transporting diesel fuel.

◆ **1 ex-U.S. 174-foot-class water tanker** Bldr: Nav. Mec. Castellamare, Italy (In serv. 1956)

ex-HQ 9118 (ex-YW 152)

**D:** 1,250 tons (fl) **S:** 9 kts **Dim:** 54.4 × 9.8 × 4.3 **A:** 2/20-mm AA (I × 2)
**M:** 1 Ansaldo diesel; 1 prop; 600 hp **Man:** 23 tot.

REMARKS: Built with U.S. funds for South Vietnam under the Offshore Procurement Program.

◆ **3 ex-U.S. Cholocco-class medium harbor tugs** Bldr: Commercial Iron Wks., Portland, Ore.

| | In serv. |
|---|---|
| ex-HQ 9550 (ex-*Poknoket,* YTM 762, ex-YTB 517) | 25-1-46 |
| ex-HQ 9551 (ex-*Hombro,* YTM 769, ex-YTB 508) | 7-7-45 |
| ex-HQ 9552 (ex-*Nootka,* YTM 771, ex-YTB 506) | 8-11-45 |

**D:** 260 tons (350 fl) **S:** 11 kts **Dim:** 30.8 × 8.5 × 3.7
**M:** 2 Enterprise diesels; 1 prop; 1,270 hp **Man:** 8 tot.

REMARKS: Reclassified YTM from YTB in 1966; transferred to South Vietnam 1971.

◆ **up to 9 ex-U.S. YTL-type small harbor tugs**

| | | |
|---|---|---|
| ex-YTL 152 | ex-YTL 245 | ex-YTL 456 |
| ex-YTL 200 | ex-YTL 423 | ex-YTL 457 |
| ex-YTL 206 | ex-YTL 452 | ex-YTL 586 |

**D:** 70 tons (80 fl) **S:** 10 kts **Dim:** 20.16 × 5.18 × 2.44
**M:** 1 Hoover-Owens-Rentschler diesel; 1 prop; 300 hp
**Electric:** 40 kw **Fuel:** 7 tons **Man:** 4 tot.

REMARKS: Built 1941–45. Four transferred to South Vietnam in 1955–56, two in 1969, and two in 1971.

◆ **2 ex-U.S. Navy repair barges (non-self-propelled)**

ex-HQ 9601 (ex-YR 24) ex-HQ 9611 (ex-YR 71)

**D:** 520 tons light (770 fl) **Dim:** 46.6 × 10.7 × 1.8

◆ **4 ex-U.S. Navy repair, berthing, and messing barges (non-self-propelled)**

| | |
|---|---|
| ex-HQ 9610 (ex-YRBM 17) | ex-HQ 9613 (ex-YRBM 21) |
| ex-HQ 9612 (ex-YRBM 16) | ex-HQ-. . . (ex-YRBM 18) |

**D:** 236 tons (310 fl) **Dim:** 34.1 × 11.0 × 0.9

REMARKS: Completed 1964–65. Ex-HQ 9613 is 498 tons (585 fl); 44.5 × 14.0 × 0.9 and was completed in 1970.

VIETNAM *(continued)*
AUXILIARIES AND SERVICE CRAFT *(continued)*

◆ **2 ex-U.S. Navy barracks craft (non-self-propelled)**

ex-HQ 9050 (ex-APL 26) ex-HQ 9051 (ex-APL 27)

**D:** 1,300 tons (2,580 fl) **Dim:** 79.6 × 15.0 × 2.6

REMARKS: Completed 1944–45.

◆ **1 ex-U.S. Navy refrigerated lighter** Bldr: Defoe SB, Bay City, Mich.

ex-HQ 490 (ex-YFR 889) (In serv. 1945)

**D:** 300 tons (660 fl) **S:** 10 kts **Dim:** 40.5 × 9.1 × 2.7
**M:** 2 G.M. diesels; 1 prop; 1,000 hp **Fuel:** 30 tons **Cargo:** 300 tons

REMARKS: Coastal cargo ship, transferred 1971.

◆ **2 ex-U.S. Navy large covered lighters**

ex-YFNB 18 ex-YFNB 28

**D:** 700 tons (2,700 fl) **Dim:** 79.6 × 14.6 × 4.0

REMARKS: Ex-HQ numbers not available. Transferred 1971. Cargo: 2,000 tons.

◆ **8 ex-U.S. Navy open lighters**

Ex-YC 791, 797, 806, 807, 1108, 1320, 1414, 1415

REMARKS: Ex YC 791, 1108, and 1320 displace 190 tons light/690 fl, others are 130 tons light/630 fl (33.5 × 9.8 × 2.4). Transferred around 1971.

◆ **2 ex-U.S. Navy floating cranes**

ex-HQ 9650 (ex-YD 230) ex-HQ 9651 (ex-YD 195)

◆ **2 ex-U.S. floating dry docks** (In serv. 1944)

ex-HQ 9600 (ex-AFDL 13) ex-HQ 9604 (ex-AFDL 22)

REMARKS: Ex-HQ 9600 has a capacity of 1,000 tons and is 61.0 × 19.5. Ex-HQ 6904 has a capacity of 1,900 tons and is 87.8 × 19.5. Both were left behind in 1975.

◆ **1 ex-U.S. water barge (non-self-propelled)**

ex-HQ 9113 (ex-YWN 153)

**D:** 220 tons (1,270 fl) **Dim:** 36.6 × 10.1 × 2.4 **Cargo:** 1,050 tons

NOTE: In addition to the ships and craft listed above, the Vietnamese Navy undoubtedly employs many smaller craft ("junks") in patrol and logistics duties. Cargo ships of up to several hundred deadweight tons capacity were built in North Vietnamese shipyards during the Vietnamese War for infiltration purposes; many of these armed craft may still be in military service.

# VIRGIN ISLANDS

**British Virgin Islands**

MERCHANT MARINE (1986): 32 ships—8,077 grt (1 tanker—818 grt)

ROYAL VIRGIN ISLANDS POLICE FORCE

◆ **1 patrol craft** Bldr: Brooke Marine, Lowestoft, U.K. (In serv. 1975)

VIRGIN CLIPPER

**D:** 15 tons (fl) **S:** 22 kts **Dim:** 12.2 × 3.7 × 0.6
**A:** 1/7.62-mm mg **Electron Equipt:** Radar: 1/Decca 101
**M:** 2 Caterpillar diesels; 2 props; 370 hp **Man:** 4 tot.

REMARKS: A replacement is planned.

◆ **2 "Sea Rider" dinghies** Bldr: Avon, U.K. (In serv. 1986)

REMARKS: Semi-rigid inflatables with 70-hp Evinrude outboards; replaced two "Sea Eagle" craft delivered 1980.

# WESTERN SAMOA

MERCHANT MARINE (1986): 6 ships—26,807 grt.

PATROL BOAT

◆ **1 Australian ASI 315 class** Bldr: Australian SB Industries, South Coogie, Western Australia (In serv. 3-88)

NAFANUA

**D:** 165 tons (fl) **S:** 20 kts **Dim:** 31.5 (28.6 wl) × 8.1 × 2.12
**A:** . . . **Electron Equipt:** Radar: 1/Furuno 1011
**M:** 2 Caterpillar 3516 diesels; 2 props; . . . hp **Electric:** 100 kw
**Fuel:** 29 tons **Range:** 2,500/12 **Man:** 3 officers, 14 men

REMARKS: Provided by Australian foreign aid. Ordered 3-10-85. Sisters being built for other Southwest Pacific nations. See illustration under Papua New Guinea. A second unit is planned.

# YEMEN

**People's Democratic Republic of Yemen (South Yemen)**

PERSONNEL (1987): About 1,000 total

MERCHANT MARINE (1986): 29 ships—12,543 grt (1 tanker—1,866 grt)

NOTE: A number of naval units were lost during the 1-86 coup. The Soviet T-58-class corvette (ex-minesweeper) has been deleted, as it was inoperable by 1984.

GUIDED-MISSILE PATROL BOATS

◆ **6 ex-Soviet OSA-II class**

**Two South Yemen Osa-IIs**—with Polnocny in background A. Zioko, 8-86

**D:** 210 tons (240 fl) **S:** 35 kts **Dim:** 38.6 × 7.6 × 2.0
**A:** 4/SS-N-2B Styx SSM (I × 4)—4/30-mm AA (II × 2)
**Electron Equipt:** Radar: 1/Square Tie, 1/Drum Tilt
**M:** 3 M504 diesels; 3 props; 15,000 hp **Range:** 500/34; 750/25 **Man:** 30 tot.

REMARKS: Transferred: 2 in 2-79 to 4-79, 3 in 1-80, 1 in 12-80, 1 in 2-83, 1 in 9-83. Two known to have been lost during 1986 coup.

TORPEDO BOATS

◆ **2 Soviet Mol class**

**D:** 170 tons (210 fl) **S:** 40 kts **Dim:** 38.6 × 7.6 × 1.8
**A:** 4/30-mm AA (II × 2)—4/533-mm TT
**Electron Equipt:** Radar: 1/Pot Drum, 1/Drum Tilt
**M:** 3 M503 diesels; 3 props; 12,000 hp **Range:** 450/34; 700/20 **Man:** 30 tot.

REMARKS: Transferred 1978. Design based on Osa-class guided-missile patrol boat. Sisters in Somali Navy.

PATROL BOATS

◆ **2 ex-Soviet Zhuk class**

**D:** 44 tons (60 fl) **S:** 34 kts **Dim:** 24.0 × 5.0 × 1.2
**A:** 4/14.5-mm mg (II × 2) **Electron Equipt:** Radar: 1/Spin Trough
**M:** 2 M50 diesels; 2 props; 2,400 hp **Range:** 700/28; 1,100/15 **Man:** 12 tot.

REMARKS: Transferred in 2-75.

AMPHIBIOUS WARFARE SHIPS

◆ **1 ex-Soviet Ropucha class** Bldr: Polnocny SY, Gdansk, Poland

**D:** 2,200 tons (3,200 fl) **S:** 18 kts **Dim:** 113.0 × 14.0 × 2.9 (aft)
**A:** 4/57-mm AA (II × 2)
**Electron Equipt:** Radar: 1/Don-2, 1/Strut Curve, 1/Muff Cob
IFF: 1/High Pole B
**M:** 2 diesels; 2 props; 10,000 hp **Range:** 3,500/16 **Man:** 70 crew + 230 troops

REMARKS: Transferred 1980. By far the largest unit in South Yemen's service. Refitted 1984–86 at Vladivostok.

YEMEN, SOUTH *(continued)*
AMPHIBIOUS WARFARE SHIPS *(continued)*

**South Yemen's Ropucha** 3-81

◆ **4 ex-Soviet Polnocny-B-class medium landing ships** Bldr: Polnocny SY, Gdansk, Poland

**D:** 800 tons (fl) **S:** 19 kts **Dim:** 74.0 × 8.6 × 2.0
**A:** 2 or 4/30-mm AA (II × 1)—2/140-mm barrage RL (XVIII × 2)—4/SA-N-5 SAM systems
**Electron Equipt:** Radar: 1/Spin Trough, 1/Drum Tilt
IFF: 1/Square Head, 1/High Pole B
**M:** 2 diesels; 2 props; 4,000 hp
**Range:** 900/18; 1,500/14 **Man:** 40 crew + 100 troops

REMARKS: Two delivered 8-73, one in 7-77 and one in 1979.

◆ **5 ex-Soviet T-4-class landing craft**

**D:** 35 tons light (93 fl) **S:** 10 kts **Dim:** 19.9 × 5.6 × 1.4
**M:** 2 Type 3D6 diesels; 2 props; 600 hp **Range:** 1,500/10

REMARKS: Transferred: 3 in 11-70, 2 in 1982. Resemble U.S. LCM(6) class.

MINISTRY OF THE INTERIOR

◆ **5 Tracker-2 class** Bldr: Fairey Marine, U.K.

**D:** 31 tons (fl) **S:** 29 kts **Dim:** 19.25 × 4.98 × 1.45
**A:** 1/20-mm AA **M:** 2 MTU 8V331 TC diesels; 2 props; 2,200 hp
**Range:** 650/25 **Man:** 11 tot.

REMARKS: Ordered 8-77; delivered 1977–78. Used in customs duties.

◆ **4 Spear class** Bldr: Fairey Marine, U.K.

**D:** 4.5 tons (fl) **S:** 26 kts **Dim:** 9.1 × 2.8 × 0.8
**A:** 3/7.62-mm mg **M:** 2 diesels; 2 props; 290 hp

REMARKS: Three delivered 20-9-75; fourth during 1978. Used in customs duties. Glass-reinforced plastic construction.

◆ **1 Interceptor class** Bldr: Fairey Marine, U.K.

REMARKS: Catamaran with two 135-hp outboard motors, can carry eight 25-man life rafts, and intended for rescue duties. Overall: 7.6 meters.

# YEMEN

## YEMEN ARAB REPUBLIC (North Yemen)

PERSONNEL (1985): Approximately 200 men, plus 250 naval port police

MERCHANT MARINE (1986): 11 ships—7,115 grt

### GUIDED-MISSILE PATROL BOATS

◆ **2 ex-Soviet OSA-II class**

**D:** 210 tons (240 fl) **S:** 35 kts **Dim:** 38.6 × 7.6 × 2.0
**A:** 4/SS-N-2B Styx SSM (I × 4)—4/30-mm AA (II × 2)
**Electron Equipt:** Radar: 1/Square Tie, 1/Drum Tilt
**M:** 3 M504 diesels; 3 props; 15,000 hp **Range:** 500/34; 750/25 **Man:** 30 tot.

REMARKS: Delivered 20-5-82.

### PATROL BOATS

◆ **3 Broadsword class** Bldr: Halter Marine, New Orleans, La. (In serv. 1978)

200 SANA'A 300 13TH JUNE 400 25TH SEPTEMBER

**13th June** 1981

**D:** 90 tons (fl) **S:** 28 kts **Dim:** 32.0 × 6.3 × 1.9
**A:** 2/23-mm AA (II × 1)—2/14.5-mm mg (II × 1)—2/12.7-mm mg (I × 2)
**Electron Equipt:** Radar: 1/Decca 914
**M:** 3 G.M. 16V71 TI diesels; 3 props; 1,400 hp **Electric:** 120 kw
**Fuel:** 16.3 tons **Man:** 14 tot.

REMARKS: Ordered 1977. Armament, added after delivery, is of Soviet origin.

◆ **9 Soviet Zhuk class**

**North Yemen Zhuk**

**D:** 48 tons (60 fl) **S:** 34 kts **Dim:** 24.6 × 5.2 × 1.2
**A:** 4/14.5-mm mg (II × 2) **Electron Equipt:** Radar: 1/Spin Trough
**M:** 2/M50F diesels; 2 props; 2,400 hp **Range:** 700/28; 1,100/15 **Man:** 12 tot.

REMARKS: Two transferred 1978, two in 1980, two in 12-84, and three in 1-87. Unlike some other units of this class, the North Yemeni units have their twin machine guns in enclosed gun houses with hemispherical covers.

### MINE COUNTERMEASURES CRAFT

◆ **2 Soviet Yevgenya class**

**D:** 80 tons (90 fl) **S:** 11 kts **Dim:** 26.2 × 6.1 × 1.5
**A:** 2/14.5 or 25-mm AA (II × 1) **Electron Equipt:** Radar: 1/Spin Trough
**M:** 2 diesels; 2 props; 600 hp **Range:** 300/10 **Man:** 10 tot.

REMARKS: Delivered 5-82. Glass-reinforced plastic construction. Export Yevgenyas normally have a twin 25-mm AA mount; uncertain in this instance.

### AMPHIBIOUS WARFARE

◆ **2 Soviet Ondatra-class landing craft**

**D:** 90 tons (140 fl) **S:** 10 kts **Dim:** 24.2 × 6.0 × 1.5
**A:** none **M:** 2 diesels; 2 props; 600 hp **Man:** 4 tot.

REMARKS: Transferred 1-83. Cargo well 13.5 × 4.0 m; bow ramp. Replaced two T-4-class landing craft transferred around 1970.

# YUGOSLAVIA

## SOCIALIST FEDERAL REPUBLIC OF YUGOSLAVIA

PERSONNEL (1987): 1,500 officers, 11,600 men (2,300 in Coast Defense Force)

MERCHANT MARINE (1986): 490 ships—2,872,613 grt
(tankers: 25 ships—308,214 grt)

NAVAL AVIATION: One squadron of 8 Soviet Ka-25 Hormone ASW helicopters, two Canadian DHC-2 Beaver STOL light transports, four Canadian CL 215 amphibians, and several license-built French SA 341H Gazelle (Partizan) helicopters may be in naval service.

The Air Force has a "Naval Cooperation Regiment," equipped with 50 RT-33 reconnaissance, MiG-21 fighter, and Jastreb attack aircraft.

COAST DEFENSE: In 1-86 Swedish RBS-15 antiship missiles were ordered to begin replacement of the existing SSC-3 Styx missiles. RBS-15 may also be carried aboard the new Kobra-class missile boats under construction.

### SUBMARINES (P = *Podmornica*)

◆ **0 (+1) Lora class** Bldr: . . .

**D:** 900 tons (surf.) **S:** . . . **Dim:** . . . × . . . × . . . **A:** . . .
**Electron Equipt:** Radar: . . .
Sonar: . . .
**M:** . . . **Range:** . . . **Man:** . . .

REMARKS: Either a "project" or an actual construction program, probably at Split. Would replace the stricken *Sutjeska* class.

◆ **2 Sava-class submarines** Bldr: Split SY

| | Laid down | L | In serv. |
|---|---|---|---|
| P 831 SAVA | 1975 | 1977 | 1978 |
| P 832 DRAVA | 1977 | 1982 | 1982 |

**Drava (P 832)** *Front*, 1-83

**D:** 770/964 tons **S:** 16 kts (sub.) **Dim:** 55.8 × 7.0 × 5.5
**A:** 6/533-mm TT—10 torpedoes or 20 mines **Endurance:** 28 days
**Electron Equipt:** Radar: . . .—Sonar: Krupp-Atlas CSU-83 suite
**M:** diesel-electric; 1 prop; 2,400 hp **Man:** 35 tot.

REMARKS: Maximum diving depth: 300 meters. Resemble the *Heroj* class, but are smaller.

◆ **3 Heroj class** Bldr: Uljanik SY, Pula

| | Laid down | L | In serv. |
|---|---|---|---|
| P 821 HEROJ | 1964 | 1967 | 1968 |
| P 822 JUNAK | 1966 | 1968 | 1969 |
| P 823 USKOK | 1968 | 1-70 | 1970 |

**D:** 1,068/1,170/1,350 tons **S:** 16/10 kts **Dim:** 64.0 × 7.2 × 5.0
**A:** 6/533-mm TT (fwd) **M:** 2 diesels, electric motors; 1 prop; 2,400 hp
**Electron Equipt:** Radar: . . .—Sonar: Krupp-Atlas . . .
EW: Stop Light intercept
**Range:** 9,700/8 **Man:** 36 tot.

REMARKS: *Heroj* (821) reported stricken 1982 after an accident; cannot be confirmed; however, the ship was operational in 1986.

**Junak (P 822)**—with Stop Light EW array raised 1984

**Uskok (P 823)** 1984

NOTE: Coastal submarines *Sutjeska* and *Neretva* are believed to have been stricken in 1986.

### MIDGET SUBMARINES (*Diverzantska Podmornica*)

◆ **3 (+ . . .) Una class** Bldr: Split SY

911 UNA (In serv. 1981) 912 ZETA (In serv. 1983) 913 SOCHA (In serv. 5-85)

**Zeta (912)** S. Breyer collection

**Zeta (912)**—crewmen fixing folding bow planes in down position
S. Breyer collection

**MIDGET SUBMARINES** *(continued)*

**D:** 76 tons surf./88 tons sub. **S:** 8.0 kts surf./11.0 sub.
**Dim:** 18.8 × 3.0 × 2.5
**A:** 6 mines or 4 R1 swimmer-delivery vehicles, externally carried
**M:** electric only: two 18-kw motors; 1 5-bladed prop
**Electronic Equipt:** Radar: none—Sonar: Krupp-Atlas PP-10 active, PSU 1-2 passive
**Range:** 250/. . . **Man:** 4 crew + 6 swimmers

Remarks: There remains some confusion over names; other sources give *Tisa* (911), *Una* (912), *Soka* (913); There may also be a fourth. The R1 swimmer-delivery vehicles each weigh 145 kg, are 3.7 m long by 0.52 diameter and have a range of 12 n.m. at 3 kts. Power is supplied by two shore-charged 128-cell, 1,450 amp./hr (5-hour rate) batteries for the *Una,* and maximum service depth is 100 m. Theoretically capable of remaining submerged for 96 hours.

◆ **4 or more Type R2, Mala-class swimmer-delivery vehicles**

**Mala (R2) class** 1984

**D:** 1.4 tons **S:** 4.4 kts **Dim:** 4.90 × 1.22 × 1.32 (1.70 fins)
**A:** 2/50-kg mines **Range:** 23/3.7
**M:** 1 electric motor; 1 prop; 6 hp **Man:** 2 tot.

Remarks: Diving depth: 60 m. Sweden has acquired one, and 6 have been sold to Libya; the U.S.S.R. may also have received examples.

**FRIGATES** (VPB—*Veliki Patrolni Brod*—Large Patrol Ship)

◆ **0 (+2) new construction** Bldr: Tito SY, Kraljevica

| | Laid down | L | In serv. | Bldr: |
|---|---|---|---|---|
| VPB 33 Kotor | 1981 | 29-5-84 | 1-87 | Uljanic SY |
| VPB 34 Pula | . . . | 1986 | . . . | Tito SY, Kraljevica |

**Kotor (VPB 33)**—artist's concept 1984

**D:** 1,850 tons (fl) **S:** 27 kts **Dim:** 96.7 (92.0 wl) × 11.2 × 3.55 (5.80 over sonar)
**A:** 4/SS-N-2C Styx (I × 4)—1/SA-N-4 SAM syst. (II × 1; 20 Gecko missiles)—2/76.2-mm DP (II × 1)—4/30-mm AA (II × 2)—2/RBU-6000 ASW RL (VII × 2)—6/. . .-mm ASW TT (III × 2)
**Electron Equipt:** Radar: 1/. . . nav.; 1/Strut Curve; 1/Palm Frond, 1/Pop Group, 1/Drum Tilt
Sonar: . . .—IFF: 1/Salt Pot A
EW: . . .
**M:** CODAG: 2 SEMT-Pielstick 12 PA6V280 diesels (4,800 hp each), 1 Soviet gas turbine (19,000 hp); 3 props (CP outboard); 28,600 hp
**Electric:** 1,350 kw **Man:** approx. 90 tot.

Remarks: These ships are apparently a modification of the design for two similar training frigates built for Indonesia and Iraq. The main propulsion diesels were ordered in 6-80 (two to be built under license in Yugoslavia), and the first was delivered 31-3-81; the propulsion concept duplicates the arrangement in the Koni class. ASW TT are probably Italian ILAS-3, with A-244 torpedoes.

◆ **2 Soviet Koni class** Bldr: Zelenodolsk SY

VPB 31 Split (In serv. 4-80) VPB 32 Koper (In serv. 19-2-83)

**Split (VPB 31)**—with Styx missiles 1983

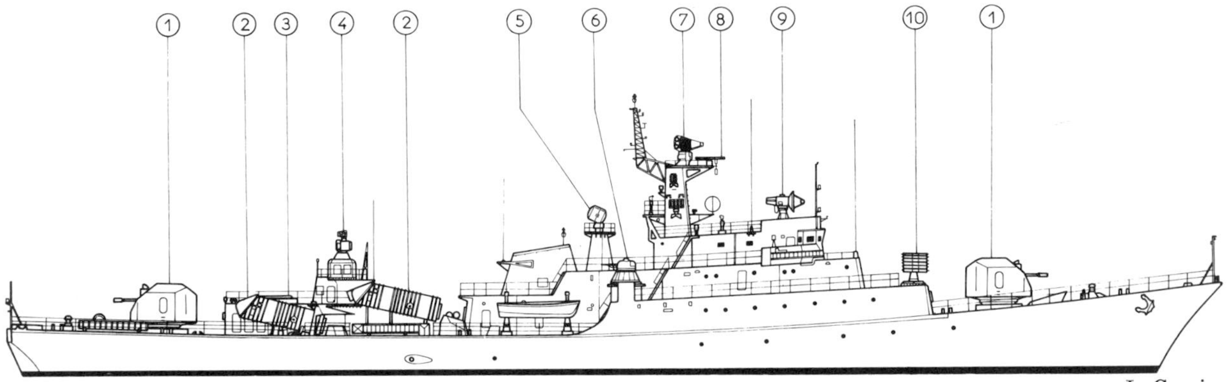


**Yugoslav Koni class** L. Gassier

1. twin 76.2-mm DP 2. launchers for SS-N-2C 3. launcher/magazine for SA-N-4 SAM system 4. Pop Group radar director for SA-N-4 5. Drum Tilt radar director for 30-mm AA 6. twin 30-mm AA 7. Strut Curve air/surface-search radar 8. Don-2 navigational/surface-search radar 9. Hawk Screech radar director for the 76.2-mm guns 10. RBU-6000 ASW RL (XII × 2)

**FRIGATES** *(continued)*

**D:** 1,440 tons light (1,600 fl) **S:** 30 kts
**Dim:** 96.40 × 12.55 × 3.48 (4.70 over sonar)
**A:** 4/SS-N-2C Styx SSM (I × 4)—1/SA-N-4 SAM syst. (II × 1, 20 Gecko missiles)—4/76.2-mm DP (II × 2)—4/30-mm AA (II × 2)—2/RBU-6000 ASW RL (XII × 2)—2/d.c. racks (12 d.c.)—mines
**Electron Equipt:** Radar: 1/Don-2, 1/Strut Curve, 1/Pop Group, 1/Hawk Screech, 1/Drum Tilt
Sonar: 1/med. freq., hull-mounted
EW: 2/Watch Dog intercept, 2 decoy RL (XVI × 2)
**M:** CODAG:1 19,000-hp gas turbine, 2 Type 68B diesels; 3 props; 35,000 hp
**Range:** 1,800/14 **Man:** 110 tot.

Remarks: New-construction units. Sisters in the Algerian, East German, Cuban, Libyan, and Soviet navies. *Koper* received Styx missiles during 1984–85; they were added to *Split* during 1982. *Koper* arrived in Yugoslavia on 5-12-83.

**CORVETTES** (PBR = *Patrolni Brod*)

◆ **2 Mornar class** Bldr: Tito SY, Kraljevica

| | Laid down | L | In serv. |
|---|---|---|---|
| PBR 551 Mornar | 1957 | 1958 | 10-9-59 |
| PBR 552 Borac | 1964 | 1965 | 1965 |

**Borac (PBR 552)** 1973

**D:** 330 tons (430 fl) **S:** 24 kts **Dim:** 51.8 × 6.97 × 3.1 (2.0 hull)
**A:** 2/40-mm AA (I × 2)—2/20-mm AA (I × 2)—4/RBU-1200 ASW RL (V × 4)—2/Mk 6 d.c. projectors—2/Mk 9 d.c. racks
**Electron Equipt:** Radar: 1/Decca 45—Sonar: 1/Tamir-11
**M:** 3 Werkspoor diesels; 3 props; 7,500 hp **Fuel:** 55 tons
**Range:** 660/24; 3,000/12 **Man:** 60 tot.

Remarks: Modernized 1970–73 at Sava Kovacevic Naval Yard, Tivat. Original two 76.2-mm DP guns, two older-model 40-mm AA, and Mousetrap ASW rocket launchers replaced by new Bofors guns and Soviet ASW rocket launchers.

◆ **1 French Le Fougueux class** Bldr: F.C. Méditerranée, Le Havre

| | Laid down | L | In serv. |
|---|---|---|---|
| PBR 581 Udarnik (ex-P 6, ex-PC 1615) | 1954 | 21-12-54 | 1-56 |

**Udarnik (PBR 581)** H. Ehlers, 4-84

**D:** 329 tons (409 fl) **S:** 18.7 kts **Dim:** 53.10 (50.9 wl) × 7.3 × 3.0 (2.1 hull)
**A:** 1/40-mm AA—2/20-mm AA (I × 2)—1/RBU-1200 ASW RL (V × 1)—2/d.c. racks
**Electron Equipt:** Radar: 1/DRBN-30—Sonar: 1/DUBA-2
**M:** 4 SEMT-Pielstick PA17V diesels; 2 props; 3,240 hp **Electric:** 120 kw
**Fuel:** 45 tons **Range:** 3,300/15; 6,350/12 **Man:** 62 tot.

Remarks: Built with U.S. Offshore Procurement Funds as U.S. PC 1615; transferred on completion. One sister in the Tunisian Navy. Engines can produce 3,840 hp for brief periods. Armament revised by 4-84.

**GUIDED-MISSILE PATROL BOATS** (RT = *Raketna Topovnjača*)

◆ **1 (+9?) Type 400, Kobra class** Bldr: Tito SY, Kraljevica

**D:** 385 tons (525 fl) **S:** 34 kts **Dim:** 54.80 (51.88 pp) × 8.96 (8.16 wl) × 2.46
**A:** 4/SS-N-2C Styx SSM—1/76-mm OTO Melara DP—2/40-mm Breda Dardo AA (II × 1)—8/20-mm AA (IV × 2)
**M:** 4 MTU 20V538 TB92 diesels; 4 props; 14,000 hp
**Range:** . . . **Endurance:** 15 days **Man:** . . .

Remarks: A missile "corvette" class intended to begin replacement of the elderly Osa-I class. Also reported as being built for Libya. Chaff rocket launchers will be mounted on the sides of the 76-mm mount. First unit may have been completed 1985. May have Swedish RBS-15 SSM vice SS-N-2C Styx, in which case 8 may be carried.

◆ **6 Rade Končar (Type 211) class** Bldr: Tito SY, Kraljevica

| | L | In serv. |
|---|---|---|
| RT 401 Rade Končar | 15-10-76 | 4-77 |
| RT 402 Vlado Četkovič | 28-8-77 | 3-78 |
| RT 403 Ramiz Sadiku | 1978 | 10-9-78 |
| RT 404 Hasan Zahirovič Lasa | 1979 | 11-79 |
| RT 405 Jordan Nikolov-Orce | 1979 | 8-79 |
| RT 406 Ante Banina | 1979 | 11-80 |

**Rade Končar (RT 401)** 1977

**Rade Končar (RT 401)** 1977

**D:** 242 tons (. . . fl) **S:** 39 kts (27 sust.) **Dim:** 45.0 × 8.0 × 1.8 (2.5 props)
**A:** 2/SS-N-2B Styx SSM—2/57-mm Bofors DP (I × 2)
**Electron Equipt:** 1/Decca 1226—1/9LV200 system
**M:** CODAG: 2 Rolls-Royce Proteus gas turbines, 4,500 hp each; 2 MTU 20V538 TB 92 diesels, 3,600 hp each; 4 CP props; 16,200 hp
**Range:** 880/23; 1,650/15 **Man:** 5 officers, 10 petty officers, 15 men
**Electric:** 300 kVA **Endurance:** 7 days

Remarks: Of Yugoslav design, using Swedish (Svensk Phillips) fire control and guns and Soviet missiles; RT 401 has 9LV200 Mk I, later ships have 9LV200 Mk II. Have a Soviet Square Head IFF interrogator. Styx missiles chosen over the Exocet originally planned, probably for economic reasons. Steel hull, aluminum superstructure. Have NBC warfare protection.

◆ **10 ex-Soviet Osa-I class** (RC = *Raketni Čamac*)

RC 301 Mitar Acev
RC 302 Vlado Bagat
RC 303 Petar Drapšin
RC 304 Steven Filipovič
RC 305 Velimir Škorpik
RC 306 Nikola Martinovič
RC 307 Josip Mazar
RC 308 Karlo Rojc
RC 309 Franc Rozman-Stane
RC 310 Zikaca Jovanovič-Španac

**GUIDED-MISSILE PATROL BOATS** *(continued)*

**Mitar Acev (RC 301)**

**D:** 175 tons (209 fl) **S:** 35 kts **Dim:** 38.6 × 7.6 × 1.8
**A:** 4/SS-N-2 Styx SSM—4/30-mm AA (II × 2)
**Electron Equipt:** Radar: 1/Square Tie, 1/Drum Tilt
IFF: 1/High Pole B, 2/Square Head
**M:** 3 M503A diesels; 3 props; 12,000 hp **Range:** 500/34; 750/25
**Man:** 25 tot.

Remarks: Transferred 1965–69. Reported to be showing their age. Can be operated at 220 tons full load, with 11 tons extra fuel.

**TORPEDO BOATS** (TČ = *Torpedni Čamac*)

◆ **14 Soviet Shershen class** (In serv. 1966–71) Bldrs: 4 in U.S.S.R.; others: Tito SY, Kraljevica

| | | |
|---|---|---|
| TČ 211 Pionir | TČ 216 Jadran | TČ 221 Strilko |
| TČ 212 Partizan | TČ 217 Kornat | TČ 222 Partizan-II |
| TČ 213 Proleter | TČ 218 Biokovac | TČ 223 Napredak |
| TČ 214 Topčider | TČ 219 Sloga | TČ 224 Pionir III |
| TČ 215 Ivan | TČ 220 Crvena Zvijezda | |

**Strilko (TČ 221)** 1980

**D:** 145 tons (170 fl) **S:** 45 kts **Dim:** 34.0 × 6.8 × 1.5
**A:** 4/30-mm AA (II × 2)—4/533-mm TT—mines
**Electron Equipt:** Radar: 1/Pot Drum, 1/Drum Tilt
Sonar: 1/High Pole B, 1/Square Head
**M:** 3 M503A diesels; 3 props; 12,000 hp **Range:** 450/34; 700/20
**Man:** 22 tot.

Remarks: Ten built in Yugoslavia under license, after four were transferred in 1965. Unlike Soviet units, have no depth-charge racks.

**PATROL BOATS** (PČ = *Patrolni Čamac*)

◆ **. . . Type 80 class** Bldr: . . .

**Type 80 class (without 20-mm AA)** 1984

**D:** 80 tons **S:** 32 kts (26 sust.) **Dim:** 27.35 × 6.55 × 1.15 (2.20 props)
**A:** 1/40-mm AA—4/20-mm AA (IV × 1)
**Electron Equipt:** Radar: 1/. . . nav. **Man:** 17 tot.
**M:** 3 diesels; 3 props; 4,350 hp **Range:** 400/25 **Endurance:** 5 days

Remarks: Reduced edition of Mirna design; offered for foreign sale. Has four illumination/chaff RL on foredeck.

◆ **11 Type 240 Mirna class** (In serv. 1981–82) Bldr: Kraljevica SY

| | | | |
|---|---|---|---|
| PČ 171 Biokovo | PČ 174 Učka | PČ 177 Frusk-gora | PČ 180 Zelengora |
| PČ 172 Phorse | PČ 175 Crmec | PČ 178 Kosmaju | PČ 181 Cer |
| PČ 173 Koprivnik | PČ 176 Mukos | PČ 179 Kozul | |

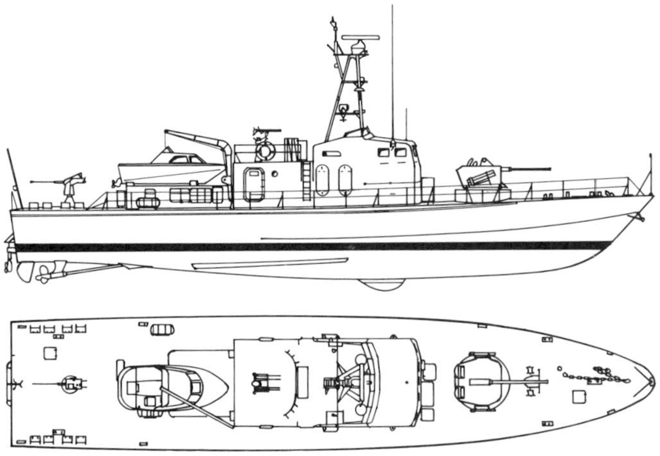

**Mirna-class patrol boat**

**D:** 120 tons (. . . fl) **S:** 30 kts **Dim:** 32.00 × 6.68 × 1.60 (2.30 max.)
**A:** 1/40-mm Bofors L70 AA—1/20-mm AA—8/Type MDB-MT3 d.c.
**Electron Equipt:** Radar: 1/. . . nav.—Sonar: high-freq. set
**M:** 2 SEMT-Pielstick 12 PA4 200GDS diesels; 2 props; 6,000 hp—electric motors for low speeds (6 kts)
**Electric:** . . . **Range:** 400/20 **Man:** 3 officers, 4 petty officers, 12 men

Remarks: The first 10 propulsion diesels were ordered in 1979, for license production in Yugoslavia. Endurance at 20 kts can be increased to 530 n.m. in emergencies. Peacetime endurance is four days, wartime: 8 days. Have 4-rail chaff launcher amidships. There are 4 chaff or illumination rocket rails on the sides of the 40-mm AA.

◆ **7 Type 131 coastal patrol craft** Bldr: Trogir SY (In serv. 1965–68)

| | | |
|---|---|---|
| PČ 132 Kalnik | PČ 135 Grudnik | PČ 137 Kamenar |
| PČ 133 Velebit | PČ 136 Romanija | PČ 140 Kožuf |
| PČ 134 Grandičar | | |

**Grudnik (PČ 135)**

**D:** 85 tons (120 fl) **S:** 22 kts **Dim:** 32.0 × 5.5 × 2.5
**A:** 6/20-mm Hispano Suiza HS831 AA (III × 2)
**Electron Equipt:** Radar: 1/Kelvin-Hughes 14/9
**M:** 2 MTU MB820 Db diesels; 2 props; 1,600 hp

Remarks: May serve in the Maritime Border Brigade, an organization similar to a coast guard. Sisters *Cer* (PČ 138) and *Durmitor* transferred to Malta 31-3-82. Several others have been scrapped: Type 80 class appears intended as their replacements.

## PATROL CRAFT

◆ **. . . Type 20 coastal and riverine**

**D:** 55 tons **S:** 16 kts **Dim:** 21.78 (20.06 wl) × 5.29 × 1.20
**A:** 2/20-mm AA (I × 2)—mines **Electron Equipt:** Radar: 1/Decca 110
**M:** 2 diesels; 2 props; 1,156 hp **Range:** 200/15 **Man:** 10 tot.

Remarks: Hull numbers in the 200-series.

◆ **. . . Type 18 coastal and riverine**

**Type 18 patrol craft** 1984

**D:** 29 tons (fl) **S:** 20 kts **Dim:** 18.70 × 3.60 × 0.90 mean
**A:** 2/20-mm AA (I × 2)—9/7.62-mm light mg (I × 9)
**Electron Equipt:** Radar: 1/Decca 110
**M:** 2 diesels; 2 props; 752 hp **Range:** 480/17 **Man:** 9 crew + 40 troops

Remarks: Intended for patrol, troop transport, and logistic support duties, with up to 4 tons of cargo

◆ **3 or more Type 16 coastal and riverine**

PČ 302 PČ 303 PČ 304

**Type 16 patrol craft** 1984

**D:** 23 tons (fl) **S:** 15 kts **Dim:** 17.00 × 3.60 × 0.85 mean
**A:** 1/20-mm AA—7/7.62-mm light mg (I × 9)
**Electron Equipt:** Radar: 1/Decca 110
**M:** 2 diesels; 2 props; 464 hp **Range:** 340/15
**Man:** 7 crew + 30 troops or frogmen

Remarks: Intended for patrol, troop transport, and logistic support duties, with up to 3 tons of cargo.

◆ **5 or more Type 15-class riverine and lake**

PČ 15-1 through PČ 15-5

**PČ 15-5 and two sisters** 1984

**D:** 19.5 tons (fl) **S:** 16 kts **Dim:** 16.87 × 3.90 × 0.65 (0.70 props)
**A:** 1/20-mm AA—2/7.62-mm mg (I × 2) **Electron Equipt:** Radar: 1/Decca 110
**M:** 2 diesels; 2 props; 330 hp **Range:** 160/12 **Man:** 6 tot.

## MINE WARFARE SHIPS (M = *Minolovac*)

◆ **4 French Sirius-class coastal minesweepers** Bldrs: M 161: Mali Losinj SY, Yugoslavia; others: A. Normand, Le Havre, France

| | In serv. |
|---|---|
| M 151 Vukov Klanac (ex-*Hrabri*, ex-MSC 229) | 9-57 |
| M 152 Podgora (ex-*Smeli*, ex-MSC 230) | 9-57 |
| M 153 Blitvenica (ex-*Slobodni*, ex-MSC 231) | 9-57 |
| M 161 Gradac (ex-*Snazhi*) | 1960 |

**D:** 400 tons (440 fl) **S:** 15 kts (sweeping: 11.5)
**Dim:** 46.4 (42.7 pp) × 8.55 × 2.5 **A:** 2/20-mm AA (II × 2)
**Electron Equipt:** Radar: 1/DRBN-30—Sonar: Plessey 193M
**M:** 2 SEMT-Pielstick 16 PA1-175 diesels; 2 props; 2,000 hp **Electric:** 375 kw
**Fuel:** 48 tons **Range:** 3,000/10 **Man:** 40 tot.

Remarks: First three built with U.S. Offshore Procurement funds. Wooden-planked hulls on metal framing. Equipped with Plessey 193M minehunting sonar, French PAP-104 remote-controlled minehunting/disposal submersibles, and Decca Hifix precision navigation systems, commencing 1981.

◆ **4 British "Ham"-class minesweepers** Bldr: Yugoslavia (In serv. 1964–66)

M 141 Milset (ex-MSI 98) M 143 Iž (ex-MSI 100)
M 142 Brsec (ex-MSI 99) M 144 Olib (ex-MSI 101)

**D:** 123 tons (164 fl) **S:** 14 kts **Dim:** 32.43 × 6.45 × 1.7
**A:** 1/40-mm **Electron Equipt:** Radar: 1/Decca 45
**M:** 2 Paxman YHAXM diesels; 2 props; 1,100 hp **Fuel:** 15 tons
**Range:** 1,500/12; 2,000/9 **Man:** 22 tot.

Remarks: Built under U.S. Offshore Procurement Program. Composite construction: wooden planking over a metal-framed hull.

◆ **6 117-class inshore minesweepers** Bldr: Yugoslavia, 1966–68

ML 117 N . . . ML 119 Maun ML 121 Gradac
ML 118 N . . . ML 120 Grajac ML 122 Iret

**D:** 120 tons (131 fl) **S:** 12 kts **Dim:** 30.0 × 5.5 × 1.5
**A:** 1/20-mm AA—2/12.7-mm mg (I × 2) **Electron Equipt:** Radar: 1/Decca 45
**M:** 2 G.M. diesels; 1,000 hp **Man:** 25 tot.

Remarks: Also used for coastal patrol. ML 117 is used as a coastal survey ship.

◆ **7 Nestin-class Type 50 river minesweepers** Bldr: Brodotehnika, Belgrade (In serv. 1976–80)

| | L | | L |
|---|---|---|---|
| RML 331 Nestin | 20-12-75 | RML 335 Vučedol | 1979 |
| RML 332 Motajica | 18-12-76 | RML 336 Djerdap | 1980 |
| RML 333 Belegis | 1-77 | RML 337 Panonsko More | 1980 |
| RML 334 Bosut | 1978 | | |

**D:** 68 tons (78 fl) **S:** 12 kts **Dim:** 27.00 × 6.50 × 1.05 (1.15 max.)
**A:** 5/20-mm AA (III × 1, I × 2)—24 small mines
**Electron Equipt:** Radar: 1/Decca 101
**M:** 2 diesels; 2 props; 520 hp **Range:** 864/10.8 **Man:** 17 tot.

Remarks: RML = *Recni Minolovac.* M 331 launched 20-12-75, M 332 launched 18-12-76, and M 333 launched 1-77. Hull of light metal alloy. Sweep gear includes Type PEAM magnetic and acoustic sweep, Type AEL-1 explosive sweep, and Types MDL-1 and MDL-2 mechanical sweeps. Two illumination chaff rocket launchers are fitted. Used on the Danube. Three also built for Iraq and one for Hungary.

MINE WARFARE SHIPS *(continued)*

**Nestin (RML 331)** 1978

### AMPHIBIOUS WARFARE SHIPS

NOTE: The new Type PO multipurpose transports can also be used as landing ships.

◆ **17 DTK 211-class landing craft** Bldr: Yugoslavia (In serv. 1950s)

DTK 212, 213, 215, 216, 219, 221, 223, 224, 225, 226, 228, 229, 232, 233, 234, 237, GOLOR

**DTK 213** L. & L. Van Ginderen, 6-84

**D:** 240 tons (410 fl) **S:** 10.3 kts **Dim:** 49.8 × 8.6 × 1.6 (2.1 max.)
**A:** 3/20-mm AA (III × 1) **M:** 3 Gray Marine 64HN9 diesels; 3 props; 625 hp
**Range:** 500/9.3 **Man:** 27 tot.

REMARKS: DTK = *Desantni Tenkonosac.* Near-duplicates of the World War II German MFP-D class. Nearly all have been equipped with 1-m-wide hull sponsons, extending beam to 8.6 meters and providing space for two mine rails with a total capacity of up to 100 small mines. Bow ramp. Can carry 140 tons of vehicles or 200 men. Seven additional units have been discarded. Unit now named *Golor* is probably considered an auxiliary.

◆ **4 RTK 401 class** (In serv. 1950s)

**D:** 227 tons (350 fl) **S:** 10.3 kts **Dim:** 46.5 × 6.5 × 1.3 (max.)
**A:** 5/20-mm AA (III × 1, I × 2)—2/mortars
**M:** 3 G.M. 64HN9 diesels; 3 props; 678 hp **Range:** 500/9

REMARKS: RTK = *Rečni Tenkonosac* (River Tank Landing Craft). Similar to the DTM 211 class; used on the Danube River. No mine sponsons.

◆ **18 DJČ 601-class (Type 21) landing craft** Bldr: Gleben SY, Vela Luka, Korčula (In serv. 1976–77)

DJČ 601 to DJČ 628

**D:** 32 tons (fl) **S:** 23.5 kts **Dim:** 21.20 × 4.84 × 1.07 (1.58 props)
**A:** 1/20-mm AA **Electron Equipt:** Radar: 1/Decca 101 **Man:** 6 crew
**M:** 1 MTU 12V331 TC81 diesel; 2 props; 1,450 hp **Range:** 320/22

REMARKS: DJC = *Desantni Jurišni Čamac.* Glass-reinforced plastic construction. Bow ramp. Can carry 40 troops or 6 tons in 32-m$^2$ cargo area. Offered for export also.

◆ **. . . Type 11 vehicle/personnel landing craft**

**Type 11** 1984

**D:** 4.8 tons (fl) **S:** 23 kts **Dim:** 11.30 × 3.00 × 0.30
**M:** 2 diesels; 2 waterjets *or* 2 outdrives; . . . hp **Range:** 100/15 **Man:** 2 tot.

REMARKS: Glass-reinforced plastic construction. Can carry two jeeps or a squad of troops. Have a small navigational radar.

### AUXILIARY SHIPS

◆ **1 Soviet Moma-class hydrographic ship** Bldr: Gdansk, Poland, 1971

PH 33 ANDRIJA MOHOROVIČIĆ

**Andrija Mohorovičič (PH 33)** 1971

**D:** 1,260 tons (1,540 fl) **S:** 17 kts **Dim:** 73.3 × 10.8 × 3.8
**Electron Equipt:** Radar: 1/Don-2 **Man:** 56 tot.
**M:** 2 Zgoda-Sulzer 6TD48 diesels; 2 CP props; 3,600 hp **Range:** 8,700/11

REMARKS: Transferred in 1972. Carries one survey launch. Five-ton crane for navigational buoy handling. Four laboratories totaling 35 m$^2$ deck space. Used for oceanographic research, hydrographic surveys, and buoy tending. PH = *Pomoćni Hidrografiski Brod* (Seagoing Hydrographic Ship).

◆ **1 submarine rescue and salvage ship** Bldr: Tito SY, Belgrade (In serv. 10-9-76)

PS 12 SPASILAC

**D:** 1,590 tons (fl) **S:** 13.4 kts **Dim:** 55.50 × 12.00 × 3.84 (4.34 max.)
**A:** 10/20-mm AA (IV × 2, I × 2) **Electric:** 540 kVA
**Electron Equipt:** Radar: 1/ . . . nav.—Sonar: . . .
**M:** 2 diesels; 2 Kort-nozzle props; 4,340 hp **Range:** 4,000/13.4
**Man:** 53 tot. (72 accomm.)

REMARKS: Resembles an oilfield supply vessel; low freeboard aft. Sister *Aka* is in the Iraqi Navy, and another has been sold to Libya. Equipped for underwater cutting and welding, towing, carrying up to 250 tons deck cargo, transferring 490 tons cargo fuel, 48 tons cargo water, and 5 tons lube oil. Also capable of salvage lifting, fire-fighting, and other salvage tasks. Can support divers to 300 m with a 3-section decompression chamber. Also has capability to support a small rescue submersible. Has a bow-thruster and can lay a 4-point moor. PS = *Pomoćni Spasilečki Brod* (Seagoing Rescue Ship).

◆ **1 salvage ship** Bldr: Howaldtswerke, Kiel (In serv. 1929)

PS 11 (ex-*Spasilac*)

**D:** 740 tons **S:** 14.5 kts **Dim:** 53.6 × 8.8 × 4.0
**M:** 1 set triple-expansion reciprocating steam; 1 prop; 2,000 hp **Boilers:** 2

REMARKS: Not scrapped as previously reported when new *Spasilac* completed in 1976.

◆ **1 cadet-training ship** Bldr: Ansaldo, Genoa (In serv. 1938)

GALEB (ex-*Kuchuk,* ex-*Ramb III*)

**Galeb** L. & L. Van Ginderen, 8-83

**D:** 5,182 tons (5,700 fl) **S:** 16 kts **Dim:** 121.2 (116.9 pp) × 15.2 × 5.6
**A:** 4/40-mm AA (I × 4)—8/20-mm AA (IV × 2)
**M:** 2 Burmeister & Wain diesels; 2 props; 7,200 hp **Range:** 20,000/16

REMARKS: Begun as a commercial banana carrier; used as an auxiliary cruiser and minelayer by the Italian Navy during World War II. Ceded to Yugoslavia after the war. Has been used as the presidential yacht, but is mostly used as a cadet-training ship. Retains old German quadruple 20-mm AA mounts; may still be usable as a minelayer. Formerly referred to as a *Minopolagac* (Minelayer).

## AUXILIARY SHIPS *(continued)*

◆ **1 missile-boat tender and command ship** Bldr: . . . , Yugoslavia (In serv. 1956)

PB 25 Vis

**D:** 510 tons (680 fl) **S:** 17 kts **Dim:** 57.0 × 8.5 × 3.5
**A:** 1/40-mm AA—2/20-mm AA (I × 2) **M:** 2 diesels; 2 props; 1,900 hp

Remarks: Resembles a yacht; primarily an administrative flagship. PB = *Pomoćni Brod* (Auxiliary Ship).

◆ **1 topsail training schooner** Bldr: Blohm + Voss, Hamburg

Jadran (In serv. 1932)

**Jadran** Yugoslav Navy

**D:** 720 tons (800 fl) **S:** 14.5 sail/9.5 diesel kts **Dim:** 60.0 × 8.8 × 4.2
**M:** 12 Linke-Hoffman diesel; 375 hp **Sail area:** 933 $m^2$

Remarks: Accommodations for 100 cadets and 20 instructors.

◆ **1 riverine command ship** Bldr: Bordotehnika, Belgrade

PB 36 Sabač (In serv. 1985)

**Sabač (PB 36)**—at launch *Front*, 1985

**D:** approx. 200 tons (fl) **S:** . . . **Dim:** . . . × . . . × . . .
**A:** . . . **Electron Equipt:** Radar: 1/Decca 110
**M:** 2 diesels; 2 props; . . . hp **Range:** . . . **Man:** . . .

Remarks: Intended to replace or supplement Danube River Flotilla flagship *Kozara*. Patrol-boat-type hull, with superstructure set well aft.

◆ **1 riverine command ship** Bldr: Linzer Schiffswerft, Austria (In serv. 1940)

Kozara (ex-U.S. *Oregon*, ex-German *Brünhild*)

**D:** 535 tons (693 fl) **S:** 12.4 kts **Dim:** 67.0 × 9.5 × 1.4
**A:** 9/20-mm AA (III × 3) **Fuel:** 44 tons
**M:** 2 Deutz RV6M545 diesels; 2 props; 800 hp

Remarks: Taken over by U.S. in immediate postwar period, then turned over to Yugoslavia. Used as a floating hotel until 1960, when taken over by the navy. In 1962 recommissioned as flagship of the Danube River Flotilla. Painted blue and white and home-ported at Bosanka Gradiška.

## SERVICE CRAFT

◆ **4 PN 13-class fuel tankers** Bldr: Yugoslavia (In serv. 1955–56)

PN 13 PN 14 PN 15 PN 16

**D:** 420 tons (650 fl) **S:** 7 kts **Dim:** 43.2 × 7.0 × 4.2
**M:** 1 Burmeister & Wain diesel; 1 prop; 300 hp **Range:** 1,500/7
**Cargo:** 300 tons

Remarks: Sister PN 17 transferred to Sudan in 1969. PN = *Pomoćni Naftaš* (Oil Fuel Auxiliary).

◆ **2 PN 24-class fuel tankers** Bldr: Split SY (In serv. early 1950s)

PN 24 PN 25

**D:** 300 tons (430 fl) **S:** 7 kts **Dim:** 46.4 × 7.2 × 3.2
**M:** 1 Burmeister & Wain diesel; 1 prop; 300 hp

◆ **3 PT 71-class cargo lighters** Bldr: Split SY (In serv. 1950s)

PT 71 Medusa PT 72 Jastoc PT 73 N . . .

**D:** 310 tons (428 fl) **S:** 7 kts **Dim:** 43.1 × 7.2 × 4.85
**M:** 1 Burmeister & Wain diesel; 1 prop; 300 hp

Remarks: PT = *Pomoćni Transporter.* A fourth, PT 74, has been stricken.

◆ **3 PT 61-class cargo lighters** Bldr: Pula and Sibenik SYs (In serv. 1951–59)

PT 64 PT 65 PT 66

**D:** 695 tons (fl) **S:** 7 kts **Dim:** 46.4 × 7.2 × 3.2
**M:** 1 Burmeister & Wain diesel; 1 prop; 300 hp

◆ **3 Type PO multipurpose transports** Bldr: . . .

PO 91 PO 92 PO 93

**PO 91**—with bow visor open, ramp extended 1984

**D:** 600 tons (860 fl) **S:** 16 kts (sust.) **Dim:** 58.20 × 11.00 × 2.75 (mean)
**A:** 1/40-mm AA—8/20-mm (IV × 2) **Electron Equipt:** Radar: 1/. . . nav.
**M:** 2 diesels; 2 CP props; 3,480 hp **Range:** 1,500/16
**Man:** 43 crew + 150 fully equipped troops, 6 vehicle drivers
**Endurance:** 10 days

Remarks: Referred to as the Lubin class by NATO. Intended to supply combatants with missiles, torpedoes, mines, and other ordnance, using two slewing cranes on upper deck. Continuous cargo deck can accommodate up to 6 tanks; has a visor-type bow and extendable bow ramp. PO = *Pomoćni Oružar* (Ammunition Auxiliary).

**YUGOSLAVIA** *(continued)*
**SERVICE CRAFT** *(continued)*

◆ **2 PO 52-class ammunition lighters** Bldr: Split SY, 1950s

PO 55 PO 56

**D:** 695 tons (fl) **S:** 7 kts **Dim:** 46.4 × 7.2 × 3.2
**M:** 1 Burmeister & Wain diesel; 1 prop; 300 hp

REMARKS: PO = *Pomoćni Oružar*. Sisters PO 52, 53, 54 discarded.

◆ **1 water tanker** Bldr: Yugoslavia (In serv. 1950s)

PV 16

**D:** 200 tons (600 fl) **S:** 7.5 kts **Dim:** 44.0 × 7.9 × 3.2
**M:** 1 diesel; 1 prop; 300 hp
**Range:** 1,500/7.5

REMARKS: Cargo: 380 tons. PV = *Pomoćni Vodonosac*.

◆ **4 PR 37-class coastal tugs** (In serv. 1950s)

PR 36 DUPIN PR 37 ZUBATAC PR 38 N . . . PR 39 N . . .

**D:** 550 tons (fl) **S:** 11 kts **Dim:** 32.0 × 8.0 × 5.0 **M:** diesels

REMARKS: Originally reciprocating steam-propelled; recently re-engined with diesels. PR = *Pomorski Remorker* (Auxiliary Tug).

◆ **8 LR 67-class harbor tugs** (In serv. 1960s)

LR 67 LR 68 LR 69 LR 70 LR 71 LR 72 LR 73 LR 74

REMARKS: LR = *Lučki Remorker* (Harbor Tug).

◆ **. . . diving tenders, survey craft, and utility transports**

Inshore survey craft version L. & L. Van Ginderen, 1987

**D:** 43–46 tons (fl) **S:** 12 kts **Dim:** 20.50 × 4.50 × 1.42
**A:** 2/20-mm AA (I × 2) **Electron Equipt:** Radar 1/Decca 101
**M:** 2 diesels; 2 props; 304 hp **Range:** 400/12
**Man:** diving tender: 6 crew + 4 divers; transport: 60 crew + 70 troops

REMARKS: Diving tender displaces 46 tons (fl). Wooden construction. Transport version has 55 $m^3$ for 15 tons cargo in lieu of the 70 troops. Armament is not usually aboard.

# ZAIRE

## REPUBLIC OF ZAIRE

PERSONNEL (1987): Approx. 900 officers and men, plus 600 marines

MERCHANT MARINE (1986): 31 ships—65,833 grt

### PATROL BOATS

◆ **5 Chinese Shanghai-II class**

**D:** 122.5 tons (134.8 fl) **S:** 28.5 kts **Dim:** 38.78 × 5.41 × 1.49 (1.554 max.)
**A:** 4/37-mm AA (II × 2)—4/25-mm AA (II × 2)
**Electron Equipt:** Radar: 1/Pot Head
**M:** 2 M50F-4, 1,200-hp diesels; 2 Type 1206, 910-hp diesels; 4 props; 4,220 hp
**Range:** 750/16.5 **Endurance:** 7 days **Electric:** 39 kw **Man:** 36 tot.

REMARKS: Two operable units delivered 2-87. Three others, inoperable, are to be repaired; they, and a stricken fourth unit, were delivered 1976–78. Intended for coastal patrol duties at the mouth of the Congo River.

### PATROL CRAFT

◆ **up to 25 Arcoa class** Bldr: Arcoa SY, France (In serv. 1975–81)

**D:** 2 tons (fl) **S:** 30 kts **Dim:** 7.68 × 3.04 × 0.80 **M:** 2 diesels; 320 hp

REMARKS: Original 12 ordered in 7-74; 14 more delivered by 11-80, another 15 delivered 1981. For use on lakes and rivers. GRP construction.

◆ **5 ex-U.S. Swift Mk-II class** Bldr: Swiftships, Morgan City, La. (In serv. 1971)

**D:** 19.2 tons (fl) **S:** 25 kts **Dim:** 15.64 × 4.14 × 1.07
**A:** 6/12.7-mm mg (II × 1, I × 4) **M:** 2 G.M. 12V71N diesels; 2 props; 860 hp
**Range:** 400/24 **Man:** 12 tot.

REMARKS: Based at Kalemie, Lake Tanganyika. Aluminum construction. In poor condition; one other has been stricken.

NOTE: There are a number of additional small riverine patrol and logistics support craft. Three North Korean-built torpedo boats delivered 1974 are no longer in service.

# ZANZIBAR

Although part of the United Republic of Tanzania, Zanzibar has internal autonomy and its own armed forces.

◆ **4 patrol craft** Bldr: Vosper Thornycroft, U.K.

**D:** 70 tons **S:** 24.5 kts **Dim:** 22.9 × 6.0 × 1.5 **A:** 2/20-mm AA (I × 2)
**M:** 2 diesels; 2 props; 1,840 hp **Range:** 800/20 **Man:** 11 tot.

REMARKS: The first two units were delivered 6-7-73, the last two in 1974. Glass-reinforced plastic construction; Keith Nelson design.

# ZIMBABWE

PERSONNEL: . . .

POLICE

### PATROL CRAFT

◆ **2 (+ . . .) small lake patrol craft** (In serv. 1986)

KF 596 N . . . KF 597 CHIBATANIDZA MATUNHU BINGA

REMARKS: Aluminum police craft; shipped to Africa 6-86. No details available.

**KF 596** L. & L. Van Ginderen, 6-86

# INDEX OF SHIPS

All ships are indexed by their full names, e.g., Almirante Guillermo Brown.

| NAME | Pages |
|---|---|

# ADDENDA

**Through 1 February 1988**

## ALGERIA

The first of an expected two Soviet Kilo-class submarines for Algeria departed the Baltic on 15-9-87; characteristics and appearance as for the standard Soviet units. The two Romeo-class submarines on loan will be returned, presumably for scrapping in the U.S.S.R.

The first of the Bulgarian-designed patrol boats, described as being 58 m o.a., began trials mid-1987.

## ANGOLA

Two Soviet Yevgenya-class inshore minesweepers were delivered during 9-87. The range of the ex-Portuguese gunboats of the *Argos* class is 4,000/12. Only one Soviet T-4-class and 4 Portuguese LDM-400-class landing craft remain in service; one 9.14-m LDP-100-class and three 12.80-m LDP-200-class landing craft are available, however. Also reported in naval service are three small cargo ships, of 35 m, 56 m, and 59 m o.a., respectively. Two Brazilian EMB-111 coastal surveillance aircraft are to deliver during 1988, partly paid for through the sale of Angola's sole F-27 Maritime patrol aircraft.

## ARGENTINA

MEKO 140-class frigate *Spiro* (P 6) was commissioned 24-11-87; the last two ships of this class are for sale. Several Brazilian Embraer EMB-312 Tucano training aircraft are to be diverted to the Argentine Navy as part of a larger order from the Air Force.

## AUSTRALIA

The new Type 471 submarines are to be 74 m o.a. and displace 2,700 tons submerged. The diesel generator sets are to employ SEMT-Pielstick diesels driving Jeumont-Schneider motor generator sets. The bow and stern of the first boat will be built at Malmö, Sweden. Modernization refit of *Oxley* (S 57) was completed 8-5-87.

The government Williamstown Dockyard has been sold private to Australian Marine Engineering Corporation (AMEC), which also received the contract to complete the two U.S. *Oliver Hazard Perry*-class guided-missile frigates under construction there; as of late 1987, the first of these was reported to be only about 12 percent complete since keel-laying 12-7-85, due to labor disputes; the second unit will be named *Newcastle* (F 06). Despite the difficulties of building complex warships in Australia, the co-production program for eight new frigates for Australia and four for New Zealand continues, with the "short list" of prospective designs reduced to the Dutch M-class and a variant of the Blohm + Voss MEKO-200 PN as of 2-88; the MEKO-200 is the rumored favorite. *Brisbane* (D 41) completed her modernization late in 1987. *Shoalwater* (M 81) was launched 20-6-87; four more craft of the *Rushcutter* (M 81) class have been ordered, with completions to come one per year 1990–93. *Curlew* (M 1121) has been extended in commission into 1989. A towed helicopter mine-disposal system is being developed for use by the R.A.N.'s Sea King helicopters. One Wessex helicopter was lost during 6-87.

Survey ship *Moresby* (A 573) is to strike during 1993. Four 35-m-o.a. catamaran inshore survey craft were ordered late in 1987 from EGLO Engineering, Port Adelaide; to carry a crew of 12, the craft will be equipped with the HYDAPS automatic data processing and logging system. The first, *Paluma,* is to complete 11-88, followed by *Mermaid* (in serv. . . .-89), *Shepparton* (in serv. . . .-89), and *Benalla,* the last to complete 11-89. **Dim:** 36.7 o.a. × 13.7 × . . . . **M:** 2 diesels; 2 props; . . . hp. **Man:** 2 officers, 10 men. To base at Cairns and work in pairs assisting *Moresby* (A 573) and *Flinders* (A 312) in shallow-water surveys in northern Australia area. Contract tenders have gone out for a 6- to 9,000-dwt tanker for conversion as an underway replenishment ship. A helicopter landing deck was added to *Jervis Bay* (AGT 203) during 6-87. The sail-training ship *Young Endeavour* arrived on her delivery voyage 25-1-87, as a gift from the U.K. to Australia in honor of the 200th anniversary of the latter's founding; the brigantine is to be operated by the R.A.N. for the training of up to 24 youth aged 16–18.

**D:** 200 tons (fl) **S:** 14 kts (sail), 10 kts (power)
**Dim:** 44.00 (31.00 hull, 28.30 wl) × 7.80 × 4.00
**M:** 2 diesels; 1 prop; . . . hp **Man:** 8 R.A.N., 24 trainees

Remarks: 173 grt. Began delivery voyage 3-8-87. Offered to Australia 11-1-86. Sail area: 110 m sq.

**Young Endeavour** *The Navy,* 8-87

**Brolga** R. Gillett, 2-88

Patrol boat *Fremantle* (P 203) replaced *Advance* (P 83) as reserve training ship at Sydney on 6-2-88. P 83 stricken for display at the Australian National Maritime Museum. In 6-88 *Warrnambool* (P 204) will replace *Bayonet* (P 101) as reserve training ship at Melbourne.

Fishing boat *Lumen* acquired and renamed *Brolga* (not commissioned) for use in auxiliary minesweeper trials, 2-88; will be retained until 1990.

## BANGLADESH

A small tanker, *Khan Jahan Ali* (A 515) is in service (see photo); no characteristics data available.

**Khan Jahan Ali (A 515)** G. Gyssels, 6-87

# BELGIUM

Minehunters *Bouvesse* (M 909) and *Breydel* (M 906), sent to the Persian Gulf with tender *Zinnia* (A 961), were given two additional single 12.7-mm mg atop the pilothouse superstructure, as well as MARISAT SATCOMM equipment. *Fuchsia* (M 919) began trials 12-1-88.

**Fuchsia (M 919)**—on trials L. & L. Van Ginderen, 1-88

# BENIN

Patrol boat *Patriote* was launched 1-88 by Soc. Bretonne de Constructions Naval (SBCN), Loctudy.

**D:** 70 tons (fl) **S:** 35+ kts **Dim:** 38.00 (36.20 pp) × 6.80 × 1.30
**A:** 1/20-mm AA—2/12.7-mm mg (1 × 2) **Electron Equipt:** Radar: . . . .
**M:** 3 Baudouin 12P15-2SR7 diesels; 3 props; 3,600 hp **Man:** 23 tot.

Remarks: Wood and epoxy construction. Earlier reports indicated waterjet propulsion.

# BOTSWANA

Land-locked Botswana was scheduled to be the recipient of two U.S. Napco Raider 7-m patrol craft under a Fiscal Year 1988 Military Aid Program grant; each would carry 2/12.7-mm mg.

# BRAZIL

Additional Sea Lynx helicopters, equipped with MEL Supersearcher radar and Rolls-Royce Gem 42 engines are planned for acquisition for use from frigates. The first three of six Super Puma helicopters was delivered 8-87; 15 total are planned. The nine Wasp helicopters are equipped to employ Avibras LM-70/7 rocket pods. Carrier *Minas Gerais* (A 11) was inactive during 1987 with recurrent catapult problems.

Submarine *Tupi* was launched 28-4-87 for delivery 7-88 by Howaldtswerke; *Tamoio,* the first Type 1400 to be built at Rio, will be launched in 1990 or 1991 for delivery 12-91. The Type 1400 class will have Krupp-Atlas DBQS-21 sonar suites and employ the Ferranti KAFS action data system, a commercial variant of the Royal Navy's DCC system. In view of the slow progress in constructing license-built diesel submarines in Brazil, it does not seem likely that the widely publicized plan to build nuclear-powered submarines of Brazilian design will reach fruition for several decades, at best. The announced planned characteristics for such a craft are: 2,500 tons surfaced (2,700 sub.); one 12 MW pressurized-water reactor, with two turbo-alternators and one motor; a speed of 25–30 kts; 6/533-mm torpedo tubes with 12 total weapons, and a diving depth of 280 m.

Construction of a polar icebreaker is planned. One 8,000-dwt underway replenishment oiler (to replace the unsatisfactory *Marajo*) was ordered 3-87 from Ishikawajima do Brasil-Estaleiros SA, Rio. A large oceangoing tug named *Almirante Hess* has been acquired.

# BRUNEI DARUSSALEM

The first three of seven 14.5-m patrol craft for the Marine Police, PDB 12–14, were delivered 5-10-87 by Singapore SB & Eng.

**PDB 13** Singapore SB & Eng., 10-87

# CAMEROON

The two large patrol boats planned for construction in the U.S.A. may be delayed or canceled for lack of U.S. foreign aid financing. Six 9.1-m patrol craft were completed 1986–87 by Societé Africaine d'Étude de la Réalisation Industrielle (SAERI), at Douala; no data available.

# CANADA

Navy: The Westland-Agusta EH.101 helicopter has been selected as the Sea King replacement. No decision on the "winner" in the nuclear submarine program contest between the U.K.-Vickers *Trafalgar* class and the French *Améthyste* class had been announced by end 1-88.

Six additional *Halifax*- or "Town"-class frigates were ordered from St. Johns SB, New Brunswick, in 12-87; these may be 10 m longer than the first group to provide greater range, missile capacity, and accommodations for female crew. *Ville de Quebec* (FFH 332) was reported laid down 4-87, but otherwise there has been little progress officially reported on the first six ships of the *Halifax* class.

Oceanographic ship *Endeavour* (AGOR 171) is CANTASS trials ship, with *Annapolis* (DDE 265) having had an operational SQR-501 TASS system installed during her 8-85 to 9-86 refit, and sister *Nipigon* (DDE 266) to complete refit with the system in mid-1988.

Coast Guard: Planned new construction in addition to the "Polar 8" arctic icebreaker on which work is to begin 1-89 includes: two Type 1000 Light Icebreaker/Navigational Aid Tenders for delivery in the early 1990s; one Type 900 Small Ice-strengthened Navaids Tender for delivery 1990; one Type 700 Special River Navaids Tender for the Hay River (to replace *Eckaloo*) to deliver fall 1988; two Type 600 Large Search-and-Rescue Cutters to deliver mid-1989 and late 1990; and two Type 500 Intermediate Search-and-Rescue Cutters to deliver 1990. *Louis St. Laurent* is in refit at Halifax from 1987–89. Three Type 100 Small Search-and-Rescue Craft were delivered during 1986 by Matsumoto, Vancouver: *Mallard* (in serv. 28-2-86), *Skua* (in serv. 14-3-86), and *Osprey* (in serv. 3-5-86):

**D:** 15 tons (fl) **S:** 26 kts **Dim:** 12.40 × 4.12 × 1.24
**Electron Equipt:** Radar: 1/Decca . . .
**M:** 2 Mitsubishi S6B diesels; 2 props; . . . hp **Range:** 312/26 **Man:** 3 tot.

Remarks: Data supersede those in the text.

**Edward Cornwallis**—with telescoping hangar extended
L. & L. Van Ginderen, 2-87

**Bartlett**—note landing craft in davits abreast stack
L. & L. Van Ginderen, 8-87

Air-cushion vehicle AP 1-88, delivered 15-7-87, by BHC, Cowes, has the following characteristics:

**D:** 44 tons (fl) **S:** 50 kts loaded **Dim:** 24.5 × 11.0 × . . .
**Electron Equipt:** Radar: 1/Decca RM 914C
**M:** 4 Deutz BF 12L513CP diesels; 2 Hoffman CP airscrew props, 6 lift fans; . . . hp
**Range:** . . . **Man:** 12 tot. **Cargo:** 11-ton payload.

REMARKS: Aluminum construction, rigid-sidewall air-cushion vehicle.

# CHILE

British "County"-class destroyer *Fife* transferred 12-8-87 as *Blanco Encalada* (14) and sailed for Chile 14-9-87 with MM 38 Exocet missiles aboard; the Sea Slug SAM system, removed during *Fife*'s tenure as cadet training ship, was not replaced.

Two ice-strengthened oilfield tug/supply vessels were purchased late 1987 and departed Southampton for Chile on 14-12-87:

| | Bldr | In serv. |
|---|---|---|
| ATF 65 JANEQUEO (ex-*Maersk Transporter*) | L.H. Salthammer Baybyggeri A/S, Vestnes, Denmark | 1974 |
| ATF 66 GALVARINA (ex-*Maersk Traveller*) | Aukra Bruk A/S, Aukra, Denmark | 1974 |

**Janequeo**—with deckload of cargo containers L. & L. Van Ginderen, 12-87

**D:** approx. 1,600 tons (fl) **S:** 15 kts **Dim:** 58.32 (52.20 pp) × 12.63 × 3.97
**Electron Equipt:** Radar: 1/. . . nav.
**M:** 2 8-cyl. Atlas-Mek diesels; 2 CP props; . . . hp—bow-thruster
**Range:** . . . **Man:** . . .

Two steel-construction Fairey Marintechnik 33-m "Protector" patrol boats were ordered during 1987 for use as pilot boats by the Chilean government.

**D:** 100 tons (fl) **S:** 30 kts (26 sust.)
**Dim:** 33.00 (28.96 wl) × 6.73 × 1.95 (props)
**A:** . . . **Electron Equipt:** Radar: 1/Furuno FR-701
**M:** 3 G.M. 16 V 149 TIB diesels; 3 props; 5,400 hp
**Electric:** 100 kw (2 × 50 kw) **Range:** 1,400/14 **Fuel:** 16 tons **Man:** . . .

# CHINA

**Xia-class ballistic-missile submarine**—showing 12 missile tubes and general resemblance to both the Han-class SSN and to early U.S. SSBNs
*Ships of the World,* 1987

Electronic warfare equipment from Italy's Elettronica is being added to frigates and destroyers. Two sets of French Thomson-Sintra SS12 VDS lightweight variable-depth sonars were bought in 1986 for trials installation on two Hainan-class subchasers. Britain's Racal signed a contract in 8-87 as weapon-system authority for fisheries protection ships, offshore patrol vessels, antisubmarine ships, and multi-role surface patrol ships to be built in China. An official statement reports that a "large underwater weapons experimental ship provides the Chinese Navy with the capability to conduct oceangoing deepwater weapon experiments."

**Top to bottom: Rice Screen 3-D radar, Type 756 navigational radar, and Fog Lamp SAM control radar on a Jiangdong-class frigate**
*Defense Technology,* 1987

**Top to bottom: Rice Lamp gunfire-control radar, Fog Lamp SAM control radar, and twin HQ 61 SAM launcher on stern of Zhongdong (Jiangdong class)** *Defense Technology,* 1987

# DENMARK

Two Sea Lynx Mk 90 helicopters originally ordered for Argentina were purchased 1987 from the U.K., in part to replace a Mk 80 lost in 9-85. Of the three Norwegian submarines designated for purchase by Denmark, *Stadt* (307) grounded early in 1987 while still in Norwegian service and was stricken as being too difficult to repair; her replacement has not yet been named. Frigates *Peder Skram* (F 352) and *Herluf Trolle* (F 353) were placed in reserve in 12-87, with a small maintenance crew; neither is expected to see further active service. The projected fisheries protection frigates are now expected to displace 3,500 tons full load and to be 100 m o.a. by 14-m beam. The first of two (F 357) is to deliver during 1989, although no building contract has yet been announced.

*Flyvefisken,* the first of the StanFlex 300 multipurpose hulls, began trials in 10-87 but will not be fully operational until 1989. The second ship of the class was to be laid down in 2-88 for delivery 1-90, and further construction is to continue at two per year, with the seventh delivering in 1993. Initial armament of the prototype is a standard OTO Melara 76-mm Compact forward (to be replaced by a 120 rd/min "Super Rapid" mount) and four Harpoon SSM; an 8-round lightweight RAM SAM may be installed aft later. The PEAB 9LV 200 Mk 3 weapons-control system employs two electro-optical directors with t.v. and infrared trackers. The propulsion system is described as employing a General Motors 500-hp 12V71 diesel to supply hydraulic power to the ship's three screws for quiet running at up to 8 kts and also providing hydraulic power to windmill the centerline fixed-pitch LM 500 gas-turbine-powered propeller when the ship is running on diesels alone. Three 250-hp G.M. 6V71 diesels drive the three approx. 200-kw ship's-service generator sets. Radars include a Plessey AWS-6 air/surface-search set and a Terma Scanter navigation set, while the EW suite is by Racal, and the ships will have U.S. WSC-3 communications equipment. The crew in missile-boat configuration is four officers, three senior petty officers, and 12 non-rated. Displacement in minelaying configuration will be 400 tons (fl).

Twelve 28-m-o.a. steel-hulled patrol craft are to be ordered for the Home Guard to replace older craft. Each will have 2/7.62-mm mg mounts, with provision for installing a 20-mm AA; max. speed will be 13 kts, and the crew will number 12.

**Beskyterren (F 340)**—with AWS-6 radar in radome G. Olsen, 6-87

**Hvidbjørnen (F 348)**—with Lynx helo on deck G. Olsen, 10-86

**Small dockyard tug Hermod** G. Olsen, 10-86

# ECUADOR

Ecuador is studying a proposal to purchase a Spanish package with 125-ton Bazán "Piranha"-class patrol boats and a smaller, GRP-hulled patrol craft.

◆ **2 (+4) 44-ft aluminum-hulled patrol boats** Bldr: Halter Marine, New Orleans, La. (In serv. 1987–88)

**44-ft patrol boat** Halter Marine, 1987

**D:** . . . **S:** . . . **Dim:** 13.41 × 4.12 × 2.08
**A:** . . . **Electron Equipt:** Radar: 1/Furuno 2400
**M:** 2 Detroit Diesel 8V71 TI diesels; 2 props; . . . hp
**Fuel:** 1.6 tons **Man:** 1 officer, 4 enlisted

REMARKS: Two built in the U.S.A., the other four to be assembled from "kits" in Ecuador. To be used for coastal patrol, rescue, drug interdiction, and fisheries patrol.

# EL SALVADOR

In 1987, with U.S. financial aid, five 12.2-m monohull and five 9.1-m catamaran patrol craft were ordered from Mercougar, North Miami, Florida. Both classes will be powered by two 300-hp Ford Merlin 6-cyl. diesels driving Arneson surface-piercing outdrives. The monohulls, for coastal patrol, will have a range of 300 n.m., while the catamarans, for river work, will have a range of 400 n.m.; one catamaran is equipped as a hospital craft. If the craft are successful, 20 additional monohulls and 10 more catamarans (5 as hospital craft) will be ordered.

On 17-12-87 ten 41-ft patrol craft were ordered from MonArk for El Salvador under the U.S. Military Aid Program.

**GC 8** J. Forster, 1986

# EQUATORIAL GUINEA

A U.S. 105-ft patrol boat from Lantana Boatyard, Lantana, Florida, is to be provided under foreign aid if funds are available under Fiscal Year 1988; armed with 2/12.7-mm mg (I × 2) and 2/7.62-mm mg (I × 2), the craft would be similar to sisters in Honduran, Jamaican, and Grenadan service.

# ETHIOPIA

The former Dutch minesweeper MS 41 has been renumbered A 04, indicating demotion to auxiliary status. The two Soviet Turya-class hydrofoil torpedoboats are numbered HTB 112 and HTB 113. Patrol boat PC 16 has become P 205, and PC 17 is now numbered P 206. TR 74 has become A 05. Cargo ship *Ras Dedgen* has become A 03; the ship was built in 1961 by Rheinstall Nordseewerke, Emden: D: 138.72 × 18.11 × 8.77; 1 diesel, 7,000 hp, 16 kts; 6,615 grt/9,513 dwt.

# FALKLAND ISLANDS

Two U.K. *Aberdovey*-class tenders, in service in the Falklands, were transferred to the Falkland Island government in 1987: *Beaulieu* (A 99), and *Blakeney* (A 104); characteristics in the Great Britain section.

# FIJI

Two 99-ton, 33-m oilfield crewboats were reportedly purchased in the U.S. during 1987 for anti-smuggling patrol. The 848-grt oceanographic research ship *Eugene McDermott II* was purchased 4-87 and renamed *Babele;* the ship was built by Carrington Slipway, Tomago, Australia.

# FINLAND

The four "Helsinki-II" missile boats ordered 21-8-87 from Hollming, Rauma, will be 40.0 m overall by 7.0-m beam and will be powered by two 4,000-hp MTU 16V538 TB92 diesels driving waterjets. The first will deliver in 1990 and the last in 1993. They will have the PEAB 9LV 200 Mk 3 weapons-control system, PEAB-MEL 9EW 300 EW system with MEL Matilda E intercept equipment and two fixed decoy RL (either 32 chaff rockets or 12 infrared/16 chaff rockets each). Armament will include 1/40-mm AA, 4 RBS-15F SSM, and a minelaying capability.

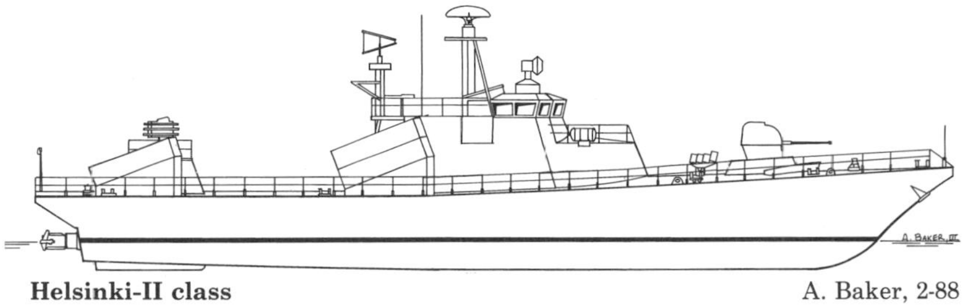

**Helsinki-II class** A. Baker, 2-88

Truck-mounted RBS-15 missiles were ordered during 1987 from Sweden for coast defense purposes.

The oil-spill recovery ship *Halli* (899) was completed 24-8-87 by Hollming, Rauma, for the Board of Navigation, to be operated by a naval crew:

**D:** . . . **S:** 11.3 kts **Dim:** 60.50 × 12.40 × . . . (5.60 moulded depth)
**M:** 2 Wärtsilä Vasa 6R22 diesels; 2 Aquamaster swiveling props; 2,650 hp
**Range:** 3,000/11.3 **Man:** . . .

Remarks: 1,400 grt/1,200 dwt. Employs MacGregor-Navire MacLORI recovery system to sweep a 30-m-wide path at up to 1.5 kts, transporting the waste oil in a 360-$m^3$ tank. In addition, the ship has an 11-m bow ramp and can accommodate vehicles of up to 48 tons so that the ship can also act as a coastal transport and landing craft.

**Unknown Finnish naval auxiliary 93** L. & L. Van Ginderen, 1987

# FRANCE

Following the planned completion of her modernization in 7-88, the carrier *Foch* (R 99) is to conduct compatibility trials with the U.S. F/A-18 Hornet fighter-bomber as a possible replacement for the overaged F-8E Crusader; as an alternative to the F/A-18, Dassault is proposing to rehabilitate 20 F-8E as an interim interceptor until the new naval variant of Rafale can be ready in the mid-1990s.

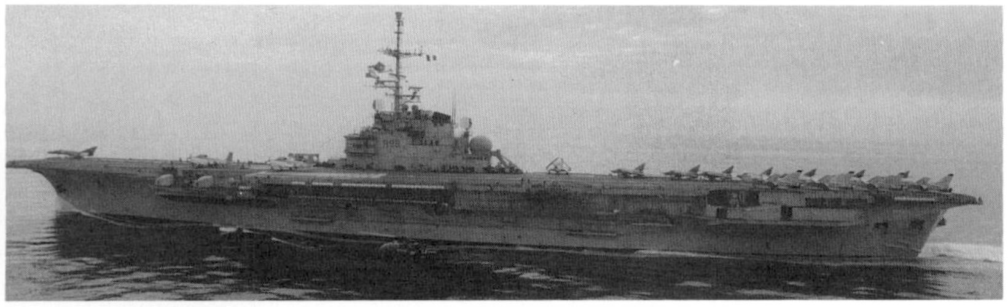

**Clemenceau (R 99)** ECPA, 8-87

Refit of the ballistic-missile submarine *Le Tonnant* (S 614) to launch M4 missiles with TN 71 warheads was completed 19-10-87.

The first of three FL 25-class frigates in the current 5-year plan is to be ordered during 1988 and the third in 1991; ultimately up to ten may be built to replace the *Commandant Rivière* class. P 400 ("Super PATRA")-class patrol boat completion dates include: *La Gracieuse* (P 687) on 26-6-87, *La Railleuse* (P 689) on 24-4-87, *La Rieuse* (P 690) on 15-5-87, and *La Tapageuse* (P 691) in 1-88. A second *Sterne*-class 200-n.m.-economic-zone patrol boat was to be ordered late in 1987; the ship may be built to the improved design now offered with 2 SACM UD 33V16M7 or UD 45V12M7 diesels (2,960 or 3,150 hp each) for a maximum speed of 24 kts and a range of 1,300/24 or 4,700/13 on 84 $m^3$ fuel; normal displacement is given as 313 tons, and a crew of 17 would be carried. Mine-countermeasures diver-support ship *Styx* (M 614) was launched 3-3-87.

**Cassard (D 614)** French Navy, 7-87

LCM(8)-class landing craft CTM 18 was ordered 4-87. Large landing craft CDIC 9051 was delivered 5-87 by SFCN, Villeneuve-la-Garenne, with two SACM UD 3012VMI diesels providing 1,080 hp total; L 9052 was launched 10-9-87.

The fifth *Durance*-class replenishment oiler, laid down 3-5-85 on speculation for possible foreign sale, was purchased at launch 3-10-87 for the French Navy and is to be completed 7-88. All five ships of the U.S. AN 93-class net and mooring buoy tenders were stricken during 10-87: *Cigale* (A 760), *Criquet* (A 761), *Fourmi* (A 762), *Grillon* (A 763), and *Scarabée* (A 764). A 760, A 762, and A 763 were replaced at St. Nazaire by the chartered tugs *Bahran* and *Cyrus,* while A 761 and A 764 were replaced at Toulon by the moorings tug *Albacore,* chartered from Feronica International Shipping:

**D:** . . . **S:** . . . **Dim:** 56.90 × 14.5 × . . .
**M:** 3 diesels; 3 props; 4,350 hp—2/340-hp thrusters
**Man:** 4 officers, 4 men

Remarks: Has 70-ton crane.

The former *Sirius*-class minesweeper *Bételgeuse* (A 747) was still in use as a trials ship in 1987, not stricken in 1982 as previously reported.

**Bételgeuse (A 747)** M. Louagie, 6-87

**Girelle**—chartered tug for rescue duty French Navy, 3-87

**Mérou**—chartered tug for rescue duty French Navy, 1987

# GABON

Construction of the planned second "Super PATRA" patrol boat from France has reportedly been canceled.

# WEST GERMANY

*U 29* (S 178), the first Type 206 submarine to undergo Type 206A modernization, arrived at Howaldtswerke 9-6-87, with completion for trials scheduled for 12-87 and recommissioning scheduled for 7-88. *U 23* (S 172) arrived 18-7-87 for the same work at Thyssen Nordseewerke, Emden. The last of the Type 206 submarines to be modernized is to complete 2-92. The proposed Type 211 replacement submarine for the Type 206 class may be canceled.

An additional four modified versions of the Type 122 (*Bremen*)-class guided-missile frigates are to be ordered during 1988 as an interim program until the NATO NFR 90 program is ready; the first of the four Type 123-class ships is to complete in 1994. *Augsburg* (F 213) launched 17-9-87; her sister *Lübeck* (F 214) launched 15-10-87. F 213 and F 214 are to receive British SCOT 1A SATCOMM systems.

Type 343 minesweeper M 1092 is named *Hameln*. Type 341 minesweeper *Pluto* (M 1092) was stricken 1-7-87; *Herkules* (M 1095) was stricken 21-8-87, and *Wega* (M 1069) is to strike during 1988.

Names have now been assigned to all 28 LCM(8)-class landing craft as follows:

| | | |
|---|---|---|
| LCM 1 Seetaucher | LCM 11 Huchen | LCM 21 Hummer (L 780) |
| LCM 2 Seenadel | LCM 12 Sprotte | LCM 22 Krill (L 781) |
| LCM 3 Seedrache | LCM 13 Sardine | LCM 23 Krabbe (L 782) |
| LCM 4 Seespinne | LCM 14 Sardelle | LCM 24 Auster (L 783) |
| LCM 5 Seeotter | LCM 15 Hering (A 1408) | LCM 25 Muschel (L 784) |
| LCM 6 Seezunge | LCM 16 Orfe | LCM 26 Koralle (L 785) |
| LCM 7 Seelilie | LCM 17 Maräne (A 1409) | LCM 27 Garnelle (L 786) |
| LCM 8 Seefeder | LCM 18 Saibling | LCM 28 Languste (L 787) |
| LCM 9 Seerose | LCM 19 Stint | |
| LCM 10 Seenelke | LCM 20 Aesche | |

Note: The auxiliary series pendant numbers assigned LCM 15 and LCM 17 duplicate those assigned to trials ships SP 1 and *Wilhelm Pullwer*.

A large number of auxiliary and service craft had their pendant numbers changed during 1987 from the "Y" service-craft series to the "A" auxiliary category or vice versa. These include: Type 726 repair ships *Odin* and *Wotan* from A 512 and A 513 to Y 847 and Y 848, respectively; Type 850 intelligence collector *Holnis* from Y 836 to A 836; Type 705 water tankers *FW 1* through *FW 6* from Y 864 through Y 869 to A 1403 through A 1406; submarine rescue craft *Stier* from Y 849 to M 1053 (possibly indicating use as a mine-clearance diving tender); magnetic research ship *Walther von Ledebur* from Y 841 to A 1410; Type 741 net tenders *SP 1* and *Wilhelm Pullwer* from Y 837 and Y 838 to A 1408 and A 1409, respectively; Type 754 diving-tender tugs *Baltrum, Juist,* and *Langeoog* from Y 1661, Y 1644, and Y 1665 to A 1439, A 1440, and A 1441, respectively; small diving tender *TB 1* from Y 1678 to M 1050; and Type 392 diving tender *Hansa* from Y 806 to M 1052.

Type 442B intelligence collector *Oker* (A 53) stricken 4-12-87. Type 423 intelligence collector *Oste* (A 52) launched 15-5-87 for completion first quarter 1988; *Oker* (A 51) launched 24-9-87 for completion third quarter 1988; and *Alster* (A 51) to lay down early 1988 for delivery 1989. All three are powered by 2 Deutz-MWM 8 BV.16.M.628 diesels, driving two, 6-bladed, fixed-pitch props for 8,800 hp total and a 15-kt maximum speed; for low speeds, the propellers are each driven by one 380-hp electric motor. Collection equipment includes Krupp-Atlas sonar, and EW gear covering the 30 MHz to 40 GHz band.

Target service craft *Kor 2* (ex-torpedoboat *Hermelin*) stricken 25-9-87. Fisheries protection ship *Anton Dohrn* stricken 2-87.

# GREAT BRITAIN

Commencement of government funding to develop the new long-range SUGW—Surface-launched Underwater Guided Weapon—to replace the now-departed Ikara has been delayed three years, due to budgetary constraints, leaving the Royal Navy with no long-range ASW weapons-delivery system other than helicopters until well into the 1990s at best. Some 21 sets of Wallop Barricade 18-rail decoy rocket launchers were ordered in 1987 for smaller ships, to be installed two or four launchers per ship.

The following sonars are in development:

- Type 2057 A towed passive linear array to replace 2031Z on surface ships, from Plessey and GEC.
- Type 2058 Towed sound source for acoustic ranges and a proposed component of the Vosper-Thornycroft Sea Serpent multi-influence towed mine-countermeasures array.
- Type 2059 An add-on to the Type 193M minehunting sonar to permit tracking the PAP-104 submersible minehunting devices; already in service.
- Type 2074 Fully integrated bow sonar array for new nuclear-powered attack submarines to replace the Type 2020 and its Type 2027 acoustic processor; Ferranti and Plessey are competing.
- Type 2075 Hull-mounted suite for Batch 2 *Upholder*-class diesel submarines, for delivery 1991-on in place of Type 2040.

Carrier *Invincible* (R 05) will not recommission until some five months after completion of her modernization overhaul, to save on crew costs. *Illustrious* (R 06) carried 12 Sea King HC.4 troop-carrying helicopters, 4 HAS.5 ASW Sea Kings, and no Sea Harriers during amphibious exercise "Purple Warrior" in 1987.

The seven Sea King helicopters first announced as about to be ordered in 9-86 were finally ordered 12-87 for delivery beginning 12-89; some will be HC.4 troop carriers and others the first built-for-the-purpose HAS.6 ASW version. The first two Sea Lynx HAS.3 began modernization early 1988 with Sea Owl forward-looking IR in place of the radar and CAE ASQ-504(V) MAD gear. The last Wessex HU.5 and Wasp HAS.1 helicopters are to be stricken by March or April 1988, leaving several helicopter-capable frigates and auxiliaries without Wasps.

*Conqueror* (S 48) completed a 16-week overhaul 11-9-87 with new prototype 2075 sonar, displays, computers, etc., for a two-year trial period. *Unseen* (S . . .) laid down 12-8-87. *Sealion* (S 07) stricken 14-12-87. *Orpheus* (S 11), stricken 16-9-87, is replacing *Finwhale* (S 05, stricken 1978) as dockside training hulk at HMS *Dolphin*.

U.S. Mk 15 Mod. 0 CIWS (20-mm Vulcan Phalanx) has been added to *York* (D 98) and *Exeter* (D 89) in place of the twin 30-mm AA mounts abreast the stack; all but one Type 42 series guided-missile destroyer will have Mk 15 CIWS by the end of 1988, although the extra weight is reported to be causing cracking problems.

**Bristol (D 23)**—as cadet-training ship L. Grazioli, 10-87

Type 22 Batch 3 frigate *Cornwall* (F 99) delivered 5-12-87; sisters *Campbeltown* (F 86) launched 7-10-87, and *Chatham* (F . . .) launched 20-1-88, the latter as the last ship to be launched from Swan Hunter's Neptune yard. These ships have the CACS 5 action-data system and have a meteorological facility; F 99 has a crew of 273, plus accommodations for an admiral's staff of 20.

**Cornwall (F 99)** Royal Navy, 12-87

**Active (F 171)**—with ASW TT, 4 20-mm AA L. & L. Van Ginderen, 12-87

Of the four unmodified "Broad-beam" *Leander*-class frigates, three are to be stricken by 31-3-89: *Achilles* (F 12), *Diomede* (F 16), and *Ariadne* (F 72); F 12 and F 16 are to be offered to Greece for sale. *Naiad* (F 39), stricken 29-4-87, is to become stationary trials ship. Both remaining *Rothesay*-class frigates, *Rothesay* (F 107) and *Plymouth* (F 126) were to strike by 31-3-88. Two of the five *Peacock*-class gunboats were to be withdrawn from Hong Kong during 1988, possibly for loan to Brunei Darussalem. The "Isles"-class patrol boats are now equipped with helicopter-type MIR.2 "Orangecrop" intercept arrays. Former Falklands patrol ship *Guardian* (P 245) was sold to a Venezuelan firm by private shipbreakers late in 1987.

Minehunter *Sandown* to launch 18-4-88. Patrol craft *Pursuer* (P 273) commissioned 19-3-88. Patrol boats *Swallow* and *Swift* to be for sale late 1988.

**Achilles (F 12)** L. & L. Van Ginderen, 11-87

**Euryalus (F 15)**—to strike during 1988, along with sister *Arethusa* (F 38) L. Grazioli, 10-87

"Hunt"-class minehunter *Berkeley* (M 40) delivered 14-1-88, and sister *Quorn* (M 41) launched 23-1-88; both have been offered to Saudi Arabia, which has requested offers to construct a class of eight minehunters from several European builders. Sisters *Brecon* (M 29), *Brocklesby* (M 33), *Bicester* (M 36), and *Hurworth* (M 39) were equipped with 2/20-mm BMARC AA, 2/7.62-mm mg, MEL Matilda intercept gear, Irwin DLF-2 "Replica" decoy equipment, 2 Barricade decoy RL, Type 2059 sonar to assist in controlling PAP-104 mine-disposal submersibles, and additional communications equipment before deploying to the Persian Gulf during 9-87. Two additional "River"-class minesweepers were assigned to the Fisheries Protection Squadron during late 1987 to free "Ton"-class ships for mine-countermeasures duties when the latter relieved "Hunts" going to the Mideast. Mine-countermeasures support ship/exercise minelayer *Abdiel* (N 21) was given additional equipment similar to the "Hunts" she accompanied to the Mideast, plus SCOT SATCOMM equipment; the ship is no longer to be stricken on 31-3-88 as earlier planned.

**Berkeley (M 40)**—on trials, 30-mm AA forward L. & L. Van Ginderen, 12-87

Landing ship *Sir Lancelot* (L 3029) may be lengthened like *Sir Tristram* (L 3505). *Sir Galahad* bears pendant L 3005 and was accepted on 25-11-87.

**Sir Galahad (L 3005)** Royal Navy, 11-87

Survey ship *Herald* (A 138) was to relieve *Abdiel* (N 21) as Persian Gulf minehunter support ship in 4-88. *Hecla* (A 133) and *Hecate* (A 137) are now to be retained in service until funds are available to replace them.

The second "Fort"-class replenishment ship, *Fort George* (A . . .), was ordered from Swan Hunter in 12-87. Helicopter training ship *Argus* (A 135) was accepted 3-3-88.

**Argus (A 135)** Royal Navy, 1987

**Argus (A 135)**—on trials Harland & Wolff, 1987

Antarctic patrol ship *Endurance* (A 171) sailed for the Falkland Islands 25-11-87 with two Lynx helicopters aboard in her enlarged hangar. The refit of the Royal Yacht *Britannia* (A 00) ended 12-10-87. "Wild Duck"-class moorings tender *Mandarin* (P 192) paid off to reserve 14-12-87.

"Oil"-class coastal tanker *Oilpress* (Y 21) entered reserve 9-5-87, as she was not configured to transport distillate fuel, only heavy oil. *Cartmel*-class tender *Cartmel* (A 350) was transferred to the Royal Naval Auxiliary Service (RNXS) during 12-87; sister *Glencoe* (A 392) replaced the damaged "Ham"-class tender *Portisham* (M 2781) as RNXS training ship on 15-9-87, with *Portisham* relegated to accommodations hulk status pending possible repairs. *Aberdovey*-class tenders *Aberdovey* (A 99) and *Blakeney* (A 104) were transferred to the Falkland Island government during 1987.

British Army Royal Corps of Transport: *Arromanches*-class landing craft *Agheila* (L 112) in service 12-6-87, and sister *Audemer* (L 113) launched 24-6-87. Tugs *Bridget* (A 323) and *Brenda* (A 335) were sold private early in 1987.

Department of Agriculture and Fisheries for Scotland: *Sulisker*-class patrol ship *Norna* was launched 11-9-87; the research ship of the same name has been stricken. Patrol ship *Jura* stricken 1-88.

**Audemer (L 113)** L. & L. Van Ginderen, 11-87

# GREECE

Greece may purchase three of the six ex-Dutch Br 1150 Atlantic Mk 1 maritime-patrol aircraft returned to France in 1987. Twelve new ASW helicopters are to be acquired, either Super Puma, Agusta ASH-3H Sea King, Sikorsky S-70B, Westland Sea King, or Westland-Agusta EH.101 aircraft. One Greek destroyer reportedly has been fitted with U.S. Harpoon missiles. Greece will build two or more Giles-Thornycroft "Osprey 55"-class patrol vessels under license from Danyard, Frederikshavn, similar to those built for Senegal and Morocco but equipped with 2 MTU 1163 series diesels for 26-kt speeds. The first of five new LSTs was laid down 4-87 at Eleusis SY: 4,400 tons with helicopter decks fore and aft, bow and stern ramps, and a turntable on the vehicle deck.

Three yard oilers ordered 1-86 from Hellenic SY, Skaramanga, are to deliver 6-88. Five oil barges from Eleusis SY were delivered 9-87. A floating dry dock of 6,000-ton capacity and 145-m length o.a., is to deliver 12-88 from Eleusis SY with technical aid from Götaverken, Arendal, Sweden.

**Aktion (N 04)** L. & L. Van Ginderen, 9-87

# GUATEMALA

**Subteniente Osorio Saravia (P-852)** PH1 J. Hilton, USN, 3-86

# GUINEA-BISSAU

Two or three old Chinese "Shantou"-class patrol boats were delivered 3-86:

**D:** 80 tons (fl) **S:** 28 kts **Dim:** 25.1 × 6.0 × 1.8
**A:** 4/37-mm AA (11 × 2)—2/14.5-mm mg (1 × 2)
**Electron Equipt:** Radar: 1/Skin Head
**M:** 2 Type 3D 12, 300-hp diesels and 2 M50, 1,200-hp diesels; 4 props; 3,000 hp

# INDIA

The present massive naval buildup is officially stated to include four to six nuclear-powered submarines, up to 10 Soviet Kashin-class guided-missile destroyers, and 6 Indian Project 15-class large frigates, with India also attempting to acquire 3 Soviet *Sovremennyy*-class destroyers. Also included are the 5 Kilo-class submarines, 12 DP-25-class corvettes (*Khukri* class), 24 Tarantul-class missile boats (16 to build in India), 8 *Magar*-class landing ships, and a total force of four underway replenishment ships. The first Tarantul-I, *Nirvik,* delivered from U.S.S.R. 2-88; the second of five is named *Ranvital.*

India's first nuclear-powered submarine, *Chakra,* was commissioned on loan from the U.S.S.R. at Vladivostok on 5-1-88 and arrived in Indian waters during 2-88; partially crewed with Soviet instructors, the Charlie-I-class ship can carry missiles in its 8 inclined tubes. Four to six additional nuclear-powered submarines are to be acquired from the U.S.S.R., class unreported. The second of five Kilo-class submarines, named *Sindhudhvaj* (S 56) arrived 10-87.

**Sindhudhvaj (S 56)** L. Grazioli, 9-87

During the reactivation in the U.K. of the carrier *Viraat* (ex-*Hermes*), various aircraft landing aids were added, including DAPS (Deck Approach Projector System), HAPI (Horizon Approach Path Indicator), and CTL (an all-weather approach system). The ship's machinery was overhauled and the boilers converted to burn distillate fuel, and the NBC warfare protection system was enhanced. The Indian Navy envisions using *Viraat* as an attack carrier with up to 30 Sea Harrier V/STOL fighters aboard, while the older and smaller *Vikrant* would carry up to 20 Sea King HC.4 troop assault helicopters.

**Viraat (R 22)** L. & L. Van Ginderen, 7-87

The landing ships of the *Magar* class are reported to be based on the design of the British *Sir Bedivere* class, with similar basic characteristics.

# INDONESIA

The Netherlands frigate *Van Galen* (F 803) was transferred to Indonesia 2-11-87; her sister *Van Nes* will be renamed *Oswald Sianaan* on transfer in 11-88. The third Lürssen PB 57 patrol boat for the Navy and the third PB 57 for the Customs Service were both delivered on 1-10-87.

**Pulau Rengat**—running trials; note second Rheinmetall 20-mm AA mount aft (minus barrel) L. & L. Van Ginderen, 12-87

## IRAN

France was reported in 1-88 to be discussing the equipping of the surviving Combattante-II-class missile boats with Exocet missiles, while at the same time, China was reported to have delivered both land-launched Silkworm antiship missiles and the ship-launched version as well. North Korea has transferred several Chaho-class patrol boats. In addition to the units listed in the text, the following ships, originally ostensibly purchased for commercial purposes, may have a naval function:

◆ **3 coastal tankers** Bldr: Ravenstein SY, Deest, the Netherlands (In serv. 1983)

IRAN PARAK IRAN SHALAK IRAN YOUSHAT

**D:** approx. 750 tons (fl) **S:** 10 kts **Dim:** 40.01 (38.82 pp) × 10.01 × 2.60
**M:** 2 G.M. 6V71 diesels; 2 props; 730 hp **Fuel:** 5 tons **Electric:** 12 kw

REMARKS: 400 grt/540 dwt.

◆ **2 small general-purpose tenders** Bldr: Damen SY, Hardinxveld, the Netherlands

HENDIJAN (L: 21-5-87) KALAT (L: 22-5-87)

REMARKS: 439 grt. No other data available.

On 19-4-88 U.S. forces sank the guided-missile boat *Joshan,* the frigate *Sahand,* and at least one Boghammar boat, and seriously damaged the frigate *Sabalan* and up to two additional Boghammars.

**Iran Ajr**—just after capture by U.S. Navy forces, 22-9-87; note mines on deck beneath cargo boom, mg on bridge wing PH3 H. Cleveland, USN

**A "Boghammar Boat"** Boghammar, 1987

## IRAQ

In 1-88 it was reported that of all the units ordered from Italy, only helicopter corvettes *Mussa ben Nussair* (F 210) and *Tariq ibn Ziad* (F 212), the oiler *Agnadeen* (A 102), and the 6,000-ton floating dry dock were actually the property of Iraq, the other new frigates and corvettes remaining in Italy as the property of their builder, Fincantieri; the oiler and the dry dock are moored at Alexandria, while F 21 and F 212 remained in Italian waters.

## IRELAND

The Irish Navy had 874 total personnel as of 31-7-87. Fuel barge *Chowl* was up for sale in 10-87; she had been built in 1924 but was reengined with a 180 Volvo diesel in recent years. *Chowl* was described as being 23.0 × 5.5 × 1.5 and of 102 grt.

## ISRAEL

If built, the first of the "Sa'ar V"-class missile corvettes would be named *Lahav.* There was no indication of any progress toward signing contracts for the submarine/missile-boat program as of 31-1-88.

## ITALY

**Sagittario (F 565)**—with radome atop pilothouse L. Grazioli, 11-87

**MCC 1102 (A 5371)**—new MTC series are similar L. Grazioli, 11-87

CUSTOMS SERVICE (*Guardia di Finanza*): Two 320-ton offshore patrol boats were ordered from Fincantieri, Muggiano, in 8-87; to deliver 1989, they will be 51.0 m o.a., be capable of 28 kts, and be armed with a Breda 30-mm AA controlled by a Elsag Pegaso optronic director. Patrol boats *Bigliani* (G.80) and *Cavaglia* (G.81) were delivered 10-10-87; displacing 85 tons (fl), they can reach 45 kts (40 kts continuous) on the 7,680 hp from two MTU 16V396 TB94 diesels and have a range of 1,200 n.m. at 18 kts. The Breda 30-mm AA is controlled by an Elsag Medusa optronic director. The craft are 26.40 × 6.95 × 1.06.

**Bigliani (G.80)**—on trials L. Grazioli, 7-87

# JAPAN

Under the Fiscal Year 1988 Budget approved 31-1-87, the Maritime Self-Defense Force will build: 1 7,200-ton Aegis guided-missile destroyer, 1 "1,900-ton" frigate, 1 2,400-ton submarine, 2 490-ton minehunters, 2 260-ton tugs, 1 310-ton water tanker, 2 490-ton fuel tankers, 2 270-ton diesel fuel tankers, and 2 25-ton launches. Aircraft approved for the JMSDF included: 9 P-3C Orion, 1 EP-3C EW Orion, 1 US-1A SAR amphibian, 3 KM-2 trainers, 1 U-36A Learjet target service aircraft, and 12 SH-60J ASW helicopters.

Characteristics for several of the major new programs have been further refined. Basic dimensions for the new "2,400-ton" submarine are now: 80.0 × 10.8 m, and the crew will total 75. Basic data for the Aegis guided-missile destroyer are now:

**D:** 7,200 tons (approx. 8,800 fl) **S:** 30 kts **Dim:** 161.0 × 21.0 × 6.1 (hull)
**A:** 2/Mk 41 vertical-launch systems (29 Standard SM-2 MR and ASROC missiles fwd, 61 aft)—8/Harpoon SSM (IV × 2)—1/127-mm OTO Melara DP—2/20-mm Mk 15 CIWS—6/324-mm ASW TT (III × 2)—platform only for 1/SH-60J ASW helicopter
**Electron Equipt:** Radar: 1/OPS-19C nav., 1/OPS-28 surf.-search, 1/SPY-1D multipurpose, 3/Mk 99 illuminators, 1/FCS-2-21 GFCS
Sonar: OQS-101 hull-mounted, SQR-19A (V) TACTASS
EW: NOLQ-2 integrated system, 4/Mk 36 SRBOC decoy RL (VI × 4)
**M:** 4 G.E. LM-2500 gas turbines; 2 CP props; 100,000 hp

Remarks: The design has grown considerably and now resembles an enlarged and improved U.S. Navy *Arleigh Burke* (DDG 51)-class destroyer. Some members of the U.S. Congress have shown considerable reluctance for the U.S. to transfer the Aegis technology to Japan, demanding that the ships be built in the U.S., although roughly half the cost of each will be spent in the U.S. even if the ships are built in Japan, as planned.

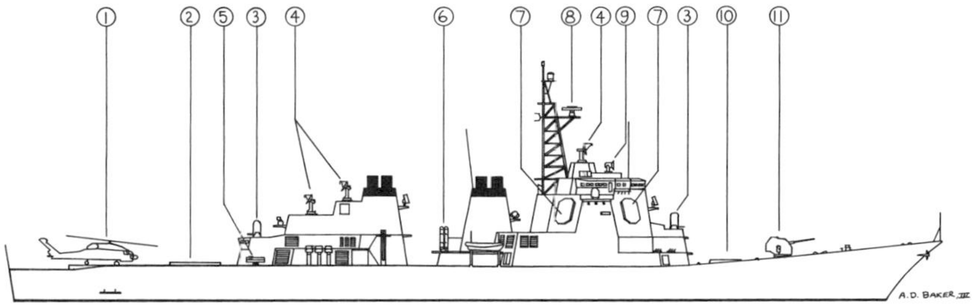


**Japan's Aegis Destroyer** A. Baker
1. SH-60J ASW helicopter 2. aft Mk 41 VLS (61 missiles) 3. 20-mm Mk 15 CIWS 4. Mk 99 illuminators 5. ASW TT 6. Harpoon SSM (IV × 2) 7. SPY-1D Aegis radar 8. OPS-28C radar 9. FCS-2-21 GFCS 10. forward Mk 41 VLS (29 missiles) 11. 127-mm OTO Melara DP

The "1,900-ton" frigate design has also evolved:

**D:** 2,000 tons (approx. 2,500 fl) **S:** 27 kts **Dim:** 109.0 × 13.4 × 3.8 (hull)
**A:** 8/Harpoon SSM (IV × 2)—1/76-mm OTO Melara DP—1/20-mm Mk 15 CIWS—1/Mk 112 ASROC ASW RL (VIII × 1)
**Electron Equipt:** Radar: 1/OPS-28, 1/OPS-14C, 1/FCS-2-21
Sonar: . . . .—EW: . . .
**M:** CODOG: 2/Rolls-Royce SM 1A Spey gas turbines or 2/Mitsubishi S12U diesels; 2 CP props; 27,000 hp
**Man:** 120 tot.

Remarks: The layout has been refined, with the CIWS occupying a central position on the otherwise empty fantail; a U.S. RAM SAM system is no longer part of the armament package. The ASROC is located amidships, between two stacks, and the Harpoon launch cells are located atop an after deckhouse.

The new "420-ton" utility landing craft, the first of which, LCU 1 (LCU 2001), was launched 1-10-87, are now given as:

**D:** 420 tons **S:** 12 kts **Dim:** 52.0 × 8.7 × 1.6
**A:** 1/20-mm JM-61-MB gatling AA **Electron Equipt:** Radar: 1/. . .
**M:** 2 Mitsubishi S6U-MTK diesels; 2 props; 3,000 hp **Man:** 28 tot.

**LCU 1 (LCU 2001)**—at launch *Ships of the World,* 10-87

Data for the new target service training ship, ATS 4202, which was launched 31-7-87 by Nippon Kokan, Tsurumi, are now given as:

**D:** 2,200 tons (approx. 3,200 fl) **S:** 20 kts **Dim:** 101.0 × 16.5 × 4.0
**A:** 1/76-mm OTO Melara DP—. . .
**Electron Equipt:** Radar: . . .—Sonar: . . .
**M:** 2 . . . diesels: 2 props; 9,100 hp **Man:** 150 tot.

Remarks: Like *Azuma* (ATS 4201), will launch and control drones, in this case the Northrop BQM-34J Chukar II, using a launch ramp on the stern. Will also have the TCATS target control system.

*Yamagiri* (DD 152), the second unit of the *Asagiri* (DD 151) class, was launched 8-10-87; *Amagiri* (DD 154) was launched 9-9-87; DD 153 is named *Yugiri.* Note that the after superstructure arrangement differs from that in the drawing in the text, the Harpoon launchers having been raised one deck and the after stack uptakes having been reoriented athwartships.

**Asagiri (DD 151)** JMSDF, 1987

*Isuzu*-class frigate *Mogami* (DE 212) was renumbered as a training ship, TV 3505, and special-use auxiliary, former destroyer *Teruzuki* (ASU 7012, ex-DD 162), was redesignated TV 3504 in mid-1987 when they replaced former destroyers *Isonami* (TV 3505, ex-DD 104) and *Shikinami* (TV 3503, ex-DD 106), which were stricken. *Mogami* has had her variable-depth sonar removed and the quadruple 533-mm torpedo-tube mount abaft the stack replaced by a deckhouse. Former submarine chaser *Hiyodori* (PC 320) was reconfigured as a yacht to replace the stricken *Hayabusa* (ASY 91) and was renumbered ASY 92. *Hatsushima*-class minehunter/minesweepers *Ogishima* (MSC 666) and *Moroshima* (MSC 667) were launched 10-6-87 and 11-6-87, respectively, and both were commissioned 19-12-87. Yard tug YT 25 was stricken during 1987.

Maritime Safety Agency *Mizuho*-class High Endurance Cutter PLH 22 was laid down 3-10-87 by Nippon Kokan, Tsurumi.

# SOUTH KOREA

Current plans call for license construction of four 1,400-ton submarines with West German Howaldtswerke assistance. South Korea is reported to have one 175-ton coastal submarine of indigenous design and construction, named *Tolgorae* (KSS 1).

# MALAWI

SFCN, Villeneuve-la-Garenne, France, is building a 70-ton, 21-m survey launch for service on Lake Malawi; the craft will be powered by two Baudouin 6F 11 SR diesels for a 10.5-kt maximum speed.

# MARSHALL ISLANDS

The patrol boat *Ionmeto* illustrated in the text is the former U.S. Gulf Coast oilfield crewboat *Southern Light,* refitted for fisheries protection duties during 1987 at Halter Shipyard, New Orleans. The 30.48-m craft was given new radars, mounting positions for machine-guns, and had the fuel capacity increased from 2,400 gallons to 9,000 gallons; the crew totals 12. Also transferred to the Marshall Islands in 1987 were two former U.S. Navy harbor utility craft (YFU), from the U.S. Department of the Interior, which had acquired them on 1-12-84; the craft, which were to be used for inter-island transport by the Marshall Islands government, were from the group YFU 71, 72, 76, or 77, built by Pacific Coast Engineering Co., Alameda, California in the late 1960s:

**D:** 220 tons (380 fl) **S:** 8 kts **Dim:** 38.10 × 10.97 × 2.29 **Electric:** 120 kw
**M:** 4 G.M. 6-71 diesels; 2 props; 1,000 hp

# MAURETANIA

French-built 18-m patrol craft *Sloughi* was discarded 1986.

# MAURITIUS

Seaborne forces were reorganized 24-7-87 as the National Coast Guard Organization for territorial waters patrol, search-and-rescue, and fisheries protection duties. In addition to the patrol boat *Amar,* there are one 15-m launch and two Indian-built *Mandowi*-class patrol launches (four more are to be supplied by India, it was announced on 24-7-87):

**D:** . . . **S:** 22 kts **Dim:** 12.50 × . . . × . . . **A:** 1/7.62-mm mg
**Range:** 240/12 **Electron Equipt:** Radar: 1/Decca 17
**M:** 2 Caterpillar diesels; 2 props; 750 hp

# MOROCCO

The first, *El Lahiq,* of Morocco's two "Osprey 55" patrol boats was reported launched 10-87 by Danyard, Frederikshavn, Denmark.

# NETHERLANDS

The Netherlands Navy mine-countermeasures ships sent to the Persian Gulf were equipped with U.S. Stinger short-range, shoulder-launched SAMs for self-protection. Harbor tugs *Hunze* (A 876) and *Rotte* (A 877) of the *Linge* class were reported completed during 10-87, and tug *Berkel* (Y 8037) was stricken 23-9-87. Torpedo lighter Y 8512 was stricken 23-9-87, and former U.S. Coast Guard utility launch Y 8217 was returned to the U.S. for disposal 21-9-87. New mooring pontoon Y 8578 was delivered 20-10-87.

# NEW ZEALAND

Update of the original five RNZAF P.-3B Orions to "Phase-I" configuration was completed 1986; during 1988 to 1991, all six will be further updated under "Phase-II." Although plans still call for the delivery of the first of four joint Australian-New Zealand frigates in the mid-1990s, as a hedge a contract was let to Y-ARD in 10-87 to study service life extension of frigates *Wellington* (F 69) and *Canterbury* (F 421) into the next century. Delivery of the new replenishment oiler *Endeavour* has been delayed, probably until March or April 1988, due to severe problems with the propulsion plant discovered on trials in 12-87. Eight Racal HYDLAPS (Hydrographic Automated Logging And Processing Systems) have been purchased for use on *Monowai* (A 06), *Takapu* (A 07), *Tarapunga* (A 08), and three 10.3-m, 7-ton survey launches, with the other two systems for shore service.

# NIGERIA

Difficulties have been experienced in obtaining export licenses for the two *Lerici*-class minehunters constructed in Italy, at least delaying their delivery well into 1988.

# NORWAY

Norway's order for P-3C Orion maritime-patrol aircraft was for four units; five of the existing P-3Bs are being sold to Spain for rehabilitation and further service, while Norway's other two P-3Bs are to be retained in support of the Norwegian Coast Guard.

**Alta (M 314)** L. & L. Van Ginderen, 1-88

# PAPUA NEW GUINEA

Australian-built ASI 315-class patrol boat *Dreger* (P 02) was completed 29-10-87, not 17-10-87, as indicated in the text.

**Dreger (P 02)** LSPH W. McBride, RAN, 11-87

# PERU

**Peru's refitted cruiser** L. & L. Van Ginderen, 1-88

The cruiser under modernization in the Netherlands, the former *Almirante Grau,* departed the Netherlands 22-1-88. During reconstruction, H.S.A.'s LW-08 was added atop the after mast, DA-08 atop the foremast, two STIR-24 and two STIR-18 fire-control radars replaced the original gun-control systems, and Dagaie and Sagaie decoy RL were added. The new antiship missile-launch positions amidships (four per side) were empty on departure, but it is reported that Otomat is to be fitted in Peru, rather than the originally planned MM 40 Exocet. The light AA guns were not replaced, but two depth-charge racks were retained on the stern. The ship departed still officially nameless, her former name having been conferred on her sister ship during her absence; the new name *General Garzoni* was reported in the Netherlands press.

# SAUDI ARABIA

Saudi Arabia has requested offers from European shipbuilders for the construction of up to eight modern minehunters and may take advantage of the presence of Dutch-built "Tripartite," British "Hunt," and Italian *Lerici*-class minehunters in the Persian Gulf to study the relative merits of each design.

# SINGAPORE

Guided-missile patrol boats of the Lürssen-designed FPB 45 class were being equipped with four Harpoon SSM, mounted in pairs and launching athwartships, late in 1987; the Harpoon launchers replace the triple, trainable Gabriel-I SSM launcher, and the two single, fixed Gabriel-I launchers have been retained. The first unit to be thus fitted was *Sea Hawk* (P 80).

# SPAIN

The nine remaining Bell AH-1G helicopters in naval service were returned to the U.S. late in 1987. Spain agreed to purchase five ex-Royal Norwegian Air Force P-3B Orion long-range patrol aircraft for rehabilitation and further service late in 1987.

**Dedalo (R 01)**—with the first two Spanish AEW Sea Kings on deck, along with three ASW Sea Kings L. Grazioli, 11-87

# SRI LANKA

The first of what was described as "12" Israeli-built "Super Dvora"-class patrol boats arrived in Sri Lanka during 12-87.

# U.S.S.R.

Yet another converted version of the Yankee-class former ballistic-missile submarine appeared in the form of an apparent specialized SS-N-21 strategic cruise-missile launcher. This variant has been lengthened to about 140 m overall, raising the submerged displacement to the neighborhood of 11,500 tons. The increased length is in part accounted for by a new mid-body section said to contain facilities for the horizontal launch of from 20 to 40 SS-N-21 missiles, leaving the six bow tubes still available for torpedo weapons. The new section is reportedly "pinched," presumably to accommodate the muzzle ends of angled-out launching tubes. The original SS-N-6 ballistic-missile-associated raised casing is still present, but the sail has been lengthened by about 3 m and is more streamlined.

**Yankee SS-N-21 cruise-missile launching conversion** R. Nor. A.F., 1987

**Delta-IV class**—note tube at top of rudder, pyramidal shape at the break of the casing, and the apparent auxiliary fins mounted well forward of the stern and barely protruding above the waterline R. Nor. A.F., 1985

**Delta-II class** U.S. Navy, 1986

A Charlie-I-class nuclear-powered cruise-missile submarine was loaned to the Indian Navy for training and commissioned as *Chakra* at Vladivostok on 5-1-88, thus depleting the Pacific Ocean Fleet of one unit of that class; presumably, the SS-N-7 antiship cruise missiles were not included in the loan package, and India stated that nuclear weapons were not aboard. India is also to receive four to six additional Soviet nuclear-powered submarines. If these are newly built (as have been nearly all Soviet ships previously transferred to India), then the already slowed output of nuclear submarines for the Soviet Navy will probably decline further; if the Indian submarines are "used," then the Soviet fleet of such ships will be decreased.

**Bambuk-class intelligence collector Kamchatka** JMSDF, 12-87

The new Bambuk (NATO nickname)-class "Intelligence collector" *Kamchatka* seen in the photograph on the previous page may in fact have some other function: the Soviets have not previously provided helicopter facilities in an intelligence ship, there is already another similar-sized intelligence-collection-ship class in current production (the Vishnaya class), and few intelligence-related antennas are evident. The tall and massive tower structure amidships may possibly house the mechanism for lowering an acoustic device beneath the hull. The pendant number is in the SSV-series (SSV-591) indicating an intelligence or communications-command role, however. (SSV = *Sudno Svyazy,* "Communications Vessel").

**SSV-33**—nuclear-powered space-event, missile-tracking, and naval command ship M.O.D., Bonn

The massive new multipurpose SSV-33 is probably powered by the same propulsion plant as the slightly smaller *Kirov*-class missile cruisers, with the amidships tower displaying the vents for two approximately nuclear reactors and the after tower housing the uptakes from "conventional" boilers. The wide splitting of the propulsion system in the twin-screwed ship gives credence to the belief that, in the *Kirov* plant, the boilers are an entirely separate source of steam, rather than acting as superheaters for the saturated steam from the reactor plant; separate turbines for each system would be required. The staggering number of antennas and radomes visible include systems previously associated with satellite communications and tracking, and missile-range tracking. Rather than just being an enlarged, greater-endurance version of the conventionally powered *Marshal Nedelin,* however, SSV-33 appears to have an order of magnitude greater capacity for communications and command functions, as witness the large number of liferafts for a crew of nearly 900, to the *Marshal Nedelin's* roughly 200. The use of specialized command and communications ships dates back at least to the 1950s in the Soviet Navy, and SSV-33 probably is intended to perform a flagship role in wartime and a space and missile experimentation mission in peacetime.

**Schmel-class river patrol boat 162** E. Seiche, 4-85

The U.S. Director of Naval Intelligence, in open testimony on 1 March 1988, reported that during 1987 the U.S.S.R. had launched eight submarines: 1 Akula SSN (the third), 1 Victor-III SSN (the 22nd), one Oscar SSGN, four Kilo SS (the 17th through 20th, with three intended for export), and a Beluga-class non-nuclear-powered experimental submarine. No ballistic-missile submarines were launched during the year, the fifth Typhoon having entered the water late in 1986, but the fifth Delta-IV SSBN was launched early in 1988. The U.S. believes that some Delta-IVs will be home-ported in the Pacific Ocean Fleet "within the next couple of years." The first Akula SSN, launched in 1984, was stated still to be in a trials status. The SS-N-21 strategic cruise missile was said to have become operational in 1988, with the modified Yankee, Akula, Sierra, and Victor-classes "assessed to be the most likely operational platforms." No new class of SSGN for the SS-NX-24 has yet been launched, but the first unit is expected by 3-89.

The carrier *Baku* was said to have become operational in 1987 (although it has not yet deployed from the Black Sea), while the new large carrier *Leonid Brezhnev* should carry out first trials in 1989. The *Brezhnev* is expected to carry the new Yak-41 VSTOL fighter and by 1992 may employ the Flanker-B Variant 2 CTOL fighter.

Other surface programs were reported moving slowly: *Kalinin,* the third *Kirov,* is still fitting out, and the fourth remains on the ways. The third *Slava* is still fitting out, and the fourth is on the ways. The eleventh *Sovremennyy* has been launched, and six more are under construction (something of a surprise, considering the obsolescence of the design—some may be for export), while *Udaloy* number nine has been launched and three more are on the ways. Construction of a new class of frigate began last year at Kaliningrad Shipyard as a possible follow-on to

**SSV 10**—Danube River flagship E. Seiche, 4-85

the Krivak class, and a new amphibious landing ship, possibly a third *Ivan Rogov,* is being built at the same yard. Two WIG (Wing-In-Ground effect) classes are in production: Utka, powered by eight turbofan engines and mounting six SS-N-22 antiship missiles (the second is believed being built), and Orlan, optimized for amphibious warfare and capable of carrying 100 troops or wheeled cargo.

Reported Soviet Naval Aviation developments included the announcement of a new seaplane, designated "TAG-D," with a possible ASW/surveillance/mining role, and further deployments of the Bear-J VLF communications relay aircraft, which first entered service in 1985. The current version of the Tu-142 Bear-F, the Mod. 4, was said to have "increased capability over its predecessors."

Press reports indicate that the U.S.S.R. ordered four 55-m Osprey-class patrol boats from Danyard, Frederikshavn, Denmark, on 11-11-87; if true, these are the first Western combatants for the U.S.S.R. since World War II.

# U.S.A.

As a means of meeting the reduced operating budget available in 1988–89, it is planned in FY 88-89 to decommission the six frigates of the *Brooke* (FFG 1) class and the ten frigates of the similar *Garcia* (FF 1040) class; since funds are unlikely to be available for proper pre-inactivation overhauls, the decommissionings would be tantamount to striking the ships, which, due to their complex turbopressurized boiler propulsion plants and generally obsolescent equipment (other than for ASW), are unlikely to make attractive foreign sales prospects. Most of the 16 frigates are in the Pacific Fleet. There was no word on the fate of the very similar *Glover* (FF 1098) or the older and less-capable *Bronstein* (FF 1037) and *McCloy* (FF 1038).

On 21-8-85 the Naval Underwater Weapons Experimental Station at Keyport, Washington, purchased the former Seattle Union College training ship *Trident* for the purpose of converting the ship into a torpedo-range service ship. The *Trident* had begun life as the U.S. Army mine planter *Lieutenant William G. Sylvester* in 1942, was later transferred to the Navy as the *Obstructor* (ACM 7), and was then passed to the Coast Guard, which used the ship as the buoy tender *Heather* (WLB 331, ex-WAGL 331) from 1-2-47 to 15-12-67, when it was donated to the college and renamed *Trident.* The ship remains idle and unconverted at Keyport under the name *Ex-Heather:*

◆ **1 former U.S. Army mine planter** Bldr: Marietta Mfgr., Point Pleasant, West Virginia (L: 1942)

. . . Ex-Heather (ex-*Trident,* ex-*Heather* (WLB 331), ex-*Obstructor* (ACM 7), ex-*Lieutenant William G. Sylvester*)

**D:** 868 tons light (1,323 fl) **S:** 12 kts **Dim:** 57.51 (51.41 pp) × 11.28 × 3.91
**M:** 2 sets Skinner Uniflow reciprocating steam; 2 props; 1,300 hp
**Boilers:** 2 Combustion Eng.; 17 kg/cm$^2$ **Range:** 2,375/11.5; 3,000/8
**Man:** 3 officers, 49 men

Remarks: Planned conversion included replacement of the steam propulsion plant with two Caterpillar D379 diesels (625 hp each) for a 12-kt maximum speed; installation of an Omnithruster 400-hp bow-thruster; installation of two underwater Mk 59 533-mm SSN 608-class torpedo tubes and facilities for storing and post-firing rework for ten 7-meter-long torpedoes; addition of a triple Mk 32 ASW torpedo-tube mount above decks; installation of four cranes for torpedo handling and recovery; renewal of all wiring; and rehabilitation of accommodations for a planned crew of 30. With the ordering of new torpedo trials ships YTT 8 and 9 in 1987, it is unlikely that *Ex-Heather* will be reactivated.

The FY 89 budget request submitted in February 1988 included 1 Trident SSBN, 3 SSNs (2 SSN 688 class and the prototype *Seawolf*), 3 DDG 51-class guided-missile destroyers, 2 MHC 51-class coastal minehunters, 1 LHD 1-class amphibious assault ship, 1 AOE 6-class replenishment ship, 2 T-AO 187-class oilers, 3 T-AGOS 19-class SWATH ocean-surveillance ships, and 1 oceanographic research ship; no yardcraft were requested.

Aircraft requested were 12 F-14D Tomcat, 72 F/A-18C/D Hornet, 24 AV-8B Harrier, 9 EA-6B Prowler, 6 E-2C Hawkeye, 14 C/MH-53E Super Stallion/Sea Dragon, 6 SH-60B Seahawk, 18 SH-60F Seahawk, 24 T-45 Goshawk, and 7 E-6A Hermes; no A-6F, AH-1W, C-2, P-3C, KC-130, HH-60H, VH-60, or MV-22 aircraft were requested.